FOREWORD

The **HarperCollins Compac**wo kinds of language help, arran asy look-up. In the top section of ext which gives help with spelling on of each page provides a thes

The dictionary text includes over 45,000 definitions and gives spelling help for all irregular forms of words. Pronunciation help is also given for words considered difficult or confusing. Center dots, as in **"ab•sinthe"** and **"mol•lusk"**, are used to indicate divisions between syllables. Alternative spellings are shown by placing the variants side by side (**amok, amuk**) but if the divergence in spelling is very great there is a separate entry.

The thesaurus text offers 130,000 synonyms. As part of an innovative design, key synonyms have been put in bold and placed first in each list of synonyms. This layout enables you to see at once which sense of the word is being referred to, which is particularly helpful when a main entry word has a number of different senses. It also gives you an idea of which synonym is the closest alternative to the word you have looked up.

This new book also takes account of recent changes in the language, with new terms like **cybersquatting**, **digital television**, **dotcom**, **DVD**, **e-commerce**, **GMO**, **twenty-four-seven**, **webcam**, and **webcast**.

The **HarperCollins Compact Dictionary & Thesaurus** is thus a uniquely helpful book, providing spelling, meaning, and a wide choice of alternative words together in a single source. The combined text makes it an invaluable language reference book, and an ideal companion for everyone who wants to increase their command of English.

GUIDE TO THE TEXT

DICTIONARY

Headword → **cav·al·cade** [KAV-əl-kayd] *n* **1** column or procession of riders. **2** series.

cav·a·lier [kav-ə-LEER] *adj* **1** careless, disdainful. ♦ *n* **2** courtly gentleman. **3** *obs* horseman. ← **Sense numbers**

cav·al·ry [KAV-əl-ree] *n, pl* **-ries** mounted troops. ← **Spelling help**

Part of speech labels → **cave** [kayv] *n* **1** hollow place in the earth. **2** den. **cav·ern** [KAV-ərn] *n* deep cave. **cav·ern·ous** *adj* **cav·i·ty** *n, pl* **-ties** hollow. **cave·man** *n* prehistoric cave dweller. **cave in 1** fall inward. **2** submit. **3** give in.

cav·i·ar [KAV-ee-ahr] *n* salted sturgeon roe.

cav·il [KAV-əl] *vi* **-iled, -il·ing** find fault without sufficient reason, make trifling objections. **cav·il·ing** *n* **cav·il·er** *n*

cav·i·ta·tion [kav-i-TAY-shən] *n* rapid formation of cavities or bubbles. **cav·i·tate** *vi* **-tat·ed, -tat·ing** undergo cavitation. ← **Definition**

ca·vort [kə-VORT] *vi* prance, frisk.

caw [kaw] *n* **1** crow's cry. ♦ *vi* **2** cry so.

cay·enne pepper [kī-EN] *n* pungent red pepper.

Cd *Chem.* cadmium.

CD 1 compact disk. **2** certificate of deposit. **CD-R** compact disk recordable. **CD-ROM** compact disk storing digitized read-only data. **CD-RW** compact disk read-write.

THESAURUS

Headword → **caution** *n* **1 = care**, alertness, carefulness, circumspection, deliberation, discretion, forethought, heed, prudence, vigilance, watchfulness **2 = warning**, admonition, advice, counsel, injunction ♦ *v* **3 = warn**, admonish, advise, tip off, urge

cautious *adj* **= careful**, cagey (*inf*), chary, circumspect, guarded, judicious, prudent, tentative, wary ← **Usage label**

cavalcade *n* **= parade**, array, march-past, procession, spectacle, train

cavalier *adj* **= haughty**, arrogant, disdainful, lofty, lordly, offhand, scornful, supercilious

cavalry *n* **= horsemen**, horse, mounted troops

Key synonym → **cave** *n* **= hollow**, cavern, cavity, den, grotto

cavern *n* **= cave**, hollow, pothole

cavernous *adj* **= deep**, hollow, sunken, yawning

cavity *n* **= hollow**, crater, dent, gap, hole, pit

cease *v* **= stop**, break off, conclude, discontinue, end, finish, halt, leave off, refrain, terminate

ceaseless *adj* **= continual**, constant,

GUIDE TO THE TEXT

DICTIONARY

Pronunciation

cease [sees] *v* **ceased, ceas·ing** bring or come to an end. **cease'less** *adj*

ce·dar [SEE-dər] *n* **1** large evergreen tree. **2** its wood.

cede [seed] *vt* **ced·ed, ced·ing** yield, give up, transfer, esp. of territory.

ce·dil·la [si-DIL-ə] *n* hooklike mark placed under a letter *c* to show the sound of *s*.

ceil·ing [SEE-ling] *n* **1** inner, upper surface of a room. **2** maximum price, wage, etc. **3** *Aviation* lower level of clouds. **4** limit of height to which aircraft can climb.

Subject field label

cel·e·brate [SEL-ə-brayt] *v* **-brat·ed, -brat·ing 1** rejoice or have festivities to mark (happy day, event, etc.). ◆ *vt* **2** observe (birthday, etc.). **3** perform (religious ceremony, etc.). **4** praise publicly. **cel'e·brant** *n* **celebrated** *adj* famous. **cel·e·bra'tion** *n* **ce·leb'ri·ty** *n, pl* **-ties 1** famous person. **2** fame.

Derived word

ce·ler·i·ty [sə-LER-i-tee] *n* swiftness.

cel·er·y [SEL-ə-ree] *n* vegetable with long juicy edible stalks.

ce·les·tial [sə-LES-chəl] *adj* **1** heavenly, divine. **2** of the sky.

cel·i·ba·cy [SEL-ə-bə-see] *n* sexual abstinence. **cel'i·bate** [-bit] *n, adj*

cell [sel] *n* **1** small room, esp. in prison. **2**

THESAURUS

endless, eternal, everlasting, incessant, interminable, never-ending, nonstop, perpetual, twenty-four-seven (*sl*), unremitting

Synonyms

Idioms and phrases

cede *v* **= surrender**, concede, hand over, make over, relinquish, renounce, resign, transfer, yield

celebrate *v* **1 = rejoice**, commemorate, drink to, keep, kill the fatted calf, observe, put the flags out, toast **2 = perform**, bless, honor, solemnize

Sense numbers

celebrated *adj* **= well-known**, acclaimed, distinguished, eminent, famous, illustrious, notable, popular, prominent, renowned

celebration *n* **1 = party**, festival, festivity, gala, jubilee, merrymaking, red-letter day, revelry **2 = performance**, anniversary, commemoration, honoring, observance, remembrance, solemnization

Part of speech label

celebrity *n* **1 = personality**, big name, big shot (*inf*), dignitary, luminary, star, superstar, V.I.P. **2 = fame**, distinction, notability, prestige, prominence, renown, reputation, repute, stardom

celestial *adj* **= heavenly**, angelic, astral, divine, ethereal, spiritual, sublime,

ABBREVIATIONS USED IN THE DICTIONARY

abbrev	abbreviation	m	meter(s)
adj	adjective	*masc*	masculine
adv	adverb	Math	Mathematics
Afr	Africa(n)	mm	millimeter(s)
Amer	America(n)	Mus	Music
Aust	Australia(n)	N	North
Brit	Britain, British	*n*	noun
Canad	Canada, Canadian	*n, pl*	plural noun
cent	century	N.Z.	New Zealand
Chem	Chemistry	*obs*	obsolete, obsolescent
cm	centimeter(s)	*offens*	offensive
comb	combining	oft	often
comp	comparative	orig	originally
conj	conjunction	*pers*	person
cu	cubic	pert	pertaining
dial	dialect	*pl*	plural
dim	diminutive	*poss*	possessive
e.g.	for example	*pp*	past participle
esp	especially	*prep*	preposition
fem	feminine	*pres t*	present tense
fig	figuratively	*pron*	pronoun
Fr	French	*pr p*	present participle
g	gram(s)	*pt*	past tense
Ger	German	R.C.	Roman Catholic
Gr	Greek	*refl*	reflexive
Hist	History	Russ	Russian
i.e.	that is	S	South
impers	impersonal	*sing*	singular
ind	indicative	*sl*	slang
inf	informal	Sp	Spanish
interj	interjection	sq	square
intr	intransitive	*sup*	superlative
It	Italian	*tr*	transitive
k	kilogram(s)	usu	usually
km	kilometer(s)	*v*	verb
l	liter(s)	*v aux*	auxiliary verb
Lat	Latin	*vi*	intransitive verb
lit	literally	*vt*	transitive verb

A a

a *adj* indefinite article, used before a noun being mentioned for the first time.

aard·vark [AHRD-vahrk] *n* S African mammal feeding on ants and termites.

a·back [ə-BAK] *adv* **taken aback** startled.

ab·a·cus [AB-ə-kəs] *n* **1** counting device of beads on wire frame. **2** flat tablet at top of architectural column.

ab·a·lo·ne [ab-ə-LOH-nee] *n* edible shellfish, yielding mother-of-pearl.

a·ban·don [ə-BAN-dən] *vt* **1** desert. **2** give up altogether. ♦ *n* **3** freedom from inhibitions, etc. **a·ban'doned** *adj* **1** deserted, forsaken. **2** uninhibited. **3** wicked.

a·base [ə-BAYS] *vt* **-based, -bas·ing** humiliate, degrade. **a·base'ment** *n*

a·bash [ə-BASH] *vt* (usu. passive) confuse, make ashamed. **a·bash'ment** *n*

a·bate [ə-BAYT] *v* **-bat·ed, -bat·ing** make or become less, diminish. **a·bate'ment** *n*

ab·at·toir [AB-ə-twahr] *n* slaughterhouse.

ab·bey [AB-ee] *n, pl* **-beys 1** dwelling place of community of monks or nuns. **2** church of an abbey.

ab·bot [AB-ət] *n* (*fem* **ab'bess**) head of abbey or monastery.

ab·bre·vi·ate [ə-BREE-vee-ayt] *vt* **-at·ed, -at·ing** shorten, abridge. **ab·bre·vi·a'tion** *n* shortened form of word or phrase.

ab·di·cate [AB-di-kayt] *v* **-cat·ed, -cat·ing** formally give up (throne, etc.). **ab·di·ca'tion** *n*

ab·do·men [AB-də-mən] *n* belly. **ab·dom'i·nal** *adj*

ab·duct [ab-DUKT] *vt* carry off, kidnap. **ab·duc'tion** *n*

ab·er·ra·tion [ab-ə-RAY-shən] *n* **1** deviation from what is normal. **2** flaw. **3** lapse. **ab·er·rant** [ə-BER-ənt] *adj*

a·bet [ə-BET] *vt* **-bet·ted, -bet·ting** assist, encourage, esp. in doing wrong. **a·bet'tor, -ter** *n*

a·bey·ance [ə-BAY-əns] *n* condition of not being in use or action.

ab·hor' *vt* **-horred, -hor·ring** dislike strongly, loathe. **ab·hor'rent** *adj* hateful.

a·bide [ə-BID] *v* **a·bode'** *or* **a·bid'ed,**

THESAURUS

abandon *v* **1** = **leave**, desert, forsake, strand **2** = **give up**, relinquish, surrender, yield ♦ *n* **3** = **wildness**, recklessness

abandonment *n* = **leaving**, dereliction, desertion, forsaking

abashed *adj* = **embarrassed**, ashamed, chagrined, disconcerted, dismayed, humiliated, mortified, shamefaced, taken aback

abate *v* = **decrease**, decline, diminish, dwindle, fade, lessen, let up, moderate, relax, slacken, subside, weaken

abbey *n* = **monastery**, convent, friary, nunnery, priory

abbreviate *v* = **shorten**, abridge, compress, condense, contract, cut, reduce, summarize

abbreviation *n* = **shortening**, abridgment, contraction, reduction, summary, synopsis

abdicate *v* = **give up**, abandon, quit, relinquish, renounce, resign, step down

(*inf*)

abdication *n* = **giving up**, abandonment, quitting, renunciation, resignation, retirement, surrender

abduct *v* = **kidnap**, carry off, seize, snatch (*sl*)

abduction *n* = **kidnaping**, carrying off, seizure

aberration *n* = **oddity**, abnormality, anomaly, defect, irregularity, lapse, peculiarity, quirk

abet *v* = **help**, aid, assist, connive at, support

abeyance *n* **in abeyance** = **shelved**, hanging fire, on ice (*inf*), pending, suspended

abhor *v* = **hate**, abominate, detest, loathe, shrink from, shudder at

abhorrent *adj* = **hateful**, abominable, disgusting, distasteful, hated, horrid, loathsome, offensive, repulsive, scuzzy (*sl*)

a·bid·ing ♦ vt **1** endure, put up with. ♦ vi **2** obs stay, reside. **abide by** obey.

a·bil·i·ty [ə-BIL-i-tee] n, pl -ties **1** competence, power. **2** talent.

ab·ject [AB-jekt] adj **1** humiliated, wretched. **2** despicable. **ab·ject'ness** n

ab·jure [ab-JOOR] vt -jured, -jur·ing give up by oath, renounce. **ab·ju·ra'tion** n

a·blaze [ə-BLAYZ] adj burning.

a·ble [AY-bəl] adj capable, competent. **a'bled** adj having a range of physical powers as specified, e.g. differently abled. **a'bly** adv **a'ble-bod'ied** adj

ab·lu·tion [ə-BLOO-shən] n (usu. pl) act of washing (oneself).

ab·ne·gate [AB-ni-gayt] vt -gat·ed, -gat·ing give up, renounce. **ab·ne·ga'tion** n

ab·nor·mal [ab-NOR-məl] adj **1** irregular. **2** not usual or typical. **3** freakish, odd. **ab·nor·mal'i·ty** n, pl -ties **ab·nor'mal·ly** adv

a·board [ə-BORD] adv on board, on ship, train, or aircraft.

a·bode [ə-BOHD] n **1** home. **2** dwelling. **3** pt./pp. of ABIDE.

ab·ol·ish [ə-BOL-ish] vt do away with. **ab·o·li'tion** n **ab·o·li'tion·ist** n one who wishes to do away with something, esp. slavery.

a·bom·i·nate [ə-BOM-ə-nayt] vt -nat·ed, -nat·ing detest. **a·bom'i·na·ble** adj **a·bom·i·na'tion** n **1** loathing. **2** the object loathed. **abominable snowman** large legendary apelike creature said to inhabit the Himalayas.

ab·o·rig·i·nal [ab-ə-RIJ-ə-nl] adj **1** (of people, etc.) original or earliest known in an area. **2** of, relating to aborigines. **ab·o·rig'i·ne** [-ə-nee] n **1** one of race of people inhabiting an area when European settlers arrived. **2** original inhabitant of country, etc. **3** (A-) one of a race of people originally inhabiting Australia.

a·bort [ə-BORT] v **1** (cause to) end prematurely (esp. pregnancy). ♦ vi **2** give birth to dead fetus. **3** fail. **a·bor'tion** n **1** operation to terminate pregnancy. **2** something deformed. **a·bor'tion·ist** n one who performs abortion, esp. illegally. **a·bor'tive** adj unsuccessful.

a·bound [ə-BOWND] v **1** be plentiful. **2** overflow. **a·bound'ing** adj

a·bout [ə-BOWT] adv **1** on all sides. **2** nearly. **3** up and down. **4** out, on the move. ♦ prep **5** around. **6** near. **7** concerning. **8** ready to. **about turn** reversal, complete change.

——————[THESAURUS]——————

abide v = **tolerate**, accept, bear, endure, put up with, stand, suffer

abide by v = **obey**, agree to, comply with, conform to, follow, observe, submit to

abiding adj = **everlasting**, continuing, enduring, lasting, permanent, persistent, unchanging

ability n = **skill**, aptitude, capability, competence, expertise, proficiency, talent

abject adj **1** = **miserable**, deplorable, forlorn, hopeless, pitiable, wretched **2** = **servile**, cringing, degraded, fawning, grovelling, submissive

ablaze adj = **on fire**, aflame, alight, blazing, burning, fiery, flaming, ignited, lighted

able adj = **capable**, accomplished, competent, efficient, proficient, qualified, skillful

able-bodied adj = **strong**, fit, healthy, robust, sound, sturdy

abnormal adj = **unusual**, atypical, exceptional, extraordinary, irregular, odd, peculiar, strange, uncommon

abnormality n = **oddity**, deformity, exception, irregularity, peculiarity, singularity, strangeness

abode n = **home**, domicile, dwelling, habitat, habitation, house, lodging, pad (sl, dated), quarters, residence

abolish v = **do away with**, annul, cancel, destroy, eliminate, end, eradicate, put an end to, quash, rescind, revoke, stamp out

abolition n = **ending**, cancellation, destruction, elimination, end, extermination, termination, wiping out

abominable adj = **terrible**, despicable, detestable, disgusting, hateful, horrible, horrid, lousy (sl), repulsive, revolting, scuzzy (sl), vile

abort v **1** = **terminate** (a pregnancy), miscarry **2** = **stop**, arrest, ax (inf), call off, check, end, fail, halt, terminate

abortion n = **termination**, deliberate miscarriage, miscarriage

abortive adj = **failed**, fruitless, futile, ineffectual, miscarried, unsuccessful, useless, vain

abound v = **be plentiful**, flourish, proliferate, swarm, swell, teem, thrive

abounding adj = **plentiful**, abundant, bountiful, copious, full, profuse, prolific, rich

a·bove [ə-BUV] *adv* **1** higher up. ◆ *prep* **2** over. **3** higher than, more than. **4** beyond.

a·brade [ə-BRAYD] *vt* **-brad·ed, -brad·ing** rub off, scrape away.

a·bra·sion [ə-BRAY-zhən] *n* **1** place scraped or worn by rubbing (e.g. on skin). **2** scraping, rubbing. **a·bra·sive** [-siv] *n* **1** substance for grinding, polishing, etc. ◆ *adj* **2** causing abrasion. **3** grating. **a·bra·sive·ness** *n* tendency to annoy.

a·breast [ə-BREST] *adv* **1** side by side. **2** keeping up with.

a·bridge [ə-BRIJ] *vt* cut short, abbreviate. **a·bridg'ment** *n*

a·broad [ə-BRAWD] *adv* **1** to or in a foreign country. **2** at large.

ab·ro·gate [AB-rə-gayt] *vt* cancel, repeal. **ab·ro·ga'tion** *n*

ab·rupt [ə-BRUPT] *adj* **1** sudden. **2** blunt. **3** hasty. **4** steep.

abs [ABZ] *pl n inf* abdominal muscles.

ab·scess [AB-ses] *n* gathering of pus in any part of the body.

ab·scis·sa [ab-SIS-ə] *n, pl* **-sae** [-see] *Math.* distance of point from the axis of coordinates.

ab·scond [ab-SKOND] *vi* leave secretly, esp. having stolen something.

ab·sent [AB-sənt] *adj* **1** away. **2** not attentive. ◆ *vt* [ab-SENT] **3** keep away. **ab'sence** *n* **ab·sen·tee'** *n* one who stays away esp. habitually. **ab·sen·tee'ism** *n* persistent absence from work, etc.

ab·sinthe [AB-sinth] *n* potent aniseed-flavored liqueur.

ab·so·lute [AB-sə-loot] *adj* **1** complete. **2** not limited, unconditional. **3** pure, e.g. *absolute alcohol.* ◆ *n* **ab'so·lute·ly** *adv* **1** completely. ◆ *interj* [-LOOT-lee] **2** certainly.

ab·solve [ab-ZOLV] *vt* **-solved, -solv·ing** free from, pardon, acquit. **ab·so·lu'tion** [-sə-LOO-shən] *n*

ab·sorb' *vt* **1** suck up, drink in. **2** engage, occupy (attention, etc.). **3** receive impact. **ab·sorb'ent** *adj* **ab·sorp'tion** *n*

ab·stain [ab-STAYN] *vi* keep from, refrain

THESAURUS

about *prep* **1** = **regarding**, as regards, concerning, dealing with, on, referring to, relating to **2** = **near**, adjacent to, beside, circa *(used with dates)*, close to, nearby ◆ *adv* **3** = **nearly**, almost, approaching, approximately, around, close to, more or less, roughly

above *prep* = **over**, beyond, exceeding, higher than, on top of, upon

above board *adj* = **honest**, fair, genuine, legitimate, square, straight

abrasion *n Medical* = **graze**, chafe, scrape, scratch, scuff, surface injury

abrasive *adj* **1** = **unpleasant**, caustic, cutting, galling, grating, irritating, rough, sharp **2** = **rough**, chafing, grating, scraping, scratchy

abreast *adj* **1** = **alongside**, beside, side by side **2 abreast of** = **informed about**, acquainted with, *au courant* with *au fait* with, conversant with, familiar with, in the picture about, in touch with, keeping one's finger on the pulse of, knowledgeable about, up to date with, up to speed with

abridge *v* = **shorten**, abbreviate, condense, cut, decrease, reduce, summarize

abroad *adv* = **overseas**, in foreign lands, out of the country

abrupt *adj* **1** = **sudden**, precipitate, quick, surprising, unexpected **2** = **curt**, brusque,

gruff, impatient, rude, short, terse

abscond *v* = **flee**, clear out, disappear, escape, make off, run off, steal away

absence *n* **1** = **nonattendance**, absenteeism, truancy **2** = **lack**, deficiency, need, omission, unavailability, want

absent *adj* **1** = **missing**, away, elsewhere, gone, nonexistent, out, unavailable **2** = **absent-minded**, blank, distracted, inattentive, oblivious, preoccupied, vacant, vague ◆ *v* **3 absent oneself** = **stay away**, keep away, play truant, withdraw

absent-minded *adj* = **vague**, distracted, dreaming, forgetful, inattentive, preoccupied, unaware

absolute *adj* **1** = **total**, complete, outright, perfect, pure, sheer, thorough, utter **2** = **supreme**, full, sovereign, unbounded, unconditional, unlimited, unrestricted

absolutely *adv* = **totally**, completely, entirely, fully, one hundred per cent, perfectly, utterly, wholly

absolution *n* = **forgiveness**, deliverance, exculpation, exoneration, mercy, pardon, release

absolve *v* = **forgive**, deliver, exculpate, excuse, let off, pardon, release, set free

absorb *v* **1** = **soak up**, consume, digest, imbibe, incorporate, receive, suck up, take in **2** = **preoccupy**, captivate, engage, engross, fascinate, rivet

from drinking alcohol, voting, etc.
ab·sten'tion n **ab'sti·nence** n

ab·ste·mi·ous [ab-STEE-mee-əs] adj sparing in food or esp. drink, temperate. **ab·ste'mi·ous·ness** n

ab·stract [ab-STRAKT] adj 1 existing only in the mind. 2 not concrete. 3 (of art) not representational. ◆ n [AB strakt] 4 summary, abridgment. ◆ vt [ab-STRAKT] 5 draw from, remove. 6 steal. **ab·stract'ed** adj preoccupied. **ab·strac'tion** n

ab·struse [ab-STROOS] adj obscure, difficult to understand, profound.

ab·surd' adj contrary to reason. **ab·surd'i·ty** n

a·bun·dance [ə-BUN-dəns] n great amount. **a·bun'dant** adj plentiful.

a·buse [ə-BYOOZ] vt -bused, -bus·ing 1 misuse. 2 address rudely. ◆ n (ə-BYOOS). **a·bu'sive** [-siv] adj **a·bu'sive·ness** n

a·but [ə-BUT] vi -but·ted, -but·ting adjoin, border on. **a·but'ment** n support, esp. of bridge or arch.

a·bys·mal [ə-BIZ-məl] adj 1 immeasurable, very great. 2 inf extremely bad. **a·bys'mal·ly** adv

absorbed adj 1 = **preoccupied**, captivated, engrossed, fascinated, immersed, involved, lost, rapt, riveted, wrapped up 2 = **digested**, assimilated, incorporated, received, soaked up

absorbent adj = **permeable**, porous, receptive, spongy

absorbing adj = **fascinating**, captivating, engrossing, gripping, interesting, intriguing, riveting, spellbinding

absorption n 1 = **soaking up**, assimilation, consumption, digestion, incorporation, sucking up 2 = **concentration**, fascination, immersion, intentness, involvement, preoccupation

abstain v = **refrain**, avoid, decline, deny (oneself), desist, fast, forbear, forgo, give up, keep from

abstemious adj = **self-denying**, ascetic, austere, frugal, moderate, sober, temperate

abstention n = **refusal**, abstaining, abstinence, avoidance, forbearance, refraining, self-control, self-denial, self-restraint

abstinence n = **self-denial**, abstemiousness, avoidance, forbearance, moderation, self-restraint, soberness, teetotalism, temperance

abstinent adj = **self-denying**, abstaining, abstemious, forbearing, moderate, self-controlled, sober, temperate

abstract adj 1 = **theoretical**, abstruse, general, hypothetical, indefinite, notional, recondite ◆ n 2 = **summary**, abridgment, digest, epitome, outline, précis, résumé, synopsis ◆ v 3 = **summarize**, abbreviate, abridge, condense, digest, epitomize, outline, précis, shorten 4 = **remove**, detach, extract, isolate, separate, take away, take out, withdraw

abstraction n 1 = **idea**, concept, formula, generalization, hypothesis, notion, theorem, theory, thought 2 = **absent-mindedness**, absence, dreaminess, inattention, pensiveness, preoccupation, remoteness, woolgathering

abstruse adj = **obscure**, arcane, complex, deep, enigmatic, esoteric, recondite, unfathomable, vague

absurd adj = **ridiculous**, crazy (inf), farcical, foolish, idiotic, illogical, inane, incongruous, irrational, ludicrous, nonsensical, preposterous, senseless, silly, stupid, unreasonable

absurdity n = **ridiculousness**, farce, folly, foolishness, incongruity, joke, nonsense, silliness, stupidity

abundance n = **plenty**, affluence, bounty, copiousness, exuberance, fullness, profusion

abundant adj = **plentiful**, ample, bountiful, copious, exuberant, filled, full, luxuriant, profuse, rich, teeming

abuse n 1 = **ill-treatment**, damage, exploitation, harm, hurt, injury, maltreatment, manhandling 2 = **insults**, blame, castigation, censure, defamation, derision, disparagement, invective, reproach, scolding, vilification 3 = **misuse**, misapplication ◆ v 4 = **ill-treat**, damage, exploit, harm, hurt, injure, maltreat, misuse, take advantage of 5 = **insult**, castigate, curse, defame, disparage, malign, scold, vilify

abusive adj 1 = **insulting**, censorious, defamatory, disparaging, libelous, offensive, reproachful, rude, scathing 2 = **harmful**, brutal, cruel, destructive, hurtful, injurious, rough

abysmal adj = **terrible**, appalling, awful, bad, dire, dreadful

a·byss [ə-BIS] n very deep gulf or pit.
Ac Chem actinium.
a·cad·e·my [ə-KAD-ə-mee] n, pl -mies 1
society to advance arts or sciences. 2
institution for specialized training. 3
secondary school. **ac·a·dem·ic**
[ak-ə-DEM-ik] adj 1 of academy, university,
etc. 2 theoretical.
ac·cede [ak-SEED] vi -ced·ed, -ced·ing 1
agree, consent. 2 attain (office, right, etc.).
ac·cel·er·ate [ak-SEL-ə-rayt] v -at·ed,
-at·ing (cause to) increase speed, hasten.
ac·cel·er·a'tion n **ac·cel'er·a·tor** n
mechanism to increase speed, esp. in
automobile.
ac·cent [AK-sent] n 1 stress or pitch in
speaking. 2 mark to show such stress. 3
local or national style of pronunciation. 4
particular attention or emphasis. ♦ vt

ac·cen·tu·ate [ak-SEN-choo-ayt] vt -at·ed,
-at·ing stress, emphasize.
ac·cept [ak-SEPT] vt 1 take, receive. 2
admit, believe. 3 agree to. **ac·cept'a·ble** adj
ac·cept'ance n
ac·cess [AK-ses] n act, right, or means of
entry. **ac·ces'si·ble** adj easy to approach.
ac·ces·sion [ak-SESH-ən] n 1 attaining of
office, right, etc. 2 increase, addition.
ac·ces·so·ry [ak-SES-ə-ree] n, pl -ries 1
additional or supplementary part of
automobile, woman's dress, etc. 2 person
inciting or assisting in crime. ♦ adj 3
contributory, assisting.
ac·ci·dent [AK-si-dənt] n 1 event
happening by chance. 2 misfortune or
mishap, esp. causing injury. 3 nonessential
quality. **ac·ci·den'tal** adj
ac·claim [ə-KLAYM] vt 1 applaud, praise. ♦

——————————— THESAURUS ———————————

abyss n = **pit**, chasm, crevasse, fissure,
gorge, gulf, void
academic adj 1 = **scholarly**, bookish,
erudite, highbrow, learned, literary,
studious 2 = **hypothetical**, abstract,
conjectural, impractical, notional,
speculative, theoretical ♦ n 3 = **scholar**,
academician, don, fellow, lecturer, master,
professor, tutor
accede v 1 = **agree**, accept, acquiesce,
admit, assent, comply, concede, concur,
consent, endorse, grant 2 = **inherit**,
assume, attain, come to, enter upon,
succeed, succeed to (as heir)
accelerate v = **speed up**, advance,
expedite, further, hasten, hurry, quicken
acceleration n = **speeding up**, hastening,
hurrying, quickening, stepping up (inf)
accent n 1 = **pronunciation**, articulation,
brogue, enunciation, inflection, intonation,
modulation, tone 2 = **emphasis**, beat,
cadence, force, pitch, rhythm, stress,
timbre ♦ v 3 = **emphasize**, accentuate,
stress, underline, underscore
accentuate v = **emphasize**, accent, draw
attention to, foreground, highlight, stress,
underline, underscore
accept v 1 = **receive**, acquire, gain, get,
obtain, secure, take 2 = **agree to**, admit,
approve, believe, concur with, consent to,
cooperate with, recognize
acceptable adj = **satisfactory**, adequate,
admissible, all right, fair, moderate,
passable, tolerable
acceptance n 1 = **accepting**, acquiring,

gaining, getting, obtaining, receipt,
securing, taking 2 = **agreement**,
acknowledgment, acquiescence,
admission, adoption, approval, assent,
concurrence, consent, cooperation,
recognition
accepted adj = **agreed**, acknowledged,
approved, common, conventional,
customary, established, normal,
recognized, traditional
access n = **entrance**, admission,
admittance, approach, entry, passage,
path, road
accessibility n 1 = **handiness**, availability,
nearness, possibility, readiness 2 =
approachability, affability, cordiality,
friendliness, informality 3 = **openness**,
susceptibility
accessible adj 1 = **handy**, achievable, at
hand, attainable, available, near, nearby,
obtainable, reachable 2 = **approachable**,
affable, available, cordial, friendly, informal
3 = **open**, exposed, liable, susceptible,
vulnerable, wide-open
accessory n 1 = **addition**,
accompaniment, adjunct, adornment,
appendage, attachment, decoration, extra,
supplement, trimming 2 = **accomplice**,
abettor, assistant, associate (in crime),
colleague, confederate, helper, partner
accident n 1 = **misfortune**, calamity,
collision, crash, disaster, misadventure,
mishap 2 = **chance**, fate, fluke, fortuity,
fortune, hazard, luck
accidental adj = **unintentional**, casual,

n **2** applause. **ac·cla·ma·tion** n
ac·cli·mate [AK-klə-mayt] v **-mat·ed,
-mat·ing** acclimatize.
ac·cli·ma·tize [ə-KLĪ-mə-tīz] v **-tized,
-tiz·ing** accustom to new climate or
environment. **ac·cli·ma·ti·za'tion** n
ac·co·lade [AK-ə-layd] n **1** praise, public
approval. **2** award, honor. **3** token of
award of knighthood, etc.
ac·com·mo·date [ə-KOM-ə-dayt] vt
-dat·ed, -dat·ing 1 supply, esp. with board
and lodging. **2** oblige. **3** harmonize, adapt.
ac·com'mo·dat·ing adj obliging.
ac·com·mo·da'tions pl n lodgings.
ac·com·pa·ny [ə-KUM-pə-nee] vt **-nied,**

-ny·ing **1** go with. **2** supplement. **3** occur
with. **4** provide a musical accompaniment.
ac·com'pa·ni·ment n that which
accompanies, esp. in music, part that goes
with solos, etc. **ac·com'pa·nist** n
ac·com·plice [ə-KOM-plis] n one assisting
another in criminal deed.
ac·com·plish [ə-KOM-plish] vt **1** carry out.
2 finish. **ac·com'plished** adj **1** complete,
perfect. **2** proficient. **ac·com'plish·ment** n
1 completion. **2** personal ability.
ac·cord [ə-KORD] n **1** agreement,
harmony. ◆ v **2** (cause to) be in accord
with. ◆ vt **3** grant. **ac·cord'ing·ly** adv **1** as
the circumstances suggest. **2** therefore.

chance, fortuitous, haphazard,
inadvertent, incidental, random,
unexpected, unforeseen, unlooked-for,
unplanned
accidentally adv = **unintentionally**, by
accident, by chance, fortuitously,
haphazardly, inadvertently, incidentally,
randomly, unwittingly
acclaim v **1** = **praise**, applaud, approve,
celebrate, cheer, clap, commend, exalt,
hail, honor, salute ◆ n **2** = **praise**,
acclamation, applause, approval,
celebration, commendation, honor, kudos
acclamation n = **praise**, acclaim,
adulation, approval, ovation, plaudit,
tribute
acclimatization n = **adaptation**,
adjustment, habituation, inurement,
naturalization
acclimatize v = **adapt**, accommodate,
accustom, adjust, get used to, habituate,
inure, naturalize
accolade n = **praise**, acclaim, applause,
approval, commendation, compliment,
ovation, recognition, tribute
accommodate v **1** = **house**, cater for,
entertain, lodge, put up, shelter **2** = **help**,
aid, assist, oblige, serve **3** = **adapt**, adjust,
comply, conform, fit, harmonize, modify,
reconcile, settle
accommodating adj = **helpful**,
considerate, cooperative, friendly,
hospitable, kind, obliging, polite, unselfish,
willing
accommodation n = **housing**, board,
house, lodging(s), quarters, shelter
accompaniment n **1** = **supplement**,
accessory, companion, complement **2** =
backing music, backing

accompany v **1** = **go with**, attend,
chaperon, conduct, convoy, escort, hold
(someone's) hand **2** = **occur with**, belong
to, come with, follow, go together with,
supplement
accompanying adj = **additional**,
associated, attached, attendant,
complementary, related, supplementary
accomplice n = **helper**, abettor, accessory,
ally, assistant, associate, collaborator,
colleague, henchman, partner
accomplish v = **do**, achieve, attain, bring
about, carry out, complete, effect,
execute, finish, fulfill, manage, perform,
produce
accomplished adj = **skilled**, expert,
gifted, masterly, polished, practiced,
proficient, talented
accomplishment n **1** = **completion**,
bringing about, carrying out, conclusion,
execution, finishing, fulfillment,
performance **2** = **achievement**, act, coup,
deed, exploit, feat, stroke, triumph
accord n **1** = **agreement**, conformity,
correspondence, harmony, rapport,
sympathy, unison ◆ v **2** = **fit**, agree,
conform, correspond, harmonize, match,
suit, tally
accordingly adv **1** = **appropriately**,
correspondingly, fitly, properly, suitably
2 = **consequently**, as a result, ergo, hence,
in consequence, so, therefore, thus
according to adv **1** = **as stated by**, as
believed by, as maintained by, in the light
of, on the authority of, on the report of **2** =
in keeping with, after, after the manner
of, consistent with, in accordance with, in
compliance with, in line with, in the
manner of

ac·cor·di·on [ə-KOR-dee-ən] n portable musical instrument with keys, metal reeds and a bellows.

ac·cost [ə-KAWST] vt approach and speak to, often aggressively.

ac·count [ə-KOWNT] n 1 report, description. 2 importance, value. 3 statement of moneys received, paid, or owed. 4 person's money held in bank. 5 credit available to person at store, etc. ◆ vt 6 reckon. 7 judge. ◆ vi 8 give reason, answer (for). **ac·count'a·ble** adj responsible. **ac·count'an·cy** n keeping, preparation of business accounts, financial records, etc. **ac·count'ant** n one practicing accountancy. **ac·count'ing** n skill or practice of keeping and preparing business accounts. ◆ adj

ac·cred·it·ed [ə-KRED-i-tid] adj authorized, officially recognized.

ac·cre·tion [ə-KREE-shən] n 1 growth. 2 something added on.

ac·crue [ə-KROO] vi -crued, -cru·ing 1 be added. 2 result.

ac·cu·mu·late [ə-KYOO-myə-layt] v -lat·ed, -lat·ing 1 gather, become gathered in increasing quantity. 2 collect. **ac·cu·mu·la'tion** n

ac·cu·rate [AK-yər-it] adj exact, correct, without errors. **ac'cu·ra·cy** n

ac·curs·ed [ə-KUR-sid] adj 1 under a curse. 2 hateful, detestable.

ac·cuse [ə-KYOOZ] vt -cused, -cus·ing 1 charge with wrongdoing. 2 blame. **ac·cu·sa·tion** [ak-yə-ZAY-shən] n **ac·cu'sa·tive** n grammatical case indicating the direct object. **ac·cu'sa·to·ry** adj

ac·cus·tom [ə-KUS-təm] vt make used to, familiarize. **ac·cus'tomed** adj 1 usual. 2 used (to). 3 in the habit (of).

ace n 1 the one at dice, cards, dominoes. 2 Tennis winning serve untouched by

———————— THESAURUS ————————

accost v = approach, buttonhole, confront, greet, hail

account n 1 = description, explanation, narrative, report, statement, story, tale, version 2 Commerce = statement, balance, bill, books, charge, invoice, reckoning, register, score, tally 3 = importance, consequence, honor, note, significance, standing, value, worth ◆ v 4 = consider, count, estimate, judge, rate, reckon, regard, think, value

accountability n = responsibility, answerability, chargeability, culpability, liability

accountable adj = responsible, amenable, answerable, charged with, liable, obligated, obliged

accountant n = auditor, bean counter (inf), book-keeper

account for v = explain, answer for, clarify, clear up, elucidate, illuminate, justify, rationalize

accredited adj = authorized, appointed, certified, empowered, endorsed, guaranteed, licensed, official, recognized

accrue v = increase, accumulate, amass, arise, be added, build up, collect, enlarge, flow, follow, grow

accumulate v = collect, accrue, amass, build up, gather, hoard, increase, pile up, store

accumulation n = collection, build-up, gathering, heap, hoard, increase, mass,

pile, stack, stock, stockpile, store

accuracy n = exactness, accurateness, authenticity, carefulness, closeness, correctness, fidelity, precision, strictness, truthfulness, veracity

accurate adj = exact, authentic, close, correct, faithful, precise, scrupulous, strict, true, unerring

accurately adv = exactly, authentically, closely, correctly, faithfully, precisely, scrupulously, strictly, to the letter, truly, unerringly

accursed adj 1 = cursed, bewitched, condemned, damned, doomed, hopeless, ill-fated, ill-omened, jinxed, unfortunate, unlucky, wretched 2 = hateful, abominable, despicable, detestable, execrable, hellish, horrible, lousy (sl), scuzzy (sl)

accusation n = charge, allegation, complaint, denunciation, incrimination, indictment, recrimination

accuse v = charge, blame, censure, denounce, impeach, impute, incriminate, indict

accustom v = adapt, acclimatize, acquaint, discipline, exercise, familiarize, train

accustomed adj 1 = usual, common, conventional, customary, established, everyday, expected, habitual, normal, ordinary, regular, traditional 2 = used, acclimatized, acquainted, adapted, familiar, familiarized, given to, in the habit

opponent. **3** very successful fighter pilot. ◆
vt **aced, ac·ing 4** score an ace. **5** *Golf* make
hole in one. **6** *inf* make grade of A.

a·cer·bi·ty [ə-SUR-bi-tee] *n* **1** severity,
sharpness. **2** sour tasting. **a·cerb'** *adj*

ac·e·tate [AS-i-tayt] *n* **1** salt or ester of
acetic acid. **2** synthetic textile fiber.

a·ce·tic [ə-SEE-tik] *adj* derived from or
having the nature of vinegar.

ac·e·tone [AS-i-tohn] *n* colorless liquid
used as a solvent.

a·cet·y·lene [ə-SET-l-een] *n* colorless,
flammable gas used esp. in welding
metals.

ache [ayk] *n* **1** continuous pain. ◆ *vi* **ached,
ach·ing 2** to be in pain.

a·chieve [ə-CHEEV] *vt* **-chieved, -chiev·ing
1** accomplish, perform successfully. **2** gain.
a·chieve'ment *n* something accomplished.

ac·id [AS-id] *adj* **1** sharp, sour. ◆ *n* **2** sour
substance. **3** *Chem.* one of a class of
compounds that combine with bases
(alkalis, oxides, etc.) to form salts. **a·cid'ic**
adj **a·cid'i·fy** *vt* **-fied, -fy·ing a·cid'i·ty** *n*
a·cid'u·lous *adj* caustic. **acid rain** rain

acidified by atmospheric pollution. **acid
test** conclusive test of value.

ac·knowl·edge [ak-NOL-ij] *vt* **-edged,
-edg·ing 1** admit, own to knowing,
recognize. **2** say one has received.
ac·knowl'edg·ment *n*

ac·me [AK-mee] *n* highest point.

ac·ne [AK-nee] *n* pimply skin disease.

ac·o·lyte [AK-ə-lit] *n* follower or attendant,
esp. of priest.

a·cous·tic [ə-KOO-stik] *adj* pert. to sound
and to hearing. **a·cous'tics** *n* **1** science of
sounds. ◆ *pl* **2** features of room or building
as regards sounds heard within it.

ac·quaint [ə-KWAYNT] *vt* **1** make familiar,
inform. **ac·quaint'ance** *n* **1** person known.
2 personal knowledge.

ac·qui·esce [ak-wee-ES] *vi* **-esced, -esc·ing**
agree, consent without complaint.
ac·qui·es'cence *n*

ac·quire [ə-KWIR] *vt* **-quired, -quir·ing**
gain, get. **ac·qui·si·tion** [ak-wə-ZISH-ən] *n*
1 act of getting. **2** material gain.
ac·quis'i·tive *adj* desirous of gaining.

ac·quit [ə-KWIT] *vt* **-quit·ted, -quit·ting 1**

of, trained

ace *n* **1** *Cards, dice, etc.* = **one**, single point
2 *Inf* = **expert**, champion, master, star,
virtuoso, wizard (*inf*)

ache *v* **1** = **hurt**, pain, pound, smart, suffer,
throb, twinge ◆ *n* **2** = **pain**, hurt, pang,
pounding, soreness, suffering, throbbing

achieve *v* = **attain**, accomplish, acquire,
bring about, carry out, complete, do,
execute, fulfill, gain, get, obtain, perform

achievement *n* = **accomplishment**, act,
deed, effort, exploit, feat, feather in one's
cap, stroke

acid *adj* **1** = **sour**, acerbic, acrid, pungent,
tart, vinegary **2** = **sharp**, biting, bitter,
caustic, cutting, harsh, trenchant, vitriolic

acidity *n* **1** = **sourness**, acerbity, pungency,
tartness **2** = **sharpness**, bitterness,
harshness

acknowledge *v* **1** = **accept**, admit, allow,
concede, confess, declare, grant, own,
profess, recognize, yield **2** = **greet**,
address, hail, notice, recognize, salute **3** =
reply to, answer, notice, react to,
recognize, respond to, return

acknowledged *adj* = **accepted**,
accredited, approved, confessed, declared,
professed, recognized, returned

acknowledgment *n* **1** = **acceptance**,

admission, allowing, confession,
declaration, profession, realization,
yielding **2** = **greeting**, addressing, hail,
hailing, notice, recognition, salutation,
salute **3** = **appreciation**, answer, credit,
gratitude, kudos, reaction, recognition,
reply, response, return, thanks

acquaint *v* = **tell**, disclose, divulge,
enlighten, familiarize, inform, let
(someone) know, notify, reveal

acquaintance *n* **1** = **associate**, colleague,
contact **2** = **knowledge**, awareness,
experience, familiarity, fellowship,
relationship, understanding

acquainted with *adj* = **familiar with**, alive
to, apprised of, *au fait* with aware of,
conscious of, experienced in, informed of,
knowledgeable about, versed in

acquiesce *v* = **agree**, accede, accept,
allow, approve, assent, comply, concur,
conform, consent, give in, go along with,
submit, yield

acquiescence *n* = **agreement**,
acceptance, approval, assent, compliance,
conformity, consent, giving in, obedience,
submission, yielding

acquire *v* = **get**, amass, attain, buy, collect,
earn, gain, gather, obtain, receive, secure,
win

declare innocent. **2** settle, discharge, as a debt. **3** behave (oneself). **ac·quit'tal** n declaration of innocence in court.

a·cre [AY-kər] n **1** measure of land, 43,560 square feet. ♦ pl **2** lands, estates. **3** inf large area or plenty of. **a'cre·age** n the extent of land in acres.

ac·rid [AK-rid] adj **1** pungent, sharp. **2** irritating.

ac·ri·mo·ny [AK-rə-moh-nee] n bitterness of feeling or language. **ac·ri·mo'ni·ous** adj

ac·ro·bat [AK-rə-bat] n one skilled in gymnastic feats, esp. as entertainer in circus, etc. **ac·ro·bat'ic** adj **ac·ro·bat'ics** pl n activities requiring agility.

ac·ro·nym [AK-rə-nim] n word formed from initial letters of other words, such as NATO.

a·crop·o·lis [ə-KROP-ə-lis] n citadel, esp. in ancient Greece.

a·cross [ə-KRAWS] adv, prep **1** crosswise. **2** from side to side. **3** on or to the other side. **4 get, put it across** explain, make (something) understood.

a·cros·tic [ə-KRAW-stik] n word puzzle (or verse) in which the first, middle, or last letters of each line spell a word or words.

a·cryl·ic [ə-KRIL-ik] n variety of synthetic materials, esp. paint and textiles.

act [akt] n **1** thing done, deed. **2** doing. **3** law or decree. **4** section of a play. ♦ v **5** perform, as in a play. ♦ vi **6** exert force, work, as mechanism. **7** behave. **act'ing** n **1** performance of a part. ♦ adj **2** temporarily performing the duties of. **ac'tion** n **1** operation. **2** deed. **3** gesture. **4** expenditure of energy. **5** battle. **6** lawsuit. **ac'tion·a·ble** adj subject to lawsuit. **ac'ti·vate** vt **-vat·ed, -vat·ing 1** to make active. **2** make radioactive. **3** make chemically active. **ac·ti·va'tion** n **ac'tive** adj **1** moving, working. **2** brisk, energetic. **ac'ti·vist** n one who takes (direct) action to achieve political or social ends. **ac·tiv'i·ty** n **ac·tor, ac·tress** n one who acts in a play, film, etc.

ac·tin·i·um [ak-TIN-ee-əm] n radioactive element occurring as decay product of uranium.

ac·tu·al [AK-choo-əl] adj **1** existing in the

THESAURUS

acquisition n **1** = **possession**, buy, gain, prize, property, purchase **2** = **acquiring**, attainment, gaining, procurement

acquisitive adj = **greedy**, avaricious, avid, covetous, grabbing, grasping, predatory, rapacious

acquit v **1** = **clear**, discharge, free, liberate, release, vindicate **2** = **behave**, bear, comport, conduct, perform

acquittal n = **clearance**, absolution, deliverance, discharge, exoneration, liberation, release, relief, vindication

acrid adj = **pungent**, bitter, caustic, harsh, sharp, vitriolic

acrimonious adj = **bitter**, caustic, irascible, petulant, rancorous, spiteful, splenetic, testy

acrimony n = **bitterness**, harshness, ill will, irascibility, rancor, virulence

act n **1** = **deed**, accomplishment, achievement, action, exploit, feat, performance, undertaking **2** = **law**, bill, decree, edict, enactment, measure, ordinance, resolution, statute **3** = **performance**, routine, show, sketch, turn **4** = **pretense**, affectation, attitude, front, performance, pose, posture, show ♦ v **5** = **do**, carry out, enact, execute, function, operate, perform, take effect, work **6** =

perform, act out, impersonate, mimic, play, play or take the part of, portray, represent

act for v = **stand in for**, cover for, deputize for, fill in for, replace, represent, substitute for, take the place of

acting n **1** = **performance**, characterization, impersonation, performing, playing, portrayal, stagecraft, theater ♦ adj **2** = **temporary**, interim, pro tem, provisional, substitute, surrogate

action n **1** = **deed**, accomplishment, achievement, act, exploit, feat, performance **2** = **lawsuit**, case, litigation, proceeding, prosecution, suit **3** = **energy**, activity, force, liveliness, spirit, vigor, vim, vitality **4** = **movement**, activity, functioning, motion, operation, process, working **5** = **battle**, clash, combat, conflict, contest, encounter, engagement, fight, skirmish, sortie

activate v = **start**, arouse, energize, galvanize, initiate, mobilize, move, rouse, set in motion, stir

active adj **1** = **busy**, bustling, hard-working, involved, occupied, on the go (inf), on the move, strenuous **2** = **energetic**, alert, animated, industrious, lively, quick, sprightly, spry, vigorous **3** = **in operation**, present. 2 real. **ac·tu·al'i·ty** n **ac'tu·al·ly** adv really, indeed.

ac·tu·ar·y [AK-choo-ar-ee] n, pl **-ar·ies** statistician who calculates insurance risks, premiums, etc. **ac·tu·ar'i·al** adj

ac·tu·ate [AK-choo-ayt] vt **-at·ed, -at·ing** 1 activate. 2 motivate. **ac'tu·a·tor** n mechanism for controlling or moving something indirectly.

a·cu·i·ty [ə-KYOO-i-tee] n keenness, esp. in vision or thought.

a·cu·men [ə-KYOO-mən] n sharpness of wit, perception, penetration.

ac·u·punc·ture [AK-yə-pungk-chər] n medical treatment involving insertion of needles at various points on the body.

a·cute [ə-KYOOT] adj 1 keen, shrewd. 2 sharp. 3 severe. 4 of angle, less than 90°. ◆ n 5 accent (´) over a letter to indicate the quality or length of its sound, as in café. **a·cute'ness** n

ad·age [AD-ij] n much used wise saying, proverb.

a·da·gio [ə-DAH-joh] adv, n, pl **-gios** Mus. leisurely, slow (passage).

ad·a·mant [AD-ə-mənt] adj very hard, unyielding. **ad·a·man'tine** [-MAN-teen] adj

Adam's apple [AD-əmz] projecting part at front of the throat, the thyroid cartilage.

a·dapt [ə-DAPT] vt 1 alter for new use. 2 fit, modify. 3 change. **a·dapt'a·ble** adj **ad·ap·ta'tion** n **a·dapt'er, -tor** n device for connecting several electrical appliances to single socket.

add v 1 join. 2 increase by. 3 say further. **ad·di·tion** [ə-DISH-ən] n **ad·di'tion·al** adj **ad'di·tive** n something added, esp. to food.

ad·den·dum [ə-DEN-dəm] n, pl **-da** [-də] thing to be added.

ad·der [AD-ər] n small poisonous snake.

ad·dict [AD-ikt] n one who has become dependent on something, esp. drugs. **ad·dict'ed** adj **ad·dic'tion** n **ad·dic'tive** adj causing addiction.

ad·dle [AD-l] v **-dled, -dling** make or

acting, at work, effectual, in action, in force, operative, working

activist n = **militant**, organizer, partisan

activity n 1 = **action**, animation, bustle, exercise, exertion, hustle, labor, motion, movement 2 = **pursuit**, hobby, interest, pastime, project, scheme

actor n = **performer**, actress, player, Thespian

actress n = **performer**, actor, leading lady, player, starlet, Thespian

actual adj = **definite**, concrete, factual, physical, positive, real, substantial, tangible

actually adv = **really**, as a matter of fact, indeed, in fact, in point of fact, in reality, in truth, literally, truly

act up v Inf = **make a fuss**, have a fit, horse around, misbehave, raise Cain, raise hell

acumen n = **judgment**, astuteness, cleverness, ingenuity, insight, intelligence, perspicacity, shrewdness

acute adj 1 = **serious**, critical, crucial, dangerous, grave, important, severe, urgent 2 = **sharp**, excruciating, fierce, intense, piercing, powerful, severe, shooting, violent 3 = **perceptive**, astute, clever, insightful, keen, observant, sensitive, sharp, smart

acuteness n 1 = **seriousness**, gravity, importance, severity, urgency 2 = **perceptiveness**, astuteness, cleverness,

discrimination, insight, perspicacity, sharpness

adamant adj = **determined**, firm, fixed, obdurate, resolute, stubborn, unbending, uncompromising

adapt v = **adjust**, acclimatize, accommodate, alter, change, conform, convert, modify, remodel, tailor

adaptability n = **flexibility**, changeability, resilience, versatility

adaptable adj = **flexible**, adjustable, changeable, compliant, easy-going, plastic, pliant, resilient, versatile

adaptation n 1 = **acclimatization**, familiarization, naturalization 2 = **conversion**, adjustment, alteration, change, modification, transformation, variation, version

add v 1 = **count up**, add up, compute, reckon, total, tot up 2 = **include**, adjoin, affix, append, attach, augment, supplement

addendum n = **addition**, appendage, appendix, attachment, extension, extra, postscript, supplement

addict n 1 = **junkie**, fiend (inf), freak (inf) 2 = **fan**, adherent, buff (inf), devotee, enthusiast, follower, nut (sl)

addicted adj = **hooked** (sl), absorbed, accustomed, dedicated, dependent, devoted, habituated become rotten, muddled.

ad·dress [ə-DRES, AD-res] *n* **1** direction on letter. **2** place where one lives. **3** *Computers* number giving the location of a piece of stored information. **4** speech. ◆ *vt* **5** mark destination, as on envelope. **6** speak to. **7** direct. **8** dispatch. **address ball** *Golf* adjust club before striking ball. **ad·dress·ee'** *n* person addressed.

ad·duce [ə-DOOS] *vt* **-duced, -duc·ing 1** offer as proof. **2** cite. **ad·duc'i·ble** *adj*

ad·e·noids [AD-n-oidz] *pl n* tissue at back of nose and throat, sometimes obstructing breathing.

a·dept [ə-DEPT] *adj* **1** skilled. ◆ *n* [AD-ept] **2** expert.

ad·e·quate [AD-i-kwit] *adj* **1** sufficient, enough, suitable. **2** not outstanding. **ad'e·qua·cy** *n*

ad·here [ad-HEER] *vi* **-hered, -her·ing 1** stick to. **2** be firm in opinion, etc. **ad·her'ent** *n, adj* **ad·he'sion** [-HEE-zhən] *n* **ad·he'sive** [-siv] *adj, n*

ad hoc [ad-HOK] *adj, adv* **1** for a particular occasion only. **2** improvised.

a·dieu [ə-DYOO] *interj* farewell. ◆ *n, pl* **a·dieus, a·dieux** [ə-DYOOZ] act of taking leave.

ad in·fi·ni·tum [in-fə-NĪ-təm] *Lat* endlessly.

ad·i·pose [AD-ə-pohs] *adj* of fat, fatty.

ad·ja·cent [ə-JAY-sənt] *adj* lying near, next (to).

ad·jec·tive [AJ-ik-tiv] *n* word that modifies or limits a noun. **ad·jec·ti'val** [-TĪ-vəl] *adj* of adjective.

ad·join [ə-JOIN] *v* **1** be next to. **2** join. **ad·join'ing** *adj* next to, near.

ad·journ [ə-JURN] *v* **1** postpone temporarily, as meeting. **2** *inf* move elsewhere.

ad·judge [ə-JUJ] *vt* **-judged, -judg·ing 1** declare. **2** decide. **3** award.

ad·ju·di·cate [ə-JOO-di-kayt] *v* **-cat·ed, -cat·ing 1** try, judge. **2** sit in judgment. **ad·ju·di·ca'tion** *n*

──── THESAURUS ────

addiction *n* = **dependence**, craving, enslavement, habit, obsession

addition *n* **1** = **inclusion**, adding, amplification, attachment, augmentation, enlargement, extension, increasing **2** = **extra**, addendum, additive, appendage, appendix, extension, gain, increase, increment, supplement **3** = **counting up**, adding up, computation, totalling, totting up **4 in addition (to)** = **as well (as)**, additionally, also, besides, into the bargain, moreover, over and above, to boot, too

additional *adj* = **extra**, added, fresh, further, new, other, spare, supplementary

address *n* **1** = **location**, abode, dwelling, home, house, residence, situation, whereabouts **2** = **speech**, discourse, dissertation, lecture, oration, sermon, talk ◆ *v* **3** = **speak to**, approach, greet, hail, talk to **4 address (oneself) to** = **concentrate on**, apply (oneself) to, attend to, devote (oneself) to, engage in, focus on, take care of

add up *v* = **count up**, add, compute, count, reckon, total, tot up

adept *adj* **1** = **skillful**, able, accomplished, adroit, expert, practiced, proficient, skilled, versed ◆ *n* **2** = **expert**, genius, hotshot (*inf*), master

adequacy *n* = **sufficiency**, capability, competence, fairness, suitability, tolerability

adequate *adj* = **enough**, competent, fair, satisfactory, sufficient, tolerable, up to scratch (*inf*)

adhere *v* = **stick**, attach, cleave, cling, fasten, fix, glue, hold fast, paste

adherent *n* = **supporter**, admirer, devotee, disciple, fan, follower, upholder

adhesive *adj* **1** = **sticky**, clinging, cohesive, gluey, glutinous, tenacious ◆ *n* **2** = **glue**, cement, gum, paste

adieu *n* = **good-bye**, farewell, leave-taking, parting, valediction

adjacent *adj* = **next**, adjoining, beside, bordering, cheek by jowl, close, near, neighboring, next door, touching

adjoin *v* = **connect**, border, join, link, touch

adjoining *adj* = **connecting**, abutting, adjacent, bordering, neighboring, next door, touching

adjourn *v* = **postpone**, defer, delay, discontinue, interrupt, put off, suspend

adjournment *n* = **postponement**, delay, discontinuation, interruption, putting off, recess, suspension

adjudicate *v* = **judge**, adjudge, arbitrate, decide, determine, mediate, referee, settle, umpire

adjudication *n* = **judgment**, arbitration, conclusion, decision, finding,

ad·junct [AJ-ungkt] *adj* **1** joined, added. ◆ *n* **2** person or thing added or subordinate.

ad·jure [ə-JOOR] *vt* **-jured, -jur·ing** beg, earnestly entreat. **ad·ju·ra·tion** [aj-ə-RAY-shən] *n*

ad·just [ə-JUST] *vt* **1** make suitable, adapt. **2** alter slightly, regulate. ◆ *vi* **3** adapt or conform to new conditions, etc. **ad·just'a·ble** *adj*

ad·ju·tant [AJ-ə-tənt] *n* military officer who assists superiors. **ad'ju·tan·cy** *n* office, rank of adjutant.

ad-lib *v* **-libbed, -lib·bing** improvise and speak spontaneously. **ad lib** *n* such speech, etc.

ad·min·is·ter [ad-MIN-ə-stər] *vt* **1** manage, look after. **2** dispense, as justice, etc. **3** apply. **ad·min·is·tra'tion** *n* **ad·min'is·tra·tive** *adj*

ad·mi·ral [AD-mər-əl] *n* naval officer of highest sea rank. **ad'mi·ral·ty** *n Law* court having jurisdiction over maritime matters.

ad·mire [ad-MĪR] *vt* **-mired, -mir·ing 1** look on with wonder and pleasure. **2** respect highly. **ad'mi·ra·ble** *adj* **ad'mi·ra·bly** *adv*

ad·mi·ra·tion *n* **ad·mir'er** *n* **ad·mir'ing·ly** *adv*

ad·mit [ad-MIT] *vt* **-mit·ted, -mit·ting 1** confess. **2** accept as true. **3** allow. **4** let in. **ad·mis'si·ble** *adj* **ad·mis'sion** *n* **1** permission to enter. **2** entrance fee. **3** confession. **ad·mit'tance** *n* permission to enter. **ad·mit'ted·ly** *adv*

ad·mix·ture [ad-MIKS-chər] *n* **1** mixture. **2** ingredient.

ad·mon·ish [ad-MON-ish] *vt* **1** reprove. **2** advise. **3** warn. **4** exhort. **ad·mo·ni'tion** [-mə-NISH-ən] *n* **ad·mon'i·to·ry** *adj*

ad nau·se·am [NAW-zee-əm] *Lat* to a boring or disgusting extent.

a·do [ə-DOO] *n* fuss.

a·do·be [ə-DOH-bee] *n* sun-dried brick.

ad·o·les·cence [ad-l-ES-əns] *n* period of life just before maturity. **ad·o·les'cent** *n* a youth. ◆ *adj*

a·dopt [ə-DOPT] *vt* **1** take into relationship, esp. as one's child. **2** take up, as principle, resolution. **a·dop'tion** *n* **a·dop'tive** *adj* that which adopts or is adopted.

a·dore [ə-DOR] *v* **-dored, -dor·ing 1** love

—————————— THESAURUS ——————————

pronouncement, ruling, settlement, verdict

adjust *v* = **alter**, accustom, adapt, make conform, modify

adjustable *adj* = **alterable**, adaptable, flexible, malleable, modifiable, movable

adjustment *n* **1** = **alteration**, adaptation, modification, redress, regulation, tuning **2** = **acclimatization**, orientation, settling in

ad-lib *v* = **improvise**, busk, extemporize, make up, speak off the cuff, wing it (*inf*)

administer *v* **1** = **manage**, conduct, control, direct, govern, handle, oversee, run, supervise **2** = **give**, apply, dispense, impose, mete out, perform, provide

administration *n* = **management**, application, conduct, control, direction, government, running, supervision

administrative *adj* = **managerial**, directorial, executive, governmental, organizational, regulatory, supervisory

administrator *n* = **manager**, bureaucrat, executive, official, organizer, supervisor

admirable *adj* = **excellent**, commendable, exquisite, fine, laudable, praiseworthy, wonderful, worthy

admiration *n* = **regard**, amazement, appreciation, approval, esteem, praise, respect, wonder

admire *v* **1** = **respect**, appreciate, approve, esteem, look up to, praise, prize, think highly of, value **2** = **marvel at**, appreciate, delight in, take pleasure in, wonder at

admirer *n* **1** = **suitor**, beau, boyfriend, lover, sweetheart, wooer **2** = **fan**, devotee, disciple, enthusiast, follower, partisan, supporter

admissible *adj* = **permissible**, acceptable, allowable, passable, tolerable

admission *n* **1** = **entrance**, acceptance, access, admittance, entrée, entry, initiation, introduction **2** = **confession**, acknowledgment, allowance, declaration, disclosure, divulgence, revelation

admit *v* **1** = **confess**, acknowledge, declare, disclose, divulge, fess up (*inf*), own, reveal **2** = **allow**, agree, grant, let, permit, recognize **3** = **let in**, accept, allow, give access, initiate, introduce, receive, take in

admonish *v* = **reprimand**, berate, chide, rebuke, scold, slap on the wrist, tell off (*inf*)

adolescence *n* **1** = **youth**, boyhood, girlhood, minority, teens **2** = **youthfulness**, childishness, immaturity

adolescent *adj* **1** = **young**, boyish, girlish, immature, juvenile, puerile, teenage, youthful ◆ *n* **2** = **youth**, juvenile, minor, teenager, youngster

intensely. **2** worship. **a·dor·a·ble** *adj*
ad·o·ra'tion *n*

a·dorn [ə-DORN] *vt* beautify, embellish,
deck. **a·dorn'ment** *n* ornament,
decoration.

ad·re·nal [ə-DREEN-l] *adj* near the kidney.
adrenal glands glands covering the top of
the kidneys. **a·dren·a·line** [-DREN-l-in] *n* **1**
hormone secreted by adrenal glands. **2** this
substance used as drug.

a·drift [ə-DRIFT] *adj, adv* **1** drifting free. **2** *inf*
detached. **3** *inf* off course.

a·droit [ə-DROIT] *adj* **1** skillful, expert. **2**
clever. **a·droit'ness** *n* dexterity.

ad·sorb [ad-SORB] *v* (of gas, vapor)
condense and form thin film on surface.
ad·sorb'ent *adj, n* **ad·sorp'tion** *n*

ad·u·la·tion [aj-ə-LAY-shən] *n* flattery.
ad'u·late *vt* **-lat·ed, -lat·ing** flatter.
ad'u·la·to·ry *adj*

a·dult [ə-DULT] *adj* **1** grown-up, mature. ◆
n **2** grown-up person. **3** full-grown animal
or plant.

a·dul·ter·ate [ə-DUL-tə-rayt] *vt* **-at·ed,
-at·ing** make impure by addition.
a·dul'ter·ant *n*

a·dul·ter·y [ə-DUL-tə-ree] *n* sexual
unfaithfulness of a husband or wife.
a·dul'ter·er, a·dul'ter·ess *n* **a·dul'ter·ous**
adj

ad·vance [ad-VANS] *v* **-vanced, -vanc·ing**
◆ *vt* **1** bring forward. **2** suggest. **3**
encourage. **4** pay beforehand. **5** *Auto.* to
time spark earlier in engine cycle. ◆ *vi* **6** go
forward. **7** improve in position or value. ◆
n **8** movement forward. **9** improvement.
10 a loan. ◆ *pl* **11** personal approach(es) to
gain favor, etc. ◆ *adj* **12** ahead in time or
position. **ad·vanced'** *adj* **1** at a late stage. **2**
not elementary. **3** ahead of the times.
ad·vance'ment *n* promotion.

ad·van·tage [ad-VAN-tij] *n* **1** superiority. **2**
more favorable position or state. **3** benefit.
ad·van·ta'geous [-vən-TAY-jəs] *adj*

ad·vent [AD-vent] *n* **1** a coming, arrival. **2**
(**A-**) the four weeks before Christmas. **the**

THESAURUS

adopt *v* **1** = **foster**, take in **2** = **choose**,
assume, espouse, follow, maintain, take up

adoption *n* **1** = **fostering**, adopting, taking
in **2** = **choice**, appropriation, assumption,
embracing, endorsement, espousal,
selection, taking up

adorable *adj* = **lovable**, appealing,
attractive, charming, cute, dear, delightful,
fetching, pleasing

adore *v* = **love**, admire, cherish, dote on,
esteem, exalt, glorify, honor, idolize, put
on a pedestal (*inf*), revere, worship

adoring *adj* = **loving**, admiring,
affectionate, devoted, doting, fond

adorn *v* = **decorate**, array, embellish,
festoon

adornment *n* = **decoration**, accessory,
embellishment, festoon, frill, frippery,
ornament, supplement, trimming

adrift *adj* **1** = **drifting**, afloat, unanchored,
unmoored **2** = **aimless**, directionless,
goalless, purposeless ◆ *adv* **3** = **wrong**,
amiss, astray, off course

adroit *adj* = **skillful**, adept, clever, deft,
dexterous, expert, masterful, neat,
proficient, skilled

adulation *n* = **worship**, fawning, fulsome
praise, servile flattery, sycophancy

adult *n* **1** = **grown-up**, grown *or* grown-up
person (man *or* woman), person of mature
age ◆ *adj* **2** = **fully grown**, full grown, fully

developed, grown-up, mature, of age, ripe

advance *v* **1** = **progress**, come forward, go
on, hasten, make inroads, proceed, speed
2 = **benefit**, further, improve, prosper **3** =
suggest, offer, present, proffer, put
forward, submit **4** = **lend**, pay beforehand,
supply on credit ◆ *n* **5** = **progress**,
advancement, development, forward
movement, headway, inroads, onward
movement **6** = **improvement**,
breakthrough, gain, growth, progress,
promotion, step **7** = **loan**, credit, deposit,
down payment, prepayment, retainer
8 advances = **overtures**, approach,
approaches, moves, proposals, proposition
◆ *adj* **9** = **prior**, beforehand, early, forward,
in front **10 in advance** = **beforehand**,
ahead, earlier, previously

advanced *adj* = **foremost**, ahead,
avant-garde, forward, higher, leading,
precocious, progressive

advancement *n* = **promotion**,
betterment, gain, improvement,
preferment, progress, rise

advantage *n* = **benefit**, ascendancy,
dominance, good, help, lead, precedence,
profit, superiority, sway

advantageous *adj* **1** = **beneficial**,
convenient, expedient, helpful, of service,
profitable, useful, valuable, worthwhile **2** =
superior, dominant, dominating,

Advent the coming of Christ. **Ad'vent·ist** n one of number of Christian sects believing in imminent return of Christ.

ad·ven·ti·tious [ad-vən-TISH-əs] adj 1 added. 2 accidental, casual.

ad·ven·ture [ad-VEN-chər] n 1 risk. 2 bold exploit. 3 remarkable happening. 4 enterprise. 5 commercial speculation **ad·ven·tur·er, ad·ven·tur·ess** n one who seeks adventures. 1 one who lives on his wits. **ad·ven'tur·ous** adj

ad·verb [AD-vurb] n word used with verb, adjective, or other adverb to modify meaning. **ad·ver'bi·al** adj

ad·verse [ad-VURS] adj 1 opposed to. 2 hostile. 3 unfavorable, bringing harm. **ad'ver·sar·y** n, pl **-sar·ies** enemy. **ad·verse'ly** adv **ad·ver'si·ty** n distress, misfortune.

ad·ver·tise [AD-vər-tīz] v **-tised, -tis·ing** ◆ vt 1 publicize. 2 make known. 3 give notice of, esp. in newspapers, etc. ◆ vi make public request (for). **ad·ver·tise'ment** n **ad'ver·tis·ing** adj, n

ad·vice [ad-VĪS] n 1 opinion given. 2 counsel. 3 information. 4 (formal) notification.

ad·vise [ad-VĪZ] vt **-vised, -vis·ing** 1 offer advice. 2 recommend a line of conduct. 3 give notice (of). **ad·vis'a·ble** adj expedient.

ad·vised' adj considered, deliberate, e.g. well-advised. **ad·vis'ed·ly** [-zid-lee] adv **ad·vi'ser** n **ad·vi'so·ry** adj

ad·vo·cate [AD-və-kit] n 1 one who pleads the cause of another, esp. in court of law. 2 attorney. ◆ vt [-kayt] 3 uphold, recommend. **ad'vo·ca·cy** [-kə-see] n

ae·gis [EE-jis] n sponsorship, protection (orig. shield of Zeus).

aer·ate [AIR-ayt] vt **-at·ed, -at·ing** 1 charge liquid with gas, as effervescent drink. 2 expose to air. **aer·a'tion** n **aer'a·tor** n apparatus for charging liquid with gas.

aer·i·al [AIR-ee-əl] adj 1 of the air. 2 operating in or from the air. 3 pertaining to aircraft. ◆ n 4 part of radio, etc. receiving or sending radio waves.

aer·ie, aer·y n see EYRIE.

aero- comb. form air or aircraft, e.g. aerodynamics.

aer·o·bat·ics [air-ə-BAT-iks] pl n stunt flying.

aer·o·bics [air-OH-biks] n exercise system designed to increase the amount of oxygen in the blood.

aer·o·dy·nam·ics [air-oh-dī-NAM-iks] n study of air flow, esp. around moving solid bodies.

aer·o·naut [AIR-ə-nawt] n pilot or navigator of lighter-than-air craft.

——— THESAURUS ———

favorable, win-win (inf)

adventure n = **escapade**, enterprise, experience, exploit, incident, occurrence, undertaking, venture

adventurer n 1 = **mercenary**, charlatan, fortune-hunter, gambler, opportunist, rogue, speculator 2 = **hero**, daredevil, heroine, knight-errant, traveler, voyager

adventurous adj = **daring**, bold, daredevil, enterprising, intrepid, reckless

adversary n = **opponent**, antagonist, competitor, contestant, enemy, foe, rival

adverse adj = **unfavorable**, contrary, detrimental, hostile, inopportune, negative, opposing

adversity n = **hardship**, affliction, bad luck, disaster, distress, hard times, misfortune, reverse, trouble

advertise v = **publicize**, announce, inform, make known, notify, plug (inf), promote, tout

advertisement n = **notice**, ad (inf), announcement, blurb, circular, commercial, plug (inf), poster

advice n = **guidance**, counsel, help, opinion, recommendation, suggestion

advisability n = **wisdom**, appropriateness, aptness, desirability, expediency, fitness, propriety, prudence, suitability

advisable adj = **wise**, appropriate, desirable, expedient, fitting, politic, prudent, recommended, seemly, sensible

advise v 1 = **recommend**, admonish, caution, commend, counsel, prescribe, suggest, urge 2 = **notify**, acquaint, apprise, inform, make known, report, tell, warn

adviser n = **guide**, aide, confidant or (fem.) confidante, consultant, counselor, helper, mentor, right-hand man

advisory adj = **advising**, consultative, counseling, helping, recommending

advocate v 1 = **recommend**, advise, argue for, campaign for, champion, commend, encourage, promote, propose, support, uphold ◆ n 2 = **supporter**, campaigner, champion, counselor, defender, promoter, proponent, spokesman, upholder 3 Law = **lawyer**, attorney, barrister, counsel

aer·o·nau·tics *n* science of air navigation and flying in general. **aer·o·nau·ti·cal** *adj*

aer·o·sol [AIR-ə-sawl] *n* (substance dispensed as fine spray from) pressurized can.

aer·o·space [AIR-oh-spays] *n* Earth's atmosphere and space beyond. ◆ *adj*

aes·thet·ic [es-THET-ik] *adj* relating to principles of beauty, taste and art. **aes·thet·ics** *n* study of art, taste, etc. **aes·thete** [ES-theet] *n* one who affects extravagant love of art.

a·far [ə-FAHR] *adv* from, at, or to, a great distance.

af·fa·ble [AF-ə-bəl] *adj* easy to speak to, polite and friendly. **af·fa·bil'i·ty** *n*

af·fair [ə-FAIR] *n* 1 thing done or attended to. 2 business. 3 happening. 4 sexual liaison. ◆ *pl* 5 personal or business interests. 6 matters of public interest.

af·fect [ə-FEKT] *vt* 1 act on, influence. 2 move feelings. 3 make show of, make pretense. 4 assume. 5 have liking for. **affect** [AF-ekt] *n Psychology* emotion, feeling, desire. **af·fec·ta'tion** *n* show, pretense. **af·fect'ed** *adj* 1 making a

pretense. 2 moved. 3 acted upon. **af·fect'ing** *adj* moving the feelings. **af·fec'tion** *n* fondness, love. **af·fec'tion·ate** *adj*

af·fi·da·vit [af-i-DAY-vit] *n* written statement under oath.

af·fil·i·ate [ə-FIL-ee-ayt] *vt* -**at·ed, -at·ing 1** connect, attach, as society to federation, etc. 2 adopt. ◆ *n* [-ee-it] 3 affiliated organization.

af·fin·i·ty [ə-FIN-i-tee] *n, pl* -**ties 1** natural liking. 2 resemblance. 3 relationship by marriage. 4 chemical attraction.

af·firm [ə-FURM] *v* 1 assert positively, declare. 2 maintain statement. 3 make solemn declaration. **af·fir·ma'tion** *n* **af·firm'a·tive** *adj* 1 asserting. ◆ *n* 2 word of assent.

af·fix [ə-FIKS] *vt* 1 fasten (to). 2 attach, append. ◆ *n* [AF-fiks] 3 addition, esp. to word, as suffix, prefix.

af·flict [ə-FLIKT] *vt* 1 give pain or grief to, distress. 2 trouble, vex. **af·flic'tion** *n*

af·flu·ent [AF-loo-ənt] *adj* 1 wealthy. 2 abundant. ◆ *n* 3 tributary stream. **af'flu·ence** *n* wealth, abundance.

THESAURUS

affable *adj* = **friendly**, amiable, amicable, approachable, congenial, cordial, courteous, genial, pleasant, sociable, urbane

affair *n* 1 = **event**, activity, business, episode, happening, incident, matter, occurrence 2 = **relationship**, amour, intrigue, liaison, romance

affect[1] *v* 1 = **influence**, act on, alter, bear upon, change, concern, impinge upon, relate to 2 = **move**, disturb, overcome, perturb, stir, touch, upset

affect[2] *v* = **put on**, adopt, aspire to, assume, contrive, feign, imitate, pretend, simulate

affectation *n* = **pretense**, act, artificiality, assumed manners, façade, insincerity, pose, pretentiousness, show

affected *adj* = **pretended**, artificial, contrived, feigned, insincere, mannered, phoney *or* phony (*inf*), put-on, unnatural

affecting *adj* = **moving**, pathetic, pitiful, poignant, sad, touching

affection *n* = **fondness**, attachment, care, feeling, goodwill, kindness, liking, love, tenderness, warmth

affectionate *adj* = **fond**, attached, caring, devoted, doting, friendly, kind, loving,

tender, warm-hearted

affiliate *v* = **join**, ally, amalgamate, associate, band together, combine, incorporate, link, unite

affinity *n* 1 = **attraction**, fondness, inclination, leaning, liking, partiality, rapport, sympathy 2 = **similarity**, analogy, closeness, connection, correspondence, kinship, likeness, relationship, resemblance

affirm *v* = **declare**, assert, certify, confirm, maintain, pronounce, state, swear, testify

affirmation *n* = **declaration**, assertion, certification, confirmation, oath, pronouncement, statement, testimony

affirmative *adj* = **agreeing**, approving, assenting, concurring, confirming, consenting, corroborative, favorable, positive

afflict *v* = **torment**, distress, grieve, harass, hurt, oppress, pain, plague, trouble

affliction *n* = **suffering**, adversity, curse, disease, hardship, misfortune, ordeal, plague, scourge, torment, trial, trouble, woe

affluence *n* = **wealth**, abundance, fortune, opulence, plenty, prosperity, riches

affluent *adj* = **wealthy**, loaded (*sl*), moneyed, opulent, prosperous, rich,

af·ford [ə-FORD] *vt* **1** be able to buy. **2** be able to spare the time, etc. **3** produce, yield, furnish.

af·front [ə-FRUNT] *vt* **1** insult openly. ◆ *n* **2** insult. **3** offense.

a·field [ə-FEELD] *adv* **1** away from home. **2** in or on the field.

a·fire [ə-FIR] *adv* on fire.

a·flame [ə-FLAYM] *adv* burning.

a·float [ə-FLOHT] *adv* **1** floating. **2** at sea. **3** in circulation.

a·foot [ə-FUUT] *adv* **1** astir. **2** on foot.

a·fore [ə-FOR] *prep, adv* before, usually in compounds, e.g. aforesaid; aforethought.

a·foul [ə-FOWL] *adj, adv* into difficulty (with).

a·fraid [ə-FRAYD] *adj* **1** frightened. **2** regretful.

a·fresh [ə-FRESH] *adv* again, anew.

Af·ri·can [AF-ri-kən] *adj* **1** belonging to Africa. ◆ *n* **2** native of Africa.
African-American *n* **1** American of African descent. ◆ *adj* **2** of African-Americans.

Af·ri·kaans [af-ri-KAHNS] *n* language used in S. Africa, derived from 17th cent. Dutch. **Af·ri·ka'ner** *n* white native of S. Afr. with Afrikaans as mother tongue.

aft *adv* toward stern of ship or tail of aircraft.

af·ter [AF-tər] *adv* **1** later. **2** behind. ◆ *prep* **3** behind. **4** later than. **5** on the model of. **6** pursuing. ◆ *conj* **7** at a later time than. ◆ *adj* **8** behind. **9** later. **10** nearer stern of ship or tail of aircraft.

af'ter·birth [-burth] *n* membrane expelled after a birth.

af'ter·care [-kair] *n* care, esp. medical, bestowed on person after period of treatment.

af'ter·ef·fect [-ə-fekt] *n* subsequent effect of deed, event, etc.

af'ter·glow [-gloh] *n* **1** light after sunset. **2** reflection of past emotion.

af'ter·math *n* result, consequence.

af·ter·noon' *n* time from noon to evening.

af'ter·taste [-tayst] *n* taste remaining or recurring after eating or drinking something.

af'ter·thought [-thawt] *n* idea occurring later.

af'ter·ward(s) [-wərd, -wərdz] *adv* later.

Ag *Chem.* silver.

a·gain [ə-GEN] *adv* **1** once more. **2** in addition. **3** back, in return. **4** besides.

a·gainst [ə-GENST] *prep* **1** in opposition to. **2** in contact with. **3** opposite. **4** in readiness for.

a·gape [ə-GAYP] *adj, adv* open-mouthed as in wonder, etc.

ag·ate [AG-it] *n* colored, semiprecious, decorative form of quartz.

age [ayj] *n* **1** length of time person or thing has existed. **2** time of life. **3** period of history. **4** maturity. **5** long time. ◆ *v* **aged**, **ag·ing 6** make or grow old. **aged** [AY-jid, ayjd] *adj* **1** old. ◆ *pl.* [AY-jid] **2** old people. **aging** *n, adj* **age'less** *adj* not growing old, not showing signs of age. **age-old** *adj* ancient.

a·gen·da [ə-JEN-də] *n* **1** things to be done.

---

well-heeled (*inf*), well-off, well-to-do

afford *v* **1** *As in* can afford = spare, bear, manage, stand, sustain **2** = give, offer, produce, provide, render, supply, yield

affordable *adj* = inexpensive, cheap, economical, low-cost, moderate, modest, reasonable

affront *n* **1** = insult, offense, outrage, provocation, slap in the face (*inf*), slight, slur ◆ *v* **2** = offend, anger, annoy, displease, insult, outrage, provoke, slight

aflame *adj* = burning, ablaze, alight, blazing, fiery, flaming, lit, on fire

afoot *adv* = going on, abroad, brewing, current, happening, in preparation, in progress, on the go (*inf*), up (*inf*)

afraid *adj* **1** = scared, apprehensive, cowardly, faint-hearted, fearful, frightened, nervous, wired (*sl*) **2** = sorry, regretful,

unhappy

afresh *adv* = again, anew, newly, once again, once more, over again

after *adv* = following, afterwards, behind, below, later, subsequently, succeeding, thereafter

aftermath *n* = effects, aftereffects, consequences, end result, outcome, results, sequel, upshot, wake

again *adv* **1** = once more, afresh, anew, another time **2** = also, besides, furthermore, in addition, moreover

against *prep* **1** = beside, abutting, facing, in contact with, on, opposite to, touching, upon **2** = opposed to, anti (*inf*), averse to, hostile to, in defiance of, in opposition to, resisting, versus **3** = in preparation for, in anticipation of, in expectation of, in provision for

2 program of business meeting.

a·gent [AY-jənt] *n* **1** one authorized to carry on business or affairs for another. **2** person or thing producing effect. **3** cause. **4** natural force. **a'gen·cy** *n* **1** instrumentality. **2** business, place of business, of agent.

agent pro·vo·ca·teur [prə-vok-ə-TUR] *n*, *pl* **agents pro·vo·ca·teur** *Fr* police or secret service spy.

ag·glu·ti·nate [ə-GLOOT-n-ayt] *vt* **-nat·ed, -nat·ing 1** unite with glue, etc. **2** form words into compounds. ◆ *adj* [-n-it] **3** united, as by glue. **ag·glu·ti·na'tion** *n*

ag·gran·dize [ə-GRAN-dīz] *vt* **-dized, -diz·ing** make greater in size, power, or rank. **ag·gran'dize·ment** [-diz-mənt] *n*

ag·gra·vate [AG-rə-vayt] *vt* **-vat·ed, -vat·ing 1** make worse or more severe. **2** *inf* annoy. **ag·gra·va'tion** *n*

ag·gre·gate [AG-ri-gayt] *vt* **-gat·ed, -gat·ing 1** gather into mass. ◆ *adj* [-git] **2** gathered thus. ◆ *n* [-git] **3** mass, sum total. **4** rock consisting of mixture of minerals. **5** mixture of gravel, etc. for concrete. **ag·gre·ga'tion** *n*

ag·gres·sion [ə-GRESH-ən] *n* **1** unprovoked attack. **2** hostile activity. **ag·gres'sive** *adj* **ag·gres'sive·ness** *n* **ag·gres'sor** *n*

ag·grieve [ə-GREEV] *vt* **-grieved, -griev·ing** pain, injure.

a·ghast [ə-GAST] *adj* struck, stupefied with horror or terror.

ag·ile [AJ-əl] *adj* **1** nimble. **2** active. **3** quick. **a·gil'i·ty** *n*

ag·i·tate [AJ-i-tayt] *v* **-tat·ed, -tat·ing** ◆ *vt* **1** disturb, excite. **2** to keep in motion, stir, shake up. **3** trouble. ◆ *vi* **4** stir up public opinion (for or against). **ag'i·ta·tor** *n*

a·glow [ə-GLOH] *adj* glowing.

THESAURUS

age *n* **1** = **time**, date, day(s), duration, epoch, era, generation, lifetime, period, span **2** = **old age**, advancing years, decline (of life), majority, maturity, senescence, senility, seniority ◆ *v* **3** = **grow old**, decline, deteriorate, mature, mellow, ripen

aged *adj* = **old**, ancient, antiquated, antique, elderly, getting on, gray

agency *n* **1** = **business**, bureau, department, office, organization **2** *Old-fashioned* = **medium**, activity, means, mechanism

agenda *n* = **list**, calendar, diary, plan, program, schedule, timetable

agent *n* **1** = **representative**, envoy, go-between, negotiator, rep (*inf*), surrogate **2** = **worker**, author, doer, mover, operator, performer **3** = **force**, agency, cause, instrument, means, power, vehicle

aggravate *v* **1** = **make worse**, exacerbate, exaggerate, increase, inflame, intensify, magnify, worsen **2** *Inf* = **annoy**, bother, get on one's nerves (*inf*), irritate, nettle, provoke

aggravation *n* **1** = **worsening**, exacerbation, exaggeration, heightening, increase, inflaming, intensification, magnification **2** *Inf* = **annoyance**, exasperation, gall, grief (*inf*), hassle (*inf*), irritation, provocation

aggregate *n* **1** = **total**, accumulation, amount, body, bulk, collection, combination, mass, pile, sum, whole ◆ *adj* **2** = **total**, accumulated, collected, combined, composite, cumulative, mixed ◆ *v* **3** = **combine**, accumulate, amass, assemble, collect, heap, mix, pile

aggression *n* **1** = **hostility**, antagonism, belligerence, destructiveness, pugnacity **2** = **attack**, assault, injury, invasion, offensive, onslaught, raid

aggressive *adj* **1** = **hostile**, belligerent, destructive, offensive, pugnacious, quarrelsome **2** = **forceful**, assertive, bold, dynamic, energetic, enterprising, militant, pushy (*inf*), vigorous

aggressor *n* = **attacker**, assailant, assaulter, invader

aggrieved *adj* = **hurt**, afflicted, distressed, disturbed, harmed, injured, unhappy, wronged

aghast *adj* = **horrified**, amazed, appalled, astonished, astounded, awestruck, confounded, shocked, startled, stunned

agile *adj* **1** = **nimble**, active, brisk, lithe, quick, sprightly, spry, supple, swift **2** = **acute**, alert, bright (*inf*), lively, quick-witted, sharp

agility *n* = **nimbleness**, litheness, liveliness, quickness, suppleness, swiftness

agitate *v* **1** = **upset**, disconcert, distract, excite, fluster, perturb, trouble, unnerve, worry **2** = **stir**, beat, convulse, disturb, rouse, shake, toss

agitation *n* **1** = **turmoil**, clamor, commotion, confusion, disturbance, excitement, ferment, trouble, upheaval **2** =

ag·nos·tic [ag-NOS-tik] *n* **1** person who believes that it is impossible to know whether God exists. ♦ *adj* **2** of this theory. **ag·nos'ti·cism** *n*

a·go [ə-goh] *adv* in the past.

a·gog [ə-GOG] *adj, adv* eager, astir.

ag·o·ny [AG-ə-nee] *n, pl* **-nies** extreme suffering of mind or body, violent struggle. **ag'o·nize** *vi* **-nized, -niz·ing 1** suffer agony. **2** worry greatly. **agony column** newspaper or magazine feature column containing advertisements relating to personal problems, esp. to missing friends or relatives.

ag·o·ra·pho·bi·a [ag-ər-ə-FOH-bee-ə] *n* abnormal fear of open spaces.

a·grar·i·an [ə-GRAIR-ee-ən] *adj* of agriculture, land or its management.

a·gree [ə-GREE] *v* **-greed, -gree·ing 1** be of same opinion. **2** consent. **3** harmonize. **4** settle suit. **a·gree'a·ble** *adj* **1** willing. **2** pleasant. **a·gree'ment** *n* **1** concord. **2** contract.

ag·ri·cul·ture [AG-ri-kul-chər] *n* art, practice of cultivating land. **ag·ri·cul'tur·al** *adj*

a·gron·o·my [ə-GRON-ə-mee] *n* the study of the management of the land and the scientific cultivation of crops. **a·gron'o·mist** *n*

a·ground [ə-GROWND] *adv* (of boat) touching bottom.

a·head [ə-HED] *adv* **1** in front. **2** forward. **3** in advance.

a·hoy [ə-HOI] *interj* shout used at sea for hailing.

aid [ayd] *vt* **1** to help. ♦ *n* **2** help, support, assistance.

aide [ayd] *n* person acting as an assistant.

aide-de-camp [AYD-də-KAMP] *n, pl* **aides-de-camp** [AYD-də-KAMP] military officer personally assisting superior.

AIDS acquired immune deficiency syndrome.

ail [ayl] *vt* **1** trouble, afflict, disturb. ♦ *vi* **2** be ill. **ail'ing** *adj* sickly. **ail'ment** *n* illness.

ai·ler·on [AY-lə-ron] *n* movable section of wing of aircraft that gives lateral control.

aim [aym] *v* **1** give direction to weapon, etc. **2** direct effort toward, try to. ♦ *n* **3** direction. **4** object, purpose. **aim'less** *adj* without purpose.

———[THESAURUS]———

turbulence, convulsion, disturbance, shaking, stirring, tossing

agitator *n* = **troublemaker**, agent provocateur, firebrand, instigator, rabble-rouser, revolutionary, stirrer (*inf*)

agog *adj* = **eager**, avid, curious, enthralled, enthusiastic, excited, expectant, impatient, in suspense, wired (*sl*)

agonize *v* = **suffer**, be distressed, be in agony, be in anguish, go through the mill, labor, strain, struggle, worry

agony *n* = **suffering**, anguish, distress, misery, pain, throes, torment, torture

agree *v* **1** = **consent**, assent, be of the same opinion, comply, concur, see eye to eye **2** = **get on (together)**, coincide, conform, correspond, match, tally

agreeable *adj* **1** = **pleasant**, delightful, enjoyable, gratifying, likable *or* likeable, pleasing, satisfying, to one's taste **2** = **consenting**, amenable, approving, complying, concurring, in accord, onside (*inf*), sympathetic, well-disposed, willing

agreement *n* **1** = **assent**, agreeing, compliance, concord, concurrence, consent, harmony, union, unison **2** = **correspondence**, compatibility, conformity, congruity, consistency,

similarity **3** = **contract**, arrangement, bargain, covenant, deal (*inf*), pact, settlement, treaty, understanding

agricultural *adj* = **farming**, agrarian, country, rural, rustic

agriculture *n* = **farming**, cultivation, culture, husbandry, tillage

aground *adv* = **beached**, ashore, foundered, grounded, high and dry, on the rocks, stranded, stuck

ahead *adv* = **in front**, at an advantage, at the head, before, in advance, in the lead, leading, to the fore, winning

aid *n* **1** = **help**, assistance, benefit, encouragement, favor, promotion, relief, service, support ♦ *v* **2** = **help**, assist, encourage, favor, promote, serve, subsidize, support, sustain

aide *n* = **assistant**, attendant, helper, right-hand man, second, supporter

ailing *adj* = **ill**, indisposed, infirm, poorly, sick, under the weather (*inf*), unwell, weak

ailment *n* = **illness**, affliction, complaint, disease, disorder, infirmity, malady, sickness

aim *v* **1** = **intend**, attempt, endeavor, mean, plan, point, propose, seek, set one's sights on, strive, try ♦ *n* **2** = **intention**, ambition,

ain't [aynt] *nonstandard* **1** am not. **2** is not. **3** are not. **4** has not. **5** have not.

air *n* **1** mixture of gases we breathe, the atmosphere. **2** breeze. **3** tune. **4** manner. ◆ *pl* **5** affected manners. ◆ *vt* **6** expose to air to dry or ventilate. **air'i·ly** *adv* **air'i·ness** *n* **air'ing** *v* **1** time spent in the open air. **2** exposure to public view. **3** radio or TV broadcast. **air'less** *adj* stuffy. **air'y** *adj* **air·i·er, air·i·est air'borne** *adj* flying, in the air. **air'bag** *n* safety device in car which inflates automatically in an accident to protect the driver or passenger. **air brake 1** brake worked by compressed air. **2** method of slowing down an aircraft. **air'brush** *n* atomizer spraying paint by compressed air. **air'-con·di·tion** *vt* maintain constant stream of clean fresh air in building at correct temperature. **air conditioner** *n* **air'craft** *n* **1** collective name for flying machines. **2** airplane. **aircraft carrier** warship with a long flat deck for the launching and landing of aircraft. **air cushion** pocket of air supporting hovercraft. **air'field** *n* landing and takeoff area for aircraft. **air force** military organization of country for air warfare. **air gun** gun discharged by force of compressed air. **air'lift** *n* transport of goods, etc. by aircraft. **air'line** *n* company operating aircraft. **air'lock** *n* **1** air bubble obstructing flow of liquid in pipe. **2** airtight chamber. **air pocket** less dense air that causes airplane to drop suddenly. **air'port** *n* station for civilian aircraft. **air pump** machine to extract or supply air. **air raid** attack by aircraft. **air shaft** passage for air into a mine, etc. **air'ship** *n* lighter-than-air flying machine with means of propulsion and steering. **air'sick·ness** *n* nausea caused by motion of aircraft in flight. **air'speed** *n* speed of aircraft relative to air. **air'strip** *n* small airfield with only one runway. **air'tight** *adj* not allowing passage of air. **air'way** *n* regular aircraft route. **air'wor·thy** *adj* fit for service in air. **air'wor·thi·ness** *n*

air'plane [-playn] *n* heavier-than-air flying machine.

aisle [īl] *n* passageway separating seating areas in church, theater, etc.

a·jar [ə-JAHR] *adv* partly open.

a·kim·bo [ə-KIM-boh] *adv* with hands on hips and elbows outward.

a·kin [ə-KIN] *adj* **1** related by blood. **2** alike, having like qualities.

Al *Chem.* aluminum.

al·a·bas·ter [AL-ə-bas-tər] *n* soft, white, semitransparent stone. **al·a·bas'trine** [-BAS-trin] *adj* of, like this.

à la carte [ah lə KAHRT] selected freely from the menu.

a·lac·ri·ty [ə-LAK-ri-tee] *n* quickness, briskness, readiness.

à la mode [ah lə MOHD] **1** in fashion. **2** topped with ice cream.

a·larm [ə-LAHRM] *n* **1** sudden fright. **2** apprehension. **3** notice of danger. **4** bell, buzzer. **5** call to arms. ◆ *vt* **6** frighten. **7** warn of danger. **a·larm'ist** *n* one given to prophesying danger or exciting alarm esp. needlessly.

THESAURUS

aspiration, desire, goal, objective, plan, purpose, target

aimless *adj* = **purposeless**, directionless, pointless, random, stray

air *n* **1** = **atmosphere**, heavens, sky **2** = **wind**, breeze, draft, zephyr **3** = **manner**, appearance, atmosphere, aura, demeanor, impression, look, mood **4** = **tune**, aria, lay, melody, song ◆ *v* **5** = **publicize**, circulate, display, exhibit, express, give vent to, make known, make public, reveal, voice **6** = **ventilate**, aerate, expose, freshen

airborne *adj* = **flying**, floating, gliding, hovering, in flight, in the air, on the wing

airing *n* **1** = **ventilation**, aeration, drying, freshening **2** = **exposure**, circulation, display, dissemination, expression, publicity, utterance, vent

airless *adj* = **stuffy**, close, heavy, muggy, oppressive, stifling, suffocating, sultry

airs *pl n* = **affectation**, arrogance, haughtiness, hauteur, pomposity, pretensions, superciliousness

airy *adj* **1** = **well-ventilated**, fresh, light, open, spacious, uncluttered **2** = **light-hearted**, blithe, cheerful, high-spirited, jaunty, lively, sprightly

aisle *n* = **passageway**, alley, corridor, gangway, lane, passage, path

alacrity *n* = **eagerness**, alertness, enthusiasm, promptness, quickness, readiness, speed, willingness, zeal

alarm *n* **1** = **fear**, anxiety, apprehension, consternation, fright, nervousness, panic, scare, trepidation **2** = **danger signal**, alarm bell, alert, bell, distress signal, hooter,

a·las [ə-LAS] *interj* cry of grief, pity, or concern.

al·ba·tross [AL-bə-traws] *n* **1** large oceanic bird, of petrel family. **2** someone or something thought to make accomplishment difficult.

al·be·it [awl-BEE-it] *conj* although.

al·bi·no [al-BĪ-noh] *n, pl* **nos** person or animal with white skin and hair, and pink eyes, due to lack of pigment. **al·bi·nism** [AL-bə-niz-əm] *n*

al·bum [AL-bəm] *n* **1** book of blank leaves, for photographs, stamps, autographs, etc. **2** one or more long-playing phonograph records or tape recordings.

al·bu·men [al-BYOO-mən] *n* egg white.

al·bu·min [al-BYOO-mən] *n* constituent of animal and vegetable matter, found nearly pure in white of egg.

al·che·my [AL-kə-mee] *n* medieval chemistry, esp. attempts to turn base metals into gold and find elixir of life. **al'che·mist** *n*

al·co·hol [AL-kə-hawl] *n* **1** intoxicating fermented liquor. **2** class of organic chemical substances. **al·co·hol'ic** *adj* **1** of alcohol. ◆ *n* **2** one addicted to alcoholic drink. **al'co·hol·ism** *n* disease, alcohol poisoning.

al·cove [AL-kohv] *n* recessed section of a room.

ale [ayl] *n* fermented malt liquor, type of beer, orig. without hops.

a·lert [ə-LURT] *adj* **1** watchful. **2** brisk, active. ◆ *n* **3** warning of sudden attack or surprise. ◆ *vt* **4** warn, esp. of danger. **5** draw attention to. **a·lert'ness** *n* **on the alert** watchful.

al·fal·fa [al-FAL-fə] *n* plant widely used as fodder.

al·fres·co [al-FRES-koh] *adv, adj* in the open air.

al·gae [AL-jee] *pl. n, sing* **-ga** [-gə] various water plants, including seaweed.

al·ge·bra [AL-jə-brə] *n* method of calculating, using symbols to represent quantities and to show relations between them, making a kind of abstract arithmetic. **al·ge·bra'ic** [-BRAY-ik] *adj*

ALGOL, Algol [AL-gol] *Computers* algorithmic oriented language.

al·go·rithm [AL-gə-rith-əm] *n* procedural model for complicated calculations.

a·li·as [AY-lee-əs] *adv* **1** otherwise known as. ◆ *n, pl* **-as·es 2** assumed name.

al·i·bi [AL-ə-bī] *n* **1** plea of being somewhere else when crime was committed. **2** *inf* excuse.

a·li·en [AY-lee-ən] *adj* **1** foreign. **2** different in nature. **3** repugnant (to). ◆ *n* **4** foreigner. **a'li·en·a·ble** *adj* able to be transferred to another owner. **a'li·en·ate** [-ə-nayt] *vt* **-at·ed, -at·ing 1** estrange. **2** transfer. **a·li·en·a'tion** *n*

a·light¹ [ə-LĪT] *vi* **1** get down. **2** land, settle.

a·light² *adj* lit up.

a·lign [ə-LĪN] *vt* bring into line or

siren, warning ◆ *v* **3** = **frighten**, daunt, dismay, distress, give (someone) a fright (*inf*), panic, scare, startle, unnerve

alarming *adj* = **frightening**, daunting, distressing, disturbing, scaring, shocking, startling, unnerving

alcoholic *n* **1** = **drunkard**, dipsomaniac, drinker, drunk, inebriate, tippler, toper, wino (*inf*) ◆ *adj* **2** = **intoxicating**, brewed, distilled, fermented, hard, strong

alcove *n* = **recess**, bay, compartment, corner, cubbyhole, cubicle, niche, nook

alert *adj* **1** = **watchful**, attentive, awake, circumspect, heedful, observant, on guard, on one's toes, on the lookout, vigilant, wide-awake ◆ *n* **2** = **warning**, alarm, signal, siren ◆ *v* **3** = **warn**, alarm, forewarn, inform, notify, signal

alertness *n* = **watchfulness**, attentiveness, heedfulness, liveliness, vigilance

alias *adv* **1** = **also known as**, also called, otherwise, otherwise known as ◆ *n* **2** = **pseudonym**, assumed name, nom de guerre, nom de plume, pen name, stage name

alibi *n* = **excuse**, defense, explanation, justification, plea, pretext, reason

alien *adj* **1** = **foreign**, exotic, incongruous, strange, unfamiliar ◆ *n* **2** = **foreigner**, newcomer, outsider, stranger

alienate *v* = **set against**, disaffect, estrange, make unfriendly, shut out, turn away

alienation *n* = **setting against**, disaffection, estrangement, remoteness, separation, turning away

alight¹ *v* **1** = **get off**, descend, disembark, dismount, get down **2** = **land**, come down, come to rest, descend, light, perch, settle, touch down agreement.

a·like [ə-LĪK] adj **1** like, similar. ♦ adv **2** in the same way.

al·i·men·ta·ry [al-ə-MEN-tə-ree] adj of food. **alimentary canal** food passage in body.

al·i·mo·ny [AL-ə-moh-nee] n allowance paid under court order to separated or divorced spouse.

a·live [ə-LĪV] adj **1** living. **2** active. **3** aware. **4** swarming.

al·ka·li [AL-kə-lī] n, pl -**lis** substance that combines with acid and neutralizes it, forming a salt. **al'ka·line** adj **al·ka·lin'i·ty** n

all [awl] adj **1** the whole of, every one of. ♦ adv **2** wholly, entirely. ♦ n **3** the whole. **4** everything, everyone. ♦ pron **5** everything, everyone. **all fours** hands and feet. **all in** exhausted. **all'-a·round'** adj showing ability in many fields. **all right 1** satisfactory. **2** well, safe. **3** pleasing. **4** very well. **5** beyond doubt.

Al·lah [AH-lə] n Muslim name for the Supreme Being.

al·lay [ə-LAY] vt lighten, relieve, calm, soothe.

al·lege [ə-LEJ] vt -**leged**, -**leg·ing 1** state without or before proof. **2** produce as argument. **al·le·ga·tion** [al-i-GAY-shən] n **al·leged'** adj **al·leg·ed·ly** adv

al·le·giance [ə-LEE-jəns] n **1** duty of a subject or citizen to sovereign or government. **2** loyalty (to person or cause).

al·le·go·ry [AL-i-gor-ee] n, pl -**ries 1** story with a meaning other than literal one. **2** description of one thing under image of another. **al·le·gor'i·cal** adj

al·le·gret·to [al-i-GRET-oh] adv, adj, n Mus. lively (passage) but not so quick as allegro.

al·le·gro [ə-LEG-roh] adv, adj, n Mus. fast (passage).

al·ler·gy [AL-ər-jee] n, pl -**gies** abnormal sensitivity to some food or substance harmless to most people. **al'ler·gen** n substance capable of inducing an allergy. **al·ler·gic** [ə-LUR-jik] adj **1** having or caused by an allergy. **2** inf having an aversion (to).

al·le·vi·ate [ə-LEE-vee-ayt] vt -**at·ed**, -**at·ing 1** ease, lessen, mitigate. **2** make light. **al·le·vi·a'tion** n

al·ley [AL-ee] n, pl -**leys 1** narrow street esp. through the middle of a block. **2** walk, path. **3** hardwood lane for bowling. **4**

THESAURUS

alight[2] adj **1** = **on fire**, ablaze, aflame, blazing, burning, fiery, flaming, lighted, lit **2** = **lit up**, bright, brilliant, illuminated, shining

align v **1** = **ally**, affiliate, agree, associate, cooperate, join, side, sympathize **2** = **line up**, even up, order, range, regulate, straighten

alignment n **1** = **alliance**, affiliation, agreement, association, cooperation, sympathy, union **2** = **lining up**, adjustment, arrangement, evening up, order, straightening up

alike adj **1** = **similar**, akin, analogous, corresponding, identical, of a piece, parallel, resembling, the same ♦ adv **2** = **similarly**, analogously, correspondingly, equally, evenly, identically, uniformly

alive adj **1** = **living**, animate, breathing, in the land of the living (inf), subsisting **2** = **in existence**, active, existing, extant, functioning, in force, operative **3** = **lively**, active, alert, animated, energetic, full of life, vital, vivacious

all adj **1** = **the whole of**, every bit of, the complete, the entire, the sum of, the totality of, the total of **2** = **every**, each, each and every, every one of, every single **3** = **complete**, entire, full, greatest, perfect, total, utter ♦ adv **4** = **completely**, altogether, entirely, fully, totally, utterly, wholly ♦ n **5** = **whole amount**, aggregate, entirety, everything, sum total, total, totality, utmost

allegation n = **claim**, accusation, affirmation, assertion, charge, declaration, statement

allege v = **claim**, affirm, assert, charge, declare, maintain, state

alleged adj **1** = **stated**, affirmed, asserted, declared, described, designated **2** = **supposed**, doubtful, dubious, ostensible, professed, purported, so-called, unproved

allegiance n = **loyalty**, constancy, devotion, faithfulness, fidelity, obedience

allegorical adj = **symbolic**, emblematic, figurative, symbolizing

allegory n = **symbol**, fable, myth, parable, story, symbolism, tale

allergic adj = **sensitive**, affected by, hypersensitive, susceptible

allergy n = **sensitivity**, antipathy, hypersensitivity, susceptibility

alleviate v = **ease**, allay, lessen, lighten,

building housing bowling lanes.

al·li·ance [ə-LĪ-əns] *n* **1** state of being allied. **2** union between families by marriage, and states by treaty. **3** confederation.

al·li·ga·tor [AL-i-gay-tər] *n* **1** animal of crocodile family. **2** leather made from its hide.

al·lit·er·a·tion [ə-lit-ə-RAY-shən] *n* beginning of two or more words in close succession with same sound, e.g *Sing a Song of Sixpence*. **al·lit·er·a·tive** *adj*

al·lo·cate [AL-ə-kayt] *vt* **-cat·ed, -cat·ing 1** assign as a share. **2** designate. **al·lo·ca'tion** *n*

al·lo·mor·phism [al-ə-MOR-fiz-əm] *n* **1** variation of form without change in essential nature. **2** variation of crystalline form of chemical compound. **al'lo·morph** *n* **al·lo·morph'ic** *adj*

al·lop·a·thy [ə-LOP-ə-thee] *n* **1** orthodox practice of medicine. **2** opposite of homeopathy.

al·lot [ə-LOT] *vt* **-lot·ted, -lot·ting 1** distribute as shares. **2** give out. **al·lot'ment** *n* **1** distribution. **2** portion of land rented for cultivation. **3** portion of land, pay, etc. allotted.

al·low [ə-LOW] *vt* **1** let happen. **2** permit. **3** acknowledge. **4** set aside. ◆ *vi* **5** (usu. with *for*) take into account. **al·low'a·ble** *adj* **al·low'ance** *n* portion or amount allowed, esp. at regular times.

al·loy [AL-oi] *n* **1** mixture of two or more metals. ◆ *vt* **2** [ə-LOI] mix metals, debase.

all right see ALL.

all·spice [AWL-spīs] *n* **1** berry of West Indian tree. **2** the tree. **3** aromatic spice prepared from its berries.

al·lude [ə-LOOD] *vi* **-lud·ed, -lud·ing 1** mention lightly, hint at, make indirect reference to. **2** refer to. **al·lu'sion** [-LOO-zhən] *n* **al·lu'sive** [-siv] *adj*

al·lure [ə-LOOR] *vt* **-lured, -lur·ing 1** entice, win over, fascinate. ◆ *n* **2** attractiveness. **al·lur'ing** *adj* charming, seductive.

moderate, reduce, relieve, soothe

alley *n* = **passage**, alleyway, backstreet, lane, passageway, pathway, walk

alliance *n* = **union**, affiliation, agreement, association, coalition, combination, confederation, connection, federation, league, marriage, pact, partnership, treaty

allied *adj* = **united**, affiliated, associated, combined, connected, in league, linked, related

allocate *v* = **assign**, allot, allow, apportion, budget, designate, earmark, mete, set aside, share out

allocation *n* = **assignment**, allotment, allowance, lot, portion, quota, ration, share

allot *v* = **assign**, allocate, apportion, budget, designate, earmark, mete, set aside, share out

allotment *n* **1** = **plot**, kitchen garden, patch, tract **2** = **assignment**, allocation, allowance, grant, portion, quota, ration, share, stint

all-out *adj* = **total**, complete, exhaustive, full, full-scale, maximum, thoroughgoing, undivided, unremitting, unrestrained

allow *v* **1** = **permit**, approve, authorize, enable, endure, let, sanction, stand, suffer, tolerate **2** = **give**, allocate, allot, assign, grant, provide, set aside, spare **3** = **acknowledge**, admit, concede, confess, grant, own

allowable *adj* = **permissible**, acceptable, admissible, all right, appropriate, suitable, tolerable

allowance *n* **1** = **portion**, allocation, amount, grant, lot, quota, ration, share, stint **2** = **concession**, deduction, discount, rebate, reduction

allow for *v* = **take into account**, consider, make allowances for, make concessions for, make provision for, plan for, provide for, take into consideration

alloy *n* **1** = **mixture**, admixture, amalgam, blend, combination, composite, compound, hybrid ◆ *v* **2** = **mix**, amalgamate, blend, combine, compound, fuse

all right *adj* **1** = **satisfactory**, acceptable, adequate, average, fair, O.K. or okay (*inf*), standard, up to scratch (*inf*) **2** = **O.K. or okay** (*inf*), healthy, safe, sound, unharmed, uninjured, well, whole

allude *v* = **refer**, hint, imply, intimate, mention, suggest, touch upon

allure *n* **1** = **attractiveness**, appeal, attraction, charm, enchantment, enticement, glamour, lure, persuasion, seductiveness, temptation ◆ *v* **2** = **attract**, captivate, charm, enchant, entice, lure, persuade, seduce, tempt, win over

alluring *adj* = **attractive**, beguiling,

al·lu·vi·al [ə-LOO-vee-əl] *adj* deposited by rivers. **al·lu'vi·on** [-vee-ən] *n* land formed by washed-up deposit. **al·lu'vi·um** [-vee-əm] *n, pl* **-vi·a** [-vee-ə] water-borne matter deposited by rivers, floods, etc.

al·ly [ə-LĪ] *vt* **-lied, -ly·ing 1** join in relationship by treaty, marriage, or friendship, etc. ♦ *n* [AL-ī] *pl* **-lies 2** country or ruler bound to another by treaty. **3** confederate.

al·ma ma·ter [AL-mə MAH-tər] **1** one's school, college, or university. **2** its song or hymn.

al·ma·nac [AWL-mə-nak] *n* yearly publication with detailed information on tides, events, etc.

al·might·y [awl-MĪ-tee] *adj* **1** having all power, omnipotent. **2** *inf* very great. **The Almighty** God.

al·mond [AH-mənd] *n* **1** kernel of the fruit of a tree related to the peach. **2** tree that bears it.

al·most [AWL-mohst] *adv* very nearly, all but.

alms [ahmz] *pl n* gifts to the poor.

al·oe [AL-oh] *n* **1** genus of plants of medicinal value. ♦ *pl* **2** bitter drug made from plant.

a·loft [ə-LAWFT] *adv* **1** on high. **2** overhead. **3** in ship's rigging.

a·lone [ə-LOHN] *adj* **1** single, solitary. ♦ *adv* **2** separately, only.

a·long [ə-LAWNG] *adv* **1** lengthwise. **2** together (with). **3** forward. ♦ *prep* **4** over the length of. **a·long'side'** *adv, prep* beside.

a·loof [ə-LOOF] *adv* **1** withdrawn. **2** at a distance. **3** apart. ♦ *adj* **4** uninvolved. **a·loof'ness** *n*

al·o·pe·ci·a [al-ə-PEESH-ə] *n* baldness.

a·loud [ə-LOWD] *adj* **1** in a voice loud enough to be heard. ♦ *adv* **2** loudly. **3** audibly.

alp *n* high mountain. **Alps** *pl* esp. mountains of Switzerland. **al·pine** [AL-pīn] *adj* **1** of, growing on, high mountains. **2** (A-) of the Alps. ♦ *n* **3** mountain plant. **al·pin·ist** [AL-pə-nist] *n* mountain climber. **al'pen·stock** [-pən-stok] *n* iron-tipped staff used by climbers.

al·pac·a [al-PAK-ə] *n* **1** Peruvian llama. **2** its wool. **3** cloth made from this.

al·pha·bet [AL-fə-bet] *n* the set of letters used in writing a language. **al·pha·bet'i·cal** *adj* in the standard order of the letters.

al·read·y [awl-RED-ee] *adv* **1** before, previously. **2** sooner than expected.

al·so [AWL-soh] *adv* **1** as well, too. **2** besides, moreover.

al·tar [AWL-tər] *n* **1** raised place, stone, etc., on which sacrifices are offered. **2** in Christian church, table on which priest consecrates the eucharist elements. **al'tar·cloth** *n* **al'tar·piece** *n* **al'tar rails** *n* **altar boy** *n* acolyte.

al·ter [AWL-tər] *v* **1** change, make or become different. **2** castrate, spay (animal). **al'ter·a·ble** *adj* **al'ter·a·bly** *adv* **al·ter·a'tion** *n*

al·ter·ca·tion [awl-tər-KAY-shən] *n* dispute,

—— THESAURUS ——

captivating, come-hither, fetching, glamorous, seductive, tempting

allusion *n* = **reference**, casual remark, hint, implication, innuendo, insinuation, intimation, mention, suggestion

ally *n* **1** = **partner**, accomplice, associate, collaborator, colleague, friend, helper, homeboy (*sl*), homegirl (*sl*) ♦ *v* **2** = **unite**, associate, collaborate, combine, join, join forces, unify

almighty *adj* **1** = **all-powerful**, absolute, invincible, omnipotent, supreme, unlimited **2** *Inf* = **great**, enormous, excessive, intense, loud, severe, terrible

almost *adv* = **nearly**, about, approximately, close to, just about, not quite, on the brink of, practically, virtually

alone *adj* = **by oneself**, apart, detached, isolated, lonely, only, separate, single, solitary, unaccompanied

aloof *adj* = **distant**, detached, haughty, remote, standoffish, supercilious, unapproachable, unfriendly

aloud *adv* = **out loud**, audibly, clearly, distinctly, intelligibly, plainly

already *adv* = **before now**, at present, before, by now, by then, even now, heretofore, just now, previously

also *adv* = **too**, additionally, and, as well, besides, further, furthermore, in addition, into the bargain, moreover, to boot

alter *v* = **change**, adapt, adjust, amend, convert, modify, reform, revise, transform, turn, vary

alteration *n* = **change**, adaptation, adjustment, amendment, conversion, difference, modification, reformation, revision, transformation, variation wrangling, noisy controversy.

al·ter e·go [AWL-tər EE-goh] **1** second self. **2** close friend.

al·ter·nate [AWL-tər-nayt] v **-nat·ed, -nat·ing** occur or cause to occur by turns. **al'ter·nate** [-nit] adj, n (one) after the other, by turns. **al·ter·na·tive** [awl-TUR-nə-tiv] n **1** one of two choices. ◆ adj **2** offering or expressing a choice. **al'ter·na·tor** n electric generator for producing alternating current. **alternative medicine** treatment of disease by non-traditional methods such as homeopathy and acupuncture.

al·though [awl-THOH] conj despite the fact that.

al·tim·e·ter [al-TIM-i-tər] n instrument for measuring height.

al·ti·tude [AL-ti-tood] n height, eminence, elevation, loftiness.

al·to [AL-toh] n, pl **-tos** Mus. **1** male singing voice or instrument above tenor. **2** contralto.

al·to·geth·er [awl-tə-GETH-ər] adv **1** entirely. **2** on the whole. **3** in total. **in the altogether** nude.

al·tru·ism [AL-troo-iz-əm] n principle of living and acting for good of others. **al'tru·ist** n **al·tru·is'tic** adj

a·lu·mi·num [ə-LOO-mə-nəm] n light nonrusting metal resembling silver. **a·lu·mi·na** n oxide of aluminum.

a·lum·na [ə-LUM-nə] n, pl **-nae** [-nee] girl or woman graduate of a particular school, college, or university.

a·lum·nus [ə-LUM-nəs] n, pl **-ni** [-nī] graduate of a particular school, college, or university.

al·ways [AWL-wayz] adv **1** at all times. **2** forever.

am first person sing. pres. ind. of BE

Am Chem. americium.

A.M., a.m. ante meridiem: before noon.

a·mal·gam [ə-MAL-gəm] n **1** compound of mercury and another metal. **2** soft, plastic mixture. **3** combination of elements.

a·mal·ga·mate [ə-MAL-gə-mayt] v **-mat·ed, -mat·ing** mix, combine or cause to combine. **a·mal·ga·ma'tion** n

a·man·u·en·sis [ə-man-yoo-EN-sis] n, pl **-ses** [-seez] **1** one who writes from dictation. **2** copyist, secretary.

a·mass [ə-MAS] v collect in quantity.

am·a·teur [AM-ə-chuur] n **1** one who carries on an art, study, game, etc. for the love of it, not for money. **2** unskilled practitioner. **am·a·teur'ish** adj imperfect, untrained.

am·a·to·ry [AM-ə-tor-ee] adj relating to love.

a·maze [ə-MAYZ] vt **-mazed, -maz·ing** surprise greatly, astound. **a·maze'ment** n **amazing** adj

Am·a·zon [AM-ə-zon] n **1** female warrior of

| THESAURUS |

alternate v **1 = change**, act reciprocally, fluctuate, interchange, oscillate, rotate, substitute, take turns ◆ adj **2 = every other**, alternating, every second, interchanging, rotating

alternative n **1 = choice**, option, other (of two), preference, recourse, selection, substitute ◆ adj **2 = different**, alternate, another, other, second, substitute

alternatively adv **= or**, as an alternative, if not, instead, on the other hand, otherwise

although conj **= though**, albeit, despite the fact that, even if, even though, notwithstanding, while

altogether adv **1 = completely**, absolutely, fully, perfectly, quite, thoroughly, totally, utterly, wholly **2 = on the whole**, all in all, all things considered, as a whole, collectively, generally, in general **3 = in total**, all told, everything included, in all, in sum, taken together

altruistic adj **= selfless**, benevolent,

charitable, generous, humanitarian, philanthropic, public-spirited, self-sacrificing, unselfish

always adv **= continually**, consistently, constantly, eternally, evermore, every time, forever, invariably, perpetually, repeatedly, twenty-four-seven (sl), without exception

amalgamate v **= combine**, ally, blend, fuse, incorporate, integrate, merge, mingle, unite

amalgamation n **= combination**, blend, coalition, compound, fusion, joining, merger, mixture, union

amass v **= collect**, accumulate, assemble, compile, gather, hoard, pile up

amateur n **= nonprofessional**, dabbler, dilettante, layman

amateurish adj **= unprofessional**, amateur, bungling, clumsy, crude, inexpert, unaccomplished

amaze v **= astonish**, alarm, astound, bewilder, dumbfound, shock, stagger,

legend. **2** tall, strong woman.
Am·a·zo'ni·an [-ZOH-nee-ən] *adj*

am·bas·sa·dor [am-BAS-ə-dər] *n* senior diplomatic representative sent by one government to another. **am·bas·sa·do'ri·al** *adj*

am·ber [AM-bər] *n* **1** yellowish, translucent fossil resin. ♦ *adj* **2** made of, colored like amber.

am·ber·gris [AM-bər-gris] *n* waxy substance secreted by the sperm whale, used in making perfumes.

am·bi·dex·trous [am-bi-DEK-strəs] *adj* able to use both hands with equal ease. **am·bi·dex·ter'i·ty** *n*

am·bi·ence, -ance [AM-bee-əns] *n* atmosphere of a place.

am·bi·ent [AM-bee-ənt] *adj* surrounding.

am·big·u·ous [am-BIG-yoo-əs] *adj* **1** having more than one meaning. **2** obscure. **am·bi·gu'i·ty** *n*

am·bi·tion [am-BISH-ən] *n* **1** desire for power, fame, honor. **2** the object of that desire. **am·bi'tious** *adj*

am·biv·a·lence [am-BIV-ə-ləns] *n* simultaneous existence of two conflicting desires, opinions, etc. **am·biv'a·lent** *adj*

am·ble [AM-bəl] *vi* **-bled, -bling 1** move along easily and gently. **2** move at an easy pace. ♦ *n* **3** this movement or pace.

am·bro·sia [am-BROH-zhə] *n Mythology* **1** food of the gods. **2** anything smelling, tasting particularly good.

am·bu·lance [AM-byə-ləns] *n* conveyance for sick or injured.

am·bush [AM-buush] *n* **1** a lying in wait (for). ♦ *vt* **2** waylay, attack from hiding, lie in wait for.

a·mel·io·rate [ə-MEEL-yə-rayt] *v* **-rat·ed, -rat·ing** make better, improve. **a·mel·io·ra'tion** *n*

a·men [AY-MEN] *interj* **1** surely. **2** so let it be.

a·me·na·ble [ə-MEE-nə-bəl] *adj* **1** easy to be led or controlled. **2** subject to, liable. **a·me'na·bly** *adv*

a·mend [ə-MEND] *vi* **1** grow better. ♦ *vt* **2** correct. **3** improve. **4** alter in detail, as bill in legislature, etc. **a·mend'ment** *n* **a·mends'** *pl n* reparation.

a·men·i·ty [ə-MEN-i-tee] *n, pl* **-ties** useful or pleasant facility or service.

A·mer·i·can [ə-MER-i-kən] *adj* of, relating to, the North American continent or the United States of America.

am·e·thyst [AM-ə-thist] *n* **1** bluish-violet precious stone. **2** its color.

a·mi·a·ble [AY-mee-ə-bəl] *adj* friendly, kindly. **a·mi·a·bil'i·ty** *n*

am·i·ca·ble [AM-i-kə-bəl] *adj* friendly.

startle, stun, surprise

amazement *n* = **astonishment**, admiration, bewilderment, confusion, perplexity, shock, surprise, wonder

amazing *adj* = **astonishing**, astounding, breathtaking, eye-opening, overwhelming, staggering, startling, stunning, surprising

ambassador *n* = **representative**, agent, consul, deputy, diplomat, envoy, legate, minister

ambiguity *n* = **vagueness**, doubt, dubiousness, equivocation, obscurity, uncertainty

ambiguous *adj* = **unclear**, dubious, enigmatic, equivocal, inconclusive, indefinite, indeterminate, obscure, vague

ambition *n* **1** = **enterprise**, aspiration, desire, drive, eagerness, longing, striving, yearning, zeal **2** = **goal**, aim, aspiration, desire, dream, hope, intent, objective, purpose, wish

ambitious *adj* = **enterprising**, aspiring, avid, eager, hopeful, intent, purposeful, striving, zealous

ambivalent *adj* = **undecided**, contradictory, doubtful, equivocal, in two minds, uncertain, wavering

amble *v* = **stroll**, dawdle, meander, mosey (*inf*), ramble, saunter, walk, wander

ambush *n* **1** = **trap**, lying in wait, waylaying ♦ *v* **2** = **trap**, attack, bushwhack (*U.S.*), ensnare, surprise, waylay

amenable *adj* = **receptive**, able to be influenced, acquiescent, agreeable, open, persuadable, responsive, susceptible

amend *v* = **change**, alter, correct, fix, improve, mend, modify, reform, remedy, repair, revise

amendment *n* **1** = **change**, alteration, correction, emendation, improvement, modification, reform, remedy, repair, revision **2** = **alteration**, addendum, addition, attachment, clarification

amends *pl n As in* **make amends for** = **compensation**, atonement, recompense, redress, reparation, restitution, satisfaction

amenity *n* = **facility**, advantage, comfort, convenience, service

am·i·ca·bil'i·ty n

a·mid [ə-MID], **a·midst** [ə-MIDST] prep **1** in the middle of, among. **2** during.

a·mid·ships [ə-MID-ships] adv near, toward, middle of ship.

a·mi·no acid [ə-MEE-noh] organic compound found in protein.

a·miss [ə-MIS] adj **1** wrong. ♦ adv **2** faultily, badly. **take amiss** be offended (by).

am·i·ty [AM-i-tee] n friendship.

am·me·ter [AM-mee-tər] n instrument for measuring electric current.

am·mo·nia [ə-MOHN-yə] n pungent alkaline gas containing hydrogen and nitrogen.

am·mo·nite [AM-ə-nīt] n whorled fossil shell like ram's horn.

am·mu·ni·tion [am-yə-NISH-ən] n **1** any projectiles (bullets, rockets, etc.) that can be discharged from a weapon. **2** facts that can be used in an argument.

am·ne·sia [am-NEE-zhə] n loss of memory.

am·nes·ty [AM-nə-stee] n, pl **-ties 1** general pardon. ♦ vt **-tied, -ty·ing 2** grant this.

am·ni·ot·ic fluid [am-nee-OT-ik] fluid surrounding fetus in womb.

a·moe·ba [ə-MEE-bə] n, pl **-bas** microscopic single-celled animal found in ponds, etc. and able to change its shape.

a·mok, a·muck [ə-MUK] adv **run amok** rush about in murderous frenzy.

a·mong [ə-MUNG], **a·mongst** [ə-MUNGST] prep mixed with, in the midst of, of. the number of, between.

a·mor·al [ay-MOR-əl] adj nonmoral, having no moral qualities. **a·mo·ral·i·ty** [ay-mə-RAL-i-tee] n

am·o·rous [AM-ər-əs] adj **1** inclined to love. **2** in love. **am'o·rous·ness** n

a·mor·phous [ə-MOR-fəs] adj without distinct shape.

a·mor·tize [AM-ər-tīz] vt pay off a debt by a sinking fund. **am'or·tiz·a·ble** adj

a·mount [ə-MOWNT] vi **1** come, be equal (to). ♦ n **2** quantity. **3** sum total.

a·mour [ə-MOOR] n (illicit) love affair.

am·pere [AM-peer] n unit of electric current. **am·per·age** [AM-pə-rij] n strength of current in amperes.

am·per·sand [AM-pər-sand] n the character (&), meaning and.

am·phet·a·mine [am-FET-ə-meen] n synthetic liquid used medicinally as stimulant, a dangerous drug if misused.

am·phib·i·ous [am-FIB-ee-əs] adj living or operating both on land and in water. **am·phib'i·an** n **1** animal that lives first in water then on land. **2** vehicle able to travel on land or water. **3** aircraft that can alight on land and water.

am·phi·the·a·ter [AM-fə-thee-ə-tər] n **1** building with tiers of seats rising around an arena. **2** room with gallery above from which one can observe surgical operations, etc.

am·pho·ra [AM-fər-ə] n, pl **-rae** [-ree] two-handled vessel of ancient Greece and Rome.

am·ple [AM-pəl] adj **1** big enough. **2** large,

———————| THESAURUS |———————

amiable adj = **pleasant**, affable, agreeable, charming, congenial, engaging, friendly, genial, likable or likeable, lovable

amicable adj = **friendly**, amiable, civil, cordial, courteous, harmonious, neighborly, peaceful, sociable

amid, amidst prep = **in the middle of**, among, amongst, in the midst of, in the thick of, surrounded by

amiss adv **1** = **wrongly**, erroneously, improperly, inappropriately, incorrectly, mistakenly, unsuitably **2** As in take (something) amiss = **as an insult**, as offensive, out of turn, wrongly ♦ adj **3** = **wrong**, awry, faulty, incorrect, mistaken, untoward

ammunition n = **munitions**, armaments, explosives, powder, rounds, shells, shot

amnesty n = **general pardon**, absolution,

dispensation, forgiveness, immunity, remission (of penalty), reprieve

amok, amuck adv As in run amok = **madly**, berserk, destructively, ferociously, in a frenzy, murderously, savagely, uncontrollably, violently, wildly

among, amongst prep **1** = **in the midst of**, amid, amidst, in the middle of, in the thick of, surrounded by, together with, with **2** = **in the group of**, in the class of, in the company of, in the number of, out of **3** = **to each of**, between

amorous adj = **loving**, erotic, impassioned, in love, lustful, passionate, tender

amount n = **quantity**, expanse, extent, magnitude, mass, measure, number, supply, volume

amount to v = **add up to**, become, come to, develop into, equal, mean, total spacious. **am'ply** *adv*

am·pli·fy [AM-plə-fī] *vt* **-fied, -fy·ing 1** increase. **2** make bigger, louder, etc. **am·pli·fi·ca'tion** *n* **am'pli·fi·er** *n*

am·pli·tude [AM-pli-tood] *n* **1** spaciousness, width. **2** maximum departure from average of alternating current, etc. **amplitude modulation 1** modulation of amplitude of radio carrier wave. **2** broadcasting system using this.

am·pule [AM-pyool] *n* container for hypodermic dose.

am·pu·tate [AM-pyə-tayt] *vi* **-tat·ed, -tat·ing** cut off (limb, etc.). **am·pu·ta'tion** *n*

amuck see AMOK.

am·u·let [AM-yə-lit] *n* something carried or worn as a charm.

a·muse [ə-MYOOZ] *vt* **-mused, -mus·ing** divert. **1** occupy pleasantly. **2** cause to laugh or smile. **a·muse'ment** *n* entertainment, pastime.

an *adj* form of a used before vowels, and sometimes before *h*, e.g. *an hour.*

an·a·bol·ic ster·oid [an-ə-BOL-ik STEER-oid] any of various hormones used by athletes to encourage muscle growth.

a·nach·ro·nism [ə-NAK-rə-niz-əm] *n* **1** mistake of time, by which something is put in wrong historical period. **2** something out-of-date.

an·a·con·da [an-ə-KON-də] *n* large semi-aquatic snake that kills by constriction.

an·a·gram [AN-ə-gram] *n* word or sentence made by reordering the letters of another word or sentence, such as *ant* from *tan.*

anal see ANUS.

an·al·ge·si·a [an-l-JEE-zee-ə] *n* absence of pain. **an·al·ge'sic** *adj, n* (drug) relieving pain.

a·na·log [AN-ə-log] *n* **1** physical object or quantity used to measure or represent another quantity. **2** something that is analogous to something else. ◆ *adj* **3** displaying information by means of a dial.

a·nal·o·gy [ə-NAL-ə-jee] *n, pl* **-gies 1** agreement or likeness in certain respects. **2** correspondence. **a·nal'o·gize** *v* **-gized, -giz·ing** explain by analogy. **a·nal'o·gous** [-ə-gəs] *adj* **1** similar. **2** parallel.

a·nal·y·sis [ə-NAL-ə-sis] *n, pl* **-ses** [-seez] separation into elements or components. **an·a·lyze** [AN-l-īz] *vt* **-lyzed, -lyz·ing 1** examine critically. **2** determine the constituent parts. **an·a·lyst** [AN-l-ist] *n* **1** one skilled in analysis, esp. chemical analysis. **2** psychoanalyst. **an·a·lyt·ic·al** [an-l-IT-i-kəl], **an·a·lyt·ic** [an-l-IT-ik] *adj*

an·ar·chy [AN-ər-kee] *n* **1** lawlessness. **2** lack of government in a country. **3** confusion. **an·ar·chic** [an-AHR-kik] *adj* **an'ar·chism** *n* **an'ar·chist** *n* one who opposes all government.

—————— THESAURUS ——————

ample *adj* = **plenty**, abundant, bountiful, copious, expansive, extensive, full, generous, lavish, plentiful, profuse

amplify *v* **1** = **explain**, develop, elaborate, enlarge, expand, flesh out, go into detail **2** = **increase**, enlarge, expand, extend, heighten, intensify, magnify, strengthen, widen

amply *adv* = **fully**, abundantly, completely, copiously, generously, profusely, richly

amputate *v* = **cut off**, curtail, lop, remove, separate, sever, truncate

amuck see AMOK

amuse *v* = **entertain**, charm, cheer, delight, interest, please, tickle

amusement *n* **1** = **entertainment**, cheer, enjoyment, fun, merriment, mirth, pleasure **2** = **entertainment**, diversion, game, hobby, joke, pastime, recreation, sport

amusing *adj* = **funny**, comical, droll, enjoyable, entertaining, humorous, interesting, witty

analogy *n* = **similarity**, comparison, correlation, correspondence, likeness, parallel, relation, resemblance

analysis *n* = **examination**, breakdown, dissection, inquiry, investigation, perusal, scrutiny, sifting, test

analytic, analytical *adj* = **rational**, inquiring, inquisitive, investigative, logical, organized, problem-solving, systematic

analyze *v* **1** = **examine**, evaluate, investigate, research, test, work over **2** = **break down**, dissect, divide, resolve, separate, sift through

anarchic *adj* = **lawless**, chaotic, disorganized, rebellious, riotous, ungoverned

anarchist *n* = **revolutionary**, insurgent, nihilist, rebel, terrorist

anarchy *n* = **lawlessness**, chaos, confusion, disorder, disorganization, revolution, riot

a·nath·e·ma [ə-NATH-ə-mə] *n, pl* **-mas 1** anything detested, hateful. **2** ban of the church. **3** curse. **a·nath'e·ma·tize** *vt* **-tized, -tiz·ing**

a·nat·o·my [ə-NAT-ə-mee] *n* **1** science of structure of the body. **2** detailed analysis. **3** the body. **an·a·tom'i·cal** *adj*

an·ces·tor [AN-ses-tər] *n* **1** person from whom another is descended. **2** early type of later form or product. **an·ces'tral** *adj* **an'ces·try** *n*

an·chor [ANG-kər] *n* **1** heavy (usu. hooked) implement dropped on cable, chain, etc. to bottom of sea, etc. to secure vessel. **2** *Radio and TV* principal announcer in program of news, sports, etc. ♦ *vt* **3** fasten by or as with anchor. **4** perform as anchor. **an'chor·age** *n* act of, place of anchoring.

an·cho·rite [ANG-kə-rīt] *n* hermit, recluse.

an·cho·vy [AN-choh-vee] *n, pl* (**-vies**) small fish of herring family.

an·cient [AYN-shənt] *adj* **1** belonging to former age. **2** old. **3** timeworn. ♦ *n* **4** one who lived in an earlier age. **ancient history 1** history of ancient times. **2** common knowledge.

an·cil·lar·y [AN-sə-ler-ee] *adj, n, pl* **-ies** subordinate, subservient, auxiliary.

and *conj* joins words, phrases, clauses, and sentences to introduce a consequence, etc.

an·dan·te [ahn-DAHN-tay] *adv, n Mus.* moderately slow (passage).

and·i·ron [AND-ī-ərn] *n* steel bar or bracket for supporting logs in a fireplace.

an·drog·y·nous [an-DROJ-ə-nəs] *adj* having characteristics of both male and female.

an·ec·dote [AN-ik-doht] *n* very short story dealing with single incident. **an'ec·do·tal** *adj* **an·ec·do'tal·ist** *n* one given to recounting anecdotes.

a·ne·mi·a [ə-NEE-mee-ə] *n* deficiency in number of red blood cells. **a·ne'mic** *adj* **1** suffering from anemia. **2** pale, sickly.

an·e·mom·e·ter [an-ə-MOM-i-tər] *n* wind gauge.

a·nem·o·ne [ə-NEM-ə-nee] *n* flower related to buttercup. **sea anemone** plantlike sea animal.

an·er·oid [AN-ə-roid] *adj* denoting a barometer that measures atmospheric pressure without use of mercury or other liquid.

an·es·the·si·ol·o·gy [an-is-thee-zi-OL-ə-jee] *n* branch of medicine dealing with anesthetics.

an·es·thet·ic [an-əs-THET-ik] *n, adj* (drug) causing loss of sensation. **an·es·the·sia** [-THEE-zhə] *n* loss of sensation.

an·es·the·tist [ə-NES-thi-tist] *n* expert in use of anesthetics. **an·es'the·tize** *vt* **-tized, -tiz·ing**

an·eu·rysm, an·eu·rism [AN-yə-riz-əm] *n* swelling out of a part of an artery.

a·new [ə-NOO] *adv* afresh, again.

an·gel [AYN-jəl] *n* **1** divine messenger. **2** ministering or attendant spirit. **3** person with the qualities of such a spirit, as gentleness, purity, etc. **an·gel'ic** *adj*

An·ge·lus [AN-jə-ləs] *n* **1** devotional service in R.C. Church in memory of the Incarnation, said at morning, noon and sunset. **2** bell announcing the time for this service.

an·ger [ANG-gər] *n* **1** strong emotion excited by a real or supposed injury. **2**

———————| THESAURUS |———————

anatomy *n* **1** = **examination**, analysis, dissection, division, inquiry, investigation, study **2** = **structure**, build, composition, frame, framework, make-up

ancestor *n* = **forefather**, forebear, forerunner, precursor, predecessor

ancient *adj* = **old**, aged, antique, archaic, old-fashioned, primeval, primordial, timeworn

ancillary *adj* = **supplementary**, additional, auxiliary, extra, secondary, subordinate, subsidiary, supporting

and *conj* = **also**, along with, as well as, furthermore, in addition to, including, moreover, plus, together with

anecdote *n* = **story**, reminiscence, short story, sketch, tale, urban legend, yarn

anemic *adj* = **pale**, ashen, colorless, feeble, pallid, sickly, wan, weak

anesthetic *n* **1** = **painkiller**, analgesic, anodyne, narcotic, opiate, sedative, soporific ♦ *adj* **2** = **pain-killing**, analgesic, anodyne, deadening, dulling, numbing, sedative, soporific

angel *n* **1** = **divine messenger**, archangel, cherub, seraph **2** *Inf* = **dear**, beauty, darling, gem, jewel, paragon, saint, treasure

angelic *adj* **1** = **pure**, adorable, beautiful, entrancing, lovely, saintly, virtuous **2** = **heavenly**, celestial, cherubic, ethereal, seraphic wrath. **3** rage. ◆ *vt* **4** excite to wrath. **5** enrage. **an'gri·ly** *adv* **an'gry** *adj* **1** full of anger. **2** inflamed.

an·gi·na (pec·to·ris) [an-JĪ-nə PEK-tər-is] *n* severe pain accompanying some heart diseases.

an·gle¹ [ANG-gəl] *vi* **-gled, -gling** fish with hook and line. **an'gler** *n*

angle² *n* **1** meeting of two lines or surfaces. **2** corner. **3** point of view. **4** *inf* devious motive. ◆ *vt* **5** bend at an angle.

An·gli·can [ANG-gli-kən] *adj, n* (member) of the Church of England. **An'gli·can·ism** *n*

An·gli·cize [ANG-glə-sīz] *vt* **-cized, -ciz·ing** **1** express in English. **2** turn into English form. **An'gli·cism** *n* English idiom or peculiarity.

Anglo- *comb. form* **1** English, e.g. *Anglo-Scottish.* **2** British, e.g. *Anglo-American.*

an·glo·phil·ia [ang-glə-FIL-ee-ə] *n* excessive admiration for English. **an'glo·phile** [-fil] *n*

An·glo·pho·bi·a [ang-glə-FOH-bee-ə] *n* dislike of England, etc. **an'glo·phobe** *n*

an·go·ra [ang-GOR-ə] *n* **1** variety of goat, cat, or rabbit with long silky hair. **2** hair of the angora goat or rabbit. **3** cloth made from this hair.

an·gos·tu·ra bark [ang-gə-STOOR-ə] *n* bitter bark of certain S American trees, used as flavoring in alcoholic drinks.

angst [ankst] *n* feeling of anxiety.

ang·strom [ANG-strəm] *n* unit of length

for measuring wavelengths of electromagnetic radiation.

an·guish [ANG-gwish] *n* **1** great mental or bodily pain. ◆ *v* **2** suffer this pain. **3** cause to suffer it.

an·gu·lar [ANG-gyə-lər] *adj* **1** (of people) bony, awkward. **2** having angles. **3** measured by an angle. **an·gu·lar'i·ty** *n*

an·hy·drous [an-HĪ-drəs] *adj* (of chemical substances) free from water.

an·i·line [AN-l-in] *n* product of coal tar or indigo that yields dyes.

an·i·mal [AN-ə-məl] *n* **1** living creature, having sensation and power of voluntary motion. **2** beast. ◆ *adj* **3** of, pert. to animals. **4** sensual. **an·i·mal·cule** [an-ə-MAL-kyool] *n* very small animal, esp. one that cannot be seen by naked eye. **animal husbandry** branch of agriculture concerned with raising domestic animals.

an·i·mate [AN-ə-mayt] *vt* **-mat·ed, -mat·ing 1** give life to. **2** enliven. **3** inspire. **4** actuate. **5** make cartoon film of. **an'i·mat·ed** *adj* **1** lively. **2** in form of cartoons. **an·i·ma'tion** *n* **1** life, vigor. **2** cartoon film.

an·i·mism [AN-ə-miz-əm] *n* primitive religion, belief that natural effects are due to spirits, that inanimate things have spirits. **an'i·mist** *n*

an·i·mos·i·ty [an-ə-MOS-i-tee] *n, pl* **-ties** hostility, enmity.

an·i·mus [AN-ə-məs] *n* **1** hatred. **2** animosity.

THESAURUS

anger *n* **1 = rage**, annoyance, displeasure, exasperation, fury, ire, outrage, resentment, temper, wrath ◆ *v* **2 = madden**, annoy, displease, enrage, exasperate, gall, incense, infuriate, outrage, rile, vex

angle¹ *n* **1 = intersection**, bend, corner, crook, edge, elbow, nook, point **2 = point of view**, approach, aspect, outlook, perspective, position, side, slant, standpoint, viewpoint

angle² *v* **= fish**, cast

angry *adj* **= furious**, annoyed, cross, displeased, enraged, exasperated, incensed, infuriated, irate, mad, outraged, resentful

angst *n* **= anxiety**, apprehension, unease, worry

anguish *n* **= suffering**, agony, distress, grief, heartache, misery, pain, sorrow, torment, woe

animal *n* **1 = creature**, beast, brute **2** *Applied to a person* **= brute**, barbarian, beast, monster, savage, wild man ◆ *adj* **3 = physical**, bestial, bodily, brutish, carnal, gross, sensual

animate *v* **1 = enliven**, energize, excite, fire, inspire, invigorate, kindle, move, stimulate ◆ *adj* **2 = living**, alive, alive and kicking, breathing, live, moving

animated *adj* **= lively**, ebullient, energetic, enthusiastic, excited, passionate, spirited, vivacious, wired (*sl*)

animation *n* **= liveliness**, ebullience, energy, enthusiasm, excitement, fervor, passion, spirit, verve, vivacity, zest

animosity *n* **= hostility**, acrimony, antipathy, bitterness, enmity, hatred, ill will, malevolence, malice, rancor, resentment

an·i·on [AN-ī-ən] *n* ion with negative charge.

an·ise [AN-is] *n* plant with aromatic seeds, which are used for flavoring.

an·i·seed [AN-ə-seed] *n* the licorice-flavored seed of anise.

an·kle [ANG-kəl] *n* joint between foot and leg. **an·klet** [ANG klit] *n* **1** ankle-ornament. **2** short sock reaching just above the ankle.

an·nals [AN-lz] *pl n* historical records of events. **an'nal·ist** *n*

an·neal [ə-NEEL] *vt* **1** toughen (metal or glass) by heating and slow cooling. **2** temper.

an·ne·lid [AN-l-id] *n* one of class of invertebrate animals, including the earthworm, etc.

an·nex [ə-NEKS] *vt* **1** add, append, attach. **2** take possession of (esp. territory). **an·nex·a·tion** [an-ik-SAY-shən] *n* annex *n* [AN-eks] **1** supplementary building. **2** something added.

an·ni·hi·late [ə-NĪ-ə-layt] *vt* -lat·ed, -lat·ing reduce to nothing, destroy utterly. **an·ni·hi·la'tion** *n*

an·ni·ver·sa·ry [an-ə-VUR-sə-ree] *n* **1** yearly return of a date. **2** celebration of this.

an·no Dom·i·ni [AN-oh DOM-ə-nee] *Lat* in the year of our Lord.

an·no·tate [AN-ə-tayt] *vt* -tat·ed, -tat·ing make notes upon, comment. **an·no·ta'tion** *n*

an·nounce [ə-NOWNS] *vt* -nounced, -nounc·ing make known, proclaim. **an·nounce'ment** *n* **an·nounc'er** *n*

broadcaster who announces items in program, introduces speakers, etc.

an·noy [ə-NOI] *vt* **1** vex. **2** make slightly angry. **3** tease. **an·noy'ance** *n*

an·nu·al [AN-yoo-əl] *adj* **1** yearly. **2** of, for a year. ♦ *n* **3** plant that completes its life cycle in a year. **4** book published each year. **an'nu·al·ly** *adv*

an·nu·i·ty [ə-NOO-i-tee] *n, pl* -ties sum or grant paid every year. **an·nu'i·tant** [-tnt] *n* holder of annuity.

an·nul [ə-NUL] *vt* -nulled, -nul·ling make void, cancel, abolish.

an·nu·lar [AN-yə-lər] *adj* ring-shaped. **an'nu·lat·ed** [-lay-tid] *adj* formed in rings. **an'nu·let** [-lit] *n* small ring or molding in shape of ring.

An·nun·ci·a·tion [ə-nun-see-AY-shən] *n* **1** angel's announcement of Incarnation to the Virgin Mary (**a**-) **2** announcing. **3** announcement. **an·nun'ci·ate** *vt* -at·ed, -at·ing proclaim, announce.

an·ode [AN-ohd] *n Electricity* **1** the positive electrode or terminal. **an·o·dize** [AN-ə-dīz] *vt* cover (metal object) with protective film by using it as an anode in electrolysis.

an·o·dyne [AN-ə-dīn] *adj* **1** relieving pain, soothing. ♦ *n* **2** pain-relieving drug. **3** something that soothes.

a·noint [ə-NOINT] *vt* **1** smear with oil or ointment. **2** consecrate with oil. **a·noint'ment** *n* **1** the Anointed. **2** the Messiah.

a·nom·a·lous [ə-NOM-ə-ləs] *adj* irregular, abnormal. **a·nom'a·ly** *n, pl* -lies **1** irregularity. **2** deviation from rule.

annals *pl n* = **records**, accounts, archives, chronicles, history

annex *v* **1** = **seize**, acquire, appropriate, conquer, occupy, take over **2** = **join**, add, adjoin, attach, connect, fasten

annihilate *v* = **destroy**, abolish, decimate, eradicate, exterminate, extinguish, obliterate, wipe out

announce *v* = **make known**, advertise, broadcast, declare, disclose, proclaim, report, reveal, tell

announcement *n* = **statement**, advertisement, broadcast, bulletin, communiqué, declaration, proclamation, report, revelation

announcer *n* = **presenter**, broadcaster, commentator, master of ceremonies, newscaster, newsreader, reporter

annoy *v* = **irritate**, anger, bother, displease, disturb, exasperate, get on one's nerves (*inf*), hassle (*inf*), madden, molest, pester, plague, trouble, vex

annoyance *n* **1** = **irritation**, anger, bother, hassle (*inf*), nuisance, trouble **2** = **nuisance**, bore, bother, drag (*inf*), pain (*inf*)

annoying *adj* = **irritating**, disturbing, exasperating, maddening, troublesome

annual *adj* = **yearly**, once a year, yearlong

annually *adv* = **yearly**, by the year, once a year, per annum, per year

annul *v* = **invalidate**, abolish, cancel, declare or render null and void, negate, nullify, repeal, retract

anoint *v* = **consecrate**, bless, hallow, sanctify

anomalous *adj* = **unusual**, abnormal,

a·non [ə-NON] *adv obs* **1** in a short time, soon. **2** now and then.

a·non·y·mous [ə-NON-ə-məs] *adj* nameless, esp. without an author's name. **an·o·nym·i·ty** [an-ə-NIM-i-tee] *n*

an·o·rak [AN-ə-rak] *n* **1** lightweight, warm, waterproof, usu. hooded jacket. **2** parka.

an·o·rex·i·a ner·vo·sa [an-ə-REK-see-ə nur-VOH-sə] *n* psychological disorder characterized by fear of becoming fat and refusal to eat.

an·oth·er [ə-NUTH-ər] *pron, adj* **1** one other. **2** a different one. **3** one more.

an·ser·ine [AN-sə-rīn] *adj* **1** of or like a goose. **2** silly.

an·swer [AN-sər] *v* **1** reply (to). **2** solve. **3** reply correctly. **4** pay. **5** meet. **6** be accountable (for, to). **7** match. **8** satisfy, suit. ◆ *n* **9** reply. **10** solution. **an'swer·a·ble** *adj* accountable. **answering machine** apparatus for answering a telephone automatically and recording messages.

ant *n* small social insect, proverbial for industry. **ant'eat·er** *n* animal that feeds on ants by means of a long, sticky tongue. **ant'hill** the mound raised by ants.

an·tag·o·nist [an-TAG-ə-nist] *n* opponent, adversary. **an·tag'o·nism** *n* **an·tag·o·nis'tic** *adj* **an·tag'o·nize** *vt* **-nized, -niz·ing** arouse hostility in.

Ant·arc·tic [ant-AHRK-tik] *adj* **1** south polar. ◆ *n* **2** these regions.

an·te [AN-tee] *n* **1** player's stake in poker. ◆ *vt* **-ted, -te·ing 2** (often with *up*) stake.

ante- *prefix* before in time or position, e.g. *antedate; antechamber.*

an·te·ced·ent [an-tə-SEED-nt] *adj, n* (thing) going before.

an·te·di·lu·vi·an [an-tee-di-LOO-vee-ən] *adj* **1** before the Flood. **2** ancient.

an·te·lope [AN-tl-ohp] *n* deer-like ruminant animal, remarkable for grace and speed.

ante me·rid·i·em [AN-tee mə-RID-ee-əm] *Lat* before noon.

an·ten·na [an-TEN-ə] *n, pl* **-nae** [-nee] **1** insect's feeler. **2** aerial.

an·te·pe·nult [an-tee-PEE-nult] *n* last syllable but two in a word. **an·te·pe·nul'ti·mate** *adj, n*

an·te·ri·or [an-TEER-ee-ər] *adj* **1** to the front. **2** before.

an·them [AN-thəm] *n* **1** song of loyalty, esp. to a country. **2** Scripture passage set to music. **3** piece of sacred music, originally sung in alternate parts by two choirs.

an·ther [AN-thər] *n* in flower, part at top of stamen containing pollen.

an·thol·o·gy [an-THOL-ə-jee] *n, pl* **-gies** collection of poems, literary extracts, etc. **an·thol'o·gist** *n* maker of such. **an·thol'o·gize** *vt* **-gized, -giz·ing** compile or publish in an anthology.

an·thra·cite [AN-thrə-sīt] *n* hard coal burning slowly almost without flame or smoke.

an·thrax [AN-thraks] *n* **1** malignant disease in cattle, communicable to people. **2** sore caused by this.

an·thro·poid [AN-thrə-poid] *adj* **1** like man. ◆ *n* **2** ape resembling human being.

an·thro·pol·o·gy [an-thrə-POL-ə-jee] *n* scientific study of origins, development of

eccentric, exceptional, incongruous, inconsistent, irregular, odd, peculiar

anomaly *n* = **irregularity**, abnormality, eccentricity, exception, incongruity, inconsistency, oddity, peculiarity

anonymous *adj* = **unnamed**, incognito, nameless, unacknowledged, uncredited, unidentified, unknown, unsigned

answer *v* **1** = **reply**, explain, react, resolve, respond, retort, return, solve ◆ *n* **2** = **reply**, comeback, defense, explanation, reaction, rejoinder, response, retort, return, riposte, solution

answerable *adj* (usually with *for* or *to*) = **responsible**, accountable, amenable, chargeable, liable, subject, to blame

answer for *v* = **be responsible for**, be

accountable for, be answerable for, be chargeable for, be liable for, be to blame for

antagonism *n* = **hostility**, antipathy, conflict, discord, dissension, friction, opposition, rivalry

antagonist *n* = **opponent**, adversary, competitor, contender, enemy, foe, rival

antagonistic *adj* = **hostile**, at odds, at variance, conflicting, incompatible, in dispute, opposed, unfriendly

antagonize *v* = **annoy**, anger, get on one's nerves (*inf*), hassle (*inf*), irritate, offend

anthem *n* **1** = **hymn**, canticle, carol, chant, chorale, psalm **2** = **song of praise**, paean

anthology *n* = **collection**, compendium, compilation, miscellany, selection, treasury

human race. **an·thro·po·log'i·cal**
[-pə-LOJ-i-kəl] *adj* **an·thro·pol'o·gist** *n*
an·thro·po·mor·phize
[an-thrə-pə-MOR-fiz] *vt* **-pized, -piz·ing**
ascribe human attributes to God or an
animal. **an·thro·po·mor'phic** *adj*
anti- *prefix* **1** against, opposed to, e.g.
anti-war. **2** opposite to, e.g. *anticlimax.* **3**
counteracting, e.g. *antifreeze.*
an·ti·bi·ot·ic [an-ti-bī-OT-ik] *n* any of
various chemical, fungal or synthetic
substances, esp. penicillin, used against
bacterial infection. ♦ *adj*
an·ti·bod·y [AN-ti-bod-ee] *n* substance in,
or introduced into, blood serum that
counteracts the growth and harmful action
of bacteria.
an·tic·i·pate [an-TIS-ə-payt] *vt* **-pat·ed,
-pat·ing 1** expect. **2** take or consider
beforehand. **3** foresee. **4** enjoy in advance.
an·tic·i·pa'tion *n* **an·tic'i·pa·to·ry**
[-pə-tor-ee] *adj*
an·ti·cli·max [an-ti-KLĪ-maks] *n* sudden
descent to the trivial or ludicrous.
an·ti·cli·mac'tic *adj*
an·tics [AN-tiks] *pl n* absurd or grotesque
movements or acts.
an·ti·cy·clone [an-tee-SĪ-klohn] *n* system
of winds moving around center of high
barometric pressure.
an·ti·dote [AN-ti-doht] *n* counteracting
remedy.
an·ti·freeze [AN-ti-freez] *n* liquid added to
water to lower its freezing point, as in
automobile radiators.
an·ti·gen [AN-ti-jən] *n* substance
stimulating production of antibodies in the

blood.
an·ti·his·ta·mine [an-ti-HIS-tə-meen] *n*
drug used esp. to treat allergies.
an·ti·mo·ny [AN-tə-moh-nee] *n* brittle,
bluish-white metal.
an·tip·a·thy [an-TIP-ə-thee] *n, pl* **-thies**
dislike, aversion.
an·ti·per·spi·rant [an-ti-PUR-spər-ənt] *n*
substance used to reduce sweating.
an·ti·phon [AN-tə-fon] *n* **1** composition in
which verses, lines are sung alternately by
two choirs. **2** anthem. **an·tiph·o·nal**
[an-TIF-ə-nl] *adj*
an·tip·o·des [an-TIP-ə-deez] *pl n* countries,
peoples on opposite side of the globe
(often refers to Aust. and N Zealand).
an·tip·o·de'an *adj*
an·ti·pope [AN-ti-pohp] *n* pope elected in
opposition to the one regularly chosen.
passé
an·tique [an-TEEK] *n* **1** relic of former
times, usu. a piece of furniture, etc. that is
collected. ♦ *adj* **2** ancient. **3** old-fashioned.
an·ti·quar'i·an *n* student or collector of old
things. **an'ti·quat·ed** *adj* out-of-date.
an·tiq·ui·ty [an-TIK-wi-tee] *n* **1** great age. **2**
former times.
an·ti·Se·mit·ic [an-tee-sə-MIT-ik] *adj*
hostile or discriminating against Jews.
an·ti·Sem'i·tism *n* **an·ti·Sem'ite** *n*
an·ti·sep·tic [an-tə-SEPT-tik] *n, adj*
(substance) preventing infection. ♦ *adj* free
from infection.
an·tith·e·sis [an-TITH-ə-sis] *n, pl* **-ses**
[-seez] **1** direct opposite. **2** contrast. **3**
opposition of ideas. **an·ti·thet'i·cal** *adj*
an·ti·tox·in [an-ti-TOK-sin] *n* serum used

┤ T H E S A U R U S ├

anticipate *v* = **expect**, await, foresee,
foretell, hope for, look forward to, predict,
prepare for
anticipation *n* = **expectation**, expectancy,
foresight, forethought, premonition,
prescience
anticlimax *n* = **disappointment**, bathos,
comedown (*inf*), letdown
antics *pl n* = **clowning**, escapades,
horseplay, mischief, playfulness, pranks,
tomfoolery, tricks
antidote *n* = **cure**, countermeasure,
remedy
antipathy *n* = **hostility**, aversion, bad
blood, dislike, enmity, hatred, ill will
antiquated *adj* = **obsolete**, antique,
archaic, dated, old-fashioned, out-of-date,

antique *n* **1** = **period piece**, bygone,
heirloom, relic ♦ *adj* **2** = **vintage**,
antiquarian, classic, olden **3** =
old-fashioned, archaic, obsolete, outdated
antiquity *n* **1** = **old age**, age, ancientness,
elderliness, oldness **2** = **distant past**,
ancient times, olden days, time
immemorial
antiseptic *adj* **1** = **hygienic**, clean,
germ-free, pure, sanitary, sterile,
uncontaminated ♦ *n* **2** = **disinfectant**,
germicide, purifier
antisocial *adj* **1** = **unsociable**, alienated,
misanthropic, reserved, retiring,
uncommunicative, unfriendly, withdrawn
2 = **disruptive**, antagonistic, belligerent,
disorderly, hostile, menacing, rebellious,

to neutralize disease poisons.

an·ti·trust [an-ti-TRUST] *adj* (of laws) opposing business monopolies.

an·ti·tus·sive [an-ti-TUS-iv] *n, adj* (substance) controlling or preventing coughing.

an·ti·ven·in [an-tee-VEN-in] *n* antitoxin to counteract specific venom, esp. of snake or spider.

ant·ler [ANT-lər] *n* branching horn of certain deer.

an·to·nym [AN-tə-nim] *n* word of opposite meaning to another, e.g. *cold* is an antonym of *hot*.

a·nus [AY-nəs] *n* the lower opening of the bowels. **a'nal** *adj*

an'vil *n* heavy iron block with steel face on which a blacksmith hammers metal into shape.

anx·ious [ANGK-shəs] *adj* 1 troubled, uneasy. 2 concerned. **anx·i·e·ty** [ang-ZĪ-ə-tee]

an·y [EN-ee] *adj* [pron.] 1 one indefinitely. 2 some. 3 every. **an'y·bod·y** *n* **an'y·how** *adv* **an'y·one** *n* **an'y·thing** *n* **an'y·way** *adv* **an'y·where** *adv*

a·or·ta [ay-OR-tə] *n* great artery rising from left ventricle of heart. **a·or'tal** *adj*

a·pace [ə-PAYS] *adv* swiftly.

a·part [ə-PAHRT] *adv* 1 separately, aside. 2 in pieces.

a·part·heid [ə-PAHRT-hayt] *n* former official government policy of racial segregation in S Africa.

a·part·ment [ə-PAHRT-mənt] *n* room or suite of rooms in larger building used for dwelling.

ap·a·thy [AP-ə-thee] *n, pl* **-thies** 1 indifference. 2 lack of emotion. **ap·a·thet'ic** *adj*

ape [ayp] *n* 1 tailless monkey such as the chimpanzee or gorilla. 2 coarse, clumsy person. 3 imitator. ◆ *vt* **aped, ap·ing** 4 imitate.

a·pe·ri·od·ic [ay-peer-ee-OD-ik] *adj* *Electricity* having no natural period or frequency.

a·pe·ri·tif [ə-per-i-TEEF] *n* alcoholic appetizer.

ap·er·ture [AP-ər-chər] *n* opening, hole.

a·pex [AY-peks] *n, pl* **a·pex·es** 1 top, peak. 2 vertex.

a·pha·sia [ə-FAY-zhə] *n* dumbness, or loss of speech control, due to disease of the brain.

a·phe·li·on [ə-FEE-lee-ən] *n* point of planet's orbit farthest from the sun.

a·phid [AY-fid] *n* any of various sap-sucking insects.

a·phis [AY-fis] *n, pl* **a·phi·des** [AY-fi-deez] an aphid.

aph·o·rism [AF-ə-riz-əm] *n* maxim, pithy saying. **aph·o·ris'tic** [-RIS-tik] *adj*

aph·ro·dis·i·ac [af-rə-DEE-zee-ak] *adj* 1 exciting sexual desire. ◆ *n* 2 substance that so excites.

a·pi·ar·y [AY-pee-er-ee] *n, pl* **-ar·ies** place where bees are kept. **a'pi·a·rist** *n* beekeeper. **a'pi·cul·ture** *n*

a·piece [ə-PEES] *adv* for each.

a·plomb [ə-PLOM] *n* self-possession, coolness, assurance.

──── THESAURUS ────

uncooperative

antithesis *n* = **opposite**, contrary, contrast, converse, inverse, reverse

anxiety *n* = **uneasiness**, angst, apprehension, concern, foreboding, misgiving, nervousness, tension, trepidation, worry

anxious *adj* 1 = **uneasy**, apprehensive, concerned, fearful, in suspense, nervous, on tenterhooks, tense, troubled, wired (*sl*), worried 2 = **eager**, desirous, impatient, intent, keen, yearning

apart *adv* 1 = **to pieces**, asunder, in bits, in pieces, to bits 2 = **separate**, alone, aside, away, by oneself, isolated, to one side 3 apart from = **except for**, aside from, besides, but, excluding, not counting, other than, save

apartment *n* = **room**, accommodation, flat, living quarters, penthouse, quarters, rooms, suite

apathetic *adj* = **uninterested**, cool, indifferent, passive, phlegmatic, unconcerned

apathy *n* = **lack of interest**, coolness, indifference, inertia, nonchalance, passivity, torpor, unconcern

apex *n* = **highest point**, crest, crown, culmination, peak, pinnacle, point, summit, top

apiece *adv* = **each**, for each, from each, individually, respectively, separately, to each

aplomb *n* = **self-possession**, calmness, composure, confidence, level-headedness, poise, sang-froid, self-assurance,

a·poc·a·lypse [ə-POK-ə-lips] *n* **1** prophetic revelation esp. of future of the world. **2** (A-) revelation to St. John, recounted in last book of the New Testament. **a·poc·a·lyp'tic** *adj*

a·poc·ry·pha [ə-POK-rə-fə] *pl n* **1** religious writing of doubtful authenticity. **2** (A-) collective name for 14 books originally in the Old Testament. **a·poc'ry·phal** *adj* spurious.

ap·o·gee [AP-ə-jee] *n* **1** point farthest from Earth in orbit of moon or satellite. **2** climax. **3** highest point.

a·pol·o·gy [ə-POL-ə-jee] *n, pl* **-gies 1** acknowledgment of offense and expression of regret. **2** written or spoken defense. **3** (with *for*) poor substitute. **a·pol·o·get'ic** *adj* **a·pol·o·get'ics** *n* branch of theology charged with defense of Christianity. **a·pol'o·gist** *n* **a·pol'o·gize** *vi* **-gized, -giz·ing**

ap·o·plex·y [AP-ə-plek-see] *n* **1** loss of sense and often paralysis caused by broken or blocked blood vessel in the brain. **2** a stroke. **ap·o·plec'tic** *adj*

a·pos·ta·sy [ə-POS-tə-see] *n, pl* **-sies** abandonment of one's religious or other faith. **a·pos'tate** [-tayt] *n, adj*

a pos·te·ri·o·ri [ay po-steer-ee-OR-ī] *adj* **1** denoting form of inductive reasoning that arrives at causes from effects. **2** empirical.

a·pos·tle [ə-POS-əl] *n* **1** ardent supporter. **2** leader of reform (A-) **3** one sent to preach the Gospel, esp. one of the first disciples of Jesus. **4** founder of Christian church in a country. **ap·os·tol'ic** *adj*

a·pos·tro·phe [ə-POS-trə-fee] *n* **1** a mark (') showing the omission of a letter or letters in a word. **2** digression to appeal to someone dead or absent.

ap·o·thegm [AP-ə-them] *n* terse saying, maxim.

a·poth·e·o·sis [ə-poth-ee-OH-sis] *n, pl* **-ses** [-seez] deification, act of raising any person or thing into a god.

ap·pall [ə-PAWL] *vt* dismay, terrify. **ap·pall'ing** *adj inf* dreadful, terrible.

ap·pa·rat·us [ap-ə-RAT-əs] *n* **1** equipment, tools, instruments, for performing any experiment, operation, etc. **2** means by which something operates.

ap·par·el [ə-PAR-əl] *n* **1** clothing. ♦ *vt* **-eled, -el·ing 2** clothe.

ap·par·ent [ə-PAR-ənt] *adj* **1** seeming. **2** obvious. **3** acknowledged, e.g. *heir apparent.*

ap·pa·ri·tion [ap-ə-RISH-ən] *n* appearance, esp. of ghost.

ap·peal [ə-PEEL] *vi* (with *to*) call upon, make earnest request. **1** be attractive. **2** refer to, have recourse to. **3** apply to higher court. ♦ *n* **4** request, reference, supplication. **ap·peal'ing** *adj* **1** making appeal. **2** pleasant, attractive. **ap·pel'lant** [-PEL-ənt] *n* one who appeals to higher court. **ap·pel'late** [-it] *adj* of appeals.

———[THESAURUS]———

self-confidence

apocryphal *adj* = **dubious**, doubtful, legendary, mythical, questionable, unauthenticated, unsubstantiated

apologetic *adj* = **regretful**, contrite, penitent, remorseful, rueful, sorry

apologize *v* = **say sorry**, ask forgiveness, beg pardon, express regret

apology *n* **1** = **defense**, acknowledgment, confession, excuse, explanation, justification, plea **2** *As in* **an apology for** = **mockery**, caricature, excuse, imitation, travesty

apostle *n* **1** = **evangelist**, herald, messenger, missionary, preacher **2** = **supporter**, advocate, champion, pioneer, propagandist, proponent

apotheosis *n* = **deification**, elevation, exaltation, glorification, idealization, idolization

appall *v* = **horrify**, alarm, daunt,

dishearten, dismay, frighten, outrage, shock, unnerve

appalling *adj* = **horrifying**, alarming, awful, daunting, dreadful, fearful, frightful, horrible, shocking, terrifying

apparatus *n* **1** = **equipment**, appliance, contraption (*inf*), device, gear, machinery, mechanism, tackle, tools **2** = **organization**, bureaucracy, chain of command, hierarchy, network, setup (*inf*), structure, system

apparent *adj* **1** = **obvious**, discernible, distinct, evident, manifest, marked, unmistakable, visible **2** = **seeming**, ostensible, outward, superficial

apparently *adv* = **it appears that**, it seems that, on the face of it, ostensibly, outwardly, seemingly, superficially

apparition *n* = **ghost**, chimera, phantom, specter, spirit, wraith

appeal *v* **1** = **plead**, ask, beg, call upon,

ap·pear [ə-PEER] *vi* **1** become visible or present. **2** seem, be plain. **3** be seen in public. **ap·pear'ance** *n* **1** an appearing. **2** aspect. **3** pretense.

ap·pease [ə-PEEZ] *vt* **-peased, -peas·ing** pacify, quiet, allay, satisfy. **ap·pease'ment** *n*

appellant see APPEAL.

ap·pel·la·tion [ap-ə-LAY-shən] *n* name.

ap·pend [ə-PEND] *vt* join on, add. **ap·pend'age** *n*

ap·pen·di·ci·tis [ə-pen-də-SĪ-tis] *n* inflammation of vermiform appendix.

ap·pen·dix [ə-PEN-diks] *n, pl* **-di·ces** [-də-seez] **1** subsidiary addition to book, etc. **2** *Anatomy* projection, esp. the small worm-shaped part of the intestine.

ap·per·cep·tion [ap-ər-SEP-shən] *n* **1** perception. **2** apprehension. **3** the mind's perception of itself as a conscious agent.

ap·per·tain [ap-ər-TAYN] *vi* belong, relate to, be appropriate.

ap·pe·tite [AP-i-tīt] *n* desire, inclination, esp. desire for food. **ap'pe·tiz·er** *n* something stimulating to appetite.

ap'pe·tiz·ing *adj*

ap·plaud [ə-PLAWD] *vt* **1** praise by handclapping. **2** praise loudly. **ap·plause'** [-PLAWZ] *n* loud approval.

ap·ple [AP-əl] *n* **1** round, firm, fleshy fruit. **2** tree bearing it.

ap·plet [AP-lət] *n Computers* computing program that runs within a page on the World Wide Web.

ap·pli·ance [ə-PLĪ-əns] *n* piece of equipment esp. electrical.

ap·pli·qué [ap-li-KAY] *n* **1** ornaments, embroidery, etc., secured to surface of material. ♦ *vt* **-quéd, -qué·ing 2** ornament thus.

ap·ply [ə-PLĪ] *v* **-plied, -ply·ing** ♦ *vt* **1** utilize, employ. **2** lay or place on. **3** administer, devote. ♦ *vi* **4** have reference (to). **5** make request (to). **ap'pli·ca·ble** *adj* relevant. **ap'pli·cant** *n* **ap·pli·ca'tion** *n* **1** applying something for a particular use. **2** relevance. **3** request for a job, etc. **4** concentration, diligence. **applied** *adj* (of skill, science, etc.) put to practical use.

ap·point [ə-POINT] *vt* **1** name, assign to a

entreat, pray, request **2 = attract**, allure, charm, entice, fascinate, interest, please, tempt ♦ *n* **3 = plea**, application, entreaty, petition, prayer, request, supplication **4 = attraction**, allure, beauty, charm, fascination

appealing *adj* **= attractive**, alluring, charming, desirable, engaging, winsome

appear *v* **1 = come into view**, be present, come out, come to light, crop up (*inf*), emerge, occur, show up (*inf*), surface, turn up **2 = look (like** *or* **as if)**, occur, seem, strike one as

appearance *n* **1 = arrival**, coming, emergence, introduction, presence **2 = look**, demeanor, expression, figure, form, looks, manner, mien (*literary*) **3 = impression**, front, guise, illusion, image, outward show, pretense, semblance

appease *v* **1 = pacify**, calm, conciliate, mollify, placate, quiet, satisfy, soothe **2 = ease**, allay, alleviate, calm, relieve, soothe

appeasement *n* **1 = pacification**, accommodation, compromise, concession, conciliation, mollification, placation **2 = easing**, alleviation, lessening, relieving, soothing

appendage *n* **= attachment**, accessory, addition, supplement

appendix *n* **= supplement**, addendum, addition, adjunct, appendage, postscript

appetite *n* **= desire**, craving, demand, hunger, liking, longing, passion, relish, stomach, taste, yearning

appetizing *adj* **= delicious**, appealing, inviting, mouthwatering, palatable, succulent, tasty, tempting, yummy (*inf*)

applaud *v* **= clap**, acclaim, approve, cheer, commend, compliment, encourage, extol, praise

applause *n* **= ovation**, accolade, approval, big hand, cheers, clapping, hand, praise

appliance *n* **= device**, apparatus, gadget, implement, instrument, machine, mechanism, tool

applicable *adj* **= appropriate**, apt, fitting, pertinent, relevant, suitable, useful

applicant *n* **= candidate**, claimant, inquirer

application *n* **1 = request**, appeal, claim, inquiry, petition, requisition **2 = effort**, commitment, dedication, diligence, hard work, industry, perseverance

apply *v* **1 = request**, appeal, claim, inquire, petition, put in, requisition **2 = use**, bring to bear, carry out, employ, exercise, exert, implement, practice, utilize **3 = put on**, cover with, lay on, paint, place, smear, spread on **4 = be relevant**, be applicable,

job or position. **2** fix, settle. **3** equip.
ap·point'ment *n* **1** engagement to meet. **2** (selection for a) position. ◆ *pl* **3** equipment, furnishings.

ap·por·tion [ə-POR-shən] *vt* divide out in shares. **ap·por'tion·ment** *n*

ap·po·site [AP-ə-zit] *adj* suitable, apt. **ap'po·site·ness** *n* **ap·po·si'tion** [-ZISH-ən] *n* **1** proximity. **2** the placing of one word beside another that it describes.

ap·praise [ə-PRAYZ] *vt* **-praised, -prais·ing** set price on, estimate value of. **ap·prais'al** *n* **ap·prais'er** *n*

ap·pre·ci·ate [ə-PREE-shee-ayt] *v* **-at·ed, -at·ing** ◆ *vt* **1** value at true worth. **2** be

grateful for. **3** understand. **4** enjoy. ◆ *vi* **5** rise in value. **ap·pre'ci·a·ble** [-shə-bəl] *adj* **1** estimable. **2** substantial. **ap·pre'ci·a·bly** *adv* **ap·pre·ci·a'tion** *n* **ap·pre'cia·tive** [-shə-tiv] *adj* capable of expressing pleasurable recognition.

ap·pre·hend [ap-ri-HEND] *vt* **1** arrest, seize by authority. **2** take hold of. **3** recognize, understand. **4** dread. **ap·pre·hen'si·ble** [-HEN-sə-bəl] *adj* **ap·pre·hen'sion** [-shən] *n* **1** dread, anxiety. **2** arrest. **3** conception. **4** ability to understand. **ap·pre·hen'sive** [-siv] *adj* **ap·pre·hen'sive·ly** *adv*

ap·pren·tice [ə-PREN-tis] *n* **1** person learning a trade under specified

——————| THESAURUS |——————

be appropriate, bear upon, be fitting, fit, pertain, refer, relate **5 apply oneself** = **try**, be diligent, buckle down (*inf*), commit oneself, concentrate, dedicate oneself, devote oneself, persevere, work hard

appoint *v* **1** = **assign**, choose, commission, delegate, elect, name, nominate, select **2** = **decide**, allot, arrange, assign, choose, designate, establish, fix, set **3** = **equip**, fit out, furnish, provide, supply

appointed *adj* **1** = **assigned**, chosen, delegated, elected, named, nominated, selected **2** = **decided**, allotted, arranged, assigned, chosen, designated, established, fixed, set **3** = **equipped**, fitted out, furnished, provided, supplied

appointment *n* **1** = **meeting**, arrangement, assignation, date, engagement, interview, rendezvous **2** = **selection**, assignment, choice, election, naming, nomination **3** = **job**, assignment, office, place, position, post, situation **4 appointments** = **fittings**, fixtures, furnishings, gear, outfit, paraphernalia, trappings

apportion *v* = **divide**, allocate, allot, assign, dispense, distribute, dole out, ration out, share

apportionment *n* = **division**, allocation, allotment, assignment, dispensing, distribution, doling out, rationing out, sharing

apposite *adj* = **appropriate**, applicable, apt, fitting, pertinent, relevant, suitable, to the point

appraisal *n* = **assessment**, estimate, estimation, evaluation, judgment, opinion

appraise *v* = **assess**, estimate, evaluate, gauge, judge, rate, review, value

appreciable *adj* = **significant**, considerable, definite, discernible, evident, marked, noticeable, obvious, pronounced, substantial

appreciate *v* **1** = **value**, admire, enjoy, like, prize, rate highly, respect, treasure **2** = **be aware of**, perceive, realize, recognize, sympathize with, take account of, understand **3** = **be grateful for**, be appreciative, be indebted, be obliged, be thankful for, give thanks for **4** = **increase**, enhance, gain, grow, improve, rise

appreciation *n* **1** = **gratitude**, acknowledgment, gratefulness, indebtedness, obligation, thankfulness, thanks **2** = **awareness**, admiration, comprehension, enjoyment, perception, realization, recognition, sensitivity, sympathy, understanding **3** = **increase**, enhancement, gain, growth, improvement, rise

appreciative *adj* **1** = **grateful**, beholden, indebted, obliged, thankful **2** = **aware**, admiring, enthusiastic, respectful, responsive, sensitive, sympathetic, understanding

apprehend *v* **1** = **arrest**, capture, catch, seize, take prisoner **2** = **understand**, comprehend, conceive, get the picture, grasp, perceive, realize, recognize

apprehension *n* **1** = **anxiety**, alarm, concern, dread, fear, foreboding, suspicion, trepidation, worry **2** = **arrest**, capture, catching, seizure, taking **3** = **awareness**, comprehension, grasp, perception, understanding

apprehensive *adj* = **anxious**, concerned, foreboding, nervous, uneasy, wired (*sl*), worried

conditions. **2** novice. ◆ *vt* **-ticed, -tic·ing 3** bind, set to work, as apprentice.
ap·pren'tice·ship *n*

ap·prise [ə-PRĪZ] *vt* **-prised, -pris·ing** inform.

ap·proach [ə-PROHCH] *v* **1** draw near (to). **2** set about. **3** address request to. **4** approximate to. **5** make advances to. ◆ *n* **6** a drawing near. **7** means of reaching or doing. **8** approximation. **9** (oft. pl) friendly or amatory overture(s). **ap·proach'a·ble** *adj*

ap·pro·ba·tion [ap-rə-BAY-shən] *n* approval.

ap·pro·pri·ate [ə-PROH-pree-ayt] *vt* **-at·ed, -at·ing 1** take for oneself. **2** put aside for particular purpose. ◆ *adj* [-it] suitable, fitting. **ap·pro'pri·ate·ness** [-it-nis] *n* **ap·pro·pri·a'tion** *n* **1** act of setting apart for purpose. **2** legislative vote of money.

ap·prove [ə-PROOV] *vt* **-proved, -prov·ing 1** think well of, commend. **2** authorize, agree to. **ap·prov'al** *n* **ap·prov'ing·ly** *adv*

ap·prox·i·mate [ə-PROK-sə-mit] *adj* **1** very near, nearly correct. **2** inexact, imprecise. ◆ *v* [-mayt] **-mat·ed, -mat·ing** ◆ *vt* **3** bring close. ◆ *vi* **4** come near. **5** be almost the same as. **ap·prox'i·mate·ly** *adv*

ap·pur·te·nance [ə-PUR-tn-əns] *n* **1** thing that appertains to. **2** accessory.

après-ski [ah-pray-SKEE] *n* social activities after day's skiing.

ap·ri·cot [AP-ri-kot] *n* **1** orange-colored fruit related to the plum. ◆ *adj* **2** of the color of the fruit.

A·pril fool [AY-prəl] butt of a joke or trick played on April Fools' Day, April 1.

a pri·o·ri [ay-prī-OR-ī] *adj* **1** denoting deductive reasoning from general principle to expected facts or effects. **2** denoting knowledge gained independently of experience.

a·pron [AY-prən] *n* **1** cloth, piece of leather, etc., worn in front to protect clothes, or as part of costume. **2** in theater, strip of stage before curtain. **3** on airfield, paved area where aircraft stand, are refueled, etc. **4** *fig* any of a variety of things resembling these.

ap·ro·pos [ap-rə-POH] *adv* **1** to the purpose. **2** with reference to. ◆ *adj* **3** apt, appropriate. *apropos* of concerning.

apse [aps] *n* arched recess, esp. in a church.

apt *adj* **1** suitable. **2** likely. **3** prompt, quick-witted. **4** dexterous. **ap·ti·tude** [AP-ti-tood] *n* capacity, fitness. **apt'ly** *adv* **apt'ness** *n*

aq·ua·ma·rine [ak-wə-mə-REEN] *n* **1**

THESAURUS

apprentice *n* = **trainee**, beginner, learner, novice, probationer, pupil, student

approach *v* **1** = **move towards**, come close, come near, draw near, near, reach **2** = **make a proposal to**, appeal to, apply to, make overtures to, sound out **3** = **set about**, begin work on, commence, embark on, enter upon, make a start, undertake ◆ *n* **4** = **coming**, advance, arrival, drawing near, nearing **5** (often plural) = **proposal**, advance, appeal, application, invitation, offer, overture, proposition **6** = **access**, avenue, entrance, passage, road, way **7** = **way**, manner, means, method, style, technique **8** = **likeness**, approximation, semblance

approachable *adj* **1** = **friendly**, affable, congenial, cordial, open, sociable **2** = **accessible**, attainable, reachable

appropriate *adj* **1** = **suitable**, apt, befitting, fitting, pertinent, relevant, to the point, well-suited ◆ *v* **2** = **seize**, commandeer, confiscate, impound, take possession of, usurp **3** = **steal**, embezzle, filch, misappropriate, pilfer, pocket **4** = **set aside**, allocate, allot, apportion, assign, devote, earmark

approval *n* **1** = **consent**, agreement, assent, authorization, blessing, endorsement, permission, recommendation, sanction **2** = **favor**, acclaim, admiration, applause, appreciation, esteem, good opinion, praise, respect

approve *v* **1** = **favor**, admire, commend, have a good opinion of, like, praise, regard highly, respect **2** = **agree to**, allow, assent to, authorize, consent to, endorse, pass, permit, ratify, recommend, sanction

approximate *adj* **1** = **close**, near **2** = **rough**, estimated, inexact, loose ◆ *v* **3** = **come close**, approach, border on, come near, reach, resemble, touch, verge on

approximately *adv* = **almost**, about, around, circa (*used with dates*), close to, in the region of, just about, more or less, nearly, roughly

approximation *n* = **guess**, conjecture, estimate, estimation, guesswork, rough calculation, rough idea

apron *n* = **pinafore**

apt *adj* **1** = **inclined**, disposed, given, liable, precious stone, a transparent beryl. ♦ *adj* **2** greenish-blue, sea-colored.

aq·ua·plane [AK-wə-playn] *n* **1** plank or boat towed by fast motorboat and ridden by person standing on it. ♦ *vi* **-planed, -plan·ing 2** ride on aquaplane. **3** (of automobile) be in contact with water on road, not with road surface. **aquaplaning** *n*

a·quar·i·um [ə-KWAIR-ee-əm] *n, pl* **-i·ums** tank or pond for keeping water animals or plants.

a·quat·ic [ə-KWAT-ik] *adj* living, growing, done in or on water. **a·quat'ics** *pl. n* water sports.

aq·ua·vit [AH-kwə-veet] *n* Scandinavian liquor usu. flavored with caraway seeds.

aq·ue·duct [AK-wi-dukt] *n* **1** artificial channel for water, esp. one like a bridge. **2** conduit.

a·que·ous [AY-kwee-əs] *adj* of, like, containing water.

aq·ui·fer [AK-wə-fər] *n* geological formation containing or conveying ground water.

aq·ui·line [AK-wə-līn] *adj* **1** relating to eagle. **2** hooked like an eagle's beak.

Ar *Chem.* argon.

Ar·ab [AR-əb] *n* **1** general term for inhabitants of Middle Eastern countries. **2** Arabian horse. **Ar'a·bic** *n* language of Arabs. ♦ *adj* **Ar'ab·ist** *n* specialist in Arabic language or in Arabic culture.

ar·a·besque [ar-ə-BESK] *n* **1** classical ballet position. **2** fanciful painted or carved ornament of Arabian origin. ♦ *adj*

ar·a·ble [AR-ə-bəl] *adj* suitable for plowing or planting crops.

a·rach·nid [ə-RAK-nid] *n* one of the Arachnida (spiders, scorpions, and mites).

a·rach'noid *adj*

ar·bi·ter [AHR-bi-tər] *n* judge, umpire. **ar·bi·trar'i·ly** [-TRER-ə-lee] *adv* **ar'bi·trar·y** *adj* **1** not bound by rules, despotic. **2** random. **ar'bi·trate** [-trayt] *v* **1** decide dispute. **2** submit to, settle by arbitration. **3** act as an umpire. **ar·bi·tra'tion** *n* hearing, settling of disputes, esp. industrial and legal, by impartial referee. **ar'bi·tra·tor** *n*

ar·bor [AHR-bər] *n* leafy glade, etc., sheltered by trees.

ar·bo·re·al [ahr-BOR-ee-əl] *adj* relating to trees. **ar·bo·re'tum** [-bə-REE-təm] *n, pl* **-tums** place for cultivating specimens of trees. **ar·bo·ri·cul·ture** [AHR-bər-i-kul-chər] *n* forestry, cultivation of trees. **ar'bor·ist** *n*

ar·bor vi·tae [ahr-bər VĪ-tee] a kind of evergreen conifer.

arc [ahrk] *n* **1** part of circumference of circle or similar curve. **2** luminous electric discharge between two conductors. **arc lamp, light** light source in which an arc between two electrodes produces intense white illumination.

ar·cade [ahr-KAYD] *n* **1** row of arches on pillars. **2** covered walk or avenue, esp. lined by shops.

ar·cane [ahr-KAYN] *adj* **1** mysterious. **2** esoteric.

arch[1] [ahrch] *n* **1** curved structure in building, supporting itself over open space by pressure of stones one against the other. **2** any similar structure. **3** a curved shape. **4** curved part of sole of the foot. ♦ *v* **5** form, make into, an arch. **arched** *adj* **arch'way** *n*

arch[2] *adj* **1** chief. **2** experienced, expert. **3** superior, knowing, coyly playful. **arch'ly** *adv* **arch'ness** *n*

——————| THESAURUS |——————

likely, of a mind, prone, ready **2 = appropriate**, fitting, pertinent, relevant, suitable, to the point **3 = gifted**, clever, quick, sharp, smart, talented

aptitude *n* **1 = tendency**, inclination, leaning, predilection, proclivity, propensity **2 = gift**, ability, capability, faculty, intelligence, proficiency, talent

arable *adj* **= productive**, farmable, fertile, fruitful

arbiter *n* **1 = judge**, adjudicator, arbitrator, referee, umpire **2 = authority**, controller, dictator, expert, governor, lord, master, pundit, ruler

arbitrary *adj* **= random**, capricious,

chance, erratic, inconsistent, personal, subjective, whimsical

arbitrate *v* **= settle**, adjudicate, decide, determine, judge, mediate, pass judgment, referee, umpire

arbitration *n* **= settlement**, adjudication, decision, determination, judgment

arbitrator *n* **= judge**, adjudicator, arbiter, referee, umpire

arc *n* **= curve**, arch, bend, bow, crescent, half-moon

arcade *n* **= gallery**, cloister, colonnade, portico

arcane *adj* **= mysterious**, esoteric, hidden, occult, recondite, secret

arch- *comb. form* chief, principal, e.g. *archenemy.*

ar·cha·ic [ahr-KAY-ik] *adj* old, primitive. **ar·cha·ism** [AHR-kee-iz-əm] *n* obsolete word or phrase.
passé

arch·bish·op [ahrch-BISH-əp] *n* chief bishop. **arch·bish·op·ric** *n*

ar·che·ol·o·gy [ahr-kee-OL-ə-jee] *n* study of ancient times from remains of art, implements, etc. **ar·che·o·log'i·cal** *adj* **ar·che·ol'o·gist** *n*

ar·cher·y [AHR-chə-ree] *n* skill, sport of shooting with bow and arrow. **arch'er** *n*

ar·che·type [AHR-ki-tīp] *n* **1** prototype. **2** perfect specimen. **ar·che·ty'pal** [-TĪ-pəl] *adj*

ar·chi·pel·a·go [ahr-kə-PEL-ə-goh] *n, pl* **-goes, -gos 1** group of islands. **2** sea with many small islands, esp. Aegean.

ar·chi·tect [AHR-ki-tekt] *n* **1** one qualified to design and supervise construction of buildings. **2** contriver. **ar·chi·tec'tur·al** [-TEK-chər-əl] *adj* **ar'chi·tec·ture** *n*

ar·chive [AHR-kīv] *n* **1** (oft. pl) collection of records, documents, etc. about an institution, family, etc. **2** place where these are kept. **3** *Computers* data put on tape or disk for long-term storage. ◆ *vt* **4** store in an archive. **ar·chi'val** *adj* **ar'chi·vist** [-kə-vist] *n*

Arc·tic [AHRK-tik] *adj* of northern polar regions. **2** (a-) very cold. ◆ *n* **3** region around north pole.

ar·dent [AHR-dnt] *adj* **1** fiery. **2** passionate. **ar'dent·ly** *adv* **ar'dor** [-dər] *n* **1** enthusiasm. **2** zeal.

ar·du·ous [AHR-joo-əs] *adj* laborious, hard to accomplish, difficult, strenuous.

are¹ [ahr] *pres. ind. pl.* of BE.

are² [air] *n* unit of measure, 100 square meters.

ar·e·a [AIR-ee-ə] *n* **1** extent, expanse of any surface. **2** two-dimensional expanse enclosed by boundary (area of square, circle, etc.). **3** region. **4** part, section. **5** subject, field of activity.

a·re·na [ə-REE-nə] *n* **1** enclosure for sports events, etc. **2** space in middle of amphitheater or stadium. **3** sphere, scene of conflict.

ar·gon [AHR-gon] *n* a gas, inert constituent of air.

ar·go·sy [AHR-gə-see] *n, pl* **-sies** *Poet.* large richly-laden merchant ship.

ar·got [AHR-goh] *n* slang.

ar·gue [AHR-gyoo] *v* **-gued, -gu·ing** ◆ *vi* **1** quarrel, dispute. **2** prove. **3** offer reasons. ◆ *vt* **4** prove by reasoning. **5** discuss. **ar'gu·a·ble** *adj* **ar'gu·ment** *n* **1** quarrel. **2** reasoning. **3** discussion. **4** theme.

———— THESAURUS ————

arch¹ *n* **1** = **curve**, archway, dome, span, vault **2** = **curve**, arc, bend, bow, hump, semicircle ◆ *v* **3** = **curve**, arc, bend, bow, bridge, span

arch² *adj* = **playful**, frolicsome, mischievous, pert, roguish, saucy, sly, waggish

archaic *adj* **1** = **old**, ancient, antique, bygone, olden (*archaic*), primitive **2** = **old-fashioned**, antiquated, behind the times, obsolete, outmoded, out of date,

archetypal *adj* **1** = **typical**, classic, ideal, model, standard **2** = **original**, prototypic *or* prototypical

archetype *n* **1** = **standard**, model, paradigm, pattern, prime example **2** = **original**, prototype

architect *n* = **designer**, master builder, planner

architecture *n* **1** = **design**, building, construction, planning **2** = **structure**, construction, design, framework, make-up, style

archive *n* **1** = **record office**, museum, registry, repository **2 archives** = **records**,

annals, chronicles, documents, papers, rolls

arctic *adj Inf* = **freezing**, chilly, cold, frigid, frozen, glacial, icy

Arctic *adj* = **polar**, far-northern, hyperborean

ardent *adj* **1** = **passionate**, amorous, hot-blooded, impassioned, intense, lusty **2** = **enthusiastic**, avid, eager, keen, zealous

ardor *n* **1** = **passion**, fervor, intensity, spirit, vehemence, warmth **2** = **enthusiasm**, avidity, eagerness, keenness, zeal

arduous *adj* = **difficult**, exhausting, fatiguing, grueling, laborious, onerous, punishing, rigorous, strenuous, taxing, tiring

area *n* **1** = **region**, district, locality, neighborhood, zone **2** = **part**, portion, section, sector **3** = **field**, department, domain, province, realm, sphere, territory

arena *n* **1** = **ring**, amphitheater, bowl, enclosure, field, ground, stadium **2** = **sphere**, area, domain, field, province,

ar·gu·men·ta·tion n **ar·gu·men'ta·tive** adj
a·ri·a [AHR-ee-ə] n air or rhythmical song in cantata, opera, etc.
ar'id adj **1** parched with heat, dry. **2** dull. **a·rid·i·ty** [ə-RID-i-tee] n
a·right [ə-RĪT] adv rightly.
a·rise [ə-RĪZ] vi **a·rose**, **a·ris·en** [ə-RIZ-ən], **a·ris·ing** I come about. **2** got up **3** rise (up), ascend.
ar·is·toc·ra·cy [ar-ə-STOK-rə-see] n, pl **-cies 1** government by the best in birth or fortune. **2** nobility. **3** upper classes. **a·ris·to·crat** [ə-RIS-tə-krat] n **a·ris·to·crat'ic** adj **1** noble. **2** elegant.
a·rith·me·tic [ə-RITH-mə-tik] n **1** science of numbers. **2** art of reckoning by figures. **ar·ith·met'ic** adj **ar·ith·met'i·cal·ly** adv
ark [ahrk] n **1** Noah's vessel. **2** (**A-**) coffer containing scrolls of the Torah.
arm¹ [ahrm] n **1** limb extending from shoulder to wrist. **2** anything projecting from main body, as branch of sea, supporting rail of chair, etc. **arm'chair** n **arm'ful** n, pl **-fuls arm'hole** n **arm'pit** n hollow under arm at shoulder.
arm-twisting n use of personal pressure to

achieve a desired result.
arm² vt **1** supply with weapons, furnish. **2** prepare bomb, etc. for use. ♦ vi **3** take up arms. ♦ n **4** weapon. **5** branch of army. ♦ pl **6** weapons. **7** war, military exploits. **8** official heraldic symbols. **ar'ma·ment** n
ar·ma·da [ahr-MAH-də] n large number of ships or aircraft.
ar·ma·dil·lo [ahr-mə-DIL-oh] n, pl **-los** small Amer. animal protected by bands of bony plates.
ar·ma·ture [AHR-mə-chər] n **1** revolving structure in electric motor, generator. **2** framework used by a sculptor to support modeling clay, etc.
ar·mi·stice [AHR-mə-stis] n truce, suspension of fighting.
ar·mor [AHR-mər] n **1** defensive covering or dress. **2** plating of tanks, warships, etc. **3** armored fighting vehicles, as tanks. **ar'mor·y** n, pl **-mor·ies**
ar·my [AHR-mee] n, pl **-mies 1** large body of soldiers armed for warfare and under military command. **2** host. **3** great number.
a·ro·ma [ə-ROH-mə] n **1** sweet smell. **2**

realm, sector, territory
argue v **1 = discuss**, assert, claim, debate, dispute, maintain, reason, remonstrate **2 = quarrel**, bicker, disagree, dispute, fall out (inf), fight, squabble
argument n **1 = quarrel**, clash, controversy, disagreement, dispute, feud, fight, row, squabble **2 = discussion**, assertion, claim, debate, dispute, plea, questioning, remonstration **3 = reason**, argumentation, case, defense, dialectic, ground(s), line of reasoning, logic, polemic, reasoning
argumentative adj **= quarrelsome**, belligerent, combative, contentious, contrary, disputatious, litigious, opinionated
arid adj **1 = dry**, barren, desert, parched, sterile, torrid, waterless **2 = boring**, dreary, dry, dull, tedious, tiresome, uninspired, uninteresting
arise v **1 = happen**, begin, emerge, ensue, follow, occur, result, start, stem **2 = get up**, get to one's feet, go up, rise, stand up, wake up
aristocracy n **= upper class**, elite, gentry, nobility, patricians, peerage, ruling class
aristocrat adj **= noble**, grandee, lady, lord,

patrician, peer, peeress
aristocratic n **= upper-class**, blue-blooded, elite, gentlemanly, lordly, noble, patrician, titled
arm¹ n **= upper limb**, appendage, limb
arm² v Especially with weapons **= equip**, accouter, array, deck out, furnish, issue with, provide, supply
armada n **= fleet**, flotilla, navy, squadron
armaments pl n **= weapons**, ammunition, arms, guns, materiel, munitions, ordnance, weaponry
armed adj **= carrying weapons**, equipped, fitted out, primed, protected
armistice n **= truce**, ceasefire, peace, suspension of hostilities
armor n **= protection**, armor plate, covering, sheathing, shield
armored adj **= protected**, armor-plated, bombproof, bulletproof, ironclad, mailed, steel-plated
arms pl n **1 = weapons**, armaments, firearms, guns, instruments of war, ordnance, weaponry **2 = heraldry**, blazonry, crest, escutcheon, insignia
army n **1 = soldiers**, armed force, legions, military, military force, soldiery, troops **2 = vast number**, array, horde, host,

fragrance. **3** peculiar charm. **ar·o·mat·ic** [ar-ə-MAT-ik] *adj*

a·rose pt. of ARISE.

a·round [ə-ROWND] *prep* **1** on all sides of. **2** somewhere in or near. **3** approximately (of time). ◆ *adv* **4** on every side. **5** in a circle. **6** here and there, nowhere in particular. **7** *inf* present in or at some place.

a·rouse [ə-ROWZ] *vt* **-roused, -rous·ing** awaken, stimulate.

ar·peg·gi·o [ahr-PEJ-ee-oh] *n, pl* **-gi·os** *Mus.* **1** notes sounded in quick succession, not together. **2** chord so played.

ar·raign [ə-RAYN] *vt* accuse, indict, put on trial. **ar·raign'ment** *n*

ar·range [ə-RAYNJ] *v* **-ranged, -rang·ing 1** set in order. **2** make agreement. **3** adjust. **4** plan. **5** adapt, as music. **6** settle, as dispute. **ar·range'ment** *n*

ar·rant [AR-ənt] *adj* downright, notorious.

ar·ras [AR-əs] *n* tapestry.

ar·ray [ə-RAY] *n* **1** order, esp. military order. **2** dress. **3** imposing show, splendor. ◆ *vt* **4** set in order. **5** dress, equip, adorn.

ar·rears [ə-REERZ] *pl n* amount unpaid or undone.

ar·rest [ə-REST] *vt* **1** detain by legal authority. **2** stop. **3** catch attention. ◆ *n* **4** seizure by warrant. **5** making prisoner. **ar·rest'ing** *adj* attracting attention, striking. **ar·rest'er** *n* **1** person who arrests. **2** mechanism to stop or slow moving object.

ar·rive [ə-RĪV] *vi* **-rived, -riv·ing 1** reach destination. **2** (with *at*) reach, attain. **3** *inf* succeed. **ar·ri'val** *n*

ar·ro·gance [AR-ə-gəns] *n* aggressive conceit. **ar'ro·gant** *adj* **1** proud. **2** overbearing.

ar·ro·gate [AR-ə-gayt] *vt* **-gat·ed, -gat·ing**

multitude, pack, swarm, throng

aroma *n* = **scent**, bouquet, fragrance, odor, perfume, redolence, savor, smell

aromatic *adj* = **fragrant**, balmy, perfumed, pungent, redolent, savory, spicy, sweet-scented, sweet-smelling

around *prep* **1** = **surrounding**, about, encircling, enclosing, encompassing, on all sides of **2** = **approximately**, about, circa (*used with dates*), roughly ◆ *adv* **3** = **everywhere**, about, all over, here and there, in all directions, on all sides, throughout, to and fro **4** = **near**, at hand, close, close at hand, nearby, nigh (*archaic or dialect*)

arouse *v* **1** = **stimulate**, excite, incite, instigate, provoke, spur, stir up, summon up, whip up **2** = **awaken**, rouse, waken, wake up

arrange *v* **1** = **plan**, construct, contrive, devise, fix up, organize, prepare **2** = **agree**, adjust, come to terms, compromise, determine, settle **3** = **put in order**, classify, group, line up, order, organize, position, sort **4** = **adapt**, instrument, orchestrate, score

arrangement *n* **1** (*often plural*) = **plan**, organization, planning, preparation, provision, schedule **2** = **agreement**, adjustment, compact, compromise, deal, settlement, terms **3** = **order**, alignment, classification, form, organization, structure, system **4** = **adaptation**, instrumentation, interpretation, orchestration, score, version

array *n* **1** = **arrangement**, collection, display, exhibition, formation, line-up, parade, show, supply **2** *Poetic* = **clothing**, apparel, attire, clothes, dress, finery, garments, regalia ◆ *v* **3** = **arrange**, display, exhibit, group, parade, range, show **4** = **dress**, adorn, attire, clothe, deck, decorate, festoon

arrest *v* **1** = **capture**, apprehend, catch, detain, seize, take prisoner **2** = **stop**, block, delay, end, inhibit, interrupt, obstruct, slow, suppress **3** = **grip**, absorb, engage, engross, fascinate, hold, intrigue, occupy ◆ *n* **4** = **capture**, bust (*inf*), detention, seizure **5** = **stopping**, blockage, delay, end, hindrance, interruption, obstruction, suppression

arresting *adj* = **striking**, cool (*inf*), engaging, impressive, noticeable, outstanding, phat (*sl*), remarkable, stunning, surprising

arrival *n* **1** = **coming**, advent, appearance, arriving, entrance, happening, occurrence, taking place **2** = **newcomer**, caller, entrant, incomer, visitor

arrive *v* **1** = **come**, appear, enter, get to, reach, show up (*inf*), turn up **2** *Inf* = **succeed**, become famous, make good, make it (*inf*), make the grade (*inf*)

arrogance *n* = **conceit**, disdainfulness, haughtiness, high-handedness, insolence, pride, superciliousness, swagger

arrogant *adj* = **conceited**, disdainful, haughty, high-handed, overbearing, seize or claim without right.

ar·row [AR-oh] *n* **1** pointed shaft shot from bow. **ar'row·head** *n* **1** head of arrow. **2** any triangular shape.

ar·row·root [AR-oh-root] *n* nutritious starch from W Indian plant, used as a food.

ar·se·nal [AHR-sə-nl] *n* **1** place for manufacture, storage weapons and ammunition. **2** *fig* repertoire (of skills, skilled personnel, etc.).

ar·se·nic [AHR-sə-nik] *n* **1** soft, gray, metallic element. **2** its oxide, a powerful poison. **ar'se·nate** [-nayt] *n* **ar·sen'i·cal** *adj*

ar·son [AHR-sən] *n* crime of intentionally setting property on fire.

art [ahrt] *n* **1** skill. **2** human skill as opposed to nature. **3** creative skill in painting, poetry, music, etc. **4** any of the works produced thus. **5** profession, craft. **6** knack. **7** contrivance, cunning, trick. **8** system of rules. ◆ *pl* **9** certain branches of learning, languages, history, etc., as distinct from natural science. **10** wiles. **art'ful** *adj* wily. **art'ful·ly** *adv* **art'ist** *n* **1** one who practices fine art, esp. painting. **2** one who makes a fine art of a craft. **ar·tiste'** [-TEEST] *n* professional entertainer, singer, dancer, etc. **ar·tis'tic** *adj* **art'ist·ry** *n* **art'less** *adj* natural, frank. **art'less·ness** *n* **art'y** *adj* **art·i·er, art·i·est** ostentatiously artistic.

ar·te·ri·o·scle·ro·sis
[ahr-teer-ee-oh-sklə-ROH-sis] *n* hardening of the arteries. **ar·te·ri·o·scle·rot'ic** *adj*

ar·ter·y [AHR-tə-ree] *n, pl* **-ter·ies 1** one of the vessels carrying blood from heart. **2** any main channel of communications. **ar·te'ri·al** [-TEER-ee-əl] *adj* **1** pert. to an artery. **2** (of a route) major.

ar·te·sian [ahr-TEE-zhən] *adj* describes deep well in which water rises by internal pressure.

ar·thri·tis [ahr-THRĪ-tis] *n* painful inflammation of joint(s). **ar·thrit'ic** [-THRIT-ik] *adj, n*

ar·thro·pod [AHR-thrə-pod] *n* **1** invertebrate with jointed limbs and segmented body e.g. **2** insect, spider.

ar·ti·choke [AHR-ti-chohk] *n* thistle-like perennial, edible flower.

ar·ti·cle [AHR-ti-kəl] *n* **1** item, object. **2** short written piece. **3** paragraph, section. **4** *Grammar* any of the words *the, a,* or *an.* **5** clause in a contract. **6** rule, condition.

ar·tic·u·late [ahr-TIK-yə-lit] *adj* **1** able to express oneself fluently. **2** jointed. **3** of speech, clear, distinct. ◆ *v* [-layt] **-lat·ed, -lat·ing** ◆ *vt* **4** joint. **5** utter distinctly. ◆ *vi* **6** speak. **ar·tic'u·late·ly** *adv* **ar·tic·u·la'tion** *n*

ar·ti·fact [AHR-tə-fakt] *n* something made by a person, esp. by hand.

ar·ti·fice [AHR-tə-fis] *n* contrivance, trick, cunning, skill. **ar·tif'i·cer** [-TIF-ə-sər] *n* craftsperson. **ar·ti·fi'cial** [-FISH-əl] *adj* **1** manufactured, synthetic. **2** insincere. **ar·ti·fi'cial·ly** *adv* **artificial intelligence** ability of machines, esp. computers, to imitate intelligent human behavior. **artificial respiration** method of restarting person's breathing after it has stopped.

ar·til·ler·y [ahr-TIL-ə-ree] *n* **1** large guns on wheels. **2** the troops that use them.

ar·ti·san [AHR-tə-zən] *n* craftsperson, skilled mechanic, manual worker.

ar·tiste see ART.

proud, scornful, supercilious

arrow *n* **1** = **dart**, bolt, flight, quarrel, shaft (*archaic*) **2** = **pointer**, indicator

arsenal *n* = **armory**, ammunition dump, arms depot, ordnance depot, stockpile, store, storehouse, supply

art *n* = **skill**, craft, expertise, ingenuity, mastery, virtuosity

artful *adj* = **cunning**, clever, crafty, shrewd, sly, smart, wily

article *n* **1** = **piece**, composition, discourse, essay, feature, item, paper, story, treatise **2** = **thing**, commodity, item, object, piece, substance, unit **3** = **clause**, item, paragraph, part, passage, point, portion, section

articulate *adj* **1** = **expressive**, clear, coherent, eloquent, fluent, lucid, well-spoken ◆ *v* **2** = **express**, enunciate, pronounce, say, speak, state, talk, utter, voice

artifice *n* **1** = **trick**, contrivance, device, machination, maneuver, stratagem, subterfuge, tactic **2** = **cleverness**, ingenuity, inventiveness, skill

artificial *adj* **1** = **synthetic**, man-made, manufactured, non-natural, plastic **2** = **fake**, bogus, counterfeit, imitation, mock, sham, simulated **3** = **insincere**, affected, contrived, false, feigned, forced, phoney *or* phony (*inf*), unnatural

artillery *n* = **big guns**, battery, cannon, cannonry, gunnery, ordnance

artisan *n* = **craftsman**, journeyman,

Ar·y·an [AIR-ee-ən] *adj* relating to Indo-European family of nations and languages.

As *Chem.* arsenic.

as [az] *adv, conj* 1 denoting: comparison. 2 similarity. 3 equality. 4 identity. 5 concurrence. 6 reason.

as·bes·tos [as-BES-təs] *n* fibrous mineral that does not burn. **as·bes·to·sis** [as-bes-STOH-sis] *n* lung disease caused by inhalation of asbestos fiber.

as·cend [ə-SEND] *vi* 1 climb, rise. ♦ *vt* 2 walk up, climb, mount. **as·cend'an·cy** *n* control, dominance. **as·cend'ant** *adj* rising. **as·cen'sion** [-shən] *n* **as·cent'** *n* rise.

as·cer·tain [as-ər-TAYN] *v* get to know, find out, determine. **as·cer·tain'a·ble** *adj*

as·cet·ic [ə-SET-ik] *n* 1 one who practices severe self-denial. ♦ *adj* 2 rigidly abstinent, austere. **as·cet'i·cism** [-ə-siz-əm] *n*

ASCII [ASS-kee] *n* a code for transmitting data between computers.

a·scor·bic acid [ə-SKOR-bik] vitamin C, present in green vegetables, citrus fruits, etc.

as·cribe [ə-SKRĪB] *vt* **-cribed, -crib·ing** attribute, impute, assign. **as·crib'a·ble** *adj*

a·sep·tic [ə-SEP-tik] *adj* germ-free. **a·sep'sis** *n*

a·sex·u·al [ay-SEK-shoo-əl] *adj* without sex.

ash[1] *n* 1 dust or remains of anything burned. ♦ *pl* 2 ruins. 3 remains after burning, esp. of a human body after cremation. **ash'en** *adj* 1 like ashes. 2 pale.

ash[2] *n* 1 deciduous timber tree. 2 its wood. **ash'en** *adj*

a·shamed [ə-SHAYMD] *adj* affected with shame, abashed.

a·shore [ə-SHOR] *adv* on shore.

Ash Wednesday first day of Lent.

A·sian [AY-zhən] *adj* 1 pert. to continent of Asia. ♦ *n* 2 native of Asia or descendant of one. **A·si·at·ic** [-zhee-AT-ik] *adj*

a·side [ə-SĪD] *adv* 1 to or on one side. 2 privately. ♦ *n* 3 words spoken in an undertone not to be heard by some person present.

as·i·nine [AS-ə-nīn] *adj* of or like an ass, silly. **as·i·nin'i·ty** [-NIN-i-tee] *n*

ask *vt* 1 request, require, question, invite. ♦ *vi* 2 make inquiry or request.

a·skance [ə-SKANS] *adv* 1 sideways, awry. 2 with a side look or meaning. **look askance** view with suspicion.

a·skew [ə-SKYOO] *adv* aside, awry.

a·sleep [ə-SLEEP] *adj, adv* sleeping, at rest.

THESAURUS

---

mechanic, skilled workman, technician

artistic *adj* = **creative**, aesthetic, beautiful, cultured, elegant, refined, sophisticated, stylish, tasteful

artistry *n* = **skill**, brilliance, craftsmanship, creativity, finesse, mastery, proficiency, virtuosity

artless *adj* 1 = **straightforward**, frank, guileless, open, plain 2 = **natural**, homely, plain, pure, simple, unadorned, unaffected, unpretentious

as *conj* 1 = **when**, at the time that, during the time that, just as, while 2 = **in the way that**, in the manner that, like 3 = **what**, that which 4 = **since**, because, considering that, seeing that 5 = **for instance**, like, such as ♦ *prep* 6 = **being**, in the character of, in the role of, under the name of

ascend *v* = **move up**, climb, go up, mount, scale

ascent *n* 1 = **rise**, ascending, ascension, climb, mounting, rising, scaling, upward movement 2 = **upward slope**, gradient, incline, ramp, rise, rising ground

ascertain *v* = **find out**, confirm, determine, discover, establish, learn

ascetic *n* 1 = **monk**, abstainer, hermit, nun, recluse ♦ *adj* 2 = **self-denying**, abstinent, austere, celibate, frugal, puritanical, self-disciplined

ascribe *v* = **attribute**, assign, charge, credit, impute, put down, refer, set down

ashamed *adj* = **embarrassed**, distressed, guilty, humiliated, mortified, remorseful, shamefaced, sheepish, sorry

ashen *adj* = **pale**, colorless, gray, leaden, like death warmed over (*inf*), pallid, wan, white

ashore *adv* = **on land**, aground, landwards, on dry land, on the beach, on the shore, shorewards, to the shore

aside *adv* 1 = **to one side**, apart, beside, on one side, out of the way, privately, separately, to the side ♦ *n* 2 = **interpolation**, parenthesis

asinine *adj* = **stupid**, fatuous, foolish, idiotic, imbecilic, moronic, senseless

ask *v* 1 = **inquire**, interrogate, query, question, quiz 2 = **request**, appeal, beg, demand, plead, seek 3 = **invite**, bid, summon

askew *adv* 1 = **crookedly**, aslant, awry,

asp *n* small venomous snake.

as·par·a·gus [ə-SPA-rə-gəs] *n* plant whose young shoots are a table delicacy.

as·pect [AS-pekt] *n* look, view, appearance, expression.

as·pen [AS-pən] *n* type of poplar tree.

as·per·i·ty [ə-SPER-i-tee] *n*, *pl* **-ties 1** roughness. **2** harshness **3** coldness.

as·per·sion [ə-SPUR-zhən] *n* **cast aspersions on** make derogatory remarks about.

as·phalt [AS-fawlt] *n* black, hard bituminous substance used for road surfaces, etc.

as·phyx·i·a [as-FIK-see-ə] *n* suffocation. **as·phyx·i·ate** [-ayt] *v* **-at·ed, -at·ing as·phyx·i·a·tion** *n*

as·pic [AS-pik] *n* jelly used to coat or make a mold of meat, eggs, fish, etc.

as·pire [ə-SPĪR] *vi* **-pired, -pir·ing 1** desire eagerly. **2** aim at high things. **3** rise to great height. **as·pi·rant** [AS-pər-ənt] *n* **1** one who aspires. **2** candidate. **as·pi·rate** [-pə-rayt] *vt* pronounce with full breathing, as *h*. **as·pir·ing** *adj*

as·pi·rin [AS-pər-in] *n* (a tablet of) drug used to allay pain and fever.

ass *n* **1** quadruped of horse family. **2** stupid person.

as·sail [ə-SAYL] *vt* attack, assault. **as·sail'a·ble** *adj* **as·sail'ant** *n*

as·sas·sin [ə-SAS-in] *n* **1** one who kills, esp. prominent person, by treacherous violence. **2** murderer. **as·sas'si·nate** *vt* **-nat·ed, -nat·ing as·sas·si·na'tion** *n*

as·sault [ə-SAWLT] *n* **1** attack, esp. sudden. ◆ *vt* **2** attack.

as·say [ə-SAY] *vt* **1** test, esp. proportions of metals in alloy or ore. ◆ *n* [AS-ay] **2** analysis, esp. of metals. **3** trial, test.

as·sem·ble [ə-SEM-bəl] *v* **-bled, -bling 1** meet, bring together. **2** collect. **3** put together (of machinery, etc.). **as·sem'blage** [-blij] *n* **as·sem'bly** *n, pl* **-blies 1** gathering, meeting. **2** assembling. **assembly line** sequence of machines, workers in factory assembling product.

as·sent [ə-SENT] *vi* **1** concur, agree. ◆ *n* **2** acquiescence, agreement, compliance.

as·sert [ə-SURT] *vt* declare strongly, insist upon. **as·ser'tion** *n* **as·sert'ive** *adj* **as·ser'tive·ly** *adv*

obliquely, off-center, to one side ◆ *adj* **2 = crooked**, awry, cockeyed (*inf*), lopsided, oblique, off-center

asleep *adj* **= sleeping**, dormant, dozing, fast asleep, napping, slumbering, snoozing (*inf*), sound asleep

aspect *n* **1 = feature**, angle, facet, side **2 = position**, outlook, point of view, prospect, scene, situation, view **3 = appearance**, air, attitude, bearing, condition, demeanor, expression, look, manner

asphyxiate *v* **= suffocate**, choke, smother, stifle, strangle, strangulate, throttle

aspiration *n* **= aim**, ambition, desire, dream, goal, hope, objective, wish

aspire *v* **= aim**, desire, dream, hope, long, seek, set one's heart on, wish

aspiring *adj* **= hopeful**, ambitious, eager, longing, wannabe (*inf*), would-be

ass *n* **1 = donkey 2 = fool**, blockhead, dork (*sl*), halfwit, idiot, jackass, oaf, schmuck (*sl*)

assail *v* **= attack**, assault, fall upon, set upon

assailant *n* **= attacker**, aggressor, assailer, assaulter, invader

assassin *n* **= murderer**, executioner, hatchet man (*sl*), hit man (*sl*), killer,

liquidator, slayer

assassinate *v* **= murder**, eliminate (*sl*), hit (*sl*), kill, liquidate, slay, take out (*sl*)

assault *n* **1 = attack**, charge, invasion, offensive, onslaught ◆ *v* **2 = attack**, beset, fall upon, set about, set upon, strike at

assemble *v* **1 = gather**, amass, bring together, call together, collect, come together, congregate, meet, muster, rally **2 = put together**, build up, connect, construct, fabricate, fit together, join, piece together, set up

assembly *n* **1 = gathering**, collection, company, conference, congress, council, crowd, group, mass, meeting **2 = putting together**, building up, connecting, construction, piecing together, setting up

assent *n* **1 = agreement**, acceptance, approval, compliance, concurrence, consent, permission, sanction ◆ *v* **2 = agree**, allow, approve, consent, grant, permit

assert *v* **1 = state**, affirm, declare, maintain, profess, pronounce, swear **2 = insist upon**, claim, defend, press, put forward, stand up for, stress, uphold **3 assert oneself = be forceful**, exert one's influence, make one's presence felt, put

as·sess [ə-SES] *vt* **1** fix value. **2** evaluate, estimate, esp. for taxation. **3** fix amount (of tax or fine). **4** tax or fine. **as·sess'ment** *n* **as·ses'sor** *n*

as·set [AS-et] *n* **1** valuable or useful person, thing. ◆ *pl* **2** property available to pay debts, esp. of insolvent debtor.

as·sid·u·ous [ə-SIJ-oo-əs] *adj* persevering, attentive, diligent. **as·si·du·i·ty** [as-i-DOO-i-tee] *n*

as·sign [ə-SĪN] *vt* **1** appoint to job, etc. **2** allot, apportion, fix. **3** ascribe. **4** transfer. **as·sign'a·ble** *adj* **as·sig·na·tion** [as-ig-NAY-shən] *n* **1** secret meeting. **2** appointment to meet. **as·sign'ment** *n* **1** act of assigning. **2** allotted duty.

as·sim·i·late [ə-SIM-ə-layt] *vt* **-lat·ed, -lat·ing 1** learn and understand. **2** make similar. **3** absorb into the system.

as·sim·i·la'tion *n*

as·sist [ə-SIST] *v* **1** give help. **2** aid. **as·sis'tance** *n* **as·sis'tant** *n* helper.

as·so·ci·ate [ə-SOH-shee-ayt] *v* **-at·ed, -at·ing** ◆ *vt* **1** link, connect, esp. as ideas in mind. **2** join. ◆ *vi* **3** formerly, keep company with. **4** combine, unite. ◆ *n* [-it] **5** companion, partner. **6** friend, ally. **7** subordinate member of association. ◆ *adj* **8** affiliated. **as·so·ci·a'tion** *n* society, club.

as·sort [ə-SORT] *vt* **1** classify, arrange. ◆ *vi* **2** match, agree with, harmonize. **as·sort'ed** *adj* mixed. **as·sort'ment** *n*

as·suage [ə-SWAYJ] *vt* **-suaged, -suag·ing 1** soften, pacify. **2** soothe.

as·sume [ə-SOOM] *vt* **-sumed, -sum·ing 1** take for granted. **2** pretend. **3** take upon oneself. **4** claim. **as·sump'tion** [-SUMP-shən] *n*

oneself forward, put one's foot down (*inf*)

assertion *n* **1** = **statement**, claim, declaration, pronouncement **2** = **insistence**, maintenance, stressing

assertive *adj* = **confident**, aggressive, domineering, emphatic, feisty (*inf*), forceful, insistent, positive, pushy (*inf*), strong-willed

assess *v* **1** = **judge**, appraise, estimate, evaluate, rate, size up (*inf*), value, weigh **2** = **evaluate**, fix, impose, levy, rate, tax, value

assessment *n* **1** = **judgment**, appraisal, estimate, evaluation, rating, valuation **2** = **evaluation**, charge, fee, levy, rating, toll, valuation

asset *n* **1** = **benefit**, advantage, aid, blessing, boon, feather in one's cap, help, resource, service **2 assets** = **property**, capital, estate, funds, goods, money, possessions, resources, wealth

assiduous *adj* = **diligent**, hard-working, indefatigable, industrious, persevering, persistent, unflagging

assign *v* **1** = **select**, appoint, choose, delegate, designate, name, nominate **2** = **give**, allocate, allot, apportion, consign, distribute, give out, grant **3** = **attribute**, accredit, ascribe, put down

assignation *n* **1** = **secret meeting**, clandestine meeting, illicit meeting, rendezvous, tryst **2** = **selection**, appointment, assignment, choice, delegation, designation, nomination

assignment *n* = **task**, appointment, commission, duty, job, mission, position, post, responsibility

assimilate *v* **1** = **learn**, absorb, digest, incorporate, take in **2** = **adjust**, adapt, blend in, mingle

assist *v* = **help**, abet, aid, cooperate, lend a helping hand, serve, support

assistance *n* = **help**, aid, backing, cooperation, helping hand, support

assistant *n* = **helper**, accomplice, aide, ally, colleague, right-hand man, second, supporter

associate *v* **1** = **connect**, ally, combine, identify, join, link, lump together **2** = **mix**, accompany, consort, hobnob, mingle, socialize ◆ *n* **3** = **partner**, collaborator, colleague, confederate, co-worker **4** = **friend**, ally, companion, comrade, homeboy (*sl*), homegirl (*sl*)

association *n* **1** = **group**, alliance, band, club, coalition, federation, league, organization, society **2** = **connection**, blend, combination, joining, juxtaposition, mixture, pairing, union

assorted *adj* = **various**, different, diverse, miscellaneous, mixed, motley, sundry, varied

assortment *n* = **variety**, array, choice, collection, jumble, medley, mixture, selection

assume *v* **1** = **take for granted**, believe, expect, fancy, imagine, infer, presume, suppose, surmise, think **2** = **take on**, accept, enter upon, put on, shoulder, take over **3** = **put on**, adopt, affect, feign,

as·sure [ə-SHOOR] vt **-sured, -sur·ing 1** tell positively, promise. **2** make sure. **3** insure against loss, esp. of life. **4** affirm. **as·sured'** adj sure. **as·sur'ed·ly** [-id-lee] adv

as·ter·isk [AS-tə-risk] n **1** star (*) used in printing. ◆ vt **2** mark thus.

a·stern [ə-STURN] adv **1** in, behind the stern. **2** backward in direction.

as·ter·oid [AS-tə-roid] n **1** small planet. ◆ adj **2** star-shaped.

asth·ma [AZ-mə] n illness in which one has difficulty in breathing. **asth·mat·ic** adj, n

a·stig·ma·tism [ə-STIG-mə-tiz-əm] n inability of lens (esp. of eye) to focus properly. **as·tig·mat·ic** [as-tig-MAT-ik] adj

a·stir [ə-STUR] adv **1** on the move. **2** out of bed. **3** in excitement.

as·ton·ish [ə-STON-ish] vt amaze, surprise. **as·ton·ish·ing** adj **as·ton·ish·ment** n

as·tound [ə-STOWND] vt **1** astonish greatly. **2** stun with amazement. **as·tound'ing** adj startling.

as·tra·khan [AS-trə-kən] n lambskin with curled wool.

as·tral [AS-trəl] adj of the stars or spirit world.

a·stray [ə-STRAY] adv off the right path, wanderingly.

a·stride [ə-STRĪD] adv with the legs apart, straddling.

as·trin·gent [ə-STRIN-jənt] adj **1** severe, harsh. **2** sharp. **3** constricting (body tissues, blood vessels, etc.). ◆ n **4** astringent substance.

as·trol·o·gy [ə-STROL-ə-jee] n **1** foretelling of events by stars. **2** medieval astronomy. **as·trol·o·ger** n **as·tro·log'i·cal** adj

as·tro·naut [AS-trə-nawt] n one trained for travel in space.

as·tron·o·my [ə-STRON-ə-mee] n scientific study of heavenly bodies. **as·tron'o·mer** n **as·tro·nom'i·cal** [-trə-NOM-i-kəl] adj **1** very large. **2** of astronomy. **astronomical unit** unit of distance used in astronomy equal to the mean distance between Earth and the sun.

as·tro·phys·ics [as-troh-FIZ-iks] n the science of the chemical and physical characteristics of heavenly bodies. **as·tro·phys'i·cist** n

as·tute [ə-STOOT] adj perceptive, shrewd. **as·tute'ly** adv **as·tute'ness** n

a·sun·der [ə-SUN-dər] adv **1** apart. **2** in pieces.

a·sy·lum [ə-SĪ-ləm] n **1** refuge, sanctuary, place of safety. **2** old name for hospital for mentally ill.

a·sym·me·try [ay-SIM-i-tree] n lack of

——————— THESAURUS ———————

imitate, impersonate, mimic, pretend to, simulate

assumed adj **1 = false**, bogus, counterfeit, fake, fictitious, made-up, make-believe **2 = taken for granted**, accepted, expected, hypothetical, presumed, presupposed, supposed, surmised

assumption n **1 = presumption**, belief, conjecture, guess, hypothesis, inference, supposition, surmise **2 = taking on**, acceptance, acquisition, adoption, entering upon, putting on, shouldering, takeover, taking up **3 = taking**, acquisition, appropriation, seizure, takeover

assurance n **1 = assertion**, declaration, guarantee, oath, pledge, promise, statement, vow, word **2 = confidence**, boldness, certainty, conviction, faith, nerve, poise, self-confidence

assure v **1 = promise**, certify, confirm, declare confidently, give one's word to, guarantee, pledge, swear, vow **2 = convince**, comfort, embolden, encourage, hearten, persuade, reassure **3 = make certain**, clinch, complete, confirm, ensure, guarantee, make sure, seal, secure

assured adj **1 = confident**, certain, poised, positive, self-assured, self-confident, sure of oneself **2 = certain**, beyond doubt, confirmed, ensured, fixed, guaranteed, in the bag (sl), secure, settled, sure

astonish v **= amaze**, astound, bewilder, confound, daze, dumbfound, stagger, stun, surprise

astonishing adj **= amazing**, astounding, bewildering, breathtaking, brilliant, sensational (inf), staggering, stunning, surprising

astonishment n **= amazement**, awe, bewilderment, confusion, consternation, surprise, wonder, wonderment

astounding adj **= amazing**, astonishing, bewildering, breathtaking, brilliant, cool (inf), impressive, phat (sl), sensational (inf), staggering, stunning, surprising

astray adj, adv **= off the right track**, adrift, amiss, lost, off, off course, off the mark, off the subject

astute adj **= intelligent**, canny, clever, crafty, cunning, perceptive, sagacious,

symmetry. **a·sym·met·ric** [-sə-MET-rik] *adj*
as·ymp·tote [AS-im-toht] *n* straight line that continually approaches a curve, but never meets it.

at *prep, adv* **1** denoting: location in space or time. **2** rate. **3** condition or state. **4** amount. **5** direction. **6** cause.
At *Chem.* astatine.

at·a·vism [AT-ə-viz-əm] *n* appearance of ancestral, not parental, characteristics in human beings, animals or plants. **at·a·vis'tic** *adj*

a·tax·i·a [ə-TAK-see-ə] *n* lack of muscular coordination.

ate [ayt] pt. of EAT.

at·el·ier [at-l-YAY] *n* workshop, artist's studio.

a·the·ism [AY-thee-iz-əm] *n* belief that there is no God. **a'the·ist** *n* **a·the·is'tic** *adj*

ath·lete [ATH-leet] *n* **1** one trained for physical exercises, feats or contests of strength. **2** one good at sports. **ath·let'ic** *adj* **ath·let'ics** *pl n* sports such as running, jumping, throwing, etc. **ath·let'i·cal·ly** *adv*

a·thwart [ə-THWORT] *prep* **1** across. ♦ *adv* **2** across, esp. obliquely.

at·las [AT-ləs] *n* volume of maps.

at·mos·phere [AT-məs-feer] *n* **1** mass of gas surrounding heavenly body, esp. Earth. **2** prevailing tone or mood (of place, etc.). **3** unit of pressure in cgs system. **at·mos·pher'ic** [-FER-ik] *adj* **at·mos·pher'ics** *pl n* **1** noises in radio reception due to electrical disturbance in the atmosphere. **2** *Politics* mood or atmosphere.

at·oll [AT-awl] *n* ring-shaped coral island enclosing lagoon.

at·om [AT-əm] *n* **1** smallest unit of matter that can enter into chemical combination. **2** any very small particle. **a·tom·ic** [ə-TOM-ik] *adj* of, arising from atoms. **at·o·mic·i·ty** [at-ə-MIS-i-tee] *n* number of atoms in molecule of an element. **at'om·ize** *vt* **-ized, -iz·ing** reduce to atoms or small particles. **at'om·iz·er** *n* instrument for discharging liquids in a fine spray. **atom(ic) bomb** one whose immense power derives from nuclear fission or fusion, nuclear bomb. **atomic energy** nuclear energy. **atomic number** the number of protons in the nucleus of an atom. **atomic reactor** see also REACTOR. **atomic weight** the weight of an atom of an element relative to that of carbon 12.

a·tone [ə-TOHN] *vi* **-toned, -ton·ing 1** make reparation, amends (for). **2** expiate. **3** give satisfaction. **a·tone'ment** *n*

a·ton·ic [ay-TON-ik] *adj* unaccented.

a·top [ə-TOP] *adv* **1** at or on the top. **2** above.

a·tro·cious [ə-TROH-shəs] *adj* **1** extremely cruel or wicked. **2** horrifying. **3** very bad. **a·troc'i·ty** [-TROS-i-tee] *n, pl* **-ties** wickedness.

at·ro·phy [A-trə-fee] *n* **1** wasting away, emaciation. ♦ *vi* **-phied, -phy·ing 2** waste away, become useless. **atrophied** *adj*

sharp, shrewd, subtle
asylum *n* **1** = **refuge**, harbor, haven, preserve, retreat, safety, sanctuary, shelter **2** *Old-fashioned* = **mental hospital**, funny farm (*sl*), hospital, institution, madhouse (*inf*), psychiatric hospital, psychiatric ward

atheism *n* = **nonbelief**, disbelief, godlessness, heathenism, infidelity, irreligion, paganism, skepticism, unbelief

atheist *n* = **nonbeliever**, disbeliever, heathen, infidel, pagan, skeptic, unbeliever

athlete *n* = **sportsperson**, competitor, contestant, gymnast, player, runner, sportsman, sportswoman

athletic *adj* = **fit**, active, energetic, muscular, powerful, strapping, strong, sturdy

athletics *pl n* = **sports**, contests, exercises, gymnastics, races, track and field events

atmosphere *n* **1** = **air**, aerosphere, heavens, sky **2** = **feeling**, ambience, character, climate, environment, mood, spirit, surroundings, tone

atom *n* = **particle**, bit, dot, molecule, speck, spot, trace

atone *v* (usually with *for*) = **make amends**, compensate, do penance, make redress, make reparation, make up for, pay for, recompense, redress

atonement *n* = **amends**, compensation, penance, recompense, redress, reparation, restitution

atrocious *adj* **1** = **cruel**, barbaric, brutal, fiendish, infernal, monstrous, savage, vicious, wicked **2** *Inf* = **shocking**, appalling, detestable, grievous, horrible, horrifying, terrible

atrocity *n* **1** = **cruelty**, barbarity, brutality, fiendishness, horror, savagery, viciousness, wickedness **2** = **act of cruelty**,

DICTIONARY

at·tach [ə-TACH] v (mainly tr) **1** join, fasten. **2** unite. **3** be connected with. **4** attribute. **5** appoint. **6** seize by law. **at·tached'** adj (with to) fond of. **at·tach'ment** n

at·ta·ché [a-ta-SHAY] n, pl **-chés** specialist attached to diplomatic mission. **attaché case** small suitcase for papers.

at·tack [ə-TAK] vt **1** take action against (in war, etc.). **2** criticize. **3** set about with vigor. **4** affect adversely. ◆ n **5** attacking action. **6** bout of sickness.

at·tain [ə-TAYN] vt **1** arrive at. **2** reach, gain by effort, accomplish. **at·tain'a·ble** adj **at·tain'ment** n esp. personal accomplishment.

at·tain·der [ə-TAYN-dər] n Hist. loss of civil rights usu. through conviction of treason.

at·tar [AT-ər] n a fragrant oil made esp. from rose petals.

at·tempt [ə-TEMPT] vt **1** try, endeavor. ◆ n **2** trial, effort.

at·tend [ə-TEND] vt **1** be present at. **2** accompany. ◆ vi **3** (with to) take care of. **4** give the mind (to), pay attention to. **at·tend'ance** n **1** an attending. **2** presence. **3** persons attending. **at·tend·ee** [ə-ten-DEE] n **at·tend'ant** n, adj **at·ten'tion** n **1** notice. **2** heed. **3** act of attending. **4** care. **5** courtesy. **at·ten'tive** adj **at·ten'tive·ness** n

at·ten·u·ate [ə-TEN yoo-ayt] v **-at·ed, -at·ing 1** weaken or become weak. **2** make or become thin. **at·ten'u·at·ed** adj **at·ten·u·a'tion** n reduction of intensity. **at·ten'u·a·tor** n device for attenuating, esp. for reducing the amplitude of an electrical signal.

at·test [ə-TEST] vt bear witness to, certify. **at·tes·ta·tion** [a-tes-TAY-shən] n formal confirmation by oath, etc.

at·tic [AT-ik] n space within roof where ceiling follows line of roof. **Attic** adj **1** of Attica, Athens. **2** (of literary or artistic style) pure, refined, elegant.

at·tire [ə-TIR] vt **-tired, -tir·ing 1** dress,

THESAURUS

abomination, crime, evil, horror, outrage
attach v **1** = **connect**, add, couple, fasten, fix, join, link, secure, stick, tie **2** = **put**, ascribe, assign, associate, attribute, connect
attached adj **1** = **spoken for**, accompanied, engaged, married, partnered **2 attached to** = **fond of**, affectionate towards, devoted to, full of regard for
attachment n **1** = **fondness**, affection, affinity, attraction, liking, regard **2** = **accessory**, accouterment, extension, extra, fitting, fixture, supplement
attack v **1** = **assault**, invade, raid, set upon, storm, strike (at) **2** = **criticize**, abuse, blame, censure, put down, vilify ◆ n **3** = **assault**, campaign, charge, foray, incursion, invasion, offensive, onslaught, raid, strike **4** = **criticism**, abuse, blame, censure, denigration, stick (sl), vilification **5** = **bout**, convulsion, fit, paroxysm, seizure, spasm, stroke
attacker n = **assailant**, aggressor, assaulter, intruder, invader, raider
attain v = **achieve**, accomplish, acquire, complete, fulfill, gain, get, obtain, reach
attainment n = **achievement**, accomplishment, completion, feat
attempt v **1** = **try**, endeavor, seek, strive, undertake, venture ◆ n **2** = **try**, bid, crack

(inf), effort, go (inf), shot (inf), stab (inf), trial
attend v **1** = **be present**, appear, frequent, go to, haunt, put in an appearance, show oneself, turn up, visit **2** = **look after**, care for, mind, minister to, nurse, take care of, tend **3** = **pay attention**, hear, heed, listen, mark, note, observe, pay heed **4 attend to** = **apply oneself to**, concentrate on, devote oneself to, get to work on, look after, occupy oneself with, see to, take care of
attendance n **1** = **presence**, appearance, attending, being there **2** = **turnout**, audience, crowd, gate, house, number present
attendant n **1** = **assistant**, aide, companion, escort, follower, guard, helper, servant ◆ adj **2** = **accompanying**, accessory, associated, concomitant, consequent, related
attention n **1** = **concentration**, deliberation, heed, intentness, mind, scrutiny, thinking, thought **2** = **notice**, awareness, consciousness, consideration, observation, recognition, regard **3** = **care**, concern, looking after, ministration, treatment
attentive adj **1** = **intent**, alert, awake, careful, concentrating, heedful, mindful, observant, studious, watchful **2** = **considerate**, courteous, helpful, kind,

array. ◆ n 2 dress, clothing.
at·ti·tude [AT-i-tood] n 1 mental view, opinion. 2 posture, pose. 3 disposition, behavior. **at·ti·tu'di·nize** vi -nized, -niz·ing assume affected attitudes.
at·tor·ney [ə-TUR-nee] n, pl -neys one legally appointed to act for another, esp. a lawyer. **attorney-at-law** n, pl -neys-at-law a lawyer.
at·tract [ə-TRAKT] v 1 draw (attention, etc.). 2 arouse interest of. 3 cause to come closer (as magnet, etc.). **at·trac'tion** n 1 power to attract. 2 something offered so as to interest, please. **at·trac'tive** adj **at·trac'tive·ness** n
at·trib·ute [ə-TRIB-yoot] vt -ut·ed, -ut·ing 1 regard as belonging to or produced by. ◆ n 2 [A-trə-byoot] quality, property or characteristic of anything. **at·trib'ut·a·ble** adj **at·tri·bu'tion** n
at·tri·tion [ə-TRISH-ən] n 1 wearing away of strength, friction. 2 rubbing away, friction.
at·tune [ə-TOON] vt -tuned, -tun·ing 1 tune, harmonize. 2 make accordant.
Au Chem. gold.
au·burn [AW-bərn] adj 1 reddish brown. ◆ n 2 this color.
au cou·rant [oh koo-RAHN] 1 up-to-date. 2 acquainted with.
auc·tion [AWK-shən] n 1 public sale in which bidder offers increase of price over another and what is sold goes to one who bids highest. ◆ v **auc·tion·eer'** n **auction bridge** card game. **Dutch auction** one in which price starts high and is reduced until purchaser is found.
au·da·cious [aw-DAY-shəs] adj 1 bold. 2 daring, impudent. **au·dac'i·ty** [-DAS-i-tee] n
au·di·ble [AW-də-bəl] adj able to be heard. **au'di·bly** adv
au·di·ence [AW-dee-əns] n 1 assembly of spectators or listeners. 2 act of hearing. 3 judicial hearing. 4 formal interview.
audio- comb. form relating to sound or hearing.
au·di·o·phile [AW-dee-ə-fil] n one who is enthusiastic about sound reproduction, esp. of music.
au·di·o·vis·u·al [aw-dee-oh-VIZH-oo-əl] adj (esp. of teaching aids) involving both sight and hearing.
au·dit [AW-dit] n 1 formal examination or settlement of financial accounts. ◆ vt 2 examine such accounts. **au'di·tor** n
au·di·tion [aw-DISH-ən] n 1 screen or other test of prospective performer. 2 hearing. ◆ vt 3 conduct such a test. **au·di·to'ri·um** n, pl -ri·ums 1 hall. 2 place where audience sits. **au'di·to·ry** adj pert. to sense of hearing.
auf Wie·der·seh·en [owf VEE-dər-zay-ən] Ger goodbye.
au·ger [AW-gər] n carpenter's tool for boring holes, large gimlet.
aught [awt] pron obs anything whatever.
aug·ment [awg-MENT] v increase, enlarge. **aug·men·ta'tion** n **aug·ment'a·ble** adj able

obliging, polite, respectful, thoughtful
attic[1] n = loft, garret
attire n = clothes, apparel, costume, dress, garb, garments, outfit, robes, wear
attitude n 1 = disposition, approach, frame of mind, mood, opinion, outlook, perspective, point of view, position, stance 2 = position, pose, posture, stance
attract v = appeal to, allure, charm, draw, enchant, entice, lure, pull (inf), tempt
attraction n = appeal, allure, charm, enticement, fascination, lure, magnetism, pull (inf), temptation
attractive adj = appealing, alluring, charming, fair, fetching, good-looking, handsome, inviting, lovely, pleasant, pretty, tempting
attribute v 1 = ascribe, assign, charge, credit, put down to, refer, set down to, trace to ◆ n 2 = quality, aspect, character, characteristic, facet, feature, peculiarity, property, trait
attune v = accustom, adapt, adjust, familiarize, harmonize, regulate
audacious adj 1 = daring, bold, brave, courageous, fearless, intrepid, rash, reckless 2 = cheeky, brazen, defiant, impertinent, impudent, insolent, presumptuous, shameless
audacity n 1 = daring, boldness, bravery, courage, fearlessness, nerve, rashness, recklessness 2 = cheek, chutzpah (inf), effrontery, impertinence, impudence, insolence, nerve
audible adj = clear, detectable, discernible, distinct, hearable, perceptible
audience n 1 = spectators, assembly, crowd, gallery, gathering, listeners, onlookers, turnout, viewers 2 = interview, consultation, hearing, meeting, reception

to increase in force or size.

au grat·in [oh GRAHT-n] cooked or baked to form light crust.

au·gur [AW-gər] n **1** among the Romans, soothsayer. ♦ v **2** be a sign of future events, foretell. **au'gu·ry** [-gyə-ree] n **1** divination from omens, etc. **2** omen.

au·gust [aw-GUST] adj majestic, dignified. **au·gust'ly** adv

auk [awk] n northern web-footed seabird with short wings used only as paddles.

aunt [ant] n father's or mother's sister, uncle's wife.

au pair [oh PAIR] n young foreign person, usu. a girl, who receives free board and lodging and usu. an allowance in return for housework, etc.

au·ra [OR-ə] n, pl **-ras 1** quality, air, atmosphere considered distinctive of person or thing. **2** medical symptom warning of impending epileptic seizure, etc.

au·ral [OR-əl] adj of, by ear. **au'ral·ly** adv

au·re·ole [OR-ee-ohl] n **1** gold disk around head in sacred pictures. **2** halo.

au re·voir [oh rə-VWAHR] Fr goodbye.

au·ri·cle [OR-i-kəl] n **1** outside ear. **2** an upper cavity of heart. **au·ric·u·lar** [aw-RIK-yə-lər] adj **1** of the auricle. **2** aural.

au·rif·er·ous [aw-RIF-ər-əs] adj gold-bearing.

au·ro·ra [aw-ROR-ə] n, pl **-ras 1** dawn. **2** lights in the atmosphere seen radiating from regions of the poles. **aurora bo·re·al·is** [bor-ee-AL-is] the northern lights. **aurora aus·tra·lis** [aw-STRAY-lis] the southern lights.

aus·cul·ta·tion [aw-skəl-TAY-shən] n listening to sounds of heart and lungs with stethoscope.

aus·pice [AW-spiss-siz] pl n **under the auspices of** with the support and approval of.

aus·pi·cious [aw-SPISH-əs] adj of good omen, favorable.

aus·tere [aw STEER] adj **1** harsh, strict, severe. **2** without luxury. **aus·tere'ly** adv **aus·ter·i·ty** [aw-STER-i-tee] n

aus·tral [AW-strəl] adj southern. **Austral** adj Australian.

Aus·tral·a·sian [aw-strə-LAY-zhən] adj, n (native or inhabitant) of Australasia (Australia, N Zealand and adjacent islands).

Aus·tral·ian [aw-STRAY-lyən] n, adj (native or inhabitant) of Australia.

au·tar·chy [AW-tahr-kee] n, pl **-chies** despotism, absolute power, dictatorship.

au·then·tic [aw-THEN-tik] adj **1** real, genuine, true. **2** trustworthy. **au·then'ti·cal·ly** adv **au·then'ti·cate** [-ti-kayt] vt **1** make valid, confirm. **2** establish truth, authorship, etc. of. **au·then·tic'i·ty** n

au·thor [AW-thər] n **1** writer of book. **2** originator, constructor.

au·thor·i·ty [ə-THOR-i-tee] n, pl **-ties 1** legal power or right. **2** delegated power. **3** influence. **4** permission. **5** expert. **6** body or board in control, esp. in pl. **au·thor'i·ta·tive** [-tay-tiv] adj **au·thor'i·ta·tive·ly** adv **au·thor·i·za'tion** n **au'thor·ize** vt **-ized, -iz·ing 1** empower. **2** permit, sanction.

aura n = **air**, ambience, atmosphere, feeling, mood, quality, tone

auspicious adj = **favorable**, bright, encouraging, felicitous, hopeful, promising

austere adj **1** = **stern**, forbidding, formal, serious, severe, solemn, strict **2** = **ascetic**, abstemious, puritanical, self-disciplined, sober, solemn, strait-laced, strict **3** = **plain**, bleak, harsh, homely, simple, spare, Spartan, stark

austerity n **1** = **sternness**, formality, inflexibility, rigor, seriousness, severity, solemnity, stiffness, strictness **2** = **asceticism**, puritanism, self-denial, self-discipline, sobriety **3** = **plainness**, simplicity, starkness

authentic adj = **genuine**, actual, authoritative, bona fide, legitimate, pure, real, true-to-life, valid

authenticity n = **genuineness**, accuracy, certainty, faithfulness, legitimacy, purity, truthfulness, validity

author n **1** = **writer**, composer, creator **2** = **creator**, architect, designer, father, founder, inventor, originator, producer

authoritarian adj **1** = **strict**, autocratic, dictatorial, doctrinaire, dogmatic, severe, tyrannical ♦ n **2** = **disciplinarian**, absolutist, autocrat, despot, dictator, tyrant

authoritative adj **1** = **reliable**, accurate, authentic, definitive, dependable, trustworthy, valid **2** = **commanding**, assertive, imperious, imposing, masterly, self-assured

au·tis·tic [aw-TIS-tik] *adj* withdrawn and divorced from reality. **au'tism** *n* this condition.

auto- *comb. form* self-, e.g. *autobiography*.

au·to [AW-toh] *n* automobile.

au·to·bi·og·ra·phy [aw-tə-bī-OG-rə-fee] *n, pl* **-phies** life of person written by that person. **au·to·bi·o·graph'i·cal** *adj*

au·toch·thon [aw-TOK-thən] *n* **1** primitive or original inhabitant. **2** native plant or animal. **au·toch'tho·nous** *adj* indigenous, native.

au·to·crat [AW-tə-krat] *n* **1** absolute ruler. **2** despotic person. **au·toc'ra·cy** [-TOK-rə-see] *n, pl* **-cies au·to·crat'ic** *adj*

au·to·er·o·tism [aw-toh-ER-ə-tiz-əm] *n* self-produced sexual arousal.

au·to·gi·ro [aw-tə-JĪ-roh] *n, pl* **-ros** aircraft like helicopter using horizontal airscrew for vertical ascent and descent.

au·to·graph [AW-tə-graf] *n* **1** a signature. **2** one's own handwriting. ◆ *vt* **3** sign.

au·to·in·tox·i·ca·tion [aw-toh-in-tok-si-KAY-shən] *n* poisoning of tissues of the body as a result of the absorption of bodily waste.

au·to·mate [AW-tə-mayt] *vt* **-mat·ed, -mat·ing 1** make manufacturing process, etc. **2** automatic. **au·to·ma'tion** *n* use of automatic devices in industrial production.

au·to·mat·ic [aw-tə-MAT-ik] *adj* **1** operated or controlled mechanically. **2** done without conscious thought. ◆ *adj, n* **3** self-loading (weapon). **au·to·mat'i·cal·ly** *adv* **au·tom'a·ton** *n, pl* **-ta** [-tə] self-acting machine, esp. simulating a human being.

au·to·mo·bile [aw-tə-mə-BEEL] *n* motor car.

au·ton·o·my [aw-TON-ə-mee] *n, pl* **-mies** self-government. **au·ton'o·mous** *adj*

au·top·sy [AW-top-see] *n, pl* **-sies** postmortem examination to determine cause of death.

au·to·sug·ges·tion [aw-toh-səg-JES-chən] *n* process of influencing the mind (toward health, etc.) conducted by oneself.

au·tumn [AW-təm] *n, adj* (typical of) the season after summer. **au·tum·nal** [aw-TUM-nl] *adj* typical of the onset of winter.

aux·il·ia·ry [awg-ZIL-yə-ree] *adj* **1** helping, subsidiary. ◆ *n, pl* **-ries 2** something subsidiary, as troops. **4** verb used to form tenses of others.

a·vail [ə-VAYL] *v* **1** be of use, advantage, value (to). ◆ *v* **2** use or advantage, esp. in *to no avail*. **a·vail·a·bil'i·ty** *n* **a·vail'a·ble** *adj* **1** obtainable. **2** accessible. **avail oneself of** make use of.

av·a·lanche [AV-ə-lanch] *n* **1** mass of

authority *n* **1** = **power**, command, control, direction, influence, supremacy, sway, weight **2** (usually plural) = **powers that be**, administration, government, management, officialdom, police, the Establishment **3** = **expert**, connoisseur, judge, master, professional, specialist

authorization *n* = **permission**, a blank check, approval, leave, license, permit, warrant

authorize *v* **1** = **empower**, accredit, commission, enable, entitle, give authority **2** = **permit**, allow, approve, give authority for, license, sanction, warrant

autocracy *n* = **dictatorship**, absolutism, despotism, tyranny

autocrat *n* = **dictator**, absolutist, despot, tyrant

autocratic *adj* = **dictatorial**, absolute, all-powerful, despotic, domineering, imperious, tyrannical

automatic *adj* **1** = **mechanical**, automated, mechanized, push-button, self-propelling **2** = **involuntary**, instinctive,

mechanical, natural, reflex, spontaneous, unconscious, unwilled

autonomous *adj* = **self-ruling**, free, independent, self-determining, self-governing, sovereign

autonomy *n* = **independence**, freedom, home rule, self-determination, self-government, self-rule, sovereignty

auxiliary *adj* **1** = **supplementary**, back-up, emergency, fall-back, reserve, secondary, subsidiary, substitute **2** = **supporting**, accessory, aiding, ancillary, assisting, helping ◆ *n* **3** = **backup**, reserve **4** = **helper**, assistant, associate, companion, subordinate, supporter

avail *v* **1** = **benefit**, aid, assist, be of advantage, be useful, help, profit ◆ *n* **2** = **benefit**, advantage, aid, good, help, profit, use

availability *n* = **accessibility**, attainability, handiness, readiness

available *adj* = **accessible**, at hand, at one's disposal, free, handy, on tap, ready, to hand snow, ice, sliding down mountain. **2** a sudden overwhelming quantity of anything.

a•vant-garde [ah-vahnt-GAHRD] *adj* markedly experimental or in advance.

av•a•rice [AV-ə-ris] *n* greed for wealth. **av•a•ri•cious** [-RISH-əs] *adj*

a•vast [ə-VAST] *interj Nautical* stop.

av•a•tar [AV-ə-tahr] *n Hinduism* descent of god to Earth in bodily form.

a•venge [ə-VENJ] *vt* **-venged, -veng•ing** take vengeance on behalf of (person) or on account of (thing). **a•veng'er** *n*

av•e•nue [AV-ə-nyoo] *n* **1** route. **2** a way of approach, a channel.

a•ver [ə-VUR] *vt* **-verred, -ver•ring** affirm, assert.

av•er•age [AV-rij] *n* **1** the mean value or quantity of a number of values or quantities. ♦ *adj* **2** calculated as an average. **3** medium, ordinary. ♦ *v* **-aged, -ag•ing** ♦ *vt* **4** fix or calculate a mean. ♦ *vi* **5** exist in or form a mean.

a•verse [ə-VURS] *adj* disinclined, unwilling. **a•ver'sion** [-zhən] *n* **1** dislike. **2** person or thing disliked.

a•vert [ə-VURT] *vt* **1** turn away. **2** ward off.

a•vi•ar•y [AY-vee-er-ee] *n, pl* **-ar•ies** enclosure for birds. **a'vi•a•rist** *n*

a•vi•a•tion [ay-vee-AY-shən] *n* **1** art of flying aircraft. **2** transport by aircraft. **a'vi•a•tor** *n*

av•id [AV-id] *adj* **1** keen, enthusiastic. **2** greedy (for). **a•vid'i•ty** *n* **av'id•ly** *adv*

av•o•ca•do [av-ə-KAH-doh] *n* **1** tropical tree. **2** its green-skinned edible fruit, alligator pear.

av•o•ca•tion [av-ə-KAY-shən] *n* **1** vocation. **2** employment, business.

a•void [ə-VOID] *vt* **1** keep away from. **2** refrain from. **3** not allow to happen. **a•void'a•ble** *adj* **a•void'ance** *n*

av•oir•du•pois [av-ər-də-POIZ] *n* system of weights used in many English-speaking countries based on pounds and ounces.

a•vow [ə-VOW] *vt* **1** declare. **2** admit. **a•vow'a•ble** *adj* **a•vow'al** *n* **a•vowed'** *adj* **a•vow'ed•ly** *adv*

a•vun•cu•lar [ə-VUNG-kyə-lər] *adj* like or of an uncle esp. in manner.

a•wait [ə-WAYT] *vt* **1** wait or stay for. **2** be in store for.

——— THESAURUS ———

avalanche *n* **1** = **snow-slide**, landslide, landslip **2** = **flood**, barrage, deluge, inundation, torrent

avant-garde *adj* = **progressive**, experimental, ground-breaking, innovative, pioneering, unconventional

avarice *n* = **greed**, covetousness, meanness, miserliness, niggardliness, parsimony, stinginess

avaricious *adj* = **grasping**, covetous, greedy, mean, miserly, niggardly, parsimonious, stingy

avenge *v* = **get revenge for**, get even for (*inf*), hit back, punish, repay, retaliate

avenue *n* = **street**, approach, boulevard, course, drive, passage, path, road, route, way

average *n* **1** = **usual**, mean, medium, midpoint, norm, normal, par, standard **2 on average** = **usually**, as a rule, for the most part, generally, normally, typically ♦ *adj* **3** = **usual**, commonplace, fair, general, normal, ordinary, regular, standard, typical **4** = **mean**, intermediate, median, medium, middle ♦ *v* **5** = **make on average**, balance out to, be on average, do on average, even out to

averse *adj* = **opposed**, disinclined, hostile,

ill-disposed, loath, reluctant, unwilling

aversion *n* = **hatred**, animosity, antipathy, disinclination, dislike, hostility, revulsion, unwillingness

avert *v* **1** = **turn away**, turn aside **2** = **ward off**, avoid, fend off, forestall, frustrate, preclude, prevent, stave off

aviator *n* = **pilot**, aeronaut, airman, flyer

avid *adj* **1** = **enthusiastic**, ardent, devoted, eager, fanatical, intense, keen, passionate, zealous **2** = **insatiable**, grasping, greedy, hungry, rapacious, ravenous, thirsty, voracious

avoid *v* **1** = **refrain from**, dodge, duck (out of) (*inf*), eschew, fight shy of, shirk **2** = **prevent**, avert **3** = **keep away from**, bypass, dodge, elude, escape, evade, shun, steer clear of

avoidance *n* = **evasion**, dodging, eluding, escape, keeping away, shunning, steering clear

avowed *adj* **1** = **declared**, open, professed, self-proclaimed, sworn **2** = **confessed**, acknowledged, admitted

await *v* **1** = **wait for**, abide, anticipate, expect, look for, look forward to, stay for **2** = **be in store for**, attend, be in readiness for, be prepared for, be ready for, wait for

a·wake [ə-WAYK] v **a·wak·ing, a·woke, a·wok·en 1** emerge or rouse from sleep. **2** become or cause to become alert. **a·wak'en·ing** n

a·wak·en [ə-WAY-kən] vt arouse (feelings, etc.) or cause to remember (memories, etc.).

a·ward [ə-WORD] vt **1** to give formally (esp. a prize or punishment). ♦ n **2** prize. **3** judicial decision, amount awarded.

a·ware [ə-WAIR] adj informed, conscious. **a·ware'ness** n

a·wash [ə-WOSH] adv **1** level with the surface of water. **2** filled or overflowing with water. **awash in** marked by an abundance of.

a·way [ə-WAY] adv **1** absent, apart, at a distance, out of the way. ♦ adj **2** Sports. played on opponent's grounds.

awe [aw] n dread mingled with reverence. **awe'some** [-səm] adj **awe'some·ly** adv **awe'some·ness** n **awe'struck** adj filled with awe.

aw·ful [AW-fəl] adj **1** very bad, unpleasant. **2** inspiring awe. **3** inf very great. **aw'ful·ly** adv **1** in an unpleasant way. **2** inf very much.

a·while [ə-HWĪL] adv for a time.

awk·ward [AWK-wərd] adj **1** clumsy, ungainly. **2** difficult. **3** inconvenient. **4** embarrassed. **awk'ward·ly** adv **awk'ward·ness** n

awl n pointed tool for marking or boring wood, leather, etc.

awn·ing n (canvas, etc.) roof or shelter, to protect from weather.

awoke pt./pp. of AWAKE.

a·wry [ə-RĪ] adv **1** crookedly. **2** amiss. **3** at a slant. ♦ adj **4** crooked, distorted. **5** wrong.

ax, axe [aks] n **1** tool with handle and heavy, sharp blade for chopping. **2** inf dismissal from employment, etc. ♦ vt **axed, ax·ing 3** inf dismiss, dispense with.

ax·iom [AK-see-əm] n **1** received or

THESAURUS

awake adj **1** = **not sleeping**, aroused, awakened, aware, conscious, wakeful, wide-awake **2** = **alert**, alive, attentive, aware, heedful, observant, on the lookout, vigilant, watchful ♦ v **3** = **wake up**, awaken, rouse, wake **4** = **alert**, arouse, kindle, provoke, revive, stimulate, stir up

awaken v **1** = **awake**, arouse, revive, rouse, wake **2** = **alert**, kindle, provoke, stimulate, stir up

awakening n = **waking up**, arousal, revival, rousing, stimulation, stirring up

award v **1** = **give**, bestow, confer, endow, grant, hand out, present ♦ n **2** = **prize**, decoration, gift, grant, trophy

aware adj **1** aware of = **knowing about**, acquainted with, conscious of, conversant with, familiar with, mindful of **2** = **informed**, enlightened, in the picture, knowledgeable

awareness n = **knowledge**, consciousness, familiarity, perception, realization, recognition, understanding

away adv **1** = **off**, abroad, elsewhere, from here, from home, hence **2** = **at a distance**, apart, far, remote **3** = **aside**, out of the way, to one side **4** = **continuously**, incessantly, interminably, relentlessly, repeatedly, uninterruptedly, unremittingly ♦ adj **5** = **not present**, abroad, absent, elsewhere, gone, not at home, not here, out

awe n **1** = **wonder**, admiration, amazement, astonishment, dread, fear, horror, respect, reverence, terror ♦ v **2** = **impress**, amaze, astonish, frighten, horrify, intimidate, stun, terrify

awesome adj **1** = **awe-inspiring**, amazing, astonishing, breathtaking, cool (inf), formidable, impressive, intimidating, phat (sl), stunning **2** Inf = **first-class**, choice, elite, excellent, first-rate, hand-picked, superior, world-class

awful adj **1** = **terrible**, abysmal, appalling, deplorable, dreadful, frightful, ghastly, horrendous

awfully adv **1** = **badly**, disgracefully, dreadfully, reprehensibly, unforgivably, unpleasantly, woefully, wretchedly **2** Inf = **very**, dreadfully, exceedingly, exceptionally, extremely, greatly, immensely, terribly

awkward adj **1** = **clumsy**, gauche, gawky, inelegant, lumbering, uncoordinated, ungainly **2** = **unmanageable**, clunky (inf), cumbersome, difficult, inconvenient, troublesome, unwieldy **3** = **embarrassing**, delicate, difficult, ill at ease, inconvenient, uncomfortable

awkwardness n **1** = **clumsiness**, gawkiness, inelegance, ungainliness **2** = **unwieldiness**, difficulty, inconvenience **3** = **embarrassment**, delicacy, difficulty, inconvenience

accepted principle. **2** self-evident truth.
ax·i·o·mat'ic adj
ax·is [AK-sis] n, pl **ax·es** [AK-seez] **1**
(imaginary) line around which a body
spins. **2** line or column about which parts
are arranged. **ax'i·al** adj **ax'i·al·ly** adv
Ax·is n coalition of Germany, Italy and
Japan, 1936–45.
ax·le [AK-səl] n shaft on which wheel turns.
a·ya·tol·lah [ah-yə-TOH-lə] adj one of a
class of Islamic religious leaders.
aye [ī] adv **1** yes. ◆ n **2** affirmative answer or
vote. ◆ pl **3** those voting for motion.
a·zal·ea [ə-ZAYL-yə] n any of group of
shrubby plants of the rhododendron
genus.
az·i·muth [AZ-ə-məth] n **1** vertical arc from
zenith to horizon. **2** angular distance of
this from meridian.
Az·tec [AZ-tek] adj, n (member) of people
ruling Mexico before Spanish conquest.
az·ure [AZH-ər] n **1** sky-blue color. **2** clear
sky. ◆ adj **3** sky-blue.

———————— THESAURUS ————————

ax n **1** = **hatchet**, adz, chopper **2 the ax** Inf
= **dismissal**, termination, the boot (sl), the
chop (sl) ◆ v **3** Inf = **cut back**, cancel,
dismiss, dispense with, eliminate, fire (inf),
get rid of, remove, sack (inf)
axiom n = **principle**, adage, aphorism,
dictum, maxim, precept, truism

axiomatic adj = **self-evident**, accepted,
assumed, certain, given, granted, manifest,
understood
axis n = **pivot**, axle, center line, shaft,
spindle
axle n = **shaft**, axis, pin, pivot, rod, spindle

B b

B *Chem.* boron.

Ba *Chem.* barium.

bab·ble [BAB-əl] *v* **-bled, -bling 1** speak foolishly, incoherently, or childishly. ◆ *n* **2** foolish, confused talk. **bab'bler** *n*

babe [bayb] *n* **1** baby. **2** guileless person.

ba·bel [BAY-bəl] *n* confused noise or scene, uproar.

ba·boon [ba-BOON] *n* large monkey of Africa and Asia.

ba·by [BAY-bee] *n, pl* **-bies** very young child, infant. **ba'by·ish** *adj* **ba'by-sit** *v* **-sat, -sit·ting ba'by-sit·ter** *n* one who cares for children when parents are out.

bac·ca·lau·re·ate [bak-ə-LOR-ee-it] *n* **1** degree of bachelor. **2** service held at college or university awarding degree. **3** sermon delivered at this service.

bac·ca·rat [BAH-kə-rah] *n* gambling card game.

bach·e·lor [BACH-lər] *n* **1** unmarried man. **2** holder of lowest four-year college or university degree.

ba·cil·lus [bə-SIL-əs] *n, pl* **-cil·li** [-SIL-ī] minute organism sometimes causing disease.

back [bak] *n* **1** hinder part of anything, e.g. human body. **2** part opposite front. **3** part or side of something farther away or less used. **4** (position of) player in football and other games behind other (forward) players. ◆ *adj* **5** situated behind. **6** earlier. ◆ *adv* **7** at, to the back. **8** in, into the past. **9** in return. ◆ *vi* **10** move backward. ◆ *vt* **11** support. **12** put wager on. **13** provide with back or backing. **back'er** *n* **1** one supporting another, esp. in contest or election campaign. **2** one betting on horse, etc. in race. **back'ing** *n* **1** support. **2** material to protect the back of something. **back'ward, back'wards** *adv* **1** to the rear.

2 to the past. **3** to worse state. **back'ward** *adj* **1** directed toward the rear. **2** (of a country, region or people) retarded in economic development. **3** behind in education. **4** reluctant, bashful. **back'ward·ness** *n* **back'bite** *vt* **-bit, -bit·ten, -bit·ing** slander absent person. **back'bit·er** *n* **back'biting** *n* **back'bone** *n* spinal column. **back'date** *vt* **-dat·ed, -dat·ing** make effective from earlier date. **back'drop** *n* painted cloth at back of stage. **back'fire** *vi* **-fired, -fir·ing 1** ignite at wrong time, as fuel in cylinder of internal-combustion engine. **2** (of plan, scheme, etc.) fail to work, esp. to the detriment of the instigator. **3** ignite wrongly, as gas burner, etc. **back'gam·mon** [-gam-ən] *n* game played with counters and dice. **back'ground** *n* **1** space behind chief figures of picture, etc. **2** past history of person. **back'hand** *n* stroke with hand turned backward. **back'hand·ed** *adj* (of compliment, etc.) with second, uncomplimentary meaning. **back'lash** *n* sudden and adverse reaction. **back'log** *n* accumulation of work, etc. to be dealt with. **back'pack** *n* type of knapsack. ◆ *vi* **-packed, -pack·ing 2** hike with this. **back'side** *n* buttocks. **back'slash** *n* backward-sloping diagonal mark (\). **back'slide** *vi* **-slid** *or* **-slid·den, -slid·ing** fall back in faith or morals. **back'stroke** *n* swimming stroke performed on the back. **back'talk** *n* impudent or insolent answer. **back'up** *n* **1** a support or reinforcement. **2** a reserve or substitute. **back up** *v* **1** support. **2** *Computers* make a copy of (a data file), esp. as a security copy. **back'wash** *n* **1** water thrown back by ship's propellers, etc. **2** a backward current. **3** a reaction. **back'wa·ter** *n* **1** still

---

THESAURUS

babble *v* **1** = **gabble**, burble, chatter, jabber, prattle **2** = **gibber**, gurgle ◆ *n* **3** = **gabble**, burble, drivel, gibberish

baby *n* **1** = **infant**, babe, babe in arms, child, newborn child ◆ *adj* **2** = **small**, little, mini, miniature, minute, teeny-weeny, tiny, wee

babyish *adj* = **childish**, foolish, immature,

water fed by back flow of stream. **2**
backward or isolated place or condition.
back'woods' *pl n* **1** remote forest areas. **2**
remote or backward area.

ba·con [BAY-kən] *n* cured and smoked
meat from side of pig.

bac·te·ri·a [bak-TEER-ee-ə] *pl n, sing* **-ri·um**
microscopic organisms, some causing
disease. **bac·te'ri·al** *adj* **bac·te·ri·cide**
[-TEER-ə-sīd] *n* substance that destroys
bacteria. **bac·te·ri·ol'o·gist** [-OL-ə-jist] *n*
bac·te·ri·ol'o·gy *n* study of bacteria.

bad *adj* **worse, worst 1** of poor quality. **2**

faulty. **3** evil. **4** immoral. **5** offensive. **6**
severe. **7** rotten, decayed. **bad'ly** *adv*
bad'ness *n* **bad-mouth** *vt sl* speak
unfavourably about.

bade [bad] pt. of BID.

badge [baj] *n* distinguishing emblem or
sign.

badg·er [BAJ-ər] *n* **1** burrowing night
animal, about the size of fox. **2** its pelt or
fur. ◆ *vt* **3** pester, worry.

bad·i·nage [bad-n-AHZH] *n* **1** playful talk,
banter.

bad·min·ton [BAD-min-tn] *n* game like

infantile, juvenile, puerile, sissy, spoiled
back *n* **1** = **rear**, end, far end, hind part,
hindquarters, reverse, stern, tail end
2 behind one's back = **secretly**, covertly,
deceitfully, sneakily, surreptitiously ◆ *v* **3** =
move back, back off, backtrack, go back,
retire, retreat, reverse, turn tail, withdraw
4 = **support**, advocate, assist, champion,
endorse, promote, sponsor ◆ *adj* **5** = **rear**,
end, hind, hindmost, posterior, tail **6** =
previous, delayed, earlier, elapsed, former,
overdue, past
backbiting *n* = **slander**, bitchiness (*sl*),
cattiness (*inf*), defamation, disparagement,
gossip, malice, scandalmongering,
spitefulness
backbone *n* **1** *Medical* = **spinal column**,
spine, vertebrae, vertebral column **2** =
strength of character, character, courage,
determination, fortitude, grit, nerve, pluck,
resolution
backbreaking *adj* = **exhausting**, arduous,
crushing, grueling, hard, laborious,
punishing, strenuous
back down *v* = **give in**, accede, admit
defeat, back-pedal, concede, surrender,
withdraw, yield
backer *n* = **supporter**, advocate, angel
(*inf*), benefactor, patron, promoter,
second, sponsor, subscriber
backfire *v* = **fail**, boomerang, disappoint,
flop (*inf*), miscarry, rebound, recoil
background *n* = **history**, circumstances,
culture, education, environment,
grounding, tradition, upbringing
backing *n* = **support**, aid, assistance,
encouragement, endorsement, moral
support, patronage, sponsorship
backlash *n* = **reaction**, counteraction,
recoil, repercussion, resistance, response,
retaliation

backlog *n* = **build-up**, accumulation,
excess, hoard, reserve, stock, supply
back out *v* (often with *of*) = **withdraw**,
abandon, cancel, excuse oneself, give up,
go back on, quit, resign, retreat, wimp out
(*sl*)
backslide *v* = **relapse**, go astray, go
wrong, lapse, revert, slip, stray, weaken
backslider *n* = **relapser**, apostate,
deserter, recidivist, recreant, renegade,
turncoat
back up *v* = **support**, aid, assist, bolster,
confirm, corroborate, reinforce, second,
stand by, substantiate
backward *adj* = **slow**, behind, dull,
retarded, subnormal, underdeveloped,
undeveloped
backwards, backward *adv* = **towards
the rear**, behind, in reverse, rearward
bacteria *pl n* = **microorganisms**, bacilli,
bugs (*sl*), germs, microbes, pathogens,
viruses
bad *adj* **1** = **inferior**, defective, faulty,
imperfect, inadequate, lousy (*sl*), poor,
substandard, unsatisfactory **2** = **harmful**,
damaging, dangerous, deleterious,
detrimental, hurtful, ruinous, unhealthy
3 = **evil**, corrupt, criminal, immoral, mean,
sinful, wicked, wrong **4** = **naughty**,
disobedient, mischievous, unruly **5** =
rotten, decayed, moldy, putrid, rancid,
sour, spoiled **6** = **unfavorable**, adverse,
distressing, gloomy, grim, troubled,
unfortunate, unpleasant
badge *n* = **mark**, brand, device, emblem,
identification, insignia, sign, stamp, token
badger *v* = **pester**, bully, goad, harass,
hound, importune, nag, plague, torment
badinage *n* = **wordplay**, banter, mockery,
pleasantry, repartee, teasing
badly *adv* **1** = **poorly**, carelessly,

tennis, played with rackets and
shuttlecocks over high net.

baf·fle [BAF-əl] vt **-fled, -fling** check,
frustrate, bewilder. **baffling** adj **baffle** n
device to regulate or divert flow of liquid,
gas, sound waves, etc.

bag n **1** sack, pouch. **2** measure of quantity.
3 woman's handbag. **4** offens unattractive
woman. ◆ v **bagged, bag·ging** ◆ vi **5** swell
out. **6** bulge. **7** sag. ◆ vt **8** put in bag. **9** kill
as game, etc. **bag'gy** adj **-gi·er, -gi·est**
loose, drooping. **bag lady** homeless
woman who carries her possessions in
shopping bags, etc. **bag'man** n, pl **-men**
person who collects and distributes illicitly
obtained money for another.

bag·a·telle [bag-ə-TEL] n **1** trifle. **2** game
like billiards.

bag·gage [BAG-ij] n **1** suitcases, etc.,
packed for journey. **2** offens woman.

bag·pipe [BAG-pīp] n (oft. pl) musical wind
instrument, of windbag and pipes.
bag'pip·er n

bail¹ [bayl] n Law **1** security given for
person's reappearance in court. **2** one
giving such security. ◆ vt **3** release, or
obtain release of, on security. **4** inf help a
person, firm, etc. out of trouble.

bail² vt empty out water from boat. **bail out**
1 leave aircraft by parachute. **2** give up on
or abandon something.

bail·iff [BAY-lif] n minor court officer.

bail·i·wick [BAY-li-wik] n a person's
domain or special area of competence.

bait [bayt] n **1** food to entice fish. **2** any lure
or enticement. ◆ vt **3** set a lure. **4** annoy,
persecute.

baize [bayz] n smooth woolen cloth.

bake [bayk] v **baked, bak·ing** ◆ vt **1** cook or
harden by dry heat. ◆ vi **2** make bread,
cakes, etc. **3** be scorched or tanned. **bak'er**
n **bak'er·y** n **baking** n **baking powder**
leavening agent containing sodium
bicarbonate, etc. used in making baked
goods.

bal·a·cla·va [bal-ə-KLAH-və] n close-fitting
woolen helmet, covering head and neck.

bal·a·lai·ka [bal-ə-LĪ-kə] n Russian musical
instrument, like guitar.

bal·ance [BAL-əns] n **1** pair of scales. **2**
equilibrium. **3** surplus. **4** sum due on an
account. **5** difference between two sums. ◆
vt **-anced, -anc·ing 6** weigh. **7** bring to
equilibrium. **balance sheet** tabular
statement of assets and liabilities. **balance
wheel** regulating wheel of watch.

bal·co·ny [BAL-kə-nee] n, pl **-nies 1** railed
platform outside window. **2** upper seats in
theater.

bald [bawld] adj **1** hairless. **2** plain. **3** bare.
bald'ing adj becoming bald. **bald'ness** n

bale [bayl] n **1** bundle or package. ◆ vt

imperfectly, inadequately, incorrectly,
ineptly, wrongly **2 = unfavorably**,
unfortunately, unsuccessfully **3 = severely**,
deeply, desperately, exceedingly,
extremely, greatly, intensely, seriously

bad-mouth v Sl **= criticize**, abuse, deride,
insult, malign, mock, slander

baffle v **= puzzle**, bewilder, confound,
confuse, flummox, mystify, nonplus,
perplex, stump

bag n **1 = container**, receptacle, sac, sack ◆
v **2 = catch**, acquire, capture, kill, land,
shoot, trap

baggage n **= luggage**, accoutrements,
bags, belongings, equipment, gear,
paraphernalia, suitcases, things

baggy adj **= loose**, bulging, droopy,
floppy, ill-fitting, oversize, roomy, sagging,
slack

bail¹ n Law **= security**, bond, guarantee,
pledge, surety, warranty

bail out v **1 = help**, aid, relieve, rescue,
save (someone's) bacon (inf) **2 = escape**,

quit, retreat, withdraw

bait n **1 = lure**, allurement, attraction,
decoy, enticement, incentive, inducement,
snare, temptation ◆ v **2 = tease**, annoy,
bother, harass, hassle (inf), hound, irritate,
persecute, torment

baked adj **= dry**, arid, desiccated, parched,
scorched, seared, sun-baked, torrid

balance n **1 = stability**, composure,
equanimity, poise, self-control,
self-possession, steadiness **2 = equilibrium**,
correspondence, equity, equivalence,
evenness, parity, symmetry **3 = remainder**,
difference, residue, rest, surplus ◆ v **4 =
stabilize**, level, match, parallel, steady **5 =
compare**, assess, consider, deliberate,
estimate, evaluate, weigh **6** Accounting **=
calculate**, compute, settle, square, tally,
total

balcony n **1 = terrace**, veranda **2 = upper
circle**, gallery, gods

bald adj **1 = hairless**, baldheaded, depilated
2 = plain, blunt, direct, forthright,

baled, bal·ing 2 make into bundles or pack into cartons. **bal'er** *n* machine that does this.

ba·leen [bə-LEEN] *n* whalebone.

bale·ful [BAYL-fəl] *adj* menacing. **bale'ful·ly** *adv*

balk [bawk] *vi* **1** swerve, pull up. **2** *Baseball* commit a balk. ♦ *vt* **3** thwart, hinder. **4** shirk. ♦ *n* **5** hindrance. **6** rafter, beam. **7** *Baseball* illegal motion of pitcher before releasing it to batter. **balk at 1** recoil. **2** stop short.

ball[1] [bawl] *n* **1** anything round. **2** globe, sphere, esp. as used in games. **3** a ball as pitched. **4** bullet. ♦ *vi* **5** clog, gather into a mass. **ball bearings** hardened steel balls used to lessen friction on bearings. **ball'park** *n* **1** stadium used for baseball games. **2** *inf* approximate range. ♦ *adj* **3** *inf* approximate. **ball'point, ball'point pen** pen with tiny ball bearing as nib.

ball[2] *n* **1** formal social gathering for dancing. **2** *inf* a very good time. **ball'room** *n*

bal·lad [BAL-əd] *n* **1** narrative poem. **2** simple song.

bal·lade [bə-LAHD] *n* **1** short poem with refrain and envoi. **2** piece of music.

bal·last [BAL-əst] *n* **1** heavy material put in ship to give steadiness. **2** that which renders anything steady. ♦ *vt* **3** load with ballast, steady.

bal·let [ba-LAY] *n* theatrical presentation of dancing and miming to musical accompaniment. **bal·le·ri·na** [bal-ə-REE-nə] *n*

bal·lis·tic [bə-LIS-tik] *adj* moving as, or

pertaining to motion of, a projectile. **bal·lis'tics** *n* scientific study of ballistic motion.

bal·loon [bə-LOON] *n* **1** large bag filled with air or gas to make it rise in the air. ♦ *vi* **2** puff out. **3** increase rapidly. **bal·loon'ing** *n* **bal·loon'ist** *n*

bal·lot [BAL-ət] *n* **1** method of voting secretly, usually by marking ballot paper and putting it into box. ♦ *vi* **2** vote or decide by ballot. **ballot box** box into which voting papers are dropped on completion.

bal·ly·hoo [BAL-ee-hoo] *n* **1** noisy confusion or uproar. **2** flamboyant, exaggerated publicity or advertising.

balm [bahm] *n* **1** aromatic substance, healing or soothing ointment. **2** anything soothing. **balm'y** *adj* **balm·i·er, balm·i·est** **1** soothing. **2** (of climate) mild. **3** (of a person) foolish. **balm'i·ness** *n*

ba·lo·ney [bə-LOW-nee] *n inf* nonsense.

bal·sa [BAWL-sə] *n* Amer. tree with light but strong wood.

bal·sam [BAWL-səm] *n* **1** resinous aromatic substance obtained from various trees and shrubs. **2** soothing ointment. **bal·sam'ic** *adj*

Baltimore oriole oriole of eastern N Amer.

bal·us·ter [BAL-ə-stər] *n* short pillar used as support to rail of staircase, etc. **bal'us·trade** [-strayd] *n* row of short pillars topped by rail.

bam·boo' *n, pl* **-boos** large tropical treelike reed.

bam·boo·zle [bam-BOO-zəl] *vt* **-zled,**

——————| THESAURUS |——————

straightforward, unadorned, unvarnished

balderdash *n* = **nonsense**, claptrap (*inf*), drivel, garbage (*inf*), gibberish, hogwash, hot air (*inf*), rubbish

baldness *n* **1** = **hairlessness**, alopecia (*Pathology*), baldheadedness **2** = **plainness**, austerity, bluntness, severity, simplicity

balk *v* **1** = **recoil**, evade, flinch, hesitate, jib, refuse, resist, shirk, shrink from **2** = **foil**, check, counteract, defeat, frustrate, hinder, obstruct, prevent, thwart

ball *n* = **sphere**, drop, globe, globule, orb, pellet, spheroid

ballast *n* = **counterbalance**, balance, counterweight, equilibrium, sandbag, stability, stabilizer, weight

balloon *v* = **swell**, billow, blow up, dilate,

distend, expand, grow rapidly, inflate, puff out

ballot *n* = **vote**, election, poll, polling, voting

ballyhoo *n* = **fuss**, babble, commotion, hubbub, hue and cry, hullabaloo, noise, racket, to-do

balm *n* **1** = **ointment**, balsam, cream, embrocation, emollient, lotion, salve, unguent **2** = **comfort**, anodyne, consolation, curative, palliative, restorative, solace

balmy *adj* = **mild**, clement, pleasant, summery, temperate

baloney *n Inf* = **nonsense**, claptrap (*inf*), crap (*sl*), drivel, garbage, hogwash, poppycock (*inf*), rubbish, stuff and

-zling mystify, hoodwink.

ban vt **banned, ban·ning 1** prohibit, forbid, outlaw. ♦ n **2** prohibition. **3** proclamation. **banns** pl n proclamation of marriage.

ba·nal [bə-NAL] adj commonplace, trivial, trite. **ba·nal'i·ty** n

ba·nan·a [bə-NAN-ə] n **1** tropical treelike plant. **2** its fruit.

band¹ n **1** strip used to bind. **2** range of values, frequencies, etc., between two limits. **band·age** [BAN-dij] n strip of cloth for binding wound.

band² n **1** company, group. **2** company of musicians. ♦ v **3** bind together. **band'mas·ter** n **band'stand** n

ban·dan·na [ban-DAN-ə] n large decorated handkerchief.

band·box [BAND-boks] n **1** light box of cardboard for hats, etc. **2** theater or other public structure of small interior dimensions.

ban·deau [ban-DOH] n, pl **-deaux** [-DOHZ] **1** band, ribbon for the hair. **2** narrow bra or top.

ban'dit n **1** outlaw. **2** robber, brigand.

ban·do·leer [ban-də-LEER] n shoulder belt for cartridges.

band·wag·on [BAND-wag-ən] n climb, jump, party, **get on the bandwagon** join something that seems sure of success.

ban·dy [BAN-dee] vt **-died, -dy·ing** beat to and fro, toss from one to another.

ban'dy-leg·ged [-leg-id] adj bowlegged, having legs curving outward.

bane [bayn] n **1** poison. **2** person or thing causing misery or distress. **bane'ful** adj

bang¹ n **1** sudden loud noise, explosion. **2** heavy blow. ♦ vt **3** make loud noise. **4** beat. **5** strike violently, slam.

bang² n (usu pl) fringe of hair cut straight across forehead.

ban·gle [BANG-gəl] n ring worn on arm or leg.

ban'ish vt **1** condemn to exile. **2** drive away. **3** dismiss. **ban'ish·ment** n exile.

ban·is·ter [BAN-ə-stər] n handrail held up by balusters.

ban·jo [BAN-joh] n, pl **-jos** musical instrument like guitar, with circular body. **ban'jo·ist** n

bank¹ [bangk] n **1** mound or ridge of earth. **2** edge of river, lake, etc. **3** rising ground in sea. ♦ v **4** enclose with ridge. **5** pile up. **6** (of aircraft) tilt inward in turning.

bank² n **1** establishment for keeping, lending, exchanging, etc. money. **2** any supply or store for future use, as a **blood bank**. ♦ vt **3** put in bank. ♦ vi **4** keep with bank. **bank'er** n **bank'ing** n **bank teller** bank cashier. **bank'note** n written promise of payment acceptable as money. **bank on** rely on.

bank³ n arrangement of switches, keys, oars, etc. in a row or in tiers.

nonsense, trash, tripe (inf)

bamboozle v Inf **1 = cheat**, con (inf), deceive, dupe, fool, hoodwink, swindle, trick **2 = puzzle**, baffle, befuddle, confound, confuse, mystify, perplex, stump

ban v **1 = prohibit**, banish, bar, block, boycott, disallow, disqualify, exclude, forbid, outlaw ♦ n **2 = prohibition**, boycott, disqualification, embargo, restriction, taboo

banal adj **= unoriginal**, hackneyed, humdrum, mundane, pedestrian, stale, stereotyped, trite, unimaginative

band¹ n **1 = ensemble**, combo, group, orchestra **2 = gang**, body, company, group, party, posse (inf)

band² n **= strip**, belt, bond, chain, cord, ribbon, strap

bandage n **1 = dressing**, compress, gauze, plaster ♦ v **2 = dress**, bind, cover, swathe

bandit n **= robber**, desperado, highwayman, marauder, outlaw, thief

bane n **= plague**, bête noire, curse, nuisance, pest, ruin, scourge, torment

bang n **1 = explosion**, clang, clap, clash, pop, slam, thud, thump **2 = blow**, bump, cuff, knock, punch, smack, stroke, whack ♦ v **3 = hit**, belt (inf), clatter, knock, slam, strike, thump **4 = explode**, boom, clang, resound, thump, thunder ♦ adv **5 = hard**, abruptly, headlong, noisily, suddenly **6 = straight**, precisely, slap, smack

banish v **1 = expel**, deport, eject, evict, exile, outlaw **2 = get rid of**, ban, cast out, discard, dismiss, oust, remove

banishment n **= expulsion**, deportation, exile, expatriation, transportation

banisters pl n **= railing**, balusters, balustrade, handrail, rail

bank¹ n **1 = storehouse**, depository, repository **2 = store**, accumulation, fund, hoard, reserve, reservoir, savings, stock, stockpile ♦ v **3 = save**, deposit, keep

bank·rupt [BANGK-rupt] *n* **1** one who fails in business, insolvent debtor. ◆ *adj* **2** financially ruined. **3** broken. **4** destitute. ◆ *vt* **5** make, cause to be, bankrupt. **bank'rupt·cy** *n*

ban·ner [BAN-ər] *n* **1** long strip with slogan, etc. **2** placard. **3** flag used as ensign.

banns *n* see BAN.

ban·quet [BANG-kwit] *n* **1** feast. ◆ *vi* **2** feast. ◆ *vt* **3** treat with feast.

ban·quette [bang-KET] *n* **1** upholstered bench usu. along a wall. **2** raised firing step behind parapet.

ban'shee *n* (in Irish folklore) female spirit with a wail portending death.

ban·tam [BAN-təm] *n* **1** dwarf variety of domestic fowl. **2** person of diminutive stature. **ban'tam·weight** *n* boxer weighing no more than 118 pounds.

ban·ter [BAN-tər] *vt* **1** make fun of. ◆ *n* **2** light, teasing language.

Ban·tu [BAN-too] *n* **1** collective name for large group of related tribes in Africa. **2** family of languages spoken by Bantu peoples.

ban·yan [BAN-yən] *n* Indian fig tree with spreading branches that take root.

ba·o·bab [BAY-oh-bab] *n* Afr. tree with thick trunk and angular branches.

Bap'tist *n* member of Protestant Christian denomination believing in necessity of baptism by immersion, esp. of adults. **baptist** *n* one who baptizes.

bap·tize [BAP-tīz] *vt* **-tized, -tiz·ing 1** immerse in, sprinkle with water ceremonially. **2** christen. **bap'tism** [-tiz-əm] *n* **bap·tis'mal** [-TIZ-məl] *adj* **bap'tist·ry** *n, pl* **-ries** place where baptism is performed.

bar¹ [bahr] *n* **1** rod or block of any substance. **2** obstacle. **3** bank of sand at mouth of river. **4** rail in law court. **5** body of lawyers. **6** room or counter where drinks are served, esp. in hotel, etc. **7** unit of music. ◆ *vt* **barred, bar·ring 8** fasten. **9** obstruct. **10** exclude. ◆ *prep* **11** except. **barring** *prep* excepting. **bar code** arrangement of numbers and parallel lines on package, electronically scanned at checkout to give price, etc. **bar'maid** *n* **bar'ten·der** *n*

bar² *n* unit of pressure.

barb [bahrb] *n* **1** sharp point curving backward behind main point of spear, fishhook, etc. **2** cutting remark. **barbed** *adj* **barbed wire** fencing wire with barbs at close intervals.

bar·ba·rous [BAHR-bər-əs] *adj* savage, brutal, uncivilized. **bar·bar'ian** [-BAIR-ee-ən] *n* **bar·bar'ic** *adj* **bar'ba·rism** *n* **bar·bar'i·ty** *n*

bank² *n* **1** = **mound**, banking, embankment, heap, mass, pile, ridge **2** = **side**, brink, edge, margin, shore ◆ *v* **3** = **pile**, amass, heap, mass, mound, stack **4** = **tilt**, camber, cant, heel, incline, pitch, slant, slope, tip

bank³ *n* = **row**, array, file, group, line, rank, sequence, series, succession

bankrupt *adj* = **insolvent**, broke (*inf*), destitute, impoverished, in queer street, in the red, ruined, wiped out (*inf*)

bankruptcy *n* = **insolvency**, disaster, failure, liquidation, ruin

banner *n* = **flag**, colors, ensign, pennant, placard, standard, streamer

banquet *n* = **feast**, dinner, meal, repast, revel, treat

banter *v* **1** = **joke**, jest, kid (*inf*), rib (*inf*), taunt, tease ◆ *n* **2** = **joking**, badinage, jesting, kidding (*inf*), repartee, teasing, wordplay

baptism *n Christianity* = **christening**, immersion, purification, sprinkling

baptize *v Christianity* = **purify**, cleanse, immerse

bar *n* **1** = **rod**, paling, palisade, pole, rail, shaft, stake, stick **2** = **obstacle**, barricade, barrier, block, deterrent, hindrance, impediment, obstruction, stop **3** = **public house**, canteen, counter, inn, saloon, tavern, watering hole (*facetious sl*) ◆ *v* **4** = **fasten**, barricade, bolt, latch, lock, secure **5** = **obstruct**, hinder, prevent, restrain **6** = **exclude**, ban, black, blackball, forbid, keep out, prohibit

Bar *n* **the Bar** *Law* = **barristers**, body of lawyers, counsel, court, judgment, tribunal

barb *n* **1** = **dig**, affront, cut, gibe, insult, sarcasm, scoff, sneer **2** = **point**, bristle, prickle, prong, quill, spike, spur, thorn

barbarian *n* **1** = **savage**, brute, yahoo **2** = **lout**, bigot, boor, philistine

barbaric *adj* **1** = **uncivilized**, primitive, rude, wild **2** = **brutal**, barbarous, coarse, crude, cruel, fierce, inhuman, savage

barbarism *n* = **savagery**, coarseness,

bar·be·cue [BAHR-bi-kyoo] *n* **1** food cooked outdoors over hot charcoal. **2** fireplace, grill used for this. ◆ *vt* **-cued, cu·ing 3** cook meat, etc. in this manner.

bar·ber [BAHR-bər] *n* **1** one whose job is to cut hair and shave beards. ◆ *v* **-bered, -ber·ing 2** perform this service.

bar·bi·tu·rate [bahr-BICH-ər-it] *n* derivative of barbituric acid used as sedative drug.

bar·ca·role [BAHR-kə-rohl] *n* **1** gondolier's song. **2** music imitative of this.

bard [bahrd] *n* **1** Celtic poet. **2** wandering minstrel. **3** poet. **the Bard of Avon** Shakespeare.

bare [bair] *adj* **bar·er, bar·est 1** uncovered. **2** naked. **3** plain. **4** scanty. ◆ *vt* **bared, bar·ing** make bare. **bare'ly** *adv* only just, scarcely. **bare'back, -backed** *adj* on unsaddled horse. **bare'faced** *adj* shameless.

barf *v sl* vomit.

bar·gain [BAHR-gən] *n* **1** something bought at price favorable to purchaser. **2** contract, agreement. ◆ *vi* **3** haggle, negotiate. **4** make bargain.

barge [bahrj] *n* **1** flat-bottomed freight boat propelled by towing. **2** roomy pleasure boat. ◆ *vi* **3** inf **barged, barg·ing 3** interrupt. **4** inf bump (into), push.

bar·i·tone [BAR-i-tohn] *n* **1** (singer with) second lowest adult male voice. ◆ *adj* **2** written for or possessing this vocal range.

bar·i·um [BA-ree-əm] *n* white metallic element.

bark¹ [bahrk] *n* **1** sharp loud cry of dog, etc. ◆ *v* **2** make, utter with such sound. **bark'er** *n* one who stands outside entrance to a circus, etc. calling out its attractions. **bark up the wrong tree 1** misdirect one's efforts. **2** pursue a wrong course.

bark² *n* **1** outer layer of trunk, branches of tree. ◆ *vt* **2** strip bark from. **3** rub off (skin), graze (shins, etc.).

bark³ *n* sailing ship, esp. large, three-masted one.

bar·ley [BAHR-lee] *n* grain used for food and making malt. **bar'ley·corn** *n* a grain of barley. **John Barleycorn** personification of intoxicating liquor.

bar mitz·vah [bahr MITS-və] *n* **1** Jewish boy at age 13 who participates in religious ceremony signifying entry into adulthood. **2** the ceremony.

barn [bahrn] *n* building to store grain, hay, etc. **barn dance** (party with) country music and dancing. **barn'yard** *n* area adjoining barn. **barnyard humor** earthy or smutty humor.

bar·na·cle [BAHR-nə-kəl] *n* shellfish that adheres to rocks, logs, ships' bottoms, etc.

ba·rom·e·ter [bə-ROM-i-tər] *n* instrument to measure pressure of atmosphere. **bar·o·met·ric** [bar-ə-ME-trik] *adj* **bar·o·graph** [BA-rə-graf] *n* recording barometer.

bar·on [BA-rən] *n* **1** member of lowest rank of peerage in Great Britain. **2** powerful businessman. **bar'o·ness** *n* **bar'o·ny** *n* **ba·ro·ni·al** [-ROH-nee-əl] *adj*

——————————| THESAURUS |——————————

crudity

barbarous *adj* **1** = **uncivilized**, barbarian, brutish, primitive, rough, rude, savage, uncouth, wild **2** = **brutal**, barbaric, cruel, ferocious, heartless, inhuman, monstrous, ruthless, vicious

barbed *adj* **1** = **cutting**, critical, hostile, hurtful, nasty, pointed, scathing, unkind **2** = **spiked**, hooked, jagged, prickly, spiny, thorny

bare *adj* **1** = **naked**, nude, stripped, unclad, unclothed, uncovered, undressed, without a stitch on (*inf*) **2** = **plain**, bald, basic, sheer, simple, stark, unembellished **3** = **simple**, austere, spare, spartan, unadorned, unembellished

barefaced *adj* **1** = **obvious**, blatant, flagrant, open, transparent, unconcealed **2** = **shameless**, audacious, bold, brash,

brazen, impudent, insolent

barely *adv* = **only just**, almost, at a push, by the skin of one's teeth, hardly, just, scarcely

barf *v Sl* = **vomit**, heave, puke (*sl*), retch, spew, throw up (*inf*), toss one's cookies (*sl*) ◆ *n* = **vomit**, puke, sick

bargain *n* **1** = **agreement**, arrangement, contract, pact, pledge, promise **2** = **good buy**, (cheap) purchase, discount, giveaway, good deal, reduction, steal (*inf*) ◆ *v* **3** = **negotiate**, agree, contract, covenant, promise, stipulate, transact

barge *n* = **canal boat**, flatboat, lighter, narrow boat

bark¹ *n, v* = **yap**, bay, growl, howl, snarl, woof, yelp

bark² *n* = **covering**, casing, cortex (*Anatomy, botany*), crust, husk, rind, skin

bar·on·et [BA-rə-nit] n lowest British hereditary title, below baron but above knight. **bar'o·net·cy** n

ba·roque [bə-ROHK] adj extravagantly ornamented, esp. in architecture and music. **baroque pearl** one irregularly shaped.

bar·rack [BA-rək] n (usu. in pl) **1** building for housing soldiers. **2** bare, barnlike building. ♦ vt **3** house in barracks.

bar·ra·cu·da [ba-rə-KOO-də] n type of large, elongated, predatory fish, mostly tropical.

bar·rage [bə-RAHZH] n **1** heavy artillery fire. **2** continuous and heavy delivery, esp. of questions, etc.

bar·rel [BA-rəl] n **1** round wooden vessel, made of curved staves bound with hoops. **2** its capacity. **3** great amount or number. **4** anything long and hollow, as tube of gun, etc. ♦ v **-reled, -rel·ing 5** put in barrel. **6** move at high speed. **bar'rel·ful** n, pl **-fuls 1** as much, as many, as a barrel can hold. **2** large amount or number. **over a barrel** helpless.

bar·ren [BA-rən] adj **1** unfruitful, sterile. **2** unprofitable. **3** dull. **bar'ren·ness** n

bar·ri·cade [BA-ri-kayd] n **1** improvised fortification, barrier. ♦ vt **-cad·ed, -cad·ing 2** to protect by building barrier. **3** block.

bar·ri·er [BAR-ee-ər] n fence, obstruction, obstacle, boundary. **barrier reef** coral reef lying parallel to shore.

bar·row¹ [BA-roh] n **1** small wheeled handcart. **2** wheelbarrow.

barrow² n castrated male swine.

barrow³ n burial mound of earth or stones.

bar·ter [BAHR-tər] v **1** trade by exchange of goods. ♦ n **2** trade by the exchange of goods.

bar·y·on [BA-ree-on] n Physics elementary particle of matter.

ba·salt [bə-SAWLT] n dark-colored, hard, compact, igneous rock. **ba·sal'tic** adj

base¹ [bays] n **1** bottom, foundation. **2** starting point. **3** center of operations. **4** fixed point. **5** Chem. compound that combines with an acid to form a salt. **6** medium into which other substances are mixed. ♦ vt **based, bas·ing 7** found, establish. **base'less** adj **base'ment** n lowest floor of building, partly or entirely below ground.

base² adj **-er, -est 1** low, mean. **2** despicable. **base'ly** adv **base'ness** n

base·ball [BAYS-bawl] n **1** game played with bat and ball between teams of 9 (sometimes 10) players. **2** the ball they use.

ba·sen·ji [bə-SEN-jee] n small African hunting dog that seldom barks.

bash v inf **1** strike violently. ♦ n **2** blow. **3** attempt. **4** festive party.

bash·ful [BASH-fəl] adj shy, modest. **bash'ful·ly** adv

BASIC [BAY-sik] computer programing

——————| THESAURUS |——————

barracks pl n = **camp**, billet, encampment, garrison, quarters

barrage n **1** = **torrent**, burst, deluge, hail, mass, onslaught, plethora, stream **2** Military = **bombardment**, battery, cannonade, fusillade, gunfire, salvo, shelling, volley

barren adj **1** = **infertile**, childless, sterile **2** = **unproductive**, arid, desert, desolate, dry, empty, unfruitful, waste

barricade n **1** = **barrier**, blockade, bulwark, fence, obstruction, palisade, rampart, stockade ♦ v **2** = **bar**, block, blockade, defend, fortify, obstruct, protect, shut in

barrier n **1** = **barricade**, bar, blockade, boundary, fence, obstacle, obstruction, wall **2** = **hindrance**, difficulty, drawback, handicap, hurdle, obstacle, restriction, stumbling block

barter v = **trade**, bargain, drive a hard bargain, exchange, haggle, sell, swap, traffic

base¹ n **1** = **bottom**, bed, foot, foundation, pedestal, rest, stand, support **2** = **basis**, core, essence, heart, key, origin, root, source **3** = **center**, camp, headquarters, home, post, settlement, starting point, station ♦ v **4** = **found**, build, construct, depend, derive, establish, ground, hinge **5** = **place**, locate, post, station

base² adj **1** = **dishonorable**, contemptible, despicable, disreputable, evil, immoral, lousy (sl), scuzzy (sl), shameful, sordid, wicked **2** = **counterfeit**, alloyed, debased, fake, forged, fraudulent, impure

baseless adj = **unfounded**, groundless, unconfirmed, uncorroborated, ungrounded, unjustified, unsubstantiated, unsupported

bash v Inf = **hit**, belt (inf), smash, sock (sl), strike, wallop (inf)

bashful adj = **shy**, blushing, coy, diffident,

language that uses common English words.

ba·sic [BAY-sik] *adj* **1** relating to, serving as base. **2** fundamental. **3** necessary. **ba'si·cal·ly** *adv*

ba·sil·i·ca [bə-SIL-i-kə] *n* type of church with long hall and pillars.

bas·i·lisk [BAS-ə-lisk] *n* **1** legendary small fire-breathing dragon. **2** type of tropical lizard related to iguanas.

ba·sin [BAY-sən] *n* **1** deep circular dish. **2** harbor. **3** land drained by river.

basis [BAY-sis] *n, pl* **-ses** [-seez] **1** foundation. **2** principal constituent.

bask *vi* lie in warmth and sunshine.

bas·ket [BAS-kit] *n* vessel made of woven cane, straw, etc. **bas'ket·ry** [-ki-tree] **bas'ket·ball** *n* **1** ball game played by two teams of 5 players who score points by throwing ball through baskets suspended above ends of playing area. **2** the ball they use.

Basque [bask] *n* **1** one of a people from W Pyrenees. **2** their language.

bas-re·lief [bah-ri-LEEF] *n* sculpture with figures standing out slightly from background.

bass[1] [bays] *n* **1** lowest part in music. **2** bass singer or voice. ◆ *adj*

bass[2] [bas] *n* any of large variety of freshwater or seawater fishes.

bas·set hound [BAS-it] *n* type of smooth-haired short-legged dog.

bas·soon [bə-SOON] *n* woodwind instrument of low tone. **bas·soon'ist** *n*

bas·tard [BAS-tərd] *n* **1** child born of unmarried parents. **2** *sl* person, esp. a man, e.g. *a lucky bastard.* ◆ *adj* **3** illegitimate. **4** spurious.

baste[1] [bayst] *vt* **bast·ed, bast·ing 1** moisten (meat) during cooking with hot fat. **2** beat severely. **bast'er** *n*

baste[2] *vt* **bast·ed, bast·ing** sew loosely, tack.

bas·ti·na·do [bas-tə-NAY-doh] *n, pl* **-does 1** beating with stick, etc. esp. on soles of feet. ◆ *vt* **-doed, -do·ing**

bas·tion [BAS-chən] *n* **1** projecting part of fortification, tower. **2** strong defense or bulwark.

bat[1] *n* **1** any of various types of clubs used to hit ball in certain sports, e.g. baseball. ◆ *v* **bat·ted, bat·ting 2** strike with bat or use bat in sport. **batting** *n* performance with bat.

bat[2] *n* nocturnal mouselike flying animal.

bat[3] *vt* **bat·ted, bat·ting** flutter (one's eyelids).

batch [bach] *n* group or set of similar objects, esp. cakes, etc. baked together.

bat·ed [BAY-tid] *adj* **with bated breath** anxiously.

bath *n* **1** vessel or place to bathe in. **2** water for bathing. **3** act of bathing. **bath'house** *n* building with dressing and washing facilities for bathers. **bath'room** *n* room with toilet and washing facilities. **take a bath** *sl* experience serious, esp. financial, losses in a venture.

bathe [bay*th*] *v* **bathed, bath'ing 1** apply liquid. **2** wash. **3** immerse in water. ◆ *n* **bath'er** *n*

ba·thos [BAY-thos] *n* ludicrous descent from the elevated to the ordinary in writing or speech.

ba·tik [bə-TEEK] *n* dyeing process using

reserved, reticent, retiring, timid

basic *adj* = **essential**, elementary, fundamental, key, necessary, primary, vital

basically *adv* = **essentially**, at heart, fundamentally, inherently, in substance, intrinsically, mostly, primarily

basics *pl n* = **essentials**, ABCs, brass tacks (*inf*), fundamentals, nitty-gritty (*inf*), nuts and bolts (*inf*), principles, rudiments

basis *n* = **foundation**, base, bottom, footing, ground, groundwork, support

bask *v* = **lie in**, laze, loll, lounge, relax, sunbathe, swim in

bass *adj* = **deep**, deep-toned, low, low-pitched, resonant, sonorous

bastard *n* **1** *Inf, offens* = **rogue**, miscreant,

reprobate, scoundrel, villain, wretch **2** = **illegitimate child**, love child, natural child

bastion *n* = **stronghold**, bulwark, citadel, defense, fortress, mainstay, prop, rock, support, tower of strength

bat *n, v* = **hit**, bang, smack, strike, swat, thump, wallop (*inf*), whack

batch *n* = **group**, amount, assemblage, bunch, collection, crowd, lot, pack, quantity, set

bath *n* **1** = **wash**, cleansing, douche, scrubbing, shower, soak, tub ◆ *v* **2** = **wash**, bathe, clean, douse, scrub down, shower, soak

bathe *v* **1** = **wash**, cleanse, rinse, soak **2** = **cover**, flood, immerse, steep, suffuse wax.

ba·ton [bə-TON] *n* stick, esp. of conductor, marshal, member of relay team.

ba·tra·chi·an [bə-TRAY-kee-ən] *n, adj* (of) any amphibian, esp. frog or toad.

bat·tal·ion [bə-TAL-yən] *n* **1** military unit consisting of three or more companies. **2** *fig* a large group.

bat·ten[1] [BAT-n] *n* **1** narrow piece of board, strip of wood. ◆ *vt* **2** (esp. with *down*) fasten, make secure.

batten[2] *vi* (usu. with *on*) thrive, esp. at someone else's expense.

bat·ter [BAT-ər] *vt* **1** strike continuously. ◆ *n* **2** mixture of flour, eggs, liquid, used in cooking.

bat·ter·y [BAT-ə-ree] *n, pl* **-ter·ies 1** connected group of electrical cells. **2** any electrical cell. **3** number of similar things occurring together. **4** *Law* assault by beating. **5** number of guns. **6** place where they are mounted. **7** unit of artillery. **8** *Baseball* pitcher and catcher as a unit.

bat·ting [BAT-ing] *n* cotton or wool fiber as stuffing or lining.

bat·tle [BAT-l] *n* **1** fight between armies, combat. ◆ *vi* **-tled, -tling 2** fight, struggle. **battle-ax** *n sl* sharp-tempered, domineering woman.

bat·tle·ment [BAT-l-mənt] *n* wall, parapet on fortification with openings for cannon.

bat·tle·ship [BAT-l-ship] *n* heavily armed and armored fighting ship of the largest and heaviest class.

bat·ty [BAT-ee] *adj inf* **-ti·er, -ti·est** crazy, silly.

bau·ble [BAW-bəl] *n* showy trinket.

baud [bawd] *n* unit of data transmission speed.

baux·ite [BAWK-sīt] *n* mineral yielding aluminum.

bawd *n* **1** prostitute. **2** brothel keeper. **bawd·y** *adj* **bawd·i·er, bawd·i·est** obscene, lewd.

bawl *vi* **1** cry. **2** shout. ◆ *n* **3** loud shout or cry. **bawl out** *vt inf* reprimand severely.

bay[1] *n* **1** wide inlet of sea. **2** space between two columns. **3** recess. **bay window** window projecting from a wall.

bay[2] *n* **1** bark. **2** cry of hounds in pursuit. ◆ *v* **3** bark (at). **at bay** cornered.

bay[3] *n* laurel tree.

bay[4] *adj* **1** reddish-brown. ◆ *n* **2** horse with body of this color and black mane.

bay·o·net [BAY-ə-nit] *n* **1** stabbing weapon fixed to rifle. ◆ *vt* **-net·ed, -net·ing 2** stab with this.

bay·ou [BĪ-oo] *n, pl* **-ous** marshy inlet or outlet of lake, river, etc., usu. sluggish.

ba·zaar [bə-ZAHR] *n* **1** market (esp. in Orient). **2** sale of goods for charity.

ba·zoo·ka [bə-ZOO-kə] *n* antitank rocket launcher.

be *v*, *present sing 1st person* **am**. *2nd person* **are**. *3rd person* **is**. *present pl* **are**. *past sing 1st person* **was**. *2nd person* **were**. *3rd person* **was**. *past pl* **were**. *present participle* **being**. *past participle* **been 1** exist or live. **2** pay a visit, e.g. *have you been to Spain?* **3** take place, e.g. *my birthday was last Monday.* **4**

baton *n* = **stick**, club, crook, mace, rod, scepter, staff, truncheon, wand

batten[1] *v* (usually with *down*) = **fasten**, board up, clamp down, cover up, fix, nail down, secure, tighten

batter *v* = **beat**, buffet, clobber (*sl*), pelt, pound, pummel, thrash, wallop (*inf*)

battery *n* = **artillery**, cannon, cannonry, gun emplacements, guns

battle *n* **1** = **fight**, action, attack, combat, encounter, engagement, hostilities, skirmish **2** = **conflict**, campaign, contest, crusade, dispute, struggle ◆ *v* **3** = **struggle**, argue, clamor, dispute, fight, lock horns, strive, war

battlefield *n* = **battleground**, combat zone, field, field of battle, front

battleship *n* = **warship**, gunboat, man-of-war

batty *adj* = **crazy**, absent-minded, bonkers (*inf*), daft (*inf*), eccentric, mad, odd, peculiar

bauble *n* = **trinket**, bagatelle, gewgaw, gimcrack, knick-knack, plaything, toy, trifle

baulk see BALK

bawdy *adj* = **rude**, coarse, dirty, indecent, lascivious, lecherous, lewd, ribald, salacious, smutty

bawl *v* **1** = **cry**, blubber, sob, wail, weep **2** = **shout**, bellow, call, clamor, howl, roar, yell

bay[1] *n* = **inlet**, bight, cove, gulf, natural harbor, sound

bay[2] *n* = **recess**, alcove, compartment, niche, nook, opening

bay[3] *v* = **howl**, bark, clamor, cry, growl, yelp

bazaar *n* **1** = **fair**, bring-and-buy, fête, sale of work **2** = **market**, exchange, used as a linking between the subject of a sentence and its complement, e.g. *John is a musician.* **5** forms the progressive present tense, e.g. *the man is running.* **6** forms the passive voice of all transitive verbs, e.g. *a good movie is being shown on television tonight.*

Be *Chem.* beryllium.

beach [beech] *n* **1** shore of sea. ♦ *vt* **2** run boat on shore. **beach'comb·er** [-koh-mər] *n* **1** one who habitually searches shore debris for items of value. **2** loafer spending days aimlessly on beach. **beach'head** *n* **1** area on beach captured from enemy. **2** base for operations. **3** foothold.

bea·con [BEE-kən] *n* **1** signal fire. **2** lighthouse, buoy. **3** (radio) signal used for navigation.

bead [beed] *n* **1** little ball pierced for threading on string of necklace, rosary, etc. **2** drop of liquid. **3** narrow molding. ♦ *vt* **4** string together or furnish with beads. **bead'ing** *n* **bead'y** *adj* **bead·i·er, bead·i·est** small and bright.

bea·gle [BEE-gəl] *n* small hound.

beak [beek] *n* **1** projecting horny jaws of bird. **2** anything pointed or projecting. **3** *sl* nose.

beak·er [BEE-kər] *n* **1** large drinking cup. **2** glass vessel used by chemists.

beam [beem] *n* **1** long squared piece of wood. **2** ship's cross timber, side, or width. **3** ray of light, etc. **4** broad smile. **5** bar of a balance. ♦ *vt* **6** aim light, radio waves, etc. (to). ♦ *vi* **7** shine. **8** smile benignly.

bean [been] *n* **1** any of various leguminous plants or their seeds. **2** head. **full of beans** *inf* lively. **bean sprout** edible sprout of newly germinated bean, esp. mung bean.

bear[1] [bair] *vt* **bore, borne** *or* **born, bear·ing 1** carry. **2** support. **3** produce. **4** endure. **5** press (upon). **bear'er** *n*

bear[2] *n* **1** heavy carnivorous quadruped. **2** other bearlike animals, such as the koala. **bear'skin** *n* tall fur helmet.

beard [beerd] *n* **1** hair on chin. ♦ *vt* **2** oppose boldly.

bear·ing [BAIR-ing] *n* **1** support or guide for mechanical part, esp. one reducing friction. **2** relevance. **3** behavior. **4** direction. **5** relative position.

beast [beest] *n* **1** animal. **2** four-footed animal. **3** brutal man. **beast'li·ness** *n* **beast'ly** *adj*

beat [beet] *v* **beat, beat·en, beat·ing** ♦ *vt* **1** strike repeatedly. **2** overcome. **3** surpass. **4** stir vigorously with striking action. **5** flap (wings). **6** make, wear (path). ♦ *vi* **7** throb.

marketplace

be *v* = **exist**, be alive, breathe, inhabit, live

beach *n* = **shore**, coast, sands, seashore, seaside, water's edge

beached *adj* = **stranded**, abandoned, aground, ashore, deserted, grounded, high and dry, marooned, wrecked

beacon *n* = **signal**, beam, bonfire, flare, lighthouse, sign, watchtower

bead *n* = **drop**, blob, bubble, dot, droplet, globule, pellet, pill

beady *adj* = **bright**, gleaming, glinting, glittering, sharp, shining

beak *n* = **bill**, mandible, neb (*archaic or dialect*), nib

beam *n* **1** = **smile**, grin **2** = **ray**, gleam, glimmer, glint, glow, shaft, streak, stream **3** = **rafter**, girder, joist, plank, spar, support, timber ♦ *v* **4** = **smile**, grin **5** = **radiate**, glare, gleam, glitter, glow, shine **6** = **send out**, broadcast, emit, transmit

bear *v* **1** = **support**, have, hold, maintain, possess, shoulder, sustain, uphold **2** = **carry**, bring, convey, move, take, transport **3** = **produce**, beget, breed, bring forth,

engender, generate, give birth to, yield **4** = **tolerate**, abide, allow, brook, endure, permit, put up with (*inf*), stomach, suffer

bearable *adj* = **tolerable**, admissible, endurable, manageable, passable, sufferable, supportable, sustainable

bearer *n* = **carrier**, agent, conveyor, messenger, porter, runner, servant

bearing *n* **1** (usually with *on* or *upon*) = **relevance**, application, connection, import, pertinence, reference, relation, significance **2** = **manner**, air, aspect, attitude, behavior, demeanor, deportment, posture

bearings *pl n* = **position**, aim, course, direction, location, orientation, situation, track, way, whereabouts

bear out *v* = **support**, confirm, corroborate, endorse, justify, prove, substantiate, uphold, vindicate

beast *n* **1** = **animal**, brute, creature **2** = **brute**, barbarian, fiend, monster, ogre, sadist, savage, swine

beastly *adj* = **unpleasant**, awful, disagreeable, horrid, mean, nasty, rotten

8 sail against wind. ◆ n 9 stroke. 10 pulsation. 11 appointed course. 12 basic rhythmic unit in piece of music. ◆ adj sl 13 exhausted. **beat'er** n 1 instrument for beating. 2 one who rouses game for shooters.

be·at·i·fy [bee-AT-ə-fī] vt -fied, -fy·ing 1 make happy. 2 R.C. Church pronounce in eternal happiness (first step in canonization). **be·a·tif·ic** [bee-ə-TIF-ik] adj **be·at·i·fi·ca'tion** n **be·at'i·tude** n blessedness.

beau [boh] n, pl **beaux** [bohz] suitor.

Beau·fort scale [BOH-fərt] system of indicating wind strength (from 0, calm, to 17, hurricane).

beau·ty [BYOO-tee] n, pl -ties 1 loveliness, grace. 2 beautiful person or thing. **beau·ti·cian** [byoo-TISH-ən] n one who gives treatment in beauty parlor. **beau'ti·ful** adj **beau'ti·fy** [-tə-fī] vt -fied, -fy·ing beauty parlor establishment offering hairdressing, manicure, etc.

bea·ver [BEE-vər] n 1 amphibious rodent. 2 its fur. 3 exceptionally hard-working person.

be·calmed [bi-KAHMD] adj (of ship) motionless through lack of wind.

became pt. of BECOME.

be·cause [bi-KAWZ] adv, conj by reason of, since.

beck [bek] n **at someone's beck and call** subject to someone's slightest whim.

beck·on [BEK-ən] v summon or lure by silent signal.

be·come [bi-KUM] v **be·came, be·come, be·com·ing** ◆ vi 1 come to be. ◆ vt 2 suit. **becoming** adj 1 suitable to. 2 proper.

bed n 1 piece of furniture for sleeping on. 2 garden plot. 3 supporting stratum. 4 bottom of river. 5 layer, stratum. ◆ vt **bed·ded, bed·ding** 6 lay in a bed. 7 plant. **bedding** n **bed'bug** n wingless bug infesting beds and sucking blood. **bed'pan** n container used as toilet by bedridden person. **bed'rid·den** adj confined to bed by age or sickness. **bed'rock** n 1 solid rock beneath the surface soil. 2 basic facts or principles. **bed'room** n **bed'spread** [-spred] n cover for bed when not in use. **bed'stead** [-sted] n framework of a bed.

be·dev·il [bi-DEV-əl] vt -iled, -il·ing 1 confuse. 2 torment. **be·dev'il·ment** n

bed·lam [BED-ləm] n noisy confused scene.

THESAURUS

beat v 1 = **hit**, bang, batter, buffet, knock, pound, strike, thrash 2 = **flap**, flutter 3 = **throb**, palpitate, pound, pulsate, quake, thump, vibrate 4 = **defeat**, conquer, outdo, overcome, overwhelm, surpass, vanquish ◆ n 5 = **throb**, palpitation, pulsation, pulse 6 = **route**, circuit, course, path, rounds, way 7 = **rhythm**, accent, cadence, meter, stress, time

beaten adj 1 = **stirred**, blended, foamy, frothy, mixed, whipped, whisked 2 = **defeated**, cowed, overcome, overwhelmed, thwarted, vanquished

beat up v Inf = **assault**, attack, batter, beat the living daylights out of (inf), knock about or around, pound, pulverize, thrash

beau n 1 Old-fashioned = **boyfriend**, admirer, fiancé, lover, suitor, sweetheart 2 = **dandy**, coxcomb, fop, gallant, ladies' man

beautiful adj = **attractive**, charming, delightful, exquisite, fair, fine, gorgeous, handsome, lovely, pleasing

beautify v = **make beautiful**, adorn, decorate, embellish, festoon, garnish, glamorize, ornament

beauty n 1 = **attractiveness**, charm,

comeliness, elegance, exquisiteness, glamour, grace, handsomeness, loveliness 2 = **belle**, good-looker, lovely (sl), stunner (inf)

becalmed adj = **still**, motionless, settled, stranded, stuck

because conj = **since**, as, by reason of, in that, on account of, owing to, thanks to

beckon v = **gesture**, bid, gesticulate, motion, nod, signal, summon, wave at

become v 1 = **come to be**, alter to, be transformed into, change into, develop into, grow into, mature into, ripen into 2 = **suit**, embellish, enhance, fit, flatter, set off

becoming adj 1 = **appropriate**, compatible, fitting, in keeping, proper, seemly, suitable, worthy 2 = **flattering**, attractive, comely, enhancing, graceful, neat, pretty, tasteful

bed n 1 = **bedstead**, berth, bunk, cot, couch, divan 2 = **plot**, area, border, garden, patch, row, strip 3 = **bottom**, base, foundation, groundwork

bedevil v 1 = **torment**, afflict, distress, harass, plague, trouble, vex, worry 2 = **confuse**, confound

bedlam n = **pandemonium**, chaos,

Bed·ou·in [BED-oo-in] *n* **1** nomadic Arab of the desert. **2** nomad.

be·drag·gle [bi-DRAG-əl] *vt* **-gled, -gling** dirty by trailing in wet or mud.

bee *n* insect that makes honey. **bee'hive** *n* **bee'line** *n* shortest route. **bees'wax** *n* wax secreted by bees. **bee in one's bonnet** an obsession.

beech *n* **1** tree with smooth grayish bark and small nuts. **2** its wood.

beef *n* **1** flesh of cattle raised and killed for eating. **2** *inf* complaint. ◆ *vi inf* **3** complain. **beef'y** *adj* **beef·i·er, beef·i·est** fleshy, stolid. **beef'burg·er** *n* hamburger.

been pp. of BE.

beep *n* **1** short, loud sound of automobile horn, etc. ◆ *v* **2** make this sound. **beep'er** *n* small portable electronic signaling device.

beer *n* fermented alcoholic drink made from hops and malt. **beer'y** *adj* **beer·i·er, beer·i·est** affected by, smelling of, beer.

beet *n* any of various plants with root used for food or extraction of sugar.

bee·tle [BEET-l] *n* class of insect with hard upper-wing cases closed over the back for protection. **bee·tle-browed** [browd] *adj* with prominent brows.

be·fall [bi-FAWL] *v* **be·fell, be·fall·en,** **be·fall·ing** happen (to).

be·fit [bi-FIT] *vt* **be·fit·ted, be·fit·ting** be suitable to.

be·fog [bi-FOG] *vt* **-fogged, -fog·ging** perplex, confuse.

be·fore [bi-FOR] *prep* **1** in front of. **2** in presence of. **3** in preference to. **4** earlier than. ◆ *adv* **5** earlier. **6** in front. ◆ *conj* **7** sooner than. **be·fore'hand** *adv* previously.

be·foul [bi-FOWL] *vt* make filthy.

be·friend [bi-FREND] *vt* make friend of.

beg *v* **begged, beg·ging** ◆ *vt* **1** ask earnestly, beseech. ◆ *vi* **2** ask for or live on charity. **beg·gar** [BEG-ər] *n*

began pt. of BEGIN.

be·get [bi-GET] *vt* **be·got** or **be·gat,** **be·got·ten** or **be·got, be·get·ting** *obs* produce, generate.

be·gin [bi-GIN] *v* **be·gan, be·gun,** **be·gin·ning 1** (cause to) start. **2** initiate. **3** originate. **be·gin'ner** *n* novice.

be·go·nia [bi-GOHN-yə] *n* genus of tropical plant.

be·got pt./pp. of BEGET.

be·grudge [bi-GRUJ] *vt* **-grudged,** **-grudg·ing** grudge, envy anyone the possession of.

be·guile [bi-GĪL] *vt* **-guiled, -guil·ing 1**

━━━━ THESAURUS ━━━━

commotion, confusion, furor, tumult, turmoil, uproar

bedraggled *adj* = **messy**, dirty, dishevelled, disordered, muddied, scuzzy (*sl*), unkempt, untidy

bedridden *adj* = **confined to bed**, confined, flat on one's back, incapacitated, laid up (*inf*)

bedrock *n* **1** = **bottom**, bed, foundation, rock bottom, substratum, substructure **2** = **basics**, basis, core, essentials, fundamentals, nuts and bolts (*inf*), roots

beefy *adj Inf* = **brawny**, bulky, hulking, muscular, stocky, strapping, sturdy, thickset

befall *v* = **happen**, chance, come to pass, fall, occur, take place, transpire (*inf*)

befitting *adj* = **appropriate**, apposite, becoming, fit, fitting, proper, right, seemly, suitable

before *prep* **1** = **ahead of**, in advance of, in front of **2** = **earlier than**, in advance of, prior to **3** = **in the presence of**, in front of ◆ *adv* **4** = **previously**, ahead, earlier, formerly, in advance, sooner **5** = **in front**, ahead

beforehand *adv* = **in advance**, ahead of time, already, before, earlier, in anticipation, previously, sooner

befriend *v* = **help**, aid, assist, back, encourage, side with, stand by, support, welcome

beg *v* **1** = **scrounge**, cadge, seek charity, solicit charity, sponge on **2** = **implore**, beseech, entreat, petition, plead, request, solicit

beggar *n* = **tramp**, bag lady, bum (*inf*), down-and-out, pauper, vagrant

beggarly *adj* = **poor**, destitute, impoverished, indigent, needy, poverty-stricken

begin *v* **1** = **start**, commence, embark on, initiate, instigate, institute, prepare, set about **2** = **happen**, appear, arise, come into being, emerge, originate, start

beginner *n* = **novice**, amateur, apprentice, learner, neophyte, rookie (*inf*), starter, trainee, tyro

beginning *n* **1** = **start**, birth, commencement, inauguration, inception, initiation, onset, opening, origin, outset **2** = **seed**, fount, germ, root charm, fascinate. **2** amuse. **3** deceive. **beguiling** *adj*

be·gun pp. of BEGIN.

be·half [bi-HAF] *n* **on behalf of** in the interest of or for the benefit of.

be·have [bi-HAYV] *vi* **-haved, -hav·ing** act, function in particular way. **be·hav·ior** [bi-HAYV-yər] *n* conduct. **behave oneself** conduct oneself well.

be·head [bi-HED] *vt* cut off head.

be·held pt./pp. of BEHOLD.

be·hest [bi-HEST] *n* charge, command.

be·hind [bi-HĪND] *prep* **1** farther back or earlier than. **2** in support of. ♦ *adv* **3** in the rear. **behind-the-scenes** kept or made in secret.

be·hold [bi-HOHLD] *vt* **be·held, be·hold·ing** watch, see. **be·hold'er** *n*

be·hol·den [bi-HOHL-dən] *adj* bound in gratitude.

be·hoove [bi-HOOV] *vi* **-hooved, -hoov·ing** be necessary or fitting for.

beige [bayzh] *n* color of undyed woolen cloth.

be·ing [BEE-ing] *n* **1** existence. **2** that which exists. **3** creature. **4** pr. p. of BE.

bel *n* unit for comparing two power levels.

be·la·bor [bi-LAY-bər] *vt* **1** beat soundly. **2** discuss (a subject) endlessly.

be·lat·ed [bi-LAY-tid] *adj* **1** late. **2** too late.

be·lay [bi-LAY] *vt* fasten rope to peg, pin, etc.

belch *vi* **1** void gas by mouth. ♦ *vt* **2** eject violently. **3** cast up. ♦ *n* **4** emission of gas, etc.

be·lea·guer [bi-LEE-gər] *vt* besiege.

bel·fry [BEL-free] *n, pl* **-fries** bell tower.

be·lie [bi-LĪ] *vt* **-lied, -ly·ing 1** contradict. **2** misrepresent.

be·lieve [bi-LEEV] *v* **-lieved, -liev·ing** ♦ *vt* **1** regard as true or real. ♦ *vi* **2** have faith. **be·lief'** *n* **be·liev'a·ble** *adj* credible. **be·liev'er** *n* esp. one of same religious faith.

be·lit·tle [bi-LIT-l] *vt* **-tled, -tling** regard, speak of, as having little worth or value.

──────── THESAURUS ────────

begrudge *v* = **resent**, be jealous, be reluctant, be stingy, envy, grudge

beguile *v* **1** = **fool**, cheat, deceive, delude, dupe, hoodwink, mislead, take for a ride (*inf*), trick **2** = **charm**, amuse, distract, divert, engross, entertain, occupy

beguiling *adj* = **charming**, alluring, attractive, bewitching, captivating, enchanting, enthralling, intriguing

behave *v* **1** = **act**, function, operate, perform, run, work **2** = **conduct oneself properly**, act correctly, keep one's nose clean, mind one's manners

behavior *n* **1** = **conduct**, actions, bearing, demeanor, deportment, manner, manners, ways **2** = **action**, functioning, operation, performance

behind *prep* **1** = **after**, at the back of, at the heels of, at the rear of, following, later than **2** = **causing**, at the bottom of, initiating, instigating, responsible for **3** = **supporting**, backing, for, in agreement, on the side of ♦ *adv* **4** = **after**, afterwards, following, in the wake (of), next, subsequently **5** = **overdue**, behindhand, in arrears, in debt ♦ *n* **6** *Inf* = **bottom**, butt, buttocks, posterior

behold *v* = **look at**, observe, perceive, regard, survey, view, watch, witness

beholden *adj* = **indebted**, bound, grateful, obliged, owing, under obligation

being *n* **1** = **existence**, life, reality **2** = **nature**, entity, essence, soul, spirit, substance **3** = **creature**, human being, individual, living thing

belated *adj* = **late**, behindhand, behind time, delayed, late in the day, overdue, tardy

belch *v* **1** = **burp** (*inf*), hiccup **2** = **emit**, discharge, disgorge, erupt, give off, spew forth, vent

beleaguered *adj* **1** = **harassed**, badgered, hassled (*inf*), persecuted, pestered, plagued, put upon, vexed **2** = **besieged**, assailed, beset, blockaded, hemmed in, surrounded

belief *n* **1** = **trust**, assurance, confidence, conviction, feeling, impression, judgment, notion, opinion **2** = **faith**, credo, creed, doctrine, dogma, ideology, principles, tenet

believable *adj* = **credible**, authentic, imaginable, likely, plausible, possible, probable, trustworthy

believe *v* **1** = **accept**, be certain of, be convinced of, credit, depend on, have faith in, rely on, swear by, trust **2** = **think**, assume, gather, imagine, judge, presume, reckon, speculate, suppose

believer *n* = **follower**, adherent, convert, devotee, disciple, supporter, upholder, zealot

be·lit'tler n

bell n **1** hollow metal instrument giving ringing sound when struck. **2** electrical device emitting ring or buzz as signal. **bell'hop** n hotel employee who carries luggage, conducts guests to rooms, etc.

bel·la·don·na [bel-ə-DON-ə] n deadly nightshade.

belle [bel] n beautiful woman, reigning beauty.

bel·li·cose [BEL-i-kohs] adj warlike.

bel·lig·er·ent [bə-LIJ-ər-ənt] adj **1** hostile, aggressive. **2** making war. ◆ n **3** warring person or nation.

bel·low [BEL-oh] vi **1** roar like bull. **2** shout. ◆ n **3** roar of bull. **4** any deep cry or shout.

bel·lows [BEL-ohz] pl n instrument for creating stream of air.

bel·ly [BEL-ee] n, pl -lies **1** part of body that contains intestines. **2** stomach. ◆ v -lied, -ly·ing **3** swell out. **belly laugh** n hearty laugh.

be·long [bi-LAWNG] vi **1** be the property or attribute of. **2** be a member or inhabitant of. **3** have an allotted place. **4** pertain to. **be·long'ings** pl n personal possessions.

be·lov·ed [bi-LUV-id or bi-LUVD] adj **1** much loved. ◆ n **2** dear one.

be·low [bi-LOH] adv **1** beneath. ◆ prep **2** lower than.

belt n **1** band. **2** girdle. **3** zone or district. ◆ vt **4** surround, fasten with belt. **5** mark with band. **6** inf thrash.

be·moan [bi-MOHN] vt grieve over (loss, etc.).

be·muse [bi-MYOOZ] v -mused, -mus·ing confuse, bewilder.

bench n **1** long seat. **2** seat or body of judges, etc. ◆ vt **3** provide with benches. **bench'mark** n fixed point, criterion.

bend v bent, bend·ing **1** (cause to) form a curve. ◆ n **2** curve. **the bends** pl n decompression sickness. **bend over backward** exert oneself to the utmost.

be·neath [bi-NEETH] prep **1** under, lower than. ◆ adv **2** below.

ben·e·dic·tion [ben-i-DIK-shən] n invocation of divine blessing.

THESAURUS

belittle v = **disparage**, decry, denigrate, deprecate, deride, deride, scoff at, scorn, sneer at

belligerent adj **1** = **aggressive**, bellicose, combative, hostile, pugnacious, unfriendly, warlike, warring ◆ n **2** = **fighter**, combatant, warring nation

bellow n, v = **shout**, bawl, clamor, cry, howl, roar, scream, shriek, yell

belly n **1** = **stomach**, abdomen, gut, insides (inf), paunch, potbelly, tummy ◆ v **2** = **swell out**, billow, bulge, fill, spread, swell

bellyful n = **surfeit**, enough, excess, glut, plateful, plenty, satiety, too much

belonging n = **relationship**, acceptance, affinity, association, attachment, fellowship, inclusion, loyalty, rapport

belongings pl n = **possessions**, accouterments, chattels, effects, gear, goods, paraphernalia, personal property, stuff, things

belong to v **1** = **be the property of**, be at the disposal of, be held by, be owned by **2** = **be a member of**, be affiliated to, be allied to, be associated with, be included in

beloved adj = **dear**, admired, adored, darling, loved, pet, precious, prized, treasured, worshipped

below prep **1** = **lesser**, inferior, subject, subordinate **2** = **less than**, lower than ◆ adv **3** = **lower**, beneath, down, under, underneath

belt n **1** = **waistband**, band, cummerbund, girdle, girth, sash **2** Geography = **zone**, area, district, layer, region, stretch, strip, tract

bemoan v = **lament**, bewail, deplore, grieve for, mourn, regret, rue, weep for

bemused adj = **puzzled**, at sea, bewildered, confused, flummoxed, muddled, nonplussed, perplexed

bench n **1** = **seat**, form, pew, settle, stall **2** = **worktable**, board, counter, table, trestle table, workbench **3** the bench = **court**, courtroom, judges, judiciary, magistrates, tribunal

benchmark n = **reference point**, criterion, gauge, level, measure, model, norm, par, standard, yardstick

bend v **1** = **curve**, arc, arch, bow, lean, turn, twist, veer ◆ n **2** = **curve**, angle, arc, arch, bow, corner, loop, turn, twist

beneath prep **1** = **under**, below, lower than, underneath **2** = **inferior to**, below, less than **3** = **unworthy of**, unbefitting ◆ adv **4** = **underneath**, below, in a lower place

benefactor n = **supporter**, backer, donor, helper, patron, philanthropist, sponsor, well-wisher

beneficial adj = **helpful**, advantageous,

ben·e·fit [BEN-ə-fit] n 1 advantage, favor, profit, good. 2 money paid by a government or business, etc. to unemployed, etc. ♦ v -**fit·ed**, -**fit·ing** 3 do good to. 4 receive good. **ben'e·fac·tor** n 1 one who helps or does good to others. 2 patron. **ben'e·fice** [-ə-fis] n an ecclesiastical livelihood. **be·nef·i·cence** n **be·nef·i·cent** adj 1 doing good. 2 kind. **ben·e·fi'cial** [-FISH-əl] adj advantageous, helpful. **ben·e·fi'ci·ar·y** n, pl -**ar·ies** benefit society organization providing life insurance, sickness benefit, etc., to its members, and often also social activities.

be·nev·o·lent [bə-NEV-ə-lənt] adj kindly, charitable. **be·nev'o·lence** n

be·night·ed [bi-NĪ-tid] adj ignorant, uncultured.

be·nign [bi-NĪN] adj kindly, mild, favorable. **be·nign'ly** adv

bent 1 pt./pp. of BEND. ♦ adj 2 curved. 3 resolved (on). ♦ n 5 inclination, personal propensity.

be·numb [bi-NUM] vt make numb, deaden.

ben·zene [BEN-zeen] n one of group of related flammable liquids used in chemistry and as solvents, cleaning agents, etc.

be·queath [bi-KWEETH] vt leave property, etc. by will. **be·quest** [bi-KWEST] n 1 bequeathing. 2 legacy.

be·rate [bi-RAYT] vt -**rat·ed**, -**rat·ing** scold harshly.

be·reave [bi-REEV] vt -**reaved**, -**reft**, -**reav·ing** deprive of, esp. by death. **be·reave'ment** n loss, esp. by death.

be·ret [bə-RAY] n round, close-fitting hat.

ber·i·ber·i [ber-ee-BER-ee] n tropical disease caused by vitamin B deficiency.

ber·ke·li·um [bər-KEE-lee-əm] n artificial radioactive metallic element.

ber·ry [BER-ee] n, pl -**ries** 1 small juicy stoneless fruit. ♦ vi -**ried**, -**ry·ing** 2 look for, pick, berries.

ber·serk [bər-SURK] adj frenzied.

berth [burth] n 1 ship's mooring place. 2 place to sleep on ship or train. ♦ vt 3 to moor.

ber·yl [BER-əl] n variety of crystalline mineral including aquamarine and emerald.

be·ryl·li·um [bə-RIL-ee-əm] n strong brittle metallic element.

be·seech [bi-SEECH] vt -**sought** or -**seeched**, -**seech·ing** entreat, implore.

be·set [bi-SET] vt -**set**, -**set·ting** assail, surround with danger, problems.

be·side [bi-SĪD] adv, prep 1 by the side of, near. 2 distinct from. **be·sides'** adv, prep in addition (to).

be·siege [bi-SEEJ] vt -**sieged**, -**sieg·ing**

————— THESAURUS —————

benign, favorable, profitable, useful, valuable, wholesome, win-win (inf)

beneficiary n = **recipient**, heir, inheritor, payee, receiver

benefit n 1 = **help**, advantage, aid, asset, assistance, favor, good, profit ♦ v 2 = **help**, aid, assist, avail, enhance, further, improve, profit

benevolent adj = **kind**, altruistic, benign, caring, charitable, generous, philanthropic

benign adj 1 = **kindly**, amiable, friendly, genial, kind, obliging, sympathetic 2 Medical = **harmless**, curable, remediable

bent adj 1 = **curved**, angled, arched, bowed, crooked, hunched, stooped, twisted 2 **bent on** = **determined to**, disposed to, fixed on, inclined to, insistent on, predisposed to, resolved on, set on ♦ n 3 = **inclination**, ability, aptitude, leaning, penchant, preference, propensity, tendency

bequeath v = **leave**, bestow, endow, entrust, give, grant, hand down, impart, pass on, will

bequest n = **legacy**, bestowal, endowment, estate, gift, inheritance, settlement

berate v = **scold**, castigate, censure, chide, criticize, harangue, rebuke, reprimand, reprove, tell off (inf), upbraid

bereavement n = **loss**, affliction, death, deprivation, misfortune, tribulation

bereft adj = **deprived**, devoid, lacking, parted from, robbed of, wanting

berserk adv = **crazy**, amok, enraged, frantic, frenzied, mad, raging, wild

berth n 1 = **bunk**, bed, billet, hammock 2 Nautical = **anchorage**, dock, harbor, haven, pier, port, quay, wharf ♦ v 3 Nautical = **anchor**, dock, drop anchor, land, moor, tie up

beseech v = **beg**, ask, call upon, entreat, implore, plead, pray, solicit

beset v = **plague**, bedevil, harass, pester, trouble

beside prep 1 = **next to**, abreast of,

surround (with armed forces, etc.).

be·sot·ted [bi-SOT-id] *adj* **1** drunk. **2** foolish. **3** infatuated.

besought *pt./pp.* of BESEECH.

be·speak [bi-SPEEK] *vt* **-spoke, -spok·en,, -speak·ing** engage beforehand.

best *adj, adv* **1** sup. of GOOD or WELL. ◆ *vt* **2** defeat. **best seller 1** book or other product sold in great numbers. **2** author of one or more of these books.

bes·tial [BES-chəl] *adj* like a beast, brutish. **bes·ti·al'i·ty** [-chee-AL-i-tee] *n*

be·stir [bi-STUR] *vt* **-stirred, -stir·ring** rouse (oneself) to activity.

be·stow [bi-STOH] *vt* give, confer. **be·stow'al** *n*

be·stride [bi-STRĪD] *vt* **-strode** or **-strid, -strid·den** or **-strid, -strid·ing** sit or stand over with legs apart, mount horse.

bet *v* **bet** or **bet·ted, bet·ting 1** agree to pay money, etc. if wrong (or win if right) in guessing result of contest, etc. ◆ *n* **2** money risked in this way.

be·tel [BEET-l] *n* species of pepper. **betel nut** the nut of the betel palm.

bête noire [bet NWAHR] *n, pl* **bêtes noires** *Fr* pet aversion.

be·tide [bi-TĪD] *v* **-tid·ed, -tid·ing** happen (to).

be·to·ken [bi-TOH-kən] *vt* be a sign of.

be·tray [bi-TRAY] *vt* **1** be disloyal to, esp. by assisting an enemy. **2** reveal, divulge. **3** show signs of. **be·tray'al** *n* **be·tray'er** *n*

be·troth [bi-TROH*TH*] *vt* promise to marry. **be·troth'al** *n* **be·trothed'** *n, adj*

bet·ter [BET-ər] *adj, adv* **1** comp. of GOOD or WELL. ◆ *v* **2** improve. **bet'ter·ment** *n*

be·tween [bi-TWEEN] *prep, adv* **1** in the intermediate part in space or time. **2** indicating reciprocal relation or comparison.

be·twixt [bi-TWIKST] *prep, adv obs* between.

bev·el [BEV-əl] *n* **1** surface not at right angle to another. **2** slant. ◆ *v* **-eled, -el·ing 3** slope, slant. **4** cut on slant. **bev'eled** *adj* slanted.

bev·er·age [BEV-rij] *n* drink.

adjacent to, alongside, at the side of, close to, near, nearby, neighboring **2 beside oneself = distraught**, apoplectic, at the end of one's tether, demented, desperate, frantic, frenzied, out of one's mind, unhinged

besides *adv* **1 = too**, also, as well, further, furthermore, in addition, into the bargain, moreover, otherwise, what's more ◆ *prep* **2 = apart from**, barring, excepting, excluding, in addition to, other than, over and above, without

besiege *v* **1 = surround**, blockade, encircle, hem in, lay siege to, shut in **2 = harass**, badger, harry, hassle (*inf*), hound, nag, pester, plague

besotted *adj* **= infatuated**, doting, hypnotized, smitten, spellbound

best *adj* **1 = finest**, foremost, leading, most excellent, outstanding, pre-eminent, principal, supreme, unsurpassed ◆ *adv* **2 = most highly**, extremely, greatly, most deeply, most fully ◆ *n* **3 = finest**, cream, *crème de la crème*, elite, flower, pick, prime, top

bestial *adj* **= brutal**, barbaric, beastly, brutish, inhuman, savage, sordid

bestow *v* **= present**, award, commit, give, grant, hand out, impart, lavish

bet *n* **1 = gamble**, long shot, risk, speculation, stake, venture, wager ◆ *v* **2 = gamble**, chance, hazard, risk, speculate, stake, venture, wager

betoken *v* **= indicate**, bode, denote, promise, represent, signify, suggest

betray *v* **1 = be disloyal**, be treacherous, be unfaithful, break one's promise, double-cross (*inf*), inform on or against, sell out (*inf*), stab in the back **2 = give away**, disclose, divulge, expose, let slip, reveal, uncover, unmask

betrayal *n* **1 = disloyalty**, deception, double-cross (*inf*), sell-out (*inf*), treachery, treason, trickery **2 = giving away**, disclosure, divulgence, revelation

better *adj* **1 = superior**, excelling, finer, greater, higher-quality, more desirable, preferable, surpassing **2 = well**, cured, fully recovered, on the mend (*inf*), recovering, stronger ◆ *adv* **3 = in a more excellent manner**, in a superior way, more advantageously, more attractively, more competently, more effectively **4 = to a greater degree**, more completely, more thoroughly ◆ *v* **5 = improve**, enhance, further, raise

between *prep* **= amidst**, among, betwixt, in the middle of, mid

beverage *n* **= drink**, liquid, liquor, refreshment

bev·y [BEV-ee] *n, pl* **bev·ies** flock or group.
be·wail [bi-WAYL] *vt* lament.
be·ware [bi-WAIR] *vi* be on one's guard, take care.
be·wil·der [bi-WIL-dər] *vt* puzzle, confuse. **be·wil'der·ing** *adj* **be·wil'der·ment** *n*
be·witch [bi-WICH] *vt* **1** cast spell over. **2** charm, fascinate. **be·witch'ing** *adj*
be·yond [bee-OND] *adv* **1** farther away. **2** besides. ◆ *prep* **3** on the farther side of. **4** later than. **5** surpassing, out of reach of.
Bh *Chem.* bohrium.
Bi *Chem.* bismuth.
bi·as [BĪ-əs] *n, pl* **-as·es 1** personal slant. **2** inclination or preference. **3** onesided inclination. ◆ *vt* **-ased, -as·ing 4** influence, affect. **bi'ased** *adj* prejudiced.
bib *n* **1** cloth put under child's chin to protect clothes when eating. **2** part of apron or overalls above waist.
Bi·ble [BĪ-bəl] *n* the sacred writings of Christianity and Judaism. **bible** *n fig* book or journal considered unchallengeably authoritative. **Bib·li·cal** [BIB-li-kəl] *adj*
bib·li·og·ra·phy [bib-lee-OG-rə-fee] *n, pl* **-phies 1** list of books on a subject. **2** history and description of books. **bib·li·og'ra·pher** *n*
bib·li·o·phile [BIB-lee-ə-fīl] *n* lover, collector of books.
bib·u·lous [BIB-yə-ləs] *adj* given to drinking.
bi·cam·er·al [bī-KAM-ər-əl] *adj* (of a legislature) having two chambers.

bi·car·bo·nate [bī-KAHR-bə-nit] *n* chemical compound releasing carbon dioxide when mixed with acid.
bi·cen·ten·ni·al [bī-sen-TEN-ee-əl] *n* **1** two hundredth anniversary. **2** its celebration. ◆ *adj* **3** relating to this.
bi·ceps [BĪ-seps] *n* two-headed muscle, esp. muscle of upper arm.
bick·er [BIK-ər] *vi, n* quarrel over petty things. **bick'er·ing** *n*
bi·cy·cle [BĪ-si-kəl] *n* vehicle with two wheels, one in front of other, pedaled by rider. **bi'cy·clist** *n*
bid *vt* **bade, bid** *or* **bid·den, bid·ding 1** offer. **2** say. **3** command. **4** invite. ◆ *n* **5** offer, esp. of price. **6** try. **bid'der** *n*
bide [bīd] *v* **bid·ed, bid·ing** *vi* **1** remain. **2** dwell. ◆ *vt* **3** await. **bid'ing** *n*
bi·det [bi-DAY] *n* low basin for washing genital area.
bi·en·ni·al [bī-EN-ee-əl] *adj* **1** happening every two years. **2** lasting two years. ◆ *n* **3** plant living two years. **bi·en'ni·um** [-əm] *n* period of two years.
bier [beer] *n* **1** frame for bearing dead to grave. **2** stand for holding dead. **3** coffin and its stand.
bi·fo·cal [bī-FOH-kəl] *adj* having two different focal lengths. **bi·fo'cals** *pl n* eyeglasses having bifocal lenses for near and distant vision.
big *adj* **big·ger, big·gest** of great or considerable size, height, number, power, etc. **big cheese** *inf* important person.

bevy *n* = **group**, band, bunch (*inf*), collection, company, crowd, gathering, pack, troupe
bewail *v* = **lament**, bemoan, cry over, deplore, grieve for, moan, mourn, regret
beware *v* = **be careful**, be cautious, be wary, guard against, heed, look out, mind, take heed, watch out
bewilder *v* = **confound**, baffle, bemuse, confuse, flummox, mystify, nonplus, perplex, puzzle
bewildered *adj* = **confused**, at a loss, at sea, baffled, flummoxed, mystified, nonplussed, perplexed, puzzled
bewitch *v* = **enchant**, beguile, captivate, charm, enrapture, entrance, fascinate, hypnotize
bewitched *adj* = **enchanted**, charmed, entranced, fascinated, mesmerized, spellbound, under a spell

beyond *prep* **1** = **past**, above, apart from, at a distance, away from, over **2** = **exceeding**, out of reach of, superior to, surpassing
bias *n* **1** = **prejudice**, favoritism, inclination, leaning, partiality, tendency ◆ *v* **2** = **prejudice**, distort, influence, predispose, slant, sway, twist, warp, weight
biased *adj* = **prejudiced**, distorted, one-sided, partial, slanted, weighted
bicker *v* = **quarrel**, argue, disagree, dispute, fight, squabble, wrangle
bid *v* **1** = **offer**, proffer, propose, submit, tender **2** = **say**, call, greet, tell, wish **3** = **tell**, ask, command, direct, instruct, order, require ◆ *n* **4** = **offer**, advance, amount, price, proposal, sum, tender **5** = **attempt**, crack (*inf*), effort, go (*inf*), stab (*inf*), try
bidding *n* = **order**, beck and call, command, direction, instruction, request,

big'head *n inf* conceit. **big'head'ed** *adj* **big shot** *inf* important or influential person. **big'-time** *adv inf* very much, to a great extent.

big·a·my [BIG-ə-mee] *n, pl* **-mies** crime of marrying a person while one is still legally married to someone else. **big'a·mist** *n*

bight [bīt] *n* **1** curve or loop in rope. **2** long curved shoreline or water bounded by it.

big·ot [BIG-ət] *n* person intolerant or not receptive to ideas of others (esp. on religion, race, etc.). **big'ot·ed** *adj* **big'ot·ry** *n*

bike [bīk] *n* short for bicycle or motor bike.

bi·ki·ni [bi-KEE-nee] *n, pl* **-nis** woman's brief two-piece swimming costume.

bi·lat·er·al [bī-LAT-ər-əl] *adj* two-sided.

bile [bīl] *n* **1** fluid secreted by the liver. **2** anger, ill temper. **bil·ious** [BIL-yəs] *adj* nauseous, nauseating. **bil'ious·ness** *n*

bilge [bilj] *n* **1** bottom of ship's hull. **2** dirty water collecting there. **3** *inf* nonsense.

bi·lin·gual [bī-LING-gwəl] *adj* speaking, or written in, two languages. **bi·lin'gual·ism** *n*

bill[1] *n* **1** written account of charges. **2** draft of legislative act. **3** poster. **4** commercial document. **5** paper money. ♦ *vt* **6** present account of charges. **7** announce by advertisement. **bill'ing** *n* degree of importance (esp. in theater, etc.). **bill'board** *n* large panel for outdoor advertising.

bill[2] *n* **1** bird's beak. ♦ *vi* **2** touch bills, as doves. **3** caress affectionately.

bil·let [BIL-it] *n* **1** civilian quarters for troops. **2** resting place. ♦ *vt* **3** quarter, as troops.

bil·let-doux [bil-ee-DOO] *n, pl* **billets-doux** [bil-ee-DOOZ] love letter.

bil·liards [BIL-yərdz] *n* game played on table with balls and cues.

bil·lion [BIL-yən] *n* thousand millions.

bil·low [BIL-oh] *n* **1** great swelling wave. ♦ *vi* **2** surge. **3** swell out.

bi·month·ly [bī-MUNTH-lee] *adv, adj* **1** every two months. **2** oft. twice a month.

bin *n* box, etc. used for storage.

bi·na·ry [BĪ-nə-ree] *adj* **1** composed of, characterized by, two. **2** dual.

bind [bīnd] *v* **bound, bind·ing** ♦ *vt* **1** tie fast. **2** tie around, gird. **3** tie together. **4** oblige. **5** seal. **6** constrain. **7** bandage. **8** cohere. **9** unite. **10** put (book) into cover. **bind'er** *n* one who, or that which binds. **bind'er·y** *n, pl* **-er·ies bind'ing** *n* **1** cover of book. **2** tape for hem, etc.

---

summons

big *adj* **1** = **large**, enormous, extensive, great, huge, immense, massive, substantial, vast **2** = **important**, eminent, influential, leading, main, powerful, prominent, significant **3** = **grown-up**, adult, elder, grown, mature **4** = **generous**, altruistic, benevolent, gracious, magnanimous, noble, unselfish

big cheese *n Inf* = **manager**, boss (*inf*), bossman (*sl*), foreman, head honcho (*sl*), overseer, superintendent, supervisor

bighead *n Inf* = **boaster**, braggart, know-all (*inf*)

bigheaded *adj* = **boastful**, arrogant, cocky, conceited, egotistic, immodest, overconfident, swollen-headed

bigot *n* = **fanatic**, racist, sectarian, zealot

bigoted *adj* = **intolerant**, biased, dogmatic, narrow-minded, opinionated, prejudiced, sectarian

bigotry *n* = **intolerance**, bias, discrimination, dogmatism, fanaticism, narrow-mindedness, prejudice, sectarianism

bill[1] *n* **1** = **charges**, account, invoice, reckoning, score, statement, tally **2** = **proposal**, measure, piece of legislation, projected law **3** = **advertisement**, bulletin, circular, handbill, handout, leaflet, notice, placard, poster **4** = **list**, agenda, card, catalog, inventory, listing, program, roster, schedule ♦ *v* **5** = **charge**, debit, invoice **6** = **advertise**, announce, give advance notice of, post

bill[2] *n* = **beak**, mandible, neb (*archaic or dialect*), nib

billet *v* **1** = **quarter**, accommodate, berth, station ♦ *n* **2** = **quarters**, accommodation, barracks, lodging

billow *n* **1** = **wave**, breaker, crest, roller, surge, swell, tide ♦ *v* **2** = **surge**, balloon, belly, puff up, rise up, roll, swell

bind *v* **1** = **secure**, fasten, hitch, lash, strap, tie **2** = **oblige**, compel, constrain, engage, force, necessitate, require ♦ *n Inf* **3** = **nuisance**, bore, drag (*inf*), pain in the neck (*inf*) **4** = **difficulty**, dilemma, quandary, spot (*inf*)

binding *adj* = **compulsory**, indissoluble, irrevocable, mandatory, necessary, obligatory, unalterable

binge [binj] n inf **1** excessive indulgence in eating or drinking. **2** spree.

bin·go [BING-goh] n game of chance in which numbers drawn are matched with those on a card.

bin·na·cle [BIN-ə-kəl] n box holding ship's compass.

bin·oc·u·lar [bə-NOK-yə-lər] adj seeing with, made for, both eyes. **bin·oc'u·lars** pl n telescope made for both eyes.

bi·no·mi·al [bī-NOH-mee-əl] adj, n (denoting) algebraic expression consisting of two terms.

bio- comb. form life or living organisms, e.g. biology.

bi·o·de·grad·a·ble [bī-oh-di-GRAY-də-bəl] adj capable of decomposition by natural means.

bi·o·di·ver·si·ty [bī-oh-dī-VURZ-ə-tee] n existence of a wide variety of species in their natural environment.

bi·og·ra·phy [bī-OG-rə-fee] n, pl -phies story of one person's life. **bi·og'ra·pher** n **bi·o·graph'i·cal** adj

bi·ol·o·gy [bī-OL-ə-jee] n study of living organisms. **bi·o·log'i·cal** adj **bi·ol'o·gist** n

bi·on·ics [bī-ON-iks] n study of relation of biological and electronic processes. **bionic** adj having physical functions controlled, augmented by electronic equipment.

bi·op·sy [BĪ-op-see] n, pl -sies examination of tissue removed surgically from a living body.

bi·o·rhythm [BĪ-oh-rith-əm] n cyclically recurring pattern of physiological states.

bi·o·ter·ror·ism [bī-oh-TER-ər-iz-əm] n use of viruses, bacteria, etc by terrorists. **bi·o·ter'ror·ist** n

bi·par·ti·san [bī-PAHR-tə-zən] adj consisting of or supported by two political parties.

bi·par·tite [bī-PAHR-tīt] adj consisting of two parts, parties.

bi·ped [BĪ-ped] n two-footed animal.

bi·plane [BĪ-playn] n airplane with two

pairs of wings.

birch [burch] n **1** tree with silvery bark. **2** rod for punishment, made of birch twigs. ◆ vt **3** flog. **birch'en** adj

bird [burd] n **1** feathered animal. ◆ vi **2** observe or identify wild birds as a hobby. **bird'brain** n stupid person.

bird·ie [BUR-dee] n. v Golf (make) score of one under par for a hole.

bi·ret·ta [bə-RET-ə] n square cap with three or four ridges worn usu. by Catholic clergy.

birth [burth] n **1** bearing, or the being born, of offspring. **2** parentage, origin. **birth control** limitation of childbearing usu. by artificial means. **birth'mark** n blemish, stain, formed on skin before birth. **birth'right** n right one has by birth.

bis·cuit [BIS-kit] n quick bread made from spoonful of rolled dough.

bi·sect [bī-SEKT] vt divide into two equal parts.

bi·sex·ual [bī-SEK-shoo-əl] adj **1** sexually attracted to both men and women. **2** of both sexes.

bish·op [BISH-əp] n **1** clergyman typically governing diocese. **2** chess piece. **bish'op·ric** n diocese or office of a bishop.

bis·muth [BIZ-məth] n reddish-white metal used in medicine, etc.

bi·son [BĪ-sən] n **1** large wild ox. **2** N Amer. buffalo.

bis·tro [BIS-troh] n, pl -tros small restaurant.

bit¹ n **1** fragment, piece. **2** biting, cutting part of tool. **3** mouthpiece of horse's bridle.

bit² pt./pp. of BITE.

bit³ n Computers smallest unit of information.

bitch [bich] n **1** female dog, fox or wolf. **2** offens spiteful woman. **3** inf complaint. ◆ vi inf **4** complain. **bitch'y** adj **bitch·i·er**, **bitch·i·est bitch'i·ness** n

bite [bīt] vt bit, bit·ten, bit·ing **1** cut into

binge n Inf = **bout**, feast, fling, orgy, spree

biography n = **life story**, account, curriculum vitae, CV, life, memoir, profile, record

birth n **1** = **childbirth**, delivery, nativity, parturition **2** = **ancestry**, background, blood, breeding, lineage, parentage, pedigree, stock

bisect v = **cut in two**, cross, cut across,

divide in two, halve, intersect, separate, split

bit¹ n = **piece**, crumb, fragment, grain, morsel, part, scrap, speck

bit² n = **curb**, brake, check, restraint, snaffle

bitch n **1** Inf = **complaint**, gripe (inf), grouse, grumble, objection, protest ◆ v **2** Inf = **complain**, bemoan, gripe (inf), grouse, grumble, lament, object esp. with teeth. **2** grip. **3** rise to bait. **4** etch with acid. ◆ *n* **5** act of biting. **6** wound so made. **7** mouthful. **biting** *adj* having power to bite.

bit·ter [BIT-ər] *adj* **-er, -est 1** sharp, sour tasting. **2** unpleasant. **3** (of person) angry, resentful. **4** sarcastic. **bit'ter·ly** *adv* **bit'ter·ness** *n* **bit'ters** *pl n* essence of bitter usu. aromatic herbs. **bitter end** final extremity.

bi·tu·men [bi-TOO-mən] *n* viscous substance occurring in asphalt, tar, etc. **bi·tu'mi·nous coal** coal yielding much bitumen on burning.

bi·valve [BĪ-valv] *adj* **1** having a double shell. ◆ *n* **2** mollusk with such shell.

biv·ou·ac [BIV-oo-ak] *n* **1** temporary encampment of soldiers, hikers, etc. ◆ *vi* **-acked, -ack·ing 2** pass the night in temporary camp.

bi·zarre [bi-ZAHR] *adj* unusual, weird.

Bk *Chem.* berkelium.

blab *v* **blabbed, blab·bing 1** reveal secrets. **2** chatter idly. ◆ *n* **3** chatter. **blab·ber** *v* **-bered, -ber·ing** blab.

black [blak] *adj* **1** of the darkest color. **2** without light. **3** dark. **4** evil. **5** somber. **6** dishonorable. ◆ *n* **7** darkest color. **8** black dye, clothing, etc. **9** (**B-**) person of

dark-skinned race. **10** African-American. **black'en** *v* **black'ing** *n* substance used for blacking and cleaning leather, etc. **black'ball** *vt* vote against, exclude. **black'bird** *n* common American black bird. **black'board** *n* dark-colored surface for writing on with chalk. **black box** *inf* name for FLIGHT RECORDER. **black economy** illegally undeclared income. **black'head** *n* dark, fatty plug blocking pore in skin. **black'list** *n* **1** list of people, organizations considered suspicious, untrustworthy, etc. ◆ *vt* **2** put on blacklist. **Black Ma·ri·a** [mə-RĪ-ə] police van for transporting prisoners. **black market** illegal buying and selling of goods. **black widow** highly poisonous N Amer. spider.

black·guard [BLAG-ahrd] *n* scoundrel.

black·mail [BLAK-mayl] *vt* **1** extort money from (a person) by threats. ◆ *n* **2** act of blackmailing. **3** money extorted thus. **black'mail·er** *n*

black·out [BLAK-owt] *n* **1** complete failure of electricity supply. **2** sudden turning off of all staglights. **3** state of temporary unconsciousness. **4** obscuring of all lights as precaution against night air attack. **black out** *vi* lose consciousness, memory, or vision temporarily.

━━━━ THESAURUS ━━━━

bitchy *adj Inf* = **spiteful**, backbiting, catty (*inf*), mean, nasty, snide, vindictive

bite *v* **1** = **cut**, chew, gnaw, nip, pierce, pinch, snap, tear, wound ◆ *n* **2** = **wound**, nip, pinch, prick, smarting, sting, tooth marks **3** = **snack**, food, light meal, morsel, mouthful, piece, refreshment, taste

biting *adj* **1** = **piercing**, bitter, cutting, harsh, penetrating, sharp **2** = **sarcastic**, caustic, cutting, incisive, mordant, scathing, stinging, trenchant, vitriolic

bitter *adj* **1** = **sour**, acid, acrid, astringent, harsh, sharp, tart, unsweetened, vinegary **2** = **resentful**, acrimonious, begrudging, hostile, sore, sour, sullen **3** = **freezing**, biting, fierce, intense, severe, stinging

bitterness *n* **1** = **sourness**, acerbity, acidity, sharpness, tartness **2** = **resentment**, acrimony, animosity, asperity, grudge, hostility, rancor, sarcasm

bizarre *adj* = **strange**, eccentric, extraordinary, fantastic, freakish, ludicrous, outlandish, peculiar, unusual, weird, zany

blab *v* = **tell**, blurt out, disclose, divulge, give away, let slip, let the cat out of the

bag, reveal, spill the beans (*inf*)

black *adj* **1** = **dark**, dusky, ebony, jet, raven, sable, swarthy **2** = **hopeless**, depressing, dismal, foreboding, gloomy, ominous, sad, somber **3** = **angry**, furious, hostile, menacing, resentful, sullen, threatening **4** = **wicked**, bad, evil, iniquitous, nefarious, villainous ◆ *v* **5** = **boycott**, ban, bar, blacklist

blacken *v* **1** = **darken**, befoul, begrime, cloud, dirty, make black, smudge, soil **2** = **discredit**, defame, denigrate, malign, slander, smear, smirch, vilify

blacklist *v* = **exclude**, ban, bar, boycott, debar, expel, reject, snub

black magic *n* = **witchcraft**, black art, diabolism, necromancy, sorcery, voodoo, wizardry

blackmail *n* **1** = **threat**, extortion, hush money (*sl*), intimidation, ransom ◆ *v* **2** = **threaten**, coerce, compel, demand, extort, hold to ransom, intimidate, squeeze

blackness *n* = **darkness**, duskiness, gloom, murkiness, swarthiness

blackout *n* **1** = **unconsciousness**, coma,

black·smith [BLAK-smith] *n* smith who works in iron.

blad·der [BLAD-ər] *n* membranous bag to contain liquid, esp. urinary bladder.

blade [blayd] *n* **1** edge, cutting part of knife or tool. **2** leaf of grass, etc. **3** sword. **4** *obs* dashing fellow. **5** flat of oar.

blame [blaym] *n* **1** censure. **2** culpability. ♦ *vt* blamed, blam·ing **3** find fault with. **4** censure. **blame'less** *adj* blame'wor·thy [-wur-*thee*] *adj*

blanch *v* **1** whiten, bleach, take color out of. **2** (of foodstuffs) briefly boil or fry. **3** turn pale.

bland *adj* -er, -est **1** devoid of distinctive characteristics. **2** smooth in manner.

blan·dish *vt* **1** coax. **2** flatter. **bland'ish·ment** *n*

blank *adj* **1** without marks or writing. **2** empty. **3** vacant, confused. **4** (of verse) without rhyme. ♦ *n* **5** empty space. **6** void. **7** cartridge containing no bullet.

blan·ket [BLANG-kit] *n* **1** thick woven covering for bed, horse, etc. **2** concealing cover. ♦ *vt* **3** cover with blanket. **4** cover, stifle.

blare [blair] *v* blared, blar·ing **1** sound loudly and harshly. ♦ *n* **2** such sound.

blar·ney [BLAHR-nee] *n* flattering talk.

bla·sé [blah-ZAY] *adj* **1** indifferent through familiarity. **2** bored.

blas·pheme [blas-FEEM] *v* show contempt for God or sacred things, esp. in speech. **blas·phem'er** *n* **blas'phe·mous** [-fə-məs] *adj* **blas'phe·my** *n*

blast *n* **1** explosion. **2** high-pressure wave of air coming from an explosion. **3** current of air. **4** gust of wind or air. **5** loud sound. **6** reprimand. **7** *sl* riotous party. ♦ *vt* **8** blow up. **9** remove, open, etc. by explosion. **10** blight. **11** ruin. **blast furnace** furnace for smelting ore, using blast of heated air.

bla·tant [BLAYT-nt] *adj* obvious. **bla'tan·cy** *n*

blaze¹ [blayz] *n* **1** strong fire or flame. **2** brightness. **3** outburst. ♦ *vi* blazed, blaz·ing **4** burn strongly. **5** be very angry.

blaze² *v* blazed, blaz·ing **1** (mark trees to) establish trail. ♦ *n* **2** mark on tree. **3** white mark on horse's face.

blaze³ *vt* blazed, blaz·ing proclaim.

blaz·er [BLAY-zər] *n* type of sports jacket.

— THESAURUS —

faint, loss of consciousness, oblivion, swoon **2** = **noncommunication**, censorship, radio silence, secrecy, suppression, withholding news

blame *v* **1** = **hold responsible**, accuse, censure, chide, condemn, criticize, find fault with, reproach ♦ *n* **2** = **responsibility**, accountability, culpability, fault, guilt, liability, onus

blameless *adj* = **innocent**, above suspicion, clean, faultless, guiltless, immaculate, impeccable, irreproachable, perfect, unblemished, virtuous

blameworthy *adj* = **reprehensible**, discreditable, disreputable, indefensible, inexcusable, iniquitous, reproachable, shameful

bland *adj* = **dull**, boring, flat, humdrum, insipid, tasteless, unexciting, uninspiring, vapid

blank *adj* **1** = **unmarked**, bare, clean, clear, empty, plain, void, white **2** = **expressionless**, deadpan, empty, impassive, poker-faced (*inf*), vacant, vague ♦ *n* **3** = **empty space**, emptiness, gap, nothingness, space, vacancy, vacuum, void

blanket *n* **1** = **cover**, coverlet, rug **2** = **covering**, carpet, cloak, coat, layer,

mantle, sheet ♦ *v* **3** = **cover**, cloak, coat, conceal, hide, mask, obscure, suppress

blare *v* = **sound out**, blast, clamor, clang, resound, roar, scream, trumpet

blasé *adj* = **indifferent**, apathetic, lukewarm, nonchalant, offhand, unconcerned

blaspheme *v* = **curse**, abuse, damn, desecrate, execrate, profane, revile, swear

blasphemous *adj* = **irreverent**, godless, impious, irreligious, profane, sacrilegious, ungodly

blasphemy *n* = **irreverence**, cursing, desecration, execration, impiety, profanity, sacrilege, swearing

blast *n* **1** = **explosion**, bang, burst, crash, detonation, discharge, eruption, outburst, salvo, volley **2** = **gust**, gale, squall, storm, strong breeze, tempest **3** = **blare**, blow, clang, honk, peal, scream, toot, wail ♦ *v* **4** = **blow up**, break up, burst, demolish, destroy, explode, put paid to, ruin, shatter

blatant *adj* = **obvious**, brazen, conspicuous, flagrant, glaring, obtrusive, ostentatious, overt

blaze *n* **1** = **fire**, bonfire, conflagration, flames **2** = **glare**, beam, brilliance, flare, flash, gleam, glitter, glow, light, radiance ♦

bla·zon [BLAY-zən] *vt* make public, proclaim.

bleach [bleech] *v* **1** make or become white. ◆ *n* **2** bleaching substance.

bleak [bleek] *adj* **-er, -est 1** cold and cheerless. **2** exposed. **bleak'ly** *adv* **bleak'ness** *n*

blear·y [BLEER-ee] *adj* **blear·i·er, blear·i·est** (of the eyes) dimmed, as with tears, sleep.

bleat [bleet] *v* **1** cry, as sheep. **2** say, speak, plaintively. ◆ *n* **3** sheep's cry.

bleed *v* **bled, bleed·ing 1** lose blood. **2** draw blood or liquid from. **3** extort money from.

bleep *n* **1** short high-pitched sound e.g. from electronic device. ◆ *vt* **2** obscure sound e.g. of TV program by making bleep. **bleep·er** *n* small portable radio receiver that makes a bleeping signal.

blem·ish *n* **1** defect. **2** stain. ◆ *vt* **3** make (something) defective, dirty, etc. **blem'ished** *adj*

blend *vt* **1** mix. ◆ *n* **2** mixture. **blend'er** *n* one who, that which blends, esp. electrical kitchen appliance for mixing food.

bless *vt* **blessed** or **blest, bless·ing 1** consecrate. **2** give thanks to. **3** ask God's favor for. **4** (usu. passive) endow (with). **5** glorify. **6** make happy. **bless'ed** [-id] *adj* **blessing** *n* **1** (ceremony asking for) God's protection, aid. **2** short prayer. **3** approval. **4** welcome event, benefit.

blew pt. of BLOW.

blight [blīt] *n* **1** plant disease. **2** harmful influence. ◆ *vt* **3** injure as with blight.

blimp *n* small, nonrigid airship used for observing.

blind [blīnd] *adj* **1** unable to see. **2** heedless, random. **3** dim. **4** closed at one end. **5** *sl* very drunk. ◆ *vt* **6** deprive of sight. ◆ *n* **7** something cutting off light. **8** window screen. **9** pretext. **10** place of concealment for hunters. **blind'ly** *adv* **blind'ness** *n* **blind flying** navigation of aircraft by use of instruments alone. **blind'fold** *vt* cover the eyes of so as to prevent vision. ◆ *n, adj* **blind-man's buff** game in which one player is blindfolded.

blink [blingk] *vi* **1** wink. **2** twinkle. **3** shine intermittently. ◆ *n* **4** gleam. **blink'ers** *pl n*

THESAURUS

---

v **3** = **burn**, fire, flame **4** = **shine**, beam, flare, flash, glare, gleam, glow

bleach *v* = **whiten**, blanch, fade, grow pale, lighten, wash out

bleak *adj* **1** = **exposed**, bare, barren, desolate, unsheltered, weather-beaten, windswept **2** = **dismal**, cheerless, depressing, discouraging, dreary, gloomy, grim, hopeless, joyless, somber

bleary *adj* = **dim**, blurred, blurry, foggy, fuzzy, hazy, indistinct, misty, murky

bleed *v* **1** = **lose blood**, flow, gush, ooze, run, shed blood, spurt **2** = **draw** or **take blood**, extract, leech **3** *Inf* = **extort**, drain, exhaust, fleece, milk, squeeze

blemish *n* **1** = **mark**, blot, defect, disfigurement, fault, flaw, imperfection, smudge, stain, taint ◆ *v* **2** = **stain**, damage, disfigure, impair, injure, mar, mark, spoil, sully, taint, tarnish

blend *v* **1** = **mix**, amalgamate, combine, compound, merge, mingle, unite **2** = **go well**, complement, fit, go with, harmonize, suit ◆ *n* **3** = **mixture**, alloy, amalgamation, combination, compound, concoction, mix, synthesis, union

bless *v* **1** = **sanctify**, anoint, consecrate, dedicate, exalt, hallow, ordain **2** = **grant**, bestow, favor, give, grace, provide

blessed *adj* = **holy**, adored, beatified, divine, hallowed, revered, sacred, sanctified

blessing *n* **1** = **benediction**, benison, commendation, consecration, dedication, grace, invocation, thanksgiving **2** = **approval**, backing, consent, favor, good wishes, leave, permission, sanction, support **3** = **benefit**, favor, gift, godsend, good fortune, help, kindness, service, windfall

blight *n* **1** = **curse**, affliction, bane, contamination, corruption, evil, plague, pollution, scourge, woe **2** = **disease**, canker, decay, fungus, infestation, mildew, pest, pestilence, rot ◆ *v* **3** = **frustrate**, crush, dash, disappoint, mar, ruin, spoil, undo, wreck

blind *adj* **1** = **sightless**, eyeless, unseeing, unsighted, visionless **2** = **unaware of**, careless, heedless, ignorant, inattentive, inconsiderate, indifferent, insensitive, oblivious, unconscious of **3** = **unreasoning**, indiscriminate, prejudiced ◆ *n* **4** = **cover**, camouflage, cloak, façade, feint, front, mask, masquerade, screen, smoke screen

blindly *adv* **1** = **thoughtlessly**, carelessly, heedlessly, inconsiderately, recklessly, senselessly **2** = **aimlessly**, at random, leather flaps to prevent horse from seeing to the side. **blink at** see, know about, but ignore. **on the blink** *inf* not working (properly).

blip *n* 1 repetitive sound or visible pulse, e.g. on radar screen. ♦ *vt* **blipped, blip·ping** 2 bleep.

bliss *n* perfect happiness. **bliss'ful** *adj* **bliss'ful·ly** *adv*

blis·ter [BLIS-tər] *n* 1 bubble on skin. 2 surface swelling, e.g. on paint. ♦ *v* 3 form blisters (on). **blis'ter·ing** *adj* (of verbal attack) bitter. **blister pack** package for goods with hard, raised, transparent cover.

blithe [blīth] *adj* 1 happy, gay. 2 heedless. **blithe'ly** *adv* **blithe'ness** *n*

blitz [blits] *n* sudden, concentrated attack. **blitz'krieg** [-kreeg] *n* 1 sudden concentrated military attack. 2 war conducted in this way.

bliz·zard [BLIZ-ərd] *n* blinding storm of wind and snow.

bloat [bloht] *v* 1 puff or swell out. ♦ *n* 2 distention of stomach of cow, etc. by gas. **bloat'ed** *adj* swollen.

blob *n* 1 soft mass, esp. drop of liquid. 2 shapeless form.

bloc [blok] *n* (political) grouping of people or countries.

block [blok] *n* 1 solid piece of wood, stone, etc. 2 *Hist.* rectangular piece of wood on

which people were beheaded. 3 obstacle. 4 stoppage. 5 pulley with frame. 6 group of buildings. 7 urban area enclosed by intersecting streets. ♦ *vt* 8 obstruct, stop up. 9 shape on block. 10 sketch (in). **block'age** *n* obstruction. **block'head** *n* fool, simpleton. **block letters** written capital letters.

block·ade [blo-KAYD] *n* physical prevention of access, esp. to port, etc. ♦ *vt* **-ad·ed, -ad·ing**

blonde, (*masc*) **blond** *adj, n* fair-haired (person).

blood [blud] *n* 1 red fluid in veins. 2 race. 3 kindred. 4 good parentage. 5 temperament. 6 passion. ♦ *vt* 7 initiate (into hunting, war, etc.). **blood'less** *adj* **blood'y -i-er, -i-est** 1 covered in blood. 2 slaughterous. ♦ *adj, adv* 3 *sl* a common intensifier. ♦ *v* 4 make bloody. **blood bank** (institution managing) store of human blood preserved for transfusion. **blood'cur·dling** *adj* horrifying. **blood'hound** *n* breed of large hound noted for keen powers of scent. **blood'shed** *n* slaughter, killing. **blood'shot** *adj* inflamed (said of eyes). **blood sport** sport in which animals are killed, e.g. fox hunting. **blood'suck·er** *n* 1 parasite (e.g. mosquito) living on host's blood. 2 parasitic person. **blood test** examination of

indiscriminately, instinctively

blink *v* 1 = **wink**, bat, flutter 2 = **flicker**, flash, gleam, glimmer, shine, twinkle, wink ♦ *n* 3 **on the blink** *Sl* = **not working (properly)**, faulty, malfunctioning, out of action, out of order, playing up

bliss *n* = **joy**, beatitude, blessedness, blissfulness, ecstasy, euphoria, felicity, gladness, happiness, heaven, nirvana, paradise, rapture

blissful *adj* = **joyful**, ecstatic, elated, enraptured, euphoric, happy, heavenly (*inf*), rapturous

blister *n* = **sore**, abscess, boil, carbuncle, cyst, pimple, pustule, swelling

blithe *adj* = **heedless**, careless, casual, indifferent, nonchalant, thoughtless, unconcerned, untroubled

blitz *n* = **attack**, assault, blitzkrieg, bombardment, campaign, offensive, onslaught, raid, strike

blizzard *n* = **snowstorm**, blast, gale, squall, storm, tempest

bloat *v* = **puff up**, balloon, blow up, dilate, distend, enlarge, expand, inflate, swell

blob *n* = **drop**, ball, bead, bubble, dab, droplet, globule, lump, mass

bloc *n* = **group**, alliance, axis, coalition, faction, league, union

block *n* 1 = **piece**, brick, chunk, hunk, ingot, lump, mass 2 = **obstruction**, bar, barrier, blockage, hindrance, impediment, jam, obstacle ♦ *v* 3 = **obstruct**, choke, clog, close, plug, stem the flow, stop up 4 = **stop**, bar, check, halt, hinder, impede, obstruct, thwart

blockade *n* = **stoppage**, barricade, barrier, block, hindrance, impediment, obstacle, obstruction, restriction, siege

blockage *n* = **obstruction**, block, impediment, occlusion, stoppage

blockhead *n* = **idiot**, chump (*inf*), dork (*sl*), dunce, fool, nitwit, schmuck (*sl*), thickhead

blond, blonde *adj* = **fair**, fair-haired, fair-skinned, flaxen, golden-haired, light, sample of blood. **blood'thirst·y** *adj* murderous, cruel. **blood transfusion** transfer of blood from one person into another.

bloom *n* 1 flower of plant. 2 blossoming. 3 prime, perfection. 4 glow. 5 powdery deposit on fruit. ◆ *vi* 6 be in flower. 7 flourish.

bloom·er [BLOO-mər] *n inf* 1 plant in bloom. 2 person reaching full competence. 3 person reaching puberty. 4 ludicrous mistake.

bloo·mers [BLOO-mərz] *pl n* girls' or women's wide, baggy underpants.

blos·som [BLOS-əm] *n* 1 flower. 2 flower bud. ◆ *vi* 3 flower. 4 develop.

blot *n* 1 spot, stain. 2 disgrace. ◆ *vt* -ted, -ting 3 spot, stain. 4 obliterate. 5 detract from. 6 soak up ink, etc. from. **blot'ter** *n* **blotting paper** soft absorbent paper for soaking up ink.

blotch [bloch] *n* 1 dark spot on skin. ◆ *vt* 2 make spotted. **blotch'y** *adj* **blotch·i·er, blotch·i·est**

blouse [blows] *n* light, loose upper garment.

blow[1] [bloh] *v* blew, blown, blow·ing ◆ *vi* 1 make a current of air. 2 pant. 3 emit sound. ◆ *vt* 4 drive air upon or into. 5 drive by current of air. 6 sound. 7 spout (of whales). 8 fan. 9 *sl* squander. ◆ *n* 10 blast. 11 gale. **blow-dry** *vt* -dried, -dry·ing style hair after washing using stream of hot air. **blow fly** fly that infects food, etc. **blow'pipe** *n* dart tube. **blow'out** *n* 1 sudden puncture in tire. 2 uncontrolled escape of oil, gas, from well. 3 *sl* festive party. **blow up** 1 explode. 2 inflate. 3 enlarge (photograph). 4 *inf* lose one's temper.

blow[2] *n* 1 stroke, knock. 2 sudden misfortune, loss.

blown pp. of BLOW[1].

blows·y [BLOW-zee] *adj* blows·i·er, blows·i·est 1 slovenly, sluttish. 2 red-faced.

blub·ber [BLUB-ər] *vi* 1 weep. ◆ *n* 2 fat of whales. 3 weeping.

bludg·eon [BLUJ-ən] *n* 1 short thick club. ◆ *vt* 2 strike with one. 3 coerce (someone into).

---

tow-headed

blood *n* 1 = **lifeblood**, gore, vital fluid 2 = **family**, ancestry, birth, descent, extraction, kinship, lineage, relations

bloodcurdling *adj* = **terrifying**, appalling, chilling, dreadful, fearful, frightening, hair-raising, horrendous, horrifying, scaring, spine-chilling

bloodshed *n* = **killing**, blood bath, blood-letting, butchery, carnage, gore, massacre, murder, slaughter, slaying

bloodthirsty *adj* = **cruel**, barbarous, brutal, cut-throat, ferocious, gory, murderous, savage, vicious, warlike

bloody *adj* 1 = **bloodstained**, bleeding, blood-soaked, blood-spattered, gaping, raw 2 = **cruel**, ferocious, fierce, sanguinary, savage

bloom *n* 1 = **flower**, blossom, blossoming, bud, efflorescence, opening (*of flowers*) 2 = **prime**, beauty, flourishing, freshness, glow, health, heyday, luster, radiance, vigor ◆ *v* 3 = **blossom**, blow, bud, burgeon, open, sprout 4 = **flourish**, develop, fare well, grow, prosper, succeed, thrive, wax

blossom *n* 1 = **flower**, bloom, bud, floret, flowers ◆ *v* 2 = **flower**, bloom, burgeon 3 = **grow**, bloom, develop, flourish, mature,

progress, prosper, thrive

blot *n* 1 = **spot**, blotch, mark, patch, smear, smudge, speck, splodge 2 = **stain**, blemish, defect, fault, flaw, scar, spot, taint ◆ *v* 3 = **stain**, disgrace, mark, smirch, smudge, spoil, spot, sully, tarnish 4 = **soak up**, absorb, dry, take up 5 **blot out**: a = **obliterate**, darken, destroy, eclipse, efface, obscure, shadow b = **erase**, cancel, expunge

blow[1] *v* 1 = **carry**, buffet, drive, fling, flutter, move, sweep, waft 2 = **exhale**, breathe, pant, puff 3 = **play**, blare, mouth, pipe, sound, toot, trumpet, vibrate

blow[2] *n* 1 = **knock**, bang, clout (*inf*), punch, smack, sock (*sl*), stroke, thump, wallop (*inf*), whack 2 = **setback**, bombshell, calamity, catastrophe, disappointment, disaster, misfortune, reverse, shock

blow out *v* 1 = **put out**, extinguish, snuff 2 = **burst**, erupt, explode, rupture, shatter

blow up *v* 1 = **explode**, blast, blow sky-high, bomb, burst, detonate, rupture, shatter 2 = **inflate**, bloat, distend, enlarge, expand, fill, puff up, pump up, swell 3 *Inf* = **lose one's temper**, become angry, erupt, fly off the handle (*inf*), hit the roof (*inf*), rage, see red (*inf*)

blue [bloo] *adj* **blu·er, blu·est 1** of the color of sky or shades of that color. **2** livid. **3** depressed. **4** indecent. ◆ *n* **5** the color. **6** dye or pigment. ◆ *vt* **blued, blu·ing 7** make blue. **8** dip in blue liquid. **blues** *pl n inf* **1** depression. **2** song in slow tempo originating with Amer. Blacks, employed in jazz music. **blu·ish** *adj* **blue baby** baby born with bluish skin caused by heart defect. **blue blood** (person of) royal or aristocratic descent. **blue-col·lar** *adj* denoting factory workers. **blue jeans** pants made usu. of blue denim. **blue-pen·cil** *vt* **-ciled, -cil·ing** alter, delete parts of, esp. to censor. **blue'print** *n* **1** copy of drawing. **2** original plan. **blue'stock·ing** *n* scholarly, intellectual woman.

bluff¹ *n* **1** cliff, steep bank. ◆ *adj* **-er, -est 2** hearty. **3** blunt. **4** steep. **5** abrupt.

bluff² *vt* **1** deceive by pretense of strength. ◆ *n* **2** pretense.

blu·ing [BLOO-ing] *n* indigo powder used in laundering.

blun·der [BLUN-dər] *n* **1** clumsy mistake. ◆ *vi* **2** make stupid mistake. **3** act clumsily.

blun·der·buss [BLUN-dər-bus] *n* obsolete short gun with wide bore.

blunt *adj* **-er, -est 1** not sharp. **2** (of speech) abrupt. ◆ *vt* **3** make blunt. **blunt'ly** *adv* **blunt'ness** *n*

blur *v* **blurred, blur·ring 1** make, become less distinct. ◆ *n* **2** something vague, indistinct. **blur'ry** *adj* **-ri·er, -ri·est**

blurb *n* statement advertising, recommending book, etc.

blurt *vt* (usu. with *out*) utter suddenly or unadvisedly.

blush *vi* **1** become red in face. **2** be ashamed. **3** redden. ◆ *n* **4** this effect.

blus·ter [BLUS-tər] *vi, n* (indulge in) noisy, aggressive behavior. **blus'ter·ing, -ter·y** *adj* (of wind, etc.) noisy and gusty.

bo·a [BOH-ə] *n, pl* **bo·as 1** large, nonvenomous snake, esp. boa constrictor. **2** long scarf of fur or feathers.

boar [bor] *n* **1** male pig. **2** wild pig.

board [bord] *n* **1** broad, flat piece of wood. **2** sheet of rigid material for specific purpose. **3** table. **4** meals. **5** group of people who administer company. **6** governing body. **7** thick, stiff paper. ◆ *pl* **8** stage. ◆ *vt* **9** cover with planks. **10** supply food daily. **11** enter ship, etc. ◆ *vi* **12** take daily meals. **board'er** *n* **board·ing house**

THESAURUS

---

bludgeon *n* **1 = club**, cudgel, truncheon ◆ *v* **2 = club**, beat up, cudgel, knock down, strike **3 = bully**, bulldoze (*inf*), coerce, force, railroad (*inf*), steamroller

blue *adj* **1 = azure**, cerulean, cobalt, cyan, navy, sapphire, sky-colored, ultramarine **2 = depressed**, dejected, despondent, downcast, low, melancholy, sad, unhappy **3 = smutty**, indecent, lewd, obscene, risqué, X-rated (*inf*)

blueprint *n* **= plan**, design, draft, outline, pattern, pilot scheme, prototype, sketch

blues *pl n* **= depression**, doldrums, dumps (*inf*), gloom, low spirits, melancholy, unhappiness

bluff¹ *v* **1 = deceive**, con, delude, fake, feign, mislead, pretend, pull the wool over someone's eyes ◆ *n* **2 = deception**, bluster, bravado, deceit, fraud, humbug, pretense, sham, subterfuge

bluff² *n* **1 = precipice**, bank, cliff, crag, escarpment, headland, peak, promontory, ridge ◆ *adj* **2 = hearty**, blunt, blustering, genial, good-natured, open, outspoken, plain-spoken

blunder *n* **1 = mistake**, bloomer (*inf*), faux pas, foul-up (*sl*), indiscretion **2 = error**,

fault, inaccuracy, mistake, oversight, slip, slip-up (*inf*) ◆ *v* **3 = make a mistake**, botch, bungle, err, foul up (*sl*), slip up (*inf*) **4 = stumble**, bumble, flounder

blunt *adj* **1 = dull**, dulled, edgeless, pointless, rounded, unsharpened **2 = forthright**, bluff, brusque, frank, outspoken, plain-spoken, rude, straightforward, tactless ◆ *v* **3 = dull**, dampen, deaden, numb, soften, take the edge off, water down, weaken

blur *v* **1 = make indistinct**, cloud, darken, make hazy, make vague, mask, obscure ◆ *n* **2 = indistinctness**, confusion, fog, haze, obscurity

blurt out *v* **= exclaim**, disclose, let the cat out of the bag, reveal, spill the beans (*inf*), tell all, utter suddenly

blush *v* **1 = turn red**, color, flush, go red (as a beetroot), redden, turn scarlet ◆ *n* **2 = reddening**, color, flush, glow, pink tinge, rosiness, rosy tint, ruddiness

bluster *v* **1 = roar**, bully, domineer, hector, rant, storm ◆ *n* **2 = hot air** (*inf*), bluff, bombast, bravado

blustery *adj* **= gusty**, boisterous, inclement, squally, stormy, tempestuous, lodging house where meals may be had. **boarding school** school providing living accommodation for pupils. **board'room** n room where board of company or governing body meets. **above board** beyond suspicion. **on board** aboard.

boast [bohst] vi **1** speak too much in praise of oneself, one's possessions. ♦ vt **2** brag of. **3** have to show. ♦ n **4** something boasted (of). **boast'er** n **boast'ful** adj

boat [boht] n **1** small open vessel. **2** ship. ♦ vi **3** sail about in boat. **boat'ing** n **boat'swain** [BOH-sən] n ship's petty officer in charge of maintenance.

bob v bobbed, **bob-bing** ♦ vi **1** move up and down. ♦ vt **2** move jerkily. **3** cut (women's) hair short. ♦ n **4** short, jerking motion. **5** short hair style. **6** weight on pendulum, etc. **bobbed** adj

bob·bin [BOB-in] n cylinder on which thread is wound.

bob·ble [BOB-əl] v, n Baseball **-bled, -bling** **1** fumble. ♦ n **2** fumbled ball.

bob·cat [BOB-kat] n N Amer. lynx.

bob·o·link [BOB-ə-lingk] n Amer. songbird.

bode [bohd] vt **bod-ed, bod-ing** be an omen of.

bod·ice [BOD-is] n upper part of woman's dress.

bod·y [BOD-ee] n, pl **bod-ies 1** entire frame of person or animal. **2** main part of such frame. **3** corpse. **4** main part of anything. **5** substance. **6** mass. **7** person. **8** number of

persons united or organized. **9** matter, opposed to spirit. **bod'i·ly** adj, adv **bod'y·guard** n escort to protect important person. **body stocking** undergarment covering body, oft. including arms and legs. **bod'y·work** n **1** body of motor vehicle. **2** repair of this.

Boer [bor] n a S Afr. of Dutch or Huguenot descent.

bof·fo [BOF-oh] adj sl **1** excellent. **2** highly successful.

bog n wet, soft ground. **bog'gy** adj **-gi-er, -gi-est** marshy. **bog down** stick as in a bog.

bo·gey [BOH-gee] n **1** evil or mischievous spirit. **2** source of fear. **3** Golf one stroke over par on a hole. **bo'gey·man** n

bog·gle [BOG-əl] v **-gled, -gling** ♦ vi **1** be surprised. **2** be baffled. ♦ vt **3** overwhelm with wonder. **4** bewilder.

bo·gus [BOH-gəs] adj sham, false.

bo·he·mi·an [boh-HEE-mee-ən] adj **1** unconventional. ♦ n **2** one who leads an unsettled life. **bo·he'mi·a** n district, social circles of bohemians.

boil[1] vi **1** change from liquid to gas, esp. by heating. **2** become cooked by boiling. **3** bubble. **4** be agitated. **5** seethe. **6** inf be hot. **7** inf be angry. ♦ vt **8** cause to boil. **9** cook by boiling. ♦ n **10** boiling state. **boil'er** n vessel for boiling. **boil'er·mak·er** n **1** repairman, worker on boilers. **2** whiskey with beer chaser. **boil·ing point 1**

violent, wild, windy

board n **1** = **plank**, panel, piece of timber, slat, timber **2** = **directors**, advisers, committee, conclave, council, panel, trustees **3** = **meals**, daily meals, provisions, victuals ♦ v **4** = **get on**, embark, enter, mount **5** = **lodge**, put up, quarter, room

boast v **1** = **brag**, blow one's own trumpet, crow, strut, swagger, talk big (sl), vaunt **2** = **possess**, be proud of, congratulate oneself on, exhibit, flatter oneself, pride oneself on, show off ♦ n **3** = **brag**, avowal

boastful adj = **bragging**, cocky, conceited, crowing, egotistical, full of oneself, swaggering, swollen-headed, vaunting

bob v = **duck**, bounce, hop, nod, oscillate, wiggle, wobble

bode v = **portend**, augur, be an omen of, forebode, foretell, predict, signify, threaten

bodily adj = **physical**, actual, carnal, corporal, corporeal, material, substantial,

tangible

body n **1** = **physique**, build, figure, form, frame, shape **2** = **torso**, trunk **3** = **corpse**, cadaver, carcass, dead body, remains, stiff (sl) **4** = **organization**, association, band, bloc, collection, company, confederation, congress, corporation, society **5** = **main part**, bulk, essence, mass, material, matter, substance

bog n = **marsh**, fen, mire, morass, quagmire, slough, swamp, wetlands

bogey n = **bugbear**, bête noire, bugaboo, nightmare

bogus adj = **fake**, artificial, counterfeit, false, forged, fraudulent, imitation, phoney or phony (inf), sham

bohemian adj **1** = **unconventional**, alternative, artistic, arty (inf), left bank, nonconformist, offbeat, unorthodox ♦ n **2** = **nonconformist**, beatnik, dropout, hippie, iconoclast temperature at which boiling occurs. **2** point at which anger becomes uncontrollable.

boil² *n* inflamed suppurating swelling on skin.

bois·ter·ous [BOI-stər-əs] *adj* **1** wild. **2** noisy. **3** turbulent. **bois'ter·ous·ness** *n*

bold [bohld] *adj* **-er, -est 1** daring, fearless. **2** presumptuous. **3** striking, prominent. **bold'ly** *adv* **bold'ness** *n* **bold'face** *n* Printing heavy-faced type.

bole [bohl] *n* trunk of a tree.

bo·le·ro [bə-LAIR-oh] *n, pl* **-ros 1** Spanish dance. **2** short loose jacket.

boll [bohl] *n* seed capsule of cotton, flax, etc. **boll weevil** beetle infesting the cotton plant.

Bol·she·vik [BOHL-shə-vik] *n* violent revolutionary, esp. member of Russian group active in overthrow of czarist regime.

bol·ster [BOHL-stər] *vt* **1** support, uphold. ◆ *n* **2** long pillow. **3** pad, support.

bolt [bohlt] *n* **1** bar or pin (esp. with thread for nut). **2** rush. **3** discharge of lightning. **4** roll of cloth. ◆ *vt* **5** fasten with bolt. **6** swallow hastily. ◆ *vi* **7** rush away. **8** break from control.

bomb [bom] *n* **1** explosive projectile. **2** any explosive device. **3** a failure. ◆ *vt* **4** attack

with bombs. **the bomb** nuclear bomb.

bom·bard' *vt* **1** shell. **2** attack (verbally).

bom·bar·dier' [-bər-DEER] *n* person in military aircraft who aims and releases bombs. **bom·bard'ment** *n* **bomb'er** *n* **1** aircraft capable of carrying bombs. **2** person using bombs illegally. **bomb'shell** *n* **1** shell of bomb. **2** surprise. **3** *inf* very attractive woman.

bom'bast *n* **1** pompous language. **2** pomposity. **bom·bas'tic** *adj*

bo·na fide [BOH-nə fīd] *Lat* **1** genuine(ly). **2** sincere(ly). **bona fi·des** [Fī-deez] good faith, sincerity.

bo·nan·za [bə-NAN-zə] *n* sudden good luck or wealth.

bond *n* **1** that which binds. **2** link, union. **3** written promise to pay money or carry out contract. ◆ *vt* **4** bind. **5** store goods until duty is paid on them. **bond'ed** *adj* **1** placed in bond. **2** mortgaged. **bonds'man** [-mən] *n* Law one whose work is to enter into bonds as surety.

bond·age [BON-dij] *n* slavery.

bone [bohn] *n* **1** hard substance forming animal's skeleton. **2** piece of this. ◆ *v* **boned, bon·ing** ◆ *vt* **3** take out bone. ◆ *vi* **4** *inf* (with *up*) study hard. **bone'less** *adj* **bon'y** *adj* **bon·i·er, bon·i·est** **bone'head** *n* *inf* stupid person.

boil¹ *v* = **bubble**, effervesce, fizz, foam, froth, seethe

boil² *n* = **pustule**, blister, carbuncle, gathering, swelling, tumor, ulcer

boisterous *adj* = **unruly**, disorderly, loud, noisy, riotous, rollicking, rowdy, unrestrained, vociferous, wild

bold *adj* **1** = **fearless**, adventurous, audacious, brave, courageous, daring, enterprising, heroic, intrepid, valiant **2** = **impudent**, barefaced, brazen, cheeky, confident, forward, insolent, rude, shameless

bolster *v* = **support**, augment, boost, help, reinforce, shore up, strengthen

bolt *n* **1** = **bar**, catch, fastener, latch, lock, sliding bar **2** = **pin**, peg, rivet, rod ◆ *v* **3** = **run away**, abscond, dash, escape, flee, fly, make a break (for it), run for it **4** = **lock**, bar, fasten, latch, secure **5** = **gobble**, cram, devour, gorge, gulp, guzzle, stuff, swallow whole, wolf

bomb *n* **1** = **explosive**, device, grenade, mine, missile, projectile, rocket, shell,

torpedo ◆ *v* **2** = **blow up**, attack, blow sky-high, bombard, destroy, shell, strafe, torpedo

bombard *v* **1** = **bomb**, assault, blitz, fire upon, open fire, pound, shell, strafe **2** = **attack**, assail, beset, besiege, harass, hound, pester

bombardment *n* = **bombing**, assault, attack, barrage, blitz, fusillade, shelling

bombastic *adj* = **grandiloquent**, grandiose, high-flown, inflated, pompous, verbose, wordy

bona fide *adj* = **genuine**, actual, authentic, honest, kosher (*inf*), legitimate, real, true

bond *n* **1** = **fastening**, chain, cord, fetter, ligature, manacle, shackle, tie **2** = **tie**, affiliation, affinity, attachment, connection, link, relation, union **3** = **agreement**, contract, covenant, guarantee, obligation, pledge, promise, word ◆ *v* **4** = **hold together**, bind, connect, fasten, fix together, glue, paste

bondage *n* = **slavery**, captivity, confinement, enslavement, imprisonment,

bon•fire [BON-fīr] *n* large outdoor fire.

bon•go [BONG-goh] *n, pl* **-gos, -goes** small drum, usu. one of a pair, played with the fingers.

bon•net [BON-it] *n* hat (usu. with strings).

bon•sai [BON-sī] *n* (art of growing) dwarf trees, shrubs.

bo•nus [BOH-nəs] *n, pl* **-nus•es** extra (oft. unexpected) payment or gift.

boob *n* 1 fool. 2 *sl* female breast.

boo•by [BOO-bee] *n, pl* **-bies** 1 fool. 2 tropical marine bird. **booby hatch** *inf* insane asylum. **booby prize** mock prize for poor performance. **booby trap** 1 harmless-looking object that explodes when disturbed. 2 form of practical joke.

boog•ie-woog•ie [BUUG-ee-WUUG-ee] *n* kind of jazz piano playing, emphasizing a rolling bass in syncopated eighth notes.

book [buuk] *n* 1 collection of sheets of paper bound together. 2 literary work. 3 main division of this. ♦ *vt* 4 reserve (table, ticket, etc.). 5 charge with legal offense. 6 enter name in book. 7 schedule engagements for. **book'ing** *n* 1 scheduled performance for entertainer, etc. 2 reservation. **book'ie** *n inf* bookmaker. **book'ish** *adj* studious, fond of reading. **book'keep•ing** *n* systematic recording of business transactions. **book'keep•er** *n* **book'let** *n* **book'mak•er** *n* one whose work is taking bets (also **book'ie**). **book'mark** *n* 1 strip of some material put between the pages of a book to mark a place. 2 *Computers.* identifier put on a website that enables the user to return to it quickly and easily. ♦ *vt* 3 *Computers.* identify and store a website so that one can return to it quickly and easily. **book'worm** *n* great reader.

boom[1] *n* 1 sudden commercial activity. 2 prosperity. ♦ *vi* 3 become active, prosperous.

boom[2] *vi, n* (make) loud, deep sound.

boom[3] *n* 1 long spar, as for stretching the bottom of a sail. 2 barrier across harbor, river, etc. 3 pole carrying overhead microphone, etc.

boo•mer•ang [BOO-mə-rang] *n* 1 curved wooden missile of Aust. Aborigines that returns to the thrower. ♦ *vi* 2 recoil. 3 return unexpectedly. 4 backfire.

boon *n* something helpful, favor.

boon•docks [BOON-doks] *pl n* rural, backward area.

boon•dog•gle [BOON-dog-əl] *n, vi* **-gled, -gling** (do) work of no practical value performed merely to appear busy.

boor *n* rude person. **boor'ish** *adj* **boor'ish•ness** *n*

boost *n* 1 encouragement, help. 2 upward push. 3 increase. ♦ *vt* **boost'er** *n* person or thing that supports, increases power, etc.

boot *n* 1 covering for the foot and ankle. 2 *inf* kick. ♦ *vt* *inf* 3 kick. 4 start up (a computer). **boot'ed** *adj*

booth *n* 1 stall. 2 cubicle.

boot'leg *v* **-legged, -leg•ging** make, carry, sell illicit goods, esp. alcohol. ♦ *adj* **boot'leg•ger** *n*

boo•ty [BOO-tee] *n, pl* **-ties** plunder, spoil.

THESAURUS

subjugation

bonus *n* = **extra**, dividend, gift, icing on the cake, plus, premium, prize, reward

bony *adj* = **thin**, emaciated, gaunt, lean, scrawny, skin and bone, skinny

book *n* 1 = **work**, publication, title, tome, tract, volume 2 = **notebook**, album, diary, exercise book, jotter, pad ♦ *v* 3 = **reserve**, arrange for, charter, engage, make reservations, organize, program, schedule 4 = **note**, enter, list, log, mark down, put down, record, register, write down

booklet *n* = **brochure**, leaflet, pamphlet

boom *v* 1 = **bang**, blast, crash, explode, resound, reverberate, roar, roll, rumble, thunder 2 = **flourish**, develop, expand, grow, increase, intensify, prosper, strengthen, swell, thrive ♦ *n* 3 = **bang**, blast, burst, clap, crash, explosion, roar,

rumble, thunder 4 = **expansion**, boost, development, growth, improvement, increase, jump, upsurge, upswing, upturn

boon[1] *n* = **benefit**, advantage, blessing, favor, gift, godsend, manna from heaven, windfall

boorish *adj* = **loutish**, churlish, coarse, crude, oafish, uncivilized, uncouth, vulgar

boost *n* 1 = **help**, encouragement, praise, promotion 2 = **rise**, addition, expansion, improvement, increase, increment, jump ♦ *v* 3 = **increase**, add to, amplify, develop, enlarge, expand, heighten, raise 4 = **advertise**, encourage, foster, further, hype, plug (*inf*), praise, promote

boot *v* = **kick**, drive, drop-kick, knock, punt, shove

booty *n* = **plunder**, gains, haul, loot, prey, spoils, swag (*sl*), takings, winnings

booze [booz] *n, vi inf* **boozed, booz·ing 1** (consume) alcoholic drink. **2** drinking spree. **booz'er** *n inf* person fond of drinking.

bo·rax [BOR-aks] *n* white soluble substance, compound of boron. **bo·rac·ic** [bə-RAS-ik] *adj*

bor·der [BOR-dər] *n* **1** margin. **2** frontier. **3** limit. **4** strip of garden. ♦ *v* **5** provide with border. **6** adjoin.

bore¹ [bor] *vt* **bored, bor·ing 1** pierce, making a hole. ♦ *n* **2** hole. **3** caliber of gun. **bor'er** *n* **1** instrument for making holes. **2** insect that bores holes.

bore² *vt* **bored, bor·ing 1** make weary by repetition, etc. ♦ *n* **2** tiresome person or thing. **bore'dom** [-dəm] *n*

bore³ pt. of BEAR.

borne, born pp. of BEAR.

bo·ron [BOR-on] *n* chemical element used in hardening steel, etc.

bor·ough [BUR-oh] *n* political subdivision in some states.

bor·row [BOR-oh] *vt* **1** obtain on loan or trust. **2** appropriate.

bor'zoi *n* breed of tall hound with long, silky coat.

bos·om [BUUZ-əm] *n* **1** human breast. **2** seat of passions and feelings.

boss¹ [baws] *n* **1** person in charge of or employing others. ♦ *vt* **2** be in charge of. **3** be domineering over. **boss'y** *adj* **boss·i·er, boss·i·est** overbearing.

boss² *n* **1** knob or stud. **2** raised ornament. ♦ *vt* **3** emboss.

bo·sun [BOH-sən] *n* boatswain.

bot·a·ny [BOT-n-ee] *n* study of plants. **bo·tan·i·cal** [bə-TAN-ik-əl] *adj* **bot'a·nist** *n* **botanical garden** garden for exhibition and study of plants.

botch [boch] *vt* spoil by clumsiness.

both [bohth] *adj, pron* **1** the two. ♦ *adv, conj* **2** as well.

both·er [BOTH-ər] *vt* **1** pester. **2** perplex. ♦ *vi, n* **3** fuss, trouble.

bot·tle [BOT-l] *n* **1** vessel for holding liquid. **2** its contents. ♦ *vt* **-tled, -tling 3** put into bottle. **4** restrain. **bot'tler** *n* **bot'tle·neck** *n* **1** narrow outlet that impedes smooth flow of traffic or production of goods. **2** person who hampers flow of work, information, etc.

bot·tom [BOT-əm] *n* **1** lowest part of anything. **2** bed of sea, river, etc. **3** buttocks. ♦ *vt* **4** put bottom to. **5** base (upon). **6** get to bottom of. **bot'tom·less** *adj* **bottom line 1** last line of financial statement. **2** crucial or deciding factor.

———————| THESAURUS |———————

border *n* **1 = frontier**, borderline, boundary, line, march **2 = edge**, bounds, brink, limits, margin, rim, verge ♦ *v* **3 = edge**, bind, decorate, fringe, hem, rim, trim

bore¹ *v* **= drill**, burrow, gouge out, mine, penetrate, perforate, pierce, sink, tunnel

bore² *v* **1 = tire**, be tedious, fatigue, jade, pall on, send to sleep, wear out, weary ♦ *n* **2 = nuisance**, geek (*sl*), pain (*inf*) **3 = pain** (*inf*), yawn (*inf*)

bored *adj* **= fed up**, listless, tired, uninterested, wearied

boredom *n* **= tedium**, apathy, ennui, flatness, monotony, sameness, tediousness, weariness, world-weariness

boring *adj* **= uninteresting**, dull, flat, humdrum, mind-numbing, monotonous, tedious, tiresome

borrow *v* **1 = take on loan**, cadge, scrounge (*inf*), use temporarily **2 = steal**, adopt, copy, obtain, plagiarize, take, usurp

bosom *n* **1 = breast**, bust, chest ♦ *adj* **2 = intimate**, boon, cherished, close, confidential, dear, very dear

boss¹ *n Inf* **= head**, chief, director, employer, leader, manager, master, supervisor

boss² *n* **= stud**, knob, point, protuberance, tip

boss around *v Inf* **= domineer**, bully, dominate, oppress, order, push around (*sl*)

bossy *adj* **= domineering**, arrogant, authoritarian, autocratic, dictatorial, hectoring, high-handed, imperious, overbearing, tyrannical

botch *v* **1 = spoil**, blunder, bungle, foul up (*sl*), mar, mess up, screw up (*inf*) ♦ *n* **2 = mess**, blunder, bungle, failure

bother *v* **1 = trouble**, alarm, concern, disturb, harass, hassle (*inf*), inconvenience, pester, plague, worry ♦ *n* **2 = trouble**, difficulty, fuss, hassle (*inf*), inconvenience, irritation, nuisance, problem, worry

bottleneck *n* **= hold-up**, block, blockage, congestion, impediment, jam, obstacle, obstruction

bottle up *v* **= suppress**, check, contain, curb, keep back, restrict, shut in, trap

bottom *n* **1 = lowest part**, base, bed,

bot·u·lism [BOCH-ə-liz-əm] *n* kind of food poisoning.

bou·clé [boo-KLAY] *n* looped yarn giving knobby effect.

bou·doir [BOO-dwahr] *n* woman's bedroom, private sitting room.

bough [rhymes with **cow**] *n* branch of tree.

bought pt./pp. of BUY.

boul·der [BOHL-dər] *n* large weather-worn rounded stone.

boul·e·vard [BUUL-ə-vahrd] *n* broad street or promenade.

bounce [bowns] *v* **bounced, bounc·ing 1** (cause to) rebound (repeatedly) on impact, as a ball. ◆ *n* **2** rebounding. **3** quality in object causing this. **4** *inf* vitality, vigor. **bounc'er** *n* esp. one employed to evict undesirables (forcibly). **bounc'ing** *adj* vigorous, robust. **bounc'y** *adj* **bounc·i·er, bounc·i·est** lively.

bound¹ [bownd] *n, vt* limit. **bound'a·ry** *n, pl* **-ries bound'ed** *adj* **bound'less** *adj*

bound² *vi, n* spring, leap.

bound³ *adj* on a specified course, e.g. *homeward bound.*

bound⁴ 1 pt./pp. of BIND. ◆ *adj* **2** committed. **3** certain. **4** tied.

boun·ty [BOWN-tee] *n, pl* **-ties 1** liberality.

2 gift. **3** premium. **boun'te·ous** [-tee-əs], **boun'ti·ful** *adj* liberal, generous.

bou·quet [boo-KAY] *n* **1** bunch of flowers. **2** perfume of wine. **3** compliment.

bour·bon [BUR-bən] *n* whiskey made from corn, malt and rye.

bour·geois [buur-ZHWAH] *n, adj disparaging* **1** middle class. **2** smugly conventional (person). **bourgeoisie** [buur-zhwah-ZEE] *n* middle classes.

bout [bowt] *n* **1** contest, fight. **2** period of time spent doing something.

bou·tique [boo-TEEK] *n* small shop, esp. one selling clothes.

bo·vine [BOH-vīn] *adj* **1** of cattle. **2** oxlike. **3** stolid, dull.

bow¹ [boh] *n* **1** weapon for shooting arrows. **2** implement for playing violin, etc. **3** ornamental knot of ribbon, etc. **4** bend, bent line. ◆ *v* **5** bend. **bow'leg·ged** [-leg-id] *adj* having legs curved outward. **bow window** one with outward curve.

bow² [rhymes with **cow**] *vi* **1** bend body in respect, assent, etc. **2** submit. ◆ *vt* **3** bend downward. **4** cause to stoop. **5** crush. ◆ *n*

bow³ [rhymes with **cow**] *n* **1** fore end of ship. **2** prow. **3** rower nearest bow.

<hr>

THESAURUS

depths, floor, foot, foundation **2 = underside**, lower side, sole, underneath **3 = buttocks**, backside, behind (*inf*), posterior, rear, rump, seat, tush (*sl*) ◆ *adj* **4 = lowest**, last

bottomless *adj* **= unlimited**, boundless, deep, fathomless, immeasurable, inexhaustible, infinite, unfathomable

bounce *v* **1 = rebound**, bob, bound, jump, leap, recoil, ricochet, spring ◆ *n* **2** *Inf* **= life**, dynamism, energy, go (*inf*), liveliness, vigor, vivacity, zip (*inf*) **3 = springiness**, elasticity, give, recoil, resilience, spring

bound¹ *adj* **1 = tied**, cased, fastened, fixed, pinioned, secured, tied up **2 = certain**, destined, doomed, fated, sure **3 = obliged**, beholden, committed, compelled, constrained, duty-bound, forced, pledged, required

bound² *v* **= limit**, confine, demarcate, encircle, enclose, hem in, restrain, restrict, surround

bound³ *v, n* **= leap**, bob, bounce, gambol, hurdle, jump, skip, spring, vault

boundary *n* **= limits**, barrier, border, borderline, brink, edge, extremity, fringe,

frontier, margin

boundless *adj* **= unlimited**, endless, immense, incalculable, inexhaustible, infinite, unconfined, untold, vast

bounds¹ *pl n* **= boundary**, border, confine, edge, extremity, limit, rim, verge

bountiful *adj Literary* **1 = plentiful**, abundant, ample, bounteous, copious, exuberant, lavish, luxuriant, prolific **2 = generous**, liberal, magnanimous, open-handed, prodigal, unstinting

bounty *n Literary* **1 = generosity**, benevolence, charity, kindness, largesse *or* largess, liberality, philanthropy **2 = reward**, bonus, gift, present

bouquet *n* **1 = bunch of flowers**, buttonhole, corsage, garland, nosegay, posy, spray, wreath **2 = aroma**, fragrance, perfume, redolence, savor, scent

bourgeois *adj* **= middle-class**, conventional, hidebound, materialistic, traditional

bout *n* **1 = period**, fit, spell, stint, term, turn **2 = fight**, boxing match, competition, contest, encounter, engagement, match, set-to, struggle

bowd·ler·ize [BOHD-lə-rīz] *vt* **-ized, -iz·ing** expurgate, censor.

bow·el [BOW-əl] *n* (oft. pl) **1** part of intestine (esp. with reference to defecation). **2** inside of anything.

bow·er [BOW-ər] *n* shady retreat, arbor.

bowl¹ [bohl] *n* **1** round vessel, deep basin. **2** drinking cup. **3** hollow.

bowl² *n* **1** wooden ball. ♦ *pl* **2** outdoor game played with such balls. ♦ *v* **3** roll or throw ball in various ways. **bowl'ing** *n* indoor game, played usu. with large, heavy balls. **bowling green** place where bowls is played. **bowling alley** place where bowling is played.

box¹ [boks] *n* (wooden) container, usu. rectangular with lid. **1** its contents. **2** small enclosure. **3** any boxlike cubicle, shelter or receptacle. ♦ *vt* **4** put in box. **5** confine.

box² *v* **1** fight with fists, esp. with padded gloves on. ♦ *vt* **2** strike. ♦ *n* **3** blow. **box'er** *n* **1** one who boxes. **2** breed of pug-faced large dog.

boy [boi] *n* **1** male child. **2** young man. **boy'hood** [-huud] *n*

boy·cott [BOI-kot] *vt* refuse to deal with or participate in. ♦ *n*

Br *Chem.* bromine.

bra [brah] *n* brassiere.

brace [brays] *n* **1** tool for boring. **2** clasp, clamp. **3** pair, couple. **4** strut, support. ♦ *pl* **5** dental appliance worn to help straighten teeth. ♦ *vt* **braced, brac·ing 6** steady (oneself) as before a blow. **7** support, make

firm. **bracing** *adj* invigorating. **brace'let** *n* **1** ornament for the arm. ♦ *pl* **2** *sl* handcuffs.

brack·et [BRAK-it] *n* **1** support for shelf, etc. **2** group. ♦ *pl* **3** marks [ ], used to enclose words, etc. ♦ *vt* **4** enclose in brackets. **5** connect.

brack·ish [BRAK-ish] *adj* (of water) slightly salty.

bract [brakt] *n* small scalelike leaf

brad *n* small nail.

brag *vi* **bragged, brag·ging 1** boast. ♦ *n* **2** boastful talk. **brag'gart** [-ərt] *n*

Brah·man [BRAY-mən] *n* breed of beef cattle.

Brah·min [BRAH-min] *n* **1** member of priestly Hindu caste. **2** socially or intellectually aloof person.

braid [brayd] *vt* **1** interweave (hair, thread, etc.). **2** trim with braid. ♦ *n* **3** length of anything interwoven or plaited. **4** ornamental tape.

Braille [brayl] *n* system of printing for blind, with raised dots instead of letters.

brain [brayn] *n* **1** mass of nerve tissue in head. **2** intellect. ♦ *vt* **3** kill by hitting on head. **brain'less** *adj* **brain'y** *adj* **brain·i·er, brain·i·est brain'child** *n* invention. **brain'storm** *n* **1** sudden mental aberration. **2** sudden clever idea. ♦ *v* **3** practice, subject to, brainstorming. **brain'storm·ing** *n* technique for coming upon innovative ideas. **brain trust** group of experts without official status who advise government officials. **brain'wash** *vt* change, distort a

bow¹ *v* **1 = bend,** bob, droop, genuflect, nod, stoop **2 = give in,** acquiesce, comply, concede, defer, kowtow, relent, submit, succumb, surrender, yield ♦ *n* **3 = bend,** bob, genuflexion, kowtow, nod, obeisance

bow² *n Nautical* **= prow,** beak, fore, head, stem

bowels *pl n* **1 = guts,** entrails, innards (*inf*), insides (*inf*), intestines, viscera, vitals **2 = depths,** belly, core, deep, hold, inside, interior

bowl¹ *n* **= basin,** dish, vessel

bowl² *v* **= throw,** fling, hurl, pitch

box¹ *n* **1 = container,** carton, case, casket, chest, pack, package, receptacle, trunk ♦ *v* **2 = pack,** package, wrap

box² *v* **= fight,** exchange blows, spar

boxer *n* **= fighter,** prizefighter, pugilist, sparring partner

boy *n* **= lad,** fellow, junior, schoolboy,

stripling, youngster, youth

boycott *v* **= embargo,** ban, bar, black, exclude, outlaw, prohibit, refuse, reject

boyfriend *n* **= sweetheart,** admirer, beau, date, lover, man, suitor

boyish *adj* **= youthful,** adolescent, childish, immature, juvenile, puerile, young

brace *n* **1 = support,** bolster, bracket, buttress, prop, reinforcement, stay, strut, truss ♦ *v* **2 = support,** bolster, buttress, fortify, reinforce, steady, strengthen

bracing *adj* **= refreshing,** brisk, crisp, exhilarating, fresh, invigorating, stimulating

brag *v* **= boast,** blow one's own trumpet, bluster, crow, swagger, talk big (*sl*), vaunt

braggart *n* **= boaster,** bigmouth (*sl*), bragger, show-off (*inf*)

braid *v* **= interweave,** entwine, interlace, intertwine, lace, plait, twine, weave person's ideas or beliefs. **brain wave** electrical impulse in brain.

braise [brayz] *vt* **braised, brais·ing** cook slowly in covered pan.

brake [brayk] *n* **1** instrument for retarding motion of wheel on vehicle. ◆ *vt* **braked, brak·ing 2** apply brake to.

bram·ble [BRAM-bəl] *n* prickly shrub. **bram'bly** *adj* **-bli·er, -bli·est**

bran *n* sifted husks of cereal grain.

branch *n* **1** limb of tree. **2** offshoot or subsidiary part of something larger or primary. ◆ *vi* **3** bear branches. **4** diverge. **5** spread. **branched branch'less** *adj*

brand *n* **1** trademark. **2** class of goods. **3** particular kind, sort. **4** mark made by hot iron. **5** burning piece of wood. **6** sword. **7** mark of disgrace. ◆ *vt* **8** burn with iron. **9** mark. **10** stigmatize. **brand-new** *adj* absolutely new.

bran·dish *vt* **1** flourish, wave (weapon, etc.).

bran·dy [BRAN-dee] *n, pl* **-dies 1** alcoholic liquor distilled from wine or fruit juice. ◆ *vt* **-died, -dy·ing 2** flavor or preserve with brandy.

brash *adj* **-er, -est** bold, impudent.

brass *n* **1** alloy of copper and zinc. **2** group of brass wind instruments forming part of orchestra or band. **3** *inf* (military) officers. ◆ *adj* **brass'y** *adj* **brass·i·er, brass·i·est 1** showy. **2** harsh. **brass'i·ness** *n*

bras·siere [brə-ZEER] *n* woman's undergarment, supporting breasts, bra.

brat *n* contemptuous term for a child.

bra·va·do [brə-VAH-doh] *n* showy display of boldness.

brave [brayv] *adj* **brav·er, brav·est 1** bold, courageous. **2** splendid, fine. ◆ *n* **3** N Amer. Indian warrior. ◆ *vt* **braved, brav·ing 4** defy, meet boldly. **brav'er·y** *n, pl* **-er·ies**

bra·vo [BRAH-voh] *interj* well done!

brawl *vi* fight noisily. ◆ *n* **brawl'er** *n*

brawn *n* **1** muscle. **2** strength. **brawn'y** *adj* **brawn·i·er, brawn·i·est** muscular.

bray *n* **1** donkey's cry. ◆ *vi* **2** utter this. **3** give out harsh or loud sounds.

braze [brayz] *vt* **brazed, braz·ing** solder with alloy of brass or zinc.

bra·zen [BRAY-zən] *adj* **1** of, like brass. **2** impudent, shameless. ◆ *vt* **3** (usu. with *out* or *through*) face, carry through with impudence. **bra'zen·ness** *n* effrontery.

bra·zier [BRAY-zhər] *n* **1** pan for burning charcoal or coals. **2** brassworker.

breach [breech] *n* **1** break, opening. **2** breaking of rule, duty, etc. **3** quarrel. ◆ *vt* **4** make a gap in. **5** break (rule, etc.).

THESAURUS

brainless *adj* = **stupid**, foolish, idiotic, inane, mindless, senseless, thoughtless, witless

brains *pl n* = **intelligence**, intellect, sense, understanding

brainy *adj Inf* = **intelligent**, bright, brilliant, clever, smart

brake *n* **1** = **control**, check, constraint, curb, rein, restraint ◆ *v* **2** = **slow**, check, decelerate, halt, moderate, reduce speed, slacken, stop

branch *n* **1** = **bough**, arm, limb, offshoot, shoot, spray, sprig **2** = **division**, chapter, department, office, part, section, subdivision, subsection, wing

brand *n* **1** = **label**, emblem, hallmark, logo, mark, marker, sign, stamp, symbol, trademark **2** = **kind**, cast, class, grade, make, quality, sort, species, type, variety ◆ *v* **3** = **mark**, burn, burn in, label, scar, stamp **4** = **stigmatize**, censure, denounce, discredit, disgrace, expose, mark

brandish *v* = **wave**, display, exhibit, flaunt, flourish, parade, raise, shake, swing, wield

brash *adj* = **bold**, brazen, cocky, impertinent, impudent, insolent, pushy (*inf*), rude

bravado *n* = **swagger**, bluster, boastfulness, boasting, bombast, swashbuckling, vaunting

brave *adj* **1** = **courageous**, bold, daring, fearless, heroic, intrepid, plucky, resolute, valiant ◆ *v* **2** = **confront**, defy, endure, face, stand up to, suffer, tackle, withstand

bravery *n* = **courage**, boldness, daring, fearlessness, fortitude, heroism, intrepidity, mettle, pluck, spirit, valor

brawl *n* **1** = **fight**, affray (*Law*), altercation, clash, dispute, fracas, fray, melee *or* mêlée, rumpus, scuffle, skirmish ◆ *v* **2** = **fight**, scrap (*inf*), scuffle, tussle, wrestle

brawn *n* = **muscle**, beef (*inf*), might, muscles, power, strength, vigor

brawny *adj* = **muscular**, beefy (*inf*), hefty (*inf*), lusty, powerful, strapping, strong, sturdy, well-built

brazen *adj* = **bold**, audacious, barefaced, brash, defiant, impudent, insolent, shameless, unabashed, unashamed

breach *n* **1** = **nonobservance**,

bread [bred] *n* **1** food made of flour or meal baked. **2** food. **3** *sl* money. **bread'fruit** *n* breadlike fruit found in Pacific islands. **bread'win·ner** *n* person who works to support family.

breadth [bredth] *n* **1** extent across, width. **2** largeness of view, mind.

break [brayk] *v* **broke, bro·ken, break·ing** ◆ *vt* **1** part by force. **2** shatter. **3** burst, destroy. **4** fail to observe. **5** disclose. **6** interrupt. **7** surpass. **8** make bankrupt. **9** relax. **10** mitigate. **11** accustom (horse) to being ridden. **12** decipher (code). ◆ *vi* **13** become broken, shattered, divided. **14** open, appear. **15** come suddenly. **16** crack, give way. **17** part, fall out. **18** (of voice) change in tone, pitch. ◆ *n* **19** fracture. **20** gap. **21** opening. **22** separation. **23** interruption. **24** respite. **25** interval. **26** *inf* opportunity. **27** dawn. **28** *Pool* opening shot in a game. **29** *Boxing* separation after a clinch. **break'a·ble** *adj* **break'age** *n* **break'er** *n* **1** person or device that breaks, for example an electrical circuit. **2** wave beating on rocks or shore. **break dance** *n* acrobatic dance style associated with hip-hop. ◆ *vi* **break'down** *n* **1** collapse, as nervous breakdown. **2** failure to function effectively. **3** analysis. **break·fast** [BREK-fəst] *n* first meal of the day. **break'-in** *n* illegal entering of building, esp. by thieves. **break'neck** *adj* dangerous. **break'through** *n* important advance. **break'wa·ter** *n* barrier to break force of waves.

breast [brest] *n* **1** human chest. **2** milk-secreting gland on chest of human female. **3** seat of the affections. **4** any protuberance. ◆ *vt* **5** face, oppose. **6** reach summit of. **breast'stroke** *n* stroke in swimming.

breath [breth] *n* **1** air used by lungs. **2** life. **3** respiration. **4** slight breeze. **breathe** [breeth] *v* **breathed, breath·ing** ◆ *vi* **1** inhale and exhale air from lungs. **2** live. **3** pause, rest. ◆ *vt* **4** inhale and exhale. **5** utter softly, whisper. **breath'er** [-thər] *n* short rest. **breath·less** [BRETH-lis] *adj* **breath'tak·ing** *adj* causing awe or excitement.

——————| THESAURUS |——————

contravention, infraction, infringement, noncompliance, transgression, trespass, violation **2 = crack**, cleft, fissure, gap, opening, rift, rupture, split

bread *n* **1 = food**, fare, nourishment, sustenance **2** *Sl* **= money**, cash, dough (*sl*)

breadth *n* **1 = width**, broadness, latitude, span, spread, wideness **2 = extent**, compass, expanse, range, scale, scope

break *v* **1 = separate**, burst, crack, destroy, disintegrate, fracture, fragment, shatter, smash, snap, split, tear **2 = disobey**, breach, contravene, disregard, infringe, renege on, transgress, violate **3 = reveal**, announce, disclose, divulge, impart, inform, let out, make public, proclaim, tell **4 = stop**, abandon, cut, discontinue, give up, interrupt, pause, rest, suspend **5 = weaken**, demoralize, dispirit, subdue, tame, undermine **6** *Of a record, etc.* **= beat**, better, exceed, excel, go beyond, outdo, outstrip, surpass, top ◆ *n* **7 = division**, crack, fissure, fracture, gap, hole, opening, split, tear **8 = rest**, breather (*inf*), hiatus, interlude, intermission, interruption, interval, let-up (*inf*), lull, pause, respite **9** *Inf* **= stroke of luck**, advantage, chance, fortune, opening, opportunity

breakable *adj* **= fragile**, brittle, crumbly, delicate, flimsy, frail, frangible, friable

breakdown *n* **= collapse**, disintegration, disruption, failure, mishap, stoppage

break down *v* **1 = collapse**, come unstuck, fail, seize up, stop, stop working **2 = be overcome**, crack up (*inf*), go to pieces

break-in *n* **= burglary**, breaking and entering, robbery

break off *v* **1 = detach**, divide, part, pull off, separate, sever, snap off, splinter **2 = stop**, cease, desist, discontinue, end, finish, halt, pull the plug on, suspend, terminate

break out *v* **= begin**, appear, arise, commence, emerge, happen, occur, set in, spring up, start

breakthrough *n* **= development**, advance, discovery, find, invention, leap, progress, quantum leap, step forward

break up *v* **1 = separate**, dissolve, divide, divorce, part, scatter, sever, split **2 = stop**, adjourn, disband, dismantle, end, suspend, terminate

breast *n* **= bosom**, bust, chest, front, teat, udder

breath *n* **= respiration**, breathing, exhalation, gasp, gulp, inhalation, pant, wheeze

Breath·a·lyz·er [BRETH-ə-lī-zər] *n* ® device that estimates amount of alcohol in breath.

bred *pt./pp.* of BREED.

breech *n* **1** buttocks. **2** hinder part of anything, esp. gun. **breech'load·er** *n*

breed *v* **bred**, **breed·ing** ♦ *vt* **1** generate, bring forth, give rise to. **2** rear. ♦ *vi* **3** be produced. **4** be with young. ♦ *n* **5** offspring produced. **6** race, kind. **breeding** *n* **1** producing. **2** manners. **3** ancestry. **breeder reactor** nuclear reactor producing more fissionable material than it consumes.

breeze [breez] *n* gentle wind. **breez'i·ly** *adv* **breez'y** *adj* **breez·i·er**, **breez·i·est 1** windy. **2** jovial, lively. **3** casual. **in a breeze** easily.

breth·ren [BRETH-rən] *obs* pl. of BROTHER.

breve [breev] *n* long musical note.

bre·vi·ar·y [BREE-vee-er-ee] *n, pl* **-ar·ies** book of daily prayers, hymns, etc.

brev·i·ty [BREV-i-tee] *n* **1** conciseness of expression. **2** short duration.

brew [broo] *vt* **1** prepare liquor, as beer from malt, etc. **2** make drink, as tea, by infusion. **3** plot, contrive. ♦ *vi* **4** be in preparation. ♦ *n* **5** beverage produced by brewing. **brew'er** *n* **brew'er·y** *n*

bri·ar¹, bri·er [BRĪ-ər] *n* prickly shrub, esp. the wild rose.

briar², brier *n* European shrub. **briar pipe** pipe made from its root.

bribe [brīb] *n* **1** anything offered or given to someone to gain favor, influence. ♦ *vt* **bribed**, **brib·ing 2** influence by bribe. **brib'er·y** *n, pl* **-er·ies**

bric-a-brac [BRIK-ə-brak] *n* miscellaneous small objects, used for ornament.

brick [brik] *n* **1** oblong mass of hardened clay used in building. **2** good-hearted person. ♦ *vt* **3** build, block, etc. with bricks.

bride [brīd] *n* woman about to be, or just, married. **brid'al** *adj* of, relating to, a bride or wedding. **bride'groom** *n* man about to be, or just, married. **brides'maid** *n*

bridge¹ [brij] *n* **1** structure for crossing river, etc. **2** something joining or supporting other parts. **3** raised narrow platform on ship. **4** upper part of nose. **5** part of violin supporting strings. ♦ *vt* **bridged**, **bridg·ing 6** make bridge over,

━━━━━━━━━━━━━━━ THESAURUS ━━━━━━━━━━━━━━━

breathe *v* **1 = inhale and exhale**, draw in, gasp, gulp, pant, puff, respire, wheeze **2 = whisper**, murmur, sigh

breather *n Inf* **= rest**, break, breathing space, halt, pause, recess, respite

breathless *adj* **1 = out of breath**, gasping, gulping, panting, short-winded, spent, wheezing **2 = excited**, eager, on tenterhooks, open-mouthed, wired (*sl*), with bated breath

breathtaking *adj* **= amazing**, astonishing, awe-inspiring, cool (*inf*), exciting, impressive, magnificent, phat (*sl*), sensational, stunning (*inf*), thrilling

breed *v* **1 = reproduce**, bear, bring forth, hatch, multiply, procreate, produce, propagate **2 = bring up**, cultivate, develop, nourish, nurture, raise, rear **3 = produce**, arouse, bring about, cause, create, generate, give rise to, stir up ♦ *n* **4 = variety**, pedigree, race, species, stock, strain, type **5 = kind**, brand, sort, stamp, type, variety

breeding *n* **1 = upbringing**, ancestry, cultivation, development, lineage, nurture, raising, rearing, reproduction, training **2 = refinement**, conduct, courtesy, cultivation, culture, polish, sophistication, urbanity

breeze *n* **1 = light wind**, air, breath of wind, current of air, draft, gust, waft, zephyr ♦ *v* **2 = move briskly**, flit, glide, hurry, pass, sail, sweep

breezy *adj* **1 = windy**, airy, blowy, blustery, fresh, gusty, squally **2 = carefree**, blithe, casual, easy-going, free and easy, jaunty, light-hearted, lively, sprightly

brevity *n* **1 = shortness**, briefness, impermanence, transience, transitoriness **2 = conciseness**, crispness, curtness, economy, pithiness, succinctness, terseness

brew *v* **1 = make** (*beer*), boil, ferment, infuse (*tea*), soak, steep, stew **2 = develop**, foment, form, gather, start, stir up ♦ *n* **3 = drink**, beverage, blend, concoction, infusion, liquor, mixture, preparation

bribe *v* **1 = buy off**, corrupt, grease the palm *or* hand of (*sl*), pay off (*inf*), reward, suborn ♦ *n* **2 = inducement**, allurement, backhander (*sl*), enticement, kickback, pay-off (*inf*), sweetener (*sl*)

bribery *n* **= buying off**, corruption, inducement, palm-greasing (*sl*), payola (*inf*)

bric-a-brac *n* **= knick-knacks**, baubles, curios, ornaments, trinkets

bridal *adj* **= matrimonial**, conjugal, connubial, marital, marriage, nuptial, span.

bridge² *n* card game.

bri·dle [BRĪD-l] *n* **1** headgear of horse harness. **2** curb. ◆ *v* **-dled, -dling 3** *vt* **4** put on bridle. **5** restrain. ◆ *vi* **6** show resentment. **bridle path** path suitable for riding horses.

brief [breef] *adj* **-er, -est 1** short in duration. **2** concise. **3** scanty. ◆ *n* **4** summary of case for judge or lawyer's use. **5** papal letter. **6** instructions. ◆ *pl* **7** underpants. **8** panties. ◆ *vt* **9** give instructions, information. **brief'ly** *adv* **brief'case** *n* hand case for carrying papers. **brief·ing book** one prepared to provide (participant) information on meeting, etc.

brier see BRIAR.

brig *n* **1** two-masted, square-rigged ship. **2** *inf* ship's jail, guardhouse.

bri·gade [bri-GAYD] *n* **1** subdivision of army. **2** organized band. **brig·a·dier'**

gen·er·al [-ə-DEER] one-star general.

brig·an·tine [BRIG-ən-teen] *n* two-masted vessel, with square-rigged foremast and fore-and-aft mainmast.

bright [brīt] *adj* **-er, -est 1** shining. **2** full of light. **3** cheerful. **4** clever. **bright'en** *v*

bril·liant [BRIL-yənt] *adj* **1** shining. **2** sparkling. **3** splendid. **4** very intelligent or clever. **5** distinguished. **bril'liance** *n*

brim *n* margin, edge, esp. of river, cup, hat. **brim·ful** *adj* **brim'less** *adj* **brim'ming** *adj* **1** to the brim. **2** until it can hold no more.

brim·stone [BRIM-stohn] *n* sulfur.

brin·dled [BRIN-dld] *adj* brownish with streaks of other color. **brin'dle** *n* **1** this color. **2** a brindled animal.

brine [brīn] *n* salt water. **brin'y** *adj* **brin·i·er, brin·i·est 1** very salty. ◆ *n* *inf* **2** the sea.

bring *vt* **brought, bring·ing 1** fetch. **2** carry with one. **3** cause to come.

brink [bringk] *n* **1** edge of steep place. **2**

wedding

bridge *n* **1** = **arch**, flyover, overpass, span, viaduct ◆ *v* **2** = **connect**, join, link, span

bridle *n* **1** = **curb**, check, control, rein, restraint ◆ *v* **2** = **get angry**, be indignant, bristle, draw (oneself) up, get one's back up, raise one's hackles, rear up

brief *adj* **1** = **short**, ephemeral, fleeting, momentary, quick, short-lived, swift, transitory ◆ *n* **2** = **summary**, abridgment, abstract, digest, epitome, outline, précis, sketch, synopsis ◆ *v* **3** = **inform**, advise, explain, fill in (*inf*), instruct, keep posted, prepare, prime, put (someone) in the picture (*inf*)

briefing *n* = **instructions**, conference, directions, guidance, information, preparation, priming, rundown

briefly *adv* = **shortly**, concisely, hastily, hurriedly, in a nutshell, in brief, momentarily, quickly

brigade *n* = **group**, band, company, corps, force, organization, outfit, squad, team, troop, unit

bright *adj* **1** = **shining**, brilliant, dazzling, gleaming, glowing, luminous, lustrous, radiant, shimmering, vivid **2** = **intelligent**, astute, aware, clever, inventive, quick-witted, sharp, smart, wide-awake **3** = **sunny**, clear, cloudless, fair, limpid, lucid, pleasant, translucent, transparent, unclouded

brighten *v* = **make brighter**, gleam, glow,

illuminate, lighten, light up, shine

brightness *n* **1** = **shine**, brilliance, glare, incandescence, intensity, light, luminosity, radiance, vividness **2** = **intelligence**, acuity, cleverness, quickness, sharpness, smartness

brilliance *n* **1** = **brightness**, dazzle, intensity, luminosity, luster, radiance, sparkle, vividness **2** = **talent**, cleverness, distinction, excellence, genius, greatness, inventiveness, wisdom **3** = **splendor**, éclat, glamour, grandeur, illustriousness, magnificence

brilliant *adj* **1** = **shining**, bright, dazzling, glittering, intense, luminous, radiant, sparkling, vivid **2** = **splendid**, celebrated, famous, glorious, illustrious, magnificent, notable, outstanding, superb **3** = **intelligent**, clever, expert, gifted, intellectual, inventive, masterly, penetrating, profound, talented

brim *n* **1** = **rim**, border, brink, edge, lip, margin, skirt, verge ◆ *v* **2** = **be full**, fill, fill up, hold no more, overflow, run over, spill, well over

bring *v* **1** = **take**, bear, carry, conduct, convey, deliver, escort, fetch, guide, lead, transfer, transport **2** = **cause**, contribute to, create, effect, inflict, occasion, produce, result in, wreak

bring about *v* = **cause**, accomplish, achieve, create, effect, generate, give rise to, make happen, produce

bring off *v* = **accomplish**, achieve, carry

verge, margin. **brink'man·ship** n
technique of attempting to gain
advantage through maneuvering
dangerous situation to limit of tolerance.
bri·quette [bri-KET] n block of compressed
coal dust.
brisk adj -er, -est active, vigorous. **brisk'ly**
adv **brisk'ness** n
bris·ket [BRIS-kit] n cut of meat from breast
of animal.
bris·tle [BRIS-əl] n 1 short stiff hair. ♦ vi
-tled, -tling 2 stand erect. 3 show temper.
bris'tly adj -tli·er, -tli·est
brit·tle [BRIT-l] adj 1 easily broken, fragile. 2
curt, irritable. **brit'tle·ness** n
broach [brohch] vt 1 pierce (cask). 2 open,
begin.
broad [brawd] adj -er, -est 1 wide,
spacious, open. 2 plain, obvious. 3 coarse.
4 general. 5 tolerant. 6 (of pronunciation)
dialectal. **broad'en** vt **broad'ly** adv

broad'ness n **broad'cast** vt -cast or
-cast·ed, -cast·ing 1 transmit by radio or
television. 2 make widely known. 3 scatter,
as seed. ♦ n 4 radio or TV program.
broad'cast·er n **broad'loom** n, adj (carpet)
woven on wide loom. **broad'-mind·ed**
[-MĪN-did] adj 1 tolerant. 2 generous.
broad'side n 1 discharge of all guns on
one side. 2 strong (verbal) attack.
bro·cade [broh-KAYD] n rich woven fabric
with raised design.
broc·co·li [BROK-ə-lee] n type of cabbage.
bro·chette [broh-SHET] n 1 small spit. 2
skewer.
bro·chure [broh-SHUUR] n pamphlet,
booklet.
brogue [brohg] n 1 stout shoe. 2 dialect,
esp. Irish accent.
broil vt 1 cook over hot coals. 2 grill. ♦ vi 3
be heated.
broke 1 see BREAK. ♦ adj 2 inf penniless.

——————————— THESAURUS ———————————

off, execute, perform, pull off, succeed
bring up v 1 = **rear**, breed, develop,
educate, form, nurture, raise, support,
teach, train 2 = **mention**, allude to,
broach, introduce, move, propose, put
forward, raise
brink n = **edge**, border, boundary, brim,
fringe, frontier, limit, lip, margin, rim, skirt,
threshold, verge
brisk adj = **lively**, active, bustling, busy,
energetic, quick, sprightly, spry, vigorous
briskly adv = **quickly**, actively, apace,
efficiently, energetically, promptly, rapidly,
readily, smartly
bristle n 1 = **hair**, barb, prickle, spine,
stubble, thorn, whisker ♦ v 2 = **stand up**,
rise, stand on end 3 = **be angry**, bridle,
flare up, rage, see red, seethe
bristly adj = **hairy**, prickly, rough, stubbly
brittle adj = **fragile**, breakable, crisp,
crumbling, crumbly, delicate, frail,
frangible, friable
broach v 1 = **bring up**, introduce, mention,
open up, propose, raise the subject, speak
of, suggest, talk of, touch on 2 = **open**,
crack, draw off, pierce, puncture, start,
tap, uncork
broad adj 1 = **wide**, ample, expansive,
extensive, generous, large, roomy,
spacious, vast, voluminous, widespread 2 =
general, all-embracing, comprehensive,
encyclopedic, inclusive, sweeping, wide,
wide-ranging

broadcast n 1 = **transmission**, program,
show, telecast ♦ v 2 = **transmit**, air, beam,
cable, put on the air, radio, relay, show,
televise 3 = **make public**, advertise,
announce, circulate, proclaim, publish,
report, spread
broaden v = **expand**, develop, enlarge,
extend, increase, spread, stretch,
supplement, swell, widen
broad-minded adj = **tolerant**,
free-thinking, indulgent, liberal,
open-minded, permissive, unbiased,
unbigoted, unprejudiced
broadside n = **attack**, assault, battering,
bombardment, censure, criticism,
denunciation, diatribe
brochure n = **booklet**, advertisement,
circular, folder, handbill, hand-out, leaflet,
mailshot, pamphlet
broke adj Inf = **penniless**, bankrupt, bust
(inf), down and out, down on one's luck
(inf), impoverished, insolvent, in the red,
ruined, short
broken adj 1 = **smashed**, burst, fractured,
fragmented, ruptured, separated, severed,
shattered 2 = **interrupted**, discontinuous,
erratic, fragmentary, incomplete,
intermittent, spasmodic 3 = **not working**,
defective, imperfect, kaput (inf), on the
blink (sl), out of order 4 = **imperfect**,
disjointed, halting, hesitating, stammering
brokenhearted adj = **heartbroken**,
desolate, devastated, disconsolate,

bro·ker [BROH-kər] n **1** one employed to buy and sell for others. **2** dealer. **bro'ker·age** n **1** business of broker. **2** payment to broker.

bro·mide [BROH-mīd] n **1** chemical compound used in medicine and photography. **2** hackneyed, commonplace statement. **bro·mid'ic** [-MID-ik] adj lacking in originality

bro·mine [BROH-meen] n liquid element used in production of chemicals.

bron·chus [BRONG-kəs] n, pl **-chi** [-kee] branch of windpipe. **bron'chi·al** adj **bron·chi'tis** [-KĪ-tis] n inflammation of bronchi.

bron·co [BRONG-koh] n, pl **-cos** N Amer. half-tamed horse.

bron·to·sau·rus [bron-tə-SOR-əs] n very large herbivorous dinosaur.

bronze [bronz] n **1** alloy of copper and tin. ♦ adj **2** made of, or colored like, bronze. ♦ vt **3** bronzed, bronz·ing **3** give appearance of bronze to.

brooch [brohch] n ornamental pin or fastening.

brood n **1** family of young, esp. of birds. **2** tribe, race. ♦ v **3** slt, as hen on eggs. **4** meditate, fret over. **brood'y** adj **brood·i·er, brood·i·est** moody, sullen.

brook[1] [bruuk] n small stream.

brook[2] vt put up with, endure, tolerate.

broom n **1** brush for sweeping. **2** yellow-flowered shrub. **broom'stick** n handle of broom.

broth [brawth] n **1** thick soup. **2** stock.

broth·el [BROTH-əl] n house of prostitution.

broth·er [BRUTH-ər] n **1** son of same parents. **2** one closely united with another. **broth'er·hood** [-huud] n **1** relationship. **2** fraternity, company. **broth'er·ly** adj **broth'er-in-law** n **1** brother of husband or wife. **2** husband of sister.

brought pt./pp. of BRING.

brow n **1** ridge over eyes. **2** forehead. **3** eyebrow. **4** edge of hill. **brow'beat** vt **-beat, -beat·en, -beat·ing** bully.

brown adj **-er, -est 1** of dark color inclining to red or yellow. ♦ n **2** the color. ♦ v **3** make, become brown. **browned off** sl **1** angry. **2** fed up.

Brown·ie [BROW-nee] n **1** Girl Scout 7 to 10 years old. **2** (b-) **3** small, nutted square of chocolate cake. **Brownie point** notional mark to one's credit for being seen to do the right thing.

browse [browz] vi **browsed, brows·ing 1** look through (book, articles for sale, etc.) in a casual manner. **2** feed on shoots and leaves. **3** Computers read hypertext, esp. on the Internet. **brows'er** n Computers. software package that enables a user to read hypertext, esp. on the Internet.

bruise [brooz] vt **bruised, bruis·ing 1** injure without breaking skin. ♦ n **2** contusion, discoloration caused by blow. **bruis'er** n inf strong, tough person.

brunch n inf breakfast and lunch

——————| THESAURUS |——————

grief-stricken, inconsolable, miserable, sorrowful, wretched

broker n = **dealer**, agent, factor, go-between, intermediary, middleman, negotiator

bronze adj = **reddish-brown**, brownish, chestnut, copper, rust, tan

brood n **1** = **offspring**, clutch, family, issue, litter, progeny ♦ v **2** = **think upon**, agonize, dwell upon, mope, mull over, muse, ponder, ruminate

brook[1] n = **stream**, beck, rill, rivulet, watercourse

brother n **1** = **sibling**, blood brother, kin, kinsman, relation, relative **2** = **monk**, cleric, friar

brotherhood n **1** = **fellowship**, brotherliness, camaraderie, companionship, comradeship, friendliness, kinship **2** = **association**, alliance,

community, fraternity, guild, league, order, society, union

brotherly adj = **kind**, affectionate, altruistic, amicable, benevolent, cordial, fraternal, friendly, neighborly, philanthropic, sympathetic

browbeat v = **bully**, badger, coerce, dragoon, hector, intimidate, ride roughshod over, threaten, tyrannize

brown adj **1** = **brunette**, auburn, bay, bronze, chestnut, chocolate, coffee, dun, hazel, sunburned, tan, tanned, tawny, umber ♦ v **2** = **fry**, cook, grill, sauté, seal, sear

browse v **1** = **skim**, dip into, examine cursorily, flip through, glance at, leaf through, look round, look through, peruse, scan, survey **2** = **graze**, chow down (sl), eat, feed, nibble

bruise v **1** = **discolor**, damage, injure, mar,

combined.

bru·nette [broo-NET] n 1 person of dark complexion and hair. ♦ adj 2 dark brown.

brunt n 1 shock of attack, chief stress. 2 first blow.

brush n 1 device with bristles, hairs, wires, etc. used for cleaning, painting, etc. 2 act, instance of brushing. 3 brief contact. 4 skirmish, fight. 5 bushy tail, bushy haircut. 6 dense growth of bushes, shrubs, etc. 7 (carbon) device taking electric current from moving to stationary parts of generator, etc. ♦ v 8 apply, remove, clean, with brush. 9 touch, discuss lightly. **brush'off** n inf 1 dismissal. 2 refusal. 3 snub. 4 rebuff. **brush'fire** n fire in area of bushes, shrubs, etc. **brush'wood** n 1 broken-off branches. 2 land covered with scrub.

brusque [brusk] adj rough in manner, curt, blunt.

brute [broot] n 1 any animal except man. 2 crude, vicious person. ♦ adj 3 animal. 4 sensual, stupid. 5 physical. **bru'tal** adj **bru·tal'i·ty** n **bru'tal·ize** vt -ized, -iz·ing **brut'ish** adj bestial, gross.

Btu British thermal unit.

bub·ble [BUB-əl] n 1 hollow globe of liquid, blown out with air. 2 something insubstantial, not serious. 3 transparent dome. ♦ vi -bled, -bling 4 rise in bubbles. 5 make gurgling sound.

bu·bon·ic plague [byoo-BON-ik playg] n acute infectious disease characterized by swellings and fever.

buc·ca·neer [buk-ə-NEER] n 1 pirate. 2 unscrupulous adventurer. **buc·ca·neer'ing** n

buck [buk] n 1 male deer, or other male animal. 2 act of bucking. 3 sl dollar. ♦ v 4 of horse, attempt to throw rider by jumping upward, etc. 5 resist, oppose (something). **buck'shot** n lead shot in shotgun shell. **buck-teeth** pl n projecting upper teeth. **pass the buck** shift blame or responsibility to another person.

buck·et [BUK-it] n 1 vessel, round with arched handle, for water, etc. 2 anything resembling this. **buck'et·ful** n, pl -fuls **bucket seat** seat with back shaped to occupier's figure.

buck·le [BUK-əl] n 1 metal clasp for fastening belt, strap, etc. ♦ v -led, -ling ♦ vt 2 fasten with buckle. ♦ vi 3 warp, bend. **buckle down** start work.

bu·col·ic [byoo-KOL-ik] adj rustic.

bud n 1 shoot or sprout on plant containing unopened leaf, flower, etc. ♦ v bud·ded, bud·ding ♦ vi 2 begin to grow. ♦ vt 3 to graft.

THESAURUS

mark, pound ♦ n 2 = **discoloration**, black mark, blemish, contusion, injury, mark, swelling

brunt n = **full force**, burden, force, impact, pressure, shock, strain, stress, thrust, violence

brush[1] n 1 = **broom**, besom, sweeper 2 = **encounter**, clash, conflict, confrontation, skirmish, tussle ♦ v 3 = **clean**, buff, paint, polish, sweep, wash 4 = **touch**, flick, glance, graze, kiss, scrape, stroke, sweep

brush[2] n = **shrubs**, brushwood, bushes, copse, scrub, thicket, undergrowth

brush off v Sl = **ignore**, blow off (sl), disdain, dismiss, disregard, reject, repudiate, scorn, snub, spurn

brush up v = **revise**, bone up (inf), cram, go over, polish up, read up, refresh one's memory, relearn, study

brusque adj = **curt**, abrupt, discourteous, gruff, impolite, sharp, short, surly, terse

brutal adj 1 = **cruel**, bloodthirsty, heartless, inhuman, ruthless, savage, uncivilized, vicious 2 = **harsh**, callous, gruff, impolite,

insensitive, rough, rude, severe

brutality n = **cruelty**, atrocity, barbarism, bloodthirstiness, ferocity, inhumanity, ruthlessness, savagery, viciousness

brute n 1 = **savage**, barbarian, beast, devil, fiend, monster, sadist, swine 2 = **animal**, beast, creature, wild animal ♦ adj 3 = **mindless**, bodily, carnal, fleshly, instinctive, physical, senseless, unthinking

bubble n 1 = **air ball**, bead, blister, blob, drop, droplet, globule ♦ v 2 = **foam**, boil, effervesce, fizz, froth, percolate, seethe, sparkle 3 = **gurgle**, babble, burble, murmur, ripple, trickle

bubbly adj 1 = **lively**, animated, bouncy, elated, excited, happy, merry, sparky, wired (sl) 2 = **frothy**, carbonated, effervescent, fizzy, foamy, sparkling

buccaneer n = **pirate**, corsair, freebooter, privateer, sea-rover

buckle n 1 = **fastener**, catch, clasp, clip, hasp ♦ v 2 = **fasten**, clasp, close, hook, secure 3 = **distort**, bend, bulge, cave in, collapse, contort, crumple, fold, twist,

Bud·dhism [BOO-diz-əm] n religion founded in India by Buddha. **Bud'dhist** adj, n

bud·dy [BUD-ee] n inf pl **-dies** pal, chum.

budge [buj] vi **budged, budg·ing** move, stir.

budg·et [BUJ-it] n 1 annual financial statement. 2 plan of systematic spending. ♦ vi **0** prepare financial statement. 4 plan financially.

buff[1] n 1 light yellow color. 2 bare skin. 3 polishing pad. ♦ vt 4 polish.

buff[2] n inf expert on some subject.

buf·fa·lo [BUF-ə-loh] n, pl **-los, -loes** any of several species of large oxen.

buff·er [BUF-ər] n 1 contrivance to lessen shock of concussion. 2 person, country that shields another against annoyance, etc.

buf·fet[1] [BUF-it] n 1 blow, slap. 2 misfortune. ♦ vt 3 strike with blows. 4 contend against. **buf'fet·ing** n

buf·fet[2] [bə-FAY] n 1 refreshment bar. 2 meal at which guests serve themselves. 3 sideboard.

buf·foon [bə-FOON] n 1 clown. 2 fool. **buf·foon'er·y** n clowning.

bug n 1 any small insect. 2 inf disease,

infection. 3 concealed listening device. ♦ vt **bugged, bug·ging** 4 install secret microphone, etc. 5 inf annoy.

bug·a·boo [BUG-ə-boo] n, pl **-boos** something that causes fear or worry.

bug·bear [BUG-bair] n 1 object of needless terror. 2 nuisance.

bug·ger [BUG-ər] n 1 vulg sodomite. 2 inf worthless person. 3 inf lad.

bu·gle [BYOO-gəl] n instrument like trumpet. **bu'gler** n

build [bild] v **built, build·ing** 1 make, construct, by putting together parts or materials. ♦ n 2 make, form. 3 physique. **build'ing** n

bulb n 1 modified leaf bud emitting roots from base, e.g. onion. 2 anything resembling this. 3 globe surrounding filament of electric light. ♦ vi 4 form bulbs. **bul'bous** adj

bulge [bulj] n 1 swelling, protuberance. 2 temporary increase. ♦ vi **bulged, bulg·ing** 3 swell out. **bulg'i·ness** n

bu·li·mi·a [byoo-LEE-mee-ə] n disorder characterized by compulsive overeating followed by self-induced vomiting. **bu·li'mic** [byoo-LEE-mik] adj, n

bulk n 1 size. 2 volume. 3 greater part. 4

warp

bud n 1 = **shoot**, embryo, germ, sprout ♦ v 2 = **develop**, burgeon, burst forth, grow, shoot, sprout

budding adj = **developing**, beginning, burgeoning, embryonic, fledgling, growing, incipient, nascent, potential, promising

budge v = **move**, dislodge, push, shift, stir

budget n 1 = **allowance**, allocation, cost, finances, funds, means, resources ♦ v 2 = **plan**, allocate, apportion, cost, estimate, ration

buff[1] adj 1 = **yellowish-brown**, sandy, straw, tan, yellowish ♦ v 2 = **polish**, brush, burnish, rub, shine, smooth

buff[2] n Inf = **expert**, addict, admirer, aficionado, connoisseur, devotee, enthusiast, fan

buffer n = **safeguard**, bulwark, bumper, cushion, fender, intermediary, screen, shield, shock absorber

buffet[1] n = **snack bar**, brasserie, café, cafeteria, refreshment counter, sideboard

buffet[2] v = **batter**, beat, bump, knock, pound, pummel, strike, thump, wallop

(inf)

buffoon n = **clown**, comedian, comic, fool, harlequin, jester, joker, wag

bug n 1 Inf = **illness**, disease, infection, virus 2 = **fault**, defect, error, flaw, glitch, gremlin ♦ v 3 Inf = **annoy**, bother, disturb, get on one's nerves (inf), hassle (inf), irritate, pester, vex 4 = **tap**, eavesdrop, listen in, spy

bugbear n = **pet hate**, bane, bête noire, bogey, dread, horror, nightmare

build v 1 = **construct**, assemble, erect, fabricate, form, make, put up, raise ♦ n 2 = **physique**, body, figure, form, frame, shape, structure

building n = **structure**, domicile, dwelling, edifice, house

build-up n = **increase**, accumulation, development, enlargement, escalation, expansion, gain, growth

bulbous adj = **bulging**, bloated, convex, rounded, swelling, swollen

bulge n 1 = **swelling**, bump, hump, lump, projection, protrusion, protuberance 2 = **increase**, boost, intensification, rise, surge ♦ v 3 = **swell out**, dilate, distend, expand,

cargo. ◆ *vi* **5** be of weight or importance.
bulk'i·ness *n* **bulk'y** *adj* **bulk·i·er, bulk·i·est**
bulk·head [BULK-hed] *n* partition in
interior of ship.
bull[1] [buul] *n* **1** male of cattle. **2** male of
various other animals. **bull'dog** *n* thickset
breed of dog. **bull'doze** [-dohz] *v* **-dozed,
-doz·ing bull'doz·er** *n* powerful tractor
with blade for excavating, etc. **bul'lock**
[-lək] *n* castrated bull. **bull's'-eye** *n, pl*
-eyes middle part of target.
bull[2] *n* papal edict.
bull[3] *n sl* **1** nonsense. ◆ *v* **2** talk nonsense
(to).
bul·let [BUUL-it] *n* projectile discharged
from rifle, pistol, etc.
bul·le·tin [BUUL-i-tn] *n* official report.
bul·lion [BUUL-yən] *n* gold or silver in
mass.
bul·ly [BUUL-ee] *n, pl* **-lies 1** one who hurts,
persecutes, or intimidates weaker people.
◆ *vt* **-lied, -ly·ing 2** intimidate, overawe. **3**
ill-treat. ◆ *adj, interj* **4** first-rate.
bul·rush [BUUL-rush] *n* tall reedlike marsh
plant with brown velvety spike.
bul·wark [BUUL-wərk] *n* **1** rampart. **2** any
defense or means of security. **3** raised side
of ship. **4** breakwater.

bum *n* **1** loafer, scrounger. ◆ *vt inf*
bummed, bum·ming 2 get by scrounging.
◆ *adj sl* **3** worthless. **4** inferior. **5** disabled.
bum·ble [BUM-bəl] *v* **-bled, -bling** perform
clumsily. **bum'bler** *n*
bum·ble·bee [BUM-bəl-bee] *n* large bee.
bump *n* **1** heavy blow, dull in sound. **2**
swelling caused by blow. **3** protuberance.
4 sudden movement. ◆ *vt* **5** strike or push
against. **bump'er** *n* **1** horizontal bar at
front and rear of automobile to protect
against damage. **2** full glass. ◆ *adj* **3** full,
abundant. **bump off** *sl* murder.
bump·kin [BUMP-kin] *n* rustic.
bump·tious [BUMP-shəs] *adj* offensively
self-assertive.
bun *n* **1** small, round bread or cake. **2** round
knot of hair. **3** *sl* enough liquor to make
one drunk.
bunch *n* **1** number of things tied or
growing together. **2** cluster. **3** tuft, knot. **4**
group, party. ◆ *vt* **5** put together in bunch.
◆ *vi* **6** gather together.
bun·dle [BUN-dl] *n* **1** package. **2** number of
things tied together. **3** *sl* lot of money. ◆ *vt*
-dled, -dling 4 tie in bundle. **5** send (off)
without ceremony.
bung *n* **1** stopper for cask. **2** large cork. ◆ *vt*

project, protrude, puff out, stick out
bulk *n* **1 = size**, dimensions, immensity,
largeness, magnitude, substance, volume,
weight **2 = main part**, better part, body,
lion's share, majority, mass, most, nearly
all, preponderance
bulky *adj* **= large**, big, cumbersome, heavy,
hulking, massive, substantial, unwieldy,
voluminous, weighty
bulldoze *v* **= demolish**, flatten, level, raze
bullet *n* **= projectile**, ball, missile, pellet,
shot, slug
bulletin *n* **= announcement**, account,
communication, communiqué, dispatch,
message, news flash, notification, report,
statement
bully *n* **1 = persecutor**, browbeater, bully
boy, coercer, intimidator, oppressor,
ruffian, tormentor, tough ◆ *v* **2 =**
persecute, browbeat, coerce, domineer,
hector, intimidate, oppress, push around
(*sl*), terrorize, tyrannize
bulwark *n* **1 = fortification**, bastion,
buttress, defense, embankment, partition,
rampart **2 = defense**, buffer, guard,
mainstay, safeguard, security, support

bumbling *adj* **= clumsy**, awkward,
blundering, bungling, incompetent,
inefficient, inept, maladroit, muddled
bump *v* **1 = knock**, bang, collide (with),
crash, hit, slam, smash into, strike **2 = jerk**,
bounce, jolt, rattle, shake ◆ *n* **3 = knock**,
bang, blow, collision, crash, impact, jolt,
thud, thump **4 = lump**, bulge, contusion,
hump, nodule, protuberance, swelling
bumper *adj* **= exceptional**, abundant,
bountiful, excellent, jumbo (*inf*), massive,
whopping (*inf*)
bumpkin *n* **= yokel**, country bumpkin, hick
(*inf*), hillbilly, peasant, redneck (*sl*), rustic
bumptious *adj* **= cocky**, arrogant, brash,
conceited, forward, full of oneself,
overconfident, pushy (*inf*), self-assertive
bumpy *adj* **= rough**, bouncy, choppy,
jarring, jerky, jolting, rutted, uneven
bunch *n* **1 = number**, assortment, batch,
bundle, clump, cluster, collection, heap,
lot, mass, pile **2 = group**, band, crowd,
flock, gang, gathering, party, team ◆ *v* **3 =**
group, assemble, bundle, cluster, collect,
huddle, mass, pack
bundle *n* **1 = bunch**, assortment, batch,

3 stop up, seal, close. **bung'hole** n

bun·ga·low [BUNG-gə-loh] n one-storied house.

bun·gle [BUNG-gəl] v **-gled, -gling** ♦ vt **1** do badly from lack of skill, botch. ♦ vi **2** act clumsily, awkwardly. ♦ n **3** blunder, muddle. **bun'gler** n

bun·ion [BUN-yən] n inflamed swelling on foot or toe.

bunk[1] [bungk] n **1** narrow, shelflike bed. ♦ vi **2** stay the night (with). **bunk bed** one of pair of beds constructed one above the other.

bunk[2] n bunkum.

bun·ker [BUNG-kər] n **1** large storage container for oil, coal, etc. **2** sandy hollow on golf course. **3** (military) underground defensive position.

bun·ko [BUNG-koh] n, pl **-kos** swindling scheme or game.

bun·kum [BUNG-kəm] n nonsense.

bun·ny [BUN-ee] n inf pl **-nies** rabbit.

Bun·sen burner [BUN-sən] gas burner, producing great heat, used for chemical experiments.

bun'ting[1] n material for flags.

bunting[2] n bird with short, stout bill.

bu·oy [BOO-ee] n **1** floating marker anchored in sea. **2** lifebuoy. ♦ vt **3** mark

with buoy. **4** keep from sinking. **5** support. **buoy·an·cy** [BOI-ən-see] n **buoy'ant** adj

bur·ble [BUR-bəl] vi **-bled, -bling 1** gurgle, as stream or baby. **2** talk idly.

bur·den [BUR-dn] n **1** load. **2** weight, cargo. **3** anything difficult to bear. ♦ vt **4** load, encumber. **burd'en·some** [-səm] adj

bu·reau [BYUUR-oh] n, pl **-reaus, -reaux** [-rohz] **1** office. **2** government department. **bu·reau·ra·cy** [byuu-ROK-rə-see] n, pl **-cies 1** government by officials. **2** body of officials. **bu·reau·crat** [BYUUR-ə-krat] n

bur·geon [BUR-jən] vi **1** bud. **2** develop rapidly.

burg·er [BUR-gər] n hamburger.

bur·gess [BUR-jis] n member of colonial Maryland or Virginia legislature.

bur·glar [BUR-glər] n one who enters building to commit theft. **bur'gla·ry** [-glə-ree] n **bur'gle** [-gəl] vt **-gled, -gling**

Bur·gun·dy [BUR-gən-dee] n, pl **-dies 1** red or white wine produced in Burgundy, France. **2** (b-) similar wine made elsewhere. **bur·gun·dy** adj dark-purplish red.

bur'lap n coarse canvas.

bur·lesque [bər-LESK] n **1** (artistic) caricature. **2** ludicrous imitation. **3** provocative and humorous stage show. ♦

collection, group, heap, mass, pile, stack ♦ v **2** (with out, off, into, etc.) = **push**, hurry, hustle, rush, shove, throw, thrust

bundle up v = **wrap up**, swathe

bungle v = **mess up**, blow (sl), blunder, botch, foul up, make a mess of, muff, ruin, spoil

bungling adj = **incompetent**, blundering, clumsy, inept, maladroit

bunk[1], **bunkum** n Inf = **nonsense**, balderdash, baloney (inf), garbage (inf), hogwash, hot air (inf), moonshine, poppycock (inf), rubbish, stuff and nonsense, twaddle

buoy n **1** = **marker**, beacon, float, guide, signal ♦ v **2 buoy up** = **encourage**, boost, cheer, cheer up, hearten, keep afloat, lift, raise, support, sustain

buoyancy n **1** = **lightness**, weightlessness **2** = **cheerfulness**, animation, bounce (inf), good humor, high spirits, liveliness

buoyant adj **1** = **floating**, afloat, light, weightless **2** = **cheerful**, carefree, chirpy (inf), happy, jaunty, light-hearted, upbeat (inf)

burden n **1** = **load**, encumbrance, weight **2** = **trouble**, affliction, millstone, onus, responsibility, strain, weight, worry ♦ v **3** = **weigh down**, bother, handicap, load, oppress, saddle with, tax, worry

bureau n **1** = **office**, agency, branch, department, division, service **2** = **desk**, writing desk

bureaucracy n **1** = **government**, administration, authorities, civil service, corridors of power, officials, the system **2** = **red tape**, officialdom, regulations

bureaucrat n = **official**, administrator, civil servant, functionary, mandarin, officer, public servant

burglar n = **housebreaker**, cat burglar, filcher, pilferer, robber, sneak thief, thief

burglary n = **breaking and entering**, break-in, housebreaking, larceny, robbery, stealing, theft, thieving

burial n = **interment**, entombment, exequies, funeral, obsequies

buried adj **1** = **interred**, entombed, laid to rest **2** = **hidden**, concealed, private, sequestered, tucked away

vt **-lesqued, -lesqu·ing 4** caricature.
bur·ly [BUR-lee] *adj* **-li·er, -li·est** sturdy, stout, robust.
burn *v* **burned** *or* **burnt, burn·ing** ♦ *vt* **1** destroy or injure by fire. **2** record data on (a CD). ♦ *vi* **3** be or feel hot. **4** be consumed by fire. ♦ *n* **5** injury, mark caused by fire.
bur·nish *vt* **1** make bright by rubbing. **2** polish. ♦ *n* **3** gloss, luster.
burp *v inf* belch (esp. of baby). ♦ *n*
burr[1] *n* soft trilling sound given to letter *r* in some dialects.
burr[2] *n* rough edge left after cutting, drilling, etc.
burr[3] *n* head of plant with prickles or hooks.
bur·ro [BUR-oh] *n, pl* **-ros** small donkey.
bur·row [BUR-oh] *n* **1** hole dug by rabbit, etc. ♦ *vt* **2** make holes in ground. **3** bore. **4** conceal oneself.
bur·sar [BUR-sər] *n* official managing finances of college, monastery, etc.
burst *v* **burst, burst·ing** ♦ *vi* **1** fly asunder. **2** break into pieces. **3** rend. **4** break suddenly into some expression of feeling. ♦ *vt* **5** shatter, break violently. ♦ *n* **6** bursting. **7** explosion. **8** outbreak. **9** spurt.
bur·y [BER-ee] *vt* **bur·ied, bur·y·ing 1** put underground. **2** inter. **3** conceal. **bur'i·al** *n, adj*
bus *n* **1** large motor vehicle for passengers. ♦ *v* **2** travel or transport by bus. **3** work as busboy. **bus'man's holiday** vacation spent in an activity closely resembling one's work.
bus·boy [BUS-boi] *n* waiter's helper in public dining room.
bush [buush] *n* **1** shrub. **2** woodland, thicket. **3** uncleared country, backwoods, interior. **bushed** *adj inf* tired out. **bush'y** *adj* **bush·i·er, bush·i·est** shaggy. **bush jacket** shirtlike jacket with patch pockets.
bush·el [BUUSH-əl] *n* dry measure of eight gallons.
busi·ness [BIZ-nis] *n* **1** profession. **2** commercial or industrial establishment. **3** commerce, trade. **4** responsibility, affair, matter. **5** work.

burlesque *n* **1** = **parody**, caricature, mockery, satire, spoof (*inf*), travesty ♦ *v* **2** = **satirize**, ape, caricature, exaggerate, imitate, lampoon, make a monkey out of, make fun of, mock, parody, ridicule, spoof (*inf*), travesty

burly *adj* = **brawny**, beefy (*inf*), big, bulky, hefty, hulking, stocky, stout, sturdy, thickset, well-built

burn *v* **1** = **be on fire**, be ablaze, blaze, flame, flare, glow, go up in flames, smoke **2** = **set on fire**, char, ignite, incinerate, kindle, light, parch, scorch, sear, singe, toast **3** = **be passionate**, be angry, be aroused, be inflamed, fume, seethe, simmer, smolder

burning *adj* **1** = **intense**, ardent, eager, fervent, impassioned, passionate, vehement **2** = **crucial**, acute, compelling, critical, essential, important, pressing, significant, urgent, vital **3** = **blazing**, fiery, flaming, flashing, gleaming, glowing, illuminated, scorching, smoldering

burnish *v* = **polish**, brighten, buff, furbish, glaze, rub up, shine, smooth

burrow *n* **1** = **hole**, den, lair, retreat, shelter, tunnel ♦ *v* **2** = **dig**, delve, excavate, hollow out, scoop out, tunnel

burst *v* **1** = **explode**, blow up, break, crack, puncture, rupture, shatter, split, tear apart **2** = **rush**, barge, break, break out, erupt, gush forth, run, spout ♦ *n* **3** = **explosion**, bang, blast, blowout, break, crack, discharge, rupture, split **4** = **rush**, gush, gust, outbreak, outburst, outpouring, spate, spurt, surge, torrent ♦ *adj* **5** = **ruptured**, flat, punctured, rent, split

bury *v* **1** = **inter**, consign to the grave, entomb, inhume, lay to rest **2** = **embed**, engulf, submerge **3** = **hide**, conceal, cover, enshroud, secrete, stow away

bush *n* **1** = **shrub**, hedge, plant, shrubbery, thicket **2 the bush** = **the wild**, backwoods, brush, scrub, scrubland, woodland

bushy *adj* = **thick**, bristling, fluffy, fuzzy, luxuriant, rough, shaggy, unruly

busily *adv* = **actively**, assiduously, briskly, diligently, energetically, industriously, purposefully, speedily, strenuously

business *n* **1** = **trade**, bargaining, commerce, dealings, industry, manufacturing, selling, transaction **2** = **establishment**, company, concern, corporation, enterprise, firm, organization, venture **3** = **profession**, career, employment, function, job, line, occupation, trade, vocation, work **4** = **concern**, affair, assignment, duty, problem, responsibility, task

businesslike *adj* = **efficient**, methodical,

bust[1] *n* **1** sculpture of head and shoulders of human body. **2** woman's breasts.

bust[2] *v inf* **1** burst. **2** make, become bankrupt. ♦ *vt sl* **3** raid. **4** arrest. ♦ *adj inf* **5** broken. **6** bankrupt. ♦ *n* **7** *sl* police raid or arrest. **8** *inf* punch.

bus·tle[1] [BUS-əl] *vi* **-tled, -tling 1** be noisily busy, active. ♦ *n* **2** fuss, commotion.

buctle[2] *n Hist.* pad worn by ladies to support back of the skirt.

bus·y [BIZ-ee] *adj* **bus·i·er, bus·i·est 1** actively employed. **2** full of activity. ♦ *vt* **bus·ied, bus·y·ing 3** occupy. **bus'y·bod·y** *n, pl* **-bod·ies** meddler.

but *prep, conj* **1** without. **2** except. **3** only. **4** yet. **5** still. **6** besides.

bu·tane [BYOO-tayn] *n* gas used for fuel.

butch [buuch] *adj, n sl* markedly or aggressively masculine (person).

butch·er [BUUCH-ər] *n* **1** one who kills, dresses animals for food, or sells meat. **2** bloody, savage man. ♦ *vt* **3** slaughter, murder. **4** spoil work. **butch'er·y** *n*

but·ler [BUT-lər] *n* chief male servant.

butt[1] *n* **1** the thick end. **2** target. **3** object of ridicule. **4** bottom or unused end of

anything. ♦ *v* **5** lie, be placed end on to.

butt[2] *v* **1** strike with head. **2** push. ♦ *n* **3** blow with head, as of sheep. **butt in** *inf* interfere, meddle. **butt·in'sky** *n, pl* **-skies** *sl* meddler.

but·ter [BUT-ər] *n* **1** fatty substance got from cream by churning. ♦ *vt* **2** spread with or as if with butter. **3** flatter.

but·ter·fly [BUT-ər-flī] *n, pl* **-flies 1** insect with large wings. **2** inconstant person. **3** stroke in swimming. ♦ *vt* **-flied, -fly·ing 4** split (foodstuff) into shape resembling butterfly.

but·ter·milk [BUT-ər-milk] *n* milk that remains after churning.

but·tock [BUT-ək] *n* (usu. pl) rump, protruding hinder part.

but·ton [BUT-n] *n* **1** knob, stud for fastening dress. **2** knob that operates doorbell, machine, etc. ♦ *vt* **3** fasten with buttons. **but'ton·hole** *n* **1** slit in garment to pass button through as fastening. ♦ *vt* **-holed, -hol·ing 2** detain (unwilling) person in conversation.

but·tress [BU-tris] *n* **1** structure to support wall. **2** prop. ♦ *vt*

──────── THESAURUS ────────

orderly, organized, practical, professional, systematic, thorough, well-ordered

businessman *n* = **executive**, capitalist, employer, entrepreneur, financier, industrialist, merchant, tradesman, tycoon

bust[1] *n* = **bosom**, breast, chest, front, torso

bust[2] *Inf* *v* **1** = **break**, burst, fracture, rupture **2** = **arrest**, catch, raid, search ♦ *adj* **3 go bust** = **go bankrupt**, become insolvent, be ruined, fail

bustle *v* **1** = **hurry**, fuss, hasten, rush, scamper, scurry, scuttle ♦ *n* **2** = **activity**, ado, commotion, excitement, flurry, fuss, hurly-burly, stir, to-do

bustling *adj* = **busy**, active, buzzing, crowded, full, humming, lively, swarming, teeming

busy *adj* **1** = **occupied**, active, employed, engaged, hard at work, industrious, on duty, rushed off one's feet, working **2** = **lively**, energetic, exacting, full, hectic, hustling ♦ *v* **3** = **occupy**, absorb, employ, engage, engross, immerse, interest

busybody *n* = **nosy rosy** (*U.S. inf*), gossip, meddler, snooper, stirrer (*inf*), troublemaker

but *conj* **1** = **however**, further, moreover, nevertheless, on the contrary, on the other

hand, still, yet ♦ *prep* **2** = **except**, bar, barring, excepting, excluding, notwithstanding, save, with the exception of ♦ *adv* **3** = **only**, just, merely, simply, singly, solely

butcher *n* **1** = **murderer**, destroyer, killer, slaughterer, slayer ♦ *v* **2** = **slaughter**, carve, clean, cut, cut up, dress, joint, prepare **3** = **kill**, assassinate, cut down, destroy, exterminate, liquidate, massacre, put to the sword, slaughter, slay

butt[1] *n* **1** = **end**, haft, handle, hilt, shaft, shank, stock **2** = **stub**, cigarette end, leftover, tip *Inf* = **buttocks**, behind (*inf*), bottom, *derrière* (*euphemistic*), rump (*inf*), tush (*sl*)

butt[2] *n* = **target**, dupe, laughing stock, victim

butt[3] *v, n* **1** *With or of the head or horns* = **knock**, bump, poke, prod, push, ram, shove, thrust ♦ *v* **2** = **butt in** = **interfere**, chip in (*inf*), cut in, interrupt, intrude, meddle, put one's oar in, stick one's nose in

butt[4] *n* = **cask**, barrel

buttonhole *v* = **detain**, accost, bore, catch, grab, importune, take aside, waylay

buttress *n* **1** = **support**, brace, mainstay, prop, reinforcement, stanchion, strut ♦ *v*

bux·om [BUK-səm] *adj* **1** full of health, plump, gay. **2** large-breasted.

buy [bī] *vt* **bought, buy·ing 1** get by payment, purchase. **2** bribe. **buy'er** *n*

buzz *vi* **1** make humming sound. ♦ *n* **2** humming sound of bees. **3** *inf* telephone call. **buzz'er** *n* any apparatus that makes buzzing sound. **buzz word** *inf* word, oft. orig. jargon, that becomes fashionable.

buz·zard [BUZ-ərd] *n* bird of prey of hawk family.

by [bī] *prep* **1** near. **2** along. **3** across. **4** past. **5** during. **6** not later than. **7** through use or agency of. **8** in units of. ♦ *adv* **9** near. **10** away, aside. **11** past. **by and by** soon, in the future. **by and large 1** on the whole. **2** speaking generally. **come by** obtain.

bye [bī] *n Sports* in early round of a tournament, a situation in which player, team not paired with opponent advances to next round without playing.

by·gone [BĪ-gawn] *adj* **1** past, former. ♦ *n* (oft. pl) **2** past occurrence.

by·law [BĪ-law] *n* law, regulation made by an organization.

by·line [BĪ-līn] *n* printed line identifying author of news story, article, etc.

by·pass [BĪ-pas] *n* **1** road for diversion of traffic from crowded centers. **2** secondary channel carrying fluid around a part and back to the main stream. ♦ *vt*

by·play [BĪ-play] *n* diversion, action apart from main action of play.

byte [bīt] *n Computers* sequence of bits processed as single unit of information.

by·word [BĪ-wurd] *n* a well-known name, saying.

——————[THESAURUS]——————

2 = support, back up, bolster, prop up, reinforce, shore up, strengthen, sustain, uphold

buxom *adj* **= plump**, ample, bosomy, busty, curvaceous, healthy, voluptuous, well-rounded

buy *v* **1 = purchase**, acquire, get, invest in, obtain, pay for, procure, shop for ♦ *n* **2 = purchase**, acquisition, bargain, deal

by *prep* **1 = via**, by way of, over **2 = through**, through the agency of **3 = near**, along, beside, close to, next to, past ♦ *adv* **4 = near**, at hand, close, handy, in reach

5 = past, aside, away, to one side

bygone *adj* **= past**, antiquated, extinct, forgotten, former, lost, of old, olden

bypass *v* **= go round**, avoid, circumvent, depart from, detour round, deviate from, get round, give a wide berth to, pass round

bystander *n* **= onlooker**, eyewitness, looker-on, observer, passer-by, spectator, viewer, watcher, witness

byword *n* **= saying**, adage, maxim, motto, precept, proverb, slogan

C c

C 1 *Chem.* Carbon. **2** Celsius.

Ca *Chem.* calcium.

cab *n* **1** taxi. **2** driver's enclosed compartment on locomotive, truck, etc. **cab'driv·er** *n* **cab'stand** *n* place where taxis may wait to be hired.

ca·bal [kə-BAL] *n* **1** small group of intriguers. **2** secret plot.

cab·a·ret [kab-ə-RAY] *n* night club.

cab·bage [KAB-ij] *n* green vegetable with usu. round head of leaves.

ca·ber [KAY-bər] *n* pole tossed as trial of strength at Scottish games.

cab·in [KAB-in] *n* **1** hut, shed. **2** small room esp. in ship. **cabin cruiser** power boat with cabin, bunks, etc.

cab·i·net [KAB-ə-nit] *n* **1** piece of furniture with drawers or shelves. **2** outer case of television, radio, etc. **3** body of advisers to head of state. **cab'i·net·mak·er** *n* artisan who makes fine furniture.

ca·ble [KAY-bəl] *n* **1** strong rope. **2** wire or bundle of wires conveying electric power, telegraph signals, etc. **3** message sent by this. **4** cable TV. ♦ *v* -**bled, -bling 5** telegraph by cable. **ca'ble·gram** *n* cabled message. **cable TV** TV service conveyed by cable to subscribers.

ca·boo·dle [kə-BOOD-l] *n inf* **the whole caboodle** the whole lot.

ca·boose [kə-BOOS] *n* (usu. last) car of freight train, for use by train crew.

ca·ca·o [kə-KAH-oh] *n* tropical tree from the seeds of which chocolate and cocoa are made.

cache [kash] *n* **1** secret hiding place. **2** store of food, arms, etc.

ca·chet [ka-SHAY] *n* **1** mark, stamp. **2** mark of authenticity. **3** prestige, distinction.

cack·le [KAK-əl] *vi* -**led, -ling 1** make chattering noise, as hen. ♦ *n* **2** cackling noise or laughter. **3** empty chatter.

ca·coph·o·ny [kə-KOF-ə-nee] *n, pl* -**nies 1** disagreeable sound. **2** discord of sounds. **ca·coph'o·nous** *adj*

cac·tus [KAK-təs] *n, pl* -**ti** [-tī] spiny succulent plant.

cad *n* dishonorable, ungentlemanly person.

ca·dav·er [kə-DAV-ər] *n* corpse. **ca·dav'er·ous** *adj* **1** corpselike. **2** sickly-looking. **3** gaunt.

cad·die [KAD-ee] *n* person hired to carry golfer's clubs, find the ball, etc.

ca·dence [KAYD-ns] *n* fall or modulation of voice in music, speech, or verse.

ca·den·za [kə-DEN-zə] *n Mus.* elaborate passage for solo instrument or singer.

ca·det [kə-DET] *n* youth in training, esp. for officer status in armed forces.

cadge [kaj] *v* **cadged, cadg·ing** get (food, money, etc.) by begging. **cadg'er** *n* sponger.

cad·mi·um [KAD-mee-əm] *n* metallic element.

ca·dre [KAD-ree] *n* nucleus or framework, esp. skeleton of military unit.

Cae·sar·e·an section [si-ZAIR-ee-ən] surgical incision through abdominal wall to deliver a baby.

ca·fé [ka-FAY] *n* **1** small or inexpensive restaurant serving light refreshments. **2** bar. **caf·e·te·ri·a** [kaf-ə-TEE-ree-ə] *n* restaurant designed for self-service.

caf·feine [ka-FEEN] *n* stimulating alkaloid

THESAURUS

cab *n* = **taxi**, hackney carriage, minicab, taxicab

cabal *n* **1** = **clique**, caucus, conclave, faction, league, party, set **2** = **plot**, conspiracy, intrigue, machination, scheme

cabin *n* **1** = **room**, berth, compartment, quarters **2** = **hut**, chalet, cottage, lodge, shack, shanty, shed

cabinet *n* = **cupboard**, case, chiffonier, closet, commode, dresser, escritoire, locker

Cabinet *n* = **council**, administration, assembly, counselors, ministry

caddish *adj* = **ungentlemanly**, despicable, ill-bred, lousy (*sl*), low, scuzzy (*sl*), unmannerly

café *n* = **snack bar**, brasserie, cafeteria,

found in tea and coffee plants.

caf·tan [KAF-tan] *n* **1** long coatlike Eastern garment. **2** imitation of it, esp. as woman's long, loose dress with sleeves.

cage [kayj] *n* **1** enclosure, box with bars or wires, esp. for keeping animals or birds. **2** place of confinement. **3** enclosed platform of elevator, esp. in mine. ◆ *vt* **caged, cag·ing 4** put in cage, confine. **cag'ey** *adj* **cag·i·er, cag·i·est** wary, shrewd.

ca·hoots [kə-HOOTS] *pl n sl* partnership, as **in cahoots with.**

cairn [kairn] *n* heap of stones, esp. as monument or landmark.

cais·son [KAY-son] *n* **1** chamber for working under water. **2** apparatus for lifting vessel out of the water. **3** ammunition wagon. **caisson disease** the bends.

ca·jole [kə-JOHL] *vt* **-joled, -jol·ing** persuade by flattery, wheedle. **ca·jol'er** *n*

cake [kayk] *n* **1** baked, sweetened, bread-like food. **2** compact mass. ◆ *v* **caked, cak·ing 3** make into a cake. **4** harden (as of mud).

cal·a·boose [KAL-ə-boos] *n inf* jail.

cal·a·mine [KAL-ə-mīn] *n* pink powder used medicinally in soothing ointment.

ca·lam·i·ty [kə-LAM-i-tee] *n, pl* **-ties 1** great misfortune. **2** deep distress, disaster. **ca·lam'i·tous** *adj*

cal·ci·um [KAL-see-əm] *n* metallic element, the basis of lime. **cal·car'e·ous** [-KAIR-ee-əs] *adj* containing lime. **cal'ci·fy** *v* **-fied, -fy·ing** convert, be converted, to lime.

cal·cu·late [KAL-kyə-layt] *v* **-lat·ed, -lat·ing**
◆ *vt* **1** estimate. **2** compute. ◆ *vi* **3** make reckonings. **cal'cu·lat·ing** *adj* **1** able to perform calculations. **2** shrewd, designing, scheming. **cal'cu·la·tor** *n* electronic or mechanical device for making calculations. **cal'cu·lus** *n, pl* **-li** [-lī] **1** branch of mathematics. **2** stone in body.

cal·en·dar [KAL-ən-dər] *n* **1** table of months and days in the year. **2** list of events, documents. **3** register.

calf[1] [kaf] *n, pl* **calves** [kavz] **1** young of cow and of other animals. **2** leather made of calf's skin. **calve** [kav] *vi* **calved, calv·ing** give birth to calf.

calf[2] *n, pl* **calves** fleshy back part of leg below knee.

cal·i·ber [KAL-ə-bər] *n* **1** size of bore of gun. **2** capacity, character. **cal'i·brate** [-brayt] *vt* **-brat·ed, -brat·ing** mark scale of measuring instrument, etc. **cal·i·bra'tion** *n*

cal·i·co [KAL-i-koh] *n, pl* **-coes, -cos** printed cotton fabric.

cal·i·per [KAL-ə-pər] *n* **1** instrument for measuring diameters. **2** thickness, esp. of tree, paper.

cal·is·then·ics [kal-əs-THEN-iks] *pl n* light gymnastic exercises.

call [kawl] *vt* **1** speak loudly to attract attention. **2** summon. **3** (oft. with *up*) telephone. **4** name. ◆ *vi* **5** shout. **6** pay visit. ◆ *n* **7** shout. **8** animal's cry. **9** visit. **10** inner urge, summons, as to be minister, etc. **11** need, demand. **call'ing** *n* vocation, profession. **call box** outdoor telephone for calling police or fire department. **call girl** prostitute who accepts appointments by telephone. **call up 1** summon to serve in

──────── THESAURUS ────────

coffee bar, coffee shop, lunchroom, restaurant, tearoom

cage *n* = **enclosure**, pen, pound

cagey *adj Inf* = **wary**, careful, cautious, chary, discreet, guarded, noncommittal, shrewd, wily

cajole *v* = **persuade**, brown-nose (*sl*), coax, flatter, seduce, sweet-talk (*inf*), wheedle

cake *n* **1** = **block**, bar, cube, loaf, lump, mass, slab ◆ *v* **2** = **encrust**, bake, coagulate, congeal, solidify

calamitous *adj* = **disastrous**, cataclysmic, catastrophic, deadly, devastating, dire, fatal, ruinous, tragic

calamity *n* = **disaster**, cataclysm, catastrophe, misadventure, misfortune, mishap, ruin, tragedy, tribulation

calculate *v* **1** = **work out**, compute, count, determine, enumerate, estimate, figure, reckon **2** = **plan**, aim, design, intend

calculated *adj* = **deliberate**, considered, intended, intentional, planned, premeditated, purposeful

calculating *adj* = **scheming**, crafty, cunning, devious, Machiavellian, manipulative, sharp, shrewd, sly

calculation *n* **1** = **working out**, answer, computation, estimate, forecast, judgment, reckoning, result **2** = **planning**, contrivance, deliberation, discretion, foresight, forethought, precaution

caliber *n* **1** = **worth**, ability, capacity, distinction, merit, quality, stature, talent **2** = **diameter**, bore, gauge, measure army. **2** imagine.

cal·lig·ra·phy [kə-LIG-rə-fee] *n* handwriting, penmanship. **cal·li·graph'ic** *adj*

cal·lous [KAL-əs] *adj* hardened, unfeeling. **cal'lous·ness** *n*

cal·low [KAL-oh] *adj* **1** inexperienced. **2** immature.

cal·lus [KAL-əs] *n, pl* **-lus·es** area of thick, hardened skin.

calm [kahm] *adj* **-er, -est 1** still, quiet, tranquil. ◆ *n* **2** stillness. **3** tranquility. **4** absence of wind. ◆ *v* **5** become, make, still or quiet. **calm'ly** *adv*

cal·o·rie [KAL-ə-ree] *n* **1** unit of heat. **2** unit of energy obtained from foods. **cal·o·rif'ic** *adj* heat-making. **cal·o·rim'e·ter** *n*

cal·u·met [KAL-yə-met] *n* **1** tobacco pipe of N Amer. Indians. **2** peace pipe.

cal·um·ny [KAL-əm-nee] *n, pl* **-nies 1** slander, false accusation. **ca·lum'ni·ate** *vt* **-at·ed, -at·ing ca·lum·ni·a'tion** *n*

ca·lyp·so [kə-LIP-soh] *n, pl* **-sos** (West Indies) improvised song on topical subject.

ca·lyx [KAY-liks] *n, pl* **-lyx·es** covering of bud.

cam [kam] *n* device to change rotary to reciprocating motion. **cam'shaft** *n* in motor vehicles, rotating shaft to which cams are fixed to lift valves.

ca·ma·ra·de·rie [kah-mə-RAH-də-ree] *n* spirit of comradeship, trust.

cam·ber [KAM-bər] *n* **1** convexity on upper surface of road, bridge, etc. **2** curvature of

aircraft wing. **3** setting of motor vehicle wheels closer together at bottom than at top.

cam·bric [KAYM-brik] *n* fine white linen or cotton cloth.

cam·cord·er [KAM-kor-dər] *n* combined portable video camera and recorder.

came pt. of COME.

cam·el [KAM-əl] *n* animal of Asia and Africa, with humped back, used as beast of burden.

cam·e·o [KAM-ee-oh] *n, pl* **-e·os 1** medallion, brooch, etc. with profile head or design carved in relief. **2** single brief scene or appearance in film, etc. by well-known performer.

cam·er·a [KAM-ər-ə] *n* apparatus used to make photographs. **cam'er·a·man** *n* photographer, esp. for TV or film. **camera ob·scu·ra** [ob-SKYUUR-ə] darkened chamber in which views of external objects are shown on sheet by means of lenses. **in camera** (of legal proceedings, etc.) conducted in private.

cam·i·sole [KAM-ə-sohl] *n* woman's short sleeveless undergarment.

cam·ou·flage [KAM-ə-flah*zh*] *n* **1** disguise, means of deceiving enemy observation, e.g. by paint, screen. ◆ *vt* **-flaged, -flag·ing** disguise.

camp [kamp] *n* **1** (place for) tents of hikers, army, etc. **2** cabins, etc. for temporary accommodation. **3** group supporting political party, etc. ◆ *adj* **4** *inf* consciously

---- THESAURUS ----

call *v* **1** = **name**, christen, describe as, designate, dub, entitle, label, style, term **2** = **cry**, arouse, hail, rouse, shout, yell **3** = **phone**, telephone **4** = **summon**, assemble, convene, gather, muster, rally ◆ *n* **5** = **cry**, hail, scream, shout, signal, whoop, yell **6** = **summons**, appeal, command, demand, invitation, notice, order, plea, request **7** = **need**, cause, excuse, grounds, justification, occasion, reason

call for *v* **1** = **require**, demand, entail, involve, necessitate, need, occasion, suggest **2** = **fetch**, collect, pick up

calling *n* = **profession**, career, life's work, mission, trade, vocation

call on *v* = **visit**, drop in on, look in on, look up, see

callous *adj* = **heartless**, cold, hard-boiled, hardened, hardhearted, insensitive, uncaring, unfeeling

callow *adj* = **inexperienced**, green, guileless, immature, naive, raw, unsophisticated

calm *adj* **1** = **cool**, collected, composed, dispassionate, relaxed, sedate, self-possessed, unemotional **2** = **still**, balmy, mild, quiet, serene, smooth, tranquil, windless ◆ *n* **3** = **peacefulness**, hush, peace, quiet, repose, serenity, stillness ◆ *v* **4** = **quieten**, hush, mollify, placate, relax, soothe

calmness *n* **1** = **coolness**, composure, cool (*sl*), equanimity, impassivity, poise, sang-froid, self-possession **2** = **peacefulness**, calm, hush, quiet, repose, restfulness, serenity, stillness, tranquility

camouflage *n* **1** = **disguise**, blind, cloak, concealment, cover, mask, masquerade, screen, subterfuge ◆ *v* **2** = **disguise**, cloak, conceal, cover, hide, mask, obfuscate, artificial. ◆ vi **5** form or lodge in a camp.

cam·paign [kam-PAYN] n **1** series of coordinated activities for some purpose, e.g. political or military campaign. ◆ vi **2** serve in campaign. **cam·paign'er** n

cam·pa·nol·o·gy [kam-pə-NOL-ə-jee] n art of ringing bells musically.

cam·phor [KAM-fər] n solid essential oil with aromatic taste and smell. **cam'phor·at·ed** adj

cam·pus [KAM-pəs] n, pl **-pus·es** grounds of college or university.

can¹ [kan] vi **could.** pt **1** be able. **2** have the power. **3** be allowed.

can² n **1** container, usu. metal, for liquids, foods. ◆ v **canned, can·ning 2** put in can. **3** prepare (food) for canning. **canned** adj **1** preserved in jar or can. **2** (of music, TV or radio programs, etc.) previously recorded. **can'ner·y** n, pl **-ner·ies** factory where food is canned.

Can·a·da Day [KAN-ə-də] July 1st, anniversary of establishment of Confederation in 1867.

Canada goose large grayish-brown N Amer. goose.

Ca·na·di·an [kə-NAY-dee-ən] n, adj (native) of Canada.

ca·nal [kə-NAL] n **1** artificial watercourse. **2** duct in body. **can·al·ize** [KAN-l-īz] vt **-ized, -iz·ing 1** convert into canal. **2** direct (thoughts, energies, etc.) into one channel.

can·a·pé [KAN-ə-pay] n small piece of toast, etc. with cheese, etc. topping.

ca·nar·y [kə-NAIR-ee] n, pl **-nar·ies** yellow singing bird.

ca·nas·ta [kə-NAS-tə] n card game played with two packs.

can·can [KAN-kan] n high-kicking (orig. French music-hall) dance.

can·cel [KAN-səl] vt **-celed, -cel·ing 1** cross out. **2** annul. **3** invalidate. **4** call off. **can·cel·la'tion** n

can·cer [KAN-sər] n malignant growth or tumor. **can'cer·ous** adj

can·de·la [kan-DEE-lə] n basic unit of luminous intensity.

can·did [KAN-did] adj **1** frank, open, impartial. **can'did·ly** adv **can'dor** [-dər] n frankness.

can·di·date [KAN-di-dayt] n **1** one who seeks office, employment, etc. **2** person taking examination or test. **can'di·da·cy** [-də-see] n, pl **-cies**

can·dle [KAN-dl] n **1** stick of wax with wick. **2** light. **can·de·la'brum** [-AH-brəm] pl **-bra** [-brə] n large, branched candle holder. **can'dle·pow·er** n unit for measuring light. **can't hold a candle to** compare unfavorably with.

can·dy [KAN-dee] n, pl **-dies 1** crystallized sugar. **2** confectionery in general. ◆ v **-died, -dy·ing 3** preserve with sugar. **4** become encrusted with sugar.

cane [kayn] n **1** stem of small palm or large grass. **2** walking stick. ◆ vt **caned, can·ing 3** beat with cane.

ca·nine [KAY-nīn] adj like, pert. to, dog. **canine tooth** one of four sharp, pointed teeth, two in each jaw.

can·is·ter [KAN-ə-stər] n container, oft. of metal, for storing dry food.

can·ker [KANG-kər] n **1** spreading sore. **2** thing that eats away, destroys, corrupts. **canker sore** painful ulcer esp. in mouth.

————— THESAURUS —————

obscure, screen, veil

camp¹ n = **camp site,** bivouac, camping ground, encampment, tents

camp² adj Inf = **effeminate,** affected, artificial, mannered, ostentatious, posturing

campaign n = **operation,** attack, crusade, drive, expedition, movement, offensive, push

canal n = **waterway,** channel, conduit, duct, passage, watercourse

cancel v **1** = **call off,** abolish, abort, annul, delete, do away with, eliminate, erase, expunge, obliterate, repeal, revoke
2 cancel out = **make up for,** balance out, compensate for, counterbalance,

neutralize, nullify, offset

cancellation n = **abandonment,** abolition, annulment, deletion, elimination, repeal, revocation

cancer n = **growth,** corruption, malignancy, pestilence, sickness, tumor

candid adj = **honest,** blunt, forthright, frank, open, outspoken, plain, straightforward, truthful

candidate n = **contender,** applicant, claimant, competitor, contestant, entrant, nominee, runner

candor n = **honesty,** directness, forthrightness, frankness, openness, outspokenness, straightforwardness, truthfulness

can·na·bis [KAN-ə-bis] *n* **1** hemp plant. **2** drug derived from this. **3** marijuana. **4** hashish.

can·nel·lo·ni [kan-I-OH-nee] *n* tubular pieces of pasta filled with meat, etc.

can·ni·bal [KAN-ə-bəl] *n* **1** one who eats human flesh. ◆ *adj* **2** relating to this practice. **can'ni·bal·ism** *n* **can'ni·bal·ize** *vt* **-ized, -iz·ing** use parts from one machine, etc. to repair another.

can·non [KAN-ən] *n*, *pl* **-nons** or **-non** large gun. **can'non·ball** *n*

can·not [KAN-ot] negative form of CAN[1].

can·ny [KAN-ee] *adj* **-ni·er, -ni·est** **1** shrewd. **2** cautious. **3** crafty. **can'ni·ly** *adv*

ca·noe [kə-NOO] *n*, *pl* **-noes** very light boat propelled with paddle or paddles. **ca·noe'ist** *n*

can·on[1] [KAN-ən] *n* **1** law or rule, esp. of church. **2** standard. **3** body of books accepted as genuine. **4** list of saints. **can·on·i·za'tion** *n* **can'on·ize** *vt* **-ized, -iz·ing** enroll in list of saints.

canon[2] *n* church dignitary, member of cathedral or collegiate chapter or staff. **ca·non'i·cal** *adj* **ca·non'i·cals** *pl n* canonical vestments.

can·o·py [KAN-ə-pee] *n*, *pl* **-pies** **1** covering over throne, bed, etc. **2** any overhanging shelter. ◆ *vt* **-pied, -py·ing** **3** cover with canopy.

cant[1] [kant] *n* **1** hypocritical speech. **2** whining. **3** language of a sect. **4** technical jargon. **5** slang, esp. of thieves.

cant[2] *v* **cant·ed, cant·ing** **1** tilt, slope. **2** bevel.

can·ta·loupe [KAN-tl-ohp] *n* variety of muskmelon.

can·tan·ker·ous [kan-TANG-kər-əs] *adj* ill-natured, quarrelsome.

can·ta·ta [kən-TAH-tə] *n* choral work like, but shorter than, oratorio.

can·teen [kan-TEEN] *n* **1** flask for carrying water. **2** place in factory, school, etc. where light meals are provided. **3** post exchange.

can·ter [KAN-tər] *n* **1** easy gallop. ◆ *v* **2** move at, make to canter.

can·ti·le·ver *n* **1** beam, girder, etc. fixed at one end only. ◆ *vi* **2** project like a cantilever. ◆ *vt* **3** build to project in this manner.

can·to [KAN-toh] *n*, *pl* **-tos** division of a poem.

can·ton [KAN-tn] *n* division of country, esp. Swiss federal state.

can·ton·ment [kan-TON-mənt] *n* quarters for troops.

can·tor [KAN-tər] *n* chief singer of liturgy in synagogue.

can·vas [KAN-vəs] *n* **1** coarse cloth used for sails, painting on, etc. **2** sails of ship. **3** picture.

can·vass [KAN-vəs] *vt* **1** solicit votes, contributions, etc. **2** discuss, examine. ◆ *n* **3** solicitation.

can·yon [KAN-yən] *n* deep gorge.

cap [kap] *n* **1** covering for head. **2** lid, top, or other covering. ◆ *vt* **capped, cap·ping** **3** put a limit on. **4** outdo. **5** seal (a well).

ca·pa·ble [KAY-pə-bəl] *adj* **1** able, gifted. **2** competent. **3** having the capacity, power. **ca·pa·bil'i·ty** *n*

ca·pac·i·ty [kə-PAS-i-tee] *n*, *pl* **-ties** **1**

——————— THESAURUS ———————

canker *n* = **disease**, bane, blight, cancer, corruption, infection, rot, scourge, sore, ulcer

cannon *n* = **gun**, big gun, field gun, mortar

canny *adj* = **shrewd**, astute, careful, cautious, clever, judicious, prudent, wise

canon *n* **1** = **rule**, criterion, dictate, formula, precept, principle, regulation, standard, statute, yardstick **2** = **list**, catalog, roll

canopy *n* = **awning**, covering, shade, sunshade

cant[1] *n* **1** = **hypocrisy**, humbug, insincerity, lip service, pretense, pretentiousness, sanctimoniousness **2** = **jargon**, argot, lingo, patter, slang, vernacular

cant[2] *v* = **tilt**, angle, bevel, incline, rise, slant, slope

cantankerous *adj* = **bad-tempered**, choleric, contrary, disagreeable, grumpy, irascible, irritable, testy, waspish

canter *n* **1** = **jog**, amble, dogtrot, lope ◆ *v* **2** = **jog**, amble, lope

canvass *v* **1** = **campaign**, electioneer, solicit, solicit votes **2** = **poll**, examine, inspect, investigate, scrutinize, study ◆ *n* **3** = **poll**, examination, investigation, scrutiny, survey, tally

cap *v* = **beat**, better, crown, eclipse, exceed, outdo, outstrip, surpass, top, transcend

capability *n* = **ability**, capacity, competence, means, potential, power, proficiency, qualification(s), wherewithal

capable *adj* = **able**, accomplished,

power of holding or grasping. **2** room. **3** volume. **4** character. **5** ability, power of mind. **ca·pa'cious** [-PAY-shəs] *adj* roomy. **ca·pac'i·tance** *n* (measure of) ability of system to store electric charge. **ca·pac'i·tor** *n*

cape[1] [kayp] *n* covering for shoulders.

cape[2] *n* point of land running into sea, headland. **Cape Cod** common type of cottage in Mass. and elsewhere in Northeast.

ca·per[1] [KAY-pər] *n* **1** skip. **2** frolic. **3** escapade. ♦ *vi* **4** skip, dance.

caper[2] *n* pickled flower bud of Sicilian shrub.

cap·il·lar·y [KAP-ə-ler-ee] *adj* **1** hairlike. ♦ *n*, *pl* **-lar·ies 2** tube with very small bore, esp. small blood vessel.

cap·i·tal [KAP-i-tl] *n* **1** chief town. **2** money, stock, funds. **3** large-sized letter. **4** headpiece of column. ♦ *adj* **5** involving or punishable by death. **6** serious. **7** chief. **8** leading. **9** excellent. **cap'i·tal·ism** *n* economic system based on private ownership of industry. **cap'i·tal·ist** *n* **1** owner of capital. **2** supporter of capitalism. ♦ *adj* **3** run by, possessing, capital, as capitalist state. **cap'i·tal·ize** *v* **-ized, -iz·ing 1** convert into capital. **2** (with *on*) turn to advantage.

Cap·i·tol [KAP-i-tl] *n* **1** building in which US Congress meets. **2** (c-) a state legislature building.

ca·pit·u·late [kə-PICH-ə-layt] *vi* **-lat·ed, -lat·ing** surrender on terms, give in. **ca·pit·u·la'tion** *n*

ca·pon [KAY-pon] *n* castrated male fowl fattened for eating. **ca'pon·ize** *vt* **-ized, -iz·ing**

cap·puc·ci·no [kap-ə-CHEE-noh] *n* espresso coffee with steamed milk.

ca·price [kə-PREES] *n* whim, freak. **ca·pri'cious** [-PRISH-əs] *adj*

cap·size [KAP-sīz] *v* **-sized, -siz·ing** ♦ *vt* **1** (of boat) upset. ♦ *vi* **2** be overturned.

cap·stan [KAP-stən] *n* machine to wind cable, esp. to hoist anchor.

cap·sule [KAP-səl] *n* **1** gelatin case for dose of medicine or drug. **2** any small enclosed area or container. **3** seed vessel of plant. **cap'sul·ize** *vt* **-ized, -iz·ing 1** enclose in a capsule. **2** put (news or information) in concise form.

cap·tain [KAP-tən] *n* **1** commander of ship or company of soldiers. **2** leader, chief. ♦ *vt* **3** be captain of.

cap·tion [KAP-shən] *n* heading, title of article, picture, etc.

cap·tious [KAP-shəs] *adj* **1** ready to find fault. **2** critical. **3** peevish. **cap'tious·ness** *n*

competent, efficient, gifted, proficient, qualified, talented

capacious *adj* = **spacious**, broad, commodious, expansive, extensive, roomy, sizable *or* sizeable, substantial, vast, voluminous, wide

capacity *n* **1** = **size**, amplitude, compass, dimensions, extent, magnitude, range, room, scope, space, volume **2** = **ability**, aptitude, aptness, capability, competence, facility, genius, gift **3** = **function**, office, position, post, province, role, sphere

cape *n* = **headland**, head, peninsula, point, promontory

caper *n* **1** = **escapade**, antic, high jinks, jape, lark (*inf*), mischief, practical joke, prank, stunt ♦ *v* **2** = **dance**, bound, cavort, frolic, gambol, jump, skip, spring, trip

capital *n* **1** = **money**, assets, cash, finances, funds, investment(s), means, principal, resources, wealth, wherewithal ♦ *adj* **2** = **principal**, cardinal, major, prime, vital **3** *Old-fashioned* = **first-rate**, excellent, fine, splendid, sterling, superb

capitalism *n* = **private enterprise**, free enterprise, laissez faire *or* laisser faire, private ownership

capitalize on *v* = **take advantage of**, benefit from, cash in on (*inf*), exploit, gain from, make the most of, profit from

capitulate *v* = **give in**, come to terms, give up, relent, submit, succumb, surrender, yield

caprice *n* = **whim**, fad, fancy, fickleness, impulse, inconstancy, notion, whimsy

capricious *adj* = **unpredictable**, changeful, erratic, fickle, fitful, impulsive, inconsistent, inconstant, mercurial, variable, wayward, whimsical

capsize *v* = **overturn**, invert, keel over, tip over, turn over, turn turtle, upset

capsule *n* **1** = **pill**, lozenge, tablet **2** *Botany* = **pod**, case, receptacle, seed case, sheath, shell, vessel

captain *n* = **leader**, boss (*inf*), chief, commander, head, master, skipper

captivate *v* = **charm**, allure, attract, beguile, bewitch, enchant, enrapture,

cap•tive [KAP-tiv] *n* **1** prisoner. ◆ *adj* **2** taken, imprisoned. **cap'ti•vate** *vt* **-vat•ed, -vat•ing** fascinate. **cap'ti•vat•ing** *adj* delightful. **cap•tiv'i•ty** *n*

cap•ture [KAP-chər] *vt* **-tured, -tur•ing 1** seize, make prisoner. ◆ *n* **2** seizure, taking. **cap'tor** *n*

car [kahr] *n* **1** automobile. **2** passenger compartment, as in cable car. **3** vehicle running on rails. **car park** area, building where vehicles may be left for a time.

ca•rafe [kə-RAF] *n* glass water bottle for the table, decanter.

car•a•mel [KAR-ə-məl] *n* **1** burned sugar or syrup for cooking. **2** type of confectionery. **car'a•mel•ize** *v* **-ized, -iz•ing 1** change (sugar, etc.) into caramel. **2** become caramel.

car•at [KAR-ət] *n* **1** small weight used for gold, diamonds, etc. **2** proportional measure of twenty-fourths used to state fineness of gold.

car•a•van [KAR-ə-van] *n* company of merchants traveling together for safety in the East.

car•a•way [KAR-ə-way] *n* plant whose seeds are used as a spice in bread, etc.

car•bide [KAHR-bīd] *n* compound of carbon with an element, esp. calcium carbide.

car•bine [KAHR-been] *n* light rifle.

car•bo•hy•drate [kahr-boh-HĪ-drayt] *n* any of large group of compounds containing carbon, hydrogen and oxygen, esp. sugars and starches as components of food.

car•bol•ic ac•id [kahr-BOL-ik] disinfectant derived from coal tar.

car•bon [KAHR-bən] *n* nonmetallic element, substance of pure charcoal, found in all organic matter. **car'bon•ate** *n* salt of carbonic acid. **car•bon'ic** *adj* **car'bon•ize** *vt* **-ized, -iz•ing** carbonic acid **1**

carbon dioxide. **2** compound formed by carbon dioxide and water. **carbon dioxide** colorless gas exhaled in respiration of animals. **carbon paper** paper coated with a dark, waxy pigment, used for duplicating written or typed matter, producing **carbon copy**.

car•bo•run•dum [kahr-bə-RUN-dəm] *n* artificial silicate of carbon.

car•bun•cle [KAHR-bung-kəl] *n* inflamed ulcer, boil or tumor.

car•bu•re•tor [KAHR-bə-ray-tər] *n* device for vaporizing and mixing gasoline with air in internal combustion engine.

car•cass [KAHR-kəs] *n* **1** dead animal body. **2** orig. skeleton.

car•cin•o•gen [kahr-SIN-ə-jən] *n* substance producing cancer.

car•ci•no•ma [kahr-sə-NOH-mə] *n, pl* **-mas** a cancer.

card¹ [kahrd] *n* **1** thick, stiff paper. **2** piece of this giving identification, etc. **3** greeting card. **4** one of the 48 or 52 playing cards making up a pack. **5** *inf* a character, eccentric. ◆ *pl n* **6** any card game. **card'board** *n* thin, stiff board made of paper pulp.

card² *n* **1** instrument for combing wool, etc. ◆ *vt* **2** comb.

car•di•ac [KAHR-dee-ak] *adj* **1** pert. to the heart. ◆ *n* **2** person with heart disease. **car'di•o•graph** [-ə-graf] *n* instrument that records movements of the heart. **car'di•o•gram** *n* graph of such.

car•di•gan [KAHR-di-gən] *n* knitted sweater opening in front.

car•di•nal [KAHR-dn-l] *adj* **1** chief, principal. ◆ *n* **2** highest rank, next to the Pope in Cath. church. **3** N Amer. finch, male of which is bright red in summer. **cardinal numbers** 1, 2, 3, etc. **cardinal points** N, S, E, W.

enthrall, entrance, fascinate, infatuate, mesmerize

captive *n* **1 = prisoner**, convict, detainee, hostage, internee, prisoner of war, slave ◆ *adj* **2 = confined**, caged, enslaved, ensnared, imprisoned, incarcerated, locked up, penned, restricted, subjugated

captivity *n* **= confinement**, bondage, custody, detention, imprisonment, incarceration, internment, slavery

capture *v* **1 = catch**, apprehend, arrest, bag, collar (*inf*), secure, seize, take, take

prisoner ◆ *n* **2 = catching**, apprehension, arrest, imprisonment, seizure, taking, taking captive, trapping

car *n* **1 = vehicle**, auto, automobile, clunker (*inf*), jalopy (*inf*), machine, motor, motorcar, wheels (*inf*) **2 = (railway) carriage**, buffet car, cable car, coach, dining car, sleeping car, van

carcass *n* **= body**, cadaver (*Medical*), corpse, dead body, framework, hulk, remains, shell, skeleton

cardinal *adj* **= principal**, capital, central,

care [kair] *vi* **cared, car·ing 1** be anxious. **2** have regard or liking (for). **3** look after. **4** be disposed to. ◆ *n* **5** attention. **6** pains, heed. **7** charge, protection. **8** anxiety. **9** caution. **care'free** *adj* **care'ful** *adj* **care'less** *adj* **care'tak·er** *n* **1** person in charge of premises. ◆ *adj* **2** temporary, interim.

ca·reen [kə-REEN] *vt* **1** cause ship to list. **2** lay ship over on its side for cleaning and repair. ◆ *vi* **3** keel over. **4** sway dangerously.

ca·reer [kə-REER] *n* **1** course through life. **2** profession. **3** rapid motion. ◆ *vi* **4** run or move at full speed.

ca·ress [kə-RES] *vt* **1** fondle, embrace, treat with affection. ◆ *n* **2** act or expression of affection.

car·et [KAR-it] *n* mark (∧) showing where to insert something omitted.

car·go [KAHR-goh] *n, pl* **-goes** load, freight, carried by ship, plane, etc.

car·i·bou [KAR-ə-boo] *n* N Amer. reindeer.

car·i·ca·ture [KAR-i-kə-chər] *n* **1** likeness exaggerated or distorted to appear ridiculous. ◆ *vt* **-tured, -tur·ing 2** portray in this way. **car'i·ca·tur·ist** *n*

car·ies [KAIR-eez] *n* tooth decay.

car·il·lon [KAIR-ə-lon] *n* **1** set of bells usu. hung in tower and played by set of keys, pedals, etc. **2** tune so played.

car·min·a·tive [kahr-MIN-ə-tiv] *n* **1** medicine to remedy flatulence. ◆ *adj* **2** acting as this.

car·mine [KAHR-min] *n* **1** brilliant red color (prepared from cochineal). ◆ *adj* **2** of this color.

car·nage [KAHR-nij] *n* slaughter.

car·nal [KAHR-nl] *adj* **1** fleshly, sensual. **2** worldly.

car·na·tion [kahr-NAY-shən] *n* **1** cultivated flower. **2** flesh color.

car·ni·val [KAHR-nə-vəl] *n* **1** festive occasion. **2** traveling fair. **3** show or display for amusement.

car·niv·o·rous [kahr-NIV-ər-əs] *adj* flesh-eating. **car'ni·vore** [-nə-vor] *n*

car·ob [KAR-əb] *n* Mediterranean tree with edible pods.

chief, essential, first, fundamental, key, leading, main, paramount, primary

care *v* **1** = **be concerned**, be bothered, be interested, mind ◆ *n* **2** = **caution**, attention, carefulness, consideration, forethought, heed, management, pains, prudence, vigilance, watchfulness **3** = **protection**, charge, control, custody, guardianship, keeping, management, supervision **4** = **worry**, anxiety, concern, disquiet, perplexity, pressure, responsibility, stress, trouble

career *n* **1** = **occupation**, calling, employment, life's work, livelihood, pursuit, vocation ◆ *v* **2** = **rush**, barrel (along) (*inf*), bolt, dash, hurtle, race, speed, tear

care for *v* **1** = **look after**, attend, foster, mind, minister to, nurse, protect, provide for, tend, watch over **2** = **like**, be fond of, desire, enjoy, love, prize, take to, want

carefree *adj* = **untroubled**, blithe, breezy, cheerful, easy-going, halcyon, happy-go-lucky, light-hearted

careful *adj* **1** = **cautious**, chary, circumspect, discreet, prudent, scrupulous, thoughtful, thrifty **2** = **thorough**, conscientious, meticulous, painstaking, particular, precise

careless *adj* **1** = **slapdash**, cavalier,

inaccurate, irresponsible, lackadaisical, neglectful, offhand, slipshod, sloppy (*inf*) **2** = **negligent**, absent-minded, forgetful, hasty, remiss, thoughtless, unthinking **3** = **nonchalant**, artless, casual, unstudied

carelessness *n* = **negligence**, indiscretion, irresponsibility, laxity, neglect, omission, slackness, sloppiness (*inf*), thoughtlessness

caress *v* **1** = **stroke**, cuddle, embrace, fondle, hug, kiss, make out (*inf*), neck (*inf*), nuzzle, pet ◆ *n* **2** = **stroke**, cuddle, embrace, fondling, hug, kiss, pat

caretaker *n* = **warden**, concierge, curator, custodian, janitor, keeper, porter, superintendent, watchman

cargo *n* = **load**, baggage, consignment, contents, freight, goods, merchandise, shipment

caricature *n* **1** = **parody**, burlesque, cartoon, distortion, farce, lampoon, satire, travesty ◆ *v* **2** = **parody**, burlesque, distort, lampoon, mimic, mock, ridicule, satirize

carnage *n* = **slaughter**, blood bath, bloodshed, butchery, havoc, holocaust, massacre, mass murder, murder, shambles

carnal *adj* = **sexual**, erotic, fleshly, lascivious, lewd, libidinous, lustful, sensual

carnival *n* = **festival**, celebration, fair, fête, fiesta, gala, holiday, jamboree, jubilee, merrymaking, revelry

car·ol [KAR-əl] *n* **1** song or hymn of joy or praise (esp. Christmas carol). ◆ *vi* **-oled, -ol·ing 2** sing (carols).

car·om [KAR-əm] *n* **1** billiard stroke, hitting both object balls with one's own. ◆ *vi* **2** make this stroke. **3** rebound, collide.

ca·rouse [kə-ROWZ] *vi* **-roused, -rous·ing** have merry drinking spree. ◆ *n* **ca·rous'er** *n*

car·ou·sel [kar ə SEL] *n* merry go round.

carp[1] [kahrp] *n* freshwater fish.

carp[2] *vi* complain about small faults or errors. **carp'ing** *adj*

car·pen·ter [KAHR-pən-tər] *n* **1** worker in timber as in building, etc. **car'pen·try** [-tree] *n* this art.

car·pet [KAHR-pit] *n* **1** heavy fabric for covering floor. ◆ *vt* **2** cover floor. **car'pet·bag** *n* traveling bag. **car'pet·bag·ger** *n* political adventurer. **on the carpet** called up for censure.

car·riage [KA-rij] *n* **1** bearing, conduct. **2** horse-drawn vehicle. **3** act, cost, of carrying.

car·ri·on [KA-ree-ən] *n* rotting dead flesh.

car·rot [KA-rət] *n* **1** plant with orange-red edible root. **2** inducement. **car'rot·top** *n* person with red hair.

car·ry [KA-ree] *v* **-ried, -ry·ing** ◆ *vt* **1** convey, transport. **2** capture, win. **3** effect. **4** behave. ◆ *vi* **5** (of projectile, sound) reach. ◆ *n* **6** range. **car'ri·er** *n* **1** one that carries goods. **2** immune person who communicates a disease to others. **3** aircraft carrier. **4** kind of pigeon. **carry on 1** continue. **2** *inf* fuss unnecessarily.

cart [kahrt] *n* **1** open (two-wheeled) vehicle, esp. pulled by horse. ◆ *vt* **2** convey in cart.

3 carry with effort. **cart'er** *n* **cart'horse** *n* **cart'wheel** *n* **1** large, spoked wheel. **2** sideways somersault. **cart'wright** *n* maker of carts.

carte blanche [kahrt blanch] *n, pl* **cartes blanches** [kahrts blanch] complete discretion or authority.

car·tel [kahr-TEL] *n* **1** commercial combination for the purpose of fixing prices, output, etc. **2** alliance of political parties, etc. to further common aims.

Car·te·sian [kahr-TEE-zhən] *adj* **1** pert. to the French philosopher René Descartes (1596-1650) or his system of coordinates. ◆ *n* **2** an adherent of his philosophy.

car·ti·lage [KAHR-tl-ij] *n* **1** firm elastic tissue in the body. **2** gristle. **car·ti·lag'i·nous** *adj*

car·tog·ra·phy [kahr-TOG-rə-fee] *n* map making. **car·tog'ra·pher** *n*

car·ton [KAHR-tn] *n* cardboard or plastic container.

car·toon [kahr-TOON] *n* **1** drawing, esp. humorous or satirical. **2** sequence of drawings telling story. **3** animated cartoon.

car·tridge [KAHR-trij] *n* **1** case containing charge for gun. **2** container for film, magnetic tape, etc. **3** unit in head of phonograph pickup.

carve [kahrv] *vt* **carved, carv·ing 1** cut. **2** hew. **3** sculpture. **4** engrave. **5** cut in pieces or slices (meat). **carv'er** *n*

car·y·at·id [kar-ee-AT-id] *n* supporting column in shape of female figure.

cas·cade [kas-KAYD] *n* **1** waterfall. **2** anything resembling this. ◆ *vi* **-cad·ed, -cad·ing 3** fall in cascades.

case[1] [kays] *n* **1** instance. **2** event,

carol *n* = **song**, chorus, ditty, hymn, lay

carp *v* = **find fault**, cavil, complain, criticize, pick holes, quibble, reproach

carpenter *n* = **joiner**, cabinet-maker, woodworker

carriage *n* **1** = **vehicle**, cab, coach, conveyance **2** = **bearing**, air, behavior, comportment, conduct, demeanor, deportment, gait, manner, posture

carry *v* **1** = **transport**, bear, bring, conduct, convey, fetch, haul, lug, move, relay, take, transfer **2** = **win**, accomplish, capture, effect, gain, secure

carry on *v* = **continue**, endure, keep going, last, maintain, perpetuate, persevere, persist

carry out *v* = **perform**, accomplish,

achieve, carry through, effect, execute, fulfill, implement, realize

carton *n* = **box**, case, container, pack, package, packet

cartoon *n* **1** = **drawing**, caricature, comic strip, lampoon, parody, satire, sketch **2** = **animation**, animated cartoon, animated film

cartridge *n* **1** = **shell**, charge, round **2** = **container**, capsule, case, cassette, cylinder, magazine

carve *v* = **cut**, chip, chisel, engrave, etch, hew, mold, sculpt, slice, whittle

cascade *n* **1** = **waterfall**, avalanche, cataract, deluge, downpour, falls, flood, fountain, outpouring, shower, torrent ◆ *v* **2** = **flow**, descend, fall, flood, gush, circumstance. **3** question at issue. **4** state of affairs, condition. **5** arguments supporting particular action, etc. **6** *Med.* patient under treatment. **7** law suit. **8** grounds for suit. **9** grammatical relation of words in sentence.

case² *n* **1** box, sheath, covering. **2** receptacle. **3** box and contents. ♦ *vt* **cased, cas·ing 4** put in a case. **case'hard·en** *vt* **1** harden by carbonizing the surface of (esp. iron) by converting into steel. **2** make hard, callous.

case·ment [KAYS-mənt] *n* window opening on hinges.

cash [kash] *n* **1** money, bills and coin. ♦ *vt* **2** turn into or exchange for money. **cash·ier** [ka-SHEER] *n* one in charge of receiving and paying of money. **cash dispenser** computerized device outside a bank for supplying cash. **cash register** till that records amount of money put in.

cash·ier [ka-SHEER] *vt* dismiss from office or service.

cash·mere [KAZH-meer] *n* **1** fine soft fabric. **2** yarn made from goat's wool.

ca·si·no [kə-SEE-noh] *n, pl* **-nos 1** building, institution for gambling. **2** type of card game.

cask [kask] *n* **1** barrel. **2** container for wine.

cas·ket [KAS-kit] *n* **1** small case for jewels, etc. **2** coffin.

Cas·san·dra [kə-SAN-drə] *n* prophet of misfortune or disaster.

cas·se·role [KAS-ə-rohl] *n* **1** fireproof cooking and serving dish. **2** food cooked in this.

cas·sette [kə-SET] *n* plastic container for film, magnetic tape, etc.

cas·sock [KAS-ək] *n* long tunic worn by clergymen.

cast [kast] *v* **1** throw or fling. **2** shed. **3** throw down. **4** deposit (a vote). **5** allot, as parts in play. **6** mold, as metal. ♦ *n* **7** throw. **8** distance thrown. **9** squint. **10** mold. **11** that which is shed or ejected. **12** set of actors. **13** type or quality. **cast'ing** *n* **cast'a·way** *n* shipwrecked person. **cast-iron** *adj* **1** made of a hard but brittle type of iron. **2** definite, unchallengeable.

cas·ta·nets [kas-tə-NETS] *pl n* (in Spanish dancing) two small curved pieces of wood, etc. clicked together in hand.

caste [kast] *n* **1** section of society in India. **2** social rank.

cast·er [KAS-tər] *n* **1** container for salt, etc. with perforated top. **2** small swiveled wheel on table leg, etc.

cas·ti·gate [KAS-ti-gayt] *vt* **-gat·ed, -gat·ing 1** punish, rebuke severely, correct. **2** chastise. **cas'ti·ga·tor** *n*

cas·tle [KAS-əl] *n* **1** fortress. **2** mansion. **3** chess piece. **castle in the air** pipe dream.

cas·tor oil [KAS-tər] vegetable medicinal oil.

cas·trate [KAS-trayt] *vt* **-trat·ed, -trat·ing 1** remove testicles, deprive of power of

overflow, pitch, plunge, pour, spill, surge, teem, tumble

case¹ *n* **1** = **instance**, example, illustration, occasion, occurrence, specimen **2** = **situation**, circumstance(s), condition, context, contingency, event, position, state **3** *Law* = **lawsuit**, action, dispute, proceedings, suit, trial

case² *n* **1** = **container**, box, canister, carton, casket, chest, crate, holder, receptacle, suitcase, tray **2** = **covering**, capsule, casing, envelope, jacket, sheath, shell, wrapper

cash *n* = **money**, coinage, currency, dough (*sl*), funds, notes, ready money, silver

cashier¹ *n* = **teller**, bank clerk, banker, bursar, clerk, purser, treasurer

cashier² *v* = **dismiss**, discard, discharge, drum out, expel, give the boot to (*sl*)

casket *n* = **box**, case, chest, coffer, jewel box

cast *n* **1** = **actors**, characters, company,

dramatis personae, players, troupe **2** = **type**, complexion, manner, stamp, style ♦ *v* **3** = **choose**, allot, appoint, assign, name, pick, select **4** = **give out**, bestow, deposit, diffuse, distribute, emit, radiate, scatter, shed, spread **5** = **form**, found, model, mold, set, shape **6** = **throw**, fling, hurl, launch, pitch, sling, thrust, toss

caste *n* = **class**, estate, grade, order, rank, social order, status, stratum

castigate *v* = **reprimand**, berate, censure, chastise, criticize, lambast(e), rebuke, scold

cast-iron *adj* = **certain**, copper-bottomed, definite, established, fixed, guaranteed, settled

castle *n* = **fortress**, chateau, citadel, keep, palace, stronghold, tower

cast-off *adj* **1** = **unwanted**, discarded, rejected, scrapped, surplus to requirements, unneeded, useless ♦ *n* **2** = **reject**, discard, failure, outcast, second

generation. **2** deprive of vigor. **cas·tra'tion**
n

cas·tra·to [ka-STRAH-toh] *n, pl* **-ti** [-tee]
singer castrated in boyhood to preserve
soprano or alto voice.

cas·u·al [KAZH-oo-əl] *adj* **1** accidental. **2**
unforeseen. **3** occasional. **4** unconcerned.
5 informal. **cas'u·al·ty** *n, pl* **-ties 1** person
killed or injured in accident, war, etc. **2**
thing lost, destroyed, in accident, etc.

cas·u·ist [KAZH-oo-ist] *n* **1** one who studies
and solves moral problems. **2** quibbler.
cas'u·ist·ry *n*

cat [kat] *n* any of various feline animals,
including, e.g. small domesticated furred
animal, and lions, tigers, etc. **cat'ty** *adj*
-ti·er, -ti·est spiteful. **cat'call** *n* derisive cry.
cat'fish *n* mainly freshwater fish with
catlike whiskers. **cat'kin** *n* drooping flower
spike. **cat'nap** *vi, n* doze. **cat's'-eye** *n, pl*
-eyes glass reflector set in road to reflect
beams from automobile headlights.
cat'walk *n* narrow, raised path or plank.

ca·tab·o·lism [kə-TAB-ə-liz-əm] *n* breaking
down of complex molecules, destructive
metabolism.

cat·a·clysm [KAT-ə-kliz-əm] *n* (disastrous)
upheaval. **1** deluge. **cat·a·clys'mic** *adj*

cat·a·comb [KAT-ə-kohm] *n* **1**
underground gallery for burial. ♦ *pl* **2** series
of underground tunnels and caves.

cat·a·lep·sy [KAT-l-ep-see] *n* condition of
unconsciousness with rigidity of muscles.
cat·a·lep'tic *adj*

cat·a·log [KAT-l-awg] *n* **1** descriptive list. ♦
vt **2** make such list of. **3** enter in catalog.

cat·a·lyst [KAT-l-ist] *n* **1** substance causing
or assisting a chemical reaction without

taking part in it. **2** person or thing that
precipitates event or change. **cat'a·lyze**
[-l-īz] *vt* **-lyzed, -lyz·ing ca·tal'y·sis** *n*
cat·a·lyt'ic *adj* **catalytic converter** type of
antipollution device for automotive
exhaust system.

cat·a·ma·ran [kat-ə-mə-RAN] *n* **1** type of
sailing boat with twin hulls. **2** raft of logs.

cat·a·pult [KAT-ə-pult] *n* **1** small forked
stick with elastic sling used for throwing
stones. **2** *Hist.* engine of war for hurling
arrows, stones, etc. **3** launching device. ♦
vt

cat·a·ract [KAT-ə-rakt] *n* **1** waterfall. **2**
downpour. **3** disease of eye.

ca·tas·tro·phe [kə-TAS-trə-fee] *n* **1** great
disaster, calamity. **2** culmination of a
tragedy. **cat·a·stroph'ic** *adj*

catch [kach] *v* **caught, catch·ing** ♦ *vt* **1** take
hold of, seize, understand. **2** hear. **3**
contract (disease). **4** be in time for. **5**
surprise, detect. ♦ *vi* **6** be contagious. **7** get
entangled. **8** begin to burn. ♦ *n* **9** seizure.
10 thing that holds, stops, etc. **11** what is
caught. **12** *inf* snag, disadvantage. **13** form
of musical composition. **14** thing, person
worth catching, esp. as spouse. **catch'er** *n*
catching *adj* **catch'y** *adj* **catch·i·er,**
catch·i·est 1 pleasant, memorable. **2** tricky.
catch'word *n* popular phrase or idea.
catch 22 inescapable dilemma. **catch·ment**
area 1 drainage basin, area in which
rainfall collects to form the supply of river,
etc. **2** area from which people are
allocated to a particular social service
agency, hospital, etc. **catch-as-catch-can**
adj using any method that can be applied.
cat·e·chize [KAT-i-kīz] *vt* **-chized, -chiz·ing**

castrate *v* = **neuter**, emasculate, geld
casual *adj* **1** = **careless**, blasé, cursory,
lackadaisical, nonchalant, offhand, relaxed,
unconcerned **2** = **occasional**, accidental,
chance, incidental, irregular, random,
unexpected **3** = **informal**, non-dressy,
sporty
casualty *n* = **victim**, death, fatality, loss,
sufferer, wounded
cat *n* = **feline**, kitty (*inf*), puss (*inf*), pussy
(*inf*), tabby
catacombs *pl n* = **vault**, crypt, tomb
catalog *n* **1** = **list**, directory, gazetteer,
index, inventory, record, register, roll,
roster, schedule ♦ *v* **2** = **list**, accession,
alphabetize, classify, file, index, inventory,

register, tabulate
catapult *n* **1** = **sling**, slingshot (*U.S.*) ♦ *v* **2** =
shoot, heave, hurl, pitch, plunge, propel
catastrophe *n* = **disaster**, adversity,
calamity, cataclysm, fiasco, misfortune,
tragedy, trouble
catcall *n* = **jeer**, boo, gibe, hiss, raspberry,
whistle
catch *v* **1** = **seize**, clutch, get, grab, grasp,
grip, lay hold of, snatch, take **2** = **capture**,
apprehend, arrest, ensnare, entrap, snare
3 = **discover**, catch in the act, detect,
expose, find out, surprise, take unawares,
unmask **4** = **contract**, develop, get, go
down with, incur, succumb to, suffer from
5 = **make out**, comprehend, discern, get,

1 instruct by question and answer. **2** question. **cat'e·chism** n **1** such instruction. **cat'e·chist** n

cat·e·go·ry [KAT-i-gohr-ee] n, pl **-ries** class, order, division. **cat·e·gor'i·cal** adj **1** positive. **2** of category. **cat·e·gor'i·cal·ly** adv **cat'e·go·rize** vt **-ized, -iz·ing**

ca·ter [KAY-tər] vi provide what is required or desired, esp. food, etc. **ca'ter·er** n

cat·er·pil·lar [KAT-ə-pil-ər] n hairy grub of moth or butterfly.

cat·er·waul [KAT-ər-wawl] vi **1** wail, howl. **2** argue noisily.

ca·the·dral [kə-THEE-drəl] n **1** principal church of diocese. ◆ adj **2** pert. to, containing cathedral.

cath·ode [KATH-ohd] n negative electrode. **cathode rays** stream of electrons.

cath·o·lic [KATH-lik] adj **1** universal. **2** including whole body of Christians. **3** (C-) relating to Catholic Church. ◆ n **4** C- adherent of Catholic Church. **Ca·thol·i·cism** [kə-THOL-ə-siz-əm] n **cath·o·lic·i·ty** [kath-ə-LIS-i-tee] n

CAT scan [kat skan] computerized axial tomography (also **CT scan**).

cat·tle [KAT-l] pl n beasts of pasture, esp. steers, cows. **cat'tle·man** n **cattle guard** heavy grid over ditch in road to prevent passage of livestock.

Cau·ca·sian [kaw-KAY-zhən] adj, n (of, pert. to) light-complexioned racial group of mankind. **Cau'ca·soid** [-kə-soid] adj, n

cau·cus [KAW-kəs] n group, meeting, esp. of members of political party, with power to decide policy, etc.

caught pt./pp. of CATCH.

caul·dron [KAWL-drən] n large pot used for boiling.

cau·li·flow·er [KAW-li-flow-ər] n variety of cabbage with edible white flowering head.

caulk [kawk] vt stop up cracks (orig. of ship) with waterproof filler. **caulk'er** n **caulk'ing** n **caulking compound** filler used in caulking.

cause [kawz] n **1** that which produces an effect. **2** reason, origin. **3** motive, purpose. **4** charity, movement. **5** lawsuit. ◆ vt **caused, caus·ing 6** bring about, make happen. **caus'al** adj **cau·sal'i·ty** n **cau·sa'tion** n **cause'less** adj groundless.

cause cé·lè·bre [kawz sə-LEB-rə] n, pl **causes cé·lè·bres** [kawz sə-LEB-rəz] great controversy e.g. famous legal case.

cause·way [KAWZ-way] n **1** raised way over marsh, etc. **2** highway.

caus·tic [KAW-stik] adj **1** burning. **2** bitter, severe. ◆ n **3** corrosive substance. **caus'ti·cal·ly** adv

cau·ter·ize [KAW-tə-rīz] vt **-ized, -iz·ing** burn with caustic or hot iron. **cau·ter·i·za'tion** n

cau·tion [KAW-shən] n **1** heedfulness, care. **2** warning. ◆ vt **3** warn. **cau'tion·ar·y** adj containing warning or precept. **cau'tious** adj

———————— THESAURUS ————————

grasp, hear, perceive, recognize, sense, take in ◆ n **6** = **fastener**, bolt, clasp, clip, latch **7** = **drawback**, disadvantage, fly in the ointment, hitch, snag, stumbling block, trap, trick

catching adj = **infectious**, communicable, contagious, transferable, transmittable

catch on v = **understand**, comprehend, find out, get the picture, grasp, see, see through

catchword n = **slogan**, byword, motto, password, watchword

catchy adj = **memorable**, captivating, haunting, popular

categorical adj = **absolute**, downright, emphatic, explicit, express, positive, unambiguous, unconditional, unequivocal, unqualified, unreserved

category n = **class**, classification, department, division, grade, grouping, heading, section, sort, type

cater v = **provide**, furnish, outfit, purvey, supply

cattle pl n = **cows**, beasts, bovines, livestock, stock

catty adj = **spiteful**, backbiting, bitchy (inf), malevolent, malicious, rancorous, shrewish, snide, venomous

cause n **1** = **origin**, agent, beginning, creator, genesis, mainspring, maker, producer, root, source, spring **2** = **reason**, basis, grounds, incentive, inducement, justification, motivation, motive, purpose **3** = **aim**, belief, conviction, enterprise, ideal, movement, principle ◆ v **4** = **produce**, bring about, create, generate, give rise to, incite, induce, lead to, result in

caustic adj **1** = **burning**, acrid, astringent, biting, corroding, corrosive, mordant, vitriolic **2** = **sarcastic**, acrimonious, cutting, pungent, scathing, stinging, trenchant, virulent, vitriolic

cav·al·cade [KAV-əl-kayd] *n* **1** column or procession of riders. **2** series.

cav·a·lier [kav-ə-LEER] *adj* **1** careless, disdainful. ◆ *n* **2** courtly gentleman. **3** *obs* horseman.

cav·al·ry [KAV-əl-ree] *n, pl* **-ries** mounted troops.

cave [kayv] *n* **1** hollow place in the earth. **2** den. **cav·ern** [KAV-ərn] *n* deep cave **cav'ern·ous** *adj* **cav'i·ty** *n, pl* **-ties** hollow. **cave'man** *n* prehistoric cave dweller. **cave in 1** fall inward. **2** submit. **3** give in.

cav·i·ar [KAV-ee-ahr] *n* salted sturgeon roe.

cav·il [KAV-əl] *vi* **-iled, -il·ing** find fault without sufficient reason, make trifling objections. **cav'il·ing** *n* **cav'il·er** *n*

cav·i·ta·tion [kav-i-TAY-shən] *n* rapid formation of cavities or bubbles. **cav'i·tate** *vi* **-tat·ed, -tat·ing** undergo cavitation.

ca·vort [kə-VORT] *vi* prance, frisk.

caw [kaw] *n* **1** crow's cry. ◆ *vi* **2** cry so.

cay·enne pepper [kī-EN] *n* pungent red pepper.

Cd *Chem.* cadmium.

CD 1 compact disk. **2** certificate of deposit. **CD-R** compact disk recordable. **CD-ROM** compact disk storing digitized read-only data. **CD-RW** compact disk read-write.

cease [sees] *v* **ceased, ceas·ing** bring or come to an end. **cease'less** *adj*

ce·dar [SEE-dər] *n* **1** large evergreen tree. **2** its wood.

cede [seed] *vt* **ced·ed, ced·ing** yield, give up, transfer, esp. of territory.

ce·dil·la [si-DIL-ə] *n* hooklike mark placed under a letter *c* to show the sound of *s*.

ceil·ing [SEE·ling] *n* **1** inner, upper surface of a room. **2** maximum price, wage, etc. **3** *Aviation* lower level of clouds. **4** limit of height to which aircraft can climb.

cel·e·brate [SEL-ə-brayt] *v* **-brat·ed, -brat·ing 1** rejoice or have festivities to mark (happy day, event, etc.). ◆ *vt* **2** observe (birthday, etc.). **3** perform (religious ceremony, etc.). **4** praise publicly. **cel'e·brant** *n* **celebrated** *adj* famous. **cel·e·bra'tion** *n* **ce·leb'ri·ty** *n, pl* **-ties 1** famous person. **2** fame.

ce·ler·i·ty [sə-LER-i-tee] *n* swiftness.

cel·er·y [SEL-ə-ree] *n* vegetable with long juicy edible stalks.

ce·les·tial [sə-LES-chəl] *adj* **1** heavenly, divine. **2** of the sky.

cel·i·ba·cy [SEL-ə-bə-see] *n* sexual abstinence. **cel'i·bate** [-bit] *n, adj*

cell [sel] *n* **1** small room, esp. in prison. **2**

caution *n* **1 = care**, alertness, carefulness, circumspection, deliberation, discretion, forethought, heed, prudence, vigilance, watchfulness **2 = warning**, admonition, advice, counsel, injunction ◆ *v* **3 = warn**, admonish, advise, tip off, urge

cautious *adj* **= careful**, cagey (*inf*), chary, circumspect, guarded, judicious, prudent, tentative, wary

cavalcade *n* **= parade**, array, march-past, procession, spectacle, train

cavalier *adj* **= haughty**, arrogant, disdainful, lofty, lordly, offhand, scornful, supercilious

cavalry *n* **= horsemen**, horse, mounted troops

cave *n* **= hollow**, cavern, cavity, den, grotto

cavern *n* **= cave**, hollow, pothole

cavernous *adj* **= deep**, hollow, sunken, yawning

cavity *n* **= hollow**, crater, dent, gap, hole, pit

cease *v* **= stop**, break off, conclude, discontinue, end, finish, halt, leave off, refrain, terminate

ceaseless *adj* **= continual**, constant,

endless, eternal, everlasting, incessant, interminable, never-ending, nonstop, perpetual, twenty-four-seven (*sl*), unremitting

cede *v* **= surrender**, concede, hand over, make over, relinquish, renounce, resign, transfer, yield

celebrate *v* **1 = rejoice**, commemorate, drink to, keep, kill the fatted calf, observe, put the flags out, toast **2 = perform**, bless, honor, solemnize

celebrated *adj* **= well-known**, acclaimed, distinguished, eminent, famous, illustrious, notable, popular, prominent, renowned

celebration *n* **1 = party**, festival, festivity, gala, jubilee, merrymaking, red-letter day, revelry **2 = performance**, anniversary, commemoration, honoring, observance, remembrance, solemnization

celebrity *n* **1 = personality**, big name, big shot (*inf*), dignitary, luminary, star, superstar, V.I.P. **2 = fame**, distinction, notability, prestige, prominence, renown, reputation, repute, stardom

celestial *adj* **= heavenly**, angelic, astral, divine, ethereal, spiritual, sublime, small cavity. **3** minute, basic unit of living matter. **4** device converting chemical energy into electrical energy. **5** small local group operating as nucleus of larger political or religious organization. **cel·lu·lar** [SEL-yə-lər] *adj* **cell phone, cellular phone** telephone, such as a car phone, operating by radio communication via a network of transmitters each serving a small area.

cel·lar [SEL-ər] *n* **1** underground room or story. **2** stock of wine. **3** wine cellar.

cel·lo [CHEL-oh] *n, pl* **-los** stringed instrument of violin family.

cel·lo·phane [SEL-ə-fayn] *n* transparent wrapping.

cel·lu·loid [SEL-yə-loid] *n* **1** synthetic plastic substance with wide range of uses. **2** motion-picture film.

cel·lu·lose [SEL-yə-lohs] *n* **1** substance of vegetable cell wall. **2** group of carbohydrates.

Cel·si·us [SEL-see-əs] *adj, n* (of) scale of temperature from 0° (melting point of ice) to 100° (boiling point of water).

Celt·ic [KEL-tik, SEL-] *n* **1** branch of language including Gaelic and Welsh. ◆ *adj* **2** of, or relating to the Celtic peoples or languages.

ce·ment [si-MENT] *n* **1** fine mortar. **2** adhesive, glue. ◆ *vt* **3** unite with cement. **4** join firmly.

cem·e·ter·y [SEM-i-ter-ee] *n, pl* **-ter·ies** burial ground.

cen·o·taph [SEN-ə-taf] *n* monument to one buried elsewhere.

cen·ser [SEN-sər] *n* pan in which incense is burned.

cen·sor [SEN-sər] *n* one authorized to examine films, books, etc. and suppress all or part if considered morally or otherwise

unacceptable. ◆ *vt* **cen·so·ri·al** [sen-SOHR-ee-əl] *adj* of censor. **cen·so·ri·ous** *adj* faultfinding. **cen'sor·ship** *n*

cen·sure [SEN-shər] *n* **1** blame. **2** harsh criticism. ◆ *vt* **-sured, -sur·ing 3** blame. **4** criticize harshly.

cen·sus [SEN-səs] *n, pl* **-sus·es** official counting of people, things, etc.

cent [sent] *n* hundredth part of dollar, etc.

cen·taur [SEN-tor] *n* mythical creature, half man, half horse.

cen·ten·ar·y [sen-TEN-ə-ree] *n, adj* centennial. **cen·te·nar·i·an** [sen-tn-AIR-ee-ən] *n* person a hundred years old.

cen·ten·ni·al [sen-TEN-ee-əl] *adj* **1** lasting, happening every hundred years. ◆ *n* **2** 100 years. **3** celebration of hundredth anniversary.

cen·ter [SEN-tər] *n* **1** midpoint. **2** pivot, axis. **3** point to or from which things move or are drawn. **4** place for specific organization or activity. **cen'tral** [-trəl] *adj* **cen·tral'i·ty** *n* **cen'tral·ize** *vt* **-ized, -iz·ing 1** bring to a center. **2** concentrate under one control. **cen'tral·ly** *adv* **cen·trif'.u·gal** [-TRIF-yə-gəl] *adj* tending away from center. **cen·trip'e·tal** [-TRIP-i-tl] *adj* tending toward center. **central heating** method of heating building from one central source. **central processing unit** *Computers* part of a computer that performs logical and arithmetical operations.

cen·ti·grade [SEN-ti-grayd] *adj* **1** another name for Celsius. **2** having one hundred degrees.

cen·ti·me·ter [SEN-tə-mee-tər] *n* hundredth part of meter.

cen·ti·pede [SEN-tə-peed] *n* small

—————— THESAURUS ——————

supernatural

celibacy *n* = **chastity**, continence, purity, virginity

cell *n* **1** = **room**, cavity, chamber, compartment, cubicle, dungeon, stall **2** = **unit**, caucus, core, coterie, group, nucleus

cement *n* **1** = **mortar**, adhesive, glue, gum, paste, plaster, sealant ◆ *v* **2** = **stick together**, attach, bind, bond, combine, glue, join, plaster, seal, unite, weld

cemetery *n* = **graveyard**, burial ground, churchyard, God's acre, necropolis

censor *v* = **cut**, blue-pencil, bowdlerize, expurgate

censorious *adj* = **critical**, captious, carping, cavilling, condemnatory, disapproving, disparaging, fault-finding, hypercritical, scathing, severe

censure *n* **1** = **disapproval**, blame, condemnation, criticism, obloquy, rebuke, reprimand, reproach, reproof, stick (*sl*) ◆ *v* **2** = **criticize**, blame, castigate, condemn, denounce, rap over the knuckles, rebuke, reprimand, reproach, scold, slap on the wrist

center *n* **1** = **middle**, core, focus, heart, hub, kernel, midpoint, nucleus, pivot ◆ *v* **2** = **focus**, cluster, concentrate, converge, segmented animal with many legs.

cen·tu·ry [SEN-chə-ree] *n, pl* **-ries 1** 100 years. **2** any set of 100.

CEO chief executive officer.

ce·ram·ic [sə-RAM-ik] *n* **1** hard brittle material of baked clay. **2** object made of this. ♦ *adj* **ce·ram·ic** *n* **1** hard brittle material made by heating clay to a very high temperature. **2** object made of this. ♦ *pl* **3** art of producing ceramic objects. ♦ *adj* **4** made of ceramic.

ce·re·al [SEER-ee-əl] *n* **1** any edible grain, such as wheat, rice, etc. **2** (breakfast) food made from grain. ♦ *adj*

ce·re·bral [sə-REE-brəl] *adj* pert. to brain or intellect.

cer·e·mo·ny [SER-ə-moh-nee] *n, pl* **-nies 1** formal observance. **2** sacred rite. **3** courteous act. **cer·e·mo'ni·al** *adj, n* **cer·e·mo'ni·ous** *adj*

ce·rise [sə-REES] *n, adj* clear, pinkish red.

cer·tain [SUR-tn] *adj* **1** sure. **2** settled, inevitable. **3** some, one. **4** of moderate (quantity, degree, etc.). **cer'tain·ly** *adv* **cer'tain·ty** *n, pl* **-ties cer'ti·tude** *n* confidence.

cer·ti·fy [SUR-tə-fī] *vt* **-fied, -fy·ing 1** declare formally. **2** endorse, guarantee. **3** declare legally insane. **cer·tif'i·cate** [-kit] *n* **1** written declaration. ♦ *vt* [-kayt] **-cat·ed, -cat·ing 2** give written declaration.

cer·ti·fi·ca'tion *n*

ce·ru·le·an [sə-ROO-lee-ən] *adj* **1** sky blue. **2** deep blue.

cer·vix [SUR-viks] *n, pl* **-vix·es** neck, esp. of womb. **cer'vi·cal** *adj*

ces·sa·tion [se-SAY-shən] *n* ceasing or stopping, pause.

ces·sion [SESH-ən] *n* yielding up.

cess·pit [SES-pit] *n* pit for receiving sewage or other refuse.

cess·pool [SES-pool] *n* **1** catch basin in which sewage collects. **2** filthy place. **3** place of moral filth.

Cf *Chem.* californium.

cf. compare.

CFC chlorofluorocarbon.

cgs units metric system of units based on *centimeter, gram, second.*

chad *n* small pieces removed during the punching of holes in punch cards, printer paper, etc.

chafe [chayf] *vt* **chafed, chaf·ing 1** make sore or worn by rubbing. **2** make warm by rubbing. **3** vex, irritate.

chaff *n* **1** husks of corn. **2** worthless matter. **3** banter. ♦ *v* **4** tease good-naturedly.

cha·grin [shə-GRIN] *n* **1** vexation, disappointment. ♦ *vt* **2** embarrass. **3** annoy. **4** disappoint.

chain [chayn] *n* **1** series of connected links or rings. **2** thing that binds. **3** connected

revolve

central *adj* **1** = **middle**, inner, interior, mean, median, mid **2** = **main**, chief, essential, focal, fundamental, key, primary, principal

centralize *v* = **unify**, concentrate, condense, incorporate, rationalize, streamline

ceremonial *adj* **1** = **ritual**, formal, liturgical, ritualistic, solemn, stately ♦ *n* **2** = **ritual**, ceremony, formality, rite, solemnity

ceremonious *adj* = **formal**, civil, courteous, deferential, dignified, punctilious, solemn, stately, stiff

ceremony *n* **1** = **ritual**, commemoration, function, observance, parade, rite, service, show, solemnities **2** = **formality**, ceremonial, decorum, etiquette, niceties, pomp, propriety, protocol

certain *adj* **1** = **sure**, assured, confident, convinced, positive, satisfied **2** = **known**, conclusive, incontrovertible, irrefutable, true, undeniable, unequivocal **3** =

inevitable, bound, definite, destined, fated, inescapable, sure **4** = **fixed**, decided, definite, established, settled

certainly *adv* = **definitely**, assuredly, indisputably, indubitably, surely, truly, undeniably, undoubtedly, without doubt

certainty *n* **1** = **sureness**, assurance, confidence, conviction, faith, positiveness, trust, validity **2** = **fact**, reality, sure thing (*inf*), truth

certificate *n* = **document**, authorization, credential(s), diploma, license, testimonial, voucher, warrant

certify *v* = **confirm**, assure, attest, authenticate, declare, guarantee, testify, validate, verify

chafe *v* **1** = **rub**, abrade, rasp, scrape, scratch **2** = **be annoyed**, be impatient, fret, fume, rage, worry

chaff[1] *n* = **waste**, dregs, husks, refuse, remains, rubbish, trash

chaff[2] *v* = **tease**, mock, rib (*inf*), ridicule, scoff, taunt series of things or events. **4** surveyor's measure. ◆ *vt* **5** fasten with a chain. **6** confine. **7** restrain.

chair *n* **1** movable seat, with back, for one person. **2** seat of authority. **3** professorship. ◆ *vt* **4** preside over. **5** carry in triumph. **chair'lift** *n* series of chairs fixed to cable for conveying people (esp. skiers) up mountain. **chair'per·son, -wom·an, -man** *n* one who presides over meeting. **chair'man·ship** *n*

chaise [shayz] *n* light horse-drawn carriage. **chaise longue** [lawng] sofa.

chal·ced·o·ny [kal-SED-n-ee] *n* whitish, bluish-white variety of quartz.

cha·let [sha-LAY] *n* **1** Swiss wooden house. **2** house in this style.

chal·ice [CHAL-is] *n* **1** cup or bowl. **2** communion cup.

chalk [chawk] *n* **1** white substance, carbonate of lime. **2** crayon. ◆ *v* **3** rub, draw, mark with chalk. **chalk'y** *adj* **chalk·i·er, chalk·i·est**

chal·lenge [CHAL-inj] *vt* **-lenged, -leng·ing 1** call to fight or account. **2** dispute. **3** stimulate. **4** object to. **5** claim. ◆ *n* **chal'lenged** *adj* disabled as specified, e.g. *physically challenged; mentally challenged.* **chal'leng·er** *n* **chal'leng·ing** *adj* difficult but stimulating.

cham·ber [CHAYM-bər] *n* **1** room for assembly. **2** assembly, body of legislators. **3** compartment. **4** cavity. **5** *obs* room. **6** chamber pot. ◆ *pl* **7** office of lawyer or judge. **8** lodgings. **cham'ber·lain** [-lin] *n* official at court of a monarch having charge of domestic and ceremonial affairs. **cham'ber·maid** *n* female servant with care

of bedrooms. **chamber music** music for performance by a few instruments. **chamber pot** vessel for urine.

cha·me·le·on [kə-MEEL-yən] *n* small lizard famous for its power of changing color.

cham·fer [CHAM-fər] *vt* **1** groove. **2** bevel. **3** flute. ◆ *n* **4** groove.

cham·ois [SHAM-ee] *n* **1** goatlike mountain antelope. **2** a soft pliable leather.

champ[1] *v* **1** munch (food) noisily, as horse. **2** be nervous, impatient.

champ[2] *n* short for CHAMPION.

cham·pagne [sham-PAYN] *n* **1** light, sparkling white wine from Champagne region of France. **2** similar wine made elsewhere.

cham·pi·on [CHAM-pee-ən] *n* **1** one that excels all others. **2** defender of a cause. **3** one who fights for another. **4** hero. ◆ *vt* **5** fight for, maintain. **cham'pi·on·ship** *n*

chance [chans] *n* **1** unpredictable course of events. **2** fortune, luck. **3** opportunity. **4** possibility. **5** risk. **6** probability. ◆ *v* **chanced, chanc·ing** ◆ *vt* **7** risk. ◆ *vi* **8** happen. ◆ *adj* **9** casual, unexpected. **chanc'y** *adj* **chanc·i·er, chanc·i·est** risky.

chan·cel [CHAN-səl] *n* part of a church where altar is.

chan·cel·lor [CHAN-sə-lər] *n* **1** high officer of state. **2** head of university, state educational system.

chan·cer·y [CHAN-sə-ree] *n, pl* **-ies** court of equity.

chan·de·lier [shan-dl-EER] *n* hanging frame with branches for holding lights.

change [chaynj] *v* **changed, chang·ing 1** alter, make or become different. **2** put on (different clothes, fresh coverings). ◆ *vt* **3**

THESAURUS

chain *n* **1** = **link**, bond, coupling, fetter, manacle, shackle **2** = **series**, progression, sequence, set, string, succession, train ◆ *v* **3** = **bind**, confine, enslave, fetter, handcuff, manacle, restrain, shackle, tether

chairman *n* = **director**, chairperson, chairwoman, master of ceremonies, president, speaker, spokesman

challenge *n* **1** = **test**, confrontation, provocation, question, trial, ultimatum ◆ *v* **2** = **test**, confront, defy, dispute, object to, question, tackle, throw down the gauntlet

chamber *n* **1** = **room**, apartment, bedroom, compartment, cubicle, enclosure, hall **2** = **council**, assembly, legislative body, legislature

champion *n* **1** = **winner**, conqueror, hero, title holder, victor **2** = **defender**, backer, guardian, patron, protector, upholder ◆ *v* **3** = **support**, advocate, back, commend, defend, encourage, espouse, fight for, promote, uphold

chance *n* **1** = **probability**, likelihood, odds, possibility, prospect **2** = **opportunity**, occasion, opening, time **3** = **luck**, accident, coincidence, destiny, fate, fortune, providence **4** = **risk**, gamble, hazard, jeopardy, speculation, uncertainty ◆ *v* **5** = **risk**, endanger, gamble, hazard, jeopardize, stake, try, venture, wager

chancy *adj Sl* = **dangerous**, difficult, hazardous, perilous, risky put or give for another. **4** exchange, interchange. ◆ *n* **5** alteration, variation. **6** variety. **7** conversion of money. **8** small money, coins. **9** balance received on payment. **change'a·ble** *adj* **change'less** *adj* **change'ling** *n* child exchanged for another.

chan·nel [CHAN-l] *n* **1** bed of stream. **2** strait. **3** deeper part of strait, bay, harbor. **4** groove. **5** means of passing or conveying. **6** band of radio frequencies. **7** TV broadcasting station. ◆ *vt* **8** groove, furrow. **9** guide, convey.

chant *n* **1** simple song or melody. **2** rhythmic or repetitious slogan. ◆ *v* **3** sing or utter chant. **4** speak monotonously or repetitiously.

chan·tey [SHAN-tee] *n* sailor's song with chorus.

chan·ti·cleer [CHAN-tə-kleer] *n* rooster.

cha·os [KAY-os] *n* **1** disorder, confusion. **2** state of universe before Creation. **cha·ot'ic** *adj* **cha·ot'i·cal·ly** *adv*

chap[1] *v* **chapped, chap·ping** of skin, become dry, raw and cracked, esp. by exposure to cold and wind. **chapped** *adj*

chap[2] *n inf* fellow, man.

chap·el [CHAP-əl] *n* **1** private church. **2** subordinate place of worship. **3** division of

church with its own altar. **4** place of worship used by a nonconforming Christian group. **5** print shop.

chap·er·on, chaperone [SHAP-ə-rohn] *n* **1** one who attends young unmarried woman in public as protector. ◆ *vt* **-oned, -on·ing 2** attend in this way.

chap·lain [CHAP-lin] *n* clergyman attached to chapel, regiment, warship, institution, etc. **chap'lain·cy** *n* office or term of chaplain.

chaps *pl n* cowboy's leggings of thick leather.

chap·ter [CHAP-tər] *n* **1** division of book. **2** section, heading. **3** assembly of clergy, bishop's council, etc. **4** organized branch of society, fraternity.

char [chahr] *vt* **charred, char·ring** scorch, burn to charcoal. **charred** *adj*

char·ac·ter [KAR-ik-tər] *n* **1** nature. **2** total of qualities making up individuality. **3** moral qualities. **4** reputation of possessing them. **5** statement of qualities of person. **6** an eccentric. **7** personality in play or novel. **8** letter, sign, or any distinctive mark. **9** essential feature. **char·ac·ter·is'tic** *adj, n* **char·ac·ter·is'ti·cal·ly** *adv* **char'ac·ter·ize** *vt* **-ized, -iz·ing 1** mark out, distinguish. **2** describe by peculiar qualities.

| THESAURUS |

change *n* **1** = **alteration**, difference, innovation, metamorphosis, modification, mutation, revolution, transformation, transition **2** = **variety**, break (*inf*), departure, diversion, novelty, variation **3** = **exchange**, conversion, interchange, substitution, swap, trade ◆ *v* **4** = **alter**, convert, modify, mutate, reform, reorganize, restyle, shift, transform, vary **5** = **exchange**, barter, convert, interchange, replace, substitute, swap, trade

changeable *adj* = **variable**, erratic, fickle, inconstant, irregular, mobile, mutable, protean, shifting, unsettled, unstable, volatile, wavering

channel *n* **1** = **route**, approach, artery, avenue, course, means, medium, path, way **2** = **passage**, canal, conduit, duct, furrow, groove, gutter, route, strait ◆ *v* **3** = **direct**, conduct, convey, guide, transmit

chant *v* **1** = **sing**, carol, chorus, descant, intone, recite, warble ◆ *n* **2** = **song**, carol, chorus, melody, psalm

chaos *n* = **disorder**, anarchy, bedlam,

confusion, disorganization, lawlessness, mayhem, pandemonium, tumult

chaotic *adj* = **disordered**, anarchic, confused, deranged, disorganized, lawless, riotous, topsy-turvy, tumultuous, uncontrolled

chap *n Inf* = **fellow**, character, guy (*inf*), individual, man, person

chaperone *n* **1** = **escort**, companion ◆ *v* **2** = **escort**, accompany, attend, protect, safeguard, shepherd, watch over

chapter *n* = **section**, clause, division, episode, part, period, phase, stage, topic

character *n* **1** = **nature**, attributes, caliber, complexion, disposition, personality, quality, temperament, type **2** = **reputation**, honor, integrity, rectitude, strength, uprightness **3** = **role**, part, persona, portrayal **4** = **eccentric**, card (*inf*), oddball, original **5** = **symbol**, device, figure, hieroglyph, letter, mark, rune, sign

characteristic *n* **1** = **feature**, attribute, faculty, idiosyncrasy, mark, peculiarity, property, quality, quirk, trait ◆ *adj* **2** = **typical**, distinctive, distinguishing,

char·ade [shə-RAYD] *n* **1** absurd act. **2** travesty. ◆ *pl* **3** word-guessing parlor game with syllables of word acted.

char·coal [CHAHR-kohl] *n* **1** black residue of wood, bones, etc., produced by smothered burning. **2** charred wood.

charge [chahrj] *v* **charged, charg·ing** ◆ *vt* **1** ask as price. **2** bring accusation against. **3** lay task on. **4** command. **5** attack. **6** deliver injunction. **7** fill with electricity. **8** fill, load. ◆ *vi* **9** make onrush, attack. ◆ *n* **10** cost, price. **11** accusation. **12** attack, onrush. **13** command, exhortation. **14** accumulation of electricity. ◆ *pl* **15** expenses. **charge'a·ble** *adj* **charg'er** *n* **1** strong, fast battle horse. **2** that which charges, esp. electrically.

char·i·ot [CHAR-ee-ət] *n* two-wheeled vehicle used in ancient fighting. **char·i·ot·eer'** *n*

cha·ris·ma [kə-RIZ-mə] *n* special power of person to inspire fascination, loyalty, etc. **char·is·mat·ic** [kar-iz-MAT-ik] *adj*

char·i·ty [CHAR-i-tee] *n*, *pl* **-ties 1** the giving of help, money, etc. to those in need. **2** organization for doing this. **3** the money, etc. given. **4** love, kindness. **5** disposition to think kindly of others. **char'i·ta·ble** *adj*

char·la·tan [SHAHR-lə-tn] *n* quack, impostor.

charm [chahrm] *n* **1** attractiveness. **2** anything that fascinates. **3** amulet. **4** magic spell. ◆ *vt* **5** bewitch. **6** delight, attract. **charmed** *adj* **charm'ing** *adj*

char·nel house [CHAHR-nl] *n* vault for bones of the dead.

chart [chahrt] *n* **1** map of sea. **2** diagram or tabulated statement. ◆ *vt* **3** map. **4** represent on chart.

char·ter [CHAHR-tər] *n* **1** document granting privileges, etc. ◆ *vt* **2** let or hire. **3** establish by charter.

char·wom·an [CHAHR-wuum-ən] *n* woman paid to clean office, house, etc.

char·y [CHAIR-ee] *adj* **char·i·er, char·i·est** cautious, sparing. **char'i·ly** *adv* **char'i·ness** *n* caution.

——————— THESAURUS ———————

idiosyncratic, individual, peculiar, representative, singular, special, symbolic, symptomatic

characterize *v* = **identify**, brand, distinguish, indicate, mark, represent, stamp, typify

charade *n* = **pretense**, fake, farce, pantomime, parody, travesty

charge *v* **1** = **accuse**, arraign, blame, impeach, incriminate, indict **2** = **rush**, assail, assault, attack, stampede, storm **3** = **fill**, load **4** = **command**, bid, commit, demand, entrust, instruct, order, require ◆ *n* **5** = **price**, amount, cost, expenditure, expense, outlay, payment, rate, toll **6** = **accusation**, allegation, imputation, indictment **7** = **rush**, assault, attack, onset, onslaught, sortie, stampede **8** = **care**, custody, duty, office, responsibility, safekeeping, trust **9** = **ward 10** = **instruction**, command, demand, direction, injunction, mandate, order, precept

charisma *n* = **charm**, allure, attraction, lure, magnetism, personality

charismatic *adj* = **charming**, alluring, attractive, enticing, influential, magnetic

charitable *adj* **1** = **tolerant**, considerate, favorable, forgiving, humane, indulgent, kindly, lenient, magnanimous,

sympathetic, understanding **2** = **generous**, beneficent, benevolent, bountiful, kind, lavish, liberal, philanthropic

charity *n* **1** = **donations**, assistance, benefaction, contributions, endowment, fund, gift, hand-out, help, largesse *or* largess, philanthropy, relief **2** = **kindness**, altruism, benevolence, compassion, fellow feeling, generosity, goodwill, humanity, indulgence

charlatan *n* = **fraud**, cheat, con man (*inf*), fake, impostor, phoney *or* phony (*inf*), pretender, quack, sham, swindler

charm *n* **1** = **attraction**, allure, appeal, fascination, magnetism **2** = **spell**, enchantment, magic, sorcery **3** = **talisman**, amulet, fetish, trinket ◆ *v* **4** = **attract**, allure, beguile, bewitch, captivate, delight, enchant, enrapture, entrance, fascinate, mesmerize, win over

charming *adj* = **attractive**, appealing, captivating, cute, delightful, fetching, likable *or* likeable, pleasing, seductive, winsome

chart *n* **1** = **table**, blueprint, diagram, graph, map, plan ◆ *v* **2** = **plot**, delineate, draft, map out, outline, shape, sketch

charter *n* **1** = **document**, contract, deed, license, permit, prerogative ◆ *v* **2** = **hire**, commission, employ, lease, rent **3** =

chase¹ [chays] *vt* **chased, chas·ing 1**
hunt, pursue. **2** drive from, away, into, etc.
♦ *n* **3** pursuit, hunting. **4** the hunted. **5**
hunting ground. **chas'er** *n* drink of beer,
soda, etc., taken after straight whiskey.

chase² *vt* **chased, chas·ing** ornament,
engrave (metal). **chas'er** *n* **chas'ing** *n*

chasm [KAZ-əm] *n* **1** deep cleft, fissure. **2**
abyss.

chas·sis [CHAS-ee] *n, pl* **chassis** [-eez]
frame, wheels and machinery of motor
vehicle on which body is supported.

chaste [chayst] *adj* **1** virginal. **2** pure. **3**
modest. **4** virtuous. **chas·ti·ty** [CHAS-ti-tee]
n

chas·ten [CHAY-sən] *vt* **1** correct by
punishment. **2** restrain, subdue.
chas'tened *adj* **chas·tise** [chas-TĪZ] *vt*
-tised, -tis·ing inflict punishment on.

chas·u·ble [CHAZ-yə-bəl] *n* priest's long
sleeveless outer vestment.

chat *vi* **chat·ted, chat·ting 1** talk idly, or
familiarly. ♦ *n* **2** familiar idle talk.
chat'room *n* site on the Internet where
users have group discussions by e-mail.

châ·teau [shat-TOH] *n, pl* **-teaus** *or* **-teaux**
[-TOHZ] (esp. in France) castle, country
house.

chat·tel [CHAT-l] *n* any movable property.

chat·ter [CHAT-ər] *vi* **1** talk idly or rapidly.
2 rattle teeth. ♦ *n* **3** idle talk. **chat'ter·er** *n*
chat'terbox *n* one who chatters

incessantly.

chauf·feur [SHOH-fər] *n* **1** paid driver of
automobile. ♦ *vt* **2** perform this work.

chau·vin·ism [SHOH-və-niz-əm] *n*
aggressive patriotism. **male chauvinism**
smug sense of male superiority over
women. **chau'vin·ist** *n*

cheap [cheep] *adj* **-er, -est 1** low in price. **2**
inexpensive. **3** easily obtained. **4** of little
value or estimation. **5** mean, inferior.
cheap'en *vt*

cheat [cheet] *vt* **1** deceive, defraud,
swindle, impose upon. ♦ *vi* **2** practice
deceit to gain advantage. **3** (oft. followed
by *on*) be sexually unfaithful. **cheat,
cheat'er** *n* one who cheats. **cheat'ers** *pl n*
sl eyeglasses.

check [chek] *vt* **1** stop. **2** restrain. **3** hinder.
4 repress. **5** control. **6** examine for
accuracy, quality, etc. ♦ *n* **7** repulse. **8**
stoppage. **9** restraint. **10** brief examination
for correctness or accuracy. **11** pattern of
squares on fabric. **12** threat to king at
chess. **13** written order to banker to pay
money from one's account. **14** printed slip
of paper used for this. **check'book** *n* book
of checks. **check'mate** *n* **1** *Chess* final
winning move. **2** any overthrow, defeat. ♦
vt **-mat·ed, -mat·ing 3** *Chess* make
game-ending move. **4** defeat. **check'out** *n*
counter in supermarket where customers
pay. **check'up** *n* examination (esp.

——————— THESAURUS ———————

authorize, sanction

chase *v* **1** = **pursue**, course, follow, hunt,
run after, stalk, track **2** = **drive away**, drive,
expel, hound, put to flight ♦ *n* **3** = **pursuit**,
hunt, hunting, race

chasm *n* = **gulf**, abyss, crater, crevasse,
fissure, gap, gorge, ravine

chaste *adj* = **pure**, immaculate, innocent,
modest, simple, unaffected, undefiled,
virtuous

chasten *v* = **subdue**, chastise, correct,
discipline, humble, humiliate, put in one's
place, tame

chastise *v* **1** = **scold**, berate, castigate,
censure, correct, discipline, upbraid
2 *Old-fashioned* = **beat**, flog, lash, lick (*inf*),
punish, scourge, whip

chastity *n* = **purity**, celibacy, continence,
innocence, maidenhood, modesty,
virginity, virtue

chat *n* **1** = **talk**, chatter, conversation,
gossip, heart-to-heart, natter, tête-à-tête ♦

v **2** = **talk**, chatter, chew the fat (*sl*),
gossip, jaw (*sl*), natter

chatter *n* **1** = **prattle**, babble, blather, chat,
gab (*inf*), gossip ♦ *v* **2** = **prattle**, babble,
blather, chat, chew the fat (*sl*), gab (*inf*),
gossip, schmooze (*sl*)

cheap *adj* **1** = **inexpensive**, bargain,
cut-price, economical, keen, low-cost,
low-priced, reasonable, reduced **2** =
inferior, common, poor, second-rate,
shoddy, tatty, tawdry, two a penny,
worthless

cheapen *v* = **degrade**, belittle, debase,
demean, denigrate, depreciate, devalue,
discredit, disparage, lower

cheat *v* **1** = **deceive**, beguile, con (*inf*),
defraud, double-cross (*inf*), dupe, fleece,
fool, mislead, rip off (*sl*), swindle, trick ♦ *n*
2 = **deceiver**, charlatan, con man (*inf*),
double-crosser (*inf*), shark, sharper,
swindler, trickster **3** = **deception**, deceit,
fraud, rip-off (*sl*), scam (*sl*), swindle,

medical) to see if all is in order.

checked [chekt] *adj* having pattern of small squares.

check·er [CHEK-ər] *n* **1** marking as on checkerboard. **2** playing piece in game of checkers. ◆ *vt* **3** mark in squares. **4** variegate. **check'ered** *adj* **1** marked in squares. **2** uneven, varied. **check'ers** *n* game played on checkered board of 64 squares with flat round playing pieces. **check'er·board** *n*

Ched·dar [CHED-ər] *n* smooth hard cheese.

cheek *n* **1** side of face below eye. **2** impudence. **3** buttock. ◆ *vt inf* **4** address impudently. **cheek by jowl** in close intimacy.

cheep *vi, n* (utter) high-pitched cry, as of young bird.

cheer *vt* **1** comfort. **2** gladden. **3** encourage by shouts. ◆ *vi* **4** shout applause. ◆ *n* **5** shout of approval. **6** happiness, good spirits. **7** mood. **cheer'ful** *adj* **cheer'i·ly** *adv* **cheer'less** *adj*

cheese [cheez] *n* curd of milk coagulated, separated from the whey and pressed. **chees'y** *adj* **chees·i·er, chees·i·est** **1** suggesting cheese in aroma, etc. **2** *sl* cheap, shabby. **cheese'cake** *n* **1** cake made with cottage or cream cheese and oft. with fruit mixture. **2** *inf* photograph of shapely, scantily clad woman. **cheese'cloth** *n* loosely woven cotton

cloth.

chee·tah [CHEE-tə] *n* large, swift, spotted feline animal.

chef [shef] *n* head cook, esp. in restaurant.

chef-d'oeu·vre [shay-DUR-vr] *Fr* masterpiece.

chem·is·try [KEM-ə-stree] *n* **1** science concerned with properties of substances and their combinations and reactions. **2** interaction of one personality with another. **chem'i·cal** *n, adj* **chem'ist** *n* one trained in chemistry.

che·mo·ther·a·py [kee-moh-THER-ə-pee] *n* treatment of disease by chemical means.

che·nille [shə-NEEL] *n* soft yarn, fabric of silk, wool, etc.

cher'ish *vt* **1** treat with affection. **2** protect. **3** foster.

che·root [shə-ROOT] *n* cigar with both ends open.

cher·ry [CHER-ee] *n* **1** small red fruit with stone. **2** tree bearing it. ◆ *adj* **3** ruddy, bright red.

cher·ub [CHER-əb] *n, pl* **cher·u·bim, cher·ubs 1** winged creature with human face. **2** angel. **che·ru·bic** [chə-ROO-bik] *adj*

cher·vil [CHUR-vil] *n* an herb.

chess *n* game of skill played by two with 32 pieces on checkered board of 64 squares. **chess'board** *n* **chess'man** *n, pl* **-men** piece used in chess.

chest *n* **1** upper part of trunk of body. **2** large, strong box. **chest of drawers** piece

---

THESAURUS

---

trickery

check *v* **1** = **examine**, inquire into, inspect, investigate, look at, make sure, monitor, research, scrutinize, study, test, vet **2** = **stop**, delay, halt, hinder, impede, inhibit, limit, obstruct, restrain, retard ◆ *n* **3** = **examination**, inspection, investigation, once-over (*inf*), research, scrutiny, test **4** = **stoppage**, constraint, control, curb, damper, hindrance, impediment, limitation, obstacle, obstruction, restraint

cheeky *adj* = **impudent**, audacious, disrespectful, forward, impertinent, insolent, insulting, pert, saucy

cheer *v* **1** = **applaud**, acclaim, clap, hail **2** = **cheer up**, brighten, buoy up, comfort, encourage, gladden, hearten, uplift ◆ *n* **3** = **applause**, acclamation, ovation, plaudits

cheerful *adj* = **happy**, buoyant, cheery, chirpy (*inf*), enthusiastic, jaunty, jolly, light-hearted, merry, optimistic, upbeat

(*inf*)

cheerfulness *n* = **happiness**, buoyancy, exuberance, gaiety, geniality, good cheer, good humor, high spirits, jauntiness, light-heartedness

cheerless *adj* = **gloomy**, bleak, desolate, dismal, drab, dreary, forlorn, miserable, somber, woeful

cheer up *v* **1** = **comfort**, encourage, enliven, gladden, hearten **2** = **take heart**, buck up (*inf*), perk up, rally

cheery *adj* = **cheerful**, breezy, carefree, chirpy (*inf*), genial, good-humored, happy, jovial, upbeat (*inf*)

chemist *n* = **pharmacist**, apothecary (*obs*), dispenser

cherish *v* **1** = **cling to**, cleave to, encourage, entertain, foster, harbor, hold dear, nurture, prize, sustain, treasure **2** = **care for**, comfort, hold dear, love, nurse, shelter, support of furniture containing drawers.

chest·nut [CHES-nut] *n* **1** large reddish-brown nut growing in prickly husk. **2** tree bearing it. **3** horse of chestnut color. **4** old joke. ♦ *adj* **5** reddish-brown.

chev·ron [SHEV-ran] *n Military* V-shaped band of braid worn on sleeve to designate rank.

chew [choo] *v* grind with teeth. ♦ *n* **chew'y** *adj* **chew·i·er, chew·i·est** firm, sticky when chewed.

chi·an·ti [kee-AHN-tee] *n* dry red Italian wine.

chic [sheek] *adj* **-er, -est** stylish, elegant. ♦ *n* **chi·can·er·y** [shi-KAY-na-ree] *n, pl* **-er·ies 1** quibbling. **2** trick, artifice.

chick [chik], **chick·en** [CHIK-an] *n* **1** young of birds, esp. of hen. **2** *sl, oft offens* **3** girl, young woman. **chicken feed** trifling amount of money. **chick'en-heart·ed** *adj* cowardly. **chick'en·pox** *n* infectious disease, esp. of children. **chick'pea** *n* **1** legume bearing pods containing pealike seeds. **2** seed of this plant.

chic·o·ry [CHIK-a-ree] *n* **1** salad plant. **2** ground root of the plant used with, or instead of, coffee.

chide [chīd] *vt* **chid·ed** or **chid, chid·ed** or **chid chid·den, chid·ing** scold, reprove, censure.

chief [cheef] *n* **1** head or principal person. ♦ *adj* **2** principal, foremost, leading. **chief'ly** *adv* **chief'tain** [-tan] *n* **1** leader, chief of clan or tribe.

chif·fon [shi-FON] *n* thin gauzy material.

chi·gnon [SHEEN-yon] *n* roll, knot, of hair worn at back of head.

chi·hua·hua [chi-WAH-wah] *n* breed of tiny dog, orig. from Mexico.

chil·blain [CHIL-blayn] *n* inflamed sore on hands, legs, etc., due to cold.

child [chīld] *n, pl* **chil·dren** [CHIL-dran] **1** young human being. **2** offspring. **child'ish** *adj* **1** of or like a child. **2** silly. **3** trifling. **child'ish·ly** *adv* **child'less** *adj* **child'like** *adj* **1** of or like a child. **2** innocent. **3** frank. **4** docile. **child'birth** *n* **child'hood** *n* period between childhood and puberty. **child's play** very easy task.

chil·i [CHIL-ee] *n, pl* **chil·ies 1** small red hot-tasting seed pod. **2** plant producing it. **3** chili con carne. **chili con carne** [kon KAHR-nee] Mexican-style dish of chilies or chili powder, ground beef, onions, etc.

chill *n* **1** coldness. **2** cold with shivering. **3** anything that damps, discourages. ♦ *v* **4** make, become cold (esp. food, drink). **chill'i·ness** *n* **chill'y** *adj* **chill-i·er, chill-i·est chill out** *sl* **1** relax, calm down. **2** spend time in trivial occupations. **3** keep company (with).

chime [chīm] *n* **1** sound of bell. **2** harmonious, ringing sound. ♦ *v* **chimed, chim·ing** ♦ *vi* **3** ring harmoniously. **4** agree.

THESAURUS

chest *n* = **box**, case, casket, coffer, crate, strongbox, trunk

chew *v* = **bite**, champ, chomp, crunch, gnaw, grind, masticate, munch

chewy *adj* = **tough**, as tough as old boots, leathery

chic *adj* = **stylish**, cool (*inf*), elegant, fashionable, phat (*sl*), smart, trendy (*inf*)

chide *v Old-fashioned* = **scold**, admonish, berate, censure, criticize, lecture, rebuke, reprimand, reproach, reprove, tell off (*inf*)

chief *n* **1** = **head**, boss (*inf*), captain, commander, director, governor, leader, manager, master, principal, ruler ♦ *adj* **2** = **primary**, foremost, highest, key, leading, main, predominant, pre-eminent, premier, prime, principal, supreme, uppermost

chiefly *adv* **1** = **especially**, above all, essentially, primarily, principally **2** = **mainly**, in general, in the main, largely, mostly, on the whole, predominantly, usually

child *n* = **youngster**, babe, baby, juvenile, kid (*inf*), minor, offspring, toddler, tot

childbirth *n* = **child-bearing**, confinement, delivery, labor, lying-in, parturition, travail

childhood *n* = **youth**, boyhood *or* girlhood, immaturity, infancy, minority, schooldays

childish *adj* = **immature**, boyish *or* girlish, foolish, infantile, juvenile, puerile, young

childlike *adj* = **innocent**, artless, guileless, ingenuous, naive, simple, trusting

chill *n* **1** = **cold**, bite, coldness, coolness, crispness, frigidity, nip, rawness, sharpness ♦ *v* **2** = **cool**, freeze, refrigerate **3** = **dishearten**, dampen, deject, depress, discourage, dismay ♦ *adj* **4** = **cold**, biting, bleak, chilly, freezing, frigid, raw, sharp, wintry

chilly *adj* **1** = **cool**, brisk, crisp, drafty, fresh, nippy, penetrating, sharp **2** = **unfriendly**, frigid, hostile, unresponsive, unsympathetic, unwelcoming

♦ vt **5** strike (bells). **chime in** break into a conversation to express an opinion.

chi·me·ra [ki-MEER-ə] n **1** fabled monster, made up of parts of various animals. **2** wild fancy. **chi·mer'i·cal** [-MER-i-kəl] adj fanciful.

chim·ney [CHIM-nee] n, pl **-neys 1** a passage for smoke. **2** narrow vertical cleft in rock.

chim·pan·zee [chim-pan-ZEE] n gregarious, intelligent ape of Africa.

chin n part of face below mouth.

chi·na [CHĪ-nə] n **1** fine earthenware, porcelain. **2** cups, saucers, etc. collectively.

chin·chil·la [chin-CHIL-ə] n **1** S Amer. rodent with soft, gray fur. **2** its fur.

chine [chīn] n **1** backbone. **2** cut of meat including backbone. **3** ridge or crest of land. **4** intersection of bottom and side of boat.

chink¹ [chingk] n cleft, crack.

chink² n **1** light metallic sound. ♦ v **2** (cause to) make this sound.

chintz [chints] n cotton cloth printed in colored designs.

chip n **1** splinter. **2** place where piece has been broken off. **3** tiny wafer of silicon forming integrated circuit in computer, etc. ♦ v **chipped, chip·ping 4** vt **5** chop into small pieces. **6** break small pieces from. **7** shape by cutting off pieces. ♦ vi **8** break off. **chip in 1** contribute. **2** butt in.

chip·munk [CHIP-mungk] n small, striped N Amer. squirrel.

chi·rop·o·dist [ki-ROP-ə-dist] n one who treats disorders of feet. **chi·rop'o·dy** n

chi·ro·prac·tor [KĪ-rə-prak-tər] n one skilled in treating bodily disorders by manipulation, massage, etc. **chi·ro·prac'tic** n

chirp [churp] n **1** short, sharp cry of bird. ♦ vi **2** make this sound. **chirp'y** adj inf **chirp·i·er, chirp·i·est** happy.

chis·el [CHIZ-əl] n **1** cutting tool, usu. bar of steel with edge across main axis. ♦ vt **-eled, -el·ing 2** cut, carve with chisel. **3** sl cheat.

chit¹ n **1** signed note for money owed. **2** informal receipt.

chit² n child, esp. young girl.

chiv·al·ry [SHIV-əl-ree] n **1** bravery and courtesy. **2** medieval system of knighthood. **chiv'al·rous** adj

chive [chīv] n herb with mild onion flavor.

chlo·rine [KLOR-een] n nonmetallic element, yellowish-green poison gas, used as disinfectant. **chlo'rate** [-ayt] n salt of chloric acid. **chlo'ric** adj **chlo'ride** n **1** compound of chlorine. **2** bleaching agent. **chlo·ri·nate** [KLOR-ə-nayt] vt **-nat·ed, -nat·ing 1** disinfect. **2** purify with chlorine.

chlo·ro·fluo·ro·car·bon [klor-ə-fluur-ə-KAHR-bən] n (also **CFC**) any of various gaseous compounds of carbon, hydrogen, chlorine, and fluorine, used in refrigerators and aerosol propellants, some of which break down the ozone in the atmosphere.

chlo·ro·form [KLOR-ə-form] n **1** volatile liquid formerly used as anesthetic. ♦ vt **2** render insensible with it.

chlo·ro·phyll [KLOR-ə-fil] n green coloring matter in plants.

chock [chok] n block or wedge to prevent heavy object from rolling or sliding. **chock'-full** adj packed full.

choc·o·late [CHAWK-lit] n **1** paste from ground cacao seeds. **2** candy, drink made from this. ♦ adj **3** dark brown.

choice [chois] n **1** act or power of choosing. **2** alternative. **3** thing or person chosen. ♦ adj **4** select, fine, worthy of being chosen.

choir [kwīr] n **1** company of singers, esp. in church. **2** part of church set aside for them.

choke [chohk] v **choked, chok·ing** ♦ vt **1** hinder, stop the breathing of. **2** smother,

——— THESAURUS ———

chime v, n = ring, clang, jingle, peal, sound, tinkle, toll

china n = pottery, ceramics, crockery, porcelain, service, tableware, ware

chink n = opening, aperture, cleft, crack, cranny, crevice, fissure, gap

chip n **1** = scratch, fragment, nick, notch, shard, shaving, sliver, wafer ♦ v **2** = nick, chisel, damage, gash, whittle

chirp v = chirrup, cheep, peep, pipe, tweet, twitter, warble

chivalrous adj = courteous, bold, brave, courageous, gallant, gentlemanly, honorable, valiant

chivalry n = courtesy, courage, gallantry, gentlemanliness, knight-errantry, knighthood, politeness

choice n **1** = option, alternative, pick, preference, say **2** = selection, range, variety ♦ adj **3** = best, elite, excellent, stifle. **3** obstruct. ♦ *vi* **4** suffer choking. ♦ *n* **5** act, noise of choking. **6** device in carburetor to increase richness of fuel-air mixture.

chol·er [KOL-ər] *n* bile, anger. **chol'er·ic** *adj* irritable.

chol·er·a [KOL-ər-ə] *n* deadly infectious disease marked by vomiting and diarrhea.

cho·les·ter·ol [kə-LES-tə-rawl] *n* substance found in animal tissue and fat.

chomp *v* chew noisily.

choose [chooz] *v* **chose, cho·sen, choos·ing** ♦ *vt* **1** pick out, select. **2** take by preference. ♦ *vi* **3** decide, think fit. **choos'y** *adj* **choos·i·er, choos·i·est** fussy.

chop *vt* **chopped, chop·ping 1** cut with blow. **2** hack. ♦ *n* **3** hewing blow. **4** slice of meat containing rib or other bone. **chop'per** *n* **1** short axe. **2** *inf* helicopter. **chop'py** *adj* **-pi·er, -pi·est** (of sea) having short, broken waves.

chops *pl n* jaw, mouth.

chop·sticks [CHOP-stiks] *pl n* implements used by Chinese and others for eating food.

cho·ral [KOR-əl] *adj* of, for, sung by, a choir.

cho·rale [kə-RAL] *n* slow, stately hymn tune.

chord [kord] *n* **1** emotional response, esp. of sympathy. **2** simultaneous sounding of musical notes. **3** straight line joining ends of arc.

chore [chor] *n* **1** (unpleasant) task. **2** odd job.

cho·re·og·ra·phy [kor-ee-OG-rə-fee] *n* **1** art of arranging dances, esp. ballet. **2** art, notation of ballet dancing. **cho·re·og·ra·pher** *n* **cho·re·o·graph·ic** *adj*

chor·tle [CHOR-tl] *vi* **-tled, -tling** chuckle happily. ♦ *n*

cho·rus [KOR-əs] *n* **1** group of singers. **2** combination of voices singing together. **3** refrain. ♦ *vt* **-rused, -rus·ing 4** sing or say together. **chor'is·ter** *n*

chose pt. of CHOOSE. **cho'sen** pp. of CHOOSE.

chow[1] *inf* ♦ *n* **1** food. ♦ *vi* **2** (oft. with *down*) eat heartily. **chow'hound** *n sl* glutton.

chow[2] *n* thick-coated dog with curled tail, orig. from China.

chow·der [CHOW-dər] *n* **1** thick soup of seafood, vegetables, etc. **2** soup resembling it, such as corn chowder.

Christ [krīst] *n* Jesus of Nazareth, regarded by Christians as the Messiah.

Chris·tian [KRIS-chən] *n* **1** follower of Christ. ♦ *adj* **2** following Christ. **3** relating to Christ or his religion. **chris'ten** [-ən] *vt* baptize, give name to. **Chris'ten·dom** [-ən-dəm] *n* all the Christian world. **Chris·ti·an·i·ty** [-chee-AN-i-tee] *n* religion of Christ. **Christian** name name given at baptism. **Christian Science** religious system founded by Mary Baker Eddy.

Christ·mas [KRIS-məs] *n* festival of birth of Christ.

chro·mat·ic [kroh-MAT-ik] *adj* **1** of color. **2** *Mus.* of scale proceeding by semitones.

chro·ma·tin [KROH-mə-tin] *n* part of protoplasmic substance in nucleus of cells that takes color in staining tests.

chrome [krohm], **chro'mi·um** [-mee-əm] *n* metal used in alloys and for plating.

chro·mo·some [KROH-mə-sohm] *n* microscopic gene-carrying body in the tissue of a cell.

Chron. Chronicles.

chron·ic [KRON-ik] *adj* **1** lasting a long time. **2** habitual.

chron·i·cle [KRON-i-kəl] *n* **1** record of events in order of time. **2** account. ♦ *vt* **-cled, -cling 3** record. **chron'i·cler** *n*

chro·nol·o·gy [krə-NOL-ə-jee] *n, pl* **-gies 1**

exclusive, prime, rare, select

choke *v* **1** = **strangle**, asphyxiate, gag, overpower, smother, stifle, suffocate, suppress, throttle **2** = **block**, bar, bung, clog, congest, constrict, obstruct, stop

choose *v* = **pick**, adopt, designate, elect, opt for, prefer, select, settle upon

choosy *adj* = **fussy**, discriminating, faddy, fastidious, finicky, particular, picky (*inf*), selective

chop *v* = **cut**, cleave, fell, hack, hew, lop, sever

chore *n* = **task**, burden, duty, errand, job

chortle *v, n* = **chuckle**, cackle, crow, guffaw

chorus *n* **1** = **choir**, choristers, ensemble, singers, vocalists **2** = **refrain**, burden, response, strain **3** = **unison**, accord, concert, harmony

christen *v* **1** = **baptize 2** = **name**, call, designate, dub, style, term, title

Christmas *n* = **festive season**, Noel, Xmas, Yule, Yuletide

chronicle *n* **1** = **record**, account, annals, diary, history, journal, narrative, register, determination of sequence of past events. **2** arrangement in order of occurrence. **3** account of events, reference work arranged in order of time. **chron•o•log•i•cal** [kron-I-OJ-i-kəl] *adj* arranged in order of time.

chro•nom•e•ter [krə-NOM-i-tər] *n* **1** instrument for measuring time exactly. **2** watch.

chrys•a•lis [KRIS-ə-lis] *n*, *pl* **chry•sal•i•des** [kri-SAL-i-deez] **1** resting state of insect between grub and butterfly, etc. **2** case enclosing it.

chry•san•the•mum [kri-SAN-thə-məm] *n* garden flower of various colors.

chub•by [CHUB-ee] *adj* **-bi•er, -bi•est** plump.

chuck¹ [chuk] *vt inf* **1** throw. **2** pat affectionately (under chin). **3** give up, reject.

chuck² *n* **1** cut of beef. **2** device for gripping, adjusting bit in power drill, etc.

chuck•le [CHUK-əl] *vi* **-led, -ling 1** laugh softly. ♦ *n* **2** such laugh.

chuk•ker [CHUK-ər] *n* period of play in game of polo.

chum *n inf* close friend. **chum'my** *adj* **-mi•er, -mi•est**

chunk [chungk] *n* thick, solid piece. **chunk'y** *adj* **chunk•i•er, chunk•i•est**

church *n* **1** building for Christian worship. **2** (C-) whole body or sect of Christians. **3** clergy. **church'ward•en** *n* **1** officer who represents interests of Anglican parish. **2** long clay pipe. **church'yard** *n*

churl *n* **1** rustic. **2** rude, boorish person. **churl'ish** *adj* **churl'ish•ness** *n*

churn *n* **1** vessel for making butter. ♦ *v* **2** shake up, stir (liquid) violently. **3** make (butter) in churn. **4** (of a stockbroker) trade (stocks) excessively to increase commissions.

chute [shoot] *n* **1** slide for sending down parcels, coal, etc. **2** channel. **3** narrow

passageway, e.g. for spraying, counting cattle, sheep, etc. **4** *inf* short for PARACHUTE.

chut•ney [CHUT-nee] *n* condiment of fruit, spices, etc.

chutz•pah [HUUT-spə] *n* **1** shameless audacity. **2** gall.

ci•ca•da [si-KAY-də] *n* cricketlike insect.

cic•a•trix [SIK-ə-triks] *n* scar of healed wound.

cic•e•ro•ne [sis-ə-ROH-nee] *n* guide for sightseers.

ci•der [SĪ-dər] *n* drink made from apples. **hard cider** cider after fermentation. **soft cider** cider before fermentation.

ci•gar [si-GAHR] *n* roll of tobacco leaves for smoking. **cig•a•rette** [sig-ə-RET] *n* finely cut tobacco rolled in paper for smoking.

ci•lan•tro [si-LAN-troh, -LAHN-] *n* coriander.

cinch [sinch] *n inf* **1** easy task, certainty. **2** strong girth used on saddle.

cin•der [SIN-dər] *n* remains of burned coal.

cin•e•ma [SIN-ə-mə] *n* **1** building used for showing of motion pictures. **2** these generally or collectively.

cin•na•mon [SIN-ə-mən] *n* **1** spice got from bark of Asian tree. **2** the tree. ♦ *adj* **3** light-brown color.

ci•pher [SĪ-fər] *n* **1** secret writing. **2** arithmetical symbol. **3** person of no importance. **4** monogram. ♦ *vt* **5** write in cipher.

cir•ca [SUR-kə] *Lat* about, approximately.

cir•cle [SUR-kəl] *n* **1** perfectly round figure. **2** ring. **3** *Theater* balcony or tier of seats above main level of auditorium. **4** group, society with common interest. **5** class of society. ♦ *v* **-cled, -cling** ♦ *vt* **6** surround. ♦ *vi* **7** move in circle. **cir'cu•lar** [-kyə-lər] *adj* **1** round. ♦ *n* **2** in a circle. ♦ *n* **3** letter, etc. intended for wide distribution. **cir'cu•late** [-kyə-layt] *v* **-lat•ed, -lat•ing** ♦ *vi* **1** move around. **2** pass from hand to hand or place

---

THESAURUS

story ♦ *v* **2** = **record**, enter, narrate, put on record, recount, register, relate, report, set down, tell

chubby *adj* = **plump**, buxom, flabby, portly, rotund, round, stout, tubby

chuckle *v* = **laugh**, chortle, crow, exult, giggle, snigger, titter

chum *n Inf* = **friend**, companion, comrade, crony, homeboy (*sl*), homegirl (*sl*), pal (*inf*)

chunk *n* = **piece**, block, dollop (*inf*), hunk, lump, mass, nugget, portion, slab

churlish *adj* = **rude**, brusque, harsh, ill-tempered, impolite, sullen, surly, uncivil

churn *v* = **stir up**, agitate, beat, convulse, swirl, toss

cinema *n* = **films**, big screen (*inf*), flicks (*sl*), motion pictures, movies, pictures

cipher *n* **1** = **code**, cryptograph **2** = **nobody**, nonentity to place. ◆ vt **3** send around. **cir·cu·la·tion** n **1** flow of blood from, and back to, heart. **2** act of moving around. **3** extent of sale of newspaper, etc. **cir'cu·la·to·ry** adj

cir·cuit [SUR-kit] n **1** complete round or course. **2** area. **3** path of electric current. **4** round of visitation, esp. of judges. **5** series of sporting events. **6** district. **cir·cu·i·tous** [sər KYOO i təs] adj roundabout, indirect. **cir'cuit·ry** n electrical circuit(s).

cir·cum·cise [SUR-kəm-sīz] vt **-cised, -cis·ing** cut off foreskin of (penis). **cir·cum·ci'sion** [-SIZH-ən] n

cir·cum·fer·ence [sər-KUM-fər-əns] n boundary line, esp. of circle.

cir·cum·flex [SUR-kəm-fleks] n accent (ˆ) over vowel to indicate length of its sound.

cir·cum·lo·cu·tion [sur-kəm-loh-KYOO-shən] n roundabout speech.

cir·cum·nav·i·gate [sur-kəm-NAV-i-gayt] vt **-gat·ed, -gat·ing** sail or fly right around.

cir·cum·scribe [SUR-kəm-skrīb] vt **-scribed, -scrib·ing** confine, bound, limit, hamper.

cir·cum·spect [SUR-kəm-spekt] adj watchful, cautious, prudent. **cir·cum·spec'tion** n

cir·cum·stance [SUR-kəm-stans] n **1** detail. **2** event. **3** matter of fact. ◆ pl **4** state of affairs. **5** condition in life, esp. financial. **6** surroundings or things accompanying an action. **cir·cum·stan'tial** adj **1** depending on detail or circumstances. **2** detailed,

minute. **3** incidental.

cir·cum·vent [sur-kəm-VENT] vt outwit, evade, get round. **cir·cum·ven'tion** n

cir·cus [SUR-kəs] n, pl **-cus·es 1** (performance of) traveling group of acrobats, clowns, performing animals, etc. **2** circular structure for public shows.

cir·rho·sis [si-ROH-sis] n any of various chronic progressive diseases of liver. **cir·rhot'ic** [-ROT-ik] adj

cir·rus [SIR-əs] n, pl **cirrus** high wispy cloud.

cis·tern [SIS-tərn] n water tank, esp. for rain water.

cit·a·del [SIT-ə-dl] n fortress in, near, or commanding a city.

cite [sīt] vt **cit·ed, cit·ing 1** quote. **2** bring forward as proof. **ci·ta·tion** [sī-TAY-shən] n **1** quoting. **2** commendation for bravery, etc.

cit·i·zen [SIT-ə-zən] n **1** native, naturalized member of state, nation, etc. **2** inhabitant of city. **cit'i·zen·ship** n

cit·ron [SI-trən] n **1** fruit like a lemon. **2** the tree. **cit'ric** adj of the acid of lemon or citron. **cit·rus fruit** citrons, lemons, limes, oranges, etc.

cit·y [SIT-ee] n, pl **cit·ies** a large town.

civ·et [SIV-it] n strong, musky perfume. **civet cat** catlike animal producing it.

civ·ic [SIV-ik] adj **1** pert. to city or citizen. **civ'ics** n study of the responsibilities and rights of citizenship.

civ·il [SIV-əl] adj **1** relating to citizens of

circle n **1** = **ring**, disc, globe, orb, sphere **2** = **group**, clique, club, company, coterie, set, society ◆ v **3** = **go round**, circumnavigate, circumscribe, encircle, enclose, envelop, ring, surround

circuit n = **course**, journey, lap, orbit, revolution, route, tour, track

circuitous adj = **indirect**, labyrinthine, meandering, oblique, rambling, roundabout, tortuous, winding

circular adj **1** = **round**, ring-shaped, rotund, spherical **2** = **orbital**, circuitous, cyclical ◆ n **3** = **advertisement**, notice

circulate v **1** = **spread**, broadcast, disseminate, distribute, issue, make known, promulgate, publicize, publish **2** = **flow**, gyrate, radiate, revolve, rotate

circulation n **1** = **bloodstream 2** = **flow**, circling, motion, rotation **3** = **distribution**, currency, dissemination, spread,

transmission

circumference n = **boundary**, border, edge, extremity, limits, outline, perimeter, periphery, rim

circumstance n = **event**, accident, condition, contingency, happening, incident, occurrence, particular, respect, situation

circumstances pl n = **situation**, means, position, state, state of affairs, station, status

cistern n = **tank**, basin, reservoir, sink, vat

citadel n = **fortress**, bastion, fortification, keep, stronghold, tower

cite v = **quote**, adduce, advance, allude to, enumerate, extract, mention, name, specify

citizen n = **inhabitant**, denizen, dweller, resident, subject, townsman

city n = **town**, conurbation, metropolis,

state. **2** not military. **3** refined, polite. **4** *Law* not criminal. **ci·vil·ian** [si-VIL-yən] *n* nonmilitary person. **ci·vil·i·ty** *n, pl* **-ties civ'il·ly** *adv* **civil service** service responsible for the public administration of the government of a city, state, or country. **civ·i·lize** [SIV-ə-līz] *vt* **-lized, -liz·ing 1** bring out of barbarism. **2** refine. **civ·i·li·za'tion** *n*

Cl *Chem.* chlorine.

clack [klak] *n* sound, as of two pieces of wood striking together. ◆ *v*

clad pt./pp. of CLOTHE.

clad·ding [KLAD-ing] *n* metal bonded to inner core of another metal, as protection against corrosion.

claim [klaym] *vt* **1** demand as right. **2** assert. **3** call for. ◆ *n* **4** demand for thing supposed due. **5** right. **6** thing claimed. **7** plot of mining land marked out by stakes as required by law. **claim'ant** [-mənt] *n*

clair·voy·ance [klair-VOI-əns] *n* power of seeing things not present to senses, second sight. **clair·voy'ant** *n, adj*

clam [klam] *n* edible mollusk.

clam·ber [KLAM-bər] *vi* to climb with difficulty or awkwardly.

clam·my [KLAM-ee] *adj* **-mi·er, -mi·est** moist and sticky. **clam'mi·ness** *n*

clam·or [KLAM-ər] *n* **1** loud shouting, outcry, noise. ◆ *vi* **2** shout, call noisily (for).

clam'or·ous *adj*

clamp [klamp] *n* **1** tool for holding or compressing. ◆ *vt* **2** fasten, strengthen with or as with clamp.

clan [klan] *n* **1** tribe or collection of families under chief and of common ancestry. **2** faction, group. **clan'nish** *adj*

clan·des·tine [klan-DES-tin] *adj* **1** secret. **2** sly.

clang [klang] *v* **1** (cause to) make loud ringing sound. ◆ *n* **2** loud ringing sound.

clank [klangk] *n* **1** short sound as of pieces of metal struck together. ◆ *v* **2** cause, move with, such sound.

clap[1] [klap] *v* **clapped, clap·ping 1** (cause to) strike with noise. **2** strike (hands) together. **3** applaud. ◆ *vt* **4** pat. **5** place or put quickly. ◆ *n* **6** hard, explosive sound. **7** slap. **clap'per** *n* **clap'trap** *n* empty words.

clap[2] *n sl* gonorrhea.

clar·et [KLAR-it] *n* **1** a dry dark red wine of Bordeaux. **2** similar wine made elsewhere.

clar·i·fy [KLAR-ə-fī] *v* **-fied, -fy·ing 1** make or become clear, pure, or more easily understood. **clar·i·fi·ca'tion** *n* **clar'i·ty** *n* clearness.

clar·i·net [klar-ə-NET] *n* woodwind musical instrument.

clar·i·on [KLAR-ee-ən] *n* **1** clear-sounding trumpet. **2** rousing sound.

municipality

civic *adj* = **public**, communal, local, municipal

civil *adj* **1** = **civic**, domestic, municipal, political **2** = **polite**, affable, courteous, obliging, refined, urbane, well-mannered

civilization *n* **1** = **culture**, advancement, cultivation, development, education, enlightenment, progress, refinement, sophistication **2** = **society**, community, nation, people, polity

civilize *v* = **cultivate**, educate, enlighten, refine, sophisticate, tame

civilized *adj* = **cultured**, educated, enlightened, humane, polite, sophisticated, tolerant, urbane

claim *v* **1** = **assert**, allege, challenge, insist, maintain, profess, uphold **2** = **demand**, ask, call for, insist, need, require ◆ *n* **3** = **assertion**, affirmation, allegation, pretension, privilege, protestation **4** = **demand**, application, call, petition, request, requirement **5** = **right**, title

clairvoyant *n* **1** = **psychic**, diviner,

fortune-teller, visionary ◆ *adj* **2** = **psychic**, extrasensory, second-sighted, telepathic, visionary

clamber *v* = **climb**, claw, scale, scrabble, scramble, shin

clammy *adj* = **moist**, close, damp, dank, sticky, sweaty

clamor *n* = **noise**, commotion, din, hubbub, outcry, racket, shouting, uproar

clamp *n* **1** = **vice**, bracket, fastener, grip, press ◆ *v* **2** = **fasten**, brace, fix, make fast, secure

clan *n* = **family**, brotherhood, faction, fraternity, group, society, tribe

clandestine *adj* = **secret**, cloak-and-dagger, concealed, covert, furtive, private, stealthy, surreptitious, underground

clap *v* = **applaud**, acclaim, cheer

clarification *n* = **explanation**, elucidation, exposition, illumination, interpretation, simplification

clarify *v* = **explain**, clear up, elucidate, illuminate, interpret, make plain, simplify,

clash [klash] *n* **1** loud noise, as of weapons striking. **2** conflict, collision. ◆ *vi* **3** make clash. **4** come into conflict. **5** (of events) coincide. **6** (of colors) look ugly together. ◆ *vt* **7** strike together to make clash.

clasp [klasp] *n* **1** hook or other means of fastening. **2** embrace. ◆ *vt* **3** fasten. **4** embrace, grasp.

class [klas] *n* **1** any division, order, kind, sort. **2** rank. **3** group of school pupils, etc. taught together. **4** division by merit. **5** quality. **6** *inf* excellence or elegance. ◆ *vt* **7** assign to proper division. **clas'si·fy** [-ə-fī] *vt* **-fied, -fy·ing 1** arrange methodically in classes. **clas·si·fi·ca'tion** *n* **clas·si·fied** *adj* **1** arranged in classes. **2** secret. **3** (of advertisements) arranged under headings in newspapers, etc. **class'y** *adj* **class·i·er, class·i·est** *inf* stylish, elegant.

clas·sic [KLAS-ik] *adj* **1** of first rank. **2** of highest rank generally, but esp. of art. **3** refined. **4** typical. **5** famous. ◆ *n* **6** (literary) work of recognized excellence. ◆ *pl* **7** ancient Latin and Greek literature. **clas'si·cal** *adj* **1** of Greek and Roman literature, art, culture. **2** of classic quality. **3** *Mus.* of established standards of form,

complexity, etc. **clas'si·cism** *n* **clas'si·cist** *n*

clat·ter [KLAT-ər] *n* **1** rattling noise. **2** noisy conversation. ◆ *v* **3** (cause to) make clatter.

clause [klawz] *n* **1** part of sentence, containing verb. **2** article in formal document as treaty, contract, etc.

claus·tro·pho·bia [klaw-strə-FOH-bee-ə] *n* abnormal fear of confined spaces.

clav·i·chord [KLAV-i-kord] *n* musical instrument with keyboard, forerunner of piano.

clav·i·cle [KLAV-i-kəl] *n* collarbone.

claw [klaw] *n* **1** sharp hooked nail of bird or beast. **2** foot of bird of prey. **3** clawlike article. ◆ *vt* **4** tear with claws. **5** grip.

clay [klay] *n* **1** fine-grained earth, plastic when wet, hardening when baked. **2** earth.

clean [kleen] *adj* **-er, -est 1** free from dirt, stain, or defilement. **2** pure. **3** guiltless. **4** trim, shapely. ◆ *adv* **-er, -est 5** so as to leave no dirt. **6** entirely. ◆ *vt* **7** free from dirt. **clean·li·ness** [KLEN-lee-nis] *n* **clean·ly** [KLEN-lee] *adv, adj* **-li·er, -li·est** clean. **cleanse** [klenz] *vt* **cleansed, cleans·ing** make clean. **come clean** *inf* confess.

THESAURUS

throw *or* shed light on

clarity *n* = **clearness**, definition, limpidity, lucidity, precision, simplicity, transparency

clash *v* **1** = **conflict**, cross swords, feud, grapple, lock horns, quarrel, war, wrangle **2** = **crash**, bang, clang, clank, clatter, jangle, jar, rattle ◆ *n* **3** = **conflict**, brush, collision, confrontation, difference of opinion, disagreement, fight, showdown (*inf*)

clasp *n* **1** = **fastening**, brooch, buckle, catch, clip, fastener, grip, hook, pin **2** = **grasp**, embrace, grip, hold, hug ◆ *v* **3** = **grasp**, clutch, embrace, grip, hold, hug, press, seize, squeeze **4** = **fasten**, connect

class *n* **1** = **group**, category, division, genre, kind, set, sort, type ◆ *v* **2** = **classify**, brand, categorize, designate, grade, group, label, rate

classic *adj* **1** = **definitive**, archetypal, exemplary, ideal, model, quintessential, standard **2** = **typical**, characteristic, regular, standard, time-honored, usual **3** = **best**, consummate, finest, first-rate, masterly, world-class **4** = **lasting**, abiding, ageless, deathless, enduring, immortal, undying ◆ *n* **5** = **standard**, exemplar,

masterpiece, model, paradigm, prototype **6** comical *Inf* = **hilarious**, hysterical, ludicrous, uproarious

classical *adj* = **pure**, elegant, harmonious, refined, restrained, symmetrical, understated, well-proportioned

classification *n* = **categorization**, analysis, arrangement, grading, sorting, taxonomy

classify *v* = **categorize**, arrange, catalog, grade, pigeonhole, rank, sort, systematize, tabulate

classy *adj Inf* = **high-class**, elegant, exclusive, ritzy, stylish, superior, swanky, top-drawer, up-market

clause *n* = **section**, article, chapter, condition, paragraph, part, passage

claw *n* **1** = **nail**, pincer, talon, tentacle ◆ *v* **2** = **scratch**, dig, lacerate, maul, rip, scrape, tear

clean *adj* **1** = **pure**, flawless, fresh, immaculate, impeccable, spotless, unblemished, unsullied **2** = **hygienic**, antiseptic, decontaminated, purified, sterile, sterilized, uncontaminated, unpolluted **3** = **moral**, chaste, decent, good, honorable, innocent, pure, respectable, upright, virtuous **4** =

clear [kleer] *adj* **-er, -est 1** pure, undimmed, bright. **2** free from cloud. **3** transparent. **4** plain, distinct. **5** without defect or drawback. **6** unimpeded. ♦ *adv* **-er, -est 7** brightly. **8** wholly, quite. ♦ *vt* **9** make clear. **10** acquit. **11** pass over or through. **12** make as profit. **13** free from obstruction, debt, difficulty. ♦ *vi* **14** become clear, bright, free, transparent. **clear'ance** *n* **1** making clear. **2** removal of obstructions, surplus stock, etc. **3** certificate that ship has been cleared at custom house. **4** space for moving part, vehicle, to pass within, through or past something. **clear'ing** *n* land cleared of trees. **clear'ly** *adv* **clear'head·ed** [-hed-id] *adj* discerning.

cleat [kleet] *n* **1** wedge. **2** piece of wood or iron with two projecting ends round which ropes are made fast. **3** (on shoes) projecting piece to furnish a grip. ♦ *pl* **4** shoes equipped with cleats.

cleave[1] [kleev] *v* **cleft, cleaved** or **clove; cleft, cleaved** or **clo·ven; cleav·ing** ♦ *vt* **1** split asunder. ♦ *vi* **2** crack, part asunder. **cleav'age** *n* **1** space between a woman's breasts, as revealed by a low-cut dress, top, etc. **2** division, split. **cleav'er** *n* butcher's heavy knife with a square blade.

cleave[2] *vi* **cleaved, cleav·ing 1** stick, adhere. **2** be loyal.

clef *n* Mus. mark showing pitch of music on staff.

cleft *n* **1** crack, fissure, chasm. **2** opening made by cleaving. **3** pt./pp. of CLEAVE[1].

clem·ent [KLEM-ənt] *adj* **1** merciful. **2** gentle. **3** mild. **clem'en·cy** *n*

clench *vt* **1** set firmly together. **2** grasp, close (fist).

cler·gy [KLUR-jee] *n* body of ordained ministers in a religion. **cler'gy·man** *n*

cler·ic [KLER-ik] *n* member of clergy.

cler·i·cal [KLER-i-kəl] *adj* **1** of clergy. **2** of, connected with, office work.

clerk [klurk] *n* **1** employee who keeps files, etc. in an office. **2** officer in charge of records, correspondence, etc. of court, government department, etc. **3** sales or service employee.

clev·er [KLEV-ər] *adj* **1** quick to understand. **2** able, skillful, adroit. **clev'er·ly** *adv* **clev'er·ness** *n*

cli·ché [klee-SHAY] *n*, *pl* **-chés** stereotyped hackneyed phrase.

click[1] [klik] *n* **1** short, sharp sound, as of latch in door. **2** catch. ♦ *vi* **3** make this sound. ♦ *v* **4** (usu. foll. by *on*) Computers.

THESAURUS

complete, conclusive, decisive, entire, final, perfect, thorough, total, unimpaired, whole ♦ *v* **5 = cleanse**, disinfect, launder, purge, purify, rinse, sanitize, scour, scrub, wash

cleanse *v* = **clean**, absolve, clear, purge, purify, rinse, scour, scrub, wash

cleanser *n* = **detergent**, disinfectant, purifier, scourer, soap, solvent

clear *adj* **1 = certain**, convinced, decided, definite, positive, resolved, satisfied, sure **2 = obvious**, apparent, blatant, comprehensible, conspicuous, distinct, evident, manifest, palpable, plain, pronounced, recognizable, unmistakable **3 = transparent**, crystalline, glassy, limpid, pellucid, see-through, translucent **4 = bright**, cloudless, fair, fine, light, luminous, shining, sunny, unclouded **5 = unobstructed**, empty, free, open, smooth, unhindered, unimpeded **6 = unblemished**, clean, immaculate, innocent, pure, untarnished ♦ *v* **7 = unblock**, disentangle, extricate, free, loosen, open, rid, unload **8 = pass over**, jump, leap, miss, vault **9 = brighten**, break up, lighten **10 = clean**,

cleanse, erase, purify, refine, sweep away, tidy (up), wipe **11 = absolve**, acquit, excuse, exonerate, justify, vindicate **12 = gain**, acquire, earn, make, reap, secure

clear-cut *adj* = **straightforward**, black-and-white, cut-and-dried (*inf*), definite, explicit, plain, precise, specific, unambiguous, unequivocal

clearly *adv* = **obviously**, beyond doubt, distinctly, evidently, markedly, openly, overtly, undeniably, undoubtedly

clergy *n* = **priesthood**, churchmen, clergymen, clerics, holy orders, ministry, the cloth

clergyman *n* = **minister**, chaplain, cleric, man of God, man of the cloth, padre, parson, pastor, priest, vicar

clever *adj* = **intelligent**, bright, gifted, ingenious, knowledgeable, quick-witted, resourceful, shrewd, smart, talented

cleverness *n* = **intelligence**, ability, brains, ingenuity, quick wits, resourcefulness, shrewdness, smartness

cliché *n* = **platitude**, banality, commonplace, hackneyed phrase, stereotype, truism

press and release (button on a mouse).
click² vi **1** sl be a success. **2** inf become
clear. **3** inf strike up friendship.

cli·ent [KLĪ-ənt] n **1** customer. **2** one who
employs professional person. **3** Computers.
program or work station that requests data
from a server. **cli·en·tele'** [-ən-TEL'] n body
of clients.

cliff [klif] n steep rock face. **cliff'hang·er** n
tense situation.

cli·mate [KLĪ-mit] n **1** condition of region
with regard to weather. **2** prevailing
feeling, atmosphere. **cli·mat'ic** adj of
climate.

cli·max [KLĪ-maks] n **1** highest point,
culmination. **2** point of greatest
excitement, tension in story, etc.
cli·mac'tic adj

climb [klīm] v **1** go up or ascend. **2**
progress with difficulty. **3** creep up,
mount. **4** slope upwards.

clinch [klinch] vt **1** clench. **2** settle,
conclude (an agreement). ◆ vi (in boxing)
hold opponent close with arm or arms. **3** sl
embrace, kiss passionately. ◆ n **4**
clinching. **5** sl embrace. **clinch'er** n inf
something decisive.

cling vi clung, cling·ing **1** adhere. **2** be
firmly attached to. **3** be dependent.

clin·ic [KLIN-ik] n **1** hospital facility for
examination, treatment of outpatients. **2**
medical training session with hospital
patients as subjects. **clin'i·cal** [-ikəl] adj **1** relating
to clinic, care of sick, etc. **2** objective,
unemotional. **3** bare, plain. **clinical
thermometer** used for taking body

temperature.

clink¹ [klingk] n **1** sharp metallic sound. ◆ v
2 (cause to) make this sound.

clink² n sl prison.

clink·er [KLING-kər] n **1** fused coal residues
from fire or furnace. **2** hard brick.

clip¹ vt clipped, clip·ping **1** cut with scissors.
2 cut short. **3** sl cheat. ◆ n **4** inf sharp blow.
clip'per n

clip² n device for gripping or holding
together, esp. hair, clothing, etc.

clip·per [KLIP-ər] n fast commercial sailing
ship.

clique [kleek] n **1** small exclusive set. **2**
faction, group of people. **cli'quish** adj
cli'quish·ness n

clit·o·ris [KLIT-ər-is] n small erectile part of
female genitals.

cloak [klohk] n **1** loose outer garment. **2**
disguise, pretext. ◆ vt **3** cover with cloak. **4**
disguise, conceal.

clob·ber [KLOB-ər] vt inf **1** beat, batter. **2**
defeat utterly.

clock [klok] n **1** instrument for measuring
time. **2** device with dial for recording or
measuring. **clock'wise** adv, adj **1** in the
direction that the hands of a clock rotate.
clock'work n mechanism similar to that of
a clock, as in a windup toy. **clock in** or **on,
out** or **off** record arrival, or departure, on
automatic time recorder.

clod [klod] n **1** lump of earth. **2** blockhead.
clod'dish adj

clog [klog] vt clogged, clog·ging **1** hamper,
impede, choke up. ◆ n **2** obstruction,
impediment. **3** wooden-soled shoe.

—————| THESAURUS |—————

client n = **customer**, applicant, buyer,
consumer, patient, patron, shopper

clientele n = **customers**, business, clients,
following, market, patronage, regulars,
trade

cliff n = **rock face**, bluff, crag, escarpment,
overhang, precipice, scar, scarp

climactic adj = **crucial**, critical, decisive,
paramount, peak

climate n = **weather**, temperature

climax n = **culmination**, height, highlight,
high point, peak, summit, top, zenith

climb v = **ascend**, clamber, mount, rise,
scale, shin up, soar, top

climb down v **1** = **descend**, dismount **2** =
back down, eat one's words, retract,
retreat

clinch v = **settle**, conclude, confirm,

decide, determine, seal, secure, set the seal
on, sew up (inf)

cling v = **stick**, adhere, clasp, clutch,
embrace, grasp, grip, hug

clinical adj = **unemotional**, analytic, cold,
detached, dispassionate, impersonal,
objective, scientific

clip¹ v **1** = **trim**, crop, curtail, cut, pare,
prune, shear, shorten, snip ◆ n, v **2** Inf =
smack, clout (inf), cuff, knock, punch,
strike, thump, wallop (inf), whack

clip² v = **attach**, fasten, fix, hold, pin, staple

clique n = **group**, cabal, circle, coterie,
faction, gang, set

cloak n **1** = **cape**, coat, mantle, wrap ◆ v **2** =
cover, camouflage, conceal, disguise, hide,
mask, obscure, screen, veil

clog v = **obstruct**, block, congest, hinder,

cloi·son·né [kloi-zə-NAY] n enamel decoration in compartments formed by small strips of metal. ◆ adj

clois·ter [KLOI-stər] n 1 covered pillared arcade. 2 monastery or convent. **clois'tered** adj confined, secluded, sheltered.

clone [klohn] n 1 group of organisms, cells of same genetic constitution as another, derived by asexual reproduction, as graft of plant, etc. 2 person closely resembling another in appearance, behavior, etc. ◆ v **cloned, clon·ing**

clop [klop] vi **clopped, clop·ping** move, sound, as horse's hooves.

close¹ [klohs] adj **clos·er, clos·est** 1 adjacent, near. 2 compact. 3 crowded. 4 affectionate, intimate. 5 almost equal. 6 careful, searching. 7 confined. 8 secret. 9 unventilated, stifling. 10 reticent. 11 niggardly. 12 strict, restricted. ◆ adv 13 nearly. 14 tightly. **close'ly** adv **close'fist'ed** adj 1 mean. 2 avaricious. **close'up** n close view, esp. portion of motion picture.

close² [klohz] v **closed, clos·ing** ◆ vt 1 shut. 2 stop up. 3 prevent access to. 4 finish. ◆ vi 5 come together. 6 grapple. ◆ n 7 end. **closed season** when it is illegal to kill certain kinds of game and fish. **closed shop** place of work in which all workers

must belong to a union.

clos·et [KLOZ-it] n 1 small room, etc. for storing clothing. 2 small private room. ◆ vt 3 shut up in private room, esp. for conference. **clos'et·ful** n, pl **-fuls**

clo·sure [KLOH-zhər] n 1 act of closing. 2 (sense of contentment experienced after) resolution of a significant event or relationship in a person's life. 3 cloture.

clot [klot] n 1 mass or lump. 2 Med. coagulated mass of blood. ◆ v **clot·ted, clot·ting** 3 form into lumps. 4 coagulate.

cloth [klawth] n 1 woven fabric. **clothes** [klohthz] pl n 1 dress. 2 bed coverings. **clothe** [klohth] vt **clothed** or **clad, cloth·ing** put clothes on. **clo·thier** [KLOH-thyər] n **cloth·ing** [KLOH-thing] n

clo·ture [KLOH-chər] n ending of debate by majority vote or other authority.

cloud [klowd] n 1 condensed water vapor floating in air. 2 state of gloom. 3 multitude. ◆ vt 4 overshadow, dim, darken. ◆ vi 5 become cloudy. **cloud'less** adj **cloud'y** adj **cloud·i·er, cloud·i·est**

clout [klowt] n inf 1 blow. 2 influence, power. ◆ vt 3 strike.

clove¹ [klohv] n 1 dried flower bud of tropical tree, used as spice. 2 one of small bulbs making up compound bulb.

clove² pt. of CLEAVE¹. **clo'ven** pp. of CLEAVE¹.

————— THESAURUS —————

impede, jam

close¹ v 1 = **shut**, bar, block, lock, plug, seal, secure, stop up 2 = **end**, cease, complete, conclude, finish, shut down, terminate, wind up 3 = **connect**, come together, couple, fuse, join, unite ◆ n 4 = **end**, completion, conclusion, culmination, denouement, ending, finale, finish

close² adj 1 = **near**, adjacent, adjoining, at hand, cheek by jowl, handy, impending, nearby, neighboring, nigh 2 = **intimate**, attached, confidential, dear, devoted, familiar, inseparable, loving 3 = **careful**, detailed, intense, minute, painstaking, rigorous, thorough 4 = **compact**, congested, crowded, dense, impenetrable, jam-packed, packed, tight 5 = **stifling**, airless, heavy, humid, muggy, oppressive, stuffy, suffocating, sweltering 6 = **secretive**, private, reticent, secret, taciturn, uncommunicative 7 = **mean**, miserly, stingy

closed adj 1 = **shut**, fastened, locked, out

of service, sealed 2 = **exclusive**, restricted 3 = **finished**, concluded, decided, ended, over, resolved, settled, terminated

cloth n = **fabric**, material, textiles

clothe v = **dress**, array, attire, cover, drape, equip, fit out, garb, robe, swathe

clothes pl n = **clothing**, apparel, attire, costume, dress, garb, garments, gear (inf), outfit, wardrobe, wear

clothing n = **clothes**, apparel, attire, costume, dress, garb, garments, gear (inf), outfit, wardrobe, wear

cloud n 1 = **mist**, gloom, haze, murk, vapor ◆ v 2 = **obscure**, becloud, darken, dim, eclipse, obfuscate, overshadow, shade, shadow, veil 3 = **confuse**, disorient, distort, impair, muddle, muddy the waters

cloudy adj 1 = **dull**, dim, gloomy, leaden, louring or lowering, overcast, somber, sunless 2 = **opaque**, muddy, murky

clout Inf n 1 = **influence**, authority, power, prestige, pull, weight ◆ v 2 = **hit**, clobber (sl), punch, sock (sl), strike, thump, wallop

clo·ver [KLOH-vər] n low-growing forage plant. **be in clover** be in luxury.

clown [klown] n 1 comic entertainer in circus. 2 jester, fool.

cloy [kloi] vt weary by sweetness, sameness, etc.

club [klub] n 1 thick stick. 2 bat, stick used in some games. 3 association for pursuance of common interest. 4 building used by such association. 5 one of the suits at cards. ◆ v **clubbed, club·bing 6** strike with club. **7** combine for a common object. **club foot** deformed foot.

cluck [kluk] vi, n (make) noise of hen.

clue [kloo] n indication, esp. of solution of mystery or puzzle. **not have a clue** be ignorant or incompetent.

clump¹ [klump] n 1 cluster of trees or plants. 2 compact mass.

clump² vi walk, tread heavily. ◆ n

clum·sy [KLUM-zee] adj **-si·er, -si·est 1** awkward, unwieldy, ungainly. **2** badly made or arranged. **clum'si·ly** adv **clum'si·ness** n

clung pt./pp. of CLING.

clunk [klungk] n (sound of) blow or something falling.

clus·ter [KLUS-tər] n 1 group, bunch. ◆ v 2 gather, grow in cluster.

clutch¹ [kluch] v 1 grasp eagerly. 2 snatch

(at). ◆ n 3 grasp, tight grip. 4 device enabling two rotating shafts to be connected and disconnected at will.

clutch² n 1 set of eggs hatched at one time. 2 brood of chickens.

clut·ter [KLUT-ər] v 1 strew. 2 crowd together in disorder. ◆ n 3 disordered, obstructive mass of objects.

Cm Chem. curium

Co Chem. cobalt.

coach [kohch] n 1 large four-wheeled carriage. 2 railway carriage. 3 class of airline travel. 4 tutor, instructor. ◆ vt 5 instruct.

co·ag·u·late [koh-AG-yə-layt] v **-lat·ed, -lat·ing 1** curdle, clot, form into a mass. 2 congeal, solidify. **co·ag·u·la'tion** n

coal [kohl] n 1 mineral consisting of carbonized vegetable matter, used as fuel. 2 glowing ember. ◆ v 3 supply with or take in coal. **coal'field** n area in which coal is found.

co·a·lesce [koh-ə-LES] vi **-lesced, -lesc·ing** unite, merge. **co·a·les'cence** n

co·a·li·tion [koh-ə-LISH-ən] n alliance, esp. of political parties.

coarse [kors] adj **coars·er, coars·est 1** rough, harsh. 2 unrefined. 3 indecent. **coarse'ness** n

coast [kohst] n 1 seashore. ◆ v 2 move

THESAURUS

(inf)

clown n 1 = **comedian**, buffoon, comic, fool, harlequin, jester, joker, prankster ◆ v 2 = **play the fool**, act the fool, jest, mess about

club n 1 = **association**, company, fraternity, group, guild, lodge, set, society, union 2 = **stick**, bat, bludgeon, cudgel, truncheon ◆ v 3 = **beat**, bash, batter, bludgeon, hammer, pummel, strike

clue n = **indication**, evidence, hint, lead, pointer, sign, suggestion, suspicion, trace

clueless adj = **stupid**, dim, dull, half-witted, simple, slow, thick, unintelligent, witless

clump n 1 = **cluster**, bunch, bundle, group, mass ◆ v 2 = **stomp**, lumber, plod, thud, thump, tramp

clumsy adj = **awkward**, bumbling, gauche, gawky, lumbering, maladroit, ponderous, uncoordinated, ungainly, unwieldy

cluster n 1 = **gathering**, assemblage, batch, bunch, clump, collection, group, knot ◆ v 2 = **gather**, assemble, bunch,

collect, flock, group

clutch v = **seize**, catch, clasp, cling to, embrace, grab, grasp, grip, snatch

clutches pl n = **power**, claws, control, custody, grasp, grip, hands, keeping, possession, sway

clutter v 1 = **litter**, scatter, strew ◆ n 2 = **untidiness**, confusion, disarray, disorder, jumble, litter, mess, muddle

coach n 1 = **bus**, car, carriage, charabanc, vehicle 2 = **instructor**, handler, teacher, trainer, tutor ◆ v 3 = **instruct**, drill, exercise, prepare, train, tutor

coalesce v = **blend**, amalgamate, combine, fuse, incorporate, integrate, merge, mix, unite

coalition n = **alliance**, amalgamation, association, bloc, combination, confederation, conjunction, fusion, merger, union

coarse adj 1 = **rough**, crude, homespun, impure, unfinished, unpolished, unprocessed, unpurified, unrefined 2 = **vulgar**, earthy, improper, indecent, under momentum. **3** proceed without making much effort. **4** sail by the coast. **coast'er** *n* **1** small ship. **2** that which, one who, coasts. **3** small table mat for glasses, etc.

coat [koht] *n* **1** sleeved outer garment. **2** animal's fur or feathers. **3** covering layer. ◆ *vt* **4** cover with layer. **5** clothe. **coat of arms** armorial bearings.

coax [kohks] *vt* wheedle, cajole, persuade, force gently.

co·ax·i·al [koh-AK-see-əl] *adj* having the same axis. **co·ax'i·al·ly** *adv*

co·balt [KOH-bawlt] *n* **1** metallic element. **2** blue pigment from it.

cob·ble [KOB-əl] *vt* **-bled, -bling 1** patch roughly. **2** mend shoes. ◆ *n* **3** round stone. **cob'bler** *n* shoe mender.

co·bra [KOH-brə] *n* venomous, hooded snake of Asia and Africa.

cob'web *n* spider's web.

co·caine [koh-KAYN] *n* addictive narcotic drug used medicinally as anesthetic.

coch·i·neal [koch-ə-NEEL] *n* scarlet dye from Mexican insect.

cock [kok] *n* **1** male bird, esp. of domestic fowl. **2** tap for liquids. **3** hammer of gun. **4** its position drawn back. ◆ *vt* **5** draw back (gun hammer) to firing position. **6** raise, turn in alert or jaunty manner. **cock'eyed** [-īd] *adj* **1** crosseyed. **2** with a squint. **3** askew. **cock'fight** *n* staged fight between roosters.

cock·a·trice [KOK-ə-tris] *n* fabulous animal similar to basilisk.

cock·chaf·er [KOK-chay-fər] *n* large, flying beetle.

cock·le [KOK-əl] *n* shellfish.

Cock·ney [KOK-nee] *n, pl* **-neys 1** native of East End of London. **2** urban dialect of London or its East End.

cock·pit [KOK-pit] *n* **1** pilot's seat, compartment in small aircraft. **2** driver's

seat in racing car. **3** orig. enclosure for cockfighting.

cock·roach [KOK-rohch] *n* kind of insect, household pest.

cock·tail [KOK-tayl] *n* short drink of whiskey, gin, etc. with flavorings, etc.

cock·y [KOK-ee] *adj* **cock·i·er, cock·i·est** conceited, pert. **cock'i·ness** *n*

co·coa [KOH-koh] *n* **1** powder made from seed of cacao (tropical) tree. **2** drink made from the powder.

co·co·nut [KOH-kə-nut] *n* **1** tropical palm. **2** very large, hard nut from this palm.

co·coon [kə-KOON] *n* **1** sheath of insect in chrysalis stage. **2** any protective covering.

co·da [KOH-də] *n Mus.* final part of musical composition.

cod·dle [KOD-l] *vt* **-dled, -dling 1** overprotect, pamper. **2** cook (eggs) lightly.

code [kohd] *n* **1** system of letters, symbols and rules for their association to transmit messages secretly or briefly. **2** scheme of conduct. **3** collection of laws. **cod'i·fy** [KOD-] *vt* **-fied, -fy·ing cod·i·fi·ca'tion** *n*

co·deine [KOH-deen] *n* alkaline sedative, analgesic drug.

co·de·pend·ent [koh-di-PEND-dənt] *adj* of a relationship involving an addict. ◆ *n* **co·de·pen'den·cy** *n*

co·dex [KOH-deks] *n, pl* **-di·ces** [-də-seez] ancient manuscript volume, esp. of Bible, etc.

codg·er [KOJ-ər] *n inf* man, esp. old.

cod·i·cil [KOD-ə-səl] *n* addition to will.

co·ed·u·ca·tion·al [koh-ej-ə-KAY-shə-nl] *adj* of education of boys and girls together in mixed classes. **co·ed** [koh-ed] *n* (female student at) coeducational school. ◆ *adj*

co·ef·fi·cient [koh-ə-FISH-ənt] *n Math.* numerical or constant factor.

co·erce [koh-URS] *vt* **-erced, -erc·ing** compel, force. **co·er'cion** [-UR-shən] *n* forcible compulsion or restraint.

indelicate, ribald, rude, smutty

coarseness *n* **1** = **roughness**, crudity, unevenness **2** = **vulgarity**, bawdiness, crudity, earthiness, indelicacy, ribaldry, smut, uncouthness

coast *n* **1** = **shore**, beach, border, coastline, seaboard, seaside ◆ *v* **2** = **cruise**, drift, freewheel, glide, sail, taxi

coat *n* **1** = **fur**, fleece, hair, hide, pelt, skin, wool **2** = **layer**, coating, covering, overlay ◆ *v* **3** = **cover**, apply, plaster, smear, spread

coax *v* = **persuade**, allure, cajole, entice, prevail upon, sweet-talk (*inf*), talk into, wheedle

cocktail *n* = **mixture**, blend, combination, mix

cocky *adj* = **overconfident**, arrogant, brash, cocksure, conceited, egotistical, full of oneself, swaggering, vain

code *n* **1** = **cipher**, cryptograph **2** = **principles**, canon, convention, custom, ethics, etiquette, manners, maxim,

co·ex·ist [koh-ig-ZIST] *vi* exist together. **co·ex·ist'ence** *n*

cof·fee [KAW-fee] *n* **1** seeds of tropical shrub. **2** drink made from roasting and grinding these.

cof·fer [KAW-fər] *n* **1** chest for valuables. **2** treasury, funds.

cof·fer·dam [KAW-fər-dam] *n* watertight structure enabling construction work to be done underwater.

cof·fin [KAW-fin] *n* box for corpse.

cog [kog] *n* **1** one of series of teeth on rim of wheel. **2** person, thing forming small part of big process, organization, etc.

co·gent [KOH-jənt] *adj* convincing, compelling, persuasive. **co'gen·cy** *n*

cog·i·tate [KOJ-i-tayt] *vi* **-tat·ed, -tat·ing** think, reflect, ponder.

co·gnac [KOHN-yak] *n* French brandy.

cog·nate [KOG-nayt] *adj* of same stock, related, kindred.

cog·ni·tion [kog-NISH-ən] *n* act or faculty of knowing. **cog'ni·tive** *adj*

cog·ni·zance [KOG-nə-zəns] *n* knowledge, perception. **cog'ni·zant** *adj*

co·gno·scen·ti [kon-yə-SHEN-tee] *pl n* people with knowledge in particular field, esp. arts.

co·hab·it [koh-HAB-it] *vi* live together as husband and wife.

co·here [koh-HEER] *vi* **-hered, -her·ing** stick together, be consistent. **co·her'ence** *n* **co·her'ent** *adj* **1** capable of logical speech, thought. **2** connected, making sense. **3** sticking together. **co·he'sion** [-HEE-zhən] *n* cohering. **co·he'sive** *adj*

co·hort [KOH-hort] *n* **1** troop. **2** associate.

coif·feur [kwah-FUUR] *n* hairdresser.

coif·fure [kwah-FYUUR] *n* hairstyle.

coil [koil] *vt* **1** lay in rings. **2** twist into

winding shape. ◆ *vi* **3** twist, take up a winding shape or spiral. ◆ *n* **4** series of rings. **5** device in vehicle, etc. to transform low-voltage direct current to higher voltage for ignition purposes. **6** contraceptive device inserted in womb.

coin [koin] *n* **1** piece of money. **2** money. ◆ *vt* **3** make into money, stamp. **4** invent. **coin'age** *n* **1** coining. **2** coins collectively. **coin money** *inf* make money rapidly.

co·in·cide [koh-in-SID] *vi* **-cid·ed, -cid·ing 1** happen together. **2** agree exactly. **co·in'ci·dence** [-si-dəns] *n* **co·in'ci·dent** *adj* coinciding. **co·in·ci·den'tal** *adj*

co·i·tus [KOH-i-təs], **co·i·tion** [koh-ISH-ən] *n* sexual intercourse.

coke¹ [kohk] *n* residue left from distillation of coal, used as fuel.

coke² *n sl* cocaine.

Col. Colossians.

co·la [KOH-lə] *n* **1** tropical tree. **2** its nut, used to flavor drink.

col·an·der [KUL-ən-dər] *n* culinary strainer perforated with small holes.

cold [kohld] *adj* **-er, -est 1** lacking heat. **2** indifferent, unmoved, apathetic. **3** dispiriting. **4** reserved or unfriendly. **5** (of colors) giving an impression of coldness. ◆ *n* **6** lack of heat. **7** illness, marked by runny nose, etc. **cold'ly** *adv* **cold'-blood·ed** *adj* **1** lacking pity, mercy. **2** having body temperature that varies with that of the surroundings. **cold chisel** toughened steel chisel. **cold feet** fear. **cold storage** method of preserving perishable foods, etc. by keeping them at artificially reduced temperature. **cold turkey** *sl* abrupt halt in use of addictive drug, etc. **cold war** economic, diplomatic but nonmilitary hostility.

──────| THESAURUS |──────

regulations, rules, system

cogent *adj* = **convincing**, compelling, effective, forceful, influential, potent, powerful, strong, weighty

cogitate *v* = **think**, consider, contemplate, deliberate, meditate, mull over, muse, ponder, reflect, ruminate

coherent *adj* **1** = **consistent**, logical, lucid, meaningful, orderly, organized, rational, reasoned, systematic **2** = **intelligible**, articulate, comprehensible

coil *v* = **wind**, curl, loop, snake, spiral, twine, twist, wreathe, writhe

coin *n* **1** = **money**, cash, change, copper,

silver, specie ◆ *v* **2** = **invent**, create, fabricate, forge, make up, mint, mold, originate

coincide *v* **1** = **occur simultaneously**, be concurrent, coexist, synchronize **2** = **agree**, accord, concur, correspond, harmonize, match, square, tally

coincidence *n* **1** = **chance**, accident, fluke, happy accident, luck, stroke of luck **2** = **coinciding**, concurrence, conjunction, correlation, correspondence

coincidental *adj* = **chance**, accidental, casual, fluky (*inf*), fortuitous, unintentional, unplanned

cole·slaw [KOHL-slaw] *n* salad dish based on shredded cabbage.

col·ic [KOL-ik] *n* severe pains in the intestines. **co·li·tis** [kə-LĪ-tis] *n* inflammation of the colon.

col·lab·o·rate [kə-LAB-ə-rayt] *vi* **-rat·ed, -rat·ing** work with another on a project. **col·lab'o·ra·tor** *n* one who works with another, esp. one who aids an enemy in occupation of his own country.

col·lage [kə-LAH*ZH*] *n* (artistic) composition of bits and pieces stuck together on background.

col·lapse [kə-LAPS] *vi* **-lapsed, -laps·ing** 1 fall. 2 give way. 3 lose strength, fail. ♦ *n* 4 act of collapsing. 5 breakdown. **col·laps'i·ble** *adj*

col·lar [KOL-ər] *n* 1 band, part of garment, worn round neck. 2 *inf* police arrest. ♦ *vt* 3 seize by collar. 4 *inf* capture, seize. **col'lar·bone** *n* bone from shoulder to breastbone.

col·late [kə-LAYT] *vt* **-lat·ed, -lat·ing** 1 compare carefully. 2 place in order (as printed sheets for binding). **col·la'tion** *n* 1 collating. 2 light meal.

col·lat·er·al [kə-LAT-ər-əl] *n* 1 security pledged for repayment of loan. ♦ *adj* 2 accompanying. 3 side by side. 4 of same stock but different line. 5 subordinate. **collateral damage** unintentional civilian casualties or damage to civilian property caused by military action.

col·league [KOL-eeg] *n* associate, companion in office or employment, fellow worker.

col·lect [kə-LEKT] *vt* 1 gather, bring together. ♦ *vi* 2 come together. 3 *inf* receive money. **col·lect'ed** *adj* 1 calm. 2 gathered. **col·lec'tion** *n* **col·lec'tive** *n* factory, farm, etc., run on principles of collectivism. ♦ *adj* **col·lec'tiv·ism** *n* theory that a government should own all means of production.

col·lege [KOL-ij] *n* 1 place of higher education. 2 society of scholars. 3 association. **col·le·giate** [kə-LEE-jit] *adj* **col·le·gian** *n* student.

col·lide [kə-LĪD] *vi* **-lid·ed, -lid·ing** 1 strike or dash together. 2 come into conflict. **col·li'sion** [-LIZH-ən] *n* colliding.

col·lo·di·on [kə-LOH-dee-ən] *n* chemical solution used in photography and medicine.

col·loid [KOL-oid] *n* suspension of particles in a solution.

THESAURUS

cold *adj* 1 = **chilly**, arctic, bleak, cool, freezing, frigid, frosty, frozen, icy, wintry 2 = **unfriendly**, aloof, distant, frigid, indifferent, reserved, standoffish ♦ *n* 3 = **coldness**, chill, frigidity, frostiness, iciness

cold-blooded *adj* = **callous**, dispassionate, heartless, ruthless, steely, stony-hearted, unemotional, unfeeling

collaborate *v* 1 = **work together**, cooperate, join forces, participate, play ball (*inf*), team up 2 = **conspire**, collude, cooperate, fraternize

collaboration *n* = **teamwork**, alliance, association, cooperation, partnership

collaborator *n* 1 = **co-worker**, associate, colleague, confederate, partner, team-mate 2 = **traitor**, fraternizer, quisling, turncoat

collapse *v* 1 = **fall down**, cave in, crumple, fall, fall apart at the seams, give way, subside 2 = **fail**, come to nothing, fold, founder, go belly-up (*inf*) ♦ *n* 3 = **falling down**, cave-in, disintegration, falling apart, ruin, subsidence 4 = **failure**, downfall, flop, slump 5 = **faint**, breakdown, exhaustion, prostration

collar *v Inf* = **seize**, apprehend, arrest, capture, catch, grab, nail (*inf*)

colleague *n* = **fellow worker**, ally, assistant, associate, collaborator, comrade, helper, partner, team-mate, workmate

collect *v* 1 = **assemble**, cluster, congregate, convene, converge, flock together, rally 2 = **gather**, accumulate, amass, assemble, heap, hoard, save, stockpile

collected *adj* = **calm**, composed, cool, poised, self-possessed, serene, unperturbed, unruffled

collection *n* 1 = **accumulation**, anthology, compilation, heap, hoard, mass, pile, set, stockpile, store 2 = **group**, assembly, assortment, cluster, company, crowd 3 = **contribution**, alms, offering, offertory

collective *adj* = **combined**, aggregate, composite, corporate, cumulative, joint, shared, unified, united

collide *v* 1 = **crash**, clash, come into collision, meet head-on 2 = **conflict**, clash

collision *n* 1 = **crash**, accident, bump, impact, pile-up (*inf*), smash 2 = **conflict**, clash, confrontation, encounter,

col·lo·qui·al [kə-LOH-kwee-əl] *adj* pert. to or used in informal conversation. **col·lo'qui·al·ism** *n* **col·lo·quy** [KOL-ə-kwee] *n, pl* **-quies 1** conversation. **2** dialogue.

col·lu·sion [kə-LOO-zhən] *n* secret agreement for a fraudulent purpose, esp. in legal proceedings. **col·lu'sive** [-siv] *adj*

co·logne [kə-LOHN] *n* perfumed liquid.

co·lon[1] [KOH-lən] *n* mark (:) indicating break in a sentence.

colon[2] *n* part of large intestine from cecum to rectum.

colo·nel [KUR-nl] *n* commander of regiment or battalion.

col·on·nade [kol-ə-NAYD] *n* row of columns.

col·o·ny [KOL-ə-nee] *n, pl* **-nies 1** body of people who settle in new country but remain subject to parent country. **2** country so settled. **3** distinctive group living together. **co·lo·ni·al** [kə-LOH-nee-əl] *adj* of colony. **col'o·nist** *n* **col·o·ni·za'tion** *n* **col'o·nize** *vt* **-nized, -niz·ing**

col·or [KUL-ər] *n* **1** hue, tint. **2** complexion. **3** paint. **4** pigment. **5** *fig* semblance, pretext. **6** timbre, quality. **7** mood. ◆ *pl* **8** flag. **9** distinguishing symbol. ◆ *vt* **10** stain, dye, paint, give color to. **11** disguise. **12** influence or distort. ◆ *vi* **13** become colored. **14** blush. **col·or·a'tion** *n* **col'or·ful** *adj* **1** with bright or varied colors. **2**

distinctive.

co·los·sus [kə-LOS-əs] *n, pl* **-los·si** [-LOS-ī] **1** huge statue. **2** something, somebody very large. **co·los'sal** *adj* huge, gigantic.

colt [kohlt] *n* young male horse.

col·umn [KOL-əm] *n* **1** long vertical cylinder, pillar. **2** support. **3** division of page. **4** body of troops. **co·lum·nar** [kə-LUM-nər] *adj* **col'um·nist** *n* journalist writing regular feature for newspaper.

com-, con- *prefix* together, jointly, e.g. *commingle*.

co·ma [KOH-mə] *n* state of unconsciousness. **co'ma·tose** [-tohs] *adj*

comb [kohm] *n* **1** toothed instrument for tidying, arranging, ornamenting hair. **2** rooster's crest. **3** mass of honey cells. ◆ *vt* **4** use comb on. **5** search with great care.

com·bat [KOM-bat] *n* **1** fight or struggle. ◆ *vt* [kəm-BAT] **2** fight, contest. **com·bat·ant** [kəm-BAT-nt] *n* **com·bat'ive** *adj*

com·bine [kəm-BĪN] *v* **1** join together. **2** ally. ◆ *n* [KOM-bīn] trust, syndicate, esp. of businesses, trade organizations, etc. **com·bi·na·tion** [kom-bə-NAY-shən] *n* **com'bine** *n* machine to harvest and thresh grain in one operation.

com·bus·tion [kəm-BUS-chən] *n* process of burning. **com·bus'ti·ble** *adj*

come [kum] *vi* **came, come, com·ing 1** approach, arrive, move toward. **2** reach. **3**

opposition, skirmish

colloquial *adj* = **informal**, conversational, demotic, everyday, familiar, idiomatic, vernacular

colony *n* = **settlement**, community, dependency, dominion, outpost, possession, province, satellite state, territory

color *n* **1** = **hue**, colorant, dye, paint, pigment, shade, tint ◆ *v* **2** = **paint**, dye, stain, tinge, tint **3** = **blush**, flush, redden

colorful *adj* **1** = **bright**, brilliant, multicolored, psychedelic, variegated **2** = **interesting**, distinctive, graphic, lively, picturesque, rich, vivid

colorless *adj* **1** = **drab**, achromatic, anemic, ashen, bleached, faded, wan, washed out **2** = **uninteresting**, characterless, dreary, dull, insipid, lackluster, vapid

colossal *adj* = **huge**, enormous, gigantic, immense, mammoth, massive, monumental, prodigious, vast

column *n* **1** = **pillar**, obelisk, post, shaft, support, upright **2** = **line**, cavalcade, file, procession, rank, row

coma *n* = **unconsciousness**, oblivion, stupor, trance

comb *v* **1** = **untangle**, arrange, dress, groom **2** = **search**, forage, hunt, rake, ransack, rummage, scour, sift

combat *n* **1** = **fight**, action, battle, conflict, contest, encounter, engagement, skirmish, struggle, war, warfare ◆ *v* **2** = **fight**, defy, do battle with, oppose, resist, withstand

combatant *n* = **fighter**, adversary, antagonist, enemy, opponent, soldier, warrior

combination *n* **1** = **mixture**, amalgamation, blend, coalescence, composite, connection, mix **2** = **association**, alliance, coalition, confederation, consortium, federation, syndicate, union

combine *v* = **join together**, amalgamate, blend, connect, integrate, link, merge, happen to. **4** occur. **5** be available. **6** originate (from). **7** become. **8** turn out to be. **come'back** n inf **1** return to active life after retirement. **2** retort. **come'down** n **1** setback. **2** descent in social status.

com·e·dy [KOM-i-dee] n, pl **-dies 1** dramatic or other work of light, amusing character. **2** humor. **co·me·di·an** [kə-MEE-dee-ən] n **1** entertainer who tells jokes, etc. **2** actor in comedy.

come·ly [KUM-lee] adj fair, pretty, good-looking. **come'li·ness** n

co·mes·ti·bles [kə-MES-tə-bəlz] n food.

com·et [KOM-it] n luminous heavenly body consisting of diffuse head, nucleus and long tail.

com·fort [KUM-fərt] n **1** well-being. **2** ease. **3** consolation. **4** means of consolation or satisfaction. ♦ vt **5** soothe. **6** cheer, gladden, console. **com·fort·a·ble** [KUMF-tə-bəl] adj **1** free from pain, etc. **2**

inf financially secure. **com'fort·a·bly** adv **com'fort·er** n **1** one who comforts. **2** woolen scarf. **3** quilt.

com·ic [KOM-ik] adj **1** relating to comedy. **2** funny, laughable. ♦ n **3** comedian. **4** magazine consisting of strip cartoons. **com'i·cal** adj

com·ma [KOM-ə] n punctuation mark (,) separating parts of sentence.

com·mand [kə-MAND] vt **1** order. **2** rule. **3** compel. **4** have in one's power. **5** overlook, dominate. ♦ vi **6** exercise rule. ♦ n **7** order. **8** power of controlling, ruling, dominating, overlooking. **9** knowledge, mastery. **10** post of one commanding. **11** district commanded, jurisdiction. **com'man·dant** [KOM-ən-dant] n **com·man·deer'** vt seize for military use, appropriate. **com·mand'er** n **com·mand'ing** adj **1** in command. **2** with air of authority. **com·mand'ment** n **com·man·do** [kə-MAN-doh] n, pl **-dos**

mix, pool, unite

come v **1** = **move towards**, advance, approach, draw near, near **2** = **arrive**, appear, enter, materialize, reach, show up (inf), turn up (inf) **3** = **happen**, fall, occur, take place **4** = **result**, arise, emanate, emerge, flow, issue, originate **5** = **reach**, extend **6** = **be available**, be made, be offered, be on offer, be produced

come about v = **happen**, arise, befall, come to pass, occur, result, take place, transpire (inf)

come across v = **find**, bump into (inf), chance upon, discover, encounter, meet, notice, stumble upon, unearth

comeback n **1** Inf = **return**, rally, rebound, recovery, resurgence, revival, triumph **2** = **response**, rejoinder, reply, retaliation, retort, riposte

come back v = **return**, reappear, recur, re-enter

comedian n = **comic**, card (inf), clown, funny man, humorist, jester, joker, wag, wit

comedown n **1** = **decline**, deflation, demotion, reverse **2** Inf = **disappointment**, anticlimax, blow, humiliation, letdown

comedy n = **humor**, farce, fun, hilarity, jesting, joking, light entertainment

comfort n **1** = **luxury**, cosiness, ease, opulence, snugness, wellbeing **2** = **relief**, compensation, consolation, help, succor, support ♦ v **3** = **console**, commiserate

with, hearten, reassure, soothe

comfortable adj **1** = **relaxing**, agreeable, convenient, cozy, homely, homey, pleasant, restful, snug **2** = **happy**, at ease, at home, contented, gratified, relaxed, serene **3** Inf = **well-off**, affluent, in clover (inf), prosperous, well-to-do

comforting adj = **consoling**, cheering, consolatory, encouraging, heart-warming, reassuring, soothing

comic adj **1** = **funny**, amusing, comical, droll, farcical, humorous, jocular, witty ♦ n **2** = **comedian**, buffoon, clown, funny man, humorist, jester, wag, wit

comical adj = **funny**, amusing, comic, droll, farcical, hilarious, humorous, priceless, side-splitting

coming adj **1** = **approaching**, at hand, forthcoming, imminent, impending, in store, near, nigh ♦ n **2** = **arrival**, advent, approach

command v **1** = **order**, bid, charge, compel, demand, direct, require **2** = **have authority over**, control, dominate, govern, handle, head, lead, manage, rule, supervise ♦ n **3** = **order**, commandment, decree, demand, directive, instruction, requirement, ultimatum **4** = **authority**, charge, control, government, management, mastery, power, rule, supervision

commandeer v = **seize**, appropriate, confiscate, requisition, sequester, (member of) special military unit trained for airborne, amphibious attack.

com·mem·o·rate [kə-MEM-ə-rayt] *vt* **-rat·ed, -rat·ing 1** celebrate, keep in memory by ceremony. **2** be a memorial of. **com·mem·o·ra'tion** *n* **com·mem'o·ra·tive** *adj*

com·mence [kə-MENS] *v* **-menced, -menc·ing** begin. **com·mence'ment** *n* **1** beginning. **2** graduation of students.

com·mend [kə-MEND] *vt* **1** praise. **2** commit, entrust. **com·mend'a·ble** *adj* **com·men·da'tion** *n*

com·men·su·rate [kə-MEN-sər-it] *adj* **1** equal in size or length of time. **2** in proportion, adequate.

com·ment [KOM-ent] *n* **1** remark, criticism. **2** gossip. **3** note, explanation. ◆ *vi* **4** remark, note. **5** annotate, criticize. **com'men·tar·y** *n, pl* **-tar·ies 1** explanatory notes or comments. **2** spoken accompaniment to film, etc. **com'men·ta·tor** *n* author, speaker of commentary.

com·merce [KOM-ərs] *n* **1** buying and

selling. **2** dealings. **3** trade. **com·mer·cial** [kə-MUR-shəl] *adj* **1** of, concerning, business, trade, profit, etc. ◆ *n* **2** advertisement on radio or TV.

com·mis·er·ate [kə-MIZ-ə-rayt] *vt* **-at·ed, -at·ing** pity, condole, sympathize with.

com·mis·sion [kə-MISH-ən] *n* **1** something entrusted to be done. **2** delegated authority. **3** body entrusted with some special duty. **4** payment by percentage for doing something. **5** warrant, esp. presidential warrant, giving authority. **6** document appointing person to officer's rank. **7** doing, committing. ◆ *vt* **8** charge with duty or task. **9** *Military* confer a rank. **10** give order for. **com·mis'sion·er** *n* **1** one empowered to act by commission or warrant. **2** member of commission or government board. **3** administrative head of professional sport.

com·mit [kə-MIT] *vt* **-mit·ted, -mit·ting 1** entrust, give in charge. **2** perpetrate, be guilty of. **3** pledge, promise. **4** compromise, entangle. **5** place in prison or mental institution. **com·mit'ment** *n*

sequestrate

commander *n* = **officer**, boss (*inf*), captain, chief, commanding officer, head, leader, ruler

commanding *adj* = **controlling**, advantageous, decisive, dominant, dominating, superior

commemorate *v* = **remember**, celebrate, honor, immortalize, pay tribute to, salute

commemoration *n* = **remembrance**, ceremony, honoring, memorial service, tribute

commence *v* = **begin**, embark on, enter upon, initiate, open, originate, start

commend *v* = **praise**, acclaim, applaud, approve, compliment, extol, recommend, speak highly of

commendable *adj* = **praiseworthy**, admirable, creditable, deserving, estimable, exemplary, laudable, meritorious, worthy

commendation *n* = **praise**, acclaim, acclamation, approbation, approval, credit, encouragement, good opinion, kudos, panegyric, recommendation

comment *n* **1** = **remark**, observation, statement **2** = **note**, annotation, commentary, explanation, exposition, illustration ◆ *v* **3** = **remark**, mention, note,

observe, point out, say, utter **4** = **annotate**, elucidate, explain, interpret

commentary *n* **1** = **narration**, description, voice-over **2** = **notes**, analysis, critique, explanation, review, treatise

commentator *n* **1** = **reporter**, special correspondent, sportscaster **2** = **critic**, annotator, interpreter

commerce *n* = **trade**, business, dealing, exchange, traffic

commercial *adj* **1** = **mercantile**, trading **2** = **materialistic**, mercenary, profit-making ◆ *n* **3** = **advertisement**, ad (*inf*), announcement, plug (*inf*)

commiserate *v* = **sympathize**, console, feel for, pity

commission *n* **1** = **duty**, errand, mandate, mission, task **2** = **fee**, cut, percentage, rake-off (*sl*), royalties **3** = **committee**, board, commissioners, delegation, deputation, representatives ◆ *v* **4** = **appoint**, authorize, contract, delegate, depute, empower, engage, nominate, order, sanction

commit *v* **1** = **do**, carry out, enact, execute, perform, perpetrate **2** = **put in custody**, confine, imprison

commitment *n* **1** = **dedication**, devotion, involvement, loyalty **2** = **responsibility**,

com·mit·tee [kə-MIT-ee] *n* body appointed, elected for special business usu. from larger body.

com·mode [kə-MOHD] *n* **1** chest of drawers. **2** toilet.

com·mo·di·ous [kə-MOH-dee-əs] *adj* roomy.

com·mod·i·ty [kə-MOD-i-tee] *n, pl* **-ties 1** article of trade. **2** anything useful.

com·mon [KOM-ən] *adj* **1** shared by or belonging to all, or to several. **2** public, general. **3** ordinary, usual, frequent. **4** inferior. **5** vulgar. ◆ *n* **6** land belonging to community. ◆ *pl* **7** ordinary people. **8** (C-) lower house of British parliament. **com'mon·ly** *adv* **Common Market** former name for EUROPEAN UNION. **com'mon·place** *adj* **1** ordinary, everyday. ◆ *n* **2** trite remark. **3** anything occurring frequently. **common sense** sound, practical understanding. **com'mon·wealth** *n* **1** republic. **2** state of the US. **3** federation of self-governing countries.

com·mo·tion [kə-MOH-shən] *n* stir, disturbance, tumult.

com·mune¹ [kə-MYOON] *vi* **-muned, -mun·ing** converse together intimately. **com·mun·ion** *n* **1** sharing of thoughts, feelings, etc. **2** fellowship. **3** body with common faith. **4** (C-) participation in sacrament of the Lord's Supper. **5** (C-) that sacrament, Eucharist.

com·mune² [KOM-yoon] *n* group of families, individuals living together and sharing property, responsibility, etc. **com·mu·nal** [kə-MYOON-l] *adj* for common use.

com·mu·ni·cate [kə-MYOO-ni-kayt] *v* **-cat·ed, -cat·ing** ◆ *vt* **1** impart, convey. **2** reveal. ◆ *vi* **3** give or exchange information. **4** have connecting passage, door. **5** receive Communion. **com·mu'ni·ca·ble** *adj* **com·mu'ni·cant** *n* one who receives Communion. **com·mu·ni·ca'tion** *n* **1** act of giving, esp. information. **2** information, message. **3** (usu pl) passage (road, railway, etc.), or means of exchanging messages (radio, mail, etc.) between places. ◆ *pl* **4** connections between military base and front. **com·mu'ni·ca·tive** *adj* free with information.

com·mu·ni·qué [kə-myoo-ni-KAY] *n* official announcement.

com·mu·nism [KOM-yə-niz-əm] *n* doctrine that all goods, means of production, etc., should be property of community. **com'mu·nist** *n, adj*

com·mu·ni·ty [kə-MYOO-ni-tee] *n, pl* **-ties 1** body of people with something in common, e.g. neighborhood, religion, etc. **2** society, the public. **3** joint ownership. **4** similarity, agreement.

com·mute [kə-MYOOT] *v* **-mut·ed, -mut·ing** ◆ *vi* **1** travel daily some distance

━━━━━ THESAURUS ━━━━━

duty, engagement, liability, obligation, tie

common *adj* **1** = **average**, commonplace, conventional, customary, everyday, familiar, frequent, habitual, ordinary, regular, routine, standard, stock, usual **2** = **popular**, accepted, general, prevailing, prevalent, universal, widespread **3** = **collective**, communal, popular, public, social **4** = **vulgar**, coarse, inferior, plebeian

commonplace *adj* **1** = **everyday**, banal, common, humdrum, mundane, obvious, ordinary, widespread ◆ *n* **2** = **cliché**, banality, platitude, truism

common sense *n* = **good sense**, horse sense, level-headedness, native intelligence, prudence, sound judgment, wit

commotion *n* = **disturbance**, disorder, excitement, furor, fuss, hue and cry, rumpus, tumult, turmoil, upheaval, uproar

communal *adj* = **public**, collective, general, joint, shared

commune *n* = **community**, collective, cooperative, kibbutz

commune with *v* = **contemplate**, meditate on, muse on, ponder, reflect on

communicate *v* = **make known**, convey, declare, disclose, impart, inform, pass on, proclaim, transmit

communication *n* **1** = **passing on**, contact, conversation, correspondence, dissemination, link, transmission **2** = **message**, announcement, disclosure, dispatch, information, news, report, statement, word

communicative *adj* = **talkative**, chatty, expansive, forthcoming, frank, informative, loquacious, open, outgoing, voluble

Communism *n* = **socialism**, Bolshevism, collectivism, Marxism, state socialism

Communist *n* = **socialist**, Bolshevik, collectivist, Marxist, Red (*inf*)

community *n* = **society**, brotherhood, commonwealth, company, general public, to work. ♦ vt 2 exchange. 3 change (punishment, etc.) into something less severe. 4 change (payment, etc.) into another form. ♦ n 5 journey made by commuting. **com·mu·ta·tion** [kom-yə-TAY-shən] n **com·mu·ta·tor** n device to change alternating electric current into direct current. **com·mut'er** n one who daily travels some distance to work.

com·pact[1] [kəm-PAKT] adj 1 neatly arranged or packed. 2 solid, concentrated. 3 terse. ♦ v 4 make, become compact. 5 compress. **com·pact'ness** n **compact disk** [KOM-pakt] small disk on which sound is recorded as series of metallic pits enclosed in polyvinyl chloride and played back by optical scanning by laser.

com·pact[2] [KOM-pakt] n small case to hold face powder, powder puff and mirror.

com·pact[3] [KOM-pakt] n agreement, covenant, treaty, contract.

com·pan·ion[1] [kəm-PAN-yən] n 1 chum, fellow, comrade, associate. 2 person employed to live with another. **com·pan·ion·a·ble** adj

companion[2] n 1 raised cover over staircase from deck to cabin of ship. 2 deck skylight.

com·pan·ion·way n staircase from deck to cabin.

com·pa·ny [KUM-pə-nee] n, pl -nies 1 gathering of persons. 2 companionship, fellowship. 3 guests. 4 business firm. 5 division of regiment under captain. 6 crew of ship. 7 actors in play.

com·pare [kəm-PAIR] vt -pared, -par·ing 1 notice or point out likenesses and differences of things. 2 liken. 3 make comparative and superlative of adjective or adverb. ♦ vi 4 be like. 5 compete with. **com·pa·ra·bil·i·ty** [kom-pər-ə-BIL-i-tee] n **com·pa·ra·ble** adj **com·par'a·tive** adj 1 that may be compared. 2 not absolute. 3 relative, partial. 4 Grammar denoting form of adjective, adverb, indicating "more". ♦ n **com·par'a·tive·ly** adv **com·par'i·son** n act of comparing.

com·part·ment [kəm-PAHRT-mənt] n 1 division or part divided off. 2 section.

com·pass [KUM-pəs] n 1 instrument for showing the north. 2 instrument for drawing circles. 3 circumference, measurement around. 4 space, area. 5 scope, reach. ♦ vt 6 surround. 7 comprehend. 8 attain, accomplish.

com·pas·sion [kəm-PASH-ən] n pity,

people, populace, public, residents, state

commuter n = daily traveler, straphanger (inf), suburbanite

compact[1] adj 1 = closely packed, compressed, condensed, dense, pressed together, solid, thick 2 = brief, compendious, concise, succinct, terse, to the point ♦ v 3 = pack closely, compress, condense, cram, stuff, tamp

compact[2] n = agreement, arrangement, bargain, bond, contract, covenant, deal, pact, treaty, understanding

companion n 1 = friend, accomplice, ally, associate, colleague, comrade, consort, homeboy (sl), homegirl (sl), mate (inf), partner 2 = escort, aide, assistant, attendant, chaperon, squire

companionship n = fellowship, camaraderie, company, comradeship, conviviality, esprit de corps, friendship, rapport, togetherness

company n 1 = business, association, concern, corporation, establishment, firm, house, partnership, syndicate 2 = group, assembly, band, collection, community, crowd, gathering, party, set 3 = guests,

callers, party, visitors

comparable adj 1 = on a par, a match for, as good as, commensurate, equal, equivalent, in a class with, on a level playing field (inf), proportionate, tantamount 2 = similar, akin, alike, analogous, cognate, corresponding, cut from the same cloth, of a piece, related

comparative adj = relative, by comparison, qualified

compare v 1 = weigh, balance, contrast, juxtapose, set against 2 (usually with with) = be on a par with, approach, bear comparison, be in the same class as, be the equal of, compete with, equal, hold a candle to, match 3 compare to = liken to, correlate to, equate to, identify with, mention in the same breath as, parallel, resemble

comparison n 1 = contrast, distinction, juxtaposition 2 = similarity, analogy, comparability, correlation, likeness, resemblance

compartment n = section, alcove, bay, berth, booth, carriage, cubbyhole, cubicle, locker, niche, pigeonhole

sympathy. **com·pas'sion·ate** [-it] *adj*
com·pat·i·ble [kəm-PAT-ə-bəl] *adj* **1** capable of harmonious existence. **2** consistent, agreeing with. **com·pat·i·bil'i·ty** *adv*
com·pa·tri·ot [kəm-PAY-tree-ət] *n* fellow countryman. ♦ *adj*
com·pel [kəm-PEL] *vt* **-pelled, -pel·ling 1** force, oblige. **2** bring about by force.
com·pen·di·um [kəm-PEN-dee-əm] *n, pl* **-di·ums** abridgment, summary. **com·pen'di·ous** *adj* brief but inclusive.
com·pen·sate [KOM-pən-sayt] *vt* **-sat·ed, -sat·ing 1** make up for. **2** recompense suitably. **3** reward. **com·pen·sa'tion** *n*
com·pete [kəm-PEET] *vi* **-pet·ed, -pet·ing 1** (oft. with *with*) strive in rivalry, contend for, vie with. **com·pe·ti·tion** [kom-pi-TISH-ən] *n* **com·pet'i·tive** [kəm-]

adj **com·pet'i·tor** *n*
com·pe·tent [KOM-pi-tənt] *adj* **1** able, skillful. **2** properly qualified. **3** proper, due, legitimate. **4** suitable, sufficient.
com·pe·tence *n* efficiency.
com·pile [kəm-PĪL] *vt* **-piled, -pil·ing 1** make up (e.g. book) from various sources or materials. **2** gather, put together.
com·pi·la·tion [kom-pə-LAY-shən] *n* **com·pil'er** *n*
com·pla·cent [kəm-PLAY-sənt] *adj* **1** self-satisfied. **2** pleased or gratified.
com·pla'cen·cy *n*
com·plain [kəm-PLAYN] *vi* **1** grumble. **2** bring charge, make known a grievance. **3** (with *of*) make known that one is suffering from. **com·plaint'** *n* **1** statement of a wrong, grievance. **2** ailment, illness.
com·plain'ant *n*

compass *n* = **range**, area, boundary, circumference, extent, field, limit, reach, realm, scope
compassion *n* = **sympathy**, condolence, fellow feeling, humanity, kindness, mercy, pity, sorrow, tender-heartedness, tenderness, understanding
compassionate *adj* = **sympathetic**, benevolent, charitable, humane, humanitarian, kind-hearted, merciful, pitying, tender-hearted, understanding
compatibility *n* = **harmony**, affinity, agreement, concord, empathy, like-mindedness, rapport, sympathy
compatible *adj* = **harmonious**, adaptable, congruous, consistent, in harmony, in keeping, suitable
compel *v* = **force**, coerce, constrain, dragoon, impel, make, oblige, railroad (*inf*)
compelling *adj* **1** = **fascinating**, enchanting, enthralling, gripping, hypnotic, irresistible, mesmeric, spellbinding **2** = **pressing**, binding, coercive, imperative, overriding, peremptory, unavoidable, urgent **3** = **convincing**, cogent, conclusive, forceful, irrefutable, powerful, telling, weighty
compensate *v* **1** = **recompense**, atone, make amends, make good, refund, reimburse, remunerate, repay **2** = **cancel (out)**, balance, counteract, counterbalance, make up for, offset, redress
compensation *n* = **recompense**, amends, atonement, damages, reimbursement,

remuneration, reparation, restitution, satisfaction
compete *v* = **contend**, be in the running, challenge, contest, fight, strive, struggle, vie
competence *n* = **ability**, capability, capacity, expertise, fitness, proficiency, skill, suitability
competent *adj* = **able**, adequate, capable, fit, proficient, qualified, suitable
competition *n* **1** = **rivalry**, opposition, strife, struggle **2** = **contest**, championship, event, head-to-head, puzzle, quiz, tournament **3** = **opposition**, challengers, field, rivals
competitive *adj* **1** = **cut-throat**, aggressive, antagonistic, at odds, dog-eat-dog, opposing, rival **2** = **ambitious**, combative
competitor *n* = **contestant**, adversary, antagonist, challenger, opponent, rival
compilation *n* = **collection**, accumulation, anthology, assemblage, assortment, treasury
compile *v* = **put together**, accumulate, amass, collect, cull, garner, gather, marshal, organize
complacency *n* = **self-satisfaction**, contentment, satisfaction, smugness
complacent *adj* = **self-satisfied**, contented, pleased with oneself, resting on one's laurels, satisfied, serene, smug, unconcerned
complain *v* = **find fault**, bemoan, bewail, carp, deplore, groan, grouse, grumble,

com·ple·ment [KOM-plə-mənt] *n* **1**
something making up a whole. **2** full
allowance, equipment, etc. ◆ *vt* **3** add to,
make complete. **com·ple·men'ta·ry** *adj*

com·plete [kəm-PLEET] *adj* **1** full, perfect. **2**
finished, ended. **3** entire. **4** thorough. ◆ *vt*
-plet·ed, -plet·ing 5 make whole, perfect. **6**
finish. **com·plete'ly** *adv* **com·ple'tion** *n*

com·plex [kəm-PLEKS] *adj* **1** intricate,
compound, involved. ◆ *n* [KOM-pleks] **2**
complicated whole. **3** group of related
buildings. **4** psychological abnormality,
obsession. **com·plex'i·ty** *n*

com·plex·ion [kəm-PLEK-shən] *n* **1** look,
color, of skin, esp. of face, appearance. **2**
aspect, character. **3** disposition.

compliant see COMPLY.

com·pli·cate [KOM-pli-kayt] *vt* **-cat·ed,
-cat·ing 1** make intricate, involved,
difficult. **2** mix up. **com·pli·ca'tion** *n*

com·plic·i·ty [kəm-PLIS-i-tee] *n, pl* **-ties**
partnership in wrongdoing.

com·pli·ment [KOM-plə-mənt] *n* **1**
expression of regard, praise. **2** flattering
speech. ◆ *pl* **3** expression of courtesy,
formal greetings. ◆ *vt* **4** praise,
congratulate. **com·pli·men'ta·ry** *adj* **1**
expressing praise. **2** free of charge.

com·ply [kəm-PLĪ] *vi* **-plied, -ply·ing**
consent, yield, do as asked. **com·pli'ance** *n*
com·pli'ant *adj*

com·po·nent [kəm-POH-nənt] *n* **1** part,

lament, moan, whine

complaint *n* **1** = **criticism**, charge,
grievance, gripe (*inf*), grouse, grumble,
lament, moan, protest **2** = **illness**,
affliction, ailment, disease, disorder,
malady, sickness, upset

complement *n* **1** = **completion**,
companion, consummation, counterpart,
finishing touch, rounding-off, supplement
2 = **total**, aggregate, capacity, entirety,
quota, totality, wholeness ◆ *v* **3** =
complete, cap (*inf*), crown, round off, set
off

complementary *adj* = **completing**,
companion, corresponding,
interdependent, interrelating, matched,
reciprocal

complete *adj* **1** = **total**, absolute,
consummate, outright, perfect, thorough,
thoroughgoing, utter **2** = **finished**,
accomplished, achieved, concluded,
ended **3** = **entire**, all, faultless, full, intact,
plenary, unbroken, whole ◆ *v* **4** = **finish**,
close, conclude, crown, end, finalize,
round off, settle, wind up (*inf*), wrap up
(*inf*)

completely *adv* = **totally**, absolutely,
altogether, entirely, every inch, fully, hook,
line and sinker, in full, lock, stock and
barrel, one hundred per cent, perfectly,
thoroughly, utterly, wholly

completion *n* = **finishing**, bitter end,
close, conclusion, culmination, end,
fruition, fulfillment

complex *adj* **1** = **compound**, composite,
heterogeneous, manifold, multifarious,
multiple **2** = **complicated**, convoluted,
elaborate, intricate, involved, labyrinthine,

tangled, tortuous ◆ *n* **3** = **structure**,
aggregate, composite, network,
organization, scheme, system **4** =
obsession, fixation, fixed idea, *idée fixe*,
phobia, preoccupation

complexion *n* **1** = **skin**, color, coloring,
hue, pigmentation, skin tone **2** = **nature**,
appearance, aspect, character, guise, light,
look, make-up

complexity *n* = **complication**, elaboration,
entanglement, intricacy, involvement,
ramification

complicate *v* = **make difficult**, confuse,
entangle, involve, muddle, ravel

complicated *adj* **1** = **difficult**, involved,
perplexing, problematic, puzzling,
troublesome **2** = **involved**, complex,
convoluted, elaborate, intricate,
labyrinthine

complication *n* **1** = **complexity**,
confusion, entanglement, intricacy, web
2 = **problem**, difficulty, drawback,
embarrassment, obstacle, snag

compliment *n* **1** = **praise**, bouquet,
commendation, congratulations, eulogy,
flattery, honor, tribute ◆ *v* **2** = **praise**,
brown-nose (*sl*), commend, congratulate,
extol, flatter, pay tribute to, salute, speak
highly of

complimentary *adj* **1** = **flattering**,
appreciative, approving, commendatory,
congratulatory, laudatory **2** = **free**,
courtesy, donated, gratis, gratuitous,
honorary, on the house

compliments *pl n* = **greetings**, good
wishes, regards, remembrances, respects,
salutation

comply *v* = **obey**, abide by, acquiesce,

element, constituent of whole. ♦ *adj* **2** composing, making up.

com•port [kəm-PORT] *v* **1** agree. **2** behave.

com•pose [kəm-POHZ] *vt* **-posed, -pos•ing 1** arrange, put in order. **2** write, invent. **3** make up. **4** calm. **5** settle, adjust. **com•posed'** *adj* calm. **com•pos'er** *n* one who composes, esp. music. **com•po•site** [kəm-POZ-it] *adj* made up of distinct parts. **com•po•si•tion** [kom-pə-ZISH-ən] *n* **com•pos•i•tor** [kəm-POZ-i-tər] *n* typesetter, one who arranges type for printing. **com•po•sure** [kəm-POH-zhər] *n* calmness.

com•pos men•tis [KOM-pəs MEN-tis] *Lat* of sound mind.

com•post [KOM-pohst] *n* fertilizing mixture of decayed vegetable matter for soil.

com•pote [KOM-poht] *n* fruit stewed or preserved in syrup.

com•pound¹ [KOM-pownd] *n* **1** mixture, blend. **2** substance, word, made up of parts. ♦ *adj* **3** not simple. **4** composite, mixed. ♦ *vt* [kəm-POWND] **5** mix, make up, put together. **6** intensify, make worse. **7** compromise, settle debt by partial payment.

com•pound² [KOM-pownd] *n* (fenced or walled) enclosure containing houses, etc.

com•pre•hend [kom-pri-HEND] *vt* **1** understand, take in. **2** include, comprise. **com•pre•hen'si•ble** *adj* **com•pre•hen'sion** *n* **com•pre•hen'sive** *adj* **1** wide, full. **2** taking in much.

com•press [kəm-PRES] *vt* **1** squeeze together. **2** make smaller in size, bulk. ♦ *n* [KOM-pres] pad of cloth applied to wound, inflamed part, etc. **com•press'i•ble** *adj* **com•pres•sion** [kəm-PRESH-ən] *n* in internal combustion engine, squeezing in of explosive charge before ignition, to give additional force. **com•pres'sor** *n* esp. machine to compress air, gas.

com•prise [kəm-PRIZ] *vt* **-prised, -pris•ing** include, contain.

com•pro•mise [KOM-prə-mīz] *n* **1** meeting halfway, coming to terms by giving up part of claim. **2** middle course. ♦ *v* **-mised, -mis•ing 3** settle (dispute) by making concessions. ♦ *vt* **4** expose to risk or suspicion.

THESAURUS

adhere to, conform to, follow, observe, submit, toe the line

component *n* **1 = part**, constituent, element, ingredient, item, piece, unit ♦ *adj* **2 = constituent**, inherent, intrinsic

compose *v* **1 = put together**, build, comprise, constitute, construct, fashion, form, make, make up **2 = create**, contrive, devise, invent, produce, write **3 = calm**, collect, control, pacify, placate, quiet, soothe **4 = arrange**, adjust

composed *adj* **= calm**, at ease, collected, cool, level-headed, poised, relaxed, sedate, self-possessed, serene, unflappable

composition *n* **1 = creation**, compilation, fashioning, formation, formulation, making, production, putting together **2 = design**, arrangement, configuration, formation, layout, make-up, organization, structure **3 = essay**, exercise, literary work, opus, piece, treatise, work

composure *n* **= calmness**, aplomb, equanimity, poise, sang-froid, self-assurance, self-possession, serenity

compound *n* **1 = combination**, alloy, amalgam, blend, composite, fusion, medley, mixture, synthesis ♦ *v* **2 = combine**, amalgamate, blend, intermingle, mix, synthesize, unite **3 = intensify**, add to, aggravate, augment, complicate, exacerbate, heighten, magnify, worsen ♦ *adj* **4 = complex**, composite, intricate, multiple

comprehend *v* **= understand**, apprehend, conceive, fathom, grasp, know, make out, perceive, see, take in

comprehensible *adj* **= understandable**, clear, coherent, conceivable, explicit, intelligible, plain

comprehension *n* **= understanding**, conception, discernment, grasp, intelligence, perception, realization

comprehensive *adj* **= broad**, all-embracing, all-inclusive, blanket, complete, encyclopedic, exhaustive, full, inclusive, thorough

compress *v* **= squeeze**, abbreviate, concentrate, condense, contract, crush, press, shorten, squash

comprise *v* **1 = be composed of**, consist of, contain, embrace, encompass, include, take in **2 = make up**, compose, constitute, form

compromise *n* **1 = give-and-take**, accommodation, adjustment, agreement, concession, settlement, trade-off ♦ *v* **2 =**

comp•trol•ler [kən-TROH-lər] *n* controller (in some titles).

com•pul•sion [kəm-PUL-shən] *n* **1** act of compelling. **2** irresistible impulse. **com•pul•sive** *adj* **com•pul•so•ri•ly** [-sə-rə-lee] *adv* **com•pul•so•ry** *adj* not optional.

com•punc•tion [kəm-PUNGK-shən] *n* regret for wrongdoing.

com•pute [kəm-PYOOT] *vt* **-put•ed, -put•ing** reckon, calculate, esp. using computer. **com•pu•ta•tion** [kom-pyə-TAY-shən] *n* reckoning, estimate. **com•put'er** *n* electronic device for storing, retrieving information and performing calculations. **com•put'er•ize** *v* **-ized, -iz•ing** equip with, perform by computer.

com•rade [KOM-rad] *n* chum, companion, friend. **com'rade•ship** *n* **com'rade•ly** *adj*

con¹ [kon] *v inf* **conned, con•ning 1** swindle, defraud. **2** cajole.

con² *vt* **conned, con•ning** direct steering (of ship).

con- *prefix* see COM-.

con•cat•e•nate [kon-KAT-n-ayt] *vt* **-nat•ed, -nat•ing** link together. **con•cat•e•na'tion** *n* connected chain (as of circumstances).

con•cave [kon-KAYV] *adj* hollow, rounded inward. **con•cav'i•ty** *n*

con•ceal [kən-SEEL] *vt* hide, keep secret.

con•cede [kən-SEED] *vt* **-ced•ed, -ced•ing 1** admit, admit truth of. **2** grant, allow, yield.

con•ceit [kən-SEET] *n* **1** vanity, overweening opinion of oneself. **2** far-fetched comparison. **con•ceit'ed** *adj*

con•ceive [kən-SEEV] *v* **-ceived, -ceiv•ing 1** think of, imagine. **2** believe. **3** form in the mind. **4** become pregnant. **con•ceiv'a•ble** *adj*

con•cen•trate [KON-sən-trayt] *v* **-trat•ed, -trat•ing ♦** *vt* **1** focus (one's efforts, etc.). **2** increase in strength. **3** reduce to small space. ♦ *vi* **4** devote all attention. **5** come together. ♦ *n* **6** concentrated material or solution. **con•cen•tra'tion** *n* **concentration camp** prison camp, esp. one in Nazi Germany.

con•cen•tric [kən-SEN-trik] *adj* having the

meet halfway, adjust, agree, concede, give and take, go fifty-fifty (*inf*), settle, strike a balance **3 = dishonor**, discredit, embarrass, expose, jeopardize, prejudice, weaken

compulsion *n* **1 = urge**, drive, necessity, need, obsession, preoccupation **2 = force**, coercion, constraint, demand, duress, obligation, pressure, urgency

compulsive *adj* **= irresistible**, compelling, driving, neurotic, obsessive, overwhelming, uncontrollable, urgent

compulsory *adj* **= obligatory**, binding, *de rigueur*, forced, imperative, mandatory, required, requisite

compute *v* **= calculate**, add up, count, enumerate, figure out, reckon, tally, total

comrade *n* **= companion**, ally, associate, colleague, co-worker, fellow, friend, homeboy (*sl*), homegirl (*sl*), partner

con *Inf n* **1 = swindle**, deception, fraud, scam (*sl*), sting (*inf*), trick ♦ *v* **2 = swindle**, cheat, deceive, defraud, double-cross (*inf*), dupe, hoodwink, rip off (*sl*), trick

concave *adj* **= hollow**, indented

conceal *v* **= hide**, bury, camouflage, cover, disguise, mask, obscure, screen

concede *v* **1 = admit**, accept, acknowledge, allow, confess, grant, own **2 = give up**, cede, hand over, relinquish, surrender, yield

conceit *n* **= self-importance**, arrogance, egotism, narcissism, pride, swagger, vanity

conceited *adj* **= self-important**, arrogant, bigheaded (*inf*), cocky, egotistical, full of oneself, immodest, narcissistic, too big for one's boots *or* breeches, vain

conceivable *adj* **= imaginable**, believable, credible, possible, thinkable

conceive *v* **1 = imagine**, believe, comprehend, envisage, fancy, suppose, think, understand **2 = think up**, contrive, create, design, devise, formulate **3 = become pregnant**, become impregnated

concentrate *v* **1 = focus one's attention on**, be engrossed in, put one's mind to, rack one's brains **2 = focus**, bring to bear, center, cluster, converge **3 = gather**, accumulate, cluster, collect, congregate, huddle

concentrated *adj* **1 = intense**, all-out (*inf*), deep, hard, intensive **2 = condensed**, boiled down, evaporated, reduced, rich, thickened, undiluted

concentration *n* **1 = single-mindedness**, absorption, application, heed **2 = focusing**, bringing to bear, centralization, centring, consolidation, convergence, intensification **3 = convergence**, accumulation, aggregation, cluster, same center.

con·cept [KON-sept] *n* **1** abstract idea. **2** mental expression. **con·cep·tu·al** [kən-SEP-choo-əl] *adj*

con·cep·tion [kən-SEP-shən] *n* **1** idea, notion. **2** act of conceiving.

con·cern [kən-SURN] *vt* **1** relate, apply to. **2** interest, affect, trouble. **3** (with *in* or *with*) involve (oneself). ◆ *n* **4** affair. **5** regard, worry. **6** importance. **7** business, enterprise. **con·cerned'** *adj* **1** connected with. **2** interested. **3** worried. **4** involved. **con·cern'ing** *prep* respecting, about.

con·cert [KON-surt] *n* **1** musical entertainment. **2** harmony, agreement. ◆ *vt* [kən-SURT] **3** arrange, plan together. **con·cert'ed** *adj* **1** mutually arranged, planned. **2** determined. **con·cer·ti·na** [kon-sər-TEE-nə] *n* musical instrument with bellows and keys. **con·cer·to** [kən-CHER-toh] *n, pl* **-tos** musical composition for solo instrument and orchestra.

con·ces·sion [kən-SESH-ən] *n* **1** act of conceding. **2** thing conceded. **3** grant. **4** special privilege.

conch [kongk] *n* seashell. **con·chol·o·gy** [kong-KOL-ə-jee] *n* study, collection of shells and shellfish.

con·cierge [kon-see-AIRZH] *n* in France esp., caretaker, doorkeeper.

con·cil·i·ate [kən-SIL-ee-ayt] *vt* **-at·ed, -at·ing** pacify, win over from hostility. **con·cil'i·a·tor** *n* **con·cil'i·a·to·ry** *adj*

con·cise [kən-SĪS] *adj* brief, terse. **con·cise'ly** *adv* **con·cise'ness** *n*

con·clave [KON-klayv] *n* **1** private meeting. **2** assembly for election of a pope.

con·clude [kən-KLOOD] *v* **-clud·ed, -clud·ing** ◆ *vt* **1** end, finish. **2** deduce. **3** settle. ◆ *vi* **4** come to end. **5** decide. **con·clu·sion** [-KLOO-zhən] *n* **con·clu'sive** *adj* decisive, convincing.

con·coct [kən-KOKT] *vt* **1** make mixture, prepare with various ingredients. **2** make up. **3** contrive, plan. **con·coc'tion** *n*

━━━━━━ THESAURUS ━━━━━━

collection, horde, mass

concept *n* = **idea**, abstraction, conception, conceptualization, hypothesis, image, notion, theory, view

conception *n* **1** = **idea**, concept, design, image, notion, plan **2** = **impregnation**, fertilization, germination, insemination

concern *n* **1** = **worry**, anxiety, apprehension, burden, care, disquiet, distress **2** = **importance**, bearing, interest, relevance **3** = **business**, affair, interest, job, responsibility, task **4** = **business**, company, corporation, enterprise, establishment, firm, organization ◆ *v* **5** = **worry**, bother, disquiet, distress, disturb, make anxious, perturb, trouble **6** = **be relevant to**, affect, apply to, bear on, interest, involve, pertain to, regard, touch

concerned *adj* **1** = **involved**, active, implicated, interested, mixed up, privy to **2** = **worried**, anxious, bothered, distressed, disturbed, troubled, uneasy, upset

concerning *prep* = **regarding**, about, apropos of, as regards, on the subject of, re, relating to, respecting, touching, with reference to

concession *n* **1** = **grant**, adjustment, allowance, boon, compromise, indulgence, permit, privilege, sop **2** = **conceding**, acknowledgment, admission, assent, confession, surrender, yielding

conciliate *v* = **pacify**, appease, clear the air, mediate, mollify, placate, reconcile, soothe, win over

conciliation *n* = **pacification**, appeasement, mollification, placation, reconciliation, soothing

conciliatory *adj* = **pacifying**, appeasing, mollifying, pacific, peaceable, placatory

concise *adj* = **brief**, compendious, condensed, laconic, pithy, short, succinct, terse

conclude *v* **1** = **decide**, assume, deduce, gather, infer, judge, surmise, work out **2** = **end**, cease, close, complete, finish, round off, terminate, wind up **3** = **accomplish**, bring about, carry out, effect, pull off

conclusion *n* **1** = **decision**, conviction, deduction, inference, judgment, opinion, verdict **2** = **end**, bitter end, close, completion, ending, finale, finish, result, termination **3** = **outcome**, consequence, culmination, end result, result, upshot

conclusive *adj* = **decisive**, clinching, convincing, definite, final, irrefutable, ultimate, unanswerable

concoct *v* = **make up**, brew, contrive, devise, formulate, hatch, invent, prepare, think up

concoction *n* = **mixture**, blend, brew, combination, compound, creation, preparation

con·com·i·tant [kon-KOM-i-tənt] *adj*
accompanying.

con·cord [KON-kord] *n* **1** agreement. **2** harmony. ♦ *vi* [kən-KORD] **3** agree.
con·cord'ance [-əns] *n* **1** agreement. **2** index to words of book (esp. Bible).

con·course [KON-kors] *n* **1** crowd. **2** large, open place in public area. **3** boulevard.

con·crete [KON-kreet] *n* **1** mixture of sand, cement, etc., used in building. ♦ *adj* **2** made of concrete. **3** particular, specific. **4** perceptible, actual. **5** solid. **con·crete'ly** *adv*

con·cu·bine [KONG-kyə-bīn] *n* **1** woman living with man as his wife, but not married to him. **2** mistress. **con·cu·bi·nage** [kon-KYOO-bə-nij] *n*

con·cu·pis·cence [kon-KYOO-pi-səns] *n* lust.

con·cur [kən-KUR] *vi* **-curred, -cur·ring 1** agree, express agreement. **2** happen together. **3** coincide. **con·cur'rence** *n* **con·cur'rent** *adj* **con·cur'rent·ly** *adv* at the same time.

con·cus·sion [kən-KUSH-ən] *n* **1** brain injury. **2** physical shock.

con·demn [kən-DEM] *vt* **1** blame. **2** find guilty. **3** doom. **4** find, declare unfit for use. **con·dem·na·tion** [kon-dem-NAY-shən]

n **con·dem'na·to·ry** *adj*

con·dense [kən-DENS] *v* **-densed, -dens·ing** ♦ *vt* **1** concentrate, make more solid. **2** turn from gas into liquid. **3** pack into few words. ♦ *vi* **4** turn from gas to liquid. **con·den·sa·tion** [kon-den-SAY-shən] *n* **con·dens'er** *n* **1** *Electricity* apparatus for storing electrical energy, a capacitor. **2** apparatus for reducing gas to liquid form. **3** a lens or mirror for focusing light.

con·de·scend [kon-də-SEND] *vi* **1** treat graciously one regarded as inferior. **2** do something below one's dignity.
con·de·scend'ing *adj* **con·de·scen'sion** *n*

con·di·ment [KON-də-mənt] *n* sauce, seasoning for food.

con·di·tion [kən-DISH-ən] *n* **1** state or circumstances of anything. **2** thing on which statement or happening or existing depends. **3** stipulation, prerequisite. **4** health, physical fitness. **5** rank. ♦ *vt* **6** accustom. **7** regulate. **8** make fit, healthy. **9** be essential to happening or existence of. **10** stipulate. **con·di'tion·al** *adj* **1** dependent on circumstances or events. ♦ *n Grammar* **2** form of verbs.

con·do [KON-doh] *n, pl* **-dos** condominium (building).

con·dole [kən-DOHL] *vi* **-doled, -dol·ing 1**

THESAURUS

concrete *adj* **1** = **specific**, definite, explicit **2** = **real**, actual, factual, material, sensible, substantial, tangible

concur *v* = **agree**, acquiesce, assent, consent

condemn *v* **1** = **disapprove**, blame, censure, damn, denounce, reproach, reprove, upbraid **2** = **sentence**, convict, damn, doom, pass sentence on

condemnation *n* **1** = **disapproval**, blame, censure, denunciation, reproach, reproof, stricture **2** = **sentence**, conviction, damnation, doom, judgment

condensation *n* **1** = **distillation**, liquefaction, precipitate, precipitation **2** = **abridgment**, contraction, digest, précis, synopsis **3** = **concentration**, compression, consolidation, crystallization, curtailment, reduction

condense *v* **1** = **abridge**, abbreviate, compress, concentrate, epitomize, shorten, summarize **2** = **concentrate**, boil down, reduce, thicken

condensed *adj* **1** = **abridged**, compressed, concentrated, shortened, shrunken,

slimmed-down, summarized **2** = **concentrated**, boiled down, reduced, thickened

condescend *v* **1** = **patronize**, talk down to **2** = **lower oneself**, bend, deign, humble *or* demean oneself, see fit, stoop

condescending *adj* = **patronizing**, disdainful, lofty, lordly, snobbish, snooty (*inf*), supercilious, superior

condition *n* **1** = **state**, circumstances, lie of the land, position, shape, situation, state of affairs **2** = **requirement**, limitation, prerequisite, proviso, qualification, restriction, rider, stipulation, terms **3** = **health**, fettle, fitness, kilter, order, shape, state of health, trim **4** = **ailment**, complaint, infirmity, malady, problem, weakness ♦ *v* **5** = **accustom**, adapt, equip, prepare, ready, tone up, train, work out

conditional *adj* = **dependent**, contingent, limited, provisional, qualified, subject to, with reservations

conditions *pl n* = **circumstances**, environment, milieu, situation, surroundings, way of life grieve with, offer sympathy. **2** commiserate with. **con·do'lence** n

con·dom [KON-dəm] n sheathlike usu. rubber contraceptive device worn by man.

con·do·min·i·um [kon-də-MIN-ee-əm] n **1** joint rule by two or more countries. **2** building with apartments, offices, etc. **3** individually owned.

con·done [kən-DOHN] vt **-doned, don·ing** overlook, forgive, treat as not existing.

con·duce [kən-DOOS] vi **-duced, -duc·ing 1** help, promote. **2** tend toward. **con·du'cive** adj

con·duct [KON-dukt] n **1** behavior. **2** management. ◆ vt [kən-DUKT] **3** escort, guide. **4** lead, direct. **5** manage. **6** transmit (heat, electricity). **con·duc'tion** n **con·duc'tive** adj **con·duc·tiv'i·ty** n **con·duc'tor** n **1** employee on bus, train, etc. who collects fares. **2** director of orchestra. **3** one who leads, guides. **4** substance capable of transmitting heat, electricity, etc.

con·du·it [KON-doo-it] n channel or pipe for conveying water, electric cables, etc.

cone [kohn] n **1** solid figure with circular base, tapering to a point. **2** fruit of pine, fir, etc. **con·ic** [KON-ik], **con'i·cal** adj

con·fab·u·late [kən-FAB-yə-layt] vi **-lat·ed, -lat·ing** chat. **con·fab** [KON-fab] n inf shortened form of confabulation. **con·fab·u·la'tion** n confidential conversation.

con·fec·tion [kən-FEK-shən] n **1** prepared delicacy, esp. something sweet. **2** candy.

con·fec'tion·er n dealer in candies, fancy cakes, etc. **con·fec'tion·er·y** n **1** confectioner's shop. **2** things confectioner sells.

con·fed·er·ate [kən-FED-ər-it] n **1** ally. **2** accomplice. ◆ v [-ə-rayt] **-at·ed, -at·ing 3** unite. **con·fed'er·a·cy** n **con·fed·er·a'tion** n alliance of political units.

con·fer [kən-FUR] v **-ferred, -fer·ring** ◆ vt **1** grant, give. **2** bestow. ◆ vi **4** talk with, take advice. **con·fer·ence** [KON-fər-əns] n meeting for consultation or deliberation.

con·fess [kən-FES] vt **1** admit, own. **2** (of priest) hear sins of. ◆ vi **3** acknowledge. **4** declare one's sins orally to priest. **con·fes'sion** [-FESH-ən] n **con·fes'sion·al** n confessor's stall. **con·fes'sor** n priest who hears confessions.

con·fet·ti [kən-FET-ee] n small bits of colored paper for throwing at weddings.

con·fide [kən-FĪD] v **-fid·ed, -fid·ing** ◆ vi **1** (with in) tell secrets, trust. ◆ vt **2** entrust. **con·fi·dant** [KON-fi-dant] n (fem **con·fi·dante**) one entrusted with secrets. **con'fi·dence** n **1** trust. **2** boldness, assurance. **3** intimacy. **4** something confided, secret. **con'fi·dent** adj **con·fi·den'tial** [-shəl] adj **1** private. **2** secret. **3** entrusted with another's confidences. **con'fi·dent·ly** adv **confidence game** con game, swindle in which victim entrusts money, etc. to thief, believed honest.

con·fig·u·ra·tion [kən-fig-yə-RAY-shən] n

condone v = **overlook**, excuse, forgive, let pass, look the other way, make allowance for, pardon, turn a blind eye to

conduct n **1** = **behavior**, attitude, bearing, demeanor, deportment, manners, ways **2** = **management**, administration, control, direction, guidance, handling, organization, running, supervision ◆ v **3** = **carry out**, administer, control, direct, handle, manage, organize, preside over, run, supervise **4** = **behave**, acquit, act, carry, comport, deport **5** = **accompany**, convey, escort, guide, lead, steer, usher

confederacy n = **union**, alliance, coalition, confederation, federation, league

confer v **1** = **discuss**, consult, converse, deliberate, discourse, talk **2** = **grant**, accord, award, bestow, give, hand out, present

conference n = **meeting**, colloquium, congress, consultation, convention, discussion, forum, seminar, symposium

confess v **1** = **admit**, acknowledge, come clean (inf), concede, confide, disclose, divulge, fess up (inf), own up **2** = **declare**, affirm, assert, confirm, profess, reveal

confession n = **admission**, acknowledgment, disclosure, exposure, revelation, unbosoming

confidant, confidante n = **close friend**, alter ego, bosom friend, crony, familiar, intimate

confide v **1** = **tell**, admit, confess, disclose, divulge, impart, reveal, whisper **2** Formal = **entrust**, commend, commit, consign

confidence n **1** = **trust**, belief, credence, dependence, faith, reliance **2** = **self-assurance**, aplomb, assurance, shape, aspect, conformation, arrangement.

con·fine [kən-FĪN] *vt* **-fined, fin·ing 1** keep within bounds. **2** keep in house, bed, etc. **3** shut up, imprison. **con·fines** [KON-finz] *pl n* boundaries, limits. **confine'ment** *n* **1** esp. childbirth. **2** imprisonment.

con·firm [kən-FURM] *vt* **1** make sure, verify. **2** strengthen, settle. **3** make valid, ratify. **4** administer confirmation to. **con·fir·ma·tion** [kon-fər-MAY-shən] *n* **1** making strong, certain. **2** Christian rite administered to confirm vows made at baptism. **3** Jewish ceremony to admit boys, girls to adult status. **con·firm'a·to·ry** *adj* **1** tending to confirm or establish. **2** corroborative. **con·firmed'** *adj* (of habit, etc.) long-established.

con·fis·cate [KON-fə-skayt] *vt* **-cat·ed, -cat·ing** seize by authority. **con·fis·ca'tion** *n* **con·fis·ca·to·ry** [kən-FIS-kə-tor-ee] *adj*

con·fla·gra·tion [kon-flə-GRAY-shən] *n* great destructive fire.

con·flict [KON-flikt] *n* **1** struggle, trial of strength. **2** disagreement. ♦ *vi* [kən-FLIKT] **3** be at odds with, be inconsistent with. **4** clash.

con·flu·ence [KON-floo-əns] *n* **1** union of streams. **2** meeting place. **con·flu·ent** *adj*

con·form [kən-FORM] *v* **1** comply with accepted standards, conventions, etc. **2** adapt to rule, pattern, custom, etc. **con·for·ma·tion** [kon-for-MAY-shən] *n* structure, adaptation. **con·form'ist** *n* one who conforms, esp. excessively. **con·form'i·ty** *n* compliance.

con·found [kon-FOWND] *vt* **1** baffle, perplex. **2** confuse. **3** defeat. **con·found'ed** *adj* old-fashioned damned.

con·front [kən-FRUNT] *vt* **1** face. **2** bring face to face with. **con·fron·ta·tion** [kon-frən-TAY-shən] *n*

boldness, courage, firmness, nerve, self-possession **3 in confidence = in secrecy**, between you and me (and the gatepost), confidentially, privately

confident *adj* **1 = certain**, convinced, counting on, positive, satisfied, secure, sure **2 = self-assured**, assured, bold, dauntless, fearless, self-reliant

confidential *adj* **= secret**, classified, hush-hush (*inf*), intimate, off the record, private, privy

confidentially *adv* **= in secret**, behind closed doors, between ourselves, in camera, in confidence, personally, privately, sub rosa

confine *v* **= restrict**, cage, enclose, hem in, hold back, imprison, incarcerate, intern, keep, limit, shut up

confinement *n* **= imprisonment**, custody, detention, incarceration, internment

confines *pl n* **= limits**, boundaries, bounds, circumference, edge, precincts

confirm *v* **1 = prove**, authenticate, bear out, corroborate, endorse, ratify, substantiate, validate, verify **2 = strengthen**, buttress, establish, fix, fortify, reinforce

confirmation *n* **1 = proof**, authentication, corroboration, evidence, substantiation, testimony, validation, verification **2 = sanction**, acceptance, agreement, approval, assent, endorsement, ratification

confirmed *adj* **= long-established**, chronic, dyed-in-the-wool, habitual, hardened, ingrained, inveterate, seasoned

confiscate *v* **= seize**, appropriate, commandeer, impound, sequester, sequestrate

confiscation *n* **= seizure**, appropriation, forfeiture, impounding, sequestration, takeover

conflict *n* **1 = opposition**, antagonism, difference, disagreement, discord, dissension, friction, hostility, strife **2 = battle**, clash, combat, contest, encounter, fight, strife, war ♦ *v* **3 = be incompatible**, be at variance, clash, collide, differ, disagree, interfere

conflicting *adj* **= incompatible**, antagonistic, clashing, contradictory, contrary, discordant, inconsistent, opposing, paradoxical

conform *v* **1 = comply**, adapt, adjust, fall in with, follow, obey, toe the line **2 = agree**, accord, correspond, harmonize, match, suit, tally

conformist *n* **= traditionalist**, stick-in-the-mud (*inf*), yes man

conformity *n* **= compliance**, conventionality, observance, orthodoxy, traditionalism

confound *v* **= bewilder**, astound, baffle, confuse, dumbfound, flummox, mystify, nonplus, perplex

confront *v* **= face**, accost, challenge, defy, encounter, oppose, stand up to, tackle

con·fuse [kən-FYOOZ] *vt* **-fused, -fus·ing 1** bewilder. **2** jumble. **3** make unclear. **4** mistake (one thing) for another. **5** disconcert. **con·fu'sion** *n*

con·geal [kən-JEEL] *v* solidify by cooling or freezing.

con·gen·ial [kən-JEEN-yəl] *adj* **1** pleasant, to one's liking. **2** of similar disposition, tastes, etc. **con·ge·ni·al'i·ty** *n*

con·gen·i·tal [kən-JEN-i-tl] *adj* **1** existing at birth. **2** dating from birth.

con·ge·ries [KON-jə-reez] *n, sing and pl.* collection or mass of small bodies, conglomeration.

con·gest [kən-JEST] *v* overcrowd or clog. **con·ges'tion** *n* abnormal accumulation, overcrowding. **con·gest'ed** *adj*

con·glom·er·ate [kən-GLOM-ər-it] *n* **1** thing, substance (esp. rock) composed of mixture of other, smaller elements or pieces. **2** business organization comprising many companies. ♦ *v* [-ə-rayt] **-at·ed, -at·ing 3** gather together. ♦ *adj* **con·glom·er·a'tion** *n*

con·grat·u·late [kən-GRACH-ə-layt] *vt* **-lat·ed, -lat·ing** express pleasure at good fortune, success, etc. **con·grat·u·la'tion** *n* **con·grat'u·la·to·ry** *adj*

con·gre·gate [KONG-gri-gayt] *v* **-gat·ed, -gat·ing 1** assemble. **2** collect, flock together. **con·gre·ga'tion** *n* assembly, esp. for worship. **con·gre·ga'tion·al** *adj* **con·gre·ga'tion·al·ism** *n* form of Protestant church organization in which local churches are self-governing.

con·gress [KONG-gris] *n* **1** meeting. **2** sexual intercourse. **3** formal assembly for discussion. **4** legislative body. **con·gres·sion·al** [kən-GRESH-ə-nl] *adj* **con'gress·man** *n* member of US House of Representatives.

con·gru·ent [KONG-groo-ənt] *adj* **1** suitable, accordant. **2** fitting together, esp. triangles. **con'gru·ence** *n* **con·gru'i·ty** *n* **con'gru·ous** *adj*

conic see CONE.

con·i·fer [KON-ə-fər] *n* cone-bearing tree, as fir, pine, etc. **co·nif·er·ous** [koh-NIF-ər-əs] *adj*

con·jec·ture [kən-JEK-chər] *n* **1** guess, guesswork. ♦ *v* **-tured, -tur·ing 2** guess, surmise. **con·jec'tur·al** *adj*

confrontation *n* = **conflict**, contest, encounter, fight, head-to-head, showdown (*inf*)

confuse *v* **1** = **mix up**, disarrange, disorder, jumble, mingle, ravel **2** = **bewilder**, baffle, bemuse, faze, flummox, mystify, nonplus, perplex, puzzle **3** = **disconcert**, discompose, disorient, fluster, rattle (*inf*), throw off balance, unnerve, upset

confused *adj* **1** = **bewildered**, at sea, baffled, disorientated, flummoxed, muddled, nonplussed, perplexed, puzzled, taken aback **2** = **disordered**, chaotic, disorganized, in disarray, jumbled, mixed up, topsy-turvy, untidy

confusing *adj* = **bewildering**, baffling, contradictory, disconcerting, misleading, perplexing, puzzling, unclear

confusion *n* **1** = **bewilderment**, disorientation, mystification, perplexity, puzzlement **2** = **disorder**, chaos, commotion, jumble, mess, muddle, shambles, turmoil, untidiness, upheaval

congenial *adj* **1** = **pleasant**, affable, agreeable, companionable, favorable, friendly, genial, kindly **2** = **compatible**, kindred, like-minded, sympathetic, well-suited

congenital *adj* = **inborn**, immanent, inbred, inherent, innate, natural

congested *adj* **1** = **overcrowded**, crowded, teeming **2** = **clogged**, blocked-up, crammed, jammed, overfilled, overflowing, packed, stuffed

congestion *n* **1** = **overcrowding**, crowding **2** = **clogging**, bottleneck, jam, surfeit

congratulate *v* = **compliment**, pat on the back, wish joy to

congratulations *pl n, interj* = **good wishes**, best wishes, compliments, felicitations, greetings

congregate *v* = **come together**, assemble, collect, convene, converge, flock, gather, mass, meet

congregation *n* = **assembly**, brethren, crowd, fellowship, flock, multitude, throng

congress *n* = **meeting**, assembly, caucus, conclave, conference, convention, council, legislature, parliament

conjecture *n* **1** = **guess**, hypothesis, shot in the dark, speculation, supposition, surmise, theory ♦ *v* **2** = **guess**, hypothesize, imagine, speculate, suppose, surmise, theorize

con·join·ed twins [kən-JOIND twinz] *pl n* the technical name for SIAMESE TWINS.

con·ju·gal [KON-jə-gəl] *adj* 1 relating to marriage. 2 between married persons. **con·ju·gal'i·ty** *n*

con·ju·gate [KON-jə-gayt] *v* **-gat·ed, -gat·ing** inflect verb in its various forms (past, present, etc.). **con·ju·ga'tion** *n*

con·junc·tion [kən JUNCK shən] *n* 1 union. 2 simultaneous happening. 3 part of speech joining words, phrases, etc. **con·junc'tive** *adj*

con·junc·ti·va [kon-jungk-TĪ-və] *n* mucous membrane lining eyelid. **con·junc·ti·vi·tis** [kən-jungk-tə-VĪ-tis] *n* inflammation of this.

con·jure [KON-jər] *v* **-jured, -jur·ing** 1 produce magic effects. 2 perform tricks by sleight of hand, etc. 3 invoke devils. 4 [kən-JUUR] implore earnestly. **con·jur·a·tion** [kon-jə-RAY-shən] *n* **con'jur·er** *n*

conk [kongk] *vt inf* strike (esp. on head). **conk out** *vi inf* 1 break down, stall. 2 faint. 3 fall asleep.

con·nect [kə-NEKT] *v* 1 join together, unite. 2 associate in the mind. **con·nec'tion** *n* 1 association. 2 train, etc. timed to enable passengers to transfer from another. 3 family relation. 4 social, commercial, etc. relationship. **con·nec'tive** *adj* **connecting rod** part of engine that

transfers motion from piston to crankshaft.

con·ning tower [KON-ing] raised observation tower containing the periscope on a submarine.

con·nive [kə-NĪV] *vi* **-nived, -niv·ing** 1 plot, conspire. 2 assent, refrain from preventing or forbidding. **con·niv'ance** *n*

con·nois·seur [kon-ə-SUR] *n* 1 critical expert in matters of taste, esp. fine arts. 2 competent judge.

con·note [kə-NOHT] *vt* **-not·ed, -not·ing** imply, mean in addition to primary meaning. **con·no·ta·tion** [kon-ə-TAY-shən] *n*

con·nu·bi·al [kə-NOO-bee-əl] *adj* of marriage.

con·quer [KONG-kər] *vt* 1 win by force of arms, overcome. 2 defeat. ◆ *vi* 3 be victorious. **con'quer·or** *n* **con·quest** [KON-kwest] *n*

con·san·guin·i·ty [kon-sang-GWIN-i-tee] *n* kinship. **con·san·guin'e·ous** *adj*

con·science [KON-shəns] *n* sense of right or wrong governing person's words and actions. **con·sci·en'tious** [-shee-EN-shəs] *adj* 1 scrupulous. 2 obedient to the dictates of conscience. **con·sci·en'tious·ly** *adv* **conscientious objector** one who refuses military service on moral or religious grounds.

con·scious [KON-shəs] *adj* 1 aware. 2

——[THESAURUS]——

conjugal *adj* = **marital**, bridal, connubial, married, matrimonial, nuptial, wedded

conjure *v* = **perform tricks**, juggle

conjurer, conjuror *n* = **magician**, illusionist, sorcerer, wizard

conjure up *v* = **bring to mind**, contrive, create, evoke, produce as if by magic, recall, recollect

connect *v* = **link**, affix, attach, couple, fasten, join, unite

connected *adj* = **linked**, affiliated, akin, allied, associated, combined, coupled, joined, related, united

connection *n* 1 = **association**, affinity, bond, liaison, tie, relationship, relevance, tie-in 2 = **link**, alliance, association, attachment, coupling, fastening, junction, tie, union 3 = **contact**, acquaintance, ally, associate, friend, homeboy (*sl*), homegirl (*sl*), sponsor

connivance *n* = **collusion**, abetting, complicity, conspiring, tacit consent

connive *v* 1 = **conspire**, collude, cook up

(*inf*), intrigue, plot, scheme 2 = **connive at** = **turn a blind eye to**, abet, disregard, let pass, look the other way, overlook, wink at

connoisseur *n* = **expert**, aficionado, appreciator, authority, buff (*inf*), devotee, judge

conquer *v* 1 = **defeat**, beat, crush, get the better of, master, overcome, overpower, overthrow, quell, subjugate, vanquish 2 = **seize**, acquire, annex, obtain, occupy, overrun, win

conqueror *n* = **winner**, conquistador, defeater, master, subjugator, vanquisher, victor

conquest *n* 1 = **defeat**, mastery, overthrow, rout, triumph, victory 2 = **takeover**, annexation, coup, invasion, occupation, subjugation

conscience *n* = **principles**, moral sense, scruples, sense of right and wrong, still small voice

conscientious *adj* = **thorough**, careful, diligent, exact, faithful, meticulous,

awake to one's surroundings and identity.
3 deliberate, intentional. **con'scious·ly** *adv*
con'scious·ness *n* being conscious.

con·script [KON-skript] *n* **1** one
compulsorily enlisted for military service. ◆
vt [kən-SKRIPT] **2** enrol (someone) for
compulsory military service. **con·scrip'tion**
n

con·se·crate [KON-si-krayt] *vt* **-crat·ed,**
-crat·ing make sacred. **con·se·cra'tion** *n*

con·sec·u·tive [kən-SEK-yə-tiv] *adj* in
unbroken succession.

con·sen·sus [kən-SEN-səs] *n* widespread
agreement, unanimity.

con·sent [kən-SENT] *vi* **1** agree to, comply.
◆ *n* **2** acquiescence. **3** permission. **4**
agreement.

con·se·quence [KON-si-kwens] *n* **1** result,
effect, outcome. **2** that which naturally
follows. **3** significance, importance.
con'se·quent *adj* **con·se·quen'tial** *adj*
important. **con'se·quent·ly** *adv* therefore,
as a result.

con·serv·a·to·ry [kən-SUR-və-tor-ee] *n, pl*

-ries 1 school for teaching music or
painting, etc. **2** greenhouse.

con·serve [kən-SURV] *vt* **-served, -serv·ing**
1 keep from change or decay. **2** preserve. **3**
maintain. ◆ *n* [KON-surv] **4** jam, preserved
fruit, etc. **con·ser·va·tion**
[kon-sər-VAY-shən] *n* protection, careful
management of natural resources and
environment. **con·ser·va'tion·ist** *n, adj*
con·serv'a·tive *adj* **1** tending or wishing to
conserve. **2** moderate. ◆ *n* **3** *Politics* one
who desires to preserve institutions of
country against change and innovation. **4**
one opposed to hasty changes or
innovations. **con·serv'a·tism** *n*

con·sid·er [kən-SID-ər] *vt* **1** think over. **2**
examine. **3** make allowance for. **4** be of
opinion that. **5** discuss. **con·sid'er·a·ble** *adj*
1 important. **2** somewhat large.
con·sid'er·ate [-it] *adj* thoughtful for
others' feelings, careful. **con·sid'er·ate·ly**
adv **con·sid·er·a'tion** *n* **1** deliberation. **2**
point of importance. **3** thoughtfulness. **4**
bribe, recompense.

painstaking, particular, punctilious
conscious *adj* **1 = aware**, alert, alive to,
awake, responsive, sensible, sentient **2 =**
deliberate, calculated, intentional,
knowing, premeditated, self-conscious,
studied, willful
consciousness *n* **= awareness**,
apprehension, knowledge, realization,
recognition, sensibility
consecrate *v* **= sanctify**, dedicate, devote,
hallow, ordain, set apart, venerate
consecutive *adj* **= successive**, in
sequence, in turn, running, sequential,
succeeding, uninterrupted
consensus *n* **= agreement**, assent,
common consent, concord, general
agreement, harmony, unanimity, unity
consent *n* **1 = agreement**, acquiescence,
approval, assent, compliance, go-ahead
(*inf*), O.K. *or* okay (*inf*), permission,
sanction ◆ *v* **2 = agree**, acquiesce, allow,
approve, assent, concur, permit
consequence *n* **1 = result**, effect, end
result, issue, outcome, repercussion,
sequel, upshot **2 = importance**, account,
concern, import, moment, significance,
value, weight
consequent *adj* **= following**, ensuing,
resultant, resulting, subsequent, successive
consequently *adv* **= as a result**,

accordingly, ergo, hence, subsequently,
therefore, thus
conservation *n* **= protection**,
guardianship, husbandry, maintenance,
preservation, safeguarding, safekeeping,
saving, upkeep
conservative *adj* **1 = traditional**, cautious,
conventional, die-hard, hidebound,
reactionary, sober ◆ *n* **2 = traditionalist**,
reactionary, stick-in-the-mud (*inf*)
conserve *v* **= protect**, hoard, husband,
keep, nurse, preserve, save, store up, take
care of, use sparingly
consider *v* **1 = think**, believe, deem, hold
to be, judge, rate, regard as **2 = think**
about, cogitate, contemplate, deliberate,
meditate, ponder, reflect, ruminate, turn
over in one's mind, weigh **3 = bear in**
mind, keep in view, make allowance for,
reckon with, remember, respect, take into
account
considerable *adj* **= large**, appreciable,
goodly, great, marked, noticeable,
plentiful, sizable *or* sizeable, substantial
considerably *adv* **= greatly**, appreciably,
markedly, noticeably, remarkably,
significantly, substantially, very much
considerate *adj* **= thoughtful**, attentive,
concerned, kindly, mindful, obliging,
patient, tactful, unselfish

con•sign [kən-SĪN] vt **1** commit, hand over. **2** entrust to carrier. **con•sign•ee** [kon-sī-NEE], **con•sign'or** n **con•sign'ment** n goods consigned.

con•sist [kən-SIST] vi **1** be composed of. **2** (with in) have as basis. **3** agree with, be compatible. **con•sist'en•cy** n **1** agreement. **2** harmony. **3** degree of firmness. **con•sist'ent** adj **1** unchanging, constant. **2** agreeing (with).

con•sis•to•ry [kən-SIS-tə-ree] n, pl **-ries** ecclesiastical court or council, esp. of pope and cardinals.

con•sole¹ [kən-SOHL] vt **-soled, -sol•ing** comfort, cheer in distress. **con•so•la•tion** [kon-sə-LAY-shən] n

con•sole² [KON-sohl] n **1** bracket supporting shelf. **2** keyboard, stops, etc., of organ. **3** cabinet for TV, radio, etc.

con•sol•i•date [kən-SOL-i-dayt] vt **-dat•ed, -dat•ing 1** combine into connected whole. **2** make firm, secure. **con•sol•i•da'tion** n

con•som•mé [kon-sə-MAY] n clear meat soup.

con•so•nant [KON-sə-nənt] n **1** sound making a syllable only with vowel. **2** non-vowel. ♦ adj **3** agreeing with, in accord. **con'so•nance** n

con•sort [kən-SORT] vi **1** associate, keep company with. ♦ n [KON-sort] **2** husband, wife, esp. of ruler. **3** ship sailing with another. **con•sor'ti•um** [SOR choo əm] n, pl **-ti•a** [-shee-ə] n association of banks, companies, etc.

con•spic•u•ous [kən-SPIK-yoo-əs] adj **1** striking, noticeable, outstanding. **2** prominent. **3** eminent.

con•spire [kən-SPĪR] vi **-spired, -spir•ing 1** combine for evil purpose. **2** plot, devise. **con•spir'a•cy** [-SPIR-ə-see] n, pl **-cies** **con•spir'a•tor** n **con•spir•a•to'ri•al** adj

con•stant [KON-stənt] adj **1** fixed, unchanging. **2** steadfast. **3** always duly happening or continuing. ♦ n **4** quantity that does not vary. **con'stan•cy** n **1** steadfastness. **2** loyalty.

consideration n **1 = thought**, analysis, deliberation, discussion, examination, reflection, review, scrutiny **2 = factor**, concern, issue, point **3 = thoughtfulness**, concern, considerateness, kindness, respect, tact **4 = payment**, fee, recompense, remuneration, reward, tip

considering prep **= taking into account**, in the light of, in view of

consignment n **= shipment**, batch, delivery, goods

consist v **1 consist of = be made up of**, amount to, be composed of, comprise, contain, embody, include, incorporate, involve **2 consist in = lie in**, be expressed by, be found or contained in, inhere in, reside in

consistency n **1 = texture**, compactness, density, firmness, thickness, viscosity **2 = constancy**, evenness, regularity, steadfastness, steadiness, uniformity

consistent adj **1 = unchanging**, constant, dependable, persistent, regular, steady, true to type, undeviating **2 = agreeing**, coherent, compatible, congruous, consonant, harmonious, logical

consolation n **= comfort**, cheer, encouragement, help, relief, solace, succor, support

console v **= comfort**, calm, cheer, encourage, express sympathy for, soothe

consolidate v **1 = strengthen**, fortify, reinforce, secure, stabilize **2 = combine**, amalgamate, federate, fuse, join, unite

consort v **1 = associate**, fraternize, go around with, hang about, around or out with, keep company, mix ♦ n **2 = spouse**, companion, husband, partner, wife

conspicuous adj **1 = obvious**, blatant, clear, evident, noticeable, patent, salient **2 = noteworthy**, illustrious, notable, outstanding, prominent, remarkable, salient, signal, striking

conspiracy n **= plot**, collusion, intrigue, machination, scheme, treason

conspirator n **= plotter**, conspirer, intriguer, schemer, traitor

conspire v **1 = plot**, contrive, intrigue, machinate, maneuver, plan, scheme **2 = work together**, combine, concur, contribute, cooperate, tend

constant adj **1 = continuous**, ceaseless, incessant, interminable, nonstop, perpetual, sustained, twenty-four-seven (sl), unrelenting **2 = unchanging**, even, fixed, invariable, permanent, stable, steady, uniform, unvarying **3 = faithful**, devoted, loyal, stalwart, staunch, true, trustworthy, trusty

constantly adv **= continuously**, all the time, always, continually, endlessly, incessantly, interminably, invariably,

con·stel·la·tion [kon-stə-LAY-shən] *n* group of stars.

con·ster·na·tion [kon-stər-NAY-shən] *n* **1** alarm, dismay, panic. **con'ster·nate** *v* **-nat·ed, -nat·ing**

con·sti·pa·tion [kon-stə-PAY-shən] *n* difficulty in emptying bowels. **con'sti·pate** *vt* **-pat·ed, -pat·ing** affect with this disorder.

con·stit·u·ent [kən-STICH-oo-ənt] *adj* **1** going toward making up whole. **2** having power to make, alter constitution of a government. ◆ *n* **3** component part. **4** element. **5** voter. **con·stit'u·en·cy** *n* body of constituents, supporters.

con·sti·tute [KON-sti-toot] *vt* **-tut·ed, -tut·ing 1** compose, set up, establish, form. **2** make into, found, give form to. **con·sti·tu'tion** *n* **1** structure, composition. **2** health. **3** character, disposition. **4** principles on which country, state is governed. **con·sti·tu'tion·al** *adj* **1** pert. to constitution. **2** in harmony with political constitution. ◆ *n* **3** walk taken for health's sake.

con·strain [kən-STRAYN] *vt* **1** force, compel. **con·straint'** *n* **1** compulsion. **2** restraint. **3** embarrassment, tension.

con·stric·tion [kən-STRIK-shən] *n* compression, squeezing together. **con·strict'** *vt* **con·stric'tive** *adj*

con·stric'tor *n* **1** that which constricts. **2** see also BOA.

con·struct [kən-STRUKT] *vt* **1** make, build, form. **2** put together. **3** compose. **con·struct** [KON-strukt] *n* **con·struc'tion** *n* **con·struc'tive** *adj* **1** serving to improve. **2** positive.

con·strue [kən-STROO] *vt* **-strued, -stru·ing 1** interpret. **2** deduce. **3** analyze grammatically.

con·sul [KON-səl] *n* **1** official appointed by a government to represent it in a foreign country. **2** in ancient Rome, one of the chief magistrates. **con'su·lar** *adj* **con'su·late** [-lit] *n*

con·sult [kən-SULT] *v* seek counsel, advice, information from. **con·sult'ant** *n* specialist, expert. **con·sul·ta·tion** [kon-səl-TAY-shən] *n* **1** consulting. **2** appointment to seek professional advice, esp. of doctor, lawyer. **con·sul·ta·tive** [kən-SUL-tə-tiv] *adj* **1** having privilege of consulting, but not of voting. **2** advisory.

con·sume [kən-SOOM] *vt* **-sumed, -sum·ing 1** eat or drink. **2** engross, possess. **3** use up. **4** destroy. **con·sum'er** *n* **1** buyer or user of commodity. **2** one who consumes. **con·sump'tion** [-SUMP-shən] *n* **1** using up. **2** destruction. **3** *old-fashioned* pulmonary tuberculosis. **con·sump'tive** *adj, n*

nonstop, perpetually, twenty-four-seven (*sl*)

consternation *n* = **dismay**, alarm, anxiety, distress, dread, fear, trepidation

constituent *n* **1** = **voter**, elector **2** = **component**, element, factor, ingredient, part, unit ◆ *adj* **3** = **component**, basic, elemental, essential, integral

constitute *v* = **make up**, compose, comprise, establish, form, found, set up

constitution *n* **1** = **health**, build, character, disposition, physique **2** = **structure**, composition, form, make-up, nature

constitutional *adj* **1** = **statutory**, chartered, vested ◆ *n* **2** = **walk**, airing, stroll, turn

constrain *v* **1** = **force**, bind, coerce, compel, impel, necessitate, oblige, pressurize **2** = **restrict**, check, confine, constrict, curb, restrain, straiten

constraint *n* **1** = **restriction**, check, curb, deterrent, hindrance, limitation, rein **2** =

force, coercion, compulsion, necessity, pressure, restraint

construct *v* = **build**, assemble, compose, create, fashion, form, make, manufacture, put together, shape

construction *n* **1** = **building**, composition, creation, edifice **2** = **interpretation**, explanation, inference, reading, rendering

constructive *adj* = **helpful**, positive, practical, productive, useful, valuable

consult *v* = **ask**, compare notes, confer, pick (someone's) brains, question, refer to, take counsel, turn to

consultant *n* = **specialist**, adviser, authority

consultation *n* = **seminar**, appointment, conference, council, deliberation, dialogue, discussion, examination, hearing, interview, meeting, session

consume *v* **1** = **eat**, chow down (*sl*), devour, eat up, gobble (up), put away, swallow **2** = **use up**, absorb, dissipate, exhaust, expend, spend, squander, waste

con·sum·mate [KON-sə-mayt] *vt* **-mat·ed,** **-mat·ing 1** perfect. **2** fulfill. **3** complete (esp. marriage by sexual intercourse). ◆ *adj* [kən-SUM-it] **4** of greatest perfection or completeness. **con·sum'mate·ly** *adv* **con·sum·ma'tion** *n*

con·tact [KON-takt] *n* **1** touching. **2** being in touch. **3** junction of two or more electrical conductors. **4** useful acquaintance. ◆ *vt* **contact lens** lens fitting over eyeball to correct defect of vision.

con·ta·gion [kən-TAY-jən] *n* **1** passing on of disease by touch, contact. **2** contagious disease. **3** harmful physical or moral influence. **con·ta'gious** *adj* communicable by contact, catching.

con·tain [kən-TAYN] *vt* **1** hold. **2** have room for. **3** include, comprise. **4** restrain (oneself). **con·tain'er** *n* **1** box, etc. for holding. **2** large cargo-carrying standard-sized receptacle for various modes of transport.

con·tam·i·nate [kən-TAM-ə-nayt] *vt* **-nat·ed, -nat·ing 1** stain, pollute, infect. **2**

make radioactive. **con·tam·i·na'tion** *n* pollution.

con·tem·plate [KON-təm-playt] *vt* **-plat·ed, -plat·ing 1** reflect, meditate on. **2** gaze upon. **3** intend. **con·tem·pla'tion** *n* **1** thoughtful consideration. **2** spiritual meditation. **con·tem·pla·tive** [kən-TEM-plə-tiv] *adj, n*

con·tem·po·rar·y [kən-TEM-pə-rer-ee] *adj* **1** existing or lasting at same time. **2** of same age. **3** modern. ◆ *n, pl* **-rar·ies 4** one existing at same time as another. **con·tem·po·ra'ne·ous** [-RAY-nee-əs] *adj*

con·tempt [kən-TEMPT] *n* **1** feeling that something is worthless, despicable, etc. **2** expression of this feeling. **3** state of being despised, disregarded. **4** willful disrespect of authority.

con·tend [kən-TEND] *vi* **1** strive, fight. **2** dispute. ◆ *vt* **3** maintain (that). **con·ten'tion** *n* **1** strife. **2** debate. **3** subject matter of dispute. **con·ten'tious** *adj* **1** quarrelsome. **2** causing dispute.

con·tent¹ [KON-tent] *n* **1** that contained.

——— THESAURUS ———

3 = **destroy**, annihilate, demolish, devastate, lay waste, ravage **4** (often passive) = **obsess**, absorb, dominate, eat up, engross, monopolize, preoccupy

consumer *n* = **buyer**, customer, purchaser, shopper, user

consummate *v* **1** = **complete**, accomplish, conclude, crown, end, finish, fulfill ◆ *adj* **2** = **skilled**, accomplished, matchless, perfect, polished, practiced, superb, supreme **3** = **complete**, absolute, conspicuous, extreme, supreme, total, utter

consumption *n* **1** = **using up**, depletion, diminution, dissipation, exhaustion, expenditure, loss, waste **2** *Old-fashioned* = **tuberculosis**, T.B.

contact *n* **1** = **communication**, association, connection **2** = **touch**, contiguity **3** = **acquaintance**, connection ◆ *v* **4** = **get** or **be in touch with**, approach, call, communicate with, reach, speak to, write to

contagious *adj* = **infectious**, catching, communicable, spreading, transmissible

contain *v* **1** = **hold**, accommodate, enclose, have capacity for, incorporate, seat **2** = **include**, comprehend, comprise, consist of, embody, embrace, involve **3** = **restrain**, control, curb, hold back, hold in, keep a

tight rein on, repress, stifle

container *n* = **holder**, receptacle, repository, vessel

contaminate *v* = **pollute**, adulterate, befoul, corrupt, defile, infect, stain, taint, tarnish

contamination *n* = **pollution**, contagion, corruption, defilement, impurity, infection, poisoning, taint

contemplate *v* **1** = **think about**, consider, deliberate, meditate, muse over, ponder, reflect upon, ruminate (upon) **2** = **consider**, envisage, expect, foresee, intend, plan, think of **3** = **look at**, examine, eye up, gaze at, inspect, regard, stare at, study, survey, view

contemporary *adj* **1** = **coexisting**, concurrent, contemporaneous **2** = **modern**, à la mode, current, newfangled, present, present-day, recent, up-to-date ◆ *n* **3** = **peer**, fellow

contempt *n* = **scorn**, derision, disdain, disregard, disrespect, mockery, neglect, slight

contemptible *adj* = **despicable**, detestable, ignominious, lousy (*sl*), measly, paltry, pitiful, scuzzy (*sl*), shameful, worthless

contemptuous *adj* = **scornful**, arrogant, condescending, derisive, disdainful,

2 holding capacity. ◆ *pl* **3** that contained. **4** index of topics in book.

con·tent² [kən-TENT] *adj* **1** satisfied. **2** willing (to). ◆ *vt* **3** satisfy. ◆ *n* **4** satisfaction. **con·tent'ed** *adj*

con·ter·mi·nous [kən-TUR-mə-nəs] *adj* **1** of the same extent (in time, etc.). **2** meeting along a common boundary. **3** meeting end to end. **co·ter'mi·nous** *adj*

con·test [KON-test] *n* **1** competition. **2** conflict. ◆ *vt* [kən-TEST] **3** dispute, debate. **4** fight or compete for. **con·test'a·ble** *adj* **con·test'ant** *n*

con·text [KON-tekst] *n* **1** words coming before, after a word or passage. **2** conditions and circumstances of event, fact, etc. **con·tex·tu·al** [kən-TEKS-choo-əl] *adj*

con·tig·u·ous [kən-TIG-yoo-əs] *adj* touching, near. **con·ti·gu'i·ty** *n*

con·ti·nent¹ [KON-tə-nənt] *n* large continuous mass of land. **con·ti·nen'tal** *adj*

continent² *adj* **1** able to control one's urination and defecation. **2** sexually chaste. **con'ti·nence** *n*

con·tin·gent [kən-TIN-jənt] *adj* **1** depending (on). **2** possible. **3** accidental. ◆ *n* **4** group (of troops, supporters, etc.). **5** part of or representative of a larger group. **con·tin'gen·cy** *n*

con·tin·ue [kən-TIN-yoo] *v* **-ued, -u·ing 1** remain, keep in existence. **2** carry on, last, go on. **3** resume. **4** prolong. **con·tin'u·al** *adj* **con·tin·u·a'tion** *n* **1** extension, extra part. **2** resumption. **3** constant succession, prolongation. **con·ti·nu'i·ty** *n* **1** logical sequence. **2** state of being continuous. **con·tin'u·ous** *adj*

con·tort [kən-TORT] *vt* twist out of normal shape. **con·tor'tion** *n* **con·tor'tion·ist** *n*

THESAURUS

haughty, sneering, supercilious, withering

contend *v* **1** = **compete**, clash, contest, fight, jostle, strive, struggle, vie **2** = **argue**, affirm, allege, assert, dispute, hold, maintain

content¹ *n* **1** = **meaning**, essence, gist, significance, substance **2** = **amount**, capacity, load, measure, size, volume

content² *adj* **1** = **satisfied**, agreeable, at ease, comfortable, contented, fulfilled, willing to accept ◆ *v* **2** = **satisfy**, appease, humor, indulge, mollify, placate, please ◆ *n* **3** = **satisfaction**, comfort, contentment, ease, gratification, peace of mind, pleasure

contented *adj* = **satisfied**, comfortable, content, glad, gratified, happy, pleased, serene, thankful

contentious *adj* = **argumentative**, bickering, captious, cavilling, disputatious, quarrelsome, querulous, wrangling

contentment *n* = **satisfaction**, comfort, content, ease, equanimity, fulfillment, happiness, peace, pleasure, serenity

contents *pl n* = **constituents**, elements, ingredients, load

contest *n* **1** = **competition**, game, match, tournament, trial **2** = **struggle**, battle, combat, conflict, controversy, dispute, fight ◆ *v* **3** = **dispute**, argue, call in or into question, challenge, debate, doubt, object to, oppose, question **4** = **compete**, contend, fight, strive, vie

contestant *n* = **competitor**, candidate, contender, entrant, participant, player

context *n* **1** = **circumstances**, ambience, conditions, situation **2** = **frame of reference**, background, connection, framework, relation

contingency *n* = **possibility**, accident, chance, emergency, event, eventuality, happening, incident

continual *adj* = **constant**, frequent, incessant, interminable, recurrent, regular, repeated, twenty-four-seven (*sl*), unremitting

continually *adv* = **constantly**, all the time, always, forever, incessantly, interminably, nonstop, persistently, repeatedly, twenty-four-seven (*sl*)

continuation *n* **1** = **continuing**, perpetuation, prolongation, resumption **2** = **addition**, extension, furtherance, postscript, sequel, supplement

continue *v* **1** = **remain**, abide, carry on, endure, last, live on, persist, stay, survive **2** = **keep on**, carry on, go on, maintain, persevere, persist in, stick at, sustain **3** = **resume**, carry on, pick up where one left off, proceed, recommence, return to, take up

continuing *adj* = **lasting**, enduring, in progress, ongoing, sustained

continuity *n* = **sequence**, cohesion, connection, flow, progression, succession

continuous *adj* = **constant**, extended, prolonged, twenty-four-seven (*sl*), unbroken, unceasing, undivided, uninterrupted

one who contorts own body to entertain.
con·tour [KON-tuur] *n* **1** outline, shape,
esp. of mountains, coast, etc. **2** (also
contour line) line on map drawn through
places of same height.
contra- *prefix* against or contrasting, e.g.
contradistinction; contrapuntal.
con·tra·band [KON-trə-band] *n* **1**
smuggled goods. **2** illegal traffic in such
goods. ♦ *adj* **3** prohibited by law.
con·tra·cep·tion [kon-trə-SEP-shən] *n*
prevention of conception usu. by artificial
means, birth control. **con·tra·cep'tive** *adj,*
n
con·tract [kən-TRAKT] *v* **1** make or become
smaller, shorter. **2** enter into agreement. **3**
agree upon. ♦ *vt* **4** incur, become affected
by. ♦ *n* [KON-trakt] bargain, agreement. **5**
formal document recording agreement. **6**
agreement enforceable by law.
con·tract'ed *adj* drawn together.
con·trac·tile [kən-TRAK-tl] *adj* tending to
contract. **con·trac'tion** *n* **con·trac'tor** *n*
one making contract, esp. builder.
con·trac'tu·al [-choo-əl] *adj*
con·tra·dict [kon-trə-DIKT] *vt* **1** deny. **2** be
at variance or inconsistent with.
con·tra·dic'tion *n* **con·tra·dic'to·ry** *adj*
con·tral·to [kən-TRAL-toh] *n, pl* -tos lowest
of female voices.

con·trap·tion [kən-TRAP-shən] *n* **1** gadget.
2 device. **3** construction, device often
overelaborate or eccentric.
con·tra·pun·tal [kon-trə-PUN-tl] *adj Mus.*
pert. to counterpoint.
con·trar·y [KON-trer-ee] *adj* **1** opposed. **2**
opposite, other. **3** [kən-TRAIR-ee] perverse,
obstinate. ♦ *n* **4** something the exact
opposite of another. ♦ *adv* **5** in opposition.
con'trar·i·ness *n*
con·trast [kən-TRAST] *vt* **1** bring out
differences. **2** set in opposition for
comparison. ♦ *vi* **3** show great difference. ♦
n [KON-trast] **4** striking difference. **5** *TV*
sharpness of image.
con·tra·vene [kon-trə-VEEN] *vt* -vened,
-ven·ing **1** transgress, infringe. **2** conflict
with. **3** contradict. **con·tra·ven'tion** *n*
con·tre·temps [KON-trə-tahn] *n*
unexpected and embarrassing event or
mishap.
con·trib·ute [kən-TRIB-yoot] *v* -ut·ed,
-ut·ing **1** give, pay to common fund. **2**
help to occur. **3** write for the press.
con·tri·bu·tion [kon-trə-BYOO-shən] *n*
con·trib'u·tive *adj* **con·trib'u·tor** *n* **1** one
who writes articles for newspapers, etc. **2**
one who donates. **con·trib'u·to·ry** *adj* **1**
partly responsible. **2** giving to pension
fund, etc.

——————| THESAURUS |——————

contraband *n* **1** = **smuggling**,
black-marketing, bootlegging, trafficking ♦
adj **2** = **smuggled**, banned, bootleg,
forbidden, hot (*inf*), illegal, illicit,
prohibited, unlawful
contract *n* **1** = **agreement**, arrangement,
bargain, commitment, covenant, pact,
settlement ♦ *v* **2** = **agree**, bargain, come to
terms, commit oneself, covenant,
negotiate, pledge **3** = **shorten**, abbreviate,
curtail, diminish, dwindle, lessen, narrow,
reduce, shrink, shrivel **4** = **catch**, acquire,
be afflicted with, develop, get, go down
with, incur
contraction *n* = **shortening**, abbreviation,
compression, narrowing, reduction,
shrinkage, shriveling, tightening
contradict *v* = **deny**, be at variance with,
belie, challenge, controvert, fly in the face
of, negate, rebut
contradiction *n* = **denial**, conflict,
contravention, incongruity, inconsistency,
negation, opposite
contradictory *adj* = **inconsistent**,

conflicting, contrary, incompatible,
opposed, opposite, paradoxical
contraption *n Inf* = **device**, apparatus,
contrivance, gadget, instrument,
mechanism
contrary *n* **1** = **opposite**, antithesis,
converse, reverse ♦ *adj* **2** = **opposed**,
adverse, clashing, contradictory, counter,
discordant, hostile, inconsistent, opposite,
paradoxical **3** = **perverse**, awkward,
cantankerous, difficult, disobliging,
intractable, obstinate, unaccommodating
contrast *n* **1** = **difference**, comparison,
disparity, dissimilarity, distinction,
divergence, foil, opposition ♦ *v* **2** =
differentiate, compare, differ, distinguish,
oppose, set in opposition, set off
contribute *v* **1** = **give**, add, bestow, chip in
(*inf*), donate, provide, subscribe, supply
2 contribute to = **be partly responsible
for**, be conducive to, be instrumental in,
help, lead to, tend to
contribution *n* = **gift**, addition, donation,
grant, input, offering, subscription

con·trite [kən-TRĪT] *adj* remorseful for wrongdoing, penitent. **con·trite'ly** *adv* **con·tri'tion** [-TRISH-ən] *n*

con·trive [kən-TRĪV] *vt* -**trived, -triv·ing 1** manage. **2** devise, invent, design. **con·triv'ance** *n* artifice or device. **con·trived'** *adj* obviously planned, artificial.

con·trol [kən-TROHL] *vt* -**trolled, -trol·ling 1** command, dominate. **2** regulate. **3** direct, check, test. ◆ *n* **4** power to direct or determine. **5** curb, check. **6** standard of comparison in experiment. ◆ *pl* **7** system of instruments to control automobile, aircraft, etc. **con·trol'la·ble** *adj* **con·trol'ler** *n* **1** one who controls. **2** official controlling expenditure. **control tower** tower in airport from which takeoffs and landings are directed.

con·tro·ver·sy [KON-trə-vur-see] *n, pl* -**sies** dispute, debate, esp. over public issues. **con·tro·ver'sial** *adj* **con'tro·vert** *vt* **1** deny. **2** argue. **con·tro·vert'i·ble** *adj*

con·tu·ma·cy [KON-tuu-mə-see] *n, pl* -**cies** stubborn disobedience. **con·tu·ma'cious** [-MAY-shəs] *adj*

con·tu·me·ly [kon-TUU-mə-lee] *n, pl* -**lies** insulting language or treatment. **con·tu·me'li·ous** [-MEE-lee-əs] *adj* abusive, insolent.

con·tu·sion [kən-TOO-zhən] *n* bruise.

co·nun·drum [kə-NUN-drəm] *n* riddle, esp. with punning answer.

con·ur·ba·tion [kon-ər-BAY-shən] *n* densely populated urban sprawl formed by spreading of towns.

con·va·lesce [kon-və-LES] *vi* -**lesced, -lesc·ing** recover health after illness, operation, etc. **con·va·les'cence** *n* **con·va·les'cent** *adj, n*

con·vec·tion [kən-VEK-shən] *n* transmission, esp. of heat, by currents in liquids or gases. **con·vec'tor** *n* **con·vec'tive** *adj*

con·vene [kən-VEEN] *vt* -**vened, -ven·ing** call together, assemble, convoke. **con·ven'tion** *n* **1** assembly. **2** treaty, agreement. **3** rule. **4** practice based on agreement. **5** accepted usage. **con·ven'tion·al** *adj* **1** (slavishly) observing customs of society. **2** customary. **3** (of weapons, war, etc.) not nuclear.

con·ven·ient [kən-VEEN-yənt] *adj* **1** handy. **2** favorable to needs, comfort. **3** well adapted to one's purpose. **con·ven'ience** *n* **1** ease, comfort, suitability. ◆ *adj* **2** (of food) quick to prepare.

contributor *n* = **giver**, donor, patron, subscriber, supporter

contrite *adj* = **sorry**, chastened, conscience-stricken, humble, penitent, regretful, remorseful, repentant, sorrowful

contrivance *n* **1** = **device**, apparatus, appliance, contraption, gadget, implement, instrument, invention, machine, mechanism **2** = **plan**, intrigue, machination, plot, ruse, scheme, stratagem, trick

contrive *v* **1** = **bring about**, arrange, effect, manage, maneuver, plan, plot, scheme, succeed **2** = **devise**, concoct, construct, create, design, fabricate, improvise, invent, manufacture

contrived *adj* = **forced**, artificial, elaborate, labored, overdone, planned, strained, unnatural

control *n* **1** = **power**, authority, charge, command, guidance, management, oversight, supervision, supremacy **2** = **restraint**, brake, check, curb, limitation, regulation ◆ *v* **3** = **have power over**, administer, command, direct, govern, handle, have charge of, manage, manipulate, supervise **4** = **restrain**, check, constrain, contain, curb, hold back, limit, repress, subdue

controls *pl n* = **instruments**, console, control panel, dash, dashboard, dials

controversial *adj* = **disputed**, at issue, contentious, debatable, disputable, open to question, under discussion

controversy *n* = **argument**, altercation, debate, dispute, quarrel, row, squabble, wrangling

convalescence *n* = **recovery**, improvement, recuperation, rehabilitation, return to health

convalescent *adj* = **recovering**, getting better, improving, mending, on the mend, recuperating

convene *v* = **gather**, assemble, bring together, call, come together, congregate, convoke, meet, summon

convenience *n* **1** = **availability**, accessibility, advantage, appropriateness, benefit, fitness, suitability, usefulness, utility **2** = **appliance**, amenity, comfort, facility, help, labor-saving device

convenient *adj* **1** = **useful**, appropriate, fit,

con·vent [KON-vent] *n* **1** religious community, esp. of nuns. **2** their building.

con·verge [kən-VURJ] *vi* **-verged, -verg·ing** approach, tend to meet. **con·ver'gence, -gen·cy** *n* **con·ver'gent** *adj*

con·ver·sant [kən-VUR-sənt] *adj* acquainted, familiar (with), versed in.

conversation see CONVERSE[1].

con·verse[1] [kən VURS] *vi* **versed, -vers·ing** talk (with). **con·ver·sa'tion** *n* **con·ver·sa'tion·al** *adj*

con·verse[2] [KON-vurs] *adj* **1** opposite, turned around, reversed. ♦ *n* **2** the opposite, contrary.

con·vert [kən-VURT] *vt* **1** apply to another purpose. **2** change. **3** transform. **4** cause to adopt (another) religion, opinion. **5** *Football* make a conversion. ♦ *n* [KON-vurt] **6** converted person. **con·ver'sion** [-zhən] *n* **1** change of state. **2** unauthorized appropriation. **3** change of opinion, religion, or party. **4** *Football* extra point scored after a touchdown. **con·vert'er** *n* **1** one who, that which converts. **2** electrical device for changing alternating current into direct current. **3** vessel in which molten metal is refined. **con·vert'i·ble** *n* car with folding roof. ♦ *adj*

con·vex [kon-VEKS] *adj* **1** curved outward. **2** of a rounded form. **con·vex'i·ty** *n*

con·vey [kən-VAY] *vt* **1** carry, transport. **2** impart, communicate. **3** *Law* make over, transfer. **con·vey'ance** *n* **1** carrying. **2** vehicle. **3** act by which title to property is transferred. **con·vey'or belt** continuous moving belt for transporting things, esp. in factory.

con·vict [kən-VIKT] *vt* **1** prove or declare guilty. ♦ *n* [KON-vikt] **2** person found guilty of crime. **3** criminal serving prison sentence. **con·vic'tion** *n* **1** verdict of guilty. **2** being convinced, firm belief, state of being sure.

con·vince [kən-VINS] *vt* **-vinced, -vinc·ing** **1** firmly persuade, satisfy by evidence or argument. **con·vinc'ing** *adj* capable of compelling belief, effective.

con·viv·i·al [kən-VIV-ee-əl] *adj* sociable, festive, jovial. **con·viv·i·al'i·ty** *n*

con·voke [kən-VOHK] *vt* **-voked, -vok·ing** call together. **con·vo·ca·tion** [kon-və-KAY-shən] *n* calling together,

handy, helpful, labor-saving, serviceable, suitable, timely **2** = **nearby**, accessible, at hand, available, close at hand, handy, just round the corner, within reach

convention *n* **1** = **custom**, code, etiquette, practice, propriety, protocol, tradition, usage **2** = **agreement**, bargain, contract, pact, protocol, treaty **3** = **assembly**, conference, congress, convocation, council, meeting

conventional *adj* **1** = **ordinary**, accepted, customary, normal, orthodox, regular, standard, traditional, usual **2** = **unoriginal**, banal, hackneyed, prosaic, routine, stereotyped

converge *v* = **come together**, coincide, combine, gather, join, meet, merge

conversation *n* = **talk**, chat, conference, dialogue, discourse, discussion, gossip, tête-à-tête

converse[1] *v* = **talk**, chat, chew the fat (*sl*), commune, confer, discourse, exchange views

converse[2] *n* **1** = **opposite**, antithesis, contrary, obverse, other side of the coin, reverse ♦ *adj* **2** = **opposite**, contrary, counter, reverse, reversed, transposed

conversion *n* **1** = **change**, metamorphosis, transformation **2** = **adaptation**, alteration, modification, reconstruction, remodeling, reorganization

convert *v* **1** = **change**, alter, transform, transpose, turn **2** = **adapt**, apply, customize, modify, remodel, reorganize, restyle, revise **3** = **reform**, convince, proselytize ♦ *n* **4** = **neophyte**, disciple, proselyte

convex *adj* = **rounded**, bulging, gibbous, protuberant

convey *v* **1** = **communicate**, disclose, impart, make known, relate, reveal, tell **2** = **carry**, bear, bring, conduct, fetch, guide, move, send, transport

convict *v* **1** = **find guilty**, condemn, imprison, pronounce guilty, sentence ♦ *n* **2** = **prisoner**, criminal, culprit, felon, jailbird, lag (*sl*)

conviction *n* **1** = **belief**, creed, faith, opinion, persuasion, principle, tenet, view **2** = **confidence**, assurance, certainty, certitude, firmness, reliance

convince *v* = **persuade**, assure, bring round, prevail upon, satisfy, sway, win over

convincing *adj* = **persuasive**, cogent, conclusive, credible, impressive, plausible, assembly, esp. of clergy, college faculty, etc.

con·vo·lute [KON-və-loot] vt **-lut·ed, -lut·ing** twist, coil, tangle. **con'vo·lut·ed** adj **con·vo·lu'tion** n

con·voy [KON-voi] n **1** party (of ships, troops, trucks, etc.) traveling together for protection. ◆ vt **2** escort for protection.

con·vulse [kən-VULS] vt **-vulsed, -vuls·ing 1** shake violently. **2** affect with violent involuntary contractions of muscles. **con·vul'sion** n **1** violent upheaval. ◆ pl **2** spasms. **3** fits of laughter or hysteria. **con·vul'sive** adj

coo [koo] n **1** cry of doves. ◆ vi **cooed, coo·ing** make such cry.

cook [kuuk] vt **1** prepare (food) for table, esp. by heat. **2** inf falsify (accounts, etc.). ◆ vi **3** undergo cooking. **4** act as cook. ◆ n **5** one who prepares food for table. **cook'er** n cooking apparatus. **cook'ie** n small cake made from sweet dough. **cook'out** n (party featuring) meal cooked and served outdoors. **cook up** inf **1** invent, plan. **2** prepare (meal).

cool [kool] adj **1** moderately cold. **2** unexcited, calm. **3** lacking friendliness or interest. **4** inf calmly insolent. **5** inf sophisticated, elegant. ◆ v **6** make, become cool. ◆ n **7** cool time, place, etc. **8** inf calmness, composure. **cool'ant** n fluid used for cooling tool, machinery, etc. **cool'er** n **1** vessel in which liquids are cooled. **2** iced drink usu. with wine or whiskey base. **3** sl jail. **cool one's heels** be kept waiting, esp. because of deliberate discourtesy.

coon [koon] n raccoon.

coop [koop] n **1** cage or pen for pigeons, etc. ◆ vt **2** shut up in a coop. **3** confine.

co-op [KOH-op] n **1** cooperative enterprise. **2** apartment or business run by one.

coop·er [KOO-pər] n one who makes casks.

co·op·er·ate [koh-OP-ə-rayt] vi **-at·ed, -at·ing** work together. **co·op·er·a'tion** n **co·op'er·a·tive** adj **1** willing to cooperate. **2** (of an enterprise) owned collectively and managed for joint economic benefit. ◆ n **3** cooperative organization.

co·opt [koh-OPT] vt **1** preempt, appropriate as one's own. **2** elect by votes of existing members.

co·or·di·nate [koh-OR-dn-ayt] vt **-nat·ed, -nat·ing 1** bring into order as parts of whole. **2** place in same rank. **3** put into harmony. ◆ n [-it] **4** Math. any of set of numbers defining location of point. ◆ adj **5** equal in degree, status, etc. **co·or·di·na'tion** n

coot [koot] n **1** small black water fowl. **2** inf silly (old) person.

cop [kop] vt sl **copped, cop·ping 1** catch. ◆ n **2** inf policeman. **cop a plea** sl plead guilty in return for light sentence.

cope [kohp] vi **coped, cop·ing** deal successfully (with).

Co·per·ni·can [koh-PUR-ni-kən] adj pert. to Copernicus, Polish astronomer (1473-1543), or to his system.

cop·ing [KOH-ping] n top course of wall, usu. sloping to throw off rain.

co·pi·ous [KOH-pee-əs] adj **1** abundant. **2** plentiful. **3** full, ample.

cop·per[1] [KOP-ər] n **1** reddish-brown

powerful, telling

convulse v = **shake**, agitate, churn up, derange, disorder, disturb, twist, work

convulsion n = **spasm**, contraction, cramp, fit, paroxysm, seizure

cool adj **1** = **cold**, chilled, chilly, nippy, refreshing **2** = **calm**, collected, composed, relaxed, sedate, self-controlled, self-possessed, unemotional, unruffled **3** = **unfriendly**, aloof, distant, indifferent, lukewarm, offhand, standoffish, unenthusiastic, unwelcoming **4** Inf = **fashionable**, hip, phat (sl), trendy (inf) ◆ v **5** = **chill**, cool off, freeze, lose heat, refrigerate ◆ n **6** Sl = **calmness**, composure, control, poise, self-control, self-discipline, self-possession, temper

cooperate v = **work together**, collaborate, combine, conspire, coordinate, join forces, pool resources, pull together

cooperation n = **teamwork**, collaboration, combined effort, esprit de corps, give-and-take, unity

cooperative adj **1** = **helpful**, accommodating, obliging, onside (inf), responsive, supportive **2** = **shared**, collective, combined, joint

coordinate v = **bring together**, harmonize, integrate, match, organize, synchronize, systematize

cope v **1** = **manage**, carry on, get by (inf), hold one's own, make the grade, struggle through, survive **2** cope with = **deal with**, contend with, grapple with, handle, malleable ductile metal. **2** bronze money, coin. ◆ *vt* **3** cover with copper. **copper beech** tree with reddish leaves.

cop'per·plate [-playt] *n* **1** plate of copper for engraving, etching. **2** print from this. **3** copybook writing. **4** first-class handwriting.

copper[2] *n sl* policeman.

co·pra [KOH-prə] *n* dried coconut kernels.

copse [kops] *n* a wood of small trees.

cop·u·la [KOP-yə-lə] *n, pl* **-las 1** word, esp. verb acting as connecting link in sentence. **2** connection, tie.

cop·u·late [KOP-yə-layt] *vi* **-lat·ed, -lat·ing** unite sexually. **cop·u·la'tion** *n*

cop·y [KOP-ee] *n, pl* **cop·ies 1** imitation. **2** single specimen of book. **3** matter for printing. ◆ *vt* **cop·ied, cop·y·ing 4** make copy of. **5** imitate. **6** transcribe. **7** follow an example. **cop'y·right** *n* **1** legal exclusive right to print and publish book, article, work of art, etc. ◆ *vt* **2** protect by copyright. **cop'y·writ·er** *n* one who writes advertisements.

co·quette [koh-KET] *n* woman who flirts. **co·quet·ry** [KOH-ki-tree] *n* **co·quet'tish** *adj*

Cor. Corinthians.

cor·al [KOR-əl] *n* **1** hard substance made by sea polyps and forming growths, islands, reefs. **2** ornament of coral. ◆ *adj* **3** made of coral. **4** of deep pink color.

cord [kord] *n* **1** thin rope or thick string. **2** rib on cloth. **3** ribbed fabric. ◆ *vt* **4** fasten with cord. **cord'age** *n*

cor·date [KOR-dayt] *adj* heart-shaped.

cor·dial [KOR-jəl] *adj* **1** hearty, sincere, warm. ◆ *n* **2** sweet, fruit-flavored alcoholic drink. **3** liqueur. **cor·di·al·i·ty** [kor-jee-AL-i-tee] *n* warmth.

cord·ite [KOR-dīt] *n* explosive compound.

cor·don [KOR-dn] *n* **1** chain of troops or police. **2** fruit tree grown as single stem. ◆ *vt* **3** form cordon around.

cor·don bleu [kor-DAWN BLUU] *adj* (esp. of food preparation) of highest standard.

cor·du·roy [KOR-də-roi] *n* cotton fabric

with velvety, ribbed surface.

core [kor] *n* **1** horny seed case of apple and other fruits. **2** central or innermost part of anything. ◆ *vt* **cored, cor·ing 3** take out the core.

co·re·spond·ent [koh-ri-SPON-dənt] *n* one cited in divorce case, alleged to have committed adultery with the respondent.

cor·gi [KOR-gee] *n* short-legged sturdy dog.

co·ri·an·der [KOR-ee-an-dər] *n* plant grown for its aromatic seeds and leaves.

Co·rin·thi·an [kə-RIN-thee-ən] *adj* **1** of Corinth. **2** of Corinthian order of architecture, ornate Greek. ◆ *pl* **3** books in New Testament.

cork [kork] *n* **1** bark of an evergreen Mediterranean oak tree. **2** piece of it or other material, esp. used as stopper for bottle, etc. ◆ *vt* **3** stop up with cork. **cork'age** *n* charge for opening wine bottles in restaurant. **cork'er** *n sl* something, someone outstanding. **cork'screw** *n* tool for pulling out corks.

corn[1] [korn] *n* **1** (kernels of) sweet corn, corn on the cob. **2** *inf* oversentimental, trite quality in play, film, etc. ◆ *vt* **3** preserve (meat) with salt or brine. **corn'y** *adj* **corn·i·er, corn·i·est** *inf* trite, oversentimental, hackneyed. **corn'cob** *n* ear of sweet corn. **corn'flour** *n* finely ground corn. **corn'flow·er** *n* blue flower, oft. growing in grainfields.

corn[2] *n* painful horny growth on foot or toe.

cor·ne·a [KOR-nee-ə] *n* transparent membrane covering front of eye.

cor·ner [KOR-nər] *n* **1** part of room where two sides meet. **2** remote or humble place. **3** point where two walls, streets, etc. meet. **4** angle, projection. **5** *Business* buying up of whole existing stock of commodity, shares. ◆ *vt* **6** drive into position of difficulty, or leaving no escape. **7** establish monopoly. ◆ *vi* **8** turn around corner. **cor'ner·stone** *n*

struggle with, weather, wrestle with

copious *adj* = **abundant**, ample, bountiful, extensive, full, lavish, plentiful, profuse

copy *n* **1** = **reproduction**, counterfeit, duplicate, facsimile, forgery, imitation, likeness, model, replica ◆ *v* **2** = **reproduce**, counterfeit, duplicate, replicate, transcribe **3** = **imitate**, ape, emulate, follow, mimic, mirror, repeat

cord *n* = **rope**, line, string, twine

cordial *adj* = **warm**, affable, agreeable, cheerful, congenial, friendly, genial, hearty, sociable

cordon *n* **1** = **chain**, barrier, line, ring ◆ *v* **2 cordon off** = **surround**, close off, encircle, enclose, fence off, isolate, picket, separate

core *n* = **center**, crux, essence, gist, heart,

indispensable part, basis. **corner kick** *Soccer* free kick from corner of field.

cor·net [kor-NET] *n* trumpet with valves.

cor·nice [KOR-nis] *n* **1** projection near top of wall. **2** ornamental, carved molding below ceiling.

cor·nu·co·pia [kor-nə-KOH-pee-ə] *n* symbol of plenty, consisting of goat's horn, overflowing with fruit and flowers.

co·rol·la [kə-ROL-ə] *n* flower's inner envelope of petals.

cor·ol·lar·y [KOR-ə-ler-ee] *n*, *pl* **-lar·ies 1** inference from a preceding statement. **2** deduction. **3** result.

co·ro·na [kə-ROH-nə] *n*, *pl* **-nas 1** halo around heavenly body. **2** flat projecting part of cornice. **3** top or crown.

cor·o·nar·y [KOR-ə-ner-ee] *adj* **1** of blood vessels surrounding heart. ◆ *n*, *pl* **-nar·ies 2** coronary thrombosis. **coronary thrombosis** disease of the heart.

cor·o·na·tion [kor-ə-NAY-shən] *n* ceremony of crowning a sovereign.

cor·o·ner [KOR-ə-nər] *n* officer who holds inquests on bodies of persons supposed killed by violence, accident, etc.

cor·o·net [KOR-ə-net] *n* small crown.

cor·po·ral[1] [KOR-pər-əl] *adj* **1** of the body. **2** material, not spiritual. **corporal punishment** (flogging, etc.) of physical nature.

corporal[2] *n* noncommissioned officer below sergeant.

cor·po·ra·tion [kor-pə-RAY-shən] *n* **1** association, body of persons legally authorized to act as an individual. **2** authorities of town or city. **cor'po·rate** [-rit] *adj*

cor·po·re·al [kor-POR-ee-əl] *adj* **1** of the body, material. **2** tangible.

corps [kor] *n*, *pl* **corps** [korz] **1** military force, body of troops. **2** any organized body of persons.

corpse [korps] *n* dead body.

cor·pu·lent [KOR-pyə-lənt] *adj* fat. **cor'pu·lence** *n*

cor·pus [KOR-pəs] *n* **1** collection or body of works, esp. by single author. **2** main part or body of something.

cor·pus·cle [KOR-pə-səl] *n* minute organism or particle, esp. red and white corpuscles of blood.

cor·ral [kə-RAL] *n* enclosure for cattle, or for defense. ◆ *vt* **-raled, -ral·ing**

cor·rect [kə-REKT] *vt* **1** set right. **2** indicate errors in. **3** rebuke, punish. **4** counteract, rectify. ◆ *adj* **5** right, exact, accurate. **6** in accordance with facts or standards. **cor·rec'tion** *n* **cor·rec'tive** *n*, *adj*

cor·re·late [KOR-ə-layt] *vt* **-lat·ed, -lat·ing 1** bring into reciprocal relation. ◆ *n* [-lit] **2** either of two things or words necessarily implying the other. **cor·re·la'tion** *n* **cor·rel·a·tive** [kə-REL-ə-tiv] *adj*, *n*

cor·re·spond [kor-ə-SPOND] *vi* **1** be in agreement, be consistent with. **2** be similar (to). **3** exchange letters. **cor·re·spond'ence** *n* **1** agreement, corresponding. **2** similarity.

THESAURUS

kernel, nub, nucleus, pith

corner *n* **1** = **angle**, bend, crook, joint **2** = **space**, hideaway, hideout, nook, retreat ◆ *v* **3** = **trap**, run to earth **4** *As in* **corner the market** = **monopolize**, dominate, engross, hog (*sl*)

corny *adj Sl* = **unoriginal**, banal, dull, hackneyed, old-fashioned, old hat, stale, stereotyped, trite

corporation *n* **1** = **business**, association, corporate body, society **2** = **town council**, civic authorities, council, municipal authorities

corps *n* = **team**, band, company, detachment, division, regiment, squadron, troop, unit

corpse *n* = **body**, cadaver, carcass, remains, stiff (*sl*)

correct *adj* **1** = **true**, accurate, exact, faultless, flawless, O.K. *or* okay (*inf*),

precise, right **2** = **proper**, acceptable, appropriate, fitting, kosher (*inf*), O.K. *or* okay (*inf*), seemly, standard ◆ *v* **3** = **rectify**, adjust, amend, cure, emend, redress, reform, remedy, right **4** = **punish**, admonish, chasten, chastise, chide, discipline, rebuke, reprimand, reprove

correction *n* **1** = **rectification**, adjustment, alteration, amendment, emendation, improvement, modification **2** = **punishment**, admonition, castigation, chastisement, discipline, reformation, reproof

correctly *adv* = **rightly**, accurately, perfectly, precisely, properly, right

correctness *n* **1** = **truth**, accuracy, exactitude, exactness, faultlessness, fidelity, preciseness, precision, regularity **2** = **decorum**, civility, good breeding, propriety, seemliness

3 exchange of letters. **4** letters received.
cor·re·spond'ent *n* **1** writer of letters. **2** one employed by newspaper, etc. to report on particular topic, country, etc.

cor·ri·dor [KOR-i-dər] *n* **1** passage in building, etc. **2** strip of territory (or air route) not under control of country through which it passes. **3** densely populated area incl. two or more major cities.

cor·ri·gen·dum [kor-i-JEN-dəm] *n, pl* **-da** [-də] thing to be corrected.

cor·rob·o·rate [kə-ROB-ə-rayt] *vt* **-rat·ed, -rat·ing** confirm, support (statement, etc.). **cor·rob·o·ra'tion** *n* **cor·rob'o·ra·tive** *adj*

cor·rode [kə-ROHD] *vt* **-rod·ed, -rod·ing** eat, wear away, eat into (by chemical action, disease, etc.). **cor·ro'sion** [-ROH-*zh*ən] *n* **cor·ro'sive** *adj*

cor·ru·gate [KOR-ə-gayt] *v* **-gat·ed, -gat·ing** wrinkle, bend into wavy ridges.

cor·rupt [kə-RUPT] *adj* **1** lacking integrity. **2** open to, or involving, bribery. **3** wicked. **4** spoiled by mistakes, altered for the worse (of words, literary passages, etc.). ◆ *vt* **5** make evil, pervert. **6** bribe. **7** make rotten. **cor·rupt'i·ble** *adj* **cor·rup'tion** *n*

cor·sage [kor-SAH*ZH*] *n* (flower, spray, worn on) bodice of woman's dress.

cor·sair [kor-sair] *n* pirate (ship).

cor·set [KOR-sit] *n* close-fitting undergarment stiffened to give support or shape to the body.

cor·tege [kor-TE*ZH*] *n* formal (funeral) procession.

cor·tex [KOR-teks] *n, pl* **-ti·ces** [-tə-seez] *Anatomy* **1** outer layer. **2** bark. **3** sheath. **cor'ti·cal** *adj*

cor·ti·sone [KOR-tə-zohn] *n* synthetic hormone used in the treatment of a variety of diseases.

cor·vette [kor-VET] *n* lightly armed warship for escort and antisubmarine duties.

co·sine [KOH-sīn] *n* in a right triangle, the ratio of a side adjacent to a given angle and the hypotenuse.

cos·met·ic [koz-MET-ik] *n* **1** preparation to beautify or improve skin, hair, etc. ◆ *adj* **2** designed to improve appearance only.

cos·mic [KOZ-mik] *adj* **1** relating to the universe. **2** of the vastness of the universe. **cos·mog'ra·pher** *n* **cos·mog'ra·phy** *n* description or mapping of the universe. **cos·mo·log·i·cal** [koz-mə-LOJ-i-kəl] *adj* **cos·mol'o·gy** *n* the science or study of the universe.

cosmic rays high-energy electromagnetic rays from space.

cos·mo·naut [KOZ-mə-nawt] *n* the Russian name for an astronaut.

cos·mo·pol·i·tan [koz-mə-POL-i-tn] *n* **1** person who has lived and traveled in many countries. ◆ *adj* **2** familiar with many countries. **3** sophisticated. **4** free from

correspond *v* **1** = **be consistent**, accord, agree, conform, fit, harmonize, match, square, tally **2** = **communicate**, exchange letters, keep in touch, write

correspondence *n* **1** = **letters**, communication, mail, post, writing **2** = **relation**, agreement, coincidence, comparison, conformity, correlation, harmony, match, similarity

correspondent *n* **1** = **letter writer**, pen friend *or* pal **2** = **reporter**, contributor, journalist

corresponding *adj* = **related**, analogous, answering, complementary, equivalent, matching, reciprocal, similar

corridor *n* = **passage**, aisle, alley, hallway, passageway

corroborate *v* = **support**, authenticate, back up, bear out, confirm, endorse, ratify, substantiate, validate

corrode *v* = **eat away**, consume, corrupt, erode, gnaw, oxidize, rust, wear away

corrosive *adj* = **corroding**, caustic, consuming, erosive, virulent, vitriolic, wasting, wearing

corrupt *adj* **1** = **dishonest**, bent (*sl*), bribable, crooked (*inf*), fraudulent, unprincipled, unscrupulous, venal **2** = **depraved**, debased, degenerate, dissolute, profligate, vicious **3** = **distorted**, altered, doctored, falsified ◆ *v* **4** = **bribe**, buy off, entice, fix (*inf*), grease (someone's) palm (*sl*), lure, suborn **5** = **deprave**, debauch, pervert, subvert **6** = **distort**, doctor, tamper with

corruption *n* **1** = **dishonesty**, bribery, extortion, fraud, shady dealings (*inf*), unscrupulousness, venality **2** = **depravity**, decadence, evil, immorality, perversion, vice, wickedness **3** = **distortion**, doctoring, falsification

corset *n* = **girdle**, belt, bodice

cosmetic *adj* = **beautifying**, nonessential, superficial, surface national prejudice.

cos·mos[1] [KOZ-məs] *n* the world or universe considered as an ordered system.

cosmos[2] *n, pl* **-mos** plant cultivated for brightly colored flowers.

cos·sack [KOS-ak] *n* member of tribe in SE Russia.

cost [kawst] *n* **1** price. **2** cost price. **3** expenditure of time, labor, etc. ◆ *pl* **4** expenses of lawsuit. ◆ *vt* **cost, cost·ing 5** have as price. **6** entail payment, or loss, or sacrifice of. **costing** *n* system of calculating cost of production, sale. **cost'li·ness** *n* **cost'ly** *adj* **-li·er, -li·est 1** valuable. **2** expensive. **cost price** price at which article is bought by one intending to resell it.

cos·tal [KOS-tl] *adj* pert. to side of body or ribs.

cos·tume [KOS-toom] *n* **1** style of dress of particular place or time, or for particular activity. **2** theatrical clothes. **cos'tum·er** *n* dealer in costumes. **costume jewelry** inexpensive jewelry.

cot [kot] *n* narrow, usu. collapsible bed.

cote [koht] *n* **1** shelter, shed for animals or birds, e.g. *dovecote*.

co·te·rie [KOH-tə-ree] *n* **1** exclusive group of people with common interests. **2** social clique.

coterminous see CONTERMINOUS.

cot·tage [KOT-ij] *n* small house. **cottage cheese** mild, soft cheese. **cottage industry** industry in which workers work in their own homes.

cot·ter [KOT-ər] *n* pin, wedge, etc. to prevent relative motion of two parts of machine, etc.

cot·ton [KOT-n] *n* **1** plant. **2** white downy fibrous covering of its seeds. **3** thread or cloth made of this. **cotton (on) to** begin to like, understand (idea, person, etc.).

cot·y·le·don [kot-l-EED-n] *n* primary leaf of plant embryos.

couch [kowch] *n* **1** piece of furniture for sitting or reclining on by day, sofa. ◆ *vt* **2** put into (words), phrase. **3** cause to lie down. **couch potato** *inf* lazy person whose only hobby is watching television. **on the couch** under psychiatric treatment.

cou·gar [KOO-gər] *n* mountain lion.

cough [kawf] *vi* **1** expel air from lungs with sudden effort and noise, often to remove obstruction. ◆ *n* **2** act of coughing.

could pt. of CAN[1].

cou·lomb [KOO-lom] *n* unit of quantity of electricity.

coun·cil [KOWN-səl] *n* **1** deliberative or administrative body. **2** one of its meetings. **3** local governing authority of town, etc. **coun'ci·lor** *n* member of council.

coun·sel [KOWN-səl] *n* **1** advice, deliberation or debate. **2** lawyer or lawyers. **3** plan, policy. ◆ *vt* **4** advise, recommend. **coun'se·lor** *n* **1** adviser. **2** lawyer. **keep one's counsel** keep a secret.

count[1] [kownt] *vt* **1** reckon, calculate, number. **2** include. **3** consider to be. ◆ *vi* **4** be reckoned in. **5** depend (on). **6** be of importance. ◆ *n* **7** reckoning. **8** total number reached by counting. **9** item in list of charges or indictment. **10** act of counting. **count'less** *adj* too many to be

cosmic *adj* = **universal**, stellar

cosmopolitan *adj* **1** = **sophisticated**, broad-minded, catholic, open-minded, universal, urbane, well-traveled, worldly-wise ◆ *n* **2** = **man** *or* **woman of the world**, jet-setter, sophisticate

cost *n* **1** = **price**, amount, charge, damage (*inf*), expense, outlay, payment, worth **2** = **loss**, damage, detriment, expense, harm, hurt, injury, penalty, sacrifice, suffering ◆ *v* **3** = **sell at**, come to, command a price of, set (someone) back (*inf*) **4** = **lose**, do disservice to, harm, hurt, injure

costly *adj* **1** = **expensive**, dear, exorbitant, extortionate, highly-priced, steep (*inf*), stiff **2** = **damaging**, catastrophic, deleterious, disastrous, harmful, loss-making, ruinous

costs *pl n* = **expenses**, budget, outgoings, overheads

costume *n* = **outfit**, apparel, attire, clothing, dress, ensemble, garb, livery, uniform

cottage *n* = **cabin**, chalet, hut, lodge, shack

cough *n* **1** = **frog** *or* **tickle in one's throat**, bark, hack ◆ *v* **2** = **clear one's throat**, bark, hack

council *n* = **governing body**, assembly, board, cabinet, committee, conference, congress, convention, panel, parliament

counsel *n* **1** = **advice**, direction, guidance, information, recommendation, suggestion, warning **2** = **legal adviser**, advocate, attorney, barrister, lawyer ◆ *v* **3** = **advise**, advocate, exhort, instruct, recommend, urge, warn counted.

count[2] *n* European nobleman of rank corresponding to that of British earl.

coun·te·nance [KOWN-tn-əns] *n* **1** face, its expression. **2** support, approval. ◆ *vt* **-nanced, -nanc·ing 3** give support, approve.

count·er[1] [KOWN-tər] *n* **1** horizontal surface in bank, store, etc., on which business is transacted. **2** work surface in kitchen. **3** disk, token used for counting or scoring, esp. in board games. **coun'ter·top** flat upper surface of counter, display case, etc.

coun·ter[2] *adv* **1** in opposite direction. **2** contrary. ◆ *vi* **3** oppose, contradict. **4** *Fencing* parry. ◆ *n* **5** parry.

counter- *prefix* **1** opposite, against, e.g. *counterattack.* **2** complementary, corresponding, e.g. *counterpart.*

coun·ter·act [kown-tər-AKT] *vt* neutralize or hinder.

coun·ter·at·tack [KOWN-tər-ə-tak] *v, n* attack after enemy's advance.

coun·ter·bal·ance [KOWN-tər-bal-əns] *n* weight balancing or neutralizing another. ◆ *vt* **-anced, anc·ing**

coun·ter·feit [KOWN-tər-fit] *adj* **1** sham, forged. ◆ *n* **2** imitation, forgery. ◆ *vt* **3**

imitate with intent to deceive. **4** forge.

coun·ter·mand [kown-tər-MAND] *vt* cancel (previous order).

coun·ter·part [KOWN-tər-pahrt] *n* **1** thing so like another as to be mistaken for it. **2** something complementary to or correlative of another.

coun·ter·point [KOWN-tər-point] *n* **1** melody added as accompaniment to given melody. **2** art of so adding melodies.

coun·ter·sign [KOWN-tər-sin] *vt* **1** sign document already signed by another. **2** ratify. ◆ *n Military* **3** secret sign.

coun·ter·sink [KOWN-tər-singk] *v* **-sunk, -sink·ing** enlarge upper part of hole (drilled in wood, etc.) to take head of screw, bolt, etc. below surface.

count'ess *n* wife or widow of count or earl.

coun·try [KUN-tree] *n, pl* **-tries 1** region, district. **2** territory of nation. **3** land of birth, residence, etc. **4** rural districts as opposed to city. **5** nation. **coun'tri·fied** [-fid] *adj* rural in manner or appearance. **coun'try·man** *n* **1** rustic. **2** compatriot. **country music** popular music based on Amer. folk music. **coun'try·side** *n* **1** rural district. **2** its inhabitants.

coun·ty [KOWN-tee] *n, pl* **-ties** division of a

——————————| THESAURUS |——————————

count *v* **1** = **add (up),** calculate, compute, enumerate, number, reckon, tally, tot up **2** = **matter,** be important, carry weight, rate, signify, tell, weigh **3** = **consider,** deem, judge, look upon, rate, regard, think **4** = **take into account** *or* **consideration,** include, number among ◆ *n* **5** = **calculation,** computation, enumeration, numbering, poll, reckoning, sum, tally

counter *v* **1** = **retaliate,** answer, hit back, meet, oppose, parry, resist, respond, ward off ◆ *adv* **2** = **opposite to,** against, at variance with, contrariwise, conversely, in defiance of, versus

counteract *v* = **act against,** foil, frustrate, negate, neutralize, offset, resist, thwart

counterbalance *v* = **offset,** balance, compensate, make up for, set off

counterfeit *adj* **1** = **fake,** bogus, false, forged, imitation, phoney *or* phony (*inf*), sham, simulated ◆ *n* **2** = **fake,** copy, forgery, fraud, imitation, phoney *or* phony (*inf*), reproduction, sham ◆ *v* **3** = **fake,** copy, fabricate, feign, forge, imitate,

impersonate, pretend, sham, simulate

countermand *v* = **cancel,** annul, override, repeal, rescind, retract, reverse, revoke

counterpart *n* = **opposite number,** complement, equal, fellow, match, mate, supplement, tally, twin

countless *adj* = **innumerable,** endless, immeasurable, incalculable, infinite, legion, limitless, myriad, numberless, uncountable, untold

count on *or* **upon** *v* = **depend on,** bank on, believe (in), lean on, pin one's faith on, reckon on, rely on, take for granted, take on trust, trust

country *n* **1** = **nation,** commonwealth, kingdom, people, realm, state **2** = **territory,** land, region, terrain **3** = **people,** citizens, community, inhabitants, nation, populace, public, society **4** = **countryside,** backwoods, farmland, green belt, outback (*Austral. & N.Z.*), provinces, sticks (*inf*)

countryside *n* = **country,** farmland, green belt, outback (*Austral. & N.Z.*), outdoors, sticks (*inf*)

count up *v* = **add,** reckon up, sum, tally,

state.

coup [koo] *n, pl* **coups** [kooz] **1** successful stroke, move or gamble. **2** coup d'état. **coup d'é·tat** [koo-day-TAH] sudden, violent seizure of government.

cou·ple [KUP-əl] *n* **1** two, pair. **2** husband and wife. **3** any two persons. ◆ *v* **-pled, -pling** ◆ *vt* **4** connect, fasten together. **5** associate, connect in the mind. ◆ *vi* **6** join, associate. **cou'plet** *n* two lines of verse, esp. rhyming and of equal length. **cou'pling** *n* connection.

cou·pon [KOO-pon] *n* **1** ticket or voucher entitling holder to discount, gift, etc. **2** detachable slip used as order form.

cour·age [KUR-ij] *n* bravery, boldness. **cou·ra·geous** [kə-RAY-jəs] *adj*

cour·i·er [KUUR-ee-ər] *n* express messenger.

course [kors] *n* **1** movement in space or time. **2** direction of movement. **3** successive development, sequence. **4** line of conduct or action. **5** series of lessons, exercises, etc. **6** any of successive parts of meal. **7** continuous line of masonry at particular level in building. **8** area where golf is played. **9** track or ground on which a race is run. ◆ *v* **coursed, cours·ing** ◆ *vt* **10** hunt. ◆ *vi* **11** run swiftly, gallop about. **12** (of blood) circulate.

court [kort] *n* **1** space enclosed by buildings, yard. **2** area marked off or enclosed for playing various games. **3** retinue and establishment of sovereign. **4** body with judicial powers, place where it meets, one of its sittings. **5** attention, homage, flattery. ◆ *vt* **6** woo, try to win or attract. **7** seek, invite. **cour·ti·er** [KOR-tee-ər] *n* one who frequents royal court. **court'li·ness** *n* **court'ly** *adj* **-li·er, -li·est** **1** ceremoniously polite. **2** characteristic of a court. **court martial** *n, pl* **courts martial** court of naval or military officers for trying naval or military offenses. **court'yard** *n* paved space enclosed by buildings or walls.

cour·te·san [KOR-tə-zən] *n* **1** court mistress. **2** high-class prostitute.

cour·te·sy [KUR-tə-see] *n, pl* **-sies** **1** politeness, good manners. **2** act of civility. **cour'te·ous** *adj* polite.

court·ship [KORT-ship] *n* wooing.

————————{ THESAURUS }————————

total

county *n* = **province**, shire

coup *n* = **masterstroke**, accomplishment, action, deed, exploit, feat, maneuver, stunt

couple *n* **1** = **pair**, brace, duo, two, twosome ◆ *v* **2** = **link**, connect, hitch, join, marry, pair, unite, wed, yoke

coupon *n* = **slip**, card, certificate, ticket, token, voucher

courage *n* = **bravery**, daring, fearlessness, gallantry, heroism, mettle, nerve, pluck, resolution, valor

courageous *adj* = **brave**, bold, daring, fearless, gallant, gritty, intrepid, lion-hearted, stouthearted, valiant

courier *n* **1** = **guide**, representative **2** = **messenger**, bearer, carrier, envoy, runner

course *n* **1** = **classes**, curriculum, lectures, program, schedule **2** = **progression**, development, flow, movement, order, progress, sequence, unfolding **3** = **route**, direction, line, passage, path, road, track, trajectory, way **4** = **racecourse**, cinder track, circuit **5** = **procedure**, behavior, conduct, manner, method, mode, plan, policy, program **6** = **period**, duration, lapse, passage, passing, sweep, term, time **7** of course = **naturally**, certainly,

definitely, indubitably, needless to say, obviously, undoubtedly, without a doubt ◆ *v* **8** = **run**, flow, gush, race, speed, stream, surge **9** = **hunt**, chase, follow, pursue, stalk

court *n* **1** = **law court**, bar, bench, tribunal **2** = **courtyard**, cloister, piazza, plaza, quad (*inf*), quadrangle, square, yard **3** = **palace**, hall, manor **4** = **royal household**, attendants, cortege, entourage, retinue, suite, train ◆ *v* **5** = **woo**, date, go (out) with, run after, serenade, set one's cap at, take out, walk out with **6** = **cultivate**, brown-nose (*sl*), curry favor with, fawn upon, flatter, pander to, seek, solicit **7** = **invite**, attract, bring about, incite, prompt, provoke, seek

courteous *adj* = **polite**, affable, attentive, civil, gallant, gracious, refined, respectful, urbane, well-mannered

courtesy *n* **1** = **politeness**, affability, civility, courteousness, gallantry, good manners, graciousness, urbanity **2** = **favor**, benevolence, indulgence, kindness

courtier *n* = **attendant**, follower, squire

courtly *adj* = **ceremonious**, chivalrous, dignified, elegant, formal, gallant, polished, refined, stately, urbane

courtyard *n* = **yard**, enclosure, quad,

cous·in [KUZ-ən] n son or daughter of uncle or aunt.

cove [kohv] n small inlet of coast, sheltered bay.

cov·en [KUV-ən] n gathering of witches.

cov·e·nant [KUV-ə-nənt] n **1** contract, mutual agreement. **2** compact. ◆ v **3** agree to a covenant.

cov·er [KUV-ər] vt **1** place or spread over. **2** extend, spread. **3** bring upon (oneself). **4** screen, protect. **5** travel over. **6** include. **7** be sufficient. **8** point a gun at. ◆ n **9** lid, wrapper, envelope, binding, screen, anything that covers. **cov'er·age** n amount, extent covered. **cov'er·let** n bedspread. **cover girl** attractive model whose picture appears on magazine cover.

co·vert [KOH-vərt] adj **1** secret, veiled, concealed, sly. ◆ n [KUV-ərt] **2** thicket, place sheltering game.

cov·et [KUV-it] vt **1** long to possess, esp. what belongs to another. **cov'et·ous** adj greedy.

cov·ey [KUV-ee] n, pl **-eys** brood of partridges or quail.

cow[1] [kow] n **1** mature female of cattle

and of certain other mammals, such as the elephant or seal. **cow'boy** n **1** ranch hand in charge of cattle on western plains of US. **2** inf reckless driver, etc.

cow[2] vt frighten into submission, overawe, subdue.

cow·ard [KOW-ərd] n one who lacks courage, shrinks from danger. **cow'ard·ice** [dis] n **cow'ard·ly** adj

cow·er [KOW-ər] vi crouch, shrink in fear.

cowl [kowl] n **1** monk's hooded cloak. **2** its hood. **3** cowling.

cowl·ing [KOW-ling] n covering for aircraft engine.

cow·rie [KOW-ree] n brightly colored sea shell.

cox·swain [KOK-sən] n **1** steersman of boat. **cox** v inf act as coxswain.

coy [koi] adj **-er, -est** (pretending to be) shy, modest. **coy'ness** n

coy·o·te [kī-OH-tee] n N Amer. prairie wolf.

co·zy [KOH-zee] adj **-zi·er, -zi·est 1** snug, comfortable, sheltered. **2** suggesting conspiratorial intimacy. **co'zi·ly** adv **co'zi·ness** n

CPU Computers. central processing unit.

————| THESAURUS |————

quadrangle

cove[1] n = **bay**, anchorage, inlet, sound

covenant n **1** = **promise**, agreement, arrangement, commitment, contract, pact, pledge ◆ v **2** = **promise**, agree, contract, pledge, stipulate, undertake

cover v **1** = **clothe**, dress, envelop, put on, wrap **2** = **overlay**, coat, daub, encase, envelop **3** = **submerge**, engulf, flood, overrun, wash over **4** = **conceal**, cloak, disguise, enshroud, hide, mask, obscure, shroud, veil **5** = **travel over**, cross, pass through or over, traverse **6** = **protect**, defend, guard, shield **7** = **report**, describe, investigate, narrate, relate, tell of, write up ◆ n **8** = **covering**, canopy, case, coating, envelope, jacket, lid, top, wrapper **9** = **disguise**, façade, front, mask, pretext, screen, smoke screen, veil **10** = **protection**, camouflage, concealment, defense, guard, shelter, shield **11** = **insurance**, compensation, indemnity, protection, reimbursement

covering adj **1** = **explanatory**, accompanying, descriptive, introductory ◆ n **2** = **cover**, blanket, casing, coating, layer, wrapping

cover-up n = **concealment**, complicity,

conspiracy, front, smoke screen, whitewash (inf)

cover up v = **conceal**, draw a veil over, hide, hush up, suppress, sweep under the carpet, whitewash (inf)

covet v = **long for**, aspire to, crave, desire, envy, lust after, set one's heart on, yearn for

covetous adj = **envious**, acquisitive, avaricious, close-fisted, grasping, greedy, jealous, rapacious, yearning

coward n = **wimp** (inf), chicken (sl), scaredy-cat (inf), yellow-belly (sl)

cowardice n = **faint-heartedness**, fearfulness, spinelessness, weakness

cowardly adj = **faint-hearted**, chicken (sl), craven, fearful, scared, soft, spineless, timorous, weak, yellow (inf)

cowboy n = **cowhand**, cattleman, drover, gaucho (S. American), herdsman, rancher, stockman

cower v = **cringe**, draw back, flinch, grovel, quail, shrink, tremble

coy adj = **shy**, bashful, demure, modest, reserved, retiring, shrinking, timid

cozy adj = **snug**, comfortable, comfy (inf), homely, homey, intimate, sheltered, tucked up, warm

Cr *Chem.* chromium.

crab [krab] *n* **1** edible crustacean with ten legs, noted for sidelong and backward walk. **2** type of louse. ♦ *vi* **crabbed, crab·bing 3** catch crabs. **4** move sideways. **crab-bed** [KRAB-id] *adj* of handwriting, hard to read. **crab'by** *adj* **-bi·er, -bi·est** irritable.

crack [krak] *vt* **1** break, split partially. **2** break with sharp noise. **3** cause to make sharp noise, as of whip, rifle, etc. **4** break down, yield. **5** *inf* tell (joke). **6** solve, decipher. ♦ *vi* **7** make sharp noise. **8** split, fissure. **9** of the voice, lose clearness when changing from boy's to man's. ♦ *n* **10** sharp explosive noise. **11** split, fissure. **12** flaw. **13** *inf* joke, esp. sarcastic. **14** chat. **15** *sl* pure, highly addictive form of cocaine. ♦ *adj* **16** *inf* special, smart, of great reputation for skill or fashion. **crack'er** *n* **1** thin dry biscuit. **2 (C-)** *sl, offens* native or inhabitant of Georgia. **crack'le** [-əl] *n* **1** sound of repeated small cracks. ♦ *vi* **-led, -ling 2** make this sound. **crack'ling** *n* **1** crackle. **2** crisp skin of roast pork, etc.

cra·dle [KRAYD-l] *n* **1** infant's bed (on rockers). **2** *fig* earliest resting place or home. **3** supporting framework. ♦ *vt* **-dled, -dling 4** hold or rock as in a cradle. **5** cherish.

craft¹ [kraft] *n* **1** skill, ability, esp. manual ability. **2** cunning. **3** skilled trade. **4** members of a trade. **craft'i·ly** *adv* **craft'y** *adj* **craft·i·er, craft·i·est** cunning, shrewd. **crafts·man** *n* **crafts·man·ship** *n*

craft² *n* **1** vessel. **2** ship.

crag [krag] *n* **1** steep rugged rock. **crag'gy** *adj* **-gi·er, -gi·est** rugged.

cram [kram] *vt* **crammed, cram·ming 1** fill quite full. **2** stuff, force. **3** pack tightly. ♦ *vi* **4** feed to excess. **5** prepare quickly for examination.

cramp [kramp] *n* **1** painful muscular contraction. **2** clamp for holding masonry, wood, etc. together. ♦ *vt* **3** restrict or hamper. **4** hem in, keep within too narrow limits.

cram·pon [KRAM-pon] *n* spike in shoe for mountain climbing esp. on ice.

crane [krayn] *n* **1** wading bird with long legs, neck, and bill. **2** machine for moving heavy weights. ♦ *vi* **craned, cran·ing 3** stretch neck to see.

cra·ni·um [KRAY-nee-əm] *n* skull. **cra'ni·al** *adj*

crank [krangk] *n* **1** arm at right angles to axis, for turning main shaft, changing reciprocal into rotary motion, etc. **2** *inf* eccentric person, faddist. ♦ *v* **3** start (engine) by turning crank. **crank'y** *adj*

━━━━━ THESAURUS ━━━━━

crack *v* **1 = break,** burst, cleave, fracture, snap, splinter, split **2 = snap,** burst, crash, detonate, explode, pop, ring **3 = give in,** break down, collapse, give way, go to pieces, lose control, succumb, yield **4** *Inf* **= hit,** clip (*inf*), clout (*inf*), cuff, slap, smack, whack **5 = solve,** decipher, fathom, get the answer to, work out ♦ *n* **6 = snap,** burst, clap, crash, explosion, pop, report **7 = break,** chink, cleft, cranny, crevice, fissure, fracture, gap, rift **8** *Inf* **= blow,** clip (*inf*), clout (*inf*), cuff, slap, smack, whack **9** *Inf* **= joke,** dig, funny remark, gag (*inf*), jibe, quip, wisecrack (*inf*), witticism

crackdown *n* **= suppression,** clampdown, crushing, repression

cracked *adj* **= broken,** chipped, damaged, defective, faulty, flawed, imperfect, split

cradle *n* **1 = crib,** bassinet, cot **2 = birthplace,** beginning, fount, fountainhead, origin, source, spring, wellspring ♦ *v* **3 = hold,** lull, nestle, nurse, rock, support

craft *n* **1 = occupation,** business, employment, handicraft, pursuit, trade, vocation, work **2 = skill,** ability, aptitude, art, artistry, expertise, ingenuity, know-how (*inf*), technique, workmanship **3 = vessel,** aircraft, boat, plane, ship, spacecraft

craftsman *n* **= skilled worker,** artisan, maker, master, smith, technician, wright

craftsmanship *n* **= workmanship,** artistry, expertise, mastery, technique

crafty *adj* **= cunning,** artful, calculating, devious, sharp, shrewd, sly, subtle, wily

crag *n* **= rock,** bluff, peak, pinnacle, tor

cram *v* **1 = stuff,** compress, force, jam, pack in, press, shove, squeeze **2 = overeat,** glut, gorge, satiate, stuff **3 = study,** bone up (*inf*), review

cramp¹ *n* **= spasm,** ache, contraction, convulsion, pain, pang, stitch, twinge

cramp² *v* **= restrict,** constrain, hamper, handicap, hinder, impede, inhibit, obstruct

cramped *adj* **= closed in,** confined, congested, crowded, hemmed in, overcrowded, packed, uncomfortable crank·i·er, crank·i·est 1 bad-tempered. 2 eccentric. crank'shaft n principal shaft of engine.

cran·ny [KRAN-ee] n, pl -nies small opening, chink. cran'nied adj

crap [krap] n gambling game played with two dice (also craps).

crape [krayp] n crepe, esp. when used for mourning clothes.

crash [krash] v (cause to) make loud noise. 1 (cause to) fall with crash. ◆ vi 2 break, smash. 3 collapse, fail, esp. financially. 4 cause (aircraft) to hit land or water. 5 collide with (another car, etc.). 6 move noisily or violently. ◆ vi 7 (of computer system or program) fail suddenly because of malfunction. ◆ n 8 loud, violent fall or impact. 9 collision, esp. between vehicles. 10 sudden, uncontrolled descent of aircraft to land. 11 sudden collapse or downfall, esp. of economy. 12 bankruptcy. ◆ adj 13 requiring, using, great effort to achieve results quickly. crash helmet helmet worn by motorcyclists, etc. to protect head.

crass [kras] adj -er, -est 1 grossly stupid. 2 insensitive. crass'ness n

crate [krayt] n large (usu. wooden) container for packing goods.

cra·ter [KRAY-tər] n 1 mouth of volcano. 2 bowl-shaped cavity, esp. one made by explosion of large shell, bomb, mine, etc.

cra·vat [krə-VAT] n man's neckband or scarf.

crave [krayv] v craved, crav·ing 1 have very strong desire for, long for. ◆ vt 2 ask humbly. 3 beg. craving n

cra·ven [KRAY-vən] adj 1 cowardly, abject, spineless. ◆ n 2 coward. cra'ven·ness n

craw [kraw] n 1 bird's or animal's stomach. 2 bird's crop.

crawl [krawl] vi 1 move on belly or on hands and knees. 2 move very slowly. 3 ingratiate oneself, cringe. 4 swim with crawl stroke. 5 be overrun (with). ◆ n 6 crawling motion. 7 very slow walk. 8 racing stroke at swimming.

cray·fish [KRAY-fish] n edible freshwater crustacean like lobster (also cray'fish).

cray·on [KRAY-on] n stick or pencil of colored chalk, wax, etc.

craze [krayz] n 1 short-lived current fashion. 2 strong desire or passion, mania. 3 madness. crazed adj 1 demented. 2 (of porcelain) having fine cracks. cra'zy adj -zi·er, -zi·est 1 insane. 2 very foolish. 3 madly eager (for). crazy quilt 1 patchwork quilt of irregular patches. 2 jumble.

creak [kreek] n 1 harsh grating noise. ◆ vi 2 make creaking sound.

cream [kreem] n 1 fatty part of milk. 2 various foods, dishes, resembling cream. 3 cosmetic, etc. with creamlike consistency. 4 yellowish-white color. 5 best part of anything. ◆ vt 6 take cream from. 7 take

cranny n = crevice, chink, cleft, crack, fissure, gap, hole, opening

crash n 1 = collision, accident, bump, pile-up (inf), smash, wreck 2 = smash, bang, boom, clang, clash, clatter, din, racket, thunder 3 = depression, downfall, failure, ruin ◆ v 4 = collide, bump (into), crash-land (an aircraft), drive into, have an accident, hit, plow into, wreck 5 = collapse, be ruined, fail, fold, fold up, go belly up (inf), go bust (inf), go to the wall, go under 6 = hurtle, fall headlong, give way, lurch, overbalance, plunge, topple

crass adj = insensitive, boorish, gross, indelicate, oafish, stupid, unrefined, witless

crate n = container, box, case, packing case, tea chest

crater n = hollow, depression, dip

crave v 1 = long for, desire, hanker after, hope for, lust after, want, yearn for 2 = beg, ask, beseech, entreat, implore, petition, plead for, pray for, seek, solicit, supplicate

craving n = longing, appetite, desire, hankering, hope, hunger, thirst, yearning, yen (inf)

crawl v 1 = creep, advance slowly, inch, slither, worm one's way, wriggle, writhe 2 = grovel, brown-nose (sl), creep, fawn, humble oneself, kiss ass (sl), toady 3 = be full of, be alive, be overrun (sl), swarm, teem

craze n = fad, enthusiasm, fashion, infatuation, mania, rage, trend, vogue

crazy adj 1 = ridiculous, absurd, foolish, idiotic, ill-conceived, ludicrous, nonsensical, preposterous, senseless 2 = fanatical, devoted, enthusiastic, infatuated, mad, passionate, wild (inf) 3 = insane, crazed, demented, deranged, mad, nuts (sl), out of one's mind, unbalanced

creak v = squeak, grate, grind, groan,

best part from. **8** beat to creamy consistency. **cream'y** *adj* **cream·i·er, cream·i·est**

crease [krees] *n* **1** line made by folding. **2** wrinkle. **3** *Ice Hockey* marked rectangular area in front of goal cage. **4** superficial bullet wound. ♦ *v* **creased, creas·ing 5** make, develop creases.

cre·ate [kree-AYT] *v* **-at·ed, -at·ing** ♦ *vt* **1** bring into being. **2** give rise to. **3** make. ♦ *vi* **4** *inf* make a fuss. **cre·a'tion** *n* **cre·a'tive** *adj* **cre·a'tor** *n*

crea·ture [KREE-chər] *n* **1** living being. **2** thing created. **3** dependent, tool (of another). **creature comforts** bodily comforts.

crèche [kresh] *n* representation of the Nativity scene.

cre·dence [KREED-ns] *n* **1** belief, credit. **2** small table for bread and wine of the Eucharist.

cre·den·tials [kri-DEN-shəlz] *pl n* **1** testimonials. **2** letters of introduction, esp. those given to ambassador.

cred·i·ble [KRED-ə-bəl] *adj* **1** worthy of belief. **2** trustworthy. **cred·i·bil'i·ty** *n*

cred·it [KRED-it] *n* **1** commendation, approval. **2** source, cause, of honor. **3** belief, trust. **4** good name. **5** influence, honor or power based on trust of others. **6** system of allowing customers to take goods for later payment. **7** money at one's disposal in bank, etc. **8** side of ledger on which such sums are entered. **9** reputation for financial reliability. ♦ *pl* **10** list of those responsible for production of film, etc. ♦ *vt* **11** attribute, believe that person has. **12** believe. **13** put on credit side of account. **cred'it·a·ble** *adj* bringing honor. **cred'i·tor** *n* one to whom debt is due.

cred·u·lous [KREJ-ə-ləs] *adj* too easy of belief, easily deceived or imposed on,

———————— THESAURUS ————————

scrape, scratch, screech

cream *n* **1** = **lotion**, cosmetic, emulsion, essence, liniment, oil, ointment, paste, salve, unguent **2** = **best**, *crème de la crème*, elite, flower, pick, prime ♦ *adj* **3** = **off-white**, yellowish-white

creamy *adj* = **smooth**, buttery, milky, rich, soft, velvety

crease *n* **1** = **line**, corrugation, fold, groove, ridge, wrinkle ♦ *v* **2** = **wrinkle**, corrugate, crumple, double up, fold, rumple, screw up

create *v* **1** = **make**, compose, devise, formulate, invent, originate, produce, spawn **2** = **cause**, bring about, lead to, occasion **3** = **appoint**, constitute, establish, install, invest, make, set up

creation *n* **1** = **making**, conception, formation, generation, genesis, procreation **2** = **setting up**, development, establishment, formation, foundation, inception, institution, production **3** = **invention**, achievement, brainchild (*inf*), concoction, handiwork, magnum opus, *pièce de résistance*, production **4** = **universe**, cosmos, nature, world

creative *adj* = **imaginative**, artistic, clever, gifted, ingenious, inspired, inventive, original, visionary

creativity *n* = **imagination**, cleverness, ingenuity, inspiration, inventiveness, originality

creator *n* = **maker**, architect, author,

designer, father, inventor, originator, prime mover

creature *n* **1** = **living thing**, animal, beast, being, brute **2** = **person**, human being, individual, man, mortal, soul, woman

credentials *pl n* = **certification**, authorization, document, license, papers, passport, reference(s), testimonial

credibility *n* = **believability**, integrity, plausibility, reliability, trustworthiness

credible *adj* **1** = **believable**, conceivable, imaginable, likely, plausible, possible, probable, reasonable, thinkable **2** = **reliable**, dependable, honest, sincere, trustworthy, trusty

credit *n* **1** = **praise**, acclaim, acknowledgment, approval, commendation, honor, kudos, recognition, tribute **2** *As in* **be a credit to** = **source of satisfaction** *or* **pride**, feather in one's cap, honor **3** = **prestige**, esteem, good name, influence, position, regard, reputation, repute, standing, status **4** = **belief**, confidence, credence, faith, reliance, trust **5 on credit** = **on account**, by deferred payment, by installments, on the card ♦ *v* **6** = **believe**, accept, have faith in, rely on, trust **7** **credit with** = **attribute to**, ascribe to, assign to, impute to

creditable *adj* = **praiseworthy**, admirable, commendable, honorable, laudable, reputable, respectable, worthy

credulity *n* = **gullibility**, blind faith,

gullible. **cre·du·li·ty** [krə-DOO-li-tee] n

creed [kreed] n 1 formal statement of religious beliefs. 2 statement, system of beliefs or principles.

creek [kreek] n narrow inlet on seacoast.

creel [kreel] n angler's fishing basket.

creep [kreep] vi **crept, creep·ing** 1 make way along ground, as snake. 2 move with stealthy, slow movements. 3 crawl. 4 act in servile way. 5 of skin or flesh, feel shrinking, shivering sensation, due to fear or repugnance. ◆ n 6 creeping. 7 sl repulsive person. ◆ pl 8 feeling of fear or repugnance. **creep'er** n creeping or climbing plant, such as ivy. **creep'y** adj **creep·i·er, creep·i·est** inf 1 uncanny, unpleasant. 2 causing flesh to creep.

cre·ma·tion [kri-MAY-shən] n burning as means of disposing of corpses. **cre·mate** [KREE-mayt] vt **-mat·ed, -mat·ing cre·ma·to·ri·um** [kree-mə-TOR-ee-əm] n place for cremation.

cre·ole [KREE-ohl] n 1 hybrid language. 2 (C-) native born W Indian, Latin American, of European descent.

cre·o·sote [KREE-ə-soht] n 1 oily antiseptic liquid distilled from coal or wood tar, used for preserving wood. ◆ vt **-sot·ed, -sot·ing** 2 coat or impregnate with creosote.

crepe [krayp] n 1 fabric with crimped surface. 2 crape. 3 thin, light pancake. **crepe rubber** rough-surfaced rubber used for soles of shoes.

crept pt./pp. of CREEP.

cre·scen·do [kri-SHEN-doh] n gradual increase of loudness, esp. in music. ◆ adj, adv

cres·cent [KRES-ənt] n (shape of) moon as seen in first or last quarter. 1 any figure of this shape. 2 curved portion of a street.

crest [krest] n 1 comb or tuft on bird's or animal's head. 2 plume on top of helmet. 3 top of mountain, ridge, wave, etc. 4 badge above shield of coat of arms, also used separately on seal, plate, etc. ◆ vi 5 crown. ◆ vt 6 reach top of. **crest'fall·en** adj cast down by failure, dejected.

cre·ta·ceous [kri-TAY-shəs] adj chalky.

cre·tin [KREET-n] n 1 offens stupid or mentally defective person. 2 obs person afflicted with deficiency in thyroid gland causing physical and mental retardation.

cre·vasse [kri-VAS] n deep open chasm, esp. in glacier.

crev·ice [KREV-is] n cleft, fissure, chink.

crew [kroo] n 1 ship's, boat's or aircraft's company, excluding passengers. 2 inf gang or set. ◆ v 3 serve as crew. **crew cut** closely cropped haircut.

crew·el [KROO-əl] n fine worsted yarn, used in needlework and embroidery.

crib [krib] n 1 child's cot. 2 barred rack used for fodder. 3 plagiarism. 4 translation used by students, sometimes illicitly. ◆ vt **cribbed, crib·bing** 5 confine in small space. 6 copy unfairly.

crib·bage [KRIB-ij] n card game for two, three, or four players.

crick [krik] n spasm or cramp in muscles, esp. in neck.

——————— THESAURUS ———————

credulousness, naivety

creed n = **belief**, articles of faith, catechism, credo, doctrine, dogma, principles

creek n = **stream**, bayou, brook, rivulet, runnel, tributary, watercourse

creep v 1 = **sneak**, approach unnoticed, skulk, slink, steal, tiptoe 2 = **crawl**, glide, slither, squirm, wriggle, writhe ◆ n 3 Sl = **brown-noser** (sl), crawler (sl), scuzzbucket (sl), sneak, sycophant, toady 4 Sl = **jerk**, loser, lowlife, pervert, scumbag (sl), scuzzbucket (sl)

creeper n = **climbing plant**, rambler, runner, trailing plant, vine

creeps pl n **give one the creeps** Inf = **disgust**, frighten, make one's hair stand on end, make one squirm, repel, repulse, scare

creepy adj Inf = **disturbing**, eerie,

frightening, hair-raising, macabre, menacing, scary (inf), sinister

crescent n = **meniscus**, new moon, sickle

crest n 1 = **top**, apex, crown, highest point, peak, pinnacle, ridge, summit 2 = **tuft**, comb, crown, mane, plume 3 = **emblem**, badge, bearings, device, insignia, symbol

crestfallen adj = **disappointed**, dejected, depressed, despondent, discouraged, disheartened, downcast, downhearted

crevice n = **gap**, chink, cleft, crack, cranny, fissure, hole, opening, slit

crew n 1 = **(ship's) company**, hands, (ship's) complement 2 = **team**, corps, gang, posse, squad 3 Inf = **crowd**, band, bunch (inf), gang, horde, mob, pack, set

crib n 1 = **cradle**, bassinet, bed, cot 2 = **manger**, rack, stall ◆ v 3 Inf = **copy**, cheat, pirate, plagiarize, purloin, steal

crick•et[1] [KRIK-it] *n* chirping insect.
cricket[2] *n* outdoor game played with bats, ball and wickets by teams of eleven a side. **crick'et•er** *n*
crime [krīm] *n* 1 violation of law (usu. a serious offense). 2 wicked or forbidden act. 3 *inf* something to be regretted. **crim•i•nal** [KRIM-ə-nl] *adj, n* **crim•i•nal'i•ty** *n* **crim•i•nol'o•gy** *n* study of crime and criminals.
crimp [krimp] *vt* 1 pinch into tiny parallel pleats. 2 wrinkle.
crim•son [KRIM-zən] *adj, n* (of) rich deep red.
cringe [krinj] *vi* **cringed, cring•ing** 1 shrink, cower. 2 behave obsequiously.
crin•kle [KRING-kəl] *v, n* **-kled, -kling** wrinkle.
crin•o•line [KRIN-l-in] *n* hooped petticoat or skirt of stiff material.
crip•ple [KRIP-əl] *n* 1 *offens* one not having normal use of limbs, disabled or deformed person. ◆ *vt* **-pled, -pling** 2 maim, disable, impair. 3 weaken, lessen efficiency of.
cri•sis [KRĪ-sis] *n, pl* **-ses** [-seez] 1 turning point or decisive moment, esp. in illness. 2

time of acute danger or difficulty.
crisp [krisp] *adj* **-er, -est** 1 brittle but firm. 2 brisk, decided. 3 clear-cut. 4 fresh, invigorating. 5 crackling. 6 of hair, curly. ◆ *n* 7 dessert of fruit baked with a crunchy mixture. **crisp'er** *n* refrigerator compartment for storing salads, etc.
cri•te•ri•on [krī-TEER-ee-ən] *n, pl* **-ri•a** [-ree-ə] standard of judgment.
crit•i•cal [KRIT-i-kəl] *adj* 1 faultfinding. 2 discerning. 3 skilled in or given to judging. 4 of great importance, crucial, decisive. **crit'ic** *n* 1 one who passes judgment. 2 writer expert in judging works of literature, art, etc. **crit'i•cism** *n* **crit'i•cize** *vt* **-cized, ciz•ing critique** [kri-TEEK] *n* critical essay, carefully written criticism.
croak [krohk] *v* 1 utter deep hoarse cry, as raven, frog. 2 talk dismally. ◆ *vi* 3 *sl* die. ◆ *n* 4 deep hoarse cry.
cro•chet [kroh-SHAY] *n* 1 kind of handicraft like knitting, done with small hooked needle. ◆ *v* 2 do, make such work.
crock [krok] *n* 1 earthenware jar or pot. 2 broken piece of earthenware. **crock'er•y** *n* earthenware dishes, utensils, etc.

crime *n* 1 = **offense**, felony, misdeed, misdemeanor, transgression, trespass, unlawful act, violation 2 = **lawbreaking**, corruption, illegality, misconduct, vice, wrongdoing
criminal *n* 1 = **lawbreaker**, convict, crook (*inf*), culprit, felon, offender, sinner, villain ◆ *adj* 2 = **unlawful**, corrupt, crooked (*inf*), illegal, illicit, immoral, lawless, wicked, wrong 3 = **disgraceful**, deplorable, foolish, preposterous, ridiculous, scandalous, senseless
cringe *v* = **shrink**, cower, draw back, flinch, recoil, shy, wince
cripple *v* 1 = **disable**, hamstring, incapacitate, lame, maim, paralyze, weaken 2 = **damage**, destroy, impair, put out of action, put paid to, ruin, spoil
crippled *adj* = **disabled**, challenged, handicapped, incapacitated, laid up (*inf*), lame, paralyzed
crisis *n* 1 = **critical point**, climax, crunch (*inf*), crux, culmination, height, moment of truth, turning point 2 = **emergency**, deep water, dire straits, meltdown (*inf*), panic stations (*inf*), plight, predicament, trouble
crisp *adj* 1 = **crunchy**, brittle, crispy, crumbly, firm, fresh 2 = **clean**, neat, smart,

spruce, tidy, trim, well-groomed, well-pressed 3 = **bracing**, brisk, fresh, invigorating, refreshing
criterion *n* = **standard**, bench mark, gauge, measure, principle, rule, test, touchstone, yardstick
critic *n* 1 = **judge**, analyst, authority, commentator, connoisseur, expert, pundit, reviewer 2 = **fault-finder**, attacker, detractor, knocker (*inf*)
critical *adj* 1 = **crucial**, all-important, decisive, pivotal, precarious, pressing, serious, urgent, vital 2 = **disparaging**, captious, censorious, derogatory, disapproving, fault-finding, nagging, nit-picking (*inf*), scathing 3 = **analytical**, discerning, discriminating, fastidious, judicious, penetrating, perceptive
criticism *n* 1 = **fault-finding**, bad press, censure, character assassination, disapproval, disparagement, flak (*inf*), stick (*sl*) 2 = **analysis**, appraisal, appreciation, assessment, comment, commentary, critique, evaluation, judgment
criticize *v* = **find fault with**, carp, censure, condemn, disapprove of, disparage, knock (*inf*), put down
croak *v* = **squawk**, caw, grunt, utter or

croc·o·dile [KROK-ə-dīl] *n* 1 large amphibious reptile. **crocodile tears** insincere grief.

crois·sant [krwah-SAHN] *n* buttery, crescent-shaped roll of leavened dough or puff pastry.

crone [krohn] *n* witchlike old woman.

cro·ny [KROH-nee] *n, pl* **-nies** intimate friend

crook [kruuk] *n* 1 hooked staff. 2 any hook, bend, sharp turn. 3 *inf* swindler, criminal. **crook·ed** *adj* 1 bent, twisted. 2 deformed. 3 dishonest.

croon [kroon] *v* hum, sing in soft, low tone. **croon·er** *n*

crop [krop] *n* 1 produce of cultivation of any plant or plants. 2 harvest. 3 pouch in bird's gullet. 4 stock of whip. 5 hunting whip. 6 short haircut. ◆ *v* **cropped, crop·ping** 7 cut short. 8 raise, produce or occupy land with crop. 9 (of animals) bite, eat down. 10 poll or clip. **crop'-dust·ing** *n* spreading fungicide, etc. on crops from aircraft. **crop up** *inf* happen unexpectedly.

cro·quet [kroh-KAY] *n* lawn game played with balls, wooden mallets and hoops.

cro·quette [kroh-KET] *n* breaded, fried ball of minced meat, fish, etc.

cro·sier [KROH-zhər] *n* bishop's or abbot's staff.

cross [kraws] *n* 1 structure or symbol of two intersecting lines or pieces (at right angles). 2 such a structure of wood as means of execution by tying or nailing victim to it. 3 symbol of Christian faith. 4 any thing or mark in the shape of cross. 5 misfortune, annoyance, affliction. 6 intermixture of breeds, hybrid. ◆ *v* 7 move or go across (something). 8 intersect. 9 meet and pass. ◆ *vt* 10 mark with lines across. 11 (with *out*) delete. 12 place or put in form of cross. 13 make sign of cross on or over. 14 modify breed of animals or plants by intermixture. 15 thwart. 16 oppose. ◆ *adj* 17 out of temper, angry. 18 peevish, perverse. 19 transverse. 20 intersecting. 21 contrary. 22 adverse. **cross'ing** *n* 1 intersection of roads, rails, etc. 2 part of street where pedestrians are expected to cross. **cross'ly** *adv* **cross'wise** *adv, adj* **cross'bow** [-boh] *n* bow fixed across wooden shoulder stock. **cross'breed** *n* breed produced from parents of different breeds. **cross-country** *adj, n* (long race) held over open ground. **cross'-ex·am·ine** *vt* examine witness already examined by other side. **cross'-eyed** *adj* having eye(s) turning inward. **cross'-fer·ti·li·za·tion** *n* fertilization of one plant by pollen of another. **cross'-grained'** *adj* having fibers running diagonally, etc. 1 perverse. **cross'-ref'er·ence** *n* reference within text to another part of text. **cross section** 1 transverse section. 2 group of people fully representative of a nation, community, etc. **cross'word puzzle** puzzle built up of intersecting words, of which some letters are common, the words being indicated by clues.

speak huskily, wheeze

crook *n* = **criminal**, cheat, racketeer, robber, rogue, shark, swindler, thief, villain

crooked *adj* 1 = **bent**, curved, deformed, distorted, hooked, irregular, misshapen, out of shape, twisted, warped, zigzag 2 = **at an angle**, askew, awry, lopsided, off-center, slanting, squint, uneven 3 = **dishonest**, bent (*sl*), corrupt, criminal, fraudulent, illegal, shady (*inf*), underhand, unlawful

croon *v* = **sing**, hum, purr, warble

crop *n* 1 = **produce**, fruits, gathering, harvest, reaping, vintage, yield ◆ *v* 2 = **cut**, clip, lop, pare, prune, shear, snip, trim 3 = **graze**, browse, nibble

crop up *v* = **happen**, appear, arise, emerge, occur, spring up, turn up

cross *v* 1 = **go across**, bridge, cut across, extend over, move across, pass over, span, traverse 2 = **intersect**, crisscross, intertwine 3 = **oppose**, block, impede, interfere, obstruct, resist 4 = **interbreed**, blend, crossbreed, cross-fertilize, cross-pollinate, hybridize, intercross, mix, mongrelize ◆ *n* 5 = **crucifix**, rood 6 = **crossroads**, crossing, intersection, junction 7 = **mixture**, amalgam, blend, combination 8 = **trouble**, affliction, burden, grief, load, misfortune, trial, tribulation, woe, worry ◆ *adj* 9 = **angry**, annoyed, grumpy, ill-tempered, in a bad mood, irascible, put out, short 10 = **transverse**, crosswise, diagonal, intersecting

cross-examine *v* = **question**, grill (*inf*), interrogate, pump, quiz

cross out *or* **off** *v* = **strike off** *or* **out**, blue-pencil, cancel, delete, eliminate, score

crotch [kroch] n **1** angle between legs, genital area. **2** fork.

crotch·et [KROCH-it] n musical note, equal to half the length of a minim.

crotch·et·y [KROCH-i-tee] adj **1** peevish. **2** irritable.

crouch [krowch] vi **1** bend low. **2** huddle down close to ground. **3** stoop servilely, cringe. ♦ n

croup [kroop] n throat disease of children, with cough.

crou·pi·er [KROO-pee-ər] n person dealing cards, collecting money, etc. at gambling table.

crow[1] [kroh] n large black scavenging bird. **crow's'-foot** n wrinkle at corner of eye. **crow's'-nest** n lookout platform high on ship's mast.

crow[2] vi **1** utter rooster's cry. **2** boast one's happiness or superiority. ♦ n **3** rooster's cry.

crow·bar [KROH-bahr] n iron or steel bar, usu. wedge-shaped, for levering.

crowd [krowd] n **1** throng, mass. ♦ vi **2** flock together. ♦ vt **3** cram, force, thrust, pack. **4** fill with people. **crowd out** exclude by excess already in.

crown [krown] n **1** monarch's headdress. **2** wreath for head. **3** monarch. **4** monarchy. **5** royal power. **6** various foreign coins. **7** top of head. **8** summit, top. **9** completion or perfection of thing. ♦ vt **10** put crown on. **11** confer title. **12** occur as culmination of series of events. **13** inf hit on head. **crown prince** heir to throne.

cru·cial [KROO-shəl] adj **1** decisive, critical. **2** inf very important.

cru·ci·ble [KROO-sə-bəl] n small melting pot.

cru·ci·fy [KROO-sə-fī] vt **-fied, -fy·ing 1** put to death on cross. **2** treat cruelly. **3** inf ridicule. **cru'ci·fix** [-fiks] n **1** cross. **2** image of (Christ on the) Cross. **cru·ci·fix'ion** n

crude [krood] adj **crud·er, crud·est 1** lacking taste, vulgar. **2** in natural or raw state, unrefined. **3** rough, unfinished. **cru'di·ty** n, pl **-ties**

cru·el [KROO-əl] adj **-er, -est 1** delighting in others' pain. **2** causing pain or suffering. **cru'el·ly** adv **cru'el·ty** n, pl **-ties**

THESAURUS

crouch v = **bend down**, bow, duck, hunch, kneel, squat, stoop

crow v = **gloat**, blow one's own trumpet, boast, brag, exult, strut, swagger, triumph

crowd n **1** = **multitude**, army, horde, host, mass, mob, swarm, throng **2** = **group**, bunch (inf), circle, clique, lot, set **3** = **audience**, attendance, gate, house, spectators ♦ v **4** = **flock**, congregate, gather, mass, stream, surge, swarm, throng **5** = **squeeze**, bundle, congest, cram, pack, pile

crowded adj = **packed**, busy, congested, cramped, full, jam-packed, swarming, teeming

crown n **1** = **coronet**, circlet, diadem, tiara **2** = **laurel wreath**, garland, honor, laurels, prize, trophy, wreath **3** = **high point**, apex, crest, pinnacle, summit, tip, top ♦ v **4** = **honor**, adorn, dignify, festoon **5** = **cap**, be the climax or culmination of, complete, finish, perfect, put the finishing touch to, round off, top **6** Sl = **strike**, belt (inf), box, hit over the head, punch

Crown n **1** = **monarchy**, royalty, sovereignty **2** = **monarch**, emperor or empress, king or queen, ruler, sovereign

crucial adj **1** = **vital**, essential, high-priority, important, momentous, pressing, urgent **2** = **critical**, central, decisive, pivotal

crucify v = **execute**, persecute, torment, torture

crude adj **1** = **primitive**, clumsy, makeshift, rough, rough-and-ready, rudimentary, unpolished **2** = **vulgar**, coarse, dirty, gross, indecent, obscene, off-color, scuzzy (sl), smutty, tasteless, uncouth **3** = **unrefined**, natural, raw, unprocessed

crudely adv = **vulgarly**, bluntly, coarsely, impolitely, roughly, rudely, tastelessly

crudity n **1** = **roughness**, clumsiness, crudeness **2** = **vulgarity**, coarseness, impropriety, indecency, indelicacy, obscenity, smuttiness

cruel adj **1** = **brutal**, barbarous, callous, hard-hearted, heartless, inhumane, malevolent, sadistic, spiteful, unkind, vicious **2** = **merciless**, pitiless, ruthless, unrelenting

cruelly adv **1** = **brutally**, barbarously, callously, heartlessly, in cold blood, mercilessly, pitilessly, sadistically, spitefully **2** = **bitterly**, deeply, fearfully, grievously, monstrously, severely

cruelty n = **brutality**, barbarity, callousness, depravity, fiendishness, inhumanity, mercilessness, ruthlessness, spitefulness

cru·et [KROO-it] n 1 small container for salt, pepper, vinegar, oil, etc. 2 stand holding such containers.

cruise [krooz] vi **cruised, cruis·ing** 1 travel about in a ship for pleasure, etc. 2 (of vehicle, aircraft) travel at safe, average speed. ♦ n 3 cruising voyage. **cruis·er** n 1 ship that cruises. 2 warship lighter and faster than battleship. **cruise missile** subsonic missile guided throughout its flight.

crumb [krum] n 1 small particle, fragment, esp. of bread. ♦ vt 2 reduce to, break into, cover with crumbs.

crum·ble [KRUM-bəl] v **-bled, -bling** 1 break into small fragments, disintegrate, crush. 2 perish, decay. ♦ vi 3 fall apart or away. **crum'bly** adj **-bli·er, -bli·est**

crum·my [KRUM-ee] adj sl **-mi·er, -mi·est** inferior, contemptible.

crum·ple [KRUM-pəl] v **-pled, -pling** 1 (cause to) collapse. 2 make or become crushed, wrinkled, creased.

crunch [krunch] n 1 sound made by chewing crisp food, treading on gravel, hard snow, etc. 2 inf critical moment or situation. ♦ v 3 make crunching sound.

cru·sade [kroo-SAYD] n 1 medieval Christian war to recover Holy Land. 2 campaign against something believed to be evil. 3 concerted action to further a cause. ♦ vi **-sad·ed, -sad·ing cru·sad'er** n

crush¹ [krush] vt 1 compress so as to break, bruise, crumple. 2 break to small pieces. 3 defeat utterly, overthrow. ♦ n 4 act of crushing. 5 crowd of people, etc.

crush² n inf infatuation.

crust [krust] n 1 hard outer part of bread. 2 similar hard outer casing on anything. ♦ v 3 cover with, form, crust. **crust'i·ly** adv **crust'y** adj **crust·i·er, crust·i·est** 1 having, or like, crust. 2 harsh, surly. 3 rude.

crus·ta·cean [kru-STAY-shən] n hard-shelled animal, e.g. crab, lobster. ♦ adj

crutch [kruch] n 1 staff with crosspiece to go under armpit of lame person, device resembling this. 2 support. 3 groin, crotch.

crux [kruks] n, pl **-es** 1 that on which a decision turns. 2 anything that puzzles very much.

cry [krī] v **cried, cry·ing** ♦ vi 1 weep. 2 wail. 3 utter call. 4 shout. 5 clamor or beg (for). ♦ vt 6 utter loudly, proclaim. ♦ n 7 loud utterance. 8 scream, wail, shout. 9 call of animal. 10 fit of weeping. 11 watchword.

cry·o·gen·ics [krī-ə-JEN-iks] n branch of physics concerned with phenomena at very low temperatures. **cry·o·gen'ic** adj

crypt [kript] n vault, esp. under church. **cryp'tic** adj secret, mysterious. **cryp'ti·cal·ly** adv **cryp'to·gram** n piece of writing in code. **cryp·tog'ra·phy** n art of writing, decoding ciphers.

crys·tal [KRIS-tl] n 1 clear transparent mineral. 2 very clear glass. 3 cut-glass

——————| THESAURUS |——————

cruise n 1 = **sail**, boat trip, sea trip, voyage ♦ v 2 = **sail**, coast, voyage 3 = **travel along**, coast, drift, keep a steady pace

crumb n = **bit**, fragment, grain, morsel, scrap, shred, soupçon

crumble v 1 = **disintegrate**, collapse, decay, degenerate, deteriorate, fall apart, go to pieces, go to rack and ruin, tumble down 2 = **crush**, fragment, granulate, grind, pound, powder, pulverize

crummy adj Inf 1 = **despicable**, contemptible, lousy (sl), mean, scuzzy (sl) 2 = **inferior**, deficient, inadequate, lousy (sl), of poor quality, poor, substandard 3 = **unwell**, below par, off color, under the weather (inf)

crumple v 1 = **crush**, crease, rumple, screw up, scrumple, wrinkle 2 = **collapse**, break down, cave in, fall, give way, go to pieces

crunch v 1 = **chomp**, champ, chew noisily, grind, munch ♦ n 2 Inf = **critical point**, crisis, crux, emergency, moment of truth, test

crusade n = **campaign**, cause, drive, movement, push

crush v 1 = **squash**, break, compress, press, pulverize, squeeze 2 = **overcome**, conquer, overpower, overwhelm, put down, quell, stamp out, subdue 3 = **humiliate**, abash, mortify, put down (sl), quash, shame ♦ n 4 = **crowd**, huddle, jam

crust n = **layer**, coating, covering, shell, skin, surface

crusty adj 1 = **crispy**, hard 2 = **irritable**, cantankerous, cross, gruff, prickly, short-tempered, testy

cry v 1 = **weep**, blubber, shed tears, snivel, sob 2 = **shout**, bawl, bellow, call out, exclaim, howl, roar, scream, shriek, yell ♦ n 3 = **weeping**, blubbering, snivelling, sob, sobbing, weep 4 = **shout**, bellow, call, exclamation, howl, roar, scream, screech, ware. **4** characteristic form assumed by many substances, with definite internal structure and external shape of symmetrically arranged plane surfaces. **crys·tal·line** [-tl-in] *adj* **crys·tal·li·za'tion** *n* **crys·tal·lize** *v* **-lized, -liz·ing 1** form into crystals. **2** become definite.

Cs *Chem.* cesium.

Cu *Chem.* copper.

cub [kub] *n* **1** young of fox and other animals. **2** cub scout. ◆ *v* **cubbed, cub·bing 3** bring forth cubs. **cub scout** member of junior division of the Boy Scouts.

cub·by·hole [KUB-ee-hohl] *n* **1** small, enclosed space or room. **2** pigeonhole.

cube [kyoob] *n* **1** regular solid figure contained by six equal square sides. **2** cube-shaped block. **3** product obtained by multiplying number by itself twice. ◆ *vt* **cubed, cub·ing 4** multiply thus. **cu'bic** *adj* **cub'ism** *n* style of art in which objects are presented as assemblage of geometrical shapes. **cub'ist** *n, adj*

cu·bi·cle [KYOO-bi-kəl] *n* partially or totally enclosed section of room, as in study hall.

cu·bit [KYOO-bit] *n* old measure of length, about 18 inches.

cuck·old [KUK-əld] *n* man whose wife has committed adultery. ◆ *vt*

cuck·oo [KOO-koo] *n, pl* **-oos 1** migratory bird that deposits its eggs in the nests of other birds. **2** its call. ◆ *adj sl* **3** crazy. ◆ *vi* **-ooed, -oo·ing**

cu·cum·ber [KYOO-kum-bər] *n* **1** plant with long fleshy green fruit. **2** the fruit, used in salad.

cud [kud] *n* food that ruminant animal brings back into mouth to chew again. **chew the cud** reflect, meditate.

cud·dle [KUD-l] *v* **-dled, -dling** ◆ *vt* **1** hug.

◆ *vi* **2** lie close and snug, nestle. ◆ *n*

cudg·el [KUJ-əl] *n* **1** short thick stick. ◆ *vt* **-eled, -el·ing 2** beat with cudgel.

cue¹ [kyoo] *n* **1** last words of actor's speech, etc. as signal to another to act or speak. **2** signal, hint, example for action.

cue² *n* long tapering rod used in pool, billiards, etc.

cuff¹ [kuf] *n* **1** ending of sleeve. **2** wristband. **off the cuff** *inf* without preparation.

cuff² *vt* **1** strike with open hand. ◆ *n* **2** blow with hand.

cui·sine [kwi-ZEEN] *n* **1** style of cooking. **2** menu, food offered by restaurant, etc.

cul-de-sac [KUL-də-SAK] *n, pl* **culs-** [kulz-] **1** street, lane open only at one end. **2** blind alley.

cu·li·nar·y [KYOO-lə-ner-ee] *adj* of, for, suitable for, cooking or kitchen.

cull [kul] *vt* **1** gather, select. **2** take out selected animals from herd. ◆ *n* **3** something culled.

cul·mi·nate [KUL-mə-nayt] *vi* **-nat·ed, -nat·ing 1** reach highest point. **2** come to climax, to a head. **cul·mi·na'tion** *n*

cul·pa·ble [KUL-pə-bəl] *adj* blameworthy. **cul·pa·bil'i·ty** *n*

cul·prit [KUL-prit] *n* one guilty of usu. minor offense.

cult [kult] *n* **1** system of religious worship. **2** pursuit of, devotion to, some person, thing, or activity. **cult'ism** *n* practices of a religious cult. **cult'ist** *n*

cul·ti·vate [KUL-tə-vayt] *vt* **-vat·ed, -vat·ing 1** till and prepare (soil) to raise crops. **2** develop, improve, refine. **3** devote attention to, cherish. **4** practice. **5** foster. **cul·ti·va'tion** *n*

cul·ture [KUL-chər] *n* **1** state of manners,

━━━━━ |̲T̲H̲E̲S̲A̲U̲R̲U̲S̲| ━━━━━

shriek, yell **5 = appeal**, plea

cub *n* **= young**, offspring, whelp

cuckoo *adj Sl* **= insane**, bonkers (*inf*), crazy, daft (*inf*), foolish, idiotic, nuts (*sl*), out of one's mind, stupid

cuddle *v* **= hug**, bill and coo, cosset, embrace, fondle, pet, snuggle

cudgel *n* **= club**, baton, bludgeon, stick, truncheon

cue *n* **= signal**, catchword, hint, key, prompting, reminder, sign, suggestion

cul-de-sac *n* **= dead end**, blind alley

culminate *v* **= end up**, climax, close, come to a climax, come to a head, conclude,

finish, wind up

culmination *n* **= climax**, acme, conclusion, consummation, finale, peak, pinnacle, zenith

culpable *adj* **= blameworthy**, at fault, found wanting, guilty, in the wrong, to blame, wrong

culprit *n* **= offender**, criminal, evildoer, felon, guilty party, miscreant, transgressor, wrongdoer

cult *n* **1 = sect**, clique, faction, religion, school **2 = devotion**, idolization, worship

cultivate *v* **1 = farm**, plant, plow, tend, till, work **2 = develop**, foster, improve,

taste, and intellectual development at a time or place. **2** cultivating. **3** artificial rearing. **4** set of bacteria so reared.
cul'tur·al adj **cul'tured** adj refined, showing culture. **cultured pearl** pearl artificially induced to grow in oyster shell.
cul·vert [KUL-vərt] n tunneled drain for passage of water under road, railroad, etc.
oum·bor·oome [KUM bər ɔəm] adj awkward, unwieldy.
cu·mu·la·tive [KYOO-myə-lə-tiv] adj **1** becoming greater by successive additions. **2** representing the sum of many items.
cu·mu·lus [KYOO-myə-ləs] n, pl **-li** [-lī] cloud shaped in rounded white woolly masses.
cu·ne·i·form [kyoo-NEE-ə-form] adj wedge-shaped, esp. of ancient Babylonian writing.
cun·ning [KUN-ing] adj **1** crafty, sly. **2** ingenious. **3** cute. ◆ n **4** skill in deceit or evasion. **5** skill, ingenuity.
cup [kup] n **1** small drinking vessel with handle at one side. **2** any small drinking vessel. **3** contents of cup. **4** various cup-shaped formations, cavities, sockets, etc. **5** cup-shaped trophy as prize. **6** portion or lot. **7** iced drink of wine and other ingredients. ◆ vt **cupped, cup·ping 8** shape as cup (hands, etc.). **cup·ful** n, pl **-fuls cup·board** [KUB-ərd] n piece of furniture, recess in room, with door, for storage.
Cu·pid [KYOO-pid] n god of love.

cu·pid·i·ty [kyoo-PID-i-tee] n **1** greed for possessions. **2** covetousness.
cu·po·la [KYOO-pə-lə] n dome.
cu·pre·ous [KYOO-pree-əs] adj of, containing, copper.
cur [kur] n **1** dog of mixed breed. **2** surly, contemptible, or mean person.
cu·ra·re [kyuu-RAHR-ee] n poisonous resin of S Amer. tree, now used as muscle relaxant in medicine.
cu·rate [KYUUR-it] n parish priest. **cu'ra·cy** n office or term of office of curate.
cur·a·tive [KYUUR-ə-tiv] adj tending to cure disease. ◆ n medicine.
cu·ra·tor [kyuur-AY-tər] n person in charge, esp. of museum, library, etc.
curb [kurb] n **1** check, restraint. **2** chain or strap passing under horse's lower jaw and giving powerful control with reins. **3** edging, esp. of stone or concrete, along street, path, etc. ◆ vt **4** restrain. **5** apply curb to.
curd [kurd] n **1** coagulated milk. **cur·dle** [KUR-dl] v **-dled, -dling 1** turn into curd, coagulate.
cure [kyuur] vt **cured, cur·ing 1** heal, restore to health. **2** remedy. **3** preserve (fish, skins, etc.). ◆ n **4** remedy. **5** course of medical treatment. **6** successful treatment, restoration to health. **cur'a·ble** adj
cu·rette [kyuu-RET] n surgical instrument for removing dead tissue, etc. from some body cavities. **cu·ret·tage** [kyuur-i-TAHZH] n

──────[THESAURUS]──────

promote, refine **3** = **court**, dance attendance upon, run after, seek out
cultivation n **1** = **farming**, gardening, husbandry, planting, plowing, tillage **2** = **development**, encouragement, fostering, furtherance, nurture, patronage, promotion, support
cultural adj = **artistic**, civilizing, edifying, educational, enlightening, enriching, humane, liberal
culture n **1** = **civilization**, customs, lifestyle, mores, society, way of life **2** = **refinement**, education, enlightenment, good taste, sophistication, urbanity **3** = **farming**, cultivation, husbandry
cultured adj = **refined**, educated, enlightened, highbrow, sophisticated, urbane, well-informed, well-read
culvert n = **drain**, channel, conduit, gutter, watercourse

cumbersome adj = **awkward**, bulky, burdensome, heavy, unmanageable, unwieldy, weighty
cunning adj **1** = **crafty**, artful, devious, Machiavellian, sharp, shifty, sly, wily **2** = **skillful**, imaginative, ingenious ◆ n **3** = **craftiness**, artfulness, deviousness, guile, slyness, trickery **4** = **skill**, artifice, cleverness, ingenuity, subtlety
cup n **1** = **mug**, beaker, bowl, chalice, goblet, teacup **2** = **trophy**
cupboard n = **cabinet**, press
curb n **1** = **restraint**, brake, bridle, check, control, deterrent, limitation, rein ◆ v **2** = **restrain**, check, control, hinder, impede, inhibit, restrict, retard, suppress
cure v **1** = **make better**, correct, ease, heal, mend, relieve, remedy, restore **2** = **preserve**, dry, pickle, salt, smoke ◆ n **3** = **remedy**, antidote, medicine, nostrum,

cur·few [KUR-fyoo] *n* **1** official regulation restricting or prohibiting movement of people, esp. at night. **2** time set as deadline by such regulation.

cu·rie [KYUUR-ee] *n* standard unit of radium emanation.

cu·ri·o [KYUUR-ee-oh] *n, pl* **-ri·os** rare or curious thing of the kind sought for collections.

cu·ri·ous [KYUUR-ee-əs] *adj* **1** eager to know, inquisitive. **2** prying. **3** puzzling, strange, odd. **cu·ri·os'i·ty** *n, pl* **-ties 1** eagerness to know. **2** inquisitiveness. **3** strange or rare thing.

cu·ri·um [KYUUR-ee-əm] *n* element produced from plutonium.

curl [kurl] *vi* **1** take spiral or curved shape or path. ◆ *vt* **2** bend into spiral or curved shape. ◆ *n* **3** spiral lock of hair. **4** spiral, curved state, form or motion. **curl'ing** *n* target game played with large rounded stones on ice. **curl'y** *adj* **curl·i·er, curl·i·est**

cur·mudg·eon [kər-MUJ-ən] *n* surly or miserly person.

cur·rent [KUR-ənt] *adj* **1** of immediate present, going on. **2** up-to-date, not yet superseded. **3** in circulation or general use. ◆ *n* **4** body of water or air in motion. **5** tendency, drift. **6** transmission of electricity through conductor. **cur'ren·cy** *n* **1** money in use. **2** state of being in use. **3** time during which thing is current.

cur·ric·u·lum [kə-RIK-yə-ləm] *n, pl* **-la** [-lə] specified course of study.

cur·ry¹ [KUR-ee] *n, pl* **-ries 1** highly-flavored, pungent condiment. **2** meat, etc. dish flavored with curry. ◆ *vt* **-ried, -ry·ing 3** prepare, flavor dish with curry.

curry² *vt* **-ried, -ry·ing 1** groom (horse) with comb. **2** dress (leather). **curry favor** try to win favor unworthily, ingratiate oneself.

curse [kurs] *n* **1** profane or obscene expression of anger, etc. **2** utterance expressing extreme ill toward some person or thing. **3** affliction, misfortune, scourge. ◆ *v* **cursed, curs·ing 4** utter curse, swear (at). **5** afflict. **curs·ed** [KUR-sid] *adj* **1** hateful. **2** wicked. **3** deserving of, or under, a curse.

cur·sive [KUR-siv] *adj, n* (written in) running script, with letters joined.

cur·so·ry [KUR-sə-ree] *adj* rapid, hasty, not detailed, superficial. **cur'so·ri·ly** *adv*

curt [kurt] *adj* **-er, -est** short, rudely brief, abrupt. **curt'ness** *n*

cur·tail [kər-TAYL] *vt* cut short, diminish.

cur·tain [KUR-tn] *n* **1** hanging drapery at window, etc. **2** cloth hung as screen. **3** screen separating audience and stage in theater. **4** end to act or scene, etc. ◆ *pl* **5** *sl* death. ◆ *vt* **6** provide, cover with curtain.

panacea, treatment

curiosity *n* **1** = **inquisitiveness**, interest, nosiness (*inf*), prying, snooping (*inf*) **2** = **oddity**, freak, novelty, phenomenon, rarity, sight, spectacle, wonder

curious *adj* **1** = **inquiring**, inquisitive, interested, questioning, searching **2** = **inquisitive**, meddling, nosy (*inf*), prying **3** = **unusual**, bizarre, extraordinary, mysterious, novel, odd, peculiar, rare, strange, unexpected

curl *v* **1** = **twirl**, bend, coil, curve, loop, spiral, turn, twist, wind ◆ *n* **2** = **twist**, coil, kink, ringlet, spiral, whorl

curly *adj* = **curling**, crinkly, curled, frizzy, fuzzy, wavy, winding

currency *n* **1** = **money**, coinage, coins, notes **2** = **acceptance**, circulation, exposure, popularity, prevalence, vogue

current *adj* **1** = **present**, contemporary, cool (*inf*), fashionable, in fashion, in vogue, phat (*sl*), present-day, trendy (*inf*), up-to-date **2** = **prevalent**, accepted, common, customary, in circulation, popular, topical, widespread ◆ *n* **3** = **flow**, course, draft, jet, progression, river, stream, tide, undertow **4** = **mood**, atmosphere, feeling, tendency, trend, undercurrent

curse *v* **1** = **swear**, blaspheme, cuss (*inf*), take the Lord's name in vain **2** = **damn**, anathematize, excommunicate ◆ *n* **3** = **oath**, blasphemy, expletive, obscenity, swearing, swearword **4** = **denunciation**, anathema, ban, excommunication, hoodoo (*inf*), jinx **5** = **affliction**, bane, hardship, plague, scourge, torment, trouble

cursed *adj* = **damned**, accursed, bedevilled, doomed, ill-fated

curt *adj* = **short**, abrupt, blunt, brief, brusque, gruff, monosyllabic, succinct, terse

curtail *v* = **cut short**, cut back, decrease, diminish, dock, lessen, reduce, shorten, truncate

curtain call return to stage by performers to acknowledge applause.

curt·sy [KURT-see] n, pl **-sies 1** woman's bow or respectful gesture made by bending knees and lowering body. ◆ vi **-sied, sy·ing**

curve [kurv] n **1** line of which no part is straight. **2** bent line or part. ◆ v **3** bend into curve. **cur·va'ceous** [-VAY-shəs] adj shapely. **cur'va·ture** [-və-chər] n **1** a bending. **2** bent shape.

cush·ion [KUUSH-ən] n **1** bag filled with soft stuffing or air, to support or ease body. **2** any soft pad or support. **3** resilient rim of pool table. ◆ vt **4** provide, protect with cushion. **5** lessen effects of.

cush·y adj **cush·i·er, cush·i·est** inf easy.

cusp [kusp] n **1** pointed end, esp. of tooth. **2** Astrology point marking the beginning of a house or sign. **cus'pid** n pointed tooth.

cus·pi·dor [KUS-pi-dor] n spittoon.

cus·tard [KUS-tərd] n dessert made of eggs, sugar and milk.

cus·to·dy [KUS-tə-dee] n, pl **-dies** safekeeping, guardianship, imprisonment. **cus·to'di·an** n keeper, caretaker.

cus·tom [KUS-təm] n **1** habit. **2** practice. **3** fashion, usage. **4** business patronage. **5** tax. ◆ pl **6** duties levied on imports. **7** government department that collects these. **8** area in airport, etc. where customs

officials examine baggage for dutiable goods. **cus·tom·ar'i·ly** adv **cus'tom·ar·y** adj usual, habitual. **cus'tom·er** n **1** one who enters store to buy, esp. regularly. **2** purchaser.

cut [kut] vt **cut, cut·ting 1** sever, penetrate, wound, divide, or separate with pressure of edge or edged instrument. **2** pare, detach, trim, or shape by cutting. **3** divide. **4** intersect. **5** reduce, decrease. **6** abridge. **7** inf ignore (person). **8** strike (with whip, etc.). **9** inf deliberately stay away from. ◆ n **10** act of cutting. **11** stroke. **12** blow, wound (of knife, whip, etc.). **13** reduction, decrease. **14** fashion, shape. **15** incision. **16** engraving. **17** piece cut off. **18** division. **19** excavation (for road, canal, etc.) through high ground. **20** inf share, esp. of profits. **cut'ter** n **1** one who, that which, cuts. **2** ship's boat for carrying stores, etc. **3** small armed government boat. **cut'ting** n **1** act of cutting, thing cut off or out. **2** shoot, twig of plant. ◆ adj **3** sarcastic, unkind. **cut'throat** adj **1** merciless. ◆ n **2** murderer. **cut dead** refuse to recognize an acquaintance.

cu·ta·ne·ous [kyoo-TAY-nee-əs] adj of skin.

cute [kyoot] adj **cut·er, cut·est** appealing, attractive, pretty.

cu·ti·cle [KYOO-ti-kəl] n dead skin, esp. at base of fingernail.

curtain n = **hanging**, drape

curve n **1** = **bend**, arc, curvature, loop, trajectory, turn ◆ v **2** = **bend**, arc, arch, coil, hook, spiral, swerve, turn, twist, wind

curved adj = **bent**, arched, bowed, rounded, serpentine, sinuous, twisted

cushion n **1** = **pillow**, beanbag, bolster, hassock, headrest, pad ◆ v **2** = **soften**, dampen, deaden, muffle, stifle, suppress

custody n **1** = **safekeeping**, care, charge, keeping, protection, supervision **2** = **imprisonment**, confinement, detention, incarceration

custom n **1** = **tradition**, convention, policy, practice, ritual, rule, usage **2** = **habit**, practice, procedure, routine, way, wont **3** = **customers**, patronage, trade

customary adj = **usual**, accepted, accustomed, common, conventional, established, normal, ordinary, routine, traditional

customer n = **client**, buyer, consumer, patron, purchaser, regular (inf), shopper

customs pl n = **duty**, import charges, tariff, tax, toll

cut v **1** = **penetrate**, chop, pierce, score, sever, slash, slice, slit, wound **2** = **divide**, bisect, dissect, slice, split **3** = **trim**, clip, hew, lop, mow, pare, prune, shave, snip **4** = **abridge**, abbreviate, condense, curtail, delete, shorten **5** = **reduce**, contract, cut back, decrease, diminish, lower, slash, slim (down) **6** = **shape**, carve, chisel, engrave, fashion, form, sculpt, whittle **7** = **hurt**, insult, put down, snub, sting, wound ◆ n **8** = **incision**, gash, laceration, nick, slash, slit, stroke, wound **9** = **reduction**, cutback, decrease, fall, lowering, saving **10** Inf = **share**, percentage, piece, portion, section, slice **11** = **style**, fashion, look, shape

cutback n = **reduction**, cut, decrease, economy, lessening, retrenchment

cut down v **1** = **fell**, hew, level, lop **2** = **reduce**, decrease, lessen, lower

cute adj = **appealing**, attractive, charming, delightful, engaging, lovable, sweet,

cut·lass [KUT-ləs] *n* short broad-bladed sword.

cut·ler·y [KUT-lə-ree] *n* knives, forks, spoons, etc.

cut·let [KUT-lit] *n* small piece of meat broiled or fried.

cy·a·nide [SĪ-ə-nīd] *n* extremely poisonous chemical compound.

cy·a·no·sis [sī-ə-NOH-sis] *n* blueness of the skin. **cy·a·not'ic** *adj*

cyber- [SĪ-bər] *comb. form* indicating computers, e.g. *cyberspace.*

cy·ber·net·ics [sī-bər-NET-iks] *n* comparative study of control mechanisms of electronic and biological systems.

cy·ber·space [SĪ-bər-spays] *n* hypothetical environment containing all the data stored in computers.

cy·ber·squat·ting [SĪ-bər-skwot-ing] *n* registering an Internet domain name belonging to another person in the hope of selling it to them for a profit. **cy'ber·squat·ter** *n*

cy·cle [SĪ-kəl] *n* **1** recurrent series or period. **2** rotation of events. **3** complete series or period. **4** development following course of stages. **5** series of poems, etc. **6** bicycle. ♦ *vi* **-cled, -cling 7** move in cycles. **8** ride bicycle. **cy'clist** *n* bicycle rider.

cy·clone [SĪ-klohn] *n* **1** system of winds moving around center of low pressure. **2** circular storm. **cy·clon'ic** [-KLON-ik] *adj*

cy·clo·tron [SĪ-klə-tron] *n* powerful apparatus that accelerates the circular movement of subatomic particles in a magnetic field, used for work in nuclear disintegration.

cyg·net [SIG-nit] *n* young swan.

cyl·in·der [SIL-in-dər] *n* **1** roller-shaped solid or hollow body, of uniform diameter. **2** piston chamber of engine. **cy·lin'dri·cal** *adj*

cym·bal [SIM-bəl] *n* one of pair of two brass plates struck together to produce ringing or clashing sound in music.

cyn·ic [SIN-ik] *n* one who expects, believes, the worst about people, their motives, or outcome of events. **cyn'i·cal** *adj* **cyn'i·cism** *n* being cynical.

cy·no·sure [SĪN-ə-shuur] *n* center of attraction.

cyst [sist] *n* sac containing liquid secretion or pus. **cys'tic** *adj* **1** of cysts. **2** of the bladder. **cys·ti'tis** *n* inflammation of bladder.

Czar [zahr] *n Hist* emperor of Russia. **Cza·ri·na** [zah-REE-nə] *n* wife of Czar.

────── THESAURUS ──────

winning, winsome

cut in *v* = interrupt, break in, butt in, intervene, intrude

cut off *v* **1** = separate, isolate, sever **2** = interrupt, disconnect, intercept

cut out *v* = stop, cease, give up, refrain from

cutthroat *adj* **1** = competitive, dog-eat-dog, fierce, relentless, ruthless, unprincipled ♦ *n* **2** = murderer, assassin, butcher, executioner, hit man (*sl*), killer

cutting *adj* = hurtful, acrimonious, barbed, bitter, caustic, malicious, sarcastic, scathing, vitriolic, wounding

cycle *n* = era, circle, period, phase, revolution, rotation

cynic *n* = skeptic, doubter, misanthrope, misanthropist, pessimist, scoffer

cynical *adj* = skeptical, contemptuous, derisive, distrustful, misanthropic, mocking, pessimistic, scoffing, scornful, unbelieving

cynicism *n* = skepticism, disbelief, doubt, misanthropy, pessimism

D d

D *Chem.* deuterium.

dab *vt* **dabbed, dab·bing 1** apply with momentary pressure, esp. anything wet and soft. **2** strike feebly. ♦ *n* **3** smear. **4** slight blow or tap. **5** small mass.

dab·ble [DAB-əl] *vi* **-bled, -bling 1** splash about. **2** be desultory student or amateur (in). **dab'bler** *n*

dac·tyl [DAK-til] *n* metrical foot of one long followed by two short syllables.

dad·dy [DAD-ee] *n inf pl* **-dies** father.

da·do [DAY-doh] *n, pl* **-dos** lower part of room wall when lined or painted separately.

dag·ger [DAG-ər] *n* short, edged stabbing weapon.

da·guerre·o·type [də-GAIR-ə-tīp] *n* **1** early photographic process. **2** photograph by it.

dahl·ia [DAL-yə] *n* garden plant of various colors.

dai·ly [DAY-lee] *adj* **1** done, occurring, published every day. ♦ *adv* **2** every day. ♦ *n, pl* **-lies 3** daily newspaper.

dain·ty [DAYN-tee] *adj* **daint·i·er, daint·i·est 1** delicate. **2** elegant, choice. **3** pretty and neat. **4** fastidious. ♦ *n, pl* **-ties 5** delicacy. **dain'ti·ly** *adv* **dain'ti·ness** *n*

dair·y [DAIR-ee] *n, pl* **-ries** place for processing milk and its products. **dair'y·ing** *n*

da·is [DAY-is] *n* raised platform, usually at end of hall.

dai·sy [DAY-zee] *n, pl* **-sies** flower with yellow center and white petals.

Da·lai La·ma [DAH-lī-LAH-mə] *n* head of Buddhist hierarchy in Tibet.

dale [dayl] *n* valley.

dal·ly [DAL-ee] *vi* **-lied, -ly·ing 1** trifle, spend time in idleness or amusement. **2** loiter. **dal'li·ance** *n*

Dal·ma·tian [dal-MAY-shən] *n* large dog, white with black spots.

dam[1] *n* **1** barrier to hold back flow of waters. **2** water so collected. ♦ *vt* **dammed, dam'ming 3** hold with or as with dam.

dam[2] *n* female parent (used of animals).

dam·age [DAM-ij] *n* **1** injury, harm, loss. ♦ *pl* **2** sum claimed or adjudged in compensation for injury. ♦ *vt* **-maged, -mag·ing 3** harm.

dam·ask [DAM-əsk] *n* **1** figured woven material of silk or linen, esp. white table linen with design shown up by light. **2** color of damask rose, velvety red.

dame [daym] *n* **1** *obs* lady. **2** *sl* woman.

damn [dam] *v* **damned, damn·ing** ♦ *vt* **1** condemn to hell. **2** be the ruin of. **3** give hostile reception to. ♦ *vi* **4** curse. ♦ *interj* **5** expression of annoyance, impatience, etc. **dam'na·ble** *adj* **1** deserving damnation. **2**

THESAURUS

dab *v* **1** = **pat**, daub, stipple, tap, touch ♦ *n* **2** = **spot**, bit, drop, pat, smudge, speck **3** = **pat**, flick, stroke, tap, touch

dabble *v* **1** = **play at**, dip into, potter, tinker, trifle (with) **2** = **splash**, dip

daft *adj Inf* **1** = **foolish**, absurd, asinine, bonkers (*inf*), crackpot (*inf*), crazy, idiotic, silly, stupid, witless **2** = **crazy**, bonkers (*sl*), demented, deranged, insane, nuts (*sl*), touched, unhinged

dagger *n* = **knife**, bayonet, dirk, stiletto

daily *adj* **1** = **everyday**, diurnal, quotidian ♦ *adv* **2** = **every day**, day by day, once a day

dainty *adj* = **delicate**, charming, elegant, exquisite, fine, graceful, neat, petite, pretty

dam *n* **1** = **barrier**, barrage, embankment, obstruction, wall ♦ *v* **2** = **block up**, barricade, hold back, obstruct, restrict

damage *v* **1** = **harm**, hurt, impair, injure, ruin, spoil, weaken, wreck ♦ *n* **2** = **harm**, destruction, detriment, devastation, hurt, injury, loss, suffering **3** *Inf* = **cost**, bill, charge, expense

damages *pl n Law* = **compensation**, fine, reimbursement, reparation, satisfaction

damaging *adj* = **harmful**, deleterious, detrimental, disadvantageous, hurtful, injurious, ruinous

dame *n* = **noblewoman**, baroness, dowager, *grande dame*, lady, peeress hateful, annoying. **dam·na·tion** n

damp adj **1** moist. **2** slightly moist. ◆ n **3** diffused moisture. **4** in coal mines, dangerous gas. ◆ vt **5** make damp. **6** (often with down) deaden, discourage. **damp'en** v **1** make, become damp. ◆ vt **2** stifle, deaden. **damp'er** n **1** anything that discourages or depresses. **2** plate in a flue to control draft.

Dan. Daniel.

dance [dans] v **danced, danc·ing** ◆ vi **1** move with measured rhythmic steps, usu. to music. **2** be in lively movement. **3** bob up and down. ◆ vt **4** perform (dance). **5** cause to dance. ◆ n **6** lively, rhythmical movement. **7** arrangement of such movements. **8** tune for them. **9** social gathering for the purpose of dancing. **danc'er** n **dan·seuse** [dahn-SUUZ] n female battle dancer.

dan·de·li·on [DAN-dl-ī-ən] n yellow-flowered wild plant.

dan·der [DAN-dər] n inf temper, fighting spirit.

dan·druff [DAN-drəf] n dead skin in small scales on the scalp, in hair.

dan·dy [DAN-dee] n, pl **-dies 1** man excessively concerned with smartness of dress. ◆ adj **2** inf excellent.

dan·ger [DAYN-jər] n **1** liability or exposure to harm. **2** risk, peril. **dan'ger·ous** adj

dan·gle [DANG-gəl] v **-gled, -gling 1** hang loosely and swaying. **2** hold suspended. **3** tempt with.

dank [dangk] adj **-er, -est** unpleasantly damp and chilly. **dank'ness** n

dap·per [DAP-ər] adj neat and precise, esp. in dress, spruce.

dap·ple [DAP-əl] v **-pled, -pling** mark with spots. **dappled** adj **1** spotted. **2** mottled. **3** variegated. **dapple-gray** adj (of horse) gray marked with darker spots.

dare [dair] vt **dared, dar·ing 1** venture, have courage (to). **2** challenge. ◆ n **3** challenge. **daring** adj **1** bold. ◆ n **2** adventurous courage. **dare'dev·il** adj, n reckless (person).

dark [dahrk] adj **-er, -est 1** without light. **2** gloomy. **3** deep in tint. **4** dim, secret. **5** unenlightened. **6** wicked. ◆ n **7** absence of light or color or knowledge. **dark'en** v **dark'ness** n **dark horse 1** somebody, something, esp. competitor in race, about whom little is known. **dark'room** n **1** darkened room for processing film.

dar·ling [DAHR-ling] adj, n much loved or

——————— THESAURUS ———————

damn v **1 = condemn**, blast, censure, criticize, denounce, put down **2 = sentence**, condemn, doom

damnation n **= condemnation**, anathema, damning, denunciation, doom

damned adj **1 = doomed**, accursed, condemned, lost **2** Sl **= detestable**, confounded, hateful, infernal, loathsome

damp adj **1 = moist**, clammy, dank, dewy, drizzly, humid, soggy, sopping, wet ◆ n **2 = moisture**, dampness, dankness, drizzle ◆ v **3 = moisten**, dampen, wet **4 damp down = reduce**, allay, check, curb, diminish, inhibit, pour cold water on, stifle

dampen v **1 = reduce**, check, dull, lessen, moderate, restrain, stifle **2 = moisten**, make damp, spray, wet

damper n As in **put a damper on = discouragement**, cold water (inf), hindrance, restraint, wet blanket (inf)

dance v **1 = prance**, hop, jig, skip, sway, trip, whirl ◆ n **2 = ball**, disco, discotheque, hop (inf, dated), social

dancer n **= ballerina**, Terpsichorean

danger n **= peril**, hazard, jeopardy, menace, pitfall, risk, threat, vulnerability

dangerous adj **= perilous**, breakneck, chancy (inf), hazardous, insecure, precarious, risky, unsafe, vulnerable

dangerously adv **= perilously**, alarmingly, hazardously, precariously, recklessly, riskily, unsafely

dangle v **1 = hang**, flap, hang down, sway, swing, trail **2 = wave**, brandish, flaunt, flourish

dapper adj **= neat**, smart, soigné or soignée, spruce, spry, trim, well-groomed, well turned out

dare v **1 = risk**, hazard, make bold, presume, venture **2 = challenge**, defy, goad, provoke, taunt, throw down the gauntlet ◆ n **3 = challenge**, provocation, taunt

daredevil n **1 = adventurer**, desperado, exhibitionist, show-off (inf), stunt man ◆ adj **2 = daring**, adventurous, audacious, bold, death-defying, reckless

daring adj **1 = brave**, adventurous, audacious, bold, daredevil, fearless, intrepid, reckless, venturesome ◆ n **2 = bravery**, audacity, boldness, courage, fearlessness, nerve (inf), pluck, temerity very lovable (person).

darn¹ [dahrn] *vt* **1** mend by filling (hole) with yarn. ♦ *n* **2** place so mended.
  darn'ing *n*

darn² *interj* mild expletive.

dart [dahrt] *n* **1** small light pointed missile. **2** darting motion. **3** small seam or intake in garment. ♦ *pl* **4** indoor game played with numbered target and miniature darts. ♦ *vt* **5** cast, throw rapidly (dart glance, etc.). ♦ *vi* **6** go rapidly or abruptly.

dash *vt* **1** smash, throw, thrust, send with violence. **2** cast down. **3** tinge, flavor, mix. ♦ *vi* **4** move, go with great speed or violence. ♦ *n* **5** rush. **6** vigor. **7** smartness. **8** small quantity, tinge. **9** stroke (-) between words. **dash'ing** *adj* spirited, showy. **dash'board** *n* in car, etc., instrument panel in front of driver.

da·shi·ki [də-SHEE-kee] *n, pl* **-kis** loose pullover garment, orig. African.

das·tard [DAS-tərd] *n obs* contemptible, sneaking coward. **das'tard·ly** *adj*

da·ta [DAY-tə] *n* **1** information consisting of observations, measurements, or facts. **2** numbers, digits, etc., stored by a computer. **database** systematized collection of data that can be manipulated

by data-processing system for specific purpose. **data processing** handling of data by computer.

date¹ [dayt] *n* **1** day of the month. **2** statement on document of its time of writing. **3** time of occurrence. **4** period of work of art, etc. **5** engagement, appointment. ♦ *v* **dat·ed, dat·ing** ♦ *vt* mark with date. **7** refer to date. **8** reveal age of. **9** *inf* accompany on social outing. ♦ *vi* **10** exist (from). **11** betray time or period of origin, become old-fashioned. **date'less** *adj* **1** without date. **2** immemorial.

date² *n* **1** sweet, single-stone fruit of palm. **2** the palm.

da·tive [DAY-tiv] *n* case indicating indirect object, etc.

da·tum *n, pl* **da·ta** single piece of information in the form of a fact or statistic.

daub [dawb] *vt* **1** coat, plaster, paint coarsely or roughly. ♦ *n* **2** crude picture. **3** smear. **daub'er** *n*

daugh·ter [DAW-tər] *n* one's female child. **daugh'ter-in-law** *n, pl* **daugh'ters-in-law** son's wife.

daunt [dawnt] *vt* frighten, esp. into giving up purpose. **daunt'less** *adj* intrepid,

──────── THESAURUS ────────

dark *adj* **1** = **dim**, dingy, murky, shadowy, shady, sunless, unlit **2** = **black**, dark-coloured, dusky, ebony, sable, swarthy **3** = **gloomy**, bleak, dismal, grim, morose, mournful, sad, somber **4** = **evil**, foul, infernal, sinister, vile, wicked **5** = **secret**, concealed, hidden, mysterious ♦ *n* **6** = **darkness**, dimness, dusk, gloom, murk, obscurity, semi-darkness **7** = **night**, evening, nightfall, night-time, twilight

darken *v* = **make dark**, blacken, dim, obscure, overshadow

darkness *n* = **dark**, blackness, duskiness, gloom, murk, nightfall, shade, shadows

darling *n* **1** = **beloved**, dear, dearest, love, sweetheart, truelove ♦ *adj* **2** = **beloved**, adored, cherished, dear, precious, treasured

darn *v* **1** = **mend**, cobble up, patch, repair, sew up, stitch ♦ *n* **2** = **mend**, invisible repair, patch, reinforcement

dart *v* = **dash**, fly, race, run, rush, shoot, spring, sprint, tear

dash *v* **1** = **rush**, bolt, fly, hurry, race, run, speed, sprint, tear **2** = **throw**, cast, fling, hurl, slam, sling **3** = **crash**, break, destroy,

shatter, smash, splinter **4** = **frustrate**, blight, foil, ruin, spoil, thwart, undo ♦ *n* **5** = **rush**, dart, race, run, sortie, sprint, spurt **6** = **little**, bit, drop, hint, pinch, soupçon, sprinkling, tinge, touch **7** = **style**, brio, élan, flair, flourish, panache, spirit, verve

dashing *adj* **1** = **bold**, debonair, gallant, lively, spirited, swashbuckling **2** = **stylish**, elegant, flamboyant, jaunty, showy, smart, sporty

data *n* = **information**, details, facts, figures, statistics

date *n* **1** = **time**, age, epoch, era, period, stage **2** = **appointment**, assignation, engagement, meeting, rendezvous, tryst **3** = **partner**, escort, friend ♦ *v* **4** = **put a date on**, assign a date to, fix the period of **5** = **become old-fashioned**, be dated, show one's age **6** date from *or* date back to = **come from**, bear a date of, belong to, exist from, originate in

dated *adj* = **old-fashioned**, obsolete, old hat, outdated, outmoded, out of date, passé, unfashionable

daub *v* = **smear**, coat, cover, paint, plaster, slap on (*inf*) fearless.

dav·en·port [DAV-ən-port] *n* **1** small writing table with drawers. **2** large couch or settee.

Da·vy Jones's locker [DAY-vee JOHN-ziz] bottom of sea, considered as sailors' grave.

daw·dle [DAWD-l] *vi* **-dled, -dling 1** idle, waste time, loiter. **daw'dler** *n*

dawn *n* **1** first light, daybreak. **2** first gleam or beginning of anything. ◆ *vi* **3** begin to grow light. **4** appear, begin. **5** (begin to) be understood.

day *n* **1** period of 24 hours. **2** time when sun is above horizon. **3** point or unit of time. **4** daylight. **5** part of day occupied by certain activity, time period. **6** special or designated day. **day'break** *n* dawn. **day'-care center** place providing daytime care, meals, etc. for preschool children, etc. **day'dream** *n* idle fancy. ◆ *vi* **day'light** *n* **1** natural light. **2** dawn. ◆ *pl* **3** consciousness, wits. **daylight saving** in summer, time set one hour ahead of local standard time, giving extra daylight in evenings. **day'time** *n* time between sunrise and sunset.

daze [dayz] *vt* **dazed, daz·ing 1** stupefy, stun, bewilder. ◆ *n* **2** stupefied or bewildered state.

daz·zle [DAZ-əl] *vt* **-zled, -zling 1** blind, confuse or overpower with brightness, light, brilliant display or prospects. ◆ *n* **2** brightness that dazzles the vision.

Db *Chem.* dubnium.

D-day [DEE-day] day selected for start of something, orig. the Allied invasion of Europe on June 6th 1944.

de- *prefix* indicating: **1** removal, e.g. *dethrone*. **2** reversal, e.g. *declassify*. **3** departure, e.g. *decamp*.

dea·con [DEE-kən] *n* **1** in hierarchical churches, member of the clergy next below priest. **2** in other churches, one who superintends secular affairs. **dea'con·ess** *n, fem.*

dead [ded] *adj* **-er, -est 1** no longer alive. **2** obsolete. **3** numb, without sensation. **4** no longer functioning, extinguished. **5** lacking luster or movement or vigor. **6** sure, complete. ◆ *adv* **7** utterly. **the dead** dead person or persons. **dead'en** *vt* **dead'ly** *adj* **-li·er, -li·est 1** fatal. **2** deathlike. ◆ *adv* **3** as if dead. **dead'beat** *n inf* **1** one who avoids payment of debts. **2** lazy, useless person. **dead'head** *n* **1** log sticking out of water as hindrance to navigation. **2** boring person. **3** train, aircraft, etc. operating empty, as when returning to terminal. **dead heat** race in which competitors finish exactly

daunting *adj* = **intimidating**, alarming, demoralizing, disconcerting, discouraging, disheartening, frightening, unnerving

dauntless *adj* = **fearless**, bold, doughty, gallant, indomitable, intrepid, resolute, stouthearted, undaunted, unflinching

dawdle *v* = **waste time**, dally, delay, drag one's feet or heels, hang about, idle, loaf, loiter, trail

dawn *n* **1** = **daybreak**, aurora (*poetic*), cockcrow, crack of dawn, daylight, morning, sunrise, sunup **2** = **beginning**, advent, birth, emergence, genesis, origin, rise, start ◆ *v* **3** = **grow light**, break, brighten, lighten **4** = **begin**, appear, develop, emerge, originate, rise, unfold **5 dawn on** *or* **upon** = **hit**, become apparent, come into one's head, come to mind, occur, register (*inf*), strike

day *n* **1** = **twenty-four hours**, daylight, daytime **2** = **point in time**, date, time **3** = **time**, age, epoch, era, heyday, period, zenith

daybreak *n* = **dawn**, break of day,

cockcrow, crack of dawn, first light, morning, sunrise, sunup

daydream *n* **1** = **fantasy**, dream, fancy, imagining, pipe dream, reverie, wish ◆ *v* **2** = **fantasize**, dream, envision, fancy, imagine, muse

daylight *n* = **sunlight**, light of day, sunshine

daze *v* **1** = **stun**, benumb, numb, paralyze, shock, stupefy ◆ *n* **2** = **shock**, bewilderment, confusion, distraction, stupor, trance, trancelike state

dazed *adj* = **shocked**, bewildered, confused, disorientated, dizzy, muddled, punch-drunk, staggered, stunned

dazzle *v* **1** = **impress**, amaze, astonish, bowl over (*inf*), overpower, overwhelm, take one's breath away **2** = **blind**, bedazzle, blur, confuse, daze **3** = **splendor**, brilliance, glitter, magnificence, razzmatazz (*sl*), sparkle

dazzling *adj* = **splendid**, brilliant, glittering, glorious, scintillating, sensational (*inf*), sparkling, stunning, virtuoso even. **dead letter 1** rule no longer observed. **2** letter that post office cannot deliver. **dead'line** n limit of time allowed. **dead'lock** n standstill. **dead'pan** adj expressionless. **dead reckoning** calculation of ship's position from log and compass, when observations cannot be taken. **dead set 1** absolutely. **2** resolute attack. **dead of night** time of greatest stillness and darkness.

deaf [def] adj **-er, -est 1** wholly or partly without hearing. **2** unwilling to listen. **deaf'en** vt make deaf.

deal [deel] v **dealt, deal'ing** ♦ vt **1** distribute, give out. **2** inflict. ♦ vi **3** act. **4** treat. **5** do business (with, in). ♦ n **6** agreement. **7** treatment. **8** share. **9** business transaction. **deal'er** n **1** one who deals (esp. cards). **2** trader. **deal'ings** pl n transactions or relations with others. **deal**

with handle, act toward (someone).

dean [deen] n **1** university or college official. **2** head of cathedral chapter.

dear [deer] adj **1** beloved. **2** precious. **3** costly, expensive. ♦ n **4** beloved one. ♦ adv **5** at a high price. **dear'ly** adv

dearth [durth] n scarcity.

death [deth] n **1** dying. **2** end of life. **3** end, extinction. **4** annihilation. **5 (D-)** personification of death, as skeleton. **death'less** adj immortal. **death'ly** adj, adv like death. **death mask** cast of person's face taken after death. **death'watch** n vigil at dying person's bedside.

de·ba·cle [day-BAH-kəl] n utter collapse, rout, disaster.

de·bar [di-BAHR] vt **-barred, -bar'ring 1** shut out from. **2** stop. **3** prohibit. **4** preclude.

de·bark [di-BAHRK] v disembark.

dead adj **1 = deceased**, defunct, departed, extinct, late, passed away, perished **2 = not working**, inactive, inoperative, stagnant, unemployed, useless **3 = numb**, inert, paralyzed **4 = total**, absolute, complete, outright, thorough, unqualified, utter **5** Inf **= exhausted**, spent, tired, worn out **6 = boring**, dull, flat, uninteresting ♦ n **7 = middle**, depth, midst

deaden v **= reduce**, alleviate, blunt, cushion, diminish, dull, lessen, muffle, smother, stifle, suppress, weaken

deadline n **= time limit**, cutoff point, limit, target date

deadlock n **1 = draw**, dead heat, tie **2 = impasse**, gridlock, stalemate, standoff, standstill

deadlocked adj **1 = even**, equal, level, neck and neck, on a level playing field (inf) **2 = gridlocked**, at an impasse, at a standstill

deadly adj **= lethal**, dangerous, death-dealing, deathly, fatal, malignant, mortal

deadpan adj **= expressionless**, blank, impassive, inexpressive, inscrutable, poker-faced, straight-faced

deaf adj **1 = hard of hearing**, stone deaf, without hearing **2 = oblivious**, indifferent, unconcerned, unhearing, unmoved

deafen v **= make deaf**, din, drown out, split or burst the eardrums

deafening adj **= ear-piercing**, booming, ear-splitting, overpowering, piercing,

resounding, ringing, thunderous

deal n **1 = agreement**, arrangement, bargain, contract, pact, transaction, understanding **2 = amount**, degree, extent, portion, quantity, share ♦ v **3 = sell**, bargain, buy and sell, do business, negotiate, stock, trade, traffic

dealer n **= trader**, merchant, purveyor, supplier, tradesman, wholesaler

deal out v **= distribute**, allot, apportion, assign, dispense, dole out, give, mete out, share

deal with v **1 = handle**, attend to, cope with, get to grips with, manage, see to, take care of, treat **2 = be concerned with**, consider

dear n **1 = beloved**, angel, darling, loved one, precious, treasure ♦ adj **2 = beloved**, cherished, close, favorite, intimate, precious, prized, treasured **3 = expensive**, at a premium, costly, high-priced, overpriced, pricey (inf)

dearly adv **1 = very much**, extremely, greatly, profoundly **2 = at great cost**, at a high price

dearth n **= scarcity**, deficiency, inadequacy, insufficiency, lack, paucity, poverty, shortage, want

death n **1 = dying**, demise, departure, end, exit, passing **2 = destruction**, downfall, extinction, finish, ruin, undoing

deathly adj **= deathlike**, ghastly, grim, pale, pallid, wan

debacle n **= disaster**, catastrophe,

de·base [di-BASE] *vt* **-based, -bas·ing 1** lower in value, quality or character. **2** adulterate coinage. **de·base'ment** *n*

de·bate [di-BAYT] *v* **-bat·ed, -bat·ing 1** argue, discuss, esp. in a formal assembly. **2** consider. ♦ *n* **3** discussion. **4** controversy. **de·bat'a·ble** *adj*

de·bauch [di-BAWCH] *vt* **1** lead into a life of depraved self-indulgence. ♦ *n* **2** bout of sensual indulgence. **de·bauch·ee** [deb-aw-CHEE] *n* dissipated person. **de·bauch'er·y** *n*

de·ben·ture [di-BEN-chər] *n* bond of company or corporation.

de·bil·i·ty [di-BIL-i-tee] *n, pl* **-ties 1** feebleness, esp. of health. **2** languor. **de·bil'i·tate** *vt* weaken, enervate.

deb'it *n Accounting* **1** entry in account of sum owed. **2** side of ledger in which such sums are entered. ♦ *vt* **3** charge, enter as due.

deb·o·nair [deb-ə-NAIR] *adj* suave, genial, affable.

de·brief [dee-BREEF] *v* of soldier, etc., report to superior on result of mission.

de·bris [də-BREE] *n* fragments, rubbish.

debt [det] *n* **1** what is owed. **2** state of owing. **debt'or** *n*

debug [dee-BUG] *vt* **1** *inf* find and remove defects in (computer program). **2** remove concealed microphones from (room or telephone).

de·bunk [di-BUNGK] *vt* expose falseness,

pretentiousness of, esp. by ridicule.

de·but [day-BYOO] *n* first appearance in public. **deb·u·tante** [DEB-yuu-tahnt] *n* young woman making official debut into society.

deca- *comb. form* ten, e.g. *decagon.*

dec·ade [DEK-ayd] *n* **1** period of ten years. **2** set of ten.

dec·a·dent [DEK-ə-dənt] *adj* **1** declining, deteriorating. **2** morally corrupt. **dec'a·dence** *n*

de·caf·fein·at·ed [dee-KAF-ə-nay-tid] *adj* (of coffee) with the caffeine removed.

dec·a·gon [DEK-ə-gon] *n* figure of 10 angles.

dec·a·he·dron [dek-ə-HEE-drən] *n* solid of 10 faces.

de·cal·ci·fy [dee-KAL-si-fī] *vt* **-fied, -fy·ing** deprive of lime, as bones or teeth.

Dec·a·logue [DEK-ə-lawg] *n* the Ten Commandments.

de·camp [di-KAMP] *vi* make off, break camp, abscond.

de·cant [di-KANT] *vt* pour off (liquid, as wine) to leave sediment. **de·cant'er** *n* stoppered bottle for wine or whiskey.

de·cap·i·tate [di-KAP-i-tayt] *vt* behead. **de·cap·i·ta'tion** *n*

de·cath·lon [di-KATH-lon] *n* athletic contest with ten events.

de·cay [di-KAY] *v* **1** rot, decompose. **2** fall off, decline. ♦ *n* **3** rotting. **4** a falling away, break up.

collapse, defeat, fiasco, reversal, rout

debase *v* = **degrade**, cheapen, devalue, lower, reduce

debatable *adj* = **doubtful**, arguable, controversial, dubious, moot, problematical, questionable, uncertain

debate *n* **1** = **discussion**, argument, contention, controversy, dispute ♦ *v* **2** = **discuss**, argue, dispute, question **3** = **consider**, deliberate, ponder, reflect, ruminate, weigh

debauchery *n* = **depravity**, dissipation, dissoluteness, excess, indulgence, intemperance, lewdness, overindulgence

debonair *adj* = **elegant**, charming, courteous, dashing, refined, smooth, suave, urbane, well-bred

debrief *v* = **interrogate**, cross-examine, examine, probe, question, quiz

debris *n* = **remains**, bits, detritus, fragments, rubble, ruins, waste, wreckage

debt *n* **1** = **debit**, commitment, liability, obligation **2 in debt** = **owing**, in arrears, in the red (*inf*), liable

debtor *n* = **borrower**, mortgagor

debunk *v* = **expose**, cut down to size, deflate, disparage, mock, ridicule, show up

debut *n* = **introduction**, beginning, bow, coming out, entrance, first appearance, initiation, presentation

decadence *n* = **degeneration**, corruption, decay, decline, deterioration, dissipation, dissolution

decadent *adj* = **degenerate**, corrupt, decaying, declining, dissolute, immoral, self-indulgent

decapitate *v* = **behead**, execute, guillotine

decay *v* **1** = **decline**, crumble, deteriorate, disintegrate, dwindle, shrivel, wane, waste away, wither **1** = **rot**, corrode, decompose, perish, putrefy ♦ *n* **3** = **decline**, collapse, degeneration, deterioration, fading, failing,

de·cease [di-SEES] *n* **1** death. ◆ *vi* **-ceased, -ceas·ing 2** die. **deceased** *adj* **1** dead. ◆ *n* **2** person lately dead.

de·ceive [di-SEEV] *vt* **-ceived, -ceiv·ing** mislead, delude, cheat. **de·ceit'** *n* **1** fraud. **2** duplicity. **de·ceit'ful** *adj*

de·cel·er·ate [dee-SEL-ə-rayt] *vi* **-at·ed, -at·ing** slow down.

de·cen·ni·al [di-SEN-ee-əl] *adj* of period of ten years.

de·cent [DEE-sənt] *adj* **1** respectable. **2** fitting, seemly. **3** not obscene. **4** adequate. **5** *inf* kind. **de'cen·cy** *n*

de·cen·tral·ize [dee-SEN-trə-līz] *vt* **-ized, -iz·ing** divide (government, organization) among local centers.

de·cep·tion [di-SEP-shən] *n* **1** deceiving. **2** illusion. **3** fraud. **4** trick. **de·cep'tive** *adj* **1** misleading. **2** apt to mislead.

deci- *comb. form* one tenth, e.g. *decimetre*.

dec·i·bel [DES-ə-bəl] *n* unit for measuring intensity of a sound.

de·cide [di-SĪD] *v* **-cid·ed, -cid·ing** ◆ *vt* **1** settle, determine, bring to resolution. **2** give judgment. ◆ *vi* **3** come to a decision,

conclusion. **de·cid'ed** *adj* **1** unmistakable. **2** settled. **3** resolute. **de·cid'ed·ly** *adv* certainly, undoubtedly. **de·cis'ion** [-SIZH-ən] *n* **de·ci'sive** *adj* **de·ci'sive·ness** *n*

de·cid·u·ous [di-SIJ-oo-əs] *adj* **1** of trees, losing leaves annually. **2** of antlers, teeth, etc. being shed at the end of a period of growth.

dec·i·mal [DES-ə-məl] *adj* **1** relating to tenths. **2** proceeding by tens. ◆ *n* **3** decimal fraction. **decimal system** system of weights and measures, or coinage, in which value of each denomination is ten times the one below it.

dec·i·mate [DES-ə-mayt] *vt* **-mat·ed, -mat·ing** destroy or kill a tenth of, large proportion of. **dec·i·ma'tion** *n*

de·ci·pher [di-SĪ-fər] *vt* **1** make out meaning of. **2** decode. **de·ci'pher·a·ble** *adj*

deck [dek] *n* **1** platform or floor, esp. one covering whole or part of ship's hull. **2** cassette deck. **3** pack of playing cards. **4** *sl* small packet of a narcotic. ◆ *vt* **5** array, decorate. **deck chair** folding chair made of canvas suspended in wooden frame.

———— THESAURUS ————

wasting, withering **4** = **rot**, caries, decomposition, gangrene, putrefaction

decease *n Formal* = **death**, demise, departure, dying, release

deceased *adj* = **dead**, defunct, departed, expired, former, late, lifeless

deceit *n* = **dishonesty**, cheating, chicanery, deception, fraud, lying, pretense, treachery, trickery

deceitful *adj* = **dishonest**, deceptive, down and dirty (*inf*), false, fraudulent, sneaky, treacherous, two-faced, untrustworthy

deceive *v* = **dupe** (*inf*), cheat, con (*inf*), fool, hoodwink, mislead, swindle, trick

deceiver *n* = **liar**, cheat, con man (*inf*), double-dealer, fraud, impostor, swindler, trickster

decency *n* = **respectability**, civility, correctness, courtesy, decorum, etiquette, modesty, propriety

decent *adj* **1** = **reasonable**, adequate, ample, fair, passable, satisfactory, sufficient, tolerable **2** = **respectable**, chaste, decorous, modest, proper, pure **3** = **proper**, appropriate, becoming, befitting, fitting, seemly, suitable **4** *Inf* = **kind**, accommodating, courteous, friendly, generous, gracious, helpful, obliging, thoughtful

deception *n* **1** = **trickery**, cunning, deceit, fraud, guile, legerdemain, treachery **2** = **trick**, bluff, decoy, hoax, illusion, lie, ruse, subterfuge

deceptive *adj* = **misleading**, ambiguous, deceitful, dishonest, false, fraudulent, illusory, unreliable

decide *v* = **reach** *or* **come to a decision**, adjudge, adjudicate, choose, conclude, determine, make up one's mind, resolve

decidedly *adv* = **definitely**, clearly, distinctly, downright, positively, unequivocally, unmistakably

decimate *v* = **devastate**, ravage, wreak havoc on

decipher *v* = **figure out** (*inf*), crack, decode, deduce, interpret, make out, read, solve

decision *n* **1** = **judgment**, arbitration, conclusion, finding, resolution, ruling, sentence, verdict **2** = **decisiveness**, determination, firmness, purpose, resolution, resolve, strength of mind *or* will

decisive *adj* **1** = **influential**, conclusive, critical, crucial, fateful, momentous, significant **2** = **resolute**, decided, determined, firm, forceful, incisive, strong-minded, trenchant

deck *v* = **decorate**, adorn, array, beautify,

de·claim [di-KLAYM] v 1 speak dramatically, rhetorically or passionately. 2 protest loudly. **dec·la·ma·tion** [dek-lə-MAY-shən] n **de·clam'a·to·ry** adj

de·clare [di-KLAIR] v -clared, -clar·ing ♦ vt 1 announce formally. 2 state emphatically. 3 show. 4 name (as liable to customs duty). ♦ vi 5 take sides (for). 6 Bridge bid (a suit or no trump). **dec·la·ra·tion** [dek-lə-RAY-shən] n **de·clar'a·tive** adj **de·clar'er** n Bridge person who plays the contract.

de·cline [di-KLĪN] v -clined, -clin·ing 1 refuse. 2 slope, bend or sink downward. 3 deteriorate gradually. 4 grow smaller, diminish. 5 list the case endings of nouns, pronouns, adjectives. ♦ n 6 gradual deterioration. 7 movement downward. 8 diminution. 9 downward slope. **de·clen·sion** n 1 in grammar, set of nouns, pronouns, etc. 2 falling off. 3 declining. **de·clin'a·ble** adj **dec·li·na'tion** n 1 sloping away, deviation. 2 angle.

de·cliv·i·ty [di-KLIV-i-tee] n downward slope.

de·code [dee-KOHD] vt -cod·ed, -cod·ing put in intelligible terms a message in code or secret alphabet.

dé·colle·té [day-kol-TAY] adj (of women's garment) having a low-cut neckline. **dé·colle·tage'** [-TAHZH] n low-cut neckline.

de·com·mis·sion [dee-kə-MISH-ən] vt 1 dismantle (nuclear reactor, industrial plant) sufficiently to abandon safely. 2 remove (ship) from service.

de·com·pose [dee-kəm-POHZ] v -posed, -pos·ing 1 separate into elements. 2 rot. **de·com·po·si·tion** [dee-kom-pə-ZISH-ən] n decay.

de·com·press [dee-kəm-PRES] vt 1 free from pressure. 2 return to condition of normal atmospheric pressure. **de·com·pres'sion** n

de·con·ges·tant [dee-kən-JES-tənt] adj, n (drug) relieving (esp. nasal) congestion.

de·con·tam·i·nate [dee-kən-TAM-ə-nayt] vt -nat·ed, -nat·ing free from contamination e.g. from poisons, radioactive substances.

de·con·trol [dee-kən-TROHL] vt -trolled, -trol·ling release from government control.

dé·cor [day-KOR] n 1 decorative scheme of a room, etc. 2 stage decoration, scenery.

dec·o·rate [DEK-ə-rayt] vt -rat·ed, -rat·ing 1 beautify by additions. 2 select paint, furniture, etc. for room, apartment, etc. 3 award (medal, etc.). **dec·o·ra'tion** n **dec'o·ra·tive** [-rə-tiv] adj

de·co·rum [di-KOR-əm] n seemly behavior, propriety, decency. **dec·o·rous** [DEK-ə-rəs] adj

de·coy [DEE-koi] n 1 something used to

clothe, dress, embellish, festoon

declaim v 1 = **orate**, harangue, hold forth, lecture, proclaim, rant, recite, speak 2 **declaim against** = **protest against**, attack, decry, denounce, inveigh, rail

declaration n 1 = **statement**, acknowledgment, affirmation, assertion, avowal, disclosure, protestation, revelation, testimony 2 = **announcement**, edict, notification, proclamation, profession, pronouncement

declare v 1 = **state**, affirm, announce, assert, claim, maintain, proclaim, profess, pronounce, swear, utter 2 = **make known**, confess, disclose, reveal, show

decline v 1 = **lessen**, decrease, diminish, dwindle, ebb, fade, fall off, shrink, sink, wane 2 = **deteriorate**, decay, degenerate, droop, languish, pine, weaken, worsen 3 = **refuse**, abstain, avoid, reject, say 'no', turn down ♦ n 4 = **lessening**, downturn, drop, dwindling, falling off, recession, slump 5 = **deterioration**, decay, degeneration,

failing, weakening, worsening

decode v = **decipher**, crack, decrypt, interpret, solve, unscramble, work out

decompose v = **rot**, break up, crumble, decay, fall apart, fester, putrefy

decor n = **decoration**, color scheme, furnishing style, ornamentation

decorate v 1 = **adorn**, beautify, embellish, festoon, grace, ornament, trim 2 = **renovate**, do up (inf), color, furbish, paint, paper, wallpaper 3 = **pin a medal on**, cite, confer an honor on or upon

decoration n 1 = **adornment**, beautification, elaboration, embellishment, enrichment, ornamentation, trimming 2 = **ornament**, bauble, frill, garnish, trimmings 3 = **medal**, award, badge, ribbon, star

decorative adj = **ornamental**, beautifying, fancy, nonfunctional, pretty

decorous adj = **proper**, becoming, correct, decent, dignified, fitting, polite, seemly, well-behaved

decorum n = **propriety**, decency, dignity,

entrap others or to distract their attention. 2 bait, lure. ◆ v [di-KOI] 3 lure, be lured as with decoy.

de·crease [di-KREES] v **-creased, -creas·ing** 1 diminish, lessen. ◆ n [DEE-krees] 2 lessening.

de·cree [di-KREE] n 1 order having the force of law. 2 edict. ◆ v **-creed, -cree·ing** 3 determine judicially. 4 order.

dec·re·ment [DEK-rə-mənt] n 1 act or state of decreasing. 2 quantity lost by decrease.

de·crep·it [di-KREP-it] adj 1 old and feeble. 2 broken down, worn out. **de·crep'i·tude** n

de·cry [di-KRĪ] vt **-cried, -cry·ing** disparage.

ded·i·cate [DED-i-kayt] vt **-cat·ed, -cat·ing** 1 commit wholly to special purpose or cause. 2 inscribe or address (book, etc.). 3 devote to God's service. **ded·i·ca'tion** n **ded'i·ca·to·ry** [-kə-tor-ee] adj

de·duce [di-DOOS] vt **-duced, -duc·ing** 1 draw as conclusion from facts. **de·duct** [di-DUKT] vt take away, subtract.

de·duct'i·ble adj **de·duc'tion** n 1 deducting. 2 amount subtracted. 3 conclusion deduced. 4 inference from general to particular. **de·duc'tive** adj

deed n 1 action or fact. 2 exploit. 3 legal document.

deem vt judge, consider, regard.

deep adj **-er, -est** 1 extending far down, in or back. 2 at, of given depth. 3 profound. 4 heartfelt. 5 hard to fathom. 6 cunning. 7 engrossed, immersed. 8 of color, dark and rich. 9 of sound, low and full. ◆ n 10 deep place. 11 the sea. ◆ adv 12 far down, etc. **deep'en** vt **deep'ly** adv **deep freeze** condition or period of suspended activity.

deer n, pl **deer** family of ruminant animals typically with antlers in male. **deer'stalk·er** n 1 one who stalks deer. 2 kind of cloth hat with visor in front and behind.

de·face [di-FAYS] vt **-faced, -fac·ing** 1 spoil or mar surface. 2 disfigure. **de·face'ment** n

de fac·to [day FAK-toh] Lat existing in fact,

—————| THESAURUS |—————

etiquette, good manners, politeness, protocol, respectability

decoy n 1 = **lure**, bait, enticement, inducement, pretense, trap ◆ v 2 = **lure**, deceive, ensnare, entice, entrap, seduce, tempt

decrease v 1 = **lessen**, cut down, decline, diminish, drop, dwindle, lower, reduce, shrink, subside ◆ n 2 = **lessening**, contraction, cutback, decline, dwindling, falling off, loss, reduction, subsidence

decree n 1 = **law**, act, command, edict, order, proclamation, ruling, statute ◆ v 2 = **order**, command, demand, ordain, prescribe, proclaim, pronounce, rule

decrepit adj 1 = **weak**, aged, doddering, feeble, frail, infirm 2 = **worn-out**, battered, beat-up (inf), broken-down, dilapidated, ramshackle, rickety, run-down, tumbledown, weather-beaten

decry v = **condemn**, belittle, criticize, denigrate, denounce, discredit, disparage, put down, run down

dedicate v 1 = **devote**, commit, give over to, pledge, surrender 2 = **inscribe**, address

dedicated adj = **devoted**, committed, enthusiastic, purposeful, single-minded, wholehearted, zealous

dedication n 1 = **devotion**, adherence, allegiance, commitment, faithfulness, loyalty, single-mindedness, wholeheartedness 2 = **inscription**, address,

message

deduce v = **conclude**, draw, gather, glean, infer, reason, take to mean, understand

deduct v = **subtract**, decrease by, knock off (inf), reduce by, remove, take away, take off

deduction n 1 = **subtraction**, decrease, diminution, discount, reduction, withdrawal 2 = **conclusion**, assumption, finding, inference, reasoning, result

deed n 1 = **action**, achievement, act, exploit, fact, feat, performance 2 Law = **document**, contract, title

deep adj 1 = **wide**, bottomless, broad, far, profound, unfathomable, yawning 2 = **mysterious**, abstract, abstruse, arcane, esoteric, hidden, obscure, recondite, secret 3 = **intense**, extreme, grave, great, profound, serious (inf), unqualified 4 = **absorbed**, engrossed, immersed, lost, preoccupied, rapt 5 = **dark**, intense, rich, strong, vivid 6 = **low**, bass, booming, low-pitched, resonant, sonorous ◆ n 7 **the deep** Poetic = **ocean**, briny (inf), high seas, main, sea

deepen v = **intensify**, grow, increase, magnify, reinforce, strengthen

deeply adv 1 = **thoroughly**, completely, gravely, profoundly, seriously, severely, to the core, to the heart, to the quick 2 = **intensely**, acutely, affectingly, distressingly, feelingly, mournfully,

whether legally recognized or not.
de·fal·ca·tion [dee-fal-KAY-shən] *n* **1** misappropriation of money held by trustee, etc. **2** the money taken. **de·fal·cate** [di-FAL-kayt] *vi* **-cat·ed, -cat·ing**

de·fame [di-FAYM] *vt* **-famed, -fam·ing** speak ill of, dishonor by slander or rumor. **def·a·ma·tion** [def-ə-MAY-shən] *n* **de·fam'a·to·ry** *adj*

de·fault [di-FAWLT] *n* **1** failure, neglect to act, appear or pay. **2** *Computers.* instruction to a computer to select a particular option unless the user specifies otherwise. ♦ *v* **3** fail (to pay). **de·fault'er** *n* one who defaults.

de·feat [di-FEET] *vt* **1** overcome, vanquish. **2** thwart. ♦ *n* **3** overthrow. **4** lose battle or encounter. **5** frustration. **de·feat'ism** *n* attitude tending to accept defeat. **de·feat'ist** *n, adj*

def·e·cate [DEF-i-kayt] *vt* **-cat·ed, -cat·ing 1** empty the bowels. **2** clear of impurities.

def·e·ca'tion *n*

de·fect [DEE-fekt] *n* **1** lack, blemish, failing. ♦ *vi* [di-FEKT] **2** desert one's country, cause, etc., esp. to join opponents. **de·fec'tion** *n* abandonment of duty or allegiance. **de·fec'tive** *adj* **1** incomplete. **2** faulty.

de·fend [di-FEND] *vt* **1** protect, ward off attack. **2** support by argument, evidence. **3** (try to) maintain (title, etc.) against challenger. **de·fense'** *n* **de·fend'ant** *n* person accused in court. **de·fend'er** *n* **de·fen'si·ble** *adj* **de·fen'sive** *adj* **1** serving for defense. ♦ *n* **2** position or attitude of defense.

de·fer¹ [di-FUR] *vt* **-ferred, -fer·ring** put off, postpone. **de·fer'ment, de·fer'ral** *n*

de·fer² [di-FUR] *vi* **-ferred, -fer·ring** submit to opinion or judgment of another. **def'er·ence** *n* respectful submission to views, etc. of another. **def·er·en'tial** [-shəl] *adj*

---

movingly, passionately, sadly

deface *v* = **vandalize**, damage, deform, disfigure, mar, mutilate, spoil, tarnish

de facto *adv* **1** = **in fact**, actually, in effect, in reality, really ♦ *adj* **2** = **actual**, existing, real

defame *v* = **slander**, bad-mouth (*sl*), cast aspersions on, denigrate, discredit, disparage, knock (*inf*), libel, malign, smear

default *n* **1** = **failure**, deficiency, dereliction, evasion, lapse, neglect, nonpayment, omission ♦ *v* **2** = **fail**, dodge, evade, neglect

defeat *v* **1** = **beat**, conquer, crush, master, overwhelm, rout, trounce, vanquish, wipe the floor with (*inf*) **2** = **frustrate**, baffle, balk, confound, foil, get the better of, ruin, thwart ♦ *n* **3** = **conquest**, beating, overthrow, rout **4** = **frustration**, failure, rebuff, reverse, setback, thwarting

defeatist *n* **1** = **pessimist**, prophet of doom, quitter ♦ *adj* **2** = **pessimistic**

defect *n* **1** = **imperfection**, blemish, blotch, error, failing, fault, flaw, spot, taint ♦ *v* **2** = **desert**, abandon, change sides, go over, rebel, revolt, walk out on (*inf*)

defection *n* = **desertion**, apostasy, rebellion

defective *adj* = **faulty**, broken, deficient, flawed, imperfect, not working, on the blink (*sl*), out of order

defector *n* = **deserter**, apostate, renegade, turncoat

defend *v* **1** = **protect**, cover, guard, keep safe, preserve, safeguard, screen, shelter, shield **2** = **support**, champion, endorse, justify, speak up for, stand up for, stick up for (*inf*), uphold, vindicate

defendant *n* = **the accused**, defense, offender, prisoner at the bar, respondent

defender *n* **1** = **protector**, bodyguard, escort, guard **2** = **supporter**, advocate, champion, sponsor

defense *n* **1** = **protection**, cover, guard, immunity, resistance, safeguard, security, shelter **2** = **shield**, barricade, bulwark, buttress, fortification, rampart **3** = **argument**, excuse, explanation, justification, plea, vindication **4** *Law* = **plea**, alibi, denial, rebuttal, testimony

defenseless *adj* = **helpless**, exposed, naked, powerless, unarmed, unguarded, unprotected, vulnerable, wide open

defensive *adj* = **on guard**, on the defensive, protective, uptight (*inf*), watchful

defer¹ *v* = **postpone**, delay, hold over, procrastinate, put off, put on ice, shelve, suspend

defer² *v* = **comply**, accede, bow, capitulate, give in, give way to, submit, yield

deference *n* = **respect**, attention, civility, consideration, courtesy, honor, politeness, regard, reverence

defiance, defiant see DEFY.

de·fi·cient [di-FISH-ənt] *adj* lacking or falling short in something, insufficient. **de·fi·cien·cy** *n* **def·i·cit** [DEF-ə-sit] *n* **1** amount by which sum of money is too small. **2** lack, shortage.

de·file¹ [di-FĪL] *vt* **-filed, -fil·ing 1** make dirty, pollute, soil. **2** sully. **3** desecrate.

de·file² *n* **1** narrow pass or valley. ♦ *vi* **filed, -fil·ing 2** march in file.

de·fine [di-FĪN] *vt* **-fined, -fin·ing 1** state contents or meaning of. **2** show clearly the form. **3** lay down clearly, fix. **4** mark out. **de·fin·a·ble** *adj* **def·i·ni·tion** [-NISH-ən] *n* **def'i·nite** [-nit] *adj* **1** exact, defined. **2** clear, specific. **3** certain, sure. **de·fin'i·tive** *adj* conclusive, to be looked on as final.

de·flate [di-FLAYT] *v* **-flat·ed, -flat·ing 1** (cause to) collapse by release of gas from. **2** take away (person's) self-esteem. **3** *Economics* cause deflation. **de·fla'tion** *n* **1** deflating. **2** *Economics* reduction of economic and industrial activity.

de·fla'tion·ar·y *adj*

de·flect [di-FLEKT] *v* (cause to) turn from straight course. **de·flec'tion** *n*

de·flow·er [di-FLOW-ər] *vt* deprive of virginity, innocence, etc. **def·lo·ra'tion** *n*

de·fo·li·ate [dee-FOH-lee-ayt] *v* **-at·ed, -at·ing** (cause to) lose leaves, esp. by action of chemicals. **defo'li·ant** *n* **de·fo·li·a'tion** *n*

de·form [di-FORM] *vt* **1** spoil shape of. **2** make ugly. **3** disfigure. **de·formed'** *adj* **de·form'i·ty** *n, pl* **-ties**

de·fraud [di-FRAWD] *vt* cheat, swindle.

de·fray [di-FRAY] *vt* provide money for (expenses, etc.).

de·frock [dee-FROK] *vt* deprive (priest, minister) of ecclesiastical status.

de·frost [di-FRAWST] *v* **1** make, become free of frost, ice. **2** thaw.

deft *adj* **-er, -est** skillful, adroit. **deft'ly** *adv* **deft'ness** *n*

de·funct [di-FUNGKT] *adj* dead, obsolete.

de·fuse [dee-FYOOZ] *vt* **-fused, -fus·ing 1**

deferential *adj* = **respectful**, ingratiating, obedient, obeisant, obsequious, polite, reverential, submissive

defiance *n* = **resistance**, confrontation, contempt, disobedience, disregard, insolence, insubordination, opposition, rebelliousness

defiant *adj* = **resisting**, audacious, bold, daring, disobedient, insolent, insubordinate, mutinous, provocative, rebellious

deficiency *n* **1** = **lack**, absence, dearth, deficit, scarcity, shortage **2** = **failing**, defect, demerit, fault, flaw, frailty, imperfection, shortcoming, weakness

deficient *adj* **1** = **lacking**, inadequate, insufficient, meager, scant, scarce, short, skimpy, wanting **2** = **unsatisfactory**, defective, faulty, flawed, impaired, imperfect, incomplete, inferior, lousy (*sl*), weak

deficit *n* = **shortfall**, arrears, deficiency, loss, shortage

define *v* **1** = **describe**, characterize, designate, explain, expound, interpret, specify, spell out **2** = **mark out**, bound, circumscribe, delineate, demarcate, limit, outline

definite *adj* **1** = **clear**, black-and-white, cut-and-dried (*inf*), exact, fixed, marked, particular, precise, specific **2** = **certain**,

assured, decided, guaranteed, positive, settled, sure

definitely *adv* = **certainly**, absolutely, categorically, clearly, positively, surely, undeniably, unmistakably, unquestionably, without doubt

definition *n* **1** = **explanation**, clarification, elucidation, exposition, statement of meaning **2** = **sharpness**, clarity, contrast, distinctness, focus, precision

definitive *adj* **1** = **final**, absolute, complete, conclusive, decisive **2** = **authoritative**, exhaustive, perfect, reliable, ultimate

deflate *v* **1** = **collapse**, empty, exhaust, flatten, puncture, shrink **2** = **humiliate**, chasten, disconcert, dispirit, humble, mortify, put down (*sl*), squash **3** *Economics* = **reduce**, depress, devalue, diminish

deflect *v* = **turn aside**, bend, deviate, diverge, glance off, ricochet, swerve, veer

deflection *n* = **deviation**, bend, divergence, swerve

deform *v* **1** = **distort**, buckle, contort, gnarl, mangle, misshape, twist, warp **2** = **disfigure**, deface, maim, mar, mutilate, ruin, spoil

deformity *n* = **abnormality**, defect, disfigurement, malformation

defraud *v* = **cheat**, con (*inf*), embezzle, fleece, pilfer, rip off (*sl*), swindle, trick

deft *adj* = **skillful**, adept, adroit, agile,

remove fuse of bomb, etc. **2** remove
tension (from situation, etc.).

de·fy [di-FĪ] vt **-fied, -fy·ing 1** challenge,
resist successfully. **2** disregard. **de·fi'ance** n
resistance. **de·fi'ant** adj **1** openly and
aggressively hostile. **2** insolent.

de·gauss [dee-GOWS] vt neutralize
magnetic field (of ship's hull, electronic
apparatus, etc.).

de·gen·er·ate [di-JEN-ə-rayt] vi **-rat·ed,
-rat·ing 1** deteriorate to lower mental,
moral, or physical level. ♦ adj [-rit] **2** fallen
away in quality. ♦ n [-rit] **3** degenerate
person. **de·gen'er·a·cy** n

de·grade [di-GRAYD] v **-grad·ed, -grad·ing**
♦ vt **1** dishonor. **2** debase. **3** reduce to
lower rank. ♦ vi **4** decompose chemically.
de·grad'a·ble adj capable of chemical,
biological decomposition. **de·grad'ed** adj
shamed, humiliated. **deg·ra·da'tion** n

de·gree [di-GREE] n **1** step, stage in
process, scale, relative rank, order,
condition, manner, way. **2** academic title
conferred by university or college. **3** unit of
measurement of temperature or angle.
third degree severe, lengthy examination,
esp. of accused person by police, to
extract information, confession.

de·hu·mid·i·fy [dee-hyoo-MID-ə-fī] vt
-fied, -fy·ing extract moisture from.

de·hy·drate [dee-HĪ-drayt] vt **-drat·ed,
-drat·ing** remove moisture from.

de·hy·dra'tion n

de·ice [dee-ĪS] vt **-iced, -ic·ing** to dislodge
ice from (e.g. windshield) or prevent its
forming.

de·i·fy [DEE-ə-fī] vt **-fied, -fy·ing 1** make
god of. **2** treat, worship as god.
de·i·fi·ca'tion n

deign [dayn] vt **1** condescend, stoop. **2**
think fit.

de·ism [DEE-iz-əm] n belief in god but not
in revelation. **de'ist** n **de·i·ty** [DEE-i-tee] n,
pl **-ties 1** divine status or attributes. **2** a
god.

dé·jà vu [DAY-zhah VOO] Fr experience of
perceiving new situation as if it had
occurred before.

de·ject [di-JEKT] vt dishearten, cast down,
depress. **de·ject'ed** adj **de·jec'tion** n

de ju·re [di JUUR-ee] Lat in law, by right.

de·lay [di-LAY] vt **1** postpone, hold back. ♦
vi **2** be tardy, linger. ♦ n **3** act or instance
of delaying. **4** interval of time between
events.

de·lec·ta·ble [di-LEK-tə-bəl] adj delightful
delicious. **de·lec·ta·tion** [dee-lek-TAY-shən]
n pleasure.

del·e·gate [DEL-i-git] n **1** person chosen to
represent another. ♦ vt [-gayt] **-gat·ed,
-gat·ing 2** send as deputy. **3** commit
(authority, business, etc.) to a deputy.
del·e·ga'tion n

de·lete [di-LEET] vt **-let·ed, -let·ing** remove,

dexterous, expert, neat, nimble, proficient

defunct adj **1** = **dead**, deceased, departed,
extinct, gone **2** = **obsolete**, bygone,
expired, inoperative, invalid, nonexistent,
out of commission

defy v = **resist**, brave, confront, disregard,
flout, scorn, slight, spurn

degenerate adj **1** = **depraved**, corrupt,
debauched, decadent, dissolute, immoral,
low, perverted ♦ v **2** = **worsen**, decay,
decline, decrease, deteriorate, fall off,
lapse, sink, slip

degradation n **1** = **disgrace**, discredit,
dishonor, humiliation, ignominy,
mortification, shame **2** = **deterioration**,
decline, degeneration, demotion,
downgrading

degrade v **1** = **disgrace**, debase, demean,
discredit, dishonor, humble, humiliate,
shame **2** = **demote**, downgrade, lower

degrading adj = **demeaning**,
dishonorable, humiliating, shameful,

undignified, unworthy

degree n = **stage**, grade, notch, point,
rung, step, unit

deity n = **god**, divinity, goddess, godhead,
idol, immortal, supreme being

dejected adj = **downhearted**, crestfallen,
depressed, despondent, disconsolate,
disheartened, downcast, glum, miserable,
sad

dejection n = **low spirits**, depression,
despair, despondency, doldrums,
downheartedness, gloom, melancholy,
sadness, sorrow, unhappiness

de jure adv = **legally**, by right, rightfully

delay v **1** = **put off**, defer, hold over,
postpone, procrastinate, shelve, suspend
2 = **hold up**, bog down, detain, hinder,
hold back, impede, obstruct, set back,
slow up ♦ n **3** = **putting off**, deferment,
postponement, procrastination,
suspension **4** = **hold-up**, hindrance,
impediment, interruption, interval,

cancel, erase. **de·le'tion** n

del·e·te·ri·ous [del-i-TEER-ee-əs] *adj* harmful, injurious.

de·lib·er·ate [di-LIB-ər-it] *adj* **1** intentional. **2** well considered. **3** without haste, slow. ◆ *v* [-rayt] **-rat·ed, -rat·ing 4** consider, debate. **de·lib·er·a'tion** n

del·i·cate [DEL-i-kit] *adj* **1** exquisite. **2** not robust, fragile. **3** sensitive. **4** requiring tact **5** deft. **del'i·ca·cy** n

del·i·ca·tes·sen [del-i-kə-TES-ən] n **1** store selling ready-to-eat foods. **2** the food sold.

de·li·cious [di-LISH-əs] *adj* delightful, pleasing to senses, esp. taste.

de·light [di-LĪT] *vt* **1** please greatly. ◆ *vi* **2** take great pleasure (in). ◆ n **3** great pleasure. **de·light'ful** *adj* **1** charming.

de·lin·e·ate [di-LIN-ee-ayt] *vt* **-at·ed, -at·ing 1** portray by drawing or description. **2** represent accurately. **de·lin·e·a'tion** n

de·lin·quent [di-LING-kwənt] n someone, esp. young person, guilty of delinquency. ◆ *adj* **de·lin'quen·cy** n, pl **-cies** (minor) offense or misdeed.

del·i·quesce [del-i-KWES] *vi* **-quesced, -quesc·ing** become liquid. **del·i·ques'cence** n **del·i·ques'cent** *adj*

de·lir·i·um [di-LEER-ee-əm] n **1** disorder of the mind, esp. in feverish illness. **2** violent excitement. **de·lir'i·ous** *adj* **1** raving. **2** light-headed, wildly excited.

setback, stoppage, wait

delegate n **1 = representative**, agent, ambassador, commissioner, deputy, envoy, legate ◆ *v* **2 = entrust**, assign, consign, devolve, give, hand over, pass on, transfer **3 = appoint**, accredit, authorize, commission, depute, designate, empower, mandate

delegation n **1 = deputation**, commission, contingent, embassy, envoys, legation, mission **2 = devolution**, assignment, commissioning, committal

delete *v* **= remove**, cancel, cross out, efface, erase, expunge, obliterate, rub out, strike out

deliberate *adj* **1 = intentional**, calculated, conscious, planned, prearranged, premeditated, purposeful, willful **2 = unhurried**, careful, cautious, circumspect, measured, methodical, ponderous, slow, thoughtful ◆ *v* **3 = consider**, cogitate, consult, debate, discuss, meditate, ponder, reflect, think, weigh

deliberately *adv* **= intentionally**, by design, calculatingly, consciously, in cold blood, knowingly, on purpose, willfully, wittingly

deliberation n **1 = consideration**, calculation, circumspection, forethought, meditation, reflection, thought **2 = discussion**, conference, consultation, debate

delicacy n **1 = fineness**, accuracy, daintiness, elegance, exquisiteness, lightness, precision, subtlety **2 = fragility**, flimsiness, frailty, slenderness, tenderness, weakness **3 = treat**, dainty, luxury, savory, tidbit **4 = fastidiousness**, discrimination,

finesse, purity, refinement, sensibility, taste **5 = sensitivity**, sensitiveness, tact

delicate *adj* **1 = fine**, deft, elegant, exquisite, graceful, precise, skilled, subtle **2 = subtle**, choice, dainty, delicious, fine, savory, tender, yummy (*inf*) **3 = fragile**, flimsy, frail, slender, slight, tender, weak **4 = considerate**, diplomatic, discreet, sensitive, tactful

delicately *adv* **1 = finely**, daintily, deftly, elegantly, exquisitely, gracefully, precisely, skillfully, subtly **2 = tactfully**, diplomatically, sensitively

delicious *adj* **= delectable**, appetizing, choice, dainty, mouthwatering, savory, tasty, toothsome, yummy (*inf*)

delight n **1 = pleasure**, ecstasy, enjoyment, gladness, glee, happiness, joy, rapture ◆ *v* **2 = please**, amuse, charm, cheer, enchant, gratify, thrill **3 delight in = take pleasure in**, appreciate, enjoy, feast on, like, love, relish, revel in, savor

delighted *adj* **= pleased**, ecstatic, elated, enchanted, happy, joyous, jubilant, overjoyed, thrilled

delightful *adj* **= pleasant**, agreeable, charming, delectable, enchanting, enjoyable, pleasurable, rapturous, thrilling

delinquent n **= criminal**, culprit, lawbreaker, miscreant, offender, villain, wrongdoer

delirious *adj* **1 = mad**, crazy, demented, deranged, incoherent, insane, raving, unhinged **2 = ecstatic**, beside oneself, carried away, excited, frantic, frenzied, hysterical, wild, wired (*sl*)

delirium n **1 = madness**, derangement, hallucination, insanity, raving **2 = frenzy**,

de·liv·er [di-LIV-ər] *vt* **1** carry (goods, etc.) to destination. **2** hand over. **3** release. **4** give birth or assist in birth (of). **5** utter or present (speech, etc.). **de·liv'er·ance** *n* rescue. **de·liv'er·y** *n*

Del·phic [DEL-fik] *adj* pert. to Delphi or to the oracle of Apollo.

del·ta [DEL-tə] *n* **1** alluvial tract where river at mouth breaks into several streams. **2** fourth letter in the Greek alphabet. **3** shape of this letter.

de·lude [di-LOOD] *vt* **-lud·ed, -lud·ing 1** deceive. **2** mislead. **de·lu'sion** [-zhən] *n*

del·uge [DEL-yooj] *n* **1** flood, great flow, rush, downpour, cloudburst. ♦ *vt* **-uged, -ug·ing 2** flood, overwhelm.

deluxe [də-LUKS] *adj* **1** rich, sumptuous. **2** superior in quality.

delve [delv] *v* **delved, delv·ing 1** (with *into*) search intensively. **2** dig.

de·mag·net·ize [dee-MAG-ni-tīz] *vt* **-tized, -tiz·ing** deprive of magnetic polarity.

dem·a·gogue [DEM-ə-gog] *n* mob leader or agitator. **dem·a·gog'ic** [-GOJ-ik] *adj*

dem'a·go·gy [-goh-jee] *n*

de·mand [di-MAND] *vt* **1** ask as giving an order. **2** ask as by right. **3** call for as due, right or necessary. ♦ *n* **4** urgent request, claim, requirement. **5** call for (specific commodity). **de·mand'ing** *adj* requiring great skill, patience, etc.

de·mar·cate [di-MAHR-kayt] *vt* **-cat·ed, -cat·ing** mark boundaries or limits of. **de·mar·ca'tion** *n*

de·mean [di-MEEN] *vt* degrade, lower, humiliate.

de·mean·or [di-MEEN-ər] *n* conduct, bearing, behavior.

de·men·ted [di-MEN-tid] *adj* **1** mad, crazy. **2** beside oneself. **de·men'tia** [-shə] *n* form of insanity.

de·mer·it [di-MER-it] *n* **1** bad mark. **2** undesirable quality.

demi- *comb. form* half, e.g. *demigod*.

de·mil·i·ta·rize [dee-MIL-i-tə-rīz] *vt* **-rized, -riz·ing** prohibit military presence or function in (an area).

dem·i·monde [DEM-ee-mond] *n* **1** class of

———— THESAURUS ————

ecstasy, fever, hysteria, passion

deliver *v* **1** = **carry**, bear, bring, cart, convey, distribute, transport **2** = **hand over**, commit, give up, grant, make over, relinquish, surrender, transfer, turn over, yield **3** = **give**, announce, declare, present, read, utter **4** = **release**, emancipate, free, liberate, loose, ransom, rescue, save **5** = **strike**, administer, aim, deal, direct, give, inflict, launch

deliverance *n* = **release**, emancipation, escape, liberation, ransom, redemption, rescue, salvation

delivery *n* **1** = **handing over**, consignment, conveyance, dispatch, distribution, surrender, transfer, transmission **2** = **speech**, articulation, elocution, enunciation, intonation, utterance **3** = **childbirth**, confinement, labor, parturition

delude *v* = **deceive**, beguile, dupe, fool, hoodwink, kid (*inf*), mislead, trick

deluge *n* **1** = **flood**, cataclysm, downpour, inundation, overflowing, spate, torrent **2** = **rush**, avalanche, barrage, flood, spate, torrent ♦ *v* **3** = **flood**, douse, drench, drown, inundate, soak, submerge, swamp **4** = **overwhelm**, engulf, inundate, overload, overrun, swamp

delusion *n* = **misconception**, error, fallacy, false impression, fancy, hallucination,

illusion, misapprehension, mistake

deluxe *adj* = **luxurious**, costly, exclusive, expensive, grand, opulent, select, special, splendid, superior

delve *v* = **research**, burrow, explore, ferret out, forage, investigate, look into, probe, rummage, search

demagogue *n* = **agitator**, firebrand, rabble-rouser

demand *v* **1** = **request**, ask, challenge, inquire, interrogate, question **2** = **require**, call for, cry out for, entail, involve, necessitate, need, want **3** = **claim**, exact, expect, insist on, order ♦ *n* **4** = **request**, inquiry, order, question, requisition **5** = **need**, call, claim, market, requirement, want

demanding *adj* = **difficult**, challenging, exacting, hard, taxing, tough, trying, wearing

demarcation *n* = **delimitation**, differentiation, distinction, division, separation

demean *v* = **lower**, abase, debase, degrade, descend, humble, stoop

demeanor *n* = **behavior**, air, bearing, carriage, comportment, conduct, deportment, manner

demented *adj* = **mad**, crazed, crazy, deranged, frenzied, insane, maniacal, women of doubtful reputation. **2** group behaving with doubtful legality, etc.

de·mise [di-MĪZ] *n* **1** death. **2** conveyance by will or bequest. **3** transfer of sovereignty on death or abdication.

dem·i·urge [DEM-ee-urj] *n* name given in some philosophies (esp. Platonic) to the creator of the world and man.

dem·o [DEM-oh] *n inf* short for DEMONSTRATION.

de·mo·bi·lize [dee-MOH-bə-līz] *vt* **-lized, -liz·ing 1** disband (troops). **2** discharge (soldier).

de·moc·ra·cy [di-MOK-rə-see] *n, pl* **-cies 1** government by the people or their elected representatives. **2** country so governed. **dem·o·crat** [DEM-ə-krat] *n* advocate of democracy. **dem·o·crat·ic** *adj* **1** connected with democracy. **2** favoring popular rights. **de·moc·ra·tize** *vt* **-tized, -tiz·ing**

de·mog·ra·phy [di-MOG-rə-fee] *n* study of population statistics, as births, deaths, diseases. **dem·o·graph·ic** [dem-ə-GRAF-ik] *adj*

de·mol·ish [di-MOL-ish] *vt* **1** knock to pieces. **2** destroy utterly, raze. **dem·o·li·tion** [dem-ə-LISH-ən] *n*

de·mon [DEE-mən] *n* **1** devil, evil spirit. **2** very cruel or malignant person. **3** person very good at or devoted to a given activity. **de·mo·ni·ac** [di-MOH-nee-ak] *n* one

possessed with a devil. **de·mo·ni·a·cal** [dee-mə-NĪ-ə-kəl] *adj* **de·mon·ic** [di-MON-ik] *adj* of the nature of a devil. **de·mon·ol·o·gy** [dee-] *n* study of demons.

dem·on·strate [DEM-ən-strayt] *v* **-strat·ed, -strat·ing ♦** *vt* **1** show by reasoning, prove. **2** describe, explain by specimens or experiments. **♦** *vi* **3** make exhibition of support, protest, etc, by public parade, demonstration. **4** make show of armed force. **de·mon·stra·ble** [di-MON-strə-bəl] *adj* **dem·on·stra'tion** *n* **1** making clear, proving by evidence. **2** exhibition and description. **3** organized public expression of opinion. **4** display of armed force. **de·mon'stra·tive** *adj* **1** expressing feelings, emotions easily and unreservedly. **2** pointing out. **3** conclusive. **dem'on·stra·tor** *n* **1** one who demonstrates equipment, products, etc. **2** one who takes part in a public demonstration.

de·mor·al·ize [di-MOR-ə-līz] *vt* **-ized, -iz·ing 1** deprive of courage and discipline. **2** undermine morally. **de·mor·al·i·za'tion** *n*

de·mote [di-MOHT] *vt* **-mot·ed, -mot·ing** reduce in status or rank. **de·mo'tion** *n*

de·mur [di-MUR] *vi* **-murred, -mur·ring** make difficulties, object. **de·mur'ral** *n* **1** raising of objection. **2** objection raised. **de·mur'rer** *n*

———| THESAURUS |———

unbalanced, unhinged

demise *n* **1** = **failure**, collapse, downfall, end, fall, ruin **2** *Euphemistic* = **death**, decease, departure

democracy *n* = **self-government**, commonwealth, republic

democratic *adj* = **self-governing**, autonomous, egalitarian, popular, populist, representative

demolish *v* **1** = **knock down**, bulldoze, destroy, dismantle, flatten, level, raze, tear down **2** = **defeat**, annihilate, destroy, overthrow, overturn, undo, wreck

demolition *n* = **knocking down**, bulldozing, destruction, explosion, levelling, razing, tearing down, wrecking

demon *n* **1** = **evil spirit**, devil, fiend, ghoul, goblin, malignant spirit **2** = **wizard**, ace (*inf*), fiend, master

demonic, demoniac, demoniacal *adj* **1** = **devilish**, diabolic, diabolical, fiendish, hellish, infernal, satanic **2** = **frenzied**, crazed, frantic, frenetic, furious, hectic,

maniacal, manic

demonstrable *adj* = **provable**, evident, irrefutable, obvious, palpable, self-evident, unmistakable, verifiable

demonstrate *v* **1** = **prove**, display, exhibit, indicate, manifest, show, testify to **2** = **show how**, describe, explain, illustrate, make clear, teach **3** = **march**, parade, picket, protest, rally

demonstration *n* **1** = **march**, mass lobby, parade, picket, protest, rally, sit-in **2** = **explanation**, description, exposition, presentation, test, trial **3** = **proof**, confirmation, display, evidence, exhibition, expression, illustration, testimony

demoralize *v* = **dishearten**, deject, depress, discourage, dispirit, undermine, unnerve, weaken

demote *v* = **downgrade**, degrade, kick downstairs (*sl*), lower in rank, relegate

demur *v* **1** = **object**, balk, dispute, hesitate, protest, refuse, take exception, waver **♦** *n* **2** *As in* **without demur** = **objection**,

de·mure [di-MYUUR] *adj* **-mur·er, -mur·est** reserved, quiet. **de·mure'ly** *adv*

den *n* **1** cave or hole of wild beast. **2** lair. **3** small room, esp. study. **4** site, haunt.

de·na·tion·a·lize [dee-NASH-ə-nl-īz] *vt* **-lized, -liz·ing** return (an industry) from public to private ownership.

de·na·ture [dee-NAY-chər] *vt* **-tured, -tur·ing** deprive of essential qualities, adulterate. **denatured alcohol** alcohol made undrinkable.

den·gue [DENG-gee] *n* an infectious tropical fever.

denial see DENY.

de·nier [DEN-yər] *n* unit of weight of silk and synthetic yarn.

den·i·grate [DEN-i-grayt] *vt* **-grat·ed, -grat·ing** belittle or disparage character of.

den·im [DEN-əm] *n* **1** strong twilled cotton fabric for trousers, overalls, etc. ♦ *pl* **2** garment made of this.

den·i·zen [DEN-ə-zən] *n* inhabitant.

de·nom·i·nate [di-NOM-ə-nayt] *vt* **-nat·ed, -nat·ing** give name to. **de·nom·i·na'tion** *n* **1** distinctly named church or sect. **2** name, esp. of class or group. **de·nom·i·na'tion·al** *adj* **de·nom'i·na·tor** *n* Arithmetic divisor in fraction.

de·note [di-NOHT] *vt* **-not·ed, -not·ing 1** stand for, be the name of. **2** mark, indicate, show. **de·no·ta·tion** [dee-noh-TAY-shən] *n* esp. explicit meaning of word or phrase.

de·noue·ment [day-noo-MAHN] *n* **1** unraveling of dramatic plot. **2** final solution of mystery.

de·nounce [di-NOWNS] *vt* **-nounced, -nounc·ing 1** speak violently against. **2** accuse. **3** terminate (treaty). **de·nun·ci·a'tion** *n* denouncing.

dense [dens] *adj* **dens·er, dens·est 1** thick, compact. **2** stupid. **den'si·ty** *n*, *pl* **-ties** mass per unit of volume.

dent *n* **1** hollow or mark left by blow or pressure. ♦ *vt* **2** make dent in. **3** mark with dent.

den·tal [DEN-tl] *adj* **1** of, pert. to teeth or dentistry. **2** pronounced by applying tongue to teeth. **den'ti·frice** [-fris] *n* powder, paste, or wash for cleaning teeth. **den'tist** *n* one skilled in care, repair of teeth. **den'tis·try** *n* art of dentist. **den·ti'tion** *n* **1** teething. **2** arrangement of teeth. **den'ture** [-chər] *n* (usu *pl*) set of false teeth. **dental floss** soft thread, oft. waxed, for cleaning between teeth.

den·tine [DEN-teen] *n* the hard bonelike part of a tooth.

de·nude [di-NOOD] *vt* **-nud·ed, -nud·ing 1** strip, make bare. **2** expose (rock) by erosion of plants, soil, etc.

denunciation see DENOUNCE.

de·ny [di-NĪ] *vt* **-nied, -ny·ing 1** declare untrue. **2** contradict. **3** reject, disown. **4** refuse to give. **5** refuse. **6** (reflex) abstain from. **de·ni'a·ble** *adj* **de·ni'al** *n*

de·o·dor·ize [dee-OH-də-rīz] *vt* **-ized,**

—— THESAURUS ——

compunction, dissent, hesitation, misgiving, protest, qualm

demure *adj* = **shy**, diffident, modest, reserved, reticent, retiring, sedate, unassuming

den *n* **1** = **lair**, cave, cavern, haunt, hideout, hole, shelter **2** *Chiefly U.S.* = **study**, cubbyhole, hideaway, living room, retreat, sanctuary, sanctum

denial *n* **1** = **negation**, contradiction, dissent, renunciation, repudiation, retraction **2** = **refusal**, prohibition, rebuff, rejection, repulse, veto

denigrate *v* = **disparage**, bad-mouth (*sl*), belittle, knock (*inf*), malign, run down, slander, vilify

denomination *n* **1** = **religious group**, belief, creed, persuasion, school, sect **2** = **unit**, grade, size, value

denote *v* = **indicate**, betoken, designate,

express, imply, mark, mean, show, signify

denounce *v* = **condemn**, accuse, attack, censure, denunciate, revile, stigmatize, vilify

dense *adj* **1** = **thick**, close-knit, compact, condensed, heavy, impenetrable, opaque, solid **2** = **stupid**, dull, obtuse, slow-witted, stolid, thick

density *n* = **tightness**, bulk, compactness, consistency, denseness, impenetrability, mass, solidity, thickness

dent *n* **1** = **hollow**, chip, crater, depression, dimple, dip, impression, indentation, pit ♦ *v* **2** = **make a dent in**, gouge, hollow, press in, push in

deny *v* **1** = **contradict**, disagree with, disprove, rebuff, rebut, refute **2** = **refuse**, begrudge, disallow, forbid, reject, turn down, withhold **3** = **renounce**, disclaim, disown, recant, repudiate, retract

-iz·ing rid of smell or mask smell of.
de·o'dor·ant n de·o'dor·iz·er n

de·ox·i·dize [dee-OK-si-dīz] vt -dized,
-diz·ing deprive of oxygen.

de·part [di-PAHRT] vi 1 go away. 2 start
out, set forth. 3 deviate, vary. 4 die.
de·par'ture [-chər] n

de·part·ment [di-PAHRT-mənt] n 1
division. 2 branch. 3 province.
de·part·men'tal adj

de·pend [di-PEND] vi (usu. with on) 1 rely
entirely. 2 live. 3 be contingent, await
settlement or decision. de·pend'a·ble adj
reliable. de·pend'ent n 1 one for whose
maintenance another is responsible. ♦ adj 2
depending on. de·pend'ence n
de·pend'en·cy n 1 dependence. 2 subject
territory.

de·pict [di-PIKT] vt 1 give picture of. 2
describe in words. de·pic'tion n

de·pil·a·to·ry [di-PIL-ə-tor-ee] n, pl -ries
substance that removes unwanted hair. ♦
adj

de·plete [di-PLEET] vt -plet·ed, -plet·ing 1
empty. 2 reduce. 3 exhaust. de·ple'tion n

de·plore [di-PLOR] vt -plored, -plor·ing 1
lament, regret. 2 deprecate, complain of.
de·plor'a·ble adj 1 lamentable. 2
disgraceful.

de·ploy [di-PLOI] v 1 of troops, ships,
aircraft (cause to) adopt battle formation.
2 arrange. de·ploy'ment n

de·po·nent [di-POH-nənt] adj 1 of verb,
having passive form but active meaning. ♦
n 2 deponent verb. 3 one who makes
statement under oath.

de·pop·u·late [di-POP-yə-layt] v -lat·ed,
-lat·ing (cause to) be reduced in
population. de·pop·u·la'tion n

de·port [di-PORT] vt expel from foreign
country, banish. de·por·ta'tion [dee-] n

de·port·ment [di-PORT-mənt] n behavior,
conduct, bearing. de·port' v behave, carry
(oneself).

de·pose [di-POHZ] v -posed, -pos·ing ♦ vt
1 remove from office, esp. of ruler. ♦ vi 2
make statement under oath, give
evidence. de·pos'al n removal from office.

de·pos·it [di-POZ-it] vt 1 set down, esp.
carefully. 2 give into safekeeping, esp. in

depart v 1 = leave, absent (oneself),
disappear, exit, go, go away, quit, retire,
retreat, withdraw 2 = deviate, differ,
digress, diverge, stray, swerve, turn aside,
vary, veer

department n = section, branch, bureau,
division, office, station, subdivision, unit

departure n 1 = leaving, exit, exodus,
going, going away, leave-taking, removal,
retirement, withdrawal 2 = divergence,
deviation, digression, variation 3 = shift,
change, difference, innovation, novelty,
whole new ball game (inf)

depend v 1 = trust in, bank on, count on,
lean on, reckon on, rely upon, turn to 2 =
be determined by, be based on, be
contingent on, be subject to, be
subordinate to, hang on, hinge on, rest
on, revolve around

dependable adj = reliable, faithful,
reputable, responsible, staunch, steady,
sure, trustworthy, trusty, unfailing

dependant n = relative, child, minor,
protégé, subordinate

dependent adj 1 = relying on, defenseless,
helpless, reliant, vulnerable, weak
2 dependent on or upon = determined by,
conditional on, contingent on, depending
on, influenced by, subject to

depict v 1 = draw, delineate, illustrate,
outline, paint, picture, portray, sketch 2 =
describe, characterize, narrate, outline,
represent

depiction n = representation, delineation,
description, picture, portrayal, sketch

deplete v = use up, consume, drain,
empty, exhaust, expend, impoverish,
lessen, reduce

deplorable adj 1 = regrettable, grievous,
lamentable, pitiable, sad, unfortunate,
wretched 2 = disgraceful, dishonorable,
reprehensible, scandalous, shameful

deplore v = disapprove of, abhor, censure,
condemn, denounce, object to, take a dim
view of

deploy v = position, arrange, set out,
station, use, utilize

deployment n = position, arrangement,
organization, spread, stationing, use,
utilization

deport v 1 = expel, banish, exile,
expatriate, extradite, oust 2 deport oneself
= behave, acquit oneself, act, bear oneself,
carry oneself, comport oneself, conduct
oneself, hold oneself

depose v 1 = remove from office, demote,
dethrone, dismiss, displace, oust 2 Law =
testify, avouch, declare, make a deposition

bank. **3** let fall (as sediment). ◆ *n* **4** thing deposited. **5** money given in part payment or as security. **6** sediment. **dep·o·si·tion** [dep-ə-ZISH-ən] *n* **1** statement written and attested. **2** act of deposing or depositing. **de·pos'i·tor** *n* **de·pos'i·to·ry** *n, pl* **-ries** place for safekeeping.

dep·ot [DEE-poh] *n* **1** storehouse. **2** building for storage and servicing of buses, trains, etc. **3** railroad, bus station.

de·prave [di-PRAYV] *vt* **-praved, -prav·ing** make bad, corrupt, pervert. **de·prav'i·ty** *n, pl* **-ties** wickedness, viciousness.

dep·re·cate [DEP-ri-kayt] *vt* **-cat·ed, -cat·ing** **1** express disapproval of. **2** advise against. **dep·re·ca'tion** *n* **dep·re·ca·to·ry** *adj*

de·pre·ci·ate [di-PREE-shee-ayt] *v* **-at·ed, -at·ing** ◆ *vt* **1** lower price, value or purchasing power of. **2** belittle. ◆ *vi* **3** fall in value. **de·pre·ci·a'tion** *n*

dep·re·da·tion [dep-ri-DAY-shən] *n* plundering, pillage. **dep're·date** *vt* **-dat·ed, -dat·ing** plunder, despoil.

de·press [di-PRES] *vt* **1** affect with low spirits. **2** lower, in level or activity. **de·pres'sion** [-PRESH-ən] *n* **1** hollow. **2** low spirits, dejection, despondency. **3** poor condition of business, slump. **de·pres'sant** *adj, n*

de·prive [di-PRĪV] *vt* **-prived, -priv·ing** strip, dispossess. **dep·ri·va·tion** [dep-rə-VAY-shən] *n* **deprived** *adj* lacking adequate food, care, amenities, etc.

depth *n* (degree of) deepness. **1** deep place, abyss. **2** intensity (of color, feeling). **3** profundity (of mind). **depth charge** bomb for use against submarines.

de·pute [di-PYOOT] **-put·ed, -put·ing** ◆ *vt* **1** allot. **2** appoint as an agent or substitute. **dep·u·ta·tion** [dep-yə-TAY-shən] *n* persons sent to speak for others. **dep'u·tize** *vi* **-tized, -tiz·ing** **1** act for another. ◆ *vt* **2** depute. **dep'u·ty** *n, pl* **-ties** **1** assistant. **2**

THESAURUS

deposit *v* **1** = **put**, drop, lay, locate, place **2** = **store**, bank, consign, entrust, lodge ◆ *n* **3** = **down payment**, installment, part payment, pledge, retainer, security, stake **4** = **sediment**, accumulation, dregs, lees, precipitate, silt

depot *n* **1** = **storehouse**, depository, repository, warehouse **2** = **bus station**, garage, terminus

depraved *adj* = **corrupt**, degenerate, dissolute, evil, immoral, sinful, vicious, vile, wicked

depravity *n* = **corruption**, debauchery, evil, immorality, sinfulness, vice, wickedness

depreciate *v* **1** = **devalue**, decrease, deflate, lessen, lose value, lower, reduce **2** = **disparage**, belittle, denigrate, deride, detract, run down, scorn, sneer at

depreciation *n* **1** = **devaluation**, deflation, depression, drop, fall, slump **2** = **disparagement**, belittlement, denigration, deprecation, detraction

depress *v* **1** = **sadden**, deject, discourage, dishearten, dispirit, make despondent, oppress, weigh down **2** = **lower**, cheapen, depreciate, devalue, diminish, downgrade, lessen, reduce **3** = **press down**, flatten, level, lower, push down

depressed *adj* **1** = **low-spirited**, blue, dejected, despondent, discouraged, dispirited, downcast, downhearted, fed up, sad, unhappy **2** = **poverty-stricken**, deprived, disadvantaged, needy, poor, run-down **3** = **lowered**, cheapened, depreciated, devalued, weakened **4** = **sunken**, concave, hollow, indented, recessed

depressing *adj* = **bleak**, discouraging, disheartening, dismal, dispiriting, gloomy, harrowing, sad, saddening

depression *n* **1** = **low spirits**, dejection, despair, despondency, downheartedness, dumps (*inf*), gloominess, melancholy, sadness, the blues **2** = **recession**, economic decline, hard or bad times, inactivity, slump, stagnation **3** = **hollow**, bowl, cavity, dent, dimple, dip, indentation, pit, valley

deprivation *n* **1** = **withholding**, denial, dispossession, expropriation, removal, withdrawal **2** = **want**, destitution, distress, hardship, need, privation

deprive *v* = **withhold**, bereave, despoil, dispossess, rob, strip

deprived *adj* = **poor**, bereft, destitute, disadvantaged, down at heel, in need, lacking, needy

depth *n* **1** = **deepness**, drop, extent, measure **2** = **insight**, astuteness, discernment, penetration, profoundness, profundity, sagacity, wisdom

deputation *n* = **delegation**, commission, embassy, envoys, legation

de·rail [dee-RAYL] v (cause to) go off the rails, as train, etc. **de·rail'ment** n

de·rail·leur [di-RAY-lər] n gear-changing mechanism for bicycles.

de·range [di-RAYNJ] vt **-ranged, -rang·ing** 1 put out of place, out of order. 2 upset. 3 make insane. **de·range'ment** n

der·by [DUR bee] n 1 horserace, esp Kentucky Derby, held at Churchill Downs, Kentucky. 2 contest between teams of skaters, etc. 3 man's low-crowned stiff felt hat.

de·reg·u·late [dee-REG-yə-layt] vt **-lat·ed, -lat·ing** remove regulations or controls from.

der·e·lict [DER-ə-likt] adj 1 abandoned, forsaken. 2 falling into ruins, dilapidated. ◆ n 3 social outcast, vagrant. 4 abandoned property, ship, etc. **der·e·lic'tion** n 1 neglect (of duty). 2 abandoning.

de·ride [di-RĪD] vt **-rid·ed, -rid·ing** speak of or treat with contempt, ridicule. **de·ri'sion** [-RIZH-ən] n ridicule. **de·ri'sive** [-RĪ-siv] adj

de ri·gueur [də ri-GUR] Fr required by etiquette, fashion or custom.

de·rive [di-RĪV] vt **-rived, -riv·ing** 1 deduce, get from. 2 show origin of. ◆ vi 3 issue, be descended (from). **der·i·va·tion** [der-ə-VAY-shən] n **de·riv·a·tive** [di-RIV-ə-tiv] adj, n

der·ma·ti·tis [dur-mə-TĪ-tis] n inflammation of skin.

der·ma·tol·o·gy [dur-mə-TOL-ə-jee] n science of skin. **der·ma·tol'o·gist** n physician specializing in skin diseases.

de·ro·gate [DER-ə-gayt] v **-gat·ed, -gat·ing** ◆ vt 1 disparage. ◆ vi 2 detract.

de·rog·a·to·ry [di-ROG-ə-tor-ee] adj disparaging, belittling, intentionally offensive.

der·rick [DER-ik] n 1 hoisting machine. 2 framework over oil well, etc.

der·ring-do [DER-ing DOO] n (act of) spirited bravery, boldness.

der·rin·ger [DER-in-jər] n short-barreled pocket pistol.

der·vish [DUR-vish] n member of Muslim ascetic order, noted for frenzied, whirling dance.

des·cant [DES-kant] n 1 Mus. decorative variation sung as accompaniment to basic melody. ◆ vi [des-KANT] 2 Mus. sing or play a descant. 3 talk about in detail. 4 dwell (on) at length.

de·scend [di-SEND] vi 1 come or go down. 2 slope down. 3 stoop, condescend. 4 spring from (ancestor, etc.). 5 pass to heir, be transmitted. 6 swoop on or attack. ◆ vt 7 go or come down. **de·scend'ant** n person descended from an ancestor. **de·scent'** n

de·scribe [di-SKRĪB] vt **-scribed, -scrib·ing** 1 give detailed account of. 2 pronounce or label. 3 trace out (geometric figure, etc.). **de·scrip·tion** [-SKRIP-shən] n 1 detailed

deputize v = **stand in for**, act for, take the place of, understudy

deputy n = **substitute**, delegate, legate, lieutenant, number two, proxy, representative, second-in-command, surrogate

deranged adj = **mad**, crazed, crazy, demented, distracted, insane, irrational, unbalanced, unhinged

derelict adj 1 = **abandoned**, deserted, dilapidated, discarded, forsaken, neglected, ruined ◆ n 2 = **tramp**, bag lady, down-and-out, outcast, vagrant

deride v = **mock**, disdain, disparage, insult, jeer, ridicule, scoff, scorn, sneer, taunt

derisory adj = **ridiculous**, contemptible, insulting, laughable, lousy (sl), ludicrous, outrageous, preposterous

derivation n = **origin**, beginning, foundation, root, source

derive from v = **come from**, arise from,

emanate from, flow from, issue from, originate from, proceed from, spring from, stem from

derogatory adj = **disparaging**, belittling, defamatory, offensive, slighting, uncomplimentary, unfavorable, unflattering

descend v 1 = **move down**, drop, fall, go down, plummet, plunge, sink, subside, tumble 2 = **slope**, dip, incline, slant 3 = **lower oneself**, degenerate, deteriorate, stoop 4 **be descended** = **originate**, be handed down, be passed down, derive, issue, proceed, spring 5 **descend on** = **attack**, arrive, invade, raid, swoop

descent n 1 = **coming down**, drop, fall, plunge, swoop 2 = **slope**, declivity, dip, drop, incline, slant 3 = **ancestry**, extraction, family tree, genealogy, lineage, origin, parentage 4 = **decline**, degeneration, deterioration account. **2** marking out. **3** kind, sort, species. **de·scrip'tive** adj

de·scry [di-SKRĪ] vt **-scried, -scry·ing** make out, catch sight of, esp. at a distance espy.

des·e·crate [DES-i-krayt] vt **-crat·ed, -crat·ing 1** violate sanctity of. **2** profane. **3** convert to evil use. **des·e·cra'tion** n

des·ert¹ [DEZ-ərt] n **1** uninhabited and barren region. ◆ adj **2** barren, uninhabited, desolate.

de·sert² [di-ZURT] vt **1** abandon, forsake, leave. ◆ vi **2** run away from service, esp. of soldiers, sailors, etc. **de·sert'er** n **de·ser'tion** n

de·sert³ [di-ZURT] n (usu pl) **1** what is due as reward or punishment. **2** merit, virtue.

de·serve [di-ZURV] vt **-served, -serv·ing 1** show oneself worthy of. **2** have by conduct a claim to. **de·serv'ed·ly** adv **de·serv'ing** adj worthy (of reward, etc.).

deshabille n see DISHABILLE.

des·ic·cate [DES-i-kayt] v **-cat·ed, -cat·ing 1** dry. **2** dry up.

de·sid·er·a·tum [di-sid-ə-RAH-təm] n, pl **-ta** [-tə] something lacked and wanted.

de·sign [di-ZĪN] vt **1** make working drawings for. **2** sketch. **3** plan out. **4** intend, select for. ◆ n **5** outline sketch. **6** working plan. **7** art of making decorative patterns, etc. **8** project, purpose, mental plan. **de·sign'ed·ly** adv on purpose. **de·sign'er** n esp. one who draws designs for manufacturers or selects typefaces, etc. for books, etc. **de·sign'ing** adj crafty, scheming.

des·ig·nate [DEZ-ig-nayt] vt **-nat·ed, -nat·ing 1** name, pick out, appoint to office. ◆ adj [-nit] **2** appointed but not yet installed. **des·ig·na'tion** n name, appellation.

de·sire [di-ZĪR] vt **-sired, -sir·ing 1** wish, long for. **2** ask for, entreat. ◆ n **3** longing, craving. **4** expressed wish, request. **5** sexual appetite. **6** something wished for or requested. **de·sir'a·ble** adj worth desiring. **de·sir'ous** adj filled with desire.

de·sist [di-ZIST] vi cease, stop.

describe v **1** = **relate**, depict, explain, express, narrate, portray, recount, report, tell **2** = **trace**, delineate, draw, mark out, outline

description n **1** = **account**, depiction, explanation, narrative, portrayal, report, representation, sketch **2** = **kind**, brand, category, class, order, sort, type, variety

descriptive adj = **graphic**, detailed, explanatory, expressive, illustrative, pictorial, picturesque, vivid

desert¹ n = **wilderness**, solitude, waste, wasteland, wilds

desert² v = **abandon**, abscond, forsake, jilt, leave, leave stranded, maroon, quit, strand, walk out on (inf)

deserted adj = **abandoned**, derelict, desolate, empty, forsaken, neglected, unoccupied, vacant

deserter n = **defector**, absconder, escapee, fugitive, renegade, runaway, traitor, truant

desertion n = **abandonment**, absconding, apostasy, betrayal, defection, dereliction, escape, evasion, flight, relinquishment

deserve v = **merit**, be entitled to, be worthy of, earn, justify, rate, warrant

deserved adj = **well-earned**, due, earned, fitting, justified, merited, proper, rightful, warranted

deserving adj = **worthy**, commendable, estimable, laudable, meritorious, praiseworthy, righteous

design v **1** = **plan**, draft, draw, outline, sketch, trace **2** = **create**, conceive, fabricate, fashion, invent, originate, think up **3** = **intend**, aim, mean, plan, propose, purpose ◆ n **4** = **plan**, blueprint, draft, drawing, model, outline, scheme, sketch **5** = **arrangement**, construction, form, organization, pattern, shape, style **6** = **intention**, aim, end, goal, object, objective, purpose, target

designate v **1** = **name**, call, dub, entitle, label, style, term **2** = **appoint**, assign, choose, delegate, depute, nominate, select

designation n = **name**, description, label, mark, title

designer n = **creator**, architect, deviser, inventor, originator, planner

desirable adj **1** = **worthwhile**, advantageous, advisable, beneficial, good, preferable, profitable, win-win (inf) **2** = **attractive**, adorable, alluring, fetching, glamorous, seductive, sexy (inf)

desire v **1** = **want**, crave, hanker after, hope for, long for, set one's heart on, thirst for, wish for, yearn for ◆ n **2** = **wish**, aspiration, craving, hankering, hope, longing, thirst, want **3** = **lust**, appetite, libido, passion

desk n 1 table or other piece of furniture designed for reading or writing. 2 counter. 3 editorial section of newspaper, etc. covering specific subject. 4 section of State Department having responsibility for particular operations.

des·o·late [DES-ə-lit] adj 1 uninhabited. 2 neglected, barren, ruinous. 3 solitary. 4 dreary, dismal, forlorn. ◆ vt [-layt] -lat·ed, -lat·ing 5 depopulate, lay waste. 6 overwhelm with grief. **des·o·la'tion** n

de·spair [di-SPAIR] vi 1 lose hope. ◆ n 2 loss of all hope. 3 cause of this. 4 despondency.

despatch see DISPATCH.

des·pe·rate [DES-pər-it] adj 1 reckless from despair. 2 difficult or dangerous. 3 frantic. 4 hopelessly bad. 5 leaving no room for hope. **des·per·a'do** [-pə-RAH-doh] n, pl -dos reckless, lawless person. **des'per·ate·ly** adv **des·per·a'tion** n

de·spise [di-SPIZ] vt -spised, -spis·ing look down on as contemptible, inferior. **des·pi·ca·ble** [DES-pi-kə-bəl] adj base, contemptible, vile.

de·spite [di-SPIT] prep in spite of.

de·spoil [di-SPOIL] vt plunder, rob, strip of. **de·spo·li·a·tion** [di-spoh-lee-AY-shən] n

de·spond·ent [di-SPON-dənt] adj dejected, depressed. **de·spond'en·cy** n

des·pot [DES-pət] n tyrant, oppressor. **des·pot·ic** [di-SPOT-ik] adj **des'pot·ism** n autocratic government, tyranny.

des·sert [di-ZURT] n course of pastry, fruit, etc. served at end of meal.

des·ti·na·tion [des-tə-NAY-shən] n 1 place a person or thing is bound for. 2 goal. 3 purpose.

des·tine [DES-tin] vt -tined, -tin·ing 1 ordain or fix beforehand. 2 set apart, devote.

———————— THESAURUS ————————

desist v = **stop**, break off, cease, discontinue, end, forbear, leave off, pause, refrain from

desolate adj 1 = **uninhabited**, bare, barren, bleak, dreary, godforsaken, solitary, wild 2 = **miserable**, dejected, despondent, disconsolate, downcast, forlorn, gloomy, wretched ◆ v 3 = **lay waste**, depopulate, despoil, destroy, devastate, lay low, pillage, plunder, ravage, ruin 4 = **deject**, depress, dishearten, dismay, distress, grieve

desolation n 1 = **ruin**, destruction, devastation, havoc 2 = **bleakness**, barrenness, isolation, solitude 3 = **misery**, anguish, dejection, despair, distress, gloom, sadness, woe, wretchedness

despair n 1 = **despondency**, anguish, dejection, depression, desperation, gloom, hopelessness, misery, wretchedness ◆ v 2 = **lose hope**, give up, lose heart

despairing adj = **hopeless**, dejected, desperate, despondent, disconsolate, frantic, grief-stricken, inconsolable, miserable, wretched

despatch see DISPATCH

desperado n = **criminal**, bandit, lawbreaker, outlaw, villain

desperate adj 1 = **reckless**, audacious, daring, frantic, furious, risky 2 = **grave**, drastic, extreme, urgent

desperately adv 1 = **gravely**, badly, dangerously, perilously, seriously, severely

2 = **hopelessly**, appallingly, fearfully, frightfully, shockingly

desperation n 1 = **recklessness**, foolhardiness, frenzy, impetuosity, madness, rashness 2 = **misery**, agony, anguish, despair, hopelessness, trouble, unhappiness, worry

despicable adj = **contemptible**, detestable, disgraceful, hateful, lousy (sl), mean, scuzzy (sl), shameful, sordid, vile, worthless, wretched

despise v = **look down on**, abhor, detest, loathe, revile, scorn

despite prep = **in spite of**, against, even with, in the face of, in the teeth of, notwithstanding, regardless of, undeterred by

despondency n = **dejection**, depression, despair, desperation, gloom, low spirits, melancholy, misery, sadness

despondent adj = **dejected**, depressed, disconsolate, disheartened, dispirited, downhearted, glum, in despair, sad, sorrowful

despot n = **tyrant**, autocrat, dictator, oppressor

despotic adj = **tyrannical**, authoritarian, autocratic, dictatorial, domineering, imperious, oppressive

despotism n = **tyranny**, autocracy, dictatorship, oppression, totalitarianism

destination n = **journey's end**, haven, resting-place, station, stop, terminus

destined adj = **fated**, bound, certain,

des·ti·ny [DES-tə-nee] *n, pl* **-nies 1** course of events or person's fate. **2** the power that foreordains.

des·ti·tute [DES-ti-toot] *adj* **1** in absolute want. **2** in great need, devoid (of). **3** penniless. **des·ti·tu'tion** *n*

de·stroy [di-STROI] *vt* **1** ruin. **2** pull to pieces. **3** undo. **4** put an end to. **5** demolish. **6** annihilate. **de·stroy'er** *n* **1** one who destroys. **2** small, swift, heavily armed warship. **de·struct** [di-STRUKT] *v* **1** destroy (one's own missile, etc.) for safety. **2** be destroyed. **de·struct'i·ble** *adj* **de·struc'tion** *n* **1** ruin, overthrow. **2** death. **de·struc'tive** *adj* **1** destroying. **2** negative, not constructive.

des·ue·tude [DES-wi-tood] *n* disuse, discontinuance.

des·ul·to·ry [DES-əl-tor-ee] *adj* **1** passing, changing fitfully from one thing to another. **2** aimless. **3** unmethodical.

de·tach [di-TACH] *vt* unfasten, disconnect, separate. **de·tach'a·ble** *adj* **de·tached'** *adj* **1** standing apart, isolated. **2** impersonal, disinterested. **de·tach'ment** *n* **1** aloofness.

de·tail [di-TAYL, DEE-tayl] *n* **1** particular. **2** small or unimportant part. **3** treatment of anything item by item. **4** party or personnel assigned for duty in military unit. ♦ *vt* **5** relate in full. **6** appoint for duty.

de·tain [di-TAYN] *vt* **1** keep under restraint. **2** hinder. **3** keep waiting. **de·ten'tion** *n* **1** confinement. **2** arrest. **3** detaining.

de·tect [di-TEKT] *vt* find out or discover existence, presence, nature or identity of. **de·tec'tion** *n* **de·tec'tive** *n* **1** police officer or private agent employed in detecting crime. ♦ *adj* **2** employed in detection. **de·tec'tor** *n* esp. mechanical sensing device or device for detecting radio signals, etc.

dé·tente [day-TAHNT] *n* lessening of tension in political or international affairs.

detention *n* see DETAIN.

de·ter [di-TUR] *vt* **-terred, -ter·ring 1** discourage, frighten. **2** hinder, prevent. **de·ter'rent** *adj, n*

de·ter·gent [di-TUR-jənt] *n* **1** cleansing,

───── THESAURUS ─────

doomed, intended, meant, predestined

destiny *n* = **fate**, doom, fortune, karma, kismet, lot, portion

destitute *adj* = **penniless**, down and out, down on one's luck (*inf*), impoverished, indigent, insolvent, moneyless, penurious, poor, poverty-stricken

destroy *v* = **ruin**, annihilate, crush, demolish, devastate, eradicate, shatter, wipe out, wreck

destruction *n* = **ruin**, annihilation, demolition, devastation, eradication, extermination, havoc, slaughter, wreckage

destructive *adj* = **damaging**, calamitous, catastrophic, deadly, devastating, fatal, harmful, lethal, ruinous

detach *v* = **separate**, cut off, disconnect, disengage, divide, remove, sever, tear off, unfasten

detached *adj* **1** = **separate**, disconnected, discrete, unconnected **2** = **uninvolved**, disinterested, dispassionate, impartial, impersonal, neutral, objective, reserved, unbiased

detachment *n* **1** = **indifference**, aloofness, coolness, nonchalance, remoteness, unconcern **2** = **impartiality**, fairness, neutrality, objectivity **3** *Military* = **unit**, body, force, party, patrol, squad, task force

detail *n* **1** = **point**, aspect, component, element, fact, factor, feature, particular, respect **2** = **fine point**, nicety, particular, triviality **3** *Military* = **party**, assignment, body, detachment, duty, fatigue, force, squad ♦ *v* **4** = **list**, catalog, enumerate, itemize, recite, recount, rehearse, relate, tabulate **5** = **appoint**, allocate, assign, charge, commission, delegate, send

detailed *adj* = **comprehensive**, blow-by-blow, exhaustive, full, intricate, minute, particular, thorough

detain *v* **1** = **delay**, check, hinder, hold up, impede, keep back, retard, slow up (*or* down) **2** = **hold**, arrest, confine, intern, restrain

detect *v* **1** = **notice**, ascertain, identify, note, observe, perceive, recognize, spot **2** = **discover**, find, track down, uncover, unmask

detective *n* = **investigator**, cop (*sl*), gumshoe (*sl*), private eye, private investigator, sleuth (*inf*)

detention *n* = **imprisonment**, confinement, custody, incarceration, quarantine

deter *v* = **discourage**, dissuade, frighten, inhibit from, intimidate, prevent, put off, stop, talk out of purifying substance. ◆ adj 2 having cleansing power.

de•te•ri•o•rate [di-TEER-ee-ə-rayt] v -rat•ed, -rat•ing become or make worse. de•te•ri•o•ra'tion n

de•ter•mine [di-TUR-min] v -mined, -min•ing ◆ vt 1 make up one's mind, decide. 2 fix as known. 3 bring to a decision. 4 be deciding factor in. 5 Law end. ◆ vi 6 come to an end. 7 come to a decision. de•ter'mi•nant adj, n de•ter'mi•nate [-nit] adj fixed in scope or nature. de•ter•mi•na'tion n 1 determining. 2 firm or resolute conduct or purpose. 3 resolve. determined adj resolute. de•ter'min•ism n theory that human action is settled by forces independent of human will.

de•test [di-TEST] vt hate, loathe. de•test'a•ble adj de•tes•ta•tion [dee-te-STAY-shən] n

de•throne [dee-THROHN] vt -throned, -thron•ing remove from throne, depose.

det•o•nate [DET-n-ayt] v of bomb, mine, explosives, etc., (cause to) explode. det•o•na'tion n det'o•na•tor n mechanical, electrical device, or small amount of explosive, used to set off main explosive charge.

de•tour [DEE-tuur] n 1 course that leaves main route to rejoin it later. 2 roundabout way. ◆ vi

de•tox [DEE-toks] inf ◆ n 1 treatment to rid the body of poisonous substances. ◆ v [dee-TOKS] 2 undergo or subject to such treatment.

de•tract [di-TRAKT] v take away (a part) from, diminish. de•trac'tor n

det•ri•ment [DE-trə-mənt] n harm done, loss, damage. det•ri•men'tal adj damaging, injurious.

de•tri•tus [di-TRĪ-təs] n 1 worn-down matter such as gravel, or rock debris. 2 debris.

de trop [də TROH] Fr not wanted, superfluous.

deuce [doos] n 1 two. 2 playing card with two spots. 3 Tennis forty all. 4 in exclamatory phrases, the devil.

Deut. Deuteronomy.

deu•te•ri•um [doo-TEER-ee-əm] n isotope of hydrogen twice as heavy as the normal gas.

de•val•ue [dee-VAL-yoo] -ued, -u•ing ◆ v 1 (of currency) reduce or be reduced in value. 2 reduce the value or worth of. de•val•u•a'tion n

dev•as•tate [DEV-ə-stayt] vt -tat•ed, -tat•ing 1 lay waste. 2 ravage. 3 inf overwhelm. dev•as•ta'tion n

de•vel•op [di-VEL-əp] vt 1 bring to maturity. 2 elaborate. 3 bring forth, bring out. 4 evolve. 5 treat photographic plate or film to bring out image. 6 improve value or change use of (land) by building, etc. ◆ vi 7 grow to maturer state. de•vel'op•er n 1 one who develops land. 2 chemical for developing film. de•vel'op•ment n

detergent n = cleaner, cleanser

deteriorate v = decline, degenerate, go downhill (inf), lower, slump, worsen

determination n = tenacity, dedication, doggedness, fortitude, perseverance, persistence, resolve, single-mindedness, steadfastness, willpower

determine v 1 = settle, conclude, decide, end, finish, ordain, regulate 2 = find out, ascertain, detect, discover, learn, verify, work out 3 = decide, choose, elect, make up one's mind, resolve

determined adj = resolute, dogged, firm, intent, persevering, persistent, single-minded, steadfast, tenacious, unwavering

deterrent n = discouragement, check, curb, disincentive, hindrance, impediment, obstacle, restraint

detest v = hate, abhor, abominate, despise, dislike intensely, loathe, recoil from

detonate v = explode, blast, blow up, discharge, set off, trigger

detour n = diversion, bypass, circuitous or indirect route, roundabout way

detract v = lessen, devaluate, diminish, lower, reduce, take away from

detriment n = damage, disadvantage, disservice, harm, hurt, impairment, injury, loss

detrimental adj = damaging, adverse, deleterious, destructive, disadvantageous, harmful, prejudicial, unfavorable

devastate v = destroy, demolish, lay waste, level, ravage, raze, ruin, sack, wreck

devastating adj = overwhelming, cutting, overpowering, savage, trenchant, vitriolic, withering

devastation n = destruction, demolition,

de·vi·ate [DEE-vee-ayt] *vi* **-at·ed, -at·ing** leave the way, turn aside, diverge. **de·vi·ant** *n, adj* (person) deviating from normal esp. in sexual practices. **de·vi·a'tion** *n* **de'vi·ous** *adj* **1** deceitful, underhanded. **2** roundabout, rambling. **3** erring.

de·vice [di-VĪS] *n* **1** contrivance, invention. **2** apparatus. **3** stratagem. **4** scheme, plot. **5** heraldic or emblematic figure or design.

dev·il [DEV-əl] *n* **1** personified spirit of evil. **2** superhuman evil being. **3** person of great wickedness, cruelty, etc. **4** *inf* fellow. **5** *inf* something difficult or annoying. **6** energy, dash, unconquerable spirit. **7** *inf* rogue, rascal. ♦ *vt* **-iled, -il·ing 8** prepare (eggs, etc.) with spicy seasoning. **dev'il·ish** *adj* **1** like, of the devil. **2** evil. ♦ *adv* **3** *inf* very, extremely. **dev'il·try** *n, pl* **-tries 1** wickedness. **2** wild and reckless mischief, revelry, high spirits. **dev'il-may-care'** *adj* happy-go-lucky. **devil's advocate 1** one who advocates opposing, unpopular view, usu. for sake of argument. **2** *Catholic*

Church one appointed to state disqualifications of person who has been proposed for sainthood.

devious *adj* see DEVIATE.

de·vise [di-VĪZ] *vt* **-vised, -vis·ing 1** plan, contrive. **2** invent. **3** plot. **4** leave by will.

de·void [di-VOID] *adj* (usu. with *of*) empty, lacking, free from.

de·volve [di-VOLV] *vi* **-volved, -volv·ing 1** pass or fall (to, upon). ♦ *vt* **2** throw (duty, etc.) on to another. **dev·o·lu·tion** [dev-ə-LOO-shən] *n* devolving, esp. transfer of authority from central to regional government.

de·vote [di-VOHT] *vt* **-vot·ed, -vot·ing** set apart, give up exclusively (to person, purpose, etc.). **devoted** *adj* loving, attached. **dev·o·tee** [dev-ə-TEE] *n* **1** ardent enthusiast. **2** zealous worshiper. **de·vo'tion** *n* **1** deep affection, loyalty. **2** dedication. **3** religious earnestness. ♦ *pl* **4** prayers, religious exercises. **de·vo'tion·al** *adj*

de·vour [di-VOWR] *vt* **1** eat greedily. **2** consume, destroy. **3** read, gaze at eagerly.

THESAURUS

desolation, havoc, ruin

develop *v* **1** = **advance**, evolve, flourish, grow, mature, progress, prosper, ripen **2** = **form**, breed, establish, generate, invent, originate **3** = **expand**, amplify, augment, broaden, elaborate, enlarge, unfold, work out

development *n* **1** = **growth**, advance, evolution, expansion, improvement, increase, progress, spread **2** = **event**, happening, incident, occurrence, result, turn of events, upshot

deviant *adj* **1** = **perverted**, kinky (*sl*), sick (*inf*), twisted, warped ♦ *n* **2** = **pervert**, freak, misfit

deviate *v* = **differ**, depart, diverge, stray, swerve, veer, wander

deviation *n* = **departure**, digression, discrepancy, disparity, divergence, inconsistency, irregularity, shift, variation

device *n* **1** = **gadget**, apparatus, appliance, contraption, implement, instrument, machine, tool **2** = **ploy**, gambit, maneuver, plan, scheme, stratagem, trick, wile

devil *n* **1 the Devil** = **Satan**, Beelzebub, Evil One, Lucifer, Mephistopheles, Prince of Darkness **2** = **brute**, beast, demon, fiend, monster, ogre, terror **3** = **scamp**, rascal, rogue, scoundrel **4** = **person**, beggar, creature, thing, wretch

devilish *adj* = **fiendish**, atrocious, damnable, detestable, diabolical, hellish, infernal, satanic, wicked

devious *adj* **1** = **sly**, calculating, deceitful, dishonest, double-dealing, insincere, scheming, surreptitious, underhand, wily **2** = **indirect**, circuitous, rambling, roundabout

devise *v* = **work out**, conceive, construct, contrive, design, dream up, formulate, invent, think up

devoid *adj* = **lacking**, bereft, deficient, destitute, empty, free from, wanting, without

devote *v* = **dedicate**, allot, apply, assign, commit, give, pledge, reserve, set apart

devoted *adj* = **dedicated**, ardent, committed, constant, devout, faithful, loyal, staunch, steadfast, true

devotee *n* = **enthusiast**, adherent, admirer, aficionado, buff (*inf*), disciple, fan, fanatic, follower, supporter

devotion *n* **1** = **dedication**, adherence, allegiance, commitment, constancy, faithfulness, fidelity, loyalty **2** = **love**, affection, attachment, fondness, passion **3** = **devoutness**, godliness, holiness, piety, reverence, spirituality **4 devotions** = **prayers**, church service, divine office, religious observance

de·vout [di-VOWT] *adj* **1** earnestly religious, pious. **2** sincere, heartfelt.

dew [doo] *n* **1** moisture from air deposited as small drops on cool surface between nightfall and morning. **2** any beaded moisture. ♦ *vt* **3** wet with or as with dew. **dew'y** *adj* **dew·i·er, dew·i·est dew'claw** *n* partly developed inner toe of dogs. **dew'lap** *n* fold of loose skin hanging from neck.

dex·ter·i·ty [dek-STER-i-tee] *n* manual skill, neatness, deftness, adroitness. **dex'ter·ous** *adj* showing dexterity, skillful.

dex·trose [DEK-strohs] *n* white, soluble, sweet-tasting crystalline solid, occurring naturally in fruit, honey, animal tissue.

dia- *prefix* through.

di·a·be·tes [dī-ə-BEE-tis] *n* various disorders characterized by excretion of abnormal amount of urine in which body fails to store and utilize glucose. **di·a·bet'ic** *n, adj*

di·a·bol·ic [dī-ə-BOL-ik], **di·a·bol'i·cal** *adj* **1** devilish. **2** *inf* very bad. **di·a·bol'i·cal·ly** *adv*

di·a·crit·ic [dī-ə-KRIT-ik] *n* sign above letter or character indicating special phonetic value, etc. **di·a·crit'i·cal** *adj* **1** of a diacritic. **2** showing a distinction.

di·a·dem [DĪ-ə-dem] *n* a crown.

di·ag·no·sis [dī-əg-NOH-sis] *n, pl* **-ses** [-seez] identification of disease from symptoms. **di'ag·nose** [-nohz] *vt* **-nosed, -nos·ing di·ag·nos'tic** [-NOS-tik] *adj*

di·ag·o·nal [dī-AG-ə-nl] *adj* **1** from corner to corner. **2** oblique. ♦ *n* **3** line from corner to corner. **di·ag'o·nal·ly** *adv*

di·a·gram [DĪ-ə-gram] *n* drawing, figure in lines, to illustrate something being expounded. **di·a·gram·mat'i·cal·ly** *adv*

di·al [DĪ-əl] *n* **1** face of clock, etc. **2** plate marked with graduations on which a pointer moves (as on a meter, radio, scale, etc.). **3** numbered disk on front of telephone. ♦ *vt* **4** operate telephone. **5** indicate on dial.

di·a·lect [DĪ-ə-lekt] *n* **1** characteristic speech of region. **2** local variety of a language. **di·a·lec'tal** *adj*

di·a·lec·tic [dī-ə-LEK-tik] *n* art of arguing. **di·a·lec'ti·cal** *adj* **di·a·lec·ti'cian** [-TISH-ən] *n* **1** logician. **2** reasoner.

di·a·logue [DĪ-ə-lawg] *n* **1** conversation between two or more (persons). **2** representation of such conversation in drama, novel, etc. **3** discussion between representatives of two governments, etc.

di·al·y·sis [dī-AL-ə-sis] *n, pl* **-ses** [-seez] *Med.* filtering of blood through membrane to remove waste products.

di·am·e·ter [dī-AM-i-tər] *n* **1** (length of) straight line from side to side of figure or body (esp. circle) through center. **2** thickness. **di·a·met'ri·cal** *adj* opposite. **di·a·met'ri·cal·ly** *adv*

di·a·mond [DĪ-mənd] *n* **1** very hard and brilliant precious stone, also used in industry. **2** rhomboid figure. **3** suit at cards. **4** playing field in baseball. **diamond jubilee** sixtieth anniversary of an event. **diamond wedding** sixtieth anniversary of a wedding.

di·a·pa·son [dī-ə-PAY-zən] *n* **1** fundamental organ stop. **2** compass of voice or instrument.

————— THESAURUS —————

devour *v* **1** = **eat**, chow down (*sl*), consume, gobble, gulp, guzzle, polish off (*inf*), swallow, wolf **2** = **destroy**, annihilate, consume, ravage, waste, wipe out **3** = **enjoy**, read compulsively *or* voraciously, take in

devout *adj* = **religious**, godly, holy, orthodox, pious, prayerful, pure, reverent, saintly

dexterity *n* **1** = **skill**, adroitness, deftness, expertise, finesse, nimbleness, proficiency, touch **2** = **cleverness**, ability, aptitude, ingenuity

diabolical *adj Inf* = **dreadful**, abysmal, appalling, atrocious, hellish, outrageous, shocking, terrible

diagnose *v* = **identify**, analyze, determine, distinguish, interpret, pinpoint, pronounce, recognize

diagnosis *n* **1** = **examination**, analysis, investigation, scrutiny **2** = **opinion**, conclusion, interpretation, pronouncement

diagonal *adj* = **slanting**, angled, cross, crossways, crosswise, oblique

diagonally *adv* = **aslant**, at an angle, cornerwise, crosswise, obliquely

diagram *n* = **plan**, chart, drawing, figure, graph, representation, sketch

dialect *n* = **language**, brogue, idiom, jargon, patois, provincialism, speech, vernacular

dialogue *n* = **conversation**, communication, conference, discourse, discussion

di·a·per [DĪ-pər] *n* **1** garment of absorbent material to absorb an infant's excrement. ◆ *vt* **2** put a diaper on.

di·aph·a·nous [dī-AF-ə-nəs] *adj* transparent.

di·a·pho·ret·ic [dī-ə-fə-RET-ik] *n* drug promoting perspiration. ◆ *adj*

di·a·phragm [DĪ-ə-fram] *n* **1** muscular partition dividing two cavities of body, midriff. **2** plate or disk wholly or partly closing tube or opening. **3** any thin dividing or covering membrane.

di·ar·rhe·a [dī-ə-REE-ə] *n* excessive looseness of the bowels.

di·a·ry [DĪ-ə-ree] *n, pl* **-ries 1** daily record of events or thoughts. **2** book for this. **3** book for noting appointments, memoranda, etc. **di'a·rist** *n* writer of diary.

di·as·to·le [dī-AS-tl-ee] *n* dilatation of the chambers of the heart.

di·a·ther·my [DĪ-ə-thur-mee] *n* heating of body tissues with electric current for medical or surgical purposes.

di·a·tom [DĪ-ə-tom] *n* one of order of microscopic algae. **di·a·tom'ic** *adj* of two atoms.

di·a·ton·ic [dī-ə-TON-ik] *adj Mus.* **1** pert. to regular major and minor scales. **2** (of melody) composed in such a scale.

di·a·tribe [DĪ-ə-trīb] *n* violently bitter verbal attack, invective, denunciation.

dice [dīs] *n, pl* **dice 1** small cube each of whose sides has a different number of spots (1 to 6), used in games of chance. ◆ *v* **diced, dic·ing** ◆ *vi* **2** gamble with dice. ◆ *vt* **3** *Cookery* cut vegetables into small cubes. **dic'er** *n* **dic'ey** *adj* **dic·i·er, dic·i·est**

inf dangerous, risky.

di·chot·o·my [dī-KOT-ə-mee] *n, pl* **-mies** division into two parts.

dic·tate [DIK-tayt] *v* **-tat·ed, -tat·ing 1** say or read for another to transcribe. **2** prescribe, lay down. **3** impose (as terms). ◆ *n* **4** bidding. **dic·ta'tion** *n* **dic·ta·tor** *n* absolute ruler. **dic·ta·to'ri·al** *adj* **1** despotic. **2** overbearing. **dic·ta·tor·ship** *n*

dic·tion [DIK-shən] *n* **1** choice and use of words. **2** enunciation.

dic·tion·ar·y [DIK-shə-ner-ee] *n, pl* **-ar·ies 1** book setting forth, alphabetically, words of language with meanings, etc. **2** reference book with items in alphabetical order.

dic·tum [DIK-təm] *n, pl* **-ta** [-tə] pronouncement, saying, maxim.

did pt. of DO.

di·dac·tic [dī-DAK-tik] *adj* **1** designed to instruct. **2** (of people) opinionated, dictatorial.

die¹ [dī] *vi* **died, dy·ing 1** cease to live. **2** come to an end. **3** stop functioning. **4** *inf* be nearly overcome (with laughter, etc.). **5** *inf* look forward (to). **die'hard** *n* one who resists (reform, etc.) to the end.

die² see DICE.

die³ *n* **1** shaped block of hard material to form metal in forge, press, etc. **2** tool for cutting thread on pipe, etc.

di·e·lec·tric [dī-i-LEK-trik] *n* **1** substance through or across which electric induction takes place. **2** nonconductor. **3** insulator.

di·er·e·sis [dī-ER-ə-sis] *n, pl* **-ses** [-seez] mark (¨) placed over vowel to show that it is sounded separately from preceding one, for example in *Noël*.

THESAURUS

diary *n* = **journal**, appointment book, chronicle, daily record, engagement book, Filofax (*Trademark*)

dictate *v* **1** = **speak**, read out, say, utter **2** = **order**, command, decree, demand, direct, impose, lay down the law, pronounce ◆ *n* **3** = **command**, decree, demand, direction, edict, fiat, injunction, order **4** = **principle**, code, law, rule

dictator *n* = **absolute ruler**, autocrat, despot, oppressor, tyrant

dictatorial *adj* **1** = **absolute**, arbitrary, autocratic, despotic, totalitarian, tyrannical, unlimited, unrestricted **2** = **domineering**, authoritarian, bossy (*inf*), imperious, oppressive, overbearing

dictatorship *n* = **absolute rule**,

absolutism, authoritarianism, autocracy, despotism, totalitarianism, tyranny

diction *n* = **pronunciation**, articulation, delivery, elocution, enunciation, fluency, inflection, intonation, speech

dictionary *n* = **wordbook**, glossary, lexicon, vocabulary

die *v* **1** = **pass away**, breathe one's last, croak (*sl*), expire, give up the ghost, kick the bucket (*sl*), perish, snuff it (*sl*) **2** = **dwindle**, decay, decline, fade, sink, subside, wane, wilt, wither **3** = **stop**, break down, fade out or away, fail, fizzle out, halt, lose power, peter out, run down **4** be **dying** = **long**, ache, be eager, desire, hunger, pine for, yearn

die-hard *n* = **reactionary**, fanatic, old

die·sel [DEE-zəl] *adj* **1** pert. to internal-combustion engine using oil as fuel. ◆ *n* **2** this engine. **3** vehicle powered by it.

di·et [DĪ-it] *n* **1** restricted or regulated course of feeding. **2** kind of food lived on. **3** food. ◆ *vi* **4** follow a dietary regimen, as to lose weight. **di'e·ta·ry** *adj* **1** relating to diet. ◆ *n* **2** a regulated diet. **di·e·tet'ic** *adj* **di·e·tet'ics** *n* science of diet. **di·e·ti'tian** [-TISH-ən] *n* one skilled in dietetics. **dietary fiber** fibrous substances in fruit and vegetables, consumption of which aids digestion.

diet² *n* **1** parliament of some countries. **2** formal assembly.

dif·fer [DIF-ər] *vi* **1** be unlike. **2** disagree. **dif'fer·ence** *n* **1** unlikeness. **2** degree or point of unlikeness. **3** disagreement. **4** remainder left after subtraction. **dif'fer·ent** *adj* unlike.

dif·fer·en·tial [dif-ə-REN-shəl] *adj* **1** varying with circumstances. **2** special. **3** *Math.* pert. to an infinitesimal change in variable quantity. **4** *Physics* relating to difference between sets of motions acting in the same direction or between pressures, etc. ◆ *n* **5** *Math.* infinitesimal difference between two consecutive states of variable quantity. **6** mechanism in automobile, etc. permitting back wheels to revolve at different speeds when rounding corner. **7** difference between rates of pay for different types of labor. **dif·fer·en·ti·ate** [-shee-ayt] *v* **-at·ed, -at·ing** ◆ *vt* **1** serve to distinguish between, make different ◆ *vi* **2** discriminate. **dif·fer·en·ti·a'tion** *n* **differential calculus** method of calculating relative rate of change for continuously varying quantities.

dif·fi·cult [DIF-i-kult] *adj* **1** requiring effort, skill, etc. to do or understand, not easy. **2** obscure. **dif'fi·cul·ty** *n, pl* **-ties 1** being difficult. **2** difficult task, problem. **3** embarrassment. **4** hindrance. **5** obscurity. **6** trouble.

dif·fi·dent [DIF-i-dənt] *adj* lacking confidence, timid, shy. **dif'fi·dence** *n* shyness.

dif·fract [di-FRAKT] *vi* break up, esp. of rays of light, sound waves. **dif·frac'tion** [-FRAK-shən] *n* deflection of ray of light, electromagnetic wave caused by an obstacle.

——— THESAURUS ———

fogey, stick-in-the-mud (*inf*)

diet¹ *n* **1** = **food**, fare, nourishment, nutriment, provisions, rations, sustenance, victuals **2** = **regime**, abstinence, fast, regimen ◆ *v* **3** = **slim**, abstain, eat sparingly, fast, lose weight

diet² *n* = **council**, chamber, congress, convention, legislature, meeting, parliament

differ *v* **1** = **be dissimilar**, contradict, contrast, depart from, diverge, run counter to, stand apart, vary **2** = **disagree**, clash, contend, debate, demur, dispute, dissent, oppose, take exception, take issue

difference *n* **1** = **dissimilarity**, alteration, change, contrast, discrepancy, disparity, diversity, variation, variety **2** = **disagreement**, argument, clash, conflict, contretemps, debate, dispute, quarrel **3** = **remainder**, balance, rest, result

different *adj* **1** = **unlike**, altered, changed, contrasting, disparate, dissimilar, divergent, inconsistent, opposed **2** = **various**, assorted, diverse, miscellaneous, sundry, varied **3** = **unusual**, atypical, distinctive, extraordinary, peculiar, singular, special, strange, uncommon

differentiate *v* **1** = **distinguish**, contrast, discriminate, make a distinction, mark off, separate, set off or apart, tell apart **2** = **make different**, adapt, alter, change, convert, modify, transform

difficult *adj* **1** = **hard**, arduous, demanding, formidable, laborious, onerous, strenuous, uphill **2** = **problematical**, abstruse, baffling, complex, complicated, intricate, involved, knotty, obscure **3** = **hard to please**, demanding, fastidious, fussy, perverse, refractory, unaccommodating

difficulty *n* **1** = **laboriousness**, arduousness, awkwardness, hardship, strain, strenuousness, tribulation **2** = **predicament**, dilemma, embarrassment, hot water (*inf*), jam (*inf*), mess, plight, quandary, trouble **3** = **problem**, complication, hindrance, hurdle, impediment, obstacle, pitfall, snag, stumbling block

diffidence *n* = **shyness**, bashfulness, hesitancy, insecurity, modesty, reserve, self-consciousness, timidity

diffident *adj* = **shy**, bashful, doubtful, hesitant, insecure, modest, reserved, self-conscious, timid, unassertive,

dif·fuse [di-FYOOZ] vt **-fused, -fus·ing 1** spread abroad. ◆ adj [-FYOOS] **2** widely spread. **3** loose, verbose, wordy. **dif·fuse'ly** adv **1** loosely. **2** wordily. **dif·fu'sion** [-zhən] n **dif·fu'sive** adj

dig v **dug, dig·ging** ◆ vi **1** work with spade. **2** search, investigate. ◆ vt **3** turn up with spade. **4** hollow out, make hole in. **5** excavate. **6** thrust into. **7** discover by searching. **8** sl understand. ◆ n **9** archaeological excavation. **10** thrust. **11** gibe, taunt. **dig'ger** n

di·gest [di-JEST] vt **1** prepare (food) in stomach, etc. for assimilation. **2** bring into handy form by sorting, tabulating, summarizing. **3** reflect on. **4** absorb. ◆ vi **5** of food, undergo digestion. ◆ n [DĪ-jest] **6** methodical summary, of laws, research, etc. **7** magazine containing condensed version of articles, etc. already published elsewhere. **di·gest'i·ble** adj **di·ges'tion** n digesting.

dig·it [DIJ-it] n **1** finger or toe. **2** any of the numbers 0 to 9. **dig'it·al** adj **1** of, resembling digits. **2** performed with fingers. **3** displaying information (time, etc.) by numbers rather than by pointer on dial. **4** of, relating to device that can write, read, or store information represented in numerical form. **digital recording** sound recording process that converts audio signals into pulses corresponding to

voltage level. **digital television** television in which the picture is transmitted in digital form and then decoded.

dig·i·tal·is [dij-i-TAL-is] n drug made from foxglove.

dig·ni·ty [DIG-ni-tee] n, pl **-ties 1** stateliness, gravity. **2** worthiness, excellence, repute. **3** honorable office or title. **dig'ni·fy** vt **-fied, -fy·ing** give dignity to. **dignified** adj stately, majestic. **dig'ni·ta·ry** [-ter-ee] n, pl **-tar·ies** holder of high office.

di·gress [di-GRES] vi turn from main course, esp. to deviate from subject in speaking or writing. **di·gres'sion** n

di·he·dral [dī-HEE-drəl] adj having two plane faces or sides.

dike [dīk] n **1** embankment to prevent flooding. **2** ditch.

di·lap·i·dat·ed [di-LAP-i-day-tid] adj **1** in ruins. **2** decayed.

dil·a·ta·tion [dil-ə-TAY-shən] n widening of body aperture for medical treatment, for example for curettage.

di·late [dī-LAYT] v **-lat·ed, -lat·ing** ◆ vt **1** widen, expand. ◆ vi **2** expand. **3** talk or write at length (on). **di·la'tion** n

dil·a·to·ry [DIL-ə-tor-ee] adj tardy, slow, belated. **dil'a·to·ri·ness** n delay.

di·lem·ma [di-LEM-ə] n **1** position in fact or argument offering choice only between unwelcome alternatives. **2** predicament.

THESAURUS

unassuming

dig v **1** = **excavate**, burrow, delve, hollow out, mine, quarry, scoop, tunnel **2** = **investigate**, delve, dig down, go into, probe, research, search **3** (with out or up) = **find**, discover, expose, uncover, unearth, uproot **4** = **poke**, drive, jab, prod, punch, thrust ◆ n **5** = **poke**, jab, prod, punch, thrust **6** = **cutting remark**, barb, gibe, insult, sneer, sneer, taunt, wisecrack (inf)

digest v **1** = **ingest**, absorb, assimilate, dissolve, incorporate **2** = **take in**, absorb, consider, contemplate, grasp, study, understand ◆ n **3** = **summary**, abridgment, abstract, epitome, précis, résumé, synopsis

digestion n = **ingestion**, absorption, assimilation, conversion, incorporation, transformation

dignified adj = **distinguished**, formal, grave, imposing, noble, reserved, solemn, stately

dignitary n = **public figure**, high-up (inf),

notable, personage, pillar of society, V.I.P., worthy

dignity n **1** = **decorum**, courtliness, grandeur, gravity, loftiness, majesty, nobility, solemnity, stateliness **2** = **honor**, eminence, importance, rank, respectability, standing, status **3** = **self-importance**, pride, self-esteem, self-respect

digress v = **wander**, depart, deviate, diverge, drift, get off the point or subject, go off at a tangent, ramble, stray

digression n = **departure**, aside, detour, deviation, divergence, diversion, straying, wandering

dilapidated adj = **ruined**, broken-down, crumbling, decrepit, in ruins, ramshackle, rickety, run-down, tumbledown

dilate v = **enlarge**, broaden, expand, puff out, stretch, swell, widen

dilatory adj = **time-wasting**, delaying, lingering, procrastinating, slow, sluggish,

dil·et·tante [DIL-i-tahnt] *n* **1** person with taste and knowledge of fine arts as pastime. **2** dabbler. ◆ *adj* **3** amateur, desultory. **dil'et·tant·ism** *n*

dil·i·gent [DIL-i-jənt] *adj* unremitting in effort, industrious, hardworking. **dil'i·gence** *n*

di·lute [di-LOOT] *vt* **-lut·ed, -lut·ing 1** reduce (liquid) in strength, esp. by adding water. **2** thin. **3** reduce in force, effect, etc. ◆ *adj* **4** weakened thus. **di·lu'tion** *n*

dim *adj* **dim·mer, dim·mest 1** indistinct, faint, not bright. **2** mentally dull. **3** unfavorable. ◆ *v* **dimmed, dim·ming 4** make, grow dim. **dim'ly** *adv* **dim'mer** *n* device for dimming electric lights. **dim'ness** *n*

dime [dīm] *n* 10-cent piece, coin of US and Canada.

di·men·sion [di-MEN-shən] *n* **1** measurement, size. **2** aspect. **fourth dimension 1** *Physics* time. **2** supernatural, fictional dimension additional to those of length, breadth, thickness.

di·min·ish *v* lessen. **dim·i·nu·tion** [dim-ə-NOO-shən] *n* **di·min·u·tive** [di-MIN-yə-tiv] *adj* **1** very small. ◆ *n* **2** derivative word, affix implying smallness.

di·min·u·en·do [di-min-yoo-EN-doh] *adj, adv Mus.* of sound, dying away.

dim·ple [DIM-pəl] *n* **1** small hollow in surface of skin, esp. of cheek. **2** any small hollow. ◆ *v* **-pled, -pling 3** mark with, show dimples.

din *n* **1** continuous roar of confused noises. ◆ *vt* **dinned, din·ning 2** repeat to weariness, ram (fact, opinion, etc.) into.

dine [dīn] *v* **dined, din·ing** ◆ *vi* **1** eat esp. dinner. ◆ *vt* **2** give dinner to. **din'er** *n* **1** one who dines. **2** informal usu. cheap restaurant. **dining room** room where meals are eaten.

din·ghy [DING-gee] *n, pl* **-ghies 1** small open boat. **2** inflatable life raft.

din·go [DING-goh] *n, pl* **-goes** Aust. wild dog.

din·gy [DIN-jee] *adj* **-gi·er, -gi·est** dirty-looking, shabby. **din'gi·ness** *n*

din·ner [DIN-ər] *n* **1** chief meal of the day. **2** official banquet.

di·no·saur [DI-nə-sor] *n* extinct reptile, often of gigantic size.

dint *n* force, power. **by dint of** by means of.

di·o·cese [DI-ə-sis] *n* ecclesiastical district under jurisdiction of bishop. **di·oc·e·san** [dī-OS-ə-sən] *adj* having jurisdiction over diocese.

di·ode [DI-ohd] *n Electronics* device for converting alternating current to direct current.

di·op·ter [dī-OP-tər] *n* unit for measuring refractive power of lens.

di·o·ram·a [dī-ə-RAM-ə] *n* miniature three-dimensional scene, esp. as museum exhibit.

di·ox·ide [dī-OK-sīd] *n* oxide with two

———— THESAURUS ————

tardy, tarrying

dilemma *n* = **predicament**, difficulty, mess, plight, problem, puzzle, quandary, spot (*inf*)

dilettante *n* = **amateur**, aesthete, dabbler, trifler

diligence *n* = **application**, attention, care, industry, laboriousness, perseverance

diligent *adj* = **hard-working**, assiduous, attentive, careful, conscientious, industrious, painstaking, persistent, studious, tireless

dilute *v* **1** = **water down**, adulterate, cut, make thinner, thin (out), weaken **2** = **reduce**, attenuate, decrease, diffuse, diminish, lessen, mitigate, temper, weaken

dim *adj* **1** = **poorly lit**, cloudy, dark, gray, overcast, shadowy, tenebrous **2** = **unclear**, bleary, blurred, faint, fuzzy, ill-defined, indistinct, obscured, shadowy **3 take a dim view** = **disapprove**, be displeased, be

skeptical, look askance, reject, suspect, take exception, view with disfavor ◆ *v* **4** = **dull**, blur, cloud, darken, fade, obscure

dimension *n* (often plural) = **measurement**, amplitude, bulk, capacity, extent, proportions, size, volume

diminish *v* **1** = **decrease**, curtail, cut, lessen, lower, reduce, shrink **2** = **dwindle**, decline, die out, recede, subside, wane

diminutive *adj* = **small**, little, mini, miniature, minute, petite, tiny, undersized

din *n* **1** = **noise**, clamor, clatter, commotion, crash, pandemonium, racket, row, uproar ◆ *v* **2 din (something) into (someone)** = **instill**, drum into, go on at, hammer into, inculcate, instruct, teach

dine *v* = **eat**, banquet, chow down (*sl*), feast, lunch, sup

dingy *adj* = **dull**, dark, dim, drab, dreary, gloomy, murky, obscure, somber

dinner *n* = **meal**, banquet, feast, main

parts of oxygen to one of the other constituents.

di·ox·in [dī-OK-sin] *n* extremely toxic byproduct of the manufacture of certain herbicides and bactericides.

dip *v* dipped, dip·ping ♦ *vt* **1** put partly or for a moment into liquid. **2** immerse, involve. **3** lower and raise again. **4** take up in ladle, bucket, etc. ♦ *vi* **5** plunge partially or temporarily. **6** go down, sink. **7** slope downward. ♦ *n* **8** act of dipping. **9** brief swim. **10** liquid chemical in which livestock are immersed to treat insect pests, etc. **11** downward slope. **12** hollow. **13** creamy mixture in which cracker, etc. is dipped before being eaten. **dip into** glance at (book, etc.).

diph·the·ri·a [dif-THEER-ee-ə] *n* infectious disease of throat with membranous growth.

diph·thong [DIF-thawng] *n* union of two vowel sounds in single compound sound.

di·plo·ma [di-PLOH-mə] *n, pl* **-mas 1** document vouching for person's proficiency. **2** title to degree, honor, etc.

di·plo·ma·cy [di-PLOH-mə-see] *n* **1** management of international relations. **2** skill in negotiation. **3** tactful, adroit dealing. **dip·lo·mat** [DIP-lə-mat] *n* one engaged in official diplomacy. **dip·lo·mat'ic** *adj* **di·plo'ma·tist** *n* tactful person.

di·plo·pi·a [di-PLOH-pee-ə] *n* double vision.

di·po·lar [dī-POH-lər] *adj* having two poles.

di·pole [DĪ-pohl] *n* type of radio and television antenna.

dip·per [DIP-ər] *n* ladle, bucket, scoop.

dip·so·ma·ni·a [dip-sə-MAY-nee-ə] *n* uncontrollable craving for alcohol. **dip·so·ma'ni·ac** *n* victim of this.

dip·tych [DIP-tik] *n* **1** ancient tablet hinged in the middle, folding together like a book. **2** painting, carving on two hinged panels.

dire [dīr] *adj* dir·er, dir·est **1** terrible. **2** urgent.

di·rect [di-REKT] *vt* **1** control, manage, order. **2** point out the way. **3** aim, point, turn. **4** address (letter, etc.). **5** supervise actors, etc. in play or film. ♦ *adj* **6** frank, straightforward. **7** straight. **8** going straight to the point. **9** immediate. **10** lineal. **di·rec'tion** *n* **1** directing. **2** aim, course of movement. **3** address, instruction. **di·rec'tive** *adj*, **di·rec'tor** *n* **1** one who directs, esp. a film. **2** member of board of directors of company. **di·rec'to·rate** [-tər-it] *n* **1** body of directors. **2** office of director. **di·rec'to·ry** *n, pl* **-ries 1** book of names, addresses, streets, etc. **2** *Computers.* area of a disk containing the names and locations of the files it currently holds. **direction finder** radio receiver that determines the direction of incoming waves.

dirge [durj] *n* song of mourning.

————————— THESAURUS —————————

dip *v* **1 = plunge**, bathe, douse, duck, dunk, immerse **2 = slope**, decline, descend, drop (down), fall, lower, sink, subside ♦ *n* **3 = plunge**, douche, drenching, ducking, immersion, soaking **4 = bathe**, dive, plunge, swim **5 = hollow**, basin, concavity, depression, hole, incline, slope **6 = drop**, decline, fall, lowering, sag, slip, slump

dip into *v* **= sample**, browse, glance at, peruse, skim

diplomacy *n* **1 = statesmanship**, international negotiation, statecraft **2 = tact**, artfulness, craft, delicacy, discretion, finesse, savoir-faire, skill, subtlety

diplomat *n* **= negotiator**, conciliator, go-between, mediator, moderator, politician, tactician

diplomatic *adj* **= tactful**, adept, discreet, polite, politic, prudent, sensitive, subtle

dire *adj* **1 = disastrous**, awful, calamitous, catastrophic, horrible, ruinous, terrible, woeful **2 = desperate**, critical, crucial, drastic, extreme, now or never, pressing, urgent **3 = grim**, dismal, dreadful, fearful, gloomy, ominous, portentous

direct *adj* **1 = straight**, nonstop, not crooked, shortest, through, unbroken, uninterrupted **2 = immediate**, face-to-face, first-hand, head-on, personal **3 = honest**, candid, frank, open, plain-spoken, straight, straightforward, upfront (*inf*) **4 = explicit**, absolute, blunt, categorical, downright, express, plain, point-blank, unambiguous, unequivocal ♦ *v* **5 = control**, conduct, guide, handle, lead, manage, oversee, run, supervise **6 = order**, bid, charge, command, demand, dictate, instruct **7 = guide**, indicate, lead, point in the direction of, point the way, show **8 = address**, label, mail, route, send **9 = aim**, focus, level, point, train

dir·i·gi·ble [DIR-i-jə-bəl] *adj* **1** steerable. ♦ *n* **2** airship.

dirt [durt] *n* **1** filth. **2** soil, earth. **3** obscene material. **4** contamination. **dirt'i·ness** *n* **dirt'y** *adj* **-i·er, -i·est 1** unclean, filthy. **2** obscene. **3** unfair. **4** dishonest.

dis- *prefix* indicating: **1** reversal, e.g. *disconnect*. **2** negation or lack, e.g. *dissimilar; disgrace* **3** removal or release, e.g. *disembowel*.

dis·a·ble [dis-AY-bəl] *vt* **-bled, -bling** make ineffective, unfit, or incapable. **dis·a'bled** *adj* lacking a physical power, such as the ability to walk. **dis·a·bil'i·ty** *n, pl* **-ties 1** incapacity. **2** drawback.

dis·a·buse [dis-ə-BYOOZ] *vt* **-bused, -bus·ing 1** undeceive, disillusion. **2** free

from error.

dis·ad·van·tage [dis-əd-VAN-tij] *n* **1** drawback. **2** hindrance. **3** detriment. ♦ *vt* **-taged, -tag·ing 4** handicap. **disadvantaged** *adj* deprived, discriminated against, underprivileged. **dis·ad·van·ta·geous** [-TAY-jəs] *adj*

dis·af·fect·ed [dis-ə-FEK-tid] *adj* ill-disposed, alienated, estranged. **dis·af·fec'tion** *n*

dis·a·gree [dis-ə-GREE] *vt* **-greed, -gree·ing 1** be at variance. **2** conflict. **3** (of food, etc.) have bad effect on. **dis·a·gree'ment** *n* **1** difference of opinion. **2** discord. **3** discrepancy. **dis·a·gree'a·ble** *adj* unpleasant.

dis·al·low [dis-ə-LOW] *vt* reject as untrue

——— THESAURUS ———

direction *n* **1 = way**, aim, bearing, course, line, path, road, route, track **2 = management**, administration, charge, command, control, guidance, leadership, order, supervision

directions *pl n* **= instructions**, briefing, guidance, guidelines, plan, recommendation, regulations

directive *n* **= order**, command, decree, edict, injunction, instruction, mandate, regulation, ruling

directly *adv* **1 = straight**, by the shortest route, exactly, in a beeline, precisely, unswervingly, without deviation **2 = honestly**, openly, plainly, point-blank, straightforwardly, truthfully, unequivocally **3 = at once**, as soon as possible, forthwith, immediately, promptly, right away, straightaway

director *n* **= controller**, administrator, chief, executive, governor, head, leader, manager, supervisor

dirge *n* **= lament**, dead march, elegy, funeral song, requiem, threnody

dirt *n* **1 = filth**, dust, grime, impurity, muck, mud **2 = soil**, clay, earth, loam **3 = obscenity**, indecency, pornography, sleaze, smut

dirty *adj* **1 = filthy**, foul, grimy, grubby, messy, mucky, muddy, polluted, scuzzy (*sl*), soiled, unclean **2 = dishonest**, crooked, fraudulent, illegal, lowdown (*sl*), scuzzy (*sl*), treacherous, unfair, unscrupulous, unsporting **3 = obscene**, blue, indecent, pornographic, salacious, scuzzy (*sl*), sleazy, smutty, X-rated **4** As in a **dirty look = angry**, annoyed, bitter,

choked, indignant, offended, resentful, scorching ♦ *v* **5 = soil**, blacken, defile, foul, muddy, pollute, smirch, spoil, stain

disability *n* **1 = handicap**, affliction, ailment, complaint, defect, disorder, impairment, infirmity, malady **2 = incapacity**, inability, unfitness

disable *v* **1 = handicap**, cripple, damage, enfeeble, immobilize, impair, incapacitate, paralyze **2 = disqualify**, invalidate, render *or* declare incapable

disabled *adj* **= handicapped**, challenged (*inf*), crippled, incapacitated, infirm, lame, paralyzed, weakened

disadvantage *n* **1 = harm**, damage, detriment, disservice, hurt, injury, loss, prejudice **2 = drawback**, downside, handicap, inconvenience, nuisance, snag, trouble

disagree *v* **1 = differ (in opinion)**, argue, clash, cross swords, dispute, dissent, object, quarrel, take issue with **2 = conflict**, be dissimilar, contradict, counter, differ, diverge, run counter to, vary **3 = make ill**, bother, discomfort, distress, hurt, nauseate, sicken, trouble, upset

disagreeable *adj* **1 = nasty**, disgusting, displeasing, distasteful, objectionable, obnoxious, offensive, repugnant, repulsive, scuzzy (*sl*), unpleasant **2 = rude**, bad-tempered, churlish, difficult, disobliging, irritable, surly, unpleasant

disagreement *n* **1 = incompatibility**, difference, discrepancy, disparity, dissimilarity, divergence, incongruity, variance **2 = argument**, altercation, clash, conflict, dispute, dissent, quarrel, row, or invalid.

dis·ap·pear [dis-ə-PEER] vi **1** vanish. **2** cease to exist. **3** be lost. **dis·ap·pear'ance** n

dis·ap·point [dis-ə-POINT] vt fail to fulfill (hope), frustrate. **dis·ap·point'ment** n

dis·ap·prove vi (foll. by of) consider wrong or bad. **dis·ap·prov'al** n

dis·arm [dis-AHRM] v **1** deprive of arms or weapons. **2** reduce country's war weapons. **3** win over. **dis·ar'ma·ment** n **dis·arm'ing** adj removing hostility, suspicion.

dis·ar·range v throw into disorder.

dis·ar·ray [dis-ə-RAY] vt **1** throw into disorder, derange. ◆ n **2** disorderliness, esp. of clothing.

dis·as·ter [di-ZAS-tər] n **1** calamity, sudden or great misfortune. **dis·as'trous** adj calamitous.

dis·band' v (cause to) cease to function as a group.

dis·bar [dis-BAHR] vt **-barred, -bar·ring** Law expel from the bar.

dis·be·lieve' vt **1** reject as false. ◆ vi **2** (foll. by in) have no faith in (in). **dis·be·lief'** n

dis·burse [dis-BURS] vt **-bursed, -burs·ing** pay out (money). **dis·burse'ment** n

disc see DISK. **disc jockey** person who introduces and plays pop records on a radio program or at a disco.

dis·card [di-SKAHRD] v **1** reject. **2** give up. **3** cast off, dismiss.

dis·cern [di-SURN] vt **1** make out. **2** distinguish. **dis·cern'i·ble** adj **dis·cern'ing** adj **1** discriminating. **2** penetrating. **dis·cern'ment** n insight.

dis·charge [dis-CHAHRJ] vt **-charged, -charg·ing 1** release. **2** dismiss. **3** emit. **4** perform (duties), fulfill (obligations). **5** let go. **6** fire off. **7** unload. **8** pay. ◆ n [DIS-chahrj] **9** discharging. **10** being discharged. **11** release. **12** matter emitted. **13** document certifying release, payment, etc.

dis·ci·ple [di-SĪ-pəl] n follower, one who

THESAURUS

squabble

disallow v = **reject**, disavow, dismiss, disown, rebuff, refuse, repudiate

disappear v **1** = **vanish**, evanesce, fade away, pass, recede **2** = **cease**, die out, dissolve, evaporate, leave no trace, melt away, pass away, perish

disappearance n = **vanishing**, departure, eclipse, evanescence, evaporation, going, melting, passing

disappoint v = **let down**, disenchant, disgruntle, dishearten, disillusion, dismay, dissatisfy, fail

disappointed adj = **let down**, cast down, despondent, discouraged, disenchanted, disgruntled, dissatisfied, downhearted, frustrated

disappointing adj = **unsatisfactory**, depressing, disconcerting, discouraging, inadequate, insufficient, lousy (sl), sad, sorry

disappointment n **1** = **frustration**, chagrin, discontent, discouragement, disenchantment, disillusionment, dissatisfaction, regret **2** = **letdown**, blow, calamity, choker (inf), misfortune, setback

disapproval n = **displeasure**, censure, condemnation, criticism, denunciation, dissatisfaction, objection, reproach

disapprove v = **condemn**, deplore, dislike, find unacceptable, frown on, look down one's nose at (inf), object to, reject, take a

dim view of, take exception to

disarm v **1** = **render defenseless**, disable **2** = **win over**, persuade, set at ease **3** = **demilitarize**, deactivate, demobilize, disband

disarmament n = **arms reduction**, arms limitation, de-escalation, demilitarization, demobilization

disarming adj = **charming**, irresistible, likable or likeable, persuasive, winning

disarrange v = **disorder**, confuse, disorganize, disturb, jumble (up), mess (up), scatter, shake (up), shuffle

disarray n **1** = **confusion**, disorder, disorganization, disunity, indiscipline, unruliness **2** = **untidiness**, chaos, clutter, jumble, mess, muddle, shambles

disaster n = **catastrophe**, adversity, calamity, cataclysm, misfortune, ruin, tragedy, trouble

disastrous adj = **terrible**, calamitous, cataclysmic, catastrophic, devastating, fatal, ruinous, tragic

disbelief n = **skepticism**, distrust, doubt, dubiety, incredulity, mistrust, unbelief

discard v = **get rid of**, abandon, cast aside, dispense with, dispose of, drop, dump (inf), jettison, reject, throw away or out

discharge v **1** = **release**, allow to go, clear, free, liberate, pardon, set free **2** = **dismiss**, cashier, discard, expel, fire (inf), oust, remove, sack (inf) **3** = **fire**, detonate, takes another as teacher and model.

dis·ci·pline [DIS-ə-plin] *n* **1** training that produces orderliness, obedience, self-control. **2** result of such training in order, conduct, etc. **3** system of rules, etc. ◆ *vt* **-plined, -plin·ing 4** train. **5** punish. **dis·ci·pli·nar'i·an** *n* one who enforces rigid discipline. **dis'ci·pli·nar·y** *adj*

dis·claim [dis-KLAYM] *vt* deny, renounce. **dis·claim'er** *n* repudiation, denial.

dis·close [di-SKLOHZ] *vt* **-closed, -clos·ing 1** allow to be seen. **2** make known. **dis·clo'sure** [-zhər] *n* revelation.

dis·col·or [dis-KUL-ər] *vt* alter color of, stain. **dis·col·or·a'tion** *n*

dis·com·fit [dis-KUM-fit] *vt* embarrass, disconcert, baffle. **dis·com'fi·ture** [-fi-chər] *n*

dis·com·pose' *vt* disturb, upset. **dis·com·po'sure** *n*

dis·con·cert [dis-kən-SURT] *vt* ruffle, confuse, upset, embarrass.

dis·con·nect' *vt* **1** undo or break the connection between (two things). **2** stop the supply of electricity or gas of.

dis·con·so·late [dis-KON-sə-lit] *adj* unhappy, downcast, forlorn.

dis·con·tent' *n* lack of contentment. **dis·con·tent'ed** *adj* **dis·con·tent'ment** *n*

dis·con·tin·ue *v* come or bring to an end. **dis·con·ti'nu·ous** *adj* characterized by interruptions. **dis·con·ti·nu'i·ty** *n*

dis·cord [DIS-kord] *n* **1** strife. **2** difference, dissension. **3** disagreement of sounds. **dis·cord'ant** *adj*

dis·co·theque [DIS-kə-tek] *n* club, etc. for

explode, let loose (*inf*), let off, set off, shoot **4 = pour forth**, dispense, emit, exude, give off, leak, ooze, release **5 = carry out**, accomplish, do, execute, fulfill, observe, perform **6 = pay**, clear, honor, meet, relieve, satisfy, settle, square up ◆ *n* **7 = release**, acquittal, clearance, liberation, pardon **8 = dismissal**, demobilization, ejection **9 = firing**, blast, burst, detonation, explosion, report, salvo, shot, volley **10 = emission**, excretion, ooze, pus, secretion, seepage, suppuration

disciple *n* **= follower**, adherent, apostle, devotee, pupil, student, supporter

disciplinarian *n* **= authoritarian**, despot, martinet, stickler, taskmaster, tyrant

discipline *n* **1 = training**, drill, exercise, method, practice, regimen, regulation **2 = punishment**, castigation, chastisement, correction **3 = self-control**, conduct, control, orderliness, regulation, restraint, strictness **4 = field of study**, area, branch of knowledge, course, curriculum, speciality, subject ◆ *v* **5 = train**, bring up, drill, educate, exercise, prepare **6 = punish**, bring to book, castigate, chasten, chastise, correct, penalize, reprimand, reprove

disclose *v* **1 = make known**, broadcast, communicate, confess, divulge, let slip, publish, relate, reveal **2 = show**, bring to light, expose, lay bare, reveal, uncover, unveil

disclosure *n* **= revelation**, acknowledgment, admission, announcement, confession, declaration,

divulgence, leak, publication

discolor *v* **= stain**, fade, mark, soil, streak, tarnish, tinge

discomfort *n* **1 = pain**, ache, hurt, irritation, malaise, soreness **2 = uneasiness**, annoyance, distress, hardship, irritation, nuisance, trouble

disconcert *v* **= disturb**, faze, fluster, perturb, rattle (*inf*), take aback, unsettle, upset, worry

disconcerting *adj* **= disturbing**, alarming, awkward, bewildering, confusing, distracting, embarrassing, perplexing, upsetting

disconnect *v* **= cut off**, detach, disengage, divide, part, separate, sever, take apart, uncouple

disconnected *adj* **= illogical**, confused, disjointed, incoherent, jumbled, mixed-up, rambling, unintelligible

disconsolate *adj* **= inconsolable**, crushed, dejected, desolate, forlorn, grief-stricken, heartbroken, miserable, wretched

discontent *n* **= dissatisfaction**, displeasure, envy, regret, restlessness, uneasiness, unhappiness

discontented *adj* **= dissatisfied**, disaffected, disgruntled, displeased, exasperated, fed up, unhappy, vexed

discontinue *v* **= stop**, abandon, break off, cease, drop, end, give up, quit, suspend, terminate

discord *n* **1 = disagreement**, conflict, dissension, disunity, division, friction, incompatibility, strife **2 = disharmony**, cacophony, din, dissonance, harshness, dancing to recorded music.

dis·count [dis-KOWNT] vt **1** consider as possibility but reject as unsuitable, inappropriate, etc. **2** deduct (amount, percentage) from usual price. **3** sell at reduced price. ◆ n [DIS-kownt] **4** amount deducted from price, expressed as cash amount or percentage.

dis·coun·te·nance [dis-KOWN-tn-əns] vt **-nanced, -nanc·ing 1** abash. **2** discourage. **3** frown upon.

dis·cour·age [dis-SKUR-ij] vt **-aged, -ag·ing 1** reduce confidence of. **2** deter. **3** show disapproval of.

dis·course [DIS-kors] n **1** conversation. **2** speech, treatise, sermon. ◆ vi [dis-KORS] **-coursed, -cours·ing 3** speak, converse, lecture.

dis·cour·te·sy n showing bad manners.

dis·cour·te·ous·ly adv

dis·cov·er [di-SKUV-ər] vt (be the first to) find out, light upon. **1** make known. **dis·cov·er·a·ble** adj **dis·cov·er·er** n **dis·cov·er·y** n, pl **-er·ies**

dis·cred·it [dis-KRED-it] vt **1** damage reputation of. **2** cast doubt on. **3** reject as untrue. ◆ n **4** disgrace. **5** doubt. **dis·cred·it·a·ble** adj

dis·creet [di-SKREET] adj prudent, circumspect. **dis·creet'ness** n

dis·crep·an·cy [di-SKREP-ən-see] n, pl **-cies** conflict, variation, as between figures. **dis·crep'ant** adj

dis·crete [di-SKREET] adj separate, disunited, discontinuous.

dis·cre·tion [di-SKRESH-ən] n **1** quality of being discreet. **2** prudence. **3** freedom to act as one chooses. **dis·cre'tion·ar·y** adj

jarring, racket, tumult

discordant adj **1** = **disagreeing**, at odds, clashing, conflicting, contradictory, contrary, different, incompatible **2** = **inharmonious**, cacophonous, dissonant, grating, harsh, jarring, shrill, strident

discount v **1** = **leave out**, brush off (sl), disbelieve, disregard, ignore, overlook, pass over **2** = **deduct**, lower, mark down, reduce, take off ◆ n **3** = **deduction**, concession, cut, rebate, reduction

discourage v **1** = **dishearten**, dampen, deject, demoralize, depress, dispirit, intimidate, overawe, put a damper on **2** = **put off**, deter, dissuade, inhibit, prevent, talk out of

discouraged adj = **put off**, crestfallen, deterred, disheartened, dismayed, dispirited, downcast, down in the mouth, glum

discouragement n **1** = **loss of confidence**, dejection, depression, despair, despondency, disappointment, dismay, downheartedness **2** = **deterrent**, damper, disincentive, hindrance, impediment, obstacle, opposition, setback

discouraging adj = **disheartening**, dampening, daunting, depressing, disappointing, dispiriting, unfavorable

discourse n **1** = **conversation**, chat, communication, dialogue, discussion, seminar, speech, talk **2** = **speech**, dissertation, essay, homily, lecture, oration, sermon, treatise ◆ v **3** = **hold forth**, expatiate, speak, talk

discourteous adj = **rude**, bad-mannered, boorish, disrespectful, ill-mannered, impolite, insolent, offhand, ungentlemanly, ungracious

discourtesy n **1** = **rudeness**, bad manners, disrespectfulness, impertinence, impoliteness, incivility, insolence **2** = **insult**, affront, cold shoulder, kick in the teeth (sl), rebuff, slight, snub

discover v **1** = **find**, come across, come upon, dig up, locate, turn up, uncover, unearth **2** = **find out**, ascertain, detect, learn, notice, perceive, realize, recognize, uncover

discovery n **1** = **finding**, detection, disclosure, exploration, location, revelation, uncovering **2** = **breakthrough**, find, innovation, invention, secret

discredit v **1** = **disgrace**, bring into disrepute, defame, dishonor, disparage, slander, smear, vilify **2** = **doubt**, challenge, deny, disbelieve, discount, dispute, distrust, mistrust, question ◆ n **3** = **disgrace**, dishonor, disrepute, ignominy, ill-repute, scandal, shame, stigma

discreditable adj = **disgraceful**, dishonorable, ignominious, reprehensible, scandalous, shameful, unworthy

discreet adj = **tactful**, careful, cautious, circumspect, considerate, diplomatic, guarded, judicious, prudent, wary

discrepancy n = **disagreement**, conflict, contradiction, difference, disparity, divergence, incongruity, inconsistency, variation

dis·crim·i·nate [di-SKRIM-ə-nayt] *vi* **-nat·ed, -nat·ing 1** single out for special favor or disfavor. **2** distinguish between. **3** be discerning. **dis·crim·i·na'tion** *n*

dis·cur·sive [di-SKUR-siv] *adj* passing from subject to subject, rambling.

dis·cus [DIS-kəs] *n* disk-shaped object thrown in athletic competition.

dis·cuss [di SKUS] *vt* **1** exchange opinions about. **2** debate. **dis·cus'sion** *n*

dis·dain [dis-DAYN] *n* **1** scorn, contempt. ♦ *vt* **2** scorn. **dis·dain'ful** *adj*

dis·ease [di-ZEEZ] *n* **1** illness. **2** disorder of health.

dis·em·bark *v* get off a ship, aircraft, or bus. **dis·em·bar·ka'tion** *n*

dis·em·bod·ied [dis-em-BOD-eed] *adj* (of spirit) released from bodily form.

dis·em·bow·el [dis-em-BOW-əl] *vt* take out entrails of.

dis·en·chant·ed [dis-en-CHAN-tid] *adj* disillusioned.

dis·en·gage' *v* release from a connection. **dis·en·gage'ment** *n*

dis·en·tan·gle *v* release from entanglement or confusion.

dis·es·tab'lish *vt* remove state support from (a church etc.). **dis·es·tab'lish·ment** *n*

dis·fa'vor *n* disapproval or dislike.

dis·fig·ure [dis-FIG-yər] *vt* **-ured, -ur·ing** mar appearance of. **dis·fig·ur·a'tion** *n* **dis·fig'ure·ment** *n* blemish, defect.

dis·gorge [dis-GORJ] *vt* **-gorged, -gorg·ing 1** vomit. **2** give up.

dis·grace [dis-GRAYS] *n* **1** shame, loss of reputation, dishonor. ♦ *vt* **-graced, -grac·ing 2** bring shame or discredit upon. **dis·grace'ful** *adj* shameful.

dis·grun·tled [dis-GRUN-tld] *adj* **1** vexed. **2** put out.

dis·guise [dis-GĪZ] *vt* **-guised, -guis·ing 1**

discretion *n* **1 = tact**, carefulness, caution, consideration, diplomacy, judiciousness, prudence, wariness **2 = choice**, inclination, pleasure, preference, volition, will

discriminate *v* **1 = show prejudice**, favor, show bias, single out, treat as inferior, treat differently, victimize **2 = differentiate**, distinguish, draw a distinction, segregate, separate, tell the difference

discriminating *adj* **= discerning**, cultivated, fastidious, particular, refined, selective, tasteful

discrimination *n* **1 = prejudice**, bias, bigotry, favoritism, intolerance, unfairness **2 = discernment**, judgment, perception, refinement, subtlety, taste

discuss *v* **= talk about**, argue, confer, consider, converse, debate, deliberate, examine

discussion *n* **= talk**, analysis, argument, conference, consultation, conversation, debate, deliberation, dialogue, discourse, exchange

disdain *n* **1 = contempt**, arrogance, derision, haughtiness, scorn, superciliousness ♦ *v* **2 = scorn**, deride, disregard, look down on, reject, slight, sneer at, spurn

disdainful *adj* **= contemptuous**, aloof, arrogant, derisive, haughty, proud, scornful, sneering, supercilious, superior

disease *n* **= illness**, affliction, ailment, complaint, condition, disorder, infection, infirmity, malady, sickness

diseased *adj* **= sick**, ailing, infected, rotten, sickly, unhealthy, unsound, unwell, unwholesome

disembark *v* **= land**, alight, arrive, get off, go ashore, step out of

disenchanted *adj* **= disillusioned**, cynical, disappointed, indifferent, jaundiced, let down, sick of, soured

disenchantment *n* **= disillusionment**, disappointment, disillusion, rude awakening

disengage *v* **= release**, disentangle, extricate, free, loosen, set free, unloose, untie

disentangle *v* **= untangle**, disconnect, disengage, extricate, free, loose, unravel

disfavor *n* **= disapproval**, disapprobation, dislike, displeasure

disfigure *v* **= damage**, blemish, deface, deform, distort, mar, mutilate, scar

disgorge *v* **= vomit**, discharge, eject, empty, expel

disgrace *n* **1 = shame**, degradation, dishonor, disrepute, ignominy, infamy, odium, opprobrium **2 = stain**, blemish, blot, reproach, scandal, slur, stigma ♦ *v* **3 = bring shame upon**, degrade, discredit, dishonor, humiliate, shame, sully, taint

disgraceful *adj* **= shameful**, contemptible, detestable, dishonorable, disreputable, ignominious, lousy (*sl*), scandalous, shocking, unworthy change appearance of, make unrecognizable. **2** conceal, cloak. **3** misrepresent. ◆ *n* **4** false appearance. **5** device to conceal identity.

dis·gust' *n* **1** violent distaste, loathing, repugnance. ◆ *vt* **2** affect with loathing.

dish *n* **1** shallow vessel for food. **2** portion or variety of food. **3** contents of dish. **4** *sl* attractive person. **dish out** *inf* **1** put in dish. **2** serve up. **3** dispense (money, abuse, etc.).

dis·ha·bille [dis-ə-BEEL] *n* state of being partly or carelessly dressed.

dis·har'mo·ny *n* lack of agreement, discord.

dis·heart'en *vt* weaken or destroy the hope, courage, or enthusiasm of.

di·shev·eled [di-SHEV-əld] *adj* **1** with disordered hair. **2** ruffled, untidy, unkempt.

dis·hon'est *adj* not honest or fair. **dis·hon'est·ly** *adv* **dis·hon'es·ty** *n*

dis·hon'or *vt* **1** treat with disrespect. **2** refuse to cash (a check). ◆ *n* **3** lack of respect. **4** state of shame or disgrace. **5** something that causes a loss of honor. **dis·hon'or·a·ble** *adj* **dis·hon'or·a·bly** *adv*

dis·il·lu·sion [dis-i-LOO-zhən] *vt* destroy ideals, illusions, or false ideas of. ◆ *n*

dis·in·fect·ant [dis-in-FEK-tənt] *n* substance that prevents or removes infection. **dis·in·fect'** *vt*

dis·in·for·ma·tion [dis-in-fər-MAY-shən] *n* false information intended to deceive or mislead.

dis·in·gen·u·ous [dis-in-JEN-yoo-əs] *adj* not sincere or frank.

dis·in·her·it [dis-in-HE-rit] *vt* to deprive of inheritance.

dis·in·te·grate [dis-IN-tə-grayt] *v* **-grat·ed,**

THESAURUS

disgruntled *adj* = **discontented**, annoyed, displeased, dissatisfied, grumpy, irritated, peeved, put out, vexed

disguise *v* **1** = **hide**, camouflage, cloak, conceal, cover, mask, screen, shroud, veil **2** = **misrepresent**, fake, falsify ◆ *n* **3** = **costume**, camouflage, cover, mask, screen, veil **4** = **façade**, deception, dissimulation, front, pretense, semblance, trickery, veneer

disguised *adj* = **in disguise**, camouflaged, covert, fake, false, feigned, incognito, masked, undercover

disgust *n* **1** = **loathing**, abhorrence, aversion, dislike, distaste, hatred, nausea, repugnance, repulsion, revulsion ◆ *v* **2** = **sicken**, displease, nauseate, offend, put off, repel, revolt

disgusted *adj* = **sickened**, appalled, nauseated, offended, repulsed, scandalized

disgusting *adj* = **sickening**, foul, gross, loathsome, nauseating, offensive, repellent, repugnant, revolting

dish *n* **1** = **bowl**, plate, platter, salver **2** = **food**, fare, recipe

dishearten *v* = **discourage**, cast down, deject, depress, deter, dismay, dispirit, put a damper on

disheveled *adj* = **untidy**, bedraggled, disordered, messy, ruffled, rumpled, tousled, uncombed, unkempt

dishonest *adj* = **deceitful**, bent (*sl*), cheating, corrupt, crooked (*inf*), disreputable, double-dealing, false, lying,

treacherous

dishonesty *n* = **deceit**, cheating, chicanery, corruption, fraud, treachery, trickery, unscrupulousness

dishonor *v* **1** = **shame**, debase, debauch, defame, degrade, discredit, disgrace, sully ◆ *n* **2** = **shame**, discredit, disgrace, disrepute, ignominy, infamy, obloquy, reproach, scandal **3** = **insult**, abuse, affront, discourtesy, indignity, offense, outrage, sacrilege, slight

dishonorable *adj* **1** = **shameful**, contemptible, despicable, discreditable, disgraceful, ignominious, infamous, lousy (*sl*), scandalous, scuzzy (*sl*) **2** = **untrustworthy**, corrupt, disreputable, shameless, treacherous, unprincipled, unscrupulous

disillusioned *adj* = **disenchanted**, disabused, disappointed, enlightened, undeceived

disinclination *n* = **reluctance**, aversion, dislike, hesitance, objection, opposition, repugnance, resistance, unwillingness

disinclined *adj* = **reluctant**, averse, hesitating, loath, not in the mood, opposed, resistant, unwilling

disinfect *v* = **sterilize**, clean, cleanse, decontaminate, deodorize, fumigate, purify, sanitize

disinfectant *n* = **antiseptic**, germicide, sterilizer

disinherit *v Law* = **cut off**, disown, dispossess, oust, repudiate

-grat·ing break up, fall to pieces.
dis·in·te·gra·tion n

dis·in·ter' vt -ter·ring, -terred 1 dig up. 2 reveal, make known.

dis·in·ter·est [dis-IN-trist] n freedom from bias or involvement. **dis·in·ter·est·ed** adj

dis·joint' vt 1 put out of joint. 2 break the natural order or logical arrangement of. **dis·joint'ed** adj 1 (of discourse) incoherent 2 disconnected.

disk n 1 thin, flat, circular object like a coin. 2 Computers storage device, consisting of a disk coated with a magnetic layer, used to record and retrieve data. 3 a phonograph record. **disk drive** Computers controller and mechanism for reading and writing data on computer disks. **disk harrow** harrow that cuts the soil with inclined disks. **disk jockey, disc jockey** person who introduces and plays pop records on a radio program or at a disco.

dis·lo·cate [DIS-loh-kayt] vt -cat·ed, -cat·ing 1 put out of joint (e.g. dislocate shoulder). 2 disrupt, displace.

dis·lo·ca'tion n

dis·lodge [dis-LOJ] vt -lodged, -lodg·ing drive out or remove from hiding place or previous position.

dis·loy·al adj not loyal, deserting one's allegiance. **dis·loy'al·ty** n

dis·mal [DIZ-məl] adj 1 depressing. 2 depressed. 3 cheerless, dreary, gloomy. **dis'mal·ly** adv

dis·man·tle [dis-MAN-tl] vt -tled, -tling take apart. **dis·man'tle·ment** n

dis·may' vt 1 dishearten, daunt. ♦ n 2 consternation, horrified amazement. 3 apprehension.

dis·mem·ber [dis-MEM-bər] vt 1 tear or cut limb from limb. 2 divide, partition. **dis·mem'ber·ment** n

dis·miss' vt 1 remove, discharge from employment. 2 send away. 3 reject. **dis·miss'al** n

dis·mount' v get off a horse or bicycle.

dis·o·bey [dis-ə-BAY] v refuse or fail to obey. **dis·o·be'di·ence** [-BEE-dee-əns] n

dis·o·blige [dis-ə-BLĪJ] vt -bliged, -blig·ing

disintegrate v = **break up**, break apart, crumble, fall apart, go to pieces, separate, shatter, splinter

disinterest n = **impartiality**, detachment, fairness, neutrality

disinterested adj = **impartial**, detached, dispassionate, even-handed, impersonal, neutral, objective, unbiased, unprejudiced

disjointed adj = **incoherent**, confused, disconnected, disordered, rambling

dislike v 1 = **be averse to**, despise, detest, disapprove, hate, loathe, not be able to bear or abide or stand, object to, take a dim view of ♦ n 2 = **aversion**, animosity, antipathy, disapproval, disinclination, displeasure, distaste, enmity, hostility, repugnance

dislodge v = **displace**, disturb, extricate, force out, knock loose, oust, remove, uproot

disloyal adj = **treacherous**, faithless, false, subversive, traitorous, two-faced, unfaithful, untrustworthy

disloyalty n = **treachery**, breach of trust, deceitfulness, double-dealing, falseness, inconstancy, infidelity, treason, unfaithfulness

dismal adj = **gloomy**, bleak, cheerless, dark, depressing, discouraging, dreary, forlorn, somber, wretched

dismantle v = **take apart**, demolish, disassemble, strip, take to pieces

dismay v 1 = **alarm**, appall, distress, frighten, horrify, paralyze, scare, terrify, unnerve 2 = **disappoint**, daunt, discourage, dishearten, disillusion, dispirit, put off ♦ n 3 = **alarm**, anxiety, apprehension, consternation, dread, fear, horror, trepidation 4 = **disappointment**, chagrin, discouragement, disillusionment

dismember v = **cut into pieces**, amputate, dissect, mutilate, sever

dismiss v 1 = **sack** (inf), ax (inf), cashier, discharge, fire (inf), give notice to, give (someone) their marching orders, lay off, remove 2 = **let go**, disperse, dissolve, free, release, send away 3 = **put out of one's mind**, banish, discard, dispel, disregard, lay aside, reject, set aside

dismissal n = **the sack** (inf), expulsion, marching orders (inf), notice, removal, the boot (sl)

disobedience n = **defiance**, indiscipline, insubordination, mutiny, noncompliance, nonobservance, recalcitrance, revolt, unruliness, waywardness

disobedient adj = **defiant**, contrary, disorderly, insubordinate, intractable, naughty, refractory, undisciplined, unruly, wayward disregard the wishes, preferences of.

dis·or·der [dis-OR-dər] *n* **1** disarray, confusion, disturbance. **2** upset of health, ailment. ◆ *vt* **3** upset order of. **4** disturb health of. **dis·or·der·ly** *adj* **1** untidy. **2** unruly.

dis·or·gan·ize *vt* disrupt the arrangement or system of. **dis·or·gan·i·za'tion** *n*

dis·o·ri·ent [dis-OR-ee-ənt] *vt* cause to lose one's bearings, confuse.

dis·own [dis-OHN] *vt* refuse to acknowledge.

dis·par·age [di-SPAR-ij] *vt* **-aged, -ag·ing 1** speak slightingly of. **2** belittle. **dis·par'age·ment** *n*

dis·pa·rate [DIS-pər-it] *adj* **1** essentially different, unrelated. **dis·par'i·ty** *n, pl* **-ties 1** inequality. **2** incongruity.

dis·pas·sion·ate [dis-PASH-ə-nit] *adj* **1** unswayed by passion. **2** calm, impartial.

dis·patch [di-SPACH] *vt* **1** send off to destination or on an errand. **2** send off. **3** finish off, get done with speed. **4** *inf* eat up. **5** kill. ◆ *n* **6** sending off. **7** efficient speed. **8** official message, report.

dis·pel [di-SPEL] *vt* **-pelled, -pel·ling** clear,

drive away, scatter.

dis·pense [di-SPENS] *vt* **-pensed, -pens·ing 1** deal out. **2** make up (medicine). **3** administer (justice). **4** grant exemption from. **dis·pen·sa·ble** *adj* **dis·pen·sa·ry** *n, pl* **-ries** place where medical aid is given. **dis·pen·sa'tion** *n* **1** act of dispensing. **2** license or exemption. **3** provision of nature or providence. **dis·pens'er** *n* **dispense with 1** do away with. **2** manage without.

dis·perse [di-SPURS] *vt* **-persed, -pers·ing** scatter. **dispersed** *adj* **1** scattered. **2** placed here and there. **dis·per'sal, dis·per'sion** [-zhən] *n*

dis·pir·it·ed [di-SPIR-i-tid] *adj* dejected, disheartened. **dis·pir'it·ing** *adj*

dis·place [dis-PLAYS] *vt* **-placed, -plac·ing 1** move from its place. **2** remove from office. **3** take place of. **dis·place'ment** *n* **1** displacing. **2** weight of liquid displaced by a solid in it.

dis·play [di-SPLAY] *vt* **1** spread out for show. **2** show, expose to view. ◆ *n* **3** displaying. **4** parade. **5** show, exhibition. **6** ostentation.

dis·please [dis-PLEEZ] *v* **-pleased,**

disobey *v* = **refuse to obey**, contravene, defy, disregard, flout, ignore, infringe, rebel, violate

disorder *n* **1** = **untidiness**, chaos, clutter, confusion, disarray, jumble, mess, muddle, shambles **2** = **disturbance**, commotion, riot, turmoil, unrest, unruliness, uproar **3** = **illness**, affliction, ailment, complaint, disease, malady, sickness

disorderly *adj* **1** = **untidy**, chaotic, confused, disorganized, jumbled, messy **2** = **unruly**, disruptive, indisciplined, lawless, riotous, rowdy, tumultuous, turbulent, ungovernable

disorganized *adj* = **muddled**, chaotic, confused, disordered, haphazard, jumbled, unsystematic

disown *v* = **deny**, cast off, disavow, disclaim, reject, renounce, repudiate

disparage *v* = **run down**, belittle, denigrate, deprecate, deride, malign, put down, ridicule, slander, vilify

dispassionate *adj* **1** = **unemotional**, calm, collected, composed, cool, imperturbable, serene, unruffled **2** = **objective**, detached, disinterested, fair, impartial, impersonal, neutral, unbiased, unprejudiced

dispatch, despatch *v* **1** = **send**, consign,

dismiss, hasten **2** = **carry out**, discharge, dispose of, finish, perform, settle **3** = **murder**, assassinate, execute, kill, slaughter, slay ◆ *n* **4** = **message**, account, bulletin, communication, communiqué, news, report, story

dispel *v* = **drive away**, banish, chase away, dismiss, disperse, eliminate, expel

dispense *v* **1** = **distribute**, allocate, allot, apportion, deal out, dole out, share **2** = **prepare**, measure, mix, supply **3** = **administer**, apply, carry out, enforce, execute, implement, operate **4 dispense with: a** = **do away with**, abolish, brush aside, cancel, dispose of, get rid of **b** = **do without**, abstain from, forgo, give up, relinquish

disperse *v* **1** = **scatter**, broadcast, diffuse, disseminate, distribute, spread, strew **2** = **break up**, disband, dissolve, scatter, separate

dispirited *adj* = **disheartened**, crestfallen, dejected, depressed, despondent, discouraged, downcast, gloomy, glum, sad

displace *v* **1** = **move**, disturb, misplace, shift, transpose **2** = **replace**, oust, succeed, supersede, supplant, take the place of

display *v* **1** = **show**, demonstrate, disclose,

pleas·ing 1 offend. **2** annoy. **dis·pleas'ure** [-PLEZH-ər] *n* anger, vexation.

dis·port [di-SPORT] *v refl* gambol, amuse oneself, frolic.

dis·pose [di-SPOHZ] *v* **-posed, -pos·ing** ♦ *vt* **1** arrange. **2** distribute. **3** incline. **4** adjust. ♦ *vi* **5** determine. **dis·pos'a·ble** *adj* designed to be thrown away after use. **dis·pos'al** *n* **dis·po·si·tion** [dis-pə-ZISH-ən] *n* **1** inclination. **2** temperament. **3** arrangement. **4** plan. **dispose of 1** sell, get rid of. **2** have authority over, deal with.

dis·pos·sess [dis-pə-ZES] *vt* cause to give up possession (of).

dis·pro·por·tion *n* lack of proportion or equality. **dis·pro·por'tion·ate** *adj*

dis·prove' *vt* show (an assertion or claim) to be incorrect.

dis·pute [di-SPYOOT] *v* **-put·ed, -put·ing** ♦ *vi* **1** debate, discuss. ♦ *vt* **2** call in question. **3** debate, argue. **4** oppose, contest. **dis·put'a·ble** *adj* **dis·pu'tant** *n* **dis·pu·ta'tious** *adj* **1** argumentative. **2** quarrelsome.

dis·qual·i·fy [dis-KWOL-ə-fī] *vt* **-fied, -fy·ing** make ineligible, unfit for some special purpose.

dis·qui·et [dis-KWĪ-it] *n* **1** anxiety, uneasiness. ♦ *vt* **2** cause (someone) to feel this.

dis·qui·si·tion [dis-kwə-ZISH-ən] *n* learned or elaborate treatise, discourse or essay.

dis·re·pute' *n* loss or lack of good reputation. **dis·rep'u·ta·ble** *adj* having or causing a bad reputation.

dis·re·spect' *n* lack of respect.

————————— THESAURUS —————————

exhibit, expose, manifest, present, reveal **2 = show off**, flaunt, flourish, parade, vaunt ♦ *n* **3 = exhibition**, array, demonstration, presentation, revelation, show **4 = show**, flourish, ostentation, pageant, parade, pomp, spectacle

displease *v* **= annoy**, anger, irk, irritate, offend, pique, put out, upset, vex

displeasure *n* **= annoyance**, anger, disapproval, dissatisfaction, distaste, indignation, irritation, resentment

disposable *adj* **1 = throwaway**, biodegradable, nonreturnable **2 = available**, consumable, expendable

disposal *n* **1 = throwing away**, discarding, dumping (*inf*), ejection, jettisoning, removal, riddance, scrapping **2 at one's disposal = available**, at one's service, consumable, expendable, free for use

dispose *v* **= arrange**, array, distribute, group, marshal, order, place, put

dispose of *v* **1 = get rid of**, destroy, discard, dump (*inf*), jettison, scrap, throw out *or* away, unload **2 = deal with**, decide, determine, end, finish with, settle

disposition *n* **1 = character**, constitution, make-up, nature, spirit, temper, temperament **2 = tendency**, bent, bias, habit, inclination, leaning, proclivity, propensity **3 = arrangement**, classification, distribution, grouping, ordering, organization, placement

disproportion *n* **= inequality**, asymmetry, discrepancy, disparity, imbalance, lopsidedness, unevenness

disproportionate *adj* **= unequal**, excessive, inordinate, out of proportion, unbalanced, uneven, unreasonable

disprove *v* **= prove false**, contradict, discredit, expose, give the lie to, invalidate, negate, rebut, refute

dispute *n* **1 = disagreement**, altercation, argument, conflict, feud, quarrel **2 = argument**, contention, controversy, debate, discussion, dissension ♦ *v* **3 = doubt**, challenge, contest, contradict, deny, impugn, question, rebut **4 = argue**, clash, cross swords, debate, quarrel, squabble

disqualification *n* **= ban**, elimination, exclusion, ineligibility, rejection

disqualified *adj* **= ineligible**, debarred, eliminated, knocked out, out of the running

disqualify *v* **= ban**, debar, declare ineligible, preclude, prohibit, rule out

disquiet *n* **1 = uneasiness**, alarm, anxiety, concern, disturbance, foreboding, nervousness, trepidation, worry ♦ *v* **2 = make uneasy**, bother, concern, disturb, perturb, trouble, unsettle, upset, worry

disregard *v* **1 = ignore**, brush aside *or* away, discount, make light of, neglect, overlook, pass over, pay no heed to, turn a blind eye to ♦ *n* **2 = inattention**, contempt, disdain, disrespect, indifference, neglect, negligence, oversight

disrepair *n* **= dilapidation**, collapse, decay, deterioration, ruination

disreputable *adj* **= discreditable**, dishonorable, ignominious, infamous, louche, notorious, scandalous, shady (*inf*),

dis·re·spect'ful *adj*

dis·rupt' *vt* **1** interrupt. **2** throw into turmoil or disorder. **dis·rup'tion** *n*
  dis·rup'tive *adj*

dis·sat·is·fied *adj* not pleased or contented. **dis·sat·is·fac'tion** *n*

dis·sect [di-SEKT] *vt* **1** cut up (body, organism) for detailed examination. **2** examine or criticize in detail. **dis·sec'tion** *n*

dis·sem·ble [di-SEM-bəl] *v* **-bled, -bling 1** conceal, disguise (feelings, etc.). **2** act the hypocrite. **dis·sem'bler** *n*

dis·sem·i·nate [di-SEM-ə-nayt] *vt* **-nat·ed, -nat·ing** spread abroad, scatter.
  dis·sem·i·na'tion *n*

dis·sent [di-SENT] *vi* **1** differ in opinion. **2** express such difference. **3** disagree with doctrine, etc. of established church, etc. ◆ *n* **4** such disagreement. **dis·sent'er** *n*

dis·ser·ta·tion [dis-ər-TAY-shən] *n* **1** written thesis. **2** formal discourse.

dis·serv·ice [dis-SUR-vis] *n* ill turn, wrong, injury.

dis·si·dent [DIS-i-dənt] *n, adj* (one) not in agreement, esp. with government.
  dis·si·dence *n* **1** dissent. **2** disagreement.

dis·sim·i·lar *adj* not alike, different.
  dis·sim·i·lar'i·ty *n*

dis·sim·u·late [di-SIM-yə-layt] *v* **-lat·ed, -lat·ing 1** pretend not to have. **2** practice deceit. **dis·sim·u·la'tion** *n*

dis·si·pate [DIS-ə-payt] *vt* **-pat·ed, -pat·ing 1** scatter. **2** waste, squander. **dis'si·pat·ed** *adj* **1** indulging in pleasure without restraint, dissolute. **2** scattered, wasted.
  dis·si·pa'tion *n* **1** scattering. **2** frivolous, dissolute way of life.

dis·so·ci·ate [di-SOH-shee-ayt] *v* **-at·ed, -at·ing 1** separate, sever. **2** disconnect.

dis·so·lute [DIS-ə-loot] *adj* lacking

THESAURUS

shameful

disrepute *n* = **discredit**, disgrace, dishonour, ignominy, ill repute, infamy, obloquy, shame, unpopularity

disrespect *n* = **contempt**, cheek, impertinence, impoliteness, impudence, insolence, irreverence, lack of respect, rudeness, sauce

disrespectful *adj* = **contemptuous**, cheeky, discourteous, impertinent, impolite, impudent, insolent, insulting, irreverent, rude

disrupt *v* **1** = **disturb**, confuse, disorder, disorganize, spoil, upset **2** = **interrupt**, break up or into, interfere with, intrude, obstruct, unsettle, upset

disruption *n* = **disturbance**, interference, interruption, stoppage

disruptive *adj* = **disturbing**, disorderly, distracting, troublesome, unruly, unsettling, upsetting

dissatisfaction *n* = **discontent**, annoyance, chagrin, disappointment, displeasure, frustration, irritation, resentment, unhappiness

dissatisfied *adj* = **discontented**, disappointed, disgruntled, displeased, fed up, frustrated, unhappy, unsatisfied

dissect *v* **1** = **cut up** or **apart**, anatomize, dismember, lay open **2** = **analyze**, break down, explore, inspect, investigate, research, scrutinize, study

disseminate *v* = **spread**, broadcast, circulate, disperse, distribute, publicize, scatter

dissension *n* = **disagreement**, conflict, discord, dispute, dissent, friction, quarrel, row, strife

dissent *v* **1** = **disagree**, differ, object, protest, refuse, withhold assent or approval ◆ *n* **2** = **disagreement**, discord, dissension, objection, opposition, refusal, resistance

dissenter *n* = **objector**, dissident, nonconformist

dissertation *n* = **thesis**, critique, discourse, disquisition, essay, exposition, treatise

disservice *n* = **bad turn**, harm, injury, injustice, unkindness, wrong

dissident *adj* **1** = **dissenting**, disagreeing, discordant, heterodox, nonconformist ◆ *n* **2** = **protester**, agitator, dissenter, rebel

dissimilar *adj* = **different**, disparate, divergent, diverse, heterogeneous, unlike, unrelated, various

dissipate *v* **1** = **squander**, consume, deplete, expend, fritter away, run through, spend, waste **2** = **disperse**, disappear, dispel, dissolve, drive away, evaporate, scatter, vanish

dissipation *n* **1** = **dispersal**, disappearance, disintegration, dissolution, scattering, vanishing **2** = **debauchery**, dissoluteness, excess, extravagance, indulgence, intemperance, prodigality, profligacy, wantonness, waste

dissociate *v* **1** = **break away**, break off, part company, quit **2** = **separate**, detach, restraint, esp. lax in morals.

dis•so•lu•tion [dis-ə-LOO-shən] n 1 breakup. 2 termination of legislature, meeting or legal relationship. 3 destruction. 4 death.

dis•solve [di-ZOLV] v -solved, -solv•ing ♦ vt 1 absorb or melt in fluid. 2 break up, put an end to, annul. ♦ vi 3 melt in fluid. 4 disappear, vanish. 5 break up, scatter. **dis•sol•u•ble** [di-SOL-yə-bəl] adj capable of being dissolved.

dis•so•nant [DIS-ə-nənt] adj jarring, discordant. **dis'so•nance** n

dis•suade [di-SWAYD] vt -suad•ed, -suad•ing advise to refrain, persuade not to. **dis•sua'sion** [-zhən] n **dis•sua'sive** adj

dis•taff [DIS-taf] n cleft stick to hold wool, etc., for spinning. **distaff side 1** maternal side. 2 female line.

dis•tance [DIS-təns] n 1 amount of space between two things. 2 remoteness. 3 aloofness, reserve. ♦ vt -tanced, -tanc•ing 4 hold or place at distance. **dis'tant** adj 1 far off, remote. 2 haughty, cold.

dis•taste [dis-TAYST] n 1 dislike of food or drink. 2 aversion, disgust. **dis•taste'ful** adj

unpleasant, displeasing to feelings. **dis•taste'ful•ness** n

dis•tem•per [dis-TEM-pər] n 1 disease of dogs. 2 method of painting on plaster without oil. 3 paint used for this. ♦ vt 4 paint with distemper.

dis•tend [di-STEND] v swell out by pressure from within, inflate. **dis•ten'sion** n

dis•tich [DIS-tik] n couplet

dis•till [di-STIL] vt 1 vaporize and recondense a liquid. 2 purify, separate, concentrate liquids by this method. 3 fig extract quality of. ♦ vi 4 trickle down. **dis•til•late** [DIS-tə-lit] n distilled liquid, esp. as fuel for some engines. **dis•till'er** n one who distills, esp. manufacturer of whiskey.

dis•tinct [di-STINGKT] adj 1 clear, easily seen. 2 definite. 3 separate, different. **dis•tinc'tion** n 1 point of difference. 2 act of distinguishing. 3 eminence, repute, high honor, high quality. **dis•tinc'tive** adj characteristic. **dis•tinct'ly** adv

dis•tin•guish [di-STING-gwish] vt 1 make difference in. 2 recognize, make out. 3 honor. 4 (usu refl) make prominent or honored. 5 classify. ♦ vi (usu with between

disconnect, distance, divorce, isolate, segregate, set apart

dissolute adj = **immoral**, debauched, degenerate, depraved, dissipated, profligate, rakish, wanton, wild

dissolution n 1 = **breaking up**, disintegration, division, parting, separation 2 = **adjournment**, discontinuation, end, finish, suspension, termination

dissolve v 1 = **melt**, deliquesce, fuse, liquefy, soften, thaw 2 = **end**, break up, discontinue, suspend, terminate, wind up

dissuade v = **deter**, advise against, discourage, put off, remonstrate, talk out of, warn

distance n 1 = **space**, extent, gap, interval, length, range, span, stretch 2 = **reserve**, aloofness, coldness, coolness, remoteness, restraint, stiffness 3 **in the distance** = **far off**, afar, far away, on the horizon, yonder ♦ v 4 **distance oneself** = **separate oneself**, be distanced from, dissociate oneself

distant adj 1 = **far-off**, abroad, far, faraway, far-flung, outlying, out-of-the-way, remote 2 = **apart**, dispersed, distinct, scattered, separate 3 = **reserved**, aloof, cool, reticent, standoffish, unapproachable, unfriendly, withdrawn

distaste n = **dislike**, aversion, disgust, horror, loathing, odium, repugnance, revulsion

distasteful adj = **unpleasant**, disagreeable, objectionable, offensive, repugnant, repulsive, scuzzy (sl), uninviting, unpalatable, unsavory

distill v = **extract**, condense, purify, refine

distinct adj 1 = **different**, detached, discrete, individual, separate, unconnected 2 = **definite**, clear, decided, evident, marked, noticeable, obvious, palpable, unmistakable, well-defined

distinction n 1 = **differentiation**, discernment, discrimination, perception, separation 2 = **feature**, characteristic, distinctiveness, individuality, mark, particularity, peculiarity, quality 3 = **difference**, contrast, differential, division, separation 4 = **excellence**, eminence, fame, greatness, honor, importance, merit, prominence, repute

distinctive adj = **characteristic**, idiosyncratic, individual, original, peculiar, singular, special, typical, unique

distinctly adv = **definitely**, clearly, decidedly, markedly, noticeably, obviously, patently, plainly, unmistakably or *among*) **6** draw distinction, grasp difference. **dis·tin'guish·a·ble** *adj* **dis·tin'guished** *adj* **1** dignified. **2** famous, eminent.

dis·tort [di-STORT] *vt* **1** put out of shape, deform. **2** misrepresent. **3** garble, falsify. **dis·tor'tion** *n*

dis·tract [di-STRAKT] *vt* **1** draw attention of (someone) away from work, etc. **2** divert. **3** perplex, bewilder, drive mad. **dis·trac'tion** *n*

dis·traught [di-STRAWT] *adj* **1** bewildered, crazed with grief. **2** frantic, distracted.

dis·tress [di-STRES] *n* **1** severe trouble, mental pain. **2** severe pressure of hunger, fatigue or want. ♦ *vt* **3** afflict, give mental pain. **dis·tress'ful** *adj*

dis·trib·ute [di-STRIB-yoot] *vt* **-ut·ed, -ut·ing 1** deal out, dispense. **2** spread, dispose at intervals. **3** classify. **dis·tri·bu'tion** *n* **dis·trib'u·tive** *adj* **dis·trib'u·tor** *n* rotary switch distributing electricity in automotive engine.

dis·trict [DIS-trikt] *n* **1** region, locality. **2** portion of territory.

dis·trust' *v* **1** regard as untrustworthy. ♦ *n* **2** feeling of suspicion or doubt. **dis·trust'ful** *adj*

dis·turb' *vt* trouble, agitate, unsettle, derange. **dis·turb'ance** *n*

————— THESAURUS —————

distinguish *v* **1** = **differentiate**, ascertain, decide, determine, discriminate, judge, tell apart, tell the difference **2** = **characterize**, categorize, classify, mark, separate, set apart, single out **3** = **make out**, discern, know, perceive, pick out, recognize, see, tell

distinguished *adj* = **eminent**, acclaimed, celebrated, famed, famous, illustrious, noted, renowned, well-known

distort *v* **1** = **misrepresent**, bias, color, falsify, pervert, slant, twist **2** = **deform**, bend, buckle, contort, disfigure, misshape, twist, warp

distortion *n* **1** = **misrepresentation**, bias, falsification, perversion, slant **2** = **deformity**, bend, buckle, contortion, crookedness, malformation, twist, warp

distract *v* **1** = **divert**, draw away, sidetrack, turn aside **2** = **amuse**, beguile, engross, entertain, occupy

distracted *adj* = **agitated**, at sea, flustered, harassed, in a flap (*inf*), perplexed, puzzled, troubled

distraction *n* **1** = **diversion**, disturbance, interference, interruption **2** = **entertainment**, amusement, diversion, pastime, recreation **3** = **agitation**, bewilderment, commotion, confusion, discord, disorder, disturbance

distraught *adj* = **frantic**, agitated, beside oneself, desperate, distracted, distressed, out of one's mind, overwrought, worked-up

distress *n* **1** = **worry**, grief, heartache, misery, pain, sorrow, suffering, torment, wretchedness **2** = **need**, adversity, difficulties, hardship, misfortune, poverty, privation, trouble ♦ *v* **3** = **upset**, disturb, grieve, harass, sadden, torment, trouble, worry

distressed *adj* **1** = **upset**, agitated, distracted, distraught, tormented, troubled, worried, wretched **2** = **poverty-stricken**, destitute, down at heel, indigent, needy, poor, straitened

distressing *adj* = **upsetting**, disturbing, harrowing, heart-breaking, painful, sad, worrying

distribute *v* **1** = **hand out**, circulate, convey, deliver, pass round **2** = **share**, allocate, allot, apportion, deal, dispense, dole out

distribution *n* **1** = **delivery**, dealing, handling, mailing, transportation **2** = **sharing**, allocation, allotment, apportionment, division **3** = **classification**, arrangement, grouping, organization, placement

district *n* = **area**, locale, locality, neighborhood, parish, quarter, region, sector, vicinity

distrust *v* **1** = **suspect**, be suspicious of, be wary of, disbelieve, doubt, mistrust, question, smell a rat (*inf*) ♦ *n* **2** = **suspicion**, disbelief, doubt, misgiving, mistrust, question, skepticism, wariness

disturb *v* **1** = **interrupt**, bother, butt in on, disrupt, interfere with, intrude on, pester **2** = **upset**, alarm, distress, fluster, harass, perturb, trouble, unnerve, unsettle, worry **3** = **muddle**, disarrange, disorder

disturbance *n* **1** = **interruption**, annoyance, bother, distraction, intrusion **2** = **disorder**, brawl, commotion, fracas, fray, rumpus

disturbed *adj* **1** *Psychiatry* = **unbalanced**, disordered, maladjusted, neurotic,

dis·use [dis-YOOS] n state of being no longer used. **dis·used'** [-YOOZD] adj

ditch [dich] n 1 long narrow hollow dug in ground for drainage, etc. ♦ v 2 make, repair ditches. 3 run car, etc. into ditch. ♦ vt 4 sl abandon, discard.

dith·er [DITH-ər] vi 1 be uncertain or indecisive. ♦ n 2 this state.

dith·y·ramb [DITH-ə-ram] n ancient Greek hymn sung in honor of Dionysus.

dit·to [DIT-oh] n, pl -tos same, aforesaid (used to avoid repetition in lists, etc.).

dit·ty [DIT-ee] n, pl -ties simple song.

di·u·ret·ic [dī-ə-RET-ik] adj 1 increasing the discharge of urine. ♦ n 2 substance with this property.

di·ur·nal [dī-UR-nəl] adj 1 daily. 2 in or of daytime. 3 taking a day.

di·va·lent [dī-VAY-lənt] adj capable of combining with two atoms of hydrogen or their equivalent.

di·van' n bed, couch without back or head.

dive [dīv] vi **dived** or **dove, div·ing** 1 plunge under surface of water. 2 descend suddenly. 3 disappear. 4 go deep down into. 5 reach quickly. ♦ n 6 act of diving. 7 sl disreputable bar, club, etc. **div'er** n one who descends into deep water. **dive bomber** aircraft that attacks after diving

steeply.

di·verge [di-VURJ] vi **-verged, -verg·ing** 1 get farther apart. 2 separate. **di·ver'gence** n **di·ver'gent** adj

di·vers [DĪ-vərz] adj obs some, various.

di·verse [di-VURS] adj different, varied. **di·ver·si·ty** n, pl **-ties** 1 quality of being different or varied. 2 range of difference. **di·ver·si·fy** vt **-fied, -fy·ing** 1 make diverse or varied. 2 give variety to. **di·ver·si·fi·ca'tion** n

di·vert [di-VURT] vt 1 turn aside, ward off. 2 amuse, entertain. **di·ver'sion** [-zhən] n 1 a diverting. 2 official detour for traffic when main route is closed. 3 amusement.

di·vest' vt 1 unclothe, strip. 2 dispossess, deprive. 3 sell off.

di·vide [di-VĪD] v **-vid·ed, -vid·ing** ♦ vt 1 make into two or more parts, split up, separate. 2 distribute, share. 3 diverge in opinion. 4 classify. ♦ vi 5 become separated. 6 part into two groups for voting, etc. ♦ n 7 division esp. between adjacent drainage areas. **div'i·dend** n 1 share of profits, of money divided among shareholders, etc. 2 number to be divided by another. **di·vid'ers** pl n pair of compasses.

di·vine [di-VĪN] adj **-vin·er, -vin·est** 1 of,

troubled, upset 2 = **worried**, anxious, apprehensive, bothered, concerned, nervous, troubled, uneasy, upset, wired (sl)

disturbing adj = **worrying**, alarming, disconcerting, distressing, frightening, harrowing, startling, unsettling, upsetting

disuse n = **neglect**, abandonment, decay, idleness

ditch n 1 = **channel**, drain, dyke, furrow, gully, moat, trench, watercourse ♦ v 2 Sl = **get rid of**, abandon, discard, dispose of, drop, dump (inf), jettison, scrap, throw out or overboard

dither v 1 = **vacillate**, hesitate, hum and haw, shillyshally (inf), teeter, waver ♦ n 2 = **flutter**, flap (inf), fluster, tizzy (inf)

dive v 1 = **plunge**, descend, dip, drop, duck, nose-dive, plummet, swoop ♦ n 2 = **plunge**, jump, leap, lunge, nose dive, spring

diverge v 1 = **separate**, branch, divide, fork, part, split, spread 2 = **deviate**, depart, digress, meander, stray, turn aside, wander

diverse adj 1 = **various**, assorted, manifold,

miscellaneous, of every description, several, sundry, varied 2 = **different**, discrete, disparate, dissimilar, distinct, divergent, separate, unlike, varying

diversify v = **vary**, branch out, change, expand, have a finger in every pie, spread out

diversion n = **pastime**, amusement, distraction, entertainment, game, recreation, relaxation, sport

diversity n = **difference**, distinctiveness, diverseness, heterogeneity, multiplicity, range, variety

divert v 1 = **redirect**, avert, deflect, switch, turn aside 2 = **distract**, draw or lead away from, lead astray, sidetrack 3 = **entertain**, amuse, beguile, delight, gratify, regale

diverting adj = **entertaining**, amusing, beguiling, enjoyable, fun, humorous, pleasant

divide v 1 = **separate**, bisect, cut (up), part, partition, segregate, split 2 = **share**, allocate, allot, deal out, dispense, distribute 3 = **cause to disagree**, break up, come between, estrange, split pert. to, proceeding from, God. **2** sacred. **3** heavenly. ♦ *n* **4** theologian. **5** clergyman. ♦ *v* **-vined, -vin·ing** guess. **6** predict, foresee, tell by inspiration or magic. **di·vi·na·tion** [div-ə-NAY-shən] *n* divining. **di·vine·ly** *adv* **di·vin·er** *n* **di·vin·i·ty** *n* **1** quality of being divine. **2** god. **3** theology. **divining rod** [forked] stick, etc. said to move when held over ground where water is present]

di·vi·sion [di-VIZH-ən] *n* **1** act of dividing. **2** part of whole. **3** barrier. **4** section. **5** difference in opinion, etc. **6** *Math.* method of finding how many times one number is contained in another. **7** army unit. **8** separation, disunion. **di·vis·i·ble** *adj* capable of division. **di·vi·sive** [-VĪ-siv] *adj* causing disagreement. **di·vi·sor** [-VĪ-zər] *n Math.* number that divides dividend.

di·vorce [di-VORS] *n* **1** legal dissolution of marriage. **2** complete separation, disunion. ♦ *vt* **-vorced, -vorc·ing** **3** dissolve marriage. **4** separate. **5** sunder. **di·vor·cee'** [-SAY] *n*

div·ot [DIV-ət] *n* piece of turf.

di·vulge [di-VULJ] *vt* **-vulged, -vulg·ing** reveal, let out (secret).

Dix·ie [DIK-see] *n* southern states of the US.

diz·zy [DIZ-ee] *adj* **-zi·er, -zi·est 1** feeling dazed, unsteady, as if about to fall. **2** causing or fit to cause dizziness, as speed,

etc. **3** *inf* silly. ♦ *v* **-zied, -zy·ing** **4** make dizzy. **diz'zi·ly** *adv* **diz'zi·ness** *n*

DJ *n* **1** disc jockey. ♦ *v* **DJ'd, DJ'·ing** **2** act as DJ.

DNA *n* deoxyribonucleic acid, the main constituent of the chromosomes of all organisms.

do[1] [doo] *v* **did, done, do·ing** ♦ *vt* **1** perform, effect, transact, bring about, finish. **2** work at. **3** work out, solve. **4** suit. **5** cover (distance). **6** provide, prepare. **7** *inf* cheat, trick. **8** frustrate. **9** look after. ♦ *vi* **10** act. **11** manage. **12** work. **13** fare. **14** serve, suffice. **15** happen. ♦ *v aux* **16** makes negative and interrogative sentences and expresses emphasis. ♦ *n inf* **17** celebration, festivity. **do away with** destroy. **do up 1** fasten. **2** renovate. **do with 1** need. **2** make use of. **do without** deny oneself.

do[2] [doh] *n* first sol-fa note.

doc·ile [DOS-əl] *adj* willing to obey, submissive.

dock[1] [dok] *n* **1** artificial enclosure near harbor for loading or repairing ships. **2** platform for loading and unloading trucks. ♦ *v* **3** of vessel, put or go into dock. **4** (of spacecraft) link or be linked together in space. **dock'er** *n* longshoreman. **dock'yard** *n* enclosure with docks, for building or

━━━━━━━━━━━━━━━━━ THESAURUS ━━━━━━━━━━━━━━━━━

dividend *n* = **bonus**, cut (*inf*), divvy (*inf*), extra, gain, plus, portion, share, surplus

divine *adj* **1** = **heavenly**, angelic, celestial, godlike, holy, spiritual, superhuman, supernatural **2** = **sacred**, consecrated, holy, religious, sanctified, spiritual **3** *Inf* = **wonderful**, beautiful, excellent, glorious, marvelous, perfect, splendid, superlative ♦ *v* **4** = **infer**, apprehend, deduce, discern, guess, perceive, suppose, surmise

divinity *n* **1** = **theology**, religion, religious studies **2** = **god** *or* **goddess**, deity, guardian spirit, spirit **3** = **godliness**, deity, divine nature, holiness, sanctity

divisible *adj* = **dividable**, separable, splittable

division *n* **1** = **separation**, cutting up, dividing, partition, splitting up **2** = **sharing**, allotment, apportionment, distribution **3** = **part**, branch, category, class, department, group, section **4** = **disagreement**, difference of opinion, discord, rupture, split, variance

divorce *n* **1** = **separation**, annulment, dissolution, split-up ♦ *v* **2** = **separate**,

disconnect, dissociate, dissolve (*marriage*), divide, part, sever, split up

divulge *v* = **make known**, confess, declare, disclose, let slip, proclaim, reveal, tell

dizzy *adj* **1** = **giddy**, faint, light-headed, off balance, reeling, shaky, swimming, wobbly, woozy (*inf*) **2** = **confused**, at sea, befuddled, bemused, bewildered, dazed, dazzled, muddled

do *v* **1** = **perform**, accomplish, achieve, carry out, complete, execute **2** = **be adequate**, be sufficient, cut the mustard, pass muster, satisfy, suffice **3** = **get ready**, arrange, fix, look after, prepare, see to **4** = **solve**, decipher, decode, figure out, puzzle out, resolve, work out **5** = **cause**, bring about, create, effect, produce

do away with *v* **1** = **kill**, exterminate, murder, slay **2** = **get rid of**, abolish, discard, discontinue, eliminate, put an end to, put paid to, remove

docile *adj* = **submissive**, amenable, biddable, compliant, manageable, obedient, pliant

docility *n* = **submissiveness**, compliance,

repairing ships.

dock[2] n 1 solid part of animal's tail. 2 cut end, stump. ◆ vt 3 cut short, esp. tail. 4 curtail, deduct (an amount) from.

dock[3] n enclosure in criminal court for prisoner.

dock·et [DOK-it] n 1 agenda. 2 list of court cases to be heard. ◆ vt 3 place on docket.

doc·tor [DOK-tər] n 1 medical practitioner. 2 one holding university's highest degree in any faculty. ◆ vt 3 treat medically. 4 repair, mend. 5 falsify (accounts, etc.). **doc·tor·al** [-əl] adj **doc·tor·ate** [-it] n

doc·trine [DOK-trin] n 1 what is taught. 2 teaching of church, school, or person. 3 belief, opinion, dogma. **doc·tri·naire'** [-trə-NAIR] adj stubbornly insistent on applying theory without regard for circumstances. ◆ n **doc'.tri·nal** adj

doc·u·ment [DOK-yə-mənt] n 1 piece of paper, etc. providing information or evidence. ◆ vt 2 furnish with proofs, illustrations, certificates. **doc·u·men·ta·ry** adj, n, pl -**ries** (of) type of film, TV program dealing with real life, not fiction. **doc·u·men·ta·tion** n

dod·der [DOD-ər] vi totter or tremble, as with age.

dodge [doj] v 1 avoid or attempt to avoid (blow, discovery, etc.) as by moving quickly. 2 evade questions by cleverness. ◆ n 3 trick, artifice. 4 ingenious method. 5 act of dodging. **dodg'er** n 1 shifty person. 2 evader.

do·do [DOH-doh] n, pl -**dos** 1 large extinct bird. 2 person with old-fashioned ideas.

doe [doh] n female of deer, hare, rabbit.

Doe [doh] n **John** or **Jane Doe** unknown or unidentified person.

does [duz] third pers. sing., pres. ind. active of DO.

doff [dof] vt 1 take off (hat, clothing). 2 discard, lay aside.

dog [dawg] n 1 domesticated carnivorous four-legged mammal. 2 person (in contempt, abuse or playfully). 3 name given to various mechanical contrivances for gripping, holding. 4 device with tooth that penetrates or grips object and detains it. 5 andiron or firedog. 6 sl ugly person. 7 sl thing of extremely poor quality. 8 inf a fellow. ◆ vt **dogged, dog-ging** 9 follow steadily or closely. **dog'ged** [-gid] adj persistent, resolute, tenacious. **dog'gy** adj -**gi·er, -gi·est dog days** 1 hot season of the rising of Dog Star. 2 period of inactivity. **dog'-ear** n 1 turned-down corner of page in book. ◆ vt 2 turn down corners of pages. **dog'-eat-dog'** n action based on complete cynicism, ruthless competition. **dog'fight** n 1 skirmish between fighter planes. 2 savage contest characterized by disregard of rules. **doggy bag** bag in which diner may take leftovers (ostensibly for dog). **dog'house** n kennel. **in the doghouse** inf in disfavor. **dog'leg** n sharp bend or angle. **dog's age** quite a long time. **Dog Star** star Sirius. **go to the dogs** degenerate.

doge [dohj] n formerly, chief magistrate in Venice.

─────┤ THESAURUS ├─────

manageability, meekness, obedience

dock[1] n 1 = **wharf**, harbor, pier, quay, waterfront ◆ v 2 = **moor**, anchor, berth, drop anchor, land, put in, tie up 3 Of spacecraft = **link up**, couple, hook up, join, rendezvous, unite

dock[2] v 1 = **deduct**, decrease, diminish, lessen, reduce, subtract, withhold 2 = **cut off**, clip, crop, curtail, cut short, shorten

doctor n 1 = **G.P.**, general practitioner, medic (inf), medical practitioner, physician ◆ v 2 = **change**, alter, disguise, falsify, misrepresent, pervert, tamper with 3 = **add to**, adulterate, cut, dilute, mix with, spike, water down

doctrinaire adj = **dogmatic**, biased, fanatical, inflexible, insistent, opinionated, rigid

doctrine n = **teaching**, article of faith, belief, conviction, creed, dogma, opinion, precept, principle, tenet

document n 1 = **paper**, certificate, record, report ◆ v 2 = **support**, authenticate, certify, corroborate, detail, substantiate, validate, verify

dodge v 1 = **duck**, dart, sidestep, swerve, turn aside 2 = **evade**, avoid, elude, get out of, shirk

dog n 1 = **hound**, canine, cur, man's best friend, pooch (sl) 2 **go to the dogs** Inf = **go to ruin**, degenerate, deteriorate, go down the drain, go to pot ◆ v 3 = **trouble**, follow, haunt, hound, plague, pursue, stalk, track, trail

dogged adj = **determined**, indefatigable, obstinate, persistent, resolute, steadfast, stubborn, tenacious, unflagging, unshakable

dog·ger·el [DAW-gər-əl] n slipshod, unpoetic or trivial verse.

do·gie [DOH-gee] n motherless calf.

dog·ma [DAWG-mə] n, pl **-mas 1** article of belief, esp. one laid down authoritatively by church. **2** body of beliefs. **dog·mat·ic** adj **1** asserting opinions with arrogance. **2** relating to dogma. **dog·mat·i·cal·ly** adv **dog·ma·tism** n arrogant assertion of opinion.

doi·ly [DOI-lee] n, pl **-lies** small cloth, paper, piece of lace to place under cake, dish, etc.

Dol·by [DOHL-bee] n ® system used in tape recording to reduce unwanted noise.

dol·ce [DOHL-chay] adj Music sweet.

dol·drums [DOHL-drəmz] pl n **1** state of depression, dumps. **2** region of light winds and calms near the equator.

dole [dohl] n **1** charitable allotment, gift. ◆ vt **doled, dol·ing 2** (usu. with out) deal out sparingly.

dole·ful [DOHL-fəl] adj dreary, mournful. **dole'ful·ly** adv

doll [dol] n **1** child's toy image of human being. **2** sl attractive person. ◆ v **3** dress (up) in latest fashion or smartly.

dol·lar [DOL-ər] n standard monetary unit of many countries, esp. US and Canada.

dol·lop [DOL-əp] n inf **1** semisolid lump. **2** unmeasured amount, a dash.

dol·ly [DOL-ee] n, pl **-lies 1** doll. **2** wheeled support for film, TV camera. **3** platform on wheels for moving heavy objects. **4** various metal devices used as aids in hammering, riveting.

dol·men [DOHL-mən] n **1** prehistoric monument. **2** stone table.

do·lo·mite [DOH-lə-mīt] n a type of limestone.

do·lor [DOH-lər] n grief, sadness, distress. **dol'or·ous** [DOL-] adj

dol·phin [DOL-fin] n sea mammal, smaller than whale, with beaklike snout.

dolt [dohlt] n stupid fellow. **dolt'ish** adj

do·main [doh-MAYN] n **1** lands held or ruled over. **2** sphere, field of influence. **3** province. **4** Computers. group of computers with the same name on the Internet.

dome [dohm] n **1** a rounded vault forming a roof. **2** something of this shape.

Domes·day Book [DOOMZ-day] record of survey of England in 1086.

do·mes·tic [də-MES-tik] adj **1** of, in the home. **2** homeloving. **3** (of animals) tamed, kept by man. **4** of, in one's own country, not foreign. ◆ n **5** household servant. **do·mes'ti·cate** [-kayt] vt **-cat·ed, -cat·ing 1** tame (animals). **2** accustom to home life. **3** adapt to an environment. **do·mes·tic·i·ty** [doh-me-STIS-i-tee] n

dom·i·cile [DOM-ə-sīl] n person's regular place of abode. **dom'i·ciled** adj living.

dom·i·nate [DOM-ə-nayt] vt **-nat·ed, -nat·ing 1** rule, control, sway. **2** of heights, overlook. ◆ vi **3** control, be the most powerful or influential member or part of something. **dom'i·nant** adj **dom·i·na'tion** n **dom·i·neer'** v act imperiously, tyrannize.

Do·min·i·can [də-MIN-i-kən] n **1** priest or

dogma n = **doctrine**, belief, credo, creed, opinion, teachings

dogmatic adj = **opinionated**, arrogant, assertive, doctrinaire, emphatic, obdurate, overbearing

doldrums n the doldrums = **inactivity**, depression, dumps (inf), gloom, listlessness, malaise

dole v dole out = **give out**, allocate, allot, apportion, assign, dispense, distribute, hand out

dollop n = **lump**, helping, portion, scoop, serving

dolt n = **idiot**, ass, blockhead, chump (inf), dope (inf), dork (sl), dunce, fool, oaf, schmuck (sl)

domestic adj **1** = **home**, family, household, private **2** = **home-loving**, domesticated, homely, housewifely, stay-at-home **3** = domesticated, house-trained, pet, tame, trained **4** = **native**, indigenous, internal ◆ n **5** = **servant**, charwoman, daily, help, maid

dominant adj **1** = **controlling**, assertive, authoritative, commanding, governing, ruling, superior, supreme **2** = **main**, chief, predominant, pre-eminent, primary, principal, prominent

dominate v **1** = **control**, direct, govern, have the whip hand over, monopolize, rule, tyrannize **2** = **tower above**, loom over, overlook, stand head and shoulders above, stand over, survey

domination n = **control**, ascendancy, authority, command, influence, power, rule, superiority, supremacy

domineering adj = **overbearing**, arrogant, authoritarian, bossy (inf), dictatorial, high-handed, imperious, oppressive, nun of the order of St. Dominic. ◆ *adj* **2** pert. to this order.

do·min·ion [də-MIN-yən] *n* **1** sovereignty, rule. **2** territory of government.

dom·i·noes [DOM-ə-nohz] *n* game played with 28 oblong flat pieces marked on one side with 0 to 6 spots on each half of the face. **dom·i·no** *n* **1** one of these pieces. **2** cloak with eye mask for masquerading.

don[1] *vt* donned, don·ning put on (clothes).

don[2] *n* **1** in English universities, fellow or tutor of college. **2** Spanish title, Sir. **3** in Mafia, head of a family or syndicate.

do·nate [DOH-nayt] *vt* **-nat·ed, -nat·ing** give. **do·na'tion** *n* gift to fund. **do·nor** [DOH-nər] *n* **donor card** specifying organs that may be used for transplant after cardholder's death.

done pp. of DO.

don·key [DONG-kee] *n, pl* **-keys 1** ass. **2** stupid or obstinate person. **donkey engine** auxiliary engine. **don'key·work** *n* drudgery.

donned pt./pp. of DON.

doo·dle [DOOD-l] *vi* **-dled, -dling** scribble absentmindedly. ◆ *n*

doom *n* **1** fate, destiny. **2** ruin. **3** judicial sentence, condemnation. **4** the Last Judgment. ◆ *vt* **5** sentence, condemn. **6** destine to destruction or suffering. **dooms'day** *n* the day of the Last Judgment.

door [dor] *n* hinged or sliding barrier to close any entrance. **door'way** *n* entrance with or without door.

dope [dohp] *n* **1** kind of varnish. **2** *sl* drug, esp. illegal, narcotic drug. **3** *inf*

information. **4** *inf* stupid person. ◆ *vt* **doped, dop·ing 5** drug (esp. of racehorses). **dop·ey** [DOH-pee] *adj* **dop·i·er, dop·i·est** *inf* **1** foolish. **2** drugged. **3** half-asleep.

Dop·pler effect [DOP-lər] shift in frequency of sound, light, other waves when emitting source moves closer or farther from the observer.

Dor·ic [DOR-ik] *n* **1** dialect of Dorians. **2** style of Greek architecture. **3** rustic dialect. ◆ *adj* **Do·ri·an** [DOR-ee-ən] *adj, n* (member) of early Greek race.

dork [dork] *n* **1** *vulg sl* penis. **2** *sl* stupid or clumsy person. ◆ *adj* **dork·i·er, dork·i·est**

dor·mant [DOR-mənt] *adj* **1** not active, in state of suspension. **2** sleeping. **dor'man·cy** *n*

dor·mer [DOR-mər] *n* **1** upright window set in sloping roof. **2** such a projecting structure.

dor·mi·to·ry [DOR-mi-tor-ee] *n, pl* **-ries** sleeping room with many beds. **dormitory suburb** suburb whose inhabitants commute to work.

dor·mouse [DOR-mows] *n* small hibernating mouselike rodent.

dor·sal [DOR-səl] *adj* of, on back.

do·ry [DOR-ee] *n, pl* **-ries** flat-bottomed boat with high bow and flaring sides.

dose [dohs] *n* **1** amount (of drug, etc.) administered at one time. **2** *inf* instance or period of something unpleasant, esp. disease. ◆ *vt* **dosed, dos·ing 3** give doses to. **dos'age** *n*

dos·si·er [DOS-ee-ay] *n* set of papers on some particular subject or event.

──── THESAURUS ────

tyrannical

dominion *n* **1** = **control**, authority, command, jurisdiction, power, rule, sovereignty, supremacy **2** = **kingdom**, country, domain, empire, realm, territory

don *v* = **put on**, clothe oneself in, dress in, get into, pull on, slip on *or* into

donate *v* = **give**, contribute, make a gift of, present, subscribe

donation *n* = **contribution**, gift, grant, hand-out, offering, present, subscription

donor *n* = **giver**, benefactor, contributor, donator, philanthropist

doom *n* **1** = **destruction**, catastrophe, downfall, fate, fortune, lot, ruin ◆ *v* **2** = **condemn**, consign, damn, destine, sentence

doomed *adj* = **condemned**, bewitched, cursed, fated, hopeless, ill-fated, ill-omened, luckless, star-crossed

door *n* = **opening**, doorway, entrance, entry, exit

dope *n* **1** *Sl* = **drug**, narcotic, opiate **2** *Inf* = **idiot**, dimwit (*inf*), doofus (*sl*), dork (*sl*), dunce, dweeb (*sl*), fool, nitwit (*inf*), schmuck (*sl*) ◆ *v* **3** = **drug**, anesthetize, knock out, narcotize, sedate, stupefy

dork *n* *Sl* = **idiot**, doofus (*sl*), dope (*sl*), dunce, dweeb (*sl*), fool, geek (*sl*), nerd

dormant *adj* = **inactive**, asleep, hibernating, inert, inoperative, latent, sleeping, slumbering, suspended

dose *n* = **quantity**, dosage, draft, measure, portion, potion, prescription

dot n 1 small spot, mark. ◆ vt **dot·ted,
dot·ting** 2 mark with dot(s). 3 sprinkle.
dot'ty adj inf **-ti·er, -ti·est** 1 eccentric. 2
crazy. 3 (with about) inf extremely fond of.
dot'com, dot-com n company that
conducts most of its business on the
Internet.

dote [doht] vi **dot·ed, dot·ing** 1 (with on or
upon) be passionately fond of. 2 be silly or
weak-minded. **dot'age** [-ij] n senility.
do'tard [-tərd] n **dot'ing** adj blindly
affectionate.

dotty see DOT.

dou·ble [DUB-əl] adj 1 of two parts, layers,
etc., folded. 2 twice as much or many. 3 of
two kinds. 4 designed for two users. 5
ambiguous. 6 deceitful. ◆ adv 7 twice. 8 to
twice the amount or extent. 9 in a pair. ◆ n
10 person or thing exactly like, or
mistakable for, another. 11 quantity twice
as much as another. 12 sharp turn. 13
running pace. ◆ v **-bled, -bling** 14 make,
become double. 15 increase twofold. 16
fold in two. 17 turn sharply. 18 get around,
sail around. **dou'bly** adv **double agent** spy
employed simultaneously by two opposing
sides. **double bass** largest and
lowest-toned instrument in violin form.
dou'ble-cross' v betray, swindle a
colleague. **dou'ble-cross'er** n
dou'ble-deal'ing n artifice, duplicity.

double Dutch sl incomprehensible talk,
gibberish. **double dutch** form of the game
of jump rope. **double glazing** two panes of
glass in a window to insulate against cold,
sound, etc. **dou'ble-head'er** n Sports two
games played consecutively on same day
in same stadium. **dou'ble-quick'** adj, adv
very fast. **double take** delayed reaction to
a remark, situation, etc. **dou'ble-talk** n, vt
(engage in) intentionally garbled speech.

dou·ble en·ten·dre [DUB-əl
ahn-TAHN-drə] n, pl **-dres** [-drəz] word or
phrase with two meanings, one usu.
indelicate.

dou·blet [DUB-lit] n close-fitting body
garment formerly worn by men.

dou·bloon [du-BLOON] n ancient Spanish
gold coin.

doubt [dowt] vt 1 hesitate to believe. 2 call
in question. 3 suspect. ◆ vi 4 be wavering
or uncertain in belief or opinion. ◆ n 5
uncertainty, wavering in belief. 6 state of
affairs giving cause for uncertainty.
doubt'ful adj **doubt'less** adv

douche [doosh] n 1 jet or spray of water
applied to (part of) body. 2 device for
douching. ◆ vt **douched, douch·ing** 3 give
douche to.

dough [doh] n 1 flour or meal kneaded
with water. 2 sl money. **dough'nut** n
sweetened and fried, usu. ring-shaped,

THESAURUS

dot n 1 = **spot**, fleck, jot, mark, point,
speck, speckle 2 **on the dot = on time**,
exactly, on the button (inf), precisely,
promptly, punctually, to the minute ◆ v
3 = **spot**, dab, dabble, fleck, speckle,
sprinkle, stipple, stud

dotage n = **senility**, decrepitude,
feebleness, imbecility, old age, second
childhood, weakness

dote on or **upon** v = **adore**, admire, hold
dear, idolize, lavish affection on, prize,
treasure

doting adj = **adoring**, devoted, fond,
foolish, indulgent, lovesick

double adj 1 = **twice**, coupled, dual,
duplicate, in pairs, paired, twin, twofold ◆
v 2 = **multiply**, duplicate, enlarge, grow,
increase, magnify ◆ n 3 = **twin**, clone,
dead ringer (sl), Doppelgänger, duplicate,
lookalike, replica, spitting image (inf) 4 **at**
or **on the double = quickly**, at full speed,
briskly, immediately, posthaste, without
delay

double-cross v = **betray**, cheat, defraud,
hoodwink, mislead, swindle, trick,
two-time (inf)

doubt n 1 = **uncertainty**, hesitancy,
hesitation, indecision, irresolution, lack of
conviction, suspense 2 = **suspicion**,
apprehension, distrust, misgiving, mistrust,
qualm, skepticism ◆ v 3 = **be uncertain**, be
dubious, demur, fluctuate, hesitate,
scruple, vacillate, waver 4 = **suspect**,
discredit, distrust, fear, lack confidence in,
mistrust, query, question

doubtful adj 1 = **unlikely**, debatable,
dubious, equivocal, improbable,
problematic(al), questionable, unclear 2 =
unsure, distrustful, hesitating, in two
minds (inf), skeptical, suspicious, tentative,
uncertain, unconvinced, wavering

doubtless adv 1 = **certainly**, assuredly,
indisputably, of course, surely,
undoubtedly, unquestionably, without
doubt 2 = **probably**, apparently, most
likely, ostensibly, presumably, seemingly,

piece of dough.

dough•ty [DOW-tee] *adj* **-ti•er, -ti•est**
valiant. **dough'ti•ness** *n* boldness.

dour [duur] *adj* grim, stubborn, severe.

douse [dows] *vt* **doused, dous•ing 1** thrust
into water. **2** extinguish (light).

dove [duv] *n* **1** bird of pigeon family. **2**
person opposed to war. **dove'cote** [-koht]
n house for doves. **dove'tail** *n* **1** joint made
with fan-shaped tenon. ◆ *v* **2** fit closely,
neatly, firmly together.

dow•a•ger [DOW-ə-jər] *n* **1** widow with
title or property derived from deceased
husband. **2** dignified elderly woman, esp.
with wealth or social prominence.

dow•dy [DOW-dee] *adj* **-di•er, -di•est 1**
unattractively or shabbily dressed. ◆ *n* **2**
woman so dressed.

dow•el [DOW-əl] *n* wooden, metal peg,
esp. joining two adjacent parts.

dow•er [DOW-ər] *n* **1** widow's share for life
of husband's estate. ◆ *vt* **2** endow. **dow'ry**
n **1** property wife brings to husband at
marriage. **2** any endowment.

down[1] *adv* **1** to, in, or toward, lower
position. **2** below the horizon. **3** (of
payment) on the spot, immediate. ◆ *prep* **4**

from higher to lower part of. **5** at lower
part of. **6** along. ◆ *adj* **7** depressed,
miserable. ◆ *vt* **8** knock, pull, push down. **9**
inf drink, esp. quickly. **down'ward** *adj, adv*
down'wards *adv* **down'cast** *adj* **1**
dejected. **2** looking down. **down'er** *n sl* **1**
barbiturate, tranquillizer, or narcotic. **2**
state of depression. **down'load** *vt* transfer
(data) from the memory of one computer
to that of another. **down'pour** *n* heavy
rainfall. **down'right** *adj* **1** plain,
straightforward. ◆ *adv* **2** quite, thoroughly.
down-stage *adj, adv* at, to front of stage.
down'-and-out' finished, defeated. **down
in the mouth** dejected, discouraged.
down East New England, esp. the state of
Maine. **down under** Australia and New
Zealand.

down[2] *n* **1** soft underfeathers, hair or fiber.
2 fluff. **down'y** *adj* **down-i-er, down-i-est**

Down syndrome genetic disorder
characterized by degree of mental and
physical retardation.

dowry see DOWER.

dowse [dowz] *v* **dowsed, dows•ing** use
divining rod. **dows'er** *n* water diviner.

dox•ol•o•gy [dok-SOL-ə-jee] *n* short hymn

supposedly

dour *adj* = **gloomy**, dismal, dreary,
forbidding, grim, morose, sour, sullen,
unfriendly

dowdy *adj* = **frumpy**, dingy, drab, dumpy
(*inf*), frowzy, homely (*U.S.*), shabby,
unfashionable

do without *v* = **manage without**, abstain
from, dispense with, forgo, get along
without, give up, kick (*inf*)

down *adj* **1** = **depressed**, dejected,
disheartened, downcast, low, miserable,
sad, unhappy ◆ *v* **2** *Inf* = **swallow**, drain,
drink (down), gulp, put away, toss off ◆ *n*
3 be down on *Inf* = **be antagonistic** or
hostile to, bear a grudge towards, be
prejudiced against, be set against, have it
in for (*sl*)

down-and-out *n* **1** = **tramp**, bag lady,
beggar, derelict, pauper, vagabond,
vagrant ◆ *adj* **2** = **destitute**, derelict, down
on one's luck (*inf*), impoverished,
penniless, short, without two pennies to
rub together (*inf*)

downcast *adj* = **dejected**, crestfallen,
depressed, despondent, disappointed,
disconsolate, discouraged, disheartened,

dismayed, dispirited

downer *n Inf* = **moaner**, killjoy, pessimist,
prophet of doom, sourpuss (*inf*),
spoilsport, wet blanket (*inf*)

downfall *n* = **ruin**, collapse, destruction,
disgrace, fall, overthrow, undoing

downgrade *v* = **demote**, degrade,
humble, lower or reduce in rank, take
down a peg (*inf*)

downhearted *adj* = **dejected**, crestfallen,
depressed, despondent, discouraged,
disheartened, dispirited, downcast, sad,
unhappy

downpour *n* = **rainstorm**, cloudburst,
deluge, flood, inundation, torrential rain

downright *adj* = **complete**, absolute,
out-and-out, outright, plain,
thoroughgoing, total, undisguised,
unqualified, utter

down-to-earth *adj* = **sensible**,
matter-of-fact, no-nonsense, plain-spoken,
practical, realistic, sane, unsentimental

downtrodden *adj* = **oppressed**, exploited,
helpless, subjugated, subservient,
tyrannized

downward *adj* = **descending**, declining,
earthward, heading down, sliding, slipping

of praise to God.

doy·en [doi-EN] n senior member of a body or profession. **doyenne** n, fem.

doze [dohz] vi dozed, doz·ing 1 sleep drowsily, be half-asleep. ◆ n 2 nap.

doz·en [DUZ-ən] n (set of) twelve.

drab adj 1 dull, monotonous. 2 of a dingy brown color. ◆ n 3 mud color. 4 slut, prostitute.

drach·ma [DRAK-mə] n, pl **-mas** former monetary unit of Greece.

Dra·co·ni·an [dray-KOH-nee-ən] adj 1 like the laws of Draco. 2 (d-) very harsh, cruel.

draft[1] n 1 design, sketch. 2 preliminary plan or layout for work to be executed. 3 rough copy of document. 4 order for money. 5 current of air between apertures in room, etc. 6 act or action of drawing. 7 act or action of drinking. 8 amount drunk at once. 9 inhaling. 10 depth of ship in water. ◆ vt 11 make sketch, plan, or rough design of. 12 make rough copy of (writing, etc.). ◆ adj 13 of beer, etc., for drawing. 14 drawn. **draft'y** adj draft·i·er, draft·i·est full of air currents. **draft horse** horse for vehicles carrying heavy loads. **drafts'man** n, pl **-men** one who makes drawings, plans, etc. **drafts'man·ship** n

draft[2] vt 1 select for compulsory military service. 2 select (professional athlete) by draft. 3 compel (person) to serve.

drag v dragged, drag·ging ◆ vt 1 pull along with difficulty or friction. 2 trail, go heavily. 3 sweep with net or grapnels. 4 protract. 5 Computers. move (an image) on screen by use of the mouse. ◆ vi 6 lag, trail. 7 be tediously protracted. ◆ n 8 check on progress. 9 checked motion. 10 sledge,

net, grapnel, rake. 11 sl influence. 12 sl tedious person or thing. 13 sl women's clothes worn by (transvestite) man. **drag'ster** n 1 automobile designed, modified for drag racing. 2 driver of such car. **drag'net** n 1 fishing net to be dragged along sea floor. 2 comprehensive search, esp. by police for criminal, etc. **drag race** automobile race where cars are timed over measured distance.

drag·on [DRAG-ən] n 1 mythical fire-breathing monster, like winged crocodile. 2 type of large lizard. **drag'on·fly** n, pl **-flies** long-bodied insect with gauzy wings.

dra·goon [drə-GOON] n 1 formerly, cavalryman of certain regiments. ◆ vt 2 oppress. 3 coerce.

drain [drayn] vt 1 draw off (liquid) by pipes, ditches, etc. 2 dry. 3 drink to dregs. 4 empty, exhaust. ◆ vi 5 flow off or away. 6 become rid of liquid. ◆ n 7 channel for removing liquid. 8 sewer. 9 depletion, strain. **drain'age** [-ij] n

drake [drayk] n male duck.

dram n 1 small draft of strong drink. 2 unit of weight, one eighth of fluid ounce, one sixteenth of avoirdupois ounce.

dra·ma [DRAH-mə] n 1 stage play. 2 art or literature of plays. 3 playlike series of events. **dra·mat·ic** [drə-MAT-ik] adj 1 pert. to drama. 2 suitable for stage representation. 3 with force and vividness of drama. 4 striking. 5 tense. 6 exciting. **dram'a·tist** n writer of plays. **dram·a·ti·za'tion** n **dram'a·tize** vt **-tized, -tiz·ing** adapt story, novel for acting.

dram·a·tur·gy [DRAM-ə-tur-jee] n the

───────────────── THESAURUS ─────────────────

doze v 1 = **nap**, nod off (inf), sleep, slumber, snooze (inf) ◆ n 2 = **nap**, catnap, forty winks (inf), shuteye (sl), siesta, snooze (inf)

drab adj = **dull**, dingy, dismal, dreary, flat, gloomy, shabby, somber

draft[1] n 1 = **outline**, abstract, plan, rough, sketch, version 2 = **order**, bill (of exchange), check, postal order ◆ v 3 = **outline**, compose, design, draw, draw up, formulate, plan, sketch

draft[2] n 1 = **breeze**, current, flow, movement, puff 2 = **drink**, cup, dose, potion, quantity

drag v 1 = **pull**, draw, haul, lug, tow, trail, tug 2 **drag on** or **out** = **last**, draw out,

extend, keep going, lengthen, persist, prolong, protract, spin out, stretch out ◆ n 3 Inf = **nuisance**, annoyance, bore, bother, downer (inf), pain (inf), pest

dragoon v = **force**, browbeat, bully, coerce, compel, constrain, drive, impel, intimidate, railroad (inf)

drain n 1 = **pipe**, channel, conduit, culvert, ditch, duct, sewer, sink, trench 2 = **reduction**, depletion, drag, exhaustion, sap, strain, withdrawal ◆ v 3 = **remove**, bleed, draw off, dry, empty, pump off or out, tap, withdraw 4 = **flow out**, effuse, exude, leak, ooze, seep, trickle, well out 5 = **drink up**, finish, gulp down, quaff, swallow 6 = **exhaust**, consume, deplete,

technique of writing and producing plays.
dram'a·tur·gist n playwright.

drape [drayp] vt **draped, drap·ing 1** cover,
adorn with cloth. **2** arrange in graceful
folds. **dra·per·y** [DRAY-pə-ree] n, pl **-per·ies**
covering, curtain, etc. of cloth.

dras·tic [DRAS-tik] adj **1** extreme, forceful.
2 severe.

draw v **drew, drawn, draw·ing ♦** vt **1** pull,
pull along, haul. **2** inhale. **3** entice. **4**
delineate, portray with pencil, etc. **5** frame,
compose, draft, write. **6** attract. **7** bring
(upon, out, etc.). **8** get by lot. **9** of ship,
require (depth of water). **10** take from
(well, barrel, etc.). **11** receive (money). **12**
bend (bow). ♦ vi **13** pull, shrink. **14** attract.
15 make, admit current of air. **16** make
pictures with pencil, etc. **17** finish game in
tie. **18** write orders for money. **19** come,
approach (near). ♦ n **20** act of drawing. **21**
casting of lots. **22** unfinished game, tie.
draw'er n **1** one who or that which draws.
2 sliding box in table or chest. ♦ pl **3**
undergarment for the lower body.

draw'ing n **1** art of depicting in line. **2**
sketch so done. **3** action of verb.
draw'back n **1** anything that takes away
from satisfaction. **2** snag. **draw'bridge** n
hinged bridge to pull up. **drawing room**
living room, sitting room. **draw near**
approach. **draw out** lengthen. **draw up 1**
arrange. **2** come to a halt.

drawl v **1** speak slowly. ♦ n **2** such speech.

drawn pp. of DRAW.

dread [dred] vt **1** fear greatly. ♦ n **2** awe,
terror. ♦ adj **3** feared, awful. **dread'ful** adj
disagreeable, shocking or bad. **dread'locks**
pl n Rastafarian hair style of long matted or
tightly curled strands. **dread'nought** n
large battleship mounting heavy guns.

dream [dreem] n **1** vision during sleep. **2**
fancy, reverie, aspiration. **3** very pleasant
idea, person, thing. ♦ v **dreamed** or
dreamt, dream·ing ♦ vi **4** have dreams. ♦
vt **5** see, imagine in dreams. **6** think of as
possible. **dream'y** adj **dream·i·er,**
dream·i·est 1 given to daydreams,
impractical, vague. **2** inf wonderful.

dissipate, empty, sap, strain, use up
drama n **1 = play**, dramatization, show,
stage show **2 = theater**, acting,
dramaturgy, stagecraft **3 = excitement**,
crisis, histrionics, scene, spectacle, turmoil
dramatic adj **1 = theatrical**, dramaturgical,
Thespian **2 = powerful**, expressive,
impressive, moving, striking, vivid **3 =
exciting**, breathtaking, climactic,
electrifying, melodramatic, sensational,
suspenseful, tense, thrilling
dramatist n **= playwright**, dramaturge,
screenwriter, scriptwriter
dramatize v **= exaggerate**, lay it on (thick)
(sl), overdo, overstate, play to the gallery
drape v **= cover**, cloak, fold, swathe, wrap
drastic adj **= extreme**, desperate, dire,
forceful, harsh, radical, severe, strong
draw v **1 = sketch**, depict, design, map
out, mark out, outline, paint, portray, trace
2 = pull, drag, haul, tow, tug **3 = take out**,
extract, pull out **4 = attract**, allure, elicit,
entice, evoke, induce, influence, invite,
persuade **5 = deduce**, derive, infer, make,
take ♦ n **6** Inf **= attraction**, enticement,
lure, pull (inf) **7 = tie**, dead heat, deadlock,
gridlock, impasse, stalemate
drawback n **= disadvantage**, deficiency,
difficulty, downside, flaw, handicap, hitch,
snag, stumbling block

drawing n **= picture**, cartoon, depiction,
illustration, outline, portrayal,
representation, sketch, study
drawn adj **= tense**, haggard, pinched,
stressed, tired, worn
draw on v **= make use of**, employ, exploit,
extract, fall back on, have recourse to, rely
on, take from, use
draw out v **= extend**, drag out, lengthen,
make longer, prolong, protract, spin out,
stretch, string out
draw up v **1 = draft**, compose, formulate,
frame, prepare, write out **2 = halt**, bring to
a stop, pull up, stop
dread v **1 = fear**, cringe at, have cold feet
(inf), quail, shrink from, shudder, tremble ♦
n **2 = fear**, alarm, apprehension, dismay,
fright, horror, terror, trepidation
dreadful adj **= terrible**, abysmal, appalling,
atrocious, awful, fearful, frightful, hideous,
horrible, shocking
dream n **1 = vision**, delusion, hallucination,
illusion, imagination, trance **2 =
daydream**, fantasy, pipe dream **3 =
ambition**, aim, aspiration, desire, goal,
hope, wish **4 = delight**, beauty, gem, joy,
marvel, pleasure, treasure ♦ v **5 = have
dreams**, conjure up, envisage, fancy,
hallucinate, imagine, think, visualize **6 =
daydream**, build castles in the air or in

drear·y [DREER-ee] *adj* **drear·i·er,**
drear·i·est dismal, dull. **drear'i·ly** *adv*
drear'i·ness *n* gloom.
dredge[1] [drej] *v* **dredged, dredg·ing 1**
bring up mud, etc., from sea bottom. **2**
deepen channel by dredge. **3** search for,
produce obscure, remote, unlikely
material. ♦ *n* **4** form of scoop or grab.
dredg'er *n* ship for dredging.
dredge[2] *vt* sprinkle with flour, etc. **dredg'er**
n
dregs [dregz] *pl n* **1** sediment, grounds. **2**
worthless part.
drench *vt* **1** wet thoroughly, soak. **2** make
(an animal) take dose of medicine. ♦ *n* **3**
soaking. **4** dose for animal.
dress *vt* **1** clothe. **2** array for show. **3** trim,
smooth, prepare surface of. **4** prepare
(food) for market or table. **5** put dressing
on (wound). **6** align (troops). ♦ *vi* **7** put on
one's clothes. **8** form in proper line. ♦ *n* **9**
one-piece garment for woman. **10**
clothing. **11** clothing for ceremonial
evening wear. **dress'er** *n* **1** one who
dresses, esp. actors or actresses. **2** chest of
drawers, oft. with mirror. **dress'ing** *n*
something applied to something else, as
sauce to food, ointment to wound,
manure to land, etc. **dress'y** *adj* **dress·i·er,**
dress·i·est 1 stylish. **2** fond of dress. **dress
circle** usu. first gallery in theater. **dressing
down** *inf* scolding. **dressing gown**
coat-shaped garment worn over pyjamas
or nightdress. **dressing room** room used
for changing clothes, esp. backstage in a
theater. **dressing table** piece of bedroom
furniture with a mirror and drawers.
dress'mak·er *n*
dres·sage [drə-SAHZH] *n* method of
training horse in special maneuvers to
show obedience.
drew pt. of DRAW.
drib·ble [DRIB-əl] *v* **-bled, -bling 1** flow in
drops, trickle. **2** run at the mouth. **3**
Basketball work ball forward with short
bounces. **4** *Soccer* work ball forward with
short kicks. ♦ *n* **5** trickle, drop. **drib'let** *n*
small portion or installment.
drift *vi* **1** be carried as by current of air,
water. **2** move aimlessly or passively. ♦ *n* **3**
process of being driven by current. **4** slow
current or course. **5** deviation from course.
6 tendency. **7** speaker's, writer's meaning.
8 wind-heaped mass of snow, sand, etc. **9**
material driven or carried by water. **drift'er**
n **1** one who, that which drifts. **2** *inf*
aimless person with no fixed job, etc.
drift'wood [-wuud] *n* wood washed
ashore by sea.
drill[1] *n* **1** boring tool or machine. **2** exercise
of soldiers or others in handling of arms
and maneuvers. **3** repeated routine in
teaching. ♦ *vt* **4** bore, pierce hole. **5**
exercise in military and other routine. ♦ *vi* **6**
practice routine.
drill[2] *n* **1** machine for sowing seed. **2** small
furrow for seed. **3** row of plants. ♦ *vt* **4** sow
seed in drills or furrows.
drill[3] *n* coarsely woven twilled fabric.
drink [dringk] *v* **drank, drunk, drink·ing 1**

Spain, fantasize, stargaze
dreamer *n* = **idealist**, daydreamer,
escapist, fantasist, utopian, visionary,
Walter Mitty
dreamy *adj* **1** = **vague**, absent, abstracted,
daydreaming, faraway, pensive,
preoccupied, with one's head in the clouds
2 = **impractical**, airy-fairy, fanciful,
imaginary, quixotic, speculative
dreary *adj* = **dull**, boring, drab, humdrum,
monotonous, tedious, tiresome,
uneventful, wearisome
dregs *pl n* **1** = **sediment**, deposit, dross,
grounds, lees, residue, residuum, scum,
waste **2** = **scum**, good-for-nothings,
rabble, riffraff
drench *v* = **soak**, drown, flood, inundate,
saturate, souse, steep, swamp, wet
dress *n* **1** = **frock**, gown, outfit, robe **2** =

clothing, apparel, attire, clothes, costume,
garb, garments, togs ♦ *v* **3** = **put on**, attire,
change, clothe, don, garb, robe, slip on or
into **4** = **bandage**, bind up, plaster, treat
5 = **arrange**, adjust, align, get ready,
prepare, straighten
dressmaker *n* = **seamstress**, couturier,
tailor
dribble *v* **1** = **run**, drip, drop, fall in drops,
leak, ooze, seep, trickle **2** = **drool**, drivel,
slaver, slobber
drift *v* **1** = **float**, be carried along, coast, go
(aimlessly), meander, stray, waft, wander
2 = **pile up**, accumulate, amass, bank up,
drive, gather ♦ *n* **3** = **pile**, accumulation,
bank, heap, mass, mound **4** = **meaning**,
direction, gist, import, intention, purport,
significance, tendency, thrust
drifter *n* = **wanderer**, beachcomber, bum

swallow liquid. **2** absorb. **3** take intoxicating liquor, esp. to excess. ◆ n **4** liquid for drinking. **5** portion of this. **6** act of drinking. **7** intoxicating liquor. **8** excessive use of it. **drink'a·ble** adj **drink to, drink the health of** express good wishes, etc. by drinking a toast to.

drip v **dripped, drip·ping 1** fall or let fall in drops. ◆ n **2** act of dripping. **3** drop. **4** Med intravenous administration of solution. **5** sl dull, insipid person. **dripping** n **1** melted fat that drips from roasting meat. ◆ adj **2** very wet. **drip-dry** [-drī] adj (of fabric) drying free of creases if hung up while wet.

drive [drīv] v **drove, driv·en, driv·ing** ◆ vt **1** urge in some direction. **2** make move and steer (vehicle, animal, etc.). **3** urge, impel. **4** fix by blows, as nail. **5** chase. **6** convey in vehicle. **7** hit a ball with force as in golf, baseball. ◆ vi **8** keep machine, animal, going. **9** steer it. **10** be conveyed in vehicle. **11** rush, dash, drift fast. ◆ n **12** act, action of driving. **13** journey in vehicle. **14** private road leading to house. **15** capacity for getting things done. **16** united effort, campaign. **17** energy. **18** forceful stroke in golf, baseball. **driv'er** n **1** one that drives. **2**

golf club. **drive time** time in the morning or evening when people drive to and from work.

driv·el [DRIV-əl] vi **1** run at the mouth or nose. **2** talk nonsense. ◆ n **3** silly nonsense.

driz·zle [DRIZ-əl] vi **-zled, -zling 1** rain in fine drops. ◆ n **2** fine, light rain.

drogue [drohg] n **1** any funnel-like device, esp. of canvas, used as sea anchor. **2** small parachute. **3** wind indicator. **4** windsock towed behind target aircraft. **5** funnel-shaped device on end of refueling hose of tanker aircraft to receive probe of aircraft being refueled.

droll [drohl] adj **-er, -est** funny, odd, comical. **droll'ness** n **drol'ly** adv

drone [drohn] n **1** male of honey bee. **2** lazy idler. **3** deep humming. **4** bass pipe of bagpipe. **5** its note. ◆ v **droned, dron·ing 6** hum. **7** talk in monotonous tone.

drool vi to slaver, drivel.

droop vi **1** hang down. **2** wilt, flag. ◆ vt **3** let hang down. ◆ n **4** drooping condition. **droop'y** adj **droop-i-er, droop-i-est**

drop n **1** globule of liquid. **2** very small quantity. **3** fall, descent. **4** distance through which thing falls. **5** thing that

(inf), hobo, itinerant, rolling stone, vagrant
drill n **1** = **boring tool**, bit, borer, gimlet **2** = **training**, discipline, exercise, instruction, practice, preparation, repetition ◆ v **3** = **bore**, penetrate, perforate, pierce, puncture, sink in **4** = **train**, coach, discipline, exercise, instruct, practice, rehearse, teach

drink v **1** = **swallow**, gulp, guzzle, imbibe, quaff, sip, suck, sup **2** = **booze** (inf), hit the bottle (inf), tipple, tope ◆ n **3** = **beverage**, liquid, potion, refreshment **4** = **alcohol**, booze (inf), hooch or hootch, liquor, spirits, the bottle (inf) **5** = **glass**, cup, draft

drip v **1** = **drop**, dribble, exude, plop, splash, sprinkle, trickle ◆ n **2** = **drop**, dribble, leak, trickle **3** Inf = **weakling**, mama's boy (inf)

drive v **1** = **operate**, direct, guide, handle, manage, motor, ride, steer, travel **2** = **goad**, coerce, constrain, force, press, prod, prompt, spur **3** = **push**, hurl, hurtle, impel, propel, send, urge **4** = **push**, hammer, ram, thrust ◆ n **5** = **run**, excursion, jaunt, journey, outing, ride, spin (inf), trip **6** = **campaign**, action, appeal, crusade, effort, push (inf) **7** = **initiative**, ambition, energy,

enterprise, get-up-and-go (inf), motivation, vigor, zip (inf)
drivel n **1** = **nonsense**, garbage (inf), gibberish, hogwash, hot air (inf), poppycock (inf), rubbish, trash ◆ v **2** = **babble**, blether, gab (inf), prate, ramble

driving adj = **forceful**, compelling, dynamic, energetic, sweeping, vigorous, violent

drizzle n **1** = **fine rain**, mist ◆ v **2** = **rain**, shower, spot or spit with rain, spray, sprinkle

droll adj = **amusing**, comical, entertaining, funny, humorous, jocular, waggish, whimsical

drone[1] v **1** = **hum**, buzz, purr, thrum, vibrate, whirr **2 drone on** = **speak monotonously**, be boring, chant, intone, spout, talk interminably ◆ n **3** = **hum**, buzz, murmuring, purr, thrum, vibration, whirring

drool v **1** = **dribble**, drivel, salivate, slaver, slobber, water at the mouth **2 drool over** = **gloat over**, dote on, gush, make much of, rave about (inf)

droop v = **sag**, bend, dangle, drop, fall down, hang (down), sink

falls, as gallows platform. ◆ *v* **dropped,
drop·ping** ◆ *vt* **6** let fall. **7** let fall in drops.
8 utter casually. **9** set down, unload. **10**
discontinue. ◆ *vi* **11** fall. **12** fall in drops. **13**
lapse. **14** come or go casually. **drop'let** *n*
drop'pings *pl n* dung of birds, rabbits, etc.
drop'out *n* person who fails to complete
course of study or one who rejects
conventional society.

dross [draws] *n* **1** scum of molten metal. **2**
impurity, refuse. **3** anything of little or no
value.

drought [drowt] *n* long spell of dry
weather.

drove[1] [drohv] pt. of DRIVE.

drove[2] *n* herd, flock, crowd, esp. in motion.
drov'er *n* driver of cattle.

drown *v* **1** die or be killed by immersion in
liquid. **2** get rid of as by submerging in
liquid. **3** make sound inaudible by louder
sound.

drow·sy [DROW-zee] *adj* **-si·er, -si·est 1**
half-asleep. **2** lulling. **3** dull. **drowse** *vi*
drow'si·ly *adv* **drow'si·ness** *n*

drub *vt* **drubbed, drub·bing** thrash, beat.
drubbing *n* beating.

drudge [druj] *vi* **1** work at menial or
distasteful tasks, slave. ◆ *n* **2** one who
drudges, hack. **drudg'er·y** *n*, *pl* **-er·ies**

drug *n* **1** medical substance. **2** narcotic. **3**
merchandise that is unsalable because of
overproduction. ◆ *vt* **drugged, drug·ging 4**
mix drugs with. **5** administer drug to, esp.
one inducing unconsciousness. **drug'store**
n pharmacy where wide variety of goods is
available. **drug·gist** *n*

dru·id [DROO-id] *n* (**D-**) member of ancient
order of Celtic priests.

drum *n* **1** percussion instrument of skin
stretched over round hollow frame, played
by beating with sticks. **2** various things
shaped like drum. **3** part of ear. ◆ *v*
drummed, drum·ming 4 play drum. **5** tap,
thump continuously. **drum'mer** *n* **1** one
who plays drum. **2** traveling salesman.
drum'head *n* part of drum that is struck.
drumhead court-martial summary one
held at war front. **drum major** leader of
military band. **drum'stick** *n* **1** stick for
beating drum. **2** lower joint of cooked
fowl's leg. **drum out** expel from military
service, etc.

drunk [drungk] *adj* **-er, -est 1** overcome by
strong drink. **2** *fig* under influence of
strong emotion. **drunk'ard** [-ərd] *n* one
given to excessive drinking. **drunk'en** *adj* **1**
drunk. **2** caused by, showing intoxication.
drunk'en·ness *n*

———— THESAURUS ————

drop *v* **1 = fall**, decline, descend, diminish,
plummet, plunge, sink, tumble **2 = drip**,
dribble, fall in drops, trickle **3 =
discontinue**, ax (*inf*), give up, kick (*inf*),
quit, relinquish ◆ *n* **4 = droplet**, bead,
bubble, drip, globule, pearl, tear **5 = dash**,
mouthful, shot (*inf*), sip, spot, swig (*inf*),
trace, trickle **6 = decrease**, cut, decline,
deterioration, downturn, fall-off, lowering,
reduction, slump **7 = fall**, descent, plunge

drop off *v* **1 = set down**, deliver, leave, let
off **2** *Inf* **= fall asleep**, doze (off), have forty
winks (*inf*), nod (off), snooze (*inf*) **3 =
decrease**, decline, diminish, dwindle, fall
off, lessen, slacken

drop out *v* **= leave**, abandon, fall by the
wayside, give up, quit, stop, withdraw

drought *n* **= dry spell**, aridity, dehydration,
dryness

drove *n* **= herd**, collection, company,
crowd, flock, horde, mob, multitude,
swarm, throng

drown *v* **1 = drench**, deluge, engulf, flood,
go under, immerse, inundate, sink,
submerge, swamp **2 = overpower**,

deaden, muffle, obliterate, overcome,
overwhelm, stifle, swallow up, wipe out

drowsy *adj* **= sleepy**, dopey (*sl*), dozy, half
asleep, heavy, lethargic, somnolent, tired,
torpid

drudge *n* **= menial**, factotum, servant,
slave, toiler, worker

drudgery *n* **= menial labor**, donkey-work,
grind (*inf*), hard work, labor, slog, toil

drug *n* **1 = medication**, medicament,
medicine, physic, poison, remedy **2 = dope**
(*sl*), narcotic, opiate, stimulant ◆ *v* **3 =
dose**, administer a drug, dope (*sl*),
medicate, treat **4 = knock out**, anesthetize,
deaden, numb, poison, stupefy

drum *v* **1 = beat**, pulsate, rap, reverberate,
tap, tattoo, throb **2 drum into = drive
home**, din into, hammer away, harp on,
instill into, reiterate

drunk *adj* **1 = intoxicated**, drunken,
inebriated, plastered (*sl*), tipsy, under the
influence (*inf*) ◆ *n* **2 = drunkard**, alcoholic,
boozer (*inf*), inebriate, lush (*sl*), wino (*inf*)

drunkard *n* **= drinker**, alcoholic,
dipsomaniac, drunk, lush (*sl*), tippler, wino

dry [drī] *adj* **dri·er, dri·est 1** without moisture. **2** rainless. **3** not yielding milk, or other liquid. **4** cold, unfriendly. **5** caustically witty. **6** having prohibition of alcoholic drink. **7** uninteresting. **8** needing effort to study. **9** lacking sweetness (as wines). ♦ *v* **dried, dry·ing 10** remove water, moisture. **11** become dry. **12** evaporate. **dri'ly** *adv* **dry'ness** *n* **dry'er** *n* **1** person or thing that dries. **2** apparatus for removing moisture. **dry battery** electric battery without liquid. **dry'-clean** *v* clean clothes with solvent other than water. **dry'-clean·er** *n* **dry ice** solid carbon dioxide. **dry'point 1** needle for engraving without acid. **2** engraving so made. **dry rot** fungoid decay in wood. **dry run** practice, rehearsal in simulated conditions.

dry·ad [DRĪ-əd] *n* wood nymph.

du·al [DOO-əl] *adj* **1** twofold. **2** of two, double, forming pair. **du'al·ism** *n* recognition of two independent powers or principles, e.g. good and evil, mind and matter. **du·al'i·ty** *n*

dub *vt* **dubbed, dub·bing 1** give title to. **2** confer knighthood on. **3** provide film with soundtrack not in original language. **4** smear with grease, dubbin. **dub'bin, dub'bing** *n* grease for making leather supple.

du·bi·ous [DOO-bee-əs] *adj* **1** causing doubt, not clear or decided. **2** of suspect character. **du·bi·e·ty** [-BĪ-i-tee] *n* **-ties** uncertainty, doubt.

du·cal [DOO-kəl] *adj* of, like a duke.

duch·ess [DUCH-is] *n* duke's wife or widow.

duch·y [DUCH-ee] *n, pl* **duch·ies** territory of duke, dukedom.

duck[1] [duk] *n* **1** common swimming bird. ♦ *v* **2** plunge (someone) under water. **3** bob down. **duck'ling** *n* **duck'billed platypus** see PLATYPUS.

duck[2] *n* **1** strong linen or cotton fabric ♦ *pl* **2** trousers of it.

duct [dukt] *n* channel, tube. **duc·tile** [DUK-tl] *adj* **1** capable of being drawn into wire. **2** flexible and tough. **3** easily led. **duc·til'i·ty** *n* **duct'less** *adj* (of glands) secreting directly certain substances essential to health.

dud *n* **1** futile, worthless person or thing. **2** shell that fails to explode. ♦ *adj* **3** worthless.

dude [dood] *n* **1** city man, esp. Easterner in the West. **2** *sl* fellow. **dude ranch** ranch operating as vacation resort.

dudg·eon [DUJ-ən] *n* anger, indignation, resentment.

duds [dudz] *pl n inf* clothes.

due [doo] *adj* **1** owing. **2** proper to be given, inflicted, etc. **3** adequate, fitting. **4** under engagement to arrive, be present. **5** timed for. ♦ *adv* (with points of compass) exactly. ♦ *n* **6** person's right. **7** (usu *pl*) charge, fee, etc. **du'ly** *adv* **1** properly. **2** fitly. **3** rightly. **4** punctually. **due to 1** attributable to. **2** caused by.

du·el [DOO-əl] *n* **1** arranged fight with deadly weapons, between two persons. **2**

——————| THESAURUS |——————

(*inf*)

drunkenness *n* = **intoxication**, alcoholism, bibulousness, dipsomania, inebriation, insobriety, intemperance

dry *adj* **1** = **dehydrated**, arid, barren, desiccated, dried up, parched, thirsty **2** = **dull**, boring, dreary, monotonous, plain, tedious, tiresome, uninteresting **3** = **sarcastic**, deadpan, droll, low-key, sly ♦ *v* **4** = **dehydrate**, dehumidify, desiccate, drain, make dry, parch, sear

dry out or **up** *v* = **become dry**, harden, shrivel up, wilt, wither, wizen

dual *adj* = **twofold**, binary, double, duplex, duplicate, matched, paired, twin

dubious *adj* **1** = **suspect**, fishy (*inf*), questionable, suspicious, unreliable, untrustworthy **2** = **unsure**, doubtful, hesitant, skeptical, uncertain,

unconvinced, undecided, wavering

duck *v* **1** = **bob**, bend, bow, crouch, dodge, drop, lower, stoop **2** = **plunge**, dip, dive, douse, dunk, immerse, souse, submerge, wet **3** *Inf* = **dodge**, avoid, escape, evade, shirk, shun, sidestep

dud *Inf n* **1** = **failure**, flop (*inf*), washout (*inf*) ♦ *adj* **2** = **useless**, broken, failed, inoperative, worthless

dudgeon *n* **in high dudgeon** = **indignant**, angry, choked, fuming, offended, resentful, ticked off (*inf*), vexed

due *adj* **1** = **expected**, scheduled **2** = **payable**, in arrears, outstanding, owed, owing, unpaid **3** = **fitting**, appropriate, deserved, justified, merited, proper, rightful, suitable, well-earned ♦ *n* **4** = **right(s)**, deserts, merits, privilege ♦ *adv* **5** = **directly**, dead, exactly, straight,

keen two-sided contest. ♦ vi **-eled, -el·ing 3**
fight in duel. **du'el·ist** n

du·en·na [doo-EN-ə] n in Spain or
Portugal, elderly governess, guardian,
chaperone.

du·et [doo-ET] n piece of music for two
performers.

duff n sl buttocks.

duf·fel [DUF-əl] n **1** coarse woolen cloth. **2**
coat of this.

duff·er [DUF-ər] n inf **1** stupid inefficient
person. **2** inept golfer.

dug¹ pt./pp. of DIG.

dug² n udder, teat of animal.

dug·out [DUG-owt] n **1** covered excavation
to provide shelter for troops, etc. **2** canoe
of hollowed-out tree. **3** Baseball roofed
structure with bench for players when not
on the field.

duke [dook] n **1** in Great Britain, peer of
rank next below prince. **2** ruler of duchy.
duch'ess n, fem. **duke'dom** [-dəm] n

dukes [dooks] pl n sl fists.

dul·cet [DUL-sit] adj (of sounds) sweet,
melodious.

dul·ci·mer [DUL-sə-mər] n stringed
instrument played with light hammers,
ancestor of piano.

dull adj **-er, -est 1** stupid. **2** insensible. **3**
sluggish. **4** tedious. **5** lacking liveliness or

variety. **6** gloomy, overcast. ♦ v **7** make or
become dull. **dull'ard** [-ərd] n

duly see DUE.

dumb [dum] adj **-er, -est 1** incapable of
speech. **2** silent. **3** inf stupid. **dumb'ly** adv
dumb'ness n **dumb'bell** n **1** weight for
exercises. **2** dolt. **dumb·found'** vt confound
into silence.

dumb down vt make less intellectually
demanding or sophisticated. **dumb show**
gestures without speech.

dum'dum n soft-nosed bullet that expands
on impact.

dum·my [DUM-ee] n, pl **-mies 1** tailor's,
dressmaker's model. **2** imitation object. **3**
Cards hand exposed on table and played
by partner. ♦ adj **4** sham, bogus. **dummy
up** inf to keep silent.

dump vt **1** throw down in mass. **2** deposit.
3 unload. **4** send (low-priced goods) for
sale abroad. ♦ n **5** place where garbage is
dumped. **6** inf dirty, unpleasant place. **7**
temporary depot of stores or munitions. ♦
pl **8** low spirits, dejection. **dump'ling** n **1**
small round mass of boiled or steamed
dough. **2** dessert of fruit wrapped in
dough and baked. **dump truck** truck for
hauling and dumping sand, stone, etc.
dump'y adj **dump·i·er, dump·i·est** short,
stout.

───── THESAURUS ─────

undeviatingly

duel n **1** = **single combat**, affair of honor
2 = **contest**, clash, competition,
encounter, engagement, fight,
head-to-head, rivalry ♦ v **3** = **fight**, clash,
compete, contend, contest, lock horns,
rival, struggle, vie with

dues pl n = **membership fee**, charge,
charges, contribution, fee, levy

dull adj **1** = **boring**, dreary, dumpy (inf), flat,
frowzy, homely (U.S.), humdrum,
monotonous, plain, tedious, uninteresting
2 = **stupid**, dense, dim-witted (inf), slow,
thick, unintelligent **3** = **cloudy**, dim,
dismal, gloomy, leaden, overcast **4** =
lifeless, apathetic, blank, indifferent,
listless, passionless, unresponsive **5** = **blunt**,
blunted, unsharpened ♦ v **6** = **relieve**,
allay, alleviate, blunt, lessen, moderate,
soften, take the edge off

duly adv **1** = **properly**, accordingly,
appropriately, befittingly, correctly,
decorously, deservedly, fittingly, rightfully,
suitably **2** = **on time**, at the proper time,

punctually

dumb adj **1** = **mute**, mum, silent,
soundless, speechless, tongue-tied,
voiceless, wordless **2** Inf = **stupid**, asinine,
dense, dim-witted (inf), dull, foolish, thick,
unintelligent

dumbfounded adj = **amazed**, astonished,
astounded, flabbergasted (inf), lost for
words, nonplussed, overwhelmed,
speechless, staggered, stunned

dummy n **1** = **model**, figure, form,
manikin, mannequin **2** = **copy**, counterfeit,
duplicate, imitation, sham, substitute **3** Sl =
fool, blockhead, dork (sl), dunce, idiot,
nitwit (inf), oaf, schmuck (sl), simpleton ♦
adj **4** = **imitation**, artificial, bogus, fake,
false, mock, phoney or phony (inf), sham,
simulated

dump v **1** = **drop**, deposit, fling down, let
fall, throw down **2** = **get rid of**, dispose of,
ditch (sl), empty out, jettison, scrap, throw
away or out, tip, unload ♦ n **3** = **rubbish
tip**, junkyard, refuse heap, rubbish heap,
tip **4** Inf = **pigsty**, hovel, mess, slum

dun[1] *vt* **dunned, dun·ning 1** persistently demand payment of debts. ✦ *n* **2** one who duns. **3** urgent request for payment.

dun[2] *adj* **1** of dull grayish brown. ✦ *n* **2** this color. **3** dun horse.

dunce [duns] *n* slow learner, stupid pupil.

dune [doon] *n* sandhill on coast or desert.

dung *n* **1** excrement of animals. **2** manure. ✦ *vt* **3** fertilize or spread with manure.

dun·ga·ree [dung-gə-REE] *n* **1** blue denim. ✦ *pl* **2** work clothes, etc. of this material.

dun·geon [DUN-jən] *n* **1** underground cell or vault for prisoners. **2** formerly, tower or keep of castle.

dunk [dungk] *vt* **1** dip bread, etc. in liquid before eating it. **2** submerge. **dunk shot** *Basketball* shot made by jumping high to thrust ball through basket.

dun·nage [DUN-ij] *n* padding, loose material for packing cargo.

du·o [DOO-oh] *n, pl* **du·os** pair of performers, etc.

du·o·dec·i·mal [doo-ə-DES-ə-məl] *adj* **1** computed by twelves. **2** twelfth.

du·o·dec·i·mo [doo-ə-DES-ə-moh] *n, pl* **-mos 1** size of book in which each sheet is folded into 12 leaves before cutting. **2** book of this size. ✦ *adj* **3** of this size.

du·o·de·num [doo-ə-DEE-nəm] *n* upper part of small intestine. **du·o·de'nal** *adj*

dupe [doop] *n* **1** victim of delusion or sharp practice. ✦ *vt* **duped, dup·ing 2** deceive for advantage, impose upon.

du·plex [DOO-pleks] *adj* **1** twofold. ✦ *n* **2** apartment with rooms on two floors. **3** two-family house.

du·pli·cate [DOO-pli-kayt] *vt* **-cat·ed, -cat·ing 1** make exact copy of. **2** double. ✦ *adj* [-kit] **3** double. **4** exactly the same as something else. ✦ *n* **5** exact copy. **du'pli·ca·tor** *n* machine for making copies (of typewritten matter, etc.). **du·plic'i·ty** [-PLIS-i-tee] *n, pl* **-ties** deceitfulness, double-dealing, bad faith.

du·ra·ble [DUUR ə bəl] *adj* lasting, resisting wear. **du·ra·bil'i·ty** *n*

du·ra·tion [duu-RAY-shən] *n* time thing lasts.

du·ress [duu-RES] *n* compulsion by use of force or threats.

dur·ing [DUUR-ing] *prep* throughout, in the time of, in the course of.

dusk *n* **1** darker stage of twilight. **2** partial darkness. **dusk'y** *adj* **dusk·i·er, dusk·i·est 1** dark. **2** dark-colored.

dust *n* **1** fine particles, powder of earth or other matter, lying on surface or blown along by wind. **2** ashes of the dead. ✦ *vt* **3** sprinkle with powder, fertilizer, etc. **4** rid of dust. **dust'er** *n* **1** cloth for removing dust. **2** housecoat. **dust'y** *adj* **dust·i·er, dust·i·est** covered with dust. **dust'bowl** [-bohl] *n* area in which dust storms have carried away the top soil.

Dutch [duch] *adj* pert. to the Netherlands, its inhabitants, its language. **Dutch courage** drunken bravado. **Dutch treat** one where each person pays own share.

du·ty [DOO-tee] *n, pl* **-ties 1** moral or legal obligation. **2** that which is due. **3** tax on goods. **4** military service. **5** one's proper employment. **du'te·ous** *adj* **du'ti·a·ble** *adj*

——————————————| THESAURUS |——————————————

dumpy *adj Inf* = **dowdy**, frowzy, frumpy, homely (*U.S.*), unfashionable

dunce *n* = **simpleton**, blockhead, dunderhead, ignoramus, moron, thickhead

dungeon *n* = **prison**, cage, cell, oubliette, vault

duplicate *adj* **1** = **identical**, corresponding, matched, matching, twin, twofold ✦ *n* **2** = **copy**, carbon copy, clone, double, facsimile, photocopy, replica, reproduction ✦ *v* **3** = **copy**, clone, double, repeat, replicate, reproduce

durability *n* = **durableness**, constancy, endurance, imperishability, permanence, persistence

durable *adj* = **long-lasting**, dependable, enduring, hard-wearing, persistent, reliable, resistant, strong, sturdy, tough

duration *n* = **length**, extent, period, span, spell, stretch, term, time

duress *n* = **pressure**, coercion, compulsion, constraint, threat

dusk *n* = **twilight**, dark, evening, eventide, gloaming (*Scot. or poetic*), nightfall, sundown, sunset

dusky *adj* **1** = **dark**, dark-complexioned, sable, swarthy **2** = **dim**, cloudy, gloomy, murky, obscure, shadowy, shady, tenebrous, twilit

dust *n* **1** = **grime**, grit, particles, powder ✦ *v* **2** = **sprinkle**, cover, dredge, powder, scatter, sift, spray, spread

dusty *adj* = **dirty**, grubby, scuzzy (*sl*), sooty, unclean, unswept

dutiful *adj* = **conscientious**, devoted, obedient, respectful, reverential, liable to customs duty. **du·ti·ful** *adj*

du·vet [doo-VAY] *n* quilt filled with down or artificial fiber.

DVD Digital Versatile *or* Video Disk.

dwarf [dworf] *n, pl* **dwarfs** *or* **dwarves** [dworvz] **1** very undersized person. **2** mythological, small, manlike creature. ◆ *adj* **3** unusually small, stunted. ◆ *vt* **4** make seem small by contrast. **5** make stunted.

dwell *vi* **dwelt** *or* **dwelled, dwell·ing 1** live, make one's abode (in). **2** fix one's attention, write or speak at length (on). **dweller** *n* **dwell'ing** *n* house.

dwin·dle [DWIN-dl] *vi* **-dled, -dling** grow less, waste away, decline.

Dy *Chem.* dysprosium.

dye [dī] *vt* **dyed, dye·ing** impregnate (cloth, etc.) with coloring matter. **1** color thus. ◆ *n* **2** coloring matter in solution or that can be dissolved for dyeing. **3** tinge, color. **dy'er** *n*

dyke[1] [dīk] *n* wall built to prevent flooding.

dyke[2] *n sl, often offens* lesbian.

dy·nam·ics [dī-NAM-iks] *n* **1** branch of physics dealing with force as producing or affecting motion. ◆ *pl* **2** forces that produce change in a system. **dy·nam'ic** *adj*

1 of, relating to motive force, force in operation. **2** energetic and forceful. **dy·nam'i·cal·ly** *adv*

dy·na·mite [DĪ-nə-mīt] *n* **1** high explosive mixture. ◆ *vt* **-mit·ed, -mit·ing 2** blow up with this. ◆ *adj* **3** *inf* topnotch.

dy·na·mo [DĪ-nə-moh] *n, pl* **-mos** machine to convert mechanical into electrical energy, generator of electricity. **dy·na·mom'e·ter** *n* instrument to measure energy expended.

dy·nas·ty [DĪ-nə-stee] *n, pl* **-ties** line, family, succession of hereditary rulers. **dy'nast** *n* ruler. **dy·nas'tic** *adj* of dynasty.

dyne [dīn] *n* cgs unit of force.

dys·en·ter·y [DIS-ən-ter-ee] *n* infection of intestine causing severe diarrhea.

dys·func·tion [dis-FUNGK-shən] *n* abnormal, impaired functioning, esp. of bodily organ.

dys·lex·i·a [dis-LEK-see-ə] *n* impaired ability to read, caused by condition of the brain. **dys·lex'ic** *adj, n*

dys·pep·sia [dis-PEP-see-ə] *n* indigestion. **dys·pep'tic** *adj, n*

dys·tro·phy [DIS-trə-fee] *n* wasting of body tissues, esp. muscles.

THESAURUS

submissive

duty *n* **1** = **responsibility**, assignment, function, job, obligation, role, task, work **2** = **loyalty**, allegiance, deference, obedience, respect, reverence **3** = **tax**, excise, levy, tariff, toll **4 on duty** = **at work**, busy, engaged, on active service

dwarf *v* **1** = **tower above** *or* **over**, diminish, dominate, overshadow ◆ *adj* **2** = **miniature**, baby, bonsai, diminutive, small, tiny, undersized ◆ *n* **3** = **midget**, Lilliputian, pygmy *or* pigmy, Tom Thumb

dweeb *n Sl* = **idiot**, doofus (*sl*), dope (*sl*), dunce, fool, geek, slang, nerd

dwell *v* = **live**, abide, inhabit, lodge, reside

dwelling *n* = **home**, abode, domicile,

habitation, house, lodging, pad (*sl*), quarters, residence

dwindle *v* = **lessen**, decline, decrease, die away, diminish, fade, peter out, shrink, subside, taper off, wane

dye *n* **1** = **coloring**, color, colorant, pigment, stain, tinge, tint ◆ *v* **2** = **color**, pigment, stain, tinge, tint

dying *adj* = **expiring**, at death's door, failing, *in extremis*, moribund, not long for this world

dynamic *adj* = **energetic**, forceful, go-ahead, go-getting (*inf*), high-powered, lively, powerful, vital

dynasty *n* = **empire**, government, house, regime, rule, sovereignty

E e

e- *prefix* electronic, e.g. *e-mail; e-tail.*
each [eech] *adj, pron* every one taken separately.
ea·ger [EE-gər] *adj* 1 having a strong wish (for something). 2 keen, impatient. **ea·ger·ness** *n*
ea·gle [EE-gəl] *n* 1 large bird with keen sight that preys on small birds and animals. 2 *Golf* score of two strokes under par for a hole. **ea·glet** [EE-glit] *n* young eagle.
ear¹ [eer] *n* 1 organ of hearing, esp. external part of it. 2 sense of hearing. 3 sensitiveness to sounds. 4 attention. **ear'ache** *n* acute pain in ear. **ear'mark** *vt* assign, reserve for definite purpose. **ear'phone** *n* receiver for radio, etc. held to or put in ear. **ear'ring** *n* ornament for lobe of the ear. **ear'shot** *n* hearing distance.
ear² *n* spike, head of corn.
earl [url] *n* British nobleman ranking next below marquis.
ear·ly [UR-lee] *adj, adv* -**li·er, -li·est** 1 before expected or usual time. 2 in first part, near or nearer beginning of some portion of time.
earn [urn] *vt* 1 obtain by work or merit. 2 gain. **earn'ings** *pl n*
ear·nest¹ [UR-nist] *adj* serious, ardent, sincere. **in earnest** serious, determined.
earnest² *n* 1 money paid over in token to bind bargain, pledge. 2 token, foretaste.
earth [urth] *n* 1 (E-) planet or world we live on. 2 ground, dry land. 3 mold, soil, mineral. **earth'en** *adj* made of clay or earth. **earth'ly** *adj* possible, feasible. **earth'y** *adj* **earth·i·er, earth·i·est** 1 of earth. 2 uninhibited. 3 vulgar. **earth'en·ware** *n* (vessels of) baked clay. **earth'quake** *n* convulsion of Earth's surface.
ease [eez] *n* 1 comfort. 2 freedom from constraint, annoyance, awkwardness, pain or trouble. 3 idleness. ♦ *v* **eased, eas·ing** 4 reduce burden. 5 give bodily or mental ease to. 6 slacken. 7 (cause to) move carefully or gradually. 8 relieve of pain. **ease'ment** *n Law* right of way, etc., over another's land. **eas'i·ly** *adv* **eas'y** *adj* **eas·i·er, eas·i·est** 1 not difficult. 2 free from pain, care, constraint or anxiety. 3

THESAURUS

each *adj* 1 = **every** ♦ *pron* 2 = **every one**, each and every one, each one, one and all ♦ *adv* 3 = **apiece**, for each, individually, per capita, per head, per person, respectively, to each
eager *adj* = **keen**, agog, anxious, athirst, avid, enthusiastic, fervent, gung ho (*sl*), hungry, impatient, longing
eagerness *n* = **keenness**, ardor, enthusiasm, fervor, hunger, impatience, thirst, yearning, zeal
ear *n* = **sensitivity**, appreciation, discrimination, perception, taste
early *adj* 1 = **premature**, advanced, forward, untimely 2 = **primitive**, primeval, primordial, undeveloped, young ♦ *adv* 3 = **too soon**, ahead of time, beforehand, in advance, in good time, prematurely
earmark *v* = **set aside**, allocate, designate, flag, label, mark out, reserve

earn *v* 1 = **make**, bring in, collect, gain, get, gross, net, receive 2 = **deserve**, acquire, attain, be entitled to, be worthy of, merit, rate, warrant, win
earnest¹ *adj* 1 = **serious**, grave, intent, resolute, resolved, sincere, solemn, thoughtful ♦ *n* 2 *As in* **in earnest** = **seriousness**, sincerity, truth
earnings *pl n* = **income**, pay, proceeds, profits, receipts, remuneration, salary, takings, wages
earth *n* 1 = **world**, globe, orb, planet, sphere 2 = **soil**, clay, dirt, ground, land, turf
earthenware *n* = **crockery**, ceramics, pots, pottery, terracotta
earthly *adj* = **worldly**, human, material, mortal, secular, temporal
earthy *adj* = **crude**, bawdy, coarse, raunchy (*sl*), ribald, robust, uninhibited,

compliant. **4** characterized by low demand. **5** fitting loosely. **6** *inf* having no preference for any particular course of action. **easy-going** *adj* **1** not fussy. **2** indolent.

ea·sel [EE-zəl] *n* frame to support picture, etc.

east [eest] *n* **1** part of horizon where sun rises. **2** (**E-**) eastern lands, Orient. ◆ *adj* **3** on, in, or near, east. **4** coming from east. ◆ *adv* **5** from, or to, east. **east'er·ly** *adj, adv* from, or to, east. **east'ern** *adj* of, dwelling in, east. **east'ern·er** *n* **east'ward** *adj, adv, n* **east'ward, east'wards** *adv*

Eas·ter [EE-stər] *n* annual festival of the resurrection of Christ.

easy see EASE.

eat [eet] *v* **ate, eat·en, eat·ing 1** chew and swallow. **2** consume, destroy. **3** gnaw. **4** wear away.

eaves [eevz] *pl n* overhanging edges of roof. **eaves'drop** *v* **-dropped, -drop·ping** listen secretly. **eaves'drop·per** *n*

ebb *vi* **1** flow back. **2** decay. ◆ *n* **3** flowing back of tide. **4** decline, decay. **at a low ebb** in a state of weakness.

eb·on·y [EB-ə-nee] *n* **-on·ies 1** hard black

wood. ◆ *adj* **2** made of, black as ebony.

e-book [EE-buuk] *n* book in the form of a file that can be downloaded to a computer via the Internet.

e·bul·lient [i-BUUL-yənt] *adj* **1** exuberant. **2** boiling. **e·bul'lience** *n* **eb·ul·li·tion** [eb-ə-LISH-ən] *n* **1** boiling. **2** effervescence. **3** outburst.

ec·cen·tric [ik-SEN-trik] *adj* **1** odd, unconventional. **2** irregular. **3** not placed, or not having axis placed, centrally. **4** not circular (in orbit). ◆ *n* **5** odd, unconventional person. **6** mechanical device to change circular into to-and-fro movement. **ec·cen·tric'i·ty** *n*

Eccles. Ecclesiastes.

ec·cle·si·as·tic [i-klee-zee-AS-tik] *n* **1** clergyman. ◆ *adj* **2** of, relating to the Christian Church. **ec·cle·si·as'ti·cal** *adj*

ech·e·lon [ESH-ə-lon] *n* **1** level, grade, of responsibility or command. **2** formation of troops, planes, etc. in parallel divisions each slightly to left or right of the one in front.

ech·o [EK-oh] *n, pl* **ech·oes 1** repetition of sounds by reflection. **2** close imitation. ◆ *v* **ech·oed, ech·o·ing** ◆ *vt* **3** repeat as echo,

unsophisticated

ease *n* **1** = **easiness**, effortlessness, facility, readiness, simplicity **2** = **content**, comfort, happiness, peace, peace of mind, quiet, serenity, tranquillity **3** = **rest**, leisure, relaxation, repose, restfulness ◆ *v* **4** = **relieve**, alleviate, calm, comfort, lessen, lighten, relax, soothe **5** = **move carefully**, edge, inch, maneuver, slide, slip

easily *adv* = **without difficulty**, comfortably, effortlessly, readily, smoothly, with ease, with one hand tied behind one's back

easy *adj* **1** = **not difficult**, a piece of cake (*inf*), child's play (*inf*), effortless, no trouble, painless, plain sailing, simple, straightforward, uncomplicated, undemanding **2** = **carefree**, comfortable, leisurely, peaceful, quiet, relaxed, serene, tranquil, untroubled **3** = **tolerant**, easy-going, indulgent, lenient, mild, permissive, unoppressive

easy-going *adj* = **relaxed**, carefree, casual, easy, even-tempered, happy-go-lucky, laid-back (*inf*), nonchalant, placid, tolerant, undemanding

eat *v* **1** = **consume**, chew, devour, gobble,

ingest, munch, scoff (*sl*), swallow **2** = **have a meal**, chow down (*sl*), dine, feed, take nourishment **3** = **destroy**, corrode, decay, dissolve, erode, rot, waste away, wear away

eavesdrop *v* = **listen in**, monitor, overhear, snoop (*inf*), spy

ebb *v* **1** = **flow back**, go out, recede, retire, retreat, subside, wane, withdraw **2** = **decline**, decrease, diminish, dwindle, fade away, fall away, flag, lessen, peter out ◆ *n* **3** = **flowing back**, going out, low tide, low water, retreat, subsidence, wane, withdrawal

eccentric *adj* **1** = **odd**, freakish, idiosyncratic, irregular, outlandish, peculiar, quirky, strange, unconventional ◆ *n* **2** = **crank** (*inf*), character (*inf*), nonconformist, oddball (*inf*), weirdo or weirdie (*inf*)

eccentricity *n* = **oddity**, abnormality, caprice, capriciousness, foible, idiosyncrasy, irregularity, peculiarity, quirk

ecclesiastic *n* **1** = **clergyman**, churchman, cleric, holy man, man of the cloth, minister, parson, pastor, priest ◆ *adj* **2** (also **ecclesiastical**) = **clerical**, divine, holy, send back the sound of. **4** imitate closely. ◆ *vi* **5** resound. **6** be repeated. **echo sounding** system of ascertaining depth of water by measuring time required to receive an echo from sea bottom or submerged object.

éclair [ee-KLAIR] *n* finger-shaped, chocolate-frosted cake filled with whipped cream or custard.

éclat [ay-KLAH] *n* splendor, renown, acclamation.

e·clec·tic [i-KLEK-tik] *adj* **1** selecting. **2** borrowing one's philosophy from various sources. **3** catholic in views or taste. ◆ *n* **e·clec'ti·cism** *n*

e·clipse [i-KLIPS] *n* **1** blotting out of sun, moon, etc. by another heavenly body. **2** obscurity. ◆ *vt* -**clipsed**, -**clips·ing 3** obscure, hide. **4** surpass. **e·clip'tic** *adj* **1** of eclipse. ◆ *n* **2** apparent path of sun.

e·col·o·gy [i-KOL-ə-jee] *n* science of plants and animals in relation to their environment. **ec·o·log'i·cal** *adj* **e·col'o·gist** *n* specialist in or advocate of ecological studies.

e·com·merce *n* business transactions conducted on the Internet.

e·con·o·my [i-KON-ə-mee] *n, pl* -**mies 1** careful management of resources to avoid unnecessary expenditure or waste. **2** sparing, restrained or efficient use. **3** system of interrelationship of money, industry and employment in a country. **ec·o·nom'ic** *adj* **1** of economics. **2** profitable. **3** economical. **ec·o·nom'i·cal** *adj* **1** not wasteful of money, time, effort, etc. **2** frugal. **ec·o·nom'ics** *n* **1** study of

economies of nations. **2** financial aspects. **e·con'o·mist** *n* specialist in economics. **e·con'o·mize** *v* -**mized**, -**miz·ing** limit or reduce expense, waste, etc.

ec·ru [EK-roo] *n, adj* (of) color of unbleached linen.

ec·sta·sy [EK-stə-see] *n, pl* -**sies 1** exalted state of feeling, mystic trance. **2** frenzy. **3** (E-) *sl* powerful drug that can produce hallucinations. **ec·stat·ic** [ik-STAT-ik] *adj* **ec·stat'i·cal·ly** *adv*

ec·u·men·i·cal [ek-yuu-MEN-i-kəl] *adj* **1** of the Christian Church throughout the world, esp. with regard to its unity. **2** interdenominational. **3** universal. **ec·u·men'i·cism** *n*

ec·ze·ma [EK-sə-mə] *n* skin disease.

ed·dy [ED-ee] *n, pl* -**dies 1** small whirl in water, smoke, etc. ◆ *vi* -**died**, -**dy·ing 2** move in whirls.

e·del·weiss [AY-dəl-vīs] *n* white-flowered alpine plant.

e·de·ma [i-DEE-mə] *n* **1** an abnormal excess of fluid in tissues, organs. **2** swelling due to this.

E·den [EE-dən] *n* **1** garden in which Adam and Eve were placed at the Creation. **2** any delightful, happy place or condition.

edge [ej] *n* **1** border, boundary. **2** cutting side of blade. **3** sharpness. **4** advantage. **5** acrimony, bitterness. ◆ *v* **edged**, **edg·ing** ◆ *vt* **6** sharpen, give edge or border to. **7** move gradually. ◆ *vi* **8** advance sideways or gradually. **edge'ways, -wise** *adv* **edg'ing** *n* **edg'y** *adj* **edg·i·er, edg·i·est** irritable, sharp or keen in temper. **on edge 1** nervous, irritable. **2** excited.

————— THESAURUS —————

pastoral, priestly, religious, spiritual

echo *n* **1** = **repetition**, answer, reverberation **2** = **copy**, imitation, mirror image, parallel, reflection, reiteration, reproduction ◆ *v* **3** = **repeat**, resound, reverberate **4** = **copy**, ape, imitate, mirror, parallel, recall, reflect, resemble

eclipse *n* **1** = **obscuring**, darkening, dimming, extinction, shading ◆ *v* **2** = **surpass**, exceed, excel, outdo, outshine, put in the shade (*inf*), transcend

economic *adj* **1** = **financial**, commercial, industrial **2** = **profitable**, money-making, productive, profit-making, remunerative, viable

economical *adj* **1** = **thrifty**, careful, frugal, prudent, scrimping, sparing **2** =

cost-effective, efficient, money-saving, sparing, time-saving **3** = **inexpensive**, cheap, low-priced, modest, reasonable

economize *v* = **cut back**, be economical, be frugal, draw in one's horns, retrench, save, scrimp, tighten one's belt

economy *n* = **thrift**, frugality, husbandry, parsimony, prudence, restraint

ecstasy *n* = **rapture**, bliss, delight, elation, euphoria, fervor, joy, seventh heaven

ecstatic *adj* = **rapturous**, blissful, elated, enraptured, entranced, euphoric, in seventh heaven, joyous, on cloud nine (*inf*), overjoyed

eddy *n* **1** = **swirl**, counter-current, counterflow, undertow, vortex, whirlpool ◆ *v* **2** = **swirl**, whirl

ed•i•ble [ED-ə-bəl] *adj* eatable, fit for eating.

e•dict [EE-dikt] *n* order proclaimed by authority, decree.

ed•i•fice [ED-ə-fis] *n* building, esp. big one.

ed•i•fy [ED-ə-fī] *vt* **-fied, -fy•ing** improve morally, instruct. **ed•i•fi•ca'tion** *n* improvement of the mind or morals.

ed'it *vt* prepare book, film, tape, etc. for publication or broadcast. **e•di•tion** [i-DISH-ən] *n* **1** form in which something is published. **2** number of copies of new publication printed at one time. **ed•i•to'ri•al** *adj* **1** of editor. ◆ *n* **2** article stating opinion of newspaper, etc.

ed•u•cate [EJ-uu-kayt] *vt* **-cat•ed, -cat•ing 1** provide schooling for. **2** teach. **3** train mentally and morally. **4** train. **5** improve, develop. **ed•u•ca'tion** *n* **ed•u•ca'tion•al** *adj* **ed'u•ca•tive** *adj* **ed'u•ca•tor** *n*

e•duce [i-DOOS] *vt* **-duced, -duc•ing 1** bring out, elicit, develop. **2** infer, deduce.

ee•rie [EER-ee] *adj* **-ri•er, -ri•est 1** weird, uncanny. **2** causing superstitious fear.

ef•face [i-FAYS] *vt* **-faced, -fac•ing** wipe or rub out. **ef•face'a•ble** *adj*

ef•fect [i-FEKT] *n* **1** result, consequence. **2** efficacy. **3** impression. **4** condition of being operative. ◆ *pl* **5** movable property. **6** lighting, sounds, etc. to accompany film, broadcast, etc. ◆ *vt* **7** bring about, accomplish. **ef•fec'tive** *adj* **1** having power to produce effects. **2** in effect, operative. **3** serviceable. **4** powerful. **5** striking. **ef•fec'tive•ly** *adv* **ef•fec'tu•al** [-choo-əl] *adj* **1** successful in producing desired effect. **2** satisfactory. **3** efficacious. **ef•fec'tu•ate** [-choo-ayt] *vt* **-at•ed, -at•ing** bring about, effect.

ef•fem•i•nate [i-FEM-ə-nit] *adj* womanish, unmanly. **ef•fem'i•na•cy** *n*

ef•fer•ent [EF-ər-ənt] *adj* conveying

THESAURUS

edge *n* **1** = **border**, boundary, brink, fringe, limit, outline, perimeter, rim, side, verge **2** = **sharpness**, bite, effectiveness, force, incisiveness, keenness, point **3** *As in* **have the edge on** = **advantage**, ascendancy, dominance, lead, superiority, upper hand **4** **on edge** = **nervous**, apprehensive, edgy, ill at ease, impatient, irritable, keyed up, on tenterhooks, tense, wired (*sl*) ◆ *v* **5** = **border**, fringe, hem **6** = **inch**, creep, ease, sidle, steal

edgy *adj* = **nervous**, anxious, ill at ease, irritable, keyed up, on edge, on tenterhooks, restive, tense, wired (*sl*)

edible *adj* = **eatable**, digestible, fit to eat, good, harmless, palatable, wholesome

edict *n* = **decree**, act, command, injunction, law, order, proclamation, ruling

edifice *n* = **building**, construction, erection, house, structure

edify *v* = **instruct**, educate, enlighten, guide, improve, inform, nurture, school, teach

edit *v* = **revise**, adapt, condense, correct, emend, polish, rewrite

edition *n* = **version**, copy, impression, issue, number, printing, program (*TV, Radio*), volume

educate *v* = **teach**, civilize, develop, discipline, enlighten, improve, inform, instruct, school, train, tutor

educated *adj* **1** = **taught**, coached, informed, instructed, nurtured, schooled, tutored **2** = **cultured**, civilized, cultivated, enlightened, knowledgeable, learned, refined, sophisticated

education *n* = **teaching**, development, discipline, enlightenment, instruction, nurture, schooling, training, tuition

educational *adj* = **instructive**, cultural, edifying, educative, enlightening, improving, informative

eerie *adj* = **frightening**, creepy (*inf*), ghostly, mysterious, scary (*inf*), spooky (*inf*), strange, uncanny, unearthly, weird

efface *v* = **obliterate**, blot out, cancel, delete, destroy, eradicate, erase, expunge, rub out, wipe out

effect *n* **1** = **result**, conclusion, consequence, end result, event, outcome, upshot **2** = **operation**, action, enforcement, execution, force, implementation **3** = **impression**, essence, impact, sense, significance, tenor ◆ *v* **4** = **bring about**, accomplish, achieve, complete, execute, fulfill, perform, produce

effective *adj* **1** = **efficient**, active, adequate, capable, competent, productive, serviceable, useful **2** = **in operation**, active, current, in effect, in force, operative **3** = **powerful**, cogent, compelling, convincing, forceful, impressive, persuasive, telling

effects *pl n* = **belongings**, gear, goods, paraphernalia, possessions, property, outward or away.

ef·fer·vesce [ef-ər-VES] vi **-vesced,**
-vesc·ing 1 give off bubbles. **2** be in high
spirits. **ef·fer·ves'cent** adj

ef·fete [i-FEET] adj worn out, feeble.

ef·fi·ca·cious [ef-i-KAY-shəs] adj **1**
producing or sure to produce desired
effect. **2** effective. **3** powerful. **4** adequate.
ef'fi·ca·cy [-kə-see] n **-cies 1** potency. **2**
force. **3** efficiency.

ef·fi·cient [i-FISH-ənt] adj **1** capable,
competent, producing effect. **ef·fi'cien·cy**
n, pl **-cies**

ef·fi·gy [EF-i-jee] n, pl **-gies** image, likeness.

ef·flo·resce [ef-lə-RES] vi **-resced, -res·cing**
burst into flower. **ef·flo·res'cence** n

ef·flu·ent [EF-loo-ənt] n **1** liquid discharged
as waste. **2** stream flowing from larger
stream, lake, etc. ♦ adj **3** flowing out.
ef·flu·vi·um [i-FLOO-vee-əm] n, pl **-vi·a**
something flowing out invisibly, esp.
affecting lungs or sense of smell.

ef·fort [EF-ərt] n exertion, endeavor,
attempt or something achieved.
ef'fort·less adj

ef·fron·ter·y [i-FRUN-tə-ree] n, pl **-ter·ies**
brazen impudence.

ef·ful·gent [i-FUL-jənt] adj radiant, shining
brightly. **ef·ful'gence** n

ef·fu·sion [i-FYOO-zhən] n (unrestrained)
outpouring. **ef·fuse** [i-FYOOZ] v **-fused,**
-fus·ing 1 pour out, shed. **2** radiate.
ef·fu'sive [-siv] adj gushing,
demonstrative.

e.g. for example.

e·gal·i·tar·i·an [i gal i TAIR ee ən] adj **1**
believing that all people should be equal. **2**
promoting this ideal. ♦ n

egg[1] n oval or round object produced by
female of bird, etc., from which young
emerge, esp. egg of domestic hen, used as
food. **egg'plant** n **1** egg-shaped dark
purple fruit. **2** plant bearing it.

egg[2] vt **egg on 1** encourage, urge. **2** incite.

e·go [EE-goh] n, pl **e·gos 1** the self. **2** the
conscious thinking subject. **3** one's image
of oneself. **4** morale. **e'go·ism** n **1**
systematic selfishness. **2** theory that bases
morality on self-interest. **e'go·tism** n **1**
selfishness. **2** self-conceit. **e'go·tist,**
eg'o·ist n **e·go·tis'tic, e·go·is'tic** adj
e·go·cen'tric adj **1** self-centered. **2** egoistic.
3 centered in the ego.

e·gre·gious [i-GREE-jəs] adj **1**

things

effeminate adj = **womanly**, camp (inf),
feminine, sissy, soft, tender, unmanly,
weak, womanish

effervescent adj **1** = **bubbling**,
carbonated, fizzy, foaming, frothy,
sparkling **2** = **lively**, animated, bubbly,
ebullient, enthusiastic, exuberant,
irrepressible, vivacious

effete adj = **decadent**, dissipated,
enfeebled, feeble, ineffectual, spoiled,
weak

efficacious adj = **effective**, adequate,
efficient, operative, potent, powerful,
productive, successful, useful

efficiency n = **competence**, adeptness,
capability, economy, effectiveness, power,
productivity, proficiency

efficient adj = **competent**, businesslike,
capable, economic, effective, organized,
productive, proficient, well-organized,
workmanlike

effigy n = **likeness**, dummy, figure, guy,
icon, idol, image, picture, portrait,
representation, statue

effluent n = **waste**, effluvium, pollutant,
sewage

effort n **1** = **exertion**, application, elbow
grease (facetious), endeavor, energy, pains,
struggle, toil, trouble, work **2** = **attempt**,
endeavor, essay, go (inf), shot (inf), stab
(inf), try

effortless adj = **easy**, painless, plain
sailing, simple, smooth, uncomplicated,
undemanding

effrontery n = **insolence**, arrogance,
audacity, brazenness, cheek (inf),
impertinence, impudence, nerve,
presumption, temerity

effusive adj = **demonstrative**, ebullient,
expansive, exuberant, gushing, lavish,
unreserved, unrestrained

egg on v = **encourage**, exhort, goad,
incite, prod, prompt, push, spur, urge

egocentric adj = **self-centered**, egoistic,
egoistical, egotistic, egotistical, selfish

egotism, egoism n = **self-centeredness**,
conceitedness, narcissism, self-absorption,
self-esteem, self-importance, self-interest,
selfishness, vanity

egotist, egoist n = **egomaniac**, bighead
(inf), boaster, braggart, narcissist

egotistic, egotistical, egoistic or
egoistical adj = **self-centered**, boasting,

outstandingly bad, blatant. **2** absurdly obvious, esp. of mistake, etc.

e·gress [EE-gres] *n* **1** way out. **2** departure.

e·gret [EE-grit] *n* one of several white herons.

ei·der [Ī-dər] *n* **1** any of several northern sea ducks. **2** eiderdown. **ei'der·down** *n* **1** its breast feathers. **2** quilt (stuffed with feathers).

eight [ayt] *n* **1** cardinal number one above seven. **2** crew of eight-oared shell. ◆ *adj* **eight·een'** *adj*, *n* **1** eight more than ten. **eight·eenth'** *adj*, *n* eighth [ayth] *adj*, *n* ordinal number. **eighth** *adj*, *n* **eight'y** *adj*, *n*, *pl* **eight·ies** ten times eight. **figure eight 1** a skating figure. **2** any figure shaped as 8.

ei·ther [EE-*th*ər] *adj*, *pron* **1** one or the other. **2** one of two. **3** each. ◆ *adv*, *conj* **4** bringing in first of alternatives or strengthening an added negation.

e·jac·u·late [i-JAK-yə-layt] *v* **-lat·ed, -lat·ing 1** eject (semen). **2** exclaim, utter suddenly. **e·jac·u·la'tion** *n*

e·ject [i-JEKT] *vt* **1** throw out. **2** expel, drive out. **e·jec'tion** *n*

eke out [eek] *vt* **1** make (supply) last, esp. by frugal use. **2** supply deficiencies of. **3** make with difficulty (a living, etc.).

e·lab·o·rate [i-LAB-ər-it] *adj* **1** carefully worked out, detailed. **2** complicated. ◆ *v* [-ayt] **-rat·ed, -rat·ing** ◆ *vi* **3** expand (upon). ◆ *vt* **4** work out in detail. **5** take pains with.

élan [ay-LAHN] *n* **1** dash. **2** ardor. **3** impetuosity. **élan vi·tal** [vee-TAL] esp. in Bergsonian philosophy, the creative force within an organism that is responsible for growth, change, etc.

e·lapse [i-LAPS] *vi* **-lapsed, -laps·ing** of time, pass.

e·las·tic [i-LAS-tik] *adj* **1** resuming normal shape after distortion, springy. **2** flexible. ◆ *n* **3** tape, fabric, containing interwoven strands of flexible rubber, etc. **e·las'ti·cized** [-sīzd] *adj* **e·las·tic'i·ty** *n*

e·la·tion [i-LAY-shən] *n* **1** high spirits. **2** pride. **e·late** [i-LAYT] *vt* **-lat·ed, -lat·ing 1** (usu. passive) be elated, etc. **2** raise the spirits of. **3** make happy. **4** exhilarate.

el·bow [EL-boh] *n* **1** joint between fore and upper parts of arm (esp. outer part of it). **2** part of sleeve covering this. **3** something resembling this, esp. angular pipe fitting. ◆ *vt* **4** shove, strike with elbow. **elbow grease** hard work. **elbow room** *n* sufficient room.

eld·er¹ [EL-dər] *adj* **1** older, senior. **2** comp. of OLD. ◆ *n* **3** person of greater age. **4** old person. **5** official of certain churches. **el'der·ly** *adj* growing old. **eld'est** *adj* **1** oldest. **2** sup. of OLD.

el·der² *n* white-flowered tree or shrub.

El Do·ra·do [el də-RAH-doh] *n* fictitious country rich in gold.

e·lect [i-LEKT] *vt* **1** choose by vote. **2** choose. ◆ *adj* **3** appointed but not yet in office. **4** chosen, select, choice. **e·lec'tion** *n* choosing, esp. by voting. **e·lec·tion·eer'** *vi* work in political campaign. **e·lec'tive** *adj* appointed, filled, or chosen by election. **e·lec'tor** *n* one who elects. **e·lec'tor·al** *adj*

———[THESAURUS]———

conceited, egocentric, full of oneself, narcissistic, self-absorbed, self-important, vain

egress *n Formal* = **exit**, departure, exodus, way out, withdrawal

eject *v* = **throw out**, banish, drive out, evict, expel, oust, remove, turn out

ejection *n* = **expulsion**, banishment, deportation, eviction, exile, removal

eke out *v* = **be sparing with**, economize on, husband, stretch out

elaborate *adj* **1** = **detailed**, intricate, minute, painstaking, precise, studied, thorough **2** = **complicated**, complex, fancy, fussy, involved, ornamented, ornate ◆ *v* **3** = **expand (upon)**, add detail, amplify, develop, embellish, enlarge, flesh out

elapse *v* = **pass**, glide by, go by, lapse, roll by, slip away

elastic *adj* **1** = **stretchy**, plastic, pliable, pliant, resilient, rubbery, springy, supple, tensile **2** = **adaptable**, accommodating, adjustable, compliant, flexible, supple, tolerant, variable, yielding

elated *adj* = **joyful**, delighted, ecstatic, euphoric, exhilarated, gleeful, jubilant, overjoyed

elation *n* = **joy**, bliss, delight, ecstasy, euphoria, exhilaration, glee, high spirits, jubilation, rapture

elbow *n* **1** = **joint**, angle ◆ *v* **2** = **push**, jostle, knock, nudge, shove

elbow room *n* = **scope**, freedom, latitude, leeway, play, room, space

elder *adj* **1** = **older**, first-born, senior ◆ *n* **2** = **older person**, senior

electoral college body of electors chosen by voters to elect President and Vice President. **e·lec'tor·ate** *n* body of persons entitled to vote.

e·lec·tric·i·ty [i-lek-TRIS-i-tee] *n* **1** form of energy associated with stationary or moving electrons or other charged particles. **2** electric current or charge. **3** science dealing with electricity. **e·lec'tric** *adj* **1** derived from, produced by, producing, transmitting or powered by electricity. **2** excited, emotionally charged. **e·lec'tri·cal** *adj* **e·lec·tri'cian** *n* one trained in installation, etc. of electrical wiring and devices. **e·lec·tri·fi·ca'tion** *n* **e·lec'tri·fy** *vt* **-fied, -fy·ing electric chair** chair in which criminals sentenced to death are electrocuted. **electric organ** *Mus.* organ in which sound is produced by electric devices instead of wind.

electro- *comb. form* operated by or caused by electricity, e.g. *electrocute*.

e·lec·tro·car·di·o·graph [i-lek-troh-KAHR-dee-ə-graf] *n* instrument for recording electrical activity of heart. **e·lec·tro·car'di·o·gram** *n* tracing produced by this.

e·lec·tro·cute [i-LEK-trə-kyoot] *vt* **-cut·ed, -cut·ing** execute, kill by electricity. **e·lec·tro·cu'tion** *n*

e·lec·trode [i-LEK-trohd] *n* conductor by which electric current enters or leaves battery, vacuum tube, etc.

e·lec·tro·en·ceph·a·lo·graph [i-lek-troh-en-SEF-ə-lə-graf] *n* instrument for recording electrical activity of brain. **e·lec·tro·en·ceph'a·lo·gram** *n* tracing produced by this.

e·lec·tro·lyte [i-LEK-trə-līt] *n* solution, molten substance that conducts electricity.

e·lec·tro·lyt'ic [-LIT-ik] *adj*

e·lec·tro·lyze [i-LEK-trə-līz] *vt* **-lyzed, -lyz·ing** decompose by electricity. **e·lec·trol'y·sis** [-TROL-ə-sis] *n*

e·lec·tro·mag·net [i-lek-troh-MAG-nit] *n* magnet containing coil of wire through which electric current is passed. **e·lec·tro·mag·net'ic** *adj*

e·lec·tron [i-LEK-tron] *n* one of fundamental particles of matter identified with unit of charge of negative electricity and essential component of the atom. **e·lec·tron'ic** *adj* **1** of electrons or electronics. **2** using devices, such as semiconductors, transistors or vacuum tubes, dependent on action of electrons. **electronic mail** see E-MAIL. **e·lec·tron'ics** *n* **1** technology concerned with development of electronic devices and circuits. **2** science of behavior and control of electrons. **electron volt** unit of energy used in nuclear physics.

e·lec·tro·plate [i-LEK-trə-playt] *vt* **-plat·ed, -plat·ing 1** coat with silver, etc. by electrolysis. ◆ *n* **2** articles electroplated.

el·e·gant [EL-ə-gənt] *adj* **1** graceful, tasteful. **2** refined. **el'e·gance** *n*

el·e·gy [EL-ə-jee] *n, pl* **-gies** lament for the dead in poem or song. **el·e·gi·ac** [el-ə-JĪ-ək] *adj* **1** suited to elegies. **2** plaintive.

el·e·ment [EL-ə-mənt] *n* **1** substance that cannot be separated into other substances by ordinary chemical techniques. **2** component part. **3** small amount, trace. **4** heating wire in electric kettle, stove, etc. **5** proper abode or sphere. **6** *pl* powers of atmosphere. **7** rudiments, first principles. **el·e·men'tal** *adj* **1** fundamental. **2** of powers of nature. **el·e·men'ta·ry** *adj* rudimentary, simple.

──── THESAURUS ────

elect *v* = **choose**, appoint, determine, opt for, pick, prefer, select, settle on, vote

election *n* = **voting**, appointment, choice, judgment, preference, selection, vote

elector *n* = **voter**, constituent, selector

electric *adj* = **charged**, dynamic, exciting, rousing, stimulating, stirring, tense, thrilling

electrify *v* = **startle**, astound, excite, galvanize, invigorate, jolt, shock, stir, thrill

elegance *n* = **style**, dignity, exquisiteness, grace, gracefulness, grandeur, luxury, refinement, taste

elegant *adj* = **stylish**, chic, delicate, exquisite, fine, graceful, handsome, polished, refined, tasteful

element *n* **1** = **component**, constituent, factor, ingredient, part, section, subdivision, unit **2** *As in* **in one's element** = **environment**, domain, field, habitat, medium, milieu, sphere

elementary *adj* = **simple**, clear, easy, plain, rudimentary, straightforward, uncomplicated

elements *pl n* **1** = **basics**, essentials, foundations, fundamentals, nuts and bolts (*inf*), principles, rudiments **2** = **weather conditions**, atmospheric conditions,

el·e·phant [EL-ə-fənt] *n* huge four-footed, thick-skinned animal with ivory tusks and long trunk. **el·e·phan·ti·a·sis** *n* disease with hardening of skin and enlargement of legs, etc. **el·e·phan'tine** [-FAN-teen] *adj* unwieldy, clumsy, heavily big.

el·e·vate [EL-ə-vayt] *vt* **-vat·ed, -vat·ing** raise, lift up, exalt. **el·e·va'tion** *n* **1** raising. **2** height, esp. above sea level. **3** angle above horizon, as of gun. **4** drawing of one side of building, etc. **el'e·va·tor** *n* cage raised and lowered in vertical shaft to transport people, etc.

e·lev·en [i-LEV-ən] *n* **1** number next above 10. **2** team of 11 persons. ◆ *adj* **e·lev'en·fold** *adj, adv* **e·lev'enth** *adj* the ordinal number. **eleventh hour** latest possible time.

elf *n, pl* **elves 1** fairy. **2** woodland sprite. **elf'in** *adj* **1** roguish, mischievous.

e·lic·it [i-LIS-it] *vt* **1** draw out, evoke. **2** bring to light.

e·lide [i-LID] *vt* **e·lid·ed, e·lid·ing** omit in pronunciation a vowel or syllable. **e·li·sion** [i-LIZH-ən] *n*

el·i·gi·ble [EL-ə-jə-bəl] *adj* **1** fit or. **2** qualified to be chosen. **3** suitable, desirable. **el·i·gi·bil'i·ty** *n*

e·lim·i·nate [i-LIM-ə-nayt] *vt* **-nat·ed, -nat·ing** remove, get rid of, set aside. **e·lim·i·na'tion** *n*

elision see ELIDE.

e·lite [i-LEET] *n* **1** choice or select body. **2** the pick or best part of society. **3** typewriter type size (12 letters to inch). ◆ *adj* **e·lit'ism** *n* **e·lit'ist** *n*

e·lix·ir [i-LIK-sər] *n* **1** preparation sought by alchemists to change base metals into gold, or to prolong life. **2** panacea.

elk *n* large deer.

el·lipse [i-LIPS] *n* oval. **el·lip'ti·cal** *adj*

el·lip·sis [i-LIP-sis] *n, pl* **-ses** [-seez] **1** omission of parts of word or sentence. **2** mark (. . .) indicating this.

el·o·cu·tion [el-ə-KYOO-shən] *n* art of public speaking, voice management. **el·o·cu'tion·ist** *n* teacher of this.

e·lon·gate [i-LAWNG-gayt] *vt* **-gat·ed, -gat·ing** lengthen, extend, prolong. **e·lon·ga'tion** *n*

e·lope [i-LOHP] *vi* **-loped, -lop·ing 1** run away from home with lover. **2** do this with intention of marrying. **e·lope'ment** *n*

el·o·quence [EL-ə-kwəns] *n* fluent, powerful use of language. **el'o·quent** *adj*

else [els] *adv* **1** besides, instead. **2** otherwise, if not. **else·where** *adv* in or to some other place.

e·lu·ci·date [i-LOO-si-dayt] *vt* **-dat·ed, -dat·ing** throw light upon, explain. **e·lu·ci·da'tion** *n*

e·lude [i-LOOD] *vt* **-lud·ed, -lud·ing 1**

THESAURUS

powers of nature

elevate *v* **1 = raise**, heighten, hoist, lift, lift up, uplift **2 = promote**, advance, aggrandize, exalt, prefer, upgrade

elevated *adj* **= high-minded**, dignified, exalted, grand, high-flown, inflated, lofty, noble, sublime

elevation *n* **1 = promotion**, advancement, aggrandizement, exaltation, preferment, upgrading **2 = altitude**, height

elicit *v* **1 = bring about**, bring forth, bring out, bring to light, call forth, cause, derive, evolve, give rise to **2 = obtain**, draw out, evoke, exact, extort, extract, wrest

eligible *adj* **= qualified**, acceptable, appropriate, desirable, fit, preferable, proper, suitable, worthy

eliminate *v* **= get rid of**, cut out, dispose of, do away with, eradicate, exterminate, remove, stamp out, take out

elite *n* **= best**, aristocracy, cream, *crème de la crème*, flower, nobility, pick, upper class

elitist *adj* **= snobbish**, exclusive, selective

elixir *n* **= panacea**, nostrum

elocution *n* **= diction**, articulation, declamation, delivery, enunciation, oratory, pronunciation, speech, speechmaking

elongate *v* **= make longer**, draw out, extend, lengthen, prolong, protract, stretch

elope *v* **= run away**, abscond, bolt, decamp, disappear, escape, leave, run off, slip away, steal away

eloquence *n* **= expressiveness**, expression, fluency, forcefulness, oratory, persuasiveness, rhetoric, way with words

eloquent *adj* **1 = silver-tongued**, articulate, fluent, forceful, moving, persuasive, stirring, well-expressed **2 = expressive**, meaningful, suggestive, telling, vivid

elsewhere *adv* **= in** or **to another place**, abroad, away, hence (*archaic*), not here, somewhere else

elucidate *v* **= clarify**, clear up, explain,

escape, slip away from, dodge. **2** baffle.
e·lu'sion n **1** act of eluding. **2** evasion.
e·lu'sive adj difficult to catch hold of,
deceptive. **e·lu'sive·ness** n
elves, elvish see ELF.
em n Printing the square of any size of type.
em- prefix see EN-.
e·ma·ci·ate [i-MAY-see-ayt] v **-at·ed,**
-at·ing make or become abnormally thin.
e·ma·ci·a'tion n
e-mail, e·mail n **1** (also **electronic mail**)
sending of messages between computer
terminals or other electronic devices. ♦ v **2**
communicate in this way.
e·a·nate [EM-ə-nayt] vi **-nat·ed, -nat·ing**
issue, proceed from, originate.
em·a·na'tion n
e·man·ci·pate [i-MAN-sə-payt] vt **-pat·ed,**
-pat·ing set free. **e·man·ci·pa'tion** n **1** act
of setting free, esp. from social, legal
restraint. **2** state of being set free.
e·man'ci·pa·tor n
e·mas·cu·late [i-MAS-kyə-layt] vt **-lat·ed,**
-lat·ing 1 castrate. **2** enfeeble, weaken.
e·mas·cu·la'tion n
em·balm [em-BAHM] vt preserve corpse
from decay by use of chemicals, herbs, etc.

em·balm'er n
em·bank·ment [em-BANGK-mənt] n
artificial mound carrying road, railway, or
serving to dam water.
em·bar·go [em-BAHR-goh] n, pl **-goes 1**
order stopping movement of ships. **2**
suspension of commerce. **3** ban. ♦ vt
-goed, -go·ing put under embargo.
em·bark [em-BAHRK] v **1** put, go, on board
ship, aircraft, etc. **2** commence new project, venture, etc.
em·bar·ka'tion n
em·bar·rass [em-BAR-əs] vt **1** perplex,
disconcert. **2** abash. **3** confuse. **4**
encumber. **em·bar'rass·ment** n
em·bas·sy [EM-bə-see] n, pl **-sies 1** office,
work or official residence of ambassador. **2**
deputation.
em·bed' vt **-bed·ded, -bed·ding** fix fast in
something solid.
em·bel·lish vt adorn, enrich.
em·bel'lish·ment n
em·ber [EM-bər] n **1** glowing cinder. ♦ pl **2**
red-hot ashes.
em·bez·zle [em-BEZ-əl] vt **-zled, -zling**
divert fraudulently, misappropriate (money
in trust, etc.). **em·bez'zle·ment** n

explicate, expound, illuminate, illustrate,
make plain, shed or throw light upon, spell
out
elude v **1 = escape**, avoid, dodge, duck
(inf), evade, flee, get away from, outrun
2 = baffle, be beyond (someone),
confound, escape, foil, frustrate, puzzle,
stump, thwart
elusive adj **1 = difficult to catch**, shifty,
slippery, tricky **2 = indefinable**, fleeting,
intangible, subtle, transient, transitory
emaciated adj **= skeletal**, cadaverous,
gaunt, haggard, lean, pinched, scrawny,
thin, undernourished, wasted
emanate v **= flow**, arise, come forth,
derive, emerge, issue, originate, proceed,
spring, stem
emancipate v **= free**, deliver, liberate,
release, set free, unchain, unfetter
emancipation n **= freedom**, deliverance,
liberation, liberty, release
embalm v **= preserve**, mummify
embargo n **1 = ban**, bar, boycott,
interdiction, prohibition, restraint,
restriction, stoppage ♦ v **2 = ban**, bar,
block, boycott, prohibit, restrict, stop
embark v **1 = go aboard**, board ship, take

ship **2 embark on** or **upon = begin**,
commence, enter, launch, plunge into, set
about, set out, start, take up
embarrass v **= shame**, discomfit,
disconcert, distress, fluster, humiliate,
mortify, show up (inf)
embarrassed adj **= ashamed**, awkward,
blushing, discomfited, disconcerted,
humiliated, mortified, red-faced,
self-conscious, sheepish
embarrassing adj **= humiliating**,
awkward, compromising, discomfiting,
disconcerting, mortifying, sensitive,
shameful, toe-curling (inf), uncomfortable
embarrassment n **1 = shame**,
awkwardness, bashfulness, distress,
humiliation, mortification,
self-consciousness, showing up (inf) **2 =**
predicament, bind (inf), difficulty, mess,
pickle (inf), scrape (inf)
embellish v **= decorate**, adorn, beautify,
elaborate, embroider, enhance, enrich,
festoon, ornament
embellishment n **= decoration**,
adornment, elaboration, embroidery,
enhancement, enrichment, exaggeration,
ornament, ornamentation

em·bez'zler n

em·bit·ter [em-BIT-ər] vt make bitter. **em·bit·ter·ment** n

em·bla·zon [em-BLAY-zən] vt adorn richly, esp. heraldically.

em·blem [EM-bləm] n **1** symbol. **2** badge, device. **em·ble·mat'ic** adj

em·bod·y [em-BOD-ee] vt -bod·ied, -bod·y·ing **1** give body, concrete expression to. **2** represent, include, be expression of. **em·bod'i·ment** n

em·bo·lism [EM-bə-liz-əm] n Med. obstruction of artery by blood clot or air bubble.

em·boss [em-BAWS] vt mold, stamp or carve in relief.

em·brace [em-BRAYS] vt -braced, -brac·ing **1** clasp in arms, hug. **2** seize, avail oneself of, accept. **3** comprise. ◆ n

em·bra·sure [em-BRAY-zhər] n **1** opening in wall for cannon. **2** beveling of wall at sides of window.

em·bro·ca·tion [em-brə-KAY-shən] n lotion for rubbing limbs, etc. to relieve pain. **em'bro·cate** vt -cat·ed, -cat·ing apply lotion, etc.

em·broi·der [em-BROI-dər] vt **1** ornament with needlework. **2** embellish, exaggerate (story). **em·broi'der·y** n

em·broil' vt **1** bring into confusion. **2** involve in hostility. **em·broil'ment** n

em·bry·o [EM-bree-oh] n, pl -os **1** unborn or undeveloped offspring, germ. **2** undeveloped thing. **em·bry·ol'o·gist** n **em·bry·ol'o·gy** n **em·bry·on'ic** adj

e·mend [i-MEND] vt remove errors from, correct. **e·men·da'tion** n

em·er·ald [EM-ər-əld] n **1** bright green precious stone. ◆ adj **2** of the color of emerald.

e·merge [i-MURJ] vi -merged, -merg·ing **1** come up, out. **2** rise to notice. **3** come into view. **4** come out on inquiry. **e·mer'gence** n **e·mer'gent** adj

e·mer·gen·cy [i-MUR-jən-see] n, pl -cies **1** sudden unforeseen thing or event needing prompt action. **2** difficult situation. **3** exigency, crisis.

e·mer·i·tus [i-MER-i-təs] adj retired, honorably discharged but retaining one's title (e.g. professor) on honorary basis.

em·er·y [EM-ər-ee] n hard mineral used for polishing. **emery board** cardboard coated with powdered emery.

e·met·ic [i-MET-ik] n, adj (medicine or agent) causing vomiting.

em·i·grate [EM-i-grayt] vt -grat·ed, -grat·ing go and settle in another country. **em'i·grant** [-grənt] n **em·i·gra'tion** n

é·mi·gré [EM-i-gray] n, pl -grés emigrant,

embezzle v = **misappropriate**, appropriate, filch, misuse, peculate, pilfer, purloin, rip off (sl), steal

embezzlement n = **misappropriation**, appropriation, filching, fraud, misuse, peculation, pilfering, stealing, theft

embittered adj = **resentful**, angry, bitter, disaffected, disillusioned, rancorous, soured, with a chip on one's shoulder (inf)

emblem n = **symbol**, badge, crest, image, insignia, mark, sign, token

embodiment n = **personification**, epitome, example, exemplar, expression, incarnation, representation, symbol

embody v **1** = **personify**, exemplify, manifest, represent, stand for, symbolize, typify **2** = **incorporate**, collect, combine, comprise, contain, include

embolden v = **encourage**, fire, inflame, invigorate, rouse, stimulate, stir, strengthen

embrace v **1** = **hug**, clasp, cuddle, envelop, hold, seize, squeeze, take or hold in one's arms **2** = **accept**, adopt, espouse, seize,

take on board, take up, welcome **3** = **include**, comprehend, comprise, contain, cover, encompass, involve, take in ◆ n **4** = **hug**, clasp, clinch (sl), cuddle, squeeze

embroil v = **involve**, enmesh, ensnare, entangle, implicate, incriminate, mire, mix up

embryo n = **germ**, beginning, nucleus, root, rudiment

emend v = **revise**, amend, correct, edit, improve, rectify

emendation n = **revision**, amendment, correction, editing, improvement, rectification

emerge v **1** = **come into view**, appear, arise, come forth, emanate, issue, rise, spring up, surface **2** = **become apparent**, become known, come out, come out in the wash, come to light, crop up, transpire

emergence n = **coming**, advent, appearance, arrival, development, materialization, rise

emergency n = **crisis**, danger, difficulty, extremity, necessity, plight, predicament, esp. one forced to leave native land for political reasons.

em·i·nent [EM-ə-nənt] *adj* **1** distinguished, notable. **em'i·nence** *n* **1** distinction. **2** height. **3** rank. **4** fame. **5** rising ground. **6** (E-) title of cardinal. **em'i·nent·ly** *adv* **é·mi·nence grise** [ay-mee-nahns GREEZ] *Fr* person wielding unofficial power, oft. surreptitiously

em·is·sar·y [EM-ə-ser-ee] *n, pl* -**sar·ies** agent, representative (esp. of government) sent on mission.

e·mit [i-MIT] *vt* -**mit·ted**, -**mit·ting** give out, put forth. **e·mis'sion** *n* **e·mit'ter** *n*

e·mol·lient [i-MOL-yənt] *adj* **1** softening, soothing. ◆ *n* **2** ointment or other softening application.

e·mol·u·ment [i-MOL-yə-mənt] *n* salary, pay, profit from work.

e·mot·i·con [i-MOH-ti-kon] *n* series of keyed characters, used esp. in e-mail, to indicate an emotion.

e·mo·tion [i-MOH-shən] *n* mental agitation, excited state of feeling, as joy, fear, etc. **e·mo'tion·al** *adj* **1** given to emotion. **2** appealing to the emotions.

e·mo·tive *adj* tending to arouse emotion.

em·pa·thy [EM-pə-thee] *n* power of understanding, imaginatively entering into, another's feelings.

em·per·or [EM-pər-ər] *n* ruler of an empire. **em'press** [-pris] *n, fem.*

em·pha·sis [EM-fə-sis] *n, pl* -**ses** [-seez] **1** importance attached. **2** stress on words. **3** vigor of speech, expression. **em'pha·size** *vt* -**sized**, -**siz·ing em·phat'ic** [-FAT-ik] *adj* **1** forceful, decided. **2** stressed.

em·pire [EM-pīr] *n* large territory, esp. aggregate of territories or peoples under supreme ruler, supreme control.

em·pir·i·cal [em-PIR-i-kəl] *adj* relying on experiment or experience, not on theory. **em·pir'i·cal·ly** *adv* **em·pir'i·cist** [-ə-sist] *n* one who relies solely on experience and observation. **em·pir'i·cism** *n*

em·place·ment [em-PLAYS-mənt] *n* **1** putting in position. **2** gun platform.

em·ploy [em-PLOI] *vt* **1** provide work for (a person) in return for money, hire. **2** keep busy. **3** use. **em·ploy·ee'** *n* **em·ploy'er** *n* **em·ploy'ment** *n* **1** an employing, being employed. **2** work, trade. **3** occupation.

——————| THESAURUS |——————

quandary, scrape (*inf*)

emigrate *v* = **move abroad**, migrate, move

emigration *n* = **departure**, exodus, migration

eminence *n* = **prominence**, distinction, esteem, fame, greatness, importance, note, prestige, renown, repute

eminent *adj* = **prominent**, celebrated, distinguished, esteemed, famous, high-ranking, illustrious, noted, renowned, well-known

emission *n* = **giving off** *or* **out**, discharge, ejaculation, ejection, exhalation, radiation, shedding, transmission

emit *v* = **give off**, cast out, discharge, eject, emanate, exude, radiate, send out, transmit

emotion *n* = **feeling**, ardor, excitement, fervor, passion, sensation, sentiment, vehemence, warmth

emotional *adj* **1** = **sensitive**, demonstrative, excitable, hot-blooded, passionate, sentimental, temperamental **2** = **moving**, affecting, emotive, heart-warming, poignant, sentimental, stirring, touching

emotive *adj* = **sensitive**, controversial, delicate, touchy

emphasis *n* = **stress**, accent, attention, force, importance, priority, prominence, significance, weight

emphasize *v* = **stress**, accentuate, dwell on, give priority to, highlight, lay stress on, play up, press home, underline

emphatic *adj* = **forceful**, categorical, definite, insistent, positive, pronounced, resounding, unequivocal, unmistakable, vigorous

empire *n* = **kingdom**, commonwealth, domain, realm

empirical *adj* = **first-hand**, experiential, experimental, observed, practical, pragmatic

employ *v* **1** = **hire**, commission, engage, enlist, retain, take on **2** = **keep busy**, engage, fill, make use of, occupy, take up, use up **3** = **use**, apply, bring to bear, exercise, exert, make use of, ply, put to use, utilize ◆ *n* **4** *As in* **in the employ of** = **service**, employment, engagement, hire

employed *adj* = **working**, active, busy, engaged, in a job, in employment, in work, occupied

employee *n* = **worker**, hand, job-holder, staff member, wage-earner, workman

employer *n* = **boss** (*inf*), company, firm,

em·po·ri·um [em-POHR-ee-əm] *n, pl*
-ri·ums 1 large store, esp. one carrying
general merchandise. **2** center of
commerce.

em·pow·er [em-POW-ər] *vt* enable,
authorize. **em·pow·er·ment** *n*

empress see EMPEROR.

emp·ty [EM-tee] *adj* **-ti·er, -ti·est 1**
containing nothing. **2** unoccupied. **3**
senseless. **4** vain, foolish. ◆ *v* **-tied, -ty·ing 5**
make, become devoid of content. **6**
discharge (contents) into. **emp'ties** *pl n*
empty boxes, bottles, etc. **emp'ti·ness** *n*

e·mu [EE-myoo] *n* large Aust. flightless bird
like ostrich.

em·u·late [EM-yə-layt] *vt* **-lat·ed, -lat·ing 1**
strive to equal or excel. **2** imitate.
em·u·la'tion *n* **1** rivalry. **2** competition.
em'u·la·tive *adj* **em'u·la·tor** *n*

e·mul·sion [i-MUL-shən] *n* **1** light-sensitive
coating of film. **2** milky liquid with oily or
resinous particles in suspension. **3** paint,
etc. in this form. **e·mul'si·fi·er** *n* **e·mul'si·fy**
vt **-fied, -fy·ing**

en *n Printing* unit of measurement, half an
em.

en-, em- *prefix* put in, into, or on, e.g.
enrage.

en·a·ble [en-AY-bəl] *vt* **-bled, -bling** make
able, authorize, empower, supply with
means (to do something).

en·act [en-AKT] *vi* **1** make law. **2** act part.
en·act'ment *n*

e·nam·el [i-NAM-əl] *n* **1** glasslike coating
applied to metal, etc. to preserve surface. **2**
coating of teeth. **3** any hard outer coating.
◆ *vt* **-eled, -el·ing**

e·nam·or [i-NAM-ər] *vt* **1** inspire with love.
2 charm. **3** bewitch.

en·camp [en-KAMP] *v* set up (in) camp.
en·camp'ment *n* camp.

en·cap·su·late [en-KAP-sə-layt] *vt* **-lat·ed,
-lat·ing 1** enclose in capsule. **2** put in
concise or abridged form.
en·cap·su·la'tion *n*

en·ceph·a·lo·gram [en-SEF-ə-lə-gram] *n*
X-ray photograph of brain.

en·chant' *vt* bewitch, delight. **en·chant'er**
n **en·chant'ress** *n, fem.* **en·chant'ment** *n*

en·chi·la·da [en-chə-LAH-də] *n* rolled
tortilla filled with sauce of meat, etc.

en·cir·cle [en-SUR-kəl] *vt* **-cled, -cling 1**

THESAURUS

owner, patron, proprietor
employment *n* **1 = taking on,**
engagement, enlistment, hire, retaining
2 = use, application, exercise, exertion,
utilization **3 = job,** line, occupation,
profession, trade, vocation, work
emporium *n Old-fashioned* **= shop,** bazaar,
market, mart, store, warehouse
empower *v* **= enable,** allow, authorize,
commission, delegate, entitle, license,
permit, qualify, sanction, warrant
emptiness *n* **1 = bareness,** blankness,
desolation, vacancy, vacuum, void, waste
2 = purposelessness, banality, futility,
hollowness, inanity, meaninglessness,
senselessness, vanity, worthlessness **3 =
insincerity,** cheapness, hollowness,
idleness
empty *adj* **1 = bare,** blank, clear, deserted,
desolate, hollow, unfurnished,
uninhabited, unoccupied, vacant, void **2 =
purposeless,** banal, fruitless, futile, hollow,
inane, meaningless, senseless, vain,
worthless **3 = insincere,** cheap, hollow,
idle ◆ *v* **4 = evacuate,** clear, drain, exhaust,
pour out, unload, vacate, void
empty-headed *adj* **= scatterbrained,**
brainless, dizzy (*inf*), featherbrained,

harebrained, silly, vacuous
emulate *v* **= imitate,** compete with, copy,
echo, follow, mimic, rival
enable *v* **= allow,** authorize, empower,
entitle, license, permit, qualify, sanction,
warrant
enact *v* **1 = establish,** authorize, command,
decree, legislate, ordain, order, proclaim,
sanction **2 = perform,** act out, depict, play,
play the part of, portray, represent
enamored *adj* **= in love,** captivated,
charmed, enraptured, fond, infatuated,
smitten, taken
encampment *n* **= camp,** base, bivouac,
camping ground, campsite, cantonment,
quarters, tents
encapsulate *v* **= sum up,** abridge,
compress, condense, digest, epitomize,
précis, summarize
enchant *v* **= fascinate,** beguile, bewitch,
captivate, charm, delight, enrapture,
enthrall, ravish, spellbind
enchanter *n* **= sorcerer,** conjurer,
magician, magus, necromancer, warlock,
witch, wizard
enchanting *adj* **= fascinating,** alluring,
attractive, bewitching, captivating,
charming, delightful, entrancing, lovely,

surround. **2** enfold. **3** go around so as to surround.

en•clave [EN-klayv] n **1** portion of territory entirely surrounded by foreign land. **2** distinct area or group isolated within larger one.

en•close [en-KLOHZ] vt **-closed, -clos•ing 1** shut in. **2** surround. **3** envelop. **4** place in with something else (in letter, etc.) **en•clo'sure** [-zhər] n

en•co•mi•um [en-KOH-mee-əm] n **-mi•ums 1** formal praise. **2** eulogy. **en•co'mi•ast** n one who composes encomiums.

en•com•pass [en-KUM-pəs] vt surround, encircle, contain.

en•core [ONG-kor] interj **1** again, once more. ◆ n **2** call for repetition of song, etc. **3** the repetition.

en•coun•ter [en-KOWN-tər] vt **1** meet unexpectedly. **2** meet in conflict. **3** be faced with (difficulty, etc.). ◆ n

en•cour•age [en-KUR-ij] vt **-aged, -ag•ing 1** hearten, animate, inspire with hope. **2** embolden. **en•cour'age•ment** n

en•croach [en-KROHCH] vi **1** intrude (on) as usurper. **2** trespass. **en•croach'ment** n

en•crust [en-KRUST] v incrust. **en•crus•ta'tion** n

en•cum•ber [en-KUM-bər] vt **1** hamper. **2** burden. **en•cum'brance** n impediment, burden.

en•cyc•li•cal [en-SIK-li-kəl] adj **1** sent to many persons or places. ◆ n **2** circular letter, esp. papal letter to all Catholic bishops

en•cy•clo•pe•dia [en-sī-klə-PEE-dee-ə] n book, set of books of information on all subjects, or on every branch of subject, usu. arranged alphabetically. **en•cy•clo•pe'dic** adj

end n **1** limit. **2** extremity. **3** conclusion, finishing. **4** fragment. **5** latter part. **6** death. **7** event, issue. **8** purpose, aim. **9** Football one of two linemen stationed farthest from the center. ◆ v **10** put an end to. **11** come to an end, finish. **end'ing** n **end'less** adj **end'pa•pers** pl n blank pages at beginning and end of book.

en•dear [en-DEER] vt to make dear or beloved. **en•dear'ing** adj **en•dear'ment** n **1** loving word. **2** tender affection.

en•deav•or [en-DEV-ər] vi **1** try, strive after. ◆ n **2** attempt, effort.

pleasant

enclose v **1** = **surround**, bound, encase, encircle, fence, hem in, shut in, wall in **2** = **send with**, include, insert, put in

encompass v **1** = **surround**, circle, encircle, enclose, envelop, ring **2** = **include**, admit, comprise, contain, cover, embrace, hold, incorporate, take in

encounter v **1** = **meet**, bump into (inf), chance upon, come upon, confront, experience, face, run across ◆ n **2** = **meeting**, brush, confrontation, rendezvous **3** = **battle**, clash, conflict, contest, head-to-head, run-in (inf)

encourage v **1** = **inspire**, buoy up, cheer, comfort, console, embolden, hearten, reassure **2** = **spur**, advocate, egg on, foster, promote, prompt, support, urge

encouragement n = **inspiration**, cheer, incitement, promotion, reassurance, stimulation, stimulus, support

encouraging adj = **promising**, bright, cheerful, comforting, good, heartening, hopeful, reassuring, rosy

encroach v = **intrude**, impinge, infringe, invade, make inroads, overstep, trespass, usurp

encumber v = **burden**, hamper, handicap, hinder, impede, inconvenience, obstruct, saddle, weigh down

end n **1** = **extremity**, boundary, edge, extent, extreme, limit, point, terminus, tip **2** = **finish**, cessation, close, closure, ending, expiration, expiry, stop, termination **3** = **conclusion**, culmination, denouement, ending, finale, resolution **4** = **remnant**, butt, fragment, leftover, oddment, remainder, scrap, stub **5** = **destruction**, death, demise, doom, extermination, extinction, ruin **6** = **purpose**, aim, goal, intention, object, objective, point, reason ◆ v **7** = **finish**, cease, close, conclude, culminate, stop, terminate, wind up

endanger v = **put at risk**, compromise, imperil, jeopardize, put in danger, risk, threaten

endearing adj = **attractive**, captivating, charming, cute, engaging, lovable, sweet, winning

endearment n = **loving word**, sweet nothing

endeavor v **1** = **try**, aim, aspire, attempt, labor, make an effort, strive, struggle, take

en·dem·ic [en-DEM-ik] *adj* **1** found only among a particular people or in a particular place. ♦ *n* **2** endemic disease.

en·dive [EN-dīv] *n* curly-leaved plant used in salad.

endo- *comb. form* within, e.g. *endocrine*.

en·do·car·di·um [en-doh-KAHR-dee-əm] *n* lining membrane of the heart.
en·do·car·di·tis [-dī-tis] *n* inflammation of this.

en·do·crine [EN-də-krin] *adj* of those glands (thyroid, pituitary, etc.) that secrete hormones directly into bloodstream.
en·do·cri·nol'o·gy *n* science dealing with endocrine glands.

en·dorse [en-DORS] *vt* **-dorsed, -dors·ing** **1** sanction. **2** confirm. **3** write (esp. sign name) on back of. **en·dorse'ment** *n*

en·dow' *vt* **1** provide permanent income for. **2** furnish (with). **en·dow'ment** *n*

en·dure [en-DUUR] *v* **-dured, -dur·ing** **1** undergo. **2** tolerate, bear. **3** last. **en·dur'a·ble** *adj* **en·dur'ance** *n* act or power of enduring.

en·e·ma [EN-ə-mə] *n* medicine, liquid injected into rectum.

en·e·my [EN-ə-mee] *n, pl* **-mies 1** hostile person. **2** opponent. **3** armed foe. **4** hostile force.

en·er·gy [EN-ər-jee] *n, pl* **-gies 1** vigor, force, activity. **2** source(s) of energy, as oil, coal, etc. **3** capacity of machine, battery, etc. for work or output of power.
en·er·get'ic *adj* **en'er·gize -gized, -giz·ing** ♦ *vt* give vigor to.

en·er·vate [EN-ər-vayt] *vt* **-vat·ed, -vat·ing** weaken, deprive of vigor. **en·er·va'tion** *n* lassitude, weakness.

en·fee·ble [en-FEE-bəl] *vt* **-bled, -bling** weaken, debilitate.

en·fi·lade [EN-fi-layd] *n* fire from artillery, sweeping line from end to end.

en·force [en-FORS] *vt* **1** compel obedience to. **2** impose (action) upon. **3** drive home. **en·force'a·ble** *adj*

en·fran·chise [en-FRAN-chīz] *vt* **-chised, -chis·ing 1** give right of voting to. **2** give legislative representation to. **3** set free.
en·fran'chise·ment [-chiz-mənt] *n*

en·gage [en-GAYJ] ♦ *vt* **1** employ. **2** reserve, hire. **3** bind by contract or promise. **4** order. **5** pledge oneself. **6** betroth. **7** undertake. **8** attract. **9** occupy. **10** bring into conflict. **11** interlock. ♦ *vi* **12** employ oneself (in). **13** promise. **14** begin to fight. **en·gaged'** *adj* **1** betrothed. **2** in use. **3** occupied, busy. **en·gage'ment** *n* **engaging** *adj* charming.

——— THESAURUS ———

pains ♦ *n* **2 = effort**, attempt, enterprise, trial, try, undertaking, venture

ending *n* **= finish**, cessation, close, completion, conclusion, culmination, denouement, end, finale

endless *adj* **= eternal**, boundless, continual, everlasting, incessant, infinite, interminable, unlimited

endorse *v* **1 = approve**, advocate, authorize, back, champion, promote, ratify, recommend, support **2 = sign**, countersign

endorsement *n* **1 = approval**, advocacy, approbation, authorization, backing, favor, ratification, recommendation, seal of approval, support **2 = signature**, countersignature

endow *v* **= provide**, award, bequeath, bestow, confer, donate, finance, fund, give

endowment *n* **= provision**, award, benefaction, bequest, donation, gift, grant, legacy

endurable *adj* **= bearable**, acceptable, sufferable, sustainable, tolerable

endurance *n* **1 = staying power**, fortitude,

patience, perseverance, persistence, resolution, stamina, strength, tenacity, toleration **2 = permanence**, continuity, durability, duration, longevity, stability

endure *v* **1 = bear**, cope with, experience, stand, suffer, sustain, undergo, withstand **2 = last**, continue, live on, persist, remain, stand, stay, survive

enduring *adj* **= long-lasting**, abiding, continuing, lasting, perennial, persistent, steadfast, unfaltering, unwavering

enemy *n* **= foe**, adversary, antagonist, competitor, opponent, rival, the opposition, the other side

energetic *adj* **= vigorous**, active, animated, dynamic, forceful, indefatigable, lively, strenuous, tireless

energy *n* **= vigor**, drive, forcefulness, get-up-and-go (*inf*), liveliness, pep, stamina, verve, vitality

enforce *v* **= impose**, administer, apply, carry out, execute, implement, insist on, prosecute, put into effect

engage *v* **1 = participate**, embark on, enter into, join, set about, take part, undertake

en·gen·der [en-JEN-dər] *vt* **1** give rise to. **2** beget. **3** rouse.

en·gine [EN-jin] *n* **1** any machine to convert energy into mechanical work, as steam or gasoline engine. **2** railroad locomotive. **3** fire engine. **en·gi·neer'** *n* **1** one who is in charge of engines, machinery, etc. or construction work (e.g. roads, bridges). **2** one who originates, organizes something. **3** one trained and skilled in engineering. ◆ *vt* **4** construct as engineer. **5** contrive. **en·gi·neer'ing** *n*

Eng·lish [ING-glish] *n* **1** the language of the US, Britain, most parts of the British Commonwealth and certain other countries. **2** the people of England. ◆ *adj* **3** relating to England.

engrain *vt* see INGRAIN.

en·grave [en-GRAYV] *vt* **-graved, -grav·ing** **1** cut in lines on metal for printing. **2** carve, incise. **3** impress deeply. **en·grav'er** *n* **en·grav'ing** *n* copy of picture printed from engraved plate.

en·gross [en-GROHS] *vt* **1** absorb (attention). **2** occupy wholly. **3** write out in large letters or in legal form. **4** monopolize.

en·gulf' *vt* swallow up.

en·hance [en-HANS] *vt* **-hanced, -hanc·ing** heighten, intensify, increase value or attractiveness. **en·hance'ment** *n*

e·nig·ma [ə-NIG-mə] *n, pl* **-mas 1** puzzling thing or person. **2** riddle. **en·ig·mat'ic** *adj*

en·join' *vt* **1** command. **2** impose, prescribe.

en·joy [en-JOI] *vt* **1** delight in. **2** take pleasure in. **3** have use or benefit of. ◆ *v refl* **4** be happy. **en·joy'a·ble** *adj*

en·large [en-LAHRJ] *v* **-larged, -larg·ing** ◆ *vt* **1** make bigger. **2** reproduce on larger scale, as photograph. ◆ *vi* **3** grow bigger. **4** talk, write about, in greater detail. **en·large'a·ble** *adj* **en·large'ment** *n* **en·larg'er** *n* optical instrument for enlarging photographs.

en·light·en [en-LI-tən] *vt* **1** give

———| THESAURUS |———

2 = **occupy**, absorb, engross, grip, involve, preoccupy **3** = **captivate**, arrest, catch, fix, gain **4** = **employ**, appoint, enlist, enroll, hire, retain, take on **5** *Military* = **begin battle with**, assail, attack, encounter, fall on, join battle with, meet, take on **6** = **set going**, activate, apply, bring into operation, energize, switch on

engaged *adj* **1** = **betrothed** (*archaic*), affianced, pledged, promised, spoken for **2** = **occupied**, busy, employed, in use, tied up, unavailable

engagement *n* **1** = **appointment**, arrangement, commitment, date, meeting **2** = **betrothal**, troth (*archaic*) **3** = **battle**, action, combat, conflict, encounter, fight

engaging *adj* = **charming**, agreeable, attractive, fetching (*inf*), likable *or* likeable, pleasing, winning, winsome

engender *v* = **produce**, breed, cause, create, generate, give rise to, induce, instigate, lead to

engine *n* = **machine**, mechanism, motor

engineer *v* = **bring about**, contrive, create, devise, effect, mastermind, plan, plot, scheme

engrave *v* **1** = **carve**, chisel, cut, etch, inscribe **2** = **fix**, embed, impress, imprint, ingrain, lodge

engraving *n* = **carving**, etching, inscription, plate, woodcut

engross *v* = **absorb**, engage, immerse, involve, occupy, preoccupy

engrossed *adj* = **absorbed**, caught up, enthralled, fascinated, gripped, immersed, lost, preoccupied, rapt, riveted

engulf *v* = **immerse**, envelop, inundate, overrun, overwhelm, submerge, swallow up, swamp

enhance *v* = **improve**, add to, boost, heighten, increase, lift, reinforce, strengthen, swell

enigma *n* = **mystery**, conundrum, problem, puzzle, riddle, teaser

enigmatic *adj* = **mysterious**, ambiguous, cryptic, equivocal, inscrutable, obscure, puzzling, unfathomable

enjoy *v* **1** = **take pleasure in** *or* **from**, appreciate, be entertained by, be pleased with, delight in, like, relish **2** = **have**, be blessed *or* favored with, experience, have the benefit of, own, possess, reap the benefits of, use

enjoyable *adj* = **pleasurable**, agreeable, delightful, entertaining, gratifying, pleasant, satisfying, to one's liking

enjoyment *n* = **pleasure**, amusement, delectation, delight, entertainment, fun, gratification, happiness, joy, relish

enlarge *v* **1** = **increase**, add to, amplify, broaden, expand, extend, grow, magnify, swell, widen **2** enlarge on = **expand on**, information to. **2** instruct, inform, shed light on. **en·light'en·ment** *n*

en·list' *v* engage as soldier or helper. **en·list'ment** *n*

en·liv·en [en-LĪ-vən] *vt* brighten, make more lively, animate.

en masse [ahn MAS] *adv* **1** in a group, body. **2** all together.

en·mesh' *vt* entangle.

en·mi·ty [EN-mi-tee] *n, pl* **-ties** ill will, hostility.

en·no·ble [en-NOH-bəl] *vt* **-bled, -bling** make noble, elevate. **en·no·ble·ment** *n*

en·nui [ahn-WEE] *n* boredom.

e·nor·mous [i-NOR-məs] *adj* very big, vast. **e·nor·mi·ty** *n* **1** a gross offense. **2** great wickedness. **3** *inf* great size.

e·nough [i-NUF] *adj* **1** as much or as many as need be. **2** sufficient. ◆ *n* **3** sufficient quantity. ◆ *adv* **4** (just) sufficiently.

enquire see INQUIRE.

en·rap·ture [en-RAP-chər] *vt* **-tured, -tur·ing 1** delight excessively. **2** charm.

en·rich' *vt* **1** make rich. **2** add to.

en·rich'ment *n*

en·roll [en-ROHL] *vt* **1** write name of on roll or list. **2** engage, enlist, take in as member. **3** enter, record. ◆ *vi* **4** become member. **en·roll'ment** *n*

en route [ahn ROOT] *Fr* on the way.

en·sconce [en-SKONS] *vt* **-sconced, -sconc·ing 1** place snugly. **2** establish in safety.

en·sem·ble [ahn-SAHM-bəl] *n* **1** whole. **2** all parts taken together. **3** woman's complete outfit. **4** company of actors, dancers, etc. **5** *Mus.* group of soloists performing together. **6** *Mus.* concerted passage. **7** general effect.

en·shrine [en-SHRĪN] *vt* **-shrined, -shrin·ing** set in shrine, preserve with great care and sacred affection.

en·sign [EN-sin] *n* **1** naval or military flag. **2** badge. **3** *Navy, Coast Guard* lowest commissioned officer.

ensilage see SILAGE.

en·slave [en-SLAYV] *vt* **-slaved, -slav·ing** make into slave. **en·slave'ment** *n*

THESAURUS

descant on, develop, elaborate on, expatiate on, give further details about

enlighten *v* = **inform**, advise, cause to understand, counsel, edify, educate, instruct, make aware, teach

enlightened *adj* = **informed**, aware, civilized, cultivated, educated, knowledgeable, open-minded, reasonable, sophisticated

enlightenment *n* = **understanding**, awareness, comprehension, education, insight, instruction, knowledge, learning, wisdom

enlist *v* **1** = **join up**, enroll, enter (into), join, muster, register, sign up, volunteer **2** = **obtain**, engage, procure, recruit

enliven *v* = **cheer up**, animate, excite, inspire, invigorate, pep up, rouse, spark, stimulate, vitalize

enmity *n* = **hostility**, acrimony, animosity, bad blood, bitterness, hatred, ill will, malice

ennoble *v* = **dignify**, aggrandize, elevate, enhance, exalt, glorify, honor, magnify, raise

enormity *n* **1** = **wickedness**, atrocity, depravity, monstrousness, outrageousness, vileness, villainy **2** = **atrocity**, abomination, crime, disgrace, evil, horror, monstrosity, outrage **3** *Inf* = **hugeness**, greatness, immensity, magnitude, vastness

enormous *adj* = **huge**, colossal, gigantic, gross, immense, mammoth, massive, mountainous, tremendous, vast

enough *adj* **1** = **sufficient**, abundant, adequate, ample, plenty ◆ *n* **2** = **sufficiency**, abundance, adequacy, ample supply, plenty, right amount ◆ *adv* **3** = **sufficiently**, abundantly, adequately, amply, reasonably, satisfactorily, tolerably

enquire see INQUIRE

enquiry see INQUIRY

enrage *v* = **anger**, exasperate, incense, inflame, infuriate, madden

enrich *v* **1** = **enhance**, augment, develop, improve, refine, supplement **2** = **make rich**, make wealthy

enroll *v* = **enlist**, accept, admit, join up, recruit, register, sign up *or* on, take on

enrollment *n* = **enlistment**, acceptance, admission, engagement, matriculation, recruitment, registration

en route *adv* = **on** *or* **along the way**, in transit, on the road

ensemble *n* **1** = **whole**, aggregate, collection, entirety, set, sum, total, totality **2** = **outfit**, costume, get-up (*inf*), suit **3** = **group**, band, cast, chorus, company, troupe

ensign *n* = **flag**, banner, colors, jack,

bondage.

en·snare [en-SNAIR] vt **-snared, -snar·ing 1** capture in snare or trap. **2** trick into false position. **3** entangle.

en·sue [en-SOO] vi **-sued, -su·ing** follow, happen after.

en·sure [en-SHUUR] vt **-sured, -sur·ing 1** make safe or sure. **2** make certain to happen. **3** secure.

en·tail [en-TAYL] vt **1** involve as result, necessitate. **2** Law restrict ownership of property to designated line of heirs. **en·tail'ment** n

en·tan·gle [en-TANG-gəl] vt **-gled, -gling 1** ensnare. **2** perplex. **en·tan'gle·ment** n

en·tente [ahn-TAHNT] n friendly understanding between nations.

en·ter [EN-tər] vt **1** go, come into. **2** penetrate. **3** join. **4** write in, register. ♦ vi **5** go, come in, join, begin. **en'trance** [-trəns] n **1** going, coming in. **2** door, passage to enter. **3** right to enter. **4** fee paid for this. **en'trant** n one who enters, esp. contest. **en'try** n, pl **-tries 1** entrance. **2** entering. **3** item entered, e.g. in account, list.

en·ter·ic [en-TER-ik] adj of or relating to the intestines. **en·ter·i'tis** n inflammation of intestines.

en·ter·prise [EN-tər-priz] n **1** bold or difficult undertaking. **2** bold spirit. **3** force of character in launching out. **4** business, company. **en'ter·pris·ing** adj

en·ter·tain [en-tər-TAYN] vt **1** amuse, divert. **2** receive as guest. **3** maintain. **4** consider favorable, take into consideration. **en·ter·tain'er** n

en·thrall [en-THRAWL] vt captivate, thrill, hold spellbound.

en·thu·si·asm [en-THOO-zee-az-əm] n ardent eagerness, zeal. **en·thuse'** v (cause to) show enthusiasm. **en·thu·si·ast** n ardent supporter of. **en·thu·si·as'tic** adj

en·tice [en-TĪS] vt **-ticed, -tic·ing** allure, attract, inveigle, tempt. **en·tic'ing** adj alluring.

en·tire [en-TĪR] adj whole, complete, unbroken. **en·tire'ly** adv **en·tire'ty** n, pl **-ties**

en·ti·tle [en-TĪ-təl] vt **-tled, -tling 1** give claim to. **2** qualify. **3** give title to.

———————[THESAURUS]———————

pennant, pennon, standard, streamer

ensue v = **follow**, arise, come next, derive, flow, issue, proceed, result, stem

ensure v **1** = **make certain**, certify, confirm, effect, guarantee, make sure, secure, warrant **2** = **protect**, guard, make safe, safeguard, secure

entail v = **involve**, bring about, call for, demand, give rise to, necessitate, occasion, require

entangle v **1** = **tangle**, catch, embroil, enmesh, ensnare, entrap, implicate, snag, snare, trap **2** = **mix up**, complicate, confuse, jumble, muddle, perplex, puzzle

enter v **1** = **come** or **go in** or **into**, arrive, make an entrance, pass into, penetrate, pierce **2** = **join**, commence, embark upon, enlist, enroll, set out on, start, take up **3** = **record**, inscribe, list, log, note, register, set down, take down

enterprise n **1** = **firm**, business, company, concern, establishment, operation **2** = **undertaking**, adventure, effort, endeavor, operation, plan, program, project, venture **3** = **initiative**, adventurousness, boldness, daring, drive, energy, enthusiasm, resourcefulness

enterprising adj = **resourceful**, adventurous, bold, daring, energetic, enthusiastic, go-ahead, intrepid, spirited

entertain v **1** = **amuse**, charm, cheer, delight, please, regale **2** = **show hospitality to**, accommodate, be host to, harbor, have company, lodge, put up, treat **3** = **consider**, conceive, contemplate, imagine, keep in mind, think about

entertaining adj = **enjoyable**, amusing, cheering, diverting, funny, humorous, interesting, pleasant, pleasurable

entertainment n = **enjoyment**, amusement, fun, leisure activity, pastime, pleasure, recreation, sport, treat

enthrall v = **fascinate**, captivate, charm, enchant, enrapture, entrance, grip, mesmerize

enthusiasm n = **keenness**, eagerness, fervor, interest, passion, relish, zeal, zest

enthusiast n = **lover**, aficionado, buff (inf), devotee, fan, fanatic, follower, supporter

enthusiastic adj = **keen**, avid, eager, fervent, gung ho (sl), passionate, vigorous, wholehearted, zealous

entice v = **attract**, allure, cajole, coax, lead on, lure, persuade, seduce, tempt

entire adj = **whole**, complete, full, gross, total

entirely adv = **completely**, absolutely, altogether, fully, in every respect,

en·ti·ty [EN-ti-tee] *n, pl* **-ties 1** thing's being or existence. **2** reality. **3** thing having real existence.

en·to·mol·o·gy [en-tə-MOL-ə-jee] *n* study of insects. **en·to·mol'o·gist** *n*

en·tou·rage [ahn-tuu-RAHZH] *n* **1** associates, retinue. **2** surroundings.

en·trails [EN-traylz] *pl n* **1** bowels, intestines. **2** inner parts.

en·trance¹ *n* see ENTER.

en·trance² [en-TRANS] *vt* **-tranced, -tranc·ing 1** delight. **2** throw into a trance.

en·treat [en-TREET] *vt* **1** ask earnestly. **2** beg, implore. **en·treat'y** *n, pl* **-treat·ies** earnest request.

en·trée [AHN-tray] *n* **1** main course of meal. **2** right of access, admission.

en·trench' *vt* **1** establish in fortified position with trenches. **2** establish firmly.

en·tre·pre·neur [ahn-trə-prə-NUR] *n* person who attempts to profit by risk and initiative.

en·tro·py [EN-trə-pee] *n* **1** unavailability of the heat energy of a system for mechanical work. **2** measurement of this.

en·trust' *vt* **1** commit, charge with. **2** put into care or protection of.

en·twine [en-TWĪN] *vt* **-twined, -twin·ing 1** interweave. **2** wreathe with. **3** embrace.

e·nu·mer·ate [i-NOO-mə-rayt] *vt* **-at·ed, -at·ing 1** mention one by one. **2** count. **e·nu·mer·a'tion** *n* **e·nu'mer·a·tor** *n*

e·nun·ci·ate [i-NUN-see-ayt] *vt* **-at·ed, -at·ing 1** state clearly. **2** proclaim. **3** pronounce. **e·nun·ci·a'tion** *n*

en·vel·op [en-VEL-əp] *vt* **1** wrap up, enclose, surround. **2** encircle. **en·vel'op·ment** *n*

en·ve·lope [EN-və-lohp] *n* **1** folded, gummed cover of letter. **2** covering, wrapper.

en·ven·om [en-VEN-əm] *vt* **1** put poison, venom in. **2** embitter.

en·vi·ron [en-VĪ-rən] *vt* **1** surround. **en·vi'ron·ment** *n* **2** conditions of life or growth.

thoroughly, totally, utterly, wholly

entitle *v* **1** = **give the right to**, allow, authorize, empower, enable, license, permit **2** = **call**, christen, dub, label, name, term, title

entity *n* = **thing**, being, creature, individual, object, organism, substance

entourage *n* = **retinue**, associates, attendants, company, court, escort, followers, staff, train

entrails *pl n* = **intestines**, bowels, guts, innards (*inf*), insides (*inf*), offal, viscera

entrance¹ *n* **1** = **way in**, access, door, doorway, entry, gate, opening, passage **2** = **appearance**, arrival, coming in, entry, introduction **3** = **admission**, access, admittance, entrée, entry, permission to enter

entrance² *v* **1** = **enchant**, bewitch, captivate, charm, delight, enrapture, enthrall, fascinate **2** = **mesmerize**, hypnotize, put in a trance

entrant *n* = **competitor**, candidate, contestant, entry, participant, player

entreaty *n* = **plea**, appeal, earnest request, exhortation, petition, prayer, request, supplication

entrenched *adj* = **fixed**, deep-rooted, deep-seated, ineradicable, ingrained, rooted, set, unshakable, well-established

entrepreneur *n* = **businessman** or **businesswoman**, impresario, industrialist, magnate, tycoon

entrust *v* = **give custody of**, assign, commit, confide, delegate, deliver, hand over, turn over

entry *n* **1** = **way in**, access, door, doorway, entrance, gate, opening, passage **2** = **coming in**, appearance, entering, entrance, initiation, introduction **3** = **admission**, access, entrance, entrée, permission to enter **4** = **record**, account, item, listing, note

entwine *v* = **twist**, interlace, interweave, knit, plait, twine, weave, wind

enumerate *v* = **list**, cite, itemize, mention, name, quote, recite, recount, relate, spell out

enunciate *v* **1** = **pronounce**, articulate, enounce, say, sound, speak, utter, vocalize, voice **2** = **state**, declare, proclaim, promulgate, pronounce, propound, publish

envelop *v* = **enclose**, cloak, cover, encase, encircle, engulf, shroud, surround, wrap

envelope *n* = **wrapping**, case, casing, cover, covering, jacket, wrapper

enviable *adj* = **desirable**, advantageous, favored, fortunate, lucky, privileged, to die for (*inf*), win-win (*inf*)

envious *adj* = **covetous**, green with envy, grudging, jealous, resentful en·vi·ron·men·tal *adj* en·vi·ron·men·tal·ist *n* ecologist. **en·vi·rons** *pl n* districts around (town, etc.), outskirts.

en·vis·age [en-VIZ-ij] *vt* **-aged, -ag·ing 1** conceive of as possibility. **2** visualize.

en·voy [EN-voi] *n* **1** messenger, representative. **2** diplomatic agent of rank below ambassador.

en·vy [EN-vee] *n, pl* **-vies 1** bitter contemplation of another's good fortune. **2** object of this feeling. ◆ *vt* **-vied, -vy·ing** grudge another's good fortune, success or qualities. **3** feel envy of. **en·vi·a·ble** *adj* arousing envy. **en·vi·ous** *adj* full of envy.

en·zyme [EN-zīm] *n* any of group of complex proteins produced by living cells and acting as catalysts in biochemical reactions.

e·on [EE-ən] *n* age, very long period of time.

ep·au·lette [EP-ə-let] *n* shoulder ornament on uniform.

Eph. Ephesians.

e·phem·er·al [i-FEM-ər-əl] *adj* short-lived, transient. **e·phem·er·a** [i-FEM-ər-ə] *pl n* items designed to last only for a short time, such as programmes or posters.

epi-, eph- (or before a vowel) **ep-** *prefix* upon, during, e.g. *epitaph; ephemeral; epoch.*

ep·ic [EP-ik] *n* **1** long poem or story telling of achievements of hero or heroes. **2** film, etc. about heroic deeds. ◆ *adj* **3** of, like, an epic. **4** impressive, grand.

ep·i·cene [EP-i-seen] *adj* **1** common to both sexes. **2** effeminate. **3** weak. ◆ *n* **4** epicene person or thing.

ep·i·cen·ter [EP-i-sen-tər] *n* focus of earthquake.

ep·i·cure [EP-i-kyuur] *n* one delighting in

eating and drinking. **ep·i·cu·re·an** *adj* **1** of Epicurus, who taught that pleasure, in the shape of practice of virtue, was highest good. **2** given to refined sensuous enjoyment. ◆ *n* **3** such person or philosopher. **ep·i·cu·re·an·ism** *n*

ep·i·dem·ic [ep-i-DEM-ik] *adj* (esp. of disease) prevalent and spreading rapidly. **1** widespread. ◆ *n*

ep·i·der·mis [ep-i-DUR-mis] *n* outer skin.

ep·i·du·ral [ep-i-DUUR-əl] *n, adj* (of) spinal anesthetic used esp. for relief of pain during childbirth.

ep·i·glot·tis [ep-i-GLOT-is] *n, pl* **-tis·es** cartilage that covers opening of larynx in swallowing. **ep·i·glot·tal** [-GLOT-əl] *adj*

ep·i·gone [EP-i-gohn] *n* imitative follower.

ep'i·gram *n* concise, witty poem or saying. **ep·i·gram·mat·ic** [-grə-MAT-ik] *adj* **ep·i·gram'ma·tist** [-GRAM-ə-tist] *n*

ep·i·graph [EP-i-graf] *n* inscription.

ep·i·lep·sy [EP-ə-lep-see] *n* disorder of nervous system causing convulsions. **ep·i·lep'tic** *n* **1** sufferer from this. ◆ *adj* **2** of, subject to, this.

ep·i·logue [EP-ə-lawg] *n* short speech or poem at end, esp. of play.

E·piph·a·ny [i-PIF-ə-nee] *n, pl* **-nies 1** festival of the announcement of Christ to the Magi, celebrated January 6. **2** (e-) sudden intuitive perception or insight.

e·pis·co·pal [i-PIS-kə-pəl] *adj* **1** of bishop. **2** ruled by bishops. **e·pis'co·pa·cy** [-pə-see] *n* government by body of bishops. **E·pis·co·pa'li·an** [-PAYL-yən] *adj, n* (member, adherent) of Episcopalian church. **e·pis'co·pate** [-kə-pit] *n* **1** bishop's office, see, or duration of office. **2** body of bishops.

ep·i·sode [EP-ə-sohd] *n* **1** incident. **2**

environment *n* = surroundings, atmosphere, background, conditions, habitat, medium, setting, situation

environmental *adj* = ecological, green

environmentalist *n* = conservationist, ecologist, green

environs *pl n* = surrounding area, district, locality, neighborhood, outskirts, precincts, suburbs, vicinity

envisage *v* **1** = imagine, conceive (of), conceptualize, contemplate, fancy, picture, think up, visualize **2** = foresee, anticipate, envision, predict, see

envoy *n* = messenger, agent, ambassador,

courier, delegate, diplomat, emissary, intermediary, representative

envy *n* **1** = covetousness, enviousness, jealousy, resentfulness, resentment ◆ *v* **2** = covet, be envious (of), begrudge, be jealous (of), grudge, resent

ephemeral *adj* = brief, fleeting, momentary, passing, short-lived, temporary, transient, transitory

epidemic *n* = spread, contagion, growth, outbreak, plague, rash, upsurge, wave

epigram *n* = witticism, aphorism, bon mot, quip

epilogue *n* = conclusion, coda, concluding

section of (serialized) book, TV program, etc. **ep·i·sod·ic** [-SOD-ik] *adj*

e·pis·te·mol·o·gy [i-pis-tə-MOL-ə-jee] *n* study of source, nature and limitations of knowledge. **e·pis·te·mo·log·i·cal** *adj*

e·pis·tle [i-PIS-əl] *n* **1** letter, esp. of apostle. **2** poem in letter form. **e·pis·to·lar·y** [-tə-ler-ee] *adj*

e·pi·taph [EP-i-taf] *n* memorial inscription on tomb.

ep·i·thet [EP-ə-thet] *n* additional, descriptive word or name.

e·pit·o·me [i-PIT-ə-mee] *n* **1** embodiment, typical example. **2** summary. **e·pit·o·mize** [-ə-mīz] *vt* **-mized, -miz·ing** typify.

ep·och [EP-ək] *n* **1** beginning of period. **2** period, era, esp. one of notable events. **ep·o·chal** [-ə-kəl] *adj*

eq·ua·ble [EK-wə-bəl] *adj* **1** even-tempered, placid. **2** uniform, not easily disturbed. **eq·ua·bly** *adv* **eq·ua·bil·i·ty** *n*

e·qual [EE-kwəl] *adj* **1** the same in number, size, merit, etc. **2** identical. **3** fit or qualified. **4** evenly balanced. ◆ *n* **5** one equal to another. ◆ *vt* **6** be equal to. **e·qual·i·ty** [i-KWOL-i-tee] *n, pl* **-ties 1** state of being equal. **2** uniformity. **e'qual·ize** *v*

-ized, -iz·ing make, become, equal. **e'qual·ly** *adv* **equal opportunity** nondiscrimination as to sex, race, etc. in employment, pay, etc.

e·qua·nim·i·ty [ee-kwə-NIM-i-tee] *n* calmness, composure, steadiness.

e·quate [i-KWAYT] *vt* **-quat·ed, -quat·ing 1** make equal. **2** bring to a common standard. **e·qua'tion** [-zhən] *n* **1** equating of two mathematical expressions. **2** balancing.

e·qua·tor [i-KWAY-tər] *n* imaginary circle around Earth equidistant from the poles. **e·qua·to·ri·al** [ee-kwə-TOR-ee-əl] *adj*

e·ques·tri·an [i-KWES-tree-ən] *adj* **1** of, skilled in, horseback riding. **2** mounted on horse. ◆ *n* **3** rider.

equi- *comb. form* equal, at equal, e.g. *equidistant.*

e·qui·an·gu·lar [ee-kwee-ANG-gyə-lər] *adj* having equal angles.

e·qui·lat·er·al [ee-kwə-LAT-ər-əl] *adj* having equal sides.

e·qui·lib·ri·um [ee-kwə-LIB-ree-əm] *n* state of steadiness, equipoise or stability.

e·quine [EE-kwīn] *adj* of, like a horse.

e·qui·nox [EE-kwə-noks] *n* **1** time when sun crosses equator and day and night are

———————— THESAURUS ————————

speech, postscript

episode *n* **1** = **event**, adventure, affair, escapade, experience, happening, incident, matter, occurrence **2** = **part**, chapter, installment, passage, scene, section

epistle *n* = **letter**, communication, message, missive, note

epitaph *n* = **monument**, inscription

epithet *n* = **name**, appellation, description, designation, moniker or monicker (*sl*), nickname, sobriquet, tag, title

epitome *n* = **personification**, archetype, embodiment, essence, quintessence, representation, type, typical example

epitomize *v* = **typify**, embody, exemplify, illustrate, personify, represent, symbolize

epoch *n* = **era**, age, date, period, time

equable *adj* = **even-tempered**, calm, composed, easy-going, imperturbable, level-headed, placid, serene, unflappable (*inf*)

equal *adj* **1** = **identical**, alike, corresponding, equivalent, the same, uniform **2** = **regular**, symmetrical, uniform, unvarying **3** = **even**, balanced, evenly

matched, fifty-fifty (*inf*) **4** = **fair**, egalitarian, even-handed, impartial, just, on a level playing field (*inf*), unbiased **5 equal to** = **capable of**, competent to, fit for, good enough for, ready for, strong enough, suitable for, up to ◆ *n* **6** = **match**, counterpart, equivalent, rival, twin ◆ *v* **7** = **match**, amount to, be tantamount to, correspond to, equate, level, parallel, tie with

equality *n* **1** = **sameness**, balance, correspondence, equivalence, evenness, identity, likeness, similarity, uniformity **2** = **fairness**, egalitarianism, equal opportunity, parity

equalize *v* = **make equal**, balance, equal, even up, level, match, regularize, smooth, square, standardize

equate *v* = **make** or **be equal**, be commensurate, compare, correspond with or to, liken, mention in the same breath, parallel

equation *n* = **equating**, comparison, correspondence, parallel

equilibrium *n* = **stability**, balance, equipoise, evenness, rest, steadiness, equal. 2 either point at which sun crosses equator.

e·quip [i-KWIP] vt **-quipped, -quip·ping** supply, fit out, array. **e·quip'ment** n

eq·ui·poise [EK-wə-poiz] n 1 perfect balance. 2 counterpoise. 3 equanimity.

eq·ui·ty [EK-wə-tee] n, pl **-ties** 1 fairness. 2 use of principles of justice to supplement law. 3 system of law so made. **eq'ui·ta·ble** adj fair, reasonable, just.

e·quiv·a·lent [i-KWIV-ə-lənt] adj 1 equal in value. 2 having the same meaning or result. 3 tantamount. 4 corresponding. **e·quiv'a·lence** n **e·quiv'a·len·cy** n

e·quiv·o·cal [i-KWIV-ə-kəl] adj 1 of double or doubtful meaning. 2 questionable. 3 liable to suspicion. **e·quiv'o·cate** vi **-cat·ed, -cat·ing** use equivocal words to mislead. **e·quiv·o·ca'tion** n

Er Chem. erbium.

e·ra [EER-ə] n 1 system of time in which years are numbered from particular event. 2 time of the event. 3 memorable date, period.

e·rad·i·cate [i-RAD-i-kayt] vt **-cat·ed, -cat·ing** 1 wipe out, exterminate. 2 root out. **e·rad'i·ca·ble** adj **e·rad·i·ca'tion** n

e·rase [i-RAYS] vt **-rased, -ras·ing** 1 rub out. 2 remove, e.g. recording from magnetic tape. **e·ra'ser** n **e·ra'sure** [-shər] n

ere [air] prep, conj Poet. 1 before. 2 sooner than.

e·rect [i-REKT] adj 1 upright. ♦ vt 2 set up. 3 build. **e·rec'tile** [-tl] adj **e·rec'tion** n esp. an erect penis. **e·rec'tor** n

erg [urg] n cgs unit of work or energy.

er·go·nom·ics [ur-gə-NOM-iks] n study of relationship between workers and their environment.

er·got [UR-gət] n 1 disease of grain. 2 diseased seed used as drug. **er'got·ism** n disease caused by eating ergot-infested grain.

er·mine [UR-min] n 1 weasel in northern regions, esp. in winter. 2 its white winter fur.

e·rode [i-ROHD] vt **-rod·ed, -rod·ing** 1 wear away. 2 eat into. **e·ro'sion** [-zhən] n

e·rog·e·nous [i-ROJ-ə-nəs] adj sensitive to sexual stimulation.

e·rot·ic [i-ROT-ik] adj relating to, or treating of, sexual pleasure. **e·rot'i·ca** [-ə-kə] n sexual literature or art. **e·rot'i·cism** [-ə-sizm] n

err [er] vi 1 make mistakes. 2 be wrong. 3 sin. **er·rat·ic** [i-RAT-ik] adj irregular in movement, conduct, etc. **er·rat'i·cal·ly** adv **er·ra·tum** [i-RAH-təm] n, pl **-ta** [-tə] printing mistake noted for correction. **er·ro·ne·ous** [i-ROH-nee-əs] adj mistaken, wrong. **er'ror** n 1 mistake. 2 wrong opinion. 3 sin.

———————— THESAURUS ————————

symmetry

equip v = supply, arm, array, fit out, furnish, provide, stock

equipment n = tools, accouterments, apparatus, gear, paraphernalia, stuff, supplies, tackle

equitable adj = fair, even-handed, honest, impartial, just, proper, reasonable, unbiased

equivalence n = equality, correspondence, evenness, parity, sameness, similarity

equivalent n 1 = equal, counterpart, match, opposite number, parallel, twin ♦ adj 2 = equal, alike, commensurate, comparable, corresponding, interchangeable, of a piece, on a level playing field (inf), same, similar, tantamount

equivocal adj = ambiguous, evasive, indefinite, indeterminate, misleading, oblique, obscure, uncertain, vague

era n = age, date, day or days, epoch,

generation, period, time

eradicate v = wipe out, annihilate, destroy, eliminate, erase, exterminate, extinguish, obliterate, remove, root out

erase v = wipe out, blot, cancel, delete, expunge, obliterate, remove, rub out

erect v 1 = build, construct, put up, raise, set up 2 = found, create, establish, form, initiate, institute, organize, set up ♦ adj 3 = upright, elevated, perpendicular, pricked-up, stiff, straight, vertical

erode v = wear down or away, abrade, consume, corrode, destroy, deteriorate, disintegrate, eat away, grind down

erosion n = deterioration, abrasion, attrition, destruction, disintegration, eating away, grinding down, wearing down or away

erotic adj = sexual, amatory, carnal, lustful, seductive, sensual, sexy (inf), voluptuous

err v = make a mistake, blunder, go wrong, miscalculate, misjudge, mistake, slip up (inf)

er·rand [ER-ənd] n **1** short journey for simple business. **2** the business, mission of messenger. **3** purpose.

er·rant [ER-ənt] adj **1** wandering in search of adventure. **2** erring. **er'ran·cy** n, pl -**cies** erring state or conduct. **er'rant·ry** n, pl -**ries** state or conduct of knight errant.

erst·while [URST-hwīl] adj of times past, former.

er·u·dite [ER-yə-dīt] adj learned. **er·u·di'tion** [-DISH-ən] n learning.

e·rupt [i-RUPT] vi burst out. **e·rup'tion** n **1** bursting out, esp. volcanic outbreak. **2** rash on the skin.

er·y·sip·e·las [er-ə-SIP-ə-ləs] n acute skin infection.

Es Chem. einsteinium.

es·ca·late [ES-kə-layt] v -**lat·ed**, -**lat·ing** increase, be increased, in extent, intensity, etc.

es·ca·la·tor [ES-kə-lay-tər] n moving staircase.

es·cape [i-SKAYP] v -**caped**, -**cap·ing** ♦ vi **1** get free. **2** get off safely. **3** go unpunished. **4** find way out. ♦ vt **5** elude. **6** be forgotten by. ♦ n **7** escaping. **es'ca·pade** n wild (mischievous) adventure. **es·cap'ism** [-KAYP-izm] n taking refuge in fantasy to avoid facing disagreeable facts.

es·carp·ment [i-SKAHRP-mənt] n steep hillside.

es·cha·tol·o·gy [es-kə-TOL-ə-jee] n study of death, judgment and last things. **es·cha·to·log'i·cal** adj

es·chew [es-CHOO] vt avoid, abstain from, shun.

es·cort [ES-kort] n **1** armed guard for traveler, etc. **2** person or persons accompanying another. **es·cort'** vt

es·cri·toire [es-kri-TWAHR] n type of writing desk.

es·cutch·eon [i-SKUCH-ən] n **1** shield with coat of arms. **2** ornamental plate around keyhole, etc.

Es·ki·mo [ES-kə-moh] n, pl -**mos** **1** member of the aboriginal race inhabiting N Canada, Greenland, Alaska, and E Siberia. **2** their language. Note that many of the peoples traditionally called **Eskimos** prefer to call themselves **Inuit**.

e·soph·a·gus [i-SOF-ə-gəs] n, pl -**gi** [-jī] canal from mouth to stomach. **1** gullet. **e·soph·a·ge'al** [-JEE-əl] adj

es·o·ter·ic [es-ə-TER-ik] adj **1** abstruse, obscure. **2** secret. **3** restricted to initiates.

ESP extrasensory perception.

es·pal·ier [i-SPAL-yər] n **1** shrub, (fruit) tree trained to grow flat, as against wall, etc. **2** trellis for this.

es·pe·cial [i-SPESH-əl] adj **1** preeminent, more than ordinary. **2** particular. **es·pe'cial·ly** adv

---

THESAURUS

errand n = **job**, charge, commission, message, mission, task

erratic adj = **unpredictable**, changeable, inconsistent, irregular, uneven, unreliable, unstable, variable, wayward

erroneous adj = **incorrect**, fallacious, false, faulty, flawed, invalid, mistaken, unsound, wrong

error n = **mistake**, bloomer (inf), blunder, miscalculation, oversight, slip, solecism

erstwhile adj = **former**, bygone, late, old, once, one-time, past, previous, sometime

erudite adj = **learned**, cultivated, cultured, educated, knowledgeable, scholarly, well-educated, well-read

erupt v **1** = **explode**, belch forth, blow up, burst out, gush, pour forth, spew forth or out, spout, throw off **2** Medical = **break out**, appear

eruption n **1** = **explosion**, discharge, ejection, flare-up, outbreak, outburst **2** Medical = **inflammation**, outbreak, rash

escalate v = **increase**, expand, extend, grow, heighten, intensify, mount, rise

escapade n = **adventure**, antic, caper, prank, scrape (inf), stunt

escape v **1** = **get away**, abscond, bolt, break free or out, flee, fly, make one's getaway, run away or off, slip away **2** = **avoid**, dodge, duck, elude, evade, pass, shun, slip **3** = **leak**, emanate, exude, flow, gush, issue, pour forth, seep ♦ n **4** = **getaway**, break, break-out, flight **5** = **avoidance**, circumvention, evasion **6** = **relaxation**, distraction, diversion, pastime, recreation **7** = **leak**, emanation, emission, seepage

escort n **1** = **guard**, bodyguard, convoy, cortege, entourage, retinue, train **2** = **companion**, attendant, beau, chaperon, guide, partner ♦ v **3** = **accompany**, chaperon, conduct, guide, lead, partner, shepherd, usher

especial adj Formal = **exceptional**, noteworthy, outstanding, principal, special, uncommon, unusual

Es•pe•ran•to [es-pə-RAHN-toh] *n* artificial language designed for universal use.

es•pi•o•nage [ES-pee-ə-nah*zh*] *n* **1** spying. **2** use of secret agents.

es•pla•nade [ES-plə-nahd] *n* level space, esp. one used as public promenade.

es•pouse [i-SPOWZ] *vt* -poused, -pous•ing **1** support, embrace (cause, etc.). **2** marry. **es•pous'al** *n*

es•pres•so [e-SPRES-oh] *n* **1** strong coffee made by forcing steam through ground coffee beans. **2** cup of espresso.

es•prit [e-SPREE] *n* **1** spirit. **2** animation. **esprit de corps** [də kor] attachment, loyalty to the society, etc., one belongs to.

es•py [i-SPĪ] *vt* -pied, -py•ing catch sight of.

es•quire [ES-kwīr] *n* **1** gentleman's courtesy title used on letters. **2** formerly, a squire.

es•say *n* **1** prose composition. **2** short treatise. **3** attempt. **es•say'** *vt* -sayed, -say'ing **1** try, attempt. **2** test. **es•say•ist** *n*

es•sence [ES-əns] *n* **1** all that makes thing what it is. **2** existence, being. **3** entity, reality. **4** extract got by distillation. **es•sen•tial** [ə-SEN-shəl] *adj* **1** necessary, indispensable. **2** inherent. **3** of, constituting essence of thing. ◆ *n* **4** indispensable element. **5** chief point.

es•tab•lish [i-STAB-lish] *vt* **1** make secure. **2** set up. **3** settle. **4** prove. **es•tab'lish•ment** *n* **1** establishing. **2** permanent organized body. **3** place of business together with its employees, equipment, etc. **4** household. **5** public institution. **established church** church officially recognized as national institution. **the Establishment** *n* group, class of people holding authority within a profession, society, etc.

es•tate [i-STAYT] *n* **1** landed property. **2** person's property. **3** deceased person's property. **4** class as part of nation. **5** rank, state, condition of life.

es•teem [i-STEEM] *vt* **1** think highly of. **2** consider. ◆ *n* **3** favorable opinion, regard, respect.

es•ter [ES-tər] *n Chem.* organic compound produced by reaction between acid and alcohol.

es•ti•mate [ES-tə-mayt] *vt* -mat•ed, -mat•ing **1** form approximate idea of (amounts, measurements, etc.). **2** form opinion of. **3** quote probable price for. ◆ *n* [-mit] **4** approximate judgment of amounts, size, etc. **5** amount, etc., arrived at. **6** opinion. **7** price quoted by contractor. **es'ti•ma•ble** *adj* worthy of regard.

———— THESAURUS ————

especially *adv* = **exceptionally**, conspicuously, markedly, notably, outstandingly, remarkably, specially, strikingly, uncommonly, unusually

espionage *n* = **spying**, counter-intelligence, intelligence, surveillance, undercover work

espousal *n* = **support**, adoption, advocacy, backing, championing, championship, defense, embracing, promotion, taking up

espouse *v* = **support**, adopt, advocate, back, champion, embrace, promote, stand up for, take up, uphold

essay *n* **1** = **composition**, article, discourse, dissertation, paper, piece, tract, treatise ◆ *v* **2** *Formal* = **attempt**, aim, endeavor, try, undertake

essence *n* **1** = **fundamental nature**, being, core, heart, nature, quintessence, soul, spirit, substance **2** = **concentrate**, distillate, extract, spirits, tincture

essential *adj* **1** = **vital**, crucial, important, indispensable, necessary, needed, requisite **2** = **fundamental**, basic, cardinal, elementary, innate, intrinsic, main,

principal ◆ *n* **3** = **prerequisite**, basic, fundamental, must, necessity, rudiment, *sine qua non*

establish *v* **1** = **create**, constitute, form, found, ground, inaugurate, institute, settle, set up **2** = **prove**, authenticate, certify, confirm, corroborate, demonstrate, substantiate, verify

establishment *n* **1** = **creation**, formation, foundation, founding, inauguration, installation, institution, organization, setting up **2** = **organization**, business, company, concern, corporation, enterprise, firm, institution, outfit (*inf*) **3 the Establishment** = **the authorities**, ruling class, the powers that be, the system

estate *n* **1** = **lands**, area, domain, holdings, manor, property **2** *Law* = **property**, assets, belongings, effects, fortune, goods, possessions, wealth

esteem *n* **1** = **respect**, admiration, credit, estimation, good opinion, honor, kudos, regard, reverence, veneration ◆ *v* **2** = **respect**, admire, love, prize, regard highly, revere, think highly of, treasure, value **3** = **consider**, believe, deem, estimate, judge,

es·ti·ma'tion *n* opinion, judgment, esteem.

es·ti·vate [ES-tə-vayt] *vi* -**vat·ed**, -**vat·ing** spend the summer.

es·trange [i-STRAYNJ] *vt* -**tranged**, -**trang·ing 1** lose affection of. **2** alienate. **es·trange'ment** *n*

es·tro·gen [ES-trə-jən] *n* hormone in females esp. controlling changes, cycles, in reproductive organs. **es·tro·gen·ic** *adj*

es·tu·ar·y [ES-choo-er-ee] *n, pl* -**ar·ies** tidal mouth of river, inlet.

e-tail *n* selling of goods via the Internet.

etc. et cetera.

et cet·er·a [et SET-ər-ə] **1** and the rest, and others. **2** or the like. **etceteras** *pl n* miscellaneous extra things or people.

etch [ech] *vt* **1** make engraving by eating away surface of metal plate with acids, etc. **2** imprint vividly. **etch'er** *n* **etch'ing** *n*

e·ter·nal [i-TUR-nəl] *adj* **1** without beginning or end. **2** everlasting. **3** changeless. **e·ter'ni·ty** *n, pl* -**ties**

e·ther [EE-thər] *n* **1** colorless volatile liquid used as anesthetic. **2** intangible fluid formerly supposed to fill all space. **3** the clear sky, region above clouds. **e·the·re·al** [i-THEER-ee-əl] *adj* **1** light, airy. **2** heavenly, spirit-like.

eth·i·cal [ETH-i-kəl] *adj* relating to morals. **eth'i·cal·ly** *adv* **eth'ics** *n* **1** science of morals. **2** moral principles, rules of conduct.

eth·nic [ETH-nik] *adj* of race or relating to classification of humans into social, cultural, etc., groups. **eth·nog'ra·phy** [-NOG-rə-fee] *n* description of human races. **eth·nol'o·gy** *n* study of human races. **ethnic cleansing** expulsion or extermination of other ethnic groups by the dominant ethnic group in an area.

e·thos [EE-thos] *n* distinctive character, spirit, etc. of people, culture, etc.

eth·yl [ETH-əl] *n* of, consisting of, or containing the hydrocarbon group C_2H_5. **eth'y·lene** [-leen] *n* poisonous gas used as anesthetic and fuel.

e·ti·ol·o·gy [ee-tee-OL-ə-jee] *n, pl* -**gies** study of causes, esp. inquiry into origin of disease. **e·ti·o·log'i·cal** *adj*

et·i·quette [ET-i-kit] *n* conventional code of conduct or behavior.

é·tude [AY-tood] *n* short musical composition, study, intended often as technical exercise.

et·y·mol·o·gy [et-ə-MOL-ə-jee] *n* **1** tracing, account of, formation of word's origin, development. **2** study of this. **et·y·mo·log'i·cal** *adj* **et·y·mol'o·gist** *n*

eu-, ev- *comb. form* well, e.g. *eugenic; euphony; evangelist.*

Eu *Chem.* europium.

eu·ca·lyp·tus [yoo-kə-LIP-təs] *n* mostly Aust. genus of tree, the gum tree, yielding timber and oil, used medicinally from leaves.

—————{ THESAURUS }—————

reckon, regard, think, view

estimate *v* **1 = calculate roughly,** assess, evaluate, gauge, guess, judge, number, reckon, value **2 = form an opinion,** believe, conjecture, consider, judge, rank, rate, reckon, surmise ◆ *n* **3 = approximate calculation,** assessment, ballpark figure (*inf*), guess, guesstimate (*inf*), judgment, valuation **4 = opinion,** appraisal, assessment, belief, estimation, judgment

estimation *n* **= opinion,** appraisal, appreciation, assessment, belief, consideration, considered opinion, judgment, view

estuary *n* **= inlet,** creek, firth, fjord, mouth

et cetera *adv* **1 = and so on,** and so forth ◆ *n* **2 = and the rest,** and others, and the like, et al.

etch *v* **= cut,** carve, eat into, engrave, impress, imprint, inscribe, stamp

etching *n* **= print,** carving, engraving,

impression, imprint, inscription

eternal *adj* **1 = everlasting,** endless, immortal, infinite, never-ending, perpetual, timeless, unceasing, unending **2 = permanent,** deathless, enduring, immutable, imperishable, indestructible, lasting, unchanging

eternity *n* **1 = infinity,** ages, endlessness, immortality, perpetuity, timelessness **2** *Theology* **= the afterlife,** heaven, paradise, the hereafter, the next world

ethical *adj* **= moral,** conscientious, fair, good, honorable, just, principled, proper, right, upright, virtuous

ethics *pl n* **= moral code,** conscience, morality, moral philosophy, moral values, principles, rules of conduct, standards

ethnic *adj* **= cultural,** folk, indigenous, national, native, racial, traditional

etiquette *n* **= good** *or* **proper behavior,** civility, courtesy, decorum, formalities,

Eu·cha·rist [YOO-kə-rist] *n* **1** Christian sacrament of the Lord's Supper. **2** the consecrated elements. **3** (e-) thanksgiving.

eu·gen·ic [yoo-JEN-ik] *adj* relating to, or tending toward, production of fine offspring. **eu·gen·ics** *n* this science.

eu·lo·gy [YOO-lə-jee] *n, pl* **-gies 1** speech or writing in praise of person esp. dead person. **2** praise. **eu·lo·gist** *n* **eu·lo·gize** [-jīz] *vt* **-gized, -giz·ing**

eu·nuch [YOO-nək] *n* castrated man, esp. formerly one employed in harem.

eu·phe·mism [YOO-fə-miz-əm] *n* **1** substitution of mild term for offensive or hurtful one. **2** instance of this. **eu·phe·mis·tic** *adj* **eu·phe·mis·ti·cal·ly** *adv*

eu·pho·ny [YOO-fə-nee] *n, pl* **-nies** pleasantness of sound. **eu·phon·ic** [-FON-ik] *adj* **eu·pho·ni·ous** [-FOH-nee-əs] *adj* pleasing to ear.

eu·pho·ria [yoo-FOR-ee-ə] *n* sense of well-being or elation. **eu·phor·ic** *adj*

eu·phu·ism [YOO-fyoo-iz-əm] *n* affected high-flown manner of writing, esp. in imitation of Lyly's *Euphues* (1580). **eu·phu·is·tic** *adj*

Eu·ra·sian [yuu-RAY-zhən] *adj* **1** of mixed European and Asiatic descent. **2** of Europe and Asia. ◆ *n* **3** one of this descent.

eu·re·ka [yuu-REE-kə] *interj* exclamation of triumph at finding something.

eu·ro *n, pl* **eu·ros** unit of the single currency of the European Union.

Euro- *comb. form* Europe or European, e.g. *Euroland.*

Eu·ro·land *n* (also **Eurozone**) the countries within the European Union that have adopted the euro.

Eu·ro·pe·an [yuur-ə-PEE-ən] *n, adj* (native) of Europe. **European Union** (also **EU**) economic and political association of a number of European nations.

Eu·sta·chian tube [yoo-STAY-shən] passage leading from pharynx to middle ear.

eu·tha·na·sia [yoo-thə-NAY-zhə] *n* **1** gentle, painless death. **2** putting to death in this way, esp. to relieve suffering.

e·vac·u·ate [i-VAK-yoo-ayt] *vt* **-at·ed, -at·ing 1** empty. **2** withdraw from. **3** discharge. **e·vac·u·a'tion** *n* **e·vac·u·ee'** *n* person moved from dangerous area esp. in time of war.

e·vade [i-VAYD] *vt* **-vad·ed, -vad·ing 1** avoid, escape from. **2** elude. **e·va'sion** [-zhən] *n* **1** subterfuge. **2** excuse. **3** equivocation. **e·va'sive** *adj* elusive, not straightforward.

e·val·u·ate [i-VAL-yoo-ayt] *vt* **-at·ed, -at·ing** find or judge value of. **e·val·u·a'tion** *n*

ev·a·nesce [ev-ə-NES] *vi* **-nesced, -nesc·ing** fade away. **ev·a·nes'cence** *n* **ev·a·nes'cent** *adj* fleeting, transient.

e·van·gel·i·cal [ee-van-JEL-i-kəl] *adj* **1** of, or according to, gospel teaching. **2** of Protestant sect that stresses salvation by faith. ◆ *n* **3** member of evangelical sect. **e·van·ge·lism** *n* **e·van·ge·list** *n* **1** writer of one of the four gospels. **2** ardent, zealous preacher of the gospel. **3** revivalist. **e·van·ge·lize** *vt* **-lized, -liz·ing 1** preach gospel to. **2** convert.

e·vap·o·rate [i-VAP-ə-rayt] *v* **-rat·ed, -rat·ing** ◆ *vi* **1** turn into, pass off in, vapor. ◆ *vt* **2** turn into vapor. **e·vap·o·ra'tion** *n*

evasion see EVADE.

eve [eev] *n* **1** evening before (holiday, etc.). **2** time just before (event, etc.).

e·ven [EE-vən] *adj* **1** flat, smooth. **2** uniform in quality, equal in amount, balanced. **3** divisible by two. **4** impartial. ◆ *vt* **5** make even. **6** smooth. **7** equalize. ◆ *adv* **8**

——— THESAURUS ———

manners, politeness, propriety, protocol

euphoria *n* = **elation**, ecstasy, exaltation, exhilaration, intoxication, joy, jubilation, rapture

evacuate *v* = **clear**, abandon, desert, forsake, leave, move out, pull out, quit, vacate, withdraw

evade *v* **1** = **avoid**, dodge, duck, elude, escape, get away from, sidestep, steer clear of **2** = **avoid answering**, equivocate, fend off, fudge, hedge, parry

evaluate *v* = **assess**, appraise, calculate, estimate, gauge, judge, rate, reckon, size

up (*inf*), weigh

evaporate *v* **1** = **dry up**, dehydrate, desiccate, dry, vaporize **2** = **disappear**, dematerialize, dissolve, fade away, melt away, vanish

evasion *n* **1** = **avoidance**, dodging, escape **2** = **deception**, equivocation, evasiveness, prevarication

evasive *adj* = **deceptive**, cagey (*inf*), equivocating, indirect, oblique, prevaricating, shifty, slippery

eve *n* **1** = **night before**, day before, vigil **2** = **brink**, edge, point, threshold, verge equally. **9** simply. **10** notwithstanding. **11** (used to express emphasis).

eve·ning [EEV-ning] *n* **1** the close of day or early part of night. **2** decline, end.

e·vent [i-VENT] *n* **1** happening. **2** notable occurrence. **3** issue, result. **4** any one contest in series in sports program. **e·vent'ful** *adj* full of exciting events. **e·ven'tu·al** [-choo-əl] *adj* **1** resulting in the end. **2** ultimate. **3** final. **e·ven·tu·al'i·ty** [-AL-i-tee] *n* possible event. **e·ven'tu·ate** *vi* **-at·ed, -at·ing 1** turn out. **2** happen. **3** end.

ev·er [EV-ər] *adv* **1** always. **2** constantly. **3** at any time. **ev'er·green** *n, adj* (tree or shrub) bearing foliage throughout year. **ev·er·more'** *adv*

eve·ry [EV-ree] *adj* **1** each of all. **2** all possible. **eve'ry·bod·y** *pron* **eve'ry·day** *adj* usual, ordinary. **eve'ry·one** *pron* **eve'ry·thing** *pron, n* **eve'ry·where** *adv* in all places.

e·vict [i-VIKT] *vt* expel by legal process, turn out. **e·vic'tion** [-shən] *n*

ev·i·dent [EV-i-dənt] *adj* plain, obvious. **ev'i·dence** *n* **1** ground of belief. **2** sign, indication. **3** testimony. ◆ *vt* **-denced, -denc·ing** indicate, prove. **ev·i·den'tial** *adj* **ev'i·dent·ly** *adv* in evidence conspicuous.

e·vil [EE-vəl] *adj* **1** bad, harmful. ◆ *n* **2** what is bad or harmful. **3** sin. **e·vil·ly** *adv* **e·vil·do·er** *n* sinner.

e·vince [i-VINS] *vt* **-vinced, -vinc·ing** show,

THESAURUS

even *adj* **1** = **level**, flat, horizontal, parallel, smooth, steady, straight, true, uniform **2** = **regular**, constant, smooth, steady, unbroken, uniform, uninterrupted, unvarying, unwavering **3** = **equal**, comparable, fifty-fifty (*inf*), identical, level, like, matching, neck and neck, on a level playing field (*inf*), on a par, similar, tied **4** = **calm**, composed, cool, even-tempered, imperturbable, placid, unruffled, well-balanced **5 get even (with)** = **pay back**, give tit for tat, reciprocate, repay, requite, retaliate

evening *n* = **dusk**, gloaming (*Scot. or poetic*), twilight

event *n* **1** = **incident**, affair, business, circumstance, episode, experience, happening, occasion, occurrence **2** = **competition**, bout, contest, game, tournament

even-tempered *adj* = **calm**, composed, cool, imperturbable, level-headed, placid, tranquil, unexcitable, unruffled

eventful *adj* = **exciting**, active, busy, dramatic, full, lively, memorable, remarkable

eventual *adj* = **final**, concluding, overall, ultimate

eventuality *n* = **possibility**, case, chance, contingency, event, likelihood, probability

eventually *adv* = **in the end**, after all, at the end of the day, finally, one day, some time, ultimately, when all is said and done

ever *adv* **1** = **at any time**, at all, at any period, at any point, by any chance, in any case, on any occasion **2** = **always**, at all times, constantly, continually, evermore, for ever, perpetually, twenty-four-seven

(*sl*)

everlasting *adj* = **eternal**, endless, immortal, indestructible, never-ending, perpetual, timeless, undying

evermore *adv* = **for ever**, always, eternally, ever, to the end of time

every *adj* = **each**, all, each one

everybody *pron* = **everyone**, all and sundry, each one, each person, every person, one and all, the whole world

everyday *adj* = **common**, customary, mundane, ordinary, routine, stock, usual, workaday

everyone *pron* = **everybody**, all and sundry, each one, each person, every person, one and all, the whole world

everything *pron* = **all**, each thing, the lot, the whole lot

everywhere *adv* = **to** *or* **in every place,** all around, all over, far and wide *or* near, high and low, in every nook and cranny, the world over, ubiquitously

evict *v* = **expel**, boot out (*inf*), eject, kick out (*inf*), oust, remove, throw out, turn out

evidence *n* **1** = **proof**, confirmation, corroboration, demonstration, grounds, indication, sign, substantiation, testimony ◆ *v* **2** = **show**, demonstrate, display, exhibit, indicate, prove, reveal, signify, witness

evident *adj* = **obvious**, apparent, clear, manifest, noticeable, perceptible, plain, unmistakable, visible

evidently *adv* **1** = **obviously**, clearly, manifestly, plainly, undoubtedly, unmistakably, without question **2** = **apparently**, ostensibly, outwardly, seemingly, to all appearances indicate.

e·voke [i-VOHK] vt -voked, -vok·ing 1 draw forth. 2 call to mind. **ev·o·ca·tion** [ev-ə-KAY-shən] n **e·voc·a·tive** [i-VOK-ə-tiv] adj

e·volve [i-VOLV] v -volved, -volv·ing 1 develop or cause to develop gradually. ◆ vi 2 undergo slow changes in process of growth. **ev·o·lu·tion** [ev-ə-LOO-shən] n 1 evolving. 2 development of species from earlier forms. **ev·o·lu·tion·ar·y** adj **ev·o·lu·tion·ist** n one who supports theory of evolution.

ewe [yoo] n female sheep.

ew·er [YOO-ər] n pitcher with wide spout.

Ex. Exodus.

ex-, e-, ef- prefix out from, from, out of, formerly, e.g. exclaim; evade; effusive; exodus.

ex·ac·er·bate [ig-ZAS-ər-bayt] vt -bat·ed, -bat·ing aggravate, embitter, make worse. **ex·ac·er·ba·tion** n

ex·act [ig-ZAKT] adj 1 precise, accurate, strictly correct. ◆ vt 2 demand, extort. 3 insist upon. 4 enforce. **ex·act·ing** adj making rigorous or excessive demands. **ex·ac·tion** n 1 act of exacting. 2 that which is exacted, as excessive work, etc. 3 oppressive demand. **ex·act·ly** adv **ex·act·ness** n 1 accuracy. 2 precision.

ex·ag·ger·ate [ig-ZAJ-ə-rayt] vt -at·ed, -at·ing 1 magnify beyond truth, overstate. 2 enlarge. 3 overestimate. **ex·ag·ger·a'tion** n

ex·alt [ig-ZAWLT] vt 1 raise up. 2 praise. 3 make noble, dignify. **ex·al·ta·tion** [eg-zawl-TAY-shən] n 1 an exalting. 2 elevation in rank, dignity or position. 3 rapture.

ex·am·ine [ig-ZAM-in] vt -ined, -in·ing 1 investigate. 2 look at closely. 3 ask questions of. 4 test knowledge or proficiency of. 5 inquire into. **ex·am·i·na'tion** n **ex·am'in·er** n

ex·am·ple [ig-ZAM-pəl] n 1 thing illustrating general rule. 2 specimen. 3 model. 4 warning, precedent, instance.

ex·as·per·ate [ig-ZAS-pə-rayt] vt -at·ed,

evil n 1 = **wickedness**, badness, depravity, malignity, sin, vice, villainy, wrongdoing 2 = **harm**, affliction, disaster, hurt, ill, injury, mischief, misfortune, suffering, woe ◆ adj 3 = **wicked**, bad, depraved, immoral, malevolent, malicious, sinful, villainous 4 = **harmful**, calamitous, catastrophic, destructive, dire, disastrous, pernicious, ruinous 5 = **offensive**, foul, noxious, pestilential, unpleasant, vile

evoke v = **recall**, arouse, awaken, call, give rise to, induce, rekindle, stir up, summon up

evolution n = **development**, expansion, growth, increase, maturation, progress, unfolding, working out

evolve v = **develop**, expand, grow, increase, mature, progress, unfold, work out

exact adj 1 = **accurate**, correct, definite, faultless, precise, right, specific, true, unerring ◆ v 2 = **demand**, claim, command, compel, extort, extract, force

exacting adj = **demanding**, difficult, hard, harsh, rigorous, severe, strict, stringent, taxing, tough

exactly adv 1 = **precisely**, accurately, correctly, explicitly, faithfully, scrupulously, truthfully, unerringly 2 = **in every respect**, absolutely, indeed, precisely, quite,

specifically, to the letter

exactness n = **precision**, accuracy, correctness, exactitude, rigorousness, scrupulousness, strictness, veracity

exaggerate v = **overstate**, amplify, embellish, embroider, enlarge, overemphasize, overestimate

exaggeration n = **overstatement**, amplification, embellishment, enlargement, hyperbole, overemphasis, overestimation

exalt v 1 = **praise**, acclaim, extol, glorify, idolize, set on a pedestal, worship 2 = **raise**, advance, elevate, ennoble, honor, promote, upgrade

exaltation n 1 = **praise**, acclaim, glorification, idolization, reverence, tribute, worship 2 = **rise**, advancement, elevation, ennoblement, promotion, upgrading

exalted adj = **high-ranking**, dignified, eminent, grand, honored, lofty, prestigious

examination n 1 = **inspection**, analysis, exploration, interrogation, investigation, research, scrutiny, study, test 2 = **questioning**, inquiry, inquisition, probe, quiz, test

examine v 1 = **inspect**, analyze, explore, investigate, peruse, scrutinize, study, survey 2 = **question**, cross-examine, grill (inf), inquire, interrogate, quiz, test

-at·ing **1** irritate, enrage. **2** intensify, make worse. **ex·as·per·a'tion** n

ex·ca·vate [EKS-kə-vayt] vt **-vat·ed, -vat·ing 1** hollow out. **2** make hole by digging. **3** unearth. **ex·ca·va'tion** n

ex·ceed [ik-SEED] vt **1** be greater than. **2** do more than authorized. **3** go beyond. **4** surpass. **ex·ceed'ing·ly** adv **1** very. **2** greatly.

ex·cel [ik-SEL] v **-celled, -cel·ling ♦** vt **1** surpass, be better than. **♦** vi **2** be very good, preeminent. **ex'cel·lence** n **ex'cel·len·cy** n title borne by certain high officials. **ex'cel·lent** adj very good.

ex·cept [ik-SEPT] prep **1** not including. **2** but. **♦** vt **3** leave or take out. **4** exclude. **ex·cept'ing** prep not including. **ex·cep'tion** n **1** thing excepted, not included in a rule. **2** objection. **ex·cep'tion·a·ble** adj open to objection. **ex·cep'tion·al** adj not ordinary, esp. much above average.

ex·cerpt [EK-surpt] n quoted or extracted passage from book, etc. **ex·cerpt'** vt extract, quote (passage from book, etc.).

ex·cess [EK-ses] n **1** an exceeding. **2** amount by which thing exceeds. **3** too great amount. **4** intemperance or immoderate conduct. **ex·ces'sive** [-siv] adj

ex·change [iks-CHAYNJ] vt **-changed, -chang·ing 1** give (something) in return for something else. **2** barter. **♦** n **3** giving one thing and receiving another. **4** giving or receiving currency of one country for that of another. **5** thing given for another. **6** building where merchants, dealers meet for business. **7** central telephone office. **ex·change'a·ble** adj

ex·cheq·uer [eks-CHEK-ər] n **1** treasury, e.g. of a government. **2** inf personal funds.

ex·cise[1] [EK-sīz] n tax levied on domestic goods during manufacture or before sale.

ex·cise[2] [ik-SĪZ] vt **-cised, -cis·ing** cut out, cut away. **ex·ci·sion** [ek-SIZH-ən] n

ex·cite [ik-SĪT] vt **-cit·ed, -cit·ing 1** arouse to

example n **1** = **specimen**, case, illustration, instance, sample **2** = **model**, archetype, ideal, paradigm, paragon, prototype, standard **3** = **warning**, caution, lesson

exasperate v = **irritate**, anger, annoy, enrage, incense, inflame, infuriate, madden, pique

exasperation n = **irritation**, anger, annoyance, fury, pique, provocation, rage, wrath

excavate v = **dig out**, burrow, delve, dig up, mine, quarry, tunnel, uncover, unearth

exceed v **1** = **surpass**, beat, better, cap (inf), eclipse, outdo, outstrip, overtake, pass, top **2** = **go over the limit of**, go over the top, overstep

exceedingly adv = **extremely**, enormously, exceptionally, extraordinarily, hugely, superlatively, surpassingly, unusually, very

excel v **1** = **be superior**, beat, eclipse, outdo, outshine, surpass, transcend **2 excel in** or **at** = **be good at**, be proficient in, be skillful at, be talented at, shine at, show talent in

excellence n = **high quality**, distinction, eminence, goodness, greatness, merit, pre-eminence, superiority, supremacy

excellent adj = **outstanding**, brilliant, exquisite, fine, first-class, first-rate, good, great, superb, superlative, world-class

except prep **1** (also **except for**) = **apart from**, barring, besides, but, excepting, excluding, omitting, other than, saving, with the exception of **♦** v **2** = **exclude**, leave out, omit, pass over

exception n **1** = **special case**, anomaly, deviation, freak, inconsistency, irregularity, oddity, peculiarity **2** = **exclusion**, leaving out, omission, passing over

exceptional adj **1** = **special**, abnormal, atypical, extraordinary, irregular, odd, peculiar, strange, unusual **2** = **remarkable**, excellent, extraordinary, marvelous, outstanding, phenomenal, prodigious, special, superior

excerpt n = **extract**, fragment, part, passage, piece, quotation, section, selection

excess n **1** = **surfeit**, glut, overload, superabundance, superfluity, surplus, too much **2** = **overindulgence**, debauchery, dissipation, dissoluteness, extravagance, intemperance, prodigality

excessive adj = **immoderate**, disproportionate, exaggerated, extreme, inordinate, overmuch, superfluous, too much, undue, unfair, unreasonable

exchange v **1** = **interchange**, barter, change, convert into, swap, switch, trade **♦** n **2** = **interchange**, barter, quid pro quo, reciprocity, substitution, swap, switch, tit for tat, trade

excitable adj = **nervous**, emotional, highly

strong emotion, stimulate. **2** rouse up, set in motion. **3** *Electricity* energize to produce electric activity or a magnetic field. **ex·cit'a·ble** *adj* **ex·ci·ta·tion** [ek-si-TAY-shən] *n* **ex·cite'ment** *n* **ex·cit'ing** *adj* **1** thrilling. **2** rousing to action.

ex·claim [ik-SKLAYM] *v* speak suddenly, cry out. **ex·cla·ma·tion** [ek-sklə-MAY-shən] *n* **ex·clam·a·to·ry** [ik-SKLAM-ə-tor-ee] *adj*

ex·clude [ik-SKLOOD] *vt* **-clud·ed, -clud·ing 1** shut out. **2** debar from. **3** reject, not consider. **ex·clu·sion** [-zhən] *n* **ex·clu'sive** *adj* **1** excluding. **2** inclined to keep out (from society, etc.). **3** sole, only. **4** select. ◆ *n* **5** something exclusive, esp. story appearing only in one newspaper. **ex·clu'sive·ly** *adv*

ex·com·mu·ni·cate [eks-kə-MYOO-ni-kayt] *vt* **-cat·ed, -cat·ing** to cut off from the sacraments of the Church. **ex·com·mu·ni·ca'tion** *n*

ex·cre·ment [EKS-krə-mənt] *n* **1** waste matter from body, esp. from bowels. **2** dung. **ex·cre·ta** [ik-SKREE-tə] *n* excrement. **ex·crete'** *vi* **-cret·ed, -cret·ing** discharge from the system. **ex·cre'tion** *n* **ex'cre·to·ry** *adj*

ex·cres·cent [ik-SKRES-ənt] *adj* **1** growing out of. **2** redundant. **ex·cres'cence** *n* unnatural outgrowth.

ex·cru·ci·ate [ik-SKROO-shee-ayt] *vt* **-at·ed, -at·ing** torment acutely, torture in body or mind.

ex·cul·pate [EK-skul-payt] *vt* **-pat·ed, -pat·ing** free from blame, acquit. **ex·cul·pa'tion** *n* **ex·cul'pa·to·ry** *adj*

ex·cur·sion [ik-SKUR-zhən] *n* **1** journey, ramble, trip for pleasure. **2** digression.

ex·cuse [ik-SKYOOZ] *vt* **-cused, -cus·ing 1** forgive, overlook. **2** try to clear from blame. **3** gain exemption. **4** set free, remit. ◆ *n* [-SKYOOS] **5** that which serves to excuse. **6** apology. **ex·cus·a·ble** [ik-SKYOO-zə-bəl] *adj*

ex·e·cra·ble [EK-si-krə-bəl] *adj* abominable, hatefully bad.

ex·e·cute [EK-si-kyoot] *vt* **-cut·ed, -cut·ing 1** inflict capital punishment on, kill. **2** carry out, perform. **3** make, produce. **4** sign (document). **ex·e·cu'tion** *n* **ex·e·cu'tion·er** *n* one employed to execute criminals. **ex·ec'u·tive** *n* **1** person in administrative position. **2** executive body. **3** executive

strung, hot-headed, mercurial, quick-tempered, temperamental, volatile, wired (*sl*)
excite *v* = **arouse**, animate, galvanize, inflame, inspire, provoke, rouse, stir up, thrill
excitement *n* = **agitation**, action, activity, animation, commotion, furor, passion, thrill
exciting *adj* = **stimulating**, dramatic, electrifying, exhilarating, rousing, sensational, stirring, thrilling
exclaim *v* = **cry out**, call out, declare, proclaim, shout, utter, yell
exclamation *n* = **cry**, call, interjection, outcry, shout, utterance, yell
exclude *v* **1** = **keep out**, ban, bar, boycott, disallow, forbid, prohibit, refuse, shut out **2** = **leave out**, count out, eliminate, ignore, omit, pass over, reject, rule out, set aside
exclusion *n* **1** = **ban**, bar, boycott, disqualification, embargo, prohibition, veto **2** = **elimination**, omission, rejection
exclusive *adj* **1** = **sole**, absolute, complete, entire, full, total, undivided, whole **2** = **limited**, confined, peculiar, restricted,

unique **3** = **select**, chic, cliquish, cool (*inf*), fashionable, phat (*sl*), restricted, snobbish, up-market
excommunicate *v* = **expel**, anathematize, ban, banish, cast out, denounce, exclude, repudiate
excruciating *adj* = **agonizing**, harrowing, insufferable, intense, piercing, severe, unbearable, violent
exculpate *v* = **absolve**, acquit, clear, discharge, excuse, exonerate, pardon, vindicate
excursion *n* = **trip**, day trip, expedition, jaunt, journey, outing, pleasure trip, ramble, tour
excusable *adj* = **forgivable**, allowable, defensible, justifiable, pardonable, permissible, understandable, warrantable
excuse *n* **1** = **justification**, apology, defense, explanation, grounds, mitigation, plea, reason, vindication ◆ *v* **2** = **justify**, apologize for, defend, explain, mitigate, vindicate **3** = **forgive**, acquit, exculpate, exonerate, make allowances for, overlook, pardon, tolerate, turn a blind eye to **4** = **free**, absolve, discharge, exempt, let off, release, relieve, spare

branch of government. ◆ adj **4** carrying into effect, esp. of branch of government executing laws. **ex·ec·u·tor** [ig-ZEK-yə-tər] n person appointed to carry out provisions of a will. **-u·trix** n, fem.

ex·e·ge·sis [ek-si-JEE-sis] n, pl **-ses** [-seez] explanation, esp. of Scripture. **ex'e·gete** [-jeet] one skilled in exegesis.

ex·em·plar [ig-ZEM-plər] n model type. **ex·em'pla·ry** [-plə-ree] adj **1** fit to be imitated, serving as example. **2** commendable. **3** typical.

ex·em·pli·fy [ig-ZEM-plə-fī] vt **-fied, -fy·ing 1** serve as example of. **2** illustrate. **3** exhibit. **4** make attested copy of. **ex·em·pli·fi·ca'tion** n

ex·empt [ig-ZEMPT] vt **1** free from. **2** excuse. ◆ adj **3** freed from, not liable for. **4** not affected by. **ex·emp'tion** n

ex·e·quies [EK-si-kweez] pl n funeral rites or procession.

ex·er·cise [EK-sər-sīz] v **-cised, -cis·ing** ◆ vt **1** use, employ. **2** give exercise to. **3** carry out, discharge. **4** trouble, harass. ◆ vi **5** take exercise. ◆ n **6** use of limbs for health. **7** practice for training. **8** task for training. **9** lesson. **10** employment. **11** use (of limbs, mind, etc.).

ex·ert [ig-ZURT] vt **1** apply (oneself) diligently, make effort. **2** bring to bear. **ex·er'tion** n effort, physical activity.

ex·hale [eks-HAYL] v **-haled, -hal·ing 1** breathe out. **2** give, pass off as vapor.

ex·haust [ig-ZAWST] vt **1** tire out. **2** use up. **3** empty. **4** draw off. **5** treat, discuss thoroughly. ◆ n **6** used steam or fluid from engine. **7** waste gases from internal combustion engine. **8** passage for, or coming out of this. **ex·haust'i·ble** adj **ex·haus'tion** [-chən] n **1** state of extreme fatigue. **2** limit of endurance. **ex·haus'tive** adj **1** thorough. **2** comprehensive.

THESAURUS

execute v **1 = put to death**, behead, electrocute, guillotine, hang, kill, shoot **2 = carry out**, accomplish, administer, discharge, effect, enact, implement, perform, prosecute

execution n **1 = carrying out**, accomplishment, administration, enactment, enforcement, implementation, operation, performance, prosecution **2 = killing**, capital punishment, hanging

executioner n **1 = hangman**, headsman **2 = killer**, assassin, exterminator, hit man (sl), liquidator, murderer, slayer

executive n **1 = administrator**, director, manager, official **2 = administration**, directorate, directors, government, hierarchy, leadership, management ◆ adj **3 = administrative**, controlling, decision-making, directing, governing, managerial

exemplary adj **1 = ideal**, admirable, commendable, excellent, fine, good, model, praiseworthy **2 = warning**, cautionary

exemplify v **= show**, demonstrate, display, embody, exhibit, illustrate, represent, serve as an example of

exempt adj **1 = immune**, excepted, excused, free, not liable, released, spared ◆ v **2 = grant immunity**, absolve, discharge, excuse, free, let off, release, relieve, spare

exemption n **= immunity**, absolution, discharge, dispensation, exception, exoneration, freedom, release

exercise n **1 = exertion**, activity, effort, labor, toil, training, work, work-out **2 = task**, drill, lesson, practice, problem **3 = use**, application, discharge, fulfillment, implementation, practice, utilization ◆ v **4 = put to use**, apply, bring to bear, employ, exert, use, utilize **5 = train**, practice, work out

exert v **1 = use**, apply, bring to bear, employ, exercise, make use of, utilize, wield **2 exert oneself = make an effort**, apply oneself, do one's best, endeavor, labor, strain, strive, struggle, toil, work

exertion n **= effort**, elbow grease (facetious), endeavor, exercise, industry, strain, struggle, toil

exhaust v **1 = tire out**, debilitate, drain, enervate, enfeeble, fatigue, sap, weaken, wear out **2 = use up**, consume, deplete, dissipate, expend, run through, spend, squander, waste

exhausted adj **1 = worn out**, debilitated, done in (inf), drained, fatigued, spent, tired out **2 = used up**, consumed, depleted, dissipated, expended, finished, spent, squandered, wasted

exhausting adj **= tiring**, backbreaking, debilitating, grueling, laborious, punishing, sapping, strenuous, taxing

exhaustion n **1 = tiredness**, debilitation, fatigue, weariness **2 = depletion**, consumption, emptying, using up

ex·hib·it [ig-ZIB-it] *vt* **1** show, display. **2** manifest. **3** show publicly (often in competition). ◆ *n* **4** thing shown, esp. in competition or as evidence in court. **ex·hi·bi·tion** [ek-sə-BISH-ən] *n* **1** display, act of displaying. **2** public show (of works of art, etc.). **ex·hi·bi'tion·ist** *n* one with compulsive desire to draw attention to self or to expose genitals publicly. **ex·hib'i·tor** *n* one who exhibits, esp. in show.

ex·hil·a·rate [ig-ZIL-ə-rayt] *vt* **-rat·ed, -rat·ing** enliven, gladden. **ex·hil·a·ra'tion** *n* high spirits, enlivenment.

ex·hort [ig-ZORT] *vt* urge, admonish earnestly. **ex·hor·ta·tion** [eg-zor-TAY-shən] *n* **ex·hort'er** *n*

ex·hume [ig-ZOOM] *vt* **-humed, -hum·ing** unearth what has been buried, disinter. **ex·hu·ma·tion** [eks-hyuu-MAY-shən] *n*

ex·i·gent [EK-si-jənt] *adj* **1** exacting. **2** urgent, pressing. **ex·i·gen·cy** *n, pl* **-cies 1** pressing need. **2** emergency.

ex·ig·u·ous [ig-ZIG-yoo-əs] *adj* scanty, meager.

ex·ile [EG-zīl] *n* **1** banishment, expulsion from one's own country. **2** long absence abroad. **3** one banished or permanently living away from own home or country. ◆ *vt* **-iled, -il·ing 4** banish, expel.

ex·ist [ig-ZIST] *vi* be, have being, live.

ex·ist'ence *n* **ex·ist'ent** *adj*

ex·is·ten·tial·ism [eg-zi-STEN-shə-liz-əm] *n* philosophy stressing importance of personal responsibility and the free agency of the individual in a seemingly meaningless universe.

ex·it [EG-zit] *n* **1** way out. **2** going out. **3** death. **4** actor's departure from stage. ◆ *vi* **5** go out.

ex li·bris [eks LEE-bris] *Lat* from the library of.

ex·o·crine [EK-sə-krin] *adj* of gland (e.g. salivary, sweat) secreting its products through ducts.

ex·o·dus [EK-sə-dəs] *n* **1** departure, esp. of crowd. **2** (**E-**) second book of Old Testament. **the Exodus** departure of Israelites from Egypt.

ex of·fi·ci·o [eks ə-FISH-ee-oh] *Lat* by right of position or office.

ex·on·er·ate [ig-ZON-ə-rayt] *vt* **-at·ed, -at·ing 1** free, declare free, from blame. **2** exculpate. **3** acquit. **ex·on·er·a'tion** *n*

ex·or·bi·tant [ig-ZOR-bi-tənt] *adj* very excessive, inordinate, immoderate. **ex·or'bi·tance** *n*

ex·or·cise [EK-sor-sīz] *vt* **-cised, -cis·ing 1** cast out (evil spirits) by invocation. **2** free person of evil spirits. **ex'or·cism** *n* **ex'or·cist** *n*

━━━━━━ THESAURUS ━━━━━━

exhaustive *adj* = **thorough**, all-embracing, complete, comprehensive, extensive, full-scale, in-depth, intensive

exhibit *v* = **display**, demonstrate, express, indicate, manifest, parade, put on view, reveal, show

exhibition *n* = **display**, demonstration, exposition, performance, presentation, representation, show, spectacle

exhilarating *adj* = **exciting**, breathtaking, enlivening, invigorating, stimulating, thrilling

exhort *v* = **urge**, advise, beseech, call upon, entreat, persuade, press, spur

exhume *v* = **dig up**, disentomb, disinter, unearth

exigency *n* = **need**, constraint, demand, necessity, requirement

exile *n* **1** = **banishment**, deportation, expatriation, expulsion **2** = **expatriate**, deportee, émigré, outcast, refugee ◆ *v* **3** = **banish**, deport, drive out, eject, expatriate, expel

exist *v* **1** = **be**, be present, endure, live,

occur, survive **2** = **survive**, eke out a living, get along or by, keep one's head above water, stay alive, subsist

existence *n* = **being**, actuality, life, subsistence

existent *adj* = **in existence**, alive, existing, extant, living, present, standing, surviving

exit *n* **1** = **way out**, door, gate, outlet **2** = **departure**, exodus, farewell, going, good-bye, leave-taking, retreat, withdrawal ◆ *v* **3** = **depart**, go away, go offstage (*Theatre*), go out, leave, make tracks, retire, retreat, take one's leave, withdraw

exodus *n* = **departure**, evacuation, exit, flight, going out, leaving, migration, retreat, withdrawal

exonerate *v* = **clear**, absolve, acquit, discharge, exculpate, excuse, justify, pardon, vindicate

exorbitant *adj* = **excessive**, extortionate, extravagant, immoderate, inordinate, outrageous, preposterous, unreasonable

exorcise *v* = **drive out**, cast out, deliver

ex·ot·ic [ig-ZOT-ik] *adj* **1** brought in from abroad, foreign. **2** rare, unusual, having strange or bizarre allure. ◆ *n* **3** exotic plant, etc. **ex·ot'i·ca** [-i-kə] *pl n* (collection of) exotic objects. **ex·ot'i·cism** *n* **exotic dancer** stripper.

ex·pand [ik-SPAND] *v* increase, spread out, dilate, develop. **ex·pand'a·ble, -i·ble** *adj* **ex·panse'** *n* **1** wide space. **2** open stretch of land. **ex·pan'si·ble** *adj* **ex·pan'sion** *n* **ex·pan'sive** *adj* **1** wide. **2** extensive. **3** friendly, talkative.

ex·pa·ti·ate [ik-SPAY-shee-ayt] *vi* **-at·ed, -at·ing 1** speak or write at great length (on). **2** enlarge (upon). **ex·pa·ti·a'tion** *n*

ex·pa·tri·ate [eks-PAY-tree-ayt] *vt* **-at·ed, -at·ing 1** banish. **2** exile. **3** withdraw (oneself) from one's native land. ◆ *adj, n* (-tree-it). **ex·pa·tri·a'tion** *n*

ex·pect [ik-SPEKT] *vt* **1** regard as probable. **2** look forward to. **3** await, hope. **ex·pect'an·cy** *n* **1** state or act of expecting. **2** that which is expected. **3** hope. **ex·pect'ant** *adj* looking or waiting for, esp. for birth of child. **ex·pect'ant·ly** *adv* **ex·pec·ta'tion** [ek-spek-TAY-shən] *n* **1** act

or state of expecting. **2** prospect of future good. **3** what is expected. **4** promise. **5** value of something expected. ◆ *pl* **6** prospect of fortune or profit esp. by inheritance.

ex·pec·to·rate [ik-SPEK-tə-rayt] *v* **-rat·ed, -rat·ing** spit out (phlegm, etc.). **ex·pec·to·ra'tion** *n*

ex·pe·di·ent [ik-SPEE-dee-ənt] *adj* **1** fitting, advisable. **2** politic. **3** suitable. **4** convenient. ◆ *n* **5** something suitable, useful, esp. in emergency. **ex·pe'di·en·cy** *n*

ex·pe·dite [EK-spi-dīt] *vt* **1** help on, hasten. **2** dispatch. **ex·pe·di'tion** [-DISH-ən] *n* **1** journey for definite (often scientific or military) purpose. **2** people, equipment engaged in expedition. **3** excursion. **4** promptness. **ex·pe·di'tion·ar·y** *adj* **ex·pe·di'tious** *adj* prompt, speedy.

ex·pel [ik-SPEL] *vt* **-pelled, -pel·ling 1** drive, cast out. **2** exclude. **3** discharge. **ex·pul'sion** *n*

ex·pend [ik-SPEND] *vt* **1** spend, pay out. **2** use up. **ex·pend'a·ble** *adj* likely, or meant, to be used up or destroyed. **ex·pend'i·ture** [-i-chər] *n* **ex·pense'** *n* **1** cost. **2** (cause of)

———— THESAURUS ————

(from), expel, purify

exotic *adj* **1** = **unusual**, colorful, fascinating, glamorous, mysterious, strange, striking, unfamiliar **2** = **foreign**, alien, external, imported, naturalized

expand *v* **1** = **increase**, amplify, broaden, develop, enlarge, extend, grow, magnify, swell, widen **2** = **spread (out)**, diffuse, stretch (out), unfold, unfurl, unravel, unroll **3 expand on** = **go into detail about**, amplify, develop, elaborate on, embellish, enlarge on, expatiate on, expound on, flesh out

expanse *n* = **area**, breadth, extent, range, space, stretch, sweep, tract

expansion *n* = **increase**, amplification, development, enlargement, growth, magnification, opening out, spread

expansive *adj* **1** = **wide**, broad, extensive, far-reaching, voluminous, wide-ranging, widespread **2** = **talkative**, affable, communicative, effusive, friendly, loquacious, open, outgoing, sociable, unreserved

expatriate *adj* **1** = **exiled**, banished, emigrant, émigré ◆ *n* **2** = **exile**, emigrant, émigré, refugee

expect *v* **1** = **think**, assume, believe,

imagine, presume, reckon, suppose, surmise, trust **2** = **look forward to**, anticipate, await, contemplate, envisage, hope for, predict, watch for **3** = **require**, call for, demand, insist on, want

expectant *adj* **1** = **expecting**, anticipating, apprehensive, eager, hopeful, in suspense, ready, watchful **2** = **pregnant**, expecting (*inf*), gravid

expectation *n* **1** = **probability**, assumption, belief, conjecture, forecast, likelihood, presumption, supposition **2** = **anticipation**, apprehension, expectancy, hope, promise, suspense

expediency *n* = **suitability**, advisability, benefit, convenience, pragmatism, profitability, prudence, usefulness, utility

expedient *n* **1** = **means**, contrivance, device, makeshift, measure, method, resort, scheme, stopgap ◆ *adj* **2** = **advantageous**, appropriate, beneficial, convenient, effective, helpful, opportune, practical, suitable, useful, win-win (*inf*)

expedition *n* = **journey**, excursion, mission, quest, safari, tour, trek, voyage

expel *v* **1** = **drive out**, belch, cast out, discharge, eject, remove, spew **2** = **dismiss**, ban, banish, chuck out (*sl*), drum spending. ♦ *pl* **3** charges, outlay incurred. **ex·pen'sive** *adj*

ex·pe·ri·ence [ik-SPEER-ee-əns] *n* **1** observation of facts as source of knowledge. **2** being affected consciously by event. **3** the event. **4** knowledge, skill, gained from life, by contact with facts and events. ♦ *vt* **-enced, -enc·ing 5** undergo, suffer, meet with. **experienced** *adj* skilled, expert, capable. **ex·pe·ri·en·tial** [ik-speer-ee-EN-shəl] *adj*

ex·per·i·ment [ik-SPER-ə-mənt] *n* **1** test, trial, something done in the hope that it may succeed, or to test hypothesis, principle, etc. ♦ *vi* **2** conduct experiment. **ex·per·i·men'tal** *adj*

ex·pert [EK-spurt] *n* **1** one skillful, knowledgeable, in something. **2** authority. ♦ *adj* **3** practiced, skillful. **ex·per·tise** [ek-spər-TEEZ] *n* **1** expertness. **2** know-how.

ex·pi·ate [EK-spee-ayt] *vt* **-at·ed, -at·ing 1** pay penalty for. **2** make amends for.

ex·pi·a'tion *n* **ex'pi·a·to·ry** [-ə-tor-ee] *adj*

ex·pire [ik-SPĪR] *vi* **-pired, -pir·ing 1** come to an end. **2** give out breath. **3** die. ♦ *vt* **4** breathe out. **ex·pi·ra·tion** *n*

ex·plain [ik-SPLAYN] *vt* **1** make clear, intelligible. **2** interpret. **3** elucidate. **4** give details of. **5** account for. **ex·pla·na·tion** [ek-splə-NAY-shən] *n* **ex·plan'a·to·ry** *adj*

ex·ple·tive [EK-spli-tiv] *n* **1** exclamation. **2** exclamatory oath. ♦ *adj* **3** serving only to fill out sentence, etc.

ex·pli·ca·ble [EK-splik-ə-bəl] *adj* explainable. **ex'pli·cate** *vt* **-cat·ed, -cat·ing** develop, explain. **ex'pli·ca·to·ry** *adj*

ex·plic·it [ik-SPLIS-it] *adj* **1** stated in detail. **2** stated, not merely implied. **3** outspoken. **4** clear, plain. **5** unequivocal.

ex·plode [ik-SPLOHD] *v* **-plod·ed, -plod·ing** ♦ *vi* **1** go off with bang. **2** burst violently. **3** (of population) increase rapidly. ♦ *vt* **4** make explode. **5** discredit, expose (a theory, etc.). **ex·plo'sion** [-zhən] *n* **ex·plo'sive** *adj, n*

out, evict, exclude, exile, throw out

expend *v* = **spend**, consume, dissipate, exhaust, go through, pay out, use (up)

expendable *adj* = **dispensable**, inessential, nonessential, replaceable, unimportant, unnecessary

expenditure *n* = **spending**, consumption, cost, expense, outgoings, outlay, output, payment

expense *n* = **cost**, charge, expenditure, loss, outlay, payment, spending

expensive *adj* = **dear**, costly, exorbitant, extravagant, high-priced, lavish, overpriced, steep (*inf*), stiff

experience *n* **1** = **knowledge**, contact, exposure, familiarity, involvement, participation, practice, training **2** = **event**, adventure, affair, encounter, episode, happening, incident, occurrence ♦ *v* **3** = **undergo**, encounter, endure, face, feel, go through, live through, sample, taste

experienced *adj* = **knowledgeable**, accomplished, expert, practiced, seasoned, tested, tried, veteran, well-versed

experiment *n* **1** = **test**, examination, experimentation, investigation, procedure, proof, research, trial, trial run ♦ *v* **2** = **test**, examine, investigate, put to the test, research, sample, try, verify

experimental *adj* = **test**, exploratory, pilot, preliminary, probationary,

provisional, speculative, tentative, trial, trial-and-error

expert *n* **1** = **master**, authority, connoisseur, past master, professional, specialist, virtuoso ♦ *adj* **2** = **skillful**, adept, adroit, experienced, masterly, practiced, professional, proficient, qualified, virtuoso

expertise *n* = **skill**, adroitness, command, facility, judgment, know-how (*inf*), knowledge, mastery, proficiency

expire *v* **1** = **finish**, cease, close, come to an end, conclude, end, lapse, run out, stop, terminate **2** = **breathe out**, emit, exhale, expel **3** = **die**, depart, kick the bucket (*inf*), pass away or on, perish

explain *v* **1** = **make clear** *or* **plain**, clarify, clear up, define, describe, elucidate, expound, resolve, teach **2** = **account for**, excuse, give a reason for, justify

explanation *n* **1** = **reason**, account, answer, excuse, justification, motive, vindication **2** = **description**, clarification, definition, elucidation, illustration, interpretation

explanatory *adj* = **descriptive**, illustrative, interpretive

explicit *adj* = **clear**, categorical, definite, frank, precise, specific, straightforward, unambiguous

explode *v* **1** = **blow up**, burst, detonate, discharge, erupt, go off, set off, shatter **2** =

ex·ploit [EK-sploit] *n* **1** brilliant feat, deed. ◆ *vt* [ik-SPLOIT] **2** turn to advantage. **3** make use of for one's own ends. **ex·ploi·ta·tion** [ek-] *n*

ex·plore [ik-SPLOHR] *vt* **-plored, -plor·ing 1** investigate. **2** examine. **3** scrutinize. **4** examine (country, etc.) by going through it. **ex·plo·ra·tion** [ek-splə-RAY-shən] *n* **ex·plor·a·to·ry** [ik-SPLOR-ə-tor-ee] *adj* **ex·plor'er** *n*

explosion see EXPLODE.

exponent see EXPOUND.

ex·port [ik-SPORT] *vt* **1** send (goods) out of the country. ◆ *n, adj* [EK-sport] **ex·por·ta·tion** [-TAY-shən] *n* **ex·port'er** *n*

ex·pose [ik-SPOHZ] *vt* **-posed, -pos·ing 1** exhibit. **2** disclose, reveal. **3** lay open (to). **4** leave unprotected. **5** expose photographic plate or film to light. **ex·po·sure** [-zhər] *n*

ex·po·sé [ek-spoh-ZAY] *n* newspaper article, etc., disclosing scandal, crime, etc.

exposition see EXPOUND.

ex·pos·tu·late [ik-SPOS-chə-layt] *vi* **-lat·ed, -lat·ing 1** remonstrate. **2** reason with (in a kindly manner). **ex·pos·tu·la'tion** *n*

ex·pound [ik-SPOWND] *vt* explain, interpret. **ex·po·nent** [ik-SPOH-nənt] *n* **1** one who expounds or promotes (idea, cause, etc.). **2** performer, executant. **3** *Math.* small, raised number showing the power of a factor. **ex·po·nen·tial** [ek-spə-NEN-shəl] *adj* **ex·po·si·tion** [-ZISH-ən] *n* **1** explanation, description. **2** exhibition of goods, etc. **ex·pos·i·tor** [ik-SPOZ-i-tər] *n* one who explains, interpreter. **ex·pos'i·to·ry** *adj* explanatory.

ex·press [ik-SPRES] *vt* **1** put into words. **2** make known or understood by words, behavior, etc. **3** squeeze out. ◆ *adj* **4** definitely stated. **5** specially designed. **6** clear. **7** positive. **8** speedy. **9** of train, fast and making few stops. ◆ *adv* **10** by express. **11** with speed. ◆ *n* **12** express train. **13** rapid parcel delivery service. **ex·press'i·ble** *adj* **ex·pres·sion** [-shən] *n* **1** expressing. **2** word, phrase. **3** look, aspect. **4** feeling. **5** utterance. **ex·pres·sion·ism** *n* theory that art depends on expression of artist's creative self, not on mere reproduction. **ex·pres·sive** *adj* **ex·press'ly** *adv* **ex·pres·sive·ness** *n*

THESAURUS

disprove, debunk, discredit, give the lie to, invalidate, refute, repudiate

exploit *v* **1** = **take advantage of**, abuse, manipulate, milk, misuse, play on *or* upon **2** = **make the best use of**, capitalize on, cash in on (*inf*), profit by *or* from, use, utilize ◆ *n* **3** = **feat**, accomplishment, achievement, adventure, attainment, deed, escapade, stunt

exploitation *n* = **misuse**, abuse, manipulation

exploration *n* **1** = **investigation**, analysis, examination, inquiry, inspection, research, scrutiny, search **2** = **expedition**, reconnaissance, survey, tour, travel, trip

exploratory *adj* = **investigative**, experimental, fact-finding, probing, searching, trial

explore *v* **1** = **investigate**, examine, inquire into, inspect, look into, probe, research, search **2** = **travel**, reconnoiter, scout, survey, tour

explosion *n* **1** = **bang**, blast, burst, clap, crack, detonation, discharge, report **2** = **outburst**, eruption, fit, outbreak

explosive *adj* **1** = **unstable**, volatile **2** = **violent**, fiery, stormy, touchy, vehement

exponent *n* **1** = **advocate**, backer, champion, defender, promoter, proponent, supporter, upholder **2** = **performer**, player

expose *v* **1** = **uncover**, display, exhibit, present, reveal, show, unveil **2** = **make vulnerable**, endanger, imperil, jeopardize, lay open, leave open, subject

exposed *adj* **1** = **unconcealed**, bare, on display, on show, on view, revealed, uncovered **2** = **unsheltered**, open, unprotected **3** = **vulnerable**, in peril, laid bare, susceptible, wide open

exposure *n* = **publicity**, display, exhibition, presentation, revelation, showing, uncovering, unveiling

expound *v* = **explain**, describe, elucidate, interpret, set forth, spell out, unfold

express *v* **1** = **state**, articulate, communicate, declare, phrase, put into words, say, utter, voice, word **2** = **show**, convey, exhibit, indicate, intimate, make known, represent, reveal, signify, stand for, symbolize ◆ *adj* **3** = **explicit**, categorical, clear, definite, distinct, plain, unambiguous **4** = **specific**, clear-cut, especial, particular, singular, special **5** = **fast**, direct, high-speed, nonstop, rapid, speedy, swift

ex·pro·pri·ate [eks-PROH-pree-ayt] *vt* **-at·ed, -at·ing 1** dispossess. **2** take out of owner's hands. **ex·pro·pri·a'tion** *n*

expulsion see EXPEL.

ex·punge [ik-SPUNJ] *vt* **-punged, -pung·ing** strike out, erase.

ex·pur·gate [EK-spər-gayt] *vt* **-gat·ed, -gat·ing** remove objectionable parts (from book, etc.), purge. **ex·pur·ga'tion** *n*

ex·quis·ite [EK-skwiz-it] *adj* **1** of extreme beauty or delicacy. **2** keen, acute. **3** keenly sensitive. **ex·quis'ite·ly** *adv*

ex·tant [EK-stənt] *adj* still existing.

ex·tem·po·re [ik-STEM-pə-ree] *adj, adv* without previous thought or preparation. **ex·tem·po·ra'ne·ous** *adj* **ex·tem'po·rize** *vt* **-rized, -riz·ing 1** speak without preparation. **2** devise for the occasion.

ex·tend [ik-STEND] *vt* **1** stretch out, lengthen. **2** prolong in duration. **3** widen in area, scope. **4** accord, grant. ◆ *vi* **5** reach. **6** cover area. **7** have range or scope. **8** become larger or wider. **ex·tend'i·ble** or **-a·ble, ex·ten'si·ble** *adj* **ex·ten·sile** [ik-STEN-səl] *adj* that can be extended.

ex·ten·sion *n* **1** stretching out, prolongation or enlargement. **2** expansion. **3** continuation, additional part, as of telephone, etc. **ex·ten'sive** *adj* wide, large, comprehensive. **ex·ten'sor** *n* straightening muscle. **ex·tent'** *n* **1** space or degree to which thing is extended. **2** size. **3** compass. **4** volume.

ex·ten·u·ate [ik STEN yoo ayt] *vt* -at ed, -at·ing **1** make less blameworthy, lessen. **2** mitigate. **ex·ten·u·a'tion** *n*

ex·te·ri·or [ik-STEER-ee-ər] *n* **1** the outside. **2** outward appearance. ◆ *adj* **3** outer, outward, external.

ex·ter·mi·nate [ik-STUR-mə-nayt] *vt* -nat·ed, -nat·ing destroy utterly, annihilate, root out, eliminate. **ex·ter·mi·na'tion** *n* **ex·ter'mi·na·tor** *n* destroyer.

ex·ter·nal [ik-STUR-nəl] *adj* outside, outward. **ex·ter·nal·ly** *adv*

ex·tinct [ik-STINGKT] *adj* **1** having died out or come to an end. **2** no longer existing. **3** quenched, no longer burning. **ex·tinc'tion** *n*

ex·tin·guish [ik-STING-gwish] *vt* **1** put out,

expression *n* **1** = **statement**, announcement, communication, declaration, utterance **2** = **indication**, demonstration, exhibition, manifestation, representation, show, sign, symbol, token **3** = **look**, air, appearance, aspect, countenance, face **4** = **phrase**, idiom, locution, remark, term, turn of phrase, word

expressive *adj* = **vivid**, eloquent, moving, poignant, striking, telling

expressly *adv* **1** = **definitely**, categorically, clearly, distinctly, explicitly, in no uncertain terms, plainly, unambiguously **2** = **specifically**, especially, particularly, specially

expulsion *n* = **ejection**, banishment, dismissal, eviction, exclusion, removal

exquisite *adj* **1** = **beautiful**, attractive, charming, comely, lovely, pleasing, striking **2** = **fine**, beautiful, dainty, delicate, elegant, lovely, precious **3** = **intense**, acute, keen, sharp

extempore *adv, adj* = **impromptu**, ad lib, freely, improvised, offhand, off the cuff (*inf*), spontaneously, unpremeditated, unprepared

extend *v* **1** = **make longer**, drag out, draw out, lengthen, prolong, spin out, spread

out, stretch **2** = **last**, carry on, continue, go on **3** = **widen**, add to, augment, broaden, enhance, enlarge, expand, increase, supplement **4** = **offer**, confer, impart, present, proffer

extension *n* **1** = **annex**, addition, appendage, appendix, supplement **2** = **lengthening**, broadening, development, enlargement, expansion, increase, spread, widening

extensive *adj* = **wide**, broad, far-flung, far-reaching, large-scale, pervasive, spacious, vast, voluminous, widespread

extent *n* = **size**, amount, area, breadth, expanse, length, stretch, volume, width

extenuating *adj* = **mitigating**, justifying, moderating, qualifying

exterior *n* **1** = **outside**, coating, covering, façade, face, shell, skin, surface ◆ *adj* **2** = **outside**, external, outer, outermost, outward, surface

exterminate *v* = **destroy**, abolish, annihilate, eliminate, eradicate

external *adj* **1** = **outer**, exterior, outermost, outside, outward, surface **2** = **outside**, alien, extrinsic, foreign

extinct *adj* = **dead**, defunct, gone, lost, vanished

extinction *n* = **dying out**, abolition,

quench. **2** wipe out. **ex·tin'guish·er** *n* device, esp. spraying liquid or foam, used to put out fires.

ex·tir·pate [EK-stər-payt] *vt* **-pat·ed, -pat·ing** root out, destroy utterly. **ex·tir·pa'tion** *n* **ex'tir·pa·tor** *n*

ex·tol [ik-STOHL] *vt* **-tolled, -tol·ling** praise highly.

ex·tort [ik-STORT] *vt* **1** get by force or threats. **2** wring out. **3** exact. **ex·tor'tion** *n*

ex·tra [EK-strə] *adj* **1** additional. **2** larger, better, than usual. ◆ *adv* **3** additionally. **4** more than usually. ◆ *n* **5** extra thing. **6** something charged as additional. **7** *Films* actor hired for crowd scenes.

extra- *prefix* outside or beyond an area or scope, e.g. *extradition*; *extramural*; *extraterritorial.*

ex·tract [ik-STRAKT] *vt* **1** take out, esp. by force. **2** obtain against person's will. **3** get by pressure, distillation, etc. **4** deduce, derive. **5** copy out, quote. ◆ *n* [EK-strakt] **6** passage from book, film, etc. **7** matter got by distillation. **8** concentrated solution. **ex·trac'tion** *n* **1** extracting, esp. of tooth. **2** ancestry.

ex·tra·di·tion [ek-strə-DISH-ən] *n* delivery, under treaty, of foreign fugitive from justice to authorities concerned. **ex'tra·dite** [-dīt] *vt* **-dit·ed, -dit·ing** give or obtain such delivery.

ex·tra·mur·al [ek-strə-MYUUR-əl] *adj* **1** connected with but outside normal courses, etc. of college or school. **2** situated outside walls or boundaries of a place.

ex·tra·ne·ous [ik-STRAY-nee-əs] *adj* **1** not essential. **2** irrelevant. **3** added from without, not belonging.

ex·tra·or·di·na·ry [ik-STROR-dn-er-ee] *adj* **1** out of the usual course. **2** additional. **3** unusual, surprising, exceptional.

ex·trap·o·late [ik-STRAP-ə-layt] *vt* **-lat·ed, -lat·ing** **1** infer something not known from known facts. **2** *Math.* estimate a value beyond known values.

ex·tra·sen·so·ry [ek-strə-SEN-sə-ree] *adj* of perception apparently gained without use of known senses.

ex·tra·ter·res·tri·al [ek-strə-tə-RES-tree-əl] *adj* of, or from outside Earth's atmosphere.

ex·trav·a·gant [ik-STRAV-ə-gənt] *adj* **1** wasteful. **2** exorbitant. **3** wild, absurd. **ex·trav'a·gance** *n* **ex·trav'a·gant·ly** *adv* **ex·trav·a·gan'za** [-GAN-zə] *n* elaborate, lavish, entertainment, display, etc.

extravert see EXTROVERT.

ex·treme [ik-STREEM] *adj* **-trem·er, -trem·est** **1** of high or highest degree. **2** severe. **3** going beyond moderation. **4** at the end. **5** outermost. ◆ *n* **6** utmost degree. **7** thing at one end or the other, first and last of series. **ex·trem'ist** *n* advocate of extreme measures. **ex·trem'i·ty**

annihilation, destruction, eradication, extermination, obliteration, oblivion

extinguish *v* **1** = **put out**, blow out, douse, quench, smother, snuff out, stifle **2** = **destroy**, annihilate, eliminate, end, eradicate, exterminate, remove, wipe out

extol *v* = **praise**, acclaim, commend, eulogize, exalt, glorify, sing the praises of

extort *v* = **force**, blackmail, bully, coerce, extract, squeeze

extortionate *adj* = **exorbitant**, excessive, extravagant, inflated, outrageous, preposterous, sky-high, unreasonable

extra *adj* **1** = **additional**, added, ancillary, auxiliary, further, more, supplementary **2** = **surplus**, excess, leftover, redundant, spare, superfluous, unused ◆ *n* **3** = **addition**, accessory, attachment, bonus, extension, supplement ◆ *adv* **4** = **exceptionally**, especially, extraordinarily, extremely, particularly, remarkably, uncommonly, unusually

extract *v* **1** = **pull out**, draw, pluck out, pull, remove, take out, uproot, withdraw **2** = **derive**, draw, elicit, glean, obtain ◆ *n* **3** = **passage**, citation, clipping, cutting, excerpt, quotation, selection **4** = **essence**, concentrate, distillation, juice

extraneous *adj* = **irrelevant**, beside the point, immaterial, inappropriate, off the subject, unconnected, unrelated

extraordinary *adj* = **unusual**, amazing, exceptional, fantastic, outstanding, phenomenal, remarkable, strange, uncommon

extravagance *n* **1** = **waste**, lavishness, overspending, prodigality, profligacy, squandering, wastefulness **2** = **excess**, exaggeration, outrageousness, preposterousness, wildness

extravagant *adj* **1** = **wasteful**, lavish, prodigal, profligate, spendthrift **2** = **excessive**, outrageous, over the top (*sl*), preposterous, reckless, unreasonable

[-TREM-i-tee] *n*, *pl* **-ties 1** farthest point. ◆ *pl* **2** hands and feet. **3** utmost distress. **4** extreme measures. **extreme sport** any of various sports with a high risk of injury or death.

ex·tri·cate [EK-stri-kayt] *vt* **-cat·ed, -cat·ing** disentangle, unravel, set free. **ex·tri·ca'tion** *n*

ex·trin·sic [ik-STRIN-sik] *adj* accessory, not belonging to, not intrinsic. **ex·trin'si·cal·ly** *adv*

ex·tro·vert [EK-strə-vurt] *n* one who is interested in other people and things rather than own feelings. **ex·tro·ver'sion** [-VUR-zhən] *n*

ex·trude [ik-STROOD] *vt* **-trud·ed, -trud·ing 1** squeeze, force out. **2** (esp. of molten metal or plastic, etc.) shape by squeezing through suitable nozzle or die.

ex·u·ber·ant [ig-ZOO-bər-ənt] *adj* **1** high-spirited, vivacious. **2** prolific, abundant, luxurious. **ex·u'ber·ance** *n*

ex·ude [ig-ZOOD] *v* **-ud·ed, -ud·ing** ◆ *vi* **1** ooze out. ◆ *vt* **2** give off (moisture).

ex·ult [ig-ZULT] *vi* rejoice, triumph.

exult'an·cy *n* **ex·ult'ant** *adj* triumphant. **ex·ul·ta·tion** [eg-zul-TAY-shən] *n*

eye [ī] *n* **1** organ of sight. **2** look, glance. **3** attention. **4** aperture. **5** view. **6** judgment. **7** watch, vigilance. **8** thing, mark resembling eye. **9** slit in needle for thread. ◆ *vt* **eyed, ey·ing 10** look at. **11** observe. **eye'less** *adj* **eye'ball** *n* ball of eye. **eye'brow** *n* fringe of hair above eye. **eye'glass** *n* **1** glass to assist sight. **2** monocle. **eye'lash** *n* hair fringing eyelid. **eye'let** *n* small hole for rope, etc. to pass through. **eye'lid** *n* lid or cover of eye. **eye'o·pen·er** *n* **1** surprising news. **2** revealing statement. **eye shadow** colored cosmetic put on around the eyes. **eye'sore** *n* **1** ugly object. **2** thing that annoys one to see. **eye'tooth** *n* canine tooth. **eye'wash** *n* *inf* deceptive talk, etc., nonsense. **eye'wit·ness** *n* one who actually sees something and can give firsthand account of it.

ey·rie [AIR-ee] *n* **1** nest of bird of prey, esp. eagle. **2** high dwelling place.

extreme *adj* **1 = maximum**, acute, great, highest, intense, severe, supreme, ultimate, utmost **2 = severe**, drastic, harsh, radical, rigid, strict, uncompromising **3 = excessive**, fanatical, immoderate, radical **4 = farthest**, far-off, most distant, outermost, remotest ◆ *n* **5 = limit**, boundary, edge, end, extremity, pole

extremely *adv* **= very**, awfully (*inf*), exceedingly, exceptionally, extraordinarily, severely, terribly, uncommonly, unusually

extremist *n* **= fanatic**, die-hard, radical, zealot

extremity *n* **1 = limit**, border, boundary, edge, extreme, frontier, pinnacle, tip **2 = crisis**, adversity, dire straits, disaster, emergency, exigency, trouble

3 extremities = hands and feet, fingers and toes, limbs

extricate *v* **= free**, disengage, disentangle, get out, release, remove, rescue, wriggle out of

extrovert *adj* **= outgoing**, exuberant, gregarious, sociable

exuberance *n* **1 = high spirits**, cheerfulness, ebullience, enthusiasm, liveliness, spirit, vitality, vivacity, zest **2 = luxuriance**, abundance, copiousness, lavishness, profusion

exuberant *adj* **1 = high-spirited**, animated, cheerful, ebullient, energetic, enthusiastic, lively, spirited, vivacious **2 = luxuriant**, abundant, copious, lavish, plentiful, profuse

exult *v* **= be joyful**, be overjoyed, celebrate, jump for joy, rejoice

eye *n* **1 = eyeball**, optic (*inf*) **2 = appreciation**, discernment, discrimination, judgment, perception, recognition, taste ◆ *v* **3 = look at**, check out (*inf*), contemplate, inspect, study, survey, view, watch

eyesight *n* **= vision**, perception, sight

eyesore *n* **= mess**, blemish, blot, disfigurement, horror, monstrosity, sight (*inf*)

eyewitness *n* **= observer**, bystander, onlooker, passer-by, spectator, viewer, witness

F f

F *Chem.* fluorine.

fa [fah] *n* fourth sol-fa note.

fa·ble [FAY-bəl] *n* **1** short story with moral, esp. one with animals as characters. **2** tale. **3** legend. **4** fiction or lie. ◆ *vt* **5** invent, tell fables about. **fab'u·list** *n* writer of fables. **fab'u·lous** [-yə-ləs] *adj* **1** amazing. **2** *inf* extremely good. **3** told of in fables. **4** unhistorical.

fab·ric [FAB-rik] *n* **1** cloth. **2** texture. **3** frame, structure. **fab'ri·cate** *vt* **-cat·ed, -cat·ing 1** build. **2** frame. **3** construct. **4** invent (lie, etc.). **5** forge (document). **fab·ri·ca'tion** *n*

fa·cade [fə-SAHD] *n* **1** front of building. **2** *fig* outward appearance.

face [fays] *n* **1** front of head. **2** distorted expression. **3** outward appearance. **4** front, upper surface, or chief side of anything. **5** dial of a clock, etc. **6** dignity. ◆ *v* **faced,**

fac·ing ◆ *vt* **7** look or front toward. **8** meet (boldly). **9** give a covering surface. ◆ *vi* **10** turn. **fac·et** [FAS-it] *n* **1** one side of many-sided body, esp. cut gem. **2** one aspect. **fa·cial** [FAY-shəl] *adj* **1** pert. to face. ◆ *n* **2** cosmetic treatment for face. **fac'ings** *pl n* lining for decoration or reinforcement, sewn on collar, cuff, etc. **face'less** *adj* **1** without a face. **2** anonymous. **face'lift·ing** *n* operation to tighten skin of face to remove wrinkles.

fa·ce·tious [fə-SEE-shəs] *adj* **1** (sarcastically) witty. **2** humorous, given to jesting, esp. at inappropriate time.

facia *n* see FASCIA.

fac·ile [FAS-il] *adj* **1** easy. **2** working easily. **3** easygoing. **4** superficial, silly. **fa·cil'i·tate** *vt* make easy, help. **fa·cil'i·ta·tor** *n* **fa·cil'i·ty** *n*, *pl* **-ties 1** easiness, dexterity. ◆ *pl* **2** good conditions. **3** means, equipment for doing

---

THESAURUS

fable *n* **1 = story**, allegory, legend, myth, parable, tale **2 = fiction**, fabrication, fantasy, fish story (*inf*), invention, tall tale (*inf*), urban legend, yarn (*inf*)

fabric *n* **1 = cloth**, material, stuff, textile, web **2 = framework**, constitution, construction, foundations, make-up, organization, structure

fabricate *v* **1 = make up**, concoct, devise, fake, falsify, feign, forge, invent, trump up **2 = build**, assemble, construct, erect, form, make, manufacture, shape

fabrication *n* **1 = forgery**, concoction, fake, falsehood, fiction, invention, lie, myth **2 = construction**, assembly, building, erection, manufacture, production

fabulous *adj* **1** *Inf* **= wonderful**, brilliant, fantastic (*inf*), marvelous, out-of-this-world (*inf*), sensational (*inf*), spectacular, superb **2 = astounding**, amazing, breathtaking, inconceivable, incredible, phenomenal, unbelievable **3 = legendary**, apocryphal, fantastic, fictitious, imaginary, invented, made-up, mythical, unreal

façade *n* **= appearance**, exterior, face, front, guise, mask, pretense, semblance, show

face *n* **1 = countenance**, features, mug (*sl*), visage **2 = expression**, appearance, aspect, look **3 = scowl**, frown, grimace, pout, smirk **4 = façade**, appearance, display, exterior, front, mask, show **5 = side**, exterior, front, outside, surface **6 = self-respect**, authority, dignity, honor, image, prestige, reputation, standing, status ◆ *v* **7 = meet**, brave, come up against, confront, deal with, encounter, experience, oppose, tackle **8 = look onto**, be opposite, front onto, overlook **9 = coat**, clad, cover, dress, finish

faceless *adj* **= impersonal**, anonymous, remote

facet *n* **= aspect**, angle, face, part, phase, plane, side, slant, surface

facetious *adj* **= funny**, amusing, comical, droll, flippant, frivolous, humorous, jocular, playful, tongue in cheek

face up to *v* **= accept**, acknowledge, come to terms with, confront, cope with, deal with, meet head-on, tackle something.

fac·sim·i·le [fak-SIM-ə-lee] *n* an exact copy.

fact [fakt] *n* **1** thing known to be true. **2** deed. **3** reality. **fac'tu·al** [-choo-əl] *adj*

fac·tion [FAK-shən] *n* **1** (dissenting) minority group within larger body. **2** dissension. **fac'tious** *adj* of or producing factions.

fac·ti·tious [fak-TISH-əs] *adj* **1** artificial. **2** specially made up. **3** unreal.

fac·tor [FAK-tər] *n* **1** something contributing to a result. **2** one of numbers that multiplied together give a given number. **3** agent, dealer. **4** business that provides money to finance commerce. **fac·to·tum** [-TOH-təm] *n* one performing all types of work.

fac·to·ry [FAK-tə-ree] *n* building in which things are manufactured.

fac·ul·ty [FAK-əl-tee] *n, pl* **-ties 1** inherent power. **2** power of the mind. **3** ability, aptitude. **4** staff of school, college or university. **5** department of university.

fad *n* **1** short-lived fashion. **2** whim. **fad'dish** *adj* **fad'dism** *n* **fad'dist** *n*

fade [fayd] *v* **fad·ed, fad·ing ♦** *vi* **1** lose color, strength. **2** wither. **3** grow dim. **4** disappear gradually. **♦** *vt* **5** cause to fade. **fade'-in, -out** *n* **1** *Radio* variation in strength of signals. **2** *TV, Film* gradual appearance and disappearance of picture.

fag *n sl, offens* short for FAGGOT (sense 2).

fag·got [FAG-ət] *n* **1** bundle of sticks for fuel, etc. **2** *sl, offens* male homosexual.

Fahr·en·heit [FAR ən hīt] *adj* measured by thermometric scale with freezing point of water 32°, boiling point 212°.

fa·ience [FAY-ahns] *n* glazed earthenware or china.

fail [fayl] *vi* **1** be unsuccessful. **2** stop operating or working. **3** be below the required standard. **4** be insufficient. **5** run short. **6** be wanting in need. **7** lose power. **8** die away. **9** become bankrupt. **♦** *vt* **10** disappoint, give no help to. **11** neglect, forget to do. **12** judge (student) to be below required standard. **fail'ing** *n* **1** deficiency. **2** fault. **♦** *prep* **3** in default of. **fail'ure** *n* **fail'-safe** *adj* of device ensuring safety or remedy of malfunction in machine, weapon, etc. **without fail 1** in spite of every difficulty. **2** certainly.

faint [faynt] *adj* **-er, -est 1** feeble, dim, pale.

——————| T H E S A U R U S |——————

facile *adj* = **superficial**, cursory, glib, hasty, shallow, slick

facilitate *v* = **promote**, expedite, forward, further, help, make easy, pave the way for, speed up

facility *n* **1** = **skill**, ability, adroitness, dexterity, ease, efficiency, effortlessness, fluency, proficiency **2** (often plural) = **equipment**, advantage, aid, amenity, appliance, convenience, means, opportunity, resource

facsimile *n* = **copy**, carbon copy, duplicate, fax, photocopy, print, replica, reproduction, transcript

fact *n* **1** = **event**, act, deed, *fait accompli*, happening, incident, occurrence, performance **2** = **truth**, certainty, reality

faction *n* **1** = **group**, bloc, cabal, clique, contingent, coterie, gang, party, set, splinter group **2** = **dissension**, conflict, disagreement, discord, disunity, division, infighting, rebellion

factor *n* = **element**, aspect, cause, component, consideration, influence, item, part

factory *n* = **works**, mill, plant

factual *adj* = **true**, authentic, correct, exact, genuine, precise, real, true-to-life

faculties *pl n* = **powers**, capabilities, intelligence, reason, senses, wits

faculty *n* **1** = **ability**, aptitude, capacity, facility, power, propensity, skill **2** = **department**, school

fad *n* = **craze**, fashion, mania, rage, trend, vogue, whim

fade *v* **1** = **pale**, bleach, discolor, lose color, wash out **2** = **dwindle**, decline, die away, disappear, dissolve, melt away, vanish, wane

faded *adj* = **discolored**, bleached, dull, indistinct, pale, washed out

fading *adj* = **declining**, decreasing, disappearing, dying, on the decline, vanishing

fail *v* **1** = **be unsuccessful**, bite the dust, break down, come to grief, come unstuck, fall, fizzle out (*inf*), flop (*inf*), founder, miscarry, misfire **2** = **disappoint**, abandon, desert, forget, forsake, let down, neglect, omit **3** = **give out**, conk out (*inf*), cut out, die, peter out, stop working **4** = **go bankrupt**, become insolvent, close down, fold (*inf*), go broke (*inf*), go bust (*inf*), go into receivership, go out of business, go to

2 weak. 3 dizzy, about to lose consciousness. ◆ vi 4 lose consciousness temporarily.

fair¹ adj **-er, -est 1** just, impartial. **2** according to rules, legitimate. **3** blond. **4** beautiful. **5** ample. **6** of moderate quality or amount. **7** unblemished. **8** plausible. **9** middling. **10** (of weather) favorable. ◆ adv **11** honestly. **fair'ing** n Aviation streamlined structure, or any part so shaped that it provides streamlined form. **fair'ly** adv **fair'ness** n **fair'way** n **1** Golf trimmed turf between tee and green. **2** navigable channel.

fair² n **1** traveling entertainment with sideshows, amusements, etc. **2** large exhibition of farm, commercial or industrial products. **3** periodical market often with amusements. **fair'ground** n

fair·y [FAIR-ee] n, pl **fair·ies 1** imaginary small creature with powers of magic. **2** sl, offens male homosexual. ◆ adj **3** of fairies. **4** like fairy, beautiful and delicate, imaginary. **fair'y·land** n **fair'y-tale** adj of or like fairy tale. **fairy tale** story of imaginary beings and happenings, esp. as told to children.

fait ac·com·pli [fay ta-kawn-PLEE] n, pl **faits accomplis** [fe za-kawn-PLEE] Fr something already done that cannot be altered.

faith [fayth] n **1** trust. **2** belief. **3** belief without proof. **4** religion. **5** promise. **6** loyalty, constancy. **faith'ful** adj constant, true. **faith'ful·ly** adv **faith'less** adj

fa·ji·tas [fa-HEE-taz] pl n Mexican dish of soft tortillas wrapped around fried strips meat or vegetables.

fake [fayk] vt **faked, fak·ing 1** conceal defects of by artifice. **2** touch up. **3** counterfeit. ◆ n **4** fraudulent object,

the wall, go under ◆ n **5 without fail** = **regularly**, conscientiously, constantly, dependably, like clockwork, punctually, religiously, twenty-four-seven (sl), without exception

failing n **1** = **weakness**, blemish, defect, deficiency, drawback, fault, flaw, imperfection, shortcoming ◆ prep **2** = **in the absence of**, in default of, lacking

failure n **1** = **defeat**, breakdown, collapse, downfall, fiasco, lack of success, miscarriage, overthrow **2** = **loser**, dead duck (sl), disappointment, dud (inf), flop (inf), nonstarter, washout (inf) **3** = **bankruptcy**, crash, downfall, insolvency, liquidation, ruin

faint adj **1** = **dim**, distant, faded, indistinct, low, muted, soft, subdued, vague **2** = **slight**, feeble, remote, unenthusiastic, weak **3** = **dizzy**, exhausted, giddy, light-headed, muzzy, weak, woozy (inf) ◆ v **4** = **pass out**, black out, collapse, keel over (inf), lose consciousness, swoon (literary) ◆ n **5** = **blackout**, collapse, swoon (literary), unconsciousness

faintly adv **1** = **softly**, feebly, in a whisper, indistinctly, weakly **2** = **slightly**, a little, dimly, somewhat

fair¹ adj **1** = **unbiased**, above board, equitable, even-handed, honest, impartial, just, lawful, legitimate, proper, unprejudiced **2** = **light**, blond, blonde, fair-haired, flaxen-haired, towheaded **3** = **respectable**, adequate, average, decent,

moderate, O.K. or okay (inf), passable, reasonable, satisfactory, tolerable **4** = **beautiful**, bonny, comely, handsome, lovely, pretty **5** = **fine**, bright, clear, cloudless, dry, sunny, unclouded

fair² n = **carnival**, bazaar, festival, fête, gala, show

fairly adv **1** = **moderately**, adequately, pretty well, quite, rather, reasonably, somewhat, tolerably **2** = **deservedly**, equitably, honestly, impartially, justly, objectively, properly, without fear or favor **3** = **positively**, absolutely, really

fairness n = **impartiality**, decency, disinterestedness, equitableness, equity, justice, legitimacy, rightfulness

fairy n = **sprite**, brownie, elf, imp, leprechaun, peri, pixie, Robin Goodfellow

fairy tale or **fairy story** n **1** = **folk tale**, romance **2** = **lie**, cock-and-bull story (inf), fabrication, fiction, invention, tall tale (inf), untruth

faith n **1** = **confidence**, assurance, conviction, credence, credit, dependence, reliance, trust **2** = **religion**, belief, church, communion, creed, denomination, dogma, persuasion **3** = **allegiance**, constancy, faithfulness, fidelity, loyalty

faithful adj **1** = **loyal**, constant, dependable, devoted, reliable, staunch, steadfast, true, trusty **2** = **accurate**, close, exact, precise, strict, true

faithless adj = **disloyal**, false, fickle, inconstant, traitorous, treacherous, person, act. ◆ *adj* **fak'er** *n* **1** one who deals in fakes. **2** swindler.

fa·kir [fə-KEER] *n* **1** member of Islamic religious order. **2** Hindu ascetic.

fa·la·fel [fə-LAH-fəl] *n* seasoned croquette of flour or ground chick peas.

fal·con [FAL-kən] *n* small bird of prey, esp. trained in hawking for sport. **fal'con·er** *n* one who keeps, trains, or hunts with falcons. **fal'con·ry** *n* hawking.

fall [fawl] *vi* **fell, fall·en 1** drop, come down freely. **2** become lower. **3** decrease. **4** hang down. **5** come to the ground, cease to stand. **6** perish. **7** collapse. **8** be captured. **9** revert. **10** lapse. **11** be uttered. **12** become. **13** happen. ◆ *n* **14** falling. **15** amount that falls. **16** amount of descent. **17** decrease. **18** collapse, ruin. **19** drop. **20** (oft pl) cascade. **21** cadence. **22** yielding to temptation. **23** autumn. **fall'out** *n* **1** radioactive particles spread as result of nuclear explosion. **2** incidental effect or outcome. **fall for 1** *inf* fall in love with. **2** *inf* be taken in by.

fal·la·cy [FAL-ə-see] *n, pl* **-cies 1** incorrect, misleading opinion or argument. **2** flaw in logic. **3** illusion. **fal·la·cious** [fə-LAY-shəs]

adj **fal·li·bil'i·ty** *n* **fal'li·ble** *adj* liable to error.

fallen pp. of FALL.

Fal·lo·pi·an tube [fə-LOH-pee-ən] *n* either of a pair of tubes through which egg cells pass from ovary to womb.

fal·low[1] [FAL-oh] *adj* **1** plowed and harrowed but left without crop. **2** uncultivated. **3** neglected.

fallow[2] *adj* brown or reddish yellow. **fallow deer** deer of this color.

false [fawls] *adj* **fals·er, fals·est 1** wrong, erroneous. **2** deceptive. **3** faithless. **4** sham, artificial. **false'ly** *adv* **false'ness** *n* faithlessness. **fal·si·fi·ca'tion** *n* **fal'si·fy** *vt* **-fied, -fy·ing 1** alter fraudulently. **2** misrepresent. **fal'si·ty** *n, pl* **-ties false'hood** *n* lie.

fal·set·to [fawl-SET-oh] *n, pl* **-tos** forced voice above natural range.

Fal·staff·i·an [fawl-STAF-ee-ən] *adj* **1** like Shakespeare's Falstaff. **2** fat. **3** convivial. **4** boasting.

fal·ter [FAWL-tər] *vi* **1** hesitate. **2** waver. **3** stumble. **fal'ter·ing·ly** *adv*

fame [faym] *n* **1** reputation. **2** renown. **famed** *adj* **fa'mous** *adj* **1** widely known. **2**

unfaithful, unreliable

fake *v* **1** = **forge**, copy, counterfeit, fabricate, feign, pretend, put on, sham, simulate ◆ *n* **2** = **impostor**, charlatan, copy, forgery, fraud, hoax, imitation, reproduction, sham ◆ *adj* **3** = **artificial**, counterfeit, false, forged, imitation, mock, phoney *or* phony (*inf*), sham

fall *v* **1** = **descend**, cascade, collapse, dive, drop, plummet, plunge, sink, subside, tumble **2** = **decrease**, decline, diminish, drop, dwindle, go down, lessen, slump, subside **3** = **be overthrown**, capitulate, pass into enemy hands, succumb, surrender **4** = **die**, be killed, meet one's end, perish **5** = **occur**, befall, chance, come about, come to pass, happen, take place **6** = **slope**, fall away, incline **7** = **lapse**, err, go astray, offend, sin, transgress, trespass ◆ *n* **8** = **descent**, dive, drop, nose dive, plummet, plunge, slip, tumble **9** = **decrease**, cut, decline, dip, drop, lessening, lowering, reduction, slump **10** = **collapse**, capitulation, defeat, destruction, downfall, overthrow, ruin **11** = **lapse**, sin, transgression

fallacy *n* = **error**, delusion, falsehood, flaw,

misapprehension, misconception, mistake, untruth

fallible *adj* = **imperfect**, erring, frail, ignorant, uncertain, weak

fall out *v* = **argue**, clash, come to blows, differ, disagree, fight, quarrel, squabble

fallow *adj* = **uncultivated**, dormant, idle, inactive, resting, unplanted, unused

false *adj* **1** = **incorrect**, erroneous, faulty, inaccurate, inexact, invalid, lying, mistaken, wrong **2** = **untrue**, lying, unreliable, unsound, untruthful **3** = **artificial**, bogus, counterfeit, fake, forged, imitation, sham, simulated **4** = **deceptive**, deceitful, fallacious, fraudulent, hypocritical, misleading, trumped up

falsehood *n* **1** = **untruthfulness**, deceit, deception, dishonesty, dissimulation, mendacity **2** = **lie**, fabrication, fib, fiction, story, untruth

falsify *v* = **forge**, alter, counterfeit, distort, doctor, fake, misrepresent, tamper with

falter *v* = **hesitate**, stammer, stumble, stutter, totter, vacillate, waver

faltering *adj* = **hesitant**, broken, irresolute, stammering, tentative, timid, uncertain, weak excellent.

fa·mil·i·ar [fə-MIL-yər] *adj* **1** well-known. **2** frequent, customary. **3** intimate. **4** closely acquainted. **5** unceremonious. **6** impertinent, too friendly. ♦ *n* **7** familiar friend. **8** familiar demon. **fa·mil·i·ar'·i·ty** *n*, *pl* -**ties fa·mil'iar·ize** *vt* -**ized**, -**iz·ing**

fam·i·ly [FAM-ə-lee] *n*, *pl* -**lies 1** group of parents and children, or near relatives. **2** person's children. **3** all descendants of common ancestor. **4** household. **5** group of allied objects. **fa·mil·ial** [fə-MIL-yəl] *adj* **family leave** unpaid work leave for family reasons.

fam·ine [FAM-in] *n* **1** extreme scarcity of food. **2** starvation. **fam'ished** *adj* very hungry.

famous see FAME.

fan[1] *n* **1** instrument for producing current of air, esp. for ventilating or cooling. **2** folding object of paper, etc., used, esp. formerly, for cooling the face. **3** outspread feathers of a bird's tail. ♦ *v* **fanned**, **fan·ning 4** spread out like fan. ♦ *vt* **5** blow or cool with fan. **fan'light** *n* (fan-shaped) window over door.

fan[2] *n inf* **1** devoted admirer. **2** an enthusiast, particularly of a sport, etc.

fa·nat·ic [fə-NAT-ik] *adj* **1** filled with abnormal enthusiasm, esp. in religion. ♦ *n* **2** fanatic person. **fa·nat'ical** *adj* **fa·nat'i·cism** *n*

fan·cy [FAN-see] *adj* -**ci·er**, -**ci·est 1** ornamental, not plain. **2** of whimsical or arbitrary kind. ♦ *n*, *pl* -**cies 3** whim, caprice. **4** liking, inclination. **5** imagination. **6** mental image. ♦ *vt* -**cied**, -**cy·ing 7** imagine. **8** be inclined to believe. **9** *inf* have a liking for. **fan'ci·er** *n* one with liking and expert knowledge (respecting some specific thing). **fan'ci·ful** *adj* **fan'ci·ful·ly** *adv*

fan·dan·go [fan-DANG-goh] *n*, *pl* -**goes 1** lively Spanish dance with castanets. **2** music for this dance.

fan·fare [FAN-fair] *n* **1** a flourish of trumpets or bugles. **2** ostentatious display.

fang *n* **1** snake's poison tooth. **2** long, pointed tooth.

fan·tail [FAN-tayl] *n* **1** (kind of bird with) fan-shaped tail. **2** projecting part of ship's stern.

—————— THESAURUS ——————

fame *n* = **prominence**, celebrity, glory, honor, kudos, renown, reputation, repute, stardom

familiar *adj* **1** = **well-known**, accustomed, common, customary, frequent, ordinary, recognizable, routine **2** = **friendly**, amicable, close, easy, intimate, relaxed **3** = **disrespectful**, bold, forward, impudent, intrusive, presumptuous

familiarity *n* **1** = **acquaintance**, awareness, experience, grasp, understanding **2** = **friendliness**, ease, informality, intimacy, openness, sociability **3** = **disrespect**, boldness, forwardness, presumption

familiarize *v* = **accustom**, habituate, instruct, inure, school, season, train

family *n* **1** = **relations**, folk (*inf*), household, kin, kith and kin, one's nearest and dearest, one's own flesh and blood, relatives **2** = **clan**, dynasty, house, race, tribe **3** = **group**, class, genre, network, subdivision, system

famine *n* = **hunger**, dearth, scarcity, starvation

famished *adj* = **starving**, ravenous, voracious

famous *adj* = **well-known**, acclaimed, celebrated, distinguished, eminent, illustrious, legendary, noted, prominent, renowned

fan[1] *n* **1** = **blower**, air conditioner, ventilator ♦ *v* **2** = **blow**, air-condition, cool, refresh, ventilate

fan[2] *n* = **supporter**, admirer, aficionado, buff (*inf*), devotee, enthusiast, follower, lover

fanatic *n* = **extremist**, activist, bigot, militant, zealot

fanatical *adj* = **passionate**, bigoted, extreme, fervent, frenzied, immoderate, obsessive, overenthusiastic, wild, zealous

fanciful *adj* = **unreal**, imaginary, mythical, romantic, visionary, whimsical, wild

fancy *adj* **1** = **elaborate**, baroque, decorative, embellished, extravagant, intricate, ornamental, ornate ♦ *n* **2** = **whim**, caprice, desire, humor, idea, impulse, inclination, notion, thought, urge **3** = **delusion**, chimera, daydream, dream, fantasy, vision ♦ *v* **4** = **suppose**, believe, conjecture, imagine, reckon, think, think likely **5** = **wish for**, crave, desire, hanker after, hope for, long for, thirst for, yearn for

fantasize *v* = **daydream**, dream, envision, imagine

fan·ta·sy [FAN-tə-see] *n, pl* **-sies 1** power of imagination, esp. extravagant. **2** mental image. **3** fanciful invention or design. **fan·ta·sia** [-TAY-zhə] *n* fanciful musical composition. **fan·ta·size** *v* -sized, -siz·ing **fan·tas·tic** *adj* **1** quaint, grotesque, extremely fanciful, wild. **2** *inf* very good. **3** *inf* very large. **fan·tas·ti·cal·ly** *adv*

FAQ *Internet,* frequently asked question or questions.

far [fahr] *adv* **far·ther** or **fur·ther, far·thest** or **fur·thest 1** at or to a great distance, or advanced point. **2** at or to a remote time. **3** by very much. ◆ *adj* **4** distant. **5** more distant. **far'·fetched'** *adj* incredible.

far·ad [FA-rəd] *n* unit of electrical capacity.

farce [fahrs] *n* **1** comedy of boisterous humor. **2** absurd and futile proceeding. **far'ci·cal** *adj* ludicrous.

fare [fair] *n* **1** charge for passenger's transport. **2** passenger. **3** food. ◆ *vi* **fared, far·ing 4** get on. **5** happen. **6** travel, progress. **fare·well'** *interj* **1** goodbye. ◆ *n* **2** leave-taking.

far·i·na·ceous [far-ə-NAY-shəs] *adj* **1** mealy, starchy. **2** made of flour or meal.

farm [fahrm] *n* **1** tract of land for cultivation or rearing livestock. **2** unit of land, water, for growing or rearing a particular crop, animal, etc. ◆ *v* **3** cultivate (land). **4** rear livestock (on farm). **farm'er** *n* **farm'house** *n* **farm'yard** *n* **farm out 1** send (work) to be done by others. **2** put into care of others.

far·o [FAIR-oh] *n* card game.

far·ra·go [fə-RAH-goh] *n, pl* **-gos** medley, hodgepodge.

far·row [FA-roh] *n* **1** litter of pigs. ◆ *v* **2** produce this.

fart [fahrt] *n vulg* (audible) emission of gas from anus. ◆ *vi*

far·ther [FAHR-thər] *adv, adj* **1** further. **2** comp. of FAR. **far'thest** *adv, adj* **1** furthest. **2** sup. of FAR.

fas·ces [FAS-eez] *pl n* **1** bundle of rods bound together around ax, forming Roman badge of authority. **2** emblem of Italian fascists.

fas·cia [FAY-shə] *n, pl* **-cias 1** *Architecture* long flat surface between moldings under eaves. **2** face of wood or stone in a building.

fas·ci·nate [FAS-ə-nayt] *vt* -nat·ed, -nat·ing **1** attract and delight by arousing interest and curiosity. **2** render motionless, as with a fixed stare. **fas·ci·na'tion** *n*

fas·cism [FASH-iz-əm] *n* **1** authoritarian political system opposed to democracy and liberalism. **2** behavior (esp. by those in authority) supposedly typical of this

——————| THESAURUS |——————

fantastic *adj* **1** *Inf* = **excellent,** awesome (*sl*), first-rate, marvelous, sensational (*inf*), superb, wonderful **2** = **strange,** fanciful, grotesque, outlandish **3** = **unrealistic,** extravagant, far-fetched, ludicrous, ridiculous, wild **4** = **implausible,** absurd, cock-and-bull (*inf*), incredible, preposterous, unlikely

fantasy *n* **1** = **imagination,** creativity, fancy, invention, originality **2** = **daydream,** dream, flight of fancy, illusion, mirage, pipe dream, reverie, vision

far *adv* **1** = **a long way,** afar, a good way, a great distance, deep, miles **2** = **much,** considerably, decidedly, extremely, greatly, incomparably, very much ◆ *adj* **3** = **remote,** distant, faraway, far-flung, far-off, outlying, out-of-the-way

farce *n* **1** = **comedy,** buffoonery, burlesque, satire, slapstick **2** = **mockery,** joke, nonsense, parody, sham, travesty

farcical *adj* = **ludicrous,** absurd, comic, derisory, laughable, nonsensical, preposterous, ridiculous, risible

fare *n* **1** = **charge,** price, ticket money **2** = **food,** provisions, rations, sustenance, victuals ◆ *v* **3** = **get on,** do, get along, make out, manage, prosper

farewell *n* = **good-bye,** adieu, departure, leave-taking, parting, sendoff (*inf*), valediction

far-fetched *adj* = **unconvincing,** cock-and-bull (*inf*), fantastic, implausible, incredible, preposterous, unbelievable, unlikely, unrealistic

farm *n* **1** = **smallholding,** farmstead, grange, homestead, plantation, ranch ◆ *v* **2** = **cultivate,** plant, work

fascinate *v* = **intrigue,** absorb, beguile, captivate, engross, enthrall, entrance, hold spellbound, rivet, transfix

fascinating *adj* = **gripping,** alluring, captivating, compelling, engaging, engrossing, enticing, intriguing, irresistible, riveting

fascination *n* = **attraction,** allure, charm, enchantment, lure, magic, magnetism, pull

system. **fas'cist** *adj, n* **fa·scis·tic**
[fə-SHIS-tik] *adj*
fash·ion [FASH-ən] *n* (latest) style, esp. of
dress, etc. **1** manner, mode. **2** form, type.
♦ *vt* **3** shape, make. **fash'ion·a·ble** *adj*
fash'ion·a·bly *adv*
fast¹ *adj* **-er, -est 1** (capable of) moving
quickly. **2** permitting, providing, rapid
progress. **3** ahead of true time. **4** firm,
steady. **5** permanent. ♦ *adv* **6** rapidly. **7**
tightly. **fast'ness** *n* **1** fast state. **2** fortress,
stronghold. **fast'back** *n* car with back
forming continuous slope from roof to
rear. **fast food** food, esp. hamburgers,
etc., prepared and served very quickly.
fast² *vi* **fast·ed, fast·ing** go without food, or
some kinds of food. ♦ *n* **fasting** *n*
fas·ten [FAS-ən] *vt* **1** attach, fix, secure. ♦ *vi*
2 become joined. **3** seize (upon).
fas·tid·i·ous [fa-STID-ee-əs] *adj* **1** hard to
please. **2** discriminating. **3** particular.
fat *n* **1** oily animal substance. **2** fat part. ♦
adj **fat·ter, fat·test 3** having too much fat.
4 containing fat, greasy. **5** profitable. **6**
fertile. **fat'ten** *vt* **1** feed (animals) for
slaughter. ♦ *vi* **2** become fat. **fat'ness** *n*

fat'ty *adj* **-ti·er, -i·est 1** containing fat. ♦ *n,
pl* **-ties 2** *inf* fat person. **fat'head** *n sl* dolt,
fool. **fat farm** resort for helping people
lose weight.
fate [fayt] *n* **1** power supposed to
predetermine events. **2** goddess of destiny.
3 destiny. **4** person's appointed lot or
condition. **5** death or destruction. ♦ *vt*
fat·ed, fat·ing 6 preordain. **fa'tal** *adj* **1**
deadly, ending in death. **2** destructive. **3**
disastrous. **4** inevitable. **fa'tal·ism** *n* **1** belief
that everything is predetermined. **2**
submission to fate. **fa'tal·ist** *n* **fa·tal·is'tic**
adj **fa·tal'i·ty** *n, pl* **-ties 1** accident resulting
in death. **2** person killed in war, accident.
fa'tal·ly *adv* **fate'ful** *adj* fraught with
destiny, prophetic.
fa·ther [FAH-thər] *n* **1** male parent. **2**
forefather, ancestor. **3** (F-) God. **4**
originator, early leader. **5** priest, confessor.
6 oldest member of a society. ♦ *vt* **7** beget.
8 originate. **9** pass as father or author of.
10 act as father to. **fa'ther·hood** *n*
fa'ther·less *adj* **fa'ther·ly** *adj* **fa·ther-in-law**
n husband's or wife's father.
fath·om [FATH-əm] *n* **1** measure of six feet

———— THESAURUS ————

fashion *n* **1** = **style**, craze, custom, fad,
look, mode, rage, trend, vogue **2** =
method, manner, mode, style, way ♦ *v* **3** =
make, construct, create, forge, form,
manufacture, mold, shape
fashionable *adj* = **popular**, à la mode,
chic, cool (*inf*), in (*inf*), in vogue, modern,
phat (*sl*), stylish, trendy (*inf*), up-to-date,
with it (*inf*)
fast¹ *adj* **1** = **quick**, brisk, fleet, flying, hasty,
rapid, speedy, swift **2** = **fixed**, close,
fastened, firm, immovable, secure, sound,
steadfast, tight **3** = **dissipated**, dissolute,
extravagant, loose, profligate, reckless,
self-indulgent, wanton, wild ♦ *adv* **4** =
quickly, hastily, hurriedly, in haste, like
lightning, rapidly, speedily, swiftly **5** =
soundly, deeply, firmly, fixedly, securely,
tightly
fast² *v* **1** = **go hungry**, abstain, deny
oneself, go without food ♦ *n* **2** = **fasting**,
abstinence
fasten *v* = **fix**, affix, attach, bind, connect,
join, link, secure, tie
fat *adj* **1** = **overweight**, corpulent, heavy,
obese, plump, portly, rotund, stout, tubby
2 = **fatty**, adipose, greasy, oily, oleaginous
♦ *n* **3** = **fatness**, blubber, bulk, corpulence,

flab, flesh, lard (*sl*), obesity, paunch, spare
tire (*inf*)
fatal *adj* **1** = **lethal**, deadly, final, incurable,
killing, malignant, mortal, terminal **2** =
ruinous, baleful, baneful, calamitous,
catastrophic, disastrous
fatality *n* = **death**, casualty, loss, mortality
fate *n* **1** = **destiny**, chance, divine will,
fortune, kismet, nemesis, predestination,
providence **2** = **fortune**, cup, horoscope,
lot, portion, stars
fated *adj* = **destined**, doomed,
foreordained, inescapable, inevitable,
predestined, preordained, sure, written
fateful *adj* **1** = **crucial**, critical, decisive,
important, portentous, significant **2** =
disastrous, deadly, destructive, fatal,
lethal, ominous, ruinous
father *n* **1** = **parent**, dad (*inf*), daddy (*inf*),
old man (*inf*), pa (*inf*), papa (*old-fashioned
inf*), pater (*old-fashioned inf, chiefly Brit.*),
pop (*inf*), sire **2** = **forefather**, ancestor,
forebear, predecessor, progenitor **3** =
founder, architect, author, creator,
inventor, maker, originator, prime mover
4 = **priest**, padre (*inf*), pastor ♦ *v* **5** = **sire**,
beget, get, procreate
fatherland *n* = **homeland**, motherland,

of water. ◆ vt **2** sound (water). **3** get to bottom of, understand. **fath'om·a·ble** adj **fath'om·less** adj too deep to fathom.

fa·tigue [fə-TEEG] n **1** weariness. **2** toil. **3** weakness of metals, etc., subjected to stress. **4** soldier's nonmilitary duty. ◆ pl **5** clothing worn for such duty. ◆ vt **-tigued, -tigu·ing 6** weary.

fat·u·ous [FACH-oo-əs] adj very silly, idiotic. **fat'u·ous·ness** n

fau·cet [FAW-sit] n **1** device for controlling flow of liquid. **2** tap.

fault [fawlt] n **1** defect. **2** flaw. **3** misdeed. **4** blame, culpability. **5** blunder. **6** mistake. **7** Tennis ball wrongly served. **8** Geology break in strata. ◆ v **9** find fault in. **10** (cause to) undergo or commit fault. **fault'i·ly** adv **fault'less** adj **fault'y** adj **fault·i·er, fault·i·est**

faun [fawn] n mythological woodland being with tail and horns.

fau·na [FAW-nə] n, pl **-nas** or **-nae** [-nee] animals of region or period collectively.

faux pas [foh-PAH] n, pl **faux pas** [-PAHZ] social blunder or indiscretion.

fa·vor [FAY-vər] n **1** goodwill. **2** approval. **3** special kindness. **4** partiality. ◆ pl **5** sexual intimacy granted by woman. **6** small party gift for a guest. ◆ vt **7** regard or treat with favor. **8** oblige. **9** treat with partiality. **10** aid. **11** support. **12** resemble. **fa'vor·a·ble** adj **fa'vor·ite** [-it] n **1** favored person or thing. **2** horse, team, etc. expected to win race (or game). ◆ adj **3** chosen, preferred. **fa'vor·it·ism** n practice of showing undue preference.

fawn[1] n **1** young deer. ◆ adj **2** light yellowish brown.

fawn[2] vi **1** of person, cringe, court favor servilely. **2** esp. of dog, show affection by wagging tail and groveling.

fax [faks] n **1** facsimile. ◆ vt **2** transmit

————————| THESAURUS |————————

native land

fatherly adj = **paternal**, affectionate, benevolent, benign, kindly, patriarchal, protective, supportive

fathom v = **understand**, comprehend, get to the bottom of, grasp, interpret

fatigue n **1** = **tiredness**, heaviness, languor, lethargy, listlessness ◆ v **2** = **tire**, drain, exhaust, take it out of (inf), weaken, wear out, weary

fatten v **1** = **grow fat**, expand, gain weight, put on weight, spread, swell, thicken **2** (often with up) = **feed up**, build up, feed, nourish, overfeed, stuff

fatty adj = **greasy**, adipose, fat, oily, oleaginous, rich

fatuous adj = **foolish**, brainless, idiotic, inane, ludicrous, mindless, moronic, silly, stupid, witless

fault n **1** = **flaw**, blemish, defect, deficiency, failing, imperfection, shortcoming, weakness, weak point **2** = **mistake**, blunder, error, indiscretion, lapse, oversight, slip **3** = **responsibility**, accountability, culpability, liability **4 at fault** = **guilty**, answerable, blamable, culpable, in the wrong, responsible, to blame **5 find fault with** = **criticize**, carp at, complain, pick holes in, pull to pieces, quibble, take to task **6 to a fault** = **excessively**, immoderately, in the extreme, overmuch, unduly ◆ v **7** = **criticize**, blame, censure, find fault with,

hold (someone) responsible, impugn

faultless adj = **flawless**, correct, exemplary, foolproof, impeccable, model, perfect, unblemished

faulty adj = **defective**, broken, damaged, flawed, impaired, imperfect, incorrect, malfunctioning, out of order, unsound

favor n **1** = **approval**, approbation, backing, good opinion, goodwill, patronage, support **2** = **good turn**, benefit, boon, courtesy, indulgence, kindness, service ◆ v **3** = **side with**, indulge, reward, smile upon **4** = **advocate**, approve, champion, commend, encourage, incline towards, prefer, support

favorable adj **1** = **advantageous**, auspicious, beneficial, encouraging, helpful, opportune, promising, propitious, suitable, win-win (inf) **2** = **positive**, affirmative, agreeable, approving, encouraging, enthusiastic, reassuring, sympathetic

favorably adv **1** = **advantageously**, auspiciously, conveniently, fortunately, opportunely, profitably, to one's advantage, well **2** = **positively**, approvingly, enthusiastically, helpfully, with approval

favorite adj **1** = **preferred**, best-loved, choice, dearest, esteemed, favored ◆ n **2** = **darling**, beloved, blue-eyed boy (inf), idol, pet, teacher's pet, the apple of one's eye

fawn[1] v (often with on or upon) = **curry**

facsimile of (printed matter, etc.) electronically.

faze [fayz] vt **fazed, faz·ing 1** fluster. **2** daunt.

Fe Chem. iron.

fear [feer] n **1** dread, alarm, anxiety, unpleasant emotion caused by coming evil or danger. ◆ vi **2** have this feeling, be afraid. ◆ vt **3** regard with fear. **4** hesitate, shrink from. **5** revere. **fear'ful** adj **fear'ful·ly** adv **fear'less** adj intrepid. **fear'some** adj terrifying.

fea·si·ble [FEE-zə-bəl] adj **1** able to be done. **2** likely. **fea·si·bil'i·ty** n

feast [feest] n **1** banquet, lavish meal. **2** religious anniversary. **3** something very pleasant, sumptuous. ◆ vi **4** partake of banquet, fare sumptuously. ◆ vt **5** regale with feast. **6** provide delight for.

feat [feet] n **1** notable deed. **2** surprising or striking feat.

feath·er [FETH-ər] n **1** one of the barbed shafts that form covering of birds. **2** anything resembling this. ◆ vt **3** provide, line with feathers. ◆ vi **4** grow feathers. ◆ v **5** turn (oar, propeller) edgewise. **feath'er·y** adj **feath·er·weight** n **1** very light person (esp. boxer) or thing. **2** inf person of small consequence or ability. **feather one's nest** enrich oneself. **in fine feather** in good form.

fea·ture [FEE-chər] n **1** (usu pl) part of face. **2** characteristic or notable part of anything. **3** main or special item. ◆ v **-tured, -tur·ing 4** give prominence to. **5** present in leading role in a film. **6** give prominence to. ◆ vi **7** be prominent (in). **fea·ture·less** adj without striking features.

fe·brile [FEE-brəl] adj **1** of fever. **2** feverish.

fe·ces [FEE-seez] pl n excrement, waste matter. **fe·cal** [-kəl] adj

feck·less [FEK-lis] adj spiritless, weak, irresponsible. **feck'less·ness** n

fec·u·lent [FEK-yə-lənt] adj full of sediment, turbid, foul. **fec'u·lence** n

fe·cund [FEE-kund] adj fertile, fruitful, fertilizing. **fe·cun·date** vt **-dat·ed, -dat·ing** fertilize, impregnate. **fe·cun·di·ty** [fi-KUN-di-tee] n

fed pt./pp. of FEED. **fed up** bored,

THESAURUS

favor, brown-nose (sl), crawl, creep, cringe, dance attendance, flatter, grovel, ingratiate oneself, kiss ass (sl), kowtow, pander to

fawn² adj = **beige**, buff, grayish-brown, neutral

fawning adj = **obsequious**, crawling, cringing, deferential, flattering, grovelling, servile, sycophantic

fear n **1** = **alarm**, apprehensiveness, dread, fright, horror, panic, terror, trepidation **2** = **bugbear**, bête noire, bogey, horror, nightmare, specter ◆ v **3** = **be afraid**, dread, shake in one's shoes, shudder at, take fright, tremble at **4 fear for** = **worry about**, be anxious about, feel concern for

fearful adj **1** = **scared**, afraid, alarmed, frightened, jumpy, nervous, timid, timorous, uneasy, wired (sl) **2** = **frightful**, awful, dire, dreadful, gruesome, hair-raising, horrendous, horrific, terrible

fearfully adv **1** = **nervously**, apprehensively, diffidently, timidly, timorously, uneasily **2** = **very**, awfully, exceedingly, excessively, frightfully, terribly, tremendously

fearless adj = **brave**, bold, courageous, dauntless, indomitable, intrepid, plucky, unafraid, undaunted, valiant

fearsome adj = **terrifying**, awe-inspiring, daunting, formidable, frightening, horrifying, menacing, unnerving

feasible adj = **possible**, achievable, attainable, likely, practicable, reasonable, viable, workable

feast n **1** = **banquet**, dinner, repast, spread (inf), treat **2** = **festival**, celebration, fête, holiday, holy day, red-letter day, saint's day **3** = **treat**, delight, enjoyment, gratification, pleasure ◆ v **4** = **eat one's fill**, gorge, gormandize, indulge, overindulge, pig out (sl), wine and dine

feat n = **accomplishment**, achievement, act, attainment, deed, exploit, performance

feathers pl n = **plumage**, down, plumes

feature n **1** = **aspect**, characteristic, facet, factor, hallmark, peculiarity, property, quality, trait **2** = **highlight**, attraction, main item, speciality **3** = **article**, column, item, piece, report, story ◆ v **4** = **spotlight**, emphasize, foreground, give prominence to, play up, present, star

features pl n = **face**, countenance, lineaments, physiognomy

feckless adj = **irresponsible**, good-for-nothing, hopeless, incompetent, ineffectual, shiftless, worthless dissatisfied.

fed·er·al [FED-ər-əl] *adj* of, or like, the government of countries that are united but retain internal independence of the separate states. **fed'er·al·ism** *n* **fed'er·ate** [-ə-rayt] *v* **-at·ed, -at·ing** form into, become, a federation. **fed·er·a'tion** *n* **1** league. **2** federal union.

fee *n* payment for professional and other services.

fee·ble [FEE-bəl] *adj* **-bler, -blest 1** weak. **2** lacking strength or effectiveness, insipid. **fee'bly** *adv*

feed *v* **fed, feed·ing 1** give food to. **2** supply, support. **3** take food. ◆ *n* **4** feeding. **5** fodder, pasturage. **6** allowance of fodder. **7** material supplied to machine. **8** part of machine taking in material. **feed'er** *n* one who or that which feeds. **feed'back** *n* **1** return of part of output of electrical circuit or loudspeakers. **2** information received in response to inquiry, etc. **feed'lot** *n* area, building where cattle are fattened for market.

feel *v* **felt, feel·ing 1** perceive, examine by touch. **2** experience. **3** proceed, find (one's way) cautiously. **4** be sensitive to. **5** show emotion (for). **6** believe, consider. ◆ *n* **7** act or instance of feeling. **8** quality or impression of something perceived by feeling. **9** sense of touch. **feel'er** *n* **1** special organ of touch in some animals. **2**

proposal put forward to test others' opinions. **3** that which feels. **feel'ing** *n* **1** sense of touch. **2** ability to feel. **3** physical sensation. **4** emotion. **5** sympathy, tenderness. **6** conviction or opinion not solely based on reason. ◆ *adj* **8** sensitive, sympathetic, heartfelt. **feel like** have an inclination for.

feet see FOOT. **feet of clay** hidden flaw in person's character.

feign [fayn] *v* pretend, sham.

feint [faynt] *n* **1** sham attack or blow meant to deceive opponent. **2** semblance, pretense. ◆ *vi* **3** make feint.

feist·y [FĪ-stee] *adj* **feist·i·er, feist·i·est 1** spirited, spunky, plucky. **2** ill-tempered. **feist'i·ness** *n*

feld·spar [FELD-spahr] *n* crystalline mineral found in granite, etc.

fe·lic·i·ty [fi-LIS-i-tee] *n, pl* **-ties 1** great happiness, bliss. **2** appropriateness of wording. **fe·lic'i·tate** *vt* **-tat·ed, -tat·ing** congratulate. **fe·lic·i·ta'tion** *pl n* congratulations. **fe·lic'i·tous** *adj* **1** apt, well-chosen. **2** happy.

fe·line [FEE-lin] *adj* **1** of cats. **2** catlike.

fell[1] pt. of FALL.

fell[2] *vt* **1** knock down. **2** cut down (tree).

fell[3] *adj* fierce, terrible.

fell[4] *n* skin or hide with hair.

fel·low [FEL-oh] *n* **1** *inf* man, boy. **2** person.

federation *n* = **union**, alliance, amalgamation, association, coalition, combination, league, syndicate

fed up *adj* = **dissatisfied**, bored, depressed, discontented, down in the mouth, glum, sick and tired (*inf*), tired

fee *n* = **charge**, bill, payment, remuneration, toll

feeble *adj* **1** = **weak**, debilitated, doddering, effete, frail, infirm, puny, sickly, weedy (*inf*) **2** = **unconvincing**, flimsy, inadequate, insufficient, lame, lousy (*sl*), paltry, pathetic, poor, tame, thin

feebleness *n* = **weakness**, effeteness, frailty, infirmity, languor, lassitude, sickliness

feed *v* **1** = **cater for**, nourish, provide for, provision, supply, sustain, victual, wine and dine **2** (sometimes with *on*) = **eat**, chow down (*sl*), devour, exist on, live on, partake of ◆ *n* **3** = **food**, fodder, pasturage, provender **4** *Inf* = **meal**, feast, repast,

spread (*inf*)

feel *v* **1** = **touch**, caress, finger, fondle, handle, manipulate, paw, stroke **2** = **experience**, be aware of, notice, observe, perceive **3** = **sense**, be convinced, intuit **4** = **believe**, consider, deem, hold, judge, think ◆ *n* **5** = **texture**, finish, surface, touch **6** = **impression**, air, ambience, atmosphere, feeling, quality, sense

feeler *n* **1** = **antenna**, tentacle, whisker **2** = **approach**, advance, probe

feeling *n* **1** = **emotion**, ardor, fervor, intensity, passion, sentiment, warmth **2** = **impression**, hunch, idea, inkling, notion, presentiment, sense, suspicion **3** = **opinion**, inclination, instinct, point of view, view **4** = **sympathy**, compassion, concern, empathy, pity, sensibility, sensitivity, understanding **5** = **sense of touch**, perception, sensation **6** = **atmosphere**, air, ambience, aura, feel, mood, quality

fell[1] *v* = **cut down**, cut, demolish, hew,

3 comrade, associate. **4** counterpart. **5** like thing. **6** member (of society). **7** student granted university fellowship. ◆ *adj* **8** of the same class, associated. **fel′low·ship** *n* **1** fraternity. **2** friendship. **3** (in university, etc.) research post or special scholarship.

fel·on [FEL-ən] *n* one guilty of felony. **fe·lo·ni·ous** [fə-LOH-nee-əs] *adj* **fel′o·ny** *n*, *pl* **-nies** serious crime.

felt[1] pt./pp. of FEEL.

felt[2] *n* **1** soft, matted fabric made by bonding fibers chemically and by pressure. **2** thing made of this. ◆ *vt* **3** make into, or cover with, felt. ◆ *vi* **4** become matted like felt. **felt′-tip pen** pen with writing point made of pressed fibers.

fe·male [FEE-mayl] *adj* **1** of sex that bears offspring. **2** relating to this sex. ◆ *n* **3** one of this sex.

fem·i·nine [FEM-ə-nin] *adj* **1** of women. **2** womanly. **3** class or type of grammatical inflection in some languages. **fem′i·nism** *n* advocacy of equal rights for women. **fem′i·nist** *n*, *adj* **fem·i·nin′i·ty** *n*

femme fa·tale [FAHM fat-TAHL] *n*, *pl* **femmes fa·tales** *Fr* alluring woman who leads men into dangerous situations by her charm.

fem·o·ral [FEM-ər-əl] *adj* of the thigh.

fe·mur [FEE-mər] *n* thigh bone.

fen *n* tract of marshy land, swamp.

fence [fens] *n* **1** structure of wire, wood, etc. enclosing an area. **2** (machinery) guard, guide. **3** *sl* dealer in stolen property. ◆ *v* **fenced, fenc·ing 4** erect fence. **5** enclose. **6** fight (as sport) with swords. **7** avoid question, etc. **8** *sl* deal in stolen property. **fencing** *n* art of swordplay.

fend *vt* **1** ward off, repel. ◆ *vi* **2** provide (for oneself, etc.). **fend′er** *n* **1** low metal frame in front of fireplace. **2** name for various protective devices. **3** frame. **4** edge. **5** buffer. **6** mudguard of car. **fender bender** *inf* collision between automobiles causing minor damage.

fen·es·tra·tion [fen-ə-STRAY-shən] *n* **1** arrangement of windows in a building. **2** (in medicine) perforation in a structure. **3** operation to create this.

feng shui [FUNG SHWAY] *n* Chinese art of deciding the best design or position of a grave, building, furniture, etc., in order to bring good luck.

fe·ral[1] [FER-əl] *adj* wild, uncultivated.

feral[2] *adj* **1** funereal, gloomy. **2** causing death.

fer·ment [FUR-ment] *n* **1** leaven, substance causing thing to ferment. **2** excitement, tumult. ◆ *v* [fər-MENT] **3** (cause to) undergo chemical change with effervescence, liberation of heat and alteration of properties, e.g. process set up in dough by yeast. **4** (cause to) become excited. **fer·men·ta·tion** [fur-] *n*

fern [furn] *n* plant with feathery fronds.

fe·ro·cious [fə-ROH-shəs] *adj* fierce, savage, cruel. **fe·roc′i·ty** [-ROS-i-tee] *n*

fer·ret [FER-it] *n* **1** tamed animal like weasel, used to catch rabbits, rats, etc. ◆ *vt* **2** drive out with ferrets. **3** search out. ◆ *vi* **4** search about, rummage.

fer·ric [FER-ik], **fer·rous** [FER-əs] *adj* pert. to, containing, iron. **fer·ru·gi·nous** [fə-ROO-jə-nəs] *adj* **1** containing iron. **2** reddish-brown. **fer·ro·con′crete** *n* reinforced concrete (strengthened by

---

THESAURUS

knock down, level

fellow *n* **1** = **man**, chap (*inf*), character, guy (*inf*), individual, person **2** = **associate**, colleague, companion, comrade, partner, peer

fellowship *n* **1** = **camaraderie**, brotherhood, companionship, sociability **2** = **society**, association, brotherhood, club, fraternity, guild, league, order

feminine *adj* = **womanly**, delicate, gentle, ladylike, soft, tender

femme fatale ◆ *n* = **seductress**, enchantress, siren, succubus, vamp (*inf*)

fen *n* = **marsh**, bog, morass, quagmire, slough, swamp

fence *n* **1** = **barrier**, barricade, defense,

hedge, palisade, railings, rampart, wall ◆ *v* **2** (often with *in* or *off*) = **enclose**, bound, confine, encircle, pen, protect, surround **3** = **evade**, dodge, equivocate, parry

ferment *n* = **commotion**, disruption, excitement, frenzy, furor, stir, tumult, turmoil, unrest, uproar

ferocious *adj* **1** = **fierce**, predatory, rapacious, ravening, savage, violent, wild **2** = **cruel**, barbaric, bloodthirsty, brutal, ruthless, vicious

ferocity *n* = **savagery**, bloodthirstiness, brutality, cruelty, fierceness, viciousness, wildness

ferret out *v* = **track down**, dig up, discover, elicit, root out, search out, trace, framework of metal).

Fer·ris wheel [FER-is] in amusement park, large, vertical wheel with seats for riding.

fer·rule [FER-əl] n metal cap to strengthen end of stick, etc.

fer·ry [FER-ee] n, pl **-ries 1** boat, etc. for transporting people, vehicles, across body of water, esp. as repeated or regular service. ◆ v **-ried**, **-ry·ing 2** carry, travel, by ferry. **3** deliver (airplanes, etc.) by air.

fer·tile [FUR-tl] adj (capable of) producing offspring, bearing crops, etc. **1** fruitful, producing abundantly. **2** inventive. **fer·til·i·ty** [fər-TIL-i-tee] n **fer·ti·li·za'tion** n **fer·ti·lize** vt **-lized**, **-liz·ing** make fertile. **fer'til·iz·er** n

fer·vent [FUR-vənt], **fer·vid** [-vid] adj ardent, vehement, intense. **fer'ven·cy** n **fer'vent·ly** adv **fer'vor** [-vər] n

fes·cue [FES-kyoo] n grass for pasture or lawns, with stiff narrow leaves.

fes·tal [FES-tl] adj **1** of feast or holiday. **2** merry.

fes·ter [FES-tər] v **1** (cause to) form pus. ◆ vi **2** rankle. **3** become embittered.

fes·ti·val [FES-tə-vəl] n **1** day, period set aside for celebration, esp. of religious feast. **2** organized series of events, performances, etc. usu. in one place. **fes·tive** [-tiv] adj **1** joyous, merry. **2** of feast. **fes·tiv'i·ty** n **1** gaiety, mirth. **2** rejoicing. ◆ pl **3** celebrations.

fe·stoon' n **1** chain of flowers, ribbons, etc. hung in curve between two points. ◆ vt **2** form, adorn with festoons.

fetch [fech] vt **1** go and bring. **2** draw forth. **3** be sold for. **4** attract. ◆ n **5** act of fetching. **fetch'ing** adj attractive.

fete [fayt] n, pl **fetes 1** gala, bazaar, etc., esp. one held out of doors. **2** festival, holiday, celebration. ◆ vt **fet·ed**, **fet·ing 3** feast. **4** honor with festive entertainment.

fet'id adj stinking.

fet·ish n **1** (inanimate) object believed to have magical powers. **2** excessive attention to something. **3** object, activity, to which excessive devotion is paid. **4** form of behaviour in which sexual pleasure is derived from looking at or handling an inanimate object. **fet'ish·ism** n **fet'ish·ist** n

fet·lock [FET-lok] n projection behind and above horse's hoof, or tuft of hair on this.

fet·ter [FET-ər] n **1** chain or shackle for feet. **2** check, restraint. ◆ pl **3** captivity. ◆ vt **4** chain up. **5** restrain, hamper.

fet·tle [FET-l] n condition, state of health.

fe·tus [FEE-təs] n, pl **-tus·es** fully developed young in womb or egg. **fe·tal** [FEET-l] adj

feud [fyood] n **1** bitter, lasting, mutual hostility, esp. between two families or tribes. **2** vendetta. ◆ vi **3** carry on feud.

feu·dal [FYOOD-l] adj of, like, medieval social and economic system based on holding land from superior in return for

unearth

ferry n **1** = **ferry boat**, packet, packet boat ◆ v **2** = **carry**, chauffeur, convey, run, ship, shuttle, transport

fertile adj = **rich**, abundant, fecund, fruitful, luxuriant, plentiful, productive, prolific, teeming

fertility n = **fruitfulness**, abundance, fecundity, luxuriance, productiveness, richness

fertilizer n = **compost**, dressing, dung, manure

fervent, fervid adj = **ardent**, devout, earnest, enthusiastic, heartfelt, impassioned, intense, vehement

fervor n = **intensity**, ardor, enthusiasm, excitement, passion, vehemence, warmth, zeal

fester v **1** = **decay**, putrefy, suppurate, ulcerate **2** = **intensify**, aggravate, smolder

festival n **1** = **celebration**, carnival, entertainment, fête, gala, jubilee **2** = **holy**

day, anniversary, commemoration, feast, fête, fiesta, holiday, red-letter day, saint's day

festive adj = **celebratory**, cheery, convivial, happy, jovial, joyful, joyous, jubilant, merry

festivity n (often plural) = **celebration**, entertainment, festival, party

festoon v = **decorate**, array, deck, drape, garland, hang, swathe, wreathe

fetch v **1** = **bring**, carry, convey, deliver, get, go for, obtain, retrieve, transport **2** = **sell for**, bring in, earn, go for, make, realize, yield

fetching adj = **attractive**, alluring, captivating, charming, cute, enticing, winsome

fetish n **1** = **fixation**, mania, obsession, thing (inf) **2** = **talisman**, amulet

feud n **1** = **hostility**, argument, conflict, disagreement, enmity, quarrel, rivalry, row, vendetta ◆ v **2** = **quarrel**, bicker, clash, contend, dispute, fall out, row, service. **feu'dal·ism** n

fe·ver [FEE-vər] n 1 condition of illness with high body temperature. 2 intense nervous excitement. **fe'vered, fe'ver·ish** adj 1 having fever. 2 accompanied by, caused by, fever. 3 in a state of restless excitement. **fe'ver·ish·ly** adv fever pitch 1 very fast pace. 2 intense excitement.

few [fyoo] adj **-er, -est** 1 not many. ♦ n 2 small number. **quite a few** several.

fey [fay] adj 1 supernatural, unreal. 2 enchanted.

fez n, pl **fez·zes** red, brimless, orig. Turkish tasseled cap.

fi·an·cé [fee-ahn-SAY] n man engaged to be married. **fi·an·cée** n, fem.

fi·as·co [fee-AS-koh] n, pl **-cos** breakdown, total failure.

fi·at [FEE-aht] n 1 decree. 2 official permission.

fib n 1 trivial lie, falsehood. ♦ vt **fibbed, fib·bing** 2 tell fib. **fib'ber** n

fi·ber [FI-bər] n 1 filament forming part of animal or plant tissue. 2 substance that can be spun (e.g. wool, cotton). **fi'brous** adj made of fiber. **fi'ber·board** n building material of compressed plant fibers. **fi'ber·glass** n material made of fine glass fibers. **fiber optics** use of bundles of long transparent glass fibers in transmitting light.

fib·u·la [FIB-yə-lə] n slender outer bone of lower leg. **fib'u·lar** adj

fick·le [FIK-əl] adj changeable, inconstant. **fick'le·ness** n

fic·tion [FIK-shən] n 1 prose, literary works of the imagination. 2 invented statement or story. **fic'tion·al** adj **fic·ti'tious** [-TISH-əs] adj 1 not genuine, false. 2 imaginary. 3 assumed.

fid·dle [FID-l] n 1 violin. ♦ v **-dled, -dling** ♦ vi 2 play fiddle. 3 make idle movements, fidget, trifle. **fid'dle·sticks** interj nonsense.

Fi·de·i De·fen·sor [FEE-de-ee de-FEN-sor] Lat defender of the faith.

fi·del·i·ty [fi-DEL-i-tee] n, pl **-ties** 1 (conjugal) faithfulness. 2 quality of sound reproduction.

fidg·et [FIJ-it] vi 1 move restlessly. 2 be uneasy. ♦ n 3 (oft pl) nervous restlessness, restless mood. 4 one who fidgets. **fidg'et·y** adj

fi·du·ci·ar·y [fi-DOO-shee-er-ee] adj 1 held, given in trust. 2 relating to trustee. ♦ n 3 trustee.

fief [feef] n Hist. land held of a superior in return for service. **fief'dom** [-dəm] n 1 estate of a feudal lord. 2 inf organization,

squabble, war

fever n = **excitement**, agitation, delirium, ferment, fervor, frenzy, restlessness

feverish adj 1 = **hot**, febrile, fevered, flushed, inflamed, pyretic (Medical) 2 = **excited**, agitated, frantic, frenetic, frenzied, overwrought, restless, wired (sl)

few adj = **not many**, meager, negligible, rare, scanty, scarcely any, sparse, sporadic

fiasco n = **debacle**, catastrophe, disaster, failure, mess, washout (inf)

fib n = **lie**, fiction, story, untruth, white lie

fiber n 1 = **thread**, filament, pile, strand, texture, wisp 2 = **essence**, nature, quality, spirit, substance 3 As in **moral fiber** = **resolution**, stamina, strength, toughness

fickle adj = **changeable**, capricious, faithless, inconstant, irresolute, temperamental, unfaithful, variable, volatile

fiction n 1 = **tale**, fantasy, legend, myth, novel, romance, story, yarn (inf) 2 = **lie**, cock and bull story (inf), fabrication, falsehood, invention, tall tale (inf), untruth, urban legend

fictional adj = **imaginary**, invented, legendary, made-up, nonexistent, unreal

fictitious adj = **false**, bogus, fabricated, imaginary, invented, made-up, make-believe, mythical, untrue

fiddle v 1 = **fidget**, finger, interfere with, mess about or around, play, tamper with, tinker ♦ n 2 = **violin** 3 **fit as a fiddle** = **healthy**, blooming, hale and hearty, in fine fettle, in good form, in good shape, in rude health, in the pink, sound, strong

fiddling adj = **trivial**, futile, insignificant, pettifogging, petty, trifling

fidelity n 1 = **loyalty**, allegiance, constancy, dependability, devotion, faithfulness, staunchness, trustworthiness 2 = **accuracy**, closeness, correspondence, exactness, faithfulness, precision, scrupulousness

fidget v 1 = **move restlessly**, fiddle (inf), fret, squirm, twitch ♦ n 2 **the fidgets** = **restlessness**, fidgetiness, jitters (inf), nervousness, unease, uneasiness

fidgety adj = **restless**, antsy (sl), impatient, jittery (inf), jumpy, nervous, on edge, restive, twitchy (inf), uneasy, wired (sl) etc. owned by controlled by one person.

field [feeld] *n* **1** area of (farming) land. **2** enclosed piece of land. **3** tract of land rich in specified product (e.g. gold field). **4** players in a game or sport collectively. **5** all competitors but the favorite. **6** battlefield. **7** area over which electric, gravitational, magnetic force can be exerted. **8** sphere of knowledge. **9** range, area of operation. ♦ *v Baseball* **10** stop and return ball. **11** send player, team, on to field. **field'er** *n* **field day 1** day of outdoor activities. **2** important occasion. **field events** throwing and jumping events in athletics. **field glasses** binoculars. **field hockey** hockey played on field, as distinct from ice hockey. **field marshal** (in some countries) army officer of highest rank. **field'work** *n* research, practical work, conducted away from the classroom, laboratory, etc. **field of view** area covered in telescope, camera, etc.

fiend [feend] *n* **1** demon, devil. **2** wicked person. **3** person very fond of or addicted to something, e.g. *fresh-air fiend; drug fiend.* **fiend'ish** *adj* wicked, difficult, unpleasant.

fierce [feers] *adj* **fierc·er, fierc·est 1** savage, wild, violent. **2** rough. **3** severe. **4** intense. **fierce'ly** *adv* **fierce'ness** *n*

fier·y [FI-ə-ree] *adj* **fier·i·er, fier·i·est 1** consisting of fire. **2** blazing, glowing, flashing. **3** irritable. **4** spirited. **fier'i·ness** *n*

fi·es·ta [fee-ES-tə] *n* (religious) celebration, carnival.

fife [fīf] *n* **1** high-pitched flute. ♦ *v* **2** play on fife. **fif'er** *n*

fifteen, fifth, fifty see FIVE.

fig *n* **1** soft, pear-shaped fruit. **2** tree bearing it.

fight [fīt] *v* **fought, fight·ing 1** contend with in battle or in single combat. **2** maintain against opponent. **3** settle by combat. ♦ *n* **fight'er** *n* **1** one who fights. **2** prizefighter. **3** aircraft designed for destroying other aircraft.

fig·ment [FIG-mənt] *n* invention, purely imaginary thing.

fig·ure [FIG-yər] *n* **1** numerical symbol. **2** amount, number. **3** form, shape. **4** bodily shape. **5** appearance, esp. conspicuous appearance. **6** space enclosed by lines, or surfaces. **7** diagram, illustration. **8** likeness. **9** image. **10** pattern, movement in dancing, skating, etc. **11** abnormal form of expression for effect in speech, e.g. metaphor. ♦ *v* **-ured, -ur·ing** ♦ *vt* **12** calculate, estimate. **13** represent by picture or diagram. **14** ornament. ♦ *vi* **15** (oft. with *in*) show, appear, be conspicuous, be included. **fig'ur·a·tive** *adj* **1** metaphorical. **2** full of figures of speech. **fig'ur·a·tive·ly** *adv* **fig·ur·ine'** [-REEN] *n* statuette. **fig'ure·head** *n* **1** nominal leader. **2** ornamental figure under bowsprit of ship.

field *n* **1** = **meadow**, grassland, green, lea (*poetic*), pasture **2** = **competitors**, applicants, candidates, competition, contestants, entrants, possibilities, runners **3** = **speciality**, area, department, discipline, domain, line, province, territory ♦ *v* **4** = **retrieve**, catch, pick up, return, stop **5** = **deal with**, deflect, handle, turn aside

fiend *n* **1** = **demon**, devil, evil spirit **2** = **brute**, barbarian, beast, ghoul, monster, ogre, savage **3** *Inf* = **enthusiast**, addict, fanatic, freak (*inf*), maniac

fiendish *adj* = **wicked**, cruel, devilish, diabolical, hellish, infernal, malignant, monstrous, satanic, unspeakable

fierce *adj* **1** = **wild**, brutal, cruel, dangerous, ferocious, fiery, menacing, savage, vicious **2** = **strong**, furious, howling, inclement, powerful, raging, stormy, tempestuous, violent **3** = **intense**, cut-throat, keen, relentless, strong

fiercely *adv* = **ferociously**, furiously, passionately, savagely, tempestuously, tigerishly, tooth and nail, viciously, with no holds barred

fiery *adj* **1** = **burning**, ablaze, afire, aflame, blazing, flaming, on fire **2** = **excitable**, fierce, hot-headed, impetuous, irascible, irritable, passionate

fight *v* **1** = **battle**, box, clash, combat, do battle, grapple, spar, struggle, tussle, wrestle **2** = **oppose**, contest, defy, dispute, make a stand against, resist, stand up to, withstand **3** = **engage in**, carry on, conduct, prosecute, wage ♦ *n* **4** = **conflict**, battle, clash, contest, dispute, duel, encounter, struggle, tussle **5** = **resistance**, belligerence, militancy, pluck, spirit

fighter *n* **1** = **soldier**, fighting man, man-at-arms, warrior **2** = **boxer**, prize fighter, pugilist

fight off *v* = **repel**, beat off, keep *or* hold at bay, repress, repulse, resist, stave off, ward

fil·a·ment [FIL-ə-mənt] *n* **1** fine wire in electric light bulb and vacuum tube that is heated by electric current. **2** threadlike body.

filch *vt* steal, pilfer.

file¹ [fīl] *n* **1** box, folder, clip, etc. holding papers for reference. **2** papers so kept. **3** information about specific person, subject. **4** orderly line, as of soldiers, one behind the other. **5** *Computers.* organized collection of related material. ◆ *v* **filed, fil·ing** ◆ *vt* **6** arrange (papers, etc.) and put them away for reference. **7** transmit (e.g. tax return). **8** *Law* place on records of a court. **9** bring suit in law court. ◆ *vi* **10** march in file. **filing** *n* **single file** single line of people one behind the other.

file² *n* **1** roughened tool for smoothing or shaping. ◆ *vt* **filed, fil·ing 2** apply file to, smooth, polish. **filing** *n* **1** action of using file. **2** scrap of metal removed by file.

filet see FILLET.

fil·i·al [FIL-ee-əl] *adj* of, befitting, son or daughter.

fil·i·bus·ter [FIL-ə-bus-tər] *n* process of obstructing legislation by using delaying tactics. ◆ *vi*

fil·i·gree [FIL-i-gree] *n* fine tracery or openwork of metal, usu. gold or silver wire.

fill *vt* **1** make full. **2** occupy completely. **3** hold, discharge duties of. **4** stop up. **5** satisfy. **6** fulfill. ◆ *vi* **7** become full. ◆ *n* **8** full supply. **9** as much as desired. **10** soil, etc., to bring area of ground up to required level. **fill·ing** *n* **filling station** business selling oil, gasoline, etc. **fill the bill** *inf* supply all that is wanted.

fil·let [fi-LAY] *n* **1** boneless slice of meat, fish. **2** narrow strip. ◆ *vt* **3** cut into fillets, bone.

fil·lip [FIL-əp] *n* **1** stimulus. **2** sudden release of finger bent against thumb. **3** snap so produced.

fil·ly [FIL-ee] *n, pl* **-lies 1** young female horse. **2** *inf* girl, young woman.

film *n* **1** sequence of images projected on screen, creating illusion of movement. **2** story, etc. presented thus, and shown in movie theater or on TV. **3** sensitized celluloid roll used in photography, cinematography. **4** thin skin or layer. **5** dimness on eyes. **6** slight haze. ◆ *adj* **7** connected with movies. ◆ *vt* **8** photograph with movie camera. **9** make movie of (scene, story, etc.). ◆ *v* **10** cover, become covered, with film. **film'y** *adj* **film·i·er, film·i·est 1** membranous. **2** gauzy. **film star** popular movie actor or actress.

fil·ter [FIL-tər] *n* **1** cloth or other material,

THESAURUS

off

figure *n* **1** = **number**, character, digit, numeral, symbol **2** = **amount**, cost, price, sum, total, value **3** = **shape**, body, build, frame, physique, proportions **4** = **diagram**, design, drawing, illustration, pattern, representation, sketch **5** = **character**, big name, celebrity, dignitary, personality ◆ *v* **6** = **calculate**, compute, count, reckon, tally, tot up, work out **7** (usually with *in*) = **feature**, act, appear, be featured, contribute to, play a part

figurehead *n* = **front man**, mouthpiece, puppet, titular *or* nominal head

figure out *v* **1** = **calculate**, compute, reckon, work out **2** = **understand**, comprehend, decipher, fathom, make out, see

filch *v* = **steal**, embezzle, misappropriate, pilfer, pinch (*inf*), take, thieve, walk off with

file¹ *n* **1** = **folder**, case, data, documents, dossier, information, portfolio **2** = **line**, column, queue, row ◆ *v* **3** = **register**,

document, enter, pigeonhole, put in place, record **4** = **march**, parade, troop

file² *v* = **smooth**, abrade, polish, rasp, rub, scrape, shape

fill *v* **1** = **stuff**, cram, crowd, glut, pack, stock, supply, swell **2** = **saturate**, charge, imbue, impregnate, pervade, suffuse **3** = **plug**, block, bung, close, cork, seal, stop **4** = **perform**, carry out, discharge, execute, fulfill, hold, occupy ◆ *n* **5** **one's fill** = **sufficient**, all one wants, ample, enough, plenty

filler *n* = **padding**, makeweight, stopgap

fill in *v* **1** = **inform**, acquaint, apprise, bring up to date, give the facts *or* background **2** = **replace**, deputize, represent, stand in, sub, substitute, take the place of

filling *n* **1** = **stuffing**, contents, filler, inside, insides, padding, wadding ◆ *adj* **2** = **satisfying**, ample, heavy, square, substantial

fill out *v* = **complete**, answer, fill in, fill up

film *n* **1** = **movie**, flick (*sl*), motion picture **2** = **layer**, coating, covering, dusting, or a device, permitting fluid to pass but retaining solid particles. **2** anything performing similar function. ♦ *vt* **3** act as filter, or as if passing through filter. ♦ *vi* **4** pass slowly (through). **fil·trate** [FIL-trayt] *n* filtered gas or liquid. **fil·tra'tion** *n*

filth *n* **1** disgusting dirt. **2** pollution. **3** obscenity. **filth'i·ly** *adv* **filth'i·ness** *n* **filth'y** *adj* **filth·i·er, filth·i·est 1** unclean. **2** foul.

fin *n* **1** propelling or steering organ of fish. **2** vertical tailplane of an airplane. **3** *sl* five-dollar bill.

fi·nal [FĪN-l] *adj* **1** at the end. **2** conclusive. ♦ *n* **3** game, heat, examination, etc., coming at end of series or school term. **fi·na·le** [fi-NAL-ee] *n* **1** closing part of musical composition, opera, etc. **2** termination. **fi·nal·i·ty** [fī-NAL-i-tee] *n* **fi'na·lize** *v* **-lized, -liz·ing fi'nal·ly** *adv*

fi·nance [fi-NANS] *n* **1** management of money. ♦ *pl* **2** money resources. ♦ *vt* **-nanced, nanc·ing 3** find capital for. **fi·nan'cial** [-shəl] *adj* of finance. **fin·an·cier'** [-SEER] *n*

finch *n* one of family of small songbirds.

find [find] *vt* **found, find·ing 1** come across. **2** light upon, obtain. **3** recognize. **4** experience, discover. **5** discover by searching. **6** ascertain. **7** supply (as funds). **8** *Law* give a verdict. ♦ *n* **9** finding. **10** (valuable) thing found. **find'er** *n* **finding** *n* judicial verdict.

fine¹ [fīn] *adj* **fin·er, fin·est 1** choice, of high quality. **2** delicate, subtle. **3** pure. **4** in small particles. **5** slender. **6** excellent. **7** handsome. **8** showy. **9** *inf* healthy, at ease, comfortable. **10** free of rain. ♦ *vt* **fined, fin·ing 11** make clear or pure. **12** refine. **13** thin. **fine'ly** *adv* **fine'ness** *n* **fin'er·y** *n, pl* **-er·ies** showy dress. **fi·nesse** [fi-NES] *n* elegant, skillful management. **fine art** art produced for its aesthetic value. **fine-tune** *vt* make fine adjustments to for optimum performance.

fine² *n* **1** sum fixed as penalty. ♦ *vt* **fined, fin·ing 2** punish by fine. **in fine 1** in conclusion. **2** in brief.

fin·ger [FING-gər] *n* **1** one of the jointed

membrane, skin, tissue ♦ *v* **3 = photograph**, shoot, take, video, videotape

filter *n* **1 = sieve**, gauze, membrane, mesh, riddle, strainer ♦ *v* **2 = purify**, clarify, filtrate, refine, screen, sieve, sift, strain, winnow **3 = trickle**, dribble, escape, exude, leak, ooze, penetrate, percolate, seep

filth *n* **1 = dirt**, excrement, grime, muck, refuse, sewage, slime, sludge, squalor **2 = obscenity**, impurity, indecency, pornography, smut, vulgarity

filthy *adj* **1 = dirty**, foul, polluted, putrid, slimy, squalid, unclean **2 = muddy**, begrimed, blackened, grimy, grubby, scuzzy (*sl*) **3 = obscene**, corrupt, depraved, impure, indecent, lewd, licentious, pornographic, smutty, X-rated

final *adj* **1 = last**, closing, concluding, latest, terminal, ultimate **2 = definitive**, absolute, conclusive, decided, definite, incontrovertible, irrevocable, settled

finale *n* **= ending**, climax, close, conclusion, culmination, denouement, epilogue

finalize *v* **= complete**, clinch, conclude, decide, settle, tie up, wind up, work out, wrap up (*inf*)

finally *adv* **1 = eventually**, at last, at length, at long last, in the end, lastly, ultimately **2 = in conclusion**, in summary, to conclude

finance *n* **1 = economics**, accounts, banking, business, commerce, investment, money ♦ *v* **2 = fund**, back, bankroll, guarantee, pay for, subsidize, support, underwrite

finances *pl n* **= resources**, affairs, assets, capital, cash, funds, money, wherewithal

financial *adj* **= economic**, fiscal, monetary, pecuniary

find *v* **1 = discover**, come across, encounter, hit upon, locate, meet, recognize, spot, uncover **2 = perceive**, detect, discover, learn, note, notice, observe, realize ♦ *n* **3 = discovery**, acquisition, asset, bargain, catch, good buy

find out *v* **1 = learn**, detect, discover, note, observe, perceive, realize **2 = detect**, catch, disclose, expose, reveal, uncover, unmask

fine¹ *adj* **1 = excellent**, accomplished, exceptional, exquisite, first-rate, magnificent, masterly, outstanding, splendid, superior **2 = sunny**, balmy, bright, clear, clement, cloudless, dry, fair, pleasant **3 = satisfactory**, acceptable, all right, convenient, good, O.K. or okay (*inf*), suitable **4 = delicate**, dainty, elegant, expensive, exquisite, fragile, quality **5 = subtle**, abstruse, acute, hairsplitting, branches of the hand. **2** various things like this. ◆ vt **3** touch or handle with fingers. **4** sl inform against (a criminal). **fin'ger·ing** n **1** manner or act of touching. **2** choice of fingers, as in playing musical instrument. **3** indication of this. **fin'ger·board** n part of violin, etc. against which fingers are placed. **fin'ger·print** n impression of tip of finger, esp. as used for identifying criminals.

fin·i·al [FIN-ee-ol] n ornament at apex of gable, spire, furniture, etc.

fin·ick·y [FIN-i-kee] adj **-ick·i·er, -ick·i·est 1** fastidious, fussy. **2** too fine.

fin'is Lat end, esp. of book.

fin'ish v (mainly tr) **1** bring, come to an end, conclude. **2** complete. **3** perfect. **4** kill. ◆ n **5** end. **6** way in which thing is finished of furniture, e.g. oak finish. **7** final appearance.

fi·nite [FI-nīt] adj bounded, limited.

fiord see FJORD.

fir [fur] n **1** kind of coniferous resinous tree. **2** its wood.

fire [fīr] n **1** state of burning, combustion, flame, glow. **2** mass of burning fuel. **3** destructive burning, conflagration. **4** burning fuel for heating a room, etc. **5** ardor, keenness, spirit. **6** shooting of firearms. ◆ v **fired, fir·ing** ◆ vt **7** discharge (firearm). **8** propel from firearm. **9** inf dismiss from employment. **10** bake. **11** make burn. **12** supply with fuel. **13** inspire. **14** explode. ◆ vi **15** discharge firearm. **16** begin to burn. **17** become excited. **fire'arm** n gun, rifle, pistol, etc. **fire'brand** n **1** burning piece of wood. **2** energetic (troublesome) person. **fire'break** [-brayk] n strip of cleared land to arrest progress of forest or grass fire. **fire'bug** n inf person who practices arson. **fire department** organized body of personnel and equipment to put out fires and rescue those in danger. **fire drill** rehearsal of procedures for escape from fire. **fire engine** vehicle with apparatus for extinguishing fires. **fire escape** means, esp. metal stairs, for escaping from burning buildings. **fire'fight·er** n **1** member of fire department. **2** person employed to fight forest fires. **fire'fly** n, pl **-flies** insect giving off phosphorescent glow. **fire'guard** n protective grating in front of fire. **fire irons** tongs, poker and shovel. **fire'man** n, pl **fire'men 1** firefighter. **2** stoker. **3** assistant to locomotive driver. **fire'place** n recess in room for fire. **fire house** building housing fire department equipment and personnel. **fire'work** n **1** device to give spectacular effects by explosions and colored sparks. ◆ pl **2** show of fireworks. **3** outburst of temper, anger. **firing squad** group of soldiers ordered to execute an offender by shooting.

minute, nice, precise, sharp **6 = slender**, diaphanous, flimsy, gauzy, gossamer, light, sheer, thin

fine² n **1 = penalty**, damages, forfeit, punishment ◆ v **2 = penalize**, punish

finery n **= splendor**, frippery, gear (inf), glad rags (inf), ornaments, showiness, Sunday best, trappings, trinkets

finesse n **= skill**, adeptness, adroitness, craft, delicacy, diplomacy, discretion, savoir-faire, sophistication, subtlety, tact

finger v **= touch**, feel, fiddle with (inf), handle, manipulate, maul, paw (inf), toy with

finish v **1 = stop**, cease, close, complete, conclude, end, round off, terminate, wind up, wrap up (inf) **2 = consume**, devour, dispose of, eat, empty, exhaust, use up **3 = destroy**, bring down, defeat, dispose of, exterminate, overcome, put an end to, put paid to, rout, ruin **4 = perfect**, polish, refine **5 = coat**, gild, lacquer, polish, stain,

texture, veneer, wax ◆ n **6 = end**, cessation, close, completion, conclusion, culmination, denouement, finale, run-in **7 = defeat**, annihilation, curtains (inf), death, end, end of the road, ruin **8 = surface**, luster, patina, polish, shine, smoothness, texture

finished adj **1 = polished**, accomplished, perfected, professional, refined **2 = over**, closed, complete, done, ended, finalized, through **3 = spent**, done, drained, empty, exhausted, used up **4 = ruined**, defeated, done for (inf), doomed, lost, through, undone, wiped out

finite adj **= limited**, bounded, circumscribed, delimited, demarcated, restricted

fire n **1 = flames**, blaze, combustion, conflagration, inferno **2 = bombardment**, barrage, cannonade, flak, fusillade, hail, salvo, shelling, sniping, volley **3 = passion**, ardor, eagerness, enthusiasm, excitement,

fir·kin [FUR-kin] n small cask.

firm [furm] adj -er, -est 1 solid, fixed, stable. 2 steadfast. 3 resolute. 4 settled. ♦ v 5 make, become firm. ♦ n 6 commercial enterprise. 7 partnership.

fir·ma·ment [FUR-mə-mənt] n expanse of sky, heavens.

first [furst] adj 1 earliest in time or order. 2 foremost in rank or position. 3 most excellent. 4 highest, chief. ♦ n 5 beginning. 6 first occurrence of something. 7 Baseball first base. ♦ adv 8 before others in time, order, etc. **first'ly** adv **first aid** help given to injured person before arrival of doctor. **first-hand** adj obtained directly from the first source. **first mate, first officer** officer of merchant vessel immediately below captain. **first-rate** adj of highest class or quality. **first-strike** adj (of a nuclear missile) for use in an opening attack to destroy enemy nuclear weapons.

fis·cal [FIS-kəl] adj of (government) finances.

fish n, pl **fish** or **fish·es** 1 vertebrate cold-blooded animal with gills, living in water. 2 its flesh as food. ♦ v 3 (attempt to) catch fish. 4 search (for). 5 try to get information indirectly. **fish'er** n **fish'er·y** n, pl -er·ies 1 business of fishing. 2 fishing ground. **fish'y** adj **fish·i·er, fish·i·est** 1 of, like, or full of fish. 2 dubious, open to suspicion. 3 unsafe. **fish'er·man** n one who catches fish for a living or for pleasure. **fish'plate** n piece of metal holding wooden beams, etc. together. **fish stick** small piece of fish covered in breadcrumbs.

fis·sure [FISH-ər] n cleft, split, cleavage. **fis'sile** [-əl] adj 1 capable of splitting. 2 tending to split. **fis·sion** [FISH-ən] n 1 splitting. 2 reproduction by division of living cells with two parts, each of which becomes complete organism. 3 splitting of atomic nucleus with release of large amount of energy. **fis'sio·n·able** adj capable of undergoing nuclear fission. **fis·sip·a·rous** [fi-SIP-ər-əs] adj reproducing by fission.

fist n clenched hand. **fist'i·cuffs** pl n fighting.

fis·tu·la [FIS-chuu-lə] n, pl -las pipelike ulcer.

fit¹ v **fit·ted** or **fit, fit·ting** ♦ vt 1 be suited to. 2 be properly adjusted to. 3 arrange,

———————— THESAURUS ————————

fervor, intensity, sparkle, spirit, verve, vigor ♦ v 4 = **shoot**, detonate, discharge, explode, let off, pull the trigger, set off, shell 5 = **inspire**, animate, enliven, excite, galvanize, impassion, inflame, rouse, stir 6 = **dismiss**, cashier, discharge, make redundant, sack (inf), show the door

firebrand n = **rabble-rouser**, agitator, demagogue, incendiary, instigator, tub-thumper

fireworks pl n 1 = **pyrotechnics**, illuminations 2 = **rage**, hysterics, row, storm, trouble, uproar

firm¹ adj 1 = **hard**, dense, inflexible, rigid, set, solid, solidified, stiff, unyielding 2 = **secure**, embedded, fast, fixed, immovable, rooted, stable, steady, tight, unshakable 3 = **definite**, adamant, inflexible, resolute, resolved, set on, unbending, unshakable, unyielding

firm² n = **company**, association, business, concern, conglomerate, corporation, enterprise, organization, partnership

firmly adv 1 = **securely**, immovably, like a rock, steadily, tightly, unflinchingly, unshakably 2 = **resolutely**, staunchly, steadfastly, unchangeably, unwaveringly

firmness n 1 = **hardness**, inelasticity, inflexibility, resistance, rigidity, solidity, stiffness 2 = **resolve**, constancy, inflexibility, resolution, staunchness, steadfastness

first adj 1 = **foremost**, chief, head, highest, leading, pre-eminent, prime, principal, ruling 2 = **earliest**, initial, introductory, maiden, opening, original, premier, primordial 3 = **elementary**, basic, cardinal, fundamental, key, primary, rudimentary ♦ n 4 As in **from the first** = **start**, beginning, commencement, inception, introduction, outset, starting point ♦ adv 5 = **beforehand**, at the beginning, at the outset, firstly, initially, in the first place, to begin with, to start with

first-rate adj = **excellent**, crack (sl), elite, exceptional, first class, outstanding, superb, superlative, top-notch (inf), world-class

fishy adj 1 Inf = **suspicious**, dubious, funny (inf), implausible, odd, questionable, suspect, unlikely 2 = **fishlike**, piscatorial, piscatory, piscine

fissure n = **crack**, breach, cleft, crevice, fault, fracture, opening, rift, rupture, split adjust, apply, insert. **4** supply, furnish. ◆ *vi* **5** be correctly adjusted or adapted. **6** be of right size. ◆ *adj* **fit·ter, fit·test 7** well-suited, worthy. **8** qualified. **9** proper, becoming. **10** ready. **11** in good condition or health. ◆ *n* **12** way anything fits, its style. **13** adjustment. **fit'ly** *adv* **fit'ment** *n* piece of equipment. **fit'ness** *n* **fitter** *n* **1** one who, that which, makes fit. **2** one who supervises making and fitting of garments. **3** mechanic skilled in fitting up metal work. **fitting** *adj* **1** appropriate, suitable. **2** proper. ◆ *n* **3** fixture. **4** apparatus. **5** action of fitting.

fit² *n* **1** seizure with convulsions, spasms, loss of consciousness, etc., as of epilepsy, hysteria, etc. **2** sudden passing attack of illness. **3** passing state, mood. **fit'ful** *adj* spasmodic, capricious. **fit'ful·ly** *adv*

five [fīv] *adj, n* cardinal number after four. **fifth** *adj, n* ordinal number. **fifth'ly** *adv* **fif'teen** *adj, n* ten plus five. **fif'teenth** *adj, n* **fif'ti·eth** *adj, n* **fif'ty** *adj, n, pl* **-ties** five tens. **fifth column** organization spying for enemy within country at war.

fix [fiks] *vt* **1** fasten, make firm or stable. **2** set, establish. **3** appoint, assign, determine. **4** make fast. **5** repair. **6** *inf* influence the outcome of unfairly or by deception. **7** bribe. **8** *sl* treat someone vengefully. ◆ *vi* **9** become firm or solidified. **10** determine. ◆ *n* **11** difficult situation. **12** position of ship, aircraft ascertained by radar, observation, etc. **13** *sl* dose of narcotic drug. **fix·a'tion** *n* **1** act of fixing. **2** preoccupation, obsession. **3** situation of being set in some way of acting or thinking. **fix'a·tive** *adj* capable of, or tending to fix. ◆ *n* **fix'ed·ly** [-sid-lee] *adv* intently. **fix'ture** [-chər] *n* **1** thing fixed in position. **2** thing attached to house. **3** sporting event that takes place regularly. **4** person long-established in a place. **fix up** arrange. **fix (someone) up** attend to person's needs, esp. arrange date.

fizz *vi* **1** hiss, splutter. ◆ *n* **2** hissing noise. **3** effervescent liquid such as champagne. **fiz'zle** [-əl] *vi* **-zled, -zling 1** splutter weakly. ◆ *n* **2** fizzling noise. **3** fiasco. **fizzle out** *inf* come to nothing, fail.

fjord [fyord] *n* (esp. in Norway) long, narrow inlet of sea.

flab·ber·gast [FLAB-ər-gast] *vt* overwhelm with astonishment.

flab·by [FLAB-ee] *adj* **-bi·er, -bi·est 1**

THESAURUS

fit¹ *v* **1** = **match**, accord, belong, conform, correspond, meet, suit, tally **2** = **prepare**, arm, equip, fit out, provide **3** = **adapt**, adjust, alter, arrange, customize, modify, shape ◆ *adj* **4** = **appropriate**, apt, becoming, correct, fitting, proper, right, seemly, suitable **5** = **healthy**, able-bodied, hale, in good shape, robust, strapping, trim, well

fit² *n* **1** = **seizure**, attack, bout, convulsion, paroxysm, spasm **2** = **outbreak**, bout, burst, outburst, spell

fitful *adj* = **irregular**, broken, desultory, disturbed, inconstant, intermittent, spasmodic, sporadic, uneven

fitness *n* **1** = **appropriateness**, aptness, competence, eligibility, propriety, readiness, suitability **2** = **health**, good condition, good health, robustness, strength, vigor

fitting *adj* **1** = **appropriate**, apposite, becoming, correct, decent, proper, right, seemly, suitable ◆ *n* **2** = **accessory**, attachment, component, part, piece, unit

fix *v* **1** = **place**, embed, establish, implant, install, locate, plant, position, set **2** = **fasten**, attach, bind, connect, link, secure, stick, tie **3** = **decide**, agree on, arrange, arrive at, determine, establish, set, settle, specify **4** = **repair**, correct, mend, patch up, put to rights, see to **5** = **focus**, direct **6** *Inf* = **manipulate**, influence, rig ◆ *n* **7** *Inf* = **predicament**, difficulty, dilemma, embarrassment, mess, pickle (*inf*), plight, quandary

fixation *n* = **preoccupation**, complex, hang-up (*inf*), idée fixe, infatuation, mania, obsession, thing (*inf*)

fixed *adj* **1** = **permanent**, established, immovable, rigid, rooted, secure, set **2** = **intent**, resolute, steady, unwavering **3** = **agreed**, arranged, decided, definite, established, planned, resolved, settled

fix up *v* **1** = **arrange**, agree on, fix, organize, plan, settle, sort out **2** (often with *with*) = **provide**, arrange for, bring about, lay on

fizz *v* = **bubble**, effervesce, fizzle, froth, hiss, sparkle, sputter

fizzy *adj* = **bubbly**, bubbling, carbonated, effervescent, gassy, sparkling

flabbergasted *adj* = **astonished**, amazed, astounded, dumbfounded, lost for words, overwhelmed, speechless, staggered, hanging loose, limp. **2** out of condition, too fat. **3** feeble. **4** yielding. **flab** *n inf* unsightly fat on the body. **flab'bi·ness** *n*

flac·cid [FLAK-sid] *adj* flabby, lacking firmness. **flac·cid'i·ty** *n*

flag¹ *n* **1** banner, piece of bunting attached to staff or halyard as standard or signal. ♦ *vt* **flagged, flag·ging 2** inform by flag signals. **Flag Day** June 14. **flag'ship** *n* **1** admiral's ship. **2** most important ship of fleet. **flag'staff** *n* pole for flag.

flag² *n* **1** flat slab of stone. ♦ *pl* **2** pavement of flags. ♦ *vt* **flagged, flag·ging 3** pave with flags. **flag'stone** *n*

flag³ *vi* **flagged, flag·ging 1** droop, fade. **2** lose vigor.

flag·el·late [FLAJ-ə-layt] *vt* **-lat·ed, -lat·ing** scourge, flog. **flag'el·lant** [-lənt] *n* one who scourges self, esp. in religious penance. **flag·el·la'tion** *n* **flag'el·la·tor** *n*

flag·eo·let [flaj-ə-LET] *n* small flutelike instrument.

flag·on [FLAG-ən] *n* large bottle of wine, etc.

fla·grant [FLAY-grənt] *adj* glaring, scandalous, blatant. **fla'gran·cy** *n*

flail [flayl] *n* **1** instrument for threshing grain by hand. ♦ *v* **2** beat with, move as, flail.

flair *n* **1** natural ability. **2** elegance.

flak *n* **1** antiaircraft fire. **2** *inf* adverse criticism.

flake [flayk] *n* **1** small, thin piece, esp. particle of snow. **2** piece chipped off. ♦ *v*

flaked, flak·ing **3** (cause to) peel off in flakes. **flak'y** *adj* **flak·i·er, flak·i·est 1** of or like flakes. **2** *sl* eccentric. **flake out** *inf* collapse, sleep from exhaustion.

flam·boy·ant [flam-BOI-ənt] *adj* **1** florid, gorgeous, showy. **2** exuberant, ostentatious.

flame [flaym] *n* **1** burning gas, esp. above fire. **2** visible burning. **3** passion, esp. love. **4** *inf* sweetheart. **5** *inf* an abusive message sent by e-mail. ♦ *v* **flamed, flam·ing 6** give out flames, blaze. **7** shine. **8** burst out. **9** *inf* to send an abusive message by e-mail.

fla·men·co [flə-MENG-koh] *n* **1** Spanish dance to guitar. **2** music for this.

fla·min·go [flə-MING-goh] *n, pl* **-gos** or **-goes** large pink to scarlet bird with long neck and legs.

flam·ma·ble [FLAM-ə-bəl] *adj* liable to catch fire,inflammable.

flan *n* **1** open sweet dessert with caramel topping. **2** tartlike pastry.

flange [flanj] *n* **1** projecting flat rim, collar, or rib. ♦ *v* **flanged, flang·ing 2** provide with or take form of flange.

flank [flangk] *n* **1** part of side between hips and ribs. **2** side of anything, e.g. body of troops. ♦ *vt* **3** guard or strengthen on flank. **4** attack or take in flank. **5** be at, move along either side of.

flan·nel [FLAN-l] *n* soft woolen fabric for clothing, esp. trousers. **flan'nel·mouth** *n* person of slow, thick speech or deceptively smooth speech.

stunned

flabby *adj* = **limp**, baggy, drooping, flaccid, floppy, loose, pendulous, sagging

flag¹ *n* **1** = **banner**, colors, ensign, pennant, pennon, standard, streamer ♦ *v* **2** = **mark**, indicate, label, note **3** (sometimes with *down*) = **hail**, signal, warn, wave

flag² *v* = **weaken**, abate, droop, fade, languish, peter out, sag, wane, weary, wilt

flagging *adj* = **fading**, declining, deteriorating, faltering, waning, weakening, wilting

flagrant *adj* = **outrageous**, barefaced, blatant, brazen, glaring, heinous, scandalous, shameless

flagstone *n* = **paving stone**, block, flag, slab

flail *v* = **thrash**, beat, thresh, windmill

flair *n* **1** = **ability**, aptitude, faculty, feel, genius, gift, knack, mastery, talent **2** =

style, chic, dash, discernment, elegance, panache, stylishness, taste

flake *n* **1** = **wafer**, layer, peeling, scale, shaving, sliver ♦ *v* **2** = **blister**, chip, peel (off)

flake out *v* = **collapse**, faint, keel over, pass out

flamboyant *adj* **1** = **extravagant**, dashing, elaborate, florid, ornate, ostentatious, showy, swashbuckling, theatrical **2** = **colorful**, brilliant, dazzling, glamorous, glitzy (*sl*)

flame *n* **1** = **fire**, blaze, brightness, light **2** *Inf* = **sweetheart**, beau, boyfriend, girlfriend, heart-throb (*Brit.*), lover ♦ *v* **3** = **burn**, blaze, flare, flash, glare, glow, shine

flaming *adj* = **burning**, ablaze, blazing, fiery, glowing, raging, red-hot

flank *n* **1** = **side**, hip, loin, thigh **2** = **wing**, side

flap *v* **flapped, flap·ping 1** move (wings, arms, etc.) as bird flying. **2** (cause to) sway. **3** strike with flat object. **4** *sl* be agitated, flustered. ◆ *n* **5** act of flapping. **6** broad piece of anything hanging from hinge or loosely from one side. **7** movable part of aircraft wing. **8** *inf* state of excitement or panic. **flap'pa·ble** *adj inf* easily confused, esp. under stress.

flare [flair] *vi* **flared, flar·ing 1** blaze with unsteady flame. **2** *inf* (with *up*) burst suddenly into anger. **3** spread outward, as bottom of skirt. ◆ *n* **4** instance of flaring. **5** signal light.

flash *n* **1** sudden burst of light or flame. **2** sudden short blaze. **3** very short time. **4** brief news item. **5** display. ◆ *vi* **6** break into sudden flame. **7** gleam. **8** burst into view. **9** move very fast. **10** appear suddenly. **11** *sl* expose oneself indecently. ◆ *vt* **12** cause to gleam. **13** emit (light, etc.) suddenly. **flash'er** *n* **1** thing that flashes. **2** *sl* one who indecently exposes self. **flash'back** *n* break in continuity of book, play or film, to introduce what has taken place previously. **flash'y** *adj* **flash-i-er, flash-i-est** showy, sham. **flash point 1** temperature at which a vapor ignites. **2** point at which violence or anger breaks out.

flask *n* **1** long-necked bottle for scientific use. **2** metal or glass pocket bottle.

flat¹ *adj* **flat·ter, flat·test 1** level. **2** spread out. **3** at full length. **4** smooth. **5** downright. **6** dull, lifeless. **7** *Mus.* below true pitch. **8** (of vehicle tire) deflated, punctured. ◆ *n* **9** what is flat. **10** *Mus.* note half tone below natural pitch. **flat'ly** *adv* **flat'ness** *n* **flat'ten** *vt* **flat feet** feet with abnormally flattened arches. **flat'foot** *n, pl* **-foots** *sl* police officer. **flat race** horse race over level ground with no jumps. **flat rate** the same price in all cases. **flat out** at, with maximum speed or effort.

flat² *n* apartment.

flat·ter [FLAT-ər] *vt* **1** fawn on. **2** praise insincerely. **3** inspire unfounded belief. **4** gratify (senses). **5** represent too favorably. **flat'ter·er** *n* **flat'ter·y** *n, pl* **-ter·ies**

flat·u·lent [FLACH-ə-lənt] *adj* **1** suffering from, generating (excess) gases in intestines. **2** pretentious. **flat'u·lence** *n* **1** flatulent condition. **2** verbosity, emptiness.

flaunt [flawnt] *v* **1** show off. **2** wave proudly.

THESAURUS

flap *v* **1** = **flutter**, beat, flail, shake, thrash, vibrate, wag, wave ◆ *n* **2** = **flutter**, beating, shaking, swinging, swish, waving

flare *v* **1** = **blaze**, burn up, flicker, glare **2** = **widen**, broaden, spread out ◆ *n* **3** = **flame**, blaze, burst, flash, flicker, glare

flare up *v* = **lose one's temper**, blow one's top (*inf*), boil over, explode, fly off the handle (*inf*), throw a tantrum

flash *n* **1** = **blaze**, burst, dazzle, flare, flicker, gleam, shimmer, spark, streak **2** = **moment**, instant, jiffy (*inf*), second, split second, trice, twinkling of an eye ◆ *v* **3** = **blaze**, flare, flicker, glare, gleam, shimmer, sparkle, twinkle **4** = **speed**, dart, dash, fly, race, shoot, streak, whistle, zoom **5** = **show**, display, exhibit, expose, flaunt, flourish

flashy *adj* = **showy**, flamboyant, garish, gaudy, glitzy (*sl*), jazzy (*inf*), ostentatious, snazzy (*inf*)

flat¹ *adj* **1** = **even**, horizontal, level, levelled, low, smooth **2** = **dull**, boring, dead, lackluster, lifeless, monotonous, tedious, tiresome, uninteresting **3** = **absolute**, categorical, downright, explicit, out-and-out, positive, unequivocal,

unqualified **4** = **punctured**, blown out, burst, collapsed, deflated, empty ◆ *adv* **5** = **completely**, absolutely, categorically, exactly, point blank, precisely, utterly **6 flat out** = **at full speed**, all out, at full tilt, for all one is worth

flat² *n* = **apartment**, rooms

flatly *adv* = **absolutely**, categorically, completely, positively, unhesitatingly

flatness *n* **1** = **evenness**, smoothness, uniformity **2** = **dullness**, monotony, tedium

flatten *v* = **level**, compress, even out, iron out, raze, smooth off, squash, trample

flatter *v* **1** = **praise**, brown-nose (*sl*), butter up, compliment, pander to, sweet-talk (*inf*), wheedle **2** = **suit**, become, do something for, enhance, set off, show to advantage

flattering *adj* **1** = **becoming**, effective, enhancing, kind, well-chosen **2** = **ingratiating**, adulatory, complimentary, fawning, fulsome, laudatory

flattery *n* = **obsequiousness**, adulation, blandishment, fawning, servility, sweet-talk (*inf*), sycophancy

flaunt *v* = **show off**, brandish, display,

flautist *n* see FLUTE.

fla·vor [FLAY-vər] *n* **1** mixed sensation of smell and taste. **2** distinctive taste, savor. **3** undefinable characteristic, quality of anything. ♦ *vt* **4** give flavor to. **5** season. **fla'vor·ing** *n* **fla'vor·ful** *adj*

flaw *n* **1** crack. **2** defect, blemish. ♦ *vt* **3** make flaw in. **flaw'less** *adj* perfect.

flax [flaks] *n* **1** plant grown for its textile fiber and seeds. **2** its fibers, spun into linen thread. **flax'en** *adj* **1** of flax. **2** light yellow or straw-colored.

flay *vt* **1** strip skin off. **2** criticize severely.

flea [flee] *n* small, wingless, jumping, blood-sucking insect. **flea'bag** *n* sl **1** worthless racehorse, unkempt dog, etc. **2** shabby hotel, etc. **flea'bite** *n* **1** insect's bite. **2** trifling injury. **3** trifle. **flea'-bit·ten** *adj* **1** bitten by flea. **2** mean, worthless. **3** scruffy. **flea market** market, usu. held outdoors, for used articles, cheap goods.

fleck [flek] *n* **1** small mark, streak, or particle. ♦ *vt* **2** mark with flecks.

fled pt./pp. of FLEE.

fledged [flejd] *adj* **1** (of birds) able to fly. **2** experienced, trained. **fledg'ling** *n* **1** young bird. **2** inexperienced person.

flee *v* fled, flee·ing run away from.

fleece [fleez] *n* **1** sheep's wool. ♦ *vt* fleeced, fleec·ing **2** rob. **fleec'y** *adj* fleec·i·er, fleec·i·est resembling wool.

fleet¹ *n* **1** number of warships organized as

unit. **2** number of ships, automobiles, etc. operating together.

fleet² *adj* -er, -est swift, nimble. **fleet'ing** *adj* passing, transient. **fleet'ing·ly** *adv*

flesh *n* **1** soft part, muscular substance, between skin and bone. **2** in plants, pulp. **3** fat. **4** person's family. **flesh'ly** *adj* -li·er, -li·est carnal, material. **flesh'y** *adj* flesh·i·er, flesh·i·est plump, pulpy. **flesh'pots** *pl n* (places catering to) self-indulgent living. **in the flesh** in person, actually present.

fleur-de-lis [flur-dl-EE] *n*, *pl* **fleurs-de-lis** [-dl-EEZ] heraldic lily with three petals.

flew pt. of FLY.

flex [fleks] *n* **1** act of flexing. ♦ *v* **2** bend, be bent. **flex·i·bil'i·ty** *n* **flex'i·ble** *adj* **1** easily bent. **2** manageable. **3** adaptable.
flex'time *n* system permitting variation in starting and finishing times of work, providing agreed total time is worked over a specified period.

flib·ber·ti·gib·bet [FLIB-ər-tee-jib-it] *n* flighty, chattering person.

flick [flik] *vt* **1** strike lightly, jerk. ♦ *n* **2** light blow. **3** jerk. **4** sl motion picture.

flick·er [FLIK-ər] *vi* **1** burn, shine, unsteadily. **2** waver, quiver. ♦ *n* **3** unsteady light or movement.

flight [flīt] *n* **1** act or manner of flying through air. **2** number flying together, as birds. **3** journey in aircraft. **4** air force unit

————— THESAURUS —————

exhibit, flash about, flourish, parade, sport (inf)

flavor *n* **1** = **taste**, aroma, flavoring, piquancy, relish, savor, seasoning, smack, tang, zest **2** = **quality**, character, essence, feel, feeling, style, tinge, tone ♦ *v* **3** = **season**, ginger up, imbue, infuse, leaven, spice

flaw *n* = **weakness**, blemish, chink in one's armor, defect, failing, fault, imperfection, weak spot

flawed *adj* = **damaged**, blemished, defective, erroneous, faulty, imperfect, unsound

flawless *adj* = **perfect**, faultless, impeccable, spotless, unblemished, unsullied

flee *v* = **run away**, bolt, depart, escape, fly, make one's getaway, take flight, take off (inf), take to one's heels, turn tail

fleet¹ *n* = **navy**, armada, flotilla, task force

fleeting *adj* = **momentary**, brief,

ephemeral, passing, short-lived, temporary, transient, transitory

flesh *n* **1** = **meat**, brawn, fat, tissue, weight **2** = **human nature**, carnality, flesh and blood **3** one's own flesh and blood = **family**, blood, kin, kinsfolk, kith and kin, relations, relatives

flexibility *n* = **adaptability**, adjustability, elasticity, give (inf), pliability, pliancy, resilience, springiness

flexible *adj* **1** = **pliable**, elastic, lithe, plastic, pliant, springy, stretchy, supple **2** = **adaptable**, adjustable, discretionary, open, variable

flick *v* **1** = **strike**, dab, flip, hit, tap, touch **2** flick through = **browse**, flip through, glance at, skim, skip, thumb

flicker *v* **1** = **twinkle**, flare, flash, glimmer, gutter, shimmer, sparkle **2** = **flutter**, quiver, vibrate, waver ♦ *n* **3** = **glimmer**, flare, flash, gleam, spark **4** = **trace**, breath, glimmer, iota, spark of command. **5** power of flying. **6** swift movement or passage. **7** sally. **8** distance flown. **9** stairs between two landings. **10** running away. **flight recorder** electronic device in aircraft storing information about its flight.

flight·y [FLĪ-tee] *adj* **flight·i·er, flight·i·est** frivolous, erratic.

flim·sy [FLIM-zee] *adj* **-si·er, -si·est 1** frail, weak, thin. **2** easily destroyed. **flim'si·ness** *n*

flinch *vi* shrink, draw back, wince.

fling *v* **flung, fling·ing.** *mainly tr* **1** throw, send, move, with force. ◆ *n* **2** throw. **3** hasty attempt. **4** spell of indulgence. **5** vigorous dance.

flint *n* **1** hard steel-gray stone. **2** piece of this. **3** hard substance used (as flint) for striking fire. **flint'y** *adj* **flint·i·er, flint·i·est 1** like or consisting of flint. **2** hard, cruel.

flip *v* **flipped, flip·ping 1** throw or flick lightly. **2** turn over. **3** *sl* react with astonishment, become irrational. ◆ *n* **4** instance, act, of flipping. **5** drink with beaten egg. **flip'pan·cy** *n, pl* **-cies flip'pant** *adj* treating serious things lightly. **flip'per** *n* **1** limb, fin for swimming. ◆ *pl* **2** fin-shaped rubber devices worn on feet to help in swimming.

flirt [flurt] *vi* **1** toy, play with another's affections. **2** trifle, toy (with). ◆ *n* **3** person who flirts. **flir·ta'tion** [-TAY-shən] *n* **flir·ta'tious** *adj*

flit *vi* **flit·ted, flit·ting 1** pass lightly and rapidly. **2** dart. **3** *inf* go away hastily, secretly.

flitch [flich] *n* side of bacon.

float [floht] *vi* **1** rest, drift on surface of liquid. **2** be suspended freely. **3** move aimlessly. ◆ *vt* **4** of liquid, support, bear alone. **5** in commerce, get (company) started. **6** obtain loan. ◆ *n* **7** light object used to help someone or something float. **8** motor vehicle carrying tableau, etc., in parade. **9** uncollected checks, etc. in process of transfer between banks, etc. **flo·ta'tion** *n* act of floating, esp. floating of business venture.

floc·cu·late [FLOK-yə-layt] *vt* **-lat·ed, -lat·ing** form into masses of particles. **floc'cu·lant** [-lənt] *n* chemical for accomplishing this.

floc·cu·lent [FLOK-yə-lənt] *adj* like tufts of wool.

flock¹ [flok] *n* **1** number of animals of one kind together. **2** *fig* body of people. **3** religious congregation. ◆ *vi* **4** gather in a crowd.

flock² *n* **1** lock, tuft of wool, etc. **2** wool refuse for stuffing cushions, etc.

floe [floh] *n* sheet of floating ice.

flog *vt* **flogged, flog·ging 1** beat with whip,

flight¹ *n* **1** *Of air travel* = **journey**, trip, voyage **2** = **aviation**, aeronautics, flying **3** = **flock**, cloud, formation, squadron, swarm, unit

flight² *n* = **escape**, departure, exit, exodus, fleeing, getaway, retreat, running away

flimsy *adj* **1** = **fragile**, delicate, frail, insubstantial, makeshift, rickety, shaky **2** = **thin**, gauzy, gossamer, light, sheer, transparent **3** = **unconvincing**, feeble, implausible, inadequate, lousy (*sl*), pathetic, poor, unsatisfactory, weak

flinch *v* = **recoil**, cower, cringe, draw back, quail, shy, shrink, shy away, wince

fling *v* **1** = **throw**, cast, catapult, heave, hurl, propel, sling, toss ◆ *n* **2** = **binge** (*inf*), bash, good time, party, spree

flip *v, n* = **toss**, flick, snap, spin, throw

flippancy *n* = **frivolity**, impertinence, irreverence, levity, pertness, sauciness

flippant *adj* = **frivolous**, cheeky, disrespectful, glib, impertinent, irreverent, offhand, superficial

flirt *v* **1** = **lead on**, hit on (*sl*), make advances, make eyes at, philander **2** (usually with *with*) = **toy with**, consider, dabble in, entertain, expose oneself to, give a thought to, play with, trifle with ◆ *n* **3** = **tease**, coquette, heart-breaker, hussy, philanderer

flirtatious *adj* = **teasing**, amorous, come-hither, coquettish, coy, enticing, flirty, provocative, sportive

float *v* **1** = **be buoyant**, hang, hover **2** = **glide**, bob, drift, move gently, sail, slide, slip along **3** = **launch**, get going, promote, set up

floating *adj* **1** = **buoyant**, afloat, buoyed up, sailing, swimming **2** = **fluctuating**, free, movable, unattached, variable, wandering

flock *n* **1** = **herd**, colony, drove, flight, gaggle, skein **2** = **crowd**, collection, company, congregation, gathering, group, herd, host, mass ◆ *v* **3** = **gather**, collect, congregate, converge, crowd, herd, stick, etc. **2** *sl* sell, esp. vigorously.

flood [flud] *n* **1** inundation, overflow of water. **2** rising of tide. **3** outpouring. **4** flowing water. ◆ *vt* **5** inundate. **6** cover, fill with water. **7** arrive, move, etc. in great numbers. **flood'gate** *n* gate, sluice for letting water in or out. **flood'light** *n* broad, intense beam of artificial light. **flood'lit** *adj* **flood tide** the rising tide.

floor [flor] *n* **1** lower surface of room. **2** set of rooms on one level, story. **3** flat space. **4** (right to speak in) meeting or legislative chamber. **5** lower limit. ◆ *vt* **6** supply with floor. **7** knock down. **8** confound. **floor'ing** *n* material for floors. **floor show** entertainment in nightclub, etc.

flop *vi* **flopped, flop·ping 1** bend, fall, collapse loosely, carelessly. **2** fall flat on floor, on water, etc. **3** *inf* go to sleep. **4** *inf* fail. ◆ *n* **5** flopping movement or sound. **6** *inf* failure. **flop'pi·ness** *n* **flop'py** *adj* **-pi·er, -pi·est** limp, unsteady. **flop'house** *n* run-down rooming house. **floppy disk** *Computers* flexible magnetic disk that stores information.

flo·ra [FLOR-ə] *n* **1** plants of a region. **2** list of them. **flor'al** *adj* of flowers. **flo·res'cence** [-əns] *n* state or time of flowering. **flo·ret** [FLOR-it] *n* small flower forming part of composite flower. **flo'ri·cul·ture** *n* cultivation of flowers. **flo·ri·cul'tur·ist** *n* **flo'rist** *n* dealer in flowers.

flor'id *adj* **1** with red, flushed complexion. **2** ornate.

floss [flaws] *n* **1** mass of fine, silky fibers. **2** fluff. **floss'y** *adj* **floss·i·er, floss·i·est 1** light and downy. **2** excessively fancy.

flotation see FLOAT.

flo·til·la [floh-TIL-ə] *n* fleet of small vessels, esp. naval vessels.

flot·sam [FLOT-səm] *n* **1** floating wreckage. **2** discarded waste objects. **3** penniless population of city, etc.

flounce[1] [flowns] *vi* **flounced, flounc·ing 1** go, move abruptly and impatiently. ◆ *n* **2** fling, jerk of body or limb.

flounce[2] *n* ornamental gathered strip on woman's garment.

floun·der[1] [FLOWN-dər] *vi* **1** plunge and struggle, esp. in water or mud. **2** proceed in bungling, hesitating manner. ◆ *n* **3** act of floundering.

flounder[2] *n* type of flatfish.

flour [FLOW-ər] *n* **1** powder prepared by sifting and grinding wheat, etc. **2** fine soft powder. ◆ *vt* **3** sprinkle with flour.

flour·ish [FLUR-ish] *vi* **1** thrive. **2** be in the prime. ◆ *vt* **3** brandish, display. **4** wave about. ◆ *n* **5** ornamental curve. **6** showy gesture in speech, etc. **7** waving of hand, weapon, etc. **8** fanfare (of trumpets).

flout [flowt] *vt* **1** show contempt for, mock. **2** defy.

flow [floh] *vi* **1** glide along as stream. **2** circulate, as the blood. **3** move easily. **4**

————————— THESAURUS —————————

huddle, mass, throng

flog *v* = **beat**, flagellate, flay, lash, scourge, thrash, trounce, whack, whip

flood *n* **1** = **deluge**, downpour, inundation, overflow, spate, tide, torrent **2** = **abundance**, flow, glut, profusion, rush, stream, torrent ◆ *v* **3** = **immerse**, drown, inundate, overflow, pour over, submerge, swamp **4** = **engulf**, overwhelm, surge, swarm, sweep **5** = **oversupply**, choke, fill, glut, saturate

floor *n* **1** = **tier**, level, stage, story ◆ *v* **2** = **knock down**, deck (*sl*), prostrate **3** *Inf* = **bewilder**, baffle, confound, defeat, disconcert, dumbfound, perplex, puzzle, stump (*inf*)

flop *v* **1** = **fall**, collapse, dangle, droop, drop, sag, slump **2** *Inf* = **fail**, come unstuck, fall flat, fold (*inf*), founder, go belly-up (*sl*), misfire ◆ *n* **3** *Inf* = **failure**, debacle, disaster, fiasco, nonstarter, washout (*inf*)

floppy *adj* = **droopy**, baggy, flaccid, limp, loose, pendulous, sagging, soft

floral *adj* = **flowery**, flower-patterned

florid *adj* **1** = **flushed**, blowsy, high-colored, rubicund, ruddy **2** = **flowery**, baroque, flamboyant, fussy, high-flown, ornate, overelaborate

flotsam *n* = **debris**, detritus, jetsam, junk, odds and ends, wreckage

flounder *v* = **fumble**, grope, struggle, stumble, thrash, toss

flourish *v* **1** = **prosper**, bloom, blossom, boom, flower, grow, increase, succeed, thrive **2** = **wave**, brandish, display, flaunt, shake, wield ◆ *n* **3** = **wave**, display, fanfare, parade, show **4** = **ornamentation**, curlicue, decoration, embellishment, plume, sweep

flourishing *adj* = **successful**, blooming, going places, in the pink, luxuriant, prospering, rampant, thriving

flout *v* = **defy**, laugh in the face of, mock,

move in waves. **5** hang loose. **6** be present in abundance. ♦ *n* **7** act, instance of flowing. **8** quantity that flows. **9** rise of tide. **10** ample supply. **flow chart** diagram showing sequence of operations in industrial, etc. process.

flow·er [FLOW-ər] *n* **1** colored (not green) part of plant from which fruit is developed. **2** bloom, blossom. **3** ornamentation. **4** choicest part, pick. ♦ *vi* **5** produce flowers. **6** bloom. **7** come to prime condition. ♦ *vt* **8** ornament with flowers. **flow'er·et** *n* small flower. **flow'er·y** *adj* **-er·i·er, -er·i·est** **1** abounding in flowers. **2** full of fine words, ornamented with figures of speech. **flower girl 1** girl selling flowers. **2** young girl designated to attend bride at wedding ceremony.

flown pp. of FLY.

flu *n* short for INFLUENZA.

fluc·tu·ate [FLUK-choo-ayt] *v* **-at·ed, -at·ing** vary, rise and fall, undulate. **fluc·tu·a'tion** *n*

flue [floo] *n* passage or pipe for smoke or hot air, chimney.

flu·ent [FLOO-ənt] *adj* **1** speaking, writing a given language easily and well. **2** easy, graceful.

fluff *n* **1** soft, feathery stuff. **2** down. **3** *inf* mistake. **4** *inf* anything insubstantial. ♦ *v* **5** make or become soft, light. **6** *inf* make mistake. **fluff'y** *adj* **fluff·i·er, fluff·i·est**

flu·id [FLOO-id] *adj* **1** flowing easily, not solid. ♦ *n* **2** gas or liquid. **flu·id'i·ty** *n* **fluid ounce** one sixteenth of a pint.

fluke¹ [flook] *n* **1** flat triangular point of

anchor. ♦ *pl* **2** whale's tail.

fluke² *n* **1** stroke of luck, accident. **fluk'y** *adj* **fluk·i·er, fluk·i·est** **1** uncertain. **2** got by luck.

fluke³ *n* **1** type of flatfish. **2** parasitic worm.

flume [floom] *n* narrow (artificial) channel for water.

flum·mer·y [FLUM-ə-ree] *n*, *pl* **-mer·ies** **1** nonsense, idle talk, humbug. **2** dish of milk, flour, eggs, etc.

flum·mox [FLUM-əks] *vt inf* bewilder, perplex.

flung pt./pp. of FLING.

flun·ky [FLUNG-kee] *n*, *pl* **-kies** **1** servant, esp. liveried manservant. **2** assistant doing menial work. **3** servile person.

fluo·res·cence [fluu-RES-əns] *n* emission of light or other radiation from substance when bombarded by particles (electrons, etc. or other radiation, as in fluorescent lamp). **fluo·res'cent** *adj*

fluor·ide [FLUUR-īd] *n* salt containing fluorine, esp. as added to domestic water supply as protection against tooth decay. **fluor'i·date** *vt* **-dat·ed, -dat·ing** treat with fluoride. **fluor·i·da'tion** *n* **fluor'ine** [-een] *n* nonmetallic element, yellowish gas.

flur·ry [FLUR-ee] *n*, *pl* **-ries** **1** squall, gust. **2** bustle, commotion. **3** fluttering (as of snowflakes). ♦ *vt* **-ried, -ry·ing** **4** agitate, bewilder, fluster.

flush¹ *vi* **1** blush. **2** of skin, redden. **3** flow suddenly or violently. **4** be excited. ♦ *vt* **5** send water through (a toilet or pipe) so as to clean it. **6** excite. ♦ *n* **7** reddening, blush. **8** rush of water. **9** excitement. **10**

THESAURUS

scoff at, scorn, sneer at, spurn

flow *v* **1 = run**, circulate, course, move, roll **2 = pour**, cascade, flood, gush, rush, stream, surge, sweep **3 = result**, arise, emanate, emerge, issue, proceed, spring ♦ *n* **4 = tide**, course, current, drift, flood, flux, outpouring, spate, stream

flower *n* **1 = bloom**, blossom, efflorescence **2 = elite**, best, cream, crème de la crème, pick ♦ *v* **3 = blossom**, bloom, flourish, mature, open, unfold

flowery *adj* **= ornate**, baroque, embellished, fancy, florid, high-flown

flowing *adj* **1 = streaming**, falling, gushing, rolling, rushing, smooth, sweeping **2 = fluent**, continuous, easy, smooth, unbroken, uninterrupted

fluctuate *v* **= change**, alternate, oscillate,

seesaw, shift, swing, vary, veer, waver

fluency *n* **= ease**, articulateness, assurance, command, control, facility, glibness, readiness, slickness, smoothness

fluent *adj* **= smooth**, articulate, easy, effortless, flowing, natural, voluble, well-versed

fluff *n* **= fuzz**, down, nap, pile

fluffy *adj* **= soft**, downy, feathery, fleecy, fuzzy

fluid *n* **1 = liquid**, liquor, solution ♦ *adj* **2 = liquid**, flowing, liquefied, melted, molten, runny, watery

fluke *n* **= lucky break**, accident, chance, coincidence, quirk of fate, serendipity, stroke of luck

flurry *n* **1 = commotion**, ado, bustle, disturbance, excitement, flutter, fuss, stir elation. **11** glow of color. **12** freshness, vigor. ◆ *adj* **13** full, in flood. **14** well supplied. **15** level with surrounding surface.

flush² *v* (cause to) leave cover and take flight.

flush³ *n* set of cards all of one suit.

flus•ter [FLUS-tər] *v* make or become nervous, agitated. ◆ *n*

flute [floot] *n* **1** wind instrument of tube with holes stopped by fingers or keys and blowhole in side. **2** groove, channel. ◆ *v* **flut•ed, flut•ing** ◆ *vi* **3** play on flute. ◆ *vt* **4** make grooves in. **flut'ist, flaut'ist** [FLOWT-] *n* flute player.

flut•ter [FLUT-ər] *v* **1** flap (as wings) rapidly without flight or in short flights. **2** quiver. **3** be or make excited, agitated. ◆ *n* **4** flapping movement. **5** nervous agitation.

flu•vi•al [FLOO-vee-əl] *adj* of rivers.

flux [fluks] *n* **1** discharge. **2** constant succession of changes. **3** substance mixed with metal to clean, aid adhesion in soldering, etc. **4** measure of strength in magnetic field.

fly¹ [flī] *v* **flew, flown, fly•ing 1** move through air on wings or in aircraft. **2** pass quickly (through air). **3** float loosely. **4** spring, rush. **5** flee, run away. ◆ *vt* **6** operate aircraft. **7** cause to fly. **8** set flying. ◆ *vi* **9** run from. ◆ *n* **10** (zipper or buttons fastening) opening in trousers. **11** flap in garment or tent. **12** flying. **flying** *adj* hurried, brief. **fly'fish** *v* fish with artificial fly as lure. **flying boat** airplane fitted with floats instead of landing wheels. **flying buttress** *Architecture* arched or slanting

structure attached at only one point to a mass of masonry. **flying colors** conspicuous success. **flying fish** fish with winglike fins used for gliding above the sea. **flying saucer** unidentified (disk-shaped) flying object, supposedly from outer space. **flying squad** special detachment of police, etc., ready to act quickly. **fly'leaf** *n*, *pl* **-leaves** blank leaf at beginning or end of book. **fly'o•ver** *n* formation of aircraft in flight for observation from ground. **fly'wheel** *n* heavy wheel regulating speed of machine.

fly² *n*, *pl* **flies** two-winged insect, esp. common housefly. **fly'catch•er** *n* small insect-eating songbird.

Fm *Chem.* fermium.

foal [fohl] *n* **1** young of horse, ass, etc. ◆ *v* **2** bear (foal).

foam [fohm] *n* **1** collection of small bubbles on liquid. **2** froth of saliva or sweat. **3** light cellular solid used for insulation, packing, etc. ◆ *v* (cause to) produce foam. **4** be very angry. **foam'y** *adj* **foam•i•er, foam•i•est**

fob *n* **1** short watch chain. **2** small pocket in waistband of trousers or vest.

fob off *v* **fobbed, fob•bing 1** ignore, dismiss someone or something in offhand (insulting) manner. **2** dispose of.

foci pl. of FOCUS.

fo•cus [FOH-kəs] *n*, *pl* **-cus•es** or **-ci** [-sī] **1** point at which rays meet after being reflected or refracted. **2** state of optical image when it is clearly defined. **3** state of instrument producing such image. **4** point of convergence. **5** point on which interest, activity is centered. ◆ *v* **-cused, -cus•ing** ◆

2 = gust, squall

flush¹ *v* **1 = blush,** color, glow, go red, redden **2 = rinse out,** cleanse, flood, hose down, wash out ◆ *n* **3 = blush,** color, glow, redness, rosiness

flush² *adj* **1 = level,** even, flat, square, true **2** *Inf* **= wealthy,** in the money (*inf*), moneyed, rich, well-heeled (*inf*), well-off

flushed *adj* **= blushing,** crimson, embarrassed, glowing, hot, red, rosy, ruddy

fluster *v* **1 = upset,** agitate, bother, confuse, disturb, perturb, rattle (*inf*), ruffle, unnerve ◆ *n* **2 = turmoil,** disturbance, dither, flap (*inf*), flurry, flutter, furor

flutter *v* **1 = beat,** flap, palpitate, quiver, ripple, tremble, vibrate, waver ◆ *n* **2 =**

vibration, palpitation, quiver, shiver, shudder, tremble, tremor, twitching **3 = agitation,** commotion, confusion, dither, excitement, fluster

fly¹ *v* **1 = take wing,** flit, flutter, hover, sail, soar, wing **2 = pilot,** control, maneuver, operate **3 = display,** flap, float, flutter, show, wave **4 = pass,** elapse, flit, glide, pass swiftly, roll on, run its course, slip away **5 = rush,** career, dart, dash, hurry, race, shoot, speed, sprint, tear **6 = flee,** escape, get away, run for it, skedaddle (*inf*), take to one's heels

flying *adj* **= hurried,** brief, fleeting, hasty, rushed, short-lived, transitory

foam *n* **1 = froth,** bubbles, head, lather, spray, spume, suds ◆ *v* **2 = bubble,** boil, vt **6** bring to focus, adjust. **7** concentrate. ◆ vi **8** come to focus. **9** converge. **fo'cal** [-kəl] adj of, at focus.

fod•der [FOD-ər] n bulk food for livestock.

foe [foh] n enemy.

fog n **1** thick mist. **2** dense watery vapor in lower atmosphere. **3** cloud of anything reducing visibility. **4** stupor. ◆ vt **fogged, fog•ging 5** cover in fog. **6** puzzle. **fog'gy** adj **-gi•er, -gi•est fog'horn** n instrument to warn ships in fog.

fo•gy [FOH-gee] n, pl **-gies** old-fashioned person.

foi•ble [FOI-bəl] n minor weakness, idiosyncrasy.

foil[1] vt **1** baffle, defeat, frustrate. ◆ n **2** blunt sword, with button on point for fencing.

foil[2] n **1** metal in thin sheet. **2** anything or person that sets off another to advantage.

foist vt (usu. with on or upon) sell, pass off inferior or unwanted thing as valuable.

fold[1] [fohld] vt **1** double up, bend part of. **2** interlace (arms). **3** wrap up. **4** clasp (in arms). **5** Cookery mix gently. ◆ vi **6** become folded. **7** admit of being folded. **8** inf fail. ◆ n **9** folding. **10** coil. **11** winding. **12** line made by folding. **13** crease. **14** foldlike geological formation. **fold'er** n binder, file for loose papers.

fold[2] n **1** enclosure for sheep. **2** body of believers, church.

fo•li•age [FOH-lee-ij] n leaves collectively,

leafage. **fo•li•a'ceous** [-AY-shəs] adj of or like leaf. **fo'li•ate** [-it] adj leaflike, having leaves.

fo•li•o [FOH-lee-oh] n, pl **-li•os 1** sheet of paper folded in half to make two leaves of book. **2** book of largest common size made up of such sheets. **3** page numbered on one side only. **4** page number.

folk [fohk] n **1** people in general. **2** family, relatives. **3** race of people. **folk dance** traditional country dance. **folk'lore** n tradition, customs, beliefs popularly held. **folk song** music originating among a people.

fol•li•cle [FOL-i-kəl] n **1** small cavity, sac. **2** seed vessel.

fol•low [FOL-oh] v **1** go or come after. ◆ vt **2** accompany, attend on. **3** keep to (path, etc.). **4** take as guide, conform to. **5** engage in. **6** have a keen interest in. **7** be consequent on. **8** grasp meaning of. ◆ vi **9** come next. **10** result. **fol'low•er** n disciple, supporter. **fol'low•ing** adj **1** about to be mentioned. ◆ n **2** body of supporters. **fol'low-through** n in ball games, continuation of stroke after impact with ball. **fol'low-up** n something done to reinforce initial action.

fol•ly [FOL-ee] n, pl **-lies 1** foolishness. **2** foolish action, idea, etc. **3** useless, extravagant structure.

fo•ment [foh-MENT] vt **1** foster, stir up. **2**

effervesce, fizz, froth, lather

focus n **1** = **center**, focal point, heart, hub, target ◆ v **2** = **concentrate**, aim, center, direct, fix, pinpoint, spotlight, zoom in

foe n = **enemy**, adversary, antagonist, opponent, rival

fog n = **mist**, gloom, miasma, murk, smog

foggy adj = **misty**, cloudy, dim, hazy, indistinct, murky, smoggy, vaporous

foil[1] v = **thwart**, balk, counter, defeat, disappoint, frustrate, nullify, stop

foil[2] n = **contrast**, antithesis, complement

foist v = **impose**, fob off, palm off, pass off, sneak in, unload

fold v **1** = **bend**, crease, double over **2** Inf = **go bankrupt**, collapse, crash, fail, go bust (inf), go to the wall, go under, shut down ◆ n **3** = **crease**, bend, furrow, overlap, pleat, wrinkle

folder n = **file**, binder, envelope, portfolio

folk n = **people**, clan, family, kin, kindred, race, tribe

follow v **1** = **come after**, come next, succeed, supersede, supplant, take the place of **2** = **pursue**, chase, dog, hound, hunt, shadow, stalk, track, trail **3** = **accompany**, attend, escort, tag along **4** = **obey**, be guided by, conform, heed, observe **5** = **understand**, appreciate, catch on (inf), comprehend, fathom, grasp, realize, take in **6** = **result**, arise, develop, ensue, flow, issue, proceed, spring **7** = **be interested in**, cultivate, keep abreast of, support

follower n = **supporter**, adherent, apostle, devotee, disciple, fan, pupil

following adj **1** = **next**, consequent, ensuing, later, subsequent, succeeding, successive ◆ n **2** = **supporters**, clientele, coterie, entourage, fans, retinue, suite, train

folly n = **foolishness**, imprudence, indiscretion, lunacy, madness, nonsense, rashness, stupidity bathe with warm lotions.

fond *adj* **-er, -est** tender, loving. **fond'ly** *adv*
fond'ness *n* fond of having liking for.

fon·dant [FON-dənt] *n* **1** soft sugar mixture
for candies. **2** candy made of this.

fon·dle [FON-dl] *vt* **-dled, -dling** caress.

fon·due [fon-DOO] *n* Swiss dish of cheese
and seasonings into which pieces of bread,
etc. are dipped.

font *n* **1** bowl for baptismal water usu. on
pedestal. **2** productive source. **3**
assortment of printing type of one size.

fon·ta·nel [fon-tn-EL] *n* soft, membraneous
gap between bones of baby's skull.

food *n* **1** solid nourishment. **2** what one
eats. **3** mental or spiritual nourishment.
food additive natural or synthetic
substance added to commercially
processed food as preservative or to add
color, flavor, etc. **food processor** electric
kitchen appliance for automatic chopping,
blending, etc. of foodstuffs. **food'stuff** *n*
food.

fool *n* **1** silly, empty-headed person. **2** dupe.
3 simpleton. **4** *Hist.* jester, clown. ◆ *vt* **5**
delude. **6** dupe. ◆ *vi* **7** act as fool. **fool'er·y**
n, pl **-er·ies 1** habitual folly. **2** act of playing
the fool. **3** absurdity. **fool'har·di·ness** *n*
fool'har·dy *adj* **-di·er, -di·est** foolishly
adventurous. **fool'ish** *adj* ill-considered,
silly, stupid. **fool'proof** *adj* proof against
failure. **fool's cap** jester's or dunce's cap.
fools'cap *n* inexpensive paper, esp.

legal-size (formerly with fool's cap as
watermark).

foot [fuut] *n, pl* **feet 1** lowest part of leg,
from ankle down. **2** lowest part of
anything, base, stand. **3** end of bed, etc. **4**
measure of twelve inches. **5** division of line
of verse. ◆ *v* (usu. tr) **6** dance. **foot it** *inf*
walk. **foot the bill** pay the entire cost.
foot'age *n* **1** length in feet. **2** length,
extent, of film used. **foot'ing** *n* **1** basis,
foundation. **2** firm standing, relations,
conditions. ◆ *pl* **3** (concrete) foundations
for walls of buildings. **foot-and-mouth
disease** infectious viral disease in sheep,
cattle, etc. **foot'ball** *n* **1** game played with
inflated oval ball. **2** the ball. **foot'ball pool**
form of gambling on results of football
games. **foot brake** brake operated by
pressure on foot pedal. **foot fault** *Tennis*
fault of overstepping baseline while
serving. **foot'hold** *n* **1** place affording
secure grip for the foot. **2** secure position
from which progress may be made.
foot'lights *pl n* lights across front of stage.
foot'loose *adj* free of any ties. **foot'note** *n*
note of reference or explanation printed at
foot of page. **foot-pound** *n* unit of
measurement of work in fps system.
foot'print *n* mark left by foot. **playing
foot'sie** flirting or sharing a surreptitious
intimacy. **foot'slog** *vi* **-slogged, slogging**
walk, go on foot. **foot'slog·ger** *n*

fop *n* man excessively concerned with

————————| THESAURUS |————————

fond *adj* **1 = loving**, adoring, affectionate,
amorous, caring, devoted, doting,
indulgent, tender, warm **2 = foolish**,
deluded, delusive, empty, naive,
overoptimistic, vain **3 fond of = keen on**,
addicted to, attached to, enamored of,
having a soft spot for, hooked on, into
(*inf*), partial to

fondle *v* **= caress**, cuddle, dandle, pat, pet,
stroke

fondly *adv* **1 = lovingly**, affectionately,
dearly, indulgently, possessively, tenderly,
with affection **2 = foolishly**, credulously,
naively, stupidly, vainly

fondness *n* **1 = liking**, attachment, fancy,
love, partiality, penchant, soft spot, taste,
weakness **2 = devotion**, affection,
attachment, kindness, love, tenderness

food *n* **= nourishment**, cuisine, diet, fare,
grub (*sl*), nutrition, rations, refreshment

fool *n* **1 = simpleton**, blockhead, dork (*sl*),

dunce, halfwit, idiot, ignoramus, imbecile
(*inf*), schmuck (*sl*) **2 = dupe**, fall guy (*inf*),
laughing stock, mug (*Brit. sl*), stooge (*sl*),
sucker (*sl*) **3 = clown**, buffoon, harlequin,
jester ◆ *v* **4 = deceive**, beguile, con (*inf*),
delude, dupe, hoodwink, mislead, take in,
trick

foolhardy *adj* **= rash**, hot-headed,
impetuous, imprudent, irresponsible,
reckless

foolish *adj* **= unwise**, absurd, ill-judged,
imprudent, injudicious, senseless, silly

foolishly *adv* **= unwisely**, idiotically,
ill-advisedly, imprudently, injudiciously,
mistakenly, stupidly

foolishness *n* **= stupidity**, absurdity, folly,
imprudence, indiscretion, irresponsibility,
silliness, weakness

foolproof *adj* **= infallible**, certain,
guaranteed, safe, sure-fire (*inf*),
unassailable, unbreakable

fashion. **fop'per·y** *n*, *pl* **-per·ies fop'pish** *adj*

for *prep* **1** intended to reach, directed or belonging to. **2** because of. **3** instead of. **4** toward. **5** on account of. **6** in favor of. **7** respecting. **8** during. **9** in search of. **10** in payment of. **11** in the character of. **12** in spite of. ◆ *conj* **13** because. **in for it** *inf* liable to punishment or blame.

for- *prefix* from, away, against, e.g. *forswear; forbid.*

for·age [FOR-ij] *n* **1** food for cattle and horses. ◆ *vi* **-aged, -ag·ing 2** collect forage. **3** make roving search.

for'ay *n* **1** raid, inroad. ◆ *vi* **2** make one.

for·bear [for-BAIR] *v* **-bore, -borne, -bear·ing** cease or refrain (from doing something). **for·bear'ance** *n* self-control, patience.

for·bid [fər-BID] *vt* **-bade** or **-bad, -bid** or **-bid·den, -bid** or **-bid·ding 1** prohibit. **2** refuse to allow. **forbidding** *adj* uninviting, threatening.

force [fors] *n* **1** strength, power. **2** compulsion. **3** that which tends to produce a change in a physical system. **4** mental or moral strength. **5** body of troops, police, etc. **6** group of people organized for particular task or duty. **7** effectiveness, operative state. **8** violence. ◆ *vt* **forced, forc·ing 9** constrain, compel. **10** produce by effort, strength. **11** break open. **12** urge, strain. **13** drive. **14** hasten maturity of. **forced** *adj* **1** accomplished by great effort. **2** compulsory. **3** unnatural. **4** strained. **5** excessive. **force'ful** *adj* powerful, persuasive. **for'ci·ble** *adj* **1** done by force. **2** efficacious, compelling, impressive. **3** strong. **for'ci·bly** *adv*

for·ceps [FOR-səps] *pl n* surgical pincers.

ford *n* shallow place where river may be crossed. ◆ *vt* **ford'a·ble** *adj*

fore[1] [for] *adj* **1** in front. ◆ *n* **2** front part.

fore[2] *interj* golfer's warning.

fore- *prefix* **1** before in time or rank, e.g. *forefather.* **2** at the front, e.g. *forecourt.*

fore-and-aft [FOR-ənd-AFT] *adj* placed in line from bow to stern of ship.

fore·arm [FOR-ahrm] *n* **1** arm between wrist and elbow. ◆ *vt* [for-AHRM] **2** arm beforehand.

fore·bear [FOR-bair] *n* ancestor.

fore·bode [for-BOHD] *vt* **-bod·ed, -bod·ing** indicate in advance. **foreboding** *n* anticipation of evil.

fore·cast [FOR-kast] *vt* **1** estimate

---

footing *n* **1** = **basis**, foundation, groundwork **2** = **relationship**, grade, position, rank, standing, status

footstep *n* = **step**, footfall, tread

forage *v* **1** = **search**, cast about, explore, hunt, rummage, scour, seek ◆ *n* **2** *Cattle, etc.* = **fodder**, feed, food, provender

foray *n* = **raid**, incursion, inroad, invasion, sally, sortie, swoop

forbear *v* = **refrain**, abstain, cease, desist, hold back, keep from, restrain oneself, stop

forbearance *n* = **patience**, long-suffering, moderation, resignation, restraint, self-control, temperance, tolerance

forbearing *adj* = **patient**, forgiving, indulgent, lenient, long-suffering, merciful, moderate, tolerant

forbid *v* = **prohibit**, ban, disallow, exclude, outlaw, preclude, rule out, veto

forbidden *adj* = **prohibited**, banned, outlawed, out of bounds, proscribed, taboo, vetoed

forbidding *adj* = **threatening**, daunting, frightening, hostile, menacing, ominous, sinister, unfriendly

force *n* **1** = **power**, energy, impulse, might, momentum, pressure, strength, vigor **2** = **compulsion**, arm-twisting (*inf*), coercion, constraint, duress, pressure, violence **3** = **intensity**, emphasis, fierceness, vehemence, vigor **4** = **army**, host, legion, patrol, regiment, squad, troop, unit **5** in **force: a** = **valid**, binding, current, effective, in operation, operative, working **b** = **in great numbers**, all together, in full strength ◆ *v* **6** = **compel**, coerce, constrain, dragoon, drive, impel, make, oblige, press, pressurize **7** = **break open**, blast, prise, wrench, wrest **8** = **push**, propel, thrust

forced *adj* **1** = **compulsory**, conscripted, enforced, involuntary, mandatory, obligatory **2** = **false**, affected, artificial, contrived, insincere, labored, stiff, strained, unnatural, wooden

forceful *adj* = **powerful**, cogent, compelling, convincing, dynamic, effective, persuasive

forcible *adj* **1** = **violent**, aggressive, armed, coercive, compulsory **2** = **strong**, compelling, energetic, forceful, potent, powerful, weighty

forebear *n* = **ancestor**, father, forefather,

beforehand (esp. weather). **2** prophesy. ◆
n **3** prediction.

fore·castle [FOHK-səl] *n* **1** forward raised
part of ship. **2** sailors' quarters.

fore·close [for-KLOHZ] *vt* **-closed,
-clos·ing 1** take away power of redeeming
(mortgage). **2** prevent, shut out, bar.
fore·clo·sure [-zhər] *n*

fore·court [FOR-kort] *n* **1** courtyard, open
space, in front of building. **2** *Tennis* part of
court between service line and net.

fore·fa·ther [FOR-fah-thər] *n* ancestor.

fore·fin·ger [FOR-fing-gər] *n* finger next to
thumb, index finger.

foregather see FORGATHER.

fore·go [for-GOH] *vt* **-went, -gone, -go·ing**
precede in time, place. **foregoing** *adj*
going before, preceding. **foregone** *adj* **1**
determined beforehand. **2** preceding.
foregone conclusion result that might
have been foreseen.

fore·ground [FOR-grownd] *n* part of view,
esp. in picture, nearest observer.

fore·hand [FOR-hand] *adj* of stroke in
racquet games made with inner side of
wrist leading.

fore·head [FOR-id] *n* part of face above
eyebrows and between temples.

for·eign [FOR-in] *adj* **1** not of, or in, one's
own country. **2** relating to, or connected
with other countries. **3** irrelevant. **4**
coming from outside. **5** unfamiliar,
strange. **for'eign·er** *n*

fore·man [FOR-mən] *n, pl* **-men 1** one in
charge of work. **2** leader of jury.

fore·mast [FOR-mast] *n* mast nearest bow.

fore·most [FOR-mohst] *adj, adv* first in
time, place, importance, etc.

fore·noon [FOR-noon] *n* morning.

fo·ren·sic [fə-REN-sik] *adj* of courts of law.
forensic medicine application of medical
knowledge in legal matters.

fore·play [FOR-play] *n* sexual stimulation
before intercourse.

fore·run·ner [FOR-run-ər] *n* one that goes
before, precursor.

fore·see [for-SEE] *vt* **-saw, -seen, -see·ing**
see beforehand.

fore·shad·ow [for-SHAD-oh] *vt* show,
suggest beforehand, be a type of.

fore·short·en [for-SHOR-tn] *vt* **1** draw
(object) so that it appears shortened. **2**
make shorter.

fore·sight [FOR-sīt] *n* **1** foreseeing. **2** care
for future.

fore·skin [FOR-skin] *n* skin that covers end
of penis.

for·est [FOR-ist] *n* **1** area with heavy
growth of trees and plants. **2** these trees. **3**
fig something resembling forest. ◆ *vt* **4**
plant, create forest (in an area). **for'est·er** *n*
one skilled in forestry. **for'est·ry** *n* study,
management of forest planting and
maintenance.

fore·stall [for-STAWL] *vt* **1** anticipate. **2**
prevent, guard against in advance.

fore·taste [FOR-tayst] *n* **1** anticipation. **2**
taste beforehand.

fore·tell [for-TEL] *vt* **-told, -tel·ling**
prophesy.

fore·thought [FOR-thawt] *n* thoughtful
consideration of future events.

forerunner, predecessor

foreboding *n* = **dread**, anxiety,
apprehension, apprehensiveness, chill,
fear, misgiving, premonition, presentiment

forecast *v* **1** = **predict**, anticipate, augur,
divine, foresee, foretell, prophesy ◆ *n* **2** =
prediction, conjecture, guess, prognosis,
prophecy

forefather *n* = **ancestor**, father, forebear,
forerunner, predecessor

forefront *n* = **lead**, center, fore,
foreground, front, prominence, spearhead,
vanguard

foregoing *adj* = **preceding**, above,
antecedent, anterior, former, previous,
prior

foreign *adj* = **alien**, exotic, external,
imported, remote, strange, unfamiliar,

unknown

foreigner *n* = **alien**, immigrant, incomer,
stranger

foremost *adj* = **leading**, chief, highest,
paramount, pre-eminent, primary, prime,
principal, supreme

forerunner *n* = **precursor**, envoy,
harbinger, herald, prototype

foresee *v* = **anticipate**, envisage, forecast,
foretell, predict, prophesy

foreshadow *v* = **predict**, augur, forebode,
indicate, portend, prefigure, presage,
promise, signal

foresight *n* = **anticipation**, far-sightedness,
forethought, precaution, preparedness,
prescience, prudence

foretell *v* = **predict**, forecast, forewarn,
presage, prognosticate, prophesy

for·ev·er [for-EV-ər] *adv* **1** always. **2** eternally. **3** *inf* for a long time.

fore·warn [for-WORN] *vt* warn, caution in advance.

forewent see FOREGO.

fore·word [FOR-wurd] *n* preface.

for·feit [FOR-fit] *n* **1** thing lost by crime or fault. **2** penalty, fine. ◆ *adj* **3** lost by crime or fault. ◆ *vt* **4** lose by penalty. **for'fei·ture** [-fi-chər] *n*

for·gath·er [for-GATH-ər] *vi* meet together, assemble, associate.

forge¹ [forj] *n* **1** place where metal is worked, smithy. **2** furnace, workshop for melting or refining metal. ◆ *vt* **forged, forg·ing 3** shape (metal) by heating in fire and hammering. **4** make, shape, invent. **5** make a fraudulent imitation of thing. **6** counterfeit. **forg'er** *n* **for'ger·y** *n, pl* **-ger·ies 1** forged artwork, document, currency, etc. **2** the making of it.

forge² *vi* **forged, forg·ing** advance steadily.

for·get [fər-GET] *vt* **-got, -got·ten** *or* **-got, -get·ting** lose memory of, neglect, overlook. **for·get'ful** *adj* liable to forget.

for·give [fər-GIV] *v* **-gave, -giv·en, -giv·ing 1** cease to blame or hold resentment against. **2** pardon. **for·give'ness** *n*

for·go [for-GOH] *vt* **-went, -gone, -go·ing 1** go without. **2** give up.

forgot, forgotten see FORGET.

fork *n* **1** pronged instrument for eating food. **2** pronged tool for digging or lifting. **3** division into branches. **4** point of this division. **5** one of the branches. ◆ *vi* **6** branch. ◆ *vt* **7** dig, lift, throw, with fork. **8** make fork-shaped. **fork out** *inf* pay (reluctantly).

for·lorn' *adj* **1** forsaken. **2** desperate. **forlorn hope** anything undertaken with little hope of success.

form *n* **1** shape, visible appearance. **2** visible person or animal. **3** structure. **4** nature. **5** species, kind. **6** regularly drawn up document, esp. printed one with blanks for particulars. **7** condition, good condition. **8** customary way of doing things. **9** set order of words. **10** *Printing* frame for type. ◆ *vt* **11** shape, mold, arrange, organize. **12** train, shape in the mind, conceive. **13** go to make up, make part of. ◆ *vi* **14** come into existence or shape. **for·ma'tion** *n* **1** forming. **2** thing formed. **3** structure, shape, arrangement. **4** military order. **form'a·tive** *adj* **1** of, relating to, development. **2** serving or tending to

---

THESAURUS

forethought *n* = **anticipation**, far-sightedness, foresight, precaution, providence, provision, prudence

forever *adv* **1** = **evermore**, always, for all time, for keeps, in perpetuity, till Doomsday, till the cows come home (*inf*) **2** = **constantly**, all the time, continually, endlessly, eternally, incessantly, interminably, perpetually, twenty-four-seven (*sl*), unremittingly

forewarn *v* = **caution**, advise, alert, apprise, give fair warning, put on guard, tip off

forfeit *n* **1** = **penalty**, damages, fine, forfeiture, loss ◆ *v* **2** = **lose**, be deprived of, be stripped of, give up, relinquish, renounce, say good-bye to, surrender

forge *v* **1** = **create**, construct, devise, fashion, form, frame, make, mold, shape, work **2** = **falsify**, copy, counterfeit, fake, feign, imitate

forgery *n* **1** = **fraudulence**, coining, counterfeiting, falsification, fraudulent imitation **2** = **fake**, counterfeit, falsification, imitation, phoney or phony (*inf*), sham

forget *v* = **neglect**, leave behind, lose sight

of, omit, overlook

forgetful *adj* = **absent-minded**, careless, inattentive, neglectful, oblivious, unmindful, vague

forgive *v* = **excuse**, absolve, acquit, condone, exonerate, let bygones be bygones, let off (*inf*), pardon

forgiveness *n* = **pardon**, absolution, acquittal, amnesty, exoneration, mercy, remission

forgiving *adj* = **merciful**, clement, compassionate, forbearing, lenient, magnanimous, soft-hearted, tolerant

forgo *v* = **give up**, abandon, do without, relinquish, renounce, resign, surrender, waive, yield

forgotten *adj* = **left behind**, bygone, lost, omitted, past, past recall, unremembered

fork *v* = **branch**, bifurcate, diverge, divide, part, split

forked *adj* = **branching**, angled, bifurcate(d), branched, divided, pronged, split, zigzag

forlorn *adj* = **miserable**, disconsolate, down in the dumps (*inf*), helpless, hopeless, pathetic, pitiful, unhappy, form. **3** used in forming. **form'less** adj

for·mal [FOR-məl] adj **1** ceremonial, according to rule. **2** of outward form or routine. **3** of, for, formal occasions. **4** according to rule that does not matter. **5** precise. **6** stiff. ◆ n **7** formal dance. **for'mal·ism** n **1** quality of being formal. **2** exclusive concern for form, structure, technique in an activity. **for·mal'i·ty** n, pl **-ties 1** observance required by custom or etiquette. **2** condition or quality of being formal. **3** conformity to custom. **4** conventionality, mere form. **5** in art, precision, stiffness, as opposed to originality.

for·mal·de·hyde [for-MAL-də-hīd] n colorless, poisonous, pungent gas, used in making antiseptics and in chemistry. **for'ma·lin** [-mə-lin] n solution of formaldehyde in water, used as disinfectant, preservative, etc.

for'mat n **1** size and shape of book. **2** organization of TV show, etc.

for·mer [FOR-mər] adj **1** earlier in time. **2** of past times. **3** first named. ◆ pron **4** first named thing or person or fact. **for'mer·ly** adv previously.

for·mi·da·ble [FOR-mi-də-bəl] adj **1** to be feared. **2** overwhelming, terrible, redoubtable. **3** likely to be difficult, serious. **for'mi·da·bly** adv

for·mu·la [FOR-myə-lə] n, pl **-las** or **-lae** [-lee] **1** set form of words setting forth principle, method or rule for doing, producing something. **2** substance so prepared. **3** specific category of racing car. **4** recipe. **5** group of numbers, letters, or symbols expressing a scientific or mathematical rule. **for'mu·late** [-layt] vt **-lat·ed, -lat·ing 1** reduce to, express in formula, or in definite form. **2** devise. **for·mu·la'tion** n

for·ni·ca·tion [for-ni-KAY-shən] n sexual intercourse outside marriage. **for'ni·cate** vi **-cat·ed, -cat·ing**

for·sake [for-SAYK] vt **-sook, -sak·en, -sak·ing 1** abandon, desert. **2** give up.

for·sooth' adv obs in truth.

for·swear [for-SWAIR] vt **-swore, -sworn, -swear·ing 1** renounce, deny. **2** refl perjure.

for·syth·i·a [for-SITH-ee-ə] n widely cultivated shrub with yellow flowers.

fort n fortified place, stronghold.

woebegone, wretched

form n **1** = **shape**, appearance, configuration, formation, pattern, structure **2** = **type**, kind, sort, style, variety **3** = **condition**, fettle, fitness, health, shape, trim **4** = **procedure**, convention, custom, etiquette, protocol **5** = **document**, application, paper, sheet **6** = **class**, grade, rank ◆ v **7** = **make**, build, construct, create, fashion, forge, mold, produce, shape **8** = **arrange**, combine, draw up, organize **9** = **take shape**, appear, become visible, come into being, crystallize, grow, materialize, rise **10** = **develop**, acquire, contract, cultivate, pick up **11** = **constitute**, compose, comprise, make up

formal adj **1** = **official**, ceremonial, ritualistic, solemn **2** = **conventional**, affected, correct, precise, stiff, unbending

formality n **1** = **convention**, custom, procedure, red tape, rite, ritual **2** = **correctness**, decorum, etiquette, protocol

format n = **style**, appearance, arrangement, construction, form, layout, look, make-up, plan, type

formation n **1** = **establishment**, constitution, development, forming,

generation, genesis, manufacture, production **2** = **pattern**, arrangement, configuration, design, grouping, structure

formative adj = **developmental**, influential

former adj = **previous**, earlier, erstwhile, one-time, prior

formerly adv = **previously**, at one time, before, lately, once

formidable adj **1** = **intimidating**, daunting, dismaying, fearful, frightful, menacing, terrifying, threatening **2** = **impressive**, awesome, cool (inf), great, mighty, phat (sl), powerful, redoubtable, terrific (inf), tremendous

formula n = **method**, blueprint, precept, principle, procedure, recipe, rule

formulate v **1** = **define**, detail, express, frame, give form to, set down, specify, systematize **2** = **devise**, develop, forge, invent, map out, originate, plan, work out

forsake v **1** = **desert**, abandon, disown, leave in the lurch, strand **2** = **give up**, forgo, relinquish, renounce, set aside, surrender, yield

forsaken adj = **deserted**, abandoned, disowned, forlorn, left in the lurch, marooned, outcast, stranded

forte¹ [fort] *n* one's strong point, that in which one excels.

for·te² [FOR-tay] *adv Mus.* loudly. **for·tis·si·mo** *adv Mus.* very loudly.

forth *adv* onward, into view. **forth·com'ing** *adj* **1** about to come. **2** ready when wanted. **3** willing to talk, communicative. **forth·with'** *adv* at once, immediately.

forth·right [FORTH-rīt] *adj* **1** direct. **2** outspoken.

fortieth see FOUR.

for·ti·fy [FOR-tə-fī] *vt* **-fied, -fy·ing 1** strengthen. **2** provide with defensive works. **for·ti·fi·ca'tion** *n*

for·ti·tude [FOR-ti-tood] *n* courage in adversity or pain, endurance.

fort·night [FORT-nīt] *n* two weeks. **fort'night·ly** *adv*

FORTRAN [FOR-tran] *Computers* a programming language for mathematical and scientific purposes.

for·tress [FOR-tris] *n* large fort or fortified town.

for·tu·i·tous [for-TOO-i-təs] *adj* accidental, by chance. **for·tu'i·tous·ly** *adv*

for·tune [FOR-chən] *n* **1** good luck, prosperity. **2** wealth. **3** stock of wealth. **4** chance, luck. **for'tu·nate** [-nit] *adj* **for'tu·nate·ly** *adv* **fortune hunter** person seeking fortune, esp. by marriage. **fortuneteller** *n* one who predicts a person's future.

forty see FOUR.

fo·rum [FOR-əm] *n* (place or medium for) meeting, assembly for open discussion or debate.

for·ward [FOR-wərd] *adj* **1** lying in front of. **2** onward. **3** presumptuous, impudent. **4** advanced, progressive. **5** relating to the future. ♦ *n* **6** player placed in forward position in various team games, e.g. basketball. ♦ *adv* **7** toward the future. **8** toward the front, to the front, into view. **9** at, in fore part of ship. **10** onward, so as to make progress. ♦ *vt* **11** help forward. **12** send, dispatch. **for'ward·ly** *adv* pertly. **for'ward·ness** *n* **for'wards** [-wərdz] *adv* **forward slash** forward-sloping diagonal mark (/).

forwent see FORGO.

fos·sil [FOS-əl] *n* **1** remnant or impression of animal or plant, esp. prehistoric one,

fort *n* **1** = **fortress**, blockhouse, camp, castle, citadel, fortification, garrison, stronghold **2 hold the fort** = **stand in**, carry on, keep things on an even keel, take over the reins

forte *n* = **speciality**, gift, métier, strength, strong point, talent

forth *adv* = **forward**, ahead, away, onward, out, outward

forthcoming *adj* **1** = **approaching**, coming, expected, future, imminent, impending, prospective, upcoming **2** = **accessible**, at hand, available, in evidence, obtainable, on tap (*inf*), ready **3** = **communicative**, chatty, expansive, free, informative, open, sociable, talkative, unreserved

forthright *adj* = **outspoken**, blunt, candid, direct, frank, open, plain-spoken, straightforward, upfront (*inf*)

forthwith *adv* = **at once**, directly, immediately, instantly, quickly, right away, straightaway, without delay

fortification *n* **1** = **defense**, bastion, fastness, fort, fortress, protection, stronghold **2** = **strengthening**, reinforcement

fortify *v* = **strengthen**, augment, buttress,

protect, reinforce, shore up, support

fortitude *n* = **courage**, backbone, bravery, fearlessness, grit, perseverance, resolution, strength, valor

fortress *n* = **castle**, citadel, fastness, fort, redoubt, stronghold

fortunate *adj* **1** = **lucky**, favored, in luck, successful, well-off **2** = **favorable**, advantageous, convenient, expedient, felicitous, fortuitous, helpful, opportune, providential, timely, win-win (*inf*)

fortunately *adv* = **luckily**, by a happy chance, by good luck, happily, providentially

fortune *n* **1** = **wealth**, affluence, opulence, possessions, property, prosperity, riches, treasure **2** = **luck**, chance, destiny, fate, kismet, providence **3 fortunes** = **destiny**, adventures, experiences, history, lot, success

forward *adj* **1** = **leading**, advance, first, foremost, front, head **2** = **presumptuous**, bold, brash, brazen, cheeky, familiar, impertinent, impudent, pushy (*inf*) **3** = **well-developed**, advanced, precocious, premature ♦ *adv* **4** = **ahead**, forth, on, onward ♦ *v* **5** = **promote**, advance, assist, expedite, further, hasten, hurry **6** = **send**, preserved in earth. **2** *inf* person, idea, etc. that is outdated and incapable of change. **fos'sil·ize** *v* **-ized, -iz·ing 1** turn into fossil. **2** petrify.

fos·ter [FAW-stər] *vt* **1** promote growth or development of. **2** bring up child, esp. not one's own. ♦ *adj* **3** of or involved in fostering a child, e.g. *foster parents*.

fought pt./pp. of FIGHT.

foul [fowl] *adj* **-er, -est 1** loathsome, offensive. **2** stinking. **3** dirty. **4** unfair. **5** wet, rough. **6** obscene, disgustingly abusive. **7** charged with harmful matter, clogged, choked. ♦ *n* **8** act of unfair play. **9** the breaking of a rule. ♦ *adv* **10** unfairly. ♦ *v* (mainly tr) **11** make, become foul. **12** jam. **13** collide with. **foul'ly** *adv*

found¹ [fownd] pt./pp. of FIND.

found² *vt* **1** establish, institute. **2** lay base of. **3** base, ground. **foun·da'tion** *n* **1** basis. **2** base, lowest part of building. **3** founding. **4** endowed institution, etc. **found'er** *n* **foundation stone** one of stones forming foundation of building, esp. stone laid with public ceremony.

found³ *vt* **1** melt and run into mold. **2** cast. **found'er** *n* **found'ry** *n, pl* **-ries 1** place for casting. **2** art of this.

found·er [FOWN-dər] *vi* **1** collapse. **2** sink. **3** become stuck as in mud, etc.

found·ling [FOWND-ling] *n* deserted infant.

fount [fownt] *n* fountain.

foun·tain [FOWN-tn] *n* **1** jet of water, esp. ornamental one. **2** spring. **3** source. **foun'tain·head** [-hed] *n* source. **fountain pen** pen with ink reservoir.

four [for] *n, adj* cardinal number next after three. **fourth** *adj* the ordinal number. **fourth'ly** *adv* **for'ti·eth** *adj* **for'ty** *adj, n, pl* **-ties** four tens. **four'teen'** *n, adj* four plus ten. **four·teenth'** *adj* **four-stroke** *adj* describing an internal-combustion engine firing once every four strokes of piston. **four'post·er** *n* bed with four posts for curtains, etc. **four'some** *n* **1** group of four people. **2** game or dance for four people. **four'square** *adj* firm, steady. **on all fours** on hands and knees. **401K** employer-run savings plan for retirement.

fowl *n* **1** domestic rooster or hen. **2** bird, its flesh. ♦ *vi* **3** hunt wild birds. **fowling piece** shotgun for fowling.

fox [foks] *n* **1** red bushy-tailed animal. **2** its fur. **3** cunning person. ♦ *vt* **4** perplex. **5** discolor (paper) with brown spots. **6** mislead. ♦ *vi* **7** act craftily. **8** sham. **fox'y** *adj* **fox·i·er, fox·i·est 1** foxlike. **2** *sl* sexually appealing. **3** attractive. **fox'hole** *n* in war, small trench giving protection. **fox'hound** *n* dog bred for hunting foxes. **fox terrier** small dog now mainly kept as a pet. **fox'trot** *n* (music for) ballroom dance. ♦ *v*

foy·er [FOI-ər] *n* **1** entrance hall in theaters, hotels, etc. **2** vestibule.

Fr *Chem.* francium.

fra·cas [FRAY-kəs] *n* **1** noisy quarrel. **2** uproar, brawl.

dispatch, post, send on

foster *v* **1** = **promote**, cultivate, encourage, feed, nurture, stimulate, support, uphold **2** = **bring up**, mother, nurse, raise, rear, take care of

foul *adj* **1** = **dirty**, fetid, filthy, funky (*sl*), malodorous, nauseating, putrid, repulsive, scuzzy (*sl*), squalid, stinking, unclean **2** = **obscene**, abusive, blue, coarse, indecent, lewd, profane, scurrilous, vulgar **3** = **offensive**, abhorrent, despicable, detestable, disgraceful, lousy (*sl*), scandalous, scuzzy (*sl*), shameful, wicked **4** = **unfair**, crooked, dishonest, fraudulent, shady (*inf*), underhand, unscrupulous ♦ *v* **5** = **pollute**, besmirch, contaminate, defile, dirty, stain, sully, taint

found *v* = **establish**, constitute, create, inaugurate, institute, organize, originate, set up, start

foundation *n* **1** = **groundwork**, base, basis, bedrock, bottom, footing, substructure, underpinning **2** = **setting up**, endowment, establishment, inauguration, institution, organization, settlement

founder¹ *n* = **initiator**, architect, author, beginner, father, inventor, originator

founder² *v* **1** = **sink**, be lost, go down, go to the bottom, submerge **2** = **fail**, break down, collapse, come to grief, come unstuck, fall through, miscarry, misfire **3** = **stumble**, lurch, sprawl, stagger, trip

foundling *n* = **stray**, orphan, outcast, waif

fountain *n* **1** = **jet**, font, fount, reservoir, spout, spray, spring, well **2** = **source**, cause, derivation, fount, fountainhead, origin, wellspring

foyer *n* = **entrance hall**, antechamber, anteroom, lobby, reception area, vestibule

fracas *n* = **brawl**, affray (*Law*), disturbance,

frac·tion [FRAK-shən] *n* **1** numerical quantity not an integer. **2** fragment, piece. **frac'tion·al** *adj* **1** constituting a fraction. **2** forming but a small part. **3** insignificant.

frac·tious [FRAK-shəs] *adj* unruly, irritable.

frac·ture [FRAK-chər] *n* **1** breakage, part broken. **2** breaking of bone. **3** breach, rupture. ◆ *v* **-tured, -tur·ing 4** break.

frag·ile [FRAJ-əl] *adj* **1** breakable. **2** frail. **3** delicate. **fra·gil'i·ty** *n*

frag·ment [FRAG-mənt] *n* **1** piece broken off. **2** small portion, incomplete part. ◆ *v* (-ment). **frag'men·tar·y** [-te-ree] *adj*

fra·grant [FRAY-grənt] *adj* sweet-smelling. **fra'grance** *n* scent.

frail [frayl] *adj* **-er, -est 1** fragile, delicate. **2** infirm. **3** in weak health. **4** morally weak. **frail'ly** *adv* **frail'ty** *n, pl* **-ties**

frame [fraym] *n* **1** that in which thing is set, as square of wood around picture, etc. **2** structure. **3** build of body. **4** constitution. **5** mood. **6** individual exposure on strip of film. ◆ *vt* **7** put together, make. **8** adapt. **9** put into words. **10** put into frame. **11** bring false charge against. **frame-up** *n inf* plot, manufactured evidence. **frame'work** *n* **1**

structure into which completing parts can be fitted. **2** supporting work.

franc [frangk] *n* monetary unit of Switzerland and (formerly) France.

fran·chise [FRAN-chīz] *n* **1** right of voting. **2** citizenship. **3** privilege or right, esp. right to sell certain goods. ◆ *v* **-chised, -chis·ing**

fran·gi·pane [FRAN-jə-payn] *n* **1** type of pastry cake. **2** its filling.

fran·gi·pan·i [fran-jə-PAN-ee] *n* **1** tropical American shrub. **2** perfume made of its flower.

frank [frangk] *adj* **-er, -est 1** candid, outspoken. **2** sincere. ◆ *n* **3** official mark on letter either canceling stamp or ensuring delivery without stamp. ◆ *vt* **4** mark letter thus. **frank'ly** *adv* candidly. **frank'ness** *n*

frank·furt·er [FRANGK-fər-tər] *n* smoked sausage, hot dog.

frank·in·cense [FRANG-kin-sens] *n* aromatic gum resin burned as incense.

fran·tic [FRAN-tik] *adj* **1** distracted with rage, grief, joy, etc. **2** frenzied. **fran'ti·cal·ly** *adv*

fra·ter·nal [frə-TUR-nl] *adj* of brother, brotherly. **fra·ter'nal·ly** *adv* **fra·ter'ni·ty** *n,*

melee *or* mêlée, riot, rumpus, scuffle, skirmish

fraction *n* = **piece**, part, percentage, portion, section, segment, share, slice

fractious *adj* = **irritable**, captious, cross, petulant, querulous, refractory, testy, tetchy, touchy

fracture *n* **1** = **break**, cleft, crack, fissure, opening, rift, rupture, split ◆ *v* **2** = **break**, crack, rupture, splinter, split

fragile *adj* = **delicate**, breakable, brittle, dainty, fine, flimsy, frail, frangible, weak

fragment *n* **1** = **piece**, bit, chip, particle, portion, scrap, shred, sliver ◆ *v* **2** = **break**, break up, come apart, come to pieces, crumble, disintegrate, shatter, splinter, split up

fragmentary *adj* = **incomplete**, bitty, broken, disconnected, incoherent, partial, piecemeal, scattered, scrappy, sketchy

fragrance *n* = **scent**, aroma, balm, bouquet, fragrancy, perfume, redolence, smell, sweet odor

fragrant *adj* = **perfumed**, aromatic, balmy, odorous, redolent, sweet-scented, sweet-smelling

frail *adj* = **weak**, delicate, feeble, flimsy, fragile, infirm, insubstantial, puny,

vulnerable

frailty *n* = **feebleness**, fallibility, frailness, infirmity, susceptibility, weakness

frame *n* **1** = **casing**, construction, framework, shell, structure **2** = **physique**, anatomy, body, build, carcass **3** **frame of mind** = **mood**, attitude, disposition, humor, outlook, state, temper ◆ *v* **4** = **construct**, assemble, build, make, manufacture, put together **5** = **draft**, compose, devise, draw up, formulate, map out, sketch **6** = **mount**, case, enclose, surround

framework *n* = **structure**, foundation, frame, groundwork, plan, shell, skeleton, the bare bones

frank *adj* = **honest**, blunt, candid, direct, forthright, open, outspoken, plain-spoken, sincere, straightforward, truthful

frankly *adv* **1** = **honestly**, candidly, in truth, to be honest **2** = **openly**, bluntly, directly, freely, plainly, without reserve

frankness *n* = **outspokenness**, bluntness, candor, forthrightness, openness, plain speaking, truthfulness

frantic *adj* **1** = **furious**, at the end of one's tether, berserk, beside oneself, distracted, distraught, wild **2** = **hectic**, desperate,

pl **-ties 1** brotherliness. **2** brotherhood. **3** college society. **frat·er·ni·za'tion** *n*
frat'er·nize *vi* **-nized, -niz·ing** to associate, make friends. **frat·ri·cid'al** [-SĪD-əl] *adj*
frat'ri·cide *n* killing, killer of brother or sister.

fraud [frawd] *n* **1** criminal deception. **2** swindle, imposture. **fraud·u·lence** [FRAW-jə-ləns] *n* **fraud'u·lent** *adj*

fraught [frawt] *adj* filled (with), involving.

fray[1] *n* **1** fight. **2** noisy quarrel.

fray[2] *v* **1** wear through by rubbing. **2** make, become ragged at edge.

fraz·zle [FRAZ-əl] *inf* ◆ *v* **-zled, -zling 1** make or become exhausted. **2** make or become irritated. ◆ *n* **3** exhausted state.

freak [freek] *n* abnormal person, animal, thing. ◆ *adj* **freak'ish** *adj* **freak'y** *adj*
freak·i·er, freak·i·est freak out *sl* (cause to) hallucinate, be wildly excited, etc.

freck·le [FREK-əl] *n* **1** light brown spot on skin, esp. caused by sun. **2** any small spot. ◆ *v* **-led, -ling 3** bring, come out in freckles.

free *adj* **fre·er, fre·est 1** able to act at will, not under compulsion or restraint. **2** not restricted or affected by. **3** not subject to cost or tax. **4** independent. **5** not exact or literal. **6** generous. **7** not in use. **8** (of

person) not occupied, having no appointment. **9** loose, not fixed. ◆ *vt* **freed, free·ing** set at liberty. **10** remove (obstacles, pain, etc.). **11** rid (of).
free'dom *n* **free'ly** *adv* **free-for-all** *n* brawl.
free'hand *adj* drawn without guiding instruments. **free'lance** [-lans] *adj, n* (of) self-employed, unattached person.
Free·ma·son [-may-sən] *n* member of secret fraternity for mutual help.
freemasonry *n* **1** principles of Freemasons. **2** fellowship, secret brotherhood.
free'-range *adj* (of livestock and poultry) kept, produced in natural, nonintensive conditions. **free space** region that has no gravitational and electromagnetic fields.
free speech right to express opinions publicly. **free-swinging** *adj* recklessly daring. **free·think'er** *n* skeptic who forms own opinions, esp. in religion. **free trade** international trade free of protective tariffs.
free'way *n* express highway.
freeze [freez] *v* **froze, fro·zen, freez·ing 1** change (by reduction of temperature) from liquid to solid, as water to ice. ◆ *vt* **2** preserve (food, etc.) by extreme cold, as in freezer. **3** fix (prices, etc.). ◆ *vi* **4** feel very cold. **5** become rigid as with fear. **6** stop.

———————| T H E S A U R U S |———————

fraught (*inf*), frenetic, frenzied
fraternity *n* **1** = **club**, association, brotherhood, circle, company, guild, league, union **2** = **companionship**, brotherhood, camaraderie, fellowship, kinship
fraternize *v* = **associate**, consort, cooperate, hobnob, keep company, mingle, mix, socialize
fraud *n* **1** = **deception**, chicanery, deceit, double-dealing, duplicity, sharp practice, swindling, treachery, trickery **2** = **impostor**, charlatan, fake, fraudster, hoaxer, phoney *or* phony (*inf*), pretender, swindler
fraudulent *adj* = **deceitful**, crooked (*inf*), dishonest, double-dealing, duplicitous, sham, swindling, treacherous
fray[1] *v* = **wear thin**, chafe, rub, wear
freak *n* **1** = **oddity**, aberration, anomaly, malformation, monstrosity, weirdo *or* weirdie (*inf*) **2** = **enthusiast**, addict, aficionado, buff (*inf*), devotee, fan, fanatic, fiend (*inf*), nut (*sl*) ◆ *adj* **3** = **abnormal**, exceptional, unparalleled, unusual
free *adj* **1** = **for nothing**, complimentary, for

free (*inf*), free of charge, gratis, gratuitous, on the house, unpaid, without charge **2** = **at liberty**, at large, footloose, independent, liberated, loose, on the loose, unfettered **3** = **allowed**, able, clear, permitted, unimpeded, unrestricted **4** = **available**, empty, idle, spare, unemployed, unoccupied, unused, vacant **5** = **generous**, lavish, liberal, unsparing, unstinting ◆ *v* **6** = **release**, deliver, let out, liberate, loose, set free, turn loose, unchain, untie **7** = **extricate**, cut loose, disengage, disentangle, rescue
freedom *n* **1** = **liberty**, deliverance, emancipation, independence, release **2** = **opportunity**, a blank check, carte blanche, discretion, free rein, latitude, license
free-for-all *n* = **fight**, brawl, fracas, melee *or* mêlée, riot, row, scrimmage
freely *adv* **1** = **willingly**, of one's own accord, of one's own free will, spontaneously, voluntarily, without prompting **2** = **openly**, candidly, frankly, plainly, unreservedly, without reserve **3** = **abundantly**, amply, copiously, extravagantly, lavishly, liberally,

freez'er n insulated cabinet for long-term storage of perishable foodstuffs. **frozen** adj of assets, etc., unrealizable. **freezing point** temperature at which liquid becomes solid.

freight [frayt] n 1 commercial transport (esp. by rail, ship). 2 cost of this. 3 goods so carried. ◆ vt 4 send as or by freight. **freight'er** n

French n 1 language spoken by people of France. ◆ adj 2 of, or pertaining to France. **French dressing** salad dressing. **French fries** deep-fried strips of potato. **French horn** musical wind instrument. **French leave** unauthorized leave. **French window** window extended to floor level and used as door.

fre·net·ic [frə-NET-ik] adj frenzied.

fren·zy [FREN-zee] n, pl -zies 1 violent mental derangement. 2 wild excitement. **fren'zied** adj

fre·quent [FREE-kwənt] adj 1 happening often. 2 common. 3 numerous. ◆ vt [fri-KWENT] 4 go often to. **fre'quen·cy** n, pl -cies 1 rate of occurrence. 2 in radio, etc. cycles per second of alternating current. **fre·quen·ta·tive** [fri-KWEN-tə-tiv] adj expressing repetition.

fres·co [FRES-koh] n, pl -coes 1 method of painting in water color on plaster of wall before it dries. 2 painting done thus.

fresh adj -er, -est 1 not stale. 2 new. 3 additional. 4 different. 5 recent. 6 inexperienced. 7 pure. 8 not pickled, frozen, etc. 9 not faded or dimmed. 10 not tired. 11 of wind, strong. 12 inf impudent. 13 forward. **fresh'en** v **fresh'et** n 1 rush of water at river mouth. 2 flood of river water. **fresh'ly** adv **fresh'man** n first-year high school or college student.

fret[1] v **fret·ted, fret·ting** 1 be irritated, worry. ◆ n 2 irritation. **fret'ful** adj irritable, (easily) upset.

fret[2] n 1 repetitive geometrical pattern. 2 small bar on fingerboard of guitar, etc. ◆ vt **fret·ted, fret·ting** 3 ornament with carved pattern. **fret saw** saw with narrow blade and fine teeth, used for fretwork. **fret'work** n carved or open woodwork in ornamental patterns and devices.

Freud·i·an [FROI-dee-ən] adj pert. to Austrian psychologist Sigmund Freud, or his theories.

fri·a·ble [FRĪ-ə-bəl] adj easily crumbled. **fri·a·bil'i·ty,** n

fri·ar [FRĪ-ər] n member of mendicant religious order. **fri'ar·y** n house of friars.

fric·as·see [frik-ə-SEE] n 1 dish of pieces of chicken or meat, fried or stewed and served with rich sauce. ◆ vt **-seed, -see·ing** 2 cook thus.

fric·tion [FRIK-shən] n 1 rubbing. 2 resistance met with by body moving over another. 3 clash of wills, etc.,

---

THESAURUS

unstintingly

freeze v 1 = **chill**, harden, ice over or up, stiffen 2 = **suspend**, fix, hold up, inhibit, peg, stop

freezing adj = **icy**, arctic, biting, bitter, chill, frosty, glacial, raw, wintry

freight n 1 = **transportation**, carriage, conveyance, shipment 2 = **cargo**, burden, consignment, goods, load, merchandise, payload

French adj = **Gallic**

frenzied adj = **furious**, distracted, feverish, frantic, frenetic, rabid, uncontrolled, wild

frenzy n = **fury**, derangement, hysteria, paroxysm, passion, rage, seizure

frequent adj 1 = **common**, customary, everyday, familiar, habitual, persistent, recurrent, repeated, usual ◆ v 2 = **visit**, attend, be found at, hang out at (inf), haunt, patronize

frequently adv = **often**, commonly, habitually, many times, much, not

infrequently, repeatedly

fresh adj 1 = **new**, different, modern, novel, original, recent, up-to-date 2 = **additional**, added, auxiliary, extra, further, more, other, supplementary 3 = **invigorating**, bracing, brisk, clean, cool, crisp, pure, refreshing, unpolluted 4 = **lively**, alert, energetic, keen, refreshed, sprightly, spry, vigorous 5 = **natural**, unprocessed 6 Inf = **cheeky**, disrespectful, familiar, forward, impudent, insolent, presumptuous

freshen v = **refresh**, enliven, freshen up, liven up, restore, revitalize

freshness n 1 = **novelty**, inventiveness, newness, originality 2 = **cleanness**, brightness, clearness, glow, shine, sparkle, vigor, wholesomeness

fret v = **worry**, agonize, brood, grieve, lose sleep over, upset or distress oneself

fretful adj = **irritable**, crotchety, edgy, fractious, querulous, short-tempered, testy, touchy, uneasy disagreement. **fric'tion·al** *adj*

fried pt./pp. of FRY.

friend [frend] *n* **1** one well known to another and regarded with affection and loyalty. **2** intimate associate. **3** supporter. **4** (F-) Quaker. **friend'less** *adj* **friend'li·ness** *n* **friend'ly** *adj* **-li·er, -li·est 1** having disposition of a friend, kind. **2** favorable. **friend'ship** *n* **friendly fire** *Military* shooting or bombing that injures or kills comrades or allies.

frieze [freez] *n* ornamental band, strip (on wall).

frig·ate [FRIG-it] *n* **1** old (sailing) warship corresponding to modern cruiser. **2** fast warship equipped for escort and antisubmarine duties.

fright [frīt] *n* **1** sudden fear. **2** shock. **3** alarm. **4** grotesque or ludicrous person or thing. **fright'en** *vt* **1** cause fear, fright in. **fright'ful** *adj* **1** terrible, calamitous. **2** shocking. **3** *inf* very great, very large. **fright'ful·ly** *adv inf* **1** terribly. **2** very.

frig·id [FRIJ-id] *adj* **1** formal, dull. **2** (sexually) unfeeling. **3** cold. **fri·gid'i·ty** *n* **frig'id·ly** *adv*

frill *n* **1** fluted strip of fabric gathered at one edge. **2** ruff of hair, feathers around neck of dog, bird, etc. **3** fringe. **4** unnecessary words, politeness. **5** superfluous thing. **6** adornment. ♦ *vt* **7** make into, decorate with frill.

fringe [frinj] *n* **1** ornamental edge of hanging threads, tassels, etc. **2** anything like this. **3** edge, limit. ♦ *vt* **fringed, fring·ing 4** adorn with, serve as, fringe. **fringe benefit** benefit provided in addition to regular pay.

frip·per·y [FRIP-ə-ree] *n, pl* **-per·ies 1** finery. **2** trivia.

fris·bee [FRIZ-bee] *n* ® disk-shaped object for throwing and catching as a sport or pastime.

frisk *vi* **1** move, leap, playfully. ♦ *vt* **2** wave briskly. **3** search (person) for concealed weapons, etc. ♦ *n* **frisk'y** *adj* **frisk·i·er, frisk·i·est**

frit·ter[1] [FRIT-ər] *vt* waste. **fritter away** throw away, waste.

fritter[2] *n* small deep-fried cake of batter oft. containing corn.

friv·o·lous [FRI-ə-ləs] *adj* **1** not serious,

friction *n* **1** = **rubbing**, abrasion, chafing, grating, rasping, resistance, scraping **2** = **hostility**, animosity, bad blood, conflict, disagreement, discord, dissension, resentment

friend *n* **1** = **companion**, buddy (*inf*), chum (*inf*), comrade, homeboy (*sl*), homegirl (*sl*), pal (*inf*), playmate **2** = **supporter**, ally, associate, patron, well-wisher

friendliness *n* = **kindliness**, affability, amiability, congeniality, conviviality, geniality, neighborliness, sociability, warmth

friendly *adj* = **sociable**, affectionate, amicable, buddy-buddy (*inf*), close, familiar, helpful, intimate, neighborly, on good terms, pally (*inf*), sympathetic, welcoming

friendship *n* = **goodwill**, affection, amity, attachment, concord, familiarity, friendliness, harmony, intimacy

fright *n* = **fear**, alarm, consternation, dread, horror, panic, scare, shock, trepidation

frighten *v* = **scare**, alarm, intimidate, petrify, shock, startle, terrify, terrorize, unnerve

frightened *adj* = **afraid**, alarmed, petrified, scared, scared stiff, startled, terrified, terrorized, terror-stricken

frightening *adj* = **terrifying**, alarming, fearful, fearsome, horrifying, menacing, scary (*inf*), shocking, unnerving

frightful *adj* = **terrifying**, alarming, awful, dreadful, fearful, ghastly, horrendous, horrible, terrible, traumatic

frigid *adj* **1** = **cold**, arctic, frosty, frozen, glacial, icy, wintry **2** = **forbidding**, aloof, austere, formal, unapproachable, unfeeling, unresponsive

frills *pl n* = **trimmings**, additions, bells and whistles, embellishments, extras, frippery, fuss, ornamentation, ostentation

fringe *n* **1** = **border**, edging, hem, trimming **2** = **edge**, borderline, limits, margin, outskirts, perimeter, periphery ♦ *adj* **3** = **unofficial**, unconventional, unorthodox

frisk *v* **1** = **frolic**, caper, cavort, gambol, jump, play, prance, skip, trip **2** = **search**, check, inspect, run over, shake down (*U.S. sl*)

frisky *adj* = **lively**, coltish, frolicsome, high-spirited, kittenish, playful, sportive

fritter away *v* = **waste**, dissipate, idle away, misspend, run through, spend like water, squander unimportant. **2** flippant. **fri·vol'i·ty** n

frizz vt **1** curl into small crisp curls. ◆ n **2** frizzed hair. **friz'zy** adj **-zi·er, -zi·est**

fro [froh] adv away, only in to and fro.

frock [frok] n **1** woman's dress. **2** various similar garments. ◆ vt **3** dress with frock. **4** invest with office of priest.

frog[1] n tailless amphibious animal developed from tadpole. **frog'man** n swimmer equipped for swimming, working, underwater.

frog[2] n **1** ornamental coat fastening of button and loop. **2** (military) attachment to belt to carry sword.

frol·ic [FROL-ik] n **1** merrymaking. ◆ vi **-icked, -ick·ing 2** behave playfully. **frol'ic·some** adj

from [frum] prep expressing point of departure, source, distance, cause, change of state, etc.

frond n plant organ consisting of stem and foliage, usually with fruit forms, esp. in ferns.

front [frunt] n **1** fore part. **2** position directly before or ahead. **3** battle line or area. **4** *Meteorology* dividing line between two air masses of different characteristics. **5** outward aspect, bearing. **6** inf something serving as a respectable cover for another, usu. criminal, activity. **7** field of activity. **8** group with common goal. ◆ v **9** look, face. **10** inf be a cover for. ◆ adj **11** of, at the front. **front'age** [-ij] n **1** front of building. **2** property line along street, lake, etc.

fron'tal [-əl] adj **fron'tier** [-TEER] n part of country that borders on another. **fron'tis·piece** n illustration facing title page of book.

frost [frawst] n **1** frozen dew or mist. **2** act or state of freezing. **3** weather in which temperature falls below point at which water turns to ice. ◆ v **4** cover, be covered with frost or something similar in appearance. **5** give slightly roughened surface. **frost'i·ly** adv **frost'y** adj **frost·i·er, frost·i·est 1** accompanied by frost. **2** chilly. **3** cold. **4** unfriendly. **frost'bite** n destruction by cold of tissue, esp. of fingers, ears, etc.

froth [frawth] n **1** collection of small bubbles, foam. **2** scum. **3** idle talk. ◆ v **4** (cause to) foam. **froth'i·ly** adv **froth'y** adj **froth·i·er, froth·i·est**

frown vi wrinkle brows. ◆ n

frowz·y [FROW-zee] adj **frowz·i·er, frowz·i·est** dirty, unkempt.

froze pt. of FREEZE. **frozen** pp. of FREEZE.

fruc·ti·fy [FRUK-tə-fī] v **-fied, -fy·ing** (cause to) bear fruit.

fru·gal [FROO-gəl] adj **1** sparing. **2** thrifty, economical. **3** meager. **fru·gal'i·ty** n

fruit [froot] n **1** seed and its envelope, esp. edible one. **2** vegetable product. **3** (usu in pl) result, benefit. ◆ vi **4** bear fruit. **fruit'ful** [-fəl] adj **fru·i·tion** [froo-ISH-ən] n **1** enjoyment. **2** realization of hopes. **fruit'less** adj **fruit'y** adj **fruit·i·er, fruit·i·est**

frump n dowdy woman. **frump'ish** adj

frivolity n = **fun**, flippancy, frivolousness, gaiety, levity, light-heartedness, silliness, superficiality, triviality

frivolous adj **1** = **flippant**, childish, foolish, idle, juvenile, puerile, silly, superficial **2** = **trivial**, minor, petty, shallow, trifling, unimportant

frolic v **1** = **play**, caper, cavort, frisk, gambol, lark, make merry, romp, sport ◆ **2** = **revel**, antic, game, lark, romp, spree

frolicsome adj = **playful**, coltish, frisky, kittenish, lively, merry, sportive

front n **1** = **exterior**, façade, face, foreground, frontage **2** = **forefront**, front line, head, lead, vanguard **3** = **disguise**, blind, cover, cover-up, façade, mask, pretext, show ◆ adj **4** = **first**, foremost, head, lead, leading, topmost ◆ v **5** = **face onto**, look over or onto, overlook

frontier n = **boundary**, borderline, edge,

limit, perimeter, verge

frost n = **hoarfrost**, freeze, rime

frosty adj **1** = **cold**, chilly, frozen, icy, wintry **2** = **unfriendly**, discouraging, frigid, standoffish, unenthusiastic, unwelcoming

froth n **1** = **foam**, bubbles, effervescence, head, lather, scum, spume, suds ◆ v **2** = **fizz**, bubble over, come to a head, effervesce, foam, lather

frothy adj = **foamy**, foaming, sudsy

frown v **1** = **scowl**, glare, glower, knit one's brows, look daggers, lour or lower **2 frown on** = **disapprove of**, discourage, dislike, look askance at, take a dim view of

frozen adj = **icy**, arctic, chilled, frigid, frosted, icebound, ice-cold, ice-covered, numb

frugal adj = **thrifty**, abstemious, careful, economical, niggardly, parsimonious, prudent, sparing

frump·y adj frump·i·er, frump·i·est

frus·trate [FRUS-trayt] vt -trat·ed, -trat·ing 1 thwart, balk. 2 baffle, disappoint. **frus·tra'tion** n

fry¹ [frī] v fried, fry·ing 1 cook with fat. 2 be cooked thus. 3 sl be executed by electrocution.

fry² n, pl fry young of fish. **small fry** young or insignificant beings.

fuch·sia [FYOO-shə] n ornamental shrub with purple-red flowers.

fud·dle [FUD-l] v -dled, -dling 1 (cause to) be intoxicated, confused. ◆ n 2 this state.

fudge¹ [fuj] n soft, variously flavored candy.

fudge² vt fudged, fudg·ing 1 make, do carelessly or dishonestly. 2 fake.

fuel [FYOO-əl] n 1 material for burning as source of heat or power. 2 something that nourishes. ◆ vt 3 provide with fuel.

fu·gi·tive [FYOO-ji-tiv] n 1 one who flees, esp. from arrest or pursuit. ◆ adj 2 fleeing,

elusive.

fugue [fyoog] n musical composition in which themes are repeated in different parts.

Füh·rer [FYUUR-ər] n Ger leader: title used by Hitler as Nazi dictator.

ful·crum [FUUL-krəm] n, pl -crums point on which a lever is placed for support.

ful·fill [fuul-FIL] vi 1 satisfy. 2 carry out. 3 obey. 4 satisfy (desire, etc.). **ful·fill'ment** n

full [fuul] adj -er, -est 1 containing as much as possible. 2 abundant. 3 complete. 4 ample. 5 plump. 6 (of garment) of ample cut. ◆ adv 7 very. 8 quite. 9 exactly. **ful'ly** adv **full'ness** n **ful·some** [FUUL-səm] adj excessive. **full-blown'** [-BLOHN] adj fully developed.

ful·mi·nate [FUL-mə-nayt] vi -nat·ed, -nat·ing 1 (esp. with against) criticize harshly. ◆ n 2 chemical compound exploding readily. **ful·mi·na'tion** n

fulsome see FULL.

─────── THESAURUS ───────

fruit n 1 = **produce**, crop, harvest, product, yield 2 = **result**, advantage, benefit, consequence, effect, end result, outcome, profit, return, reward

fruitful adj = **useful**, advantageous, beneficial, effective, productive, profitable, rewarding, successful, win-win (inf), worthwhile

fruition n = **maturity**, attainment, completion, fulfillment, materialization, perfection, realization, ripeness

fruitless adj = **useless**, futile, ineffectual, pointless, profitless, unavailing, unproductive, unprofitable, unsuccessful, vain

frustrate v = **thwart**, balk, block, check, counter, defeat, disappoint, foil, forestall, nullify, stymie

frustrated adj = **disappointed**, discouraged, disheartened, embittered, resentful

frustration n 1 = **obstruction**, blocking, circumvention, foiling, thwarting 2 = **annoyance**, disappointment, dissatisfaction, grievance, irritation, resentment, vexation

fuel n = **incitement**, ammunition, provocation

fugitive n 1 = **runaway**, deserter, escapee, refugee ◆ adj 2 = **momentary**, brief, ephemeral, fleeting, passing, short-lived, temporary, transient, transitory

fulfill v 1 = **achieve**, accomplish, carry out, complete, perform, realize, satisfy 2 = **comply with**, answer, conform to, fill, meet, obey

fulfillment n = **achievement**, accomplishment, attainment, completion, consummation, implementation, realization

full adj 1 = **saturated**, brimming, complete, filled, loaded, replete, satiated, stocked 2 = **plentiful**, abundant, adequate, ample, comprehensive, exhaustive, extensive, generous 3 = **rich**, clear, deep, distinct, loud, resonant, rounded 4 = **plump**, buxom, curvaceous, rounded, voluptuous 5 = **loose**, baggy, capacious, large, puffy, voluminous ◆ n 6 **in full** = **completely**, in its entirety, in total, without exception

full-blooded adj = **vigorous**, hearty, lusty, red-blooded, virile

fullness n 1 = **plenty**, abundance, copiousness, fill, profusion, satiety, saturation, sufficiency 2 = **richness**, clearness, loudness, resonance, strength

full-scale adj = **major**, all-out, comprehensive, exhaustive, in-depth, sweeping, thorough, thoroughgoing, wide-ranging

fully adv = **totally**, altogether, completely, entirely, in all respects, one hundred per cent, perfectly, thoroughly, utterly, wholly

fulsome adj = **insincere**, excessive,

fum·ble [FUM-bəl] v -bled, -bling 1 grope about. 2 handle awkwardly. 3 in football, etc., drop (ball). ◆ n 4 awkward attempt.

fume [fyoom] vi 1 be angry. 2 emit smoke or vapor. ◆ n 3 smoke. 4 vapor. **fu'mi·gate** vt -gat·ed, -gat·ing apply fumes or smoke to, esp. for disinfection. **fu'mi·ga·tor** n

fun n anything enjoyable, amusing, etc. **fun'ni·ly** adv **fun'ny** adj -ni·er, -ni·est 1 comical. 2 odd. 3 difficult to explain.

func·tion [FUNGK-shən] n 1 work a thing is designed to do. 2 (large) social event. 3 duty. 4 profession. 5 Math. quantity whose value depends on varying value of another. ◆ vi 6 operate, work. **func'tion·al** adj 1 having a special purpose. 2 practical, necessary. 3 capable of operating. **func'tion·ar·y** n, pl -ar·ies official.

fund n 1 stock or sum of money. 2 supply, store. ◆ pl 3 money resources. ◆ vt 4 (in financial, business dealings) provide or obtain funds in various ways.

fun·da·men·tal [fun-də-MEN-tl] adj 1 of, affecting, or serving as, the base. 2 essential, primary. ◆ n 3 basic rule or fact. **fun'da·ment** [-mənt] n 1 buttocks. 2 foundation. **fun·da·men'tal·ism** n **fun·da·men'tal·ist** n one laying stress on

belief in literal and verbal inspiration of Bible and other traditional creeds.

fu·ner·al [FYOO-nər-əl] n (ceremony associated with) burial or cremation of dead. **fu·ne're·al** [-NEE-ree-əl] adj 1 like a funeral. 2 dark. 3 gloomy.

fun·gi·ble [FUN-jə-bəl] adj (of assets) freely exchangeable.

fun·gus [FUNG-gəs] n, pl -gi [-jī] **-gus·es** plant without leaves, flowers, or roots, as mushroom, mold. **fun'gal** adj **fun'gous** adj **fun'gi·cide** [-jə-sīd] n fungus destroyer.

fu·nic·u·lar [fyoo-NIK-yə-lər] n cable railway on mountainside with two counterbalanced cars.

funk [fungk] n style of dance music with strong beat. **funk'y** adj funk·i·er, funk·i·est 1 (of music) having a strong beat. 2 sl unconventional. 3 sl fetid.

fun·nel [FUN-l] n 1 cone-shaped vessel or tube. 2 chimney of locomotive or ship. 3 ventilating shaft. ◆ v -neled, -nel·ing 4 (cause to) move as through funnel. 5 concentrate, focus.

funny see FUN.

fur n 1 soft hair of animal. 2 garment, etc. 3 of dressed skins with such hair. 4 furlike coating. ◆ vt furred, fur·ring 5 cover with

————— THESAURUS —————

extravagant, immoderate, inordinate, sycophantic, unctuous

fumble v = grope, feel around, flounder, scrabble

fume v = rage, get hot under the collar (inf), rant, see red (inf), seethe, smolder, storm

fumes pl n = smoke, exhaust, gas, pollution, smog, vapor

fumigate v = disinfect, clean out or up, cleanse, purify, sanitize, sterilize

fuming adj = angry, enraged, in a rage, incensed, on the warpath (inf), raging, seething, up in arms

fun n 1 = enjoyment, amusement, entertainment, jollity, merriment, mirth, pleasure, recreation, sport 2 make fun of = mock, lampoon, laugh at, parody, poke fun at, ridicule, satirize ◆ adj 3 = enjoyable, amusing, convivial, diverting, entertaining, lively, witty

function n 1 = purpose, business, duty, job, mission, raison d'être, responsibility, role, task 2 = reception, affair, gathering, social occasion ◆ v 3 = work, act, behave, do duty, go, operate, perform, run

functional adj 1 = practical, hard-wearing, serviceable, useful, utilitarian 2 = working, operative

fund n 1 = reserve, kitty, pool, stock, store, supply ◆ v 2 = finance, pay for, subsidize, support

fundamental adj 1 = essential, basic, cardinal, central, elementary, key, primary, principal, rudimentary, underlying ◆ n 2 = principle, axiom, cornerstone, law, rudiment, rule

fundamentally adv = essentially, at bottom, at heart, basically, intrinsically, primarily, radically

funds pl n = money, capital, cash, finance, ready money, resources, savings, the wherewithal

funeral n = burial, cremation, inhumation, interment, obsequies

funnel v = channel, conduct, convey, direct, filter, move, pass, pour

funny adj 1 = humorous, amusing, comic, comical, droll, entertaining, hilarious, riotous, side-splitting, witty 2 = peculiar, curious, mysterious, odd, queer, strange, suspicious, unusual, weird fur. **fur'ri·er** n 1 dealer in furs. 2 repairer, dresser of furs. **fur'ry** adj -ri·er, -ri·est of, like fur.

fur'bish vt clean up.

fu·ri·ous [FYUUR-ee-əs] adj 1 extremely angry. **fu'ri·ous·ly** adv

furl vt roll up and bind (sail, umbrella, etc.).

fur·long [FUR-lawng] n eighth of mile.

fur·lough [FUR-loh] n leave of absence, esp. to soldier.

fur·nace [FUR-nis] n 1 apparatus for applying great heat to metals. 2 closed fireplace for heating boiler, etc. 3 hot place.

fur'nish vt 1 fit up house with furniture. 2 equip. 3 supply, yield. **fur'ni·ture** [-chər] n movable contents of a house or room.

fu·ror [FYUUR-or] n 1 public outburst, esp. of protest. 2 sudden enthusiasm.

fur·row [FUR-oh] n 1 trench as made by plow. 2 groove. ◆ vt 3 make furrows in.

fur·ther [FUR-thər] adv 1 more. 2 in addition. 3 at or to a greater distance or extent. ◆ adj 4 additional. 5 more distant. 6 comp. of FAR. ◆ vt 7 help forward. 8 promote. **fur'ther·ance** n **fur'ther·more** adv besides. **fur'thest** adj sup. of FAR. ◆ adv **fur'ther·most** adj

fur·tive [FUR-tiv] adj stealthy, sly, secret. **fur'tive·ly** adv

fu·ry [FYUUR-ee] n, pl -ries 1 wild rage, violent anger. 2 violence of storm, etc. 3 usu. snake-haired avenging deity.

fuse [fyooz] v **fused, fus·ing** 1 blend by melting. 2 melt with heat. 3 amalgamate. ◆ n 4 (also **fuze**) soft wire, with low melting point, used as safety device in electrical systems. 5 device (orig. combustible cord) for igniting bomb, etc. **fu'si·ble** [-zə-bəl] adj **fu·sion** [FYOO-zhən] n 1 melting. 2 state of being melted. 3 union of things, as atomic nuclei, as if melted together.

fu·se·lage [FYOO-sə-lahzh] n body of aircraft.

fu·sil·lade [FYOO-sə-layd] n continuous discharge of firearms.

fuss n 1 needless bustle or concern. 2 complaint. 3 objection. ◆ vi 4 make fuss. **fuss'i·ly** adv **fuss'i·ness** n **fuss'y** adj **fuss·i·er, fuss·i·est** 1 particular. 2 hard to please. 3 overmeticulous. 4 overelaborate.

fus·tian [FUS-chən] n 1 thick cotton cloth. 2 inflated language.

fus·ty [FUS-tee] adj -ti·er, -ti·est 1 moldy. 2 smelling of damp. 3 old-fashioned. **fus'ti·ness** n

fu·tile [FYOOT-l] adj useless, ineffectual, trifling. **fu·til'i·ty** n, pl -ties

fu·ton [FOO-ton] n Japanese padded quilt,

─── | THESAURUS | ───

furious adj 1 = **angry**, beside oneself, enraged, fuming, incensed, infuriated, livid (inf), raging, up in arms 2 = **violent**, fierce, intense, savage, turbulent, unrestrained, vehement

furnish v 1 = **decorate**, equip, fit out, stock 2 = **supply**, give, grant, hand out, offer, present, provide

furniture n = **household goods**, appliances, fittings, furnishings, goods, possessions, things (inf)

furor n = **disturbance**, commotion, hullabaloo, outcry, stir, to-do, uproar

furrow n 1 = **groove**, channel, crease, hollow, line, rut, seam, trench, wrinkle ◆ v 2 = **wrinkle**, corrugate, crease, draw together, knit

further adv 1 = **in addition**, additionally, also, besides, furthermore, into the bargain, moreover, to boot ◆ adj 2 = **additional**, extra, fresh, more, new, other, supplementary ◆ v 3 = **promote**, advance, assist, encourage, forward, help, lend support to, work for

furthermore adv = **besides**, additionally, as well, further, in addition, into the bargain, moreover, to boot, too

furthest adj = **most distant**, extreme, farthest, furthermost, outmost, remotest, ultimate

furtive adj = **sly**, clandestine, conspiratorial, secretive, sneaky, stealthy, surreptitious, underhand, under-the-table

fury n 1 = **anger**, frenzy, impetuosity, madness, passion, rage, wrath 2 = **violence**, ferocity, fierceness, force, intensity, savagery, severity, vehemence

fuss n 1 = **bother**, ado, commotion, excitement, palaver, stir, to-do 2 = **argument**, complaint, furor, objection, row, squabble, trouble ◆ v 3 = **worry**, fidget, fret, get worked up, take pains

fussy adj 1 = **hard to please**, choosy (inf), difficult, fastidious, finicky, nit-picking (inf), particular, picky (inf) 2 = **overelaborate**, busy, cluttered, overworked, rococo

fusty adj = **stale**, airless, damp, mildewed, moldering, musty, stuffy laid on floor as bed.

fu·ture [FYOO-chər] *n* **1** time to come. **2** what will happen. **3** tense of verb indicating this. **4** likelihood of development. ♦ *adj* **5** that will be. **6** of, relating to, time to come. **fu'tur·ism** *n* movement in art marked by revolt against tradition. **fu'tur·ist** *n, adj* **fu·tur·ist'ic** *adj*

ultramodern. **fu·tu'ri·ty** [-TUUR-i-tee] *n, pl* -ties future time.

fuze see FUSE.

fuzz *n* **1** fluff. **2** fluffy or frizzed hair. **3** blur. **4** *sl* police (officer). **fuzz'y** *adj* **fuzz·i·er, fuzz·i·est** **1** fluffy, frizzy. **2** blurred, indistinct.

futile *adj* = **useless**, fruitless, ineffectual, unavailing, unprofitable, unsuccessful, vain, worthless

futility *n* = **uselessness**, emptiness, hollowness, ineffectiveness

future *n* **1** = **hereafter**, time to come **2** = **outlook**, expectation, prospect ♦ *adj* **3** =

forthcoming, approaching, coming, fated, impending, later, subsequent, to come

fuzzy *adj* **1** = **fluffy**, downy, frizzy, woolly **2** = **indistinct**, bleary, blurred, distorted, ill-defined, obscure, out of focus, unclear, vague

G g

Ga *Chem.* gallium.

gab·ar·dine, gab·er·dine [GAB-ər-deen] *n* **1** fine twill cloth like serge. **2** *Hist.* loose outer garment worn by Orthodox Jews.

gab·ble [GAB-əl] *v* **-bled, -bling 1** talk, utter inarticulately or too fast. ♦ *n* **2** such talk. **gab** *n, v* **gabbed, gab·bing** *inf* talk, chatter. **gab'by** *adj* **-bi·er, -bi·est** *inf* talkative. **gift of gab** eloquence, loquacity.

ga·ble [GAY-bəl] *n* triangular upper part of wall at end of ridged roof.

gad *vi* **gad·ded, gad·ding. gad about, around** go around in search of pleasure. **gad'a·bout** *n* pleasure seeker.

gad·fly [GAD-flī] *n, pl* **-flies 1** cattle-biting fly. **2** worrying person.

gadg·et [GAJ-it] *n* **1** small mechanical device. **2** object valued for its novelty or ingenuity. **gadg'et·ry** *n*

Gael [gayl] *n* one who speaks Gaelic. **Gael'ic** *n* **1** language of Ireland and Scottish Highlands. ♦ *adj* **2** of Gaels, their language or customs.

gaff *n* **1** stick with iron hook for landing fish. **2** spar for top of fore-and-aft sail. ♦ *vt* **3** seize (fish) with gaff.

gaffe [gaf] *n* **1** blunder. **2** tactless remark.

gaf·fer [GAF-ər] *n* **1** *inf* old man. **2** senior electrician on a TV or movie set.

gag¹ *v* **gagged, gag·ging 1** stop up (person's mouth) with cloth, etc. **2** retch, choke. ♦ *n* **3** cloth, etc. put into, tied across mouth.

gag² *n* joke, funny story.

ga·ga [GAH-gah] *adj inf* **1** foolishly enthusiastic. **2** infatuated.

gage¹ [gayj] *n* **1** pledge, thing given as security. **2** challenge, or something symbolizing one.

gage² see GAUGE.

gag·gle [GAG-əl] *n* **1** flock of geese. **2** *inf* disorderly crowd.

gaiety see GAY.

gain [gayn] *vt* **1** obtain, secure. **2** obtain as profit. **3** win. **4** earn. **5** reach. ♦ *vi* **6** increase, improve. **7** get nearer. **8** (of watch, clock) operate too fast. ♦ *n* **9** profit. **10** increase, improvement. **gain'ful·ly** *adv* **1** profitably. **2** for a wage, salary.

gain·say [GAYN-say] *vt* **-said, -say·ing**

─────────────── **THESAURUS** ───────────────

gabble *v* **1** = **prattle**, babble, blabber, gibber, gush, jabber, spout ♦ *n* **2** = **gibberish**, babble, blabber, chatter, drivel, prattle, twaddle

gadabout *n* = **pleasure-seeker**, gallivanter, rambler, rover, wanderer

gadget *n* = **device**, appliance, contraption (*inf*), contrivance, gizmo (*sl*), instrument, invention, thing, tool

gaffe *n* = **blunder**, bloomer (*inf*), faux pas, indiscretion, lapse, mistake, slip, solecism

gag¹ *v* **1** = **suppress**, curb, muffle, muzzle, quiet, silence, stifle, stop up **2** = **retch**, barf (*sl*), heave, puke (*sl*), spew, throw up (*inf*), toss one's cookies (*sl*), vomit

gag² *n* = **joke**, crack (*sl*), funny (*inf*), hoax, jest, wisecrack (*inf*), witticism

gaiety *n* **1** = **cheerfulness**, blitheness, exhilaration, glee, high spirits, jollity, light-heartedness, merriment, mirth **2** =

merrymaking, conviviality, festivity, fun, jollification, revelry

gaily *adv* **1** = **cheerfully**, blithely, gleefully, happily, joyfully, light-heartedly, merrily **2** = **colorfully**, brightly, brilliantly, flamboyantly, flashily, gaudily, showily

gain *v* **1** = **obtain**, acquire, attain, capture, collect, gather, get, land, pick up, secure, win **2** = **reach**, arrive at, attain, come to, get to **3 gain on** = **get nearer**, approach, catch up with, close, narrow the gap, overtake ♦ *n* **4** = **profit**, advantage, benefit, dividend, return, yield **5** = **increase**, advance, growth, improvement, progress, rise

gainful *adj* = **profitable**, advantageous, beneficial, fruitful, lucrative, productive, remunerative, rewarding, useful, win-win (*inf*), worthwhile

gains *pl n* = **profits**, earnings, prize,

deny, contradict.

gait [gayt] *n* **1** manner of walking. **2** pace.

Gal. Galatians.

ga·la [GAY-lə] *n* **1** festive occasion. **2** celebration. **3** special entertainment. ♦ *adj* **4** festive. **5** showy.

gal·ax·y [GAL-ək-see] *n, pl* **-ax·ies 1** system of stars bound by gravitational forces. **2** splendid gathering, esp. of famous people. **ga·lac·tic** [gə-LAK-tik] *adj*

gale [gayl] *n* **1** strong wind. **2** *inf* loud outburst, esp. of laughter.

gall¹ [gawl] *n inf* **1** impudence. **2** bitterness. **gall'blad·der** *n* sac attached to liver, reservoir for bile. **gall'stone** *n* hard secretion in gallbladder or ducts leading from it.

gall² *n* **1** painful swelling, esp. on horse. **2** sore caused by chafing. ♦ *vt* **3** make sore by rubbing. **4** vex, irritate.

gall³ *n* abnormal growth or excrescence on trees, etc.

gal·lant [GAL-ənt] *adj* **1** fine, stately, brave. **2** [gə-LANT] chivalrous, very attentive to women. ♦ *n* **3** [gə-LANT] lover, suitor. **4** dashing, fashionable young man. **gal'lant·ly** *adv* **gal'lant·ry** *n, pl* **-ries**

gal·le·on [GAL-ee-ən] *n* large, high-built sailing ship of war.

gal·ler·y [GAL-ə-ree] *n, pl* **-ler·ies 1** covered walk with side openings, colonnade. **2** platform or projecting upper floor in theater, etc. **3** group of spectators. **4** long, narrow platform on outside of building. **5** room or rooms for special purposes, e.g. showing works of art. **6** passage in wall, open to interior of building.

gal·ley [GAL-ee] *n, pl* **-leys 1** one-decked vessel with sails and oars, usu. rowed by slaves or criminals. **2** kitchen of ship or aircraft. **3** printer's tray for composed type. **galley proof** printer's proof before being made up into pages. **galley slave 1** one condemned to row in galley. **2** drudge.

Gal·lic [GAL-ik] *adj* **1** of ancient Gaul. **2** French. **Gal'li·cism** *n* French word or idiom.

gal·li·um [GAL-ee-əm] *n* soft, gray metal of great fusibility.

gal·li·vant [GAL-ə-vant] *vi* gad about.

gal·lon [GAL-ən] *n* liquid measure of four quarts (3.7853 liters).

gal·lop [GAL-əp] *v* **1** go, ride at gallop. **2** move fast. ♦ *n* **3** horse's fastest pace with all four feet off ground together in each stride. **4** ride at this pace. **gal'lop·ing** *adj* **1** at a gallop. **2** speedy, swift.

gal·lows [GAL-ohz] *n* structure, usu. of two upright beams and crossbar, esp. for hanging criminals.

Gal·lup poll [GAL-əp] *n* method of finding out public opinion by questioning a cross section of the population.

ga·loot [gə-LOOT] *n inf* silly, clumsy person.

ga·lore [gə-LOR] *adv* in plenty.

ga·losh·es [gə-LOSH-əz] *pl n* waterproof overshoes.

proceeds, revenue, takings, winnings

gainsay *v* = **contradict**, contravene, controvert, deny, disagree with, dispute, rebut, retract

gait *n* = **walk**, bearing, carriage, pace, step, stride, tread

gala *n* = **festival**, carnival, celebration, festivity, fête, jamboree, pageant

gale *n* **1** = **storm**, blast, cyclone, hurricane, squall, tempest, tornado, typhoon **2** = **outburst**, burst, eruption, explosion, fit, howl, outbreak, peal, shout, shriek

gall¹ *n* **1** *Inf* = **impudence**, brazenness, cheek (*inf*), chutzpah (*inf*), effrontery, impertinence, insolence, nerve (*inf*) **2** = **bitterness**, acrimony, animosity, bile, hostility, rancor

gall² *v* **1** = **scrape**, abrade, chafe, irritate **2** = **annoy**, exasperate, irk, irritate, provoke, rankle, vex

gallant *adj* **1** = **brave**, bold, courageous, heroic, honorable, intrepid, manly, noble, valiant **2** = **chivalrous**, attentive, courteous, gentlemanly, gracious, noble, polite

gallantry *n* **1** = **bravery**, boldness, courage, heroism, intrepidity, manliness, spirit, valor **2** = **attentiveness**, chivalry, courteousness, courtesy, gentlemanliness, graciousness, nobility, politeness

galling *adj* = **annoying**, bitter, exasperating, irksome, irritating, provoking, vexatious

gallivant *v* = **wander**, gad about, ramble, roam, rove

gallop *v* = **run**, bolt, career, dash, hurry, race, rush, speed, sprint

galore *adv* = **in abundance**, all over the place, aplenty, everywhere, in great quantity, in great numbers, in profusion,

gal·van·ic [gal-VAN-ik] *adj* **1** of, producing, concerning electric current, esp. when produced chemically. **2** *inf* resembling effect of electric shock, startling. **gal'va·nize** [-və-nīz] *vt* **-nized, -niz·ing 1** stimulate to action. **2** excite, startle. **3** cover (iron, etc.) with protective zinc coating.

gam'bit *n* **1** *Chess* opening involving sacrifice of a piece. **2** any opening maneuver, comment, etc. intended to secure an advantage.

gam·ble [GAM-bəl] *vi* **-bled, -bling 1** play games of chance to win money. **2** act on expectation of something. ◆ *n* **3** risky undertaking. **4** bet, wager. **gam'bler** *n*

gam·bol [GAM-bəl] *vi* **-boled, -bol·ing** skip, jump playfully. ◆ *n* **1** frolic.

game¹ [gaym] *n* **1** diversion, pastime. **2** jest. **3** contest for amusement. **4** scheme, strategy. **5** animals or birds hunted. **6** their flesh. ◆ *adj* **game·er, game·est 7** brave. **8** willing. **game'ster** *n* gambler. **game'cock** *n* rooster bred for fighting. **game'keep·er** *n* person employed to breed game, prevent poaching.

game² *adj* lame, crippled (leg).

gam·ete [GAM-eet] *n Biology* a sexual cell that unites with another for reproduction or the formation of a new individual.

gam·ma [GAM-ə] *n* third letter of the Greek alphabet. **gamma ray** a very penetrative electromagnetic ray.

gam·mon [GAM-ən] *n* **1** cured or smoked ham. **2** lower end of side of bacon.

gam·ut [GAM-ət] *n* whole range or scale (orig. of musical notes).

gan·der [GAN-dər] *n* **1** male goose. **2** *sl* a quick look.

gang *n* **1** (criminal) group. **2** organized group of persons working together. ◆ *vi* **3** (esp. with *together*) form gang. **gang up** *vi* form an alliance (against).

gang'ling *adj* lanky, awkward in movement.

gan·gli·on [GANG-glee-ən] *n, pl* **-gli·a** [-glee-ə] nerve nucleus.

gang·plank [GANG-plangk] *n* portable bridge for boarding or leaving vessel.

gan·grene [GANG-green] *n* death or decay of body tissue as a result of disease or injury. **gan'gre·nous** [-grə-nəs] *adj*

gang·sta rap [GANG-sta] *n* a style of rap music featuring lyrics that are anti-authority and often derogatory to women.

gang·ster [GANG-stər] *n* **1** member of criminal gang. **2** notorious or hardened criminal.

gang'way *n* **1** bridge from ship to shore. **2** anything similar. ◆ *interj* **3** make way!

gan·try [GAN-tree] *n, pl* **-tries 1** structure to support crane, railway signals, etc. **2** framework beside rocket on launching pad.

gap *n* **1** breach, opening, interval. **2** cleft. **3** empty space.

gape [gayp] *vi* **gaped, gap·ing 1** stare in wonder. **2** open mouth wide, as in yawning. **3** be, become wide open.

——— THESAURUS ———

to spare

galvanize *v* = **stimulate**, electrify, excite, inspire, invigorate, jolt, provoke, spur, stir

gamble *v* **1** = **bet**, game, play, wager **2** = **risk**, chance, hazard, speculate, stick one's neck out (*inf*), take a chance ◆ *n* **3** = **risk**, chance, leap in the dark, lottery, speculation, uncertainty, venture **4** = **bet**, wager

gambol *v* **1** = **frolic**, caper, cavort, frisk, hop, jump, prance, skip ◆ *n* **2** = **frolic**, caper, hop, jump, prance, skip

game¹ *n* **1** = **pastime**, amusement, distraction, diversion, entertainment, lark, recreation, sport **2** = **match**, competition, contest, event, head-to-head, meeting, tournament **3** = **wild animals**, prey, quarry **4** = **scheme**, design, plan, plot, ploy, stratagem, tactic, trick ◆ *adj* **5** = **brave**,

courageous, gallant, gritty, intrepid, persistent, plucky, spirited **6** = **willing**, desirous, eager, interested, keen, prepared, ready

gamut *n* = **range**, area, catalog, compass, field, scale, scope, series, sweep

gang *n* = **group**, band, clique, club, company, coterie, crowd, mob, pack, squad, team

gangling *adj* = **tall**, angular, awkward, lanky, rangy, rawboned, spindly

gangster *n* = **racketeer**, crook (*inf*), hood (*sl*), hoodlum, mobster (*sl*)

gap *n* **1** = **opening**, break, chink, cleft, crack, hole, space **2** = **interval**, breathing space, hiatus, interlude, intermission, interruption, lacuna, lull, pause, respite **3** = **difference**, disagreement, disparity, divergence, inconsistency

ga·rage [gə-RAH*ZH*] *n* **1** (part of) building to house automobiles. **2** refueling and repair center for them. ◆ *vt* **-raged, -rag·ing 3** leave automobile in garage.

garb [gahrb] *n* **1** dress. **2** fashion of dress. ◆ *vt* **3** dress, clothe.

gar·bage [GAHR-bij] *n* **1** rubbish. **2** refuse. **garbage can** large, usu. cylindrical container for household rubbish.

gar·ble [GAHR-bəl] *vt* **-bled, -bling** jumble or distort (story, account, etc.).

gar·den [GAHR-dn] *n* **1** ground for growing flowers, fruit, or vegetables. ◆ *vi* **2** cultivate garden. **gar·den·er** [GAHRD-nər] *n* **gar·den·ing** [GAHRD-ning] *n*

gar·de·nia [gahr-DEE-nyə] *n* (sub)tropical shrub, with fragrant white or yellow flowers.

gar·gan·tu·an [gahr-GAN-choo-ən] *adj* immense, enormous, huge.

gar·gle [GAHR-gəl] *v* **-gled, -gling** ◆ *vi* **1** wash throat with liquid kept moving by the breath. ◆ *vt* **2** wash (throat) thus. ◆ *n* **3** gargling. **4** preparation for this purpose.

gar·goyle [GAHR-goil] *n* carved (grotesque) face on waterspout, esp. on Gothic church.

gar·ish [GAIR-ish] *adj* **1** showy. **2** gaudy.

gar·land [GAHR-lənd] *n* **1** wreath of flowers worn or hung as decoration. ◆ *vt* **2** decorate with garlands.

gar·lic [GAHR-lik] *n* (bulb of) plant with strong smell and taste, used in cooking and seasoning.

gar·ment [GAHR-mənt] *n* **1** article of clothing. ◆ *pl* **2** clothes.

gar·ner [GAHR-nər] *vt* store up, collect, as if

in granary.

gar·net [GAHR-nit] *n* red semiprecious stone.

gar·nish [GAHR-nish] *vt* **1** adorn, decorate (esp. food). ◆ *n* **2** material for this.

gar·ret [GAR-it] *n* small (usu. wretched) room on top floor, attic.

gar·ri·son [GAR-ə-sən] *n* **1** troops stationed in town, fort, etc. **2** fortified place. ◆ *vt* **3** furnish or occupy with garrison.

gar·rote [gə-ROHT] *n* **1** capital punishment by strangling. **2** apparatus for this. ◆ *vt* **-rot·ed, -rot·ing 3** execute, kill thus. **gar·rot'er** *n*

gar·ru·lous [GAR-ə-ləs] *adj* (frivolously) talkative. **gar·ru·li·ty** [gə-ROO-li-tee] *n* loquacity.

gar·ter [GAHR-tər] *n* band worn around leg to hold up sock or stocking. **garter snake** type of harmless snake.

gas *n, pl* **-es 1** airlike substance, esp. one that does not liquefy or solidify at ordinary temperatures. **2** fossil fuel in form of gas, used for heating or lighting. **3** gaseous anesthetic. **4** poisonous or irritant substance dispersed through atmosphere in warfare, etc. **5** gasoline. **6** automobile accelerator. **7** *sl* idle, boastful talk. ◆ *v* **gassed, gas·sing 8** project gas over. **9** poison with gas. **10** fill with gas. **11** *sl* talk idly, boastfully. **gas'e·ous** [-ee-əs] *adj* of, like gas. **gass'y** *adj* **-si·er, -si·est** filled with gas. **gas'bag** *n sl* person who talks idly. **gas mask** mask with chemical filter to guard against poisoning by gas.

gash *n* **1** gaping wound, slash. ◆ *vt* **2** cut deeply.

gape *v* **1** = **stare**, gawk, goggle, wonder **2** = **open**, crack, split, yawn

gaping *adj* = **wide**, broad, cavernous, great, open, vast, wide open, yawning

garbage *n* = **rubbish**, litter, refuse, trash, waste

garbled *adj* = **jumbled**, confused, distorted, double-Dutch, incomprehensible, mixed up, unintelligible

garish *adj* = **gaudy**, brash, brassy, flashy, loud, showy, tacky (*inf*), tasteless, vulgar

garland *n* **1** = **wreath**, bays, chaplet, crown, festoon, honors, laurels ◆ *v* **2** = **adorn**, crown, deck, festoon, wreathe

garments *pl n* = **clothes**, apparel, attire, clothing, costume, dress, garb, gear (*sl*), outfit, uniform

garner *v* = **collect**, accumulate, amass, gather, hoard, save, stockpile, store, stow away

garnish *v* **1** = **decorate**, adorn, embellish, enhance, ornament, set off, trim ◆ *n* **2** = **decoration**, adornment, embellishment, enhancement, ornamentation, trimming

garrison *n* **1** = **troops**, armed force, command, detachment, unit **2** = **fort**, base, camp, encampment, fortification, fortress, post, station, stronghold ◆ *v* **3** = **station**, assign, position, post, put on duty

garrulous *adj* = **talkative**, chatty, gossiping, loquacious, prattling, verbose, voluble

gash *v* **1** = **cut**, gouge, lacerate, slash, slit, split, tear, wound ◆ *n* **2** = **cut**, gouge,

gas·ket [GAS-kit] *n* rubber, neoprene, etc. used as seal between metal faces, esp. in engines.

gas·o·hol [GAS-ə-hawl] *n* mixture of gasoline and ethyl alcohol used as fuel for automobiles.

gas·o·line [gas-ə-LEEN] *n* refined petroleum used in automobiles, etc.

gasp *vi* **1** catch breath with open mouth, as in exhaustion or surprise. ◆ *n* **2** convulsive catching of breath.

gas·tric [GAS-trik] *adj* of stomach. **gas·tro·nom·i·cal** [-trə-NOM-ə-kəl] *adj* **gas·tron·o·my** [ga-STRON-ə-mee] *n* art of good eating.

gas·tro·en·ter·i·tis [gas-troh-en-tə-RĪ-tis] *n* inflammation of stomach and intestines.

gas·tro·pod [GAS-trə-pod] *n* mollusk, e.g. snail, with disklike organ of locomotion on ventral surface.

gate [gayt] *n* **1** opening in wall, fence, etc. **2** barrier for closing it. **3** sluice. **4** any entrance or way out. **5** (entrance money paid by) those attending sports event. **gate'-crash·er** *n inf* person who enters sports event, social function, etc. uninvited.

gath·er [GATH-ər] *v* (cause to) assemble. **1** increase gradually. **2** draw together. ◆ *vt* **3** collect. **4** learn, understand. **5** draw material into small tucks or folds. **gath·er·ing** *n* assembly.

gauche [gohsh] *adj* tactless, blundering. **gau·che·rie** *n* awkwardness, clumsiness.

gau·cho [GOW-choh] *n, pl* **-chos** cowboy of S Amer. pampas.

gaud [gawd] *n* showy ornament. **gaud'i·ly** *adv* **gaud'iness** *n* **gaud'y** *adj* **gaud·i·er, gaud·i·est** showy in tasteless way.

gauge, gage [gayj] *n* **1** standard measure, as of diameter of wire, thickness of sheet metal, etc. **2** distance between rails of railway. **3** capacity, extent. **4** instrument for measuring such things as wire, rainfall, height of water in boiler, etc. ◆ *vt* **gauged, gaug·ing 5** measure. **6** estimate.

gaunt [gawnt] *adj* **-er, -est** extremely lean, haggard.

gaunt·let [GAWNT-lit] *n* **1** armored glove. **2** glove covering part of arm. **3 run the gauntlet** formerly, run as punishment between two lines of men striking at runner with sticks, etc. **4** be exposed to criticism or unpleasant treatment. **5** undergo ordeal. **throw down the gauntlet** offer challenge.

gauss [gows] *n* unit of density of magnetic field.

gauze [gawz] *n* **1** thin transparent fabric of silk, wire, etc. **2** this as surgical dressing.

gave pt. of GIVE.

gav·el [GAV-əl] *n* mallet of presiding officer or auctioneer.

ga·votte [gə-VOT] *n* **1** lively dance. **2** music for it.

gawk *vi* stare stupidly. **gawk'y** *adj* **gawk·i·er, gawk·i·est** clumsy, awkward.

gay *adj* **-er, -est 1** homosexual. **2** merry. **3** lively. **4** cheerful. **5** bright. **6** lighthearted. **7** showy. **8** given to pleasure. ◆ *n* **9** homosexual. **gai'e·ty** *n, pl* **-ties gai'ly** *adv*

gaze [gayz] *vi* **gazed, gaz·ing** look fixedly. ◆

incision, laceration, slash, slit, split, tear, wound

gasp *v* **1** = **gulp**, blow, catch one's breath, choke, pant, puff ◆ *n* **2** = **gulp**, exclamation, pant, puff, sharp intake of breath

gate *n* = **barrier**, door, entrance, exit, gateway, opening, passage, portal

gather *v* **1** = **assemble**, accumulate, amass, collect, garner, mass, muster, stockpile **2** = **learn**, assume, conclude, deduce, hear, infer, surmise, understand **3** = **pick**, cull, garner, glean, harvest, pluck, reap, select **4** = **intensify**, deepen, expand, grow, heighten, increase, rise, swell, thicken **5** = **fold**, pleat, tuck

gathering *n* = **assembly**, company, conclave, congress, convention, crowd, group, meeting

gauche *adj* = **awkward**, clumsy, ill-mannered, inelegant, tactless, unsophisticated

gaudy *adj* = **garish**, bright, flashy, loud, showy, tacky (*inf*), tasteless, vulgar

gauge *v* **1** = **measure**, ascertain, calculate, check, compute, count, determine, weigh **2** = **judge**, adjudge, appraise, assess, estimate, evaluate, guess, rate, reckon, value ◆ *n* **3** = **indicator**, criterion, guide, guideline, measure, meter, standard, test, touchstone, yardstick

gaunt *adj* = **emaciated**, angular, anorexic, bony, cadaverous, lean, pinched, scrawny, skeletal, skinny, spare

gawky *adj* = **awkward**, clumsy, gauche, loutish, lumbering, maladroit, ungainly *n*

ga·ze·bo [gə-ZEE-boh] *n* summerhouse, small roofed structure, with extensive view.

ga·zelle [gə-ZEL] *n* small graceful antelope.

ga·zette [gə-ZET] *n* name for newspaper.

gaz·et·teer' *n* geographical dictionary.

ga·zil·lion [gə-ZIL-yən] *n inf* extremely large unspecified number.

Gd *Chem.* gadolinium.

Ge *Chem.* germanium.

gear [geer] *n* **1** set of wheels working together, esp. by engaging cogs. **2** connection by which engine, motor, etc. is brought into work. **3** arrangement by which driving wheel of cycle, automobile, etc. performs more or fewer revolutions relative to pedals, pistons, etc. **4** equipment. **5** clothing. **6** goods, utensils. **7** apparatus, tackle, tools. **8** rigging. **9** harness. ♦ *vt* **10** adapt (one thing) so as to conform with another. **11** provide with gear. **12** put in gear. **gear'box** *n* case protecting gearing of bicycle, automobile, etc. **in gear** connected up and ready for work. **out of gear** disconnected.

geek *n inf* boring, unattractive person.

geese [gees] pl. of GOOSE.

gee·zer [GEE-zər] *n sl* (old, eccentric) man.

ge·fil·te fish [gə-FIL-tə] in Jewish cookery, a dish of various freshwater fish chopped and blended with eggs, matzo meal, etc.

Gei·ger count·er [GI-gər] *n* instrument for detecting radioactivity, cosmic radiation and charged atomic particles.

gei·sha [GAY-shə] *n* in Japan, professional female entertainer and companion for men.

gel [jel] *n* **1** jelly-like substance. ♦ *vi* **gelled,**

gel·ling 2 form a gel. **3** jell.

gel·a·tin [JEL-ə-tn] *n* **1** substance prepared from animal bones, etc., producing edible jelly. **2** anything resembling this.

ge·lat·i·nous [jə-LAT-n-əs] *adj* like gelatin or jelly.

geld *vt* castrate. **geld'ing** *n* castrated horse.

gel·id [JEL-id] *adj* very cold.

gem [jem] *n* **1** precious stone, esp. when cut and polished. **2** treasure. ♦ *vt* **gemmed, gem·ming 3** adorn with gems.

Gen. Genesis.

gen·darme [ZHAHN-dahrm] *n* policeman in France.

gen·der [JEN-dər] *n* **1** sex, male or female. **2** grammatical classification of nouns, according to sex (actual or attributed).

gene [jeen] *n* biological factor determining inherited characteristics.

ge·ne·al·o·gy [jee-nee-AL-ə-jee] *n, pl* **-gies 1** account of descent from ancestors. **2** pedigree. **3** study of pedigrees. **ge·ne·a·log'i·cal** [-LOJ-ə-kəl] *adj*

genera pl. of GENUS.

gen·er·al [JEN-ər-əl] *adj* **1** common, widespread. **2** not particular or specific. **3** applicable to all or most. **4** usual, prevalent. **5** miscellaneous. **6** dealing with main element only. **7** vague, indefinite. ♦ *n* **8** army officer of rank above colonel. **gen·er·al'i·ty** *n, pl* **-ties 1** general principle. **2** vague statement. **3** indefiniteness. **gen·er·al·i·za'tion** *n* **1** general conclusion from particular instance. **2** inference. **gen'er·al·ize** *v* **-ized, -iz·ing** ♦ *vt* **1** reduce to general laws. ♦ *vi* **2** draw general conclusions. **general practitioner** physician with practice not restricted to particular branch of medicine.

—————— THESAURUS ——————

gay *adj* **1** = **homosexual**, bent (*inf*, *derogatory*), lesbian, queer (*inf*, *derogatory*) **2** = **carefree**, blithe, cheerful, jovial, light-hearted, lively, merry, sparkling **3** = **colorful**, bright, brilliant, flamboyant, flashy, rich, showy, vivid ♦ *n* **4** = **homosexual**, lesbian

gaze *v* **1** = **stare**, gape, look, regard, view, watch, wonder ♦ *n* **2** = **stare**, fixed look, look

gazette *n* = **newspaper**, journal, news-sheet, paper, periodical

gear *n* **1** = **cog**, cogwheel, gearwheel **2** = **mechanism**, cogs, machinery, works **3** = **equipment**, accouterments, apparatus,

instruments, paraphernalia, supplies, tackle, tools **4** = **clothing**, clothes, costume, dress, garments, outfit, togs, wear ♦ *v* **5** = **equip**, adapt, adjust, fit

geek *n Sl* = **bore**, anorak (*inf*), dork (*sl*), drip (*inf*), obsessive, trainspotter (*inf*), wonk (*inf*)

gelatinous *adj* = **jelly-like**, gluey, glutinous, gummy, sticky, viscous

gelid *adj* = **cold**, arctic, chilly, freezing, frigid, frosty, frozen, glacial, ice-cold, icy

gem *n* **1** = **precious stone**, jewel, stone **2** = **prize**, jewel, masterpiece, pearl, treasure

general *adj* **1** = **common**, accepted, broad, extensive, popular, prevalent, public, universal, widespread **2** = **imprecise**,

gen·er·ate [JEN-ə-rayt] *vt* **-at·ed, -at·ing 1** bring into being. **2** produce. **gen·er·a'tion** *n* **1** bringing into being. **2** all persons born about same time. **3** average time between two such generations (about 30 years). **gen'er·a·tor** *n* **1** apparatus for producing (steam, electricity, etc.). **2** begetter.

ge·ner·ic [ji-NER-ik] *adj* belonging to, characteristic of class or genus. **ge·ner'i·cal·ly** *adv* **generic drug** one sold without brand name.

gen·er·ous [JEN-ər-əs] *adj* **1** liberal, free in giving. **2** abundant. **gen·er·os'i·ty** *n, pl* **-ties**

gen·e·sis [JEN-ə-sis] *n, pl* **-ses** [-seez] **1** origin. **2** mode of formation. **3** (**G-**) first book of Bible.

ge·net·ics [jə-NET-iks] *n* scientific study of heredity and variation in organisms. **ge·net'ic** *adj* **ge·net'i·cist** *n* **genetic engineering** deliberate modification of heredity characteristics by treatment of DNA to transfer selected genes.

gen·ial [JEEN-yəl] *adj* **1** cheerful, warm in behavior. **2** mild, conducive to growth. **ge·ni·al'i·ty** *n*

ge·nie [JEE-nee] *n* in fairy tales, servant appearing by, and working, magic.

gen·i·tal [JEN-i-tl] *adj* relating to sexual organs or reproduction. **gen'i·tals** *pl n* the sexual organs.

gen·i·tive [JEN-i-tiv] *adj, n* possessive (case).

gen·ius [JEEN-yəs] *n* **1** (person with) exceptional power or ability, esp. of mind. **2** distinctive spirit or nature (of nation, etc.).

gen·o·cide [JEN-ə-sīd] *n* murder of a nationality or ethnic group.

gen·re [ZHAHN-rə] *n* **1** kind. **2** sort. **3** style. **4** painting of homely scene.

gen·teel [jen-TEEL] *adj* **1** well-bred. **2** stylish. **3** affectedly proper.

gen·tile [JEN-tīl] *adj, n* non-Jewish (person).

gen·tle [JEN-tl] *adj* **-tler, -tlest 1** mild, quiet, not rough or severe. **2** soft and soothing. **3** courteous. **4** moderate. **5** gradual. **6** wellborn. **gen·til'i·ty** *n* respectability, (pretentious) politeness. **gen'tle·ness** *n* **1** quality of being gentle. **2** tenderness. **gent'ly** *adv* **gen·tri·fi·ca'tion** *n* buying of properties in run-down urban neighborhoods by affluent people, thus increasing property values but displacing less affluent residents and owners of small businesses. **gent'ry** *n* wellborn people. **gen'tle·man** *n* **1** well-bred man. **2** man of good social position. **3** man (used as a

─── THESAURUS ───

approximate, ill-defined, indefinite, inexact, loose, unspecific, vague **3 = universal**, across-the-board, blanket, collective, comprehensive, indiscriminate, miscellaneous, sweeping, total

generally *adv* **1 = usually**, as a rule, by and large, customarily, normally, on the whole, ordinarily, typically **2 = commonly**, extensively, popularly, publicly, universally, widely

generate *v* **= produce**, breed, cause, create, engender, give rise to, make, propagate

generation *n* **1 = production**, creation, formation, genesis, propagation, reproduction **2 = age group**, breed, crop **3 = age**, epoch, era, period, time

generic *adj* **= collective**, blanket, common, comprehensive, general, inclusive, universal, wide

generosity *n* **1 = charity**, beneficence, bounty, kindness, largesse *or* largess, liberality, munificence, open-handedness **2 = unselfishness**, goodness, high-mindedness, magnanimity, nobleness

generous *adj* **1 = charitable**, beneficent, bountiful, hospitable, kind, lavish, liberal, open-handed, unstinting **2 = unselfish**, big-hearted, good, high-minded, lofty, magnanimous, noble **3 = plentiful**, abundant, ample, copious, full, lavish, liberal, rich, unstinting

genesis *n* **= beginning**, birth, creation, formation, inception, origin, start

genial *adj* **= cheerful**, affable, agreeable, amiable, congenial, friendly, good-natured, jovial, pleasant, warm

geniality *n* **= cheerfulness**, affability, agreeableness, amiability, conviviality, cordiality, friendliness, good cheer, joviality, warmth

genius *n* **1 = master**, brainbox, expert, hotshot (*inf*), maestro, mastermind, savant, virtuoso, whiz (*inf*) **2 = brilliance**, ability, aptitude, bent, capacity, flair, gift, knack, talent

genre *n* **= type**, category, class, group, kind, sort, species, style

genteel *adj* **= refined**, courteous, cultured, elegant, gentlemanly, ladylike, polite,

gen'tle·man·ly *adj* **gentlemen's agreement 1** agreement binding by honor but not valid in law. **2** unwritten law in private club, etc. to discriminate against members of certain groups. **gen'tri·fy** *v* **-fied, -fy·ing** change by gentrification, undergo this change.

gen·u·flect [JEN-yə-flekt] *vi* bend knee, esp. in worship. **gen·u·flec'tion** *n*

gen·u·ine [JEN-yoo-in] *adj* **1** real, true, not sham, authentic. **2** sincere. **3** pure.

ge·nus [JEE-nəs] *n, pl* **gen·e·ra** [JEN-ər-ə] class, order, group (esp. of insects, animals, etc.) with common characteristics usu. comprising several species.

ge·o·cen·tric [jee-oh-SEN-trik] *adj Astronomy* **1** measured, seen from Earth. **2** having Earth as center.

ge·ode [JEE-ohd] *n* **1** cavity lined with crystals. **2** stone containing this.

ge·o·des·ic [jee-ə-DES-ik] *adj* of geometry of curved surfaces. **geodesic dome** light but strong hemispherical construction formed from set of polygons.

ge·og·ra·phy [jee-OG-rə-fee] *n, pl* **-phies** science of Earth's form, physical features, climate, population, etc. **ge·og'ra·pher** *n*

ge·ol·o·gy [jee-OL-ə-jee] *n* science of Earth's crust, rocks, strata, etc. **ge·o·log'i·cal** *adj*

ge·om·e·try [jee-OM-i-tree] *n* science of properties and relations of lines, surfaces, etc. **ge·o·met'ric** *adj*

ge·o·phys·ics [jee-oh-FIZ-iks] *n* science dealing with physics of Earth. **ge·o·phys'i·cal** *adj*

ge·o·sta·tion·ar·y

[jee-oh-STAY-shə-ner-ee] *adj* (of satellite) in orbit around Earth so satellite remains over same point on surface.

ger·bil [JUR-bəl] *n* burrowing, desert rodent of Asia and Africa.

ger·i·at·rics [jer-ee-A-triks] *n* branch of medicine dealing with old age and its diseases. **ger·i·at'ric** *adj* old. ♦ *n* **2** *sl* old person.

germ [jurm] *n* **1** microbe, esp. causing disease. **2** elementary thing. **3** rudiment of new organism, of animal or plant. **ger'mi·cide** [-mə-sīd] *n* substance for destroying disease germs.

Ger·man [JUR-mən] *n, adj* (language or native) of Germany. **German measles** rubella, mild disease with symptoms like measles.

german *adj* **1** of the same parents. **2** closely akin, e.g. *brother-german*.

ger·mane [jər-MAYN] *adj* relevant, pertinent.

ger·mi·nate [JUR-mə-nayt] *v* **-nat·ed, -nat·ing** (cause to) sprout or begin to grow.

ger·ry·man·der [JER-i-man-dər] *vt* manipulate election districts so as to favor one side.

ger·und [JER-ənd] *n* noun formed from verb, such as *living*.

ges·ta·tion [je-STAY-shən] *n* **1** carrying of young in womb between conception and birth. **2** this period.

ges·tic·u·late [je-STIK-yə-layt] *vi* use expressive movements of hands and arms when speaking.

ges·ture [JES-chər] *n* **1** movement to

respectable, urbane, well-mannered

gentle *adj* **1** = **sweet-tempered**, compassionate, humane, kindly, meek, mild, placid, tender **2** = **moderate**, light, mild, muted, slight, soft, soothing **3** = **gradual**, easy, imperceptible, light, mild, moderate, slight, slow **4** = **tame**, biddable, broken, docile, manageable, placid, tractable

gentlemanly *adj* = **polite**, civil, courteous, gallant, genteel, honorable, refined, urbane, well-mannered

gentleness *n* = **tenderness**, compassion, kindness, mildness, softness, sweetness

gentry *n* = **nobility**, aristocracy, elite, upper class, upper crust (*inf*)

genuine *adj* **1** = **authentic**, actual, bona fide, legitimate, real, the real McCoy, true, veritable **2** = **sincere**, candid, earnest, frank, heartfelt, honest, unaffected, unfeigned

germ *n* **1** = **microbe**, bacterium, bug (*inf*), microorganism, virus **2** = **beginning**, embryo, origin, root, rudiment, seed, source, spark

germane *adj* = **relevant**, apposite, appropriate, apropos, connected, fitting, material, pertinent, related, to the point *or* purpose

germinate *v* = **sprout**, bud, develop, generate, grow, originate, shoot, swell, vegetate

gesticulate *v* = **signal**, gesture, indicate, make a sign, motion, sign, wave convey meaning. **2** indication of state of mind. ◆ *vi* **-tured, -tur·ing 3** make such a movement.

get *v* **got** or **got·ten, get·ting** ◆ *vt* **1** obtain, procure. **2** contract. **3** catch. **4** earn. **5** cause to go or come. **6** bring into position or state. **7** induce. **8** engender. **9** be in possession of, have (to do). **10** *inf* understand. ◆ *vi* **11** succeed in coming or going. **12** reach, attain. **13** become. **get'a·way** *n* escape. **get across** be understood. **get at 1** gain access to. **2** annoy. **3** criticize. **4** influence.

gey·ser [GĪ-zər] *n* hot spring throwing up spout of water from time to time.

ghast·ly [GAST-lee] *adj inf* **-li·er, -li·est 1** unpleasant. **2** deathlike, pallid. **3** horrible. ◆ *adv* **4** horribly.

gher·kin [GUR-kin] *n* small cucumber used in pickling.

ghet·to [GET-oh] *n, pl* **-tos** densely populated (esp. by one racial or ethnic group) slum area. **ghet'to·blast·er** *n inf* large portable cassette or CD player and radio.

ghost [gohst] *n* **1** spirit, dead person appearing again. **2** specter. **3** semblance. **4** faint trace. **5** one who writes work to appear under another's name, ghostwriter. ◆ *v* **6** (also **ghost'write**) write another's work, speeches, etc. **ghost'ly** *adj*

ghoul [gool] *n* **1** malevolent spirit. **2** person with morbid interests. **3** fiend. **ghoul'ish** *adj* **1** of or like ghoul. **2** horrible.

gi·ant [JĪ-ənt] *n* **1** mythical being of superhuman size. **2** very tall person, plant, etc. ◆ *adj* **3** huge. **gi·gan'tic** *adj* enormous, huge.

gib·ber [JIB-ər] *vi* make meaningless sounds with mouth, jabber, chatter. **gib'ber·ish** *n* meaningless speech or words.

gib·bet [JIB-it] *n* **1** gallows. **2** post with arm on which executed criminal was hung. **3** death by hanging. ◆ *vt* **4** hang on gibbet. **5** hold up to scorn.

gib·bon [GIB-ən] *n* type of ape.

gibe [jīb] *v* **gibed, gib·ing 1** utter taunts. **2** mock. **3** jeer. ◆ *n* **4** insulting remark.

gesture *n* **1** = **signal**, action, gesticulation, indication, motion, sign ◆ *v* **2** = **signal**, gesticulate, indicate, motion, sign, wave

get *v* **1** = **obtain**, acquire, attain, fetch, gain, land, net, pick up, procure, receive, secure, win **2** = **contract**, catch, come down with, fall victim to, take **3** = **capture**, grab, lay hold of, seize, take **4** = **become**, come to be, grow, turn **5** = **understand**, catch, comprehend, fathom, follow, perceive, see, take in, work out **6** = **persuade**, convince, induce, influence, prevail upon **7** *Inf* = **annoy**, bug (*inf*), gall, irritate, upset, vex

get across *v* **1** = **cross**, ford, negotiate, pass over, traverse **2** = **communicate**, bring home to, convey, impart, make clear or understood, put over, transmit

get along *v* = **be friendly**, agree, be compatible, click (*sl*), concur, hit it off (*inf*)

get at *v* **1** = **gain access to**, acquire, attain, come to grips with, get hold of, reach **2** = **imply**, hint, intend, lead up to, mean, suggest **3** = **criticize**, attack, blame, find fault with, nag, pick on

getaway *n* = **escape**, break, break-out, flight

get by *v* = **manage**, cope, exist, fare, get along, keep one's head above water, make both ends meet, survive

get off *v* = **leave**, alight, depart, descend, disembark, dismount, escape, exit

get on *v* = **board**, ascend, climb, embark, mount

get over *v* = **recover from**, come round, get better, mend, pull through, rally, revive, survive

ghastly *adj* = **horrible**, dreadful, frightful, gruesome, hideous, horrendous, loathsome, shocking, terrible, terrifying

ghost *n* **1** = **spirit**, apparition, phantom, poltergeist, soul, specter, spook (*inf*), wraith **2** = **trace**, glimmer, hint, possibility, semblance, shadow, suggestion

ghostly *adj* = **supernatural**, eerie, ghostlike, phantom, spectral, spooky (*inf*), unearthly, wraithlike

ghoulish *adj* = **macabre**, disgusting, grisly, gruesome, morbid, sick (*inf*), unwholesome

giant *n* **1** = **ogre**, colossus, monster, titan ◆ *adj* **2** = **huge**, colossal, enormous, gargantuan, gigantic, immense, mammoth, titanic, vast

gibberish *n* = **nonsense**, babble, drivel, gobbledygook (*inf*), mumbo jumbo, twaddle

gibe, jibe *v* **1** = **taunt**, jeer, make fun of, mock, poke fun at, ridicule, scoff, scorn, sneer ◆ *n* **2** = **taunt**, barb, crack (*sl*), dig,

gib·lets [JIB-lits] *pl n* internal edible parts of fowl, such as liver, gizzard, etc.

gid·dy [GID-ee] *adj* **-di·er, -di·est 1** dizzy, feeling as if about to fall. **2** liable to cause this feeling. **3** flighty, frivolous. **gid'di·ness** *n*

gift *n* **1** thing given, present. **2** faculty, power. ♦ *vt* **3** present (with). **4** endow, bestow. **gift'ed** *adj* talented.

gig *n* **1** light, two-wheeled carriage. **2** *inf* single booking of musicians to play at club, etc.

giga- *prefix* **1** denoting 10⁹, e.g. *gigavolt.* **2** *Computers* denoting 230, e.g. *gigabyte.*

gigantic see GIANT.

gig·gle [GIG-əl] *vi* **-gled, -gling 1** laugh nervously, foolishly. ♦ *n* **2** such a laugh.

gig·o·lo [JIG-ə-loh] *n, pl* **-los** man kept, paid, by (older) woman to be her escort, lover.

gild *vt* **gilded** *or* **gilt, gild·ing 1** put thin layer of gold on. **2** make falsely attractive. **gilt** *adj* **1** gilded. ♦ *n* **2** thin layer of gold put on.

gill [jil] *n* liquid measure, quarter of pint.

gills [gillz] *pl n* breathing organs in fish and other water creatures.

gim·bals [JIM-bəlz] *pl n* pivoted rings, for keeping things, e.g. compass, horizontal at sea or in space.

gim·let [GIM-lit] *n* **1** boring tool, usu. with screw point. **2** drink of vodka or gin with lime juice.

gim·mick [GIM-ik] *n* clever device, stratagem, etc., esp. one designed to attract attention or publicity.

gimp *n* **1** narrow fabric or braid used as edging or trimming. **2** *sl* a limp. **3** *sl* person who limps.

gin¹ [jin] *n* alcoholic liquor flavored with juniper berries.

gin² *n* **1** primitive engine in which vertical shaft is turned to drive horizontal beam in a circle. **2** machine for separating cotton from seeds.

gin·ger [JIN-jər] *n* **1** plant with pungent spicy root used in cooking, etc. **2** the root. **3** *inf* spirit, mettle. **4** light reddish-yellow color. ♦ *vt* **5** stimulate. **gin'ger·y** *adj* **1** of, like ginger. **2** spicy. **3** high-spirited. **4** reddish. **ginger ale, beer** ginger-flavored soft drink. **gin'ger·bread** *n* cake, cookie flavored with ginger.

gin·ger·ly [JIN-jər-lee] *adv* cautiously, warily, reluctantly.

ging·ham [GING-əm] *n* cotton cloth, usu. checked, woven from dyed yarn.

gink·go [GING-koh] *n, pl* **-goes** large Chinese shade tree.

gin·seng [JIN-seng] *n* (root of) plant believed to have tonic and energy-giving properties.

gi·raffe [jə-RAF] *n* Afr. ruminant animal, with spotted coat and very long neck and legs.

gird [gurd] *vt* **gird·ed** *or* **girt, gird·ing 1** put belt around. **2** fasten clothes thus. **3** equip with, or belt on, a sword. **4** prepare (oneself). **5** encircle. **gird'er** *n* large beam, esp. of steel.

gir·dle [GURD-l] *n* **1** corset. **2** waistband. **3** anything that surrounds, encircles. ♦ *vt* **-dled, -dling 4** surround, encircle. **5** remove bark (of tree) from a band around it.

girl [gurl] *n* **1** female child. **2** young

jeer, sarcasm, scoffing, sneer

giddiness *n* = **dizziness**, faintness, light-headedness, vertigo

giddy *adj* = **dizzy**, dizzying, faint, light-headed, reeling, unsteady, vertiginous

gift *n* **1** = **donation**, bequest, bonus, contribution, grant, hand-out, legacy, offering, present **2** = **talent**, ability, capability, capacity, flair, genius, knack, power

gifted *adj* = **talented**, able, accomplished, brilliant, capable, clever, expert, ingenious, masterly, skilled

gigantic *adj* = **enormous**, colossal, giant, huge, immense, mammoth, stupendous, titanic, tremendous

giggle *v, n* = **laugh**, cackle, chortle, chuckle, snigger, titter, twitter

gild *v* = **embellish**, adorn, beautify, brighten, coat, dress up, embroider, enhance, ornament

gimmick *n* = **stunt**, contrivance, device, dodge, ploy, scheme

gingerly *adv* = **cautiously**, carefully, charily, circumspectly, hesitantly, reluctantly, suspiciously, timidly, warily

gird¹ *v* = **surround**, encircle, enclose, encompass, enfold, hem in, ring

girdle *n* **1** = **belt**, band, cummerbund, sash, waistband ♦ *v* **2** = **surround**, bound, encircle, enclose, encompass, gird, ring (formerly, an unmarried) woman. **girl'hood** [-huud] n

girt pt./pp. of GIRD.

girth [gurth] n 1 measurement around thing. 2 leather or cloth band put around horse to hold saddle, etc. ◆ vt 3 surround, secure, with girth. 4 girdle.

gist [jist] n substance, main point (of remarks, etc.).

give [giv] v gave, giv·en, giv·ing ◆ vt 1 bestow, confer ownership of, make present of. 2 deliver. 3 impart. 4 assign. 5 yield, supply. 6 utter. 7 emit. 8 be host of (party, etc.). 9 make over. 10 cause to have. ◆ vi 11 yield, give way, move. ◆ n 12 yielding, elasticity. **give'a·way** n 1 act of giving something away. 2 what is given away. 3 telltale sign. **give up** 1 acknowledge defeat. 2 abandon.

giz·zard [GIZ-ərd] n part of bird's stomach.

gla·brous [GLAY-brəs] adj 1 smooth. 2 without hairs or any unevenness.

gla·cier [GLAY-shər] n river of ice, slow-moving mass of ice formed by accumulated snow in mountain valleys.

gla·cial adj 1 of ice, or of glaciers. 2 very cold. **gla·ci·a'tion** n

glad adj -der, -dest 1 pleased. 2 happy, joyous. 3 giving joy. **glad'den** vt make glad. **glad'ly** adv **glad rags** inf dressy clothes for party, etc.

glade [glayd] n clear, grassy space in wood or forest.

glad·i·a·tor [GLAD ee ay tər] n trained fighter in ancient Roman arena.

glam·our [GLAM-ər] n alluring charm, fascination. **glam'or·ize** vt -ized, -iz·ing make appear glamorous. **glam'or·ous** adj

glance [glans] vi glanced, glanc·ing 1 look rapidly or briefly. 2 allude, touch. 3 glide off something struck. 4 pass quickly. ◆ n 5 brief look. 6 flash. 7 gleam. 8 sudden (deflected) blow.

gland n one of various small organs controlling different bodily functions by chemical means. **glan·du·lar** [GLAN-jə-lər] adj

glare [glair] vi glared, glar·ing 1 look fiercely. 2 shine brightly, intensely. 3 be conspicuous. ◆ n

————— THESAURUS —————

girl n = **female child**, damsel (archaic), daughter, lass, maid (archaic), maiden (archaic), miss

girth n = **circumference**, bulk, measure, size

gist n = **point**, core, essence, force, idea, meaning, sense, significance, substance

give v 1 = **present**, award, contribute, deliver, donate, grant, hand over or out, provide, supply 2 = **announce**, communicate, issue, notify, pronounce, transmit, utter 3 = **concede**, grant, hand over, relinquish, surrender, yield 4 = **produce**, cause, engender, make, occasion

give away v = **reveal**, betray, disclose, divulge, expose, leak, let out, let slip, uncover

give in v = **admit defeat**, capitulate, collapse, concede, quit, submit, succumb, surrender, yield

give off v = **emit**, discharge, exude, produce, release, send out, throw out

give out v = **emit**, discharge, exude, produce, release, send out, throw out

give up v = **abandon**, call it a day or night, cease, desist, leave off, quit, relinquish, renounce, stop, surrender

glad adj 1 = **happy**, contented, delighted, gratified, joyful, overjoyed, pleased 2 =

pleasing, cheerful, cheering, gratifying, pleasant

gladden v = **please**, cheer, delight, gratify, hearten

gladly adv = **happily**, cheerfully, freely, gleefully, readily, willingly, with pleasure

gladness n = **happiness**, cheerfulness, delight, gaiety, glee, high spirits, joy, mirth, pleasure

glamorous adj = **elegant**, attractive, dazzling, exciting, fascinating, glittering, glossy, prestigious, smart

glamour n = **charm**, allure, appeal, attraction, beauty, enchantment, fascination, prestige

glance v 1 = **look**, glimpse, peek, peep, scan, view 2 = **gleam**, flash, glimmer, glint, glisten, glitter, reflect, shimmer, shine, twinkle ◆ n 3 = **look**, glimpse, peek, peep, view

glare v 1 = **scowl**, frown, glower, look daggers, lour or lower 2 = **dazzle**, blaze, flame, flare ◆ n 3 = **scowl**, black look, dirty look, frown, glower, lour or lower 4 = **dazzle**, blaze, brilliance, flame, glow

glaring adj 1 = **conspicuous**, blatant, flagrant, gross, manifest, obvious, outrageous, unconcealed 2 = **dazzling**, blazing, bright, garish, glowing

glass n 1 hard transparent substance made by fusing sand, soda, potash, etc. 2 things made of it. 3 tumbler. 4 its contents. 5 lens. 6 mirror. 7 spyglass. ◆ pl 8 eyeglasses. **glass'i·ness** n **glass'y** adj **glass·i·er, glass·i·est** 1 like glass. 2 expressionless. **glass wool** insulating fabric of spun glass.

glau·co·ma [glow-KOH-mə] n eye disease.

glaze [glayz] v **glazed, glaz·ing** ◆ vt 1 furnish with glass. 2 cover with glassy substance. ◆ vi 3 become glassy. ◆ n 4 transparent coating. 5 substance used for this. 6 glossy surface. **gla·zier** [GLAY-zhər] n one who glazes windows.

gleam [gleem] n 1 slight or passing beam of light. 2 faint or momentary show. ◆ vi 3 give out gleams.

glean [gleen] v 1 pick up (facts, etc.). 2 gather, pick up, orig. after reapers in grainfields. **glean'er** n

glee n 1 mirth, merriment. 2 musical composition for three or more voices. **glee'ful** adj **glee club** chorus organized for singing choral music.

glen n narrow valley, usu. wooded and with a stream.

glib adj **-ber, -best** 1 fluent but insincere or superficial. 2 plausible. **glib'ness** n

glide [glīd] vi **glid·ed, glid·ing** 1 pass smoothly and continuously. 2 of airplane, move without use of engines. ◆ n 3 smooth, silent movement. 4 Mus. sounds made in passing from tone to tone. **glid'er** n 1 aircraft without engine that moves through the action of gravity and air currents. 2 porch swing. **glid'ing** n sport of flying gliders.

glim·mer [GLIM-ər] vi 1 shine faintly, flicker. ◆ n **glim'mer·ing** n 1 faint gleam of light. 2 faint idea, notion.

glimpse [glimps] n 1 brief or incomplete view. ◆ vt **glimpsed, glimps·ing** 2 catch glimpse of.

glint v 1 flash, glance, glitter. 2 reflect. ◆ n

glis·ten [GLIS-ən] vi gleam by reflecting light.

glitch [glich] n small problem that stops something from working properly.

glit·ter [GLIT-ər] vi 1 shine with bright quivering light, sparkle. 2 be showy. ◆ n 3 luster. 4 sparkle.

gloam·ing [GLOH-ming] n evening twilight.

gloat [gloht] vi regard, dwell on with smugness or malicious satisfaction.

glob n soft lump or mass.

glassy adj 1 = **transparent**, clear, glossy, shiny, slippery, smooth 2 = **expressionless**, blank, cold, dull, empty, fixed, glazed, lifeless, vacant

glaze v 1 = **coat**, enamel, gloss, lacquer, polish, varnish ◆ n 2 = **coat**, enamel, finish, gloss, lacquer, luster, patina, polish, shine, varnish

gleam n 1 = **glow**, beam, flash, glimmer, ray, sparkle 2 = **trace**, flicker, glimmer, hint, inkling, suggestion ◆ v 3 = **shine**, flash, glimmer, glint, glisten, glitter, glow, shimmer, sparkle

glee n = **delight**, elation, exhilaration, exuberance, exultation, joy, merriment, triumph

gleeful adj = **delighted**, elated, exuberant, exultant, joyful, jubilant, overjoyed, triumphant

glib adj = **smooth**, easy, fluent, insincere, plausible, quick, ready, slick, suave, voluble

glide v = **slide**, coast, drift, float, flow, roll, run, sail, skate, slip

glimmer v 1 = **flicker**, blink, gleam, glisten, glitter, glow, shimmer, shine, sparkle, twinkle ◆ n 2 = **gleam**, blink, flicker, glow,

ray, shimmer, sparkle, twinkle 3 = **trace**, flicker, gleam, hint, suggestion

glimpse n 1 = **look**, glance, peek, peep, sight, sighting ◆ v 2 = **catch sight of**, espy, sight, spot, spy, view

glint v 1 = **gleam**, flash, glimmer, glitter, shine, sparkle, twinkle ◆ n 2 = **gleam**, flash, glimmer, glitter, shine, sparkle, twinkle, twinkling

glisten v = **gleam**, flash, glance, glare, glimmer, glint, glitter, shimmer, shine, sparkle, twinkle

glitch n = **problem**, blip, difficulty, gremlin, hitch, interruption, malfunction, snag

glitter v 1 = **shine**, flash, glare, gleam, glimmer, glint, glisten, shimmer, sparkle, twinkle ◆ n 2 = **shine**, brightness, flash, glare, gleam, radiance, sheen, shimmer, sparkle 3 = **glamour**, display, gaudiness, pageantry, show, showiness, splendor, tinsel

gloat v = **relish**, brag, crow, drool, exult, glory, revel in, rub it in (inf), triumph

global adj 1 = **worldwide**, international, planetary, universal, world 2 = **comprehensive**, all-inclusive, exhaustive,

globe [glohb] *n* **1** sphere with map of Earth or stars. **2** heavenly sphere, esp. Earth. **3** ball, sphere. **glob'al** *adj* **1** of globe. **2** relating to whole world. **glob·al·i·za'tion** [gloh-bəl-ī-ZAY-shən] *n* broadening the scope, application, influence, or effect of something to the entire world. **glob'u·lar** [-yə-lər] *adj* globe-shaped. **glob'ule** [-yool] *n* **1** small round particle. **2** drop. **glob'u·lin** *n* kind of simple protein. **global warming** increase in overall temperature worldwide believed to be caused by pollutants. **globe'trot·ter** *n* (habitual) world traveler.

glock·en·spiel [GLOK-ən-speel] *n* percussion instrument of metal bars struck with hammers.

gloom *n* **1** darkness. **2** melancholy, depression. **gloom'y** *adj* **gloom·i·er, gloom·i·est**

glo·ry [GLOR-ee] *n* **1** renown, honorable fame. **2** splendor. **3** exalted or prosperous state. **4** heavenly bliss. ◆ *vi* **-ried, -ry·ing 1** take pride (in). **glor'i·fy** *vt* **-fied, -fy·ing 1** make glorious. **2** invest with glory. **glo'ri·ous** *adj* **1** illustrious. **2** splendid. **3** excellent. **4** delightful.

gloss¹ *n* **1** surface shine, luster. ◆ *vt* **2** put gloss on. **3** (esp. with *over*) (try to) cover up, pass over (fault, error). **gloss'i·ness** *n* **gloss'y** *adj* **gloss·i·er, gloss·i·est 1** smooth, shiny. ◆ *n* **2** photograph printed on shiny paper.

gloss² *n* **1** marginal interpretation of word. **2** comment, explanation. ◆ *vt* **3** interpret. **4** comment. **5** explain away. **glos'sa·ry** *n, pl* **-ries** dictionary, vocabulary of special words.

glot'tis *n* human vocal apparatus, larynx. **glot'tal** [GLOT-l] *adj*

glove [gluv] *n* **1** covering for the hand. ◆ *vt* **gloved, glov·ing 2** cover with, or as with glove. **glove compartment** storage area in dashboard of automobile. **the gloves** boxing gloves.

glow [gloh] *vi* **1** give out light and heat without flames. **2** shine. **3** experience well-being or satisfaction. **4** be or look hot. **5** burn with emotion. ◆ *n* **6** shining heat. **7** warmth of color. **8** feeling of well-being. **9** ardor. **glow·worm** [GLOH-wurm] *n* female insect giving out green light. **glow·er** [GLOW-ər] *vi* scowl.

general, total, unlimited

globe *n* = **sphere**, ball, earth, orb, planet, world

globule *n* = **droplet**, bead, bubble, drop, particle, pearl, pellet

gloom *n* **1** = **darkness**, blackness, dark, dusk, murk, obscurity, shade, shadow, twilight **2** = **depression**, dejection, despondency, low spirits, melancholy, sorrow, unhappiness, woe

gloomy *adj* **1** = **dark**, black, dim, dismal, dreary, dull, gray, murky, somber **2** = **depressing**, bad, cheerless, disheartening, dispiriting, dreary, sad, somber **3** = **miserable**, crestfallen, dejected, dispirited, downcast, downhearted, glum, melancholy, morose, pessimistic, sad

glorify *v* **1** = **enhance**, aggrandize, dignify, elevate, ennoble, magnify **2** = **worship**, adore, bless, exalt, honor, idolize, pay homage to, revere, venerate **3** = **praise**, celebrate, eulogize, extol, sing *or* sound the praises of

glorious *adj* **1** = **famous**, celebrated, distinguished, eminent, honored, illustrious, magnificent, majestic, renowned **2** = **splendid**, beautiful, brilliant, dazzling, gorgeous, shining, superb **3** =

delightful, excellent, fine, gorgeous, marvelous, wonderful

glory *n* **1** = **honor**, dignity, distinction, eminence, fame, kudos, praise, prestige, renown **2** = **splendor**, grandeur, greatness, magnificence, majesty, nobility, pageantry, pomp ◆ *v* **3** = **triumph**, boast, exult, pride oneself, relish, revel, take delight

gloss¹ *n* = **shine**, brightness, gleam, luster, patina, polish, sheen, veneer

gloss² *n* **1** = **comment**, annotation, commentary, elucidation, explanation, footnote, interpretation, note, translation ◆ *v* **2** = **interpret**, annotate, comment, elucidate, explain, translate

glossy *adj* = **shiny**, bright, glassy, glazed, lustrous, polished, shining, silky

glow *v* **1** = **shine**, brighten, burn, gleam, glimmer, redden, smolder ◆ *n* **2** = **light**, burning, gleam, glimmer, luminosity, phosphorescence **3** = **radiance**, brightness, brilliance, effulgence, splendor, vividness

glower *v* **1** = **scowl**, frown, give a dirty look, glare, look daggers, lour *or* lower ◆ *n* **2** = **scowl**, black look, dirty look, frown, glare, lour *or* lower

glowing *adj* **1** = **bright**, aglow, flaming, luminous, radiant **2** = **complimentary**,

glu•cose [GLOO-kohs] n type of sugar found in fruit, etc.

glue [gloo] n 1 any natural or synthetic adhesive. 2 any sticky substance. ◆ vt **glued, glu•ing** 3 fasten (as if) with glue. **glue sniffing** practice of inhaling fumes of glue for intoxicating or hallucinatory effects.

glum adj **glum•mer, glum•mest** sullen, moody, gloomy.

glut n 1 surfeit, excessive amount. ◆ vt **glut•ted, glut•ting** 2 feed, gratify to the full or to excess. 3 overstock.

glu•ten [GLOOT-n] n protein present in cereal grain. **glu'ti•nous** adj sticky, gluey.

glut•ton [GLUT-n] n 1 greedy person. 2 one with great liking or capacity for something, esp. food and drink. **glut'ton•ous** adj like glutton, greedy. **glut'ton•y** n

glyc•er•in [GLIS-ər-in] n colorless sweet liquid with wide application in chemistry and industry.

GM genetically modified.

GMO genetically modified organism.

gnarled [nahrld] adj knobby, rugged, twisted.

gnash [nash] v grind (teeth) together as in anger or pain.

gnat [nat] n small, biting, two-winged fly.

gnaw [naw] v 1 bite or chew steadily. 2 (esp. with at) cause distress to.

gneiss [nīs] n coarse-grained metamorphic rock.

gnome [nohm] n 1 legendary creature like small old man. 2 international financier. **gnom'ish** adj

gno•mic [NOH-mik] adj of or like an aphorism.

gnos•tic [NOS-tik] adj of, relating to knowledge, esp. spiritual knowledge.

gnu [noo] n S Afr. antelope somewhat like ox.

go [goh] vi **went, gone, go•ing** 1 move along, make way. 2 be moving. 3 depart. 4 function. 5 make specified sound. 6 fail, give way, break down. 7 elapse. 8 be kept, put. 9 be able to be put. 10 result. 11 contribute to result. 12 tend to. 13 be accepted, have force. 14 become. ◆ n 15 going. 16 energy, vigor. 17 attempt. 18 turn. **go-go dancer** dancer, usu. scantily dressed, who performs rhythmic and oft. erotic modern dance routines, esp. in nightclub.

goad [gohd] n 1 spiked stick for driving cattle. 2 anything that urges to action. 3 incentive. ◆ vt 4 urge on. 5 torment.

goal [gohl] n 1 end of race. 2 object of effort. 3 posts through which ball is to be driven in various games. 4 the score so made.

goat [goht] n four-footed animal with long hair, horns and beard. **goat•ee'** n beard like goat's. **get someone's goat** inf annoy (someone).

gob n 1 lump. 2 sl sailor. **gob•ble** [GOB-əl] vt **-bled, -bling** eat hastily, noisily or greedily.

gob•ble n 1 throaty, gurgling cry of male

adulatory, ecstatic, enthusiastic, laudatory, rave (inf), rhapsodic

glue n 1 = **adhesive**, cement, gum, paste ◆ v 2 = **stick**, affix, cement, fix, gum, paste, seal

glum adj = **gloomy**, crestfallen, dejected, doleful, low, morose, pessimistic, sullen

glut n 1 = **surfeit**, excess, oversupply, plethora, saturation, superfluity, surplus ◆ v 2 = **saturate**, choke, clog, deluge, flood, inundate, overload, oversupply

glutton n = **gourmand**, pig (inf)

gluttonous adj = **greedy**, gormandizing, insatiable, piggish, ravenous, voracious

gluttony n = **greed**, gormandizing, greediness, voracity

gnarled adj = **twisted**, contorted, knotted, knotty, rough, rugged, weather-beaten, wrinkled

gnaw v = **bite**, chew, munch, nibble

go v 1 = **move**, advance, journey, make for, pass, proceed, set off, travel 2 = **leave**, depart, make tracks, move out, slope off, withdraw 3 = **function**, move, operate, perform, run, work 4 = **contribute**, lead to, serve, tend, work towards 5 = **harmonize**, agree, blend, chime, complement, correspond, fit, match, suit 6 = **elapse**, expire, flow, lapse, pass, slip away ◆ n 7 = **attempt**, bid, crack (inf), effort, shot (inf), try, turn 8 inf = **energy**, drive, force, life, spirit, verve, vigor, vitality, vivacity

goad v 1 = **provoke**, drive, egg on, exhort, incite, prod, prompt, spur ◆ n 2 = **provocation**, impetus, incentive, incitement, irritation, spur, stimulus, urge

goal n = **aim**, ambition, end, intention, object, objective, purpose, target turkey. ◆ vi -**bled, -bling 2** make such a noise.

gob·ble·dy·gook, -de·gook
[GOB-əl-dee-guuk] n pretentious, usu. incomprehensible language, esp. as used by officials.

gob·let [GOB-lit] n drinking cup.

gob·lin n Folklore small, usu. malevolent being.

god n **1** superhuman being worshipped as having supernatural power. **2** object of worship, idol. **3** (G-) in monotheistic religions, the Supreme Being, creator and ruler of universe. **god'dess** n, fem. **god'like** adj **god'li·ness** n **god'ly** adj **-li·er, -li·est** devout, pious. **god'child** n child for whom a person stands as godparent. **god'father** n **god'mother** n **god'parent** n sponsor at baptism. **God-fearing** adj religious, good. **god'for·sak·en** [-fər-say-kən] adj hopeless, dismal. **God'head** n divine nature or deity. **god'send** n something unexpected and welcome.

gog·gle [GOG-əl] vi **-gled, -gling 1** (of eyes) bulge. **2** stare. ◆ pl n **3** protective eyeglasses.

goi·ter [GOI-tər] n neck swelling due to enlargement of thyroid gland.

go-kart, go-cart see KART.

gold [gohld] n **1** yellow precious metal. **2** coins of this. **3** wealth. **4** beautiful or precious thing. **5** color of gold. ◆ adj **6** of, like gold. **gold'en** adj gold digger inf woman skillful in extracting money from men. **golden mean** middle way between extremes. **gold'en·rod** n tall plant with golden flower spikes. **golden rule** important principle. **golden wedding** fiftieth wedding anniversary. **gold'field** n place where gold deposits are known to exist. **gold'finch** n bird with yellow feathers. **gold'fish** n any of various ornamental pond or aquarium fish. **gold standard** financial arrangement whereby currencies of countries accepting it are expressed in fixed terms of gold.

golf n **1** outdoor game in which small hard ball is struck with clubs into a succession of holes. ◆ vi **2** play this game.

go·nad [GOH-nad] n gland producing gametes.

gon·do·la [GON-dl-ə] n Venetian canal boat. **gon·do·lier'** n rower of gondola.

gone [gawn] pp. of GO.

gong n **1** metal plate with turned rim that resounds as bell when struck with soft mallet. **2** anything used thus.

gon·or·rhea [gon-ə-REE-ə] n a venereal disease.

good [guud] adj **bet·ter, best 1** commendable. **2** right. **3** proper. **4** excellent. **5** beneficial. **6** well-behaved. **7** virtuous. **8** kind. **9** safe. **10** adequate. **11** sound. **12** valid. ◆ n **13** benefit. **14** well-being. **15** profit. ◆ pl **16** property. **17** wares. **good'ly** adj large, considerable. **good'ness** n good will **1** kindly feeling, heartiness. **2** value of a business in reputation, etc. over and above its tangible assets.

THESAURUS

gobble v = **devour**, bolt, cram, gorge, gulp, guzzle, stuff, swallow, wolf

gobbledygook n = **nonsense**, babble, cant, gabble, gibberish, hocus-pocus, jargon, mumbo jumbo, twaddle

go-between n = **intermediary**, agent, broker, dealer, mediator, medium, middleman

godforsaken adj = **desolate**, abandoned, bleak, deserted, dismal, dreary, forlorn, gloomy, lonely, remote, wretched

godlike adj = **divine**, celestial, heavenly, superhuman, transcendent

godly adj = **devout**, god-fearing, good, holy, pious, religious, righteous, saintly

godsend n = **blessing**, boon, manna, stroke of luck, windfall

go for v **1** = **favor**, admire, be attracted to, be fond of, choose, like, prefer **2** = **attack**, assail, assault, launch oneself at, rush upon, set about or upon, spring upon

golden adj **1** = **yellow**, blond or blonde, flaxen **2** = **successful**, flourishing, glorious, halcyon, happy, prosperous, rich **3** = **promising**, excellent, favorable, opportune

gone adj **1** = **finished**, elapsed, ended, over, past **2** = **missing**, absent, astray, away, lacking, lost, vanished

good adj **1** = **pleasing**, acceptable, admirable, excellent, fine, first-class, first-rate, great, satisfactory, splendid, superior **2** = **praiseworthy**, admirable, ethical, honest, honorable, moral, righteous, trustworthy, upright, virtuous, worthy **3** = **expert**, able, accomplished, adept, adroit, clever, competent, proficient, skilled, talented **4** = **beneficial**, advantageous, convenient, favorable,

good-bye [guud-Bī] *interj, n* form of address on parting.

goof *n inf* **1** mistake. **2** stupid person. ◆ *vi* **3** make mistake. **goof'y** *adj* **goof·i·er, goof·i·est** silly.

goon *n sl* **1** stupid, awkward fellow. **2** *inf* hired thug, hoodlum.

goose *n sl* **1** web-footed bird. **2** its flesh. **3** simpleton. **goose flesh** bristling of skin due to cold, fright. **goose step** formal parade step.

go·pher [GOH-fər] *n* various species of Amer. burrowing rodents. **gopher ball** *Baseball sl* pitched ball hit for home run.

gore[1] [gor] *n* (dried) blood from wound. **gor'y** *adj* **gor·i·er, gor·i·est**

gore[2] *vt* **gored, gor·ing** pierce with horns.

gore[3] *n* **1** triangular piece inserted to shape garment. ◆ *vt* **gored, gor·ing 2** shape thus.

gorge [gorj] *n* **1** ravine. **2** disgust, resentment. ◆ *vi* **gorged, gorg·ing 3** feed greedily.

gor·geous [GOR-jəs] *adj* **1** splendid, showy, dazzling. **2** *inf* extremely pleasing.

gor·gon [GOR-gən] *n* **1** terrifying or repulsive woman. **2** (**G**-) in Greek mythology, any of three sisters whose appearance turned any viewer to stone.

go·ril·la [gə-RIL-ə] *n* largest anthropoid ape, found in Afr.

gor·mand·ize [GOR-mən-dīz] *vt* **-ized, -iz·ing** eat hurriedly or like a glutton.

gory see GORE[1].

gos'hawk *n* large hawk.

gos·ling [GOZ-ling] *n* young goose.

gos·pel [GOS-pəl] *n* **1** unquestionable truth. **2** (**G**-) any of first four books of New Testament.

gos·sa·mer [GOS-ə-mər] *n* **1** filmy substance like spider's web. **2** thin gauze or silk fabric.

gos·sip [GOS-əp] *n* **1** idle (malicious) talk

THESAURUS

fitting, helpful, profitable, suitable, useful, wholesome, win-win (*inf*) **5 = kind**, altruistic, benevolent, charitable, friendly, humane, kind-hearted, kindly, merciful, obliging **6 = valid**, authentic, bona fide, genuine, legitimate, proper, real, true **7 = well-behaved**, dutiful, obedient, orderly, polite, well-mannered **8 = full**, adequate, ample, complete, considerable, extensive, large, substantial, sufficient ◆ *n* **9 = benefit**, advantage, gain, interest, profit, use, usefulness, welfare, wellbeing **10 = virtue**, excellence, goodness, merit, morality, rectitude, right, righteousness, worth **11 for good = permanently**, finally, for ever, irrevocably, once and for all

good-bye *n* **= farewell**, adieu, leave-taking, parting

good-for-nothing *n* **1 = idler**, couch potato (*sl*), slacker (*inf*), waster, wastrel ◆ *adj* **2 = worthless**, feckless, idle, irresponsible, useless

goodly *adj* **= considerable**, ample, large, significant, sizable *or* sizeable, substantial, tidy (*inf*)

goodness *n* **1 = excellence**, merit, quality, superiority, value, worth **2 = kindness**, benevolence, friendliness, generosity, goodwill, humaneness, kind-heartedness, kindliness, mercy **3 = virtue**, honesty, honor, integrity, merit, morality, probity, rectitude, righteousness, uprightness **4 = benefit**, advantage, salubriousness, wholesomeness

goods *pl n* **1 = property**, belongings, chattels, effects, gear, paraphernalia, possessions, things, trappings **2 = merchandise**, commodities, stock, stuff, wares

goodwill *n* **= friendliness**, amity, benevolence, friendship, heartiness, kindliness

go off *v* **1 = explode**, blow up, detonate, fire **2 = leave**, decamp, depart, go away, move out, part, quit, slope off

go out *v* **1 = leave**, depart, exit **2 = be extinguished**, die out, expire, fade out

go over *v* **= examine**, inspect, rehearse, reiterate, review, revise, study, work over

gore[1] *n* **= blood**, bloodshed, butchery, carnage, slaughter

gore[2] *v* **= pierce**, impale, transfix, wound

gorge[1] *n* **1 = ravine**, canyon, chasm, cleft, defile, fissure, pass ◆ *v* **2 = overeat**, cram, devour, feed, glut, gobble, gulp, guzzle, stuff, wolf

gorgeous *adj* **1 = beautiful**, dazzling, elegant, magnificent, ravishing, splendid, stunning (*inf*), sumptuous, superb **2** *Inf* **= pleasing**, delightful, enjoyable, exquisite, fine, glorious, good, lovely

gory *adj* **= bloodthirsty**, blood-soaked, bloodstained, bloody, murderous, sanguinary

gospel *n* **1 = truth**, certainty, fact, the last word **2 = doctrine**, credo, creed, message,

about other persons, esp. regardless of fact. **2** one who talks thus. ◆ *vi* **-siped, -sip·ing 3** engage in gossip. **4** chatter.
got see GET.
Goth·ic [GOTH-ik] *adj* **1** *Architecture* of the pointed arch style common in Europe from twelfth to sixteenth century. **2** of Goths. **3** barbarous. **4** gloomy. **5** grotesque. **6** (of type) German black letter.
gouge [gowj] *vt* **gouged, goug·ing 1** scoop out. **2** force out. **3** extort from. **4** overcharge. ◆ *n* **5** chisel with curved cutting edge.
gou·lash [GOO-lahsh] *n* stew of meat and vegetables seasoned with paprika, etc.
gourd [gord] *n* **1** trailing or climbing plant. **2** its large fleshy fruit. **3** its rind as vessel.
gour·mand [guur-MAHND] *n* glutton.
gour·met [guur-MAY] *n* **1** connoisseur of wine, food. **2** epicure.
gout [gowt] *n* disease with inflammation, esp. of joints.
gov·ern [GUV-ərn] *vt* **1** rule, direct, guide, control. **2** decide or determine. **3** be followed by (grammatical case, etc.). **gov'ern·a·ble** *adj* **gov'ern·ess** *n* woman teacher in private household.
gov'ern·ment *n* exercise of political authority in directing a people, country,

etc. **1** system by which community is ruled. **2** body of people in charge of government of country. **3** executive power. **4** control. **5** direction. **6** exercise of authority. **gov'ern·or** *n* **1** one who governs, esp. one invested with supreme authority in a state, etc. **2** chief administrator of an institution. **3** member of committee responsible for an organization or institution. **4** regulator for speed of engine.
gown *n* **1** loose flowing outer garment. **2** woman's (long) dress. **3** official robe, as in university, etc.
grab *vt* **grabbed, grab·bing 1** grasp suddenly. **2** snatch. ◆ *n* **3** sudden clutch. **4** quick attempt to seize. **5** device or implement for clutching.
grace [grays] *n* **1** charm, elegance. **2** accomplishment. **3** goodwill, favor. **4** sense of propriety. **5** postponement granted. **6** short thanksgiving before or after meal. ◆ *vt* **graced, grac·ing 7** add grace to, honor. **grace'ful** *adj* **grace'less** *adj* **1** shameless, depraved. **gra'cious** [-shəs] *adj* **1** favorable. **2** kind. **3** pleasing. **4** indulgent, beneficent, condescending. **grace note** *Mus.* melodic ornament.
grade [grayd] *n* **1** step, stage. **2** degree of

news, revelation, tidings
gossip *n* **1** = **idle talk**, blether, chitchat, hearsay, scandal, small talk, tittle-tattle **2** = **busybody**, chatterbox (*inf*), chatterer, gossipmonger, scandalmonger, tattler, telltale ◆ *v* **3** = **chat**, blether, chew the fat (*sl*), gabble, jaw (*sl*), prate, prattle, tattle
go through *v* **1** = **suffer**, bear, brave, endure, experience, tolerate, undergo, withstand **2** = **examine**, check, explore, forage, hunt, look, search
gouge *v* **1** = **scoop**, chisel, claw, cut, dig (out), hollow (out) ◆ *n* **2** = **gash**, cut, furrow, groove, hollow, scoop, scratch, trench
gourmet *n* = **connoisseur**, *bon vivant*, epicure, foodie (*inf*), gastronome
govern *v* **1** = **rule**, administer, command, control, direct, guide, handle, lead, manage, order **2** = **restrain**, check, control, curb, discipline, hold in check, master, regulate, subdue, tame
government *n* **1** = **rule**, administration, authority, governance, sovereignty, statecraft **2** = **executive**, administration,

ministry, powers-that-be, regime
governor *n* = **leader**, administrator, chief, commander, controller, director, executive, head, manager, ruler
gown *n* = **dress**, costume, frock, garb, garment, habit, robe
grab *v* = **snatch**, capture, catch, catch *or* take hold of, clutch, grasp, grip, pluck, seize, snap up
grace *n* **1** = **elegance**, attractiveness, beauty, charm, comeliness, ease, gracefulness, poise, polish, refinement, tastefulness **2** = **goodwill**, benefaction, benevolence, favor, generosity, goodness, kindliness, kindness **3** = **manners**, consideration, decency, decorum, etiquette, propriety, tact **4** = **indulgence**, mercy, pardon, reprieve **5** = **prayer**, benediction, blessing, thanks, thanksgiving ◆ *v* **6** = **honor**, adorn, decorate, dignify, embellish, enhance, enrich, favor, ornament, set off
graceful *adj* = **elegant**, beautiful, charming, comely, easy, pleasing, tasteful
gracious *adj* = **kind**, charitable, civil,

rank, etc. **3** class. **4** mark, rating. **5** slope. ◆ *vt* **grad•ed, grad•ing 6** arrange in classes. **7** assign grade to. **8** level ground, move earth with grader. **gra•da'tion** *n* **1** series of degrees or steps. **2** each of them. **3** arrangement in steps. **4** in painting, gradual passing from one shade, etc. to another. **grad'er** *n* esp. machine with wide blade used in road making. **make the grade** succeed.

gra•di•ent [GRAY-dee-ənt] *n* (degree of) slope.

grad•u•al [GRAJ-oo-əl] *adj* **1** taking place by degrees. **2** slow and steady. **3** not steep. **grad'u•al•ly** *adv*

grad•u•ate [GRAJ-oo-ayt] *v* -**at•ed, -at•ing** ◆ *vi* **1** receive diploma or degree on completing course of study. ◆ *vt* **2** divide into degrees. **3** mark, arrange according to scale. ◆ *n* [-it] **4** holder of diploma or degree. **grad•u•a'tion** *n*

graf•fi•ti [grə-FEE-tee] *pl n* words or drawings scribbled or sprayed on walls etc.

graft[1] *n* **1** shoot of plant set in stalk of another. **2** the process. **3** surgical transplant of skin, tissue. ◆ *vt* **4** insert (shoot) in another stalk. **5** transplant (living tissue in surgery).

graft[2] *n inf* **1** self-advancement, profit by unfair means, esp. through official or political privilege. **2** bribe. **3** swindle.

grail [grayl] *n* cup or dish used by Christ at the Last Supper (also **Holy Grail**).

grain [grayn] *n* **1** seed, fruit of cereal plant. **2** wheat and allied plants. **3** small hard particle. **4** unit of weight, 0.0648 gram. **5** texture. **6** arrangement of fibers. **7** any very small amount. **8** natural temperament or disposition.

gram *n* unit of weight (equivalent to 0.035 ounce) in metric system, one thousandth of a kilogram.

gram•mar [GRAM-ər] *n* **1** science of structure and usage of language. **2** book on this. **3** correct use of words. **gram•mar•i•an** [grə-MAIR-ee-ən] *n* **gram•mat'i•cal** *adj* according to grammar. **grammar school** elementary school.

gra•na•ry [GRAY-nə-ree] *n, pl* -**ries** storehouse for grain. **1** rich grain-growing region.

grand *adj* -**er, -est 1** imposing. **2** magnificent. **3** majestic. **4** noble. **5** splendid. **6** eminent. **7** lofty. **8** chief, of chief importance. **9** final (total). **gran•deur** [GRAN-jər] *n* **1** nobility. **2** magnificence. **3** dignity. **gran•dil'o•quence** *n* **gran•dil'o•quent** *adj* pompous in speech. **gran•di•ose** [-dee-ohs] *adj* **1** imposing. **2** affectedly grand. **3** striking. **grand'child** *n* child of one's child. **grand'daugh•ter** *n* female grandchild. **grand'fa•ther** *n* male grandparent. **grand'moth•er** *n* female grandparent. **grand'par•ent** *n* parent of one's parent. **grand piano** large harp-shaped piano with horizontal strings. **grand'son** *n* male grandchild. **grand'stand** *n* structure with tiered seats for spectators.

grange [graynj] *n* farm with its farmhouse

THESAURUS

considerate, cordial, courteous, friendly, polite, well-mannered

grade *n* **1** = **level**, category, class, degree, echelon, group, rank, stage ◆ *v* **2** = **classify**, arrange, class, group, order, range, rank, rate, sort

gradient *n* = **slope**, bank, declivity, grade, hill, incline, rise

gradual *adj* = **steady**, gentle, graduated, piecemeal, progressive, regular, slow, unhurried

gradually *adv* = **steadily**, by degrees, gently, little by little, progressively, slowly, step by step, unhurriedly

graduate *v* **1** = **mark off**, calibrate, grade, measure out, proportion, regulate **2** = **classify**, arrange, grade, group, order, rank, sort

graft *n* **1** = **shoot**, bud, implant, scion, splice, sprout ◆ *v* **2** = **transplant**, affix, implant, ingraft, insert, join, splice

grain *n* **1** = **cereals**, corn **2** = **seed**, grist, kernel **3** = **bit**, fragment, granule, modicum, morsel, particle, piece, scrap, speck, trace **4** = **texture**, fiber, nap, pattern, surface, weave **5** *As in* **go against the grain** = **inclination**, character, disposition, humor, make-up, temper

grand *adj* **1** = **impressive**, dignified, grandiose, great, imposing, large, magnificent, regal, splendid, stately, sublime **2** = **excellent**, cool (*inf*), fine, first-class, great (*inf*), outstanding, phat (*sl*), splendid, wonderful

grandeur *n* = **splendor**, dignity, magnificence, majesty, nobility, pomp, stateliness, sublimity

grandiose *adj* **1** = **pretentious**, affected,

and farm buildings.

gran·ite [GRAN-it] *n* hard crystalline igneous rock. **gran'ite·like** *adj*

gran·ny [GRAN-ee] *n, pl* **-nies** *inf* grandmother.

grant *vt* **1** consent to fulfill (request). **2** permit. **3** bestow. **4** admit. ◆ *n* **5** sum of money provided by government or other source for specific purpose, as education. **6** gift. **7** allowance, concession.

gran·ule [GRAN-yool] *n* **1** small grain. **2** small particle. **gran'u·lar** [-yǝ-lǝr] *adj* of or like grains.

grape [grayp] *n* fruit of vine. **grape'shot** *n* bullets scattering when fired. **grape'vine** [-vīn] *n* **1** grape-bearing vine. **2** *inf* unofficial means of conveying information.

grape·fruit [GRAYP-froot] *n* subtropical citrus fruit.

graph [graf] *n* **1** drawing depicting relation of different numbers, quantities, etc. ◆ *vt* **2** represent by graph.

graph·ic [GRAF-ik] *adj* **1** vividly descriptive. **2** of, in, relating to, writing, drawing, painting, etc. **graphics** *pl n* diagrams, graphs, etc., esp. as used on a TV programme or computer screen. **graph'i·cal·ly** *adv* **graph'ite** [-īt] *n* form of carbon (used in pencils). **graph·ol'o·gy** *n* study of handwriting.

grap·nel [GRAP-nl] *n* **1** hooked iron instrument for seizing anything. **2** small anchor with several flukes.

grap·ple [GRAP-ǝl] *v* **-pled, -pling** **1** come to grips with, wrestle. **2** cope or contend. ◆ *n* **3** grappling. **4** grapnel.

grasp *v* (try, struggle to) seize hold. **1** understand. ◆ *n* **2** act of grasping. **3** grip. **4** comprehension. **grasp'ing** *adj* greedy, avaricious.

grass *n* **1** common type of plant with jointed stems and long narrow leaves (including cereals, bamboo, etc.). **2** such plants grown as lawn. **3** pasture. **4** *sl* marijuana. ◆ *vt* **5** cover with grass. **grass'hop·per** *n* **1** jumping, chirping insect. **grass roots** **1** ordinary people. **2** fundamentals. **grass-roots** *adj* coming from ordinary people, the rank and file.

grate¹ [grayt] *n* framework of metal bars for holding fuel in fireplace. **grat'ing** *n* framework of parallel or latticed bars covering opening.

grate² *v* **grat·ed, grat·ing** ◆ *vt* **1** rub into small bits on rough surface. ◆ *vi* **2** rub with harsh noise. **3** have irritating effect. **grat'er** *n* utensil with rough surface for reducing substance to small particles. **grating** *adj* **1** harsh. **2** irritating.

grate·ful [GRAYT-fǝl] *adj* **1** thankful. **2** appreciative. **3** pleasing. **grat·i·tude** [GRAT-ǝ-tood] *n* sense of being thankful for favor.

grat·i·fy [GRAT-ǝ-fī] *vt* **-fied, -fy·ing** **1** satisfy. **2** please. **3** indulge. **grat·i·fi·ca'tion** *n*

bombastic, extravagant, flamboyant, high-flown, ostentatious, pompous, showy **2 = imposing**, grand, impressive, lofty, magnificent, majestic, monumental, stately

grant *v* **1 = consent to**, accede to, agree to, allow, permit **2 = give**, allocate, allot, assign, award, donate, hand out, present **3 = admit**, acknowledge, concede ◆ *n* **4 = award**, allowance, donation, endowment, gift, hand-out, present, subsidy

granule *n* **= grain**, atom, crumb, fragment, molecule, particle, speck

graphic *adj* **1 = vivid**, clear, detailed, explicit, expressive, lively, lucid, striking **2 = pictorial**, diagrammatic, visual

grapple *v* **1 = grip**, clutch, grab, grasp, seize, wrestle **2 = deal with**, address oneself to, confront, get to grips with, struggle, tackle, take on

grasp *v* **1 = grip**, catch, clasp, clinch, clutch, grab, grapple, hold, lay or take

hold of, seize, snatch **2 = understand**, catch on, catch *or* get the drift of, comprehend, get, realize, see, take in ◆ *n* **3 = grip**, clasp, clutches, embrace, hold, possession, tenure **4 = control**, power, reach, scope ◆ **5 = understanding**, awareness, comprehension, grip, knowledge, mastery

grasping *adj* **= greedy**, acquisitive, avaricious, covetous, rapacious

grate *v* **1 = shred**, mince, pulverize, triturate **2 = scrape**, creak, grind, rasp, rub, scratch **3 = annoy**, exasperate, get on one's nerves (*inf*), irritate, jar, rankle, set one's teeth on edge

grateful *adj* **= thankful**, appreciative, beholden, indebted, obliged

gratification *n* **= satisfaction**, delight, enjoyment, fulfillment, indulgence, pleasure, relish, reward, thrill

gratify *v* **= please**, delight, give pleasure,

gratin see AU GRATIN.

grat'is adv, adj free, for nothing.

gra·tu·i·tous [grə-TOO-i-təs] adj 1 given free. 2 uncalled for. **gra·tu'i·tous·ly** adv **gra·tu'i·ty** n, pl **-ties** a tip.

grave¹ [grayv] n 1 hole dug to bury corpse. 2 death. **grave'stone** n monument on grave. **grave'yard** n

grave² adj **grav·er, grav·est** 1 serious, weighty. 2 dignified, solemn. 3 plain, dark in color. 4 deep in note. **grave'ly** adv

grave³ n accent (`) over vowel to indicate special sound quality.

grav·el [GRAV-əl] n 1 small stones. 2 coarse sand. ◆ vt **-eled, -el·ing** 3 cover with gravel. **grav'el·ly** adj

grav·en [GRAY-vən] adj carved, engraved.

grav·i·tate [GRAV-i-tayt] vi **-tat·ed, -tat·ing** 1 move by gravity. 2 tend (toward) center of attraction. 3 sink, settle down. **grav·i·ta'tion** n

grav·i·ty [GRAV-i-tee] n, pl **-ties** 1 force of attraction of one body for another, esp. of objects to Earth. 2 heaviness. 3 importance. 4 seriousness. 5 staidness.

gra·vy [GRAY-vee] n, pl **-vies** 1 juices from meat in cooking. 2 sauce for food made from these. 3 thing of value obtained unexpectedly.

gray adj 1 between black and white, as ashes or lead. 2 clouded. 3 dismal. 4 turning white. 5 aged. 6 intermediate, indeterminate. ◆ n 7 gray color. 8 gray or white horse.

graze¹ [grayz] v **grazed, graz·ing** feed on grass, pasture.

graze² vt **grazed, graz·ing** 1 touch lightly in passing, scratch, scrape. ◆ n 2 grazing. 3 abrasion.

grease [grees] n 1 soft melted fat of animals. 2 thick oil as lubricant. ◆ vt **greased, greas·ing** 3 apply grease to. **greas'i·ness** n **greas'y** adj **greas·i·er, greas·i·est** grease gun appliance for injecting grease into machinery. **grease monkey** inf mechanic. **grease'paint** n theatrical makeup.

great [grayt] adj **-er, -est** 1 large, big. 2 important. 3 preeminent, distinguished. 4 inf excellent. **great-** prefix one generation older or younger than, e.g. great-grandfather. **great'ly** adv **great'ness** n **Great Dane** breed of very large dog.

Gre·cian [GREE-shən] adj of (ancient)

THESAURUS

gladden, humor, requite, satisfy

grating¹ adj = **irritating**, annoying, discordant, displeasing, harsh, jarring, offensive, raucous, strident, unpleasant

grating² n = **grille**, grate, grid, gridiron, lattice, trellis

gratitude n = **thankfulness**, appreciation, gratefulness, indebtedness, obligation, recognition, thanks

gratuitous adj 1 = **free**, complimentary, gratis, spontaneous, unasked-for, unpaid, unrewarded, voluntary 2 = **unjustified**, baseless, causeless, groundless, needless, superfluous, uncalled-for, unmerited, unnecessary, unwarranted, wanton

gratuity n = **tip**, bonus, donation, gift, largesse or largess, reward

grave¹ n = **burying place**, crypt, mausoleum, pit, sepulcher, tomb, vault

grave² adj 1 = **solemn**, dignified, dour, earnest, serious, sober, somber, unsmiling 2 = **important**, acute, critical, dangerous, pressing, serious, severe, threatening, urgent

graveyard n = **cemetery**, burial ground, charnel house, churchyard, necropolis

gravity n 1 = **importance**, acuteness, momentousness, perilousness, seriousness, severity, significance, urgency, weightiness 2 = **solemnity**, dignity, earnestness, gravitas, seriousness, sobriety

gray adj 1 = **pale**, ashen, pallid, wan 2 = **dismal**, dark, depressing, dim, drab, dreary, dull, gloomy 3 = **characterless**, anonymous, colorless, dull

graze¹ v = **feed**, browse, crop, pasture

graze² v 1 = **touch**, brush, glance off, rub, scrape, shave, skim 2 = **scratch**, abrade, chafe, scrape, skin ◆ n 3 = **scratch**, abrasion, scrape

greasy adj = **fatty**, oily, oleaginous, slimy, slippery

great adj 1 = **large**, big, enormous, gigantic, huge, immense, prodigious, vast, voluminous 2 = **important**, critical, crucial, momentous, serious, significant 3 = **famous**, eminent, illustrious, noteworthy, outstanding, prominent, remarkable, renowned 4 inf = **excellent**, fantastic (inf), fine, marvelous, superb, terrific (inf), tremendous (inf), wonderful

greatly adv = **very much**, considerably, enormously, exceedingly, hugely, immensely, remarkably, tremendously,

Greece.

greed *n* excessive consumption of, desire for, food, wealth. **greed'y** *adj* **greed·i·er, greed·i·est 1** gluttonous. **2** eagerly desirous. **3** voracious. **4** covetous. **greed·i·ly** *adv*

Greek *n* **1** native language of Greece. ◆ *adj* **2** of Greece or Greek.

green *adj* **1** of color between blue and yellow. **2** grass-colored. **3** emerald. **4** unripe. **5** inexperienced. **6** gullible. **7** envious. ◆ *n* **8** color. **9** area of grass, esp. in golf, for putting. ◆ *pl* **10** green vegetables. **green'er·y** *n, pl* **-er·ies** vegetation. **green belt** area of farms, open country around a community. **green'horn** *n* **1** inexperienced person. **2** *sl* recent immigrant, newcomer. **green'house** *n, pl* **-hous·es** [-how-ziz] (usu.) glass house for rearing plants. **greenhouse effect** rise in the temperature of the earth caused by heat absorbed from the sun being unable to leave the atmosphere. **green'room** *n* room for actors, TV performers, when offstage. **green thumb** talent for gardening.

greet *vt* **1** meet with expressions of welcome. **2** accost, salute. **3** receive. **greet'ing** *n*

gre·gar·i·ous [gri-GAIR-ee-əs] *adj* **1** fond of company, sociable. **2** living in flocks.

gre·gar'i·ous·ness *n*

grem'lin *n* imaginary being blamed for mechanical and other troubles.

gre·nade [gri-NAYD] *n* explosive shell or bomb, thrown by hand or shot from rifle.

gren·a·dine [gren-ə-DEEN] *n* syrup made from pomegranate juice, for sweetening and coloring drinks.

grew pt. of GROW.

grey·hound [GRAY-hownd] *n* swift slender dog used in racing.

grid *n* **1** network of horizontal and vertical lines, bars, etc. **2** any interconnecting system of links. **3** regional network of electricity supply.

grid·dle [GRID-l] *n* **1** frying pan, flat iron plate for cooking. **grid'dle·cake** *n* pancake.

grid·i·ron [GRID-ī-ərn] *n* **1** frame of metal bars for grilling. **2** (field of play for) football.

grid·lock [GRID-lok] *n* **1** situation where traffic is not moving. **2** point in a dispute at which no agreement can be reached. **grid'locked** *adj*

grief [greef] *n* deep sorrow. **griev·ance** [GREE-vəns] *n* real or imaginary ground of complaint. **grieve** *v* **grieved, griev·ing** ◆ *vi* **1** feel grief. ◆ *vt* **2** cause grief to. **griev'ous** *adj* **1** painful, oppressive. **2** very serious.

grif·fin, grif·fon [GRIF-in] *n* fabulous

——— | THESAURUS | ———

vastly

greatness *n* **1** = **immensity**, enormity, hugeness, magnitude, prodigiousness, size, vastness **2** = **importance**, gravity, momentousness, seriousness, significance, urgency, weight **3** = **fame**, celebrity, distinction, eminence, glory, grandeur, illustriousness, kudos, note, renown

greed, greediness *n* **1** = **gluttony**, edacity, esurience, gormandizing, hunger, voracity **2** = **avarice**, acquisitiveness, avidity, covetousness, craving, desire, longing, selfishness

greedy *adj* **1** = **gluttonous**, gormandizing, hungry, insatiable, piggish, ravenous, voracious **2** = **grasping**, acquisitive, avaricious, avid, covetous, craving, desirous, rapacious, selfish

green *adj* **1** = **leafy**, grassy, verdant **2** = **ecological**, conservationist, environment-friendly, non-polluting, ozone-friendly **3** = **immature**, gullible, inexperienced, naive, new, raw, untrained, wet behind the ears (*inf*) **4** = **jealous**,

covetous, envious, grudging, resentful ◆ *n* **5** = **lawn**, common, sward, turf

greet *v* = **welcome**, accost, address, compliment, hail, meet, receive, salute

greeting *n* = **welcome**, address, reception, salutation, salute

gregarious *adj* = **outgoing**, affable, companionable, convivial, cordial, friendly, sociable, social

gridlock *n* = **standstill**, deadlock, impasse, stalemate

grief *n* = **sadness**, anguish, distress, heartache, misery, regret, remorse, sorrow, suffering, woe

grievance *n* = **complaint**, ax to grind, gripe (*inf*), injury, injustice

grieve *v* **1** = **mourn**, complain, deplore, lament, regret, rue, suffer, weep **2** = **sadden**, afflict, distress, hurt, injure, pain, wound

grievous *adj* **1** = **painful**, dreadful, grave, harmful, severe **2** = **deplorable**, atrocious, dreadful, monstrous, offensive, outrageous, shameful, shocking monster with eagle's head and wings and lion's body.

grill n 1 grated utensil for broiling meat, etc. 2 food cooked on grill. 3 grillroom. ♦ v 4 cook (food) on grill. 5 subject to severe questioning. **grill'ing** n severe cross-examination. **grill'room** n restaurant specializing in grilled food.

grille [gril] n grating, crosswork of bars over opening.

grim adj **grim·mer, grim·mest** 1 stern. 2 of stern or forbidding aspect, relentless. 3 joyless.

grim·ace [GRIM-əs] n 1 wry face. ♦ vi **-aced, -ac·ing** 2 make wry face.

grime [grīm] n 1 ingrained dirt, soot. ♦ vt **grimed, grim·ing** 2 soil. 3 dirty. 4 blacken. **grim'y** adj **grim·i·er, grim·i·est**

grin vi **grinned, grin·ning** 1 show teeth, as in laughter. ♦ n 2 grinning smile.

grind [grīnd] v **ground, grind·ing** 1 crush to powder. 2 oppress. 3 make sharp, smooth. 4 grate. ♦ vi 5 perform action of grinding. 6 inf (with away) work (esp. study) hard. 7 grate. ♦ n inf 8 hard work, excessively diligent student. 9 action of grinding.

grin·go [GRING-goh] n, pl **-gos** in Mexico, contemptuous name for foreigner, esp. American or Englishman.

grip n 1 firm hold, grasp. 2 grasping power. 3 mastery. 4 handle. 5 suitcase or traveling bag. ♦ vt **gripped, grip·ping** 6 grasp or hold tightly. 7 hold interest or attention of.

gripe [grīp] vi inf **griped, grip·ing** 1 complain (persistently). ♦ n 2 inf complaint. ♦ pl 3 intestinal pain.

gris·ly [GRIZ-lee] adj **-li·er, -li·est** grim, causing terror, ghastly.

grist n grain to be ground. **grist for one's mill** something that can be turned to advantage.

gris·tle [GRIS-əl] n cartilage, tough flexible tissue.

grit n 1 rough particles of sand. 2 coarse sandstone. 3 courage. ♦ pl 4 hominy, etc. coarsely ground and cooked as breakfast food. ♦ vt **grit·ted, grit·ting** 5 clench, grind (teeth). **grit'ty** adj **-ti·er, -ti·est**

griz·zle [GRIZ-əl] v **-zled, -zling** make, become gray. **griz'zly** large Amer. bear (also **grizzly bear**).

groan [grohn] vi 1 make low, deep sound of grief or pain. 2 be in pain or overburdened. ♦ n

groats [grohts] n hulled grain or kernels of oats, wheat, etc. broken into fragments.

gro·cer [GROH-sər] n dealer in foodstuffs. **gro'cer·ies** pl n commodities sold by a grocer. **gro'cer·y** n, pl **-cer·ies** trade, premises of grocer.

grog·gy [GROG-ee] adj inf **-gi·er, -gi·est** unsteady, shaky, weak.

groin n 1 fold where legs meet abdomen. 2 euphemism for genitals.

groom n 1 person caring for horses. 2 bridegroom. ♦ vt 3 tend or look after. 4 brush or clean (esp. horse). 5 train

———————————— THESAURUS ————————————

grim adj = **forbidding**, formidable, harsh, merciless, ruthless, severe, sinister, stern, terrible

grimace n 1 = **scowl**, face, frown, sneer ♦ v 2 = **scowl**, frown, lour or lower, make a face or faces, sneer

grime n = **dirt**, filth, grease, smut, soot

grimy adj = **dirty**, filthy, foul, grubby, scuzzy (sl), soiled, sooty, unclean

grind v 1 = **crush**, abrade, granulate, grate, mill, pound, powder, pulverize, triturate 2 = **smooth**, polish, sand, sharpen, whet 3 = **scrape**, gnash, grate ♦ n 4 Inf = **hard work**, chore, drudgery, labor, sweat (inf), toil

grip n 1 = **clasp**, hold 2 = **control**, clutches, domination, influence, possession, power 3 = **understanding**, command, comprehension, grasp, mastery ♦ v 4 = **grasp**, clasp, clutch, hold, seize, take hold

of 5 = **engross**, absorb, enthrall, entrance, fascinate, hold, mesmerize, rivet

gripping adj = **fascinating**, compelling, engrossing, enthralling, entrancing, exciting, riveting, spellbinding, thrilling

grisly adj = **gruesome**, appalling, awful, dreadful, ghastly, horrible, macabre, shocking, terrifying

grit n 1 = **gravel**, dust, pebbles, sand 2 = **courage**, backbone, determination, fortitude, guts (inf), perseverance, resolution, spirit, tenacity ♦ v 3 = **grind**, clench, gnash, grate

gritty adj 1 = **rough**, dusty, granular, gravelly, rasping, sandy 2 = **courageous**, brave, determined, dogged, plucky, resolute, spirited, steadfast, tenacious

groan n 1 = **moan**, cry, sigh, whine ♦ v 2 = **moan**, cry, sigh, whine

groggy adj = **dizzy**, confused, dazed, faint,

(someone for something). **well-groomed** adj neat, smart.

groove [groov] n 1 narrow channel, hollow, esp. cut by tool. 2 rut, routine. ◆ vt **grooved, groov·ing** 3 cut groove in. **groov'y** adj sl **groov·i·er, groov·i·est** attractive, exciting.

grope [grohp] vi **groped, grop·ing** feel about, search blindly.

gros·beak [GROHS-beek] n finch with large powerful bill.

gross [grohs] adj **-er, -est** 1 very fat. 2 total, not net. 3 coarse. 4 indecent. 5 flagrant. 6 thick, rank. ◆ n 7 twelve dozen. **gross out** sl disgust, sicken.

gro·tesque [groh-TESK] adj (horribly) distorted. 1 absurd. ◆ n 2 grotesque person, thing.

grot·to [GROT-oh] n, pl **-toes** small picturesque cave.

grouch [growch] n inf 1 persistent grumbler. 2 discontented mood. ◆ vi 3 grumble, be peevish.

ground¹ [grownd] n 1 surface of Earth. 2 soil, earth. 3 reason, motive. 4 coating to work on with paint. 5 background, main surface worked on in painting, embroidery, etc. 6 special area. 7 bottom

of sea. ◆ pl 8 dregs. 9 land around house and belonging to it. ◆ vt 10 establish. 11 instruct (in elements). 12 place on ground. ◆ vi 13 run ashore. 14 strike ground. **ground'ed** adj 1 of aircraft or pilot, unable or not permitted to fly. 2 inf of child, punished by restriction of activities. **ground'ing** n basic general knowledge of a subject. **ground'less** adj without reason. **ground'speed** n aircraft's speed in relation to ground.

ground² pt./pp. of GRIND.

group [groop] n 1 number of persons or things near together, or placed or classified together. 2 small musical band of players or singers. 3 class. 4 two or more figures forming one artistic design. ◆ v 5 place, fall into group.

grouse¹ [grows] n, pl **grouse** 1 game bird. 2 its flesh.

grouse² vi **groused, grous·ing** 1 grumble, complain. ◆ n 2 complaint. **grous'er** n grumbler.

grout [growt] n 1 thin fluid mortar. ◆ vt 2 fill up with grout.

grove [grohv] n small group of trees.

grov·el [GRUV-əl] vi **-eled, -el·ing** 1 abase oneself. 2 lie or crawl facedown.

shaky, unsteady, weak, wobbly

groom n 1 = **stableman**, stableboy ◆ v 2 = **smarten up**, clean, preen, primp, spruce up, tidy 3 = **rub down**, brush, clean, curry, tend 4 = **train**, coach, drill, educate, make ready, nurture, prepare, prime, ready

groove n = **indentation**, channel, cut, flute, furrow, hollow, rut, trench, trough

grope v = **feel**, cast about, fish, flounder, forage, fumble, scrabble, search

gross adj 1 = **fat**, corpulent, hulking, obese, overweight 2 = **total**, aggregate, before deductions, before tax, entire, whole 3 = **vulgar**, coarse, crude, indelicate, obscene, offensive 4 = **blatant**, flagrant, grievous, heinous, rank, sheer, unmitigated, utter ◆ v 5 = **earn**, bring in, make, rake in (inf), take

grotesque adj = **unnatural**, bizarre, deformed, distorted, fantastic, freakish, outlandish, preposterous, strange

ground n 1 = **earth**, dry land, land, soil, terra firma, terrain, turf 2 = **stadium**, arena, field, park, pitch 3 (often plural) = **land**, estate, fields, gardens, terrain, territory 4 (usually plural) = **dregs**, deposit, lees, sediment 5 **grounds** = **reason**, basis,

cause, excuse, foundation, justification, motive, occasion, pretext, rationale ◆ v 6 = **base**, establish, fix, found, set, settle 7 = **instruct**, acquaint with, familiarize with, initiate, teach, train, tutor

groundless adj = **unjustified**, baseless, empty, idle, uncalled-for, unfounded, unwarranted

groundwork n = **preliminaries**, foundation, fundamentals, preparation, spadework, underpinnings

group n 1 = **set**, band, bunch, cluster, collection, crowd, gang, pack, party ◆ v 2 = **arrange**, bracket, class, classify, marshal, order, sort

grouse v 1 = **complain**, bellyache (sl), carp, gripe (inf), grumble, moan, whine ◆ n 2 = **complaint**, grievance, gripe (inf), grouch (inf), grumble, moan, objection, protest

grove n = **wood**, coppice, copse, covert, plantation, spinney, thicket

grovel v = **humble oneself**, abase oneself, bow and scrape, brown-nose (sl), crawl, creep, cringe, demean oneself, fawn, kiss ass (sl), kowtow, toady

grow [groh] *v* **grew, grown, grow·ing** ♦ *vi*
1 develop naturally. **2** increase in size,
height, etc. **3** be produced. **4** become by
degrees. ♦ *vt* **5** produce by cultivation.
growth *n* **1** growing. **2** increase. **3** what
has grown or is growing. **grown-up** *adj*
grownup *n* adult.

growl *vi* **1** make low guttural sound of
anger. **2** rumble. **3** murmur, complain. ♦ *n*

grub *v* **grubbed, grub·bing 1** dig
superficially. **2** root up. **3** dig, rummage. **4**
plod. **5** drudge. ♦ *n* **6** larva of insect. **7** *sl*
food. **grub'by** *adj* **-bi·er, -bi·est** dirty.

grudge [gruj] *vt* **grudged, grudg·ing 1** be
unwilling to give, allow. ♦ *n* **2** ill will.

gru·el [GROO-əl] *n* food of cereal boiled in
milk or water. **gru'el·ing** *adj, n* exhausting,
severe (experience).

grue·some [GROO-səm] *adj* fearful,
horrible, grisly. **grue'some·ness** *n*

gruff *adj* **-er, -est** rough in manner or voice,
surly. **gruff'ness** *n*

grum·ble [GRUM-bəl] *vi* **-bled, -bling 1**
complain. **2** rumble, murmur. **3** make
growling sounds. ♦ *n* **4** complaint. **5** low
growl.

grump·y [GRUM-pee] *adj* **grump·i·er,
grump·i·est** ill-tempered, surly.

grump'i·ness *n*

grunge [grunj] *n* **1** style of rock music with
a fuzzy guitar sound. **2** deliberately untidy
and uncoordinated fashion style.

grunt *vi* **1** make sound characteristic of pig.
♦ *n* **2** pig's sound. **3** gruff noise.

G-string [JEE-string] *n* **1** very small
covering for genitals. **2** *Mus.* string tuned
to G.

gua·no [GWAH-noh] *n* manure of seabird.

guar·an·tee [gar-ən-TEE] *n* **1** formal
assurance (esp. in writing) that product,
etc. will meet certain standards, last for
given time, etc. ♦ *vt* **-teed, -tee'ing 2** give
guarantee of, for something. **3** secure
(against risk, etc.). **guar'an·tor** *n* one who
guarantees. **guar'an·ty** *n, pl* **-ties**

guard [gahrd] *vt* **1** protect, defend. ♦ *vi* **2**
be careful, take precautions (against). ♦ *n* **3**
person, group that protects, supervises,
keeps watch. **4** sentry. **5** soldiers protecting
anything. **6** official in charge of train. **7**
protection. **8** screen for enclosing anything
dangerous. **9** protector. **10** posture of
defense. **guard'i·an** [-ee-ən] *n* **1** keeper,
protector. **2** person having custody of
infant, etc. **guard'i·an·ship** *n* care.
guard'house *n* place for stationing those

grow *v* **1 = increase**, develop, enlarge,
expand, get bigger, multiply, spread,
stretch, swell **2 = originate**, arise, issue,
spring, stem **3 = improve**, advance,
flourish, progress, prosper, succeed, thrive
4 = become, come to be, get, turn **5 =
cultivate**, breed, farm, nurture, produce,
propagate, raise

grown-up *adj* **1 = mature**, adult,
fully-grown, of age ♦ *n* **2 = adult**, man,
woman

growth *n* **1 = increase**, development,
enlargement, expansion, multiplication,
proliferation, stretching **2 = improvement**,
advance, expansion, progress, prosperity,
rise, success **3** *Medical* **= tumor**, lump

grub *n* **1 = larva**, caterpillar, maggot **2** *Sl* **=
food**, rations, sustenance, victuals ♦ *v* **3 =
dig up**, burrow, pull up, root (*inf*) **4 =
search**, ferret, forage, hunt, rummage,
scour, uncover, unearth

grubby *adj* **= dirty**, filthy, grimy, messy,
mucky, scuzzy (*sl*), seedy, shabby, sordid,
squalid, unwashed

grudge *v* **1 = resent**, begrudge, complain,
covet, envy, mind ♦ *n* **2 = resentment**,

animosity, antipathy, bitterness, dislike,
enmity, grievance, rancor

grueling *adj* **= exhausting**, arduous,
backbreaking, demanding, laborious,
punishing, severe, strenuous, taxing, tiring

gruesome *adj* **= horrific**, ghastly, grim,
grisly, horrible, macabre, shocking, terrible

gruff *adj* **1 = surly**, bad-tempered, brusque,
churlish, grumpy, rough, rude, sullen,
ungracious **2 = hoarse**, croaking, guttural,
harsh, husky, low, rasping, rough, throaty

grumble *v* **1 = complain**, bleat, carp, gripe
(*inf*), grouch (*inf*), grouse, moan, whine **2 =
rumble**, growl, gurgle, murmur, mutter,
roar ♦ *n* **3 = complaint**, grievance, gripe
(*inf*), grouch (*inf*), grouse, moan,
objection, protest **4 = rumble**, growl,
gurgle, murmur, muttering, roar

grumpy *adj* **= irritable**, cantankerous,
crotchety, ill-tempered, peevish, sulky,
sullen, surly, testy

guarantee *n* **1 = assurance**, bond,
certainty, pledge, promise, security, surety,
warranty, word of honor ♦ *v* **2 = make
certain**, assure, certify, ensure, pledge,
promise, secure, vouch for, warrant

on guard or for prisoners.

gua·va [GWAH-və] n tropical tree with fruit used to make jelly.

Guern·sey [GURN-zee] n, pl **-seys** breed of cattle.

guer·ril·la [gə-RIL-ə] n member of irregular armed force, esp. fighting established force, government, etc. ♦ adj

guess [ges] vt **1** estimate without calculation. **2** conjecture, suppose. **3** consider, think. ♦ vi **4** form conjectures. ♦ n

guest [gest] n **1** one entertained at another's house. **2** one living in hotel. **guest'house** n small house for guests, separate from main house.

guff n inf **1** silly talk. **2** insolent talk.

guf·faw [gə-FAW] n **1** crude noisy laugh. ♦ vi **2** laugh in this way.

guide [gīd] n **1** one who shows the way. **2** adviser. **3** book of instruction or information. **4** contrivance for directing motion. ♦ vt **guid·ed, guid·ing 5** lead, act as guide to. **6** arrange. **guid'ance** [-əns] n **guided missile** missile whose flight path is controlled by radio signals or programmed homing mechanism.

guild [gild] n **1** organization, club. **2** society for mutual help, or with common object. **3** Hist. society of merchants or tradesmen.

guile [gīl] n cunning, deceit. **guile'ful** adj **guile'less** adj sincere, straightforward.

guil·lo·tine [GIL-ə-teen] n **1** machine for beheading. ♦ vt **-tined, -tin·ing 2** behead.

guilt [gilt] n **1** fact, state of having done wrong. **2** responsibility for criminal or moral offense. **guilt'less** adj innocent. **guilt'y** adj **guilt·i·er, guilt·i·est** having committed an offense.

guin·ea pig [GIN-ee] n **1** rodent originating in S Amer. **2** inf person used in experiments.

guise [gīz] n external appearance, esp. one

———————| THESAURUS |———————

guard v **1** = **watch over**, defend, mind, preserve, protect, safeguard, secure, shield ♦ n **2** = **protector**, custodian, defender, lookout, picket, sentinel, sentry, warden, watch, watchman **3** = **protection**, buffer, defense, safeguard, screen, security, shield **4** off guard = **unprepared**, napping, unready, unwary **5** on guard = **prepared**, alert, cautious, circumspect, on the alert, on the lookout, ready, vigilant, wary, watchful

guarded adj = **cautious**, cagey (inf), careful, circumspect, noncommittal, prudent, reserved, reticent, suspicious, wary

guardian n = **keeper**, champion, curator, custodian, defender, guard, protector, warden

guerrilla n = **freedom fighter**, partisan, underground fighter

guess v **1** = **estimate**, conjecture, hypothesize, predict, speculate, work out **2** = **suppose**, believe, conjecture, fancy, imagine, judge, reckon, suspect, think ♦ n **3** = **prediction**, conjecture, hypothesis, shot in the dark, speculation, supposition, theory

guesswork n = **speculation**, conjecture, estimation, supposition, surmise, theory

guest n = **visitor**, boarder, caller, company, lodger, visitant

guidance n = **advice**, counseling, direction, help, instruction, leadership, management, teaching

guide n **1** = **escort**, adviser, conductor, counselor, leader, mentor, teacher, usher **2** = **model**, example, ideal, inspiration, paradigm, standard **3** = **pointer**, beacon, guiding light, landmark, lodestar, marker, sign, signpost **4** = **guidebook**, Baedeker, catalog, directory, handbook, instructions, key, manual ♦ v **5** = **lead**, accompany, conduct, direct, escort, shepherd, show the way, usher **6** = **steer**, command, control, direct, handle, manage, maneuver **7** = **supervise**, advise, counsel, influence, instruct, oversee, superintend, teach, train

guild n = **society**, association, brotherhood, club, company, corporation, fellowship, fraternity, league, lodge, order, organization, union

guile n = **cunning**, artifice, cleverness, craft, deceit, slyness, trickery, wiliness

guilt n **1** = **culpability**, blame, guiltiness, misconduct, responsibility, sinfulness, wickedness, wrongdoing **2** = **remorse**, contrition, guilty conscience, regret, self-reproach, shame, stigma

guiltless adj = **innocent**, blameless, clean (sl), irreproachable, pure, sinless, spotless, squeaky-clean, untainted

guilty adj **1** = **responsible**, at fault, blameworthy, culpable, reprehensible, sinful, to blame, wrong **2** = **remorseful**, ashamed, conscience-stricken, contrite, regretful, rueful, shamefaced, sheepish, assumed.

gui·tar [gi-TAHR] n usu. six-stringed instrument played by plucking or strumming. **gui·tar'ist** n

gulch n 1 ravine. 2 gully.

gulf n 1 large inlet of the sea. 2 chasm. 3 large gap.

gull[1] n long-winged web-footed seabird.

gull[2] n 1 dupe, fool. ◆ vt 2 dupe, cheat. **gul·li·bil'i·ty** n **gul'li·ble** adj easily imposed on, credulous.

gul·let [GUL-it] n food passage from mouth to stomach.

gul·ly [GUL-ee] n, pl **-lies** channel or ravine worn by water.

gulp vt 1 swallow eagerly. ◆ vi 2 gasp, choke.

gum[1] n 1 firm flesh in which teeth are set. ◆ vt **gummed, gum·ming** 2 chew with the gums.

gum[2] n 1 sticky substance issuing from certain trees. 2 an adhesive. 3 chewing gum. 4 gum tree, eucalyptus. ◆ vt **gummed, gum·ming** 5 stick with gum. **gum'my** adj **-mi·er, -mi·est gum'shoe** n 1 shoe of rubber. 2 sl detective. **gum tree** any species of eucalyptus. **gum up the works** sl impede progress.

gump·tion [GUM-shən] n 1 resourcefulness. 2 shrewdness, sense.

gun n 1 weapon with metal tube from which missiles are discharged by explosion. 2 cannon, pistol, etc. ◆ v **gunned, gun·ning** 3 shoot. 4 pursue, as with gun. 5 race engine (of car). **gun'ner** n

gun'ner·y n use or science of large guns. **gun'boat** n small warship. **gun dog** (breed of) dog used to retrieve, etc. game.

gun'man n armed criminal. **gun'met·al** n alloy of copper and tin or zinc, formerly used for guns. **gun'pow·der** n explosive mixture of saltpeter, sulfur, charcoal.

gun'shot n 1 shot or range of gun. ◆ adj 2 caused by missile from gun. **gun'wale, gun'nel** [GUN-l] n upper edge of ship's side.

gunk [gungk] n inf any sticky, oily matter.

gun·ny [GUN-ee] n, pl **-nies** strong, coarse sacking made from jute.

gup·py [GUP-ee] n, pl **-pies** small colorful aquarium fish.

gur·gle [GUR-gəl] n 1 bubbling noise. ◆ vi **-gled, -gling** 2 utter, flow with gurgle.

gur·ney [GUR-nee] n, pl **-neys** wheeled bed.

gu·ru [GUUR-oo] n a spiritual teacher, esp. in India.

gush vi 1 flow out suddenly and copiously, spurt. ◆ n 2 sudden and copious flow. 3 effusiveness. **gush'er** n 1 gushing person. 2 oil well.

gus·set [GUS-it] n triangle or diamond-shaped piece of material let into garment. **gus'set·ed** adj

gust n 1 sudden blast of wind. 2 burst of rain, anger, passion, etc. **gust'y** adj **gust·i·er, gust·i·est**

gus·to [GUS-toh] n enjoyment, zest.

gut n 1 (oft. pl) entrails, intestines. 2 material made from guts of animals, e.g.

sorry

guise n = **form**, appearance, aspect, demeanor, disguise, mode, pretense, semblance, shape

gulf n 1 = **bay**, bight, sea inlet 2 = **chasm**, abyss, gap, opening, rift, separation, split, void

gullibility n = **credulity**, innocence, naivety, simplicity

gullible adj = **naive**, born yesterday, credulous, innocent, simple, trusting, unsuspecting, wet behind the ears (inf)

gully n = **channel**, ditch, gutter, watercourse

gulp v 1 = **swallow**, devour, gobble, guzzle, quaff, swig (inf), swill, wolf 2 = **gasp**, choke, swallow ◆ n 3 = **swallow**, draft, mouthful, swig (inf)

gum n 1 = **glue**, adhesive, cement, paste,

resin ◆ v 2 = **stick**, affix, cement, glue, paste

gun n = **firearm**, handgun, piece (sl), pistol, revolver, rifle, saturday night special (sl)

gunman n = **terrorist**, bandit, gunslinger (sl), killer

gurgle v 1 = **murmur**, babble, bubble, lap, plash, purl, ripple, splash ◆ n 2 = **murmur**, babble, purl, ripple

guru n = **teacher**, authority, leader, master, mentor, sage, Svengali, tutor

gush v 1 = **flow**, cascade, flood, pour, run, rush, spout, spurt, stream 2 = **enthuse**, babble, chatter, effervesce, effuse, overstate, spout ◆ n 3 = **stream**, cascade, flood, flow, jet, rush, spout, spurt, torrent

gust n 1 = **blast**, blow, breeze, puff, rush, squall ◆ v 2 = **blow**, blast, squall

gusto n = **relish**, delight, enjoyment,

for violin strings, etc. ◆ *pl inf* **3** essential, fundamental part. **4** courage. ◆ *vt* **gut·ted**, **gut·ting 5** remove guts from (fish, etc.). **6** remove, destroy contents of (house). **guts'y** *adj inf* **guts·i·er**, **guts·i·est 1** courageous. **2** vigorous.

gut·ter [GUT-ər] *n* **1** shallow trough for carrying off water from roof or side of street. ◆ *vt* **2** make channels in ◆ *vi* **3** flow in streams. **4** of candle, melt away by wax forming channels and running down. **gutter press** journalism that relies on sensationalism. **gut'ter·snipe** [-snīp] *n* neglected slum child.

gut·tur·al [GUT-ər-əl] *adj* **1** of, relating to, or produced in, the throat. ◆ *n* **2** guttural sound or letter.

guy[1] [gī] *n* **1** *inf* person (usu. male). ◆ *vt* **guyed**, **guy·ing 2** make fun of. **3** ridicule. **wise guy** *inf, usu. disparaging* clever person.

guy[2] *n* rope, chain, etc. to steady, secure something, e.g. tent. ◆ *vt* **guyed**, **guy·ing 1** keep in position by guy.

guz·zle [GUZ-əl] *v* **-zled**, **-zling** eat or drink greedily. ◆ *n*

gym [jim] *n* short for GYMNASIUM or GYMNASTICS.

gym·kha·na [jim-KAH-nə] *n* **1** competition or display of horse riding or gymnastics. **2** place for this.

gym·na·si·um [jim-NAY-zee-əm] *n* place equipped for muscular exercises, athletic training. **gym'nast** *n* expert in gymnastics. **gym·nas'tics** *pl n* muscular exercises, with or without apparatus, e.g. parallel bars.

gy·ne·col·o·gy [gī ni KOL ə jee] *n* branch of medicine dealing with functions and diseases of women. **gy·ne·col'o·gist** *n*

gyp·sum [JIP-səm] *n* crystalline sulfate of lime, a source of plaster.

Gyp·sy [JIP-see] *n, pl* **-sies** one of a wandering people originally from NW India, Romany.

gy·rate [JĪ-rayt] *vi* **-rat·ed**, **-rat·ing** move in circle, spirally, revolve. **gy·ra'tion** *n*

gy·ro·com·pass [Jī-roh-kum-pəs] *n* compass using gyroscope.

gy·ro·scope [Jī-rə-skohp] *n* disk or wheel so mounted as to be able to rotate about any axis, esp. to keep disk (with compass, etc.) level despite movement of ship, etc. **gy·ro·scop'ic** [-SKOP-ik] *adj*

gy·ro·sta·bi·liz·er [jī-rə-STAY-bə-lī-zər] *n* gyroscopic device to prevent rolling of ship or airplane.

———————| THESAURUS |———————

enthusiasm, fervor, pleasure, verve, zeal
gut *n* **1** *Inf* = **paunch**, belly, potbelly, spare tire (*sl*) **2 guts:** **a** = **intestines**, belly, bowels, entrails, innards (*inf*), insides (*inf*), stomach, viscera **b** *Inf* = **courage**, audacity, backbone, daring, mettle, nerve, pluck, spirit ◆ *v* **3** = **disembowel**, clean **4** = **ravage**, clean out, despoil, empty ◆ *adj* **5** *As in* **gut reaction** = **instinctive**, basic, heartfelt, intuitive, involuntary, natural, spontaneous, unthinking, visceral
gutsy *adj* = **brave**, bold, courageous,

determined, gritty, indomitable, plucky, resolute, spirited
gutter *n* = **drain**, channel, conduit, ditch, sluice, trench, trough
guttural *adj* = **throaty**, deep, gravelly, gruff, hoarse, husky, rasping, rough, thick
guy *n Inf* = **man**, chap, dude (*sl*), fellow, lad, person
guzzle *v* = **devour**, bolt, cram, drink, gobble, stuff (oneself), swill, wolf
Gypsy *n* = **traveler**, Bohemian, nomad, rambler, roamer, Romany, rover, wanderer

H h

H *Chem.* hydrogen.

ha·be·as cor·pus [HAY-bee-əs KOR-pəs] *n* writ issued to produce prisoner in court.

hab·er·dash·er [HAB-ər-dash-ər] *n* dealer in articles of dress, ribbons, pins, needles, etc. **hab'er·dash·er·y** *n* **-er·ies**

hab·it *n* **1** settled tendency or practice. **2** constitution. **3** customary apparel esp. of nun or monk. **4** woman's riding dress. **ha·bit·u·al** [hə-BICH-oo-əl] *adj* **1** formed or acquired by habit. **2** usual, customary. **ha·bit·u·ate** [-ayt] *vt* **-at·ed, -at·ing** accustom. **ha·bit·u·a'tion** *n* **ha·bit·u·é** [-oo-ay] *n* constant visitor.

hab·it·a·ble [HAB-i-tə-bəl] *adj* fit to live in. **hab·i·tat** *n* natural home (of animal, etc.). **hab·i·ta'tion** [-TAY-shən] *n* dwelling place.

ha·ci·en·da [hah-see-EN-də] *n, pl* **-das** ranch or large estate in Sp. Amer.

hack¹ [hak] *vt* **1** cut, chop (at) violently. **2** *inf* utter harsh, dry cough. **3** *sl* deal or cope with. ♦ *n* **hack'er** *n sl* person who through personal computer breaks into computer system of company or government. **hack around** *sl* pass time idly.

hack² *n* **1** drudge, esp. writer of inferior literary works. **2** cabdriver. **hack'work** *n* dull, repetitive work.

hack·le [HAK-əl] *n* **1** neck feathers of rooster, etc. ♦ *pl* **2** hairs on back of neck of dog and other animals that are raised in anger.

hack·ney [HAK-nee] *n, pl* **-neys** harness horse, carriage, coach kept for hire.

hack·neyed [HAK-need] *adj* (of words, etc.) stale, trite because of overuse.

hack·saw [HAK-saw] *n* handsaw for cutting metal.

had pt./pp. of HAVE.

Ha·des [HAY-deez] *n Greek myth* underworld home of the dead.

haft *n* **1** handle (of knife, etc.). ♦ *vt* **2** fit with one.

hag *n* **1** ugly old woman. **2** witch.

hag·gard [HAG-ərd] *adj* **1** wild-looking. **2** anxious, careworn.

hag·gis *n* Scottish dish made from sheep's heart, lungs, liver, chopped with oatmeal, suet, onion, etc., and boiled in the stomach.

hag·gle [HAG-əl] *vi* **-gled, -gling** bargain, wrangle over price. ♦ *n*

hag·i·ol·o·gy [hag-ee-OL-ə-jee] *n, pl* **-gies** literature of the lives of saints. **hag·i·og'ra·pher** [-rə-fər] *n* **hag·i·og'ra·phy** *n, pl* **-phies** writing of this.

hail¹ [hayl] *n* (shower of) pellets of ice. **1** intense shower, barrage. ♦ *v* **2** pour down as shower of hail. **hail'stone** *n*

hail² *vt* **1** greet (esp. enthusiastically). **2** acclaim, acknowledge. **3** call. ♦ *vi* **4** come (from).

THESAURUS

habit *n* **1** = **mannerism**, custom, practice, proclivity, propensity, quirk, tendency, way **2** = **addiction**, dependence

habitation *n* **1** = **dwelling**, abode, domicile, home, house, living quarters, lodging, quarters, residence **2** = **occupancy**, inhabitance, occupation, tenancy

habitual *adj* = **customary**, accustomed, familiar, normal, regular, routine, standard, traditional, usual

hack¹ *v* = **cut**, chop, hew, lacerate, mangle, mutilate, slash

hack² *n* **1** = **scribbler**, literary hack, penny-a-liner **2** = **horse**, crock, nag

hackneyed *adj* = **unoriginal**, clichéd, commonplace, overworked, stale, stereotyped, stock, threadbare, tired, trite

hag *n* = **witch**, crone, harridan

haggard *adj* = **gaunt**, careworn, drawn, emaciated, pinched, thin, wan

haggle *v* = **bargain**, barter, beat down

hail¹ *n* **1** = **bombardment**, barrage, downpour, rain, shower, storm, volley ♦ *v* **2** = **rain down on**, batter, beat down upon, bombard, pelt, rain, shower

hail² *v* **1** = **greet**, acclaim, acknowledge, applaud, cheer, honor, salute, welcome

hair *n* **1** filament growing from skin of animal, as covering of person's head. **2** such filaments collectively. **hair'i·ness** *n* **hair'y** *adj* **hair·i·er, hair·i·est hair'do** [-doo] *n, pl* **-dos** way of styling hair. **hair'dress·er** *n* one who attends to and cuts hair, esp. women's hair. **hair'line** *adj, n* **1** very fine (line). **2** lower edge of human hair e.g. on forehead. **hair'pin** *n* pin for keeping hair in place. **hairpin bend** U-shaped turn in road. **hair'split·ting** *n* making of overly fine distinctions. **hair'spring** *n* very fine, delicate spring in timepiece. **hair trigger** trigger operated by light touch. **hair-trigger** *adj* easily set off, e.g. *a hair-trigger temper.*

hal·cy·on [HAL-see-ən] *n* bird fabled to calm the sea and to breed on floating nest. **halcyon days** time of peace and happiness.

hale [hayl] *adj* **hal·er, hal·est** robust, healthy, e.g. *hale and hearty.*

half [haf] *n, pl* **halves** [havz] **1** either of two equal parts of thing. ♦ *adj* **2** forming half. ♦ *adv* **3** to the extent of half. **half'back** *n Football* one of two players lining up on each side of fullback. **half-baked** *adj* **1** underdone. **2** *inf* immature, silly. **half'-breed** *n offens* person with parents of different races. **half'-broth·er** *n* brother by one parent only. **half-cocked** *adj* ill-prepared. **half-heart·ed** *adj*

unenthusiastic. **half'-life** *n, pl* **-lives** time taken for half the atoms in radioactive material to decay. **half nel'son** hold in wrestling. **half'-sis·ter** *n* sister by one parent only. **half'time** *n Sports* rest period between two halves of a game. **half'tone** *n* illustration printed by photoengraving from plate, showing lights and shadows by means of minute dots. **half vol·ley** *Sport* striking of a ball the moment it bounces. **half'wit** *n* **1** feeble-minded person. **2** stupid person.

hal·i·but [HAL-ə-bət] *n* large edible flatfish.

hal·i·to·sis [hal-i-TOH-sis] *n* bad-smelling breath.

hall [hawl] *n* (entrance) passage. **1** large room or building belonging to particular group or used for particular purpose esp. public assembly.

hal·le·lu·jah [hal-ə-LOO-yə] *n, interj* exclamation of praise to God.

hall'mark [HAWL-mahrk] *n* **1** mark used to indicate standard of tested gold and silver. **2** mark of excellence. **3** distinguishing feature.

hal·low [HAL-oh] *vt* make, or honor as holy. **Hal·low·een** [hal-ə-WEEN] *n* the evening of Oct. 31st, the day before All Saints' Day.

hal·lu·ci·nate [hə-LOO-sə-nayt] *vi* **-nat·ed, -nat·ing** suffer illusions. **hal·lu·ci·na'tion** *n* illusion. **hal·lu'ci·na·to·ry** *adj*

——————| THESAURUS |——————

2 = **flag down**, signal to, wave down **3** hail from = **come from**, be a native of, be born in, originate in

hair *n* = **locks**, head of hair, mane, mop, shock, tresses

hairdresser *n* = **stylist**, barber, coiffeur *or* coiffeuse

hair-raising *adj* = **frightening**, alarming, bloodcurdling, horrifying, scary, shocking, spine-chilling, terrifying

hairstyle *n* = **haircut**, coiffure, cut, hairdo, style

hairy *adj* = **shaggy**, bushy, furry, hirsute, stubbly, unshaven, woolly

halcyon *adj* **1** = **peaceful**, calm, gentle, quiet, serene, tranquil, undisturbed **2** *As in* **halcyon days** = **happy**, carefree, flourishing, golden, palmy, prosperous

hale *adj* = **healthy**, able-bodied, fit, flourishing, in the pink, robust, sound, strong, vigorous, well

half *n* **1** = **equal part**, fifty per cent,

hemisphere, portion, section ♦ *adj* **2** = **partial**, halved, limited, moderate ♦ *adv* **3** = **partially**, in part, partly

half-baked *adj* = **ill-judged**, ill-conceived, impractical, poorly planned, short-sighted, unformed, unthought out *or* through

half-hearted *adj* = **unenthusiastic**, apathetic, indifferent, lackluster, listless, lukewarm, perfunctory, tame

halfway *adv* **1** = **midway**, to *or* in the middle ♦ *adj* **2** = **midway**, central, equidistant, intermediate, mid, middle

halfwit *n* = **fool**, airhead (*sl*), dork (*sl*), dunderhead, idiot, imbecile (*inf*), moron, schmuck (*sl*), simpleton

hall *n* **1** = **entrance hall**, corridor, entry, foyer, hallway, lobby, passage, passageway, vestibule **2** = **meeting place**, assembly room, auditorium, chamber, concert hall

hallmark *n* **1** = **seal**, device, endorsement, mark, sign, stamp, symbol **2** = **indication**,

hal·lu·ci·no·gen [-jən] n drug inducing hallucinations.

ha·lo [HAY-loh] n, pl **-los, -loes 1** circle of light around moon, sun, etc. **2** disk of light around saint's head in picture. **3** ideal glory attaching to person. ♦ vt **-loed, -lo·ing 4** surround with halo.

halt[1] [hawlt] n **1** interruption or end to progress, etc. (esp. as command to stop marching). ♦ v **2** (cause to) stop.

halt[2] vi falter, fail. **halt'ing** adj hesitant, lame.

hal·ter [HAWL-tər] n **1** rope or strap with headgear to fasten horses or cattle. **2** low-cut dress style with strap passing behind neck. ♦ vt **3** put halter on, fasten with one.

halve [hav] vt **halved, halv·ing 1** cut in half. **2** reduce to half. **3** share.

hal·yard [HAL-yərd] n rope for raising sail, signal flags, etc.

ham n **1** meat (esp. salted or smoked) from thigh of pig. **2** actor adopting exaggerated, unconvincing style. **3** amateur radio enthusiast. **4 ham it up** overact. **ham'string** n **1** tendon at back of knee. ♦ vt **-strung, -string·ing 2** cripple by cutting this. **3** render useless. **4** thwart.

ham·burg·er [HAM-burg-gər] n broiled, fried patty of ground beef, esp. served in bread roll.

ham·let [HAM-lit] n small village.

ham·mer [HAM-ər] n **1** tool usu. with heavy head at end of handle, for beating, driving nails, etc. **2** machine for same purposes. **3** contrivance for exploding charge of gun. **4** auctioneer's mallet. **5** heavy metal ball on wire thrown in sports. ♦ v **6** strike with, or as with, hammer. **ham'mer·head** [-hed] n shark with wide, flattened head. **ham'mer·toe** n deformed toe. **hammer out** solve problem by painstaking work.

ham·mock [HAM-ək] n bed of canvas, etc., hung on cords.

ham·per[1] [HAM-pər] n **1** large covered basket, such as for laundry. **2** large parcel, box, etc. of food, wines, etc., esp. one sent as gift.

ham·per[2] vt impede, obstruct movements of.

ham·ster [HAM-stər] n type of rodent, sometimes kept as pet.

ham'strung adj **1** crippled, thwarted. **2** see HAM.

hand n **1** extremity of arm beyond wrist. **2** side, quarter, direction. **3** style of writing. **4** cards dealt to player. **5** measure of four inches. **6** manual worker. **7** sailor. **8** help, aid. **9** pointer on dial. **10** applause. ♦ vt **11** pass. **12** deliver. **13** hold out. **hand'ful** n, pl **-fuls 1** small amount or number. **2** inf person, thing causing problems. **hand'i·ly** adv **hand'i·ness** n dexterity. **2** state of being near, available. **hand'y** adj **hand·i·er, hand·i·est 1** convenient. **2** clever with the hands. **hand'bag** n **1** woman's bag for personal articles. **2** bag for carrying in hand. **hand'bill** n small printed notice. **hand'book** n small reference or instruction book. **hand'cuff** n fetter for wrist, usu. joined in pair. ♦ vt **2** secure thus. **hand'i·craft** n manual occupation or skill. **hand'i·work** n thing done by particular person. **hand·ker·chief** [HANG-kər-chif] n small square of fabric carried in pocket for wiping nose, etc. **hand'out** n **1** inf money, food, etc. given free. **2** pamphlet giving news, information, etc. **hands-on** adj involving practical experience of equipment. **hand'stand** n act of supporting body in upside-down position by hands alone. **hand'writ·ing** n way person writes. **hand'y·man** n **1** one employed to do various tasks. **2** one skilled in odd jobs. **hand in glove** very intimate.

THESAURUS

sure sign, telltale sign

hallucination n = **illusion**, apparition, delusion, dream, fantasy, figment of the imagination, mirage, vision

halo n = **ring of light**, aura, corona, nimbus, radiance

halt[1] v **1** = **stop**, break off, cease, come to an end, desist, rest, stand still, wait **2** = **end**, block, bring to an end, check, curb, cut short, nip in the bud, terminate ♦ n **3** = **stop**, close, end, pause, standstill,

stoppage

halting adj = **faltering**, awkward, hesitant, labored, stammering, stumbling, stuttering

halve v = **bisect**, cut in half, divide equally, share equally, split in two

hammer v **1** = **hit**, bang, beat, drive, knock, strike, tap **2** Inf = **defeat**, beat, drub, run rings around (inf), thrash, trounce, wipe the floor with (inf)

hamper v = **hinder**, frustrate, hamstring, handicap, impede, interfere with, obstruct,

hand·i·cap [HAN-dee-kap] *n* **1** something that hampers or hinders. **2** race, contest in which chances are equalized by weights carried, golf strokes, etc. **3** condition so imposed. **4** any physical disability. ◆ *vt* **-capped, -cap·ping 5** hamper. **6** impose handicap on. **7** attempt to predict winner of race, game. **handicapped** *dated* physically or mentally disabled.

han·dle [HAN-dl] *n* **1** part of thing to hold it by. ◆ *vi* **-dled, -dling 2** touch, feel with hands. **3** manage. **4** deal with. **5** trade. **han'dle·bars** *pl n* curved metal bars used to steer bicycle, motorbike, etc. **handlebar mustache** one resembling handlebar.

hand·some [HAN-səm] *adj* **1** of fine appearance. **2** generous. **3** ample.

hang *v* hung *or* hanged, hang·ing ◆ *vt* **1** suspend. **2** kill by suspension by neck. **3** attach, set up (wallpaper, doors, etc.). ◆ *vi*

4 be suspended, cling. **hang'er** *n* frame on which clothes, etc. can be hung. **hang'dog** *adj* sullen, dejected. **hang glider** glider like large kite, with pilot hanging in frame below. **hang gliding** *n* **hang'man** *n* executioner. **hang'o·ver** *n* aftereffects of too much drinking. **hang out** *inf* reside, frequent. **hang-up** *n sl* **1** persistent emotional problem. **2** preoccupation.

hang·ar [HANG-ər] *n* large shed for aircraft.

hank [hangk] *n* coil, skein, length, esp. as measure of yarn.

hank·er [HANG-kər] *vi* (oft. with *after* or *for*) crave.

han·ky-pan·ky [HANG-kee-PANG-kee] *n* *inf* **1** trickery. **2** illicit sexual relations.

han·som [HAN-səm] *n* two-wheeled horse-drawn cab for two to ride inside with driver mounted up behind.

hap·haz·ard [hap-HAZ-ərd] *adj* random,

——————| THESAURUS |——————

prevent, restrict

hand *n* **1 = palm**, fist, mitt (*sl*), paw (*inf*) **2 = hired man**, artisan, craftsman, employee, laborer, operative, worker, workman **3 = penmanship**, calligraphy, handwriting, script **4 = ovation**, clap, round of applause **5 at** *or* **on hand = nearby**, at one's fingertips, available, close, handy, near, ready, within reach ◆ *v* **6 = pass**, deliver, hand over

handbook *n* **= guidebook**, Baedeker, guide, instruction book, manual

handcuff *v* **= shackle**, fetter, manacle

handcuffs *pl n* **= shackles**, cuffs (*inf*), fetters, manacles

handful *n* **= few**, small number, smattering, sprinkling

handicap *n* **1 = disadvantage**, barrier, drawback, hindrance, impediment, limitation, obstacle, restriction, stumbling block **2 = advantage**, head start **3 = disability**, defect, impairment ◆ *v* **4 = restrict**, burden, encumber, hamper, hamstring, hinder, hold back, impede, limit

handicraft *n* **= craftsmanship**, art, craft, handiwork, skill, workmanship

handiwork *n* **= creation**, achievement, design, invention, product, production

handle *n* **1 = grip**, haft, hilt, stock ◆ *v* **2 = hold**, feel, finger, grasp, pick up, touch **3 = control**, direct, guide, manage, maneuver, manipulate **4 = deal with**, cope with, manage

hand-out *n* **1 = charity**, alms **2 = leaflet**, bulletin, circular, literature (*inf*), mailshot, press release

handsome *adj* **1 = good-looking**, attractive, comely, elegant, gorgeous, personable, well-proportioned **2 = large**, abundant, ample, considerable, generous, liberal, plentiful, sizable *or* sizeable

handwriting *n* **= penmanship**, calligraphy, hand, scrawl, script

handy *adj* **1 = available**, accessible, at hand, at one's fingertips, close, convenient, nearby, on hand, within reach **2 = useful**, convenient, easy to use, helpful, manageable, neat, practical, serviceable, user-friendly **3 = skillful**, adept, adroit, deft, dexterous, expert, proficient, skilled

hang *v* **1 = suspend**, dangle, droop **2 = execute**, lynch, string up (*inf*) ◆ *n* **3 get the hang of = grasp**, comprehend, understand

hang back *v* **= hesitate**, be reluctant, demur, hold back, recoil

hangdog *adj* **= guilty**, cowed, cringing, defeated, downcast, furtive, shamefaced, wretched

hangover *n* **= aftereffects**, crapulence, morning after (*inf*)

hang-up *n* **= preoccupation**, block, difficulty, inhibition, obsession, problem, thing (*inf*)

hank *n* **= coil**, length, loop, piece, roll, skein

hanker *v* (with *for* or *after*) **= desire**, crave, hunger, itch, long, lust, pine, thirst, yearn careless.

hap•less [HAP-lis] *adj* unlucky.

hap•pen [HAP-ən] *vi* **1** come about, occur. **2** chance to do. **hap'pen•ing** *n* occurrence, event.

hap•py *adj* **-pi•er, -pi•est 1** glad, content. **2** lucky, fortunate. **3** apt. **hap'pi•ly** *adv* **hap'pi•ness** *n* **hap'py-go-luck'y** *adj* casual, lighthearted.

ha•ra-ki•ri [HAHR-ə-KEER-ee] *n* in Japan, ritual suicide by disemboweling.

ha•rangue [hə-RANG] *n* **1** vehement speech. **2** tirade. ◆ *v* **-rangued, -rangu•ing**

ha•rass [hə-RAS] *vt* worry, trouble, torment. **ha•rass'ment** *n*

har•bin•ger [HAHR-bin-jər] *n* **1** one who announces another's approach. **2** forerunner, herald.

har•bor [HAHR-bər] *n* **1** shelter for ships. **2** shelter. ◆ *v* **3** give shelter, protection to. **4** maintain (secretly) esp. grudge, etc.

hard [hahrd] *adj* **-er, -est 1** firm, resisting pressure. **2** solid. **3** difficult to understand. **4** harsh, unfeeling. **5** difficult to bear. **6** practical, shrewd. **7** heavy. **8** strenuous. **9** of water, not making lather well with soap. **10** of drugs, highly addictive. ◆ *adv* **11** vigorously. **12** with difficulty. **13** close. **hard'en** *v* **hard'ly** *adv* **1** unkindly, harshly. **2** scarcely, not quite. **3** only just. **hard'ship** *n* **1** bad luck. **2** severe toil, suffering. **3** instance of this. **hard'ball** *n* **1** baseball. **2** *inf* forceful or ruthless methods of achieving a goal. **hard-boiled** *adj* **1** boiled so long as to be hard. **2** *inf* of person, unemotional, unsentimental. **hard copy 1** computer output printed on paper. **2** original paper document. **hard disk** *Computers.* rigid data-storage disk in a sealed container. **hard-hat** *n* *inf* construction worker. **hard'head'ed** *adj* shrewd. **hard-pressed** *adj* heavily burdened. **hard'ware** *n* **1** tools, implements. **2** necessary (parts of) machinery. **3** *Computers* mechanical and electronic parts. **hard'wood** *n* wood from deciduous trees. **hard of hearing** rather deaf. **hard up** very short of money.

THESAURUS

haphazard *adj* = **disorganized**, aimless, casual, hit or miss (*inf*), indiscriminate, random, slapdash

happen *v* **1** = **occur**, come about, come to pass, develop, result, take place, transpire (*inf*) **2** = **chance**, turn out

happening *n* = **event**, affair, episode, experience, incident, occurrence, proceeding

happily *adv* **1** = **willingly**, freely, gladly, with pleasure **2** = **joyfully**, blithely, cheerfully, gaily, gleefully, joyously, merrily **3** = **luckily**, fortunately, opportunely, providentially

happiness *n* = **joy**, bliss, cheerfulness, contentment, delight, ecstasy, elation, jubilation, pleasure, satisfaction

happy *adj* **1** = **joyful**, blissful, cheerful, content, delighted, ecstatic, elated, glad, jubilant, merry, overjoyed, pleased, thrilled **2** = **fortunate**, advantageous, auspicious, favorable, lucky, timely, win-win (*inf*)

happy-go-lucky *adj* = **carefree**, blithe, easy-going, light-hearted, nonchalant, unconcerned, untroubled

harangue *v* **1** = **rant**, address, declaim, exhort, hold forth, lecture, spout (*inf*) ◆ *n* **2** = **speech**, address, declamation, diatribe, exhortation, tirade

harass *v* = **annoy**, bother, harry, hassle (*inf*), hound, persecute, pester, plague, trouble, vex

harassed *adj* = **worried**, careworn, distraught, hassled (*inf*), strained, tormented, troubled, under pressure, vexed

harassment *n* = **trouble**, annoyance, bother, hassle (*inf*), irritation, nuisance, persecution, pestering

harbor *n* **1** = **port**, anchorage, haven ◆ *v* **2** = **shelter**, hide, protect, provide refuge, shield **3** = **maintain**, cling to, entertain, foster, hold, nurse, nurture, retain

hard *adj* **1** = **solid**, firm, inflexible, rigid, rocklike, stiff, strong, tough, unyielding **2** = **strenuous**, arduous, backbreaking, exacting, exhausting, laborious, rigorous, tough **3** = **difficult**, complicated, intricate, involved, knotty, perplexing, puzzling, thorny **4** = **unfeeling**, callous, cold, cruel, hardhearted, pitiless, stern, unkind, unsympathetic **5** = **painful**, disagreeable, distressing, grievous, intolerable, unpleasant ◆ *adv* **6** = **energetically**, fiercely, forcefully, forcibly, heavily, intensely, powerfully, severely, sharply, strongly, vigorously, violently, with all one's might, with might and main **7** = **diligently**, doggedly, industriously, persistently, steadily, untiringly

har·dy [HAHR-dee] *adj* **-di·er, -di·est 1** robust, vigorous. **2** bold. **3** of plants, able to grow in the open all the year round. **har'di·hood** [-huud] *n* extreme boldness, audacity. **hard'i·ly** *adv* **har'di·ness** *n*

hare [hair] *n* animal like large rabbit, with longer legs and ears, noted for speed. **hare'brained** *adj* rash, wild. **hare'lip** *n* fissure of upper lip

har·em [HAIR-əm] *n* **1** women's part of Muslim dwelling. **2** one man's wives and concubines.

hark [hahrk] *vi* listen. **hark back** return to previous subject of discussion.

har·le·quin [HAHR-lə-kwin] *n* stock comic character, esp. masked clown in diamond-patterned costume. **har·le·quin·ade'** [-NAYD] *n* **1** scene in pantomime. **2** buffoonery.

har·lot [HAHR-lət] *n* whore, prostitute. **har'lot·ry** *n*

harm [hahrm] *n* **1** damage, injury. ◆ *vt* **2** cause harm to. **harm'ful** *adj* **harm'less** *adj* unable or unlikely to hurt.

har·mo·ny [HAHR-mə-nee] *n, pl* **-nies 1** agreement. **2** concord. **3** peace. **4** combination of notes to make chords. **5** melodious sound. **har·mon'ic** *adj* **1** of harmony. ◆ *n* **2** tone or note whose frequency is a multiple of its pitch. **har·mon'ics** *n* science of musical sounds. **har·mon'i·ca** *n* various musical instruments, but esp. mouth organ. **har·mo'ni·ous** *adj* **har'mo·nize** [-mə-nīz] *v* **niaed, ni·a·ing** ◆ *vt* **1** bring into harmony. **2** cause to agree. **3** reconcile. ◆ *vi* **4** be in harmony.

har·ness [HAHR-nis] *n* **1** equipment for attaching horse to cart, plow, etc. **2** any such equipment. ◆ *vt* **3** put on, in harness. **4** utilize energy or power of (waterfall, etc.).

harp [hahrp] *n* **1** musical instrument of strings played by hand. ◆ *vi* **2** play on harp. **3** dwell (on) persistently. **harp'ist** *n* **harp'si·chord** [-si-kord] *n* stringed instrument like piano.

har·poon [hahr-POON] *n* **1** barbed spear with rope attached for catching whales. ◆ *vt* **2** catch, kill with this. **har·poon'er** *n* **harpoon gun** gun for firing harpoon in whaling.

<hr>

THESAURUS

hard-boiled *adj* = **tough**, cynical, hard-nosed (*inf*), matter-of-fact, practical, realistic, unsentimental

harden *v* **1** = **solidify**, anneal, bake, cake, freeze, set, stiffen **2** = **accustom**, habituate, inure, season, train

hardened *adj* **1** = **habitual**, chronic, incorrigible, inveterate, shameless **2** = **accustomed**, habituated, inured, seasoned, toughened

hard-headed *adj* = **sensible**, level-headed, practical, pragmatic, realistic, shrewd, tough, unsentimental

hardhearted *adj* = **unsympathetic**, callous, cold, hard, heartless, insensitive, uncaring, unfeeling

hardiness *n* = **resilience**, resolution, robustness, ruggedness, sturdiness, toughness

hardly *adv* = **barely**, just, only just, scarcely, with difficulty

hardship *n* = **suffering**, adversity, difficulty, misfortune, need, privation, tribulation

hard up *adj* = **poor**, broke (*inf*), impecunious, impoverished, on the breadline, out of pocket, penniless, short, strapped for cash (*inf*)

hardy *adj* = **strong**, robust, rugged, sound, stout, sturdy, tough

harm *v* **1** = **injure**, abuse, damage, hurt, ill-treat, maltreat, ruin, spoil, wound ◆ *n* **2** = **injury**, abuse, damage, hurt, ill, loss, mischief, misfortune

harmful *adj* = **destructive**, damaging, deleterious, detrimental, hurtful, injurious, noxious, pernicious

harmless *adj* = **innocuous**, gentle, innocent, inoffensive, nontoxic, safe, unobjectionable

harmonious *adj* **1** = **melodious**, agreeable, concordant, consonant, dulcet, mellifluous, musical, sweet-sounding, tuneful **2** = **friendly**, agreeable, amicable, compatible, congenial, cordial, sympathetic

harmonize *v* = **blend**, chime with, cohere, coordinate, correspond, match, tally, tone in with

harmony *n* **1** = **agreement**, accord, amicability, compatibility, concord, cooperation, friendship, peace, rapport, sympathy **2** = **tunefulness**, euphony, melody, tune, unison

harness *n* **1** = **equipment**, gear, tack, tackle ◆ *v* **2** = **exploit**, channel, control,

Har·py [HAHR-pee] *n, pl* **-pies 1** monster with body of woman and wings and claws of bird. **2** (h-) cruel, grasping person.

har·ri·dan [HAHR-i-dn] *n* shrewish old woman, hag.

har·row [HAR-oh] *n* **1** implement for smoothing, leveling or stirring up soil. ♦ *vt* **2** draw harrow over. **3** distress greatly. **har'row·ing** *adj* **1** heartrending. **2** distressful.

har·ry [HAR-ee] *vt* **-ried, -ry·ing 1** harass. **2** ravage.

harsh [hahrsh] *adj* **-er, -est 1** rough, discordant. **2** severe. **3** unfeeling. **harsh·ness** *n*

har·um-scar·um [HAIR-əm-SKAIR-əm] *adj* **1** reckless, wild. **2** disorganized.

har·vest [HAHR-vist] *n* (season for) gathering in grain. **1** gathering. **2** crop. **3** product of action. ♦ *vt* **4** reap and gather in.

has [haz] third person sing. pres. indicative of HAVE.

hash *n* **1** dish of hashed meat, etc. **2** *inf* short for HASHISH. **3** mess, jumble. ♦ *vt* **4** cut up small, chop. **5** mix up.

hash·ish [hash-EESH] *n* resinous extract of Indian hemp, esp. used as hallucinogen.

hasp *n* **1** clasp passing over a staple for fastening door, etc. ♦ *vt* **2** fasten, secure with hasp.

has·sle [HAS-əl] *n inf* **1** quarrel. **2** a lot of bother, trouble. ♦ *v* **-sled, -sling**

has·sock [HAS-ək] *n* **1** cushion used as footstool, ottoman. **2** tuft of grass.

haste [hayst] *n* **1** speed, quickness, hurry. ♦ *v* **hast·ed, hast·ing** ♦ *vi* **2** hasten. **has·ten** [HAY-sən] *v* (cause to) hurry, increase speed. **hast'i·ly** *adv* **hast'y** *adj* **hast·i·er, hast·i·est**

hat *n* head covering, usu. with brim. **hat'ter** *n* dealer in, maker of hats. **hat trick** any three successive achievements, esp. in sports.

hatch[1] [hach] *v* **1** of young, esp. of birds, (cause to) emerge from egg. **2** contrive, devise. **hatch'er·y** *n, pl* **-er·ies**

hatch[2] *n* **1** hatchway. **2** trapdoor over it. **3** lower half of divided door. **hatch'back** *n* automobile with single lifting door in rear. **hatch'way** *n* opening in deck of ship, etc.

hatch[3] *vt* **1** engrave or draw lines on for shading. **2** shade with parallel lines.

hatch·et [HACH-it] *n* small ax. **hatchet job** malicious verbal attack. **hatchet man 1** person carrying out unpleasant assignments for another. **2** professional assassin. **bury the hatchet** make peace.

hate [hayt] *vt* **hat·ed, hat·ing 1** dislike strongly. **2** bear malice toward. ♦ *n* **3** this feeling. **4** that which is hated. **hate'ful** *adj* detestable. **ha·tred** [HAY-trid] *n* extreme dislike, active ill will.

haugh·ty [HAW-tee] *adj* **-ti·er, -ti·est**

———— THESAURUS ————

employ, mobilize, utilize

harrowing *adj* = **distressing**, agonizing, disturbing, heart-rending, nerve-racking, painful, terrifying, tormenting, traumatic

harry *v* = **pester**, badger, bother, chivvy, harass, hassle (*inf*), molest, plague

harsh *adj* **1** = **raucous**, discordant, dissonant, grating, guttural, rasping, rough, strident **2** = **severe**, austere, cruel, draconian, drastic, pitiless, punitive, ruthless, stern

harshly *adv* = **severely**, brutally, cruelly, roughly, sternly, strictly

harshness *n* = **severity**, asperity, austerity, brutality, rigor, roughness, sternness

harvest *n* **1** = **crop**, produce, yield ♦ *v* **2** = **gather**, mow, pick, pluck, reap

hassle *n* **1** = **argument**, bickering, disagreement, dispute, fight, quarrel, row, squabble **2** = **trouble**, bother, difficulty, grief (*inf*), inconvenience, problem ♦ *v* **3** = **bother**, annoy, badger, bug (*inf*), harass,

hound, pester

haste *n* **1** = **speed**, alacrity, quickness, rapidity, swiftness, urgency, velocity **2** = **rush**, hurry, hustle, impetuosity

hasten *v* = **rush**, dash, fly, hurry (up), make haste, race, scurry, speed

hastily *adv* **1** = **speedily**, promptly, quickly, rapidly **2** = **hurriedly**, impetuously, precipitately, rashly

hasty *adj* **1** = **speedy**, brisk, hurried, prompt, rapid, swift, urgent **2** = **impetuous**, impulsive, precipitate, rash, thoughtless

hatch *v* **1** = **incubate**, breed, bring forth, brood **2** = **devise**, conceive, concoct, contrive, cook up (*inf*), design, dream up (*inf*), think up

hate *v* **1** = **detest**, abhor, despise, dislike, loathe, recoil from **2** = **be unwilling**, be loath, be reluctant, be sorry, dislike, feel disinclined, shrink from ♦ *n* **3** = **dislike**, animosity, antipathy, aversion, detestation, proud, arrogant. **haugh'ti·ness** n

haul [hawl] vt **1** pull, drag with effort. ◆ vi **2** of wind, shift in direction. ◆ n **3** hauling. **4** what is hauled. **5** catch of fish. **6** acquisition. **7** distance (to be) covered. **haul·age** [HAW-lij] n **1** carrying of loads. **2** charge for this. **haul'er** n firm, person that transports goods by road.

haunch [hawnch] n **1** human hip or fleshy hindquarter of animal. **2** leg and loin of animal as food.

haunt [hawnt] vt **1** visit regularly. **2** visit in form of ghost. **3** recur to. ◆ n **4** esp. place frequently visited. **haunt'ed** adj **1** frequented by ghosts. **2** worried.

hau·teur [hoh-TUR] n **1** haughty spirit. **2** arrogance.

have [hav] vt **had, hav·ing 1** hold, possess. **2** be possessed, affected with. **3** be obliged (to do). **4** cheat, outwit. **5** engage in, obtain. **6** contain. **7** allow. **8** cause to be done. **9** give birth to. **10** used to form past tenses (with a past participle), e.g. *we have looked; she had done enough.*

ha·ven [HAY-vən] n place of safety.

hav·er·sack [HAV-ər-sak] n canvas bag for provisions, etc. carried on back or shoulder

when hiking, etc.

hav·oc [HAV-ək] n **1** devastation, ruin. **2** inf confusion, chaos.

hawk[1] n **1** bird of prey smaller than eagle. **2** supporter, advocate, of warlike policies. ◆ vi **3** hunt with hawks. **4** attack like hawk.

hawk[2] vt offer (goods) for sale, as in street. **hawk'er** n

hawk[3] vi clear throat noisily.

haw·ser [HAW-zər] n large rope or cable.

hay n grass mown and dried. **hay'cock** n conical pile of hay for drying. **hay fever** allergic reaction to pollen, dust, etc. **hay'stack** n large pile of hay. **hay'wire** adj **1** crazy. **2** disorganized.

haz·ard [HAZ-ərd] n **1** chance. **2** risk, danger. ◆ vt **3** expose to risk. **4** run risk of. **haz'ard·ous** adj risky.

haze [hayz] n **1** mist, often due to heat. **2** obscurity. **ha'zy** adj **-zi·er, -zi·est 1** misty. **2** obscured. **3** vague.

ha·zel [HAY-zəl] n **1** bush or small tree bearing nuts. **2** yellowish-brown color of the nuts. ◆ adj **3** light brown.

He Chem. helium.

he [hee] pron **1** third person masculine pronoun. **2** person, animal already referred

————— THESAURUS —————

enmity, hatred, hostility, loathing

hateful adj = **despicable**, abhorrent, detestable, horrible, loathsome, lousy (sl), obnoxious, odious, offensive, repellent, repugnant, repulsive, scuzzy (sl)

hatred n = **dislike**, animosity, antipathy, aversion, detestation, enmity, hate, repugnance, revulsion

haughty adj = **proud**, arrogant, conceited, contemptuous, disdainful, imperious, scornful, snooty (inf), stuck-up (inf), supercilious

haul v **1** = **drag**, draw, heave, lug, pull, tug ◆ n **2** = **gain**, booty, catch, harvest, loot, spoils, takings, yield

haunt v **1** = **plague**, obsess, possess, prey on, recur, stay with, torment, trouble, weigh on ◆ n **2** = **meeting place**, hangout (inf), rendezvous, stamping ground

haunted adj **1** = **possessed**, cursed, eerie, ghostly, jinxed, spooky (inf) **2** = **preoccupied**, obsessed, plagued, tormented, troubled, worried

haunting adj = **poignant**, evocative, nostalgic, persistent, unforgettable

have v **1** = **possess**, hold, keep, obtain, own, retain **2** = **receive**, accept, acquire,

gain, get, obtain, procure, secure, take **3** = **experience**, endure, enjoy, feel, meet with, suffer, sustain, undergo **4** = **give birth to**, bear, beget, bring forth, deliver **5** have to = **be obliged**, be bound, be compelled, be forced, have got to, must, ought, should

haven n = **sanctuary**, asylum, refuge, retreat, sanctum, shelter

havoc n = **disorder**, chaos, confusion, disruption, mayhem, shambles

haywire adj As in go haywire = **topsy-turvy**, chaotic, confused, disordered, disorganized, mixed up, out of order, shambolic (inf)

hazard n **1** = **danger**, jeopardy, peril, pitfall, risk, threat ◆ v **2** = **jeopardize**, endanger, expose, imperil, risk, threaten **3** As in hazard a guess = **conjecture**, advance, offer, presume, throw out, venture, volunteer

hazardous adj = **dangerous**, difficult, insecure, perilous, precarious, risky, unsafe

haze n = **mist**, cloud, fog, obscurity, vapor

hazy adj **1** = **misty**, cloudy, dim, dull, foggy, overcast **2** = **vague**, fuzzy, ill-defined, indefinite, indistinct, muddled,

to. ◆ *comb. form* **3** male, e.g. *he-goat.*
head [hed] *n* **1** upper part of person's or animal's body, containing mouth, sense organs and brain. **2** upper part of anything. **3** chief of organization, school, etc. **4** chief part. **5** aptitude, capacity. **6** crisis. **7** leader. **8** title. **9** headland. **10** person, animal considered as unit. **11** white froth on beer, etc. **12** *inf* headache. **13** *sl* addict, habitual user of drug. ◆ *adj* **14** chief, principal. **15** of wind, contrary. ◆ *vt* **16** be at the top, head of. **17** lead, direct. **18** provide with head. **19** hit (ball) with head. ◆ *vi* **20** make for. **21** form a head. **head'er** *n* **1** headfirst plunge. **2** brick laid with end in face of wall. **3** action of striking ball with head. **head'ing** *n* title. **heads** *adv inf* with obverse side (of coin) uppermost. **head'y** *adj* **head·i·er, head·i·est** apt to intoxicate or excite. **head'ache** [-ayk] *n* **1** continuous pain in head. **2** worrying circumstance. **head'board** *n* vertical board at head of bed. **head'land** [-lənd] *n* promontory. **head'light** *n* powerful lamp carried on front of locomotive, motor vehicle, etc. **head'line** *n* news summary, in large type in newspaper. **head'long** *adv* head foremost, in rush. **head'quar·ters** *pl n* **1** residence of commander-in-chief. **2** center of operations. **head'stone** *n* gravestone. **head'strong** *adj* self-willed. **head'way** *n* advance, progress.
heal [heel] *v* make or become well. **health** [helth] *n* **1** soundness of body. **2** condition of body. **3** toast drunk in person's honor. **health'i·ly** *adv* **health'y** *adj* **health·i·er, health·i·est** **1** of strong constitution. **2** of or producing good health, well-being, etc. **3** vigorous. **health food** vegetarian food, organically grown, eaten for dietary value.
heap [heep] *n* **1** pile of things lying one on another. **2** great quantity. ◆ *vt* **3** pile, load with.
hear [heer] *v* **heard** [hurd], **hear·ing 1** perceive by ear. **2** listen to. **3** *Law* try (case). **4** heed. **5** perceive sound. **6** learn. **hear'ing** *n* **1** ability to hear. **2** earshot. **3** judicial examination. **hear'say** *n* rumor. ◆ *adj*
heark·en [HAHR-kən] *vi* listen.

THESAURUS

nebulous, uncertain, unclear
head *n* **1** = **skull**, crown, noodle (*sl*), nut (*sl*), pate **2** = **leader**, boss (*inf*), captain, chief, commander, director, manager, master, principal, supervisor **3** = **top**, crest, crown, peak, pinnacle, summit, tip **4** = **brain**, brains (*inf*), intellect, intelligence, mind, thought, understanding **5 go to one's head** = **excite**, intoxicate, make conceited, puff up **6 head over heels** = **uncontrollably**, completely, intensely, thoroughly, utterly, wholeheartedly ◆ *adj* **7** = **chief**, arch, first, leading, main, pre-eminent, premier, prime, principal, supreme ◆ *v* **8** = **lead**, be *or* go first, cap, crown, lead the way, precede, top **9** = **control**, be in charge of, command, direct, govern, guide, lead, manage, run **10** = **make for**, aim, go to, make a beeline for, point, set off for, set out, start towards, steer, turn
headache *n* **1** = **migraine**, neuralgia **2** = **problem**, bane, bother, inconvenience, nuisance, trouble, vexation, worry
heading *n* = **title**, caption, headline, name, rubric
headlong *adv, adj* **1** = **headfirst**, head-on ◆ *adv* **2** = **hastily**, heedlessly, helter-skelter, hurriedly, pell-mell, precipitately, rashly, thoughtlessly ◆ *adj* **3** = **hasty**, breakneck, dangerous, impetuous, impulsive, inconsiderate, precipitate, reckless, thoughtless
headstrong *adj* = **obstinate**, foolhardy, heedless, impulsive, perverse, pig-headed, self-willed, stubborn, unruly, willful
headway *n* = **progress**, advance, improvement, progression, way
heady *adj* **1** = **inebriating**, intoxicating, potent, strong **2** = **exciting**, exhilarating, intoxicating, stimulating, thrilling
heal *v* = **cure**, make well, mend, regenerate, remedy, restore, treat
health *n* **1** = **wellbeing**, fitness, good condition, healthiness, robustness, soundness, strength, vigor **2** = **condition**, constitution, fettle, shape, state
healthy *adj* **1** = **well**, active, fit, hale and hearty, in fine fettle, in good shape (*inf*), in the pink, robust, strong **2** = **wholesome**, beneficial, hygienic, invigorating, nourishing, nutritious, salubrious, salutary
heap *n* **1** = **pile**, accumulation, collection, hoard, lot, mass, mound, stack **2** (often plural) = **a lot**, great deal, lots (*inf*), mass, plenty, pot(s) (*inf*), stack(s), tons ◆ *v* **3** = **pile**, accumulate, amass, collect, gather, hoard, stack **4** = **confer**, assign, bestow,

hearse [hurs] *n* funeral carriage for coffin.
heart [hahrt] *n* **1** organ that makes blood
circulate. **2** seat of emotions and
affections. **3** mind, soul, courage. **4** central
part. **5** playing card marked with figure of
heart. **6** one of these marks. **heart'en** *v*
make, become cheerful. **heart'i·ly** *adv*
heart'less [-lis] *adj* unfeeling. **heart'y** *adj*
heart·i·er, heart·i·est 3 friendly, **2** vigorous,
3 in good health. **4** satisfying the appetite.
heart attack sudden severe malfunction of
heart. **heart'burn** *n* pain in upper intestine.
heart'rend·ing *adj* **1** overwhelming with
grief. **2** agonizing. **heart'throb** *n* object of
infatuation. **heart'-to-heart'** *adj* frank,
sincere. **by heart** by memory.
hearth [hahrth] *n* **1** floor of fireplace. **2** part
of room where fire is made. **3** home.
heat [heet] *n* **1** hotness. **2** sensation of this.
3 hot weather or climate. **4** warmth of
feeling, anger, etc. **5** sexual excitement

caused by readiness to mate in female
animals. **6** one of many races, etc. to
decide persons to compete in finals. ◆ *v* **7**
make, become hot. **heat'ed** *adj* esp. angry.
heath [heeth] *n* **1** tract of wasteland. **2**
low-growing evergreen shrub.
hea·then [HEE-*th*ən] *adj* **1** not adhering to
a religious system. **2** pagan. **3** barbarous. **4**
unenlightened. ◆ *n* **5** heathen person.
hea'then·ish *adj* **1** of or like heathen. **2**
rough. **3** barbarous.
heath·er [HE*th*-ər] *n* shrub growing on
heaths and mountains.
heave [heev] *v* **heaved, heav·ing** ◆ *vt* **1** lift
with effort. **2** throw (something heavy). **3**
utter (sigh). ◆ *vi* **4** swell, rise. **5** vomit. ◆ *n*
heav·en [HEV-ən] *n* **1** abode of God. **2**
place of bliss. **3** (also pl) sky. **heav'en·ly** *adj*
1 lovely, delightful, divine. **2** beautiful. **3** of
or like heaven.
heav·y [HEV-ee] *adj* **heav·i·er, heav·i·est 1**

———— THESAURUS ————

load, shower upon
hear *v* **1 = listen to**, catch, overhear **2 =
learn**, ascertain, discover, find out, gather,
get wind of (*inf*), pick up **3** *Law* **= try**,
examine, investigate, judge
hearing *n* **= inquiry**, industrial tribunal,
investigation, review, trial
hearsay *n* **= rumor**, gossip, idle talk,
report, tittle-tattle, word of mouth
heart *n* **1 = nature**, character, disposition,
soul, temperament **2 = bravery**, courage,
fortitude, pluck, purpose, resolution, spirit,
will **3 = center**, core, hub, middle, nucleus,
quintessence **4 by heart = by memory**, by
rote, off pat, parrot-fashion (*inf*), pat, word
for word
heartache *n* **= sorrow**, agony, anguish,
despair, distress, grief, heartbreak, pain,
remorse, suffering, torment, torture
heartbreak *n* **= grief**, anguish, desolation,
despair, misery, pain, sorrow, suffering
heartbreaking *adj* **= tragic**, agonizing,
distressing, harrowing, heart-rending,
pitiful, poignant, sad
heartbroken *adj* **= miserable**,
brokenhearted, crushed, desolate,
despondent, disconsolate, dispirited,
heartsick
heartfelt *adj* **= sincere**, deep, devout,
earnest, genuine, honest, profound,
unfeigned, wholehearted
heartily *adv* **= enthusiastically**, eagerly,
earnestly, resolutely, vigorously, zealously

heartless *adj* **= cruel**, callous, cold, hard,
hardhearted, merciless, pitiless, uncaring,
unfeeling
heart-rending *adj* **= moving**, affecting,
distressing, harrowing, heartbreaking,
poignant, sad, tragic
hearty *adj* **1 = friendly**, back-slapping,
ebullient, effusive, enthusiastic, genial,
jovial, warm **2 = substantial**, ample, filling,
nourishing, sizable *or* sizeable, solid, square
heat *v* **1 = warm up**, make hot, reheat ◆ *n*
2 = hotness, high temperature, warmth
3 = intensity, excitement, fervor, fury,
passion, vehemence
heated *adj* **= angry**, excited, fierce,
frenzied, furious, impassioned, intense,
passionate, stormy, vehement
heathen *n* **1 = unbeliever**, infidel, pagan ◆
adj **2 = pagan**, godless, idolatrous,
irreligious
heave *v* **1 = lift**, drag (up), haul (up), hoist,
pull (up), raise, tug **2 = throw**, cast, fling,
hurl, pitch, send, sling, toss **3 = sigh**,
groan, puff **4 = vomit**, barf (*sl*), gag, retch,
spew, throw up (*inf*)
heaven *n* **1 = paradise**, bliss, Elysium *or*
Elysian fields (*Greek myth*), hereafter, life
everlasting, next world, nirvana (*Buddhism,
Hinduism*), Zion (*Christianity*) **2 =
happiness**, bliss, ecstasy, paradise,
rapture, seventh heaven, utopia **3 the
heavens = sky**, ether, firmament
heavenly *adj* **1 = beautiful**, blissful,

weighty, striking, falling with force. **2** dense. **3** sluggish. **4** difficult, severe. **5** sorrowful. **6** serious. **7** dull. **8** *sl* serious, excellent. **heav'i·ly** *adv* **heav'i·ness** *n*

heavy industry basic, large-scale industry producing metal, machinery, etc. **heavy metal** rock music with strong beat and amplified instrumental effects. **heavy water** deuterium oxide, water in which normal hydrogen content has been replaced by deuterium.

Heb. Hebrews.

He·brew [HEE-broo] *n* **1** member of an ancient Semitic people. **2** their language. **3** its modern form, used in Israel.

heck·le [HEK-əl] *v* **-led, -ling** interrupt or try to annoy (speaker) by questions, taunts, etc.

hect-, hecto- *comb. form* one hundred, e.g. *hectoliter; hectometer.*

hec·tare [HEK-tahr] *n* one hundred ares (10,000 square meters, 2.471 acres).

hec·tic [HEK-tik] *adj* rushed, busy.

hec·tor [HEK-tər] *v* **1** bully, bluster. ◆ *n* **2** bully.

hedge [hej] *n* **1** fence of bushes. ◆ *v* **hedged, hedg·ing** ◆ *vt* **2** surround with hedge. **3** obstruct. **4** hem in. **5** bet on both sides. ◆ *vi* **6** make hedge. **7** be evasive. **8** secure against loss. **hedge'hog** *n* small animal covered with spines.

he·don·ism [HEED-n-iz-əm] *n* doctrine that pleasure is the chief good. **he'don·ist** *n*

heed *vt* take notice of, care for. **heed'ful** *adj* **heed'less** *adj* careless.

heel[1] *n* **1** hinder part of foot. **2** part of shoe supporting this. **3** undesirable person. ◆ *vt* **4** supply with heel. **5** touch ground with heel. ◆ *vi* **6** of dog, follow at one's heels.

heel[2] *v* **1** of ship, (cause to) lean to one side. ◆ *n* **2** heeling, list.

heft·y [HEF-tee] *adj* **heft·i·er, heft·i·est 1** bulky. **2** weighty. **3** strong.

he·gem·o·ny [hi-JEM-ə-nee] *n, pl* **-nies** leadership, political domination.

heif·er [HEF-ər] *n* young cow.

height [hīt] *n* **1** measure from base to top. **2** quality of being high. **3** elevation. **4** highest degree. **5** (oft. pl) area of high ground. **6 heights** extremes, e.g. *dizzy heights of success.* **height'en** *vt* **1** make higher. **2** intensify.

hei·nous [HAY-nəs] *adj* atrocious, extremely wicked, detestable.

heir [air] *n* person entitled to inherit property or rank. **heir'ess** *n, fem.* **heir'loom** *n* thing that has been in family for generations.

held pt./pp. of HOLD.

hel·i·cal [HEL-i-kəl] *adj* spiral.

hel·i·cop·ter [HEL-i-kop-tər] *n* aircraft

——————— THESAURUS ———————

delightful, divine (*inf*), exquisite, lovely, ravishing, sublime, wonderful **2 = celestial**, angelic, blessed, divine, holy, immortal

heavily *adv* **1 = ponderously**, awkwardly, clumsily, weightily **2 = densely**, closely, compactly, thickly **3 = considerably**, a great deal, copiously, excessively, to excess, very much

heaviness *n* **= weight**, gravity, heftiness, ponderousness

heavy *adj* **1 = weighty**, bulky, hefty, massive, ponderous **2 = considerable**, abundant, copious, excessive, large, profuse

heckle *v* **= jeer**, boo, disrupt, interrupt, shout down, taunt

hectic *adj* **= frantic**, animated, chaotic, feverish, frenetic, heated, turbulent

hedge *n* **1 = barrier**, boundary, screen, windbreak ◆ *v* **2 = dodge**, duck, equivocate, evade, prevaricate, sidestep, temporize **3 = insure**, cover, guard, protect, safeguard, shield

heed *n* **1 = care**, attention, caution, mind, notice, regard, respect, thought ◆ *v* **2 = pay attention to**, bear in mind, consider, follow, listen to, note, obey, observe, take notice of

heedless *adj* **= careless**, foolhardy, inattentive, oblivious, thoughtless, unmindful

heel *n Sl* **= swine**, louse, rat, scumbag, scuzzbucket (*sl*), skunk

heel over *v* **= lean over**, keel over, list, tilt

hefty *adj* **= strong**, big, burly, hulking, massive, muscular, robust, strapping

height *n* **1 = altitude**, elevation, highness, loftiness, stature, tallness **2 = peak**, apex, crest, crown, pinnacle, summit, top, zenith **3 = culmination**, climax, limit, maximum, ultimate

heighten *v* **= intensify**, add to, amplify, enhance, improve, increase, magnify, sharpen, strengthen

heir *n* **= successor**, beneficiary, heiress (*fem*), inheritor, next in line made to rise vertically by pull of rotating blades turning horizontally. **hel'i·port** *n* airport for helicopters.

helio- *comb. form* sun, e.g. *heliograph*.

he·li·o·graph [HEE-lee-ə-graf] *n* signaling apparatus employing a mirror to reflect sun's rays.

he·li·o·ther·a·py [hee-lee-oh-THER-ə-pee] *n* therapeutic use of sunlight.

he·li·o·trope [HEE-lee-ə-trohp] *n* **1** plant with purple flowers. **2** color of the flowers. **he·li·o·trop'ic** [-TROP-ik] *adj* growing, turning toward source of light.

he·li·um [HEE-lee-əm] *n* very light, nonflammable gaseous element.

he·lix [HEE-liks] *n* spiral.

hell *n* **1** abode of the damned. **2** abode of the dead generally. **3** place or state of wickedness, or misery, or torture. **hell'ish** *adj*

Hel·len·ic [he-LEN-ik] *adj* pert. to inhabitants of Greece.

hel·lo [he-LOH] *interj* expression of greeting or surprise.

helm *n* tiller, wheel for turning ship's rudder.

hel·met [HEL-mit] *n* defensive or protective covering for head.

help *vt* **1** aid, assist. **2** support. **3** succor. **4** remedy, prevent. ◆ *n* **5** assistance or support. **help'ful** *adj* **help'ing** *n* single portion of food taken at a meal. **help'less**

[-lis] *adj* **1** useless, incompetent. **2** unaided. **3** unable to help. **help'mate, -meet** *n* **1** helpful companion. **2** husband or wife.

hel·ter-skel·ter [HEL-tər-SKEL-tər] *adv, adj, n* (in) hurry and confusion.

hem *n* **1** border of cloth, esp. one made by turning over edge and sewing it down. ◆ *vt* **hemmed, hem·ming 2** sew thus. **3** confine, shut in. **hem'stitch** *n* ornamental stitch. ◆ *vt*

hemi- *comb. form* half, e.g. *hemisphere*.

hem·i·ple·gi·a [hem-i-PLEE-jə] *n* paralysis of one side of body. **hem·i·ple'gic** *adj, n*

hem·i·sphere [HEM-i-sfeer] *n* **1** half sphere. **2** half of celestial sphere. **3** half of Earth. **hem·i·spher'i·cal** [-sfe-rə-kəl] *adj*

hem·lock [HEM-lok] *n* **1** poisonous plant. **2** poison extracted from it. **3** evergreen of pine family.

hemo-, hema- *comb. form* blood, e.g. *hemophilia*.

he·mo·glo·bin [HEE-mə-gloh-bin] *n* coloring and oxygen-bearing matter of red blood corpuscles.

he·mo·phil·i·a [hee-mə-FIL-ee-ə] *n* hereditary tendency to intensive bleeding as blood fails to clot. **he·mo·phil'i·ac** *n*

hem·or·rhage [HEM-ər-ij] *n* **1** profuse bleeding. ◆ *vi* **-rhaged, -rhag·ing 2** bleed profusely. **3** lose assets, esp. in large amounts.

hem·or·rhoids [HEM-ə-roidz] *pl n* swollen

THESAURUS

hell *n* **1** = underworld, abyss, fire and brimstone, Hades (*Greek myth*), hellfire, inferno, nether world **2** = torment, agony, anguish, misery, nightmare, ordeal, suffering, wretchedness

hellish *adj* = devilish, damnable, diabolical, fiendish, infernal

hello *interj* = welcome, good afternoon, good evening, good morning, greetings

helm *n* **1** = tiller, rudder, wheel **2** at the helm = in charge, at the wheel, in command, in control, in the driving seat, in the saddle

help *v* **1** = aid, abet, assist, cooperate, lend a hand, succor, support **2** = improve, alleviate, ameliorate, ease, facilitate, mitigate, relieve **3** = refrain from, avoid, keep from, prevent, resist ◆ *n* **4** = assistance, advice, aid, cooperation, guidance, helping hand, support

helper *n* = assistant, adjutant, aide, ally, attendant, collaborator, helpmate, mate,

partner, right-hand man, second, supporter

helpful *adj* **1** = useful, advantageous, beneficial, constructive, practical, profitable, timely, win-win (*inf*) **2** = cooperative, accommodating, considerate, friendly, kind, neighborly, supportive, sympathetic

helping *n* = portion, dollop (*inf*), piece, plateful, ration, serving

helpless *adj* = weak, challenged, disabled, impotent, incapable, infirm, paralyzed, powerless

helter-skelter *adj* **1** = haphazard, confused, disordered, hit-or-miss, jumbled, muddled, random, topsy-turvy ◆ *adv* **2** = carelessly, anyhow, hastily, headlong, hurriedly, pell-mell, rashly, recklessly, wildly

hem *n* **1** = edge, border, fringe, margin, trimming ◆ *v* **2 hem in** = surround, beset, circumscribe, confine, enclose, restrict, veins in rectum (also **piles**).

hemp n **1** Indian plant. **2** its fiber used for rope, etc. **3** any of several narcotic drugs made from varieties of hemp. **hemp'en** [-pən] adj made of hemp or rope.

hen n female of domestic fowl and others. **hen'peck** vt (of a woman) harass (a man, esp. husband) by nagging.

hence [hens] adv **1** from this point. **2** for this reason. **hence·for'ward**, **hence'forth** adv from now onward.

hench·man [HENCH-mən] n **1** trusty follower. **2** unscrupulous supporter.

hen·na [HEN-ə] n **1** flowering shrub. **2** reddish dye made from it.

hen·o·the·ism [HEN-ə-thee-iz-əm] n belief in one god (of several) as special god of one's family, tribe, etc.

hen·ry [HEN-ree] n, pl **-ries** SI unit of electrical inductance.

he·pat·ic [hi-PAT-ik] adj pert. to the liver. **hep·a·ti·tis** [hep-ə-TĪ-tis] n inflammation of the liver.

hepta- comb. form seven, e.g. heptagon.

hep·ta·gon [HEP-tə-gon] n figure with seven angles. **hep·tag'o·nal** adj

her [hur] adj objective and possessive case of SHE. **hers** pron of her. **her·self'** pron emphatic form of SHE.

her·ald [HER-əld] n **1** messenger, envoy. **2** officer who makes royal proclamations, arranges ceremonies, etc. ♦ vt **3** announce. **4** proclaim approach of. **he·ral·dic** [hi-RAL-dik] adj **her'ald·ry** n study of (right to have) heraldic bearings.

herb [urb] n **1** plant with soft stem that dies down after flowering. **2** plant of which parts are used in cookery or medicine. **her·ba·ceous** [hur-BAY-shəs] adj **1** of, like herbs. **2** perennially flowering. **herb·al** [HUR-bəl] adj **1** of herbs. ♦ n **2** book on herbs. **herb'al·ist** n **1** writer on herbs. **2** collector, dealer in medicinal herbs. **herb'i·cide** [-sīd] n chemical that destroys plants. **her·biv'o·rous** [-ə-rəs] adj feeding on plants.

Her·cu·les [HUR-kyə-leez] n mythical hero noted for strength. **her·cu·le'an** [-kyə-LEE-ən] adj **1** requiring great strength, courage. **2** hard to perform.

herd [hurd] n **1** company of animals, usu. of same species, feeding or traveling together. ♦ v **2** crowd together. ♦ vt **3** tend (herd). **herds·man** [HURDZ-mən] n

here [heer] adv **1** in this place. **2** at or to this point. **here·af'ter** adv **1** in time to come. ♦ n **2** future existence after death. **here·to·fore'** [-tə-FOR] adv before.

he·red·i·ty [hə-RED-i-tee] n tendency of organism to transmit its nature to its descendants. **he·red'i·tar·y** [-ter-ee] adj **1** descending by inheritance. **2** holding office by inheritance. **3** that can be transmitted from one generation to another.

her·e·sy [HER-ə-see] n, pl **-sies** [-seez] opinion contrary to orthodox opinion or belief. **her'e·tic** n one holding opinions contrary to orthodox faith. **he·ret'i·cal** [-kəl] adj

her·it·age [HER-i-tij] n **1** what may be or is inherited. **2** anything from past, esp. owned or handed down by tradition. **her'it·a·ble** adj that can be inherited.

shut in

hence conj = **therefore**, ergo, for this reason, on that account, thus

henchman n = **attendant**, associate, bodyguard, follower, minder (sl), right-hand man, sidekick (sl), subordinate, supporter

henpecked adj = **bullied**, browbeaten, dominated, meek, subjugated, timid

herald n **1** = **messenger**, crier **2** = **forerunner**, harbinger, indication, omen, precursor, sign, signal, token ♦ v **3** = **indicate**, foretoken, portend, presage, promise, show, usher in

herd n **1** = **multitude**, collection, crowd, drove, flock, horde, mass, mob, swarm, throng ♦ v **2** = **congregate**, assemble, collect, flock, gather, huddle, muster, rally

hereafter adv **1** = **in future**, from now on, hence, henceforth, henceforward ♦ n **2** = **afterlife**, life after death, next world

hereditary adj **1** = **genetic**, inborn, inbred, inheritable, transmissible **2** = **inherited**, ancestral, traditional

heredity n = **genetics**, constitution, genetic make-up, inheritance

heresy n = **dissidence**, apostasy, heterodoxy, iconoclasm, unorthodoxy

heretic n = **dissident**, apostate, dissenter, nonconformist, renegade, revisionist

heretical adj = **unorthodox**, heterodox, iconoclastic, idolatrous, impious, revisionist

heritage n = **inheritance**, bequest, birthright, endowment, legacy, tradition

her·maph·ro·dite [hur-MAF-rə-dīt] *n* person, animal with characteristics or reproductive organs of both sexes.

her·met·ic [hur-MET-ik] *adj* sealed so as to be airtight. **her·met'i·cal·ly** *adv*

her·mit [HUR-mit] *n* one living in solitude, esp. from religious motives. **her'mit·age** [-tij] *n* this person's abode.

her·ni·a [HUR-nee-ə] *n* projection of (part of) organ through lining encasing it.

he·ro [HEER-oh] *n, pl* **-roes 1** one greatly regarded for achievements or qualities. **2** principal character in poem, play, story. **3** illustrious warrior. **4** demigod. **her·o·ine** [HER-oh-in] *n, fem.* **he·ro'ic** [hi-ROH-ik] *adj* **1** of, like hero. **2** courageous, daring. **he·ro'i·cal·ly** *adv* **he·ro'ics** *pl n* extravagant behavior. **her'o·ism** *n* **1** qualities of hero. **2** courage, boldness. **hero sandwich** large sandwich of meats, etc. on loaf of Italian bread. **hero worship 1** admiration of heroes or of great men. **2** excessive admiration of others.

her·o·in [HER-oh-in] *n* white crystalline derivative of morphine, a highly addictive narcotic.

her·on [HER-ən] *n* long-legged wading bird.

her·pes [HUR-peez] *n* any of several diseases, including shingles and cold sores.

her'ring *n* important food fish of northern hemisphere.

hertz [hurts] *n, pl* **hertz** SI unit of frequency.

hes·i·tate [HEZ-i-tayt] *vi* **-tat·ed, -tat·ing 1** hold back. **2** feel, or show indecision. **3** be reluctant. **hes'i·tan·cy** [-tən-see] *n* **hes·i·ta'tion** *n* **1** wavering. **2** doubt. **3** stammering. **hes'i·tant** *adj* undecided,

pausing.

hetero- *comb. form* other or different, e.g. *heterosexual.*

het·er·o·dox [HET-ər-ə-doks] *adj* not orthodox. **het'er·o·dox·y** *n, pl* **-dox·ies**

het·er·o·ge·ne·ous [het-ər-ə-JEE-nee-əs] *adj* composed of diverse elements. **het·er·o·ge·ne'i·ty** [-jə-NEE-i-tee] *n*

het·er·o·sex·u·al [het-ər-ə-SEK-shoo-əl] *n* person sexually attracted to members of the opposite sex.

heu·ris·tic [hyuu-RIS-tik] *adj* serving to find out or to stimulate investigation.

hew [hyoo] *v* hewed *or* hewn, hew·ing chop, cut with axe. **hew'er** *n*

hex [heks] *n* **1** magic spell. ♦ *v* **2** bewitch.

hex-, hexa- *comb. form* six, e.g. *hexagon.*

hex·a·gon [HEK-sə-gon] *n* figure with six angles. **hex·ag'o·nal** *adj*

hex·am·e·ter [hek-SAM-i-tər] *n* line of verse of six feet.

hey·day [HAY-day] *n* bloom, prime.

Hf *Chem.* hafnium.

Hg *Chem.* mercury.

hi·a·tus [hī-AY-təs] *n, pl* **-tus·es** break or gap where something is missing.

hi·ber·nate [HĪ-bər-nayt] *vi* **-nat·ed, -nat·ing** pass the winter, esp. in a torpid state. **hi·ber·na'tion** *n*

hi·bis·cus [hī-BIS-kəs] *n* flowering (sub)tropical shrub.

hic·cup [HIK-up] *n* **1** spasm of the breathing organs with an abrupt cough-like sound. ♦ *vi* **-cupped, -cup·ping 2** have this.

hick [hik] *adj inf* **1** rustic. **2** unsophisticated. ♦ *n* **3** person, place like this.

hick·o·ry [HIK-ə-ree] *n, pl* **-o·ries 1** N Amer. nut-bearing tree. **2** its tough wood.

hermit *n* = **recluse**, anchorite, eremite, loner (*inf*), monk

hero *n* **1** = **idol**, champion, conqueror, star, superstar, victor **2** = **leading man**, protagonist

heroic *adj* = **courageous**, brave, daring, fearless, gallant, intrepid, lion-hearted, valiant

heroine *n* = **leading lady**, diva, prima donna, protagonist

heroism *n* = **bravery**, courage, courageousness, fearlessness, gallantry, intrepidity, valor

hesitant *adj* = **uncertain**, diffident, doubtful, half-hearted, halting, irresolute,

reluctant, unsure, vacillating, wavering

hesitate *v* **1** = **delay**, dither, doubt, hum and haw, pause, vacillate, wait **2** = **be reluctant**, balk, be unwilling, demur, hang back, scruple, shrink from, think twice

hesitation *n* **1** = **indecision**, delay, doubt, hesitancy, irresolution, uncertainty, vacillation **2** = **reluctance**, misgiving(s), qualm(s), scruple(s), unwillingness

hew *v* **1** = **cut**, ax, chop, hack, lop, split **2** = **carve**, fashion, form, make, model, sculpt, sculpture, shape, smooth

heyday *n* = **prime**, bloom, pink, prime of life, salad days

hiatus *n* = **pause**, break, discontinuity, gap,

hide¹ [hīd] *v* **hid, hid·den** *or* **hid, hid·ing ◆** *vt* **1** put, keep out of sight. **2** conceal, keep secret. **◆** *vi* **3** conceal oneself. **hide'out** *n* hiding place.

hide² *n* skin of animal. **hid'ing** *n sl* thrashing. **hide'bound** *adj* **1** restricted, esp. by petty rules, etc. **2** narrow-minded.

hid·e·ous [HID-ee-əs] *adj* repulsive, revolting.

hi·er·ar·chy [HĪ-ə-rahr-kee] *n, pl* **-chies** system of persons or things arranged in graded order. **hi·er·ar'chi·cal** *adj*

hi·er·o·glyph·ic [hī-ər-ə-GLIF-ik] *adj* **1** of a system of picture writing, as used in ancient Egypt. **◆** *n* **2** symbol representing object, concept or sound. **3** symbol, picture, difficult to decipher. **hi'er·o·glyph** *n*

hi-fi [HĪ-FĪ] *adj* **1** short for HIGH-FIDELITY. **◆** *n* **2** high-fidelity equipment.

high [hī] *adj* **-er, -est 1** tall, lofty. **2** far up. **3** of roads, main. **4** of meat, tainted. **5** of sound, acute in pitch. **6** expensive. **7** of great importance, quality, or rank. **8** *inf* in state of euphoria, esp. induced by alcohol or drugs. **◆** *adv* **9** far up. **10** strongly, to a great extent. **11** at, to a high pitch. **12** at a high rate. **high'ly** *adv* **high'ness** *n* **1** quality of being high. **2** (H-) **3** title of prince and princess. **high'brow** *n* **1** intellectual, esp. intellectual snob. **◆** *adj* **2** intellectual. **3** difficult. **4** serious. **high'-fi·del'i·ty** *adj* of high-quality sound-reproducing equipment. **high-flown** *adj* extravagant, bombastic. **high'-hand'ed** *adj* domineering, dogmatic. **high'land** [-lənd] *n* relatively high ground. **High'land** *adj* of, from the highlands of Scotland. **high'light** *n* **1** lightest or brightest area in painting, photograph, etc. **2** outstanding feature. **◆** *vt* **3** bring into prominence. **high'-rise** *adj, n* (of) building that has many stories and elevators. **high'-sound'ing** *adj* pompous, imposing. **high-strung** *adj* excitable, nervous.

high-tech *adj* same as HI-TECH. **high time** latest possible time. **high'way** *n* main road. **highway robbery** *inf* exorbitant fee or charge. **high'way·man** [-mən] *n* (formerly) robber on road, esp. mounted.

hi·jack [HĪ-jak] *vt* **1** divert or wrongfully take command of a vehicle (esp. aircraft) or its contents or passengers. **2** rob. **hi'jack·er** *n*

THESAURUS

interruption, interval, respite, space
hidden *adj* = **concealed**, clandestine, covert, latent, secret, under wraps, unseen, veiled
hide¹ *v* **1** = **conceal**, secrete, stash (*inf*) **2** = **go into hiding**, go to ground, go underground, hole up, lie low, take cover **3** = **disguise**, camouflage, cloak, conceal, cover, mask, obscure, shroud, veil **4** = **suppress**, draw a veil over, hush up, keep dark, keep secret, keep under one's hat, withhold
hide² *n* = **skin**, pelt
hidebound *adj* = **conventional**, narrow-minded, rigid, set in one's ways, strait-laced, ultraconservative
hideous *adj* = **ugly**, ghastly, grim, grisly, grotesque, gruesome, monstrous, repulsive, revolting, scuzzy (*sl*), unsightly
hideout *n* = **hideaway**, den, hiding place, lair, shelter
hierarchy *n* = **grading**, pecking order, ranking
high *adj* **1** = **tall**, elevated, lofty, soaring, steep, towering **2** = **extreme**, excessive, extraordinary, great, intensified, sharp, strong **3** = **important**, arch, chief, eminent, exalted, powerful, superior **4** *Inf* = **intoxicated**, stoned (*sl*), tripping (*inf*) **5** = **high-pitched**, acute, penetrating, piercing, piping, sharp, shrill, strident **◆** *adv* **6** = **aloft**, at great height, far up, way up
highbrow *n* **1** = **intellectual**, aesthete, egghead (*inf*), scholar **◆** *adj* **2** = **intellectual**, bookish, cultivated, cultured, sophisticated
high-flown *adj* = **extravagant**, elaborate, exaggerated, florid, grandiose, inflated, lofty, overblown, pretentious
high-handed *adj* = **dictatorial**, despotic, domineering, imperious, oppressive, overbearing, tyrannical, willful
highlight *n* **1** = **feature**, climax, focal point, focus, high point, high spot, peak **◆** *v* **2** = **emphasize**, accent, accentuate, bring to the fore, show up, spotlight, stress, underline
highly *adv* = **extremely**, exceptionally, greatly, immensely, tremendously, vastly, very, very much
highly strung *adj* = **nervous**, edgy, excitable, neurotic, sensitive, stressed, temperamental, tense, twitchy (*inf*), wired (*sl*)

hike [hīk] v **hiked, hik·ing** ◆ vi **1** walk a long way (for pleasure) in country. ◆ vt **2** pull (up), hitch. ◆ n **hik'er** n

hi·lar·i·ty [hi-LAR-i-tee] n cheerfulness, gaiety. **hi·lar'i·ous** adj

hill n **1** natural elevation, small mountain. **2** mound. **hill'ock** [-ək] n little hill. **hill'y** adj **hill·i·er, hill·i·est hill'bil·ly** n, pl **-lies** offens unsophisticated country person.

hilt n handle of sword, etc. **up to the hilt** completely.

him pron objective case of pronoun HE. **him·self'** pron emphatic form of HE.

hind¹ [hīnd] n female of deer.

hind² adj at the back, posterior (also **hind·er**) [HIN-dər]

hin·der [HIN-dər] vt obstruct, impede, delay. **hin'drance** [-drəns] n

Hin·di [HIN-dee] n language of N central India. **Hin'du** [-doo] n person who adheres to Hinduism. **Hin'du·ism** the dominant religion of India.

hinge [hinj] n **1** movable joint, as that on which door hangs. ◆ v **hinged, hing·ing** ◆ vt **2** attach with, or as with, hinge. ◆ vi **3** turn, depend on.

hint n **1** slight indication or suggestion. ◆ v **2** give hint of.

hin·ter·land [HIN-tər-land] n district lying behind coast, or near city, port, etc.

hip n **1** either side of body below waist and above thigh. **2** angle formed where

sloping sides of roof meet. **3** fruit of rose, esp. wild.

hip-hop [HIP-hop] n pop-culture movement involving rap music, graffiti, and break dancing.

hip·pie [HIP-ee] n (formerly) (young) person whose behavior, dress, etc. implies rejection of conventional values.

hip·po·pot·a·mus [hip-ə-POT-ə-məs] n, pl **-mus·es** or **-mi** [-mī] large Afr. animal living in and near rivers.

hire [hīr] vt **hired, hir·ing 1** obtain temporary use of by payment. **2** engage for wage. ◆ n **3** hiring or being hired. **4** payment for use of thing. **hire'ling** n one who works for wages.

hir·sute [HUR-soot] adj hairy.

his [hiz] pron, adj belonging to him.

His·pan·ic [hi-SPAN-ik] adj **1** relating to Spain or to Spanish-speaking Central and S. America. ◆ n **2** Spanish-speaking person. **3** U.S. resident of Hispanic descent.

his'pid adj **1** rough with bristles or minute spines. **2** bristly, shaggy.

hiss vi **1** make sharp sound of letter S, esp. in disapproval. ◆ vt **2** express disapproval, deride thus. ◆ n

his·ta·mine [HIS-tə-meen] n substance released by body tissues, sometimes creating allergic reactions.

his·tol·o·gy [hi-STOL-ə-jee] n science that treats of minute structure of organic

hijack v = **seize**, commandeer, expropriate, take over

hike n **1** = **walk**, march, ramble, tramp, trek ◆ v **2** = **walk**, back-pack, ramble, tramp **3 hike up** = **raise**, hitch up, jack up, lift, pull up

hilarious adj = **funny**, amusing, comical, entertaining, humorous, rollicking, side-splitting, uproarious

hilarity n = **laughter**, amusement, exhilaration, glee, high spirits, jollity, merriment, mirth

hill n = **mount**, fell, height, hillock, hilltop, knoll, mound, tor

hillock n = **mound**, hummock, knoll

hilly adj = **mountainous**, rolling, undulating

hilt n = **handle**, grip, haft, handgrip

hinder v = **obstruct**, block, check, delay, encumber, frustrate, hamper, handicap, hold up or back, impede, interrupt, stop

hindmost adj = **last**, final, furthest, furthest behind, rearmost, trailing

hindrance n = **obstacle**, barrier, deterrent, difficulty, drawback, handicap, hitch, impediment, obstruction, restriction, snag, stumbling block

hinge v = **depend**, be contingent, hang, pivot, rest, revolve around, turn

hint n **1** = **indication**, allusion, clue, implication, innuendo, insinuation, intimation, suggestion **2** = **advice**, help, pointer, suggestion, tip **3** = **trace**, dash, suggestion, suspicion, tinge, touch, undertone ◆ v **4** = **suggest**, imply, indicate, insinuate, intimate

hippie n = **bohemian**, beatnik, dropout

hire v **1** = **employ**, appoint, commission, engage, sign up, take on **2** = **rent**, charter, engage, lease, let ◆ n **3** = **rental**, charge, cost, fee, price, rent

hiss n **1** = **sibilation**, buzz, hissing **2** = **catcall**, boo, jeer ◆ v **3** = **whistle**, sibilate, wheeze, whirr, whiz **4** = **jeer**, boo, deride, tissues.

his·to·ry [HIS-tə-ree] *n, pl* **-ries 1** record of past events. **2** study of these. **3** past events. **4** train of events, public or private. **5** course of life or existence. **6** systematic account of phenomena. **his·to'ri·an** *n* writer of history. **his·tor'ic** *adj* noted in history. **his·tor'i·cal** *adj* **1** of, based on, history. **2** belonging to past. **his·tor·ic'i·ty** [-tə-RIS-i-tee] *n* historical authenticity. **his·to·ri·og'ra·pher** *n* **1** official historian. **2** one who studies historical method. **his·to·ri·og'ra·phy** *n* methods of historical research.

his·tri·on·ic [his-tree-ON-ik] *adj* excessively theatrical, insincere, artificial in manner. **his·tri·on'ics** *n* behavior like this.

hit *v* **hit, hit·ting** ◆ *vt* **1** strike with blow or missile. **2** affect injuriously. **3** find. ◆ *vi* **4** strike. **5** light (upon). ◆ *n* **6** blow. **7** success. **8** *Computers.* single visit to a website or single result of a search. **hit'ter** *n* hit man *sl* hired assassin. **hit it off** *inf* get along with (person). **hit or miss** haphazard(ly). **hit the hay** *inf* go to bed. **hit the road** *inf* **1** proceed on journey. **2** depart.

hitch [hich] *vt* **1** fasten with loop, etc. **2** raise, move with jerk. ◆ *vi* **3** be caught or fastened. ◆ *n* **4** difficulty. **5** knot, fastening. **6** jerk. **hitch'hike** *vi* **-hiked, -hik·ing** travel by begging free rides.

hi-tech *n* **1** technology requiring sophisticated scientific equipment and engineering techniques. **2** interior design using features of industrial equipment. ◆ *adj*

hith·er [HITH-ər] *adv* to or toward this place. **hith'er·to** *adv* up to now or to this time.

hive [hīv] *n* **1** structure in which bees live or are housed. **2** *fig* place swarming with busy occupants. ◆ *v* **hived, hiv·ing 3** gather, place bees, in hive.

hives [hīvz] *pl n* eruptive skin disease.

Ho *Chem.* holmium.

hoard [hord] *n* **1** stock, store, esp. hidden away. ◆ *vt* **2** amass and hide away. **3** store.

hoarse [hors] *adj* **hoars·er, hoars·est** rough, harsh sounding, husky.

hoar·y [HOR-ee] *adj* **hoar·i·er, hoar·i·est 1** gray with age. **2** grayish-white. **3** of great antiquity. **4** venerable. **hoar'frost** *n* frozen dew.

hoax [hohks] *n* **1** practical joke. **2** deceptive trick. ◆ *vt* **3** play trick on. **4** deceive. **hoax'er** *n*

hob *n* **1** projection or shelf at side or back of fireplace, used for keeping food warm. **2** tool for cutting gear teeth, etc. **hob'nail** [-nayl] *n* large-headed nail for boot soles.

hoot, mock

historic *adj* = **significant**, epoch-making, extraordinary, famous, ground-breaking, momentous, notable, outstanding, remarkable

historical *adj* = **factual**, actual, attested, authentic, documented, real

history *n* **1** = **chronicle**, account, annals, narrative, recital, record, story **2** = **the past**, antiquity, olden days, yesterday, yesteryear

hit *v* **1** = **strike**, bang, beat, clout (*inf*), knock, slap, smack, thump, wallop (*inf*), whack **2** = **collide with**, bang into, bump, clash with, crash against, run into, smash into **3** = **reach**, accomplish, achieve, arrive at, attain, gain **4** = **affect**, damage, devastate, impact on, influence, leave a mark on, overwhelm, touch **5 hit it off** *Inf* = **get on (well)**, be on good terms, click (*sl*), get on like a house on fire (*inf*) ◆ *n* **6** = **stroke**, belt (*inf*), blow, clout (*inf*), knock, rap, slap, smack, wallop (*inf*) **7** = **success**, sensation, smash (*inf*), triumph, winner

hit-and-miss *adj* = **haphazard**, aimless, casual, disorganized, indiscriminate, random, undirected, uneven

hitch *n* **1** = **problem**, catch, difficulty, drawback, hindrance, hold-up, impediment, obstacle, snag ◆ *v* **2** = **fasten**, attach, connect, couple, harness, join, tether, tie **3** *Inf* = **hitchhike**, thumb a lift **4 hitch up** = **pull up**, jerk, tug, yank

hitherto *adv* = **previously**, heretofore, so far, thus far, until now

hit on *v* = **think up**, arrive at, discover, invent, light upon, strike upon, stumble on

hoard *n* **1** = **store**, accumulation, cache, fund, pile, reserve, stockpile, supply, treasure-trove ◆ *v* **2** = **save**, accumulate, amass, collect, gather, lay up, put by, stash away (*inf*), stockpile, store

hoarse *adj* = **raucous**, croaky, grating, gravelly, gruff, guttural, husky, rasping, rough, throaty

hoax *n* **1** = **trick**, con (*inf*), deception, fraud, practical joke, prank, spoof (*inf*), swindle ◆ *v* **2** = **deceive**, con (*sl*), dupe, fool,

hob·ble [HOB-əl] v **-bled, -bling** ◆ vi **1** walk lamely. ◆ vt **2** tie legs together (of horse, etc.). **3** impede, hamper. ◆ n **4** straps or ropes put on an animal's legs to prevent it from straying. **5** limping gait.

hob·by [HOB-ee] n, pl **-bies** favorite occupation as pastime. **hob'by·horse** n **1** toy horse. **2** favorite topic, preoccupation.

hob'gob·lin n mischievous fairy.

hob'nob vi **-nobbed, -nob·bing** associate, be familiar (with).

ho·bo [HOH-boh] n, pl **-boes** shiftless, wandering person.

hock [hok] n **1** backward-pointing joint on leg of horse, etc., corresponding to human ankle. ◆ vt **2** disable by cutting tendons of hock, hamstring.

hock·ey [HOK-ee] n **1** team game played on a field with ball and curved sticks. **2** ice hockey.

ho·cus-po·cus [HOH-kəs-POH-kəs] n **1** trickery. **2** mystifying jargon.

hod n small trough on a pole for carrying mortar, bricks, etc.

hoe [hoh] n **1** tool for weeding, breaking ground, etc. ◆ vt **hoed, hoe·ing**

hog [hawg] n **1** pig, esp. castrated male for fattening. **2** greedy, dirty person. ◆ vt **hogged, hog·ging** inf **3** eat, use (something) selfishly. **hogs·head** [HAWGZ-hed] n **1** large cask. **2** liquid

measure of 63 to 140 gallons (238 to 530 liters). **hog'tie** vt **-tied, -ty·ing 1** hobble. **2** hamper. **hog'wash** n **1** nonsense. **2** pig food.

ho·gan [HOH-gən] n Navajo Indian dwelling of earth, branches, etc.

hoi pol·loi [HOI pə-LOI] n **1** the common mass of people. **2** the masses.

hoist vt raise aloft, raise with tackle, etc.

ho·key·po·key [HO-kee-PO-kee] n kind of playful dance or its music.

hold[1] [hohld] v **held, hold·ing** ◆ vt **1** keep fast, grasp. **2** support in or with hands, etc. **3** maintain in position. **4** have capacity for. **5** own, occupy. **6** carry on. **7** detain. **8** celebrate. **9** keep back. **10** believe. ◆ vi **11** cling. **12** not to give away. **13** abide (by). **14** keep (to). **15** last, proceed, be in force. **16** occur. ◆ n **17** grasp. **18** influence. **hold'ing** n (oft pl) property, as land or stocks and bonds. **hold'up** n **1** armed robbery. **2** delay.

hold[2] n space in ship or aircraft for cargo.

hole [hohl] n **1** hollow place, cavity. **2** perforation. **3** opening. **4** inf unattractive place. **5** inf difficult situation. ◆ v **holed, hol·ing 6** make holes in. **7** go into a hole. **8** drive into a hole.

hol'i·day n day or other period of rest from work, etc., esp. spent away from home.

hol·low [HOL-oh] adj **-er, -est 1** having a

hoodwink, swindle, trick

hobby n = **pastime**, diversion, (leisure) activity, leisure pursuit, relaxation

hobnob v = **socialize**, associate, consort, fraternize, hang about, hang out (inf), keep company, mingle, mix

hoist v **1** = **raise**, elevate, erect, heave, lift ◆ n **2** = **lift**, crane, elevator, winch

hold v **1** = **own**, have, keep, maintain, occupy, possess, retain **2** = **grasp**, clasp, cling, clutch, cradle, embrace, enfold, grip **3** = **restrain**, confine, detain, impound, imprison **4** = **consider**, assume, believe, deem, judge, presume, reckon, regard, think **5** = **convene**, call, conduct, preside over, run **6** = **accommodate**, contain, have a capacity for, seat, take ◆ n **7** = **grip**, clasp, grasp **8** = **foothold**, footing, support **9** = **control**, influence, mastery

holder n **1** = **owner**, bearer, keeper, possessor, proprietor **2** = **case**, container, cover

hold forth v = **speak**, declaim, discourse,

go on, lecture, preach, spiel (inf), spout (inf)

hold-up n **1** = **delay**, bottleneck, hitch, setback, snag, stoppage, traffic jam, wait **2** = **robbery**, mugging (inf), stick-up (sl), theft

hold up v **1** = **delay**, detain, hinder, retard, set back, slow down, stop **2** = **support**, prop, shore up, sustain **3** = **rob**, mug (inf), waylay

hold with v = **approve of**, agree to or with, be in favor of, countenance, subscribe to, support

hole n **1** = **opening**, aperture, breach, crack, fissure, gap, orifice, perforation, puncture, tear, vent **2** = **cavity**, cave, cavern, chamber, hollow, pit **3** = **burrow**, den, earth, lair, shelter **4** inf = **hovel**, dive (sl), dump (inf), slum

holiday n **1** = **vacation**, break, leave, recess, time off **2** = **festival**, celebration, feast, fête, gala

holiness n = **divinity**, godliness, piety,

cavity, not solid. **2** empty. **3** false. **4** insincere. **5** not full-toned. ◆ *n* **6** cavity, hole, valley. ◆ *vt* **7** make hollow, make hole in. **8** excavate.

hol•ly [HOL-ee] *n, pl* **-lies** [-leez] evergreen shrub usu. with prickly leaves and red berries.

hol•o•caust [HOL-ə-kawst] *n* **1** great destruction of life, esp. by fire. **2** (H-) **3** mass slaughter of Jews in Nazi concentration camps during World War II.

hol'o•gram [HOL-ə-gram] *n a* three-dimensional photographic image.

hol•o•graph [HOL-ə-graf] *n* document wholly written by the signer.

ho•log•ra•phy [hə-LOG-rə-fee] *n* science of using lasers to produce a photographic record that can reproduce a three-dimensional image.

hol•ster [HOHL-stər] *n* case for pistol, hung from belt, etc.

ho•ly [HOH-lee] *adj* **-li•er, -li•est 1** belonging, devoted to God. **2** free from sin. **3** divine. **4** consecrated. **ho'li•ness** *n* **1** sanctity. **2** (H-) **3** Pope's title. **holy day** day of religious festival. **Holy Communion** service of the Eucharist. **Holy Week** that before Easter Sunday.

hom•age [HOM-ij] *n* **1** tribute, respect, reverence. **2** formal acknowledgment of allegiance.

home [hohm] *n* **1** dwelling place. **2** residence. **3** native place. **4** institution for the elderly, infirm, etc. ◆ *adj* **5** of, connected with, home. **6** native. ◆ *adv* **7** to, at one's home. **8** to the point. ◆ *v* **homed, hom•ing 9** direct or be directed onto a point or target. **home'boy** *n sl* close friend. **home fries** boiled potatoes, sliced and fried in butter, etc. **home'less** *adj* **home'ly** *adj* **-li•er, -li•est 1** unpretentious. **2** warm and domesticated. **3** plain. **home'ward** [-wərd] *adj, adv* **home'wards** *adv* **home-brew** *n* alcoholic drink made at home, esp. beer. **home'sick** *adj* depressed by absence from home. **home'spun** *adj* **1** domestic. **2** simple. ◆ *n* **3** cloth made of homespun yarn. **home'stead** [-sted] *n* house with outbuildings, esp. on farm. **home'stead•er** *n* **home'work** *n* school work done usu. at home. **bring home to** impress deeply upon. **home free** sure of success. **home page** *n Internet*. introductory information about a website with links to the information or services provided.

ho•me•op•a•thy [hoh-mee-OP-ə-thee] *n* treatment of disease by small doses of what would produce symptoms in healthy person. **ho•me•o•path'ic** *adj*

————— THESAURUS —————

purity, righteousness, sacredness, saintliness, sanctity, spirituality

hollow *adj* **1 = empty**, unfilled, vacant, void **2 = deep**, dull, low, muted, reverberant **3 = worthless**, fruitless, futile, meaningless, pointless, useless, vain ◆ *n* **4 = cavity**, basin, bowl, crater, depression, hole, pit, trough **5 = valley**, dale, dell, dingle, glen ◆ *v* **6 = scoop**, dig, excavate, gouge

holocaust *n* **= genocide**, annihilation, conflagration, destruction, devastation, massacre

holy *adj* **1 = devout**, god-fearing, godly, pious, pure, religious, righteous, saintly, virtuous **2 = sacred**, blessed, consecrated, hallowed, sacrosanct, sanctified, venerable

homage *n* **= respect**, adoration, adulation, deference, devotion, honor, reverence, worship

home *n* **1 = house**, abode, domicile, dwelling, habitation, pad (*sl, dated*), residence **2 = birthplace**, home town **3 at home: a = in**, available, present **b = at**

ease, comfortable, familiar, relaxed **4 bring home to = make clear**, drive home, emphasize, impress upon, press home ◆ *adj* **5 = domestic**, familiar, internal, local, native

homeboy *or* **home girl** *n Sl* **= friend**, buddy (*inf*), chum (*inf*), comrade, crony, pal (*inf*)

homeland *n* **= native land**, country of origin, fatherland, mother country, motherland

homeless *adj* **1 = destitute**, displaced, dispossessed, down-and-out, down on one's luck (*inf*) ◆ *n* **2 the homeless = vagrants**, squatters

homely *adj U.S.* **= dowdy**, dumpy (*inf*), frowzy, frumpy, ugly, unattractive, unfashionable

homespun *adj* **= unsophisticated**, coarse, dumpy (*inf*), homely (*U.S.*), home-made, plain, rough

homey *adj* **= comfortable**, cozy, friendly, homespun, modest, ordinary, plain, simple, welcoming

hom·i·cide [HOM-ə-sīd] *n* **1** killing of human being. **2** killer. **hom·i·cid'al** *adj*

hom·i·ly [HOM-ə-lee] *n, pl* **-lies** [-leez] **1** sermon. **2** religious discourse. **hom·i·let'ic** *adj* of sermons. **hom·i·let'ics** *n* art of preaching.

Ho·mo [HOH-moh] *n* genus to which modern man belongs.

homo- *comb. form* same, like, e.g. *homophone; homosexual.*

ho·mo·ge·ne·ous [hoh-mə-JEE-nee-əs] *adj* **1** formed of uniform parts. **2** similar, uniform. **3** of the same nature. **ho·mo·ge·ne'i·ty** *n* **ho·mog·e·nize** [hə-MOJ-ə-nīz] *vt* **-nized, -niz·ing 1** break up fat globules in milk and cream to distribute them evenly. **2** make uniform or similar.

ho·mol·o·gous [hə-MOL-ə-gəs] *adj* having the same relation, relative position, etc. **ho·mo·logue** [HOH-mə-lawg] *n* homologous thing.

hom·o·nym [HOM-ə-nim] *n* word of same form as another, but of different sense.

ho·mo·sex·u·al [hoh-mə-SEK-shoo-əl] *n* person sexually attracted to members of the same sex. ♦ *adj* **ho·mo·sex·u·al'i·ty** *n* **ho·mo·pho'bi·a** [-PHOH-bee-ə] *n* hate or fear of homosexuals and homosexuality.

hone [hohn] *n* **1** whetstone for sharpening razors, etc. ♦ *vt* **honed, hon·ing 2** sharpen on one.

hon·est [ON-ist] *adj* **1** not cheating, lying, stealing, etc. **2** genuine. **3** without pretension. **hon'est·y** *n* quality of being honest.

hon·ey [HUN-ee] *n, pl* **-eys** sweet fluid made by bees. **hon'ey·comb** [-kohm] *n* **1** wax structure in hexagonal cells in which bees place honey, eggs, etc. ♦ *vt* **2** fill with cells or perforations. **hon'ey·dew** [-doo] *n* **1** sweet sticky substance found on plants. **2** type of sweet melon. **hon'ey·moon** *n* **1** holiday taken by newly wedded couple. **2** any new relationship with initial period of harmony. ♦ *vi* **3** spend one's honeymoon.

honk [hongk] *n* **1** call of goose. **2** any sound like this, esp. sound of automobile horn. ♦ *vi* **3** make this sound. ♦ *vt* **4** cause (automobile horn) to sound.

hon·or [ON-ər] *n* **1** personal integrity. **2** renown. **3** reputation. **4** sense of what is right or due. **5** chastity. **6** high rank or position. **7** source, cause of honor. **8** pleasure, privilege. ♦ *pl* **9** mark of respect. **10** distinction in examination. ♦ *vt* **11** respect highly. **12** confer honor on. **13** accept or pay (bill, etc.) when due. **hon'or·a·ble** *adj* **hon·o·rar'i·um** *n, pl* **-rar·i·a** a fee. **hon'or·ar·y** *adj* **1** conferred for the sake of honor only. **2** holding position without pay or usual requirements. **3** giving services without pay. **hon·or·if'ic** *adj* **1** conferring, indicating honor. ♦ *n* **2** in certain languages, form used to show respect, esp. in direct address.

homicidal *adj* = **murderous**, deadly, lethal, maniacal, mortal

homicide *n* **1** = **murder**, bloodshed, killing, manslaughter, slaying **2** = **murderer**, killer, slayer

homily *n* = **sermon**, address, discourse, lecture, preaching

homogeneity *n* = **uniformity**, consistency, correspondence, sameness, similarity

homogeneous *adj* = **uniform**, akin, alike, analogous, comparable, consistent, identical, similar, unvarying

hone *v* = **sharpen**, edge, file, grind, point, polish, whet

honest *adj* **1** = **trustworthy**, ethical, honorable, law-abiding, reputable, scrupulous, truthful, upright, virtuous **2** = **open**, candid, direct, forthright, frank, plain, sincere, upfront (*inf*)

honestly *adv* **1** = **ethically**, by fair means, cleanly, honorably, lawfully, legally **2** = **frankly**, candidly, in all sincerity, plainly, straight (out), to one's face, truthfully

honesty *n* **1** = **integrity**, honor, incorruptibility, morality, probity, rectitude, scrupulousness, trustworthiness, truthfulness, uprightness, virtue **2** = **frankness**, bluntness, candor, openness, outspokenness, sincerity, straightforwardness

honor *n* **1** = **glory**, credit, dignity, distinction, fame, kudos, prestige, renown, reputation **2** = **tribute**, accolade, commendation, homage, praise, recognition **3** = **fairness**, decency, goodness, honesty, integrity, morality, probity, rectitude **4** = **privilege**, compliment, credit, pleasure ♦ *v* **5** = **respect**, adore, appreciate, esteem, prize, value **6** = **fulfill**, be true to, carry out, discharge, keep, live up to, observe **7** =

hood[1] [huud] n 1 covering for head and neck, often part of cloak or gown. 2 hoodlike thing, as covering of engine compartment of automobile, etc. **hood'ed** adj covered with or shaped like a hood. **hood'wink** vt deceive.

hood[2] n sl hoodlum.

hood·lum [HUUD-ləm] n 1 gangster. 2 street ruffian.

hoo'doo n cause of bad luck.

hoof [huuf] n, pl hoofs or hooves horny casing of foot of horse, etc. **on the hoof** [of livestock] alive]

hoo-ha [HOO-hah] n 1 uproar. ◆ interj 2 exclamation expressing excitement or surprise.

hook [huuk] n 1 bent piece of metal, etc., for catching hold, hanging up, etc. 2 something resembling hook in shape or function. 3 curved cutting tool. 4 enticement. 5 Boxing blow delivered with elbow bent. ◆ vt 6 grasp, catch, hold, as with hook. 7 fasten with hook. 8 Golf drive (ball) widely to the left (of right-handed golfer, and vice versa). **hooked** adj 1 shaped like hook. 2 caught. 3 inf addicted to. 4 sl married. **hook'er** n sl prostitute. **hook'up** n linking of radio, television stations. **hook'worm** [-wurm] n parasitic worm infesting humans and animals.

hook·ah [HUUK-ə] n oriental pipe in which smoke is drawn through cooling water and long tube.

hoo·li·gan [HOO-li-gən] n 1 violent, irresponsible (young) person. 2 ruffian. **hoo'li·gan·ism** n

hoop n 1 rigid circular band of metal, wood, etc. such a band used for binding barrel, etc., for use as a toy, or for jumping through as in circus acts. ◆ vt 2 bind with hoops. 3 encircle. **put through the hoops** inf subject to ordeal or test.

hoop·la [HOOP-lah] n inf 1 excitement. 2 hullabaloo.

hoot n 1 owl's cry or similar sound. 2 cry of disapproval or derision. 3 sl funny person or thing. ◆ vi 4 utter hoot (esp. in derision). ◆ vt 5 assail (someone) with derisive cries. 6 drive (someone) away by hooting.

hop[1] vi hopped, hop·ping 1 spring on one foot. 2 inf move quickly. ◆ n 3 leap, skip. 4 one stage of journey. **hop'scotch** [-skoch] n children's game of hopping in pattern drawn on ground.

hop[2] n 1 climbing plant with bitter cones used to flavor beer, etc. ◆ pl 2 the cones.

hope [hohp] n 1 expectation of something desired. 2 thing that gives, or object of, this feeling. ◆ v hoped, hop·ing 3 feel hope (for). **hope'ful** adj **hope'less** adj young hopeful promising boy or girl.

hop·per [HOP-ər] n 1 one who hops. 2 device for feeding material into mill or machine or grain into truck, etc. **hopper car** railroad freight car, usu. open at top and containing one or more hoppers, for transport and discharge of grain, etc.

horde [hord] n large crowd (esp. moving

acclaim, commemorate, commend, decorate, praise 8 = **accept**, acknowledge, pass, pay, take

honorable adj = **respected**, creditable, estimable, reputable, respectable, virtuous

honorary adj = **nominal**, complimentary, in name or title only, titular, unofficial, unpaid

hoodwink v = **deceive**, con (inf), delude, dupe, fool, mislead, swindle, trick

hook n 1 = **fastener**, catch, clasp, link, peg ◆ v 2 = **fasten**, clasp, fix, secure 3 = **catch**, ensnare, entrap, snare, trap

hooked adj 1 = **bent**, aquiline, curved, hook-shaped 2 = **addicted**, devoted, enamored, obsessed, taken, turned on (sl)

hooligan n = **delinquent**, lager lout, ruffian, vandal

hooliganism n = **delinquency**, disorder, loutishness, rowdiness, vandalism, violence

hoop n = **ring**, band, circlet, girdle, loop, wheel

hoot n 1 = **cry**, call, toot 2 = **catcall**, boo, hiss, jeer ◆ v 3 = **jeer**, boo, hiss, howl down

hop v 1 = **jump**, bound, caper, leap, skip, spring, trip, vault ◆ n 2 = **jump**, bounce, bound, leap, skip, spring, step, vault

hope v 1 = **desire**, aspire, cross one's fingers, long, look forward to, set one's heart on ◆ n 2 = **desire**, ambition, assumption, dream, expectation, longing

hopeful adj 1 = **optimistic**, buoyant, confident, expectant, looking forward to, sanguine 2 = **promising**, auspicious, bright, encouraging, heartening, reassuring, rosy

hopefully adv = **optimistically**, confidently, expectantly

hopeless adj = **pointless**, futile, impossible, no-win, unattainable, useless, together).

ho·ri·zon [hə-RĪ-zən] *n* **1** boundary of part of Earth seen from any given point. **2** lines where Earth and sky seem to meet. **3** boundary of mental outlook. **hor·i·zon·tal** [hor-ə-ZON-tl] *adj* parallel with horizon, level.

hor·mone [HOR-mohn] *n* **1** substance secreted by certain glands that stimulates organs of the body. **2** synthetic substance with same effect.

horn *n* **1** hard projection on heads of certain animals, e.g. cattle. **2** substance of it. **3** various things made of, or resembling it. **4** *Music* wind instrument orig. made of a horn. **5** device (esp. in car) emitting sound as alarm, warning, etc. **horned** *adj* having horns. **horn'y** *adj* **horn·i·er, horn·i·est 1** hornlike. **2** *sl* lustful. **horn'pipe** *n* lively dance, esp. associated with sailors.

hor·net [HOR-nit] *n* large insect of wasp family. **hornet's nest** much opposition, animosity.

hor·o·scope [HOR-ə-skohp] *n* **1** observation of, or scheme showing disposition of planets, etc. at given moment, esp. birth, by which character and abilities of individual are predicted. **2** telling of person's fortune by this method.

hor·ren·dous [haw-REN-dəs] *adj* horrific.

hor·ror [HOR-ər] *n* **1** terror. **2** loathing, fear of. **3** its cause. **hor'ri·ble** *adj* exciting horror, hideous, shocking. **hor'ri·bly** *adv* **hor'rid** *adj* **1** unpleasant, repulsive. **2** *inf* unkind. **hor'ri·fy** *vt* **-fied, -fy·ing** move to horror. **hor·rif'ic** *adj* particularly horrible.

hors d'oeu·vre [or-DURV] *n, pl* **-vres** [-DURVZ] small appetizer served before main meal.

horse [hors] *n* **1** four-legged animal used for riding and work. **2** cavalry. **3** vaulting horse. **4** frame for support. **5** *sl* heroin. ◆ *vt* **horsed, hors·ing 6** provide with horse or horses. **hors'y** *adj* **hors·i·er, hors·i·est 1** having to do with horses. **2** devoted to horses or horse racing. **horse'fly** *n, pl* **-flies** large bloodsucking fly. **horse laugh** harsh boisterous laugh usu. expressing derision. **horse'man** [-mən], **-wom·an** *n* rider on horse. **horse'play** *n* rough, boisterous play. **horse'pow·er** *n* unit of power of engine, etc., 550 foot-pounds per second. **horse'shoe** [-shoo] *n* **1** protective U-shaped piece of iron nailed to horse's hoof. **2** thing so shaped. **horse around** *sl* play roughly, boisterously.

hor·ti·cul·ture [HOR-ti-kul-chər] *n* art or science of gardening. **hor·ti·cul'tur·al** *adj*

Hos. Hosea.

ho·san·na [hoh-ZAN-ə] *n, pl* **-nas** cry of praise, adoration.

hose [hohz] *n* **1** flexible tube for conveying liquid or gas. **2** stockings. ◆ *vt* **hosed, hos·ing 3** water with hose. **ho'sier·y** *n* stockings or socks.

hos·pice [HOS-pis] *n* **1** traveler's house of rest kept by religious order. **2** residence for care of terminally ill.

hos·pi·tal [HOS-pi-tl] *n* institution for care of sick. **hos·pi·tal·i·za'tion** *n* **hos'pi·tal·ize** *vt* **-ized, -iz·ing** to place for care in a hospital.

vain

horde *n* = **crowd**, band, drove, gang, host, mob, multitude, pack, swarm, throng

horizon *n* = **skyline**, vista

horizontal *adj* = **level**, flat, parallel

horrible *adj* **1** = **terrifying**, appalling, dreadful, frightful, ghastly, grim, grisly, gruesome, hideous, repulsive, revolting, shocking **2** = **unpleasant**, awful, cruel, disagreeable, dreadful, horrid, lousy (*sl*), mean, nasty, scuzzy (*sl*), terrible

horrid *adj* **1** = **unpleasant**, awful, disagreeable, dreadful, horrible, terrible **2** = **unkind**, beastly (*inf*), cruel, mean, nasty

horrific *adj* = **terrifying**, appalling, awful, dreadful, frightful, ghastly, grisly, horrendous, horrifying, shocking

horrify *v* **1** = **terrify**, alarm, frighten,

intimidate, make one's hair stand on end, petrify, scare **2** = **shock**, appall, dismay, outrage, sicken

horror *n* **1** = **terror**, alarm, consternation, dread, fear, fright, panic **2** = **hatred**, aversion, detestation, disgust, loathing, odium, repugnance, revulsion

horse *n* = **nag**, colt, filly, mare, mount, stallion, steed (*archaic or literary*)

horseman *n* = **rider**, cavalier, cavalryman, dragoon, equestrian

horseplay *n* = **buffoonery**, clowning, fooling around, high jinks, pranks, romping, rough-and-tumble, skylarking (*inf*)

hospitable *adj* = **welcoming**, cordial, friendly, generous, gracious, kind, liberal, sociable

hos·pi·tal·i·ty [hos-pi-TAL-i-tee] *n, pl* **-ties** friendly and liberal reception of strangers or guests. **hos'pi·ta·ble** *adj* welcoming, kindly.

host[1] [hohst] *n* **1** one who entertains another. **2** master of ceremonies of show. **3** animal, plant on which parasite lives. **4** *Computers.* computer that provides data or connectivity to others on a network. ♦ *vt* **5** act as a host. **-ess** *n, fem.*

host[2] *n* large number.

Host *n* consecrated bread of the Eucharist.

hos·tage [HOS-tij] *n* person taken or given as pledge or security.

hos·tel [HOS-tl] *n* building providing accommodation at low cost for particular category of people, as students, or the homeless.

hos·tile [HOS-tl] *adj* **1** opposed, antagonistic. **2** warlike. **3** of an enemy. **4** unfriendly. **hos·til'i·ty** *n* enmity. **hos·til'i·ties** *pl n* acts of warfare.

hot *adj* **hot·ter, hot·test** **1** of high temperature, very warm, giving or feeling heat. **2** angry. **3** severe. **4** recent, new. **5** much favored. **6** spicy. **7** *sl* good, quick, smart, lucky, successful. **8** *sl* stolen. **hot'ly** *adv* **hot'ness** *n* **hot air** *inf* boastful, empty talk. **hot'bed** *n* **1** bed of earth heated by manure and grass for young plants. **2** any place encouraging growth. **3** center of activity. **hot'-blood·ed** [-blud-id] *adj* passionate, excitable. **hot dog** frankfurter

(in split bread roll). **hot'foot** [-fuut] *v, adv* (go) quickly. **hot'head** [-hed] *n* hasty, intemperate person. **hot'house** *n* **1** forcing house for plants. **2** heated building for cultivating tropical plants in cold or temperate climates. **hot line** direct communication link between heads of governments, etc. **hot pants** **1** extremely brief and close-fitting pants for women. **2** *sl* strong sexual desire. **hot'plate** *n* **1** heated plate on electric cooker. **2** portable device for keeping food warm.

ho·tel [hoh-TEL] *n* commercial establishment providing lodging.

hound [hownd] *n* **1** hunting dog. ♦ *vt* **2** chase, urge, pursue.

hour [owr] *n* **1** twenty-fourth part of day. **2** sixty minutes. **3** time of day. **4** appointed time. ♦ *pl* **5** fixed periods for work, prayers, etc. **6** book of prayers. **hour'ly** *adv* **1** every hour. **2** frequently. ♦ *adj* **3** frequent. **4** happening every hour. **hour'glass** *n* instrument using dropping sand or mercury to indicate passage of an hour.

hou·ri [HUUR-ee] *n, pl* **-ris** beautiful virgin provided in the Muslim paradise.

house [hows] *n, pl* **hous·es** [HOW-ziz] **1** building for human habitation. **2** building for other specified purpose. **3** legislative or other assembly. **4** family. **5** business firm. **6** theater audience, performance. ♦ *vt* [howz] **housed, hous·ing** **7** give or receive shelter, lodging or storage. **8** cover or

hospitality *n* = **welcome**, conviviality, cordiality, friendliness, neighborliness, sociability, warmth

host[1] *n* **1** = **master of ceremonies**, entertainer, innkeeper, landlord *or* landlady, proprietor **2** = **presenter**, anchorman *or* anchorwoman ♦ *v* **3** = **present**, front (*inf*), introduce

host[2] *n* = **multitude**, army, array, drove, horde, legion, myriad, swarm, throng

hostage *n* = **prisoner**, captive, pawn

hostile *adj* **1** = **opposed**, antagonistic, belligerent, contrary, ill-disposed, rancorous **2** = **unfriendly**, adverse, inhospitable, unsympathetic, unwelcoming

hostilities *pl n* = **warfare**, conflict, fighting, war

hostility *n* = **opposition**, animosity, antipathy, enmity, hatred, ill will, malice, resentment, unfriendliness

hot *adj* **1** = **heated**, boiling, roasting, scalding, scorching, searing, steaming, sultry, sweltering, torrid, warm **2** = **spicy**, biting, peppery, piquant, pungent, sharp **3** = **fierce**, fiery, intense, passionate, raging, stormy, violent **4** = **recent**, fresh, just out, latest, new, up to the minute **5** = **popular**, approved, favored, in demand, in vogue, sought-after

hot air *n* = **empty talk**, bombast, claptrap (*inf*), guff (*sl*), verbiage, wind

hot-blooded *adj* = **passionate**, ardent, excitable, fiery, impulsive, spirited, temperamental, wild

hot-headed *adj* = **rash**, fiery, foolhardy, hasty, hot-tempered, impetuous, quick-tempered, reckless, volatile

hot water *n* (usually preceded by *in*) *Inf* = **predicament**, dilemma, fix (*inf*), jam (*inf*), mess, scrape (*inf*), spot (*inf*), tight spot

hound *v* = **harass**, badger, goad, harry,

contain. **housing** n 1 (providing of) houses. 2 part or structure designed to cover, protect, contain. **house'boat** n boat for living in on river, etc. **house'break•er** [-brayk-ər] n burglar. **house'coat** n woman's long loose garment for casual wear at home. **house'hold** n inmates of house collectively. **house'hold•er** n 1 occupier of house as own dwelling. 2 head of household. **house'-hus•band** n man who runs a household. **house'keep•er** n person managing affairs of household. **house'keep•ing** n running household. **house'warm•ing** n party to celebrate entry into new house. **house'wife** n woman who runs a household.

hov•el [HUV-əl] n mean dwelling.

hov•er [HUV-ər] vi 1 hang in the air (of bird, etc.). 2 loiter. 3 be in state of indecision. **hov'er•craft** n type of craft that can travel over land and sea on a cushion of air.

how adv 1 in what way. 2 by what means. 3 in what condition. 4 to what degree. 5 (in direct or dependent question). **how•ev'er** conj 1 nevertheless. ◆ adv 2 in whatever way, degree. 3 all the same.

how•dah [HOW-də] n (canopied) seat on elephant's back.

how•itz•er [HOW-it-sər] n short gun firing shells at high elevation.

howl vi 1 utter long loud cry. ◆ n 2 such cry. **howl'er** n 1 one that howls. 2

embarrassing mistake.

hoy•den [HOID-n] n wild, boisterous girl, tomboy.

Hs Chem. hassium.

HTML Computers hypertext markup language: text description language that is used on the World Wide Web.

hub n 1 middle part of wheel, from which spokes radiate. 2 central point of activity.

hub'bub n 1 confused noise of many voices. 2 uproar.

huck•ster [HUK-stər] n 1 retailer, peddler. 2 person using aggressive or questionable methods of selling. ◆ vt 3 sell goods thus.

hud•dle [HUD-l] n 1 crowded mass. 2 inf impromptu conference, esp. of offensive football team during game. ◆ v -dled, -dling 3 heap, crowd together. 4 hunch. 5 confer.

hue [hyoo] n color, complexion.

hue and cry 1 public uproar, outcry. 2 loud outcry usually in pursuit of wrongdoer.

huff n 1 passing mood of anger. ◆ v 2 make or become angry, resentful. ◆ vi 3 blow, puff heavily. **huff'i•ly** adv **huff'y** adj **huff•i•er, huff•i•est**

hug vt **hugged, hug•ging** 1 clasp tightly in the arms. 2 cling. 3 keep close to. ◆ n 4 fond embrace.

huge [hyooj] adj very big. **huge'ly** adv very much.

hu•la [HOO-lə] n native dance of Hawaii.

impel, persecute, pester, provoke

house n 1 = **home**, abode, domicile, dwelling, habitation, homestead, pad (sl, dated), residence 2 = **family**, household 3 = **dynasty**, clan, tribe 4 = **firm**, business, company, organization, outfit (inf) 5 = **assembly**, Commons, legislative body, parliament 6 on the house = **free**, for nothing, gratis ◆ v 7 = **accommodate**, billet, harbor, lodge, put up, quarter, take in 8 = **contain**, cover, keep, protect, sheathe, shelter, store

household n = **family**, home, house

householder n = **occupant**, homeowner, resident, tenant

housing n 1 = **accommodation**, dwellings, homes, houses 2 = **case**, casing, container, cover, covering, enclosure, sheath

hovel n = **hut**, cabin, den, hole, shack, shanty, shed

hover v 1 = **float**, drift, flutter, fly, hang 2 =

linger, hang about 3 = **waver**, dither, fluctuate, oscillate, vacillate

however adv = **nevertheless**, after all, anyhow, but, nonetheless, notwithstanding, still, though, yet

howl n 1 = **cry**, bawl, bay, clamor, groan, roar, scream, shriek, wail ◆ v 2 = **cry**, bawl, bellow, roar, scream, shriek, wail, weep, yell

hub n = **center**, core, focal point, focus, heart, middle, nerve center

huddle v 1 = **crowd**, cluster, converge, flock, gather, press, throng 2 = **curl up**, crouch, hunch up ◆ n 3 Inf = **conference**, discussion, meeting, powwow

hue n = **color**, dye, shade, tinge, tint, tone

hug v 1 = **clasp**, cuddle, embrace, enfold, hold close, squeeze, take in one's arms ◆ n 2 = **embrace**, bear hug, clasp, clinch (sl), squeeze

huge adj = **large**, colossal, enormous,

hulk *n* body of abandoned vessel. **1** large, unwieldy thing. **hulk'ing** *adj* unwieldy, bulky.

hull *n* **1** frame, body of ship. **2** calyx of strawberry, raspberry, or similar fruit. **3** shell, husk. ◆ *vt* **4** remove shell, hull.

hul·la·ba·loo [HUL-ə-bə-loo] *n, pl* **-loos** uproar, clamor, row.

hum *v* hummed, hum·ming ◆ *vi* **1** make low continuous sound as bee. **2** be very active. ◆ *vt* **3** sing with closed lips. ◆ *n* **4** humming sound. **5** smell. **6** great activity. **7** in radio, disturbance affecting reception. **hum'ming·bird** *n* very small bird whose wings make humming noise.

hu·man [HYOO-mən] *adj* **1** of people. **2** relating to, characteristic of, people's nature. **hu·mane'** [-MAYN] *adj* **1** benevolent, kind. **2** merciful. **hu'man·ism** *n* **1** belief in human effort rather than religion. **2** interest in human welfare and affairs. **3** classical literary culture. **hu'man·ist** *n* **hu·man·i·tar'i·an** *n* philanthropist. ◆ *adj* **hu·man'i·ty** *n, pl* **-ties**

[-teez] **1** human nature. **2** human race. **3** kindliness. ◆ *pl* **4** study of literature, philosophy, the arts. **hu'man·ize** *vt* **-ized, -iz·ing 1** make human. **2** civilize. **hu'man·ly** *adv* **hu'man·kind** [-kīnd] *n* human race as a whole.

hum·ble [HUM-bəl] *adj* **-bler, -blest 1** lowly, modest. ◆ *vt* **-bled, -bling 2** bring low, abase, humiliate. **hum'bly** *adv*

hum'bug *n* **1** impostor. **2** sham, nonsense, deception. ◆ *vt* **-bugged, -bug·ging 3** deceive. **4** defraud.

hum·ding·er [HUM-DING-ər] *n inf* excellent person or thing.

hum'drum *adj* commonplace, dull, monotonous.

hu·mer·us [HYOO-mər-əs] *n, pl* **-mer·i** [-mə-rī] long bone of upper arm.

hu·mid [HYOO-mid] *adj* moist, damp. **hu·mid'i·fi·er** *n* device for increasing amount of water vapor in air in room, etc. **hu·mid'i·fy** *vt* **-fied, -fy·ing hu·mid'i·ty** *n*

hu·mil·i·ate [hyoo-MIL-ee-ayt] *vt* **-at·ed, -at·ing** lower dignity of, abase, mortify.

THESAURUS

gigantic, immense, mammoth, massive, monumental, tremendous, vast

hulk *n* **1 = wreck,** frame, hull, shell, shipwreck **2 = oaf,** lout, lubber, lump (*inf*)

hull *n* = **frame,** body, casing, covering, framework

hum *v* **1 = murmur,** buzz, drone, purr, throb, thrum, vibrate, whir **2 = be busy,** bustle, buzz, pulsate, pulse, stir

human *adj* **1 = mortal,** manlike ◆ *n* **2 = human being,** creature, individual, man *or* woman, mortal, person, soul

humane *adj* = **kind,** benign, compassionate, forgiving, good-natured, merciful, sympathetic, tender, understanding

humanitarian *adj* **1 = compassionate,** altruistic, benevolent, charitable, humane, philanthropic, public-spirited ◆ *n* **2 = philanthropist,** altruist, benefactor, Good Samaritan

humanity *n* **1 = human race,** Homo sapiens, humankind, man, mankind, people **2 = human nature,** mortality **3 = sympathy,** charity, compassion, fellow feeling, kind-heartedness, kindness, mercy, philanthropy

humanize *v* = **civilize,** educate, enlighten, improve, soften, tame

humble *adj* **1 = modest,** meek,

self-effacing, unassuming, unostentatious, unpretentious **2 = lowly,** mean, modest, obscure, ordinary, plebeian, poor, simple, undistinguished ◆ *v* **3 = humiliate,** chasten, crush, disgrace, put (someone) in their place, subdue, take down a peg (*inf*)

humbug *n* **1 = fraud,** charlatan, con man (*inf*), faker, impostor, phoney *or* phony (*inf*), swindler, trickster **2 = nonsense,** baloney (*inf*), cant, claptrap (*inf*), hypocrisy, quackery, rubbish **3 = killjoy,** scrooge (*inf*), spoilsport, wet blanket (*inf*)

humdrum *adj* = **dull,** banal, boring, dreary, monotonous, mundane, ordinary, tedious, tiresome, uneventful

humid *adj* = **damp,** clammy, dank, moist, muggy, steamy, sticky, sultry, wet

humidity *n* = **damp,** clamminess, dampness, dankness, moistness, moisture, mugginess, wetness

humiliate *v* = **embarrass,** bring low, chasten, crush, degrade, humble, mortify, put down, put (someone) in their place, shame

humiliating *adj* = **embarrassing,** crushing, degrading, humbling, ignominious, mortifying, shaming

humiliation *n* = **embarrassment,** degradation, disgrace, dishonor, humbling, ignominy, indignity, loss of

hu·mil·i·ty [hyoo-MIL-i-tee] *n* **1** state of being humble. **2** meekness.

hum·mock [HUM-ək] *n* **1** low knoll, hillock. **2** ridge of ice.

hum·mus [HEW-mus] *n* creamy dip of Middle East origin, made from puréed chickpeas.

hu·mor [HYOO-mər] *n* **1** faculty of saying or perceiving what excites amusement. **2** state of mind, mood. **3** temperament. **4** *obs* one of four chief fluids of body. ◆ *vt* **5** gratify, indulge. **hu'mor·ist** *n* person who acts, speaks, writes humorously. **hu'mor·ous** *adj* **1** funny. **2** amusing.

hump *n* **1** normal or deforming lump, esp. on back. **2** hillock. ◆ *vt* **3** make hump-shaped. **4** *inf* exert (oneself), hurry. **5** *sl* carry or heave. **hump'back** *n* person with hump. **hump'backed** *adj* having a hump.

hu·mus [HYOO-məs] *n* decayed vegetable and animal mold.

hunch *n inf* **1** intuition or premonition. **2** hump. ◆ *vt* **3** thrust, bend into hump. **hunch'back** *n* humpback.

hun·dred [HUN-drid] *n, adj* cardinal number, ten times ten. **hun'dredth** [-dridth] *adj* the ordinal number. **hun'dred·fold** *adj, adv* **hun'dred·weight** *n* weight of 100 lbs. (45.359 kg).

hung **1** pt./pp. of HANG. ◆ *adj* **2** (of jury, etc.) unable to decide. **3** not having majority. **hung'o'ver** *adj inf* experiencing a hangover. **hung up** *inf* **1** delayed. **2** stymied. **3** baffled. **hung up on** *sl* obsessed by.

hun·ger [HUNG-gər] *n* **1** discomfort, exhaustion from lack of food. **2** strong desire. ◆ *vi* **hun'gri·ly** *adv* **hun'gry** *adj* **-gri·er, -gri·est** having keen appetite. **hunger strike** refusal of all food, as a protest.

hunk [hungk] *n* **1** thick piece. **2** *sl* attractive man with excellent physique.

hunt *v* **1** seek out to kill or capture for sport or food. **2** search (for). ◆ *n* **3** chase, search. **4** track of country hunted over. **5** (party organized for) hunting. **6** pack of hounds. **7** hunting club. **hunt'er** *n* **1** one who hunts. **2** horse, dog bred for hunting. **-ress** *n, fem.*

hur·dle [HUR-dl] *n* **1** portable frame of bars for temporary fences or for jumping over. **2** obstacle. ◆ *vi* **-dled, -dling 3** race over hurdles. **hurdles** *n* a race over hurdles. **hurd'ler** *n*

hurl *vt* throw violently. **hurl·y-burl·y** [HUR-lee-BUR-lee] *n, pl* **-burl·ies** loud confusion.

hur·rah [hə-RAH], **hur·ray** [-RAY] *interj* exclamation of joy or applause. **last hurrah** final occasion of achievement.

face, mortification, put-down, shame
humility *n* = **modesty**, humbleness, lowliness, meekness, submissiveness, unpretentiousness

humor *n* **1** = **funniness**, amusement, comedy, drollery, facetiousness, fun, jocularity, ludicrousness **2** = **joking**, comedy, farce, jesting, pleasantry, wisecracks (*inf*), wit, witticisms **3** = **mood**, disposition, frame of mind, spirits, temper ◆ *v* **4** = **indulge**, accommodate, flatter, go along with, gratify, mollify, pander to

humorist *n* = **comedian**, card (*inf*), comic, funny man, jester, joker, wag, wit

humorous *adj* = **funny**, amusing, comic, comical, droll, entertaining, jocular, playful, waggish, witty

hump *n* = **lump**, bulge, bump, mound, projection, protrusion, protuberance, swelling

hunch *n* **1** = **feeling**, idea, impression, inkling, intuition, premonition, presentiment, suspicion ◆ *v* **2** = **draw in**, arch, bend, curve

hunger *n* **1** = **famine**, starvation **2** = **appetite**, emptiness, hungriness, ravenousness **3** = **desire**, ache, appetite, craving, itch, lust, thirst, yearning ◆ *v* **4** = **want**, ache, crave, desire, hanker, itch, long, thirst, wish, yearn

hungry *adj* **1** = **empty**, famished, ravenous, starved, starving, voracious **2** = **eager**, athirst, avid, covetous, craving, desirous, greedy, keen, yearning

hunk *n* = **lump**, block, chunk, mass, nugget, piece, slab, wedge

hunt *v* **1** = **stalk**, chase, hound, pursue, track, trail **2** = **search**, ferret about, forage, look, scour, seek ◆ *n* **3** = **search**, chase, hunting, investigation, pursuit, quest

hurdle *n* **1** = **fence**, barricade, barrier **2** = **obstacle**, barrier, difficulty, handicap, hazard, hindrance, impediment, obstruction, stumbling block

hurl *v* = **throw**, cast, fling, heave, launch, let fly, pitch, propel, sling, toss

hur·ri·cane [HUR-i-kayn] *n* very strong, potentially destructive wind or storm. **hurricane lamp** lamp with glass chimney around flame.

hur·ry [HUR-ee] *v* **-ried, -ry·ing 1** (cause to) move or act in great haste. ♦ *n, pl* **-ries 2** undue haste. **3** eagerness. **hur'ried·ly** *adv*

hurt *v* hurt, hurt·ing ♦ *vt* **1** injure, damage, give pain to, wound feelings of. **2** distress. ♦ *vi inf* **3** feel pain. ♦ *n* **4** wound, injury, harm. **hurt'ful** *adj*

hur·tle [HUR-tl] *vi* **-tled, -tling 1** move rapidly. **2** rush violently. **3** whirl.

hus·band [HUZ-bənd] *n* **1** married man. ♦ *vt* **2** economize. **3** use to best advantage. **hus'band·ry** [-dree] *n* **1** farming. **2** economy.

hush *v* **1** make or be silent. ♦ *n* **2** stillness. **3** quietness. **hush-hush** *adj inf* secret. **hush up 1** suppress rumors, information. **2** make secret.

husk *n* **1** dry covering of certain seeds and fruits. **2** worthless outside part. ♦ *vt* **3** remove husk from. **husk'y** *adj* **husk·i·er, husk·i·est 1** rough in tone. **2** hoarse. **3** dry as husk, dry in the throat. **4** of, full of, husks. **5** big and strong.

husk·y [HUS-kee] *n, pl* **husk·ies** Arctic sledge dog with thick hair and curled tail.

hus·sy [HUS-ee] *n, pl* **-sies 1** brazen or immoral woman. **2** impudent girl or young woman.

hus·tings [HUS-tingz] *pl n* **1** any place from which political campaign speeches are made. **2** political campaigning.

hus·tle [HUS-əl] *v* **-tled, -tling 1** push about, jostle, hurry. ♦ *vi* **2** *sl* solicit clients esp. for prostitution. ♦ *n* **hus·tler** [HUS-lər] **1** industrious person. **2** *sl* prostitute.

hut *n* any small house or shelter, usu. of wood or metal.

hutch [huch] *n* boxlike pen for rabbits, etc.

hy·brid [HĪ-brid] *n* **1** offspring of two plants or animals of different species. **2** mongrel. ♦ *adj* **3** crossbred. **hy'brid·ism** *n* **hy'brid·ize** *v* **-ized, -iz·ing 1** make hybrid. **2** crossbreed.

hy·dra [HĪ-drə] *n, pl* **-dras** [-drəz] fabulous many-headed water serpent. **1** any persistent problem. **2** freshwater polyp. **hy'dra-head·ed** *adj* **1** hard to understand, root out.

hy·dran·gea [hī-DRAYN-jə] *n* ornamental shrub with pink, blue, or white flowers.

hy·drant [HĪ-drənt] *n* water pipe with nozzle for hose.

hy·drau·lic [hī-DRAW-lik] *adj* concerned with, operated by, pressure transmitted through liquid in pipe. **hy·drau'lics** *n* science of mechanical properties of liquid in motion.

hydro- *comb. form* **1** water, e.g.

THESAURUS

hurricane *n* = **storm**, cyclone, gale, tempest, tornado, twister, typhoon

hurried *adj* = **hasty**, brief, cursory, perfunctory, quick, rushed, short, speedy, swift

hurry *v* **1** = **rush**, dash, fly, get a move on (*inf*), make haste, scoot, scurry, step on it (*inf*) ♦ *n* **2** = **urgency**, flurry, haste, quickness, rush, speed

hurt *v* **1** = **harm**, bruise, damage, disable, impair, injure, mar, spoil, wound **2** = **ache**, be sore, be tender, burn, smart, sting, throb **3** = **sadden**, annoy, distress, grieve, pain, upset, wound ♦ *n* **4** = **distress**, discomfort, pain, pang, soreness, suffering ♦ *adj* **5** = **injured**, bruised, cut, damaged, harmed, scarred, wounded **6** = **offended**, aggrieved, crushed, wounded

hurtful *adj* = **unkind**, cruel, cutting, damaging, destructive, malicious, nasty, spiteful, upsetting, wounding

hurtle *v* = **rush**, charge, crash, fly, plunge, race, shoot, speed, stampede, tear

husband *n* **1** = **partner**, better half (*humorous*), mate, spouse ♦ *v* **2** = **economize**, budget, conserve, hoard, save, store

husbandry *n* **1** = **farming**, agriculture, cultivation, tillage **2** = **thrift**, economy, frugality

hush *v* **1** = **quieten**, mute, muzzle, shush, silence ♦ *n* **2** = **quiet**, calm, peace, silence, stillness, tranquillity

hush-hush *adj* = **secret**, classified, confidential, restricted, top-secret, under wraps

husky *adj* **1** = **hoarse**, croaky, gruff, guttural, harsh, raucous, rough, throaty **2** = **muscular**, burly, hefty, powerful, rugged, stocky, strapping, thickset

hustle *v* = **jostle**, elbow, force, jog, push, shove

hut *n* = **shed**, cabin, den, hovel, lean-to, shanty, shelter

hybrid *n* = **crossbreed**, amalgam, composite, compound, cross, half-breed, *hydroelectric.* **2** presence of hydrogen, e.g. *hydrocarbon.*

hy·dro·car·bon [hī-drə-KAHR-bən] *n* compound of hydrogen and carbon.

hy·dro·chlor·ic ac·id [hī-drə-KLOR-ik] strong colorless acid used in many industrial and laboratory processes.

hy·dro·dy·nam·ics [hī-droh-dī-NAM-iks] *n* science of the motions of system wholly or partly fluid.

hy·dro·e·lec·tric [hī-droh-i-LEK-trik] *adj* pert. to generation of electricity by use of water.

hy·dro·foil [HĪ-drə-foil] *n* fast, light vessel with hull raised out of water at speed by action of vanes in water.

hy·dro·gen [HĪ-drə-jən] *n* colorless gas that combines with oxygen to form water. **hydrogen bomb** atom bomb of enormous power in which hydrogen nuclei are converted into helium nuclei. **hydrogen peroxide** colorless liquid used as antiseptic and bleach.

hy·drog·ra·phy [hī-DROG-rə-fee] *n* description of waters of the earth. **hy·dro·graph·ic** *adj*

hy·drol·y·sis [hī-DROL-ə-sis] *n* decomposition of chemical compound reacting with water.

hy·drom·e·ter [hī-DROM-i-tər] *n* device for measuring relative density of liquid.

hy·dro·pho·bi·a [hī-drə-FOH-bee-ə] *n* **1** aversion to water, esp. as symptom of rabies. **2** rabies.

hy·dro·plane [HĪ-drə-playn] *n* **1** light skimming motorboat. **2** seaplane. **3** vane controlling motion of submarine, etc.

hy·dro·pon·ics [hī-drə-PON-iks] *n* science of cultivating plants in water without using soil.

hy·dro·ther·a·py [hī-drə-THER-ə-pee] *n* *Med.* treatment of disease by external application of water.

hy·drous [HĪ-drəs] *adj* containing water.

hy·e·na [hī-EE-nə] *n* wild animal related to dog.

hy·giene [HĪ-jeen] *n* **1** principles and practice of health and cleanliness. **2** study of these principles. **hy·gi·en·ic** [hī-jee-EN-ik] *adj* **hy·gien'ist** [-JEE-nist] *n*

hy·grom·e·ter [hī-GROM-i-tər] *n* instrument for measuring humidity of air.

hy·gro·scop·ic [hī-grə-SKOP-ik] *adj* readily absorbing moisture from the atmosphere.

hy·men [HĪ-mən] *n* **1** membrane partly covering vagina of virgin. **2** (**H-**) **3** Greek god of marriage.

hymn [him] *n* **1** song of praise, esp. to God. ♦ *vt* **2** praise in song. **hym·nal** [HIM-nl] *adj* **1** of hymns. ♦ *n* **2** book of hymns (also **hymn book**).

hype¹ [hīp] *n sl* **1** hypodermic syringe. **2** drug addict.

hype² *n inf* **1** deception, racket. **2** intensive publicity. ♦ *v* **hyped, hyp·ing 3** *inf* promote (a product) using intensive publicity.

hyper- *comb. form* over, above, excessively, e.g. *hyperactive.*

hy·per·bo·la [hī-PUR-bə-lə] *n* curve produced when cone is cut by plane making larger angle with the base than the side makes.

hy·per·bo·le [hī-PUR-bə-lee] *n* rhetorical exaggeration. **hy·per·bol'ic** *adj*

hy·per·bo·re·an [hī-pər-BOR-ee-ən] *adj, n* (inhabitant) of extreme north.

hy·per·crit·i·cal [hī-pər-KRIT-i-kəl] *adj* too critical.

hy·per·link [HĪ-pər-lingk] *n Computers* link from a hypertext file that gives users instant access to related material in another file.

hy·per·sen·si·tive [hī-pər-SEN-si-tiv] *adj* unduly vulnerable emotionally or physically.

hy·per·ten·sion [hī-pər-TEN-shən] *n* abnormally high blood pressure.

hy·per·text [HĪ-pər-tekst] *n* computer software and hardware that allows users to store and view text and move between related items easily.

hy·phen [HĪ-fən] *n* short line (-) indicating that two words or syllables are to be connected. **hy·phen·ate** [-nayt] *vt* **-at·ed, -at·ing** join by a hyphen.

hyp·no·sis [HIP-noh-sis] *n, pl* **-ses** [-seez] induced state like deep sleep in which subject acts on external suggestion. **hyp·not'ic** *adj* **1** of hypnosis or of the person or thing producing it. **2** like

mixture, mongrel

hygiene *n* = **cleanliness**, sanitation

hygienic *adj* = **clean**, aseptic, disinfected, germ-free, healthy, pure, sanitary, sterile

hymn *n* = **anthem**, carol, chant, paean, psalm

hype *n* = **publicity**, ballyhoo (*inf*), brouhaha, plugging (*inf*), promotion,

something that induces hypnosis.
hyp·no·tism [HIP-nə-tiz-əm] *n* **hyp'no·tist** *n* **hyp·no·tize** *vt* **-tized, -tiz·ing** **1** affect with hypnosis. **2** affect in way resembling hypnotic state.

hy·po [HĪ-poh] *n* short for hyposulfite (sodium thiosulfate), used as fixer in developing photographs.

hypo-, hyph-, hyp- *comb. forms* under, below, less, e.g. *hypothermia.*

hy·po·al·ler·gen·ic [hī-poh-al-ər-JEN-ik] *adj* (of cosmetics, etc.) not likely to cause allergic reaction.

hy·po·chon·dri·a [hī-pə-KON-dree-ə] *n* morbid depression, without cause, about one's own health. **hy·po·chon'dri·ac** *adj, n*

hy·poc·ri·sy [hi-POK-rə-see] *n, pl* **-sies** [-seez] assuming of false appearance of virtue. **1** insincerity. **hyp·o·crite** [HIP-ə-krit] *n* **hyp·o·crit'i·cal** *adj*

hy·po·der·mic [hī-pə-DUR-mik] *adj* **1** introduced, injected beneath the skin. ♦ *n* **2** hypodermic syringe or needle.

hy·po·gas·tric [hī-pə-GAS-trik] *adj* relating to, situated in, lower part of abdomen.

hy·pot·e·nuse [hī-POT-n-oos] *n* side of a right triangle opposite the right angle.

hy·po·ther·mi·a [hī-pə-THUR-mee-ə] *n* condition of having body temperature reduced to dangerously low level.

hy·poth·e·sis [hī-POTH-ə-sis] *n, pl* **-ses** [-seez] suggested explanation of something. **1** assumption as basis of reasoning. **hy·po·thet'i·cal** *adj* **hy·poth'e·size** [-POTH-ə-sīz] *v* **-sized, -siz·ing**

hypso- *comb. form* height, e.g. *hypsometry.*

hyp·sog·ra·phy [hip-SOG-rə-fee] *n* branch of geography dealing with altitudes.

hyp·som·e·ter [hip-SOM-i-tər] *n* instrument for measuring altitudes. **hyp·som'e·try** [-tree] *n* science of measuring altitudes.

hys·ter·ec·to·my [his-tə-REK-tə-mee] *n, pl* **-mies** surgical operation for removing the uterus.

hys·ter·e·sis [his-tə-REE-sis] *n Physics* lag or delay in changes in variable property of a system.

hys·te·ri·a [hi-STER-ee-ə] *n* **1** mental disorder with emotional outbursts. **2** any frenzied emotional state. **3** fit of crying or laughing. **hys·ter'i·cal** *adj* **hys·ter'ics** *pl n* **1** fits of hysteria. **2** *inf* uncontrollable laughter.

Hz hertz.

—————————| THESAURUS |—————————

razzmatazz (*sl*)

hypnotic *adj* = **mesmeric**, mesmerizing, sleep-inducing, soothing, soporific, spellbinding

hypnotize *v* = **mesmerize**, put in a trance, put to sleep

hypocrisy *n* = **insincerity**, cant, deceitfulness, deception, duplicity, pretense

hypocrite *n* = **fraud**, charlatan, deceiver, impostor, phoney *or* phony (*inf*), pretender

hypocritical *adj* = **insincere**, canting, deceitful, duplicitous, false, fraudulent, phoney *or* phony (*inf*), sanctimonious,
two-faced

hypothesis *n* = **assumption**, postulate, premise, proposition, supposition, theory, thesis

hypothetical *adj* = **theoretical**, academic, assumed, conjectural, imaginary, putative, speculative, supposed

hysteria *n* = **frenzy**, agitation, delirium, hysterics, madness, panic

hysterical *adj* **1** = **frenzied**, crazed, distracted, distraught, frantic, overwrought, raving **2** *Inf* = **hilarious**, comical, side-splitting, uproarious

I i

I *Chem.* iodine.

I *pron* the pronoun of the first person singular.

i·amb [Ī-amb] *n* metrical foot of short and long syllable. **i·am'bic** *adj*

i·bex [Ī-beks] *n, pl* **-bex·es** wild goat with large horns.

ibid. [IB-id] (referring to a book, page, or passage already mentioned) in the same place.

i·bis [Ī-bis] *n* storklike bird.

ice [īs] *n* 1 frozen water. 2 frozen dessert made of sweetened water and fruit flavoring. ◆ *v* **iced, ic·ing** 3 cover, become covered with ice. 4 cool with ice. 5 cover with icing. **i'ci·cle** [-sə-kəl] *n* tapering spike of ice hanging where water has dripped. **i'ci·ly** *adv* in icy manner. **I'ci·ness** *n* **i'cing** *n* mixture of sugar and water, etc. used to decorate cakes. **i'cy** *adj* **i·ci·er, i·ci·est** 1 covered with ice. 2 cold. 3 chilling. **ice'berg** [-burg] *n* large floating mass of ice. **ice cream** sweetened frozen dessert made from cream, eggs, etc. **ice floe** [-floh] *n* sheet of floating ice. **ice hockey** team game played on ice with puck.

ich·thy·ol·o·gy [ik-thee-OL-ə-jee] *n* scientific study of fish.

icicle see ICE.

i·con [Ī-kon] *n* 1 image, representation, esp. of religious figure. 2 graphic representing a function, activated by clicking on. **i·con·o·clast** *n* 1 one who attacks established principles, etc. 2 breaker of icons. **i·con·o·clas'tic** *adj* **i·co·nog'ra·phy** *n* 1 icons collectively. 2 study of icons.

id *n Psychoanalysis* the mind's instinctive energies.

i·de·a [ī-DEE-ə] *n* 1 notion in the mind. 2 conception. 3 vague belief. 4 plan, aim. **i·de'al** *n* 1 conception of something that is perfect. 2 perfect person or thing. ◆ *adj* 3 perfect. 4 visionary. 5 existing only in idea. **i·de'al·ism** *n* 1 tendency to seek perfection in everything. 2 philosophy that mind is the only reality. **i·de'al·ist** *n* 1 one who holds doctrine of idealism. 2 one who strives after the ideal. 3 impractical person. **i·de·al·is'tic** *adj* **i·de'al·ize** *vt* **-ized, -iz·ing** portray as ideal.

i·dem [Ī-dem] *Lat* the same.

i·den·ti·ty [ī-DEN-ti-tee] *n, pl* **-ties** 1 individuality. 2 being the same, exactly alike. **i·den'ti·cal** *adj* very same.

THESAURUS
---

icy *adj* **1** = **cold**, biting, bitter, chill, chilly, freezing, frosty, ice-cold, raw **2** = **slippery**, glassy, slippy (*inf or dialect*) **3** = **unfriendly**, aloof, cold, distant, frigid, frosty, unwelcoming

idea *n* **1** = **thought**, concept, impression, perception **2** = **belief**, conviction, notion, opinion, teaching, view **3** = **plan**, aim, intention, object, objective, purpose

ideal *adj* **1** = **perfect**, archetypal, classic, complete, consummate, model, quintessential, supreme ◆ *n* **2** = **model**, last word, paradigm, paragon, pattern, perfection, prototype, standard

idealist *n* = **romantic**, dreamer, Utopian, visionary

idealistic *adj* = **perfectionist**, impracticable, optimistic, romantic, starry-eyed, Utopian, visionary

idealize *v* = **romanticize**, apotheosize, ennoble, exalt, glorify, magnify, put on a pedestal, worship

ideally *adv* = **in a perfect world**, all things being equal, if one had one's way

identical *adj* = **alike**, duplicate, indistinguishable, interchangeable, matching, twin

identification *n* **1** = **recognition**, naming, pinpointing **2** = **empathy**, association, connection, fellow feeling, involvement, rapport, relationship, sympathy

identify *v* **1** = **recognize**, diagnose, make out, name, pick out, pinpoint, place, point out, put one's finger on (*inf*), spot **2 identify with** = **relate to**, associate with, empathize with, feel for, respond to

i·den'ti·fi·a·ble *adj* **i·den'ti·fy** *v* **-fied, -fy·ing** **1** establish identity of. **2** associate (oneself) with. **3** treat as identical.

id·e·o·graph [ID-ee-ə-graf] *n* picture, symbol, figure, etc., suggesting an object without naming it (also **id'e·o·gram**).

i·de·ol·o·gy [ī-dee-OL-ə-jee] *n, pl* **-gies** body of ideas, beliefs of group, nation, etc. **i·de·o·log'i·cal** *adj* **i'de·o·logue** [-lawg] *n* zealous advocate of an ideology.

ides [īdz] *n* (in the Ancient Roman calendar) the 15th of March, May, July, or October, or the 13th of other months.

idiocy see IDIOT.

id·i·om [ID-ee-əm] *n* **1** way of expression natural or peculiar to a language or group. **2** characteristic style of expression. **id·i·o·mat'ic** *adj* **1** using idioms. **2** colloquial.

id·i·o·syn·cra·sy [id-ee-ə-SING-krə-see] *n* peculiarity of mind, temper or disposition in a person. **id·i·o·syn·crat'ic** [-oh-sing-KRAT-ik] *adj*

id·i·ot [ID-ee-ət] *n* foolish, senseless person. **id'i·o·cy** [-ə-see] *n* **id·i·ot'ic** *adj* utterly senseless or stupid.

i·dle [ĪD-l] *adj* **-dler, -dlest 1** unemployed. **2** lazy. **3** useless, vain, groundless. ♦ *vi* **-dled, -dling 4** be idle. **5** (of engine) run slowly

with gears disengaged. ♦ *vt* **6** (esp. with *away*) waste. **i'dle·ness** *n* **i'dler** *n* **i'dly** *adv*

i·dol [ĪD-l] *n* **1** image of deity as object of worship. **2** object of excessive devotion. **i·dol'a·ter** *n* worshiper of idols. **i·dol'a·trous** [-trəs] *adj* **i·dol'a·try** *n* **i'dol·ize** *vt* **-ized, -iz·ing 1** love or venerate to excess. **2** make an idol of.

i·dyll [ĪD-l] *n* short descriptive poem of picturesque or charming scene or episode, esp. of rustic life. **i·dyl·lic** [ī-DIL-ik] *adj* **1** of, like, idyll. **2** delightful.

i.e. that is to say.

if *conj* **1** on condition or supposition that. **2** whether. **3** although. ♦ *n* **4** uncertainty or doubt, e.g. *no ifs, ands, or buts.* **if'fy** [-ee] *adj inf* **-fi·er, -fi·est** dubious.

ig·loo *n* dome-shaped Inuit house of snow and ice.

ig·ne·ous [IG-nee-əs] *adj* esp. of rocks, formed as molten rock cools and hardens.

ig·nite [ig-NĪT] *v* **-nit·ed, -nit·ing** (cause to) burn. **ig·ni'tion** [-NISH-ən] *n* **1** act of kindling or setting on fire. **2** in internal combustion engine, means of firing explosive mixture, usu. electric spark.

ig·no·ble [ig-NOH-bəl] *adj* **1** mean, base. **2** of low birth. **ig·no'bly** *adv*

ig·no·min·y [IG-nə-min-ee] *n, pl* **-min·ies 1**

━━━━━━ THESAURUS ━━━━━━

identity *n* **1** = **existence**, individuality, personality, self **2** = **sameness**, correspondence, unity

idiocy *n* = **foolishness**, asininity, fatuousness, imbecility, inanity, insanity, lunacy, senselessness

idiom *n* **1** = **phrase**, expression, turn of phrase **2** = **language**, jargon, parlance, style, vernacular

idiosyncrasy *n* = **peculiarity**, characteristic, eccentricity, mannerism, oddity, quirk, trick

idiot *n* = **fool**, chump, cretin (*offens*), dork (*sl*), dunderhead, halfwit, imbecile, moron, schmuck (*sl*), simpleton

idiotic *adj* = **foolish**, asinine, bonkers (*inf*), crazy, daft (*inf*), foolhardy, harebrained, insane, moronic, senseless, stupid

idle *adj* **1** = **inactive**, redundant, unemployed, unoccupied, unused, vacant **2** = **lazy**, good-for-nothing, indolent, lackadaisical, shiftless, slothful, sluggish **3** = **useless**, fruitless, futile, groundless, ineffective, pointless, unavailing, unsuccessful, vain, worthless ♦ *v* **4** (often

with *away*) = **laze**, dally, dawdle, kill time, loaf, loiter, lounge, potter

idleness *n* **1** = **inactivity**, inaction, leisure, time on one's hands, unemployment **2** = **laziness**, inertia, shiftlessness, sloth, sluggishness, torpor

idol *n* **1** = **graven image**, deity, god **2** = **hero**, beloved, darling, favorite, pet, pin-up (*sl*)

idolatry *n* = **adoration**, adulation, exaltation, glorification

idolize *v* = **worship**, adore, dote upon, exalt, glorify, hero-worship, look up to, love, revere, venerate

idyllic *adj* = **idealized**, charming, halcyon, heavenly, ideal, picturesque, unspoiled

if *conj* = **provided**, assuming, on condition that, providing, supposing

ignite *v* **1** = **catch fire**, burn, burst into flames, flare up, inflame, take fire **2** = **set fire to**, kindle, light, set alight, torch

ignominious *adj* = **humiliating**, discreditable, disgraceful, dishonorable, indecorous, inglorious, shameful, sorry, undignified

dishonor, disgrace. **2** shameful act.
ig·no·min·i·ous [-ee-əs] *adj*

ig·nore [ig-NOR] *vt* **-nored, -nor·ing**
disregard, leave out of account.
ig·no·ra'mus [-RA-məs] *n, pl* **-mus·es**
ignorant person. **ig'no·rance** [-rəns] *n* lack
of knowledge. **ig'no·rant** *adj* **1** lacking
knowledge. **2** uneducated. **3** unaware.

i·gua·na [i-GWAH-nə] *n* large tropical
American lizard.

il- *prefix* same as IN-¹ or IN-².

il·e·um [IL-ee-əm] *n* lower part of small
intestine. **il'e·ac** *adj*

ilk *adj* same. **of that ilk** of the same type or
class.

ill *adj* **1** not in good health. **2** bad, evil. **3**
faulty. **4** unfavorable. ♦ *n* **5** evil, harm. **6**
mild disease. ♦ *adv* **7** badly. **8** hardly, with
difficulty. **ill'ness** *n* **ill'-ad·vised'** *adj* **1**
imprudent. **2** injudicious. **ill'·fat'ed**
[-FAY-tid] *adj* unfortunate. **ill'·fa'vored**

[-FAY-vərd] *adj* **1** ugly, deformed. **2**
offensive. **ill'-got·ten** *adj* obtained
dishonestly. **ill'·man'nered** *adj* boorish,
uncivil. **ill-timed** *adj* inopportune. **ill-treat**
vt treat cruelly. **ill will** unkind feeling,
hostility.

il·le·gal *adj* against the law. **il·le'gal·ly** *adv*
il·le·gal'i·ty *n, pl* **-ties**

il·leg'i·ble *adj* unable to be read or
deciphered. **il·leg·i·bil'i·ty** *n*

il·le·git·i·mate [il-i-JIT-ə-mit] *adj* **1** born
out of wedlock. **2** unlawful. **3** not regular.
♦ *n* **4** bastard.

il·lic'it [i-LIS-it] *adj* **1** illegal. **2** prohibited,
forbidden.

il·lit·er·ate [i-LIT-ər-it] *adj* **1** not literate. **2**
unable to read or write. ♦ *n* **3** illiterate
person. **il·lit'er·a·cy** *n*

il·log'i·cal *adj* **1** unreasonable. **2** not
logical.

il·lu·mi·nate [i-LOO-mə-nayt] *vt* **-nat·ed,**

THESAURUS

ignominy *n* = **disgrace**, discredit,
dishonor, disrepute, humiliation, infamy,
obloquy, shame, stigma
ignorance *n* = **unawareness**,
inexperience, innocence, unconsciousness,
unfamiliarity
ignorant *adj* **1** = **uninformed**, benighted,
inexperienced, innocent, oblivious,
unaware, unconscious, unenlightened,
uninitiated, unwitting **2** = **uneducated**,
illiterate **3** = **insensitive**, crass, half-baked
(*inf*), rude
ignore *v* = **overlook**, blow off (*sl*),
discount, disregard, neglect, pass over,
reject, take no notice of, turn a blind eye
to
ill *adj* **1** = **unwell**, ailing, diseased,
indisposed, infirm, off-color, sick, under
the weather (*inf*), unhealthy **2** = **harmful**,
bad, damaging, deleterious, detrimental,
evil, foul, injurious, unfortunate ♦ *n* **3** =
harm, affliction, hardship, hurt, injury,
misery, misfortune, trouble,
unpleasantness, woe ♦ *adv* **4** = **badly**,
inauspiciously, poorly, unfavorably,
unfortunately, unluckily **5** = **hardly**, barely,
by no means, scantily
ill-advised *adj* = **misguided**, foolhardy,
ill-considered, ill-judged, imprudent,
incautious, injudicious, rash, reckless,
thoughtless, unwise
ill-disposed *adj* = **unfriendly**, antagonistic,
disobliging, hostile, inimical,

uncooperative, unwelcoming
illegal *adj* = **unlawful**, banned, criminal,
felonious, forbidden, illicit, outlawed,
prohibited, unauthorized, unlicensed
illegality *n* = **crime**, felony, illegitimacy,
lawlessness, wrong
illegible *adj* = **indecipherable**, obscure,
scrawled, unreadable
illegitimate *adj* **1** = **unlawful**, illegal, illicit,
improper, unauthorized **2** = **born out of
wedlock**, bastard
ill-fated *adj* = **doomed**, hapless,
ill-omened, ill-starred, luckless,
star-crossed, unfortunate, unhappy,
unlucky
illicit *adj* **1** = **illegal**, criminal, felonious,
illegitimate, prohibited, unauthorized,
unlawful, unlicensed **2** = **forbidden**,
clandestine, furtive, guilty, immoral,
improper
illiterate *adj* = **uneducated**, ignorant,
uncultured, untaught, untutored
ill-mannered *adj* = **rude**, badly behaved,
boorish, churlish, discourteous, impolite,
insolent, loutish, uncouth
illness *n* = **disease**, affliction, ailment,
disorder, infirmity, malady, sickness
illogical *adj* = **irrational**, absurd,
inconsistent, invalid, meaningless,
senseless, unreasonable, unscientific,
unsound
ill-treat *v* = **abuse**, damage, harm, injure,
maltreat, mishandle, misuse, oppress

-nat·ing 1 light up. 2 clarify. 3 decorate
with lights. 4 decorate with gold and
colors. il·lu·mi·na'tion n il·lu'mine vt
-mined, -min·ing illuminate.
il·lu·sion [i-LOO-zhən] n deceptive
appearance or belief. il·lu'sion·ist n
conjurer. il·lu'so·ry [-LOO-sə-ree] adj
deceptive.
il·lus·trate [IL-ə-strayt] vt -trat·ed, -trat·ing
1 provide with pictures or examples. 2
exemplify. il·lus·tra'tion n 1 picture,
diagram. 2 example. 3 act of illustrating.
il·lus'tra·tive adj providing explanation.
il·lus·tri·ous [i-LUS-tree-əs] adj 1 famous. 2
distinguished. 3 exalted.
im- prefix same as IN-¹ or IN-².
im·age [IM-ij] n 1 representation or likeness
of person or thing. 2 optical counterpart,
as in mirror. 3 double, copy. 4 general
impression. 5 mental picture created by
words, esp. in literature. ♦ vt -aged,

-mag·ing 6 make image of. 7 reflect.
im'age·ry n images collectively, esp. in
literature.
im·ag·ine [i-MAJ-in] vt 1 picture to oneself.
2 think. 3 conjecture. im·ag'i·na·ble adj
im·ag'i·nar·y adj existing only in fancy.
im·ag·i·na'tion n 1 faculty of making
mental images of things not present. 2
fancy. 3 resourcefulness. im·ag'i·na·tive adj
i·mam [i-MAHM] n Islamic minister or
priest.
im·bal·ance [im-BAL-əns] n lack of
balance, proportion.
im·be·cile [IM-bə-sil] n 1 idiot. ♦ adj 2
idiotic. im·be·cil'i·ty n
im·bibe [im-BĪB] v -bibed, -bib·ing ♦ vt 1
drink in. 2 absorb. ♦ vi 3 drink.
im·bri·cate [IM-brə-kit] adj lying over each
other in regular order, like tiles or shingles
on roof. im·bri·ca'tion n
im·bro·glio [im-BROHL-yoh] n, pl -glios 1

─────────── THESAURUS ───────────

illuminate v 1 = **light up**, brighten 2 =
explain, clarify, clear up, elucidate,
enlighten, interpret, make clear, shed light
on
illuminating adj = **informative**,
enlightening, explanatory, helpful,
instructive, revealing
illumination n 1 = **light**, brightness,
lighting, radiance 2 = **enlightenment**,
clarification, insight, revelation
illusion n 1 = **fantasy**, chimera, daydream,
figment of the imagination, hallucination,
mirage, will-o'-the-wisp 2 =
misconception, deception, delusion, error,
fallacy, misapprehension
illusory adj = **unreal**, chimerical, deceptive,
delusive, fallacious, false, hallucinatory,
mistaken, sham
illustrate v = **demonstrate**, bring home,
elucidate, emphasize, explain, point up,
show
illustrated adj = **pictorial**, decorated,
graphic
illustration n 1 = **example**, case, instance,
specimen 2 = **picture**, decoration, figure,
plate, sketch
illustrious adj = **famous**, celebrated,
distinguished, eminent, glorious, great,
notable, prominent, renowned
ill will n = **hostility**, animosity, bad blood,
dislike, enmity, hatred, malice, rancor,
resentment, venom
image n 1 = **representation**, effigy, figure,

icon, idol, likeness, picture, portrait, statue
2 = **replica**, counterpart, (dead) ringer (sl),
Doppelgänger, double, facsimile, spitting
image (inf) 3 = **concept**, idea, impression,
mental picture, perception
imaginable adj = **possible**, believable,
comprehensible, conceivable, credible,
likely, plausible
imaginary adj = **fictional**, fictitious,
hypothetical, illusory, imagined, invented,
made-up, nonexistent, unreal
imagination n 1 = **creativity**, enterprise,
ingenuity, invention, inventiveness,
originality, resourcefulness, vision 2 =
unreality, illusion, supposition
imaginative adj = **creative**, clever,
enterprising, ingenious, inspired, inventive,
original
imagine v 1 = **envisage**, conceive,
conceptualize, conjure up, picture, plan,
think of, think up, visualize 2 = **believe**,
assume, conjecture, fancy, guess (inf),
infer, suppose, surmise, suspect, take it,
think
imbecile n 1 = **idiot**, chump, cretin (offens),
dork (sl), fool, halfwit, moron, schmuck
(sl), thickhead ♦ adj 2 = **stupid**, asinine,
fatuous, feeble-minded, foolish, idiotic,
moronic, thick, witless
imbibe v 1 = **drink**, consume, knock back
(inf), quaff, sink (inf), swallow, swig (inf)
2 Literary = **absorb**, acquire, assimilate,
gain, gather, ingest, receive, take in

disagreement. **2** complicated situation, plot.

im·bue [im-BYOO] *vt* **-bued, -bu·ing 1** inspire. **2** saturate.

im·i·tate [IM-i-tayt] *vt* **-tat·ed, -tat·ing 1** take as model. **2** mimic, copy. **im'i·ta·ble** *adj* **im·i·ta'tion** *n* **1** act of imitating. **2** copy of original. **3** likeness. **4** counterfeit. **im'i·ta·tive** *adj* **im'i·ta·tor** *n*

im·mac·u·late [im-AK-yə-lit] *adj* **1** spotless. **2** pure. **3** unsullied.

im·ma·nent [IM-mə-nənt] *adj* abiding in, inherent. **im'ma·nence** *n*

im·ma·te·ri·al [im-ə-TEER-ee-əl] *adj* **1** unimportant, trifling. **2** not consisting of matter. **3** spiritual.

im·ma·ture' *adj* **1** not fully developed. **2** lacking wisdom or stability because of youth. **im·ma·tu'ri·ty** *n*

im·me·di·ate [i-MEE-dee-it] *adj* **1** occurring at once. **2** direct, not separated by others. **im·me'di·a·cy** *n*

im·me·mo·ri·al [im-ə-MOR-ee-əl] *adj* beyond memory.

im·mense [i-MENS] *adj* huge, vast. **im·men'si·ty** *n* vastness.

im·merse [i-MURS] *vt* **-mersed, -mers·ing 1** dip, plunge, into liquid. **2** involve. **3** engross. **im·mer'sion** [-zhən] *n* immersing. **immersion heater** *n* electric appliance for heating liquid in which it is immersed.

im·mi·grate [IM-i-grayt] *vi* **-grat·ed, -grat·ing** come into country as settler. **im'mi·grant** [-grənt] *n, adj* **im·mi·gra'tion** *n*

im·mi·nent [IM-ə-nənt] *adj* **1** liable to happen soon. **2** close at hand. **im'mi·nence** *n*

im·mo'bile *adj* **1** not moving. **2** unable to move. **im·mo·bil'i·ty** *n* **im·mo'bi·lize** *vt* make unable to move or work.

im·mod'er·ate *adj* excessive or

——— THESAURUS ———

imbroglio *n* = **complication**, embarrassment, entanglement, involvement, misunderstanding, quandary

imitate *v* = **copy**, ape, echo, emulate, follow, mimic, mirror, repeat, simulate

imitation *n* **1** = **mimicry**, counterfeiting, duplication, likeness, resemblance, simulation **2** = **replica**, fake, forgery, impersonation, impression, reproduction, sham, substitution ◆ *adj* **3** = **artificial**, dummy, ersatz, man-made, mock, phoney *or* phony (*inf*), reproduction, sham, simulated, synthetic

imitative *adj* = **derivative**, copycat (*inf*), mimetic, parrot-like, second-hand, simulated, unoriginal

imitator *n* = **impersonator**, copier, copycat (*inf*), impressionist, mimic, parrot

immaculate *adj* **1** = **clean**, neat, spick-and-span, spotless, spruce, squeaky-clean **2** = **flawless**, above reproach, faultless, impeccable, perfect, unblemished, unexceptionable, untarnished

immaterial *adj* = **irrelevant**, extraneous, inconsequential, inessential, insignificant, of no importance, trivial, unimportant

immature *adj* **1** = **young**, adolescent, undeveloped, unformed, unripe **2** = **childish**, callow, inexperienced, infantile, juvenile, puerile

immaturity *n* **1** = **unripeness**, greenness, imperfection, rawness, unpreparedness **2** =

childishness, callowness, inexperience, puerility

immediate *adj* **1** = **instant**, instantaneous **2** = **nearest**, close, direct, near, next

immediately *adv* = **at once**, directly, forthwith, instantly, now, promptly, right away, straight away, this instant, without delay

immense *adj* = **huge**, colossal, enormous, extensive, gigantic, great, massive, monumental, stupendous, tremendous, vast

immensity *n* = **size**, bulk, enormity, expanse, extent, greatness, hugeness, magnitude, vastness

immerse *v* **1** = **plunge**, bathe, dip, douse, duck, dunk, sink, submerge **2** = **engross**, absorb, busy, engage, involve, occupy, take up

immersion *n* **1** = **dipping**, dousing, ducking, dunking, plunging, submerging **2** = **involvement**, absorption, concentration, preoccupation

immigrant *n* = **settler**, incomer, newcomer

imminent *adj* = **near**, at hand, close, coming, forthcoming, gathering, impending, in the pipeline, looming

immobile *adj* = **stationary**, at a standstill, at rest, fixed, immovable, motionless, rigid, rooted, static, still, stock-still, unmoving

immobility *n* = **stillness**, fixity, inertness,

unreasonable.

im·mod·est *adj* **1** behaving in an indecent or improper manner. **2** behaving in a boastful or conceited manner. **im·mod'es·ty** *n*

im·mo·late [IM-ə-layt] *vt* **-lat·ed, -lat·ing** kill, sacrifice. **im·mo·la'tion** *n*

im·mor·al [i-MOR-əl] *adj* **1** corrupt. **2** promiscuous. **3** indecent. **4** unethical. **im·mor'al·i·ty** *n, pl* **-ties**

im·mor·tal [i-MOR-tl] *adj* **1** deathless. **2** famed for all time. ◆ *n* **3** immortal being. **4** god. **5** one whose fame will last. **im·mor·tal'i·ty** *n* **im·mor'tal·ize** *vt* **-ized, -iz·ing**

im·mov'a·ble *adj* **1** unable to be moved. **2** unwilling to change one's opinions or beliefs. **3** not affected by feeling, emotionless.

im·mune [i-MYOON] *adj* **1** proof (against a disease, etc.). **2** secure, exempt. **im·mu'ni·ty** *n* **1** state of being immune. **2**

freedom from prosecution, etc.

im·mu·ni·za'tion *n* process of making immune to disease. **im'mu·nize** *vt* **-nized, -niz·ing** make immune. **im·mu·nol'o·gy** *n* branch of biology concerned with study of immunity.

im·mu·ta·ble [i-MYOO-tə-bəl] *adj* unchangeable.

imp *n* **1** little devil. **2** mischievous child.

im·pact [IM-pakt] *n* **1** collision. **2** profound effect. **impact** [im-PAKT] *vt* drive, press.

im·pair' *vt* weaken, damage. **im·pair'ment** *n*

im·pal·a [im-PAL-ə] *n, pl* **-pal·as** antelope of Africa.

im·pale [im-PAYL] *vt* **-paled, -pal·ing 1** pierce with sharp instrument. **2** make helpless as if pierced through.

im·part [im-PAHRT] *vt* **1** communicate (information, etc.). **2** give.

im·par·tial [im-PAHR-shəl] *adj* **1** not biased or prejudiced. **2** fair. **im·par·ti·al'i·ty** *n*

motionlessness, stability, steadiness

immobilize *v* = **paralyze**, bring to a standstill, cripple, disable, freeze, halt, stop, transfix

immoderate *adj* = **excessive**, exaggerated, exorbitant, extravagant, extreme, inordinate, over the top (*sl*), undue, unjustified, unreasonable

immoral *adj* = **wicked**, bad, corrupt, debauched, depraved, dissolute, indecent, sinful, unethical, unprincipled, wrong

immorality *n* = **wickedness**, corruption, debauchery, depravity, dissoluteness, sin, vice, wrong

immortal *adj* **1** = **eternal**, deathless, enduring, everlasting, imperishable, lasting, perennial, undying ◆ *n* **2** = **god**, goddess **3** = **great**, genius, hero

immortality *n* **1** = **eternity**, everlasting life, perpetuity **2** = **fame**, celebrity, glory, greatness, renown

immortalize *v* = **commemorate**, celebrate, exalt, glorify

immovable *adj* **1** = **fixed**, firm, immutable, jammed, secure, set, stable, stationary, stuck **2** = **inflexible**, adamant, obdurate, resolute, steadfast, unshakable, unwavering, unyielding

immune *adj* = **exempt**, clear, free, invulnerable, proof (against), protected, resistant, safe, unaffected

immunity *n* **1** = **exemption**, amnesty,

freedom, indemnity, invulnerability, license, release **2** = **resistance**, immunization, protection

immunize *v* = **vaccinate**, inoculate, protect, safeguard

imp *n* **1** = **demon**, devil, sprite **2** = **rascal**, brat, minx, rogue, scamp

impact *n* **1** = **collision**, blow, bump, contact, crash, jolt, knock, smash, stroke, thump **2** = **effect**, consequences, impression, influence, repercussions, significance ◆ *v* **3** = **hit**, clash, collide, crash, crush, strike

impair *v* = **worsen**, blunt, damage, decrease, diminish, harm, hinder, injure, lessen, reduce, undermine, weaken

impaired *adj* = **damaged**, defective, faulty, flawed, imperfect, unsound

impart *v* **1** = **communicate**, convey, disclose, divulge, make known, pass on, relate, reveal, tell **2** = **give**, accord, afford, bestow, confer, grant, lend, yield

impartial *adj* = **neutral**, detached, disinterested, equitable, even-handed, fair, just, objective, open-minded, unbiased, unprejudiced

impartiality *n* = **neutrality**, detachment, disinterestedness, dispassion, equity, even-handedness, fairness, objectivity, open-mindedness

impassable *adj* = **blocked**, closed, impenetrable, obstructed

im·passe [IM-pas] *n* **1** deadlock. **2** place, situation, from which there is no outlet.

im·pas·sioned [im-PASH-ənd] *adj* deeply moved, ardent.

im·pas·sive [im-PAS-iv] *adj* **1** showing no emotion. **2** calm. **im·pas·siv'i·ty** *n*

im·pa'tient *adj* **1** irritable at any delay or difficulty. **2** restless (to have or do something). **im·pa'tience** *n*

im·peach [im-PEECH] *vt* **1** charge with crime. **2** call to account. **3** *Law* challenge credibility of (a witness). **im·peach'a·ble** *adj*

im·pec·ca·ble [im-PEK-ə-bəl] *adj* without flaw or error.

im·pe·cu·ni·ous [im-pi-KYOO-nee-əs] *adj* poor. **im·pe·cu'ni·ous·ness** *n* **im·pe·cu·ni·os'i·ty** *n*

im·pede [im-PEED] *vt* **-ped·ed, -ped·ing** hinder. **im·ped'ance** *n Electricity* measure of opposition offered to flow of alternating current. **im·ped'i·ment** [-PED-ə-mənt] *n* **1** obstruction. **2** defect.

im·pel' *vt* **-pelled, -pel·ling 1** induce, incite. **2** drive, force. **im·pel'ler** *n*

im·pend' *vi* **1** threaten. **2** be imminent. **3** hang over. **im·pend'ing** *adj*

im·per·a·tive [im-PER-ə-tiv] *adj* **1** necessary. **2** peremptory. **3** expressing command. ◆ *n* **4** imperative mood.

im·per·cep'ti·ble *adj* too slight or gradual to be noticed.

im·per'fect *adj* **1** having faults or mistakes. **2** not complete. **3** *Grammar* denoting a tense of verbs describing continuous, incomplete, or repeated past actions. ◆ *n* **4** *Grammar* imperfect tense. **im·per·fec'tion** *n*

im·pe·ri·al [im-PEER-ee-əl] *adj* **1** of empire, or emperor. **2** majestic. **im·pe'ri·al·ism** *n* extension of empire. **1** belief in colonial empire. **im·pe'ri·al·ist** *n*

im·per·il [im-PER-əl] *vt* **-iled, -il·ing** bring into peril, endanger.

im·pe·ri·ous [im-PEER-ee-əs] *adj* **1** domineering. **2** haughty. **3** dictatorial. **im·pe'ri·ous·ness** *n*

im·per·son·al [im-PUR-sə-nl] *adj* **1** objective, having no personal significance. **2** devoid of human warmth, personality, etc. **3** (of verb) without personal subject. **im·per·son·al'i·ty** *n*

im·per·son·ate [im-PUR-sə-nayt] *vt* **-at·ed, -at·ing 1** pretend to be (another person). **2** play the part of. **im·per·son·a'tion** *n*

impasse *n* = **deadlock**, dead end, gridlock, stalemate, standoff, standstill

impassioned *adj* = **intense**, animated, fervent, fiery, heated, inspired, passionate, rousing, stirring

impatience *n* **1** = **haste**, impetuosity, intolerance, rashness **2** = **restlessness**, agitation, anxiety, eagerness, edginess, fretfulness, nervousness, uneasiness

impatient *adj* **1** = **hasty**, demanding, hot-tempered, impetuous, intolerant **2** = **restless**, eager, edgy, fretful, straining at the leash

impeach *v* = **charge**, accuse, arraign, indict

impeccable *adj* = **faultless**, blameless, flawless, immaculate, irreproachable, perfect, unblemished, unimpeachable

impecunious *adj* = **poor**, broke (*inf*), destitute, down and out, down on one's luck (*inf*), indigent, insolvent, penniless, poverty-stricken

impede *v* = **hinder**, block, check, disrupt, hamper, hold up, obstruct, slow (down), thwart

impediment *n* = **obstacle**, barrier, difficulty, encumbrance, hindrance, obstruction, snag, stumbling block

impel *v* = **force**, compel, constrain, drive, induce, oblige, push, require

impending *adj* = **looming**, approaching, coming, forthcoming, gathering, imminent, in the pipeline, near, upcoming

impenetrable *adj* **1** = **solid**, dense, impassable, impermeable, impervious, inviolable, thick **2** = **incomprehensible**, arcane, enigmatic, inscrutable, mysterious, obscure, unfathomable, unintelligible

imperative *adj* = **urgent**, crucial, essential, pressing, vital

imperceptible *adj* = **undetectable**, faint, indiscernible, microscopic, minute, slight, small, subtle, tiny

imperfect *adj* = **flawed**, damaged, defective, faulty, impaired, incomplete, limited, unfinished

imperfection *n* = **fault**, blemish, defect, deficiency, failing, flaw, frailty, shortcoming, taint, weakness

imperial *adj* = **royal**, kingly, majestic, princely, queenly, regal, sovereign

imperil *v* = **endanger**, expose, jeopardize, risk

impersonal *adj* = **remote**, aloof, cold, detached, dispassionate, formal, inhuman,

DICTIONARY

im·per·ti·nent [im-PUR-tn-ənt] *adj* insolent, rude. **im·per'ti·nence** *n*

im·per·turb·a·ble [im-pər-TUR-bə-bəl] *adj* calm, not excitable.

im·per·vi·ous [im-PUR-vee-əs] *adj* **1** not affording passage. **2** impenetrable (to feeling, argument, etc.).

im·pe·ti·go [im-pi-TĪ-goh] *n* contagious skin disease.

im·pet·u·ous [im-PECH-oo-əs] *adj* likely to act without consideration, rash. **im·pet·u·os'i·ty** *n*

im·pe·tus [IM-pi-təs] *n* **1** force with which body moves. **2** impulse.

im·pinge [im-PINJ] *vi* **pinged**, **-ping·ing 1** encroach (upon). **2** collide (with). **im·pinge'ment** *n*

im·pi·ous [IM-pee-əs] *adj* irreverent, profane, wicked. **im·pi'e·ty** [-PĪ-i-tee] *n*

im·plac·a·ble [im-PLAK-ə-bəl] *adj* not to be appeased. **2** unyielding. **im·plac·a·bil'i·ty** *n*

im·plant' *vt* insert, fix. **im'plant** *n* **1** *Dentistry* artificial tooth implanted permanently in jaw. **2** implanted breast enhancement.

im·ple·ment [IM-plə-mənt] *n* **1** tool, instrument, utensil. ♦ *vt* [-ment] **2** carry out (instructions, etc.). **3** put into effect.

im·pli·cate [IM-pli-kayt] *vt* **-cat·ed, -cat·ing 1** involve, include. **2** entangle. **3** imply. **im·pli·ca'tion** *n* something implied.

im·plic·it [-PLIS-it] *adj* implied but not expressed. **2** absolute and unreserved.

im·plore [im-PLOR] *vt* **-plored, -plor·ing** entreat earnestly.

im·ply [im-PLĪ] *vt* **-plied, -ply·ing 1** indicate by hint, suggest. **2** mean.

im·po·lite' *adj* showing bad manners.

im·port' *vt* **1** bring in, introduce (esp.

THESAURUS

neutral

impersonate *v* = **imitate**, ape, do (*inf*), masquerade as, mimic, pass oneself off as, pose as (*inf*)

impersonation *n* = **imitation**, caricature, impression, mimicry, parody

impertinence *n* = **rudeness**, brazenness, cheek (*inf*), disrespect, effrontery, front, impudence, insolence, nerve (*inf*), presumption

impertinent *adj* = **rude**, brazen, cheeky (*inf*), disrespectful, impolite, impudent, insolent, presumptuous

imperturbable *adj* = **calm**, collected, composed, cool, nerveless, self-possessed, serene, unexcitable, unflappable (*inf*), unruffled

impervious *adj* **1** = **sealed**, impassable, impenetrable, impermeable, resistant **2** = **unaffected**, immune, invulnerable, proof against, unmoved, untouched

impetuosity *n* = **haste**, impulsiveness, precipitateness, rashness

impetuous *adj* = **rash**, hasty, impulsive, precipitate, unthinking

impetus *n* **1** = **incentive**, catalyst, goad, impulse, motivation, push, spur, stimulus **2** = **force**, energy, momentum, power

impinge *v* **1** = **encroach**, infringe, invade, obtrude, trespass, violate **2** = **affect**, bear upon, have a bearing on, impact, influence, relate to, touch

impious *adj* = **sacrilegious**, blasphemous, godless, irreligious, irreverent, profane,

sinful, ungodly, unholy, wicked

impish *adj* = **mischievous**, devilish, puckish, rascally, roguish, sportive, waggish

implacable *adj* = **unyielding**, inflexible, intractable, merciless, pitiless, unbending, uncompromising, unforgiving

implant *v* **1** = **instill**, inculcate, infuse **2** = **insert**, fix, graft

implement *v* **1** = **carry out**, bring about, complete, effect, enforce, execute, fulfill, perform, realize ♦ *n* **2** = **tool**, apparatus, appliance, device, gadget, instrument, utensil

implicate *v* = **incriminate**, associate, embroil, entangle, include, inculpate, involve

implication *n* = **suggestion**, inference, innuendo, meaning, overtone, presumption, significance

implicit *adj* **1** = **implied**, inferred, latent, tacit, taken for granted, undeclared, understood, unspoken **2** = **absolute**, constant, firm, fixed, full, steadfast, unqualified, unreserved, wholehearted

implied *adj* = **unspoken**, hinted at, implicit, indirect, suggested, tacit, undeclared, unexpressed, unstated

implore *v* = **beg**, beseech, entreat, importune, plead with, pray

imply *v* **1** = **hint**, insinuate, intimate, signify, suggest **2** = **entail**, indicate, involve, mean, point to, presuppose

impolite *adj* = **bad-mannered**,

goods from foreign country). **2** imply. **im'port** n **1** thing imported. **2** meaning. **3** importance. **im·port'er** n

im·por·tant [im-POR-tnt] *adj* **1** of great consequence. **2** momentous. **3** pompous. **im·por'tance** n

im·por·tune [im-por-TOON] *vt* **-tuned, -tun·ing** request, demand persistently. **im·por'tu·nate** [-POR-chə nit] *adj* persistent. **im·por·tu'ni·ty** n

im·pose [im-POHZ] *vt* **-posed, -pos·ing 1** levy (tax, duty, etc., upon). ◆ *vi* **2** take advantage (of), practice deceit on. **im·pos'ing** *adj* impressive. **im·po·si'tion** n **1** that which is imposed. **2** tax. **3** burden. **4** deception. **im'post** n duty, tax on imports.

im·pos·si·ble [im-POS-ə-bəl] *adj* **1** incapable of being done or experienced. **2** absurd. **3** unreasonable. **im·pos·si·bil'i·ty** n, *pl* **-ties**

im·pos·tor [im-POS-tər] n deceiver, one who assumes false identity.

im·po·tent [IM-pə-tənt] *adj* **1** powerless. **2** (of males) incapable of sexual intercourse. **im'po·tence** n

im·pound [im-POWND] *vt* **1** take legal possession of and, often, place in a pound (automobile, animal, etc.). **2** confiscate.

im·pov·er·ish [im-POV-ər-ish] *vt* make poor or weak. **im·pov'er·ish·ment** n

im·prac·ti·ca·ble *adj* incapable of being put into practice.

im·prac·ti·cal *adj* not sensible.

im·pre·ca·tion [im-pri-KAY-shən] n **1** invoking of evil. **2** curse. **im'pre·cate** *vt* **-cat·ed, -cat·ing**

im·preg·na·ble [im-PREG-nə-bəl] *adj* **1** proof against attack. **2** unassailable. **3** unable to be broken into. **im·preg·na·bil'i·ty** n

discourteous, disrespectful, ill-mannered, insolent, loutish, rude, uncouth

impoliteness n = **bad manners**, boorishness, churlishness, discourtesy, disrespect, insolence, rudeness

import v **1** = **bring in**, introduce ◆ n **2** = **meaning**, drift, gist, implication, intention, sense, significance, thrust **3** = **importance**, consequence, magnitude, moment, significance, substance, weight

importance n **1** = **significance**, concern, consequence, import, interest, moment, substance, usefulness, value, weight **2** = **prestige**, distinction, eminence, esteem, influence, prominence, standing, status

important adj **1** = **significant**, far-reaching, momentous, seminal, serious, substantial, urgent, weighty **2** = **powerful**, eminent, high-ranking, influential, noteworthy, pre-eminent, prominent

importunate adj = **persistent**, demanding, dogged, insistent, pressing, urgent

impose v **1** = **establish**, decree, fix, institute, introduce, levy, ordain **2** = **inflict**, appoint, enforce, saddle (someone) with

imposing adj = **impressive**, commanding, dignified, grand, majestic, stately, striking

imposition n **1** = **application**, introduction, levying **2** = **intrusion**, liberty, presumption

impossibility n = **hopelessness**, impracticability, inability

impossible adj **1** = **unattainable**, impracticable, inconceivable, out of the question, unachievable, unobtainable, unthinkable **2** = **absurd**, ludicrous, outrageous, preposterous, unreasonable

impostor n = **impersonator**, charlatan, deceiver, fake, fraud, phoney or phony (inf), pretender, sham, trickster

impotence n = **powerlessness**, feebleness, frailty, helplessness, inability, incapacity, incompetence, ineffectiveness, paralysis, uselessness, weakness

impotent adj = **powerless**, feeble, frail, helpless, incapable, incapacitated, incompetent, ineffective, paralyzed, weak

impoverish v **1** = **bankrupt**, beggar, break, ruin **2** = **diminish**, deplete, drain, exhaust, reduce, sap, use up, wear out

impoverished adj = **poor**, bankrupt, destitute, impecunious, needy, penurious, poverty-stricken

impracticable adj = **unfeasible**, impossible, out of the question, unachievable, unattainable, unworkable

impractical adj **1** = **unworkable**, impossible, impracticable, inoperable, nonviable, unrealistic, wild **2** = **idealistic**, romantic, starry-eyed, unrealistic

imprecise adj = **indefinite**, equivocal, hazy, ill-defined, indeterminate, inexact, inexplicit, loose, rough, vague, woolly

impregnable adj = **invulnerable**, impenetrable, indestructible, invincible, secure, unassailable, unbeatable, unconquerable

im·preg·nate [im-PREG-nayt] *vt* **-nat·ed,** **-nat·ing 1** saturate, infuse. **2** make pregnant. **im·preg·na'tion** *n*

im·pre·sa·ri·o [im-prə-SAHR-ee-oh] *n, pl* **-ri·os 1** organizer of public entertainment. **2** manager of opera, ballet, etc.

im·press'[1] *vt* **1** affect deeply, usu. favorably. **2** imprint, stamp. **3** fix. ♦ *n* [IM-pres] **4** act of impressing. **5** mark impressed. **im·pres'sion** *n* **1** effect produced, esp. on mind. **2** notion, belief. **3** imprint. **4** a printing. **5** total of copies printed at once. **6** printed copy. **im·pres'sion·a·ble** *adj* susceptible to external influences. **im·pres'sion·ism** *n* art style that renders general effect without detail. **im·pres'sion·ist** *n* **im·pres'sive** *adj* making deep impression.

im·press'[2] *vt* press into service.

im·pri·ma·tur [im-pri-MAH-tər] *n* **1** license to print book, etc. **2** sanction, approval.

im'print *n* **1** mark made by pressure. **2** characteristic mark. ♦ *vt* [im-PRINT] **3** produce mark. **4** stamp. **5** fix in mind.

im·pris·on [im-PRIZ-ən] *vt* put in prison. **im·pris'on·ment** *n*

im·prob'a·ble *adj* not likely to be true or to happen. **im·prob·a·bil'i·ty** *n, pl* **-ties**

im·promp·tu [im-PROMP-too] *adv, adj* **1** on the spur of the moment. **2** unrehearsed.

im·prop'er *adj* **1** indecent. **2** incorrect or irregular. **improper fraction** fraction in which the numerator is larger than the denominator, as in ⅝.

im·pro·pri'e·ty *n, pl* **-ties** unsuitable or slightly improper behaviour.

im·prove [im-PROOV] *v* **-proved, -prov·ing** make or become better in quality, standard, value, etc. **im·prove'ment** *n*

im·prov·i·dent [im-PROV-i-dənt] *adj* **1** thriftless. **2** negligent. **3** imprudent. **im·prov'i·dence** *n*

im·pro·vise [IM-prə-vīz] *v* **-vised, -vis·ing 1** make use of materials at hand. **2** compose, utter without preparation.

——————— THESAURUS ———————

impregnate *v* **1** = **saturate**, infuse, permeate, soak, steep, suffuse **2** = **fertilize**, inseminate, make pregnant

impress *v* **1** = **excite**, affect, inspire, make an impression, move, stir, strike, touch **2** = **stress**, bring home to, emphasize, fix, inculcate, instill into **3** = **imprint**, emboss, engrave, indent, mark, print, stamp

impression *n* **1** = **effect**, feeling, impact, influence, reaction **2** = **idea**, belief, conviction, feeling, hunch, notion, sense, suspicion **3** = **mark**, dent, hollow, imprint, indentation, outline, stamp **4** = **imitation**, impersonation, parody

impressionable *adj* = **suggestible**, gullible, ingenuous, open, receptive, responsive, sensitive, susceptible, vulnerable

impressive *adj* = **grand**, awesome, cool (*inf*), dramatic, exciting, moving, phat (*sl*), powerful, stirring, striking

imprint *n* **1** = **mark**, impression, indentation, sign, stamp ♦ *v* **2** = **fix**, engrave, etch, impress, print, stamp

imprison *v* = **jail**, confine, detain, incarcerate, intern, lock up, put away, send down (*inf*)

imprisoned *adj* = **jailed**, behind bars, captive, confined, incarcerated, in jail, inside (*sl*), locked up, under lock and key

imprisonment *n* = **custody**, confinement, detention, incarceration

improbability *n* = **doubt**, dubiety, uncertainty, unlikelihood

improbable *adj* = **doubtful**, dubious, fanciful, far-fetched, implausible, questionable, unconvincing, unlikely, weak

impromptu *adj* = **unprepared**, ad-lib, extemporaneous, improvised, offhand, off the cuff (*inf*), spontaneous, unrehearsed, unscripted

improper *adj* **1** = **indecent**, risqué, smutty, suggestive, unbecoming, unseemly, untoward, vulgar **2** = **unwarranted**, inappropriate, out of place, uncalled-for, unfit, unsuitable

impropriety *n* = **indecency**, bad taste, incongruity, vulgarity

improve *v* **1** = **enhance**, advance, better, correct, help, rectify, touch up, upgrade **2** = **progress**, develop, make strides, pick up, rally, rise

improvement *n* **1** = **enhancement**, advancement, betterment **2** = **progress**, development, rally, recovery, upswing

improvident *adj* = **imprudent**, careless, negligent, prodigal, profligate, reckless, short-sighted, spendthrift, thoughtless, wasteful

improvisation *n* **1** = **spontaneity**, ad-libbing, extemporizing, invention **2** = **makeshift**, ad-lib, expedient

im·prov·i·sa·tion [-ZAY-shən] n

im·pu·dent [IM-pyə-dənt] adj disrespectful, impertinent. **im'pu·dence** n

im·pugn [im-PYOON] vt **-pugned, -pugn·ing** call in question, challenge as false.

im·pulse [IM-puls] n **1** sudden inclination to act. **2** sudden application of force. **3** motion caused by it. **4** stimulation of nerve moving muscle. **im·pul'sion** n impulse, usu. in its first sense. **im·pul'sive** adj given to acting without reflection, rash.

im·pu·ni·ty [im-PYOO-ni-tee] n freedom, exemption from injurious consequences or punishment.

im·pure' adj **1** having dirty or unwanted substances mixed in. **2** immoral, obscene. **im·pu'ri·ty** n, pl **-ties**

im·pute [im-PYOOT] vt **-put·ed, -put·ing** ascribe, attribute to. **im·pu·ta'tion** n **1** that

which is imputed as a charge or fault. **2** reproach, censure.

in prep **1** expresses inclusion within limits of space, time, circumstance, sphere, etc. ♦ adv **2** in or into some state, place, etc. **3** inf in vogue, etc. ♦ adj **4** inf fashionable.

In Chem. indium.

in-[1], il-, im-, ir- prefix **1** not, non, e.g. incredible. **2** lack of, e.g. inexperience.

in-[2], il-, im-, ir- prefix in, into, towards, within, on, e.g. infiltrate.

in·a·bil'i·ty n lack of means or skill to do something.

in·ac'cu·rate adj not correct. **in·ac'cu·ra·cy** n, pl **-cies**

in·ad'e·quate adj **1** not enough. **2** not good enough. **in·ad'e·qua·cy** n, pl **-cies**

in·ad·vert·ent [in-əd-VUR-tnt] adj **1** not attentive. **2** negligent. **3** unintentional. **in·ad·vert'ence** n

improvise v **1 = extemporize**, ad-lib, busk, invent, play it by ear (inf), speak off the cuff (inf), wing it (inf) **2 = concoct**, contrive, devise, throw together

imprudent adj **= unwise**, careless, foolhardy, ill-advised, ill-considered, ill-judged, injudicious, irresponsible, rash, reckless

impudence n **= boldness**, audacity, brazenness, cheek (inf), effrontery, impertinence, insolence, nerve (inf), presumption, shamelessness

impudent adj **= bold**, audacious, brazen, cheeky (inf), impertinent, insolent, pert, presumptuous, rude, shameless

impulse n **= urge**, caprice, feeling, inclination, notion, whim, wish

impulsive adj **= instinctive**, devil-may-care, hasty, impetuous, intuitive, passionate, precipitate, rash, spontaneous

impunity n **= security**, dispensation, exemption, freedom, immunity, liberty, license, permission

impure adj **1 = unrefined**, adulterated, debased, dirty, mixed **2 = contaminated**, defiled, dirty, infected, polluted, tainted **3 = immoral**, corrupt, indecent, lascivious, lewd, licentious, obscene, unchaste

impurity n **= contamination**, defilement, dirtiness, infection, pollution, taint

imputation n **= blame**, accusation, aspersion, censure, insinuation, reproach, slander, slur

inability n **= incapability**, disability,

disqualification, impotence, inadequacy, incapacity, incompetence, ineptitude, powerlessness

inaccessible adj **= out of reach**, impassable, out of the way, remote, unapproachable, unattainable, unreachable

inaccuracy n **= error**, defect, erratum, fault, lapse, mistake

inaccurate adj **= incorrect**, defective, erroneous, faulty, imprecise, mistaken, out, unreliable, unsound, wrong

inactive adj **= unused**, dormant, idle, inoperative, unemployed, unoccupied

inactivity n **= immobility**, dormancy, hibernation, inaction, passivity, unemployment

inadequacy n **1 = shortage**, dearth, insufficiency, meagerness, paucity, poverty, scantiness **2 = incompetence**, deficiency, inability, incapacity, ineffectiveness **3 = shortcoming**, defect, failing, imperfection, weakness

inadequate adj **1 = insufficient**, meager, scant, sketchy, sparse **2 = incompetent**, deficient, faulty, found wanting, incapable, lousy (sl), not up to scratch (inf), unqualified

inadmissible adj **= unacceptable**, inappropriate, irrelevant, unallowable

inadvertently adv **= unintentionally**, accidentally, by accident, by mistake, involuntarily, mistakenly, unwittingly

inadvisable adj **= unwise**, ill-advised,

in·ane [i-NAYN] *adj* foolish, silly, vacant. **in·a·ni·tion** [-NISH-ən] *n* **1** exhaustion. **2** silliness. **in·an'i·ty** *n*

in·an·i·mate [in-AN-ə-mit] *adj* **1** lacking qualities of living beings. **2** appearing dead. **3** lacking vitality.

in·ap·pro'pri·ate *adj* not suitable.

in·as·much as [in-əz-MUCH] *conj* because or in so far as.

in·au·gu·rate [in-AW-gyə-rayt] *vt* **-rat·ed, -rat·ing 1** begin, initiate the use of, esp. with ceremony. **2** admit to office. **in·au'gu·ral** *adj* **in·au·gu·ra'tion** *n* **1** act of inaugurating. **2** ceremony to celebrate the initiation or admittance of.

in·aus·pi·cious [in-aw-SPISH-əs] *adj* **1** not auspicious. **2** unlucky. **3** unfavorable. **in·aus·pi'cious·ly** *adv*

in·board [IN-bord] *adj* inside hull or bulwarks.

in'born *adj* **1** existing from birth. **2** inherent.

in'breed *vt* **-bred, -breed·ing** breed from union of closely related individuals. **in'bred** *adj* **1** produced as result of inbreeding. **2** inborn, ingrained.

in·cal·cu·la·ble [in-KAL-kyə-lə-bəl] *adj* **1** beyond calculation. **2** very great.

in cam·er·a [KAM-ə-rə] in secret or private session.

in·can·des·cent [in-kən-DES-ənt] *adj* **1** glowing with heat, shining. **2** of artificial light, produced by glowing filament. **in·can·des'cence** *n*

in·can·ta·tion [in-kan-TAY-shən] *n* magic spell or formula, charm.

in·ca·pa·ble *adj* **1** (foll. by *of*) unable (to do something). **2** incompetent.

in·ca·pac·i·tate [in-kə-PAS-i-tayt] *vt* **-tat·ed, -tat·ing 1** disable. **2** make unfit. **3** disqualify. **in·ca·pac'i·ty** *n*

in·car·cer·ate [in-KAHR-sə-rayt] *vt* **-at·ed, -at·ing** imprison. **in·car·cer·a'tion** *n*

in·car·nate [in-KAR-nayt] *vt* **-nat·ed,**

THESAURUS

---

impolitic, imprudent, inexpedient, injudicious

inane *adj* = **senseless**, empty, fatuous, frivolous, futile, idiotic, mindless, silly, stupid, vacuous

inanimate *adj* = **lifeless**, cold, dead, defunct, extinct, inert

inapplicable *adj* = **irrelevant**, inappropriate, unsuitable

inappropriate *adj* = **unsuitable**, improper, incongruous, out of place, unbecoming, unbefitting, unfitting, unseemly, untimely

inarticulate *adj* = **faltering**, halting, hesitant, poorly spoken

inattention *n* = **neglect**, absent-mindedness, carelessness, daydreaming, inattentiveness, preoccupation, thoughtlessness

inattentive *adj* = **preoccupied**, careless, distracted, dreamy, negligent, unobservant, vague

inaudible *adj* = **indistinct**, low, mumbling, out of earshot, stifled, unheard

inaugural *adj* = **first**, initial, introductory, maiden, opening

inaugurate *v* **1** = **launch**, begin, commence, get under way, initiate, institute, introduce, set in motion **2** = **invest**, induct, install

inauguration *n* **1** = **launch**, initiation, institution, opening, setting up **2** = **investiture**, induction, installation

inauspicious *adj* = **unpromising**, bad, discouraging, ill-omened, ominous, unfavorable, unfortunate, unlucky, unpropitious

inborn *adj* = **natural**, congenital, hereditary, inbred, ingrained, inherent, innate, instinctive, intuitive, native

inbred *adj* = **innate**, constitutional, deep-seated, ingrained, inherent, native, natural

incalculable *adj* = **countless**, boundless, infinite, innumerable, limitless, numberless, untold, vast

incantation *n* = **chant**, charm, formula, invocation, spell

incapable *adj* **1** = **incompetent**, feeble, inadequate, ineffective, inept, inexpert, insufficient, lousy (*sl*), unfit, unqualified, weak **2** = **unable**, helpless, impotent, powerless

incapacitate *v* = **disable**, cripple, immobilize, lay up (*inf*), paralyze, put out of action (*inf*)

incapacitated *adj* = **indisposed**, hors de combat, immobilized, laid up (*inf*), out of action (*inf*), unfit

incapacity *n* = **inability**, impotence, inadequacy, incapability, incompetency, ineffectiveness, powerlessness, unfitness, weakness

incarcerate *v* = **imprison**, confine, detain, impound, intern, jail, lock up, throw in jail

-nat·ing 1 embody in flesh, esp. in human form. ♦ adj [-nit] 2 embodied in flesh, in human form. 3 typified. in·car·na'tion n

in·cen·di·ar·y [in-SEN-dee-er-ee] adj 1 of malicious setting on fire of property. 2 creating strife, violence, etc. 3 designed to cause fires. ♦ n 4 arsonist. 5 agitator. 6 bomb, etc. filled with inflammatory substance.

in·cense¹ [in-SENS] vt -censed, -cens·ing enrage.

in·cense² [IN-sens] n 1 gum, spice giving perfume when burned. 2 its smoke. ♦ vt -censed, -cens·ing 3 burn incense to. 4 perfume it with it.

in·cen·tive [in-SEN-tiv] n 1 something that arouses to effort or action. 2 stimulus.

in·cep·tion [in-SEP-shən] n beginning. in·cep'tive [-tiv] adj

in·ces·sant [in-SES-ənt] adj unceasing.

in·cest [IN-sest] n sexual intercourse between two people too closely related to marry. in·ces'tu·ous [-SES-choo-əs] adj

inch n 1 one twelfth of foot, or 2.54 centimeters. ♦ v 2 move very slowly.

in·cho·ate [in-KOH-it] adj 1 just begun. 2 undeveloped.

in·ci·dent [IN-si-dənt] n 1 event, occurrence. ♦ adj 2 naturally attaching to. 3 striking, falling (upon). in'ci·dence n 1 degree, extent or frequency of occurrence. 2 a falling on, or affecting. in·ci·den'tal adj occurring as a minor part or an inevitable accompaniment or by chance. in·ci·den'tal·ly adv 1 by chance. 2 by the way. in·ci·den'tals pl. n accompanying items.

in·cin·er·ate [in-SIN-ə-rayt] vt -at·ed, -at·ing 1 burn up completely. 2 reduce to ashes. in·cin'er·a·tor n

in·cip·i·ent [in-SIP-ee-ənt] adj beginning.

in·cise [in-SIZ] vt -cised, -cis·ing 1 cut into. 2 engrave. in·ci'sion [in-SIZH-ən] n in·ci'sive adj 1 keen or biting (of remark, etc.). 2 sharp. in·ci'sor n cutting tooth.

in·cite [in-SIT] vt -cit·ed, -cit·ing urge, stir up. in·cite'ment n

in·clem·ent [in-KLEM-ənt] adj of weather, stormy, severe, cold. in·clem'en·cy n

in·cline [in-KLIN] v -clined, -clin·ing 1 lean,

incarceration n = imprisonment, captivity, confinement, detention, internment

incarnate adj = personified, embodied, typified

incarnation n = embodiment, epitome, manifestation, personification, type

incense¹ v = anger, enrage, inflame, infuriate, irritate, madden, make one's hackles rise, rile (inf)

incensed adj = angry, enraged, fuming, furious, indignant, infuriated, irate, maddened, steamed up (sl), up in arms

incentive n = encouragement, bait, carrot (inf), enticement, inducement, lure, motivation, spur, stimulus

inception n = beginning, birth, commencement, dawn, initiation, origin, outset, start

incessant adj = endless, ceaseless, constant, continual, eternal, interminable, never-ending, nonstop, perpetual, twenty-four-seven (sl), unceasing, unending

incessantly adv = endlessly, ceaselessly, constantly, continually, eternally, interminably, nonstop, perpetually, persistently, twenty-four-seven (sl)

incident n 1 = happening, adventure, episode, event, fact, matter, occasion, occurrence 2 = disturbance, clash, commotion, confrontation, contretemps, scene

incidental adj = secondary, ancillary, minor, nonessential, occasional, subordinate, subsidiary

incidentally adv = parenthetically, by the bye, by the way, in passing

incinerate v = burn up, carbonize, char, cremate, reduce to ashes

incipient adj = beginning, commencing, developing, embryonic, inchoate, nascent, starting

incision n = cut, gash, notch, opening, slash, slit

incisive adj = penetrating, acute, keen, perspicacious, piercing, trenchant

incite v = provoke, encourage, foment, inflame, instigate, spur, stimulate, stir up, urge, whip up

incitement n = provocation, agitation, encouragement, impetus, instigation, prompting, spur, stimulus

incivility n = rudeness, bad manners, boorishness, discourteousness, discourtesy, disrespect, ill-breeding, impoliteness

inclement adj = stormy, foul, harsh, intemperate, rough, severe, tempestuous slope. **2** (cause to) be disposed. **3** bend or lower (the head, etc.). ♦ n [IN-klīn] **4** slope. **in·cli·na·tion** n **1** liking, tendency or preference. **2** sloping surface. **3** degree of deviation.

in·clude [in-KLOOD] vt **-clud·ed, -clud·ing 1** have as (part of) contents. **2** comprise. **3** add in. **4** take in. **in·clu·sion** [-zhən] n **in·clu·sive** adj including (everything).

in·cog·ni·to [in-kog-NEE-toh] adv, adj **1** under assumed identity. ♦ n, pl **-tos 2** assumed identity.

in·co·her·ent [in-koh-HEER-ənt] adj **1** lacking clarity, disorganized. **2** inarticulate. **in·co·her·ence** n

in·come [IN-kum] n **1** amount of money, esp. annual, from salary, investments, etc. **2** receipts. **income tax** personal, corporate tax levied on annual income.

in·com·ing [IN-kum-ing] adj **1** coming in.

2 about to come into office. **3** next.

in·com·mode [in-kə-MOHD] vt **-mod·ed, -mod·ing 1** trouble, inconvenience. **2** disturb. **in·com·mo'di·ous** adj **1** cramped. **2** inconvenient.

in·com·mu·ni·ca·do [in-kə-MYOO-ni-kah-doh] adj, adv deprived (by force or by choice) of communication with others.

in·com'pa·ra·ble adj beyond comparison, unequalled.

in·com·pat'i·ble adj inconsistent or conflicting. **in·com·pat·i·bil'i·ty** n

in·com'pe·tent adj not having the necessary ability or skill to do something. **in·com'pe·tence** n

in·con·gru·ous [in-KONG-groo-əs] adj **1** not appropriate. **2** inconsistent, absurd. **in·con·gru'i·ty** n

in·con·se·quen·tial [in-kon-si-KWEN-shəl]

THESAURUS

inclination n **1** = **tendency**, disposition, liking, partiality, penchant, predilection, predisposition, prejudice, proclivity, proneness, propensity **2** = **slope**, angle, gradient, incline, pitch, slant, tilt

incline v **1** = **predispose**, influence, persuade, prejudice, sway **2** = **slope**, lean, slant, tilt, tip, veer ♦ n **3** = **slope**, ascent, descent, dip, grade, gradient, rise

inclined adj = **disposed**, apt, given, liable, likely, minded, predisposed, prone, willing

include v **1** = **contain**, comprise, cover, embrace, encompass, incorporate, involve, subsume, take in **2** = **introduce**, add, enter, insert

inclusion n = **addition**, incorporation, insertion

inclusive adj = **comprehensive**, across-the-board, all-embracing, blanket, general, global, sweeping, umbrella

incognito adj = **in disguise**, disguised, under an assumed name, unknown, unrecognized

incoherence n = **unintelligibility**, disjointedness, inarticulateness

incoherent adj = **unintelligible**, confused, disjointed, disordered, inarticulate, inconsistent, jumbled, muddled, rambling, stammering, stuttering

income n = **revenue**, earnings, pay, proceeds, profits, receipts, salary, takings, wages

incoming adj = **arriving**, approaching, entering, homeward, landing, new,

returning

incomparable adj = **unequaled**, beyond compare, inimitable, matchless, peerless, superlative, supreme, transcendent, unmatched, unparalleled, unrivaled

incompatible adj = **inconsistent**, conflicting, contradictory, incongruous, mismatched, unsuited

incompetence n = **ineptitude**, inability, inadequacy, incapability, incapacity, ineffectiveness, unfitness, uselessness

incompetent adj = **inept**, bungling, floundering, incapable, ineffectual, inexpert, unfit, useless

incomplete adj = **unfinished**, deficient, fragmentary, imperfect, partial, wanting

incomprehensible adj = **unintelligible**, baffling, beyond one's grasp, impenetrable, obscure, opaque, perplexing, puzzling, unfathomable

inconceivable adj = **unimaginable**, beyond belief, incomprehensible, incredible, mind-boggling (inf), out of the question, unbelievable, unheard-of, unthinkable

inconclusive adj = **indecisive**, ambiguous, indeterminate, open, unconvincing, undecided, up in the air (inf), vague

incongruity n = **inappropriateness**, conflict, discrepancy, disparity, incompatibility, inconsistency, unsuitability

incongruous adj = **inappropriate**, discordant, improper, incompatible, out of keeping, out of place, unbecoming, *adj* **1** illogical. **2** irrelevant, trivial.

in·con·sid·er·ate *adj* not considering other people.

in·con·sist·ent *adj* **1** changeable in behaviour or mood. **2** containing contradictory elements. **3** not in accordance. **in·con·sist·en·cy** *n, pl* **-cies**

in·con·tro·vert·i·ble [in kon tro VUR to bol] *adj* **1** undeniable. **2** indisputable.

in·con·ven·ience *n* **1** trouble or difficulty. ◆ *v* **2** cause trouble or difficulty to. **in·con·ven·ient** *adj*

in·cor·po·rate [in-KOR-pə-rayt] *vt* **-rat·ed, -rat·ing 1** include. **2** unite into one body. **3** form into corporation.

in·cor·ri·gi·ble [in-KOR-i-jə-bəl] *adj* **1**

beyond correction or reform. **2** firmly rooted.

in·crease [in-KREES] *v* **-creased, -creas·ing 1** make or become greater in size, number, etc. ◆ *n* [IN-krees] **2** growth, enlargement, profit. **in·creas·ing·ly** *adv* more and more.

in·cred·i·ble [in-KRED-ə-bəl] *adj* **1** unbelievable. **2** *inf* marvelous, amazing.

in·cred·u·lous [in-KREJ-ə-ləs] *adj* unbelieving. **in·cre·du·li·ty** [-krə-DOO-lə-tee] *n*

in·cre·ment [IN-krə-mənt] *n* increase, esp. one of a series. **in·cre·men·tal** *adj*

in·crim·i·nate [in-KRIM-ə-nayt] *vt* **-nat·ed, -nat·ing 1** imply guilt of. **2** accuse of crime. **in·crim·i·na·to·ry** *adj*

in·crust [in-KRUST] *v* cover with or form a

unsuitable

inconsiderable *adj* = **insignificant**, inconsequential, minor, negligible, slight, small, trifling, trivial, unimportant

inconsiderate *adj* = **selfish**, indelicate, insensitive, rude, tactless, thoughtless, unkind, unthinking

inconsistency *n* **1** = **incompatibility**, disagreement, discrepancy, disparity, divergence, incongruity, variance **2** = **unreliability**, fickleness, instability, unpredictability, unsteadiness

inconsistent *adj* **1** = **incompatible**, at odds, conflicting, contradictory, discordant, incongruous, irreconcilable, out of step **2** = **changeable**, capricious, erratic, fickle, unpredictable, unstable, unsteady, variable

inconsolable *adj* = **heartbroken**, brokenhearted, desolate, despairing

inconspicuous *adj* = **unobtrusive**, camouflaged, hidden, insignificant, ordinary, plain, unassuming, unnoticeable, unostentatious

incontrovertible *adj* = **indisputable**, certain, established, incontestable, indubitable, irrefutable, positive, sure, undeniable, unquestionable

inconvenience *n* **1** = **trouble**, awkwardness, bother, difficulty, disadvantage, disruption, disturbance, fuss, hindrance, nuisance ◆ *v* **2** = **trouble**, bother, discommode, disrupt, disturb, put out, upset

inconvenient *adj* = **troublesome**, awkward, bothersome, disadvantageous, disturbing, inopportune, unsuitable,

untimely

incorporate *v* = **include**, absorb, assimilate, blend, combine, integrate, merge, subsume

incorrect *adj* = **false**, erroneous, faulty, flawed, inaccurate, mistaken, untrue, wrong

incorrigible *adj* = **incurable**, hardened, hopeless, intractable, inveterate, irredeemable, unreformed

incorruptible *adj* **1** = **honest**, above suspicion, straight, trustworthy, upright **2** = **imperishable**, everlasting, undecaying

increase *v* **1** = **grow**, advance, boost, develop, enlarge, escalate, expand, extend, multiply, raise, spread, swell ◆ *n* **2** = **growth**, development, enlargement, escalation, expansion, extension, gain, increment, rise, upturn

increasingly *adv* = **progressively**, more and more

incredible *adj* **1** = **implausible**, beyond belief, far-fetched, improbable, inconceivable, preposterous, unbelievable, unimaginable, unthinkable **2** *inf* = **amazing**, astonishing, astounding, extraordinary, prodigious, sensational (*inf*), wonderful

incredulity *n* = **disbelief**, distrust, doubt, skepticism

incredulous *adj* = **disbelieving**, distrustful, doubtful, dubious, skeptical, suspicious, unbelieving, unconvinced

increment *n* = **increase**, accrual, addition, advancement, augmentation, enlargement, gain, step up, supplement

incriminate *v* = **implicate**, accuse, blame,

crust or hard covering.

in·cu·bate [IN-kyə-bayt] *vt* **-bat·ed, -bat·ing 1** provide (eggs, embryos, bacteria, etc.) with heat or other favorable condition for development. ◆ *vi* **2** develop in this way. **in·cu·ba'tion** *n* **in·cu·ba·tor** *n* apparatus for artificially hatching eggs, for rearing premature babies.

in·cu·bus [IN-kyə-bəs] *n, pl* **-bi** [-bī] **1** nightmare or obsession. **2** orig. demon believed to afflict sleeping person.

in·cul·cate [in-KUL-kayt] *vt* **-cat·ed, -cat·ing** impress on the mind. **in·cul·ca'tion** *n*

in·cum·bent [in-KUM-bənt] *adj* **1** lying, resting (on). ◆ *n* **2** holder of office, esp. elective office in government. **in·cum'ben·cy** *n* **1** obligation. **2** office or tenure of incumbent. **it is incumbent on** it is the duty of.

in·cur [in-KUR] *vt* **-curred, -cur·ring** fall into, bring upon oneself. **in·cur'sion** [-zhən] *n* invasion, penetration.

in·cur'a·ble *adj* **1** not able to be cured. **2** not willing or able to change. **in·cur'a·bly** *adv*

in·debt·ed [in-DET-id] *adj* **1** owing gratitude for help, favors, etc. **2** owing money. **in·debt'ed·ness** *n*

in·de'cent *adj* **1** morally or sexually offensive. **2** unsuitable or unseemly. **in·de'cen·cy** *n*

in·de·ci'sive *adj* unable to make decisions. **in·de·cis'ion** *n*

in·deed' *adv* **1** in truth. **2** really. **3** in fact. **4** certainly. ◆ *interj* **5** denoting surprise, doubt, etc.

in·de·fat·i·ga·ble [in-di-FAT-i-gə-bəl] *adj* untiring. **in·de·fat'i·ga·bly** *adv*

in·de·fen·si·ble [in-di-FEN-sə-bəl] *adj* not justifiable or defensible.

in·def'i·nite *adj* **1** without exact limits. **2** vague, unclear. **indefinite article** *Grammar* the word *a* or *an*.

in·del·i·ble [in-DEL-ə-bəl] *adj* **1** that cannot be blotted out, effaced or erased. **2** producing such a mark. **in·del'i·bly** *adv*

in·del·i·cate [in-DEL-i-kit] *adj* coarse, embarrassing, tasteless.

in·dem·ni·ty [in-DEM-ni-tee] *n, pl* **-ties 1** compensation. **2** security against loss. **in·dem·ni·fi·ca'tion** *n* **in·dem'ni·fy** [-fī] *vt* **-fied, -fy·ing 1** give indemnity to. **2** compensate.

in·dent' *v* **1** set in (from margin, etc.). **2**

──── THESAURUS ────

charge, impeach, inculpate, involve

incumbent *adj* = **obligatory**, binding, compulsory, mandatory, necessary

incur *v* = **earn**, arouse, bring (upon oneself), draw, expose oneself to, gain, meet with, provoke

incurable *adj* = **fatal**, inoperable, irremediable, terminal

indebted *adj* = **grateful**, beholden, in debt, obligated, obliged, under an obligation

indecency *n* = **obscenity**, immodesty, impropriety, impurity, indelicacy, lewdness, licentiousness, pornography, vulgarity

indecent *adj* **1** = **lewd**, crude, dirty, filthy, immodest, improper, impure, licentious, pornographic, salacious, scuzzy (*sl*), X-rated **2** = **unbecoming**, in bad taste, indecorous, unseemly, vulgar

indecipherable *adj* = **illegible**, indistinguishable, unintelligible, unreadable

indecision *n* = **hesitation**, dithering, doubt, indecisiveness, uncertainty, vacillation, wavering

indecisive *adj* = **hesitating**, dithering, faltering, in two minds (*inf*), tentative, uncertain, undecided, vacillating, wavering

indeed *adv* = **really**, actually, certainly, in truth, truly, undoubtedly

indefensible *adj* = **unforgivable**, inexcusable, unjustifiable, unpardonable, untenable, unwarrantable, wrong

indefinable *adj* = **inexpressible**, impalpable, indescribable

indefinite *adj* = **unclear**, doubtful, equivocal, ill-defined, imprecise, indeterminate, inexact, uncertain, unfixed, vague

indefinitely *adv* = **endlessly**, ad infinitum, continually, for ever

indelible *adj* = **permanent**, enduring, indestructible, ineradicable, ingrained, lasting

indelicate *adj* = **offensive**, coarse, crude, embarrassing, immodest, off-color, risqué, rude, suggestive, tasteless, vulgar

indemnify *v* **1** = **insure**, guarantee, protect, secure, underwrite **2** = **compensate**, reimburse, remunerate, repair, repay

indemnity *n* **1** = **insurance**, guarantee, protection, security **2** = **compensation**, redress, reimbursement, remuneration, make notches in. ♦ n [IN-dent] **3** indentation. **4** notch. **in•den•ta'tion** n **in•den'ture** n **1** contract, esp. one binding apprentice to master. **2** indentation. ♦ vt **-tured, -tur•ing 3** bind by indenture.

in•de•pend•ent [in-di-PEN-dənt] adj **1** not subject to others. **2** self-reliant. **3** free. **4** valid in itself. **5** politically of no party. **in•de•pend'ence** n **1** being independent. **2** self-reliance. **3** self-support.

in•de•scrib•a•ble [in-di-SKRĪ-bə-bəl] adj **1** beyond description. **2** too intense, etc. for words. **in•de•scrib'a•bly** adv

in•de•ter•mi•nate [in-di-TUR-mə-nit] adj **1** uncertain. **2** inconclusive. **3** incalculable.

in•dex [IN-deks] n, pl **-dex•es, -di•ces** [-də-seez] **1** alphabetical list of references, usu. at end of book. **2** pointer, indicator. **3** Math. exponent. **4** Economics quantity indicating relative level of wages, prices, etc. compared with date established as standard. ♦ vt **5** provide book with index. **6** insert in index. **7** adjust wages, prices, etc. to reflect change in some economic indicator.

In•di•an [IN-dee-ən] n **1** native of India. **2** oft offens person descended from indigenous peoples of N America. ♦ adj

in•di•cate [IN-di-kayt] vt **-cat•ed, -cat•ing 1** point out. **2** state briefly. **3** signify. **in•di•ca'tion** n **1** sign. **2** token. **3** explanation. **in•dic'a•tive** adj **1** pointing to. **2** Grammar stating fact. **in'di•ca•tor** n **1** one who, that which, indicates. **2** on vehicle, flashing light showing driver's intention to turn.

in•dict [in-DĪT] vt accuse, esp. by legal process. **in•dict'ment** [-mənt] n

in•dif•fer•ent [in-DIF-ər-ənt] adj **1** uninterested. **2** unimportant. **3** neither good nor bad. **4** inferior. **5** neutral. **in•dif'fer•ence** n

in•dig•e•nous [in-DIJ-ə-nəs] adj born in or natural to a country.

in•di•gent [IN-di-jənt] adj poor, needy. **in'di•gence** n poverty.

in•di•ges•tion [in-di-JES-chən] n (discomfort, pain caused by) difficulty in digesting food. **in•di•gest'i•ble** adj

in•dig•nant [in-DIG-nənt] adj **1** moved by anger and scorn. **2** angered by sense of injury or injustice. **in•dig•na'tion** n **in•dig'ni•ty** n humiliation, insult, slight.

in•di•go [IN-də-goh] n, pl **-gos 1** blue dye

THESAURUS

---

reparation, restitution

independence n = **freedom**, autonomy, liberty, self-reliance, self-rule, self-sufficiency, sovereignty

independent adj **1** = **free**, liberated, separate, unconstrained, uncontrolled **2** = **self-governing**, autonomous, nonaligned, self-determining, sovereign **3** = **self-sufficient**, liberated, self-contained, self-reliant, self-supporting

independently adv = **separately**, alone, autonomously, by oneself, individually, on one's own, solo, unaided

indescribable adj = **unutterable**, beyond description, beyond words, indefinable, inexpressible

indestructible adj = **permanent**, enduring, everlasting, immortal, imperishable, incorruptible, indelible, indissoluble, lasting, unbreakable

indeterminate adj = **uncertain**, imprecise, indefinite, inexact, undefined, unfixed, unspecified, unstipulated, vague

indicate v **1** = **signify**, betoken, denote, imply, manifest, point to, reveal, suggest **2** = **point out**, designate, specify **3** = **show**, display, express, read, record, register

indication n = **sign**, clue, evidence, hint, inkling, intimation, manifestation, mark, suggestion, symptom

indicative adj = **suggestive**, pointing to, significant, symptomatic

indicator n = **sign**, gauge, guide, mark, meter, pointer, signal, symbol

indict v = **charge**, accuse, arraign, impeach, prosecute, summon

indictment n = **charge**, accusation, allegation, impeachment, prosecution, summons

indifference n = **disregard**, aloofness, apathy, coldness, coolness, detachment, inattention, negligence, nonchalance, unconcern

indifferent adj **1** = **unconcerned**, aloof, callous, cold, cool, detached, impervious, inattentive, uninterested, unmoved, unsympathetic **2** = **mediocre**, moderate, ordinary, passable, so-so (inf), undistinguished

indigestion n = **heartburn**, dyspepsia, upset stomach

indignant adj = **resentful**, angry, disgruntled, exasperated, incensed, irate, peeved (inf), riled, scornful, ticked off (inf), obtained from plant. **2** the plant. ♦ *adj* **3** deep blue.

in·di·rect' *adj* **1** done or caused by someone or something else. **2** not by a straight route.

in·dis·creet' *adj* incautious or tactless in revealing secrets. **in·dis·cre'tion** *n*

in·dis·crim·i·nate [in-di-SKRIM-ə-nit] *adj* **1** lacking discrimination. **2** jumbled.

in·dis·pen·sa·ble [in-di-SPEN-sə-bəl] *adj* **1** necessary. **2** essential.

in·dis·po·si·tion [in-dis-pə-ZISH-ən] *n* **1** sickness. **2** disinclination. **in·dis·posed'** [-POHZD] *adj* **1** unwell, not fit. **2** disinclined.

in·dis·sol·u·ble [in-di-SOL-yə-bəl] *adj* permanent.

in·di·um [IN-dee-əm] *n* soft silver-white metallic element.

in·di·vid·u·al [in-də-VIJ-oo-əl] *adj* **1** single. **2** characteristic of single person or thing. **3** distinctive. ♦ *n* **4** single person or thing.

in·di·vid·u·al·ism *n* principle of asserting one's independence. **in·di·vid·u·al·ist** *n*

in·di·vid·u·al'i·ty *n* **1** distinctive character. **2** personality. **in·di·vid·u·al·ize** *vt* **-ized, -iz·ing** make (or treat) as individual. **in·di·vid·u·al·ly** *adv* singly.

in·doc·tri·nate [in-DOK-trə-nayt] *vt* **-nat·ed, -nat·ing** implant beliefs in the mind of.

in·do·lent [IN-dl-ənt] *adj* lazy. **in'do·lence** *n*

in·dom·i·ta·ble [in-DOM-i-tə-bəl] *adj* unyielding.

in·door [IN-dor] *adj* **1** within doors. **2** under cover. **in·doors** [in-DORZ] *adv*

in·du·bi·ta·ble [in-DOO-bi-tə-bəl] *adj* **1** beyond doubt. **2** certain. **in·du'bi·ta·bly** *adv*

in·duce [in-DOOS] *vt* **-duced, -duc·ing 1** persuade. **2** bring on. **3** cause. **4** produce by induction. **in·duce'ment** *n* incentive, attraction.

THESAURUS

up in arms (*inf*)

indignation *n* = **resentment**, anger, exasperation, pique, rage, scorn, umbrage

indignity *n* = **humiliation**, affront, dishonor, disrespect, injury, insult, opprobrium, slight, snub

indirect *adj* **1** = **circuitous**, long-drawn-out, meandering, oblique, rambling, roundabout, tortuous, wandering **2** = **incidental**, secondary, subsidiary, unintended

indiscreet *adj* = **tactless**, impolitic, imprudent, incautious, injudicious, naive, rash, reckless, unwise

indiscretion *n* = **mistake**, error, faux pas, folly, foolishness, gaffe, lapse, slip

indiscriminate *adj* = **random**, careless, desultory, general, uncritical, undiscriminating, unsystematic, wholesale

indispensable *adj* = **essential**, crucial, imperative, key, necessary, needed, requisite, vital

indisposed *adj* = **ill**, ailing, sick, under the weather, unwell

indisposition *n* = **illness**, ailment, ill health, sickness

indisputable *adj* = **undeniable**, beyond doubt, certain, incontestable, incontrovertible, indubitable, irrefutable, unquestionable

indistinct *adj* = **unclear**, blurred, faint, fuzzy, hazy, ill-defined, indeterminate,

shadowy, undefined, vague

individual *adj* **1** = **personal**, characteristic, distinctive, exclusive, idiosyncratic, own, particular, peculiar, singular, special, specific, unique ♦ *n* **2** = **person**, being, character, creature, soul, unit

individualist *n* = **maverick**, freethinker, independent, loner, lone wolf, nonconformist, original

individuality *n* = **distinctiveness**, character, originality, personality, separateness, singularity, uniqueness

individually *adv* = **separately**, apart, independently, one at a time, one by one, singly

indoctrinate *v* = **train**, brainwash, drill, ground, imbue, initiate, instruct, school, teach

indoctrination *n* = **training**, brainwashing, drilling, grounding, inculcation, instruction, schooling

indolent *adj* = **lazy**, idle, inactive, inert, languid, lethargic, listless, slothful, sluggish, workshy

indomitable *adj* = **invincible**, bold, resolute, staunch, steadfast, unbeatable, unconquerable, unflinching, unyielding

indubitable *adj* = **certain**, incontestable, incontrovertible, indisputable, irrefutable, obvious, sure, undeniable, unquestionable

induce *v* **1** = **persuade**, convince, encourage, incite, influence, instigate,

in·duct [in-DUKT] *vt* install in office.
in·duc'tion *n* **1** an inducting. **2** general inference from particular instances. **3** production of electric or magnetic state in body by its being near (not touching) electrified or magnetized body.
in·duc'tance [-təns] *n* **in·duc'tive** *adj*

in·dulge [in-DULJ] *vt* **-dulged, -dulg·ing 1** gratify. **2** give free course to. **3** pamper. **4** spoil. **in·dul'gence** [-jəns] *n* **1** an indulging. **2** extravagance. **3** something granted as a favor or privilege. **4** *R.C. Church* remission of temporal punishment due after absolution. **in·dul'gent** [-jənt] *adj*

in·dus·try [IN-də-stree] *n* **1** manufacture, processing, etc. of goods. **2** branch of this. **3** diligence. **4** habitual hard work.
in·dus'tri·al *adj* of industries, trades.
in·dus'tri·al·ize *vt* **-ized, -iz·ing**
in·dus'tri·ous [-tree-əs] *adj* diligent.

in·e·bri·ate [in-EE-bree-ayt] *vt* **-at·ed, -at·ing 1** make drunk. **2** intoxicate. ◆ *adj* [-bree-it] **3** drunken. ◆ *n* **4** habitual

drunkard. **in·e·bri·a'tion** *n* drunkenness.
in·ed·i·ble [in-ED-ə-bəl] *adj* **1** not eatable. **2** unfit for food.
in·ed·u·ca·ble [in-EJ-uu-kə-bəl] *adj* incapable of being educated, e.g. through mental retardation.
in·ef·fa·ble [in-EF-ə-bəl] *adj* **1** too great or sacred for words. **2** unutterable.
in·ef·fa·bil'i·ty *n*
in·ef·fi'cient *adj* unable to perform a task or function to the best advantage.
in·ef·fi'cien·cy *n*
in·el·i·gi·ble [in-EL-i-jə-bəl] *adj* not fit or qualified (for something). **in·el·i·gi·bil'i·ty** *n*
in·ept' *adj* **1** absurd. **2** out of place. **3** clumsy. **in·ept'i·tude** *n*
in·ert [in-URT] *adj* **1** without power of action or resistance. **2** slow, sluggish. **3** chemically unreactive. **in·er'tia** [-UR-shə] *n* **1** inactivity. **2** property by which matter continues in its existing state of rest or motion in straight line, unless that state is changed by external force.

———— THESAURUS ————

prevail upon, prompt, talk into **2 = cause**, bring about, effect, engender, generate, give rise to, lead to, occasion, produce
inducement *n* **= incentive**, attraction, bait, carrot (*inf*), encouragement, incitement, lure, reward
indulge *v* **1 = gratify**, feed, give way to, pander to, satisfy, yield to **2 = spoil**, cosset, give in to, go along with, humor, pamper
indulgence *n* **1 = gratification**, appeasement, fulfillment, satiation, satisfaction **2 = luxury**, extravagance, favor, privilege, treat **3 = tolerance**, forbearance, patience, understanding
indulgent *adj* **= lenient**, compliant, easy-going, forbearing, kindly, liberal, permissive, tolerant, understanding
industrialist *n* **= capitalist**, big businessman, captain of industry, magnate, manufacturer, tycoon
industrious *adj* **= hard-working**, busy, conscientious, diligent, energetic, persistent, purposeful, tireless, zealous
industry *n* **1 = business**, commerce, manufacturing, production, trade **2 = effort**, activity, application, diligence, labor, tirelessness, toil, zeal
inebriated *adj* **= drunk**, crocked (*sl*), intoxicated, paralytic (*inf*), plastered (*sl*), three sheets to the wind (*sl*), tipsy, under the influence (*inf*)

ineffective *adj* **= useless**, fruitless, futile, idle, impotent, inefficient, unavailing, unproductive, vain, worthless
ineffectual *adj* **= weak**, feeble, impotent, inadequate, incompetent, ineffective, inept, lousy (*sl*)
inefficiency *n* **= incompetence**, carelessness, disorganization, muddle, slackness, sloppiness
inefficient *adj* **= incompetent**, disorganized, ineffectual, inept, wasteful, weak
ineligible *adj* **= unqualified**, disqualified, ruled out, unacceptable, unfit, unsuitable
inept *adj* **= incompetent**, bumbling, bungling, clumsy, inexpert, maladroit
ineptitude *n* **= incompetence**, clumsiness, inexpertness, unfitness
inequality *n* **= disparity**, bias, difference, disproportion, diversity, irregularity, prejudice, unevenness
inequitable *adj* **= unfair**, biased, discriminatory, one-sided, partial, partisan, preferential, prejudiced, unjust
inert *adj* **= inactive**, dead, dormant, immobile, lifeless, motionless, static, still, unreactive, unresponsive
inertia *n* **= inactivity**, apathy, immobility, lethargy, listlessness, passivity, sloth, unresponsiveness
inescapable *adj* **= unavoidable**, certain,

in·es·ti·ma·ble [in-ES-tə-mə-bəl] *adj* too good, too great, to be estimated.

in·ev·i·ta·ble [in-EV-i-tə-bəl] *adj* **1** unavoidable. **2** sure to happen. **in·ev·i·ta·bil'i·ty** *n*

in·ex·o·ra·ble [in-EK-sər-ə-bəl] *adj* relentless. **in·ex'o·ra·bly** *adv*

in·ex·pe'ri·enced *adj* having no knowledge or experience of a particular situation, activity, etc. **in·ex·pe'ri·ence** *n*

in·ex·pli·ca·ble [in-EK-spli-kə-bəl] *adj* impossible to explain.

in ex·tre·mis [eks-TREE-mis] *Lat* at the point of death.

in·fal·li·ble [in-FAL-ə-bəl] *adj* **1** unerring. **2** not liable to fail. **3** certain, sure. **in·fal·li·bil'i·ty** *n*

in·fa·mous [IN-fə-məs] *adj* **1** notorious. **2** shocking. **in'fa·my** [-mee] *n, pl* **-mies**

in·fant [IN-fənt] *n* very young child.

in'fan·cy *n* **in·fan'ti·cide** [-FAN-tə-sīd] *n* **1** murder of newborn child. **2** person guilty of this. **in'fan·tile** [-fən-tīl] *adj* childish.

in·fan·try [IN-fən-tree] *n, pl* **-tries** foot soldiers.

in·fat·u·ate [in-FACH-oo-ayt] *vt* **-at·ed, -at·ing** inspire with folly or foolish passion. **in·fat'u·at·ed** *adj* foolishly enamored. **in·fat·u·a'tion** *n*

in·fect [in-FEKT] *vt* **1** affect (with disease). **2** contaminate. **in·fec'tion** [-shən] *n* **in·fec'tious** [-shəs] *adj* catching, spreading, pestilential.

in·fer [in-FUR] *vt* **-ferred, -fer·ring** deduce, conclude. **in'fer·ence** [-fər-əns] *n* **in·fer·en'tial** [-fər-EN-shəl] *adj* deduced.

in·fe·ri·or [in-FEER-ee-ər] *adj* **1** of poor quality. **2** lower. ◆ *n* **3** one lower (in rank, etc.). **in·fe·ri·or'i·ty** *n* **inferiority complex** *Psychoanalysis* intense sense of inferiority.

THESAURUS

destined, fated, ineluctable, inevitable, inexorable, sure

inestimable *adj* = **incalculable**, immeasurable, invaluable, precious, priceless, prodigious

inevitable *adj* = **unavoidable**, assured, certain, destined, fixed, ineluctable, inescapable, inexorable, sure

inevitably *adv* = **unavoidably**, as a result, automatically, certainly, necessarily, of necessity, perforce, surely, willy-nilly

inexcusable *adj* = **unforgivable**, indefensible, outrageous, unjustifiable, unpardonable, unwarrantable

inexorable *adj* = **unrelenting**, inescapable, relentless, remorseless, unbending, unyielding

inexpensive *adj* = **cheap**, bargain, budget, economical, modest, reasonable

inexperience *n* = **unfamiliarity**, callowness, greenness, ignorance, newness, rawness

inexperienced *adj* = **immature**, callow, green, new, raw, unpracticed, untried, unversed

inexpert *adj* = **amateurish**, bungling, clumsy, inept, maladroit, unpracticed, unprofessional, unskilled

inexplicable *adj* = **unaccountable**, baffling, enigmatic, incomprehensible, insoluble, mysterious, mystifying, strange, unfathomable, unintelligible

inextricably *adv* = **inseparably**, indissolubly, indistinguishably, intricately,

irretrievably, totally

infallibility *n* = **perfection**, impeccability, omniscience, supremacy, unerringness

infallible *adj* = **foolproof**, certain, dependable, reliable, sure, sure-fire (*inf*), trustworthy, unbeatable, unfailing

infamous *adj* = **notorious**, disreputable, ignominious, ill-famed

infancy *n* = **beginnings**, cradle, dawn, inception, origins, outset, start

infant *n* = **baby**, babe, child, minor, toddler, tot

infantile *adj* = **childish**, babyish, immature, puerile

infatuate *v* = **obsess**, besot, bewitch, captivate, enchant, enrapture, fascinate

infatuated *adj* = **obsessed**, besotted, bewitched, captivated, carried away, enamored, enraptured, fascinated, possessed, smitten (*inf*), spellbound

infatuation *n* = **obsession**, crush (*inf*), fixation, madness, passion, thing (*inf*)

infect *v* = **contaminate**, affect, blight, corrupt, defile, poison, pollute, taint

infection *n* = **contamination**, contagion, corruption, defilement, poison, pollution, virus

infectious *adj* = **catching**, communicable, contagious, spreading, transmittable, virulent

infer *v* = **deduce**, conclude, derive, gather, presume, surmise, understand

inference *n* = **deduction**, assumption, conclusion, presumption, reading, surmise

in·fer·nal [in-FUR-nl] *adj* **1** devilish. **2** hellish. **3** *inf* irritating, confounded.

in·fer·no [in-FUR-noh] *n* **1** region of hell. **2** great destructive fire.

in·fer·tile *adj* **1** unable to produce offspring. **2** (of soil) barren, not productive. **in·fer·tile** *n*

in·fest' *vt* inhabit or overrun in dangerously or unpleasantly large numbers. **in·fes·ta'tion** *n*

in·fi·del·i·ty [in-fi-DEL-i-tee] *n* **1** unfaithfulness. **2** religious disbelief. **3** disloyalty. **4** treachery. **in'fi·del** [-dl] *n* unbeliever. ♦ *adj*

in·fil·trate [in-FIL-trayt] *v* **-trat·ed, -trat·ing** **1** trickle through. **2** cause to pass through pores. **3** gain access surreptitiously. **in·fil·tra'tion** *n*

in·fi·nite [IN-fə-nit] *adj* boundless. **in'fi·nite·ly** *adv* exceedingly. **in·fin·i·tes'i·mal** [-TES-ə-məl] *adj* extremely, infinitely small. **in·fin'i·ty** *n* unlimited and endless extent.

in·fin·i·tive [in-FIN-i-tiv] *adj Grammar* **1** in form expressing notion of verb without

limitation of tense, person, or number. ♦ *n* **2** verb in this form. **3** the form.

in·firm [in-FURM] *adj* **1** physically weak. **2** mentally weak. **3** irresolute. **in·fir'ma·ry** [-mə-ree] *n* **1** hospital. **2** dispensary. **in·fir'mi·ty** *n, pl* **-ties**

in·flame [in-FLAYM] *v* **-flamed, -flam·ing** **1** rouse to anger, excitement. **2** cause inflammation in. **3** become inflamed. **in·flam·ma·bil'i·ty** *n* **in·flam'ma·ble** *adj* easily set on fire. **2** excitable. **in·flam·ma'tion** *n* infection of part of the body, with pain, heat, swelling, and redness.

in·flate [in-FLAYT] *v* **-flat·ed, -flat·ing** **1** blow up with air, gas. **2** swell. **3** cause economic inflation. **4** raise price, esp. artificially. **in·fla'tion** *n* increase in prices and fall in value of money. **in·fla'tion·ar·y** *adj*

in·flect [in-FLEKT] *vt* **1** modify (words) to show grammatical relationships. **2** bend inward. **in·flec'tion** *n* **1** modification of word. **2** modulation of voice.

in·flex·i·ble [in-FLEK-sə-bəl] *adj* **1** incapable

———— THESAURUS ————

inferior *adj* **1** = **lower**, lesser, menial, minor, secondary, subordinate, subsidiary ♦ *n* **2** = **underling**, junior, menial, subordinate

inferiority *n* **1** = **inadequacy**, deficiency, imperfection, insignificance, mediocrity, shoddiness, worthlessness **2** = **subservience**, abasement, lowliness, subordination

infernal *adj* = **devilish**, accursed, damnable, damned, diabolical, fiendish, hellish, satanic

infertile *adj* = **barren**, sterile, unfruitful, unproductive

infertility *n* = **sterility**, barrenness, infecundity, unproductiveness

infest *v* = **overrun**, beset, invade, penetrate, permeate, ravage, swarm, throng

infested *adj* = **overrun**, alive, crawling, ravaged, ridden, swarming, teeming

infiltrate *v* = **penetrate**, filter through, insinuate oneself, make inroads (into), percolate, permeate, pervade, sneak in (*inf*)

infinite *adj* = **never-ending**, boundless, eternal, everlasting, illimitable, immeasurable, inexhaustible, limitless, measureless, unbounded

infinitesimal *adj* = **microscopic**, insignificant, minuscule, minute, negligible, teeny, tiny, unnoticeable

infinity *n* = **eternity**, boundlessness, endlessness, immensity, vastness

infirm *adj* = **frail**, ailing, debilitated, decrepit, doddering, enfeebled, failing, feeble, weak

infirmity *n* = **frailty**, decrepitude, ill health, sickliness, vulnerability

inflame *v* = **enrage**, anger, arouse, excite, incense, infuriate, madden, provoke, rouse, stimulate

inflamed *adj* = **sore**, fevered, hot, infected, red, swollen

inflammable *adj* = **flammable**, combustible, incendiary

inflammation *n* = **soreness**, painfulness, rash, redness, tenderness

inflammatory *adj* = **provocative**, explosive, fiery, intemperate, like a red rag to a bull, rabble-rousing

inflate *v* = **expand**, bloat, blow up, dilate, distend, enlarge, increase, puff up *or* out, pump up, swell

inflated *adj* = **exaggerated**, ostentatious, overblown, swollen

inflation *n* = **expansion**, enlargement, escalation, extension, increase, rise, of being bent. **2** stern. **in·flex·i·bil'i·ty** n

in·flict [in-FLIKT] vt impose, deliver forcibly. **in·flic'tion** n **1** inflicting. **2** punishment.

in·flu·ence [IN-floo-əns] n **1** effect of one person or thing on another. **2** power of person or thing having an effect. **3** thing, person exercising this. ◆ vt **-enced, -enc·ing 4** sway. **5** induce. **6** affect. **in·flu·en'tial** adj

in·flu·en·za [in-floo-EN-zə] n contagious feverish respiratory virus disease.

in·flux [IN-fluks] n **1** a flowing in. **2** inflow.

in·form' vt **1** tell. **2** animate. ◆ vi **3** give information (about). **in·form'ant** [-ənt] n one who tells. **in·for·ma'tion** n what is told, knowledge. **in·form'a·tive** adj **in·fo·mer'cial** [in-foh-MUR-shəl] n TV commercial advertising something in an informative way. **information superhighway** worldwide network of computers sharing information at high speed. **information technology** use of computers and electronic technology to store and communicate information.

in·for'mal adj **1** relaxed and friendly. **2** appropriate for everyday life or use. **in·for·mal'i·ty** n

infraction n see INFRINGE.

in·fra·red [in-frə-RED] adj denoting rays below red end of visible spectrum.

in·fra·struc·ture [IN-frə-struk-chər] n basic structure or fixed capital items of an organization or economic system.

in·fre'quent adj not happening often.

in·fringe [in-FRINJ] vt **-fringed, -fring·ing** transgress, break. **in·fringe'ment** n **in·frac'tion** n **1** breach. **2** violation.

in·fu·ri·ate [in-FYUUR-ee-ayt] vt **-at·ed, -at·ing** enrage.

in·fuse [in-FYOOZ] v **-fused, -fus·ing 1** soak to extract flavor, etc. **2** instill, charge. **in·fu'sion** [-FYOO-zhən] n **1** an infusing. **2** liquid extract obtained.

in·gen·ious [in-JEEN-yəs] adj **1** clever at contriving. **2** cleverly contrived. **in·ge·nu'i·ty** [-jə-NOO-ə-tee] n

in·gé·nue [AN-zhə-noo] n **1** artless girl or young woman. **2** actress playing such a part.

in·gen·u·ous [in-JEN-yoo-əs] adj **1** frank. **2**

---

spread, swelling

inflexibility n = **obstinacy**, intransigence, obduracy

inflexible adj **1** = **obstinate**, implacable, intractable, obdurate, resolute, set in one's ways, steadfast, stubborn, unbending, uncompromising **2** = **inelastic**, hard, rigid, stiff, taut

inflict v = **impose**, administer, apply, deliver, levy, mete or deal out, visit, wreak

infliction n = **imposition**, administration, perpetration, wreaking

influence n **1** = **effect**, authority, control, domination, magnetism, pressure, weight **2** = **power**, clout (inf), hold, importance, leverage, prestige, pull (inf) ◆ v **3** = **affect**, control, direct, guide, manipulate, sway

influential adj = **important**, authoritative, instrumental, leading, potent, powerful, significant, telling, weighty

influx n = **arrival**, incursion, inrush, inundation, invasion, rush

inform v **1** = **tell**, advise, communicate, enlighten, instruct, notify, teach, tip off **2** = **incriminate**, betray, blow the whistle on (inf), denounce, inculpate, squeal (sl)

informal adj = **relaxed**, casual, colloquial, cozy, easy, familiar, homey, natural, simple, unofficial

informality n = **familiarity**, casualness, ease, naturalness, relaxation, simplicity

information n = **facts**, data, intelligence, knowledge, message, news, notice, report

informative adj = **instructive**, chatty, communicative, edifying, educational, enlightening, forthcoming, illuminating, revealing

informed adj = **knowledgeable**, enlightened, erudite, expert, familiar, in the picture, learned, up to date, versed, well-read

informer n = **betrayer**, accuser, Judas, sneak, stool pigeon

infrequent adj = **occasional**, few and far between, once in a blue moon, rare, sporadic, uncommon, unusual

infringe v = **break**, contravene, disobey, transgress, violate

infringement n = **contravention**, breach, infraction, transgression, trespass, violation

infuriate v = **enrage**, anger, exasperate, incense, irritate, madden, provoke, rile

infuriating adj = **annoying**, exasperating, galling, irritating, maddening, mortifying, provoking, vexatious

ingenious adj = **creative**, bright, brilliant, clever, crafty, inventive, original, resourceful, shrewd naive, innocent. **in·gen'u·ous·ness** n

in·ges·tion [in-JES-chən] n act of introducing food into the body.

in·got [ING-gət] n brick of cast metal, esp. gold.

in·grain [in-GRAYN] vt implant deeply. **in·grained'** adj **1** deep-rooted. **2** inveterate.

in·gra·ti·ate [in-GRAY-shee-ayt] v refl get (oneself) into favor. **in·gra'ti·at·ing·ly** adv

in·grat'i·tude n lack of gratitude or thanks.

in·gre·di·ent [in-GREE-dee-ənt] n component part of a mixture.

in'gress n entry, means, right of entrance.

in·hab'it vt dwell in. **in·hab'it·a·ble** adj **in·hab'it·ant** [-i-tənt] n

in·hale [in-HAYL] v **-haled, -hal·ing** breathe in (air, etc.). **in·ha·la'tion** n esp. medical preparation for inhaling. **in·ha'ler** n **1** person who inhales. **2** (also **in'ha·la·tor**) device producing, and assisting inhalation

of therapeutic vapors.

in·here [in-HEER] vi **-hered, -her·ing 1** of qualities, exist (in). **2** of rights, be vested (in person). **in·her'ent** [-HEER-ənt] adj existing as an inseparable part.

in·her'it vt **1** receive as heir. **2** derive from parents. ♦ vi **3** succeed as heir. **in·her'it·ance** [-əns] n

in·hib'it vt **1** restrain (impulse, desire, etc.). **2** hinder (action). **3** forbid. **in·hi·bi'tion** n **1** repression of emotion, instinct. **2** a stopping or retarding. **in·hib'i·to·ry** adj

in·hos·pi'ta·ble adj **1** not welcoming, unfriendly. **2** difficult to live in, harsh.

in·hu·man [in-HYOO-mən] adj **1** cruel, brutal. **2** not human. **in·hu·man'i·ty** n

in·im·i·cal [i-NIM-i-kəl] adj **1** unfavorable (to). **2** unfriendly. **3** hostile.

in·im·i·ta·ble [i-NIM-i-tə-bəl] adj defying imitation. **in·im'i·ta·bly** adv

in·iq·ui·ty [i-NIK-wi-tee] n, pl **-ties 1** gross

ingenuity n = **originality**, cleverness, flair, genius, gift, inventiveness, resourcefulness, sharpness, shrewdness

ingenuous adj = **naive**, artless, guileless, honest, innocent, open, plain, simple, sincere, trusting, unsophisticated

inglorious adj = **dishonorable**, discreditable, disgraceful, disreputable, ignoble, ignominious, infamous, shameful, unheroic

ingratiate v = **pander to**, brown-nose (sl), crawl, curry favor, fawn, flatter, grovel, insinuate oneself, kiss ass (sl), toady

ingratiating adj = **sycophantic**, crawling, fawning, flattering, humble, obsequious, servile, toadying, unctuous

ingratitude n = **ungratefulness**, thanklessness

ingredient n = **component**, constituent, element, part

inhabit v = **live**, abide, dwell, occupy, populate, reside

inhabitant n = **dweller**, citizen, denizen, inmate, native, occupant, occupier, resident, tenant

inhabited adj = **populated**, colonized, developed, occupied, peopled, settled, tenanted

inhale v = **breathe in**, draw in, gasp, respire, suck in

inherent adj = **innate**, essential, hereditary, inborn, inbred, inbuilt, ingrained, inherited, intrinsic, native, natural

inherit v = **be left**, come into, fall heir to, succeed to

inheritance n = **legacy**, bequest, birthright, heritage, patrimony

inhibit v = **restrain**, check, constrain, curb, discourage, frustrate, hinder, hold back or in, impede, obstruct

inhibited adj = **shy**, constrained, guarded, repressed, reserved, reticent, self-conscious, subdued

inhibition n = **shyness**, block, hang-up (inf), reserve, restraint, reticence, self-consciousness

inhospitable adj **1** = **unwelcoming**, cool, uncongenial, unfriendly, unreceptive, unsociable, xenophobic **2** = **bleak**, barren, desolate, forbidding, godforsaken, hostile

inhuman adj = **cruel**, barbaric, brutal, cold-blooded, heartless, merciless, pitiless, ruthless, savage, unfeeling

inhumane adj = **cruel**, brutal, heartless, pitiless, unfeeling, unkind, unsympathetic

inhumanity n = **cruelty**, atrocity, barbarism, brutality, heartlessness, pitilessness, ruthlessness, unkindness

inimical adj = **hostile**, adverse, antagonistic, ill-disposed, opposed, unfavorable, unfriendly, unwelcoming

inimitable adj = **unique**, consummate, incomparable, matchless, peerless, unparalleled, unrivaled

iniquitous adj = **wicked**, criminal, evil, immoral, reprehensible, sinful, unjust injustice. **2** wickedness, sin. **in·iq'ui·tous** *adj* unfair, sinful, unjust.

in·i·tial [i-NISH-əl] *adj* **1** of, occurring at the beginning. ♦ *n* **2** initial letter, esp. of person's name. ♦ *vt* **-tialed, -tial·ing 3** mark, sign with one's initials.

in·i·ti·ate [i-NISH-ee-ayt] *vt* **-at·ed, -at·ing 1** originate. **2** begin. **3** admit into closed society. **4** instruct in elements (of). ♦ *n* [-ee-it] **5** initiated person. **in·i·ti·a'tion** *n* **in·i'ti·a·tive** *n* **1** first step, lead. **2** ability to act independently. ♦ *adj* **3** originating.

in·ject [in-JEKT] *vt* introduce (esp. fluid, medicine, etc. with syringe). **in·jec'tion** *n*

in·junc·tion [in-JUNGK-shən] *n* **1** judicial order to restrain. **2** authoritative order.

in·ju·ry [IN-jə-ree] *n, pl* **-ries 1** physical damage or harm. **2** wrong. **in·jure** [IN-jər] *vt* **-jured, -jur·ing** do harm or damage to. **in·ju'ri·ous** [-JUU-ree-əs] *adj*

in·jus·tice [in-JUS-tis] *n* **1** want of justice. **2** wrong. **3** injury. **4** unjust act.

ink *n* **1** fluid used for writing or printing. ♦ *vt* **2** mark with ink. **3** cover, smear with it. **ink·ling** [INGK-ling] *n* hint, slight

knowledge or suspicion.

inlaid see INLAY.

in·land *n* **1** interior of country. ♦ *adj* [IN-lənd] **2** in this. **3** away from the sea. **4** within a country. ♦ *adv* [IN-land] **5** in or toward the inland.

in'-law *n* relative by marriage esp. mother-in-law and father-in-law.

in'lay *vt* **-laid, -lay·ing 1** embed. **2** decorate with inset pattern. ♦ *n* **3** inlaid piece or pattern.

in'let *n* **1** entrance. **2** small arm of sea, lake, etc. **3** piece inserted.

in lo·co pa·ren·tis [LOH-koh pə-REN-tis] *Lat* in place of a parent.

in·mate [IN-mayt] *n* occupant, esp. of prison, hospital, etc.

in·most [IN-mohst] *adj* **1** most inward, deepest. **2** most secret.

inn *n* **1** restaurant or tavern. **2** country hotel. **inn'keep·er** *n*

in·nards [IN-ərdz] *pl n* internal organs or working parts.

in·nate [i-NAYT] *adj* **1** inborn. **2** inherent.

in·ner [IN-ər] *adj* lying within. **in'ner·most**

━━━━━━ THESAURUS ━━━━━━

iniquity *n* = **wickedness**, abomination, evil, injustice, sin, wrong

initial *adj* = **first**, beginning, incipient, introductory, opening, primary

initially *adv* = **at first**, at *or* in the beginning, first, firstly, originally, primarily

initiate *v* **1** = **begin**, commence, get under way, kick off (*inf*), launch, open, originate, set in motion, start **2** = **induct**, indoctrinate, introduce, invest **3** = **instruct**, acquaint with, coach, familiarize with, teach, train ♦ *n* **4** = **novice**, beginner, convert, entrant, learner, member, probationer

initiation *n* = **introduction**, debut, enrollment, entrance, inauguration, induction, installation, investiture

initiative *n* **1** = **first step**, advantage, first move, lead **2** = **resourcefulness**, ambition, drive, dynamism, enterprise, get-up-and-go (*inf*), leadership

inject *v* **1** = **vaccinate**, inoculate **2** = **introduce**, bring in, infuse, insert, instill

injection *n* **1** = **vaccination**, inoculation, shot (*inf*) **2** = **introduction**, dose, infusion, insertion

injudicious *adj* = **unwise**, foolish, ill-advised, ill-judged, impolitic, imprudent, incautious, inexpedient, rash, unthinking

injunction *n* = **order**, command, exhortation, instruction, mandate, precept, ruling

injure *v* = **hurt**, damage, harm, impair, ruin, spoil, undermine, wound

injured *adj* = **hurt**, broken, challenged, damaged, disabled, undermined, weakened, wounded

injury *n* = **harm**, damage, detriment, disservice, hurt, ill, trauma (*Pathology*), wound, wrong

injustice *n* = **unfairness**, bias, discrimination, inequality, inequity, iniquity, oppression, partisanship, prejudice, wrong

inkling *n* = **suspicion**, clue, conception, hint, idea, indication, intimation, notion, suggestion, whisper

inland *adj* = **interior**, domestic, internal, upcountry

inlet *n* = **bay**, bight, creek, firth *or* frith (*Scot.*), fjord, passage

inmost *or* **innermost** *adj* = **deepest**, basic, central, essential, intimate, personal, private, secret

innate *adj* = **inborn**, congenital, constitutional, essential, inbred, ingrained, inherent, instinctive, intuitive, native, natural *adj* **inner tube** rubber air tube of pneumatic tire.

in·ning *n Sports* **1** side's turn at bat. **2** spell, turn.

in·no·cent [IN-ə-sənt] *adj* **1** pure. **2** guiltless. **3** harmless. ♦ *n* **4** innocent person, esp. young child. **in·'no·cence** *n*

in·noc·u·ous [i-NOK-yoo-əs] *adj* harmless.

in·no·vate [IN-ə-vayt] *vt* **-vat·ed. -vat·ing** introduce changes, new things. **in·no·va'tion** *n*

in·nu·en·do [in-yoo-EN-doh] *n, pl* **-dos 1** allusive remark, hint. **2** indirect accusation.

in·nu·mer·a·ble [i-NOO-mər-ə-bəl] *adj* **1** countless. **2** very numerous.

in·oc·u·late [i-NOK-yə-layt] *vt* **-lat·ed, -lat·ing** immunize by injecting vaccine. **in·oc·u·la'tion** *n*

in·of·fen·sive *adj* causing no harm.

in·op·er·a·ble [in-OP-ər-ə-bəl] *adj* **1** unworkable. **2** *Med.* that cannot be operated on. **in·op'er·a·tive** *adj* **1** not operative. **2** ineffective.

in·op·por·tune [in-op-ər-TOON] *adj* badly timed.

in·or·di·nate [in-OR-dn-it] *adj* excessive.

in·or·gan·ic [in-or-GAN-ik] *adj* **1** not having structure or characteristics of living organisms. **2** of substances without carbon.

in·pa·tient [IN-pay-shənt] *n* patient who stays in hospital.

in·put [IN-puut] *n* **1** act of putting in. **2** that which is put in, as resource needed for industrial production, etc. **3** data, etc. fed into a computer.

in·quest [IN-kwest] *n* **1** legal or judicial inquiry presided over by a coroner. **2** detailed inquiry or discussion.

in·quire [in-KWIR] *vi* **-quired, -quir·ing** seek information. **in·quir'er** *n* **in·quir'y** *n, pl* **-quir·ies 1** question. **2** investigation.

in·qui·si·tion [in-kwə-ZISH-ən] *n* **1** searching investigation, official inquiry. **2** (I-) *Hist.* organization within the Catholic Church for suppressing heresy. **in·quis'i·tor** [-KWIZ-ə-tər] *n*

in·quis·i·tive [in-KWIZ-i-tiv] *adj* **1** curious.

————————| THESAURUS |————————

inner *adj* **1 = inside**, central, interior, internal, inward, middle **2 = private**, hidden, intimate, personal, repressed, secret, unrevealed

innkeeper *n* **= publican**, host *or* hostess, hotelier, landlord *or* landlady, mine host

innocence *n* **1 = guiltlessness**, blamelessness, clean hands, incorruptibility, probity, purity, uprightness, virtue **2 = harmlessness**, innocuousness, inoffensiveness **3 = inexperience**, artlessness, credulousness, gullibility, ingenuousness, naivety, simplicity, unworldliness

innocent *adj* **1 = not guilty**, blameless, guiltless, honest, in the clear, uninvolved **2 = harmless**, innocuous, inoffensive, unobjectionable, well-intentioned, well-meant **3 = naive**, artless, childlike, credulous, gullible, ingenuous, open, simple, unworldly

innovation *n* **= modernization**, alteration, change, departure, introduction, newness, novelty, variation

innuendo *n* **= insinuation**, aspersion, hint, implication, imputation, intimation, overtone, suggestion, whisper

innumerable *adj* **= countless**, beyond number, incalculable, infinite, multitudinous, myriad, numberless, numerous, unnumbered, untold

inoffensive *adj* **= harmless**, innocent, innocuous, mild, quiet, retiring, unobjectionable, unobtrusive

inoperative *adj* **= out of action**, broken, defective, ineffective, invalid, null and void, out of order, out of service, useless

inopportune *adj* **= inconvenient**, ill-chosen, ill-timed, inappropriate, unfavorable, unfortunate, unpropitious, unseasonable, unsuitable, untimely

inordinate *adj* **= excessive**, disproportionate, extravagant, immoderate, intemperate, preposterous, unconscionable, undue, unreasonable, unwarranted

inorganic *adj* **= artificial**, chemical, man-made

inquest *n* **= inquiry**, inquisition, investigation, probe

inquire *v* **1 = investigate**, examine, explore, look into, make inquiries, probe, research **2** (also **enquire**) **= ask**, query, question

inquiry *n* **1 = investigation**, examination, exploration, inquest, interrogation, probe, research, study, survey **2** (also **enquiry**) **= question**, query

inquisition *n* **= investigation**, cross-examination, examination, grilling

2 prying.

in·road [IN-rohd] n 1 incursion. 2 encroachment.

in·sane [in-SAYN] adj 1 mentally deranged. 2 crazy, senseless. **in·sane'ly** adv 1 like a lunatic, madly. 2 excessively. **in·san'i·ty** n

in·san'i·tar·y adj dirty or unhealthy.

in·sa·tia·ble [in-SAY-shə-bəl] adj incapable of being satisfied.

in·scribe [in-SKRĪB] vt -scribed, -scrib·ing 1 write, engrave (in or on something). 2 mark. 3 dedicate. 4 trace (figure) within another. **in·scrip'tion** n 1 inscribing. 2 words inscribed on monument, etc.

in·scru·ta·ble [in-SKROO-tə-bəl] adj 1 mysterious, impenetrable. 2 affording no explanation. **in·scru·ta·bil'i·ty** n

in·sect [IN-sekt] n small invertebrate animal with six legs, usu. segmented body and two or four wings. **in·sec'ti·cide** [-sīd] n preparation for killing insects. **in·sec·tiv'o·rous** adj insect-eating.

in·se·cure [in-si-KYUUR] adj 1 not safe or firm. 2 anxious, not confident.

in·sem·i·nate [in-SEM-ə-nayt] vt -nat·ed, -nat·ing implant semen into. **artificial insemination** impregnation of the female by artificial means.

in·sen·sate [in-SEN-sayt] adj 1 without sensation, unconscious. 2 unfeeling.

in·sen·si·ble [in-SEN-sə-bəl] adj 1 unconscious. 2 without feeling. 3 not aware. 4 not perceptible. **in·sen'si·bly** adv imperceptibly.

in·sen·si·tive adj unaware of or ignoring other people's feelings. **in·sen·si·tiv'i·ty** n

in·sert [in-SURT] vt 1 introduce. 2 place or put (in, into, between). ◆ n [IN-surt] 3 something inserted. **in·ser'tion** [-shən] n

in·set n something extra inserted esp. as decoration. **in·set'** vt -set, -set·ting

in·shore [IN-shor] adj 1 near shore. ◆ adv 2 toward shore.

in·side [IN-sīd] n 1 inner side, surface, or part. 2 inner circle of influence. 3 sl confidential information. ◆ pl 4 inf internal parts of body. ◆ adj 5 of, in, or on, inside. ◆ adv [in-SĪD] 6 in or into the inside. 7 sl in prison. ◆ prep 8 within, on inner side.

in·sid·i·ous [in-SID-ee-əs] adj 1 stealthy, treacherous. 2 unseen but deadly.

in·sight [IN-sīt] n deep understanding.

──────── THESAURUS ────────

(inf), inquest, inquiry, questioning, third degree (inf)

inquisitive adj = **curious**, inquiring, nosy (inf), probing, prying, questioning

insane adj 1 = **mad**, crazed, crazy, demented, deranged, mentally ill, out of one's mind, unhinged 2 = **stupid**, bonkers (inf), daft (inf), foolish, idiotic, impractical, irrational, irresponsible, preposterous, senseless

insanitary adj = **unhealthy**, dirty, disease-ridden, filthy, infested, insalubrious, polluted, scuzzy (sl), unclean, unhygienic

insanity n 1 = **madness**, delirium, dementia, mental disorder, mental illness 2 = **stupidity**, folly, irresponsibility, lunacy, senselessness

insatiable adj = **unquenchable**, greedy, intemperate, rapacious, ravenous, voracious

inscribe v = **carve**, cut, engrave, etch, impress, imprint

inscription n = **engraving**, dedication, legend, words

inscrutable adj 1 = **enigmatic**, blank, deadpan, impenetrable, poker-faced (inf) 2 = **mysterious**, hidden,

incomprehensible, inexplicable, unexplainable, unfathomable, unintelligible

insecure adj 1 = **anxious**, afraid, uncertain, unsure 2 = **unsafe**, defenseless, exposed, unguarded, unprotected, vulnerable, wide-open

insecurity n = **anxiety**, fear, uncertainty, worry

insensible adj = **unaware**, impervious, oblivious, unaffected, unconscious, unmindful

insensitive adj = **unfeeling**, callous, hardened, indifferent, thick-skinned, tough, uncaring, unconcerned

inseparable adj 1 = **indivisible**, indissoluble 2 = **devoted**, bosom, close, intimate

insert v = **enter**, embed, implant, introduce, place, put, stick in

insertion n = **inclusion**, addition, implant, interpolation, introduction, supplement

inside adj 1 = **inner**, interior, internal, inward 2 = **confidential**, classified, exclusive, internal, private, restricted, secret ◆ adv 3 = **indoors**, under cover, within ◆ n 4 = **interior**, contents 5 **insides** Inf = **stomach**, belly, bowels, entrails, guts,

in·sig·ni·a [in-SIG-nee-ə] *n, pl* **-ni·as, -ni·a** badge or emblem of honor or office.

in·sig·nif'i·cant *adj* not important. **in·sig·nif'i·cance** *n*

in·sin·cere' *adj* showing false feelings, not genuine. **in·sin·cer'i·ty** *n, pl* **-ties**

in·sin·u·ate [in-SIN-yoo-ayt] *vt* **-at·ed, -at·ing 1** hint. **2** work oneself into favor. **3** introduce gradually or subtly. **in·sin·u·a'tion** *n*

in·sip'id *adj* dull, tasteless, spiritless.

in·sist' *vi* **1** demand persistently. **2** maintain. **3** emphasize. **in·sist'ence** *n* **in·sist'ent** *adj*

in si·tu [SĪ-too] *Lat* in its original place or position.

in·so·lent [IN-sə-lənt] *adj* arrogantly impudent. **in'so·lence** *n*

in·sol'vent *adj* unable to pay one's debts. **in·sol'ven·cy** *n*

in·som·ni·a [in-SOM-nee-ə] *n* sleeplessness. **in·som'ni·ac** [-nee-ak] *adj, n*

in·so·much [in-sə-MUCH] *adv* to such an extent.

in·sou·ci·ant [in-SOO-see-ənt] *adj* indifferent, careless, unconcerned. **in·sou'ci·ance** *n*

in·spect [in-SPEKT] *vt* examine closely or officially. **in·spec'tion** *n* **in·spec'tor** *n* **1** one who inspects. **2** high-ranking police or fire officer.

in·spire [in-SPĪR] *vt* **-spired, -spir·ing 1** animate, invigorate. **2** arouse, create feeling, thought. **3** give rise to. **4** breathe in, inhale. **in·spi·ra'tion** *n* **1** good idea. **2** creative influence or stimulus.

————— THESAURUS —————

innards (*inf*), viscera, vitals

insidious *adj* = **stealthy**, deceptive, sly, smooth, sneaking, subtle, surreptitious

insight *n* = **understanding**, awareness, comprehension, discernment, judgment, observation, penetration, perception, perspicacity, vision

insignia *n* = **badge**, crest, emblem, symbol

insignificance *n* = **unimportance**, inconsequence, irrelevance, meaninglessness, pettiness, triviality, worthlessness

insignificant *adj* = **unimportant**, inconsequential, irrelevant, meaningless, minor, nondescript, paltry, petty, trifling, trivial

insincere *adj* = **deceitful**, dishonest, disingenuous, duplicitous, false, hollow, hypocritical, lying, two-faced, untruthful

insincerity *n* = **deceitfulness**, dishonesty, dissimulation, duplicity, hypocrisy, pretense, untruthfulness

insinuate *v* **1** = **imply**, allude, hint, indicate, intimate, suggest **2** = **ingratiate**, curry favor, get in with, worm or work one's way in

insinuation *n* = **implication**, allusion, aspersion, hint, innuendo, slur, suggestion

insipid *adj* **1** = **bland**, anemic, characterless, colorless, prosaic, uninteresting, vapid, wishy-washy (*inf*) **2** = **tasteless**, bland, flavorless, unappetizing, watery

insist *v* **1** = **demand**, lay down the law, put one's foot down (*inf*), require **2** = **assert**, aver, claim, maintain, reiterate, repeat,

swear, vow

insistence *n* = **persistence**, emphasis, importunity, stress

insistent *adj* = **persistent**, dogged, emphatic, importunate, incessant, persevering, unrelenting, urgent

insolence *n* = **rudeness**, boldness, cheek (*inf*), disrespect, effrontery, impertinence, impudence

insolent *adj* = **rude**, bold, contemptuous, impertinent, impudent, insubordinate, insulting

insoluble *adj* = **inexplicable**, baffling, impenetrable, indecipherable, mysterious, unaccountable, unfathomable, unsolvable

insolvency *n* = **bankruptcy**, failure, liquidation, ruin

insolvent *adj* = **bankrupt**, broke (*inf*), failed, gone bust (*inf*), gone to the wall, in receivership, ruined

insomnia *n* = **sleeplessness**, wakefulness

inspect *v* = **examine**, check, go over or through, investigate, look over, scrutinize, survey, vet

inspection *n* = **examination**, check, checkup, investigation, once-over (*inf*), review, scrutiny, search, survey

inspector *n* = **examiner**, censor, investigator, overseer, scrutinizer, superintendent, supervisor

inspiration *n* **1** = **influence**, muse, spur, stimulus **2** = **revelation**, creativity, illumination, insight

inspire *v* **1** = **stimulate**, animate, encourage, enliven, galvanize, influence, spur **2** = **arouse**, enkindle, excite, give rise

in·stall [in-STAWL] *vt* 1 have (apparatus) put in. 2 establish. 3 place (person in office, etc.) with ceremony. **in·stal·la'tion** *n* 1 act of installing. 2 that which is installed.

in·stall·ment [in-STAWL-mənt] *n* 1 payment of part of debt. 2 any of parts of a whole delivered in succession.

in·stance [IN-stəns] *n* 1 example. 2 particular case. 3 request. ◆ *vt* **-stanced, -stanc·ing** 4 cite.

in·stant [IN-stənt] *n* 1 moment, point of time. ◆ *adj* 2 immediate. 3 urgent. 4 (of foods) requiring little preparation. **in·stan·ta'ne·ous** *adj* happening in an instant. **in·stan'ter** *adv* at once. **in'stant·ly** *adv* at once.

in·stead [in-STED] *adv* 1 in place (of). 2 as a substitute.

in'step *n* top of foot between toes and ankle.

in·sti·gate [IN-sti-gayt] *vt* **-gat·ed, -gat·ing** 1 incite, urge. 2 bring about. **in·sti·ga'tion** *n*

in·still' *vt* 1 implant. 2 inculcate. **in·still'ment** *n*

in·stinct [IN-stingkt] *n* 1 inborn impulse or propensity. 2 unconscious skill. 3 intuition. **in·stinc'tive** *adj*

in·sti·tute [IN-sti-toot] *vt* **-tut·ed, -tut·ing** 1 establish, found. 2 appoint. 3 set in motion. ◆ *n* 4 society for promoting some public goal, esp. scientific. 5 its building. **in·sti·tu'tion** *n* 1 an instituting. 2 establishment for care or education, hospital, college, etc. 3 an established custom or law. 4 *inf* a well-established person. **in·sti·tu'tion·al** *adj* 1 of institutions. 2 routine. **in·sti·tu'tion·al·ize** *vt* **-ized, -iz·ing** 1 place in an institution esp. for care

to, produce

inspired *adj* 1 = **brilliant**, cool (*inf*), dazzling, impressive, memorable, outstanding, phat (*sl*), superlative, thrilling, wonderful 2 = **uplifted**, elated, enthused, exhilarated, stimulated

inspiring *adj* = **uplifting**, exciting, exhilarating, heartening, moving, rousing, stimulating, stirring

instability *n* = **unpredictability**, changeableness, fickleness, fluctuation, impermanence, inconstancy, insecurity, unsteadiness, variability, volatility, wavering

install *v* 1 = **set up**, fix, lay, lodge, place, position, put in, station 2 = **induct**, establish, inaugurate, institute, introduce, invest 3 = **settle**, ensconce, position

installation *n* 1 = **setting up**, establishment, fitting, installment, placing, positioning 2 = **induction**, inauguration, investiture 3 = **equipment**, machinery, plant, system

installment *n* = **portion**, chapter, division, episode, part, repayment, section

instance *n* 1 = **example**, case, illustration, occasion, occurrence, situation ◆ *v* 2 = **quote**, adduce, cite, mention, name, specify

instant *n* 1 = **second**, flash, jiffy (*inf*), moment, split second, trice, twinkling of an eye (*inf*) 2 = **juncture**, moment, occasion, point, time ◆ *adj* 3 = **immediate**, direct, instantaneous, on-the-spot,

prompt, quick, split-second 4 = **precooked**, convenience, fast, ready-mixed

instantaneous *adj* = **immediate**, direct, instant, on-the-spot, prompt

instantaneously *adv* = **immediately**, at once, instantly, in the twinkling of an eye (*inf*), on the spot, promptly, straight away

instantly *adv* = **immediately**, at once, directly, instantaneously, now, right away, straight away, this minute

instead *adv* 1 = **rather**, alternatively, in lieu, in preference, on second thoughts, preferably 2 **instead of** = **in place of**, in lieu of, rather than

instigate *v* = **provoke**, bring about, incite, influence, initiate, prompt, set off, start, stimulate, trigger

instigation *n* = **prompting**, behest, bidding, encouragement, incentive, incitement, urging

instigator *n* = **ringleader**, agitator, leader, motivator, prime mover, troublemaker

instill *v* = **introduce**, engender, imbue, implant, inculcate, infuse, insinuate

instinct *n* = **intuition**, faculty, gift, impulse, knack, predisposition, proclivity, talent, tendency

instinctive *adj* = **inborn**, automatic, inherent, innate, intuitive, involuntary, natural, reflex, spontaneous, unpremeditated, visceral

instinctively *adv* = **intuitively**, automatically, by instinct, involuntarily, of mentally ill. **2** make or become an institution.

in·struct [in-STRUKT] *vt* **1** teach. **2** inform. **3** order. **4** brief (jury, lawyer). **in·struc'tion** *n* **1** teaching. **2** order. ♦ *pl* **3** directions. **in·struc'tive** *adj* **1** informative. **2** useful.

in·stru·ment [IN-strə-mənt] *n* **1** tool, implement, means, person, thing used to make, do, measure, etc. **2** mechanism for producing musical sound. **3** legal document. **in·stru·men'tal** *adj* **1** acting as instrument or means. **2** helpful. **3** belonging to, produced by musical instruments. **in·stru·men'tal·ist** *n* player of musical instrument. **in·stru·men·tal'i·ty** *n*, *pl* **-ties** agency, means. **in·stru·men·ta'tion** *n* arrangement of music for instruments.

in·sub·or·di·nate [in-sə-BOR-dn-it] *adj* **1** not submissive. **2** mutinous, rebellious. **in·sub·or·di·na'tion** *n*

in·su·lar [IN-sə-lər] *adj* **1** of an island. **2** remote, detached. **3** narrow-minded or prejudiced. **in·su·lar'i·ty** *n*

in·su·late [IN-sə-layt] *vt* **-lat·ed**, **-lat·ing 1** prevent or reduce transfer of electricity, heat, sound, etc. **2** isolate, detach. **in·su·la'tion** *n*

in·su·lin [IN-sə-lin] *n* pancreatic hormone, used in treating diabetes.

in·sult' *vt* **1** behave rudely to. **2** offend. ♦ *n* [IN-sult] **3** offensive remark. **4** affront. **in·sult'ing** *adj*

in·su·per·a·ble [in-SOO-pər-ə-bəl] *adj* **1** that cannot be overcome or surmounted. **2** unconquerable.

in·sure [in-SHUUR] *v* **-sured**, **-sur·ing 1**

naturally, without thinking

institute *n* **1** = **society**, academy, association, college, foundation, guild, institution, school ♦ *v* **2** = **establish**, fix, found, initiate, introduce, launch, organize, originate, pioneer, set up, start

institution *n* **1** = **establishment**, academy, college, foundation, institute, school, society **2** = **custom**, convention, law, practice, ritual, rule, tradition

institutional *adj* = **conventional**, accepted, established, formal, orthodox

instruct *v* **1** = **order**, bid, charge, command, direct, enjoin, tell **2** = **teach**, coach, drill, educate, ground, school, train, tutor

instruction *n* **1** = **teaching**, coaching, education, grounding, guidance, lesson(s), schooling, training, tuition **2** = **order**, command, demand, directive, injunction, mandate, ruling

instructions *pl n* = **orders**, advice, directions, guidance, information, key, recommendations, rules

instructive *adj* = **informative**, edifying, educational, enlightening, helpful, illuminating, revealing, useful

instructor *n* = **teacher**, adviser, coach, demonstrator, guide, mentor, trainer, tutor

instrument *n* **1** = **tool**, apparatus, appliance, contraption (*inf*), device, gadget, implement, mechanism **2** = **means**, agency, agent, mechanism, medium, organ, vehicle

instrumental *adj* = **active**, contributory,

helpful, influential, involved, useful

insubordinate *adj* = **disobedient**, defiant, disorderly, mutinous, rebellious, recalcitrant, refractory, undisciplined, ungovernable, unruly

insubordination *n* = **disobedience**, defiance, indiscipline, insurrection, mutiny, rebellion, recalcitrance, revolt

insubstantial *adj* = **flimsy**, feeble, frail, poor, slight, tenuous, thin, weak

insufferable *adj* = **unbearable**, detestable, dreadful, impossible, insupportable, intolerable, unendurable

insufficient *adj* = **inadequate**, deficient, incapable, lacking, scant, short

insular *adj* = **narrow-minded**, blinkered, circumscribed, inward-looking, limited, narrow, parochial, petty, provincial

insulate *v* = **isolate**, close off, cocoon, cushion, cut off, protect, sequester, shield

insult *v* **1** = **offend**, abuse, affront, call names, put down, slander, slight, snub ♦ *n* **2** = **abuse**, affront, aspersion, insolence, offense, put-down, slap in the face (*inf*), slight, snub

insulting *adj* = **offensive**, abusive, contemptuous, degrading, disparaging, insolent, rude, scurrilous

insuperable *adj* = **insurmountable**, impassable, invincible, unconquerable

insupportable *adj* **1** = **intolerable**, insufferable, unbearable, unendurable **2** = **unjustifiable**, indefensible, untenable

insurance *n* = **protection**, assurance, cover, guarantee, indemnity, safeguard, security, warranty contract for payment in event of loss, death, etc., by payment of premiums. **2** make such contract about. **3** make safe (against). **in·sur'a·ble** *adj* **in·sur'ance** *n* **in·sur'er** *n* **1** insurance policy. **2** contract of insurance.

in·sur·gent [in-SUR-jənt] *adj* **1** in revolt. ◆ *n* **2** rebel. **in·sur'gence, in·sur·rec'tion** *n* revolt.

in·tact [in-TAKT] *adj* **1** untouched. **2** uninjured.

in·tagl·io [in-TAL-yoh] *n, pl* **-tagl·ios 1** engraved design. **2** gem so cut.

in·take [IN-tayk] *n* **1** what is taken in. **2** quantity taken in. **3** opening for taking in. **4** in car, air passage into carburetor.

in·tan'gi·ble [IN-ti-grəl] *adj* not clear or definite enough to be seen or felt easily.

in·te·ger [IN-ti-jər] *n* **1** whole number. **2** whole of anything.

in·te·gral [IN-ti-grəl] *adj* constituting an essential part of a whole. **in·te·grate** *vt* **-grat·ed, -grat·ing 1** combine into one whole. **2** unify diverse elements (of community, etc.). **in·te·gra'tion** *n* **integral calculus** branch of mathematics of changing quantities that calculates total effects of the change. **integrated circuit** tiny electronic circuit, usu. on silicon chip.

in·teg·ri·ty [in-TEG-ri-tee] *n* **1** honesty. **2** original perfect state.

in·teg·u·ment [in-TEG-yə-mənt] *n* natural covering, skin, rind, husk.

in·tel·lect [IN-tl-ekt] *n* power of thinking and reasoning. **in·tel·lec'tu·al** *adj* **1** of, appealing to intellect. **2** having good intellect. ◆ *n* **3** one endowed with intellect and attracted to intellectual things.

in·tel·li·gent [in-TEL-i-jənt] *adj* **1** having, showing good intellect. **2** quick at understanding. **3** informed. **in·tel'li·gence** *n* **1** quickness of understanding. **2** mental power or ability. **3** intellect. **4** information, news, esp. military information. **in·tel·li·gent'si·a** [-JENT-see-ə] *n* intellectual or cultured classes. **in·tel'li·gi·ble** [-jə-bəl] *adj* understandable.

in·tem·per·ate [in-TEM-pər-it] *adj* **1** drinking alcohol to excess. **2** immoderate. **3** unrestrained. **in·tem'per·ance** [-əns] *n*

in·tend' *vt* propose, mean (to do, say, etc.). **in·tend'ed** *adj* **1** planned, future. ◆ *n* **2** *inf* proposed spouse.

in·tense [in-TENS] *adj* **1** very strong or

insure *v* = **protect**, assure, cover, guarantee, indemnify, underwrite, warrant

insurgent *n* **1** = **rebel**, insurrectionist, mutineer, revolutionary, rioter ◆ *adj* **2** = **rebellious**, disobedient, insubordinate, mutinous, revolting, revolutionary, riotous, seditious

insurmountable *adj* = **insuperable**, hopeless, impassable, impossible, invincible, overwhelming, unconquerable

insurrection *n* = **rebellion**, coup, insurgency, mutiny, revolt, revolution, riot, uprising

intact *adj* = **undamaged**, complete, entire, perfect, sound, unbroken, unharmed, unimpaired, unscathed, whole

integral *adj* = **essential**, basic, component, constituent, fundamental, indispensable, intrinsic, necessary

integrate *v* = **combine**, amalgamate, assimilate, blend, fuse, incorporate, join, merge, unite

integration *n* = **assimilation**, amalgamation, blending, combining, fusing, incorporation, mixing, unification

integrity *n* **1** = **honesty**, goodness, honor, incorruptibility, principle, probity, purity,

rectitude, uprightness, virtue **2** = **unity**, coherence, cohesion, completeness, soundness, wholeness

intellect *n* = **intelligence**, brains (*inf*), judgment, mind, reason, sense, understanding

intellectual *adj* **1** = **scholarly**, bookish, cerebral, highbrow, intelligent, studious, thoughtful ◆ *n* **2** = **thinker**, academic, egghead (*inf*), highbrow

intelligence *n* **1** = **understanding**, acumen, brain power, brains (*inf*), cleverness, comprehension, intellect, perception, sense **2** = **information**, data, facts, findings, knowledge, news, notification, report

intelligent *adj* = **clever**, brainy (*inf*), bright, enlightened, perspicacious, quick-witted, sharp, smart, well-informed

intelligentsia *n* = **intellectuals**, highbrows, literati

intelligible *adj* = **understandable**, clear, comprehensible, distinct, lucid, open, plain

intemperate *adj* = **excessive**, extreme, immoderate, profligate, self-indulgent, unbridled, unrestrained, wild

intend *v* = **plan**, aim, have in mind *or* view,

acute. **2** emotional. **in·ten·si·fi·ca'tion** n
in·ten·si·fy v **-fied, -fy·ing** make or
become stronger. **2** increase. **in·ten'si·ty** n
1 intense quality. **2** strength. **in·ten'sive**
adj characterized by intensity or emphasis
on specified factor.

in·tent' n **1** purpose. ◆ adj **2** concentrating
(on). **3** resolved, bent. **4** preoccupied,
absorbed. **in·ten'tion** n purpose, aim.
in·ten'tion·al adj

in·ter [in-TUR] vt **-terred, -ter·ring** bury.
in·ter'ment n

inter- prefix between, among, mutually,
e.g. *interglacial; interrelation.*

in·ter·act [in-tər-AKT] vi act on each other.
in·ter·ac'tion n

in·ter·cede [in-tər-SEED] vi **-ced·ed,
-ced·ing 1** plead in favor of. **2** mediate.
in·ter·ces'sion n

in·ter·cept [in-tər-SEPT] vt **1** cut off. **2**
seize, stop in transit. **in·ter·cep'tion** n
in·ter·cept'or, -er n **1** one who, that which
intercepts. **2** fast fighter plane, missile, etc.

in·ter·change [in-tər-CHAYNJ] v **-changed,
-chang·ing 1** (cause to) exchange places. ◆

n [IN-tər-chaynj] **2** interchanging. **3**
highway intersection. **in·ter·change'a·ble**
adj able to be exchanged in position or
use.

in·ter·con·ti·nen·tal [in-tər-kon-tn-EN-təl]
adj **1** connecting continents. **2** (of missile)
able to reach one continent from another.

in·ter·course [IN-tər-kors] n **1** mutual
dealings. **2** communication. **3** sexual
joining of two people. **4** copulation.

in·ter·dict [IN-tər-dikt] n **1** in Catholic
church, decree restraining faithful from
receiving certain sacraments. **2** formal
prohibition. **in·ter·dict'** vt **1** prohibit,
forbid. **2** restrain. **in·ter·dic'tion** n

in·ter·est [IN-tər-ist] n **1** concern, curiosity.
2 thing exciting this. **3** sum paid for use of
borrowed money. **4** legal concern. **5** right,
advantage, share. ◆ vt **6** excite, cause to
feel interest. **in'ter·est·ing** adj

in·ter·face [IN-tər-fays] n area, surface,
boundary linking two systems.

in·ter·fere [in-tər-FEER] vi **-fered, -fer·ing 1**
meddle, intervene. **2** clash. **in·ter·fer'ence**
n **1** act of interfering. **2** *Radio* interruption

———————— THESAURUS ————————

mean, propose, purpose

intense adj **1 = extreme,** acute, deep,
excessive, fierce, great, powerful,
profound, severe **2 = passionate,** ardent,
fanatical, fervent, fierce, heightened,
impassioned, vehement

intensify v **= increase,** add to, aggravate,
deepen, escalate, heighten, magnify,
redouble, reinforce, sharpen, strengthen

intensity n **= force,** ardor, emotion,
fanaticism, fervor, fierceness, passion,
strength, vehemence, vigor

intensive adj **= concentrated,**
comprehensive, demanding, exhaustive,
in-depth, thorough, thoroughgoing

intent n **1 = intention,** aim, design, end,
goal, meaning, object, objective, plan,
purpose ◆ adj **2 = attentive,** absorbed,
determined, eager, engrossed,
preoccupied, rapt, resolved, steadfast,
watchful

intention n **= purpose,** aim, design, end,
goal, idea, object, objective, point, target

intentional adj **= deliberate,** calculated,
intended, meant, planned, premeditated,
willful

intentionally adv **= deliberately,**
designedly, on purpose, willfully

inter v **= bury,** entomb, lay to rest

intercede v **= mediate,** arbitrate,
intervene, plead

intercept v **= seize,** block, catch, cut off,
head off, interrupt, obstruct, stop

interchange v **1 = switch,** alternate,
exchange, reciprocate, swap ◆ n **2 =
junction,** intersection

interchangeable adj **= identical,**
equivalent, exchangeable, reciprocal,
synonymous

intercourse n **1 = communication,**
commerce, contact, dealings **2 = sexual
intercourse,** carnal knowledge, coitus,
copulation, sex

interest n **1 = curiosity,** attention,
concern, notice, regard **2 = hobby,**
activity, diversion, pastime, preoccupation,
pursuit **3 = advantage,** benefit, good,
profit **4 = stake,** claim, investment, right,
share ◆ v **5 = intrigue,** attract, catch one's
eye, divert, engross, fascinate

interested adj **1 = curious,** attracted,
drawn, excited, fascinated, keen **2 =
involved,** concerned, implicated

interesting adj **= intriguing,** absorbing,
appealing, attractive, compelling,
engaging, engrossing, gripping,
stimulating, thought-provoking

interface n **= connection,** border,

in·ter·fer·on [in-tər-FEER-on] *n* a cellular protein that stops development of an invading virus.

in·ter·im [IN-tər-əm] *n* 1 meantime. ◆ *adj* 2 temporary, intervening.

in·te·ri·or [in-TEER-ee-ər] *adj* 1 inner. 2 inland. 3 indoors. ◆ *n* 4 inside. 5 inland region.

in·ter·ject [in-tər-JEKT] *vt* interpose (remark, etc.). **in·ter·jec'tion** *n* 1 exclamation. 2 interjected remark.

in·ter·lard [in-tər-LAHRD] *v* intersperse.

in·ter·loc·u·tor [in-tər-LOK-yə-tər] *n* 1 one who takes part in conversation. 2 middle man in line of minstrel performers. **in·ter·loc'u·to·ry** *adj* of a court decree, issued before the final decision in an action.

in·ter·lop·er [IN-tər-lohp-ər] *n* 1 one intruding upon another's affairs. 2 intruder.

in·ter·lude [IN-tər-lood] *n* 1 interval (in play, etc.). 2 something filling an interval.

in·ter·mar·ry [in-tər-MAR-ee] *vi* -ried, -ry·ing 1 (of families, races, religions) become related by marriage. 2 marry within one's family. **in·ter·mar'riage** *n*

in·ter·me·di·ate [in-tər-MEE-dee-it] *adj* 1 coming between. 2 interposed.

in·ter·me'di·ar·y *n*

in·ter·mez·zo [in-tər-MET-soh] *n, pl* -zos short performance between acts of play or opera.

in·ter·mi·na·ble [in-TUR-mə-nə-bəl] *adj* endless. **in·ter'mi·na·bly** *adv*

in·ter·mis·sion [in-tər-MISH-ən] *n* short interval between parts of a concert, play, etc. **in·ter·mit'tent** *adj* occurring at intervals.

in·tern[1] [in-TURN] *vt* confine to special area or camp. **in·tern'ment** *n* **in·tern·ee'** *n*

in·tern[2], **in·terne** [IN-turn] *n* 1 recent medical school graduate residing in hospital and working under supervision as member of staff. 2 trainee in occupation or profession. **in'tern·ship** *n*

in·ter·nal [in-TUR-nl] *adj* 1 inward. 2 interior. 3 within (a country, organization). **internal combustion** process of exploding mixture of air and fuel within engine cylinder.

in·ter·na·tion·al [in-tər-NASH-ə-nl] *adj* 1 of relations between nations. ◆ *n* 2 labor union, etc. with units, members, in more than one country.

in·ter·ne·cine [in-tər-NEE-seen] *adj* 1 mutually destructive. 2 deadly.

In·ter·net, in·ter·net [IN-tər-net] *n* large international public access computer network.

boundary, frontier, link

interfere *v* 1 = **intrude**, butt in, intervene, meddle, stick one's oar in (*inf*), tamper 2 (often with *with*) = **conflict**, clash, hamper, handicap, hinder, impede, inhibit, obstruct

interference *n* 1 = **intrusion**, intervention, meddling, prying 2 = **conflict**, clashing, collision, obstruction, opposition

interim *adj* = **temporary**, acting, caretaker, improvised, makeshift, provisional, stopgap

interior *n* 1 = **inside**, center, core, heart ◆ *adj* 2 = **inside**, inner, internal, inward 3 = **mental**, hidden, inner, intimate, personal, private, secret, spiritual

interloper *n* = **trespasser**, gate-crasher (*inf*), intruder, meddler

interlude *n* = **interval**, break, breathing space, delay, hiatus, intermission, pause, respite, rest, spell, stoppage

intermediary *n* = **mediator**, agent, broker, go-between, middleman

intermediate *adj* = **middle**, halfway,

in-between (*inf*), intervening, mid, midway, transitional

interment *n* = **burial**, funeral

interminable *adj* = **endless**, ceaseless, everlasting, infinite, long-drawn-out, long-winded, never-ending, perpetual, protracted

intermingle *v* = **mix**, blend, combine, fuse, interlace, intermix, interweave, merge

intermission *n* = **interval**, break, interlude, pause, recess, respite, rest, stoppage

intermittent *adj* = **periodic**, broken, fitful, irregular, occasional, spasmodic, sporadic

intern *v* = **imprison**, confine, detain, hold, hold in custody

internal *adj* 1 = **inner**, inside, interior 2 = **domestic**, civic, home, in-house, intramural

international *adj* = **universal**, cosmopolitan, global, intercontinental, worldwide

in·ter·po·late [in-TUR-pə-layt] *vt* **-lat·ed,**
-lat·ing 1 insert new (esp. misleading)
matter (in book, etc.). **2** interject (remark).
3 *Math.* estimate a value between known
values. **in·ter·po·la'tion** *n*

in·ter·pose [in-tər-POHZ] *v* **-posed,**
-pos·ing ♦ *vt* **1** insert. **2** say as interruption.
3 put in the way. **♦** *vi* **4** intervene. **5**
obstruct. **in·ter·po·si'tion** [-pə-ZISH-ən] *n*

in·ter·pret [in-TUR-prit] *v* **1** explain. **2**
translate, esp. orally. **3** *Art* render,
represent. **in·ter·pre·ta'tion** *n*

in·ter·reg·num [in-tər-REG-nəm] *n, pl*
-nums 1 interval between reigns. **2** gap in
continuity.

in·ter·ro·gate [in-TER-ə-gayt] *vt* **-gat·ed,**
-gat·ing question, esp. closely or officially.
in·ter·ro·ga'tion *n* **in·ter·rog'a·tive** *adj* **1**
questioning. **♦** *n* **2** word used in asking
question. **in·ter·rog'a·to·ry** *adj* **1** of inquiry.
♦ *n* **2** question, set of questions.

in·ter·rupt [in-tə-RUPT] *v* **1** break in
(upon). **2** stop the course of. **3** block.
in·ter·rup'tion *n*

in·ter·sect [in-tər-SEKT] *vt* **1** divide by
passing across or through. **♦** *vi* **2** meet and
cross. **in·ter·sec'tion** *n* point where lines,
roads cross.

in·ter·sperse [in-tər-SPURS] *vt* **-spersed,**
-spers·ing sprinkle (something with or
something among or in).

in·ter·stel·lar [in-tər-STEL-ər] *adj* (of the
space) between stars.

in·ter·stice [in-TUR-stis] *n, pl* **-stic·es**
[-sə-seez] chink, gap, crevice. **in·ter·sti'tial**
[-STISH-əl] *adj*

in·ter·val [IN-tər-vəl] *n* **1** intervening time
or space. **2** pause, break. **3** short period
between parts of play, concert, etc. **4**
difference (of pitch).

in·ter·vene [in-tər-VEEN] *vi* **-vened,**
-ven·ing 1 come into a situation in order to
change it. **2** be, come between or among.
3 occur in meantime. **4** interpose.
in·ter·ven'tion *n*

in·tes·tate [in-TES-tayt] *adj* **1** not having
made a will. **♦** *n* **2** person dying intestate.
in·tes'ta·cy [-tə-see] *n*

in·tes·tine [in-TES-tin] *n* (usu *pl*) lower part
of alimentary canal between stomach and
anus. **in·tes'ti·nal** *adj* of bowels.

in·ti·mate¹ [IN-tə-mit] *adj* **1** closely
acquainted, familiar. **2** private. **3** extensive.
4 having sexual relations (with). **♦** *n* **5**
intimate friend. **in'ti·ma·cy** [-mə-see] *n*

in·ti·mate² [IN-tə-mayt] *vt* **-mat·ed,**
-mat·ing 1 imply. **2** announce.
in·ti·ma'tion *n* notice.

Internet *n* = information superhighway,
cyberspace, the net (*inf*), the web (*inf*),
World Wide Web

interpose *v* = **interrupt**, insert, interject,
put one's oar in

interpret *v* = **explain**, construe, decipher,
decode, elucidate, make sense of, render,
translate

interpretation *n* = **explanation**, analysis,
clarification, elucidation, exposition,
portrayal, rendition, translation, version

interpreter *n* = **translator**, commentator

interrogate *v* = **question**, cross-examine,
examine, grill (*inf*), investigate, pump, quiz

interrogation *n* = **questioning**,
cross-examination, examination, grilling
(*inf*), inquiry, inquisition, third degree (*inf*)

interrupt *v* **1** = **intrude**, barge in (*inf*),
break in, butt in, disturb, heckle, interfere
(with) **2** = **suspend**, break off, cut short,
delay, discontinue, hold up, lay aside, stop

interruption *n* = **stoppage**, break,
disruption, disturbance, hitch, intrusion,
pause, suspension

intersection *n* = **junction**, crossing,

crossroads, interchange

interval *n* = **break**, delay, gap, interlude,
intermission, pause, respite, rest, space,
spell

intervene *v* **1** = **involve oneself**, arbitrate,
intercede, interfere, intrude, lend a hand,
mediate, step in (*inf*) **2** = **happen**, befall,
come to pass, ensue, occur, take place

intervention *n* = **mediation**, agency,
interference, intrusion

interview *n* **1** = **meeting**, audience,
conference, consultation, dialogue, press
conference, talk **♦** *v* **2** = **question**,
examine, interrogate, talk to

interviewer *n* = **questioner**, examiner,
interrogator, investigator, reporter

intestines *pl n* = **guts**, bowels, entrails,
innards (*inf*), insides (*inf*), viscera

intimacy *n* = **familiarity**, closeness,
confidentiality

intimate¹ *adj* **1** = **close**, bosom,
buddy-buddy (*inf*), confidential, dear,
near, thick (*inf*) **2** = **personal**, confidential,
private, secret **3** = **detailed**, deep,
exhaustive, first-hand, immediate,

in·tim·i·date [in-TIM-i-dayt] *vt* -dat·ed, -dat·ing 1 frighten into submission. 2 deter by threats. **in·tim·i·da'tion** *n*

in·to [IN-too] *prep* 1 expresses motion to a point within. 2 indicates change of state. 3 indicates coming up against, encountering. 4 indicates arithmetical division.

in·tol'er·a·ble *adj* more than can be endured.

in·tone [in-TOHN] *vt* -toned, -ton·ing 1 chant. 2 recite in monotone. **in·to·na'tion** *n* 1 modulation of voice. 2 intoning. 3 accent.

in·tox·i·cate [in-TOK-si-kayt] *vt* -cat·ed, -cat·ing 1 make drunk. 2 excite to excess. **in·tox'i·cant** [-kənt] *adj, n* intoxicating (liquor).

intr. intransitive.

intra- *prefix* within, e.g. *intravenous*.

in·trac·ta·ble [in-TRAK-tə-bəl] *adj* 1 difficult to influence. 2 hard to control.

in·tra·net [IN-trə-net] *n Computers* local network that makes use of Internet technology.

in·tran·si·gent [in-TRAN-si-jənt] *adj* uncompromising, obstinate.

in·tra·u·ter·ine [in-trə-YOO-tər-in] *adj* within the womb.

in·tra·ve·nous [in-trə-VEE-nəs] *adj* into a vein.

in·trep·id *adj* fearless, undaunted. **in·tre·pid'i·ty** *n*

in·tri·cate [IN-tri-kit] *adj* involved, puzzlingly entangled. **in'tri·ca·cy** *n, pl* -cies

in·trigue [in-TREEG] *n* 1 underhanded plot. 2 secret love affair. ◆ *v* -trigued, -tri·guing ◆ *vi* 3 carry on intrigue. ◆ *vt* 4 interest, puzzle.

in·trin·sic [in-TRIN-sik] *adj* inherent,

---

in-depth, profound 4 = **snug**, comfy (*inf*), cozy, friendly, homey, warm ◆ *n* 5 = **friend**, close friend, confidant *or* (*fem.*) confidante, (constant) companion, crony, homeboy (*sl*), homegirl (*sl*), soul mate

intimate² *v* 1 = **suggest**, hint, imply, indicate, insinuate 2 = **announce**, communicate, declare, make known, state

intimately *adv* 1 = **confidingly**, affectionately, confidentially, familiarly, personally, tenderly, warmly 2 = **in detail**, fully, inside out, thoroughly, very well

intimation *n* 1 = **hint**, allusion, indication, inkling, insinuation, reminder, suggestion, warning 2 = **announcement**, communication, declaration, notice

intimidate *v* = **frighten**, browbeat, bully, coerce, daunt, overawe, scare, subdue, terrorize, threaten

intimidation *n* = **bullying**, arm-twisting (*inf*), browbeating, coercion, menaces, pressure, terrorization, threat(s)

intolerable *adj* = **unbearable**, excruciating, impossible, insufferable, insupportable, painful, unendurable

intolerance *n* = **narrow-mindedness**, bigotry, chauvinism, discrimination, dogmatism, fanaticism, illiberality, prejudice

intolerant *adj* = **narrow-minded**, bigoted, chauvinistic, dictatorial, dogmatic, fanatical, illiberal, prejudiced, small-minded

intone *v* = **recite**, chant

intoxicated *adj* 1 = **drunk**, drunken, inebriated, paralytic (*inf*), plastered (*sl*), tipsy, under the influence (*inf*) 2 = **euphoric**, dizzy, elated, enraptured, excited, exhilarated, high (*inf*), wired (*sl*)

intoxicating *adj* 1 = **alcoholic**, strong 2 = **exciting**, exhilarating, heady, thrilling

intoxication *n* 1 = **drunkenness**, inebriation, insobriety, tipsiness 2 = **excitement**, delirium, elation, euphoria, exhilaration

intransigent *adj* = **uncompromising**, hardline, intractable, obdurate, obstinate, stiff-necked, stubborn, unbending, unyielding

intrepid *adj* = **fearless**, audacious, bold, brave, courageous, daring, gallant, plucky, stouthearted, valiant

intricacy *n* = **complexity**, complication, convolutions, elaborateness

intricate *adj* = **complicated**, complex, convoluted, elaborate, fancy, involved, labyrinthine, tangled, tortuous

intrigue *v* 1 = **interest**, attract, fascinate, rivet, titillate 2 = **plot**, connive, conspire, machinate, maneuver, scheme ◆ *n* 3 = **plot**, chicanery, collusion, conspiracy, machination, maneuver, scheme, stratagem, wile 4 = **affair**, amour, intimacy, liaison, romance

intriguing *adj* = **interesting**, beguiling, compelling, diverting, exciting, fascinating, tantalizing, titillating essential. **in·trin'si·cal·ly** adv

intro- prefix into, within, e.g. introduce; introvert.

in·tro·duce [in-trə-DOOS] vt -duced, -duc·ing 1 make acquainted. 2 present. 3 bring in. 4 bring forward. 5 bring into practice. 6 insert. **in·tro·duc'tion** n 1 an introducing. 2 presentation of one person to another. 3 preliminary section or treatment. **in·tro·duc'to·ry** adj preliminary.

in·tro·spec·tion n [in-trə-SPEK-shən] examination of one's own thoughts. **in·tro·spec'tive** adj

in·tro·vert [IN-trə-vurt] n Psychoanalysis one who looks inward rather than at the external world. **in·tro·ver'sion** [-zhən] n **in'tro·vert·ed** adj

in·trude [in-TROOD] v -trud·ed, -trud·ing thrust (oneself) in uninvited. **in·tru'sion** [-zhən] n **in·tru'sive** adj

in·tu·i·tion [in-too-ISH-ən] n 1 immediate

mental apprehension without reasoning. 2 immediate insight. **in·tu'it** v **in·tu'i·tive** adj

In·u·it [IN-oo-it] n one of race of indigenous people of Alaska, N Canada, and Greenland. ◆ adj

in·un·date [IN-ən-dayt] vt -dat·ed, -dat·ing 1 flood. 2 overwhelm. **in·un·da'tion** n

in·ure [in-YUUR] vt -ured, -ur·ing accustom, esp. to hardship, danger, etc.

in·vade [in-VAYD] vt -vad·ed, -vad·ing 1 enter by force with hostile intent. 2 overrun. 3 pervade. **in·va'sion** [-zhən] n

in·va·lid[1] [IN-və-lid] n 1 one suffering from chronic ill health. ◆ adj 2 ill, suffering from sickness or injury. ◆ v 3 become an invalid. 4 retire from active service because of illness, etc.

in·val·id[2] [in-VAL-id] adj not valid.

in·val·u·a·ble [in-VAL-yoo-ə-bəl] adj priceless.

invasion see INVADE.

———————— THESAURUS ————————

intrinsic adj = **inborn**, basic, built-in, congenital, constitutional, essential, fundamental, inbred, inherent, native, natural

introduce v 1 = **present**, acquaint, familiarize, make known 2 = **bring in**, establish, found, initiate, institute, launch, pioneer, set up, start 3 = **bring up**, advance, air, broach, moot, put forward, submit 4 = **insert**, add, inject, put in, throw in (inf)

introduction n 1 = **launch**, establishment, inauguration, institution, pioneering 2 = **opening**, foreword, intro (inf), lead-in, preamble, preface, prelude, prologue

introductory adj = **preliminary**, first, inaugural, initial, opening, preparatory

introspective adj = **inward-looking**, brooding, contemplative, introverted, meditative, pensive

introverted adj = **introspective**, inner-directed, inward-looking, self-contained, withdrawn

intrude v = **interfere**, butt in, encroach, infringe, interrupt, meddle, push in, trespass

intruder n = **trespasser**, gate-crasher (inf), infiltrator, interloper, invader, prowler

intrusion n = **invasion**, encroachment, infringement, interference, interruption, trespass, violation

intrusive adj = **interfering**, impertinent, importunate, meddlesome, nosy (inf),

presumptuous, pushy (inf), uncalled-for, unwanted

intuition n = **instinct**, hunch, insight, perception, presentiment, sixth sense

intuitive adj = **instinctive**, innate, spontaneous, untaught

inundate v = **flood**, drown, engulf, immerse, overflow, overrun, overwhelm, submerge, swamp

invade v 1 = **attack**, assault, burst in, descend upon, encroach, infringe, make inroads, occupy, raid, violate 2 = **infest**, overrun, permeate, pervade, swarm over

invader n = **attacker**, aggressor, plunderer, raider, trespasser

invalid[1] adj 1 = **disabled**, ailing, bedridden, challenged, frail, ill, infirm, sick ◆ n 2 = **patient**, convalescent, valetudinarian

invalid[2] adj = **null and void**, fallacious, false, illogical, inoperative, irrational, unfounded, unsound, void, worthless

invalidate v = **nullify**, annul, cancel, overthrow, undermine, undo

invaluable adj = **precious**, inestimable, priceless, valuable, worth one's or its weight in gold

invariably adv = **consistently**, always, customarily, day in, day out, habitually, perpetually, regularly, unfailingly, without exception

invasion n 1 = **attack**, assault, campaign, foray, incursion, inroad, offensive, onslaught, raid 2 = **intrusion**, breach,

in•veigh [in-VAY] *vi* speak violently (against). **in•vec'tive** *n* abusive speech or writing, vituperation.

in•vei•gle [in-VAY-gəl] *vt* **-gled, -gling** entice, seduce, wheedle.

in•vent' *vt* **1** devise, originate. **2** fabricate (falsehoods, etc.). **in•ven'tion** *n* **1** that which is invented. **2** ability to invent. **3** contrivance. **4** deceit. **5** lie. **in•vent'ive** *adj* **1** resourceful. **2** creative. **in•ven'tor** *n*

in•ven•to•ry [IN-vən-tor-ee] *n, pl* **-ries 1** detailed list of goods, etc. ♦ *vt* **-ried, -ry•ing 2** make list of.

in•vert [in-VURT] *vt* **1** turn upside down. **2** reverse position, relations of. **in•verse'** *adj* **1** inverted. **2** opposite. ♦ *n* **in•verse'ly** *adv* **in•ver'sion** [-zhən] *n*

in•ver•te•brate [in-VUR-tə-brit] *n* **1** animal having no vertebral column. ♦ *adj* **2** spineless.

in•vest' *vt* **1** lay out (money, time, effort, etc.) for profit or advantage. **2** install. **3** endow. **4** *Poet.* cover as with garment.

in•ves'ti•ture [-chər] *n* formal installation of person in office or rank. **in•vest'ment** *n* **1** investing. **2** money invested. **3** stocks, bonds, etc. bought.

in•ves•ti•gate [in-VES-ti-gayt] *v* **1** inquire into. **2** examine. **in•ves•ti•ga'tion** *n*

in•vet•er•ate [in-VET-ər-it] *adj* **1** deep-rooted. **2** long established, confirmed.

in•vid•i•ous [in-VID-ee-əs] *adj* likely to cause ill will or envy.

in•vig•or•ate [in-VIG-ə-rayt] *vt* **-at•ed, -at•ing** give vigor to, strengthen.

in•vin•ci•ble [in-VIN-sə-bəl] *adj* unconquerable. **in•vin•ci•bil'i•ty** *n*

in•vi•o•la•ble [in-Vl-ə-lə-bəl] *adj* **1** not to be profaned. **2** sacred. **3** unalterable. **in•vi'o•late** [-ə-lit] *adj* **1** unhurt. **2** unprofaned. **3** unbroken.

in•vis'i•ble *adj* not able to be seen. **in•vis•i•bil'i•ty** *n*

THESAURUS

encroachment, infraction, infringement, usurpation, violation

invective *n* = **abuse**, censure, denunciation, diatribe, tirade, tongue-lashing, vilification, vituperation

invent *v* **1** = **create**, coin, conceive, design, devise, discover, formulate, improvise, originate, think up **2** = **make up**, concoct, cook up (*inf*), fabricate, feign, forge, manufacture, trump up

invention *n* **1** = **creation**, brainchild (*inf*), contraption, contrivance, design, device, discovery, gadget, instrument **2** = **creativity**, genius, imagination, ingenuity, inventiveness, originality, resourcefulness **3** = **fiction**, fabrication, falsehood, fantasy, forgery, lie, untruth, yarn

inventive *adj* = **creative**, fertile, imaginative, ingenious, innovative, inspired, original, resourceful

inventor *n* = **creator**, architect, author, coiner, designer, maker, originator

inventory *n* = **list**, account, catalog, file, record, register, roll, roster

inverse *adj* = **opposite**, contrary, converse, reverse, reversed, transposed

invert *v* = **overturn**, reverse, transpose, upset, upturn

invest *v* **1** = **spend**, advance, devote, lay out, put in, sink **2** = **empower**, authorize, charge, license, sanction, vest

investigate *v* = **examine**, explore, go into,

inquire into, inspect, look into, probe, research, study

investigation *n* = **examination**, exploration, inquest, inquiry, inspection, probe, review, search, study, survey

investigator *n* = **examiner**, gumshoe (*sl*), inquirer, (private) detective, private eye (*inf*), researcher, sleuth

investiture *n* = **installation**, enthronement, inauguration, induction, ordination

investment *n* **1** = **transaction**, speculation, venture **2** = **stake**, ante (*inf*), contribution

inveterate *adj* = **long-standing**, chronic, confirmed, deep-seated, dyed-in-the-wool, entrenched, habitual, hardened, incorrigible, incurable

invidious *adj* = **undesirable**, hateful

invigorate *v* = **refresh**, energize, enliven, exhilarate, fortify, galvanize, liven up, revitalize, stimulate

invincible *adj* = **unbeatable**, impregnable, indestructible, indomitable, insuperable, invulnerable, unassailable, unconquerable

inviolable *adj* = **sacrosanct**, hallowed, holy, inalienable, sacred, unalterable

inviolate *adj* = **intact**, entire, pure, unbroken, undefiled, unhurt, unpolluted, unsullied, untouched, whole

invisible *adj* = **unseen**, imperceptible, indiscernible

in·vite [in-VĪT] *vt* **-vit·ed, -vit·ing 1** request the company of. **2** ask courteously. **3** ask for. **4** attract, call forth. ◆ *n* [IN-vīt] **5** *inf* an invitation. **in·vi·ta'tion** *n*

in·voice [IN-vois] *n* **1** itemized bill for goods or services sold. ◆ *vt* **-voiced, -voic·ing 2** make or present an invoice.

in·voke [in-VOHK] *vt* **-voked, -vok·ing 1** call on. **2** appeal to. **3** ask earnestly for. **4** summon. **in·vo·ca'tion** *n*

in·vol·un·tar·y [in-VOL-ən-ter-ee] *adj* **1** not done willingly. **2** unintentional. **3** instinctive.

in·vo·lute [IN-və-loot] *adj* **1** complex. **2** coiled spirally. **3** (also **in·vo·lut'ed**) rolled inward.

in·volve [in-VOLV] *vt* **-volved, -volv·ing 1** include. **2** entail. **3** implicate (person). **4** concern. **5** entangle. **involved** *adj* **1** complicated. **2** concerned (in).

in·vul·ner·a·ble *adj* not able to be wounded or harmed.

in·ward [IN-wərd] *adj* **1** internal. **2** situated within. **3** spiritual, mental. ◆ *adv* (also **in'wards**) **4** toward the inside. **5** into the mind. **in'ward·ly** *adv* **1** in the mind. **2** internally.

i·o·dine [Ī-ə-dīn] *n* nonmetallic element found in seaweed and used in antiseptic solution, photography, etc. **i'o·dize** *vt* **-dized, -diz·ing** treat or react with iodine.

i·on [Ī-ən] *n* electrically charged atom or group of atoms. **i·on'ic** *adj* **i·on·i·za'tion** *n* **i'on·ize** *vt* **-ized, -iz·ing** change into ions. **i·on'o·sphere** *n* region of atmosphere about 50 to 250 miles (80 to 400 km) above Earth.

I·on·ic [ī-ON-ik] *adj Architecture* distinguished by scroll-like decoration on columns.

i·o·ta [ī-OH-tə] *n* **1** the Greek letter *i*. **2** (usu. with *not*) very small amount.

ip·so fac·to [IP-soh FAK-toh] *Lat* by that very fact.

Ir *Chem.* iridium.

ir- *prefix* same as IN-¹ or IN-².

ire [īr] *n* anger, wrath. **i·ras·ci·ble** [i-RAS-ə-bəl] *adj* hot-tempered. **i·ras'ci·bly** *adv* **i·rate** [ī-RAYT] *adj* angry.

ir·i·des·cent [ir-i-DES-ənt] *adj* exhibiting changing colors like those of the rainbow. **ir·i·des'cence** *n*

i·rid·i·um [i-RID-ee-əm] *n* very hard, corrosion-resistant metallic element.

i·ris [Ī-ris] *n* **1** circular membrane of eye containing pupil. **2** plant with sword-shaped leaves and showy flowers.

irk [urk] *vt* irritate, vex. **irk'some** [-sum] *adj* tiresome.

i·ron [Ī-ərn] *n* **1** metallic element, much used for tools, etc., and the raw material of steel. **2** tool, etc., of this metal. **3** appliance used, when heated, to smooth cloth. **4** metal-headed golf club. ◆ *pl* **5** fetters. ◆ *adj*

——————— THESAURUS ———————

invitation *n* = **request**, call, invite (*inf*), summons

invite *v* **1** = **request**, ask, beg, bid, summon **2** = **encourage**, ask for (*inf*), attract, court, entice, provoke, tempt, welcome

inviting *adj* = **tempting**, alluring, appealing, attractive, enticing, mouthwatering, seductive, welcoming

invocation *n* = **appeal**, entreaty, petition, prayer, supplication

invoke *v* **1** = **call upon**, appeal to, beg, beseech, entreat, implore, petition, pray, supplicate **2** = **apply**, implement, initiate, put into effect, resort to, use

involuntary *adj* = **unintentional**, automatic, instinctive, reflex, spontaneous, unconscious, uncontrolled, unthinking

involve *v* **1** = **entail**, imply, mean, necessitate, presuppose, require **2** = **concern**, affect, draw in, implicate, touch

involved *adj* **1** = **complicated**, complex, confusing, convoluted, elaborate, intricate, labyrinthine, tangled, tortuous **2** = **concerned**, caught (up), implicated, mixed up in or with, participating, taking part

involvement *n* = **connection**, association, commitment, interest, participation

invulnerable *adj* = **safe**, impenetrable, indestructible, insusceptible, invincible, proof against, secure, unassailable

inward *adj* **1** = **incoming**, entering, inbound, ingoing **2** = **internal**, inner, inside, interior **3** = **private**, confidential, hidden, inmost, innermost, personal, secret

inwardly *adv* = **privately**, at heart, deep down, inside, secretly

irate *adj* = **angry**, annoyed, cross, enraged, furious, incensed, indignant, infuriated, livid

irksome *adj* = **irritating**, annoying, bothersome, disagreeable, exasperating, tiresome, troublesome, trying, vexing,

6 of, like, iron. **7** inflexible, unyielding. **8** robust. ◆ *v* **9** smooth, cover, fetter, etc., with iron or an iron. **i'ron-clad** *adj* protected with or as with iron. **iron curtain** any barrier that separates communities or ideologies. **iron lung** apparatus for administering artificial respiration.

i·ro·ny [Ī-rə-nee] *n, pl* **-nies 1** (usu. humorous or mildly sarcastic) use of words to mean the opposite of what is said. **2** event, situation opposite of that expected. **i·ron'ic** *adj* of, using, irony.

ir·ra·di·ate [i-RAY-dee-ayt] *vt* **-at·ed, -at·ing 1** treat by irradiation. **2** shine upon, throw light upon, light up. **ir·ra·di·a'tion** *n* impregnation by X-rays, light rays.

ir·ra'tion·al *adj* not based on or not using logical reasoning.

ir·re·fran·gi·ble [ir-i-FRAN-jə-bəl] *adj* **1** inviolable. **2** in optics, not susceptible to refraction.

ir·ref·u·ta·ble [i-REF-yə-tə-bəl] *adj* that cannot be refuted, disproved.

ir·reg·u·lar *adj* **1** not regular or even. **2** not conforming to accepted practice. **3** (of a word) not following the typical pattern of formation in a language. **ir·reg·u·lar'i·ty** *n, pl* **-ties**

ir·rel'e·vant *adj* not connected with the matter in hand. **ir·rel'e·vance** *n*

ir·rep·a·ra·ble [i-REP-ər-ə-bəl] *adj* not able to be repaired or remedied.

ir·re·place'a·ble *adj* impossible to replace.

ir·re·sist'i·ble *adj* too attractive or strong to resist.

ir·res'o·lute *adj* unable to make decisions.

ir·re·spec·tive [ir-i-SPEK-tiv] *adj* without taking account of (of).

ir·re·spon'si·ble *adj* not showing or not done with due care for the consequences of one's actions or attitudes.

ir·rev·o·ca·ble [i-REV-ə-kə-bəl] *adj* not able to be changed, undone, altered.

ir·ri·gate [IR-i-gayt] *vt* **-gat·ed, -gat·ing** water by artificial channels, pipes, etc. **ir·ri·ga'tion** *n*

wearisome

iron *adj* **1** = **ferrous**, chalybeate, ferric **2** = **inflexible**, adamant, hard, implacable, indomitable, rigid, steely, strong, tough, unbending, unyielding

ironic *adj* **1** = **sarcastic**, double-edged, mocking, sardonic, satirical, with tongue in cheek, wry **2** = **paradoxical**, incongruous

iron out *v* = **settle**, clear up, get rid of, put right, reconcile, resolve, smooth over, sort out, straighten out

irony *n* **1** = **sarcasm**, mockery, satire **2** = **paradox**, incongruity

irrational *adj* = **illogical**, absurd, crazy, nonsensical, preposterous, unreasonable

irrefutable *adj* = **undeniable**, certain, incontestable, incontrovertible, indisputable, indubitable, sure, unquestionable

irregular *adj* **1** = **variable**, erratic, fitful, haphazard, occasional, random, spasmodic, sporadic, unsystematic **2** = **unconventional**, abnormal, exceptional, extraordinary, peculiar, unofficial, unorthodox, unusual **3** = **uneven**, asymmetrical, bumpy, crooked, jagged, lopsided, ragged, rough

irregularity *n* **1** = **uncertainty**, desultoriness, disorganization, haphazardness **2** = **abnormality**, anomaly, oddity, peculiarity, unorthodoxy **3** =

unevenness, asymmetry, bumpiness, jaggedness, lopsidedness, raggedness, roughness

irrelevant *adj* = **unconnected**, beside the point, extraneous, immaterial, impertinent, inapplicable, inappropriate, neither here nor there, unrelated

irreparable *adj* = **beyond repair**, incurable, irremediable, irretrievable, irreversible

irrepressible *adj* = **ebullient**, boisterous, buoyant, effervescent, unstoppable

irreproachable *adj* = **blameless**, beyond reproach, faultless, impeccable, innocent, perfect, pure, unimpeachable

irresistible *adj* = **overwhelming**, compelling, compulsive, overpowering, urgent

irresponsible *adj* = **immature**, careless, reckless, scatterbrained, shiftless, thoughtless, unreliable, untrustworthy

irreverent *adj* = **disrespectful**, cheeky (*inf*), flippant, iconoclastic, impertinent, impudent, mocking, tongue-in-cheek

irreversible *adj* = **irrevocable**, final, incurable, irreparable, unalterable

irrevocable *adj* = **fixed**, fated, immutable, irreversible, predestined, predetermined, settled, unalterable

irrigate *v* = **water**, flood, inundate, moisten, wet

ir·ri·tate [IR-i-tayt] *vt* **-tat·ed, -tat·ing 1** annoy. **2** inflame. **3** stimulate. **ir'ri·ta·ble** *adj* easily annoyed. **ir'ri·tant** *adj, n* (person or thing) causing irritation. **ir·ri·ta'tion** *n*

Is. Isaiah.

is [iz] third person singular, present indicative of BE.

Is·lam [iz-LAHM] *n* Muslim faith or world. **Is·lam'ic** *adj*

is·land [Ī-lənd] *n* **1** piece of land surrounded by water. **2** raised area for pedestrians in middle of road.

isle [īl] *n* island. **is·let** [Ī-lit] *n* little island.

i·so·bar [Ī-sə-bahr] *n* line on map connecting places of equal mean barometric pressure.

i·so·late [Ī-sə-layt] *vt* **-lat·ed, -lat·ing** place apart or alone. **i·so·la'tion** *n* **i·so·la'tion·ism** *n* policy of not participating in international affairs.

i·so·mer [Ī-sə-mər] *n* substance with same molecules as another but different atomic arrangement. **i·so·mer'ic** *adj*

i·so·met·ric [ī-sə-ME-trik] *adj* **1** having equal dimensions. **2** relating to muscular contraction without movement. **i·so·met'rics** *pl n* system of isometric exercises.

i·sos·ce·les [ī-SOS-ə-leez] *adj* of triangle, having two sides equal.

i·so·therm [Ī-sə-thurm] *n* line on map connecting points of equal mean temperature.

i·so·tope [Ī-sə-tohp] *n* atom of element having a different nuclear mass and atomic weight from other atoms in same element. **i·so·top'ic** *adj*

ISP Internet service provider: business providing its customers with connection to the Internet.

is·sue [ISH-oo] *n* **1** sending or giving out officially or publicly. **2** number or amount so given out. **3** discharge. **4** offspring, children. **5** topic of discussion. **6** question, dispute. **7** outcome, result. ◆ *v* **-sued, -su·ing** ◆ *vi* **8** go out. **9** result in. **10** arise (from). ◆ *vt* **11** emit, give out, send out. **12** distribute, publish.

isth·mus [IS-məs] *n* neck of land between two seas.

it *pron* neuter pronoun of the third person. **its** *adj* belonging to it. **it's 1** it is. **2** it has. **it·self'** *pron* emphatic form of IT.

i·tal·ic [i-TAL-ik] *adj* of type, sloping. **i·tal'ics** *pl n* this type, now used for emphasis, etc. **i·tal'i·cize** [-sīz] *vt* put in italics.

itch [ich] *vi, n* (feel) irritation in the skin. **itch'y** *adj* **itch·i·er, itch·i·est**

i·tem [Ī-təm] *n* **1** single thing in list,

THESAURUS

irritability *n* = **bad temper**, ill humor, impatience, irascibility, prickliness, testiness, tetchiness, touchiness

irritable *adj* = **bad-tempered**, cantankerous, crotchety, ill-tempered, irascible, oversensitive, prickly, testy, tetchy, touchy

irritate *v* **1** = **annoy**, anger, bother, exasperate, get on one's nerves (*inf*), infuriate, needle (*inf*), nettle, rankle with, try one's patience **2** = **rub**, chafe, inflame, pain

irritated *adj* = **annoyed**, angry, bothered, cross, exasperated, nettled, piqued, put out, vexed

irritating *adj* = **annoying**, disturbing, infuriating, irksome, maddening, nagging, troublesome, trying

irritation *n* **1** = **annoyance**, anger, displeasure, exasperation, indignation, resentment, testiness, vexation **2** = **nuisance**, drag (*inf*), irritant, pain in the neck (*inf*), thorn in one's flesh

island *n* = **isle**, atoll, cay *or* key, islet

isolate *v* = **separate**, cut off, detach, disconnect, insulate, segregate, set apart

isolated *adj* = **remote**, hidden, lonely, off the beaten track, outlying, out-of-the-way, secluded

isolation *n* = **separation**, detachment, remoteness, seclusion, segregation, solitude

issue *n* **1** = **topic**, bone of contention, matter, point, problem, question, subject **2** = **outcome**, consequence, effect, end result, result, upshot **3** = **edition**, copy, number, printing **4** = **children**, descendants, heirs, offspring, progeny **5 take issue** = **disagree**, challenge, dispute, object, oppose, raise an objection, take exception ◆ *v* **6** = **publish**, announce, broadcast, circulate, deliver, distribute, give out, put out, release

isthmus *n* = **strip**, spit

itch *n* **1** = **irritation**, itchiness, prickling, tingling **2** = **desire**, craving, hankering, hunger, longing, lust, passion, yearning, yen (*inf*) ◆ *v* **3** = **prickle**, irritate, tickle, collection, etc. **2** piece of information. **3** entry in account, etc. **i'tem·ize** *vt* **-ized, -iz·ing**

it·er·ate [IT-ə-rayt] *vt* **-at·ed, -at·ing** repeat. **it·er·a'tion** *n* **it'er·a·tive** *adj*

i·tin·er·ant [ī-TIN-ər-ənt] *adj* **1** traveling from place to place. **2** working for a short time in various places. **3** traveling on circuit. **i·tin'er·ar·y** *n, pl* **-ar·ies 1** record, line of travel. **2** route. **3** guidebook.

i·vo·ry [Ī-və-ree] *n, pl* **-ries** hard white substance of the tusks of elephants, etc. **ivory tower** seclusion, remoteness.

i·vy [Ī-vee] *n, pl* **-vies** climbing evergreen plant. **i'vied** *adj* covered with ivy.

THESAURUS

tingle **4 = long**, ache, crave, hanker, hunger, lust, pine, yearn

itchy *adj* **= impatient**, eager, edgy, fidgety, restive, restless, unsettled

item *n* **1 = detail**, article, component, entry, matter, particular, point, thing **2 = report**, account, article, bulletin, dispatch, feature, note, notice, paragraph, piece

itinerant *adj* **= wandering**, migratory, nomadic, peripatetic, roaming, roving, traveling, vagrant

itinerary *n* **= schedule**, program, route, timetable

J j

jab *vt* **jabbed, jab·bing 1** poke roughly. **2** thrust, stab abruptly. ◆ *n* **3** poke. **4** punch.

jab·ber [JAB-ər] *v* **1** chatter. **2** utter, talk rapidly, incoherently. **Jab'ber·wock·y** *n* nonsense, esp. in verse.

jack [jak] *n* **1** fellow, man. **2** *inf* sailor. **3** male of some animals. **4** device for lifting heavy weight, esp. automobile. **5** playing card with picture of soldier or servant. **6** socket and plug connection for electrical equipment. **7** small flag, esp. national, at sea. ◆ *vt* (usu. with *up*) lift (an object) with a jack. **jack-of-all-trades** *pl* **jacks** person adept at many kinds of work.

jack·al [JAK-əl] *n* wild, gregarious animal of Asia and Africa closely allied to dog.

jack·ass [JAK-as] *n* **1** male donkey. **2** blockhead.

jack·et [JAK-it] *n* **1** outer garment, short coat. **2** outer casing, cover.

jack·knife [JAK-nīf] *n*, *pl* **-knives 1** clasp knife. **2** dive with sharp bend at waist in midair. ◆ *v* **-knifed, -knif·ing** bend sharply, e.g. an articulated truck forming a sharp angle with its trailer.

jack·pot [JAK-pot] *n* **1** large prize. **2** accumulated stakes, as in poker.

jac·quard [JAK-ahrd] *n* fabric in which design is incorporated into the weave.

Ja·cuz·zi [jə-KOO-zee] *n* ® **1** device that swirls water in a bath. **2** bath with this device.

jade¹ [jayd] *n* **1** ornamental semiprecious stone, usu. dark green. **2** this color.

jade² *n* **1** sorry or worn-out horse. **2** disreputable woman. **jad'ed** *adj* tired and unenthusiastic.

jag *n* **1** sharp or ragged projection. **2** spree. **jag'ged** [-id] *adj*

jag·uar [JAG-wahr] *n* large S Amer. spotted cat.

jail [jayl] *n* **1** building for confinement of criminals or suspects. ◆ *v* **2** send to, confine in prison. **jail'bait** [-bayt] *n* *sl* underage girl with whom sexual intercourse is considered a crime. **jail'er** *n* **jail'bird** *n* hardened criminal.

ja·lop·y [jə-LOP-ee] *n*, *pl* **-lop·ies** *inf* old car.

jam *vt* **jammed, jam·ming 1** pack together. **2** (cause to) stick together and become unworkable. **3** apply fiercely. **4** squeeze. **5** *Radio* block (another station) with impulses of equal wavelength. ◆ *n* **6** fruit preserved by boiling with sugar. **7** crush. **8** delay of traffic. **9** awkward situation. **jam-packed** *adj* filled to capacity. **jam session** [improvised] jazz session]

jamb [jam] *n* side post of arch, door, etc.

jam·bo·ree [jam-bə-REE] *n* **1** large gathering or rally of scouts. **2** spree, celebration.

jan·gle [JANG-gəl] *v* **-gled, -gling 1** (cause to) sound harshly, as bell. **2** (of nerves) irritate. ◆ *n* **3** harsh sound.

THESAURUS

jab *v*, *n* = **poke**, dig, lunge, nudge, prod, punch, stab, tap, thrust

jabber *v* = **chatter**, babble, blether, gabble, mumble, ramble, yap (*inf*)

jacket *n* = **covering**, case, casing, coat, sheath, skin, wrapper, wrapping

jackpot *n* = **prize**, award, bonanza, reward, winnings

jack up *v* = **raise**, elevate, hoist, lift, lift up

jaded *adj* = **tired**, exhausted, fatigued, spent, weary

jagged *adj* = **uneven**, barbed, craggy, indented, ragged, serrated, spiked, toothed

jail *n* **1** = **prison**, penitentiary, reformatory, slammer (*sl*) ◆ *v* **2** = **imprison**, confine, detain, incarcerate, lock up, send down

jailer *n* = **guard**, keeper, warden

jam *v* **1** = **pack**, cram, force, press, ram, squeeze, stuff, wedge **2** = **crowd**, crush, throng **3** = **congest**, block, clog, obstruct, stall, stick ◆ *n* **4** = **predicament**, deep water, fix (*inf*), hot water, pickle (*inf*), tight spot, trouble

jamboree *n* = **festival**, carnival, celebration, festivity, fête, revelry, spree

jan·i·tor [JAN-i-tər] n custodian, cleaner.

jar¹ [jahr] n **1** round vessel of glass, earthenware, etc. **2** inf drink of beer, whiskey, etc.

jar² v **jarred, jar·ring 1** (cause to) vibrate suddenly, violently. **2** have disturbing, painful effect on. ◆ n **3** jarring sound. **4** shock, etc.

jar·gon [JAHR-gən] n **1** specialized language concerned with particular subject. **2** pretentious or nonsensical language.

jas·per [JAS-pər] n red, yellow, dark green or brown quartz.

jaun·dice [JAWN-dis] n **1** disease marked by yellowness of skin. **2** bitterness, ill humor. **3** prejudice. ◆ v **-diced, -dic·ing 4** make, become prejudiced, bitter, etc.

jaunt [jawnt] n **1** short pleasure trip. ◆ vi **2** make one.

jaun·ty [JAWN-tee] adj **-ti·er, -ti·est 1** sprightly. **2** brisk. **3** smart, trim. **jaun'ti·ly** adv

Java [JAH-və] n ® computer programming language that is widely used on the Internet.

jave·lin [JAV-lin] n spear, esp. for throwing in sporting events.

jaw n **1** one of bones in which teeth are set. **2** pl mouth. **3** fig narrow opening of a gorge or valley. **4** gripping part of vise, etc. ◆ vi **5** sl talk lengthily.

jay n noisy bird of brilliant plumage. **jay'walk·er** n careless pedestrian. **jay'walk** vi

jazz n syncopated music and dance. **jazz'y** adj **-jazz·i·er, jazz·i·est** flashy, showy. **jazz up 1** play as jazz. **2** make more lively, appealing.

jeal·ous [JEL-əs] adj **1** distrustful of the faithfulness (of). **2** envious. **3** suspiciously watchful.

jeans [jeenz] pl n casual trousers, esp. of denim.

jeer v **1** scoff, deride. ◆ n **2** scoff, taunt, gibe.

Je·ho·vah [ji-HO-və] n God.

je·june [ji-JOON] adj **1** simple, naive. **2** meager.

jell v **1** congeal. **2** assume definite form.

jel·ly [JEL-ee] n, pl **-lies 1** semitransparent food made with gelatin, becoming softly stiff as it cools. **2** anything of the consistency of this. **jel'ly·fish** n jellylike small sea animal.

jeop·ard·y [JEP-ər-dee] n danger. **jeop'ard·ize** vt **-ized, -iz·ing** endanger.

Jer. Jeremiah.

jerk [jurk] n **1** sharp, abruptly stopped movement. **2** twitch. **3** sharp pull. **4** sl stupid person, inconsequential person. ◆ v **5** move or throw with a jerk. **jerk'i·ly** adv **jerk'y** adj **jerk·i·er, jerk·i·est** uneven, spasmodic.

THESAURUS

jangle v = **rattle**, chime, clank, clash, clatter, jingle, vibrate

janitor n = **caretaker**, concierge, custodian, doorkeeper, porter

jar¹ n = **pot**, container, crock, jug, pitcher, urn, vase

jar² v **1** = **jolt**, bump, convulse, rattle, rock, shake, vibrate **2** = **irritate**, annoy, get on one's nerves (inf), grate, irk, nettle, offend ◆ n **3** = **jolt**, bump, convulsion, shock, vibration

jargon n = **parlance**, argot, idiom, usage

jaundiced adj **1** = **cynical**, skeptical **2** = **bitter**, envious, hostile, jealous, resentful, spiteful, suspicious

jaunt n = **outing**, airing, excursion, expedition, ramble, stroll, tour, trip

jaunty adj = **sprightly**, buoyant, carefree, high-spirited, lively, perky, self-confident, sparky

jaw v = **talk**, chat, chatter, chew the fat (sl), gossip, spout

jaws pl n = **opening**, entrance, mouth

jazz up v = **enliven**, animate, enhance, improve

jazzy adj = **flashy**, fancy, gaudy, snazzy (inf)

jealous adj **1** = **envious**, covetous, desirous, green, grudging, resentful **2** = **wary**, mistrustful, protective, suspicious, vigilant, watchful

jealousy n = **envy**, covetousness, mistrust, possessiveness, resentment, spite, suspicion

jeans pl n = **denims**, Levis (Trademark)

jeer v **1** = **scoff**, barrack, deride, gibe, heckle, mock, ridicule, taunt ◆ n **2** = **taunt**, abuse, boo, catcall, derision, gibe, ridicule

jell v **1** = **solidify**, congeal, harden, set, thicken **2** = **take shape**, come together, crystallize, materialize

jeopardize v = **endanger**, chance, expose, gamble, imperil, risk, stake, venture

jeopardy n = **danger**, insecurity, peril, risk, vulnerability

jer·sey [JUR-zee] *n, pl* **-seys 1** knitted sweater. **2** machine-knitted fabric. **3** (J-) breed of cow.

jest *n, vi* joke. **jest'er** *n Hist.* professional clown at court.

Jes·u·it [JEZH-oo-it] *n* member of Society of Jesus, order founded by Ignatius Loyola in 1534. **Jes·u·it'i·cal** *adj* **1** of Jesuits. **2** (j-) crafty, using overly subtle reasoning.

jet¹ *n* **1** stream of liquid, gas, etc., esp. shot from small hole. **2** the small hole. **3** spout, nozzle. **4** aircraft driven by jet propulsion. ◆ *v* **jet·ted, -jet·ting 5** throw out. **6** shoot forth. **jet-black** *adj* deep black. **jet lag** fatigue caused by crossing time zones in jet aircraft. **jet propulsion** propulsion by thrust provided by jet of gas or liquid. **jet ski** small self-propelled vehicle resembling a scooter, which skims across water on a flat keel.

jet² *n* hard black mineral capable of brilliant polish.

jet·sam [JET-səm] *n* goods thrown out to lighten ship and later washed ashore. **jet'ti·son** [-tə-sən] *vt* **1** abandon. **2** throw overboard.

jet·ty [JET-ee] *n* **-ties** small pier, wharf.

Jew [joo] *n* **1** one of Hebrew ancestry. **2** one who practices Judaism. **Jew'ish** *adj* **Jew'ry** *n* the Jews. **jew's harp** *n* small musical instrument held between teeth and played by finger.

jew·el [JOO-əl] *n* **1** precious stone. **2** ornament containing one. **3** precious thing. **jew'el·er** *n* dealer in jewels.

jew'el·ry *n*

jib *n* **1** triangular sail set forward of mast. **2** projecting arm of crane or derrick.

jibe see GIBE.

jif·fy [JIF-ee] *n, pl* **-fies** *inf* very short period of time.

jig *n* **1** lively dance. **2** music for it. **3** small mechanical device. **4** guide for cutting, etc. **5** *Angling* any of various lures. ◆ *vi* **jigged, jig·ging 6** dance jig. **7** make jerky up-and-down movements. **jig'saw** *n* machine-mounted saw for cutting curves, etc. **jigsaw puzzle** picture stuck on board and cut into interlocking pieces with jigsaw.

jig·ger [JIG-ər] *n* small glass holding and pouring measure of whiskey, etc.

jig·gle [JIG-əl] *v* **-gled, -gling** move (up and down, etc.) with short jerky movements.

jilt *vt* cast off (lover).

jim·my [JIM-ee] *n, pl* **-mies 1** short steel crowbar. ◆ *vt* **-mied, -my·ing 2** force open with a jimmy, etc.

jin·gle [JING-gəl] *n* **1** mixed metallic noise, as of shaken chain. **2** catchy, rhythmic verse, song, etc. ◆ *v* **-gled, -gling 3** (cause to) make jingling sound.

jin·go·ism [JING-goh-iz-əm] *n* chauvinism. **jin·go·is'tic** *adj*

jinks [jingks] *pl n* **high jinks** boisterous merrymaking.

jinx [jingks] *n* **1** force, person, thing bringing bad luck. ◆ *v* **2** be or put a jinx on.

jit·ters [JIT-ərz] *pl n* worried nervousness,

---

jerk *v, n* = **tug**, jolt, lurch, pull, thrust, twitch, wrench, yank

jerky *adj* = **bumpy**, convulsive, jolting, jumpy, shaky, spasmodic, twitchy

jest *n* **1** = **joke**, bon mot, crack (*sl*), jape, pleasantry, prank, quip, wisecrack (*inf*), witticism ◆ *v* **2** = **joke**, kid (*inf*), mock, quip, tease

jester *n* = **clown**, buffoon, fool, harlequin

jet¹ *adj* = **black**, coal-black, ebony, inky, pitch-black, raven, sable

jet² *n* **1** = **stream**, flow, fountain, gush, spout, spray, spring **2** = **nozzle**, atomizer, sprayer, sprinkler ◆ *v* **3** = **fly**, soar, zoom

jettison *v* = **abandon**, discard, dump, eject, expel, scrap, throw overboard, unload

jetty *n* = **pier**, breakwater, dock, groyne, mole, quay, wharf

jewel *n* **1** = **gemstone**, ornament, rock (*sl*), sparkler (*inf*) **2** = **rarity**, collector's item, find, gem, pearl, treasure, wonder

jewelry *n* = **jewels**, finery, gems, ornaments, regalia, treasure, trinkets

jib *v* = **refuse**, balk, recoil, retreat, shrink, stop short

jibe see GIBE

jiffy *n Sl* = **instant**, blink of an eye (*inf*), flash, heartbeat (*inf*), second, two shakes of a lamb's tail (*sl*)

jig *v* = **skip**, bob, bounce, caper, prance, wiggle

jingle *n* **1** = **rattle**, clang, clink, reverberation, ringing, tinkle **2** = **song**, chorus, ditty, melody, tune ◆ *v* **3** = **ring**, chime, clatter, clink, jangle, rattle, tinkle

jinx *n* **1** = **curse**, evil eye (*inf*), hex (*inf*), hoodoo (*inf*), nemesis ◆ *v* **2** = **curse**, bewitch, hex (*inf*) anxiety. **jit'ter·y** adj **-ter·i·er, -ter·i·est** nervous.

jiujitsu n see JUJITSU.

jive [jīv] n 1 (dance performed to) swing music, esp. of 1950's. ◆ v **jived, jiv·ing** 2 play, dance to, swing music. 3 sl tease. 4 fool.

job n 1 piece of work, task. 2 position, office. 3 inf difficult task. 4 sl a crime, esp. robbery. **job'ber** n wholesale merchant. **job'less** [-lis] adj, pl. n unemployed (people).

jock·ey [JOK-ee] n, pl **-eys** 1 professional rider in horse races. ◆ v **-eyed, -ey·ing** 2 (esp. with for) maneuver.

jo·cose [joh-KOHS] adj waggish, humorous. **jo·cos'i·ty** [-KOS-i-tee] n **joc'u·lar** [-yə-lər] adj 1 joking. 2 given to joking. **joc·u·lar'i·ty** n

joc·und [JOK-ənd] adj merry, cheerful. **jo·cun·di·ty** [joh-KUN-di-tee] n, pl **-ties**

jodh·purs [JOD-pərz] pl n tight-legged riding breeches.

jog v **jogged, jog·ging** ◆ vi 1 run slowly or move at trot, esp. for physical exercise. ◆ vt 2 jar, nudge. 3 remind, stimulate. ◆ n 4 jogging. **jog'ger** n jogging n

jog·gle [JOG-əl] v **-gled, -gling** 1 move to and fro in jerks. 2 shake.

John [jon] n 1 name. 2 (j-) sl toilet. 3 sl prostitute's customer.

joie de vi·vre [zhwad VEE-vrə] Fr

enjoyment of life, ebullience.

join vt 1 put together, fasten, unite. 2 become a member (of). ◆ vi 3 become united, connected. 4 (with up) enlist. 5 take part (in). ◆ n 6 joining. 7 place of joining, seam. **join'er** n 1 maker of finished woodwork. 2 one who joins.

joint n 1 arrangement by which two things fit together, rigidly or loosely. 2 place of this. 3 sl house, place, etc. 4 sl disreputable bar or nightclub. 5 sl marijuana cigarette. ◆ adj 6 common. 7 shared by two or more. ◆ vt 8 connect by joints. 9 divide at the joints. **joint'ly** adv **out of joint** 1 dislocated. 2 disorganized.

joist n one of the parallel beams stretched from wall to wall on which to fix floor or ceiling.

joke [johk] n 1 thing said or done to cause laughter. 2 something not in earnest, or ridiculous. ◆ vi **joked, jok·ing** 3 make jokes. **jok'er** n 1 one who jokes. 2 inf fellow. 3 extra card in pack, counting as highest card in some games.

jol·ly [JOL-ee] adj **-li·er, -li·est** 1 jovial, festive, merry. ◆ vt **-lied, -ly·ing** 3 (esp. with along) (try to) make person, occasion, etc. happier.

jolt [johlt] n 1 sudden jerk. 2 bump. 3 shock. 4 inf a strong drink. ◆ v 5 move, shake with jolts.

joss [jos] n Chinese idol. **joss house**

jitters pl n = **nerves**, anxiety, butterflies (in one's stomach) (inf), cold feet (inf), fidgets, nervousness, the shakes (inf)

jittery adj = **nervous**, agitated, anxious, fidgety, jumpy, shaky, trembling, twitchy (inf), wired (sl)

job n 1 = **task**, assignment, chore, duty, enterprise, errand, undertaking, venture 2 = **occupation**, business, calling, career, employment, livelihood, profession, vocation

jobless adj = **unemployed**, idle, inactive, out of work, unoccupied

jocular adj = **humorous**, amusing, droll, facetious, funny, joking, jovial, playful, sportive, teasing, waggish

jog v 1 = **nudge**, prod, push, shake, stir 2 = **run**, canter, lope, trot

John Doe n Inf = **man in the street**, average guy, average person, know-nothing (sl)

joie de vivre ◆ n = **enthusiasm**,

ebullience, enjoyment, gusto, relish, zest

join v 1 = **connect**, add, append, attach, combine, couple, fasten, link, unite 2 = **enroll**, enlist, enter, sign up

joint adj 1 = **shared**, collective, combined, communal, cooperative, joined, mutual, united ◆ n 2 = **junction**, connection, hinge, intersection, nexus, node ◆ v 3 = **divide**, carve, cut up, dissect, segment, sever

jointly adv = **collectively**, as one, in common, in conjunction, in league, in partnership, mutually, together

joke n 1 = **jest**, gag (inf), jape, prank, pun, quip, wisecrack (inf), witticism 2 = **clown**, buffoon, laughing stock ◆ v 3 = **jest**, banter, kid (inf), mock, play the fool, quip, taunt, tease

joker n = **comedian**, buffoon, clown, comic, humorist, jester, prankster, trickster, wag, wit

jolly adj = **happy**, cheerful, chirpy (inf), genial, jovial, merry, playful, sprightly,

Chinese temple. **joss stick** stick of Chinese incense.

jos·tle [JOS-əl] *v* **-tled, -tling** knock or push against.

jot *n* **1** small amount, whit. ◆ *vt* **jot·ted, jot·ting** **2** write briefly. **3** make note of. **jot'ting** *n* **1** quick note. **2** memorandum.

joule [jool] *n Electricity* unit of work or energy.

jour·nal [JUR-nl] *n* **1** daily newspaper or other periodical. **2** daily record. **3** logbook. **4** part of axle or shaft resting on the bearings. **jour·nal·ese'** [-EEZ] *n* **1** journalist's jargon. **2** style full of clichés. **jour'nal·ism** *n* editing, writing in periodicals.

jour·ney [JUR-nee] *n, pl* **-neys** **1** going to a place, excursion. **2** distance traveled. ◆ *vi* **-neyed, -ney·ing** **3** travel.

joust [jowst] *n Hist.* **1** encounter with lances between two mounted knights. ◆ *vi* **2** engage in joust.

jo·vi·al [JOH-vee-əl] *adj* convivial, merry, gay. **jo·vi·al'i·ty** *n*

jowl *n* **1** cheek, jaw. **2** outside of throat when prominent.

joy [joi] *n* **1** gladness, pleasure, delight. **2** cause of this. **joy'ful** [-fuul] *adj* **joy'less** [-lis] *adj* **joy'ride** *n* (high-speed) automobile trip. **joy'stick** *n inf* control stick of aircraft or computer device.

ju'bi·lant [JOO-bə-lənt] *adj* exultant. **ju·bi·la'tion** *n*

ju·bi·lee [JOO-bə-lee] *n* time of rejoicing, esp. 25th (silver) or 50th (golden) anniversary.

Jud. Judges.

Ju·da·ic [joo-DAY-ik] *adj* Jewish. **Ju'da·ism** *n*

judge [juj] *n* **1** officer appointed to try cases in law courts. **2** one who decides in a dispute, contest, etc. **3** one able to form a reliable opinion, arbiter. **4** umpire. **5** in Jewish history, ruler. ◆ *v* **judged, judg·ing** ◆ *vi* **6** act as judge. ◆ *vt* **7** act as judge of. **8** try, estimate. **9** decide. **judg'ment** *n* **1** faculty of judging. **2** sentence of court. **3** opinion. **4** misfortune regarded as sign of divine displeasure.

ju·di·ca·ture [JOO-di-kə-chər] *n* **1** administration of justice. **2** body of judges. **ju·di'cial** [-DISH-əl] *adj* **1** of or by a court or

———— THESAURUS ————

upbeat (*inf*)

jolt *n* **1** = **jerk**, bump, jar, jog, jump, lurch, shake, start **2** = **surprise**, blow, bolt from the blue, bombshell, setback, shock ◆ *v* **3** = **jerk**, jar, jog, jostle, knock, push, shake, shove **4** = **surprise**, discompose, disturb, perturb, stagger, startle, stun

jostle *v* = **push**, bump, elbow, hustle, jog, jolt, shake, shove

jot *v* **1** = **note down**, list, record, scribble ◆ *n* **2** = **bit**, fraction, grain, morsel, scrap, speck

journal *n* **1** = **newspaper**, daily, gazette, magazine, monthly, periodical, weekly **2** = **diary**, chronicle, log, record

journalist *n* = **reporter**, broadcaster, columnist, commentator, correspondent, hack, newsman *or* newswoman, pressman

journey *n* **1** = **trip**, excursion, expedition, odyssey, pilgrimage, tour, trek, voyage ◆ *v* **2** = **travel**, go, proceed, roam, rove, tour, traverse, trek, voyage, wander

jovial *adj* = **cheerful**, animated, cheery, convivial, happy, jolly, merry, mirthful

joy *n* = **delight**, bliss, ecstasy, elation, gaiety, glee, pleasure, rapture, satisfaction

joyful *adj* = **delighted**, elated, enraptured, glad, gratified, happy, jubilant, merry,

pleased

joyless *adj* = **unhappy**, cheerless, depressed, dismal, dreary, gloomy, miserable, sad

joyous *adj* = **joyful**, festive, merry, rapturous

jubilant *adj* = **overjoyed**, elated, enraptured, euphoric, exuberant, exultant, thrilled, triumphant

jubilation *n* = **joy**, celebration, ecstasy, elation, excitement, exultation, festivity, triumph

jubilee *n* = **celebration**, festival, festivity, holiday

judge *n* **1** = **referee**, adjudicator, arbiter, arbitrator, moderator, umpire **2** = **critic**, arbiter, assessor, authority, connoisseur, expert **3** = **magistrate**, justice ◆ *v* **4** = **arbitrate**, adjudicate, decide, mediate, referee, umpire **5** = **consider**, appraise, assess, esteem, estimate, evaluate, rate, value

judgment *n* **1** = **sense**, acumen, discernment, discrimination, prudence, shrewdness, understanding, wisdom **2** = **verdict**, arbitration, decision, decree, finding, ruling, sentence **3** = **opinion**, appraisal, assessment, belief, diagnosis, judge. **2** proper to a judge. **3** discriminating. **ju·di'ci·ar·y** [-shee-er-ee] *n*, *pl* **-ar·ies** system of courts and judges. **ju·di'cious** [-shəs] *adj* well-judged, sensible, prudent.

ju·do [JOO-doh] *n* modern sport derived from jujitsu.

jug *n* **1** vessel for liquids, with handle and small spout. **2** its contents. **3** *sl* prison. ◆ *vt* jugged, jug·ging **4** stew (esp. hare) in jug.

jug·ger·naut [JUG-ər-nawt] *n* large overpowering, destructive force.

jug·gle [JUG-əl] *v* **-gled**, **-gling 1** throw and catch (several objects) so most are in the air simultaneously. **2** manage, manipulate (accounts, etc.) to deceive. ◆ *n* **jug'gler** *n*

jug·u·lar vein [JUG-yə-lər] one of three large veins of the neck returning blood from the head.

juice [joos] *n* **1** liquid part of vegetable, fruit, or meat. **2** *sl* electric current. **3** *sl* fuel used to run engine. **4** vigor, vitality. **juic'y** *adj* **juic·i·er**, **juic·i·est 1** succulent. **2** scandalous, improper.

ju·jit·su [joo-JIT-soo] *n* the Japanese art of wrestling and self-defense.

ju·jube [JOO-joo-bee] *n* **1** lozenge of gelatin, sugar, etc. **2** a fruit.

ju·lep [JOO-lip] *n* **1** sweet drink. **2** medicated drink.

Jul·ian [JOOL-yən] *adj* of Julius Caesar. **Julian calendar** calendar as adjusted by Julius Caesar in 46 B.C., in which the year was made to consist of 365 days, 6 hours,

instead of 365 days.

ju·li·enne [joo-lee-EN] *n* **1** kind of clear soup. ◆ *adj* **2** of food, cut into thin strips or small pieces. ◆ *vt*

jum·ble [JUM-bəl] *vt* **-bled**, **-bling 1** mingle, mix in confusion. ◆ *n* **2** confused heap, muddle.

jum·bo [JUM-boh] *n inf* **1** elephant. **2** anything very large.

jump *v* **1** (cause to) spring, leap (over). **2** move hastily. **3** pass or skip (over). ◆ *vi* **4** move hastily. **5** rise steeply. **6** parachute from aircraft. **7** start, jerk (with astonishment, etc.). **8** of faulty film, etc., make abrupt movements. ◆ *vt* **9** come off (tracks, rails, etc.). **10** attack without warning. ◆ *n* **11** act of jumping. **12** obstacle to be jumped. **13** distance, height jumped. **14** sudden nervous jerk or start. **15** sudden rise in prices. **jump'er** *n* **1** one who, that which jumps. **2** sleeveless dress. **3** electric cable to connect discharged car battery to external battery to aid starting of engine. **jump'y** *adj* **jump·i·er**, **jump·i·est** nervous. **jump'suit** *n* one-piece garment of trousers and top.

junc·tion [JUNGK-shən] *n* **1** railroad station, etc. where lines, routes join. **2** place of joining. **3** joining.

junc·ture [JUNGK-chər] *n* state of affairs.

jun·gle [JUNG-gəl] *n* **1** tangled vegetation of equatorial forest. **2** land covered with it. **3** tangled mass. **4** condition of intense competition, struggle for survival.

THESAURUS

estimate, finding, valuation, view

judicial *adj* = **legal**, official

judicious *adj* = **sensible**, astute, careful, discriminating, enlightened, prudent, shrewd, thoughtful, well-judged, wise

jug *n* = **container**, carafe, crock, ewer, jar, pitcher, urn, vessel

juggle *v* = **manipulate**, alter, change, maneuver, modify

juice *n* = **liquid**, extract, fluid, liquor, nectar, sap

juicy *adj* **1** = **moist**, lush, succulent **2** = **interesting**, colorful, provocative, racy, risqué, sensational, spicy (*inf*), suggestive, vivid

jumble *n* **1** = **muddle**, clutter, confusion, disarray, disorder, mess, mishmash, mixture ◆ *v* **2** = **mix**, confuse, disorder, disorganize, mistake, muddle, shuffle

jumbo *adj* = **giant**, gigantic, huge,

immense, large, oversized

jump *v* **1** = **leap**, bounce, bound, hop, hurdle, skip, spring, vault **2** = **recoil**, flinch, jerk, start, wince **3** = **miss**, avoid, evade, omit, skip **4** = **increase**, advance, ascend, escalate, rise, surge ◆ *n* **5** = **leap**, bound, hop, skip, spring, vault **6** = **interruption**, break, gap, hiatus, lacuna, space **7** = **rise**, advance, increase, increment, upsurge, upturn

jumped-up *adj* = **conceited**, arrogant, insolent, overbearing, pompous, presumptuous

jumpy *adj* = **nervous**, agitated, anxious, apprehensive, fidgety, jittery (*inf*), on edge, restless, tense, wired (*sl*)

junction *n* = **connection**, coupling, linking, union

juncture *n* = **moment**, occasion, point, time

jun·ior [JOON-yər] *adj* **1** younger. **2** of lower standing. ♦ *n* **3** junior person.

ju·ni·per [JOON-ə-pər] *n* evergreen shrub with berries yielding oil of juniper, used for medicine and gin making.

junk¹ [jungk] *n* **1** discarded, useless objects. **2** *inf* nonsense. **3** *sl* narcotic drug esp. heroin. **junk'ie** *n, pl* **-junk·ies** *inf* drug addict. **junk food** food, oft. of low nutritional value, eaten in addition to or instead of regular meals. **junk mail** unsolicited mail advertising goods or services.

junk² *n* Chinese sailing vessel.

jun·ket [JUNG-kit] *n* **1** curdled milk flavored and sweetened. **2** pleasure trip esp. one paid for by others. ♦ *vi* **3** go on a junket.

jun·ta [HUUN-tə] *n* group of military officers holding power in a country.

Ju·pi·ter [JOO-pi-tər] *n* **1** Roman chief of gods. **2** largest of the planets.

ju·ris·dic·tion [juur-is-DIK-shən] *n* **1** administration of justice. **2** authority. **3** territory covered by it. **ju·ris·pru'dence** [-PROO-dəns] *n* science of, skill in, law. **ju'rist** *n* one skilled in law.

ju·ry [JUUR-ee] *n, pl* **-ries 1** body of persons sworn to render verdict in court of law. **2** body of judges of competition. **ju'ror** *n* member of jury.

just *adj* **1** fair. **2** upright, honest. **3** proper, right, equitable. ♦ *adv* **4** exactly. **5** barely. **6** at this instant. **7** merely, only. **8** really. **jus'tice** *n* **1** quality of being just. **2** fairness. **3** judicial proceedings. **4** judge, magistrate. **jus'ti·fy** *vt* **fied, fy ing 1** prove right, true or innocent. **2** vindicate. **3** excuse. **jus·ti·fi·a·ble** *adj*

jut *vi* **jut·ted, jut·ting 1** project, stick out. ♦ *n* **2** projection.

jute [joot] *n* fiber of certain plants, used for rope, canvas, etc.

ju·ve·nile [JOO-və-nl] *adj* **1** young. **2** of, for young children. **3** immature. ♦ *n* **4** young person, child, male actor. **ju·ve·nil'i·a** *pl n* works produced in author's youth. **juvenile court** court dealing with young offenders or children in need of care. **juvenile delinquent** young person guilty of some offense, antisocial behavior, etc.

jux·ta·pose [JUK-stə-pohz] *vt* **-posed, -pos·ing** put side by side. **jux·ta·po·si'tion** *n* contiguity, being side by side.

═══════THESAURUS═══════

junior *adj* = **minor**, inferior, lesser, lower, secondary, subordinate, younger

junk *n* = **rubbish**, clutter, debris, litter, odds and ends, refuse, scrap, trash, waste

jurisdiction *n* **1** = **authority**, command, control, influence, power, rule **2** = **range**, area, bounds, compass, field, province, scope, sphere

just *adv* **1** = **exactly**, absolutely, completely, entirely, perfectly, precisely **2** = **recently**, hardly, lately, only now, scarcely **3** = **merely**, by the skin of one's teeth, only, simply, solely ♦ *adj* **4** = **fair**, conscientious, equitable, fair-minded, good, honest, upright, virtuous **5** = **proper**, appropriate, apt, deserved, due, fitting, justified, merited, rightful

justice *n* **1** = **fairness**, equity, honesty, integrity, law, legality, legitimacy, right **2** = **judge**, magistrate

justifiable *adj* = **reasonable**, acceptable, defensible, excusable, legitimate, sensible, understandable, valid, warrantable

justification *n* **1** = **explanation**, defense, excuse, rationalization, vindication **2** = **reason**, basis, grounds, warrant

justify *v* = **explain**, defend, exculpate, excuse, exonerate, support, uphold, vindicate, warrant

justly *adv* = **properly**, correctly, equitably, fairly, lawfully

jut *v* = **stick out**, bulge, extend, overhang, poke, project, protrude

juvenile *adj* **1** = **young**, babyish, callow, childish, immature, inexperienced, infantile, puerile, youthful ♦ *n* **2** = **child**, adolescent, boy, girl, infant, minor, youth

juxtaposition *n* = **proximity**, adjacency, closeness, contact, nearness, propinquity, vicinity

K k

K 1 Kelvin. **2** *Chem.* potassium.

ka·bob [kə-BOB], **ke·bab** [kə-BAB] *n* dish of small pieces of meat, tomatoes, etc. grilled on skewers.

kale [kayl] *n* type of cabbage.

ka·lei·do·scope [kə-LĪ-də-skohp] *n* **1** optical toy for producing changing symmetrical patterns by multiple reflections of colored glass chips, etc., in inclined mirrors enclosed in tube. **2** any complex, frequently changing pattern. **ka·lei·do·scop·ic** [-SKOP-ik] *adj* swiftly changing.

ka·mi·ka·ze [kah-mi-KAH-zə] *n* suicidal attack, esp. as in World War II, by Japanese pilots.

kan·ga·roo [kang-gə-ROO] *n, pl* **-roos** Aust. marsupial with very strongly developed hind legs for jumping. **kangaroo court** irregular, illegal court.

ka·pok [KAY-pok] *n* **1** tropical tree. **2** fiber from its seed pods used to stuff cushions, etc.

ka·put [kah-PUUT] *adj sl* ruined, out of order, no good.

ka·ra·te [kə-RAH-tee] *n* Japanese system of unarmed combat using feet, hands, elbows, etc. as weapons in a variety of ways.

kar·ma [KAHR-mə] *n Buddhism, Hinduism* one's actions seen as affecting fate for next reincarnation.

kart [kahrt] *n* miniature low-powered racing car (also **go-kart**).

kay·ak [KĪ-ak] *n* **1** Inuit canoe made of sealskins stretched over frame. **2** any canoe of this design.

ka·zoo [kə-ZOO] *n, pl* **-zoos** cigar-shaped musical instrument producing nasal sound.

kbyte *Computers* kilobyte.

kebab, kebob see KABOB.

ked·ger·ee [KEJ-ə-ree] *n* East Indian dish of fish cooked with rice, eggs, etc.

keel *n* lowest longitudinal support on which ship is built. **keel'haul** *vt* **1** formerly, punish by hauling under keel of ship. **2** rebuke severely. **keel over 1** turn upside down. **2** collapse suddenly.

keen[1] *adj* **-er, -est 1** sharp. **2** acute. **3** eager. **4** shrewd, strong. **keen'ly** *adv* **keen'ness** *n*

keen[2] *n* **1** funeral lament. ◆ *vi* **2** wail over the dead.

keep *v* **kept, keep·ing 1** retain possession of, not lose. **2** store. **3** cause to continue. **4** take charge of. **5** maintain, detain. **6** provide upkeep. **7** reserve. **8** remain good. **9** remain. **10** continue. ◆ *n* **11** living or support. **12** charge or care. **13** central tower of castle, stronghold. **keep'er** *n* **keep'ing** *n* **1** harmony, agreement. **2** care, charge, possession. **keep'sake** *n* thing treasured for sake of giver.

THESAURUS

kamikaze *adj* = **self-destructive**, foolhardy, suicidal

keel over *v* = **collapse**, black out (*inf*), faint, pass out

keen[1] *adj* **1** = **eager**, ardent, avid, enthusiastic, impassioned, intense, zealous **2** = **sharp**, cutting, incisive, razor-like **3** = **astute**, canny, clever, perceptive, quick, shrewd, wise

keenness *n* = **eagerness**, ardor, enthusiasm, fervor, intensity, passion, zeal, zest

keep *v* **1** = **retain**, conserve, control, hold, maintain, possess, preserve **2** = **store**,

carry, deposit, hold, place, stack, stock **3** = **look after**, care for, guard, maintain, manage, mind, protect, tend, watch over **4** = **support**, feed, maintain, provide for, subsidize, sustain **5** = **detain**, delay, hinder, hold back, keep back, obstruct, prevent, restrain ◆ *n* **6** = **board**, food, living, maintenance **7** = **tower**, castle

keeper *n* = **guardian**, attendant, caretaker, curator, custodian, guard, preserver, steward, warden

keeping *n* **1** = **care**, charge, custody, guardianship, possession, protection, safekeeping **2** *As in* **in keeping with** =

keg *n* small barrel usu. holding 5 to 10 gallons (19 to 38 liters).

kelp *n* **1** large seaweed. **2** its ashes, yielding iodine.

Kel·vin *adj* **1** of thermometric scale starting at absolute zero (-273.15° Celsius). ♦ *n* **2** SI unit of temperature.

ken *n* **1** range of knowledge. ♦ *vt* **kenned** or **kent, ken·ning 2** *Scot* know

ken·do [KEN-doh] *n* Japanese sport of fencing, using bamboo staves.

ken·nel [KEN-l] *n* **1** house, shelter for dog. **2** (oft. pl) place for breeding, boarding dogs. ♦ *vt* **-neled, -nel·ing 3** put into kennel.

kept pt./pp. of KEEP.

ker·chief [KUR-chif] *n* **1** square scarf used as head covering. **2** handkerchief.

ker·nel [KUR-nl] *n* **1** inner seed of nut or fruit stone. **2** central, essential part.

ker·o·sene [KER-ə-seen] *n* fuel distilled from petroleum or coal and shale.

ketch [kech] *n* two-masted sailing vessel.

ketch·up [KECH-əp] *n* condiment of vinegar, tomatoes, etc.

ket·tle [KET-l] *n* metal vessel with spout and handle, esp. for boiling water. **ket·tle·drum** *n* musical instrument made of membrane stretched over copper, brass, etc. hemisphere. **a fine kettle of fish** awkward situation, mess.

key [kee] *n* **1** instrument for operating lock, winding clock, etc. **2** something providing control, explanation, means of achieving an end, etc. **3** *Mus.* set of related notes. **4** operating lever of typewriter, piano, computer, etc. **5** mode of thought. ♦ *vt* **6** (also **key in**) enter (text) using a keyboard. **7** provide symbols on map, etc. to assist identification of positions on it. ♦ *adj* **8** vital. **9** most important. **key·board** [-bord] *n* set of keys on piano, computer, etc. **key·hole** *n* **1** hole for inserting key into lock. **2** any shape resembling this. **key·note** [-noht] *n* **1** dominant idea. **2** basic note of musical key. **key·pad** *n* small keyboard with push buttons. **key·stone** *n* central stone of arch that locks all in position.

khak·i [KAK-ee] *adj* **1** dull yellowish-brown. ♦ *n, pl* **khakis 2** khaki cloth. **3** (usu. pl) military uniform.

Khmer [kmair] *n* member of a people of Cambodia.

Ki. Kings.

kib·ble [KIB-əl] *vt* **-bled, -bling 1** grind into small pieces. ♦ *n* **2** dry dog food prepared in this way.

kib·butz [ki-BUUTS] *n* in Israel, Jewish communal agricultural settlement. **kib·butz·nik** *n* member of kibbutz.

ki·bosh [KĪ-bosh] *n inf* nonsense. **to put the kibosh on 1** silence. **2** check. **3** defeat.

kick [kik] *vi* **1** strike out with foot. **2** score with a kick. **3** be recalcitrant. **4** recoil. ♦ *vt* **5** strike or hit with foot. **6** *sl* free oneself of (drug habit, etc.). ♦ *n* **7** foot blow. **8** recoil. **9** excitement, thrill. **kick·back** *n* **1** strong reaction. **2** money paid illegally for favors done, etc. **kick off** *v* **1** start game of football. **2** begin (discussion, etc.). **kick-start** *v* start motorcycle engine, etc. by pedal that is kicked downward.

kid *n* **1** young goat. **2** leather of its skin. **3** *inf* child. ♦ *v* **kid·ded, kid·ding 4** (of a goat) give birth. **5** *inf* tease, deceive. **6** *inf* behave, speak in fun.

kid·nap *vt* **-napped, -nap·ping** seize and hold for ransom. **kid·nap·per** *n*

kid·ney [KID-nee] *n, pl* **-neys 1** either of the

agreement, accord, balance, compliance, conformity, correspondence, harmony, observance, proportion

keepsake *n* = **souvenir,** memento, relic, reminder, symbol, token

keep up *v* = **maintain,** continue, keep pace, preserve, sustain

keg *n* = **barrel,** cask, drum, vat

kernel *n* = **essence,** core, germ, gist, nub, pith, substance

key *n* **1** = **opener,** latchkey **2** = **answer,** explanation, solution ♦ *adj* **3** = **essential,** crucial, decisive, fundamental, important, leading, main, major, pivotal, principal

key in *v* = **type,** enter, input, keyboard

keynote *n* = **heart,** center, core, essence, gist, substance, theme

kick *v* **1** = **boot,** punt **2** *Inf* = **give up,** abandon, desist from, leave off, quit, stop ♦ *n* **3** *Inf* = **thrill,** buzz (*sl*), pleasure, stimulation

kick off *v* = **begin,** commence, get the show on the road, initiate, open, start

kick out *v* = **dismiss,** eject, evict, expel, get rid of, remove, sack (*inf*)

kid¹ *n Inf* = **child,** baby, infant, minor, teenager, tot, youngster, youth

kid² *v* = **tease,** delude, fool, hoax, jest, joke,

pair of organs that secrete urine. **2** animal kidney used as food. **3** nature, kind. **kidney bean** common bean, kidney-shaped at maturity.

kill vt **1** deprive of life. **2** destroy. **3** neutralize. **4** pass (time). **5** weaken or dilute. **6** inf tire, exhaust. **7** inf cause to suffer pain. **8** inf quash, defeat, veto. ◆ n **9** act of killing. **10** animals, etc. killed in hunt. **11** enemy troops, aircraft, etc. killed or destroyed in combat. **kill'er** n one who, that which, kills. **kill'ing** adj inf **1** very tiring. **2** very funny. ◆ n **3** sudden success, esp. on stock market.

kiln n furnace, oven.

kil·o [KEE-loh] n short for KILOGRAM.

kilo- comb. form one thousand, e.g. kiloliter; kilometer.

kil·o·byte [KIL-ə-bīt] n Computers **1** 1,024 bytes. **2** (loosely) one thousand bytes.

kil·o·gram [KIL-ə-gram] n weight of one thousand grams.

kil·o·hertz [KIL-ə-hurts] n one thousand cycles per second.

kil·o·watt [KIL-ə-wot] n Electricity one thousand watts.

kilt n short, usu. tartan, skirt, deeply pleated, worn orig. by Scottish Highlanders. **kilt'ed** adj

ki·mo·no [kə-MOH-nə] n, pl **-nos 1** loose, wide-sleeved Japanese robe, fastened with sash. **2** woman's garment like this.

kin n family, relatives. ◆ adj related by blood. **kin'dred** [-drid] n **1** relationship. **2** relatives. ◆ adj **3** similar. **4** related. **kin'folk** [-fohk] n **kin'ship** n

kind [kīnd] n **1** genus, sort, class. ◆ adj **-er, -est 2** sympathetic, considerate. **3** good, benevolent. **4** gentle. **kind'li·ness** n **kind'ly** adj **-li·er, -li·est** kind, genial. ◆ adv **kind'ness** n **kind'heart·ed** adj **in kind 1** (of payment) in goods rather than money. **2** with something similar.

kin·der·gar·ten [KIN-dər-gahr-tn] n class, school for children of about four to six years old.

kin·dle [KIN-dl] v **-dled, -dling** ◆ vt **1** set on fire. **2** inspire, excite. ◆ vi **3** catch fire. **kind'ling** n small wood to kindle fires.

ki·net·ic [ki-NET-ik] adj of motion in relation to force. **ki·net'ics** n the branch of mechanics concerned with the study of bodies in motion.

king n **1** male sovereign ruler of independent country. **2** monarch. **3** piece in game of chess. **4** playing card with picture of a king. **5** Checkers two pieces on top of one another, allowed freedom of movement. **king'ly** adj **-li·er, -li·est** royal. **2** appropriate to a king. **king'dom** [-dəm]

THESAURUS

pretend, trick

kidnap v = **abduct**, capture, hijack, hold to ransom, seize

kill v **1** = **slay**, assassinate, butcher, destroy, execute, exterminate, liquidate, massacre, murder, slaughter **2** = **suppress**, extinguish, halt, quash, quell, scotch, smother, stifle, stop

killer n = **assassin**, butcher, cut-throat, executioner, exterminator, gunman, hit man (sl), murderer, slayer

killing n **1** = **slaughter**, bloodshed, carnage, extermination, homicide, manslaughter, massacre, murder, slaying **2** Inf = **bonanza**, cleanup (inf), coup, gain, profit, success, windfall

killjoy n = **spoilsport**, dampener, wet blanket (inf)

kin n = **family**, kindred, kinsfolk, relations, relatives

kind¹ adj = **considerate**, benign, charitable, compassionate, courteous, friendly, generous, humane, kindly, obliging, philanthropic, tender-hearted

kind² n = **class**, brand, breed, family, set, sort, species, variety

kind-hearted adj = **sympathetic**, altruistic, compassionate, considerate, generous, good-natured, helpful, humane, kind, tender-hearted

kindle v **1** = **set fire to**, ignite, inflame, light **2** = **arouse**, awaken, induce, inspire, provoke, rouse, stimulate, stir

kindliness n = **kindness**, amiability, benevolence, charity, compassion, friendliness, gentleness, humanity, kind-heartedness

kindly adj **1** = **good-natured**, benevolent, benign, compassionate, helpful, kind, pleasant, sympathetic, warm ◆ adv **2** = **politely**, agreeably, cordially, graciously, tenderly, thoughtfully

kindness n = **goodwill**, benevolence, charity, compassion, generosity, humanity, kindliness, philanthropy, understanding

kindred adj **1** = **similar**, akin, corresponding, like, matching, related ◆ n **2** = **family**, kin, kinsfolk, relations, relatives n **1** country ruled by king. **2** realm. **3** sphere. **king'fish** n **1** any of several types of fish. **2** inf person in position of authority. **king'pin** n **1** swivel pin. **2** central or front pin in bowling. **3** inf chief thing or person. **king-size, king-sized** adj inf **1** large. **2** larger than standard size.

kink [kingk] n **1** tight twist in rope, wire, hair, etc. **2** crick, as of neck. **3** inf eccentricity. ◆ v **4** make, become kinked. **5** put, make kink in. **6** twist. **kink'y** adj **kink·i·er, kink·i·est 1** full of kinks. **2** inf eccentric, esp. given to deviant (sexual) practices.

ki·osk [KEE-osk] n small, sometimes movable booth selling soft drinks, cigarettes, newspapers, etc.

kip·per [KIP-ər] vt **1** cure (fish) by splitting open, rubbing with salt, and drying or smoking. ◆ n **2** kippered fish.

kirsch [keersh] n brandy made from cherries.

kis·met [KIZ-mit] n fate, destiny.

kiss n **1** touch or caress with lips. **2** light touch. ◆ v **kiss'er** n **1** one who kisses. **2** sl mouth or face. **kissing kin** relative(s) familiar enough to greet with polite kiss. **kiss of death** apparently friendly ruinous act.

kit n **1** outfit, equipment. **2** personal effects, esp. of traveler. **3** set of pieces of equipment sold ready to be assembled. **kit bag** small bag for holding soldier's or traveler's kit.

kitch·en [KICH-ən] n room used for cooking. **kitch·en·ette'** n small compact kitchen. **kitchen garden** garden for raising vegetables, herbs, etc. **kitchen sink 1** sink in kitchen. **2** final item imaginable.

kite [kīt] n **1** light papered frame flown in wind. **2** large hawk. **3** check drawn against nonexistent funds. ◆ vt **kit·ed, kit·ing 4** use check in this way. **5** cash or pass such a check.

kith n **kith and kin** friends and relatives.

kitsch [kich] n vulgarized, pretentious art, literature, etc., usu. with popular, sentimental appeal.

kit·ten [KIT-n] n young cat.

kit·ty [KIT-ee] n, pl **-ties 1** short for KITTEN. **2** in some card games, pool of money. **3** communal fund.

ki·wi [KEE-wee] n, pl **-wis 1** any N.Z. flightless bird of the genus *Apteryx*. **2** inf New Zealander. **kiwi fruit** fuzzy fruit of Asian climbing plant, the Chinese gooseberry.

klax·on [KLAK-sən] n powerful electric horn, used as warning signal.

klep·to·ma·ni·a [klep-tə-MAY-nee-ə] n compulsive tendency to steal for the sake of theft. **klep·to·ma'ni·ac** n

knack [nak] n **1** acquired facility or dexterity. **2** trick. **3** habit.

knap·sack [NAP-sak] n soldier's or traveler's bag to strap to the back, rucksack.

knave [nayv] n **1** jack at cards. **2** obs rogue. **knav'er·y** n villainy. **knav'ish** adj

knead [need] vt **1** work (flour) into dough. **2** work, massage.

knee [nee] n **1** joint between thigh and lower leg. **2** part of garment covering knee. ◆ vt **kneed, knee·ing** strike, push with knee. **knee'cap** n bone in front of knee.

kneel [neel] vi **knelt** or **kneeled, kneel·ing** fall, rest on knees.

——————| THESAURUS |——————

king n = **ruler**, emperor, monarch, sovereign

kingdom n = **country**, nation, realm, state, territory

kink n **1** = **twist**, bend, coil, wrinkle **2** = **quirk**, eccentricity, fetish, foible, idiosyncrasy, vagary, whim

kinky adj **1** Sl = **weird**, eccentric, odd, outlandish, peculiar, queer, quirky, strange **2** = **twisted**, coiled, curled, tangled

kinship n **1** = **relation**, consanguinity, kin, ties of blood **2** = **similarity**, affinity, association, connection, correspondence, relationship

kiosk n = **booth**, bookstall, counter, newsstand, stall, stand

kiss v **1** = **osculate**, neck (inf), peck (inf) **2** = **brush**, glance, graze, scrape, touch ◆ n **3** = **osculation**, peck (inf), smacker (sl), smooch (sl)

kit n = **equipment**, apparatus, gear, paraphernalia, tackle, tools

knack n = **skill**, ability, aptitude, capacity, expertise, facility, gift, propensity, talent, trick

knave n = **rogue**, rascal, scoundrel, villain

knead v = **squeeze**, form, manipulate, massage, mold, press, rub, shape, work

kneel v = **genuflect**, get (down) on one's knees, stoop

knell [nel] *n* **1** sound of a bell, esp. at funeral or death. **2** portent of doom.

knew pt. of KNOW.

knick·ers [NIK-ərz] *pl n* loose-fitting short trousers gathered in at knee.

knick-knack [NIK-nak] *n* small ornament or toy.

knife [nīf] *n, pl* **knives 1** cutting blade, esp. one in handle, used as implement or weapon. ◆ *vt* **knifed, knif·ing 2** cut or stab with knife. **knife edge** critical, possibly dangerous situation.

knight [nīt] *n Brit* **1** man of rank below baronet, having right to prefix *Sir* to his name. **2** member of medieval order of chivalry. **3** champion. **4** piece in chess. ◆ *vt* **5** confer knighthood on. **knight'hood** [-huud] *n*

knish *n* turnover filled with potato, meat, etc. and fried or baked.

knit [nit] *v* **knit'ted** *or* **knit, knit·ting 1** form (garment, etc.) by putting together series of loops in wool or other yarn. **2** draw together. **3** unite. **knit'ting** *n* **1** knitted work. **2** act of knitting.

knob [nob] *n* rounded lump, esp. at end or on surface of anything. **knob·by** *adj* **-bi·er, -bi·est**

knock [nok] *vt* **1** strike, hit. **2** *inf* disparage. **3** rap audibly. **4** (of engine) make metallic noise, ping. ◆ *n* **5** blow, rap. **knock'er** *n* **1** metal appliance for knocking on door. **2** who or what knocks. **knock-kneed** *adj*

having incurved legs. **knocked out** exhausted, tired, worn out. **knock off 1** *inf* cease work. **2** *inf* copy, plagiarize. **3** *sl* kill. **4** *sl* steal. **knock out** *inf* **1** render (opponent) unconscious. **2** overwhelm, amaze. **3** make (something) hurriedly. **knock'out** *n* **1** blow, etc. that renders unconscious. **2** *inf* person or thing overwhelmingly attractive. **knock up** *sl* make pregnant.

knoll [nohl] *n* small rounded hill, mound.

knot [not] *n* **1** fastening of strands by looping and pulling tight. **2** cluster. **3** small closely knit group. **4** tie, bond. **5** hard lump, esp. of wood where branch joins or has joined in. **6** unit of speed used by ships, equal to one nautical mile per hour. **7** difficulty. ◆ *vt* **knot·ted, knot·ting 8** tie with knot, in knots. **knot'ty** *adj* **-ti·er, -ti·est 1** full of knots. **2** puzzling, difficult. **knot'hole** [-hohl] *n* hole in wood where knot has been.

know [noh] *v* **knew, known, know·ing** ◆ *vt* **1** be aware of, have information about, be acquainted with, recognize, have experience, understand. ◆ *vi* **2** have information or understanding. **know'ing** *adj* cunning, shrewd. **know'ing·ly** *adv* **1** shrewdly. **2** deliberately. **knowl·edge** [NOL-ij] *n* **1** knowing. **2** what one knows. **3** learning. **knowl'edge·a·ble** *adj* intelligent, well-informed. **know-how** *n* practical knowledge, experience, aptitude. **in the know** informed.

THESAURUS

knell *n* = **ringing**, chime, peal, sound, toll

knick-knack *n* = **trinket**, bagatelle, bauble, bric-a-brac, plaything, trifle

knife *n* **1** = **blade**, cutter ◆ *v* **2** = **cut**, lacerate, pierce, slash, stab, wound

knit *v* **1** = **join**, bind, fasten, intertwine, link, tie, unite, weave **2** = **wrinkle**, crease, furrow, knot, pucker

knob *n* = **lump**, bump, hump, knot, projection, protrusion, stud

knock *v* **1** = **hit**, belt (*inf*), cuff, punch, rap, smack, strike, thump **2** *Inf* = **criticize**, abuse, belittle, censure, condemn, denigrate, deprecate, disparage, find fault, run down ◆ *n* **3** = **blow**, clip, clout (*inf*), cuff, rap, slap, smack, thump **4** = **setback**, defeat, failure, rebuff, rejection, reversal

knock down *v* = **demolish**, destroy, fell, level, raze

knock off *v* **1** = **stop work**, clock off, clock out, finish **2** = **steal**, pinch, rob, thieve

knockout *n* **1** = **killer blow**, coup de grâce, KO or K.O. (*sl*) **2** = **success**, hit, sensation, smash, smash hit, triumph, winner

knot *n* **1** = **connection**, bond, joint, ligature, loop, tie **2** = **cluster**, bunch, clump, collection ◆ *v* **3** = **tie**, bind, loop, secure, tether

know *v* **1** = **realize**, comprehend, feel certain, notice, perceive, recognize, see, understand **2** = **be acquainted with**, be familiar with, have dealings with, have knowledge of, recognize

know-how *n* = **capability**, ability, aptitude, expertise, ingenuity, knack, knowledge, savoir-faire, skill, talent

knowing *adj* = **meaningful**, expressive, significant

knowingly *adv* = **deliberately**, consciously, intentionally, on purpose, purposely, willfully, wittingly

knowledge *n* **1** = **learning**, education,

knuck•le [nuk-əl] *n* **1** bone at finger joint. **2** knee joint of calf or pig. ♦ *vt* **-led, -ling** strike with knuckles. **knuckle ball** *Baseball* pitch delivered by holding ball by thumb and first joints or tips of first two or three fingers. **knuckle-dust•er** *n* metal appliances worn on knuckles to add force to blow, brass knuckles. **knuckle down** get down (to work) **knuckle under** yield, submit.

knurled [nurld] *adj* **1** serrated. **2** gnarled.

ko•a•la [koh-AH-lə] *n* marsupial Aust. animal, native bear.

kohl *n* powdered antimony used orig. in Eastern countries for darkening the eyelids.

kohl•ra•bi [kohl-RAH-bee] *n, pl* **-bies** type of cabbage with edible stem.

ko•peck [KOH-pek] *n* monetary unit of Russia and Belarus, one hundredth of ruble.

Ko•ran [kə-RAN] *n* sacred book of Muslims.

ko•sher [KOH-shər] *adj* **1** permitted, clean, good, as of food, etc., conforming to the Jewish dietary law. **2** *inf* legitimate, authentic. ♦ *n* **3** *inf* kosher food. ♦ *vt* **4** make (food, etc.) kosher.

kow•tow *n* **1** former Chinese custom of touching ground with head in respect. **2** submission. ♦ *vi* **3** (esp. with *to*) prostrate oneself. **4** be obsequious, fawn on.

Kr *Chem.* krypton.

Krem'lin *n* central government of Russia and, formerly, the Soviet Union.

krill [kril] *n, pl* **krill** small shrimplike marine animal.

kryp•ton [KRIP-ton] *n* rare gaseous element, present in atmosphere.

ku•dos [KOO-dohz] *n* **1** honor. **2** acclaim.

ku•du [KOO-doo] *n* Afr. antelope with spiral horns.

ku•lak [kuu-LAHK] *n* independent well-to-do Russian peasant of Czarist times.

kum•quat [KUM-kwot] *n* **1** small Chinese tree. **2** its round orange fruit.

kung fu [kung foo] Chinese martial art combining techniques of judo and karate.

Kwan•zaa [KWAHN-zə, -zah] *n* African-American festival held from December 26 through January 1.

enlightenment, erudition, instruction, intelligence, scholarship, wisdom **2 = acquaintance**, cognizance, familiarity, intimacy

knowledgeable *adj* **1 = well-informed**, *au fait*, aware, clued-up (*inf*), cognizant, conversant, experienced, familiar, in the know (*inf*) **2 = intelligent**, educated, erudite, learned, scholarly

known *adj* **= famous**, acknowledged, avowed, celebrated, noted, recognized, well-known

knuckle under *v* **= give way**, accede, acquiesce, capitulate, cave in (*inf*), give in, submit, succumb, surrender, yield

kudos *n* **= praise**, acclaim, applause, credit, laudation, plaudits, recognition

L l

la see LAH.
La *Chem.* lanthanum.
la·bel [LAY-bəl] *n* **1** slip of paper, metal, etc., fixed to object to give information about it. **2** brief, descriptive phrase or term. ◆ *vt* **-beled, -bel·ing**
la·bi·al [LAY-bee-əl] *adj* **1** of the lips. **2** pronounced with the lips. ◆ *n* **3** labial consonant.
la·bor [LAY-bər] *n* **1** exertion of body or mind. **2** task. **3** workers collectively. **4** effort, pain, of childbirth or time taken for this. ◆ *vi* **5** work hard. **6** strive. **7** maintain normal motion with difficulty. **8** (esp. of ship) be tossed heavily. ◆ *vt* **9** elaborate. **10** stress to excess. **la'bored** *adj* uttered, done, with difficulty. **la'bor·er** *n* one who labors, esp. person doing manual work for wages. **la·bo·ri·ous** [lə-BOR-ee-əs] *adj* tedious.
lab·o·ra·to·ry [LAB-rə-tor-ee] *n* place for scientific investigations or for manufacture of chemicals.
lab·ra·dor [LAB-rə-dor] *n* breed of large, smooth-coated retriever dog.

lab·y·rinth [LAB-ə-rinth] *n* **1** network of tortuous passages, maze. **2** inexplicable difficulty. **3** perplexity. **lab·y·rin'thine** [-RIN-thin] *adj*
lace [lays] *n* **1** fine patterned openwork fabric. **2** cord, usu. one of pair, to draw edges together, e.g. to tighten shoes, etc. **3** ornamental braid. ◆ *vt* **4** fasten with laces. **5** flavor with whiskey, etc. **lac'y** *adj* **lac·i·er, lac·i·est** fine, like lace.
lac·er·ate [LAS-ə-rayt] *vt* **-at·ed, -at·ing 1** tear, mangle. **2** distress. **lac·er·a'tion** *n*
lach·ry·mal [LAK-rə-məl] *adj* of tears. **lach·ry·ma·to·ry** [-mə-tor-ee] *adj* causing tears or inflammation of eyes. **lach·ry·mose** [-mohs] *adj* tearful.
lack [lak] *n* **1** deficiency, need. ◆ *vt* **2** need, be short of. **lack'lus·ter** *adj* lacking brilliance or vitality.
lack·a·dai·si·cal [lak-ə-DAY-zi-kəl] *adj* **1** languid, listless. **2** lazy, careless.
lack·ey [LAK-ee] *n, pl* **-eys 1** servile follower. **2** footman. ◆ *v* **-eyed, -ey·ing 3** be, or play, the lackey. **4** wait upon.
la·con·ic [lə-KON-ik] *adj* **1** using, expressed

THESAURUS

label *n* **1 = tag**, marker, sticker, ticket ◆ *v* **2 = mark**, stamp, tag
labor *n* **1 = work**, industry, toil **2 = workers**, employees, hands, laborers, workforce **3 = childbirth**, delivery, parturition ◆ *v* **4 = work**, endeavor, slave, strive, struggle, sweat (*inf*), toil **5** (usually with *under*) **= be disadvantaged**, be a victim of, be burdened by, suffer **6 = overemphasize**, dwell on, elaborate, overdo, strain
labored *adj* **= forced**, awkward, difficult, heavy, stiff, strained
laborer *n* **= worker**, blue-collar worker, drudge, hand, manual worker
laborious *adj* **= hard**, arduous, backbreaking, exhausting, onerous, strenuous, tiring, tough, wearisome
labyrinth *n* **= maze**, intricacy, jungle, tangle

lace *n* **1 = netting**, filigree, openwork **2 = cord**, bootlace, shoelace, string, tie ◆ *v* **3 = fasten**, bind, do up, thread, tie **4 = mix in**, add to, fortify, spike
lacerate *v* **= tear**, claw, cut, gash, mangle, rip, slash, wound
laceration *n* **= cut**, gash, rent, rip, slash, tear, wound
lack *n* **1 = shortage**, absence, dearth, deficiency, need, scarcity, want ◆ *v* **2 = need**, be deficient in, be short of, be without, miss, require, want
lackadaisical *adj* **1 = lethargic**, apathetic, dull, half-hearted, indifferent, languid, listless **2 = lazy**, abstracted, dreamy, idle, indolent, inert
lackey *n* **1 = hanger-on**, brown-noser (*sl*), flatterer, minion, sycophant, toady, yes man **2 = manservant**, attendant, flunky, footman, valet

in few words. **2** brief, terse. **3** offhand, not caring. **la·con'i·cal·ly** *adv*

lac·quer [LAK-ər] *n* **1** hard varnish. ♦ *vt* **2** coat with this.

la·crosse [lə-KRAWS] *n* ball game played with long-handled racket, or crosse.

lac·tic [LAK-tik] *adj* of milk. **lac'tate** *vi* **-tat·ed, -tat·ing** secrete milk. **lac·ta'tion** *n* **lac'tose** [-tohs] *n* white crystalline substance occurring in milk.

la·cu·na [lə-KYOO-nə] *n, pl* **-nae** [-nee] gap, missing part, esp. in document or series.

lad *n* boy, young fellow.

lad·der [LAD-ər] *n* **1** frame of two poles connected by crossbars called rungs, used for climbing. **2** flaw in stockings, caused by running of torn stitch.

lade [layd] *vt* **lad·ed** *or* **lad·en, lad·ing 1** load. **2** ship. **3** burden, weigh down. **lad'ing** *n* cargo, freight.

la·dle [LAYD-l] *n* **1** spoon with long handle for large bowl. ♦ *vt* **-dled, -dling 2** serve out liquid with a ladle.

la·dy [LAY-dee] *n, pl* **-dies 1** female counterpart of gentleman. **2** polite term for a woman. **3** title of some women of rank. **la'dy·like** *adj* **1** gracious. **2** well-mannered. **Our Lady** the Virgin Mary. **la'dy·fin·ger** *n* small sponge cake in shape of finger. **lady-of-the-night** *n, pl* **ladies-** prostitute.

lag[1] *vi* **lagged, lag·ging 1** go too slowly, fall behind. ♦ *n* **2** lagging, interval of time between events. **lag'gard** [-ərd] *n* one who lags. **lagging** *adj* loitering, slow.

lag[2] *vt* **lagged, lag·ging** wrap boiler, pipes, etc. with insulating material. **lagging** *n* this material.

la·ger [LAH-gər] *n* **1** a light-bodied type of beer. ♦ *vt* **2** age (beer) by storing in tanks.

la·goon [lə-GOON] *n* saltwater lake,

enclosed by atoll, or separated by sandbank from sea.

lah, la *n* sixth sol-fa note.

la·ic [LAY-ik] *adj* secular, lay. **la'i·cize** [-sīz] *vt* **-cized, -ciz·ing** render secular or lay.

laid [layd] pt./pp. of LAY. **laid-back** *adj inf* relaxed.

lain [layn] pp. of LIE.

lair *n* resting place, den of animal.

lais·sez faire [les-ay FAIR] *n* **1** principle of nonintervention, esp. by government in commercial affairs. **2** indifference.

la·i·ty [LAY-i-tee] *n* lay worshipers, the people as opposed to clergy.

lake [layk] *n* expanse of inland water.

lam *n sl* **1** hasty escape. ♦ *vi sl* **lammed, lam·ming 2** run away fast. **3** escape. **on the lam** *sl* **1** escaping. **2** hiding esp. from police.

Lam. Lamentations.

la·ma [LAH-mə] *n* Buddhist priest in Tibet or Mongolia. **la'ma·ser·y** *n* monastery of lamas.

lamb [lam] *n* **1** young of the sheep. **2** its meat. **3** innocent or helpless creature. ♦ *vi* (of sheep). **4** give birth to lamb. **lamb'like** *adj* meek, gentle.

lam·baste [lam-BAYST] *vt* **-bast·ed, -bast·ing** beat, reprimand.

lam·bent [LAM-bənt] *adj* **1** (of flame) flickering softly. **2** glowing.

lame [laym] *adj* **lam·er, lam·est 1** crippled in a limb, esp. leg. **2** limping. **3** (of excuse, etc.) unconvincing. ♦ *vt* **lamed, lam·ing 4** cripple. **lame duck 1** official serving out term of office while waiting for elected successor to assume office. **2** disabled, weak person or thing.

la·mé [la-MAY] *n, adj* (fabric) interwoven with gold or silver thread.

la·ment [lə-MENT] *v* **1** feel, express sorrow

———————[THESAURUS]———————

lackluster *adj* = **flat**, drab, dull, leaden, lifeless, muted, prosaic, uninspired, vapid

laconic *adj* = **terse**, brief, concise, curt, monosyllabic, pithy, short, succinct

lad *n* = **boy**, fellow, guy (*inf*), juvenile, kid (*inf*), youngster, youth

laden *adj* = **loaded**, burdened, charged, encumbered, full, weighed down

lady *n* **1** = **gentlewoman**, dame **2** = **woman**, female

ladylike *adj* = **refined**, elegant, genteel, modest, polite, proper, respectable, sophisticated, well-bred

lag *v* = **hang back**, dawdle, delay, linger, loiter, straggle, tarry, trail

laggard *n* = **straggler**, dawdler, idler, loiterer, slowpoke (*inf*), sluggard, snail

laid-back *adj* = **relaxed**, casual, easy-going, free and easy, unflappable (*inf*), unhurried

lair *n* = **nest**, burrow, den, earth, hole

laissez faire *n* = **nonintervention**, free enterprise, free trade

lake *n* = **pond**, basin, lagoon, mere, pool, reservoir, tarn

lame *adj* **1** = **disabled**, challenged, crippled, game, handicapped, hobbling, (for). ♦ *n* **2** passionate expression of grief. **3** song of grief. **lam·en·ta·ble** [LAM-] *adj* deplorable. **lam·en·ta'tion** *n*

lam·i·na [LAM-ə-nə] *n, pl* **-nas** thin plate, scale, flake. **lam'i·nate** [-nayt] *v* **-nat·ed, -nat·ing 1** make (sheet of material) by bonding together two or more thin sheets. **2** split, beat, form into thin sheets. **3** cover with thin sheet of material. ♦ *n* [-nit] **4** laminated sheet. **lam·i·na'tion** *n*

lamp *n* **1** any of various. **2** appliances (esp. electrical) that produce light, heat, radiation, etc. **3** formerly, vessel holding oil burned by wick for lighting. **lamp'black** *n* pigment made from soot. **lamp'light** *n* **lamp'post** *n* post supporting lamp in street.

lam·poon' *n* **1** satire ridiculing person, literary work, etc. ♦ *vt* **2** satirize, ridicule. **lam·poon'ist** *n*

lam·prey [LAM-pree] *n, pl* **-preys** fish like an eel with a round sucking mouth.

lance [lans] *n* **1** horseman's spear. ♦ *vt* **lanced, lanc·ing 2** pierce with lance or lancet. **lan'ce·o·late** [-see-ə-layt] *adj* lance-shaped, tapering. **lanc'er** *n* formerly, cavalry soldier armed with lance. **lan'cet** [-sit] *n* pointed two-edged surgical knife.

land *n* **1** solid part of Earth's surface. **2** ground, soil. **3** country. **4** property consisting of land. ♦ *pl* **5** estates. ♦ *vi* **6** come to land, disembark. **7** bring an aircraft from air to land or water. **8** alight, step down. **9** arrive on ground. ♦ *vt* **10** bring to land. **11** come or bring to some point or condition. **12** *inf* obtain. **13** catch. **land'ed** *adj* possessing, consisting of lands. **land'ing** *n* **1** act of landing. **2** platform between flights of stairs. **land'fall** *n* ship's approach to land at end of voyage. **land'locked** *adj* enclosed by land. **land'lord, -la·dy** *n* **1** person who lets land or houses, etc. **2** owner of apartment house, etc. **land'lub·ber** *n* person ignorant of the sea and ships. **land'mark** *n* **1** boundary mark, conspicuous object, as guide for direction, etc. **2** event, decision, etc. considered as important stage in development of something. **land'scape** *n* **1** piece of inland scenery. **2** picture of it. **3** prospect. ♦ *v* **-scaped, -scap·ing 4** create, arrange, garden, park, etc. **landscape gardener** *n* person who designs gardens or parks so that they look attractive. **land'slide** *n* **1** falling of soil, rock, etc. down mountainside. **2** overwhelming electoral victory.

lane [layn] *n* **1** narrow road or street. **2** specified route followed by shipping or aircraft. **3** area of road for one stream of traffic.

lan·guage [LANG-gwij] *n* **1** system of sounds, symbols, etc. for communicating thought. **2** specialized vocabulary used by a particular group. **3** style of speech or expression. **4** system of words and symbols for computer programming.

lan·guish [LANG-gwish] *vi* **1** be or become

limping **2 = unconvincing**, feeble, flimsy, inadequate, lousy (*sl*), pathetic, poor, thin, unsatisfactory, weak

lament *v* **1 = complain**, bemoan, bewail, deplore, grieve, mourn, regret, sorrow, wail, weep ♦ *n* **2 = complaint**, lamentation, moan, wailing **3 = dirge**, elegy, requiem, threnody

lamentable *adj* **= regrettable**, deplorable, distressing, grievous, mournful, tragic, unfortunate, woeful

lampoon *n* **1 = satire**, burlesque, caricature, parody, spoof (*inf*) ♦ *v* **2 = ridicule**, caricature, make fun of, mock, parody, satirize

land *n* **1 = ground**, dry land, earth, terra firma **2 = soil**, dirt, ground, loam **3 = countryside**, farmland **4 = property**, estate, grounds, realty **5 = country**, district, nation, province, region, territory, tract ♦ *v* **6 = arrive**, alight, come to rest, disembark, dock, touch down **7 = end up**, turn up, wind up **8** *Inf* **= obtain**, acquire, gain, get, secure, win

landlord *n* **1 = innkeeper**, host, hotelier **2 = owner**, freeholder, lessor, proprietor

landmark *n* **1 = feature**, monument **2 = milestone**, turning point, watershed

landscape *n* **= scenery**, countryside, outlook, panorama, prospect, scene, view, vista

landslide *n* **1 = rockfall**, avalanche, landslip ♦ *adj* **2 = overwhelming**, conclusive, decisive, runaway

lane *n* **= road**, alley, footpath, passageway, path, pathway, street, way

language *n* **1 = speech**, communication, discourse, expression, parlance, talk **2 = tongue**, dialect, patois, vernacular

languid *adj* **1 = lazy**, indifferent,

DICTIONARY

weak or faint. **2** be in depressing or painful conditions. **3** droop, pine. **lan'guid** *adj* **1** lacking energy, interest. **2** spiritless, dull. **lan'guor** [-gər] *n* **1** want of energy or interest. **2** faintness. **3** tender mood. **4** softness of atmosphere. **lan'guor·ous** *adj*

lank [langk] *adj* **1** lean and tall. **2** straight and limp. **lank'y** *adj* **lank·i·er, lank·i·est**

lan·o·lin [LAN-l-in] *n* grease from wool used in ointments, etc.

lan·tern [LAN-tərn] *n* **1** transparent case for lamp or candle. **2** erection on dome or roof to let out smoke, admit light.

lan·tha·num [LAN-thə-nəm] *n* silvery-white ductile metallic element.

lan·yard [LAN-yərd] *n* **1** short cord for securing knife or whistle. **2** short nautical rope. **3** cord for firing cannon.

lap¹ *n* **1** the part between waist and knees of a person when sitting. **2** *fig* place where anything lies securely. **3** single circuit of racetrack, track. **4** stage or part of journey. **5** single turn of wound thread, etc. ◆ *vt* **lapped, lap·ping 6** enfold, wrap around. **7** overtake opponent to be one or more circuits ahead. **lap dog** *n* small pet dog. **lap'top** *adj* **1** (of a computer) small and light enough to be held on the user's lap. ◆ *n* **2** such a computer.

lap² *vt* **lapped, lap·ping 1** drink by scooping up with tongue. **2** (of waves, etc.) beat softly.

la·pel [lə-PEL] *n* part of front of a jacket or coat folded back toward shoulders.

lap·i·dar·y [LAP-i-der-ee] *adj* **1** of stones. **2** engraved on stone. **3** exhibiting extreme refinement. **4** concise and dignified. ◆ *n, pl* **-dar·ies 5** cutter, engraver of stones.

lap·is laz·u·li [LAP-is LAZ-uu-lee] bright blue stone or pigment.

lapse [laps] *n* **1** fall (in standard, condition, virtue, etc.). **2** slip. **3** mistake. **4** passing (of time, etc.). ◆ *vi* **lapsed, laps·ing 5** fall away. **6** end, esp. through disuse.

lar·board [LAHR-bord] *n, adj* old term for port (side of ship).

lar·ce·ny [LAHR-sə-nee] *n, pl* **-nies** theft.

lard [lahrd] *n* **1** prepared pig fat. ◆ *vt* **2** insert strips of bacon in (meat). **3** intersperse, decorate (speech with strange words, etc.).

lar·der [LAHR-dər] *n* storeroom for food.

large [lahrj] *adj* **1** broad in range or area. **2** great in size, number, etc. **3** liberal. **4** generous. ◆ *adv* **5** in a big way. **large'ly** *adv* **lar·gess', lar·gesse'** *n* **1** bounty. **2** gift. **3** donation. **at large 1** free, not confined. **2** in general. **3** fully.

lar·go [LAHR-goh] *adv Mus.* slow and dignified.

lar·i·at [LAR-ee-ət] *n* lasso.

lark¹ [lahrk] *n* small brown songbird, skylark.

lark² *n* **1** frolic, spree. ◆ *vi* **2** indulge in lark.

THESAURUS

lackadaisical, languorous, listless, unenthusiastic **2** = **lethargic**, dull, heavy, sluggish, torpid

languish *v* **1** = **weaken**, decline, droop, fade, fail, faint, flag, wilt, wither **2** (often with *for*) = **pine**, desire, hanker, hunger, long, yearn **3** = **be neglected**, be abandoned, rot, suffer, waste away

lank *adj* **1** = **limp**, lifeless, straggling **2** = **thin**, emaciated, gaunt, lean, scrawny, skinny, slender, slim, spare

lanky *adj* = **gangling**, angular, bony, gaunt, rangy, spare, tall

lap¹ *n* = **circuit**, circle, loop, orbit, tour

lap² *v* **1** = **ripple**, gurgle, plash, purl, splash, swish, wash **2** = **drink**, lick, sip, sup

lapse *n* **1** = **mistake**, error, failing, fault, indiscretion, negligence, omission, oversight, slip **2** = **interval**, break, breathing space, gap, intermission, interruption, lull, pause **3** = **drop**, decline, deterioration, fall ◆ *v* **4** = **drop**, decline,

degenerate, deteriorate, fall, sink, slide, slip **5** = **end**, expire, run out, stop, terminate

lapsed *adj* = **out of date**, discontinued, ended, expired, finished, invalid, run out

large *adj* **1** = **big**, considerable, enormous, gigantic, great, huge, immense, massive, monumental, sizable *or* sizeable, substantial, vast **2 at large: a** = **free**, at liberty, on the loose, on the run, unconfined **b** = **in general**, as a whole, chiefly, generally, in the main, mainly **c** = **at length**, exhaustively, greatly, in full detail

largely *adv* = **mainly**, as a rule, by and large, chiefly, generally, mostly, predominantly, primarily, principally, to a great extent

large-scale *adj* = **wide-ranging**, broad, extensive, far-reaching, global, sweeping, vast, wholesale, wide

lark *n* **1** = **prank**, caper, escapade, fun, game, jape, mischief ◆ *v* **2 lark about** =

lar·va [LAHR-və] *n, pl* **-vae** [-vee] insect in immature but active stage. **lar'val** *adj*

lar·ynx [LAR-ingks] *n, pl* **-es** part of throat containing vocal cords. **lar·yn·gi'tis** [-jī-tis] *n* inflammation of this.

la·sa·gne [lə-ZAHN-yə] *n* 1 pasta formed in wide, flat sheets. 2 baked dish of this with meat, cheese, tomato sauce, etc.

las·civ'i·ous [lə-SIV-ee-əs] *adj* lustful.

la·ser [LAY-zər] *n* device for concentrating electromagnetic radiation or light of mixed frequencies into an intense, narrow, concentrated beam.

lash[1] *n* 1 stroke with whip. 2 flexible part of whip. 3 eyelash. ◆ *vt* 4 strike with whip, thong, etc. 5 dash against (as waves). 6 attack verbally, ridicule. 7 flick, wave sharply to and fro. ◆ *vi* 8 (with *out*) hit, kick.

lash[2] *vt* fasten or bind tightly with cord, etc.

las·si·tude [LAS-i-tood] *n* weariness.

las·so [LAS-oh] *n, pl* **-sos** or **-soes** rope with noose for catching cattle, etc. ◆ *vt* **-soed, -so·ing**

last[1] *adj, adv* 1 after all others, coming at the end. 2 most recent(ly). ◆ *adj* 3 only remaining. 4 sup. of LATE. ◆ *n* 5 last person or thing. **last'ly** *adv* finally.

last[2] *vi* continue, hold out, remain alive or unexhausted, endure.

last[3] *n* model of foot on which shoes are made, repaired.

latch [lach] *n* 1 fastening for door, consisting of bar, catch for it, and lever to lift it. 2 small lock with spring action. ◆ *vt* 3 fasten with latch. **latch'key** [-kee] *n*

late [layt] *adj* **lat·er** or **lat·ter, lat·est** or **last** 1 coming after the appointed time. 2 delayed. 3 that was recently but now is not. 4 recently dead. 5 recent in date. 6 of late stage of development. ◆ *adv* **lat·er, lat·est** 7 after proper time. 8 recently. 9 at, till late hour. **late'ly** *adv* not long since.

la·tent [LAYT-nt] *adj* 1 existing but not developed. 2 hidden.

lat·er·al [LAT-ər-əl] *adj* of, at, from the side. **lat'er·al·ly** *adv*

la·tex [LAY-teks] *n* sap or fluid of plants, esp. of rubber tree.

lath *n, pl* **laths** [la*th*z] thin strip of wood, or wire mesh. **lath'ing** *n*

lathe [lay*th*] *n* machine for turning object while it is being shaped.

lath·er [LA*TH*-ər] *n* 1 froth of soap and water. 2 frothy sweat. ◆ *v* 3 make frothy. 4 *inf* beat.

Lat·in [LAT-n] *n* 1 language of ancient Romans. ◆ *adj* 2 of ancient Romans, of, in their language. 3 denoting people speaking a language descended from Latin esp. Spanish. **La·ti·no** [lə-TEE-noh] *n, pl*

━━━━━━━━━┤ THESAURUS ├━━━━━━━━━

play, caper, cavort, have fun, make mischief

lash[1] *n* 1 = **blow**, hit, stripe, stroke, swipe (*inf*) ◆ *v* 2 = **whip**, beat, birch, flog, scourge, thrash 3 = **pound**, beat, buffet, dash, drum, hammer, smack, strike 4 = **scold**, attack, blast, censure, criticize, put down, upbraid

lash[2] *v* = **fasten**, bind, make fast, secure, strap, tie

lass *n* = **girl**, damsel, maid, maiden, young woman

last[1] *adj* 1 = **hindmost**, at the end, rearmost 2 = **most recent**, latest 3 = **final**, closing, concluding, terminal, ultimate ◆ *adv* 4 = **in the rear**, after, behind, bringing up the rear, in *or* at the end

last[2] *v* = **continue**, abide, carry on, endure, keep on, persist, remain, stand up, survive

lasting *adj* = **continuing**, abiding, durable, enduring, long-standing, long-term, perennial, permanent

latch *n* 1 = **fastening**, bar, bolt, catch,

hasp, hook, lock ◆ *v* 2 = **fasten**, bar, bolt, make fast, secure

late *adj* 1 = **overdue**, behind, behindhand, belated, delayed, last-minute, tardy 2 = **recent**, advanced, fresh, modern, new 3 = **dead**, deceased, defunct, departed, former, past ◆ *adv* 4 = **belatedly**, at the last minute, behindhand, behind time, dilatorily, tardily

lately *adv* = **recently**, in recent times, just now, latterly, not long ago, of late

lateness *n* = **delay**, belatedness, tardiness

latent *adj* = **hidden**, concealed, dormant, invisible, potential, undeveloped, unrealized

later *adv* = **afterwards**, after, by and by, in a while, in time, later on, subsequently, thereafter

lateral *adj* = **sideways**, edgeways, flanking

latest *adj* = **up-to-date**, cool (*inf*), current, fashionable, modern, most recent, newest, phat (*sl*), up-to-the-minute

lather *n* 1 = **froth**, bubbles, foam,

-nos person of Central or S Amer. descent.
lat·i·tude [LAT-i-tood] *n* **1** angular distance on meridian reckoned N or S from equator. **2** deviation from a standard. **3** freedom from restriction. **4** scope. ◆ *pl* **5** regions.
la·trine [lə-TREEN] *n* in army, etc., toilet.
lat·ter [LAT-ər] *adj* **1** second of two. **2** later. **3** more recent. **lat'ter·ly** *adv*
lat·tice [LAT-is] *n* **1** structure of strips of wood, metal, etc. crossing with spaces between. **2** window, gate, so made. **lat'ticed** *adj*
laud [lawd] *n* hymn, song, of praise. ◆ *vt* **laud'a·ble** *adj* praiseworthy. **laud'a·bly** *adv* **laud'a·to·ry** [-tor-ee] *adj* expressing, containing, praise.
lau·da·num [LAWD-n-əm] *n* tincture of opium.
laugh [laf] *vi* make sounds instinctively expressing amusement, merriment, or scorn. ◆ *n* **laugh'a·ble** *adj* ludicrous. **laugh'a·bly** *adv* **laugh'ter** *n* laughing gas nitrous oxide as anesthetic. **laughing stock** object of general derision.
launch¹ [lawnch] *vt* **1** set afloat. **2** set in motion. **3** start. **4** propel (missile, spacecraft) into space. **5** hurl, send. ◆ *vi* **6** enter on course. **launch'er** *n* installation, vehicle, device for launching rockets, missiles, etc.
launch² *n* large engine-driven boat.

laun·dry [LAWN-dree] *n, pl* **-dries 1** place for washing clothes, esp. as a business. **2** clothes, etc. for washing. **laun'der** *vt* wash and iron. **laun-der-ette'** *n* self-service laundry with coin-operated washing, drying machines.
lau·re·ate [LOR-ee-ət] *adj* **1** crowned with laurels. ◆ *n* **2** person honored for achievements. **poet laureate** poet honored as most eminent of country or region.
lau·rel [LOR-əl] *n* **1** glossy-leaved shrub, bay tree. ◆ *pl* **2** its leaves, emblem of victory or merit.
la·va [LAH-və] *n* molten matter thrown out by volcanoes, solidifying as it cools.
lav·a·to·ry [LAV-ə-tor-ee] *n* **-ries 1** washroom. **2** toilet.
lave [layv] *vt* **laved, lav·ing** wash, bathe.
lav·en·der [LAV-ən-dər] *n* **1** shrub with fragrant flowers. **2** color of the flowers, pale lilac.
lav·ish *adj* **1** giving or spending profusely. **2** very, too abundant. ◆ *vt* **3** spend, bestow, profusely.
law *n* **1** rule binding on community. **2** system of such rules. **3** legal science. **4** knowledge, administration of it. **5** *inf* (member of) police force. **6** general principle deduced from facts. **7** invariable sequence of events in nature. **law'ful** [-fəl] *adj* allowed by law. **law'ful·ly** *adv* **law'less** [-lis] *adj* **1** ignoring laws. **2** violent. **law'yer**

——————| T H E S A U R U S |——————

soapsuds, suds ◆ *v* **2** = **froth**, foam, soap
latitude *n* = **scope**, elbowroom, freedom, laxity, leeway, liberty, license, play
latter *adj* = **last-mentioned**, closing, concluding, last, second
latterly *adv* = **recently**, lately, of late
lattice *n* = **grid**, grating, grille, trellis
laudable *adj* = **praiseworthy**, admirable, commendable, creditable, excellent, meritorious, of note, worthy
laugh *v* **1** = **chuckle**, be in stitches, chortle, giggle, guffaw, snigger, split one's sides, titter ◆ *n* **2** = **chuckle**, chortle, giggle, guffaw, snigger, titter **3** *Inf* = **joke**, hoot (*inf*), lark, scream (*inf*)
laughable *adj* = **ridiculous**, absurd, derisory, farcical, ludicrous, nonsensical, preposterous, risible
laughing stock *n* = **figure of fun**, butt, target, victim
laugh off *v* = **disregard**, brush aside, dismiss, ignore, minimize, pooh-pooh,

shrug off
laughter *n* = **amusement**, glee, hilarity, merriment, mirth
launch *v* **1** = **propel**, discharge, dispatch, fire, project, send off, set in motion **2** = **begin**, commence, embark upon, inaugurate, initiate, instigate, introduce, open, start
laurels *pl n* = **glory**, credit, distinction, fame, honor, kudos, praise, prestige, recognition, renown
lavatory *n* = **toilet**, bathroom, latrine, powder room, (public) convenience, washroom, water closet, W.C.
lavish *adj* **1** = **plentiful**, abundant, copious, profuse, prolific **2** = **generous**, bountiful, free, liberal, munificent, open-handed, unstinting **3** = **extravagant**, exaggerated, excessive, immoderate, prodigal, unrestrained, wasteful, wild ◆ *v* **4** = **spend**, deluge, dissipate, expend, heap, pour, shower, squander, waste

n professional expert in law. **law'·a·bid·ing** [-bīd-ing] *adj* **1** obedient to laws. **2** well-behaved. **law'giv·er** *n* one who makes laws. **law'suit** [-soot] *n* prosecution of claim in court.

lawn[1] *n* stretch of carefully tended turf in garden, etc. **lawn tennis** tennis played on grass court.

lawn[2] *n* fine linen.

lawyer see LAW.

lax [laks] *adj* **1** not strict. **2** lacking precision. **3** loose, slack. **lax'a·tive** *adj* having loosening effect on bowels. ◆ *n* **lax'i·ty, lax'ness** *n* **1** slackness. **2** looseness of (moral) standards.

lay[1] *pt.* of LIE[1].

lay[2] *vt* **laid, lay·ing** deposit, set, cause to lie. **lay'er** *n* **1** single thickness of some substance, as stratum or coating on surface. **2** laying hen. **3** shoot of plant pegged down or partly covered with soil or plastic to encourage root growth. ◆ *vt* **4** propagate plants by making layers.

lay'down *n* in bridge, unbeatable hand held by declarer who plays with all cards exposed to view. **lay'out** *n* arrangement, esp. of matter for printing. **lay off** dismiss employees during slack period. **lay'off** *n* **lay on 1** provide, supply. **2** apply. **3** strike. **lay on hands** of healer, place hands on person to be cured. **lay out 1** display. **2** expend. **3** prepare for burial. **4** plan copy for printing, etc. **5** *sl* knock out. **6** *sl* criticize severely. **lay waste** devastate.

lay[3] *n* minstrel's song.

lay[4] *adj* **1** not clerical or professional. **2** of, or done, by persons not clergymen. **lay'man, lay'per·son** *n* ordinary person.

lay·ette [lay-ET] *n* clothes, etc. for newborn child.

laz·ar [LAZ-ər] *n* leper.

la·zy [LAY-zee] *adj* **-zi·er, -zi·est** averse to work, indolent. **laze** *vi* **lazed, laz·ing** indulge in laziness. **la'zi·ly** *adv* **la'zi·ness** *n*

lead[1] [leed] *v* **led, lead·ing** ◆ *vt* **1** guide, conduct. **2** persuade. **3** direct. **4** conduct

law *n* **1** = **constitution**, charter, code **2** = **rule**, act, command, commandment, decree, edict, order, ordinance, regulation, statute **3** = **principle**, axiom, canon, precept

law-abiding *adj* = **obedient**, compliant, dutiful, good, honest, honorable, lawful, orderly, peaceable

law-breaker *n* = **criminal**, convict, crook (*inf*), culprit, delinquent, felon, miscreant, offender, villain, wrongdoer

lawful *adj* = **legal**, authorized, constitutional, legalized, legitimate, licit, permissible, rightful, valid, warranted

lawless *adj* = **disorderly**, anarchic, chaotic, rebellious, riotous, unruly, wild

lawlessness *n* = **anarchy**, chaos, disorder, mob rule

lawsuit *n* = **case**, action, dispute, industrial tribunal, litigation, proceedings, prosecution, suit, trial

lawyer *n* = **legal adviser**, advocate, attorney, barrister (*chiefly Brit.*), counsel, counselor

lax *adj* = **slack**, careless, casual, lenient, negligent, overindulgent, remiss, slapdash, slipshod

lay[1] *v* **1** = **place**, deposit, leave, plant, put, set, set down, spread **2** = **arrange**, organize, position, set out **3** = **produce**, bear, deposit **4** = **put forward**, advance,

bring forward, lodge, offer, present, submit **5** = **attribute**, allocate, allot, ascribe, assign, impute **6** = **devise**, concoct, contrive, design, hatch, plan, plot, prepare, work out **7** = **bet**, gamble, give odds, hazard, risk, stake, wager

lay[2] *adj* **1** = **nonclerical**, secular **2** = **nonspecialist**, amateur, inexpert, nonprofessional

layer *n* = **tier**, row, seam, stratum, thickness

layman *n* = **amateur**, lay person, nonprofessional, outsider

layoff *n* = **dismissal**, discharge, unemployment

lay off *v* = **dismiss**, discharge, let go, pay off

lay on *v* = **provide**, cater (for), furnish, give, purvey, supply

layout *n* = **arrangement**, design, formation, outline, plan

lay out *v* **1** = **arrange**, design, display, exhibit, plan, spread out **2** *Inf* = **spend**, disburse, expend, fork out (*sl*), invest, pay, shell out (*inf*) **3** *Inf* = **knock out**, knock for six (*inf*), knock unconscious, KO or K.O. (*sl*)

laziness *n* = **idleness**, inactivity, indolence, slackness, sloth, sluggishness

lazy *adj* **1** = **idle**, inactive, indolent, inert, slack, slothful, slow, workshy **2** = **lethargic**, drowsy, languid, languorous, sleepy, slow-moving, sluggish, somnolent, torpid people. ♦ *vi* 5 be, go, play first. 6 result. 7 give access to. ♦ *n* 8 leading. 9 that which leads or is used to lead. 10 example. 11 front or principal place, role, etc. 12 cable bringing current to electric instrument. **lead'er** *n* 1 one who leads. 2 most important or prominent article in newspaper (also **leading article**). **lead'er·ship** *n* **leading question** question worded to prompt answer desired. **lead time** time between design of product and its production.

lead² [led] *n* 1 soft heavy gray metal. 2 plummet, used for sounding depths of water. 3 graphite. ♦ *vt* -ed, -ing 4 cover, weight or space with lead. **lead'en** *adj* 1 of, like lead. 2 heavy. 3 dull. **go over like a lead balloon** *sl* fail to arouse interest or support.

leaf [leef] *n, pl* **leaves** 1 organ of photosynthesis in plants, consisting of a flat, usu. green blade on stem. 2 two pages of book, etc. 3 thin sheet. 4 flap, movable part of table, etc. ♦ *vt* 5 turn through (pages, etc.) cursorily. **leaf'less** [-lis] *adj* **leaf'let** [-lit] *n* 1 small leaf. 2 single

sheet, often folded, of printed matter for distribution as e.g. notice or advertisement. **leaf'y** *adj* **leaf-i·er, leaf-i·est**

league¹ [leeg] *n* 1 agreement for mutual help. 2 parties to it. 3 federation of teams, etc. 4 *inf* class, level. ♦ *vi* **leagued, lea-guing** 5 unite in a league. 6 combine in an association. **lea'guer** *n* member of league

league² *n obs* measure of distance, about three miles.

leak [leek] *n* 1 hole, defect, that allows escape or entrance of liquid, gas, radiation, etc. 2 disclosure. ♦ *vi* 3 let fluid, etc. in or out. 4 (of fluid, etc.) find its way through leak. ♦ *vt* 5 let escape. ♦ *v* (allow to) become known little by little. **leak'age** [-ij] *n* 1 leaking. 2 gradual escape or loss. **leak'y** *adj* **leak-i·er, leak-i·est**

lean¹ [leen] *adj* -er, -est 1 lacking fat. 2 thin. 3 meager. 4 (of mixture of fuel and air) with too little fuel. ♦ *n* 5 lean part of meat, mainly muscular tissue.

lean² *v* **leaned, lean-ing** 1 rest against. 2 bend, incline. 3 tend (toward). 4 depend, rely (on). **leaning** *n* 1 tendency. **lean-to** *n*,

lead *v* 1 = **guide**, conduct, escort, pilot, precede, show the way, steer, usher 2 = **persuade**, cause, dispose, draw, incline, induce, influence, prevail, prompt 3 = **command**, direct, govern, head, manage, preside over, supervise 4 = **be ahead (of)**, blaze a trail, come first, exceed, excel, outdo, outstrip, surpass, transcend 5 = **live**, experience, have, pass, spend, undergo 6 = **result in**, bring on, cause, contribute, produce ♦ *n* 7 = **first place**, precedence, primacy, priority, supremacy, vanguard 8 = **advantage**, edge, margin, start 9 = **example**, direction, guidance, leadership, model 10 = **clue**, hint, indication, suggestion 11 = **leading role**, principal, protagonist, title role ♦ *adj* 12 = **main**, chief, first, foremost, head, leading, premier, primary, prime, principal

leader *n* = **principal**, boss (*inf*), captain, chief, chieftain, commander, director, guide, head, ringleader, ruler

leadership *n* 1 = **guidance**, direction, domination, management, running, superintendency 2 = **authority**, command, control, influence, initiative, pre-eminence, supremacy

leading *adj* = **main**, chief, dominant, first,

foremost, greatest, highest, primary, principal

lead on *v* = **entice**, beguile, deceive, draw on, lure, seduce, string along (*inf*), tempt

lead up to *v* = **introduce**, pave the way, prepare for

leaf *n* 1 = **frond**, blade 2 = **page**, folio, sheet ♦ *v* 3 **leaf through** = **browse**, flip, glance, riffle, skim, thumb (through)

leaflet *n* = **booklet**, brochure, circular, pamphlet

leafy *adj* = **green**, bosky (*literary*), shaded, shady, verdant

league *n* 1 = **association**, alliance, coalition, confederation, consortium, federation, fraternity, group, guild, partnership, union 2 = **class**, category, level

leak *n* 1 = **hole**, aperture, chink, crack, crevice, fissure, opening, puncture 2 = **drip**, leakage, percolation, seepage 3 = **disclosure**, divulgence ♦ *v* 4 = **drip**, escape, exude, ooze, pass, percolate, seep, spill, trickle 5 = **disclose**, divulge, give away, let slip, make known, make public, pass on, reveal, tell

leaky *adj* = **punctured**, cracked, holey, leaking, perforated, porous, split

pl **-tos** shed built against tree or post.
leap [leep] *v* **leaped** *or* **leapt, leap·ing 1**
spring, jump. **2** spring over. ◆ *n* **3** jump.
leap'frog *n* game in which player vaults
over another bending down. **leap year**
year with February 29th as extra day,
occurring every fourth year.
learn [lurn] *v* **learned** *or* **learnt, learn·ing 1**
gain skill, knowledge by study, practice or
teaching. **2** gain knowledge. **3** be taught. **4**
find out. **learn'ed** [LUR-nid] *adj* **1** erudite,
deeply read. **2** showing much learning.
learn'er *n* **learn'ing** *n* knowledge acquired
by study.
lease [lees] *n* **1** contract by which land or
property is rented for stated time by owner
to tenant. ◆ *vt* **leased, leas·ing 2** let, rent
by, take on lease.
leash [leesh] *n* **1** thong for holding a dog. **2**
curb. ◆ *vt* **3** hold on leash. **4** restrain.
least [leest] *adj* **1** smallest. **2** sup. of LITTLE.
◆ *n* **3** smallest one. ◆ *adv* **4** in smallest
degree.

leath·er [LETH-ər] *n* prepared skin of
animal. **leath'er·y** *adj* like leather, tough.
leave¹ [leev] *v* **left, leav·ing 1** go away
from. **2** deposit. **3** allow to remain. **4**
depart from. **5** entrust. **6** bequeath. **7** go
away, set out.
leave² *n* **1** permission. **2** permission to be
absent from work, duty. **3** period of such
absence. **4** formal parting.
leav·en [LEV-ən] *n* **1** yeast. **2** *fig*
transforming influence. ◆ *vt* **3** raise with
leaven. **4** influence. **5** modify.
lech·er [LECH-ər] *n* man given to lewdness.
lech'er·ous *adj* **1** lewd. **2** provoking lust. **3**
lascivious. **lech'er·ous·ly** *adv*
lech'er·ous·ness *n* **lech'er·y** *n, pl* **-er·ies**
lec·tern [LEK-tərn] *n* **1** reading desk, esp. in
church. **2** stand with slanted top to hold
book, notes, etc.
lec·ture [LEK-chər] *n* **1** instructive
discourse. **2** speech of reproof. ◆ *v* **-tured,
-tur·ing** *vi* **3** deliver discourse. ◆ *vt* **4**
reprove. **lec'tur·er** *n*

lean¹ *v* **1 = rest**, be supported, prop,
recline, repose **2 = bend**, heel, incline,
slant, slope, tilt, tip **3 = tend**, be disposed
to, be prone to, favor, prefer **4 lean on =
depend on**, count on, have faith in, rely
on, trust
lean² *adj* **1 = slim**, angular, bony, gaunt,
rangy, skinny, slender, spare, thin, wiry **2 =
unproductive**, barren, meager, poor,
scanty, unfruitful
leaning *n* **= tendency**, bent, bias,
disposition, inclination, partiality,
penchant, predilection, proclivity,
propensity
leap *v* **1 = jump**, bounce, bound, hop, skip,
spring ◆ *n* **2 = jump**, bound, spring, vault
3 = increase, escalation, rise, surge,
upsurge, upswing
learn *v* **1 = master**, grasp, pick up **2 =
memorize**, commit to memory, get off
pat, learn by heart **3 = discover**, ascertain,
detect, discern, find out, gather, hear,
understand
learned *adj* **= scholarly**, academic, erudite,
highbrow, intellectual, versed,
well-informed, well-read
learner *n* **= beginner**, apprentice,
neophyte, novice, tyro
learning *n* **= knowledge**, culture,
education, erudition, information, lore,
scholarship, study, wisdom

lease *v* **= hire**, charter, let, loan, rent
leash *n* **= lead**, rein, tether
least *adj* **= smallest**, fewest, lowest,
meanest, minimum, poorest, slightest,
tiniest
leathery *adj* **= tough**, hard, rough
leave¹ *v* **1 = depart**, decamp, disappear,
exit, go away, make tracks, move, pull out,
quit, retire, slope off, withdraw **2 = forget**,
leave behind, mislay **3 = cause**, deposit,
generate, produce, result in **4 = give up**,
abandon, drop, relinquish, renounce,
surrender **5 = entrust**, allot, assign, cede,
commit, consign, give over, refer **6 =
bequeath**, hand down, will
leave² *n* **1 = permission**, allowance,
authorization, concession, consent,
dispensation, freedom, liberty, sanction **2 =
holiday**, furlough, leave of absence,
sabbatical, time off, vacation **3 = parting**,
adieu, departure, farewell, good-bye,
leave-taking, retirement, withdrawal
leave out *v* **= omit**, blow off (*sl*), cast
aside, disregard, exclude, ignore, neglect,
overlook, reject
lecherous *adj* **= lustful**, lascivious, lewd,
libidinous, licentious, prurient, salacious
lecture *n* **1 = talk**, address, discourse,
instruction, lesson, speech **2 = rebuke**,
reprimand, reproof, scolding, talking-to
(*inf*), telling off (*inf*) ◆ *v* **3 = talk**, address,

ledge [lej] n 1 narrow shelf sticking out from wall, cliff, etc. 2 ridge, rock below surface of sea.

ledg·er [LEJ-ər] n 1 book of debit and credit accounts, chief account book of firm. 2 flat stone. **ledger line** Mus. short line, above or below stave.

lee n 1 shelter. 2 side of anything, esp. ship, away from wind. **lee'ward** [-wərd] adj, n 1 (on) lee side. ◆ adv 2 toward this side. **lee'way** n 1 leeward drift of ship. 2 room for free movement within limits.

leech n species of bloodsucking worm.

leek n plant like onion with long bulb and thick stem.

leer vi 1 glance with malign, sly, or lascivious expression. ◆ n 2 such glance.

lees [leez] pl n 1 sediment of wine, etc. 2 dregs.

left[1] adj 1 denotes the side that faces west when the front faces north. 2 opposite to the right. ◆ n 3 the left hand or part. 4 Politics reforming or radical party (also **left wing**) adv 5 on or toward the left. **left'ist** n, adj (person) of the political left.

left[2] pt./pp. of LEAVE.

leg n 1 one of limbs on which person or animal walks, runs, stands. 2 part of garment covering leg. 3 anything that supports, as leg of table. 4 stage of journey. **leg'gings** pl n covering of leather or other material for legs. **leg'gy** adj -gi·er, -gi·est 1 long-legged. 2 (of plants) straggling. **leg'warm·er** n one of pair of long knitted footless socks worn over tights when exercising.

leg·a·cy [LEG-ə-see] n, pl -cies 1 anything left by will, bequest. 2 thing handed down to successor.

le·gal [LEE-gəl] adj of, appointed or permitted by, or based on, law. **le·gal'i·ty** n **le·gal·ize** vt -ized, -iz·ing make legal.

leg·ate [LEG-it] n ambassador, esp. papal. **le·ga'tion** n 1 diplomatic minister and staff. 2 headquarters for these.

leg·a·tee [leg-ə-TEE] n recipient of legacy.

le·ga·to [lə-GAH-toh] adv Mus. smoothly.

leg·end [LEJ-ənd] n 1 traditional story or myth. 2 traditional literature. 3 famous, renowned, person or event. 4 inscription. **leg'end·ar·y** adj

leg·er·de·main [lej-ər-də-MAYN] n juggling, conjuring, sleight of hand, trickery.

leg·i·ble [LEJ-ə-bəl] adj easily read. **leg·i·bil'i·ty** n

le·gion [LEE-jən] n 1 body of infantry in Roman army. 2 various modern military bodies. 3 association of veterans. 4 large number. **le'gion·ar·y** adj, n **le·gion·naires'**

THESAURUS

discourse, expound, hold forth, speak, spout, teach 4 = **scold**, admonish, berate, castigate, censure, reprimand, reprove, tell off (inf)

ledge n = **shelf**, mantle, projection, ridge, sill, step

leer n, v = **grin**, gloat, goggle, ogle, smirk, squint, stare

lees pl n = **sediment**, deposit, dregs, grounds

leeway n = **room**, elbowroom, latitude, margin, play, scope, space

left adj 1 = **left-hand**, larboard (Nautical), port, sinistral 2 Of politics = **socialist**, leftist, left-wing, radical

leftover n = **remnant**, oddment, scrap

left-wing adj = **socialist**, communist, radical, red (inf)

leg n 1 = **limb**, lower limb, member, pin (inf), stump (inf) 2 = **support**, brace, prop, upright 3 = **stage**, lap, part, portion, section, segment, stretch 4 **pull someone's leg** Inf = **tease**, fool, kid (inf), make fun of, trick

legacy n = **bequest**, estate, gift, heirloom, inheritance

legal adj 1 = **legitimate**, allowed, authorized, constitutional, lawful, licit, permissible, sanctioned, valid 2 = **judicial**, forensic, juridical

legality n = **legitimacy**, lawfulness, rightfulness, validity

legalize v = **allow**, approve, authorize, decriminalize, legitimate, legitimize, license, permit, sanction, validate

legation n = **delegation**, consulate, embassy, representation

legend n 1 = **myth**, fable, fiction, folk tale, saga, story, tale 2 = **celebrity**, luminary, megastar (inf), phenomenon, prodigy 3 = **inscription**, caption, motto

legendary adj 1 = **mythical**, apocryphal, fabled, fabulous, fictitious, romantic, traditional 2 = **famous**, celebrated, famed, illustrious, immortal, renowned, well-known

legibility n = **clarity**, neatness, readability

legible adj = **clear**, decipherable, distinct,

disease [-NAIRZ] serious bacterial disease similar to pneumonia.

leg·is·la·tor [LEJ-is-lay-tər] n maker of laws. **leg'is·late** vi **-lat·ed, -lat·ing** make laws. **leg·is·la'tion** n 1 act of legislating. 2 law or laws that are made. **leg'is·la·tive** adj **leg'is·la·ture** [-chər] n body that makes laws of a country or state.

le·git·i·mate [lə-JIT-ə-mit] adj 1 born in wedlock. 2 lawful, regular. 3 fairly deduced. **le·git'i·ma·cy** [-mə-see] n **le·git'i·mize** vt **-mized, -miz·ing** make legitimate.

le·gu·mi·nous [li-GYOO-mə-nəs] adj (of plants) pod-bearing. **leg·ume** [LEG-yoom] n leguminous plant.

lei [lay] n garland of flowers.

lei·sure [LEE-zhər] n 1 freedom from occupation. 2 spare time. **lei'sure·ly** adj 1 deliberate, unhurried. ◆ adv 2 slowly. **lei'sured** adj with plenty of spare time.

leit·mo·tif [LĪT-moh-teef] n Mus. recurring theme associated with some person, situation, thought.

lem·ming [LEM-ing] n rodent of northern regions.

lem·on [LEM-ən] n 1 pale yellow acid fruit. 2 tree bearing it. 3 its color. 4 inf useless or

defective person or thing. **lem·on·ade'** [-AYD] n drink made from lemon juice.

le·mur [LEE-mər] n nocturnal animal like monkey.

lend vt **lent, lend·ing** 1 give temporary use of. 2 let out for hire or interest. 3 give, bestow. **lends itself to** is suitable for.

length [lengkth] n 1 quality of being long. 2 measurement from end to end. 3 duration. 4 extent. 5 piece of a certain length. **length'en** v 1 make, become, longer. 2 draw out. **length'i·ly** adv **length'wise** adj, adv **length'y** adj **length·i·er, length·i·est** (over)long. **at length** 1 in full detail. 2 at last.

le·ni·ent [LEE-nee-ənt] adj mild, tolerant, not strict. **le'ni·en·cy** n

len·i·ty [LEN-i-tee] n, pl **-ties** 1 mercy. 2 clemency.

lens [lenz] n, pl **-es** piece of glass or similar material with one or both sides curved, used to converge or diverge light rays in cameras, eyeglasses, telescopes, etc.

lent pt./pp. of LEND.

Lent n period of fasting from Ash Wednesday to Easter. **Lent'en** adj of, in, or suitable to Lent.

len'til n edible seed of leguminous plant.

THESAURUS

easy to read, neat, readable

legion n 1 = **army**, brigade, company, division, force, troop 2 = **multitude**, drove, horde, host, mass, myriad, number, throng

legislation n 1 = **lawmaking**, enactment, prescription, regulation 2 = **law**, act, bill, charter, measure, regulation, ruling, statute

legislative adj = **law-making**, judicial, law-giving

legislator n = **lawmaker**, lawgiver

legislature n = **parliament**, assembly, chamber, congress, senate

legitimate adj 1 = **legal**, authentic, authorized, genuine, kosher (inf), lawful, licit, rightful 2 = **reasonable**, admissible, correct, justifiable, logical, sensible, valid, warranted, well-founded ◆ v 3 = **authorize**, legalize, legitimize, permit, pronounce lawful, sanction

legitimize v = **legalize**, authorize, permit, sanction

leisure n = **spare time**, ease, freedom, free time, liberty, recreation, relaxation, rest

leisurely adj = **unhurried**, comfortable,

easy, gentle, lazy, relaxed, slow

lend v 1 = **loan**, advance 2 = **add**, bestow, confer, give, grant, impart, provide, supply 3 **lend itself to** = **suit**, be appropriate, be serviceable

length n 1 Of linear extent = **distance**, extent, longitude, measure, reach, span 2 Of time = **duration**, period, space, span, stretch, term 3 = **piece**, measure, portion, section, segment 4 **at length: a = in detail**, completely, fully, in depth, thoroughly, to the full **b = for a long time**, for ages, for hours, interminably **c = at last**, at long last, eventually, finally, in the end

lengthen v = **extend**, continue, draw out, elongate, expand, increase, prolong, protract, spin out, stretch

lengthy adj = **long**, drawn-out, extended, interminable, long-drawn-out, long-winded, prolonged, protracted, tedious

leniency n = **tolerance**, clemency, compassion, forbearance, indulgence, mercy, moderation, pity, quarter

lenient adj = **tolerant**, compassionate, forbearing, forgiving, indulgent, kind,

len·tic·u·lar *adj* like lentil.

len·to [LEN-toh] *adv Mus.* slowly.

le·o·nine [LEE-ə-nīn] *adj* like a lion.

leop·ard [LEP-ərd] *n* large, spotted, carnivorous animal of cat family, like panther.

le·o·tard [LEE-ə-tahrd] *n* tight-fitting garment covering most of body, worn by acrobats, dancers, etc.

lep·er [LEP-ər] *n* 1 one suffering from leprosy. 2 person ignored or despised. **lep'ro·sy** [-rə-see] *n* disease attacking nerves and skin resulting in loss of feeling in affected parts. **lep'rous** [-rəs] *adj*

lep·re·chaun [LEP-rə-kawn] *n* mischievous elf of Irish folklore.

les·bi·an [LEZ-bee-ən] *n* a homosexual woman. **les'bi·an·ism** *n*

lese maj·es·ty [LEEZ] *n* 1 treason. 2 taking of liberties.

le·sion [LEE-zhən] *n* injury, injurious change in texture or action of an organ of the body.

less *adj* 1 comp. of LITTLE. 2 not so much. ◆ *n* 3 smaller part, quantity. 4 a lesser amount. ◆ *adv* 5 to a smaller extent or degree. ◆ *prep* 6 after deducting, minus. **less'en** *vt* 1 diminish. 2 reduce. **less'er** *adj* 1 less. 2 smaller. 3 minor.

les·see [le-SEE] *n* one to whom lease is granted.

les·son [LES-ən] *n* 1 installment of course of instruction. 2 content of this. 3 experience that teaches. 4 portion of Scripture read in church.

les·sor [LES-or] *n* grantor of a lease.

lest *conj* 1 in order that not. 2 for fear that.

let[1] *v* let, let·ting ◆ *vt* 1 allow, enable, cause. 2 allow to escape. 3 grant use of for rent, lease. ◆ *vi* 4 be leased. ◆ *v aux* 5 used to express a proposal, command, threat, assumption.

let[2] *n* 1 in law, obstacle or hindrance. 2 in tennis, etc., minor infringement, esp. obstruction of ball by net on service, requiring replaying of point.

le·thal [LEE-thəl] *adj* deadly.

leth·ar·gy [LETH-ər-jee] *n, pl* -gies 1 apathy, want of energy or interest. 2 unnatural drowsiness. **le·thar'gic** *adj* **le·thar'gi·cal·ly** *adv*

let·ter [LET-ər] *n* 1 alphabetical symbol. 2 written message. 3 strict meaning, interpretation. ◆ *pl* 4 literature, knowledge of books. ◆ *vt* 5 mark with, in letters. **let'tered** *adj* learned. **let'ter·press** *n* 1 process of printing from raised type. 2 matter printed in this way.

let·tuce [LET-is] *n* plant grown for use in salad.

merciful, sparing

lesbian *adj* = **homosexual**, gay, sapphic

less *adj* 1 = **smaller**, shorter ◆ *prep* 2 = **minus**, excepting, lacking, subtracting, without

lessen *v* = **reduce**, contract, decrease, diminish, ease, lower, minimize, narrow, shrink

lesser *adj* = **minor**, inferior, less important, lower, secondary

lesson *n* 1 = **class**, coaching, instruction, period, schooling, teaching, tutoring 2 = **example**, deterrent, message, moral

let[1] *v* 1 = **allow**, authorize, entitle, give permission, give the go-ahead, permit, sanction, tolerate 2 = **lease**, hire, rent

let[2] *n* = **hindrance**, constraint, impediment, interference, obstacle, obstruction, prohibition, restriction

letdown *n* = **disappointment**, anticlimax, blow, comedown (*inf*), setback, washout (*inf*)

let down *v* = **disappoint**, disenchant, disillusion, dissatisfy, fail, fall short, leave in the lurch, leave stranded

lethal *adj* = **deadly**, dangerous, destructive, devastating, fatal, mortal, murderous, virulent

lethargic *adj* = **sluggish**, apathetic, drowsy, dull, languid, listless, sleepy, slothful

lethargy *n* = **sluggishness**, apathy, drowsiness, inertia, languor, lassitude, listlessness, sleepiness, sloth

let off *v* 1 = **fire**, detonate, discharge, explode 2 = **emit**, exude, give off, leak, release 3 = **excuse**, absolve, discharge, exempt, exonerate, forgive, pardon, release, spare

let on *v* = **reveal**, admit, disclose, divulge, give away, let the cat out of the bag (*inf*), make known, say

let out *v* 1 = **emit**, give vent to, produce 2 = **release**, discharge, free, let go, liberate

letter *n* 1 = **character**, sign, symbol 2 = **message**, communication, dispatch, epistle, line, missive, note

let-up *n* = **lessening**, break, breathing

leu·co·cyte [LOO-kə-sīt] *n* one of white blood corpuscles.

leu·ke·mi·a [loo-KEE-mee-ə] *n* a progressive blood disease.

Lev. Leviticus.

lev'ee¹ *n Hist.* 1 reception held by sovereign on rising. 2 reception in someone's honor.

levee² *n* river embankment, natural or artificial.

lev·el [LEV-əl] *adj* 1 horizontal. 2 even in surface. 3 consistent in style, quality, etc. ♦ *n* 4 horizontal line or surface. 5 instrument for showing, testing horizontal plane. 6 position on scale. 7 standard, grade. 8 horizontal passage in mine. ♦ *v* -eled, -el·ing 9 make level. 10 bring to same level. 11 knock down. 12 aim (gun, or, *fig* accusation, etc.). 13 *inf* (esp. with *with*) be honest, frank. **le'vel·head'ed** [-HED-id] *adj* not apt to be carried away by emotion.

lev·er [LEV-ər] *n* 1 rigid bar pivoted about a fulcrum to transfer a force with mechanical advantage. 2 handle pressed, pulled, etc. 3 to operate something. ♦ *vt* 4 pry, move, with lever. **lever'age** [-ij] *n* 1 action, power of lever. 2 influence. 3 power to accomplish something. 4 advantage.

le·vi·a·than [lə-Vī-ə-thən] *n* 1 sea monster. 2 anything huge or formidable.

lev·i·ta·tion [lev-i-TAY-shən] *n* the power of raising a solid body into the air supernaturally. **lev'i·tate** *v* -tat·ed, -tat·ing (cause to) do this.

lev·i·ty [LEV-i-tee] *n, pl* -ties 1 inclination to make a joke of serious matters, frivolity. 2 facetiousness.

lev·y [LEV-ee] *vt* **lev·ied, lev·y·ing** 1 impose (tax). 2 raise (troops). ♦ *n, pl* **lev·ies** 3 imposition or collection of taxes. 4 enrolling of troops. 5 amount, number levied.

lewd [lood] *adj* -er, -est 1 lustful. 2 indecent. **lewd'ly** *adv* **lewd'ness** *n*

lex·i·con [LEK-si-kon] *n* dictionary. **lex·i·cog'ra·pher** [-rə-fər] *n* writer of dictionaries. **lex·i·cog'ra·phy** *n*

Li *Chem.* lithium.

li·a·ble [Lī-ə-bəl] *adj* 1 answerable. 2 exposed (to). 3 subject (to). 4 likely (to). **li·a·bil'i·ty** *n* 1 state of being liable, obligation. 2 hindrance, disadvantage. 3 (*pl* -ties) debts.

li·ai·son [lee-AY-zon] *n* 1 union. 2

THESAURUS

space, interval, lull, pause, remission, respite, slackening

let up *v* = **stop**, abate, decrease, diminish, ease (up), moderate, relax, slacken, subside

level *adj* 1 = **horizontal**, flat 2 = **even**, consistent, plain, smooth, uniform 3 = **equal**, balanced, commensurate, comparable, equivalent, even, neck and neck, on a level playing field (*inf*), on a par, proportionate ♦ *v* 4 = **flatten**, even off or out, plane, smooth 5 = **equalize**, balance, even up 6 = **raze**, bulldoze, demolish, destroy, devastate, flatten, knock down, pull down, tear down 7 = **direct**, aim, focus, point, train ♦ *n* 8 = **position**, achievement, degree, grade, rank, stage, standard, standing, status 9 **on the level** *Inf* = **honest**, above board, fair, genuine, square, straight

level-headed *adj* = **steady**, balanced, calm, collected, composed, cool, sensible, unflappable (*inf*)

lever *n* 1 = **handle**, bar ♦ *v* 2 = **prise**, force

leverage *n* = **influence**, authority, clout (*inf*), pull (*inf*), weight

levity *n* = **light-heartedness**, facetiousness, flippancy, frivolity, silliness, skittishness, triviality

levy *v* 1 = **impose**, charge, collect, demand, exact 2 = **conscript**, call up, mobilize, muster, raise ♦ *n* 3 = **imposition**, assessment, collection, exaction, gathering 4 = **tax**, duty, excise, fee, tariff, toll

lewd *adj* = **indecent**, bawdy, lascivious, libidinous, licentious, lustful, obscene, pornographic, smutty, wanton, X-rated

lewdness *n* = **indecency**, bawdiness, carnality, debauchery, depravity, lasciviousness, lechery, licentiousness, obscenity, pornography, wantonness

liability *n* 1 = **responsibility**, accountability, answerability, culpability 2 = **debt**, debit, obligation 3 = **disadvantage**, burden, drawback, encumbrance, handicap, hindrance, inconvenience, millstone, nuisance

liable *adj* 1 = **responsible**, accountable, answerable, obligated 2 = **vulnerable**, exposed, open, subject, susceptible 3 = **likely**, apt, disposed, inclined, prone, tending

liaise *v* = **link**, communicate, keep contact, mediate connection. **3** intimacy, esp. secret. **4** person who keeps others in touch with one another.

li·ar [LĪ-ər] *n* one who tells lies.

li·ba·tion [lī-BAY-shən] *n* **1** drink poured as offering to the gods. **2** *facetious* **3** drink of whiskey.

li·bel [LĪ-bəl] *n* **1** published statement falsely damaging person's reputation. ◆ *vt* **-beled, -bel·ing 2** defame falsely. **li'bel·ous** *adj* defamatory.

lib·er·al [LIB-ər-əl] *adj* **1** of political party favoring democratic reforms or favoring individual freedom. **2** generous. **3** tolerant. **4** abundant. **5** (of education) designed to develop general cultural interests. ◆ *n* **6** one who has liberal ideas or opinions. **lib'er·al·ism** *n* **lib·er·al'i·ty** *n, pl* **-ties** munificence. **lib'er·al·ize** *vt* **-ized, -iz·ing**

lib·er·ate [LIB-ə-rayt] *vt* **-at·ed, -at·ing** set free. **lib·er·a'tion** *n*

lib·er·tar·i·an [lib-ər-TAIR-ee-ən] *n* believer in freedom of thought, etc., or in free will. ◆ *adj*

lib·er·tine [LIB-ər-teen] *n* **1** morally

dissolute person. ◆ *adj* **2** dissolute.

lib·er·ty [LIB-ər-tee] *n* **1** freedom. **2** (*pl* **-ties**) rights, privileges. **at liberty 1** free. **2** having the right. **3** out of work. **take liberties (with)** be presumptuous.

li·bi·do [li-BEE-doh] *n, pl* **-dos 1** life force. **2** emotional craving, esp. of sexual origin. **li·bid'i·nous** *adj* lustful.

li·brar·y [LĪ-hrer-ee] *n, pl* **-brar·ies 1** room, building where books are kept. **2** collection of books, phonograph records, etc. **3** reading, writing room in house. **li·brar'i·an** *n* keeper of library.

li·bret·to [li-BRET-oh] *n, pl* **-tos** *or* **-ti** [-tee] words of an opera. **li·bret'tist** *n*

lice *n* see LOUSE.

li·cense [LĪ-səns] *n* **1** (document, certificate, giving) leave, permission. **2** excessive liberty. **3** dissoluteness. **4** writer's, artist's intentional transgression of rules of art (also **poetic license**). **li'cense** *vt* **-censed, -cens·ing** grant license to. **li·cen·see'** *n* holder of license.

li·cen·tious [lī-SEN-shəs] *adj* **1** dissolute. **2** sexually immoral.

liaison *n* **1** = **communication**, connection, contact, hook-up, interchange **2** = **affair**, amour, entanglement, intrigue, love affair, romance

liar *n* = **falsifier**, fabricator, fibber, perjurer

libel *n* **1** = **defamation**, aspersion, calumny, denigration, smear ◆ *v* **2** = **defame**, blacken, malign, revile, slur, smear, vilify

libelous *adj* = **defamatory**, derogatory, false, injurious, malicious, scurrilous, untrue

liberal *adj* **1** = **progressive**, libertarian, radical, reformist **2** = **generous**, beneficent, bountiful, charitable, kind, open-handed, open-hearted, unstinting **3** = **tolerant**, broad-minded, indulgent, permissive **4** = **abundant**, ample, bountiful, copious, handsome, lavish, munificent, plentiful, profuse, rich

liberality *n* **1** = **generosity**, beneficence, benevolence, bounty, charity, kindness, largesse *or* largess, munificence, philanthropy **2** = **toleration**, broad-mindedness, latitude, liberalism, libertarianism, permissiveness

liberalize *v* = **relax**, ease, loosen, moderate, modify, slacken, soften

liberate *v* = **free**, deliver, emancipate, let loose, let out, release, rescue, set free

liberation *n* = **deliverance**, emancipation, freedom, freeing, liberty, release

liberator *n* = **deliverer**, emancipator, freer, redeemer, rescuer, savior

libertine *n* = **reprobate**, debauchee, lecher, profligate, rake, roué, sensualist, voluptuary, womanizer

liberty *n* **1** = **freedom**, autonomy, emancipation, immunity, independence, liberation, release, self-determination, sovereignty **2** = **impertinence**, impropriety, impudence, insolence, presumption **3 at liberty** = **free**, on the loose, unrestricted

libidinous *adj* = **lustful**, carnal, debauched, lascivious, lecherous, sensual, wanton

license *n* **1** = **certificate**, charter, permit, warrant **2** = **permission**, authority, authorization, blank check, carte blanche, dispensation, entitlement, exemption, immunity, leave, liberty, right **3** = **latitude**, freedom, independence, leeway, liberty **4** = **laxity**, excess, immoderation, indulgence, irresponsibility

license *v* = **permit**, accredit, allow, authorize, certify, empower, sanction, warrant

licentious *adj* = **promiscuous**, abandoned,

li·chen [LĪ-kən] *n* small flowerless plants forming crust on rocks, trees, etc.

lick [lik] *vt* **1** pass the tongue over. **2** touch lightly. **3** *inf* defeat. **4** *inf* flog, beat. ◆ *n* **5** act of licking. **6** small amount (esp. of work, etc.). **7** block or natural deposit of salt or other chemical licked by cattle, etc. **lick'ing** *n* **1** beating. **2** defeat.

lic·o·rice [LIK-ər-ish] *n* **1** black substance used in medicine and as a candy. **2** plant, its root from which it is obtained.

lid *n* **1** movable cover. **2** cover of the eye. **3** *sl* hat.

lie[1] [lī] *vi* **lay, lain, ly·ing 1** be horizontal, at rest. **2** be situated. **3** remain, be in certain state or position. **4** exist, be found. **5** recline. ◆ *n* **6** manner, direction, position in which thing lies. **7** of a golf ball, its position relative to difficulty of hitting it.

lie[2] *vi* **lied, ly·ing 1** make false statement knowingly. ◆ *n* **2** falsehood. **li'ar** [-ər] *n* white lie untruth said without evil intent. **give the lie to** disprove.

lien [leen] *n* right to hold another's property until claim is met.

lieu [loo] *n* place. **in lieu of** instead of.

lieu·ten·ant [loo-TEN-ənt] *n* **1** deputy. **2** *Army, Marines* rank below captain. **3** *Navy* rank below lieutenant commander. **4** police, fire department officer.

life [līf] *n, pl* **lives 1** active principle of existence of animals and plants, animate existence. **2** time of its lasting. **3** history of such existence. **4** way of living. **5** vigor,

vivacity. **life'less** [-lis] *adj* **1** dead. **2** inert. **3** dull. **life'long** *adj* lasting a lifetime. **life belt, life jacket** buoyant device to keep afloat person in danger of drowning. **life style** particular attitudes, habits, etc. of person or group. **life-support** *adj* of equipment or treatment necessary to keep a person alive. **life'time** *n* length of time person, animal, or object lives or functions.

lift *vt* **1** raise in position, status, mood, volume, etc. **2** take up and remove. **3** exalt spiritually. **4** *inf* steal. ◆ *vi* **5** rise. ◆ *n* **6** raising apparatus. **7** ride in car, etc., as passenger. **8** force of air acting at right angles on aircraft wing, so lifting it. **9** *inf* feeling of cheerfulness, uplift.

lig·a·ment [LIG-ə-mənt] *n* band of tissue joining bones. **lig'a·ture** [-chər] *n* **1** anything that binds. **2** thread for tying up blood vessels or for removing tumors.

light[1] [līt] *adj* **-er, -est 1** of, or bearing, little weight. **2** not severe. **3** gentle. **4** easy, requiring little effort. **5** trivial. **6** (of industry) producing small, usu. consumer goods, using light machinery. ◆ *adv* **7** in light manner. ◆ *v* **light-ed** *or* **lit, light·ing** ◆ *vi* **8** alight (from vehicle, etc.). **9** come by chance (upon). **light'en** *vt* reduce, remove (load, etc.). **lights** *pl n* lungs of animals as food. **light'head·ed** *adj* **1** dizzy, inclined to faint. **2** delirious. **light'heart·ed** *adj* carefree. **light'weight** *n, adj* **1** (person) of little weight or importance. **2** boxer weighing between 126 and 135 pounds

---

THESAURUS

debauched, dissolute, immoral, lascivious, lustful, sensual, wanton

lick *v* **1** = taste, lap, tongue **2** *Of flames* = flicker, dart, flick, play over, ripple, touch **3** *Sl* = beat, defeat, master, outdo, outstrip, overcome, rout, trounce, vanquish ◆ *n* **4** = dab, bit, stroke, touch **5** *Inf* = pace, clip (*inf*), rate, speed

lie[1] *v* **1** = falsify, dissimulate, equivocate, fabricate, fib, prevaricate, tell untruths ◆ *n* **2** = falsehood, deceit, fabrication, fib, fiction, invention, prevarication, untruth

lie[2] *v* **1** = recline, loll, lounge, repose, rest, sprawl, stretch out **2** = be situated, be, be placed, exist, extend

life *n* **1** = being, sentience, vitality **2** = existence, being, lifetime, span, time **3** = biography, autobiography, confessions, history, life story, memoirs, story **4** = behavior, conduct, life style, way of life **5** =

liveliness, animation, energy, high spirits, spirit, verve, vigor, vitality, vivacity, zest

lifeless *adj* **1** = dead, deceased, defunct, extinct, inanimate **2** = dull, colorless, flat, lackluster, lethargic, listless, sluggish, wooden **3** = unconscious, comatose, dead to the world (*inf*), insensible

lifelike *adj* = realistic, authentic, exact, faithful, natural, true-to-life, vivid

lifelong *adj* = long-standing, enduring, lasting, long-lasting, perennial, persistent

lifetime *n* = existence, career, day(s), span, time

lift *v* **1** = raise, draw up, elevate, hoist, pick up, uplift, upraise **2** = revoke, annul, cancel, countermand, end, remove, rescind, stop, terminate **3** = disappear, be dispelled, disperse, dissipate, vanish ◆ *n* **4** = ride, drive, run **5** = boost, encouragement, pick-me-up, shot in the arm (*inf*)

(56.7 to 61 kg).

light² *n* **1** electromagnetic radiation by which things are visible. **2** source of this, lamp. **3** window. **4** light part of anything. **5** means or act of setting fire to. **6** understanding. ♦ *pl* **7** traffic lights. ♦ *adj* **-er, -est 8** bright. **9** pale, not dark. ♦ *v* **light·ed** or **lit, light·ing 10** set burning. **11** give light to. **12** take fire. **13** brighten. **light'en** *vt* make light. **light'ing** *n* apparatus for supplying artificial light. **light'ning** *n* visible discharge of electricity in atmosphere. **light'house** *n* tower with a light to guide ships. **light-year** *n Astronomy* distance light travels in one year, about six trillion miles.

light·er [Lĭ-tar] *n* **1** device for lighting cigarettes, etc. **2** flat-bottomed boat for unloading ships.

like¹ [līk] *adj* **1** resembling. **2** similar. **3** characteristic of. ♦ *adv* **4** in the manner of. ♦ *pron* **5** similar thing. **like'li·hood** [-huud] *n* probability. **like'ly** *adj* **-li·er, -li·est 1** probable. **2** hopeful, promising. ♦ *adv* **3** probably. **lik'en** *vt* compare. **like'ness** *n* **1** resemblance. **2** portrait. **like'wise** *adv* in like manner.

like² *vt* **liked, lik·ing** find agreeable, enjoy, love. **lik'a·ble** *adj* **liking** *n* **1** fondness. **2** inclination, taste.

light¹ *n* **1** = **brightness**, brilliance, glare, gleam, glint, glow, illumination, luminosity, radiance, shine **2** = **lamp**, beacon, candle, flare, lantern, taper, torch **3** = **aspect**, angle, context, interpretation, point of view, slant, vantage point, viewpoint **4** = **match**, flame, lighter ♦ *adj* **5** = **bright**, brilliant, illuminated, luminous, lustrous, shining, well-lit **6** = **pale**, bleached, blond, faded, fair, pastel ♦ *v* **7** = **ignite**, inflame, kindle **8** = **illuminate**, brighten, light up

light² *adj* **1** = **insubstantial**, airy, buoyant, flimsy, portable, slight, underweight **2** = **weak**, faint, gentle, indistinct, mild, moderate, slight, soft **3** = **insignificant**, inconsequential, inconsiderable, scanty, slight, small, trifling, trivial **4** = **nimble**, agile, graceful, lithe, sprightly, sylphlike **5** = **light-hearted**, amusing, entertaining, frivolous, funny, humorous, witty **6** = **digestible**, frugal, modest ♦ *v* **7** = **settle**, alight, land, perch **8 light on** or **upon** = **come across**, chance upon, discover, encounter, find, happen upon, hit upon, stumble on

lighten¹ *v* = **brighten**, become light, illuminate, irradiate, light up

lighten² *v* **1** = **ease**, allay, alleviate, ameliorate, assuage, lessen, mitigate, reduce, relieve **2** = **cheer**, brighten, buoy up, lift, perk up, revive

light-headed *adj* = **faint**, dizzy, giddy, hazy, vertiginous, woozy (*inf*)

light-hearted *adj* = **carefree**, blithe, cheerful, happy-go-lucky, jolly, jovial, playful, upbeat (*inf*)

lightly *adv* **1** = **gently**, delicately, faintly, slightly, softly **2** = **moderately**, sparingly,

sparsely, thinly **3** = **easily**, effortlessly, readily, simply **4** = **carelessly**, breezily, flippantly, frivolously, heedlessly, thoughtlessly

lightweight *adj* = **unimportant**, inconsequential, insignificant, paltry, petty, slight, trifling, trivial, worthless

likable, likeable *adj* = **attractive**, agreeable, amiable, appealing, charming, engaging, nice, pleasant, sympathetic

like¹ *adj* = **similar**, akin, alike, analogous, corresponding, equivalent, identical, parallel, same

like² *v* **1** = **enjoy**, be fond of, be keen on, be partial to, delight in, go for, love, relish, revel in **2** = **admire**, appreciate, approve, cherish, esteem, hold dear, prize, take to **3** = **wish**, care to, choose, desire, fancy, feel inclined, prefer, want **4** *Inf* = **be attracted to**, be captivated by, be turned on by (*inf*), lust after, take a liking to, take to

likelihood *n* = **probability**, chance, possibility, prospect

likely *adj* **1** = **inclined**, apt, disposed, liable, prone, tending **2** = **probable**, anticipated, expected, odds-on, on the cards, to be expected **3** = **plausible**, believable, credible, feasible, possible, reasonable **4** = **promising**, hopeful, up-and-coming

liken *v* = **compare**, equate, match, parallel, relate, set beside

likeness *n* **1** = **resemblance**, affinity, correspondence, similarity **2** = **portrait**, depiction, effigy, image, picture, representation

likewise *adv* = **similarly**, in like manner, in the same way

liking *n* = **fondness**, affection, inclination,

li·lac [LĪ-lək] n 1 shrub bearing purple or white flowers. 2 pale reddish purple. ♦ adj 3 of this color.

Lil·li·pu·tian [lil-i-PYOO-shən] adj 1 diminutive. ♦ n 2 very small person.

lilt v 1 sing merrily. 2 move lightly. ♦ n 3 rhythmical effect in music, swing. lilt'ing adj

lil·y [LIL-ee] n, pl lil·ies bulbous flowering plant. lil·y-white adj 1 white. 2 pure, above reproach. 3 of an organization or community, forbidding admission to blacks.

limb¹ [lim] n 1 arm or leg. 2 wing. 3 branch of tree.

limb² n 1 edge of sun or moon. 2 edge of sextant.

lim·ber¹ [LIM-bər] n detachable front of gun carriage.

lim·ber² adj pliant, lithe. limber up loosen stiff muscles by exercise.

lim·bo¹ [LIM-boh] n, pl -bos 1 supposed region intermediate between heaven and hell for the unbaptized. 2 intermediate, indeterminate place or state.

lim·bo² n, pl -bos West Indian dance in which dancers pass under a bar.

lime¹ [līm] n 1 any of certain calcium compounds used in making fertilizer, cement. ♦ vt limed, lim·ing 2 treat (land) with lime. lime'light n 1 formerly, intense white light obtained by heating lime. 2 glare of publicity. lime'stone n sedimentary rock used in building.

lime² n small acid fruit like lemon.

lim·er·ick [LIM-ər-ik] n self-contained, nonsensical, humorous verse of five lines.

lim'it n 1 utmost extent or duration. 2 boundary. ♦ vt 3 restrict, restrain, bound. lim·i·ta'tion n lim'it·less adj

lim·ou·sine [LIM-ə-zeen] n large, luxurious car.

limp¹ adj -er, -est without firmness or stiffness. limp'ly adv

limp² vi 1 walk lamely. ♦ n 2 limping gait.

lim'pid adj 1 clear. 2 translucent. lim·pid'i·ty n

linch'pin n 1 pin to hold wheel on its axle. 2 essential person or thing.

line [līn] n 1 long narrow mark. 2 stroke made with pen, etc. 3 continuous length without breadth. 4 row. 5 series, course. 6 telephone connection. 7 progeny. 8 province of activity. 9 shipping company. 10 railroad track. 11 any class of goods. 12 cord. 13 string. 14 wire. 15 advice, guidance. ♦ vt lined, lin·ing 16 cover inside. 17 mark with lines. 18 bring into line. 19 be, form border, edge. lin'e·age [-ee-ij] n descent from, descendants of an ancestor. lin'e·al adj 1 of lines. 2 in direct line of descent. lin'e·a·ment n feature of face. lin'e·ar adj of, in lines. lin·er [LĪN-ər] n large ship or aircraft of passenger line. line dancing form of social dancing performed by rows of people to popular music. lines'man [-mən] n Sports official who helps referee, umpire. get a line on obtain all relevant information about.

lin·en [LIN-ən] adj 1 made of flax. ♦ n 2

---

love, partiality, penchant, preference, soft spot, taste, weakness

limb n 1 = part, appendage, arm, extremity, leg, member, wing 2 = branch, bough, offshoot, projection, spur

limelight n = publicity, attention, celebrity, fame, prominence, public eye, recognition, stardom, the spotlight

limit n 1 = breaking point, deadline, end, ultimate 2 = boundary, border, edge, frontier, perimeter ♦ v 3 = restrict, bound, check, circumscribe, confine, curb, ration, restrain

limitation n = restriction, check, condition, constraint, control, curb, qualification, reservation, restraint

limited adj = restricted, bounded, checked, circumscribed, confined, constrained, controlled, curbed, finite

limitless adj = infinite, boundless, countless, endless, inexhaustible, unbounded, unlimited, untold, vast

limp¹ v 1 = hobble, falter, hop, shamble, shuffle ♦ n 2 = lameness, hobble

limp² adj = floppy, drooping, flabby, flaccid, pliable, slack, soft

line¹ n 1 = stroke, band, groove, mark, score, scratch, streak, stripe 2 = wrinkle, crease, crow's foot, furrow, mark 3 = boundary, border, borderline, edge, frontier, limit 4 = string, cable, cord, rope, thread, wire 5 = trajectory, course, direction, path, route, track 6 = job, area, business, calling, employment, field, occupation, profession, specialization, trade 7 = row, column, file, procession, queue, rank 8 in line for = due for, in the running for ♦ v 9 = mark, crease, furrow, cloth made of flax. **3** linen articles collectively. **4** sheets, tablecloths, etc., or shirts (orig. made of linen).

lin·ger [LING-gər] *vi* **1** delay, loiter. **2** remain long.

lin·ge·rie [LAHN-*zh*ə-ree] *n* women's underwear or nightwear.

lin·go [LING-goh] *n inf* language, speech esp. applied to jargon and slang

lin·gua fran·ca [LING-gwə FRANG-kə] *n, pl* **-fran·cas** language used for communication between people of different mother tongues.

lin·gual [LING-gwəl] *adj* **1** of the tongue or language. ◆ *n* **2** sound made by the tongue, as *d, l, t.* **lin'guist** *n* **1** one skilled in languages or language study. **lin·guis'tic** *adj* of languages or their study.

lin·guis'tics *n* study, science of language.

lin·i·ment [LIN-ə-mənt] *n* lotion for rubbing on limbs, etc. for relieving pain.

lin·ing [LĪ-ning] *n* covering for the inside of garment, etc.

link [lingk] *n* **1** ring of a chain. **2** connection. **3** measure, one hundredth part of surveyor's chain. ◆ *vt* **4** join with, as with, link. **5** intertwine. ◆ *vi* **6** be so joined. **link'age** [-ij]

links [lingks] *pl n* golf course, esp. one by the sea.

li·no·le·um [li-NOH-lee-əm] *n* floor covering of burlap or canvas with smooth, hard, decorative coating of powdered cork, etc.

lin'seed *n* seed of flax plant.

lint *n* **1** tiny shreds of yarn. **2** bits of thread. **3** soft material for dressing wounds.

lin·tel [LIN-tl] *n* top piece of door or window.

li·on [LĪ-ən] *n* large animal of cat family. **li'on·ess** *n, fem.* **li'on·ize** *vt* **-ized, -iz·ing** treat as celebrity. **li'on·heart·ed** *adj* exceptionally brave.

lip *n* **1** upper or lower edge of the mouth. **2** edge or margin. **3** *sl* impudence. **lip gloss** cosmetic to give lips sheen. **lip'read·ing** *n* method of understanding spoken words by interpreting movements of speaker's lips. **lip service** insincere tribute or respect. **lip'stick** *n* cosmetic preparation, usu. in stick form, for coloring lips.

lip·o·suc·tion [LIP-oh-suk-shən, LĪP-oh-] *n* cosmetic operation removing fat from the body by suction.

li·queur [li-KUR] *n* alcoholic liquor flavored and sweetened.

liq·uid [LIK-wid] *adj* **1** fluid, not solid or gaseous. **2** flowing smoothly. **3** (of assets) in form of money or easily converted into money. ◆ *n* **4** substance in liquid form. **liq'ue·fy** [-wə-fī] *v* **-fied, -fy·ing** make or become liquid. **li·quid'i·ty** *n* state of being able to meet financial obligations. **liquid air, liquefied gas** air, gas reduced to liquid state on application of increased pressure at low temperature.

liq·ui·date [LIK-wi-dayt] *vt* **-dat·ed, -dat·ing** **1** pay (debt). **2** arrange affairs of, and dissolve (company). **3** wipe out, kill. **liq·ui·da'tion** *n* **1** process of clearing up financial affairs. **2** state of being bankrupt. **liq'ui·da·tor** *n* official appointed to liquidate business.

liq·uor [LIK-ər] *n* liquid, esp. an alcoholic one.

li·ra [LEER-ə] *n, pl* **-ras** monetary unit of

——————— THESAURUS ———————

rule, score **10 = border**, bound, edge, fringe

lineaments *pl n* = **features**, countenance, face, physiognomy

lined *adj* **1 = ruled**, feint **2 = wrinkled**, furrowed, wizened, worn

lines *pl n* = **words**, part, script

line-up *n* = **arrangement**, array, row, selection, team

linger *v* **1 = stay**, hang around, loiter, remain, stop, tarry, wait **2 = delay**, dally, dawdle, drag one's feet *or* heels, idle, take one's time

link *n* **1 = component**, constituent, element, member, part, piece **2 = connection**, affinity, association,

attachment, bond, relationship, tie-up ◆ *v* **3 = fasten**, attach, bind, connect, couple, join, tie, unite **4 = associate**, bracket, connect, identify, relate

lip *n* **1 = edge**, brim, brink, margin, rim **2** *Sl* = **impudence**, backchat (*inf*), cheek (*inf*), effrontery, impertinence, insolence

liquid *n* **1 = fluid**, juice, solution ◆ *adj* **2 = fluid**, aqueous, flowing, melted, molten, running, runny **3** *Of assets* = **convertible**, negotiable

liquidate *v* **1 = pay**, clear, discharge, honor, pay off, settle, square **2 = dissolve**, abolish, annul, cancel, terminate **3 = kill**, destroy, dispatch, eliminate, exterminate, get rid of, murder, wipe out (*inf*)

Turkey and (formerly) Italy.

lisle [līl] *n* fine hard-twisted cotton thread.

lisp *v* **1** speech defect in which *s* and *z* are pronounced *th*. **2** speak falteringly. ◆ *n*

lis•some [LIS-əm] *adj* supple, agile.

list[1] *n* **1** inventory, register. **2** catalog. **3** edge of cloth, selvage. ◆ *pl* **4** field for combat. ◆ *vt* **5** place on list.

list[2] *vi* **1** (of ship) lean to one side. ◆ *n* **2** inclination of ship.

lis•ten [LIS-ən] *vi* try to hear, attend to. **lis'ten•er** *n*

list•less [LIST-lis] *adj* indifferent, languid.

lit pt./pp. of LIGHT.

lit•a•ny [LIT-n-ee] *n, pl* **-nies 1** prayer with responses from congregation. **2** tedious account.

li•ter [LEE-tər] *n* measure of volume of fluid, one cubic decimeter, about 1.05 quarts.

lit•er•al [LIT-ər-əl] *adj* **1** according to sense of actual words, not figurative. **2** exact in wording. **3** of letters.

lit•er•ate [LIT-ər-it] *adj* **1** able to read and write. **2** educated. ◆ *n* **3** literate person. **lit'er•a•cy** *n* **lit•e•ra'ti** [-RAH-tee] *pl n* scholarly, literary people.

lit•er•a•ture [LIT-ər-ə-chər] *n* books and writings of a country, period or subject. **lit'er•ar•y** *adj* of or learned in literature.

lithe [līth] *adj* **lith•er, lith•est** supple, pliant. **lithe'some** [-səm] *adj* lissome, supple.

lith•i•um [LITH-ee-əm] *n* **1** one of the lightest alkaline metallic elements. **2** this substance used in treatment of depression, etc.

li•thog•ra•phy [li-THOG-rə-fee] *n* method of printing from metal or stone block using the antipathy of grease and water. **lith'o•graph** *n* **1** print so produced. ◆ *vt* **2** print thus. **li•thog'ra•pher** *n*

lit•i•gant [LIT-i-gənt] *n, adj* (person) conducting a lawsuit. **lit•i•ga'tion** *n* lawsuit.

lit•i•gate [LIT-i-gayt] *v* **-gat•ed, -gat•ing** ◆ *vt* **1** contest in law. ◆ *vi* **2** carry on a lawsuit. **li•ti'gious** [-jəs] *adj* **1** given to engaging in lawsuits. **2** disputatious. **li•ti'gious•ness** *n*

lit•mus [LIT-məs] *n* blue dye turned red by acids and restored to blue by alkali. **litmus paper** paper impregnated with litmus. **litmus test 1** use of litmus paper to test acidity or alkalinity of a solution. **2** any crucial test based on only one factor.

lit•ter [LIT-ər] *n* **1** untidy refuse. **2** odds and ends. **3** young of animal produced at one birth. **4** straw, etc. as bedding for animals. **5** portable couch. **6** kind of stretcher for wounded. ◆ *vt* **7** strew with litter. **8** bring forth.

lit•tle [LIT-l] *adj* **1** small, not much. ◆ *n* **2** small quantity. ◆ *adv* **3** slightly.

lit•to•ral [LIT-ər-əl] *adj* **1** pert. to the shore of sea, lake, ocean. ◆ *n* **2** littoral region.

THESAURUS

liquor *n* **1** = **alcohol**, booze (*inf*), drink, hard stuff (*inf*), spirits, strong drink **2** = **juice**, broth, extract, liquid, stock

list[1] *n* **1** = **register**, catalog, directory, index, inventory, record, roll, series, tally ◆ *v* **2** = **tabulate**, catalog, enter, enumerate, itemize, record, register

list[2] *v* **1** = **lean**, careen, heel over, incline, tilt, tip ◆ *n* **2** = **tilt**, cant, leaning, slant

listen *v* **1** = **hear**, attend, lend an ear, prick up one's ears **2** = **pay attention**, heed, mind, obey, observe, take notice

listless *adj* = **languid**, apathetic, indifferent, indolent, lethargic, sluggish

literacy *n* = **education**, knowledge, learning

literal *adj* **1** = **exact**, accurate, close, faithful, strict, verbatim, word for word **2** = **actual**, bona fide, genuine, plain, real, simple, true, unvarnished

literally *adv* = **strictly**, actually, exactly, faithfully, precisely, really, to the letter, truly, verbatim, word for word

literary *adj* = **well-read**, bookish, erudite, formal, learned, scholarly

literate *adj* = **educated**, informed, knowledgeable

literature *n* = **writings**, letters, lore

lithe *adj* = **supple**, flexible, limber, lissom(e), loose-limbed, pliable

litigant *n* = **claimant**, party, plaintiff

litigate *v* = **sue**, go to court, press charges, prosecute

litigation *n* = **lawsuit**, action, case, prosecution

litter *n* **1** = **rubbish**, debris, detritus, garbage, muck, refuse, trash **2** = **brood**, offspring, progeny, young ◆ *v* **3** = **clutter**, derange, disarrange, disorder, mess up **4** = **scatter**, strew

little *adj* **1** = **small**, diminutive, miniature, minute, petite, short, tiny, wee **2** = **young**, babyish, immature, infant, junior, undeveloped ◆ *adv* **3** = **hardly**, barely **4** = **rarely**, hardly ever, not often, scarcely, seldom ◆ *n* **5** = **bit**, fragment, hint, particle,

lit·ur·gy [LIT-ər-jee] *n, pl* **-gies** prescribed form of public worship. **li·tur·gi·cal** *adj*

live[1] [liv] *v* **lived, liv·ing 1** have life. **2** pass one's life. **3** continue in life. **4** continue, last. **5** dwell. **6** feed. **liv'a·ble** *adj* suitable for living in. **2** tolerable. **living** *n* **1** action of being in life. **2** people now alive. **3** way of life. **4** means of living. **5** church benefice.

live[2] [līv] *adj* **liv·er, liv·est 1** living, alive, active, vital. **2** flaming. **3** (of transmission line, etc.) carrying electric current. **4** (of broadcast) transmitted during the actual performance. **live'ly** *adj* **-li·er, -li·est** brisk, active, vivid. **live'li·ness** *n* **liv'en** *vt* (esp. with *up*) make (more) lively. **live'stock** *n* domestic animals. **live wire 1** wire carrying electric current. **2** able, very energetic person.

live·li·hood [LĪV-lee-huud] *n* **1** means of living. **2** subsistence, support.

live·long [LIV-lawng] *adj* of a period of time, lasting throughout, esp. as though forever.

liv·er [LIV-ər] *n* **1** organ secreting bile. **2** animal liver as food. **liv'er·ish** *adj* unwell, as from liver upset. **2** cross, touchy, irritable.

liv·er·y [LIV-ə-ree] *n, pl* **-er·ies 1** distinctive dress of person or group, esp. servant(s). **2** care, feeding of horses. **3** a livery stable. **livery stable** where horses are kept at a charge or hired out.

liv'id *adj* **1** of a bluish pale color. **2** discolored, as by bruising. **3** of reddish color. **4** *inf* angry, furious.

liz·ard [LIZ-ərd] *n* four-footed reptile.

Lk. Luke.

lla·ma [LAH-mə] *n* woolly-haired animal used as beast of burden in S Amer.

load [lohd] *n* **1** burden. **2** amount usu. carried at once. **3** actual load carried by vehicle. **4** resistance against which engine has to work. **5** amount of electrical energy drawn from a source. ◆ *vt* **6** put load on or into. **7** charge (gun). **8** weigh down. **load'ed** *adj* **1** carrying a load. **2** (of dice) dishonestly weighted. **3** biased. **4** (of question) containing hidden trap or implication. **5** *sl* wealthy. **6** *sl* drunk.

loadstar, -stone *n* see LODE.

loaf[1] [lohf] *n, pl* **loaves 1** mass of bread as baked. **2** shaped mass of food.

loaf[2] *vi* idle, loiter. **loaf'er** *n* idler.

loam [lohm] *n* fertile soil.

—————| THESAURUS |—————

speck, spot, touch, trace

live[1] *v* **1** = **exist**, be, be alive, breathe **2** = **persist**, last, prevail **3** = **dwell**, abide, inhabit, lodge, occupy, reside, settle **4** = **survive**, endure, get along, make ends meet, subsist, support oneself **5** = **thrive**, flourish, prosper

live[2] *adj* **1** = **living**, alive, animate, breathing **2** = **topical**, burning, controversial, current, hot, pertinent, pressing, prevalent **3** = **burning**, active, alight, blazing, glowing, hot, ignited, smoldering

livelihood *n* = **occupation**, bread and butter (*inf*), employment, job, living, work

liveliness *n* = **energy**, animation, boisterousness, dynamism, spirit, sprightliness, vitality, vivacity

lively *adj* **1** = **vigorous**, active, agile, alert, brisk, energetic, keen, perky, quick, sprightly **2** = **animated**, cheerful, chirpy (*inf*), sparky, spirited, upbeat (*inf*), vivacious **3** = **vivid**, bright, colorful, exciting, forceful, invigorating, refreshing, stimulating

liven up *v* = **stir**, animate, brighten, buck up (*inf*), enliven, perk up, rouse

liverish *adj* **1** = **sick**, bilious, queasy **2** =

irritable, crotchety, crusty, disagreeable, grumpy, ill-humored, irascible, splenetic, tetchy

livery *n* = **costume**, attire, clothing, dress, garb, regalia, suit, uniform

livid *adj* **1** *Inf* = **angry**, beside oneself, enraged, fuming, furious, incensed, indignant, infuriated, outraged **2** = **discolored**, black-and-blue, bruised, contused, purple

living *adj* **1** = **alive**, active, breathing, existing **2** = **current**, active, contemporary, extant, in use ◆ *n* **3** = **existence**, being, existing, life, subsistence **4** = **life style**, way of life

load *n* **1** = **cargo**, consignment, freight, shipment **2** = **burden**, albatross, encumbrance, millstone, onus, trouble, weight, worry ◆ *v* **3** = **fill**, cram, freight, heap, pack, pile, stack, stuff **4** = **burden**, encumber, oppress, saddle with, weigh down, worry **5** *Of firearms* = **make ready**, charge, prime

loaded *adj* **1** = **weighted**, biased, distorted **2** = **tricky**, artful, insidious, manipulative, prejudicial **3** *Sl* = **rich**, affluent, flush (*inf*), moneyed, wealthy, well-heeled (*inf*), well

loan [lohn] n **1** act of lending. **2** thing lent. **3** money borrowed at interest. **4** permission to use. ◆ v **5** grant loan of.

loath, loth [lohth] adj **1** unwilling, reluctant (to). **loathe** [lohth] vt **loathed, loath·ing** hate, abhor. **loathing** [LOHTH-ing] n **1** disgust. **2** repulsion. **loath·some** [LOHTH-səm] adj disgusting.

lob n **lobbed, lob·bing 1** in tennis, artillery, etc., ball, shell, sent high in air. ◆ v **2** hit, fire, thus.

lob·by [LOB-ee] n, pl **-bies 1** corridor into which rooms open. **2** passage or room adjacent to legislative chamber. **3** group of people who try to influence members of legislature. **lob'by·ing** n activity of this group. **lob'by·ist** n

lobe [lohb] n **1** any rounded projection. **2** subdivision of body organ. **3** soft, hanging part of ear. **lobed** adj **lob·bot·o·my** [lə-BOT-ə-mee] n, pl **-mies** surgical incision into lobe of organ, esp. brain.

lob·ster [LOB-stər] n shellfish with long tail and claws, turning red when boiled.

lo·cal [LOH-kəl] adj **1** of, existing in particular place. **2** confined to a definite spot, district or part of the body. **3** of place. **4** (of train) making many stops. ◆ n **5** person belonging to a district. **6** local branch of labor union. **7** local train. **lo·cale** [loh-KAL] n scene of event. **lo·cal'i·ty** n **1**

place, situation. **2** district. **lo'cal·ize** vt **-ized, -iz·ing** assign, restrict to definite place. **local anesthetic** one that produces insensibility in one part of body.

lo·cate [loh-KAYT] vt **-cat·ed, -cat·ing 1** attribute to a place. **2** find the place of. **3** situate. **lo·ca'tion** n **1** placing. **2** situation. **3** site of film production away from studio.

lock[1] [lok] n **1** appliance for fastening door, lid, etc. **2** mechanism for firing gun. **3** enclosure in river or canal for moving boats from one level to another. **4** air lock. **5** appliance to check the motion of a mechanism. **6** interlocking. **7** block, jam. ◆ vt **8** fasten, make secure with lock. **9** place in locked container. **10** join firmly. **11** cause to become immovable. **12** embrace closely. ◆ vi **13** become fixed or united. **14** become immovable. **lock'er** n small closet with lock. **lock'jaw** n tetanus. **lock'out** n exclusion of workmen by employers as means of coercion. **lock'smith** n one who makes and mends locks. **lock'up** n prison.

lock[2] n tress of hair.

lock·et [LOK-it] n small hinged pendant for portrait, etc.

lo·co·mo·tive [loh-kə-MOH-tiv] n **1** engine for pulling train on railway tracks. ◆ adj **2** having power of moving from place to place. **lo·co·mo'tion** n action, power of moving.

off, well-to-do

loaf[1] n = **lump**, block, cake, cube, slab

loaf[2] v = **idle**, laze, lie around, loiter, lounge around, take it easy

loan n **1** = **advance**, credit ◆ v **2** = **lend**, advance, let out

loath, loth adj = **unwilling**, averse, disinclined, opposed, reluctant

loathe v = **hate**, abhor, abominate, despise, detest, dislike

loathing n = **hatred**, abhorrence, antipathy, aversion, detestation, disgust, repugnance, repulsion, revulsion

loathsome adj = **hateful**, abhorrent, detestable, disgusting, nauseating, obnoxious, odious, offensive, repugnant, repulsive, revolting, scuzzy (sl), vile

lobby n **1** = **corridor**, entrance hall, foyer, hallway, passage, porch, vestibule **2** = **pressure group** ◆ v **3** = **campaign**, influence, persuade, press, pressure, promote, push, urge

local adj **1** = **regional**, provincial **2** =

restricted, confined, limited ◆ n **3** = **resident**, inhabitant, native

locality n **1** = **neighborhood**, area, district, neck of the woods (inf), region, vicinity **2** = **site**, locale, location, place, position, scene, setting, spot

localize v = **restrict**, circumscribe, confine, contain, delimit, limit

locate v **1** = **find**, come across, detect, discover, pin down, pinpoint, track down, unearth **2** = **place**, establish, fix, put, seat, set, settle, situate

location n = **position**, locale, place, point, site, situation, spot, venue

lock[1] n **1** = **fastening**, bolt, clasp, padlock ◆ v **2** = **fasten**, bolt, close, seal, secure, shut **3** = **unite**, clench, engage, entangle, entwine, join, link **4** = **embrace**, clasp, clutch, encircle, enclose, grasp, hug, press

lock[2] n = **strand**, curl, ringlet, tress, tuft

lockup n = **prison**, cell, jail

lock up v = **imprison**, cage, confine, detain, incarcerate, jail, put behind bars,

lo·cus [LOH-kəs] n, pl **-ci** [-sī] 1 exact place or locality. 2 curve made by all points satisfying certain mathematical condition, or by point, line or surface moving under such condition.

lo·cust [LOH-kəst] n 1 destructive winged insect. 2 N Amer. tree. 3 wood of this tree.

lo·cu·tion [loh-KYOO-shən] n 1 a phrase. 2 speech. 3 mode or style of speaking.

lode [lohd] n vein of ore. **lode'star** n 1 star that shows the way. 2 any guide on which attention is fixed. 3 Polaris. **lode'stone** n magnetic iron ore.

lodge [loj] n 1 house, cabin used seasonally or occasionally, e.g. for hunting, skiing. 2 gatekeeper's house. 3 meeting place of branch of certain fraternal organizations. 4 the branch. ◆ v **lodged, lodg·ing** ◆ vt 5 house. 6 deposit. 7 bring (a charge, etc.) against someone. ◆ vi 8 live in another's house at fixed rent. 9 come to rest (in, on). **lodg'er** n **lodgings** pl n rented room(s) in another person's house.

loft [lawft] n 1 space between top story and roof. 2 upper story of warehouse, factory, etc. typically with large unpartitioned space. 3 gallery in church, etc. ◆ vt 4 send (golf ball, etc.) high. **loft building** building in which all stories have large unobstructed space once used for manufacturing but now usu. are converted to residences. **loft'i·ly** adv haughtily. **loft'i·ness** n **loft'y** adj **loft·i·er, loft·i·est** 1 of great height. 2 elevated. 3 haughty.

log¹ [lawg] n 1 portion of felled tree stripped of branches. 2 detailed record of voyages, time traveled, etc., of ship, aircraft, etc. 3 apparatus used formerly for measuring ship's speed. ◆ vt **logged, log·ging** 4 keep a record of. 5 travel (specified distance, time). **log'ging** n cutting and transporting logs to river. **log in, out** v gain entrance to or leave a computer system by keying in a special command.

log² n logarithm.

log·a·rithm [LAW-gə-rith-əm] n one of series of arithmetical functions tabulated for use in calculation.

log·ger·head [LAW-gər-hed] n at **loggerheads** quarreling, disputing.

log·ic [LOJ-ik] n 1 art or philosophy of reasoning. 2 reasoned thought or argument. 3 coherence of various facts, events, etc. **log'i·cal** adj 1 of logic. 2 according to reason. 3 reasonable. 4 apt to reason correctly. **lo·gi·cian** [loh-JISH-ən] n

lo·gis·tics [loh-JIS-tiks] n 1 the transport, housing and feeding of troops. 2 organization of any project, operation. **lo·gis'ti·cal** adj

lo·go [LOH-goh] n, pl **-gos** company emblem or similar device.

loin n 1 part of body between ribs and hip. 2 cut of meat from this. ◆ pl 3 hips and lower abdomen. **loin'cloth** n garment covering loins only.

loi·ter [LOI-tər] vi 1 dawdle, hang about. 2 idle. **loi'ter·er** n

loll [lol] vi 1 sit, lie lazily. 2 hang out. ◆ vt 3 allow to hang out.

lone [lohn] adj solitary. **lone'ly** adj **-li·er,**

shut up

lodge n 1 = **cabin**, chalet, cottage, gatehouse, hut, shelter 2 = **society**, branch, chapter, club, group ◆ v 3 = **stay**, board, room 4 = **stick**, come to rest, imbed, implant 5 = **register**, file, put on record, submit

lodger n = **tenant**, boarder, paying guest, resident

lodging n (often plural) = **accommodation**, abode, apartments, quarters, residence, rooms, shelter

lofty adj 1 = **high**, raised, soaring, towering 2 = **noble**, dignified, distinguished, elevated, exalted, grand, illustrious, renowned 3 = **haughty**, arrogant, condescending, disdainful, patronizing, proud, supercilious

log n 1 = **stump**, block, chunk, trunk 2 = **record**, account, chart ◆ v 3 = **chop**, cut, fell, hew 4 = **record**, chart, note, register, set down

loggerheads pl n **at loggerheads** = **quarreling**, at daggers drawn, at each other's throats, at odds, feuding, in dispute, opposed

logic n = **reason**, good sense, sense

logical adj 1 = **rational**, clear, cogent, coherent, consistent, sound, valid, well-organized 2 = **reasonable**, plausible, sensible, wise

loiter v = **linger**, dally, dawdle, dilly-dally (inf), hang about or around, idle, loaf, skulk

loll v 1 = **lounge**, loaf, recline, relax, slouch, slump, sprawl 2 = **droop**, dangle, drop, flap, flop, hang, sag

-li·est 1 sad because alone. **2** unfrequented. **3** solitary, alone. **lone'li·ness** n **lon'er** n one who prefers to be alone. **lone'some** [-səm] adj

long¹ [lawng] adj **-er, -est 1** having length, esp. great length, in space or time. **2** extensive. **3** protracted. ♦ adv **4** for a long time. **long'hand** n writing in which words are written out in full by hand rather than on typewriter, etc. **long'-play'ing** adj (of record) lasting for 10 to 30 minutes because of its fine grooves. **long-range** adj **1** of the future. **2** able to travel long distances without refueling. **3** (of weapons) designed to hit distant target. **long shot** competitor, undertaking, bet, etc. with small chance of success. **long ton** 2240 lbs. **long'-wind'ed** adj tediously loquacious.

long² vi have keen desire, yearn (for).

long'ing n yearning.

lon·gev·i·ty [lon-JEV-i-tee] n **1** long existence or life. **2** length of existence or life. **3** tenure.

lon·gi·tude [LON-ji-tood] n distance east or west from prime meridian. **lon·gi·tu'di·nal** adj **1** of length or longitude. **2** lengthwise.

long·shore·man [LAWNG-SHOR-mən] n dock laborer.

look [luuk] vi **1** direct, use eyes. **2** face. **3** seem. **4** search (for). **5** hope (for). **6** (with after) take care of. ♦ n **7** looking. **8** view. **9** search. ♦ pl **10** appearance. **good looks** beauty. **look'a·like** n person who is double of another. **look'out** n **1** guard. **2** place for watching. **3** watchman. **4** object of worry, concern. **look after** tend. **look down on** despise.

loom¹ n **1** machine for weaving. **2** middle

---

lone adj = **solitary**, one, only, single, sole, unaccompanied

loneliness n = **solitude**, desolation, isolation, seclusion

lonely adj **1** = **abandoned**, destitute, forlorn, forsaken, friendless, lonesome **2** = **solitary**, alone, apart, companionless, isolated, lone, single, withdrawn **3** = **remote**, deserted, desolate, godforsaken, isolated, out-of-the-way, secluded, unfrequented, uninhabited

loner n = **individualist**, lone wolf, maverick, outsider, recluse

lonesome adj = **lonely**, companionless, desolate, dreary, forlorn, friendless, gloomy

long¹ adj **1** = **elongated**, expanded, extended, extensive, far-reaching, lengthy, spread out, stretched **2** = **prolonged**, interminable, lengthy, lingering, long-drawn-out, protracted, sustained

long² v = **desire**, crave, hanker, itch, lust, pine, want, wish, yearn

longing n = **desire**, ambition, aspiration, craving, hope, itch, thirst, urge, wish, yearning, yen (inf)

long-lived adj = **long-lasting**, enduring

long shot n = **outsider**, dark horse

long-standing adj = **established**, abiding, enduring, fixed, long-established, long-lasting, time-honored

long-suffering adj = **uncomplaining**, easy-going, forbearing, forgiving, patient, resigned, stoical, tolerant

long-winded adj = **rambling**, lengthy, long-drawn-out, prolix, prolonged, repetitious, tedious, tiresome, verbose, wordy

look v **1** = **see**, contemplate, examine, eye, gaze, glance, observe, scan, study, survey, view, watch **2** = **seem**, appear, look like, strike one as **3** = **face**, front, overlook **4** = **hope**, anticipate, await, expect, reckon on **5** = **search**, forage, hunt, seek ♦ n **6** = **view**, examination, gaze, glance, glimpse, inspection, observation, peek, sight **7** = **appearance**, air, aspect, bearing, countenance, demeanor, expression, manner, semblance

look after v = **take care of**, attend to, care for, guard, keep an eye on, mind, nurse, protect, supervise, take charge of, tend

look down on v = **disdain**, contemn, despise, scorn, sneer, spurn

look forward to v = **anticipate**, await, expect, hope for, long for, look for, wait for

lookout n **1** = **vigil**, guard, readiness, watch **2** = **watchman**, guard, sentinel, sentry **3** = **watchtower**, observation post, observatory, post

look out v = **be careful**, beware, keep an eye out, pay attention, watch out

look up v **1** = **research**, find, hunt for, search for, seek out, track down **2** = **improve**, get better, perk up, pick up, progress, shape up (inf) **3** = **visit**, call on, drop in on (inf), look in on **4 look up to** =

part of oar.

loom[2] *vi* **1** appear dimly. **2** seem ominously close. **3** assume great importance.

loon[1] *n* Amer. fish-eating diving bird.

loon[2] *n* stupid, foolish person. **loon'y** *adj* **loon·i·er, loon·i·est ♦** *n, pl* **-nies loony bin** *inf* mental hospital or ward.

loop *n* **1** figure made by curved line crossing itself. **2** similar rounded shape in cord or rope, etc. crossed on itself. **3** contraceptive coil. **4** aerial maneuver in which aircraft describes complete circle. ♦ *v* **5** form loop.

loop·hole [LOOP-hohl] *n* **1** means of evading rule without infringing it. **2** vertical slit in building wall, esp. for defense.

loose [loos] *adj* **loos·er, loos·est 1** not tight, fastened, fixed, or tense. **2** slack. **3** vague. **4** dissolute. ♦ *v* **loosed, loos·ing ♦** *vt* **5** free. **6** unfasten. **7** slacken. ♦ *vi* **8** (with *off*) shoot, let fly. **loose'ly** *adv* **loos'en** *vt* make loose. **loose'ness** *n* **on the loose 1** free. **2** on a spree.

loot *n, vt* plunder.

lop[1] *vt* **lopped, lop·ping 1** cut away twigs and branches. **2** chop off.

lop[2] *vi* **lopped, lop·ping** hang limply.

lop'-eared *adj* having drooping ears.

lop'sid·ed *adj* **1** with one side lower than the other. **2** badly balanced.

lope [lohp] *vi* **loped, lop·ing** run with long, easy strides.

lo·qua·cious [loh-KWAY-shəs] *adj* talkative. **lo·quac'i·ty** [-KWAS-ə-tee] *n*

lord *n* **1** British nobleman, peer of the realm. **2** feudal superior. **3** one ruling others. **4** owner. **5** (L-) God. ♦ *vi* **6** domineer. **lord'li·ness** *n* **lord'ly** *adj* **-li·er, -li·est 1** imperious, proud. **2** fit for a lord. **lord'ship** *n* **1** rule, ownership. **2** domain. **3** title of some noblemen.

lore [lor] *n* **1** learning. **2** body of facts and traditions.

lor·gnette [lorn-YET] *n* pair of eyeglasses mounted on long handle.

lorn *adj poet* **1** abandoned. **2** desolate.

lose [looz] *v* **lost, los·ing ♦** *vt* **1** be deprived of, fail to retain or use. **2** let slip. **3** fail to get. **4** (of clock, etc.) run slow (by specified amount). **5** be defeated in. ♦ *vi* **6** suffer loss. **loss** [laws] *n* **1** a losing. **2** what is lost. **3** harm or damage resulting from losing.

lost *adj* **1** unable to be found. **2** unable to find one's way. **3** bewildered. **4** not won. **5** not utilized.

THESAURUS

respect, admire, defer to, esteem, honor, revere

loom *v* = **appear**, bulk, emerge, hover, impend, menace, take shape, threaten

loop *n* **1** = **curve**, circle, coil, curl, ring, spiral, twirl, twist, whorl ♦ *v* **2** = **twist**, coil, curl, knot, roll, spiral, turn, wind round

loophole *n* = **let-out**, escape, excuse

loose *adj* **1** = **untied**, free, insecure, unattached, unbound, unfastened, unfettered, unrestricted **2** = **slack**, easy, relaxed, sloppy **3** = **vague**, ill-defined, imprecise, inaccurate, indistinct, inexact, rambling, random **4** = **promiscuous**, abandoned, debauched, dissipated, dissolute, fast, immoral, profligate ♦ *v* **5** = **free**, detach, disconnect, liberate, release, set free, unfasten, unleash, untie

loosen *v* **1** = **untie**, detach, separate, undo, unloose **2** = **free**, liberate, release, set free **3 loosen up** = **relax**, ease up *or* off, go easy (*inf*), let up, soften

loot *n* **1** = **plunder**, booty, goods, haul, prize, spoils, swag (*sl*) ♦ *v* **2** = **plunder**, despoil, pillage, raid, ransack, ravage, rifle, rob, sack

lopsided *adj* = **crooked**, askew, asymmetrical, awry, cockeyed, disproportionate, squint, unbalanced, uneven, warped

lord *n* **1** = **master**, commander, governor, leader, liege, overlord, ruler, superior **2** = **nobleman**, earl, noble, peer, viscount **3 Our Lord** *or* **the Lord** = **Jesus Christ**, Christ, God, Jehovah, the Almighty ♦ *v* **4 lord it over** = **order around**, boss around (*inf*), domineer, pull rank, put on airs, swagger

lordly *adj* = **proud**, arrogant, condescending, disdainful, domineering, haughty, high-handed, imperious, lofty, overbearing

lore *n* = **traditions**, beliefs, doctrine, sayings, teaching, wisdom

lose *v* **1** = **mislay**, be deprived of, drop, forget, misplace **2** = **forfeit**, miss, pass up (*inf*), yield **3** = **be defeated**, come to grief, lose out

loser *n* **1** = **failure**, also-ran, dud (*inf*), flop (*inf*) **2** = **nerd**, dork (*sl*), drip (*inf*), dweeb (*sl*), geek (*sl*)

loss *n* **1** = **defeat**, failure, forfeiture,

lot *n* **1** great number. **2** collection. **3** large quantity. **4** share. **5** fate. **6** destiny. **7** item at auction. **8** one of a set of objects used to decide something by chance, as in **to cast lots**. **9** area of land. ♦ *pl* **10** great numbers or quantity. ♦ *adv* **11** a great deal.

loth see LOATH.

lo·tion [LOH-shən] *n* liquid for washing to reduce itching, etc., improving skin, etc.

lot·ter·y [LOT-ə-ree] *n, pl* **-ter·ies 1** method of raising funds by selling tickets and prizes by chance. **2** any gamble.

lot·to [LOT-oh] *n* game of chance like bingo.

lo·tus [LOH-təs] *n, pl* **-tus·es 1** legendary plant whose fruits induce forgetfulness when eaten. **2** Egyptian water lily. **lotus position** seated cross-legged position used in yoga, etc.

loud [lowd] *adj* **-er, -est 1** strongly audible. **2** noisy. **3** obtrusive. **loud'ly** *adv* **loud'speak·er** *n* instrument for converting electrical signals into sound audible at a distance.

lounge [lownj] *vi* **lounged, loung·ing 1** sit, lie, walk, or stand in a relaxed manner. ♦ *n* **2** general waiting, relaxing area in airport, hotel, etc. **3** bar. **loung'er** *n* loafer.

louse [lows] *n, pl* **lice** a parasitic insect. **lous'y** *adj inf* **lous·i·er, lous·i·est 1** nasty, unpleasant. **2** *sl* (too) generously provided, thickly populated (with). **3** bad, poor. **4** having lice.

lout [lowt] *n* crude, oafish person. **lout'ish** *adj*

lou·ver [LOO-vər] *n* **1** one of a set of boards or slats set parallel and slanted to admit air but not rain or sunlight. **2** ventilating structure of these.

love [luv] *n* **1** warm affection. **2** benevolence. **3** charity. **4** sexual passion. **5** sweetheart. **6** *Tennis, etc.* score of zero. ♦ *v* **loved, lov·ing** ♦ *vt* **7** admire passionately. **8** delight in. ♦ *vi* **9** be in love. **lov'a·ble** *adj* **love'less** [-lis] *adj* **love'lorn** *adj* forsaken by, pining for a lover. **love'li·ness** *n* **love'ly** *adj* **-li·er, -li·est** beautiful, delightful. **loving** *adj* **1** affectionate. **2** tender. **lov'ing·ly** *adv* **loving cup 1** bowl formerly passed around at banquet. **2** large cup given as prize. **make love (to)** have sexual intercourse (with).

━━━━━━━━━━ THESAURUS ━━━━━━━━━━

mislaying, squandering, waste **2 = damage**, cost, destruction, harm, hurt, injury, ruin **3** (sometimes plural) **= deficit**, debit, debt, deficiency, depletion **4 at a loss = confused**, at one's wits' end, baffled, bewildered, helpless, nonplussed, perplexed, puzzled, stumped

lost *adj* **1 = missing**, disappeared, mislaid, misplaced, vanished, wayward **2 = off-course**, adrift, astray, at sea, disoriented, off-track

lot *n* **1 = collection**, assortment, batch, bunch (*inf*), consignment, crowd, group, quantity, set **2 = destiny**, accident, chance, doom, fate, fortune **3 a lot** *or* **lots = plenty**, abundance, a great deal, heap(s), masses (*inf*), piles (*inf*), scores, stack(s)

loth see LOATH

lotion *n* **= cream**, balm, embrocation, liniment, salve, solution

lottery *n* **1 = raffle**, drawing, sweepstakes **2 = gamble**, chance, hazard, risk, toss-up (*inf*)

loud *adj* **1 = noisy**, blaring, booming, clamorous, deafening, ear-splitting, forte (*Mus*), resounding, thundering, tumultuous, vociferous **2 = garish**, brash, flamboyant, flashy, gaudy, glaring, lurid, showy

loudly *adv* **= noisily**, deafeningly, fortissimo (*Mus*), lustily, shrilly, uproariously, vehemently, vigorously, vociferously

lounge *v* **= relax**, laze, lie about, loaf, loiter, loll, sprawl, take it easy

lousy *adj Inf* **= crummy**, awful, crappy (*sl*), inadequate, inferior, shabby, shoddy, terrible

lout *n* **= oaf**, boor, dolt, lummox (*inf*)

lovable, loveable *adj* **= endearing**, adorable, amiable, charming, cute, delightful, enchanting, likable *or* likeable, lovely, sweet

love *v* **1 = adore**, cherish, dote on, hold dear, idolize, prize, treasure, worship **2 = enjoy**, appreciate, delight in, like, relish, savor, take pleasure in ♦ *n* **3 = passion**, adoration, affection, ardor, attachment, devotion, infatuation, tenderness, warmth **4 = liking**, devotion, enjoyment, fondness, inclination, partiality, relish, soft spot, taste, weakness **5 = beloved**, darling, dear, dearest, lover, sweetheart, truelove **6 in love = enamored**, besotted, charmed, enraptured, infatuated, smitten

love affair *n* **= romance**, affair, amour, intrigue, liaison, relationship

low¹ [loh] *adj* **-er, -est 1** not tall, high or elevated. **2** humble. **3** commonplace. **4** coarse, vulgar. **5** dejected. **6** ill. **7** not loud. **8** moderate. **9** cheap. **low'er** *vt* **1** cause, allow to descend. **2** move down. **3** diminish, degrade. ◆ *adj* **4** below in position or rank. **5** at an early stage, period of development. **low'li·ness** *n* **low'ly** *adj* **-li·er, -li·est** modest, humble. **low'brow** *n* person with no intellectual or cultural interests. ◆ *adj* **low'down** *n inf* **1** inside information. ◆ *adj* **2** mean, shabby, dishonorable. **low frequency 1** in electricity any frequency of alternating current from about 30 to 300 kilohertz. **2** frequency within audible range. **low-key** [-kee] *adj* subdued, restrained, not intense. **low'land** *n* low-lying land. **low-ten·sion** *adj* carrying, operating at low voltage.

low² *vi* **1** of cattle, utter their cry, bellow. ◆ *n* **2** cry of cattle, bellow.

low·er [LOW-ər] *vi* **1** look gloomy or threatening, as sky. **2** scowl. ◆ *n* **3** scowl, frown.

loy·al [LOI-əl] *adj* faithful, true to allegiance. **loy'al·ly** *adv* **loy'al·ty** *n*

loz·enge [LOZ-inj] *n* **1** small candy or tablet of medicine. **2** rhombus, diamond figure.

Lr *Chem.* lawrencium.

LSD lysergic acid diethylamide (hallucinogenic drug).

Lu *Chem.* lutetium.

lub·ber [LUB-ər] *n* **1** clumsy fellow. **2** unskilled seaman.

lu·bri·cate [LOO-bri-kayt] *vt* **-cat·ed, -cat·ing 1** oil, grease. **2** make slippery. **lu'bri·cant** [-kənt] *n* substance used for this. **lu·bri·ca'tion** [-KAY-shən] *n* **lu·bric'i·ty** [-BRIS-i-tee] *n, pl* **-ties 1** slipperiness, smoothness. **2** lewdness.

lu·cid [LOO-sid] *adj* **1** clear. **2** easily understood. **3** sane. **lu·cid'i·ty** *n*

Lu·ci·fer [LOO-sə-fər] *n* Satan.

luck [luk] *n* **1** fortune, good or bad. **2** good fortune. **3** chance. **luck'i·ly** *adv* fortunately. **luck'less** *adj* having bad luck. **luck'y** *adj* **luck·i·er, luck·i·est** having good luck.

——————[THESAURUS]——————

lovely *adj* **1** = **attractive**, adorable, beautiful, charming, comely, exquisite, graceful, handsome, pretty **2** = **enjoyable**, agreeable, delightful, engaging, nice, pleasant, pleasing

lover *n* = **sweetheart**, admirer, beloved, boyfriend *or* girlfriend, flame (*inf*), mistress, suitor

loving *adj* = **affectionate**, amorous, dear, devoted, doting, fond, tender, warm-hearted

low¹ *adj* **1** = **small**, little, short, squat, stunted **2** = **inferior**, deficient, inadequate, lousy (*sl*), poor, second-rate, shoddy **3** = **coarse**, common, crude, disreputable, rough, rude, undignified, vulgar **4** = **dejected**, depressed, despondent, disheartened, downcast, down in the dumps (*inf*), fed up, gloomy, glum, miserable **5** = **ill**, debilitated, frail, stricken, weak **6** = **quiet**, gentle, hushed, muffled, muted, soft, subdued, whispered

lowdown *n Inf* = **information**, info (*inf*), inside story, intelligence

lower¹ *adj* **1** = **minor**, inferior, junior, lesser, secondary, second-class, smaller, subordinate **2** = **reduced**, curtailed, decreased, diminished, lessened ◆ *v* **3** = **drop**, depress, fall, let down, sink, submerge, take down **4** = **lessen**, cut, decrease, diminish, minimize, prune, reduce, slash

low-key *adj* = **subdued**, muted, quiet, restrained, toned down, understated

lowly *adj* = **humble**, meek, mild, modest, unassuming

low-spirited *adj* = **depressed**, dejected, despondent, dismal, down, down-hearted, fed up, low, miserable, sad

loyal *adj* = **faithful**, constant, dependable, devoted, dutiful, staunch, steadfast, true, trustworthy, trusty, unwavering

loyalty *n* = **faithfulness**, allegiance, constancy, dependability, devotion, fidelity, staunchness, steadfastness, trustworthiness

lubricate *v* = **oil**, grease, smear

lucid *adj* **1** = **clear**, comprehensible, explicit, intelligible, transparent **2** = **translucent**, clear, crystalline, diaphanous, glassy, limpid, pellucid, transparent **3** = **clear-headed**, all there, compos mentis, in one's right mind, rational, sane

luck *n* **1** = **fortune**, accident, chance, destiny, fate **2** = **good fortune**, advantage, blessing, godsend, prosperity, serendipity, success, windfall

luckily *adv* = **fortunately**, favorably, happily, opportunely, propitiously, providentially lu·cre [LOO-kər] n money, wealth. lu'cra·tive [-krə-tiv] adj very profitable. filthy lucre inf money.

lu·di·crous [LOO-di-krəs] adj absurd, laughable, ridiculous.

lug[1] v lugged, lug·ging ◆ vt 1 drag with effort. ◆ vi 2 pull hard.

lug[2] n 1 projection, tag serving as handle or support. 2 sl fellow, blockhead.

lug·gage [LUG-ij] n traveler's suitcases and other baggage.

lu·gu·bri·ous [luu-GOO-bree-əs] adj mournful, doleful, gloomy. lu·gu'bri·ous·ly adv

luke·warm [look-worm] adj 1 moderately warm, tepid. 2 indifferent.

lull vt 1 soothe, sing to sleep. 2 make quiet. ◆ vi 3 become quiet, subside. ◆ n 4 brief time of quiet in storm, etc. lull'a·by n, pl -bies lulling song, esp. for children.

lum·bar [LUM-bahr] adj relating to body between lower ribs and hips. lum·ba'go [-BAY-goh] n rheumatism in lower part of the back.

lum·ber [LUM-bər] n 1 sawn timber. 2 disused articles, useless rubbish. ◆ vi 3 move heavily. ◆ vt 4 convert (a number of trees) into lumber. 5 burden with something unpleasant. lum'ber·jack n logger.

lu·men [LOO-mən] n, pl -mi·na [-mə-nə] SI unit of luminous flux.

lu·mi·nous [LOO-mə-nəs] adj 1 bright. 2 shedding light. 3 glowing. 4 lucid. lu'mi·nar·y [-ner-ee] n 1 learned person. 2 prominent person. 3 heavenly body giving light. lu·mi·nes'cence [-NES-əns] n emission of light at low temperatures by process (e.g. chemical) not involving burning. lu·mi·nos'i·ty n

lump n 1 shapeless piece or mass. 2 swelling. 3 large sum. ◆ vt 4 throw together in one mass or sum. ◆ vi 5 move heavily. lump'ish adj 1 clumsy. 2 stupid. lump'y adj lump·i·er, lump·i·est 1 full of lumps. 2 uneven. lump it inf 1 put up with. 2 accept and endure.

lu·nar [LOO-nər] adj relating to the moon.

lu·na·tic [LOO-nə-tik] adj 1 insane. ◆ n 2 insane person. lu'na·cy n, pl -cies 1 lunatic fringe 1 extreme, radical section of group, etc.

lunch n 1 meal taken in the middle of the day. ◆ v 2 eat, entertain at lunch. lunch'eon [-ən] n a lunch.

lung n one of the two organs of respiration in vertebrates. lung'fish n type of fish with air-breathing lung.

lunge [lunj] vi lunged, lung·ing 1 thrust with sword, etc. ◆ n 2 such thrust. 3

luckless adj = ill-fated, cursed, doomed, hapless, hopeless, jinxed, unfortunate, unlucky

lucky adj = fortunate, advantageous, blessed, charmed, favored, serendipitous, successful, win-win (inf)

lucrative adj = profitable, advantageous, fruitful, productive, remunerative, well-paid

lucre n = money, gain, mammon, pelf, profit, riches, spoils, wealth

ludicrous adj = ridiculous, absurd, crazy, farcical, laughable, nonsensical, outlandish, preposterous, silly

luggage n = baggage, bags, cases, gear, impedimenta, paraphernalia, suitcases, things

lugubrious adj = gloomy, doleful, melancholy, mournful, sad, serious, somber, sorrowful, woebegone

lukewarm adj 1 = tepid, warm 2 = half-hearted, apathetic, cool, indifferent, unenthusiastic, unresponsive

lull v 1 = calm, allay, pacify, quell, soothe, subdue, tranquilize ◆ n 2 = respite, calm, hush, let-up (inf), pause, quiet, silence

lumber v = plod, clump, shamble, shuffle, stump, trudge, trundle, waddle

lumbering adj = awkward, clumsy, heavy, hulking, ponderous, ungainly

luminous adj = bright, glowing, illuminated, luminescent, lustrous, radiant, shining

lump[1] n 1 = piece, ball, chunk, hunk, mass, nugget 2 = swelling, bulge, bump, growth, hump, protrusion, tumor ◆ v 3 = group, collect, combine, conglomerate, consolidate, mass, pool

lumpy adj = bumpy, knobbly, uneven

lunacy n 1 = insanity, dementia, derangement, madness, mania, psychosis 2 = foolishness, absurdity, craziness, folly, foolhardiness, madness, stupidity

lunatic adj 1 = irrational, bonkers (inf), crackbrained (inf), crackpot (inf), crazy, daft, deranged, insane, mad ◆ n 2 = madman, maniac, nutcase (sl), psychopath sudden movement of body, plunge.

lu·pine[1] [LOO-pin] *n* leguminous plant with tall spikes of flowers.

lu·pine[2] [LOO-pīn] *adj* like a wolf.

lu·pus [LOO-pəs] *n* skin disease.

lurch *n* **1** sudden roll to one side. ♦ *vi* **2** stagger. **leave in the lurch** leave in difficulties.

lure [luur] *n* **1** something that entices. **2** bait. **3** power to attract. ♦ *vt* **lured, lur·ing 4** entice. **5** attract.

lu·rid [LUUR-id] *adj* **1** vivid in shocking detail, sensational. **2** pale, wan. **3** lit with unnatural glare.

lurk *vi* lie hidden. **lurk·ing** *adj* (of suspicion) not definite.

lus·cious [LUSH-əs] *adj* **1** sweet, juicy. **2** extremely pleasurable or attractive.

lush[1] *adj* **-er, -est** (of grass, etc.) luxuriant and juicy, fresh.

lush[2] *n sl* **1** heavy drinker. **2** alcoholic.

lust *n* **1** strong desire for sexual gratification. **2** any strong desire. ♦ *vi* **3** have passionate desire. **lust'ful** [-fəl] *adj* **lust·i·ly** *adv* **lust'y** *adj* **lust·i·er, lust·i·est** vigorous, healthy.

lus·ter [LUST-ər] *n* **1** gloss, sheen. **2** splendor. **3** renown. **4** glory. **5** glossy material. **6** metallic pottery glaze. **lus'trous** [-trəs] *adj* shining, luminous.

lute [loot] *n* old stringed musical instrument

played with the fingers. **lu'te·nist** *n*

lux [luks] *n, pl* **lu·ces** [LOO-seez] SI unit of illumination.

lux·u·ry [LUK-shə-ree] *n, pl* **-ries 1** possession and use of costly, choice things for enjoyment. **2** enjoyable but not necessary thing. **3** comfortable surroundings. **lux·u·ri·ance** [lug ZHUUR-ee əns] *n* abundance, proliferation. **lux·u·ri·ant** *adj* **1** growing thickly. **2** abundant. **lux·u·ri·ate** [-ayt] *vi* **-at·ed, -at·ing 1** indulge in luxury. **2** flourish profusely. **3** take delight (in). **lux·u·ri·ous** *adj* **1** fond of luxury. **2** self-indulgent. **3** sumptuous.

ly·ce·um [lī-SEE-əm] *n* **1** institution for popular education e.g. concerts, lectures. **2** public building for this purpose.

lye [lī] *n* water made alkaline with wood ashes, etc. for washing.

lying pr. p. of LIE.

lymph [limf] *n* colorless bodily fluid, mainly of white blood cells. **lym·phat'ic** *adj* **1** of lymph. **2** flabby, sluggish. ♦ *n* **3** vessel in the body conveying lymph.

lynch [linch] *vt* put to death without trial. **lynch law** procedure of self-appointed court trying and punishing esp. executing accused.

lynx [lingks] *n* animal of cat family with grey-brown mottled fur, tufted ears and a

lunge *n* **1** = **thrust**, charge, jab, pounce, spring, swing ♦ *v* **2** = **pounce**, charge, dive, leap, plunge, thrust

lurch *v* **1** = **tilt**, heave, heel, lean, list, pitch, rock, roll **2** = **stagger**, reel, stumble, sway, totter, weave

lure *v* **1** = **tempt**, allure, attract, draw, ensnare, entice, invite, seduce ♦ *n* **2** = **temptation**, allurement, attraction, bait, carrot (*inf*), enticement, incentive, inducement

lurid *adj* **1** = **sensational**, graphic, melodramatic, shocking, vivid **2** = **glaring**, intense

lurk *v* = **hide**, conceal oneself, lie in wait, prowl, skulk, slink, sneak

luscious *adj* = **delicious**, appetizing, juicy, mouth-watering, palatable, succulent, sweet, toothsome, yummy (*inf*)

lush *adj* **1** = **abundant**, dense, flourishing, green, rank, verdant **2** = **luxurious**, elaborate, extravagant, grand, lavish, opulent, ornate, palatial, plush (*inf*), sumptuous

lust *n* **1** = **lechery**, lasciviousness, lewdness, sensuality **2** = **appetite**, craving, desire, greed, longing, passion, thirst ♦ *v* **3** = **desire**, covet, crave, hunger for or after, want, yearn

luster *n* **1** = **sparkle**, gleam, glint, glitter, gloss, glow, sheen, shimmer, shine **2** = **glory**, distinction, fame, honor, kudos, prestige, renown

lusty *adj* = **vigorous**, energetic, healthy, hearty, powerful, robust, strong, sturdy, virile

luxurious *adj* = **sumptuous**, comfortable, expensive, lavish, magnificent, opulent, plush (*inf*), rich, splendid

luxury *n* **1** = **opulence**, affluence, hedonism, richness, splendor, sumptuousness **2** = **extravagance**, extra, frill, indulgence, treat

lying *n* **1** = **dishonesty**, deceit, mendacity, perjury, untruthfulness ♦ *adj* **2** = **deceitful**, dishonest, false, mendacious, perfidious, short tail.

lyre [lir] *n* instrument like harp. **lyr·ic** [LIR-ik], **lyr'i·cal** *adj* **1** of short personal poems expressing emotion. **2** of lyre. **3** meant to be sung. **lyric** *n* **1** lyric poem. ◆ *pl* **2** words of popular song. **lyr'i·cist** [-sist] *n* **1** writer of lyrics. **2** lyric poet. **wax lyrical** express great enthusiasm.

——————— THESAURUS ———————

treacherous, two-faced, untruthful
lyrical *adj* = **enthusiastic**, effusive,

impassioned, inspired, poetic, rhapsodic

M m

ma·ca·bre [mə-KAH-brə] *adj* gruesome, ghastly.

mac·ad·am [mə-KAD-əm] *n* 1 road surface made of pressed layers of small broken stones. 2 this stone.

mac·a·roon [mak-ə-ROON] *n* small cookie made of egg whites, almond paste, etc.

ma·caw [mə-KAW] *n* kind of parrot.

mace [mays] *n* spice made of the husk of the nutmeg.

Mace [mays] *n* ® liquid causing tears and nausea, used as spray for riot control.

mac·er·ate [MAS-ə-rayt] *vt* -at·ed, -at·ing 1 soften by soaking. 2 cause to waste away.

ma·chete [mə-SHET-ee] *n* broad, heavy knife used for cutting or as a weapon.

Mach·i·a·vel·li·an [mak-ee-ə-VEL-ə-ən] *adj* politically unprincipled, crafty, perfidious, subtle.

mach·i·na·tion [mak-ə-NAY-shən] *n* (usu pl) plotting, intrigue.

ma·chine [mə-SHEEN] *n* 1 apparatus combining action of several parts to apply mechanical force. 2 controlling organization. 3 mechanical appliance. 4 vehicle. ♦ *vt* -chined, -chin·ing 5 sew, print, shape, etc. with machine. **ma·chin'er·y** *n, pl* -er·ies 1 parts of machine collectively. 2 machines. **ma·chin'ist** *n* one who makes or operates machines.

ma·chis·mo [mah-CHEEZ-moh] *n* strong or exaggerated masculine pride or masculinity. **ma'cho** [-choh] *adj* 1 denoting or exhibiting such pride in masculinity. ♦ *n, pl* -chos 2 person exhibiting this.

mach (number) [mahk] *n* the ratio of the air speed of an aircraft to the velocity of sound under given conditions.

mack·er·el [MAK-ər-əl] *n* edible sea fish with blue and silver stripes.

mac·ra·mé [MAK-rə-may] *n* ornamental webbing of knotted cord.

mac·ro·bi·ot·ics [mak-roh-bī-OT-iks] *n* (with sing v) dietary system advocating grain and vegetables grown without chemical additives. **mac·ro·bi·ot'ic** *adj, n* (relating to the diet of) person practicing macrobiotics.

mac·ro·cosm [MAK-rə-koz-əm] *n* 1 the universe. 2 any large, complete system.

mad *adj* -der, -dest 1 suffering from mental disease, insane. 2 wildly foolish. 3 very enthusiastic (about). 4 excited. 5 furious, angry. **mad'den** *vt* make mad. **mad'ly** *adv* **mad'man** *n* **mad'ness** *n* 1 insanity. 2 folly.

mad·am [MAD-əm] *n* 1 polite form of address to a woman. 2 woman in charge of house. 3 woman in charge of house of prostitution.

THESAURUS

macabre *adj* = gruesome, dreadful, eerie, frightening, ghastly, ghostly, ghoulish, grim, grisly, morbid

machiavellian *adj* = scheming, astute, crafty, cunning, cynical, double-dealing, opportunist, sly, underhand, unscrupulous

machine *n* 1 = appliance, apparatus, contraption, contrivance, device, engine, instrument, mechanism, tool 2 = system, machinery, organization, setup (*inf*), structure

machinery *n* = equipment, apparatus, gear, instruments, tackle, tools

macho *adj* = manly, chauvinist, masculine, virile

mad *adj* 1 = insane, crazy (*inf*), demented, deranged, *non compos mentis*, nuts (*sl*), of unsound mind, out of one's mind, psychotic, raving, unhinged, unstable 2 = foolish, absurd, asinine, bonkers (*inf*), daft (*inf*), foolhardy, irrational, nonsensical, preposterous, senseless, wild 3 = angry, berserk, enraged, furious, incensed, livid (*inf*), wild 4 = enthusiastic, ardent, avid, crazy (*inf*), fanatical, impassioned, infatuated, wild 5 = frenzied, excited, frenetic, uncontrolled, unrestrained, wild, wired (*sl*) 6 like mad *Inf* = energetically, enthusiastically, excitedly, furiously, rapidly, speedily, violently, wildly

made pt./pp. of MAKE.

Ma·don·na [mə-DON-ə] n 1 the Virgin Mary. 2 picture or statue of her.

mad·ri·gal [MAD-ri-gəl] n 1 unaccompanied part song. 2 short love poem or song.

mael·strom [MAYL-strəm] n 1 great whirlpool. 2 turmoil.

ma·es·to·so [mī-STOH-soh] adv Mus. grandly, in majestic manner.

maes·tro [MĪ-stroh] n 1 outstanding musician, conductor. 2 man regarded as master of any art.

Ma·fi·a [MAH-fee-ə] n international secret organization engaging in crime, orig. Italian.

mag·a·zine [mag-ə-ZEEN] n 1 periodical publication with stories and articles by different writers. 2 appliance for supplying cartridges automatically to gun. 3 storehouse for explosives or arms.

ma·gen·ta [mə-JEN-tə] adj, n (of) purplish-red color.

mag·got [MAG-ət] n grub, larva of certain flies. **mag·got·y** adj infested with maggots.

Ma·gi [MAY-jī] pl n 1 priests of ancient Persia. 2 the wise men from the East at the Nativity.

mag·ic [MAJ-ik] n 1 art of supposedly invoking supernatural powers to influence events, etc. 2 any mysterious agency or power. 3 witchcraft, conjuring. ♦ adj **mag'i·cal** adj **ma·gi'cian** n one skilled in magic, wizard, conjurer, enchanter.

mag·is·trate [MAJ-ə-strayt] n 1 civil officer administering law. 2 justice of the peace. **mag·is·te'ri·al** [-STEER-ee-əl] adj 1 of, referring to magistrate. 2 authoritative. 3 weighty. **mag'is·tra·cy** [-strə-see] n, pl **-cies** 1 office of magistrate. 2 magistrates collectively.

mag·ma [MAG-mə] n 1 paste, suspension. 2 molten rock inside Earth's crust.

mag·nan·i·mous [mag-NAN-ə-məs] adj noble, generous, not petty. **mag·na·nim'i·ty** n

mag·nate [MAG-nayt] n influential or wealthy person.

mag·ne·si·um [mag-NEE-zee-əm] n metallic element. **mag·ne'sia** [-zhə] n white powder compound of this used in medicine.

mag·net [MAG-nit] n 1 piece of iron, steel having properties of attracting iron, steel

---

THESAURUS

madden v = **infuriate**, annoy, derange, drive one crazy, enrage, incense, inflame, irritate, upset

madly adv 1 = **insanely**, crazily, deliriously, distractedly, frantically, frenziedly, hysterically 2 = **foolishly**, absurdly, irrationally, ludicrously, senselessly, wildly 3 = **energetically**, excitedly, furiously, like mad (inf), recklessly, speedily, wildly 4 Inf = **passionately**, desperately, devotedly, intensely, to distraction

madman or **madwoman** n = **lunatic**, maniac, nutcase (sl), psycho (sl), psychopath

madness n 1 = **insanity**, aberration, craziness, delusion, dementia, derangement, distraction, lunacy, mania, mental illness, psychopathy, psychosis 2 = **foolishness**, absurdity, daftness (inf), folly, foolhardiness, idiocy, nonsense, preposterousness, wildness

maelstrom n 1 = **whirlpool**, vortex 2 = **turmoil**, chaos, confusion, disorder, tumult, upheaval

maestro n = **master**, expert, genius, virtuoso

magazine n 1 = **journal**, pamphlet, periodical 2 = **storehouse**, arsenal, depot, store, warehouse

magic n 1 = **sorcery**, black art, enchantment, necromancy, witchcraft, wizardry 2 = **conjuring**, illusion, legerdemain, prestidigitation, sleight of hand, trickery 3 = **charm**, allurement, enchantment, fascination, glamour, magnetism, power ♦ adj 4 (also **magical**) = **miraculous**, bewitching, charming, enchanting, entrancing, fascinating, marvelous, spellbinding

magician n = **sorcerer**, conjurer, enchanter or enchantress, illusionist, necromancer, warlock, witch, wizard

magisterial adj = **authoritative**, commanding, lordly, masterful

magistrate n = **judge**, J.P., justice, justice of the peace

magnanimity n = **generosity**, benevolence, big-heartedness, largesse or largess, nobility, selflessness, unselfishness

magnanimous adj = **generous**, big-hearted, bountiful, charitable, kind, noble, selfless, unselfish

magnate n = **tycoon**, baron, captain of industry, mogul, plutocrat and pointing north and south when suspended. **2** lodestone. **mag·net'ic** *adj* **1** with properties of magnet. **2** exerting powerful attraction. **mag·net'i·cal·ly** *adv* **mag'net·ism** [-ni-tiz-əm] *n* **1** magnetic phenomena. **2** science of this. **3** personal charm or power of attracting others. **mag'net·ize** *vt* **-ized, -iz·ing** **1** make into a magnet. **2** attract as if by magnet. **3** fascinate. **mag·ne'to** [-NEE-toh] *n, pl* **-tos** apparatus for ignition in internal combustion engine.

mag·nif·i·cent [mag-NIF-ə-sənt] *adj* **1** splendid. **2** stately, imposing. **3** excellent. **mag·nif'i·cence** *n*

mag·ni·fy [MAG-nə-fī] *v* **-fied, -fy·ing** **1** increase apparent size of, as with lens. **2** exaggerate. **3** make greater. **mag·ni·fi·ca'tion** [-KAY-shən] *n*

mag·nil·o·quent [mag-NIL-ə-kwənt] *adj* **1** speaking pompously. **2** grandiose. **mag·nil'o·quence** *n*

mag·ni·tude [MAG-ni-tood] *n* **1** importance. **2** greatness, size.

mag·num [MAG-nəm] *n* large wine bottle (approx. 1.6 quarts, 1.5 liters).

mag·pie [MAG-pī] *n* **1** black-and-white bird. **2** incessantly talkative person.

ma·ha·ra·jah [mah-hə-RAH-jə] *n* former title of some Indian princes.

ma·ha·ri·shi [mah-hə-REE-shee] *n* Hindu religious teacher or mystic.

ma·hat·ma [mə-HAHT-mə] *n Hinduism* **1** man of saintly life with supernatural

powers. **2** one endowed with great wisdom and power.

mahl·stick [MAHL-stik] *n* light stick with ball at one end, held in other hand to support working hand while painting.

maid·en [MAYD-n] *n* **1** *lit* young unmarried woman. ♦ *adj* **2** unmarried. **3** of, suited to maiden. **4** first. **5** having blank record. **maid** *n* **1** woman servant. **2** *lit* young unmarried woman. **maid'en·ly** *adj* modest. **maid'en·hair** *n* fern with delicate stalks and fronds. **maid'en·head** *n* virginity. **maiden name** woman's surname before marriage.

mail¹ [mayl] *n* **1** letters, etc. transported and delivered by the post office. **2** letters, etc. conveyed at one time. **3** the postal system. **4** train, ship, etc. carrying mail. ♦ *vt* **5** send by mail. **electronic mail** sending of messages between computer terminals (also **e-mail**).

mail² *n* armor of interlaced rings or overlapping plates. **mailed** *adj* covered with mail.

maim [maym] *vt* cripple, mutilate.

main [mayn] *adj* chief, principal, leading. ♦ *n* **2** principal pipe, line carrying water, gas, etc. **3** chief part. **4** strength, power. **5** *obs* open sea. **main'ly** *adv* for the most part, chiefly. **main'frame** *Computers* ♦ *adj* **1** denoting a high-speed general-purpose computer. ♦ *n* **2** such a computer. **main'land** *n* stretch of land that forms main part of a country. **main'mast** *n* chief mast in ship. **main'sail** *n* lowest sail of

——————| THESAURUS |——————

magnetic *adj* = **attractive**, captivating, charismatic, charming, fascinating, hypnotic, irresistible, mesmerizing, seductive

magnetism *n* = **charm**, allure, appeal, attraction, charisma, drawing power, magic, pull, seductiveness

magnification *n* = **increase**, amplification, enhancement, enlargement, expansion, heightening, intensification

magnificence *n* = **splendor**, brilliance, glory, grandeur, majesty, nobility, opulence, stateliness, sumptuousness

magnificent *adj* **1** = **splendid**, cool (*inf*), glorious, gorgeous, imposing, impressive, majestic, regal, sublime, sumptuous **2** = **excellent**, brilliant, fine, outstanding, phat (*sl*), splendid, superb

magnify *v* **1** = **enlarge**, amplify, blow up (*inf*), boost, dilate, expand, heighten,

increase, intensify **2** = **overstate**, exaggerate, inflate, overemphasize, overplay

magnitude *n* **1** = **importance**, consequence, greatness, moment, note, significance, weight **2** = **size**, amount, amplitude, extent, mass, quantity, volume

maid *n* **1** = **girl**, damsel, lass, maiden, wench **2** = **servant**, housemaid, maidservant, serving-maid

maiden *n* **1** = **girl**, damsel, lass, maid, virgin, wench ♦ *v* **2** = **unmarried**, unwed **3** = **first**, inaugural, initial, introductory

maidenly *adj* = **modest**, chaste, decent, decorous, demure, pure, virginal

mail *n* **1** = **letters**, correspondence, junk mail, post (*chiefly Brit.*) **2** = **postal service**, collection, delivery, post office ♦ *v* **3** = **post**, dispatch, forward, send, transmit

maim *v* = **cripple**, disable, hurt, injure,

mainmast. **main'spring** n 1 chief spring of watch or clock. 2 chief cause or motive. **main'stay** n 1 rope from mainmast. 2 chief support.

main·tain [mayn-TAYN] vt 1 carry on. 2 preserve. 3 support. 4 sustain. 5 keep up. 6 keep supplied. 7 affirm. 8 support by argument. 9 defend. **main'te·nance** [-tə-nəns] n 1 maintaining. 2 means of support. 3 upkeep of buildings, etc. 4 provision of money for separated or divorced spouse.

maize [mayz] n primitive corn with kernels of various colors, Indian corn.

maj·es·ty [MAJ-ə-stee] n 1 stateliness. 2 sovereignty. 3 grandeur. **ma·jes'tic** [mə-] adj 1 splendid. 2 regal. **ma·jes'ti·cal·ly** adv

ma·jor [MAY-jər] n 1 military officer ranking next above captain. 2 scale in music. 3 principal field of study at college. 4 person engaged in this. ◆ adj 5 greater in number, quality, extent. 6 significant, serious.

ma·jor'i·ty n 1 greater number. 2 larger party voting together. 3 more than half of votes cast in election. 4 coming of age. 5 rank of major. **major-do·mo** [-DOH-moh] n, pl -mos male servant in charge of large household.

make [mayk] v made, mak·ing 1 construct. 2 produce. 3 create. 4 establish. 5 appoint. 6 amount to. 7 cause to do something. 8 accomplish. 9 reach. 10 earn. 11 tend. 12 contribute. ◆ n 13 brand, type, or style. **making** n 1 creation. ◆ pl 2 necessary requirements or qualities. **make allowance for** take mitigating circumstance into consideration. **make'shift** n temporary expedient. **make'up** n 1 cosmetics. 2 characteristics. 3 layout. **make up** 1 compose. 2 complete. 3 complete. 4 compensate. 5 apply cosmetics. 6 invent. **on the make** 1 inf intent on gain. 2 sl seeking sexual relations.

mal- comb. form ill, badly, e.g. malformation;

mutilate, wound

main adj 1 = **chief**, central, essential, foremost, head, leading, pre-eminent, primary, principal ◆ n 2 = **conduit**, cable, channel, duct, line, pipe 3 **in the main** = **on the whole**, for the most part, generally, in general, mainly, mostly

mainly adv = **chiefly**, for the most part, in the main, largely, mostly, on the whole, predominantly, primarily, principally

mainstay n = **pillar**, anchor, backbone, bulwark, buttress, lynchpin, prop

mainstream adj = **conventional**, accepted, current, established, general, orthodox, prevailing, received

maintain v 1 = **keep up**, carry on, continue, perpetuate, preserve, prolong, retain, sustain 2 = **support**, care for, look after, provide for, supply, take care of 3 = **assert**, avow, claim, contend, declare, insist, profess, state

maintenance n 1 = **continuation**, carrying-on, perpetuation, prolongation 2 = **upkeep**, care, conservation, keeping, nurture, preservation, repairs 3 = **allowance**, alimony, keep, support

majestic adj = **grand**, grandiose, impressive, magnificent, monumental, regal, splendid, stately, sublime, superb

majesty n = **grandeur**, glory, magnificence, nobility, pomp, splendor, stateliness

major adj 1 = **main**, bigger, chief, greater, higher, leading, senior, supreme 2 = **important**, critical, crucial, great, notable, outstanding, serious, significant

majority n 1 = **preponderance**, best part, bulk, greater number, mass, most 2 = **adulthood**, manhood or womanhood, maturity, seniority

make v 1 = **create**, assemble, build, construct, fashion, form, manufacture, produce, put together, synthesize 2 = **produce**, accomplish, bring about, cause, create, effect, generate, give rise to, lead to 3 = **force**, cause, compel, constrain, drive, impel, induce, oblige, prevail upon, require 4 = **amount to**, add up to, compose, constitute, form 5 = **perform**, carry out, do, effect, execute 6 = **earn**, clear, gain, get, net, obtain, win 7 **make it** inf = **succeed**, arrive (inf), get on, prosper ◆ n 8 = **brand**, kind, model, sort, style, type, variety

make-believe n = **fantasy**, imagination, play-acting, pretense, unreality

make for v = **head for**, aim for, be bound for, head towards

make off v 1 = **flee**, bolt, clear out (inf), run away or off, take to one's heels 2 **make off with** = **steal**, abduct, carry off, filch, kidnap, pinch (inf), run away or off with

make out v 1 = **see**, detect, discern, discover, distinguish, perceive, recognize *malevolent.*

ma·lac·ca [mə-LAK-ə] *n* brown cane used for walking stick.

mal·a·droit [mal-ə-DROIT] *adj* clumsy, awkward.

mal·a·dy [MAL-ə-dee] *n, pl* **-dies** disease.

ma·laise [ma-LAYZ] *n* vague, unlocated feeling of bodily discomfort.

mal·a·prop·ism [MAL-ə-prop-iz-əm] *n* ludicrous misuse of word.

ma·lar·i·a [mə-LAIR-ee-ə] *n* infectious disease caused by parasite transmitted by bite of some mosquitoes. **ma·lar'i·al** *adj*

mal·con·tent [mal-kən-TENT] *adj* **1** actively discontented. ◆ *n* **2** malcontent person.

male [mayl] *adj* **1** of sex producing gametes that fertilize female gametes. **2** of men or male animals. **3** of machine part, made to fit inside corresponding recessed female part. ◆ *n* **4** male person or animal.

mal·e·dic·tion [mal-i-DIK-shən] *n* curse.

mal·e·fac·tor [MAL-ə-fak-tər] *n* criminal.

mal·ev·o·lent [mə-LEV-ə-lənt] *adj* full of ill will. **mal·ev'o·lence** *n*

mal·fea·sance [mal-FEE-zəns] *n* **1** illegal action. **2** official misconduct.

mal·ice [MAL-is] *n* **1** ill will. **2** spite. **ma·li·cious** [mə-LISH-əs] *adj* **1** intending evil or unkindness. **2** spiteful. **3** moved by hatred.

ma·lign [mə-LĪn] *adj* **1** evil in influence or effect. ◆ *vt* **2** slander, misrepresent. **ma·lig'nan·cy** [-LIG-nən-see] *n* **ma·lig'nant** *adj* **1** feeling extreme ill will. **2** (of disease) resistant to therapy. **3** tending to produce death. **ma·lig'ni·ty** *n* malignant disposition.

2 = **understand**, comprehend, decipher, fathom, follow, grasp, work out **3** = **write out**, complete, draw up, fill in *or* out **4** = **pretend**, assert, claim, let on, make as if *or* though **5** = **fare**, get on, manage

maker *n* = **manufacturer**, builder, constructor, producer

makeshift *adj* = **temporary**, expedient, provisional, stopgap, substitute

make-up *n* **1** = **cosmetics**, face (*inf*), greasepaint (*Theatre*), paint (*inf*), powder **2** = **structure**, arrangement, assembly, composition, configuration, constitution, construction, format, organization **3** = **nature**, character, constitution, disposition, temperament

make up *v* **1** = **form**, compose, comprise, constitute **2** = **invent**, coin, compose, concoct, construct, create, devise, dream up, formulate, frame, originate **3** = **complete**, fill, supply **4** = **settle**, bury the hatchet, call it quits, reconcile **5 make up for** = **compensate for**, atone for, balance, make amends for, offset, recompense

making *n* = **creation**, assembly, building, composition, construction, fabrication, manufacture, production

makings *pl n* = **beginnings**, capacity, ingredients, potential

maladjusted *adj* = **disturbed**, alienated, neurotic, unstable

maladministration *n* = **mismanagement**, corruption, dishonesty, incompetence, inefficiency, malpractice, misrule

maladroit *adj* = **clumsy**, awkward, inept, inexpert, unskillful

malady *n* = **disease**, affliction, ailment, complaint, disorder, illness, infirmity, sickness

malaise *n* = **unease**, anxiety, depression, disquiet, melancholy

malcontent *n* = **troublemaker**, agitator, mischief-maker, rebel, stirrer (*inf*)

male *adj* = **masculine**, manly, virile

malefactor *n* = **wrongdoer**, criminal, delinquent, evildoer, miscreant, offender, villain

malevolence *n* = **malice**, hate, hatred, ill will, rancor, spite, vindictiveness

malevolent *adj* = **spiteful**, hostile, ill-natured, malicious, malign, vengeful, vindictive

malformation *n* = **deformity**, distortion, misshapenness

malformed *adj* = **misshapen**, abnormal, crooked, deformed, distorted, irregular, twisted

malfunction *v* **1** = **break down**, fail, go wrong ◆ *n* **2** = **fault**, breakdown, defect, failure, flaw, glitch

malice *n* = **ill will**, animosity, enmity, evil intent, hate, hatred, malevolence, spite, vindictiveness

malicious *adj* = **spiteful**, ill-disposed, ill-natured, malevolent, rancorous, resentful, vengeful

malign *v* **1** = **disparage**, abuse, defame, denigrate, libel, run down, slander, smear, vilify ◆ *adj* **2** = **evil**, bad, destructive,

ma·lin·ger [mə-LING-gər] vi feign illness to escape duty. **ma·lin'ger·er** n

mall [mawl] n **1** level, shaded walk. **2** street, shopping area closed to vehicles.

mal·le·a·ble [MAL-ee-ə-bəl] adj **1** capable of being hammered into shape. **2** adaptable.

mal·let [MAL-it] n (wooden, etc.) hammer. **1** croquet or polo stick.

mal·nu·tri·tion [mal-noo-TRISH-ən] n inadequate nutrition.

mal·o·dor·ous [mal-OH-dər-əs] adj evil-smelling.

mal·prac·tice [mal-PRAK-tis] n immoral, careless illegal or unethical conduct.

malt [mawlt] n **1** grain used for brewing or distilling. ◆ vt **2** make into malt.

mam·bo [MAHM-boh] n, pl **-bos** Latin Amer. dance like rumba.

mam·mal [MAM-əl] n animal of type that suckles its young. **mam·ma'li·an** [-MAY-lee-ən] adj

mam·ma·ry [MAM-er-ee] adj of, relating to breast or milk-producing gland.

mam·mon [MAM-ən] n **1** wealth regarded as source of evil. **2** (**M-**) false god of covetousness.

mam·moth [MAM-əth] n **1** extinct animal like an elephant. ◆ adj **2** colossal.

man n, pl **men 1** human being. **2** person. **3** human race. **4** adult male. **5** manservant. **6** piece used in chess, etc. ◆ vt **manned, man·ning 7** supply (ship, artillery, etc.) with necessary crew. **8** fortify. **man'ful** adj brave, vigorous. **man'li·ness** n **man'ly** adj **-li·er, -li·est man'nish** adj like a man.

man·han·dle vt **-dled, -dling** treat roughly.

man·hole n opening through which person can pass to a drain, sewer, etc.

man'hood [-huud] n **man'kind'** [-KĪND] n human beings in general. **man'pow·er** n **1** power of human effort. **2** available number of workers. **man'slaugh·ter** [-slaw-tər] n culpable homicide without malice aforethought.

man·a·cle [MAN-ə-kəl] n **1** fetter, handcuff. ◆ vt **-cled, -cling 2** shackle.

man·age [MAN-ij] vt **-aged, -ag·ing 1** be in charge of, administer. **2** succeed in doing. **3** control. **4** handle, cope with. **5** conduct, carry on. **6** persuade. **man'age·a·ble** adj **man'age·ment** n **1** those who manage, as board of directors, etc. **2** administration. **3** skillful use of means. **4** conduct. **man'ag·er** n **1** one in charge of business, institution, actor, etc. **2** one who manages efficiently. **man·a·ge'ri·al** adj

man·a·tee [MAN-ə-tee] n large, plant-eating aquatic mammal.

man·da·rin [MAN-də-rin] n **1** Hist. Chinese

── THESAURUS ──

harmful, hostile, injurious, malevolent, malignant, pernicious, wicked

malignant adj **1 = harmful**, destructive, hostile, hurtful, malevolent, malign, pernicious, spiteful **2** Medical = **uncontrollable**, cancerous, dangerous, deadly, fatal, irremediable

malleable adj **1 = workable**, ductile, plastic, soft, tensile **2 = manageable**, adaptable, biddable, compliant, impressionable, pliable, tractable

malodorous adj **= smelly**, fetid, funky (sl), mephitic, nauseating, noisome, offensive, putrid, reeking, stinking

malpractice n **= misconduct**, abuse, dereliction, mismanagement, negligence

maltreat v **= abuse**, bully, harm, hurt, ill-treat, injure, mistreat

mammoth adj **= colossal**, enormous, giant, gigantic, huge, immense, massive, monumental, mountainous, prodigious

man n **1 = male**, chap (inf), dude (inf), gentleman, guy (inf) **2 = human**, human being, individual, person, soul **3 =**

mankind, Homo sapiens, humanity, humankind, human race, people **4 = manservant**, attendant, retainer, servant, valet ◆ v **5 = staff**, crew, garrison, occupy, people

manacle n **1 = handcuff**, bond, chain, fetter, iron, shackle ◆ v **2 = handcuff**, bind, chain, fetter, put in chains, shackle

manage v **1 = administer**, be in charge (of), command, conduct, direct, handle, run, supervise **2 = succeed**, accomplish, arrange, contrive, effect, engineer **3 = handle**, control, manipulate, operate, use **4 = cope**, carry on, get by (inf), make do, muddle through, survive

manageable adj **= docile**, amenable, compliant, easy, submissive

management n **1 = directors**, administration, board, employers, executive(s) **2 = administration**, command, control, direction, handling, operation, running, supervision

manager n **= supervisor**, administrator, boss (inf), director, executive, governor, high-ranking bureaucrat. **2** *fig* any high government official. **3** Chinese variety of orange.

man·date [MAN-dayt] *n* **1** command of, or commission to act for, another. **2** commission from United Nations to govern a territory. **3** instruction from electorate to representative or government. **man'dat·ed** *adj* committed to a mandate. **man'da·to·ry** [-də-tor-ee] *n* holder of a mandate. **man'da·to·ry** *adj* compulsory.

man·di·ble [MAN-də-bəl] *n* **1** lower jawbone. **2** either part of bird's beak. **man·dib'u·lar** *adj* of, like mandible.

man·do·lin [MAN-dl-in] *n* stringed musical instrument.

man·drel [MAN-drəl] *n* **1** axis on which material is supported in a lathe. **2** spindle around which metal is forged.

man'drill *n* large blue-faced baboon.

mane [mayn] *n* long hair on neck of horse, lion, etc.

ma·neu·ver [mə-NOO-vər] *n* **1** contrived, complicated, perhaps deceptive plan or action. **2** skillful management. ◆ *v* **3** employ stratagems, work adroitly. **4** (cause to) perform maneuvers.

man·ga·nese [MANG-gə-neez] *n* **1** metallic element. **2** black oxide of this.

mange [maynj] *n* skin disease of dogs, etc. **man'gy** *adj* **-gi·er, -gi·est** scruffy, shabby.

man·ger [MAYN-jər] *n* eating trough in

stable.

man·gle¹ [MANG-gəl] *n* **1** machine for pressing clothes, etc. to remove water. ◆ *vt* **-gled, -gling 2** press in mangle.

man·gle² *vt* **-gled, -gling** mutilate, spoil, hack.

man·go [MANG-goh] *n, pl* **-goes 1** tropical fruit. **2** tree bearing it.

man·grove [MANG-grohv] *n* tropical tree that grows on muddy banks of estuaries.

ma·ni·a [MAY-nee-ə] *n* **1** madness. **2** prevailing craze. **ma'ni·ac, ma·ni'a·cal, man'ic** *adj* affected by mania. **maniac** *n inf* **1** mad person. **2** wild enthusiast.

man·i·cure [MAN-i-kyuur] *n* **1** treatment and care of fingernails and hands. ◆ *vt* **-cured, -cur·ing 2** apply such treatment. **man'i·cur·ist** *n* one who does this professionally.

man·i·fest [MAN-ə-fest] *adj* **1** clearly revealed, undoubted. ◆ *vt* **2** make manifest. ◆ *n* **3** list of cargo for customs. **man·i·fes·ta'tion** *n* **man'i·fest·ly** *adv* clearly. **man·i·fes'to** *n, pl* **-toes** declaration of policy by political party, government, or movement.

man·i·fold [MAN-ə-fohld] *adj* **1** numerous and varied. ◆ *n* **2** in internal combustion engine, pipe with several outlets.

ma·nip·u·late [mə-NIP-yə-layt] *vt* **-lat·ed, -lat·ing 1** handle. **2** deal with skillfully. **3** manage. **4** falsify. **ma·nip·u·la'tion** *n* **1** act of manipulating, working by hand. **2**

——— THESAURUS ———

head, organizer

mandate *n* = **command**, commission, decree, directive, edict, instruction, order

mandatory *adj* = **compulsory**, binding, obligatory, required, requisite

maneuver *n* **1** = **stratagem**, dodge, intrigue, machination, ploy, ruse, scheme, subterfuge, tactic, trick **2** = **movement**, exercise, operation ◆ *v* **3** = **manipulate**, contrive, engineer, machinate, pull strings, scheme, wangle (*inf*) **4** = **move**, deploy, exercise

manfully *adv* = **bravely**, boldly, courageously, determinedly, gallantly, hard, resolutely, stoutly, valiantly

mangle *v* = **crush**, deform, destroy, disfigure, distort, mutilate, ruin, spoil, tear, wreck

mangy *adj* = **dirty**, moth-eaten, scuzzy (*sl*), seedy, shabby, shoddy, squalid

manhandle *v* = **rough up**, knock about or

around, maul, paw (*inf*)

manhood *n* = **manliness**, masculinity, virility

mania *n* **1** = **madness**, delirium, dementia, derangement, insanity, lunacy **2** = **obsession**, craze, fad (*inf*), fetish, fixation, passion, preoccupation, thing (*inf*)

maniac *n* **1** = **madman** or **madwoman**, lunatic, psycho (*sl*), psychopath **2** = **fanatic**, enthusiast, fan, fiend (*inf*), freak (*inf*)

manifest *adj* **1** = **obvious**, apparent, blatant, clear, conspicuous, evident, glaring, noticeable, palpable, patent ◆ *v* **2** = **display**, demonstrate, exhibit, expose, express, reveal, show

manifestation *n* = **display**, demonstration, exhibition, expression, indication, mark, show, sign, symptom

manifold *adj* = **numerous**, assorted, copious, diverse, many, multifarious, skilled use of hands. **ma·nip'u·la·tive** adj

man·na [MAN-ə] n **1** food of Israelites in the wilderness. **2** unexpected benefit.

man·ne·quin [MAN-i-kin] n **1** person who models clothes, esp. at fashion shows. **2** clothing dummy.

man·ner [MAN-ər] n **1** way thing happens or is done. **2** sort, kind. **3** custom. **4** style. ◆ pl **5** social behavior. **man'ner·ism** n person's distinctive habit, trait. **man'ner·ly** adj polite.

man·or [MAN-ər] n main house of estate or plantation. **ma·no'ri·al** adj

man·sard [MAN-sahrd] n roof with break in its slope, lower part being steeper than upper.

man·sion [MAN-shən] n large house.

man·tel [MAN-tl] n **1** structure around fireplace. **2** mantelpiece. **man'tel·piece, -shelf** n shelf at top of mantel.

man·til·la [man-TIL-ə] n in Spain, (lace) scarf worn as headdress.

man·tis n, pl **-tis·es** genus of insects including the stick insects and leaf insects.

man·tle [MAN-tl] n **1** loose cloak. **2** covering. **3** incandescent fireproof network hood around gas jet. ◆ vt **-tled, -tling 4** cover. **5** conceal. **man·tle·piece** n mantel.

man·tra [MAN-trə] n word or phrase

repeated as object of concentration in meditation.

man·u·al [MAN-yoo-əl] adj **1** of, or done with, the hands. **2** by human labor, not automatic. ◆ n **3** handbook. **4** textbook. **5** organ keyboard.

man·u·fac·ture [man-yə-FAK-chər] vt **-tured, -tur·ing 1** process, make (materials) into finished articles. **2** produce (articles). **3** invent, concoct. ◆ n **4** making of articles, materials, esp. in large quantities. **5** anything produced from raw materials. **man·u·fac'tur·er** n

ma·nure [mə-NUUR] vt **-nured, -nur·ing 1** enrich land. ◆ n **2** dung, chemical fertilizer (used to enrich land).

man·u·script [MAN-yə-skript] n **1** book, document, written by hand. **2** copy for printing. ◆ adj **3** handwritten or typed.

man·y [MEN-ee] adj **more, most 1** numerous. ◆ n, pron **2** large number.

Ma·o·ri [MAH-aw-ree] n **1** member of New Zealand aboriginal population. **2** their language.

map n **1** flat representation of Earth or some part of it, or of the heavens. ◆ vt **mapped, map·ping 2** make a map of. **3** (with out) plan.

ma·ple [MAY-pəl] n tree with broad leaves,

THESAURUS

multiple, varied, various

manipulate v **1** = **work**, handle, operate, use **2** = **influence**, control, direct, engineer, maneuver

mankind n = **people**, Homo sapiens, humanity, humankind, human race, man

manliness n = **virility**, boldness, bravery, courage, fearlessness, masculinity, valor, vigor

manly adj = **virile**, bold, brave, courageous, fearless, manful, masculine, strapping, strong, vigorous

man-made adj = **artificial**, ersatz, manufactured, mock, synthetic

manner n **1** = **behavior**, air, aspect, bearing, conduct, demeanor **2** = **style**, custom, fashion, method, mode, way **3** = **type**, brand, category, form, kind, sort, variety

mannered adj = **affected**, artificial, pretentious, stilted

mannerism n = **habit**, characteristic, foible, idiosyncrasy, peculiarity, quirk, trait, trick

manners pl n **1** = **behavior**, conduct,

demeanor **2** = **politeness**, courtesy, decorum, etiquette, p's and q's, refinement

mansion n = **residence**, hall, manor, seat, villa

mantle n **1** = **cloak**, cape, hood, shawl, wrap **2** = **covering**, blanket, canopy, curtain, pall, screen, shroud, veil

manual adj **1** = **hand-operated**, human, physical ◆ n **2** = **handbook**, bible, instructions

manufacture v **1** = **make**, assemble, build, construct, create, mass-produce, produce, put together, turn out **2** = **concoct**, cook up (inf), devise, fabricate, invent, make up, think up, trump up ◆ n **3** = **making**, assembly, construction, creation, production

manufacturer n = **maker**, builder, constructor, creator, industrialist, producer

manure n = **compost**, droppings, dung, excrement, fertilizer, muck, ordure

many adj **1** = **numerous**, abundant, countless, innumerable, manifold, myriad, umpteen (inf), various ◆ n **2** = **a lot**, heaps a variety of which (**sugar maple**) yields sugar.

ma·quis [mah-KEE] *n* **1** scrubby undergrowth of Mediterranean countries. **2** name adopted by French resistance movement in WWII.

mar [mahr] *vt* **marred, mar·ring** spoil, impair.

mar·a·bou [MAR-ə-boo] *n* **1** kind of stork. **2** its soft white lower tail feathers, formerly used to trim hats, etc. **3** kind of silk.

ma·rac·a [mə-RAH-kə] *n* percussion instrument of gourd containing dried seeds, etc.

mar·a·schi·no [mar-ə-SKEE-noh] *n* liqueur made from cherries.

mar·a·thon [MAR-ə-thon] *n* **1** long-distance race. **2** endurance contest.

ma·raud [mə-RAWD] *v* **1** make raid for plunder. **2** pillage. **ma·raud'er** *n*

mar·ble [MAHR-bəl] *n* **1** kind of limestone capable of taking polish. **2** slab of, sculpture in this. **3** small ball used in children's game. **mar'bled** *adj* **1** having mottled appearance, like marble. **2** (of beef) streaked with fat.

march [mahrch] *vi* **1** walk with military step. **2** go, progress. ♦ *vt* **3** cause to march. ♦ *n* **4** action of marching. **5** distance marched in day. **6** tune to accompany marching.

mar·chion·ess [MAHR-shə-nis] *n* wife, widow of marquis.

Mar·di Gras [MAHR-dee grah] *n* **1** festival of Shrove Tuesday. **2** revelry celebrating this.

mare [mair] *n* female horse. **mare's-nest** *n* supposed discovery that proves worthless.

mar·ga·rine [MAHR-jər-in] *n* butter substitute made from vegetable fats.

mar·gin [MAHR-jin] *n* **1** border, edge. **2** space around printed page. **3** amount allowed beyond what is necessary. **mar'gin·al** *adj*

mar·i·gold [MAR-i-gohld] *n* plant with yellow flowers.

ma·ri·jua·na [mar-ə-WAH-nə] *n* dried flowers and leaves of hemp plant, used as narcotic.

ma·ri·na [mə-REE-nə] *n* mooring facility for yachts and pleasure boats.

mar·i·nade [mar-ə-NAYD] *n* seasoned, flavored liquid used to soak fish, meat, etc. before cooking. **mar'i·nate** *vt* **-nat·ed, -nat·ing**

ma·rine [mə-REEN] *adj* **1** of the sea or shipping. **2** used at, found in sea. ♦ *n* **3** shipping, fleet. **4** soldier trained for land or sea combat. **mar'i·ner** *n* sailor.

mar·i·on·ette [mar-ee-ə-NET] *n* puppet worked with strings.

mar·i·tal [MAR-i-tl] *adj* relating to marriage.

mar·i·time [MAR-i-tīm] *adj* **1** connected with seafaring. **2** naval. **3** bordering on the sea.

mar·jo·ram [MAHR-jər-əm] *n* aromatic herb.

mark[1] [mahrk] *n* **1** line, dot, scar, etc. **2** sign, token. **3** inscription. **4** letter, number showing evaluation of schoolwork, etc. **5** indication. **6** target. ♦ *vt* **7** make a mark on. **8** be distinguishing mark of. **9** indicate. **10** notice. **11** watch. **12** assess, e.g. examination paper. ♦ *vi* **13** take notice. **mark'er** *n* **1** one who, that which marks. **2** counter used at card playing, etc. **3** *sl* an IOU. **marks'man** *n* skilled shot.

mark[2] *n* former German monetary unit.

mar·ket [MAHR-kit] *n* **1** assembly, place for

(*inf*), lots (*inf*), plenty, scores

mar *v* = **spoil**, blemish, damage, detract from, disfigure, hurt, impair, ruin, scar, stain, taint, tarnish

maraud *v* = **raid**, forage, loot, pillage, plunder, ransack, ravage

marauder *n* = **raider**, bandit, buccaneer, outlaw, plunderer

march *v* = **walk**, file, pace, parade, stride, strut ♦ *n* **2** = **walk**, routemarch, trek **3** = **progress**, advance, development, evolution, progression

margin *n* = **edge**, border, boundary, brink, perimeter, periphery, rim, side, verge

marginal *adj* **1** = **borderline**, bordering, on the edge, peripheral **2** = **insignificant**, minimal, minor, negligible, slight, small

marijuana *n* = **cannabis**, dope (*sl*), grass (*sl*), hemp, pot (*sl*)

marine *adj* = **nautical**, maritime, naval, seafaring, seagoing

mariner *n* = **sailor**, salt, sea dog, seafarer, seaman

marital *adj* = **matrimonial**, conjugal, connubial, nuptial

maritime *adj* **1** = **nautical**, marine, naval, oceanic, seafaring **2** = **coastal**, littoral, seaside buying and selling. **2** demand for goods. **3** center for trade. ◆ *vt* **4** offer or produce for sale. **mar·ket·a·ble** *adj*

mar·ma·lade [MAHR-mə-layd] *n* preserve usually made of oranges, lemons, etc.

mar·mo·re·al [mahr-MOR-ee-əl] *adj* of or like marble.

ma·roon[1] [mə-ROON] *n* **1** brownish-red. **2** firework. ◆ *adj* **3** of the color.

ma·roon[2] *vt* **1** leave (person) on deserted island or coast. **2** isolate, cut off by any means.

mar·quee [mahr-KEE] *n* **1** rooflike shelter with open sides. **2** rooflike projection above theater, etc. displaying name of play, etc. being performed.

mar·quis [MAHR-kwis] *n* nobleman of rank below duke.

mar·row [MAR-oh] *n* **1** fatty substance inside bones. **2** vital part.

mar·ry [MAR-ee] *v* -**ried**, -**ry·ing 1** join as husband and wife. **2** unite closely. **mar·riage** [MAR-ij] *n* **1** state of being married. **2** wedding. **mar·riage·a·ble** *adj*

Mars [mahrz] *n* **1** Roman god of war. **2** planet nearest but one to Earth. **Mar·tian** [MAHR-shən] *n* **1** supposed inhabitant of Mars. ◆ *adj* **2** of Mars.

marsh [mahrsh] *n* low-lying wet land. **marsh·y** *adj* **marsh·i·er**, **marsh·i·est**

mar·shal [MAHR-shəl] *n* **1** high officer of state. **2** law enforcement officer. ◆ *vt* -**shaled**, -**shal·ing 3** arrange in due order. **4** conduct with ceremony. **field marshal** in some nations, military officer of the highest rank.

marsh'mal·low [MAHRSH-mal-oh] *n* spongy candy orig. made from root of **marsh mallow**, shrubby plant growing near marshes.

mar·su·pi·al [mahr-SOO-pee-əl] *n* animal that carries its young in pouch, e.g. kangaroo. ◆ *adj*

mar·ten [MAHR-tn] *n* **1** weasel-like animal. **2** its fur.

mar·tial [MAHR-shəl] *adj* **1** relating to war. **2** warlike, brave. **court martial** see COURT. **martial law** law enforced by military authorities in times of danger or emergency.

mar'tin *n* species of swallow.

mar·ti·net [mahr-tn-ET] *n* strict disciplinarian.

mar·ti·ni [mahr-TEE-nee] *n, pl* -**nis** cocktail containing gin and vermouth.

mar·tyr [MAHR-tər] *n* **1** one put to death for not renouncing beliefs. **2** one who suffers in some cause. **3** one in constant suffering. ◆ *vt* **4** make martyr of. **mar'tyr·dom** [-dəm] *n*

mar·vel [MAHR-vəl] *vi* -**veled**, -**vel·ing 1** wonder. ◆ *n* **2** wonderful thing.

mark *n* **1** = **spot**, blemish, blot, line, scar, scratch, smudge, stain, streak **2** = **sign**, badge, device, emblem, flag, hallmark, label, symbol, token **3** = **criterion**, measure, norm, standard, yardstick **4** = **target**, aim, goal, object, objective, purpose ◆ *v* **5** = **scar**, blemish, blot, scratch, smudge, stain, streak **6** = **characterize**, brand, flag, identify, label, stamp **7** = **distinguish**, denote, exemplify, illustrate, show **8** = **observe**, attend, mind, note, notice, pay attention, pay heed, watch **9** = **grade**, appraise, assess, correct, evaluate

marked *adj* = **noticeable**, blatant, clear, conspicuous, decided, distinct, obvious, patent, prominent, pronounced, striking

markedly *adv* = **noticeable**, clearly, considerably, conspicuously, decidedly, distinctly, obviously, strikingly

market *n* **1** = **fair**, bazaar, mart ◆ *v* **2** = **sell**, retail, vend

marketable *adj* = **sought after**, in demand, salable, wanted

marksman, markswoman *n* = **sharpshooter**, crack shot (*inf*), good shot

maroon *v* = **abandon**, desert, leave, leave high and dry (*inf*), strand

marriage *n* = **wedding**, match, matrimony, nuptials, wedlock

marry *v* **1** = **wed**, get hitched (*sl*), tie the knot (*inf*) **2** = **unite**, ally, bond, join, knit, link, merge, unify, yoke

marsh *n* = **swamp**, bog, fen, morass, quagmire, slough

marshal *v* **1** = **arrange**, align, array, deploy, draw up, group, line up, order, organize **2** = **conduct**, escort, guide, lead, shepherd, usher

marshy *adj* = **swampy**, boggy, quaggy, waterlogged, wet

martial *adj* = **military**, bellicose, belligerent, warlike

martinet *n* = **disciplinarian**, stickler

martyrdom *n* = **persecution**, ordeal, suffering

mar·vel·ous *adj* **1** amazing. **2** wonderful.

mar·zi·pan [MAHR-zə-pan] *n* paste of almonds, sugar, etc. used in candies, cakes, etc.

mas·car·a [ma-SKAIR-ə] *n* cosmetic for darkening eyelashes and eyebrows.

mas·cot [MAS-kot] *n* animal, person or thing supposed to bring luck.

mas·cu·line [MAS-kyə-lin] *adj* **1** relating to males. **2** manly. **3** of the grammatical gender to which names of males belong.

mash *n* **1** grain, meal mixed with warm water. **2** warm food for horses, etc. ◆ *vt* **3** make into a mash. **4** crush into soft mass or pulp.

mask *n* **1** covering for face. **2** *Surgery* covering for nose and mouth. **3** disguise, pretense. ◆ *vt* **4** cover with mask. **5** hide, disguise.

mas·och·ism [MAS-ə-kiz-əm] *n* abnormal condition in which pleasure (esp. sexual) is derived from pain, humiliation, etc. **mas'och·ist** *n* **mas·och·is'tic** *adj*

ma·son [MAY-sən] *n* **1** worker in stone. **2** (M-) Freemason. **Ma·son'ic** *adj* of Freemasonry. **ma'son·ry** *n* **1** stonework. **2** (M-) Freemasonry.

masque [mask] *n Hist.* form of theatrical performance. **mas·quer·ade'** *n* **1** masked ball. ◆ *vi* **-ad·ed, -ad·ing 2** appear in disguise.

Mass *n* service of the Eucharist.

mass *n* **1** quantity of matter. **2** dense collection of this. **3** large quantity or number. ◆ *v* **4** form into a mass. **mas'sive** *adj* large and heavy. **mass-pro·duce'** *vt* **-duced, -duc·ing** produce standardized articles in large quantities. **mass production** manufacturing of standardized goods in large quantities. **the masses** the common people.

mas·sa·cre [MAS-ə-kər] *n* **1** indiscriminate, large-scale killing, esp. of unresisting people. ◆ *vt* **-cred, -cring 2** kill indiscriminately.

mas·sage [mə-SAH*ZH*] *n* **1** rubbing and kneading of muscles, etc. as curative treatment. ◆ *vt* **-saged, -sag·ing 2** apply this treatment to. **mas·seur'** [-SUR], *(fem)* **-seuse** [-SOOS] *n* one who practices massage.

mast *n* **1** pole for supporting ship's sails. **2** tall upright support for aerial, etc.

mas·tec·to·my [ma-STEK-tə-mee] *n, pl* **-mies** surgical removal of a breast.

mas·ter [MAS-tər] *n* **1** one in control. **2** employer. **3** head of household. **4** owner. **5** document, etc. from which copies are made. **6** captain of merchant ship. **7** expert. **8** great artist. **9** teacher. ◆ *vt* **10** overcome. **11** acquire knowledge of or skill in. **mas'ter·ful** *adj* imperious, domineering. **mas'ter·ly** *adj* showing great competence. **mas'ter·y** *n* **1** full understanding (of). **2** expertise. **3** authority. **4** victory. **master key** one that opens many different locks. **mas'ter·mind** *vt* plan, direct. ◆ *n* **mas'ter·piece** *n* outstanding work.

| THESAURUS |

marvel *v* **1** = **wonder**, be amazed, be awed, gape ◆ *n* **2** = **wonder**, miracle, phenomenon, portent, prodigy

marvelous *adj* **1** = **amazing**, astonishing, astounding, breathtaking, brilliant, extraordinary, miraculous, phenomenal, prodigious, spectacular, stupendous **2** = **excellent**, fabulous (*inf*), fantastic (*inf*), great (*inf*), splendid, superb, terrific (*inf*), wonderful

masculine *adj* = **male**, manlike, manly, mannish, virile

mask *n* **1** = **disguise**, camouflage, cover, façade, front, guise, screen, veil ◆ *v* **2** = **disguise**, camouflage, cloak, conceal, cover, hide, obscure, screen, veil

masquerade *n* **1** = **masked ball**, fancy dress party, revel **2** = **pretense**, cloak, cover-up, deception, disguise, mask, pose, screen, subterfuge ◆ *v* **3** = **pose**, disguise,

dissemble, dissimulate, impersonate, pass oneself off, pretend (to be)

mass *n* **1** = **piece**, block, chunk, hunk, lump **2** = **lot**, bunch, collection, heap, load, pile, quantity, stack **3** = **size**, bulk, greatness, magnitude ◆ *adj* **4** = **large-scale**, extensive, general, indiscriminate, wholesale, widespread ◆ *v* **5** = **gather**, accumulate, assemble, collect, congregate, rally, swarm, throng

massacre *n* **1** = **slaughter**, annihilation, blood bath, butchery, carnage, extermination, holocaust, murder ◆ *v* **2** = **slaughter**, butcher, cut to pieces, exterminate, kill, mow down, murder, wipe out

massage *n* **1** = **rub-down**, manipulation ◆ *v* **2** = **rub down**, knead, manipulate

massive *adj* = **huge**, big, colossal, enormous, gigantic, hefty, immense,

mas·tic [MAS-tik] *n* **1** gum obtained from certain trees. **2** pasty substance.

mas·ti·cate [MAS-ti-kayt] *vt* -cat·ed, -cat·ing chew. **mas·ti·ca'tion** *n*

mas'tiff *n* large dog.

mas'toid *adj* **1** nipple-shaped. ◆ *n* **2** prominence on bone behind human ear. **mas·toid·i'tis** *n* inflammation of this area.

mas·tur·bate [MAS-tər-bayt] *v* -bat·ed, -bat·ing stimulate (one's own) genital organs. **mas·tur·ba'tion** *n*

mat¹ *n* **1** small rug. **2** piece of fabric to protect another surface or to wipe feet on, etc. **3** thick tangled mass. ◆ *v* mat·ted, mat·ting form into such mass. **go to the mat** struggle unyieldingly.

mat² see MATTE.

mat·a·dor [MAT-ə-dor] *n* bullfighter who slays bulls in bullfights.

match¹ [mach] *n* **1** contest, game. **2** equal. **3** person, thing exactly corresponding to another. **4** marriage. **5** person regarded as eligible for marriage. ◆ *vt* **6** get something corresponding to (color, pattern, etc.). **7** oppose, put in competition (with). **8** arrange marriage for. **9** join (in marriage). ◆ *vi* **10** correspond. **match'less** *adj* unequaled. **match'mak·er** *n* one who schemes to bring about a marriage.

match² *n* **1** small stick with head that ignites when rubbed. **2** fuse. **match'box** *n*

mate¹ [mayt] *n* **1** husband, wife. **2** one of pair. **3** officer in merchant ship. ◆ *v* mat·ed, mat·ing **4** marry. **5** pair.

mate² *n, vt Chess* mat·ed, mat·ing checkmate.

ma·te·ri·al [mə-TEER-ee-əl] *n* **1** substance from which thing is made. **2** cloth, fabric. ◆ *adj* **3** of matter or body. **4** affecting physical well-being. **5** unspiritual. **6** important, essential. **ma·te·ri·al·ism** *n* **1** excessive interest in, desire for money and possessions. **2** doctrine that nothing but matter exists, denying independent existence of spirit. **ma·te·ri·al·is'tic** *adj* **ma·te·ri·al·ize** *v* -ized, -iz·ing **1** *vi* **2** come into existence or view. ◆ *vt* **3** make material. **ma·te·ri·al·ly** *adv* appreciably. **ma·ter·nal** [mə-TUR-nl] *adj* **1** motherly. **2**

mammoth, monumental, whopping (*inf*)

master *n* **1** = **ruler**, boss (*inf*), commander, controller, director, governor, lord, manager **2** = **expert**, ace (*inf*), doyen, genius, maestro, past master, virtuoso, wizard **3** = **teacher**, guide, guru, instructor, tutor ◆ *adj* **4** = **main**, chief, foremost, leading, predominant, prime, principal ◆ *v* **5** = **learn**, get the hang of (*inf*), grasp **6** = **overcome**, conquer, defeat, tame, triumph over, vanquish

masterful *adj* **1** = **skillful**, adroit, consummate, expert, fine, first-rate, masterly, superlative, supreme, world-class **2** = **domineering**, arrogant, bossy (*inf*), high-handed, imperious, overbearing, overweening

masterly *adj* = **skillful**, adroit, consummate, crack (*sl*), expert, first-rate, masterful, supreme, world-class

mastermind *v* **1** = **plan**, conceive, devise, direct, manage, organize ◆ *n* **2** = **organizer**, architect, brain(s) (*inf*), director, engineer, manager, planner

masterpiece *n* = **classic**, jewel, magnum opus, pièce de résistance, tour de force

mastery *n* **1** = **expertise**, finesse, know-how (*inf*), proficiency, prowess, skill, virtuosity **2** = **control**, ascendancy, command, domination, superiority, supremacy, upper hand, whip hand

match *n* **1** = **game**, bout, competition, contest, head-to-head, test, trial **2** = **equal**, counterpart, peer, rival **3** = **marriage**, alliance, pairing, partnership ◆ *v* **4** = **correspond**, accord, agree, fit, go with, harmonize, tally **5** = **rival**, compare, compete, emulate, equal, measure up to

matching *adj* = **identical**, coordinating, corresponding, equivalent, like, twin

matchless *adj* = **unequaled**, incomparable, inimitable, superlative, supreme, unmatched, unparalleled, unrivaled, unsurpassed

mate *n* **1** = **partner**, husband *or* wife, spouse **2** = **colleague**, associate, companion **3** = **assistant**, helper, subordinate ◆ *v* **4** = **pair**, breed, couple

material *n* **1** = **substance**, matter, stuff **2** = **information**, data, evidence, facts, notes **3** = **cloth**, fabric ◆ *adj* **4** = **physical**, bodily, concrete, corporeal, palpable, substantial, tangible **5** = **important**, essential, meaningful, momentous, serious, significant, vital, weighty **6** = **relevant**, applicable, apposite, apropos, germane, pertinent

materialize *v* = **occur**, appear, come

of a mother. **3** related through mother.
ma·ter·ni·ty *n* motherhood.

math·e·mat·ics [math-ə-MAT-iks] *n*
science of numbers, quantities and shapes.
math·e·mat·i·cal *adj* **math·e·ma·ti·cian**
[-TI-shən] *n*

mat·i·née [mat-n-AY] *n* afternoon
performance in theater.

maî·tre d'hô·tel [may-tər doh-TEL] *n, pl*
maî·tres [-tərz] headwaiter, owner, or
manager of hotel.

ma·tri·arch [MAY-tree-ahrk] *n* mother as
head and ruler of family. **ma·tri·ar·chy** *n, pl*
-chies society with government by women
and descent reckoned in female line.

mat·ri·cide [MA-tri-sīd] *n* **1** the crime of
killing one's mother. **2** one who does this.

ma·tric·u·late [mə-TRIK-yə-layt] *v* **-lat·ed,
-lat·ing** enroll, be enrolled as degree
candidate in a college or university.
ma·tric·u·la·tion *n*

mat·ri·mo·ny [MA-trə-moh-nee] *n*
marriage. **mat·ri·mo·ni·al** *adj*

ma·trix [MAY-triks] *n, pl* **-tri·ces** [-tri-seez]
substance, situation in which something
originates, takes form, or is enclosed. **1**
mold for casting. **2** *Math.* rectangular array
of elements set out in rows and columns.

ma·tron [MAY-trən] *n* **1** married woman
esp. of established social position. **2**
woman who superintends domestic
arrangements of public institution,
boarding school, etc. **3** woman guard in

prison, etc. **ma·tron·ly** *adj* sedate.

Matt. Matthew.

matte [mat] *adj* of photographic print, dull,
lusterless, not shiny.

mat·ter [MAT-ər] *n* **1** substance of which
thing is made. **2** physical or bodily
substance. **3** affair, business. **4** cause of
trouble. **5** substance of book, etc. ◆ *vi* **6** be
of importance, signify.

mat·tock [MAT-ək] *n* tool like pick with
ends of blades flattened for cutting,
hoeing.

mat·tress [MA-tris] *n* stuffed flat case,
often with springs, or foam rubber pad,
used as part of bed. **air mattress** inflatable
mattress usu. of rubbery material.

ma·ture [mə-CHUUR] *adj* **-tur·er, -tur·est 1**
ripe, completely developed. **2** grown-up. ◆
v **-tured, -tur·ing 3** bring, come to
maturity. ◆ *vi* (of bond, etc.) come due.
mat·u·ra·tion *n* process of maturing.
ma·tu·ri·ty *n* state of being mature.

maud·lin [MAWD-lin] *adj* weakly or
tearfully sentimental.

maul [mawl] *vt* **1** handle roughly. **2** beat or
bruise. ◆ *n* **3** heavy wooden hammer.

maulstick *n* see MAHLSTICK.

mau·so·le·um [maw-sə-LEE-əm] *n* stately
building as a tomb.

mauve [mawv] *adj, n* (of) pale purple color.

mav·er·ick [MAV-ər-ik] *n* **1** unbranded
steer, strayed cow. **2** independent,
unorthodox person.

about, come to pass, happen, take shape,
turn up

materially *adv* = **significantly**, essentially,
gravely, greatly, much, seriously,
substantially

maternal *adj* = **motherly**

maternity *n* = **motherhood**, motherliness

matrimonial *adj* = **marital**, conjugal,
connubial, nuptial

matrimony *n* = **marriage**, nuptials,
wedding ceremony, wedlock

matted *adj* = **tangled**, knotted, tousled,
uncombed

matter *n* **1** = **substance**, body, material,
stuff **2** = **situation**, affair, business,
concern, event, incident, proceeding,
question, subject, topic **3** *As in* **what's the
matter?** = **problem**, complication,
difficulty, distress, trouble, worry ◆ *v* **4** = **be
important**, carry weight, count, make a
difference, signify

matter-of-fact *adj* = **unsentimental**,
deadpan, down-to-earth, emotionless,
mundane, plain, prosaic, sober,
unimaginative

mature *adj* **1** = **grown-up**, adult,
full-grown, fully fledged, mellow, of age,
ready, ripe, seasoned ◆ *v* **2** = **develop**, age,
bloom, blossom, come of age, grow up,
mellow, ripen

maturity *n* = **adulthood**, experience,
manhood *or* womanhood, ripeness,
wisdom

maudlin *adj* = **sentimental**, mawkish,
overemotional, slushy (*inf*), tearful, weepy
(*inf*)

maul *v* **1** = **ill-treat**, abuse, manhandle,
molest, paw **2** = **tear**, batter, claw,
lacerate, mangle

maverick *n* **1** = **rebel**, dissenter, eccentric,
heretic, iconoclast, individualist,
nonconformist, protester, radical ◆ *adj* **2** =

maw *n* stomach, crop.

mawk·ish [MAW-kish] *adj* **1** weakly sentimental, maudlin. **2** sickening.

max·im [MAK-sim] *n* **1** general truth, proverb. **2** rule of conduct, principle.

max·i·mum [MAK-sə-məm] *n* **1** greatest size or number. **2** highest point. ◆ *adj* **3** greatest. **max'i·mize** *vt* **-mized, -miz·ing**

may *v, pt* **might** used as an auxiliary to express possibility, permission, opportunity, etc. **may'be** *adv* **1** perhaps. **2** possibly.

May'day *n* international radiotelephone distress signal.

may·fly [MAY-flî] *n* short-lived flying insect, found near water.

may'hem *n* **1** in law, depriving person by violence of limb, member or organ, or causing mutilation of body. **2** any violent destruction. **3** confusion.

may·on·naise [may-ə-NAYZ] *n* creamy sauce of egg yolks, etc., esp. for salads.

may·or [MAY-ər] *n* head of municipality. **may'or·al** *adj* **may'or·al·ty** [-əl-tee] *n* (time of) office of mayor.

may·pole [MAY-pohl] *n* pole set up for dancing around on **May Day** to celebrate spring.

maze [mayz] *n* **1** labyrinth. **2** network of paths, lines. **3** state of confusion.

ma·zur·ka [mə-ZUR-kə] *n* **1** lively Polish dance like polka. **2** music for it.

MC *n* master of ceremonies.

me [mee] *pron* objective case singular of first personal pronoun I.

me·a cul·pa [ME-ah KUUL-pah] *Lat* my fault.

mead·ow [MED-oh] *n* tract of grassland.

mea·ger [MEE-gər] *adj* lean, thin, scanty, insufficient.

meal[1] [meel] *n* **1** occasion when food is served and eaten. **2** the food.

meal[2] *n* grain ground to powder. **meal'y** *adj* **meal·i·er, meal·i·est mealy-mouthed** [-mowthd] *adj* euphemistic, insincere in what one says.

mean[1] [meen] *v* **meant** [ment], **mean·ing 1** intend. **2** signify. **3** have a meaning. **4** have the intention of behaving. **mean'ing** *n* **1** sense, significance. ◆ *adj* **2** expressive. **mean'ing·ful** [-fəl] *adj* of great meaning or significance. **mean'ing·less** *adj*

mean[2] *adj* **-er, -est 1** ungenerous, petty. **2** miserly, niggardly. **3** unpleasant. **4** callous. **5** shabby. **6** ashamed. **mean'ness** *n*

mean[3] *n* **1** thing that is intermediate. **2** middle point. ◆ *pl* **3** that by which thing is done. **4** money. **5** resources. ◆ *adj* **6** intermediate in time, quality, etc. **3** average. **means test** inquiry into person's means to decide eligibility for pension, grant, etc. **mean'time, -while** *adv, n* (during) time between one happening and another. **by all means** certainly. **by no means** not at all.

me·an·der [mee-AN-dər] *vi* **1** flow windingly. **2** wander aimlessly.

mea·sles [MEE-zəlz] *n* infectious disease

THESAURUS

rebel, dissenting, eccentric, heretical, iconoclastic, individualistic, nonconformist, radical

mawkish *adj* = **sentimental**, emotional, maudlin, schmaltzy (*sl*), slushy (*inf*)

maxim *n* = **saying**, adage, aphorism, axiom, dictum, motto, proverb, rule

maximum *n* **1** = **top**, ceiling, height, peak, pinnacle, summit, upper limit, utmost, zenith ◆ *adj* **2** = **greatest**, highest, most, paramount, supreme, topmost, utmost

maybe *adv* = **perhaps**, perchance (*archaic*), possibly

mayhem *n* = **chaos**, commotion, confusion, destruction, disorder, fracas, havoc, trouble, violence

maze *n* **1** = **labyrinth 2** = **web**, confusion, imbroglio, tangle

meadow *n* = **field**, grassland, lea (*poetic*), pasture

meager *adj* = **insubstantial**, inadequate, lousy (*sl*), measly, paltry, poor, puny, scanty, slight, small

meal *n Inf* = **feast**, feed, repast, spread (*inf*)

mean[1] *v* **1** = **signify**, convey, denote, express, imply, indicate, represent, spell, stand for, symbolize **2** = **intend**, aim, aspire, design, desire, plan, set out, want, wish

mean[2] *adj* **1** = **miserly**, mercenary, niggardly, parsimonious, penny-pinching, stingy, tight-fisted, ungenerous **2** = **despicable**, callous, contemptible, hard-hearted, lousy (*sl*), petty, scuzzy (*sl*), shabby, shameful, sordid, vile

mean[3] *n* **1** = **average**, balance, compromise, happy medium, middle, midpoint, norm ◆ *adj* **2** = **average**, middle, standard

meander *v* **1** = **wind**, snake, turn, zigzag

producing rash of red spots. **mea'sly** adj **-sli-er, -sli-est** inf **1** poor, wretched, stingy. **2** of measles.

meas•ure [MEZH-ər] n **1** size, quantity. **2** vessel, rod, line, etc. for ascertaining size or quantity. **3** unit of size or quantity. **4** course, plan of action. **5** law. **6** poetical rhythm. **7** musical time. **8** Poet. tune. **9** obs dance. ◆ vt **-ured, -ur•ing 10** ascertain size, quantity of. **11** be (so much) in size or quantity. **12** indicate measurement of. **13** estimate. **14** bring into competition (against). **meas'ur•a•ble** adj **meas'ured** adj **1** determined by measure. **2** steady. **3** rhythmical. **4** carefully considered. **meas'ure•ment** n **1** measuring. **2** size. ◆ pl **3** dimensions.

meat [meet] n **1** animal flesh as food. **2** food. **meat'y** adj **meat-i-er, meat-i-est 1** (tasting) of, like meat. **2** brawny. **3** full of import or interest.

Mec•ca [MEK-ə] n **1** holy city of Islam. **2** (m-) place that attracts visitors.

me•chan•ic [mə-KAN-ik] n **1** one employed in working with machinery. **2** skilled worker. ◆ pl **3** scientific theory of motion. **me•chan'i•cal** adj **1** concerned with machines or operation of them. **2** worked, produced (as though) by machine. **3** acting without thought. **me•chan'i•cal•ly** adv

mech•an•ism [MEK-ə-niz-əm] n **1** structure of machine. **2** piece of machinery. **mech'a•nize** vt **-nized, -niz•ing 1** equip with machinery. **2** make mechanical, automatic. **3** Military equip with armored vehicles.

med•al [MED-l] n piece of metal with inscription, etc. used as reward or memento. **me•dal'lion** [mə-DAL-yən] n **1** large medal. **2** various things like this in decorative work. **med'al•ist** n **1** winner of a

2 = **wander**, ramble, stroll ◆ n **3** = **curve**, bend, coil, loop, turn, twist, zigzag

meaning n = **sense**, connotation, drift, gist, message, significance, substance

meaningful adj = **significant**, important, material, purposeful, relevant, useful, valid, worthwhile

meaningless adj = **pointless**, empty, futile, inane, inconsequential, insignificant, senseless, useless, vain, worthless

meanness n **1** = **miserliness**, niggardliness, parsimony, selfishness, stinginess **2** = **pettiness**, disgracefulness, ignobility, narrow-mindedness, shabbiness, shamefulness

means pl n **1** = **method**, agency, instrument, medium, mode, process, way **2** = **money**, affluence, capital, fortune, funds, income, resources, wealth, wherewithal **3 by all means** = **certainly**, definitely, doubtlessly, of course, surely **4 by no means** = **in no way**, definitely not, not in the least, on no account

meantime, meanwhile adv = **at the same time**, concurrently, in the interim, simultaneously

measly adj = **meager**, miserable, paltry, pathetic, pitiful, poor, puny, scanty, skimpy

measurable adj = **quantifiable**, assessable, perceptible, significant

measure n **1** = **quantity**, allotment, allowance, amount, portion, quota, ration,

share **2** = **gauge**, meter, rule, scale, yardstick **3** = **action**, act, deed, expedient, maneuver, means, procedure, step **4** = **law**, act, bill, resolution, statute **5** = **rhythm**, beat, cadence, meter, verse ◆ v **6** = **quantify**, assess, calculate, calibrate, compute, determine, evaluate, gauge, weigh

measured adj **1** = **steady**, dignified, even, leisurely, regular, sedate, slow, solemn, stately, unhurried **2** = **considered**, calculated, deliberate, reasoned, sober, studied, well-thought-out

measurement n = **calculation**, assessment, calibration, computation, evaluation, mensuration, valuation

measure up to v = **fulfill the expectations**, be equal to, be suitable, come up to scratch (inf), fit or fill the bill, make the grade (inf)

meat n = **flesh**

meaty adj **1** = **brawny**, beefy (inf), burly, heavily built, heavy, muscular, solid, strapping, sturdy **2** = **interesting**, meaningful, profound, rich, significant, substantial

mechanical adj **1** = **automatic**, automated **2** = **unthinking**, automatic, cursory, impersonal, instinctive, involuntary, perfunctory, routine, unfeeling

mechanism n **1** = **machine**, apparatus, appliance, contrivance, device, instrument, tool **2** = **process**, agency, means, method, medal. **2** maker of medals.

med·dle [MED-l] *vi* **-dled, -dling** interfere, busy oneself with unnecessarily. **med'dle·some** [-səm] *adj*

me·di·a [MEE-dee-ə] *n* **1** pl. of MEDIUM. **2** used esp. of the mass media, radio, TV, etc. **media event** event staged for or exploited by mass media.

mediaeval see MEDIEVAL.

me·di·al [MEE-dee-əl] *adj* **1** in the middle. **2** pert. to a mean or average. **me'di·an** *adj, n* middle (point or line).

me·di·ate [MEE-dee-ayt] *v* **-at·ed, -at·ing** ◆ *vi* **1** intervene to reconcile. ◆ *vt* **2** bring about by mediation. ◆ *adj* **3** depending on mediation. **me·di·a'tion** *n* **1** intervention on behalf of another. **2** act of going between.

med·i·cine [MED-i-sin] *n* **1** drug or remedy for treating disease. **2** science of preventing, diagnosing, alleviating, or curing disease. **med'i·cal** [-kəl] *adj* **me·dic'a·ment** *n* remedy. **med'i·cate** [-kayt] *vt* **-cat·ed, -cat·ing** treat, impregnate with medicinal substances. **med·i·ca'tion** *n* **me·dic'i·nal** [-DIS-ə-nəl] *adj* curative.

me·di·e·val [mee-dee-EE-vəl] *adj* of Middle Ages. **me·di·e'val·ist** *n* student of the Middle Ages.

me·di·o·cre [mee-dee-OH-kər] *adj* **1** neither bad nor good, ordinary, middling. **2** second-rate. **me·di·oc'ri·ty** [-OK-rə-tee] *n*

med·i·tate [MED-i-tayt] *v* **-tat·ed, -tat·ing** ◆ *vi* **1** be occupied in thought. **2** reflect deeply on spiritual matters. **3** engage in transcendental meditation. ◆ *vt* **4** think about. **5** plan. **med·i·ta'tion** [-TAY-shən] *n* **1** thought. **2** absorption in thought. **3** religious contemplation. **med'i·ta·tive** *adj* **1** thoughtful. **2** reflective.

me·di·um [MEE-dee-əm] *adj* **1** between two qualities, degrees, etc., average. ◆ *n, pl* **-di·a** or **-di·ums 2** middle quality, degree. **3** intermediate substance conveying force. **4** means, agency of communicating news, etc. to public, as radio, newspapers, etc. **5** person through whom communication can supposedly be held with spirit world. **6** surroundings. **7** environment.

med·ley [MED-lee] *n, pl* **-leys** miscellaneous mixture.

Me·du·sa [mə-DOO-sə] *n, pl* **-sas** *Mythology* Gorgon whose head turned beholders into stone.

meek *adj* **-er, -est** submissive, humble. **meek'ly** *adv* **meek'ness** *n*

meer·schaum [MEER-shəm] *n* **1** white

———————— THESAURUS ————————

operation, procedure, system, technique

meddle *v* = **interfere**, butt in, intervene, intrude, pry, tamper

meddlesome *adj* = **interfering**, intrusive, meddling, mischievous, officious, prying

mediate *v* = **intervene**, arbitrate, conciliate, intercede, reconcile, referee, step in (*inf*), umpire

mediation *n* = **arbitration**, conciliation, intercession, intervention, reconciliation

mediator *n* = **negotiator**, arbiter, arbitrator, go-between, honest broker, intermediary, middleman, peacemaker, referee, umpire

medicinal *adj* = **therapeutic**, curative, healing, medical, remedial, restorative

medicine *n* = **remedy**, cure, drug, medicament, medication, nostrum

mediocre *adj* = **second-rate**, average, indifferent, inferior, middling, ordinary, passable, pedestrian, so-so (*inf*), undistinguished

mediocrity *n* = **insignificance**, indifference, inferiority, ordinariness, unimportance

meditate *v* **1** = **reflect**, cogitate, consider, contemplate, deliberate, muse, ponder, ruminate, think **2** = **plan**, have in mind, intend, purpose, scheme

meditation *n* = **reflection**, cogitation, contemplation, musing, pondering, rumination, study, thought

medium *adj* **1** = **middle**, average, fair, intermediate, mean, median, mediocre, middling, midway ◆ *n* **2** = **middle**, average, center, compromise, mean, midpoint **3** = **means**, agency, channel, instrument, mode, organ, vehicle, way **4** = **environment**, atmosphere, conditions, milieu, setting, surroundings **5** = **spiritualist**

medley *n* = **mixture**, assortment, farrago, jumble, *mélange*, miscellany, mishmash, mixed bag (*inf*), potpourri

meek *adj* = **submissive**, acquiescent, compliant, deferential, docile, gentle, humble, mild, modest, timid, unassuming, unpretentious

meekness *n* = **submissiveness**, acquiescence, compliance, deference, substance like clay. **2** tobacco pipe bowl of this.

meet *vt* met, **meet·ing 1** come face to face come face to face with, encounter. **2** satisfy. **3** pay. **4** converge at specified point. **5** assemble. **6** come into contact. ◆ *n* **7** meeting, esp. for sports. **meeting** *n* **1** assembly. **2** encounter.

meg·a·bit [MEG-ə-bit] *n* Computers **1** 1,010,578 bits. **2** (loosely) one million bits.

meg·a·byte [MEG-ə-bīt] *n* Computers **1** 1,048,576 bytes. **2** (loosely) one million bytes.

meg·a·lith [MEG-ə-lith] *n* great stone. **meg·a·lith·ic** *adj*

meg·a·lo·ma·ni·a [meg-ə-loh-MAY-nee-ə] *n* desire for, delusions of grandeur, power, etc.

meg·a·ton [MEG-ə-tun] *n* **1** one million tons. **2** explosive power equal to that of million tons of TNT.

meg'ohm *n* Electricity one million ohms.

mel·an·chol·y [MEL-ən-kol-ee] *n* **1** sadness, dejection, gloom. ◆ *adj* **2** gloomy, dejected. **mel·an·chol·i·a** [-KOH-lee-ə] *n* former name for DEPRESSION.

mé·lange [may-LAHNZH] *n* mixture.

mel·a·nin [MEL-ə-nin] *n* dark pigment found in hair, skin, etc. of man.

me·lee [MAY-lay] *n* **1** confused fight

among several people. **2** confusion. **3** turmoil.

mel·io·rate [MEEL-yə-rayt] *v* **-rat·ed, -rat·ing** improve. **mel·io·ra'tion** *n* **mel'io·rism** *n* doctrine that the world can be improved by human effort.

mel·lif·lu·ous [mə-LIF-loo-əs] *adj* (of sound, voice) smooth, sweet.

mel·low [MEL-oh] *adj* **-er, -est** ripe. **2** softened by age, experience. **3** soft, not harsh. **4** genial, gay. ◆ *v* **5** make, become mellow.

mel·o·dra·ma [MEL-ə-dram-ə] *n* **1** play full of sensational and startling situations, often highly emotional. **2** overly dramatic behavior, emotion. **mel·o·dra·mat·ic** [-drə-MAT-ik] *adj*

mel·o·dy [MEL-ə-dee] *n, pl* **-dies 1** series of musical notes that make tune. **2** sweet sound. **mel·o·di·ous** [mə-LOH-dee-əs] *adj* pleasing to the ear. **2** tuneful.

mel·on [MEL-ən] *n* large, fleshy, juicy fruit.

melt *v* **melt·ed** or **mol·ten, melt·ing 1** (cause to) become liquid by heat. **2** dissolve. **3** soften. **4** waste away. **5** blend (into). **6** disappear. **melting** *adj* **1** softening. **2** languishing. **3** tender.

melt'down *n* in nuclear reactor, melting of fuel rods, with possible release of radiation.

mem·ber [MEM-bər] *n* **1** any of individuals

docility, gentleness, humility, mildness, modesty, timidity

meet *v* **1** = **encounter**, bump into, chance on, come across, confront, contact, find, happen on, run across, run into **2** = **converge**, come together, connect, cross, intersect, join, link up, touch **3** = **satisfy**, answer, come up to, comply with, discharge, fulfill, match, measure up to **4** = **gather**, assemble, collect, come together, congregate, convene, muster **5** = **experience**, bear, encounter, endure, face, go through, suffer, undergo

meeting *n* **1** = **encounter**, assignation, confrontation, engagement, introduction, rendezvous, tryst **2** = **conference**, assembly, conclave, congress, convention, gathering, get-together (*inf*), reunion, session

melancholy *n* **1** = **sadness**, dejection, depression, despondency, gloom, low spirits, misery, sorrow, unhappiness ◆ *adj* **2** = **sad**, depressed, despondent, dispirited, downhearted, gloomy, glum, miserable,

mournful, sorrowful

melee, mêlée *n* = **fight**, brawl, fracas, free-for-all (*inf*), rumpus, scrimmage, scuffle, skirmish, tussle

mellifluous *adj* = **sweet**, dulcet, euphonious, honeyed, silvery, smooth, soft, soothing, sweet-sounding

mellow *adj* **1** = **soft**, delicate, full-flavored, mature, rich, ripe, sweet ◆ *v* **2** = **mature**, develop, improve, ripen, season, soften, sweeten

melodious *adj* = **tuneful**, dulcet, euphonious, harmonious, melodic, musical, sweet-sounding

melodramatic *adj* = **sensational**, blood-and-thunder, extravagant, histrionic, overdramatic, overemotional, theatrical

melody *n* **1** = **tune**, air, music, song, strain, theme **2** = **tunefulness**, euphony, harmony, melodiousness, musicality

melt *v* **1** = **dissolve**, fuse, liquefy, soften, thaw **2** (often with *away*) = **disappear**, disperse, dissolve, evanesce, evaporate, making up body or society. **2** limb. **3** any part of complex whole.

mem·brane [MEM-brayn] *n* thin flexible tissue in plant or animal body.

me·men·to [mə-MEN-toh] *n, pl* **-tos** or **-toes** thing serving to remind, souvenir.

mem·oir [MEM-wahr] *n* **1** autobiography, personal history, biography. **2** record of events.

mem·o·ry [MEM-ə-ree] *n, pl* **-ries 1** faculty of recollecting, recalling to mind. **2** recollection. **3** thing remembered. **4** length of time one can remember. **5** commemoration. **6** part or faculty of computer that stores information. **me·mo·ri·al** *adj* **1** of, preserving memory. ◆ *n* **2** thing, esp. a monument, that serves to keep in memory. **mem'or·a·ble** *adj* worthy of remembrance, noteworthy. **mem·o·ran·dum** *n, pl* **-dums** or **-da 1** note to help the memory, etc. **2** informal letter. **3** note of contract. **me·mo'ri·al·ize** *vt* **-ized, -iz·ing** commemorate. **mem'o·rize** *vt* **-ized, -iz·ing** commit to memory.

men·ace [MEN-is] *n* **1** threat. ◆ *vt* **-aced, -ac·ing 2** threaten, endanger.

mé·nage [may-NAH*ZH*] *n* persons of a household. **ménage à trois** [ah TWAH] arrangement in which three persons, e.g. two men and one woman, share sexual relations while occupying same household.

me·nag·er·ie [mə-NAJ-ə-ree] *n* exhibition, collection of wild animals.

mend *vt* **1** repair, patch. **2** reform, correct, put right. ◆ *vi* **3** improve, esp. in health. ◆ *n* **4** repaired breakage, hole. **on the mend** regaining health.

men·da·cious [men-DAY-shəs] *adj* untruthful. **men·dac'i·ty** [-DAS-i-tee] *n* (tendency to) untruthfulness.

men·di·cant [MEN-di-kənt] *adj* **1** begging. ◆ *n* **2** beggar. **men'di·can·cy** *n* begging.

me·ni·al [MEE-nee-əl] *adj* **1** of work requiring little skill. **2** of household duties or servants. **3** servile. ◆ *n* **4** servant. **5** servile person.

men·in·gi·tis [men-in-JĪ-tis] *n* inflammation of the membranes of the brain.

me·nis·cus [mə-NIS-kəs] *n* **1** curved surface of liquid. **2** curved lens.

men·o·pause [MEN-ə-pawz] *n* final cessation of menstruation.

men·stru·a·tion [men-stroo-AY-shən] *n*

fade, vanish **3** = **soften**, disarm, mollify, relax

member *n* **1** = **representative**, associate, fellow **2** = **limb**, appendage, arm, extremity, leg, part

membership *n* **1** = **members**, associates, body, fellows **2** = **participation**, belonging, enrollment, fellowship

memento *n* = **souvenir**, keepsake, memorial, relic, remembrance, reminder, token, trophy

memoir *n* = **account**, biography, essay, journal, life, monograph, narrative, record

memoirs *pl n* = **autobiography**, diary, experiences, journals, life story, memories, recollections, reminiscences

memorable *adj* = **noteworthy**, celebrated, famous, historic, momentous, notable, remarkable, significant, striking, unforgettable

memorandum *n* = **note**, communication, jotting, memo, message, minute, reminder

memorial *n* **1** = **monument**, memento, plaque, record, remembrance, souvenir ◆ *adj* **2** = **commemorative**, monumental

memorize *v* = **remember**, commit to memory, learn, learn by heart, learn by rote

memory *n* **1** = **recall**, recollection, remembrance, reminiscence, retention **2** = **commemoration**, honor, remembrance

menace *n* **1** = **threat**, intimidation, warning **2** *Inf* = **nuisance**, annoyance, pest, plague, troublemaker ◆ *v* **3** = **threaten**, bully, frighten, intimidate, loom, lour *or* lower, terrorize

menacing *adj* = **threatening**, forbidding, frightening, intimidating, looming, louring *or* lowering, ominous

mend *v* **1** = **repair**, darn, fix, patch, refit, renew, renovate, restore, retouch **2** = **improve**, ameliorate, amend, correct, emend, rectify, reform, revise **3** = **heal**, convalesce, get better, recover, recuperate ◆ *n* **4** = **repair**, darn, patch, stitch **5 on the mend** = **convalescent**, getting better, improving, recovering, recuperating

mendacious *adj* = **lying**, deceitful, deceptive, dishonest, duplicitous, fallacious, false, fraudulent, insincere, untruthful

menial *adj* **1** = **unskilled**, boring, dull, humdrum, low-status, routine ◆ *n* **2** = **servant**, attendant, drudge, flunky, lackey, approximately monthly discharge of blood and cellular debris from womb of nonpregnant woman. **men'stru•al** *adj* **men'stru•ate** *vi* **-at•ed, -at•ing**

men•su•ra•tion [men-sha-RAY-shan] *n* measuring, esp. of areas.

men•tal [MEN-tal] *adj* **1** of, done by the mind. **2** *inf* slightly mad. **men•tal'i•ty** *n* state or quality of mind.

men•thol [MEN-thawl] *n* organic compound found in peppermint, used medicinally.

men•tion [MEN-shan] *vt* **1** refer to briefly, speak of. ◆ *n* **2** acknowledgment. **3** reference to or remark about (person or thing). **men'tion•a•ble** *adj* fit or suitable to be mentioned.

men•tor *n* wise, trusted adviser, guide, teacher.

men•u [MEN-yoo] *n* **1** list of dishes to be served, or from which to order. **2** *Computers* list of options available to user.

mer•can•tile [MUR-kan-tīl] *adj* of, engaged in trade, commerce.

mer•ce•nar•y [MUR-sa-ner-ee] *adj* **1** influenced by greed. **2** working merely for reward. ◆ *n* **-nar•ies 3** hired soldier.

mer•chant [MUR-chant] *n* **1** one engaged in trade. **2** storekeeper. **mer'chan•dise** *n* merchant's wares. **mer'chant•man** [-man] *n* trading ship. **merchant navy** ships engaged in a nation's commerce.

mer•cu•ry [MUR-kya-ree] *n* **1** silvery metal, liquid at ordinary temperature, quicksilver. **2** (M-) Roman god of eloquence, messenger of the gods, etc. **3** planet nearest to sun. **mer•cu'ri•al** [-KYOO-ree-al] *adj* **1** relating to, containing mercury. **2** lively, changeable.

mer•cy [MUR-see] *n, pl* **-cies** refraining from infliction of suffering by one who has right, power to inflict it, compassion. **mer'ci•ful** [-fal] *adj* **mer'ci•less** [-lis] *adj*

mere [meer] *adj, sup* **mer•est 1** only. **2** not more than. **3** nothing but. **mere'ly** *adv*

mer•e•tri•cious [mer-i-TRISH-as] *adj* **1** superficially or garishly attractive. **2** insincere.

merge [murj] *v* **merged, merg•ing** (cause to) lose identity or be absorbed. **mer'ger** *n* **1** combination of business firms into one. **2** absorption into something greater.

me•rid•i•an [ma-RID-ee-an] *n* **1** circle of Earth passing through poles. **2** imaginary

underling

mental *adj* **1** = **intellectual**, cerebral **2** *Inf* = **insane**, deranged, disturbed, mad, mentally ill, psychotic, unbalanced, unstable

mentality *n* = **attitude**, cast of mind, character, disposition, make-up, outlook, personality, psychology

mentally *adv* = **in the mind**, in one's head, intellectually, inwardly, psychologically

mention *v* **1** = **refer to**, bring up, declare, disclose, divulge, intimate, point out, reveal, state, touch upon ◆ *n* **2** = **acknowledgment**, citation, recognition, tribute **3** = **reference**, allusion, indication, observation, remark

mentor *n* = **guide**, adviser, coach, counselor, guru, instructor, teacher, tutor

menu *n* = **bill of fare**, carte du jour

mercantile *adj* = **commercial**, trading

mercenary *adj* **1** = **greedy**, acquisitive, avaricious, grasping, money-grubbing (*inf*), sordid, venal ◆ *n* **2** = **hireling**, soldier of fortune

merchandise *n* = **goods**, commodities, produce, products, stock, wares

merchant *n* = **tradesman**, broker, dealer, purveyor, retailer, salesman, seller, shopkeeper, supplier, trader, trafficker, vendor, wholesaler

merciful *adj* = **compassionate**, clement, forgiving, generous, gracious, humane, kind, lenient, sparing, sympathetic, tender-hearted

merciless *adj* = **cruel**, barbarous, callous, hard-hearted, harsh, heartless, pitiless, ruthless, unforgiving

mercurial *adj* = **lively**, active, capricious, changeable, impulsive, irrepressible, mobile, quicksilver, spirited, sprightly, unpredictable, volatile

mercy *n* **1** = **compassion**, clemency, forbearance, forgiveness, grace, kindness, leniency, pity **2** = **blessing**, boon, godsend

mere *adj* = **simple**, bare, common, nothing more than, plain, pure, sheer

meretricious *adj* = **trashy**, flashy, garish, gaudy, gimcrack, showy, tawdry, tinsel

merge *v* = **combine**, amalgamate, blend, coalesce, converge, fuse, join, meet, mingle, mix, unite

merger *n* = **union**, amalgamation, coalition, combination, consolidation, fusion, incorporation circle in sky passing through celestial poles. **3** highest point reached by star, etc. **4** period of greatest splendor. ♦ adj **5** of meridian. **6** at peak of something.

me•ringue [mə-RANG] n **1** baked mixture of white of eggs and sugar. **2** cake of this.

mer•it n **1** excellence, worth. **2** quality of deserving reward. ♦ pl **3** excellence. ♦ vt **4** deserve. **mer•i•to'ri•ous** adj deserving praise.

mer•maid [MUR-mayd] n imaginary sea creature with upper part of woman and lower part of fish.

mer•ry [MER-ee] adj -ri•er, -ri•est joyous, cheerful. **mer'ri•ly** adv **mer'ri•ment** n

mesh n (one of the open spaces of, or wires, etc. forming) network, net. ♦ v **1** entangle, become entangled. **2** (of gears) engage. ♦ vi **3** coordinate (with).

mes•mer•ism [MEZ-mə-riz-əm] n former term for HYPNOTISM. **mes'mer•ize** vt **-ized, -iz•ing 1** hypnotize. **2** fascinate, hold spellbound.

me•son [MEE-zon] n elementary atomic particle.

mess n **1** untidy confusion. **2** trouble, difficulty. **3** place where military personnel group regularly eat together. ♦ vi **4** make mess. **5** putter (about). **6** Military eat in a mess. **mess up 1** make dirty. **2** botch. **3** spoil. **mess'y** adj **mess•i•er, mess•i•est**

mes•sage [MES-ij] n **1** communication sent. **2** meaning, moral. **mes'sen•ger** n bearer of message.

Mes•si•ah [mi-SI-ə] n **1** Jews' promised deliverer. **2** Christ. **mes•si•an'ic** [mes-ee-AN-ik] adj

Messrs [MES-ərz] pl. of MR.

met pt./pp. of MEET.

meta- comb. form change, e.g. metamorphose; metathesis.

me•tab•o•lism [mə-TAB-ə-liz-əm] n chemical process of living body. **met•a•bol'ic** adj **me•tab'o•lize** vt **-lized, -liz•ing**

met•al [MET-l] n **1** mineral substance, opaque, fusible and malleable, capable of conducting heat and electricity. **2** object made of metal. **me•tal'lic** adj **met'al•lur•gist** n **met'al•lur•gy** n scientific study of extracting, refining metals, and their structure and properties.

met•a•mor•pho•sis [met-ə-MOR-fə-sis] n, pl **-ses** change of shape, character, etc. **met•a•mor'phic** adj (esp. of rocks) changed in texture, structure by heat, pressure, etc. **met•a•mor'phose** [-fohz] vt **-phosed, -phos•ing** transform.

met•a•phor [MET-ə-for] n **1** figure of speech in which term is transferred to something it does not literally apply to. **2** instance of this. **met•a•phor'i•cal** adj

---

THESAURUS

merit n **1** = **worth**, advantage, asset, excellence, goodness, integrity, quality, strong point, talent, value, virtue ♦ v **2** = **deserve**, be entitled to, be worthy of, earn, have a right to, rate, warrant

meritorious adj = **praiseworthy**, admirable, commendable, creditable, deserving, excellent, good, laudable, virtuous, worthy

merriment n = **fun**, amusement, festivity, glee, hilarity, jollity, joviality, laughter, mirth, revelry

merry adj = **cheerful**, blithe, carefree, convivial, festive, happy, jolly, joyous

mesh n **1** = **net**, netting, network, tracery, web ♦ v **2** = **engage**, combine, connect, coordinate, dovetail, harmonize, interlock, knit

mesmerize v = **entrance**, captivate, enthrall, fascinate, grip, hold spellbound, hypnotize

mess n **1** = **disorder**, chaos, clutter, confusion, disarray, disorganization, jumble, litter, shambles, untidiness **2** = **difficulty**, dilemma, fix (inf), hot water, jam (inf), muddle, pickle (inf), plight, predicament, tight spot (inf) ♦ v **3** (often with up) = **dirty**, clutter, disarrange, dishevel, muddle, pollute, scramble **4** (often with with) = **interfere**, meddle, play, tamper, tinker

message n **1** = **communication**, bulletin, communiqué, dispatch, letter, memorandum, note, tidings, word **2** = **point**, idea, import, meaning, moral, purport, theme

messenger n = **courier**, carrier, delivery boy, emissary, envoy, errand-boy, go-between, herald, runner

messy adj = **untidy**, chaotic, cluttered, confused, dirty, disheveled, disordered, disorganized, muddled, scuzzy (sl), shambolic, sloppy (inf)

metamorphosis n = **transformation**, alteration, change, conversion, mutation, transmutation figurative.

met·a·phys·ics [met-ə-FIZ-iks] *n* branch of philosophy concerned with being and knowing.

me·tath·e·sis [mə-TATH-ə-sis] *n, pl* **-ses** [-seez] transposition, esp. of letters in word, e.g. Old English *bridd* gives modern *bird*.

mete [meet] *vt* **met·ed, met·ing** measure. **mete out 1** distribute. **2** allot as punishment.

me·te·or [MEE-tee-ər] *n* small, fast-moving celestial body, visible as streak of incandescence if it enters Earth's atmosphere. **me·te·or'ic** *adj* **1** of, like meteor. **2** brilliant but short-lived. **me'te·or·ite** *n* fallen meteor.

me·te·or·ol·o·gy [mee-tee-ə-ROL-ə-jee] *n* study of Earth's atmosphere, esp. for weather forecasting.

me·ter[1] [MEE-tər] *n* **1** unit of length in decimal system. **2** SI unit of length. **3** rhythm of poem. **met'ric** *adj* of system of weights and measures in which meter is a unit. **met'ri·cal** *adj* of measurement of poetic meter.

meter[2] *n* **1** that which measures. **2** instrument for recording consumption of gas, electricity, etc.

meth·ane [METH-ayn] *n* inflammable gas, compound of carbon and hydrogen.

meth·od [METH-əd] *n* **1** way, manner. **2** technique. **3** orderliness, system. **me·thod'i·cal** *adj* orderly. **meth·od·ol'o·gy** *n, pl* **-gies** particular method or procedure.

Meth·od·ist [METH-ə-dist] *n* member of any of the churches originated by Wesley and his followers. ♦ *adj* **Meth'od·ism** *n*

me·tic·u·lous [mə-TIK-yə-ləs] *adj* (over)particular about details.

mé·tier [MAY-tyay] *n* **1** profession, vocation. **2** one's forte.

me·ton·y·my [mi-TON-ə-mee] *n* figure of speech in which thing is replaced by another associated with it, e.g. *the Oval Office* for *the president*.

met·ro·nome [ME-trə-nohm] *n* instrument that marks musical time by means of ticking pendulum.

me·trop·o·lis [mi-TROP-ə-lis] *n, pl* **-lis·es** chief city of a country, region. **met·ro·pol'i·tan** *adj* **1** of metropolis. ♦ *n* **2** bishop with authority over other bishops of an ecclesiastical province.

met·tle [MET-l] *n* courage, spirit. **met'tle·some** [-səm] *adj* high-spirited.

mew [myoo] *n* **1** cry of cat. ♦ *vi* **2** utter this cry.

mez·za·nine [MEZ-ə-neen] *n* **1** in a theater, lowest balcony or forward part of balcony. **2** in a building, low story between two other stories, esp. between first and second stories.

mez·zo·so·pran·o [MET-soh-sə-PRAN-oh] *n, pl* **-pran·os** voice, singer between soprano and contralto.

Mg *Chem.* magnesium.

mi [mee] *n* third sol-fa note.

mi·as·ma [mī-AZ-mə] *n, pl* **-mas** unwholesome or foreboding atmosphere.

mi·ca [MĪ-kə] *n* mineral found as glittering scales, plates.

mi·crobe [MĪ-krohb] *n* **1** minute organism. **2** disease germ. **mi·cro'bi·al** *adj*

mi·cro·chip [MĪ-kroh-chip] *n* small wafer of silicon, etc. containing electronic circuits, chip.

mi·cro·com·put·er [MĪ-kroh-kəm-pyoo-tər] *n* computer having a central processing unit contained in one or more silicon chips.

mi·cro·cosm [MĪ-krə-koz-əm] *n* **1**

---

metaphor *n* = **figure of speech**, allegory, analogy, image, symbol, trope

metaphorical *adj* = **figurative**, allegorical, emblematic, symbolic

mete *v* = **distribute**, administer, apportion, assign, deal, dispense, portion

meteoric *adj* = **spectacular**, brilliant, dazzling, fast, overnight, rapid, speedy, sudden, swift

method *n* **1** = **manner**, approach, mode, modus operandi, procedure, process, routine, style, system, technique, way **2** = **orderliness**, order, organization, pattern,

planning, purpose, regularity, system

methodical *adj* = **orderly**, businesslike, deliberate, disciplined, meticulous, organized, precise, regular, structured, systematic

meticulous *adj* = **thorough**, exact, fastidious, fussy, painstaking, particular, precise, punctilious, scrupulous, strict

mettle *n* = **courage**, bravery, fortitude, gallantry, life, nerve, pluck, resolution, spirit, valor, vigor

microbe *n* = **microorganism**, bacillus, bacterium, bug (*inf*), germ, virus miniature representation, model, etc. of some larger system. **2** human beings, society as epitome of universe.

mi·cro·fi·ber [MĪ-krə-fī-bər] n very fine synthetic yarn.

mi·cro·fiche [MĪ-krə-feesh] n microfilm in sheet form.

mi·cro·film [MĪ-krə-film] n miniaturized recording of manuscript, book on roll of film.

mi·crom·e·ter [mī-KROM-i-tər] n instrument for measuring very small distances or angles.

mi·cron [MĪ-kron] n unit of length, one millionth of a meter.

mi·cro·or·gan·ism [mī-kroh-OR-gə-niz-əm] n organism of microscopic size.

mi·cro·phone [MĪ-krə-fohn] n instrument for amplifying, transmitting sounds.

mi·cro·proc·es·sor [MĪ-kroh-pros-es-ər] n integrated circuit acting as central processing unit in small computer.

mi·cro·scope [MĪ-krə-skohp] n instrument by which very small body is magnified and made visible. **mi·cro·scop·ic** [-SKOP-ik] adj **1** of microscope. **2** very small. **mi·cros·co·py** [-KROS-kə-pee] n use of microscope.

mi·cro·wave [MĪ-kroh-wayv] n **1** electromagnetic wave with wavelength of a few centimeters, used in radar, cooking, etc. **2** microwave oven.

mid adj intermediate, in the middle of. **mid'day** n noon. **mid'night** n twelve

o'clock at night. **mid'ship·man** [-mən] n student, e.g. at US Naval Academy, training for commission as naval officer. **mid'sum·mer** n **1** middle of summer. **2** summer solstice. **mid'way** adj, adv halfway. **mid'win·ter** n

mid·dle [MID-l] adj **1** equidistant from two extremes. **2** medium, intermediate. ◆ n **3** middle point or part. **mid'dling** adj **1** mediocre. **2** moderate. ◆ adv **Middle Ages** period from about 1000 AD to the 15th century. **middle class 1** social class of business, professional people, etc. **2** middle economic class. **mid'dle-class** adj **mid'dle·man** n business person between producer and consumer.

midge [mij] n gnat or similar insect.

midg·et [MIJ-it] n very small person or thing.

mid'riff n middle part of body.

midst prep **1** in the middle of. ◆ n **2** middle. **in the midst of** surrounded by, among.

mid·wife [MID-wīf] n trained person who assists at childbirth. **mid·wife'ry** [-WĪF-ə-ree] n art, practice of this.

mien [meen] n person's bearing, demeanor or appearance.

might¹ [mīt] see MAY.

might² n power, strength. **might'i·ly** adv **1** strongly. **2** powerfully. **might'y** adj **might·i·er, might·i·est 1** of great power. **2** strong. **3** valiant. **4** important. ◆ adv **5** inf very.

mi·graine [MĪ-grayn] n severe headache, oft. with nausea and other symptoms.

——— THESAURUS ———

microscopic adj = **tiny**, imperceptible, infinitesimal, invisible, minuscule, minute, negligible

midday n = **noon**, noonday, twelve o'clock

middle adj **1** = **central**, halfway, intermediate, intervening, mean, median, medium, mid ◆ n **2** = **center**, focus, halfway point, heart, midpoint, midsection, midst

middle-class adj = **bourgeois**, conventional, traditional

middling adj **1** = **mediocre**, indifferent, so-so (inf), tolerable, unexceptional, unremarkable **2** = **moderate**, adequate, all right, average, fair, medium, modest, O.K. or okay (inf), ordinary, passable, serviceable

midget n = **dwarf**, pygmy or pigmy, shrimp (inf), Tom Thumb

midnight n = **twelve o'clock**, dead of

night, middle of the night, the witching hour

midst n **in the midst of** = **among**, amidst, during, in the middle of, in the thick of, surrounded by

midway adj, adv = **halfway**, betwixt and between, in the middle

might n **1** = **power**, energy, force, strength, vigor **2 with might and main** = **forcefully**, lustily, manfully, mightily, vigorously

mightily adv **1** = **very**, decidedly, exceedingly, extremely, greatly, highly, hugely, intensely, much **2** = **powerfully**, energetically, forcefully, lustily, manfully, strongly, vigorously

mighty adj = **powerful**, forceful, lusty, robust, strapping, strong, sturdy, vigorous

migrant n **1** = **wanderer**, drifter, emigrant, immigrant, itinerant, nomad, rover,

mi·grate [MĪ-grayt] vi **-grat·ed, -grat·ing** move from one place to another. **mi'grant** [-grənt] n, adj **mi·gra'tion** n **1** act of passing from one place, condition to another. **2** number migrating together. **mi'gra·to·ry** [-grə-TOR-ee] adj **1** of, capable of migration. **2** (of animals) changing from one place to another according to season.

mild [mīld] adj **-er, -est 1** not strongly flavored. **2** gentle, merciful. **3** calm or temperate. **mild'ly** adv **mild'ness** n

mil·dew [MIL-doo] n **1** destructive fungus on plants or things exposed to damp. ♦ v **2** become tainted, affect with mildew.

mile [mīl] n measure of length, 1760 yards (1.609 km). **mile'age** n **1** distance in miles. **2** traveling expenses per mile. **3** miles traveled (per gallon of gasoline). **mile'stone** n **1** stone marker showing distance. **2** significant event, achievement.

mi·lieu [mil-YUU] n environment, condition in life.

mil·i·tar·y [MIL-i-ter-ee] adj **1** of, for, soldiers, armies or war. ♦ n **2** armed services. **mil'i·tan·cy** [-tən-see] n **mil'i·tant** adj **1** aggressive, vigorous in support of cause. **2** prepared, willing to fight. **mil'i·ta·rism** [-tə-riz-əm] n enthusiasm for military force and methods. **mil'i·ta·rize** vt **-rized, -riz·ing** convert to military use. **mi·li'tia** [-LISH-ə] n military force of citizens serving full time only in emergencies.

mil·i·tate [MIL-i-tayt] vi **-tat·ed, -tat·ing** (esp. with *against*) have strong influence, effect on.

milk n **1** white fluid with which mammals feed their young. **2** fluid in some plants. ♦ vt **3** draw milk from. **milk'y** adj **milk·i·er, milk·i·est 1** containing, like milk. **2** (of liquids) opaque, clouded. **milk'sop** n **1** weak, effeminate fellow. **2** milquetoast. **milk teeth** first set of teeth in young mammals. **Milky Way** luminous band of stars, etc. stretching across sky, the galaxy.

mill n **1** factory. **2** machine for grinding, pulverizing grain, paper, etc. ♦ vt **3** put through mill. **4** cut fine grooves across edges of (e.g. coins). ♦ vi **5** move in confused manner, as cattle or crowds of people. **mill'er** n **mill'stone** n **1** flat circular stone for grinding. **2** heavy emotional or mental burden.

mil·len·ni·um [mi-LEN-ee-əm] n, pl **-ni·a** [-nee-ə] period of a thousand years during which some claim Christ is to reign on earth. **1** period of a thousand years. **2** period of peace, happiness. **millennium bug** n Computers. software problem arising from the change in date at the start of the 21st century.

mil·let [MIL-it] n a cereal grass.

milli- comb. form **1** thousandth, e.g. *milligram*. **2** thousandth part of a gram.

mil·li·bar [MIL-ə-bahr] n unit of atmospheric pressure.

mil·li·ner [MIL-ə-nər] n maker of, dealer in women's hats, ribbons, etc. **mil'li·ner·y** n milliner's goods or work.

mil·lion [MIL-yən] n 1000 thousands. **mil·lion·aire'** n **1** owner of a million dollars, etc. or more. **2** very rich person. **mil'lionth** adj, n

mil·li·pede [MIL-ə-peed] n small

traveler ♦ adj **2 = traveling**, drifting, immigrant, itinerant, migratory, nomadic, roving, shifting, transient, vagrant, wandering

migrate v **= move**, emigrate, journey, roam, rove, travel, trek, voyage, wander

migration n **= wandering**, emigration, journey, movement, roving, travel, trek, voyage

migratory adj **= nomadic**, itinerant, migrant, peripatetic, roving, transient

mild adj **1 = gentle**, calm, docile, easy-going, equable, meek, peaceable, placid **2 = bland**, smooth **3 = calm**, balmy, moderate, temperate, tranquil, warm

mildness n **= gentleness**, calmness, clemency, docility, moderation, placidity, tranquillity, warmth

milieu n **= surroundings**, background, element, environment, locale, location, scene, setting

militant adj **= aggressive**, active, assertive, combative, vigorous

military adj **1 = warlike**, armed, martial, soldierly ♦ n **2 = armed forces**, army, forces, services

militate v militate against **= counteract**, be detrimental to, conflict with, counter, oppose, resist, tell against, weigh against

milk v **= exploit**, extract, pump, take advantage of

mill n **1 = factory**, foundry, plant, works **2 = grinder**, crusher ♦ v **3 = grind**, crush, grate, pound, powder **4 = swarm**, crowd, arthropod, like centipede, with jointed body and many pairs of legs.

milque·toast [MILK-tohst] *n* ineffectual person esp. one easily dominated.

milt *n* spawn of male fish.

mime [mīm] *n* **1** acting without the use of words. **2** actor who does this. ♦ *v* **mimed, mim·ing 3** act in mime.

mim·ic [MIM-ik] *vt* **-icked, -ick·ing 1** imitate (person, manner, etc.) esp. for satirical effect. ♦ *n* **2** one who, or animal that does this, or is adept at it. ♦ *adj* **mim'ic·ry** *n, pl* **-ries** mimicking.

min·a·ret [min-ə-RET] *n* tall slender tower of mosque.

mince [mins] *v* **minced, minc·ing** ♦ *vt* **1** cut, chop very small. **2** soften or moderate (words, etc.). ♦ *vi* **3** walk, speak in affected manner. ♦ *n* **4** something minced. **5** mincemeat. **minc'ing** *adj* affected in manner. **mince'meat** *n* mixture of minced apples, currants, spices, sometimes meat, etc. **mince pie** pie containing mincemeat or mince.

mind [mīnd] *n* **1** thinking faculties as distinguished from the body, intellectual faculties. **2** memory, attention. **3** intention. **4** taste. **5** sanity. ♦ *vt* **6** take offense at. **7** care for. **8** attend to. **9** be cautious, careful

about (something). **10** be concerned, troubled about. ♦ *vi* **11** be careful. **12** heed. **mind'ful** [fəl] *adj* **1** heedful. **2** keeping in memory. **mind'less** [-lis] *adj* stupid, careless.

mine¹ [mīn] *pron* belonging to me.

mine² *n* **1** deep hole for digging out coal, metals, etc. **2** in war, hidden deposit of explosive to blow up ship, etc. **3** land mine. **4** profitable source. ♦ *v* **mined, min·ing** ♦ *vt* **5** dig from mine. **6** make mine in or under. **7** place explosive mines in, on. ♦ *vi* **8** make, work in mine. **mi'ner** *n* one who works in a mine. **mine'field** *n* area of land or sea containing mines. **mine'lay·er** *n* ship for laying mines. **mine'sweep·er** *n* ship, helicopter for clearing away mines.

min·er·al [MIN-ər-əl] *n* **1** naturally occurring inorganic substance, esp. as obtained by mining. ♦ *adj* **2** of, containing, or like minerals. **min·er·al'o·gy** *n* science of minerals. **mineral water** water containing some mineral, esp. natural or artificial kinds for drinking.

min·e·stro·ne [min-ə-STROH-nee] *n* type of vegetable soup containing pasta.

min·gle [MING-gəl] *v* **-gled, -gling** mix, blend, unite, merge.

throng

millstone *n* **1** = **grindstone**, quernstone **2** = **burden**, affliction, albatross, encumbrance, load, weight

mime *v* = **act out**, gesture, represent, simulate

mimic *v* **1** = **imitate**, ape, caricature, do (*inf*), impersonate, parody ♦ *n* **2** = **imitator**, caricaturist, copycat (*inf*), impersonator, impressionist

mimicry *n* = **imitation**, burlesque, caricature, impersonation, mimicking, mockery, parody

mince *v* **1** = **cut**, chop, crumble, grind, hash **2** *As in* **mince one's words** = **tone down**, moderate, soften, spare, weaken

mincing *adj* = **affected**, camp (*inf*), dainty, effeminate, foppish, precious, pretentious, sissy

mind *n* **1** = **intelligence**, brain(s) (*inf*), gray matter (*inf*), intellect, reason, sense, understanding, wits **2** = **memory**, recollection, remembrance **3** = **intention**, desire, disposition, fancy, inclination, leaning, notion, urge, wish **4** = **sanity**,

judgment, marbles (*inf*), mental balance, rationality, reason, senses, wits **5 make up one's mind = decide**, choose, determine, resolve ♦ *v* **6** = **take offense**, be affronted, be bothered, care, disapprove, dislike, object, resent **7** = **pay attention**, heed, listen to, mark, note, obey, observe, pay heed to, take heed **8** = **guard**, attend to, keep an eye on, look after, take care of, tend, watch **9** = **be careful**, be cautious, be on (one's) guard, be wary, take care, watch

mindful *adj* = **aware**, alert, alive to, careful, conscious, heedful, wary, watchful

mindless *adj* = **stupid**, foolish, idiotic, inane, moronic, thoughtless, unthinking, witless

mine *n* **1** = **pit**, colliery, deposit, excavation, shaft **2** = **source**, abundance, fund, hoard, reserve, stock, store, supply, treasury, wealth ♦ *v* **3** = **dig up**, dig for, excavate, extract, hew, quarry, unearth

mingle *v* **1** = **mix**, blend, combine, intermingle, interweave, join, merge, unite **2** = **associate**, consort, fraternize, hang

min·i [MIN-ee] n **1** something small or miniature. **2** short skirt. **3** small computer. ◆ adj

min·i·a·ture [MIN-ee-ə-chər] n **1** small painted portrait. **2** anything on small scale. ◆ adj **3** small-scale, minute.

min·i·bus [MIN-ee-bus] n small bus for about fifteen passengers.

min·im [MIN-əm] n **1** unit of fluid measure, one-sixtieth of a dram. **2** Mus. note half the length of semibreve.

min·i·mize [MIN-ə-mīz] vt **-mized, -miz·ing** bring to, estimate at smallest possible amount. **min'i·mal** [-məl] adj **min'i·mum** [-məm] n, pl **-mums 1** lowest size or quantity. ◆ adj **2** least possible.

min·ion [MIN-yən] n **1** favorite. **2** servile follower.

min·is·ter [MIN-ə-stər] n **1** person in charge of government department. **2** diplomatic representative. **3** clergyman. ◆ vi **4** attend to needs of, take care of. **min·is·te'ri·al** [-STEER-ee-əl] adj **min·is·tra'tion** n rendering help, esp. to sick. **min'is·try** n, pl **-tries 1** office of clergyman. **2** body of ministers forming government. **3** act of ministering. **minister without portfolio** minister of state not in charge of specific department.

mink [mingk] n **1** variety of weasel. **2** its (brown) fur.

min·now [MIN-oh] n small freshwater fish.

mi·nor [MĪ-nər] adj **1** lesser. **2** under age. ◆ n **3** person below age of legal majority. **4** scale in music. **mi·nor·i·ty** [mi-NOR-i-tee] n **1** lesser number. **2** smaller party voting together. **3** ethical or religious group in a minority in any country. **4** state of being a minor.

Min·o·taur [MIN-ə-tor] n fabled monster, half bull, half man.

min·strel [MIN-strəl] n **1** medieval singer, musician, poet. ◆ pl **2** performers in minstrel show. **minstrel show** formerly, an entertainment of songs and jokes provided by white performers with blackened faces.

mint¹ n **1** place where money is coined. ◆ vt **2** coin, invent.

mint² n aromatic plant.

min·u·et [min-yoo-ET] n **1** stately dance. **2** music for it.

mi·nus [MĪ-nəs] prep, adj **1** less, with the deduction of, deprived of. **2** lacking. **3** negative. ◆ n **4** the sign (-) denoting subtraction.

mi·nus·cule [MIN-iss-skyool] adj very small.

mi·nute¹ [mī-NOOT] adj **-nut·er, -nut·est 1** very small. **2** precise. **mi·nute'ly** adv **mi·nu·ti·ae** [mi-NOO-shee-ee] pl n trifles, precise details.

min·ute² [MIN-it] n **1** 60th part of hour or degree. **2** moment. **3** memorandum. ◆ pl **4** record of proceedings of meeting, etc.

—————————— THESAURUS ——————————

about or around, hobnob, rub shoulders (inf), socialize

miniature adj = **small**, diminutive, little, minuscule, minute, scaled-down, tiny, toy

minimal adj = **minimum**, least, least possible, nominal, slightest, smallest, token

minimize v **1** = **reduce**, curtail, decrease, diminish, miniaturize, prune, shrink **2** = **play down**, belittle, decry, deprecate, discount, disparage, make light or little of, underrate

minimum adj **1** = **least**, least possible, lowest, minimal, slightest, smallest ◆ n **2** = **least**, lowest, nadir

minion n = **follower**, flunky, hanger-on, henchman, hireling, lackey, underling, yes man

minister n **1** = **clergyman**, cleric, parson, pastor, preacher, priest, rector, vicar ◆ v **2** = **attend**, administer, cater to, pander to, serve, take care of, tend

ministry n **1** = **department**, bureau,

council, office, quango **2** = **the priesthood**, holy orders, the church

minor adj = **small**, inconsequential, insignificant, lesser, petty, slight, trivial, unimportant ◆ n = **underage person**, adolescent, child, juvenile, teenager, youngster (inf), youth

minstrel n = **musician**, bard, singer, songstress, troubadour

mint v = **make**, cast, coin, produce, punch, stamp, strike

minuscule adj = **tiny**, diminutive, infinitesimal, little, microscopic, miniature, minute

minute¹ n = **moment**, flash, instant, jiffy (inf), second, trice

minute² adj **1** = **small**, diminutive, infinitesimal, little, microscopic, miniature, minuscule, tiny **2** = **precise**, close, critical, detailed, exact, exhaustive, meticulous, painstaking, punctilious

minutes pl n = **record**, memorandum,

minx [mingks] *n* bold, flirtatious girl.

mir·a·cle [MIR-ə-kəl] *n* **1** supernatural event. **2** marvel. **mi·rac'u·lous** *adj* **miracle play** drama (esp. medieval) based on sacred subject.

mi·rage [mi-RAHZH] *n* deceptive image in atmosphere, e.g. of lake in desert.

mire [mīr] *n* **1** swampy ground, mud. ♦ *vt* **mired, mir·ing 2** stick in, dirty with mud. **3** entangle, involve.

mir·ror [MIR-ər] *n* **1** glass or polished surface reflecting images. ♦ *vt* **2** reflect.

mirth [murth] *n* merriment, gaiety. **mirth'ful** *adj*

MIS management information system(s).

mis- *prefix* wrong(ly), bad(ly).

mis·an·thrope [MIS-ən-throhp] *n* hater of mankind. **mis·an·throp'ic** *adj*

mis·ap·pro·pri·ate [mis-ə-PROH-pree-ayt] *vt* **-at·ed, -at·ing 1** put to dishonest use. **2** embezzle.

mis·be·have' *v* behave badly. **mis·be·hav'iour** *n*

mis·cal'cu·late *vt* calculate or judge wrongly. **mis·cal·cu·la'tion** *n*

mis·car·ry [mis-KA-ree] *vi* **-ried, -ry·ing 1** bring forth young prematurely. **2** go wrong, fail. **mis·car'riage** [-KA-rij] *n*

mis·cast' *v* **-cast, -cast·ing 1** distribute acting parts wrongly. **2** assign to unsuitable role.

mis·cel·la·ne·ous [mis-ə-LAY-nee-əs] *adj* mixed, assorted. **mis'cel·la·ny** *n, pl* **-nies 1** collection of assorted writings in one book. **2** medley.

mis·chief [MIS-chif] *n* **1** annoying behavior. **2** inclination to tease, disturb. **3** harm. **4** source of harm or annoyance. **mis'chie·vous** [-chi-vəs] *adj* **1** of a child, full of pranks. **2** disposed to mischief. **3** having harmful effect.

mis·ci·ble [MIS-ə-bəl] *adj* capable of mixing.

mis·con·cep·tion [mis-kən-SEP-shən] *n* wrong idea, belief.

mis·con'duct *n* immoral or unethical

notes, proceedings, transactions, transcript

minutiae *pl n* = **details**, finer points, ins and outs, niceties, particulars, subtleties, trifles, trivia

minx *n* = **flirt**, coquette, hussy

miracle *n* = **wonder**, marvel, phenomenon, prodigy

miraculous *adj* = **wonderful**, amazing, astonishing, astounding, extraordinary, incredible, phenomenal, prodigious, unaccountable, unbelievable

mirage *n* = **illusion**, hallucination, optical illusion

mire *n* **1** = **swamp**, bog, marsh, morass, quagmire **2** = **mud**, dirt, muck, ooze, slime

mirror *n* **1** = **looking-glass**, glass, reflector ♦ *v* **2** = **reflect**, copy, echo, emulate, follow

mirth *n* = **merriment**, amusement, cheerfulness, fun, gaiety, glee, hilarity, jollity, joviality, laughter, revelry

mirthful *adj* = **merry**, blithe, cheerful, cheery, festive, happy, jolly, jovial, light-hearted, playful, sportive

misadventure *n* = **misfortune**, accident, bad luck, calamity, catastrophe, debacle, disaster, mishap, reverse, setback

misanthropic *adj* = **antisocial**, cynical, malevolent, unfriendly

misapprehend *v* = **misunderstand**, misconstrue, misinterpret, misread, mistake

misapprehension *n* = **misunderstanding**, delusion, error, fallacy, misconception, misinterpretation, mistake

misappropriate *v* = **steal**, embezzle, misspend, misuse, peculate, pocket

misbehave *v* = **act up**, be disobedient, make a fuss, make trouble, make waves

miscalculate *v* = **misjudge**, blunder, err, overestimate, overrate, slip up, underestimate, underrate

miscarriage *n* = **failure**, breakdown, error, mishap, perversion

miscarry *v* = **fail**, come to grief, fall through, go awry, go wrong, misfire

miscellaneous *adj* = **mixed**, assorted, diverse, jumbled, motley, sundry, varied, various

miscellany *n* = **assortment**, anthology, collection, jumble, medley, mélange, mixed bag, mixture, potpourri, variety

mischance *n* = **misfortune**, accident, calamity, disaster, misadventure, mishap

mischief *n* **1** = **trouble**, impishness, misbehavior, monkey business (*inf*), naughtiness, shenanigans (*inf*), waywardness **2** = **harm**, damage, evil, hurt, injury, misfortune, trouble

mischievous *adj* **1** = **naughty**, impish, playful, puckish, rascally, roguish, sportive, troublesome, wayward **2** = **malicious**, damaging, destructive, evil, harmful, behaviour.

mis·cre·ant [MIS-kree-ənt] *n* wicked person, evildoer, villain.

mis'deed *n* wrongful act.

mis·de·mean·or [mis-di-MEE-nər] *n* **1** in law, offense less grave than a felony. **2** minor offense.

mi·ser [MĪ-zər] *n* **1** hoarder of money. **2** stingy person. **mi'ser·ly** *adj* **1** avaricious. **2** niggardly.

mis·er·a·ble [MIZ-ər-ə-bəl] *adj* **1** very unhappy, wretched. **2** causing misery. **3** worthless. **4** squalid. **mis'er·y** *n, pl* **-er·ies 1** great unhappiness. **2** distress. **3** poverty.

mis'fit *n* esp. person not suited to surroundings or work.

mis·for'tune *n* (piece of) bad luck.

mis·giv'ing *n* (oft pl) feeling of fear, doubt, etc.

mis·guid·ed [mis-GĪ-did] *adj* foolish,

unreasonable.

mis'hap *n* minor accident.

mis·in·form' *vt* give incorrect information to. **mis·in·for·ma'tion** *n*

mis·judge' *v* judge wrongly or unfairly. **mis·judg'ment** *n*

mis·lay' *vt* **-laid, -lay·ing 1** put in place that cannot later be remembered. **2** place wrongly.

mis·lead [mis-LEED] *vt* **-led, -lead·ing 1** give false information to. **2** lead astray. **misleading** *adj* deceptive.

mis·man·age *vt* organize or run (something) badly. **mis·man'age·ment** *n*

mis·no·mer [mis-NOH-mər] *n* **1** wrong name or term. **2** use of this.

mi·sog·y·ny [mi-SOJ-ə-nee] *n* hatred of women. **mi·sog'y·nist** *n*

mis·place' *vt* **1** mislay. **2** put in the wrong place. **3** give (trust or affection)

——————— THESAURUS ———————

hurtful, spiteful, vicious, wicked

misconception *n* = **delusion**, error, fallacy, misapprehension, misunderstanding

misconduct *n* = **immorality**, impropriety, malpractice, mismanagement, wrongdoing

miscreant *n* = **wrongdoer**, criminal, rascal, reprobate, rogue, scoundrel, sinner, vagabond, villain

misdeed *n* = **offense**, crime, fault, misconduct, misdemeanor, sin, transgression, wrong

misdemeanor *n* = **offense**, fault, infringement, misdeed, peccadillo, transgression

miser *n* = **skinflint**, cheapskate (*inf*), niggard, penny-pincher (*inf*), Scrooge

miserable *adj* **1** = **unhappy**, dejected, depressed, despondent, disconsolate, forlorn, gloomy, sorrowful, woebegone, wretched **2** = **squalid**, deplorable, lamentable, shameful, sordid, sorry, wretched

miserly *adj* = **mean**, avaricious, grasping, niggardly, parsimonious, penny-pinching (*inf*), stingy, tightfisted, ungenerous

misery *n* = **unhappiness**, anguish, depression, desolation, despair, distress, gloom, grief, sorrow, suffering, torment, woe

misfire *v* = **fail**, fall through, go wrong, miscarry

misfit *n* = **nonconformist**, eccentric, fish

out of water (*inf*), oddball (*inf*), square peg (in a round hole) (*inf*)

misfortune *n* **1** = **bad luck**, adversity, hard luck, ill luck, infelicity **2** = **mishap**, affliction, calamity, disaster, reverse, setback, tragedy, tribulation, trouble

misgiving *n* = **unease**, anxiety, apprehension, distrust, doubt, qualm, reservation, suspicion, trepidation, uncertainty, worry

misguided *adj* = **unwise**, deluded, erroneous, ill-advised, imprudent, injudicious, misplaced, mistaken, unwarranted

mishandle *v* = **mismanage**, botch, bungle, make a mess of, mess up (*inf*), muff

mishap *n* = **accident**, calamity, misadventure, mischance, misfortune

misinform *v* = **mislead**, deceive, misdirect, misguide

misinterpret *v* = **misunderstand**, distort, misapprehend, misconceive, misconstrue, misjudge, misread, misrepresent, mistake

misjudge *v* = **miscalculate**, overestimate, overrate, underestimate, underrate

mislay *v* = **lose**, lose track of, misplace

mislead *v* = **deceive**, delude, fool, hoodwink, misdirect, misguide, misinform

misleading *adj* = **confusing**, ambiguous, deceptive, disingenuous, evasive, false

mismanage *v* = **mishandle**, botch, bungle, make a mess of, mess up, misconduct, misdirect, misgovern inappropriately.

mis'print n printing error. ♦ vt

mis•pro•nounce' v pronounce (a word) wrongly. **mis•pro•nun•ci•a'tion** n

miss vt **1** fail to hit, reach, find, catch, or notice. **2** be late for. **3** omit. **4** notice or regret absence of. **5** avoid. ♦ vi (of engine) misfire. ♦ n **6** fact, instance of missing. **miss'ing** adj **1** lost. **2** absent.

mis•sal [MIS-əl] n book containing prayers, etc. of the Mass.

mis•shap'en [mis-SHAY-pən] adj badly shaped, deformed.

mis•sile [MIS-əl] n that which may be thrown, homed to damage, destroy. **guided missile** see also GUIDE.

mis•sion [MISH-ən] n **1** specific task or duty. **2** calling in life. **3** delegation. **4** sending or being sent on some service. **5** those sent. **mis'sion•ar•y** n, pl **-ar•ies** one sent to a place, society to spread religion. ♦ adj

mis•sive [MIS-iv] n letter.

mis•spell' v spell (a word) wrongly.

mis•spent' adj wasted or misused.

mist n water vapor in fine drops. **mist'y** adj **mist•i•er, mist•i•est 1** full of mist. **2** dim. **3** obscure.

mis•take [mi-STAYK] n **1** error, blunder. ♦ v **-took** [-TUUK], **-tak•en, -tak•ing** ♦ vt **2** fail to understand. **3** form wrong opinion about. **4** take (person or thing) for another. ♦ vi **5** be in error.

mis•ter [MIS-tər] n the full form of Mr.

mis•tle•toe [MIS-əl-toh] n evergreen parasitic plant with white berries that grows on trees.

mis•tress [MIS-tris] n **1** object of man's illicit love. **2** woman with mastery or control. **3** woman owner. **4** woman teacher. **5** obs title given to married woman.

mis•un•der•stand' v fail to understand properly. **mis•un•der•stand'ing** n

———— THESAURUS ————

misplace v = lose, lose track of, mislay

misprint n = mistake, corrigendum, erratum, literal, typo (inf)

misquote v = misrepresent, falsify, twist

misrepresent v = distort, disguise, falsify, misinterpret

misrule n = disorder, anarchy, chaos, confusion, lawlessness, turmoil

miss[1] v **1** = omit, leave out, let go, overlook, pass over, skip **2** = avoid, escape, evade **3** = long for, pine for, yearn for ♦ n **4** = mistake, blunder, error, failure, omission, oversight

misshapen adj = deformed, contorted, crooked, distorted, grotesque, malformed, twisted, warped

missile n = rocket, projectile, weapon

missing adj = absent, astray, lacking, left out, lost, mislaid, misplaced, unaccounted-for

mission n = task, assignment, commission, duty, errand, job, quest, undertaking, vocation

missionary n = evangelist, apostle, preacher

missive n = letter, communication, dispatch, epistle, memorandum, message, note, report

misspent adj = wasted, dissipated, imprudent, profitless, squandered

mist n = fog, cloud, film, haze, smog, spray, steam, vapor

mistake n **1** = error, blunder, erratum, fault, faux pas, miscalculation, oversight, slip ♦ v **2** = misunderstand, misapprehend, misconstrue, misinterpret, misjudge, misread **3** = confuse with, mix up with, take for

mistaken adj = wrong, erroneous, false, faulty, inaccurate, incorrect, misguided, unsound, wide of the mark

mistakenly adv = incorrectly, by mistake, erroneously, fallaciously, falsely, inaccurately, misguidedly, wrongly

mistimed adj = inopportune, badly timed, ill-timed, untimely

mistreat v = abuse, harm, ill-treat, injure, knock about or around, maltreat, manhandle, misuse, molest

mistress n = lover, concubine, girlfriend, kept woman, paramour

mistrust v **1** = doubt, be wary of, distrust, fear, suspect ♦ n **2** = suspicion, distrust, doubt, misgiving, skepticism, uncertainty, wariness

mistrustful adj = suspicious, chary, cynical, distrustful, doubtful, fearful, hesitant, skeptical, uncertain, wary

misty adj = foggy, blurred, cloudy, dim, hazy, indistinct, murky, obscure, opaque, overcast

misunderstand v = misinterpret, be at cross-purposes, get the wrong end of the stick, misapprehend, misconstrue,

mis·use¹ *n* **1** incorrect, improper, or careless use. ◆ *vt* **2** use wrongly. **3** treat badly.

mite [mīt] *n* **1** very small insect. **2** anything very small. **3** small contribution but all one can afford.

mi·ter [MĪ-tər] *n* **1** bishop's headdress. **2** joint between two pieces of wood, etc. meeting at right angles. ◆ *vt* **3** join with, shape for a miter joint. **4** put miter on.

mit·i·gate [MIT-i-gayt] *vt* **-gat·ed, -gat·ing** make less severe. **mit·i·ga'tion** *n*

mitt *n* **1** baseball player's glove esp. for catcher, first baseman. **2** *sl* hand.

mit·ten [MIT-n] *n* glove with two compartments, one for thumb and one for fingers.

mix [miks] *vt* **1** put together, combine, blend, mingle. ◆ *vi* **2** be mixed. **3** associate. **mixed** *adj* **1** composed of different elements, races, sexes, etc. **mix'er** *n* **1** one who, that which mixes. **2** informal party intended to help guests meet one another. **mix'ture** [-chər] *n* **mixed-up** *adj* **1** confused. **2** emotionally unstable. **mix-up** *n* **1** confused situation. **2** a fight.

mks units metric system of units based on the meter, kilogram and second.

Mn *Chem.* manganese.

mne·mon·ic [ni-MON-ik] *adj* **1** helping the memory. ◆ *n* **2** something intended to help the memory.

Mo *Chem.* molybdenum.

moan [mohn] *n* **1** low murmur, usually of pain. ◆ *v* **2** utter with moan, lament.

moat [moht] *n* **1** deep wide ditch esp. around castle. ◆ *vt* **2** surround with moat.

mob *n* **1** disorderly crowd of people. **2** mixed assembly. ◆ *vt* **mobbed, mob·bing 3** attack in mob. **4** crowd around boisterously.

mo·bile [MOH-bəl] *adj* **1** capable of movement. **2** easily moved or changed. ◆ *n* [moh-BEEL] **3** hanging structure of card, plastic, etc. designed to move in air currents. **mo·bil'i·ty** *n* **mobile home** large trailer, connected to utilities at a trailer park, etc., used as a residence. **mobile phone** portable phone powered by batteries.

mo·bi·lize [MOH-bə-līz] *v* **-lized, -liz·ing 1** (of armed services) prepare for military service. ◆ *vt* **2** organize for a purpose. **mo·bi·li·za'tion** [-ZAY-shən] *n* in war time, calling up of men and women for active service.

misjudge, misread, mistake

misunderstanding *n* = **mistake**, error, misconception, misinterpretation, misjudgment, mix-up

misuse *n* **1** = **waste**, abuse, desecration, misapplication, squandering ◆ *v* **2** = **waste**, abuse, desecrate, misapply, prostitute, squander

mitigate *v* = **ease**, extenuate, lessen, lighten, moderate, soften, subdue, temper

mitigation *n* = **relief**, alleviation, diminution, extenuation, moderation, remission

mix *v* **1** = **combine**, blend, cross, fuse, intermingle, interweave, join, jumble, merge, mingle **2** = **socialize**, associate, consort, fraternize, hang out (*inf*), hobnob, mingle ◆ *n* **3** = **mixture**, alloy, amalgam, assortment, blend, combination, compound, fusion, medley

mixed *adj* **1** = **combined**, amalgamated, blended, composite, compound, joint, mingled, united **2** = **varied**, assorted, cosmopolitan, diverse, heterogeneous, miscellaneous, motley

mixed-up *adj* = **confused**, at sea,

bewildered, distraught, disturbed, maladjusted, muddled, perplexed, puzzled, upset

mixture *n* = **blend**, amalgam, assortment, brew, compound, fusion, jumble, medley, mix, potpourri, variety

mix-up *n* = **confusion**, mess, mistake, misunderstanding, muddle, tangle

mix up *v* **1** = **combine**, blend, mix **2** = **confuse**, confound, muddle

moan *n* **1** = **groan**, lament, sigh, sob, wail, whine **2** *Inf* = **grumble**, complaint, gripe (*inf*), grouch (*inf*), grouse, protest, whine ◆ *v* **3** = **groan**, lament, sigh, sob, whine **4** *Inf* = **grumble**, bleat, carp, complain, groan, grouse, whine

mob *n* **1** = **crowd**, drove, flock, horde, host, mass, multitude, pack, swarm, throng **2** *Sl* = **gang**, crew (*inf*), group, lot, set ◆ *v* **3** = **surround**, crowd around, jostle, set upon, swarm around

mobile *adj* = **movable**, itinerant, moving, peripatetic, portable, traveling, wandering

mobilize *v* = **prepare**, activate, call to arms, call up, get *or* make ready, marshal, organize, rally, ready

moc·ca·sin [MOK-ə-sin] n Amer. Indian soft shoe, usu. of deerskin.

mo·cha [MOH-kə] n 1 type of strong, dark coffee. 2 this flavor.

mock [mok] vt 1 make fun of, ridicule. 2 mimic. ◆ vi 3 scoff. ◆ n 4 act of mocking. 5 laughingstock. ◆ adj 6 sham, imitation. **mock·er·y** n, pl **-er·ies** 1 derision. 2 travesty. **mocking bird** N Amer. bird that imitates songs of others. **mock-up** n scale model.

mode [mohd] n 1 method, manner. 2 prevailing fashion.

mod·el [MOD-l] n 1 miniature representation. 2 pattern. 3 person or thing worthy of imitation. 4 person employed by artist to pose, or by dress designer to display clothing. ◆ vt **-eled, -el·ing** 5 make model of. 6 mold. 7 display (clothing) for dress designer.

mo·dem [MOH-dem] n device for connecting two computers via a telephone line.

mod·er·ate [MOD-ər-it] adj 1 not going to extremes, temperate, medium. ◆ n 2 person of moderate views. ◆ v [-ayt] 3 make, become less violent or excessive. 4 preside over meeting, etc. **mod'er·a·tor** n 1 mediator. 2 president of Presbyterian body. 3 arbitrator. 4 person presiding over panel discussion.

mod·ern [MOD-ərn] adj 1 of present or recent times. 2 in, of current fashion. ◆ n 3 person living in modern times. **mod'ern·ism** n (support of) modern tendencies, thoughts, etc. **mod·ern·i·za'tion** [-ZAY-shən] n **mod'ern·ize** [-īz] vt **-ized, -iz·ing** bring up to date.

mod·est [MOD-ist] adj 1 not overrating one's qualities or achievements. 2 shy. 3 moderate, not excessive. 4 decorous, decent. **mod'es·ty** n

mod·i·cum [MOD-i-kəm] n small quantity.

mod·i·fy [MOD-ə-fī] v (mainly tr) **-fied, -fy·ing** 1 change slightly. 2 tone down. **mod·i·fi·ca'tion** n **mod'i·fi·er** [-fī-ər] n esp. word qualifying another.

mock v 1 = **laugh at**, deride, jeer, make fun of, poke fun at, ridicule, scoff, scorn, sneer, taunt, tease 2 = **mimic**, ape, caricature, imitate, lampoon, parody, satirize ◆ adj 3 = **imitation**, artificial, dummy, fake, false, feigned, phoney or phony (inf), pretended, sham, spurious

mockery n 1 = **derision**, contempt, disdain, disrespect, insults, jeering, ridicule, scoffing, scorn 2 = **farce**, disappointment, joke, letdown

mocking adj = **scornful**, contemptuous, derisive, disdainful, disrespectful, sarcastic, sardonic, satirical, scoffing

mode n 1 = **method**, form, manner, procedure, process, style, system, technique, way 2 = **fashion**, craze, look, rage, style, trend, vogue

model n 1 = **representation**, copy, dummy, facsimile, image, imitation, miniature, mock-up, replica 2 = **pattern**, archetype, example, ideal, original, paradigm, paragon, prototype, standard 3 = **sitter**, poser, subject ◆ v 4 = **shape**, carve, design, fashion, form, mold, sculpt 5 = **show off**, display, sport (inf), wear

moderate adj 1 = **mild**, controlled, gentle, limited, middle-of-the-road, modest, reasonable, restrained, steady 2 = **average**, fair, indifferent, mediocre, middling, ordinary, passable, so-so (inf), unexceptional ◆ v 3 = **regulate**, control, curb, ease, modulate, restrain, soften, subdue, temper, tone down

moderately adv = **reasonably**, fairly, passably, quite, rather, slightly, somewhat, tolerably

moderation n = **restraint**, fairness, reasonableness, temperance

modern adj = **current**, contemporary, fresh, new, newfangled, novel, present-day, recent, up-to-date

modernity n = **novelty**, currency, freshness, innovation, newness

modernize v = **update**, make over, rejuvenate, remake, remodel, renew, renovate, revamp

modest adj 1 = **unpretentious**, bashful, coy, demure, diffident, reserved, reticent, retiring, self-effacing, shy 2 = **moderate**, fair, limited, middling, ordinary, small, unexceptional

modesty n = **reserve**, bashfulness, coyness, demureness, diffidence, humility, reticence, shyness, timidity

modicum n = **little**, bit, crumb, drop, fragment, scrap, shred, touch

modification n = **change**, adjustment, alteration, qualification, refinement, revision, variation

mod·u·late [MOJ-ə-layt] v **-lat·ed, -lat·ing**
♦ vt **1** regulate. **2** vary in tone. ♦ vi **3**
change key of music. **mod·u·la'tion** n **1**
modulating. **2** *Electronics* superimposing
signals onto high-frequency carrier.

mod·ule [MOJ-ool] n (detachable) unit,
section, component with specific function.

mo·dus op·e·ran·di [MOH-dəs
op-ə-RAN-dee] *Lat* method of operating,
tackling task.

mo·gul [MOH-gəl] n **1** important or
powerful person. **2** bump in ski slope.

mo·hair [MOH-hair] n **1** fine cloth of goat
hair. **2** hair of Angora goat.

mo·hel [MOH-əl] n in Jewish tradition,
person who performs rite of circumcision.

moi·e·ty [MOI-i-tee] n, pl **-ties** a half.

moist adj **-er, -est** damp, slightly wet.
moist'en [MOI-sən] v **mois'ture** [-chər] n
liquid, esp. diffused or in drops.

mo·lar [MOH-lər] adj **1** (of teeth) for
grinding. ♦ n **2** molar tooth.

mo·las·ses [mə-LAS-iz] n thick brown
syrup, byproduct of process of sugar
refining.

mold¹ [mohld] n **1** hollow object in which
metal, etc. is cast. **2** pattern for shaping. **3**
character. **4** shape, form. ♦ vt **5** shape or
pattern. **mold'ing** n **1** molded object. **2**
ornamental edging. **3** decoration.

mold² n fungoid growth caused by
dampness. **mold'y** adj **mold·i·er, mold·i·est**

stale, musty.

mold³ n loose soil rich in organic matter.
mold'er vi decay or cause to decay into
dust.

mole¹ [mohl] n small dark protuberant
spot on the skin.

mole² n **1** small burrowing animal. **2** spy,
informer.

mole³ n SI unit of amount of substance.

mol·e·cule [MOL-ə-kyool] n **1** simplest
freely existing chemical unit, composed of
two or more atoms. **2** very small particle.
mo·lec'u·lar adj of, inherent in molecules.

mo·lest [mə-LEST] vt **1** pester, interfere
with so as to annoy or injure. **2** make
indecent sexual advances esp. to a child.

mol·li·fy [MOL-ə-fī] vt **-fied, -fy·ing** calm
down, placate, soften. **mol·li·fi·ca'tion** n

mol·lusk [MOL-əsk] n soft-bodied, usu.
hard-shelled animal, e.g. snail, oyster.

molt [mohlt] v **1** cast or shed fur, feathers,
etc. ♦ n **2** molting.

molten see MELT.

mo·lyb·de·num [mə-LIB-də-nəm] n
silver-white metallic element.

mo·ment [MOH-mənt] n **1** very short
space of time. **2** (present) point in time.
mo·men·tar'i·ly adv **mo'men·tar·y** adj
lasting only a moment.

mo·men·tous [moh-MEN-təs] adj of great
importance.

mo·men·tum [moh-MEN-təm] n **1** force

——— THESAURUS ———

modify v **1** = **change**, adapt, adjust, alter,
convert, reform, remodel, revise, rework
2 = **tone down**, ease, lessen, lower,
moderate, qualify, restrain, soften, temper

modish adj = **fashionable**, chic,
contemporary, cool (*inf*), current, in, phat
(*sl*), smart, stylish, trendy (*inf*),
up-to-the-minute, voguish

modulate v = **adjust**, attune, balance,
regulate, tune, vary

mogul n = **tycoon**, baron, big cheese (*inf*),
big shot (*inf*), magnate, V.I.P.

moist adj = **damp**, clammy, dewy, humid,
soggy, wet

moisten v = **dampen**, damp, moisturize,
soak, water, wet

moisture n = **dampness**, dew, liquid,
water, wetness

mold¹ n **1** = **cast**, pattern, shape **2** =
design, build, construction, fashion, form,
format, kind, pattern, shape, style **3** =
nature, caliber, character, kind, quality,

sort, stamp, type ♦ v **4** = **shape**, construct,
create, fashion, forge, form, make, model,
sculpt, work **5** = **influence**, affect, control,
direct, form, make, shape

mold² n = **fungus**, blight, mildew,
mustiness

moldy adj = **stale**, bad, blighted, decaying,
fusty, mildewed, musty, rotten

molecule n = **particle**, jot, speck

molest v **1** = **annoy**, badger, beset, bother,
disturb, harass, persecute, pester, plague,
torment, worry **2** = **abuse**, attack, harm,
hurt, ill-treat, interfere with, maltreat

mollify v = **pacify**, appease, calm,
conciliate, placate, quiet, soothe, sweeten

moment n **1** = **instant**, flash, jiffy (*inf*),
second, split second, trice, twinkling **2** =
time, juncture, point, stage

momentarily adv = **briefly**, for a moment,
temporarily

momentary adj = **short-lived**, brief,
fleeting, passing, short, temporary,

of a moving body. **2** impetus gained from motion.

mon·arch [MON-ərk] *n* sovereign ruler of a country. **mo·nar'chi·cal** *adj* **mon'ar·chist** *n* supporter of monarchy. **mon'ar·chy** *n, pl* **-chies 1** nation ruled by sovereign. **2** monarch's rule.

mon·as·ter·y [MON-ə-ster-ee] *n, pl* **-ter·ies** house occupied by members of religious order. **mo·nas·tic** [mə-NAS-tik] *adj* **1** relating to monks, nuns, or monasteries. ◆ *n* **2** monk, recluse.

mon·ey [MUN-ee] *n, pl* **-eys** *or* **-ies** banknotes, coin, etc., used as medium of exchange. **mon·e·ta·rism** [MON-ə-tə-riz-əm] *n* theory that inflation is caused by increase in money supply. **mon'e·ta·rist** *n, adj* **mon'e·tar·y** *adj* **mon-eyed, -ied** [MUN-eed] *adj* rich.

mon·gol·ism [MONG-gə-liz-əm] *n* a former and non-medical name for Down SYNDROME.

mon·goose [MON-goos] *n, pl* **-goos·es** small animal of Asia and Africa noted for killing snakes.

mon·grel [MONG-grəl] *n* **1** animal, esp. dog, of mixed breed. **2** hybrid. ◆ *adj*

mon·i·tor [MON-i-tər] *n* **1** person or device that checks, controls, warns or keeps record of something. **2** pupil assisting teacher with conduct of class. **3** television set used in a studio for checking program being transmitted. **4** *Computers* cathode ray tube with screen for viewing data. **5** type of large lizard. ◆ *vt* **6** watch, check on. **mon'i·to·ry** [-tor-ee] *adj* giving warning.

monk [munk] *n* one of a religious community of men living apart under vows. **monk'ish** *adj*

mon·key [MUN-kee] *n, pl* **-keys 1** long-tailed primate. **2** mischievous child. ◆ *vi* **-keyed, -key·ing 3** meddle, fool (with). **monkey wrench** one with adjustable jaw.

mono- *comb. form* single, e.g. *monosyllabic*.

mon·o·chrome [MON-ə-krohm] *n* **1** representation in one color. ◆ *adj* **2** of one color. **mon·o·chro·mat·ic** *adj*

mon·o·cle [MON-ə-kəl] *n* single eyeglass.

mo·noc·u·lar [mə-NOK-yə-lər] *adj* one-eyed.

mo·nog·a·my [mə-NOG-ə-mee] *n* custom of being married to one person at a time. **mo·nog'a·mous** *adj*

mon·o·gram [MON-ə-gram] *n* design of one or more letters interwoven.

mon·o·graph [MON-ə-graf] *n* short scholarly book on single subject.

mon·o·lith [MON-ə-lith] *n* monument consisting of single standing stone. **mon·o·lith'ic** *adj* **1** of or like a monolith. **2** massive, inflexible.

mon·o·logue [MON-ə-lawg] *n* **1** dramatic composition with only one speaker. **2** long speech by one person.

mon·o·ma·ni·a [mon-ə-MAY-nee-ə] *n* excessive preoccupation with one thing.

transitory

momentous *adj* = **significant**, critical, crucial, fateful, historic, important, pivotal, vital, weighty

momentum *n* = **impetus**, drive, energy, force, power, propulsion, push, strength, thrust

monarch *n* = **ruler**, emperor *or* empress, king, potentate, prince *or* princess, queen, sovereign

monarchy *n* **1** = **sovereignty**, autocracy, kingship, monocracy, royalism **2** = **kingdom**, empire, principality, realm

monastery *n* = **abbey**, cloister, convent, friary, nunnery, priory

monastic *adj* = **monkish**, ascetic, cloistered, contemplative, hermit-like, reclusive, secluded, sequestered, withdrawn

monetary *adj* = **financial**, budgetary, capital, cash, fiscal, pecuniary

money *n* = **cash**, capital, coin, currency, hard cash, legal tender, riches, silver, wealth

mongrel *n* **1** = **hybrid**, cross, crossbreed, half-breed ◆ *adj* **2** = **hybrid**, crossbred

monitor *n* **1** = **watchdog**, guide, invigilator, supervisor ◆ *v* **2** = **check**, follow, keep an eye on, keep tabs on, keep track of, observe, stalk, survey, watch

monk *n* = **friar**, brother

monkey *n* **1** = **simian**, primate **2** = **rascal**, devil, imp, rogue, scamp ◆ *v* **3** = **fool**, meddle, mess, play, tinker

monolithic *adj* = **huge**, colossal, impenetrable, intractable, massive, monumental, solid

monologue *n* = **speech**, harangue, lecture, sermon, soliloquy

monopolize *v* = **control**, corner the market in, dominate, hog (*sl*), keep to oneself, take over

mo·nop·o·ly [mə-NOP-ə-lee] *n, pl* **-lies** exclusive control of commerce, privilege, etc. **mo·nop'o·lize** *vt* **-lized, -liz·ing** claim, take exclusive possession of.

mon·o·rail [MON-ə-rayl] *n* railway with cars running on or suspended from single rail.

mon·o·the·ism [MON-ə-thee-iz-əm] *n* belief in only one God.

mon·o·tone [MON-ə-tohn] *n* continuing on one note. **mo·not·o·nous** [mə-NOT-n-əs] *adj* lacking in variety, dull, wearisome. **mo·not'o·ny** *n*

mon·soon' *n* 1 seasonal wind of SE Asia. 2 very heavy rainfall season.

mon·ster [MON-stər] *n* 1 fantastic imaginary beast. 2 misshapen animal or plant. 3 very wicked person. 4 huge person, animal or thing. ♦ *adj* 5 huge. **mon·stros'i·ty** *n* 1 monstrous being. 2 deformity. 3 distortion. **mon'strous** [-strəs] *adj* 1 of, like monster. 2 unnatural. 3 enormous. 4 horrible.

mon·tage [mon-TAHZH] *n* 1 elements of two or more pictures imposed upon a single background to give a unified effect. 2 method of editing a film.

month [munth] *n* 1 one of twelve periods into which the year is divided. 2 period of moon's revolution around Earth. **month'ly** *adj* 1 happening or payable once a month. ♦ *adv* 2 once a month. ♦ *n* 3 magazine published every month.

mon·u·ment [MON-yə-mənt] *n* anything that commemorates, esp. a building or statue. **mon·u·men'tal** [-MEN-tl] *adj* 1 vast, lasting. 2 of or serving as monument.

mooch *vi sl* 1 borrow without intending to repay. 2 beg.

mood[1] *n* state of mind and feelings. **mood'y** *adj* **mood·i·er, mood·i·est** 1 gloomy, pensive. 2 changeable in mood.

mood[2] *n Grammar* form indicating function of verb.

moon *n* 1 satellite that takes lunar month to revolve around Earth. 2 any secondary planet. ♦ *vi* 3 go about dreamily. **moon'light** *n* **moon'shine** *n inf* 1 whiskey, esp. corn liquor, illicitly distilled. 2 nonsense. 3 moonlight. **moon'stone** *n* transparent semiprecious stone.

moor[1] *n* tract of open uncultivated land, often hilly and overgrown with heath.

moor[2] *v* secure (ship) with chains or ropes. **moor'ings** *pl n* 1 ropes, etc. for mooring. 2 something providing stability, security.

moose [moos] *n* N Amer. deer with large antlers.

moot *adj* 1 that is open to argument, debatable. 2 purely academic.

——————{ THESAURUS }——————

monotonous *adj* = **tedious**, boring, dull, humdrum, mind-numbing, repetitive, tiresome, unchanging, wearisome

monotony *n* = **tedium**, boredom, monotonousness, repetitiveness, routine, sameness, tediousness

monster *n* 1 = **brute**, beast, demon, devil, fiend, villain 2 = **freak**, monstrosity, mutant 3 = **giant**, colossus, mammoth, titan ♦ *adj* 4 = **huge**, colossal, enormous, gigantic, immense, mammoth, massive, stupendous, tremendous

monstrosity *n* = **eyesore**, freak, horror, monster

monstrous *adj* 1 = **unnatural**, fiendish, freakish, frightful, grotesque, gruesome, hideous, horrible 2 = **outrageous**, diabolical, disgraceful, foul, inhuman, intolerable, scandalous, shocking 3 = **huge**, colossal, enormous, immense, mammoth, massive, prodigious, stupendous, tremendous

monument *n* = **memorial**, cairn, cenotaph, commemoration, gravestone, headstone, marker, mausoleum, shrine, tombstone

monumental *adj* 1 = **important**, awesome, enormous, epoch-making, historic, majestic, memorable, significant, unforgettable 2 *Inf* = **immense**, colossal, great, massive, staggering

mood *n* = **state of mind**, disposition, frame of mind, humor, spirit, temper

moody *adj* 1 = **sullen**, gloomy, glum, ill-tempered, irritable, morose, sad, sulky, temperamental, touchy 2 = **changeable**, capricious, erratic, fickle, flighty, impulsive, mercurial, temperamental, unpredictable, volatile

moon *n* 1 = **satellite** ♦ *v* 2 = **idle**, daydream, languish, mope, waste time

moor[1] *n* = **moorland**, heath

moor[2] *v* = **tie up**, anchor, berth, dock, lash, make fast, secure

moot *adj* 1 = **debatable**, arguable, contestable, controversial, disputable, doubtful, undecided, unresolved, unsettled ♦ *v* 2 = **bring up**, broach, propose, put

mop n 1 bundle of yarn, cloth, etc. on end of stick, used for cleaning. 2 tangle (of hair, etc.). ◆ vt mopped, mop·ping 3 clean, wipe with mop or other absorbent material.

mope [mohp] vi moped, mop·ing be gloomy, apathetic.

mo·ped [MOH-ped] n light motorized bicycle.

mo·raine [mə-RAYN] n accumulated mass of debris, earth, stones, etc., deposited by glacier.

mor·al [MOR-əl] adj 1 pert. to right and wrong conduct. 2 of good conduct. ◆ n 3 practical lesson, e.g. of fable. ◆ pl 4 habits with respect to right and wrong, esp. in matters of sex. **mor·al·ist** n teacher of morality. **mo·ral·i·ty** [mə-RAL-ə-tee] n 1 good moral conduct. 2 moral goodness or badness. 3 kind of medieval drama, containing moral lesson. **mor·al·ize** v -ized, -iz·ing ◆ vi 1 write, think about moral aspect of things. ◆ vt 2 interpret morally. **moral victory** triumph that is psychological rather than practical.

mo·rale [mə-RAL] n degree of confidence, hope of person or group.

mo·rass [mə-RAS] n 1 marsh. 2 mess.

mor·a·to·ri·um [mor-ə-TOR-ee-əm] n, pl -ri·ums 1 act authorizing postponement of payments, etc. 2 delay.

mor'bid adj 1 unduly interested in death. 2 gruesome. 3 diseased.

mor·dant [MOR-dnt] adj 1 biting. 2 corrosive. 3 scathing. ◆ n 4 substance that fixes dyes.

more [mor] adj 1 greater in quantity or number. 2 comp. of MANY or MUCH. ◆ adv 3 to a greater extent. 4 in addition. ◆ pron 5 greater or additional amount or number. **more·o'ver** adv besides, further.

mor·ga·nat·ic marriage [mor-gə-NAT-ik] marriage of king or prince in which wife does not share husband's rank or possessions and children do not inherit from father.

morgue [morg] n 1 mortuary. 2 newspaper reference file or file room.

mor·i·bund [MOR-ə-bund] adj 1 dying. 2 stagnant.

Mor·mon [MOR-mən] n member of religious sect founded in US.

morn'ing n early part of day until noon. **morning-after pill** woman's contraceptive pill for use within hours after sexual intercourse. **morning glory** plant with trumpet-shaped flowers that close in late afternoon.

mo·roc·co [mə-ROK-oh] n goatskin leather.

mo·ron [MOR-on] n 1 (formerly) person with low intelligence quotient. 2 inf fool. **mo·ron'ic** adj

mo·rose [mə-ROHS] adj sullen, moody.

THESAURUS

forward, suggest

mop n 1 = squeegee, sponge, swab 2 = mane, shock, tangle, thatch

mope v = brood, fret, languish, moon, pine, sulk

mop up v = clean up, soak up, sponge, swab, wash, wipe

moral adj 1 = good, decent, ethical, high-minded, honorable, just, noble, principled, right, virtuous ◆ n 2 = lesson, meaning, message, point, significance

morale n = confidence, esprit de corps, heart, self-esteem, spirit

morality n 1 = integrity, decency, goodness, honesty, justice, righteousness, virtue 2 = standards, conduct, ethics, manners, morals, mores, philosophy, principles

morals pl n = morality, behavior, conduct, ethics, habits, integrity, manners, mores, principles, scruples, standards

morass n 1 = marsh, bog, fen, quagmire,

slough, swamp 2 = mess, confusion, mix-up, muddle, tangle

moratorium n = postponement, freeze, halt, standstill, suspension

morbid adj 1 = unwholesome, ghoulish, gloomy, melancholy, sick, somber, unhealthy 2 = gruesome, dreadful, ghastly, grisly, hideous, horrid, macabre

mordant adj = sarcastic, biting, caustic, cutting, incisive, pungent, scathing, stinging, trenchant

more adj 1 = extra, added, additional, further, new, other, supplementary ◆ adv 2 = to a greater extent, better, further, longer

moreover adv = furthermore, additionally, also, as well, besides, further, in addition, too

morgue n = mortuary

moribund adj = declining, on its last legs, stagnant, waning, weak

morning n = dawn, a.m., break of day,

morph [morf] *v* cause or undergo change of shape or appearance via computer graphic effects.

mor·phine [MOR-feen] *n* narcotic extract of opium used to induce sleep and relieve pain.

mor·phol·o·gy [mor-FOL-ə-jee] *n* **1** science of structure of organisms. **2** form and structure of words of a language.

Morse [mors] *n* system of telegraphic signaling in which letters of alphabet are represented by combinations of dots and dashes, or short and long flashes.

mor·sel [MOR-səl] *n* fragment, small piece.

mor·tal [MOR-tl] *adj* **1** subject to death. **2** causing death. ♦ *n* **3** mortal creature. **mor·tal'i·ty** *n* **1** state of being mortal. **2** great loss of life. **3** death rate. **mor'tal·ly** *adv* **1** fatally. **2** deeply, intensely.

mor·tar [MOR-tər] *n* **1** mixture of lime, sand and water for holding bricks and stones together. **2** small cannon firing over short range. **3** vessel in which substances are pounded. **mor'tar·board** [-bord] *n* square academic cap.

mort·gage [MOR-gij] *n* **1** conveyance of property as security for debt with provision that property be reconveyed on payment within agreed time. ♦ *vt* **-gaged, -gag·ing 2** convey by mortgage. **3** pledge as security. **mort·ga·gee'** *n* person to whom property is mortgaged. **mort'ga·gor, -ger** *n* person who mortgages property.

mor·ti·fy [MOR-tə-fi] *v* **-fied, -fy·ing 1** humiliate. **2** subdue by self-denial. **3** (of flesh) be affected with gangrene. **mor·ti·fi·ca'tion** [-fi-KAY-shən] *n*

mor·tise [MOR-tis] *n* **1** hole in piece of wood, etc. to receive the tongue (tenon) and end of another piece. ♦ *vt* **-tised, -tis·ing 2** make mortise in. **3** fasten by mortise and tenon.

mor·tu·ar·y [MOR-choo-er-ee] *n, pl* **-ar·ies 1** funeral parlor. ♦ *adj* **2** of, for burial. **3** pert. to death.

mo·sa·ic [moh-ZAY-ik] *n* **1** picture or pattern of small bits of colored stone, glass, etc. **2** this process of decoration.

Mo·sa·ic [moh-ZAY-ik] *adj* of Moses.

mosh *vi* dance violently and frantically with others in group at rock concert. ♦ *n*

Moslem *n* see MUSLIM.

mosque [mosk] *n* Muslim temple.

mos·qui·to [mə-SKEE-toh] *n, pl* **-toes** or **-tos** any of various kinds of flying, biting insects.

moss [maws] *n* small plant growing in masses on moist surfaces. **moss'y** *adj* **moss·i·er, moss·i·est** covered with moss.

most [mohst] *adj* **1** greatest in size, number, or degree. **2** sup. of MUCH or MANY. ♦ *n* **3** greatest number, amount, or degree. ♦ *adv* **4** in the greatest degree. **5** abbrev. of ALMOST. **most'ly** *adv* for the most part, generally, on the whole.

mo·tel [moh-TEL] *n* roadside hotel with accommodation for motorists and their vehicles.

———————| THESAURUS |———————

daybreak, forenoon, morn (*poetic*), sunrise

moron *n* = **fool**, blockhead, cretin (*offens*), dork (*sl*), dunce, dunderhead, halfwit, idiot, imbecile, oaf, schmuck (*sl*)

moronic *adj* = **idiotic**, cretinous (*offens*), foolish, halfwitted, imbecilic, mindless, stupid, unintelligent

morose *adj* = **sullen**, depressed, dour, gloomy, glum, ill-tempered, moody, sour, sulky, surly, taciturn

morsel *n* = **piece**, bit, bite, crumb, mouthful, part, scrap, soupçon, taste, tidbit

mortal *adj* **1** = **human**, ephemeral, impermanent, passing, temporal, transient, worldly **2** = **fatal**, deadly, death-dealing, destructive, killing, lethal, murderous, terminal ♦ *n* **3** = **human being**, being, earthling, human, individual, man, person, woman

mortality *n* **1** = **humanity**, impermanence,

transience **2** = **killing**, bloodshed, carnage, death, destruction, fatality

mortification *n* **1** = **humiliation**, annoyance, chagrin, discomfiture, embarrassment, shame, vexation **2** = **discipline**, abasement, chastening, control, denial, subjugation **3** *Medical* = **gangrene**, corruption, festering

mortified *adj* = **humiliated**, ashamed, chagrined, chastened, crushed, deflated, embarrassed, humbled, shamed

mortify *v* **1** = **humiliate**, chagrin, chasten, crush, deflate, embarrass, humble, shame **2** = **discipline**, abase, chasten, control, deny, subdue **3** *Of flesh* = **putrefy**, deaden, die, fester

mortuary *n* = **morgue**, funeral parlour

mostly *adv* = **generally**, as a rule, chiefly, largely, mainly, on the whole, predominantly, primarily, principally,

mo·tet [moh-TET] *n* **1** short sacred vocal composition.

moth [mawth] *n* **1** usu. nocturnal insect like butterfly. **2** its grub. **moth'ball** *n* **1** small ball of camphor or naphthalene to repel moths from stored clothing, etc. ◆ *vt* **2** put in mothballs. **3** store, postpone, etc. **moth'eat·en** *adj* **1** eaten, damaged by grub of moth. **2** decayed, scruffy.

moth·er [MUTH-ər] *n* **1** female parent. **2** head of religious community of women. ◆ *adj* **3** natural, native, inborn. ◆ *vt* **4** act as mother to. **moth'er·hood** [-huud] *n* **moth'er·ly** *adj* **mother-in-law** *n* mother of one's wife or husband. **mother of pearl** iridescent lining of certain shells.

mo·tif [moh-TEEF] *n* **1** dominating theme. **2** recurring design.

mo·tion [MOH-shən] *n* **1** process or action or way of moving. **2** proposal in meeting. **3** application to judge. ◆ *vt* **4** direct by sign. **mo'tion·less** [-lis] *adj* still, immobile.

mo·tive [MOH-tiv] *n* **1** that which makes person act in particular way. **2** inner impulse. ◆ *adj* **3** causing motion. **mo'ti·vate** *vt* **-vat·ed, -vat·ing 1** instigate. **2** incite. **mo·ti·va'tion** [-VAY-shən] *n*

mot·ley [MOT-lee] *adj* **1** miscellaneous, varied. **2** multicolored.

mo·to·cross [MOH-toh-kraws] *n* motorcycle race over rough course.

mo·tor [MOH-tər] *n* **1** that which imparts movement. **2** machine to supply motive power. **3** automobile. ◆ *vi* **4** travel by automobile. **mo'tor·ist** *n* user of automobile. **mo'tor·ize** *vt* **-ized, -iz·ing** equip with motor. **motor home** large motor vehicle with living quarters, used for recreational travel.

mot·tle [MOT-l] *vt* **-tled, -tling 1** mark with blotches, variegate. ◆ *n* **2** arrangement of blotches. **3** blotch on surface.

mot·to [MOT-oh] *n, pl* **-toes 1** saying adopted as rule of conduct. **2** short inscribed sentence. **3** word or sentence on badge or banner.

mound [mownd] *n* **1** heap of earth or stones. **2** small hill.

mount [mownt] *vi* **1** rise. **2** increase. **3** get on horseback. ◆ *vt* **4** get up on. **5** frame (picture). **6** fix, set up. **7** provide with horse. ◆ *n* **8** that on which thing is supported or fitted. **9** horse. **10** hill.

moun·tain [MOWN-tn] *n* **1** hill of great size. **2** surplus. **moun·tain·eer'** *n* one who lives among or climbs mountains.

usually

moth-eaten *adj* = **decayed**, decrepit, dilapidated, ragged, shabby, tattered, threadbare, worn-out

mother *n* **1** = **parent**, dam, ma (*inf*), mama *or* mamma (*old-fashioned inf*), mater (*old-fashioned inf, chiefly Brit.*), mom (*inf*), mommy (*inf*), old lady (*inf*) ◆ *adj* **2** = **native**, inborn, innate, natural ◆ *v* **3** = **nurture**, care for, cherish, nurse, protect, raise, rear, tend

motherly *adj* = **maternal**, affectionate, caring, comforting, loving, protective, sheltering

motif *n* **1** = **theme**, concept, idea, leitmotif, subject **2** = **design**, decoration, ornament, shape

motion *n* **1** = **movement**, flow, locomotion, mobility, move, progress, travel **2** = **proposal**, proposition, recommendation, submission, suggestion ◆ *v* **3** = **gesture**, beckon, direct, gesticulate, nod, signal, wave

motionless *adj* = **still**, fixed, frozen, immobile, paralyzed, standing, static, stationary, stock-still, transfixed, unmoving

motivate *v* = **inspire**, arouse, cause, drive, induce, move, persuade, prompt, stimulate, stir

motivation *n* = **incentive**, incitement, inducement, inspiration, motive, reason, spur, stimulus

motive *n* = **reason**, ground(s), incentive, inducement, inspiration, object, purpose, rationale, stimulus

motley *adj* **1** = **miscellaneous**, assorted, disparate, heterogeneous, mixed, varied **2** = **multicolored**, checkered, variegated

mottled *adj* = **blotchy**, dappled, flecked, piebald, speckled, spotted, stippled, streaked

motto *n* = **saying**, adage, dictum, maxim, precept, proverb, rule, slogan, watchword

mound *n* **1** = **heap**, drift, pile, rick, stack **2** = **hill**, bank, dune, embankment, hillock, knoll, rise

mount *v* **1** = **climb**, ascend, clamber up, go up, scale **2** = **bestride**, climb onto, jump on **3** = **increase**, accumulate, build, escalate, grow, intensify, multiply, pile up, swell ◆ *n* **4** = **backing**, base, frame, setting, stand, support **5** = **horse**, steed (*archaic or*

moun'tain·ous adj very high, rugged.
mountain bike bicycle with straight handlebars and broad, thick tires, for cycling over rough terrain.
moun·te·bank [MOWN-tə-bangk] n charlatan, fake.
Moun·tie [MOWN-tee] n inf member of Royal Canadian Mounted Police.
mourn [morn] v feel, show sorrow (for). **mourn'er** n **mourn'ful** [-fəl] adj 1 sad. 2 dismal. **mourn'ful·ly** adv **mourn'ing** n 1 grieving. 2 conventional signs of grief for death. 3 clothes of mourner.
mouse [mows] n, pl **mice** [mīs] 1 small rodent. 2 Computers hand-operated device for moving the cursor, clicking on icons, etc. without keying. ♦ vi 3 catch, hunt mice. 4 prowl. **mous'er** n cat used for catching mice. **mous'y** adj **mous·i·er, mous·i·est** 1 like mouse, esp. in color. 2 meek, shy.
mousse [moos] n sweet dessert of flavored cream whipped and frozen.
moustache see MUSTACHE.
mouth [mowth] n 1 opening in head for eating, speaking, etc. 2 opening into anything hollow. 3 outfall of river. 4 entrance to harbor, etc. ♦ vt [mowth] 5 declaim, esp. in public. 6 form (words) with lips without speaking. 7 take, move in mouth. **mouth'piece** n 1 end of anything placed between lips, e.g. pipe. 2 spokesman.
move [moov] v **moved, mov·ing** ♦ vt 1 change position of. 2 stir emotions of. 3 incite. 4 propose for consideration. ♦ vi 5 change places. 6 change one's dwelling, etc. 7 take action. ♦ n 8 a moving. 9 motion toward some goal. **mov'a·ble** adj, n **move'ment** n 1 process, action of moving. 2 moving parts of machine. 3 division of piece of music.
mov·ie [MOOV-ee] n inf cinema film.
mow [moh] v **mowed** or **mown, mow·ing** cut (grass, etc.). **mow'er** n person or machine that mows.
MP3, Mpeg-1 la·yer3 n Computers digital compression format used to reduce audio files to a fraction of their original size without loss of sound quality.

——| THESAURUS |——

literary)
mountain n 1 = **peak**, alp, fell (Brit.), mount 2 = **heap**, abundance, mass, mound, pile, stack, ton
mountainous adj 1 = **high**, alpine, highland, rocky, soaring, steep, towering, upland 2 = **huge**, daunting, enormous, gigantic, great, immense, mammoth, mighty, monumental
mourn v = **grieve**, bemoan, bewail, deplore, lament, rue, wail, weep
mournful adj 1 = **sad**, melancholy, piteous, plaintive, sorrowful, tragic, unhappy, woeful 2 = **dismal**, disconsolate, downcast, gloomy, grieving, heavy-hearted, lugubrious, miserable, rueful, somber
mourning n 1 = **grieving**, bereavement, grief, lamentation, weeping, woe 2 = **black**, sackcloth and ashes, widow's weeds
mouth n 1 = **lips**, jaws, maw 2 = **opening**, aperture, door, entrance, gateway, inlet, orifice
mouthful n = **taste**, bit, bite, little, morsel, sample, spoonful, swallow
mouthpiece n = **spokesperson**, agent, delegate, representative, spokesman or spokeswoman
movable adj = **portable**, detachable, mobile, transferable, transportable

move v 1 = **go**, advance, budge, proceed, progress, shift, stir 2 = **change**, shift, switch, transfer, transpose 3 = **leave**, migrate, pack one's bags (inf), quit, relocate, remove 4 = **drive**, activate, operate, propel, shift, start, turn 5 = **touch**, affect, excite, impress 6 = **incite**, cause, induce, influence, inspire, motivate, persuade, prompt, rouse 7 = **propose**, advocate, put forward, recommend, suggest, urge ♦ n 8 = **action**, maneuver, measure, ploy, step, stratagem, stroke, turn 9 = **transfer**, relocation, removal, shift
movement n 1 = **motion**, action, activity, change, development, flow, maneuver, progress, stirring 2 = **group**, campaign, crusade, drive, faction, front, grouping, organization, party 3 = **workings**, action, machinery, mechanism, works 4 Mus = **section**, division, part, passage
movie n = **film**, feature, flick (sl), picture
moving adj 1 = **emotional**, affecting, inspiring, pathetic, persuasive, poignant, stirring, touching 2 = **mobile**, movable, portable, running, unfixed
mow v = **cut**, crop, scythe, shear, trim
mow down v = **massacre**, butcher, cut down, cut to pieces, shoot down, slaughter

Mr mister.

Mrs title of married woman.

Ms title used instead of Miss or Mrs.

Mt *Chem.* meitnerium.

much *adj* **more, most 1** existing in quantity. ◆ *n* **2** large amount. **3** a great deal. **4** important matter. ◆ *adv* **5** in a great degree. **6** nearly.

mu·ci·lage [MYOO-sə-lij] *n* gum, glue.

muck [muk] *n* **1** horse, cattle dung. **2** unclean refuse. **3** insulting remarks. ◆ *vt* **4** make dirty. **muck'y** *adj* **muck·i·er, muck·i·est 1** dirty. **2** messy. **3** unpleasant. **muck out** *v* remove muck from. **muck up** *v* *inf* ruin, bungle, confuse.

mu·cus [MYOO-kəs] *n* viscid fluid secreted by mucous membrane. **mu'cous** [-kəs] *adj* **1** resembling mucus. **2** secreting mucus. **3** slimy. **mucous membrane** lining of canals and cavities of the body.

mud *n* **1** wet and soft earth. **2** *inf* slander. **mud'dy** *adj* **-di·er, -di·est**

mud·dle [MUD-əl] *vt* **-dled, -dling 1** (esp. with *up*) confuse. **2** bewilder. **3** mismanage. ◆ *n* **4** confusion. **5** tangle.

mu·ez·zin [myoo-EZ-in] *n* crier who summons Muslims to prayer.

muff¹ *n* tube-shaped covering to keep the hands warm.

muff² *vt* miss, bungle, fail in.

muf·fin *n* cup-shaped quick bread.

muf·fle [MUF-əl] *vt* **-fled, -fling** wrap up, esp. to deaden sound. **muf'fler** [-lər] *n* **1** on motor vehicles, device for accomplishing this. **2** scarf.

muf·ti [MUF-tee] *n* plain clothes as distinguished from uniform, e.g. of soldier.

mug¹ *n* drinking cup.

mug² *n* **1** *sl* face. **2** *sl* ruffian, criminal. ◆ *vt* **mugged, mug·ging 3** rob violently. **mug'ger** [-ər] *n*

mug·gy [MUG-ee] *adj* **-gi·er, -gi·est** damp and stifling.

Mu·ham·mad, Mo·ham·med [muu-HAM-əd] *n* prophet and founder of Islam. **Mu·ham·mad·an** *adj*, *n* Muslim.

mu·lat·to [mə-LAT-oh] *adj*, *n*, *pl* **-oes** (child) of one white and one black parent.

mul·ber·ry [MUL-ber-ee] *n*, *pl* **-ries 1** tree whose leaves are used to feed silkworms. **2** its purplish fruit.

mulch *n* **1** straw, leaves, etc., spread as protection for roots of plants. ◆ *vt* **2** protect thus.

mule [myool] *n* **1** animal that is cross between female horse and male donkey. **2** hybrid. **3** spinning machine. **4** small locomotive. **5** slipper. **mul'ish** *adj* obstinate.

mull *vt* **1** heat (wine) with sugar and spices. **2** think (over), ponder.

mul·lah [MUL-ə] *n* Muslim theologian.

mul·let¹ [MUL-it] *n* edible sea fish.

mul·let² *n* haircut in which the hair is short at the top and sides and long at the back.

mul·lion [MUL-yən] *n* upright dividing bar in window.

multi-, mult- *comb. form* many, e.g. *multiracial; multistory.*

mul·ti·far·i·ous [mul-tə-FAIR-ee-əs] *adj* of

THESAURUS

much *adj* **1 = great**, abundant, a lot of, ample, considerable, copious, plenty of, sizable *or* sizeable, substantial ◆ *n* **2 = a lot**, a good deal, a great deal, heaps (*inf*), lots (*inf*), plenty ◆ *adv* **3 = greatly**, a great deal, a lot, considerably, decidedly, exceedingly

muck *n* **1 = manure**, dung, ordure **2 = dirt**, filth, mire, mud, ooze, slime, sludge

mucky *adj* **= dirty**, begrimed, filthy, grimy, messy, muddy, scuzzy (*sl*)

mud *n* **= dirt**, clay, mire, ooze, silt, slime, sludge

muddle *v* **1 = jumble**, disarrange, disorder, disorganize, mess, scramble, spoil, tangle **2 = confuse**, befuddle, bewilder, confound, daze, disorient, perplex, stupefy ◆ *n* **3 = confusion**, chaos, disarray, disorder, disorganization, jumble, mess, mix-up, predicament, tangle

muddy *adj* **1 = dirty**, bespattered, grimy, mucky, mud-caked, scuzzy (*sl*), soiled **2 = boggy**, marshy, quaggy, swampy

muffle *v* **1 = wrap up**, cloak, cover, envelop, shroud, swaddle, swathe **2 = deaden**, muzzle, quieten, silence, soften, stifle, suppress

muffled *adj* **= indistinct**, faint, muted, stifled, strangled, subdued, suppressed

mug¹ *n* **= cup**, beaker, flagon, pot, tankard

mug² *n* **= face**, countenance, features, visage **1 = fool**, dork (*sl*), schmuck (*sl*), sucker (*sl*) ◆ *v* **2 = attack**, assault, beat up, rob, set about *or* upon

muggy *adj* **= humid**, clammy, close, moist, oppressive, sticky, stuffy, sultry

mull *v* **= ponder**, consider, contemplate, deliberate, meditate, reflect on, ruminate, think over, weigh various kinds or parts.

mul·ti·ple [MUL-tə-pəl] *adj* **1** having various parts. ◆ *n* **2** quantity that contains another an exact number of times. **mul·ti·pli·cand'** *n* Math. number to be multiplied. **mul·ti·pli·ca'tion** *n* **mul·ti·plic'i·ty** [-PLIS-i-tee] *n* variety, greatness in number. **mul'ti·ply** [-plī] *v* **-plied, -ply·ing 1** (cause to) increase in number, quantity, or degree. ◆ *vt* **2** combine (two numbers or quantities) by multiplication. **3** increase in number by reproduction.

mul·ti·plex [MUL-tə-pleks] *adj* Telecommunications capable of transmitting numerous messages over same wire or channel.

mul·ti·tude [MUL-ti-tood] *n* **1** great number. **2** great crowd. **3** populace. **mul·ti·tu'di·nous** *adj* very numerous.

mum *adj* silent. **mum's the word** keep silent.

mum·ble [MUM-bəl] *v* **-bled, -bling** speak indistinctly, mutter.

mum·my [MUM-ee] *n*, *pl* **-mies** embalmed body. **mum'mi·fy** *vt* **-fied, -fy·ing**

mumps *n* infectious disease marked by swelling in the glands of the neck.

munch *v* **1** chew noisily and vigorously. **2** crunch.

mun·dane [mun-DAYN] *adj* **1** ordinary, everyday. **2** belonging to this world, earthly.

mu·nic·i·pal [myuu-NIS-ə-pəl] *adj* belonging to affairs of city or town. **mu·nic·i·pal'i·ty** *n*, *pl* **-ties 1** city or town with local self-government. **2** its governing body.

mu·nif·i·cent [myoo-NIF-ə-sənt] *adj* very generous. **mu·nif'i·cence** *n* bounty.

mu·ni·tions [myoo-NISH-ənz] *pl n* military stores.

mu·ral [MYUUR-əl] *n* **1** painting on a wall. ◆ *adj* **2** of or on a wall.

mur·der [MUR-dər] *n* **1** unlawful premeditated killing of human being. ◆ *vt* **2** kill thus. **mur'der·ous** *adj*

murk *n* thick darkness. **murk'y** *adj* **murk·i·er, murk·i·est** gloomy.

mur·mur [MUR-mər] *n* **1** low, indistinct sound. ◆ *vi* **2** make such a sound. **3** complain. ◆ *vt* **4** utter in a low voice.

mus·cle [MUS-əl] *n* **1** part of body that produces movement by contracting. **2** system of muscles. **mus'cu·lar** [-kyə-lər] *adj* **1** with well-developed muscles. **2** strong. **3** of, like muscle. **mus'cle·bound** *adj* with muscles stiff through overdevelopment. **muscular dystrophy** disease with wasting of muscles. **muscle in** *inf* force one's way into. **muscle shirt** *inf* shirt that leaves full arm exposed.

muse [myooz] *vi* **mused, mus·ing 1**

multifarious *adj* = **diverse**, different, legion, manifold, many, miscellaneous, multiple, numerous, sundry, varied

multiple *adj* = **many**, manifold, multitudinous, numerous, several, sundry, various

multiply *v* **1** = **increase**, build up, expand, extend, proliferate, spread **2** = **reproduce**, breed, propagate

multitude *n* = **mass**, army, crowd, horde, host, mob, myriad, swarm, throng

munch *v* = **chew**, champ, chomp, crunch

mundane *adj* **1** = **ordinary**, banal, commonplace, day-to-day, everyday, humdrum, prosaic, routine, workaday **2** = **earthly**, mortal, secular, temporal, terrestrial, worldly

municipal *adj* = **civic**, public, urban

municipality *n* = **town**, borough, city, district, township

munificence *n* = **generosity**, beneficence, benevolence, bounty, largesse *or* largess, liberality, magnanimousness, philanthropy

munificent *adj* = **generous**, beneficent, benevolent, bountiful, lavish, liberal, magnanimous, open-handed, philanthropic, unstinting

murder *n* **1** = **killing**, assassination, bloodshed, butchery, carnage, homicide, manslaughter, massacre, slaying ◆ *v* **2** = **kill**, assassinate, bump off (*sl*), butcher, eliminate (*sl*), massacre, slaughter, slay

murderer *n* = **killer**, assassin, butcher, cut-throat, hit man (*sl*), homicide, slaughterer, slayer

murderous *adj* = **deadly**, bloodthirsty, brutal, cruel, cut-throat, ferocious, lethal, savage

murky *adj* = **dark**, cloudy, dim, dull, gloomy, gray, misty, overcast

murmur *v* **1** = **mumble**, mutter, whisper **2** = **grumble**, complain, moan (*inf*) ◆ *n* **3** = **drone**, buzzing, humming, purr, rumble, whisper

muscle *n* **1** = **tendon**, sinew **2** = **strength**, brawn, clout (*inf*), forcefulness, might, ponder. **2** consider meditatively. **3** be lost in thought.

Muse [myooz] *n* one of the nine goddesses inspiring learning and the arts.

mu•se•um [myoo-ZEE-əm] *n* place housing collection of natural, artistic, historical or scientific objects.

mush[1] *n* **1** soft pulpy mass. **2** cloying sentimentality. **mush'y** *adj* **mush•i•er, mush•i•est**

mush[2] *vi* **1** travel over snow with dog team and sled. ◆ *vt* **2** spur on (sled) dogs. ◆ *interj* **3** go!

mush'room *n* **1** fungoid growth, typically with stem and cap structure, some species edible. ◆ *vi* **2** shoot up rapidly. **3** expand. **mushroom cloud** large cloud resembling mushroom, esp. from nuclear explosion.

mu•sic [MYOO-zik] *n* **1** art form using melodious and harmonious combination of notes. **2** laws of this. **3** composition in this art. **mu'si•cal** *adj* **1** of, like music. **2** interested in, or with instinct for, music. **3** pleasant to ear. ◆ *n* **4** play, motion picture in which music plays essential part. **mu•si'cian** *n* **mu•si•col'o•gist** [-jist] *n* **mu•si•col'o•gy** *n* scientific study of music. **musical comedy** light dramatic entertainment of songs, dances, etc.

musk *n* **1** scent obtained from gland of **musk deer. 2** various plants with similar scent. **musk'y** *adj* **musk•i•er, musk•i•est musk ox** ox of Arctic Amer. **musk'rat** *n* **1** N Amer. rodent found near water. **2** its fur.

mus•ket [MUS-kit] *n Hist.* infantryman's gun. **mus•ket•eer'** *n*

Mus•lim [MUZ-lim] *n* **1** follower of religion of Islam. ◆ *adj* **2** of religion, culture, etc. of Islam.

mus•lin [MUZ-lin] *n* fine cotton fabric.

mus•sel [MUS-əl] *n* bivalve shellfish.

must[1] *v aux* **1** be obliged to, or certain to. ◆ *n* **2** something one must do.

must[2] *n* **1** newly-pressed grape juice. **2** unfermented wine.

mus•tache, mous•tache [MUS-tash] *n* hair on the upper lip.

mus'tang *n* wild horse.

mus•tard [MUS-tərd] *n* **1** powder made from the seeds of a plant, used in paste as a condiment. **2** the plant. **mustard gas** poisonous gas causing blistering, lung damage, etc.

mus•ter [MUS-tər] *v* **1** assemble. ◆ *n* **2** assembly, esp. for exercise, inspection.

mus•ty [MUS-tee] *adj* **-ti•er, -ti•est** moldy, stale. **must** *n* **mus'ti•ness** *n*

mu•tate [MYOO-tayt] *v* **-tat•ed, -tat•ing** (cause to) undergo mutation. **mu'ta•ble** [-tə-bəl] *adj* liable to change. **mu'tant** [-tənt] *n* mutated animal, plant, etc. **mu•ta'tion** [-TAY-shən] *n* change, esp. genetic change causing divergence from kind or racial type. **mu'ta•tive** *adj*

mute [myoot] *adj* **mut•er, mut•est 1** dumb. **2** silent. ◆ *n* **3** person incapable of speech. **4** *Mus.* contrivance to soften tone of instruments. **mut'ed** *adj* **1** (of sound) muffled. **2** (of light) subdued.

mu•ti•late [MYOOT-l-ayt] *vt* **-lat•ed, -lat•ing 1** deprive of a limb or other part. **2** damage. **3** deface. **mu•ti•la'tion** *n*

power, stamina, weight

muscular *adj* = **strong**, athletic, powerful, robust, sinewy, strapping, sturdy, vigorous

muse *v* = **ponder**, brood, cogitate, consider, contemplate, deliberate, meditate, mull over, reflect, ruminate

mushy *adj* **1** = **soft**, pulpy, semi-solid, slushy, squashy, squelchy **2** *Inf* = **sentimental**, maudlin, mawkish, saccharine, schmaltzy (*sl*), sloppy (*inf*), slushy (*inf*)

musical *adj* = **melodious**, dulcet, euphonious, harmonious, lyrical, melodic, sweet-sounding, tuneful

must[1] *n* = **necessity**, essential, fundamental, imperative, prerequisite, requirement, requisite, *sine qua non*

muster *v* **1** = **assemble**, call together,

convene, gather, marshal, mobilize, rally, summon ◆ *n* **2** = **assembly**, collection, congregation, convention, gathering, meeting, rally, roundup

musty *adj* = **stale**, airless, dank, funky (*sl*), fusty, mildewed, moldy, old, smelly, stuffy

mutability *n* = **change**, alteration, evolution, metamorphosis, transition, variation, vicissitude

mutable *adj* = **changeable**, adaptable, alterable, fickle, inconsistent, inconstant, unsettled, unstable, variable, volatile

mutation *n* = **change**, alteration, evolution, metamorphosis, modification, transfiguration, transformation, variation

mute *adj* = **silent**, dumb, mum, speechless, unspoken, voiceless, wordless

mutilate *v* **1** = **maim**, amputate, cut up,

mu·ti·ny [MYOOT-n-ee] *n, pl* **-nies 1** rebellion against authority, esp. against officers of disciplined body. ◆ *vi* **-nied, -ny·ing 2** commit mutiny. **mu·ti·neer'** *n* **mu'tin·ous** *adj* rebellious.

mutt *n inf* (mongrel) dog.

mut·ter [MUT-ər] *vi* **1** speak with mouth nearly closed, indistinctly. **2** grumble. ◆ *vt* **3** utter in such tones. ◆ *n* (act of) muttering.

mut·ton [MUT-ən] *n* flesh of sheep used as food. **mut·ton-chops** *pl n* side whiskers broad at jaw, narrow at temples. **mut'ton·head** [-hed] *n inf* slow-witted person.

mu·tu·al [MYOO-choo-əl] *adj* **1** done, possessed, etc., by each of two with respect to the other. **2** reciprocal. **3** common to both or all. **mu·tu·al'i·ty** *n* **mutual fund** investment company selling shares to public with repurchase on request.

muz·zle [MUZ-əl] *n* **1** mouth and nose of animal. **2** cover for these to prevent biting. **3** open end of gun. ◆ *vt* **-zled, -zling 4** put muzzle on. **5** silence, gag.

my [mī] *adj* belonging to me. **my·self'** *pron* emphatic or reflexive form of *I* or

ME.

my·col·o·gy [mī-KOL-ə-jee] *n* science of fungi.

my·o·pi·a [mī-OH-pee-ə] *n* **1** nearsightedness. **2** obtuseness. **my·op'ic** *adj*

myr·i·ad [MIR-ee-əd] *adj* **1** innumerable. ◆ *n* **2** large indefinite number.

myrrh [mur] *n* aromatic gum, formerly used as incense.

my·self *pron* **1** the reflexive form of *I* or *me*. **2** I or me in person, as distinct from anyone else, **3** my usual self.

mys·ter·y [MIS-tə-ree] *n, pl* **-teries 1** obscure or secret thing. **2** anything strange or inexplicable. **3** religious rite. **4** in Middle Ages, biblical play.

mys·te·ri·ous *adj* **1** of unknown cause or nature. **2** creating a feeling of strangeness, curiosity, or wonder.

mys·tic [MIS-tik] *n* **1** one who seeks divine, spiritual knowledge, esp. by prayer, contemplation, etc. ◆ *adj* **2** of hidden meaning, esp. in religious sense. **mys'ti·cal** *adj* **mys'ti·cism** [-siz-əm] *n*

mys·ti·fy [MIS-tə-fī] *vt* **-fied, -fy·ing** bewilder, puzzle. **mys·ti·fi·ca'tion** [-KAY-shən] *n*

——————— THESAURUS ———————

damage, disfigure, dismember, injure, lacerate, mangle **2 = distort**, adulterate, bowdlerize, censor, cut, damage, expurgate

mutinous *adj* **= rebellious**, disobedient, insubordinate, insurgent, refractory, riotous, subversive, unmanageable, unruly

mutiny *n* **1 = rebellion**, disobedience, insubordination, insurrection, revolt, revolution, riot, uprising ◆ *v* **2 = rebel**, disobey, resist, revolt, rise up

mutter *v* **= grumble**, complain, grouse, mumble, murmur, rumble

mutual *adj* **= shared**, common, interchangeable, joint, reciprocal, requited, returned

muzzle *n* **1 = jaws**, mouth, nose, snout **2 = gag**, guard ◆ *v* **3 = suppress**, censor, curb, gag, restrain, silence, stifle

myopic *adj* **= short-sighted**, near-sighted

myriad *adj* **1 = innumerable**, countless, immeasurable, incalculable, multitudinous, untold ◆ *n* **2 = multitude**, army, horde, host, swarm

mysterious *adj* **= strange**, arcane, enigmatic, inexplicable, inscrutable,

mystifying, perplexing, puzzling, secret, uncanny, unfathomable, weird

mystery *n* **= puzzle**, conundrum, enigma, problem, question, riddle, secret, teaser

mystic, mystical *adj* **= supernatural**, inscrutable, metaphysical, mysterious, occult, otherworldly, paranormal, preternatural, transcendental

mystify *v* **= puzzle**, baffle, bewilder, confound, confuse, flummox, nonplus, perplex, stump

myth *n* **1 = legend**, allegory, fable, fairy story, fiction, folk tale, saga, story, urban legend *or* myth **2 = illusion**, delusion, fancy, fantasy, figment, imagination, superstition, tall tale (*inf*)

mythical *adj* **1 = legendary**, fabled, fabulous, fairy-tale, mythological **2 = imaginary**, fabricated, fantasy, fictitious, invented, made-up, make-believe, nonexistent, pretended, unreal, untrue

mythological *adj* **= legendary**, fabulous, mythic, mythical, traditional

mythology *n* **= legend**, folklore, lore,

mys·tique [mi-STEEK] *n* aura of mystery, power, etc.

myth [mith] *n* **1** tale with supernatural characters or events. **2** invented story. **3** imaginary person or object. **myth'i·cal** *adj* **myth·o·log'i·cal** [-LOJ-ə-kəl] *adj* **my·thol'o·gy** *n, pl* **-gies 1** myths collectively. **2** study of them.

———— THESAURUS ————

tradition

mystique *n* = **fascination**, awe, charisma, charm, glamour, magic, spell

N n

N _Chem._ **1** nitrogen. **2** _Physics_ newton.

Na _Chem._ sodium.

na•bob [NAY-bob] _n_ wealthy, powerful person.

na•cre [NAY-kər] _n_ mother-of-pearl.

na•dir [NAY-dər] _n_ **1** point opposite the zenith. **2** lowest point.

nag¹ _v_ **nagged, nag•ging 1** scold or annoy constantly. **2** cause pain to constantly. ♦ _n_ **3** nagging. **4** one who nags.

nag² _n_ **1** old horse. **2** _sl_ any horse. **3** small horse for riding.

nai•ad [NAY-ad] _n_ water nymph.

nail [nayl] _n_ **1** horny shield at ends of fingers, toes. **2** claw. **3** small metal spike for fastening wood, etc. ♦ _vt_ **4** fasten with nails. **5** _inf_ catch. **hit the nail on the head** do or say the right thing.

na•ive [nah-EEV] _adj_ simple, unaffected, ingenuous. **na•ive•té** [-eev-TAY] _n_

nak•ed [NAY-kid] _adj_ **1** without clothes. **2** exposed, bare. **3** undisguised. **naked eye** the eye unassisted by any optical instrument.

name [naym] _n_ **1** word by which person, thing, etc. is denoted. **2** reputation. **3** title. **4** credit. **5** family. **6** famous person. ♦ _vt_ **named, nam•ing 7** give name to. **8** call by name. **9** entitle. **10** appoint. **11** mention. **12** specify. **name'less** [-lis] _adj_ **1** without a name. **2** indescribable. **3** too dreadful to be mentioned. **4** obscure. **name'ly** _adv_ that is to say. **name'sake** _n_ **1** person named after another. **2** person with same name as another. **name and shame** make public the name of (a wrongdoer) in order to bring public condemnation on him or her.

nap¹ _vi_ **napped, nap•ping 1** take short sleep, esp. in daytime. ♦ _n_ **2** short sleep.

nap² _n_ downy surface on cloth made by projecting fibers.

na•palm [NAY-pahm] _n_ jellied gasoline,

THESAURUS

nadir _n_ = **bottom**, depths, lowest point, minimum, rock bottom

nag¹ _v_ **1** = **scold**, annoy, badger, harass, hassle (_inf_), henpeck, irritate, pester, plague, upbraid, worry ♦ _n_ **2** = **scold**, harpy, shrew, tartar, virago

nag² _n_ = **horse**, hack

nagging _adj_ = **irritating**, persistent, scolding, shrewish, worrying

nail _v_ = **fasten**, attach, fix, hammer, join, pin, secure, tack

naive _adj_ **1** = **gullible**, callow, credulous, green, unsuspicious, wet behind the ears (_inf_) **2** = **innocent**, artless, guileless, ingenuous, open, simple, trusting, unsophisticated, unworldly

naivety, naïveté _n_ **1** = **gullibility**, callowness, credulity **2** = **innocence**, artlessness, guilelessness, inexperience, ingenuousness, naturalness, openness, simplicity

naked _adj_ = **nude**, bare, exposed, in one's birthday suit (_inf_), stripped, unclothed, undressed, without a stitch on (_inf_)

nakedness _n_ = **nudity**, bareness, undress

name _n_ **1** = **title**, designation, epithet, handle (_sl_), moniker _or_ monicker (_sl_), nickname, sobriquet, term **2** = **fame**, distinction, eminence, esteem, honor, note, praise, renown, repute ♦ _v_ **3** = **call**, baptize, christen, dub, entitle, label, style, term **4** = **nominate**, appoint, choose, designate, select, specify

named _adj_ **1** = **called**, baptized, christened, dubbed, entitled, known as, labeled, styled, termed **2** = **nominated**, appointed, chosen, designated, mentioned, picked, selected, singled out, specified

nameless _adj_ **1** = **anonymous**, unnamed, untitled **2** = **unknown**, incognito, obscure, undistinguished, unheard-of, unsung **3** = **horrible**, abominable, indescribable, unmentionable, unspeakable, unutterable

namely _adv_ = **specifically**, to wit, viz.

nap¹ _n_ **1** = **sleep**, catnap, forty winks (_inf_), rest, siesta ♦ _v_ **2** = **sleep**, catnap, doze, drop off (_inf_), nod off (_inf_), rest, snooze (_inf_) highly incendiary, used in bombs, etc.

nape [nayp] n back of neck.

naph•tha [NAF-thə] n inflammable oil distilled from coal, etc. **naph'tha•lene** [-leen] n white crystalline product distilled from coal tar, used in disinfectants, mothballs, etc.

nap•kin n cloth, paper for wiping fingers or lips at table.

nar•cis•sus [nahr-SIS-əs] n, pl **nar•cis•sus** genus of bulbous plants including daffodil, jonquil, esp. one with white flowers. **nar'cis•sism** n abnormal love and admiration of oneself. **nar'cis•sist** n

nar•cot•ic [nahr-KOT-ik] n any of a group of drugs, including morphine and opium, producing numbness and stupor, used medicinally but addictive. ◆ adj

nar•rate [NAR-ayt] vt **-rat•ed, -rat•ing** relate, recount, tell (story). **nar•ra'tion** n **nar'ra•tive** [-rə-tiv] n **1** account, story. ◆ adj **2** relating. **nar'ra•tor** [-ray-tər] n

nar•row [NAR-oh] adj **-er, -est 1** of little breadth, or width esp. in comparison to length. **2** limited. **3** barely adequate or successful. ◆ v **4** make, become narrow. **nar'rows** pl n narrow part of straits. **nar'row•ness** n **narrow-minded** adj **1** illiberal. **2** bigoted. **narrow-mindedness** n prejudice, bigotry.

na•sal [NAY-zəl] adj **1** of nose. ◆ n **2** sound partly produced in nose. **na'sal•ly** adv

nas•cent [NAYS-ənt] adj **1** just coming into existence. **2** springing up.

nas•tur•tium [nə-STUR-shəm] n garden plant with red or orange flowers.

nas•ty [NAS-tee] adj **-ti•er, -ti•est** foul, disagreeable, unpleasant. **nas'ti•ly** adv **nas'ti•ness** n

na•tal [NAYT-l] adj of birth.

na•tion [NAY-shən] n people or race organized as a country. **na'tion•al** [NASH-ə-nl] adj **1** belonging or pert. to a nation. **2** public, general. ◆ n **3** member of a nation. **na'tion•al•ism** n **1** loyalty, devotion to one's country. **2** movement for independence of country, people, ruled by another. **na•tion•al'i•ty** n, pl **-ties 1** national quality or feeling. **2** fact of belonging to particular nation. **3** member of this. **na'tion•al•ize** vt **-ized, -iz•ing** convert (private industry, resources, etc.) to government control.

na•tive [NAY-tiv] adj **1** inborn. **2** born in particular place. **3** found in pure state. **4** that was place of one's birth. ◆ n **5** one born in a place. **6** member of indigenous people of a country. **7** species of plant, animal, etc. originating in a pure place. **Native American** n **1** person descended from the

---

THESAURUS

nap[2] n = weave, down, fiber, grain, pile

napkin n = cloth, linen, wipe

narcissism n = egotism, self-love, vanity

narcotic n **1** = drug, analgesic, anesthetic, anodyne, opiate, painkiller, sedative, tranquilizer ◆ adj **2** = sedative, analgesic, calming, hypnotic, painkilling, soporific

narrate v = tell, chronicle, describe, detail, recite, recount, relate, report

narration n = telling, description, explanation, reading, recital, relation

narrative n = story, account, chronicle, history, report, statement, tale

narrator n = storyteller, author, chronicler, commentator, reporter, writer

narrow adj **1** = thin, attenuated, fine, slender, slim, spare, tapering **2** = limited, close, confined, constricted, contracted, meager, restricted, tight **3** = insular, dogmatic, illiberal, intolerant, narrow-minded, partial, prejudiced, small-minded ◆ v **4** = tighten, constrict, limit, reduce

narrowly adv = just, barely, by the skin of

one's teeth, only just, scarcely

narrow-minded adj = intolerant, bigoted, hidebound, illiberal, opinionated, parochial, prejudiced, provincial, small-minded

nastiness n = unpleasantness, malice, meanness, spitefulness

nasty adj **1** = objectionable, disagreeable, loathsome, obnoxious, offensive, unpleasant, vile **2** = spiteful, despicable, disagreeable, distasteful, lousy (sl), malicious, mean, scuzzy (sl), unpleasant, vicious, vile **3** = painful, bad, critical, dangerous, serious, severe

nation n = country, people, race, realm, society, state, tribe

national adj **1** = nationwide, countrywide, public, widespread ◆ n **2** = citizen, inhabitant, native, resident, subject

nationalism n = patriotism, allegiance, chauvinism, jingoism, loyalty

nationality n = race, birth, nation

nationwide adj = national, countrywide, general, widespread original inhabitants of the American continent. ◆ *adj* **2** of Native Americans.

na·tiv·i·ty [nə-TIV-i-tee] *n, pl* **-ties 1** birth. **2** time, circumstances of birth. **3** (N-) birth of Christ.

nat·ter [NAT-ər] *vi* talk idly.

nat·ty [NAT-ee] *adj* **ti·er, -ti·est 1** neat and smart. **2** spruce. **nat'ti·ly** *adv*

na·ture [NAY-chər] *n* **1** innate or essential qualities of person or thing. **2** class, sort. **3** life force. **4** (N-) power underlying all phenomena in material world. **5** material world as a whole. **6** natural unspoiled scenery or countryside, and plants and animals in it. **7** disposition. **8** temperament. **nat·u·ral** [NACH-ər-əl] *adj* **1** of, according to, occurring in, provided by, nature. **2** inborn. **3** normal. **4** unaffected. **5** illegitimate. ◆ *n* **6** something, somebody well suited for something. **7** *Mus.* symbol used to remove effect of sharp or flat preceding it. **nat'u·ral·ist** *n* student of natural history. **nat·u·ral·is'tic** *adj* of or imitating nature in effect or characteristics. **nat'u·ral·ize** *vt* **-ized, -iz·ing 1** admit to citizenship. **2** accustom to different climate or environment. **nat'u·ral·ly** *adv* **1** of or according to nature.

2 by nature. **3** of course. **natural history** study of animals and plants.

naught [nawt] *n* **1** nothing. **2** nought.

naugh·ty [NAW-tee] *adj* **-ti·er, -ti·est 1** disobedient, not behaving well. **2** mildly indecent, tasteless. **naugh'ti·ly** *adv*

nau·se·a [NAW-zee-ə] *n* feeling that precedes vomiting. **nau'se·ate** *vt* **-at·ed, -at·ing** sicken. **nau'seous** [NAW-shəs]. **nau'se·at·ing** *adj* **1** disgusting. **2** causing nausea.

nau·ti·cal [NAW-ti-kəl] *adj* **1** of seamen or ships. **2** marine. **nautical mile** 6080.20 feet (1853.25 meters).

nau·ti·lus [NAWT-l-əs] *n, pl* **-lus·es** univalvular shellfish.

naval see NAVY.

nave [nayv] *n* main part of church.

na·vel [NAY-vəl] *n* umbilicus, small scar, depression in middle of abdomen where umbilical cord was attached.

nav·i·gate [NAV-i-gayt] *v* **-gat·ed, -gat·ing 1** plan, direct, plot path or position of ship, etc. **2** travel. **nav'i·ga·ble** *adj* **nav·i·ga'tion** *n* **1** science of directing course of seagoing vessel, or of aircraft in flight. **2** shipping. **nav'i·ga·tor** *n* one who navigates.

na·vy [NAY-vee] *n, pl* **-vies 1** fleet. **2**

———————[THESAURUS]———————

native *adj* **1** = **local**, domestic, home, indigenous **2** = **inborn**, congenital, hereditary, inbred, ingrained, innate, instinctive, intrinsic, natural ◆ *n* **3** = **inhabitant**, aborigine, citizen, countryman, dweller, national, resident

natty *adj* = **smart**, dapper, elegant, fashionable, neat, phat (*sl*), snazzy (*inf*), spruce, stylish, trim

natural *adj* **1** = **normal**, common, everyday, legitimate, logical, ordinary, regular, typical, usual **2** = **unaffected**, genuine, ingenuous, open, real, simple, spontaneous, unpretentious, unsophisticated **3** = **innate**, characteristic, essential, inborn, inherent, instinctive, intuitive, native **4** = **pure**, organic, plain, unrefined, whole

naturalist *n* = **biologist**, botanist, ecologist, zoologist

naturalistic *adj* = **realistic**, lifelike, true-to-life

naturally *adv* **1** = **of course**, certainly **2** = **genuinely**, normally, simply, spontaneously, typically, unaffectedly, unpretentiously

nature *n* **1** = **creation**, cosmos, earth, environment, universe, world **2** = **make-up**, character, complexion, constitution, essence **3** = **kind**, category, description, sort, species, style, type, variety **4** = **temperament**, disposition, humor, mood, outlook, temper

naughty *adj* **1** = **disobedient**, bad, impish, misbehaved, mischievous, refractory, wayward, wicked, worthless **2** = **obscene**, improper, lewd, ribald, risqué, smutty, vulgar

nausea *n* = **sickness**, biliousness, queasiness, retching, squeamishness, vomiting

nauseate *v* = **sicken**, disgust, offend, repel, repulse, revolt, turn one's stomach

nauseous *adj* = **sickening**, abhorrent, disgusting, distasteful, nauseating, offensive, repugnant, repulsive, revolting, scuzzy (*sl*)

nautical *adj* = **maritime**, marine, naval

naval *adj* = **nautical**, marine, maritime

navigable *adj* **1** = **passable**, clear, negotiable, unobstructed **2** = **sailable**, controllable, dirigible warships of country with their crews and organization. ◆ *adj* **3** navy-blue. **na'val** *adj* of the navy. **navy-blue** *adj* very dark blue.

Na·zi [NAHT-see] *n* **1** member of the National Socialist political party in Germany, 1919-45. **2** one who thinks, acts, like a Nazi. ◆ *adj*

Nb *Chem.* niobium.

Nd *Chem.* neodymium.

Ne *Chem.* neon.

Ne·an·der·thal [nee-AN-dər-thawl] *adj* **1** of a type of primitive man. **2** (**n-**) primitive.

neap [neep] *adj* low. **neap tide** the low tide at the first and third quarters of the moon.

near [neer] *prep* **1** close to. ◆ *adv* **-er, -est 2** at or to a short distance. ◆ *adj* **-er, -est 3** close at hand. **4** closely related. **5** narrow, so as barely to escape. **6** stingy. **7** (of vehicles, horses, etc.) at driver's left. ◆ *v* **8** approach. **near'by** *adj* adjacent. **near'ly** *adv* **1** closely. **2** almost.

neat [neet] *adj* **-er, -est 1** tidy, orderly. **2** efficient. **3** precise, deft. **4** cleverly worded. **5** undiluted. **6** simple and elegant. **neat'ly**

adv

neb·u·la [NEB-yə-lə] *n, pl* **-lae** [-lee] *Astronomy* diffuse cloud of particles, gases. **neb'u·lous** *adj* **1** cloudy. **2** vague, indistinct.

nec·es·sar·y [NES-ə-ser-ee] *adj* **1** needful, requisite, that must be done. **2** unavoidable, inevitable. **nec'es·sar·i·ly** *adv* **ne·ces'si·tate** *vt* **-tat·ed, -tat·ing** make necessary. **ne·ces'si·tous** *adj* poor, needy, destitute. **ne·ces'si·ty** *n, pl* **-ties 1** something needed, requisite. **2** constraining power or state of affairs. **3** compulsion. **4** poverty.

neck [nek] *n* **1** part of body joining head to shoulders. **2** narrower part of a bottle, etc. **3** narrow piece of anything between wider parts. ◆ *vi* **4** *inf* embrace, cuddle. **neck'lace** [-lis] *n* ornament around the neck.

nec·ro·man·cy [NEK-rə-man-see] *n* magic, esp. by communication with dead. **nec'ro·man·cer** *n* wizard.

ne·crop·o·lis [nə-KROP-ə-lis] *n, pl* **-lis·es** cemetery.

navigate *v* = **sail**, drive, guide, handle, maneuver, pilot, steer, voyage

navigation *n* = **sailing**, helmsmanship, seamanship, voyaging

navigator *n* = **pilot**, mariner, seaman

navy *n* = **fleet**, armada, flotilla

near *adj* **1** = **close**, adjacent, adjoining, nearby, neighboring **2** = **forthcoming**, approaching, imminent, impending, in the offing, looming, nigh, upcoming

nearby *adj* = **neighboring**, adjacent, adjoining, convenient, handy

nearly *adv* = **almost**, approximately, as good as, just about, practically, roughly, virtually, well-nigh

nearness *n* = **closeness**, accessibility, availability, handiness, proximity, vicinity

near-sighted *adj* = **short-sighted**, myopic

neat *adj* **1** = **tidy**, orderly, shipshape, smart, spick-and-span, spruce, systematic, trim **2** = **elegant**, adept, adroit, deft, dexterous, efficient, graceful, nimble, skillful, stylish **3** *Of alcoholic drinks* = **straight**, pure, undiluted, unmixed

neatly *adv* **1** = **tidily**, daintily, fastidiously, methodically, smartly, sprucely, systematically **2** = **elegantly**, adeptly, adroitly, deftly, dexterously, efficiently, expertly, gracefully, nimbly, skillfully

neatness *n* **1** = **tidiness**, daintiness,

orderliness, smartness, spruceness, trimness **2** = **elegance**, adroitness, deftness, dexterity, efficiency, grace, nimbleness, skill, style

nebulous *adj* = **vague**, confused, dim, hazy, imprecise, indefinite, indistinct, shadowy, uncertain, unclear

necessarily *adv* = **certainly**, automatically, compulsorily, incontrovertibly, inevitably, inexorably, naturally, of necessity, undoubtedly

necessary *adj* **1** = **needed**, compulsory, essential, imperative, indispensable, mandatory, obligatory, required, requisite, vital **2** = **certain**, fated, inescapable, inevitable, inexorable, unavoidable

necessitate *v* = **compel**, call for, coerce, constrain, demand, force, impel, oblige, require

necessities *pl n* = **essentials**, exigencies, fundamentals, needs, requirements

necessity *n* **1** = **inevitability**, compulsion, inexorableness, obligation **2** = **need**, desideratum, essential, fundamental, prerequisite, requirement, requisite, *sine qua non*

necromancy *n* = **magic**, black magic, divination, enchantment, sorcery, witchcraft, wizardry

necropolis *n* = **cemetery**, burial ground,

nec·tar [NEK-tər] n 1 honey of flowers. 2 drink of the gods.

nec·tar·ine [nek-tə-REEN] n variety of peach.

nee [nay] adj indicating maiden name of married woman.

need vt 1 want, require. ♦ n 2 (state, instance of) want. 3 requirement. 4 necessity. 5 poverty. **need'ful** adj necessary, requisite. **need'less** adj unnecessary. **needs** adv (preceded or foll. by must) necessarily. **need'y** adj **need·i·er, need·i·est** poor, in want.

nee·dle [NEE-dl] n –dled, –dling 1 pointed pin with an eye and no head, for sewing. 2 long, pointed pin for knitting. 3 pointer of gauge, dial. 4 magnetized bar of compass. 5 stylus for record player. 6 leaf of fir, pine, etc. 7 obelisk. 8 hypodermic syringe. ♦ vt 9 inf goad, provoke. **need'le·craft, -work** n embroidery, sewing.

ne·far·i·ous [ni-FAIR-ee-əs] adj wicked.

ne·far'i·ous·ness n

ne·gate [ni-GAYT] vt **-gat·ed, -gat·ing** deny, nullify. **ne·ga'tion** n contradiction, denial.

neg·a·tive [NEG-ə-tiv] adj 1 expressing denial or refusal. 2 lacking enthusiasm, energy, interest. 3 not positive. 4 of electrical charge having the same polarity as the charge of an electron. ♦ n 5 negative word or statement. 6 Photography picture made by action of light on chemicals in which lights and shades are reversed.

ne·glect [ni-GLEKT] vt 1 disregard, take no care of. 2 fail to do. 3 omit through carelessness. ♦ n 4 fact of neglecting or being neglected. **ne·glect'ful** adj

neg·li·gee [NEG-li-zhay] n woman's light, gauzy nightgown or dressing gown.

neg·li·gence [NEG-li-jəns] n 1 neglect. 2 carelessness. **neg'li·gent** adj **neg'li·gi·ble** adj 1 able to be disregarded. 2 very small or unimportant.

—— THESAURUS ——

churchyard, graveyard

need v 1 = **require**, call for, demand, entail, lack, miss, necessitate, want ♦ n 2 = **poverty**, deprivation, destitution, inadequacy, insufficiency, lack, paucity, penury, shortage 3 = **requirement**, demand, desideratum, essential, requisite 4 = **emergency**, exigency, necessity, obligation, urgency, want

needed adj = **necessary**, called for, desired, lacked, required, wanted

needful adj = **necessary**, essential, indispensable, needed, required, requisite, stipulated, vital

needle v = **irritate**, annoy, get on one's nerves (inf), goad, harass, nag, pester, provoke, rile, taunt

needless adj = **unnecessary**, gratuitous, groundless, pointless, redundant, superfluous, uncalled-for, unwanted, useless

needlework n = **embroidery**, needlecraft, sewing, stitching, tailoring

needy adj = **poor**, deprived, destitute, disadvantaged, impoverished, penniless, poverty-stricken, underprivileged

nefarious adj = **wicked**, criminal, depraved, evil, foul, heinous, infernal, villainous

negate v 1 = **invalidate**, annul, cancel, countermand, neutralize, nullify, obviate, reverse, wipe out 2 = **deny**, contradict,

disallow, disprove, gainsay (archaic or literary), oppose, rebut, refute

negation n 1 = **cancellation**, neutralization, nullification 2 = **denial**, contradiction, converse, disavowal, inverse, opposite, rejection, renunciation, reverse

negative adj 1 = **contradictory**, contrary, denying, dissenting, opposing, refusing, rejecting, resisting 2 = **pessimistic**, cynical, gloomy, jaundiced, uncooperative, unenthusiastic, unwilling ♦ n 3 = **contradiction**, denial, refusal

neglect v 1 = **disregard**, blow off (sl), disdain, ignore, overlook, rebuff, scorn, slight, spurn 2 = **forget**, be remiss, evade, omit, pass over, shirk, skimp ♦ n 3 = **disregard**, disdain, inattention, indifference 4 = **negligence**, carelessness, dereliction, failure, laxity, oversight, slackness

neglected adj 1 = **abandoned**, derelict, overgrown 2 = **disregarded**, unappreciated, underestimated, undervalued

neglectful adj = **careless**, heedless, inattentive, indifferent, lax, negligent, remiss, thoughtless, uncaring

negligence n = **carelessness**, dereliction, disregard, inattention, indifference, laxity, neglect, slackness, thoughtlessness

negligent adj = **careless**, forgetful,

ne•go•ti•ate [ni-GOH-shee-ayt] *v* **-at•ed,**
-at•ing ◆ *vi* **1** discuss with view to mutual
settlement. ◆ *vt* **2** arrange by conference. **3**
transfer (bill, check, etc.). **4** get over, past,
around (obstacle). **ne•go'ti•a•ble** [-shə-bəl]
adj **ne•go•ti•a'tion** [-shee-AY-shən] *n* **1**
dealing with another on business. **2**
discussion. **3** transference (of bill, check,
etc.).

Ne•gro [NEE-groh] *n, pl* **-groes** *oft offens*
dark-skinned person of African ancestry. ◆
adj

neigh [nay] *n* **1** cry of horse. ◆ *vi* **2** utter this
cry.

neigh•bor [NAY-bər] *n* one who lives near
another. **neigh'bor•hood** *n* **1** district. **2**
people of a district. **3** region around about.
neigh'bor•ing *adj* situated nearby.
neigh'bor•ly *adj* **1** as or befitting a good or
friendly neighbor. **2** friendly. **3** helpful.

nei•ther [NEE-*thər*] *adj, pron* **1** not the one
or the other. ◆ *adv* **2** not on the one hand.
3 not either. ◆ *conj* **4** nor yet.

nem•e•sis [NEM-ə-sis] *n, pl* **-ses** [-seez] **1**
retribution. **2** (**N-**) the goddess of
vengeance.

neo- *comb. form* new, later, revived in
modified form, based upon, e.g.
neoclassicism.

Ne•o•lith•ic [nee-ə-LITH-ik] *adj* of the later
Stone Age.

ne•ol•o•gism [nee-OL-ə-jiz-əm] *n* newly
coined word or phrase.

ne•on [NEE-on] *n* one of the inert
constituent gases of the atmosphere, used
in illuminated signs and lights.

ne•o•phyte [NEE-ə-fit] *n* **1** new convert. **2**
beginner, novice.

neph•ew [NEF-yoo] *n* brother's or sister's
son.

ne•phri•tis [nə-FRĪ-tis] *n* inflammation of
kidneys. **ne•phro•sis** [-FROH-sis] *n*
degenerative disease of kidneys.

nep•o•tism [NEP-ə-tiz-əm] *n* undue
favoritism toward one's relations.

Nep•tune [NEP-toon] *n* **1** god of the sea. **2**
planet second farthest from sun.

nep•tu•ni•um [nep-TOO-nee-əm] *n*
synthetic metallic element.

nerd [nurd] *n sl* boring person obsessed
with a particular subject.

nerve [nurv] *n* **1** sinew, tendon. **2** fiber or
bundle of fibers conveying feeling,
impulses to motion, etc. to and from brain
and other parts of body. **3** assurance. **4**
coolness in danger. **5** audacity. **6** *pl*
irritability, unusual sensitiveness to fear,
annoyance, etc. **nerve'less** [-lis] *adj* **1**
without nerves. **2** useless. **3** weak. **4**
paralyzed. **nerv'ous** [-əs] *adj* **1** excitable. **2**
timid, apprehensive, worried. **3** of the
nerves. **nerv'y** [-ee] *adj* **nerv•i•er, nerv•i•est**
1 nervous, jumpy, irritable. **2** on edge.
nervous breakdown condition of mental,
emotional disturbance, disability.

nest *n* **1** place in which bird lays and

heedless, inattentive, neglectful, remiss,
slack, slapdash, thoughtless, unthinking

negligible *adj* = **insignificant,**
imperceptible, inconsequential, minor,
minute, small, trifling, trivial, unimportant

negotiable *adj* = **debatable,** variable

negotiate *v* **1** = **deal,** arrange, bargain,
conciliate, debate, discuss, haggle,
mediate, transact, work out **2** = **get round,**
clear, cross, get over, get past, pass,
surmount

negotiation *n* = **bargaining,** arbitration,
debate, diplomacy, discussion, haggling,
mediation, transaction, wheeling and
dealing (*inf*)

negotiator *n* = **mediator,** ambassador,
delegate, diplomat, honest broker,
intermediary, moderator

neighborhood *n* = **district,** community,
environs, locale, locality, quarter, region,
vicinity

neighboring *adj* = **nearby,** adjacent,
adjoining, bordering, connecting, near,
next, surrounding

neighborly *adj* = **helpful,** considerate,
friendly, harmonious, hospitable, kind,
obliging, sociable

nemesis *n* = **retribution,** destiny,
destruction, fate, vengeance

nepotism *n* = **favoritism,** bias, partiality,
patronage, preferential treatment

nerd *n* = **bore,** doofus (*sl*), dork (*sl*), drip
(*inf*), dweeb (*sl*), egghead (*inf*), geek (*sl*),
goober (*inf*)

nerve *n* **1** = **bravery,** courage, daring,
fearlessness, grit, guts (*inf*), pluck,
resolution, will **2** = **impudence,** audacity,
boldness, brazenness, cheek (*inf*),
impertinence, insolence, temerity ◆ *v*
3 nerve oneself = **brace oneself,** fortify
oneself, steel oneself

nerveless *adj* = **calm,** composed,

hatches its eggs. **2** animal's breeding place. **3** snug retreat. ◆ *vi* **4** make, have a nest. **nest egg** (fund of) money in reserve.

nes·tle [NES-əl] *vi* **-tled, -tling** settle comfortably, usu. pressing in or close to something.

nest'ling *n* bird too young to leave nest.

net¹ *n* **1** openwork fabric of meshes of cord, etc. **2** piece of it used to catch fish, etc. **3** (N-) short for INTERNET. ◆ *vt* **net·ted, net·ting 4** cover with, or catch in, net. **5** catch, ensnare. **netting** *n* string or wire net. **net'ball** *n* Tennis return shot that hits top of net and remains in play.

net·i·quette [NET-i-kit] *n* informal code of behaviour on the Internet.

net² *adj* **1** left after all deductions. **2** free from deduction. ◆ *vt* **net·ted, net·ting 3** gain, yield as clear profit.

neth·er [NETH-ər] *adj* lower.

ne·tsu·ke [NET-skee] *n* carved wooden or ivory toggle or button worn in Japan.

net·tle [NET-l] *n* **1** plant with stinging hairs on the leaves. ◆ *vt* **-tled, -tling 2** irritate, provoke.

net·work [NET-wurk] *n* **1** system of intersecting lines, roads, etc. **2** interconnecting group of people or things. **3** in broadcasting, group of stations

connected to transmit same programs simultaneously. **4** Computers system of interconnected computers.

neu·ral [NUUR-əl] *adj* of the nerves.

neu·ral·gia [nuu-RAL-jə] *n* pain in, along nerves, esp. of face and head. **neu·ral'gic** [-jik] *adj*

neu·ri·tis [nuu-RĪ-tis] *n* inflammation of nerves.

neu·rol·o·gy [nuu-ROL-ə-jee] *n* science, study of nerves. **neu·rol'o·gist** *n*

neu·ro·sis [nuu-ROH-sis] *n, pl* **-ses** [-seez] relatively mild mental disorder. **neu·rot'ic** *adj* **1** suffering from nervous disorder. **2** abnormally sensitive. ◆ *n* **3** neurotic person.

neu·ter [NOO-tər] *adj* **1** neither masculine nor feminine. ◆ *n* **2** neuter word. **3** neuter gender. ◆ *vt* **4** castrate, spay (domestic animals).

neu·tral [NOO-trəl] *adj* **1** taking neither side in war, dispute, etc. **2** without marked qualities. **3** belonging to neither of two classes. ◆ *n* **4** neutral nation or a citizen of one. **5** neutral gear. **neu·tral'i·ty** *n* **neu'tral·ize** *vt* **-ized, -iz·ing 1** make ineffective. **2** counterbalance. **neutral gear** in vehicle, position of gears that leaves transmission disengaged.

controlled, cool, impassive, imperturbable, self-possessed, unemotional

nerve-racking *adj* = **tense**, difficult, distressing, frightening, harrowing, stressful, trying, worrying

nerves *pl n* = **tension**, anxiety, butterflies (in one's stomach) (*inf*), cold feet (*inf*), fretfulness, nervousness, strain, stress, worry

nervous *adj* = **apprehensive**, anxious, edgy, fearful, jumpy, on edge, tense, uneasy, uptight (*inf*), wired (*sl*), worried

nervousness *n* = **anxiety**, agitation, disquiet, excitability, fluster, tension, touchiness, worry

nervy *adj* = **anxious**, agitated, fidgety, jittery (*inf*), jumpy, nervous, on edge, tense, twitchy (*inf*), wired (*sl*)

nest *n* = **refuge**, den, haunt, hideaway, retreat

nest egg *n* = **reserve**, cache, deposit, fall-back, fund(s), savings, store

nestle *v* = **snuggle**, cuddle, curl up, huddle, nuzzle

nestling *n* = **chick**, fledgling

net¹ *n* **1** = **mesh**, lattice, netting, network, openwork, tracery, web ◆ *v* **2** = **catch**, bag, capture, enmesh, ensnare, entangle, trap

net² *adj* **1** = **final**, after taxes, clear, take-home ◆ *v* **2** = **earn**, accumulate, bring in, clear, gain, make, realize, reap

nether *adj* = **lower**, below, beneath, bottom, inferior, under, underground

nettled *adj* = **irritated**, annoyed, exasperated, galled, harassed, incensed, peeved, put out, riled, vexed

network *n* = **system**, arrangement, complex, grid, labyrinth, lattice, maze, organization, structure, web

neurosis *n* = **obsession**, abnormality, affliction, derangement, instability, maladjustment, mental illness, phobia

neurotic *adj* = **unstable**, abnormal, compulsive, disturbed, maladjusted, manic, nervous, obsessive, unhealthy

neuter *v* = **castrate**, doctor (*inf*), emasculate, fix (*inf*), geld, spay

neutral *adj* **1** = **unbiased**, disinterested, even-handed, impartial, nonaligned, nonpartisan, uncommitted, uninvolved,

neu·tron [NOO-tron] *n* electrically neutral particle of the nucleus of an atom. **neutron bomb** nuclear bomb designed to destroy people but not buildings.

nev·er [NEV-ər] *adv* at no time. **nev·er·the·less'** *adv* for all that, notwithstanding.

ne·vus [NEE-vəs] *n* **1** congenital mark on skin. **2** birthmark, mole.

new [noo] *adj* **-er, -est 1** not existing before, fresh. **2** that has lately come into some state or existence. **3** unfamiliar, strange. ♦ *adv* **4** newly. **new'ly** *adv* recently, fresh. **new'ness** *n* **New Age** cultural movement originating in the 1980s, characterized by such things as alternative medicine, astrology, and meditation. **new'com·er** *n* recent arrival. **new'fang·led** [-FANG-əld] *adj* of new fashion.

new·el [NOO-əl] *n* **1** central pillar of winding staircase. **2** post at top or bottom of staircase rail.

news [nooz] *n* **1** report of recent happenings, tidings. **2** interesting fact not previously known. **news'cast** *n* news broadcast. **news'deal·er** *n* shopkeeper who sells newspapers and magazines. **news'flash** *n* brief news item, oft.

interrupting radio, TV program. **news'group** *n* **Computers** forum where subscribers exchange information about a specific subject by e-mail. **news'pa·per** *n* periodical publication containing news, advertisements, etc. **news'print** *n* paper of the kind used for newspapers, etc. **news'reel** *n* motion picture giving news. **news'room** *n* room where news is received and prepared for publication or broadcast. **news'wor·thy** [-wur-thee] *adj* **-thi·er, -thi·est** sufficiently interesting or important to be reported as news.

newt [noot] *n* small, tailed amphibious creature.

new·ton [NOOT-n] *n* SI unit of force.

next [nekst] *adj, adv* **1** nearest. **2** immediately following. **next of kin** nearest relative(s).

nex·us [NEK-səs] *n, pl* **nexus 1** tie. **2** connection, link.

Ni *Chem.* nickel.

nib·ble [NIB-əl] *v* **-bled, -bling 1** take little bites of. ♦ *n* **2** little bite.

nice [nīs] *adj* **nic·er, nic·est 1** pleasant. **2** attractive. **3** friendly, kind. **4** subtle, fine. **5** careful, exact. **6** difficult to decide. **nice'ly** *adv* **ni'ce·ty** *n, pl* **-ties 1** minute distinction or detail. **2** subtlety. **3** precision.

───── THESAURUS ─────

unprejudiced **2** = **indeterminate**, dull, indistinct, intermediate, undefined

neutrality *n* = **impartiality**, detachment, nonalignment, noninterference, noninvolvement, nonpartisanship

neutralize *v* = **counteract**, cancel, compensate for, counterbalance, frustrate, negate, nullify, offset, undo

never *adv* = **at no time**, not at all, on no account, under no circumstances

nevertheless *adv* = **nonetheless**, but, even so, (even) though, however, notwithstanding, regardless, still, yet

new *adj* **1** = **modern**, contemporary, current, fresh, ground-breaking, latest, novel, original, recent, state-of-the-art, unfamiliar, up-to-date **2** = **changed**, altered, improved, modernized, redesigned, renewed, restored **3** = **extra**, added, more, supplementary

newcomer *n* = **novice**, arrival, beginner, Johnny-come-lately (*inf*), new kid in town (*inf*), parvenu

newfangled *adj* = **new**, contemporary, cool (*inf*), fashionable, gimmicky, modern,

novel, phat (*sl*), recent, state-of-the-art

newly *adv* = **recently**, anew, freshly, just, lately, latterly

newness *n* = **novelty**, freshness, innovation, oddity, originality, strangeness, unfamiliarity, uniqueness

news *n* = **information**, bulletin, communiqué, exposé, gossip, hearsay, intelligence, latest (*inf*), report, revelation, rumor, story

newsworthy *adj* = **interesting**, important, notable, noteworthy, remarkable, significant, stimulating

next *adj* **1** = **following**, consequent, ensuing, later, subsequent, succeeding **2** = **nearest**, adjacent, adjoining, closest, neighboring ♦ *adv* **3** = **afterwards**, following, later, subsequent, thereafter

nibble *v* **1** = **bite**, eat, gnaw, munch, nip, peck, pick at ♦ *n* **2** = **snack**, bite, crumb, morsel, peck, *soupçon*, taste, tidbit

nice *adj* **1** = **pleasant**, agreeable, attractive, charming, delightful, good, pleasurable **2** = **kind**, courteous, friendly, likable *or* likeable, polite, well-mannered **3** = **neat**,

niche [nich] *n* **1** recess in wall. **2** suitable place in life, public estimation, etc.

nick [nik] *vt* **1** make notch in, indent. **2** *sl* steal. ♦ *n* **3** notch. **4** exact point of time. **in the nick of time** at the last possible moment.

nick·el [NIK-əl] *n* **1** silver-white metal much used in alloys and plating. **2** five-cent piece.

nick·name [NIK-naym] *n* familiar name added to or replacing an ordinary name.

nic·o·tine [NIK-ə-teen] *n* poisonous oily liquid in tobacco.

niece [nees] *n* brother's or sister's daughter.

nif·ty [NIFT-ee] *adj* **-ti·er, -tiest** *inf* neat or smart.

nig·gard [NIG-ərd] *n* mean, stingy person. **nig'gard·ly** *adj, adv* **nig'gard·li·ness** *n*

nig·gle [NIG-əl] *vi* **-gled, -gling 1** find fault continually. **2** annoy. **niggling** *adj* **1** petty. **2** irritating and persistent.

nigh [nī] *adj, adv, prep lit* near.

night [nīt] *n* **1** time of darkness between sunset and sunrise. **2** end of daylight. **3** dark. **night'ie** *n inf* nightgown. **night'ly** *adj* **1** happening, done every night. **2** of the night. ♦ *adv* **3** every night. **4** by night. **night'cap** *n* **1** cap worn in bed. **2** *inf* late-night (alcoholic) drink. **night'club** *n* establishment for dancing, music, etc.

open until early morning. **night'gown** *n* woman's or child's loose gown worn in bed. **night'in·gale** *n* small Old World bird that sings usu. at night. **night'mare** [-mair] *n* **1** very bad dream. **2** terrifying experience. **night'time** *n*

ni·hil·ism [NĪ-ə-liz-əm] *n* **1** rejection of all religious and moral principles. **2** opposition to all constituted authority, or government. **ni'hil·ist** *n* **ni·hil·ist'ic** *adj*

nim·ble [NIM-bəl] *adj* **-bler, -blest** agile, active, quick, dexterous. **nim'bly** *adv*

nim·bus [NIM-bəs] *n, pl* **-bi** [-bī] **-bus·es 1** rain or storm cloud. **2** cloud of glory, halo.

nine [nīn] *adj, n* cardinal number next above eight. **ninth** *adj* **ninth'ly** *adv*
nine·teen' *adj, n* nine more than ten.
nine·teenth' *adj* **nine'ty** *adj, n* nine tens.
nine'ti·eth *adj* **nine'pins** *n* game where wooden pins are set up to be knocked down by rolling ball, skittles.

nip *v* **nipped, nip·ping 1** pinch sharply. **2** detach by pinching, bite. **3** check growth (of plants) thus. **4** *inf* steal. **5** *inf* beat (opponent) by close margin hurry. ♦ *n* **6** pinch. **7** check to growth. **8** sharp coldness of weather. **9** small alcoholic drink. **nip'per** *n* **1** thing (e.g. crab's claw) that nips. **2** *inf* small boy. ♦ *pl* **3** pincers. **nip'py** *adj* **-pi·er, -pi·est** *inf* **1** cold. **2** quick.

dainty, fine, tidy, trim **4 = subtle,** careful, delicate, fastidious, fine, meticulous, precise, strict

nicely *adv* **1 = pleasantly,** acceptably, agreeably, attractively, charmingly, delightfully, pleasurably, well **2 = kindly,** amiably, commendably, courteously, politely **3 = neatly,** daintily, finely, tidily, trimly

nicety *n* **= subtlety,** daintiness, delicacy, discrimination, distinction, nuance, refinement

niche *n* **1 = alcove,** corner, hollow, nook, opening, recess **2 = position,** calling, pigeonhole (*inf*), place, slot (*inf*), vocation

nick *v* **1 = cut,** chip, dent, mark, notch, scar, score, scratch, snick ♦ *n* **2 = cut,** chip, dent, mark, notch, scar, scratch

nickname *n* **= pet name,** diminutive, epithet, label, moniker *or* monicker (*sl*), sobriquet

nifty *adj* **= neat,** attractive, chic, deft, pleasing, smart, stylish

niggard *n* **= miser,** cheapskate (*inf*),

Scrooge, skinflint

niggardly *adj* **= stingy,** avaricious, frugal, grudging, mean, miserly, parsimonious, tightfisted, ungenerous

niggle *v* **1 = worry,** annoy, irritate, rankle **2 = criticize,** carp, cavil, find fault, fuss

niggling *adj* **1 = persistent,** gnawing, irritating, troubling, worrying **2 = petty,** finicky, fussy, nit-picking (*inf*), pettifogging, picky (*inf*), quibbling

night *n* **= darkness,** dark, night-time

nightfall *n* **= evening,** dusk, sundown, sunset, twilight

nightly *adj* **1 = nocturnal,** night-time ♦ *adv* **2 = every night,** each night, night after night, nightly (*inf*)

nightmare *n* **1 = bad dream,** hallucination **2 = ordeal,** horror, torment, trial, tribulation

nil *n* **= nothing,** love, naught, none, zero

nimble *adj* **= agile,** brisk, deft, dexterous, lively, quick, sprightly, spry, swift

nimbly *adv* **= quickly,** briskly, deftly, dexterously, easily, readily, smartly, spryly,

nip·ple [NIP-əl] n **1** point of a breast, teat. **2** anything like this.

nir·va·na [nir-VAH-nə] n **1** Buddhism absolute blessedness. **2** Hinduism merging of individual in supreme spirit.

nit n egg of louse or other parasite. **nit'pick·ing** adj inf overconcerned with detail, esp. to find fault. **nit'pick** v **1** show such overconcern. **2** criticize over petty faults. **nit'wit** n inf fool. **nit·ty-grit·ty** n sl basic facts, details.

ni·tro·gen [NĪ-trə-jən] n one of the gases making up the air. **ni'trate** n compound of nitric acid and an alkali. **ni'tric** adj **ni'trous** adj **ni·trog'e·nous** [-TROJ]-ə-nəs] adj of, containing nitrogen. **ni·tro·glyc'er·in** [-troh-GLIS-ə-rin] n explosive liquid.

No Chem. nobelium.

no [noh] adj **1** not any, not a. **2** not at all. ◆ adv **3** expresses negative reply to question or request. ◆ n, pl **noes 4** refusal. **5** denial. **6** negative vote or voter. **no one** nobody. **no-go** adj sl **1** not operating. **2** canceled. **no man's land 1** waste or unclaimed land. **2** contested ground between two opposing forces. **no way** inf absolutely not.

no·bel·i·um [noh-BEL-ee-əm] n synthetic element produced from curium.

no·ble [NOH-bəl] adj **-bler, -blest 1** of the nobility. **2** showing, having high moral qualities. **3** impressive, excellent. ◆ n **4** member of the nobility. **no·bil'i·ty** n **1** in some countries, class holding special rank, usu. hereditary. **2** being noble. **no'bly** adv

no·bod·y [NOH-bod-ee] pron **1** no person. **2** no one. ◆ n, pl **-bod·ies 3** person of no importance.

noc·tur·nal [nok-TUR-nl] adj **1** of, in, by, night. **2** active by night.

noc·turne [NOK-turn] n dreamy piece of music.

nod v **nod·ded, nod·ding 1** bow head slightly and quickly in assent, command, etc. **2** let head droop with sleep. ◆ n **3** act of nodding. **nodding acquaintance** slight knowledge of person or subject. **give the nod to** inf express approval of. **nod off** fall asleep.

node [nohd] n **1** knot or knob. **2** point at which curve crosses itself. **no'dal** [-əl] adj

nod·ule [NOJ-ool] n **1** little knot. **2** rounded irregular mineral mass.

No·el [noh-EL] n **1** Christmas. **2** (n-) Christmas carol.

nog n **1** drink made with beaten eggs. **2** eggnog. **3** peg, block.

nog·gin [NOG-ən] n **1** small amount of liquor. **2** small mug. **3** inf head.

noise [noyz] n **1** any sound, esp. disturbing one. **2** clamor, din. **3** loud outcry. **4** talk or interest. ◆ vt **5** rumor. **noise'less** [-lis] adj without noise, quiet, silent. **nois'i·ly** adv **nois'y** adj **nois·i·er, nois·i·est 1** making much noise. **2** clamorous.

swiftly

nip¹ v = **pinch**, bite, squeeze, tweak

nip² n = **dram**, draft, drop, mouthful, shot (inf), sip, snifter (inf)

nippy adj = **chilly**, biting, sharp, stinging

nirvana n = **paradise**, bliss, joy, peace, serenity, tranquillity

nit-picking adj = **fussy**, captious, carping, finicky, hairsplitting, pedantic, pettifogging, quibbling

nitty-gritty n = **basics**, brass tacks (inf), core, crux, essentials, fundamentals, gist, substance

nitwit n Inf = **fool**, dimwit (inf), doofus (sl), dork (sl), dummy (sl), halfwit, oaf, schmuck (sl), simpleton

no interj **1** = **never**, nay, not at all, no way ◆ n **2** = **refusal**, denial, negation

nobility n **1** = **integrity**, honor, incorruptibility, uprightness, virtue **2** = **aristocracy**, elite, lords, nobles, patricians, peerage, upper class

noble adj **1** = **worthy**, generous, honorable, magnanimous, upright, virtuous **2** = **aristocratic**, blue-blooded, highborn, lordly, patrician, titled **3** = **great**, dignified, distinguished, grand, imposing, impressive, lofty, splendid, stately ◆ n **4** = **lord**, aristocrat, nobleman, peer

nobody pron **1** = **no-one** ◆ n **2** = **nonentity**, cipher, lightweight (inf), menial

nocturnal adj = **nightly**, night-time

nod v **1** = **acknowledge**, bow, gesture, indicate, signal **2** = **sleep**, doze, drowse, nap ◆ n **3** = **gesture**, acknowledgment, greeting, indication, sign, signal

noggin n **1** = **cup**, dram, mug, nip, tot **2** Inf = **head**, block (inf), noodle (sl), nut (sl)

no go adj = **impossible**, futile, hopeless, vain

noise n = **sound**, clamor, commotion, din, hubbub, racket, row, uproar

noiseless adj = **silent**, hushed, inaudible, mute, quiet, soundless, still

noi·some [NOI-səm] *adj* **1** disgusting. **2** noxious.

no·mad [NOH-mad] *n* **1** member of tribe with no fixed dwelling place. **2** wanderer. **no·mad·ic** *adj*

nom de plume [nom də PLOOM] *Fr* **1** writer's assumed name. **2** pen name. **3** pseudonym.

no·men·cla·ture [NOH-mən-klay-chər] *n* terminology of particular science, etc.

nom·i·nal [NOM-ə-nəl] *adj* **1** in name only. **2** (of fee, etc.) small, insignificant. **3** of a name or names. **nom'i·nal·ly** *adv* **1** in name only. **2** not really.

nom·i·nate [NOM-ə-nayt] *vt* **-nat·ed, -nat·ing 1** propose as candidate. **2** appoint to office. **nom·i·na'tion** *n* **nom'i·na·tive** [-nə-tiv] *adj, n* (of) case of nouns, pronouns when subject of verb. **nom·i·nee'** *n* candidate.

non- *prefix* indicating: **1** negation, e.g. *nonexistent.* **2** refusal or failure, e.g. *noncooperation.* **3** exclusion from a specified class, e.g. *nonfiction.* **4** lack or absence, e.g. *nonevent.*

non·a·ge·nar·i·an [non-ə-jə-NAIR-ee-ən] *adj* **1** aged between ninety and ninety-nine. ◆ *n* **2** person of such age.

non·ag·gres'sion *n* policy of not attacking other countries.

non·al·co·hol'ic *adj* containing no alcohol.

nonce [nons] *n* **for the nonce 1** for the occasion only. **2** for the present.

non·cha·lant [non-shə-LAHNT] *adj* casually unconcerned, indifferent, cool. **non'cha·lance** *n*

non·com·bat·ant [non-kəm-BAT-nt] *n* **1** civilian during war. **2** member of army who does not fight, e.g. chaplain.

non·com·mit·tal [non-kə-MIT-l] *adj* avoiding definite preference or pledge.

non com·pos men·tis [NON KOM-pohs MEN-tis] *Lat* of unsound mind.

non·con·duc'tor *n* substance that is a poor conductor of heat, electricity, or sound.

non·con·trib'u·to·ry *adj* denoting a pension scheme for employees, the premiums of which are paid entirely by the employer.

non·de·script [non-di-SKRIPT] *adj* lacking distinctive characteristics, indeterminate.

none [nun] *pron* **1** no one, not any. ◆ *adj* **2**

——— THESAURUS ———

noisome *adj* **1** = **poisonous**, bad, harmful, pernicious, pestilential, unhealthy, unwholesome **2** = **offensive**, disgusting, fetid, foul, funky (*sl*), malodorous, noxious, putrid, smelly, stinking

noisy *adj* = **loud**, boisterous, cacophonous, clamorous, deafening, ear-splitting, strident, tumultuous, uproarious, vociferous

nomad *n* = **wanderer**, drifter, itinerant, migrant, rambler, rover, vagabond

nomadic *adj* = **wandering**, itinerant, migrant, peripatetic, roaming, roving, traveling, vagrant

nom de plume *n* = **pseudonym**, alias, assumed name, nom de guerre, pen name

nomenclature *n* = **terminology**, classification, codification, phraseology, taxonomy, vocabulary

nominal *adj* **1** = **so-called**, formal, ostensible, professed, puppet, purported, supposed, theoretical, titular **2** = **small**, inconsiderable, insignificant, minimal, symbolic, token, trifling, trivial

nominate *v* = **name**, appoint, assign, choose, designate, elect, propose, recommend, select, suggest

nomination *n* = **choice**, appointment, designation, election, proposal, recommendation, selection, suggestion

nominee *n* = **candidate**, aspirant, contestant, entrant, protégé, runner

nonaligned *adj* = **neutral**, impartial, uncommitted, undecided

nonchalance *n* = **indifference**, calm, composure, equanimity, imperturbability, sang-froid, self-possession, unconcern

nonchalant *adj* = **casual**, blasé, calm, careless, indifferent, insouciant, laid-back (*inf*), offhand, unconcerned, unperturbed

noncombatant *n* = **civilian**, neutral, nonbelligerent

noncommittal *adj* = **evasive**, cautious, circumspect, equivocal, guarded, neutral, politic, temporizing, tentative, vague, wary

non compos mentis ◆ *adj* = **insane**, crazy, deranged, mentally ill, unbalanced, unhinged

nonconformist *n* = **maverick**, dissenter, eccentric, heretic, iconoclast, individualist, protester, radical, rebel

nonconformity *n* = **dissent**, eccentricity, heresy, heterodoxy

nondescript *adj* = **ordinary**,

no. ♦ *adv* **3** in no way. **none-the-less'** *adv* despite that, however.

non·en·ti·ty [non-EN-ti-tee] *n, pl* **-ties 1** insignificant person, thing. **2** nonexistent thing.

non·e·vent' *n* disappointing or insignificant occurrence.

non·ex·ist'ent *adj* not existing, imaginary. **nonexistence** *n*

non·fic'tion *n* writing that deals with facts or real events.

non·in·ter·ven'tion *n* refusal to intervene in the affairs of others.

non·pa·reil [non-pə-REL] *adj* **1** unequaled, matchless. ♦ *n* **2** person or thing unequaled or unrivaled. **3** small bead of colored sugar used to decorate cakes, etc. **4** flat round piece of chocolate covered with this sugar.

non·pay'ment *n* failure to pay money owed.

non·plus' *vt* **-plussed, -plus·sing** disconcert, confound, or bewilder completely.

non·prof·it *adj* not run with the intention of making a profit.

non·sense [NON-sens] *n* **1** lack of sense. **2** absurd language. **3** silly conduct. **non·sen'si·cal** *adj* **1** ridiculous. **2** meaningless. **3** without sense.

non se·qui·tur [non SEK-wi-tər] *Lat* statement with little or no relation to what preceded it.

non·smok'er *n* person who does not smoke. **non-smok'ing, no-smok'ing** *adj* denoting an area in which smoking is forbidden.

non·stand'ard *adj* denoting language that is not regarded as correct by educated native speakers.

non·start'er *n* person or idea that has little chance of success.

non·stick' *adj* coated with a substance that food will not stick to when cooked.

non·stop' *adj, adv* without a stop.

non·tox'ic *adj* not poisonous.

non·vi·o·lent *adj* using peaceful methods to bring about change. **non·vi·o·lence** *n*

noo·dle¹ [NOOD-l] *n* strip of pasta served in soup, etc.

noodle² *n* **1** simpleton, fool. **2** *sl* the head.

nook [nuuk] *n* sheltered corner, retreat.

noon *n* midday, twelve o'clock. **noon'day** *n* noon. **noon'tide** *n* the time about noon.

noose [noos] *n* **1** running loop. **2** snare. ♦ *vt* **noosed, noos·ing 3** catch, ensnare in noose, lasso.

nor *conj* and not.

Nor·dic [NOR-dik] *adj* pert. to peoples of Germanic stock, e.g. Scandinavians.

norm *n* **1** average level of achievement. **2** rule or authoritative standard. **3** model. **4** standard type or pattern. **nor'mal** *adj* **1** ordinary. **2** usual. **3** conforming to type. ♦ *n Geom.* **4** perpendicular. **nor'mal·ly** *adv*

north *n* **1** direction to the right of person

commonplace, dull, featureless, undistinguished, unexceptional, unremarkable

none *pron* = **not any**, nil, nobody, no-one, nothing, not one, zero

nonentity *n* = **nobody**, cipher, lightweight (*inf*), mediocrity, small fry

nonessential *adj* = **unnecessary**, dispensable, expendable, extraneous, inessential, peripheral, superfluous, unimportant

nonetheless *adv* = **nevertheless**, despite that, even so, however, in spite of that, yet

nonevent *n* = **flop** (*inf*), disappointment, dud (*inf*), failure, fiasco, washout

nonexistent *adj* = **imaginary**, chimerical, fictional, hypothetical, illusory, legendary, mythical, unreal

nonsense *n* = **rubbish**, balderdash, claptrap (*inf*), drivel, gibberish, hot air (*inf*), stupidity, tripe (*inf*), twaddle

nonsensical *adj* = **senseless**, absurd, crazy, foolish, inane, incomprehensible, irrational, meaningless, ridiculous, silly

nonstarter *n* = **dead loss**, dud (*inf*), lemon (*inf*), loser, no-hoper (*inf*), turkey (*inf*), washout (*inf*)

nonstop *adj* **1** = **continuous**, constant, endless, incessant, interminable, relentless, twenty-four-seven (*sl*), unbroken, uninterrupted ♦ *adv* **2** = **continuously**, ceaselessly, constantly, endlessly, incessantly, interminably, perpetually, relentlessly, twenty-four-seven (*sl*), unremittingly

noodle *n Sl* = **head**, common sense, gut feeling (*inf*), intuition, sense

nook *n* = **niche**, alcove, corner, cubbyhole, hideout, opening, recess, retreat

noon *n* = **midday**, high noon, noonday, noontide, twelve noon

norm *n* = **standard**, average, benchmark,

facing the sunset. **2** part of the world, of country, etc. toward this point. ◆ *adv* **3** toward or in the north. ◆ *adj* **4** to, from, or in the north. **north·er·ly** [NOR-*thər*-lee] *adj* **1** (of wind) from the north. ◆ *n* **2** a wind from the north. **north·ern** *adj* **north·ern·er** *n* person from the north. **north·ward** [NORTH-*wərd*] *adj* **north'ward(s)** *adv*

nose [nohz] *n* **1** organ of smell, used also in breathing. **2** any projection resembling a nose, as prow of ship, aircraft, etc. ◆ *v* **nosed, nos·ing 3** (cause to) move forward slowly and carefully. ◆ *vt* **4** touch with nose. **5** smell, sniff. ◆ *vi* **6** smell. **7** pry. **nos·y** *adj* **nos·i·er, nos·i·est** inquisitive. **nose'dive** *n* **1** downward sweep of aircraft. **2** any sudden sharp fall. **nose'gay** *n* bunch of flowers.

nos·tal·gia [no-STAL-jə] *n* **1** longing for return of past events. **2** homesickness. **nos·tal'gic** *adj*

nos·tril [NOS-trəl] *n* one of the two external openings of the nose.

nos·trum [NOS-trəm] *n* **1** quack medicine. **2** secret remedy.

not *adv* expressing negation, refusal, denial.

no·ta be·ne [NOH-tah BE-ne] *Lat* note well.

no·ta·ble [NOH-tə-bəl] *adj* **1** worthy of note, remarkable. ◆ *n* **2** person of distinction. **no·ta·bil'i·ty** *n, pl* **-ties 1** prominence. **2** an eminent person. **no'ta·bly** *adv*

no·ta·tion [noh-TAY-shən] *n* **1** representation of numbers, quantities, by symbols. **2** set of such symbols.

notch [noch] *n* **1** V-shaped cut or indentation. **2** *inf* step, grade. ◆ *vt* **3** make notches in.

note [noht] *n* **1** brief comment or record. **2** short letter. **3** promissory note. **4** symbol for musical sound. **5** single tone. **6** sign. **7** indication, hint. **8** fame. **9** notice. **10** regard. ◆ *pl* **11** brief jottings written down for future reference. ◆ *vt* **not·ed, not·ing 12** observe, record. **13** heed. **noted** *adj* **1** well-known. **2** celebrated. **note'book** *n* small book with blank pages for writing. **note'wor·thy** [-wur-*thee*] *adj* worth noting, remarkable.

criterion, par, pattern, rule, yardstick

normal *adj* **1 = usual**, average, common, conventional, natural, ordinary, regular, routine, standard, typical **2 = sane**, rational, reasonable, well-adjusted

normality *n* **1 = regularity**, conventionality, naturalness **2 = sanity**, balance, rationality, reason

normally *adv* **= usually**, as a rule, commonly, generally, habitually, ordinarily, regularly, typically

north *adj* **1 = northern**, Arctic, boreal, northerly, polar ◆ *adv* **2 = northward(s)**, northerly

nose *n* **1 = snout**, beak, bill, honker (*sl*), proboscis ◆ *v* **2 = ease forward**, nudge, nuzzle, push, shove **3 = pry**, meddle, snoop (*inf*)

nosegay *n* **= posy**, bouquet

nostalgia *n* **= reminiscence**, homesickness, longing, pining, regretfulness, remembrance, wistfulness, yearning

nostalgic *adj* **= sentimental**, emotional, homesick, longing, maudlin, regretful, wistful

nostrum *n* **= medicine**, cure, drug, elixir, panacea, potion, remedy, treatment

nosy *adj* **= inquisitive**, curious,

eavesdropping, interfering, intrusive, meddlesome, prying, snooping (*inf*)

notability *n* **= fame**, celebrity, distinction, eminence, esteem, renown

notable *adj* **1 = remarkable**, conspicuous, extraordinary, memorable, noteworthy, outstanding, rare, striking, uncommon, unusual ◆ *n* **2 = celebrity**, big name, dignitary, personage, V.I.P.

notably *adv* **= particularly**, especially, outstandingly, strikingly

notation *n* **= signs**, characters, code, script, symbols, system

notch *n* **1 = cut**, cleft, incision, indentation, mark, nick, score **2** *Inf* **= level**, degree, grade, step ◆ *v* **3 = cut**, indent, mark, nick, score, scratch

notch up *v* **= register**, achieve, gain, make, score

note *n* **1 = message**, comment, communication, epistle, jotting, letter, memo, memorandum, minute, remark, reminder **2 = symbol**, indication, mark, sign, token ◆ *v* **3 = see**, notice, observe, perceive **4 = mark**, denote, designate, indicate, record, register **5 = mention**, remark

notebook *n* **= jotter**, diary, exercise book, journal, notepad

noth•ing [NUTH-ing] *n* **1** no thing, not anything, nought. ♦ *adv* **2** not at all, in no way.

no•tice [NOH-tis] *n* **1** observation. **2** attention, consideration. **3** warning, intimation, announcement. **4** advance notification of intention to end a contract, etc., as of employment. **5** review. ♦ *vt* **-ticed, -tic•ing 6** observe, mention. **7** give attention to. **no'tice•a•ble** *adj* **1** conspicuous. **2** attracting attention. **3** appreciable.

no•ti•fy [NOH-tə-fī] *vt* **-fied, -fy•ing 1** report. **2** give notice of or to. **no•ti•fi•ca'tion** [-KAY-shən] *n*

no•tion [NOH-shən] *n* **1** concept. **2** opinion. **3** whim. ♦ *pl* **4** small items e.g. buttons, thread for sale in store. **no'tion•al** *adj* speculative, imaginary, abstract.

no•to•ri•ous [noh-TOR-ee-əs] *adj* **1** known for something bad. **2** well-known. **no•to•ri'e•ty** [-tə-RĪ-i-tee]) *n* discreditable publicity.

not•with•stand'ing *prep* **1** in spite of. ♦ *adv* **2** all the same. ♦ *conj* **3** although.

nou•gat [NOO-gət] *n* chewy candy containing nuts, fruit, etc.

nought [nawt] *n* **1** nothing. **2** figure 0.

noun [nown] *n* word used as name of person, idea, or thing, substantive.

nour•ish [NUR-ish] *vt* **1** feed. **2** nurture. **3** tend. **4** encourage.

nou•velle cui•sine [noo-vel kwee-ZEEN] *Fr* style of preparing and presenting food with light sauces and unusual combinations of flavors.

no•va [NOH-və] *n, pl* **-vas** star that suddenly becomes brighter then loses brightness through months or years.

nov•el¹ [NOV-əl] *n* fictitious tale in book form. **nov'el•ist** *n* writer of novels.

novel² *adj* **1** new, recent. **2** strange. **nov'el•ty** *n, pl* **-ties 1** newness. **2** something new or unusual. **3** small ornament, trinket.

no•ve•na [noh-VEE-nə] *n R.C. Church*

noted *adj* = **famous**, acclaimed, celebrated, distinguished, eminent, illustrious, notable, prominent, renowned, well-known

noteworthy *adj* = **remarkable**, exceptional, extraordinary, important, notable, outstanding, significant, unusual

nothing *n* = **nought**, emptiness, nada (*inf*), nil, nothingness, nullity, void, zero

nothingness *n* **1** = **oblivion**, nonbeing, nonexistence, nullity **2** = **insignificance**, unimportance, worthlessness

notice *n* **1** = **observation**, cognizance, consideration, heed, interest, note, regard **2** = **attention**, civility, respect **3** = **announcement**, advice, communication, instruction, intimation, news, notification, order, warning ♦ *v* **4** = **observe**, detect, discern, distinguish, mark, note, perceive, see, spot

noticeable *adj* = **obvious**, appreciable, clear, conspicuous, evident, manifest, perceptible, plain, striking

notification *n* = **announcement**, advice, declaration, information, intelligence, message, notice, statement, warning

notify *v* = **inform**, advise, alert, announce, declare, make known, publish, tell, warn

notion *n* **1** = **idea**, belief, concept, impression, inkling, opinion, sentiment, view **2** = **whim**, caprice, desire, fancy, impulse, inclination, wish

notional *adj* = **speculative**, abstract, conceptual, hypothetical, imaginary, theoretical, unreal

notoriety *n* = **scandal**, dishonor, disrepute, infamy, obloquy, opprobrium

notorious *adj* = **infamous**, dishonorable, disreputable, opprobrious, scandalous

notoriously *adv* = **infamously**, dishonorably, disreputably, opprobriously, scandalously

notwithstanding *prep* = **despite**, in spite of

nought *n* = **zero**, nil, nothing

nourish *v* **1** = **feed**, nurse, nurture, supply, sustain, tend **2** = **encourage**, comfort, cultivate, foster, maintain, promote, support

nourishing *adj* = **nutritious**, beneficial, nutritive, wholesome

nourishment *n* = **food**, nutriment, nutrition, sustenance

novel¹ *n* = **story**, fiction, narrative, romance, tale

novel² *adj* = **new**, different, fresh, innovative, original, strange, uncommon, unfamiliar, unusual

novelty *n* **1** = **newness**, freshness, innovation, oddity, originality, strangeness, surprise, unfamiliarity, uniqueness **2** = **gimmick**, curiosity, gadget **3** = **knick-knack**, bauble, memento, souvenir, prayers, services usu. extending over nine consecutive days.

nov·ice [NOV-is] n **1** one new to anything. **2** beginner. **3** candidate for admission to religious order. **no·vi·ti·ate** [noh-VISH-ee-it] n **1** probationary period. **2** part of religious house for novices. **3** novice.

now adv **1** at the present time. **2** immediately. **3** (oft. with *just*) recently. ◆ conj **4** seeing that, since. **now'a·days** adv in these times, at present.

no·where [NOH-hwair] adv not in any place or state.

no·wise [NOH-wiz] adv not in any manner or degree.

nox·ious [NOK-shəs] adj poisonous, harmful.

noz·zle [NOZ-əl] n pointed spout, esp. at end of hose.

Np Chem. neptunium.

NT New Testament.

nu·ance [NOO-ahns] n delicate shade of difference, in color, tone of voice, etc.

nub n **1** small lump. **2** main point (of story, etc.).

nu·bile [NOO-bil] adj marriageable. **nu·bil'i·ty** n

nu·cle·us [NOO-klee-əs] n, pl **-cle·i** [-klee-ī] **1** center, kernel. **2** beginning meant to receive additions. **3** core of the atom. **nu'cle·ar** [-klee-ər] adj of, pert. to atomic nucleus. **nuclear energy** energy released

by nuclear fission. **nuclear fission** disintegration of the atom. **nuclear reaction** change in structure and energy content of atomic nucleus by interaction with another nucleus, particle. **nuclear reactor** see REACTOR. **nuclear winter** period of extremely low temperatures and little light after nuclear war.

nude [nood] n **1** state of being naked. **2** (picture, statue, etc. of) naked person. ◆ adj **3** naked. **nud'ism** n practice of nudity. **nud'ist** n **nu'di·ty** n

nudge [nuj] vt **nudged, nudg·ing 1** touch slightly esp. with elbow to gain someone's attention, prod someone into action. ◆ n **2** such touch.

nu·ga·to·ry [NOO-gə-tor-ee] adj **1** trifling. **2** futile.

nug·get [NUG-it] n **1** rough lump of native gold. **2** anything of significance, value.

nui·sance [NOO-səns] n something or someone harmful, offensive, annoying or disagreeable.

null adj of no effect, void. **nul'li·fy** [-fī] vt **-fied, -fy·ing 1** cancel. **2** make useless or ineffective. **nul'li·ty** n state of being null and void.

Num. Numbers.

numb [num] adj **-er, -est 1** deprived of feeling, esp. by cold. ◆ vt **2** make numb. **3** deaden.

num·ber [NUM-bər] n **1** sum or aggregate.

---

trifle, trinket

novice n = **beginner**, amateur, apprentice, learner, newcomer, probationer, pupil, trainee

now adv **1** = **nowadays**, anymore, at the moment **2** = **immediately**, at once, instantly, promptly, straightaway **3 now and then** or **again** = **occasionally**, from time to time, infrequently, intermittently, on and off, sometimes, sporadically

nowadays adv = **now**, anymore, at the moment, in this day and age, today

noxious adj = **harmful**, deadly, destructive, foul, hurtful, injurious, poisonous, unhealthy, unwholesome

nuance n = **subtlety**, degree, distinction, gradation, nicety, refinement, shade, tinge

nubile adj = **marriageable**, ripe (inf)

nucleus n = **center**, basis, core, focus, heart, kernel, nub, pivot

nude adj = **naked**, bare, disrobed, in one's birthday suit, stark-naked, stripped,

unclad, unclothed, undressed, without a stitch on (inf)

nudge v = **push**, bump, dig, elbow, jog, poke, prod, shove, touch

nudity n = **nakedness**, bareness, deshabille, nudism, undress

nugget n = **lump**, chunk, clump, hunk, mass, piece

nuisance n = **problem**, annoyance, bother, drag (inf), hassle (inf), inconvenience, irritation, pain in the neck, pest, trouble

null adj **null and void** = **invalid**, inoperative, useless, valueless, void, worthless

nullify v = **cancel**, counteract, invalidate, negate, neutralize, obviate, render null and void, veto

nullity n = **nonexistence**, invalidity, powerlessness, uselessness, worthlessness

numb adj **1** = **unfeeling**, benumbed, dead, deadened, frozen, immobilized, insensitive, paralyzed, torpid ◆ v **2** = **deaden**, benumb, dull, freeze, immobilize,

2 word or symbol saying how many. **3** single issue of a journal, etc., issued in regular series. **4** classification as to singular or plural. **5** song, piece of music. **6** performance. **7** company, collection. **8** identifying number, as of particular house, telephone, etc. **9** *inf* measure, correct estimation of. ◆ *vt* **10** count. **11** class, reckon. **12** give a number to. **13** amount to. **num'ber·less** *adj* countless. **number crunching** *inf* large-scale processing of numerical data.

nu·mer·al [NOO-mər-əl] *n* sign or word denoting a number. **nu'mer·ate** *vt* **-at·ed, -at·ing** count. **nu·mer·a'tion** *n* **nu'mer·a·tor** *n* top part of fraction, figure showing how many of the fractional units are taken. **nu·mer'i·cal** *adj* of, in respect of, number or numbers. **nu'mer·ous** [-əs] *adj* many.

nu·mis·mat·ic [noo-miz-MAT-ik] *adj* of coins. **nu·mis·mat'ics** *n* the study of coins. **nu·mis'ma·tist** [-mə-tist] *n*

nun *n* woman living (in convent) under religious vows. **nun'ner·y** *n, pl* **-ies** convent of nuns.

nun·cu·pa·tive [NUNG-kyə-pay-tiv] *adj* **1** of a will, oral. **2** not written.

nup·tial [NUP-shəl] *adj* of, relating to marriage. **nup'tials** *pl. n* **1** marriage. **2** wedding ceremony.

nurse [nurs] *n* **1** person trained for care of sick or injured. **2** woman tending another's child. ◆ *vt* **nursed, nurs·ing 3** act as nurse to. **4** suckle. **5** pay special attention to. **6** harbor (grudge, etc.). **nurs'er·y** *n, pl* **-er·ies 1** room for children. **2** rearing place for plants. **nurs'er·y·man** [-mən] *n* one who raises plants for sale. **nursing home** institution for housing and caring for the aged or chronically ill.

nur·ture [NUR-chər] *n* **1** bringing up. **2** education. **3** rearing. **4** nourishment. ◆ *vt* **-tured, -tur·ing 5** bring up. **6** educate.

nut *n* **1** fruit consisting of hard shell and kernel. **2** hollow metal collar into which a screw fits. **3** *sl* the head. **4** *sl* eccentric or crazy person. ◆ *vi* **nut·ted, nut·ting 5** gather nuts. **nut'ty** *adj* **-ti·er, -ti·est 1** of, like nut. **2** pleasant to taste and bite. **3** *sl* insane, crazy. **4** eccentric. **nuts** *adj sl* insane. **nut'hatch** *n* small songbird. **nut'meg** *n* aromatic seed of Indian tree.

nu·tri·ent [NOO-tree-ənt] *adj* **1** nourishing. ◆ *n* **2** something nutritious.

nu·tri·ment [NOO-trə-mənt] *n* nourishing food. **nu·tri'tion** [-TRISH-ən] *n* **1** food. **2** act of nourishing. **3** study of this process. **nu·tri'tion·ist** *n* one trained in nutrition. **nu·tri'tious, nu'tri·tive** *adj* **1** nourishing. **2** promoting growth.

nuz·zle [NUZ-əl] *vi* **-zled, -zling 1** burrow,

THESAURUS

paralyze

number *n* **1** = **numeral**, character, digit, figure, integer **2** = **quantity**, aggregate, amount, collection, crowd, horde, multitude, throng **3** = **issue**, copy, edition, imprint, printing ◆ *v* **4** = **count**, account, add, calculate, compute, enumerate, include, reckon, total

numberless *adj* = **infinite**, countless, endless, innumerable, multitudinous, myriad, unnumbered, untold

numbness *n* = **deadness**, dullness, insensitivity, paralysis, torpor

numeral *n* = **number**, digit, figure, integer

numerous *adj* = **many**, abundant, copious, plentiful, profuse, several, thick on the ground

nunnery *n* = **convent**, abbey, cloister, house

nuptial *adj* = **marital**, bridal, conjugal, connubial, matrimonial

nuptials *pl n* = **wedding**, marriage, matrimony

nurse *v* **1** = **look after**, care for, minister to, tend, treat **2** = **breast-feed**, feed, nourish, nurture, suckle, wet-nurse **3** = **foster**, cherish, cultivate, encourage, harbor, preserve, promote, succor, support

nursery *n* = **creche**, kindergarten, playgroup

nurture *n* **1** = **development**, discipline, education, instruction, rearing, training, upbringing ◆ *v* **2** = **develop**, bring up, discipline, educate, instruct, rear, school, train

nut *n* **1** *Sl* = **madman**, crank (*inf*), lunatic, maniac, nutcase (*sl*), psycho (*sl*) **2** *Sl* = **head**, brain, mind, reason, senses

nutrition *n* = **food**, nourishment, nutriment, sustenance

nutritious *adj* = **nourishing**, beneficial, health-giving, invigorating, nutritive, strengthening, wholesome

nuts *adj Inf* = **insane**, deranged, disturbed, mad, mentally ill, psychotic, unbalanced, unstable press with nose. **2** nestle.

ny·lon [NĪ-lon] *n* **1** synthetic material used for fabrics, bristles, ropes, etc. ◆ *pl* **2** stockings made of this.

nymph [nimf] *n* legendary semidivine maiden of sea, woods, mountains, etc.

nym·pho·ma·ni·a [nim-fə-MAY-nee-ə] *n* abnormally intense sexual desire in women. **nym·pho·ma'ni·ac** *n*

──────┤ THESAURUS ├──────

nuzzle *v* = **snuggle**, burrow, cuddle, fondle, nestle, pet

nymph *n* = **sylph**, dryad, girl, maiden, naiad

O o

O *Chem.* oxygen.

oaf [ohf] *n* **1** lout. **2** dolt.

oak [ohk] *n* common, deciduous forest tree. **oak·en** [-in] *adj* of oak.

oa·kum [OH-kəm] *n* loose fiber, used for caulking, got by unraveling old rope.

oar [or] *n* **1** wooden lever with broad blade worked by the hands to propel boat. **2** oarsman. ◆ *v* **3** row. **oars·man** [ORZ-mən] *n, pl* **-men oars'manship** *n* skill in rowing.

o·a·sis [oh-AY-sis] *n, pl* **-ses** [-seez] **1** fertile spot in desert. **2** place serving as pleasant change from routine.

oat [oht] *n* (usu. pl) **1** grain of cereal grass. **2** the plant. **oat·en** [-in] *adj* **oat'meal** [-meel] *n*

oath [ohth] *n, pl* **oaths** [ohthz] **1** confirmation of truth of statement by naming something sacred. **2** curse.

ob·bli·ga·to [ob-li-GAH-toh] *adj, n, pl* **-tos** *or* **-ti** [-tee] **1** (in musical score) essential. **2** essential part of a musical score.

ob·du·rate [OB-duu-rit] *adj* stubborn, unyielding. **ob'du·ra·cy** [-rə-see] *n*

o·be·di·ence [oh-BEE-dee-əns] *n* submission to authority. **o·be'di·ent** *adj* **1** willing to obey. **2** compliant. **3** dutiful.

o·bei·sance [oh-BAY-səns] *n* **1** deference. **2** a bow or curtsy.

ob·e·lisk [OB-ə-lisk] *n* tapering rectangular stone column, with pyramidal apex.

o·bese [oh-BEES] *adj* very fat, corpulent. **o·be'si·ty** *n*

o·bey [oh-BAY] *vt* **1** do the bidding of. **2** act in accordance with. ◆ *vi* **3** do as ordered. **4** submit to authority.

ob·fus·cate [OB-fə-skayt] *vt* **-cat·ed, -cat·ing 1** perplex. **2** darken. **3** make obscure.

o·bit·u·ar·y [oh-BICH-oo-er-ee] *n, pl* **-ar·ies 1** notice, record of death. **2** biographical sketch of deceased person, esp. in newspaper (also **ob'it**).

ob·ject¹ [OB-jikt] *n* **1** material thing. **2** that to which feeling or action is directed. **3** end or aim. **4** *Grammar* word dependent on verb or preposition. **object lesson** lesson with practical and concrete illustration. **no object** not an obstacle or hindrance.

ob·ject² [əb-JEKT] *vt* **1** state in opposition. ◆ *vi* **2** feel dislike or reluctance to something. **ob·jec'tion** *n* **ob·jec'tion·a·ble** *adj* **1** disagreeable. **2** justly liable to objection.

ob·jec·tive [əb-JEK-tiv] *adj* **1** external to the

THESAURUS

oaf *n* = **idiot**, blockhead, clod, dolt, dork (*sl*), dunce, fool, goon, lout, moron, schmuck (*sl*)

oafish *adj* = **moronic**, dense, dim-witted (*inf*), doltish, dumb (*inf*), loutish, stupid, thick

oath *n* **1** = **promise**, affirmation, avowal, bond, pledge, vow, word **2** = **swearword**, blasphemy, curse, expletive, profanity

obdurate *adj* = **stubborn**, dogged, hard-hearted, immovable, implacable, inflexible, obstinate, pig-headed, unyielding

obedience *n* = **respect**, acquiescence, compliance, docility, observance, reverence, submissiveness, subservience

obedient *adj* = **respectful**, acquiescent,

biddable, compliant, deferential, docile, dutiful, submissive, subservient, well-trained

obelisk *n* = **column**, monolith, monument, needle, pillar, shaft

obese *adj* = **fat**, corpulent, gross, heavy, overweight, paunchy, plump, portly, rotund, stout, tubby

obesity *n* = **fatness**, bulk, corpulence, grossness, portliness, stoutness, tubbiness

obey *v* = **carry out**, abide by, act upon, adhere to, comply, conform, follow, heed, keep, observe

obfuscate *v* = **confuse**, befog, cloud, darken, muddy the waters, obscure, perplex

object¹ *n* **1** = **thing**, article, body, entity,

mind. **2** impartial. ◆ *n* **3** thing or place
aimed at. **ob·jec·tiv'i·ty** [ob-jek-TIV-] *n*
ob·jur·gate [OB-jər-gayt] *vt* **-gat·ed,**
-gat·ing scold, reprove. **ob·jur·ga'tion** *n*
ob·late [OB-layt] *adj* of a sphere, flattened
at the poles.
o·blige [ə-BLĪJ] *vt* **o·bliged, o·blig·ing 1**
bind morally or legally to do service to. **2**
compel. **ob'li·gate** *vt* **-gat·ed, -gat·ing 1**
bind esp. by legal contract. **2** put under
obligation. **ob·li·ga'tion** *n* **1** binding duty,
promise. **2** debt of gratitude. **o·blig'a·to·ry**
adj **1** required. **2** binding. **o·blig'ing** *adj*
ready to serve others, civil, helpful,
courteous.
o·blique [ə-BLEEK] *adj* **1** slanting. **2**
indirect. **o·blique'ly** *adv* **o·bliq'ui·ty**
[-BLIK-wi-tee] *n, pl* **-ties 1** slant. **2**
dishonesty. **oblique angle** one not a right

angle.
ob·lit·er·ate [ə-BLIT-ə-rayt] *vt* **-at·ed,**
-at·ing blot out, efface, destroy
completely.
ob·liv·i·on [ə-BLIV-ee-ən] *n* forgetting or
being forgotten. **ob·liv'i·ous** *adj* **1**
forgetful. **2** unaware.
ob·long [OB-lawng] *adj* **1** rectangular, with
adjacent sides unequal. ◆ *n* **2** oblong
figure.
ob·lo·quy [OB-lə-kwee] *n, pl* **-quies 1**
reproach, abuse. **2** disgrace. **3** detraction.
ob·nox·ious [əb-NOK-shəs] *adj* offensive,
disliked, odious.
o·boe [OH-boh] *n* woodwind instrument.
o'bo·ist *n*
ob·scene [əb-SEEN] *adj* indecent, lewd,
repulsive. **ob·scen'i·ty** [-SEN-i-tee] *n*
ob·scure [əb-SKYUUR] *adj* **-scur·er,**

——————| THESAURUS |——————

item, phenomenon **2** = **target**, focus,
recipient, victim **3** = **purpose**, aim, design,
end, goal, idea, intention, objective, point
object[2] *v* = **protest**, argue against, demur,
draw the line (at something), expostulate,
oppose, take exception
objection *n* = **protest**, counter-argument,
demur, doubt, opposition, remonstrance,
scruple
objectionable *adj* = **unpleasant**,
deplorable, disagreeable, intolerable,
obnoxious, offensive, regrettable,
repugnant, unseemly
objective *n* **1** = **purpose**, aim, ambition,
end, goal, intention, mark, object, target ◆
adj **2** = **unbiased**, detached, disinterested,
dispassionate, even-handed, fair, impartial,
open-minded, unprejudiced
objectively *adv* = **impartially**,
disinterestedly, dispassionately,
even-handedly, with an open mind
objectivity *n* = **impartiality**, detachment,
disinterestedness, dispassion
obligation *n* = **duty**, accountability,
burden, charge, compulsion, liability,
requirement, responsibility
obligatory *adj* = **compulsory**, binding, *de
rigueur*, essential, imperative, mandatory,
necessary, required, requisite, unavoidable
oblige *v* **1** = **compel**, bind, constrain, force,
impel, make, necessitate, require **2** =
indulge, accommodate, benefit, gratify,
please
obliged *adj* **1** = **grateful**, appreciative,
beholden, indebted, in (someone's) debt,

thankful **2** = **bound**, compelled, forced,
required
obliging *adj* = **cooperative**,
accommodating, agreeable, considerate,
good-natured, helpful, kind, polite, willing
oblique *adj* **1** = **slanting**, angled, aslant,
sloping, tilted **2** = **indirect**, backhanded,
circuitous, implied, roundabout, sidelong
obliterate *v* = **destroy**, annihilate, blot out,
efface, eradicate, erase, expunge,
extirpate, root out, wipe out
obliteration *n* = **annihilation**, elimination,
eradication, extirpation, wiping out
oblivion *n* **1** = **neglect**, abeyance,
disregard, forgetfulness **2** =
unconsciousness, insensibility,
obliviousness, unawareness
oblivious *adj* = **unaware**, forgetful,
heedless, ignorant, insensible, neglectful,
negligent, regardless, unconcerned,
unconscious, unmindful
obloquy *n* **1** = **abuse**, aspersion, attack,
blame, censure, criticism, invective,
reproach, slander, vilification **2** = **discredit**,
disgrace, dishonor, humiliation, ignominy,
infamy, shame, stigma
obnoxious *adj* = **offensive**, disagreeable,
insufferable, loathsome, nasty, nauseating,
objectionable, odious, repulsive, revolting,
scuzzy (*sl*), unpleasant
obscene *adj* **1** = **indecent**, dirty, filthy,
immoral, improper, lewd, offensive,
pornographic, salacious, scuzzy (*sl*),
X-rated **2** = **sickening**, atrocious,
disgusting, evil, heinous, loathsome,

-scur·est 1 unclear, indistinct. **2** unexplained. **3** dark, dim. **4** humble. ♦ *vt* **-scured, -scur·ing 5** make unintelligible. **6** dim. **7** conceal. **ob·scu·rant** [-SKYUUR-ənt] *n* one who opposes enlightenment or reform. **ob·scu·rant·ism** *n* **ob·scu·ri·ty** *n* **1** indistinctness. **2** lack of intelligibility. **3** darkness. **4** obscure, esp. unrecognized, place or position.

ob·se·quies [OB-si-kweez] *pl n* funeral rites.

ob·se·qui·ous [əb-SEE-kwee-əs] *adj* servile, fawning.

ob·serve [əb-ZURV] *v* **-served, -serv·ing** ♦ *vt* **1** notice, remark. **2** watch. **3** note systematically. **4** keep, follow. ♦ *vi* **5** make a remark. **ob·serv·a·ble** *adj* **ob·serv·ance** [-əns] *n* **1** paying attention. **2** keeping. **ob·serv·ant** *adj* **1** quick to notice. **2** careful in observing. **ob·ser·va·tion** *n* **1** action,

habit of observing. **2** noticing. **3** remark. **ob·serv·a·to·ry** [-və-tor-ee] *n, pl* **-ries** place for watching stars, etc.

ob·sess [əb-SES] *vt* haunt, fill the mind. **ob·ses·sion** [-SESH-ən] *n* **1** fixed idea. **2** domination of the mind by one idea. **ob·ses·sive** *adj*

ob·sid·i·an [əb-SID-ee-ən] *n* fused volcanic rock, forming hard, dark, natural glass.

ob·so·lete [ob-sə-LEET] *adj* disused, out of date. **ob·so·les·cent** [-LES-ənt] *adj* going out of use. passé

ob·sta·cle [OB-stə-kəl] *n* **1** hindrance. **2** impediment, barrier, obstruction.

ob·stet·rics [əb-STE-triks] *n* branch of medicine concerned with childbirth and care of women before and after childbirth. **ob·stet·ric** *adj* **ob·ste·tri·cian** [-shən] *n*

ob·sti·nate [OB-stə-nit] *adj* **1** stubborn. **2**

THESAURUS

outrageous, shocking, vile, wicked
obscenity *n* **1 = indecency**, coarseness, dirtiness, impropriety, lewdness, licentiousness, pornography, smut **2 = swearword**, four-letter word, profanity, vulgarism **3 = outrage**, abomination, affront, atrocity, blight, evil, offense, wrong
obscure *adj* **1 = vague**, ambiguous, arcane, confusing, cryptic, enigmatic, esoteric, mysterious, opaque, recondite **2 = indistinct**, blurred, cloudy, dim, faint, gloomy, murky, shadowy **3 = little-known**, humble, lowly, out-of-the-way, remote, undistinguished, unheard-of, unknown ♦ *v* **4 = conceal**, cover, disguise, hide, obfuscate, screen, veil
obscurity *n* **1 = darkness**, dimness, dusk, gloom, haze, shadows **2 = insignificance**, lowliness, unimportance
obsequious *adj* **= sycophantic**, cringing, deferential, fawning, flattering, grovelling, ingratiating, servile, submissive, unctuous
observable *adj* **= noticeable**, apparent, detectable, discernible, evident, obvious, perceptible, recognizable, visible
observance *n* **= honoring**, carrying out, compliance, fulfillment, performance
observant *adj* **= attentive**, alert, eagle-eyed, perceptive, quick, sharp-eyed, vigilant, watchful, wide-awake
observation *n* **1 = study**, examination, inspection, monitoring, review, scrutiny, surveillance, watching **2 = remark**,

comment, note, opinion, pronouncement, reflection, thought, utterance
observe *v* **1 = see**, detect, discern, discover, note, notice, perceive, spot, witness **2 = watch**, check, keep an eye on (*inf*), keep track of, look at, monitor, scrutinize, study, survey, view **3 = remark**, comment, mention, note, opine, say, state **4 = honor**, abide by, adhere to, comply, conform to, follow, heed, keep, obey, respect
observer *n* **= spectator**, beholder, bystander, eyewitness, fly on the wall, looker-on, onlooker, viewer, watcher, witness
obsessed *adj* **= preoccupied**, dominated, gripped, haunted, hung up on (*sl*), infatuated, troubled
obsession *n* **= preoccupation**, complex, fetish, fixation, hang-up (*inf*), infatuation, mania, phobia, thing (*inf*)
obsessive *adj* **= compulsive**, besetting, consuming, gripping, haunting
obsolescent *adj* **= waning**, ageing, declining, dying out, on the wane, on the way out, past its prime
obsolete *adj* **= extinct**, antiquated, archaic, discarded, disused, old, old-fashioned, outmoded, out of date
obstacle *n* **= difficulty**, bar, barrier, block, hindrance, hitch, hurdle, impediment, obstruction, snag, stumbling block
obstinacy *n* **= stubbornness**, doggedness, inflexibility, intransigence, obduracy,

self-willed. **3** unyielding. **4** hard to
overcome or cure. **ob'sti·na·cy** *n*

ob·strep·er·ous [əb-STREP-ər-əs] *adj*
unruly, noisy, boisterous.

ob·struct [əb-STRUKT] *vt* **1** block up. **2**
hinder. **3** impede. **ob·struc'tion** *n*
ob·struc'tion·ist *n* one who deliberately
opposes transaction of business.

ob·tain [əb-TAYN] *vt* **1** get. **2** acquire. **3**
procure by effort. ◆ *vi* **4** be customary.
ob·tain'a·ble *adj* procurable.

ob·trude [əb-TROOD] *vt* **-trud·ed, -trud·ing**
thrust forward unduly. **ob·tru'sion**
[-TROO-zhən] *n* **ob·tru'sive** *adj* forward,
pushing.

ob·tuse [əb-TOOS] *adj* **1** dull of
perception. **2** stupid. **3** greater than right
angle. **4** not pointed.

ob·verse [OB-vurs] *n* **1** a fact, idea, etc.
that is the complement of another. **2** side
of coin, medal, etc. that has the principal
design. ◆ *adj* [ob-VURS]

ob·vi·ate [OB-vee-ayt] *vt* **-at·ed, -at·ing**

remove, make unnecessary.

ob·vi·ous [OB-vee-əs] *adj* **1** clear, evident.
2 wanting in subtlety.

oc·ca·sion [ə-KAY-zhən] *n* **1** time when
thing happens. **2** reason, need. **3**
opportunity. **4** special event. ◆ *vt* **5** cause.
oc·ca'sion·al *adj* **1** happening, found now
and then. **2** produced for some special
event, e.g. *occasional music.* **oc·ca'sion·al·ly**
adv sometimes, now and then.

Oc·ci·dent [OK-si-dənt] *n* the West.
oc·ci·dent'al *adj*

oc·ci·put [OK-sə-put] *n* back of head.
oc·cip'i·tal *adj*

oc·clude [ə-KLOOD] *vt* **-clud·ed, -clud·ing**
shut in or out. **oc·clu'sion** [-zhən] *n*
oc·clu'sive *adj* serving to occlude.

oc·cult [ə-KULT] *adj* **1** secret, mysterious. **2**
supernatural. ◆ *n* **3** esoteric knowledge. ◆
vt **4** hide from view. **oc·cul·ta·tion**
[ok-əl-TAY-shən] *n* eclipse. **oc'cult·ism** *n*
study of supernatural.

oc·cu·py [OK-yə-pī] *vt* **-pied, -py·ing 1**

persistence, pig-headedness, tenacity,
willfulness

obstinate *adj* = **stubborn**, determined,
dogged, inflexible, intractable,
intransigent, pig-headed, refractory,
self-willed, strong-minded, willful

obstreperous *adj* = **unruly**, disorderly,
loud, noisy, riotous, rowdy, turbulent,
unmanageable, wild

obstruct *v* = **block**, bar, barricade, check,
hamper, hinder, impede, restrict, stop,
thwart

obstruction *n* = **obstacle**, bar, barricade,
barrier, blockage, difficulty, hindrance,
impediment

obstructive *adj* = **uncooperative**,
awkward, blocking, delaying, hindering,
restrictive, stalling, unhelpful

obtain *v* **1** = **get**, achieve, acquire, attain,
earn, gain, land, procure, secure **2** = **exist**,
be in force, be prevalent, be the case,
hold, prevail

obtainable *adj* = **available**, achievable,
attainable, on tap (*inf*), to be had

obtrusive *adj* = **noticeable**, blatant,
obvious, prominent, protruding,
protuberant, sticking out

obtuse *adj* = **slow**, dense, dull, stolid,
stupid, thick, uncomprehending

obviate *v* = **preclude**, avert, prevent,
remove

obvious *adj* = **evident**, apparent, clear,
conspicuous, distinct, indisputable,
manifest, noticeable, plain, self-evident,
undeniable, unmistakable

obviously *adv* = **clearly**, manifestly, of
course, palpably, patently, plainly,
undeniably, unmistakably, unquestionably,
without doubt

occasion *n* **1** = **time**, chance, moment,
opening, opportunity, window **2** = **event**,
affair, celebration, experience, happening,
occurrence **3** = **reason**, call, cause, excuse,
ground(s), justification, motive,
prompting, provocation ◆ *v* **4** = **cause**,
bring about, engender, generate, give rise
to, induce, inspire, lead to, produce,
prompt, provoke

occasional *adj* = **infrequent**, incidental,
intermittent, irregular, odd, rare, sporadic,
uncommon

occasionally *adv* = **sometimes**, at times,
from time to time, irregularly, now and
again, once in a while, periodically

occult *adj* = **supernatural**, arcane, esoteric,
magical, mysterious, mystical

occupancy *n* = **tenure**, possession,
residence, tenancy, use

occupant *n* = **inhabitant**, incumbent,
indweller, inmate, lessee, occupier,
resident, tenant

occupation *n* **1** = **profession**, business,

inhabit, fill. **2** employ. **3** take possession of.

oc·cu·pan·cy n **1** fact of occupying. **2** residing. **oc'cu·pant** n tenant.

oc·cu·pa'tion n **1** employment. **2** pursuit. **3** fact of occupying. **4** seizure.

oc·cu·pa'tion·al adj pert. to occupation, esp. of diseases arising from a particular occupation. **2** pert. to use of occupations, e.g. craft, hobbies, etc. as means of rehabilitation.

oc·cur [ə-KUR] vi -curred, -cur·ring **1** happen. **2** come to mind. **oc·cur'rence** n happening.

o·cean [OH-shən] n **1** great body of water. **2** large division of this. **3** the sea. **o·ce·an'ic** [-shee-AN-ik] adj **o·cea·nol·o·gy** [oh-shə-NOL-ə-jee] n branch of science that relates to ocean.

oc·e·lot [OS-ə-lot] n Amer. leopardlike cat.

o·cher [OH-kər] n **1** various earths used as yellow or brown pigments. **2** this color, from yellow to brown.

o'clock [ə-KLOK] adv by the clock.

oct-, octa-, octo- comb. form eight, e.g. octagon; octopus.

oc·ta·gon [OK-tə-gon] n plane figure with eight angles. **oc·tag'o·nal** adj

oc·tane [OK-tayn] n ingredient of gasoline. **octane number** measure of ability of gasoline to reduce engine knock.

oc·tave [OK-tiv] n Mus. **1** eighth note

above or below given note. **2** this space.

oc·ta·vo [ok-TAY-voh] n, pl **-vos** book in which each sheet is folded three times forming eight leaves.

oc·tet [ok-TET] n **1** group of eight. **2** music for eight instruments or singers.

oc·to·ge·nar·i·an [ok-tə-jə-NAIR-ee-ən] n person aged between eighty and ninety. ◆ adj

oc·to·pus [OK-tə-pəs] n mollusk with eight arms covered with suckers. **oc·to·pod** n, adj (mollusk) with eight feet.

oc·tu·ple [ok-TUU-pəl] adj **1** eight times as many or as much. **2** eightfold.

oc·u·lar [OK-yə-lər] adj of eye or sight.

OD [oh-DEE] n **1** overdose esp. of dangerous drug. **2** person who has taken overdose. ◆ v **-ed, -ing 3** take, die of, overdose.

odd adj **-er, -est 1** strange, queer. **2** incidental, random. **3** that is one in addition when the rest have been divided into equal groups. **4** not even. **5** not part of a set. **odds** pl n **1** advantage conceded in betting. **2** likelihood. **odd'i·ty** n, pl **-ties 1** odd person or thing. **2** quality of being odd. **odd'ments** [-mənts] pl n **1** remnants. **2** trifles. **odds and ends** odd fragments or scraps.

ode [ohd] n lyric poem on particular subject.

———— THESAURUS ————

calling, employment, job, line (of work), pursuit, trade, vocation, walk of life **2 = possession**, control, holding, occupancy, residence, tenancy, tenure **3 = invasion**, conquest, seizure, subjugation

occupied adj **1 = busy**, employed, engaged, working **2 = in use**, engaged, full, taken, unavailable **3 = inhabited**, lived-in, peopled, settled, tenanted

occupy v **1** (often passive) **= take up**, divert, employ, engage, engross, involve, monopolize, preoccupy, tie up **2 = live in**, dwell, inhabit, own, possess, reside in **3 = fill**, cover, permeate, pervade, take up **4 = invade**, capture, overrun, seize, take over

occur v **1 = happen**, befall, come about, crop up (inf), take place, turn up (inf) **2 = exist**, appear, be found, be present, develop, manifest itself, show itself **3 occur to = come to mind**, cross one's mind, dawn on, enter one's head, spring to mind, strike one, suggest itself

occurrence n **1 = incident**, adventure, affair, circumstance, episode, event, happening, instance **2 = existence**, appearance, development, materialization

odd adj **1 = unusual**, bizarre, extraordinary, freakish, irregular, peculiar, rare, remarkable, singular, strange **2 = occasional**, casual, incidental, irregular, periodic, random, sundry, various **3 = spare**, leftover, remaining, solitary, surplus, unmatched, unpaired

oddity n **1 = irregularity**, abnormality, anomaly, eccentricity, freak, idiosyncrasy, peculiarity, quirk **2 = misfit**, crank (inf), maverick, oddball (inf)

oddment n **= leftover**, bit, fag end, fragment, off cut, remnant, scrap, snippet

odds pl n **1 = probability**, chances, likelihood **2 at odds = in conflict**, at daggers drawn, at loggerheads, at sixes and sevens, at variance, out of line

odds and ends pl n **= scraps**, bits, bits

o·di·um [OH-dee-əm] *n* hatred, widespread dislike. **o'di·ous** *adj* hateful, repulsive, obnoxious.

o·dor [OH-dər] *n* smell. **o·dor·if·er·ous** [oh-də-RIF-ər-əs] *adj* spreading an odor. **o'dor·ize** *vt* **-ized, -iz·ing** fill with scent. **o'dor·ous** *adj* **1** fragrant. **2** scented. **o'dor·less** [-lis] *adj*

od·ys·sey [OD-ə-see] *n. pl* **-seys** any long adventurous journey.

of [əv] *prep* denotes removal, separation, ownership, attribute, material, quality.

off [awf] *adv* **1** away. ◆ *prep* **2** away from. ◆ *adj* **3** not operative. **4** canceled or postponed. **5** bad, sour, etc. **6** distant. **7** of horses, vehicles, etc., to driver's right. **off-color** *adj* **1** slightly ill. **2** risqué. **off-hand'** *adj, adv* **1** without previous thought. **2** curt. **off-line'** *adj* **1** (of a computer) not directly controlled by a central processor. **2** not connected to or done via the Internet. ◆ *adv* **off-mes·sage** *adj* not following the official line, not saying what is expected. **off-road** *adj* (of a motor vehicle) designed for use away from public roads. **off'set** *n* **1** that which

counterbalances, compensates. **2** method of printing. **off·set'** *vt* **off'spring** *n* children, issue. **in the offing** likely to happen soon.

of·fal [AW-fəl] *n* **1** edible entrails of animal. **2** refuse.

of·fend [ə-FEND] *vt* **1** hurt feelings of, displease. ◆ *vi* **2** do wrong. **of·fense'** *n* **1** wrong. **2** crime. **3** insult. **4** *Sports, military* attacking team, force. **of·fen'sive** *adj* **1** causing displeasure. **2** aggressive. ◆ *n* **3** position or movement of attack.

of·fer [AW-fər] *vt* **1** present for acceptance or refusal. **2** tender. **3** propose. **4** attempt. ◆ *vi* **5** present itself. ◆ *n* **6** offering, bid. **of'fer·er, -or** *n* **of'fer·to·ry** *n, pl* **-ies 1** offering of the bread and wine at the Eucharist. **2** collection in church service.

of·fice [AW-fis] *n* **1** room(s), building, in which business, clerical work, etc. is done. **2** commercial or professional organization. **3** official position. **4** service. **5** duty. **6** form of worship. ◆ *pl* **7** task. **8** service. **of'fi·cer** *n* **1** one in command in army, navy, etc. **2** official.

of·fi·cial [ə-FISH-əl] *adj* **1** with, by,

and pieces, debris, oddments, remnants

odious *adj* = **offensive**, detestable, horrid, loathsome, obnoxious, repulsive, revolting, scuzzy (*sl*), unpleasant

odor *n* = **smell**, aroma, bouquet, essence, fragrance, perfume, redolence, scent, stench, stink

odyssey *n* = **journey**, crusade, pilgrimage, quest, trek, voyage

off *adv* **1** = **away**, apart, aside, elsewhere, out ◆ *adj* **2** = **unavailable**, canceled, finished, gone, postponed

offbeat *adj* = **unusual**, eccentric, left-field (*inf*), novel, outré, strange, unconventional, unorthodox, way-out (*inf*)

off color *adj* = **ill**, out of sorts, peaky, poorly (*inf*), queasy, run down, sick, under the weather (*inf*), unwell

offend *v* = **insult**, affront, annoy, displease, hurt (someone's) feelings, outrage, slight, snub, upset

offended *adj* = **resentful**, affronted, disgruntled, displeased, outraged, piqued, put out (*inf*), smarting, stung, upset

offender *n* = **criminal**, crook, culprit, delinquent, lawbreaker, miscreant, sinner, transgressor, villain, wrongdoer

offense *n* **1** = **crime**, fault, misdeed,

misdemeanor, sin, transgression, trespass, wrongdoing **2** = **snub**, affront, hurt, indignity, injustice, insult, outrage, slight **3** = **annoyance**, anger, displeasure, indignation, pique, resentment, umbrage, wrath

offensive *adj* **1** = **insulting**, abusive, discourteous, disrespectful, impertinent, insolent, objectionable, rude **2** = **disagreeable**, disgusting, nauseating, obnoxious, odious, repellent, revolting, unpleasant, vile **3** = **aggressive**, attacking, invading ◆ *n* **4** = **attack**, campaign, drive, onslaught, push (*inf*)

offer *v* **1** = **bid**, proffer, tender **2** = **provide**, afford, furnish, present **3** = **propose**, advance, submit, suggest **4** = **volunteer**, come forward, offer one's services ◆ *n* **5** = **bid**, proposal, proposition, submission, suggestion, tender

offering *n* = **donation**, contribution, gift, hand-out, present, sacrifice, subscription

offhand *adj* **1** = **casual**, aloof, brusque, careless, curt, glib ◆ *adv* **2** = **impromptu**, ad lib, extempore, off the cuff (*inf*)

office *n* = **post**, function, occupation, place, responsibility, role, situation

officer *n* = **official**, agent, appointee,

authority. ♦ n 2 one holding office, esp. in public body. **of·fi'cial·dom** [-dəm] n officials collectively, or their attitudes, work, usu. in contemptuous sense.

of·fi·ci·ate [ə-FISH-ee-ayt] vi -at·ed, -at·ing 1 perform duties of office. 2 perform ceremony.

of·fi·cious [ə-FISH-əs] adj 1 objectionably persistent in offering service. 2 interfering.

of·ten [AW-fən] adv many times, frequently. **oft** adv poet often.

o·gle [OH-gəl] v o·gled, o·gling 1 stare, look (at) amorously. ♦ n 2 this look. **o'gler** n

o·gre [OH-gər] n Folklore 1 man-eating giant. 2 monster.

ohm n unit of electrical resistance. **ohm'me·ter** [-ee-tər] n

oil n 1 any of a number of viscous liquids with smooth, sticky feel and wide variety of uses. 2 petroleum. 3 any of variety of petroleum derivatives, esp. as fuel or lubricant. ♦ vt 4 lubricate with oil. 5 apply oil to. **oil'y** adj oil·i·er, oil·i·est **oil'skin** n cloth treated with oil to make it waterproof. **oiled** sl drunk.

oint·ment [OINT-mənt] n greasy preparation for healing or beautifying the skin.

OK, o·kay [oh-kay] adj, adv inf 1 all right. ♦ n, pl **OK's** 2 approval. ♦ vt **OK'd, OK'ing** 3 approve.

o·ka·pi [oh-KAH-pee] n, pl -pis Afr. animal like short-necked giraffe.

old [ohld] adj old·er, old·est or eld·er eld·est 1 aged, having lived or existed long. 2 belonging to earlier period. **old-fash'ioned** [-FASH-ənd] adj 1 in style of earlier period, out of date. 2 fond of old ways. **old maid** offens 1 elderly spinster. 2 fussy person.

o·le·ag·i·nous [oh-lee-AJ-ə-nəs] adj oily, producing oil. 2 unctuous, fawning.

ol·fac·to·ry [ohl-FAK-tə-ree] adj of smelling.

ol·i·gar·chy [OL-i-gahr-kee] n, pl -chies government by a few. **ol·i·gar'chic** adj

ol·ive [OL-iv] n 1 evergreen tree. 2 its oil-yielding fruit. 3 its wood, color. ♦ adj 4 grayish-green.

O·lym·pi·ad [ə-LIM-pee-ad] n 1 four-year period between Olympic games. 2 celebration of modern Olympic games.

om·buds·man [OM-bədz-mən] n, pl -men 1 official who investigates citizens' complaints against government. 2 person

——— THESAURUS ———

executive, functionary, office-holder, representative

official adj 1 = **authorized**, accredited, authentic, certified, formal, legitimate, licensed, proper, sanctioned ♦ n 2 = **officer**, agent, bureaucrat, executive, functionary, office bearer, representative

officiate v = **preside**, chair, conduct, manage, oversee, serve, superintend

officious adj = **interfering**, dictatorial, intrusive, meddlesome, obtrusive, overzealous, pushy (inf), self-important

offing n **in the offing** = **in prospect**, imminent, on the horizon, upcoming

offset v = **cancel out**, balance out, compensate for, counteract, counterbalance, make up for, neutralize

offshoot n = **by-product**, adjunct, appendage, development, spin-off

offspring n 1 = **child**, descendant, heir, scion, successor 2 = **children**, brood, descendants, family, heirs, issue, progeny, young

often adv = **frequently**, generally, repeatedly, time and again

ogle v = **leer**, eye up (inf)

ogre n = **monster**, bogeyman, bugbear, demon, devil, giant, specter

oil v = **lubricate**, grease

oily adj = **greasy**, fatty, oleaginous

ointment n = **lotion**, balm, cream, embrocation, emollient, liniment, salve, unguent

O.K., okay interj 1 = **all right**, agreed, right, roger, very good, very well, yes ♦ adj 2 = **all right**, acceptable, adequate, fine, good, in order, permitted, satisfactory, up to scratch (inf) ♦ v 3 = **approve**, agree to, authorize, endorse, give the green light, rubber-stamp (inf), sanction ♦ n 4 = **approval**, agreement, assent, authorization, consent, go-ahead (inf), green light, permission, sanction, say-so (inf), seal of approval

old adj 1 = **senile**, aged, ancient, decrepit, elderly, mature, venerable 2 = **antique**, antediluvian, antiquated, dated, obsolete, timeworn, one-time, previous 3 = **former**, earlier, erstwhile, one-time, previous

old-fashioned adj = **out of date**, behind the times, dated, obsolescent, obsolete, old hat, outdated, outmoded, passé, appointed to perform analogous function in a business.

o•me•ga [oh-MAY-gə] *n* **1** last letter of Greek alphabet. **2** end.

om•e•let [OM-lit] *n* dish of eggs beaten up and cooked in melted butter with other ingredients and seasoning.

o•men [OH-mən] *n* prophetic object or happening. **om•i•nous** [OM-ə-nəs] *adj* boding evil, threatening.

o•mit [oh-MIT] *vt* **o•mit•ted, o•mit•ting 1** leave out, neglect. **2** leave undone. **o•mis•sion** [-MISH-ən] *n*

omni- *comb. form* all, e.g. *omnipresent.*

om•ni•bus [OM-nə-bəs] *n* **1** bus. **2** book containing several works. ♦ *adj* **3** serving, containing several objects or subjects.

om•ni•di•rec•tion•al *adj* [om-nə-di-REK-shə-nl] in radio, denotes transmission, reception in all directions.

om•nip•o•tent [om-NIP-ə-tənt] *adj* all-powerful. **om•nip'o•tence** *n*

om•ni•pres•ent [om-nə-PREZ-ənt] *adj* present everywhere. **om•ni•pres'ence** *n*

om•nis•cient [om-NISH-ənt] *adj* knowing everything. **om•nis'cience** *n*

om•niv•o•rous [om-NIV-ər-əs] *adj* **1** devouring all foods. **2** not selective e.g. in reading.

on *prep* **1** above and touching, at, near, toward, etc. **2** attached to. **3** concerning. **4** performed upon. **5** during. **6** taking regularly. ♦ *adj* **7** operating. **8** taking place. ♦ *adv* **9** so as to be on. **10** forward. **11** continuously, etc. **12** in progress. **on•line'**

adj **1** (of a computer) directly controlled by a central processor. **2** connected to, or done via, the Internet. ♦ *adv* **on-mes'sage** *adj* following the official line, saying what is expected.

o•nan•ism [OH-nə-niz-əm] *n* masturbation.

once [wuns] *adv* **1** one time. **2** formerly. **3** ever. **once'-o•ver** *n inf* quick examination. **at once 1** immediately. **2** simultaneously.

on•co•gene [ONG-kə-jeen] *n* any of several genes that when abnormally activated can cause cancer. **on•co•gen'ic** *adj*

on•col•o•gy [ong-KOL-ə-jee] *n* **1** branch of medicine dealing with tumors. **2** study of cancer.

one [wun] *adj* **1** lowest cardinal number. **2** single. **3** united. **4** only, without others. **5** identical. ♦ *n* **6** number or figure 1. **7** single specimen. ♦ *pron* **9** particular but not stated person. **10** any person. **one'ness** *n* **1** unity. **2** uniformity. **3** singleness. **one•self'** *pron* **one'-sid•ed** *adj* **1** partial. **2** uneven. **one-way** *adj* denotes system of traffic circulation in one direction only.

on•er•ous [ON-ər-əs] *adj* burdensome.

on•ion [UN-yən] *n* edible bulb of pungent flavor. **know one's onions** *sl* know one's field, etc. thoroughly.

on•ly [OHN-lee] *adj* **1** being the one specimen. ♦ *adv* **2** solely, merely, exclusively. ♦ *conj* **3** but then, excepting that.

on•o•mas•tics [on-ə-MAS-tiks] *n* study of proper names.

unfashionable

omen *n* = **sign**, foreboding, indication, portent, premonition, presage, warning

ominous *adj* = **sinister**, fateful, foreboding, inauspicious, portentous, threatening, unpromising, unpropitious

omission *n* = **exclusion**, failure, lack, neglect, oversight

omit *v* = **leave out**, drop, eliminate, exclude, forget, neglect, overlook, pass over, skip

omnipotence *n* = **supremacy**, invincibility, mastery

omnipotent *adj* = **almighty**, all-powerful, supreme

omniscient *adj* = **all-knowing**, all-wise

once *adv* **1** = **formerly**, at one time, long ago, once upon a time, previously **2 at once: a** = **immediately**, directly, forthwith,

instantly, now, right away, straight away, this (very) minute **b** = **simultaneously**, at the same time, together

oncoming *adj* = **approaching**, advancing, forthcoming, looming, onrushing

onerous *adj* = **difficult**, burdensome, demanding, exacting, hard, heavy, laborious, oppressive, taxing

one-sided *adj* = **biased**, lopsided, partial, partisan, prejudiced, unfair, unjust

ongoing *adj* = **evolving**, continuous, developing, progressing, unfinished, unfolding

onlooker *n* = **observer**, bystander, eyewitness, looker-on, spectator, viewer, watcher, witness

only *adj* **1** = **sole**, exclusive, individual, lone, single, solitary, unique ♦ *adv* **2** = **merely**, barely, just, purely, simply

on·o·mat·o·poe·ia [on-ə-mat-ə-PEE-ə] *n* formation of a word by using sounds that resemble or suggest the object or action to be named. **on·o·mat·o·poe'ic, on·o·mat·o·po·et'ic** *adj*

on·set *n* **1** violent attack. **2** assault. **3** beginning.

on·slaught [ON-slawt] *n* attack.

on·to [ON-too] *prep* **1** on top of. **2** aware of.

on·tog·e·ny [on-TOJ-ə-nee] *n* development of an individual organism.

on·tol·o·gy [on-TOL-ə-jee] *n* science of being or reality.

o·nus [OH-nəs] *n, pl* **-nus·es** responsibility, burden.

on·ward [ON-wərd] *adj* **1** advanced or advancing. ♦ *adv* **2** in advance, ahead, forward. **on'wards** *adv*

on·yx [ON-iks] *n* variety of chalcedony.

ooze [ooz] *vi* **oozed, ooz·ing 1** pass slowly out, exude (moisture). ♦ *n* **2** sluggish flow. **3** wet mud, slime.

o·pal [OH-pəl] *n* glassy gemstone displaying variegated colors. **o·pal·es'cent** *adj*

o·paque [oh-PAYK] *adj* not allowing the passage of light, not transparent. **o·pac'i·ty** [-PAS-i-tee] *n*

op. cit. [op sit] in the work cited.

o·pen [OH-pən] *adj* **1** not shut or blocked up. **2** without lid or door. **3** bare. **4** undisguised. **5** not enclosed, covered or exclusive. **6** spread out, accessible. **7** frank, sincere. ♦ *vt* **8** set open, uncover, give access to. **9** disclose, lay bare. **10** begin. **11** make a hole in. ♦ *vi* **12** become open. **13** begin. ♦ *n* **14** clear space, unenclosed country. **15** *Sports* competition in which all may enter. **o'pen·ing** *n* **1** hole, gap. **2** beginning. **3** opportunity. ♦ *adj* **4** first. **5** initial. **o'pen·ly** *adv* without concealment. **o'pen·hand'ed** *adj* generous. **o'pen·heart'ed** *adj* frank, magnanimous. **o'pen·mind'ed** *adj* unprejudiced. **o'pen·work** *n* pattern with interstices.

op·er·a [OP-ər-ə] *n* musical drama. **op·er·at'ic** *adj* of opera. **op·er·et'ta** *n* light, comic opera.

op·er·a·tion [op-ə-RAY-shən] *n* **1** working, way things work. **2** scope. **3** act of surgery. **4** military action. **op'er·ate** *v* **-at·ed, -at·ing** ♦ *vt* **1** cause to function. **2** effect. ♦ *vi* **3** work. **4** produce an effect. **5** perform act of surgery. **6** exert power. **op·er·a'tion·al** *adj* **1** of operation(s). **2** working. **op'er·a·tive** [-ə-tiv] *adj* **1** working. ♦ *n* **2** worker, esp. with a special skill. **3** secret agent.

THESAURUS

onset *n* = **beginning**, inception, outbreak, start

onslaught *n* = **attack**, assault, blitz, charge, offensive, onrush, onset

onus *n* = **burden**, liability, load, obligation, responsibility, task

onward, onwards *adv* = **ahead**, beyond, forth, forward, in front, on

ooze[1] *v* = **seep**, drain, dribble, drip, escape, filter, leak

ooze[2] *n* = **mud**, alluvium, mire, silt, slime, sludge

opaque *adj* = **cloudy**, dim, dull, filmy, hazy, impenetrable, muddy, murky

open *adj* **1** = **unfastened**, agape, ajar, gaping, uncovered, unfolded, unfurled, unlocked, yawning **2** = **accessible**, available, free, public, unoccupied, unrestricted, vacant **3** = **unresolved**, arguable, debatable, moot, undecided, unsettled **4** = **frank**, candid, guileless, honest, sincere, transparent ♦ *v* **5** = **start**, begin, commence, inaugurate, initiate, kick off (*inf*), launch, set in motion **6** = **unfasten**, unblock, uncork, uncover, undo,

unlock, untie, unwrap **7** = **unfold**, expand, spread (out), unfurl, unroll

open-air *adj* = **outdoor**, alfresco

open-handed *adj* = **generous**, bountiful, free, lavish, liberal, munificent, unstinting

opening *n* **1** = **hole**, aperture, chink, cleft, crack, fissure, gap, orifice, perforation, slot, space **2** = **opportunity**, chance, occasion, vacancy **3** = **beginning**, commencement, dawn, inception, initiation, launch, outset, start ♦ *adj* **4** = **first**, beginning, inaugural, initial, introductory, maiden, primary

openly *adv* = **candidly**, forthrightly, frankly, overtly, plainly, unhesitatingly, unreservedly

open-minded *adj* = **tolerant**, broad-minded, impartial, liberal, reasonable, receptive, unbiased, undogmatic, unprejudiced

operate *v* **1** = **work**, act, function, go, perform, run **2** = **handle**, be in charge of, manage, maneuver, use, work

operation *n* = **procedure**, action, course, exercise, motion, movement, performance, process

o·phid·i·an [oh-FID-ee-ən] *adj, n* (reptile) of the order including snakes.

oph·thal·mic [of-THAL-mik] *adj* of eyes. **oph·thal·mol·o·gist** [-jist] *n* **oph·thal·mol·o·gy** *n* study of eye and its diseases. **oph·thal·mo·scope** [-skohp] *n* instrument for examining interior of eye.

opiate see OPIUM.

o·pin·ion [ə-PIN-yən] *n* **1** what one thinks about something. **2** belief, judgment. **o·pine** [oh-PIN] *vt* **o·pined, o·pin·ing 1** think. **2** utter opinion. **o·pin·ion·at·ed** *adj* **1** stubborn in one's opinions. **2** dogmatic.

o·pi·um [OH-pee-əm] *n* sedative-narcotic drug made from poppy. **o'pi·ate** [-it] *n* **1** drug containing opium. **2** narcotic. ◆ *adj* **3** inducing sleep. **4** soothing.

o·pos·sum [ə-POS-əm] *n* small Amer. marsupial animal, possum.

op·po·nent [ə-POH-nənt] *n* adversary, antagonist.

op·por·tune [op-ər-TOON] *adj* seasonable, well-timed. **op·por·tun'ism** *n* policy of doing what is expedient at the time regardless of principle. **op·por·tun'ist** *n, adj* **op·por·tu'ni·ty** *n, pl* **-ties 1** favorable time or condition. **2** good chance.

op·pose [ə-POHZ] *vt* **-posed, -pos·ing 1** resist, withstand. **2** contrast. **3** set against. **op·po·site** [OP-ə-zit] *adj* **1** contrary. **2** facing. **3** diametrically different. **4** adverse. ◆ *n* **5** the contrary. ◆ *prep, adv* **6** facing. **7** on the other side. **op·po·si'tion** [-ZISH-ən] *n* **1** antithesis. **2** resistance. **3** obstruction. **4** hostility. **5** group opposing another. **6** party opposing that in power.

op·press [ə-PRES] *vt* **1** govern with tyranny. **2** weigh down. **op·pres'sion** [-PRESH-ən] *n* **1** act of oppressing. **2** severity. **3** misery. **op·pres'sive** *adj* **1** tyrannical. **2** hard to bear. **3** heavy. **4** hot and tiring (of weather). **op·pres'sor** [-ər] *n*

op·pro·bri·um [ə-PROH-bree-əm] *n* disgrace. **op·pro'bri·ous** *adj* **1** reproachful. **2** shameful. **3** abusive.

opt *vi* make a choice. **op'ta·tive** [OP-tə-tiv]

———————— THESAURUS ————————

operational *adj* = **working**, functional, going, operative, prepared, ready, up and running, usable, viable, workable

operative *adj* **1** = **in force**, active, effective, functioning, in operation, operational ◆ *n* **2** = **worker**, artisan, employee, laborer

operator *n* = **worker**, conductor, driver, handler, mechanic, operative, practitioner, technician

opinion *n* = **belief**, assessment, feeling, idea, impression, judgment, point of view, sentiment, theory, view

opinionated *adj* = **dogmatic**, bigoted, cocksure, doctrinaire, overbearing, pig-headed, prejudiced, single-minded

opponent *n* = **competitor**, adversary, antagonist, challenger, contestant, enemy, foe, rival

opportune *adj* = **timely**, advantageous, appropriate, apt, auspicious, convenient, favorable, fitting, suitable, well-timed

opportunism *n* = **expediency**, exploitation, pragmatism, unscrupulousness

opportunity *n* = **chance**, moment, occasion, opening, scope, time

oppose *v* = **fight**, block, combat, counter, defy, resist, take issue with, take on, thwart, withstand

opposed *adj* = **averse**, antagonistic, clashing, conflicting, contrary, dissentient, hostile

opposing *adj* = **hostile**, conflicting, contrary, enemy, incompatible, opposite, rival

opposite *adj* **1** = **facing**, fronting **2** = **different**, antithetical, conflicting, contrary, contrasted, reverse, unlike ◆ *n* **3** = **reverse**, antithesis, contradiction, contrary, converse, inverse

opposition *n* **1** = **hostility**, antagonism, competition, disapproval, obstruction, prevention, resistance, unfriendliness **2** = **opponent**, antagonist, competition, foe, other side, rival

oppress *v* **1** = **depress**, afflict, burden, dispirit, harass, sadden, torment, vex **2** = **persecute**, abuse, maltreat, subdue, subjugate, suppress, wrong

oppressed *adj* = **downtrodden**, abused, browbeaten, disadvantaged, harassed, maltreated, tyrannized, underprivileged

oppression *n* = **persecution**, abuse, brutality, cruelty, injury, injustice, maltreatment, subjection, tyranny

oppressive *adj* **1** = **tyrannical**, brutal, cruel, despotic, harsh, inhuman, repressive, severe, unjust **2** = **sultry**, airless, close, muggy, stifling, stuffy

oppressor *n* = **persecutor**, autocrat, bully, despot, scourge, slave-driver, tormentor, tyrant *adj* expressing wish or desire.

op·tic [OP-tik] *adj* **1** of eye or sight. ◆ *n* **2** eye. **optics** *n* science of sight and light. **op'ti·cal** *adj* **optical character reader** device for scanning magnetically coded data on labels, cans, etc. **op·ti'cian** [-TISH-ən] *n* maker of, dealer in eyeglasses, contact lenses.

op·ti·mism [OP-tə-miz-əm] *n* **1** disposition to look on the bright side. **2** doctrine that good must prevail in the end. **3** belief that the world is the best possible world. **op'ti·mist** *n* **op·ti·mis'tic** *adj*

op·ti·mum [OP-tə-məm] *adj*, *n* the best, the most favorable.

op·tion [OP-shən] *n* **1** choice. **2** preference. **3** thing chosen. **4** in business, purchased privilege of either buying or selling things at specified price within specified time. **op'tion·al** *adj* leaving to choice.

op·tom·e·trist [op-TOM-i-trist] *n* person qualified to examine eyesight, prescribing corrective lenses, etc. **op·tom'e·try** *n*

op·u·lent [OP-yə-lənt] *adj* **1** rich. **2** copious. **op'u·lence** *n* riches, wealth.

o·pus [OH-pəs] *n*, *pl* **o·pus·es** or **op·er·a** [OHP-ə-rə] **1** work. **2** musical composition, e.g. *Grieg's opus 53*.

or *conj* **1** introduces alternatives. **2** if not.

or·a·cle [OR-ə-kəl] *n* **1** divine utterance, prophecy, oft. ambiguous, given at shrine of god. **2** the shrine. **3** wise or mysterious adviser. **o·rac·u·lar** [aw-RAK-yə-lər] *adj* **1** of oracle. **2** prophetic. **3** authoritative. **4** ambiguous.

o·ral [OR-əl] *adj* **1** spoken. **2** by mouth. ◆ *n* **3** spoken examination. **o'ral·ly** *adv*

or·ange [OR-inj] *n* **1** bright reddish-yellow round fruit. **2** tree bearing it. **3** fruit's color.

o·rang·u·tan [aw-RANG-uu-tan] *n* large E. Indian ape.

or·a·tor [OR-ə-tər] *n* **1** maker of speech. **2** skillful speaker. **o·ra'tion** [aw-RAY-shən] *n* formal speech. **or·a·tor'i·cal** *adj* of orator or oration. **or'a·to·ry** *n* **1** speeches. **2** eloquence. **3** small private chapel.

or·a·to·ri·o [or-ə-TOR-ee-oh] *n*, *pl* **-ri·os** semidramatic composition of sacred music.

orb *n* **1** globe, sphere. **2** eye, eyeball.

or·bit *n* **1** track of planet, satellite, comet, etc., around another heavenly body. **2** field of influence, sphere. **3** eye socket. ◆ *v* **4** move in, or put into, an orbit.

or·chard [OR-chərd] *n* **1** area for cultivation of fruit trees. **2** the trees.

or·ches·tra [OR-kə-strə] *n* **1** band of musicians. **2** place for such band in theater, etc. **or·ches'tral** *adj* **or'ches·trate** *vt* **-trat·ed, -trat·ing 1** compose or arrange music for orchestra. **2** organize, arrange.

or·chid [OR-kid] *n* genus of various

──── THESAURUS ────

opt *v* (often with *for*) = **choose**, decide (on), elect, go for, plump for, prefer

optimistic *adj* = **hopeful**, buoyant, cheerful, confident, encouraged, expectant, positive, rosy, sanguine

optimum *adj* = **ideal**, best, highest, optimal, peak, perfect, superlative

option *n* = **choice**, alternative, preference, selection

optional *adj* = **voluntary**, discretionary, elective, extra, open, possible

opulence *n* **1** = **wealth**, affluence, luxuriance, luxury, plenty, prosperity, riches **2** = **abundance**, copiousness, cornucopia, fullness, profusion, richness, superabundance

opulent *adj* **1** = **rich**, affluent, lavish, luxurious, moneyed, prosperous, sumptuous, wealthy, well-off, well-to-do **2** = **abundant**, copious, lavish, luxuriant, plentiful, profuse, prolific

opus *n* = **work**, brainchild, composition, creation, *oeuvre*, piece, production

oracle *n* **1** = **prophecy**, divination, prediction, prognostication, revelation **2** = **pundit**, adviser, authority, guru, mastermind, mentor, wizard

oral *adj* = **spoken**, verbal, vocal

oration *n* = **speech**, address, discourse, harangue, homily, lecture

orator *n* = **public speaker**, declaimer, lecturer, rhetorician, speaker

oratorical *adj* = **rhetorical**, bombastic, declamatory, eloquent, grandiloquent, high-flown, magniloquent, sonorous

oratory *n* = **eloquence**, declamation, elocution, grandiloquence, public speaking, rhetoric, speech-making

orb *n* = **sphere**, ball, circle, globe, ring

orbit *n* **1** = **path**, circle, course, cycle, revolution, rotation, trajectory **2** = **sphere of influence**, ambit, compass, domain, influence, range, reach, scope, sweep ◆ *v* **3** = **circle**, circumnavigate, encircle, revolve around

orchestrate *v* **1** = **score**, arrange **2** =

flowering plants.

or·dain [or-DAYN] vt **1** admit to religious ministry. **2** confer holy orders upon. **3** decree, enact. **4** destine. **or·di·na'tion** n

or·deal [or-DEEL] n **1** severe, trying experience. **2** Hist. form of trial by which accused underwent severe physical test.

or·der [OR-dər] n **1** regular or proper arrangement or condition. **2** sequence. **3** peaceful condition of society. **4** rank, class. **5** group. **6** command. **7** request for something to be supplied. **8** mode of procedure. **9** instruction. **10** monastic society. ◆ vt **11** request (something) to be supplied or made. **12** request (something) to be supplied or made. **13** arrange. **or'der·li·ness** n **or'der·ly** adj **1** tidy. **2** methodical. **3** well-behaved. ◆ n **4** hospital attendant. **5** soldier performing chores for officer. **or·di·nal** [OR-dn-əl] adj showing position in a series. ◆ n **2** ordinal number.

or·di·nance [OR-dn-əns] n **1** decree, rule. **2** rite, ceremony.

or·di·nar·y [OR-dn-er-ee] adj **1** usual, normal. **2** common. **3** plain. **4** commonplace. ◆ n **5** average condition. **or'di·nar·i·ly** adv

ord·nance [ORD-nəns] n **1** big guns, artillery. **2** military stores.

or·dure [OR-jər] n **1** dung. **2** filth.

ore [or] n naturally occurring mineral that yields metal.

o·reg·a·no [ə-REG-ə-noh] n herb, variety of marjoram.

or·gan [OR-gən] n **1** musical wind instrument of pipes and stops, played by keys. **2** member of animal or plant carrying out particular function. **3** means of action. **4** medium of information, esp. newspaper. **or·gan·ic** adj **1** of, derived from, living organisms. **2** of bodily organs. **3** affecting bodily organs. **4** having vital organs. **5** Chem. of compounds formed from carbon. **6** grown with fertilizers derived from animal or vegetable matter. **7** organized, systematic. **or·gan'i·cal·ly** adv **or'gan·ist** n organ player.

or·gan·ize [OR-gə-nīz] vt **-nized, -niz·ing 1**

organize, arrange, coordinate, put together, set up, stage-manage

ordain v **1** = **appoint**, anoint, consecrate, invest, nominate **2** = **order**, decree, demand, dictate, fix, lay down, legislate, prescribe, rule, will

ordeal n = **hardship**, agony, anguish, baptism of fire, nightmare, suffering, test, torture, trial, tribulation(s)

order n **1** = **instruction**, command, decree, dictate, direction, directive, injunction, law, mandate, regulation, rule **2** = **sequence**, arrangement, array, grouping, layout, line-up, progression, series, structure **3** = **tidiness**, method, neatness, orderliness, organization, pattern, regularity, symmetry, system **4** = **discipline**, calm, control, law, law and order, peace, quiet, tranquillity **5** = **request**, application, booking, commission, requisition, reservation **6** = **class**, caste, grade, position, rank, status **7** = **kind**, class, family, genre, ilk, sort, type **8** = **society**, association, brotherhood, community, company, fraternity, guild, organization ◆ v **9** = **instruct**, bid, charge, command, decree, demand, direct, require **10** = **request**, apply for, book, reserve, send away for **11** = **arrange**, catalog, classify, group, marshal, organize, sort out,

systematize

orderly adj **1** = **well-organized**, businesslike, in order, methodical, neat, regular, scientific, shipshape, systematic, tidy **2** = **well-behaved**, controlled, disciplined, law-abiding, peaceable, quiet, restrained

ordinarily adv = **usually**, as a rule, commonly, customarily, generally, habitually, in general, normally

ordinary adj **1** = **usual**, common, conventional, everyday, normal, regular, routine, standard, stock, typical **2** = **commonplace**, banal, humble, humdrum, modest, mundane, plain, unremarkable, workaday

organ n **1** = **part**, element, structure, unit **2** = **mouthpiece**, forum, medium, vehicle, voice

organic adj **1** = **natural**, animate, biological, live, living **2** = **systematic**, integrated, methodical, ordered, organized, structured

organism n = **creature**, animal, being, body, entity, structure

organization n **1** = **group**, association, body, company, confederation, corporation, institution, outfit (inf), syndicate **2** = **management**, construction, coordination, direction, organizing, give definite structure. **2** get up, arrange. **3** put into working order. **4** unite in a society. **or'gan·ism** *n* **1** organized body or system. **2** plant, animal. **or·gan·i·za'tion** *n* **1** act of organizing. **2** body of people. **3** society.

or·gasm [OR-gaz-əm] *n* sexual climax.

or·gy [OR-jee] *n, pl* **-gies 1** drunken or licentious revel, debauch. **2** act of immoderation, overindulgence.

o·ri·el [OR-ee-əl] *n* **1** projecting part of an upper room with a window. **2** the window.

o·ri·ent [OR-ee-ənt] *n* **1** (O-) East. **2** luster of best pearls. ◆ *adj* **3** rising. **4** (O-) Eastern. ◆ *vt* [OR-ee-ent] **5** place so as to face east or other known direction. **6** take bearings. **7** determine one's position. **o·ri·en'tal** *adj* **1** of, or from, the East. ◆ *n* **2** *oft offens* person from the East or of Eastern descent. **o·ri·en'tal·ist** *n* expert in Eastern languages and history. **o·ri·en·ta'tion** *n*

or·i·fice [OR-ə-fis] *n* opening, mouth of a cavity, e.g. pipe.

o·ri·ga·mi [or-i-GAH-mee] *n* Japanese art of paper folding.

or·i·gin [OR-i-jin] *n* **1** beginning. **2** source. **3** parentage.

o·rig·i·nal [ə-RIJ-ə-nl] *adj* **1** primitive, earliest. **2** new, not copied or derived. **3** thinking or acting for oneself. **4** eccentric. ◆ *n* **5** pattern, thing from which another is copied. **6** unconventional or strange person. **o·rig'i·nal·i·ty** *n* power of producing something individual to oneself. **o·rig'i·nal·ly** *adv* **1** at first. **2** in the beginning.

o·rig·i·nate [ə-RIJ-ə-nayt] *v* **-nat·ed, -nat·ing** come or bring into existence, begin. **o·rig'i·na·tor** [-tər] *n*

o·ri·ole [OR-ee-ohl] *n* any of several thrushlike birds.

O·ri·on [ə-RĪ-ən] *n* bright constellation.

or·i·son [OR-ə-zən] *n* prayer.

or·mo·lu [OR-mə-loo] *n* **1** gilded bronze. **2** gold-colored alloy. **3** articles of these.

or·na·ment [OR-nə-mənt] *n* **1** any object used to adorn or decorate. **2** decoration. ◆ *vt* [-ment] **3** adorn. **or·na·ment'al** *adj* **or·na·men·ta'tion** *n*

or·nate [or-NAYT] *adj* highly decorated or elaborate.

or·ni·thol·o·gy [or-nə-THOL-ə-jee] *n*

THESAURUS

planning, running, structuring **3 = arrangement**, chemistry, composition, format, make-up, pattern, structure, unity

organize *v* = **arrange**, classify, coordinate, group, marshal, put together, run, set up, systematize, take care of

orgy *n* **1 = revel**, bacchanalia, carousal, debauch, revelry, Saturnalia **2 = spree**, binge (*inf*), bout, excess, indulgence, overindulgence, splurge, surfeit

orient *v* = **familiarize**, acclimatize, adapt, adjust, align, get one's bearings, orientate

orientation *n* **1 = position**, bearings, direction, location **2 = familiarization**, acclimatization, adaptation, adjustment, assimilation, introduction, settling in

orifice *n* = **opening**, aperture, cleft, hole, mouth, pore, rent, vent

origin *n* **1 = root**, base, basis, derivation, fount, fountainhead, source, wellspring **2 = beginning**, birth, creation, emergence, foundation, genesis, inception, launch, start

original *adj* **1 = first**, earliest, initial, introductory, opening, primary, starting **2 = new**, fresh, ground-breaking, innovative, novel, seminal, unprecedented, unusual **3 = creative**, fertile, imaginative,

ingenious, inventive, resourceful ◆ *n* **4 = prototype**, archetype, master, model, paradigm, pattern, precedent, standard

originality *n* = **novelty**, creativity, freshness, imagination, ingenuity, innovation, inventiveness, newness, unorthodoxy

originally *adv* = **initially**, at first, first, in the beginning, to begin with

originate *v* **1 = begin**, arise, come, derive, emerge, result, rise, spring, start, stem **2 = introduce**, bring about, create, formulate, generate, institute, launch, pioneer

originator *n* = **creator**, architect, author, father *or* mother, founder, inventor, maker, pioneer

ornament *n* **1 = decoration**, accessory, adornment, bauble, embellishment, festoon, knick-knack, trimming, trinket ◆ *v* **2 = decorate**, adorn, beautify, embellish, festoon, grace, prettify

ornamental *adj* = **decorative**, attractive, beautifying, embellishing, for show, showy

ornamentation *n* = **decoration**, adornment, elaboration, embellishment, embroidery, frills, ornateness

ornate *adj* = **elaborate**, baroque, busy, decorated, fancy, florid, fussy, science of birds. **or·ni·thol'o·gist** n

o·ro·tund [OR-ə-tund] adj **1** full, clear, and musical. **2** pompous.

or·phan [OR-fən] n child bereaved of one or both parents. **or'phan·age** [-fə-nij] n institution for care of orphans.

ortho- comb. form right, correct.

or·tho·dox [OR-thə-doks] adj **1** holding accepted views. **2** conventional **or'tho·dox·y** n

or·thog·ra·phy [or-THOG-rə-fee] n correct spelling.

or·tho·pe·dic [or-thə-PEE-dik] adj for curing deformity, disorder of bones. **or·tho·pe'dics** n medical specialty dealing with this. **or·tho·pe'dist** n

Os Chem. osmium.

os·cil·late [OS-ə-layt] vi **-lat·ed, -lat·ing 1** swing to and fro. **2** waver. **3** fluctuate (regularly). **os·cil·la'tion** n **os'cil·la·tor** n **os·cil·la·to·ry** adj **os·cil'lo·scope** n electronic instrument producing visible representation of rapidly changing quantity.

os·mi·um [OZ-mee-əm] n heaviest known of metallic elements.

os·mo·sis [oz-MOH-sis] n percolation of fluids through porous partitions. **os·mot'ic** adj

os·se·ous [OS-ee-əs] adj **1** of, like bone. **2** bony. **os·si·fi·ca'tion** n **os'si·fy** [-fī] v **-fied, -fy·ing 1** turn into bone. **2** grow rigid.

os·ten·si·ble [o-STEN-sə-bəl] adj **1** apparent. **2** professed. **os·ten'si·bly** adv

os·ten·ta·tion [os-ten-TAY-shən] n show, pretentious display. **os·ten·ta'tious** adj **1** given to display. **2** showing off.

os·te·op·a·thy [os-tee-OP-ə-thee] n art of treating disease by removing structural derangement by manipulation, esp. of spine. **os'te·o·path** n one skilled in this art.

os·tra·cize [OS-trə-sīz] vt **-cized, -ciz·ing** exclude, banish from society, exile. **os'tra·cism** [-siz-əm] n social boycotting.

os·trich n large swift-running flightless Afr. bird.

oth·er [UTH-ər] adj **1** not this. **2** not the same. **3** alternative, different. ◆ pron **4** other person or thing. **oth'er·wise** adv **1** differently. **2** in another way. ◆ conj **3** else, if not.

o·ti·ose [OH-shee-ohs, OH-tee-ohs] adj **1** superfluous. **2** useless.

o·ti·tis [oh-TĪ-tis] n inflammation of the ear.

ot·ter [OT-ər] n furry aquatic fish-eating animal.

Ot·to·man [OT-ə-mən] adj **1** Turkish. ◆ n **2** Turk. **3** (**o-**) cushioned, backless seat. **4** (**o-**) cushioned footstool.

ought [awt] v aux **1** expressing duty or obligation or advisability. **2** be bound.

Oui·ja [WEE-jə] n ® board with letters and symbols used to obtain messages at seances.

ounce [owns] n a weight, sixteenth of avoirdupois pound (28.349 grams), twelfth of troy pound (31.103 grams).

our [OW-ər] adj belonging to us. **ours** pron

ornamented, overelaborate, rococo

orthodox adj = **established**, accepted, approved, conventional, customary, official, received, traditional, well-established

orthodoxy n = **conformity**, authority, conventionality, received wisdom, traditionalism

oscillate v = **fluctuate**, seesaw, sway, swing, vacillate, vary, vibrate, waver

oscillation n = **swing**, fluctuation, instability, vacillation, variation, wavering

ossify v = **harden**, fossilize, solidify, stiffen

ostensible adj = **apparent**, outward, pretended, professed, purported, seeming, so-called, superficial, supposed

ostensibly adv = **apparently**, on the face of it, professedly, seemingly, supposedly

ostentation n = **display**, affectation, exhibitionism, flamboyance, flashiness, flaunting, parade, pomp, pretentiousness, show, showing off (inf)

ostentatious adj = **pretentious**, brash, conspicuous, flamboyant, flashy, gaudy, loud, obtrusive, showy

ostracism n = **exclusion**, banishment, exile, isolation, rejection

ostracize v = **exclude**, banish, cast out, cold-shoulder, exile, give (someone) the cold shoulder, reject, shun

other adj **1** = **additional**, added, alternative, auxiliary, extra, further, more, spare, supplementary **2** = **different**, contrasting, dissimilar, distinct, diverse, separate, unrelated, variant

otherwise conj **1** = **or else**, if not, or then ◆ adv **2** = **differently**, any other way, contrarily

ounce n = **shred**, atom, crumb, drop, grain, scrap, speck, trace thing(s) belonging to us. **our·selves'** *pron* emphatic or reflexive form of WE.

oust [owst] *vt* put out, expel.

out [owt] *adv* 1 from within, away. 2 wrong. 3 on strike. ♦ *adj* 4 not worth considering. 5 not allowed. 6 unfashionable. 7 unconscious. 8 not in use, operation, etc. 9 at an end. 10 not burning. 11 *Baseball* failed to get on base. ♦ *vt* 12 *inf* name (public figure) as being homosexual. **out'er** *adj* away from the inside. **out'er·most** [-mohst] *adj* on extreme outside. **out'ing** *n* pleasure excursion. **out'ward** [-wurd] *adj, adv* **out'wards** [-wurdz] *adv*

out- *prefix* beyond, in excess, e.g. *outclass; outdistance; outsize.*

out·bal·ance [owt-BAL-əns] *vt* -anced, -anc·ing 1 outweigh. 2 exceed in weight.

out·board [OWT-bord] *adj* of boat's engine, mounted on, outside stern.

out·break [OWT-brayk] *n* sudden occurrence, esp. of disease or strife.

out·burst [OWT-burst] *n* bursting out, esp. of violent emotion.

out·cast [OWT-kast] *n* someone rejected. ♦ *adj*

out·class [owt-KLAS] *vt* excel, surpass.

out·come [OWT-kum] *n* result.

out·crop [OWT-krop] *n* 1 *Geology* rock coming out of stratum to the surface. ♦ *vi* [owt-KROP] -cropped, -crop·ping 2 come out to the surface.

out·doors [owt-DORZ] *adv* in the open air. **out'door** *adj*

out·fit [OWT-fit] *n* 1 equipment. 2 clothes and accessories. 3 *inf* group or association regarded as a unit. **out'fit·ter** *n* one who supplies clothing and accessories.

out·flank [owt-FLANGK] *vt* 1 to get beyond the flank (of enemy army). 2 circumvent. 3 outmaneuver.

out·go·ing [OWT-goh-ing] *adj* 1 departing. 2 friendly, sociable.

out·grow [owt-GROH] *vt* -grew, -grown, -grow·ing 1 become too large or too old for. 2 surpass in growth.

out·house [OWT-hows] *n* 1 outdoor toilet. 2 shed, etc. near main building.

out·land·ish [owt-LAN-dish] *adj* queer, extravagantly strange.

out·law [OWT-law] *n* 1 one beyond protection of the law. 2 exile, bandit. ♦ *vt* 3 make (someone) an outlaw. 4 ban.

━━━━━━━━━━━━━ THESAURUS ━━━━━━━━━━━

oust *v* = **expel**, depose, dislodge, displace, dispossess, eject, throw out, topple, turn out, unseat

out *adj* 1 = **away**, abroad, absent, elsewhere, gone, not at home, outside 2 = **extinguished**, at an end, dead, ended, exhausted, expired, finished, used up

outbreak *n* = **eruption**, burst, epidemic, explosion, flare-up, outburst, rash, upsurge

outburst *n* = **outpouring**, eruption, explosion, flare-up, outbreak, paroxysm, spasm, surge

outcast *n* = **pariah**, castaway, exile, leper, *persona non grata*, refugee, vagabond, wretch

outclass *v* = **surpass**, eclipse, excel, leave standing (*inf*), outdo, outshine, outstrip, overshadow, run rings around (*inf*)

outcome *n* = **result**, conclusion, consequence, end, issue, payoff (*inf*), upshot

outcry *n* = **protest**, clamor, commotion, complaint, hue and cry, hullaballoo, outburst, uproar

outdated *adj* = **old-fashioned**, antiquated, archaic, obsolete, outmoded, out of date, passé, unfashionable

outdo *v* = **surpass**, beat, best, eclipse, exceed, get the better of, outclass, outmaneuver, overcome, top, transcend

outdoor *adj* = **open-air**, alfresco, out-of-door(s), outside

outer *adj* = **external**, exposed, exterior, outlying, outside, outward, peripheral, surface

outfit *n* 1 = **costume**, clothes, ensemble, garb, get-up (*inf*), kit, suit 2 = **group**, company, crew, organization, setup (*inf*), squad, team, unit

outgoing *adj* 1 = **leaving**, departing, former, retiring, withdrawing 2 = **sociable**, approachable, communicative, expansive, extrovert, friendly, gregarious, open, warm

outgoings *pl n* = **expenses**, costs, expenditure, outlay, overheads

outing *n* = **trip**, excursion, expedition, jaunt, spin (*inf*)

outlandish *adj* = **strange**, bizarre, exotic, fantastic, far-out (*sl*), freakish, outré, preposterous, unheard-of, weird

outlaw *n* 1 = **bandit**, desperado, fugitive, highwayman, marauder, outcast, robber ♦ *v* 2 = **forbid**, ban, bar, disallow, exclude, prohibit, proscribe

out·lay [OWT-lay] *n* expenditure.

out·let [OWT-let] *n* **1** opening, vent. **2** means of release or escape. **3** market for product or service.

out·line [OWT-līn] *n* **1** rough sketch. **2** general plan. **3** lines enclosing visible figure. ♦ *vt* **-lined, lin·ing 4** sketch. **5** summarize.

out·look [OWT luuk] *n* **1** point of view. **2** probable outcome. **3** view.

out·ly·ing [OWT-lī-ing] *adj* distant, remote.

out·mod·ed [owt-MOH-did] *adj* no longer fashionable or accepted.

out·pa·tient [OWT-pay-shənt] *n* patient treated but not kept at hospital.

out·put [OWT-puut] *n* **1** quantity produced. **2** *Computers* data produced. ♦ *vt* **3** *Computers* produce (data) at the end of a process.

out·rage [OWT-rayj] *n* **1** violation of others' rights. **2** gross or violent offense or indignity. **3** anger arising from this. ♦ *vt* **-raged, rag·ing 4** offend grossly. **5** insult. **6** injure, violate. **out·ra·geous** [-RAY-jəs] *adj*

ou·tré [oo-TRAY] *adj* **1** extravagantly odd. **2** bizarre.

out·rig·ger [OWT-rig-ər] *n* **1** frame, esp. with float attached, outside boat's gunwale. **2** frame on rowing boat's side with rowlock. **3** boat with one.

out·right [OWT-rīt] *adj* **1** undisputed. **2** downright. **3** positive. ♦ *adv* [owt-rīt] **4** completely. **5** once for all. **6** openly.

out·set [OWT-set] *n* beginning.

out·side [OWT-sīd] *n* **1** exterior. ♦ *adv* [owt-SĪD] **2** not inside. **3** in the open air. ♦ *adj* [owt-SĪD] **4** on exterior. **5** remote, unlikely. **6** greatest possible, probable. **out·sid·er** *n* **1** person outside specific group. **2** contestant thought unlikely to win.

out·skirts [OWT-skurts] *pl n* outer areas,

outlay *n* = **expenditure**, cost, expenses, investment, outgoings, spending

outlet *n* **1** = **release**, avenue, channel, duct, exit, opening, vent **2** = **shop**, market, store

outline *n* **1** = **summary**, recapitulation, résumé, rundown, synopsis, thumbnail sketch **2** = **shape**, configuration, contour, delineation, figure, form, profile, silhouette ♦ *v* **3** = **summarize**, adumbrate, delineate, draft, plan, rough out, sketch (in), trace

outlive *v* = **survive**, outlast

outlook *n* **1** = **attitude**, angle, frame of mind, perspective, point of view, slant, standpoint, viewpoint **2** = **prospect**, expectations, forecast, future

outlying *adj* = **remote**, distant, far-flung, out-of-the-way, peripheral, provincial

outmoded *adj* = **old-fashioned**, anachronistic, antiquated, archaic, obsolete, out-of-date, outworn, passé, unfashionable

out-of-date *adj* = **old-fashioned**, antiquated, dated, expired, invalid, lapsed, obsolete, outmoded, outworn, passé

outpouring *n* = **stream**, cascade, effusion, flow, spate, spurt, torrent

output *n* = **production**, achievement, manufacture, productivity, yield

outrage *n* **1** = **violation**, abuse, affront, desecration, indignity, insult, offense, sacrilege, violence **2** = **indignation**, anger, fury, hurt, resentment, shock, wrath ♦ *v* **3** = **offend**, affront, incense, infuriate, madden, scandalize, shock

outrageous *adj* **1** = **offensive**, atrocious, disgraceful, flagrant, heinous, iniquitous, nefarious, unspeakable, villainous, wicked **2** = **shocking**, exorbitant, extravagant, immoderate, preposterous, scandalous, steep (*inf*), unreasonable

outré *adj* = **eccentric**, bizarre, fantastic, freakish, odd, off-the-wall (*sl*), outlandish, unconventional, weird

outright *adj* **1** = **absolute**, complete, out-and-out, perfect, thorough, thoroughgoing, total, unconditional, unmitigated, unqualified **2** = **direct**, definite, flat, straightforward, unequivocal, unqualified ♦ *adv* **3** = **absolutely**, completely, openly, overtly, straightforwardly, thoroughly, to the full

outset *n* = **beginning**, commencement, inauguration, inception, kickoff (*inf*), onset, opening, start

outshine *v* = **overshadow**, eclipse, leave *or* put in the shade, outclass, outdo, outstrip, surpass, transcend, upstage

outside *adj* **1** = **external**, exterior, extraneous, outer, outward **2** *As in an* **outside chance** = **unlikely**, distant, faint, marginal, remote, slight, slim, small ♦ *n* **3** = **surface**, exterior, façade, face, front, skin, topside

outsider *n* = **interloper**, incomer, intruder, newcomer, odd man out, stranger districts, esp. of city.

out·spok·en [OWT-SPOH-kən] *adj* frank, candid.

out·stand·ing [owt-STAN-ding] *adj* **1** excellent. **2** remarkable. **3** unsettled, unpaid.

out·strip [owt-STRIP] *vt* **-stripped, -strip·ping** outrun, surpass.

out·wit [owt-WIT] *vt* **-wit·ted, -wit·ting** get the better of by cunning.

o·val [OH-vəl] *adj* **1** egg-shaped, elliptical. ♦ *n* **2** something of this shape.

o·va·ry [OH-və-ree] *n, pl* **-ries** female egg-producing organ. **o·var·i·an** [-VAIR-ee-ən] *adj*

o·va·tion [oh-VAY-shən] *n* enthusiastic burst of applause.

ov·en [UV-ən] *n* heated chamber for baking in.

o·ver [OH-vər] *adv* **1** above, above and beyond, going beyond, in excess, too much, past, finished, in repetition, across,

downward, etc. ♦ *prep* **2** above. **3** on, upon. **4** more than, in excess of, along, etc. ♦ *adj* **5** upper, outer.

over- *prefix* **1** too much, e.g. *overeat*. **2** above, e.g. *overlord*. **3** on top, e.g. *overshoe*.

o·ver·all [OH-vər-awl] *adj, adv* **1** in total. ♦ *n* **2** coat-shaped protective garment. ♦ *pl* **3** protective garment consisting of trousers with a part extending up over the chest.

o·ver·awe' *vt* affect (someone) with an overpowering sense of awe.

o·ver·bal'ance *v* lose balance.

o·ver·bear·ing [oh-vər-BAIR-ing] *adj* domineering.

o·ver·blown [OH-vər-BLOHN] *adj* excessive, bombastic.

o·ver·board [OH-vər-bord] *adv* from a vessel into the water.

o·ver·cast [OH-vər-KAST] *adj* covered over, esp. by clouds.

o'ver·coat *n* heavy coat.

———— THESAURUS ————

outsize *adj* = **extra-large**, giant, gigantic, huge, jumbo (*inf*), mammoth, monster, oversized

outskirts *pl n* = **edge**, boundary, environs, periphery, suburbia, suburbs

outspoken *adj* = **forthright**, abrupt, blunt, explicit, frank, open, plain-spoken, unceremonious, unequivocal

outstanding *adj* **1** = **excellent**, cool (*inf*), exceptional, great, important, impressive, phat (*sl*), special, superior, superlative **2** = **unpaid**, due, payable, pending, remaining, uncollected, unsettled

outstrip *v* = **surpass**, better, eclipse, exceed, excel, outdistance, outdo, overtake, transcend

outward *adj* = **apparent**, noticeable, observable, obvious, ostensible, perceptible, surface, visible

outwardly *adv* = **ostensibly**, apparently, externally, on the face of it, on the surface, seemingly, superficially, to all intents and purposes

outweigh *v* = **override**, cancel (out), compensate for, eclipse, prevail over, take precedence over, tip the scales

outwit *v* = **outthink**, cheat, dupe, fool, get the better of, outfox, outmaneuver, outsmart (*inf*), swindle

outworn *adj* = **outdated**, antiquated, discredited, disused, hackneyed, obsolete, outmoded, out-of-date, threadbare,

worn-out

oval *adj* = **elliptical**, egg-shaped, ovoid

ovation *n* = **applause**, acclaim, acclamation, big hand, cheers, clapping, plaudits, tribute

over *prep* **1** = **on**, above, on top of, upon **2** = **exceeding**, above, in excess of, more than ♦ *adv* **3** = **above**, aloft, on high, overhead **4** = **extra**, beyond, in addition, in excess, left over ♦ *adj* **5** = **finished**, bygone, closed, completed, concluded, done (with), ended, gone, past

overact *v* = **exaggerate**, ham *or* ham up (*inf*), overdo, overplay

overall *adj* **1** = **total**, all-embracing, blanket, complete, comprehensive, general, global, inclusive ♦ *adv* **2** = **in general**, on the whole

overawe *v* = **intimidate**, abash, alarm, daunt, frighten, scare, terrify

overbalance *v* = **overturn**, capsize, keel over, slip, tip over, topple over, tumble, turn turtle

overbearing *adj* = **arrogant**, bossy (*inf*), dictatorial, domineering, haughty, high-handed, imperious, supercilious, superior

overblown *adj* = **excessive**, disproportionate, immoderate, inflated, overdone, over the top, undue

overcast *adj* = **cloudy**, dismal, dreary, dull, gray, leaden, louring *or* lowering, murky

o·ver·come [oh-vər-KUM] *vt* **-came,
-come, -com·ing 1** conquer. **2** surmount. **3**
make powerless.

o·ver·crowd' *vt* fill with more people or
things is desirable. **ov·er·crowd'ing** *n*

o·ver·do' *vt* **1** do to excess. **2** exaggerate
(something).

o'ver·dose *n* **1** excessive dose of a drug. ♦
v **2** take an overdose

o·ver·draft [OH-vər-draft] *n* withdrawal of
money in excess of credit balance on bank
account.

o·ver·due' *adj* still due after the time
allowed.

o·ver·flow' *v* **1** flow over. **2** be filled
beyond capacity. ♦ *n* **3** something that
overflows. **4** outlet for excess liquid. **5**
excess amount.

o·ver·haul [oh-vər-HAWL] *vt* **1** examine

and set in order, repair. **2** overtake. ♦ *n*
[OH-vər-hawl] **3** thorough examination,
esp. for repairs.

o·ver·head [OH-vər-hed] *adj* **1** over one's
head, above. ♦ *n* **2** expense of running a
business, over and above cost of
manufacturing and of raw materials. ♦ *adv*
[OH-vər-HED] **3** aloft, above.

o·ver·kill [OH-vər-kil] *n* capacity,
advantage greater than required.

o·ver·lap' *v* **1** share part of the same space
or period of time (as). ♦ *n* **2** area
overlapping.

o·ver·look [oh-vər-LUUK] *vt* **1** fail to notice.
2 disregard. **3** look over.

o·ver·pow'er *v* **1** subdue or overcome
(someone). **2** make helpless or ineffective.
o·ver·pow'er·ing *adj*

o·ver·re·act' *vi* react more strongly than is

THESAURUS

overcharge *v* = **cheat**, fleece, rip off (*sl*),
short-change, sting (*inf*), surcharge

overcome *v* **1** = **conquer**, beat, defeat,
master, overpower, overwhelm, prevail,
subdue, subjugate, surmount, triumph
over, vanquish ♦ *adj* **2** = **affected**, at a loss
for words, bowled over (*inf*),
overwhelmed, speechless, swept off one's
feet

overconfident *adj* = **brash**, cocksure,
foolhardy, overweening, presumptuous

overcrowded *adj* = **congested**, bursting
at the seams, choked, jam-packed,
overloaded, overpopulated, packed (out),
swarming

overdo *v* **1** = **exaggerate**, belabor, gild the
lily, go overboard (*inf*), overindulge,
overreach, overstate **2 overdo it** =
overwork, bite off more than one can
chew, burn the candle at both ends (*inf*),
overload, strain *or* overstrain oneself, wear
oneself out

overdone *adj* **1** = **excessive**, exaggerated,
fulsome, immoderate, inordinate,
overelaborate, too much, undue,
unnecessary **2** = **overcooked**, burnt,
charred, dried up, spoiled

overdue *adj* = **late**, behindhand, behind
schedule, belated, owing, tardy,
unpunctual

overeat *v* = **overindulge**, binge (*inf*),
gorge, gormandize, guzzle, pig out (*sl*),
stuff oneself

overemphasize *v* = **overstress**, belabor,
blow up out of all proportion, make a

mountain out of a molehill (*inf*),
overdramatize

overflow *v* **1** = **spill**, brim over, bubble
over, pour over, run over, well over ♦ *n* **2** =
surplus, overabundance, spilling over

overhang *v* = **project**, extend, jut, loom,
protrude, stick out

overhaul *v* **1** = **repair**, check, do up (*inf*),
examine, inspect, recondition, refurbish,
restore, service **2** = **overtake**, catch up
with, get ahead of, pass ♦ *n* **3** = **checkup**,
check, examination, inspection,
reconditioning, service

overhead *adv* **1** = **above**, aloft, in the sky,
on high, skyward, up above, upward ♦ *adj*
2 = **aerial**, overhanging, upper

overheads *pl n* = **running costs**, operating
costs

overindulgence *n* = **excess**,
immoderation, intemperance, overeating,
surfeit

overjoyed *adj* = **delighted**, elated,
euphoric, jubilant, on cloud nine (*inf*), over
the moon (*inf*), thrilled

overload *v* = **overburden**, burden,
encumber, oppress, overtax, saddle (with),
strain, weigh down

overlook *v* **1** = **forget**, disregard, miss,
neglect, omit, pass **2** = **ignore**, condone,
disregard, excuse, forgive, make
allowances for, pardon, turn a blind eye to,
wink at **3** = **have a view of**, look over *or*
out on

overpower *v* = **overwhelm**, conquer,
crush, defeat, master, overcome,

necessary.

o·ver·ride [oh-vər-RĪD] *vt* **-rode, -rid·den, -rid·ing 1** set aside, disregard. **2** cancel. **3** trample down.

o·ver·rule' *vt* **1** reverse the decision of (a person with less power). **2** reverse (someone else's decision).

o·ver·run' *v* **1** conquer rapidly. **2** spread over (a place) rapidly. **3** extend beyond a set limit.

o·ver·seas [OH-vər-SEEZ] *adj* **1** foreign. ◆ *adj, adv* [oh-vər-SEEZ] **2** to, from place over the sea.

o·ver·se·er [OH-vər-see-ər] *n* supervisor. **o·ver·see'** *vt* **-saw, -seen, -see·ing** supervise.

o·ver·shoot' *v* go beyond (a mark or target).

o·ver·sight [OH-vər-sīt] *n* **1** failure to notice. **2** mistake. **3** supervision.

o·vert [oh-VURT] *adj* open, unconcealed.

o·vert'ly *adv*

o·ver·take [oh-vər-TAYK] *vt* **-took, -tak·en, -tak·ing 1** move past (vehicle, person) traveling in same direction. **2** come up with in pursuit. **3** catch up.

o·ver·tax [oh-vər-TAKS] *vt* **1** tax too heavily. **2** impose too great a strain on.

o·ver·throw [oh-vər-THROH] *vt* **-threw, -thrown, -throw·ing 1** upset, overturn. **2** defeat. ◆ *n* [OH-vər-throh] ruin. **3** defeat. **4** fall.

o·ver·tone [OH-vər-tohn] *n* additional meaning, nuance.

o·ver·ture [OH-vər-chər] *n* **1** *Mus.* orchestral introduction. **2** opening of negotiations. **3** formal offer.

o·ver·ween·ing [OH-vər-WEE-ning] *adj* thinking too much of oneself.

o·ver·whelm [oh-vər-HWELM] *vt* **1** crush. **2** submerge, engulf. **o·ver·whelm'ing** *adj* **1** decisive. **2** irresistible.

---

overthrow, quell, subdue, subjugate, vanquish

overpowering *adj* = **irresistible**, forceful, invincible, irrefutable, overwhelming, powerful, strong

overrate *v* = **overestimate**, exaggerate, overvalue

override *v* = **overrule**, annul, cancel, countermand, nullify, outweigh, supersede

overriding *adj* = **ultimate**, dominant, paramount, predominant, primary, supreme

overrule *v* = **reverse**, alter, annul, cancel, countermand, override, overturn, repeal, rescind, veto

overrun *v* **1** = **invade**, occupy, overwhelm, rout **2** = **infest**, choke, inundate, permeate, ravage, spread over, swarm over **3** = **exceed**, go beyond, overshoot, run over *or* on

overseer *n* = **supervisor**, boss (*inf*), chief, foreman, master, superintendent

overshadow *v* **1** = **outshine**, dominate, dwarf, eclipse, leave *or* put in the shade, surpass, tower above **2** = **spoil**, blight, mar, put a damper on, ruin, temper

oversight *n* = **mistake**, blunder, carelessness, error, fault, lapse, neglect, omission, slip

overt *adj* = **open**, blatant, manifest, observable, obvious, plain, public, unconcealed, undisguised

overtake *v* **1** = **pass**, catch up with, get

past, leave behind, outdistance, outdo, outstrip, overhaul **2** = **befall**, engulf, happen, hit, overwhelm, strike

overthrow *v* **1** = **defeat**, bring down, conquer, depose, dethrone, oust, overcome, overpower, topple, unseat, vanquish ◆ *n* **2** = **downfall**, defeat, destruction, dethronement, fall, ousting, undoing, unseating

overtone *n* = **connotation**, hint, implication, innuendo, intimation, nuance, sense, suggestion, undercurrent

overture *n* **1** *Mus.* = **introduction**, opening, prelude **2 overtures** = **approach**, advance, invitation, offer, proposal, proposition

overturn *v* **1** = **tip over**, capsize, keel over, overbalance, topple, upend, upturn **2** = **overthrow**, bring down, depose, destroy, unseat

overweight *adj* = **fat**, bulky, chubby, chunky, corpulent, heavy, hefty, obese, plump, portly, stout, tubby (*inf*)

overwhelm *v* **1** = **devastate**, bowl over (*inf*), knock (someone) for six (*inf*), overcome, stagger, sweep (someone) off his *or* her feet, take (someone's) breath away **2** = **destroy**, crush, cut to pieces, massacre, overpower, overrun, rout

overwhelming *adj* = **devastating**, breathtaking, crushing, irresistible, overpowering, shattering, stunning, towering

overwork *v* **1** = **strain**, burn the midnight

o·ver·wrought [OH-vər-RAWT] *adj* **1** overexcited. **2** too elaborate.

o·vip·a·rous [oh-VIP-ər-əs] *adj* laying eggs.

ov·ule [OV-yool] *n* unfertilized seed. **ov'u·late** [-yə-layt] *vi* **-lat·ed, -lat·ing** produce, discharge (egg) from ovary.

o·vum [OH-vəm] *n, pl* **o·va** [OH-və] female egg cell, in which development of fetus takes place.

owe [oh] *vt* **owed, ow·ing** be bound to repay, be indebted for. **owing** *adj* owed, due. **owing to** caused by, as result of.

owl *n* night bird of prey. **owl'ish** *adj* resembling an owl.

own [ohn] *adj* **1** emphasizes possession. ◆ *vt* **2** possess. **3** acknowledge. ◆ *vi* **4** to confess. **own'er·ship** *n* possession.

ox [oks] *n, pl* **ox·en 1** large cloven-footed and usu. horned farm animal. **2** bull or cow. **ox'bow** [-boh] *n* **1** U-shaped harness collar of ox. **2** bow-shaped bend in river.

ox·ide [OK-sīd] *n* compound of oxygen and another element. **ox'i·dize** *v* **-dized, -diz·ing** (cause to) combine with oxide, rust.

ox·y·gen [OK-si-jən] *n* gas in atmosphere essential to life, combustion, etc. **ox'y·gen·ate** *vt* **-at·ed, -at·ing** combine or treat with oxygen.

ox·y·mo·ron [ok-si-MOR-on] *n* figure of speech in which two ideas of opposite meaning are combined to form an expressive phrase or epithet, such as *cruel kindness*.

oys·ter [OI-stər] *n* edible bivalve mollusk or shellfish.

o·zone [OH-zohn] *n* form of oxygen with pungent odor. **ozone layer** layer of upper atmosphere with concentration of ozone.

——— THESAURUS ———

oil, sweat (*inf*), work one's fingers to the bone **2 = overuse**, exhaust, exploit, fatigue, oppress, wear out, weary

overwrought *adj* **= agitated**, distracted, excited, frantic, keyed up, on edge, overexcited, tense, uptight (*inf*), wired (*sl*)

owe *v* **= be in debt**, be in arrears, be obligated *or* indebted

owing *adj* **= unpaid**, due, outstanding, overdue, owed, payable, unsettled

owing to *prep* **= because of**, as a result of, on account of

own *adj* **1 = personal**, individual, particular, private ◆ *pron* **2 hold one's own =**

compete, keep going, keep one's end up, keep one's head above water **3 on one's own = alone**, by oneself, independently, singly, unaided, unassisted, under one's own steam ◆ *v* **4 = possess**, be in possession of, enjoy, have, hold, keep, retain **5 = acknowledge**, admit, allow, concede, confess, grant, recognize **6 own up = confess**, admit, come clean, make a clean breast, tell the truth

owner *n* **= possessor**, holder, landlord *or* landlady, proprietor

ownership *n* **= possession**, dominion, title

P p

P *Chem.* phosphorus.

Pa *Chem.* protactinium.

pace [pays] *n* **1** step. **2** its length. **3** rate of movement. **4** walk, gait. ♦ *v* **paced, pac·ing 5** *vi* **6** step. ♦ *vt* **7** set speed for. **8** cross, measure with steps. **pac'er** *n* **1** one who sets the pace for another. **2** horse used for pacing in harness racing. **pace'mak·er** *n* esp. electronic device surgically implanted in those with heart disease.

pa·chin·ko [pə-CHING-koh] *n* Japanese pinball machine.

pach·y·derm [PAK-i-durm] *n* thick-skinned animal, such as an elephant. **pach·y·der'ma·tous** [-mə-təs] *adj* thick-skinned, stolid.

pac·i·fy [PAS-ə-fī] *vt* **-fied, -fy·ing 1** calm. **2** establish peace. **pa·cif'ic** *adj* **1** peaceable. **2** calm, tranquil. **pa'ci·fi·er** ring or nipple for baby to suck or chew. **pac'i·fism** *n* **pac'i·fist** *n* **1** advocate of abolition of war. **2** one who refuses to help in war.

pack [pak] *n* **1** bundle. **2** band of animals. **3** large set of people or things. **4** set of, container for, retail commodities. **5** set of playing cards. **6** mass of floating ice. ♦ *vt* **7** put together in suitcase, etc. **8** make into a bundle. **9** press tightly together, cram. **10** fill with things. **11** fill (meeting, etc.) with one's own supporters. **12** order off. **pack'age** [-ij] *n* **1** parcel. **2** set of items offered together. ♦ *vt* **-aged, -ag·ing pack'et** [-it] *n* **1** small parcel. **2** small container (and contents). **3** *inf* large sum of money. **4** small mail, passenger, freight boat. **pack'horse** *n* horse for carrying goods. **pack ice** loose floating ice that has been compacted together.

pact [pakt] *n* covenant, agreement, compact.

pad¹ *n* **1** piece of soft material used as a cushion, protection, etc. **2** block of sheets of paper. **3** foot or sole of various animals. **4** place for launching rockets. **5** *sl* residence. ♦ *vt* **pad·ded, pad·ding 6** make soft, fill in, protect, etc., with pad or padding. **7** add to dishonestly. **padding** *n* **1** material used for stuffing. **2** literary matter put in simply to increase quantity.

pad² *vi* **pad·ded, pad·ding 1** walk with soft step. **2** travel slowly. ♦ *n* **3** sound of soft footstep.

pad·dle¹ [PAD-əl] *n* **1** short oar with

THESAURUS

pace *n* **1 = step**, gait, stride, tread, walk **2 = speed**, rate, tempo, velocity ♦ *v* **3 = stride**, march, patrol, pound **4 pace out = measure**, count, mark out, step

pacifist *n* **= peace lover**, conscientious objector, dove

pacify *v* **= calm**, allay, appease, assuage, mollify, placate, propitiate, soothe

pack *v* **1 = package**, bundle, load, store, stow **2 = cram**, compress, crowd, fill, jam, press, ram, stuff **3 pack off = send away**, dismiss, send packing (*inf*) ♦ *n* **4 = bundle**, back pack, burden, kitbag, knapsack, load, parcel, rucksack **5 = packet**, package **6 = group**, band, bunch, company, crowd, flock, gang, herd, mob, troop

package *n* **1 = parcel**, box, carton, container, packet **2 = unit**, combination, whole ♦ *v* **3 = pack**, box, parcel (up), wrap

packed *adj* **= full**, chock-a-block, chock-full, crammed, crowded, filled, jammed, jam-packed

packet *n* **= package**, bag, carton, container, parcel

pack it in *v Inf* **= stop**, cease, chuck (*inf*), give up *or* over, kick (*inf*)

pack up *v* **1 = put away**, store **2** *Inf* **= stop**, finish, give up, pack it in (*inf*) **3 = break down**, conk out (*inf*), fail

pact *n* **= agreement**, alliance, bargain, covenant, deal, treaty, understanding

pad¹ *n* **1 = cushion**, buffer, protection, stuffing, wad **2 = notepad**, block, jotter, writing pad **3 = paw**, foot, sole **4** *Sl, dated* **= home**, apartment, flat, place ♦ *v* **5 = pack**, cushion, fill, protect, stuff **6 pad out**

broad blade at one or each end. ♦ v **-dled,
-dling 2** move by, as with, paddles. **3** row
gently. **paddle wheel** wheel with crosswise
blades striking water successively to propel
ship.

paddle² vt **-dled, -dling 1** walk with bare
feet in shallow water. ♦ n **2** such a walk.

pad·dock [PAD-ək] n small grass field or
enclosure.

pad·dy [PAD-ee] n, pl **-dies** rice growing or
in the husk. **paddy field** field where rice is
grown.

pad·lock [PAD-lok] n **1** detachable lock
with hinged hoop to go through staple or
ring. ♦ vt **2** fasten thus.

pae·an [PEE-ən] n song of triumph or
thanksgiving.

pa·gan [PAY-gən] adj, n heathen.
pa'gan·ism n

page¹ [payj] n **1** one side of leaf of book,
etc. **2** screenful of information from a
website or teletext service.

page² n **1** boy servant. **2** attendant. ♦ vt
paged, pag·ing 3 summon (a person), by
bleeper or loudspeaker, in order to pass on
a message. **page'boy** n hair style with hair
rolled under usu. at shoulder length.

pag·eant [PAJ-ənt] n **1** show of persons in

costume in procession, dramatic scenes,
etc., usu. illustrating history. **2** brilliant
show. **pag'eant·ry** n, pl **-ies**

pag·i·nate [PAJ-ə-nate] vt **-nat·ed, -nat·ing**
number pages of. **pag·i·na'tion** n

pa·go·da [pə-GOH-də] n pyramidal temple
or tower of Chinese or Indian type.

paid [payd] pt. of PAY. **paid-up** adj paid in
full

pail [payl] n bucket. **pail'ful** [-fəl] n, pl **-fuls**

pain [payn] n **1** bodily or mental suffering.
2 penalty or punishment. ♦ pl **3** trouble,
exertion. ♦ vt **4** inflict pain upon. **pain'ful**
[-fəl] adj **pain'less** [-lis] adj **pain'kill·er** n
drug, as aspirin, that reduces pain.
pains'tak·ing adj diligent, careful.

paint [paynt] n **1** coloring matter spread on
a surface with brushes, roller, spray gun,
etc. ♦ vt **2** portray, color, coat, or make
picture of, with paint. **3** apply makeup. **4**
describe. **paint'er** n **paint'ing** n picture in
paint.

paint·er [PAYN-tər] n line at bow of boat
for tying it up.

pair n **1** set of two, esp. existing or
generally used together. ♦ v **2** arrange in
twos. **3** group or be grouped in twos.

pais·ley [PAYZ-lee] n, pl **-leys** pattern of

THESAURUS

= **lengthen**, elaborate, fill out, flesh out,
protract, spin out, stretch

pad² v = **sneak**, creep, go barefoot, steal

padding n **1** = **filling**, packing, stuffing,
wadding **2** = **wordiness**, hot air (inf),
verbiage, verbosity

paddle¹ n **1** = **oar**, scull ♦ v **2** = **row**, propel,
pull, scull

paddle² v **1** = **wade**, slop, splash (about)
2 = **dabble**, stir

pagan adj **1** = **heathen**, idolatrous, infidel,
polytheistic ♦ n **2** = **heathen**, idolater,
infidel, polytheist

page¹ n = **folio**, leaf, sheet, side

page² n **1** = **attendant**, pageboy, servant,
squire ♦ v **2** = **call**, send for, summon

pageant n = **show**, display, parade,
procession, spectacle, tableau

pageantry n = **spectacle**, display,
grandeur, parade, pomp, show, splendor,
theatricality

pain n **1** = **hurt**, ache, discomfort, irritation,
pang, soreness, tenderness, throb, twinge
2 = **suffering**, agony, anguish, distress,
heartache, misery, torment, torture ♦ v **3** =
hurt, smart, sting, throb **4** = **distress**,

agonize, cut to the quick, grieve, hurt,
sadden, torment, torture

pained adj = **distressed**, aggrieved, hurt,
injured, offended, upset, wounded

painful adj **1** = **distressing**, disagreeable,
distasteful, grievous, unpleasant **2** = **sore**,
aching, agonizing, smarting, tender **3** =
difficult, arduous, hard, laborious,
troublesome, trying

painfully adv = **distressingly**, clearly,
dreadfully, sadly, unfortunately

painkiller n = **analgesic**, anesthetic,
anodyne, drug

painless adj = **simple**, easy, effortless, fast,
quick

pains pl n = **trouble**, bother, care,
diligence, effort

painstaking adj = **thorough**, assiduous,
careful, conscientious, diligent, meticulous,
scrupulous

paint n **1** = **coloring**, color, dye, pigment,
stain, tint ♦ v **2** = **depict**, draw, picture,
portray, represent, sketch **3** = **coat**, apply,
color, cover, daub

pair n **1** = **couple**, brace, duo, twins ♦ v **2** =
couple, bracket, join, match (up), team,

small curving shapes.

pa·ja·mas [pə-JAH-məz] *pl n* sleeping suit of loose-fitting trousers and jacket.

pal *n inf* friend.

pal·ace [PAL-is] *n* **1** residence of king, bishop, etc. **2** stately mansion. **pa·la·tial** [pə-LAY-shəl] *adj* magnificent. **pal·a·tine** [PAL-ə-tīn] *adj* with royal privileges.

pal·ate [PAL-it] *n* **1** roof of mouth. **2** sense of taste. **pal'at·a·ble** *adj* agreeable to eat. **pal'a·tal** [-təl] *adj* **1** of the palate. **2** made by placing tongue against palate.

palatial, palatine see PALACE.

pa·lav·er [pə-LAV-ər] *n* **1** fuss. **2** conference, discussion.

pale[1] [payl] *adj* **pal·er, pal·est 1** wan, dim, whitish. ◆ *vi* **paled, pal·ing** whiten. **2** lose superiority or importance.

pale[2] *n* stake, boundary. **pal'ing** *n* upright stakes making up fence. **beyond the pale** beyond limits of propriety, safety, etc.

pa·le·o·lith·ic [pay-lee-ə-LITH-ik] *adj* of the old Stone Age.

pa·le·on·tol·o·gy [pay-lee-ən-TOL-ə-jee] *n* study of past geological periods and fossils.

pal·ette [PAL-it] *n* artist's flat board for mixing colors on.

pal·i·mo·ny [PAL-ə-moh-nee] *n* alimony awarded to partner in broken romantic relationship.

pal·in·drome [PAL-in-drohm] *n* word, verse or sentence that is the same when read backward or forward.

pal·i·sade [pal-ə-SAYD] *n* **1** fence of stakes. ◆ *pl* **2** line of cliffs. ◆ *vt* **-sad·ed, -sad·ing 3** to enclose or protect with one.

pall[1] [pawl] *n* **1** cloth spread over a coffin. **2** depressing, oppressive atmosphere. **pall'bear·er** *n* one carrying, attending coffin at funeral.

pall[2] *vi* **1** become tasteless or tiresome. **2** cloy.

pal·let[1] [PAL-it] *n* **1** straw mattress. **2** small bed.

pallet[2] *n* portable platform for storing and moving goods.

pal·li·ate [PAL-ee-ayt] *vt* **-at·ed, -at·ing 1** relieve without curing. **2** excuse. **pal'li·a·tive** [-ə-tiv] *adj* **1** giving temporary or partial relief. ◆ *n* **2** that which excuses, mitigates or alleviates.

pal·lid [PAL-id] *adj* pale, wan, colorless. **pal'lor** [-ər] *n* paleness.

palm [pahm] *n* **1** inner surface of hand. **2** tropical tree. **3** leaf of the tree as symbol of victory. ◆ *vt* **4** conceal in palm of hand. **5** pass off by trickery. **palm'is·try** *n* fortune telling from lines on palm of hand. **palm'y** *adj* **palm·i·er, palm·i·est** flourishing, successful. **Palm Sunday** Sunday before Easter. **palm'top** *adj* **1** (of a computer) small enough to be held in the hand. ◆ *n* **2** such a computer.

pal·o·mi·no [pal-ə-MEE-noh] *n, pl* **-nos** golden horse with white mane and tail.

pal·pa·ble [PAL-pə-bəl] *adj* **1** obvious. **2** certain. **3** that can be touched or felt. **pal'pa·bly** *adv*

pal·pate [PAL-payt] *vt* **-pat·ed, -pat·ing** *Med.* examine by touch.

pal·pi·tate [PAL-pi-tayt] *vi* **-tat·ed, -tat·ing 1** throb. **2** pulsate violently. **pal·pi·ta'tion** *n* **1** throbbing. **2** violent, irregular beating of heart.

pal·sy [PAWL-zee] *n, pl* **-sies** paralysis, esp.

twin

pal *n Inf* = **friend**, buddy (*inf*), chum (*inf*), companion, comrade, crony, homeboy (*sl*), homegirl (*sl*)

palatable *adj* = **delicious**, appetizing, luscious, mouthwatering, tasty, yummy (*inf*)

palate *n* = **taste**, appetite, stomach

palatial *adj* = **magnificent**, grand, imposing, majestic, opulent, regal, splendid, stately

palaver *n* = **fuss**, big deal (*inf*), performance (*inf*), rigmarole, song and dance (*inf*), to-do

pale[1] *adj* **1** = **white**, ashen, bleached, colorless, faded, light, pallid, pasty, wan ◆

v **2** = **become pale**, blanch, go white, lose color, whiten

pall[1] *n* **1** = **cloud**, mantle, shadow, shroud, veil **2** = **gloom**, check, damp, damper

pall[2] *v* = **become boring**, become dull, become tedious, cloy, jade, sicken, tire, weary

pallid *adj* = **pale**, anemic, ashen, colorless, pasty, wan

pallor *n* = **paleness**, lack of color, pallidness, wanness, whiteness

palm off *v* = **fob off**, foist off, pass off

palpable *adj* = **obvious**, clear, conspicuous, evident, manifest, plain, unmistakable, visible

palpitate *v* = **beat**, flutter, pound, pulsate,

with tremors. **pal'sied** adj affected with palsy.

pal·try [PAWL-tree] adj **-tri·er, -tri·est** worthless, contemptible, trifling.

pam·pas [PAM-pəz] pl n vast grassy treeless plains in S Amer.

pam·per [PAM-pər] vt overindulge, spoil by coddling.

pam·phlet [PAM-flit] n thin unbound book usu. on some topical subject. **pam·phlet·eer'** n writer of these.

pan[1] n **1** broad, shallow vessel. **2** depression in ground, esp. where salt forms. ♦ vt **panned, pan·ning 3** wash gold ore in pan. **4** inf criticize harshly. **pan out** vi inf result, esp. successfully.

pan[2] v **panned, pan·ning** move motion picture or TV camera slowly while shooting to cover scene, follow moving object, etc.

pan-, pant-, panto- comb. form all, e.g. panacea; pan-American.

pan·a·ce·a [pan-ə-SEE-ə] n universal remedy, cure for all ills.

pa·nache [pə-NASH] n dashing style.

pan·cake [PAN-kayk] n **1** thin cake of batter fried in pan. **2** flat cake or stick of compressed makeup. ♦ vi **-caked, -cak·ing 3** Aviation make flat landing by dropping in a level position.

pan·chro·mat·ic [pan-kroh-MAT-ik] adj Photography sensitive to light of all colors.

pan·cre·as [PAN-kree-əs] n digestive gland behind stomach. **pan·cre·at'ic** adj

pan·da [PAN-də] n large black and white bearlike mammal of China.

pan·dem·ic [pan-DEM-ik] adj (of disease) occurring over wide area.

pan·de·mo·ni·um [pan-də-MOH-nee-əm] n scene of din and uproar.

pan·der [PAN-dər] v **1** (esp. with to) give gratification to (weakness or desires). ♦ n **2** pimp.

pane [payn] n single piece of glass in a window or door.

pan·e·gyr·ic [pan-ə-JIR-ik] n speech of praise. **pan·e·gyr'i·cal** adj laudatory. **pan·e·gyr'ist** n

pan·el [PAN-l] n **1** compartment of surface, usu. raised or sunk, for example in a door. **2** any distinct section of something. **3** strip of material inserted in garment. **4** group of persons as team in quiz game, etc. **5** list of jurors, doctors, etc. **6** thin board with picture on it. ♦ vt **-eled, -el·ing 7** adorn with panels. **paneling** n paneled work. **pan'el·ist** n member of panel.

pang n **1** sudden pain, sharp twinge. **2** compunction.

pan·ic [PAN-ik] n **1** sudden and infectious fear. **2** extreme fright. **3** unreasoning terror. ♦ adj **4** of fear, etc. ♦ v **-icked, -ick·ing 5** feel or cause to feel panic. **pan'ick·y** adj **1** inclined to panic. **2** nervous. **panic button** button or switch that operates safety device, for use in emergency. **panic-stricken, -struck** adj panicky.

pan·o·ply [PAN-ə-plee] n, pl **-plies** complete, magnificent array. **pan'o·plied** adj

pan·o·ram·a [pan-ə-RAM-ə] n **1** wide and complete view. **2** picture arranged around spectators or unrolled before them. **pan·o·ram'ic** adj

throb, tremble

paltry adj = **insignificant**, contemptible, despicable, inconsiderable, lousy (sl), meager, mean, measly, minor, miserable, petty, poor, puny, scuzzy (sl), slight, small, trifling, trivial, unimportant, worthless

pamper v = **spoil**, cater to, coddle, cosset, indulge, overindulge, pet

pamphlet n = **booklet**, brochure, circular, leaflet, tract

pan[1] n **1** = **pot**, container, saucepan ♦ v **2** = **sift out**, look for, search for **3** Inf = **criticize**, censure, knock (inf), slam (sl)

pan[2] v = **move**, follow, sweep, track

panacea n = **cure-all**, nostrum, universal cure

panache n = **style**, dash, élan,

flamboyance

pandemonium n = **uproar**, bedlam, chaos, confusion, din, hullabaloo, racket, rumpus, turmoil

pander v **pander to** = **indulge**, cater to, gratify, play up to (inf), please, satisfy

pang n = **twinge**, ache, pain, prick, spasm, stab, sting

panic n **1** = **fear**, alarm, fright, hysteria, scare, terror ♦ v **2** = **go to pieces**, become hysterical, lose one's nerve **3** = **alarm**, scare, unnerve

panic-stricken adj = **frightened**, frightened out of one's wits, hysterical, in a cold sweat (inf), panicky, scared, scared stiff, terrified

panoply n = **array**, attire, dress, garb,

pan·sy [PAN-zee] n, pl **-sies 1** flower, species of violet. **2** sl, offens effeminate man.

pant vi **1** gasp for breath. **2** yearn. **3** long. **4** throb. ◆ n **5** gasp.

pan·ta·loon [PAN-tl-oon] n **1** in pantomime, foolish old man who is the butt of clown. ◆ pl **2** obs baggy trousers.

pan·the·ism [PAN-thee-iz-əm] n identification of God with the universe. **pan·the·is'tic** adj **pan'the·on** [-thee-ən] n temple of all gods.

pan·ther [PAN-thər] n **1** cougar. **2** puma. **3** variety of leopard.

pant·ies [PAN-teez] pl n women's undergarment.

pan·to·mime [PAN-tə-mīm] n dramatic entertainment without speech.

pan·try [PAN-tree] n, pl **-tries** [-treez] room for storing food or utensils.

pants pl n **1** trousers. **2** undergarment for lower trunk.

pant·y·hose [PAN-tee-hohz] pl n women's one-piece garment combining stockings and panties.

pant·y·waist [PAN-tee-wayst] n inf, offens effeminate man.

pap n **1** soft food for infants, invalids, etc. **2** pulp, mash. **3** idea, book, etc. lacking substance.

pa·pa·cy [PAY-pə-see] n, pl **-cies 1** office of Pope. **2** papal system. **pa'pal** adj of, relating to, the Pope. **pa'pist** n, adj offens Roman Catholic.

pa·pa·raz·zo [pah-pə-RAHT-soh] n, pl **-raz·zi** [-RAHT-see] freelance photographer specializing in candid shots of celebrities.

pa·pa·ya [pə-PAH-yə] n **1** tree bearing melon-shaped fruit. **2** its fruit.

pa·per [PAY-pər] n **1** material made by pressing pulp of rags, straw, wood, etc., into thin, flat sheets. **2** printed sheet of paper. **3** newspaper. **4** article, essay. ◆ pl **5** documents, etc. ◆ vt **6** cover, decorate with paper. **paper over** (try to) conceal (differences, etc.) in order to preserve friendship, etc.

pa·pier-mâ·ché [PAY-pər mə-SHAY] n pulp from rags or paper mixed with size, shaped by molding and dried hard.

pa·poose [pa-POOS] n N Amer. Indian child.

pap·ri·ka [pa-PREE-kə] n (powdered seasoning prepared from) type of red pepper.

pa·py·rus [pə-PĪ-rəs] n, pl **-py·ri** [-PĪ-rī] **1** species of reed. **2** (manuscript written on) kind of paper made from this plant.

par [pahr] n **1** equality of value or standing. **2** face value (of stocks and bonds). **3** Golf estimated standard score. ◆ vt **parred, par·ring 4** Golf make par on hole or round. **par'i·ty** n **1** equality. **2** analogy.

para-, par-, pa- comb. form beside, beyond, e.g. paradigm; parallel; parody.

par·a·ble [PA-rə-bəl] n allegory, story with a moral lesson.

pa·rab·o·la [pə-RAB-ə-lə] n section of cone cut by plane parallel to the cone's side.

par·a·chute [PA-rə-shoot] n **1** apparatus extending like umbrella used to retard the descent of a falling body. ◆ v **-chut·ed, -chut·ing 2** land or cause to land by parachute. **par'a·chut·ist** n **golden parachute** employment contract for key employee of company guaranteeing substantial severance pay, etc. if company is sold.

pa·rade [pə-RAYD] n **1** display. **2** muster of troops. **3** parade ground. ◆ v **-rad·ed, -rad·ing 4** march. **5** display.

par·a·digm [PA-rə-dīm] n **1** example. **2** model. **par·a·dig·mat'ic** [-dig-MAT-ik] adj

par·a·dise [PA-rə-dīs] n **1** heaven. **2** state of bliss. **3** (**P-**) Garden of Eden.

par·a·dox [PA-rə-doks] n statement that

regalia, trappings

panorama n = **view**, prospect, vista

panoramic adj = **wide**, comprehensive, extensive, overall, sweeping

pant v = **puff**, blow, breathe, gasp, heave, wheeze

pants pl n = **trousers**, slacks

paper n **1** = **newspaper**, daily, gazette, journal **2** = **essay**, article, dissertation, report, treatise **3 papers: a** = **documents**, certificates, deeds, records **b** = **letters**, archive, diaries, documents, dossier, file, records ◆ v **4** = **wallpaper**, hang

par n = **average**, level, mean, norm, standard, usual

parable n = **lesson**, allegory, fable, moral tale, story

parade n **1** = **procession**, array, cavalcade, march, pageant **2** = **show**, display, spectacle ◆ v **3** = **flaunt**, display, exhibit, show off (inf) **4** = **march**, process

paradigm n = **model**, example, ideal,

seems absurd or self-contradictory but may be true. **par·a·dox'i·cal** adj

par·af·fin [PA-rə-fin] n waxlike or liquid hydrocarbon mixture used as fuel, solvent, in candles, etc.

par·a·gon [PA-rə-gon] n pattern or model of excellence.

par·a·graph [PA-rə-graf] n **1** section of chapter or book. **2** short notice, as in newspaper. ◆ vt **3** arrange in paragraphs.

par·a·keet [PA-rə-keet] n small kind of parrot.

par·al·lax [PA-rə-laks] n apparent difference in object's position or direction as viewed from different points.

par·al·lel [PA-rə-lel] adj **1** continuously at equal distances. **2** precisely corresponding. ◆ n **3** line equidistant from another at all points. **4** thing exactly like another. **5** comparison. **6** line of latitude. ◆ vt **-leled, -lel·ing 7** represent as similar, compare. **par'al·lel·ism** n **par·al·lel'o·gram** [-ə-gram] n four-sided plane figure with opposite sides parallel.

pa·ral·y·sis [pə-RAL-ə-sis] n, pl **-ses** [-seez] incapacity to move or feel, due to damage to nervous system. **par·a·lyze** [PA-rə-liz] vt **-lyzed, -lyz·ing 1** affect with paralysis. **2** cripple. **3** make useless or ineffectual. **par·a·lyt·ic** [-LIT-ik] adj, n (person) affected with paralysis. **infantile paralysis** poliomyelitis.

persons working in various capacities in support of medical profession. **par·a·med'ic** n

pa·ram·e·ter [pə-RAM-i-tər] n **1** measurable characteristic. **2** any constant limiting factor.

par·a·mil·i·tar·y [pa-rə-MIL-i-ter-ee] adj of civilian group organized on military lines or in support of the military.

par·a·mount [PA-rə-mownt] adj supreme, eminent, preeminent, chief.

par·a·mour [PA-rə-moor] n old-fashioned lover, esp. of a person married to someone else.

par·a·noi·a [pa-rə-NOI-ə] n mental disease with delusions of fame, grandeur, persecution. **par·a·noi'ac** adj, n **par'a·noid** adj **1** of paranoia. **2** inf exhibiting fear of persecution, etc. ◆ n

par·a·pet [PA-rə-pit] n low wall, railing along edge of balcony, bridge, etc.

par·a·pher·na·lia [pa-rə-fər-NAYL-yə] pl n **1** personal belongings. **2** odds and ends of equipment.

par·a·phrase [PA-rə-frayz] n **1** expression of meaning of passage in other words. **2** free translation. ◆ vt **-phrased, -phras·ing 3** put into other words.

par·a·ple·gi·a [pa-rə-PLEE-jee-ə] n paralysis of lower half of body. **par·a·ple'gic** n, adj

par·a·psy·chol·o·gy [pa-rə-sī-KOL-ə-jee] n study of subjects pert. to extrasensory perception, e.g. telepathy.

——————— THESAURUS ———————

pattern
paradise n **1** = **heaven**, Elysian fields, Happy Valley, Promised Land **2** = **bliss**, delight, felicity, heaven, utopia
paradox n = **contradiction**, anomaly, enigma, oddity, puzzle
paradoxical adj = **contradictory**, baffling, confounding, enigmatic, puzzling
paragon n = **model**, epitome, exemplar, ideal, nonpareil, pattern, quintessence
paragraph n = **section**, clause, item, part, passage, subdivision
parallel adj **1** = **equidistant**, alongside, side by side **2** = **matching**, analogous, corresponding, like, resembling, similar ◆ n **3** = **equivalent**, analogue, counterpart, equal, match, twin **4** = **similarity**, analogy, comparison, likeness
paralysis n **1** = **immobility**, palsy **2** = **standstill**, breakdown, halt, stoppage
paralytic adj = **paralyzed**, challenged,

crippled, disabled, incapacitated, lame, palsied
paralyze v **1** = **disable**, cripple, incapacitate, lame **2** = **immobilize**, freeze, halt, numb, petrify, stun
parameter n = **limit**, framework, limitation, restriction, specification
paramount adj = **principal**, cardinal, chief, first, foremost, main, primary, prime, supreme
paranoid adj **1** = **mentally ill**, deluded, disturbed, manic, neurotic, paranoiac, psychotic **2** Inf = **suspicious**, fearful, nervous, wired (sl), worried
paraphernalia n = **equipment**, apparatus, baggage, belongings, effects, gear, stuff, tackle, things, trappings
paraphrase n **1** = **rewording**, rephrasing, restatement ◆ v **2** = **reword**, express in other words or one's own words, rephrase, restate

par·a·site [PA-rə-sīt] n 1 animal or plant living in or on another. 2 self-interested hanger-on. **par·a·sit'ic** [-SIT-ik] adj of the nature of, living as, parasite. **par'a·sit·ism** [-si-tiz-əm] n **par·a·si·tol'o·gy** n study of animal and vegetable parasites, esp. as causes of disease.

par·a·sol [PA-rə-sawl] n lightweight umbrella used as sunshade.

par·a·troop·er [PA-rə-troo-pər] n soldier trained to descend from airplane by parachute.

par·a·ty·phoid [pa-rə-TĪ-foid] n an infectious disease similar to but distinct from typhoid fever.

par·boil [PAHR-boil] vt boil until partly cooked.

par·cel [PAHR-səl] n 1 packet of goods, esp. one enclosed in paper. 2 quantity dealt with at one time. 3 tract of land. ♦ vt -celed, -cel·ing 4 wrap up. 5 divide into, distribute in, parts.

parch [pahrch] v 1 dry by heating. 2 make, become hot and dry. 3 scorch. 4 roast slightly.

parch·ment [PAHRCH-mənt] n 1 sheep, goat, calf skin prepared for writing. 2 manuscript of this.

par·don [PAHR-dn] vt 1 forgive, excuse. ♦ n 2 forgiveness. 3 release from punishment. **par'don·a·ble** adj

pare [pair] vt pared, par·ing 1 trim, cut edge or surface of. 2 decrease bit by bit. **par'ing** n piece pared off, rind.

par·e·gor·ic [pa-ri-GOR-ik] n tincture of opium used to stop diarrhea.

par·ent [PAIR-ənt] n father or mother.

par'ent·age n descent, extraction. **pa·rent·al** [pə-REN-tl] adj **par'ent·hood** [-huud] n

pa·ren·the·sis [pə-REN-thə-sis] n word, phrase, etc. inserted in passage independently of grammatical sequence and usu. marked off by brackets, dashes, or commas. **pa·ren'the·ses** [-seez] pl n round brackets, ( ). **par·en·thet'ic·al** adj

pa·ri·ah [pə-RĪ-ə] n social outcast.

par·ish [PA-rish] n 1 district under one clergyman. 2 subdivision of county. **pa·rish'ion·er** n member, inhabitant of parish.

parity see PAR.

park [pahrk] n 1 large area of land in natural state preserved for recreational use. 2 field or stadium for sporting events. 3 large enclosed piece of ground, usu. with grass or woodland, attached to country house or for public use. 4 space in camp for military supplies. ♦ vt 5 leave for a short time. 6 maneuver (automobile, etc) into a suitable space. 7 inf engage in caressing and kissing in parked automobile.

par·ka [PAHR-kə] n warm waterproof coat with hood.

par·lance [PAHR-ləns] n 1 way of speaking, conversation. 2 idiom.

par·ley [PAHR-lee] n, pl -leys 1 meeting between leaders or representatives of opposing forces to discuss terms. ♦ vi -leyed, -ley·ing 2 hold discussion about terms.

par·lia·ment [PAHR-lə-mənt] n legislature of some countries. **par·lia·men·tar'i·an** [-TAIR-ee-ən] n expert in rules and

THESAURUS

parasite n = sponger (inf), bloodsucker (inf), hanger-on, leech, scrounger (inf)

parasitic, parasitical adj = scrounging (inf), bloodsucking (inf), sponging (inf)

parcel n 1 = package, bundle, pack ♦ v 2 (often with up) = wrap, do up, pack, package, tie up

parch v = dry up, dehydrate, desiccate, evaporate, shrivel, wither

parched adj = dried out or up, arid, dehydrated, dry, thirsty

pardon v 1 = forgive, absolve, acquit, excuse, exonerate, let off (inf), overlook ♦ n 2 = forgiveness, absolution, acquittal, amnesty, exoneration

pardonable adj = forgivable, excusable, minor, understandable, venial

pare v 1 = peel, clip, cut, shave, skin, trim 2 = cut back, crop, cut, decrease, dock, reduce

parent n = father or mother, procreator, progenitor, sire

parentage n = family, ancestry, birth, descent, lineage, pedigree, stock

pariah n = outcast, exile, undesirable, untouchable

parish n = community, church, congregation, flock

parity n = equality, consistency, equivalence, uniformity, unity

park n = parkland, estate, garden, grounds, woodland

parlance n = language, idiom, jargon, phraseology, speech, talk, tongue procedures of a legislature or other formal organization.

par·lor [PAHR-lər] *n* **1** sitting room, room for receiving company in small house. **2** place for milking cows. **3** room or building as business premises, esp. undertaker, hairdresser, etc.

Par·me·san [PAHR-mə-zahn] *n* hard dry Italian cheese for grating.

pa·ro·chi·al [pə-ROH-kee-əl] *adj* **1** narrow, provincial. **2** of a parish. **pa·ro'chi·al·ism** *n*

par·o·dy [PA-rə-dee] *n, pl* **-dies 1** composition in which author's style is made fun of by imitation. **2** travesty. ◆ *vt* **-died, -dy·ing 3** write parody of. **par'o·dist** *n*

pa·role [pə-ROHL] *n* **1** early freeing of prisoner on condition of good behavior. **2** word of honor. ◆ *vt* **-roled, rol·ing 3** place on parole.

par·ox·ysm [PA-rək-siz-əm] *n* sudden violent attack of pain, rage, laughter.

par·quet [pahr-KAY] *n* **1** flooring of wooden blocks arranged in pattern. ◆ *vt* **-queted** [-KAYD], **-quet·ing** [-KAY-ing] **2** lay a parquet.

par·ri·cide [PA-rə-sīd] *n* murder or murderer of a parent.

par·rot [PA-rət] *n* **1** bird with short hooked beak, some varieties of which can imitate speaking. **2** unintelligent imitator. ◆ *vt* **3** imitate or repeat without understanding.

par·ry [PA-ree] *vt* **-ried, -ry·ing 1** ward off, turn aside. **2** act of parrying, ◆ *n, pl* **-ries 2** act of parrying, esp. in fencing.

parse [pahrs] *vt* **parsed, pars·ing** describe (word), analyze (sentence) in terms of grammar.

par·si·mo·ny [PAHR-sə-moh-nee] *n* **1** stinginess. **2** undue economy. **par·si·mo'ni·ous** *adj* sparing.

pars·ley [PAHR-slee] *n* herb used for seasoning, garnish, etc.

pars·nip [PAHR-snip] *n* edible whitish root vegetable.

par·son [PAHR-sən] *n* **1** clergyman of parish or church. **2** clergyman. **par'son·age** *n* parson's house.

part [pahrt] *n* **1** portion, section, share. **2** division. **3** actor's role. **4** duty. ◆ *pl* **5** region. ◆ *v* **6** divide. **7** separate. **part'ing** *n* **1** division between sections of hair on head. **2** separation. **3** leave-taking. **part'ly** *adv* in part. **part song** song for several voices singing in harmony.

par·take [pahr-TAYK] *v* **-took, -tak·en, -tak·ing 1** take or have share in. **2** take food or drink.

par·tial [PAHR-shəl] *adj* **1** not general or complete. **2** prejudiced. **3** fond of. **par'tial·ly** *adv* partly. **par·ti·al·i·ty** [pahr-shee-AL-i-tee] *n* **1** favoritism. **2** fondness for.

par·tic·i·pate [pahr-TIS-ə-payt] *v* **-pat·ed,**

parliament *n* = **assembly**, congress, convention, council, legislature, senate

parliamentary *adj* = **governmental**, law-making, legislative

parlor *n Old-fashioned* = **sitting room**, drawing room, front room, living room, lounge

parochial *adj* = **provincial**, insular, limited, narrow, narrow-minded, petty, small-minded

parody *n* **1** = **satire** (*inf*), burlesque, caricature, skit, spoof (*inf*) ◆ *v* **2** = **satirize** (*inf*), burlesque, caricature

paroxysm *n* = **outburst**, attack, convulsion, fit, seizure, spasm

parrot *v* = **repeat**, copy, echo, imitate, mimic

parry *v* **1** = **ward off**, block, deflect, rebuff, repel, repulse **2** = **evade**, avoid, dodge, sidestep

parsimonious *adj* = **mean**, close, frugal, miserly, niggardly, penny-pinching (*inf*), stingy, tightfisted

parson *n* = **clergyman**, churchman, cleric, minister, pastor, preacher, priest, vicar

part *n* **1** = **piece**, bit, fraction, fragment, portion, scrap, section, share **2** = **component**, branch, constituent, division, member, unit **3** *Theatre* = **role**, character, lines **4** = **side**, behalf, cause, concern, interest **5** (*often plural*) = **region**, area, district, neighborhood, quarter, vicinity **6 in good part** = **good-naturedly**, cheerfully, well, without offense **7 in part** = **partly**, a little, in some measure, partially, somewhat ◆ *v* **8** = **divide**, break, come apart, detach, rend, separate, sever, split, tear **9** = **separate**, depart, go, go away, leave, split up, withdraw

partake *v* **1 partake of** = **consume**, chow down (*sl*), eat, take **2 partake in** = **participate in**, engage in, share in, take part in

partial *adj* **1** = **incomplete**, imperfect,

-pat·ing **1** share in. **2** take part in.
par·tic'i·pant *n* **par·tic'i·pa·to·ry** *adj*
par·ti·ci·ple [PAHR-tə-sip-əl] *n* adjective made by inflection from verb and keeping verb's relation to dependent words.
par·ti·cip'i·al *adj*
par·ti·cle [PAHR-ti-kəl] *n* **1** minute portion of matter. **2** least possible amount. **3** minor part of speech in grammar, prefix, suffix.
par·ti-col·ored [PAHR-tee-kul-ərd] *adj* differently colored in different parts, variegated.
par·tic·u·lar [pahr-TIK-yə-lər] *adj* **1** relating to one, not general. **2** distinct. **3** minute. **4** very exact. **5** fastidious. ◆ *n* **6** detail, item. ◆ *pl* **7** detailed account. **8** items of information. **par·tic'u·lar·ize** *vt* **-ized, -iz·ing** mention in detail. **par·tic'u·lar·ly** *adv*
par·ti·san [PAHR-tə-zən] *n* **1** adherent of a party. **2** guerrilla, member of resistance movement. ◆ *adj* **3** adhering to faction. **4** prejudiced.
par·ti·tion [pahr-TISH-ən] *n* **1** division. **2** interior dividing wall. ◆ *vt* **3** divide, cut into

sections.
part·ner [PAHRT-nər] *n* **1** ally or companion. **2** member of a partnership. **3** one who dances with another. **4** a husband or wife. **5** *Sport* one who plays with another against opponents. ◆ *vt* **6** be a partner of. **part'ner·ship** *n* association of persons for business, etc.
par·tridge [PAHR-trij] *n, pl* **-tridg·es** game bird of the grouse family.
par·tu·ri·tion [pahr-tyuu-RISH-ən] *n* **1** act of bringing forth young. **2** childbirth.
par·ty [PAHR-tee] *n, pl* **-ties 1** social assembly. **2** group of persons traveling or working together. **3** group of persons united in opinion. **4** side. **5** person. ◆ *adj* **6** of, belonging to, a party or faction. **party line 1** telephone line serving two or more subscribers. **2** policies of political party. **party wall** common wall separating adjoining premises.
par·ve·nu [PAHR-və-noo] *n* **1** one newly risen into position of notice, power, wealth. **2** upstart.
Pas·cal [PAS-kal] *n* high-level computer

uncompleted, unfinished **2 = biased,** discriminatory, one-sided, partisan, prejudiced, unfair, unjust
partiality *n* **1 = bias,** favoritism, preference, prejudice **2 = liking,** fondness, inclination, love, penchant, predilection, taste, weakness
partially *adv* **= partly,** fractionally, incompletely, in part, not wholly, somewhat
participant *n* **= participator,** contributor, member, player, stakeholder
participate *v* **= take part,** be involved in, join in, partake, perform, share
participation *n* **= taking part,** contribution, involvement, joining in, partaking, sharing in
particle *n* **= bit,** grain, iota, jot, mite, piece, scrap, shred, speck
particular *adj* **1 = specific,** distinct, exact, peculiar, precise, special **2 = special,** especial, exceptional, marked, notable, noteworthy, remarkable, singular, uncommon, unusual **3 = fussy,** choosy (*inf*), demanding, fastidious, finicky, picky (*inf*) ◆ *n* **4** (usually plural) **= detail,** circumstance, fact, feature, item, specification **5 in particular = especially,** distinctly, exactly, particularly, specifically

particularly *adv* **1 = especially,** exceptionally, notably, singularly, uncommonly, unusually **2 = specifically,** distinctly, especially, explicitly, expressly, in particular
parting *n* **1 = going,** farewell, good-bye **2 = division,** breaking, rift, rupture, separation, split
partisan *n* **1 = supporter,** adherent, devotee, upholder **2 = underground fighter,** guerrilla, resistance fighter ◆ *adj* **3 = prejudiced,** biased, interested, one-sided, partial, sectarian
partition *n* **1 = screen,** barrier, wall **2 = division,** segregation, separation **3 = allotment,** apportionment, distribution ◆ *v* **4 = separate,** divide, screen
partly *adv* **= partially,** slightly, somewhat
partner *n* **1 = spouse,** consort, husband *or* wife, mate, significant other (*inf*) **2 = companion,** ally, associate, colleague, comrade, helper, mate
partnership *n* **= company,** alliance, cooperative, firm, house, society, union
party *n* **1 = get-together** (*inf*), celebration, festivity, function, gathering, reception, social gathering **2 = group,** band, company, crew, gang, squad, team, unit **3 = faction,** camp, clique, coterie, league,

programming language developed as a teaching language.

pas•chal [PAS-kəl] *adj* of Passover or Easter.

pass *vt* **1** go by, beyond, through, etc. **2** exceed. **3** be accepted by. **4** undergo successfully. **5** spend. **6** transfer. **7** exchange. **8** disregard. **9** bring into force, sanction a legislative bill, etc. ◆ *vi* **10** go. **11** be transferred from one state or person to another. **12** elapse. **13** undergo examination successfully. **14** be taken as member of religious or racial group other than one's own. ◆ *n* **15** way, esp. a narrow and difficult way. **16** permit, license, authorization. **17** successful result from test. **18** condition. **19** *Sports* transfer of ball by kick or throw. **pass'a•ble** *adj* (just) acceptable. **pass'ing** *adj* **1** transitory. **2** cursory, casual. **pass off** present (something) under false pretenses. **pass up** ignore, neglect, reject.

pas•sage [PAS-ij] *n* **1** channel, opening. **2** way through, corridor. **3** part of book, etc. **4** journey, voyage, fare. **5** enactment of rule, law by legislature, etc. **6** conversation,

dispute. **7** incident.

pas•sé [pa-SAY] *adj* **1** out-of-date. **2** past the prime.

pas•sen•ger [PAS-ən-jər] *n* traveler, esp. by public conveyance.

pas•ser•ine [PAS-ər-in] *adj* of the order of perching birds.

pas'sim *Lat* everywhere, throughout.

pas•sion [PASH-ən] *n* **1** ardent desire, esp. sexual. **2** any strongly felt emotion. **3** suffering (esp. that of Christ). **pas'sion•ate** [-it] *adj* (easily) moved by strong emotions.

pas•sive [PAS-iv] *adj* **1** unresisting. **2** submissive. **3** inactive. **4** denoting grammatical voice of verb in which the subject receives the action. **pas•siv'i•ty** *n* **passive smoking** involuntary inhalation of smoke from other's cigarettes by nonsmoker.

Pass•o•ver [PAS-oh-vər] *n* Jewish spring festival commemorating exodus of Jews from Egypt.

pass'port *n* official document granting permission to pass, travel abroad, etc.

pass•word [PAS-wurd] *n* **1** word, phrase,

set, side **4** = **person**, individual, someone

pass *v* **1** = **go by** *or* **past**, elapse, go, lapse, move, proceed, run **2** = **qualify**, do, get through, graduate, succeed **3** = **spend**, fill, occupy, while away **4** = **give**, convey, deliver, hand, send, transfer **5** = **approve**, accept, decree, enact, legislate, ordain, ratify **6** = **exceed**, beat, go beyond, outdo, outstrip, surpass **7** = **end**, blow over, cease, go ◆ *n* **8** = **gap**, canyon, gorge, ravine, route **9** = **license**, authorization, passport, permit, ticket, warrant

passable *adj* = **adequate**, acceptable, all right, average, fair, mediocre, so-so (*inf*), tolerable

passage *n* **1** = **way**, alley, avenue, channel, course, path, road, route **2** = **corridor**, hall, lobby, vestibule **3** = **extract**, excerpt, piece, quotation, reading, section, text **4** = **journey**, crossing, trek, trip, voyage **5** = **safe-conduct**, freedom, permission, right

passageway *n* = **corridor**, aisle, alley, hall, hallway, lane, passage

pass away *v Euphemistic* = **die**, expire, kick the bucket (*sl*), pass on, pass over, shuffle off this mortal coil, snuff it (*inf*)

passé *adj* = **out-of-date**, dated, obsolete, old-fashioned, old hat, outdated, outmoded, unfashionable

passenger *n* = **traveler**, fare, rider

passer-by *n* = **bystander**, onlooker, witness

passing *adj* **1** = **momentary**, brief, ephemeral, fleeting, short-lived, temporary, transient, transitory **2** = **superficial**, casual, cursory, glancing, quick, short

passion *n* **1** = **love**, ardor, desire, infatuation, lust **2** = **emotion**, ardor, excitement, feeling, fervor, fire, heat, intensity, warmth, zeal **3** = **rage**, anger, fit, frenzy, fury, outburst, paroxysm, storm **4** = **mania**, bug (*inf*), craving, craze, enthusiasm, fascination, obsession

passionate *adj* **1** = **loving**, amorous, ardent, erotic, hot, lustful **2** = **emotional**, ardent, eager, fervent, fierce, heartfelt, impassioned, intense, strong

passive *adj* = **submissive**, compliant, docile, inactive, quiescent, receptive

pass off *v* = **fake**, counterfeit, make a pretense of, palm off

pass out *v* = **faint**, become unconscious, black out (*inf*), lose consciousness

pass over *v* = **disregard**, ignore, overlook, take no notice of

pass up *v* = **miss**, abstain, decline, forgo, let slip, neglect to distinguish friend from enemy. **2** countersign.

past *adj* **1** ended. **2** gone by. **3** elapsed. ◆ *n* **4** bygone times. ◆ *adv* **5** by. **6** along. ◆ *prep* **7** beyond. **8** after.

pas•ta [PAH-stə] *n* type of food, such as spaghetti, that is made in different shapes from flour and water.

paste [payst] *n* **1** soft composition, as toothpaste. **2** soft plastic mixture or adhesive. **3** fine glass to imitate gems. ◆ *vt* **past•ed, past•ing 4** fasten with paste. **past•y** *adj* **past•i•er, past•i•est 5** like paste. **2** white. **3** sickly.

pas•tel [pa-STEL] *n* **1** colored crayon. **2** art of drawing with crayons. **3** pale, delicate color. ◆ *adj* **4** delicately tinted.

pas•teur•ize [PAS-chə-rīz] *vt* **-ized, -iz•ing** sterilize by heat. **pas•teur•i•za'tion** *n*

pas•tiche [pa-STEESH] *n* **1** literary, musical, artistic work composed of parts borrowed from other works and loosely connected together. **2** work imitating another's style.

pas•tille [pa-STEEL] *n* **1** lozenge. **2** aromatic substance burned as deodorant or fumigator.

pas•time [PAS-tīm] *n* **1** that which makes time pass agreeably. **2** recreation.

pas•tor [PAS-tər] *n* **1** priest or minister in charge of a church. **pas'to•ral** *adj* **1** of, or like, shepherd's or rural life. **2** of office of pastor. ◆ *n* **3** poem describing rural life.

pas•try [PAY-stree] *n, pl* **-tries** article of food made chiefly of flour, shortening and water.

pas•ture [PAS-chər] *n* **1** grass for food of cattle. **2** ground on which cattle graze. ◆ *v* **-tured, -tur•ing 3** (cause to) graze. **pas'tur•age** *n* (right to) pasture.

pat[1] *vt* **pat•ted, pat•ting 1** tap. ◆ *n* **2** light, quick blow. **3** small mass, as of butter, beaten into shape.

pat[2] *adv* **1** exactly. **2** fluently. **3** opportunely. **4** glib. **5** exactly right.

patch [pach] *n* **1** piece of cloth sewn on garment. **2** spot. **3** plot of ground. **4** protecting pad for the eye. **5** small contrasting area. **6** short period. ◆ *vt* **7** mend. **8** repair clumsily. **patch'y** *adj* **patch•i•er, patch•i•est 1** of uneven quality. **2** full of patches. **patch'work** *n* **1** work composed of pieces sewn together. **2** jumble.

patch•ou•li [pə-CHOO-lee] *n* **1** Indian herb. **2** perfume from it.

pate [payt] *n* **1** head. **2** top of head.

pâ•té [pah-TAY] *n* spread of finely chopped liver, etc. **pâté de foie gras** [də-fwah-GRAH] one made of goose liver.

pa•tel•la [pə-TEL-ə] *n, pl* **-las** kneecap. **pa•tel'lar** *adj*

pat•ent [PAT-nt] *n* **1** document securing to person or organization exclusive right to invention. ◆ *adj* **2** open. **3** evident. **4** manifest. **5** open to public perusal, e.g. *letters patent.* ◆ *vt* **6** secure a patent. **pat•ent•ee'** *n* **1** one who has a patent. **pat'ent•ly** *adv* obviously. **patent leather** (imitation) leather processed to give hard, glossy surface.

───── THESAURUS ─────

password *n* = **signal**, key word, watchword

past *adj* **1** = **former**, ancient, bygone, early, olden, previous **2** = **over**, done, ended, finished, gone ◆ *n* **3** = **background**, history, life, past life **4 the past** = **former times**, days gone by, long ago, olden days ◆ *prep* **5** = **after**, beyond, later than **6** = **beyond**, across, by, over

paste *n* **1** = **adhesive**, cement, glue, gum ◆ *v* **2** = **stick**, cement, glue, gum

pastel *adj* = **pale**, delicate, light, muted, soft

pastiche *n* = **medley**, blend, *mélange*, miscellany, mixture

pastime *n* = **activity**, amusement, diversion, entertainment, game, hobby, recreation

pastor *n* = **clergyman**, churchman,

ecclesiastic, minister, parson, priest, rector, vicar

pastoral *adj* **1** = **rustic**, bucolic, country, rural **2** = **ecclesiastical**, clerical, ministerial, priestly

pasture *n* = **grassland**, grass, grazing, meadow

pasty *adj* = **pale**, anemic, pallid, sickly, wan

pat[1] *v* **1** = **stroke**, caress, fondle, pet, tap, touch ◆ *n* **2** = **stroke**, clap, tap

patch *n* **1** = **reinforcement 2** = **spot**, bit, scrap, shred, small piece **3** = **plot**, area, ground, land, tract ◆ *v* **4** = **mend**, cover, reinforce, repair, sew up

patchwork *n* = **mixture**, jumble, medley, pastiche

patchy *adj* = **uneven**, erratic, fitful, irregular, sketchy, spotty, variable

patent *n* **1** = **copyright**, license ◆ *adj* **2** =

pa·ter·fa·mil·i·as [pah-tər-fə-MIL-ee-əs] *n*, *pl* **-ases** father of a family.

pa·ter·nal [pə-TUR-nl] *adj* **1** fatherly. **2** of a father. **3** related through a father. **pa·ter'nal·ism** *n* authority exercised in a way that limits individual responsibility. **pa·ter·nal·is'tic** *adj* **pa·ter'ni·ty** *n* **1** relation of a father to his offspring. **2** fatherhood.

pa·ter·nos·ter [PAY tər NOS tər] *n* **1** Lord's Prayer. **2** beads of rosary.

path *n*, *pl* **paths** [pathz] **1** way or track. **2** course of action.

pa·thet·ic [pə-THET-ik] *adj* **1** affecting or moving tender emotions. **2** distressingly inadequate. **pa·thet'i·cal·ly** *adv*

path·o·gen·ic [path-ə-JEN-ik] *adj* producing disease. **path'o·gen** *n* disease-producing agent, e.g. virus.

pa·thol·o·gy [pə-THOL-ə-jee] *n* science of diseases. **path·o·log'i·cal** [-LOJ-i-kəl] *adj* **1** of the science of disease. **2** due to disease. **3** compulsively motivated. **pa·thol'o·gist** *n*

pa·thos [PAY-thos] *n* power of exciting tender emotions.

pa·tient [PAY-shənt] *adj* **1** bearing trials calmly. ♦ *n* **2** person under medical treatment. **pa'tience** *n* **1** quality of enduring. **2** card game for one player.

pat·i·na [pə-TEE-nə] *n* **1** fine layer on a surface. **2** sheen of age on woodwork.

pat·i·o [PAT-ee-oh] *n*, *pl* **-ios** (usu. paved)

area adjoining house for lounging, etc.

pat·ois [PA-twah] *n* regional dialect.

pa·tri·arch [PAY-tree-ahrk] *n* father and founder of family, esp. Biblical. **pa·tri·ar'chal** *adj* venerable.

pa·tri·cian [pə-TRISH-ən] *n* **1** noble of ancient Rome. **2** one of noble birth. ♦ *adj* **3** of noble birth.

pat·ri·cide [PA-trə-sīd] *n* murder or murderer of father.

pat·ri·mo·ny [PA-trə-moh-nee] *n*, *pl* **-nies** property inherited from ancestors.

pa·tri·ot [PAY-tree-ət] *n* one who loves own country and maintains its interests. **pa'tri·ot·ism** *n* [-ə-tiz-əm] love of, loyalty to one's country. **pa·tri·ot'ic** [-OT-ik] *adj* inspired by love of one's country.

pa·trol [pə-TROHL] *n* **1** regular circuit by guard. **2** person, small group patrolling. **3** unit of Boy Scouts or Girl Scouts. ♦ *v* **-trolled, -trol·ling 4** go around on guard, or reconnoitering.

pa·tron [PAY-trən] *n* **1** one who sponsors or aids artists, charities, etc. **2** protector. **3** regular customer. **4** guardian saint. **5** one who has disposition of benefice, etc. **pa'tron·age** *n* support given by, or position of, a patron. **pa'tron·ize** *vt* **-ized, -iz·ing 1** assume air of superiority toward. **2** frequent as customer. **3** encourage.

pat·ro·nym·ic [pa-trə-NIM-ik] *n* name

———— THESAURUS ————

obvious, apparent, clear, evident, glaring, manifest

paternal *adj* = **fatherly**, concerned, protective, solicitous

paternity *n* **1** = **fatherhood 2** = **parentage**, descent, extraction, family, lineage

path *n* **1** = **way**, footpath, road, track, trail **2** = **course**, direction, road, route, way

pathetic *adj* = **sad**, affecting, distressing, heart-rending, moving, pitiable, plaintive, poignant, tender, touching

pathos *n* = **sadness**, pitifulness, plaintiveness, poignancy

patience *n* **1** = **forbearance**, calmness, restraint, serenity, sufferance, tolerance **2** = **endurance**, constancy, fortitude, long-suffering, perseverance, resignation, stoicism, submission

patient *adj* **1** = **long-suffering**, calm, enduring, persevering, philosophical, resigned, stoical, submissive, uncomplaining **2** = **forbearing**, even-tempered, forgiving, indulgent,

lenient, mild, tolerant, understanding ♦ *n* **3** = **sick person**, case, invalid, sufferer

patriot *n* = **nationalist**, chauvinist, loyalist

patriotic *adj* = **nationalistic**, chauvinistic, jingoistic, loyal

patriotism *n* = **nationalism**, jingoism

patrol *n* **1** = **policing**, guarding, protecting, vigilance, watching **2** = **guard**, patrolman, sentinel, watch, watchman ♦ *v* **3** = **police**, guard, inspect, keep guard, keep watch, safeguard

patron *n* **1** = **supporter**, backer, benefactor, champion, friend, helper, philanthropist, sponsor **2** = **customer**, buyer, client, frequenter, habitué, shopper

patronage *n* **1** = **support**, aid, assistance, backing, help, promotion, sponsorship **2** = **custom**, business, clientele, commerce, trade, trading, traffic

patronize *v* **1** = **talk down to**, look down on **2** = **be a customer** *or* **client of**, do business with, frequent, shop at **3** = **support**, back, fund, help, maintain, derived from that of parent or an ancestor.

pat·ter [PAT-ər] *vi* **1** make noise, as sound of quick, short steps. **2** tap in quick succession. **3** pray, talk rapidly. ◆ *n* **4** quick succession of taps. **5** *inf* glib, rapid speech.

pat·tern [PAT-ərn] *n* **1** arrangement of repeated parts. **2** design. **3** shape to direct cutting of cloth, etc. **4** model. **5** specimen. ◆ *vt* **6** (with *on* or *after*) model. **7** decorate with pattern.

pat·ty [PAT-ee] *n, pl* **-ties 1** a little pie. **2** thin round piece of meat, candy, etc.

pau·ci·ty [PAW-si-tee] *n* **1** scarcity. **2** smallness of quantity. **3** fewness.

paunch [pawnch] *n* **1** belly. **2** potbelly.

pau·per [PAW-pər] *n* poor person, esp. formerly, one supported by the public. **pau'per·ism** *n* **1** destitution. **2** extreme poverty. **pau'per·ize** *vt* **-ized, -iz·ing** reduce to pauperism.

pause [pawz] *vi* **paused, paus·ing 1** cease for a time. ◆ *n* **2** stop or rest.

pave [payv] *vt* **paved, pav·ing** form surface with stone or brick. **pave'ment** [-mənt] *n* **1** paved floor, footpath. **2** material for paving. **pave the way for 1** lead up to. **2** facilitate entrance of.

pa·vil·ion [pə-VIL-yən] *n* **1** clubhouse on playing field, etc. **2** building for housing exhibition, etc. **3** large ornate tent.

paw *n* **1** foot of animal. ◆ *v* **2** scrape with forefoot. **3** handle roughly. **4** stroke with the hands.

pawn[1] *vt* **1** deposit (article) as security for money borrowed. ◆ *n* **2** article deposited. **pawn'bro·ker** *n* lender of money on goods pledged.

pawn[2] *n* **1** piece in chess. **2** *fig* person used as mere tool.

pay *v* **paid, pay·ing** ◆ *vt* **1** give money, etc., for goods or services rendered. **2** compensate. **3** give or bestow. **4** be profitable to. **5** (with *out*) release bit by bit, as rope. ◆ *vi* **6** be remunerative. **7** be profitable. **8** (with *out*) spend. ◆ *n* **9** wages. **10** paid employment. **pay'a·ble** *adj* **1** justly due. **2** profitable. **pay·ee'** *n* person to whom money is paid or due. **pay'ment** [-mənt] *n* discharge of debt. **pay'load** *n* **1** part of cargo earning revenue. **2** explosive power of missile, etc. **paying guest** boarder, lodger, esp. in private house. **pay television** programs provided for viewers who pay monthly or per-program fees.

promote, sponsor

patronizing *adj* = **condescending**, disdainful, gracious, haughty, snobbish, supercilious, superior

patter[1] *v* **1** = **tap**, beat, pat, pitter-patter **2** = **walk lightly**, scurry, scuttle, skip, trip ◆ *n* **3** = **tapping**, pattering, pitter-patter

patter[2] *n* **1** = **spiel** (*inf*), line, pitch **2** = **chatter**, gabble, jabber, nattering, prattle **3** = **jargon**, argot, cant, lingo (*inf*), patois, slang, vernacular ◆ *v* **4** = **chatter**, jabber, prate, rattle on, spout (*inf*)

pattern *n* **1** = **design**, arrangement, decoration, device, figure, motif **2** = **order**, method, plan, sequence, system **3** = **plan**, design, diagram, guide, original, stencil, template ◆ *v* **4** = **model**, copy, follow, form, imitate, mold, style

paucity *n Formal* = **scarcity**, dearth, deficiency, lack, rarity, scantiness, shortage, sparseness

paunch *n* = **belly**, pot, potbelly, spare tire (*sl*)

pauper *n* = **down-and-out**, bankrupt, beggar, mendicant, poor person

pause *v* **1** = **stop briefly**, break, cease, delay, halt, have a breather (*inf*), interrupt,

rest, take a break, wait ◆ *n* **2** = **stop**, break, breather (*inf*), cessation, gap, halt, interlude, intermission, interval, lull, respite, rest, stoppage

pave *v* = **cover**, concrete, floor, surface, tile

paw *v* = **manhandle**, grab, handle roughly, maul, molest

pawn[1] *v* = **hock** (*inf*), deposit, mortgage, pledge

pawn[2] *n* = **tool**, cat's-paw, instrument, plaything, puppet, stooge (*sl*)

pay *v* **1** = **reimburse**, compensate, give, recompense, remit, remunerate, requite, reward, settle **2** = **give**, bestow, extend, grant, hand out, present **3** = **benefit**, do good, profit, serve **4** = **be profitable**, make a return, make money **5** = **yield**, bring in, produce, return ◆ *n* **6** = **wages**, allowance, earnings, fee, income, payment, recompense, reimbursement, remuneration, reward, salary, stipend

payable *adj* = **due**, outstanding, owed, owing

pay back *v* **1** = **repay**, refund, reimburse, settle up, square **2** = **get even with** (*inf*), hit back, retaliate

payment *n* **1** = **paying**, discharge,

Pb *Chem.* lead.

pc 1 politically correct. **2** personal computer.

Pd *Chem.* palladium.

pea [pee] *n* **1** fruit, growing in pods, of climbing plant. **2** the plant. **pea-green** *adj* of shade of green like color of green peas. **pea green** this color. **pea soup 1** thick soup made of green peas. **2** *inf* thick fog.

peace [pees] *n* **1** freedom from war. **2** harmony. **3** quietness of mind. **4** calm. **5** repose. **peace'a·ble** *adj* disposed to peace. **peace'a·bly** *adv* **peace'ful** *adj* **1** free from war, tumult. **2** mild. **3** undisturbed.

peach [peech] *n* **1** stone fruit of delicate flavor. **2** *inf* person or thing very pleasant. **3** pinkish-yellow color. **peach'y** *adj* **peach·i·er, peach·i·est 1** like peach. **2** *inf* fine, excellent.

pea·cock [PEE-kok] *n* male of bird with fanlike tail, brilliantly colored. **pea'hen** *n, fem.* **pea'fowl** *n* peacock or peahen.

peak [peek] *n* **1** pointed end of anything, esp. hill's sharp top. **2** point of greatest development, etc. **3** sharp increase. **4** projecting piece on front of cap. ♦ *v* **5** (cause to) form, reach peaks. **peaked** *adj* like, having a peak. **peak·ed** [PEE-kid] sickly, wan, drawn.

peal [peel] *n* **1** loud sound or succession of loud sounds. **2** changes rung on set of bells. **3** chime. ♦ *vi* **4** sound loudly.

pea·nut [PEE-nut] *n* **1** pea-shaped nut that ripens underground. **2** the plant. ♦ *pl* **3** *inf* trifling amount of money.

pear [pair] *n* **1** tree yielding sweet, juicy fruit. **2** the fruit. **pear-shaped** *adj* shaped like a pear, heavier at the bottom than the top.

pearl [purl] *n* hard, lustrous structure found in several mollusks, esp. pearl oyster and used as jewel. **pearl'y** *adj* **pearl·i·er, pearl·i·est** like pearls.

peas·ant [PEZ-ənt] *n* **1** in certain countries, member of low social class, esp. in rural district. **2** boorish person. **peas'ant·ry** *n* peasants collectively.

peat [peet] *n* **1** decomposed vegetable substance found in bogs. **2** turf of it used for fuel. **peat moss** dried peat, used as mulch, etc.

peb·ble [PEB-əl] *n* **1** small roundish stone. **2** pale, transparent rock crystal. **3** grainy, irregular surface. ♦ *vt* **-bled, -bling 4** pave, cover with pebbles.

pe·can [pi-KAHN] *n* **1** N Amer. tree, species of hickory, allied to walnut. **2** its edible nut.

pec·ca·dil·lo [pek-ə-DIL-oh] *n, pl* **-loes 1** slight offense. **2** petty crime.

pec·ca·ry [PEK-ə-ree] *n, pl* **-ries** vicious Amer. animal allied to pig.

peck[1] [pek] *n* **1** fourth part of bushel, equal to 8.81 liters. **2** great deal.

peck[2] *v* **1** pick, strike with or as with beak. **2** nibble. ♦ *n* **3** quick kiss. **peck'ish** *adj inf* irritable.

pecs [peks] *pl n inf* pectoral muscles.

pec·tin [PEK-tin] *n* gelatinizing substance obtained from ripe fruits. **pec'tic** *adj* **1** congealing. **2** denoting pectin.

pec·to·ral [PEK-tər-əl] *adj* **1** of the breast. ♦ *n* **2** pectoral part of organ. **3** breastplate.

pec·u·late [PEK-yə-layt] *v* **-lat·ed, -lat·ing 1**

remittance, settlement **2 = remittance,** advance, deposit, installment, premium **3 = wage,** fee, hire, remuneration, reward

pay off *v* **1 = settle,** clear, discharge, pay in full, square **2 = succeed,** be effective, work

pay out *v* **= spend,** disburse, expend, fork out *or* over *or* up (*sl*), shell out (*inf*)

peace *n* **1 = stillness,** calm, calmness, hush, quiet, repose, rest, silence, tranquillity **2 = serenity,** calm, composure, contentment, repose **3 = harmony,** accord, agreement, concord **4 = truce,** armistice, treaty

peaceable *adj* **= peace-loving,** conciliatory, friendly, gentle, mild, peaceful, unwarlike

peaceful *adj* **1 = at peace,** amicable, friendly, harmonious, nonviolent **2 = calm,** placid, quiet, restful, serene, still, tranquil, undisturbed **3 = peace-loving,** conciliatory, peaceable, unwarlike

peacemaker *n* **= mediator,** arbitrator, conciliator, pacifier

peak *n* **1 = point,** apex, brow, crest, pinnacle, summit, tip, top **2 = high point,** acme, climax, crown, culmination, zenith ♦ *v* **3 = culminate,** climax, come to a head

peal *n* **1 = ring,** blast, chime, clang, clap, crash, reverberation, roar, rumble ♦ *v* **2 = ring,** chime, crash, resound, roar, rumble

peasant *n* **= rustic,** countryman

peccadillo *n* **= misdeed,** error, indiscretion, lapse, misdemeanor, slip

peck *v, n* **= pick,** dig, hit, jab, poke, prick,

embezzle. **2** steal. **pec·u·la'tion** n

pe·cu·liar [pi-KYOOL-yər] adj **1** strange. **2** particular. **3** belonging to. **pe·cu·li·ar'i·ty** n **1** oddity. **2** characteristic. **3** distinguishing feature.

pe·cu·ni·ar·y [pi-KYOO-nee-er-ee] adj relating to, or consisting of, money.

ped·a·gogue [PED-ə-gog] n **1** schoolmaster. **2** pedant. **ped·a·gog'ic** [-GOJ-ik] adj

ped·al [PED-l] n **1** something to transmit motion from foot. **2** foot lever to modify tone or swell of musical instrument. **3** Mus. note, usu. bass, held through successive harmonies. ◆ adj **4** of a foot. ◆ v -daled, -dal·ing **5** propel bicycle, etc. by using its pedals. **6** use pedal.

ped·ant [PED-ənt] n one who overvalues, or insists on, petty details of book learning, grammatical rules, etc. **pe·dan'tic** adj **ped'ant·ry** n, pl **-tries**

ped·dle [PED-l] vt **-dled, -dling** go around selling goods. **ped'dler, ped'lar** n

ped·er·ast [PED-ə-rast] n man who has homosexual relations with boy. **ped'er·as·ty** n

ped·es·tal [PED-ə-stl] n base of column, pillar. **put on a pedestal** idealize.

pe·des·tri·an [pə-DES-tree-ən] n **1** one who goes on foot. **2** walker. ◆ adj **3** going on foot. **4** commonplace. **5** dull, uninspiring.

pe·di·at·rics [pee-dee-A-triks] n branch of medicine dealing with diseases and disorders of children. **pe·di·a·tri'cian** [-ə-TRISH-ən] n

ped·i·cel [PED-ə-səl] n small, short stalk of leaf, flower or fruit.

ped·i·cure [PED-i-kyoor] n medical or cosmetic treatment of feet.

ped'i·gree n **1** register of ancestors. **2** genealogy.

ped·i·ment [PED-ə-mənt] n triangular part over Greek portico, etc. **ped·i·men'tal** [-MEN-tl] adj

pe·dom·e·ter [pə-DOM-i-tər] n instrument that measures the distance walked.

pe·dun·cle [pi-DUNG-kəl] n **1** flower stalk. **2** stalklike structure.

peek vi, n peep, glance.

peel vt **1** strip off skin, rind or any form of covering. ◆ vi **2** come off, as skin, rind. ◆ n **3** rind, skin. **peeled** adj inf of eyes, watchful. **peel'ings** pl n parings.

peep[1] vi **1** look slyly or quickly. ◆ n **2** such a look.

peep[2] vi **1** cry, as chick. **2** chirp. ◆ n **3** such a cry.

peer[1] n **1** nobleman. **2** one of the same rank, ability, etc. **peer'age** [-ij] n **1** body of peers. **2** rank of peer. **peer'ess** n, fem.

strike, tap

peculiar adj **1** = **odd**, abnormal, bizarre, curious, eccentric, extraordinary, freakish, funny, offbeat, outlandish, outré, quaint, queer, singular, strange, uncommon, unconventional, unusual, weird **2** = **specific**, characteristic, distinctive, particular, special, unique

peculiarity n **1** = **eccentricity**, abnormality, foible, idiosyncrasy, mannerism, oddity, quirk **2** = **characteristic**, attribute, feature, mark, particularity, property, quality, trait

pedagogue n = **teacher**, instructor, master or mistress, schoolmaster or schoolmistress

pedant n = **hairsplitter**, nit-picker (inf), quibbler

pedantic adj = **hairsplitting**, academic, bookish, donnish, formal, fussy, nit-picking (inf), particular, precise, punctilious

pedantry n = **hairsplitting**, punctiliousness, quibbling

peddle v = **sell**, hawk, market, push (inf), trade

peddler n = **seller**, door-to-door salesman, hawker, huckster, vendor

pedestal n = **support**, base, foot, mounting, plinth, stand

pedestrian n **1** = **walker**, foot-traveler ◆ adj **2** = **dull**, banal, boring, commonplace, humdrum, mediocre, mundane, ordinary, prosaic, uninspired

pedigree n **1** = **lineage**, ancestry, blood, breed, descent, extraction, family, family tree, genealogy, line, race, stock ◆ adj **2** = **purebred**, full-blooded, thoroughbred

peek v **1** = **glance**, look, peep ◆ n **2** = **glance**, glimpse, look, look-see (sl), peep

peel v **1** = **skin**, flake off, pare, scale, strip off ◆ n **2** = **skin**, peeling, rind

peep[1] v **1** = **peek**, look, sneak a look, steal a look ◆ n **2** = **look**, glimpse, look-see (sl), peek

peep[2] v, n = **tweet**, cheep, chirp, squeak

peephole n = **spyhole**, aperture, chink, crack, hole, opening

peer'less [-lis] *adj* without match or equal.
peer[2] *vi* look closely and intently.
peeved [peevd] *adj* sulky, irritated. **peeve** *vt* **peeved, peev·ing 1** annoy. **2** vex.
pee'vish *adj* **1** fretful. **2** irritable. **pee'vish·ly** *adv* **pee'vish·ness** [-nis] *n* annoyance.
peg *n* **1** nail or pin for joining, fastening, marking, etc. **2** (mark of) level, standard, etc. ◆ *v* **pegged, peg·ging 3** fasten with pegs. **4** stabilize (prices). **5** *inf* throw. **6** (with *away*) persevere. **take down a peg** humble (someone).
peign·oir [pain-WAHR] *n* woman's dressing gown, jacket, wrapper.
pe·jo·ra·tive [pi-JOR-ə-tiv] *adj* (of words, etc.) with unpleasant, disparaging connotation.
Pe·king·ese [pee-kə-NEEZ] *n* small Chinese dog.
pe·lag·ic [pə-LAJ-ik] *adj* of the deep sea.
pel·i·can [PEL-i-kən] *n* large, fish-eating waterfowl with large pouch beneath its bill.
pel·let [PEL-it] *n* little ball, pill.
pell-mell *adv* in utter confusion, headlong.
pel·lu·cid [pə-LOO-sid] *adj* **1** translucent. **2** clear.
pelt[1] *vt* **1** strike with missiles. ◆ *vi* **2** throw missiles. **3** rush. **4** fall persistently, as rain.
pelt[2] *n* raw hide or skin.
pel'vis *n, pl* **-vis·es** bony cavity at base of

human trunk. **pel'vic** *adj* pert. to pelvis.
pen[1] *n* **1** instrument for writing. ◆ *vt* **penned, pen·ning 2** compose. **3** write. **pen name** author's pseudonym. **pen pal** person with whom one corresponds, usu. someone whom one has never met.
pen[2] *n* **1** small enclosure, as for sheep. ◆ *vt* **penned, pen·ning 2** put, keep in enclosure.
pen[3] *n* female swan.
pe·nal [PEEN-l] *adj* of, incurring, inflicting, punishment. **pe'nal·ize** *vt* **-ized, -iz·ing 1** impose penalty on. **2** handicap. **pen'al·ty** *n, pl* **-ties 1** punishment for crime or offense. **2** forfeit. **3** *Sports* handicap or disadvantage imposed for infringement of rule, etc.
pen·ance [PEN-əns] *n* **1** suffering submitted to as expression of penitence. **2** repentance.
pen·chant [PEN-chənt] *n* inclination, decided taste.
pen·cil [PEN-səl] *n* **1** instrument as of graphite, for writing, etc. **2** *Optics* narrow beam of light. ◆ *vt* **-ciled, -cil·ing 3** paint or draw. **4** mark with pencil.
pend'ant [PEN-dənt] *n* hanging ornament. **pend'ent** *adj* **1** suspended. **2** hanging. **3** projecting.
pend'ing *prep* **1** during, until. ◆ *adj* **2** awaiting settlement. **3** undecided. **4** imminent.

————| THESAURUS |————

peer[1] *n* **1 = noble**, aristocrat, lord, nobleman **2 = equal**, compeer, fellow, like
peer[2] *v* **= squint**, gaze, inspect, peep, scan, snoop, spy
peerage *n* **= aristocracy**, lords and ladies, nobility, peers
peerless *adj* **= unequaled**, beyond compare, excellent, incomparable, matchless, outstanding, unmatched, unparalleled, unrivaled
peevish *adj* **= irritable**, cantankerous, childish, churlish, cross, crotchety, fractious, fretful, grumpy, petulant, querulous, snappy, sulky, sullen, surly
peg *v* **= fasten**, attach, fix, join, secure
pejorative *adj* **= derogatory**, deprecatory, depreciatory, disparaging, negative, uncomplimentary, unpleasant
pelt[1] *v* **1 = throw**, batter, bombard, cast, hurl, pepper, shower, sling, strike **2 = rush**, belt (*sl*), charge, dash, hurry, run fast, shoot, speed, tear **3 = pour**, bucket down

(*inf*), rain cats and dogs (*inf*), rain hard, teem
pelt[2] *n* **= coat**, fell, hide, skin
pen[1] *v* **= write**, compose, draft, draw up, jot down
pen[2] *n* **1 = enclosure**, cage, coop, fold, hutch, pound, sty ◆ *v* **2 = enclose**, cage, confine, coop up, fence in, hedge, shut up or in
penal *adj* **= disciplinary**, corrective, punitive
penalize *v* **= punish**, discipline, handicap, impose a penalty on
penalty *n* **= punishment**, fine, forfeit, handicap, price
penance *n* **= atonement**, penalty, reparation, sackcloth and ashes
penchant *n* **= liking**, bent, bias, fondness, inclination, leaning, partiality, predilection, proclivity, propensity, taste, tendency
pending *adj* **= undecided**, awaiting, imminent, impending, in the balance,

pen·du·lous [PEN-jə-ləs] *adj* hanging, swinging. **pen'du·lum** [-ləm] *n* suspended weight swinging to and fro, esp. as regulator for clock.

pen·e·trate [PEN-i-trayt] *vt* **-trat·ed, trat·ing 1** enter into. **2** pierce. **3** arrive at the meaning of. **pen·e·tra·bil'i·ty** *n* quality of being penetrable. **pen'e·tra·ble** [-trə-bəl] *adj* capable of being entered or pierced. **penetrating** *adj* **1** sharp. **2** easily heard. **3** subtle. **4** quick to understand. **pen·e·tra'tion** *n* insight, acuteness. **pen'e·tra·tive** [-tray-tiv] *adj* **1** piercing. **2** discerning.

pen·guin [PENG-gwin] *n* flightless, short-legged swimming bird.

pen·i·cil·lin [pen-ə-SIL-in] *n* antibiotic drug effective against a wide range of diseases, infections.

pen·in·su·la [pə-NINS-yə-lə] *n* portion of land nearly surrounded by water. **pen·in'su·lar** *adj*

pe·nis [PEE-nis] *n, pl* **-nis·es** male organ of copulation (and of urination) in man and many mammals.

pen·i·tent [PEN-i-tənt] *adj* **1** affected by sense of guilt. ♦ *n* **2** one that repents of sin. **pen'i·tence** *n* **1** sorrow for sin. **2** repentance. **pen·i·ten'tial** [-TEN-shəl] *adj* of, or expressing, penitence. **pen·i·ten'tia·ry** [-TEN-shə-ree] *adj* **1** relating to penance, or to the rules of penance. ♦ *n, pl* **-ries 2** prison.

pen·nant [PEN-ənt] *n* long narrow flag.

pen·non [PEN-ən] *n* small pointed or swallow-tailed flag.

pen·ny [PEN-ee] *n, pl* **-nies 1** coin, 100th part of dollar. **2** similar coin of other countries. **pen'ni·less** [-lis] *adj* **1** having no money. **2** poor. **a pretty penny** *inf* considerable amount of money.

pe·nol·o·gy [pee-NOL-ə-jee] *n* study of punishment and prevention of crime.

pen·sion [PEN-shən] *n* **1** regular payment to old people, retired public officials, workers, etc. ♦ *vt* **2** grant pension to. **pen'sion·er** *n*

pen·sive [PEN-siv] *adj* **1** thoughtful with sadness. **2** wistful.

pent *adj* shut up, kept in. **pent-up** *adj* not released, repressed.

pen·ta·gon [PEN-tə-gon] *n* plane figure having five angles. **pen·tag'o·nal** [-TAG-ə-nl] *adj*

pen·tam·e·ter [pen-TAM-i-tər] *n* verse of five metrical feet.

Pen·ta·teuch [PEN-tə-tyook] *n* first five books of Old Testament.

pen·tath·lon [pen-TATH-lən] *n* athletic contest of five events.

Pen·te·cost [PEN-ti-kawst] *n* Christian festival of seventh Sunday after Easter.

pent·house [PENT-hows] *n, pl* **-hous·es** [-howz-iz] apartment or other structure on top, or top floor, of building.

pen·tode [PEN-tohd] *n Electronics* five-electrode vacuum tube, having anode, cathode and three grids.

pe·nult [PEE-nult] *n* last syllable but one of word. **pen·ul·ti·mate** [pi-NUL-tə-mit] *adj* next before the last.

pe·num·bra [pi-NUM-brə] *n* **1** imperfect shadow. **2** in an eclipse, the partially shadowed region that surrounds the full

---

THESAURUS

undetermined, unsettled

penetrate *v* **1** = **pierce**, bore, enter, go through, prick, stab **2** = **grasp**, comprehend, decipher, fathom, figure out (*inf*), get to the bottom of, work out

penetrating *adj* **1** = **sharp**, carrying, harsh, piercing, shrill **2** = **perceptive**, acute, astute, incisive, intelligent, keen, perspicacious, quick, sharp, sharp-witted, shrewd

penetration *n* **1** = **piercing**, entrance, entry, incision, puncturing **2** = **perception**, acuteness, astuteness, insight, keenness, sharpness, shrewdness

penitence *n* = **repentance**, compunction, contrition, regret, remorse, shame, sorrow

penitent *adj* = **repentant**, abject,

apologetic, conscience-stricken, contrite, regretful, remorseful, sorry

pen name *n* = **pseudonym**, nom de plume

pennant *n* = **flag**, banner, ensign, pennon, streamer

penniless *adj* = **poor**, broke (*inf*), destitute, dirt-poor (*inf*), down and out, down on one's luck (*inf*), flat broke (*inf*), impecunious, impoverished, indigent, penurious, poverty-stricken

pension *n* = **allowance**, annuity, benefit, superannuation

pensive *adj* = **thoughtful**, contemplative, dreamy, meditative, musing, preoccupied, reflective, sad, serious, solemn, wistful

pent-up *adj* = **suppressed**, bottled up, curbed, held back, inhibited, repressed, shadow.

pen·u·ry [PEN-yə-ree] n **1** extreme poverty. **2** extreme scarcity. **pe·nu·ri·ous** [pə-NUUR-ee-əs] adj **1** niggardly, stingy. **2** poor, scanty.

peo·ple [PEE-pəl] pl n **1** persons generally. **2** community, nation. **3** race. **4** family. ◆ vt **-pled, -pling 5** stock with inhabitants. **6** populate.

pep n inf **1** vigor. **2** energy. **3** enthusiasm. ◆ vt **pepped, pep·ping 4** impart energy to. **5** speed up.

pep·per [PEP-ər] n **1** fruit of climbing plant that yields pungent aromatic spice. **2** various slightly pungent vegetables, e.g. capsicum. ◆ vt **3** season with pepper. **4** sprinkle, dot. **5** pelt with missiles. **pep·per·y** adj **1** having the qualities of pepper. **2** irritable. **pep'per·corn** n **1** dried pepper berry. **2** something trifling. **pep'per·mint** n **1** plant noted for aromatic pungent liquor distilled from it. **2** a candy flavored with this.

pep·tic [PEP-tik] adj relating to digestion or digestive juices.

per [pər] prep **1** for each. **2** by. **3** in manner of.

per-, par-, pel-, pil- prefix through, thoroughly, e.g. perfect; pellucid.

per·am·bu·late [pər-AM-byə-layt] v **-lat·ed, -lat·ing** ◆ vt **1** walk through or over. **2** traverse. ◆ vi **3** walk about. **per·am'bu·la·tor** n baby carriage.

per an·num [pər AN-əm] Lat by the year.

per·cale [pər-KAYL] n woven cotton used esp. for sheets.

per cap·i·ta [pər KAP-i-tə] Lat for each person.

per·ceive [pər-SEEV] vt **-ceived, -ceiv·ing 1** obtain knowledge of through senses. **2** observe. **3** understand. **per·ceiv'a·ble** adj **per·cep'ti·ble** adj discernible, recognizable. **per·cep'tion** n **1** faculty of perceiving. **2** intuitive judgment. **per·cep'tive** adj

per·cent·age [pər-SEN-tij] n proportion or rate per hundred. **per cent** in each hundred.

perception n see PERCEIVE.

perch[1] [purch] n freshwater fish.

perch[2] n **1** resting place, as for bird. ◆ vt **2** place, as on perch. ◆ vi **3** alight, settle on fixed body. **4** roost. **5** balance on.

per·cip·i·ent [pər-SIP-ee-ənt] adj **1** having faculty of perception. **2** perceiving. ◆ n **3** one who perceives.

per·co·late [PUR-kə-layt] v **-lat·ed, -lat·ing 1** pass through fine mesh as liquid. **2** permeate. **3** filter. **per'co·la·tor** n coffeepot with filter.

per·cus·sion [pər-KUSH-ən] n **1** collision. **2** impact. **3** vibratory shock. **percussion instrument** musical instrument played by being struck, such as drums or cymbals.

per di·em [pər DEE-əm] Lat **1** by the day. **2** for each day.

per·di·tion [pər-DISH-ən] n spiritual ruin.

per·e·gri·nate [PER-i-grə-nayt] vi **-nat·ed, -nat·ing 1** travel about. **2** roam.

per·e·grine [PER-i-grin] n type of falcon.

per·emp·to·ry [pə-REMP-tə-ree] adj **1** authoritative, imperious. **2** forbidding debate. **3** decisive.

——————| THESAURUS |——————

smothered, stifled

penury n = **poverty**, beggary, destitution, indigence, need, privation, want

people pl n **1** = **persons**, humanity, mankind, men and women, mortals **2** = **nation**, citizens, community, folk, inhabitants, population, public **3** = **family**, clan, race, tribe ◆ v **4** = **inhabit**, colonize, occupy, populate, settle

pepper n **1** = **seasoning**, flavor, spice ◆ v **2** = **sprinkle**, dot, fleck, spatter, speck **3** = **pelt**, bombard, shower

perceive v **1** = **see**, behold, discern, discover, espy, make out, note, notice, observe, recognize, spot **2** = **understand**, comprehend, gather, grasp, learn, realize, see

perceptible adj = **visible**, apparent,

appreciable, clear, detectable, discernible, evident, noticeable, observable, obvious, recognizable, tangible

perception n = **understanding**, awareness, conception, consciousness, feeling, grasp, idea, impression, notion, sensation, sense

perceptive adj = **observant**, acute, alert, astute, aware, percipient, perspicacious, quick, sharp

perch n **1** = **resting place**, branch, pole, post ◆ v **2** = **sit**, alight, balance, land, rest, roost, settle

percussion n = **impact**, blow, bump, clash, collision, crash, knock, smash, thump

peremptory adj **1** = **imperative**, absolute, binding, compelling, decisive, final, obligatory **2** = **imperious**, authoritative,

DICTIONARY

per·en·ni·al [pə-REN-ee-əl] *adj* **1** lasting through the years. **2** perpetual, unfailing. ◆ *n* **3** plant lasting more than two years.

per·fect [PUR-fikt] *adj* **1** complete. **2** finished. **3** whole. **4** unspoiled. **5** faultless. **6** correct, precise. **7** excellent. **8** of highest quality. ◆ *n* **9** tense denoting a complete act. ◆ *vt* [pər-FEKT] **10** improve. **11** finish. **12** make skillful. **per·fect'i·ble** *adj* capable of becoming perfect. **per·fec'tion** [-FEK-shən] *n* **1** state of being perfect. **2** faultlessness. **per'fect·ly** *adv*

per·fi·dy [PUR-fi-dee] *n, pl* **-dies** treachery, disloyalty. **per·fid'i·ous** *adj*

per·fo·rate [PUR-fə-rayt] *vt* **-rat·ed, -rat·ing** make hole(s) in, penetrate. **per·fo·ra'tion** *n* hole(s) made through thing.

per·force [pər-FORS] *adv* of necessity.

per·form [pər-FORM] *vt* **1** bring to completion. **2** accomplish. **3** fulfill. **4** represent on stage. ◆ *vi* **5** function. **6** act part. **7** play, as on musical instrument. **per·for'mance** [-məns] *n*

per·fume [PUR-fyoom] *n* **1** agreeable scent. **2** fragrance. ◆ *vt* **-fumed, -fum·ing 3** imbue with an agreeable odor. **4** scent. **per·fum'er** *n*

per·func·to·ry [pər-FUNGK-tə-ree] *adj* **1** superficial. **2** hasty. **3** done indifferently.

per·go·la [PUR-gə-lə] *n* **1** area covered by plants growing on trellis. **2** the trellis.

per·haps [pər-HAPS] *adv* possibly.

peri- *prefix* round, e.g. *perimeter; period; periphrasis.*

per·i·car·di·um [per-i-KAHR-dee-əm] *n, pl* **-di·a** [-dee-ə] membrane enclosing the heart. **per·i·car·di'tis** *n* inflammation of this.

per·i·he·li·on [per-ə-HEE-lee-ən] *n, pl* **-li·a** [-lee-ə] point in orbit of planet or comet nearest to sun.

per·il [PER-əl] *n* **1** danger. **2** exposure to injury. **per'il·ous** *adj* full of peril, hazardous.

pe·rim·e·ter [pə-RIM-i-tər] *n* **1** outer boundary of an area. **2** length of this.

pe·ri·od [PEER-ee-əd] *n* **1** particular portion of time. **2** a series of years. **3** single

THESAURUS

bossy (*inf*), dictatorial, dogmatic, domineering, overbearing

perennial *adj* = **lasting**, abiding, constant, continual, enduring, incessant, persistent, recurrent, twenty-four-seven (*sl*)

perfect *adj* **1** = **complete**, absolute, consummate, entire, finished, full, sheer, unmitigated, utter, whole **2** = **faultless**, flawless, immaculate, impeccable, pure, spotless, unblemished **3** = **excellent**, ideal, splendid, sublime, superb, superlative, supreme **4** = **exact**, accurate, correct, faithful, precise, true, unerring ◆ *v* **5** = **improve**, develop, polish, refine **6** = **accomplish**, achieve, carry out, complete, finish, fulfill, perform

perfection *n* **1** = **completeness**, maturity **2** = **purity**, integrity, perfectness, wholeness **3** = **excellence**, exquisiteness, sublimity, superiority **4** = **exactness**, faultlessness, precision

perfectionist *n* = **stickler**, precisionist, purist

perfectly *adv* **1** = **completely**, absolutely, altogether, fully, quite, thoroughly, totally, utterly, wholly **2** = **flawlessly**, faultlessly, ideally, impeccably, superbly, supremely, wonderfully

perfidious *adj Literary* = **treacherous**, disloyal, double-dealing, traitorous, two-faced, unfaithful

perforate *v* = **pierce**, bore, drill, penetrate, punch, puncture

perform *v* **1** = **carry out**, accomplish, achieve, complete, discharge, do, execute, fulfill, pull off, work **2** = **present**, act, enact, play, produce, put on, represent, stage

performance *n* **1** = **carrying out**, accomplishment, achievement, act, completion, execution, fulfillment, work **2** = **presentation**, acting, appearance, exhibition, gig (*inf*), play, portrayal, production, show

performer *n* = **artiste**, actor *or* actress, player, Thespian, trouper

perfume *n* = **fragrance**, aroma, bouquet, odor, scent, smell

perfunctory *adj* = **offhand**, cursory, heedless, indifferent, mechanical, routine, sketchy, superficial

perhaps *adv* = **maybe**, conceivably, feasibly, it may be, perchance (*archaic*), possibly

peril *n* = **danger**, hazard, jeopardy, menace, risk, uncertainty

perilous *adj* = **dangerous**, hazardous, precarious, risky, threatening, unsafe

perimeter *n* = **boundary**, ambit, border, bounds, circumference, confines, edge, occurrence of menstruation. **4** cycle. **5** conclusion. **6** full stop (.) at the end of a sentence. **7** complete sentence. ◆ *adj* **8** of furniture, dress, play, etc., belonging to particular time in history. **pe·ri·od·ic** *adj* recurring at regular intervals. **pe·ri·od·i·cal** *adj*, *n* **1** (of) publication issued at regular intervals. ◆ *adj* **2** of a period. **3** periodic. **pe·ri·o·dia·i·ty** [DIS i tee] *n*

per·i·pa·tet·ic [per-ə-pə-TET-ik] *adj* **1** itinerant. **2** walking, traveling about.

pe·riph·er·y [pə-RIF-ə-ree] *n*, *pl* **-er·ies 1** circumference. **2** surface, outside. **pe·riph·er·al** [-ə-rəl] *adj* **1** minor, unimportant. **2** of periphery.

pe·riph·ra·sis [pə-RIF-rə-sis] *n*, *pl* **-ses** [-seez] roundabout speech or phrase. **1** circumlocution. **per·i·phras·tic** *adj*

per·i·scope [PER-ə-skohp] *n* instrument used esp. in submarines, for giving view of objects on different level.

per·ish *vi* **1** die, waste away. **2** decay, rot. **per·ish·a·ble** *adj* **1** that will not last long. ◆ *pl n* **2** perishable food.

per·i·to·ne·um [per-i-tn-EE-əm] *n*, *pl* **-ne·ums** *or* **-to·ne·a** [-EE-ə] membrane lining internal surface of abdomen. **per·i·to·ni·tis** [-NĪ-tis] *n* inflammation of it.

per·i·win·kle [PER-i-wing-kəl] *n* **1** myrtle. **2** small edible shellfish.

per·jure [PUR-jər] *vt* **-jured, -jur·ing 1** be guilty of perjury. **per'ju·ry** *n*, *pl* **-ries 1** crime of false testimony under oath. **2** false swearing.

perk·y [PUR-kee] *adj* **perk·i·er, perk·i·est** lively, cheerful, jaunty, gay. **perk up** make, become cheerful.

per·ma·frost [PUR-mə-frawst] *n* permanently frozen ground.

per·ma·nent [PUR-mə-nənt] *adj* **1** continuing in same state. **2** lasting. **per'ma·nence, per'ma·nen·cy** *n* fixedness. **permanent wave** *n* (treatment of hair producing) long-lasting style.

per·me·ate [PUR-mee-ayt] *vt* **-at·ed, -at·ing 1** pervade, saturate. **2** pass through pores of. **per'me·a·ble** [-ə-bəl] *adj* admitting of passage of fluids.

per·mit [pər-MIT] *vt* **-mit·ted, -mit·ting 1** allow. **2** give leave to. ◆ *n* [PUR-mit] **3** license to do something. **4** written permission. **permis·si·ble** *adj* allowable. **per·mis·sion** *n* **1** authorization. **2** leave, liberty. **per·mis·sive** *adj* (too) tolerant, lenient, esp. as parent.

per·mute [pər-MYOOT] *vt* **-mut·ed,**

limit, margin, periphery

period *n* = **time**, interval, season, space, span, spell, stretch, term, while

periodic *adj* = **recurrent**, cyclical, intermittent, occasional, regular, repeated, sporadic

periodical *n* = **publication**, journal, magazine, monthly, paper, quarterly, weekly

peripheral *adj* **1** = **incidental**, inessential, irrelevant, marginal, minor, secondary, unimportant **2** = **outermost**, exterior, external, outer, outside

perish *v* **1** = **die**, be killed, expire, lose one's life, pass away **2** = **be destroyed**, collapse, decline, disappear, fall, vanish **3** = **rot**, decay, decompose, disintegrate, molder, waste

perishable *adj* = **short-lived**, decaying, decomposable

perjure *v* **perjure oneself** *Criminal law* = **commit perjury**, bear false witness, forswear, give false testimony, lie under oath, swear falsely

perjury *n* = **lying under oath**, bearing false witness, false statement, forswearing,

giving false testimony

perk *n Inf* = **bonus**, benefit, extra, fringe benefit, perquisite, plus

permanence *n* = **continuity**, constancy, continuance, durability, endurance, finality, indestructibility, perpetuity, stability

permanent *adj* = **lasting**, abiding, constant, enduring, eternal, everlasting, immutable, perpetual, persistent, stable, steadfast, twenty-four-seven (*sl*), unchanging

permeate *v* = **pervade**, charge, fill, imbue, impregnate, infiltrate, penetrate, saturate, spread through

permissible *adj* = **permitted**, acceptable, allowable, all right, authorized, lawful, legal, legitimate, O.K. or okay (*inf*)

permission *n* = **authorization**, allowance, approval, assent, consent, dispensation, go-ahead (*inf*), green light, leave, liberty, license, sanction

permissive *adj* = **tolerant**, easy-going, forbearing, free, indulgent, lax, lenient, liberal

permit *v* **1** = **allow**, authorize, consent,

-mut·ing interchange. **per·mu·ta·tion**
[pur-myuu-TAY-shən] *n* **1** mutual
transference. **2** *Math.* arrangement of a
number of quantities in every possible
order.

per·ni·cious [pər-NISH-əs] *adj* **1** wicked or
mischievous. **2** extremely hurtful. **3** having
quality of destroying or injuring.

per·o·ra·tion [per-ə-RAY-shən] *n*
concluding part of oration.

per·ox·ide [pə-ROK-sīd] *n* **1** oxide of a
given base containing greatest quantity of
oxygen. **2** short for HYDROGEN PEROXIDE.

per·pen·di·cu·lar [pur-pən-DIK-yə-lər] *adj*
1 at right angles to the plane of the
horizon. **2** at right angles to given line or
surface. **3** exactly upright. ◆ *n* **4** line falling
at right angles on another line or plane.

per·pe·trate [PUR-pi-trayt] *vt* **-trat·ed,
-trat·ing** perform or be responsible for
(something bad).

per·pet·u·al [pər-PECH-oo-əl] *adj* **1**
continuous. **2** lasting for ever.
per·pet·u·ate *vt* **at·ed, -at·ing 1** make
perpetual. **2** not to allow to be forgotten.
per·pet·u·a'tion *n* **per·pet·u·i·ty**

[pur-pi-TOO-i-tee] *n*

per·plex [pər-PLEKS] *vt* **1** puzzle. **2**
bewilder. **3** make difficult to understand.
per·plex'i·ty *n, pl* **-ties** puzzled or tangled
state.

per·qui·site [PUR-kwi-zit] *n* **1** any
incidental benefit from a certain type of
employment. **2** casual payment in addition
to salary. **3** something due as a privilege.

per se [pur SAY] *Lat* by or in itself.

per·se·cute [PUR-si-kyoot] *vt* **-cut·ed,
-cut·ing 1** oppress because of race,
religion, etc. **2** subject to persistent
ill-treatment. **per·se·cu'tion** *n*

per·se·vere [pur-sə-VEER] *vi* **-vered,
-ver·ing** persist, maintain effort.
per·se·ver'ance [-əns] *n* persistence.

per·si·flage [PUR-sə-flahzh] *n* **1** idle talk. **2**
frivolous style of treating subject.

per·sim·mon [pər-SIM-ən] *n* **1** Amer. tree.
2 its hard wood. **3** its fruit.

per·sist [pər-SIST] *vi* continue in spite of
obstacles or objections. **per·sist'ence**
[-əns] *n* **per·sist'en·cy** *n* **per·sist'ent** *adj* **1**
persisting. **2** steady. **3** persevering. **4**
lasting.

enable, entitle, give leave *or* permission,
give the green light to, grant, let, license,
sanction ◆ *n* **2 = license**, authorization,
pass, passport, permission, warrant

permutation *n* = transformation,
alteration, change, transposition

pernicious *adj* = wicked, bad, damaging,
dangerous, deadly, destructive,
detrimental, evil, fatal, harmful, hurtful,
malign, poisonous

perpendicular *adj* = upright, at right
angles to, on end, plumb, straight, vertical

perpetrate *v* = commit, carry out, do,
enact, execute, perform, wreak

perpetual *adj* **1** = everlasting, endless,
eternal, infinite, lasting, never-ending,
perennial, permanent, unchanging,
unending **2 = continual**, constant,
continuous, endless, incessant,
interminable, never-ending, persistent,
recurrent, repeated, twenty-four-seven (*sl*)

perpetuate *v* = maintain, immortalize,
keep going, preserve

perplex *v* = puzzle, baffle, bewilder,
confound, confuse, mystify, stump

perplexing *adj* = puzzling, baffling,
bewildering, complex, complicated,
confusing, difficult, enigmatic, hard,

inexplicable, mystifying

perplexity *n* **1** = puzzlement, bafflement,
bewilderment, confusion,
incomprehension, mystification **2 = puzzle**,
difficulty, fix (*inf*), mystery, paradox

perquisite *n Formal* = bonus, benefit,
dividend, extra, perk (*inf*), plus

persecute *v* **1** = victimize, afflict, ill-treat,
maltreat, oppress, torment, torture **2 =
harass**, annoy, badger, bother, hassle (*inf*),
pester, tease

perseverance *n* = persistence,
determination, diligence, doggedness,
endurance, pertinacity, resolution, tenacity

persevere *v* = keep going, carry on,
continue, go on, hang on, persist, remain,
stick at *or* to

persist *v* **1** = continue, carry on, keep up,
last, linger, remain **2 = persevere**,
continue, insist, stand firm

persistence *n* = determination,
doggedness, endurance, grit,
perseverance, pertinacity, resolution,
tenacity, tirelessness

persistent *adj* **1** = continuous, constant,
continual, endless, incessant,
never-ending, perpetual, repeated,
twenty-four-seven (*sl*) **2 = determined**,

per·snick·et·y [pər-SNIK-i-tee] *adj inf* **1** fussy. **2** fastidious about trifles. **3** snobbishly aloof. **4** requiring great care.

per·son [PUR-sən] *n* **1** individual (human) being. **2** body of human being. **3** *Grammar* classification, or one of the classes, of pronouns and verb forms according to the person speaking, spoken to, or spoken of. **per·so·na** [pər-SOH-nə] *n, pl* **-nas** assumed character. **per'son·a·ble** *adj* good-looking. **per'son·age** [-ij] *n* notable person. **per'son·al** *adj* **1** individual, private, or one's own. **2** of, relating to grammatical person. **per·son·al'i·ty** *n, pl* **-ties 1** distinctive character. **2** a celebrity. **per'son·al·ly** *adv* in person. **per'son·ate** *vt* **-at·ed, -at·ing** pass oneself off as. **personal computer** small computer used for word processing, e-mail, computer games, etc. **personal property** *Law* all property except land and interests in land that pass to heir. **personal stereo** very small portable cassette player with headphones.

per·son·i·fy [pər-SON-ə-fī] *vt* **-fied, -fy·ing**

1 represent as person. **2** typify. **per·son·i·fi·ca'tion** *n*

per·son·nel [pur-sə-NEL] *n* staff employed in a service or institution.

per·spec·tive [pər-SPEK-tiv] *n* **1** mental view. **2** art of drawing on flat surface to give effect of solidity and relative distances and sizes. **3** drawing in perspective.

per·spi·ca·cious [pur-spi-KAY-shəs] *adj* having quick mental insight. **per·spi·cac'i·ty** [-KAS-] *n*

per·spic·u·ous [pər-SPIK-yoo-əs] *adj* **1** clearly expressed. **2** lucid. **3** plain. **4** obvious. **per·spi·cu'i·ty** *n*

per·spire [pər-SPĪR] *v* **-spired, -spir·ing** sweat. **per·spi·ra'tion** [-spi-RAY-shən] *n* **1** sweating. **2** sweat.

per·suade [pər-SWAYD] *vt* **-suad·ed, -suad·ing 1** bring (one to do something) by argument, charm, etc. **2** convince. **per·sua'sion** [-SWAY-zhən] *n* **1** art, act of persuading. **2** way of thinking or belief. **per·sua'sive** *adj*

pert *adj* **-er, -est** forward, saucy.

THESAURUS

---

dogged, obdurate, obstinate, persevering, pertinacious, steadfast, steady, stubborn, tenacious, tireless, unflagging

person *n* **1** = **individual**, being, body, human, soul **2 in person** = **personally**, bodily, in the flesh, oneself

personable *adj* = **pleasant**, agreeable, amiable, attractive, charming, good-looking, handsome, likable *or* likeable, nice

personage *n* = **personality**, big shot (*inf*), celebrity, dignitary, luminary, megastar (*inf*), notable, public figure, somebody, V.I.P.

personal *adj* **1** = **private**, exclusive, individual, intimate, own, particular, peculiar, special **2** = **offensive**, derogatory, disparaging, insulting, nasty

personality *n* **1** = **nature**, character, disposition, identity, individuality, make-up, temperament **2** = **celebrity**, famous name, household name, megastar (*inf*), notable, personage, star

personally *adv* **1** = **by oneself**, alone, independently, on one's own, solely **2** = **in one's opinion**, for one's part, from one's own viewpoint, in one's books, in one's own view **3** = **individually**, individualistically, privately, specially, subjectively

personification *n* = **embodiment**, epitome, image, incarnation, portrayal, representation

personify *v* = **embody**, epitomize, exemplify, represent, symbolize, typify

personnel *n* = **employees**, helpers, human resources, people, staff, workers, workforce

perspective *n* **1** = **outlook**, angle, attitude, context, frame of reference **2** = **objectivity**, proportion, relation, relative importance, relativity

perspicacious *adj* = **perceptive**, acute, alert, astute, discerning, keen, percipient, sharp, shrewd

perspiration *n* = **sweat**, moisture, wetness

perspire *v* = **sweat**, exude, glow, pour with sweat, secrete, swelter

persuade *v* **1** = **talk into**, coax, entice, impel, incite, induce, influence, sway, urge, win over **2** = **convince**, cause to believe, satisfy

persuasion *n* **1** = **urging**, cajolery, enticement, inducement, wheedling **2** = **persuasiveness**, cogency, force, potency, power **3** = **creed**, belief, conviction, credo, faith, opinion, tenet, views **4** = **faction**, camp, denomination, party, school, school of thought, side

persuasive *adj* = **convincing**, cogent, compelling, credible, effective, eloquent,

DICTIONARY

per·tain [pər-TAYN] *vi* **1** belong, relate, have reference (to). **2** concern.

per·ti·na·cious [pur-tn-AY-shəs] *adj* obstinate, persistent. **per·ti·nac'i·ty** [-AS-i-tee] *n* doggedness, resolution.

per·ti·nent [PUR-tn-ənt] *adj* to the point. **per'ti·nence** *n* relevance.

per·turb [pər-TURB] *vt* **1** disturb greatly. **2** alarm. **per·tur·ba'tion** *n* **1** disturbance. **2** agitation of mind.

pe·ruse [pə-ROOZ] *vt* **-rused, -rus·ing** examine, read, esp. in slow and careful, or leisurely, manner. **pe·rus'al** *n*

per·vade [pər-VAYD] *vt* **-vad·ed, -vad·ing 1** spread through. **2** be rife among. **per·va'sive** *adj*

per·vert [pər-VURT] *vt* **1** turn to wrong use. **2** lead astray. ◆ *n* [PUR-vərt] **3** one who shows unhealthy abnormality, esp. in sexual matters. **per·verse** [pər-VURS] *adj* **1** obstinately or unreasonably wrong. **2** self-willed. **3** headstrong. **4** wayward. **per·ver'sion** [-VUR-zhən] *n*

pes·sa·ry [PES-ə-ree] *n, pl* **-ries 1** instrument used to support mouth and neck of uterus. **2** appliance to prevent conception. **3** medicated suppository.

pes·si·mism [PES-ə-miz-əm] *n* **1** tendency to see the worst side of things. **2** theory that everything turns to evil. **pes'si·mist** *n* **pes·si·mis'tic** *adj*

pest *n* **1** troublesome or harmful thing, person or insect. **2** plague. **pest'i·cide** [-sīd] *n* chemical for killing pests, esp. insects. **pes·tif'er·ous** [-ər-əs] *adj* **1** troublesome. **2** bringing plague.

pes·ter [PES-tər] *vt* **1** trouble or vex persistently. **2** harass.

THESAURUS

forceful, influential, plausible, sound, telling, valid, weighty

pert *adj* = **impudent**, bold, cheeky, forward, impertinent, insolent, sassy (*inf*), saucy

pertain *v* = **relate**, apply, befit, belong, be relevant, concern, refer, regard

pertinent *adj* = **relevant**, applicable, apposite, appropriate, apt, fit, fitting, germane, material, proper, to the point

pertness *n* = **impudence**, audacity, cheek (*inf*), cheekiness, effrontery, forwardness, front, impertinence, insolence, sauciness

perturb *v* = **disturb**, agitate, bother, disconcert, faze, fluster, ruffle, trouble, unsettle, vex, worry

perturbed *adj* = **disturbed**, agitated, anxious, disconcerted, flustered, shaken, troubled, uncomfortable, uneasy, worried

peruse *v* = **read**, browse, check, examine, inspect, scan, scrutinize, study

pervade *v* = **spread through**, charge, fill, imbue, infuse, penetrate, permeate, suffuse

pervasive *adj* = **widespread**, common, extensive, general, omnipresent, prevalent, rife, ubiquitous, universal

perverse *adj* **1** = **abnormal**, contrary, deviant, disobedient, improper, rebellious, refractory, troublesome, unhealthy **2** = **willful**, contrary, dogged, headstrong, intractable, intransigent, obdurate, wrong-headed **3** = **stubborn**, contrary, mulish, obstinate, pig-headed, stiff-necked, wayward **4** = **ill-natured**, churlish, cross, fractious, ill-tempered,

peevish, surly

perversion *n* **1** = **deviation**, aberration, abnormality, debauchery, depravity, immorality, kink (*sl*), kinkiness (*sl*), unnaturalness, vice **2** = **distortion**, corruption, falsification, misinterpretation, misrepresentation, twisting

perversity *n* = **contrariness**, contradictoriness, intransigence, obduracy, refractoriness, waywardness, wrong-headedness

pervert *v* **1** = **distort**, abuse, falsify, garble, misrepresent, misuse, twist, warp **2** = **corrupt**, debase, debauch, degrade, deprave, lead astray ◆ *n* **3** = **deviant**, degenerate, sicko (*inf*), weirdo *or* weirdie (*inf*)

perverted *adj* = **unnatural**, abnormal, corrupt, debased, debauched, depraved, deviant, kinky (*sl*), sick, twisted, unhealthy, warped

pessimism *n* = **gloominess**, dejection, depression, despair, despondency, distrust, gloom, hopelessness, melancholy

pessimist *n* = **wet blanket** (*inf*), cynic, defeatist, killjoy, prophet of doom, worrier

pessimistic *adj* = **gloomy**, bleak, cynical, dark, dejected, depressed, despairing, despondent, glum, hopeless, morose

pest *n* **1** = **nuisance**, annoyance, bane, bother, drag (*inf*), irritation, pain (*inf*), thorn in one's flesh, trial, vexation **2** = **infection**, blight, bug, epidemic, pestilence, plague, scourge

pester *v* = **annoy**, badger, bedevil, bother,

pes·ti·lence [PES-tl-əns] n epidemic disease, esp. bubonic plague. **pes'ti·lent** adj **1** troublesome. **2** deadly. **pes·ti·len'tial** [-LEN-shəl] adj

pes·tle [PES-əl] n instrument with which things are pounded in a mortar.

Pet. Peter.

pet n **1** animal or person kept or regarded with affection. ◆ vt **pet·ted, pet·ting 2** make pet of. **3** inf hug, embrace, fondle.

pet·al [PET-l] n white or colored leaflike part of flower. **pet'aled** adj

pe·tard [pi-TAHRD] n formerly, an explosive device. **hoist by one's own petard** ruined, destroyed by plot one intended for another.

pe·ter [PEE-tər] vi **peter out** inf disappear, lose power gradually.

pe·tit [PET-ee] adj Law small, petty.

pe·tite [pə-TEET] adj small, dainty.

pe·ti·tion [pə-TISH-ən] n **1** entreaty, request, esp.one presented to a governing body or person. ◆ vt **2** present petition to. **pe·ti'tion·er** n

pet·rel [PE-trəl] n sea bird.

pet·ri·fy [PE-trə-fī] vt **-fied, -fy·ing 1** turn to stone. **2** fig make motionless with fear. **3** make dumb with amazement. **pet·ri·fac'tion** n

pe·tro·le·um [pə-TROH-lee-əm] n unrefined oil.

pet·ti·coat [PET-ee-koht] n women's undergarment worn under skirts, dresses, etc.

pet·ti·fog·ger [PET-ee-fog-ər] n **1** quibbler. **2** unethical lawyer. **3** one given to mean dealing in small matters.

pet·ty [PET-ee] adj **-ti·er, -ti·est 1** unimportant, trivial. **2** small-minded, mean. **3** on a small scale. **petty cash** cash kept by firm to pay minor incidental expenses. **petty officer** noncommissioned officer in Navy.

pet·u·lant [PECH-ə-lənt] adj **1** given to small fits of temper. **2** peevish. **pet'u·lance** n peevishness.

pe·tu·nia [pi-TOON-yə] n plant with funnel-shaped purple or white flowers.

pew [pyoo] n **1** fixed seat in church. **2** inf chair, seat.

pew·ter [PYOO-tər] n **1** alloy of tin and lead. **2** utensil of this.

pha·lanx [FAY-langks] n, pl **-lanx·es** body of soldiers, etc. formed in close array.

phal·lus [FAL-əs] n, pl **-lus·es 1** penis. **2** symbol of it used in primitive rites. **phal'lic** adj

phan·tas·ma·go·ri·a [fan-taz-mə-GOR-ee-ə] n **1** crowd of dim or unreal figures. **2** exhibition of illusions.

phan·tom [FAN-təm] n **1** apparition. **2** specter, ghost. **3** fancied vision.

Phar·aoh [FAIR-oh] n title of ancient Egyptian kings.

————————| THESAURUS |————————

bug (inf), harass, harry, hassle (inf), nag, plague, torment

pestilence n = **plague**, epidemic, visitation

pestilent adj **1** = **annoying**, bothersome, irksome, irritating, tiresome, vexing **2** = **harmful**, detrimental, evil, injurious, pernicious **3** = **contaminated**, catching, contagious, diseased, disease-ridden, infected, infectious

pestilential adj = **deadly**, dangerous, destructive, detrimental, harmful, hazardous, injurious, pernicious

pet¹ n **1** = **favorite**, darling, idol, jewel, treasure ◆ adj **2** = **favorite**, cherished, dearest, dear to one's heart ◆ v **3** = **pamper**, baby, coddle, cosset, spoil **4** = **fondle**, caress, pat, stroke **5** = **cuddle**, kiss, make out, neck (inf), smooch (inf)

peter out v = **die out**, dwindle, ebb, fade, fail, run out, stop, taper off, wane

petite adj = **small**, dainty, delicate, elfin, little, slight

petition n **1** = **appeal**, entreaty, plea, prayer, request, solicitation, suit, supplication ◆ v **2** = **appeal**, adjure, ask, beg, beseech, entreat, plead, pray, solicit, supplicate

petrify v **1** = **terrify**, horrify, immobilize, paralyze, stun, stupefy, transfix **2** = **fossilize**, calcify, harden, turn to stone

petty adj **1** = **trivial**, contemptible, inconsiderable, insignificant, little, lousy (sl), measly (inf), negligible, paltry, slight, small, trifling, unimportant **2** = **small-minded**, mean, mean-minded, shabby, spiteful, ungenerous

petulance n = **sulkiness**, bad temper, ill humor, irritability, peevishness, pique, sullenness

petulant adj = **sulky**, bad-tempered, huffy, ill-humored, moody, peevish, sullen

phantom n **1** = **specter**, apparition, ghost, phantasm, shade (literary), spirit, spook (inf), wraith **2** = **illusion**, figment of the

phar·i·see [FA-rə-see] n 1 sanctimonious person. 2 hypocrite. **phar·i·sa·ic** [-SAY-ik] adj

phar·ma·ceu·tic [fahr-mə-SOO-tik] adj of pharmacy. **phar·ma·ceu·ti·cal** adj **phar·ma·cist** n person qualified to dispense drugs. **phar·ma·col·o·gy** [-KOL-ə-jee] n study of drugs. **phar·ma·co·poe·ia** [-kə-PEE-ə] n official book with list and directions for use of drugs. **phar·ma·cy** [-mə-see] n 1 preparation and dispensing of drugs. 2 drugstore.

phar·ynx [FA-rinks] n, pl **pha·ryn·ges** [fə-RIN-jeez] cavity forming back part of mouth and terminating in gullet. **pha·ryn·ge·al** adj

phase [fayz] n 1 any distinct or characteristic period or stage in a development or chain of events. ◆ vt **phased, phas·ing** 2 arrange, execute in stages or to coincide with something else.

pheas·ant [FEZ-ənt] n game bird with bright plumage.

phe·no·bar·bi·tal [fee-noh-BAHR-bi-tawl] n drug inducing sleep.

phe·nom·e·non [fi-NOM-ə-non] n, pl **-na** [-nə] 1 anything appearing or observed. 2 remarkable person or thing. **phe·nom·e·nal** adj 1 relating to phenomena. 2 remarkable. 3 recognizable

or evidenced by senses.

Phil. Philippians.

phil- comb. form loving, e.g. philanthropy; philosophy.

phi·lan·der [fi-LAN-dər] vi (of man) flirt with, make love to, women, esp. with no intention of marrying them. **phi·lan·der·er** n

phi·lan·thro·py [fi-LAN-thrə-pee] n, pl **-pies** 1 practice of doing good to people. 2 love of mankind. 3 a philanthropic organization. **phi·lan·throp·ic** adj 1 loving mankind. 2 benevolent. **phi·lan·thro·pist** n

phi·lat·e·ly [fi-LAT-l-ee] n stamp collecting. **phi·lat·e·list** n

phil·is·tine [FIL-ə-steen] n ignorant, smug person. ◆ adj

phi·lol·o·gy [fi-LOL-ə-jee] n science of structure and development of languages. **phi·lol·o·gist** n

phi·los·o·phy [fi-LOS-ə-fee] n 1 pursuit of wisdom. 2 study of realities and general principles. 3 system of theories on nature of things or on conduct. 4 calmness of mind. **phi·los·o·pher** n one who studies, possesses, or originates philosophy. **phil·o·soph·i·cal** adj 1 of, like philosophy. 2 wise, learned. 3 calm, stoical. **phi·los·o·phize** [-fiz] vi **-phized, -phiz·ing** 1 reason like philosopher. 2 theorize. 3 moralize.

——— THESAURUS ———

imagination, hallucination, vision

phase n = **stage**, chapter, development, juncture, period, point, position, step, time

phase out v = **wind down**, close, ease off, eliminate, pull out, remove, run down, terminate, wind up, withdraw

phenomenal adj = **extraordinary**, exceptional, fantastic, marvelous, miraculous, outstanding, prodigious, remarkable, unusual

phenomenon n 1 = **occurrence**, circumstance, episode, event, fact, happening, incident 2 = **wonder**, exception, marvel, miracle, prodigy, rarity, sensation

philanderer n = **womanizer** (inf), Casanova, Don Juan, flirt, gigolo, ladies' man, playboy, stud (sl), wolf (inf)

philanthropic adj = **humanitarian**, beneficent, benevolent, charitable, humane, kind, kind-hearted, munificent, public-spirited

philanthropist n = **humanitarian**,

benefactor, contributor, donor, giver, patron

philanthropy n = **humanitarianism**, almsgiving, beneficence, benevolence, brotherly love, charitableness, charity, generosity, kind-heartedness

philistine n 1 = **boor**, barbarian, ignoramus, lout, lowbrow, vulgarian, yahoo ◆ adj 2 = **uncultured**, boorish, ignorant, lowbrow, tasteless, uncultivated, uneducated, unrefined

philosopher n = **thinker**, logician, metaphysician, sage, theorist, wise man

philosophical adj 1 = **wise**, abstract, logical, rational, sagacious, theoretical, thoughtful 2 = **stoical**, calm, collected, composed, cool, serene, tranquil, unruffled

philosophy n 1 = **thought**, knowledge, logic, metaphysics, rationalism, reasoning, thinking, wisdom 2 = **outlook**, beliefs, convictions, doctrine, ideology, principles, tenets, thinking, values, viewpoint, world view 3 = **stoicism**, calmness, composure,

phle·bi·tis [flə-BĪ-tis] *n* inflammation of a vein.

phlegm [flem] *n* **1** viscid substance formed. **2** by mucous membrane and ejected by coughing, etc. **3** apathy, sluggishness. **phleg·mat·ic** [fleg-MAT-ik] *adj* **1** not easily agitated. **2** composed.

pho·bi·a [FOH-bee-ə] *n* **1** fear or aversion. **2** unreasoning dislike.

phoe·nix [FEE-niks] *n* **1** legendary bird. **2** unique thing.

phone [fohn] *n, v inf* telephone. **phone card** prepaid card used to pay for telephone calls. **phone tag** repeated unsuccessful attempts to contact by telephone.

pho·net·ic [fə-NET-ik] *adj* of, or relating to, vocal sounds. **pho·net·ics** *n* science of vocal sounds. **pho·ne·ti·cian** [foh-ni-TISH-ən] *n*

phono- *comb. form* sound, e.g. *phonology.*

pho·no·graph [FOH-nə-graf] *n* instrument recording and reproducing sounds, record player.

pho·ny [FOH-nee] *inf* ◆ *adj* **-ni·er, -ni·est 1** not genuine. **2** insincere. ◆ *n, pl* **pho'nies 3** phony person or thing.

phos·pho·rus [FOS-fər-əs] *n* toxic, flammable, nonmetallic element that appears luminous in the dark. **phos·phate** [FOS-fayt] *n* compound of phosphorus. **phos·pho·res'cence** *n* faint glow in the dark.

pho·to [FOH-toh] *n inf* short for PHOTOGRAPH. **photo finish** photo taken at end of race to show placing of contestants.

photo- *comb. form* light, e.g. *photometer; photosynthesis.*

pho·to·cop·y [FOH-toh-kop-ee] *n, pl* **-cop·ies** photographic reproduction. ◆ *vt* **-cop·ied, -cop·y·ing**

pho·to·e·lec·tron [foh-toh-i-LEK-tron] *n* electron liberated from metallic surface by action of beam of light.

pho·to·gen·ic [foh-tə-JEN-ik] *adj* capable of being photographed attractively.

pho·to·graph [FOH-tə-graf] *n* **1** picture made by chemical action of light on sensitive film. ◆ *vt* **2** take photograph of. **pho·tog'ra·pher** [-rə-fər] *n*

pho·to·syn·the·sis [foh-tə-SIN-thə-sis] *n* process by which green plant uses sun's energy to build up carbohydrate reserves.

phrase [frayz] *n* **1** group of words. **2** pithy expression. **3** mode of expression. ◆ *vt* **phrased, phras·ing 4** express in words. **phra·se·ol·o·gy** [fray-zee-OL-ə-jee] *n* manner of expression, choice of words. **phras·al verb** [-əl] *n* phrase consisting of verb and preposition, often with meaning different to the parts, such as *take in* meaning *deceive.*

phre·nol·o·gy [frə-NOL-ə-jee] *n* (formerly) study of skull's shape. **1** theory that character and mental powers are indicated by shape of skull. **phre·nol'o·gist** *n*

phy·lac·ter·y [fi-LAK-tə-ree] *n, pl* **-ter·ies** leather case containing religious texts worn by Jewish men during weekday morning prayers.

phys·ic [FIZ-ik] *n* **1** medicine, esp. cathartic. ◆ *pl* **2** science of properties of matter and energy. **phys'i·cal** *adj* **1** bodily, as opposed to mental or moral. **2** material. **3** of physics of body. **phy·si'cian** *n* medical doctor. **phys'i·cist** *n* one skilled in, or student of, physics.

———[THESAURUS]———

equanimity, self-possession, serenity

phlegmatic *adj* = **unemotional**, apathetic, impassive, indifferent, placid, stoical, stolid, undemonstrative, unfeeling

phobia *n* = **terror**, aversion, detestation, dread, fear, hatred, horror, loathing, repulsion, revulsion, thing (*inf*)

phone *n* **1** = **telephone**, blower (*inf*), horn (*inf*) **2** = **call** ◆ *v* **3** = **call**, get on the blower (*inf*), get on the horn (*inf*), give someone a call, make a call, telephone

phony *Inf adj* **1** = **fake**, bogus, counterfeit, ersatz, false, imitation, pseudo (*inf*), sham ◆ *n* **2** = **fake**, counterfeit, forgery, fraud, impostor, pseud (*inf*), sham

photograph *n* **1** = **picture**, photo (*inf*), print, shot, snap (*inf*), snapshot, transparency ◆ *v* **2** = **take a picture of**, film, record, shoot, snap (*inf*), take (someone's) picture

photographic *adj* **1** = **lifelike**, graphic, natural, pictorial, realistic, visual, vivid **2** *Of a person's memory* = **accurate**, exact, faithful, precise, retentive

phrase *n* **1** = **expression**, group of words, idiom, remark, saying ◆ *v* **2** = **express**, put, put into words, say, voice, word

phraseology *n* = **wording**, choice of words, expression, idiom, language, parlance, phrase, phrasing, speech, style,

phys·i·og·no·my [fiz-ee-OG-nə-mee] *n, pl* **-mies 1** judging character by face. **2** face. **3** outward appearance of something.

phys·i·ol·o·gy [fiz-ee-OL-ə-jee] *n* science of normal function of living things. **phy·si·ol'o·gist** *n*

phys·i·o·ther·a·py [fiz-ee-oh-THER-ə-pee] *n* therapeutic use of physical means, as massage, etc. **phys·i·o·ther'a·pist** *n*

phy·sique [fi-ZEEK] *n* bodily structure, constitution and development.

pi [pī] *n* Math. ratio of circumference of circle to its diameter, approx. 3.141592.

pi·an·o [pee-AN-oh] *n, pl* **-an·os 1** musical instrument with strings that are struck by hammers worked by keyboard (also **pianofor'te**). **pi·an·ist** [pee-AN-ist] *n* performer on piano.

pi·az·za [pee-AZ-ə] *n* **1** square, marketplace. **2** veranda.

pi·ca [PĪ-kə] *n* **1** printing type of 6 lines to the inch. **2** size of type, 12 point. **3** typewriter type size (10 letters to inch).

pi·ca·dor [PIK-ə-dor] *n* mounted bullfighter with lance.

pic·a·resque [pik-ə-RESK] *adj* of fiction, esp. episodic and dealing with the adventures of rogues.

pic·co·lo [PIK-ə-loh] *n, pl* **-los** small flute.

pick¹ [pik] *vt* **1** choose, select carefully. **2** pluck, gather. **3** peck at. **4** pierce with something pointed. **5** find occasion for. ♦ *n* **6** act of picking. **7** choicest part. **pick'ings** *pl n* **1** gleanings. **2** odds and ends of profit.

pick-me-up *n inf* stimulating drink, tonic.

pick'pock·et *n* one who steals from another's pocket. **pick'up** *n* device for conversion of mechanical energy into electric signals, as in record player, etc. **pickup truck** small truck with open body. **pick on** find fault with. **pick up 1** raise, lift. **2** collect. **3** improve, get better. **4** accelerate.

pick² *n* tool with curved steel crossbar and wooden shaft, for breaking up hard ground or masonry. **pick'ax** *n* pick.

pick·er·el [PIK-ər-əl] *n* small pike.

pick·et [PIK-it] *n* **1** prong, pointed stake. **2** person, esp. striker, posted outside building, etc. to prevent use of facility, deter would-be workers during strike. ♦ *vt* **3** post as picket. **4** beset with pickets. **5** tether to peg. **picket fence** fence of pickets. **picket line** line of pickets.

pick·le [PIK-əl] *n* **1** food, esp. cucumber, preserved in brine, vinegar, etc. **2** liquid used for preserving. **3** *inf* awkward situation. ♦ *pl* **4** pickled vegetables. ♦ *vt* **-led, -ling 5** preserve in pickle. **pickled** *adj sl* drunk.

———————————— THESAURUS ————————————

syntax

physical *adj* **1** = **bodily**, corporal, corporeal, earthly, fleshly, incarnate, mortal **2** = **material**, natural, palpable, real, solid, substantial, tangible

physician *n* = **doctor**, doc (*inf*), doctor of medicine, general practitioner, G.P., M.D., medic (*inf*), medical practitioner

physique *n* = **build**, body, constitution, figure, form, frame, shape, structure

pick *v* **1** = **select**, choose, decide upon, elect, fix upon, hand-pick, opt for, settle upon, single out **2** = **gather**, collect, harvest, pluck, pull **3** = **nibble**, have no appetite, peck at, play or toy with, push the food round the plate **4** = **provoke**, incite, instigate, start **5** = **open**, break into, break open, crack, force ♦ *n* **6** = **choice**, decision, option, preference, selection **7** = **the best**, crème de la crème, elect, elite, the cream

picket *n* **1** = **protester**, demonstrator, picketer **2** = **lookout**, guard, patrol, sentinel, sentry, watch **3** = **stake**, pale, paling, post, stanchion, upright ♦ *v* **4** = **blockade**, boycott, demonstrate

pickle *n* **1** *Inf* = **predicament**, bind (*inf*), difficulty, dilemma, fix (*inf*), hot water (*inf*), jam (*inf*), quandary, scrape (*inf*), tight spot ♦ *v* **2** = **preserve**, marinade, steep

pick-me-up *n Inf* = **tonic**, bracer (*inf*), refreshment, restorative, shot in the arm (*inf*), stimulant

pick on *v* = **torment**, badger, bait, bully, goad, hector, tease

pick out *v* = **identify**, discriminate, distinguish, make out, perceive, recognize, tell apart

pick up *v* **1** = **lift**, gather, grasp, raise, take up, uplift **2** = **obtain**, buy, come across, find, purchase **3** = **recover**, be on the mend, get better, improve, mend, rally, take a turn for the better, turn the corner **4** = **learn**, acquire, get the hang of (*inf*), master **5** = **collect**, call for, get

pick-up *n* = **improvement**, change for the better, rally, recovery, revival, rise, strengthening, upswing, upturn

pic·nic [PIK-nik] *n* **1** pleasure outing including meal out of doors. ♦ *vi* **-nicked, -nick·ing 2** take part in picnic.

Pict [pikt] *n* member of ancient people of NE Scotland.

pic·ture [PIK-chər] *n* **1** drawing or painting. **2** mental image. **3** beautiful or picturesque object. ♦ *pl* **4** *inf* movies. ♦ *vt* **-tured, -tur·ing 5** represent in, or as in, a picture. **pic·to'ri·al** *adj* **1** of, in, with, painting or pictures. **2** graphic. **pic·tur·esque** [pik-chə-RESK] *adj* **1** such as would be effective in picture. **2** striking, vivid.

pidg·in [PIJ-ən] *n* language, not a mother tongue, made up of elements of two or more other languages.

pie [pī] *n* baked dish of fruit, meat, etc., usu. with pastry crust.

pie·bald [PĪ-bawld] *adj* **1** irregularly marked with black and white. **2** motley. ♦ *n* **3** piebald horse or other animal.

piece [pees] *n* **1** bit, part, fragment. **2** single object. **3** literary or musical composition, etc. **4** small object used in checkers, chess, etc. **5** firearm. ♦ *vt* **pieced, piec·ing 6** mend, put together. **piece'meal** *adv* by, in, or into pieces, a bit at a time. **piece'work** *n* work paid for according to quantity produced.

pièce de ré·sis·tance [pyes də ray-zee-STAHNS] *Fr* most impressive item.

pied [pīd] *adj* **1** piebald. **2** variegated.

pie-eyed [PĪ-īd] *adj sl* drunk.

pier [peer] *n* **1** structure running into sea as landing stage. **2** piece of solid upright masonry as foundation for building, etc.

pierce [peers] *vt* **pierced, pierc·ing 1** make hole in. **2** make a way through. **piercing** *adj* **1** keen. **2** penetrating.

pi·e·ty [PĪ-i-tee] *n, pl* **-ties 1** godliness. **2** devoutness, goodness. **3** dutifulness.

pig *n* **1** wild or domesticated mammal killed for pork, ham, bacon. **2** *inf* greedy, dirty person. **3** *offens sl* policeman. **4** oblong mass of smelted metal. ♦ *vi* **pigged, pig·ging 5** of sow, produce litter. **pig'gish** *adj* **1** dirty. **2** greedy. **3** stubborn. **pig'head·ed** *adj* obstinate. **pig'skin** *n* **1** (leather made from) the skin of a pig. **2** *inf* a football. **pig'tail** *n* braid of hair hanging from back of head.

pi·geon [PIJ-ən] *n* **1** bird of many wild and domesticated varieties, often trained to carry messages. **2** *sl* dupe. **pi'geon·hole** [-hohl] *n* **1** compartment for papers in desk, etc. ♦ *vt* **-holed, -hol·ing 2** defer. **3** classify. **pi'geon-toed** [-tohd] *adj* with feet, toes turned inward.

picnic *n* = **excursion**, outdoor meal, outing

pictorial *adj* = **graphic**, illustrated, picturesque, representational, scenic

picture *n* **1** = **representation**, drawing, engraving, illustration, image, likeness, painting, photograph, portrait, print, sketch **2** = **description**, account, depiction, image, impression, report **3** = **double**, carbon copy, copy, dead ringer (*sl*), duplicate, image, likeness, lookalike, replica, spitting image (*inf*), twin **4** = **personification**, embodiment, epitome, essence **5** = **film**, flick (*sl*), motion picture, movie ♦ *v* **6** = **imagine**, conceive of, envision, see, visualize **7** = **represent**, depict, draw, illustrate, paint, photograph, show, sketch

picturesque *adj* **1** = **pretty**, attractive, beautiful, charming, quaint, scenic, striking **2** = **vivid**, colorful, graphic

piebald *adj* = **pied**, black and white, brindled, dappled, flecked, mottled, speckled, spotted

piece *n* **1** = **bit**, chunk, fragment, morsel, part, portion, quantity, segment, slice **2** =

work, article, composition, creation, item, study, work of art

piecemeal *adv* = **bit by bit**, by degrees, gradually, little by little

pier *n* **1** = **jetty**, landing place, promenade, quay, wharf **2** = **pillar**, buttress, column, pile, post, support, upright

pierce *v* = **penetrate**, bore, drill, enter, perforate, prick, puncture, spike, stab, stick into

piercing *adj* **1** *Usually of sound* = **penetrating**, ear-splitting, high-pitched, loud, sharp, shrill **2** = **keen**, alert, penetrating, perceptive, perspicacious, quick-witted, sharp, shrewd **3** *Usually of weather* = **cold**, arctic, biting, bitter, freezing, nippy, wintry **4** = **sharp**, acute, agonizing, excruciating, intense, painful, severe, stabbing

piety *n* = **holiness**, faith, godliness, piousness, religion, reverence

pig *n* **1** = **hog**, boar, porker, sow, swine **2** *Inf* = **slob** (*sl*), boor, brute, glutton, hog (*inf*), swine

pigeonhole *n* **1** = **compartment**,

pig·ment [PIG-mənt] *n* coloring matter, paint or dye.

pigmy see PYGMY.

pike[1] [pīk] *n* various types of large, predatory freshwater fish.

pike[2] *n* spear formerly used by infantry.

pi·laf [PEE-lahf] *n* Middle Eastern dish of steamed rice with spices, sometimes with meat or fowl, etc.

pi·las·ter [pi-LAS-tər] *n* square column, usu. set in wall.

pile[1] [pīl] *n* 1 heap. 2 great mass of building. ◆ *v* **piled, pil·ing** ◆ *vt* 3 heap (up), stack load. ◆ *vi* 4 (with *in* or *out*) move in a group. **atomic pile** nuclear reactor.

pile[2] *n* beam driven into the ground, esp. as foundation for building in water or wet ground. **pile driver** *n* 1 machine for driving down piles. 2 person who operates this machine.

pile[3] *n* 1 nap of cloth, esp. of velvet, carpet, etc. 2 down.

piles [pīlz] *pl n* tumors of veins of rectum, hemorrhoids.

pil·fer [PIL-fər] *v* steal in small quantities. **pil'fer·age** [-ij] *n* **pil'fer·er** *n*

pil·grim *n* 1 one who journeys to sacred place. 2 wanderer, wayfarer. **pil'grim·age** [-ij] *n*

pill *n* 1 small ball of medicine swallowed whole. 2 anything disagreeable that has to be endured. **the pill** oral contraceptive. **pill'box** *n* 1 small box for pills. 2 small

concrete fort.

pil·lage [PIL-ij] *v* **-laged, -lag·ing** 1 plunder, ravage, sack. ◆ *n* 2 seizure of goods, esp. in war. 3 plunder.

pil·lar [PIL-ər] *n* 1 slender, upright structure, column. 2 prominent supporter.

pil·lo·ry [PIL-ə-ree] *n, pl* **-ries** 1 frame with holes for head and hands in which offender was confined and exposed to public abuse and ridicule. ◆ *vt* **-ried, -ry·ing** 2 expose to ridicule and abuse. 3 set in pillory.

pil·low [PIL-oh] *n* 1 cushion for the head, esp. in bed. ◆ *vt* 2 lay on, or as on, pillow.

pi·lot [PĪ-lət] *n* 1 person qualified to fly an aircraft or spacecraft. 2 one qualified to take charge of ship entering or leaving harbor, or where knowledge of local water is needed. 3 steersman. 4 guide. ◆ *adj* 5 experimental and preliminary. ◆ *vt* 6 act as pilot to. 7 steer. **pilot light** small auxiliary flame lighting main one in gas appliance, etc.

pi·mi·en·to [pi-MYEN-toh] *n, pl* **-tos** (fruit of the) sweet red pepper (also **pi·men'to**).

pimp *n* 1 one who solicits for prostitute. ◆ *vi* 2 act as pimp.

pim·ple [PIM-pəl] *n* small pus-filled spot on the skin. **pim'ply** *adj* **-pli·er, -li·est**

pin *n* 1 short thin piece of stiff wire with point and head, for fastening. 2 wooden or metal peg or rivet. ◆ *vt* **pinned, pin·ning** 3 fasten with pin. 4 seize and hold fast.

cubbyhole, locker, niche, place, section ◆ *v* 2 = **classify**, categorize, characterize, compartmentalize, ghettoize, label, slot (*inf*) 3 = **put off**, defer, postpone, shelve

pig-headed *adj* = **stubborn**, contrary, inflexible, mulish, obstinate, self-willed, stiff-necked, unyielding

pigment *n* = **color**, coloring, dye, paint, stain, tincture, tint

pile[1] *n* 1 = **heap**, accumulation, collection, hoard, mass, mound, mountain, stack 2 = **building**, edifice, erection, structure ◆ *v* 3 = **collect**, accumulate, amass, assemble, gather, heap, hoard, stack 4 = **crowd**, crush, flock, flood, jam, pack, rush, stream

pile[2] *n* = **foundation**, beam, column, pillar, post, support, upright

pile[3] *n* = **nap**, down, fiber, fur, hair, plush

pile-up *n Inf* = **collision**, accident, crash, multiple collision, smash, smash-up (*inf*)

pilfer *v* = **steal**, appropriate, embezzle,

filch, lift (*inf*), pinch (*inf*), purloin, swipe (*sl*), take

pilgrim *n* = **traveler**, wanderer, wayfarer

pilgrimage *n* = **journey**, excursion, expedition, mission, tour, trip

pill *n* 1 = **tablet**, capsule, pellet 2 **the pill** = **oral contraceptive**

pillage *v* 1 = **plunder**, despoil, loot, maraud, raid, ransack, ravage, sack ◆ *n* 2 = **plunder**, marauding, robbery, sack, spoliation

pillar *n* 1 = **support**, column, pier, post, prop, shaft, stanchion, upright 2 = **supporter**, follower, mainstay, upholder

pillory *v* = **ridicule**, brand, denounce, stigmatize

pilot *n* 1 = **airman**, aviator, flyer 2 = **helmsman**, navigator, steersman ◆ *adj* 3 = **trial**, experimental, model, test ◆ *v* 4 = **fly**, conduct, direct, drive, guide, handle, navigate, operate, steer

pin'ball *n* table game, where small ball is shot through various hazards. **pin money** trivial sum. **pin'point** *vt* mark exactly.

pin·a·fore [PIN-ə-for] *n* **1** child's apron. **2** woman's dress with a bib top.

pince-nez [PANS-nay] *n, pl* **pince-nez** eyeglasses kept on nose by spring.

pin·cers [PIN-sərz] *pl n* **1** tool for gripping, composed of two limbs crossed and pivoted. **2** claws of lobster, etc. **pincers movement** military maneuver in which both flanks of a force are attacked simultaneously.

pinch *vt* **1** nip, squeeze. **2** stint. **3** *sl* steal. **4** *sl* arrest. ◆ *n* **5** nip. **6** as much as can be taken up between finger and thumb. **7** stress. **8** emergency. **pinch'bar** *n* crowbar.

pine[1] [pīn] *n* **1** evergreen coniferous tree. **2** its wood.

pine[2] *vi* **pined, pin·ing 1** yearn. **2** waste away with grief, etc.

pin·e·al [PIN-ee-əl] *adj* shaped like pine cone. **pineal gland** small cone-shaped gland situated at base of brain.

pine·ap·ple [PĪ-nap-əl] *n* **1** tropical plant with spiny leaves bearing large edible fruit. **2** the fruit. **3** *sl* a bomb.

ping *vi* **1** produce brief ringing sound. **2** of engine, knock.

pin·guid [PING-gwid] *adj* **1** oily. **2** fat.

pin·ion[1] [PIN-yən] *n* **1** bird's wing. ◆ *vt* **2** disable or confine by binding wings, arms, etc.

pinion[2] *n* small cogwheel.

pink [pingk] *n* **1** pale red color. **2** garden plant. **3** best condition, fitness. ◆ *adj* **4** of

color pink. ◆ *vt* **5** pierce. **6** finish edge (of fabric) with perforations or scallops.

pin·na·cle [PIN-ə-kəl] *n* **1** highest pitch or point. **2** mountain peak. **3** pointed turret on buttress or roof.

pint [pīnt] *n* liquid measure, one eighth of gallon (.568 liter).

pin·tle [PIN-tl] *n* pivot pin.

pin'up *n* picture of sexually attractive person, esp. (partly) naked.

pi·o·neer [pī-ə-NEER] *n* **1** explorer. **2** early settler. **3** originator. **4** one of advance party preparing road, etc. for troops. ◆ *vi* **5** act as pioneer or leader.

pi·ous [PĪ-əs] *adj* **1** devout. **2** righteous.

pip[1] *n* **1** seed in fruit. **2** *inf* something or someone outstanding.

pip[2] *n* **1** spot on playing cards, dice, or dominoes. **2** *inf* metal insigne on officer's shoulder showing rank.

pip[3] *n* disease of poultry.

pipe [pīp] *n* **1** tube of metal or other material. **2** tube with small bowl at end for smoking tobacco. **3** musical instrument, whistle. ◆ *pl* **4** bagpipes. ◆ *v* **piped, pip·ing 5** play on pipe. **6** utter in shrill tone. **7** convey by pipe. **8** ornament with a piping or fancy edging. **pip'er** *n* player on pipe or bagpipes. **piping** *n* **1** system of pipes. **2** fancy edging or trimming on clothes. **3** act or art of playing on pipe, esp. bagpipes. **pipe down** *inf* **1** stop making noise. **2** stop talking. **pipe dream** fanciful, impossible plan, etc. **pipe'line** *n* **1** long pipe for transporting oil, water, etc. **2** means of communications. **pipe up** *inf* **1** assert

pimple *n* = **spot**, boil, pustule, zit (*sl*)

pin *v* **1** = **fasten**, affix, attach, fix, join, secure **2** = **hold fast**, fix, hold down, immobilize, pinion

pinch *v* **1** = **squeeze**, compress, grasp, nip, press **2** = **hurt**, cramp, crush, pain **3** *Inf* = **steal**, filch, lift (*inf*), pilfer, purloin, swipe (*sl*) ◆ *n* **4** = **squeeze**, nip **5** = **dash**, bit, jot, mite, *soupçon*, speck **6** = **hardship**, crisis, difficulty, emergency, necessity, plight, predicament, strait

pinched *adj* = **thin**, drawn, gaunt, haggard, peaky, worn

pin down *v* **1** = **force**, compel, constrain, make, press, pressurize **2** = **determine**, identify, locate, name, pinpoint, specify

pine *v* **1** (often with *for*) = **long**, ache, crave, desire, eat one's heart out over, hanker,

hunger for, thirst for, wish for, yearn for **2** = **waste**, decline, fade, languish, sicken

pinion *v* = **immobilize**, bind, chain, fasten, fetter, manacle, shackle, tie

pink[1] *adj* = **rosy**, flushed, reddish, rose, roseate, salmon

pinnacle *n* = **peak**, apex, crest, crown, height, summit, top, vertex, zenith

pinpoint *v* = **identify**, define, distinguish, locate

pioneer *n* **1** = **settler**, colonist, explorer **2** = **founder**, developer, innovator, leader, trailblazer ◆ *v* **3** = **develop**, create, discover, establish, initiate, instigate, institute, invent, originate, show the way, start

pious *adj* = **religious**, devout, God-fearing, godly, holy, reverent, righteous, saintly oneself by speaking. **2** speak louder. **in the pipeline 1** yet to come. **2** in process of completion, etc.

pi·pette [pī-PET] *n* slender glass tube to transfer fluids from one vessel to another.

pip'pin *n* kind of apple.

pi·quant [PEE-kənt] *adj* **1** pungent. **2** stimulating. **pi'quan·cy** *n*

pique [peek] *n* **1** feeling of injury, baffled curiosity or resentment. ◆ *vt* **piqued, piqu·ing 2** hurt pride of. **3** irritate. **4** stimulate.

pi·qué [pi-KAY] *n* stiff ribbed cotton fabric.

pi·ra·nha [pi-RAHN-yə] *n, pl* **-nhas** small voracious freshwater fish of tropical Amer.

pi·rate [PĪ-rət] *n* **1** sea robber. **2** publisher, etc., who infringes copyright. ◆ *n, adj* **3** (person) broadcasting illegally. ◆ *vt* **-rat·ed, -rat·ing 4** use or reproduce (artistic work, etc.) illicitly. **pi'ra·cy** [-see] *n, pl* **-cies**

pir·ou·ette [pir-oo-ET] *n* **1** spinning around on the toe. ◆ *vi* **-et·ted, -et·ting 2** do this.

pissed [pist] *adj sl* angry, annoyed, or disappointed.

pis·tach·i·o [pi-STASH-ee-oh] *n, pl* **-i·os 1** small hard-shelled, sweet-tasting nut. **2** tree producing it.

pis·til [PIS-tl] *n* seed-bearing organ of flower.

pis·tol [PIS-tl] *n* **1** small firearm for one hand. ◆ *vt* **-toled, -tol·ing 2** shoot with pistol.

pis·ton [PIS-tən] *n* in internal combustion engine, steam engine, etc., cylindrical part

propelled to and fro in hollow cylinder by pressure of gas, etc. to convert reciprocating motion to rotation.

pit *n* **1** deep hole in ground. **2** mine or its shaft. **3** depression. **4** enclosure where cocks are set to fight. **5** servicing, refueling area on automobile racetrack. ◆ *vt* **pit·ted, pit·ting 6** set to fight, match. **7** mark with small dents or scars. **pit'fall** *n* **1** any hidden danger. **2** covered pit for trapping animals or people.

pitch¹ [pich] *vt* **1** cast or throw. **2** set up. **3** set the key of (a tune). ◆ *vi* **4** fall headlong. **5** of ship, plunge lengthwise. ◆ *n* **6** act of pitching. **7** degree, height, intensity. **8** slope. **9** distance propeller advances during one revolution. **10** distance between threads of screw, teeth of saw, etc. **11** acuteness of tone. **12** *Baseball* ball delivered by pitcher to batter. **13** *inf* persuasive sales talk. **pitch'er** *n Baseball* player who delivers ball to batter.

pitch'fork *n* **1** fork for lifting hay, etc. ◆ *vt* **2** throw with, as with, pitchfork. **pitch'out** *n Baseball* pitch thrown intentionally beyond batter's reach to improve catcher's chance of putting out base runner attempting to steal.

pitch² *n* **1** dark sticky substance obtained from tar or turpentine. ◆ *vt* **2** coat with this. **pitch'y** *adj* **pitch·i·er, pitch·i·est 1** covered with pitch. **2** black as pitch. **pitch-black, -dark** *adj* very dark.

pitch·blende [PICH-blend] *n* mineral

--- THESAURUS ---

pipe *n* **1** = **tube**, conduit, duct, hose, line, main, passage, pipeline ◆ *v* **2** = **whistle**, cheep, peep, play, sing, sound, warble **3** = **convey**, channel, conduct

pipe down *v Inf* = **be quiet**, hold one's tongue, hush, quieten down, shush, shut one's mouth, shut up (*inf*)

pipeline *n* = **tube**, conduit, duct, passage, pipe

piquant *adj* **1** = **spicy**, biting, pungent, savory, sharp, tangy, tart, zesty **2** = **interesting**, lively, provocative, scintillating, sparkling, stimulating

pique *n* **1** = **resentment**, annoyance, displeasure, huff, hurt feelings, irritation, offense, umbrage, wounded pride ◆ *v* **2** = **displease**, affront, annoy, get (*inf*), irk, irritate, nettle, offend, rile, sting **3** = **arouse**, excite, rouse, spur, stimulate, stir, whet

piracy *n* = **robbery**, buccaneering, freebooting, stealing, theft

pirate *n* **1** = **buccaneer**, corsair, freebooter, marauder, raider **2** = **plagiarist**, infringer, plagiarizer ◆ *v* **3** = **copy**, appropriate, plagiarize, poach, reproduce, steal

pit *n* **1** = **hole**, abyss, cavity, chasm, crater, dent, depression, hollow ◆ *v* **2** = **scar**, dent, indent, mark, pockmark

pitch *v* **1** = **throw**, cast, chuck (*inf*), fling, heave, hurl, lob (*inf*), sling, toss **2** = **set up**, erect, put up, raise, settle **3** = **fall**, dive, drop, topple, tumble **4** = **toss**, lurch, plunge, roll ◆ *n* **5** = **sports field**, field of play, ground, park **6** = **level**, degree, height, highest point, point, summit **7** = **slope**, angle, dip, gradient, incline, tilt **8** = **tone**, modulation, sound, timbre **9** = **sales talk**, patter, spiel (*inf*)

pitch-black *adj* = **jet-black**, dark, inky,

composed largely of uranium oxide, yielding radium.

pitch•er [PICH-ər] n 1 large jug. 2 see also PITCH.

pith n 1 tissue in stems and branches of certain plants. 2 essential substance, most important part. **pith'i•ly** adv **pith'y** adj **pith•i•er, pith•i•est 1** terse, cogent, concise. 2 consisting of pith.

pi•ton [PEE-ton] n metal spike used in mountain climbing.

pit•tance [PIT-ns] n 1 small allowance. 2 inadequate wages.

pi•tu•i•tar•y [pi-TOO-i-ter-ee] adj of, pert. to, the endocrine gland at base of brain.

pit•y [PIT-ee] n, pl **pit•ies 1** sympathy, sorrow for others' suffering. 2 regrettable fact. ♦ vt **pit•ied, pit•y•ing 3** feel pity for. **pit'e•ous** adj 1 deserving pity. 2 sad, wretched. **pit'i•a•ble** adj **pit'i•ful** [-i-fəl] adj 1 woeful. 2 contemptible. **pit'i•less** [-i-lis] adj 1 feeling no pity. 2 hard, merciless.

piv•ot [PIV-ət] n 1 shaft or pin on which thing turns. ♦ vt 2 furnish with pivot. ♦ vi 3 hinge on one. **piv'ot•al** [-ət-əl] adj 1 of,

acting as, pivot. 2 of crucial importance.

pix•ie [PIK-see] n 1 fairy. 2 mischievous person.

pi•zazz [pə-ZAZ] n inf sparkle, vitality, glamour.

piz•za [PEET-sə] n dish of baked disk of dough covered with cheese and tomato sauce and wide variety of garnishes. **piz•ze•ri'a** [-REE-ə] n place selling pizzas.

piz•zi•ca•to [pit-si-KAH-toh] adj Mus. played by plucking string of violin, etc., with finger.

plac•ard [PLAK-ahrd] n 1 paper or card with notice on one side for posting up or carrying, poster. ♦ vt 2 post placards on. 3 advertise, display on placards.

pla•cate [PLAY-klayt] vt -cat•ed, -cat•ing conciliate, pacify, appease. **pla•ca•to'ry** [-kə-tor-ee] adj

place [plays] n 1 locality, spot. 2 position. 3 stead. 4 duty. 5 town, village, residence, buildings. 6 office, employment. 7 seat, space. ♦ vt **placed, plac•ing 8** put in particular place. 9 set. 10 identify. 11 make (order, bet, etc.).

pitch-dark, unlit

pitch in v = **help**, chip in (inf), contribute, cooperate, do one's bit, join in, lend a hand, participate

piteous adj = **pathetic**, affecting, distressing, harrowing, heartbreaking, heart-rending, moving, pitiable, pitiful, plaintive, poignant, sad

pitfall n = **danger**, catch, difficulty, drawback, hazard, peril, snag, trap

pith n = **essence**, core, crux, gist, heart, kernel, nub, point, quintessence, salient point

pithy adj = **succinct**, brief, cogent, concise, epigrammatic, laconic, pointed, short, terse, to the point, trenchant

pitiful adj 1 = **pathetic**, distressing, grievous, harrowing, heartbreaking, heart-rending, piteous, pitiable, sad, wretched 2 = **contemptible**, abject, base, lousy (sl), low, mean, miserable, paltry, shabby, sorry

pitiless adj = **merciless**, callous, cold-blooded, cold-hearted, cruel, hardhearted, heartless, implacable, relentless, ruthless, unmerciful

pittance n = **peanuts** (sl), chicken feed (sl), drop, mite, slave wages, trifle

pity n 1 = **compassion**, charity, clemency,

fellow feeling, forbearance, kindness, mercy, sympathy 2 = **shame**, bummer (sl), crying shame, misfortune, sin ♦ v 3 = **feel sorry for**, bleed for, feel for, grieve for, have compassion for, sympathize with, weep for

pivot n 1 = **axis**, axle, fulcrum, spindle, swivel 2 = **hub**, center, heart, hinge, kingpin ♦ v 3 = **turn**, revolve, rotate, spin, swivel, twirl 4 = **rely**, be contingent, depend, hang, hinge

pivotal adj = **crucial**, central, critical, decisive, vital

pixie n = **elf**, brownie, fairy, sprite

placard n = **notice**, advertisement, bill, poster

placate v = **calm**, appease, assuage, conciliate, humor, mollify, pacify, propitiate, soothe

place n 1 = **spot**, area, location, point, position, site, venue, whereabouts 2 = **region**, district, locale, locality, neighborhood, quarter, vicinity 3 = **position**, grade, rank, station, status 4 = **space**, accommodation, room 5 = **home**, abode, domicile, dwelling, house, pad (sl, dated), property, residence 6 = **duty**, affair, charge, concern, function, prerogative, responsibility, right, role 7 = **job**,

pla·ce·bo [plə-SEE-boh] *n, pl* **-bos** sugar pill, etc. given to unsuspecting patient as active drug.

pla·cen·ta [plə-SEN-tə] *n, pl* **-tas 1** organ formed in uterus during pregnancy, providing nutrients for fetus. **2** afterbirth.

plac·id [PLAS-id] *adj* **1** calm. **2** equable. **pla·cid·i·ty** [plə-SID-i-tee] *n* mildness, quiet.

pla·gia·rism [PLAY-jə-riz-əm] *n* taking ideas, passages, etc. from an author and presenting them, unacknowledged, as one's own. **pla'gia·rize** [-rīz] *v* **-rized, -riz·ing pla'gia·rist** *n*

plague [playg] *n* **1** highly contagious disease, esp. bubonic plague. **2** nuisance. **3** affliction. ◆ *vt* **plagued, pla·guing 4** trouble, annoy.

plaid [plad] *n* **1** checked or tartan pattern. **2** fabric made of this.

plain [playn] *adj* **-er, -est 1** flat, level. **2** unobstructed, not intricate. **3** clear, obvious. **4** easily understood. **5** simple. **6** ordinary. **7** without decoration. **8** not beautiful. ◆ *n* **9** tract of level country. ◆ *adv* **10** clearly. **plain'ly** [-lee] *adv* **plain'ness** [-nis] *n* **plain clothes** civilian dress, as opposed to uniform. **plain dealing** directness and honesty in transactions. **plain sailing** unobstructed course of action. **plain speaking** frankness, candor.

plain·tiff [PLAYN-tif] *n Law* one who sues in court.

plain·tive [PLAYN-tiv] *adj* sad, mournful, melancholy.

plait [playt] *n* **1** braid of hair, straw, etc. ◆ *vt* **2** form or weave into braids.

plan *n* **1** scheme. **2** way of proceeding. **3** project, design. **4** drawing of horizontal section. **5** diagram, map. ◆ *vt* **planned, plan·ning 6** make plan of. **7** arrange beforehand.

planch·et [PLAN-chit] *n* **1** flat sheet of metal. **2** disk of metal from which coin is stamped.

plan·chette [plan-SHET] *n* small board used in spiritualism.

plane[1] [playn] *n* **1** smooth surface. **2** a level. **3** carpenter's tool for smoothing wood. ◆ *vt* **planed, plan·ing 4** make smooth with one. ◆ *adj* **5** perfectly flat or level. **plan'er** *n* planing machine.

plane[2] *v* **planed, plan·ing 1** of airplane, glide. **2** of boat, rise and partly skim over water. ◆ *n* **3** wing of airplane. **4** airplane.

━━━━━━ | THESAURUS | ━━━━━━

appointment, employment, position, post **8 take place = happen**, come about, go on, occur, transpire (*inf*) ◆ *v* **9 = put**, deposit, install, lay, locate, position, rest, set, situate, stand, station, stick (*inf*) **10 = classify**, arrange, class, grade, group, order, rank, sort **11 = identify**, know, put one's finger on, recognize, remember **12 = assign**, allocate, appoint, charge, entrust, give

placid *adj* **= calm**, collected, composed, equable, even-tempered, imperturbable, serene, tranquil, unexcitable, unruffled, untroubled

plagiarism *n* **= copying**, borrowing, infringement, piracy, theft

plagiarize *v* **= copy**, borrow, lift (*inf*), pirate, steal

plague *n* **1 = disease**, epidemic, infection, pestilence **2 = affliction**, bane, blight, curse, evil, scourge, torment ◆ *v* **3 = pester**, annoy, badger, bother, harass, harry, hassle (*inf*), tease, torment, torture, trouble, vex

plain *adj* **1 = clear**, comprehensible, distinct, evident, manifest, obvious, overt, patent, unambiguous, understandable, unmistakable, visible **2 = honest**, blunt, candid, direct, downright, forthright, frank, open, outspoken, straightforward, upfront (*inf*) **3 = unadorned**, austere, bare, basic, severe, simple, Spartan, stark, unembellished, unfussy, unornamented **4 = ugly**, dumpy (*inf*), frowzy, homely (*U.S.*), ill-favored, no oil painting (*inf*), not beautiful, unattractive, unlovely, unprepossessing **5 = ordinary**, common, commonplace, everyday, simple, unaffected, unpretentious ◆ *n* **6 = flatland**, grassland, plateau, prairie, steppe, veld

plain-spoken *adj* **= blunt**, candid, direct, downright, forthright, frank, outspoken

plaintive *adj* **= sorrowful**, heart-rending, mournful, pathetic, piteous, pitiful, sad

plan *n* **1 = scheme**, design, method, plot, program, proposal, strategy, suggestion, system **2 = diagram**, blueprint, chart, drawing, layout, map, representation, sketch ◆ *v* **3 = devise**, arrange, contrive, design, draft, formulate, organize, outline, plot, scheme, think out **4 = intend**, aim, mean, propose, purpose

plane *n* **1 = airplane**, aircraft, jet **2 = flat surface**, level surface **3 = level**, condition,

plan·et [PLAN-it] *n* heavenly body revolving around the sun. **plan'e·tar·y** [-i-ter-ee] *adj* of, like, planets.

plan·e·tar·i·um [plan-i-TAIR-ee-əm] *n* **1** an apparatus that shows the movement of sun, moon, stars and planets by projecting lights on the inside of a dome. **2** building in which the apparatus is housed.

plan·gent [PLAN-jənt] *adj* resounding.

plank [plangk] *n* **1** long flat piece of sawn timber. ♦ *vt* **2** cover with planks.

plank·ton [PLANGK-tən] *n* minute animal and vegetable organisms floating in ocean.

plant *n* **1** living organism feeding on inorganic substances and without power of locomotion. **2** such an organism that is smaller than tree or shrub. **3** equipment or machinery needed for manufacture. **4** building and equipment for manufacturing purposes. **5** complete equipment used for heating, air conditioning, etc. ♦ *vt* **6** set in ground, to grow. **7** support, establish. **8** stock with plants. **9** *sl* hide, esp. to deceive or observe. **plant'er** *n* **1** one who plants. **2** ornamental pot or stand for house plants.

plan·tain¹ [PLAN-tin] *n* low-growing weed with broad leaves.

plantain² *n* **1** tropical plant like banana. **2** its fruit.

plan·ta·tion [plan-TAY-shən] *n* **1** estate or large farm for cultivation of tobacco, cotton, etc. **2** wood of planted trees. **3** formerly, colony.

plaque [plak] *n* **1** ornamental plate, tablet. **2** plate of clasp or brooch. **3** filmy deposit on surfaces of teeth, conducive to decay.

plas·ma [PLAZ-mə] *n* clear, fluid portion of blood.

plas·ter [PLAS-tər] *n* **1** mixture of lime,

sand, etc. for coating walls, etc. **2** piece of fabric spread with medicinal or adhesive substance. ♦ *vt* **3** apply plaster to. **4** apply like plaster. **5** *inf* defeat soundly. **plas'tered** *adj sl* drunk.

plas·tic [PLAS-tik] *n* **1** any of a group of synthetic products derived from casein, cellulose, etc. that can be readily molded into any form and are extremely durable. ♦ *adj* **2** made of plastic. **3** easily molded, pliant. **4** capable of being molded. **5** produced by molding. **plas·tic·i·ty** [pla-STIS-i-tee] *n* ability to be molded. **plastic surgery** repair or reconstruction of missing or malformed parts of the body for medical or cosmetic reasons.

plate [playt] *n* **1** shallow round dish. **2** flat thin sheet of metal, glass, etc. **3** household utensils of gold or silver. **4** device for printing. **5** illustration in book. **6** set of false teeth, part of this that adheres to roof of mouth. ♦ *vt* **plat·ed, plat·ing 7** cover with thin coating of gold, silver, or other metal. **plate'ful** [-fəl] *n, pl* **-fuls plat'er** *n* **1** person who plates. **2** inferior race horse. **plate glass** kind of thick glass used for mirrors, windows, etc. **plate tec·ton'ics** *Geology* study of structure of Earth's crust, esp. movement of layers of rocks.

pla·teau [pla-TOH] *n, pl* **-teaus** [-TOHZ] **1** tract of level high land, tableland. **2** period of stability.

plat·en [PLAT-n] *n Printing* **1** plate by which paper is pressed against type. **2** roller in typewriter.

plat·form *n* **1** raised level surface or floor, stage. **2** raised area in station from which passengers board trains. **3** political program.

———————| THESAURUS |———————

degree, position ♦ *adj* **4** = **level**, even, flat, horizontal, regular, smooth ♦ *v* **5** = **skim**, glide, sail, skate

plant *n* **1** = **vegetable**, bush, flower, herb, shrub, weed **2** = **factory**, foundry, mill, shop, works, yard **3** = **machinery**, apparatus, equipment, gear ♦ *v* **4** = **sow**, put in the ground, scatter, seed, transplant **5** = **place**, establish, fix, found, insert, put, set

plaster *n* **1** = **mortar**, gypsum, plaster of Paris, stucco **2** = **bandage**, adhesive plaster, dressing, Elastoplast (*Trademark*), sticking plaster ♦ *v* **3** = **cover**, coat, daub, overlay, smear, spread

plastic *adj* **1** = **manageable**, docile, malleable, pliable, receptive, responsive, tractable **2** = **pliant**, ductile, flexible, moldable, pliable, soft, supple

plate *n* **1** = **platter**, dish, trencher (*archaic*) **2** = **helping**, course, dish, portion, serving **3** = **layer**, panel, sheet, slab **4** = **illustration**, lithograph, print ♦ *v* **5** = **coat**, cover, gild, laminate, overlay

plateau *n* **1** = **upland**, highland, table, tableland **2** = **levelling off**, level, stability, stage

platform *n* **1** = **stage**, dais, podium, rostrum, stand **2** = **policy**, manifesto, objective(s), party line, principle, program

plat·i·num [PLAT-n-əm] *n* white heavy malleable metal.

plat·i·tude [PLAT-i-tood] *n* commonplace remark. **plat·i·tu'di·nous** *adj*

Pla·ton·ic [plə-TON-ik] *adj* 1 of Plato or his philosophy. 2 (**p-**) (of love) purely spiritual, friendly.

pla·toon [plə-TOON] *n* two or more squads of soldiers employed as unit.

plat·ter [PLAT-ər] *n* flat dish.

plat·y·pus [PLAT-i-pəs] *n, pl* **-pus·es** small Aust. egg-laying amphibious mammal, with dense fur, webbed feet and ducklike bill (also **duckbilled platypus**).

plau·dit [PLAW-dit] *n* act of applause, handclapping.

plau·si·ble [PLAW-zə-bəl] *adj* 1 apparently fair or reasonable. 2 fair-spoken. **plau·si·bil'i·ty** *n*

play *vi* 1 amuse oneself. 2 take part in game. 3 behave carelessly. 4 act a part on the stage. 5 perform on musical instrument. 6 move with light or irregular motion, flicker, etc. ♦ *vt* 7 contend with in game. 8 take part in (game). 9 trifle. 10 act the part of. 11 perform (music). 12 perform on (instrument). 13 use, work (instrument). ♦ *n* 14 dramatic piece or performance. 15 sport. 16 amusement. 17 manner of action or conduct. 18 activity. 19 brisk or free movement. 20 gambling. **play'boy** *n* rich man who lives only for pleasure. **play'ful** [-fəl] *adj* lively. **play'group** [-groop] *n* group of young children playing regularly under adult supervision. **play'house** *n* 1 theater. 2 small house for children to play in. **playing card** one of set of usu. 52 cards used in card games. **playing field** extensive piece of ground for open-air games. **play'thing** *n* toy. **play'wright** [-rīt] *n* author of plays.

pla·za [PLAH-zə] *n* 1 open space or square. 2 complex of retail stores, etc.

plea [plee] *n* 1 entreaty. 2 statement of prisoner or defendant. 3 excuse. **plead** *v* **plead·ed** or **pled, plead·ing** 1 make earnest appeal. 2 address court of law. 3 bring forward as excuse or plea. **plea bargaining** procedure in which defendant agrees to plead guilty in return for leniency in sentencing, etc.

please [pleez] *v* **pleased, pleas·ing** ♦ *vt* 1

platitude *n* = **cliché**, banality, commonplace, truism

platoon *n* = **squad**, company, group, outfit (*inf*), patrol, squadron, team

platter *n* = **plate**, dish, salver, tray, trencher (*archaic*)

plaudits *pl n* = **approval**, acclaim, acclamation, applause, approbation, praise

plausible *adj* 1 = **reasonable**, believable, conceivable, credible, likely, persuasive, possible, probable, tenable 2 = **glib**, smooth, smooth-talking, smooth-tongued, specious

play *v* 1 = **amuse oneself**, entertain oneself, fool, have fun, revel, romp, sport, trifle 2 = **compete**, challenge, contend against, participate, take on, take part 3 = **act**, act the part of, perform, portray, represent ♦ *n* 4 = **drama**, comedy, dramatic piece, farce, pantomime, piece, show, stage show, tragedy 5 = **amusement**, diversion, entertainment, fun, game, pastime, recreation, sport 6 = **fun**, humor, jest, joking, lark (*inf*), prank, sport 7 = **space**, elbowroom, latitude, leeway, margin, room, scope

playboy *n* = **womanizer**, ladies' man, philanderer, rake, roué

play down *v* = **minimize**, gloss over, make light of, make little of, underplay, underrate

player *n* 1 = **sportsman** or **sportswoman**, competitor, contestant, participant 2 = **musician**, artist, instrumentalist, performer, virtuoso 3 = **performer**, actor or actress, entertainer, Thespian, trouper

playful *adj* = **lively**, frisky, impish, merry, mischievous, spirited, sportive, sprightly, vivacious

playmate *n* = **friend**, chum (*inf*), companion, comrade, pal (*inf*), playfellow

play on or **upon** *v* = **take advantage of**, abuse, capitalize on, exploit, impose on, trade on

plaything *n* = **toy**, amusement, game, pastime, trifle

play up *v* = **emphasize**, accentuate, highlight, stress, underline

plea *n* 1 = **appeal**, entreaty, intercession, petition, prayer, request, suit, supplication 2 = **excuse**, defense, explanation, justification

plead *v* = **appeal**, ask, beg, beseech, entreat, implore, petition, request

pleasant *adj* 1 = **pleasing**, agreeable, amusing, delightful, enjoyable, fine, lovely, be agreeable to. **2** gratify. **3** delight. ◆ *vi* **4** like. **5** be willing. ◆ *adv* **6** word of request.

pleas•ant [PLEZ-ənt] *adj* pleasing, agreeable. **pleas'ant•ry** [-ən-tree] *n, pl* **-ries** joke, humor. **pleas•ur•a•ble** [PLEZH-ər-ə-bəl] *adj* giving pleasure. **pleas'ure** *n* **1** enjoyment. **2** satisfaction, will, choice.

pleat [pleet] *n* **1** any of various types of fold made by doubling material back on itself. ◆ *vi* **2** make, gather into pleats.

plebe [pleeb] *n* at US military and naval academies, member of first-year class.

ple•be•ian [pli-BEE-ən] *adj* **1** belonging to the common people. **2** low or rough. ◆ *n* **3** one of the common people.

pleb•i•scite [PLEB-ə-sīt] *n* decision by direct voting of the electorate.

plec•trum [PLEK-trəm] *n, pl* **-trums** small implement for plucking strings of guitar, etc.

pledge [plej] *n* **1** promise. **2** thing given over as security. **3** toast. ◆ *vt* **pledged, pledg•ing 4** promise formally. **5** bind or secure by pledge. **6** give over as security.

Pleis•to•cene [PLĪ-stə-seen] *adj Geology* of the glacial period of formation.

ple•na•ry [PLEE-nə-ree] *adj* **1** complete, without limitations, absolute. **2** of meeting, etc., with all members present.

plen•i•po•ten•ti•ar•y [plen-ə-pə-TEN-shee-er-ee] *adj, n* (envoy) having full powers.

plen•i•tude [PLEN-i-tood] *n* completeness, abundance, entirety.

plen•ty *n, pl* **-ties 1** abundance. **2** quite enough. **plen'te•ous** [-tee-əs] *adj* **1** ample. **2** rich. **3** copious. **plen'ti•ful** [ti fəl] *adj* abundant.

ple•num [PLEE-nəm] *n, pl* **-nums 1** space as considered to be full of matter (opposed to vacuum). **2** condition of fullness. **3** space above ceiling, etc. for receiving, storing heated or cooled air.

ple•o•nasm [PLEE-ə-naz-əm] *n* use of more words than necessary. **ple•o•nas'tic** [-NAS-tik] *adj*

pleth•o•ra [PLETH-ər-ə] *n* oversupply. **ple•thor•ic** [ple-THOR-ik] *adj*

pleu•ri•sy [PLUUR-ə-see] *n* inflammation of the pleura. **pleura** *n* membrane lining the chest and covering the lungs.

plex•us [PLEK-səs] *n, pl* **-us•es** network of nerves, or fibers.

pli•a•ble [PLĪ-ə-bəl] *adj* easily bent or influenced. **pli•a•bil'i•ty** *n* **pli'an•cy** [-ən-see] *n* **pli'ant** *adj* pliable.

pli•ers [PLĪ-ərz] *pl n* tool with hinged arms

nice, pleasurable **2 = nice**, affable, agreeable, amiable, charming, congenial, engaging, friendly, genial, likable *or* likeable

pleasantry *n* **= joke**, badinage, banter, jest, quip, witticism

please *v* **= delight**, amuse, entertain, gladden, gratify, humor, indulge, satisfy, suit

pleased *adj* **= happy**, contented, delighted, euphoric, glad, gratified, over the moon *(inf)*, satisfied, thrilled

pleasing *adj* **= enjoyable**, agreeable, charming, delightful, engaging, gratifying, likable *or* likeable, pleasurable, satisfying

pleasurable *adj* **= enjoyable**, agreeable, delightful, fun, good, lovely, nice, pleasant

pleasure *n* **= happiness**, amusement, bliss, delectation, delight, enjoyment, gladness, gratification, joy, satisfaction

plebeian *adj* **1 = common**, base, coarse, low, lower-class, proletarian, uncultivated, unrefined, vulgar, working-class ◆ *n* **2 = commoner**, common man, man in the street, pleb, proletarian

pledge *n* **1 = promise**, assurance, covenant, oath, undertaking, vow, warrant, word **2 = guarantee**, bail, collateral, deposit, pawn, security, surety ◆ *v* **3 = promise**, contract, engage, give one's oath, give one's word, swear, vow

plentiful *adj* **= abundant**, ample, bountiful, copious, generous, lavish, liberal, overflowing, plenteous, profuse

plenty *n* **1 = lots** *(inf)*, abundance, enough, great deal, heap(s) *(inf)*, masses, pile(s) *(inf)*, plethora, quantity, stack(s) **2 = abundance**, affluence, copiousness, fertility, fruitfulness, plenitude, profusion, prosperity, wealth

plethora *n* **= excess**, glut, overabundance, profusion, superabundance, surfeit, surplus

pliable *adj* **1 = flexible**, bendable, bendy, malleable, plastic, pliant, supple **2 = impressionable**, adaptable, compliant, docile, easily led, pliant, receptive, responsive, susceptible, tractable

pliant *adj* **1 = flexible**, bendable, bendy, plastic, pliable, supple **2 = impressionable**, biddable, compliant, easily led, pliable, and jaws for gripping.

plight[1] [plīt] *n* **1** distressing state. **2** predicament.

plight[2] *vt* promise, engage oneself to.

Plim·soll line [PLIM-sǝl] mark on ships indicating maximum displacement permitted when loaded.

Pli·o·cene [PLĪ-ǝ-seen] *n Geology* the most recent tertiary deposits.

plod *vi* **plod·ded, plod·ding** walk or work doggedly.

plop *n* **1** sound of object falling into water. ♦ *vi* **plopped, plop·ping 2** fall with, as though with, such a sound. **3** make the sound.

plot[1] *n* **1** secret plan, conspiracy. **2** essence of story, play, etc. ♦ *v* **plot·ted, plot·ting 3** devise secretly. **4** mark position of. **5** make map of. **6** conspire.

plot[2] *n* small piece of land.

plov·er [PLUV-ǝr] *n* one of various shore birds, typically with round head, straight bill and long pointed wings.

plow *n* **1** implement for turning up soil. **2** similar implement for clearing snow, etc. ♦ *vt* **3** turn up with plow, furrow. ♦ *vi* **4** work at slowly. **plow'share** [-shair] *n* blade of plow. **plow under 1** bury beneath soil by plowing. **2** overwhelm.

ploy [ploi] *n* **1** stratagem. **2** occupation. **3** prank.

pluck [pluk] *vt* **1** pull, pick off. **2** strip from. **3** sound strings of (guitar, etc.) with

fingers, plectrum. ♦ *n* **4** courage. **5** sudden pull or tug. **pluck'y** *adj* **pluck·i·er, pluck·i·est** courageous.

plug *n* **1** thing fitting into and filling a hole. **2** *Electricity* device connecting appliance to electricity supply. **3** tobacco pressed hard. **4** *inf* recommendation, advertisement. **5** *sl* worn-out horse. ♦ *vt* **plugged, plug·ging 6** stop with plug. **7** *inf* advertise anything by constant repetition. **8** *sl* punch. **9** *sl* shoot. **plug away** work hard. **plug in** connect (electrical appliance) with power source by means of plug.

plum *n* **1** stone fruit. **2** tree bearing it. **3** choicest part, piece, position, etc. **4** dark reddish-purple color. ♦ *adj* **5** choice. **6** plum-colored.

plumage see PLUME.

plumb [plum] *n* **1** ball of lead attached to string used for sounding, finding the perpendicular, etc. ♦ *adj* **2** perpendicular. ♦ *adv* **3** perpendicularly. **4** exactly. **5** *inf* downright. **6** honestly. ♦ *vt* **7** set exactly upright. **8** find depth of. **9** reach, undergo. **10** equip with, connect to plumbing system. **plumb'er** [PLUM-ǝr] *n* worker who attends to water and sewage systems. **plumb'ing** *n* **1** trade of plumber. **2** system of water and sewage pipes. **plumb'line** *n* cord with plumb attached.

plume [ploom] *n* **1** feather. **2** ornament of feathers, etc. ♦ *vt* **plumed, plum·ing 3** furnish with plumes. **4** pride oneself.

———— THESAURUS ————

susceptible, tractable

plight[1] *n* = **difficulty**, condition, jam (*inf*), predicament, scrape (*inf*), situation, spot (*inf*), state, trouble

plod *v* **1** = **trudge**, clump, drag, lumber, tramp, tread **2** = **slog**, grind (*inf*), labor, persevere, plow through, soldier on, toil

plot[1] *n* **1** = **plan**, cabal, conspiracy, intrigue, machination, scheme, stratagem **2** = **story**, action, narrative, outline, scenario, story line, subject, theme ♦ *v* **3** = **plan**, collude, conspire, contrive, intrigue, machinate, maneuver, scheme **4** = **devise**, conceive, concoct, contrive, cook up (*inf*), design, hatch, lay **5** = **chart**, calculate, locate, map, mark, outline

plot[2] *n* = **patch**, allotment, area, ground, lot, parcel, tract

plow *v* **1** = **turn over**, cultivate, dig, till **2** (usually with *through*) = **forge**, cut, drive, plunge, press, push, wade

ploy *n* = **tactic**, device, dodge, maneuver, move, ruse, scheme, stratagem, trick, wile

pluck *v* **1** = **pull out** *or* **off**, collect, draw, gather, harvest, pick **2** = **tug**, catch, clutch, jerk, pull at, snatch, tweak, yank **3** = **strum**, finger, pick, twang ♦ *n* **4** = **courage**, backbone, boldness, bravery, grit, guts (*inf*), nerve

plucky *adj* = **courageous**, bold, brave, daring, game, gutsy (*sl*), intrepid

plug *n* **1** = **stopper**, bung, cork, spigot **2** *Inf* = **mention**, advertisement, hype, publicity, push ♦ *v* **3** = **seal**, block, bung, close, cork, fill, pack, stop, stopper, stop up, stuff **4** *Inf* = **mention**, advertise, build up, hype, promote, publicize, push

plum *adj* = **choice**, best, first-class, prize

plumb *v* **1** = **delve**, explore, fathom, gauge, go into, penetrate, probe, unravel ♦ *n* **2** = **weight**, lead, plumb bob, plummet ♦ *adv* **3** = **exactly**, bang, precisely, slap

plum·age [PLOO-mij] *n* bird's feathers collectively.

plum·met [PLUM-it] *vi* **1** plunge headlong. ◆ *n* **2** plumbline.

plump[1] *adj* **-er, -est** **1** of rounded form, moderately fat, chubby. ◆ *v* **2** make, become plump.

plump[2] *vi* **1** sit, fall abruptly. **2** (with *for*) support enthusiastically. ◆ *vt* **3** drop, throw abruptly. ◆ *adv* **4** suddenly. **5** heavily. **6** directly.

plun·der [PLUN-dər] *vt* **1** take by force. **2** rob systematically. ◆ *vi* **3** rob. ◆ *n* **4** pillage. **5** booty, spoils.

plunge [plunj] *v* **plunged, plung·ing** ◆ *vt* **1** put forcibly (into). ◆ *vi* **2** throw oneself (into). **3** enter, rush with violence. **4** descend very suddenly. ◆ *n* **5** dive. **plung'er** *n* rubber suction cap with handle to unblock drains. **take the plunge** *inf* **1** embark on risky enterprise. **2** get married.

plunk *v* **1** pluck (string of banjo, etc.). **2** drop, fall suddenly and heavily. ◆ *n*

plu·ral [PLUUR-əl] *adj* **1** of, denoting more than one person or thing. ◆ *n* **2** word in its plural form. **plu'ral·ism** *n* **1** holding of more than one office at a time. **2** coexistence of different social groups, etc., in one society. **plu·ral'i·ty** *n, pl* **-ties 1** of three or more candidates, etc. **2** largest share of votes.

plus *prep* **1** with addition of. ◆ *adj* **2** to be added. **3** positive. ◆ *n* **4** sign (+) denoting addition. **5** advantage.

plush *n* **1** fabric with long nap, long-piled velvet. ◆ *adj* **-er, -est 2** luxurious.

Plu·to [PLOO-toh] *n* **1** Greek god of the underworld. **2** farthest planet from the sun.

plu·toc·ra·cy [ploo-TOK-rə-see] *n, pl* **-cies**

1 government by the rich. **2** state ruled thus. **3** wealthy class. **plu'to·crat** [-tə-krat] *n* wealthy person.

plu·to·ni·um [ploo-TOH-nee-əm] *n* radioactive metallic element used esp. in nuclear reactors and weapons.

ply[1] [plī] *v* **plied, ply·ing 1** wield. **2** work at. **3** supply pressingly. **4** urge. **5** keep busy. **6** go to and fro, run regularly.

ply[2] *n* **1** fold or thickness. **2** strand of yarn. **ply'wood** [-wuud] *n* board of thin layers of wood glued together with grains at right angles.

Pm *Chem.* promethium.

pneu·mat·ic [nuu-MAT-ik] *adj* of, worked by, inflated with wind or air.

pneu·mo·nia [nuu-MOHN-yə] *n* inflammation of the lungs.

Po *Chem.* polonium.

poach[1] [pohch] *vt* **1** take (game) illegally. **2** trample, make swampy or soft. ◆ *vi* **3** trespass for this purpose. **4** encroach. **poach'er** *n*

poach[2] *vt* simmer (eggs, fish, etc.) gently in water, etc. **poach'er** *n*

pock [pok] *n* pustule, as in smallpox, etc. **pock'marked** *adj*

pock·et [POK-it] *n* **1** small bag inserted in garment. **2** cavity filled with ore, etc. **3** socket, cavity, pouch or hollow. **4** mass of water or air differing from that surrounding it. **5** isolated group or area. ◆ *vt* **6** put into one's pocket. **7** appropriate, steal. ◆ *adj* **8** small. **pocket money 1** small, regular allowance given to children by parents. **2** allowance for small, occasional expenses. **pocket veto** indirect veto of bill by president, governor, who retains bill unsigned until legislative adjournment.

pod *n* **1** long seed vessel, as of peas, beans,

————————| THESAURUS |————————

plume *n* = **feather**, crest, pinion, quill

plummet *v* = **plunge**, crash, descend, dive, drop down, fall, nose-dive, tumble

plump[1] *adj* = **chubby**, corpulent, dumpy, fat, roly-poly, rotund, round, stout, tubby

plunder *v* **1** = **loot**, pillage, raid, ransack, rifle, rob, sack, strip ◆ *n* **2** = **loot**, booty, ill-gotten gains, pillage, prize, spoils, swag (*sl*)

plunge *v* **1** = **throw**, cast, pitch **2** = **hurtle**, career, charge, dash, jump, rush, tear **3** = **descend**, dip, dive, drop, fall, nose-dive, plummet, sink, tumble ◆ *n* **4** = **dive**, descent, drop, fall, jump

plus *prep* **1** = **and**, added to, coupled with, with ◆ *adj* **2** = **additional**, added, add-on, extra, supplementary ◆ *n* **3** = **advantage**, asset, benefit, bonus, extra, gain, good point

plush *adj* = **luxurious**, deluxe, lavish, luxury, opulent, rich, sumptuous

ply[1] *v* **1** = **work at**, carry on, exercise, follow, practice, pursue **2** = **use**, employ, handle, manipulate, wield

poach *v* = **encroach**, appropriate, infringe, intrude, trespass

pocket *n* **1** = **pouch**, bag, compartment, receptacle, sack ◆ *v* **2** = **steal**, appropriate, etc. ◆ v **pod·ded, pod·ding** ◆ vi **2** form pods. ◆ vt **3** shell.

po·di·um [POH-dee-əm] n small raised platform.

po·em [POH-əm] n imaginative composition in rhythmic lines. **po·et** [-it] n writer of poems. **po·et·ry** n art or work of poet, verse. **po·e·sy** [-ə-see] n poetry. **po·et·ic** [-ET-ik] adj **po·et·i·cal·ly** adv **po·et·as·ter** [-as-tər] n would-be or inferior poet.

po·grom [pə-GRUM] n organized persecution and massacre, esp. of Jews.

poign·ant [POIN-yənt] adj **1** moving. **2** biting, stinging. **3** vivid. **4** pungent. **poign'an·cy** n, pl **-cies**

poin·set·ti·a [poin-SET-ee-ə] n orig. Amer. shrub, widely cultivated for its clusters of scarlet leaves, resembling petals.

point n **1** dot, mark. **2** punctuation mark. **3** item, detail. **4** unit of value. **5** position, degree, stage. **6** moment. **7** gist of an argument. **8** purpose. **9** striking or effective part or quality. **10** essential object or thing. **11** sharp end. **12** single unit in scoring. **13** headland. **14** one of direction marks of compass. **15** fine kind of lace. **16** act of pointing. **17** printing unit, one-twelfth of a pica. ◆ pl **18** electrical contacts in distributor of engine. ◆ vi **19** show direction or position by extending finger. **20** direct attention. **21** (of dog) indicate position of game by standing facing it. ◆ vt **22** aim, direct. **23** sharpen. **24** fill up joints with mortar. **25** give value to (words, etc.). **point'ed** adj **1** sharp. **2** direct, telling. **point'er** n **1** index. **2** indicating rod, etc., used for pointing. **3** indication. **4** dog trained to point. **point'less** [-lis] adj **1** blunt. **2** futile, irrelevant. **point-blank** adj **1** aimed horizontally. **2** plain, blunt. ◆ adv **3** with level aim (there being no necessity to elevate for distance). **4** at short range.

poise [poiz] n **1** composure. **2** self-possession. **3** balance, equilibrium, carriage (of body, etc.). ◆ v **poised, pois·ing** (cause to be) balanced or suspended. ◆ vt **5** hold in readiness.

poi·son [POI-zən] n **1** substance that kills or injures when introduced into living organism. ◆ vt **2** give poison to. **3** infect. **4** pervert, spoil. **poi'son·ous** adj **poison-pen**

filch, lift (inf), pilfer, purloin, take ◆ adj **3** = **small**, abridged, compact, concise, little, miniature, portable

pod n, v = **shell**, hull, husk, shuck

podium n = **platform**, dais, rostrum, stage

poem n = **verse**, lyric, ode, rhyme, song, sonnet

poet n = **bard**, lyricist, rhymer, versifier

poetic adj = **lyrical**, elegiac, lyric, metrical

poetry n = **verse**, poems, rhyme, rhyming

poignancy n **1** = **sadness**, emotion, feeling, pathos, sentiment, tenderness **2** = **sharpness**, bitterness, intensity, keenness

poignant adj = **moving**, bitter, distressing, heart-rending, intense, painful, pathetic, sad, touching

point n **1** = **essence**, crux, drift, gist, heart, import, meaning, nub, pith, question, subject, thrust **2** = **aim**, end, goal, intent, intention, motive, object, objective, purpose, reason **3** = **item**, aspect, detail, feature, particular **4** = **characteristic**, aspect, attribute, quality, respect, trait **5** = **place**, location, position, site, spot, stage **6** = **full stop**, dot, mark, period, stop **7** = **end**, apex, prong, sharp end, spike, spur, summit, tip, top **8** = **headland**, cape, head, promontory **9** = **stage**, circumstance, condition, degree, extent, position **10** = **moment**, instant, juncture, time, very minute **11** = **unit**, score, tally ◆ v **12** = **indicate**, call attention to, denote, designate, direct, show, signify **13** = **aim**, direct, level, train

point-blank adj **1** = **direct**, blunt, downright, explicit, express, plain ◆ adv **2** = **directly**, bluntly, candidly, explicitly, forthrightly, frankly, openly, plainly, straight

pointed adj **1** = **sharp**, acute, barbed, edged **2** = **cutting**, acute, biting, incisive, keen, penetrating, pertinent, sharp, telling

pointer n **1** = **hint**, advice, caution, information, recommendation, suggestion, tip **2** = **indicator**, guide, hand, needle

pointless adj = **senseless**, absurd, aimless, fruitless, futile, inane, irrelevant, meaningless, silly, stupid, useless

point out v = **mention**, allude to, bring up, identify, indicate, show, specify

poise n = **composure**, aplomb, assurance, calmness, cool (sl), dignity, presence, sang-froid, self-possession

poised adj **1** = **ready**, all set, prepared, standing by, waiting **2** = **composed**, calm, collected, dignified, self-confident,

letter malicious anonymous letter.

poke¹ [pohk] *v* **poked, pok·ing ♦** *vt* **1** push, thrust with finger, stick, etc. **2** thrust forward. **♦** *vi* **3** make thrusts. **4** pry. **♦** *n* **5** act of poking. **pok·er** *n* metal rod for poking fire. **pok·y** *adj* **pok·i·er, pok·i·est** small, confined, cramped.

poke² *n* **pig in a poke** something bought, etc. without previous inspection.

pok·er [POHK-ər] *n* card game. **poker face 1** expressionless face. **2** person with this.

polar *adj* see POLE².

Po·lar·oid [POH-lə-roid] *n* ® **1** type of plastic that polarizes light. **2** camera that develops print very quickly inside itself.

pole¹ [pohl] *n* **1** long rounded piece of wood, etc. **♦** *vt* **poled, pol·ing 2** propel with pole.

pole² *n* **1** each of the ends of axis of Earth or celestial sphere. **2** each of opposite ends of magnet, electric battery, etc. **po·lar** [POH-lər] *adj* **1** pert. to the N and S pole, or to magnetic poles. **2** directly opposite in tendency, character, etc. **po·lar·i·ty** *n* **po·lar·i·za·tion** [-ZAY-shən] *n* **po·lar·ize** *vt* **-rized, -riz·ing 1** give polarity to. **2** affect light in order to restrict vibration of its waves to certain directions. **polar bear** white Arctic bear. **poles apart** having completely opposite interests, etc.

po·lem·ic [pə-LEM-ik] *adj* **1** controversial. **♦**

n **2** war of words, argument. **po·lem'i·cal** *adj* **po·lem'i·cize** [-sīz] *vt* **-cized, -ciz·ing**

po·lice [pə-LEES] *n* **1** the civil force that maintains public order. **♦** *vt* **-liced, -lic·ing 2** keep in order. **police officer** *n* member of police force.

pol·i·cy¹ [POL-ə-see] *n, pl* **-cies 1** course of action adopted, esp. in state affairs. **2** prudence.

policy² *n, pl* **-cies** insurance contract.

po·li·o [poh-lee-oh] *n* (also **po·li·o·my·e·li·tis**) disease of spinal cord characterized by fever and possibly paralysis.

pol·ish *vt* **1** make smooth and glossy. **2** refine. **♦** *n* **3** shine. **4** polishing. **5** substance for polishing. **6** refinement.

po·lite [pə-LIT] *adj* **-lit·er, -lit·est 1** showing regard for others in manners, speech, etc. **2** refined, cultured. **po·lite'ness** *n* courtesy.

pol·i·tic [POL-i-tik] *adj* wise, shrewd, expedient, cunning. **pol'i·tics** *n* **1** art of government. **2** political affairs or life. **po·lit'i·cal** *adj* of the state or its affairs. **pol·i·ti'cian** [-TISH-ən] *n* one engaged in politics. **pol'i·ty** *n, pl* **-ties 1** form of government. **2** organized state. **3** civil government. **politically correct** (esp. of language) intended to avoid any implied prejudice.

pol·ka [POHL-kə] *n, pl* **-kas 1** lively

self-possessed, together (*inf*)

poison *n* **1** = **toxin**, bane, venom **♦** *v* **2** = **murder**, give (someone) poison, kill **3** = **contaminate**, infect, pollute **4** = **corrupt**, defile, deprave, pervert, subvert, taint, undermine, warp

poisonous *adj* **1** = **toxic**, deadly, fatal, lethal, mortal, noxious, venomous, virulent **2** = **evil**, baleful, corrupting, malicious, noxious, pernicious

poke *v* **1** = **jab**, dig, nudge, prod, push, shove, stab, stick, thrust **♦** *n* **2** = **jab**, dig, nudge, prod, thrust

poky *adj* = **small**, confined, cramped, narrow, tiny

pole¹ *n* = **rod**, bar, mast, post, shaft, spar, staff, stick

police *n* **1** = **the law** (*inf*), boys in blue (*inf*), constabulary, fuzz (*sl*), police force **♦** *v* **2** = **control**, guard, patrol, protect, regulate, watch

policeman *n* = **cop** (*sl*), constable, copper (*sl*), fuzz (*sl*), officer

policy *n* = **procedure**, action, approach, code, course, custom, plan, practice, rule, scheme

polish *v* **1** = **shine**, brighten, buff, burnish, rub, smooth, wax **2** = **perfect**, brush up, enhance, finish, improve, refine, touch up **♦** *n* **3** = **varnish**, wax **4** = **sheen**, brightness, finish, glaze, gloss, luster **5** = **style**, breeding, class (*inf*), elegance, finesse, finish, grace, refinement

polished *adj* **1** = **accomplished**, adept, expert, fine, masterly, professional, skillful, superlative **2** = **shining**, bright, burnished, gleaming, glossy, smooth **3** = **elegant**, cultivated, polite, refined, sophisticated, well-bred

polite *adj* **1** = **mannerly**, civil, complaisant, courteous, gracious, respectful, well-behaved, well-mannered **2** = **refined**, civilized, cultured, elegant, genteel, polished, sophisticated, well-bred

politeness *n* = **courtesy**, civility, courteousness, decency, etiquette,

19th-century dance. **2** music for it. **polka dot** one of pattern of bold spots on fabric, etc.

poll [pohl] n **1** voting. **2** counting of votes. **3** number of votes recorded. **4** canvassing of sample of population to determine general opinion. **5** (top of) head. ◆ pl **6** place where votes are cast. ◆ vt **7** receive (votes). **8** take votes of. **9** lop, shear. **10** cut horns from animals. ◆ vi **11** vote. **polled** adj hornless. **poll'ster** n one who conducts polls. **poll tax** (esp. formerly) tax on each person.

pol·lard [POL-ərd] n **1** hornless animal of normally horned variety. **2** tree on which a close head of young branches has been made by polling. ◆ vt **3** make a pollard of.

pol·len [POL-ən] n fertilizing dust of flower. **pol'li·nate** vt **-nat·ed, -nat·ing**

pol·lute [pə-LOOT] vt **-lut·ed, -lut·ing 1** make foul. **2** corrupt. **3** desecrate. **pol·lu'tant** [-tənt] n **pol·lu'tion** n

po·lo [POH-loh] n game like hockey played by teams of 4 players on horseback. **water polo** game played similarly by swimmers seven to a side.

pol·o·naise [pol-ə-NAYZ] n **1** Polish dance. **2** music for it.

pol·ter·geist [POHL-tər-gīst] n noisy mischievous spirit.

poly- comb. form many, e.g. polysyllabic.

pol·y·an·dry [POL-ee-an-dree] n polygamy in which woman has more than one husband. **pol·y·an'drous** adj

pol·y·chrome [POL-ee-krohm] adj **1** many colored. ◆ n **2** work of art in many colors. **pol·y·chro·mat'ic** adj

pol·y·es·ter [POL-ee-es-tər] n any of large class of synthetic materials used as plastics, textile fibers, etc.

pol·y·eth·yl·ene [pol-ee-ETH-ə-leen] n tough thermoplastic material.

po·lyg·a·my [pə-LIG-ə-mee] n custom of being married to several persons at a time. **po·lyg'a·mist** n

pol·y·glot [POL-ee-glot] adj **1** speaking, writing in several languages. ◆ n **2** person who speaks, read and writes in many languages.

pol·y·gon [POL-ee-gon] n figure with many angles or sides.

po·lyg·y·ny [pə-LIJ-ə-nee] n polygamy in which one man has more than one wife.

pol·y·he·dron [pol-ee-HEE-drən] n solid figure contained by many faces.

pol·y·math [POL-ee-math] n learned person.

pol·y·mer [POL-ə-mər] n compound, as polystyrene, that has large molecules formed from repeated units. **po·lym·er·i·za·tion** [pə-lim-ər-ə-ZAY-shən] n **po·lym'er·ize** [-LIM-ər-īz] vt **-ized, -iz·ing**

pol·yp [POL-ip] n **1** sea anemone, or allied animal. **2** tumor with branched roots.

pol·y·sty·rene [pol-ee-STĪ-reen] n synthetic material used esp. as white rigid foam for packing, etc.

pol·y·tech·nic [pol-ee-TEK-nik] n college dealing mainly with technical subjects. ◆ adj

pol·y·the·ism [POL-ee-thee-iz-əm] n belief in many gods. **pol·y·the·is'tic** adj

pol·y·un·sat·u·rat·ed [pol-ee-un-SACH-ə-ray-tid] adj of group of fats that do not form cholesterol in blood.

pol·y·u·re·thane [pol-ee-YUUR-ə-thayn] n class of synthetic materials, often in foam or flexible form.

po·made [po-MAYD] n scented ointment for hair.

po·me·gran·ate [POM-ə-gran-it] n **1** tree. **2** its fruit with thick rind containing many seeds in red pulp.

pom·mel [PUM-əl] n **1** front of saddle. **2** knob of sword hilt. ◆ vt **-meled, -mel·ing 3** pummel.

───── THESAURUS ─────

mannerliness
politic adj = **wise**, advisable, diplomatic, expedient, judicious, prudent, sensible
political adj = **governmental**, parliamentary, policy-making
politician n = **statesman**, bureaucrat, congressman, legislator, office bearer, public servant, representative
politics n = **statesmanship**, affairs of state, civics, government, political science
poll n **1** = **canvass**, ballot, census, count,

sampling, survey **2** = **vote**, figures, returns, tally, voting ◆ v **3** = **tally**, register **4** = **question**, ballot, canvass, interview, sample, survey
pollute v **1** = **contaminate**, dirty, foul, infect, poison, soil, spoil, stain, taint **2** = **defile**, corrupt, debase, debauch, deprave, desecrate, dishonor, profane, sully
pollution n = **contamination**, corruption, defilement, dirtying, foulness, impurity, taint, uncleanness

pomp n splendid display or ceremony.

pom'pom n tuft of ribbon, wool, feathers, etc., decorating hat, shoe, etc.

pomp·ous [POM-pəs] adj **1** self-important. **2** ostentatious. **3** of language, inflated, stilted. **pom·pos'i·ty** n, pl **-ties**

pon·cho [PON-choh] n, pl **-chos** loose circular cloak with hole for head.

pond n small body, pool or lake of still water.

pon·der [PON-dər] v **1** muse, meditate, think over. **2** consider, deliberate on.

pon·der·ous [PON-dər-əs] adj **1** heavy, unwieldy. **2** boring. **pon'der·a·ble** adj able to be evaluated or weighed.

pon'tiff n **1** Pope. **2** high priest. **3** bishop. **pon·tif'i·cal** adj **pon·tif'i·cate** [-kit] n dignity or office of pontiff. **pon·tif'i·cate** [-kayt] vi **-cat·ed, -cat·ing 1** speak bombastically. **2** act as pontiff.

pon·toon' n flat-bottomed boat or metal drum for use in supporting temporary bridge.

po·ny [POH-nee] n, pl **-nies 1** horse of small breed. **2** small horse. **3** very small glass. **po'ny·tail** n long hair tied in one bunch at back of head.

poo·dle [POOD-l] n pet dog with long curly hair often clipped fancifully.

pool[1] n **1** small body of still water. **2** deep

place in river or stream. **3** puddle. **4** swimming pool.

pool[2] n **1** common fund or resources. **2** group of people, e.g. typists, any of whom can work for any of several employers. **3** collective stakes in various games. **4** cartel. **5** variety of billiards. ♦ vt **6** put in common fund.

poop[1] n ship's stern.

poop[2] vt sl exhaust (someone). **poop out** sl **1** fail in something. **2** cease functioning.

poop[3] n children's sl **1** excrement. ♦ vi **2** defecate.

poop[4] n sl pertinent information.

poor [puur] adj **-er, -est 1** having little money. **2** unproductive. **3** inadequate, insignificant. **4** needy. **5** miserable, pitiable. **6** feeble. **7** not fertile. **poor'ly** adv, adj not in good health.

pop[1] v **popped, pop·ping** ♦ vi **1** make small explosive sound. **2** inf **3** go or come unexpectedly or suddenly. ♦ vt **4** cause to make small explosive sound. **5** put or place suddenly. ♦ n **6** small explosive sound. **7** inf nonalcoholic soda. **pop'corn** n **1** any kind of corn with kernels that puff up when roasted. **2** the roasted product.

pop[2] n inf **1** father. **2** old man.

pop[3] n music of general appeal, esp. to young people. ♦ adj **2** short for POPULAR.

THESAURUS

pomp n **1 = ceremony**, flourish, grandeur, magnificence, pageant, pageantry, splendor, state **2 = show**, display, grandiosity, ostentation

pomposity n **= self-importance**, affectation, airs, grandiosity, pompousness, portentousness, pretension, pretentiousness

pompous adj **1 = self-important**, arrogant, grandiose, ostentatious, pretentious, puffed up, showy **2 = grandiloquent**, boastful, bombastic, high-flown, inflated

ponder v **= think**, brood, cogitate, consider, contemplate, deliberate, meditate, mull over, muse, reflect, ruminate

ponderous adj **1 = dull**, heavy, long-winded, pedantic, tedious **2 = unwieldy**, bulky, cumbersome, heavy, huge, massive, weighty **3 = clumsy**, awkward, heavy-footed, lumbering

pontificate v **= expound**, hold forth, lay

down the law, preach, pronounce, sound off

pool[1] n **1 = pond**, lake, mere, puddle, tarn **2 = swimming pool**, swimming bath

pool[2] n **1 = syndicate**, collective, consortium, group, team, trust **2 = kitty**, bank, funds, jackpot, pot ♦ v **3 = combine**, amalgamate, join forces, league, merge, put together, share

poor adj **1 = impoverished**, broke (inf), destitute, down and out, down on one's luck (inf), hard up (inf), impecunious, indigent, needy, on the breadline, penniless, penurious, poverty-stricken, short **2 = inadequate**, deficient, incomplete, insufficient, lacking, lousy (sl), meager, measly, scant, scanty, skimpy **3 = inferior**, below par, lousy (sl), low-grade, mediocre, rotten (inf), rubbishy, second-rate, substandard, unsatisfactory **4 = unfortunate**, hapless, ill-fated, luckless, pitiable, unhappy, unlucky, wretched

poorly adv **= badly**, inadequately, incompetently, inexpertly, insufficiently,

Pope [pohp] *n* bishop of Rome and head of R.C. Church.

pop·lar [POP-lər] *n* tree noted for its slender tallness.

pop'lin *n* corded fabric usu. of cotton.

pop·pa·dom [POP-ə-dəm] *n* thin, round, crisp Indian bread.

pop·py [POP-ee] *n, pl* **-pies** bright-flowered plant yielding opium.

pop·u·lace [POP-yə-ləs] *n* **1** the common people. **2** the masses.

pop·u·lar [POP-yə-lər] *adj* **1** finding general favor. **2** of, by the people. **pop·u·lar'i·ty** *n* state or quality of being generally liked. **pop'u·lar·ize** *vt* **-ized, -iz·ing** make popular.

pop·u·late [POP-yə-layt] *vt* **-lat·ed, -lat·ing** fill with inhabitants. **pop·u·la'tion** [-LAY-shən] *n* **1** inhabitants. **2** their number. **pop'u·lous** [-ləs] *adj* thickly populated or inhabited.

pop·u·list [POP-yə-list] *adj* claiming to represent the whole of the people. ◆ *n* **pop'u·lism** [-liz-əm] *n*

por·ce·lain [POR-sə-lin] *n* fine earthenware, china.

porch *n* **1** covered approach to entrance of building. **2** veranda.

por·cine [POR-sin] *adj* of, like a pig.

por·cu·pine [POR-kyə-pīn] *n* rodent covered with long, pointed quills.

pore¹ [por] *vi* **pored, por·ing 1** fix eye or mind upon. **2** study closely.

pore² *n* minute opening, esp. in skin. **po·ros·i·ty** [pə-ROS-i-tee] *n* **por·ous** [POR-əs] *adj* **1** allowing liquid to soak through. **2** full of pores.

pork *n* pig's flesh as food. **pork'er** *n* pig raised for food. **pork'y** *adj* **pork·i·er, pork·i·est** fleshy, fat.

porn, por'no *n inf* short for PORNOGRAPHY.

por·nog·ra·phy [por-NOG-rə-fee] *n* indecent literature, films, etc. **por·nog'ra·pher** *n* **por·no·graph'ic** *adj*

por·phy·ry [POR-fə-ree] *n, pl* **-ries** reddish stone with embedded crystals.

por·poise [POR-pəs] *n* blunt-nosed sea mammal like dolphin.

por·ridge [POR-ij] *n* soft food of oatmeal, etc. boiled in water.

port¹ *n* **1** harbor, haven. **2** town with harbor.

port² *n* **1** larboard or left side of ship. ◆ *vt* **2** turn to left side of a ship.

port³ *n* strong sweet, usu. red, fortified wine from Portugal.

port⁴ *n* opening in side of ship. **port'hole** *n* small opening or window in side of ship.

port⁵ *vt Military* **1** carry rifle, etc. diagonally across body. ◆ *n* **2** this position.

port·a·ble [POR-tə-bəl] *n, adj* (something) easily carried.

unsatisfactorily, unsuccessfully

pop *v* **1** = **burst**, bang, crack, explode, go off, snap **2** = **put**, insert, push, shove, slip, stick, thrust, tuck ◆ *n* **3** = **bang**, burst, crack, explosion, noise, report

pope *n* = **Holy Father**, Bishop of Rome, pontiff, Vicar of Christ

populace *n* = **people**, general public, hoi polloi, masses, mob, multitude

popular *adj* **1** = **well-liked**, accepted, approved, cool (*inf*), fashionable, favorite, in (*inf*), in demand, in favor, liked, phat (*sl*), sought-after **2** = **common**, conventional, current, general, prevailing, prevalent, universal

popularity *n* = **favor**, acceptance, acclaim, approval, currency, esteem, regard, vogue

popularize *v* = **make popular**, disseminate, give currency to, give mass appeal, make available to all, spread, universalize

popularly *adv* = **generally**, commonly, conventionally, customarily, ordinarily, traditionally, universally, usually, widely

populate *v* = **inhabit**, colonize, live in, occupy, settle

population *n* = **inhabitants**, community, denizens, folk, natives, people, residents, society

populous *adj* = **populated**, crowded, heavily populated, overpopulated, packed, swarming, teeming

pore¹ *v* **pore over** = **study**, examine, peruse, ponder, read, scrutinize

pore² *n* = **opening**, hole, orifice, outlet

pornographic *adj* = **obscene**, blue, dirty, filthy, indecent, lewd, salacious, scuzzy (*sl*), smutty, X-rated

pornography *n* = **obscenity**, dirt, filth, indecency, porn (*inf*), smut

porous *adj* = **permeable**, absorbent, absorptive, penetrable, spongy

port *n* = **harbor**, anchorage, haven, seaport

portable *adj* = **light**, compact, convenient, easily carried, handy, manageable, movable

por·tage [POR-tij] *n* (cost of) transport.
por·tal [POR-tl] *n* **1** large doorway or imposing gate. **2** *Computers* Internet site providing links to other sites.
   portal-to-portal pay payment to worker that includes pay for all time spent on employer's premises.
port·cul·lis [port-KUL-is] *n* defense grating to raise or lower in front of castle gateway.
por·tend *vt* **1** foretell. **2** be an omen of.
   por·tent *n* **1** omen, warning. **2** marvel. **por·ten·tous** [-təs] *adj* **1** ominous. **2** threatening. **3** pompous.
por·ter [POR-tər] *n* **1** person employed to carry luggage. **2** doorkeeper.
port·fo·li·o [port-FOH-lee-oh] *n, pl* **-li·os 1** flat portable case for loose papers. **2** office of minister of state, member of cabinet.
por·ti·co [POR-ti-koh] *n, pl* **-coes** or **-cos 1** colonnade. **2** covered walk.
por·tiere [por-TYAIR] *n* heavy door curtain.
por·tion [POR-shən] *n* **1** part, share, helping. **2** destiny, lot. ◆ *vt* **3** divide into shares.
port·ly [PORT-lee] *adj* **-li·er, -li·est** bulky, stout.

port·man·teau [port-MAN-toh] *n, pl* **-teaus** leather suitcase, esp. one opening into two compartments. **portmanteau word** word made by putting together parts of other words, such as *motel* from *motor* and *hotel*.
por·tray [-trit] *vt* make pictures of, describe. **por·trait** [-trit] *n* likeness of (face of) person. **por·trai·ture** [-tri-char] *n*
por·tray·al [-əl] *n* act of portraying.
pose [pohz] *v* **posed, pos·ing** ◆ *vt* **1** place in attitude. **2** put forward. ◆ *vi* **3** assume attitude, affect or pretend to be a certain character. ◆ *n* **4** attitude, esp. one assumed for effect. **po·seur** [poh-ZUR] *n* one who assumes affected attitude to create impression.
pos·er [POH-zər] *n* puzzling question.
posh *adj inf* smart, elegant, stylish.
pos·it [POZ-it] *vt* lay down as principle.
po·si·tion [pə-ZISH-ən] *n* **1** place. **2** situation. **3** location, attitude. **4** status. **5** state of affairs. **6** employment. **7** strategic point. ◆ *vt* **8** place in position.
pos·i·tive [POZ-i-tiv] *adj* **1** certain. **2** sure. **3** definite, absolute, unquestionable. **4** utter.

THESAURUS

portend *v* = **foretell**, augur, betoken, bode, foreshadow, herald, indicate, predict, prognosticate, promise, warn of
portent *n* = **omen**, augury, forewarning, indication, prognostication, sign, warning
portentous *adj* **1** = **significant**, crucial, fateful, important, menacing, momentous, ominous **2** = **pompous**, ponderous, self-important, solemn
porter[1] *n* = **baggage attendant**, bearer, carrier
porter[2] *n* = **doorman**, caretaker, concierge, gatekeeper, janitor
portion *n* **1** = **part**, bit, fragment, morsel, piece, scrap, section, segment **2** = **share**, allocation, allotment, allowance, lot, measure, quantity, quota, ration **3** = **helping**, piece, serving **4** = **destiny**, fate, fortune, lot, luck ◆ *v* **5** **portion out** = **divide**, allocate, allot, apportion, deal, distribute, dole out, share out
portly *adj* = **stout**, burly, corpulent, fat, fleshy, heavy, large, plump
portrait *n* **1** = **picture**, image, likeness, painting, photograph, representation **2** = **description**, characterization, depiction, portrayal, profile, thumbnail sketch
portray *v* **1** = **represent**, depict, draw,

figure, illustrate, paint, picture, sketch **2** = **describe**, characterize, depict, put in words **3** = **play**, act the part of, represent
portrayal *n* = **representation**, characterization, depiction, interpretation, performance, picture
pose *v* **1** = **position**, model, sit **2** = **put on airs**, posture, show off (*inf*) **3** **pose as** = **impersonate**, masquerade as, pass oneself off as, pretend to be, profess to be ◆ *n* **4** = **posture**, attitude, bearing, position, stance **5** = **act**, affectation, air, façade, front, mannerism, posturing, pretense
poser *n* = **puzzle**, enigma, problem, question, riddle
posit *v* = **put forward**, advance, assume, postulate, presume, propound, state
position *n* **1** = **place**, area, bearings, locale, location, point, post, situation, spot, station, whereabouts **2** = **posture**, arrangement, attitude, pose, stance **3** = **attitude**, belief, opinion, outlook, point of view, slant, stance, view, viewpoint **4** = **status**, importance, place, prestige, rank, reputation, standing, station, stature **5** = **job**, duty, employment, occupation, office, place, post, role, situation ◆ *v* **6** = **place**, arrange, lay out, locate, put, set, stand

5 downright. 6 confident. 7 not negative. 8 greater than zero. 9 *Electricity* having deficiency of electrons. ♦ *n* 10 something positive. 11 *Photography* print in which lights and shadows are not reversed.

pos•i•tiv•ism *n* philosophy recognizing only matters of fact and experience. **pos•i•tiv•ist** *n* believer in this.

pos•i•tron [POZ-i-tron] *n* positive electron.

pos•se [POS-ee] *n* body of armed people, esp. for maintaining law and order.

pos•sess [pə-ZES] *vt* 1 own. 2 (of evil spirit, etc.) have mastery of. **pos•ses•sion** *n* 1 act of possessing. 2 thing possessed. 3 ownership. **pos•ses•sive** *adj* 1 of, indicating possess. 2 with excessive desire to possess, control. ♦ *n* 3 possessive case in grammar. **pos•ses•sor** *n* owner.

pos•si•ble [POS-ə-bəl] *adj* 1 that can, or may, be, exist, happen or be done. 2 worthy of consideration. ♦ *n* 3 possible candidate. **pos•si•bil'i•ty** *n, pl* **-ties** **pos'si•bly** *adv* perhaps.

pos•sum [POS-əm] *n* opossum. **play possum** pretend to be dead, asleep, etc. to deceive opponent.

post[1] [pohst] *n* 1 upright pole of timber or metal fixed firmly, usu. to support or mark something. ♦ *vt* 2 display. 3 stick up (on notice board, etc.). 4 *Computers* make

(e-mail) publicly available. **post'er** *n* 1 large advertising bill. 2 one who posts bills. **poster paints, colors** flat paints suited for posters.

post[2] *n* 1 mail. 2 collection or delivery of this. 3 office. 4 situation. 5 point, station, place of duty. 6 place where soldier is stationed. 7 place held by body of troops. 8 fort. ♦ *vt* 9 put into mailbox. 10 supply with latest information. 11 station (soldiers, etc.) in particular spot. 12 transfer (entries) to ledger. ♦ *adv* 13 with haste. **post•age** [POH-stij] *n* charge for carrying letter. **post'al** [-əl] *adj* **postal money order** written order, available at post office, for payment of sum of money. **post'card** *n* stamped card sent by mail. **post'man** [-mən] *n, pl* **-men** postal employee who collects or delivers mail. **post'mark** *n* official mark with name of office, etc. stamped on letters. **post'mas•ter** *n* official in charge of post office. **post'mis•tress** [-tris] *n, fem.* **post office** place where postal business is conducted.

post- *prefix* after, behind, later than, e.g. *postwar.*

post•date [pohst-DAYT] *vt* **-dat•ed, -dat•ing** give date later than actual date. **poste res•tante** [pohst re-STAHNT] *Fr*

positive *adj* 1 = **certain**, assured, confident, convinced, sure 2 = **definite**, absolute, categorical, certain, clear, conclusive, decisive, explicit, express, firm, real 3 = **helpful**, beneficial, constructive, practical, productive, progressive, useful

positively *adv* = **definitely**, absolutely, assuredly, categorically, certainly, emphatically, firmly, surely, unequivocally, unquestionably

possess *v* 1 = **have**, enjoy, hold, own 2 = **control**, acquire, dominate, hold, occupy, seize, take over

possessed *adj* = **crazed**, berserk, demented, frenzied, obsessed, raving

possession *n* 1 = **ownership**, control, custody, hold, occupation, tenure, title 2 **possessions** = **property**, assets, belongings, chattels, effects, estate, things

possessive *adj* = **jealous**, controlling, covetous, dominating, domineering, overprotective, selfish

possibility *n* 1 = **feasibility**, likelihood, potentiality, practicability, workableness

2 = **likelihood**, chance, hope, liability, odds, probability, prospect, risk 3 (often plural) = **potential**, capabilities, potentiality, promise, prospects, talent

possible *adj* 1 = **conceivable**, credible, hypothetical, imaginable, likely, potential 2 = **likely**, hopeful, potential, probable, promising 3 = **feasible**, attainable, doable, practicable, realizable, viable, workable

possibly *adv* = **perhaps**, maybe, perchance (*archaic*)

post[1] *n* **keep someone posted** = **notify**, advise, brief, fill in on (*inf*), inform, report to

post[2] *n* 1 = **support**, column, picket, pillar, pole, shaft, stake, upright ♦ *v* 2 = **put up**, affix, display, pin up

post[3] *n* 1 = **job**, appointment, assignment, employment, office, place, position, situation 2 = **station**, beat, place, position ♦ *v* 3 = **station**, assign, place, position, put, situate

poster *n* = **notice**, advertisement, announcement, bill, placard, public notice, direction on mail to indicate that post office should keep traveler's letters till called for.

pos·te·ri·or [po-STEER-ee-ər] *adj* **1** later, hinder. ◆ *n* **2** the buttocks.

pos·ter·i·ty [po-STER-i-tee] *n* **1** later generations. **2** descendants.

post·grad·u·ate [pohst-GRAJ-oo-it] *adj* carried on after graduation. ◆ *n*

post·hu·mous [POS-chə-məs] *adj* **1** occurring after death. **2** born after father's death. **3** published after author's death. **post'hu·mous·ly** *adv*

post·mor·tem [pohst-MOR-təm] *n* **1** medical examination of dead body. **2** evaluation after event, etc. ends. ◆ *adj* **3** taking place after death.

post·par·tum [pohst-PAHR-təm] *adj* occurring after childbirth.

post·pone [pohs-POHN] *vt* **-poned, -pon·ing** put off to later time, defer.

post·pran·di·al [pohst-PRAN-dee-əl] *adj* after a meal, esp. dinner.

post·script [POHST-skript] *n* addition to letter, book, etc.

pos·tu·lant [POS-chə-lənt] *n* candidate for admission to religious order.

pos·tu·late [POS-chə-layt] *vt* **-lat·ed, -lat·ing** **1** take for granted. **2** lay down as self-evident. **3** stipulate. ◆ *n* [-lit] **4** proposition assumed without proof. **5** prerequisite.

pos·ture [POS-chər] *n* **1** attitude, position of body. ◆ *v* **-tured, -tur·ing** **2** pose.

po·sy [POH-zee] *n, pl* **-sies 1** flower. **2** bunch of flowers.

pot *n* **1** round vessel. **2** cooking vessel. **3** trap, esp. for crabs, lobsters. **4** *sl* marijuana. **5** *inf* a lot. ◆ *vt* **pot·ted, pot·ting 6** put into,

preserve in pot. **pot·ted** *adj* **1** cooked, preserved, in a pot. **2** *sl* drunk. **pot'hole** *n* **1** pitlike cavity in rocks, usu. limestone, produced by faulting and water action. **2** hole worn in road. **pot'luck** *n* whatever is to be had (to eat). **pot'sherd** [-shurd] *n* broken fragment of pottery. **pot shot** easy or random shot.

po·ta·ble [POH-tə-bəl] *adj* drinkable. **po·ta'tion** [-TAY-shən] *n* **1** drink. **2** drinking.

pot·ash *n* **1** alkali used in soap, etc. **2** crude potassium carbonate.

po·tas·si·um [pə-TAS-ee-əm] *n* white metallic element.

po·ta·to [pə-TAY-toh] *n, pl* **-toes** plant with tubers grown for food. **hot potato** topic, etc. too threatening to bring up. **sweet potato 1** trailing plant. **2** its edible sweetish tubers.

po·tent [POHT-nt] *adj* **1** powerful, influential. **2** (of male) capable of sexual intercourse. **po'ten·cy** *n* **1** physical or moral power. **2** efficacy.

po·ten·tate [POHT-n-tayt] *n* ruler.

po·ten·tial [pə-TEN-shəl] *adj* **1** latent, that may or might but does not now exist or act. ◆ *n* **2** possibility. **3** amount of potential energy. **4** *Electricity* level of electric pressure. **po·ten·ti·al·i·ty** [-shee-AL-i-tee] *n*

po·tion [POH-shən] *n* dose of medicine or poison.

pot·pour·ri [poh-puu-REE] *n* **1** mixture of rose petals, spices, etc. **2** musical, literary medley.

pot·tage [POT-ij] *n* soup or stew.

pot·ter [POT-ər] *n* maker of earthenware vessels. **pot'ter·y** *n, pl* **-ter·ies 1** earthenware. **2** where it is made. **3** art of

sticker

posterity *n* **1 = future**, succeeding generations **2 = descendants**, children, family, heirs, issue, offspring, progeny

postpone *v* **= put off**, adjourn, defer, delay, put back, put on the back burner (*inf*), shelve, suspend

postponement *n* **= delay**, adjournment, deferment, deferral, stay, suspension

postscript *n* **= P.S.**, addition, afterthought, supplement

postulate *v* **= presuppose**, assume, hypothesize, posit, propose, suppose, take for granted, theorize

posture *n* **1 = bearing**, attitude, carriage,

disposition, set, stance ◆ *v* **2 = show off** (*inf*), affect, pose, put on airs

pot[1] *n* **= container**, bowl, pan, vessel

potency *n* **= power**, effectiveness, force, influence, might, strength

potent *adj* **1 = powerful**, authoritative, commanding, dominant, dynamic, influential **2 = strong**, forceful, mighty, powerful, vigorous

potential *adj* **1 = possible**, dormant, future, hidden, inherent, latent, likely, promising ◆ *n* **2 = ability**, aptitude, capability, capacity, possibility, potentiality, power, wherewithal

potion *n* **= concoction**, brew, dose, draft,

making it.

pouch [powch] *n* **1** small bag. **2** pocket. ◆ *vt* **3** put into one.

poul·tice [POHL-tis] *n* soft composition of cloth, bread, etc., applied hot to sore or inflamed parts of the body.

poul·try [POHL-tree] *n* domestic fowl collectively.

pounce[1] [powns] *vi* **pounced, pounc·ing** **1** spring suddenly, swoop (upon). ◆ *n* **2** swoop or sudden descent.

pounce[2] *n* fine powder used to prevent ink from spreading on unsized paper or in pattern making.

pound[1] [pownd] *vt* **1** beat, thump. **2** crush to pieces or powder. **3** walk, run heavily.

pound[2] *n* **1** unit of troy weight. **2** unit of avoirdupois weight equal to 0.453 kg. **3** monetary unit in United Kingdom.

pound[3] *n* **1** enclosure for stray animals or officially removed vehicles. **2** confined space.

pound·al [POWN-dl] *n* a unit of force in the foot-pound-second system.

pour [por] *vi* **1** come out in a stream,

crowd, etc. **2** flow freely. **3** rain heavily. ◆ *vt* **4** give out thus. **5** cause to run out.

pout [powt] *v* **1** thrust out (lips), look sulky. ◆ *n* **2** act of pouting. **pout'er** *n* pigeon with power of inflating its crop.

pov·er·ty [POV-ər-tee] *n* **1** state of being poor. **2** poorness. **3** lack of means. **4** scarcity.

pow·der [POW-dər] *n* **1** solid matter in fine dry particles. **2** medicine in this form. **3** gunpowder. **4** face powder, etc. ◆ *vt* **5** apply powder to. **6** reduce to powder. **pow'der·y** *adj*

pow·er [POW-ər] *n* **1** ability to do or act. **2** strength. **3** authority. **4** control. **5** person or thing having authority. **6** mechanical energy. **7** electricity supply. **8** rate of doing work. **9** product from continuous multiplication of number by itself. **pow'ered** *adj* having or operated by mechanical or electrical power. **pow'er·ful** [-fəl] *adj* **pow'er·less** [-lis] *adj* **pow'er·house, power station** *n* installation for generating and distributing electric power.

pow'wow *n* **1** conference. ◆ *vi* **2** confer.

elixir, mixture, philtre

pottery *n* = **ceramics**, earthenware, stoneware, terracotta

pouch *n* = **bag**, container, pocket, purse, sack

pounce *v* **1** = **spring**, attack, fall upon, jump, leap at, strike, swoop ◆ *n* **2** = **spring**, assault, attack, bound, jump, leap, swoop

pound[1] *v* **1** = **beat**, batter, belabor, clobber (*sl*), hammer, pummel, strike, thrash, thump **2** = **crush**, powder, pulverize **3** = **pulsate**, beat, palpitate, pulse, throb **4** = **stomp** (*inf*), march, thunder, tramp

pound[2] *n* = **enclosure**, compound, pen, yard

pour *v* **1** = **flow**, course, emit, gush, run, rush, spew, spout, stream **2** = **let flow**, decant, spill, splash **3** = **rain**, bucket down (*inf*), pelt (down), teem **4** = **stream**, crowd, swarm, teem, throng

pout *v* **1** = **sulk**, glower, look petulant, pull a long face ◆ *n* **2** = **sullen look**, glower, long face

poverty *n* **1** = **pennilessness**, beggary, destitution, hardship, indigence, insolvency, need, penury, privation, want **2** = **scarcity**, dearth, deficiency, insufficiency, lack, paucity, shortage

poverty-stricken *adj* = **penniless**, broke (*inf*), destitute, down and out, down on one's luck (*inf*), flat broke (*inf*), impecunious, impoverished, indigent, poor

powder *n* **1** = **dust**, fine grains, loose particles, talc ◆ *v* **2** = **dust**, cover, dredge, scatter, sprinkle, strew

powdery *adj* = **fine**, crumbly, dry, dusty, grainy, granular

power *n* **1** = **ability**, capability, capacity, competence, competency, faculty, potential **2** = **control**, ascendancy, authority, command, dominance, domination, dominion, influence, mastery, rule **3** = **authority**, authorization, license, prerogative, privilege, right, warrant **4** = **strength**, brawn, energy, force, forcefulness, intensity, might, muscle, potency, vigor

powerful *adj* **1** = **controlling**, authoritative, commanding, dominant, influential, prevailing **2** = **strong**, energetic, mighty, potent, strapping, sturdy, vigorous **3** = **persuasive**, cogent, compelling, convincing, effectual, forceful, impressive, striking, telling, weighty

powerless *adj* **1** = **defenseless**,

pox [poks] *n* **1** one of several diseases marked by pustular eruptions of skin. **2** *inf* syphilis.

Pr *Chem.* praseodymium.

prac·ti·cal [PRAK-ti-kəl] *adj* **1** given to action rather than theory. **2** relating to action or real existence. **3** useful. **4** in effect though not in name. **5** virtual. **prac'ti·cal·ly** *adv* **prac·ti·ca·ble** [-kə-həl] *adj* that can be done, used, etc. **prac·ti'tion·er** *n* one engaged in a profession.

prac·tice [PRAK-tis] *v* **-ticed, -tic·ing** ♦ *vt* **1** do repeatedly, work at to gain skill. **2** do habitually. **3** put into action. ♦ *vi* **4** exercise oneself. **5** exercise profession. **practice** *n* **1** habit. **2** mastery or skill. **3** exercise of art or profession. **4** action, not theory.

prag·mat·ic [prag-MAT-ik] *adj* **1** concerned with practical consequence. **2** of the affairs of state. **prag'ma·tism** [-mə-tiz-əm] *n* **prag'ma·tist** *n*

prair·ie [PRAIR-ee] *n* large mostly treeless tract of grassland. **prairie dog** small Amer. rodent allied to marmot. **prairie oyster 1** as remedy for hangover, a drink of raw egg usu. with seasonings. **2** as food, testis of a calf.

praise [prayz] *n* **1** commendation. **2** fact, state of being praised. ♦ *vt* **praised, prais·ing 3** express approval, admiration of. **4** speak well of. **5** glorify.

praise'wor·thy [-wur-*th*ee] *adj*

pra·line [PRAH-leen] *n* candy made of nuts with caramel covering.

prance [prans] *vi* **pranced, pranc·ing 1** swagger. **2** caper. **3** walk with bounds. ♦ *n* **4** prancing.

pran·di·al [PRAN-dee-əl] *adj* of a meal, esp. dinner.

prank [prangk] *n* mischievous trick or escapade, frolic.

pra·se·o·dym·i·um [pray-zee-oh-DIM-ee-əm] *n* rare-earth chemical element.

prate [prayt] *vi* **prat·ed, prat·ing 1** talk idly, chatter. ♦ *n* **2** idle chatter.

prat·tle [PRAT-l] *vi* **-tled, -tling 1** talk like child. ♦ *n* **2** trifling, childish talk. **prat'tler** *n* babbler.

prawn *n* edible sea crustacean like a

dependent, ineffective, subject, tied, unarmed, vulnerable **2 = helpless,** challenged, debilitated, disabled, feeble, frail, impotent, incapable, incapacitated, ineffectual, weak

practicability *n* **= feasibility,** advantage, possibility, practicality, use, usefulness, viability

practicable *adj* **= feasible,** achievable, attainable, doable, possible, viable

practical *adj* **1 = functional,** applied, empirical, experimental, factual, pragmatic, realistic, utilitarian **2 = sensible,** businesslike, down-to-earth, hard-headed, matter-of-fact, ordinary, realistic **3 = feasible,** doable, practicable, serviceable, useful, workable **4 = skilled,** accomplished, efficient, experienced, proficient

practically *adv* **1 = almost,** all but, basically, essentially, fundamentally, in effect, just about, nearly, very nearly, virtually, well-nigh **2 = sensibly,** clearly, matter-of-factly, rationally, realistically, reasonably

practice *n* **1 = custom,** habit, method, mode, routine, rule, system, tradition, usage, way, wont **2 = rehearsal,** drill, exercise, preparation, repetition, study, training **3 = profession,** business, career,

vocation, work **4 = use,** action, application, exercise, experience, operation ♦ *v* **5 = rehearse,** drill, exercise, go over, go through, prepare, repeat, study, train **6 = do,** apply, carry out, follow, observe, perform **7 = work at,** carry on, engage in, pursue

practiced *adj* **= skilled,** able, accomplished, experienced, expert, proficient, seasoned, trained, versed

pragmatic *adj* **= practical,** businesslike, down-to-earth, hard-headed, realistic, sensible, utilitarian

praise *v* **1 = approve,** acclaim, admire, applaud, cheer, compliment, congratulate, eulogize, extol, honor, laud **2 = give thanks to,** adore, bless, exalt, glorify, worship ♦ *n* **3 = approval,** acclaim, acclamation, approbation, commendation, compliment, congratulation, eulogy, kudos, plaudit, tribute **4 = thanks,** adoration, glory, homage, kudos, worship

praiseworthy *adj* **= creditable,** admirable, commendable, laudable, meritorious, worthy

prance *v* **1 = dance,** caper, cavort, frisk, gambol, romp, skip **2 = strut,** parade, show off (*inf*), stalk, swagger

prank *n* **= trick,** antic, escapade, jape, lark

shrimp.

pray *vt* **1** ask earnestly. **2** entreat. ◆ *vi* **3** offer prayers, esp. to God. **prayer** [prair] *n* **1** action, practice of praying to God. **2** earnest entreaty. **pray'er** *n* one who prays.

pre- *prefix* before, beforehand, e.g. *prenatal; prerecord; preshrunk.*

preach [preech] *vi* **1** deliver sermon. **2** give moral, religious advice. ◆ *vt* **3** set forth in religious discourse. **4** advocate. **preach'er** *n*

pre·am·ble [PREE-am-bəl] *n* introductory part of document, story, etc.

pre·car·i·ous [pri-KAIR-ee-əs] *adj* insecure, unstable, perilous.

pre·cau·tion [pri-KAW-shən] *n* **1** previous care to prevent evil or secure good. **2** preventive measure. **pre·cau'tion·ar·y** *adj*

pre·cede [pri-SEED] *v* **-ced·ed, -ced·ing** go, come before in rank, order, time, etc. **prec·e·dence** [PRES-i-dəns] *n* priority in position, rank, time, etc. **prec'e·dent** *n* previous case or occurrence taken as rule.

pre·cept [PREE-sept] *n* rule for conduct, maxim. **pre·cep'tor** *n* instructor.

pre·ces·sion [pree-SESH-ən] *n* **1** act of preceding. **2** motion of spinning body, in which the axis of rotation sweeps out a cone.

pre·cinct [PREE-singkt] *n* **1** enclosed, limited area. **2** administrative area of city, esp. of police, board of elections. ◆ *pl* **3** environs. **precinct house** police station.

pre·cious [PRE-shəs] *adj* **1** beloved, cherished. **2** of great value, highly valued. **3** rare. **pre·ci·os·i·ty** [presh-ee-OS-i-tee] *n* overrefinement in art or literature. **prec'ious·ly** *adv*

prec·i·pice [PRES-ə-pis] *n* very steep cliff or rockface. **pre·cip'i·tous** *adj* sheer.

pre·cip·i·tant [prə-SIP-i-tənt] *adj* **1** hasty, rash. **2** abrupt. **pre·cip'i·tance, -tan·cy** *n*

pre·cip·i·tate [pri-SIP-i-tayt] *vt* **-tat·ed, -tat·ing 1** hasten happening of. **2** throw headlong. **3** *Chem.* cause to be deposited in solid form from solution. ◆ *adj* [-i-tit] **4** too sudden. **5** rash, impetuous. ◆ *n* [-i-tit] **6** substance chemically precipitated. **pre·cip'i·tate·ly** [-tit-lee] *adv* **pre·cip·i·ta·tion** [-TAY-shən] *n* esp. rain, snow, etc.

pré·cis [PRAY-see] *n, pl* **pré·cis** [PRAY-seez]

THESAURUS

(*inf*), practical joke

pray *v* **1** = **say one's prayers**, offer a prayer, recite the rosary **2** = **beg**, adjure, ask, beseech, entreat, implore, petition, plead, request, solicit

prayer *n* **1** = **orison**, devotion, invocation, litany, supplication **2** = **plea**, appeal, entreaty, petition, request, supplication

preach *v* **1** = **deliver a sermon**, address, evangelize **2** = **lecture**, advocate, exhort, moralize, sermonize

preacher *n* = **clergyman**, evangelist, minister, missionary, parson

preamble *n* = **introduction**, foreword, opening statement *or* remarks, preface, prelude

precarious *adj* = **dangerous**, hazardous, insecure, perilous, risky, shaky, tricky, unreliable, unsafe, unsure

precaution *n* **1** = **safeguard**, insurance, protection, provision, safety measure **2** = **forethought**, care, caution, providence, prudence, wariness

precede *v* = **go before**, antedate, come first, head, introduce, lead, preface

precedence *n* = **priority**, antecedence, pre-eminence, primacy, rank, seniority, superiority, supremacy

precedent *n* = **instance**, antecedent, example, model, paradigm, pattern, prototype, standard

preceding *adj* = **previous**, above, aforementioned, aforesaid, earlier, foregoing, former, past, prior

precept *n* = **rule**, canon, command, commandment, decree, instruction, law, order, principle, regulation, statute

precinct *n* **1** = **enclosure**, confine, limit **2** = **area**, district, quarter, section, sector, zone

precious *adj* **1** = **valuable**, costly, dear, expensive, fine, invaluable, priceless, prized **2** = **loved**, adored, beloved, cherished, darling, dear, prized, treasured **3** = **affected**, artificial, overnice, overrefined

precipice *n* = **cliff**, bluff, crag, height, rock face

precipitate *v* **1** = **quicken**, accelerate, advance, bring on, expedite, hasten, hurry, speed up, trigger **2** = **throw**, cast, fling, hurl, launch, let fly ◆ *adj* **3** = **hasty**, heedless, impetuous, impulsive, precipitous, rash, reckless **4** = **swift**, breakneck, headlong, rapid, rushing **5** = **sudden**, abrupt, brief, quick, unexpected, without warning abstract, summary.

pre·cise [pri-SĪS] *adj* **1** definite. **2** particular. **3** exact, strictly worded. **4** careful in observance. **5** punctilious, formal. **pre·cise·ly** *adv* **pre·ci·sion** [-SIZH-ən] *n* accuracy.

pre·clude [pri-KLOOD] *vt* **-clud·ed, -clud·ing** **1** prevent from happening. **2** shut out.

pre·co·cious [pri-KOH-shəs] *adj* developed, matured early or too soon. **pre·coc'i·ty** [-KOS-i-tee], **pre·co'cious·ness** [-KOH-shəs-nis] *n*

pre·con·ceive [pree-kən-SEEV] *vt* **-ceived, -ceiv·ing** form an idea beforehand. **pre·con·cep'tion** [-SEP-shən] *n*

pre·con·di·tion [pree-kən-DISH-ən] *n* necessary or required condition.

pre·cur·sor [pri-KUR-sər] *n* forerunner. **pre·cur'sive** *adj* **pre·cur'so·ry** *adj*

pred·a·to·ry [PRED-ə-tor-ee] *adj* **1** hunting, killing other animals, etc. for food. **2** plundering. **pred'a·tor** *n* predatory animal.

pred·e·ces·sor [PRED-ə-ses-ər] *n* **1** one who precedes another in an office or position. **2** ancestor.

pre·des·tine [pri-DES-tin] *vt* **-tined, -tin·ing** decree beforehand, foreordain. **pre·des·ti·na'tion** *n*

pre·dic·a·ment [pri-DIK-ə-mənt] *n* perplexing, embarrassing or difficult situation.

pred·i·cate [PRED-i-kayt] *vt* **-cat·ed, -cat·ing** **1** affirm, assert. **2** base (on or upon). ◆ *n* [-kit] **3** that which is predicated. **4** *Grammar* statement made about a subject.

pre·dict [pri-DIKT] *vt* foretell, prophesy. **pre·dict'a·ble** *adj*

pre·di·lec·tion [pred-l-EK-shən] *n* preference, liking, partiality.

pre·dis·pose [pree-dis-POHZ] *vt* **-posed, -pos·ing** **1** incline, influence someone (toward). **2** make susceptible (to).

THESAURUS

precipitous *adj* **1** = **sheer**, abrupt, dizzy, high, perpendicular, steep **2** = **hasty**, heedless, hurried, precipitate, rash, reckless

précis *n* **1** = **summary**, abridgment, outline, résumé, synopsis ◆ *v* **2** = **summarize**, abridge, outline, shorten, sum up

precise *adj* **1** = **exact**, absolute, accurate, correct, definite, explicit, express, particular, specific, strict **2** = **strict**, careful, exact, fastidious, finicky, formal, meticulous, particular, punctilious, rigid, scrupulous, stiff

precisely *adv* = **exactly**, absolutely, accurately, correctly, just so, plumb (*inf*), smack (*inf*), square, squarely, strictly

precision *n* = **exactness**, accuracy, care, meticulousness, particularity, preciseness

preclude *v* = **prevent**, check, debar, exclude, forestall, inhibit, obviate, prohibit, rule out, stop

precocious *adj* = **advanced**, ahead, bright, developed, forward, quick, smart

preconceived *adj* = **presumed**, forejudged, prejudged, presupposed

preconception *n* = **preconceived idea** or **notion**, bias, notion, predisposition, prejudice, presupposition

precursor *n* **1** = **herald**, forerunner, harbinger, vanguard **2** = **forerunner**, antecedent, forebear, predecessor

predatory *adj* = **hunting**, carnivorous, predacious, raptorial

predecessor *n* **1** = **previous job holder**, antecedent, forerunner, precursor **2** = **ancestor**, antecedent, forebear, forefather

predestination *n* = **fate**, destiny, foreordainment, foreordination, predetermination

predestined *adj* = **fated**, doomed, meant, preordained

predetermined *adj* = **prearranged**, agreed, fixed, preplanned, set

predicament *n* = **fix** (*inf*), dilemma, jam (*inf*), mess, pinch, plight, quandary, scrape (*inf*), situation, spot (*inf*)

predict *v* = **foretell**, augur, divine, forecast, portend, prophesy

predictable *adj* = **likely**, anticipated, certain, expected, foreseeable, reliable, sure

prediction *n* = **prophecy**, augury, divination, forecast, prognosis, prognostication

predilection *n* = **liking**, bias, fondness, inclination, leaning, love, partiality, penchant, preference, propensity, taste, weakness

predispose *v* = **incline**, affect, bias, dispose, influence, lead, prejudice, prompt

predisposed *adj* = **inclined**, given, liable, minded, ready, subject, susceptible, willing

predominant *adj* = **main**, ascendant, chief, dominant, leading, paramount,

pre·dom·i·nate [pri-DOM-ə-nayt] *vi* **-nat·ed, -nat·ing 1** be main or controlling element. **pre·dom'i·nance** [-nəns] *n* **pre·dom'i·nant** *adj* chief.

pre·em·i·nent [pree-EM-ə-nənt] *adj* excelling all others, outstanding. **pre·em'i·nence** *n*

pre·empt [pree-EMPT] *vt* acquire in advance or act in advance of or to exclusion of others. **pre·emp'tive** *adj*

preen *vt* **1** trim (feathers) with beak, plume. **2** smarten oneself.

pre·fab·ri·cate [pree-FAB-ri-kayt] *vt* **-cat·ed, -cat·ing** manufacture buildings, etc. in shaped sections, for rapid assembly on the site. **pre'fab** *n* building so made.

pref·ace [PREF-is] *n* **1** introduction to book, etc. ♦ *vt* **-faced, -fac·ing 2** introduce. **pref'a·to·ry** *adj*

pre·fect [PREE-fekt] *n* person put in authority. **pre·fec·ture** [PREE-fek-chər] *n* office, residence, jurisdiction of a prefect.

pre·fer [pri-FUR] *vt* **-ferred, -fer·ring 1** like better. **2** promote. **pref·er·a·ble**

[PREF-ər-ə-bəl] *adj* more desirable. **pref'er·a·bly** *adv* **pref'er·ence** [-əns] *n* **pref·er·en'tial** [-EN-shəl] *adj* giving, receiving preference.

pre·fix [PREE-fiks] *n* **1** preposition or particle put at beginning of word or title. ♦ *vt* **2** put as introduction. **3** put before word to make compound.

preg·nant [PREG-nənt] *adj* **1** carrying fetus in womb. **2** full of meaning, significance. **3** inventive. **preg'nan·cy** *n*

pre·hen·sile [pri-HEN-sil] *adj* capable of grasping.

pre·his·tor·ic [pree-hi-STOR-ik] *adj* before period in which written history begins. **pre·his'to·ry** *n*

prej·u·dice [PREJ-ə-dis] *n* **1** preconceived opinion. **2** bias, partiality. **3** damage or injury likely to happen to person or person's rights as a result of others' action or judgment. ♦ *vt* **-diced, -dic·ing 4** influence. **5** bias. **6** injure. **prej·u·di'cial** [-DISH-əl] *adj* **1** injurious. **2** disadvantageous.

THESAURUS

prevailing, prevalent, prime, principal

predominantly *adv* = **mainly**, chiefly, for the most part, generally, largely, mostly, primarily, principally

predominate *v* = **prevail**, be most noticeable, carry weight, hold sway, outweigh, overrule, overshadow

pre-eminence *n* = **superiority**, distinction, excellence, predominance, prestige, prominence, renown, supremacy

pre-eminent *adj* = **outstanding**, chief, distinguished, excellent, foremost, incomparable, matchless, predominant, renowned, superior, supreme

pre-empt *v* = **anticipate**, appropriate, assume, usurp

preen *v* **1** *Of birds* = **clean**, plume **2** = **smarten**, dress up, spruce up, titivate **3** preen oneself (on) = **pride oneself**, congratulate oneself

preface *n* **1** = **introduction**, foreword, preamble, preliminary, prelude, prologue ♦ *v* **2** = **introduce**, begin, open, prefix

prefer *v* = **like better**, be partial to, choose, desire, fancy, favor, go for, incline towards, opt for, pick

preferable *adj* = **better**, best, chosen, favored, more desirable, superior

preferably *adv* = **rather**, by choice, first, in or for preference, sooner

preference *n* **1** = **first choice**, choice, desire, favorite, option, partiality, pick, predilection, selection **2** = **priority**, favored treatment, favoritism, first place, precedence

preferential *adj* = **privileged**, advantageous, better, favored, special

preferment *n* = **promotion**, advancement, elevation, exaltation, rise, upgrading

pregnant *adj* **1** = **expectant**, big *or* heavy with child, expecting (*inf*), with child **2** = **meaningful**, charged, eloquent, expressive, loaded, pointed, significant, telling, weighty

prehistoric *adj* = **earliest**, early, primeval, primitive, primordial

prejudge *v* = **jump to conclusions**, anticipate, presume, presuppose

prejudice *n* **1** = **bias**, partiality, preconceived notion, preconception, prejudgment **2** = **discrimination**, bigotry, chauvinism, injustice, intolerance, narrow-mindedness, unfairness ♦ *v* **3** = **bias**, color, distort, influence, poison, predispose, slant **4** = **harm**, damage, hinder, hurt, impair, injure, mar, spoil, undermine

prejudiced *adj* = **biased**, bigoted, influenced, intolerant, narrow-minded, one-sided, opinionated, unfair

prel·ate [PREL-it] *n* bishop or other church dignitary of equal or higher rank. **prel'a·cy** [-ə-see] *n* prelate's office.

pre·lim·i·nar·y [pri-LIM-ə-ner-ee] *adj* **1** preparatory, introductory. ♦ *n, pl* -**ies 2** introductory, preparatory statement, action.

prel·ude [PRAY-lood] *n* **1** *Mus.* introductory movement. **2** performance, event, etc. serving as introduction. ♦ *v* -**ud·ed, -ud·ing 3** serve as prelude, introduce.

pre·mar·i·tal [pree-MA-ri-təl] *adj* occurring before marriage.

pre·ma·ture [pree-mə-CHUUR] *adj* happening, done before proper time.

pre·med·i·tate [pri-MED-i-tayt] *vt* -**tat·ed, -tat·ing** consider, plan beforehand. **pre·med·i·ta'tion** *n*

pre·mier [pri-MEER] *n* **1** prime minister. ♦ *adj* **2** chief, foremost. **3** first. **pre·mier'ship** *n* **1** office of premier.

pre·miere [pri-MEER] *n* **1** first performance of a play, film, etc. ♦ *vi* -**miered, -mier·ing 2** have first performance.

prem·ise [PREM-is] *n* **1** *Logic* proposition from which inference is drawn. ♦ *pl* **2** house, building with its belongings. **premise** *vt* -**mised, -mis·ing** state by way of introduction.

pre·mi·um [PREE-mee-əm] *n* **1** prize, bonus. **2** sum paid for insurance. **3** excess over nominal value. **4** great value or regard.

pre·mo·ni·tion [pree-mə-NISH-ən] *n* presentiment, foreboding. **pre·mon·i·to·ry** [pri-MON-i-tor-ee] *adj*

pre·na·tal [pree-NAYT-l] *adj* occurring before birth.

pre·oc·cu·py [pree-OK-yə-pī] *vt* -**pied, -py·ing** occupy to the exclusion of other things. **pre·oc·cu·pa'tion** *n* mental concentration or absorption.

prep [prep] *n* preppy.

pre·pare [pri-PAIR] *v* -**pared, -par·ing** ♦ *vt* **1** make ready. **2** make. ♦ *vi* **3** get ready. **prep·a·ra'tion** *n* **1** making ready beforehand. **2** something that is prepared, as a medicine. **3** at school, (time spent) preparing work for lesson. **pre·par'a·to·ry** [-PA-rə-tor-ee] *adj* **1** serving to prepare. **2** introductory. **pre·par'ed·ness** [-id-nis] *n* state of being prepared. **preparatory**

prejudicial *adj* = **harmful**, damaging, deleterious, detrimental, disadvantageous, hurtful, injurious, unfavorable

preliminary *adj* **1** = **first**, initial, introductory, opening, pilot, prefatory, preparatory, prior, test, trial ♦ *n* **2** = **introduction**, beginning, opening, overture, preamble, preface, prelude, start

prelude *n* = **introduction**, beginning, foreword, overture, preamble, preface, prologue, start

premature *adj* **1** = **early**, forward, unseasonable, untimely **2** = **hasty**, ill-timed, overhasty, rash, too soon, untimely

premeditated *adj* = **planned**, calculated, conscious, considered, deliberate, intentional, willful

premeditation *n* = **planning**, design, forethought, intention, plotting, prearrangement, predetermination, purpose

premier *n* **1** = **head of government**, chancellor, chief minister, chief officer, prime minister ♦ *adj* **2** = **chief**, first, foremost, head, highest, leading, main, primary, prime, principal

premiere *n* = **first night**, debut, opening

premise *n* = **assumption**, argument, assertion, hypothesis, postulation, presupposition, proposition, supposition

premises *pl n* = **building**, establishment, place, property, site

premium *n* **1** = **bonus**, bounty, fee, perk (*inf*), perquisite, prize, reward **2 at a premium** = **in great demand**, hard to come by, in short supply, rare, scarce

premonition *n* = **feeling**, foreboding, hunch, idea, intuition, presentiment, suspicion

preoccupation *n* **1** = **obsession**, bee in one's bonnet, fixation **2** = **absorption**, absent-mindedness, abstraction, daydreaming, engrossment, immersion, reverie, woolgathering

preoccupied *adj* = **absorbed**, absent-minded, distracted, engrossed, immersed, lost in, oblivious, rapt, wrapped up

preparation *n* **1** = **groundwork**, getting ready, preparing **2** (*often plural*) = **arrangement**, measure, plan, provision **3** = **mixture**, compound, concoction, medicine

preparatory *adj* = **introductory**, opening, prefatory, preliminary, primary

school private school preparing students for college.

pre·pay [pree-PAY] vt **-paid, -pay·ing** pay or pay for beforehand. **pre·paid'** adj

pre·pon·der·ate [pri-PON-də-rayt] vi **-at·ed, -at·ing** be of greater weight or power. **pre·pon'der·ance** [-əns] n superiority of power, numbers, etc.

prep·o·si·tion [prep-ə-ZISH-ən] n word marking relation between noun or pronoun and other words. **prep·o·si'tion·al** adj

pre·pos·sess [pree-pə-ZES] vt **1** impress, esp. favorably, beforehand. **2** possess beforehand. **pre·pos·sess'ing** adj inviting favorable opinion, attractive, winning.

pre·pos·ter·ous [pri-POS-tər-əs] adj utterly absurd, foolish.

prep·py, prep·pie [PRE-pee] n **-ies** inf (person who behaves like) student or former student of preparatory school. ♦ adj

pre·puce [PRE-pyoos] n retractable fold of skin covering tip of penis, foreskin.

pre·req·ui·site [pri-REK-wə-zit] n, adj (something) required as prior condition.

pre·rog·a·tive [pri-ROG-ə-tiv] n **1** peculiar power or right, esp. as vested in ruler. ♦ adj **2** privileged.

pres·age [PRES-ij] n **1** omen, indication of something to come. ♦ vt **-aged, -ag·ing 2** foretell.

pres·by·o·pi·a [prez-bee-OH-pee-ə] n progressively diminishing ability of the eye to focus, esp. on near objects, farsightedness.

pres·by·ter [PREZ-bi-tər] n **1** elder in early Christian church. **2** priest. **3** member of a presbytery. **Pres·by·te'ri·an** adj, n (member) of Protestant church governed by lay elders. **pres'by·ter·y** n **1** church court composed of all ministers within a certain district and one or two ruling elders from each church. **2** R.C. Church rectory.

pre·science [PRESH-əns] n foreknowledge. **pres'cient** adj

pre·scribe [pri-SKRĪB] v **-scribed, -scrib·ing 1** set out rules for. **2** order. **3** ordain. **4** order use of (medicine). **pre·scrip'tion** n **1** prescribing. **2** thing prescribed. **3** written statement of it. **pre·scrip'tive** adj

pres·ent¹ [PREZ-ənt] adj **1** that is here. **2** now existing or happening. ♦ n **3** present time or tense. **pres'ence** n **1** being present. **2** appearance, bearing. **pres'ent·ly** adv **1** soon. **2** at present.

pre·sent² [pri-ZENT] vt **1** introduce formally. **2** show. **3** give. **4** offer. **5** point, aim. **pres'ent** n gift. **pre·sent'a·ble** adj fit to be seen. **pres·en·ta'tion** [-TAY-shən] n **pre·sent'er** n person who presents, esp. an award.

pre·sen·ti·ment [pri-ZEN-tə-mənt] n

———— THESAURUS ————

prepare v = **make** or **get ready,** adapt, adjust, arrange, practice, prime, train, warm up

prepared adj **1** = **ready,** arranged, in order, in readiness, primed, set **2** = **willing,** disposed, inclined

preponderance n = **predominance,** dominance, domination, extensiveness, greater numbers, greater part, lion's share, mass, prevalence, supremacy

prepossessing adj = **attractive,** appealing, charming, engaging, fetching, good-looking, handsome, likable or likeable, pleasing

preposterous adj = **ridiculous,** absurd, crazy, incredible, insane, laughable, ludicrous, nonsensical, out of the question, outrageous, unthinkable

prerequisite n **1** = **requirement,** condition, essential, must, necessity, precondition, qualification, requisite, sine qua non ♦ adj **2** = **required,** essential, indispensable, mandatory, necessary,

obligatory, requisite, vital

prerogative n = **right,** advantage, due, exemption, immunity, liberty, privilege

presage v = **portend,** augur, betoken, bode, foreshadow, foretoken, signify

prescience n = **foresight,** clairvoyance, foreknowledge, precognition, second sight

prescribe v = **order,** decree, dictate, direct, lay down, ordain, recommend, rule, set, specify, stipulate

prescription n **1** = **instruction,** direction, formula, recipe **2** = **medicine,** drug, mixture, preparation, remedy

presence n **1** = **being,** attendance, existence, inhabitance, occupancy, residence **2** = **personality,** air, appearance, aspect, aura, bearing, carriage, demeanor, poise, self-assurance

presence of mind n = **level-headedness,** calmness, composure, cool (sl), coolness, self-possession, wits

present¹ adj **1** = **here,** at hand, near, nearby, ready, there **2** = **current,**

sense of something (esp. evil) about to happen.

pre·serve [pri-ZURV] vt **-served, -serv·ing** 1 keep from harm, injury or decay. 2 maintain. 3 pickle, can. ◆ n 4 special area. 5 that which is preserved, as fruit, etc. 6 place where game is kept for private fishing, shooting. ◆ pl 7 preserved vegetables, fruit, etc. **pres·er·va'tion** n **pre·serv'a·tive** n 1 chemical put into perishable foods, drinks, etc. to keep them from going bad. ◆ adj 2 tending to preserve. 3 having quality of preserving.

pre·side [pri-ZĪD] vi **-sid·ed, -sid·ing** 1 be chairperson. 2 superintend. **pres'i·dent** [-dənt] n head of organization, company, republic, etc. **pres'i·den·cy** n, pl **-cies** **pres·i·den'tial** [-DEN-shəl] adj

press[1] vt 1 subject to push or squeeze. 2 smooth by pressure or heat. 3 urge steadily, earnestly. ◆ vi 4 bring weight to bear. 5 throng. 6 hasten. ◆ n 7 a pressing. 8 machine for pressing, esp. printing machine. 9 printing house. 10 its work or art. 11 newspapers collectively. 12 reporters, journalists. 13 crowd. 14 stress.

press'ing adj 1 urgent. 2 persistent. **press agent** person employed to advertise and secure publicity for any person, enterprise, etc. **press'man** [-mən] n printer who attends to the press.

press[2] vt force to serve esp. in navy or army. **press gang** formerly, body of men employed to press men into naval service.

pres·sure [PRESH-ər] n 1 act of pressing. 2 influence. 3 authority. 4 difficulties. 5 Physics thrust per unit area. **pres·sur·i·za'tion** [-ZAY-shən] n in aircraft, maintenance of normal atmospheric pressure at high altitudes. **pres'sur·ize** vt **-ized, -iz·ing** **pressure cooker** reinforced pot that cooks food rapidly by steam under pressure. **pressure group** organized group that exerts influence on policies, public opinion, etc.

pres·ti·dig·i·ta·tion [pres-ti-dij-i-TAY-shən] n sleight of hand. **pres·ti·dig'i·ta·tor** n

pres·tige [pre-STEEZH] n 1 reputation. 2 influence depending on it. **pres·tig'i·ous** [-STIJ-əs] adj

pres·to [PRES-toh] adv Mus. quickly.

contemporary, existent, existing, immediate, present-day ◆ n 3 **the present** = **now**, here and now, the present moment, the time being, today 4 **at present** = **just now**, at the moment, now, right now 5 **for the present** = **for now**, for the moment, for the time being, in the meantime, temporarily

present[2] n 1 = **gift**, boon, donation, endowment, grant, gratuity, hand-out, offering ◆ v 2 = **introduce**, acquaint with, make known 3 = **put on**, display, exhibit, give, show, stage 4 = **give**, award, bestow, confer, grant, hand out, hand over

presentable adj = **decent**, acceptable, becoming, fit to be seen, O.K. or okay (inf), passable, respectable, satisfactory, suitable

presentation n 1 = **giving**, award, bestowal, conferral, donation, offering 2 = **production**, demonstration, display, exhibition, performance, show

presently adv = **soon**, anon (archaic), before long, by and by, shortly

preservation n = **protection**, conservation, maintenance, safeguarding, safekeeping, safety, salvation, support

preserve v 1 = **save**, care for, conserve, defend, keep, protect, safeguard, shelter,

shield 2 = **maintain**, continue, keep, keep up, perpetuate, sustain, uphold ◆ n 3 = **area**, domain, field, realm, sphere

preside v = **run**, administer, chair, conduct, control, direct, govern, head, lead, manage, officiate

press v 1 = **force down**, compress, crush, depress, jam, mash, push, squeeze 2 = **hug**, clasp, crush, embrace, fold in one's arms, hold close, squeeze 3 = **smooth**, flatten, iron 4 = **urge**, beg, entreat, exhort, implore, petition, plead, pressurize 5 = **crowd**, flock, gather, herd, push, seethe, surge, swarm, throng ◆ n 6 **the press: a** = **newspapers**, Fleet Street, fourth estate, news media, the papers **b** = **journalists**, columnists, correspondents, newsmen, pressmen, reporters

pressing adj = **urgent**, crucial, high-priority, imperative, important, importunate, serious, vital

pressure n 1 = **force**, compressing, compression, crushing, squeezing, weight 2 = **power**, coercion, compulsion, constraint, force, influence, sway 3 = **stress**, burden, demands, hassle (inf), heat, load, strain, urgency

prestige n = **status**, credit, distinction,

pre·stressed [PREE-strest] *adj* (of concrete) containing stretched steel cables for strengthening.

pre·sume [pri-ZOOM] *v* -sumed, -sum·ing ◆ *vt* **1** take for granted. ◆ *vi* **2** take liberties. **pre·sum'a·bly** *adv* **1** probably. **2** doubtlessly. **pre·sump'tion** [-ZUM-shən] *n* **1** forward, arrogant opinion or conduct. **2** strong probability. **pre·sump'tive** *adj* that may be assumed as true or valid until contrary is proved. **pre·sump'tu·ous** [-shoo-əs] *adj* forward, impudent, taking liberties.

pre·sup·pose [pree-sə-POHZ] *vt* -posed, -pos·ing assume or take for granted beforehand. **pre·sup·po·si'tion** [-ZI-shən] *n* previous supposition.

pre·tend [pri-TEND] *vt* **1** claim or allege (something untrue). **2** make believe, as in play. ◆ *vi* **3** lay claim (to). **pre·tense'** *n* **1** simulation. **2** pretext. **pre·tend'er** *n*

claimant (to throne). **pre·ten'sion** *n* **pre·ten'tious** [-shəs] *adj* **1** making claim to special merit or importance. **2** given to outward show.

pre·ter·nat·u·ral [pree-tər-NACH-ər-əl] *adj* **1** out of ordinary way of nature. **2** abnormal, supernatural.

pre·text [PREE-tekst] *n* **1** excuse. **2** pretense.

pret·ty [PRIT-ee] *adj* -ti·er, -ti·est **1** having beauty that is attractive rather than imposing. **2** charming, etc. ◆ *adv* **3** fairly, moderately. **pret'ti·ness** [-nis] *n*

pret·zel [PRET-səl] *n* crisp, dry biscuit usu. shaped as knot or stick.

pre·vail [pri-VAYL] *vi* **1** gain mastery. **2** triumph. **3** be in fashion, generally established. **pre·vail'ing** *adj* **1** widespread. **2** predominant. **prev'a·lence** [-ləns] *n* **prev'a·lent** [-lənt] *adj* extensively existing, rife.

THESAURUS

eminence, fame, honor, importance, kudos, renown, reputation, standing

prestigious *adj* = **celebrated**, eminent, esteemed, great, illustrious, important, notable, prominent, renowned, respected

presumably *adv* = **it would seem**, apparently, in all likelihood, in all probability, on the face of it, probably, seemingly

presume *v* **1** = **believe**, assume, conjecture, guess (*inf*), infer, postulate, suppose, surmise, take for granted, think **2** = **dare**, go so far, make so bold, take the liberty, venture

presumption *n* **1** = **cheek** (*inf*), audacity, boldness, effrontery, gall (*inf*), impudence, insolence, nerve (*inf*) **2** = **probability**, basis, chance, likelihood

presumptuous *adj* = **pushy** (*inf*), audacious, bold, forward, insolent, overconfident, too big for one's boots

presuppose *v* = **presume**, assume, imply, posit, postulate, take as read, take for granted

presupposition *n* = **assumption**, belief, preconception, premise, presumption, supposition

pretend *v* **1** = **feign**, affect, allege, assume, fake, falsify, impersonate, profess, sham, simulate **2** = **make believe**, act, imagine, make up, suppose

pretended *adj* = **feigned**, bogus, counterfeit, fake, false, phoney *or* phony

(*inf*), pretend (*inf*), pseudo (*inf*), sham, so-called

pretender *n* = **claimant**, aspirant

pretense *n* **1** = **deception**, acting, charade, deceit, falsehood, feigning, sham, simulation, trickery **2** = **show**, affectation, artifice, display, façade, veneer

pretension *n* **1** = **claim**, aspiration, assumption, demand, pretense, profession **2** = **affectation**, airs, conceit, ostentation, pretentiousness, self-importance, show, snobbery, vanity

pretentious *adj* = **affected**, conceited, grandiloquent, grandiose, high-flown, inflated, mannered, ostentatious, pompous, puffed up, showy, snobbish

pretext *n* = **guise**, cloak, cover, excuse, ploy, pretense, ruse, show

pretty *adj* **1** = **attractive**, beautiful, bonny, charming, comely, fair, good-looking, lovely ◆ *adv* **2** = **fairly**, kind of (*inf*), moderately, quite, rather, reasonably, somewhat

prevail *v* **1** = **win**, be victorious, overcome, overrule, succeed, triumph **2** = **be widespread**, abound, be current, be prevalent, exist generally, predominate

prevailing *adj* **1** = **widespread**, common, cool (*inf*), current, customary, established, fashionable, general, in vogue, ordinary, phat (*sl*), popular, prevalent, usual **2** = **predominating**, dominant, main, principal, ruling

pre·var·i·cate [pri-VA-ri-kayt] vi **-cat·ed,**
-cat·ing 1 make evasive or misleading
statements. **2** lie. **pre·var'i·ca·tor** n
pre·vent [pri-VENT] vt stop, hinder.
pre·vent'a·ble adj **pre·ven'tion** [-shən] n
pre·ven'tive adj, n
pre·view [PREE-vyoo] n **1** advance
showing. **2** a showing of scenes from a
forthcoming film, etc.
pre·vi·ous [PREE-vee-əs] adj **1** earlier. **2**
preceding. **3** happening before.
pre·vi·ous·ly adv before.
prey [pray] n **1** animal hunted and killed by
carnivorous animals. **2** victim. ◆ vi **3** seize
for food. **4** treat as prey. **5** (with upon)
afflict, obsess.
price [prīs] n **1** amount, etc. for which thing
is bought or sold. **2** cost. **3** value. **4** reward.
5 odds in betting. ◆ vt **priced, pric·ing 6**
fix, ask price for. **price'less** [-lis] adj **1**
invaluable. **2** very funny. **pric'ey** [-ee] adj
pric·i·er, pric·i·est expensive.

prick [prik] vt **1** pierce slightly with sharp
point. **2** cause to feel mental pain. **3** mark
by prick. **4** erect (ears). ◆ n **5** slight hole
made by pricking. **6** pricking or being
pricked. **7** sting. **8** remorse. **9** that which
pricks. **10** sharp point. **prick'le** n **1** thorn,
spike. ◆ vi **-kled, -kling 2** feel tingling or
pricking sensation. **prick'ly** adj **-li·er, -li·est**
prickly heat inflammation of skin with
stinging pains.
pride [prīd] n **1** too high an opinion of
oneself. **2** worthy self-esteem. **3** feeling of
elation or great satisfaction. **4** something
causing this. **5** group (of lions). ◆ v refl
prid·ed, prid·ing 6 take pride.
priest [preest] n official minister of religion,
member of clergy. **priest'ess** n, fem.
priest'hood [-huud] n **priest'ly** adj **-li·er,**
-li·est
prig n self-righteous person who professes
superior culture, morality, etc. **prig'gish**
adj

———— THESAURUS ————

prevalence n = **commonness**, currency,
frequency, popularity, universality
prevalent adj = **common**, current,
customary, established, frequent, general,
popular, universal, usual, widespread
prevaricate v = **evade**, beat about the
bush, cavil, deceive, dodge, equivocate,
hedge
prevent v = **stop**, avert, avoid, foil,
forestall, frustrate, hamper, hinder,
impede, inhibit, obstruct, obviate,
preclude, thwart
prevention n = **elimination**, avoidance,
deterrence, precaution, safeguard,
thwarting
preventive adj **1** = **hindering**, hampering,
impeding, obstructive **2** = **protective**,
counteractive, deterrent, precautionary ◆ n
3 = **hindrance**, block, impediment,
obstacle, obstruction **4** = **protection**,
deterrent, prevention, remedy, safeguard,
shield
preview n = **advance showing**, foretaste,
sneak preview, taster, trailer
previous adj = **earlier**, erstwhile,
foregoing, former, past, preceding, prior
previously adv = **before**, beforehand,
earlier, formerly, hitherto, in the past, once
prey n **1** = **quarry**, game, kill **2** = **victim**,
dupe, fall guy (inf), mug (Brit. sl), target
price n **1** = **cost**, amount, charge, damage
(inf), estimate, expense, fee, figure, rate,

value, worth **2** = **consequences**, cost,
penalty, toll ◆ v **3** = **evaluate**, assess, cost,
estimate, rate, value
priceless adj **1** = **valuable**, costly, dear,
expensive, invaluable, precious **2** Inf =
hilarious, amusing, comic, droll, funny,
rib-tickling, side-splitting
pricey adj = **expensive**, costly, dear,
high-priced, steep (inf)
prick v **1** = **pierce**, jab, lance, perforate,
punch, puncture, stab **2** = **sting**, bite, itch,
prickle, smart, tingle ◆ n **3** = **puncture**,
hole, perforation, pinhole, wound
prickle n **1** = **spike**, barb, needle, point,
spine, spur, thorn ◆ v **2** = **tingle**, itch,
smart, sting **3** = **prick**, jab, stick
prickly adj **1** = **spiny**, barbed, bristly,
thorny **2** = **itchy**, crawling, scratchy, sharp,
smarting, stinging, tingling
pride n **1** = **satisfaction**, delight,
gratification, joy, pleasure **2** = **self-respect**,
dignity, honor, self-esteem, self-worth **3** =
conceit, arrogance, egotism, hubris,
pretension, pretentiousness,
self-importance, self-love, superciliousness,
vanity **4** = **gem**, jewel, pride and joy,
treasure
priest n = **clergyman**, cleric, curate, divine,
ecclesiastic, father, minister, pastor, vicar
prig n = **goody-goody** (inf), prude, puritan,
stuffed shirt (inf)
priggish adj = **self-righteous**,

prim *adj* **prim·mer, prim·mest** very restrained, formally prudish.

pri·ma·cy [PRĪ-me-see] *n* **1** state of being first in rank, grade, etc. **2** office of PRIMATE¹.

pri·ma don·na [pree-mə DON-ə] *n, pl* **donnas 1** principal female singer in opera. **2** temperamental person.

pri·ma fa·ci·e [PRĪ-mə FAY-shee] *Lat* **1** at first sight. **2** obvious.

pri·mal [PRĪ-məl] *adj* **1** of earliest age. **2** first, original. **pri·ma'ri·ly** *adv* **pri'ma·ry** *adj* **1** chief. **2** of the first stage, decision, etc. **3** elementary.

pri·mate¹ [PRĪ-mit] *n* archbishop.

primate² [PRĪ-mayt] *n* one of order of mammals including monkeys and man.

prime¹ [prīm] *adj* **1** fundamental. **2** original. **3** chief. **4** best. ◆ *n* **5** first, best part of anything. **6** youth. **7** full health and vigor. ◆ *vt* **primed, prim·ing 8** prepare (gun, engine, pump, etc.) for use. **9** fill up, e.g. with information. **prime minister** leader of parliamentary government.

prime² *vt* **primed, prim·ing** prepare for paint with preliminary coating of oil, etc. **prim'er** [PRĪM-ər] *n* paint, etc. for priming.

prim·er [PRIM-ər] *n* elementary schoolbook or manual.

pri·me·val [prī-MEE-vəl] *adj* of the earliest age of the world.

prim·i·tive [PRIM-i-tiv] *adj* **1** of an early undeveloped kind, ancient. **2** crude, rough.

pri·mo·gen·i·ture [prī-mə-JEN-i-chər] *n* rule by which real estate passes to the first born son. **pri·mo·gen'i·tor** *n* **1** earliest ancestor. **2** forefather.

pri·mor·di·al [prī-MOR-dee-əl] *adj* existing at or from the beginning.

prince [prins] *n* **1** son or (in some countries) grandson of king or queen. **2** ruler, chief. **prin'cess** *n, fem.* **prince'ly** *adj* **-li·er, -li·est 1** generous, lavish. **2** stately. **3** magnificent.

prin·ci·pal [PRIN-sə-pəl] *adj* **1** chief in importance. ◆ *n* **2** person for whom another is agent. **3** head of institution, esp. school. **4** sum of money lent and yielding interest. **5** chief actor. **prin·ci·pal'i·ty** *n* territory, dignity of prince.

prin·ci·ple [PRIN-sə-pəl] *n* **1** moral rule. **2** settled reason of action. **3** uprightness. **4** fundamental truth or element.

print *vt* **1** reproduce (words, pictures, etc., by pressing inked plates, type, blocks, etc. to paper, etc.). **2** produce thus. **3** write in imitation of this. **4** impress. **5** *Photography*

goody-goody (*inf*), holier-than-thou, prim, prudish, puritanical

prim *adj* = **prudish**, demure, fastidious, fussy, priggish, prissy (*inf*), proper, puritanical, strait-laced

prima donna *n* = **diva**, leading lady, star

primarily *adv* **1** = **chiefly**, above all, essentially, fundamentally, generally, largely, mainly, mostly, principally **2** = **at first**, at or from the start, first and foremost, initially, in the beginning, in the first place, originally

primary *adj* **1** = **chief**, cardinal, first, greatest, highest, main, paramount, prime, principal **2** = **elementary**, introductory, rudimentary, simple

prime *adj* **1** = **main**, chief, leading, predominant, pre-eminent, primary, principal **2** = **best**, choice, excellent, first-class, first-rate, highest, quality, select, top ◆ *n* **3** = **peak**, bloom, flower, height, heyday, zenith ◆ *v* **4** = **inform**, brief, clue in (*inf*), fill in (*inf*), notify, tell **5** = **prepare**, coach, get ready, make ready, train

primeval *adj* = **earliest**, ancient, early, first,

old, prehistoric, primal, primitive, primordial

primitive *adj* **1** = **early**, earliest, elementary, first, original, primary, primeval, primordial **2** = **crude**, rough, rudimentary, simple, unrefined

prince *n* = **ruler**, lord, monarch, sovereign

princely *adj* **1** = **regal**, imperial, majestic, noble, royal, sovereign **2** = **generous**, bounteous, gracious, lavish, liberal, munificent, open-handed, rich

principal *adj* **1** = **main**, cardinal, chief, essential, first, foremost, key, leading, paramount, pre-eminent, primary, prime ◆ *n* **2** = **head** (*inf*), dean, headmaster *or* headmistress, superintendent **3** = **star**, lead, leader **4** = **capital**, assets, money

principally *adv* = **mainly**, above all, chiefly, especially, largely, mostly, predominantly, primarily

principle *n* **1** = **rule**, canon, criterion, doctrine, dogma, fundamental, law, maxim, precept, standard, truth **2** = **morals**, conscience, integrity, probity, scruples, sense of honor **3 in principle** = **in**

produce pictures from negatives. **6** stamp (fabric) with colored design. ◆ n **7** printed matter. **8** printed lettering. **9** written imitation of printed type. **10** photograph. **11** impression, mark left on surface by thing that has pressed against it. **12** printed cotton fabric. **print'er** n person or device engaged in printing. **printed circuit** electronic circuit with wiring printed on an insulating base. **print'out** n printed information from computer, teleprinter, etc.

pri·or [PRĪ-ər] adj **1** earlier. ◆ n **2** chief of religious house or order. **pri'or·ess** n, fem. **pri·or'i·ty** n, pl **-ties 1** precedence. **2** something given special attention. **pri'o·ry** n, pl **-ries** monastery, convent under prior, prioress. **prior to** before, earlier.

prise [prīz] vt **prised, pris·ing 1** force open by levering. **2** obtain (information, etc.) with difficulty.

prism [PRIZ-əm] n transparent solid usu. with triangular ends and rectangular sides, used to disperse light into spectrum or refract it in optical instruments, etc. **pris·mat'ic** adj **1** of prism shape. **2** (of color) such as is produced by refraction through prism, rainbowlike, brilliant.

pris·on [PRIZ-ən] n jail. **pris'on·er** n **1** one kept in prison. **2** captive.

pris·sy [PRIS-ee] adj **-si·er, -si·est** fussy, prim.

pris·tine [pris-TEEN] adj original, primitive, unspoiled, good.

pri·vate [PRĪ-vit] adj **1** secret, not public. **2** reserved for, or belonging to, or concerning, an individual only. **3** personal. **4** secluded. **5** denoting soldier or marine of lowest rank. **6** not controlled by government. ◆ n **7** private soldier or marine. **pri'va·cy** [-vi-see] n **pri·va·tize** vt **-tized, -tiz·ing** transfer from government or public ownership to private enterprise.

pri·va·tion [prī-VAY-shən] n **1** want of comforts or necessities. **2** hardship. **3** act of depriving. **priv·a·tive** [PRIV-ə-tiv] adj of privation or negation.

priv·et [PRIV-it] n bushy shrub used for hedges.

priv·i·lege [PRIV-ə-lij] n **1** advantage or favor that only a few obtain. **2** right, advantage belonging to person or class. **priv'i·leged** adj enjoying special right or immunity.

priv·y [PRIV-ee] adj **1** admitted to knowledge of secret. ◆ n, pl **priv·ies 2** outhouse. **3** Law person having interest in an action.

prize¹ [prīz] n **1** reward given for success in competition. **2** thing striven for. **3** thing won. ◆ adj **4** winning or likely to win a prize. ◆ vt **prized, priz·ing 5** value highly. **prize'fight** n boxing match for money.

prize² n ship, property captured in (naval)

————————| THESAURUS |————————

theory, ideally, theoretically

print v **1** = **publish**, engrave, impress, imprint, issue, mark, stamp ◆ n **2** = **publication**, book, magazine, newspaper, newsprint, periodical, printed matter **3** = **reproduction**, copy, engraving, photo (inf), photograph, picture

prior adj **1** = **earlier**, foregoing, former, preceding, pre-existent, pre-existing, previous **2 prior to** = **before**, earlier than, preceding, previous to

priority n = **precedence**, pre-eminence, preference, rank, right of way, seniority

priory n = **monastery**, abbey, convent, nunnery, religious house

prison n = **jail**, clink (sl), confinement, cooler (sl), dungeon, lockup, penitentiary, slammer (sl)

prisoner n **1** = **convict**, con (sl), jailbird, lag (sl) **2** = **captive**, detainee, hostage, internee

prissy adj = **prim**, old-maidish (inf), prim

and proper, prudish, strait-laced

pristine adj = **new**, immaculate, pure, uncorrupted, undefiled, unspoiled, unsullied, untouched, virginal

privacy n = **seclusion**, isolation, retirement, retreat, solitude

private adj **1** = **exclusive**, individual, intimate, own, personal, reserved, special **2** = **secret**, clandestine, confidential, covert, hush-hush (inf), off the record, unofficial **3** = **secluded**, concealed, isolated, secret, separate, sequestered, solitary

privilege n = **right**, advantage, claim, concession, due, entitlement, freedom, liberty, prerogative

privileged adj = **special**, advantaged, elite, entitled, favored, honored

privy adj **1 privy to** = **informed of**, apprised of, aware of, cognizant of, in on, in the know about (inf), wise to (sl) ◆ n **2** = **lavatory**, latrine, outside toilet warfare.

pro¹ [proh] *adj, adv* in favor of.

pro² *n* **1** professional. ◆ *adj* **2** professional.

pro- *prefix* for, instead of, before, in front, e.g. *proconsul; pronoun; project.*

pro·ac·tive [proh-AK-tiv] *adj* taking the initiative and acting in advance, rather than simply reacting to circumstances and events.

prob·a·ble [PROB-ə-bəl] *adj* likely. **prob·a·bil'i·ty** *n* **1** likelihood. **2** anything that has appearance of truth. **prob'a·bly** *adv*

pro·bate [PROH-bayt] *n* **1** proving of authenticity of will. **2** certificate of this. **probate court** court with power over administration of estates of dead persons.

pro·ba·tion [proh-BAY-shən] *n* **1** system of releasing lawbreakers, but placing them under supervision for stated period. **2** testing of candidate before admission to full membership.

probe [prohb] *vt* **probed, prob·ing 1** search into, examine, question closely. ◆ *n* **2** that which probes, or is used to probe. **3** thorough inquiry.

pro·bi·ty [PROH-bi-tee] *n* honesty, uprightness, integrity.

prob·lem [PROB-ləm] *n* **1** matter, etc. difficult to deal with or solve. **2** question set for solution. **3** puzzle. **prob·le·mat'ic** *adj* **1** questionable. **2** uncertain. **3** disputable.

pro·bos·cis [proh-BOS-is] *n, pl* **-cis·es 1** trunk or long snout. **2** *inf* nose, esp. prominent one.

pro·ceed [prə-SEED] *vi* **1** go forward, continue. **2** be carried on. **3** take legal action. **pro·ceeds** [PROH-seedz] *pl n* amount of money or profit received. **pro·ce·dur·al** [-SEE-jər-əl] *adj* **pro·ce'dure** *n* **1** act, manner of proceeding. **2** conduct. **pro·ceed'ing** *n* **1** act or course of action. **2** transaction. ◆ *pl* **3** minutes of meeting. **4** methods of prosecuting charge, claim, etc.

proc·ess [PROS-es] *n* **1** series of actions or changes. **2** method of operation. **3** state of going on. **4** action of law. **5** outgrowth. ◆ *vt* **6** handle, treat, prepare by special method of manufacture, etc. **pro·ces·sion** [prə-SESH-ən] *n* **1** regular, orderly progress. **2** line of persons in formal order. **pro·ces'sion·al** *adj* **proc'es·sor** *n* **1** person or device that processes. **2** *Computers* same as CENTRAL PROCESSING UNIT.

pro·claim [proh-KLAYM] *vt* announce

prize¹ *n* **1** = **reward**, accolade, award, honor, trophy **2** = **winnings**, haul, jackpot, purse, stakes ◆ *adj* **3** = **champion**, award-winning, best, first-rate, outstanding, top, winning

prize² *v* = **value**, cherish, esteem, hold dear, treasure

probability *n* = **likelihood**, chance(s), expectation, liability, likeliness, odds, prospect

probable *adj* = **likely**, apparent, credible, feasible, plausible, possible, presumable, reasonable

probably *adv* = **likely**, doubtless, maybe, most likely, perchance (*archaic*), perhaps, possibly, presumably

probation *n* = **trial period**, apprenticeship, trial

probe *v* **1** = **examine**, explore, go into, investigate, look into, scrutinize, search **2** = **explore**, feel around, poke, prod ◆ *n* **3** = **examination**, detection, exploration, inquiry, investigation, scrutiny, study

problem *n* **1** = **difficulty**, complication, dilemma, dispute, predicament, quandary, trouble **2** = **puzzle**, conundrum, enigma,

poser, question, riddle

problematic *adj* = **tricky**, debatable, doubtful, dubious, problematical, puzzling

procedure *n* = **method**, action, conduct, course, custom, modus operandi, policy, practice, process, routine, strategy, system

proceed *v* **1** = **go on**, carry on, continue, go ahead, move on, press on, progress **2** = **arise**, come, derive, emanate, flow, issue, originate, result, spring, stem

proceeding *n* **1** = **action**, act, deed, measure, move, procedure, process, step **2 proceedings** = **business**, account, affairs, archives, doings, minutes, records, report, transactions

proceeds *pl n* = **income**, earnings, gain, products, profit, returns, revenue, takings, yield

process *n* **1** = **procedure**, action, course, manner, means, measure, method, operation, performance, practice, system **2** = **development**, advance, evolution, growth, movement, progress, progression ◆ *v* **3** = **handle**, deal with, fulfill

procession *n* = **parade**, cavalcade, cortege, file, march, train

publicly, declare. **proc·la·ma'tion**
[prok-lə-MAY-shən] n

pro·cliv·i·ty [proh-KLIV-i-tee] n, pl **-ties**
inclination, tendency.

pro·cras·ti·nate [proh-KRAS-tə-nayt] vi
-nat·ed, -nat·ing put off, delay.
pro·cras·ti·na'tion n **pro·cras'ti·na·tor** n

pro·cre·ate [PROH-kree-ayt] vt **-at·ed,
-at·ing** produce offspring, generate
pro·cre·a'tion n

Pro·crus·te·an [proh-KRUS-tee-ən] adj
compelling uniformity by violence.

proc·tol·o·gy [prok-TOL-ə-jee] n medical
specialty dealing with diseases of anus and
rectum.

proc·tor [PROK-tər] n **1** person appointed
to supervise students during examinations.
2 university official with administrative,
esp. disciplinary, duties.

pro·cure [prə-KYUUR] v **-cured, -cur·ing** ♦
vt **1** obtain, acquire. **2** provide. **3** bring
about. ♦ vi **4** act as pimp. **pro·cure'ment** n
pro·cur'er n **1** one who procures. **2** pimp.
pro·cur'ess n, fem.

prod vt **prod·ded, prod·ding 1** poke with

something pointed. **2** stimulate to action.
♦ n **3** prodding. **4** goad. **5** pointed
instrument.

prod·i·gal [PROD-i-gəl] adj **1** wasteful. **2**
extravagant. ♦ n **3** spendthrift.
prod·i·gal'i·ty n reckless extravagance.

prod·i·gy [PROD-i-jee] n, pl **-gies 1** person
esp. precocious child with some marvelous
gift. **2** thing causing wonder. **pro·di·gious**
[prə-DIJ-əs] adj **1** very great, immense. **2**
extraordinary. **pro·di'gious·ly** adv

pro·duce [prə-DOOS] vt **-duced, -duc·ing 1**
bring into existence. **2** yield. **3** make. **4**
bring forward. **5** manufacture. **6** exhibit. **7**
present on stage, film, TV. **8** Geometry
extend in length. ♦ n [PROD-oos] **9** that
which is yielded or made, esp. vegetables.
pro·duc'er n person who produces, esp.
play, film, etc. **prod'uct** [-əkt] n **1** result of
process of manufacture. **2** number
resulting from multiplication. **pro·duc'tion**
n **1** producing. **2** things produced.
pro·duc'tive adj **1** fertile. **2** creative. **3**
efficient. **pro·duc·tiv'i·ty** n

pro·fam·i·ly [proh-FAM-ə-lee] adj **1**

proclaim v = **declare**, advertise, announce,
circulate, herald, indicate, make known,
profess, publish

proclamation n = **declaration**,
announcement, decree, edict, notice,
notification, pronouncement, publication

procrastinate v = **delay**, dally, drag one's
feet (inf), gain time, play for time,
postpone, put off, stall, temporize

procure v = **obtain**, acquire, buy, come by,
find, gain, get, pick up, purchase, score
(sl), secure, win

prod v **1** = **poke**, dig, drive, jab, nudge,
push, shove **2** = **prompt**, egg on, goad,
impel, incite, motivate, move, rouse, spur,
stimulate, urge ♦ n **3** = **poke**, dig, jab,
nudge, push, shove **4** = **prompt**, cue,
reminder, signal, stimulus

prodigal adj = **extravagant**, excessive,
immoderate, improvident, profligate,
reckless, spendthrift, wasteful

prodigious adj **1** = **huge**, colossal,
enormous, giant, gigantic, immense,
massive, monstrous, vast **2** = **wonderful**,
amazing, exceptional, extraordinary,
fabulous, fantastic (inf), marvelous,
phenomenal, remarkable, staggering

prodigy n **1** = **genius**, mastermind, talent,
whizz (inf), wizard **2** = **wonder**, marvel,

miracle, phenomenon, sensation

produce v **1** = **cause**, bring about, effect,
generate, give rise to **2** = **bring forth**, bear,
beget, breed, deliver **3** = **show**, advance,
demonstrate, exhibit, offer, present **4** =
make, compose, construct, create,
develop, fabricate, invent, manufacture **5** =
present, direct, do, exhibit, mount, put
on, show, stage ♦ n **6** = **fruit and
vegetables**, crop, greengrocery, harvest,
product, yield

producer n **1** = **director**, impresario **2** =
maker, farmer, grower, manufacturer

product n **1** = **goods**, artefact, commodity,
creation, invention, merchandise, produce,
work **2** = **result**, consequence, effect,
outcome, upshot

production n **1** = **producing**, construction,
creation, fabrication, formation, making,
manufacture, manufacturing **2** =
presentation, direction, management,
staging

productive adj **1** = **fertile**, creative, fecund,
fruitful, inventive, plentiful, prolific, rich **2** =
useful, advantageous, beneficial,
constructive, effective, profitable,
rewarding, valuable, win-win (inf),
worthwhile

productivity n = **output**, production, work

antiabortion. **2** pro-life.
pro·fane [prə-FAYN] *adj* **1** irreverent,
blasphemous. **2** not sacred. ◆ *vt* **-faned,
-fan·ing 3** pollute, desecrate. **prof·a·na·tion**
[prof-ə-NAY-shən] *n* **pro·fan·i·ty**
[prə-FAN-i-tee] *n* profane talk or behavior,
blasphemy.
pro·fess [prə-FES] *vt* **1** affirm belief in. **2**
confess publicly. **3** assert. **4** claim, pretend.
pro·fess'ed·ly *adv* avowedly. **pro·fes·sion** *n*
1 calling or occupation, esp. learned,
scientific or artistic. **2** a professing. **3** vow
of religious faith on entering religious
order. **pro·fes·sion·al** *adj* **1** engaged in a
profession. **2** engaged in a game or sport
for money. ◆ *n* **3** member of profession. **4**
paid player. **pro·fes·sor** *n* teacher of
highest rank in college or university.
pro·fes·so·ri·al *adj*

proffer *vt, n* offer.
pro·fi·cient [prə-FISH-ənt] *adj* **1** skilled. **2**
expert. **pro·fi'cien·cy** *n*
pro·file [PROH-fil] *n* **1** outline, esp. of face,
as seen from side. **2** brief biographical
sketch.
prof·it *n* **1** money gained. **2** benefit
obtained. ◆ *v* **3** benefit. **prof·it·a·ble** *adj*
yielding profit. **prof·it·eer'** *n* **1** one who
makes excessive profits at the expense of
the public. ◆ *vi* **2** to do this.
prof·li·gate [PROF-li-git] *adj* **1** dissolute. **2**
reckless, wasteful. ◆ *n* **3** dissolute person.
prof'li·ga·cy [-li-gi-see] *n*
pro for·ma [proh FOR-mə] *Lat* **1**
prescribing a set form. **2** for the sake of
form.
pro·found [prə-FOWND] *adj* **-er, -est 1**
very learned. **2** deep. **pro·fun'di·ty** *n*

———— THESAURUS ————

rate, yield
profane *adj* **1 = sacrilegious**, disrespectful,
godless, impious, impure, irreligious,
irreverent, sinful, ungodly, wicked **2 =
crude**, blasphemous, coarse, filthy, foul,
obscene, vulgar ◆ *v* **3 = desecrate**, commit
sacrilege, debase, defile, violate
profanity *n* **1 = sacrilege**, blasphemy,
impiety, profaneness **2 = swearing**, curse,
cursing, irreverence, obscenity
profess *v* **1 = claim**, allege, fake, feign,
make out, pretend, purport **2 = state**,
admit, affirm, announce, assert, avow,
confess, declare, proclaim, vouch
professed *adj* **1 = supposed**, alleged,
ostensible, pretended, purported,
self-styled, so-called, would-be **2 =
declared**, avowed, confessed, confirmed,
proclaimed, self-acknowledged,
self-confessed
profession *n* **1 = occupation**, business,
calling, career, employment, office,
position, sphere, vocation **2 = declaration**,
affirmation, assertion, avowal, claim,
confession, statement
professional *adj* **1 = expert**, adept,
competent, efficient, experienced,
masterly, proficient, qualified, skilled ◆ *n*
2 = expert, adept, maestro, master, past
master, pro (*sl*), specialist, virtuoso
professor *n* **= teacher**, don (*Brit.*), fellow
(*Brit.*), prof (*inf*)
proficiency *n* **= skill**, ability, aptitude,
competence, dexterity, expertise, knack,
know-how (*inf*), mastery

proficient *adj* **= skilled**, able,
accomplished, adept, capable, competent,
efficient, expert, gifted, masterly, skillful
profile *n* **1 = outline**, contour, drawing,
figure, form, side view, silhouette, sketch
2 = biography, characterization, sketch,
thumbnail sketch, vignette
profit *n* **1** (often plural) **= earnings**, gain,
proceeds, receipts, return, revenue,
takings, yield **2 = benefit**, advancement,
advantage, gain, good, use, value ◆ *v* **3 =
benefit**, be of advantage to, gain, help,
improve, promote, serve **4 = make money**,
earn, gain
profitable *adj* **1 = money-making**,
commercial, cost-effective, fruitful,
lucrative, paying, remunerative,
worthwhile **2 = beneficial**, advantageous,
fruitful, productive, rewarding, useful,
valuable, win-win (*inf*), worthwhile
profiteer *n* **1 = racketeer**, exploiter ◆ *v* **2 =
racketeer**, exploit, make a quick buck (*sl*)
profligate *adj* **1 = extravagant**,
immoderate, improvident, prodigal,
reckless, spendthrift, wasteful **2 =
depraved**, debauched, degenerate,
dissolute, immoral, licentious, shameless,
wanton, wicked, wild ◆ *n* **3 = spendthrift**,
squanderer, waster, wastrel **4 =
degenerate**, debauchee, libertine, rake,
reprobate, roué
profound *adj* **1 = wise**, abstruse, deep,
learned, penetrating, philosophical,
sagacious, sage **2 = intense**, acute, deeply
felt, extreme, great, heartfelt, keen

pro·fuse [prə-FYOOS] *adj* abundant, prodigal. **pro·fu·sion** [-FYOO-zhən] *n*

prog·e·ny [PROJ-ə-nee] *n* children. **pro·gen·i·tor** [proh-JEN-i-tər] *n* ancestor.

pro·ges·ter·one [proh-JES-tə-rohn] *n* hormone that prepares uterus for pregnancy and prevents further ovulation.

prog·na·thous [prog-NAY-thəs] *adj* with projecting lower jaw.

prog·no·sis [prog-NOH-sis] *n, pl* **-ses** [-seez] **1** art of foretelling course of disease by symptoms. **2** forecast. **prog·nos·tic** *adj* **1** of, serving as prognosis. ◆ *n* **prog·nos·ti·cate** *vt* **-cat·ed, -cat·ing** foretell.

pro·gram [PROH-gram] *n* **1** plan, detailed notes of intended proceedings. **2** broadcast on radio or television. **3** detailed instructions for a computer. ◆ *vt* **-grammed, -gram·ming 4** feed program into (computer). **5** arrange detailed instructions for computer. **pro'gram·mer** *n*

prog'ress *n* **1** onward movement. **2** development. ◆ *vi* [prə-GRES] **3** go forward. **4** improve. **pro·gres·sion** *n* **1**

moving forward. **2** advance, improvement. **3** increase or decrease of numbers or magnitudes according to fixed law. **4** *Mus.* regular succession of chords. **pro·gres·sive** *adj* **1** progressing by degrees. **2** favoring political or social reform.

pro·hib·it [proh-HIB-it] *vt* forbid. **pro·hi·bi·tion** *n* **1** act of forbidding. **2** interdict. **3** interdiction of supply and consumption of alcoholic drinks. **pro·hib·i·tive** *adj* **1** tending to forbid or exclude. **2** (of prices) very high.

pro·ject [PROJ-ekt] *n* **1** plan, scheme. **2** design. ◆ *v* [prə-JEKT] *vt* **3** plan. **4** throw. **5** cause to appear on distant background. ◆ *vi* **6** stick out, protrude. **pro·jec·tile** [-JEK-til] *n* **1** heavy missile, esp. shell or ball. ◆ *adj* **2** for throwing. **pro·jec·tion** *n* **pro·jec·tion·ist** *n* operator of film projector. **pro·jec·tor** *n* **1** apparatus for projecting photographic images, films, slides on screen. **2** one that forms scheme or design.

pro·lapse [proh-LAPS] *n* **1** falling, slipping down of part of body from normal

——————— THESAURUS ———————

profuse *adj* = **plentiful**, abundant, ample, bountiful, copious, luxuriant, overflowing, prolific

profusion *n* = **abundance**, bounty, excess, extravagance, glut, plethora, quantity, surplus, wealth

progeny *n* = **children**, descendants, family, issue, lineage, offspring, posterity, race, stock, young

prognosis *n* = **forecast**, diagnosis, prediction, prognostication, projection

program *n* **1** = **schedule**, agenda, curriculum, line-up, list, listing, order of events, plan, syllabus, timetable **2** = **show**, broadcast, performance, presentation, production

progress *n* **1** = **development**, advance, breakthrough, gain, growth, headway, improvement **2** = **movement**, advance, course, passage, way **3 in progress** = **going on**, being done, happening, occurring, proceeding, taking place, under way ◆ *v* **4** = **develop**, advance, gain, grow, improve **5** = **move on**, advance, continue, go forward, make headway, proceed, travel

progression *n* **1** = **progress**, advance, advancement, furtherance, gain, headway, movement forward **2** = **sequence**, chain,

course, cycle, series, string, succession

progressive *adj* **1** = **enlightened**, advanced, avant-garde, forward-looking, liberal, modern, radical, reformist, revolutionary **2** = **growing**, advancing, continuing, developing, increasing, ongoing

prohibit *v* **1** = **forbid**, ban, debar, disallow, outlaw, proscribe, veto **2** = **prevent**, hamper, hinder, impede, restrict, stop

prohibition *n* **1** = **prevention**, constraint, exclusion, obstruction, restriction **2** = **ban**, bar, boycott, embargo, injunction, interdict, proscription, veto

prohibitive *adj* = **exorbitant**, excessive, extortionate, steep (*inf*)

project *n* **1** = **scheme** (*inf*), activity, assignment, enterprise, job, occupation, plan, task, undertaking, venture, work ◆ *v* **2** = **forecast**, calculate, estimate, extrapolate, gauge, predict, reckon **3** = **stick out**, bulge, extend, jut, overhang, protrude, stand out

projectile *n* = **missile**, bullet, rocket, shell

projection *n* **1** = **protrusion**, bulge, ledge, overhang, protuberance, ridge, shelf **2** = **forecast**, calculation, computation, estimate, estimation, extrapolation, reckoning

position. ◆ *vi* **2** fall or slip down in this way.
pro·le·tar·i·at [proh-li-TAIR-ee-ət] *n* lowest class of community, working class. **pro·le·tar'i·an** *adj, n*
pro-life *adj* see PROFAMILY.
pro·lif·er·ate [prə-LIF-ə-rayt] *v* **-at·ed, -at·ing** grow or reproduce rapidly. **pro·lif·er·a'tion** *n*
pro·lif·ic [prə-LIF-ik] *adj* **1** fruitful. **2** producing offspring.
pro·lix [proh-LIKS] *adj* wordy, long-winded. **pro·lix'i·ty** *n*
pro·logue [PROH-lawg] *n* preface, esp. speech before a play.
pro·long [prə-LAWNG] *vt* **1** lengthen. **2** protract.
prom *n* school or college dance, esp. at end of school year.
prom·e·nade [prom-ə-NAYD] *n* **1** leisurely walk. **2** place made or used for this. ◆ *vi* **-nad·ed, -nad·ing 3** take leisurely walk. **4** go up and down.
prom·i·nent [PROM-ə-nənt] *adj* **1** sticking

out. **2** conspicuous. **3** distinguished. **prom'i·nence** *n*
pro·mis·cu·ous [prə-MIS-kyoo-əs] *adj* **1** indiscriminate, esp. in sexual relations. **2** mixed without distinction. **prom·is·cu'i·ty** [-KYOO-ə-tee] *n*
prom·ise [PROM-is] *v* **-mised, -mis·ing** ◆ *vt* **1** give assurance. ◆ *vi* **2** be likely to. ◆ *n* **3** undertaking to do or not to do something. **4** potential. **prom'is·ing** *adj* showing good signs, hopeful. **prom'is·so·ry** *adj* containing promise. **promissory note** written promise to pay sum to person named, at specified time.
prom·on·to·ry [PROM-ən-tor-ee] *n, pl* **-ries** point of high land jutting out into the sea, headland.
pro·mote [prə-MOHT] *vt* **-mot·ed, -mot·ing 1** help forward. **2** move up to higher rank or position. **3** work for. **4** encourage sale of. **pro·mot'er** *n* **pro·mo'tion** *n* **1** advancement. **2** preferment.

proletarian *adj* **1** = **working-class**, common, plebeian ◆ *n* **2** = **worker**, commoner, man of the people, pleb, plebeian
proletariat *n* = **working class**, commoners, hoi polloi, laboring classes, lower classes, plebs, the common people, the masses
proliferate *v* = **increase**, breed, expand, grow rapidly, multiply
proliferation *n* = **multiplication**, expansion, increase, spread
prolific *adj* = **productive**, abundant, copious, fecund, fertile, fruitful, luxuriant, profuse
prologue *n* = **introduction**, foreword, preamble, preface, preliminary, prelude
prolong *v* = **lengthen**, continue, delay, drag out, draw out, extend, perpetuate, protract, spin out, stretch
promenade *n* **1** = **walkway**, esplanade, parade, prom **2** = **stroll**, constitutional, saunter, turn, walk ◆ *v* **3** = **stroll**, perambulate, saunter, take a walk, walk
prominence *n* **1** = **conspicuousness**, markedness **2** = **fame**, celebrity, distinction, eminence, importance, name, prestige, reputation
prominent *adj* **1** = **noticeable**, conspicuous, eye-catching, obtrusive, obvious, outstanding, pronounced **2** =

famous, distinguished, eminent, foremost, important, leading, main, notable, renowned, top, well-known
promiscuity *n* = **licentiousness**, debauchery, immorality, looseness, permissiveness, promiscuousness, wantonness
promiscuous *adj* = **licentious**, abandoned, debauched, fast, immoral, libertine, loose, wanton, wild
promise *v* **1** = **guarantee**, assure, contract, give an undertaking, give one's word, pledge, swear, take an oath, undertake, vow, warrant **2** = **seem likely**, augur, betoken, indicate, look like, show signs of, suggest ◆ *n* **3** = **guarantee**, assurance, bond, commitment, oath, pledge, undertaking, vow, word **4** = **potential**, ability, aptitude, capability, capacity, flair, talent
promising *adj* **1** = **encouraging**, auspicious, bright, favorable, hopeful, likely, propitious, reassuring, rosy **2** = **talented**, able, gifted, rising
promontory *n* = **point**, cape, foreland, head, headland
promote *v* **1** = **help**, advance, aid, assist, back, boost, encourage, forward, foster, support **2** = **raise**, elevate, exalt, upgrade **3** = **advertise**, hype, plug (*inf*), publicize, push, sell

prompt adj **-er, -est 1** done at once. **2** acting with alacrity. **3** punctual. **4** ready. ◆ v **5** urge, suggest. **6** help out (actor or speaker) by reading or suggesting next words. **prompt'er** n **prompt'ness** [-nis] n **prompt'ly** adv

prom·ul·gate [PROM-əl-gayt] vt **-gat·ed, -gat·ing** proclaim, publish. **prom·ul·ga'tion** n

prone [prohn] adj **1** lying face or front downward. **2** inclined (to). **prone'ness** [-nis] n

prong n one tine of fork or similar instrument.

pro·noun [PROH-nown] n word used to replace noun. **pro·nom'i·nal** adj pert. to, like pronoun.

pro·nounce [prə-NOWNS] v **-nounced, -nounc·ing** ◆ vt **1** utter formally. **2** form with organs of speech. **3** speak distinctly. **4** declare. ◆ vi **5** give opinion or decision. **pro·nounce'able** adj **pro·nounced'** adj strongly marked, decided. **pro·nounce'ment** n declaration. **pro·nun·ci·a'tion** n **1** way word, etc. is pronounced. **2** articulation.

pron·to [PRON-toh] adv inf at once, immediately, quickly.

proof n **1** evidence. **2** thing that proves. **3** test, demonstration. **4** trial impression from type or engraved plate. **5** Photography print from a negative. **6** standard of strength of alcoholic drink. ◆ adj **7** giving impenetrable defense against. **8** of proven strength. **proof'read** [-reed] v **-read, -read·ing** read and correct proofs. **proof'read·er** n

prop[1] vt **propped, prop·ping 1** support, sustain, hold up. ◆ n **2** pole, beam, etc. **3** used as support.

prop[2] n short for PROPELLER.

prop[3] n short for (THEATRICAL) PROPERTY.

prop·a·gan·da [prop-ə-GAN-də] n organized dissemination of information to assist or damage political cause, etc. **prop·a·gan'dist** n **prop·a·gan'dize** [-dīz] vt **-dized, -diz·ing**

prop·a·gate [prop-ə-gayt] v **-gat·ed, -gat·ing** ◆ vt **1** reproduce, breed, spread by sowing, breeding, etc. **2** transmit. ◆ vi **3** breed, multiply. **prop·a·ga'tion** n

pro·pane [PROH-payn] n colorless,

promotion n **1** = **rise**, advancement, elevation, exaltation, honor, move up, preferment, upgrading **2** = **publicity**, advertising, plugging (inf) **3** = **encouragement**, advancement, boosting, furtherance, support

prompt v **1** = **cause**, elicit, give rise to, occasion, provoke **2** = **remind**, assist, cue, help out ◆ adj **3** = **immediate**, early, instant, quick, rapid, speedy, swift, timely ◆ adv **4** Inf = **exactly**, on the dot, promptly, punctually, sharp

promptly adv = **immediately**, at once, directly, on the dot, on time, punctually, quickly, speedily, swiftly

promptness n = **swiftness**, briskness, eagerness, haste, punctuality, quickness, speed, willingness

promulgate v = **make known**, broadcast, circulate, communicate, disseminate, make public, proclaim, promote, publish, spread

prone adj **1** = **liable**, apt, bent, disposed, given, inclined, likely, predisposed, subject, susceptible, tending **2** = **face down**, flat, horizontal, prostrate, recumbent

prong n = **point**, spike, tine

pronounce v **1** = **say**, accent, articulate,

enunciate, sound, speak **2** = **declare**, affirm, announce, decree, deliver, proclaim

pronounced adj = **noticeable**, conspicuous, decided, definite, distinct, evident, marked, obvious, striking

pronouncement n = **announcement**, declaration, decree, dictum, edict, judgment, proclamation, statement

pronunciation n = **intonation**, accent, articulation, diction, enunciation, inflection, speech, stress

proof n **1** = **evidence**, authentication, confirmation, corroboration, demonstration, substantiation, testimony, verification ◆ adj **2** = **impervious**, impenetrable, repellent, resistant, strong

prop v **1** = **support**, bolster, brace, buttress, hold up, stay, sustain, uphold ◆ n **2** = **support**, brace, buttress, mainstay, stanchion, stay

propaganda n = **information**, advertising, disinformation, hype, promotion, publicity

propagate v **1** = **spread**, broadcast, circulate, disseminate, promote, promulgate, publish, transmit **2** = **reproduce**, beget, breed, engender, generate, increase, multiply, procreate, produce flammable gas from petroleum.

pro•pel [prə-PEL] *vt* **-pelled, -pel•ling** cause to move forward. **pro•pel'lant, -lent** *n* something causing propulsion, such as rocket fuel. **pro•pel'ler** *n* revolving shaft with blades for driving ship or aircraft. **pro•pul'sion** *n* act of, means of, driving forward. **pro•pul'sive, pro•pul'so•ry** *adj* 1 tending, having power to propel. 2 urging on.

pro•pen•si•ty [prə-PEN-si-tee] *n, pl* **-ties** 1 inclination or bent. 2 tendency. 3 disposition.

prop•er [PROP-ər] *adj* 1 appropriate. 2 correct. 3 conforming to etiquette, decorous. 4 strict. 5 (of noun) denoting individual person or place.

prop•er•ty [PROP-ər-tee] *n, pl* **-ties** 1 that which is owned. 2 estate whether in lands, goods, or money. 3 quality, attribute of something. 4 article used on stage in play, etc.

proph•et [PROF-it] *n* 1 inspired teacher or revealer of divine will. 2 foreteller of future. **proph'e•cy** [-ə-see] *n, pl* **-cies** prediction, prophetic utterance. **proph'e•sy** [-ə-sī] *v* **-sied, -sy•ing** 1 foretell, predict. 2 make predictions. **pro•phet'ic** *adj*

pro•phet'i•cal•ly *adv*

pro•phy•lac•tic [prof-ə-LAK-tik] *n, adj* 1 (something) done or used to ward off disease. 2 condom. **pro•phy•lax'is** *n*

pro•pin•qui•ty [proh-PING-kwi-tee] *n* nearness, proximity, close kinship.

pro•pi•ti•ate [prə-PISH-ee-ayt] *vt* **-at•ed, -at•ing** appease, gain favor of. **pro•pi'ti•a•to•ry** *adj* **pro•pi'tious** *adj* favorable, auspicious.

pro•po•nent [prə-POH-nənt] *n* one who advocates something.

pro•por•tion [prə-POR-shən] *n* 1 relative size or number. 2 comparison. 3 due relation between connected things or parts. 4 share. 5 relation. ◆ *pl* 6 dimensions. ◆ *vt* 7 arrange proportions of. **pro•por'tion•al, pro•por'tion•ate** *adj* 1 having a due proportion. 2 corresponding in size, number, etc. **pro•por'tion•al•ly** *adv*

pro•pose [prə-POHZ] *v* **-posed, -pos•ing** ◆ *vt* 1 put forward for consideration. 2 nominate. 3 intend. ◆ *vi* 4 offer marriage. **pro•pos'al** *n* **prop•o•si'tion** *n* 1 offer. 2 statement, assertion. 3 theorem. 4 suggestion of terms. 5 thing to be dealt with. 6 proposal of illicit sexual relations.

pro•pound [prə-POWND] *vt* put forward

———————— THESAURUS ————————

propel *v* = drive, force, impel, launch, push, send, shoot, shove, thrust

propensity *n* = tendency, bent, disposition, inclination, liability, penchant, predisposition, proclivity

proper *adj* 1 = suitable, appropriate, apt, becoming, befitting, fit, fitting, right 2 = correct, accepted, conventional, established, formal, orthodox, precise, right 3 = polite, decent, decorous, genteel, gentlemanly, ladylike, mannerly, respectable, seemly

properly *adv* 1 = suitably, appropriately, aptly, fittingly, rightly 2 = correctly, accurately 3 = politely, decently, respectably

property *n* 1 = possessions, assets, belongings, capital, effects, estate, goods, holdings, riches, wealth 2 = land, estate, freehold, holding, real estate 3 = quality, attribute, characteristic, feature, hallmark, trait

prophecy *n* = prediction, augury, divination, forecast, prognostication, second sight, soothsaying

prophesy *v* = predict, augur, divine,

forecast, foresee, foretell, prognosticate

prophet *n* = soothsayer, diviner, forecaster, oracle, prophesier, seer, sibyl

prophetic *adj* = predictive, oracular, prescient, prognostic, sibylline

propitious *adj* = favorable, auspicious, bright, encouraging, fortunate, happy, lucky, promising

proportion *n* 1 = relative amount, ratio, relationship 2 = balance, congruity, correspondence, harmony, symmetry 3 = part, amount, division, fraction, percentage, quota, segment, share 4 proportions = dimensions, capacity, expanse, extent, size, volume

proportional, proportionate *adj* = balanced, commensurate, compatible, consistent, corresponding, equitable, even, in proportion

proposal *n* = suggestion, bid, offer, plan, presentation, program, project, recommendation, scheme

propose *v* 1 = put forward, advance, present, submit, suggest 2 = nominate, name, present, recommend 3 = intend, aim, design, have in mind, mean, plan, for consideration or solution.

pro·pri·e·tor [prə-PRĪ-i-tər] *n* owner.
pro·pri'e·tar·y [-ter-ee] *adj* **1** belonging to owner. **2** made by firm with exclusive rights of manufacture.

pro·pri·e·ty [prə-PRĪ-i-tee] *n, pl* **-ties** properness, correct conduct, fitness.

propulsion see PROPEL.

pro ra·ta [proh RAY-tə] *Lat* in proportion

pro·sa·ic [proh-ZAY-ik] *adj* commonplace, unromantic.

pro·sce·ni·um [proh-SEE-nee-əm] *n, pl* **-ni·a** [-nee-ə] arch or opening framing stage.

pro·scribe [proh-SKRĪB] *vt* **-scribed, -scrib·ing** outlaw, condemn. **pro·scrip'tion** *n*

prose [prohz] *n* speech or writing not verse. **pros'y** *adj* **pros·i·er, pros·i·est** tedious, dull.

pros·e·cute [PROS-i-kyoot] *vt* **-cut·ed, -cut·ing** carry on, bring legal proceedings against. **pros·e·cu'tion** *n* **pros'e·cu·tor** *n*

pros·e·lyte [PROS-ə-līt] *n* convert. **pros'e·lyt·ize** [li-tīz] *vt* **-ized, -iz·ing**

pros·o·dy [PROS-ə-dee] *n* system, study of

versification. **pros'o·dist** *n*

pros·pect [PROS-pekt] *n* **1** expectation, chance for success. **2** view, outlook. **3** likely customer or subscriber. **4** mental view. ♦ *v* **5** explore, esp. for gold. **pro·spec'tive** *adj* **1** anticipated. **2** future. **pro·spec'tor** *n*

pro·spec·tus [prə-SPEK-təs] *n, pl* **-tus·es** document describing company, school, etc.

pros·per [PROS-pər] *vi* do well.
pros·per'i·ty *n, pl* **-ties** good fortune, well-being. **pros'per·ous** *adj* **1** doing well, successful. **2** flourishing, rich, well-off.

pros·tate [PROS-tayt] *n* gland accessory to male generative organs.

pros·the·sis [pros-THEE-sis] *n, pl* **-ses** [-seez] (replacement of part of body with) artificial substitute.

pros·ti·tute [PROS-ti-toot] *n* **1** one who offers sexual intercourse in return for payment. ♦ *vt* **-tut·ed, -tut·ing 2** make a prostitute of. **3** put to unworthy use.
pros·ti·tu'tion *n*

pros·trate [PROS-trayt] *adj* **1** lying flat. **2** crushed, submissive, overcome. ♦ *vt* **-trat·ed, -trat·ing 3** throw flat on ground. **4**

——————| THESAURUS |——————

scheme **4 = offer marriage**, ask for someone's hand (in marriage), pop the question (*inf*)

proposition *n* **1 = proposal**, plan, recommendation, scheme, suggestion ♦ *v* **2 = make a pass at**, accost, make an improper suggestion, solicit

propound *v* **= put forward**, advance, postulate, present, propose, submit, suggest

proprietor, proprietress *n* **= owner**, landlord *or* landlady, titleholder

propriety *n* **1 = correctness**, aptness, fitness, rightness, seemliness **2 = decorum**, courtesy, decency, etiquette, manners, politeness, respectability, seemliness

propulsion *n* **= drive**, impetus, impulse, propelling force, push, thrust

prosaic *adj* **= dull**, boring, everyday, humdrum, matter-of-fact, mundane, ordinary, pedestrian, routine, trite, unimaginative

proscribe *v* **1 = prohibit**, ban, embargo, forbid, interdict **2 = outlaw**, banish, deport, exclude, exile, expatriate, expel, ostracize

prosecute *v Law* **= put on trial**, arraign, bring to trial, indict, litigate, sue, take to

court, try

prospect *n* **1 = expectation**, anticipation, future, hope, odds, outlook, probability, promise **2** (sometimes plural) **= likelihood**, chance, possibility **3 = view**, landscape, outlook, scene, sight, spectacle, vista ♦ *v* **4 = look for**, search for, seek

prospective *adj* **= future**, anticipated, coming, destined, expected, forthcoming, imminent, intended, likely, possible, potential

prospectus *n* **= catalog**, list, outline, program, syllabus, synopsis

prosper *v* **= succeed**, advance, do well, flourish, get on, progress, thrive

prosperity *n* **= success**, affluence, fortune, good fortune, luxury, plenty, prosperousness, riches, wealth

prosperous *adj* **1 = wealthy**, affluent, moneyed, rich, well-heeled (*inf*), well-off, well-to-do **2 = successful**, booming, doing well, flourishing, fortunate, lucky, thriving

prostitute *n* **1 = whore**, call girl, fallen woman, harlot, ho (*sl*), hooker (*sl*), loose woman, streetwalker, strumpet, tart (*inf*), trollop ♦ *v* **2 = cheapen**, debase, degrade, demean, devalue, misapply, pervert, profane reduce to exhaustion. **pros·tra'tion** *n*

pro·tag·o·nist [proh-TAG-ə-nist] *n* **1** leading character. **2** principal actor. **3** champion of a cause.

pro·te·an [PROH-tee-ən] *adj* **1** variable. **2** versatile.

pro·tect [prə-TEKT] *vt* defend, guard, keep from harm. **pro·tec'tion** *n* **pro·tec'tion·ist** *n* one who advocates protecting industries by taxing competing imports. **pro·tec'tive** *adj* **pro·tec'tor** *n* **1** one who protects. **2** regent. **pro·tec'tor·ate** [-tər-it] *n* **1** relation of country to territory it protects and controls. **2** such territory. **3** office, period of protector of a country.

pro·té·gé [PROH-tə-zhay] *n* one under another's care, protection or patronage. **pro·té·gée** *n, fem.*

pro·tein [PROH-teen] *n* any of kinds of organic compounds that form most essential part of food of living creatures.

pro·test [PROH-test] *n* **1** declaration or demonstration of objection. ◆ *vi* [prə-TEST] **2** object. **3** make declaration against. **4** assert formally. **prot·es·ta·tion** [prot-ə-STAY-shən] *n* strong declaration.

Prot·es·tant [PROT-ə-stənt] *adj* **1** belonging to any branch of the Western Christian Church outside the Roman

Catholic Church. ◆ *n* **2** member of such church. **Prot'es·tant·ism** *n*

proto-, prot- *comb. form* first, e.g. *prototype.*

pro·to·col [PROH-tə-kawl] *n* **1** diplomatic etiquette. **2** draft of terms signed by parties as basis of formal treaty. **3** *Computers.* standardized format for exchanging data, esp. between different computer systems.

pro·ton [PROH-ton] *n* positively charged particle in nucleus of atom.

pro·to·plasm [PROH-tə-plaz-əm] *n* substance that is living matter of all animal and plant cells.

pro·to·type [PROH-tə-tīp] *n* **1** original, or model, after which thing is copied. **2** pattern.

pro·to·zo·an [proh-tə-ZOH-ən] *n* minute animal of lowest and simplest class.

pro·tract [proh-TRAKT] *vt* **1** lengthen. **2** prolong. **3** delay. **4** draw to scale. **pro·tract'ed** *adj* **1** long drawn out. **2** tedious. **pro·trac'tor** *n* instrument for measuring angles on paper.

pro·trude [proh-TROOD] *v* **-trud·ed, -trud·ing** stick out, project. **pro·tru'sion** [-*zh*ən] *n* **pro·tru'sive** [-siv] *adj* thrusting forward.

———————— | THESAURUS | ————————

prostrate *adj* **1 = prone**, flat, horizontal **2 = exhausted**, dejected, depressed, desolate, drained, inconsolable, overcome, spent, worn out ◆ *v* **3 = exhaust**, drain, fatigue, sap, tire, wear out, weary **4 prostrate oneself = bow down to**, abase oneself, fall at (someone's) feet, grovel, kiss ass (*sl*), kneel, kowtow

protagonist *n* **1 = supporter**, advocate, champion, exponent **2 = leading character**, central character, hero *or* heroine, principal

protect *v* **= keep safe**, defend, guard, look after, preserve, safeguard, save, screen, shelter, shield, stick up for (*inf*), support, watch over

protection *n* **1 = safety**, aegis, care, custody, defense, protecting, safeguard, safekeeping, security **2 = safeguard**, barrier, buffer, cover, guard, screen, shelter, shield

protective *adj* **= protecting**, defensive, fatherly, maternal, motherly, paternal, vigilant, watchful

protector *n* **= defender**, bodyguard,

champion, guard, guardian, patron

protest *n* **1 = objection**, complaint, dissent, outcry, protestation, remonstrance ◆ *v* **2 = object**, complain, cry out, demonstrate, demur, disagree, disapprove, express disapproval, oppose, remonstrate **3 = assert**, affirm, attest, avow, declare, insist, maintain, profess

protestation *n* **= declaration**, affirmation, avowal, profession, vow

protester *n* **= demonstrator**, agitator, rebel

protocol *n* **= code of behavior**, conventions, customs, decorum, etiquette, manners, propriety

prototype *n* **= original**, example, first, model, pattern, standard, type

protracted *adj* **= extended**, dragged out, drawn-out, long-drawn-out, prolonged, spun out

protrude *v* **= stick out**, bulge, come through, extend, jut, obtrude, project, stand out

protrusion *n* **= projection**, bulge, bump, lump, outgrowth, protuberance

pro·tu·ber·ant [proh-TOO-bər-ənt] *adj* bulging out. **pro·tu'ber·ance** [-əns] *n* bulge, swelling.

proud [prowd] *adj* **-er, -est 1** feeling or displaying pride. **2** arrogant. **3** gratified. **4** noble. **5** self-respecting. **6** stately. **proud'ly** *adv* **proud flesh** flesh growing around healing wound.

Prov. Proverbs.

prove [proov] *v* **proved** or **prov·en, prov·ing ◆** *vt* **1** establish validity of. **2** demonstrate, test. **◆** *vi* **3** turn out (to be, etc.). **4** (of dough) rise in warm place before baking. **proven** *adj* proved.

prov·e·nance [PROV-ə-nəns] *n* place of origin, source.

prov·en·der [PROV-ən-dər] *n* fodder.

prov·erb [PROV-ərb] *n* short, pithy, traditional saying in common use. **pro·ver'bi·al** [prə-VUR-bee-əl] *adj*

pro·vide [prə-VĪD] *v* **-vid·ed, -vid·ing ◆** *vi* **1** make preparation. **◆** *vt* **2** supply, equip, prepare, furnish, give. **pro·vid'er** *n* **1** provided that. **2** on condition that.

prov·i·dent [PROV-i-dənt] *adj* **1** thrifty. **2** showing foresight. **prov'i·dence** *n* **1** kindly care of God or nature. **2** foresight. **3** economy. **prov·i·den'tial** [-DEN-shəl] *adj* strikingly fortunate, lucky.

prov·ince [PROV-əns] *n* **1** division of a country, district. **2** sphere of action. **◆** *pl* **3** any part of country outside capital or largest cities. **pro·vin'cial** [prə-VIN-shəl] *adj* **1** of a province. **2** unsophisticated. **3** narrow in outlook. **◆** *n* **4** unsophisticated person. **5** inhabitant of province. **pro·vin'cial·ism** *n* **1** narrowness of outlook. **2** lack of refinement. **3** idiom peculiar to district.

pro·vi·sion [prə-VIZH-ən] *n* **1** a providing, esp. for the future. **2** thing provided. **3** *Law* article of instrument or statute. **◆** *pl* **4** food. **◆** *vt* **5** supply with food. **pro·vi'sion·al** *adj* **1** temporary. **2** conditional.

THESAURUS

protuberance *n* = **bulge**, bump, excrescence, hump, knob, lump, outgrowth, process, prominence, protrusion, swelling

proud *adj* **1** = **satisfied**, content, glad, gratified, pleased, well-pleased **2** = **conceited**, arrogant, boastful, disdainful, haughty, imperious, lordly, overbearing, self-satisfied, snobbish, supercilious

prove *v* **1** = **verify**, authenticate, confirm, demonstrate, determine, establish, justify, show, substantiate **2** = **test**, analyze, assay, check, examine, try **3** = **turn out**, come out, end up, result

proven *adj* = **established**, attested, confirmed, definite, proved, reliable, tested, verified

proverb *n* = **saying**, adage, dictum, maxim, saw

proverbial *adj* = **conventional**, acknowledged, axiomatic, current, famed, famous, legendary, notorious, traditional, typical, well-known

provide *v* **1** = **supply**, cater, equip, furnish, outfit, purvey, stock up **2** = **give**, add, afford, bring, impart, lend, present, produce, render, serve, yield **3 provide for** or **against** = **take precautions**, anticipate, forearm, plan ahead, plan for, prepare for **4 provide for** = **support**, care for, keep, maintain, sustain, take care of

providence *n* = **fate**, destiny, fortune

provident *adj* **1** = **thrifty**, economical, frugal, prudent **2** = **foresighted**, careful, cautious, discreet, far-seeing, forearmed, shrewd, vigilant, well-prepared, wise

providential *adj* = **lucky**, fortuitous, fortunate, happy, heaven-sent, opportune, timely

provider *n* **1** = **supplier**, donor, giver, source **2** = **breadwinner**, earner, supporter, wage earner

providing, provided *conj* = **on condition that**, as long as, given

province *n* **1** = **region**, colony, department, district, division, domain, patch, section, zone **2** = **area**, business, capacity, concern, duty, field, function, line, responsibility, role, sphere

provincial *adj* **1** = **rural**, country, hick (*inf*), homespun, local, rustic **2** = **narrow-minded**, insular, inward-looking, limited, narrow, parochial, small-minded, small-town, unsophisticated **◆** *n* **3** = **yokel**, country cousin, hayseed, hick (*inf*), rustic

provision *n* **1** = **supplying**, catering, equipping, furnishing, providing **2** = **condition**, clause, demand, proviso, requirement, rider, stipulation, term

provisional *adj* **1** = **temporary**, interim **2** = **conditional**, contingent, limited, qualified, tentative

provisions *pl n* = **food**, comestibles, eatables, edibles, fare, foodstuff, rations,

pro·vi·so [prə-VĪ-zoh] *n, pl* **-sos** *or* **-soes** condition.

pro·vo·ca·teur [prə-vok-ə-TUR] *n* **1** one who causes dissension, makes trouble. **2** agitator. **3** see AGENT PROVOCATEUR.

pro·voke [prə-VOHK] *vt* **-voked, -vok·ing 1** irritate. **2** incense. **3** arouse. **4** excite. **5** cause. **prov·o·ca·tion** [-ə-KAY-shən] *n* **pro·voc·a·tive** [-VOK-ə-tiv] *adj*

pro·vost [PROH-vohst] *n* **1** one who superintends or presides. **2** high administrative officer of university. **provost marshal** head of military police.

prow [rhymes with **cow**] *n* bow of vessel.

prow·ess [PROW-is] *n* **1** skill. **2** bravery, fighting capacity.

prowl *vi* roam stealthily, esp. in search of prey or booty. ◆ *n* **prowl·er** *n* **on the prowl 1** searching stealthily. **2** seeking sexual partner.

prox·i·mate [PROK-sə-mit] *adj* nearest, next, immediate. **prox·im'i·ty** *n*

prox·y [PROK-see] *n, pl* **prox·ies 1** authorized agent or substitute. **2** writing authorizing one to act as this.

prude [prood] *n* one who affects excessive modesty or propriety. **prud'er·y** *n, pl* **-er·ies prud'ish** *adj*

pru·dent [PROOD-nt] *adj* **1** careful, discreet. **2** sensible. **pru'dence** *n* **1** habit of acting with careful deliberation. **2** wisdom applied to practice. **pru·den'tial** *adj*

prune¹ [proon] *n* dried plum.

prune² *vt* **pruned, prun·ing 1** cut out dead parts, excessive branches, etc. **2** shorten, reduce.

pru·ri·ent [PRUUR-ee-ənt] *adj* **1** given to, springing from lewd thoughts. **2** having unhealthy curiosity or desire. **pru'ri·ence** *n*

pry [prī] *vi* **pried, pry·ing 1** make furtive or impertinent inquiries. **2** look curiously. **3** force open.

Ps. Psalm(s).

psalm [sahm] *n* **1** sacred song. **2** (P-) any of the sacred songs making up the Book of Psalms in the Bible. **psalm'ist** *n* writer of psalms. **psal·mo·dy** [SAHM-ə-dee] *n* art, act of singing sacred music. **psal·ter** [SAWL-tər] *n* **1** book of psalms. **2** (P-) copy of the Psalms as separate book. **psal'ter·y** [-tə-ree] *n, pl* **-ter·ies** obsolete stringed instrument like lyre.

pseu·do [SOO-doh] *adj* sham, fake.

pseudo- *comb. form* false, sham, e.g. *pseudo-Gothic; pseudoscience.*

pseu·do·nym [SOOD-n-im] *n* **1** false, fictitious name. **2** pen name.

psit·ta·co·sis [sit-ə-KOH-sis] *n* dangerous

THESAURUS

stores, supplies, victuals

proviso *n* = **condition**, clause, qualification, requirement, rider, stipulation

provocation *n* **1** = **cause**, grounds, incitement, motivation, reason, stimulus **2** = **offense**, affront, annoyance, challenge, dare, grievance, indignity, injury, insult, taunt

provocative *adj* = **offensive**, annoying, galling, goading, insulting, provoking, stimulating

provoke *v* **1** = **anger**, aggravate (*inf*), annoy, enrage, hassle (*inf*), incense, infuriate, irk, irritate, madden, rile **2** = **cause**, bring about, elicit, evoke, incite, induce, occasion, produce, promote, prompt, rouse, stir

prowess *n* **1** = **skill**, accomplishment, adeptness, aptitude, excellence, expertise, genius, mastery, talent **2** = **bravery**, courage, daring, fearlessness, heroism, mettle, valiance, valor

prowl *v* = **move stealthily**, skulk, slink, sneak, stalk, steal

proximity *n* = **nearness**, closeness

proxy *n* = **representative**, agent, delegate, deputy, factor, substitute

prudence *n* = **common sense**, care, caution, discretion, good sense, judgment, vigilance, wariness, wisdom

prudent *adj* **1** = **sensible**, careful, cautious, discerning, discreet, judicious, politic, shrewd, vigilant, wary, wise **2** = **thrifty**, canny, careful, economical, far-sighted, frugal, provident, sparing

prudish *adj* = **prim**, old-maidish (*inf*), overmodest, priggish, prissy (*inf*), proper, puritanical, starchy (*inf*), strait-laced, stuffy, Victorian

prune *v* = **cut**, clip, dock, reduce, shape, shorten, snip, trim

pry *v* = **be inquisitive**, be nosy (*inf*), interfere, intrude, meddle, poke, snoop (*inf*)

prying *adj* = **inquisitive**, curious, interfering, meddlesome, meddling, nosy (*inf*), snooping (*inf*), spying

psalm *n* = **hymn**, chant

pseudo- *adj* = **false**, artificial, fake, imitation, mock, phoney *or* phony (*inf*), infectious disease, germ of which is carried by parrots.

psy·che [SĪ-kee] *n* human mind or soul.

psych·e·del·ic [sī-ki-DEL-ik] *adj* **1** of or causing hallucinations. **2** like intense colors, etc. experienced during hallucinations.

psy·chic [SĪ-kik] *adj* **1** sensitive to phenomena lying outside range of normal experience. **2** of soul or mind. **3** that appears to be outside region of physical law. **psy·chi·a·try** [si-KĪ-ə-tree] *n* medical treatment of mental diseases. **psy·chi·a·trist** *n* **psy·cho·a·nal'y·sis** [sī-koh-] *n* method of studying and treating mental disorders. **psy·cho·an'a·lyst** *n* **psy·cho·log·i·cal** [sī-kə-LOJ-i-kəl] *adj* **1** of psychology. **2** of the mind. **psy·chol'o·gist** *n* **psy·chol'o·gy** *n* **1** study of mind. **2** person's mental makeup. **psy·chom'e·try** *n* **1** measurement, testing of psychological processes. **2** supposed ability to divine unknown persons' qualities by handling object used or worn by them. **psy'cho·path** *n* person afflicted with severe mental disorder causing him or her to commit antisocial, often violent acts. **psy·cho·path'ic** *adj* **psy·cho'sis** *n, pl* **-ses** [-seez] severe mental disorder in which person's contact with reality becomes distorted. **psy·cho'tic** *adj, n* **psy·cho·so·mat'ic** [-sə-MAT-ik] *adj* of physical disorders thought to have

psychological causes. **psy·cho·ther'a·py** *n* treatment of disease by psychological, not physical, means.

psych up [sīk] *vt* prepare (oneself or another) psychologically for action, performance, etc.

Pt *Chem.* platinum.

ptar·mi·gan [TAHR-mi-gən] *n* bird of grouse family that turns white in winter.

PT boat small, fast naval vessel used primarily for torpedoing enemy shipping.

pter·o·dac·tyl [ter-ə-DAK-til] *n* extinct flying reptile with large batlike wings.

pto·maine [TOH-mayn] *n* any of kinds of poisonous alkaloid found in decaying matter.

Pu *Chem.* plutonium.

pu·ber·ty [PYOO-bər-tee] *n* sexual maturity.

pubic [PYOO-bik] *adj* of the lower abdomen.

pub·lic [PUB-lik] *adj* **1** of or concerning the public as a whole. **2** not private. **3** open to general observation or knowledge. **4** accessible to all. **5** serving the people. ◆ *n* **6** the community or its members. **pub'lic·ly** *adv* **1** public relations. **2** promotion of good relations of an organization or business with the general public. **public school** local elementary school. **public service** government employment. **public spirit** interest in and devotion to welfare of community.

pub·li·cist [PUB-lə-sist] *n* **1** press agent. **2**

——————| THESAURUS |——————

pretended, sham, spurious

pseudonym *n* = **false name**, alias, assumed name, incognito, nom de plume, pen name

psyche *n* = **soul**, anima, individuality, mind, personality, self, spirit

psychiatrist *n* = **psychotherapist**, analyst, headshrinker (*sl*), psychoanalyst, psychologist, shrink (*sl*), therapist

psychic *adj* **1** = **supernatural**, mystic, occult **2** = **mental**, psychological, spiritual

psychological *adj* **1** = **mental**, cerebral, intellectual **2** = **imaginary**, all in the mind, irrational, psychosomatic, unreal

psychology *n* **1** = **behaviorism**, science of mind, study of personality **2** = **way of thinking**, attitude, mental make-up, mental processes, thought processes, what makes one tick

psychopath *n* = **madman**, headcase (*inf*),

lunatic, maniac, nutcase (*sl*), psychotic, sociopath

psychotic *adj* = **mad**, certifiable, demented, deranged, insane, loony (*inf*), lunatic, *non compos mentis*, unbalanced

puberty *n* = **adolescence**, pubescence, teens

public *adj* **1** = **general**, civic, common, national, popular, social, state, universal, widespread **2** = **communal**, accessible, open, unrestricted **3** = **well-known**, important, prominent, respected **4** = **plain**, acknowledged, known, obvious, open, overt, patent ◆ *n* **5** = **people**, citizens, community, electorate, everyone, nation, populace, society

publication *n* **1** = **pamphlet**, brochure, issue, leaflet, magazine, newspaper, periodical, title **2** = **announcement**, broadcasting, declaration, disclosure, writer on public concerns. **pub·lic'i·ty** n 1 process of attracting public attention. 2 attention thus gained. **pub'li·cize** vt **-cized, -ciz·ing** 1 give publicity to. 2 bring to public notice.

pub'lish vt 1 prepare and issue for sale (books, music, etc.). 2 make generally known. 3 proclaim. **pub·li·ca'tion** [-KAY-shən] n **pub'lish·er** n

puce [pyoos] adj n purplish-brown (color).

puck[1] [puk] n hard rubber disk used instead of ball in ice hockey.

puck[2] n mischievous sprite. **puck'ish** adj

puck·er [PUK-ər] v 1 gather into wrinkles. ◆ n 2 crease, fold.

pud·ding [PUUD-ing] n thick, cooked dessert, often made from flour, milk, eggs, flavoring, etc.

pud·dle [PUD-l] n 1 small pool of water. 2 rough cement for lining walls of canals, etc. ◆ vt **-dled, -dling** 3 line with puddle. 4 make muddy. **puddling** n method of converting pig iron to wrought iron by oxidizing the carbon.

pu·den·dum [pyoo-DEN-dəm] n, pl **-da** [-də] 1 external genital organs, esp. of a woman. 2 vulva.

pu·er·ile [PYOO-ər-il] adj 1 childish. 2 foolish. 3 trivial.

puff n 1 short blast of breath, wind, etc. 2 its sound. 3 type of pastry. 4 laudatory review or advertisement. ◆ vi 5 blow abruptly. 6 breathe hard. ◆ vt 7 send out in a puff. 8 blow out, inflate. 9 advertise. 10 smoke hard. **puff'y** adj **puff·i·er, puff·i·est** 1

short-winded. 2 swollen. **puff'ball** n ball-shaped fungus.

puf'fin n sea bird with large brightly-colored beak.

pug n 1 small snub-nosed dog. 2 sl boxer. **pug nose** snub nose.

pu·gi·list [PYOO-jə-list] n boxer. **pu'gi·lism** n **pu·gi·lis'tic** adj

pug·na·cious [pug-NAY-shəs] adj given to fighting. **pug·nac'i·ty** [-NAS-i-tee] n

puke [pyook] sl ◆ vi **puked, puk·ing** 1 vomit. ◆ n 2 vomit.

pul·chri·tude [PUL-kri-tood] n beauty. **pul·chri·tu'di·nous** adj

pull [puul] vt 1 exert force on object to move it toward source of force. 2 strain or stretch. 3 tear. 4 propel by rowing. ◆ n 5 act of pulling. 6 force exerted by it. 7 drink of liquor. 8 inf power, influence. **pull in** (of train) arrive. 1 attract. 2 sl arrest. **pull off** inf carry through to successful issue. **pull out** 1 withdraw. 2 extract. 3 (of train) depart. 4 (of car, etc.) move away from side of road or move out to overtake. **pull over** (of car, etc.) drive to side of road and stop. **pull someone's leg** make fun of. **pull up** 1 tear up. 2 recover lost ground. 3 improve. 4 come to a stop. 5 halt. 6 reprimand.

pul'let [PUUL-it] n young hen.

pul·ley [PUUL-ee] n, pl **-leys** wheel with groove in rim for cord, used to raise weights by downward pull.

Pull·man [PUUL-mən] ® n, pl **-mans** railroad sleeping car or parlor car.

pull·o·ver [PUUL-oh-vər] n sweater without

notification, proclamation, publishing, reporting

publicity n = **advertising**, attention, boost, hype, plug (inf), press, promotion

publicize v = **advertise**, hype, make known, play up, plug (inf), promote, push

public-spirited adj = **altruistic**, charitable, humanitarian, philanthropic, unselfish

publish v 1 = **put out**, issue, print, produce 2 = **announce**, advertise, broadcast, circulate, disclose, divulge, proclaim, publicize, reveal, spread

pucker v 1 = **wrinkle**, contract, crease, draw together, gather, knit, purse, screw up, tighten ◆ n 2 = **wrinkle**, crease, fold

puerile adj = **childish**, babyish, foolish, immature, juvenile, silly, trivial

puff n 1 = **blast**, breath, draft, gust, whiff 2 = **smoke**, drag (sl), pull ◆ v 3 = **blow**,

breathe, exhale, gasp, gulp, pant, wheeze 4 = **smoke**, drag (sl), draw, inhale, pull at or on, suck 5 (usually with up) = **swell**, bloat, dilate, distend, expand, inflate

puffy adj = **swollen**, bloated, distended, enlarged, puffed up

pugilist n = **boxer**, fighter, prizefighter

pugnacious adj = **aggressive**, belligerent, combative, hot-tempered, quarrelsome

pull v 1 = **draw**, drag, haul, jerk, tow, trail, tug, yank 2 = **strain**, dislocate, rip, sprain, stretch, tear, wrench 3 = **extract**, draw out, gather, pick, pluck, remove, take out, uproot ◆ n 4 = **tug**, jerk, twitch, yank 5 = **puff**, drag (sl), inhalation 6 Inf = **influence**, clout (inf), muscle, power, weight

pull down v = **demolish**, bulldoze, destroy, raze, remove

pull off v = **succeed**, accomplish, carry out,

fastening, to be pulled over head.

pul·mo·nar·y [PUUL-mə-ner-ee] *adj* of lungs.

pulp *n* **1** soft, moist, vegetable or animal matter. **2** flesh of fruit. **3** any soft soggy mass. ◆ *vt* **4** reduce to pulp.

pul·pit [PUUL-pit] *n* (enclosed) platform for preacher, minister, rabbi, etc.

pul·sar [PUL-sahr] *n* small dense star emitting radio waves.

pulse [puls] *n* **1** movement of blood in arteries corresponding to heartbeat, discernible to touch, for example in the wrist. **2** any regular beat or vibration. **pul·sate** [PUL-sayt] *vi* **-sat·ed, -sat·ing** throb, quiver. **pul·sa'tion** [-SAY-shən] *n*

pul·ver·ize [PUL-və-rīz] *vt* **-ized, -iz·ing 1** reduce to powder. **2** smash or demolish.

pu·ma [PYOO-mə] *n* large Amer. feline carnivore, cougar.

pum·ice [PUM-is] *n* light porous variety of lava.

pum·mel [PUM-əl] *vt* **-meled, -mel·ing** strike repeatedly with fists.

pump¹ *n* **1** appliance in which piston and handle are used for raising water, or putting in or taking out air or liquid, etc. ◆ *vt* **2** raise, put in, take out, etc. with pump. **3** empty by means of a pump. **4** extract information from. ◆ *vi* **5** work pump. **6** work like pump. **pump iron** lift weights as exercise.

pump² *n* light shoe.

pump'kin *n* any of varieties of gourd, eaten esp. as vegetable, in pie.

pun *n* **1** play on words. ◆ *vi* **punned, pun·ning 2** make one. **pun'ster** [-stər] *n*

punch¹ *n* **1** tool for perforating or stamping. **2** blow with fist. **3** vigor. ◆ *vt* **4** stamp, perforate with punch. **5** strike with fist. **pull punches 1** punch lightly. **2** *inf* lessen, withhold, criticism. **punch-drunk** *adj inf* dazed, as by repeated blows.

punch² *n* drink of spirits or wine with fruit juice, spice, etc.

punc·til·i·ous [pungk-TIL-ee-əs] *adj* **1** making much of details of etiquette. **2** very exact, particular. **punc·til'i·ous·ness** [-nis] *n*

punc·tu·al [PUNGK-choo-əl] *adj* in good time, not late, prompt. **punc·tu·al'i·ty** *n*

punc·tu·ate [PUNGK-choo-ayt] *vt* **-at·ed, -at·ing 1** put in punctuation marks. **2** interrupt at intervals. **3** emphasize. **punc·tu·a'tion** *n* marks, such as commas and colons, put in writing to assist in making sense clear.

punc·ture [PUNGK-chər] *n* **1** small hole made by sharp object, esp. in tire. **2** act of puncturing. ◆ *vt* **-tured, -tur·ing 3** prick hole in, perforate.

pun'dit *n* self-appointed expert.

pun·gent [PUN-jənt] *adj* **1** biting. **2** irritant. **3** piercing. **4** tart. **5** caustic. **pun'gen·cy** *n*

——————| THESAURUS |——————

do the trick, manage

pull out *v* = **withdraw**, depart, evacuate, leave, quit, retreat

pull through *v* = **survive**, get better, rally, recover

pulp *n* **1** = **paste**, mash, mush **2** = **flesh**, soft part ◆ *v* **3** = **crush**, mash, pulverize, squash ◆ *adj* **4** = **cheap**, lurid, rubbishy, trashy

pulsate *v* = **throb**, beat, palpitate, pound, pulse, quiver, thump

pulse *n* **1** = **beat**, beating, pulsation, rhythm, throb, throbbing, vibration ◆ *v* **2** = **beat**, pulsate, throb, vibrate

pulverize *v* **1** = **crush**, granulate, grind, mill, pound **2** = **defeat**, annihilate, crush, demolish, destroy, flatten, smash, wreck

pummel *v* = **beat**, batter, hammer, pound, punch, strike, thump

pump *v* **1** (often with *into*) = **drive**, force, inject, pour, push, send, supply **2** = **interrogate**, cross-examine, probe, quiz

pun *n* = **play on words**, double entendre, quip, witticism

punch¹ *v* **1** = **hit**, belt (*inf*), bop (*inf*), box, pummel, smash, sock (*sl*), strike ◆ *n* **2** = **blow**, bop (*inf*), hit, jab, sock (*sl*), wallop (*inf*) **3** *Inf* = **effectiveness**, bite, drive, forcefulness, impact, verve, vigor

punch² *v* = **pierce**, bore, cut, drill, perforate, prick, puncture, stamp

punctilious *adj* = **particular**, exact, finicky, formal, fussy, meticulous, nice, precise, proper, strict

punctual *adj* = **on time**, exact, on the dot, precise, prompt, timely

punctuality *n* = **promptness**, promptitude, readiness

punctuate *v* **1** = **interrupt**, break, intersperse, pepper, sprinkle **2** = **emphasize**, accentuate, stress, underline

puncture *n* **1** = **hole**, break, cut, damage, leak, nick, opening, slit **2** = **flat tire**, flat ◆ *v* **3** = **pierce**, bore, cut, nick, penetrate,

pun·ish *vt* **1** cause to suffer for offense. **2** inflict penalty on. **3** use or treat roughly. **pun·ish·a·ble** *adj* **pun·ish·ment** *n* **pu·ni·tive** [PYOO-ni-tiv] *adj* inflicting or intending to inflict punishment.

punk *adj, n* **1** inferior, rotten, worthless (person or thing). **2** petty (hoodlum). **3** (of) style of rock music.

punt¹ *n* **1** flat-bottomed square-ended boat, propelled by pushing with pole. ◆ *vt* **2** propel thus.

punt² *vt* Football **1** kick ball before it touches ground, when let fall from hands. ◆ *n* **2** such a kick.

punt³ *vi* gamble, bet. **punt·er** *n* **1** one who punts. **2** gambler.

pu·ny [PYOO-nee] *adj* **-ni·er, -ni·est** small and feeble.

pup *n* young of certain animals, such as dogs and seals.

pu·pa [PYOO-pə] *n, pl* **-pas** stage between larva and adult in metamorphosis of insect, chrysalis. **pu'pal** *adj*

pu·pil [PYOO-pəl] *n* **1** person being taught. **2** opening in iris of eye.

pup·pet [PUP-it] *n* small doll or figure of person, etc. controlled by operator's hand. **pup·pet·eer'** *n* **puppet show** show with puppets worked by hidden performer.

pup·py [PUP-ee] *n, pl* **-pies** young dog.

pur·chase [PUR-chəs] *vt* **-chased, -chas·ing** **1** buy. ◆ *n* **2** buying. **3** what is bought. **4** leverage, grip.

pur·dah [PUR-də] *n* **1** Muslim, Hindu custom of keeping women in seclusion. **2** screen, veil to achieve this.

pure [pyuur] *adj* **pur·er, pur·est 1** unmixed, untainted. **2** simple. **3** spotless. **4** faultless. **5** innocent. **6** concerned with theory only. **pure·ly** *adv* **pu·ri·fi·ca'tion** *n* **pu'ri·fy** *vt* **-fied, -fy·ing** make, become pure, clear or clean. **pur'ism** *n* excessive insistence on correctness of language. **pur'ist** *n* **pu'ri·ty** *n* state of being pure.

pu·rée [pyuu-RAY] *n* pulp, soup, of cooked fruit or vegetables put through sieve, etc. ◆ *vt* **-réed, -rée·ing**

pur·ga·to·ry [PUR-gə-tor-ee] *n* **-ries** place or state of torment, pain or distress, esp. temporary.

purge [purj] *vt* **purged, purg·ing 1** make clean, purify. **2** remove, get rid of. **3** clear out. ◆ *n* **4** act, process of purging. **5** removal of undesirable members from political party, army, etc. **pur'ga·tive** [-gə-tiv] *adj, n*

perforate, prick, rupture

pungent *adj* = **strong**, acrid, bitter, hot, peppery, piquant, sharp, sour, spicy, tart

punish *v* = **discipline**, castigate, chasten, chastise, correct, penalize, sentence

punishable *adj* = **culpable**, blameworthy, criminal, indictable

punishing *adj* = **hard**, arduous, backbreaking, exhausting, grueling, strenuous, taxing, tiring, wearing

punishment *n* = **penalty**, chastening, chastisement, correction, discipline, penance, retribution

punitive *adj* = **retaliatory**, in reprisal, retaliative

punt *v* **1** = **bet**, back, gamble, lay, stake, wager ◆ *n* **2** = **bet**, gamble, stake, wager

puny *adj* = **feeble**, frail, little, sickly, stunted, tiny, weak

pupil *n* = **learner**, beginner, disciple, novice, schoolboy or schoolgirl, student

puppet *n* **1** = **marionette**, doll, ventriloquist's dummy **2** = **pawn**, cat's-paw, instrument, mouthpiece, stooge, tool

purchase *v* **1** = **buy**, acquire, come by, gain, get, obtain, pay for, pick up, score (sl) ◆ *n* **2** = **buy**, acquisition, asset, gain, investment, possession, property **3** = **grip**, foothold, hold, leverage, support

pure *adj* **1** = **unmixed**, authentic, flawless, genuine, natural, neat, real, simple, straight, unalloyed **2** = **clean**, germ-free, sanitary, spotless, squeaky-clean, sterilized, uncontaminated, unpolluted, untainted, wholesome **3** = **innocent**, blameless, chaste, impeccable, modest, uncorrupted, unsullied, virginal, virtuous **4** = **complete**, absolute, outright, sheer, thorough, unmitigated, unqualified, utter

purely *adv* = **absolutely**, completely, entirely, exclusively, just, merely, only, simply, solely, wholly

purge *v* **1** = **get rid of**, do away with, eradicate, expel, exterminate, remove, wipe out ◆ *n* **2** = **removal**, ejection, elimination, eradication, expulsion

purify *v* **1** = **clean**, clarify, cleanse, decontaminate, disinfect, refine, sanitize, wash **2** = **absolve**, cleanse, redeem, sanctify

purist *n* = **stickler**, formalist, pedant

Pu·ri·tan [PYUUR-i-tn] n 1 *Hist.* member of extreme Protestant party. 2 **(p-)** person of extreme strictness in morals or religion. **pu·ri·tan'i·cal** adj 1 strict in the observance of religious and moral duties. 2 overscrupulous. **pu'ri·tan·ism** n

purl n 1 stitch that forms ridge in knitting. ◆ vi 2 knit in purl.

pur·loin [pər-LOIN] vt 1 steal. 2 pilfer.

pur·ple [PUR-pəl] n, adj **-pler, -plest** (of) color between crimson and violet.

pur·port [pər-PORT] vt 1 claim to be (true, etc.). 2 signify, imply. ◆ n [PUR-port] 3 meaning. 4 apparent meaning. 5 significance.

pur·pose [PUR-pəs] n 1 reason, object. 2 design. 3 aim, intention. ◆ vt **-posed, -pos·ing** 4 intend. **pur'pose·ly** adv on purpose intentionally.

purr n 1 pleased noise that cat makes. ◆ vi 2 utter this.

purse [purs] n 1 small bag for money. 2 handbag. 3 resources. 4 money as prize. ◆ v **pursed, purs·ing** ◆ vt 5 pucker in wrinkles. ◆ vi 6 become wrinkled and

drawn in. **purs'er** n ship's officer who keeps accounts.

pur·sue [pər-SOO] v **-sued, -su·ing** ◆ vt 1 run after. 2 chase. 3 aim at. 4 engage in. 5 continue. 6 follow. ◆ vi 7 go in pursuit. 8 continue. **pur·su'ance** [-əns] n carrying out. **pur·su'ant** [-ənt] adv accordingly. **pur·su'er** n **pur·suit'** [-SOOT] n 1 running after, attempt to catch. 2 occupation.

purulent adj see PUS.

pur·vey [pər-VAY] vt supply (provisions). **pur·vey'or** n

pur·view [PUR-vyoo] n scope, range.

pus n yellowish matter produced by suppuration. **pu·ru·lence** [PYUUR-ə-ləns] n **pu'ru·lent** adj 1 forming, discharging pus. 2 septic.

push [puush] vt 1 move, try to move away by pressure. 2 drive or impel. 3 sl sell (esp. narcotic drugs) illegally. ◆ vi 4 make thrust. 5 advance with steady effort. ◆ n 6 thrust. 7 persevering self-assertion. 8 big military advance. **push'er** n **push'y** adj **push·i·er, push·i·est** given to pushing oneself. **pu·sil·lan·i·mous** [pyoo-sə-LAN-ə-məs]

puritan n 1 = **moralist**, fanatic, prude, rigorist, zealot ◆ adj 2 = **strict**, ascetic, austere, moralistic, narrow-minded, prudish, severe, strait-laced

puritanical adj = **strict**, ascetic, austere, narrow-minded, proper, prudish, puritan, severe, strait-laced

purity n 1 = **cleanness**, cleanliness, faultlessness, immaculateness, pureness, wholesomeness 2 = **innocence**, chasteness, chastity, decency, honesty, integrity, virginity, virtue, virtuousness

purloin v = **steal**, appropriate, filch, pilfer, pinch (inf), swipe (sl), thieve

purport v 1 = **claim**, allege, assert, profess ◆ n 2 = **significance**, drift, gist, idea, implication, import, meaning

purpose n 1 = **reason**, aim, idea, intention, object, point 2 = **aim**, ambition, desire, end, goal, hope, intention, object, plan, wish 3 = **determination**, firmness, persistence, resolution, resolve, single-mindedness, tenacity, will 4 **on purpose** = **deliberately**, designedly, intentionally, knowingly, purposely

purposeless adj = **pointless**, aimless, empty, motiveless, needless, senseless, uncalled-for, unnecessary

purposely adv = **deliberately**, consciously,

expressly, intentionally, knowingly, on purpose, with intent

purse n 1 = **pouch**, money-bag, wallet 2 = **money**, exchequer, funds, means, resources, treasury, wealth ◆ v 3 = **pucker**, contract, pout, press together, tighten

pursue v 1 = **follow**, chase, dog, hound, hunt, hunt down, run after, shadow, stalk, tail (inf), track 2 = **try for**, aim for, desire, seek, strive for, work towards 3 = **engage in**, carry on, conduct, perform, practice 4 = **continue**, carry on, keep on, maintain, persevere in, persist in, proceed

pursuit n 1 = **pursuing**, chase, hunt, quest, search, seeking, trailing 2 = **occupation**, activity, hobby, interest, line, pastime, pleasure

purvey v = **supply**, cater, deal in, furnish, provide, sell, trade in

push v 1 = **shove**, depress, drive, press, propel, ram, thrust 2 = **make** or **force one's way**, elbow, jostle, move, shoulder, shove, squeeze, thrust 3 = **urge**, encourage, hurry, impel, incite, persuade, press, spur ◆ n 4 = **shove**, butt, nudge, thrust 5 = **drive**, ambition, dynamism, energy, enterprise, go (inf), initiative, vigor, vitality

pushed adj (often with for) = **short of**,

adj cowardly. **pu·sil·la·nim'i·ty** [-lə-NIM-ə-tee] *n*

puss [puus], **pus'sy** *n, pl* **-ses, -sies** *inf* cat.

puss·y·foot [PUUS-ee-fuut] *vi* **1** move stealthily. **2** act indecisively, procrastinate.

pus·tule [PUS-chuul] *n* pimple containing pus.

put [puut] *vt* **put, put·ting 1** place. **2** set. **3** express. **4** throw (esp. shot). ♦ *n* **5** throw. **put across** express, carry out successfully. **put off 1** postpone. **2** disconcert. **3** repel. **put up 1** erect. **2** accommodate. **3** nominate.

pu·ta·tive [PYOO-tə-tiv] *adj* reputed, supposed.

pu·trid [PYOO-trid] *adj* **1** decomposed. **2** rotten. **pu'tre·fy** [-trə-fī] *v* **-fied, -fy·ing**

make or become rotten. **pu·tre·fac'tion** *n* **pu·tres'cent** [-ənt] *adj* becoming rotten.

putsch [puuch] *n* surprise attempt to overthrow the existing power, political revolt.

putt [put] *vt* strike (golf ball) along ground in direction of hole. **putt'er** *n* **1** golf club for putting. **2** person who putts.

put·ter [PUT-ər] *vi* work, act in feeble, unsystematic way.

put·ty [PUT-ee] *n, pl* **-ties 1** paste of ground chalk and oil as used by glaziers. ♦ *vt* **-tied, -ty·ing 2** fix, fill with putty.

puz·zle [PUZ-əl] *v* **-zled, -zling 1** perplex or be perplexed. ♦ *n* **2** bewildering, perplexing question, problem or toy. **puz'zle·ment** *n*

hurried, pressed, rushed, under pressure

pushover *n* **1 = piece of cake** (*inf*), breeze (*inf*), child's play (*inf*), cinch (*sl*), picnic (*inf*), plain sailing, walkover (*inf*) **2 = sucker** (*sl*), easy game (*inf*), easy *or* soft mark (*inf*), mug (*Brit. sl*), walkover (*inf*)

pushy *adj* **= forceful**, ambitious, assertive, bold, brash, bumptious, obtrusive, presumptuous, self-assertive

pussyfoot *v* **= hedge**, beat about the bush, be noncommittal, equivocate, hum and haw, prevaricate, sit on the fence

put *v* **1 = place**, deposit, lay, position, rest, set, settle, situate **2 = express**, phrase, state, utter, word **3 = throw**, cast, fling, heave, hurl, lob, pitch, toss

put across *or* **over** *v* **= communicate**, convey, explain, get across, make clear, make oneself understood

put aside *or* **by** *v* **= save**, deposit, lay by, stockpile, store

put away *v* **1 = save**, deposit, keep, put by **2 = commit**, certify, institutionalize, lock up **3 = consume**, devour, eat up, gobble, wolf down **4 = put back**, replace, tidy away

put down *v* **1 = record**, enter, set down, take down, write down **2 = stamp out**, crush, quash, quell, repress, suppress **3** (usually with *to*) **= attribute**, ascribe, impute, set down **4 = put to sleep**, destroy, do away with, put out of its misery **5** *Sl* **= humiliate**, disparage, mortify, shame, slight, snub

put forward *v* **= recommend**, advance, nominate, propose, submit, suggest, tender

put off *v* **1 = postpone**, defer, delay, hold over, put on the back burner (*inf*), take a rain check on (*inf*) **2 = disconcert**, confuse, discomfit, dismay, faze, nonplus, perturb, throw (*inf*), unsettle **3 = discourage**, dishearten, dissuade

put on *v* **1 = don**, change into, dress, get dressed in, slip into **2 = fake**, affect, assume, feign, pretend, sham, simulate **3 = present**, do, mount, produce, show, stage **4 = add**, gain, increase by

put out *v* **1 = annoy**, anger, exasperate, irk, irritate, nettle, vex **2 = extinguish**, blow out, douse, quench **3 = inconvenience**, bother, discomfit, discommode, impose upon, incommode, trouble

putrid *adj* **= rotten**, bad, decayed, decomposed, putrefied, rancid, rotting, spoiled

putter *v* **= mess around**, dabble, dawdle, monkey around (*inf*), tinker

put up *v* **1 = erect**, build, construct, fabricate, raise **2 = accommodate**, board, house, lodge, take in **3 = recommend**, nominate, offer, present, propose, put forward, submit **4 put up with = stand**, abide, bear, endure, stand for, swallow, take, tolerate

puzzle *v* **1 = perplex**, baffle, bewilder, confound, confuse, mystify, stump ♦ *n* **2 = problem**, conundrum, enigma, mystery, paradox, poser, question, riddle

puzzled *adj* **= perplexed**, at a loss, at sea, baffled, bewildered, confused, lost, mystified

puzzlement *n* **= perplexity**, bafflement, bewilderment, confusion, doubt,

pyg·my, pig·my [PIG-mee] *n, pl* **-mies 1** abnormally undersized person. **2** (P-) member of one of dwarf peoples of Equatorial Africa. ♦ *adj* **3** undersized.

py·lon [PI-lon] *n* **1** post, tower, esp. for guiding aviators. **2** steel tower for supporting power lines.

py·or·rhe·a [pī-ə-REE-ə] *n* inflammation of the gums with discharge of pus and loosening of teeth.

pyr·a·mid [PIR-ə-mid] *n* **1** solid figure with sloping sides meeting at apex. **2** structure of this shape, esp. ancient Egyptian. **3** group of persons or things arranged, organized, like pyramid. **py·ram'i·dal** *adj*

pyre [pīr] *n* pile of wood for burning a dead body.

py·ri·tes [pī-RĪ-teez] *n, pl* **py·ri·tes** sulfide of a metal, esp. iron pyrites.

py·ro·ma·ni·ac [pī-rə-MAY-nee-ak] *n* person with uncontrollable desire to set things on fire.

py·rom·e·ter [pī-ROM-i-tər] *n* instrument for measuring very high temperature.

py·ro·tech·nics [pī rə TEK niks] *n* manufacture, display of fireworks.

Pyr·rhic victory [PIR-ik] one won at too high cost.

py·thon [PĪ-thon] *n* large nonpoisonous snake that crushes its prey.

pyx [piks] *n* vessel in which consecrated Host is preserved.

———— THESAURUS ————

mystification

puzzling *adj* = **perplexing**, abstruse, baffling, bewildering, enigmatic, incomprehensible, involved, mystifying

Q q

Q.E.D. which was to be shown or proved.
qua [kway] *prep* in the capacity of.
quack [kwak] *n* **1** harsh cry of duck. **2** pretender to medical or other skill. ♦ *vi* **3** (of duck) utter cry.
quadr-, quadri- *comb. form* four, e.g. *quadrilateral.*
quad·ran·gle [KWOD-rang-gəl] *n* **1** four-sided figure. **2** four-sided courtyard in a building. **quad·ran'gu·lar** [-gyə-lər] *adj*
quad·rant [KWOD-rənt] *n* **1** quarter of circle. **2** instrument for taking angular measurements. **quad·rat'ic** *adj* of equation, involving square of unknown quantity.
quad·ra·phon·ic [kwod-rə-FON-ik] *adj* of a sound system using four independent speakers.
quad·ri·lat·er·al [kwod-rə-LAT-ər-əl] *adj* **1** four-sided. ♦ *n* **2** four-sided figure.
quad·rille [kwo-DRIL] *n* **1** square dance. **2** music played for it.
quad·ril·lion [kwo-DRIL-yən] *n* cardinal number of 1 followed by 15 zeros.
quad·ru·man·ous [kwo-DROO-mə-nəs] *adj* of apes, etc. having four feet that can be used as hands.
quad·ru·ped [KWOD-ruu-ped] *n* four-footed animal.
quad·ru·ple [kwo-DROO-pəl] *adj* **1** fourfold. ♦ *v* **-pled, -pling** **2** make, become four times as much. **quad·ru'pli·cate** [-kit] *adj* fourfold.
quad·ru·plet [kwo-DRUP-lit] *n* one of four offspring born at one birth.
quaff [kwof] *v* drink heartily or in one swallow.
quag·mire [KWAG-mīr] *n* bog, swamp.
quail[1] [kwayl] *n* small bird of partridge family.
quail[2] *vi* **1** flinch. **2** cower.
quaint [kwaynt] *adj* **-er, -est** **1** interestingly old-fashioned or odd. **2** curious. **3** whimsical. **quaint'ness** [-nis] *n*
quake [kwayk] *vi* **quaked, quak·ing** shake, tremble.
Quak·er [KWAY-kər] *n* member of Christian sect, the **Society of Friends.**
qual·i·fy [KWOL-ə-fī] *v* **-fied, -fy·ing** **1** make oneself competent. **2** moderate. **3** limit. **4** make competent. **5** ascribe quality to. **6** describe. **qual·i·fi·ca'tion** *n* **1** thing that qualifies, attribute. **2** restriction. **3** qualifying.
qual·i·ty [KWOL-i-tee] *n, pl* **-ties** **1** attribute, characteristic, property. **2** degree of excellence. **3** rank. **qual'i·ta·tive** *adj* depending on quality.
qualm [kwahm] *n* **1** misgiving. **2** sudden

THESAURUS

quack *n* = **charlatan**, fake, fraud, humbug, impostor, mountebank, phoney *or* phony (*inf*), pretender
quaff *v* = **drink**, down, gulp, imbibe, swallow, swig (*inf*)
quagmire *n* = **bog**, fen, marsh, mire, morass, quicksand, slough, swamp
quail *v* = **shrink**, blanch, blench, cower, cringe, falter, flinch, have cold feet (*inf*), recoil, shudder
quaint *adj* **1** = **unusual**, bizarre, curious, droll, eccentric, fanciful, odd, old-fashioned, peculiar, queer, singular, strange **2** = **old-fashioned**, antiquated, old-world, picturesque
quake *v* = **shake**, move, quiver, rock, shiver, shudder, tremble, vibrate
qualification *n* **1** = **attribute**, ability, aptitude, capability, eligibility, fitness, quality, skill, suitability **2** = **condition**, caveat, limitation, modification, proviso, requirement, reservation, rider, stipulation
qualified *adj* **1** = **capable**, able, adept, competent, efficient, experienced, expert, fit, practiced, proficient, skillful, trained **2** = **restricted**, bounded, conditional, confined, contingent, limited, modified, provisional, reserved
qualify *v* **1** = **certify**, empower, equip, fit, permit, prepare, ready, train **2** = **moderate**, diminish, ease, lessen, limit, reduce, regulate, restrain, restrict, soften,

feeling of sickness, nausea.

quan·da·ry [KWAN-dree] *n, pl* **-ries** state of perplexity, puzzling situation, dilemma.

quan·ti·ty [KWON-ti-tee] *n, pl* **-ties 1** size, number, amount. **2** specified or considerable amount. **quan'ti·fy** [-fī] *vt* **-fied**, **-fy·ing** discover, express quantity of. **quan'ti·ta·tive** *adj* **quan'tum** [-təm] *n, pl* **-ta** [-tə] desired or required amount. **quantum leap, jump** *inf* sudden large change, increase, or advance. **quantum theory** theory that in radiation, energy of electrons is discharged not continuously but in discrete units, or quanta.

quar·an·tine [KWOR-ən-teen] *n* **1** isolation to prevent spreading of infection. ◆ *vt* **-tined**, **-tin·ing** put, keep in quarantine.

quark [kwork] *n Physics* any of several hypothetical particles thought to be fundamental units of matter.

quar·rel [KWOR-əl] *n* **1** angry dispute. **2** argument. ◆ *vi* **-reled**, **-rel·ing 3** argue. **4** find fault with. **quar'rel·some** [-səm] *adj*

quar·ry¹ [KWOR-ee] *n, pl* **-ries 1** object of hunt or pursuit. **2** prey.

quarry² *n, pl* **-ries 1** excavation where stone, etc. is obtained from ground for building, etc. ◆ *v* **-ried**, **-ry·ing 2** get from quarry.

quart [kwort] *n* liquid measure, quarter of gallon or 2 pints (0.964 liter).

quar·ter [KWOR-tər] *n* **1** fourth part. **2** 25 cents. **3** region, district. **4** mercy. ◆ *pl* **5** lodgings. ◆ *vt* **6** divide into quarters. **7** lodge. **quar'ter·ly** *adj* **1** happening, due, etc. each quarter of year. ◆ *n, pl* **-lies 2** quarterly periodical. **quar·tet'** *n* **1** group of four musicians. **2** music for four performers. **quar'to** *n, pl* **-tos 1** size of book in which sheets are folded into four leaves. ◆ *adj* **2** of this size. **quar'ter·deck** *n* after part of upper deck used esp. for official, ceremonial purposes. **quarter horse** small, powerful breed of horse bred for short races. **quar'ter·mas·ter** *n* officer responsible for quarters, clothing, etc.

quartz [kworts] *n* stone of pure crystalline silica. **quartz'ite** [-īt] *n* quartz rock. **quartz timepiece** watch or clock operated by a vibrating quartz crystal.

qua·sar [KWAY-zahr] *n* extremely distant starlike object emitting powerful radio waves.

quash [kwosh] *vt* **1** annul. **2** reject. **3** subdue forcibly.

quasi- [KWAY-zī] *comb. form* seemingly, resembling but not actually being, e.g. *quasi-scientific.*

quat·er·nar·y [KWOT-ər-ner-ee] *adj* **1** of the number four. **2** having four parts. **3** (**Q-**) *Geology* of most recent period after Tertiary.

quat·rain [KWO-trayn] *n* four-line stanza, esp. rhymed alternately.

temper

quality *n* **1** = **excellence**, caliber, distinction, grade, merit, position, rank, standing, status **2** = **characteristic**, aspect, attribute, condition, feature, mark, property, trait **3** = **nature**, character, kind, make, sort

qualm *n* = **misgiving**, anxiety, apprehension, compunction, disquiet, doubt, hesitation, scruple, twinge *or* pang of conscience, uneasiness

quandary *n* = **difficulty**, Catch-22, dilemma, impasse, plight, predicament, puzzle, strait

quantity *n* **1** = **amount**, lot, number, part, sum, total **2** = **size**, bulk, capacity, extent, length, magnitude, mass, measure, volume

quarrel *n* **1** = **disagreement**, argument, brawl, breach, contention, controversy, dispute, dissension, feud, fight, row, squabble, tiff ◆ *v* **2** = **disagree**, argue,

bicker, brawl, clash, differ, dispute, fall out (*inf*), fight, row, squabble

quarrelsome *adj* = **argumentative**, belligerent, combative, contentious, disputatious, pugnacious

quarry *n* = **prey**, aim, game, goal, objective, prize, victim

quarter *n* **1** = **district**, area, locality, neighborhood, part, place, province, region, side, zone **2** = **mercy**, clemency, compassion, forgiveness, leniency, pity ◆ *v* **3** = **accommodate**, billet, board, house, lodge, place, post, station

quarters *pl n* = **lodgings**, abode, barracks, billet, chambers, dwelling, habitation, residence, rooms

quash *v* **1** = **annul**, cancel, invalidate, overrule, overthrow, rescind, reverse, revoke **2** = **suppress**, beat, crush, overthrow, put down, quell, repress, squash, subdue

quasi- *adj* = **pseudo-**, apparent, seeming,

qua·ver [KWAY-vər] *vt* **1** say or sing in quavering tones. ♦ *vi* **2** tremble, shake, vibrate. ♦ *n* **3** musical note half length of crotchet. **4** quavering trill.

quay [kee] *n* **1** solid, fixed landing stage. **2** wharf.

quea·sy [KWEE-zee] *adj* **-si·er, -si·est** inclined to, or causing, sickness.

queen [kween] *n* **1** king's wife. **2** female ruler. **3** piece in chess. **4** fertile female bee, wasp, etc. **5** playing card with picture of a queen, ranking between king and jack. **6** *sl, offens* male homosexual. **queen'ly** *adj* **-li·er, -li·est**

queer [kweer] *adj* **-er, -est 1** odd, strange. **2** *sl, usu offens* homosexual. ♦ *n* **3** *sl, usu. offens* homosexual. ♦ *vt* **4** spoil. **5** interfere with.

quell [kwel] *vt* **1** crush, put down. **2** allay. **3** pacify.

quench [kwench] *vt* **1** slake. **2** extinguish, put out, suppress.

quer·u·lous [KWER-ə-ləs] *adj* fretful, peevish, whining.

que·ry [KWEER-ee] *n, pl* **-ries 1** question. **2** mark of interrogation. ♦ *vt* **-ried, -ry·ing 3** question, ask.

quest [kwest] *n, vi* search.

ques·tion [KWES-chən] *n* **1** sentence seeking for answer. **2** that which is asked. **3** interrogation. **4** inquiry. **5** problem. **6** point for debate. **7** debate, strife. ♦ *vt* **8** ask questions of, interrogate. **9** dispute. **10** doubt. **ques'tion·a·ble** *adj* doubtful, esp. not clearly true or honest. **ques·tion·naire'** *n* list of questions drawn up for formal answer.

queue [kyoo] *n* **1** line of waiting persons, vehicles. **2** sequence of computer tasks awaiting action. ♦ *vi* **queued, queu·ing 3** (with *up*) wait in line. **4** arrange computer tasks in queue.

quib·ble [KWIB-əl] *n* **1** trivial objection. ♦ *v* **-bled, -bling 2** make this.

quiche [keesh] *n* open pielike dish of cheese, etc. on light pastry shell.

quick [kwik] *adj* **-er, -est 1** rapid, swift. **2** keen. **3** brisk. **4** hasty. ♦ *n* **5** part of body sensitive to pain. **6** sensitive flesh. **the quick** *obs* living people. ♦ *adv* **1** rapidly. **quick'en** *v* make, become faster or more lively. **quick'ie** *n* **1** *inf* quick drink, etc. **quick'ly** *adv* **quick'sand** *n* loose wet sand easily yielding to pressure and engulfing

---

THESAURUS

---

semi-, so-called, would-be

quaver *v* **1** = **tremble**, flicker, flutter, quake, quiver, shake, vibrate, waver ♦ *n* **2** = **trembling**, quiver, shake, tremble, tremor, vibration

queasy *adj* **1** = **sick**, bilious, green around the gills (*inf*), ill, nauseated, off color, squeamish, upset **2** = **uneasy**, anxious, fidgety, ill at ease, restless, troubled, uncertain, worried

queen *n* **1** = **sovereign**, consort, monarch, ruler **2** = **ideal**, mistress, model, star

queer *adj* **1** = **strange**, abnormal, curious, droll, extraordinary, funny, odd, peculiar, uncommon, unusual, weird **2** = **faint**, dizzy, giddy, light-headed, queasy

quell *v* **1** = **suppress**, conquer, crush, defeat, overcome, overpower, put down, quash, subdue, vanquish **2** = **assuage**, allay, appease, calm, mollify, pacify, quiet, soothe

quench *v* **1** = **satisfy**, allay, appease, sate, satiate, slake **2** = **put out**, crush, douse, extinguish, smother, stifle, suppress

querulous *adj* = **complaining**, captious, carping, critical, discontented, dissatisfied, fault-finding, grumbling, peevish, whining

query *n* **1** = **question**, doubt, inquiry, objection, problem, suspicion ♦ *v* **2** = **doubt**, challenge, disbelieve, dispute, distrust, mistrust, suspect ♦ *n* **3** = **ask**, inquire *or* enquire, question

quest *n* = **search**, adventure, crusade, enterprise, expedition, hunt, journey, mission

question *n* **1** = **issue**, motion, point, point at issue, proposal, proposition, subject, theme, topic **2** = **difficulty**, argument, contention, controversy, dispute, doubt, problem, query **3 in question** = **under discussion**, at issue, in doubt, open to debate **4 out of the question** = **impossible**, inconceivable, unthinkable ♦ *v* **5** = **ask**, cross-examine, examine, inquire, interrogate, interview, probe, quiz **6** = **dispute**, challenge, disbelieve, doubt, mistrust, oppose, query, suspect

questionable *adj* = **dubious**, controversial, debatable, doubtful, iffy (*inf*), moot, suspect, suspicious

queue *n* = **line**, chain, file, sequence, series, string, train

quibble *v* **1** = **split hairs**, carp, cavil ♦ *n* **2** = **objection**, cavil, complaint, criticism,

persons, animals, etc. **quick'silver** n
mercury. **quick-tempered** adj irascible.
quid pro quo [KWID proh KWOH] Lat
something given in exchange.
qui·es·cent [kwee-ES-ənt] adj 1 at rest,
inactive, inert. 2 silent. **qui·es'cence** n
qui·et [KWĪ-it] adj -er, -est 1 with little or
no motion or noise. 2 undisturbed. 3 not
showy or obtrusive ◆ n 4 state of
peacefulness, absence of noise or
disturbance. ◆ v 5 make, become quiet.
qui'et·ly adv **qui'e·tude** n
quill [kwil] n 1 large feather. 2 hollow stem
of this. 3 pen, plectrum made from
feather. 4 spine of porcupine.
quilt [kwilt] n 1 padded coverlet. ◆ vt 2
stitch (two pieces of cloth) with pad
between.
quince [kwins] n 1 acid pear-shaped fruit. 2
tree bearing it.
qui·nine [KWĪ-nīn] n bitter drug made
from bark of tree, used to treat fever, and
as mixer.
quin·quen·ni·al [kwin-KWEN-ee-əl] adj
occurring once in, or lasting, five years.

quin·sy [KWIN-zee] n inflammation of
throat or tonsils.
quint [kwint] n short for QUINTUPLET.
quin·tes·sence [kwin-TES-əns] n 1 purest
form, essential feature. 2 embodiment.
quin·tes·sen'tial [-tə-SEN-shəl] adj
quin·tet [kwin-TET] n 1 set of five singers or
players. 2 composition for five voices or
instruments.
quin·tu·plet [kwin-TUP-lit] n one of five
offspring born at one birth.
quip [kwip] n, v **quipped, quip·ping** (utter)
witty saying.
quire [kwīr] n 24 sheets of writing paper.
quirk [kwurk] n 1 individual peculiarity of
character. 2 unexpected twist or turn.
quis·ling [KWIZ-ling] n traitor who aids
occupying enemy force.
quit [kwit] v **quit** or **quit·ted, quit·ting** 1
stop doing a thing. 2 depart. 3 leave, go
away from. 4 cease from. ◆ adj 5 free, rid.
quits adj on equal or even terms by
repayment, etc. **quit'tance** [KWIT-ns] n 1
discharge. 2 receipt. **quit'ter** n one lacking
perseverance.

——— THESAURUS ———

nicety, niggle
quick adj 1 = **fast**, brisk, express, fleet,
hasty, rapid, speedy, swift 2 = **brief**,
cursory, hasty, hurried, perfunctory 3 =
sudden, prompt 4 = **intelligent**, acute,
alert, astute, bright (inf), clever, perceptive,
quick-witted, sharp, shrewd, smart 5 =
deft, adept, adroit, dexterous, skillful 6 =
excitable, irascible, irritable, passionate,
testy, touchy
quicken v 1 = **speed**, accelerate, expedite,
hasten, hurry, impel, precipitate 2 =
invigorate, arouse, energize, excite, incite,
inspire, revive, stimulate, vitalize
quickly adv = **swiftly**, abruptly, apace,
briskly, fast, hastily, hurriedly, promptly,
pronto (inf), rapidly, soon, speedily
quick-tempered adj = **hot-tempered**,
choleric, fiery, irascible, irritable,
quarrelsome, testy
quick-witted adj = **clever**, alert, astute,
bright (inf), keen, perceptive, sharp,
shrewd, smart
quiet adj 1 = **silent**, hushed, inaudible, low,
noiseless, peaceful, soft, soundless 2 =
calm, mild, peaceful, placid, restful,
serene, smooth, tranquil 3 = **undisturbed**,
isolated, private, secluded, sequestered,
unfrequented 4 = **reserved**, gentle, meek,

mild, retiring, sedate, shy ◆ n 5 = **peace**,
calmness, ease, quietness, repose, rest,
serenity, silence, stillness, tranquillity
quieten v 1 = **silence**, compose, hush,
muffle, mute, quell, quiet, stifle, still, stop,
subdue 2 = **soothe**, allay, appease, blunt,
calm, deaden, dull
quietly adv 1 = **silently**, in an undertone,
inaudibly, in silence, mutely, noiselessly,
softly 2 = **calmly**, mildly, patiently,
placidly, serenely
quietness n = **peace**, calm, hush, quiet,
silence, stillness, tranquillity
quilt n = **bedspread**, continental quilt,
counterpane, coverlet, duvet, eiderdown
quintessence n = **essence**, distillation,
soul, spirit
quintessential adj = **ultimate**, archetypal,
definitive, prototypical, typical
quip n = **joke**, gibe, jest, pleasantry, retort,
riposte, sally, wisecrack (inf), witticism
quirk n = **peculiarity**, aberration,
characteristic, eccentricity, foible, habit,
idiosyncrasy, kink, mannerism, oddity, trait
quirky adj = **odd**, eccentric, idiosyncratic,
offbeat, peculiar, unusual
quit v 1 = **stop**, abandon, cease,
discontinue, drop, end, give up, halt 2 =
resign, abdicate, go, leave, pull out, retire,

quite [kwīt] *adv* **1** wholly, completely. **2** very considerably. **3** somewhat, rather. ◆ *interj* **4** exactly, just so.

quiv•er[1] [KWIV-ər] *vi* **1** shake or tremble. ◆ *n* **2** quivering. **3** vibration.

quiver[2] *n* carrying case for arrows.

quix•ot•ic [kwik-SOT-ik] *adj* unrealistically and impractically optimistic, idealistic, chivalrous.

quiz [kwiz] *n, pl* **quiz•zes 1** entertainment in which general or specific knowledge of players is tested by questions. **2** examination, interrogation. ◆ *vt* **quizzed, quiz•zing 3** question, interrogate. **quiz'zi•cal** *adj* **1** questioning. **2** mocking.

quoit [kwoit] *n* **1** ring for throwing at peg as a game. ◆ *pl* **2** the game in which quoits are tossed at a stake in the ground in attempts to encircle it.

quo•rum [KWOR-əm] *n* least number that must be present in meeting to make its transactions valid.

quo•ta [KWOH-tə] *n* **1** share to be contributed or received. **2** specified number, quantity, that may be imported or admitted.

quote [kwoht] *vt* **quot•ed, quot•ing 1** copy or repeat passages from. **2** refer to, esp. to confirm view. **3** state price for. **quot'a•ble** *adj* **quo•ta'tion** *n*

quoth [kwohth] *v obs* said.

quo•tid•i•an [kwoh-TID-ee-ən] *adj* **1** daily. **2** everyday, commonplace.

quo•tient [KWOH-shənt] *n* number resulting from dividing one number by another.

q.v. which see: used to refer a reader to another item in the same book.

THESAURUS

step down (*inf*) **3** = **depart**, go, leave, pull out

quite *adv* **1** = **somewhat**, fairly, moderately, rather, reasonably, relatively **2** = **absolutely**, completely, entirely, fully, perfectly, totally, wholly **3** = **truly**, in fact, in reality, in truth, really

quiver *v* **1** = **shake**, oscillate, quake, quaver, shiver, shudder, tremble, vibrate ◆ *n* **2** = **shake**, oscillation, shiver, shudder, tremble, tremor, vibration

quixotic *adj* = **unrealistic**, dreamy, fanciful, idealistic, impractical, romantic

quiz *n* **1** = **examination**, investigation, questioning, test ◆ *v* **2** = **question**, ask, examine, interrogate, investigate

quizzical *adj* = **mocking**, arch, questioning, sardonic, teasing

quota *n* = **share**, allowance, assignment, part, portion, ration, slice

quotation *n* **1** = **passage**, citation, excerpt, extract, quote (*inf*), reference **2** *Commerce* = **estimate**, charge, cost, figure, price, quote (*inf*), rate, tender

quote *v* = **repeat**, cite, detail, instance, name, recall, recite, recollect, refer to

R r

Ra *Chem.* radium.

rab·bet [RAB-it] *n* 1 recess, groove cut into piece of timber to join with matching piece. ◆ *vt* **-bet·ed, -bet·ing** 2 cut rabbet in.

rab·bi [RAB-ī] *n, pl* **-bis** Jewish learned man, spiritual leader, teacher. **rab·bin·i·cal** *adj*

rab'bit *n* 1 small burrowing rodent like hare. ◆ *vi* 2 hunt rabbits. **rabbit punch** 1 sharp blow to back of neck. 2 see RAREBIT.

rab·ble [RAB-əl] *n* 1 crowd of vulgar, noisy people. 2 mob.

rab'id *adj* 1 relating to or having rabies. 2 furious. 3 mad. 4 fanatical.

ra·bies [RAY-beez] *n* acute infectious viral disease transmitted by dogs, etc.

rac·coon [ra-KOON] *n* small N Amer. mammal.

race¹ [rays] *n* 1 contest of speed, as in running, swimming, etc. 2 contest, rivalry. 3 strong current of water, esp. leading to water wheel. ◆ *pl* 4 meeting for horse racing. ◆ *v* **raced, rac·ing** ◆ *vt* 5 cause to run rapidly. ◆ *vi* 6 run swiftly. 7 of engine, pedal, etc., to move rapidly and erratically, esp. on removal of resistance. **rac'er** *n* person, vehicle, animal that races.

race² *n* 1 group of people of common ancestry with distinguishing physical features (skin color, etc.). 2 species. 3 type. **ra·cial** [RAY-shəl] *adj* **rac'ism** *n* 1 belief in innate superiority of particular race. 2 antagonism toward members of different race based on this belief. **rac'ist** *adj, n*

rack¹ [rak] *n* 1 framework for displaying or holding baggage, books, hats, bottles, etc. 2 *Mechanics* straight bar with teeth on its edge, to work with pinion. 3 instrument of torture by stretching. ◆ *vt* 4 stretch on rack or wheel. 5 torture. 6 stretch, strain. **rack'ing** *adj* agonizing (pain).

rack² *n* **rack and ruin** destruction.

rack³ *n* neck or rib section of mutton, lamb, pork.

rack·et¹ [RAK-it] *n* 1 loud noise, uproar. 2 occupation by which money is made illegally. **rack·et·eer** [rak-i-TEER] *n* one making illegal profits. **rack'et·y** *adj* noisy.

racket², rac·quet [RAK-it] *n* 1 bat used in tennis, etc. ◆ *pl* 2 ball game played in paved, walled court.

rac·on·teur [rak-ən-TUR] *n* skilled storyteller.

racquet see RACKET².

rac·y [RAY-see] *adj* **rac·i·er, rac·i·est** 1 spirited. 2 lively. 3 having strong flavor. 4 spicy. 5 piquant. **rac'i·ly** *adv* **rac'i·ness** *n*

ra·dar [RAY-dahr] *n* device for finding range and direction by ultrahigh frequency point-to-point radio waves, which reflect back to their source and reveal position and nature of objects sought.

radial see RADIUS.

THESAURUS

rabble *n* = **mob**, canaille, crowd, herd, horde, swarm, throng

rabid *adj* 1 = **fanatical**, extreme, fervent, irrational, narrow-minded, zealous 2 = **mad**, hydrophobic

race¹ *n* 1 = **contest**, chase, competition, dash, pursuit, rivalry ◆ *v* 2 = **run**, career, compete, contest, dart, dash, fly, gallop, hurry, speed, tear, zoom

race² *n* = **people**, blood, folk, nation, stock, tribe, type

racial *adj* = **ethnic**, ethnological, folk, genealogical, genetic, national, tribal

rack *n* 1 = **frame**, framework, stand, structure ◆ *v* 2 = **torture**, afflict, agonize, crucify, harrow, oppress, pain, torment

racket *n* 1 = **noise**, clamor, din, disturbance, fuss, outcry, pandemonium, row 2 = **fraud**, scheme

racy *adj* 1 = **risqué**, bawdy, blue, naughty, smutty, suggestive 2 = **lively**, animated, energetic, entertaining, exciting, sparkling, spirited

radiance *n* 1 = **happiness**, delight, gaiety, joy, pleasure, rapture, warmth 2 = **brightness**, brilliance, glare, gleam, glow, light, luster, shine

radiant *adj* 1 = **happy**, blissful, delighted,

ra·di·ate [RAY-dee-ayt] v -at·ed, -at·ing 1 emit, be emitted in rays. 2 spread out from center. **ra'di·ance** [-əns] n 1 brightness. 2 splendor. **ra'di·ant** [-ənt] adj 1 beaming. 2 shining. 3 emitting rays. **ra·di·a'tion** n 1 transmission of heat, light, etc. from one body to another. 2 particles, rays, emitted in nuclear decay. 3 act of radiating. **ra'di·a·tor** n 1 that which radiates, esp. heating apparatus for rooms. 2 cooling apparatus of automobile engine.

rad·i·cal [RAD-i-kəl] adj 1 fundamental, thorough. 2 extreme. 3 of root. ◆ n 4 person of extreme (political) views. 5 number expressed as root of another. 6 group of atoms of several elements that remain unchanged in a series of chemical compounds.

ra·di·o [RAY-dee-oh] n, pl -di·os 1 use of electromagnetic waves for broadcasting, communication, etc. 2 device for receiving, amplifying radio signals. 3 broadcasting, content of radio program. ◆ vt -di·oed, -di·o·ing 4 transmit message, etc. by radio.

radio- comb. form of rays, of radiation, of radium, e.g. radiology.

ra·di·o·ac·tive [ray-dee-oh-AK-tiv] adj emitting invisible rays that penetrate matter. **ra·di·o·ac·tiv'i·ty** n

ra·di·o·gra·phy [ray-dee-OG-rə-fee] n production of image on film or plate by radiation.

ra·di·ol·o·gy [ray-dee-OL-ə-jee] n science of use of rays in medicine. **ra·di·ol'o·gist** n

ra·di·o·ther·a·py [ray-dee-oh-THER-ə-pee] n diagnosis and treatment of disease by x-rays.

rad·ish n pungent root vegetable.

ra·di·um [RAY-dee-əm] n radioactive metallic element.

ra·di·us [RAY-dee-əs] n, pl -di·i [-dee-ī] 1 straight line from center to circumference of circle. 2 outer of two bones in forearm. **ra'di·al** [-əl] adj 1 arranged like radii of circle. 2 of ray or rays. 3 of radius.

ra·dome [RAY-dohm] n dome-shaped housing for radar.

ra·don [RAY-don] n radioactive gaseous element.

raf·fi·a [RAF-fee-ə] n prepared palm fiber for making mats, etc.

raff'ish adj disreputable.

raf·fle [RAF-əl] n 1 lottery in which an article is assigned by lot to one of those buying tickets. ◆ vt -fled, -fling 2 dispose of by raffle.

raft n floating structure of logs, planks, etc.

raf·ter [RAF-tər] n one of the main beams of a roof.

raft·ing [RAF-ting] n sport of traveling on rivers by raft. **raft·er** n participant in this.

rag[1] n 1 fragment of cloth. 2 torn piece. 3 inf newspaper, etc., esp. one considered worthless. 4 piece of ragtime music. ◆ pl 5 tattered clothing. **rag·ged** [RAG-id] adj 1 shaggy. 2 torn. 3 clothed in torn clothes. 4 lacking smoothness. **rag'bag** n confused assortment. **rag'time** n style of jazz piano music.

rag[2] vt ragged, rag·ging 1 tease. 2 torment. 3 play practical jokes on.

rag·a·muf·fin [RAG-ə-muf-in] n ragged, dirty person or child.

rage [rayj] n 1 violent anger or passion. 2 fury. 3 aggressive behavior associated with a certain activity, e.g., road rage. ◆ vi raged, rag·ing 4 speak, act with fury. 5 proceed violently and without check (as storm, battle, etc.). 6 be widely and violently prevalent. **all the rage** very popular.

ecstatic, glowing, joyful, joyous, on cloud nine (inf), rapturous 2 = **bright**, brilliant, gleaming, glittering, glowing, luminous, lustrous, shining

radiate v 1 = **spread out**, branch out, diverge, issue 2 = **emit**, diffuse, give off or out, pour, scatter, send out, shed, spread

radical adj 1 = **fundamental**, basic, deep-seated, innate, natural, profound 2 = **extreme**, complete, drastic, entire, extremist, fanatical, severe, sweeping, thorough ◆ n 3 = **extremist**, fanatic, militant, revolutionary

raffle n = **draw**, lottery, sweep, sweepstake

ragamuffin n = **urchin**, guttersnipe

rage n 1 = **fury**, anger, frenzy, ire, madness, passion, rampage, wrath 2 As in all the rage = **craze**, enthusiasm, fad (inf), fashion, latest thing, trend, vogue ◆ v 3 = **be furious**, blow one's top, blow up (inf), fly off the handle, fume, go ballistic (sl), go up the wall (sl), see red, seethe, storm, wig out (sl)

ragged adj 1 = **tattered**, in rags, in tatters, shabby, tatty, threadbare, torn, unkempt 2 = **rough**, jagged, rugged, serrated,

rag·lan [RAG-lən] *adj* of sleeves that continue to the neck so that there are no shoulder seams.

ra·gout [ra-GOO] *n* highly seasoned stew of meat and vegetables.

raid [rayd] *n* **1** rush, attack. **2** foray. ♦ *vt* **3** make raid on.

rail¹ [rayl] *n* **1** horizontal bar, esp. as part of fence, track, etc. **2** *sl* line of cocaine for sniffing. **rail'ing** *n* fence, barrier made of rails supported by posts. **rail'head** [-hed] *n* farthest point to which railway line extends. **rail'road, rail'way** *n* **1** track of steel rails on which trains run. **2** company operating railroad.

rail² *vi* **1** utter abuse. **2** scoff. **3** scold. **4** reproach. **rail'ler·y** [-ə-ree] *n, pl* **-ler·ies** banter.

rail³ *n* any of kinds of marsh birds.

rai·ment [RAY-mənt] *n* clothing.

rain [rayn] *n* **1** moisture falling in drops from clouds. **2** fall of such drops. ♦ *vi* **3** fall as rain. ♦ *vt* **4** pour down like rain. **rain'y** *adj* **rain·i·er, rain·i·est rain'bow** [-boh] *n* arch of prismatic colors in sky. **rain'coat** *n* light water-resistant overcoat.

raise [rayz] *vt* **raised, rais·ing 1** lift up. **2** set up. **3** build. **4** increase. **5** elevate. **6** promote. **7** heighten, as pitch of voice. **8** breed into existence. **9** levy, collect. **10** end (siege). **raise Cain** [KAYN] be riotous,

angry, etc.

rai·sin [RAY-zin] *n* dried grape.

rai·son d'ê·tre [RAY-zohn DE-trə] *Fr* reason or justification for existence.

raj [rahj] *n* rule, sway, esp. in India. **ra'jah** *n* Indian prince or ruler.

rake¹ [rayk] *n* **1** tool with long handle and crosspiece with teeth for gathering hay, leaves, etc. ♦ *vt* **raked, rak·ing 2** gather, smooth with rake. **3** sweep, search over. **4** sweep with shot. **rake-off** *n* monetary commission, esp. illegal.

rake² *n* dissolute or dissipated man.

rake³ *n* **1** slope, esp. of ship's funnel, etc. ♦ *v* **raked, rak·ing 2** incline from perpendicular. **rak'ish** *adj* appearing dashing or speedy.

ral·ly [RAL-ee] *v* **-lied, -ly·ing 1** bring together, esp. what has been scattered, as routed army or dispersed troops. **2** come together. **3** regain health or strength, revive. ♦ *n* **4** act of rallying. **5** assembly, esp. outdoor, of any organization. **6** *Tennis* lively exchange of strokes.

ram *n* **1** male sheep. **2** hydraulic machine. **3** battering engine. ♦ *vt* **rammed, ram·ming 4** force, drive. **5** strike against with force. **6** stuff. **7** strike with ram.

RAM [ram] *Computers* random-access memory (as on a hard disk).

ram·ble [RAM-bəl] *vi* **-bled, -bling 1** walk

uneven, unfinished

raging *adj* = **furious**, beside oneself, enraged, fuming, incensed, infuriated, mad, raving, seething

rags *pl n* = **tatters**, castoffs, old clothes, tattered clothing

raid *n* **1** = **attack**, foray, incursion, inroad, invasion, sally, sortie ♦ *v* **2** = **attack**, assault, foray, invade, pillage, plunder, sack

raider *n* = **attacker**, invader, marauder, plunderer, robber, thief

railing *n* = **fence**, balustrade, barrier, paling, rails

rain *n* **1** = **rainfall**, cloudburst, deluge, downpour, drizzle, fall, raindrops, showers, torrent ♦ *v* **2** = **pour**, bucket down (*inf*), come down in buckets (*inf*), drizzle, pelt (down), rain cats and dogs, teem **3** = **fall**, deposit, drop, shower, sprinkle

rainy *adj* = **wet**, damp, drizzly, showery

raise *v* **1** = **lift**, build, elevate, erect, heave, hoist, rear, uplift **2** = **increase**, advance,

amplify, boost, enhance, enlarge, heighten, inflate, intensify, magnify, strengthen **3** = **collect**, assemble, form, gather, mass, obtain, rally, recruit **4** = **cause**, create, engender, occasion, originate, produce, provoke, start **5** = **bring up**, develop, nurture, rear **6** = **suggest**, advance, broach, introduce, moot, put forward

rake¹ *v* **1** = **gather**, collect, remove **2** = **search**, comb, scour, scrutinize

rake² *n* = **libertine**, debauchee, lecher, playboy, roué

rakish¹ *adj* = **dashing**, dapper, debonair, devil-may-care, jaunty, raffish

rally¹ *n* **1** = **gathering**, assembly, congress, convention, meeting **2** = **recovery**, improvement, recuperation, revival ♦ *v* **3** = **reassemble**, regroup, reorganize, unite **4** = **gather**, assemble, collect, convene, marshal, muster, round up, unite **5** = **recover**, get better, improve, recuperate, revive

without definite route. **2** wander. **3** talk incoherently. **4** spread in random fashion.
♦ *n* **5** rambling walk. **ram'bler** *n* **1** climbing rose. **2** one who rambles.

ram•e•kin [RAM-i-kin] *n* **1** small fireproof dish. **2** food baked in it.

ram•i•fy [RAM-ə-fī] *v* **-fied, -fy•ing 1** spread in branches, subdivide. **2** become complex. **ram•i•fi•ca'tion** *n* **1** branch, subdivision. **2** process of branching out. **3** consequence.

ra•mose [RAY-mōs] *adj* branching.

ramp *n* gradual slope joining two level surfaces.

ram•page [ram-PAYJ] *vi* **-paged, -pag•ing 1** dash about violently. ♦ *n* [RAM-payj] **2** angry or destructive behavior. **ram•pa'geous** [-jəs] *adj*

ramp•ant [RAM-pənt] *adj* **1** violent. **2** rife. **3** rearing.

ram•part [RAM-pahrt] *n* mound, wall for defense.

ram•shack•le [RAM-shak-əl] *adj* tumble-down, rickety, makeshift.

ran pt. of RUN.

ranch *n* **1** cattle farm. ♦ *vi* **2** manage one. **ranch'er** *n*

ran•cid [RAN-sid] *adj* smelling or tasting offensive, like stale fat.

ran•cor [RANG-kər] *n* bitter, inveterate hate. **ran'cor•ous** *adj* **1** malignant. **2** virulent.

ran•dom [RAN-dəm] *adj* made or done by chance, without plan. **at random** haphazard(ly).

rang pt. of RING².

range [raynj] *n* **1** limits. **2** row. **3** scope, sphere. **4** distance missile can travel. **5** distance of mark shot at. **6** place for shooting practice or rocket testing. **7** rank. **8** kitchen stove. ♦ *v* **ranged, rang•ing** ♦ *vt* **9** set in row. **10** classify. **11** roam. ♦ *vi* **12** extend. **13** roam. **14** pass from one point to another. **15** fluctuate (as prices). **rang'er** *n* official in charge of or patrolling park, etc. **rang'y** *adj* **rang•i•er, rang•i•est 1** with long, slender limbs. **2** spacious. **range'find•er** *n* instrument for finding distance away of given object.

rank¹ [rangk] *n* **1** row, line. **2** order. **3** social class. **4** status. **5** relative place or position. ♦ *vt* **6** draw up in rank, classify. ♦ *vi* **7** have rank, place. **8** have certain distinctions. **the ranks** common soldiers. **rank and file** (esp. in labor unions) great mass or majority of people.

rank² *adj* **-er, -est 1** growing too thickly, coarse. **2** offensively strong. **3** rancid. **4** vile. **5** flagrant. **rank'ly** *adv*

ran•kle [RANG-kəl] *vi* **-kled, -kling** fester,

THESAURUS

ram *v* **1** = **hit**, butt, crash, dash, drive, force, impact, smash **2** = **cram**, crowd, force, jam, stuff, thrust

ramble *v* **1** = **walk**, range, roam, rove, saunter, stray, stroll, wander **2** = **babble** ♦ *n* **3** = **walk**, hike, roaming, roving, saunter, stroll, tour

rambler *n* = **walker**, hiker, rover, wanderer, wayfarer

rambling *adj* = **long-winded**, circuitous, digressive, disconnected, discursive, disjointed, incoherent, wordy

ramification *n* **ramifications** = **consequences**, developments, results, sequel, upshot

ramp *n* = **slope**, gradient, incline, rise

rampage *v* **1** = **go berserk**, rage, run amok, run riot, storm ♦ *n* **2 on the rampage** = **berserk**, amok, out of control, raging, riotous, violent, wild

rampant *adj* **1** = **widespread**, prevalent, profuse, rife, spreading like wildfire, unchecked, uncontrolled, unrestrained **2** *Heraldry* = **upright**, erect, rearing,
standing

rampart *n* = **defense**, bastion, bulwark, fence, fortification, wall

ramshackle *adj* = **rickety**, crumbling, decrepit, derelict, flimsy, shaky, tumbledown, unsafe, unsteady

rancid *adj* = **rotten**, bad, fetid, foul, putrid, rank, sour, stale, strong-smelling, tainted

rancor *n* = **hatred**, animosity, bad blood, bitterness, hate, ill feeling, ill will

random *adj* **1** = **chance**, accidental, adventitious, casual, fortuitous, haphazard, hit or miss, incidental ♦ *n* **2 at random** = **haphazardly**, arbitrarily, by chance, randomly, unsystematically, willy-nilly

range *n* **1** = **limits**, area, bounds, orbit, province, radius, reach, scope, sphere **2** = **series**, assortment, collection, gamut, lot, selection, variety ♦ *v* **3** = **vary**, extend, reach, run, stretch **4** = **roam**, ramble, rove, traverse, wander

rangy *adj* = **long-limbed**, gangling, lanky, leggy, long-legged

rank¹ *n* **1** = **status**, caste, class, degree,

continue to cause anger, resentment or bitterness.

ran•sack [RAN-sak] *vt* **1** search thoroughly. **2** pillage, plunder.

ran•som [RAN-səm] *n* **1** release from captivity by payment. **2** amount paid. ◆ *vt* **3** pay ransom for.

rant *vi* **1** rave in violent, high-sounding language ◆ *n* **2** noisy, boisterous speech. **3** wild gaiety.

rap[1] *n* **1** smart slight blow. **2** rhythmic monologue performed to music. ◆ *v* **rapped, rap•ping 3** give rap to. **4** utter abruptly. **5** perform rhythmic monologue to music. **rap'per** *n* **1** singer of rap. **2** person or thing that raps. **take the rap** *sl* take blame, suffer punishment (for), whether guilty or not.

rap[2] *n* **not care a rap** not care at all.

ra•pa•cious [rə-PAY-shəs] *adj* **1** greedy. **2** grasping. **ra•pac'i•ty** [-PAS-i-tee] *n*

rape [rayp] *vt* **raped, rap•ing 1** force (person) to submit unwillingly to sexual intercourse. ◆ *n* **2** act of raping. **3** any

violation or abuse. **rap'ist** *n*

rap'id *adj* quick, swift. **rapids** *pl n* part of river with fast, turbulent current. **ra•pid'i•ty** *n*

ra•pi•er [RAY-pee-ər] *n* fine-bladed sword for thrusting only.

rap•ine [RAP-in] *n* plunder.

rap•port [ra-POR] *n* harmony, agreement.

rap•proche•ment [rap-rohsh-MAHN] *n* reestablishment of friendly relations, esp. between nations.

rapt *adj* engrossed, spellbound. **rap'ture** [-chər] *n* ecstasy. **rap'tur•ous** *adj*

rare[1] [rair] *adj* **rar•er, rar•est 1** uncommon. **2** infrequent. **3** of uncommon quality. **4** of atmosphere, having low density, thin. **rare'ly** *adv* seldom. **rar'i•ty** *n, pl* **-ties 1** anything rare. **2** rareness.

rare[2] *adj* **rar•er, rar•est** (of meat) lightly cooked.

rare•bit [RAIR-bit] *n* see WELSH RABBIT.

rar•e•fy [RAIR-ə-fī] *v* **-fied, -fy•ing 1** make, become thin, rare, or less dense. **2** refine.

rar•ing [RAIR-ing] *adj inf* enthusiastically

———————————— THESAURUS ————————————

division, grade, level, order, position, sort, type **2 = row**, column, file, group, line, range, series, tier ◆ *v* **3 = arrange**, align, array, dispose, line up, order, sort

rank[2] *adj* **1 = absolute**, arrant, blatant, complete, downright, flagrant, gross, sheer, thorough, total, utter **2 = foul**, bad, disgusting, funky (*sl*), noisome, noxious, offensive, rancid, revolting, smelly, stinking **3 = abundant**, dense, lush, luxuriant, profuse

rank and file *n* **= general public**, majority, mass, masses

rankle *v* **= annoy**, anger, gall, get on one's nerves (*inf*), irk, irritate, rile

ransack *v* **1 = search**, comb, explore, go through, rummage, scour, turn inside out **2 = plunder**, loot, pillage, raid, strip

ransom *n* **= payment**, money, payoff, price

rant *v* **= shout**, cry, declaim, rave, roar, yell

rap *v* **1 = hit**, crack, knock, strike, tap ◆ *n* **2 = blow**, clout (*inf*), crack, knock, tap **3** *Sl* **= punishment**, blame, responsibility

rapacious *adj* **= greedy**, avaricious, grasping, insatiable, predatory, preying, voracious

rape *v* **1 = sexually assault**, abuse, force, outrage, ravish, violate ◆ *n* **2 = sexual assault**, outrage, ravishment, violation **3 = desecration**, abuse, defilement, violation

rapid *adj* **= quick**, brisk, express, fast, hasty, hurried, prompt, speedy, swift

rapidity *n* **= speed**, alacrity, briskness, fleetness, haste, hurry, promptness, quickness, rush, swiftness, velocity

rapidly *adv* **= quickly**, briskly, fast, hastily, hurriedly, in haste, promptly, pronto (*inf*), speedily, swiftly

rapport *n* **= bond**, affinity, empathy, harmony, link, relationship, sympathy, tie, understanding

rapprochement *n* **= reconciliation**, detente, reunion

rapt *adj* **= spellbound**, absorbed, engrossed, enthralled, entranced, fascinated, gripped

rapture *n* **= ecstasy**, bliss, delight, euphoria, joy, rhapsody, seventh heaven, transport

rapturous *adj* **= ecstatic**, blissful, euphoric, in seventh heaven, joyful, overjoyed, over the moon (*inf*), transported

rare[1] *adj* **1 = uncommon**, few, infrequent, scarce, singular, sparse, strange, unusual **2 = superb**, choice, excellent, fine, great, peerless, superlative

rarefied *adj* **= exalted**, elevated, high, lofty, noble, spiritual, sublime

rarely *adv* **= seldom**, hardly, hardly ever, infrequently willing, ready.

ras·cal [RAS-kəl] *n* **1** rogue. **2** naughty (young) person. **ras·cal'i·ty** [-KAL-i-tee] *n* roguery, baseness. **ras·cal·ly** [-kəl-ee] *adj*

rash¹ *adj* **-er, -est** hasty, reckless, incautious.

rash² *n* **1** skin eruption. **2** outbreak, series of (unpleasant) occurrences.

rash·er [RASH-ər] *n* **1** serving of bacon, usu. three or four slices. **2** thin slice of bacon or ham.

rasp *n* **1** harsh, grating noise. **2** coarse file. ◆ *v* **3** scrape with rasp. **4** make scraping noise. **5** speak in grating voice. **6** grate upon. **7** irritate.

rasp·ber·ry [RAZ-ber-ee] *n* **1** red, juicy edible berry. **2** plant which bears it. **3** *inf* spluttering noise with tongue and lips to show contempt.

Ras·ta·far·i·an [ras-tə-FAIR-ee-ən] *n, adj* (member) of Jamaican cult regarding Haile Selassie, late emperor of Ethiopia, as the messiah.

rat *n* **1** small rodent. **2** *sl* contemptible person, esp. deserter, informer, etc. ◆ *vi* **rat·ted, rat·ting 3** *sl* inform (on), betray, desert, abandon. **4** hunt rats. **rat'ty** *adj sl* **-ti·er, -ti·est** mean, ill-tempered, irritable. **rat race** continual hectic competitive activity. **rat'trap** *n* **1** device for catching rats. **2** dilapidated dwelling.

ratch·et [RACH-it] *n* set of teeth on bar or wheel allowing motion in one direction only.

rate¹ [rayt] *n* **1** proportion between two things. **2** charge. **3** degree of speed, etc. ◆ *vt* **rat·ed, rat·ing 4** value. **5** estimate value of. **rat'a·ble** *adj* that can be rated or appraised.

rate² *vt* **rat·ed, rat·ing** scold, chide.

rath·er [RATH-ər] *adv* **1** to some extent. **2** preferably. **3** more willingly.

rat·i·fy [RAT-ə-fī] *vt* **-fied, -fy·ing** confirm. **rat·i·fi·ca'tion** [-fi-KAY-shən] *n*

rat·ing [RAY-ting] *n* **1** credit standing. **2** fixing a rate. **3** classification, esp. of ship, enlisted member of armed forces. **4** angry rebuke.

ra·tio [RAY-shoh] *n, pl* **-tios 1** proportion. **2** quantitative relation.

ra·ti·oc·i·nate [rash-ee-OS-ə-nayt] *vi* **-nat·ed, -nat·ing** reason. **ra·ti·oc·i·na'tion** [-NAY-shən] *n*

ra·tion [RASH-ən] *n* **1** fixed allowance of food, etc. ◆ *vt* **2** supply with, limit to certain amount.

ra·tion·al [RASH-ə-nl] *adj* **1** reasonable, sensible. **2** capable of thinking, reasoning. **ra·tion·ale'** [-NAL] *n* reasons given for actions, etc. **ra'tion·al·ism** *n* philosophy that regards reason as only guide or authority. **ra·tion·al'i·ty** *n* **ra·tion·al·i·za'tion** *n* **ra'tion·al·ize** *vt* **-ized, -iz·ing 1** justify by plausible reasoning. **2** reorganize to improve efficiency, etc.

rat·tan [ra-TAN] *n* **1** climbing palm with

raring *adj* As in **raring to** = eager, desperate, enthusiastic, impatient, keen, longing, ready

rarity *n* **1** = curio, collector's item, find, gem, treasure **2** = uncommonness, infrequency, scarcity, shortage, sparseness, strangeness, unusualness

rascal *n* = rogue, devil, good-for-nothing, imp, scamp, scoundrel, villain

rash¹ *adj* = reckless, careless, foolhardy, hasty, heedless, ill-advised, impetuous, imprudent, impulsive, incautious

rash² *n* **1** = outbreak, eruption **2** = spate, flood, outbreak, plague, series, wave

rashness *n* = recklessness, carelessness, foolhardiness, hastiness, heedlessness, indiscretion, thoughtlessness

rate¹ *n* **1** = speed, pace, tempo, velocity **2** = degree, proportion, ratio, scale, standard **3** = charge, cost, fee, figure, price **4 at any rate** = in any case, anyhow, anyway, at all

events ◆ *v* **5** = evaluate, consider, count, estimate, grade, measure, rank, reckon, value **6** = deserve, be entitled to, be worthy of, merit

rather *adv* **1** = to some extent, a little, fairly, moderately, quite, relatively, somewhat, to some degree **2** = preferably, more readily, more willingly, sooner

ratify *v* = approve, affirm, authorize, confirm, endorse, establish, sanction, uphold

rating¹ *n* = position, class, degree, grade, order, placing, rank, rate, status

ratio *n* = proportion, fraction, percentage, rate, relation

ration *n* **1** = allowance, allotment, helping, measure, part, portion, quota, share ◆ *v* **2** = limit, budget, control, restrict

rational *adj* = sane, intelligent, logical, lucid, realistic, reasonable, sensible, sound, wise jointed stems. 2 cane of this oft. used for furniture.

rat·tle [RAT-l] v **-tled, -tling** ♦ vi 1 give out succession of short sharp sounds. 2 clatter. ♦ vt 3 shake briskly causing a sharp clatter of sounds. 4 confuse, fluster. ♦ n 5 such sound. 6 instrument for making it. 7 set of horny rings in rattlesnake's tail. **rat'tle·snake** n poisonous snake

rau·cous [RAW-kəs] adj 1 hoarse. 2 harsh.

raun·chy [RAWN-chee] adj inf **-chi·er, -chi·est** 1 earthy, vulgar, sexy. 2 slovenly.

rav·age [RAV-ij] vt **-aged, -ag·ing** 1 lay waste, plunder. ♦ n 2 destruction.

rave [rayv] vi **raved, rav·ing** talk wildly in delirium or enthusiastically. ♦ n

rav·el [RAV-əl] vt **-eled, -el·ing** 1 entangle. 2 fray out. 3 disentangle.

ra·ven[1] [RAY-vən] n 1 black bird like crow. ♦ adj 2 shiny black.

raven[2] v seek prey, plunder. **rav·en·ous** [RAV-ə-nəs] adj very hungry.

ra·vine [rə-VEEN] n narrow steep-sided valley worn by stream, gorge.

ra·vi·o·li [rav-ee-OH-lee] pl n small, thin pieces of dough filled with highly seasoned, chopped meat and cooked.

rav·ish vt 1 enrapture. 2 commit rape upon. **rav'ish·ing** adj lovely, entrancing.

raw adj **-er, -est** 1 uncooked. 2 not manufactured or refined. 3 skinned. 4 inexperienced, unpracticed, as recruits. 5 sensitive. 6 chilly. **raw deal** unfair or dishonest treatment. **raw'hide** n 1 untanned hide. 2 whip of this.

ray[1] n 1 single line or narrow beam of light, heat, etc. 2 any of set of radiating lines. ♦ vi 3 come out in rays. 4 radiate.

ray[2] n marine fish, often very large, with winglike pectoral fins and whiplike tail.

ray'on n (fabric of) synthetic fiber.

raze [rayz] vt **razed, raz·ing** 1 destroy completely. 2 wipe out, delete. 3 level.

ra·zor [RAY-zər] n sharp instrument for shaving or for cutting hair.

Rb Chem. rubidium.

re[1] [ray] n second sol-fa note.

re[2] prep with reference to, concerning.

Re Chem. rhenium.

re- prefix again, e.g. re-enter; retrial.

reach [reech] vt 1 arrive at. 2 extend. 3 succeed in touching. 4 attain to. ♦ vi 5 stretch out hand. 6 extend. ♦ n 7 act of reaching. 8 power of touching. 9 grasp, scope. 10 range. 11 straight stretch of river between two bends.

rationale n = **reason**, grounds, logic, motivation, philosophy, principle, raison d'être, theory

rationalize v = **justify**, account for, excuse, vindicate

rattle v 1 = **clatter**, bang, jangle 2 = **shake**, bounce, jar, jolt, vibrate 3 Inf = **fluster**, disconcert, disturb, faze, perturb, shake, upset

raucous adj = **harsh**, grating, hoarse, loud, noisy, rough, strident

raunchy adj Sl = **sexy**, coarse, earthy, lusty, sexual, steamy (inf)

ravage v 1 = **destroy**, demolish, despoil, devastate, lay waste, ransack, ruin, spoil ♦ n 2 ravages = **damage**, destruction, devastation, havoc, ruin, ruination, spoliation

rave v 1 = **rant**, babble, be delirious, go mad (inf), rage, roar 2 = **enthuse**, be excited about (inf), be wild about (inf), gush, praise

ravenous adj = **starving**, famished, starved

ravine n = **canyon**, defile, gorge, gulch, gully, pass

raving adj = **mad**, crazed, crazy, delirious, hysterical, insane, irrational, wild

ravish v 1 = **enchant**, captivate, charm, delight, enrapture, entrance, fascinate, spellbind 2 = **rape**, abuse, force, sexually assault, violate

ravishing adj = **enchanting**, beautiful, bewitching, charming, entrancing, gorgeous, lovely

raw adj 1 = **uncooked**, fresh, natural 2 = **unrefined**, basic, coarse, crude, natural, rough, unfinished, unprocessed 3 = **inexperienced**, callow, green, immature, new 4 = **chilly**, biting, bitter, cold, freezing, piercing

ray n = **beam**, bar, flash, gleam, shaft

raze v = **destroy**, demolish, flatten, knock down, level, pull down, ruin

re prep = **concerning**, about, apropos, regarding, with reference to, with regard to

reach v 1 = **arrive at**, attain, get to, make 2 = **touch**, contact, extend to, grasp, stretch to 3 = **contact**, communicate with, get hold of, get in touch with, get through to ♦ n 4 = **range**, capacity, distance, extension, extent, grasp, influence, power,

re·act [ree-AKT] *vi* act in return, opposition or toward former state. **re·ac'tance** [-əns] *n Electricity* resistance in coil, apart from ohmic resistance, due to current reacting on itself. **re·ac'tion** [-AK-shən] *n* **1** any action resisting another. **2** counter or backward tendency. **3** response. **4** chemical or nuclear change, combination or decomposition. **re·ac'tion·ar·y** *n, adj, pl* **-ar·ies** (person) opposed to change, esp. in politics, etc. **re·ac'tive** *adj* chemically active. **re·ac'tor** *n* apparatus in which nuclear reaction is maintained and controlled to produce nuclear energy.

read [reed] *v* **read** [red], **read·ing** ◆ *vt* **1** look at and understand written or printed matter. **2** learn by reading. **3** interpret mentally. **4** read and utter. **5** interpret. **6** study. **7** understand any indicating instrument. **8** (of instrument) register. ◆ *vi* **9** be occupied in reading. **10** find mentioned in reading. **read'a·ble** *adj* that can be read, or read with pleasure. **read'er** *n* **1** one who reads. **2** university professor's assistant. **3** school textbook. **4** one who

reads manuscripts submitted to publisher.

re·ad·just' *v* adapt to a new situation. **re·ad·just'ment** *n*

re·ad·mit' *vt* **-mit·ting, -mit·ted** let (person, country, etc.) back in to a place or organization.

read·y [RED-ee] *adj* **read·i·er, read·i·est 1** prepared for use or action. **2** willing, prompt. **read'i·ly** *adv* **1** promptly. **2** willingly. **read'i·ness** [-nis] *n*

re·a·gent [ree-AY-jənt] *n* chemical substance that reacts with another and is used to detect presence of the other.

re·al [REE-əl] *adj* **1** existing in fact. **2** happening. **3** actual. **4** genuine. **5** (of property) consisting of land and houses. **re'al·ism** *n* **1** regarding things as they are. **2** artistic treatment with this outlook. **re·al·is'tic** *adj* **re·al'i·ty** *n* real existence. **re'al·ly** *adv* **re'al·ty** *n* real estate. **real estate** landed property.

re·al·ize [REE-ə-līz] *vt* **-ized, -iz·ing 1** apprehend, grasp significance of. **2** make real. **3** convert into money. **re·al·i·za'tion** *n*

realm [relm] *n* kingdom, province, domain,

———————————— THESAURUS ————————————

scope, stretch

react *v* **1** = **respond**, answer, reply **2** = **act**, behave, function, operate, proceed, work

reaction *n* **1** = **response**, answer, reply **2** = **recoil**, counteraction **3** = **conservatism**, the right

reactionary *adj* **1** = **conservative**, right-wing ◆ *n* **2** = **conservative**, die-hard, right-winger

read *v* **1** = **look at**, peruse, pore over, scan, study **2** = **interpret**, comprehend, construe, decipher, discover, see, understand **3** = **register**, display, indicate, record, show

readable *adj* **1** = **enjoyable**, entertaining, enthralling, gripping, interesting **2** = **legible**, clear, comprehensible, decipherable

readily *adv* **1** = **willingly**, eagerly, freely, gladly, promptly, quickly **2** = **easily**, effortlessly, quickly, smoothly, speedily, unhesitatingly

readiness *n* **1** = **willingness**, eagerness, keenness **2** = **ease**, adroitness, dexterity, facility, promptness

reading *n* **1** = **perusal**, examination, inspection, scrutiny, study **2** = **recital**, lesson, performance, sermon **3** = **interpretation**, grasp, impression, version

4 = **learning**, education, erudition, knowledge, scholarship

ready *adj* **1** = **prepared**, arranged, fit, organized, primed, ripe, set **2** = **willing**, agreeable, disposed, eager, glad, happy, inclined, keen, prone **3** = **prompt**, alert, bright, clever, intelligent, keen, perceptive, quick, sharp, smart **4** = **available**, accessible, convenient, handy, near, present

real *adj* = **genuine**, actual, authentic, factual, rightful, sincere, true, unfeigned, valid

realistic *adj* **1** = **practical**, common-sense, down-to-earth, level-headed, matter-of-fact, real, sensible **2** = **lifelike**, authentic, faithful, genuine, natural, true, true to life

reality *n* = **truth**, actuality, fact, realism, validity, verity

realization *n* **1** = **awareness**, cognizance, comprehension, conception, grasp, perception, recognition, understanding **2** = **achievement**, accomplishment, fulfillment

realize *v* **1** = **become aware of**, comprehend, get the message, grasp, take in, understand **2** = **achieve**, accomplish, carry out *or* through, complete, do, effect, fulfill, perform sphere.

ream[1] [reem] n 1 twenty quires or 500 sheets of paper. ◆ pl 2 large quantity of written matter.

ream[2] vt enlarge, bevel out, as hole in metal. **ream'er** n tool for this.

reap [reep] v 1 cut and gather harvest. 2 receive as fruit of previous activity. **reap'er** n

re•ap•pear' vi appear again. **re•ap•pear'ance** n

rear[1] [reer] n 1 back part. 2 part of army, procession, etc. behind others. **rear admiral** lowest flag rank in certain navies. **rear'guard** n troops protecting rear of army. **rear'most** [-mohst] adj

rear[2] vt 1 care for and educate (children). 2 breed. 3 erect. ◆ vi 4 rise, esp. on hind feet.

re•arm' v 1 arm again. ◆ vt 2 equip (army, nation, etc.) with better weapons. **re•ar'ma•ment** n

re•ar•range' vt organize differently, alter. **rearrangement** n

rea•son [REE-zən] n 1 ground, motive. 2 faculty of thinking. 3 sanity. 4 sensible or logical thought or view. ◆ vi 5 think

logically in forming conclusions. ◆ vt 6 (usu. with with) persuade by logical argument into doing, etc. **rea'son•a•ble** adj 1 sensible, not excessive. 2 suitable. 3 logical.

re•as•sure [ree-ə-SHUUR] vt -sured, -sur•ing restore confidence to.

re•bate [REE-bayt] n 1 discount, refund. ◆ vt bat•ed, -bat•ing 2 deduct.

re•bel [ri-BEL] vi -belled, -bel•ling 1 revolt, resist lawful authority, take arms against ruling power. ◆ n [REB-əl] 2 one who rebels. 3 insurgent. ◆ adj [REB-əl] 4 in rebellion. **re•bel•lion** [ri-BEL-yən] n organized open resistance to authority, revolt. **re•bel'lious** adj

re•birth' n revival or renaissance. **re•born'** adj active again after a period of inactivity.

re•boot' v to shut down and then restart (a computer system).

re•bound [ri-BOWND] vi 1 spring back. 2 misfire, esp. so as to hurt perpetrator (of plan, deed, etc.). ◆ n [REE-bownd] 3 act of springing back or recoiling. 4 return.

re•buff [ri-BUF] n 1 blunt refusal. 2 check. ◆ vt 3 repulse, snub.

really adv = truly, actually, certainly, genuinely, in actuality, indeed, in fact, positively, surely

realm n 1 = kingdom, country, domain, dominion, empire, land 2 = sphere, area, branch, department, field, province, territory, world

reap v 1 = collect, bring in, cut, garner, gather, harvest 2 = obtain, acquire, derive, gain, get

rear[1] n 1 = back, end, rearguard, stern, tail, tail end ◆ adj 2 = back, following, hind, last

rear[2] v 1 = bring up, breed, educate, foster, nurture, raise, train 2 = rise, loom, soar, tower

reason n 1 = cause, aim, goal, grounds, incentive, intention, motive, object, purpose 2 = sense(s), intellect, judgment, logic, mind, rationality, sanity, soundness, understanding ◆ v 3 = deduce, conclude, infer, make out, think, work out 4 reason with = persuade, bring round (inf), prevail upon, talk into or out of, urge, win over

reasonable adj 1 = sensible, logical, plausible, practical, sane, sober, sound, tenable, wise 2 = moderate, equitable, fair, fit, just, modest, O.K. or okay (inf), proper, right

reasoned adj = sensible, clear, logical, well-thought-out

reasoning n = thinking, analysis, logic, thought

reassure v = encourage, comfort, hearten, put or set one's mind at rest, restore confidence to

rebate n = refund, allowance, bonus, deduction, discount, reduction

rebel v 1 = revolt, mutiny, resist, rise up 2 = defy, disobey, dissent ◆ n 3 = revolutionary, insurgent, revolutionist, secessionist 4 = nonconformist, apostate, dissenter, heretic, schismatic ◆ adj 5 = rebellious, insurgent, insurrectionary, revolutionary

rebellion n 1 = resistance, mutiny, revolt, revolution, rising, uprising 2 = nonconformity, defiance, heresy, schism

rebellious adj 1 = revolutionary, disloyal, disobedient, disorderly, insurgent, mutinous, rebel, seditious, unruly 2 = defiant, difficult, refractory, resistant, unmanageable

rebound v 1 = bounce, recoil, ricochet 2 = misfire, backfire, boomerang, recoil

rebuff v 1 = reject, cold-shoulder, cut, knock back (sl), refuse, repulse, slight,

re·build' *vt* **-build'ing, -built 1** build (building, town) again, after severe damage. **2** develop (business, relationship, etc.) again after destruction or damage.

re·buke [ri-BYOOK] *vt* **-buked, -buk·ing** reprove, reprimand, find fault with. ◆ *n*

re·bus [REE-bəs] *n, pl* **-bus·es** riddle in which names of things, etc. are represented by pictures standing for syllables, etc.

re·but [ri-BUT] *vt* **-but·ted, -but·ting** refute, disprove. **re·but'tal** *n*

re·cal·ci·trant [ri-KAL-si-trənt] *adj, n* willfully disobedient (person).

re·call [ri-KAWL] *vt* **1** recollect, remember. **2** call, summon, order back. **3** annul, cancel. **4** revive, restore. ◆ *n* [REE-kawl] **5** summons to return. **6** ability to remember.

re·cant [ri-KANT] *vt* withdraw statement, opinion, etc. **re·can·ta'tion** *n*

re·ca·pit·u·late [ree-kə-PICH-ə-layt] *vt* **-lat·ed, -lat·ing 1** state again briefly. **2** repeat.

re·cap'ture *vt* **1** experience again. **2** capture again.

re·cede [ri-SEED] *vi* **-ced·ed, -ced·ing 1** go back. **2** become distant. **3** slope backward. **4** begin balding.

re·ceipt [ri-SEET] *n* **1** written acknowledgment of money received. **2** receiving or being received. ◆ *vt* **3** acknowledge payment of in writing.

re·ceive [ri-SEEV] *vt* **-ceived, -ceiv·ing 1** take, accept, get. **2** experience. **3** greet (guests). **re·ceiv'a·ble** *adj* **re·ceiv'er** *n* **1** official appointed to receive money. **2** fence, one who takes stolen goods knowing them to have been stolen. **3** equipment in telephone, radio or TV that converts electrical signals into sound, light.

re·cent [REE-sənt] *adj* **1** that has lately happened. **2** new. **re·cent·ly** *adv*

re·cep·ta·cle [ri-SEP-tə-kəl] *n* vessel, place or space, to contain anything.

re·cep·tion [ri-SEP-shən] *n* **1** receiving. **2** manner of receiving. **3** welcome. **4** formal party. **5** in broadcasting, quality of signals received. **re·cep'tion·ist** *n* person who receives guests, clients, etc.

re·cep·tive [ri-SEP-tiv] *adj* able, quick, willing to receive new ideas, suggestions, etc. **re·cep·tiv'i·ty** *n*

re·cess [REE-ses] *n* **1** niche, alcove. **2** hollow. **3** secret, hidden place. **4** remission or suspension of business. **5** vacation, holiday.

THESAURUS

snub, spurn, turn down ◆ *n* **2** = **rejection**, cold shoulder, kick in the teeth (*sl*), knock-back (*sl*), refusal, repulse, slap in the face (*inf*), slight, snub

rebuke *v* **1** = **scold**, admonish, castigate, censure, chide, reprimand, reprove, tell off (*inf*) ◆ *n* **2** = **scolding**, admonition, censure, reprimand, row, telling-off (*inf*)

rebut *v* = **disprove**, confute, invalidate, negate, overturn, prove wrong, refute

rebuttal *n* = **disproof**, confutation, invalidation, negation, refutation

recalcitrant *adj* = **disobedient**, defiant, insubordinate, refractory, unmanageable, unruly, wayward, willful

recall *v* **1** = **recollect**, bring or call to mind, evoke, remember **2** = **annul**, cancel, countermand, repeal, retract, revoke, withdraw ◆ *n* **3** = **recollection**, memory, remembrance **4** = **annulment**, cancellation, repeal, rescindment, retraction, withdrawal

recant *v* = **withdraw**, disclaim, forswear, renege, repudiate, retract, revoke, take back

recapitulate *v* = **repeat**, outline, recap

(*inf*), recount, restate, summarize

recede *v* = **fall back**, abate, ebb, regress, retire, retreat, return, subside, withdraw

receipt *n* **1** = **sales slip**, counterfoil, proof of purchase **2** = **receiving**, acceptance, delivery, reception

receive *v* **1** = **get**, accept, acquire, be given, collect, obtain, pick up, take **2** = **experience**, bear, encounter, suffer, sustain, undergo **3** = **greet**, accommodate, admit, entertain, meet, welcome

recent *adj* = **new**, current, fresh, late, modern, novel, present-day, up-to-date

recently *adv* = **newly**, currently, freshly, lately, latterly, not long ago, of late

receptacle *n* = **container**, holder, repository

reception *n* **1** = **party**, function, levee, soirée **2** = **welcome**, acknowledgment, greeting, reaction, response, treatment

receptive *adj* = **open**, amenable, interested, open-minded, open to suggestions, susceptible, sympathetic

recess *n* **1** = **alcove**, bay, corner, hollow, niche, nook **2** = **break**, holiday, intermission, interval, respite, rest, vacation

re·ces·sion [ri-SESH-ən] n 1 period of reduction in economic activity. 2 act of receding. **re·ces·sive** adj receding.

re·ces·sion·al [ri-SESH-ə-nl] n hymn sung while clergy retire.

re·cher·ché [rə-SHAIR-shay] adj 1 of studied elegance. 2 exquisite. 3 choice.

re·cid·i·vist [ri-SID-ə-vist] n one who relapses into crime.

rec·i·pe [RES-ə-pee] n 1 directions for cooking a dish. 2 prescription. 3 expedient.

re·cip·i·ent [ri-SIP-ee-ənt] adj 1 that can or does receive. ◆ n 2 one who, that which receives.

re·cip·ro·cal [ri-SIP-rə-kəl] adj 1 complementary. 2 mutual. 3 moving backward and forward. 4 alternating. **re·cip·ro·cate** [-rə-kayt] v -cat·ed, -cat·ing ◆ vt 1 give and receive mutually. 2 return. ◆ vi 3 move backward and forward. **re·ci·proc·i·ty** [res-ə-PROS-i-tee] n

re·cite [ri-SĪT] vt -cit·ed, -cit·ing repeat aloud, esp. to audience. **re·cit·al** [-əl] n 1 musical performance, usu. by one person. 2 act of reciting. 3 narration of facts, etc. 4 story. 5 public entertainment of recitations, etc. **rec·i·ta·tion** n 1 recital,

usu. from memory, of poetry or prose. 2 recountal. **rec·i·ta·tive** [res-i-tə-TEEV] n musical declamation.

reck·less [REK-lis] adj heedless, incautious.

reck·on [REK-ən] v 1 count. 2 include. 3 consider. 4 inf think, deem. 5 make calculations.

re·claim [ri-KLAYM] vt 1 make fit for cultivation. 2 bring back. 3 reform. 4 demand the return of. **rec·la·ma·tion** n

re·cline [ri-KLĪN] vi -clined, -clin·ing sit or lie back on one's side.

rec·luse [REK-loos] n 1 hermit. ◆ adj [ri-KLOOS] 2 living in seclusion, shut off from the world. **re·clu·sive** adj

rec·og·nize [REK-əg-nīz] vt -nized, -niz·ing 1 know again. 2 treat as valid. 3 notice, show appreciation of. **rec·og·ni·tion** n **rec·og·niz·a·ble** adj **re·cog·ni·zance** [ri-KOG-nə-zəns] n 1 avowal. 2 bond by which person undertakes before court to observe some condition. 3 obs recognition.

re·coil [ri-KOIL] vi 1 draw back in horror, etc. 2 go wrong so as to hurt the perpetrator. 3 rebound (esp. of gun when fired). ◆ n [REE-koil] 4 backward spring. 5 retreat. 6 recoiling.

THESAURUS

recession n = **depression**, decline, drop, slump

recipe n 1 = **directions**, ingredients, instructions 2 = **method**, formula, prescription, procedure, process, technique

reciprocal adj = **mutual**, alternate, complementary, correlative, corresponding, equivalent, exchanged, interchangeable

reciprocate v = **return**, exchange, reply, requite, respond, swap, trade

recital n 1 = **performance**, rehearsal, rendering 2 = **recitation**, account, narrative, reading, relation, statement, telling

recitation n = **recital**, lecture, passage, performance, piece, reading

recite v = **repeat**, declaim, deliver, narrate, perform, speak

reckless adj = **careless**, hasty, headlong, heedless, imprudent, mindless, precipitate, rash, thoughtless, wild

reckon v 1 = **think**, assume, believe, guess (inf), imagine, suppose 2 = **consider**, account, count, deem, esteem, judge, rate, regard 3 = **count**, add up, calculate,

compute, figure, number, tally, total

reckoning n 1 = **count**, addition, calculation, estimate 2 = **bill**, account, charge, due, score

reclaim v = **regain**, recapture, recover, redeem, reform, retrieve, salvage

recline v = **lean**, lie (down), loll, lounge, repose, rest, sprawl

recluse n = **hermit**, anchoress, anchorite, monk, solitary

reclusive adj = **solitary**, hermit-like, isolated, retiring, withdrawn

recognition n 1 = **identification**, discovery, recollection, remembrance 2 = **acceptance**, admission, allowance, confession 3 = **appreciation**, notice, respect

recognize v 1 = **identify**, know, notice, place, recall, recollect, remember, spot 2 = **accept**, admit, allow, concede, grant 3 = **appreciate**, notice, respect

recoil v 1 = **jerk back**, kick, react, rebound, spring back 2 = **draw back**, falter, quail, shrink 3 = **backfire**, boomerang, misfire, rebound ◆ n 4 = **reaction**, backlash, kick, rebound, repercussion

rec·ol·lect [rek-ə-LEKT] vt call back to mind, remember.

rec·om·mend [rek-ə-MEND] vt **1** advise, counsel. **2** praise, commend. **3** make acceptable. **rec·om·men·da'tion** n

rec·om·pense [REK-əm-pens] vt **-pensed, -pens·ing 1** reward. **2** compensate, make up for. ◆ n **3** compensation. **4** reward. **5** requital.

rec·on·cile [rek-ən-sīl] vt **-ciled, -cil·ing 1** bring back into friendship. **2** adjust, settle, harmonize. **rec·on·cil'a·ble** adj **rec·on·cil·i·a'tion** n

rec·on·dite [REK-ən-dīt] adj obscure, abstruse, little known.

re·con·di·tion [ree-kən-DISH-ən] vt restore to good condition, working order.

re·con·noi·ter [ree-kə-NOI-tər] vt **1** make preliminary survey of. **2** survey position of enemy. ◆ vi **3** make reconnaissance. **re·con·nais·sance** [ri-KON-ə-səns] n **1** examination or survey for military or engineering purposes. **2** scouting.

re·con·sid'er v think about again, consider

changing.

re·con·sti·tute [ree-KON-sti-toot] vt **-tut·ed, -tut·ing** restore (food) to former state esp. by addition of water to a concentrate.

re·con·struct' v **1** rebuild. **2** use evidence to re-create. **re·con·struc'tion** n

re·cord [REK-ərd] n **1** being recorded. **2** document or other thing that records. **3** disk with indentations that phonograph transforms into sound. **4** best recorded achievement. **5** known facts about person's past. ◆ v [ri-KORD] **6** preserve (sound, TV programs, etc.) on plastic disk, magnetic tape, etc. for reproduction on playback device. ◆ vt **7** put in writing. **8** register. **re·cord'er** n **1** one who, that which records. **2** type of flute. **re·cord'ing** n **1** process of making records from sound. **2** something recorded, e.g. radio or TV program. **record player** instrument for reproducing sound on disks. **off the record** not for publication.

re·count [ri-KOWNT] vt tell in detail.

————— THESAURUS —————

recollect v = **remember**, place, recall, summon up

recollection n = **memory**, impression, recall, remembrance, reminiscence

recommend v **1** = **advise**, advance, advocate, counsel, prescribe, propose, put forward, suggest **2** = **praise**, approve, commend, endorse

recommendation n **1** = **advice**, counsel, proposal, suggestion **2** = **praise**, advocacy, approval, commendation, endorsement, reference, sanction, testimonial

recompense v **1** = **reward**, pay, remunerate **2** = **compensate**, make up for, pay for, redress, reimburse, repay, requite ◆ n **3** = **compensation**, amends, damages, payment, remuneration, reparation, repayment, requital, restitution **4** = **reward**, payment, return, wages

reconcile v **1** = **resolve**, adjust, compose, put to rights, rectify, settle, square **2** = **reunite**, appease, conciliate, make peace between, propitiate **3** = **accept**, put up with (inf), resign oneself, submit, yield

reconciliation n = **reunion**, conciliation, pacification, reconcilement

recondite adj = **obscure**, arcane, concealed, dark, deep, difficult, hidden, mysterious, occult, profound, secret

recondition v = **restore**, do up (inf),

overhaul, remodel, renew, renovate, repair, revamp

reconnaissance n = **inspection**, exploration, investigation, observation, scan, survey

reconnoiter v = **inspect**, case (sl), explore, investigate, observe, scan, spy out, survey

reconsider v = **rethink**, reassess, review, revise, think again

reconstruct v **1** = **rebuild**, recreate, regenerate, remake, remodel, renovate, restore **2** = **deduce**, build up, piece together

record n **1** = **document**, account, chronicle, diary, entry, file, journal, log, register, report **2** = **evidence**, documentation, testimony, trace, witness **3** = **disc**, album, LP, single, vinyl **4** = **background**, career, history, performance **5** off the record = **confidential**, not for publication, private, unofficial ◆ v **6** = **write down**, chronicle, document, enter, log, minute, note, register, set down, take down **7** = **tape**, make a recording of, tape-record, video, video-tape **8** = **register**, give evidence of, indicate, say, show

recorder n = **chronicler**, archivist, clerk, diarist, historian, scribe

recording n = **record**, disc, tape, video

re•coup [ri-KOOP] *vt* **1** recompense, compensate. **2** recover what has been expended or lost.

re•course [REE-kors] *n* **1** (resorting to) source of help. **2** *Law* right of action or appeal.

re•cov•er [ri-KUV-ər] *vt* **1** regain, get back. ♦ *vi* **2** get back health. **re•cov'er•y** *n*, *pl* -er•ies

re•cre•ate' *v* make happen or exist again.

rec•re•a'tion [rek-ree-AY-shən] *n* agreeable or refreshing occupation, relaxation, amusement.

rec•re•a'tion•al *adj*

recreational vehicle large vanlike vehicle equipped to be lived in.

re•crim•i•nate [ri-KRIM-ə-nayt] *vi* -nat•ed, -nat•ing make countercharge or mutual accusation. **re•crim•i•na'tion** *n* mutual abuse and blame.

re•cru•desce [ree-kroo-DES] *vi* -desced, -desc•ing break out again. **re•cru•des'cent** *adj*

re•cruit [ri-KROOT] *n* **1** newly-enlisted soldier. **2** one newly joining society, etc. ♦ *vt* **3** enlist fresh soldiers, etc.

rec•tan•gle [REK-tang-gəl] *n* oblong four-sided figure with four right angles. **rec•tang'u•lar** *adj* shaped thus.

rec•ti•fy *vt* -fied, -fy•ing put right, correct, remedy, purify. **rec•ti•fi•ca'tion** *n* **1** act of setting right. **2** *Electricity* conversion of alternating current into direct current.

rec'ti•fi•er [-fī-ər] *n* person or thing that rectifies.

rec•ti•lin•e•ar [rek-tl-IN-ee-ər] *adj* **1** in straight line. **2** characterized by straight lines.

rec•ti•tude [REK-ti-tood] *n* **1** moral uprightness. **2** honesty of purpose.

rec•to [REK-toh] *n*, *pl* -tos right-hand page of book, front of leaf.

rec•tor [REK-tər] *n* **1** member of clergy with care of parish. **2** head of certain institutions, chiefly academic. **rec'to•ry** *n* rector's house.

rec•tum [REK-təm] *n* final section of large intestine. **rec'tal** [-tl] *adj*

re•cum•bent [ri-KUM-bənt] *adj* lying down. **re•cum'ben•cy** *n*

re•cu•per•ate [ri-KOO-pər-ayt] *v* -at•ed, -at•ing **1** restore, be restored from illness, losses, etc. **2** convalesce. **re•cu•per•a'tion** *n*

re•cur [ri-KUR] *vi* -curred, -cur•ring **1** happen again. **2** return again and again. **3** go or come back in mind. **re•cur'rence** [-əns] *n* repetition. **re•cur'rent** [-ənt] *adj*

re•cy•cle [ree-SĪ-kəl] *vt* -cled, -cling **1** reprocess a manufactured substance for use again. **2** reuse.

red *adj* **1** of color varying from crimson to orange and seen in blood, rubies, glowing fire, etc. ♦ *n* **2** the color. **3** communist. **red'den** *v* **1** make red. **2** become red. **3** flush. **red'dish** *adj* **red-blood•ed** [-blud-id] *adj* **1** vigorous. **2** virile. **red'coat** *n* in

---

THESAURUS

recount *v* = **tell**, depict, describe, narrate, recite, relate, repeat, report

recoup *v* **1** = **regain**, recover, retrieve, win back **2** = **compensate**, make up for, refund, reimburse, remunerate, repay, requite

recourse *n* = **option**, alternative, choice, expedient, remedy, resort, resource, way out

recover *v* **1** = **get better**, convalesce, get well, heal, improve, mend, rally, recuperate, revive **2** = **regain**, get back, recapture, reclaim, redeem, repossess, restore, retrieve

recovery *n* **1** = **improvement**, convalescence, healing, mending, recuperation, revival **2** = **retrieval**, reclamation, repossession, restoration

recreation *n* = **pastime**, amusement, diversion, enjoyment, entertainment, fun, hobby, leisure activity, play, relaxation, sport

recrimination *n* = **bickering**, counterattack, mutual accusation, quarrel, squabbling

recruit *v* **1** = **enlist**, draft, enroll, levy, mobilize, muster, raise **2** = **win (over)**, engage, obtain, procure ♦ *n* **3** = **beginner**, apprentice, convert, helper, initiate, learner, novice, trainee

rectify *v* = **correct**, adjust, emend, fix, improve, redress, remedy, repair, right

rectitude *n* = **morality**, decency, goodness, honesty, honor, integrity, principle, probity, virtue

recuperate *v* = **recover**, convalesce, get better, improve, mend

recur *v* = **happen again**, come again, persist, reappear, repeat, return, revert

recurrent *adj* = **periodic**, continued, frequent, habitual, recurring

recycle *v* = **reprocess**, reclaim, reuse,

American Revolution, a British soldier. **red flag** danger signal. **red-hand'ed** *adj* (caught) in the act. **red herring** topic introduced to divert attention from main issue. **red-hot 1** red with heat. **2** creating excitement. **red tape** excessive adherence to official rules. **red'wood** [-wuud] *n* giant coniferous tree of California. **in the red 1** operating at loss. **2** in debt. **see red** *inf* be very angry.

re·deem [ri-DEEM] *vt* **1** buy back. **2** set free. **3** free from sin. **4** make up for. **re·demp'tion** [-DEM-shən] *n* **re·deem'a·ble** *adj* **The Re·deem·er** Jesus Christ.

re·de·vel'op *v* rebuild or renovate (an area or building). **re·de·vel'op·ment** *n*

red·o·lent [RED-l-ənt] *adj* **1** smelling strongly, fragrant. **2** reminiscent (of). **red'o·lence** *n*

re·dou·ble [ree-DUB-əl] *v* **-bled, -bling 1** increase, multiply, intensify. **2** double a second time.

re·doubt [ri-DOWT] *n* detached outwork in fortifications.

re·doubt·a·ble [ri-DOWT-ə-bəl] *adj* dreaded, formidable.

re·dound [ri-DOWND] *vt* **1** contribute (to). **2** recoil.

re·dress [ri-DRES] *vt* **1** set right. **2** make amends for. ◆ *n* [REE-dres] **3** compensation, amends.

re·duce [ri-DOOS] *vt* **-duced, -duc·ing 1** bring down, lower. **2** lessen, weaken. **3** bring by force or necessity to some state or action. **4** slim. **5** simplify. **6** dilute. **7** *Chem.* separate substance from others with which it is combined. **re·duc'i·ble** *adj* **re·duc'tion** [-DUK-shən] *n* **reducing agent** substance used to deoxidize or lessen density of another substance.

re·dun·dant [ri-DUN-dənt] *adj* superfluous. **re·dun'dan·cy** *n*

re·ech'o *v* **-ech·o·ing, -ech·oed** echo over and over again, resound.

reed *n* **1** various marsh or water plants. **2** tall straight stem of one. **3** *Mus.* vibrating cane or metal strip of certain wind instruments. **reed'y** *adj* **reed·i·er, reed·i·est 1** full of reeds. **2** like reed instrument, harsh and thin in tone.

reef *n* **1** ridge of rock or coral near surface of sea. **2** vein of ore. **3** part of sail that can be rolled up to reduce area. ◆ *vt* **4** take in a reef of. **reef'er** *n* **1** sailor's close-fitting jacket. **2** *sl* marijuana cigarette.

reek *n* **1** strong (unpleasant) smell. ◆ *vi* **2** emit fumes. **3** smell.

reel *n* **1** spool on which film is wound. **2** *Motion Pictures* portion of film. **3** winding apparatus. **4** bobbin. **5** thread wound on

salvage, save

red *adj* **1** = **crimson**, carmine, cherry, coral, ruby, scarlet, vermilion **2** *Of hair* = **chestnut**, carroty, flame-colored, reddish, sandy, titian **3** = **flushed**, blushing, embarrassed, florid, shamefaced ◆ *n* **4 in the red** *Inf* = **in debt**, in arrears, insolvent, overdrawn **5 see red** *Inf* = **lose one's temper**, blow one's top, crack up (*inf*), fly off the handle (*inf*), go ballistic (*sl*), go mad (*inf*)

red-blooded *adj Inf* = **vigorous**, lusty, robust, strong, virile

redden *v* = **flush**, blush, color (up), crimson, go red

redeem *v* **1** = **make up for**, atone for, compensate for, make amends for **2** = **reinstate**, absolve, restore to favor **3** = **save**, deliver, emancipate, free, liberate, ransom **4** = **buy back**, reclaim, recover, regain, repurchase, retrieve

redemption *n* **1** = **compensation**, amends, atonement, reparation **2** = **salvation**, deliverance, emancipation,

liberation, release, rescue **3** = **repurchase**, reclamation, recovery, repossession, retrieval

red-handed *adj* = **in the act**, (in) flagrante delicto

redolent *adj* **1** = **reminiscent**, evocative, suggestive **2** = **scented**, aromatic, fragrant, odorous, perfumed, sweet-smelling

redoubtable *adj* = **formidable**, fearful, fearsome, mighty, powerful, strong

redress *v* **1** = **make amends for**, compensate for, make up for **2** = **put right**, adjust, balance, correct, even up, rectify, regulate ◆ *n* **3** = **amends**, atonement, compensation, payment, recompense, reparation

reduce *v* **1** = **lessen**, abate, curtail, cut down, decrease, diminish, lower, moderate, shorten, weaken **2** = **degrade**, break, bring low, downgrade, humble

redundant *adj* = **superfluous**, extra, inessential, supernumerary, surplus, unnecessary, unwanted

reek *v* **1** = **stink**, smell ◆ *n* **2** = **stink**, fetor, this. **6** lively dance. **7** music for it. **8** act of staggering. ◆ vt **9** wind on reel. **10** draw (in) by means of reel. ◆ vi **11** stagger, sway, rock. **reel off** recite, write fluently, quickly.

re·fec·to·ry [ri-FEK-tə-ree] n, pl **-ries** dining room in monastery, college, etc. **re·fec'tion** n a meal.

re·fer [ri-FUR] v **-ferred, -fer·ring** ◆ vi **1** relate (to), allude. ◆ vt **2** send to for information. **3** trace, ascribe to. **4** submit for decision. **re·fer'ral** n act, instance of referring. **ref·er·ee'** n **1** arbitrator. **2** person willing to whom scientific paper, etc. is sent for judgment of its quality, etc. **3** umpire. ◆ v **-eed, -ee·ing 4** act as referee. **ref'er·ence** [-ins] n **1** act of referring. **2** citation or direction in book. **3** appeal to judgment of another. **4** testimonial. **5** one to whom inquiries as to character, etc. may be made. **ref·er·en'dum** n, pl **-da** [-də] submitting of question to electorate.

re·fill' v **1** fill again. ◆ n **2** second or subsequent filling. **3** replacement supply of something in a permanent container.

re·fine [ri-FĪN] v **-fined, -fin·ing** purify. **re·fine'ment** n **1** subtlety. **2** improvement, elaboration. **3** fineness of feeling, taste or manners. **re·fin'er·y** n, pl **-er·ies** place for refining sugar, oil, etc.

re·fla·tion [ri-FLAY-shən] n (steps taken to produce) increase in economic activity of country, etc.

re·flect [ri-FLEKT] vt **1** throw back, esp. rays of light. **2** cast (discredit, etc.) upon. ◆ vi **3** meditate. **re·flec'tion** [-FLEK-shən] n **1** act of reflecting. **2** return of rays of heat, light, or waves of sound, from surface. **3** image of object given back by mirror, etc. **4** conscious thought. **5** meditation. **6** expression of thought. **re·flec'tive** adj **1** meditative, quiet, contemplative. **2** throwing back images. **re·flec'tor** n polished surface for reflecting light, etc.

re·flex [REE-fleks] n **1** reflex action. **2** reflected image. **3** reflected light, color, etc. ◆ adj **4** (of muscular action) involuntary. **5** reflected. **6** bent back. **re·flex·ive** [ri-FLEK-siv] adj Grammar describes verb denoting agent's action on self. **reflex action** involuntary response to (nerve) stimulation.

re·form [ri-FORM] v **1** improve. **2** abandon evil practices. **3** reconstruct. ◆ n **4** improvement. **ref·or·ma'tion** [ref-ər-MAY-shən] n **re·form'a·to·ry** n, pl **-ries** institution for reforming juvenile offenders.

re·fract [ri-FRAKT] vi change course of

odor, smell, stench

reel v **1** = **stagger**, lurch, pitch, rock, roll, sway **2** = **whirl**, revolve, spin, swirl

refer v **1** = **allude**, bring up, cite, mention, speak of **2** = **relate**, apply, belong, be relevant to, concern, pertain **3** = **consult**, apply, go, look up, turn to **4** = **direct**, guide, point, send

referee n **1** = **umpire**, adjudicator, arbiter, arbitrator, judge, ref (inf) ◆ v **2** = **umpire**, adjudicate, arbitrate, judge, mediate

reference n **1** = **citation**, allusion, mention, note, quotation **2** = **testimonial**, character, credentials, endorsement, recommendation **3** = **relevance**, applicability, bearing, connection, relation

referendum n = **public vote**, plebiscite, popular vote

refine v **1** = **purify**, clarify, cleanse, distill, filter, process **2** = **improve**, hone, perfect, polish

refined adj **1** = **cultured**, civilized, cultivated, elegant, polished, polite, well-bred **2** = **pure**, clarified, clean, distilled, filtered, processed, purified **3** =

discerning, delicate, discriminating, fastidious, fine, precise, sensitive

refinement n **1** = **sophistication**, breeding, civility, courtesy, cultivation, culture, discrimination, gentility, good breeding, polish, taste **2** = **subtlety**, fine point, nicety, nuance **3** = **purification**, clarification, cleansing, distillation, filtering, processing

reflect v **1** = **throw back**, echo, mirror, reproduce, return **2** = **show**, demonstrate, display, indicate, manifest, reveal **3** = **think**, cogitate, consider, meditate, muse, ponder, ruminate, wonder

reflection n **1** = **image**, echo, mirror image **2** = **thought**, cogitation, consideration, contemplation, idea, meditation, musing, observation, opinion, thinking

reflective adj = **thoughtful**, contemplative, meditative, pensive

reform n **1** = **improvement**, amendment, betterment, rehabilitation ◆ v **2** = **improve**, amend, correct, mend, rectify, restore **3** = **mend one's ways**, clean up one's act (inf), go straight (inf), shape up (inf), turn over a light, etc. passing from one medium to another. **re·frac'tion** n

re·frac·to·ry [ri-FRAK-tə-ree] adj **1** unmanageable. **2** difficult to treat or work. **3** Med. resistant to treatment. **4** resistant to heat.

re·frain[1] [ri-FRAYN] vi abstain (from).

re·frain[2] n **1** phrase or verse repeated regularly esp. in song or poem. **2** chorus.

re·fran·gi·ble [ri-FRAN-jə-bəl] adj that can be refracted.

re·fresh [ri-FRESH] vt **1** give freshness to. **2** revive. **3** renew. **4** brighten. **5** provide with refreshment. **re·fresh'er** n that which refreshes. **re·fresh'ment** n **1** that which refreshes, esp. food, drink. **2** restorative.

re·frig·er·ate [ri-FRIJ-ə-rayt] vt **-at·ed, -at·ing 1** freeze. **2** cool. **re·frig'er·ant** n refrigerating substance. ◆ adj **re·frig'er·a·tor** n apparatus in which foods, drinks are kept cool.

ref·uge [REF-yooj] n shelter, protection, retreat, sanctuary. **ref·u·gee** [ref-yuu-JEE] n one who seeks refuge, esp. in foreign country.

re·ful·gent [ri-FUL-jənt] adj shining, radiant. **re·ful'gence** n **re·ful'gen·cy** n

splendor.

re·fund [ri-FUND] vt **1** pay back. ◆ n [REE-fund] **2** return of money. **3** amount returned.

re·fur·bish [ree-FUR-bish] vt furbish, furnish or brighten anew.

re·fuse[1] [ri-FYOOZ] v **-fused, -fus·ing** decline, deny, reject. **re·fus'al** n **1** denial of anything demanded or offered. **2** option.

ref·use[2] [REF-yoos] n rubbish, useless matter.

re·fute [ri-FYOOT] vt **-fut·ed, -fut·ing** disprove. **re·fut'a·ble** adj **ref·u·ta·tion** [ref-yuu-TAY-shən] n

re·gal [REE-gəl] adj of, like a king. **re·ga·li·a** [ri-GAY-lee-ə] pl n **1** insignia of royalty, as used at coronation, etc. **2** emblems of high office, an order, etc. **re·gal·i·ty** [ri-GAL-i-tee] n, pl **-ties**

re·gale [ri-GAYL] vt **-galed, -gal·ing 1** give pleasure to. **2** feast.

re·gard [ri-GAHRD] vt **1** look at. **2** consider. **3** relate to. **4** heed. ◆ n **5** look. **6** attention. **7** particular respect. **8** esteem. ◆ pl **9** expression of good will. **re·gard'ful** adj heedful, careful. **re·gard'less** adj **1** heedless. ◆ adv **2** in spite of everything.

new leaf

refractory adj = **unmanageable**, difficult, disobedient, headstrong, intractable, uncontrollable, unruly, willful

refrain[1] v = **stop**, abstain, avoid, cease, desist, forbear, leave off, renounce

refrain[2] n = **chorus**, melody, tune

refresh v **1** = **revive**, brace, enliven, freshen, reinvigorate, revitalize, stimulate **2** = **stimulate**, jog, prompt, renew

refreshing adj **1** = **stimulating**, bracing, fresh, invigorating **2** = **new**, novel, original

refreshment n **refreshments** = **food and drink**, drinks, snacks, tidbits

refrigerate v = **cool**, chill, freeze, keep cold

refuge n = **shelter**, asylum, haven, hideout, protection, retreat, sanctuary

refugee n = **exile**, displaced person, émigré, escapee

refund v **1** = **repay**, pay back, reimburse, restore, return ◆ n **2** = **repayment**, reimbursement, return

refurbish v = **renovate**, clean up, do up (inf), mend, overhaul, repair, restore, revamp

refusal n = **denial**, knock-back (sl), rebuff, rejection

refuse[1] v = **reject**, decline, deny, say no, spurn, turn down, withhold

refuse[2] n = **rubbish**, garbage, junk (inf), litter, trash, waste

refute v = **disprove**, discredit, negate, overthrow, prove false, rebut

regain v **1** = **recover**, get back, recapture, recoup, retrieve, take back, win back **2** = **get back to**, reach again, return to

regal adj = **royal**, kingly or queenly, magnificent, majestic, noble, princely

regale v = **entertain**, amuse, delight, divert

regalia pl n = **emblems**, accouterments, decorations, finery, paraphernalia, trappings

regard v **1** = **consider**, believe, deem, esteem, judge, rate, see, suppose, think, view **2** = **look at**, behold, check out (inf), eye, gaze at, observe, scrutinize, view, watch **3** = **heed**, attend, listen to, mind, pay attention to, take notice of **4** as **regards** = **concerning**, pertaining to, regarding, relating to ◆ n **5** = **heed**, attention, interest, mind, notice **6** = **respect**, care, concern, consideration, esteem, thought **7** = **look**, gaze, glance, scrutiny, stare

re·gat·ta [ri-GAT-ə] n meeting for yacht or boat races.

re·gen·er·ate [ri-JEN-ə-rayt] v **-at·ed, -at·ing 1** cause spiritual rebirth. **2** reform morally. **3** reproduce, re-create. **4** reorganize. ♦ adj [-ə-rit] **5** born anew. **re·gen·er·a'tion** n **re·gen'er·a·tive** adj

re·gent [REE-jənt] n **1** ruler of kingdom during absence, minority, etc., of its monarch. ♦ adj **2** ruling. **re'gen·cy** n status, (period of) office of regent.

reg·gae [REG-ay] n style of popular West Indian music with strong beat.

reg·i·cide [REJ-ə-sīd] n **1** one who kills a king. **2** this crime.

re·gime [rə-ZHEEM] n system of government, administration.

reg·i·men [REJ-ə-mən] n **1** prescribed system of diet, etc. **2** rule.

reg·i·ment [REJ-ə-mənt] n **1** organized body of troops in charge of unit of army. ♦ vt [REJ-ə-ment] **2** discipline, organize rigidly or too strictly. **reg·i·men'tal** adj of regiment.

re·gion [REE-jən] n **1** area, district. **2** stretch of country. **3** part of the body. **4** sphere, realm. **5** administrative division of a country. **re'gion·al** adj

reg·is·ter [REJ-ə-stər] n **1** list. **2** catalogue. **3** roll. **4** device for registering. **5** written record. **6** range of voice or instrument. ♦ **7** show, be shown on meter, face, etc. ♦ vt **8** enter in register. **9** record. **10** show. **11** set down in writing. **12** *Printing, photography* cause to correspond precisely. **reg'is·trar** [-trahr] n keeper of a register esp. in college or university. **reg·is·tra'tion** n **reg'is·try** n, pl **-tries 1** registering. **2** place where registers are kept, esp. of births, marriages, deaths.

re·gorge [ri-GORJ] v **-gorged, -gorg·ing** vomit up.

re·gress [ri-GRES] vi return, revert to former place, condition, etc. ♦ n **re·gres'sion** [-shən] n **1** act of returning. **2** retrogression. **re·gres'sive** adj falling back.

re·gret [ri-GRET] vt **-gret·ted, -gret·ting 1** feel sorry, distressed for loss of or on account of. ♦ n **2** sorrow, distress for thing done or left undone or lost. **re·gret'ful** adj **re·gret'ta·ble** adj

reg·u·lar [REG-yə-lər] adj **1** normal. **2** habitual. **3** done, occurring, according to rule. **4** periodical. **5** straight, level. **6** living under rule. **7** belonging to standing army. ♦ n **8** regular soldier. **9** regular customer. **reg·u·lar'i·ty** n **reg'u·lar·ize** vt **-ized, -iz·ing**

reg·u·late [REG-yə-layt] vt **-lat·ed, -lat·ing 1**

————| THESAURUS |————

regarding prep = **concerning**, about, as regards, in or with regard to, on the subject of, re, respecting, with reference to

regardless adj **1** = **heedless**, inconsiderate, indifferent, neglectful, negligent, rash, reckless, unmindful ♦ adv **2** = **anyway**, in any case, in spite of everything, nevertheless

regards pl n = **good wishes**, best wishes, compliments, greetings, respects

regenerate v = **renew**, breathe new life into, invigorate, reawaken, reinvigorate, rejuvenate, restore, revive

regime n = **government**, leadership, management, reign, rule, system

regimented adj = **controlled**, disciplined, ordered, organized, regulated, systematized

region n = **area**, district, locality, part, place, quarter, section, sector, territory, tract, zone

regional adj = **local**, district, parochial, provincial, zonal

register n **1** = **list**, archives, catalog, chronicle, diary, file, log, record, roll, roster ♦ v **2** = **record**, catalog, chronicle, enlist, enroll, enter, list, note **3** = **show**, display, exhibit, express, indicate, manifest, mark, reveal

regress v = **revert**, backslide, degenerate, deteriorate, fall away or off, go back, lapse, relapse, return

regret v **1** = **feel sorry about**, bemoan, bewail, deplore, grieve, lament, miss, mourn, repent, rue ♦ n **2** = **sorrow**, bitterness, compunction, contrition, penitence, remorse, repentance, ruefulness

regretful adj = **sorry**, apologetic, contrite, penitent, remorseful, repentant, rueful, sad, sorrowful

regrettable adj = **unfortunate**, disappointing, distressing, lamentable, sad, shameful

regular adj **1** = **normal**, common, customary, habitual, ordinary, routine, typical, usual **2** = **even**, balanced, flat, level, smooth, straight, symmetrical, uniform **3** = **systematic**, consistent, constant, even, fixed, ordered, set, stated, steady, uniform adjust. **2** arrange. **3** direct. **4** govern. **5** put under rule. **reg·u·la'tion** n **reg'u·la·tor** n contrivance to produce uniformity of motion, as flywheel, governor, etc.

re·gur·gi·tate [ri-GUR-ji-tayt] v **1** vomit. **2** bring back (swallowed food) into mouth.

re·ha·bil·i·tate [ree-hə-BIL-i-tayt] vt **-tat·ed, -tat·ing 1** help (person) to readjust to society after a period of illness, imprisonment, etc. **2** restore to reputation or former position. **3** make fit again. **4** reinstate.

re·hash [ree-HASH] vt **1** rework, reuse. ◆ n [REE-hash] **2** old materials presented in new form.

re·hearse [ri-HURS] vt **-hearsed, -hears·ing 1** practice (play, etc.). **2** repeat aloud. **3** say over again. **4** train, drill. **re·hears'al** n

reign [rayn] n **1** period of sovereign's rule. ◆ vi **2** be ruler. **3** be supreme.

re·im·burse [ree-im-BURS] vt **1** -bursed, -burs·ing **2** refund. **3** pay back. **re·im·burse'ment** n

rein [rayn] n **1** narrow strap attached to bit to guide horse. **2** instrument for governing. ◆ vt **3** check, manage with

reins. **4** control. **give free rein to** remove restraints.

re·in·car·na·tion [ree-in-kahr-NAY-shən] n **1** rebirth of soul in successive bodies. **2** one of series of such transmigrations. **re·in·car'nate** [-KAHR-nayt] vt **-nat·ed, -nat·ing**

rein·deer [RAYN-deer] n deer, with large branched antlers, that lives in the arctic regions.

re·in·force [ree-in-FORS] vt **-forced, -forc·ing 1** strengthen with new support, material, force. **2** strengthen with additional troops, ships, etc. **re·in·force'ment** n **reinforced concrete** concrete strengthened internally by steel bars.

re·in·state [ree-in-STAYT] vt **-stat·ed, -stat·ing** replace, restore, reestablish.

re·it·er·ate [ree-IT-ə-rayt] vt **-at·ed, -at·ing** repeat again and again. **re·it·er·a'tion** n repetition. **re·it'er·a·tive** [-ər-ə-tiv] adj

re·ject [ri-JEKT] vt **1** refuse to accept. **2** put aside. **3** discard. **4** renounce. ◆ n [REE-jekt] **5** person or thing rejected as not up to standard. **re·jec'tion** n refusal.

regulate v **1** = **control**, direct, govern, guide, handle, manage, rule, run, supervise **2** = **adjust**, balance, fit, moderate, modulate, tune

regulation n **1** = **rule**, decree, dictate, edict, law, order, precept, statute **2** = **control**, direction, government, management, supervision **3** = **adjustment**, modulation, tuning

regurgitate v = **vomit**, barf (sl), disgorge, puke (sl), spew (out or up), throw up (inf)

rehabilitate v **1** = **reintegrate**, adjust **2** = **redeem**, clear, reform, restore, save

rehash v **1** = **rework**, refashion, rejig (inf), reuse, rewrite ◆ n **2** = **reworking**, new version, rearrangement, rewrite

rehearsal n = **practice**, drill, preparation, rehearsing, run-through

rehearse v = **practice**, drill, go over, prepare, recite, repeat, run through, train

reign n **1** = **rule**, command, control, dominion, monarchy, power ◆ v **2** = **rule**, be in power, command, govern, influence **3** = **be supreme**, hold sway, predominate, prevail

reimburse v = **pay back**, compensate, recompense, refund, remunerate, repay, return

rein v **1** = **control**, check, curb, halt, hold back, limit, restrain, restrict ◆ n **2** = **control**, brake, bridle, check, curb, harness, hold, restraint

reincarnation n = **rebirth**, transmigration of souls

reinforce v = **support**, bolster, emphasize, fortify, prop, strengthen, stress, supplement, toughen

reinforcement n **1** = **strengthening**, augmentation, fortification, increase **2** = **support**, brace, buttress, prop, stay **3 reinforcements** = **reserves**, additional or fresh troops, auxiliaries, support

reinstate v = **restore**, recall, re-establish, replace, return

reiterate v = **repeat**, do again, restate, say again

reject v **1** = **deny**, decline, disallow, exclude, renounce, repudiate, veto **2** = **rebuff**, jilt, refuse, repulse, say no to, spurn, turn down **3** = **discard**, eliminate, jettison, scrap, throw away or out ◆ n **4** = **castoff**, discard, failure, second

rejection n **1** = **denial**, dismissal, exclusion, renunciation, repudiation, thumbs down, veto **2** = **rebuff**, brushoff (sl), kick in the teeth (sl), knock-back (sl), refusal

re·joice [ri-JOIS] v **-joiced, -joic·ing 1** make or be joyful, merry. **2** gladden. **3** exult.

re·join [ree-JOIN] vt **1** reply. **2** join again. **re·join·der** [ri-JOIN-dər] n answer, retort.

re·ju·ve·nate [ri-JOO-və-nayt] vt **-nat·ed, -nat·ing** restore to youth. **re·ju·ve·na'tion** n **re·ju·ve·nes·cence** [ri-joo-və-NES-əns] n process of growing young again.

re·lapse [ri-LAPS] vi **-lapsed, -laps·ing 1** fall back into evil, illness, etc. ◆ n [REE-laps] **2** return of bad habits, illness, etc.

re·late [ri-LAYT] v **-lat·ed, -lat·ing** ◆ vt **1** narrate, recount. **2** establish relation between. **3** have reference or relation to. ◆ vi **4** (with to) form sympathetic relationship.

re·la·tion [ri-LAY-shən] n **1** relative quality or condition. **2** connection by blood or marriage. **3** connection between things. **4** act of relating. **5** narrative. **re·la'tion·ship** n **rel·a·tive** [REL-ə-tiv] adj **1** dependent on relation to something else, not absolute. **2** having reference or relation (to). ◆ n **3** one connected by blood or marriage. **4** relative word or thing. **rel·a·tiv'i·ty** n **1** state of being relative. **2** subject of two theories of Albert Einstein, dealing with relationships of space, time and motion, and acceleration and gravity.

re·lax [ri-LAKS] vt **1** make loose or slack. ◆ vi **2** become loosened or slack. **3** ease up from effort or attention. **4** become more friendly, less strict. **re·lax·a'tion** [ree-] n **1** relaxing recreation. **2** alleviation. **3** abatement.

re·lay [REE-lay] n **1** fresh set of people or animals relieving others. **2** *Electricity* device for making or breaking local circuit. ◆ vt **-layed, -laying 3** pass on, as message. **relay race** race between teams of which each runner races part of distance.

re·lease [ri-LEES] vt **-leased, -leas·ing 1** give up, surrender, set free. **2** permit public showing of (movie, etc.). ◆ n **3**

rejig v = **rearrange**, alter, juggle, manipulate, reorganize, tweak

rejoice v = **be glad**, be happy, be overjoyed, celebrate, exult, glory

rejoicing n = **happiness**, celebration, elation, exultation, gladness, joy, jubilation, merrymaking

rejoin v = **reply**, answer, respond, retort, riposte

rejoinder n = **reply**, answer, comeback (*inf*), response, retort, riposte

rejuvenate v = **revitalize**, breathe new life into, refresh, regenerate, reinvigorate, renew, restore

relapse v **1** = **lapse**, backslide, degenerate, fail, regress, revert, slip back **2** = **worsen**, deteriorate, fade, fail, sicken, sink, weaken ◆ n **3** = **lapse**, backsliding, regression, retrogression **4** = **worsening**, deterioration, turn for the worse, weakening

relate v **1** = **connect**, associate, correlate, couple, join, link **2** = **concern**, apply, be relevant to, have to do with, pertain, refer **3** = **tell**, describe, detail, narrate, recite, recount, report

related adj **1** = **akin**, kindred **2** = **associated**, affiliated, akin, connected, interconnected, joint, linked

relation n **1** = **connection**, bearing, bond, comparison, correlation, link **2** = **relative**, kin, kinsman *or* kinswoman **3** = **kinship**, affinity, kindred

relations pl n **1** = **dealings**, affairs, connections, contact, interaction, intercourse, relationship **2** = **family**, clan, kin, kindred, kinsfolk, kinsmen, relatives, tribe

relationship n **1** = **association**, affinity, bond, connection, kinship, rapport **2** = **affair**, liaison **3** = **connection**, correlation, link, parallel, similarity, tie-up

relative adj **1** = **dependent**, allied, associated, comparative, contingent, corresponding, proportionate, related **2** = **relevant**, applicable, apposite, appropriate, apropos, germane, pertinent ◆ n **3** = **relation**, kinsman *or* kinswoman, member of one's *or* the family

relatively adv = **comparatively**, rather, somewhat

relax v **1** = **be** *or* **feel at ease**, calm, chill out (*sl*), lighten up (*sl*), rest, take it easy, unwind **2** = **lessen**, abate, ease, ebb, let up, loosen, lower, moderate, reduce, relieve, slacken, weaken

relaxation n = **leisure**, enjoyment, fun, pleasure, recreation, rest

relaxed adj = **easy-going**, casual, comfortable, easy, free and easy, homey, informal, laid-back (*inf*), leisurely

relay n **1** = **shift**, relief, turn **2** = **message**, dispatch, transmission ◆ v **3** = **pass on**, broadcast, carry, communicate, send, setting free. **4** releasing. **5** written discharge. **6** permission to show publicly. **7** film, record, etc. newly issued.

rel·e·gate [REL-i-gayt] *vt* **-gat·ed, -gat·ing 1** banish, consign. **2** demote. **rel·e·ga'tion** *n*

re·lent [ri-LENT] *vi* give up harsh intention, become less severe. **re·lent'less** [-lis] *adj* **1** pitiless. **2** merciless.

rel·e·vant [REL-ə-vənt] *adj* having to do with the matter in hand, to the point. **rel'e·vance** *n*

reliable, reliance see RELY.

rel·ic [REL-ik] *n* **1** thing remaining, esp. as memorial of saint. **2** memento. ◆ *pl* **3** remains, traces.

re·lief [ri-LEEF] *n* **1** alleviation, end of pain, distress, etc. **2** money, food given to victims of disaster, poverty, etc. **3** release from duty. **4** one who relieves another. **5** freeing of besieged city, etc. **6** projection of carved design from surface. **7** distinctness, prominence. **re·lieve** [ri-LEEV] *vt* **-lieved, -liev·ing** bring or give relief to. **relief map** map showing elevations and depressions of country in relief.

re·li·gion [ri-LIJ-ən] *n* system of belief in, worship of a supernatural power or god. **re·li'gious** *adj* **1** pert. to religion. **2** pious. **3** conscientious. **re·li'gious·ly** *adv* **1** in religious manner. **2** scrupulously. **3** conscientiously.

re·lin·quish [ri-LING-kwish] *vt* give up, abandon.

rel·i·quar·y [REL-i-kwer-ee] *n, pl* **-quar·ies** case or shrine for holy relics.

rel·ish [REL-ish] *v* **1** enjoy, like. ◆ *n* **2** liking, gusto. **3** appetizing savory food, such as pickle. **4** taste or flavor.

re·luc·tant [ri-LUK-tənt] *adj* unwilling, loath, disinclined. **re·luc'tance** *n*

re·ly [ri-Lī] *vi* **-lied, -ly·ing 1** depend (on). **2** trust. **re·li·a·bil'i·ty** *n* **re·li'a·ble** *adj* trustworthy, dependable. **re·li·ance** [ri-Lī-əns] *n* **1** trust. **2** confidence. **3** dependence. **re·li'ant** [-ənt] *adj* **1** confident. **2** trustful.

re·main [ri-MAYN] *vi* **1** stay, be left behind. **2** continue. **3** abide. **4** last. **remains** *pl n* **1** relics, esp. of ancient buildings. **2** dead body. **re·main'der** *n* **1** rest, what is left

─────── THESAURUS ───────

release *v* **1 = set free**, discharge, drop, extricate, free, liberate, loose, unbridle, undo, unfasten **2 = acquit**, absolve, exonerate, let go, let off **3 = issue**, circulate, distribute, launch, make known, make public, publish, put out ◆ *n* **4 = liberation**, deliverance, discharge, emancipation, freedom, liberty **5 = acquittal**, absolution, exemption, exoneration **6 = issue**, proclamation, publication

relegate *v* **= demote**, downgrade

relent *v* **= be merciful**, capitulate, change one's mind, come round, have pity, show mercy, soften, yield

relentless *adj* **1 = unremitting**, incessant, nonstop, persistent, unrelenting, unrelieved **2 = merciless**, cruel, fierce, implacable, pitiless, remorseless, ruthless, unrelenting

relevant *adj* **= significant**, apposite, appropriate, apt, fitting, germane, pertinent, related, to the point

reliable *adj* **= dependable**, faithful, safe, sound, staunch, sure, true, trustworthy

reliance *n* **= trust**, belief, confidence, dependence, faith

relic *n* **= remnant**, fragment, keepsake,

memento, souvenir, trace, vestige

relief *n* **1 = ease**, comfort, cure, deliverance, mitigation, release, remedy, solace **2 = rest**, break, breather (*inf*), relaxation, respite **3 = aid**, assistance, help, succor, support

relieve *v* **1 = ease**, alleviate, assuage, calm, comfort, console, cure, mitigate, relax, soften, soothe **2 = help**, aid, assist, succor, support, sustain

religious *adj* **1 = devout**, devotional, faithful, godly, holy, pious, sacred, spiritual **2 = conscientious**, faithful, meticulous, punctilious, rigid, scrupulous

relinquish *v* **= give up**, abandon, abdicate, cede, drop, forsake, leave, let go, renounce, surrender

relish *v* **1 = enjoy**, delight in, fancy, like, revel in, savor ◆ *n* **2 = enjoyment**, fancy, fondness, gusto, liking, love, partiality, penchant, predilection, taste **3 = condiment**, sauce, seasoning **4 = flavor**, piquancy, smack, spice, tang, taste, trace

reluctance *n* **= unwillingness**, aversion, disinclination, dislike, distaste, loathing, repugnance

reluctant *adj* **= unwilling**, disinclined, hesitant, loath, unenthusiastic

rely *v* **= depend**, bank, bet, count, trust

after subtraction. ♦ *vt* **2** offer (end of consignment of goods, material, etc.) at reduced prices.

re·mand [ri-MAND] *vt* send back, esp. into custody.

re·mark [ri-MAHRK] *vi* **1** make casual comment (on). ♦ *vt* **2** comment, observe. **3** say. **4** take notice of. ♦ *n* **5** observation, comment. **re·mark'a·ble** *adj* noteworthy, unusual. **re·mark'a·bly** *adv* **1** exceedingly. **2** unusually.

re·mar·ry *v* **-ry·ing, -ried** marry again following a divorce or the death of one's previous husband or wife.

rem·e·dy [REM-i-dee] *n, pl* **-dies** means of curing, counteracting or relieving disease, trouble, etc. ♦ *vt* **-died, -dy·ing** put right. **re·me'di·a·ble** *adj* **re·me'di·al** *adj* designed, intended to correct specific disability, handicap, etc. **re·me·di·a'tion** *n*

re·mem·ber [ri-MEM-bər] *vt* **1** retain in, recall to memory. ♦ *vi* **2** have in mind. **re·mem'brance** [-brəns] *n* **1** memory. **2** token. **3** souvenir. **4** reminiscence.

re·mind [ri-MĪND] *vt* **1** cause to remember. **2** put in mind (of). **re·mind'er** *n*

rem·i·nisce [rem-ə-NIS] *vi* **-nisced, -nisc·ing** talk, write of past times, experiences, etc. **rem·i·nis'cence** *n* **1** remembering. **2** thing recollected. ♦ *pl* **3** memoirs. **rem·i·nis'cent** *adj* reminding or suggestive (of).

re·miss [ri-MIS] *adj* negligent, careless.

re·mit [ri-MIT] *v* **-mit·ted, -mit·ting 1** send money for goods, services, etc., esp. by mail. **2** refrain from exacting. **3** give up. **4** restore, return. **5** slacken. **6** forgive (sin, etc.). ♦ *n* **7** *Law* transfer of court record to another court. **re·mis'sion** *n* **1** abatement. **2** reduction in length of prison term. **3** pardon, forgiveness. **re·mit'tance** *n* **1** sending of money. **2** money sent.

rem·nant [REM-nənt] *n* **1** fragment or small piece remaining. **2** oddment.

re·mon·strate [ri-MON-strayt] *vi* **-strat·ed, -strat·ing** protest, reason with, argue. **re·mon'strance** [-strəns] *n*

re·morse [ri-MORS] *n* regret and

remain *v* **1** = **continue**, abide, dwell, endure, go on, last, persist, stand, stay, survive **2** = **stay behind**, be left, delay, linger, wait

remainder *n* = **rest**, balance, excess, leavings, remains, remnant, residue, surplus

remaining *adj* = **left-over**, lingering, outstanding, persisting, surviving, unfinished

remains *pl n* **1** = **remnants**, debris, dregs, leavings, leftovers, relics, residue, rest **2** = **body**, cadaver, carcass, corpse

remark *v* **1** = **comment**, declare, mention, observe, pass comment, reflect, say, state **2** = **notice**, espy, make out, mark, note, observe, perceive, see ♦ *n* **3** = **comment**, observation, reflection, statement, utterance

remarkable *adj* = **extraordinary**, notable, outstanding, rare, singular, striking, surprising, uncommon, unusual, wonderful

remedy *n* **1** = **cure**, medicine, nostrum, treatment ♦ *v* **2** = **put right**, correct, fix, rectify, set to rights

remember *v* **1** = **recall**, call to mind, commemorate, look back (on), recollect, reminisce, think back **2** = **bear in mind**, keep in mind

remembrance *n* **1** = **memory**, recall, recollection, reminiscence, thought **2** = **souvenir**, commemoration, keepsake, memento, memorial, monument, reminder, token

remind *v* = **call to mind**, jog one's memory, make (someone) remember, prompt

reminisce *v* = **recall**, hark back, look back, recollect, remember, think back

reminiscence *n* = **recollection**, anecdote, memoir, memory, recall, remembrance

reminiscent *adj* = **suggestive**, evocative, similar

remiss *adj* = **careless**, forgetful, heedless, lax, neglectful, negligent, thoughtless

remission *n* **1** = **pardon**, absolution, amnesty, discharge, exemption, release, reprieve **2** = **lessening**, abatement, alleviation, ebb, lull, relaxation, respite

remit *v* **1** = **send**, dispatch, forward, mail, post, transmit **2** = **cancel**, halt, repeal, rescind, stop **3** = **postpone**, defer, delay, put off, shelve, suspend ♦ *n* **4** = **instructions**, brief, guidelines, orders

remittance *n* = **payment**, allowance, fee

remnant *n* = **remainder**, end, fragment, leftovers, remains, residue, rest, trace, vestige

remonstrate *v* = **argue**, dispute, dissent,

repentance. **re·morse'ful** [-fəl] *adj*
re·morse'less [-lis] *adj* pitiless.
re·mote [ri-MOHT] *adj* **-mot·er, -mot·est 1**
far away, distant. **2** aloof. **3** slight.
re·mote'ly *adv* **remote control** control of
apparatus from a distance by electrical
device.
re·move [ri-MOOV] *v* **-moved, -mov·ing** ◆
vt **1** take away or off. **2** transfer. **3**
withdraw. ◆ *vi* **4** go away, change
residence. ◆ *n* **5** degree of difference.
re·mov·a·ble *adj* **re·mov'al** *n*
re·mu·ner·ate [ri-MYOO-nə-rayt] *vt*
reward, pay. **re·mu·ner·a'tion** *n*
re·mu'ner·a·tive *adj*
ren·ais·sance [ren-ə-SAHNS] *n* revival,
rebirth, esp. revival of learning in 14th to
16th centuries.
re·nal [REEN-l] *adj* of the kidneys.
re·nas·cent [ri-NAS-ənt] *adj* springing up
again into being.
rend *v* **rent, rend·ing 1** tear, wrench apart.
2 burst, break, split.
ren·der [REN-dər] *vt* **1** submit, present. **2**
give in return, deliver up. **3** cause to
become. **4** portray, represent. **5** melt
down. **6** cover with plaster.
ren·dez·vous [RAHN-de-voo] *n, pl*
rendezvous [-vooz] **1** meeting place. **2**
appointment. **3** haunt. **4** assignation. ◆ *vi*
-voused [-vood], **-vous·ing** [-voo-ing] **5**
meet, come together.
ren·di·tion [ren-DISH-ən] *n* **1** performance.
2 translation.
ren·e·gade [REN-i-gayd] *n* **1** deserter. **2**
outlaw. **3** rebel. ◆ *adj*
re·nege [ri-NIG] *vi* **-neged, -neg·ing 1** (usu.
with *on*) go back on (promise, etc.). **2** in
cards, break rule.
re·new [ri-NOO] *vt* **1** begin again. **2**
reaffirm. **3** make valid again. **4** make new.
5 revive. **6** restore to former state. **7**
replenish. ◆ *vi* **8** be made new. **9** grow
again. **re·new·a·bil'i·ty** *n* quality of being

──────── THESAURUS ────────

object, protest, take issue
remorse *n* = **regret**, anguish,
compunction, contrition, grief, guilt,
penitence, repentance, shame, sorrow
remorseful *adj* = **regretful**, apologetic,
ashamed, conscience-stricken, contrite,
guilty, penitent, repentant, sorry
remorseless *adj* **1** = **pitiless**, callous,
cruel, inhumane, merciless, ruthless **2** =
relentless, inexorable
remote *adj* **1** = **distant**, far, inaccessible, in
the middle of nowhere, isolated,
out-of-the-way, secluded **2** = **aloof**,
abstracted, cold, detached, distant,
reserved, standoffish, uncommunicative,
withdrawn **3** = **slight**, doubtful, dubious,
faint, outside, slender, slim, small, unlikely
removal *n* **1** = **taking away** *or* **off** *or* **out**,
dislodgment, ejection, elimination,
eradication, extraction, uprooting,
withdrawal **2** = **dismissal**, expulsion **3** =
move, departure, relocation, transfer
remove *v* **1** = **take away** *or* **off** *or* **out**,
abolish, delete, detach, displace, eject,
eliminate, erase, excise, extract, get rid of,
wipe from the face of the earth, withdraw
2 = **dismiss**, depose, dethrone, discharge,
expel, oust, throw out **3** = **move**, depart,
flit (*Scot. & Northern English dialect*),
relocate
remunerate *v* = **pay**, compensate,
recompense, reimburse, repay, requite,

reward
remuneration *n* = **payment**, earnings,
fee, income, pay, return, reward, salary,
stipend, wages
remunerative *adj* = **profitable**, economic,
lucrative, moneymaking, paying,
rewarding, worthwhile
renaissance, renascence *n* = **rebirth**,
reappearance, reawakening, renewal,
restoration, resurgence, revival
rend *v* = **tear**, rip, rupture, separate,
wrench
render *v* **1** = **make**, cause to become, leave
2 = **provide**, furnish, give, hand out, pay,
present, submit, supply, tender **3** =
portray, act, depict, do, give, perform,
play, represent
rendezvous *n* **1** = **appointment**,
assignation, date, engagement, meeting,
tryst **2** = **meeting place**, gathering point,
venue ◆ *v* **3** = **meet**, assemble, come
together, gather, join up
rendition *n* **1** = **performance**,
arrangement, interpretation, portrayal,
presentation, reading, rendering, version
2 = **translation**, interpretation, reading,
transcription, version
renegade *n* **1** = **deserter**, apostate,
defector, traitor, turncoat ◆ *adj* **2** =
rebellious, apostate, disloyal, traitorous,
unfaithful
renege *v* = **break one's word**, back out,

renewable. **re·new'a·ble** *adj* **re·new'al** *n* **1** revival, restoration. **2** regeneration.

ren·net [REN-it] *n* **1** lining membrane of calf's fourth stomach. **2** preparation from this membrane for curdling milk.

re·nounce [ri-NOWNS] *vt* **-nounced,** **-nounc·ing 1** give up, cast off, disown. **2** abjure. **3** resign, as title or claim. **re·nun·ci·a'tion** *n*

ren·o·vate [REN-a-vayt] *vt* restore, repair, renew, do up. **ren·o·va'tion** *n*

re·nown [ri-NOWN] *n* fame.

rent[1] *n* **1** payment for use of land, buildings, machines, etc. ♦ *vt* **2** hold by lease. **3** hire. **4** let. **rent·al** [RENT-əl] *n* sum payable as rent.

rent[2] *n* **1** tear. **2** fissure. **3** pt./pp. of REND.

renunciation see RENOUNCE.

rep[1] *n* fabric with corded surface for upholstery, etc.

rep[2] *adj, n* short for REPERTORY (COMPANY).

rep[3] *n* short for REPRESENTATIVE.

re·paid [ri-PAYD] pt./pp. of REPAY.

re·pair[1] [ri-PAIR] *vt* **1** make whole, sound again. **2** mend. **3** patch. **4** restore. ♦ *n* **re·pair'a·ble** *adj* **rep·a·ra·tion** [rep-ə-RAY-shən] *n* **1** repairing. **2** amends, compensation.

repair[2] *vi* resort (to), go.

rep·ar·tee [rep-ər-TEE] *n* **1** witty retort. **2** interchange of reports.

re·past [ri-PAST] *n* a meal.

re·pa·tri·ate [ri-PAY-tree-ayt] *vt* **-at·ed,** **-at·ing** send (someone) back to own country.

re·pay [ri-PAY] *vt* **-paid, -pay·ing 1** pay back, refund. **2** make return for. **re·pay'ment** *n*

re·peal [ri-PEEL] *vt* **1** revoke, annul, cancel. ♦ *n* **2** act of repealing.

re·peat [ri-PEET] *vt* **1** say, do again. **2** reproduce. **3** recur. ♦ *vi* **4** recur. **5** of food, be tasted repeatedly for some time after being eaten. ♦ *n* **6** act, instance of repeating, esp. TV show broadcast again. **re·peat'ed·ly** *adv* **1** again and again. **2** frequently. **re·peat'er** *n* **1** firearm that can be discharged many times without reloading. **2** watch that strikes hours.

rep·e·ti·tion [rep-i-TISH-ən] *n* **1** act of repeating. **2** thing repeated. **3** piece learned by heart and repeated.

rep·e·ti'tious *adj* repeated unnecessarily.

re·pet'i·tive *adj* repeated.

re·pel [ri-PEL] *vt* **-pelled, -pel·ling 1** drive back, ward off, refuse. **2** be repulsive to. **re·pel'lent** [-ənt] *adj* **1** distasteful. **2**

THESAURUS

break a promise, default, go back

renew *v* **1** = **recommence**, continue, extend, reaffirm, recreate, reopen, repeat, resume **2** = **restore**, mend, modernize, overhaul, refit, refurbish, renovate, repair **3** = **replace**, refresh, replenish, restock

renounce *v* = **give up**, abjure, deny, disown, forsake, forswear, quit, recant, relinquish, waive

renovate *v* = **restore**, do up (*inf*), modernize, overhaul, recondition, refit, refurbish, renew, repair

renown *n* = **fame**, distinction, eminence, note, reputation, repute

renowned *adj* = **famous**, celebrated, distinguished, eminent, esteemed, notable, noted, well-known

rent[1] *v* **1** = **hire**, charter, lease, let ♦ *n* **2** = **hire**, fee, lease, payment, rental

rent[2] *n* = **tear**, gash, hole, opening, rip, slash, slit, split

renunciation *n* = **giving up**, abandonment, abdication, abjuration, denial, disavowal, forswearing, rejection, relinquishment, repudiation

reorganize *v* = **rearrange**, reshuffle, restructure

repair[1] *v* **1** = **mend**, fix, heal, patch, patch up, renovate, restore ♦ *n* **2** = **mend**, darn, overhaul, patch, restoration

reparation *n* = **compensation**, atonement, damages, recompense, restitution, satisfaction

repartee *n* = **wit**, badinage, banter, riposte, wittiness, wordplay

repast *n* = **meal**, food

repay *v* **1** = **pay back**, compensate, recompense, refund, reimburse, requite, return, square **2** = **get even with** (*inf*), avenge, hit back, reciprocate, retaliate, revenge

repeal *v* **1** = **abolish**, annul, cancel, invalidate, nullify, recall, reverse, revoke ♦ *n* **2** = **abolition**, annulment, cancellation, invalidation, rescindment

repeat *v* **1** = **reiterate**, echo, replay, reproduce, rerun, reshow, restate, retell ♦ *n* **2** = **repetition**, echo, reiteration, replay, rerun, reshowing

repeatedly *adv* = **over and over**,

resisting water, etc. ♦ n 3 that which repels, esp. chemical to repel insects.

re·pent [ri-PENT] vi 1 wish one had not done something. 2 feel regret for deed or omission. ♦ vt 3 feel regret for. **re·pent'ance** [-əns] n contrition. **re·pent'ant** [-ənt] adj

re·per·cus·sion [ree-pər-KUSH-ən] n 1 indirect effect, oft. unpleasant. 2 recoil. 3 echo.

rep·er·to·ry [REP-ər-tor-ee] n, pl -ries 1 repertoire, collection. 2 store. **rep'er·toire** [-twahr] n stock of plays, songs, etc. that performer or company can give. **repertory theater** theater with permanent company producing succession of plays.

repetition, repetitious, repetitive see REPEAT.

re·pine [ri-PIN] vi -pined, -pin·ing fret, complain.

re·place [ri-PLAYS] vt -placed, -plac·ing 1 substitute for. 2 put back.

re·play [REE-play] n 1 (also **instant replay**) immediate reshowing on TV of incident in sport, esp. in slow motion. 2 replaying of a match. ♦ vt [ree-PLAY]

re·plen·ish [ri-PLEN-ish] vt fill up again. **re·plen'ish·ment** n

re·plete [ri-PLEET] adj filled, gorged.

rep·li·ca [REP-li-kə] n 1 exact copy. 2 facsimile, duplicate. **rep·li·cate** [REP-li-kayt] vt -cat·ed, -cat·ing make, be a copy of. **rep·li·ca'tion** n **rep'li·ca·ble** adj

re·ply [ri-PLĪ] v -plied, -ply·ing 1 answer or respond. ♦ n, pl -lies 2 answer or response.

re·port [ri-PORT] n 1 account, statement. 2 written statement of child's progress at school. 3 rumor. 4 repute. 5 bang. ♦ vt 6 announce, relate. 7 make, give account of. 8 take down in writing. 9 complain about. ♦ vi 10 make report. 11 act as reporter. 12 present oneself (to). **re·port'er** n one who reports, esp. for newspaper.

re·pose [ri-POHZ] n 1 peace. 2 composure.

THESAURUS

frequently, many times, often

repel v 1 = **disgust**, gross out (sl), nauseate, offend, revolt, sicken 2 = **drive off**, fight, hold off, parry, rebuff, repulse, resist, ward off

repellent adj 1 = **disgusting**, abhorrent, hateful, horrid, loathsome, nauseating, noxious, offensive, repugnant, repulsive, revolting, scuzzy (sl), sickening 2 = **proof**, impermeable, repelling, resistant

repent v = **regret**, be sorry, feel remorse, rue

repentance n = **regret**, compunction, contrition, grief, guilt, penitence, remorse

repentant adj = **regretful**, contrite, penitent, remorseful, rueful, sorry

repercussion n repercussions = **consequences**, backlash, result, sequel, side effects

repertoire n = **range**, collection, list, repertory, stock, store, supply

repetition n = **repeating**, echo, recurrence, reiteration, renewal, replication, restatement, tautology

repetitious adj = **long-winded**, prolix, tautological, tedious, verbose, wordy

repetitive adj = **monotonous**, boring, dull, mechanical, recurrent, tedious, unchanging, unvaried

rephrase v = **reword**, paraphrase, put differently

repine v = **complain**, fret, grumble, moan

replace v = **take the place of**, follow, oust, substitute, succeed, supersede, supplant, take over from

replacement n = **successor**, double, proxy, stand-in, substitute, surrogate, understudy

replenish v = **refill**, fill, provide, reload, replace, restore, top up

replete adj = **full**, crammed, filled, full up, glutted, gorged, stuffed

replica n = **duplicate**, carbon copy (inf), copy, facsimile, imitation, model, reproduction

replicate v = **copy**, duplicate, mimic, recreate, reduplicate, reproduce

reply v 1 = **answer**, counter, reciprocate, rejoin, respond, retaliate, retort ♦ n 2 = **answer**, counter, counterattack, reaction, rejoinder, response, retaliation, retort, riposte

report v 1 = **communicate**, broadcast, cover, describe, detail, inform of, narrate, pass on, recount, relate, state, tell 2 = **present oneself**, appear, arrive, come, turn up ♦ n 3 = **account**, communication, description, narrative, news, record, statement, word 4 = **article**, piece, story, write-up 5 = **rumor**, buzz, gossip, hearsay, talk 6 = **bang**, blast, boom, crack, detonation, discharge, explosion, noise, sound

reporter n = **journalist**, correspondent,

3 sleep. ♦ *v* **-posed, -pos•ing** ♦ *vi* **4** rest. ♦ *vt* **5** lay to rest. **6** place. **7** rely, lean (on). **re•pos'i•tor•y** [-POZ-i-tor-ee] *n, pl* **-tor•ies** place where valuables are deposited for safekeeping. **2** store.

rep•re•hend [rep-ri-HEND] *vt* find fault with. **rep•re•hen'si•ble** *adj* deserving censure. **2** unworthy. **rep•re•hen'sion** *n* censure.

rep•re•sent [rep-ri-ZENT] *vt* **1** stand for. **2** deputize for. **3** act, play. **4** symbolize. **5** make out to be. **6** call up by description or portrait. **rep•re•sen•ta'tion** *n* **rep•re•sent'a•tive** *n* **1** one chosen to stand for group. **2** (traveling) salesman. ♦ *adj* **3** typical.

re•press [ri-PRES] *vt* keep down or under, quell, check. **re•pres'sion** [-PRESH-ən] *n* restraint. **re•pres'sive** *adj*

re•prieve [ri-PREEV] *vt* **-prieved, -priev•ing** **1** suspend execution of (condemned person). **2** give temporary relief (to). ♦ *n* **3** postponement or cancellation of

punishment. **4** respite. **5** last-minute intervention.

rep•ri•mand [REP-rə-mand] *n* **1** sharp rebuke. ♦ *vt* **2** rebuke sharply.

re•print' *vt* **1** print further copies of (a book). ♦ *n* **2** reprinted copy.

re•pris•al [ri-PRI-zəl] *n* retaliation.

re•proach [ri-PROHCH] *vt* **1** blame, rebuke. ♦ *n* **2** scolding, upbraiding. **3** expression of this. **4** thing bringing discredit. **re•proach'ful** [-fəl] *adj*

rep•ro•bate [REP-rə-bayt] *adj* **1** depraved. **2** rejected by God. ♦ *n* **3** depraved or disreputable person. ♦ *vt* **-bat•ed, -bat•ing** **4** disapprove of, reject.

re•pro•duce [ree-prə-DOOS] *v* **-duced, -duc•ing** ♦ *vt* **1** produce copy of. **2** bring new individuals into existence. **3** re-create, produce anew. ♦ *vi* **4** propagate. **5** generate. **re•pro•duc'i•ble** *adj* **re•pro•duc'tion** *n* **1** process of reproducing. **2** that which is reproduced. **3** facsimile, as of painting, etc. **re•pro•duc'tive** *adj*

——————— THESAURUS ———————

hack (*derogatory*), pressman, writer

repose[1] *n* **1** = **peace**, ease, quietness, relaxation, respite, rest, stillness, tranquillity **2** = **composure**, calmness, poise, self-possession **3** = **sleep**, slumber ♦ *v* **4** = **rest**, lie, lie down, recline, rest upon

repository *n* = **store**, depository, storehouse, treasury, vault

reprehensible *adj* = **blameworthy**, bad, culpable, disgraceful, shameful, unworthy

represent *v* **1** = **stand for**, act for, betoken, mean, serve as, speak for, symbolize **2** = **symbolize**, embody, epitomize, exemplify, personify, typify **3** = **portray**, denote, depict, describe, illustrate, outline, picture, show

representation *n* = **portrayal**, account, depiction, description, illustration, image, likeness, model, picture, portrait

representative *n* **1** = **delegate**, agent, deputy, member, proxy, spokesman *or* spokeswoman **2** = **salesman**, agent, commercial traveler, rep ♦ *adj* **3** = **typical**, archetypal, characteristic, exemplary, symbolic

repress *v* **1** = **inhibit**, bottle up, check, control, curb, hold back, restrain, stifle, suppress **2** = **subdue**, quell, subjugate

repression *n* = **subjugation**, constraint, control, despotism, domination, restraint, suppression, tyranny

repressive *adj* = **oppressive**, absolute, authoritarian, despotic, dictatorial, tyrannical

reprieve *v* **1** = **grant a stay of execution to**, let off the hook (*sl*), pardon **2** = **relieve**, abate, allay, alleviate, mitigate, palliate ♦ *n* **3** = **stay of execution**, amnesty, deferment, pardon, postponement, remission **4** = **relief**, alleviation, mitigation, palliation, respite

reprimand *v* **1** = **blame**, censure, rap on the knuckles, rebuke, scold ♦ *n* **2** = **blame**, censure, rebuke, reproach, reproof, talking-to (*inf*)

reprisal *n* = **retaliation**, retribution, revenge, vengeance

reproach *n* **1** = **blame**, censure, condemnation, disapproval, opprobrium, rebuke ♦ *v* **2** = **blame**, censure, condemn, criticize, lambast(e), rebuke, reprimand, scold, upbraid

reproachful *adj* = **critical**, censorious, condemnatory, disapproving, fault-finding, reproving

reprobate *n* **1** = **scoundrel**, bad egg (*old-fashioned inf*), degenerate, evildoer, miscreant, profligate, rake, rascal, villain ♦ *adj* **2** = **depraved**, abandoned, bad, base, corrupt, degenerate, dissolute, immoral, sinful, wicked

reproduce *v* **1** = **copy**, duplicate, echo,

re·prove [ri-PROOV] vt **-proved, -prov·ing** censure, rebuke. **re·proof'** n

rep·tile [REP-til, REP-tīl] n cold-blooded, air breathing vertebrate with horny scales or plates, as snake, tortoise, etc. **rep·til'i·an** adj

re·pub·lic [ri-PUB-lik] n country without monarch in which supremacy of people or their elected representatives is formally acknowledged. **re·pub'li·can** adj, n

re·pu·di·ate [ri-PYOO-dee-ayt] vt **-at·ed, -at·ing 1** reject authority or validity of. **2** cast off, disown. **re·pu·di·a'tion** n

re·pug·nant [ri-PUG-nənt] adj **1** offensive. **2** distasteful. **3** contrary. **re·pug'nance** n **1** dislike, aversion. **2** incompatibility.

re·pulse [ri-PULS] vt **-pulsed, -puls·ing 1** drive back. **2** rebuff. **3** repel. ◆ n **4** driving back, rejection, rebuff. **re·pul'sion** [-shən] n **1** distaste, aversion. **2** Physics force separating two objects. **re·pul'sive** adj loathsome, disgusting.

re·pute [ri-PYOOT] vt **-put·ed, -put·ing 1** reckon, consider. ◆ n **2** reputation, credit. **rep'u·ta·ble** adj **1** of good repute. **2** respectable. **rep·u·ta'tion** n **1** estimation in which person is held. **2** character. **3** good name.

re·quest [ri-KWEST] n **1** asking. **2** thing asked for. ◆ vt **3** ask.

Req·ui·em [REK-wee-əm] n **1** Mass for the dead. **2** (r-) music for this.

re·quire [ri-KWĪR] vt **-quired, -quir·ing 1** want, need. **2** demand. **re·quire'ment** n **1** essential condition. **2** specific need. **3** want.

req·ui·site [REK-wə-zit] adj **1** necessary. **2** essential. ◆ n

req·ui·si·tion [rek-wə-ZISH-ən] n **1** formal demand, such as for materials or supplies. ◆ vt **2** demand (supplies). **3** press into service.

re·quite [ri-KWĪT] vt **-quit·ed, -quit·ing** repay.

imitate, match, mirror, recreate, repeat, replicate **2 = breed**, multiply, procreate, propagate, spawn

reproduction n **1 = breeding**, generation, increase, multiplication **2 = copy**, duplicate, facsimile, imitation, picture, print, replica

reproof n **= rebuke**, blame, censure, condemnation, criticism, reprimand, scolding

reprove v **= rebuke**, berate, blame, censure, condemn, reprimand, scold, tell off (inf)

repudiate v **= reject**, deny, disavow, disclaim, disown, renounce

repugnance n **= distaste**, abhorrence, aversion, disgust, dislike, hatred, loathing

repugnant adj **= distasteful**, abhorrent, disgusting, loathsome, nauseating, offensive, repellent, revolting, sickening, vile

repulse v **1 = drive back**, beat off, fight off, rebuff, repel, ward off **2 = rebuff**, refuse, reject, snub, spurn, turn down

repulsion n **= distaste**, abhorrence, aversion, detestation, disgust, hatred, loathing, repugnance, revulsion

repulsive adj **= disgusting**, abhorrent, foul, loathsome, nauseating, repellent, revolting, scuzzy (sl), sickening, vile

reputable adj **= respectable**, creditable, excellent, good, honorable, reliable,

trustworthy, well-thought-of, worthy

reputation n **= estimation**, character, esteem, name, renown, repute, standing, stature

repute n **= reputation**, celebrity, distinction, eminence, fame, name, renown, standing, stature

reputed adj **= supposed**, alleged, believed, considered, deemed, estimated, held, reckoned, regarded

reputedly adv **= supposedly**, allegedly, apparently, seemingly

request v **1 = ask (for)**, appeal for, demand, desire, entreat, invite, seek, solicit ◆ n **2 = asking**, appeal, call, demand, desire, entreaty, suit

require v **1 = need**, crave, desire, lack, miss, want, wish **2 = demand**, ask, bid, call upon, command, compel, exact, insist upon, oblige, order

required adj **= needed**, called for, essential, necessary, obligatory, requisite

requirement n **= necessity**, demand, essential, lack, must, need, prerequisite, stipulation, want

requisite adj **1 = necessary**, called for, essential, indispensable, needed, needful, obligatory, required ◆ n **2 = necessity**, condition, essential, must, need, prerequisite, requirement

requisition v **1 = demand**, call for, request ◆ n **2 = demand**, call, request, summons

re·scind [ri-SIND] *vt* cancel, annul. **re·scis·sion** [-SIZH-ən] *n*

res·cue [RES-kyoo] *vt* **-cued, -cu·ing** save, deliver, extricate. ◆ *n* **res'cu·er** *n*

re·search [ri-SURCH] *n* **1** investigation, esp. scientific study to discover facts. ◆ *v* **2** carry out investigations (on, into).

re·sem·ble [ri-ZEM-bəl] *vt* **-bled, -bling** be like, look like. **re·sem'blance** *n*

re·sent [ri-ZENT] *vt* **1** show, feel indignation at. **2** retain bitterness about. **re·sent'ful** [-fəl] *adj* **re·sent'ment** [-mənt] *n*

re·serve [ri-ZURV] *vt* **-served, -serv·ing 1** hold back, set aside, keep for future use. ◆ *n* **2** (also *pl*) something, esp. money, troops, etc. kept for emergencies. **3** (also **reservation**) area of land reserved for particular purpose or for use by particular group of people, etc. **4** reticence, concealment of feelings or friendliness. **re·ser·va'tion** *n* **1** reserving. **2** thing reserved. **3** doubt. **4** exception or limitation. **reserved** *adj* not showing feelings, lacking cordiality. **re·serv'ist** *n* one serving in reserve.

res·er·voir [REZ-ər-vwahr] *n* **1** enclosed area for storage of water, esp. for community supplies. **2** receptacle for liquid, gas, etc. **3** place where anything is kept in store.

re·shuf·fle *n* **1** reorganization. ◆ *v* **2** reorganize.

re·side [ri-ZID] *vi* **-sid·ed, -sid·ing** dwell permanently. **res·i·dence** [REZ-i-dəns] *n* **1** home. **2** house. **res'i·den·cy** *n* **1** dwelling. **2** position or period of medical resident. **res'i·dent** [-dənt] *adj, n* **res·i·den'tial** *adj* **1** (of part of town) consisting mainly of residences. **2** of, connected with residence. **3** providing living accommodation. **resident** physician in residence at hospital and serving on staff to obtain advanced training.

res·i·due [REZ-i-doo] *n* what is left,

——— THESAURUS ———

requital *n* = **return**, repayment

requite *v* = **return**, get even, give in return, pay (someone) back in his *or* her own coin, reciprocate, repay, respond, retaliate

rescind *v* = **annul**, cancel, countermand, declare null and void, invalidate, repeal, set aside

rescue *v* **1** = **save**, deliver, get out, liberate, recover, redeem, release, salvage ◆ *n* **2** = **liberation**, deliverance, recovery, redemption, release, salvage, salvation, saving

research *n* **1** = **investigation**, analysis, examination, exploration, probe, study ◆ *v* **2** = **investigate**, analyze, examine, explore, probe, study

resemblance *n* = **similarity**, correspondence, kinship, likeness, parallel, sameness, similitude

resemble *v* = **be like**, bear a resemblance to, be similar to, look like, mirror, parallel

resent *v* = **be bitter about**, begrudge, grudge, object to, take exception to, take offense at

resentful *adj* = **bitter**, angry, embittered, grudging, indignant, miffed (*inf*), offended, piqued, ticked off (*inf*)

resentment *n* = **bitterness**, animosity, bad blood, grudge, ill feeling, ill will, indignation, pique, rancor, umbrage

reservation *n* **1** = **doubt**, hesitancy, scruple **2** = **condition**, proviso, qualification, rider, stipulation **3** = **reserve**, preserve, sanctuary, territory

reserve *v* **1** = **keep**, hoard, hold, put by, retain, save, set aside, stockpile, store **2** = **book**, engage, prearrange, secure ◆ *n* **3** = **store**, cache, fund, hoard, reservoir, savings, stock, supply **4** = **reservation**, park, preserve, sanctuary, tract **5** = **shyness**, constraint, reservation, restraint, reticence, secretiveness, silence, taciturnity ◆ *adj* **6** = **substitute**, auxiliary, extra, fall-back, secondary, spare

reserved *adj* **1** = **uncommunicative**, restrained, reticent, retiring, secretive, shy, silent, standoffish, taciturn, undemonstrative **2** = **set aside**, booked, engaged, held, kept, restricted, retained, spoken for, taken

reservoir *n* **1** = **lake**, basin, pond, tank **2** = **store**, pool, reserves, source, stock, supply

reshuffle *n* **1** = **reorganization**, change, rearrangement, redistribution, regrouping, restructuring, revision ◆ *v* **2** = **reorganize**, change around, rearrange, redistribute, regroup, restructure, revise

reside *v* = **live**, abide, dwell, inhabit, lodge, stay

residence *n* = **home**, abode, domicile, dwelling, flat, habitation, house, lodging, place

resident *n* = **inhabitant**, citizen, local, lodger, occupant, occupier, tenant

remainder. **re·sid·u·al** [ri-ZIJ-oo-əl] *adj*
residuals *pl n* additional payments to
performers for reruns of film, TV programs,
etc. in which they appear.
re·sign [ri-ZĪN] *vt* **1** give up. ♦ *vi* **2** give up
office, employment, etc. **3** reconcile
(oneself) to. **res·ig·na'tion** [-ig-NAY-shən]
n **1** resigning. **2** being resigned,
submission. **re·signed'** [-ZĪND] *adj* content
to endure.
re·sil·ient [ri-ZIL-yənt] *adj* **1** capable of
returning to normal after stretching, etc.,
elastic. **2** (of person) recovering quickly
from shock, etc. **re·sil'ience, -ien·cy** *n*
res·in [REZ-in] *n* sticky substance formed in
and oozing from plants, esp. firs and pines.
res'in·ous [-nəs] *adj* of, like resin.
re·sist [ri-ZIST] *v* withstand, oppose.
re·sist'ance [-əns] *n* **1** act of resisting. **2**
opposition. **3** hindrance. **4** *Electricity*
opposition offered by circuit to passage of
current through it. **re·sist'ant** [-ənt] *adj*
re·sist'i·ble *adj* **re·sis·tiv'i·ty** *n* measure of

electrical resistance. **re·sist'or** *n*
component of electrical circuit producing
resistance.
res·o·lute [REZ-ə-loot] *adj* determined.
res·o·lu'tion *n* **1** resolving. **2** firmness. **3**
purpose or thing resolved upon. **4** decision
or vote of assembly.
re·solve [ri-ZOLV] *vt* **-solved, -solv·ing 1**
make up one's mind. **2** decide with effort
of will. **3** form by resolution of vote. **4**
separate component parts of. **5** make
clear. ♦ *n* **6** resolution. **7** fixed purpose.
res·o·nance [REZ-ə-nəns] *n* **1** echoing, esp.
in deep tone. **2** sound produced by body
vibrating in sympathy with neighboring
source of sound. **res'o·nant** [-nənt] *adj*
res'o·nate *vi, vt* **-nat·ed, -nat·ing**
re·sort [ri-ZORT] *vi* **1** have recourse. **2**
frequent. ♦ *n* **3** place for vacations. **4**
recourse. **5** frequented place. **6** haunt.
re·sound [ri-ZOWND] *vi* echo, ring, go on
sounding. **re·sound'ing** *adj* **1** echoing. **2**
thorough.

residual *adj* = **remaining**, leftover,
unconsumed, unused, vestigial
residue *n* = **remainder**, dregs, excess,
extra, leftovers, remains, remnant, rest,
surplus
resign *v* **1** = **quit**, abdicate, give in one's
notice, leave, step down (*inf*), vacate **2** =
give up, abandon, forgo, forsake,
relinquish, renounce, surrender, yield
3 resign oneself = **accept**, acquiesce, give
in, submit, succumb, yield
resignation *n* **1** = **leaving**, abandonment,
abdication, departure **2** = **endurance**,
acceptance, acquiescence, compliance,
nonresistance, passivity, patience,
submission, sufferance
resigned *adj* = **stoical**, compliant,
long-suffering, patient, subdued,
unresisting
resilient *adj* **1** = **tough**, buoyant, hardy,
irrepressible, strong **2** = **flexible**, elastic,
plastic, pliable, rubbery, springy, supple
resist *v* **1** = **oppose**, battle, combat, defy,
hinder, stand up to **2** = **refrain from**,
abstain from, avoid, forbear, forgo, keep
from **3** = **withstand**, be proof against
resistance *n* = **fighting**, battle, defiance,
fight, hindrance, impediment, obstruction,
opposition, struggle
resistant *adj* **1** = **impervious**, hard, proof
against, strong, tough, unaffected by **2** =

opposed, antagonistic, hostile, intractable,
intransigent, unwilling
resolute *adj* = **determined**, dogged, firm,
fixed, immovable, inflexible, set, steadfast,
strong-willed, tenacious, unshakable,
unwavering
resolution *n* **1** = **determination**,
doggedness, firmness, perseverance,
purpose, resoluteness, resolve,
steadfastness, tenacity, willpower **2** =
decision, aim, declaration, determination,
intent, intention, purpose, resolve
resolve *v* **1** = **decide**, agree, conclude,
determine, fix, intend, purpose **2** = **break
down**, analyze, reduce, separate **3** = **work
out**, answer, clear up, crack, fathom ♦ *n*
4 = **determination**, firmness, resoluteness,
resolution, steadfastness, willpower **5** =
decision, intention, objective, purpose,
resolution
resonant *adj* = **echoing**, booming,
resounding, reverberating, ringing,
sonorous
resort *v* **1 resort to** = **use**, employ, fall back
on, have recourse to, turn to, utilize ♦ *n* **2** =
holiday center, haunt, retreat, spot, tourist
center **3** = **recourse**, reference
resound *v* = **echo**, re-echo, resonate,
reverberate, ring
resounding *adj* = **echoing**, booming, full,
powerful, resonant, reverberating, ringing,

re·source [ri-ZORS, ri-SORS] *n* 1 capability, ingenuity. 2 that to which one resorts for support. 3 expedient. ♦ *pl* 4 source of economic wealth. 5 supply that can be drawn on. 6 means of support, funds. **re·source'ful** [-fəl] *adj*

re·spect [ri-SPEKT] *n* 1 deference, esteem. 2 point or aspect. 3 reference, relation. ♦ *vt* 4 treat with esteem. 5 show consideration for. **re·spect·a·bil'i·ty** *n* **re·spect'a·ble** *adj* 1 worthy of respect, decent. 2 fairly good. **re·spect'ful** *adj* **re·spect'ing** *prep* concerning. **re·spect'ive** *adj* 1 relating separately to each of those in question. 2 several, separate.

res·pi·ra·tion [res-pə-RAY-shən] *n* breathing. **res'pi·ra·tor** *n* apparatus worn over mouth and breathed through as protection against dust, poison gas, etc. or to provide artificial respiration. **res'pi·ra·to·ry** [-rə-tor-ee] *adj*

res·pite [RES-pit] *n* 1 pause. 2 interval. 3 suspension of labor. 4 delay. 5 reprieve.

re·splend·ent [ri-SPLEN-dənt] *adj* 1 brilliant, splendid. 2 shining.

re·splend'en·cy [-ən-see] *n*

re·spond [ri-SPOND] *vi* 1 answer. 2 act in answer to stimulus. 3 react. **re·spond'ent** *adj* 1 replying. ♦ *n* 2 one who answers. 3 defendant. **re·sponse'** *n* answer. **re·spon'sive** *adj* readily reacting to some influence.

re·spon·si·ble [ri-SPON-sə-bəl] *adj* 1 liable to answer for. 2 accountable. 3 dependable. 4 involving responsibility. 5 of good credit or position. **re·spon·si·bil'i·ty** *n* 1 state of being answerable. 2 duty. 3 charge. 4 obligation.

rest[1] *n* 1 repose. 2 freedom from exertion, etc. 3 that on which anything rests or leans. 4 pause, esp. in music. 5 support. ♦ *vi* 6 take rest. 7 be supported. ♦ *vt* 8 give rest to. 9 place on support. **rest'ful** [-fəl] *adj* **rest'less** [-lis] *adj* 1 offering no rest. 2 uneasy, impatient. **rest home** residential establishment providing care for aged, convalescent, etc.

rest[2] *n* 1 remainder. 2 others. ♦ *vi* 3 remain. 4 continue to be.

res·tau·rant [RES-tər-ənt] *n* commercial

THESAURUS

sonorous

resource *n* 1 = **ingenuity**, ability, capability, cleverness, initiative, inventiveness 2 = **means**, course, device, expedient, resort

resourceful *adj* = **ingenious**, able, bright, capable, clever, creative, inventive

resources *pl n* = **reserves**, assets, capital, funds, holdings, money, riches, supplies, wealth

respect *n* 1 = **regard**, admiration, consideration, deference, esteem, estimation, honor, recognition 2 = **point**, aspect, characteristic, detail, feature, matter, particular, sense, way 3 = **relation**, bearing, connection, reference, regard ♦ *v* 4 = **think highly of**, admire, defer to, esteem, have a good *or* high opinion of, honor, look up to, value 5 = **show consideration for**, abide by, adhere to, comply with, follow, heed, honor, obey, observe

respectable *adj* 1 = **honorable**, decent, estimable, good, honest, reputable, upright, worthy 2 = **reasonable**, ample, appreciable, considerable, decent, fair, sizable *or* sizeable, substantial

respectful *adj* = **polite**, civil, courteous, deferential, mannerly, reverent,

well-mannered

respective *adj* = **specific**, individual, own, particular, relevant

respite *n* = **pause**, break, cessation, halt, interval, lull, recess, relief, rest

resplendent *adj* = **brilliant**, bright, dazzling, glorious, radiant, shining, splendid

respond *v* = **answer**, react, reciprocate, rejoin, reply, retort, return

response *n* = **answer**, counterattack, feedback, reaction, rejoinder, reply, retort, return

responsibility *n* 1 = **authority**, importance, power 2 = **fault**, blame, culpability, guilt 3 = **duty**, care, charge, liability, obligation, onus 4 = **level-headedness**, conscientiousness, dependability, rationality, sensibleness, trustworthiness

responsible *adj* 1 = **in charge**, in authority, in control 2 = **to blame**, at fault, culpable, guilty 3 = **accountable**, answerable, liable 4 = **sensible**, dependable, level-headed, rational, reliable, trustworthy

responsive *adj* = **sensitive**, alive, impressionable, open, reactive, receptive, susceptible

establishment serving food.
res·tau·ra·teur' [-ə-TUR] *n* keeper of one.
res·ti·tu·tion [res-ti-TOO-shən] *n* **1** giving back or making up. **2** reparation, compensation.
res·tive [RES-tiv] *adj* **1** restless. **2** resisting control, impatient.
re·store [ri-STOR] *vt* **-stored, -stor·ing 1** build up again, repair, renew. **2** reestablish. **3** give back. **res·to·ra'tion** *n* **re·stor'a·tive** *adj* **1** restoring. ♦ *n* **2** medicine to strengthen, etc. **re·stor'er** *n*
re·strain [ri-STRAYN] *vt* **1** check, hold back. **2** prevent. **3** confine. **re·straint'** *n* restraining, control, esp. self-control.
re·strict [ri-STRIKT] *vt* limit, bound. **re·stric'tion** *n* **1** limitation. **2** restraint. **3** rule. **re·stric'tive** *adj* **re·stric'ted** *adj*

denying residence, membership to persons of certain races, ethnic groups, etc.
re·sult [ri-ZULT] *vi* **1** follow as consequence. **2** happen. **3** end. ♦ *n* **4** effect, outcome. **re·sult'ant** [-ZUL-tnt] *adj* arising as result.
re·sume [ri-ZOOM] *vt* **-sumed, -sum·ing** begin again. **ré·su·mé** [REZ-uu-may] *n* **1** summary, abstract. **2** brief statement of one's qualifications for employment, public office, etc. **re·sump'tion** [-shən] *n* **1** resuming. **2** fresh start.
re·sur·gence [ri-SUR-jəns] *n* rising again. **re·sur'gent** *adj*
res·ur·rect [rez-ə-REKT] *vt* **1** restore to life, resuscitate. **2** use once more (something discarded, etc.). **res·ur·rec'tion** *n* **1** rising again (esp. from dead). **2** revival.

═══ THESAURUS ═══

rest[1] *n* **1 = repose**, calm, inactivity, leisure, relaxation, relief, stillness, tranquillity **2 = pause**, break, cessation, halt, interlude, intermission, interval, lull, respite, stop **3 = support**, base, holder, prop, stand ♦ *v* **4 = relax**, be at ease, put one's feet up, sit down, take it easy **5 = be supported**, lean, lie, prop, recline, repose, sit

rest[2] *n* **= remainder**, balance, excess, others, remains, remnants, residue, surplus

restaurant *n* **= bistro**, café, cafeteria, diner, eatery, tearoom

restful *adj* **= relaxing**, calm, calming, peaceful, quiet, relaxed, serene, soothing, tranquil

restitution *n* **= compensation**, amends, recompense, reparation, requital

restive *adj* **= restless**, edgy, fidgety, impatient, jumpy, nervous, on edge, wired (*sl*)

restless *adj* **1 = moving**, nomadic, roving, transient, unsettled, unstable, wandering **2 = unsettled**, antsy (*sl*), edgy, fidgeting, fidgety, jumpy, nervous, on edge, restive, wired (*sl*)

restlessness *n* **1 = movement**, activity, bustle, unrest, unsettledness **2 = restiveness**, edginess, jitters (*inf*), jumpiness, nervousness

restoration *n* **1 = repair**, reconstruction, renewal, renovation, revitalization, revival **2 = reinstatement**, re-establishment, replacement, restitution, return

restore *v* **1 = repair**, fix, mend, rebuild, recondition, reconstruct, refurbish, renew, renovate **2 = revive**, build up, refresh,

revitalize, strengthen **3 = return**, bring back, give back, hand back, recover, reinstate, replace, send back **4 = reinstate**, reintroduce

restrain *v* **= hold back**, check, constrain, contain, control, curb, curtail, hamper, hinder, inhibit, restrict

restrained *adj* **= controlled**, calm, mild, moderate, self-controlled, undemonstrative

restraint *n* **1 = self-control**, control, inhibition, moderation, self-discipline, self-possession, self-restraint **2 = limitation**, ban, check, curb, embargo, interdict, limit, rein

restrict *v* **= limit**, bound, confine, contain, hamper, handicap, inhibit, regulate, restrain

restriction *n* **= limitation**, confinement, control, curb, handicap, inhibition, regulation, restraint, rule

result *n* **1 = consequence**, effect, end, end result, outcome, product, sequel, upshot ♦ *v* **2 = happen**, appear, arise, derive, develop, ensue, follow, issue, spring **3 result in = end in**, culminate in, finish with

resume *v* **= begin again**, carry on, continue, go on, proceed, reopen, restart

résumé *n* **= summary**, précis, recapitulation, rundown, synopsis

resumption *n* **= continuation**, carrying on, re-establishment, renewal, reopening, restart, resurgence

resurgence *n* **= revival**, rebirth, re-emergence, renaissance, resumption,

re·sus·ci·tate [ri-SUS-i-tayt] *vt* **-tat·ed,**
-tat·ing revive to life, consciousness.

re·tail [REE-tayl] *n* **1** sale in small quantities.
♦ *adv* **2** at retail. ♦ *v* **3** sell, be sold, retail. **4**
recount.

re·tain [ri-TAYN] *vt* **1** keep. **2** engage
services of. **re·tain'er** *n* fee to retain
professional adviser, esp. lawyer.
re·ten'tion [-shən] *n* **re·ten'tive** *adj*
capable of retaining, remembering.

re·tal·i·ate [ri-TAL-ee-ayt] *v* **-at·ed, -at·ing 1**
repay in kind. **2** revenge. **re·tal·i·a'tion** *n*
re·tal'i·a·to·ry *adj*

re·tard [ri-TAHRD] *vt* **1** make slow or late. **2**
keep back. **3** impede development of.
re·tard'ed *adj* underdeveloped, esp.
mentally. **re·tar·da'tion** *n*

retch [rech] *vi* try to vomit.

ret·i·cent [RET-ə-sənt] *adj* **1** reserved in
speech. **2** uncommunicative. **ret'i·cence** *n*

ret·i·na [RET-n-ə] *n, pl* **-nas** light-sensitive
membrane at back of eye. **ret'i·nal** *adj*
ret·i·ni'tis [-NĪ-tis] *n* inflammation of
retina.

ret·i·nue [RET-n-yoo] *n* band of followers
or attendants.

re·tire [ri-TĪR] *v* **-tired, -tir·ing** ♦ *vi* **1** give up
office or work. **2** go away. **3** withdraw. **4**
go to bed. ♦ *vt* **5** cause to retire. **retired** *adj*
that has retired from office, etc.
re·tire'ment [-mənt] *n* **re·tir'ing** *adj*
unobtrusive, shy.

re·tort [ri-TORT] *vt* **1** reply. **2** repay in kind,
retaliate. **3** hurl back (charge, etc.). ♦ *vi* **4**
reply with countercharge. ♦ *n* **5** vigorous
reply or repartee. **6** vessel with bent neck
used for distilling.

re·touch [ree-TUCH] *vt* touch up, improve
by new touches, esp. of paint, etc.

re·trace [ri-TRAYS] *vt* **-traced, -trac·ing** go
back over (a route, etc.) again.

re·tract [ri-TRAKT] *v* draw back, recant.
re·tract'a·ble *adj* **re·trac'tion** *n* drawing or
taking back, esp. of statement, etc.
re·trac'tor *n* **1** muscle. **2** surgical
instrument.

re·tread [ree-TRED] *vt* **1** restore tread to
worn rubber tire. ♦ *n* [REE-tred] **2**
retreaded tire. **3** *sl* person returned to work
after dismissal. **4** person training for new
type of work. **5** *inf* reworked old idea, etc.

re·treat [ri-TREET] *vi* **1** move back from any
position. **2** retire. ♦ *n* **3** act of, or military
signal for, retiring, withdrawal. **4** place to
which anyone retires esp. for meditation. **5**
refuge. **6** sunset call on bugle.

resurrection, return

resurrect *v* = **revive**, bring back,
reintroduce, renew

resurrection *n* = **revival**, reappearance,
rebirth, renaissance, renewal, restoration,
resurgence, return

resuscitate *v* = **revive**, bring round,
resurrect, revitalize, save

retain *v* **1** = **keep**, hold, hold back,
maintain, preserve, reserve, save **2** = **hire**,
commission, employ, engage, pay, reserve

retainer *n* **1** = **fee**, advance, deposit **2** =
servant, attendant, domestic

retaliate *v* = **pay (someone) back**, get
even with (*inf*), hit back, reciprocate, strike
back, take revenge

retaliation *n* = **revenge**, an eye for an eye,
counterblow, reciprocation, repayment,
reprisal, requital, vengeance

retard *v* = **slow down**, arrest, check, delay,
handicap, hinder, hold back *or* up,
impede, set back

retch *v* = **gag**, barf (*sl*), heave, puke (*sl*),
regurgitate, spew, throw up (*inf*), vomit

reticence *n* = **silence**, quietness, reserve,
taciturnity

reticent *adj* = **uncommunicative**,
close-lipped, quiet, reserved, silent,
taciturn, tight-lipped, unforthcoming

retinue *n* = **attendants**, aides, entourage,
escort, followers, servants

retire *v* **1** = **stop working**, give up work **2** =
withdraw, depart, exit, go away, leave **3** =
go to bed, hit the hay (*sl*), hit the sack (*sl*),
turn in (*inf*)

retirement *n* = **withdrawal**, privacy,
retreat, seclusion, solitude

retiring *adj* = **shy**, bashful, quiet, reserved,
self-effacing, timid, unassertive,
unassuming

retort *v* **1** = **reply**, answer, come back with,
counter, respond, return, riposte ♦ *n* **2** =
reply, answer, comeback (*inf*), rejoinder,
response, riposte

retract *v* **1** = **withdraw**, deny, disavow,
disclaim, eat one's words, recant, renege,
renounce, revoke, take back **2** = **draw in**,
pull back, pull in, sheathe

retreat *v* **1** = **withdraw**, back away, back
off, depart, draw back, fall back, go back,
leave, pull back ♦ *n* **2** = **withdrawal**,
departure, evacuation, flight, retirement

re·trench [ri-TRENCH] vt **1** reduce expenditure, esp. by dismissing staff. **2** cut down.

ret·ri·bu·tion [re-trə-BYOO-shən] n **1** recompense, esp. for evil deeds. **2** vengeance.

re·trieve [ri-TREEV] vt **-trieved, -triev·ing 1** fetch back again. **2** restore. **3** rescue from ruin. **4** recover, esp. information from computer. **5** regain. **re·triev'al** n **re·triev'er** n dog trained to retrieve game.

ret·ro·ac·tive [re-troh-AK-tiv] adj applying or referring to the past.

ret·ro·grade [RE-trə-grayd] adj **1** going backward, reverting. **2** reactionary. **ret·ro·gres·sion** [-GRE-shən] n **ret·ro·gres·sive** adj

ret·ro·spect [RE-trə-spekt] n looking back, survey of past. **ret·ro·spec·tion** [-SPEK-shən] n **ret·ro·spec·tive** adj

re·trous·sé [ri-troo-SAY] adj of nose, turned upward.

re·turn [ri-TURN] vi **1** go, come back. ◆ vt **2** give, send back. **3** report officially. **4** elect. ◆ n **5** returning, being returned. **6** profit. **7** official report esp. tax return.

re·un·ion [ree-YOON-yən] n gathering of people who have been apart. **re·u·nite'** v bring or come together again after a separation.

Rev. Revelations.

rev n inf **1** revolution (of engine). ◆ v **revved, rev·ving 2** (oft. with up) increase speed of revolution (of engine).

re·val·ue [ree-VAL-yoo] v **-ued, -u·ing** adjust exchange value of currency upward.

re·vamp [ree-VAMP] vt renovate, restore.

re·veal [ri-VEEL] vt **1** make known. **2** show. **rev·e·la'tion** n

rev·eil·le [REV-ə-lee] n morning bugle call, etc. to waken soldiers.

rev·el [REV-əl] vi **-eled, -el·ing 1** take pleasure (in). **2** make merry. ◆ n **3** (usu pl) merrymaking. **rev'el·ry** n festivity.

re·venge [ri-VENJ] n **1** retaliation for wrong done. **2** act that satisfies this. **3** desire for this. ◆ v **-venged, -veng·ing** vt **4** avenge. **5** make retaliation for. ◆ v refl **6** avenge oneself. **re·venge'ful** [-fəl] adj **1** vindictive. **2** resentful.

THESAURUS

3 = refuge, haven, hideaway, sanctuary, seclusion, shelter

retrench v **= cut back**, economize, make economies, save, tighten one's belt

retrenchment n **= cutback**, cost-cutting, cut, economy, saving, tightening one's belt

retribution n **= punishment**, justice, Nemesis, reckoning, reprisal, retaliation, revenge, vengeance

retrieve v **= get back**, recapture, recoup, recover, redeem, regain, restore, save, win back

retrograde adj **= declining**, backward, degenerative, deteriorating, downward, regressive, retrogressive, worsening

retrogress v **= decline**, backslide, deteriorate, go back, go downhill (inf), regress, relapse, worsen

retrospect n **= hindsight**, re-examination, review

return v **1 = come back**, go back, reappear, rebound, recur, retreat, revert, turn back **2 = put back**, re-establish, reinstate, replace, restore **3 = give back**, pay back, recompense, refund, reimburse, repay **4 = reply**, answer, respond, retort **5 = elect**, choose, vote in ◆ n **6 = restoration**, re-establishment, reinstatement **7 = reappearance**, recurrence **8 = retreat**,

rebound, recoil **9 = profit**, gain, income, interest, proceeds, revenue, takings, yield **10 = report**, account, form, list, statement, summary **11 = reply**, answer, comeback (inf), rejoinder, response, retort

revamp v **= renovate**, do up (inf), overhaul, recondition, refurbish, restore

reveal v **1 = make known**, announce, disclose, divulge, give away, impart, let out, let slip, make public, proclaim, tell **2 = show**, display, exhibit, manifest, uncover, unearth, unmask, unveil

revel v **1 = celebrate**, carouse, live it up (inf), make merry **2 revel in = enjoy**, delight in, indulge in, lap up, luxuriate in, relish, take pleasure in, thrive on ◆ n **3** (often plural) **= merrymaking**, carousal, celebration, festivity, party, spree

revelation n **= disclosure**, exhibition, exposé, exposure, news, proclamation, publication, uncovering, unearthing, unveiling

reveller n **= carouser**, merrymaker, partygoer

revelry n **= festivity**, carousal, celebration, fun, jollity, merrymaking, party, spree

revenge n **1 = retaliation**, an eye for an eye, reprisal, retribution, vengeance ◆ v **2 = avenge**, get even, hit back, repay,

rev·e·nue [REV-ən-yoo] *n* income, esp. of nation, as taxes, etc.

re·ver·ber·ate [ri-VUR-bə-rayt] *v* **-at·ed, -at·ing** echo, resound, throw back (sound, etc.).

re·vere [ri-VEER] *vt* **-vered, -ver·ing** hold in great regard or religious respect. **rev'er·ence** [-əns] *n* **1** revering. **2** awe mingled with respect and esteem. **3** veneration. **rev'er·end** [-ənd] *adj* (esp. as prefix to clergyman's name) worthy of reverence. **rev'er·ent** [-ənt] *adj* showing reverence. **rev·er·en'tial** *adj* marked by reverence.

rev·er·ie [REV-ə-ree] *n* daydream, absent-minded state.

re·verse [ri-VURS] *v* **-versed, -vers·ing 1** (of vehicle) (cause to) move backward. ◆ *vt* **2** turn upside down or other way round. **3** change completely. ◆ *n* **4** opposite, contrary. **5** side opposite, obverse. **6** defeat. **7** reverse gear. ◆ *adj* **8** opposite, contrary. **re·ver'sal** [-səl] *n* **re·vers'i·ble** *adj* **reverse gear** mechanism enabling vehicle to move backward.

re·vert [ri-VURT] *vi* **1** return to former state.

2 come back to subject. **3** refer to a second time. **4** turn backward. **re·ver'sion** [-VUR-zhən] *n* (of property) rightful passing to owner or designated heir, etc.

re·vet·ment [ri-VET-mənt] *n* facing of stone, sandbags, etc. for wall.

re·view [ri-VYOO] *vt* **1** examine. **2** look back on. **3** reconsider. **4** hold, make, write review of. ◆ *n* **5** general survey. **6** critical notice of book, etc. **7** periodical with critical articles. **8** inspection of troops. **9** revue. **re·view'er** *n* writer of reviews.

re·vile [ri-VIL] *vt* **-viled, -vil·ing** be viciously scornful of, abuse.

re·vise [ri-VIZ] *vt* **-vised, -vis·ing 1** look over and correct. **2** change, alter. **re·vi'sion** [-zhən] *n* **1** reexamination for purpose of correcting. **2** act of revising. **3** revised copy. **re·vi'sion·ism** *n* departure from generally accepted theory, interpretation. **re·vi'sion·ist** *adj, n*

re·vive [ri-VIV] *v* **-vived, -viv·ing** bring, come back to life, vigor, use, etc. **re·viv'al** [-vəl] *n* reviving, esp. of religious fervor. **re·viv'al·ist** *n* organizer of religious revival.

re·voke [ri-VOHK] *vt* **-voked, -vok·ing 1**

——————— THESAURUS ———————

retaliate, take revenge for

revenue *n* = **income**, gain, proceeds, profits, receipts, returns, takings, yield

reverberate *v* = **echo**, re-echo, resound, ring, vibrate

revere *v* = **be in awe of**, exalt, honor, look up to, respect, reverence, venerate, worship

reverence *n* = **awe**, admiration, high esteem, honor, respect, veneration, worship

reverent *adj* = **respectful**, awed, deferential, humble, reverential

reverie *n* = **daydream**, abstraction, brown study, woolgathering

reverse *v* **1** = **turn round**, invert, transpose, turn back, turn over, turn upside down, upend **2** = **change**, annul, cancel, countermand, invalidate, overrule, overthrow, overturn, quash, repeal, rescind, revoke, undo **3** = **go backwards**, back, back up, move backwards, retreat ◆ *n* **4** = **opposite**, contrary, converse, inverse **5** = **back**, other side, rear, underside, wrong side **6** = **misfortune**, adversity, affliction, blow, disappointment, failure, hardship, misadventure, mishap, reversal, setback ◆ *adj* **7** = **opposite**, contrary,

converse

revert *v* = **return**, come back, go back, resume

review *n* **1** = **critique**, commentary, criticism, evaluation, judgment, notice **2** = **magazine**, journal, periodical **3** = **survey**, analysis, examination, scrutiny, study **4** *Military* = **inspection**, march past, parade ◆ *v* **5** = **assess**, criticize, evaluate, judge, study **6** = **reconsider**, reassess, re-evaluate, re-examine, rethink, revise, think over **7** = **look back on**, recall, recollect, reflect on, remember **8** = **inspect**, examine **9** = **study**, cram (*inf*), revise (*chiefly Brit.*)

reviewer *n* = **critic**, commentator, judge

revile *v* = **malign**, abuse, bad-mouth (*sl*), denigrate, knock (*inf*), reproach, run down, vilify

revise *v* = **change**, alter, amend, correct, edit, emend, redo, review, rework, update

revision *n* = **change**, amendment, correction, emendation, updating

revival *n* = **renewal**, reawakening, rebirth, renaissance, resurgence, resurrection, revitalization

revive *v* = **revitalize**, awaken, bring round, come round, invigorate, reanimate, recover, refresh, rekindle, renew, restore take back, withdraw. **2** cancel. **rev'o·ca·ble** [-ə-kə-bəl] *adj* **rev·o·ca'tion** *n* repeal.

re·volt [ri-VOHLT] *n* **1** rebellion. ◆ *vi* **2** rise in rebellion. **3** feel disgust. ◆ *vt* **4** affect with disgust. **re·volt'ing** *adj* disgusting, horrible.

re·volve [ri-VOLV] *v* **-volved, -volv·ing** ◆ *vi* **1** turn around, rotate. **2** be centered on. ◆ *vt* **3** rotate. **rev·o·lu'tion** *n* **1** violent overthrow of government. **2** great change. **3** complete rotation, turning or spinning around. **rev·o·lu'tion·ar·y** *adj, n* **rev·o·lu'tion·ize** *vt* **-ized, -iz·ing 1** change considerably. **2** bring about revolution in.

re·volv·er [ri-VOL-vər] *n* repeating pistol with revolving cylinder.

re·vue, re·view [ri-VYOO] *n* theatrical entertainment with topical sketches and songs.

re·vul·sion [ri-VUL-shən] *n* **1** sudden violent change of feeling. **2** marked repugnance or abhorrence.

re·ward [ri-WORD] *vt* pay, make return for service, conduct, etc. ◆ *n* **re·ward'ing** *adj* giving personal satisfaction, worthwhile.

re·wind' *v* run (tape or film) back to an earlier point in order to replay.

Rf *Chem.* rutherfordium.

Rh *Chem.* rhodium.

rhap·so·dy [RAP-sə-dee] *n, pl* **-dies**

enthusiastic or high-flown (musical) composition or utterance. **rhap·sod'ic** *adj* **rhap'so·dize** [-sə-dīz] *v* **-dized, -diz·ing**

rhe·o·stat [REE-ə-stat] *n* instrument for regulating the value of the resistance in an electric circuit.

rhe·sus [REE-səs] *n* small, long-tailed monkey of S Asia. **rhesus factor, Rh factor** feature distinguishing different types of human blood.

rhet·o·ric [RET-ər-ik] *n* **1** art of effective speaking or writing. **2** artificial or exaggerated language. **rhe·tor·i·cal** [ri-TOR-i-kəl] *adj* (of question) not requiring an answer. **rhet·o·ri'cian** [-RISH-ən] *n*

rheu·ma·tism [ROO-mə-tiz-əm] *n* painful inflammation of joints or muscles. **rheu·mat·ic** [ruu-MAT-ik] *adj, n* **rheu·ma·toid** [ROO-mə-toid] *adj* of, like rheumatism.

Rh factor see RHESUS.

rhi·no·cer·os [rī-NOS-ər-əs] *n, pl* **-os·es** large thick-skinned animal with one or two horns on nose.

rho·di·um [ROH-dee-əm] *n* hard metal like platinum.

rhom·bus [ROM-bəs] *n, pl* **-bus·es** or **-bi** [-bī] equilateral but not right-angled parallelogram, diamond-shaped figure.

revoke *v* = **cancel**, annul, countermand, disclaim, invalidate, negate, nullify, obviate, quash, repeal, rescind, retract, reverse, set aside, withdraw

revolt *n* **1** = **uprising**, insurgency, insurrection, mutiny, rebellion, revolution, rising ◆ *v* **2** = **rebel**, mutiny, resist, rise **3** = **disgust**, gross out (*sl*), make one's flesh creep, nauseate, repel, repulse, sicken, turn one's stomach

revolting *adj* = **disgusting**, foul, horrible, horrid, nauseating, repellent, repugnant, repulsive, scuzzy (*sl*), sickening, yucky *or* yukky (*sl*)

revolution *n* **1** = **revolt**, coup, insurgency, mutiny, rebellion, rising **2** = **transformation**, innovation, reformation, sea change, shift, upheaval **3** = **rotation**, circle, circuit, cycle, lap, orbit, spin, turn

revolutionary *adj* **1** = **rebel**, extremist, insurgent, radical, subversive **2** = **new**, different, drastic, ground-breaking, innovative, novel, progressive, radical ◆ *n* **3** = **rebel**, insurgent, revolutionist

revolutionize *v* = **transform**, modernize, reform

revolve *v* = **rotate**, circle, go round, orbit, spin, turn, twist, wheel, whirl

revulsion *n* = **disgust**, abhorrence, detestation, loathing, repugnance, repulsion

reward *n* **1** = **payment**, bonus, bounty, premium, prize, recompense, repayment, return, wages **2** = **punishment**, just deserts, retribution ◆ *v* **3** = **pay**, compensate, recompense, remunerate, repay

rewarding *adj* = **worthwhile**, beneficial, enriching, fruitful, fulfilling, productive, profitable, satisfying, valuable

rhapsodize *v* = **enthuse**, go into ecstasies, gush, rave (*inf*)

rhetoric *n* **1** = **oratory**, eloquence **2** = **hyperbole**, bombast, grandiloquence, magniloquence, verbosity, wordiness

rhetorical *adj* = **oratorical**, bombastic, declamatory, grandiloquent, high-flown, magniloquent, verbose

rhu·barb [ROO-bahrb] n 1 garden plant of
which the fleshy stalks are cooked and
used as fruit. 2 laxative from root of allied
Chinese plant. 3 sl argument, fight.

rhyme [rīm] n 1 identity of sounds at ends
of lines of verse, or in words. 2 word or
syllable identical in sound to another. 3
verse marked by rhyme. ♦ vt **rhymed,
rhym·ing 4** make rhymes.

rhythm [RITH-əm] n measured beat or
flow, esp. of words, music, etc. **rhyth'mic**
adj **rhyth'mi·cal·ly** adv

rib[1] n 1 one of curved bones springing from
spine and forming framework of upper
part of body. 2 cut of meat including
rib(s). 3 curved timber of framework of
boat. 4 raised series of rows in knitting,
etc. ♦ vt **ribbed, rib·bing 5** furnish, mark
with ribs. 6 knit to form a rib pattern.
rib'bing n

rib[2] vt inf **ribbed, rib·bing** tease, ridicule.
rib'bing n

rib·ald [RIB-əld] adj 1 irreverent, scurrilous.
2 indecent. ♦ n 3 ribald person. **rib'ald·ry** n
vulgar, indecent talk.

rib·bon [RIB-ən] n 1 narrow band of fabric
used for trimming, tying, etc. 2 long strip
or line of anything. **ribbon development**
building of houses, etc. along main road
leading out of town, etc.

ri·bo·fla·vin [RĪ-boh-flay-vin] n form of
vitamin B.

rice [rīs] n 1 cereal plant. 2 its seeds as food.
rice paper fine (edible) Chinese paper.

rich adj **-er, -est 1** wealthy. 2 fertile. 3

abounding. 4 valuable. 5 (of food)
containing much fat or sugar. 6 mellow. 7
amusing. ♦ n 8 the wealthy classes. **rich·es**
[RICH-iz] pl n wealth. **rich'ly** adv

rick·ets [RIK-its] n disease of children
marked by softening of bones, bow legs,
etc., caused by vitamin D deficiency.
rick'et·y adj **-et·i·er, -et·i·est 1** shaky,
insecure, unstable. 2 suffering from rickets.

rick·shaw [RIK-shaw] n light two-wheeled
man-drawn Asian vehicle.

ric·o·chet [rik-ə-SHAY] vi **-cheted**
[-SHAYD], **-chet·ing** [-SHAY-ing] **1** (of
bullet) rebound or be deflected by solid
surface or water. ♦ n 2 bullet or shot to
which this happens.

rid vt **rid** or **rid·ded, rid·ding 1** clear, relieve
of. 2 free. 3 deliver. **rid·dance** [RID-ns] n 1
clearance. 2 act of ridding. 3 deliverance. 4
relief.

rid·den [RID-n] **1** pp. of RIDE. ♦ adj **2**
afflicted or affected by the thing specified,
e.g. disease-ridden.

rid·dle[1] [RID-l] n 1 question made
puzzling to test one's ingenuity. 2 enigma.
3 puzzling thing, person. ♦ vi **-dled, -dling**
4 speak in, make riddles.

rid·dle[2] vt **-dled, -dling** pierce with many
holes. **riddled** adj full of, esp. holes.

ride [rīd] v **rode, rid·den, rid·ing 1** sit on
and control or propel (horse, bicycle, etc.).
2 be carried on or across. ♦ vi **3** go on
horseback or in vehicle. 4 lie at anchor. ♦ vt
5 travel over. ♦ n 6 journey on horse, etc.,
or in any vehicle. **rid'er** n 1 one who rides.

rhyme n **1 = poetry,** ode, poem, song,
verse ♦ v **2 = sound like,** harmonize

rhythm n **= beat,** accent, cadence, lilt,
meter, pulse, swing, tempo, time

rhythmic, rhythmical adj **= cadenced,**
lilting, metrical, musical, periodic,
pulsating, throbbing

ribald adj **= rude,** bawdy, blue, broad,
coarse, earthy, naughty, obscene, racy,
smutty, vulgar

rich adj **1 = wealthy,** affluent, loaded (sl),
moneyed, prosperous, well-heeled (inf),
well-off, well-to-do **2 = well-stocked,** full,
productive, well-supplied **3 = abundant,**
abounding, ample, copious, fertile, fruitful,
lush, luxurious, plentiful, productive,
prolific **4 = full-bodied,** creamy, fatty,
luscious, succulent, sweet, tasty

riches pl n **= wealth,** affluence, assets,

fortune, plenty, resources, substance,
treasure

richly adv **1 = elaborately,** elegantly,
expensively, exquisitely, gorgeously,
lavishly, luxuriously, opulently, splendidly,
sumptuously **2 = fully,** amply,
appropriately, properly, suitably,
thoroughly, well

rickety adj **= shaky,** insecure, precarious,
ramshackle, tottering, unsound, unsteady,
wobbly

rid v **1 = free,** clear, deliver, disburden,
disencumber, make free, purge, relieve,
unburden **2 get rid of = dispose of,** dump,
eject, eliminate, expel, remove, throw
away or out

riddle[1] n **= puzzle,** conundrum, enigma,
mystery, poser, problem

riddled adj **= filled,** damaged, infested,

2 supplementary clause. 3 addition to a document.

ridge [rij] n 1 long narrow hill. 2 long, narrow elevation on surface. 3 line of meeting of two sloping surfaces. ♦ vt **ridged, ridg·ing** 4 form into ridges.

ri·dic·u·lous [ri-DIK-yə-ləs] adj deserving to be laughed at, absurd, foolish. **rid·i·cule** [RID-i-kyool] n 1 treatment of person or thing as ridiculous. ♦ vt **-culed, -cul·ing** 2 laugh at, deride.

rife [rīf] adj prevalent, common.

rif·fle [RIF-əl] v **-fled, -fling** flick through (pages, etc.).

riff'raff n rabble, disreputable people.

ri·fle [RĪ-fəl] vt **-fled, -fling** 1 search and rob. 2 ransack. 3 make spiral grooves in (gun barrel, etc.). ♦ n 4 firearm with long barrel. **rifling** n 1 arrangement of grooves in gun barrel. 2 pillaging.

rift n crack, split, cleft.

rig vt **rigged, rig·ging** 1 provide (ship) with spars, ropes, etc. 2 equip. 3 set up, esp. as makeshift. 4 arrange in dishonest way. ♦ n 5 way ship's masts and sails are arranged. 6 apparatus for drilling for oil and gas. 7 tractor-trailer truck. 8 style of dress. **rigging** n 1 ship's spars and ropes. 2 lifting tackle.

right [rīt] adj 1 just. 2 in accordance with truth and duty. 3 true. 4 correct. 5 proper. 6 of side that faces east when front is turned to north. 7 Politics (also **right wing**) conservative or reactionary. 8 straight. 9 upright. 10 of outer or more finished side of fabric. ♦ vt 11 bring back to vertical position. 12 do justice to. ♦ vi 13 come back to vertical position. ♦ n 14 claim, title, etc. allowed or due. 15 what is right, just or due. 16 conservative political party. 17 punch, blow with right hand. ♦ adv 18 straight. 19 properly. 20 very. 21 on or to right side. **right'ful** [-fəl] adj **right'ly** adv 1 right angle. 2 angle of 90 degrees. **right of way** Law 1 right to pass over someone's land. 2 path used. 3 right to driver to proceed.

right·eous [RĪ-chəs] adj 1 just, upright. 2 godly. 3 virtuous. 4 good. 5 honest.

rig·id [RIJ-id] adj 1 inflexible. 2 harsh, stiff. **ri·gid'i·ty** n

rig·ma·role [RIG-mə-rohl] n 1 meaningless

permeated, pervaded, spoilt

ride v 1 = **control**, handle, manage 2 = **travel**, be carried, go, move ♦ n 3 = **trip**, drive, jaunt, journey, lift, outing

ridicule n 1 = **mockery**, chaff, derision, gibe, jeer, laughter, raillery, scorn ♦ v 2 = **laugh at**, chaff, deride, jeer, make fun of, mock, poke fun at, sneer

ridiculous adj = **laughable**, absurd, comical, farcical, funny, ludicrous, risible, silly, stupid

rife adj = **widespread**, common, frequent, general, prevalent, rampant, ubiquitous, universal

riffraff n = **rabble**, dregs of society (sl), hoi polloi, scum of the earth (sl)

rifle v = **ransack**, burgle, go through, loot, pillage, plunder, rob, sack, strip

rift n 1 = **breach**, disagreement, division, falling out (inf), quarrel, separation, split 2 = **split**, break, cleft, crack, crevice, fault, fissure, flaw, gap, opening

rig v 1 = **fix** (inf), arrange, engineer, gerrymander, manipulate, tamper with 2 = **equip**, fit out, furnish, outfit, supply ♦ n 3 = **apparatus**, equipment, fittings, fixtures, gear, tackle

right adj 1 = **just**, equitable, ethical, fair, good, honest, lawful, moral, proper 2 = **correct**, accurate, exact, factual, genuine, precise, true, valid 3 = **proper**, appropriate, becoming, desirable, done, fit, fitting, seemly, suitable ♦ adv 4 = **correctly**, accurately, exactly, genuinely, precisely, truly 5 = **properly**, appropriately, aptly, fittingly, suitably 6 = **straight**, directly, promptly, quickly, straightaway 7 = **exactly**, precisely, squarely ♦ n 8 = **claim**, authority, business, due, freedom, liberty, license, permission, power, prerogative, privilege ♦ v 9 = **rectify**, correct, fix, put right, redress, settle, sort out, straighten

right away adv = **immediately**, at once, directly, forthwith, instantly, now, pronto (inf), straightaway

righteous adj = **virtuous**, ethical, fair, good, honest, honorable, just, moral, pure, upright

righteousness n = **virtue**, goodness, honesty, honor, integrity, justice, morality, probity, purity, rectitude, uprightness

rightful adj = **lawful**, due, just, legal, legitimate, proper, real, true, valid

rigid adj 1 = **strict**, exact, fixed, inflexible, rigorous, set, stringent, unbending, uncompromising 2 = **stiff**, inflexible, string of words. **2** long, complicated procedure.

rig·or[1] [RIG-ər] n sudden coldness attended by shivering. **rigor mor'tis** stiffening of body after death.

rigor[2] n **1** harshness, severity, strictness. **2** hardship. **rig'or·ous** adj stern, harsh, severe.

rile [rīl] vt **riled, ril·ing** inf anger, annoy

rill n small stream.

rim n **1** edge, border, margin. **2** outer ring of wheel. ♦ vt **rimmed, rim·ming 3** furnish with rim. **4** coat or encrust. **5** Basketball, golf of ball, go around basket, hole, and not drop in. **rimmed** adj bordered, edged. **rim'less** adj

rime [rīm] n hoarfrost. **rim'y** adj **rim·i·er, rim·i·est**

rind [rīnd] n outer coating of fruits, etc.

ring[1] n **1** circle of gold, etc., esp. for finger. **2** any circular band, coil, rim, etc. **3** circle of persons. **4** enclosed area, esp. roped-in square for boxing. ♦ vt **ringed, ring·ing 5** put ring round. **6** mark (bird, etc.) with ring. **ring'er** n **1** one who rings bells. **2** sl student, athlete, racehorse, etc. participating in examination, sporting event, etc. under false pretenses or fraudulently in place of another. **dead ringer** sl person, thing apparently identical

to another. **ring'lead·er** [-leed-ər] n instigator of mutiny, riot, etc. **ring'let** [-lit] n curly lock of hair. **ring'worm** [-wurm] n fungal skin disease in circular patches.

ring[2] vi **rang, rung, ring·ing 1** give out clear resonant sound, as bell. **2** resound. **3** cause (bell) to sound. **4** telephone. ♦ n **5** a ringing. **6** telephone call.

rink [ringk] n **1** sheet of ice for skating or hockey. **2** floor for roller skating.

rinse [rins] vt **rinsed, rins·ing 1** remove soap (from washed clothes, hair, etc.) by applying clean water. **2** wash lightly. ♦ n **3** a rinsing. **4** liquid to tint hair.

ri·ot [RĪ-ət] n **1** tumult, disorder. **2** loud revelry. **3** disorderly, unrestrained disturbance. **4** profusion. ♦ vi **5** make, engage in riot. **ri'ot·ous** adj unruly, rebellious, wanton.

R.I.P. rest in peace.

rip[1] vt **ripped, rip·ping 1** cut, tear away, slash, rend. ♦ n **2** rent, tear. **rip'cord** n cord pulled to open parachute. **rip'saw** n saw with coarse teeth (used for cutting wood along grain). **rip off** sl steal, cheat, overcharge. **rip'off** n sl act of stealing, overcharging, etc.

rip[2] n strong current, esp. one moving away from the shore.

ri·par·i·an [ri-PAIR-ee-ən] adj of, on banks

——————| THESAURUS |——————

unyielding

rigmarole n = **procedure**, bother, fuss, hassle (inf), nonsense, palaver

rigor n **1** = **strictness**, harshness, inflexibility, rigidity, sternness, stringency **2** = **hardship**, ordeal, privation, suffering, trial

rigorous adj = **strict**, demanding, exacting, hard, harsh, inflexible, severe, stern, stringent, tough

rig-out n = **outfit**, costume, dress, garb, gear (inf), get-up (inf), togs

rig out v **1** = **dress**, array, attire, clothe, costume **2** = **equip**, fit, furnish, outfit

rig up v = **set up**, arrange, assemble, build, construct, erect, fix up, improvise, put together, put up

rile v = **anger**, aggravate (inf), annoy, get or put one's back up, irk, irritate

rim n = **edge**, border, brim, brink, lip, margin, verge

rind n = **skin**, crust, husk, outer layer, peel

ring[1] v **1** = **chime**, clang, peal, reverberate, sound, toll **2** = **phone**, buzz (inf), call,

telephone ♦ n **3** = **chime**, knell, peal **4** = **call**, buzz (inf), phone call

ring[2] n **1** = **circle**, band, circuit, halo, hoop, loop, round **2** = **arena**, circus, enclosure, rink **3** = **gang**, association, band, cartel, circle, group, mob, syndicate ♦ v **4** = **encircle**, enclose, gird, girdle, surround

rinse v **1** = **wash**, bathe, clean, cleanse, dip, splash ♦ n **2** = **wash**, bath, dip, splash

riot n **1** = **disturbance**, anarchy, confusion, disorder, lawlessness, strife, tumult, turbulence, turmoil, upheaval **2** = **revelry**, carousal, festivity, frolic, high jinks, merrymaking **3** = **profusion**, display, extravaganza, show, splash **4 run riot: a** = **rampage**, be out of control, go wild **b** = **grow profusely**, spread like wildfire ♦ v **5** = **rampage**, go on the rampage, run riot

riotous adj **1** = **unrestrained**, boisterous, loud, noisy, uproarious, wild **2** = **unruly**, anarchic, disorderly, lawless, rebellious, rowdy, ungovernable, violent

rip v **1** = **tear**, burst, claw, cut, gash, lacerate, rend, slash, slit, split ♦ n **2** = **tear**, of river.

ripe [rīp] *adj* **rip·er, rip·est 1** ready to be reaped, eaten, etc. **2** matured. **3** (of judgment, etc.) sound. **rip'en** *v* **1** grow ripe. **2** mature.

ri·poste [ri-POHST] *n* **1** verbal retort. **2** counterstroke. **3** *Fencing* quick lunge after parry.

rip·ple [RIP-əl] *n* **1** slight wave, ruffling of surface. **2** anything like this. **3** sound like ripples of water. ◆ *v* **-pled, -pling** *vi* **4** flow, form into little waves. **5** (of sounds) rise and fall gently. ◆ *vt* **6** form ripples on.

rise [rīz] *vi* **rose, ris·en, ris·ing 1** get up. **2** move upward. **3** appear above horizon. **4** reach higher level. **5** increase in value or price. **6** rebel. **7** adjourn. **8** have its source. ◆ *n* **9** rising. **10** upslope. **11** increase, esp. of prices. **ris'er** *n* **1** one who rises, esp. from bed. **2** vertical part of stair step.

rising *n* **1** revolt. ◆ *adj* **2** increasing in rank, maturity.

ris·i·ble [RIS-ə-bəl] *adj* **1** inclined to laugh. **2** laughable. **ris·i·bil'i·ty** *n, pl* **-ties**

risk *n* **1** chance of disaster or loss. ◆ *vt* **2** venture. **3** put in jeopardy. **4** take chance of. **risk'y** *adj* **risk·i·er, risk·i·est 1**

dangerous. **2** hazardous.

ri·sot·to [ri-SAW-toh] *n* dish of rice cooked in stock with various other ingredients.

ris·qué [ri-SKAY] *adj* suggestive of indecency.

rite [rīt] *n* formal practice or custom, esp. religious. **rit·u·al** [RICH-oo-əl] *n* **1** prescribed order or book of rites. **2** regular, stereotyped action or behavior. ◆ *adj* **3** concerning rites. **rit'u·al·ism** *n* practice of ritual.

ri·val [RĪ-vəl] *n* **1** one that competes with another for favor, success, etc. ◆ *vt* **-valed, -val·ing 2** vie with. ◆ *adj* **3** in position of rival. **ri'val·ry** *n* keen competition.

riv·er [RIV-ər] *n* **1** large natural stream of water. **2** copious flow.

riv·et [RIV-it] *n* **1** bolt for fastening metal plates, the end being put through holes and then beaten flat. ◆ *vt* **-et·ed, -et·ing 2** fasten with rivets. **3** cause to be fixed or held firmly, as in surprise, horror, etc. **riv'et·er** *n*

riv·u·let [RIV-yə-lit] *n* small stream.

Rn *Chem.* radon.

roach [rohch] *n* **1** cockroach. **2** *sl* butt of marijuana cigarette.

————————— THESAURUS —————————

cut, gash, hole, laceration, rent, slash, slit, split

ripe *adj* **1** = **mature**, mellow, ready, ripened, seasoned **2** = **suitable**, auspicious, favorable, ideal, opportune, right, timely

ripen *v* = **mature**, burgeon, develop, grow ripe, season

rip-off *n* = **swindle**, cheat, con (*inf*), con trick (*inf*), fraud, scam (*sl*), theft

rip off *v Sl* = **swindle**, cheat, con (*inf*), defraud, fleece, rob

riposte *n* **1** = **retort**, answer, comeback (*inf*), rejoinder, reply, response, sally ◆ *v* **2** = **retort**, answer, come back, reply, respond

rise *v* **1** = **get up**, arise, get to one's feet, stand up **2** = **go up**, ascend, climb **3** = **advance**, get on, progress, prosper **4** = **get steeper**, ascend, go uphill, slope upwards **5** = **increase**, go up, grow, intensify, mount **6** = **rebel**, mutiny, revolt **7** = **originate**, happen, issue, occur, spring ◆ *n* **8** = **increase**, upsurge, upswing, upturn **9** = **advancement**, climb, progress, promotion **10** = **upward slope**, ascent, elevation, incline **11 give rise to** = **cause**, bring about, effect, produce, result in

risk *n* **1** = **danger**, chance, gamble, hazard,

jeopardy, peril, pitfall, possibility ◆ *v* **2** = **dare**, chance, endanger, gamble, hazard, imperil, jeopardize, venture

risky *adj* = **dangerous**, chancy (*inf*), hazardous, perilous, uncertain, unsafe

risqué *adj* = **suggestive**, bawdy, blue, improper, indelicate, naughty, racy, ribald

rite *n* = **ceremony**, custom, observance, practice, procedure, ritual

ritual *n* **1** = **ceremony**, observance, rite **2** = **custom**, convention, habit, practice, procedure, protocol, routine, tradition ◆ *adj* **3** = **ceremonial**, conventional, customary, habitual, routine

rival *n* **1** = **opponent**, adversary, competitor, contender, contestant ◆ *adj* **2** = **competing**, conflicting, opposing ◆ *v* **3** = **equal**, be a match for, come up to, compare with, compete, match

rivalry *n* = **competition**, conflict, contention, contest, opposition

river *n* **1** = **stream**, brook, creek, tributary, waterway **2** = **flow**, flood, rush, spate, torrent

riveting *adj* = **enthralling**, absorbing, captivating, engrossing, fascinating, gripping, hypnotic, spellbinding

road [rohd] n **1** track, way prepared for passengers, vehicles, etc. **2** direction, way. **3** street. **road'block** n barricade across road to stop traffic for inspection, etc. **road hog** selfish, aggressive driver. **road'run·ner** n large cuckoo of W US, Mexico, C Amer. able to run quickly. **road'side** n, adj **road'ster** n obs touring car. **road'work** [-wurk] n **1** repairs to road. **2** running, jogging along country roads as exercise for boxers. **road'worth·y** [-wur-thee] adj (of vehicle) mechanically sound. **road warrior** inf frequent business traveler.

roam [rohm] v wander about, rove. **roam'er** n

roan [rohn] adj **1** (of horses) having coat in which main color is thickly interspersed with another, esp. bay, sorrel or chestnut mixed with white or gray. ◆ n **2** roan horse.

roar [ror] v **1** make or utter loud deep hoarse sound as of lion, thunder, voice in anger, etc. ◆ n **2** such a sound. **roar'ing** adj **1** brisk and profitable. ◆ adv **2** noisily.

roast [rohst] v **1** bake, cook in closed oven. **2** cook by exposure to open fire. **3** make, be very hot. ◆ n **4** piece of meat for roasting. **5** inf roasting. ◆ adj **6** roasted. **roast'ing** n **1** severe criticism, scolding. **2** session of good-natured scolding by way of tribute to honored person.

rob vt robbed, rob·bing **1** plunder, steal from. **2** pillage, defraud. **rob'ber** n **rob'ber·y** n, pl -ber·ies

robe [rohb] n **1** long outer garment, often denoting rank or office. ◆ v robed, rob·ing ◆ vt **2** dress. ◆ vi **3** put on robes,

vestments.

rob'in n large thrush with red breast. **robin's-egg blue** pale green to light blue.

ro·bot [ROH-bot] n **1** automated machine, esp. performing functions in human manner. **2** person of machine-like efficiency. **ro·bot·ics** [roh-BOT-iks] n science of designing and using robots.

ro·bust [roh BUST] adj sturdy, strong. **ro·bust'ness** [-nis] n

roc [rok] n monstrous bird of Arabian mythology.

rock[1] [rok] n **1** stone. **2** large rugged mass of stone. **3** sl diamond, gem. **rock'er·y** n, pl -er·ies mound or grotto of stones or rocks for plants in a garden. **rock'y** adj rock·i·er, rock·i·est **1** having many rocks. **2** rugged, presenting difficulty. **rock bottom** lowest possible level. **between a rock and a hard place** between equally unattractive alternatives.

rock[2] v **1** (cause to) sway to and fro. ◆ n **2** style of pop music derived from rock-'n'-roll. **rock'er** n curved piece of wood, etc. on which thing may rock. **rocking chair** chair allowing the sitter to rock backwards and forwards. **rock-'n'-roll** n popular dance rhythm. **rock the boat** inf disrupt smooth routine of company, etc. **off one's rocker** sl insane.

rock·et [ROK-it] n **1** self-propelling device powered by burning of explosive contents (used as firework, for display, signaling, line carrying, weapon, etc.). **2** vehicle propelled by rocket engine, as weapon or carrying spacecraft. ◆ vi **3** move fast, esp. upward, as rocket. **rock'et·ry** n

——————| THESAURUS |——————

road n = **way**, course, highway, lane, motorway, path, pathway, roadway, route, track

roam v = **wander**, prowl, ramble, range, rove, stray, travel, walk

roar v **1** = **cry**, bawl, bay, bellow, howl, shout, yell **2** = **guffaw**, hoot, laugh heartily, split one's sides (inf) ◆ n **3** = **cry**, bellow, howl, outcry, shout, yell **4** = **guffaw**, hoot

rob v = **steal from**, burgle, cheat, con (inf), defraud, deprive, dispossess, hold up, loot, mug (inf), pillage, plunder, raid

robber n = **thief**, bandit, burglar, cheat, con man (inf), fraud, looter, mugger (inf), plunderer, raider, stealer

robbery n = **theft**, burglary, hold-up,

larceny, mugging (inf), pillage, plunder, raid, rip-off (sl), stealing, stick-up (sl), swindle

robe n **1** = **gown**, costume, habit ◆ v **2** = **clothe**, dress, garb

robot n = **machine**, android, automaton, mechanical man

robust adj = **strong**, fit, hale, hardy, healthy, muscular, powerful, stout, strapping, sturdy, tough, vigorous

rock[1] n = **stone**, boulder

rock[2] v **1** = **sway**, lurch, pitch, reel, roll, swing, toss **2** = **shock**, astonish, astound, shake, stagger, stun, surprise

rocky[1] adj = **rough**, craggy, rugged, stony

rocky[2] adj = **unstable**, rickety, shaky, unsteady, wobbly

ro·co·co [rə-KOH-koh] *adj* **1** of furniture, architecture, etc. having much conventional decoration in style of early 18th cent. work in France. **2** tastelessly florid.

rod *n* **1** slender straight bar, stick. **2** cane. **3** old unit of length equal to 5.5 yards.

rode pt. of RIDE.

ro·dent [ROHD-nt] *n* animal with teeth specialized for gnawing, such as a rat or squirrel.

ro·de·o [ROH-dee-oh] *n* display of skills, competition, with bareback riding, cattle handling techniques, etc.

roe [roh] *n* mass of eggs in fish.

roent·gen [RENT-gən] *n* measuring unit of radiation dose.

rogue [rohg] *n* **1** rascal, knave, scoundrel. **2** mischief-loving person or child. **3** wild beast of savage temper, living apart from herd. **ro'guish** *adj*

rois·ter [ROI-stər] *vi* be noisy, boisterous, bragging. **roist'er·er** *n* reveler.

role, rôle [rohl] *n* **1** actor's part. **2** specific task or function.

roll [rohl] *v* **1** move by turning over and over. ◆ *vt* **2** wind around. **3** smooth out with roller. ◆ *vi* **4** move, sweep along. **5** undulate. **6** of ship, swing from side to side. **7** of aircraft, turn about a line from nose to tail in flight. ◆ *n* **8** act of lying down and turning over and over or from side to side. **9** piece of paper, etc. rolled up. **10** any object thus shaped, e.g. jelly roll. **11** list, catalogue. **12** bread baked into small oval or round. **13** continuous sound, as of drums, thunder, etc. **roll'er** *n* **1** cylinder of wood, stone, metal, etc. used for pressing, crushing, smoothing, supporting things to be moved, winding thing on, etc. **2** long wave of sea. **roll call** act, time of calling over list of names, as in schools or army. **roller bearings** bearings

of hardened steel rollers. **Roll'er·blade** *n* ® roller skate with the wheels set in a straight line, mounted on a boot. **roller coaster 1** small gravity railroad in amusement park with steep ascents and descents for frightening riders. **2** any experience with similar ups and downs. **roller skate** skate with wheels instead of runner. **roller towel** loop of towel on roller. **rolling pin** cylindrical roller for pastry or dough. **rolling stock** locomotives, freight cars, etc. of railroad. **roll top** *n* **1** in desk, flexible lid sliding in grooves. **2** such a desk. **roll up 1** appear, turn up. **2** increase, accumulate.

rol·lick·ing [ROL-i-king] *adj* boisterously jovial and merry.

ro·ly-po·ly [ROH-lee-poh-lee] *adj* **1** round, plump. ◆ *n* **2** round, plump person or thing.

ROM [rom] *Computers* read-only memory (permanently recorded on a computer chip).

Rom. Romans.

Ro·man [ROH-mən] *adj* of Rome or Roman Catholic Church. **Roman Catholic** member of Roman Catholic Church. **Roman Catholic Church** the Christian church that acknowledges supremacy of the Pope. **Roman numerals** letters I, V, X, L, C, D, M used to represent numbers in manner of Romans. **roman type** plain upright letters, ordinary style of printing.

roman á clef [roh-mah-na-KLAY] *n, pl* **romans á clef** [roh-mah-na-KLAY] *Fr* novel that disguises real events and people.

ro·mance [roh-MANS] *n* **1** love affair, esp. intense and happy one. **2** mysterious or exciting quality. **3** tale of chivalry. **4** tale with scenes remote from ordinary life. **5** literature like this. **6** picturesque falsehood. ◆ *v* **-manced, -manc·ing** ◆ *vi* **7** exaggerate, fantasize. ◆ *vt* if **8** woo, court. **Romance language** any of vernacular languages of

---

THESAURUS

---

rod *n* = **stick**, bar, baton, cane, pole, shaft, staff, wand

rogue *n* = **scoundrel**, crook (*inf*), fraud, rascal, scamp, villain

role *n* **1** = **job**, capacity, duty, function, part, position, post, task **2** = **part**, character, portrayal, representation

roll *v* **1** = **turn**, go round, revolve, rotate, spin, swivel, trundle, twirl, wheel, whirl **2** = **wind**, bind, enfold, envelop, furl, swathe, wrap **3** = **flow**, run, undulate **4** = **level**,

even, flatten, press, smooth **5** = **tumble**, lurch, reel, rock, sway, toss ◆ *n* **6** = **turn**, cycle, reel, revolution, rotation, spin, twirl, wheel, whirl **7** = **register**, census, index, list, record **8** = **rumble**, boom, reverberation, roar, thunder

rollicking[1] *adj* = **boisterous**, carefree, devil-may-care, exuberant, hearty, jaunty, lively, playful

roly-poly *adj* = **plump**, buxom, chubby, fat, rounded, tubby certain countries, developed from Latin, as French, Spanish, etc. **ro·man'tic** adj **1** characterized by romance. **2** of or dealing with love. **3** of literature, etc., preferring passion and imagination to proportion and finish. ◆ n **ro·man'ti·cism** [-ti-sizm] n **ro·man'ti·cize** vi -cized, -ciz·ing

Ro·man·esque [rohm-ən-NESK] adj, n (in) style of round-arched vaulted architecture of period between Classical and Gothic.

romp vi **1** run, play wildly, joyfully. ◆ n **2** spell of romping. **3** easy victory. **romp'ers** [-ərz] pl n child's loose one-piece garment. **romp home** win easily.

ron·deau [ron-DOH] n, pl -deaux [-DOHZ] short poem with opening words used as refrain. **ron·del'** n extended rondeau. **ron·de·let** [ron-dl-ET] n short rondeau.

ron·do [RON-doh] n, pl -dos piece of music with leading theme to which return is continually made.

roof n, pl **roofs 1** outside upper covering of building. **2** top, covering part of anything. ◆ vt **3** put roof on, over.

rook¹ [ruuk] n **1** bird of crow family. ◆ vt **2** swindle, cheat. **rook'er·y** n, pl -er·ies colony of rooks.

rook² n chess piece shaped like a castle.

rook·ie [RUUK-ee] n **1** recruit, esp. in army. **2** Sports professional athlete playing in first season.

room n **1** space. **2** space enough. **3** division of house. **4** scope, opportunity. ◆ pl **5** lodgings. **room'y** adj **room·i·er, room·i·est** spacious.

roost n **1** perch for poultry. ◆ vi **2** perch. **roost'er** n **1** male of domestic fowl. **2** cock.

root¹ n **1** part of plant that grows down into earth and conveys nourishment to plant. **2** plant with edible root, such as a carrot. **3** vital part. **4** (also **roots**) source, origin, original cause of anything. **5** Anatomy embedded portion of tooth, nail, hair, etc. **6** primitive word from which other words are derived. **7** factor of a quantity that, when multiplied by itself the number of times indicated, gives the quantity. ◆ v **8** (cause to) take root. **9** pull by roots. **10** dig, burrow.

root² vi **1** cheer. **2** applaud. **3** encourage. **root'er** n

rope [rohp] n **1** thick cord. ◆ vt **roped, rop·ing 2** secure, mark off with rope. **rope in** inf entice, lure by deception.

ro·sa·ry [ROH-zə-ree] n, pl -ries **1** series of prayers. **2** string of beads for counting these prayers as they are recited. **3** rose garden, bed of roses.

rose¹ [rohz] n **1** shrub, climbing plant usu. with prickly stems and fragrant flowers. **2** the flower. **3** perforated flat nozzle for hose, watering can, etc. **4** pink color. ◆ adj **5** of this color. **ro·se·ate** [ROH-zee-it] adj rose-colored, rosy. **ro·sette** [roh-ZET] n **1** rose-shaped bunch of ribbon. **2** rose-shaped architectural ornament. **ros'y**

————— THESAURUS —————

romance n **1** = **love affair**, affair, amour, attachment, liaison, relationship **2** = **excitement**, charm, color, fascination, glamour, mystery **3** = **story**, fairy tale, fantasy, legend, love story, melodrama, tale

romantic adj **1** = **loving**, amorous, fond, passionate, sentimental, tender **2** = **idealistic**, dreamy, impractical, starry-eyed, unrealistic **3** = **exciting**, colorful, fascinating, glamorous, mysterious ◆ n **4** = **idealist**, dreamer, sentimentalist

romp v **1** = **frolic**, caper, cavort, frisk, gambol, have fun, sport **2** = **win easily**, walk it (inf), win by a mile (inf), win hands down ◆ n **3** = **frolic**, caper, lark (inf)

room n **1** = **chamber**, apartment, office **2** = **space**, area, capacity, expanse, extent, leeway, margin, range, scope **3** = **opportunity**, chance, occasion, scope

roomy adj = **spacious**, ample, broad, capacious, commodious, extensive, generous, large, sizable or sizeable, wide

root¹ n **1** = **stem**, rhizome, tuber **2** = **source**, base, bottom, cause, core, foundation, heart, nucleus, origin, seat, seed **3** **roots** = **sense of belonging**, birthplace, cradle, family, heritage, home, origins ◆ v **4** = **establish**, anchor, fasten, fix, ground, implant, moor, set, stick

root² v = **dig**, burrow, ferret

rooted adj = **deep-seated**, confirmed, deep, deeply felt, entrenched, established, firm, fixed, ingrained

root out v = **get rid of**, abolish, do away with, eliminate, eradicate, exterminate, extirpate, remove, weed out

rope n **1** = **cord**, cable, hawser, line, strand **2 know the ropes** = **be experienced**, be an old hand, be knowledgeable

rope in v = **persuade**, engage, enlist,

adj **ros·i·er, ros·i·est 1** flushed. **2** hopeful, promising. **rose-colored** *adj* **1** having color of rose. **2** unwarrantably optimistic. **rose window** circular window with series of mullions branching from center. **rose of Sharon** [SHAR-ən] low, spreading small tree or shrub with white, purplish or red flowers.

rose² pt. of RISE.

ro·sé [roh-ZAY] *n* pink wine.

rose·mar·y [ROHZ-mair-ee] *n* **1** evergreen fragrant flowering shrub. **2** its leaves and flowers used as seasoning.

Ro·si·cru·cian [roh-zi-KROO-shən] *n* member of secret order devoted to occult law. ◆ *adj* **Ro·si·cru'cian·ism** *n*

ros·in [ROZ-in] *n* resin esp. used for rubbing on bows of violins, etc.

ros·ter [ROS-tər] *n* list or plan showing turns of duty.

ros·trum [ROS-trəm] *n, pl* **-tra** [-trə] **-trums 1** platform, stage, pulpit. **2** beak or bill of a bird.

rot *v* **rot·ted, rot·ting 1** decompose naturally. **2** corrupt. ◆ *n* **3** decay, putrefaction. **4** any disease producing decomposition of tissue. **5** nonsense. **rot'ten** *adj* **1** decomposed, putrid. **2** corrupt.

ro·ta·ry [ROH-tə-ree] *adj* **1** (of movement) circular. **2** operated by rotary movement. **ro·tate** [ROH-tayt] *v* **-tat·ed, -tat·ing** (cause to) move around center or on pivot.

ro·ta'tion *n* **1** rotating. **2** regular succession. **Rotary Club** one of international association of businessmen's clubs. **Ro·tar'i·an** *n* member of such.

rote [roht] *n* habitual, mechanical repetition. **by rote** by memory.

ro·tis·ser·ie [roh-TIS-ə-ree] *n* (electrically driven) rotating spit for cooking meat.

ro·tor [ROH-tər] *n* rotating portion of a dynamo motor or turbine.

rotten see ROT.

ro·tund [roh-TUND] *adj* **1** round. **2** plump. **3** sonorous. **ro·tun'di·ty** *n*

rouble see RUBLE.

rou·é [roo-AY] *n* **1** dissolute or dissipated man. **2** rake.

rouge [roozh] *n* **1** red powder, cream used to color cheeks. ◆ *v* **rouged, roug·ing 2** color with rouge.

rough [ruf] *adj* **-er, -est 1** not smooth, of irregular surface. **2** violent, stormy, boisterous. **3** rude. **4** uncivil. **5** lacking refinement. **6** approximate. **7** in preliminary form. ◆ *vt* **8** make rough. **9** plan out approximately. **10** (with *it*) live without usual comforts, etc. ◆ *n* **11** rough condition or area. **12** sketch. **diamond in the rough** excellent, valuable but unsophisticated person. **rough'en** [-n] *vt* **rough·age** [RUF-ij] *n* unassimilated portion of food promoting proper intestinal action. **rough'house** [-hows] *n, v* **-housed, -hous·ing** fight, row.

━━━━━━━━ THESAURUS ━━━━━━━━

inveigle, involve, talk into

roster *n* = **rota**, agenda, catalog, list, register, roll, schedule, table

rostrum *n* = **stage**, dais, platform, podium, stand

rosy *adj* **1** = **pink**, red **2** = **glowing**, blooming, healthy-looking, radiant, ruddy **3** = **promising**, auspicious, bright, cheerful, encouraging, favorable, hopeful, optimistic

rot *v* **1** = **decay**, crumble, decompose, deteriorate, go bad, molder, perish, putrefy, spoil **2** = **deteriorate**, decline, waste away ◆ *n* **3** = **decay**, blight, canker, corruption, decomposition, mold, putrefaction

rotary *adj* = **revolving**, rotating, spinning, turning

rotate *v* **1** = **revolve**, go round, gyrate, pivot, reel, spin, swivel, turn, wheel **2** = **take turns**, alternate, switch

rotation *n* **1** = **revolution**, orbit, reel, spin, spinning, turn, turning, wheel **2** = **sequence**, alternation, cycle, succession, switching

rotten *adj* **1** = **decaying**, bad, corrupt, crumbling, decomposing, festering, funky (*sl*), moldy, perished, putrescent, rank, smelly, sour, stinking **2** = **corrupt**, crooked (*inf*), dishonest, dishonorable, immoral, perfidious **3** *Inf* = **despicable**, base, contemptible, dirty, lousy (*sl*), mean, nasty, scuzzy (*sl*)

rotund *adj* **1** = **round**, globular, rounded, spherical **2** = **plump**, chubby, corpulent, fat, fleshy, portly, stout, tubby

rough *adj* **1** = **uneven**, broken, bumpy, craggy, irregular, jagged, rocky, stony **2** = **ungracious**, blunt, brusque, coarse, impolite, rude, unceremonious, uncivil, uncouth, unmannerly **3** = **approximate**, estimated, general, imprecise, inexact,

rou·lette [roo-LET] *n* game of chance played with revolving dishlike wheel and ball.

round [rownd] *adj* **-er, -est 1** spherical, cylindrical, circular, curved. **2** full, complete. **3** roughly correct. **4** large, considerable. **5** plump. **6** unqualified, positive. ◆ *adv* **7** with circular or circuitous course. ◆ *n* **8** thing round in shape. **9** recurrent duties. **10** stage in competition. **11** customary course, as of postman. **12** game (of golf). **13** one of several periods in boxing match, etc. **14** cartridge for firearm. **15** rung. **16** movement in circle. ◆ *prep* **17** about. **18** on all sides of. ◆ *v* **19** make, become round. ◆ *vt* **20** move around. **round'ers** *n* British ball game resembling baseball. **round'ly** *adv* **1** plainly. **2** thoroughly. **round·a·bout'** *adj* not straightforward. **round robin** sports tournament in which all contestants play one another. **round up 1** drive (cattle) together. **2** collect and arrest criminals.

roun·de·lay [ROWN-dl-ay] *n* simple song with refrain.

rouse [rowz] *v* **roused, rous·ing** ◆ *vt* **1** wake up, stir up, excite to action. **2** cause to rise. ◆ *vi* **3** waken. **roust·a·bout** [ROWST-ə-bowt] *n* laborer working in circus, oil rig, etc.

rout [rowt] *n* **1** overwhelming defeat, disorderly retreat. **2** noisy rabble. ◆ *vt* **3** scatter and put to flight.

route [root] *n* **1** road, chosen way. **go the route** *inf* **1** see through to the end. **2** *Baseball* pitch complete game.

rou·tine [roo-TEEN] *n* **1** regularity of procedure, unvarying round. **2** regular course. ◆ *adj* **3** ordinary, regular.

roux [roo] *n* fat and flour cooked together as thickener for sauces.

rove [rohv] *v* **roved, rov·ing 1** wander, roam. **rov'er** *n* **1** one who roves. **2** pirate.

row¹ [roh] *n* **1** number of things in a straight line. **2** rank. **3** file. **4** line.

row² *v* **1** propel boat by oars. ◆ *n* **2** spell of rowing. **row'boat** *n*

row³ [rhymes with **cow**] *n* **1** dispute. **2** disturbance. ◆ *vi* **3** quarrel noisily.

row·dy [ROW-dee] *adj* **-di·er, -di·est 1**

———————| THESAURUS |———————

sketchy, vague **4 = stormy**, choppy, squally, turbulent, wild **5 = nasty**, cruel, hard, harsh, tough, unfeeling, unpleasant, violent **6 = basic**, crude, imperfect, incomplete, rudimentary, sketchy, unfinished, unpolished, unrefined **7 = unpleasant**, arduous, hard, tough, uncomfortable ◆ *v* **8 rough out = outline**, draft, plan, sketch ◆ *n* **9 = outline**, draft, mock-up, preliminary sketch

rough-and-ready *adj* **= makeshift**, crude, improvised, provisional, sketchy, stopgap, unpolished, unrefined

round *adj* **1 = spherical**, circular, curved, cylindrical, globular, rotund, rounded **2 = plump**, ample, fleshy, full, full-fleshed, rotund ◆ *v* **3 = go round**, bypass, circle, encircle, flank, skirt, turn ◆ *n* **4 = sphere**, ball, band, circle, disc, globe, orb, ring **5 = stage**, division, lap, level, period, session, turn **6 = series**, cycle, sequence, session, succession **7 = course**, beat, circuit, routine, schedule, series, tour

roundabout *adj* **= indirect**, circuitous, devious, discursive, evasive, oblique, tortuous

round off *v* **= complete**, close, conclude, finish off

roundup *n* **= gathering**, assembly,

collection, herding, marshalling, muster, rally

round up *v* **= gather**, collect, drive, group, herd, marshal, muster, rally

rouse *v* **1 = wake up**, awaken, call, rise, wake **2 = excite**, agitate, anger, animate, incite, inflame, move, provoke, stimulate, stir

rousing *adj* **= lively**, exciting, inspiring, moving, spirited, stimulating, stirring

rout *n* **1 = defeat**, beating, debacle, drubbing, overthrow, thrashing ◆ *v* **2 = defeat**, beat, conquer, crush, destroy, drub, overthrow, thrash, trounce, wipe the floor with (*inf*)

route *n* **= way**, beat, circuit, course, direction, itinerary, journey, path, road

routine *n* **1 = procedure**, custom, method, order, pattern, practice, program ◆ *adj* **2 = usual**, customary, everyday, habitual, normal, ordinary, standard, typical **3 = boring**, dull, humdrum, predictable, tedious, tiresome

rove *v* **= wander**, drift, ramble, range, roam, stray, traipse (*inf*)

row¹ *n* **= line**, bank, column, file, range, series, string

row² *n* **1 = dispute**, brawl, quarrel, squabble, tiff, trouble **2 = disturbance**, disorderly, noisy and rough. ◆ *n* **2** person like this.

roy·al [ROI-əl] *adj* **1** of, worthy of, befitting, patronized by, king or queen. **2** splendid. **roy'al·ist** *n* supporter of monarchy. **roy'al·ty** *n* **1** royal dignity or power. **2** royal persons. **3** payment to owner of land for right to work minerals, or to inventor for use of invention. **4** payment to author depending on sales.

Ru *Chem.* ruthenium.

rub *v* **rubbed, rub·bing** ◆ *vt* **1** apply pressure to with circular or backward and forward movement. **2** clean, polish, dry, thus. **3** pass hand over. **4** abrade, chafe. **5** remove by friction. ◆ *vi* **6** come into contact accompanied by friction. **7** become frayed or worn by friction. ◆ *n* **8** rubbing. **9** impediment.

rub·ber¹ [RUB-ər] *n* **1** coagulated sap of rough, elastic consistency, of certain tropical trees. **2** piece of rubber, etc. used for erasing. **3** thing for rubbing. **4** person who rubs. **5** *sl* condom. ◆ *adj* **6** of rubber. **rub'ber·ize** *vt* **-ized, -iz·ing** coat, impregnate, treat with rubber. **rub'ber·y** *adj* **rub'ber·neck** *v* gawk at. **rubber stamp** **1** device for imprinting dates, etc. **2** automatic authorization.

rubber² *n* **1** series of odd number of games or contests at various games, such as bridge. **2** two out of three games won. **rubber match** deciding contest between tied opponents.

rub·bish [RUB-ish] *n* **1** refuse, waste material, garbage. **2** anything worthless. **3** trash, nonsense. **rub'bish·y** *adj* valueless.

rub·ble [RUB-əl] *n* **1** fragments of stone, etc. **2** builders' rubbish.

ru·bel·la [roo-BEL-ə] *n* mild contagious viral disease, German measles.

ru·bi·cund [ROO-bi-kund] *adj* ruddy.

ru·ble, rou·ble [ROO-bəl] *n* unit of currency of Russia and Belarus.

ru·bric [ROO-brik] *n* **1** title, heading. **2** direction in liturgy. **3** instruction.

ru·by [ROO-bee] *n* **-bies 1** precious red gem. **2** its color. ◆ *adj* **3** of this color.

ruck·sack [RUK-sak] *n* pack carried on back, knapsack.

ruck·us [RUK-əs] *n* uproar, disturbance.

rud·der [RUD-ər] *n* flat piece hinged to boat's stern or rear of aircraft to steer by.

rud·dy [RUD-ee] *adj* **-di·er, -di·est 1** of fresh or healthy red color. **2** rosy. **3** florid.

rude [rood] *adj* **1** impolite. **2** coarse. **3** vulgar. **4** primitive. **5** roughly made. **6** uneducated. **7** sudden, violent. **rude'ly** *adv* **rude'ness** *n*

ru·di·ments [ROO-də-mənts] *pl n* elements, first principles. **ru·di·men'ta·ry** *adj*

rue¹ [roo] *v* **rued, ru·ing 1** grieve for. **2** regret. **3** deplore. **4** repent. ◆ *n* **5** sorrow. **6** repentance. **rue'ful** [-fəl] *adj* **1** sorry. **2** regretful. **3** dejected. **4** deplorable.

rue² *n* plant with evergreen bitter leaves.

ruff¹ *n* **1** starched and frilled collar. **2** natural

commotion, noise, racket, rumpus, tumult, uproar ◆ *v* **3** = **quarrel**, argue, dispute, fight, squabble, wrangle

rowdy *adj* **1** = **disorderly**, loud, noisy, rough, unruly, wild ◆ *n* **2** = **hooligan**, lout, ruffian

royal *adj* **1** = **regal**, imperial, kingly, princely, queenly, sovereign **2** = **splendid**, grand, impressive, magnificent, majestic, stately

rub *v* **1** = **polish**, clean, scour, shine, wipe **2** = **chafe**, abrade, fray, grate, scrape ◆ *n* **3** = **polish**, shine, stroke, wipe **4** = **massage**, caress, kneading

rubbish *n* **1** = **waste**, garbage, junk (*inf*), litter, lumber, refuse, scrap, trash **2** = **nonsense**, claptrap (*inf*), garbage, hogwash, hot air (*inf*), trash, tripe (*inf*)

rub out *v* = **erase**, cancel, delete, efface, obliterate, remove, wipe out

ruckus *n* *Inf* = **uproar**, commotion, disturbance, fracas, fuss, hoopla, trouble

ruddy *adj* = **rosy**, blooming, fresh, glowing, healthy, radiant, red, reddish, rosy-cheeked

rude *adj* **1** = **impolite**, abusive, cheeky, discourteous, disrespectful, ill-mannered, impertinent, impudent, insolent, insulting, uncivil, unmannerly **2** = **vulgar**, boorish, brutish, coarse, graceless, loutish, oafish, rough, uncivilized, uncouth, uncultured **3** = **unpleasant**, abrupt, harsh, sharp, startling, sudden **4** = **roughly-made**, artless, crude, inartistic, inelegant, makeshift, primitive, raw, rough, simple

rudimentary *adj* = **basic**, early, elementary, fundamental, initial, primitive, undeveloped

rudiments *pl n* = **basics**, beginnings, elements, essentials, foundation, collar of feathers, fur, etc. on some birds and animals. **3** type of shore bird. **ruf'fle** vt **-fled, -fling 1** rumple, disorder. **2** annoy, put out. **3** frill, pleat. ◆ n **4** frilled trimming.

ruff² n, v Cards trump.

ruf•fi•an [RUF-ee-ən] n violent, lawless person.

rug n **1** small, oft. shaggy or thick-piled floor mat. **2** thick woolen wrap, coverlet. **3** sl toupee, hairpiece. **rug'rat** n inf small child.

rug•by [RUG-bee] n form of football with two teams of 15 players.

rug•ged [RUG-id] adj **1** rough. **2** broken. **3** unpolished. **4** harsh, austere.

ru•in [ROO-in] n **1** decay, destruction. **2** downfall. **3** fallen or broken state. **4** loss of wealth, position, etc. ◆ pl **5** ruined buildings, etc. ◆ vt **6** reduce to ruins. **7** bring to decay or destruction. **8** spoil. **9** impoverish. **ru•in•a'tion** n **ru'in•ous** adj causing or characterized by ruin or destruction.

rule [rool] n **1** principle. **2** precept. **3** authority. **4** government. **5** what is usual. **6** control. **7** measuring stick. ◆ vt **ruled, rul•ing 8** govern. **9** decide. **10** mark with straight lines. **11** draw (line). **rul'er** n **1** one who governs. **2** stick for measuring or ruling lines.

rum n liquor distilled from sugar cane.

rum•ba [RUM-bə] n, pl **-bas 1** rhythmic dance, orig. Cuban. **2** music for it.

rum•ble [RUM-bəl] vi **-bled, -bling 1** make noise as of distant thunder, heavy vehicle, etc. **2** sl engage in gang street fight. ◆ n **3** noise like thunder, etc. **4** gang street fight.

ru•mi•nate [ROO-mə-nayt] vi **-nat•ed, -nat•ing 1** chew cud. **2** ponder over. **3** meditate. **ru'mi•nant** [-nənt] adj, n cud-chewing (animal). **ru•mi•na'tion** [-NAY-shən] n quiet meditation and reflection. **ru'mi•na•tive** [-mə-nə-tiv] adj

rum•mage [RUM-ij] v **-maged, -mag•ing** search thoroughly. ◆ n **rummage sale** sale of miscellaneous, usu. secondhand, items.

fundamentals

rue v = **regret**, be sorry for, kick oneself for, lament, mourn, repent

rueful adj = **regretful**, contrite, mournful, penitent, remorseful, repentant, sorrowful, sorry

ruffian n = **thug**, brute, bully, hoodlum, hooligan, tough

ruffle v **1** = **disarrange**, dishevel, disorder, mess up, rumple, tousle **2** = **annoy**, agitate, fluster, irritate, nettle, peeve (inf), tick off, upset

rugged adj **1** = **rough**, broken, bumpy, craggy, difficult, irregular, jagged, ragged, rocky, uneven **2** = **strong-featured**, rough-hewn, weather-beaten **3** = **tough**, brawny, burly, husky (inf), muscular, robust, strong, sturdy, well-built

ruin v **1** = **destroy**, crush, defeat, demolish, devastate, lay waste, smash, wreck **2** = **bankrupt**, impoverish, pauperize **3** = **spoil**, blow (sl), botch, damage, make a mess of, mess up, screw up (inf) ◆ n **4** = **destruction**, breakdown, collapse, defeat, devastation, downfall, fall, undoing, wreck **5** = **disrepair**, decay, disintegration, ruination, wreckage **6** = **bankruptcy**, destitution, insolvency

ruinous adj **1** = **devastating**, calamitous, catastrophic, destructive, dire, disastrous, shattering **2** = **extravagant**, crippling,

immoderate, wasteful

rule n **1** = **regulation**, axiom, canon, decree, direction, guideline, law, maxim, precept, principle, tenet **2** = **custom**, convention, habit, practice, procedure, routine, tradition **3** = **government**, authority, command, control, dominion, jurisdiction, mastery, power, regime, reign **4** as a rule = **usually**, generally, mainly, normally, on the whole, ordinarily ◆ v **5** = **govern**, be in authority, be in power, command, control, direct, reign **6** = **be prevalent**, be customary, predominate, preponderate, prevail **7** = **decree**, decide, judge, pronounce, settle

rule out v = **exclude**, ban, debar, dismiss, disqualify, eliminate, leave out, preclude, prohibit, reject

ruler n **1** = **governor**, commander, controller, head of state, king or queen, leader, lord, monarch, potentate, sovereign **2** = **measure**, rule, yardstick

ruling n **1** = **decision**, adjudication, decree, judgment, pronouncement, verdict ◆ adj **2** = **governing**, commanding, controlling, reigning **3** = **predominant**, chief, dominant, main, pre-eminent, preponderant, prevailing, principal

ruminate v = **ponder**, cogitate, consider, contemplate, deliberate, mull over, muse, reflect, think, turn over in one's mind

rum·my[1] [RUM-ee] *n* card game.
rum·my[2] [RUM-ee] *n, pl* **-mies** *sl* drunkard.
ru·mor [ROO-mər] *n* **1** hearsay, common talk, unproved statement. ♦ *vt* **2** put out as, by way of, rumor.
rump *n* **1** tail end. **2** buttocks.
rum·ple [RUM-pəl] *v, n* **-pled, -pling** crease, wrinkle.
rum·pus [RUM-pəs] *n, pl* **-us·es** **1** disturbance. **2** noise and confusion.
run *v* **ran, run, run·ning** ♦ *vi* **1** move with more rapid gait than walking. **2** go quickly. **3** flow. **4** flee. **5** compete in race, contest, election. **6** revolve. **7** continue. **8** function. **9** travel according to schedule. **10** fuse. **11** melt. **12** spread over. **13** have certain meaning. ♦ *vt* **14** cross by running. **15** expose oneself (to risk, etc.). **16** cause to run. **17** (of newspaper) print, publish. **18** transport and dispose of (smuggled goods). **19** manage. **20** operate. ♦ *n* **21** act, spell of running. **22** rush. **23** tendency, course. **24** period. **25** sequence. **26** heavy demand. **27** enclosure for domestic poultry, animals. **28** ride in car. **29** series of unraveled stitches, ladder. **30** score of one at baseball. **31** steep snow-covered course for skiing. **run'ner** *n* **1** racer. **2** messenger. **3** curved piece of wood on which sleigh slides. **4** any similar appliance. **5** slender stem of plant running along ground forming new roots at intervals. **6** strip of cloth, carpet. **running** *adj* **1** continuous. **2** consecutive. **3** flowing. **4** discharging. **5** effortless. **6** entered for race. **7** used for running. ♦ *n* **8** act of moving or flowing quickly. **9** management. **run'ny** *adj* **-ni·er, -ni·est** tending to flow or exude moisture. **run'down** *n* summary. **run-down** *adj* exhausted. **run down 1** stop working. **2** reduce. **3** exhaust. **4** denigrate. **run'way** *n* level stretch where aircraft take off and land. **in the running** having fair chance in competition.
rung[1] *n* crossbar or spoke, esp. in ladder.
rung[2] pp. of RING[2].
runt *n* **1** small animal, below usual size of

rummage *v* = **search**, delve, forage, hunt, ransack, root
rumor *n* = **story**, buzz, dirt (*sl*), gossip, hearsay, news, report, talk, whisper, word
rump *n* = **buttocks**, backside (*inf*), bottom, buns (*sl*), butt (*inf*), derrière (*euphemistic*), hindquarters, posterior, rear, rear end, seat
rumpus *n* = **commotion**, disturbance, furor, fuss, hue and cry, noise, row, uproar
run *v* **1** = **race**, bolt, dash, gallop, hurry, jog, lope, rush, scurry, sprint **2** = **flee**, beat a retreat, beat it (*sl*), bolt, escape, make a run for it, take flight, take off (*inf*), take to one's heels **3** = **move**, course, glide, go, pass, roll, skim **4** = **work**, function, go, operate, perform **5** = **manage**, administer, be in charge of, control, direct, handle, head, lead, operate **6** = **continue**, extend, go, proceed, reach, stretch **7** = **flow**, discharge, go, gush, leak, pour, spill, spout, stream **8** = **melt**, dissolve, go soft, liquefy **9** = **publish**, display, feature, print **10** = **compete**, be a candidate, contend, put oneself up for, stand, take part **11** = **smuggle**, bootleg, traffic in ♦ *n* **12** = **race**, dash, gallop, jog, rush, sprint, spurt **13** = **ride**, drive, excursion, jaunt, outing, spin (*inf*), trip **14** = **sequence**, course, period, season, series, spell, stretch, string **15** = **enclosure**, coop, pen **16 in the long run** = **eventually**, in the end, ultimately
run across *v* = **meet**, bump into, come across, encounter, run into
runaway *n* **1** = **fugitive**, deserter, escapee, refugee, truant ♦ *adj* **2** = **escaped**, fleeing, fugitive, loose, wild
run away *v* = **flee**, abscond, bolt, escape, fly the coop (*inf*), make a run for it, scram (*inf*), take to one's heels
run-down *adj* **1** = **exhausted**, below par, debilitated, drained, enervated, unhealthy, weak, weary, worn-out **2** = **dilapidated**, broken-down, decrepit, ramshackle, seedy, shabby, worn-out
run down *v* **1** = **criticize**, bad-mouth (*sl*), belittle, decry, denigrate, disparage, knock (*inf*) **2** = **reduce**, curtail, cut, cut back, decrease, downsize, trim **3** = **knock down**, hit, knock over, run into, run over **4** = **weaken**, debilitate, exhaust
run into *v* **1** = **meet**, bump into, come across *or* upon, encounter, run across **2** = **hit**, collide with, strike
runner *n* **1** = **athlete**, jogger, sprinter **2** = **messenger**, courier, dispatch bearer, errand boy
running *adj* **1** = **continuous**, constant, incessant, perpetual, twenty-four-seven (*sl*), unbroken, uninterrupted **2** = **flowing**, moving, streaming ♦ *n* **3** = **management**,

species. 2 *offens* undersized person.

ru·pee [roo-PEE] *n* monetary unit of India and Pakistan.

rup·ture [RUP-chər] *n* 1 breaking, breach. 2 hernia. ◆ *v* **-tured, tur·ing** 3 break. 4 burst, sever.

ru·ral [RUUR-əl] *adj* 1 of the country. 2 rustic.

ruse [rooz] *n* stratagem, trick.

rush[1] *vt* 1 impel, carry along violently and rapidly. 2 take by sudden assault. ◆ *vi* 3 cause to hurry. 4 move violently or rapidly. ◆ *n* 5 rushing, charge. 6 hurry. 7 eager demand for. 8 heavy current (of air, water, etc.). ◆ *adj* 9 done with speed. 10 characterized by speed. **rush hour** period at beginning and end of day when many people are traveling to and from work.

rush[2] *n* 1 marsh plant with slender pithy stem. 2 the stems as material for baskets.

rusk *n* kind of sweet raised bread esp. used for feeding babies.

rus·set [RUS-it] *adj* 1 reddish-brown. ◆ *n* 2 the color. 3 apple with skin of this color.

rust *n* 1 reddish-brown coating formed on iron by oxidation. 2 disease of plants. ◆ *v* 3

contract, affect with rust. **rust'y** *adj* **rust·i·er, rust·i·est** 1 coated with rust, of rust color. 2 out of practice. **rust'proof** *adj*

rus·tic [RUS-tik] *adj* 1 of, or as of, country people. 2 rural. 3 of rough manufacture. 4 made of untrimmed tree limbs. ◆ *n* 5 country person, peasant. **rus'ti·cate** *v* **-cat·ed, -cat·ing** ◆ *vt* 1 send to, house in, country. ◆ *vi* 2 live a country life.

rus·tle[1] [RUS-əl] *vi* **-tled, -tling** 1 make sound as of blown dead leaves, etc. ◆ *n* 2 this sound.

rustle[2] *vt* **-tled, -tling** steal (cattle). **rus'tler** *n* cattle thief.

rut[1] *n* 1 furrow made by wheel. 2 settled habit or way of living. 3 groove. **rut'ty** *adj* **-ti·er, -ti·est**

rut[2] *n* 1 periodic sexual excitement among animals. ◆ *vi* **rut·ted, rut·ting** 2 be under influence of this.

ruth·less [ROOTH-lis] *adj* pitiless, merciless.

RV *n* recreational vehicle.

rye [rī] *n* 1 grain used for forage and bread. 2 plant bearing it. 3 whisky made from rye.

————— THESAURUS —————

administration, control, direction, leadership, organization, supervision 4 = **working**, functioning, maintenance, operation, performance

runny *adj* = **flowing**, fluid, liquefied, liquid, melted, watery

run off *v* = **flee**, bolt, escape, fly the coop (*inf*), make off, run away, take flight, take to one's heels

run out *v* = **be used up**, be exhausted, dry up, end, fail, finish, give out

run over *v* 1 = **knock down**, hit, knock over, run down 2 = **go through**, check, go over, rehearse, run through

run through *v* = **rehearse**, go over, practise, read, run over

rupture *n* 1 = **break**, breach, burst, crack, fissure, rent, split, tear ◆ *v* 2 = **break**, burst, crack, separate, sever, split, tear

rural *adj* = **rustic**, agricultural, country, pastoral, sylvan

ruse *n* = **trick**, device, dodge, hoax, maneuver, ploy, stratagem, subterfuge

rush *v* 1 = **hurry**, bolt, career, dash, fly, hasten, race, run, shoot, speed, tear 2 = **push**, hurry, hustle, press 3 = **attack**, charge, storm ◆ *n* 4 = **hurry**, charge, dash,

haste, race, scramble, stampede, surge 5 = **attack**, assault, charge, onslaught ◆ *adj* 6 = **hasty**, fast, hurried, quick, rapid, swift, urgent

rust *n* 1 = **corrosion**, oxidation 2 = **mildew**, blight, mold, must, rot ◆ *v* 3 = **corrode**, oxidize

rustic *adj* 1 = **rural**, country, pastoral, sylvan 2 = **uncouth**, awkward, coarse, crude, rough ◆ *n* 3 = **yokel**, boor, bumpkin, clod, clodhopper (*inf*), hick (*inf*), hillbilly, peasant, redneck (*sl*)

rustle *v* 1 = **crackle**, crinkle, whisper ◆ *n* 2 = **crackle**, crinkling, rustling, whisper

rusty *adj* 1 = **corroded**, oxidized, rust-covered, rusted 2 = **reddish**, chestnut, coppery, reddish-brown, russet, rust-colored 3 = **out of practice**, stale, unpracticed, weak

rut *n* 1 = **groove**, furrow, indentation, track, trough, wheel mark 2 = **habit**, dead end, pattern, routine, system

ruthless *adj* = **merciless**, brutal, callous, cruel, harsh, heartless, pitiless, relentless, remorseless

rutted *adj* = **grooved**, cut, furrowed, gouged, holed, indented, marked, scored

S s

S *Chem.* sulfur.

Sab·bath [SAB-əth] *n* **1** Saturday, devoted to worship and rest from work in Judaism and certain Christian churches. **2** Sunday, observed by Christians as day of worship and rest. **sab·bat·i·cal** [sə-BAT-ə-kəl] *adj, n* (denoting) leave granted to university staff, etc. for study.

sa·ber [SAY-bər] *n* **1** curved cavalry sword. **2** fencing sword having two cutting edges and blunt point.

sa·ble [SAY-bəl] *n* **1** small weasellike animal of cold regions. **2** its fur. **3** black. ◆ *adj* **4** black.

sab·o·tage [SAB-ə-tahzh] *n* intentional damage done to roads, machines, etc., esp. secretly in war. ◆ *v* **-taged, -tag·ing** **sab·o·teur** [sab-ə-TUR] *n*

sac [sak] *n* pouchlike structure in an animal or vegetable body.

sac·cha·rin [SAK-ər-in] *n* artificial sweetener. **sac'cha·rine** [-in] *adj* excessively sweet.

sac·er·do·tal [sas-ər-DOHT-l] *adj* of priests.

sa·chet [sa-SHAY] *n* small envelope or bag, esp. one holding scented powder.

sack [sak] *n* **1** large bag, orig. of coarse material. **2** pillaging. **3** *sl* dismissal. **4** *sl* bed. ◆ *vt* **5** pillage (captured town). **6** *sl* fire (person) from a job. **sack'ing** *n* material for sacks. **sack·cloth** [SAK-klawth] *n* coarse fabric used for sacks and worn as sign of mourning.

sac·ra·ment [SAK-rə-mənt] *n* one of certain ceremonies of Christian church esp. Eucharist. **sac·ra·men'tal** *adj*

sa·cred [SAY-krid] *adj* **1** dedicated, regarded as holy. **2** set apart, reserved. **3** inviolable. **4** connected with, intended for religious use.

sac·ri·fice [SAK-rə-fīs] *n* **1** giving something up for sake of something else. **2** act of giving up. **3** thing so given up. **4** making of offering to a god. **5** thing offered. ◆ *vt* **-ficed, -fic·ing** **6** offer as sacrifice. **7** give up. **8** sell at very cheap price. **sac·ri·fi'cial** [-FISH-l] *adj*

sac·ri·lege [SAK-rə-lij] *n* misuse, desecration of something sacred. **sac·ri·leg'ious** [-LEEJ-əs] *adj* **1** profane. **2** desecrating.

sac·ro·sanct [SAK-roh-sangkt] *adj* **1** preserved by religious fear against desecration or violence. **2** inviolable.

sac·rum [SAK-rəm] *n, pl* **sac·ra** [SAK-rə] five vertebrae forming compound bone at base of spinal column.

sad *adj* **sad·der, sad·dest 1** sorrowful. **2** unsatisfactory, deplorable. **sad·den** [SAD-n] *vt* make sad.

THESAURUS

sabotage *n* **1** = **damage**, destruction, disruption, subversion, wrecking ◆ *v* **2** = **damage**, destroy, disable, disrupt, incapacitate, subvert, vandalize, wreck

saccharine *adj* = **oversweet**, cloying, honeyed, nauseating, sickly, sugary, syrupy

sack[1] *n* **1** the sack = **dismissal**, discharge, the ax (*inf*), the boot (*sl*) ◆ *v* **2** = **dismiss**, ax (*inf*), discharge, fire (*inf*)

sack[2] *n* **1** = **plundering**, looting, pillage ◆ *v* **2** = **plunder**, loot, pillage, raid, rob, ruin, strip

sacred *adj* **1** = **holy**, blessed, divine, hallowed, revered, sanctified **2** = **religious**, ecclesiastical, holy **3** = **inviolable**, protected, sacrosanct

sacrifice *n* **1** = **surrender**, loss, renunciation **2** = **offering**, oblation ◆ *v* **3** = **give up**, forego, forfeit, let go, lose, say good-bye to, surrender **4** = **offer**, immolate, offer up

sacrilege *n* = **desecration**, blasphemy, heresy, impiety, irreverence, profanation, violation

sacrilegious *adj* = **profane**, blasphemous, desecrating, impious, irreligious, irreverent

sacrosanct *adj* = **inviolable**, hallowed, inviolate, sacred, sanctified, set apart, untouchable

sad *adj* **1** = **unhappy**, blue, dejected,

sad·dle [SAD-l] n **1** rider's seat to fasten on horse, bicycle, etc. **2** anything resembling a saddle. **3** cut of mutton, venison, etc. for roasting. **4** ridge of hill. ◆ vt **-dled, -dling 5** put saddle on. **6** lay burden, responsibility on.

sa·dism [SAY-diz-əm] n form of (sexual) perversion marked by love of inflicting pain. **sa'dist** n **sa·dis·tic** [sə-DIS-tik] adj

sa·fa·ri [sə-FAH-ree] n (party making) overland (hunting) journey, esp. in Africa. **safari park** park where lions, etc. may be viewed by public from automobiles.

safe [sayf] adj **saf·er, saf·est 1** secure, protected. **2** uninjured, out of danger. **3** not involving risk. **4** trustworthy. **5** sure, reliable. **6** cautious. ◆ n **7** strong lockable container. **8** structure for storing meat, etc. **safe'ly** adv **safe'ty** n **safe-conduct** [KON-dukt] n a permit to pass somewhere. **safe'guard** [-GAHRD] n **1** protection. ◆ vt **2** protect. **safety glass** glass resistant to fragmenting when broken.

saf·fron [SAF-rən] n **1** crocus. **2** orange colored flavoring obtained from it. **3** the color. ◆ adj **4** orange.

sag vi **sagged, sagging 1** sink in middle. **2** hang sideways. **3** curve downward under pressure. **4** give way. **5** tire. **6** (of clothes) hang loosely. ◆ n **7** droop.

sa·ga [SAH-gə] n **1** legend of Norse heroes. **2** any long (heroic) story.

sa·ga·cious [sə-GAY-shəs] adj wise. **sa·gac'i·ty** [-GAS-i-tee] n

sage[1] [sayj] n **1** very wise person. ◆ adj **sag·er, sag·est 2** wise.

sage[2] n aromatic herb.

said [sed] pt./pp. of SAY.

sail [sayl] n **1** piece of fabric stretched to catch wind for propelling ship, etc. **2** act of sailing. **3** journey upon the water. **4** ships collectively. **5** arm of windmill. ◆ vi **6** travel by water. **7** move smoothly. **8** begin voyage. ◆ vt **9** navigate. **sail'or** n **1** seaman. **2** one who sails. **sail'board** [-bord] n craft used for windsurfing like surfboard with mast and single sail.

saint [saynt] n (title of) person formally recognized (esp. by R.C. Church) after death, as having gained by holy deeds a special place in heaven. **1** exceptionally good person. **saint'ed** [-id] adj **1** canonized. **2** sacred. **saint'li·ness** [-nis] n holiness. **saint'ly** adj

sake[1] [sayk] n **1** cause, account. **2** end, purpose. **for the sake of 1** on behalf of. **2** to please or benefit.

sa·ke[2] [SAH-kee] n Japanese alcoholic drink made of fermented rice.

sa·laam [sə-LAHM] n **1** bow of salutation,

depressed, doleful, down, low, low-spirited, melancholy, mournful, woebegone **2** = **tragic**, depressing, dismal, grievous, harrowing, heart-rending, moving, pathetic, pitiful, poignant, upsetting **3** = **deplorable**, bad, lamentable, sorry, wretched

sadden v = **upset**, deject, depress, distress, grieve, make sad

saddle v = **burden**, encumber, load

sadistic adj = **cruel**, barbarous, brutal, ruthless, vicious

sadness n = **unhappiness**, dejection, depression, despondency, grief, melancholy, misery, poignancy, sorrow, the blues

safe adj **1** = **secure**, impregnable, in safe hands, out of danger, out of harm's way, protected, safe and sound **2** = **unharmed**, all right, intact, O.K. or okay (inf), undamaged, unhurt, unscathed **3** = **risk-free**, certain, impregnable, secure, sound ◆ n **4** = **strongbox**, coffer, deposit box, repository, safe-deposit box, vault

safeguard v **1** = **protect**, defend, guard, look after, preserve ◆ n **2** = **protection**, defense, guard, security

safely adv = **in safety**, in one piece, safe and sound, with impunity, without risk

safety n **1** = **security**, impregnability, protection **2** = **shelter**, cover, refuge, sanctuary

sag v **1** = **sink**, bag, dip, droop, fall, give way, hang loosely, slump **2** = **tire**, droop, flag, wane, weaken, wilt

saga n = **tale**, epic, legend, narrative, story, yarn

sage n **1** = **wise man**, elder, guru, master, philosopher ◆ adj **2** = **wise**, judicious, sagacious, sapient, sensible

sail v **1** = **embark**, set sail **2** = **glide**, drift, float, fly, skim, soar, sweep, wing **3** = **pilot**, steer

sailor n = **mariner**, marine, sea dog, seafarer, seaman

saintly adj = **virtuous**, godly, holy, pious, religious, righteous, saintlike

sake n **1** = **benefit**, account, behalf, good,

mark of respect in East. ♦ vt **2** salute.

sal•able adj see SALE.

sa•la•cious [sə-LAY-shəs] adj excessively concerned with sex, lewd.

sal•ad [SAL-əd] n mixed vegetables, or fruit, used as food without cooking, oft. combined with fish, meat, etc. ♦ adj **salad days** period of youthful inexperience. **salad dressing** oil, vinegar, herbs, etc. mixed together as sauce for salad.

sal•a•man•der [SAL-ə-man-dər] n **1** variety of lizard. **2** portable space heater.

sa•la•mi [sə-LAH-mee] n variety of highly-spiced sausage.

sal•a•ry [SAL-ə-ree] n, pl **-ries** fixed regular payment to persons employed usu. in nonmanual work. **sal'a•ried** adj

sale [sayl] n **1** selling. **2** selling of goods at unusually low prices. **3** auction. **sal'a•ble** adj capable of being sold. **sales'per•son** n **1** one who sells goods, etc. in store. **2** one traveling to sell goods, esp. as representative of firm. **sales'man•ship** n art of selling or presenting goods in most effective way.

sa•li•ent [SAY-lee-ənt] adj **1** prominent, noticeable. **2** jutting out. ♦ n **3** salient angle, esp. in fortification or line of battle.

sa•line [SAY-leen] adj **1** containing, consisting of a chemical salt, esp. common salt. **2** salty. **sa•lin•i•ty** [sə-LIN-i-tee] n

sa•li•va [sə-LĪ-və] n liquid that forms in mouth, spittle. **sal•i•var•y** [SAL-ə-ver-ee] adj **sal'i•vate** v -vat•ed, -vat•ing

sal•low [SAL-oh] adj of unhealthy pale or yellowish color.

sal•ly [SAL-ee] n, pl **-lies 1** rushing out, esp. by troops. **2** outburst. **3** witty remark. ♦ vi -lied, -ly•ing **4** rush. **5** set out.

salm•on [SAM-ən] n **1** large silvery fish with orange-pink flesh valued as food. **2** color of

its flesh. ♦ adj **3** of this color.

sal•mo•nel•la [sal-mə-NEL-ə] n, pl -lae [-nee] bacteria causing disease (esp. food poisoning).

sa•lon [sə-LON] n **1** (reception room for) guests in fashionable household. **2** commercial premises of hairdressers, beauticians, etc.

sa•loon [sə-LOON] n **1** principal cabin or sitting room in passenger ship. **2** bar. **3** public room for specified use, e.g. billiards.

salt [sawlt] n **1** white powdery or granular crystalline substance consisting mainly of sodium chloride, used to season or preserve food. **2** chemical compound of acid and metal. **3** wit. ♦ vt **4** season, sprinkle with, spread, preserve with salt. **salt'y** adj **salt•i•er, salt•i•est** of, like salt. **old salt** sailor. **salt'cel•lar** [-sel-ər] n salt shaker. **salt lick** deposit, block of salt licked by game, cattle, etc. **salt pan** n depression encrusted with salt after partial draining away of water. **salt•pe•ter** [sawlt-PEE-tər] n potassium nitrate used in gunpowder. **with a pinch of salt** allowing for exaggeration. **worth one's salt** efficient.

sa•lu•bri•ous [sə-LOO-bree-əs] adj favorable to health, beneficial.

Sa•lu•ki [sə-LOO-kee] n tall hound with silky coat.

sal•u•tar•y [SAL-yə-ter-ee] adj wholesome, resulting in good.

sa•lute [sə-LOOT] v -lut•ed, -lut•ing ♦ vt **1** greet with words or sign. **2** acknowledge with praise. ♦ vi **3** perform military salute. ♦ n **4** word, sign by which one greets another. **5** motion of arm as mark of respect to superior, etc. in military usage. **6** firing of guns as military greeting of honor. **sal•u•ta'tion** [-yə-TAY-shən] n

sal•vage [SAL-vij] n **1** act of saving ship or

interest, welfare **2 = purpose**, aim, end, motive, objective, reason

salacious adj **= lascivious**, carnal, erotic, lecherous, lewd, libidinous, lustful

salary n **= pay**, earnings, income, wage, wages

sale n **1 = selling**, deal, disposal, marketing, transaction **2 for sale = available**, obtainable, on the market

salient adj **= prominent**, conspicuous, important, noticeable, outstanding, pronounced, striking

sallow adj **= wan**, anemic, pale, pallid,

pasty, sickly, unhealthy, yellowish

salt n **1 = seasoning**, flavor, relish, savor, taste **2 with a grain** or **pinch of salt = skeptically**, cynically, disbelievingly, suspiciously, with reservations ♦ adj **3 = salty**, brackish, briny, saline

salty adj **= salt**, brackish, briny, saline

salubrious adj **= healthy**, beneficial, good for one, health-giving, wholesome

salutary adj **= beneficial**, advantageous, good for one, profitable, useful, valuable

salute n **1 = greeting**, address, recognition, salutation ♦ v **2 = greet**, acknowledge, other property from danger of loss. 2 property so saved. ♦ vt -vaged, -vag·ing

sal·va·tion [sal-VAY-shən] n fact or state of being saved, esp. of soul.

salve [sav] n 1 healing ointment. ♦ vt salved, salv·ing 2 anoint with such, soothe.

sal·ver [SAL-vər] n (silver) tray for presentation of food, letters, etc.

sal·vo [SAL-voh] n, pl -vos or -voes simultaneous discharge of guns, etc.

Sam. Samuel.

Sa·mar·i·tan [sə-MAR-i-tn] n 1 native of ancient Samaria. 2 (s-) benevolent person.

sam·ba [SAM-bə] n 1 dance of S Amer. origin. 2 music for it.

same [saym] adj 1 identical, not different, unchanged. 2 uniform. 3 just mentioned previously. **same'ness** [-nis] n 1 similarity. 2 monotony.

sam·o·var [SAM-ə-vahr] n Russian tea urn.

Sam·o·yed [sam-ə-YED] n dog with thick white coat and tightly curled tail.

sam'pan n small oriental boat.

sam·ple [SAM-pəl] n 1 specimen. ♦ vt -pled, -pling 2 take, give sample of. 3 try. 4 test. 5 select. 6 use part of (old sound recording) in new recording. **sam'pler** n beginner's exercise in embroidery. **sampling** n 1 the taking of samples. 2 sample.

sam·u·rai [SAM-uu-rī] n, pl **samurai** member of ancient Japanese warrior caste.

san·a·to·ri·um [san-ə-TOR-ee-əm] n, pl -ri·ums or -ri·a [-ree-ə] 1 hospital, esp. for chronically ill. 2 health resort.

sanc·ti·fy [SANGK-tə-fī] vt -fied, -fying 1 set apart as holy. 2 free from sin.

sanc·ti·fi·ca'tion n **sanc'ti·ty** n, pl -ti·ties 1 saintliness. 2 sacredness. 3 inviolability.

sanc·tu·ar·y [-choo-er-ee] n, pl -ar·ies 1 holy place. 2 part of church nearest altar. 3 place of special holiness in synagogue. 4 place where fugitive was safe from arrest or violence. 5 place protected by law where animals, etc. can live without interference. **sanc·tum** [SANGK-təm] n 1 sacred place or shrine. 2 person's private room. **sanctum sanc·to·rum** [sangk-TOR-əm] n 1 holy of holies in Temple in Jerusalem. 2 sanctum.

sanc·ti·mo·ni·ous [sangk-tə-MOH-nee-əs] adj making a show of piety, holiness. **sanc·ti·mo'ni·ous·ness** n

sanc·tion [SANGK-shən] n 1 permission, authorization. 2 penalty for breaking law. ♦ pl 3 boycott or other coercive measure esp. by one country against another regarded as having violated a law, right, etc. ♦ vt 4 allow, authorize, permit.

sand n 1 substance consisting of small grains of rock or mineral, esp. on beach or in desert. ♦ pl 2 stretches or banks of this, usually forming seashore. ♦ vt 3 polish, smooth with sandpaper. 4 cover, mix with sand. **sand'er** n (power) tool for smoothing surfaces. **sand'y** adj sand·i·er, sand·i·est 1 like sand. 2 sand-colored. 3 consisting of, covered with sand. **sand'bag** n 1 bag filled with sand or soil, used as protection against gunfire, floodwater, etc. and as weapon. ♦ vt -bagged, -bag·ging 2 beat, hit with sandbag. 3 inf in football, tackle passer as if from ambush.

──── THESAURUS ────

address, hail, welcome 3 = **honor**, acknowledge, pay tribute or homage to, recognize

salvage v = **save**, recover, redeem, rescue, retrieve

salvation n = **saving**, deliverance, escape, preservation, redemption, rescue

salve n = **ointment**, balm, cream, emollient, lotion

same adj 1 = **aforementioned**, aforesaid 2 = **identical**, alike, corresponding, duplicate, equal, twin 3 = **unchanged**, changeless, consistent, constant, invariable, unaltered, unvarying

sample n 1 = **specimen**, example, instance, model, pattern ♦ v 2 = **test**, experience, inspect, taste, try ♦ adj 3 =

test, representative, specimen, trial

sanctify v = **consecrate**, cleanse, hallow

sanctimonious adj = **holier-than-thou**, hypocritical, pious, self-righteous, smug

sanction n 1 = **permission**, approval, authority, authorization, backing, O.K. or okay (inf), stamp or seal of approval 2 = (often plural) = **ban**, boycott, coercive measures, embargo, penalty ♦ v 3 = **permit**, allow, approve, authorize, endorse

sanctity n 1 = **sacredness**, inviolability 2 = **holiness**, godliness, goodness, grace, piety, righteousness

sanctuary n 1 = **shrine**, altar, church, temple 2 = **protection**, asylum, haven, refuge, retreat, shelter 3 = **reserve**, conservation area, national park, nature

sand'blast n jet of sand blown from a nozzle under pressure for cleaning, grinding, etc. ◆ vt **sand'pa·per** n paper with sand stuck on it for scraping or polishing wood, etc. **sand'pit, sand'box** n quantity of sand for children to play in. **sand'stone** n rock composed of sand.

san·dal [SAN-dl] n shoe consisting of sole attached by straps.

sand'wich n 1 two slices of bread with meat or other food between. 2 anything resembling this. ◆ vt 3 insert between two other things.

sane [sayn] adj **san·er, san·est 1** of sound mind. 2 sensible, rational. **san·i·ty** [SAN-i-tee] n

sang pt. of SING.

sang-froid [sahn-FRWAH] n Fr 1 composure. 2 indifference. 3 self-possession.

san·guine [SANG-gwin] adj 1 cheerful, confident. 2 ruddy in complexion. **san·gui·nar·y** [SANG-gwə-ner-ee] adj 1 accompanied by bloodshed. 2 bloodthirsty.

san·i·tar·y [SAN-i-ter-ee] adj helping protection of health against dirt, etc. **san·i·ta'tion** n measures, apparatus for preservation of public health.

sank pt. of SINK.

San'skrit n ancient language of India.

sap[1] n 1 moisture that circulates in plants. 2 energy. ◆ v sapped, sap·ping 3 drain off sap. **sap'ling** n young tree.

sap[2] v sapped, sap·ping 1 undermine. 2 destroy insidiously. 3 weaken. ◆ n 4 trench dug in order to approach or undermine enemy position. **sap'per** n [-pər] n soldier doing this.

sap[3] n sl foolish, gullible person.

sa·pi·ent [SAY-pee-ənt] adj usu. ironical 1 wise. 2 discerning. 3 shrewd. 4 knowing. **sa'pi·ence** n

Sap·phic [SAF-ik] adj 1 of Sappho, a Grecian poet. 2 denoting a kind of verse. ◆ n 3 Sapphic verse. **sap'phism** [SAF-iz-əm] n lesbianism.

sap·phire [SAF-īr] n 1 (usu. blue) precious stone. 2 deep blue. ◆ adj

sar·a·band [SAR-ə-band] n 1 slow, stately Spanish dance. 2 music for it.

sar·casm [SAHR-kaz-əm] n 1 bitter or wounding ironic remark. 2 such remarks. 3 taunt. 4 sneer. 5 irony. 6 use of such expressions. **sar·cas'tic** [-KAS-tik] adj **sar·cas'ti·cal·ly** adv

sar·coph·a·gous [sahr-KOF-ə-gəs] adj carnivorous.

sar·coph·a·gus [sahr-KOF-ə-gəs] n, pl **-gi** [-jī] stone coffin.

sar·dine [sahr-DEEN] n small fish of herring family, usu. preserved in oil.

sar·don·ic [sahr-DON-ik] adj characterized by irony, mockery or derision.

sar·don·yx [sahr-DON-iks] n gemstone, variety of chalcedony.

sar·gas·sum [sahr-GAS-əm], **sar·gas·so** [-GAS-oh] n gulfweed, type of floating seaweed.

sa·ri [SAHR-ee] n, pl **-ris** Hindu woman's robe.

sa·rong [sə-RAWNG] n skirtlike garment worn in Asian and Pacific countries.

sar·sa·pa·ril·la [sas-pə-RIL-ə] n (flavor of) drink like root beer orig. made from root of plant.

sar·to·ri·al [sahr-TOR-ee-əl] adj of tailor, tailoring, or men's clothes.

sash[1] n decorative belt, ribbon, wound around the body.

sash[2] n window frame opened by moving up and down in grooves.

THESAURUS

reserve

sane adj 1 = **rational**, all there (inf), compos mentis, in one's right mind, mentally sound, of sound mind 2 = **sensible**, balanced, judicious, level-headed, reasonable, sound

sanguine adj = **cheerful**, buoyant, confident, hopeful, optimistic

sanitary adj = **hygienic**, clean, germ-free, healthy, wholesome

sanity n 1 = **mental health**, normality, rationality, reason, saneness 2 = **good sense**, common sense, level-headedness,

rationality, sense

sap[1] n 1 = **vital fluid**, essence, lifeblood 2 Inf Sl = **fool**, dork (sl), idiot, jerk (sl), ninny, schmuck (sl), simpleton

sap[2] v = **weaken**, deplete, drain, exhaust, undermine

sarcasm n = **irony**, bitterness, cynicism, derision, mockery, satire

sarcastic adj = **ironic**, acid, biting, caustic, cutting, cynical, mocking, sardonic, satirical

sardonic adj = **mocking**, cynical, derisive, dry, ironic, sarcastic, sneering, wry

sas·sa·fras [SAS-ə-fras] *n* tree of laurel family with aromatic bark used medicinally.

sat pt./pp. of SIT.

Sa·tan [SAYT-n] *n* the devil. **sa·tan'ic** [sə-TAN-ik], **sa·tan'i·cal** *adj* devilish, fiendish.

satch·el [SACH-əl] *n* small bag, oft. with shoulder strap.

sate [sayt] *vt* **sat·ed, sat·ing** satisfy a desire or appetite fully or excessively.

sat·el·lite [SAT-l-īt] *n* **1** celestial body or manmade planet orbiting planet. **2** person, country, etc. dependent on another.

sa·ti·ate [SAY-shee-ayt] *vt* **-at·ed, at·ing 1** satisfy to the full. **2** surfeit. **sa·ti·a'tion** *n* **sa·ti·e·ty** [sə-TĪ-i-tee] *n* feeling of having had too much.

sat·in [SAT-n] *n* fabric (of silk, nylon, etc.) with glossy surface on one side. **sat'in·y** *adj* of, like satin.

sat·ire [SAT-īr] *n* **1** composition in which vice, folly or foolish person is held up to ridicule. **2** use of ridicule or sarcasm to expose vice and folly. **sa·tir·i·cal** [sə-TIR-i-kəl] *adj* **1** of nature of satire. **2** sarcastic. **3** bitter. **sat'i·rist** *n* **sat'i·rize** *vt* **-rized, -riz·ing 1** make object of satire. **2** censure thus.

sat·is·fy [SAT-is-fī] *vt* **-fied, -fy·ing 1** content, meet wishes of. **2** pay. **3** fulfill, supply adequately. **4** convince. **sat·is·fac'tion** *n* **sat·is·fac'to·ry** *adj*

sa·trap [SAY-trap] *n* **1** provincial governor in ancient Persia. **2** subordinate ruler, oft. despotic.

sat·u·rate [SACH-ə-rayt] *vt* **-rat·ed, -rat·ing 1** soak thoroughly. **2** cause to absorb maximum amount. **3** *Chem.* cause substance to combine to its full capacity with another. **4** shell or bomb heavily. **sat·u·ra'tion** *n* act, result of saturating.

Sat·urn [SAT-ərn] *n* **1** Roman god. **2** one of planets. **sat·ur·nine** [SAT-ər-nīn] *adj* **1** gloomy. **2** sluggish in temperament, dull, morose. **Sat·ur·na'li·a** [-NAY-lee-ə] *n, pl* **-li·as 1** ancient festival of Saturn. **2** (**s-**) noisy revelry, orgy.

sa·tyr [SAY-tər] *n* **1** woodland deity, part man, part goat. **2** lustful man.

sauce [saws] *n* **1** liquid added to food to enhance flavor. **2** *inf* impudence. **3** *sl* whiskey. ◆ *vt* **sauced, sauc·ing 4** add sauce to. **5** *inf* be cheeky, impudent to. **sau'ci·ly** *adv* **sau'cy** *adj* **-ci·er, -ci·est** impudent. **sauce'pan** *n* cooking pot with long handle.

sau·cer [SAW-sər] *n* **1** curved plate put under cup. **2** shallow depression.

sau·er·kraut [SOW-ər-krowt] *n* German dish of finely shredded and pickled cabbage.

sau·na [SAW-nə] *n* steam bath, orig. Finnish.

saun·ter [SAWN-tər] *vi* **1** walk in leisurely manner, stroll. ◆ *n* **2** leisurely walk or stroll.

sau·ri·an [SOR-ee-ən] *n* one of the order of

Satan *n* = **The Devil**, Beelzebub, Lord of the Flies, Lucifer, Mephistopheles, Prince of Darkness, The Evil One

satanic *adj* = **evil**, black, demonic, devilish, diabolic, fiendish, hellish, infernal, wicked

satiate *v* **1** = **glut**, cloy, gorge, jade, nauseate, overfill, stuff, surfeit **2** = **satisfy**, sate, slake

satire *n* = **mockery**, burlesque, caricature, irony, lampoon, parody, ridicule, spoof (*inf*)

satirical *adj* = **mocking**, biting, caustic, cutting, incisive, ironic

satirize *v* = **ridicule**, burlesque, deride, lampoon, parody, pillory

satisfaction *n* **1** = **contentment**, comfort, content, enjoyment, happiness, pleasure, pride, repletion, satiety **2** = **fulfillment**, achievement, assuaging, gratification

satisfactory *adj* = **adequate**, acceptable,

all right, average, fair, good enough, passable, sufficient

satisfy *v* **1** = **content**, assuage, gratify, indulge, pacify, pander to, please, quench, sate, slake **2** = **fulfill**, answer, do, meet, serve, suffice **3** = **persuade**, assure, convince, reassure

saturate *v* = **soak**, drench, imbue, souse, steep, suffuse, waterlog, wet through

saturated *adj* = **soaked**, drenched, dripping, soaking (wet), sodden, sopping (wet), waterlogged, wet through

saturnine *adj* = **gloomy**, dour, glum, grave, morose, somber

saucy *adj* **1** = **impudent**, cheeky (*inf*), forward, impertinent, insolent, pert, presumptuous, rude **2** = **jaunty**, dashing, gay, perky

saunter *v* **1** = **stroll**, amble, meander, mosey (*inf*), ramble, roam, wander ◆ *n* **2** =

reptiles including the alligator, lizard, etc.

sau·sage [SAW-sij] *n* chopped seasoned meat enclosed in thin tube of animal intestine or synthetic material. **sausage meat** meat prepared for this.

sau·té [soh-TAY] *adj* 1 cooked or browned in pan with little butter, oil, etc. ◆ *vt* **-téed, -té·ing** 2 cook in this way.

Sau·ternes [soh-TURN] *n* 1 sweet white wine from S Bordeaux, France. 2 (**s-**) similar wine made elsewhere.

sav·age [SAV-ij] *adj* 1 wild. 2 ferocious. 3 brutal. 4 uncivilized, primitive. ◆ *n* 5 member of savage tribe, barbarian. ◆ *vt* **-aged, -ag·ing** 6 attack ferociously. **sav'age·ry** *n*

sa·van·na, sa·van·nah [sə-VAN-ə]. ◆ *n* extensive open grassy plain.

sa·vant [sa-VAHNT] *n* person of learning.

save [sayv] *v* **saved, sav·ing** ◆ *vt* 1 rescue, preserve. 2 protect. 3 secure. 4 keep for future, lay by. 5 prevent need of. 6 spare. 7 except. 8 *Computers* keep (data) by moving to location for storage. ◆ *vi* 9 lay by money. ◆ *prep* 10 except. ◆ *conj* 11 but. **saving** *adj* 1 frugal. 2 thrifty. 3 delivering from sin. 4 excepting. 5 compensating. ◆ *prep* 6 except. ◆ *n* 7 economy. ◆ *pl* 8 money, earnings put by for future use.

sav·ior [SAYV-yər] *n* 1 person who rescues another. 2 (**S-**) Christ.

sa·voir-faire [sav-wahr-FAIR] *n Fr* ability to do, say, the right thing in any situation.

sa·vor [SAY-vər] *n* 1 characteristic taste. 2 flavor. 3 odor. 4 distinctive quality. ◆ *vi* 5 have particular smell or taste. 6 have suggestion (of). ◆ *vt* 7 give flavor to. 8 have flavor of. 9 enjoy, appreciate. **sa'vor·y** *adj* 1 attractive to taste or smell. 2 not sweet.

sa·vor·y [SAY-və-ree] *n, pl* **-vor·ies** aromatic herb used in cooking.

sav·vy [SAV-ee] *vt inf* **-vied, -vy·ing** 1 understand. ◆ *n* 2 wits, intelligence.

saw¹ *n* 1 tool for cutting wood, etc. by tearing it with toothed edge. ◆ *v* **sawed** or **sawn, saw·ing** 2 cut with saw. 3 make movements of sawing. **saw'dust** *n* fine wood fragments made in sawing. **saw'mill** *n* mill where timber is sawed by machine into planks, etc.

saw² pt. of SEE.

saw³ *n* wise saying, proverb.

sax·i·frage [SAK-sə-frij] *n* alpine or rock plant.

Sax·on [SAK-sən] *n* member of West Germanic people who settled widely in Europe in the early Middle Ages. ◆ *adj*

sax·o·phone [SAK-sə-fohn] *n* keyed wind instrument.

say *vt* **said** [sed], **say·ing, says** [sez] 1 speak. 2 pronounce. 3 state. 4 express. 5 take as example or as near enough. 6 form and deliver opinion. ◆ *n* 7 what one has to say. 8 chance of saying it. 9 share in decision. **saying** *n* maxim, proverb.

THESAURUS

stroll, airing, amble, ramble, turn, walk

savage *adj* 1 = **wild**, feral, undomesticated, untamed 2 = **uncultivated**, rough, rugged, uncivilized 3 = **cruel**, barbarous, bestial, bloodthirsty, brutal, ferocious, fierce, harsh, ruthless, sadistic, vicious 4 = **primitive**, rude, unspoilt ◆ *n* 5 = **lout**, boor, yahoo ◆ *v* 6 = **attack**, lacerate, mangle, maul

savagery *n* = **cruelty**, barbarity, brutality, ferocity, ruthlessness, viciousness

save *v* 1 = **rescue**, deliver, free, liberate, recover, redeem, salvage 2 = **protect**, conserve, guard, keep safe, look after, preserve, safeguard 3 = **keep**, collect, gather, hoard, hold, husband, lay by, put by, reserve, set aside, store

saving *n* 1 = **economy**, bargain, discount, reduction ◆ *adj* 2 = **redeeming**, compensatory, extenuating

savings *pl n* = **nest egg**, fund, reserves,

resources, store

savior *n* = **rescuer**, defender, deliverer, liberator, preserver, redeemer

Savior *n* = **Christ**, Jesus, Messiah, Redeemer

savoir-faire *n* = **social know-how** (*inf*), diplomacy, discretion, finesse, poise, social graces, tact, urbanity, worldliness

savor *v* 1 = **enjoy**, appreciate, delight in, luxuriate in, relish, revel in 2 (often with *of*) = **suggest**, be suggestive, show signs, smack ◆ *n* 3 = **flavor**, piquancy, relish, smack, smell, tang, taste

savory *adj* = **spicy**, appetizing, full-flavored, luscious, mouthwatering, palatable, piquant, rich, tasty

say *v* 1 = **speak**, affirm, announce, assert, declare, maintain, mention, pronounce, remark, state, utter, voice 2 = **suppose**, assume, conjecture, estimate, guess, imagine, presume, surmise 3 = **express**,

Sb *Chem.* antimony.

Sc *Chem.* scandium.

scab [skab] *n* **1** crust formed over wound. **2** skin disease. **3** disease of plants. **4** strikebreaker. **scab'by** *adj* **-bi·er**, **-bi·est**

scab·bard [SKAB-ərd] *n* sheath for sword or dagger.

scab·rous [SKAYB-rəs] *adj* **1** having rough surface. **2** thorny. **3** indecent. **4** risky.

scaf·fold [SKAF-əld] *n* **1** temporary platform for workmen. **2** gallows. **scaf'fold·ing** *n* (material for building) scaffold.

sca·lar [SKAY-lər] *n* variable quantity, e.g. time, having magnitude but no direction. ♦ *adj*

scald [skawld] *vt* **1** burn with hot liquid or steam. **2** clean, sterilize with boiling water. **3** heat (liquid) almost to boiling point. ♦ *n* **4** injury by scalding.

scale[1] *n* **1** one of the thin, overlapping plates covering fishes and reptiles. **2** thin flake. **3** incrustation that forms in boilers, etc. ♦ *v* **scaled, scal·ing** ♦ *vt* **4** remove scales from. ♦ *vi* **5** come off in scales. **scal'y** *adj* **scal·i·er, scal·i·est** resembling or covered in scales. **scale insect** plant pest covered by waxy secretion.

scale[2] *n* **1** (chiefly in *pl*) weighing instrument. ♦ *vt* **scaled, scal·ing 2** weigh in scales. **3** have weight of.

scale[3] *n* **1** graduated table or sequence of marks at regular intervals used as reference or for fixing standards, as in making measurements, in music, etc. **2** ratio of size between a thing and a model or map of it. **3** (relative) degree, extent. ♦ *vt* **scaled, scal·ing 4** climb. ♦ *adj* **5** proportionate. **scale up, down** increase *or* decrease proportionally in size.

sca·lene [SKAY-leen] *adj* (of triangle) with three unequal sides.

scal·lop [SKOL-əp] *n* **1** edible shellfish. **2** edging in small curves like edge of scallop shell. ♦ *vt* **3** shape like scallop shell. **4** cook in scallop shell *or* dish like one.

scalp [skalp] *n* **1** skin and hair of top of head. ♦ *vt* **2** cut off scalp of.

scal·pel [SKAL-pəl] *n* small surgical knife.

scam [skam] *n inf* a dishonest scheme.

scamp [skamp] *n* **1** mischievous person or child. ♦ *v* **2** do *or* make hastily or carelessly.

scamp·er [SKAM-pər] *vi* **1** run about. **2** run hastily from place to place. ♦ *n*

scam·pi [SKAM-pee] *n, pl* **scampi 1** large shrimp. **2** dish of these sautéed in oil *or* butter and garlic.

scan [skan] *v* **scanned, scan·ning 1** look at carefully, scrutinize. **2** measure or read (verse) by metrical feet. **3** examine, search by systematically varying the direction of a radar or sonar beam. **4** glance over quickly. **5** (of verse) conform to metrical rules. ♦ *n* **6** scanning. **scan'ner** *n* device, esp. electronic, that scans. **scan'sion** [-shən] *n*

scan·dal [SKAN-dl] *n* **1** action, event generally considered disgraceful. **2** malicious gossip. **scan'dal·ize** *vt* **-ized, -iz·ing** shock. **scan'dal·ous** [-dl-əs] *adj* outrageous, disgraceful.

---

communicate, convey, imply ♦ *n* **4 = chance to speak**, voice, vote **5 = influence**, authority, clout (*inf*), power, weight

saying *n* = **proverb**, adage, aphorism, axiom, dictum, maxim

scale[1] *n* = **flake**, lamina, layer, plate

scale[2] *n* **1** = **graduation**, gradation, hierarchy, ladder, progression, ranking, sequence, series, steps **2** = **ratio**, proportion **3** = **degree**, extent, range, reach, scope ♦ *v* **4** = **climb**, ascend, clamber, escalade, mount, surmount **5** = **adjust**, proportion, regulate

scam *v Sl* **1** = **cheat**, cook the books (*inf*), diddle (*inf*), fix, swindle, wangle (*inf*) ♦ *n* **2** *Sl* = **fraud**, fix, racket (*sl*), swindle

scamp *n* = **rascal**, devil, imp, monkey,

rogue, scallywag (*inf*)

scamper *v* = **run**, dart, dash, hasten, hurry, romp, scoot, scurry, scuttle

scan *v* **1** = **glance over**, check, check out (*inf*), examine, eye, look through, run one's eye over, run over, skim **2** = **scrutinize**, investigate, scour, search, survey, sweep

scandal *n* **1** = **crime**, disgrace, embarrassment, offense, sin, wrongdoing **2** = **shame**, defamation, discredit, disgrace, dishonor, ignominy, infamy, opprobrium, stigma **3** = **gossip**, aspersion, dirt, rumors, slander, talk, tattle

scandalize *v* = **shock**, affront, appall, horrify, offend, outrage

scandalous *adj* **1** = **shocking**, disgraceful, disreputable, infamous, outrageous,

scant [skant] *adj* **-er, -est** barely sufficient or not sufficient. **scant'i·ly** *adv* **scant'y** *adj* **scant·i·er, scant·i·est scant·ies** [SKAN-teez] *n* very brief underpants.

scape·goat [SKAYP-goht] *n* person bearing blame due to others. **scape'grace** [-grays] *n* 1 rascal. 2 unscrupulous person.

scap·u·la [SKAP-yə-lə] *n, pl* **-las** shoulder blade. **scap'u·lar** [-lər] *adj* 1 of scapula. ◆ *n* 2 loose sleeveless monastic garment.

scar [skar] *n* 1 mark left by healed wound, burn or sore. 2 change resulting from emotional distress. ◆ *v* **scarred, scar·ring** 3 mark, heal with scar.

scar·ab [SKA-rəb] *n* 1 sacred beetle of ancient Egypt. 2 gem cut in shape of this.

scarce [skairs] *adj* 1 hard to find. 2 existing or available in insufficient quantity. 3 uncommon. **scarce'ly** *adv* 1 only just. 2 not quite. 3 definitely or probably not. **scar'ci·ty** [-si-tee] *n*

scare [skair] *vt* **scared, scar·ing** 1 frighten. ◆ *n* 2 fright, sudden panic. **scar'y** *adj* **scar·i·er, scar·i·est scare'crow** [-kroh] *n* 1 thing set up to frighten birds from crops. 2 badly dressed or miserable looking person. **scare·mon·ger** [-mung-gər] *n* one who spreads alarming rumors.

scarf¹ [skarf] *n, pl* **scarfs** or **scarves** long narrow strip, large piece of material to put around neck, head, etc.

scarf² *n, pl* **scarfs** 1 part cut away from each of two pieces of timber to be jointed longitudinally. 2 joint so made. ◆ *vt* 3 cut or join in this way.

scar·i·fy [SKA-rə-fī] *vt* **-fied, -fy·ing** 1 scratch, cut slightly all over. 2 lacerate. 3 stir surface soil of. 4 criticize mercilessly.

scar·let [SKAHR-lit] *n* 1 a brilliant red color. 2 cloth or clothing of this color. ◆ *adj* 3 of this color. 4 immoral, esp. unchaste. **scarlet fever** infectious fever with scarlet rash.

scarp [skahrp] *n* 1 steep slope. 2 inside slope of ditch in fortifications.

scath·ing [SKAYth-ing] *adj* 1 harshly critical. 2 cutting. 3 damaging.

scat·ter [SKAT-ər] *vt* 1 throw in various directions. 2 put here and there. 3 sprinkle. ◆ *vi* 4 disperse. ◆ *n* **scat'ter·brain** [-brayn] *n* silly, careless person.

scav·enge [SKAV-inj] *v* **-enged, -eng·ing** 1 search for (anything usable) usu. among discarded material. **scav'en·ger** *n* 1 person who scavenges. 2 animal, bird that feeds on refuse.

scene [seen] *n* 1 place of action of novel, play, etc. 2 place of any action. 3 subdivision of play. 4 view. 5 episode. 6 display of strong emotion. **scen'er·y** *n, pl* **-er·ies** 1 natural features of area. 2 constructions of wood, canvas, etc. used on stage to represent a place where action is happening. **sce'nic** *adj* 1 picturesque. 2 of or on the stage. **sce·nar·i·o** [si-NAIR-ee-oh] *n, pl* **-i·os** summary of plot (of play, etc.) or plan.

scent [sent] *n* 1 distinctive smell, esp.

shameful, unseemly 2 = **slanderous**, defamatory, libelous, scurrilous, untrue

scant *adj* = **meager**, barely sufficient, little, minimal, sparse

scanty *adj* = **meager**, bare, deficient, inadequate, insufficient, lousy (*sl*), poor, scant, short, skimpy, sparse, thin

scapegoat *n* = **whipping boy**, fall guy (*inf*)

scar *n* 1 = **mark**, blemish, injury, wound ◆ *v* 2 = **mark**, damage, disfigure

scarce *adj* = **rare**, few, few and far between, infrequent, in short supply, insufficient, uncommon

scarcely *adv* 1 = **hardly**, barely 2 = **definitely not**, hardly

scarcity *n* = **shortage**, dearth, deficiency, insufficiency, lack, paucity, rareness, want

scare *v* 1 = **frighten**, alarm, dismay, intimidate, panic, shock, startle, terrify ◆ *n* 2 = **fright**, panic, shock, start, terror

scared *adj* = **frightened**, fearful, panicky, panic-stricken, petrified, shaken, startled, terrified

scary *adj* = **frightening**, alarming, chilling, creepy (*inf*), horrifying, spine-chilling, spooky (*inf*), terrifying

scathing *adj* = **critical**, biting, caustic, cutting, harsh, sarcastic, scornful, trenchant, withering

scatter *v* 1 = **throw about**, diffuse, disseminate, fling, shower, spread, sprinkle, strew 2 = **disperse**, disband, dispel, dissipate

scatterbrain *n* = **featherbrain**, butterfly, flibbertigibbet

scenario *n* = **story line**, outline, résumé, summary, synopsis

scene *n* 1 = **site**, area, locality, place, position, setting, spot 2 = **setting**, backdrop, background, location, set 3 =

pleasant one. **2** trail, clue. **3** perfume. ◆ *vt* **4** detect or track (by smell). **5** suspect, sense. **6** fill with fragrance.

scep·ter [SEP-tər] *n* **1** ornamental staff as symbol of royal power. **2** royal dignity.

sched·ule [SKEJ-uul] *n* **1** plan of procedure for a project. **2** list. **3** timetable. ◆ *vt* **-uled, -ul·ing 4** enter in schedule. **5** plan to occur at certain time. **on schedule** on time.

scho·ma [SKEE-mə] *n, pl* **-ma·ta** [-mə-tə] **-mas** overall plan or diagram. **sche·mat'ic** *adj* presented as plan or diagram. **sche·ma·tize** [-tīz] *v* **-tized, -tiz·ing**

scheme [skeem] *n* **1** plan, design. **2** project. **3** outline. ◆ *v* **schemed, schem·ing 4** devise, plan, esp. in underhand manner. **schem'er** *n*

scher·zo [SKERT-soh] *n Mus.* light playful composition.

schism [SIZ-əm] *n* (group resulting from) division in political party, church, etc. **schis·mat'ic** *n, adj*

schist [shist] *n* crystalline rock that splits into layers.

schiz·o·phre·ni·a [skit-sə-FREE-nee-ə] *n* mental disorder involving deterioration of, confusion about personality.

schiz·o·phren'ic [-FREN-ik] *adj, n* **schiz'oid** [-soid] *adj* relating to schizophrenia.

schmaltz [shmahlts] *n* excessive sentimentality. **schmaltz'y** *adj* **schmaltz·i·er, schmaltz·i·est**

schnapps [shnops] *n* **1** spirit distilled from potatoes. **2** any strong spirit.

schnit·zel [SHNIT-səl] *n* thin slice of meat, esp. veal.

scholar *n* see SCHOOL¹.

school¹ [skool] *n* **1** institution for teaching children or for giving instruction in any subject. **2** buildings of such institution. **3** group of thinkers, writers, artists, etc. with principles or methods in common. ◆ *vt* **4** educate. **5** bring under control, train. **school'man** *n* medieval philosopher. **schol'ar** [SKOL-ər] *n* **1** learned person. **2** one taught in school. **3** one quick to learn. **schol'ar·ly** *adj* learned, erudite. **schol'ar·ship** *n* **1** learning. **2** prize, grant to student for payment of school or college fees. **scho·las·tic** [skə-LAS-tik] *adj* **1** of schools or scholars, or education. **2** pedantic.

school² *n* large number (of fish, whales, etc.).

——————— THESAURUS ———————

show, display, drama, exhibition, pageant, picture, sight, spectacle **4 = act**, division, episode, part **5 = view**, landscape, panorama, prospect, vista **6 = fuss**, commotion, exhibition, performance, row, tantrum, to-do **7** *Inf* **= world**, arena, business, environment

scenery *n* **1 = landscape**, surroundings, terrain, view, vista **2** *Theatre* **= set**, backdrop, flats, setting, stage set

scenic *adj* **= picturesque**, beautiful, panoramic, spectacular, striking

scent *n* **1 = fragrance**, aroma, bouquet, odor, perfume, smell **2 = trail**, spoor, track ◆ *v* **3 = detect**, discern, nose out, sense, smell, sniff

scented *adj* **= fragrant**, aromatic, odoriferous, perfumed, sweet-smelling

schedule *n* **1 = plan**, agenda, calendar, catalog, inventory, list, program, timetable ◆ *v* **2 = plan**, appoint, arrange, book, organize, program

scheme *n* **1 = plan**, program, project, proposal, strategy, system, tactics **2 = diagram**, blueprint, chart, draft, layout, outline, pattern **3 = plot**, conspiracy, intrigue, maneuver, ploy, ruse, stratagem,

subterfuge ◆ *v* **4 = plan**, lay plans, project, work out **5 = plot**, collude, conspire, intrigue, machinate, maneuver

scheming *adj* **= calculating**, artful, conniving, cunning, sly, tricky, underhand, wily

schism *n* **= division**, breach, break, rift, rupture, separation, split

scholar *n* **1 = intellectual**, academic, savant **2 = student**, disciple, learner, pupil, schoolboy *or* schoolgirl

scholarly *adj* **= learned**, academic, bookish, erudite, intellectual, lettered, scholastic

scholarship *n* **1 = learning**, book-learning, education, erudition, knowledge **2 = bursary**, fellowship

scholastic *adj* **= learned**, academic, lettered, scholarly

school *n* **1 = academy**, college, faculty, institute, institution, seminary **2 = group**, adherents, circle, denomination, devotees, disciples, faction, followers, set ◆ *v* **3 = train**, coach, discipline, drill, educate, instruct, tutor

schooling *n* **1 = teaching**, education, tuition **2 = training**, coaching, drill,

schoon•er [SKOO-nər] n **1** fore-and-aft rigged vessel with two or more masts. **2** tall glass.

schot•tische [SHOT-ish] n **1** kind of dance. **2** music for this.

sci•at•i•ca [sī-AT-i-kə] n **1** neuralgia of hip and thigh. **2** pain in sciatic nerve. **sci•at'ic** adj **1** of the hip. **2** of sciatica.

sci•ence [SĪ-əns] n **1** systematic study and knowledge of natural or physical phenomena. **2** any branch of study concerned with observed material facts. **sci•en•tif'ic** adj **1** of the principles of science. **2** systematic. **sci•en•tif'i•cal•ly** adv **sci•en•tist** n one versed in natural sciences. **science fiction** stories set in the future making imaginative use of scientific knowledge.

scim•i•tar [SIM-i-tər] n oriental curved sword.

scin•til•late [SIN-tl-ayt] vi **-lat•ed, -lat•ing 1** sparkle. **2** be animated, witty, clever. **scin•til•la'tion** n

sci•on [SĪ-ən] n **1** descendant, heir. **2** slip for grafting.

scis•sors [SIZ-ərs] pl n cutting instrument with two crossed pivoted blades.

scle•ro•sis [skli-ROH-sis] n, pl **-ses** [-seez] a hardening of bodily organs, tissues, etc. **scle•rot'ic** [-ROT-ik] adj

scoff [skof] vt **1** express derision for. ♦ n **2** derision. **3** mocking words. **scoff'er** n

scold [skohld] v **1** find fault. **2** reprimand, be angry with. ♦ n **3** someone who does this. **scold'ing** n

sconce [skons] n bracket candlestick on wall.

scone [skohn] n small plain biscuit baked on griddle or in oven.

scoop [skoop] n **1** small shovel-like tool for ladling, hollowing out, etc. **2** inf exclusive news item. **3** inf information. ♦ vt **4** ladle out. **5** hollow out, rake in with scoop. **6** make sudden profit. **7** beat (rival newspaper, etc.).

scoot [skoot] vi inf move off quickly. **scoot'er** n **1** child's vehicle propelled by pushing on ground with one foot. **2** light motorcycle (also **motor scooter**).

scope [skohp] n **1** range of activity or application. **2** room, opportunity.

scorch [skorch] v **1** burn, be burned, on surface. **2** parch. **3** shrivel. **4** wither. ♦ n **5** slight burn. **scorch'er** n inf very hot day.

score [skor] n **1** points gained in game, competition. **2** group of 20. **3** musical notation. **4** mark or notch, esp. to keep tally. **5** reason, account. **6** grievance. ♦ pl **7** lots. ♦ v **scored, scor•ing** ♦ vt **8** gain points in game. **9** mark. **10** cross out. **11** arrange music (for). ♦ vi **12** keep tally of points. **13** succeed.

instruction

science n **1** = **discipline**, body of knowledge, branch of knowledge **2** = **skill**, art, technique

scientific adj = **systematic**, accurate, controlled, exact, mathematical, precise

scientist n = **inventor**, technophile

scintillating adj = **brilliant**, animated, bright, dazzling, exciting, glittering, lively, sparkling, stimulating

scoff[1] v = **scorn**, belittle, deride, despise, jeer, knock (inf), laugh at, mock, pooh-pooh, ridicule, sneer

scoff[2] v = **gobble (up)**, bolt, devour, gorge oneself on, gulp down, guzzle, wolf

scold v = **reprimand**, berate, castigate, censure, chew out (sl), find fault with, lecture, rebuke, reproach, reprove, tell off (inf), upbraid

scolding n = **rebuke**, lecture, row, telling-off (inf)

scoop n **1** = **ladle**, dipper, spoon **2** = **exclusive**, exposé, revelation, sensation ♦ v

3 (often with up) = **lift**, gather up, pick up, take up **4** (often with out) = **hollow**, bail, dig, empty, excavate, gouge, shovel

scope n **1** = **opportunity**, freedom, latitude, liberty, room, space **2** = **range**, area, capacity, orbit, outlook, reach, span, sphere

scorch v = **burn**, parch, roast, sear, shrivel, singe, wither

scorching adj = **burning**, baking, boiling, fiery, flaming, red-hot, roasting, searing

score n **1** = **points**, grade, mark, outcome, record, result, total **2** = **grounds**, basis, cause, ground, reason **3** = **grievance**, grudge, injury, injustice, wrong **4 scores** = **lots**, hundreds, masses, millions, multitudes, myriads, swarms ♦ v **5** = **gain**, achieve, chalk up (inf), make, notch up (inf), win **6** = **keep count**, count, record, register, tally **7** = **cut**, deface, gouge, graze, mark, scrape, scratch, slash **8** (with out or through) = **cross out**, cancel, delete, obliterate, strike out **9** Mus = **arrange**,

scorn [skorn] n 1 contempt, derision. ◆ vt 2 despise. **scorn'ful** [-fəl] adj derisive. **scorn'ful·ly** adv

scor·pi·on [SKOR-pee-ən] n small lobster-shaped animal with sting at end of jointed tail.

Scot [skot] n native of Scotland. **Scot'tish** adj **Scotch** n whisky distilled in Scotland. **Scots** adj 1 Scottish. ◆ n 2 English dialect spoken in Scotland. **Scots'man** [-mən], **Scots'wom·an** n

scotch [skoch] vt put an end to.

scot-free [skot-free] adj without harm or loss.

scoun·drel [SKOWN-drəl] n villain, blackguard. **scoun'drel·ly** adj

scour¹ [skowr] vt 1 clean, polish by rubbing. 2 clear or flush out.

scour² v move rapidly along or over (territory) in search of something.

scourge [skurj] n 1 whip, lash. 2 severe affliction. 3 pest. 4 calamity. ◆ vt scourged, scourg·ing 5 flog. 6 punish severely.

scout [skowt] n 1 one sent out to reconnoitre. 2 (S-) member of organization for young people which aims to develop character and responsibility. ◆ vi 3 go out, act as scout. 4 reconnoiter. **scout'mas·ter** n leader of troop of Boy Scouts.

scow [skow] n unpowered barge.

scowl [skowl] vi 1 frown gloomily or sullenly. ◆ n 2 angry or gloomy expression.

scrab·ble [SKRAB-əl] v -bled, -bling 1 scrape at with hands, claws in disorderly manner. ◆ n 2 (S-) ® board game in which words are formed by letter tiles.

scrag [skrag] n 1 lean person or animal. 2 lean end of a neck of mutton **scrag'gy** adj -gi·er, -gi·est thin, bony.

scrag·gly [SKRAG-lee] adj -gli·er, -gli·est untidy.

scram¹ [skram] v scrammed, scram·ming inf go away hastily, get out.

scram² n emergency shutdown of nuclear reactor. ◆ v scrammed, scram·ming

scram·ble [SKRAM-bəl] v -bled, -bling ◆ vi 1 move along or up by crawling, climbing, etc. 2 struggle with others (for). 3 (of aircraft, aircrew) take off hurriedly. ◆ vt 4 mix up. 5 cook (eggs) beaten up with milk. 6 render (speech) unintelligible by electronic means. ◆ n 7 scrambling. 8 rough climb. 9 disorderly proceeding. 10 emergency takeoff of military aircraft.

scrap [skrap] n 1 small piece or fragment. 2 leftover material. 3 inf fight. ◆ v scrapped, scrap·ping 4 break up, discard as useless. 5 fight. **scrap'py** adj -pi·er, -pi·est 1 unequal in quality. 2 badly finished. **scrap'book** [-buuk] n book in which newspaper clippings, etc. are kept.

adapt, orchestrate, set

scorn n 1 = **contempt**, derision, disdain, disparagement, mockery, sarcasm ◆ v 2 = **despise**, be above, deride, disdain, flout, reject, scoff at, slight, spurn

scornful adj = **contemptuous**, derisive, disdainful, haughty, jeering, mocking, sarcastic, sardonic, scathing, scoffing, sneering

scoundrel n = **rogue**, bastard (offens), good-for-nothing, heel (sl), miscreant, rascal, reprobate, scamp, swine, villain

scour¹ v = **rub**, abrade, buff, clean, polish, scrub, wash

scour² v = **search**, beat, comb, hunt, ransack

scourge n 1 = **affliction**, bane, curse, infliction, misfortune, pest, plague, terror, torment 2 = **whip**, cat, lash, strap, switch, thong ◆ v 3 = **afflict**, curse, plague, terrorize, torment 4 = **whip**, beat, cane, flog, horsewhip, lash, thrash

scout n 1 = **vanguard**, advance guard,

lookout, outrider, precursor, reconnoiterer ◆ v 2 = **reconnoiter**, investigate, observe, probe, spy, survey, watch

scowl v 1 = **glower**, frown, lour or lower ◆ n 2 = **glower**, black look, dirty look, frown

scrabble v = **scrape**, claw, scramble, scratch

scraggy adj = **scrawny**, angular, bony, lean, skinny

scram v = **go away**, abscond, beat it (sl), clear off (inf), get lost (inf), leave, make oneself scarce (inf), make tracks, vamoose (sl)

scramble v 1 = **struggle**, climb, crawl, scrabble, swarm 2 = **strive**, contend, jostle, push, run, rush, vie ◆ n 3 = **climb**, trek 4 = **struggle**, commotion, competition, confusion, melee or mêlée, race, rush, tussle

scrap¹ n 1 = **piece**, bit, crumb, fragment, grain, morsel, part, particle, portion, sliver, snippet 2 = **waste**, junk, off cuts 3 scraps = **leftovers**, bits, leavings, remains ◆ v 4 =

scrape [skrayp] *vt* **scraped, scrap·ing 1** rub with something sharp. **2** clean, smooth thus. **3** grate. **4** scratch. **5** rub with harsh noise. ◆ *n* **6** act, sound of scraping. **7** awkward situation, esp. as result of escapade. **scrap'er** *n* **1** instrument for scraping. **2** contrivance on which mud, etc. is scraped from shoes.

scratch [skrach] *vt* **1** score, make narrow surface wound with claws, nails, or anything pointed. **2** make marks on with pointed instruments. **3** scrape (skin) with nails to relieve itching. **4** remove, withdraw from list, race, etc. ◆ *vi* **5** use claws or nails, esp. to relieve itching. ◆ *n* **6** wound, mark or sound made by scratching. **7** line or starting point. ◆ *adj* **8** got together at short notice. **9** impromptu. **10** *Golf* without any allowance. **scratch'y** *adj* **scratch·i·er, scratch·i·est scratch hit** *Baseball* weak hit barely enabling batter to reach first base.

scrawl [skrawl] *vt* **1** write, draw untidily. ◆ *n* **2** thing scrawled. **3** careless writing.

scrawn•y [SKRAW-nee] *adj* **scrawn·i·er, scrawn·i·est** thin, bony.

scream [skreem] *vi* **1** utter piercing cry, esp. of fear, pain, etc. **2** be very obvious. ◆ *vt* **3** utter in a scream. ◆ *n* **4** shrill, piercing cry. **5** *inf* very funny person or thing.

scree [skree] *n* **1** loose shifting stones. **2** slope covered with these.

screech [skreech] *vi, n* scream.

screed [skreed] *n* **1** long (tedious) letter, passage or speech. **2** thin layer of cement. **3** in masonry, board used to make level.

screen [skreen] *n* **1** device to shelter from heat, light, draft, observation, etc. **2** anything used for such purpose. **3** mesh over doors, windows to keep out insects. **4** white or silvered surface on which photographic images are projected. **5** windscreen. **6** wooden or stone partition in church. ◆ *vt* **7** shelter, hide. **8** protect from detection. **9** show (film). **10** scrutinize. **11** examine (group of people) for presence of disease, weapons, etc. **12** examine for political motives. **13** *Electricity* protect from stray electric or magnetic fields. **screen saver** *Computers* software that produces changing images on a monitor when the computer is operating but idle. **the screen** motion pictures generally.

screw [skroo] *n* **1** (nail-like device or cylinder with) spiral thread cut to engage similar thread or to bore into material (wood, etc.) to pin or fasten. **2** anything resembling a screw in shape, esp. in spiral form. **3** propeller. **4** twist. ◆ *vt* **5** fasten with screw. **6** twist around. **7** extort. **screw'y** *adj* **screw·i·er, screw·i·est** *sl* crazy, eccentric. **screw'driv·er** *n* **1** tool for turning screws. **2** drink of vodka and orange juice. **screw up** *sl* bungle, distort.

scrib•ble [SKRIB-əl] *v* **-bled, -bling 1** write,

discard, abandon, ditch (*sl*), drop, jettison, throw away or out, write off

scrap² *Inf n* **1 = fight**, argument, battle, disagreement, dispute, quarrel, row, squabble, wrangle ◆ *v* **2 = fight**, argue, row, squabble, wrangle

scrape *v* **1 = graze**, bark, rub, scratch, scuff, skin **2 = rub**, clean, erase, remove, scour **3 = grate**, grind, rasp, scratch, squeak **4 = scrimp**, pinch, save, skimp, stint **5 scrape through = get by** (*inf*), just make it, struggle ◆ *n* **6** *Inf* **= predicament**, awkward situation, difficulty, dilemma, fix (*inf*), mess, plight, tight spot

scrapheap *n* **on the scrapheap = discarded**, ditched (*sl*), jettisoned, put out to pasture (*inf*), redundant

scrappy *adj* **= fragmentary**, bitty, disjointed, incomplete, piecemeal, sketchy, thrown together

scratch *v* **1 = mark**, claw, cut, damage, etch, grate, graze, lacerate, score, scrape

2 = withdraw, abolish, call off, cancel, delete, eliminate, erase, pull out ◆ *n* **3 = mark**, blemish, claw mark, gash, graze, laceration, scrape **4 up to scratch = adequate**, acceptable, satisfactory, sufficient, up to standard ◆ *adj* **5 = improvised**, impromptu, rough-and-ready

scrawl *v* **= scribble**, doodle, squiggle, writing

scrawny *adj* **= thin**, bony, gaunt, lean, scraggy, skin-and-bones (*inf*), skinny, undernourished

scream *v* **1 = cry**, bawl, screech, shriek, yell ◆ *n* **2 = cry**, howl, screech, shriek, yell, yelp

screech *n, v* **= cry**, scream, shriek

screen *n* **1 = cover**, awning, canopy, cloak, guard, partition, room divider, shade, shelter, shield **2 = mesh**, net ◆ *v* **3 = cover**, cloak, conceal, hide, mask, shade, veil **4 = protect**, defend, guard, shelter, shield **5 = vet**, evaluate, examine, filter, gauge, scan, sift, sort **6 = broadcast**, present, put on, draw carelessly. **2** make meaningless marks with pen or pencil. ♦ *n* **3** something scribbled.

scribe [skrīb] *n* **1** writer. **2** copyist. ♦ *v* **scribed, scrib·ing 3** scratch a line with pointed instrument.

scrim·mage [SKRIM-ij] *n* **1** scuffle. **2** *Football* a play. ♦ *v* **-maged, -mag·ing 3** engage in scrimmage.

scrimp [skrimp] *vt* **1** make too small or short. **2** treat meanly. **scrimp'y** *adj* **scrimp·i·er, scrimp·i·est**

scrip [skrip] *n* **1** written certificate esp. of holding fractional share of stock. **2** paper certificates issued in place of money.

script [skript] *n* (system or style of) handwriting. **1** written characters. **2** written text of film, play, radio or television program. ♦ *vt* **3** write a script.

scrip·ture [SKRIP-chər] *n* **1** sacred writings. **2** (S-) the Bible. **scrip'tur·al** *adj*

scrof·u·la [SKROF-yə-lə] *n* tuberculosis of lymphatic glands, esp. of neck. **scrof'u·lous** [-ləs] *adj*

scroll [skrohl] *n* **1** roll of parchment or paper. **2** list. **3** ornament shaped thus. ♦ *v* **4** *Computers.* move (text) up or down on a VDU screen.

scro·tum [SKROH-təm] *n, pl* **-tums** pouch containing testicles.

scrounge [skrownj] *v* **scrounged, scroung·ing** get without cost, by begging. **scroung'er** *n*

scrub¹ [skrub] *vt* **scrubbed, scrub·bing 1** clean with hard brush and water. **2** scour.

3 *sl* cancel, get rid of. ♦ *n* **4** scrubbing.

scrub² *n* **1** stunted trees. **2** brushwood. **scrub'by** *adj* **-bi·er, -bi·est 1** covered with scrub. **2** stunted. **3** shabby.

scruff [skruf] *n* nape (of neck).

scrum [skrum] *n* *Rugby* restarting of play in which opposing packs of forwards push against each other to gain possession of the ball.

scrunch [skrunch] *v* **1** crumple or crunch or be crumpled or crunched. ♦ *n* **2** act or sound of scrunching. **scrun'chie** [SKRUNCH-ee] *n* loop of elastic covered loosely with fabric, used to hold the hair in a ponytail.

scru·ple [SKROO-pəl] *n* **1** doubt or hesitation about what is morally right. **2** weight of 20 grains. ♦ *vi* **-pled, -pling 3** hesitate. **scru'pu·lous** [-pyə-ləs] *adj* **1** extremely conscientious. **2** thorough, attentive to small points.

scru·ti·ny [SKROOT-n-ee] *n, pl* **-nies 1** close examination. **2** critical investigation. **3** searching look. **scru'ti·nize** *vt* **-nized, -niz·ing** examine closely.

scu·ba [SKOO-bə] *n, adj* (relating to) self-contained underwater breathing apparatus.

scud [skud] *vi* **scud·ded, scud·ding 1** run fast. **2** run before wind.

scuff [skuf] *vi* **1** drag, scrape with feet in walking. ♦ *vt* **2** scrape with feet. **3** scratch (something) by scraping. ♦ *n* **4** act, sound of scuffing. ♦ *pl* **5** thong sandals. **scuffed** *adj* (of shoes) scraped or slightly grazed.

——————— THESAURUS ———————

show

screw *v* **1** = **turn**, tighten, twist **2** *Inf* (often with *out of*) = **extort**, extract, wrest, wring

screw up *v* **1** *Inf* = **bungle**, botch, make a mess of (*sl*), mess up, mishandle, spoil **2** = **distort**, contort, pucker, wrinkle

screwy *adj* = **crazy**, crackpot (*inf*), eccentric, loopy (*inf*), nutty (*sl*), odd, off-the-wall (*sl*), out to lunch (*inf*), weird

scribble *v* = **scrawl**, dash off, jot, write

scribe *n* = **copyist**, amanuensis, writer

scrimp *v* = **economize**, be frugal, save, scrape, skimp, stint, tighten one's belt

script *n* **1** = **text**, book, copy, dialogue, libretto, lines, words **2** = **handwriting**, calligraphy, penmanship, writing

Scripture *n* = **The Bible**, Holy Bible, Holy Scripture, Holy Writ, The Good Book, The Gospels, The Scriptures

scrounge *v* *Inf* = **cadge**, beg, bum (*inf*), freeload (*sl*), sponge (*inf*)

scrounger *adj* = **cadger**, freeloader (*sl*), parasite, sponger (*inf*)

scrub *v* = **scour**, clean, cleanse, rub

scruple *n* **1** = **misgiving**, compunction, doubt, hesitation, qualm, reluctance, second thoughts, uneasiness ♦ *v* **2** = **have misgivings about**, demur, doubt, have qualms about, hesitate, think twice about

scrupulous *adj* **1** = **moral**, conscientious, honorable, principled, upright **2** = **careful**, exact, fastidious, meticulous, precise, punctilious, rigorous, strict

scrutinize *v* = **examine**, explore, inspect, investigate, peruse, pore over, probe, scan, search, study

scrutiny *n* = **examination**, analysis, exploration, inspection, investigation,

scuf·fle [SKUF-əl] *vi* **-fled, -fling 1** fight in disorderly manner. **2** shuffle. ◆ *n*

scull [skul] *n* **1** oar used in stern of boat. **2** short oar used in pairs. ◆ *v* **3** propel, move by means of scull(s).

scul·ler·y [SKUL-ə-ree] *n, pl* **-ler·ies** place for washing dishes, etc. **scul·lion** [SKUL-yən] *n* **1** despicable person. **2** kitchen servant doing menial work.

sculp·ture [SKULP-chər] *n* **1** art of forming figures in relief or solid. **2** product of this art. ◆ *vt* **-tured, -tur·ing 3** represent by sculpture. **sculpt** *v* **sculp'tur·al** *adj* with qualities proper to sculpture. **sculp·tor, sculp'tress** [-tris] *n*

scum [skum] *n* **1** froth or other floating matter on liquid. **2** waste part of anything. **3** vile person(s) or thing(s). **scum'my** *adj* **-mi·er, -mi·est**

scup·per [SKUP-ər] *n* hole in ship's side level with deck to carry off water.

scurf [skurf] *n* flaky matter on scalp, dandruff. **scurf'y** *adj* **scurf·i·er, scurf·i·est**

scur·ril·ous [SKUR-ə-ləs] *adj* coarse, indecently abusive. **scur·ril·i·ty** [skə-RIL-i-tee] *n, pl* **-ties**

scur·ry [SKUR-ee] *vi* **-ried, -ry·ing 1** run hastily. ◆ *n, pl* **-ries 2** bustling haste. **3** flurry.

scur·vy [SKUR-vee] *n* **1** disease caused by lack of vitamin C. ◆ *adj* **-vi·er, -vi·est 2** afflicted with the disease. **3** mean, contemptible.

scut·tle¹ [SKUT-l] *n* fireside container for coal.

scuttle² *vi* **-tled, -tling 1** rush away. **2** run hurriedly. ◆ *n*

scuttle³ *vt* **-tled, -tling 1** make hole in ship to sink it. **2** abandon, cause to be abandoned.

scut·work [SKUT-wurk] *n inf* menial work.

scythe [sīth] *n* **1** manual implement with long curved blade for cutting grass, grain. ◆ *vt* **scythed, scyth·ing 2** cut with scythe.

Se *Chem.* selenium.

sea [see] *n* **1** mass of salt water covering greater part of Earth. **2** broad tract of this. **3** waves. **4** swell. **5** large quantity. **6** vast expanse. **sea'board** [-bord] *n* coast. **sea'far·ing** [-fair-ing] *adj* occupied in sea voyages. **sea horse** fish with bony plated body and horselike head. **sea lion** kind of large seal. **sea'man** [-mən] *n* sailor. **sea'sick·ness** *n* nausea caused by motion of ship. **sea'sick** *adj* **sea urchin** marine animal, echinus. **sea'weed** *n* plant growing in sea. **sea'wor·thy** [-wurth-ee] *adj* **-thi·er, -thi·est** in fit condition to put to sea.

seal¹ [seel] *n* **1** piece of metal or stone engraved with device for impression on wax, etc. **2** impression thus made (on letters, etc.). **3** device, material preventing passage of water, air, oil, etc. (also **seal'er**) *vt* **4** affix seal to ratify, authorize. **5** mark with stamp as evidence of some quality. **6** keep close or secret. **7** settle. **8** make watertight, airtight, etc.

seal² *n* **1** amphibious furred carnivorous mammal with flippers as limbs. ◆ *vi* **2** hunt seals. **seal'er** *n* person or ship engaged in sealing. **seal'skin** *n* skin, fur of seals.

seam [seem] *n* **1** line of junction of two edges, e.g. of two pieces of cloth, or two planks. **2** thin layer, stratum. ◆ *vt* **3** mark with furrows or wrinkles. **seam'less** [-lis] *adj* **seam'y** *adj* **seam·i·er, seam·i·est 1** sordid. **2** marked with seams. **seam'stress**

---

perusal, search, study

scuffle *v* **1** = **fight**, clash, grapple, jostle, struggle, tussle ◆ *n* **2** = **fight**, brawl, commotion, disturbance, fray, scrimmage, skirmish, tussle

sculpture *v* = **sculpt**, carve, chisel, fashion, form, hew, model, mold, shape

scum *n* **1** = **impurities**, dross, film, froth **2** = **rabble**, dregs of society, riffraff, trash

scurrilous *adj* = **slanderous**, abusive, defamatory, insulting, scandalous, vituperative

scurry *v* **1** = **hurry**, dart, dash, race, scamper, scoot, scuttle, sprint ◆ *n* **2** = **flurry**, scampering, whirl

scuttle *v* = **run**, bustle, hasten, hurry, rush, scamper, scoot, scurry

sea *n* **1** = **ocean**, main, the deep, the waves **2** = **expanse**, abundance, mass, multitude, plethora, profusion **3** at sea = **bewildered**, baffled, confused, lost, mystified, puzzled

seafaring *adj* = **nautical**, marine, maritime, naval

seal *n* **1** = **authentication**, confirmation, imprimatur, insignia, ratification, stamp ◆ *v* **2** = **close**, bung, enclose, fasten, plug, shut, stop, stopper, stop up **3** = **authenticate**, confirm, ratify, stamp, validate **4** = **settle**, clinch, conclude, consummate, finalize **5** seal off = **isolate**,

[-stris] n sewing woman.

sé•ance [SAY-ahns] n meeting at which spiritualists attempt to communicate with the dead.

sear [seer] vt 1 scorch, brand with hot iron. 2 deaden.

search [surch] v 1 look over or through to find something. 2 probe into, examine. ◆ n 3 act of searching. 4 quest. **search'ing** adj 1 keen. 2 thorough. 3 severe. **search engine** Computers Internet service enabling users to search for items of interest online. **search'light** n powerful electric light with concentrated beam.

sea•son [SEE-zən] n 1 one of four divisions of year associated with type of weather and stage of agriculture. 2 period during which this happens, grows, is active, etc. 3 proper time. ◆ vt 4 flavor with salt, herbs, etc. 5 make reliable or ready for use. 6 make experienced. **sea'son•a•ble** adj 1 appropriate for the season. 2 opportune. 3 fit. **sea'son•al** [-əl] adj depending on, varying with seasons. **sea'son•ing** n flavoring. **in season** (of an animal) in heat. **season ticket** one for series of events within a certain time.

seat [seet] n 1 thing for sitting on. 2 buttocks. 3 base. 4 right to sit (e.g. in legislature, etc.). 5 place where something

is located, centered. 6 locality of disease, trouble, etc. 7 country house. ◆ vt 8 make to sit. 9 provide sitting accommodation for. 10 install firmly.

se•ba•ceous [si-BAY-shəs] adj 1 of, pert. to fat. 2 secreting fat, oil.

se•cant [SEE-kant] n Math. 1 (secant of an angle) reciprocal of its cosine. 2 line that intersects a curve.

se•cede [si-SEED] vi -ced•ed, -ced•ing withdraw formally from federation, union, etc. **se•ces'sion** [-SESH-ən] n

se•clude [si-KLOOD] vt -clud•ed, -clud•ing guard from, remove from sight, view, contact with others. **secluded** adj 1 remote. 2 private. **se•clu'sion** [-KLOO-zhən] n

sec•ond [SEK-ənd] adj 1 next after first. 2 alternate, additional. 3 of lower quality. ◆ n 4 person or thing coming second. 5 attendant. 6 sixtieth part of minute. 7 SI unit of time. 8 moment. ◆ pl 9 inferior goods. ◆ vt 10 support. 11 support (motion in meeting) so that discussion may be in order. **sec•ond•hand'** adj 1 bought after use by another. 2 not original. **second sight** faculty of seeing events before they occur.

sec•ond•ar•y [SEK-ən-der-ee] adj 1 subsidiary, of less importance. 2 developed

put out of bounds, quarantine, segregate

seam n 1 = joint, closure 2 = layer, lode, stratum, vein 3 = ridge, furrow, line, wrinkle

sear v = scorch, burn, sizzle

search v 1 = look, comb, examine, explore, hunt, inspect, investigate, ransack, scour, scrutinize ◆ n 2 = look, examination, exploration, hunt, inspection, investigation, pursuit, quest

searching adj = keen, close, intent, penetrating, piercing, probing, quizzical, sharp

season n 1 = period, spell, term, time ◆ v 2 = flavor, enliven, pep up, salt, spice

seasonable adj = appropriate, convenient, fit, opportune, providential, suitable, timely, well-timed

seasoned adj = experienced, hardened, practiced, time-served, veteran

seasoning n = flavoring, condiment, dressing, relish, salt and pepper, sauce, spice

seat n 1 = chair, bench, pew, settle, stall,

stool 2 = center, capital, heart, hub, place, site, situation, source 3 = residence, abode, ancestral hall, house, mansion 4 = membership, chair, constituency, incumbency, place ◆ v 5 = sit, fix, install, locate, place, set, settle 6 = hold, accommodate, cater for, contain, sit, take

seating n = accommodation, chairs, places, room, seats

secede v = withdraw, break with, leave, pull out, quit, resign, split from

secluded adj = private, cloistered, cut off, isolated, lonely, out-of-the-way, sheltered, solitary

seclusion n = privacy, isolation, shelter, solitude

second¹ adj 1 = next, following, subsequent, succeeding 2 = additional, alternative, extra, further, other 3 = inferior, lesser, lower, secondary, subordinate ◆ n 4 = supporter, assistant, backer, helper ◆ v 5 = support, approve, assist, back, endorse, go along with

second² n = moment, flash, instant, jiffy

from, or dependent on, something else. **3** *Education* after primary stage. **sec'ond·ar·i·ly** *adv*

se·cret [SEE-krit] *adj* **1** kept, meant to be kept from knowledge of others. **2** hidden. **3** private. ◆ *n* **4** thing kept secret. **se'cre·cy** [-krə-see] *n, pl* **-cies** keeping or being kept secret. **se'cre·tive** *adj* **1** given to having secrets. **2** uncommunicative. **3** reticent. **se'cre·tive·ness** [-tiv-nis] *n*

sec·re·tar·y [SEK-ri-ter-ee] *n, pl* **-tar·ies 1** one employed by individual or organization to deal with papers and correspondence, keep records, prepare business, etc. **2** member of presidential cabinet. **sec·re·tar'i·al** [-TAIR-ee-əl] *adj* **sec·re·tar'i·at** [-ət] *n* **1** body of secretaries. **2** building occupied by secretarial staff.

se·crete [si-KREET] *vt* **-cret·ed, -cret·ing 1** hide. **2** conceal. **3** (of gland, etc.) collect and supply particular substance in body. **se·cre'tion** *n*

sect [sekt] *n* **1** group of people (within religious body, etc.) with common interest. **2** faction. **sec·tar'i·an** [-TAIR-ee-ən] *adj* **1** of a sect. **2** narrow-minded.

sec·tion [SEK-shən] *n* **1** part cut off. **2** division. **3** portion. **4** distinct part of city, country, people, etc. **5** cutting. **6** drawing of anything as if cut through. **sec'tion·al** *adj*

sec·tor [SEK-tər] *n* **1** part or subdivision. **2** part of circle enclosed by two radii and the arc they cut off.

sec·u·lar [SEK-yə-lər] *adj* **1** worldly. **2** lay, not religious. **3** not monastic. **4** lasting for, or occurring once in, an age. **5** centuries old. **sec'u·lar·ism** *n* **sec'u·lar·ist** *n* one who believes that religion should have no place in civil affairs. **sec·u·lar·i·za'tion** *n* **sec'u·lar·ize** *vt* **-ized, -iz·ing** transfer from religious to lay possession or use.

se·cure [si-KYOOR] *adj* **-cur·er, -cur·est 1** safe. **2** free from fear, anxiety. **3** firmly fixed. **4** certain. **5** sure, confident. ◆ *vt* **-cured, -cur·ing 6** gain possession of. **7** make safe. **8** free (creditor) from risk of loss. **9** make firm. **se·cur'i·ty** *n, pl* **-ties** state of safety. **1** protection. **2** that which secures. **3** assurance. **4** anything given as bond, caution or pledge. **5** one who becomes surety for another.

se·dan [si-DAN] *n* enclosed automobile

———————— THESAURUS ————————

(*inf*), minute, sec (*inf*), trice
secondary *adj* **1 = subordinate**, inferior, lesser, lower, minor, unimportant **2 = resultant**, contingent, derived, indirect **3 = backup**, auxiliary, fall-back, reserve, subsidiary, supporting
second-class *adj* **= inferior**, indifferent, mediocre, second-best, second-rate, undistinguished, uninspiring
second-hand *adj* **1 = used**, hand-me-down (*inf*), nearly new ◆ *adv* **2 = indirectly**
second in command *n* **= deputy**, number two, right-hand man
secondly *adv* **= next**, in the second place, second
second-rate *adj* **= inferior**, low-grade, low-quality, mediocre, poor, rubbishy, shoddy, substandard, tacky (*inf*), tawdry, two-bit (*sl*)
secrecy *n* **1 = mystery**, concealment, confidentiality, privacy, silence **2 = secretiveness**, clandestineness, covertness, furtiveness, stealth
secret *adj* **1 = concealed**, close, disguised, furtive, hidden, undercover, underground, undisclosed, unknown, unrevealed **2 =**

stealthy, secretive, sly, underhand **3 = mysterious**, abstruse, arcane, clandestine, cryptic, occult ◆ *n* **4 = mystery**, code, enigma, key **5 in secret = secretly**, slyly, surreptitiously
secrete[1] *v* **= give off**, emanate, emit, exude
secrete[2] *v* **= hide**, cache, conceal, harbor, stash (*inf*), stow
secretive *adj* **= reticent**, close, deep, reserved, tight-lipped, uncommunicative
secretly *adv* **= in secret**, clandestinely, covertly, furtively, privately, quietly, stealthily, surreptitiously
sect *n* **= group**, camp, denomination, division, faction, party, schism
sectarian *adj* **1 = narrow-minded**, bigoted, doctrinaire, dogmatic, factional, fanatical, limited, parochial, partisan ◆ *n* **2 = bigot**, dogmatist, extremist, fanatic, partisan, zealot
section *n* **1 = part**, division, fraction, installment, passage, piece, portion, segment, slice **2 = district**, area, region, sector, zone
sector *n* **= part**, area, district, division, quarter, region, zone
secular *adj* **= worldly**, civil, earthly, lay,

body with two or four doors. **sedan chair** *Hist.* closed chair for one person, carried on poles by bearers.

se·date¹ [si-DAYT] *adj* calm, collected, serious.

sedate² *vt* **-dat·ed, -dat·ing** make calm by sedative. **se·da·tion** *n* **sed·a·tive** *adj* **1** having soothing or calming effect. ♦ *n* **2** sedative drug.

sed·on·ta·ry [SED-n-ter-ee] *adj* **1** done sitting down. **2** sitting much.

Se·der [SAY-dər] *n* ritual for the first or first two nights of Passover.

sed·i·ment [SED-ə-mənt] *n* **1** matter that settles to the bottom of liquid. **2** dregs, lees. **sed·i·men'ta·ry** *adj*

se·di·tion [si-DISH-ən] *n* speech or action threatening authority of a state. **se·di'tious** [-shəs] *adj*

se·duce [SI-doos] *vt* **-duced, -duc·ing 1** persuade to commit some (wrong) deed, esp. sexual intercourse. **2** tempt. **3** attract. **se·duc'er, se·duc'tress** *n* **se·duc'tion** [-DUK-shən] *n* **se·duc'tive** *adj* **1** alluring. **2**

winning.

sed·u·lous [SEJ-ə-ləs] *adj* **1** diligent. **2** industrious. **3** persevering, persistent. **se·du·li·ty** [si-DOO-li-tee] *n*

see¹ *v* **saw, seen, see·ing 1** perceive with eyes or mentally. **2** observe. **3** watch. **4** find out. **5** reflect. **6** come to know. **7** interview. **8** make sure. **9** accompany. **10** perceive. **11** consider. **12** understand. **seeing** *conj* **1** since. **2** in view of the fact that.

see² *n* diocese, office, or jurisdiction of bishop.

seed *n* **1** reproductive germs of plants. **2** one grain of this. **3** such grains saved or used for sowing. **4** origin. **5** sperm. **6** offspring. ♦ *vt* **7** sow with seed. **8** arrange draw for tennis or other tournament, so that best players do not meet in early rounds. ♦ *vi* **9** produce seed. **seed'ling** *n* young plant raised from seed. **seed'y** *adj* **seed·i·er, seed·i·est 1** shabby. **2** gone to seed. **3** unwell, ill.

seek *v* **sought** [sawt], **seek·ing 1** make

nonspiritual, temporal

secure *adj* **1** = **safe**, immune, protected, unassailable **2** = **sure**, assured, certain, confident, easy, reassured **3** = **fixed**, fast, fastened, firm, immovable, stable, steady ♦ *v* **4** = **obtain**, acquire, gain, get, procure, score (*sl*) **5** = **fasten**, attach, bolt, chain, fix, lock, make fast, tie up

security *n* **1** = **precautions**, defense, protection, safeguards, safety measures **2** = **safety**, care, custody, refuge, safekeeping, sanctuary **3** = **sureness**, assurance, certainty, confidence, conviction, positiveness, reliance **4** = **pledge**, collateral, gage, guarantee, hostage, insurance, pawn, surety

sedate *adj* = **calm**, collected, composed, cool, dignified, serene, tranquil

sedative *adj* **1** = **calming**, anodyne, relaxing, soothing, tranquilizing ♦ *n* **2** = **tranquilizer**, anodyne, downer *or* down (*sl*)

sedentary *adj* = **inactive**, desk, desk-bound, seated, sitting

sediment *n* = **dregs**, deposit, grounds, lees, residue

sedition *n* = **rabble-rousing**, agitation, incitement to riot, subversion

seditious *adj* = **revolutionary**, dissident, mutinous, rebellious, refractory, subversive

seduce *v* **1** = **corrupt**, debauch, deflower, deprave, dishonor **2** = **tempt**, beguile, deceive, entice, inveigle, lead astray, lure, mislead

seduction *n* **1** = **corruption 2** = **temptation**, enticement, lure, snare

seductive *adj* = **alluring**, attractive, bewitching, enticing, inviting, provocative, tempting

seductress *n* = **temptress**, enchantress, *femme fatale*, siren, succubus, vamp (*inf*)

see¹ *v* **1** = **perceive**, behold, catch sight of, discern, distinguish, espy, glimpse, look, make out, notice, observe, sight, spot, witness **2** = **understand**, appreciate, comprehend, fathom, feel, follow, get, grasp, realize **3** = **find out**, ascertain, determine, discover, learn **4** = **make sure**, ensure, guarantee, make certain, see to it **5** = **consider**, decide, deliberate, reflect, think over **6** = **visit**, confer with, consult, interview, receive, speak to **7** = **go out with**, court, date (*inf*), go steady with (*inf*) **8** = **accompany**, escort, lead, show, usher, walk

seed *n* **1** = **grain**, egg, embryo, germ, kernel, ovum, pip, spore **2** = **origin**, beginning, germ, nucleus, source, start **3** = **offspring**, children, descendants, issue, progeny **4 go** *or* **run to seed** = **decline**, search or inquiry for. **2** search.

seem *vi* **1** appear (to be or to do). **2** look. **3** appear to one's judgment. **seem'ing** *adj* apparent but not real. **seem'ing·ly** *adv*

seem·ly [SEEM-lee] *adj* **-li·er, -li·est** becoming and proper. **seem'li·ness** [-nis] *n*

seen pp. of SEE.

seep *vi* trickle through slowly, as water, ooze.

seer *n* prophet.

seer·suck·er [SEER-suk-ər] *n* light cotton fabric with slightly crinkled surface.

see'saw *n* **1** game in which children sit at opposite ends of plank supported in middle and swing up and down. **2** plank used for this. ♦ *vi* **3** move up and down.

seethe [seeth] *vi* **seethed, seeth·ing 1** boil, foam. **2** be very agitated. **3** be in constant movement (as large crowd, etc.).

seg·ment [SEG-mənt] *n* **1** piece cut off. **2** section. ♦ *v* [SEG-ment] **3** to divide into segments. **seg·men·ta'tion** *n*

seg·re·gate [SEG-ri-gayt] *vt* **-gat·ed, -gat·ing 1** set apart from rest. **2** dissociate. **3** separate. **4** isolate. **seg·re·ga'tion** *n*

se·gue [SAY-gway] *vi* **-gued, -gue·ing 1** proceed from one section or piece of music to another without break. **2** make a transition smoothly e.g. from one topic of conversation to another. ♦ *n*

seis·mic [SIZ-mik] *adj* pert. to earthquakes. **seis'mo·graph** [-mə-graf] *n* instrument to record earthquakes. **seis·mo·log'ic·al** *adj* pert. to seismology. **seis·mol'o·gist** [-MOL-ə-jist] *n* one versed in seismology. **seis·mol'o·gy** *n* science concerned with study of earthquakes.

seize [seez] *v* **seized, seiz·ing** ♦ *vt* **1** grasp. **2** lay hold of. **3** capture. ♦ *vi* **4** in machine, of bearing or piston, to stick tightly through overheating. **seiz·ure** [SEE-zhər] *n* **1** act of taking, esp. by legal writ, as goods. **2** sudden onset of disease.

sel·dom [SEL-dəm] *adv* not often, rarely.

se·lect [si-LEKT] *vt* **1** pick out, choose. ♦ *adj* **2** choice, picked. **3** exclusive. **se·lec'tion** *n* **se·lec'tive** *adj* **se·lec·tiv'i·ty** *n*

se·le·ni·um [si-LEE-nee-əm] *n* nonmetallic element with photoelectric properties.

sel·e·nog·ra·phy [sel-ə-NOG-rə-fee] *n* study of surface of moon.

──────── THESAURUS ────────

decay, degenerate, deteriorate, go downhill (*inf*), go to pot, let oneself go

seedy *Inf adj* = **shabby**, dilapidated, dirty, grubby, mangy, run-down, scuzzy (*sl*), sleazy, squalid, tatty

seeing *conj* = **since**, as, inasmuch as, in view of the fact that

seek *v* **1** = **look for**, be after, follow, hunt, pursue, search for, stalk **2** = **try**, aim, aspire to, attempt, endeavor, essay, strive

seem *v* = **appear**, assume, give the impression, look

seemly *adj* = **fitting**, appropriate, becoming, correct, decent, decorous, fit, proper, suitable

seep *v* = **ooze**, exude, leak, permeate, soak, trickle, well

seer *n* = **prophet**, sibyl, soothsayer

seesaw *v* = **alternate**, fluctuate, oscillate, swing

seethe *v* **1** = **be furious**, be livid, fume, go ballistic (*sl*), rage, see red (*inf*), simmer **2** = **boil**, bubble, fizz, foam, froth

see through *v* **1** = **be undeceived by**, be wise to (*inf*), fathom, not fall for, penetrate **2 see (something) through** = **persevere (with)**, keep at, persist, stick out (*inf*) **3 see (someone) through** = **help out**, stick by, support

segment *n* = **section**, bit, division, part, piece, portion, slice, wedge

segregate *v* = **set apart**, discriminate against, dissociate, isolate, separate

segregation *n* = **separation**, apartheid, discrimination, isolation

seize *v* **1** = **grab**, catch up, clutch, grasp, grip, lay hands on, snatch, take **2** = **confiscate**, appropriate, commandeer, impound, take possession of **3** = **capture**, apprehend, arrest, catch, take captive

seizure *n* **1** = **attack**, convulsion, fit, paroxysm, spasm **2** = **capture**, apprehension, arrest **3** = **taking**, annexation, commandeering, confiscation, grabbing

seldom *adv* = **rarely**, hardly ever, infrequently, not often

select *v* **1** = **choose**, opt for, pick, single out ♦ *adj* **2** = **choice**, excellent, first-class, hand-picked, special, superior, top-notch (*inf*) **3** = **exclusive**, cliquish, elite, privileged

selection *n* **1** = **choice**, choosing, option, pick, preference **2** = **range**, assortment, choice, collection, medley, variety

selective *adj* = **particular**, careful,

self *pron, pl* **selves 1** used reflexively or to express emphasis. ♦ *adj* **2** (of color, etc.) same throughout, uniform. ♦ *n* **3** one's own person or individuality. **self'ish** *adj* **1** concerned unduly over personal profit or pleasure. **2** lacking consideration for others. **3** greedy. **self'ish·ly** *adv* **self'less** [-lis] *adj* **1** having no regard for self. **2** unselfish.

self- *prefix* used with many main words to mean: **1** of oneself or itself. **2** by, to, in, due to, for, or from the self. **3** automatic(ally). **self-ad·dressed'** *adj* addressed to the sender. **self-as·sured'** *adj* confident. **self-cen'tered** *adj* totally preoccupied with one's own concerns. **self-con'fi·dent** *adj* **self-con·tained' 1** containing everything needed, complete. **2** (of an apartment) having its own facilities. **self-con·trol'** *n* ability to control one's feelings and reactions. **self-de·fense'** *n* defending of oneself or one's property. **self-em·ployed'** *adj* earning a living from one's own business. **self-ev'i·dent** *adj* obvious without proof. **self-help'** *n* **1** use of one's own abilities to solve problems. **2** practice of solving one's problems within a group of people with similar problems. **self-in·dul'gent** *adj* tending to indulge

one's desires. **self-in'ter·est** *adj* one's own advantage. **self-rais'ing** *adj* (of flour) containing a raising agent. **self-sat'is·fied** *adj* conceited.

self-con'scious [-KON-shəs] *adj* **1** unduly aware of oneself. **2** conscious of one's acts or states.

self-de·ter·mi·na·tion [-dı-tur-mə-NAY-shən] *n* the right of person or nation to decide for itself.

self-made [-mayd] *adj* having achieved wealth, status, etc. by one's own efforts.

self-pos·sessed [-pə-ZEST] *adj* calm, composed. **self-pos·ses'sion** [-pə-ZESH-ən] *n*

self-re·spect' [-ri-SPEKT] *n* proper sense of one's own dignity and integrity.

self-right'eous [-RĪ-chəs] *adj* smugly sure of one's own virtue.

self·same [-saym] *adj* very same.

self-seek'ing *adj, n* (having) preoccupation with one's own interests.

self-serv'ice [-SUR-vis] *adj, n* (of the serving of oneself in a store or restaurant.

self-suf·fi'cient [-sə-FISH-ənt] *adj* **1** sufficient in itself. **2** relying on one's own powers.

self-will' *n* **1** obstinacy. **2** willfulness. **self-willed'** *adj* headstrong.

discerning, discriminating
self-assurance *n* = **confidence**, assertiveness, positiveness, self-confidence, self-possession
self-centered *adj* = **selfish**, egotistic, narcissistic, self-seeking
self-confidence *n* = **self-assurance**, aplomb, confidence, nerve, poise
self-confident *adj* = **self-assured**, assured, confident, poised, sure of oneself
self-conscious *adj* = **embarrassed**, awkward, bashful, diffident, ill at ease, insecure, nervous, uncomfortable, wired (*sl*)
self-control *n* = **willpower**, restraint, self-discipline, self-restraint
self-esteem *n* = **self-respect**, confidence, faith in oneself, pride, self-assurance, self-regard
self-evident *adj* = **obvious**, clear, incontrovertible, inescapable, undeniable
self-important *adj* = **conceited**, bigheaded, cocky, full of oneself, pompous, swollen-headed
self-indulgence *n* = **intemperance**,

excess, extravagance
selfish *adj* = **self-centered**, egoistic, egoistical, egotist, egotistical, greedy, self-interested, ungenerous
selfless *adj* = **unselfish**, altruistic, generous, self-denying, self-sacrificing
self-possessed *adj* = **self-assured**, collected, confident, cool, poised, unruffled
self-reliant *adj* = **independent**, self-sufficient, self-supporting
self-respect *n* = **pride**, dignity, morale, self-esteem
self-restraint *n* = **self-control**, self-command, self-discipline, willpower
self-righteous *adj* = **sanctimonious**, complacent, holier-than-thou, priggish, self-satisfied, smug, superior
self-sacrifice *n* = **selflessness**, altruism, generosity, self-denial
self-satisfied *adj* = **smug**, complacent, pleased with oneself, self-congratulatory
self-seeking *adj* = **selfish**, careerist, looking out for number one (*inf*), out for what one can get, self-interested,

sell *v* sold, sell·ing 1 hand over for a price. 2 stock, have for sale. 3 make someone accept. 4 find purchasers. 5 *inf* betray, cheat. ◆ *n* 6 *inf* hoax. **sell'er** *n* **sell'out** *n* 1 disposing of completely by selling. 2 betrayal.

selt·zer (water) [SELT-sər] *n* effervescent (mineral) water.

sel·vage [SEL-vij] *n* finished, unfraying edge of cloth.

se·man·tic [si-MAN-tik] *adj* relating to meaning of words or symbols. **se·man'tics** *n* study of linguistic meaning.

sem·a·phore [SEM-ə-for] *n* 1 post with movable arms for signaling. 2 system of signaling by human or mechanical arms.

sem·blance [SEM-bləns] *n* (false) appearance. 1 image, likeness.

se·men [SEE-mən] *n* 1 fluid carrying sperm of male animals. 2 sperm.

se·mes·ter [si-MES-tər] *n* (half-year) session of academic year in many universities, colleges.

sem·i [SEM-ī] *n inf* semitrailer.

semi- *comb. form* half, partly, not completely, e.g. *semicircle*.

sem·i·breve [SEM-ee-breev] *n* musical note half the length of a breve.

sem·i·cir·cle [SEM-i-sur-kəl] *n* half of circle. **sem·i·cir'cu·lar** [-SUR-kyə-lər] *adj*

sem·i·co·lon [SEM-i-koh-lən] *n* punctuation mark (;).

sem·i·con·duc·tor [sem-i-kən-DUK-tər] *n Physics* substance with an electrical conductivity that increases with temperature or voltage.

sem·i·de·tached [sem-ee-di-TACHT] *adj, n* (of) house joined to another on one side only.

sem·i·fi·nal [sem-ee-FĪN-l] *n* match, round, etc. before final.

sem·i·nal [SEM-ə-nl] *adj* 1 capable of developing. 2 influential, important. 3 rudimentary. 4 of semen or seed.

sem·i·nar [SEM-ə-nahr] *n* meeting of group (of students) for discussion.

sem·i·nar·y [SEM-ə-ner-ee] *n, pl* -nar·ies college for priests. **sem·i·nar'i·an** *n* student at seminary.

sem·i·pre·cious [sem-ee-PRESH-əs] *adj* (of gemstones) having less value than precious stones.

sem·i·skilled [sem-ee-SKILD] *adj* partly skilled, trained but not for specialized work.

Sem·ite [SEM-īt] *n* 1 member of ancient and modern peoples including Jews and Arabs. 2 Jew. **Se·mit·ic** [sə-MIT-ik] *adj* 1 denoting a Semite. 2 Jewish.

sem·i·tone [SEM-ee-tohn] *n* musical half tone.

sem·i·trail·er [SEM-i-tray-lər] *n* trailer used for hauling freight, having wheels at back but supported by towing vehicle in front.

sem·o·li·na [sem-ə-LEE-nə] *n* milled product of durum wheat, used for pasta, etc.

sen·ate [SEN-it] *n* 1 upper legislative body of country. 2 upper council of university, etc. **sen'a·tor** [-ə-tər] *n* **sen·a·to'ri·al** [-TOR-ee-əl] *adj*

send *vt* sent, send·ing 1 cause to go or be conveyed. 2 dispatch. 3 transmit (by radio).

se·nile [SEE-nīl] *adj* showing weakness of old age. **se·nil·i·ty** [si-NIL-i-tee] *n*

sen·ior [SEEN-yər] *adj* 1 superior in rank or standing. 2 older. ◆ *n* 3 superior. 4 elder

---

THESAURUS

self-serving

sell *v* 1 = **trade**, barter, exchange 2 = **deal in**, handle, market, peddle, retail, stock, trade in, traffic in

seller *n* = **dealer**, agent, merchant, purveyor, retailer, salesman *or* saleswoman, supplier, vendor

selling *n* = **dealing**, business, trading, traffic

sell out *v* 1 = **dispose of**, be out of stock of, get rid of, run out of 2 *Inf* = **betray**, double-cross (*inf*), sell down the river (*inf*), stab in the back

semblance *n* = **appearance**, aspect, façade, mask, pretense, resemblance, show, veneer

seminal *adj* = **influential**, formative, ground-breaking, important, innovative, original

send *v* 1 = **convey**, direct, dispatch, forward, remit, transmit 2 = **propel**, cast, fire, fling, hurl, let fly, shoot

send for *v* = **summon**, call for, order, request

sendoff *n* = **farewell**, departure, leave-taking, start, valediction

senile *adj* = **doddering**, decrepit, doting, in one's dotage

senility *n* = **dotage**, decrepitude, infirmity, loss of one's faculties, senile dementia

person. **sen·ior'i·ty** [-YOR-i-tee] *n*
se·ñor [sayn-YOR] *n* Sp title of respect, like
Mr. **se·ñor'a** *n* Mrs. **se·ño·ri·ta** [-REE-tə] *n*
Miss.

sen·sa·tion [sen-SAY-shən] *n* **1** operation
of sense, feeling, awareness. **2** excited
feeling, state of excitement. **3** exciting
event. **4** strong impression. **5** commotion.
sen·sa'tion·al *adj* **1** producing great
excitement. **2** melodramatic. **3** of
perception by senses. **sen·sa'tion·al·ism** *n*
1 use of sensational language, etc. to
arouse intense emotional excitement. **2**
doctrine that sensations are basis of all
knowledge.

sense [sens] *n* **1** any of bodily faculties of
perception or feeling. **2** sensitiveness of
any or all of these faculties. **3** ability to
perceive, mental alertness. **4**
consciousness. **5** meaning. **6** coherence,
intelligible meaning. **7** sound practical
judgment. ♦ *vt* **sensed, sens·ing 8**
perceive. **9** understand. **sense'less** [-lis] *adj*
sen·si·ble [SEN-sə-bəl] *adj* **1** reasonable,

wise. **2** perceptible by senses. **3** aware,
mindful. **4** considerable, appreciable.
sen·si·bil'i·ty *n* ability to feel esp.
emotional or moral feelings. **sen'si·bly** *adv*
sen·si·tive [SEN-sit-iv] *adj* **1** open to,
acutely affected by, external impressions. **2**
easily affected or altered. **3** easily upset by
criticism. **4** responsive to slight changes.
sen·si·tiv'i·ty *n* **sen'si·tize** [-tīz] *vt* **-tized,
-tiz·ing** make sensitive, esp. make
(photographic film, etc.) sensitive to light.
sen·sor [SEN-sər] *n* device that responds to
stimulus.
sen·so·ry [SEN-sə-ree] *adj* relating to
organs, operation, of senses.
sen·su·al [SEN-shoo-əl] *adj* **1** of senses only
and not of mind. **2** given to pursuit of
pleasures of sense. **3** self-indulgent. **4**
licentious. **sen'su·al·ist** *n*
sen·su·ous [SEN-shoo-əs] *adj* stimulating,
or apprehended by, senses esp. in
aesthetic manner.
sent pt./pp. of SEND.
sen·tence [SEN-tns] *n* **1** combination of

senior *adj* **1 = higher ranking**, superior **2 =
older**, elder
senior citizen *n* **= pensioner**, old fogey
(*sl*), old or elderly person, retired person
seniority *n* **= superiority**, precedence,
priority, rank
sensation *n* **1 = feeling**, awareness,
consciousness, impression, perception,
sense **2 = excitement**, commotion, furor,
stir, thrill
sensational *adj* **1 = dramatic**, amazing,
astounding, awesome, exciting,
melodramatic, shock-horror (*facetious*),
shocking, thrilling **2 = excellent**, awesome
(*inf*), cool (*inf*), fabulous (*inf*), impressive,
marvelous, mind-blowing (*inf*), out of this
world (*inf*), phat (*sl*), superb
sense *n* **1 = faculty**, feeling, sensation **2 =
feeling**, atmosphere, aura, awareness,
consciousness, impression, perception **3**
(*sometimes plural*) **= intelligence**, brains
(*inf*), cleverness, common sense,
judgment, reason, sagacity, sanity,
sharpness, understanding, wisdom, wit(s)
4 = meaning, drift, gist, implication,
import, significance ♦ *v* **5 = perceive**, be
aware of, discern, feel, get the impression,
pick up, realize, understand
senseless *adj* **1 = stupid**, asinine, bonkers
(*inf*), crazy, daft (*inf*), foolish, idiotic,

illogical, inane, irrational, mad, mindless,
nonsensical, pointless, ridiculous, silly **2 =
unconscious**, insensible, out, out cold,
stunned
sensibility *n* **1** (*often plural*) **= feelings**,
emotions, moral sense, sentiments,
susceptibilities **2 = sensitivity**,
responsiveness, sensitiveness, susceptibility
sensible *adj* **1 = wise**, canny,
down-to-earth, intelligent, judicious,
practical, prudent, rational, realistic, sage,
sane, shrewd, sound **2** (*usually with of*) **=
aware**, conscious, mindful, sensitive to
sensitive *adj* **1 = easily hurt**, delicate,
tender **2 = susceptible**, easily affected,
impressionable, responsive, touchy-feely
(*inf*) **3 = touchy**, easily offended, easily
upset, thin-skinned **4 = responsive**, acute,
fine, keen, precise
sensitivity *n* **= sensitiveness**, delicacy,
receptiveness, responsiveness,
susceptibility
sensual *adj* **1 = physical**, animal, bodily,
carnal, fleshly, luxurious, voluptuous **2 =
erotic**, lascivious, lecherous, lewd, lustful,
raunchy (*sl*), sexual
sensuality *n* **= eroticism**, carnality,
lasciviousness, lecherousness, lewdness,
sexiness (*inf*), voluptuousness
sensuous *adj* **= pleasurable**, gratifying,

words that is complete as expressing a thought. **2** judgment passed on criminal by court or judge. ♦ *vt* **-tenced, -tenc·ing 3** pass sentence on, condemn. **sen·ten'tial** [-TEN-shəl] *adj* **1** of sentence.

sen·ten'tious [-shəs] *adj* **1** full of axioms and maxims. **2** pithy. **3** pompously moralizing. **sen·ten'tious·ness** *n*

sen·tient [SEN-shənt] *adj* **1** capable of feeling. **2** thinking. **sen'tience** *n*

sen·ti·ment [SEN-tə-mənt] *n* **1** tendency to be moved by feeling rather than reason. **2** verbal expression of feeling. **3** mental feeling, emotion. **4** opinion. **sen·ti·men'tal** *adj* **1** given to indulgence in sentiment and in its expression. **2** weak. **3** sloppy. **sen·ti·men·tal'i·ty** *n*

sen·ti·nel [SEN-tn-l] *n* sentry.

sen·try [SEN-tree] *n, pl* **-tries** soldier on watch.

se·pal [SEE-pəl] *n* leaf or division of the calyx of a flower.

sep·a·rate [SEP-ə-rayt] *v* **-rat·ed, -rat·ing** ♦ *vt* **1** part. **2** divide. **3** sever. **4** put apart. **5** occupy place between. ♦ *vi* **6** withdraw, become parted from. ♦ *adj* [SEP-ər-it] **7** disconnected, apart, distinct, individual. **sep'a·ra·ble** *adj* **sep·a·ra'tion** [-RAY-shən] *n* **1** disconnection. **2** *Law* living apart of

married people without divorce. **sep'a·ra·tor** *n* **1** that which separates. **2** apparatus for separating cream from milk.

se·pi·a [SEE-pee-ə] *n* **1** reddish-brown pigment made from a fluid secreted by the cuttlefish. ♦ *adj* **2** of this color.

sep'sis *n* presence of pus-forming bacteria in body.

sep·ten·ni·al [sep-TEN-ee-əl] *adj* lasting, occurring every seven years.

sep·tet' *n* **1** music for seven instruments or voices. **2** group of seven performers.

sep·tic [SEP-tik] *adj* **1** of, caused by, sepsis. **2** (of wound) infected. **sep·ti·ce'mi·a** [-SEE-mee-ə] *n* blood poisoning.

sep·tu·a·ge·nar·i·an [sep-choo-ə-jə-NAIR-ee-ən] *adj* aged between seventy and eighty. ♦ *n*

sep·ul·cher [SEP-əl-kər] *n* **1** tomb. **2** burial vault. **se·pul·chral** [sə-PUL-krəl] *adj* **1** of burial, or the grave. **2** mournful. **3** gloomy. **sep'ul·ture** [-əl-chər] *n* burial.

se·quel [SEE-kwəl] *n* **1** consequence. **2** continuation, e.g. of story.

se·quence [SEE-kwəns] *n* **1** arrangement of things in successive order. **2** section, episode of motion picture. **se·quen·tial** [si-KWEN-shəl] *adj*

se·ques·ter [si-KWES-tər] *vt* **1** separate. **2**

———————— THESAURUS ————————

hedonistic, sybaritic

sentence *n* **1** = **punishment**, condemnation, decision, decree, judgment, order, ruling, verdict ♦ *v* **2** = **condemn**, doom, penalize

sententious *adj* = **pompous**, canting, judgmental, moralistic, preachifying (*inf*), sanctimonious

sentient *adj* = **feeling**, conscious, living, sensitive

sentiment *n* **1** = **emotion**, sensibility, tenderness **2** (often plural) = **feeling**, attitude, belief, idea, judgment, opinion, view **3** = **sentimentality**, emotionalism, mawkishness, romanticism

sentimental *adj* = **romantic**, emotional, maudlin, nostalgic, overemotional, schmaltzy (*sl*), slushy (*inf*), soft-hearted, touching, weepy (*inf*)

sentimentality *n* = **romanticism**, corniness (*sl*), emotionalism, mawkishness, nostalgia, schmaltz (*sl*)

sentinel *n* = **guard**, lookout, sentry, watch, watchman

separable *adj* = **distinguishable**,

detachable, divisible

separate *v* **1** = **divide**, come apart, come away, detach, disconnect, disjoin, remove, sever, split, sunder **2** = **part**, break up, disunite, diverge, divorce, estrange, part company, split up **3** = **isolate**, segregate, single out ♦ *adj* **4** = **unconnected**, detached, disconnected, divided, divorced, isolated, unattached **5** = **individual**, alone, apart, distinct, particular, single, solitary

separated *adj* = **disconnected**, apart, disassociated, disunited, divided, parted, separate, sundered

separately *adv* = **individually**, alone, apart, severally, singly

separation *n* **1** = **division**, break, disconnection, dissociation, disunion, gap **2** = **split-up**, break-up, divorce, parting, rift, split

septic *adj* = **infected**, festering, poisoned, putrefying, putrid, suppurating

sepulcher *n* = **tomb**, burial place, grave, mausoleum, vault

sequel *n* **1** = **follow-up**, continuation, development **2** = **consequence**, seclude. 3 put aside. **se·ques'trate** [-KWES-trayt] vt **-trat·ed, -trat·ing 1** confiscate. 2 divert or appropriate income of property to satisfy claims against its owner. **se·ques·tra'tion** [-TRAY-shən] n

se·quin [SEE-kwin] n **1** small ornamental metal disk or spangle on dresses, etc. **2** orig. Venetian gold coin.

se·quoi·a [si-KWOI-ə] n giant Californian coniferous tree.

se·ragl·io [si-RAL-yoh] n, pl **-ragl·ios** harem, palace, of Turkish sultan.

ser·aph [SER-əf] n, pl **-a·phim** [-ə-fim] member of highest order of angels.

ser·e·nade [ser-ə-NAYD] n **1** sentimental piece of music or song of type addressed to woman by lover esp. at evening. ♦ v **-nad·ed, -nad·ing 2** sing serenade (to someone).

ser·en·dip·i·ty [ser-ən-DIP-i-tee] n faculty of making fortunate discoveries by accident.

se·rene [sə-REEN] adj **1** calm, tranquil. **2** unclouded. **3** quiet, placid. **se·ren'i·ty** [-REN-i-tee] n

serf [surf] n one of class of medieval laborers bound to, and transferred with, land. **serf'dom** [-dəm] n

serge [surj] n strong hard-wearing twilled worsted fabric.

ser·geant [SAHR-jənt] n noncommissioned officer in Army, Marine Corps, police department. **sergeant major 1** noncommissioned Army officer serving as chief administrative assistant. **2** noncommissioned officer ranking above first sergeant in Marine Corps. **sergeant at arms** legislative, organizational officer assigned to keep order, etc.

se·ries [SEER-eez] n, pl **series 1** sequence. **2**

succession, set (e.g. of radio, TV programs with same characters, setting, but different stories). **se·ri·al** [SEER-ee-əl] n **1** story or play produced in successive episodes or installments. **2** periodical publication. ♦ adj **se'ri·al·ize** v **-ized, -iz·ing** publish, present as serial. **serial killer** murderer who commits series of murders in same pattern oft. in same locality.

ser'if n small line finishing off stroke of letter.

se·ri·ous [SEER-ee-əs] adj **1** thoughtful, solemn. **2** earnest, sincere. **3** of importance. **4** giving cause for concern.

ser·mon [SUR-mən] n **1** discourse of religious instruction or exhortation spoken or read from pulpit. **2** any similar discourse. **ser'mon·ize** vi **-ized, -iz·ing 1** talk like preacher. **2** compose sermons.

ser·pent [SUR-pənt] n snake. **serp'en·tine** [-teen] adj like, shaped like, serpent.

ser·rate [SER-ayt], **ser·rat·ed** [SER-ay-tid] adj having notched, sawlike edge. **ser·ra'tion** n

se·rum [SEER-əm] n, pl **-rums** watery animal fluid, esp. thin part of blood as used for inoculation or vaccination.

serve [surv] v **served, serv·ing** (mainly tr) **1** work for, under, another. **2** attend to customers) in store, etc. **3** provide. **4** help to (food, etc.). **5** present (food, etc.) in particular way. **6** provide with regular supply of. **7** be member of military unit. **8** pay homage to. **9** spend time doing. **10** be useful, suitable enough. **11** Tennis, etc. put (ball) into play. ♦ n Tennis, etc. act of serving ball. **ser'vant** [-vənt] n personal or domestic attendant. **ser'ver** [-vər] n **1** person who serves. **2** Computers computer or program that supplies data to other

conclusion, end, outcome, result, upshot

sequence n = **succession**, arrangement, chain, course, cycle, order, progression, series

serene adj = **calm**, composed, peaceful, tranquil, unruffled, untroubled

serenity n = **calmness**, calm, composure, peace, peacefulness, quietness, stillness, tranquillity

series n = **sequence**, chain, course, order, progression, run, set, string, succession, train

serious adj **1** = **severe**, acute, critical, dangerous **2** = **important**, crucial, fateful,

grim, momentous, no laughing matter, pressing, significant, urgent, worrying **3** = **solemn**, grave, humorless, sober, unsmiling **4** = **sincere**, earnest, genuine, honest, in earnest

seriously adv **1** = **gravely**, acutely, badly, critically, dangerously, severely **2** = **sincerely**, gravely, in earnest

seriousness n **1** = **importance**, gravity, significance, urgency **2** = **solemnity**, earnestness, gravitas, gravity

sermon n **1** = **homily**, address **2** = **lecture**, harangue, talking-to (inf)

servant n = **attendant**, domestic, help,

machines on a network. **serv·ice** [-vis] *n* **1** the act of serving, helping, assisting. **2** system organized to provide for needs of public. **3** maintenance of vehicle. **4** use. **5** readiness, availability for use. **6** set of dishes, etc. **7** form, session, of public worship. ◆ *pl* **8** armed forces. ◆ *vt* **-iced, -ic·ing 9** overhaul. **serv·ice·a·ble** *adj* **1** in working order, usable. **2** durable. **service road** narrow road giving access to houses, stores, etc. **service station** place supplying fuel, oil, maintenance for motor vehicles.

ser·vile [SUR-vil] *adj* **1** slavish, without independence. **2** cringing. **3** fawning. **4** menial. **ser·vil'i·ty** *n*

ser·vi·tude [SUR-vi-tood] *n* bondage, slavery.

ser·vo·mech·an·ism
[SUR-voh-mek-ə-niz-əm] *n* electronic device for converting small mechanical, hydraulic or other type of force into larger, esp. in steering mechanisms.

ses·a·me [SES-ə-mee] *n* plant with seeds used as herbs and for making oil.

ses·sion [SESH-ən] *n* **1** meeting of court, etc. **2** assembly. **3** continuous series of such meetings. **4** any period devoted to an activity. **5** school or university term, e.g. *summer session.*

set *v* **set, set·ting** (mainly tr) **1** put or place in specified position or condition. **2** cause to sit. **3** fix, point, put up. **4** make ready. **5** become firm or fixed. **6** establish. **7** prescribe, allot. **8** put to music. **9** of hair, arrange while wet, so that it dries in position. **10** of sun, go down. **11** have direction. ◆ *adj* **12** fixed, established. **13** deliberate. **14** formal, arranged beforehand. **15** unvarying. ◆ *n* **16** act or state of being set. **17** bearing, posture. **18** *Radio, TV* complete apparatus for reception or transmission. **19** *Theater, films* **20** organized settings and equipment to form ensemble of scene. **21** number of things, persons associated as being similar, complementary or used together. **22** *Math.* group of numbers, objects, etc. with at least one common property. **set'back** *n* anything that hinders or impedes. **set'up** *n* **1** position. **2** organization. **set up 1** establish. **2** *inf* treat, as to drinks. **3** *inf* frame, entrap. **4** *inf* lure into embarrassing, dangerous, situation. **set shot** *Basketball* shot at basket taken from standing position and relatively distant from basket. **set·tee'** *n* couch.

maid, retainer, slave

serve *v* **1 = work for**, aid, assist, attend to, help, minister to, wait on **2 = perform**, act, complete, discharge, do, fulfill **3 = provide**, deliver, dish up, present, set out, supply **4 = be adequate**, answer the purpose, be acceptable, do, function as, satisfy, suffice, suit

service *n* **1 = help**, assistance, avail, benefit, use, usefulness **2 = work**, business, duty, employment, labor, office **3 = overhaul**, check, maintenance **4 = ceremony**, observance, rite, worship ◆ *v* **5 = overhaul**, check, fine tune, go over, maintain, tune (up)

serviceable *adj* **= useful**, beneficial, functional, helpful, operative, practical, profitable, usable, utilitarian

servile *adj* **= subservient**, abject, fawning, grovelling, obsequious, sycophantic, toadying

serving *n* **= portion**, helping

session *n* **= meeting**, assembly, conference, congress, discussion, hearing, period, sitting

set¹ *v* **1 = put**, deposit, lay, locate, place,

plant, position, rest, seat, situate, station, stick **2 = prepare**, arrange, lay, make ready, spread **3 = harden**, cake, congeal, crystallize, solidify, stiffen, thicken **4 = arrange**, appoint, decide (upon), determine, establish, fix, fix up, resolve, schedule, settle, specify **5 = assign**, allot, decree, impose, ordain, prescribe, specify **6 = go down**, decline, dip, disappear, sink, subside, vanish ◆ *n* **7 = position**, attitude, bearing, carriage, posture **8 = scenery**, scene, setting, stage set ◆ *adj* **9 = fixed**, agreed, appointed, arranged, decided, definite, established, prearranged, predetermined, scheduled, settled **10 = inflexible**, hard and fast, immovable, rigid, stubborn **11 = conventional**, stereotyped, stock, traditional, unspontaneous **12 set on** *or* **upon = determined**, bent, intent, resolute

set² *n* **1 = series**, assortment, batch, collection, compendium **2 = group**, band, circle, clique, company, coterie, crowd, faction, gang

setback *n* **= hold-up**, blow, check, defeat, disappointment, hitch, misfortune, reverse

set·ter [SET-ər] *n* various breeds of gun dog.

set·ting [SET-ing] *n* **1** background. **2** surroundings. **3** scenery and other stage accessories. **4** act of fixing. **5** decorative metalwork holding precious stone, etc. in position. **6** tableware and cutlery for (single place at) table. **7** descending below horizon of sun. **8** music for song.

set·tle [SET-l] *v* -tled, -tling ◆ *vt* **1** arrange, put in order. **2** establish, make firm or secure or quiet. **3** decide upon. **4** end (dispute, etc.). **5** pay. **6** bestow (property) by legal deed. ◆ *vi* **7** come to rest. **8** subside. **9** become clear. **10** take up residence. **11** subside, sink to bottom. **12** come to agreement. **set·tle·ment** [-mənt] *n* **1** act of settling. **2** place newly inhabited. **3** money bestowed legally. **4** subsidence (of building). **set·tler** [SET-lər] *n* colonist.

sev·en [SEV-ən] *adj, n* cardinal number, next after six. **sev'enth** *adj* the ordinal number. **sev'en·teen'** *adj, n* ten and seven. **sev'en·ty** *adj, n, pl* -ties ten times seven.

sev·er [SEV-ər] *v* **1** separate, divide. **2** cut off. **sev·er·ance** [-əns] *n* **severance pay** compensation paid by a firm to an employee for loss of employment.

sev·er·al [SEV-ər-əl] *adj* **1** some, a few. **2** separate. **3** individual. **4** various. **5** different. ◆ *pron* **6** indefinite small number. **sev'er·al·ly** *adv* **1** apart from others. **2** singly.

se·vere [sə-VEER] *adj* -ver·er, -ver·est **1** strict. **2** rigorous. **3** hard to do. **4** harsh. **5** austere. **6** extreme. **se·ver'i·ty** [-VER-i-tee] *n*

sew [soh] *v* sewed, sewn *or* sewed, sew·ing **1** join with needle and thread. **2** make by sewing.

sew·age [SOO-ij] *n* refuse, waste matter, excrement conveyed in sewer. **sew'er** *n* underground drain to remove waste water and refuse. **sew'er·age** *n* **1** arrangement of sewers. **2** sewage.

sex [seks] *n* **1** state of being male or female. **2** males or females collectively. **3** sexual intercourse. ◆ *vt* **5** ascertain sex of. **sex'ism** *n* discrimination on basis of sex. **sex'ist** *n, adj* **sex·u·al** [SEK-shoo-əl] *adj* **sex'y** *adj* **sex·i·er, sex·i·est** sexual intercourse act of procreation in which male's penis is inserted into female's vagina.

———————— THESAURUS ————————

set back *v* **1** = **hold up**, delay, hinder, impede, retard, slow

set off *v* **1** = **leave**, depart, embark, start out **2** = **detonate**, explode, ignite

setting *n* = **background**, backdrop, context, location, scene, scenery, set, site, surroundings

settle *v* **1** = **put in order**, adjust, order, regulate, straighten out, work out **2** = **land**, alight, come to rest, descend, light **3** = **move to**, dwell, inhabit, live, make one's home, put down roots, reside, set up home, take up residence **4** = **colonize**, people, pioneer, populate **5** = **calm**, lull, pacify, quell, quiet, quieten, reassure, relax, relieve, soothe **6** = **pay**, clear, discharge, square (up) **7** (often with *on* or *upon*) = **decide**, agree, confirm, determine, establish, fix **8** = **resolve**, clear up, decide, put an end to, reconcile

settlement *n* **1** = **agreement**, arrangement, conclusion, confirmation, establishment, working out **2** = **payment**, clearing, discharge **3** = **colony**, community, encampment, outpost

settler *n* = **colonist**, colonizer, frontiersman, immigrant, pioneer

setup *n* = **arrangement**, conditions, organization, regime, structure, system

set up *v* **1** = **build**, assemble, construct, erect, put together, put up, raise **2** = **establish**, arrange, begin, found, initiate, institute, organize, prearrange, prepare

sever *v* **1** = **cut**, cut in two, detach, disconnect, disjoin, divide, part, separate, split **2** = **break off**, dissociate, put an end to, terminate

several *adj* = **some**, different, diverse, manifold, many, sundry, various

severe *adj* **1** = **strict**, austere, cruel, drastic, hard, harsh, oppressive, rigid, unbending **2** = **grim**, forbidding, grave, serious, stern, tight-lipped, unsmiling **3** = **intense**, acute, extreme, fierce **4** = **plain**, austere, classic, homely, restrained, simple, Spartan, unadorned, unembellished, unfussy

severely *adv* **1** = **strictly**, harshly, sharply, sternly **2** = **seriously**, acutely, badly, extremely, gravely

severity *n* = **strictness**, hardness, harshness, severeness, sternness, toughness

sex *n* **1** = **gender 2** = **(sexual) intercourse**, coition, coitus, copulation, fornication,

sex·a·ge·nar·i·an [sek-sə-jə-NAIR-ee-ən] *adj, n* (person) sixty to seventy years old.

sex·tant [SEK-stənt] *n* navigator's instrument for measuring elevations of heavenly body, etc.

sex·tet [seks-TET] *n* (composition for) six singers or players. **1** group of six.

sex·ton [SEK-stən] *n* **1** official who takes care of church building and its contents and sometimes assists in burial of dead. **2** official who takes care of synagogue and sometimes assists cantor in conducting services.

Sg *Chem.* seaborgium.

shab·by [SHAB-ee] *adj* **-bi·er, -bi·est 1** faded, worn, ragged. **2** poorly dressed. **3** mean, dishonorable. **4** stingy. **shab'bi·ly** *adv* **shab'bi·ness** [-nis] *n*

shack [shak] *n* rough hut. **shack up (with)** *sl* live (with) esp. as husband and wife without being legally married.

shack·le [SHAK-əl] *n* **1** metal ring or fastening for prisoner's wrist or ankle. **2** anything that confines. ◆ *vt* **-led, -ling 3** fasten with shackles. **4** hamper.

shade [shayd] *n* **1** partial darkness. **2** shelter, place sheltered from light, heat, etc. **3** darker part of anything. **4** depth of color. **5** tinge. **6** ghost. **7** screen. **8** anything used to screen. **9** window blind. ◆ *pl* **10** *sl* sunglasses. ◆ *vt* **shad·ed, shad·ing 11** screen from light, darken. **12** represent shades in drawing. **shad'y** *adj* **shad·i·er, shad·i·est 1** shielded from sun. **2** dim. **3** dubious. **4** dishonest. **5** dishonorable.

shad·ow [SHAD-oh] *n* **1** dark figure projected by anything that intercepts rays of light. **2** patch of shade. **3** slight trace. **4** indistinct image. **5** gloom. **6** inseparable companion. ◆ *vt* **7** cast shadow over. **8** follow and watch closely. **shad'ow·y** *adj*

shaft *n* **1** straight rod, stem, handle. **2** arrow. **3** ray, beam (of light). **4** revolving rod for transmitting power. **5** one of the bars between which horse is harnessed. **6** entrance boring of mine.

shag[1] *n* **1** matted wool or hair. **2** long-napped cloth. **3** coarse shredded tobacco. **shag'gy** *adj* **-gi·er, -gi·est 1** covered with rough hair or wool. **2** tousled. **3** unkempt.

shag[2] *vt* **shagged, shag·ging 1** chase after. **2** *Baseball* in practice, chase and catch fly balls.

shah *n* formerly, ruler of Iran.

shake [shayk] *v* **shook** [shuuk], **shak·en 1** (cause to) move with quick vibrations. **2**

---

lovemaking, sexual relations

sexual *adj* **1** = **carnal**, erotic, intimate, sensual, sexy **2** = **reproductive**, genital, procreative, sex

sexual intercourse *n* = **copulation**, carnal knowledge, coition, coitus, sex, union

sexuality *n* = **desire**, carnality, eroticism, lust, sensuality, sexiness (*inf*)

sexy *adj* = **erotic**, arousing, naughty, provocative, seductive, sensual, sensuous, suggestive, titillating

shabby *adj* **1** = **tatty**, dilapidated, mean, ragged, run-down, seedy, tattered, threadbare, worn **2** = **mean**, cheap, contemptible, despicable, dirty, dishonorable, lousy (*sl*), low, rotten (*inf*), scurvy, scuzzy (*sl*)

shack *n* = **hut**, cabin, shanty

shackle *n* **1** (often plural) = **fetter**, bond, chain, iron, leg-iron, manacle ◆ *v* **2** = **fetter**, bind, chain, manacle, put in irons

shade *n* **1** = **dimness**, dusk, gloom, gloominess, semidarkness, shadow **2** = **screen**, blind, canopy, cover, covering, curtain, shield, veil **3** = **color**, hue, tinge, tint, tone **4** = **dash**, hint, suggestion, trace **5** *Literary* = **ghost**, apparition, phantom, specter, spirit **6** put into the shade = **outshine**, eclipse, outclass, overshadow ◆ *v* **7** = **cover**, conceal, hide, obscure, protect, screen, shield, veil **8** = **darken**, cloud, dim, shadow

shadow *n* **1** = **dimness**, cover, darkness, dusk, gloom, shade **2** = **trace**, hint, suggestion, suspicion **3** = **cloud**, blight, gloom, sadness ◆ *v* **4** = **shade**, darken, overhang, screen, shield **5** = **follow**, stalk, tail (*inf*), trail

shadowy *adj* **1** = **dark**, dim, dusky, gloomy, murky, shaded, shady **2** = **vague**, dim, dreamlike, faint, ghostly, nebulous, phantom, spectral, unsubstantial

shady *adj* **1** = **shaded**, cool, dim **2** *Inf* = **crooked**, disreputable, dubious, questionable, shifty, suspect, suspicious, unethical

shaft *n* **1** = **handle**, pole, rod, shank, stem **2** = **ray**, beam, gleam

shaggy *adj* = **unkempt**, hairy, hirsute,

tremble. **3** grasp the hand (of another) in greeting. **4** upset. **5** wave, brandish. ♦ *n* **6** act of shaking. **7** vibration. **8** jolt. **9** *inf* short period of time, jiffy. **shak'i·ly** *adv* **shak'y** *adj* **shak·i·er, shak·i·est** unsteady, insecure.

shale [shayl] *n* flaky, sedimentary rock.

shall [shal] *v, pt* **should** used as an auxiliary to make the future tense or to indicate intention, obligation, or inevitability.

shal·lot [SHAL-ət] *n* kind of small onion.

shal·low [SHAL-oh] *adj* **-er, -est 1** not deep. **2** having little depth of water. **3** superficial. **4** not sincere. ♦ *n* **5** shallow place.

sham *adj, n* **1** imitation, counterfeit. ♦ *v* **shammed, sham·ming 2** pretend, feign.

sham·ble [SHAM-bəl] *vi* **-bled, -bling** walk in shuffling, awkward way.

sham·bles [SHAM-bəlz] *n* messy, disorderly thing or place.

shame [shaym] *n* **1** emotion caused by consciousness of guilt or dishonor in one's conduct or state. **2** cause of disgrace. **3** ignominy. **4** pity, hard luck. ♦ *vt* **shamed, sham·ing 5** cause to feel shame. **6** disgrace. **7** force by shame (into). **shame'ful** [-fəl] *adj* disgraceful.

shame·less [-lis] *adj* **1** with no sense of shame. **2** indecent. **shame'faced** [-faysd] *adj* ashamed.

sham·poo' *n* **1** various preparations of liquid soap for washing hair, carpets, etc. **2** this process. ♦ *vt* **-pooed, -poo·ing 3** use shampoo to wash.

sham·rock [SHAM-rok] *n* cloverlike plant with three leaves on each stem, esp. as Irish emblem.

shang·hai [SHANG-hī] *vt* **-haied, -hai·ing** force, trick someone to do something.

shank *n* **1** lower leg. **2** shinbone. **3** stem of thing. **shank of the evening** best or main part of the evening.

shan'tung *n* soft, natural Chinese silk.

shan·ty[1] [SHAN-tee] *n, pl* **-ties 1** temporary wooden building. **2** crude dwelling.

shanty[2] see CHANTEY.

shape [shayp] *n* **1** external form or appearance, esp. of a woman. **2** mold, pattern. **3** condition, esp. of physical fitness. ♦ *v* **shaped, shap·ing** ♦ *vt* **4** form, mold, fashion, make. ♦ *vi* **5** develop. **shape'less** [-lis] *adj* **shape'ly** *adj* **-li·er, -li·est** well-proportioned.

long-haired, rough, tousled, unshorn

shake *v* **1** = **vibrate**, bump, jar, jolt, quake, rock, shiver, totter, tremble **2** = **wave**, brandish, flourish **3** = **upset**, distress, disturb, frighten, rattle (*inf*), shock, unnerve ♦ *n* **4** = **vibration**, agitation, convulsion, jerk, jolt, quaking, shiver, shudder, trembling, tremor

shake up *v* **1** = **stir (up)**, agitate, churn (up), mix **2** = **upset**, disturb, shock, unsettle

shaky *adj* **1** = **unsteady**, faltering, precarious, quivery, rickety, trembling, unstable, weak **2** = **uncertain**, dubious, iffy (*inf*), questionable, suspect

shallow *adj* **1** = **superficial**, empty, slight, surface, trivial **2** = **unintelligent**, foolish, frivolous, ignorant, puerile, simple

sham *n* **1** = **phoney** *or* **phony** (*inf*), counterfeit, forgery, fraud, hoax, humbug, imitation, impostor, pretense ♦ *adj* **2** = **false**, artificial, bogus, counterfeit, feigned, imitation, mock, phoney *or* phony (*inf*), pretended, simulated ♦ *v* **3** = **fake**, affect, assume, feign, pretend, put on, simulate

shambles *n* = **chaos**, confusion, disarray, disorder, havoc, madhouse, mess, muddle

shame *n* **1** = **embarrassment**, abashment, humiliation, ignominy, mortification **2** = **disgrace**, blot, discredit, dishonor, disrepute, infamy, reproach, scandal, smear ♦ *v* **3** = **embarrass**, abash, disgrace, humble, humiliate, mortify **4** = **dishonor**, blot, debase, defile, degrade, smear, stain

shamefaced *adj* = **embarrassed**, abashed, ashamed, humiliated, mortified, red-faced, sheepish

shameful *adj* **1** = **embarrassing**, humiliating, mortifying **2** = **disgraceful**, base, dishonorable, low, mean, outrageous, scandalous, wicked

shameless *adj* = **brazen**, audacious, barefaced, flagrant, hardened, insolent, unabashed, unashamed

shanty *n* = **shack**, cabin, hut, shed

shape *n* **1** = **form**, build, configuration, contours, figure, lines, outline, profile, silhouette **2** = **pattern**, frame, model, mold **3** = **condition**, fettle, health, state, trim ♦ *v* **4** = **form**, create, fashion, make, model, mold, produce **5** = **develop**, adapt, devise, frame, modify, plan

shapeless *adj* = **formless**, amorphous, irregular, misshapen, unstructured

shard [shahrd] n broken fragment, esp. of earthenware.

share[1] [shair] n 1 portion. 2 quota. 3 lot. 4 unit of ownership in corporation. ◆ v **shared, shar·ing** 5 give, take a share. 6 join with others in doing, using, something. **share'hold·er** n

share[2] n blade of plow.

shark [shahrk] n 1 large sometimes predatory sea fish. 2 person who cheats others. 3 inf person of great ability in cards, etc.

sharp [shahrp] adj **-er, -est** 1 having keen cutting edge or fine point. 2 keen. 3 not gradual or gentle. 4 brisk. 5 clever. 6 harsh. 7 dealing cleverly but unfairly. 8 shrill. 9 strongly marked, esp. in outline. ◆ adv 10 promptly. ◆ n 11 Mus. note half a tone above natural pitch. 12 cheat, swindler (also **sharp'er**). **sharp'en** vt make sharp. **sharp'shoot·er** n marksman.

shat·ter [SHAT-ər] v 1 break in pieces. 2 ruin (plans, etc.). 3 disturb (person) greatly.

shave [shayv] v **shaved** or **shav·en, shav·ing** 1 cut close, esp. hair of face or head. 2 pare away. 3 graze. 4 reduce. ◆ n 5 shaving. **shav'ings** pl n parings. **close shave** narrow escape.

shawl n piece of fabric to cover woman's shoulders or head.

she [shee] pron 3rd person singular feminine pronoun.

sheaf [sheef] n, pl **sheaves** 1 bundle, esp. corn. 2 loose leaves of paper.

shear [sheer] vt **sheared** or **shorn, shear·ing** 1 clip hair, wool from. 2 cut through. 3 trim (e.g. hedge). 4 fracture. **shears** pl. n 1 large pair of scissors. 2 mechanical shearing, cutting instrument.

sheath [sheeth] n, pl **sheaths** [sheethz] 1 close-fitting cover, esp. for knife or sword. 2 scabbard. 3 condom. **sheathe** [sheeth] vt **sheathed, sheath·ing** put into sheath.

she·bang [shə-BANG] n inf situation, matter, esp. whole shebang.

shed[1] n roofed shelter used for storage or as workshop.

shed[2] vt **shed, shed·ding** 1 (cause to) pour forth (e.g. tears, blood). 2 cast off.

sheen n gloss.

sheep n ruminant animal bred for wool and meat. **sheep'ish** adj embarrassed, shy. **sheep-dip** n solution in which sheep are immersed to kill vermin and germs in fleece. **sheep'dog** n dog of various breeds orig. for herding sheep. **sheep'skin** n 1 skin of sheep (with fleece) used for clothing, rug or without fleece for parchment. 2 inf diploma.

sheer[1] adj **-er, -est** 1 perpendicular. 2 of material, very fine, transparent. 3 absolute, unmitigated.

sheer[2] vi 1 deviate from course. 2 swerve. 3 turn aside.

sheet[1] n 1 large piece of cotton, etc. to

── THESAURUS ──

shapely adj = **well-formed**, curvaceous, elegant, graceful, neat, trim, well-proportioned

share n 1 = **part**, allotment, allowance, contribution, due, lot, portion, quota, ration, whack (inf) ◆ v 2 = **divide**, assign, distribute, partake, participate, receive, split

sharp adj 1 = **keen**, acute, jagged, pointed, serrated, spiky 2 = **sudden**, abrupt, distinct, extreme, marked 3 = **clear**, crisp, distinct, well-defined 4 = **quick-witted**, alert, astute, bright, clever, discerning, knowing, penetrating, perceptive, quick 5 = **dishonest**, artful, crafty, cunning, sly, unscrupulous, wily 6 = **cutting**, barbed, biting, bitter, caustic, harsh, hurtful 7 = **sour**, acid, acrid, hot, piquant, pungent, tart 8 = **acute**, intense, painful, piercing, severe, shooting, stabbing ◆ adv 9 = **promptly**, exactly, on the dot, on time,

precisely, punctually

sharpen v = **whet**, edge, grind, hone

shatter v 1 = **smash**, break, burst, crack, crush, pulverize 2 = **destroy**, demolish, ruin, torpedo, wreck

shattered adj Inf = **devastated**, blown away, crushed

shave v = **trim**, crop, pare, shear

shed[1] n = **hut**, outhouse, shack

shed[2] v 1 = **give out**, cast, drop, emit, give, radiate, scatter, shower, spill 2 = **cast off**, discard, moult, slough

sheen n = **shine**, brightness, gleam, gloss, luster, polish

sheepish adj = **embarrassed**, abashed, ashamed, mortified, self-conscious, shamefaced

sheer adj 1 = **total**, absolute, complete, downright, out-and-out, pure, unmitigated, utter 2 = **steep**, abrupt, precipitous 3 = **fine**, diaphanous, gauzy, cover bed. **2** broad piece of any thin material. **3** large expanse. ◆ vt **4** cover with sheet.

sheet² n rope fastened in corner of sail. **sheet anchor** large anchor for emergency.

sheik [shayk, sheek] n Arab chief.

shek·el [SHEK-əl] n **1** monetary unit of Israel. ◆ pl **2** inf money.

shelf n, pl **shelves 1** board fixed horizontally (on wall, etc.) for holding things. **2** ledge.

shell n **1** hard outer case (esp. of egg, nut, etc.). **2** husk. **3** explosive projectile. **4** outer part of structure left when interior is removed. **5** racing shell. ◆ vt **6** take shell from. **7** take out of shell. **8** fire at with shells. **racing shell** long light racing boat for rowing by crew of one or more. **shell'fish** n **1** mollusk. **2** crustacean. **shell shock** battle fatigue, nervous disorder caused by bursting of shells or bombs. **shell out** inf pay up.

shel·lac [shə-LAK] n **1** varnish. ◆ vt **-lacked, -lack·ing 2** coat with shellac.

shel·ter [SHEL-tər] n **1** place, structure giving protection. **2** protection. **3** refuge. **4** haven. ◆ vt **5** give protection to. **6** screen. ◆ vi **7** take shelter.

shelve [shelv] v **shelved, shelv·ing** ◆ vt **1** put on a shelf. **2** put off. **3** cease to employ. **4** defer indefinitely. ◆ vi **5** slope gradually.

she·nan·i·gans [shə-NAN-i-gənz] pl n inf **1** frolicking. **2** playing tricks, etc.

shep·herd [SHEP-ərd] n **1** person who

tends sheep. ◆ vt **2** guide, watch over. **shep'herd·ess** [-is] n, fem.

sher·bet [SHUR-bit] n frozen fruit-flavored dessert like ices but with gelatin, etc. added.

sher'iff n law enforcement officer.

Sher·pa [SHUR-pə] n, pl **-pas** or **-pa** member of a Tibetan people.

sher·ry [SHER-ee] n, pl **-ries** fortified wine from S Spain.

shib·bo·leth [SHIB-ə-lith] n **1** custom, word, etc. distinguishing people of particular class or group. **2** test word, pet phrase of sect or party.

shield [sheeld] n **1** piece of armor carried on arm. **2** any protection used to stop blows, missiles, etc. **3** any protective device. **4** sports trophy. ◆ vt **5** cover, protect.

shift v (cause to) move, change position. ◆ n **1** relay of workers. **2** time of their working. **3** evasion. **4** expedient. **5** removal. **6** woman's underskirt or dress. **shift'i·ness** [-nis] n **shift'less** [-lis] adj lacking in resource or character. **shift'y** adj **shift·i·er, shift·i·est** evasive, of dubious character.

shil·le·lagh [shə-LAY-lə] n (in Ireland) cudgel.

shil·ling n **1** former Brit. coin, now 5 pence. **2** monetary unit in various countries.

shil·ly-shal·ly [SHIL-ee-shal-ee] vi **-lied, -ly·ing 1** waver. ◆ n **2** wavering, indecision.

shim·mer [SHIM-ər] vi **1** shine with

gossamer, see-through, thin, transparent

sheet n **1 = coat**, film, lamina, layer, overlay, stratum, surface, veneer **2 = piece**, panel, plate, slab **3 = expanse**, area, blanket, covering, stretch, sweep

shell n **1 = case**, husk, pod **2 = frame**, framework, hull, structure ◆ v **3 = bomb**, attack, blitz, bombard, strafe

shell out v **= pay out**, fork out (sl), give, hand over

shelter n **1 = protection**, cover, defense, guard, screen **2 = safety**, asylum, haven, refuge, retreat, sanctuary, security ◆ v **3 = protect**, cover, defend, guard, harbor, hide, safeguard, shield **4 = take shelter**, hide, seek refuge

sheltered adj **= protected**, cloistered, isolated, quiet, screened, secluded, shaded, shielded

shelve v **= postpone**, defer, freeze, put aside, put on ice, put on the back burner (inf), suspend, take a rain check on (inf)

shepherd v **= guide**, conduct, herd, steer, usher

shield n **1 = protection**, cover, defense, guard, safeguard, screen, shelter ◆ v **2 = protect**, cover, defend, guard, safeguard, screen, shelter

shift v **1 = move**, budge, displace, move around, rearrange, relocate, reposition ◆ n **2 = move**, displacement, rearrangement, shifting

shiftless adj **= lazy**, aimless, good-for-nothing, idle, lackadaisical, slothful, unambitious, unenterprising

shifty adj **= untrustworthy**, deceitful, devious, evasive, furtive, slippery, sly, tricky, underhand shin n **1** front of lower leg. ◆ v **shinned, shin·ning 2** climb with arms and legs. **shin'bone** [-bohn] n tibia.

shin'dig n inf elaborate party, dance, etc.

shine [shīn] v **shone, shin·ing 1** give out, reflect light. **2** perform very well, excel. **3** cause to shine by polishing. ◆ n **4** brightness, luster. **5** polishing. **shin'y** adj **shin·i·er, shin·i·est**

shin·gle¹ [SHIN-gəl] n **1** wooden roof and wall tile. ◆ vt **-gled, -gling 2** cover with shingles.

shingle² n mass of pebbles.

shin·gles [SHIN-gəlz] n disease causing inflammation along a nerve.

Shin·to [SHIN-toh] n native Japanese religion. **Shin'to·ism** n

ship n **1** large seagoing vessel. ◆ v **shipped, ship·ping 2** put on or send (esp. by ship). **3** embark. **4** take employment on ship. **ship'ment** [-mənt] n **1** act of shipping. **2** goods shipped. **shipping** n **1** freight transport business. **2** ships collectively. **ship'shape** [-shayp] adj orderly, trim. **ship'wreck** [-rek] n **1** destruction of a ship through storm, collision, etc. ◆ vt **2** cause to undergo shipwreck. **ship'yard** n place for building and repair of ships. **ship out 1** leave by ship. **2** inf quit, resign, be fired.

shirk [shurk] vt evade, try to avoid (duty, etc.).

shirr [shur] vt **1** gather (fabric) into parallel rows. ◆ n **2** series of gathered rows decorating a dress, blouse, etc. (also **shir'ring**).

shirt [shurt] n garment for upper part of body.

shiv n sl knife.

shiv·er¹ [SHIV-ər] vi **1** tremble, usu. with cold or fear. **2** shudder. **3** vibrate. ◆ n **4** act, state, of shivering.

shiver² v **1** splinter, break in pieces. ◆ n **2** splinter.

shoal [shohl] n **1** stretch of shallow water. **2** sandbank or bar. ◆ v **3** make, become, shallow.

shock¹ [shok] vt **1** horrify, scandalize. ◆ n **2** violent or damaging blow. **3** emotional disturbance. **4** state of weakness, illness, caused by physical or mental shock. **5** paralytic stroke. **6** collision. **7** effect on sensory nerves of electric discharge. **shock'er** n person or thing that shocks or distresses. **shock absorber** device (esp. in automobiles) to absorb shocks.

shock² n group of corn sheaves placed together.

shock³ n **1** mass of hair. ◆ adj **2** shaggy. **shock'head·ed** [-hed-id] adj

shod·dy [SHOD-ee] adj **-di·er, -di·est 1** worthless, trashy, second-rate, of poor material.

shoe [shoo] n, pl **shoes 1** covering for foot, not enclosing ankle. **2** metal rim or curved bar put on horse's hoof. **3** various protective plates or undercoverings. ◆ vt

---

THESAURUS

shimmer v **1 = gleam**, glisten, scintillate, twinkle ◆ n **2 = gleam**, iridescence

shine v **1 = gleam**, beam, flash, glare, glisten, glitter, glow, radiate, sparkle, twinkle **2 = polish**, brush, buff, burnish **3 = stand out**, be conspicuous, excel ◆ n **4 = brightness**, glare, gleam, light, radiance, shimmer, sparkle **5 = polish**, gloss, luster, sheen

shining adj **= bright**, beaming, brilliant, gleaming, glistening, luminous, radiant, shimmering, sparkling

shiny adj **= bright**, gleaming, glistening, glossy, lustrous, polished

ship n **= vessel**, boat, craft

shipshape adj **= tidy**, neat, orderly, spick-and-span, trim, well-ordered, well-organized

shirk v **= dodge**, avoid, evade, get out of, slack

shirker n **= slacker**, clock-watcher, dodger, idler

shiver¹ v **1 = tremble**, quake, quiver, shake, shudder ◆ n **2 = trembling**, flutter, quiver, shudder, tremor

shiver² v **= splinter**, break, crack, fragment, shatter, smash, smash to smithereens

shivery adj **= shaking**, chilled, chilly, cold, quaking, quivery, shaky

shock v **1 = horrify**, appall, disgust, nauseate, revolt, scandalize, sicken **2 = astound**, jolt, shake, stagger, stun, stupefy ◆ n **3 = impact**, blow, clash, collision **4 = upset**, blow, bombshell, distress, disturbance, stupefaction, stupor, trauma

shocking adj **= dreadful**, appalling, atrocious, disgraceful, disgusting, ghastly, horrifying, nauseating, outrageous, revolting, scandalous, sickening

shoddy adj **= inferior**, poor, rubbishy,

shod or **shoed, shod** or **shoed, shoe·ing 4** protect, furnish with shoe or shoes.

shoe'string adj, n very small (amount of money, etc.).

shone pt./pp. of SHINE.

shoo interj **1** go away! ◆ vt **shooed, shoo'-ing 2** drive away. **shoo'-in** n inf **1** person or thing certain to win or succeed. **2** match or contest that is easy to win.

shook [shuuk] pt. of SHAKE.

shoot v **shot, shoot·ing 1** hit, wound, kill with missile fired from weapon. **2** discharge weapon. **3** send, slide, push rapidly. **4** photograph, film. **5** hunt. **6** sprout. ◆ n **7** young branch, sprout. **8** shooting competition. **9** hunting expedition.

shop n **1** store, place for retail sale of goods and services. **2** workshop, factory. ◆ vi **shopped, shop·ping 3** visit stores to buy or examine. **shop'lift·er** n one who steals from store. **shop stew'ard** [STOO-ərd] labor union of workers in factory, etc. **talk shop** talk of one's business, etc. at unsuitable moments.

shore[1] [shor] n edge of sea or lake.

shore[2] vt **shored, shor·ing** prop (up).

shorn pp. of SHEAR.

short adj **-er, -est 1** not long. **2** not tall. **3** brief, hasty. **4** not reaching quantity or standard required. **5** wanting, lacking. **6** abrupt, rude. **7** Stock Exchange not in possession of stock shares when selling them. ◆ adv **8** suddenly, abruptly. **9** without reaching end. ◆ n **10** short film. ◆ pl **11** short trousers. **short'age** [-ij] n deficiency. **short'en** v **short'ly** adv **1** soon. **2** briefly. **short'bread** [-bred] n butter cookie. **short'cake** [-kayk] **1** cake made of butter, flour and sugar. **2** dessert of biscuit dough with fruit topping. **short circuit** Electricity connection, often accidental, of low resistance between two parts of circuit. **short'com·ing** [-kum-ing] n **1** failing. **2** defect. **short'hand** n method of rapid writing by signs or contractions. **short'-hand·ed** adj lacking the usual or necessary number of workers, helpers. **short list** selected list of candidates (esp. for job) from which final selection will be made. **short shrift** summary treatment. **short ton** (2000 lbs.). **short wave** radio wave of frequency greater than 1600 kHz.

short·en·ing [SHORT-ning] n **1** fat used to make cake, etc. rich and crumbly. **2** pr. p. of SHORTEN.

shot n **1** act of shooting. **2** missile. **3** lead in small pellets. **4** marksman. **5** try, attempt. **6** photograph. **7** short film sequence. **8** dose. **9** hypodermic injection. ◆ adj **10** woven so that color is different, according to angle of light. **11** pt./pp. of SHOOT.

should [shuud] v past tense of **shall** used as an auxiliary to make the subjunctive mood or to indicate obligation or possibility.

second-rate, slipshod, tawdry, trashy

shoot v **1** = hit, blast (sl), bring down, kill, open fire, plug (sl) **2** = fire, discharge, emit, fling, hurl, launch, project, propel **3** = speed, bolt, charge, dart, dash, fly, hurtle, race, rush, streak, tear ◆ n **4** = branch, bud, offshoot, sprig, sprout

shop n = store, boutique, emporium, hypermarket, supermarket

shore n = beach, coast, sands, seashore, strand (poetic)

shore up v = support, brace, buttress, hold, prop, reinforce, strengthen, underpin

short adj **1** = concise, brief, compressed, laconic, pithy, succinct, summary, terse **2** = small, diminutive, dumpy, little, petite, squat **3** = brief, fleeting, momentary **4** (often with of) = lacking, deficient, limited, low (on), scant, scarce, wanting **5** = abrupt, brusque, curt, discourteous,

impolite, sharp, terse, uncivil ◆ adv **6** = abruptly, suddenly, without warning

shortage n = deficiency, dearth, insufficiency, lack, paucity, scarcity, want

shortcoming n = failing, defect, fault, flaw, imperfection, weakness

shorten v = cut, abbreviate, abridge, curtail, decrease, diminish, lessen, reduce

shortly adv = soon, before long, in a little while, presently

short-sighted adj **1** = near-sighted, myopic **2** = unthinking, ill-advised, ill-considered, impolitic, impractical, improvident, imprudent, injudicious

short-tempered adj = quick-tempered, hot-tempered, impatient, irascible, testy

shot[1] n **1** = throw, discharge, lob, pot shot **2** = pellet, ball, bullet, lead, projectile, slug **3** = marksman, shooter **4** Sl = attempt, effort, endeavor, go (inf), stab (inf), try,

shoul·der [SHOHL-dər] n 1 part of body to which arm or foreleg is attached. 2 anything resembling shoulder. 3 side of road. ♦ vt 4 undertake. 5 bear (burden). 6 accept (responsibility). 7 put on one's shoulder. ♦ vi 8 make way by pushing. **shoulder blade** [blayd] shoulder bone.

shout [showt] n 1 loud cry. ♦ v 2 utter (cry, etc.) with loud voice.

shove [shuv] vt **shoved, shov·ing** 1 push. ♦ n 2 push. **shove off** inf go away.

shovel [SHUV-əl] n 1 instrument for scooping, lifting earth, etc. ♦ vt **-eled, -el·ing** 2 lift, move (as) with shovel.

show [shoh] v **showed, shown, show·ing** 1 expose to view. 2 point out. 3 display. 4 exhibit. 5 explain. 6 prove. 7 guide. 8 accord (favor, etc.). 9 appear. 10 be noticeable. ♦ n 11 display, exhibition. 12 spectacle. 13 theatrical or other entertainment. 14 indication. 15 competitive event. 16 ostentation. 17 semblance. 18 pretense. **show'i·ly** adv **show'y** adj **show·i·er, show·i·est** 1 gaudy. 2 ostentatious. **show'down** n 1 confrontation. 2 final test. **show jump·ing** horse-riding competition to demonstrate

skill in jumping obstacles. **show'man** [-mən] n, pl **-men** 1 organizer of theatrical events, circuses, etc. 2 one skilled in presenting anything in effective way. **show off** 1 exhibit to invite admiration. 2 behave in this way. **show-off** n **show up** 1 reveal. 2 expose. 3 embarrass. 4 arrive.

show·er [SHOW-ər] n 1 short fall of rain. 2 anything coming down like rain. 3 kind of bath in which person stands while being sprayed with water. 4 party to present gifts to a person, as a prospective bride. ♦ vt 5 bestow liberally. ♦ vi 6 take bath in shower. **show'er·y** adj

shrank pt. of SHRINK.

shrap·nel [SHRAP-nəl] n 1 shell filled with pellets that scatter on bursting. 2 shell splinters.

shred n 1 fragment, torn strip. 2 small amount. ♦ vt **shred** or **shred·ded, shred·ding** 2 cut, tear to shreds.

shrew [shroo] n 1 animal like mouse. 2 bad-tempered woman. 3 scold. **shrew'ish** adj nagging.

shrewd [shrood] adj **-er, -est** 1 astute, intelligent. 2 crafty. **shrewd'ness** [-nis] n

shriek [shreek] n 1 shrill cry. 2 piercing

──────── THESAURUS ────────

turn

shoulder v 1 = **bear**, accept, assume, be responsible for, carry, take on 2 = **push**, elbow, jostle, press, shove

shout n 1 = **cry**, bellow, call, roar, scream, yell ♦ v 2 = **cry (out)**, bawl, bellow, call (out), holler (inf), roar, scream, yell

shout down v = **silence**, drown, drown out, overwhelm

shove v = **push**, drive, elbow, impel, jostle, press, propel, thrust

shovel v = **move**, dredge, heap, ladle, load, scoop, toss

shove off v = **go away**, clear off (inf), depart, leave, push off (inf), scram (inf)

show v 1 = **be visible**, appear 2 = **display**, exhibit, present 3 = **prove**, clarify, demonstrate, elucidate, point out 4 = **instruct**, demonstrate, explain, teach 5 = **display**, indicate, manifest, register, reveal 6 = **guide**, accompany, attend, conduct, escort, lead ♦ n 7 = **entertainment**, presentation, production 8 = **exhibition**, array, display, fair, pageant, parade, sight, spectacle 9 = **pretense**, affectation, air, appearance, display, illusion, parade, pose

showdown n = **confrontation**, clash,

face-off (sl)

shower n 1 = **deluge**, barrage, stream, torrent, volley ♦ v 2 = **inundate**, deluge, heap, lavish, pour, rain

showman n = **performer**, entertainer

show-off n = **exhibitionist**, boaster, braggart, poseur

show off v 1 = **exhibit**, demonstrate, display, flaunt, parade 2 = **boast**, blow one's own trumpet, brag, swagger

show up v 1 = **stand out**, appear, be conspicuous, be visible 2 = **reveal**, expose, highlight, lay bare 3 Inf = **embarrass**, let down, mortify, put to shame 4 = **arrive**, appear, come, turn up

showy adj 1 = **ostentatious**, brash, flamboyant, flash (inf), flashy, over the top (inf) 2 = **gaudy**, garish, loud

shred n 1 = **strip**, bit, fragment, piece, scrap, sliver, tatter 2 = **particle**, atom, grain, iota, jot, scrap, trace

shrew n = **nag**, harpy, harridan, scold, spitfire, vixen

shrewd adj = **clever**, astute, calculating, canny, crafty, cunning, intelligent, keen, perceptive, perspicacious, sharp, smart

shrewdness n = **astuteness**, canniness,

scream. ◆ v 3 screech.

shrike [shrīk] n bird of prey with heavy hooked bill.

shrill adj 1 piercing, sharp in tone. ◆ v 2 utter in such tone. **shril'ly** adv

shrimp n 1 (pl **shrimp** or) **shrimps** small edible crustacean. 2 (pl **shrimps**) inf undersized person. ◆ vi 3 go catching shrimps.

shrine [shrīn] n place (building, tomb, alcove) of worship, usu. associated with saint.

shrink [shreenk] v **shrank** or **shrunk**, **shrunk** or **shrunk·en**, **shrink·ing** 1 become smaller. 2 retire, flinch, recoil. 3 make smaller. ◆ n sl 4 psychiatrist, psychotherapist. **shrink'age** [-ij] n

shrive [shrīv] vt **shrove** or **shrived**, **shriv·en** or **shrived**, **shriv·ing** give absolution to. **shrift** n obs 1 confession. 2 absolution.

shriv·el [SHRIV-əl] vi **-eled**, **-el·ing** shrink and wither.

shroud [shrowd] n 1 sheet, wrapping, for corpse. 2 anything that covers, envelops like shroud. ◆ pl 3 set of ropes to masthead. ◆ vt 4 put shroud on. 5 screen, veil. 6 wrap up.

Shrove Tuesday [shrohv] day before Ash Wednesday.

shrub n 1 bushy plant. 2 drink of fruit juices, etc. oft. with alcohol. **shrub'ber·y** [-ər-ee] n, pl **-ber·ies** 1 planting of shrubs. 2 shrubs collectively.

shrug v **shrugged**, **shrug·ging** 1 raise shoulders, as sign of indifference, ignorance, etc. 2 move (shoulders) thus. 3 (with off) dismiss as unimportant. ◆ n 4

shrugging.

shrunk, shrunken pp. of SHRINK.

shuck [shuk] n 1 shell, husk, pod. ◆ vt 2 remove husks, etc. from. **shucks** interj inf used as mild expression of regret.

shud·der [SHUD-ər] vi 1 shake, tremble violently, esp. with horror. ◆ n 2 shuddering, tremor.

shuf·fle [SHUF-əl] vi **-fled**, **-fling** 1 move feet without lifting them. 2 dance like this. 3 act evasively. ◆ vt 4 mix (cards). 5 (with off) evade, pass to another. ◆ n 6 shuffling. 7 rearrangement.

shun vt **shunned, shun·ning** 1 avoid. 2 keep away from.

shunt vt 1 push aside. 2 divert. 3 move (train) from one line to another.

shut v **shut, shut·ting** 1 close. 2 bar. 3 forbid entrance to. **shut'ter** [-ər] n 1 movable window screen, usu. hinged to frame. 2 device in camera admitting light as required to film or plate. **shut down** close or stop factory, machine, etc.

shut·tle [SHUT-l] n 1 instrument that threads weft between threads of warp in weaving. 2 similar appliance in sewing machine. 3 plane, bus, etc. traveling to and fro over short distance. ◆ v **-tled, -tling** 4 (cause to) move back and forth. **shut'tle·cock** n small, light cone with cork stub and fan of feathers used as a ball in badminton.

shy[1] [shī] adj **shy·er** or **shi·er, shy·est** or **shi·est** 1 awkward in company. 2 timid, bashful. 3 reluctant. 4 scarce, lacking (esp. in card games, not having enough money for bet, etc.). ◆ vi **shied, shy·ing** 5 start

discernment, judgment, perspicacity, quick wits, sharpness, smartness

shriek v, n = cry, scream, screech, squeal, yell

shrill adj = piercing, high, penetrating, sharp

shrink v 1 = decrease, contract, diminish, dwindle, grow smaller, lessen, narrow, shorten 2 = recoil, cower, cringe, draw back, flinch, quail

shrivel v = wither, dehydrate, desiccate, shrink, wilt, wizen

shroud n 1 = winding sheet, grave clothes 2 = covering, mantle, pall, screen, veil ◆ v 3 = conceal, blanket, cloak, cover, envelop, hide, screen, veil

shudder v 1 = shiver, convulse, quake,

quiver, shake, tremble ◆ n 2 = shiver, quiver, spasm, tremor

shuffle v 1 = scuffle, drag, scrape, shamble 2 = rearrange, disarrange, disorder, jumble, mix

shun v = avoid, keep away from, steer clear of

shut v = close, fasten, seal, secure, slam

shut down v 1 = stop, halt, switch off 2 = close, shut up

shut out v = exclude, bar, debar, keep out, lock out

shuttle v = go back and forth, alternate, commute, go to and fro

shut up v 1 Inf = be quiet, fall silent, gag, hold one's tongue, hush, silence 2 = confine, cage, coop up, immure, imprison, back in fear. **6** show sudden reluctance. ◆ *n, pl* **shies 7** start of fear by horse. **shy'ly** *adv* **shy'ness** [-nis] *n*

shy² *vt, n* **shied, shy·ing** throw.

shy·ster [SHĪ-stər] *n inf* dishonest, deceitful person, esp. unprofessional lawyer.

SI *Fr* Système International (d'Unités), international system of units of measurement based on units of ten.

Si *Chem.* silicon.

Si·a·mese cat [Sī-ə-MEEZ] breed of cat with blue eyes.

Siamese twins nontechnical name for CONJOINED TWINS.

sib·i·lant [SIB-ə-lənt] *adj* **1** hissing. ◆ *n* **2** speech sound with hissing effect.

sib'ling *n* person's brother or sister. ◆ *adj*

sib·yl [SIB-əl] *n* woman endowed with spirit of prophecy. **sib'yl·line** [-een] *adj* occult.

sic [sik] *Lat* thus: oft. used to call attention to a quoted mistake.

sick [sik] *adj* **-er, -est 1** inclined to vomit, vomiting. **2** not well or healthy, physically or mentally. **3** macabre, sadistic, morbid. **4** bored, tired. **5** disgusted. **sick'en** [-ən] *v* **1** make, become, sick. **2** disgust. **3** nauseate. **sick'ly** *adj* **1** unhealthy, weakly. **2** inducing nausea. **sick'ness** [-nis] *n* **sick bay** place set aside for treating sick people, esp. aboard ships.

sick·le [SIK-əl] *n* reaping hook.

side [sīd] *n* **1** one of the surfaces of object,

esp. upright inner or outer surface. **2** either surface of thing having only two. **3** part of body that is to right or left. **4** region nearer or farther than, or right or left of, dividing line, etc. **5** region. **6** aspect or part. **7** one of two parties or sets of opponents. **8** sect, faction. **9** line of descent traced through one parent. ◆ *adj* **10** at, in, the side. **11** subordinate, incidental. ◆ *vi* **sid·ed, sid·ing 12** (usu. with *with*) take up cause of. **siding** *n* short line of rails on which trains or wagons are shunted from main line. **side'board** [-bord] *n* piece of furniture for holding dishes, etc. in dining room. **side'burns** [-burnz] *pl n* man's side whiskers. **side'car** *n* **1** small car attached to side of motorcycle. **2** cocktail made with brandy, orange liqueur and lemon juice. **side'kick** *n* **1** pal. **2** assistant. **side'light** [-līt] *n* **1** esp. either of two lights on vessel for use at night. **2** item of incidental information. **side'line** *n* **1** *Sports* boundary of playing area. **2** subsidiary interest or activity. **side'long** [-lawng] *adj* **1** lateral, not directly forward. ◆ *adv* **2** obliquely. **side'man** *n, pl* **-men** instrumentalist in band. **side'track** *v* deviate from main topic. ◆ *n* **side'walk** *n* footpath beside road. **side'ways** [-wayz] *adv* **1** to or from the side. **2** laterally.

si·de·re·al [sī-DEER-ee-əl] *adj* relating to, fixed by, stars.

incarcerate

shy¹ *adj* **1 = timid**, bashful, coy, diffident, retiring, self-conscious, self-effacing, shrinking **2 = cautious**, chary, distrustful, hesitant, suspicious, wary ◆ *v* **3** (sometimes with *off* or *away*) = **recoil**, balk, draw back, flinch, start

shy² *v* = **throw**, cast, fling, hurl, pitch, sling, toss

shyness *n* = **timidity**, bashfulness, diffidence, lack of confidence, self-consciousness, timidity, timorousness

sick *adj* **1 = nauseous**, ill, nauseated, queasy **2 = unwell**, ailing, diseased, indisposed, poorly (*inf*), under the weather (*inf*) **3** *Inf* = **morbid**, black, ghoulish, macabre, sadistic **4 sick of = tired**, bored, fed up, jaded, weary

sicken *v* **1 = disgust**, gross out (*sl*), nauseate, repel, revolt, turn one's stomach **2 = fall ill**, ail, take sick

sickening *adj* = **disgusting**, distasteful,

foul, gross (*sl*), loathsome, nauseating, noisome, offensive, repulsive, revolting, scuzzy (*sl*), stomach-turning (*inf*), vile, yucky or yukky (*sl*)

sickly *adj* **1 = unhealthy**, ailing, delicate, faint, feeble, infirm, pallid, peaky, wan, weak **2 = nauseating**, cloying, mawkish

sickness *n* **1 = illness**, affliction, ailment, bug (*inf*), complaint, disease, disorder, malady **2 = nausea**, queasiness, vomiting

side *n* **1 = border**, boundary, division, edge, limit, margin, perimeter, rim, sector, verge **2 = part**, aspect, face, facet, flank, hand, surface, view **3 = party**, camp, cause, faction, sect, team **4 = point of view**, angle, opinion, position, slant, stand, standpoint, viewpoint ◆ *adj* **5 = subordinate**, ancillary, incidental, lesser, marginal, minor, secondary, subsidiary ◆ *v* **6** (usually with *with*) = **support**, ally with, favor, go along with, take the part of

sidelong *adj* = **sideways**, covert, indirect,

si·dle [SĪD-l] vi **-dled, -dling 1** move in furtive or stealthy manner. **2** move sideways.

SIDS sudden infant death syndrome, unexplained death of baby while asleep.

siege [seej] n besieging of town or fortified place.

si·en·na [see-EN-ə] n (pigment of) brownish-yellow color.

si·er·ra [see-ER-ə] n range of mountains with jagged peaks.

si·es·ta [see-ES-tə] n rest, sleep in afternoon.

sieve [siv] n **1** device with network or perforated bottom for sifting. ◆ v **sieved, siev·ing 2** sift. **3** strain.

sift vt **1** separate (e.g. with sieve) coarser portion from finer. **2** examine closely. **sift'er** n

sigh [sī] v, n (utter) long audible breath. **sigh for** yearn for, grieve for.

sight [sīt] n **1** faculty of seeing. **2** seeing. **3** thing seen. **4** view. **5** glimpse. **6** device for guiding eye. **7** spectacle. **8** inf pitiful or ridiculous or unusual object. **9** inf large number, great deal. ◆ vt **10** catch sight of. **11** adjust sights of gun, etc. **sight for sore eyes** inf person or thing one is glad to see. **sight'less** [-lis] adj **sight-read** [-reed] v **-read** [-red], **-read·ing** [-reed-ing] play, sing music without previous preparation. **sight'see** v visit (place) to look at interesting sights.

sign [sīn] n **1** mark, gesture, etc. to convey some meaning. **2** (board, placard, bearing) notice, warning, etc. **3** symbol. **4** omen. **5** evidence. ◆ vt **6** put one's signature to. **7** ratify. ◆ vi **8** make sign or gesture. **9** affix signature. **10** use symbols of sign language. **sign language** gestures used for communicating with deaf people.

sig·nal [SIG-nəl] n **1** sign to convey order or information, esp. on railroads. **2** that which in first place impels any action. **3** sequence of electrical impulses or radio waves transmitted or received. ◆ adj **4** remarkable, striking. ◆ v **-naled, -nal·ing 5** make signals to. **6** give orders, etc. by signals. **sig'nal·ize** vt **-ized, -iz·ing** make notable.

sig·na·to·ry [SIG-nə-tor-ee] n, pl **-ries** one of those who sign agreements, treaties.

sig·na·ture [SIG-nə-chər] n **1** person's name written by self. **2** act of writing it. **signature tune** theme song.

sig·net [SIG-nit] n small seal.

sig·nif·i·cant [sig-NIF-i-kənt] adj **1** revealing. **2** designed to make something known. **3** important. **sig·nif'i·cance** [-kəns] n **1** import, weight. **2** meaning. **sig·ni·fi·ca'tion** n meaning.

sig·ni·fy [SIG-nə-fī] v **-fied, -fy·ing 1** mean. **2** indicate. **3** denote. **4** imply. **5** be of importance.

---

oblique

sidestep v = **avoid**, circumvent, dodge, duck (inf), evade, skirt

sidetrack v = **divert**, deflect, distract

sideways adv **1** = **obliquely**, edgeways, laterally, sidelong, to the side ◆ adj **2** = **oblique**, sidelong

sidle v = **edge**, creep, inch, slink, sneak, steal

siesta n = **nap**, catnap, doze, forty winks (inf), sleep, snooze (inf)

sieve n **1** = **strainer**, colander ◆ v **2** = **sift**, separate, strain

sift v **1** = **sieve**, filter, separate **2** = **examine**, analyze, go through, investigate, research, scrutinize, work over

sight n **1** = **vision**, eye, eyes, eyesight, seeing **2** = **view**, appearance, perception, range of vision, visibility **3** = **spectacle**, display, exhibition, pageant, scene, show, vista **4** = **eyesore**, mess, monstrosity **5 catch sight of** = **spot**, espy, glimpse ◆ v

6 = **spot**, behold, discern, distinguish, make out, observe, perceive, see

sign n **1** = **indication**, clue, evidence, hint, mark, proof, signal, symptom, token **2** = **notice**, board, placard, warning **3** = **symbol**, badge, device, emblem, logo, mark **4** = **omen**, augury, auspice, foreboding, portent, warning ◆ v **5** = **autograph**, endorse, initial, inscribe **6** = **gesture**, beckon, gesticulate, indicate, signal

signal n **1** = **sign**, beacon, cue, gesture, indication, mark, token ◆ v **2** = **gesture**, beckon, gesticulate, indicate, motion, sign, wave

significance n **1** = **importance**, consequence, moment, relevance, weight **2** = **meaning**, force, implication(s), import, message, point, purport, sense

significant adj **1** = **important**, critical, material, momentous, noteworthy, serious, vital, weighty **2** = **meaningful**, eloquent,

si·gnor [SEEN-yor] *n* Italian title of respect, like Mr. **si·gno·ra** [sin-YOR-ə] *n* Mrs. **si·gno·ri·na** [seen-yə-REEN-ə] *n* Miss.

Sikh [seek] *n* member of Hindu religious sect.

si·lage [SĪ-lij] *n* fodder crop harvested while green and stored in state of partial fermentation.

si·lence [SĪ-ləns] *n* 1 absence of noise. 2 refraining from speech. ♦ *vt* **-lenced, -lenc·ing** 3 make silent. 4 put a stop to. **si'lenc·er** *n* device to reduce noise of firearm. **si'lent** *adj*

sil·hou·ette [sil-oo-ET] *n* 1 outline of object seen against light background. 2 profile portrait in black. ♦ *vt* **-et·ted, -et·ting** 3 show in or as if in silhouette.

sil·i·ca [SIL-i-kə] *n* naturally occurring dioxide of silicon. **si·li·ceous** [sə-LEE-shəs] *adj* **si·li·co·sis** [si-li-KOH-sis] *n* lung disease caused by inhaling silica dust over a long period.

sil·i·con [SIL-i-kən] *n* brittle metalloid element found in sand, clay, stone, widely used in chemistry, industry. **sil'i·cone** [-kohn] *n* large class of synthetic substances, related to silicon and used in chemistry, industry, medicine.

silk *n* 1 fiber made by larvae (**silkworms**) of a certain moth. 2 thread, fabric made from this. **silk'en** *adj* 1 made of, like silk. 2 soft. 3 smooth. 4 dressed in silk. **silk'i·ness** [-nis] *n*

sill *n* 1 ledge beneath window. 2 bottom part of door or window frame.

sil·ly [SIL-ee] *adj* **-li·er, -li·est** 1 foolish. 2 trivial. 3 feebleminded. **sil'li·ness** [-nis] *n*

si·lo [SĪ-loh] *n, pl* **-los** 1 pit, tower for storing fodder or grain. 2 underground missile launching site.

silt *n* 1 mud deposited by water. ♦ *v* 2 fill, be choked with silt. **silt·a'tion** *n*

sil·ver [SIL-vər] *n* 1 white precious metal. 2 things made of it. 3 silver coins. 4 cutlery. ♦ *adj* 5 made of silver. 6 resembling silver or its color. 7 having pale luster, as moon. 8 soft, melodious, as sound. 9 bright. ♦ *vt* 10 coat with silver. **sil'ver·y** *adj* **silver birch** tree having silvery white peeling bark. **silver wedding** 25th wedding anniversary.

sim·i·an [SIM-ee-ən] *adj* of, like apes.

sim·i·lar [SIM-ə-lər] *adj* resembling, like. **sim·i·lar'i·ty** *n* 1 likeness. 2 close resemblance.

sim·i·le [SIM-ə-lee] *n* comparison of one thing with another, using *as* or *like*, esp. in poetry.

si·mil·i·tude [si-MIL-i-tood] *n* 1 outward appearance, likeness. 2 guise.

sim·mer [SIM-ər] *v* 1 keep or be just bubbling or just below boiling point. 2 to be in state of suppressed anger or laughter.

sim·per [SIM-pər] *vi* smile, utter in silly or affected way. ♦ *n*

sim·ple [SIM-pəl] *adj* **-pler, -plest** 1 not complicated. 2 plain. 3 not combined or complex. 4 ordinary, mere. 5 guileless. 6 stupid. **sim'ple·ton** [-tən] *n* foolish person. **sim·plic'i·ty** [-PLIS-ə-tee] *n, pl* **-ties** simpleness, clearness, artlessness. **sim·pli·fi·ca'tion** *n* **sim'pli·fy** *vt* **-fied,**

─────── THESAURUS ───────

expressive, indicative, suggestive

signify *v* 1 = **indicate**, be a sign of, betoken, connote, denote, imply, intimate, mean, portend, suggest 2 = **matter**, be important, carry weight, count

silence *n* 1 = **quiet**, calm, hush, lull, peace, stillness 2 = **muteness**, dumbness, reticence, taciturnity ♦ *v* 3 = **quieten**, cut off, cut short, deaden, gag, muffle, quiet, stifle, still, suppress

silent *adj* 1 = **quiet**, hushed, muted, noiseless, soundless, still 2 = **mute**, dumb, speechless, taciturn, voiceless, wordless

silently *adj* = **quietly**, inaudibly, in silence, mutely, noiselessly, soundlessly, without a sound, wordlessly

silhouette *n* 1 = **outline**, form, profile, shape ♦ *v* 2 = **outline**, etch, stand out

silky *adj* = **smooth**, silken, sleek, velvety

silly *adj* = **foolish**, absurd, asinine, fatuous, idiotic, inane, ridiculous, senseless, stupid, unwise

silt *n* 1 = **sediment**, alluvium, deposit, ooze, sludge ♦ *v* 2 **silt up** = **clog**, choke, congest

similar *adj* = **alike**, analogous, close, comparable, like, resembling

similarity *n* = **resemblance**, affinity, agreement, analogy, closeness, comparability, correspondence, likeness, sameness

simmer *v* = **fume**, be angry, rage, seethe, smolder

simmer down *v* = **calm down**, control oneself, cool off or down

simper *v* = **smile coyly**, smile affectedly, smirk

-fy·ing make simple, plain or easy.
sim·plis·tic adj extremely simple, naive.
sim·ply adv **simple fraction** one in which both the numerator and the denominator are whole numbers.
sim·u·late [SIM-yə-layt] vt **-lat·ed, -lat·ing 1** make pretense of. **2** reproduce, copy, esp. conditions of particular situation. **sim·u·la·tion** n **sim·u·la·tor** n
si·mul·ta·ne·ous [sī-məl-TAY-nee-əs] adj occurring at the same time. **si·mul·ta·ne'i·ty** [-tə-NEE-i-tee] n **simulta'ne·ous·ly** adv
sin n **1** transgression of divine or moral law, esp. committed consciously. **2** offense against principle or standard. ◆ vi **sinned, sin·ning 3** commit sin. **sin'ful** [-fəl] adj **1** of nature of sin. **2** guilty of sin. **sin'ful·ly** adv
since [sins] prep **1** during or throughout period of time after. ◆ conj **2** from time when. **3** because. ◆ adv **4** from that time.
sin·cere [sin-SEER] adj **1** not hypocritical, actually moved by or feeling apparent emotions. **2** true, genuine. **3** unaffected. **sin·cere'ly** adv **sin·cer'i·ty** [-SER-i-tee] n
sine [sīn] n mathematical function, esp. ratio of length of hypotenuse to opposite side in right triangle.
si·ne·cure [SĪ-ni-kyuur] n office with pay but minimal duties.
si·ne di·e [SĪ-nee Dī-ee] Lat with no date, indefinitely postponed.
si·ne qua non [SĪ-nee kway non] Lat essential condition or requirement.
sin·ew [SIN-yoo] n **1** tough, fibrous cord joining muscle to bone. ◆ pl **2** muscles, strength. **sin'ew·y** adj **1** stringy. **2** muscular.
sing v **sang, sung, sing·ing 1** utter musical sounds. **2** hum, whistle, ring. **3** utter (words) with musical modulation. **4** celebrate in song or poetry. **sing'song** [-sawng] adj monotonously regular in tone, rhythm.
singe [sinj] vt **singed, singe·ing 1** burn surface of. ◆ n **2** act or effect of singeing.

simple adj **1 = easy**, clear, intelligible, lucid, plain, straightforward, uncomplicated, understandable, uninvolved **2 = plain**, classic, natural, unembellished, unfussy **3 = pure**, elementary, unalloyed, uncombined, unmixed **4 = artless**, childlike, guileless, ingenuous, innocent, naive, natural, sincere, unaffected, unsophisticated **5 = honest**, bald, basic, direct, frank, naked, plain, sincere, stark **6 = humble**, dumpy (inf), homely, modest, unpretentious **7 = feeble-minded**, foolish, half-witted, moronic, slow, stupid
simple-minded adj **= feeble-minded**, backward, dim-witted, foolish, idiot, idiotic, moronic, retarded, simple, stupid
simpleton n **= halfwit**, doofus (sl), dork (sl), dullard, fool, idiot, imbecile (inf), moron, schmuck (sl)
simplicity n **1 = ease**, clarity, clearness, straightforwardness **2 = plainness**, lack of adornment, purity, restraint **3 = artlessness**, candor, directness, innocence, naivety, openness
simplify v **= make simpler**, abridge, disentangle, dumb down, reduce to essentials, streamline
simply adv **1 = plainly**, clearly, directly, easily, intelligibly, naturally, straightforwardly, unpretentiously **2 = just**,

merely, only, purely, solely **3 = totally**, absolutely, completely, really, utterly, wholly
simulate v **= pretend**, act, affect, feign, put on, sham
simultaneous adj **= coinciding**, at the same time, coincident, concurrent, contemporaneous, synchronous
simultaneously adv **= at the same time**, concurrently, together
sin n **1 = wrongdoing**, crime, error, evil, guilt, iniquity, misdeed, offense, transgression ◆ v **2 = transgress**, err, fall, go astray, lapse, offend
sincere adj **= honest**, candid, earnest, frank, genuine, guileless, heartfelt, real, serious, true, unaffected
sincerely adv **= honestly**, earnestly, genuinely, in earnest, seriously, truly, wholeheartedly
sincerity n **= honesty**, candor, frankness, genuineness, seriousness, truth
sinecure n **= soft job** (inf), gravy train (sl), money for jam or old rope (inf), soft option
sinful adj **= guilty**, bad, corrupt, criminal, erring, immoral, iniquitous, wicked
sing v **1 = warble**, carol, chant, chirp, croon, pipe, trill, yodel **2 = hum**, buzz, purr, whine
singe v **= burn**, char, scorch, sear
singer n **= vocalist**, balladeer, cantor,

sin·gle [SING-gəl] *adj* **1** one only. **2** alone, separate. **3** unmarried. **4** for one. **5** formed of only one part, fold, etc. **6** wholehearted, straightforward. ◆ *n* **7** single thing. **8** phonograph record with one short item on each side. **9** *Baseball* one-base hit. ◆ *vt* **-gled, -gling 10** pick (out). **11** make single. **sin'gly** *adv* **single file** persons, things arranged in one line. **single-hand·ed** *adj* without assistance. **singles bar** bar or club that is social meeting place esp. for single people.

sin·gu·lar [SING-gyə-lər] *adj* **1** remarkable. **2** unusual. **3** unique. **4** denoting one person or thing. **sin·gu·lar'i·ty** *n, pl* **-ties** something unusual. **sin'gu·lar·ly** [-lər-lee] *adv* **1** particularly. **2** peculiarly.

sin·is·ter [SIN-ə-stər] *adj* **1** threatening. **2** evil-looking. **3** wicked. **4** unlucky. **5** *Heraldry* on bearer's left-hand side. **sin'is·trous** [-trəs] *adj* ill-omened.

sink [singk] *v* **sank** or **sunk, sunk** or **sunk·en, sink·ing 1** become submerged (in water). **2** drop, give way. **3** decline in value, health, etc. **4** penetrate (into). **5** cause to sink. **6** make by digging out. **7** invest. ◆ *n* **8** receptacle with pipe for carrying away waste water. **9** cesspool. **10** place of corruption, vice. **sink'er** *n* weight for fishing line. **sink'hole** [-hohl] *n* **1** low land where drainage collects. **2** cavity formed in rock by water. **sinking fund** money set aside at intervals for payment of particular liability at fixed date.

Sino- *comb. form* Chinese, of China, e.g. *Sino-American relations.*

sin·u·ous [SIN-yoo-əs] *adj* curving, devious, lithe. **sin·u·os'i·ty** [-OS-i-tee] *n, pl* **-ties**

si·nus [SĪ-nəs] *n, pl* **-nus·es** cavity, esp. air passages in bones of skull. **si·nus·i'tis** [-SĪ-tis] *n* inflammation of sinus.

sip *v* **sipped, sip·ping** drink in very small portions. ◆ *n*

si·phon [SĪ-fən] *n* **1** device, esp. bent tube, that uses atmospheric or gaseous pressure to draw liquid from container. ◆ *v* **2** draw off thus. **3** draw off in small amounts.

sir [sur] *n* **1** polite term of address for a man. **2** (**S-**) title of knight or baronet.

sire [sīr] *n* **1** male parent, esp. of horse or domestic animal. **2** term of address to king. ◆ *v* **sired, sir·ing 3** beget.

si·ren [SĪ-rən] *n* **1** device making loud wailing noise, esp. giving warning of danger. **2** legendary sea nymph who lured sailors to destruction. **3** alluring woman.

sir·loin [SUR-loin] *n* prime cut of loin of beef.

si·sal [SĪ-səl] *n* (fiber of) plant used in making ropes.

sis·sy [SIS-ee] *adj, n, pl* **-sies 1** weak, cowardly (person). **2** effeminate boy or man.

—————— THESAURUS ——————

chorister, crooner, minstrel, soloist

single *adj* **1** = **one**, distinct, individual, lone, only, separate, sole, solitary **2** = **individual**, exclusive, separate, undivided, unshared **3** = **simple**, unblended, unmixed **4** = **unmarried**, free, unattached, unwed ◆ *v* **5** (usually with *out*) = **pick**, choose, distinguish, fix on, pick on or out, select, separate, set apart

single-handed *adv* = **unaided**, alone, by oneself, independently, on one's own, solo, unassisted, without help

single-minded *adj* = **determined**, dedicated, dogged, fixed, unswerving

singly *adv* = **one by one**, individually, one at a time, separately

singular *adj* **1** = **single**, individual, separate, sole **2** = **remarkable**, eminent, exceptional, notable, noteworthy, outstanding **3** = **unusual**, curious, eccentric, extraordinary, odd, peculiar, queer, strange

singularly *adv* = **remarkably**, especially, exceptionally, notably, outstandingly, particularly, uncommonly, unusually

sinister *adj* = **threatening**, dire, disquieting, evil, malign, menacing, ominous

sink *v* **1** = **descend**, dip, drop, fall, founder, go down, go under, lower, plunge, submerge, subside **2** = **fall**, abate, collapse, drop, lapse, slip, subside **3** = **decline**, decay, deteriorate, diminish, dwindle, fade, fail, flag, lessen, weaken, worsen **4** = **dig**, bore, drill, drive, excavate **5** = **stoop**, be reduced to, lower oneself

sink in *v* = **be understood**, get through to, penetrate, register (*inf*)

sinner *n* = **wrongdoer**, evildoer, malefactor, miscreant, offender, transgressor

sip *v* **1** = **drink**, sample, sup, taste ◆ *n* **2** = **swallow**, drop, taste, thimbleful

sissy *n* **1** = **wimp** (*inf*), coward, mama's

sis·ter [SIS-tər] n **1** daughter of same parents. **2** woman fellow member esp. of religious body. ◆ adj **3** closely related, similar. **sis'ter·hood** [-huud] n **1** relation of sister. **2** order, band of women. **sis'ter·ly** adj **sister-in-law** n **1** sister of husband or wife. **2** brother's wife.

sit v sat, sit·ting (mainly intr) **1** adopt posture or rest on buttocks, thighs. **2** perch. **3** incubate. **4** pose for portrait. **5** occupy official position. **6** hold session. **7** remain. **8** take examination. **9** keep watch over baby, etc. **sit in** protest by refusing to move from place. **sit-in** n such protest.

si·tar [si-TAHR] n stringed musical instrument, esp. of India. **si·tar'ist** n

site [sīt] n **1** place, location. **2** space for, with, a building. **3** same as WEBSITE.

sit·u·ate [SICH-oo-ayt] v -at·ed, -at·ing **1** place, locate. **sit·u·a'tion** n **1** place, position. **2** state of affairs. **3** employment, post.

six [siks] adj, n cardinal number one more than five. **sixth** adj **1** ordinal number. ◆ n **2** sixth part. **six'teen'** n, adj six and ten. **six'ty** n, adj, pl -ties six times ten.

size[1] [sīz] n **1** bigness, dimensions. **2** one of series of standard measurements of clothes, etc. **3** inf state of affairs. ◆ vt sized, siz·ing **4** arrange according to size. **siz'a·ble, size'a·ble** adj quite large. **size up** inf assess (person, situation, etc.).

size[2] n **1** gluelike sealer, filler. ◆ vt sized,

siz·ing 2 coat, treat with size.

siz·zle [SIZ-l] v, n -zled, -zling (make) hissing, spluttering sound as of frying. **siz'zler** [-lər] n inf hot day.

skate[1] [skayt] n **1** steel blade attached to boot, for gliding over ice. ◆ vi skat·ed, skat·ing **2** glide as on skates. **skat'er** n **skate'board** n small board mounted on roller-skate wheels.

skate[2] n large marine ray.

ske·dad·dle [ski-DAD-l] vi inf -dled, -dling **1** flee. **2** run away hurriedly.

skeet n shooting sport with clay target propelled from trap to simulate flying bird.

skein [skayn] n **1** quantity of yarn, wool, etc. in loose knot. **2** flight of wildfowl.

skel·e·ton [SKEL-i-tn] n **1** bones of animal. **2** bones separated from flesh and preserved in their natural position. **3** very thin person. **4** outline, draft, framework. **5** nucleus. ◆ adj **6** reduced to a minimum. **7** drawn in outline. **8** not in detail. **skel'e·tal** [-tl] adj **skeleton key** key filed down so as to open many different locks.

skep·tic [SKEP-tik] n **1** one who maintains doubt or disbelief. **2** agnostic. **3** unbeliever. **skep'ti·cal** [-kl] adj **skep'ti·cism** [-siz-əm] n

sketch [skech] n **1** rough drawing. **2** brief account. **3** essay. **4** short humorous play. ◆ v **5** make sketch (of). **sketch'y** adj **sketch·i·er, sketch·i·est 1** omitting detail. **2** incomplete. **3** inadequate.

THESAURUS

boy, softie (inf), weakling ◆ adj **2** = **wimpish** or **wimpy** (inf), cowardly, effeminate, feeble, soft (inf), unmanly, weak

sit v **1** = **rest**, perch, settle **2** = **convene**, assemble, deliberate, meet, officiate, preside

site n **1** = **location**, place, plot, position, setting, spot **2** = **locate**, install, place, position, set, situate

situation n **1** = **state of affairs**, case, circumstances, condition, plight, state **2** = **location**, place, position, setting, site, spot **3** = **status**, rank, station **4** = **job**, employment, office, place, position, post

sizable, sizeable adj = **large**, considerable, decent, goodly, largish, respectable, substantial

size n = **dimensions**, amount, bulk, extent, immensity, magnitude, mass, proportions, range, volume

size up v = **assess**, appraise, evaluate, take stock of

sizzle v = **hiss**, crackle, frizzle, fry, spit

skedaddle v Sl = **run away**, abscond, beat it (sl), clear off (inf), disappear, flee, run for it, scram (inf), take to one's heels

skeleton n = **framework**, bare bones, draft, frame, outline, sketch, structure

skeptic n = **doubter**, cynic, disbeliever, doubting Thomas

skeptical adj = **doubtful**, cynical, disbelieving, dubious, incredulous, mistrustful, unconvinced

skepticism n = **doubt**, cynicism, disbelief, incredulity, unbelief

sketch n **1** = **drawing**, delineation, design, draft, outline, plan ◆ v **2** = **draw**, delineate, depict, draft, outline, represent, rough out

sketchy adj = **incomplete**, cursory, inadequate, perfunctory, rough, scrappy, skimpy, superficial

skew [skyoo] vi **1** move obliquely. ◆ adj **2** slanting. **3** crooked.

skew•er [SKYOO-ər] n **1** pin to fasten (meat) together. ◆ v **2** pierce or fasten (as though) with skewer.

ski [skee] n, pl **skis 1** long runner fastened to boot for sliding over snow or water. ◆ v **skied, ski•ing 2** slide on skis. **3** go skiing.

skid v **skid•ded, skid•ding 1** slide (sideways), esp. vehicle out of control with wheels not rotating. ◆ n **2** instance of this. **3** device to facilitate sliding, e.g. in moving heavy objects. **skid•dy** adj **-di•er, -di•est**

skiff n small boat.

skill n **1** practical ability, cleverness, dexterity. **skilled** adj **1** having, requiring knowledge, united with readiness and dexterity. **skill'ful** [-fəl] adj **1** expert, masterly. **2** adroit.

skil•let [SKIL-it] n small frying pan.

skim v **skimmed, skim•ming 1** remove floating matter from surface of liquid. **2** glide over lightly and rapidly. **3** read thus. **4** move thus. **skim milk, skimmed milk** milk from which cream has been removed.

skimp vt **1** give short measure. **2** do thing imperfectly. **skimp'y** adj **skimp•i•er, skimp•i•est 1** meager. **2** scanty.

skin n **1** outer covering of vertebrate body, lower animal or fruit. **2** animal skin used as material or container. **3** film on surface of cooling liquid, etc. **4** complexion. ◆ vt **skinned, skin•ning 5** remove skin of. **skin'ny** adj **-ni•er, -ni•est** thin. **skin-deep** adj **1** superficial. **2** slight. **skin diving** underwater swimming using breathing apparatus. **skin'flint** n miser, niggard. **skin graft** transplant of piece of healthy skin to wound to form new skin. **skin•tight** [-tīt] adj fitting close to skin.

skip[1] v **skipped, skip•ping 1** leap lightly. **2** jump a rope as it is swung under one. **3** pass over, omit. ◆ n **4** act of skipping.

skip[2] n large bucket, container for transporting people, materials in mines, etc.

skip•per [SKIP-ər] n **1** captain of ship, plane or team. ◆ vt **2** captain.

skirl [skurl] n sound of bagpipes.

skir•mish [SKUR-mish] n **1** fight between small parties, small battle. ◆ vi **2** fight briefly or irregularly.

skirt [skurt] n **1** woman's garment hanging from waist. **2** lower part of woman's dress, coat, etc. **3** outlying part. **4** sl, offens woman. ◆ v **5** border. **6** go around. **skirt'ing** n material for women's skirts.

skit n short satirical piece, esp. theatrical sketch.

skit'tish adj frisky, frivolous.

skit•tle [SKIT-l] n **1** bottle-shaped object used as a target in some games. ◆ pl **2** game in which players try to knock over skittles by rolling a ball at them.

skoal [skohl] interj (as a toast) to your health.

skul•dug•ger•y [skul-DUG-ə-ree] n, pl **-ger•ies** trickery.

skulk vi **1** sneak out of the way. **2** lurk. **skulk'er** n

skill n = **expertise**, ability, art, cleverness, competence, craft, dexterity, facility, knack, proficiency, skillfulness, talent, technique

skilled adj = **expert**, able, masterly, professional, proficient, skillful

skillful adj = **expert**, able, adept, adroit, clever, competent, dexterous, masterly, practiced, professional, proficient, skilled

skim v **1** = **separate**, cream **2** = **glide**, coast, float, fly, sail, soar **3** (usually with *through*) = **scan**, glance, run one's eye over

skimp v = **stint**, be mean with, be sparing with, cut corners, scamp, scrimp

skin n **1** = **hide**, fell, pelt **2** = **coating**, casing, crust, film, husk, outside, peel, rind ◆ v **3** = **peel**, flay, scrape

skin alive v Inf = **attack**, assail, assault, let have it (inf), let loose on (inf)

skinflint n = **miser**, niggard, penny-pincher (inf), Scrooge

skinny adj = **thin**, emaciated, lean, scrawny, undernourished

skip v **1** = **hop**, bob, bounce, caper, dance, flit, frisk, gambol, prance, trip **2** = **pass over**, eschew, give (something) a miss, leave out, miss out, omit

skirmish n **1** = **fight**, battle, brush, clash, conflict, encounter, fracas, scrap (inf) ◆ v **2** = **fight**, clash, collide

skirt v **1** = **border**, edge, flank **2** (often with *around or round*) = **avoid**, circumvent, evade, steer clear of

skit n **1** = **parody**, burlesque, sketch, spoof (inf) **2** = **play**, comedy, drama, performance

skittish adj = **lively**, excitable, fidgety, highly strung, jumpy, nervous, restive,

skull n bony case that encloses brain. **skull'cap** n close-fitting cap.

skunk n 1 small N Amer. animal that emits evil-smelling fluid. 2 inf mean person.

sky [skī] n, pl **skies** 1 apparently dome-shaped expanse extending upward from the horizon. 2 outer space. 3 heavenly regions. ♦ vt **skied, sky·ing** 4 inf hit, throw (ball) high. **sky'div·ing** n parachute jumping with delayed opening of parachute. **sky'light** [-līt] n window in roof or ceiling. **sky'scrap·er** [-skrayp-ər] n very tall building.

slab n thick, broad piece.

slack [slak] adj 1 loose. 2 sluggish. 3 careless, negligent. 4 not busy. ♦ n 5 loose part, as of rope. ♦ vi 6 be idle or lazy. **slack'en** v 1 become looser. 2 become slower, abate.

slacks [slaks] pl n informal trousers worn by men or women.

slag n refuse of smelted metal.

slain pp. of SLAY.

slake [slayk] vt **slaked, slak·ing** 1 satisfy (thirst, desire, etc.). 2 combine (lime) with water to produce calcium hydroxide.

sla·lom [SLAH-ləm] n, v race over winding course in skiing, automobile racing, etc.

slam v **slammed, slam·ming** 1 shut noisily. 2 bang. 3 hit. 4 dash down. 5 inf criticize harshly. ♦ n 6 (noise of) this action. **slam dunk** n 1 Basketball. forceful downward basket. 2 inf clearcut success. ♦ vt 3

slam-dunked', slam-dunk'ing Basketball. shoot (ball) in a slam dunk. **grand slam** 1 Cards winning of all tricks. 2 Sports winning of selected group of major tournaments in one year.

slan·der [SLAN-dər] n 1 false or malicious statement about person. ♦ v 2 utter such statement. **slan'der·ous** adj

slang n words, etc. or meanings of these used very informally for novelty or vividness or for the sake of unconventionality.

slant v 1 slope. 2 put at angle. 3 write, present (news, etc.) with bias. ♦ n 4 slope. 5 point of view. 6 idea. ♦ adj 7 sloping, oblique. **slant'wise** [-wīz] adv

slap n 1 blow with open hand or flat instrument. ♦ vt **slapped, slap·ping** 2 strike thus. 3 put on, down carelessly or messily. **slap'dash** adj careless and abrupt. **slap'stick** n broad boisterous comedy.

slash vt 1 gash. 2 lash. 3 cut, slit. 4 criticize unmercifully. ♦ n 5 gash. 6 cutting stroke. 7 sloping punctuation mark, either / or .

slat n narrow strip of wood or metal as in window blinds, etc.

slate [slayt] n 1 kind of stone that splits easily in flat sheets. 2 piece of this for covering roof or, formerly, for writing on. ♦ vt **slat·ed, slat·ing** 3 cover with slates.

slath·er [SLATH-ər] n inf 1 generous amount. ♦ vt inf -**ered, -er·ing** 2 spread,

wired (sl)

skulk v = **lurk**, creep, prowl, slink, sneak

sky n = **heavens**, firmament

slab n = **piece**, chunk, lump, portion, slice, wedge

slack adj 1 = **loose**, baggy, lax, limp, relaxed 2 = **negligent**, idle, inactive, lax, lazy, neglectful, remiss, slapdash, slipshod 3 = **slow**, dull, inactive, quiet, slow-moving, sluggish ♦ n 4 = **room**, excess, give (inf), leeway ♦ v 5 = **shirk**, dodge, idle

slacken v (often with off) = **lessen**, abate, decrease, diminish, drop off, moderate, reduce, relax

slacker n = **idler**, couch potato (sl), dodger, loafer, shirker

slake v = **satisfy**, assuage, quench, sate

slam v = **bang**, crash, dash, fling, hurl, smash, throw

slander n 1 = **defamation**, calumny, libel,

scandal, smear ♦ v 2 = **defame**, blacken (someone's) name, libel, malign, smear

slanderous adj = **defamatory**, damaging, libelous, malicious

slant v 1 = **slope**, bend, bevel, cant, heel, incline, lean, list, tilt 2 = **bias**, angle, color, distort, twist ♦ n 3 = **slope**, camber, gradient, incline, tilt 4 = **bias**, angle, emphasis, one-sidedness, point of view, prejudice

slanting adj = **sloping**, angled, at an angle, bent, diagonal, inclined, oblique, tilted, tilting

slap n 1 = **smack**, blow, cuff, spank ♦ v 2 = **smack**, clap, cuff, paddle (U.S. & Canad.), spank

slapdash adj = **careless**, clumsy, hasty, hurried, messy, slipshod, sloppy (inf)

slash v 1 = **cut**, gash, hack, lacerate, rend, rip, score, slit 2 = **reduce**, cut, drop, lower ♦ n 3 = **cut**, gash, incision, laceration, rent, apply thickly.

slat·tern [SLAT-ərn] *n* **1** slut. **slatt'ern·ly** *adj* **1** slovenly, untidy.

slaugh·ter [SLAW-tər] *n* **1** killing. ◆ *vt* **2** kill. **slaugh'ter·ous** *adj* **slaugh'ter·house** [-hows] *n* place for butchering animals for food.

slave [slayv] *n* **1** captive, person without freedom or personal rights. **2** one dominated by another or by a habit, etc. ◆ *vi* **slaved, slav·ing 3** work like slave. **slav'er** *n* person, ship engaged in slave traffic. **slav'er·y** *n* **slav'ish** *adj* servile.

slav·er [SLAV-ər] *vi* **1** dribble saliva from mouth. **2** fawn. ◆ *n* **3** saliva running from mouth.

slay *vt* **slew, slain, slay·ing 1** kill. **2** *inf* impress, esp. by being very funny. **slay'er** *n* killer.

slea·zy [SLEE-zee] *adj* -**zi·er, -zi·est** sordid. **sleaze** [sleez] *n* *sl* **1** sordidness. **2** contemptible person.

sled *n* **1** carriage on runners for sliding on snow. **2** toboggan. ◆ *v* **sled·ded, sled·ding**

sledge [slej] *n* **1** sledgehammer. **2** sled.

sledge·ham·mer [SLEJ-ham-ər] *n* heavy hammer with long handle.

sleek *adj* -**er, -est** glossy, smooth, shiny.

sleep *n* **1** unconscious state regularly occurring in humans and animals. **2** slumber, repose. **3** *inf* dried particles oft. found in corners of eyes after sleeping. ◆ *v* **slept, sleep·ing 4** take rest in sleep, slumber. **5** accommodate for sleeping. **sleep'er** *n* **1** one who sleeps. **2** railroad

sleeping car. **3** *inf* person, firm, etc. that succeeds unexpectedly. **sleep'i·ly** *adv* **sleep'i·ness** [-nis] *n* **sleep'less** [-lis] *adj* **sleep'y** *adj* **sleep·i·er, sleep·i·est sleeping sickness** Afr. disease spread by tsetse fly. **sleep'o·ver** *n* instance of spending the night at another person's home.

sleet *n* rain and snow or hail falling together.

sleeve [sleev] *n* **1** part of garment that covers arm. **2** case surrounding shaft. **3** phonograph record cover. ◆ *vt* **sleeved, sleev·ing 4** furnish with sleeves. **sleeved** *adj* **sleeve'less** [-lis] *adj* **have up one's sleeve** have something prepared secretly for emergency or as trick.

sleigh [slay] *n* sled.

sleight [slīt] *n* **1** dexterity. **2** trickery. **3** deviousness. **sleight of hand 1** (manual dexterity in) conjuring, juggling. **2** legerdemain.

slen·der [SLEN-dər] *adj* **1** slim, slight. **2** feeble.

slept pt./pp. of SLEEP.

sleuth [slooth] *n* **1** detective. **2** bloodhound. ◆ *vt* **3** track.

slew[1] [sloo] pt. of SLAY.

slew[2] *v* swing around.

slew[3] *n inf* large number or quantity.

slice [slīs] *n* **1** thin flat piece cut off. **2** share. **3** spatula. **4** slice of pizza. ◆ *vt* **sliced, slic·ing 5** cut into slices. **6** cut cleanly. **7** hit with bat, club, etc. at angle.

slick [slik] *adj* **1** smooth. **2** smooth-tongued. **3** flattering. **4** superficially attractive. **5** sly.

rip, slit

slaughter *v* **1 = murder**, butcher, kill, massacre, slay ◆ *n* **2 = murder**, bloodshed, butchery, carnage, killing, massacre, slaying

slaughterhouse *n* **= abattoir**

slave *n* **1 = servant**, drudge, serf, vassal ◆ *v* **2 = toil**, drudge, slog

slavery *n* **= enslavement**, bondage, captivity, servitude, subjugation

slavish *adj* **1 = servile**, abject, base, cringing, fawning, grovelling, obsequious, submissive, sycophantic **2 = imitative**, second-hand, unimaginative, unoriginal

slay *v* **= kill**, butcher, massacre, mow down, murder, slaughter

sleaze *n* **= corruption**, bribery, dishonesty, extortion, fraud, unscrupulousness, venality

sleazy *adj* **= sordid**, disreputable, low, run-down, scuzzy (*sl*), seedy, squalid

sleek *adj* **= glossy**, lustrous, shiny, smooth

sleep *n* **1 = slumber(s)**, doze, forty winks (*inf*), hibernation, nap, siesta, snooze (*inf*) ◆ *v* **2 = slumber**, catnap, doze, drowse, hibernate, snooze (*inf*), take a nap

sleepless *adj* **= wakeful**, insomniac, restless

sleepy *adj* **= drowsy**, dull, heavy, inactive, lethargic, sluggish

slender *adj* **1 = slim**, lean, narrow, slight, willowy **2 = faint**, poor, remote, slight, slim, tenuous, thin **3 = meager**, little, scant, scanty, small

sleuth *n* **= detective**, gumshoe (*sl*), private eye (*inf*), (private) investigator

slice *n* **1 = share**, cut, helping, portion, segment, sliver, wedge ◆ *v* **2 = cut**, carve,

◆ vt **6** make glossy, smooth. ◆ n **7** slippery area. **8** patch of oil on water.

slide [slīd] v **slid** or **slid·den, slid·ing 1** slip smoothly along. **2** glide, as over ice. **3** pass imperceptibly. **4** deteriorate morally. ◆ n **5** sliding. **6** surface, track for sliding. **7** sliding part of mechanism. **8** piece of glass holding object to be viewed under microscope. **9** photographic transparency. **slide rule** mathematical instrument of two parts, one of which slides upon the other, for rapid calculations. **sliding scale** schedule for automatically varying one thing (e.g. wages) according to fluctuations of another (e.g. cost of living).

slight [slīt] adj **1** small, trifling. **2** not substantial, fragile. **3** slim, slender. ◆ vt **4** disregard. **5** neglect. ◆ n **6** indifference. **7** act of discourtesy.

slim adj **slim·mer, slim·mest 1** thin. **2** slight. ◆ v **slimmed, slim·ming 3** reduce person's weight by diet and exercise. **slim'ness** n **slim'line** adj **1** appearing slim. **2** pert. to slimness.

slime [slīm] n greasy, thick, liquid mud or similar substance. **slim'y** adj **slim·i·er, slim·i·est 1** like slime. **2** fawning.

sling n **1** strap, loop with string attached at each end for hurling stone. **2** bandage for supporting wounded limb. **3** rope, belt, etc. for hoisting, carrying weights. ◆ vt **slung, sling·ing 4** throw. **5** hoist, swing by

rope.

slink vi **slunk, slink·ing** move stealthily, sneak. **slink'y** adj **slink·i·er, slink·i·est 1** sinuously graceful. **2** (of clothes, etc.) figure-hugging.

slip[1] v **slipped, slip·ping 1** (cause to) move smoothly, easily, quietly. **2** pass out of (mind, etc.). **3** (of motor vehicle clutch) engage partially, fail. ◆ vi **4** lose balance by sliding. **5** fall from person's grasp. **6** (usu. with up) make mistake. **7** decline in health, morals. ◆ vt **8** put on or take off easily, quickly. **9** let go (anchor, etc.). **10** dislocate (bone). ◆ n **11** act or occasion of slipping. **12** mistake. **13** petticoat. **14** small piece of paper. **15** plant cutting. **16** launching slope on which ships are built. **17** covering for pillow. **18** small child. **slip'shod** adj slovenly, careless. **slip'stream** n Aviation stream of air driven astern by engine.

slip[2] n clay mixed with water to creamy consistency, used for decorating ceramic ware.

slip·per [SLIP-ər] n light shoe for indoor use. **slip'pered** adj

slip·per·y [SLIP-ə-ree] adj **1** so smooth as to cause slipping or to be difficult to hold or catch. **2** changeable. **3** unreliable. **4** crafty. **5** wily.

slit vt **slit, slit·ting 1** make long straight cut in. **2** cut in strips. ◆ n

slith·er [SLITH-ər] vi slide unsteadily (down

divide, sever

slick adj **1** = **glib**, plausible, polished, smooth, specious **2** = **skillful**, adroit, deft, dexterous, polished, professional ◆ v **3** = **smooth**, plaster down, sleek

slide v = **slip**, coast, glide, skim, slither

slight adj **1** = **small**, feeble, insignificant, meager, measly, minor, paltry, scanty, trifling, trivial, unimportant **2** = **slim**, delicate, feeble, fragile, lightly-built, small, spare ◆ v **3** = **snub**, affront, blow off (sl), disdain, ignore, insult, scorn ◆ n **4** = **snub**, affront, insult, neglect, rebuff, slap in the face (inf), (the) cold shoulder

slightly adv = **a little**, somewhat

slim adj **1** = **slender**, lean, narrow, slight, svelte, thin, trim **2** = **slight**, faint, poor, remote, slender ◆ v **3** = **lose weight**, diet, reduce

slimy adj **1** = **viscous**, clammy, glutinous, oozy **2** = **obsequious**, creeping, grovelling, oily, servile, smarmy (Brit. inf), unctuous

sling v **1** = **throw**, cast, chuck (inf), fling, heave, hurl, lob (inf), shy, toss **2** = **hang**, dangle, suspend

slink v = **creep**, prowl, skulk, slip, sneak, steal

slinky adj = **figure-hugging**, clinging, close-fitting, skintight

slip[1] v **1** = **fall**, skid **2** = **slide**, glide, skate, slither **3** = **sneak**, conceal, creep, hide, steal **4** (sometimes with up) = **make a mistake**, blunder, err, miscalculate **5 let slip** = **give away**, disclose, divulge, leak, reveal ◆ n **6** = **mistake**, blunder, error, failure, fault, lapse, omission, oversight **7 give (someone) the slip** = **escape from**, dodge, elude, evade, get away from, lose (someone)

slippery adj **1** = **smooth**, glassy, greasy, icy, slippy (inf or dialect), unsafe **2** = **devious**, crafty, cunning, dishonest, evasive, shifty, tricky, untrustworthy

slipshod adj = **careless**, casual, slapdash,

slope, etc.).

sliv·er [SLIV-ər] *n* **1** thin small piece torn off something. **2** splinter.

slob *n* slovenly, coarse person.

slob·ber [SLOB-ər] *v* **1** slaver. **2** be weakly and excessively demonstrative. ◆ *n* **3** running saliva. **4** maudlin speech.

sloe [sloh] *n* blue-black, sour fruit of blackthorn. **sloe-eyed** *adj* **1** dark-eyed. **2** slanty-eyed. **sloe gin** [jin] liqueur of sloes steeped in gin.

slog *v* **slogged, slog·ging 1** hit vigorously, esp. in boxing. **2** work or study with dogged determination. **3** move, work with difficulty. ◆ *n*

slo·gan [SLOH-gən] *n* distinctive phrase (in advertising, etc.).

sloop *n* **1** small one-masted vessel. **2** *Hist.* small warship.

slop *v* **slopped, slop·ping 1** spill. **2** splash. ◆ *n* **3** spilled liquid. **4** watery food. **5** dirty liquid. ◆ *pl* **6** liquid refuse. **slop'py** *adj* **-pi·er, -pi·est 1** careless, untidy. **2** sentimental. **3** wet, muddy.

slope [slohp] *v* **sloped, slop·ing** ◆ *vt* **1** place slanting. ◆ *vi* **2** lie in, follow an inclined course. **3** go furtively. ◆ *n* **4** slant. **5** upward, downward inclination.

slosh *n* **1** watery mud, etc. ◆ *v* **2** splash. **sloshed** *adj sl* drunk.

slot *n* **1** narrow hole or depression. **2** slit for coins. ◆ *vt* **slot·ted, slot·ting 3** put in slot. **4** sort. **5** place in series, organization. **slot machine** automatic machine worked by insertion of coin.

sloth [slawth] *n* **1** sluggish S Amer. animal. **2** sluggishness. **sloth'ful** [-fəl] *adj* lazy, idle.

slouch [slowch] *vi* **1** walk, sit, etc. in lazy or ungainly, drooping manner. ◆ *n, adj* **2** (of hat) with wide, flexible brim.

slough[1] [rhymes with **cow**] *n* bog.

slough[2] [sluf] *n* **1** skin shed by snake. ◆ *v* **2** shed (skin). **3** drop off.

slov·en [SLUV-ən] *n* dirty, untidy person. **slov'en·ly** *adj* **-li·er, -li·est 1** untidy. **2** careless. **3** disorderly. ◆ *adv*

slow [sloh] *adj* **-er, -est 1** lasting a long time. **2** moving at low speed. **3** behind the true time. **4** dull. ◆ *v* **5** slacken speed (of). **slow motion** motion picture showing movement greatly slowed down. **slow'poke** [-pohk] *n* person slow in moving, acting, deciding, etc.

sludge [sluj] *n* **1** slush, ooze. **2** sewage.

───── THESAURUS ─────

sloppy (*inf*), slovenly, untidy

slit *n* **1** = **cut**, gash, incision, opening, rent, split, tear ◆ *v* **2** = **cut (open)**, gash, knife, lance, pierce, rip, slash

slither *v* = **slide**, glide, slink, slip, snake, undulate

sliver *n* = **shred**, fragment, paring, shaving, splinter

slobber *v* = **drool**, dribble, drivel, salivate, slaver

slobbish *adj* = **messy**, slovenly, unclean, unkempt, untidy

slog *v* **1** = **work**, labor, plod, plow through, slave, toil **2** = **trudge**, tramp, trek **3** = **hit**, punch, slug, sock (*sl*), strike, thump, wallop (*inf*) ◆ *n* **4** = **labor**, effort, exertion, struggle **5** = **trudge**, hike, tramp, trek

slogan *n* = **catch phrase**, catchword, motto

slop *v* **1** = **spill**, overflow, slosh (*inf*), splash ◆ *n* **2** *Inf* = **food**, grub (*sl*), mess (*sl*)

slope *n* **1** = **inclination**, gradient, incline, ramp, rise, slant, tilt ◆ *v* **2** = **slant**, drop away, fall, incline, lean, rise, tilt **3** **slope off** = **slink away**, creep away, slip away

sloping *adj* = **slanting**, inclined, leaning, oblique

sloppy *adj* **1** = **careless**, messy, slipshod, slovenly, untidy **2** = **sentimental**, gushing, mawkish, slushy (*inf*)

slot *n* **1** = **opening**, aperture, groove, hole, slit, vent **2** *Inf* = **place**, opening, position, space, time, vacancy ◆ *v* **3** = **fit in**, fit, insert

sloth *n* = **laziness**, idleness, inactivity, inertia, slackness, sluggishness, torpor

slothful *adj* = **lazy**, idle, inactive, indolent, workshy

slouch *v* = **slump**, droop, loll, stoop

slovenly *adj* = **careless**, disorderly, negligent, slack, slapdash, slipshod, sloppy (*inf*), untidy

slow *adj* **1** = **prolonged**, gradual, lingering, long-drawn-out, protracted **2** = **unhurried**, dawdling, lackadaisical, laggard, lazy, leisurely, ponderous, sluggish **3** = **late**, backward, behind, delayed, tardy **4** = **stupid**, braindead (*inf*), dense, dim, dull-witted, obtuse, retarded, thick ◆ *v* **5** (often with *up* or *down*) = **reduce speed**, brake, decelerate, handicap, hold up, retard, slacken (off)

slowly *adv* = **gradually**, leisurely, unhurriedly

slug[1] *n* **1** land snail with no shell. **2** bullet. **slug'gard** [-ərd] *n* lazy, idle person. **slug'gish** *adj* **1** slow. **2** lazy, inert. **3** not functioning well. **slug'gish·ness** *n*

slug[2] *v* **slugged, slug·ging 1** hit, slog. ◆ *n inf* **2** heavy blow. **3** shot of whiskey. **slug'ger** *n* hard-hitting boxer, baseball batter.

sluice [sloos] *n* **1** gate, door to control flow of water. ◆ *vt* **sluiced, sluic·ing 2** pour water over, through.

slum *n* **1** squalid street or neighborhood. ◆ *vi* **slummed, slum·ming 2** visit slums. **slum'lord** *n* landlord who owns buildings in slums and neglects them.

slum·ber [SLUM-bər] *vi, n* sleep. **slum'ber·er** *n*

slump *v* **1** fall heavily. **2** relax ungracefully. **3** decline suddenly in value, volume or esteem. ◆ *n* **4** sudden decline. **5** (of prices, etc.) sharp fall. **6** depression.

slung pt./pp. of SLING.

slunk pt./pp. of SLINK.

slur *vt* **slurred, slur·ring 1** pass over lightly. **2** run together (words, musical notes). **3** disparage. ◆ *n* **4** slight, stigma. **5** *Mus.* curved line above or below notes to be slurred.

slurp *v* eat, drink noisily.

slur·ry [SLUR-ee] *n, pl* **-ries** muddy liquid mixture as cement, mud, etc.

slush *n* **1** watery, muddy substance. **2** excessive sentimentality. **slush'y** *adj*

slush·i·er, slush·i·est slush fund fund for financing bribery, corruption.

slut *n offens* promiscuous woman. **slut'tish** *adj*

sly [slī] *adj* **sly·er** or **sli·er, sly·est** or **sli·est 1** cunning, wily, knowing. **2** secret, deceitful. **sly'ly, sli'ly** *adv* **sly'ness** [-nis] *n*

Sm *Chem.* samarium.

smack[1] [smak] *n* **1** taste, flavor. **2** *sl* heroin. ◆ *vi* **3** taste (of). **4** suggest.

smack[2] *vt* **1** slap. **2** open and close (lips) with loud sound. ◆ *n* **3** smacking slap. **4** crack. **5** such sound. **6** loud kiss. ◆ *adv inf* **7** squarely. **8** directly. **smack'dab'** *adv inf* smack.

smack[3] *n* small sailing vessel, usu. for fishing.

small [smawl] *adj* **-er, -est 1** little, unimportant. **2** petty. **3** short. **4** weak. **5** mean. ◆ *n* **6** small slender part esp. of the back. **small hours** hours just after midnight. **small-mind·ed** [-mīnd-id] *adj* **1** having narrow views. **2** petty. **small'pox** *n* contagious disease. **small talk** light, polite conversation.

smarm·y [SMAHR-mee] *adj* **smarm·i·er, smarm·i·est 1** unpleasantly suave. **2** fawning.

smart [smahrt] *adj* **-er, -est 1** astute. **2** brisk. **3** clever, witty. **4** impertinent. **5** trim, well dressed. **6** fashionable. **7** causing stinging pain. ◆ *v* **8** feel, cause pain. ◆ *n* **9** sharp pain. **smart'en** *vt* **smart'ly** *adv*

——————————| THESAURUS |——————————

sludge *n* = **sediment**, mire, muck, mud, ooze, residue, silt, slime

sluggish *adj* = **inactive**, dull, heavy, indolent, inert, lethargic, slothful, slow, torpid

slum *n* = **hovel**, ghetto

slumber *v* = **sleep**, doze, drowse, nap, snooze (*inf*)

slump *v* **1** = **fall**, collapse, crash, plunge, sink, slip **2** = **sag**, droop, hunch, loll, slouch ◆ *n* **3** = **fall**, collapse, crash, decline, downturn, drop, reverse, trough **4** = **recession**, depression

slur *n* = **insult**, affront, aspersion, calumny, innuendo, insinuation, smear, stain

slut *n Offens* = **tart**, ho (*sl*), trollop, whore

sly *adj* **1** = **cunning**, artful, clever, crafty, devious, scheming, secret, shifty, stealthy, subtle, underhand, wily **2** = **roguish**, arch, impish, knowing, mischievous ◆ *n* **3** **on the sly** = **secretly**, covertly, on the quiet,

privately, surreptitiously

smack *v* **1** = **slap**, clap, cuff, hit, paddle (*U.S. & Canad.*), spank, strike ◆ *n* **2** = **slap**, blow ◆ *adv* **3** *Inf* = **directly**, exactly, precisely, right, slap (*inf*), squarely, straight

small *adj* **1** = **little**, diminutive, mini, miniature, minute, petite, pygmy *or* pigmy, teeny, teeny-weeny, tiny, undersized, wee **2** = **unimportant**, insignificant, minor, negligible, paltry, petty, trifling, trivial **3** = **petty**, base, mean, narrow **4** = **modest**, humble, unpretentious

small-minded *adj* = **petty**, bigoted, intolerant, mean, narrow-minded, ungenerous

small-time *adj* = **minor**, insignificant, of no account, petty, unimportant

smarmy *adj Brit. inf* = **obsequious**, crawling, ingratiating, servile, smooth, suave, sycophantic, toadying, unctuous

smart'ness [-nis] n **smart al'eck** conceited person, know-it-all. **smart ass** sl, offens smart aleck. **smart card** plastic card with integrated circuit capable of storing and processing data, used for identification, bank and store transactions, etc.

smash vt **1** break violently. **2** strike hard. **3** ruin. **4** destroy. ♦ vi **5** break. **6** dash violently against. ♦ n **7** heavy blow. **8** collision (of vehicles, etc.). **9** total financial failure. **10** inf popular success. **smashed** adj sl very drunk or affected by drugs. **smash'er** n attractive person, thing.

smat•ter•ing [SMAT-ər-ing] n slight superficial knowledge.

smear [smeer] vt **1** rub with grease, etc. **2** smudge, spread with dirt, grease, etc. ♦ n **3** mark made thus. **4** sample of secretion for medical examination. **5** slander.

smell v **smelled** or **smelt**, **smell'ing 1** perceive by nose. **2** suspect. **3** give out odor. **4** use nose. ♦ n **5** faculty of perceiving odors by nose. **6** anything detected by sense of smell. **smell'y** adj **smell•i•er**, **smell•i•est** with strong (unpleasant) smell.

smelt[1] vt extract metal from ore. **smelt'er** n

smelt[2] n fish of salmon family.

smid•gen [SMIJ-ən] n very small amount.

smile [smīl] n **1** curving or parting of lips in pleased or amused expression. ♦ v **smiled**, **smil•ing 2** wear, assume a smile. **3** approve, favor.

smirch [smurch] vt **1** dirty, sully. **2**

disgrace, discredit. ♦ n **3** stain. **4** disgrace.

smirk [smurk] n **1** smile expressing scorn, smugness. ♦ v

smite [smīt] vt **smote**, **smit'ten** or **smit**, **smit'ing 1** strike. **2** attack. **3** afflict. **4** affect, esp. with love or fear.

smith n worker in iron, gold, etc. **smith'y** n, pl **smith•ies 1** blacksmith's workshop. **2** blacksmith.

smith•er•eens [SMITH-ər-eenz] pl n small bits.

smock [smok] n **1** loose outer garment. ♦ vt **2** gather by sewing in honeycomb pattern. **smock'ing** n

smog n mixture of smoke and fog.

smoke [smohk] n **1** cloudy mass of suspended particles that rises from fire or anything burning. **2** spell of tobacco smoking. ♦ v **smoked**, **smok•ing** ♦ vi **3** give off smoke. **4** inhale and expel tobacco smoke. ♦ vt **5** use (tobacco) by smoking. **6** expose to smoke (esp. in curing fish, etc.). **smok'er** n **1** one who smokes. **2** informal party.

smol•der [SMOHL-dər] vi **1** burn slowly without flame. **2** (of feelings) exist in suppressed state.

smooch v, n inf kiss, cuddle.

smooth [smooth] adj **1** not rough, even of surface or texture. **2** sinuous. **3** flowing. **4** calm, soft, soothing. **5** suave, plausible. **6** free from jolts. ♦ vt **7** make smooth. **8** quiet. **smooth'ly** adv

smor•gas•bord [SMOR-gəs-bord] n buffet

smart adj **1** = **clever**, acute, astute, bright, canny, ingenious, intelligent, keen, quick, sharp, shrewd **2** = **brisk**, lively, quick, vigorous ♦ v **3** = **sting**, burn, hurt ♦ n **4** = **sting**, pain, soreness

smart aleck n Inf = **know-all** (inf), smarty pants (inf), wise guy (inf)

smarten v = **tidy**, groom, put in order, put to rights, spruce up

smash v **1** = **break**, crush, demolish, pulverize, shatter **2** = **collide**, crash **3** = **destroy**, lay waste, ruin, trash (sl), wreck ♦ n **4** = **destruction**, collapse, downfall, failure, ruin **5** = **collision**, accident, crash

smattering n = **modicum**, bit, rudiments

smear v **1** = **spread over**, bedaub, coat, cover, daub, rub on **2** = **dirty**, smudge, soil, stain, sully **3** = **slander**, besmirch, blacken, malign ♦ n **4** = **smudge**, blot, blotch, daub, splotch, streak **5** = **slander**,

calumny, defamation, libel

smell v **1** = **sniff**, scent **2** = **stink**, reek ♦ n **3** = **odor**, aroma, bouquet, fragrance, perfume, scent **4** = **stink**, fetor, stench

smelly adj = **stinking**, fetid, foul, foul-smelling, funky (sl), malodorous, noisome, reeking

smirk n = **smug look**, simper

smitten adj **1** = **afflicted**, laid low, plagued, struck **2** = **infatuated**, beguiled, bewitched, captivated, charmed, enamored

smolder v = **seethe**, boil, fume, rage, simmer

smooth adj **1** = **even**, flat, flush, horizontal, level, plane **2** = **sleek**, glossy, polished, shiny, silky, soft, velvety **3** = **easy**, effortless, well-ordered **4** = **flowing**, regular, rhythmic, steady, uniform **5** = **suave**, facile, glib, persuasive, slick, meal of assorted dishes.

smote pt. of SMITE.

smoth·er [SMUTH-ər] v 1 suffocate. 2 envelop. 3 suppress. ◆ vi 4 be suffocated.

SMS Short Message Server, system for sending messages of no more than 160 characters to a cell phone.

smudge [smuj] v **smudged, smudg·ing** make smear, stain, dirty mark (on). ◆ n

smug adj **smug·ger** self-satisfied, complacent. **smug'ly** adv

smug·gle [SMUG-əl] vt **-gled, -gling** 1 import, export without paying customs duties. 2 conceal, take secretly. **smug'gler** n

smut n 1 piece of soot, particle of dirt. 2 lewd or obscene talk, etc. 3 disease of grain. ◆ vt **smut·ted, smut·ting** 4 blacken, smudge. **smut'ty** adj **-ti·er, -ti·est** 1 soiled with smut, soot. 2 obscene, lewd.

Sn Chem. tin.

snack [snak] n 1 light portion of food eaten hastily between meals. ◆ vi 2 eat thus. **snack bar** lunchroom at which light meals are served.

snag n 1 difficulty. 2 sharp protuberance. 3 hole, loop in fabric caused by sharp object. 4 obstacle (e.g. tree branch, etc. in river bed). ◆ vt **snagged, snag'ging** 5 catch, damage on snag.

snail [snayl] n 1 slow-moving mollusk with shell. 2 slow, sluggish person. **snail'like** adj **snail mail** n inf 1 conventional mail, as opposed to e-mail. 2 the conventional postal system. **snail-mail** vt send by the conventional postal system, rather than by e-mail.

snake [snayk] n 1 long scaly limbless reptile, serpent. ◆ v **snaked, snak·ing** 2 move like snake. **snak'y** adj **snak·i·er, snak·i·est** twisted or winding. **snake in the grass** hidden enemy.

snap v **snapped, snap·ping** 1 break suddenly. 2 make cracking sound. 3 bite (at) suddenly. 4 speak suddenly, angrily. ◆ n 5 act of snapping. 6 fastener. 7 snapshot. 8 inf easy task. 9 brief period, esp. of cold weather. ◆ adj 10 sudden, unplanned, arranged quickly. **snap'py** adj **-pi·er, -pi·est** 1 irritable. 2 inf quick. 3 inf well-dressed, fashionable. **snap'drag·on** n plant with flowers that can be opened like a mouth. **snap'shot** n informal photograph.

snare [snair] n (noose used as) trap. ◆ vt **snared, snar·ing** catch with one.

snarl [snahrl] n 1 growl of angry dog. 2 tangle, knot. ◆ vi 3 utter snarl. 4 grumble.

snatch [snach] v 1 make quick grab or bite (at). 2 seize, catch. ◆ n 3 grab. 4 fragment. 5 short spell.

sneak [sneek] vi **sneaked, sneak·ing** 1 slink. 2 move about furtively. 3 act in mean, underhand manner. ◆ n 4 mean, treacherous person. **sneak'ing** adj secret but persistent. **sneak pre'view** unannounced showing of movie before general release.

sneak·ers [SNEEK-ərz] pl n flexible,

smarmy (Brit. inf), unctuous, urbane 6 = **mellow**, agreeable, mild, pleasant ◆ v 7 = **flatten**, iron, level, plane, press 8 = **calm**, appease, assuage, ease, mitigate, mollify, soften

smother v 1 = **suffocate**, choke, stifle, strangle 2 = **suppress**, conceal, hide, muffle, repress, stifle

smudge v 1 = **smear**, daub, dirty, mark, smirch ◆ n 2 = **smear**, blemish, blot

smug adj = **self-satisfied**, complacent, conceited, superior

smuggler n = **trafficker**, bootlegger, runner

smutty adj = **obscene**, bawdy, blue, coarse, crude, dirty, indecent, indelicate, suggestive, vulgar

snack n = **light meal**, bite, refreshment(s)

snag n 1 = **difficulty**, catch, complication, disadvantage, downside, drawback, hitch,

obstacle, problem ◆ v 2 = **catch**, rip, tear

snap v 1 = **break**, crack, separate 2 = **crackle**, click, pop 3 = **bite at**, bite, nip, snatch 4 = **speak sharply**, bark, jump down (someone's) throat (inf), lash out at ◆ n 5 = **crackle**, pop 6 = **bite**, grab, nip ◆ adj 7 = **instant**, immediate, spur-of-the-moment, sudden

snappy adj 1 = **irritable**, cross, edgy, testy, touchy 2 = **smart**, chic, cool (inf), dapper, fashionable, phat (sl), stylish

snap up v = **seize**, grab, pounce upon, take advantage of

snare n 1 = **trap**, gin, net, noose, wire ◆ v 2 = **trap**, catch, entrap, net, seize, wire

snarl[1] v (often with up) = **tangle**, entangle, entwine, muddle, ravel

snarl-up n = **tangle**, confusion, entanglement, muddle

snatch v 1 = **seize**, clutch, grab, grasp, grip

informal sports shoes.

sneer n scornful, contemptuous expression or remark. ◆ v

sneeze [sneez] vi **sneezed, sneez·ing** emit breath through nose with sudden involuntary spasm and noise. ◆ n

snick·er [SNIK-ər] n sly, disrespectful laugh, esp. partly stifled. ◆ v

snide [snīd] adj **snid·er, snid·est** malicious, supercilious.

sniff vi **1** inhale through nose with sharp hiss. **2** (with at) express disapproval, etc. by sniffing. ◆ vt **3** take up through nose, smell. ◆ v **snif·fle** [-əl] **-fled, -fling 1** sniff noisily through nose, esp. when suffering from a cold in the head. **2** snuffle.

snig·ger [SNIG-ər] n snicker.

snip vt **snipped, snip·ping 1** cut, cut bits off. ◆ n **2** act, sound of snipping. **3** bit cut off. **4** inf small, insignificant, impertinent person. **snip·pet** [SNIP-it] n shred, fragment, clipping. **snips** pl n tool for cutting.

snipe [snīp] n **1** wading bird. ◆ v **sniped, snip·ing 2** shoot at enemy from cover. **3** (with at) criticize, attack (person) slyly. **snip'er** n

snit n irritated state of mind.

snitch [snich] vt inf **1** steal. ◆ vi **2** inform. ◆ n **3** informer.

sniv·el [SNIV-əl] vi **-eled, -el·ing 1** sniffle to show distress. **2** whine.

snob n one who pretentiously judges others by social rank, etc. **snob'ber·y** n **snob'bish** adj of or like a snob.

snook·er [SNUUK-ər] n **1** game like pool played with 21 balls. ◆ vt **2** leave (opponent) in unfavorable position. **3** place (someone) in difficult situation. **4** sl cheat.

snoop v **1** pry, meddle. **2** peer into. ◆ n **3** one who acts thus. **4** snooping.

snoot·y [SNOOT-ee] adj **snoot·i·er, snoot·i·est** inf haughty.

snooze [snooz] vi **snoozed, snooz·ing 1** take short sleep. ◆ n **2** nap.

snore [snor] vi **snored, snor·ing** breathe noisily when asleep. ◆ n

snor·kel [SNOR-kəl] n **1** tube for breathing underwater. ◆ vi **2** swim, fish using this.

snort vi **1** make (contemptuous) noise by driving breath through nostrils. **2** sl inhale drug. ◆ n **3** noise of snorting. **4** sl shot of liquor. **5** sl amount of drug inhaled.

snot n vulg mucus from nose. **snot·ty** [-tee] adj **-ti·er, -ti·est** inf arrogant.

snout [snowt] n animal's nose.

snow [snoh] n **1** frozen vapor that falls in flakes. **2** sl cocaine. ◆ v **3** fall, sprinkle as snow. **4** let fall, throw down like snow. **5** cover with snow. **6** sl overwhelm. **7** sl deceive. **snow'y** adj **snow·i·er, snow·i·est 1** of, like snow. **2** covered with snow. **3** very white. **snow'ball** n **1** snow pressed

◆ n **2** = **bit**, fragment, part, piece, snippet

sneak v **1** = **slink**, lurk, pad, skulk, slip, steal **2** = **slip**, smuggle, spirit ◆ n **3** = **informer**, telltale

sneaking adj **1** = **nagging**, persistent, uncomfortable, worrying **2** = **secret**, hidden, private, undivulged, unexpressed, unvoiced

sneaky adj = **sly**, deceitful, devious, dishonest, double-dealing, down and dirty (inf), furtive, low, mean, shifty, untrustworthy

sneer n **1** = **scorn**, derision, gibe, jeer, mockery, ridicule ◆ v **2** = **scorn**, deride, disdain, jeer, laugh, mock, ridicule

snide adj = **nasty**, cynical, disparaging, hurtful, ill-natured, malicious, sarcastic, scornful, sneering, spiteful

sniff v = **inhale**, breathe, smell

snigger n, v = **laugh**, giggle, snicker, titter

snip v **1** = **cut**, clip, crop, dock, shave, trim ◆ n **2** = **bit**, clipping, fragment, piece, scrap, shred

snipe v = **criticize**, carp, denigrate, disparage, jeer, knock (inf), put down

snippet n = **piece**, fragment, part, scrap, shred

snitch v **1** Inf = **inform on**, grass on (Brit. sl), tattle on, tell on (inf), tell tales ◆ n **2** = **informer**, tattletale, telltale

snivel v = **whine**, cry, moan, sniffle, whimper

snob n = **elitist**, highbrow, prig

snobbery n = **arrogance**, airs, pretension, pride, snobbishness

snobbish adj = **superior**, arrogant, patronizing, pretentious, snooty (inf), stuck-up (inf)

snoop v = **pry**, interfere, poke one's nose in (inf), spy

snooper n = **nosy rosy** (U.S. inf), busybody, meddler, snoop (inf)

snooze v **1** = **doze**, catnap, nap, take forty winks (inf) ◆ n **2** = **doze**, catnap, forty into hard ball for throwing. ◆ v 2 increase rapidly. 3 play, fight with snowballs. **snow blind·ness** temporary blindness due to brightness of snow. **snow'board** n board like surfboard for descending ski slopes. **snow'drift** n bank of deep snow. **snow fence** fence for erecting in winter beside exposed road. **snow job** sl attempt to deceive by flattery or exaggeration. **snow line** elevation above which snow does not melt. **snow'shoes** [-shooz] pl n shoes like rackets for traveling on snow. **snow under 1** cover and block with snow. **2** fig overwhelm.

snub vt snubbed, snub·bing 1 insult (esp. by ignoring) intentionally. ◆ n, adj 2 short and blunt. **snub-nosed** adj

snuff[1] n powdered tobacco for inhaling through nose. **up to snuff** inf up to a standard.

snuff[2] vt extinguish (esp. candle, etc.).

snuf·fle [SNUF-əl] vi -fled, -fling breathe noisily, with difficulty.

snug adj -ger, -gest warm, comfortable. **snug'gle** v -gled, -gling lie close to for warmth or affection. **snug'ly** adv

so[1] [soh] adv 1 to such an extent. 2 in such a manner. 3 very. 4 the case being such. 5 accordingly. ◆ conj 6 therefore. 7 in order that. 8 with the result that. ◆ interj 9 well! **so-called** adj called by but doubtfully deserving that name. **so long** inf goodbye.

so[2] see SOL.

soak [sohk] v 1 steep. 2 absorb. 3 drench. 4 lie in liquid. 5 sl overcharge (customer). ◆ n 6 soaking. 7 sl habitual drunkard.

soap [sohp] n 1 compound of alkali and oil used in washing. ◆ vt 2 apply soap to. **soap'y** adj soap-i-er, soap-i-est **soap opera** radio or TV serial of domestic life.

soar [sor] vi 1 fly high. 2 increase, rise (in price, etc.).

sob vi sobbed, sob·bing 1 catch breath, esp. in weeping. ◆ n 2 sobbing. **sob story** tale of personal distress told to arouse sympathy.

so·ber [SOH-bər] adj -ber-er, -ber-est 1 not drunk. 2 temperate. 3 subdued. 4 dull, plain. 5 solemn. ◆ v 6 make, become sober. **so·bri·e·ty** [sə-BRĪ-i-tee] n state of being sober.

so·bri·quet [SOH-brə-kay] n 1 nickname. 2 assumed name.

soc·cer [SOK-ər] n ball game played with feet and spherical ball.

so·cia·ble [SOH-shə-bəl] adj 1 friendly. 2 convivial. **so·cia·bil'i·ty** n

so·cial [SOH-shəl] adj 1 living in communities. 2 relating to society. 3 sociable. ◆ n 4 informal gathering. **so'cial·ite** n 1 member of fashionable society. **so'cial·ize** v -ized, -iz-ing **so'cial·ly** adv **social security** government-sponsored provision for the disabled, unemployed, aged, etc. **social work** work to improve welfare of others.

so·cial·ism [SOH-shə-liz-əm] n political system that advocates public ownership of means of production, distribution and exchange. **so'cial·ist** n, adj

---

winks (inf), nap, siesta

snub v 1 = **put down**, avoid, blow off (sl), cold-shoulder, cut (inf), humiliate, ignore, rebuff, slight ◆ n 2 = **insult**, affront, put-down, slap in the face

snug adj = **cozy**, comfortable, comfy (inf), homey, warm

snuggle v = **nestle**, cuddle, nuzzle

soak v 1 = **wet**, bathe, damp, drench, immerse, moisten, saturate, steep 2 = **penetrate**, permeate, seep 3 **soak up** = **absorb**, assimilate

soaking adj = **soaked**, drenched, dripping, saturated, sodden, sopping, streaming, wet through, wringing wet

soar v 1 = **ascend**, fly, mount, rise, wing 2 = **rise**, climb, escalate, rocket, shoot up

sob v = **cry**, howl, shed tears, weep

sober adj 1 = **abstinent**, abstemious,

moderate, temperate 2 = **serious**, composed, cool, grave, level-headed, rational, reasonable, sedate, solemn, staid, steady 3 = **plain**, dark, drab, dumpy (inf), frowzy, homely (U.S.), quiet, somber, subdued

sobriety n 1 = **abstinence**, abstemiousness, moderation, nonindulgence, soberness, temperance 2 = **seriousness**, gravity, level-headedness, solemnity, staidness, steadiness

so-called adj = **alleged**, pretended, professed, self-styled, supposed

sociable adj = **friendly**, affable, companionable, convivial, cordial, genial, gregarious, outgoing, social, warm

social adj 1 = **communal**, collective, common, community, general, group, public ◆ n 2 = **get-together** (inf),

so·ci·e·ty [sə-SĪ-i-tee] *n, pl* **-ties 1** living associated with others. **2** those so living. **3** companionship. **4** company. **5** association. **6** club. **7** fashionable people collectively.

so·ci·ol·o·gy [soh-see-OL-ə-jee] *n* study of societies.

sock¹ [sok] *n* cloth covering for foot.

sock² *vt* **1** hit. ◆ *n* **2** blow.

sock·et [SOK-it] *n* hole or recess for something to fit into.

So·crat·ic [sə-KRAT-ik] *adj* of, like Greek philosopher Socrates.

sod *n* lump of earth with grass.

so·da [SOH-də] *n* **1** compound of sodium. **2** soda water. **soda water** water charged with carbon dioxide.

sod·den [SOD-n] *adj* **1** soaked. **2** drunk. **3** heavy and lumpy.

so·di·um [SOD-dee-əm] *n* metallic alkaline element. **sodium bicarbonate** white crystalline soluble compound (also **bicarbonate of soda**).

sod·om·y [SOD-ə-mee] *n* anal intercourse. **sod·om·ite** *n*

so·fa [SOH-fə] *n* upholstered couch with back and arms, for two or more people.

soft [sawft] *adj* **-er, -est 1** yielding easily to pressure, not hard. **2** mild. **3** easy. **4** subdued. **5** quiet, gentle. **6** (too) lenient. **7** oversentimental. **8** foolish, stupid. **9** (of water) containing few mineral salts. **10** (of drugs) not liable to cause addiction.

soft·en [SAWF-ən] *v* **1** make, become soft or softer. **2** mollify. **3** lighten. **4** mitigate. **5** make less loud. **soft'ly** *adv* gently, quietly. **soft'ball** *n* (ball used in) variation of baseball using larger, softer ball. **soft drink** one that is nonalcoholic. **soft goods** nondurable goods, e.g. curtains, rugs. **soft soap** *inf* flattery. **soft'ware** *n* programs used with a computer. **soft'wood** [-wuud] *n* wood of coniferous tree.

sog·gy [SOG-ee] *adj* **-gi·er, -gi·est 1** soaked with liquid. **2** damp and heavy.

soil¹ *n* **1** earth, ground. **2** country, territory.

soil² *v* **1** make, become dirty. **2** tarnish, defile. ◆ *n* **3** dirt. **4** sewage. **5** stain.

soir·ee [swah-RAY] *n* private evening party esp. with music.

so·journ [SOH-jurn] *vi* **1** stay for a time. ◆ *n* **2** short stay. **so'journ·er** *n*

sol, so *n* fifth sol-fa note.

sol·ace [SOL-is] *n, vt* **-aced, -ac·ing** comfort in distress.

so·lar [SOH-lər] *adj* of the sun. **solar plex'us** network of nerves at pit of stomach.

so·lar·i·um [sə-LAIR-ee-əm] *n, pl* **-i·ums** room built mainly of glass to give exposure to sun.

sold pt./pp. of SELL.

sol·der [SOD-ər] *n* **1** easily-melted alloy used for joining metal. ◆ *vt* **2** join with it. **soldering iron** tool for melting and

——————| THESAURUS |——————

gathering, party

socialize *v* = **mix**, fraternize, get about *or* around, go out

society *n* **1** = **mankind**, civilization, humanity, people, the community, the public **2** = **organization**, association, circle, club, fellowship, group, guild, institute, league, order, union **3** = **upper classes**, beau monde, elite, gentry, high society **4** = **companionship**, company, fellowship, friendship

sodden *adj* = **soaked**, drenched, saturated, soggy, sopping, waterlogged

sofa *n* = **couch**, chaise longue, divan, settee

soft *adj* **1** = **pliable**, bendable, elastic, flexible, malleable, moldable, plastic, supple **2** = **yielding**, elastic, gelatinous, pulpy, spongy, squashy **3** = **velvety**, downy, feathery, fleecy, silky, smooth **4** = **quiet**, dulcet, gentle, murmured, muted, soft-toned **5** = **pale**, bland, light, mellow, pastel, subdued **6** = **dim**, dimmed, faint, restful **7** = **mild**, balmy, temperate **8** = **lenient**, easy-going, indulgent, lax, overindulgent, permissive, spineless **9** = **out of condition**, effeminate, flabby, flaccid, limp, weak **10** *Inf* = **easy**, comfortable, undemanding **11** = **kind**, compassionate, gentle, sensitive, sentimental, tenderhearted, touchy-feely (*inf*)

soften *v* = **lessen**, allay, appease, cushion, ease, mitigate, moderate, mollify, still, subdue, temper

softhearted *adj* = **kind**, charitable, compassionate, sentimental, sympathetic, tender, tenderhearted, warm-hearted

soggy *adj* = **sodden**, dripping, moist, saturated, soaked, sopping, waterlogged

soil¹ *n* **1** = **earth**, clay, dirt, dust, ground **2** = **land**, country

soil² *v* = **dirty**, befoul, besmirch, defile, foul, pollute, spot, stain, sully, tarnish

solace *n* **1** = **comfort**, consolation, relief ◆ *v* applying solder.

sol·dier [SOHL-jər] *n* **1** one serving in army. ♦ *vi* **2** serve in army. **3** *inf* loaf. **4** (with *on*) persist doggedly. **sol'dier·ly** *adj*

sole[1] [sohl] *adj* **1** one and only, unique. **2** solitary. **sole'ly** *adv* **1** alone. **2** only. **3** entirely.

sole[2] *n* **1** underside of foot. **2** underpart of shoe, etc. ♦ *vt* **soled, sol·ing 3** fit with sole.

sole[3] *n* small edible flatfish.

sol·e·cism [SOL-ə-siz-əm] *n* breach of grammar or etiquette.

sol·emn [SOL-əm] *adj* **1** serious. **2** formal. **3** impressive. **sol'emn·ly** *adv* **so·lem·ni·ty** [sə-LEM-ni-tee] *n* **sol·em·nize** [SOL-əm-nīz] *vt* **-nized, -niz·ing 1** celebrate, perform. **2** make solemn.

sol·e·noid [SOH-lə-noid] *n* coil of wire as part of electrical apparatus.

sol-fa [sohl-FAH] *n Mus.* system of syllables sol, fa, etc. sung in scale.

so·lic·it [sə-LIS-it] *vt* **1** request. **2** accost. **3** urge. **4** entice. **so·lic·i·ta'tion** *n* **so·lic'i·tor** *n* one who solicits. **so·lic'i·tous** *adj* **1** anxious. **2** eager. **3** earnest. **so·lic'i·tude** *n*

sol·id *adj* **1** not hollow. **2** compact. **3** composed of one substance. **4** firm. **5** massive. **6** reliable, sound. ♦ *n* **7** body of three dimensions. **8** substance not liquid or gas. **sol·i·dar'i·ty** *n* **1** unity of interests. **2** united condition. **so·lid'i·fy** *v* **-fied, -fy·ing 1** make, become solid or firm. **2** harden.

so·lid'i·ty *n*

so·lil·o·quy [sə-LIL-ə-kwee] *n, pl* **-quies** (esp. in drama) thoughts spoken by person while alone. **so·lil'o·quize** *vi* **-quized, -quiz·ing**

sol·ip·sism [SOL-ip-siz-əm] *n* doctrine that self is the only thing known to exist. **sol'ip·sist** *n*

sol·i·tar·y [SOL-i-ter-ee] *adj* **1** alone, single. ♦ *n* **2** hermit. **sol'i·taire** *n* **1** game for one person played with cards or with pegs set in board. **2** single precious stone set by itself. **sol'i·tude** *n* **1** state of being alone. **2** loneliness.

so·lo [SOH-loh] *n, pl* **-los 1** music for one performer. ♦ *adj* **2** not concerted. **3** unaccompanied, alone. **4** piloting airplane alone. **so'lo·ist** *n*

sol·stice [SOL-stis] *n* either shortest (winter) or longest (summer) day of year.

solve [solv] *vt* **solved, solv·ing 1** work out, explain. **2** find answer to. **sol·u·bil·i·ty** [sol-yə-BIL-i-tee] *n* **sol'u·ble** *adj* **1** capable of being dissolved in liquid. **2** able to be solved or explained. **so·lu·tion** [sə-LOO-shən] *n* **1** answer to problem. **2** dissolving. **3** liquid with something dissolved in it. **solv'a·ble** *adj* **sol'ven·cy** [-vən-see] *n* **sol'vent** *adj* **1** able to meet financial obligations. ♦ *n* **2** liquid with power of dissolving.

som·ber [SOM-bər] *adj* dark, gloomy.

2 = **comfort**, console

soldier *n* = **fighter**, man-at-arms, serviceman, trooper, warrior

sole *adj* = **only**, alone, exclusive, individual, one, single, solitary

solely *adv* = **only**, alone, completely, entirely, exclusively, merely

solemn *adj* **1** = **formal**, ceremonial, dignified, grand, grave, momentous, stately **2** = **serious**, earnest, grave, sedate, sober, staid

solemnity *n* **1** = **seriousness**, earnestness, gravity **2** = **formality**, grandeur, impressiveness, momentousness

solicitous *adj* = **concerned**, anxious, attentive, careful

solicitude *n* = **concern**, anxiety, attentiveness, care, consideration, regard

solid *adj* **1** = **firm**, compact, concrete, dense, hard **2** = **strong**, stable, sturdy, substantial, unshakable **3** = **sound**, genuine, good, pure, real, reliable **4** =

reliable, dependable, trusty, upright, upstanding, worthy

solidarity *n* = **unity**, accord, cohesion, concordance, like-mindedness, team spirit, unanimity, unification

solidify *v* = **harden**, cake, coagulate, cohere, congeal, jell, set

solitary *adj* **1** = **unsociable**, cloistered, isolated, reclusive, unsocial **2** = **single**, alone, lone, sole **3** = **lonely**, companionless, friendless, lonesome **4** = **isolated**, hidden, out-of-the-way, remote, unfrequented

solitude *n* = **isolation**, loneliness, privacy, retirement, seclusion

solution *n* **1** = **answer**, explanation, key, result **2** *Chem* = **mixture**, blend, compound, mix, solvent

solve *v* = **answer**, clear up, crack, decipher, disentangle, get to the bottom of, resolve, unravel, work out

somber *adj* **1** = **dark**, dim, drab, dull,

som·bre·ro [som-BRAIR-oh] *n, pl* **-bre·ros** wide-brimmed hat worn in Mexico, Spain, etc.

some [sum] *adj* **1** denoting an indefinite number, amount or extent. **2** one or other. **3** amount of. **4** certain. **5** approximately. ♦ *pron* **6** portion, quantity. **some'bod·y** *n* **1** some person. **2** important person. **some'how** *adv* by some means unknown. **some'thing** *n* **1** thing not clearly defined. **2** indefinite amount, quantity or degree. **-something** *comb. form* (person) of an age above a given figure, e.g. *thirtysomething*. **some'time** *adv* **1** formerly. **2** at some (past or future) time. ♦ *adj* **3** former. **some'times** *adv* **1** occasionally. **2** now and then. **some'what** [-hwot] *adv* to some extent, rather. **some'where** [-hwair] *adv*

som·er·sault [SUM-ər-sawlt] *n* tumbling head over heels.

som·nam·bu·list [som-NAM-byə-list] *n* sleepwalker. **som'nam'bu·lism** *n*

som·no·lent [SOM-nə-lənt] *adj* **1** drowsy. **2** causing sleep. **som'no·lence** *n*

son [sun] *n* male child. **son-in-law** *n* daughter's husband.

so·nar [SOH-nahr] *n* device like echo sounder.

so·na·ta [sə-NAH-tə] *n* piece of music in several movements. **son·a·ti·na** [son-ə-TEE-nə] *n* short sonata.

son et lumière [saw-nay-luu-MYAIR] *Fr* entertainment staged at night at famous place, building, giving dramatic history of it with lighting and sound effects.

song [sawng] *n* **1** singing. **2** poem, etc. for singing. **song'ster** *n* **1** singer. **2** songbird. **song'stress** [-stris] *n, fem.*

sonic [SON-ik] *adj* pert. to sound waves. **sonic boom** explosive sound caused by aircraft traveling at supersonic speed.

son·net [SON-it] *n* fourteen-line poem with definite rhyme scheme. **son·net·eer** [son-i-TEER] *n* writer of this.

so·no·rous [sə-NOR-ees, SAHN-ər-us] *adj* giving out (deep) sound, resonant. **so·nor'i·ty** *n*

soon *adv* **1** in a short time. **2** before long. **3** early, quickly.

soot [suut] *n* black powdery substance formed by burning of coal, etc. **soot'y** *adj* **soot·i·er, soot·i·est** of, like soot.

sooth *n* truth. **sooth'say·er** *n* **1** one who foretells future. **2** diviner.

soothe [sooth] *vt* **soothed, sooth·ing 1** make calm, tranquil. **2** relieve (pain, etc.).

sop *n* **1** piece of bread, etc. soaked in liquid. **2** concession, bribe. ♦ *vt* **sopped, sop·ping 3** steep in water, etc. **4** soak (up). **sopping** *adj* completely soaked.

soph·ist [SOF-ist] *n* fallacious reasoner, quibbler. **soph'ism** [-izm] *n* specious argument. **soph'ist·ry** *n*

so·phis·ti·cate [sə-FIS-ti-kayt] *vt* **-cat·ed, -cat·ing 1** make artificial, spoil, falsify, corrupt. ♦ *n* [-kit] **2** sophisticated person. **sophisticated** *adj* **1** having refined or cultured tastes, habits. **2** worldly wise. **3** superficially clever. **4** complex. **so·phis·ti·ca'tion** *n*

soph·o·more [SOF-ə-mor] *n* student in second year at high school or college. **soph·o·mor'ic** intellectually pretentious.

sop·o·rif·ic [sop-ə-RIF-ik] *adj* causing sleep (esp. by drugs).

so·pran·o [sə-PRAN-oh] *n, pl* **-pran·os 1**

─── THESAURUS ───

gloomy, sober **2 = gloomy**, dismal, doleful, grave, joyless, lugubrious, mournful, sad, sober

somebody *n* **= celebrity**, dignitary, household name, luminary, megastar (*inf*), name, notable, personage, star

someday *adv* **= eventually**, one day, one of these (fine) days, sooner or later

somehow *adv* **= one way or another**, by fair means or foul, by hook or (by) crook, by some means or other, come hell or high water (*inf*), come what may

sometimes *adv* **= occasionally**, at times, now and then

song *n* **= ballad**, air, anthem, carol, chant, chorus, ditty, hymn, number, psalm, tune

soon *adv* **= before long**, in the near future, shortly

soothe *v* **1 = calm**, allay, appease, hush, lull, mollify, pacify, quiet, still **2 = relieve**, alleviate, assuage, ease

soothing *adj* **= calming**, emollient, palliative, relaxing, restful

soothsayer *n* **= prophet**, diviner, fortune-teller, seer, sibyl

sophisticated *adj* **1 = cultured**, cosmopolitan, cultivated, refined, urbane, worldly **2 = complex**, advanced, complicated, delicate, elaborate, intricate, refined, subtle

sophistication *n* **= savoir-faire**, finesse, poise, urbanity, worldliness, worldly

highest voice in women and boys. **2** singer
with this voice. **3** musical part for it.
sor·bet [sor-BAY] *n* sherbet.
sor·cer·er [SOR-sər-ər] *n* magician.
sor'cer·ess [-ris] *n, fem.* **sor'cer·y** *n, pl* **-ies**
witchcraft, magic.
sor'did *adj* **1** mean, squalid. **2** ignoble,
base. **sor'did·ly** *adv* **sor'did·ness** [-nis] *n*
sore [sor] *adj* **sor·er, sor·est 1** painful. **2**
causing annoyance. **3** severe. **4** distressed.
5 annoyed. ♦ *adv obs* **6** grievously,
intensely. ♦ *n* **7** sore place, ulcer, boil, etc.
sore'ly *adv* **1** grievously. **2** greatly.
sor·ghum [SOR-gəm] *n* kind of grass
cultivated for grain.
sor·rel [SOR-əl] *n* **1** plant. **2** reddish-brown
color. **3** horse of this color. ♦ *adj* **4** of this
color.
sor·row [SOR-oh] *n* **1** pain of mind, grief,
sadness. ♦ *vi* **2** grieve. **sor'row·ful** [-fəl] *adj*
sor·ry [SOR-ee] *adj* **-ri·er, -ri·est 1** feeling
pity or regret. **2** distressed. **3** miserable,
wretched. **4** mean, poor. **sor'ri·ly** *adv*
sort *n* **1** kind or class. ♦ *vt* **2** classify. **sort'er**
n
sor·tie [SOR-tee] *n* sally by besieged forces.
SOS *n* **1** international code signal of
distress. **2** call for help.

so-so [SOH-soh] *adj* **1** mediocre. ♦ *adv* **2**
tolerably.
sot *n* habitual drunkard.
sot·to vo·ce [SOT-oh VOH-chee] *It* in an
undertone.
souf·flé [soo-FLAY] *n* **1** dish of eggs beaten
to froth, flavored and baked. **2** dessert like
this of various ingredients.
sough [rhymes with cow] *n* low
murmuring sound as of wind in trees.
sought [sawt] *pt./pp.* of SEEK.
soul [sohl] *n* **1** spiritual and immortal part
of human being. **2** example, pattern. **3**
person. **4** (also **soul music**) type of Black
music combining urban blues with jazz,
pop, etc. **soul'ful** [-fəl] *adj* full of emotion
or sentiment. **soul'less** [-lis] *adj* **1**
mechanical. **2** lacking sensitivity or
nobility. **3** heartless, cruel.
sound¹ [sownd] *n* **1** what is heard. **2**
noise. ♦ *vi* **3** make a sound. **4** seem. **5** give
impression of. ♦ *vt* **6** cause to sound. **7**
utter. **sound barrier** hypothetical barrier to
flight at speed of sound waves. **sound bite**
short pithy statement extracted from a
longer speech for use esp. in television or
radio news reports. **sound track** recorded
sound accompaniment of motion picture,

―――― THESAURUS ――――

wisdom
soporific *adj* **1** = **sleep-inducing**, sedative,
somnolent, tranquilizing ♦ *n* **2** = **sedative**,
narcotic, opiate, tranquilizer
sorcerer *n* = **magician**, enchanter,
necromancer, warlock, witch, wizard
sorcery *n* = **black magic**, black art,
enchantment, magic, necromancy,
witchcraft, wizardry
sordid *adj* **1** = **dirty**, filthy, foul, mean,
scuzzy (*sl*), seedy, sleazy, squalid, unclean
2 = **base**, debauched, degenerate, low,
shabby, shameful, vicious, vile **3** =
mercenary, avaricious, covetous, grasping,
selfish
sore *adj* **1** = **painful**, angry, burning,
inflamed, irritated, raw, sensitive,
smarting, tender **2** = **annoying**, severe,
sharp, troublesome **3** = **annoyed**,
aggrieved, angry, cross, hurt, irked,
irritated, pained, resentful, stung, upset **4** =
urgent, acute, critical, desperate, dire,
extreme, pressing
sorrow *n* **1** = **grief**, anguish, distress,
heartache, heartbreak, misery, mourning,
regret, sadness, unhappiness, woe **2** =

affliction, hardship, misfortune, trial,
tribulation, trouble, woe ♦ *v* **3** = **grieve**,
agonize, bemoan, be sad, bewail, lament,
mourn
sorrowful *adj* = **sad**, dejected, dismal,
doleful, grieving, miserable, mournful,
sorry, unhappy, woebegone, woeful,
wretched
sorry *adj* **1** = **regretful**, apologetic,
conscience-stricken, contrite, penitent,
remorseful, repentant, shamefaced **2** =
sympathetic, commiserative,
compassionate, full of pity, moved **3** =
wretched, deplorable, mean, miserable,
pathetic, pitiful, poor, sad
sort *n* **1** = **kind**, brand, category, class, ilk,
make, nature, order, quality, style, type,
variety ♦ *v* **2** = **arrange**, categorize, classify,
divide, grade, group, order, put in order,
rank
sort out *v* **1** = **resolve**, clarify, clear up **2** =
organize, tidy up
soul *n* **1** = **spirit**, essence, life, vital force **2** =
personification, embodiment, epitome,
essence, quintessence, type **3** = **person**,
being, body, creature, individual, man *or*

etc.

sound² adj -er, -est **1** in good condition. **2** solid. **3** of good judgment. **4** legal. **5** solvent. **6** thorough. **7** effective. **8** watertight. **9** deep. **sound'ly** adv thoroughly.

sound³ vt **1** find depth of, as water. **2** ascertain views of. **3** probe. **sound'ings** pl n measurements taken by sounding.

sound⁴ n **1** channel. **2** strait.

soup [soop] n liquid food made by boiling or simmering meat, vegetables, etc. **soup'y** adj **soup·i·er, soup·i·est 1** like soup. **2** murky. **3** sentimental.

sour [sowr] adj **1** acid. **2** gone bad. **3** rancid. **4** peevish. **5** disagreeable. ◆ v **6** make, become sour. **sour'ness** [-nis] n **sour'puss** [-puus] -inf sullen, sour-faced person.

source [sors] n **1** origin, starting point. **2** spring.

souse [rhymes with **louse**] v **soused, sous·ing 1** plunge, drench. **2** pickle. ◆ n **3** sousing. **4** brine for pickling. **5** sl drunkard. **soused** adj sl drunk.

south [sowth] n **1** cardinal point opposite north. **2** region, part of country, etc. lying to that side. ◆ adj, adv **3** (that is) toward south. **south'ward** [-wǝrd] adj, adv **south'wards** [-wǝrdz] adv **south·er·ly** [SUTH-ǝr-lee] adj **1** toward south. ◆ n, pl **-lies 2** wind from the south. **south·ern** [SUTH-ǝrn] adj in south. **south·west·er** [sowth-WES-tǝr] n wind, storm from the southwest.

sou·ve·nir [soo-vǝ-NEER] n keepsake, memento.

sov·er·eign [SOV-rin] n **1** king, queen. **2** former British gold coin worth 20 shillings. ◆ adj **3** supreme. **4** efficacious. **sov'er·eign·ty** n, pl **-ties 1** supreme power and right to exercise it. **2** dominion. **3** independent state.

so·vi·et [SOH-vee-et] n **1** formerly, elected council at various levels of government in USSR. **2** (**S-**) official or citizen of the former USSR. ◆ adj **3** of the former USSR.

sow¹ [soh] v **sowed, sown** or **sowed, sow·ing** ◆ vi **1** scatter, plant seed. ◆ vt **2** scatter, deposit (seed). **3** spread abroad.

sow² [rhymes with **cow**] n female adult pig.

soy·bean [SOI-been] n edible bean used as livestock feed, meat substitute, etc.

soy sauce [SOI saws] sauce made by fermenting soybeans in brine.

spa [spah] n **1** medicinal spring. **2** place, resort with one.

space [spays] n **1** extent. **2** room. **3** period. **4** empty place. **5** area. **6** expanse. **7** region beyond Earth's atmosphere. ◆ vt **spaced, spac·ing 8** place at intervals. **spa'cious** [-shǝs] adj roomy, extensive. **space'craft, space'ship** n vehicle for travel beyond Earth's atmosphere. **space shuttle** vehicle for repeated space flights. **space'suit** n sealed, pressurized suit worn by astronaut.

spade¹ [spayd] n tool for digging.

woman

sound¹ n **1 = noise,** din, report, reverberation, tone **2 = impression,** drift, idea, look ◆ v **3 = resound,** echo, reverberate **4 = seem,** appear, look **5 = pronounce,** announce, articulate, declare, express, utter

sound² adj **1 = perfect,** fit, healthy, intact, solid, unhurt, unimpaired, uninjured, whole **2 = sensible,** correct, logical, proper, prudent, rational, reasonable, right, trustworthy, valid, well-founded, wise **3 = deep,** unbroken, undisturbed, untroubled

sound³ v **= fathom,** plumb, probe

sound out v **= probe,** canvass, pump, question, see how the land lies

sour adj **1 = sharp,** acetic, acid, bitter, pungent, tart **2 = gone off,** curdled, gone bad, turned **3 = ill-natured,** acrimonious,

disagreeable, embittered, ill-tempered, peevish, tart, ungenerous, waspish

source n **1 = origin,** author, beginning, cause, derivation, fount, originator **2 = informant,** authority

souvenir n **= keepsake,** memento, reminder

sovereign n **1 = monarch,** chief, emperor or empress, king or queen, potentate, prince, ruler ◆ adj **2 = supreme,** absolute, imperial, kingly or queenly, principal, royal, ruling **3 = excellent,** effectual, efficacious, efficient

sovereignty n **= supreme power,** domination, kingship, primacy, supremacy

sow v **= scatter,** implant, plant, seed

space n **1 = room,** capacity, elbowroom, expanse, extent, leeway, margin, play, scope **2 = gap,** blank, distance, interval, omission **3 = time,** duration, interval,

spade·work [SPAYD-wurk] *n* arduous preparatory work.

spade² *n* leaf-shaped black symbol on playing card.

spa·ghet·ti [spə-GET-ee] *n* pasta in form of long strings.

spake [spayk] *obs* pt. of SPEAK.

spam *v* **spam·ming, spammed** *Computers.* *sl* send unsolicited e-mail simultaneously to a number of users on the Internet.

span *n* **1** space from thumb to little finger as measure. **2** extent, space. **3** stretch of arch, etc. ◆ *vt* **spanned, span·ning 4** stretch over. **5** measure with hand.

span·gle [SPANG-gəl] *n* **1** small shiny metallic ornament. ◆ *vt* **-gled, -gling 2** decorate with spangles.

span·iel [SPAN-yəl] *n* breed of dog with long ears and silky hair.

spank [spangk] *vt* slap with flat of hand, etc. esp. on buttocks. ◆ *n* **spank'ing** *n* **1** series of spanks. ◆ *adj* **2** quick, lively. **3** large, fine.

spar¹ [spahr] *n* pole, beam, esp. as part of ship's rigging.

spar² *vi* **sparred, spar·ring 1** box. **2** dispute, esp. in fun. ◆ *n* **3** sparring.

spar³ *n* any of kinds of crystalline mineral.

spare [spair] *vt* **spared, spar·ing 1** leave unhurt. **2** show mercy. **3** abstain from using. **4** do without. **5** give away. ◆ *adj* **6**

additional. **7** in reserve. **8** thin. **9** lean. **10** scanty. ◆ *n* **11** spare part (for machine).

sparing *adj* economical, careful.

spark [spahrk] *n* **1** small glowing or burning particle. **2** flash of light produced by electrical discharge. **3** vivacity, humor. **4** trace. **5** in internal-combustion engines, electric spark (in spark plug) that ignites explosive mixture in cylinder. ◆ *v* **6** emit sparks. **7** kindle, excite. **8** *obs* woo.

spar·kle [SPAHR-kəl] *vi* **-kled, -kling 1** glitter. **2** effervesce. **3** scintillate. ◆ *n* **4** small spark. glitter. **6** flash. **7** lustre. **sparkling** *adj* **1** flashing. **2** glittering. **3** brilliant. **4** lively. **5** (of wines) effervescent.

spar·row [SPA-roh] *n* small finch.

sparse [spahrs] *adj* **spars·er, spars·est** thinly scattered.

Spar·tan [SPAHR-tn] *adj* **1** hardy. **2** austere. **3** frugal. **4** undaunted.

spasm [SPAZ-əm] *n* **1** sudden convulsive (muscular) contraction. **2** sudden burst of activity, etc. **spas·mod·ic** [spaz-MOD-ik] *adj* occurring in spasms.

spas·tic [SPAS-tik] *n* **1** *oft considered offens* person who has cerebral palsy. ◆ *adj* **2** affected by involuntary muscle contractions, e.g. *spastic colon.* **3** *oft considered offens* suffering from cerebral palsy.

spat¹ pt. of **SPIT¹**.

==THESAURUS==

period, span, while

spacious *adj* = **roomy**, ample, broad, capacious, commodious, expansive, extensive, huge, large, sizable *or* sizeable

spadework *n* = **preparation**, donkey-work, groundwork, labor

span *n* **1** = **extent**, amount, distance, length, reach, spread, stretch **2** = **period**, duration, spell, term ◆ *v* **3** = **extend across**, bridge, cover, cross, link, traverse

spank *v* = **smack**, cuff, paddle (*U.S. & Canad.*), slap

spar *v* = **argue**, bicker, row, scrap (*inf*), squabble, wrangle

spare *adj* **1** = **extra**, additional, free, leftover, odd, over, superfluous, surplus, unoccupied, unused, unwanted **2** = **thin**, gaunt, lean, meager, wiry ◆ *v* **3** = **have mercy on**, be merciful to, go easy on (*inf*), leave, let off (*inf*), pardon, save from **4** = **afford**, do without, give, grant, let (someone) have, manage without, part with

spare time *n* = **leisure**, free time, odd moments

sparing *adj* = **economical**, careful, frugal, prudent, saving, thrifty

spark *n* **1** = **flicker**, flare, flash, gleam, glint **2** = **trace**, atom, hint, jot, scrap, vestige ◆ *v* **3** (often with *off*) = **start**, inspire, precipitate, provoke, set off, stimulate, trigger (off)

sparkle *v* **1** = **glitter**, dance, flash, gleam, glint, glisten, scintillate, shimmer, shine, twinkle ◆ *n* **2** = **glitter**, brilliance, flash, flicker, gleam, glint, twinkle **3** = **vivacity**, dash, élan, life, spirit, vitality

sparse *adj* = **scattered**, few and far between, meager, scanty, scarce

spartan *adj* = **austere**, ascetic, disciplined, frugal, plain, rigorous, self-denying, severe, strict

spasm *n* **1** = **convulsion**, contraction, paroxysm, twitch **2** = **burst**, eruption, fit, frenzy, outburst, seizure

spasmodic *adj* = **sporadic**, convulsive,

spat² *n* short gaiter.

spat³ *n* 1 slight quarrel. ◆ *vi* **spat·ted, spat·ting** 2 quarrel.

spate [spayt] *n* 1 rush, outpouring. 2 flood.

spa·tial [SPAY-shəl] *adj* of, in space.

spat·ter [SPAT-ər] *vt* 1 splash, cast drops over. ◆ *vi* 2 be scattered in drops. ◆ *n* 3 slight splash. 4 sprinkling.

spat·u·la [SPACH-ə-lə] *n* utensil with broad, flat blade for various purposes.

spav'in *n* injury to, growth on horse's leg. **spav'ined** *adj* lame, decrepit.

spawn *n* 1 eggs of fish, frog, etc. ◆ *vi* (of fish or frog) cast eggs. 2 produce in great numbers.

spay *vt* remove ovaries from (animal).

speak [speek] *v* **spoke, spo·ken, speak·ing** 1 utter words. 2 converse. 3 deliver discourse. 4 utter. 5 pronounce. 6 express. 7 communicate in. **speak'er** *n* 1 one who speaks. 2 one who specializes in speechmaking. 3 (**S-**) official chairman of US House of Representatives, other legislative bodies. 4 loudspeaker.

spear [speer] *n* 1 long pointed weapon. 2 slender shoot, as of asparagus. ◆ *vt* 3 transfix, pierce, wound with spear. **spear'head** [-hed] *n* leading force in attack, campaign. ◆ *vt*

spear·mint [SPEER-mint] *n* type of mint.

spec [spek] *n* **on spec** *inf* as a risk or gamble.

spe·cial [SPESH-əl] *adj* 1 beyond the usual.

2 particular, individual. 3 distinct. 4 limited. **spe'cial·ist** *n* one who devotes self to special subject or branch of subject. **spe'cial·ty** *n, pl* **-ties** special product, skill, characteristic, etc. **spe'cial·ize** *v* **-ized, -iz·ing** ◆ *vi* 1 be specialist. 2 be adapted to special function or environment. ◆ *vt* 3 make special.

spe·cie [SPEE-shee] *n* coined, as distinct from paper, money.

spe·cies [SPEE-sheez] *n, pl* **species** 1 sort, kind, esp. animals, etc. 2 class. 3 subdivision.

spe·cif·ic [spə-SIF-ik] *adj* 1 definite. 2 exact in detail. 3 characteristic of a thing or kind. **spe·cif'i·cal·ly** *adv* **spec'i·fy** *vt* **-fied, -fy·ing** state definitely or in detail. **spec·i·fi·ca'tion** [-KAY-shən] *n* detailed description of something to be made, done. **specific gravity** ratio of density of substance to that of water.

spec·i·men [SPES-ə-mən] *n* 1 part typifying whole. 2 individual example.

spe·cious [SPEE-shəs] *adj* deceptively plausible, but false. **spe'cious·ly** *adv* **spe'cious·ness** [-nis] *n*

speck [spek] *n* 1 small spot, particle. ◆ *vt* 2 spot. **speck·le** [SPEK-l] *n, vt* **-led, -ling** speck.

spec·ta·cle [SPEK-tə-kəl] *n* 1 show. 2 thing exhibited. 3 ridiculous sight. **spectacles** *pl n* eyeglasses. **spec·tac'u·lar** *adj* 1 impressive. 2 showy. 3 grand. 4

━━━ THESAURUS ━━━

erratic, fitful, intermittent, irregular, jerky

spate *n* = **flood**, deluge, flow, outpouring, rush, torrent

speak *v* 1 = **talk**, articulate, converse, express, pronounce, say, state, tell, utter 2 = **lecture**, address, declaim, discourse, hold forth

speaker *n* = **lecturer**, orator, public speaker, spokesman *or* spokeswoman, spokesperson

speak out *or* **up** *v* = **speak one's mind**, have one's say, make one's position plain, voice one's opinions

spearhead *v* = **lead**, head, initiate, launch, pioneer, set in motion, set off

special *adj* 1 = **exceptional**, extraordinary, important, memorable, significant, uncommon, unique, unusual 2 = **particular**, appropriate, distinctive, individual, precise, specific

specialist *n* = **expert**, authority, buff (*inf*),

connoisseur, consultant, master, professional

speciality *n* = **forte**, bag (*sl, dated*), métier, *pièce de résistance*, specialty

species *n* = **kind**, breed, category, class, group, sort, type, variety

specific *adj* 1 = **particular**, characteristic, distinguishing, special 2 = **definite**, clear-cut, exact, explicit, express, precise, unequivocal

specification *n* = **requirement**, condition, detail, particular, qualification, stipulation

specify *v* = **state**, define, designate, detail, indicate, mention, name, stipulate

specimen *n* = **sample**, example, exemplification, instance, model, pattern, representative, type

speck *n* 1 = **mark**, blemish, dot, fleck, mote, speckle, spot, stain 2 = **particle**, atom, bit, grain, iota, jot, mite, shred

speckled *adj* = **flecked**, dappled, dotted,

magnificent. ◆ *n* **5** lavishly produced performance. **spec·ta·tor** [SPEK-tay-tər] *n* one who looks on.

spec·ter [SPEK-tər] *n* **1** ghost. **2** image of something unpleasant. **spec·tral** [-trəl] *adj* ghostly.

spec·trum [SPEK-trəm] *n, pl* **-tra** [-trə] **1** band of colors into which beam of light can be decomposed e.g. by prism. **2** range (of e.g. opinions, occupations). **spec·tro·scope** [-trə-skohp] *n* instrument for producing, examining physical spectra.

spec·u·late [SPEK-yə-layt] *vi* **-lat·ed, -lat·ing 1** guess, conjecture. **2** engage in (risky) commercial transactions. **spec·u·la'tion** *n* **spec·u·la·tive** [-lə-tiv] *adj* given to, characterized by speculation. **spec'u·la·tor** *n*

spec·u·lum [SPEK-yə-ləm] *n, pl* **-lums 1** mirror. **2** reflector of polished metal, esp. in reflecting telescopes.

speech *n* **1** act, faculty of speaking. **2** words, language. **3** conversation. **4** discourse. **5** (formal) talk given before audience. **speech'i·fy** *vi* **-fied, -fy·ing** make speech, esp. long and tedious one. **speech'less** [-lis] *adj* **1** mute. **2** at a loss for words.

speed *n* **1** swiftness. **2** rate of progress. **3** degree of sensitivity of photographic film. **4** *sl* amphetamine. ◆ *v* **sped** *or* **speed·ed, speed·ing 5** move quickly. **6** drive vehicle at high speed. **7** further. **8** expedite. **speed'ing** *n* driving (vehicle) at high speed, esp. over legal limit. **speed'i·ly** *adv* **speed'y** *adj* **speed·i·er, speed·i·est 1** quick. **2** rapid. **3** nimble. **4** prompt. **speed'boat** *n* light fast motorboat. **speed·om'e·ter** [-OM-ə-tər] *n* instrument to show speed of vehicle. **speed'way** *n* track for automobile or motorcycle racing.

spe·le·ol·o·gy [spee-lee-OL-ə-jee] *n* study, exploring of caves. **spe·le·ol'o·gist** *n*

spell[1] *vt* **spelled** *or* **spelt, spell·ing 1** give letters of in order. **2** read letter by letter. **3** indicate, result in. **spelling** *n* **spell'check·er** *n Computers* program that finds words in a document that are not recognized as being correctly spelled. **spell out** make explicit.

spell[2] *n* **1** magic formula. **2** enchantment. **spell'bound** [-bownd] *adj* **1** enchanted. **2** entranced.

spell[3] *n* (short) period of time, work.

mottled, spotted, sprinkled

spectacle *n* **1 = sight**, curiosity, marvel, phenomenon, scene, wonder **2 = show**, display, event, exhibition, extravaganza, pageant, performance

spectacular *adj* **1 = impressive**, cool (*inf*), dazzling, dramatic, grand, magnificent, phat (*sl*), sensational, splendid, striking, stunning (*inf*) ◆ *n* **2 = show**, display, spectacle

spectator *n* **= onlooker**, bystander, looker-on, observer, viewer, watcher

specter *n* **= ghost**, apparition, phantom, spirit, vision, wraith

speculate *v* **1 = conjecture**, consider, guess, hypothesize, suppose, surmise, theorize, wonder **2 = gamble**, hazard, risk, venture

speculation *n* **1 = guesswork**, conjecture, hypothesis, opinion, supposition, surmise, theory **2 = gamble**, hazard, risk

speculative *adj* **= hypothetical**, academic, conjectural, notional, suppositional, theoretical

speech *n* **1 = communication**, conversation, dialogue, discussion, talk **2 = talk**, address, discourse, homily, lecture,

oration, spiel (*inf*) **3 = language**, articulation, dialect, diction, enunciation, idiom, jargon, parlance, tongue

speechless *adj* **1 = mute**, dumb, inarticulate, silent, wordless **2 = astounded**, aghast, amazed, dazed, shocked

speed *n* **1 = swiftness**, haste, hurry, pace, quickness, rapidity, rush, velocity ◆ *v* **2 = race**, career, gallop, hasten, hurry, make haste, rush, tear, zoom **3 = help**, advance, aid, assist, boost, expedite, facilitate

speed up *v* **= accelerate**, gather momentum, increase the tempo

speedy *adj* **= quick**, express, fast, hasty, headlong, hurried, immediate, precipitate, prompt, rapid, swift

spell[1] *v* **= indicate**, augur, imply, mean, point to, portend, signify

spell[2] *n* **1 = incantation**, charm **2 = fascination**, allure, bewitchment, enchantment, glamour, magic

spell[3] *n* **= period**, bout, course, interval, season, stretch, term, time

spellbound *adj* **= entranced**, bewitched, captivated, charmed, enthralled, fascinated, gripped, mesmerized, rapt

DICTIONARY

spend *vt* **spent, spend·ing 1** pay out. **2** pass (time) on activity, etc. **3** use up completely. **spend'thrift** *n* wasteful person.

sperm [spurm] *n* **1** male reproductive cell. **2** semen. **sper·mat'ic** *adj* of sperm. **sperm'i·cide** [-sīd] *n* drug, etc. that kills sperm.

sper·ma·cet·i [spur-mə-SET-ee] *n* white, waxy substance obtained from oil from head of sperm whale. **sperm whale** large, toothed whale.

spew [spyoo] *v* **1** vomit. **2** gush.

sphag·num [SFAG-nəm] *n* moss that grows in bogs.

sphere [sfeer] *n* **1** ball, globe. **2** range. **3** field of action. **4** status. **5** position. **6** province. **spher·i·cal** [SFER-i-kəl] *adj*

sphinc·ter [SFINGK-tər] *n* ring of muscle surrounding opening of hollow bodily organ.

sphinx [sfingks] *n, pl* **-es 1** figure in Egypt with lion's body and human head. **2** (**S-**) the great statue of this near the pyramids of Giza. **3** monster, half woman, half lion. **4** enigmatic person.

spice [spīs] *n* **1** aromatic or pungent vegetable substance. **2** spices collectively. **3** anything that adds flavor, relish, piquancy, interest, etc. ◆ *vt* **spiced, spic·ing 4** season with spices, flavor. **spic'y** *adj* **spic·i·er, spic·i·est 1** flavored with spices. **2** slightly indecent, risqué.

spick-and-span [SPIK-ən-SPAN] *adj* **1** spotlessly clean. **2** neat, smart, new-looking.

spi·der [SPĪ-dər] *n* small eight-legged creature that spins web to catch prey. **spi'der·y** *adj*

spiel [speel] *n inf* **1** glib (sales) talk. ◆ *vi* **2** deliver spiel, recite. **spiel'er** *n*

spig·ot [SPIG-ət] *n* **1** peg or plug. **2** faucet.

spike [spīk] *n* **1** sharp point. **2** sharp pointed object. **3** long flower cluster with flowers attached directly to the stalk. ◆ *vt* **spiked, spik·ing 4** pierce, fasten with spike. **5** render ineffective. **6** add alcohol to (drink).

spill *v* **spilled** or **spilt, spill·ing 1** (cause to) pour from, flow over, fall out, esp. unintentionally. **2** upset. **3** be lost or wasted. ◆ *n* **4** spillway. **5** spillage. **spill'age** [-ij] *n* amount spilled. **spill'way** *n* passageway through which excess water spills.

spin *v* **spun, spin·ning 1** (cause to) revolve rapidly. **2** whirl. **3** twist into thread. **4** prolong. **5** tell (a story). **6** fish with lure. ◆ *n* **7** spinning. **8** (of aircraft) descent in dive with continued rotation. **9** rapid run or ride. **10** *Politics* interpretation (of event, speech, etc.) to gain partisan advantage. **spinning** *n* act, process of drawing out and twisting into threads, as wool, cotton, flax, etc. **spinning wheel** household machine with large wheel turned by treadle for spinning wool, etc. into thread. **spin doctor** *inf* person who provides a favourable slant to a news item or policy on behalf of a political personality or party. **spin-dry** *vt* **-dried, -dry·ing** spin clothes in (washing) machine to remove excess water.

spin·ach [SPIN-ich] *n* dark green leafy vegetable.

spin·dle [SPIN-dl] *n* rod, axis for spinning.

THESAURUS

spend *v* **1** = **pay out**, disburse, expend, fork out (*sl*) **2** = **pass**, fill, occupy, while away **3** = **use up**, consume, dissipate, drain, empty, exhaust, run through, squander, waste

spendthrift *n* **1** = **squanderer**, big spender, profligate, spender, waster ◆ *adj* **2** = **wasteful**, extravagant, improvident, prodigal, profligate

spew *v* = **vomit**, barf (*sl*), disgorge, puke (*sl*), regurgitate, throw up (*inf*)

sphere *n* **1** = **ball**, circle, globe, globule, orb **2** = **field**, capacity, department, domain, function, patch, province, realm, scope, territory, turf (*sl*)

spherical *adj* = **round**, globe-shaped, globular, rotund

spice *n* **1** = **seasoning**, relish, savor **2** = **excitement**, color, pep, piquancy, zest, zing (*inf*)

spicy *adj* **1** = **hot**, aromatic, piquant, savory, seasoned **2** *Inf* = **scandalous**, hot (*inf*), indelicate, racy, ribald, risqué, suggestive, titillating

spike *n* **1** = **point**, barb, prong, spine ◆ *v* **2** = **impale**, spear, spit, stick

spill *v* **1** = **pour**, discharge, disgorge, overflow, slop over ◆ *n* **2** = **fall**, tumble

spin *v* **1** = **revolve**, gyrate, pirouette, reel, rotate, turn, twirl, twist, whirl **2** = **reel**, swim, whirl ◆ *n* **3** = **revolution**, gyration, roll, whirl **4** *Inf* = **drive**, joy ride (*inf*), ride

spin·dly *adj* **-dli·er, -dli·est 1** long and slender. **2** attenuated.

spin'drift *n* spray blown along surface of sea.

spine [spīn] *n* **1** backbone. **2** thin spike, esp. on fish, etc. **3** ridge. **4** back of book. **spi'nal** [-əl] *adj* **spine'less** [-lis] *adj* **1** lacking spine. **2** cowardly.

spin·et [SPIN-it] *n* **1** small piano. **2** small harpsichord.

spin·na·ker [SPIN-ə-kər] *n* large yacht sail.

spin·ster [SPIN-stər] *n* unmarried woman.

spi·ral [SPĪ-rəl] *n* **1** continuous curve drawn at ever increasing distance from fixed point. **2** anything resembling this. **3** *Football* kick or pass turning on longer axis. ◆ *v* **-raled, -ral·ing 4** of e.g. football or inflation, (cause to) take spiral course. ◆ *adj*

spire [spīr] *n* **1** pointed part of steeple. **2** pointed stem of plant.

spir'it *n* **1** life principle animating body. **2** disposition. **3** liveliness. **4** courage. **5** frame of mind. **6** essential character or meaning. **7** soul. **8** ghost. **9** liquid got by distillation, alcohol. ◆ *pl* **10** emotional state. **11** strong alcoholic drink e.g. whiskey. ◆ *vt* **12** carry away mysteriously. **spir'it·ed** [-id] *adj* lively. **spir'it·less** [-lis] *adj* listless, apathetic. **spir'it·u·al** [-choo-əl] *adj* **1** given to, interested in things of the spirit. ◆ *n* **2** religious song, hymn. **spir'it·u·al·ism** *n* belief that spirits of the dead communicate with the living. **spir'it·u·al·ist** *n*

spir'it·u·ous *adj* alcoholic. **spirit level** glass tube containing bubble in liquid, used to check horizontal, vertical surfaces.

spirt *n* see SPURT.

spit[1] *v* **spit** or **spat, spit·ting 1** eject saliva. **2** eject from mouth. ◆ *n* **3** spitting, saliva. **spit·tle** [SPIT-l] *n* saliva. **spit'ball** *n* **1** illegal pitch of baseball moistened with saliva by pitcher. **2** ball of chewed paper used as missile. **spit·toon'** *n* vessel to spit into. **spit'fire** *n* person, esp. woman or girl, with fiery temper.

spit[2] *n* **1** sharp rod to put through meat for roasting. **2** sandy point projecting into the sea. ◆ *vt* **spit·ted, spit·ting 3** thrust through.

spite [spīt] *n* **1** malice. ◆ *vt* **spit·ed, spit·ing 2** thwart spitefully. **spite'ful** [-fəl] *adj* **in spite of** *prep* **1** regardless of. **2** notwithstanding.

splash *v* **1** scatter liquid about or on, over something. **2** print, display prominently. ◆ *n* **3** sound of this. **4** patch, esp. of color. **5** (effect of) extravagant display. **6** small amount.

splat *n* wet, slapping sound.

splat·ter [SPLAT-ər] *v, n* spatter.

---

spine *n* **1** = **backbone**, spinal column, vertebrae, vertebral column **2** = **barb**, needle, quill, ray, spike, spur

spine-chilling *adj* = **frightening**, bloodcurdling, eerie, horrifying, scary (*inf*), spooky (*inf*), terrifying

spineless *adj* = **weak**, cowardly, faint-hearted, feeble, gutless (*inf*), lily-livered, soft, weak-kneed (*inf*)

spin out *v* = **prolong**, amplify, delay, drag out, draw out, extend, lengthen

spiral *n* **1** = **coil**, corkscrew, helix, whorl ◆ *adj* **2** = **coiled**, helical, whorled, winding

spirit *n* **1** = **life force**, life, soul, vital spark **2** = **feeling**, atmosphere, gist, tenor, tone **3** = **temperament**, attitude, character, disposition, outlook, temper **4** = **liveliness**, animation, brio, energy, enthusiasm, fire, force, life, mettle, vigor, zest **5** = **courage**, backbone, gameness, grit, guts (*inf*), spunk (*inf*) **6** = **essence**, intention, meaning, purport, purpose, sense, substance **7** = **ghost**, apparition, phantom, specter **8** **spirits** = **mood**, feelings, frame of mind,

morale ◆ *v* **9** (with *away* or *off*) = **remove**, abduct, abstract, carry, purloin, seize, steal, whisk

spirited *adj* = **lively**, active, animated, energetic, feisty (*inf*), mettlesome, vivacious

spiritual *adj* = **sacred**, devotional, divine, holy, religious

spit *v* **1** = **eject**, expectorate, splutter, throw out ◆ *n* **2** = **saliva**, dribble, drool, slaver, spittle

spite *n* **1** = **malice**, animosity, hatred, ill will, malevolence, spitefulness, spleen, venom **2** **in spite of** = **despite**, (even) though, notwithstanding, regardless of ◆ *v* **3** = **hurt**, annoy, harm, injure, vex

spiteful *adj* = **malicious**, bitchy (*inf*), ill-natured, malevolent, nasty, vindictive

splash *v* **1** = **scatter**, shower, slop, spatter, spray, sprinkle, wet **2** = **publicize**, broadcast, tout, trumpet ◆ *n* **3** = **dash**, burst, patch, spattering, touch **4** *Inf* = **display**, effect, impact, sensation, stir

splash out *v Inf* = **spend**, be extravagant,

splay *adj* **1** spread out. **2** slanting. **3** turned outward. ◆ *vt* **4** spread out. **5** twist outward. ◆ *n* **6** slanted surface.
splay'foot·ed [-fuut-id] *adj* flat and broad (of foot).

spleen *n* **1** organ in the abdomen. **2** anger. **3** irritable or morose temper. **sple·net·ic** [splə-NET-ik] *adj*

splen'did *adj* magnificent, brilliant, excellent. **splen'did·ly** *adv* **splen'dor** [-dər] *n*

splice [splīs] *vt* **spliced, splic·ing 1** join by interweaving strands. **2** join (wood) by overlapping. **3** *inf* join in marriage. ◆ *n* **4** spliced joint.

spline [splīn] *n* narrow groove, ridge, strip, esp. joining wood, etc.

splint *n* rigid support for broken limb, etc.

splin·ter [SPLIN-tər] *n* **1** thin fragment. ◆ *vi* **2** break into fragments, shiver. **splinter group** group that separates from main party, organization, oft. after disagreement.

split *v* **split, split'ting 1** break asunder. **2** separate. **3** divide. **4** *sl* depart. ◆ *n* **5** crack, fissure. **6** dessert of fruit, usu. banana, and ice cream.

splotch [sploch] *n, v* splash, daub.
splotch'y *adj* **splotch·i·er, splotch·i·est**

splurge [splurj] *v* **splurged, splurg·ing** spend money extravagantly. ◆ *n*

splut·ter [SPLUT-ər] *v* **1** make hissing, spitting sounds. **2** utter incoherently with spitting sounds. ◆ *n*

spoil *v* **spoiled** or **spoilt, spoil·ing 1** damage, injure. **2** damage manners or behavior of (esp. child) by indulgence. **3** pillage. **4** go bad. ◆ *n* **5** booty. **6** waste material, esp. in mining (also **spoil'age**).
spoil'er *n* slowing device on aircraft wing, etc. **spoiling for** eager for.

spoke[1] [spohk] pt. of SPEAK.
spokes'per·son, -wo·man, -man *n* one deputed to speak for others.

spoke[2] *n* radial bar of a wheel.

spoken pp. of SPEAK.

spo·li·a·tion [spoh-lee-AY-shən] *n* **1** act of spoiling. **2** robbery. **3** destruction.
spo'li·ate [-ayt] *v* **-at·ed, -at·ing** despoil, plunder, pillage.

spon'dee *n* metrical foot consisting of two long syllables.

sponge [spunj] *n* **1** marine animal. **2** its skeleton, or a synthetic substance like it, used to absorb liquids. **3** type of light cake. ◆ *v* **sponged, spong·ing** ◆ *vt* **4** wipe with sponge. ◆ *vi* **5** live meanly at expense of others. **6** cadge. **spong'er** *n* *sl* one who cadges, or lives at expense of others. **spon'gy** *adj* **-gi·er, -gi·est 1** spongelike. **2** wet and soft.

spon·sor [SPON-sər] *n* **1** one promoting, advertising something. **2** one who agrees to give money to a charity on completion of specified activity by another. **3** one taking responsibility (esp. for welfare of child at baptism, i.e. godparent). **4** guarantor. ◆ *vt* **5** act as sponsor.

THESAURUS

spare no expense, splurge
splendid *adj* **1 = marvelous**, fantastic (*inf*), first-class, glorious, great (*inf*), wonderful **2 = magnificent**, cool (*inf*), costly, gorgeous, impressive, lavish, luxurious, ornate, phat (*sl*), resplendent, rich, sumptuous, superb
splendor *n* **= magnificence**, brightness, brilliance, display, glory, grandeur, pomp, richness, show, spectacle, sumptuousness
splinter *n* **1 = sliver**, chip, flake, fragment ◆ *v* **2 = shatter**, disintegrate, fracture, split
split *v* **1 = break**, burst, come apart, come undone, crack, give way, open, rend, rip **2 = separate**, branch, cleave, disband, disunite, diverge, fork, part **3 = share out**, allocate, allot, apportion, distribute, divide, halve, partition ◆ *n* **4 = crack**, breach, division, fissure, gap, rent, rip, separation, slit, tear **5 = division**, breach, break-up,

discord, dissension, estrangement, rift, rupture, schism ◆ *adj* **6 = divided**, broken, cleft, cracked, fractured, ruptured
split up *v* **= separate**, break up, divorce, part
spoil *v* **1 = ruin**, damage, destroy, disfigure, harm, impair, injure, mar, mess up, trash (*sl*), wreck **2 = overindulge**, coddle, cosset, indulge, pamper **3 = go bad**, addle, curdle, decay, decompose, rot, turn
spoils *pl n* **= booty**, loot, plunder, prey, swag (*sl*), treasure
spoilsport *n* **= killjoy**, damper, misery (*inf*), sourpuss, wet blanket (*inf*)
spoken *adj* **= said**, expressed, oral, told, unwritten, uttered, verbal, viva voce, voiced
spokesperson *n* **= speaker**, mouthpiece, official, spin doctor (*inf*), spokesman or spokeswoman, voice

spon·sor·ship n

spon·ta·ne·ous [spon-TAY-nee-əs] adj **1** voluntary. **2** natural. **3** not forced. **4** produced without external force. **spon·ta·ne'i·ty** [-tə-NEE-i-tee] n

spoof n **1** mild satirical mockery. **2** trick, hoax. ◆ v

spook n **1** ghost. ◆ vt **2** haunt. **spook'y** adj **spook·i·er, spook·i·est**

spool n reel, bobbin.

spoon n **1** implement with shallow bowl at end of handle for carrying food to mouth, etc. ◆ vt **2** lift with spoon. **spoon'ful** [-fəl] n, pl **-fuls** [-fəlz] **spoon'fed** adj **1** fed (as if) with spoon. **2** pampered.

spoon·er·ism [SPOO-nə-riz-əm] n amusing transposition of initial consonants, such as *half-warmed fish* for *half-formed wish.*

spoor [spuur] n **1** trail of wild animals. ◆ v **2** follow spoor.

spo·rad·ic [spə-RAD-ik] adj **1** intermittent. **2** scattered, single. **spo·rad'i·cal·ly** adv

spore [spor] n minute reproductive organism of some plants and protozoans.

sport n **1** game, activity for pleasure, competition, exercise. **2** enjoyment. **3** mockery. **4** cheerful person, good loser. ◆ vt **5** wear (esp. ostentatiously). ◆ vi **6** frolic. **7** play (sport). **sport'ing** adj **1** of sport. **2** behaving with fairness, generosity.

sport'ive adj playful. **sports car** fast (open) car. **sports jacket** man's casual jacket. **sports'man** [-mən] n, pl **-men 1** one who engages in sport. **2** good loser. **sports'man·ship** n **sport utility vehicle** powerful four-wheel drive vehicle for rough terrain.

spot n **1** small mark, stain. **2** blemish, **3** pimple. **4** place. **5** (difficult) situation. ◆ vt **spot·ted, spot·ting 6** mark with spots. **7** detect. **8** observe. **9** blemish. **spot'less** [-lis] adj **1** unblemished. **2** pure. **spot'less·ly** adv **spot'ty** adj **-ti·er, -ti·est 1** with spots. **2** uneven. **spot check** random examination. **spot'light** n **1** powerful illuminating small area. **2** center of attention.

spouse [spows] n husband or wife. **spous·al** [SPOWZ-əl] n, adj (of) marriage.

spout [spowt] v **1** pour out. **2** inf speechify. ◆ n **3** projecting tube or lip for pouring liquids. **4** copious discharge.

sprain n, vt wrench or twist (of muscle, etc.).

sprang pt. of SPRING.

sprat n small sea fish.

sprawl vi **1** lie or sit about awkwardly. **2** spread in rambling, unplanned way. ◆ n **3** sprawling.

spray¹ n (device for producing) fine drops of liquid. ◆ vt sprinkle with shower of fine

---

THESAURUS

spongy adj = **porous**, absorbent

sponsor n **1** = **backer**, patron, promoter ◆ v **2** = **back**, finance, fund, patronize, promote, subsidize

spontaneous adj = **unplanned**, impromptu, impulsive, instinctive, natural, unprompted, voluntary, willing

spoof n Inf = **parody**, burlesque, caricature, mockery, satire

spooky adj = **eerie**, chilling, creepy (inf), frightening, scary (inf), spine-chilling, uncanny, unearthly, weird

sporadic adj = **intermittent**, irregular, occasional, scattered, spasmodic

sport n **1** = **game**, amusement, diversion, exercise, pastime, play, recreation **2** = **fun**, badinage, banter, jest, joking, teasing ◆ v **3** Old-fashioned, Inf = **wear**, display, exhibit, show off

sporting adj = **fair**, game (inf), sportsmanlike

sporty adj = **athletic**, energetic, outdoor

spot n **1** = **mark**, blemish, blot, blotch, scar,

smudge, speck, speckle, stain **2** = **place**, location, point, position, scene, site **3** Inf = **predicament**, difficulty, hot water (inf), mess, plight, quandary, tight spot, trouble ◆ v **4** = **see**, catch a glimpse of, catch sight of, detect, discern, espy, make out, observe, recognize, sight **5** = **mark**, dirty, fleck, mottle, smirch, soil, spatter, speckle, splodge, splotch, stain

spotless adj = **clean**, flawless, gleaming, immaculate, impeccable, pure, shining, unblemished, unstained, unsullied, untarnished

spotlight n **1** = **attention**, fame, limelight, public eye ◆ v **2** = **highlight**, accentuate, draw attention to

spotted adj = **speckled**, dappled, dotted, flecked, mottled

spouse n = **partner**, consort, husband or wife, mate, significant other (inf)

spout v = **stream**, discharge, gush, shoot, spray, spurt, surge

sprawl v = **loll**, flop, lounge, slouch, slump

drops.

spray² n **1** branch, twig with buds, flowers, etc. **2** floral ornament, brooch, etc. like this.

spread [spred] v **spread, spread'ing 1** extend. **2** stretch out. **3** open out. **4** scatter. **5** distribute. **6** unfold. **7** cover. ♦ n **8** extent. **9** increase. **10** ample meal. **11** food that can be spread on bread, etc. **spread'-ea·gle** adj with arms and legs outstretched. **spread'sheet** n computer program for manipulating figures.

spree n **1** session of overindulgence. **2** romp.

sprig n **1** small twig. **2** ornamental design like this. **3** small headless nail.

spright·ly [SPRĪT-lee] adj **-li·er, -li·est** lively, brisk. **spright'li·ness** [-nis] n

spring v **sprang, sprung, spring·ing 1** leap. **2** shoot up or forth. **3** come into being. **4** appear. **5** grow. **6** become bent or split. **7** produce unexpectedly. **8** set off (trap). ♦ n **9** leap. **10** recoil. **11** piece of coiled or bent metal with much resilience. **12** flow of water from earth. **13** first season of year. **spring'y** adj **spring·i·er, spring·i·est** elastic. **spring'board** [-bord] n **1** flexible board for diving. **2** anything that supplies impetus for action.

sprin·kle [SPRING-kəl] vt **-kled, -kling** scatter small drops on, strew. **sprin'kler** n

sprinkling n small amount or number.

sprint vt **1** run short distance at great speed. ♦ n **2** such run, race. **sprint'er** n one who sprints.

sprit n small spar set diagonally across a fore-and-aft sail in order to extend it.

sprite [sprīt] n fairy, elf.

sprock·et [SPROK-it] n **1** projection on wheel or capstan for engaging chain. **2** wheel with these.

sprout [sprowt] vi **1** put forth shoots, spring up. ♦ n **2** shoot. **Brus'sels sprout** [-səlz] n kind of miniature cabbage.

spruce¹ [sproos] n variety of fir.

spruce² [sproos] adj **spruc·er, spruc·est 1** neat in dress. ♦ v **spruced, spruc·ing 2** (with up) make (oneself) spruce.

sprung pp. of SPRING.

spry [sprī] adj **spry·er** or **spri·er, spry·est** or **spri·est** nimble, vigorous.

spud n inf potato.

spume [spyoom] n, vi **spumed, spum·ing** foam, froth.

spun pt./pp. of SPIN.

spunk n courage, spirit.

spur n **1** pricking instrument attached to horseman's heel. **2** incitement. **3** stimulus. **4** projection on rooster's leg. **5** projecting mountain range. **6** branch (road, etc.). ♦ vt **spurred, spur·ring 7** equip with spurs. **8** urge on.

spray¹ n **1 = droplets**, drizzle, fine mist **2 = aerosol**, atomizer, sprinkler ♦ v **3 = scatter**, diffuse, shower, sprinkle

spray² n **= sprig**, branch, corsage, floral arrangement

spread v **1 = open (out)**, broaden, dilate, expand, extend, sprawl, stretch, unfold, unroll, widen **2 = proliferate**, escalate, multiply **3 = circulate**, broadcast, disseminate, make known, propagate ♦ n **4 = increase**, advance, development, dispersal, dissemination, expansion, proliferation **5 = extent**, span, stretch, sweep

spree n **= binge** (inf), bacchanalia, carousal, fling, orgy, revel

sprightly adj **= lively**, active, agile, brisk, energetic, nimble, spirited, spry, vivacious

spring v **1 = jump**, bounce, bound, leap, vault **2** (often with from) **= originate**, arise, come, derive, descend, issue, proceed, start, stem **3** (often with up) **= appear**, develop, mushroom, shoot up ♦ n **4 =**

jump, bound, leap, vault **5 = elasticity**, bounce, buoyancy, flexibility, resilience

springy adj **= elastic**, bouncy, buoyant, flexible, resilient, rubbery

sprinkle v **= scatter**, dredge, dust, pepper, powder, shower, spray, strew

sprinkling n **= scattering**, dash, dusting, few, handful, sprinkle

sprint v **= race**, dart, dash, shoot, tear

sprite n **= spirit**, brownie, elf, fairy, goblin, imp, pixie

sprout v **= grow**, bud, develop, shoot, spring

spruce adj **= smart**, dapper, neat, trim, well-groomed, well turned out

spruce up v **= smarten up**, tidy, titivate

spry adj **= active**, agile, nimble, sprightly, supple

spur n **1 = stimulus**, impetus, impulse, incentive, incitement, inducement, motive **2 = goad**, prick **3 on the spur of the moment = on impulse**, impromptu, impulsively, on the spot, without planning

spu·ri·ous [SPYUUR-ee-əs] *adj* not genuine.

spurn *vt* reject with scorn, thrust aside.

spurt *v* **1** send, come out in jet. **2** rush suddenly. ◆ *n* **3** jet. **4** short sudden effort, esp. in race.

sput·nik [SPUUT-nik] *n* one of series of Russian satellites.

sput·ter [SPUT-ər] *v* splutter.

spu·tum [SPYOO-təm] *n, pl* **-ta** [-tə] spittle.

spy [spī] *n, pl* **spies 1** one who watches (esp. in rival countries, companies, etc.) and reports secretly. ◆ *v* **spied, spy·ing 2** act as spy. **3** catch sight of. **spy'glass** *n* small telescope.

squab·ble [SKWOB-əl] *vi* **-bled, -bling** engage in petty, noisy quarrel, bicker. ◆ *n*

squad [skwod] *n* small party, esp. of soldiers or police. **squad car** police patrol automobile (also **patrol car**). **squad·ron** [-rən] *n* division of an air force, fleet, or cavalry regiment.

squal·id [SKWOL-id] *adj* mean and dirty. **squal'or** [-ər] *n*

squall [skwawl] *n* **1** harsh cry. **2** sudden gust of wind. **3** short storm. ◆ *vi* **4** yell.

squan·der [SKWON-dər] *vt* spend wastefully, dissipate.

square [skwair] *n* **1** equilateral rectangle. **2** area of this shape. **3** in town, open space (of this shape). **4** product of a number multiplied by itself. **5** instrument for drawing right angles. **6** *sl* person behind the times. ◆ *adj* **7** square in form. **8** honest.

9 straight, even. **10** level, equal. **11** denoting a measure of area. **12** *inf* straightforward, honest. **13** *sl* ignorant of current trends in dress, music, etc., conservative. ◆ *v* **squared, squar·ing 14** *vt* **15** make square. **16** find square of. **17** pay. ◆ *vi* **18** fit, suit. **square'ly** *adv* **square off** get ready to dispute or fight. **square root** number that, multiplied by itself, gives number of which it is factor.

squash [skwosh] *vt* **1** crush flat. **2** pulp. **3** suppress. **4** humiliate (person). ◆ *n* **5** act of squashing. **6** (also **squash racquets**) game played with rackets and soft balls in walled court. **7** plant bearing gourds used as a vegetable.

squat [skwot] *vi* **squat·ted** *or* **squat, squat·ting 1** sit on heels. **2** act as squatter. ◆ *adj* **squat·ter, squat·test** short and thick. **squatter** *n* one who settles on land or occupies house without permission.

squaw [skwaw] *n* **1** *offens* Amer. Indian woman. **2** *sl* wife.

squawk [skwawk] *n* **1** short harsh cry, esp. of bird. ◆ *v* **2** utter this.

squeak [skweek] *v, n* (make) short shrill sound.

squeal [skweel] *n* **1** long piercing squeak. ◆ *vi* **2** make one. **3** *sl* turn informer, supply information (about another). **squeal'er** *n*

squeam·ish [SKWEEM-ish] *adj* **1** easily nauseated. **2** easily shocked. **3** overscrupulous.

——— THESAURUS ———

◆ *v* **4** = **incite**, animate, drive, goad, impel, prick, prod, prompt, stimulate, urge

spurious *adj* = **false**, artificial, bogus, fake, phoney *or* phony (*inf*), pretended, sham, specious, unauthentic

spurn *v* = **reject**, despise, disdain, rebuff, repulse, scorn, slight, snub

spurt *v* **1** = **gush**, burst, erupt, shoot, squirt, surge ◆ *n* **2** = **burst**, fit, rush, spate, surge

spy *n* **1** = **undercover agent**, mole ◆ *v* **2** = **catch sight of**, espy, glimpse, notice, observe, spot

squabble *v* **1** = **quarrel**, argue, bicker, dispute, fight, row, wrangle ◆ *n* **2** = **quarrel**, argument, disagreement, dispute, fight, row, tiff

squad *n* = **team**, band, company, crew, force, gang, group, troop

squalid *adj* = **dirty**, filthy, scuzzy (*sl*), seedy, sleazy, slummy, sordid, unclean

squalor *n* = **filth**, foulness, sleaziness, squalidness

squander *v* = **waste**, blow (*sl*), expend, fritter away, misspend, misuse, spend

square *adj* **1** = **honest**, above board, ethical, fair, genuine, kosher (*inf*), straight **2** *Inf* = **uncool**, dorky (*sl*), nerdy, unhip ◆ *v* **3** = **even up**, adjust, align, level **4** (sometimes with *up*) = **pay off**, settle **5** (often with *with*) = **agree**, correspond, fit, match, reconcile, tally

squash *v* **1** = **crush**, compress, distort, flatten, mash, press, pulp, smash **2** = **suppress**, annihilate, crush, humiliate, quell, silence

squashy *adj* = **soft**, mushy, pulpy, spongy, yielding

squawk *v* = **cry**, hoot, screech

squeak *v* = **peep**, pipe, squeal

squeal *n, v* = **scream**, screech, shriek, wail, yell

squee·gee [SKWEE-jee] *n* **1** tool with rubber blade for clearing water (from glass, etc., spreading wet paper, etc.). ◆ *vt* **-geed, -gee·ing 2** press, smooth with a squeegee.

squeeze [skweez] *vt* **squeezed, squeez·ing 1** press. **2** wring. **3** force. **4** hug. **5** subject to extortion. ◆ *n* **6** act of squeezing. **7** period of hardship, difficulty caused by financial weakness.

squelch [skwelch] *vt* **1** squash. **2** silence with crushing rebuke, etc. ◆ *vi* **3** make, walk with wet sucking sound, as in walking through mud. ◆ *n*

squib [skwib] *n* **1** small (faulty) firework. **2** short piece of writing. **3** short news story.

squid [skwid] *n* type of cuttlefish.

squig·gle [SKWIG-əl] *n* **1** wavy, wriggling mark. ◆ *vi* **-gled, -gling 2** wriggle. **3** draw squiggle.

squint [skwint] *vi* **1** look with eyes partially closed. **2** have the eyes turned in different directions. **3** glance sideways. **4** look askance. ◆ *n* **5** partially closed eyes. **6** crossed eyes. **7** *inf* a glance.

squire [skwīr] *n* country gentleman.

squirm [skwurm] *vi* **1** wriggle. **2** be embarrassed. ◆ *n*

squir·rel [SKWUR-əl] *n* **1** small graceful bushy-tailed tree animal. ◆ *vt* **-reled, -rel·ing 2** store or hide (possession) for future use.

squirt [skwurt] *v* (of liquid) force, be forced through narrow opening. ◆ *n* **1** jet. **2** *inf* short or insignificant person. **3** *inf* (impudent) youngster.

squish [skwish] *v, n* (make) soft splashing sound.

Sr *Chem.* strontium.

stab *v* **stabbed, stab·bing 1** pierce, strike (at) with pointed weapon. ◆ *n* **2** blow, wound so inflicted. **3** sudden unpleasant sensation. **4** attempt.

sta·bi·lize [STAY-bə-līz] *vt* **-ized, -iz·ing** make steady, restore to equilibrium, esp. of money values, prices and wages. **sta·bi·li·za'tion** *n* **sta'bi·liz·er** *n* device to maintain equilibrium of ship, aircraft, etc.

sta·ble[1] [STAY-bəl] *n* **1** building for horses. **2** racehorses of particular owner, establishment. **3** such establishment. ◆ *vt* **-bled, -bling 4** put into, lodge in, a stable.

stable[2] *adj* **-bler, -blest 1** firmly fixed. **2** steadfast, resolute. **sta·bil·i·ty** [stə-BIL-ə-tee] *n* **1** steadiness. **2** ability to resist change of any kind. **sta'bly** *adv*

stac·ca·to [stə-KAH-toh] *adj, adv* **1** *Mus.* with notes sharply separated. **2** abrupt.

stack [stak] *n* **1** ordered pile, heap. **2** chimney. ◆ *vt* **3** pile in stack. **4** control aircraft waiting to land so that they fly safely at different altitudes.

sta·di·um [STAY-dee-əm] *n, pl* **-di·ums** open-air or covered arena for athletics, etc.

staff[1] *n, pl* **staffs 1** body of officers or workers. **2** personnel. **3** pole. ◆ *vt* **4** employ personnel. **5** supply with personnel.

staff[2] *n, pl* **staffs** or **staves** five lines on which music is written.

stag *n* **1** adult male deer. ◆ *adj* **2** for men only, e.g. *stag party*.

stage [stayj] *n* **1** period, division of development. **2** raised floor or platform. **3** (platform of) theater. **4** scene of action. **5** stopping place of stagecoach, etc. on road, distance between two of them. **6**

squeamish *adj* **1** = **delicate**, fastidious, prudish, strait-laced **2** = **sick**, nauseous, queasy

squeeze *v* **1** = **press**, clutch, compress, crush, grip, pinch, squash, wring **2** = **cram**, crowd, force, jam, pack, press, ram, stuff **3** = **hug**, clasp, cuddle, embrace, enfold **4** = **extort**, milk, pressurize, wrest ◆ *n* **5** = **hug**, clasp, embrace **6** = **crush**, congestion, crowd, jam, press, squash

squirm *v* = **wriggle**, twist, writhe

squirt *n Inf* = **child**, baby, boy, girl, infant, kid (*inf*), minor, toddler, tot, whippersnapper (*old-fashioned*), youngster

stab *v* **1** = **pierce**, impale, jab, knife, spear, stick, thrust, transfix, wound ◆ *n* **2** = **wound**, gash, incision, jab, puncture, thrust **3** = **twinge**, ache, pang, prick **4** **make** or **have a stab at** *Inf* = **attempt**, endeavor, have a go, try

stability *n* = **firmness**, solidity, soundness, steadiness, strength

stable *adj* **1** = **firm**, constant, established, fast, fixed, immovable, lasting, permanent, secure, sound, strong **2** = **steady**, reliable, staunch, steadfast, sure

stack *n* **1** = **pile**, heap, load, mass, mound, mountain ◆ *v* **2** = **pile**, accumulate, amass, assemble, heap up, load

staff *n* **1** = **workers**, employees, personnel, team, workforce **2** = **stick**, cane, crook, pole, rod, scepter, stave, wand separate unit of space rocket, which can usu. be jettisoned. ◆ vt **staged, stag·ing 7** put (play) on stage. **8** arrange, bring about. **stag'y** adj **stag·i·er, stag·i·est 1** theatrical. **by easy stages 1** unhurriedly. **2** gradually. **stage whisper** loud whisper intended to be heard by audience.

stag·ger [STAG-ər] vi **1** walk unsteadily. ◆ vt **2** astound. **3** arrange in overlapping or alternating positions, times. **4** distribute over a period. ◆ n **5** act of staggering. **stag'gers** n **1** form of vertigo. **2** disease of horses. **stag'ger·ing** adj astounding.

stag·nate [STAG-nayt] vi **-nat·ed, -nat·ing** cease to flow or develop. **stag·na'tion** n **stag'nant** [-nənt] adj **1** sluggish. **2** not flowing. **3** foul, impure.

staid [stayd] adj of sober and quiet character, sedate. **staid'ly** adv **staid'ness** [-nis] n

stain [stayn] v **1** spot, mark. **2** apply liquid coloring to (wood, etc.). **3** bring disgrace upon. ◆ n **stain'less** adj **stainless steel** rustless steel alloy.

stairs [stairz] pl n set of steps, esp. as part of house. **stair'case, -way** n **1** structure enclosing stairs. **2** stairs. **stair'well** n vertical opening enclosing staircase.

stake [stayk] n **1** sharpened stick or post. **2** money wagered or contended for. ◆ vt **staked, stak·ing 3** secure, mark out with stakes. **4** wager, risk.

sta·lac·tite [stə-LAK-tīt] n lime deposit like icicle on roof of cave.

sta·lag·mite [stə-LAG-mīt] n lime deposit like pillar on floor of cave.

stale [stayl] adj **stal·er, stal·est** n old, lacking freshness. **2** hackneyed. **3** lacking energy, dullness through monotony. **stale'mate** n **1** Chess draw through one player being unable to move. **2** deadlock, impasse.

stalk¹ [stawk] n **1** plant's stem. **2** anything like this.

stalk² v **1** follow, approach stealthily. **2** walk in stiff and stately manner. **3** pursue persistently and, sometimes, attack (a person with whom one is obsessed). ◆ n **4** stalking. **stalk'er** n **stalk'ing-horse** n pretext.

stall [stawl] n **1** compartment in stable, etc. **2** booth for display and sale of goods. **3** seat in choir or chancel of church. **4** slowdown. ◆ v **5** put in stall. **6** stick fast. **7** (motor engine) unintentionally stop. **8** (aircraft) lose flying speed. **9** delay. **10** hinder.

stal·lion [STAL-yən] n uncastrated male horse, esp. for breeding.

stal·wart [STAWL-wərt] adj **1** strong, brave. **2** staunch. ◆ n **3** stalwart person.

sta·men [STAY-mən] n male organ of a flowering plant.

stam·i·na [STAM-ə-nə] n power of endurance, vitality.

stam·mer [STAM-ər] v **1** speak, say with repetition of syllables, stutter. ◆ n **2** habit of so speaking. **stam'mer·er** n

stamp vi **1** put down foot with force. ◆ vt **2** impress mark on. **3** affix postage stamp. **4** fix in memory. **5** reveal, characterize. ◆ n **6** stamping with foot. **7** imprinted mark. **8** appliance for marking. **9** piece of gummed paper printed with device as evidence of

———— THESAURUS ————

stage n = **point**, division, juncture, lap, leg, level, period, phase, step

stagger v **1** = **totter**, lurch, reel, sway, wobble **2** = **astound**, amaze, astonish, confound, overwhelm, shake, shock, stun, stupefy **3** = **overlap**, alternate, step

stagnant adj = **stale**, quiet, sluggish, still

stagnate v = **vegetate**, decay, decline, idle, languish, rot, rust

staid adj = **sedate**, calm, composed, grave, serious, sober, solemn, steady

stain v **1** = **mark**, blemish, blot, dirty, discolor, smirch, soil, spot, tinge ◆ n **2** = **mark**, blemish, blot, discoloration, smirch, spot **3** = **stigma**, disgrace, dishonor, shame, slur

stake¹ n = **pole**, pale, paling, palisade,

picket, post, stick

stake² n **1** = **bet**, ante, pledge, wager **2** = **interest**, concern, investment, involvement, share ◆ v **3** = **bet**, chance, gamble, hazard, risk, venture, wager

stale adj **1** = **old**, decayed, dry, flat, fusty, hard, musty, sour **2** = **unoriginal**, banal, hackneyed, overused, stereotyped, threadbare, trite, worn-out

stalk v = **pursue**, follow, haunt, hunt, shadow, track

stall v = **play for time**, hedge, temporize

stalwart adj = **strong**, staunch, stout, strapping, sturdy

stamina n = **staying power**, endurance, energy, force, power, resilience, strength

stammer v = **stutter**, falter, hesitate,

postage, etc. **10** character.

stam·pede [stam-PEED] n **1** sudden frightened rush, esp. of herd of cattle, crowd. ◆ v **-ped·ed, -ped·ing 2** cause, take part in stampede.

stance [stans] n **1** manner, position of standing. **2** attitude. **3** point of view.

stanch [stawnch] vt stop flow (of blood) from.

stan·chion [STAN-shən] n **1** upright bar, support. ◆ vt **2** make secure with stanchion.

stand v **stood** [stuud], **stand·ing 1** have, take, set in upright position. **2** remain. **3** be situated. **4** remain firm or stationary. **5** cease to move. **6** endure. **7** adhere to principles. **8** offer oneself as a candidate. **9** be symbol, etc. of. **10** provide free treat to. ◆ n **11** holding firm. **12** position. **13** halt. **14** something on which thing can be placed. **15** structure from which spectators watch sport, etc. **16** stop made by traveling entertainer, etc., e.g. *one-night stand*. **standing** n **1** reputation, status. **2**

duration. ◆ adj **3** erect. **4** permanent, lasting. **5** stagnant. **6** performed from stationary position, e.g. *standing jump*. **stand·by** [-bī] n, pl **-bys** [-bīz] someone, something that can be relied on. **stand in** act as substitute (for). **stand-in** n substitute. **stand over 1** watch closely. **2** postpone.

stand·ard [STAN-dərd] n **1** accepted example of something against which others are judged. **2** degree, quality. **3** flag. **4** weight or measure to which others must conform. **5** post. ◆ adj **6** usual, regular. **7** average. **8** of recognized authority, competence. **9** accepted as correct. **stand·ard·ize** vt **-ized, -iz·ing** regulate by a standard.

stand·off [STAND-awf] n (objectionable) aloofness. **1** *Sports* a tie. ◆ adj **2** (objectionably) aloof. **3** reserved.

stand·point n **1** point of view, opinion. **2** mental attitude.

stank pt. of STINK.

stan·nous [STAN-əs] adj of, containing tin.

pause, stumble

stamp n **1** = **imprint**, brand, earmark, hallmark, mark, signature ◆ v **2** = **trample**, crush **3** = **identify**, brand, categorize, label, mark, reveal, show to be **4** = **imprint**, impress, mark, print

stampede n = **rush**, charge, flight, rout

stamp out v = **eliminate**, crush, destroy, eradicate, put down, quell, scotch, suppress

stance n **1** = **attitude**, position, stand, standpoint, viewpoint **2** = **posture**, bearing, carriage, deportment

stand v **1** = **be upright**, be erect, be vertical, rise **2** = **put**, mount, place, position, set **3** = **exist**, be valid, continue, hold, obtain, prevail, remain **4** = **tolerate**, abide, allow, bear, brook, countenance, deal with (*sl*), endure, handle, put up with (*inf*), stomach, take ◆ n **5** = **stall**, booth, table **6** = **position**, attitude, determination, opinion, stance **7** = **support**, base, bracket, dais, platform, rack, stage, tripod

standard n **1** = **benchmark**, average, criterion, gauge, grade, guideline, measure, model, norm, yardstick **2** (often plural) = **principles**, ethics, ideals, morals **3** = **flag**, banner, ensign ◆ adj **4** = **usual**, average, basic, customary, normal, orthodox, regular, typical **5** = **accepted**,

approved, authoritative, definitive, established, official, recognized

standardize v = **bring into line**, institutionalize, regiment

stand by v **1** = **be prepared**, wait **2** = **support**, back, be loyal to, champion, take (someone's) part

stand for v **1** = **represent**, betoken, denote, indicate, mean, signify, symbolize **2** *Inf* = **tolerate**, bear, brook, endure, put up with

stand-in n = **substitute**, deputy, locum, replacement, reserve, stopgap, surrogate, understudy

stand in for v = **be a substitute for**, cover for, deputize for, represent, take the place of

standing adj **1** = **permanent**, fixed, lasting, regular **2** = **upright**, erect, vertical ◆ n **3** = **status**, eminence, footing, position, rank, reputation, repute **4** = **duration**, continuance, existence

standoffish adj = **reserved**, aloof, cold, distant, haughty, remote, unapproachable, unsociable

stand out v = **be conspicuous**, be distinct, be obvious, be prominent

standpoint n = **point of view**, angle, position, stance, viewpoint

stand up for v = **support**, champion,

stan·za [STAN-zə] *n, pl* **-zas** group of lines of verse.

sta·ple [STAY-pəl] *n* **1** U-shaped piece of metal with pointed ends to drive into wood for use as ring. **2** paper fastener. **3** main product. **4** fiber. **5** pile of wool, etc. ◆ *adj* **6** principal. **7** regularly produced or made for market. ◆ *vt* **-pled, -pling 8** fasten with staple. **9** sort, classify (wool, etc.) according to length of fibre. **sta'pler** *n* small device for fastening papers together.

star [stahr] *n* **1** celestial body, seen as twinkling point of light. **2** asterisk. **3** celebrated player, actor. **4** medal, jewel, etc. of apparent shape of star. ◆ *v* **starred, star·ring 5** adorn with stars. **6** mark (with asterisk). **7** feature as star performer. **8** play leading role in film, etc. ◆ *adj* **9** leading, most important, famous. **star'ry** *adj* **-ri·er, -ri·est** covered with stars. **star'dom** [-dəm] *n* **star'fish** *n* small star-shaped sea creature.

star·board [STAHR-bərd] *n* **1** right-hand side of ship, looking forward. ◆ *adj* **2** of, on this side.

starch *n* **1** substance forming the main food element in bread, potatoes, etc., and used mixed with water, for stiffening laundered fabrics. **2** *inf* boldness. **3** vigor. **4** energy. ◆ *vt* **5** stiffen thus. **starch'y** *adj* **starch·i·er, starch·i·est 1** containing starch. **2** stiff. **3** formal. **4** prim.

stare [stair] *vi* **stared, star·ing 1** look fixedly at. **2** gaze with eyes wide open. **3** be obvious or visible to. ◆ *n* **4** staring, fixed gaze. **stare down 1** abash by staring at. **2** defeat by staring.

stark [stahrk] *adj* **-er, -est 1** blunt, bare. **2** desolate. **3** absolute. ◆ *adv* **4** completely.

start [stahrt] *vt* **1** begin. **2** set going. ◆ *vi* **3** begin, esp. journey. **4** make sudden movement. ◆ *n* **5** beginning. **6** abrupt movement. **7** advantage of a lead in a race. **start'er** *n* **1** electric motor starting car engine. **2** competitor in, supervisor of, start of race.

star·tle [STAHR-tl] *vt* **-tled, -tling** give a fright to.

starve [stahrv] *v* **starved, starv·ing** (cause to) suffer or die from hunger. **star·va'tion** [-VAY-shən] *n*

stash *vt* **1** put away, store, hide. ◆ *n* **2** anything stashed. **3** place for this. **4** *sl* supply of illicit drugs.

state [stayt] *n* **1** condition. **2** place, situation. **3** politically organized people e.g. any of the fifty states of the USA. **4** government. **5** rank. **6** pomp. ◆ *vt* **stat·ed, stat·ing 7** express in words. **stated** *adj* **1** fixed. **2** regular. **3** settled. **state'ly** *adj* **-li·er, -li·est** dignified, lofty. **state'ment** [-mənt] *n* **1** expression in words. **2** account. **state'room** [-ruum] *n* private cabin on ship. **states'man** [-mən] *n, pl* **-men** respected political leader. **states'man·ship** *n* statesman's art.

defend, stick up for (*inf*), uphold

staple *adj* = **principal**, basic, chief, fundamental, key, main, predominant

star *n* **1** = **heavenly body 2** = **celebrity**, big name, luminary, main attraction, megastar (*inf*), name, superstar (*inf*) ◆ *adj* **3** = **leading**, brilliant, celebrated, major, prominent, well-known

stare *v* = **gaze**, eyeball (*sl*), gape, gawk, goggle, look, watch

stark *adj* **1** = **harsh**, austere, bare, barren, bleak, grim, hard, homely, plain, severe **2** = **absolute**, blunt, downright, out-and-out, pure, sheer, unmitigated, utter ◆ *adv* **3** = **absolutely**, altogether, completely, entirely, quite, utterly, wholly

start *v* **1** = **begin**, appear, arise, commence, issue, originate **2** = **set about**, embark upon, make a beginning, take the first step **3** = **set in motion**, activate, get going, initiate, instigate, kick-start, open,

originate, trigger **4** = **jump**, flinch, jerk, recoil, shy **5** = **establish**, begin, create, found, inaugurate, initiate, institute, launch, pioneer, set up ◆ *n* **6** = **beginning**, birth, dawn, foundation, inception, initiation, onset, opening, outset **7** = **advantage**, edge, head start, lead **8** = **jump**, convulsion, spasm

startle *v* = **surprise**, frighten, make (someone) jump, scare, shock

starving *adj* = **hungry**, famished, ravenous, starved

state *n* **1** = **condition**, circumstances, position, predicament, shape, situation **2** = **frame of mind**, attitude, humor, mood, spirits **3** = **country**, commonwealth, federation, government, kingdom, land, nation, republic, territory **4** = **ceremony**, display, glory, grandeur, majesty, pomp, splendor, style ◆ *v* **5** = **express**, affirm, articulate, assert, declare, expound,

stat·ic [STAT-ik] *adj* **1** motionless, inactive. **2** pert. to bodies at rest, or in equilibrium. ◆ *n* **3** electrical interference in radio reception. **stat'i·cal·ly** *adv*

sta·tion [STAY-shən] *n* **1** place where thing stops or is placed. **2** stopping place for railroad trains, buses. **3** local office for police force, fire department, etc. **4** place equipped for radio or television transmission. **5** post. **6** status. **7** position in life. ◆ *vt* **8** put in position. **sta'tion·ar·y** [-er-ee] *adj* **1** not moving, fixed. **2** not changing.

sta·tion·er [STAY-shən-ər] *n* dealer in writing materials, etc. **sta'tion·er·y** *n*

sta·tis·tic [stə-TIS-tik] *n* numerical fact collected and classified systematically. **sta·tis·tics** *n* science of classifying and interpreting numerical information. **sta·tis'ti·cal** [-kəl] *adj* **stat·is·ti·cian** [stat-i-STISH-ən] *n* one who compiles and studies statistics.

stat·ue [STACH-oo] *n* solid carved or cast image of person, animal, etc. **stat'u·ar·y** [-er-ee] *n* statues collectively. **stat·u·esque'** [-esk] *adj* **1** like statue. **2** dignified.

stat·ure [STACH-ər] *n* **1** bodily height. **2** greatness.

sta·tus [STAY-təs] *n* **1** position, rank. **2** prestige. **3** relation to others. **status quo** [kwoh] existing state of affairs.

stat·ute [STACH-oot] *n* written law. **stat'u·to·ry** [-ə-tor-ee] *adj* enacted, defined or authorized by statute.

staunch [stawnch] *adj* **-er, -est** trustworthy, loyal.

stave [stayv] *n* **1** one of the pieces forming barrel. **2** verse, stanza. **3** *Mus.* staff. ◆ *vt* **staved** *or* **stove, stav·ing** **4** break hole in. **5** ward (off).

stay¹ *v* **stayed, stay·ing** **1** remain. **2** sojourn. **3** pause. **4** wait. **5** endure. **6** stop. **7** hinder. **8** postpone. ◆ *n* **9** remaining, sojourning. **10** check. **11** restraint. **12** deterrent. **13** postponement.

stay² *n* **1** support, prop, rope supporting mast, etc. ◆ *pl* **2** formerly, laced corsets.

stead [sted] *n* place. **in stead** in place (of). **in good stead** of service.

stead·y [STED-ee] *adj* **stead·i·er, stead·i·est** **1** firm. **2** regular. **3** temperate. **4** industrious. **5** reliable. ◆ *vt* **stead·ied, stead·y·ing** **6** make steady. **stead'i·ly** *adv* **stead'i·ness** [-nis] *n* **stead'fast** [-fəst] *adj* firm, fixed, unyielding. **stead'fast·ly** *adv*

steak [stayk] *n* **1** slice of meat, esp. beef. **2** slice of fish.

steal [steel] *v* **stole, sto·len, steal·ing** **1** rob. **2** move silently. **3** take without right or leave.

present, say, specify, utter, voice
stately *adj* = **grand**, august, dignified, lofty, majestic, noble, regal, royal
statement *n* = **account**, announcement, communication, communiqué, declaration, proclamation, report
state-of-the-art *adj* = **latest**, newest, up-to-date, up-to-the-minute
static *adj* = **stationary**, fixed, immobile, motionless, still, unmoving
station *n* **1** = **headquarters**, base, depot **2** = **place**, location, position, post, seat, situation **3** = **position**, post, rank, situation, standing, status ◆ *v* **4** = **assign**, establish, install, locate, post, set
stationary *adj* = **motionless**, fixed, parked, standing, static, stock-still, unmoving
statuesque *adj* = **well-proportioned**, imposing, Junoesque
stature *n* = **importance**, eminence, prestige, prominence, rank, standing
status *n* = **position**, condition, consequence, eminence, grade, prestige,

rank, standing
staunch¹ *adj* = **loyal**, faithful, firm, sound, stalwart, steadfast, true, trusty
staunch² *v* = **stop**, check, dam, halt, stay, stem
stay¹ *v* **1** = **remain**, abide, continue, halt, linger, loiter, pause, stop, tarry, wait ◆ *n* **2** = **visit**, holiday, sojourn, stop, stopover **3** = **postponement**, deferment, delay, halt, stopping, suspension
steadfast *adj* = **firm**, faithful, fast, fixed, intent, loyal, resolute, stalwart, staunch, steady, unswerving, unwavering
steady *adj* **1** = **firm**, fixed, safe, stable **2** = **sensible**, balanced, calm, dependable, equable, level-headed, reliable, sober **3** = **continuous**, ceaseless, consistent, constant, incessant, nonstop, persistent, regular, twenty-four-seven (*sl*), unbroken, uninterrupted ◆ *v* **4** = **stabilize**, balance, brace, secure, support
steal *v* **1** = **take**, appropriate, embezzle, filch, lift (*inf*), misappropriate, pilfer, pinch (*inf*), purloin, thieve **2** = **sneak**, creep, slink,

stealth [stelth] *n* secret or underhanded procedure, behavior. **stealth'i·ly** *adv* **stealth'y** *adj* **stealth·i·er, stealth·i·est**

steam [steem] *n* **1** vapor of boiling water. **2** *inf* power, energy. ◆ *vi* **3** give off steam. **4** rise in vapor. **5** move by steam power. ◆ *vt* **6** cook or treat with steam. **steam'er** *n* **1** steam-propelled ship. **2** vessel for cooking or treating with steam. **steam engine** engine worked or propelled by steam. **steam'roll·er** *n* **1** large roller, orig. moved by steam, for leveling road surfaces, etc. **2** any great power used to crush opposition. ◆ *vt* **3** crush.

steed *n* *Poet.* horse.

steel *n* **1** hard and malleable metal made by mixing carbon in iron. **2** tool, weapon of steel. ◆ *vt* **3** harden. **steel'y** *adj* **steel·i·er, steel·i·est**

steep¹ *adj* **-er, -est 1** rising, sloping abruptly. **2** precipitous. **3** (of prices) very high or exorbitant. **4** unreasonable. **steep'en** *v* **steep'ly** *adv* **steep'ness** *n*

steep² *v* **1** soak, saturate. ◆ *n* **2** act or process of steeping. **3** the liquid used.

stee·ple [STEE-pəl] *n* church tower with spire. **stee'ple·chase** *n* **1** horse race with ditches and fences to jump. **2** foot race with hurdles, etc. to jump. **stee'ple·jack** *n* one who builds, repairs chimneys, steeples, etc.

steer¹ *vt* **1** guide, direct course of vessel, motor vehicle, etc. ◆ *vi* **2** direct one's course. **steer'age** [-ij] *n* formerly, cheapest accommodation on ship. **steer'ing wheel** wheel turned by the driver of a vehicle in order to steer it.

steer² *n* castrated bull.

stein [stīn] *n* earthenware beer mug.

ste·le [STEE-lee] *n* ancient carved stone pillar or slab.

stel·lar [STEL-ər] *adj* of stars.

stem¹ *n* **1** stalk, trunk. **2** long slender part, as in tobacco pipe. **3** part of word to which inflections are added. **4** foremost part of ship. **stem cell** *Histology.* undifferentiated embryonic cell that gives rise to specialized cells, such as blood, bone, etc.

stem² *vt* **stemmed, stem·ming** check, stop, dam up.

stench *n* evil smell.

sten·cil [STEN-səl] *n* **1** thin sheet pierced with pattern which is brushed over with paint or ink, leaving pattern on surface under it. **2** the pattern. **3** the plate. **4** pattern made. ◆ *vt* **-ciled, -cil·ing**

ste·nog·ra·phy [stə-NOG-rə-fee] *n* shorthand writing. **sten·og'ra·pher** *n* **sten·o·graph'ic** *adj*

stent *n* surgical implant to keep an artery open.

sten·to·ri·an [sten-TOR-ee-ən] *adj* (of voice) very loud.

step *v* **stepped, step·ping 1** move and set down foot. **2** proceed (in this way). **3** measure in paces. ◆ *n* **4** act of stepping. **5** sound made by stepping. **6** mark made by foot. **7** manner of walking. **8** series of foot movements forming part of dance. **9** gait. **10** pace. **11** measure, act, stage in proceeding. **12** board, rung, etc. to put foot on. **13** degree in scale. **14** mast socket. **15** promotion. ◆ *pl* **16** portable ladder with hinged prop attached, stepladder. **step'lad·der** *n* four-legged ladder having broad flat steps.

step·child [STEP-chīld] *n, pl* **-child·ren** [-CHIL-drən] **1** child of husband or wife by former marriage. **2** person, organization, idea, etc. treated improperly. **step'broth·er** *n* **step'fa·ther** *n* **step'moth·er** *n* **step'sis·ter** *n*

slip, tiptoe

stealth *n* = **secrecy**, furtiveness, slyness, sneakiness, stealthiness, surreptitiousness, unobtrusiveness

stealthy *adj* = **secret**, furtive, secretive, sneaking, surreptitious

steep¹ *adj* **1** = **sheer**, abrupt, precipitous **2** = **high**, exorbitant, extortionate, extreme, overpriced, unreasonable

steep² *v* **1** = **soak**, drench, immerse, macerate, marinate (*Cookery*), moisten, souse, submerge **2** = **saturate**, fill, imbue, infuse, permeate, pervade, suffuse

steer *v* = **direct**, conduct, control, guide, handle, pilot

stem¹ *n* **1** = **stalk**, axis, branch, shoot, trunk ◆ *v* **2** **stem from** = **originate in**, arise from, be caused by, derive from

stem² *v* = **stop**, check, curb, dam, hold back, staunch

stench *n* = **stink**, foul smell, reek, whiff

step *n* **1** = **footstep**, footfall, footprint, pace, print, stride, track **2** = **stage**, move, phase, point **3** = **action**, act, deed, expedient, means, measure, move **4** = **degree**, level, rank ◆ *v* **5** = **walk**, move,

steppe [step] *n* extensive treeless plain in European and Asiatic Russia.

stere [steer] *n* cubic meter.

ster·e·o·phon·ic [ster-ee-ə-FON-ik] *adj* (of sound) giving effect of coming from many directions. **ster'e·o** *adj, n* (of, for) stereophonic record player, etc.

ster·e·o·scop·ic [ster-ee-ə-SKOP-ik] *adj* having three-dimensional effect.

ster·e·o·type [STER-ee-ə-tīp] *n* **1** metal plate for printing cast from type. **2** something (monotonously) familiar, conventional, predictable. ♦ *vt* **-typed, -typ·ing 3** make stereotype of.

ster·ile [STER-əl] *adj* **1** unable to produce fruit, crops, young, etc. **2** free from (harmful) germs. **ste·ril·i·ty** [stə-RIL-ə-tee] *n* **ster·i·li·za'tion** *n* process or act of making sterile. **ster'i·lize** *vt* **-lized, -liz·ing** render sterile.

ster·ling [STUR-ling] *adj* **1** genuine, true. **2** of solid worth, dependable. **3** in British money. ♦ *n* **4** British money.

stern[1] [sturn] *adj* severe, strict. **stern'ly** *adv* **stern'ness** [-nis] *n*

stern[2] *n* rear part of ship.

ster·num [STUR-nəm] *n* the breast bone.

ster·to·rous [STUR-tər-əs] *adj* with sound of heavy breathing, hoarse snoring.

stet *Lat* let it stand (proofreader's direction to cancel alteration previously made).

steth·o·scope [STETH-ə-skohp] *n* instrument for listening to action of heart, lungs, etc.

Stet·son [STET-sən] *n* ℞ type of broad-brimmed felt hat esp. cowboy hat.

ste·ve·dore [STEE-vi-dor] *n* one who loads or unloads ships.

stew [stoo] *n* **1** food cooked slowly in closed vessel. **2** state of excitement, agitation or worry. ♦ *v* **3** cook by stewing. **4** worry. **stew in one's own juice** suffer consequences of one's own actions.

stew·ard [STOO-ərd] *n* **1** one who manages another's property. **2** official managing race meeting, assembly, etc. **3** attendant on ship's or aircraft's passengers. **stew'ard·ess** [-is] *n, fem.*

stick [stik] *n* **1** long, thin piece of wood. **2** anything shaped like a stick. **3** *inf* uninteresting person. ♦ *v* **stuck, stick·ing** ♦ *vt* **4** pierce, stab. **5** place, fasten, as by pins, glue. **6** protrude. **7** bewilder. **8** *inf* impose disagreeable responsibility on (someone). ♦ *vi* **9** adhere. **10** come to stop, jam. **11** remain. **12** be fastened. **13** protrude. **stick'er** *n* adhesive label, e.g. *bumper sticker.* **stick'y** *adj* **stick·i·er, stick·i·est 1** covered with, like adhesive substance. **2** (of weather) warm, humid. **3** *inf* difficult, unpleasant. **stick shift** automobile transmission with manually operated shift lever.

stick·ler [STIK-lər] *n* person who insists on something.

stiff *adj* **-er, -est 1** not easily bent or moved. **2** rigid. **3** awkward. **4** difficult. **5** thick, not fluid. **6** formal. **7** stubborn. **8** unnatural. **9** strong or fresh, as breeze. **10** *inf* excessive. ♦ *n* **11** *sl* corpse. **12** *sl* a drunk. ♦ *vt* **13** *sl* fail

---

THESAURUS

pace, tread

step in *v* = **intervene**, become involved, take action

step up *v* = **increase**, intensify, raise

stereotype *n* **1** = **formula**, pattern ♦ *v* **2** = **categorize**, pigeonhole, standardize, typecast

sterile *adj* **1** = **germ-free**, aseptic, disinfected, sterilized **2** = **barren**, bare, dry, empty, fruitless, unfruitful, unproductive

sterilize *v* = **disinfect**, fumigate, purify

sterling *adj* = **excellent**, fine, genuine, sound, superlative, true

stern *adj* = **severe**, austere, forbidding, grim, hard, harsh, inflexible, rigid, serious, strict

stick[1] *n* **1** = **cane**, baton, crook, pole, rod, staff, twig **2** *Brit. sl* = **abuse**, criticism, flak (*inf*)

stick[2] *v* **1** = **poke**, dig, jab, penetrate, pierce, prod, puncture, spear, stab, thrust, transfix **2** = **fasten**, adhere, affix, attach, bind, bond, cling, fix, glue, hold, join, paste, weld **3** (with *out, up, etc.*) = **protrude**, bulge, extend, jut, obtrude, poke, project, show **4** = **put**, deposit, lay, place, set **5** = **stay**, linger, persist, remain **6** *Sl* = **tolerate**, abide, stand, stomach, take **7 stick up for** = **defend**, champion, stand up for, support

stickler *n* = **perfectionist**, fanatic, fusspot (*inf*), purist

sticky *adj* **1** = **tacky**, adhesive, clinging, gluey, glutinous, gooey (*inf*), gummy, viscid, viscous **2** *Inf* = **difficult**, awkward, delicate, embarrassing, nasty, tricky, unpleasant **3** = **humid**, clammy, close, muggy, oppressive, sultry, sweltering

DICTIONARY

to tip (waiter, etc.). **stiff'en** [-in] v **stiff'ly** adv **stiff-necked** [-nekt] adj **1** obstinate, stubborn. **2** haughty.

sti·fle [STIF-əl] vt **-fled, -fling** smother, suppress.

stig·ma [STIG-mə] n, pl **-mas** or **-ma·ta** [-MAH-tə] distinguishing mark esp. of disgrace. **stig'ma·tize** vt **-tized, -tiz·ing** mark with stigma.

sti·let·to [sti-LET-oh] n, pl **-tos** or **-toes 1** small dagger. **2** small boring tool. ◆ adj **3** thin, pointed like a stiletto.

still¹ adj **-er, -est 1** motionless, noiseless, at rest. ◆ vt **2** quiet. ◆ adv **3** to this time. **4** yet. **5** even. ◆ n **6** photograph esp. of motion picture scene. **still'born** adj born dead. **still life** a painting of inanimate objects.

still² n apparatus for distilling.

stilt n **1** pole with footrests for walking raised from ground. **2** long post supporting building, etc. **stilt'ed** [-id] adj stiff in manner, pompous.

stim·u·lus [STIM-yə-ləs] n, pl **-li** [-lī] **1** something that rouses to activity. **2** incentive. **stim'u·lant** [-lənt] n drug, etc. acting as a stimulus. **stim'u·late** vt **-lat·ed, -lat·ing** rouse up, spur. **stim'u·lat·ing** adj acting as stimulus. **stim·u·la'tion** n

stim'u·la·tive [-lə-tiv] adj

sting v **stung, sting·ing 1** thrust sting into. **2** cause sharp pain to. **3** sl cheat, take advantage of, esp. by overcharging. **4** feel sharp pain. ◆ n (wound, pain, caused by) sharp pointed organ, often poisonous, of certain insects and animals. **5** sl illegal operation conducted by police, etc. to collect evidence against criminals.

stin·gy [STIN-jee] adj **-gi·er, -gi·est 1** mean. **2** avaricious. **3** niggardly. **stin'gi·ness** [-nis] n

stink vi **stank** or **stunk, stunk, stink·ing 1** give out strongly offensive smell. **2** inf be markedly inferior. ◆ n **3** such smell, stench. **4** inf fuss, bother. **5** scandal.

stint vt **1** be frugal, miserly to (someone) or with (something). ◆ n **2** allotted amount of work or time. **3** limitation, restriction.

sti·pend [STĪ-pend] n payment, esp. scholarship or fellowship allowance given to student. **sti·pen'di·ar·y** [-dee-er-ee] adj receiving stipend.

stip·ple [STIP-əl] vt **-pled, -pling 1** engrave, paint in dots. ◆ n **2** this process.

stip·u·late [STIP-yə-layt] vi **-lat·ed, -lat·ing** specify in making a bargain. **stip·u·la'tion** n **1** proviso. **2** condition.

THESAURUS

stiff adj **1 = inflexible,** firm, hard, inelastic, rigid, solid, taut, tense, tight, unbending, unyielding **2 = awkward,** clumsy, graceless, inelegant, jerky (inf), ungainly, ungraceful **3 = difficult,** arduous, exacting, hard, tough **4 = severe,** drastic, extreme, hard, harsh, heavy, strict **5 = unrelaxed,** artificial, constrained, forced, formal, stilted, unnatural

stiffen v **1 = brace,** reinforce, tauten, tense **2 = set,** congeal, crystallize, harden, jell, solidify, thicken

stifle v **1 = suppress,** check, hush, repress, restrain, silence, smother, stop **2 = suffocate,** asphyxiate, choke, smother, strangle

stigma n **= disgrace,** dishonor, shame, slur, smirch, stain

still adj **1 = motionless,** calm, peaceful, restful, serene, stationary, tranquil, undisturbed **2 = silent,** hushed, quiet ◆ v **3 = quieten,** allay, calm, hush, lull, pacify, quiet, settle, silence, soothe ◆ conj **4 = however,** but, nevertheless, notwithstanding, yet

stilted adj **= stiff,** constrained, forced,

unnatural, wooden

stimulant n **= pick-me-up** (inf), restorative, tonic, upper (sl)

stimulate v **= arouse,** encourage, fire, impel, incite, prompt, provoke, rouse, spur

stimulating adj **= exciting,** exhilarating, inspiring, provocative, rousing, stirring

stimulus n **= incentive,** encouragement, goad, impetus, incitement, inducement, spur

sting v **1 = hurt,** burn, pain, smart, tingle, wound **2** Inf **= cheat,** defraud, fleece, overcharge, rip off (sl), swindle

stingy adj **= mean,** miserly, niggardly, parsimonious, penny-pinching (inf), tightfisted, ungenerous

stink n **1 = stench,** fetor, foul smell ◆ v **2 = reek**

stint v **1 = be mean,** be frugal, be sparing, hold back, skimp on ◆ n **2 = share,** period, quota, shift, spell, stretch, term, time, turn

stipulate v **= specify,** agree, contract, covenant, insist upon, require, settle

stipulation n **= specification,** agreement, clause, condition, precondition, proviso, qualification, requirement

stir [stur] *v* **stirred, stir-ring 1** (begin to) move. **2** rouse. **3** cause trouble. **4** set, keep in motion. **5** excite. ◆ *n* **6** commotion, disturbance.

stir-rup [STUR-əp] *n* metal loop hung from strap for supporting foot of rider on horse.

stitch [stich] *n* **1** movement of needle in sewing, etc. **2** its result in the work. **3** sharp pain in side. **4** least fragment (of clothing). ◆ *v* **5** sew.

stock [stok] *n* **1** goods, material stored, esp. for sale or later use. **2** reserve, fund. **3** shares in, or capital of, company, etc. **4** standing, reputation. **5** farm animals (livestock). **6** plant, stem from which cuttings are taken. **7** handle of gun, tool, etc. **8** liquid broth produced by boiling meat, etc. **9** flowering plant. **10** lineage. ◆ *pl* **11** *Hist.* frame to secure feet, hands (of offender). **12** frame to support ship during construction. ◆ *adj* **13** kept in stock. **14** standard, hackneyed. ◆ *vt* **15** keep, store. **16** supply with livestock, fish, etc. **stock'y** *adj* **stock-i-er, stock-i-est** thickset. **stock'brok-er** [-brohk-ər] *n* agent for buying, selling stocks and bonds. **stock car** ordinary automobile strengthened and modified for a form of racing in which automobiles often collide. **stock ex-change** institution for buying and selling shares. **stock'pile** *v* acquire and store large quantity of (something). **stock-still** *adj* motionless. **stock'tak-ing** *n* examination, counting and valuing of goods in a store, etc. **put stock in** believe, trust.

stock-ade [sto-KAYD] *n* enclosure of stakes, barrier.

stock-ing [STOK-ing] *n* close-fitting covering for leg and foot.

stodg-y [STOJ-ee] *adj* **stodg-i-er, stodg-i-est** heavy, dull.

sto-gy [STOH-gee] *n, pl* **-gies** cheap cigar.

sto-ic [STOH-ik] *adj* **1** capable of much self-control, great endurance without complaint. ◆ *n* **2** stoical person. **sto'i-cal** [-kəl] *adj*

stoke [stohk] *v* **stoked, stok-ing** feed, tend fire or furnace. **stok'er** *n*

stole¹ [stohl] pt. of STEAL.

stole² *n* long scarf or shawl.

sto'len [stohl-ən] pp. of STEAL.

stol'id *adj* **1** hard to excite. **2** heavy, slow, apathetic.

stom-ach [STUM-ək] *n* **1** sac forming chief digestive organ in any animal. **2** appetite. **3** desire, inclination. ◆ *vt* **4** put up with.

stomp *vi* put down foot with force.

stone [stohn] *n* **1** (piece of) rock. **2** gem. **3** hard seed of fruit. **4** hard deposit formed in kidneys, bladder. **5** British unit of weight, 14 lbs. ◆ *vt* **stoned, ston-ing 6** throw stones at. **7** free (fruit) from stones. **stoned** *adj sl* stupefied by alcohol or drugs. **ston'i-ly** *adv* **ston'y** *adj* **ston-i-er, ston-i-est 1** of, like stone. **2** hard. **3** cold. **stone-broke** [-brohk] *adj* with no money left. **stone-dead** *adj* completely dead. **stone-deaf** *adj* completely deaf. **stone'wall** *v* **1** stall. **2** evade. **3** filibuster. **stone'ware** [-wair] *n* heavy common pottery.

stir *v* **1** = **mix**, agitate, beat, shake **2** = **stimulate**, arouse, awaken, excite, incite, provoke, rouse, spur ◆ *n* **3** = **commotion**, activity, bustle, disorder, disturbance, excitement, flurry, fuss

stock *n* **1** = **goods**, array, choice, commodities, merchandise, range, selection, variety, wares **2** = **supply**, fund, hoard, reserve, stockpile, store **3** = **property**, assets, capital, funds, investment **4** = **livestock**, beasts, cattle, domestic animals ◆ *adj* **5** = **standard**, conventional, customary, ordinary, regular, routine, usual **6** = **hackneyed**, banal, overused, trite ◆ *v* **7** = **sell**, deal in, handle, keep, supply, trade in **8** = **provide with**, equip, fit out, furnish, supply **9 stock up** = **store (up)**, accumulate, amass, gather, hoard, lay in,

put away, save

stocky *adj* = **thickset**, chunky, dumpy, solid, stubby, sturdy

stodgy *adj* **1** = **heavy**, filling, leaden, starchy **2** = **dull**, boring, heavy going, staid, stuffy, tedious, unexciting

stoical *adj* = **resigned**, dispassionate, impassive, long-suffering, philosophical, phlegmatic, stoic, stolid

stoicism *n* = **resignation**, acceptance, forbearance, fortitude, impassivity, long-suffering, patience, stolidity

stolid *adj* = **apathetic**, dull, lumpish, unemotional, wooden

stomach *n* **1** = **belly**, abdomen, gut (*inf*), pot, tummy (*inf*) **2** = **inclination**, appetite, desire, relish, taste ◆ *v* **3** = **bear**, abide, endure, swallow, take, tolerate

stood [stuud] pt./pp. of STAND.

stooge [stooj] n 1 performer always the butt of another's jokes. 2 anyone taken advantage of by another.

stool n 1 backless chair. 2 excrement.

stoop[1] vi 1 lean forward or down, bend. 2 swoop. 3 abase, degrade oneself. ◆ n 4 stooping carriage of the body.

stoop[2] n steps or small porch in front of house.

stop v stopped, stop-ping 1 check, bring to halt. 2 prevent. 3 interrupt. 4 suspend. 5 desist from. 6 fill up an opening. 7 cease, come to a halt. 8 stay. ◆ n 9 stopping or becoming stopped. 10 any device for altering or regulating pitch. 11 set of pipes in organ having tones of a distinct quality. **stop'page** [-ij] n **stop'per** [-ər] n plug for closing bottle, etc. **stop'gap** n temporary substitute. **stop'off, stop'o•ver** n short break in journey. **stop'watch** n one that can be stopped for exact timing e.g. of race. **pull out all the stops** use all available means.

store [stor] vt stored, stor•ing 1 stock, furnish, keep. 2 Computers enter or retain (data). ◆ n 3 retail store. 4 abundance. 5 stock. 6 place for keeping goods. 7 warehouse. ◆ pl 8 stocks of goods, provisions. **stor'age** n **in store 1** in readiness. 2 imminent.

stork n large wading bird.

storm n 1 violent weather with wind, rain, hail, sand, snow, etc. 2 assault on fortress. 3 violent outbreak, discharge. ◆ vt 4 assault. 5 take by storm. ◆ vi 6 rage. **storm'y** adj storm-i-er, storm-i-est 1 like storm. 2 (emotionally) violent.

sto•ry[1] [STOR-ee] n, pl -ries 1 (book, piece of prose, etc.) telling about events, happenings. 2 lie.

story[2] n, pl -ries horizontal division of a building.

stoup [stoop] n small basin for holy water.

stout [stowt] adj -er, -est 1 sturdy, resolute. ◆ n 3 kind of beer. **stout'ly** adv **stout'ness** [-nis] n

stove[1] [stohv] n apparatus for cooking, heating, etc.

stove[2] pt./pp. of STAVE.

stow [stoh] vt pack away. **stow'age** [-ij] n **stow'a•way** n one who hides in ship to obtain free passage.

strad•dle [STRAD-l] v -dled, -dling ◆ vt 1 bestride. ◆ vi 2 spread legs wide. ◆ n

strafe [strayf] vt strafed, straf•ing attack

stony adj = cold, blank, chilly, expressionless, hard, hostile, icy, unresponsive

stoop v 1 = bend, bow, crouch, duck, hunch, lean 2 stoop to = sink to, descend to, lower oneself by, resort to ◆ n 3 = slouch, bad posture, round-shoulderedness

stop v 1 = halt, cease, conclude, cut short, desist, discontinue, end, finish, pause, put an end to, quit, refrain, shut down, terminate 2 = prevent, arrest, forestall, hinder, hold back, impede, repress, restrain 3 = plug, block, obstruct, seal, staunch, stem 4 = stay, lodge, rest ◆ n 5 = end, cessation, finish, halt, standstill 6 = stay, break, rest 7 = station, depot, terminus

stopgap n = makeshift, improvisation, resort, substitute

stoppage n = stopping, arrest, close, closure, cutoff, halt, hindrance, shutdown, standstill

store v 1 = put by, deposit, garner, hoard, keep, put aside, reserve, save, stockpile ◆ n 2 = shop, market, mart, outlet 3 = supply,

accumulation, cache, fund, hoard, quantity, reserve, stock, stockpile 4 = repository, depository, storeroom, warehouse

storm n 1 = tempest, blizzard, gale, hurricane, squall 2 = outburst, agitation, commotion, disturbance, furor, outbreak, outcry, row, rumpus, strife, tumult, turmoil ◆ v 3 = attack, assail, assault, charge, rush 4 = rage, bluster, rant, rave, thunder 5 = rush, flounce, fly, stamp

stormy adj = wild, blustery, inclement, raging, rough, squally, turbulent, windy

story n 1 = tale, account, anecdote, history, legend, narrative, romance, yarn 2 = report, article, feature, news, news item, scoop

stout adj 1 = fat, big, bulky, burly, corpulent, fleshy, heavy, overweight, plump, portly, rotund, tubby 2 = strong, able-bodied, brawny, muscular, robust, stalwart, strapping, sturdy 3 = brave, bold, courageous, fearless, gallant, intrepid, plucky, resolute, valiant

stow v = pack, bundle, load, put away, stash (inf), store

(esp. with bullets, rockets) from air.
strag·gle [STRAG-əl] *vi* **-gled, -gling** stray, get dispersed, linger. **strag'gler** *n*
straight [strayt] *adj* **-er, -est 1** without bend. **2** honest. **3** level. **4** in order. **5** (of whiskey) undiluted, neat. **6** expressionless. **7** (of drama, actor, etc.) serious. **8** *sl* heterosexual. ♦ *n* **9** straight condition or part. ♦ *adv* **10** direct. **straight'en** [-in] *v* **straight'a·way** *adv* immediately. **straight·for'ward** [-wərd] *adj* **1** open, frank. **2** simple. **3** honest.
strain[1] [strayn] *vt* **1** stretch tightly. **2** stretch to full or to excess. **3** filter. ♦ *vi* **4** make great effort. ♦ *n* **5** stretching force. **6** violent effort. **7** injury from being strained. **8** burst of music or poetry. **9** great demand. **10** (condition caused by) overwork, worry, etc. **11** tone of speaking or writing. **strain'er** [-ər] *n* filter, sieve.
strain[2] *n* **1** breed or race. **2** type (esp. in biology). **3** trace, streak.
strait [strayt] *n* **1** channel of water connecting two larger areas of water. ♦ *pl*

2 position of difficulty or distress. ♦ *adj* **3** narrow. **4** strict. **strait'en** [-in] *vt* **1** make strait, narrow. **2** press with poverty. **strait'jack·et** *n* jacket to confine arms of violent person. **strait-laced** [-laysd] *adj* **1** austere, strict. **2** puritanical.
strand[1] *v* **1** run aground. **2** leave, be left in difficulties or helpless.
strand[2] *n* one single string or wire of rope, etc.
strange [straynj] *adj* **strang·er, strang·est 1** odd. **2** queer. **3** unaccustomed. **4** foreign. **5** uncommon. **6** wonderful. **7** singular. **stran'ger** *n* **1** unknown person. **2** foreigner. **3** one unaccustomed (to). **strange'ness** [-nis] *n*
stran·gle [STRANG-gəl] *vt* **-gled, -gling 1** kill by squeezing windpipe. **2** suppress. **stran·gu·la'tion** [-yə-LAY-shən] *n* strangling.
strap *n* **1** strip, esp. of leather. ♦ *vt* **strapped, strap·ping 2** fasten, beat with strap. **strap'ping** *adj* tall and powerful. **strap'hang·er** *n* in bus, subway car, one

———————— THESAURUS ————————

straight *adj* **1 = direct**, near, short **2 = level**, aligned, even, horizontal, right, smooth, square, true **3 = upright**, erect, plumb, vertical **4 = honest**, above board, accurate, fair, honorable, just, law-abiding, trustworthy, upright **5 = frank**, blunt, bold, candid, forthright, honest, outright, plain, straightforward **6 = successive**, consecutive, continuous, nonstop, running, solid **7 = undiluted**, neat, pure, unadulterated, unmixed **8 = orderly**, arranged, in order, neat, organized, shipshape, tidy **9** *Sl* **= conventional**, bourgeois, conservative ♦ *adv* **10 = directly**, at once, immediately, instantly
straight away *adv* **= immediately**, at once, directly, instantly, now, right away
straighten *v* **= neaten**, arrange, order, put in order, tidy (up)
straightforward *adj* **1 = honest**, candid, direct, forthright, genuine, open, sincere, truthful, upfront (*inf*) **2 = easy**, elementary, routine, simple, uncomplicated
strain[1] *v* **1 = stretch**, distend, draw tight, tauten, tighten **2 = overexert**, injure, overtax, overwork, pull, sprain, tax, tear, twist, wrench **3 = strive**, bend over backwards (*inf*), endeavor, give it one's best shot (*inf*), go for it (*inf*), knock oneself out (*inf*), labor, struggle **4 = sieve**, filter,

purify, sift ♦ *n* **5 = stress**, anxiety, burden, pressure, tension **6 = exertion**, effort, force, struggle **7 = injury**, pull, sprain, wrench
strain[2] *n* **1 = breed**, ancestry, blood, descent, extraction, family, lineage, race **2 = trace**, streak, suggestion, tendency
strained *adj* **1 = forced**, artificial, false, put on, unnatural **2 = tense**, awkward, difficult, embarrassed, stiff, uneasy
strait *n* **1** (often plural) **= channel**, narrows, sound **2 straits = difficulty**, dilemma, extremity, hardship, plight, predicament
strait-laced *adj* **= strict**, moralistic, narrow-minded, prim, proper, prudish, puritanical
strand *n* **= filament**, fiber, string, thread
stranded *adj* **1 = beached**, aground, ashore, grounded, marooned, shipwrecked **2 = helpless**, abandoned, high and dry
strange *adj* **1 = odd**, abnormal, bizarre, curious, extraordinary, peculiar, queer, uncommon, weird, wonderful **2 = unfamiliar**, alien, exotic, foreign, new, novel, unknown, untried
stranger *n* **= newcomer**, alien, foreigner, guest, incomer, outlander, visitor
strangle *v* **1 = throttle**, asphyxiate, choke, strangulate **2 = suppress**, inhibit, repress, stifle

who has to stand, steadying self with strap provided for this purpose.

strat·a·gem [STRAT-ə-jəm] n plan, trick. **strat'e·gy** n, pl **-gies 1** art of war. **2** overall plan. **strat'e·gist** n **stra·te·gic** [strə-TEE-jik] adj

strat·o·sphere [STRAT-ə-sfeer] n upper part of the atmosphere from approx. 11 km to 50 km above Earth's surface.

stra·tum [STRAY-təm] n, pl **stra·ta** [-tə] **1** layer, esp. of rock. **2** class in society. **strat'i·fy** v **-fied, -fy·ing** form, deposit in layers. **strat·i·fi·ca'tion** n

straw n **1** stalks of grain. **2** single stalk. **3** long, narrow tube used to suck up liquid. **straw·ber·ry** n **1** creeping plant producing a red, juicy fruit. **2** the fruit.

stray vi **1** wander. **2** digress. **3** get lost. ◆ adj **4** strayed. **5** occasional, scattered. ◆ n **6** stray animal.

streak [streek] n **1** long line or band. **2** element, trace. ◆ vt **3** mark with streaks. ◆ vi **4** move fast. **5** run naked in public. **streak'y** adj **streak·i·er, streak·i·est 1** having streaks. **2** striped.

stream [streem] n **1** flowing body of water or other liquid. **2** steady flow. ◆ vi **3** flow. **4** run with liquid. **5** float, wave in the air. ◆ vt **6** discharge, send in stream. **stream'er**

[-ər] n (paper) ribbon, narrow flag.

stream·lined [STREEM-līnd] adj (of train, plane, etc.) built so as to offer least resistance to air.

street n road in town, etc. usu. lined with houses. **street'car** n vehicle (esp. electrically driven and for public transport) running usu. on rails laid on roadway. **street'walk·er** n prostitute. **street'wise, -smart** adj inf adept at surviving in urban, oft. criminal, environment.

strength [strengkth] n **1** quality of being strong. **2** power. **3** capacity for exertion or endurance. **4** vehemence. **5** force. **6** full or necessary number of people. **strength'en** v make stronger, reinforce. **on the strength of 1** relying on. **2** because of.

stren·u·ous [STREN-yoo-əs] adj **1** energetic. **2** earnest.

strep·to·coc·cus [strep-tə-KOK-əs] n, pl **-coc·ci** [-KOK-sī] genus of bacteria.

strep·to·my·cin [strep-tə-MĪ-sin] n antibiotic drug.

stress n **1** emphasis. **2** strain. **3** impelling force. **4** effort. **5** tension. ◆ vt **6** emphasize. **7** accent. **8** put mechanical stress on.

stretch [strech] vt **1** extend. **2** exert to utmost. **3** tighten, pull out. **4** reach out. ◆ vi **5** reach. **6** have elasticity. ◆ n **7**

THESAURUS

strap n **1 = belt**, thong, tie ◆ v **2 = fasten**, bind, buckle, lash, secure, tie

strapping adj **= well-built**, big, brawny, husky (inf), powerful, robust, sturdy

stratagem n **= trick**, device, dodge, maneuver, plan, ploy, ruse, scheme, subterfuge

strategic adj **1 = tactical**, calculated, deliberate, diplomatic, planned, politic **2 = crucial**, cardinal, critical, decisive, important, key, vital

strategy n **= plan**, approach, policy, procedure, scheme

stray v **1 = wander**, drift, err, go astray **2 = digress**, deviate, diverge, get off the point ◆ adj **3 = lost**, abandoned, homeless, roaming, vagrant **4 = random**, accidental, chance

streak n **1 = band**, layer, line, slash, strip, stripe, stroke, vein **2 = trace**, dash, element, strain, touch, vein ◆ v **3 = speed**, dart, flash, fly, hurtle, sprint, tear, whizz (inf), zoom

stream n **1 = river**, bayou, beck, brook, rivulet, tributary **2 = flow**, course, current,

drift, run, rush, surge, tide, torrent ◆ v **3 = flow**, cascade, course, flood, gush, issue, pour, run, spill, spout

streamlined adj **= efficient**, organized, rationalized, slick, smooth-running

street n **= road**, avenue, boulevard, lane, parkway, roadway, row, terrace

strength n **1 = might**, brawn, courage, fortitude, muscle, robustness, stamina, sturdiness, toughness **2 = intensity**, effectiveness, efficacy, force, potency, power, vigor **3 = advantage**, asset, strong point

strengthen v **1 = fortify**, brace up, consolidate, harden, invigorate, restore, stiffen, toughen **2 = reinforce**, augment, bolster, brace, build up, buttress, harden, intensify, support

strenuous adj **= demanding**, arduous, hard, laborious, tough, uphill

stress n **1 = strain**, anxiety, burden, pressure, tension, trauma, worry **2 = emphasis**, force, significance, weight **3 = accent**, accentuation, beat, emphasis ◆ v **4 = emphasize**, accentuate, dwell on, stretching, being stretched, expanse. **8** spell. **stretch'er** *n* **1** person, thing that stretches. **2** appliance on which disabled person is carried. **3** bar linking legs of chair.

strew [stroo] *vt* **strewed, strewn** or **strewed, strew·ing** scatter over surface, spread.

stri·ate [STRĪ-ayt] *vt* **-at·ed, -at·ing 1** mark with streaks. **2** score. **stri·a'tion** *n* **striated** *adj* streaked, furrowed, grooved.

strick·en [STRIK-ən] *adj* **1** seriously affected by disease, grief, famine. **2** afflicted. **3** pp. of STRIKE.

strict [strikt] *adj* **-er, -est 1** stern, not lax or indulgent. **2** defined. **3** without exception.

stric·ture [STRIK-chər] *n* **1** critical remark. **2** constriction.

stride [strīd] *vi* **strode, strid·den, strid·ing 1** walk with long steps. ◆ *n* **2** single step. **3** its length. **4** regular pace. **hit one's stride** reach the level at which one consistently functions best.

stri·dent [STRĪD-nt] *adj* **1** harsh in tone. **2** loud. **3** urgent.

strife [strīf] *n* **1** conflict. **2** quarreling.

strike [strīk] *v* **struck** or **strick·en, strik·ing 1** hit (against). **2** ignite. **3** (of snake) bite. **4** arrive at, come upon. **5** of plants (cause to) take root. **6** attack. **7** hook (fish). **8** sound (time) as bell in clock, etc. **9** *Baseball* swing and miss a pitch, etc. ◆ *vt* **10** affect. **11** enter mind of. **12** discover (gold, oil, etc.). **13** dismantle, remove. **14** make (coin). ◆ *vi*

15 cease work as protest or to make demands. ◆ *n* **16** act of striking. **strik'er** *n* **striking** *adj* noteworthy, impressive. **strike it rich** meet unexpected financial success. **strike off** remove. **strike out 1** fail in a venture. **2** *Baseball* make three strikes.

string *n* (length of) thin cord or other material. **1** strand, row. **2** series. **3** fiber in plants. ◆ *pl* **4** conditions. ◆ *vt* **strung, string·ing 5** provide with, thread on string. **6** form in line, series. **stringed** *adj* (of musical instruments) furnished with strings. **string'y** *adj* **string·i·er, string·i·est 1** like string. **2** fibrous.

strin·gent [STRIN-jənt] *adj* strict, rigid, binding. **strin'gen·cy** *n* severity.

strip *v* **stripped, strip·ping 1** lay bare, take covering off. **2** dismantle. **3** deprive (of). **4** undress. ◆ *n* **5** long, narrow piece. **strip'per** *n* person who performs a striptease. **strip'tease** [-teez] *n* nightclub or theater act in which stripper undresses in time to music.

stripe [strīp] *n* **1** narrow mark, band. **2** chevron as symbol of military rank. **3** style, kind.

strip'ling *n* a youth.

strive [strīv] *vi* **strove** or **strived, striv·en** or **strived, striv·ing** try hard, struggle, contend.

strobe [strohb] *n* apparatus that produces high-intensity flashing light.

strode [strohd] pt. of STRIDE.

stroke [strohk] *n* **1** blow. **2** sudden action,

underline

stretch *v* **1** = **extend**, cover, put forth, reach, spread, unroll **2** = **pull**, distend, draw out, elongate, expand, strain, tighten ◆ *n* **3** = **expanse**, area, distance, extent, spread, tract **4** = **period**, space, spell, stint, term, time

strict *adj* **1** = **severe**, authoritarian, firm, harsh, stern, stringent **2** = **exact**, accurate, close, faithful, meticulous, precise, scrupulous, true **3** = **absolute**, total, utter

strident *adj* = **harsh**, discordant, grating, jarring, raucous, screeching, shrill

strife *n* = **conflict**, battle, clash, discord, dissension, friction, quarrel

strike *v* **1** = **walk out**, down tools, mutiny, revolt **2** = **hit**, beat, clobber (*sl*), clout (*inf*), cuff, hammer, knock, punch, slap, smack, thump, wallop (*inf*) **3** = **collide with**, bump into, hit, run into **4** = **attack**, assail, assault,

hit **5** = **occur to**, come to, dawn on or upon, hit, register (*inf*)

striking *adj* = **impressive**, conspicuous, cool (*inf*), dramatic, noticeable, outstanding, phat (*sl*)

string *n* **1** = **cord**, fiber, twine **2** = **series**, chain, file, line, procession, row, sequence, succession

stringent *adj* = **strict**, inflexible, rigid, rigorous, severe, tight, tough

stringy *adj* = **fibrous**, gristly, sinewy, tough

strip[1] *v* **1** = **undress**, disrobe, unclothe **2** = **plunder**, despoil, divest, empty, loot, pillage, ransack, rob, sack

strip[2] *n* = **piece**, band, belt, shred

strive *v* = **try**, attempt, bend over backwards (*inf*), break one's neck (*inf*), do one's best, give it one's best shot (*inf*), go all out (*inf*), knock oneself out (*inf*), labor, make an all-out effort (*inf*), struggle, toil occurrence. **3** apoplexy. **4** mark of pen, pencil, brush, etc. **5** chime of clock. **6** completed movement in series. **7** act, manner of striking (ball, etc.). **8** style, method of swimming. **9** rower sitting nearest stern setting the rate. **10** act of stroking. ◆ *vt* **stroked, strok·ing 11** set time in rowing. **12** pass hand lightly over.

stroll [strohl] *vi* walk in leisurely or idle manner. ◆ *n*

strong [strawng] *adj* **-er, -est 1** powerful, robust, healthy. **2** difficult to break. **3** noticeable. **4** intense. **5** emphatic. **6** not diluted. **7** having a certain number. **strong·hold** [-hohld] *n* fortress.

stron·ti·um [STRON-shee-əm] *n* silvery-white chemical element. **strontium 90** radioactive isotope of strontium present in fallout of nuclear explosions.

strop *n* **1** leather for sharpening razors. ◆ *vt* **stropped, strop·ping 2** sharpen on one.

strove [strohv] pt. of STRIVE.

struck pt./pp. of STRIKE.

struc·ture [STRUK-chər] *n* **1** (arrangement of parts in) construction, building, etc. **2** form. **3** organization. ◆ *vt* **-tured, -tur·ing 4** give structure to. **struc'tur·al** [-chər-əl] *adj*

strug·gle [STRUG-əl] *vi* **-gled, -gling 1** contend. **2** fight. **3** proceed, work, move with difficulty and effort. ◆ *n*

strum *v* **strummed, strum·ming** strike notes of guitar, etc.

strum·pet [STRUM-pit] *n* **1** promiscuous woman. **2** prostitute.

strung pt./pp. of STRING.

strut *vi* **strut·ted, strut·ting 1** walk affectedly or pompously. ◆ *n* **2** brace. **3** rigid support, usu. set obliquely. **4** strutting gait.

strych·nine [STRIK-nin] *n* poison obtained from nux vomica seeds.

stub *n* **1** remnant of anything, e.g. pencil, cigarette, etc. **2** retained portion of check, etc. ◆ *vt* **stubbed, stub·bing 3** strike (e.g. toes) against fixed object. **4** extinguish by pressing against surface. **stub'by** *adj* **-bi·er, -bi·est** short, broad.

stub·ble [STUB-əl] *n* **1** stumps of cut grain, etc. after cutting. **2** short growth of beard.

stub·born [STUB-ərn] *adj* unyielding, obstinate. **stub'born·ness** [-nis] *n*

stuc·co [STUK-oh] *n, pl* **-coes** or **-cos 1** plaster. ◆ *vt* **-coed, -co·ing 2** apply stucco to (wall).

stuck pt./pp. of STICK.

stud[1] *n* **1** nail with large head. **2** type of button. **3** vertical wall support. ◆ *vt* **stud'ded, stud'ding 4** set with studs. **stud'ding** *n*

stud[2] *n* **1** stallion, set of horses, kept for

stroke *v* **1** = **caress**, fondle, pet, rub ◆ *n* **2** = **apoplexy**, attack, collapse, fit, seizure **3** = **blow**, hit, knock, pat, rap, thump

stroll *v* **1** = **walk**, amble, promenade, ramble, saunter ◆ *n* **2** = **walk**, breath of air, constitutional, promenade, ramble, turn

strong *adj* **1** = **powerful**, athletic, brawny, burly, hardy, lusty, muscular, robust, strapping, sturdy, tough **2** = **durable**, hard-wearing, heavy-duty, sturdy, substantial, well-built **3** = **persuasive**, compelling, convincing, effective, potent, sound, telling, weighty, well-founded **4** = **intense**, acute, deep, fervent, fervid, fierce, firm, keen, vehement, violent, zealous **5** = **extreme**, drastic, forceful, severe **6** = **bright**, bold, brilliant, dazzling

stronghold *n* = **fortress**, bastion, bulwark, castle, citadel, fort

structure *n* **1** = **building**, construction, edifice, erection **2** = **arrangement**, configuration, construction, design, form, formation, make-up, organization ◆ *v* **3** = **arrange**, assemble, build up, design,

organize, shape

struggle *v* **1** = **strive**, exert oneself, give it one's best shot (*inf*), go all out (*inf*), knock oneself out (*inf*), labor, make an all-out effort (*inf*), strain, toil, work **2** = **fight**, battle, compete, contend, grapple, wrestle ◆ *n* **3** = **effort**, exertion, labor, pains, scramble, toil, work **4** = **fight**, battle, brush, clash, combat, conflict, contest, tussle

strut *v* = **swagger**, parade, peacock, prance

stub *n* **1** = **butt**, remainder, remnant, stump, tail, tail end **2** = **counterfoil**

stubborn *adj* = **obstinate**, dogged, headstrong, inflexible, intractable, obdurate, persistent, pig-headed, recalcitrant, tenacious, unyielding

stubby *adj* = **stocky**, chunky, dumpy, short, squat, thickset

stuck *adj* **1** = **fastened**, cemented, fast, fixed, glued, joined **2** *Inf* = **baffled**, beaten, stumped

stuck-up *adj* = **snobbish**, arrogant, bigheaded (*inf*), conceited, haughty, breeding. **2** *sl* man known for sexual prowess. **stud'book** [-buuk] *n* book giving pedigree of noted or thoroughbred animals, esp. horses. **stud farm** establishment where horses are kept for breeding.

stu·di·o [STOO-dee-oh] *n, pl* **-di·os 1** workroom of artist, photographer, etc. **2** building, room where motion pictures, TV or radio shows are made, broadcast. **3** apartment of one main room.

stud·y [STUD-ee] *v* **stud·ied, stud·y·ing 1** be engaged in learning. **2** make study of. **3** try constantly to do. **4** consider. **5** scrutinize. ◆ *n, pl* **stud·ies 6** effort to acquire knowledge. **7** subject of this. **8** room to study in. **9** book, report, etc. produced as result of study. **10** sketch. **stu·dent** [STOOD-nt] *n* one who studies, esp. at college, etc. **studied** *adj* carefully designed, premeditated. **stu·di·ous** [STOO-dee-əs] *adj* **1** fond of study. **2** thoughtful. **3** painstaking. **4** deliberate. **stu'di·ous·ly** *adv*

stuff *v* **1** pack, cram, fill (completely). **2** eat large amount. **3** fill with seasoned mixture. **4** fill (animal's skin) with material to preserve lifelike form. ◆ *n* **5** material, fabric. **6** any substance. **stuff'ing** *n* material for stuffing, esp. seasoned mixture for inserting in poultry, etc. before cooking. **stuff'y** *adj* **stuff·i·er, stuff·i·est 1** lacking fresh air. **2** dull, conventional. **stuffed shirt** pompous person.

stul·ti·fy [STUL-tə-fi] *vt* **-fied, -fy·ing** make ineffectual. **stul·ti·fi·ca'tion** *n*

stum·ble [STUM-bəl] *vi* **-bled, -bling 1** trip and nearly fall. **2** falter. ◆ *n* stumbling **block 1** obstacle.

stump *n* **1** remnant of tree, tooth, etc., when main part has been cut away. **2** part of leg or arm remaining after amputation. ◆ *vt* **3** confuse, puzzle. ◆ *vi* **4** walk heavily, noisily. **stump'y** *adj* **stump·i·er, stump·i·est** short and thickset.

stun *vt* **stunned, stun·ning 1** knock senseless. **2** amaze.

stung pt./pp. of STING.

stunk pp. of STINK.

stunt¹ *vt* **1** check growth of, dwarf. **stunt'ed** *adj* **1** underdeveloped. **2** undersized.

stunt² *n* **1** feat of dexterity or daring. **2** anything spectacular, unusual done to gain publicity.

stu·pe·fy [STOO-pə-fi] *vt* **-fied, -fy·ing 1** make insensitive, lethargic. **2** astound. **stu·pe·fac'tion** *n*

proud, snooty (*inf*)

stud *v* = **ornament**, bejewel, dot, spangle, spot

student *n* = **learner**, apprentice, disciple, pupil, scholar, trainee, undergraduate

studied *adj* = **planned**, conscious, deliberate, intentional, premeditated

studio *n* = **workshop**, atelier

studious *adj* = **scholarly**, academic, assiduous, bookish, diligent, hard-working, intellectual

study *v* **1** = **contemplate**, consider, examine, go into, ponder, pore over, read **2** = **learn**, cram (*inf*), read up, review **3** = **examine**, analyze, investigate, look into, research, scrutinize, survey ◆ *n* **4** = **learning**, application, lessons, reading, research, school work **5** = **examination**, analysis, consideration, contemplation, inquiry, inspection, investigation, review, scrutiny, survey

stuff *n* **1** = **things**, belongings, effects, equipment, gear, kit, objects, paraphernalia, possessions, tackle **2** = **substance**, essence, matter **3** = **material**, cloth, fabric, textile ◆ *v* **4** = **cram**, crowd, fill, force, jam, pack, push, ram, shove, squeeze

stuffing *n* = **filling**, packing, wadding

stuffy *adj* **1** = **airless**, close, frowsty, heavy, muggy, oppressive, stale, stifling, sultry, unventilated **2** *inf* = **staid**, dreary, dull, pompous, priggish, prim, stodgy

stumble *v* **1** = **trip**, fall, falter, lurch, reel, slip, stagger **2** (with *across, on* or *upon*) = **discover**, chance upon, come across, find

stump *v* = **baffle**, bewilder, confuse, flummox, mystify, nonplus, perplex, puzzle

stumpy *adj* = **stocky**, dumpy, short, squat, stubby, thickset

stun *v* = **overcome**, astonish, astound, bewilder, confound, confuse, overpower, shock, stagger, stupefy

stunning *adj* = **wonderful**, beautiful, cool (*inf*), dazzling, gorgeous, impressive, lovely, marvelous, phat (*sl*), sensational (*inf*), spectacular, striking

stunt *n* = **feat**, act, deed, exploit, trick

stunted *adj* = **undersized**, diminutive,

stu·pen·dous [stoo-PEN-dəs] *adj* **1** astonishing. **2** amazing. **3** huge.

stu·pid [STOO-pid] *adj* **-er, -est 1** slow-witted. **2** silly. **3** in a stupor. **stu·pid'i·ty** *n, pl* **-ties**

stu·por [STOO-pər] *n* **1** dazed state. **2** insensibility. **stu'por·ous** *adj*

stur·dy [STUR-dee] *adj* **-di·er, -di·est 1** robust, strongly built. **2** vigorous. **stur'di·ly** *adv*

stur·geon [STUR-jən] *n* fish yielding caviar.

stut·ter [STUT-ər] *v* **1** speak with difficulty. **2** stammer. ♦ *n*

sty[1] [stī] *n, pl* **sties 1** place to keep pigs in. **2** hovel, dirty place.

sty[2] *n, pl* **sties** inflammation on edge of eyelid.

Styg·i·an [STIJ-ee-ən] *adj* **1** of river Styx in Hades. **2** gloomy. **3** infernal.

style [stīl] *n* **1** manner of writing, doing, etc. **2** designation. **3** sort. **4** elegance, refinement. **5** superior manner, quality. **6** design. ♦ *vt* **styled, styl·ing 7** shape, design. **8** adapt. **9** designate. **styl'ish** *adj* fashionable. **styl'ist** *n* **1** one cultivating style in literary or other execution. **2** designer. **3** hairdresser. **styl·is'tic** *adj* **styl'ize** *vt* **-ized, -iz·ing** give conventional stylistic form to.

sty·lus [STĪ-ləs] *n, pl* **-lus·es 1** writing instrument. **2** (in record player) tiny point running in groove of record.

sty·mie [STI-mee] *vt* **-mied, -my·ing** hinder, thwart.

styp·tic [STIP-tik] *adj, n* (designating) a substance that stops bleeding.

suave [swahv] *adj* **suav·er, suav·est** smoothly polite, affable, bland. **suav'i·ty** *n*

sub 1 submarine. **2** submarine sandwich. **3** substitute. ♦ *vi inf* **subbed, sub·bing 4** serve as substitute.

sub- *prefix* under, less than, in lower position, subordinate, forming subdivision, etc., as in: *subaquatic; subheading; subnormal; subsoil.*

sub·com·mit·tee [SUB-kə-mit-ee] *n* section of committee functioning separately from main body.

sub·con·scious [sub-KON-shəs] *adj* **1** acting, existing without one's awareness. ♦ *n* **2** *Psychology* that part of the human mind unknown, or only partly known to possessor.

sub·cu·ta·ne·ous [sub-kyoo-TAY-nee-əs] *adj* under the skin.

sub·di·vide [sub-di-VĪD] *vt* **-vid·ed, -vid·ing** divide again. **sub'di·vi·sion** [-vizh-ən] *n*

sub·due [səb-DOO] *v* **-dued, -du·ing 1** overcome. **subdued'** *adj* **1** cowed, quiet. **2** (of light) not bright or intense.

little, small, tiny

stupefy *v* = **astound**, amaze, daze, dumbfound, shock, stagger, stun

stupendous *adj* **1** = **wonderful**, amazing, astounding, breathtaking, marvelous, overwhelming, sensational (*inf*), staggering, superb **2** = **huge**, colossal, enormous, gigantic, mega (*sl*), vast

stupid *adj* **1** = **unintelligent**, brainless, dense, dim, dumb (*inf*), half-witted, moronic, obtuse, simple, simple-minded, slow, slow-witted, thick **2** = **foolish**, asinine, bonkers (*inf*), daft (*inf*), idiotic, imbecilic, inane, nonsensical, pointless, rash, senseless, unintelligent **3** = **dazed**, groggy, insensate, semiconscious, stunned, stupefied

stupidity *n* **1** = **lack of intelligence**, brainlessness, denseness, dimness, dullness, imbecility, obtuseness, slowness, thickness **2** = **foolishness**, absurdity, fatuousness, folly, idiocy, inanity, lunacy, madness, silliness

stupor *n* = **daze**, coma, insensibility,

stupefaction, unconsciousness

sturdy *adj* **1** = **robust**, athletic, brawny, hardy, lusty, muscular, powerful **2** = **well-built**, durable, solid, substantial, well-made

stutter *v* = **stammer**, falter, hesitate, stumble

style *n* **1** = **design**, cut, form, manner **2** = **manner**, approach, method, mode, technique, way **3** = **elegance**, chic, élan, flair, panache, polish, smartness, sophistication, taste **4** = **type**, category, genre, kind, sort, variety **5** = **fashion**, mode, rage, trend, vogue **6** = **luxury**, affluence, comfort, ease, elegance, grandeur ♦ *v* **7** = **design**, adapt, arrange, cut, fashion, shape, tailor **8** = **call**, designate, dub, entitle, label, name, term

stylish *adj* = **smart**, chic, cool (*inf*), dressy (*inf*), fashionable, modish, phat (*sl*), trendy (*inf*), voguish

suave *adj* = **smooth**, charming, courteous, debonair, polite, sophisticated, urbane

subconscious *adj* = **hidden**, inner,

subject [SUB-jikt] n **1** theme, topic. **2** that about which something is predicated. **3** conscious self. **4** one under power of another. ◆ adj **5** owing allegiance. **6** subordinate. **7** dependent. **8** liable (to). ◆ vt [səb-JEKT] **9** cause to undergo. **10** make liable. **11** subdue. **sub·jec·tion** [-JEK-shən] n act of bringing, or state of being, under control. **sub·jec·tive** adj **1** based on personal feelings, not impartial. **2** of the self. **3** existing in the mind. **4** displaying artist's individuality. **sub·jec·tiv'i·ty** n

sub ju·di·ce [sub JOO-di-see] Lat under judicial consideration.

sub·ju·gate [SUB-jə-gayt] vt **-gat·ed, -gat·ing 1** force to submit. **2** conquer. **sub·ju·ga'tion** n

sub·junc·tive [səb-JUNGK-tiv] n **1** mood used mainly in subordinate clauses expressing wish, possibility. ◆ adj **2** in, of, that mood.

sub·let' vt **-let, -let·ting** (of tenant) let to another all or part of what tenant has rented.

sub·li·mate [SUB-lə-mayt] vt **-mat·ed, -mat·ing 1** Psychology direct energy (esp. sexual) into activities considered more socially acceptable. **2** refine. ◆ n [-mit] **3** Chem. material obtained when substance is sublimed. **sub·li·ma'tion** n **1** Psychology unconscious diversion of sexual impulses

towards new aim and activities. **2** Chem. process in which a solid changes directly into a vapor.

sub·lime [sə-BLĪM] adj **1** elevated. **2** eminent. **3** majestic. **4** inspiring awe. **5** exalted. ◆ v **-limed, -lim·ing 6** Chem. change or cause to change from solid to vapor. **sub·lime'ly** adv

sub·lim·i·nal [sub-LIM-ə-nl] adj resulting from processes of which the individual is not aware.

sub·ma·rine [sub-mə-REEN] n **1** ship that can travel below surface of sea and remain submerged for long periods. ◆ adj **2** below surface of sea. **submarine sandwich** overstuffed sandwich of meats, cheese, etc. in long loaf of Italian bread.

sub·merge [səb-MURJ] v **-merged, -merg·ing** place, go under water. **sub·mer'sion** [-MUR-zhən] n

sub·mit [səb-MIT] v **-mit·ted, -mit·ting 1** surrender. **2** put forward for consideration. **3** surrender. **4** defer. **sub·mis'sion** [-MISH-ən] n **sub·mis'sive** adj meek, obedient.

sub·or·di·nate [sə-BOR-dn-it] adj **1** of lower rank or less importance. ◆ n **2** inferior. **3** one under order of another. ◆ vt [-dn-ayt] **-nat·ed, -nat·ing** make, treat as subordinate. **sub·or·di·na'tion** [-NAY-shən] n

——————— THESAURUS ———————

intuitive, latent, repressed, subliminal

subdue v **1** = **overcome**, break, conquer, control, crush, defeat, master, overpower, quell, tame, vanquish **2** = **moderate**, mellow, quieten down, soften, suppress, tone down

subdued adj **1** = **quiet**, chastened, crestfallen, dejected, downcast, down in the mouth, sad, serious **2** = **soft**, dim, hushed, muted, quiet, subtle, toned down, unobtrusive

subject n **1** = **topic**, affair, business, issue, matter, object, point, question, substance, theme **2** = **citizen**, national, subordinate ◆ adj **3** = **subordinate**, dependent, inferior, obedient, satellite **4 subject to: a** = **liable to**, exposed to, in danger of, open to, prone to, susceptible to, vulnerable to **b** = **conditional on**, contingent on, dependent on ◆ v **5** = **put through**, expose, lay open, submit, treat

subjective adj = **personal**, biased, nonobjective, prejudiced

subjugate v = **conquer**, enslave, master, overcome, overpower, quell, subdue, suppress, vanquish

sublime adj = **noble**, elevated, exalted, glorious, grand, great, high, lofty

submerge v = **immerse**, deluge, dip, duck, engulf, flood, inundate, overflow, overwhelm, plunge, sink, swamp

submission n **1** = **surrender**, assent, capitulation, giving in, yielding **2** = **presentation**, entry, handing in, tendering **3** = **meekness**, compliance, deference, docility, obedience, passivity, resignation

submissive adj = **meek**, accommodating, acquiescent, amenable, compliant, docile, obedient, passive, pliant, tractable, unresisting, yielding

submit v **1** = **surrender**, accede, agree, capitulate, comply, endure, give in, succumb, tolerate, yield **2** = **put forward**, hand in, present, proffer, table, tender

subordinate adj **1** = **lesser**, dependent, inferior, junior, lower, minor, secondary,

sub·orn [sə-BORN] vt bribe to do evil.
sub·or·na·tion [sub-or-NAY-shən] n

sub·poe·na [sə-PEE-nə] n 1 writ requiring
attendance at court of law. ♦ vt -naed,
-na·ing 2 summon by such order.

sub·scribe [səb-SKRĪB] vt -scribed,
-scrib·ing 1 pay, promise to pay
(contribution). 2 write one's name at end
of document. **sub·scrip'tion** n 1
subscribing. 2 money paid.

sub·se·quent [SUB-si-kwənt] adj later,
following or coming after in time.

sub·ser·vi·ent [səb-SUR-vee-ənt] adj
submissive, servile. **sub·ser'vi·ence** n

sub·side [səb-SĪD] vi -sid·ed, -sid·ing 1
abate, come to an end. 2 sink. 3 settle. 4
collapse. **sub·sid'ence** n

sub·sid·i·ar·y [səb-SID-ee-er-ee] adj 1
supplementing. 2 secondary. 3 auxiliary. ♦
n, pl -ar·ies

sub·si·dize [SUB-si-dīz] vt -dized, -diz·ing 1
help financially. 2 pay grant to. **sub'si·dy**
[-dee] n, pl -dies money granted.

sub·sist [səb-SIST] vi exist, sustain life.
sub·sist'ence [-əns] n 1 the means by
which one supports life. 2 livelihood.

sub·son·ic [sub-SON-ik] adj concerning
speeds less than that of sound.

sub·stance [SUB-stəns] n 1 matter. 2
particular kind of matter. 3 chief part,
essence. 4 wealth. **sub·stan·tial**
[səb-STAN-shəl] adj 1 considerable. 2 of
real value. 3 solid, big, important. 4 really
existing. **sub·stan'ti·ate** [-shee-ayt] vt
-at·ed, -at·ing bring evidence for, confirm,
prove. **sub·stan·ti·a'tion** n **sub'stan·tive**
[-stən·tiv] adj 1 having independent
existence. 2 real, fixed. ♦ n 3 noun.

sub·sti·tute [SUB-sti-toot] v -tut·ed,
-tut·ing 1 put, serve in exchange (for). ♦ n
2 thing, person put in place of another. 3
deputy. **sub·sti·tu'tion** n

sub·sume [səb-SOOM] vt -sumed,
-sum·ing incorporate (idea, case, etc.)
under comprehensive heading,
classification.

sub·tend [səb-TEND] vt be opposite to and
delimit.

sub·ter·fuge [SUB-tər-fyooj] n trick, lying
excuse used to evade something.

sub·ter·ra·ne·an [sub-tə-RAY-nee-ən] adj
1 underground. 2 in concealment.

sub·ti·tle [SUB-tīt-l] n 1 secondary title of
book. 2 written translation of film
dialogue, superimposed on film.

sub·tle [SUT-l] adj -tler, -tlest 1 not
immediately obvious. 2 ingenious, acute. 3
crafty. 4 intricate. 5 delicate. 6 making fine
distinctions. **sub'tle·ty** [-tee] n, pl -ties

sub·tract [səb-TRAKT] vt take away,

subject ♦ n 2 = **inferior**, aide, assistant,
attendant, junior, second
subordination n = **inferiority**, inferior or
secondary status, servitude, subjection
subscribe v 1 = **donate**, contribute, give
2 = **support**, advocate, endorse
subscription n 1 = **membership fee**,
annual payment, dues 2 = **donation**,
contribution, gift
subsequent adj = **following**, after,
ensuing, later, succeeding, successive
subsequently adv = **later**, afterwards
subservient adj = **servile**, abject,
deferential, obsequious, slavish,
submissive, sycophantic
subside v 1 = **decrease**, abate, diminish,
ease, ebb, lessen, quieten, slacken, wane
2 = **sink**, cave in, collapse, drop, lower,
settle
subsidence n 1 = **sinking**, settling 2 =
decrease, abatement, easing off,
lessening, slackening
subsidiary adj = **lesser**, ancillary, auxiliary,
minor, secondary, subordinate,

supplementary
subsidize v = **fund**, finance, promote,
sponsor, support
subsidy n = **aid**, allowance, assistance,
grant, help, support
substance n 1 = **material**, body, fabric,
stuff 2 = **meaning**, essence, gist, import,
main point, significance 3 = **reality**,
actuality, concreteness 4 = **wealth**, assets,
estate, means, property, resources
substantial adj = **big**, ample, considerable,
important, large, significant, sizable or
sizeable
substantiate v = **support**, authenticate,
confirm, establish, prove, verify
substitute v 1 = **replace**, change,
exchange, interchange, swap, switch ♦ n
2 = **replacement**, agent, deputy, locum,
proxy, reserve, sub, surrogate ♦ adj 3 =
replacement, alternative, fall-back, proxy,
reserve, second, surrogate
substitution n = **replacement**, change,
exchange, swap, switch
subterfuge n = **trick**, deception, dodge,

deduct. **sub·trac'tion** [-TRAK-shən] n

sub·trop·i·cal [sub-TROP-i-kəl] adj of regions bordering on the tropics.

sub'urb n residential area on outskirts of city. **sub·ur·ban** [sə-BUR-bən] adj **sub·ur'bi·a** [-bee-ə] n suburbs of a city.

sub·ven·tion [səb-VEN-shən] n subsidy.

sub·vert [səb-VURT] vt 1 overthrow. 2 corrupt. **sub·ver'sion** [-zhən] n **sub·ver'sive** [-siv] adj

sub'way n 1 underground passage. 2 underground railroad.

suc·ceed [sək-SEED] vi 1 accomplish purpose. 2 turn out satisfactorily. 3 follow. ◆ vt 4 follow, take place of. **suc·cess'** n 1 favorable accomplishment, attainment, issue or outcome. 2 successful person or thing. **suc·cess'ful** [-fəl] adj **suc·ces·sion** [-SESH-ən] n 1 following. 2 series. 3 succeeding. **suc·ces'sive** adj 1 following in order. 2 consecutive. **suc·ces'sor** [-ər] n

suc·cinct [sək-SINGKT] adj terse, concise. **succinct'ly** adv **suc·cinct'ness** [-nis] n

suc·cor [SUK-ər] vt, n help in distress.

suc·cu·bus [SUK-yə-bəs] n, pl **-bi** [-bī] female demon fabled to have sexual intercourse with sleeping men.

suc·cu·lent [SUK-yə-lənt] adj 1 juicy, full of juice. 2 (of plant) having thick, fleshy leaves. ◆ n 3 such plant. **suc·cu·lence** [-lins] n

suc·cumb [sə-KUM] vi 1 yield, give way. 2 die.

such adj 1 of the kind or degree mentioned. 2 so great, so much. 3 so made, etc. 4 of the same kind. **such'like** adj 1 such. ◆ pron 2 other such things.

suck [suk] vt 1 draw into mouth. 2 hold (dissolve) in mouth. 3 draw in. ◆ n 4 sucking. **suck'er** n 1 person, thing that sucks. 2 organ, appliance that adheres by suction. 3 shoot coming from root or base of stem of plant. 4 inf person easily deceived or taken in.

suck·le [SUK-əl] v **-led, -ling** feed from the breast. **suck'ling** n unweaned infant.

suc·tion [SUK-shən] n 1 drawing or sucking of air or fluid. 2 force produced by difference in pressure.

sud·den [SUD-n] adj 1 done, occurring unexpectedly. 2 abrupt, hurried. **sud'den·ness** [-dən-is] n

su·dor·if·ic [soo-də-RIF-ik] adj 1 causing perspiration. ◆ n 2 medicine that produces sweat.

suds [sudz] pl n 1 froth of soap and water, lather. 2 sl beer.

sue [soo] v **sued, su·ing** ◆ vt 1 prosecute. 2

maneuver, ploy, ruse, stratagem

subtle adj 1 = **sophisticated**, delicate, refined 2 = **faint**, delicate, implied, slight, understated 3 = **crafty**, artful, cunning, devious, ingenious, shrewd, sly, wily

subtlety n 1 = **sophistication**, delicacy, refinement 2 = **cunning**, artfulness, cleverness, craftiness, deviousness, ingenuity, slyness, wiliness

subtract v = **take away**, deduct, diminish, remove, take from, take off

subversive adj 1 = **seditious**, riotous, treasonous ◆ n 2 = **dissident**, fifth columnist, saboteur, terrorist, traitor

subvert v = **overturn**, sabotage, undermine

succeed v 1 = **make it** (inf), be successful, flourish, make good, make the grade (inf), prosper, thrive, triumph, work 2 = **follow**, come next, ensue, result

success n 1 = **luck**, fame, fortune, happiness, prosperity, triumph 2 = **hit** (inf), celebrity, megastar (inf), sensation, smash (inf), star, superstar, winner

successful adj = **thriving**, booming, flourishing, fortunate, fruitful, lucky, profitable, prosperous, rewarding, top, victorious

successfully adv = **well**, favorably, victoriously, with flying colors

succession n 1 = **series**, chain, course, cycle, order, progression, run, sequence, train 2 = **taking over**, accession, assumption, inheritance

successive adj = **consecutive**, following, in succession

succinct adj = **brief**, compact, concise, laconic, pithy, terse

succor n 1 = **help**, aid, assistance ◆ v 2 = **help**, aid, assist

succulent adj = **juicy**, luscious, lush, moist

succumb v 1 = **surrender**, capitulate, give in, submit, yield 2 = **die**, fall

sucker n Sl = **fool**, dork (sl), dupe, mug (Brit. sl), pushover (sl), schmuck (sl), victim

sudden adj = **quick**, abrupt, hasty, hurried, rapid, rash, swift, unexpected

suddenly adv = **abruptly**, all of a sudden, unexpectedly seek justice from. ◆ vi 3 make application or entreaty. 4 beseech.

suede [swayd] n leather with soft, velvety finish.

su·et [SOO-it] n hard animal fat from sheep, cow, etc.

suf·fer [SUF-ər] v 1 undergo, endure, experience (pain, etc.). 2 allow. **suf'fer·a·ble** adj **suf'fer·ance** [-əns] n toleration.

suf·fice [sə-FĪS] v -ficed, -fic·ing be adequate, satisfactory (for). **suf·fi·cien·cy** [sə-FISH-ən-see] n adequate amount. **suf·fi'cient** adj enough, adequate.

suf·fix [SUF-iks] n 1 letter or word added to end of word. ◆ vt 2 add, annex to the end.

suf·fo·cate [SUF-ə-kayt] v -cat·ed, -cat·ing 1 kill, be killed by deprivation of oxygen. 2 smother.

suf·frage [SUF-rij] n vote or right of voting. **suf'fra·gist** n one claiming a right of voting. **suf·fra·gette'** n, fem.

suf·fuse [sə-FYOOZ] vt -fused, -fus·ing well up and spread over. **suf·fu'sion** [-FYOO-zhən] n

sug·ar [SHUUG-ər] n 1 sweet crystalline vegetable substance. ◆ vt 2 sweeten, make pleasant (with sugar). **sug'ar·y** adj **sugar cane** plant from whose juice sugar is obtained. **sugar daddy** inf wealthy (elderly) man who pays for (esp. sexual) favors of younger woman.

sug·gest [səg-JEST] vt 1 propose. 2 call up

the idea of. **sug·gest'i·ble** adj easily influenced. **sug·gest'ion** [-chən] n 1 hint. 2 proposal. 3 insinuation of impression, belief, etc., into mind. **sug·gest'ive** adj containing, open to suggestion, esp. of something indecent.

su·i·cide [SOO-ə-sīd] n (act of) one who takes own life. **su·i·cid'al** [-əl] adj

suit [soot] n 1 set of clothing. 2 garment worn for particular event, purpose. 3 one of four sets in pack of cards. 4 action at law. ◆ v 5 make, be fit or appropriate for. 6 be acceptable to (someone). **suit'a·ble** adj 1 fitting, proper, convenient. 2 becoming. **suit'a·bly** adv **suit'case** [-kays] n flat rectangular traveling case.

suite [sweet] n 1 matched set esp. furniture. 2 set of rooms.

suit·or [SOOT-ər] n 1 wooer. 2 one who sues. 3 petitioner.

sul·fate [SUL-fayt] n salt formed by sulfuric acid in combination with any base.

sul·fon·a·mides [sul-FON-ə-mīdz] n group of drugs used as internal germicides in treatment of many bacterial diseases.

sul·fur [SUL-fər] n pale yellow nonmetallic element. **sul·fur·ic** [sul-FYUUR-ik] adj

sulk vi 1 be silent, resentful, esp. to draw attention to oneself. ◆ n 2 this mood. **sulk'y** adj **sulk·i·er, sulk·i·est**

sul·len [SUL-ən] adj 1 unwilling to talk or be sociable, morose. 2 dismal. 3 dull.

sul·ly [SUL-ee] vt -lied, -ly·ing stain, tarnish,

——————— THESAURUS ———————

sue v Law = **take (someone) to court**, charge, indict, prosecute, summon

suffer v 1 = **undergo**, bear, endure, experience, go through, sustain 2 = **tolerate**, put up with (inf)

suffering n = **pain**, agony, anguish, discomfort, distress, hardship, misery, ordeal, torment

suffice v = **be enough**, be adequate, be sufficient, do, meet requirements, serve

sufficient adj = **adequate**, enough, satisfactory

suffocate v = **choke**, asphyxiate, smother, stifle

suggest v 1 = **recommend**, advise, advocate, prescribe, propose 2 = **bring to mind**, evoke 3 = **hint**, imply, indicate, intimate

suggestion n 1 = **recommendation**, motion, plan, proposal, proposition 2 = **hint**, breath, indication, intimation, trace,

whisper

suggestive adj = **smutty**, bawdy, blue, indelicate, provocative, racy, ribald, risqué, rude

suit n 1 = **outfit**, clothing, costume, dress, ensemble, habit 2 = **lawsuit**, action, case, cause, proceeding, prosecution, trial ◆ v 3 = **be acceptable to**, do, gratify, please, satisfy 4 = **befit**, agree, become, go with, harmonize, match, tally

suitability n = **appropriateness**, aptness, fitness, rightness

suitable adj = **appropriate**, apt, becoming, befitting, fit, fitting, proper, right, satisfactory

suite n = **rooms**, apartment

suitor n Old-fashioned = **admirer**, beau (old-fashioned), young man

sulk v = **be sullen**, be in a huff, pout

sulky adj = **huffy**, cross, disgruntled, in the sulks, moody, petulant, querulous, disgrace.

sul·tan [SUL-tn] n ruler of Muslim country. **sul·tan'a** n 1 sultan's wife or concubine. 2 kind of raisin.

sul·try [SUL-tree] adj -tri·er, -tri·est 1 (of weather) hot, humid. 2 (of person) looking sensual.

sum n 1 amount, total. 2 problem in arithmetic. ♦ v **summed, sum·ming** 3 add up. 4 make summary of main parts.

sum·ma·ry [SUM-ə-ree] n, pl -ries 1 abridgment or statement of chief points of longer document, speech, etc. 2 abstract. ♦ adj 3 done quickly. **sum·mar·i·ly** [sə-MAIR-ə-lee] adv 1 speedily. 2 abruptly. **sum'ma·rize** [-ə-rīz] vt -rized, -riz·ing 1 make summary of. 2 present briefly and concisely.

sum·mer [SUM-ər] n 1 second, warmest season. ♦ vi 2 pass the summer. **sum'mer·y** adj

sum'mit n top, peak. **summit conference** meeting of heads of governments. **sum'mit·ry** [-mi-tree] n practice, art of holding summit conferences.

sum·mon [SUM-ən] vt 1 demand attendance of. 2 call on. 3 bid witness appear in court. 4 gather up (energies, etc.). **sum'mons** n 1 call. 2 authoritative demand.

sump n place or receptacle (esp. as oil reservoir in engine) where fluid collects.

sump·tu·ous [SUMP-choo-əs] adj 1 lavish, magnificent. 2 costly. **sump'tu·ous·ness**

[-nis] n **sump'tu·ar·y** [-er-ee] adj pert. to or regulating expenditure.

sun n 1 luminous body around which Earth and other planets revolve. 2 its rays. ♦ v **sunned, sun·ning** 3 expose (self) to sun's rays. **sun'ny** adj -ni·er, -ni·est 1 like the sun. 2 warm. 3 cheerful. **sun'bath·ing** [-bayth-ing] n exposure of whole or part of body to sun's rays. **sun'beam** [-beem] n ray of sun. **sun'burn** n inflammation of skin due to excessive exposure to sun. **sun'down** n sunset. **sun'spot** n dark patch appearing temporarily on sun's surface. **sun'stroke** [-strohk] n illness caused by prolonged exposure to intensely hot sun. **sun'tan** n coloring of skin by exposure to sun.

sun·dae [SUN-day] n ice cream topped with fruit, etc.

sun·der [SUN-dər] vt separate, sever.

sun·dry [SUN-dree] adj several, various. **sun'dries** pl n odd items not mentioned in detail.

sung pp. of SING.

sunk, sunk'en [-in] pp. of SINK.

sup v **supped, sup·ping** 1 take by sips. 2 take supper. ♦ n 3 mouthful of liquid.

su·per [SOO-pər] adj 1 very good. ♦ n 2 short for SUPERINTENDENT.

super- prefix above, greater, exceeding(ly), e.g. superhuman; superman; supertanker.

su·per·a·ble [SOO-pər-ə-bəl] adj 1 capable of being overcome. 2 surmountable.

su·per·an·nu·ate [soo-pər-AN-yoo-ayt] vt

———————— THESAURUS ————————

resentful, sullen

sullen adj = **morose**, cross, dour, glowering, moody, sour, surly, unsociable

sully v = **defile**, besmirch, disgrace, dishonor, smirch, stain, tarnish

sultry adj 1 = **humid**, close, hot, muggy, oppressive, sticky, stifling 2 = **seductive**, provocative, sensual, sexy (inf)

sum n = **total**, aggregate, amount, tally, whole

summarize v = **sum up**, abridge, condense, encapsulate, epitomize, précis

summary n = **synopsis**, abridgment, outline, précis, résumé, review, rundown

summit n = **peak**, acme, apex, head, height, pinnacle, top, zenith

summon v 1 = **send for**, bid, call, invite 2 (often with up) = **gather**, draw on, muster

sumptuous adj = **luxurious**, gorgeous, grand, lavish, opulent, splendid, superb

sum up v = **summarize**, put in a nutshell, recapitulate, review

sunburned adj = **tanned**, bronzed, brown, burnt, peeling, red

sundry adj = **various**, assorted, different, miscellaneous, several, some

sunken adj 1 = **hollow**, drawn, haggard 2 = **lower**, buried, recessed, submerged

sunny adj 1 = **bright**, clear, fine, radiant, summery, sunlit, unclouded 2 = **cheerful**, buoyant, cheery, happy, joyful, light-hearted

sunrise n = **dawn**, break of day, cockcrow, daybreak

sunset n = **nightfall**, close of (the) day, dusk, eventide

super adj Inf = **excellent**, glorious, magnificent, marvelous, outstanding, sensational (inf), superb, terrific (inf), wonderful

-at·ed, -at·ing 1 pension off. **2** discharge or dismiss as too old.

su·perb [suu-PURB] *adj* splendid, grand, impressive.

su·per·charge [SOO-pər-chahrj] *vt* **-charged, -charg·ing** charge, fill to excess. **su'per·charg·er** *n* (internal-combustion engine) device to ensure complete filling of cylinder with explosive mixture when running at high speed.

su·per·cil·i·ous [soo-pər-SIL-ee-əs] *adj* displaying arrogant pride, scorn, indifference. **su·per·cil'i·ous·ness** [-nis] *n*

su·per·fi·cial [soo-pər-FISH-əl] *adj* **1** of or on surface. **2** not careful or thorough. **3** without depth, shallow.

su·per·flu·ous [suu-PUR-floo-əs] *adj* **1** extra, unnecessary. **2** excessive. **3** left over. **su·per·flu'i·ty** [-FLOO-i-tee] *n, pl* **-ties 1** superabundance. **2** unnecessary amount.

su·per·high·way [soo-pər-HI-way] *n* broad multilane highway for travel at high speeds.

su·per·in·tend [soo-pər-in-TEND] *v* **1** have charge of. **2** overlook. **3** supervise. **su·per·in·tend'ent** *n* esp. person in charge of building maintenance.

su·pe·ri·or [sə-PEER-ee-ər] *adj* **1** greater in quality or quantity. **2** upper, higher in position, rank or quality. **3** showing consciousness of being so. **su·pe·ri·or'i·ty** *n* quality of being higher, greater, or more excellent.

su·per·la·tive [sə-PUR-lə-tiv] *adj* **1** of, in highest degree or quality. **2** surpassing. **3** *Grammar* denoting form of adjective, adverb meaning *most*. ◆ *n* **4** *Grammar* superlative degree of adjective or adverb.

su·per·mar·ket [SOO-pər-mahr-kit] *n* large self-service store selling chiefly food and household goods.

su·per·mod·el [SOO-pər-mod-l] *n* famous and highly-paid fashion model.

su·per·nal [suu-PUR-nl] *adj* celestial.

su·per·nat·u·ral [soo-pər-NACH-ər-əl] *adj* **1** being beyond the powers or laws of nature. **2** miraculous. ◆ *n* **3** being, place, etc. of miraculous powers.

su·per·nu·mer·ar·y [soo-pər-NOO-mə-rer-ee] *adj* **1** in excess of normal number, extra. ◆ *n, pl* **-ar·ies 2** extra person or thing.

su·per·script [SOO-pər-skript] *n, adj* (character) printed, written above the line.

su·per·sede [soo-pər-SEED] *vt* **-sed·ed, -sed·ing 1** take the place of. **2** set aside, discard, supplant.

su·per·son·ic [soo-pər-SON-ik] *adj* denoting speed greater than that of sound.

su·per·sti·tion [soo-pər-STISH-ən] *n* religion, opinion or practice based on belief in luck or magic. **su·per·sti'tious** [-STI-shəs] *adj*

su·per·vene [soo-pər-VEEN] *vi* **-vened, -ven·ing** happen, as an interruption or

THESAURUS

superb *adj* = **splendid**, excellent, exquisite, fine, first-rate, grand, magnificent, marvelous, superior, superlative, world-class

supercilious *adj* = **scornful**, arrogant, contemptuous, disdainful, haughty, lofty, snooty (*inf*), stuck-up (*inf*)

superficial *adj* **1** = **hasty**, casual, cursory, desultory, hurried, perfunctory, sketchy, slapdash **2** = **shallow**, empty-headed, frivolous, silly, trivial **3** = **surface**, exterior, external, on the surface, slight

superfluous *adj* = **excess**, extra, left over, redundant, remaining, spare, supernumerary, surplus

superhuman *adj* **1** = **heroic**, phenomenal, prodigious **2** = **supernatural**, paranormal

superintendence *n* = **supervision**, charge, control, direction, government, management

superintendent *n* = **supervisor**, chief, controller, director, governor, inspector, manager, overseer

superior *adj* **1** = **better**, grander, greater, higher, surpassing, unrivaled **2** = **supercilious**, condescending, disdainful, haughty, lofty, lordly, patronizing, pretentious, snobbish **3** = **first-class**, choice, deluxe, excellent, exceptional, exclusive, first-rate ◆ *n* **4** = **boss** (*inf*), chief, director, manager, principal, senior, supervisor

superiority *n* = **supremacy**, advantage, ascendancy, excellence, lead, predominance

superlative *adj* = **outstanding**, excellent, supreme, unparalleled, unrivaled, unsurpassed

supernatural *adj* = **paranormal**, ghostly, hidden, miraculous, mystic, occult, psychic, spectral, uncanny, unearthly

supersede *v* = **replace**, displace, oust,

change. **su·per·ven·tion** [-shən] *n*
su·per·vise [SOO-pər-vīz] *vt* **-vised,
-vis·ing 1** oversee. **2** direct. **3** inspect and
control. **4** superintend. **su·per·vi'sion**
[-VIZH-ən] *n* **su'per·vis·or** *n*
su·pine [soo-PĪN] *adj* **1** lying on back with
face upward. **2** indolent. ♦ *n* [SOO-pīn] **3**
Latin verbal noun.
sup·per [SUP-ər] *n* (light) evening meal.
sup·plant [sə-PLANT] *vt* **1** take the place
of, esp. unfairly. **2** oust.
sup·ple [SUP-əl] *adj* **-pler, -plest 1** pliable. **2**
flexible. **3** compliant. **sup·ply** [SUP-lee] *adv*
sup·ple·ment [SUP-lə-mənt] *n* **1** thing
added to fill up, supply deficiency, esp.
extra part added to book, etc. **2** additional
number of periodical, usu. on special
subject. **3** separate, often illustrated section
published periodically with newspaper. ♦
vt **4** add to. **5** supply deficiency.
sup·ple·men'ta·ry [-tə-ree] *adj* additional.
sup·pli·ant [SUP-lee-ənt] *adj* **1** petitioning.
♦ *n* **2** petitioner.
sup·pli·cate [SUP-li-kayt] *v* **-cat·ed, -cat·ing**
beg humbly, entreat. **sup'pli·cant**

[-pli·cənt] *n* **sup·pli·ca'tion** [-KAY-shən] *n*
sup'pli·ca·to·ry [-kə-tor-ee] *adj*
sup·ply [sə-PLĪ] *vt* **-plied, -ply·ing 1** furnish.
2 make available. **3** provide. ♦ *n, pl* **-plies 4**
supplying, substitute. **5** stock, store.
sup·port [sə-PORT] *vt* **1** hold up. **2** sustain.
3 assist. ♦ *n* **4** supporting, being
supported. **5** means of support.
sup·port'a·ble *adj* **sup·port'er** *n* adherent.
sup·port'ing *adj* (of motion picture, etc.
role) less important. **sup·port'ive** *adj*
sup·pose [sə-POHZ] *vt* **-posed, -pos·ing 1**
assume as theory. **2** take for granted. **3**
accept as likely. **4** (in passive) be expected,
obliged. **5** ought. **sup·posed'** *adj*
sup·pos·ed·ly [sə-POH-zid-lee] *adv*
sup·po·si'tion [-ZISH-ən] *n* **1** assumption. **2**
belief without proof. **3** conjecture.
sup·po·si'tious *adj* **sup·pos·i·ti·tious**
[sə-poz-i-TISH-əs] *adj* **1** sham. **2** spurious. **3**
counterfeit.
sup·pos·i·to·ry [sə-POZ-i-tor-ee] *n, pl* **-ries**
medication (in capsule) for insertion in
orifice of body.
sup·press [sə-PRES] *vt* **1** put down,

supplant, take the place of, usurp
supervise *v* = **oversee**, control, direct,
handle, look after, manage, run,
superintend
supervision *n* = **superintendence**, care,
charge, control, direction, guidance,
management
supervisor *n* = **boss** (*inf*), administrator,
chief, foreman, inspector, manager,
overseer
supplant *v* = **replace**, displace, oust,
supersede, take the place of
supple *adj* = **flexible**, limber, lissom(e),
lithe, pliable, pliant
supplement *n* **1** = **addition**, add-on,
appendix, extra, insert, postscript, pull-out
♦ *v* **2** = **add**, augment, complement,
extend, reinforce
supplementary *adj* = **additional**, add-on,
ancillary, auxiliary, extra, secondary
supplication *n* = **plea**, appeal, entreaty,
petition, prayer, request
supply *v* **1** = **provide**, contribute, endow,
equip, furnish, give, grant, produce, stock,
yield ♦ *n* **2** = **store**, cache, fund, hoard,
quantity, reserve, source, stock **3** (usually
plural) = **provisions**, equipment, food,
materials, necessities, rations, stores
support *v* **1** = **bear**, brace, buttress, carry,

hold, prop, reinforce, sustain **2** = **provide
for**, finance, fund, keep, look after,
maintain, sustain **3** = **help**, aid, assist, back,
champion, defend, second, side with **4** =
bear out, confirm, corroborate,
substantiate, verify ♦ *n* **5** = **help**, aid,
assistance, backing, encouragement,
loyalty **6** = **prop**, brace, foundation, pillar,
post **7** = **supporter**, backer, mainstay,
prop, second, tower of strength **8** =
upkeep, keep, maintenance, subsistence,
sustenance
supporter *n* = **follower**, adherent,
advocate, champion, fan, friend, helper,
patron, sponsor, well-wisher
supportive *adj* = **helpful**, encouraging,
sympathetic, understanding
suppose *v* **1** = **presume**, assume,
conjecture, expect, guess (*inf*), imagine,
think **2** = **imagine**, conjecture, consider,
hypothesize, postulate, pretend
supposed *adj* **1** = **presumed**, accepted,
alleged, assumed, professed **2** (usually with
to) = **meant**, expected, obliged, required
supposedly *adv* = **allegedly**,
hypothetically, ostensibly, presumably,
theoretically
supposition *n* = **guess**, conjecture,
hypothesis, presumption, speculation,

restrain. **2** crush, stifle. **3** keep or withdraw from publication. **sup·pres'sion** [-PRESH-ən] n

sup·pu·rate [SUP-yə-rayt] vi **-rat·ed, -rat·ing** fester, form pus. **sup·pu·ra'tion** [-shən] n

supra- prefix above, over, e.g. supranational.

su·preme [sə-PREEM] adj **1** highest in authority or rank. **2** utmost. **su·prem·a·cy** [-PREM-ə-see] n position of being supreme.

sur·cease [sur-SEES] vi **-ceased, -ceas·ing 1** cease, desist. ♦ n **2** cessation.

sur·charge [SUR-chahrj] n **1** additional charge. ♦ vt [sur-CHAHRJ] **-charged, -charg·ing 2** make additional charge.

sure [shuur] adj **1** certain. **2** trustworthy. **3** without doubt. ♦ adv inf **4** certainly. **sure'ly** adv **sur·e·ty** [SHUUR-i-tee] n, pl **-ties 1** one who takes responsibility for another's obligations. **2** security against damage, etc. **3** certainty.

surf n **1** waves breaking on shore. ♦ v **2** swim in, ride surf. **3** move quickly through a medium such as the World Wide Web. **surf'ing** n this sport. **surf'er** n one who (often) goes surfing. **surf'board** n board used in surfing.

sur·face [SUR-fis] n **1** outside face of body. **2** exterior. **3** plane. **4** top, visible side. **5** superficial appearance, outward

impression. ♦ adj **6** involving the surface only. **7** going no deeper than surface. ♦ v **-faced, -fac·ing 8** (cause to) come to surface. **9** put a surface on.

sur·feit [SUR-fit] n **1** excess. **2** disgust caused by excess. ♦ v **3** feed to excess. **4** provide anything in excess.

surge [surj] n **1** wave. **2** sudden increase. **3** Electricity sudden rush of current in circuit. ♦ vi **surged, surg·ing 4** move in large waves. **5** swell, billow. **6** rise precipitately.

sur·geon [SUR-jən] n physician who performs operations. **sur'ger·y** n medical treatment by operation. **sur'gi·cal** [-kəl] adj

sur·ly [SUR-lee] adj **-li·er, -li·est 1** gloomily morose. **2** ill-natured. **3** cross and rude. **sur'li·ness** [-nis] n

sur·mise [sər-MIZ] v, n **-mised, -mis·ing** guess, conjecture.

sur·mount [sər-MOWNT] vt get over, overcome. **sur·mount'a·ble** adj

sur·name [SUR-naym] n family name.

sur·pass [sər-PAS] vt **1** go beyond. **2** excel. **3** outstrip. **sur·pass'a·ble** adj **sur·pass'ing** adj **1** excellent. **2** exceeding others.

sur·plice [SUR-plis] n loose white vestment worn by clergy and choir members.

sur'plus n what remains over in excess.

sur·prise [sər-PRĪZ] vt **-prised, -pris·ing 1** cause surprise to. **2** astonish. **3** take, come

——————| THESAURUS |——————

surmise, theory

suppress v **1** = **stop**, check, conquer, crush, overpower, put an end to, quash, quell, subdue **2** = **restrain**, conceal, contain, curb, hold in or back, repress, silence, smother, stifle

suppression n = **elimination**, check, crushing, quashing, smothering

supremacy n = **domination**, mastery, predominance, primacy, sovereignty, supreme power, sway

supreme adj = **highest**, chief, foremost, greatest, head, leading, paramount, pre-eminent, prime, principal, top, ultimate

sure adj **1** = **certain**, assured, confident, convinced, decided, definite, positive **2** = **reliable**, accurate, dependable, foolproof, infallible, undeniable, undoubted, unerring, unfailing **3** = **inevitable**, assured, bound, guaranteed, inescapable

surely adv = **undoubtedly**, certainly, definitely, doubtlessly, indubitably, unquestionably, without doubt

surface n **1** = **outside**, covering, exterior, face, side, top, veneer ♦ v **2** = **appear**, arise, come to light, come up, crop up (inf), emerge, materialize, transpire

surfeit n = **excess**, glut, plethora, superfluity

surge n **1** = **rush**, flood, flow, gush, outpouring **2** = **wave**, billow, roller, swell ♦ v **3** = **rush**, gush, heave, rise, roll

surly adj = **ill-tempered**, churlish, cross, grouchy (inf), morose, sulky, sullen, uncivil, ungracious

surmise v **1** = **guess**, conjecture, imagine, presume, speculate, suppose ♦ n **2** = **guess**, assumption, conjecture, presumption, speculation, supposition

surpass v = **outdo**, beat, eclipse, exceed, excel, outshine, outstrip, transcend

surpassing adj = **supreme**, exceptional, extraordinary, incomparable, matchless, outstanding, unrivaled

surplus n **1** = **excess**, balance, remainder, residue, surfeit ♦ adj **2** = **excess**, extra, odd, remaining, spare, superfluous upon unexpectedly. **4** startle (someone) into action thus. ◆ *vi* **n 5** what takes unawares. **6** something unexpected. **7** emotion aroused by being taken unawares.

sur·re·al·ism [sə-REE-ə-liz-əm] *n* movement in art and literature emphasizing expression of the unconscious. **sur·re'al** *adj* **sur·re·al·ist** *n, adj*

sur·ren·der [sə-REN-dər] *vt* **1** hand over, give up. ◆ *vi* **2** yield. **3** cease resistance. **4** capitulate. ◆ *n* **5** act of surrendering.

sur·rep·ti·tious [sur-əp-TISH-əs] *adj* **1** done secretly or stealthily. **2** furtive.

sur·ro·gate [SUR-ə-gayt, SUR-ə-git] *n* **1** deputy, esp. of bishop. **2** substitute. **3** judicial officer supervising probate of wills. **surrogate mother** woman who bears child on behalf of childless woman.

sur·round [sə-ROWND] *vt* **1** be, come all around, encompass. **2** encircle. **3** hem in. ◆ *n* **4** border, edging. **sur·round'ings** *pl n* conditions, scenery, etc. around a person, place, environment.

sur·tax [SUR-taks] *n* additional tax.

sur·veil·lance [sər-VAY-ləns] *n* close watch, supervision. **sur·veil'lant** *adj, n*

sur·vey [sər-VAY] *vt* **1** view, scrutinize. **2** inspect, examine. **3** measure, map (land).

◆ *n* [SUR-vay] *pl* **-veys 4** a surveying. **5** inspection. **6** report incorporating results of survey. **sur·vey'or** *n*

sur·vive [sər-VĪV] *v* **-vived, -viv·ing** ◆ *vt* **1** outlive. **2** come through alive. ◆ *vi* **3** continue to live or exist. **sur·viv'al** [-əl] *n* continuation of existence of persons, things, etc. **sur·viv'or** [-ər] *n* **1** one left alive when others have died. **2** one who continues to function despite setbacks.

sus·cep·ti·ble [sə-SEP-tə-bəl] *adj* **1** yielding readily (to). **2** capable (of). **3** impressionable. **sus·cep·ti·bil'i·ty** *n*

sus·pect [sə-SPEKT] *vt* **1** doubt innocence of. **2** have impression of existence or presence of. **3** be inclined to believe that. **4** mistrust. ◆ *adj* [SUS-pekt] **5** of suspected character. ◆ *n* [SUS-pekt] **6** suspected person.

sus·pend [sə-SPEND] *vt* **1** hang up. **2** cause to cease for a time. **3** debar from an office or privilege. **4** keep inoperative. **5** sustain in fluid. **sus·pend'ers** *pl n* straps for supporting trousers, etc.

sus·pense [sə-SPENS] *n* **1** state of uncertainty, esp. while awaiting news, an event, etc. **2** anxiety, worry. **sus·pen'sion** [-shən] *n* **1** state of being suspended. **2** springs on axle of body of vehicle. **sus·pen'so·ry** [-sə-ree] *adj*

surprise *n* **1** = **shock**, bombshell, eye-opener (*inf*), jolt, revelation **2** = **amazement**, astonishment, incredulity, wonder ◆ *v* **3** = **amaze**, astonish, stagger, stun, take aback **4** = **catch unawares** or **off-guard**, discover, spring upon, startle

surprised *adj* = **amazed**, astonished, speechless, taken by surprise, thunderstruck

surprising *adj* = **amazing**, astonishing, extraordinary, incredible, remarkable, staggering, unexpected, unusual

surrender *v* **1** = **give in**, capitulate, give way, submit, succumb, yield **2** = **give up**, abandon, cede, concede, part with, relinquish, renounce, waive, yield ◆ *n* **3** = **submission**, capitulation, relinquishment, renunciation, resignation

surreptitious *adj* = **secret**, covert, furtive, sly, stealthy, underhand

surrogate *n* = **substitute**, proxy, representative, stand-in

surround *v* = **enclose**, encircle, encompass, envelop, hem in, ring

surroundings *pl n* = **environment**, background, location, milieu, setting

surveillance *n* = **observation**, inspection, scrutiny, supervision, watch

survey *v* **1** = **look over**, contemplate, examine, inspect, observe, scan, scrutinize, view **2** = **estimate**, appraise, assess, measure, plan, plot, size up ◆ *n* **3** = **examination**, inspection, scrutiny **4** = **study**, inquiry, review

survive *v* = **remain alive**, endure, last, live on, outlast, outlive

susceptible *adj* **1** (usually with *to*) = **liable**, disposed, given, inclined, prone, subject, vulnerable **2** = **impressionable**, receptive, responsive, sensitive, suggestible

suspect *v* **1** = **believe**, consider, feel, guess, speculate, suppose **2** = **distrust**, doubt, mistrust ◆ *adj* **3** = **dubious**, doubtful, iffy (*inf*), questionable

suspend *v* **1** = **hang**, attach, dangle **2** = **postpone**, cease, cut short, defer, discontinue, interrupt, put off, shelve

suspense *n* = **uncertainty**, anxiety,

sus·pi·cion [sə-SPISH-ən] *n* **1** suspecting, being suspected. **2** slight trace.
sus·pi·cious *adj*

sus·tain [sə-STAYN] *vt* **1** keep, hold up. **2** endure. **3** keep alive. **4** confirm.
sus·tain'a·ble *adj* **sus'te·nance** [-nəns] *n* food.

su·ture [SOO-chər] *n* **1** act of sewing. **2** sewing up of a wound. **3** material used for this. **4** a joining of the bones of the skull. ♦ *vt* **-tured, -tur·ing 5** join by suture.

SUV sport utility vehicle.

su·ze·rain [SOO-zə-rin] *n* **1** sovereign with rights over autonomous state. **2** feudal lord. **su'ze·rain·ty** [-tee] *n*

svelte [svelt] *adj* **svelt·er, svelt·est 1** lightly built, slender. **2** sophisticated.

swab [swob] *n* **1** mop. **2** pad of surgical cotton, etc. for cleaning, taking specimen, etc. **3** *sl* sailor, low or unmannerly fellow. ♦ *vt* **swabbed, swab'bing 4** clean with swab.

swad·dle [SWOD-l] *vt* **-dled, -dling** swathe. **swaddling clothes** *Hist.* long strips of cloth for wrapping infant.

swag *n sl* stolen property.

swag·ger [SWAG-ər] *vi* **1** strut. **2** boast. ♦ *n* **3** strutting gait. **4** boastful, overconfident manner.

swain [swayn] *n* rustic lover.

swal·low¹ [SWOL-oh] *vt* **1** cause, allow to pass down gullet. **2** engulf. **3** suppress, keep back. **4** believe gullibly. ♦ *n* **5** act of swallowing.

swallow² *n* migratory bird with forked tail and skimming manner of flight.

swam pt. of SWIM.

swamp [swomp] *n* **1** bog. ♦ *vt* **2** entangle in swamp. **3** overwhelm. **4** flood. **swamp'y** *adj* **swamp·i·er, swamp·i·est**

swan [swon] *n* large, web-footed water bird with graceful curved neck. **swan song 1** fabled song of a swan before death. **2** last act, etc. before death.

swank [swangk] *vi* **1** swagger. **2** show off. ♦ *n* **3** smartness. **4** style. **swank'y** *adj* **swank·i·er, swank·i·est 1** smart. **2** showy.

swap [swop] *n, v* **swapped, swap·ping 1** exchange. **2** barter.

swarm [sworm] *n* **1** large cluster of insects. **2** vast crowd. ♦ *vi* (of bees) be on the move in swarm. **3** gather in large numbers.

swarth·y [SWOR-*thee*] *adj* **swarth·i·er, swarth·i·est** of dark complexion.

swash·buck·ler [SWOSH-buk-lər] *n* swaggering daredevil person.
swash'buck·ling *adj*

swas·ti·ka [SWOS-ti-kə] *n* form of cross with arms bent at right angles, used as emblem by Nazis.

swat [swot] *vt* **swat·ted, swat·ting 1** hit smartly. **2** kill, esp. insects.

swath [swoth] *n* **1** line of grass or grain cut and thrown together by scythe or mower. **2** whole sweep of scythe or mower.

swathe [swo*th*] *vt* **swathed, swath·ing** cover with wraps or bandages.

sway *v* **1** swing unsteadily. **2** (cause to) vacillate in opinion, etc. **3** influence opinion, etc. ♦ *n* **4** control. **5** power. **6** swaying motion.

——————[THESAURUS]——————

apprehension, doubt, expectation, insecurity, irresolution, tension
suspension *n* = **postponement**, abeyance, break, breaking off, deferment, discontinuation, interruption
suspicion *n* **1** = **distrust**, doubt, dubiety, misgiving, mistrust, qualm, skepticism, wariness **2** = **idea**, guess, hunch, impression, notion **3** = **trace**, hint, shade, soupçon, streak, suggestion, tinge, touch
suspicious *adj* **1** = **distrustful**, doubtful, skeptical, unbelieving, wary **2** = **suspect**, doubtful, dubious, fishy (*inf*), questionable
sustain *v* **1** = **maintain**, continue, keep up, prolong, protract **2** = **keep alive**, aid, assist, help, nourish **3** = **withstand**, bear, endure, experience, feel, suffer, undergo **4** = **support**, bear, uphold
sustained *adj* = **continuous**, constant,

nonstop, perpetual, prolonged, steady, twenty-four-seven (*sl*), unremitting
swagger *v* = **show off** (*inf*), boast, brag, parade
swallow *v* = **gulp**, chow down (*sl*), consume, devour, drink, eat, swig (*inf*)
swamp *n* **1** = **bog**, fen, marsh, mire, morass, quagmire, slough ♦ *v* **2** = **flood**, capsize, engulf, inundate, sink, submerge **3** = **overwhelm**, flood, inundate, overload
swarm *n* **1** = **multitude**, army, crowd, flock, herd, horde, host, mass, throng ♦ *v* **2** = **crowd**, flock, mass, stream, throng **3** = **teem**, abound, bristle, crawl
swarthy *adj* = **dark-skinned**, black, brown, dark, dark-complexioned, dusky
swashbuckling *adj* = **dashing**, bold, daredevil, flamboyant
swathe *v* = **wrap**, bundle up, cloak, drape,

swear [swair] v **swore, sworn, swear-ing** ◆ vt **1** promise on oath. **2** cause to take an oath. ◆ vi **3** declare. **4** use profanity.

sweat [swet] n **1** moisture oozing from, forming on skin, esp. in humans. ◆ v **sweat** or **sweat-ed, sweat-ing 2** (cause to) exude sweat. **3** toil. **4** employ at wrongfully low wages. **5** worry. **6** wait anxiously. **sweat'y** adj **sweat-i-er, sweat-i-est sweat'shirt** [-shurt] n long-sleeved cotton pullover.

sweat•er [SWET-ər] n knitted pullover or cardigan with or without sleeves.

sweep v **swept, sweep-ing** ◆ vi **1** effect cleaning with broom. **2** pass quickly or magnificently. **3** extend in continuous curve. ◆ vt **4** clean with broom. **5** carry impetuously. ◆ n **6** act of cleaning with broom. **7** sweeping motion. **8** wide curve. **9** range. **10** long oar. **11** one who cleans chimneys. **sweeping** adj **1** wide-ranging. **2** without limitations, reservations.

sweep'stakes n **1** gamble in which winner takes stakes contributed by all. **2** type of lottery. **3** risky venture promising great return.

sweet adj **-er, -est 1** tasting like sugar. **2** agreeable. **3** kind, charming. **4** fresh, fragrant. **5** in good condition. **6** tuneful. **7** gentle, dear, beloved. ◆ n **8** small piece of

sweet food. **9** something pleasant. ◆ pl **10** cake, etc. containing much sugar.

sweet'en [-in] v **sweet'en-er** [-ən-ər] n

sweet'bread [-bred] n animal's pancreas used as food. **sweet'heart** n lover.

sweetheart contract collusive contract between labor union and company benefiting latter. **sweet'meat** n sweetened delicacy e.g. small cake, candy. **sweet potato 1** trailing plant. **2** its edible, sweetish, starchy tubers. **sweet talk** inf flattery. **sweet-talk** v inf coax, flatter.

swell v **swelled, swol-len** [SWOHL-ən] **swelled, swel-ling 1** expand. ◆ vi **2** be greatly filled with pride, emotion. ◆ n **3** act of swelling or being swollen. **4** wave of sea. **5** mechanism in organ to vary volume of sound. **6** inf person of high social standing. ◆ adj inf **7** stylish, socially prominent. **8** fine.

swel•ter [SWEL-tər] vi be oppressed with heat.

swept pt./pp. of SWEEP.

swerve [swurv] vi **swerved, swerv-ing 1** swing around, change direction during motion. **2** turn aside (from duty, etc.). ◆ n **3** swerving.

swift adj **-er, -est 1** rapid, quick, ready. ◆ n **2** bird like a swallow.

swig n inf **1** large swallow of drink. ◆ v inf

THESAURUS

envelop, shroud

sway v **1** = **lean**, bend, rock, roll, swing **2** = **influence**, affect, guide, induce, persuade ◆ n **3** = **power**, authority, clout (inf), control, influence

swear v **1** = **curse**, be foul-mouthed, blaspheme **2** = **declare**, affirm, assert, attest, promise, testify, vow

swearing n = **bad language**, blasphemy, cursing, foul language, profanity

swearword n = **oath**, curse, expletive, four-letter word, obscenity, profanity

sweat n **1** = **perspiration 2** Inf = **labor**, chore, drudgery, toil **3** Inf = **worry**, agitation, anxiety, distress, panic, strain ◆ v **4** = **perspire**, glow **5** Inf = **worry**, agonize, fret, suffer, torture oneself

sweaty adj = **perspiring**, clammy, sticky

sweep v **1** = **clear**, brush, clean, remove **2** = **sail**, fly, glide, pass, skim, tear, zoom ◆ n **3** = **arc**, bend, curve, move, stroke, swing **4** = **extent**, range, scope, stretch

sweeping adj **1** = **wide-ranging**, all-embracing, all-inclusive, broad,

comprehensive, extensive, global, wide **2** = **indiscriminate**, blanket, exaggerated, overstated, unqualified, wholesale

sweet adj **1** = **sugary**, cloying, saccharine **2** = **charming**, agreeable, appealing, cute, delightful, engaging, kind, likable or likeable, lovable, winning **3** = **melodious**, dulcet, harmonious, mellow, musical **4** = **fragrant**, aromatic, clean, fresh, pure ◆ n **5** (usually plural) = **confectionery**, bonbon

sweeten v **1** = **sugar 2** = **mollify**, appease, pacify, soothe

sweetheart n = **lover**, beloved, boyfriend or girlfriend, darling, dear, love

swell v **1** = **expand**, balloon, bloat, bulge, dilate, distend, enlarge, grow, increase, rise ◆ n **2** = **wave**, billow, surge

swelling n = **enlargement**, bulge, bump, distension, inflammation, lump, protuberance

sweltering adj = **hot**, boiling, burning, oppressive, scorching, stifling

swerve v = **veer**, bend, deflect, deviate, diverge, stray, swing, turn, turn aside

swigged, swig·ging 2 drink thus.
swill v 1 drink greedily. 2 feed (pigs) with swill. ◆ n 3 liquid or wet pig food. 4 greedy drinking. 5 kitchen refuse. 6 drivel.
swim v swam, swum, swim·ming ◆ vi 1 support and move oneself in water. 2 float. 3 be flooded. 4 have feeling of dizziness. ◆ vt 5 cross by swimming. 6 compete in by swimming. ◆ n 7 spell of swimming. **swim·ming·ly** adv successfully, effortlessly.
swin·dle [SWIN-dl] n, v -dled, -dling cheat. **swind'ler** [-lər] n **swind'ling** n
swine [swīn] n, pl **swine** 1 pig. 2 contemptible person. **swin'ish** adj
swing v swung, swing·ing 1 (cause to) move to and fro. 2 (cause to) pivot, turn. 3 hang. 4 arrange, play music with (jazz) rhythm. ◆ vi 5 be hanged. 6 hit out (at). ◆ n 7 act, instance of swinging. 8 seat hung to swing on. 9 fluctuation (esp. e.g. in voting pattern). **swing'er** n sl person regarded as modern and lively or sexually promiscuous.
swipe [swīp] v swiped, swip·ing 1 strike with sweeping or glancing blow. 2 inf steal. 3 pass (a plastic card, such as a credit card) through a machine which electronically reads information on the card.
swirl [swurl] v (cause to) move with eddying motion. ◆ n such motion.
swish v (cause to) move with audible hissing sound. ◆ n 1 the sound. 2 sl effeminate homosexual male. ◆ adj 3 sl effeminate.

switch [swich] n 1 mechanism to complete or interrupt electric circuit, etc. 2 abrupt change. 3 flexible stick or twig. 4 tufted end of animal's tail. 5 type of women's hairpiece. ◆ vi 6 shift, change. 7 swing. ◆ vt 8 affect (current, etc.) with switch. 9 change abruptly. 10 strike with switch. **switch'back** n road, railway with steep rises and descents. **switch'board** [-bord] n installation for establishing or varying connections in telephone and electric circuits.
swiv·el [SWIV-əl] n 1 mechanism of two parts that can revolve the one on the other. ◆ v -eled, -el·ing 2 turn (on swivel).
swollen [SWOH-lən] pp. of SWELL.
swoon vi, n faint.
swoop vi 1 dive, as hawk. ◆ n 2 act of swooping. 3 sudden attack.
sword [sord] n weapon with long blade for cutting or thrusting.
swore v pt. of SWEAR.
sworn v 1 pp. of SWEAR. ◆ adj 2 bound by or as if by an oath, e.g. sworn enemies.
swum pp. of SWIM.
swung pt./pp. of SWING.
syb·a·rite [SIB-ə-rīt] n lover of luxury. **syb·a·rit'ic** [-RIT-ik] adj
syc·o·phant [SIK-ə-fənt] n one using flattery to gain favors. **syc·o·phan'tic** [-FAN-tik] adj **syc·o·phan·cy** [-fən-see] n
syl·la·ble [SIL-ə-bəl] n division of word as unit for pronunciation. **syl·lab'ic** adj **syl·lab'i·fy** vt -fied, -fy·ing
syl·la·bus [SIL-ə-bəs] n, pl -bus·es, -bi [-bī]

THESAURUS

swift adj = **quick**, fast, hurried, prompt, rapid, speedy
swiftly adv = **quickly**, fast, hurriedly, promptly, rapidly, speedily
swiftness n = **speed**, promptness, quickness, rapidity, speediness, velocity
swindle v 1 = **cheat**, con, defraud, fleece, rip (someone) off (sl), sting (inf), trick ◆ n 2 = **fraud**, con trick (inf), deception, racket, rip-off (sl), scam (sl)
swindler n = **cheat**, con man (inf), fraud, rogue, shark, trickster
swing v 1 = **sway**, oscillate, rock, veer, wave 2 (usually with round) = **turn**, curve, pivot, rotate, swivel 3 = **hang**, dangle, suspend ◆ n 4 = **swaying**, oscillation
swipe v 1 = **hit**, lash out at, slap, strike, wallop (inf) 2 Sl = **steal**, appropriate, filch, lift (inf), pinch (inf), purloin ◆ n 3 = **blow**,

clout (inf), cuff, slap, smack, wallop (inf)
swirl v = **whirl**, churn, eddy, spin, twist
switch n 1 = **change**, reversal, shift 2 = **exchange**, substitution, swap ◆ v 3 = **change**, deflect, deviate, divert, shift 4 = **exchange**, substitute, swap
swivel v = **turn**, pivot, revolve, rotate, spin
swollen adj = **enlarged**, bloated, distended, inflamed, puffed up
swoop v 1 = **pounce**, descend, dive, rush, stoop, sweep ◆ n 2 = **pounce**, descent, drop, lunge, plunge, rush, stoop, sweep
swop v = **exchange**, barter, interchange, switch, trade
sycophant n = **crawler**, brown-noser (sl), fawner, flatterer, toady, yes man
sycophantic adj = **obsequious**, crawling, fawning, flattering, grovelling, ingratiating, servile, slimy, smarmy (Brit.

1 outline of a course of study. **2** list of subjects studied in course.

syl·lo·gism [SIL-ə-jiz-əm] *n* form of logical reasoning consisting of two premises and conclusion. **syl·lo·gis'tic** *adj*

sylph [silf] *n* **1** slender, graceful woman. **2** sprite.

syl·van [SIL-vən] *adj* of forests, trees.

sym- see SYN-.

sym·bi·o·sis [sim-bee-OH-sis] *n, pl* **-ses** [-seez] **1** living together of two organisms of different kinds, esp. to their mutual benefit. **2** similar relationship involving people, etc. **sym·bi·ot·ic** [-OT-ik] *adj*

sym·bol [SIM-bəl] *n* **1** sign. **2** thing representing or typifying something. **sym·bol'ic** *adj* **sym·bol'i·cal·ly** *adv* **sym'bol·ism** *n* **1** use of, representation by symbols. **2** movement in art holding that work of art should express idea in symbolic form. **sym'bol·ist** *n, adj* **sym'bol·ize** *vt* **-ized, -iz·ing**

sym·me·try [SIM-ə-tree] *n, pl* **-tries 1** proportion between parts. **2** balance of arrangement between two sides. **3** order. **sym·met'ri·cal** *adj* **1** having due proportion in its parts. **2** harmonious. **3** regular.

sym·pa·thy [SIM-pə-thee] *n, pl* **-thies 1** feeling for another in pain, etc. **2** compassion, pity. **3** sharing of emotion, interest, desire, etc. **4** fellow feeling. **sym·pa·thet'ic** *adj* **sym'pa·thize** [-thīz] *vi* **-thized, -thiz·ing**

sym·pho·ny [SIM-fə-nee] *n, pl* **-nies 1** composition for full orchestra. **2** harmony of sounds. **sym·phon'ic** [-FON-ik] *adj* **sym·pho'ni·ous** [-FOH-nee-əs] *adj* harmonious.

sym·po·si·um [sim-POH-zee-əm] *n, pl* **-si·a** [-zee-ə] **1** conference, meeting. **2** discussion, writings on a given topic.

symp·tom [SIMP-təm] *n* **1** change in body indicating its state of health or disease. **2** sign, token. **symp·to·mat'ic** *adj*

syn- *prefix* with, together, alike, e.g. *synchronize; syncopate.*

syn·a·gogue [SIN-ə-gog] *n* (place of worship of) Jewish congregation.

syn·chro·nize [SING-krə-nīz] *v* **-nized, -niz·ing ♦** *vt* **1** make agree in time. ♦ *vi* **2** happen at same time. **syn·chro·ni·za'tion** *n* **syn'chro·nous** [-nis] *adj* simultaneous.

syn·co·pate [SING-kə-payt] *vt* **-pat·ed, -pat·ing** accentuate weak beat in bar of music. **syn·co·pa'tion** *n*

syn·di·cate [SIN-di-kit] *n* **1** body of people, delegates associated for some enterprise. ♦ *v* [-kayt] **-cat·ed, -cat·ing 2** form syndicate. ♦ *vt* **3** publish in many newspapers at the same time.

syn·drome [SIN-drohm] *n* **1** combination of several symptoms in disease. **2** symptom, set of symptoms or characteristics.

syn·ec·do·che [si-NEK-də-kee] *n* figure of speech by which whole of thing is put for part or part for whole, such as *sail* for *ship.*

syn·er·gy [SIN-ər-jee] *n* potential ability for people or groups to be more successful working together than on their own.

syn·od [SIN-əd] *n* **1** church council. **2** convention.

syn·o·nym [SIN-ə-nim] *n* word with (nearly) same meaning as another. **syn·on·y·mous** [si-NON-ə-məs] *adj*

syn·op·sis [si-NOP-sis] *n, pl* **-ses** [-seez] summary, outline. **syn·op'tic** *adj* **1** of, like

---

THESAURUS

inf), toadying, unctuous

syllabus *n* = **course of study**, curriculum

symbol *n* = **sign**, badge, emblem, figure, icon, image, logo, mark, representation, token

symbolic *adj* = **representative**, allegorical, emblematic, figurative

symbolize *v* = **represent**, denote, mean, personify, signify, stand for, typify

symmetrical *adj* = **balanced**, in proportion, regular

symmetry *n* = **balance**, evenness, order, proportion, regularity

sympathetic *adj* **1** = **caring**, compassionate, concerned, interested,

kind, pitying, supportive, understanding, warm **2** = **like-minded**, agreeable, companionable, compatible, congenial, friendly

sympathize *v* **1** = **feel for**, commiserate, condole, pity **2** = **agree**, side with, understand

sympathizer *n* = **supporter**, partisan, well-wisher

sympathy *n* **1** = **compassion**, commiseration, pity, understanding **2** = **agreement**, affinity, fellow feeling, rapport

symptom *n* = **sign**, expression, indication, mark, token, warning

symptomatic *adj* = **indicative**,

synopsis. **2** having same viewpoint.

syn·tax [SIN-taks] *n* part of grammar treating of arrangement of words in sentence. **syn·tac'tic** *adj*

syn·the·sis [SIN-thə-sis] *n, pl* **-ses** [-seez] putting together, combination. **syn'the·size** *v* **-sized, -siz·ing** make artificially. **syn'the·siz·er** [-sīz-ər] *n* electronic keyboard instrument capable of reproducing a wide range of musical sounds. **syn·thet'ic** *adj* **1** artificial. **2** of synthesis.

syph·i·lis [SIF-ə-lis] *n* contagious venereal disease. **syph·i·lit'ic** *adj*

sy·ringe [sə-RINJ] *n* **1** instrument for drawing in liquid by piston and forcing it out in fine stream or spray. **2** squirt. ◆ *vt* **-ringed, -ring·ing 3** spray, cleanse with syringe.

syr·up [SIR-əp] *n* **1** thick solution obtained in process of refining sugar, molasses, etc. **2** any liquid like this, esp. in consistency. **syr'up·y** *adj*

sys·tem [SIS-təm] *n* **1** complex whole, organization. **2** method. **3** classification. **sys·tem·at'ic** *adj* methodical. **sys'tem·a·tize** [-tīz] *vt* **-tized, -tiz·ing 1** reduce to system. **2** arrange methodically. **sys·tem'ic** *adj* affecting entire body or organism.

sys·to·le [SIS-tə-lee] *n* contraction of heart and arteries for expelling blood and carrying on circulation. **sys·tol·ic** [sis-TOL-ik] *adj* **1** contracting. **2** of systole.

——— THESAURUS ———

characteristic, suggestive

synthetic *adj* = **artificial**, fake, man-made

system *n* **1** = **method**, practice, procedure, routine, technique **2** = **arrangement**,

classification, organization, scheme, structure

systematic *adj* = **methodical**, efficient, orderly, organized

T t

T *Chem.* tritium. **to a T** precisely, to a nicety.
Ta *Chem.* tantalum.

tab *n* tag, label, short strap. **keep tabs on** *inf* keep watchful eye on.

tab·er·na·cle [TAB-ər-nak-əl] *n* **1** portable shrine of Israelites. **2** receptacle containing reserved Eucharist. **3** place of worship.

ta·ble [TAY-bəl] *n* **1** piece of furniture consisting of flat board supported by legs. **2** food. **3** set of facts, figures arranged in lines or columns. ♦ *vt* **-bled, -bling 4** lay on table. **5** lay aside (motion, etc.) for possible but unlikely consideration in future. **ta'ble·land** *n* plateau, high flat area. **ta'ble·spoon** *n* spoon used for serving food, etc. **under the table 1** secretly. **2** as bribe. **3** drunk.

tab·leau [ta-BLOH] *n, pl* **-leaux** *or* **-leaus** [-BLOHZ] **1** group of persons, silent and motionless, arranged to represent some scene. **2** dramatic scene.

ta·ble d'hôte [TAH-bəl DOHT] *n, pl* **ta·bles d'hôte** [TAH-bəl DOHT] *Fr* meal, with limited choice of dishes, at a fixed price.

tab·let [TAB-lit] *n* **1** pill of compressed powdered medicinal substance. **2** writing pad. **3** slab of stone, wood, etc., esp. used formerly for writing on.

tab'loid *n* (illustrated) popular small-sized newspaper usu. with terse, sensational headlines.

ta·boo [tə-BOO] *adj* **1** forbidden or disapproved of. ♦ *n, pl* **-boos 2** prohibition resulting from social conventions, etc. **3** thing prohibited. ♦ *vt* **-booed, -boo·ing 4** place under taboo.

tab·u·lar [TAB-yə-lər] *adj* shaped, arranged like a table. **tab·u·late** [-layt] *vt* **-lat·ed, -lat·ing** arrange (figures, facts, etc.) in tables.

tacho- *comb. form* speed, e.g. *tachometer.*

ta·chom·e·ter [ta-KOM-i-tər] *n* device for measuring speed, esp. of revolving shaft (e.g. in automobile) and hence revolutions per minute.

tac·it [TAS-it] *adj* **1** implied but not spoken. **2** silent. **tac'it·ly** *adv* **tac'i·turn** *adj* **1** talking little. **2** habitually silent.

tack¹ [tak] *n* **1** small nail. **2** long loose stitch. **3** *Nautical* course of ship obliquely to windward. **4** course, direction. ♦ *vt* **5** nail with tacks. **6** stitch lightly. **7** append, attach. **8** sail to windward.

tack² *n* riding harness for horses.

tack·le [TAK-əl] *n* **1** equipment, apparatus, esp. for fishing. **2** lifting appliances with ropes. **3** *Football* lineman between guard and end. ♦ *vt* **-led, -ling 4** take in hand. **5** grip, grapple with. **6** undertake to cope with, master, etc. **7** *Football* seize, bring down (ball-carrier).

tack·y [TAK-ee] *adj* **tack·i·er, tack·i·est 1**

THESAURUS

table *n* **1** = **counter**, bench, board, stand **2** = **list**, catalog, chart, diagram, record, register, roll, schedule, tabulation ♦ *v* **3** = **submit**, enter, move, propose, put forward, suggest

tableau *n* = **picture**, representation, scene, spectacle

taboo *n* **1** = **prohibition**, anathema, ban, interdict, proscription, restriction ♦ *adj* **2** = **forbidden**, anathema, banned, outlawed, prohibited, proscribed, unacceptable, unmentionable

tacit *adj* = **implied**, implicit, inferred, undeclared, understood, unexpressed, unspoken, unstated

taciturn *adj* = **uncommunicative**, quiet, reserved, reticent, silent, tight-lipped, unforthcoming, withdrawn

tack¹ *n* **1** = **nail**, drawing pin, pin ♦ *v* **2** = **fasten**, affix, attach, fix, nail, pin **3** = **stitch**, baste **4 tack on** = **append**, add, attach, tag

tack² *n* = **course**, approach, direction, heading, line, method, path, plan, procedure, way

tackle *v* **1** = **deal with**, attempt, come *or* get to grips with, embark upon, get stuck into (*inf*), set about, undertake **2** =

sticky. **2** not quite dry. **3** dowdy, shabby. **tack'i·ness** [-nis] *n*

ta·co [TAK-oh] *n* **-cos** usu. fried tortilla folded or wrapped round filling.

tact [takt] *n* **1** skill in dealing with people or situations. **2** delicate perception of the feelings of others. **tact'ful** [-fəl] *adj* **tact'less** [-lis] *adj*

tac·tics [TAK-tiks] *n* **1** art of handling troops, ships in battle. **2** adroit management of a situation. **3** plans for this. **tac·ti·cal** [TAK-ti-kəl] *adj* **tac·ti·cian** [-TISH-ən] *n*

tac·tile [TAK-til] *adj* of, relating to the sense of touch.

tad'pole [TAD-pohl] *n* immature frog, in its first state before gills and tail are absorbed.

taf·fe·ta [TAF-i-tə] *n* smooth, stiff fabric of silk, nylon, etc.

taf·fy [TAF-ee] *n, pl* **-fies** candy of molasses and sugar.

tag[1] *n* **1** label identifying or showing price of (something). **2** ragged, hanging end. **3** pointed end of shoelace, etc. **4** trite saying or quotation. **5** any appendage. ◆ *vt* **tagged, tag·ging 6** append, add (on). **7** trail (along) behind.

tag[2] *n* **1** children's game where one being chased becomes the chaser upon being touched. ◆ *vt* **tagged, tag·ging 2** touch. **tag wrestling** wrestling match for teams

of two, where one partner may replace the other upon being touched on hand.

tail [tayl] *n* **1** flexible prolongation of animal's spine. **2** lower or inferior part of anything. **3** appendage. **4** rear part of aircraft. **5** *inf* person employed to follow another. ◆ *pl* **6** reverse side of coin. **7** tail coat. ◆ *vt* **8** remove tail of. **9** *inf* follow closely, trail. **tail'ings** *pl n* waste left over from some (e.g. industrial) process. **tail'less** [-lis] *adj* **tail'board** [-bord] *n* removable or hinged rear board on truck, etc. **tail end** last part. **tail'light** *n* light carried at rear of vehicle. **tail'spin** *n* **1** spinning dive of aircraft. **2** sudden (e.g. emotional, financial) collapse. **tail'wind** *n* wind coming from behind. **tail off** diminish gradually, dwindle. **turn tail** run away.

tai·lor [TAY-lər] *n* maker of outer clothing, esp. for men. **tailor-made** *adj* **1** made by tailor. **2** well-fitting. **3** appropriate.

taint [taynt] *v* **1** affect or be affected by pollution, corruption, etc. ◆ *n* **2** defect, flaw. **3** infection, contamination.

take [tayk] *v* **took** [tuuk], **tak·en, tak·ing** ◆ *vt* **1** grasp, get hold of. **2** get. **3** receive, assume. **4** adopt. **5** accept. **6** understand. **7** consider. **8** carry, conduct. **9** use. **10** capture. **11** consume. **12** subtract. **13** require. ◆ *vi* **14** be effective. **15** please. **16**

—————— THESAURUS ——————

confront, challenge, grab, grasp, halt, intercept, seize, stop ◆ *n* **3 = challenge**, block **4 = equipment**, accouterments, apparatus, gear, paraphernalia, tools, trappings

tacky[1] *adj* = **sticky**, adhesive, gluey, gummy, wet

tacky[2] *adj Inf* = **vulgar**, cheap, off-color, scuzzy (*sl*), seedy, shabby, shoddy, sleazy, tasteless, tatty

tact *n* = **diplomacy**, consideration, delicacy, discretion, sensitivity, thoughtfulness, understanding

tactful *adj* = **diplomatic**, considerate, delicate, discreet, polite, politic, sensitive, thoughtful, understanding

tactic *n* **1 = policy**, approach, maneuver, method, move, ploy, scheme, stratagem **2 tactics** = **strategy**, campaigning, generalship, maneuvers, plans

tactical *adj* = **strategic**, cunning, diplomatic, shrewd, smart

tactician *n* = **strategist**, general,

mastermind, planner

tactless *adj* = **insensitive**, impolite, impolitic, inconsiderate, indelicate, indiscreet, thoughtless, undiplomatic, unsubtle

tag *n* **1 = label**, flap, identification, mark, marker, note, slip, tab, ticket ◆ *v* **2 = label**, mark **3** (with *along* or *on*) = **accompany**, attend, follow, shadow, stalk, tail (*inf*), trail

tail *n* **1 = extremity**, appendage, end, rear end, tailpiece **2 turn tail = run away**, cut and run, flee, retreat, run off, take to one's heels ◆ *v* **3** *Inf* = **follow**, shadow, stalk, track, trail

tailor *n* **1 = outfitter**, clothier, costumier, couturier, dressmaker, seamstress ◆ *v* **2 = adapt**, adjust, alter, customize, fashion, modify, mold, shape, style

taint *v* **1 = spoil**, blemish, contaminate, corrupt, damage, defile, pollute, ruin, stain, sully, tarnish ◆ *n* **2 = stain**, black mark, blemish, blot, defect, demerit, fault, flaw, spot

DICTIONARY

go. ◆ n **17** *Motion Pictures* (recording of) scene, sequence photographed without interruption. **18** *inf* earnings, receipts. **tak'ing** *adj* charming. **take'off** n **1** instant at which aircraft becomes airborne. **2** commencement of flight. **take after** resemble in face or character. **take down 1** write down. **2** dismantle. **3** humiliate. **take in 1** understand. **2** make (garment, etc.) smaller. **3** deceive. **take in vain 1** blaspheme. **2** be facetious. **take off 1** (of aircraft) leave ground. **2** *inf* go away. **3** *inf* mimic. **take to** become fond of.

tal·cum pow'der [TAL-kəm] n **1** powder, usu. scented, to absorb body moisture, deodorize, etc.

tale [tayl] n **1** story, narrative, report. **2** fictitious story.

tal·ent [TAL-ənt] n **1** natural ability or power. **2** ancient weight or money. **tal'ent·ed** [-id] *adj* gifted.

tal·is·man [TAL-is-mən] n, pl **-mans 1** object supposed to have magic power. **2** amulet. **tal·is·man'ic** [-MAN-ik] *adj*

talk [tawk] vi **1** express, exchange ideas, etc. in words. ◆ vt **2** express in speech, utter. **3** discuss. ◆ n **4** speech, lecture. **5** conversation. **6** rumor. **talk'a·tive** *adj* fond of talking. **talking-to** n, pl **-tos** reproof. **talk show** TV or radio program in which guests are interviewed informally.

tall [tawl] *adj* **1** high. **2** of great stature. **tall story** unlikely and probably untrue tale.

tal·low [TAL-oh] n **1** melted and clarified animal fat. ◆ vt **2** smear with this.

tal·ly [TAL-ee] vi **-lied, -ly·ing 1** correspond one with the other. **2** keep record. ◆ n, pl **-lies 3** record, account, total number.

Tal·mud [TAHL-muud] n body of Jewish law. **Tal·mud'ic** [-MUUD-ik] *adj*

tal·on [TAL-ən] n claw.

tam·bou·rine [tam-bə-REEN] n flat

THESAURUS

take v **1** = **capture**, acquire, catch, get, grasp, grip, obtain, secure, seize **2** = **accompany**, bring, conduct, convoy, escort, guide, lead, usher **3** = **carry**, bear, bring, convey, ferry, fetch, haul, transport **4** = **steal**, appropriate, misappropriate, pinch (*inf*), pocket, purloin **5** = **require**, call for, demand, necessitate, need **6** = **tolerate**, abide, bear, endure, put up with (*inf*), stand, stomach, withstand **7** = **have room for**, accept, accommodate, contain, hold **8** = **subtract**, deduct, eliminate, remove **9** = **assume**, believe, presume, regard, understand

take in v **1** = **understand**, absorb, assimilate, comprehend, digest, get the hang of (*inf*), grasp **2** = **deceive**, cheat, con (*inf*), dupe, fool, hoodwink, mislead, swindle, trick

takeoff n = **departure**, launch, liftoff

take off v **1** = **remove**, discard, peel off, strip off **2** = **lift off**, take to the air **3** *Inf* = **depart**, abscond, decamp, disappear, go, leave, slope off

takeover n = **merger**, coup, incorporation

take up v **1** = **occupy**, absorb, consume, cover, extend over, fill, use up **2** = **start**, adopt, become involved in, engage in

taking *adj* **1** = **charming**, attractive, beguiling, captivating, enchanting, engaging, fetching (*inf*), likable *or* likeable, prepossessing ◆ n **2** **takings** = **revenue**, earnings, income, proceeds, profits,

receipts, returns, take

tale n = **story**, account, anecdote, fable, legend, narrative, saga, yarn (*inf*)

talent n = **ability**, aptitude, capacity, flair, genius, gift, knack

talented *adj* = **gifted**, able, brilliant

talisman n = **charm**, amulet, fetish, lucky charm, mascot

talk v **1** = **speak**, chat, chatter, chew the fat (*sl*), communicate, converse, gossip, natter, utter **2** = **negotiate**, confabulate, confer, parley **3** = **inform**, blab, give the game away, let the cat out of the bag, tell all ◆ n **4** = **speech**, address, discourse, disquisition, lecture, oration, sermon

talkative *adj* = **loquacious**, chatty, effusive, garrulous, gossipy, long-winded, mouthy, verbose, voluble, wordy

talker n = **speaker**, chatterbox, conversationalist, lecturer, orator

talking-to n = **reprimand**, criticism, lecture, rebuke, reproach, reproof, scolding, telling-off (*inf*)

tall *adj* **1** = **high**, big, elevated, giant, lanky, lofty, soaring, towering **2** *As in* **tall tale** *Inf* = **implausible**, absurd, cock-and-bull (*inf*), exaggerated, far-fetched, incredible, preposterous, unbelievable **3** *As in* **tall order** = **difficult**, demanding, hard, unreasonable, well-nigh impossible

tally v **1** = **correspond**, accord, agree, coincide, concur, conform, fit, harmonize, match, square ◆ n **2** = **record**, count, mark, half-drum with jingling disks of metal attached.

tame [taym] *adj* **tam·er, tam·est 1** not wild, domesticated. **2** subdued. **3** uninteresting. ♦ *vt* **4** make tame. **tame'ly** *adv* **1** in a tame manner. **2** without resisting.

tamp *vt* pack, force down by repeated blows.

tam·per [TAM-pər] *vi* **1** interfere (with) improperly. **2** meddle.

tam'pon *n* plug of lint, cotton, etc. inserted in wound, body cavity, to stop flow of blood, absorb secretions, etc.

tan *n, adj* **tan·ner, tan·nest 1** (of) brown color of skin after long exposure to rays of sun, etc. ♦ *v* **tanned, tan·ning 2** (cause to) go brown. **3** (of animal hide) convert to leather by chemical treatment. **tan'ner** *n* **tan'ner·y** *n* place where hides are tanned. **tan'nic** *adj* **tan'nin** *n* vegetable substance used as tanning agent. **tan'bark** *n* bark of certain trees, yielding tannin.

tang *n* **1** strong pungent taste or smell. **2** trace, hint. **3** spike, barb. **tang'y** *adj* **tang·i·er, tang·i·est**

tan·gent [TAN-jənt] *n* **1** line that touches a curve without cutting. **2** divergent course. ♦ *adj* **3** touching, meeting without cutting. **tan·gen'tial** [-JEN-shəl] *adj* **tan·gen'tial·ly** *adv*

tan·ge·rine [tan-jə-REEN] *n* **1** citrus tree. **2** its fruit, a variety of orange.

tan·gi·ble [TAN-jə-bəl] *adj* **1** that can be touched. **2** definite. **3** palpable. **4** concrete.

tan·gle [TANG-gəl] *n* **1** confused mass or situation. ♦ *vt* **-gled, -gling 2** twist together in muddle. **3** contend (with).

tan·go [TANG-goh] *n, pl* **-gos** dance of S Amer. origin.

tank *n* **1** storage vessel for liquids or gas. **2** armored motor vehicle moving on tracks. **3** cistern. **4** reservoir. **tank'er** *n* ship, truck, etc. for carrying liquid in bulk.

tan·kard [TANG-kərd] *n* **1** large drinking cup of metal or glass. **2** its contents, esp. beer.

tannin see TAN.

tan·ta·lize [TAN-tə-līz] *vt* **-lized, -liz·ing 1** torment by appearing to offer something desired. **2** tease.

tan·ta·mount [TAN-tə-mownt] *adj* **1** equivalent in value or signification. **2** equal, amounting (to).

tan·trum [TAN-trəm] *n* childish outburst of temper.

tap¹ *v* **tapped, tap·ping 1** strike lightly but with some noise. ♦ *n* **2** slight blow, rap.

tap² *n* **1** valve with handle to regulate or stop flow of fluid in pipe, etc. **2** stopper, plug permitting liquid to be drawn from cask, etc. **3** steel tool for forming internal screw threads. ♦ *vt* **tapped, tap·ping 4** put tap in. **5** draw off with or as with tap. **6** make secret connection to telephone wire to overhear conversation on it. **7** make connection for supply of electricity at intermediate point in supply line. **8** form internal threads in.

reckoning, running total, score, total

tame *adj* **1 = domesticated**, amenable, broken, disciplined, docile, gentle, obedient, tractable **2 = submissive**, compliant, docile, manageable, meek, obedient, subdued, unresisting **3 = uninteresting**, bland, boring, dull, humdrum, insipid, unexciting, uninspiring, vapid ♦ *v* **4 = domesticate**, break in, house-train, train **5 = discipline**, bring to heel, conquer, humble, master, subdue, subjugate, suppress

tamper *v* **= interfere**, alter, fiddle (*inf*), fool about (*inf*), meddle, mess about, tinker

tangible *adj* **= definite**, actual, concrete, material, palpable, perceptible, positive, real

tangle *n* **1 = knot**, coil, entanglement, jungle, twist, web **2 = confusion**, complication, entanglement, fix (*inf*),

imbroglio, jam, mess, mix-up ♦ *v* **3 = twist**, coil, entangle, interweave, knot, mat, mesh, ravel **4** (often with *with*) **= come into conflict**, come up against, contend, contest, cross swords, dispute, lock horns

tangled *adj* **1 = twisted**, entangled, jumbled, knotted, matted, messy, snarled, tousled **2 = complicated**, complex, confused, convoluted, involved, knotty, messy, mixed-up

tangy *adj* **= sharp**, piquant, pungent, spicy, tart

tantalize *v* **= torment**, frustrate, lead on, taunt, tease, torture

tantamount *adj* **= equivalent**, commensurate, equal, synonymous

tantrum *n* **= outburst**, fit, flare-up, hysterics, temper

tap¹ *v* **1 = knock**, beat, drum, pat, rap, strike, touch ♦ *n* **2 = knock**, pat, rap, touch

DICTIONARY

tape [tayp] *n* **1** narrow long strip of fabric, paper, etc. **2** magnetic recording of music, data, etc. ◆ *vt* **taped, tap·ing 3** record (speech, music, etc.). **tape deck** device for playing magnetic tape recordings. **tape measure** tape of fabric, metal marked off in centimeters, inches, etc. **tape recorder** apparatus for recording sound on magnetized tape and playing it back. **tape'worm** [-wurm] *n* long flat worm parasitic in animals and people.

ta·per [TAY-pər] *vi* **1** become gradually thinner toward one end. ◆ *n* **2** thin candle. **3** long wick covered with wax. **4** a narrowing.

tap·es·try [TAP-ə-stree] *n, pl* **-tries** fabric decorated with designs in colors woven by needles. **tap'es·tried** *adj*

tap·i·o·ca [tap-ee-OH-kə] *n* beadlike starch made from cassava root, used esp. in puddings, as thickener, etc.

ta·pir [TAY-pər] *n* Amer. animal with elongated snout, allied to pig.

tap'root *n* large single root growing straight down.

tar¹ [tahr] *n* **1** thick black liquid distilled from coal, etc. ◆ *vt* **tarred, tar·ring 2** coat, treat (as though) with tar. **tarred with same brush** (made to appear) guilty of same misdeeds.

tar² *n inf* sailor.

tar·an·tel·la [ta-rən-TEL-ə] *n* **1** lively Italian dance. **2** music for it.

ta·ran·tu·la [tə-RAN-chuu-lə] *n, pl* **-las** any of various large (poisonous) hairy spiders.

tar·dy [TAHR-dee] *adj* **-di·er, -di·est** slow, late. **tar'di·ly** *adv*

tare [tair] *n* **1** weight of wrapping, container for goods. **2** unladen weight of vehicle.

tar·get [TAHR-git] *n* **1** mark to aim at in shooting. **2** thing aimed at. **3** object of criticism. **4** butt.

tar·iff [TA-rif] *n* **1** tax levied on imports, etc. **2** list of charges. **3** bill.

tarn [tahrn] *n* small mountain lake.

tar·nish [TAHR-nish] *v* **1** (cause to) become stained, lose shine or become dimmed or sullied. ◆ *n* **2** discoloration, blemish.

ta·ro [TAHR-oh] *n, pl* **-ros 1** plant of Pacific islands now cultivated widely. **2** its edible tuber.

ta·rot [TA-roh] *n* one of special pack of cards now used mainly in fortunetelling.

tar·pau·lin [tahr-PAW-lin] *n* (sheet of) heavy hard-wearing waterproof fabric.

tar·ry *vi* **-ried, -ry·ing 1** linger, delay. **2** stay behind.

tart¹ [tahrt] *n* **1** small pie filled with fruit, jam, etc. **2** *sl* promiscuous woman. **3** prostitute.

tart² *adj* **-er, -est 1** sour. **2** sharp. **3** bitter.

tar·tan [TAHR-tn] *n* **1** woolen cloth woven in pattern of colored checks, esp. in colors, patterns associated with Scottish clans. **2** such pattern.

tar·tar¹ [TAHR-tər] *n* **1** crust deposited on teeth. **2** deposit formed during fermentation of wine.

tartar² *n* **1** ill-tempered person, difficult to deal with. **2** (T-) member of group of peoples including Mongols and Turks.

task *n* **1** piece of work (esp. unpleasant or difficult) set or undertaken. ◆ *vt* **2** assign task to. **3** exact. **task force 1** naval or military unit dispatched to carry out specific undertaking. **2** any similar group in government, industry. **task'mas·ter** *n* (stern) overseer. **take to task** reprove.

tas·sel [TAS-əl] *n* **1** ornament of fringed

THESAURUS

tap² *n* **1** = **valve**, stopcock **2 on tap: a** *Inf* = **available**, at hand, in reserve, on hand, ready **b** = **on draft** ◆ *v* **3** = **listen in on**, bug (*inf*), eavesdrop on **4** = **draw off**, bleed, drain, siphon off

tape *n* **1** = **strip**, band, ribbon ◆ *v* **2** = **record**, tape-record, video **3** = **bind**, seal, secure, stick, wrap

taper *v* **1** = **narrow**, come to a point, thin **2 taper off** = **lessen**, decrease, die away, dwindle, fade, reduce, subside, wane, wind down

target *n* **1** = **goal**, aim, ambition, end, intention, mark, object, objective **2** = victim, butt, scapegoat

tariff *n* = **tax**, duty, excise, levy, toll

tarnish *v* **1** = **stain**, blacken, blemish, blot, darken, discolor, sully, taint ◆ *n* **2** = **stain**, blemish, blot, discoloration, spot, taint

tart¹ *n* = **pie**, pastry, tartlet

tart² *adj* = **sharp**, acid, bitter, piquant, pungent, sour, tangy, vinegary

tart³ *n* = **slut**, call girl, floozy (*sl*), ho (*sl*), prostitute, trollop, whore

task *n* **1** = **job**, assignment, chore, duty, enterprise, exercise, mission, undertaking **2 take to task** = **criticize**, blame, censure, reprimand, reproach, reprove, scold, tell

knot of threads, etc. **2** tuft. **tas'seled** adj
taste [tayst] n **1** sense by which flavor,
quality of substance is detected by the
tongue. **2** this act or sensation. **3** (brief)
experience of something. **4** small amount.
5 preference, liking. **6** power of discerning,
judging. **7** discretion, delicacy. ◆ v **tast·ed,
tast·ing 8** observe or distinguish the taste
of a substance. **9** take small amount into
mouth. **10** experience. ◆ vi **11** have specific
flavor. **taste'ful** [-fəl] adj **1** in good style. **2**
with, showing good taste. **taste'less** [-lis]
adj **tast'y** adj **tast·i·er, tast·i·est** pleasantly
or highly flavored. **taste bud** small organ
of taste on tongue.
tat v **tat·ted, tat·ting** make by tatting.
tatting n type of handmade lace.
tat·ter [TAT-ər] v **1** make or become
ragged, worn to shreds. ◆ n **2** ragged
piece.
tat·tle vi, n, v -**tled, -tling** gossip, chatter.
tat·too[1] [ta-TOO] n, pl -**toos 1** beat of
drum and bugle call. **2** military spectacle
or pageant.
tattoo[2] vt -**tooed, -too·ing 1** mark skin in
patterns, etc. by pricking and filling
punctures with indelible colored inks. ◆ n,
pl -**toos 2** mark so made.
tat·ty [TAT-ee] adj -**ti·er, -ti·est** shabby,
worn out.
taught [tawt] pt./pp. of TEACH.
taunt [tawnt] vt **1** provoke, deride with

insulting words, etc. ◆ n **2** instance of this.
3 words used for this.
taut [tawt] adj -**er, -est 1** drawn tight. **2**
under strain.
tau·tol·o·gy [taw-TOL-ə-gee] n, pl -**gies**
needless repetition of same thing in other
words in same sentence. **tau·to·log'i·cal**
[-tə-LOJ-ə-kəl] adj
lav·ern [TAV-ərn] n **1** bar. **2** inn.
taw·dry [TAW-dree] adj -**dri·er, -dri·est**
showy, but cheap and without taste,
flashy. **taw'dri·ness** [-nis] n
taw·ny [TAW-nee] adj, n -**ni·er, -ni·est** (of)
light (yellowish) brown.
tax [taks] n **1** compulsory payments by
wage earners, companies, etc. imposed by
government to raise revenue. **2** heavy
demand on something. ◆ vt **3** impose tax
on. **4** strain. **5** accuse, blame. **tax'a·ble** adj
tax·a'tion n levying of taxes. **tax'pay·er** n
tax return statement supplied to
authorities of personal income and tax
due.
tax·i [TAK-see] n, pl **tax·is 1** (also **tax'i·cab**)
motor vehicle for hire with driver. ◆ vi
tax·ied, tax·i·ing or **tax·y·ing 2** (of aircraft)
run along ground under its own power. **3**
ride in taxi.
tax·i·der·my [TAK-si-dur-mee] n art of
stuffing, mounting animal skins to give
them lifelike appearance. **tax'i·der·mist** n
tax·on·o·my [tak-SON-ə-mee] n science,

——————| THESAURUS |——————

off (inf), upbraid
taste n **1** = flavor, relish, savor, smack, tang
2 = bit, bite, dash, morsel, mouthful,
sample, soupçon, spoonful, tidbit **3** =
liking, appetite, fancy, fondness,
inclination, partiality, penchant,
predilection, preference **4** = **refinement**,
appreciation, discernment, discrimination,
elegance, judgment, sophistication, style ◆
v **5** = **distinguish**, differentiate, discern,
perceive **6** = **sample**, savor, sip, test, try
7 = **have a flavor of**, savor of, smack of **8** =
experience, encounter, know, meet with,
partake of, undergo
tasteful adj = **refined**, artistic, cultivated,
cultured, discriminating, elegant,
exquisite, in good taste, polished, stylish
tasteless adj **1** = **insipid**, bland, boring,
dull, flat, flavorless, mild, thin, weak **2** =
vulgar, crass, crude, gaudy, gross,
inelegant, off-color, tacky (inf), tawdry
tasty adj = **delicious**, appetizing,

delectable, full-flavored, luscious,
palatable, savory, toothsome, yummy (inf)
tatters n **in tatters** = **ragged**, down at
heel, in rags, in shreds, ripped, tattered,
threadbare, torn
tatty adj = **ragged**, bedraggled,
dilapidated, down at heel, neglected,
run-down, shabby, threadbare, worn
taunt v **1** = **tease**, deride, insult, jeer, mock,
provoke, ridicule, torment ◆ n **2** = **jeer**,
derision, dig, gibe, insult, provocation,
ridicule, sarcasm, teasing
taut adj = **tight**, flexed, rigid, strained,
stressed, stretched, tense
tavern n = **inn**, alehouse (archaic), bar,
hostelry, public house
tawdry adj = **vulgar**, cheap, flashy, gaudy,
gimcrack, tacky (inf), tasteless, tatty,
tinselly
tax n **1** = **charge**, duty, excise, levy, tariff,
tithe, toll ◆ v **2** = **charge**, assess, rate **3** =
strain, burden, exhaust, load, stretch, test,

practice of classification, esp. of biological organisms.

Tb *Chem.* terbium.

T-bone steak loin steak with T-shaped bone.

Tc *Chem.* technetium.

te see TI.

Te *Chem.* tellurium.

tea [tee] *n* **1** dried leaves of plant cultivated esp. in (sub)tropical Asia. **2** infusion of it as beverage. **3** various herbal beverages. **4** tea, cakes, etc. as light afternoon meal. **5** *sl* marijuana. **tea bag** small porous bag of paper containing tea leaves. **tea'spoon** *n* small spoon for stirring tea, etc.

teach [teech] *v* **taught** [tawt], **teach·ing 1** instruct. **2** educate. **3** train. **4** impart knowledge of. **5** act as teacher. **teach'er** *n*

teak [teek] *n* **1** East Indian tree. **2** very hard wood obtained from it.

teal [teel] *n* **1** type of small duck. **2** greenish-blue color.

team [teem] *n* **1** set of animals, players of game, etc. associated in activity. ◆ *vi* **2** (usu. with *up*) (cause to) make a team. **team'ster** *n* driver of truck or team of draft animals. **team spirit** subordination of individual desire for good of team. **team'work** *n* cooperative work by team acting as unit.

tear¹ [teer] *n* drop of fluid appearing in and falling from eye. **tear'ful** [-fəl] *adj* **1** inclined to weep. **2** involving tears. **tear gas** irritant gas causing abnormal watering

of eyes, and temporary blindness. **tear·jerk·er** [TEER-jur-kər] *n inf* excessively sentimental story, moving picture, etc.

tear² [tair] *v* **tore**, **torn**, **tear·ing 1** pull apart, rend. **2** become torn. **3** rush. ◆ *n* **4** hole, cut or split.

tease [teez] *vt* **teased**, **teas·ing 1** tantalize, torment, irritate, bait. **2** pull apart fibers of. ◆ *n* **3** one who teases.

teat [teet] *n* **1** nipple of female breast. **2** rubber nipple of baby's feeding bottle.

tech·ni·cal [TEK-ni-kəl] *adj* **1** of, specializing in industrial, practical or mechanical arts and applied sciences. **2** skilled in practical and mechanical arts. **3** belonging to particular art or science. **4** according to letter of the law. **tech·ni·cal'i·ty** *n* **1** point of procedure. **2** state of being technical. **tech·ni'cian** [-NISH-ən] *n* one skilled in technique of an art. **tech·nique** [tek-NEEK] *n* **1** method of performance in an art. **2** skill required for mastery of subject. **technical college** higher educational institution specializing in mechanical and industrial arts and applied science, etc. **technical knockout** *Boxing* termination of bout by referee who judges that one boxer is not fit to continue.

tech·noc·ra·cy [tek-NOK-rə-see] *n* **1** government by technical experts. **2** example of this. **tech'no·crat** [-nə-krat] *n* **tech·nol·o·gy** [tek-NOL-ə-gee] *n, pl* **-gies 1** application of practical, mechanical

---

THESAURUS

try, weaken, weary

taxing *adj* = **demanding**, exacting, exhausting, onerous, punishing, sapping, stressful, tiring, tough, trying

teach *v* = **instruct**, coach, drill, educate, enlighten, guide, inform, show, train, tutor

teacher *n* = **instructor**, coach, educator, guide, lecturer, master or mistress, mentor, schoolteacher, trainer, tutor

team *n* **1** = **group**, band, body, bunch, company, gang, line-up, set, side, squad ◆ *v* **2** (often with *up*) = **join**, band together, cooperate, couple, get together, link, unite, work together

teamwork *n* = **cooperation**, collaboration, coordination, esprit de corps, fellowship, harmony, unity

tear *v* **1** = **rip**, claw, lacerate, mangle, mutilate, pull apart, rend, rupture, scratch, shred, split **2** = **rush**, bolt, charge, dash,

fly, hurry, race, run, speed, sprint, zoom ◆ *n* **3** = **hole**, laceration, rent, rip, rupture, scratch, split

tearful *adj* = **weeping**, blubbering, crying, in tears, lachrymose, sobbing, weepy (*inf*), whimpering

tears *pl n* **1** = **crying**, blubbering, sobbing, wailing, weeping **2 in tears** = **crying**, blubbering, distressed, sobbing, weeping

tease *v* = **mock**, goad, lead on, provoke, pull someone's leg (*inf*), tantalize, taunt, torment

technical *adj* = **scientific**, hi-tech or high-tech, skilled, specialist, specialized, technological

technique *n* **1** = **method**, approach, manner, means, mode, procedure, style, system, way **2** = **skill**, artistry, craft, craftsmanship, execution, performance, proficiency, touch sciences to industry, commerce. **2** technical methods, skills, knowledge. **tech·no·log'i·cal** *adj*

tec·ton·ic [tek-TON-ik] *adj* **1** of construction or building. **2** *Geology* pert. to (forces or condition of) structure of Earth's crust. **tec·ton'ics** *n* art, science of building.

te·di·ous [TEE-dee-əs] *adj* causing fatigue or boredom, monotonous. **te'di·um** [-əm] *n* monotony.

tee *n Golf* **1** slightly raised ground from which first stroke of hole is made. **2** small peg supporting ball for this stroke. **tee off 1** make first stroke of hole in golf. **2** *sl* scold. **3** *sl* irritate.

teem *vi* **1** abound with. **2** swarm. **3** be prolific. **4** pour, rain heavily.

teens [teenz] *pl n* years of life from 13 to 19. **teen'age** *adj* **teen'ag·er** *n* person in teens.

teepee *n* see TEPEE.

tee·ter [TEE-tər] *vi* **1** seesaw or make similar movements. **2** vacillate.

teeth pl. of TOOTH.

teethe [teeth] *vi* **teethed, teeth·ing** (of baby) grow first teeth. **teething ring** ring on which baby can bite.

tee·to·tal [tee-TOHT-l] *adj* pledged to abstain from alcohol. **tee·to'tal·er** *n*

tele- *comb. form* **1** at a distance, and from far off, e.g. *telecommunications.* **2** by telephone, e.g. *telebanking.* **3** of or involving television, e.g. *telecast.*

tel·e·cast [TEL-i-kast] *v, n* **-cast** or **-cast·ed, -cast·ing** (broadcast) TV program.

tel·e·com·mu·ni·ca·tions [tel-i-kə-myoo-ni-KAY-shənz] *n* science and technology of communications by telephony, radio, TV, etc.

tel·e·gram [TEL-i-gram] *n* message sent by telegraph.

tel·e·graph [TEL-i-graf] *n* **1** electrical

apparatus for transmitting messages to a distance. **2** any signaling device for transmitting messages. ◆ *v* **3** communicate by telegraph. **tel·e·graph'ic** *adj* **te·leg'ra·pher** *n* one who works telegraph. **te·leg'ra·phy** *n* **1** science of telegraph. **2** use of telegraph.

tel·e·mar·ket·ing [tel-ə-MAHR-ki-ting] *n* selling or advertising by telephone, television.

tel·e·ol·o·gy [tel-ee-OL-ə-jee] *n* **1** doctrine of final causes. **2** belief that things happen because of the purpose or design that will be fulfilled by them.

te·lep·a·thy [tə-LEP-ə-thee] *n* action of one mind on another at a distance. **tel·e·path'ic** [-ə-PATH-ik] *adj*

tel·e·phone [tel-ə-FOHN] *n* **1** apparatus for communicating sound to hearer at a distance. ◆ *v* **-phoned, -phon·ing 2** communicate, speak by telephone. **tel·e·phon'ic** [-FON-ik] *adj* **te·leph·o·ny** [tə-LEF-ə-nee] *n*

tel·e·pho·to [TEL-ə-foh-toh] *adj* (of lens) producing magnified image of distant object.

Tel·e·Promp·Ter [TEL-ə-promp-tər] *n* ® off-camera device to enable TV performer to refer to magnified script out of sight of the cameras.

tel·e·scope [TEL-ə-skohp] *n* **1** optical instrument for magnifying images of distant objects. ◆ *v* **-scoped, -scop·ing 2** slide or drive together, esp. parts designed to fit one inside the other. **3** make smaller, shorter. **tel·e·scop'ic** [-SKOP-ik] *adj*

tel·e·text [TEL-i-tekst] *n* electronic system that shows information, news, graphics on subscribers' TV screens.

tel·e·vi·sion [TEL-ə-vizh-ən] *n* **1** system of producing on screen images of distant objects, events, etc. by electromagnetic

—————— THESAURUS ——————

tedious *adj* = **boring**, drab, dreary, dull, humdrum, irksome, laborious, mind-numbing, monotonous, tiresome, wearisome

tedium *n* = **boredom**, drabness, dreariness, dullness, monotony, routine, sameness, tediousness

teeming[1] *adj* = **full**, abundant, alive, brimming, bristling, bursting, crawling, overflowing, swarming, thick

teeming[2] *adj* = **pouring**, pelting, raining cats and dogs (*inf*)

teenager *n* = **youth**, adolescent, boy, girl, juvenile, minor

teeter *v* = **wobble**, rock, seesaw, stagger, sway, totter, waver

teetotaler *n* = **abstainer**, nondrinker

telepathy *n* = **mind-reading**, E.S.P., sixth sense

telephone *n* **1** = **phone**, handset, line ◆ *v* **2** = **call**, dial, phone

telescope *n* **1** = **glass**, spyglass ◆ *v* **2** = **shorten**, abbreviate, abridge, compress, condense, contract, shrink radiation. **2** device for receiving this transmission and converting it to optical images. **3** programs, etc. viewed on TV set. **tel'e·vise** [-vīz] *vt* **-vised, -vis·ing 1** transmit by TV. **2** make, produce as TV program.

tel·e·work·ing [TEL-i-wurk-ing] *n* use of home computers, telephones, etc., to enable a person to work from home while maintaining contact with colleagues or customers. **tel'e·work·er** *n*

tell *v* told, tel·ling ♦ *vt* **1** let know. **2** order, direct. **3** narrate, make known. **4** discern. **5** distinguish. **6** count. ♦ *vi* **7** give account. **8** be of weight, importance. **9** reveal secrets. **tel'ler** *n* **1** narrator. **2** bank cashier. **telling** *adj* effective, striking. **tell'tale** *n* **1** sneak. **2** automatic indicator. ♦ *adj* **3** revealing.

tel·lu·ri·um [te-LUUR-ee-əm] *n* nonmetallic bluish-white element. **tel·lu'ric** *adj*

tem·blor [TEM-blər] *n* earthquake.

te·mer·i·ty [tə-MER-i-tee] *n* boldness, audacity.

temp *n* *inf* one employed on temporary basis.

tem·per [TEM-pər] *n* **1** frame of mind. **2** anger, oft. noisy. **3** mental constitution. **4** degree of hardness of steel, etc. ♦ *vt* **5** restrain, qualify, moderate. **6** harden. **7** bring to proper condition.

tem·per·a [TEM-pər-ə] *n* **1** emulsion used as painting medium. ♦ *n* **2** painting made with this.

tem·per·a·ment [TEM-pər-ə-mənt] *n* **1** natural disposition. **2** emotional mood. **3** mental constitution. **tem·per·a·men'tal** *adj* **1** given to extremes of temperament, moody. **2** of, occasioned by temperament.

tem·per·ate [TEM-pər-it] *adj* **1** not extreme. **2** showing, practicing moderation. **tem'per·ance** [-əns] *n* **1** moderation. **2** abstinence, esp. from alcohol.

tem·per·a·ture [TEM-pər-ə-chər] *n* **1** degree of heat or coldness. **2** *inf* (abnormally) high body temperature.

tem·pest [TEM-pist] *n* violent storm. **tem·pes·tu·ous** [tem-PES-choo-əs] *adj* **1** turbulent. **2** violent, stormy.

tem·plate [TEM-plit] *n* mold, pattern to

THESAURUS

television *n* = **TV**, small screen (*inf*), the tube (*sl*)

tell *v* **1** = **inform**, announce, communicate, disclose, divulge, express, make known, notify, proclaim, reveal, state **2** = **instruct**, bid, call upon, command, direct, order, require, summon **3** = **describe**, chronicle, depict, narrate, portray, recount, relate, report **4** = **distinguish**, differentiate, discern, discriminate, identify **5** = **carry weight**, count, have *or* take effect, make its presence felt, register, take its toll, weigh

telling *adj* = **effective**, considerable, decisive, forceful, impressive, influential, marked, powerful, significant, striking

telling-off *n* = **reprimand**, criticism, lecture, rebuke, reproach, reproof, scolding, talking-to

tell off *v* = **reprimand**, berate, censure, chide, lecture, rebuke, reproach, scold

temerity *n* = **boldness**, audacity, chutzpah (*inf*), effrontery, front, impudence, nerve (*inf*), rashness, recklessness

temper *n* **1** = **rage**, bad mood, fury, passion, tantrum **2** = **irritability**, hot-headedness, irascibility, passion, petulance, resentment, surliness **3** = **self-control**, calmness, composure, cool

(*sl*), equanimity **4** = **frame of mind**, constitution, disposition, humor, mind, mood, nature, temperament ♦ *v* **5** = **moderate**, assuage, lessen, mitigate, mollify, restrain, soften, soothe, tone down **6** = **strengthen**, anneal, harden, toughen

temperament *n* **1** = **nature**, bent, character, constitution, disposition, humor, make-up, outlook, personality, temper **2** = **excitability**, anger, hot-headedness, moodiness, petulance, volatility

temperamental *adj* **1** = **moody**, capricious, emotional, excitable, highly strung, hypersensitive, irritable, sensitive, touchy, volatile **2** = **unreliable**, erratic, inconsistent, inconstant, unpredictable

temperance *n* **1** = **moderation**, continence, discretion, forbearance, restraint, self-control, self-discipline, self-restraint **2** = **teetotalism**, abstemiousness, abstinence, sobriety

temperate *adj* **1** = **mild**, calm, cool, fair, gentle, moderate, pleasant **2** = **self-restrained**, calm, composed, dispassionate, even-tempered, mild, moderate, reasonable, self-controlled, sensible

tempest *n* = **gale**, cyclone, hurricane,

help shape something accurately.

tem·ple[1] [TEM-pəl] *n* 1 building for worship. 2 shrine.

temple[2] *n* flat part on either side of forehead.

tem·po [TEM-poh] *n, pl* **-pos** rate, rhythm, esp. in music.

tem·po·ral [TEM-pə-rəl] *adj* 1 of time. 2 of this life or world, secular.

tem·po·rar·y [TEM-pə-rer-ee] *adj* 1 lasting, used only for a time. ◆ *n, pl* **-ies** 2 person employed on temporary basis. **tem·po·rar·i·ly** *adv*

tem·po·rize [TEM-pə-rīz] *vi* **-ized, -iz·ing** 1 use evasive action. 2 hedge. 3 gain time by negotiation, etc. 4 conform to circumstances. **tem'po·riz·er** *n*

tempt *vt* 1 try to persuade, entice, esp. to something wrong or unwise. 2 dispose, cause to be inclined to. **temp·ta·tion** [-TAY-shən] *n* 1 act of tempting. 2 thing that tempts. **tempt'er, tempt'ress** *n* **tempt'ing** *adj* attractive, inviting.

ten *n, adj* cardinal number next after nine. **tenth** *adj, n* ordinal number.

ten·a·ble [TEN-ə-bəl] *adj* able to be held, defended, maintained.

te·na·cious [tə-NAY-shəs] *adj* 1 holding fast. 2 retentive. 3 stubborn. **te·nac'i·ty** [-NAS-i-tee] *n*

ten·ant [TEN-ənt] *n* one who holds lands, house, etc. on rent or lease. **ten'an·cy** *n, pl* **-cies**

tend[1] *vi* 1 be inclined. 2 be conducive. 3 make in direction of. **ten'den·cy** [-dən-see] *n, pl* **-cies** inclination, bent. **ten·den'tious** [-DEN-shəs] *adj* 1 having, showing tendency or bias. 2 controversial.

tend[2] *vt* take care of, watch over. **tend'er** *n* 1 small boat carried by yacht or ship. 2 carriage for fuel and water attached to steam locomotive. 3 one who tends, e.g. *bartender*.

ten·der[1] [TEN-dər] *adj* 1 not tough or hard. 2 easily injured. 3 gentle, loving, affectionate. 4 delicate, soft. **ten'der·ness** [-nis] *n* **ten'der·ize** *vt* **-ized, -iz·ing** soften (meat) by pounding or by treating (it) with substance made for this purpose. **ten'der·foot** [-fuut] *n, pl* **-feet** *or* **-foots** newcomer, esp. to ranch, etc.

tender[2] *vt* 1 offer. ◆ *vi* 2 make offer or estimate. ◆ *n* 3 offer. 4 offer or estimate for contract to undertake specific work. 5 what may legally be offered in payment.

ten·don [TEN-dən] *n* sinew attaching

squall, storm, tornado, typhoon

tempestuous *adj* 1 = **stormy**, blustery, gusty, inclement, raging, squally, turbulent, windy 2 = **violent**, boisterous, emotional, furious, heated, intense, passionate, stormy, turbulent, wild

temple *n* = **shrine**, church, place of worship, sanctuary

temporarily *adv* = **briefly**, fleetingly, for the time being, momentarily, pro tem

temporary *adj* = **impermanent**, brief, ephemeral, fleeting, interim, momentary, provisional, short-lived, transitory

tempt *v* = **entice**, allure, attract, coax, invite, lead on, lure, seduce, tantalize

temptation *n* = **enticement**, allurement, inducement, lure, pull, seduction, tantalization

tempting *adj* = **enticing**, alluring, appetizing, attractive, inviting, mouthwatering, seductive, tantalizing

tenable *adj* = **sound**, arguable, believable, defensible, justifiable, plausible, rational, reasonable, viable

tenacious *adj* 1 = **firm**, clinging, forceful, immovable, iron, strong, tight, unshakable

2 = **stubborn**, adamant, determined, dogged, obdurate, obstinate, persistent, resolute, steadfast, unswerving, unyielding

tenacity *n* = **perseverance**, application, determination, doggedness, obduracy, persistence, resolve, steadfastness, stubbornness

tenancy *n* = **lease**, occupancy, possession, renting, residence

tenant *n* = **leaseholder**, inhabitant, lessee, occupant, occupier, renter, resident

tend[1] *v* 1 = **be inclined**, be apt, be liable, gravitate, have a tendency, incline, lean 2 = **go**, aim, bear, head, lead, make for, point

tend[2] *v* = **take care of**, attend, cultivate, keep, look after, maintain, manage, nurture, watch over

tendency *n* = **inclination**, disposition, leaning, liability, proclivity, proneness, propensity, susceptibility

tender[1] *adj* 1 = **gentle**, affectionate, caring, compassionate, considerate, kind, loving, sympathetic, tenderhearted, warm-hearted 2 = **vulnerable**, immature, impressionable, inexperienced, raw, sensitive, young, muscle to bone, etc. **ten·di·ni'tis** [-NĪ-tis] *n* inflammation of tendon.

ten'dril *n* **1** slender curling stem by which climbing plant clings to anything. **2** curl, as of hair.

ten·e·ment [TEN-ə-mənt] *n* run-down apartment house, esp. in slum.

ten·et [TEN-it] *n* doctrine, belief.

ten'nis *n* game in which ball is struck with racket by players on opposite sides of net, lawn tennis. **tennis elbow** strained muscle as a result of playing tennis.

ten·on [TEN-ən] *n* tongue put on end of piece of wood, etc., to fit into a mortise.

ten·or [TEN-ər] *n* **1** male voice between alto and bass. **2** music for, singer with this. **3** general course, meaning.

tense[1] [tens] *n* modification of verb to show time of action.

tense[2] *adj* **tens·er, tens·est 1** stretched tight. **2** strained. **3** taut. **4** emotionally strained. ♦ *v* **tensed, tens·ing 5** make, become tense. **ten'sile** [-səl] *adj* **1** of, relating to tension. **2** capable of being stretched. **ten'sion** [-shən] *n* **1** stretching. **2** strain when stretched. **3** emotional strain or excitement. **4** hostility, suspense. **5** *Electricity* voltage.

tent *n* portable shelter of canvas, etc.

ten·ta·cle [TEN-tə-kəl] *n* elongated, flexible organ of some animals (e.g. octopus) used for grasping, feeding, etc.

ten·ta·tive [TEN-tə-tiv] *adj* **1** done as a trial. **2** experimental, cautious.

ten·ter·hooks [TEN-tər-huuks] *pl n* **on tenterhooks** in anxious suspense.

ten·u·ous [TEN-yoo-əs] *adj* **1** flimsy, uncertain. **2** thin, fine, slender.

ten·ure [TEN-yər] *n* (length of time of) possession, holding of office, position, etc.

te·pee, tee·pee [TEE-pee] *n* N Amer. Indian cone-shaped tent of animal skins.

tep'id *adj* **1** moderately warm, lukewarm. **2** half-hearted.

te·qui·la [tə-KEE-lə] *n* Mexican alcoholic liquor.

tera- *comb. form* denoting one million million (10^{12}), e.g. *terameter*.

ter·bi·um [TUR-bee-əm] *n* rare metallic element.

ter·cen·ten·ar·y [tur-sen-TEN-ə-ree] *adj, n, pl* **-nar·ies** (of) three-hundredth anniversary.

term [turm] *n* **1** word, expression. **2** limited period of time. **3** period during which courts sit, schools are open, etc. **4** limit, end. ♦ *pl* **5** conditions. **6** mutual relationship. ♦ *vt* **7** name, designate.

ter·mi·nal [TUR-mə-nl] *adj* **1** at, forming an end. **2** pert. to, forming a terminus. **3** (of disease) ending in death. ♦ *n* **4** terminal part or structure. **5** extremity. **6** point where current enters, leaves electrical device (e.g. battery). **7** device permitting operation of computer at some distance from it.

──── THESAURUS ────

youthful **3** = **sensitive**, bruised, inflamed, painful, raw, sore

tender[2] *v* **1** = **offer**, give, hand in, present, proffer, propose, put forward, submit, volunteer ♦ *n* **2** = **offer**, bid, estimate, proposal, submission **3** *As in* **legal tender** = **currency**, money, payment

tenderness *n* **1** = **gentleness**, affection, care, compassion, consideration, kindness, love, sentimentality, sympathy, warmth **2** = **soreness**, inflammation, pain, sensitivity

tense *adj* **1** = **nervous**, anxious, apprehensive, edgy, jumpy, keyed up, on edge, on tenterhooks, strained, uptight (*inf*), wired (*sl*) **2** = **stressful**, exciting, nerve-racking, worrying **3** = **tight**, rigid, strained, stretched, taut ♦ *v* **4** = **tighten**, brace, flex, strain, stretch

tension *n* **1** = **suspense**, anxiety, apprehension, hostility, nervousness,

pressure, strain, stress, unease **2** = **tightness**, pressure, rigidity, stiffness, stress, stretching, tautness

tentative *adj* **1** = **experimental**, conjectural, indefinite, provisional, speculative, unconfirmed, unsettled **2** = **hesitant**, cautious, diffident, doubtful, faltering, timid, uncertain, undecided, unsure

tenuous *adj* = **slight**, doubtful, dubious, flimsy, insubstantial, nebulous, shaky, sketchy, weak

tepid *adj* **1** = **lukewarm**, warmish **2** = **half-hearted**, apathetic, cool, indifferent, lukewarm, unenthusiastic

term *n* **1** = **word**, expression, name, phrase, title **2** = **period**, duration, interval, season, span, spell, time, while ♦ *v* **3** = **call**, designate, dub, entitle, label, name, style

terminal *adj* **1** = **deadly**, fatal, incurable, killing, lethal, mortal **2** = **final**, concluding,

ter·mi·nate [TUR-mə-nayt] v **-nat·ed,** **-nat·ing** bring, come to an end. **ter·mi·na'tion** [-shən] n

ter·mi·nol·o·gy [tur-mə-NOL-ə-jee] n, pl **-gies** 1 set of technical terms or vocabulary. 2 study of terms.

ter·mi·nus [TUR-mə-nəs] n, pl **-ni** [-nī] 1 finishing point. 2 farthest limit. 3 railroad station, bus station, etc. at end of long-distance line.

ter·mite [TUR-mīt] n insect, some species of which feed on and damage wood (also **white ant**).

ter·race [TER-əs] n 1 raised level place. 2 level cut out of hill. 3 row, street of houses built as one block. ◆ vt **-raced, -rac·ing** 4 form into, furnish with terrace.

ter·ra cot·ta [TER-ə KOT-ə] 1 hard unglazed pottery. 2 its color, a brownish-red.

ter·ra fir·ma [FUR-mə] Lat 1 firm ground. 2 dry land.

ter·rain [tə-RAYN] n area of ground, esp. with reference to its physical character.

ter·ra·pin [TER-ə-pin] n type of aquatic tortoise.

ter·rar·i·um [tə-RAIR-ee-əm] n, pl **-i·ums** enclosed container in which small plants,

animals are kept.

ter·raz·zo [tə-RAZ-oh] n floor, wall finish of chips of stone set in mortar and polished.

ter·res·tri·al [tə-RES-tree-əl] adj 1 of the earth. 2 of, living on land.

ter·ri·ble [TER-ə-bəl] adj 1 serious. 2 dreadful, frightful. 3 excessive. 4 causing fear. **ter·ri·bly** adv

ter·ri·er [TER-ee-ər] n small dog of various breeds, orig. for following quarry into burrow.

ter·rif·ic [tə-RIF-ik] adj 1 very great. 2 inf good, excellent. 3 terrible, awe-inspiring.

ter·ri·fy [TER-ə-fī] vt **-fied, -fy·ing** fill with fear, dread.

ter·ri·to·ry [TER-i-tor-ee] n, pl **-ries** 1 region. 2 geographical area under control of a political unit, esp. a sovereign state. 3 area of knowledge. **ter·ri·to'ri·al** adj

ter·ror [TER-ər] n 1 great fear. 2 inf troublesome person or thing. **ter'ror·ism** n 1 use of violence, intimidation to achieve ends. 2 state of terror. **ter'ror·ist** n, adj **ter'ror·ize** vt **-ized, -iz·ing** force, oppress by fear, violence.

terse [turs] adj **ters·er, ters·est** 1 expressed in few words, concise. 2 abrupt.

ter·ti·ar·y [TUR-shee-er-ee] adj 1 third in

———— THESAURUS ————

extreme, last, ultimate, utmost ◆ n 3 = **terminus,** depot, end of the line, station
terminate v = **end,** abort, cease, close, complete, conclude, discontinue, finish, stop
termination n = **ending,** abortion, cessation, conclusion, discontinuation, end, finish
terminology n = **language,** jargon, nomenclature, phraseology, terms, vocabulary
terminus n = **end of the line,** depot, garage, last stop, station
terms pl n 1 = **conditions,** particulars, provisions, provisos, qualifications, specifications, stipulations 2 = **relationship,** footing, relations, standing, status
terrain n = **ground,** country, going, land, landscape, topography
terrestrial adj = **earthly,** global, worldly
terrible adj 1 = **serious,** dangerous, desperate, extreme, severe 2 = **bad,** abysmal, awful, dire, dreadful, poor, rotten (inf) 3 = **fearful,** dreadful, frightful, horrendous, horrible, horrifying,

monstrous, shocking, terrifying
terribly adv = **extremely,** awfully (inf), decidedly, desperately, exceedingly, seriously, thoroughly, very
terrific adj 1 = **great,** enormous, fearful, gigantic, huge, intense, tremendous 2 Inf = **excellent,** amazing, brilliant, fantastic (inf), magnificent, marvelous, outstanding, sensational (inf), stupendous, superb, wonderful
terrified adj = **frightened,** alarmed, appalled, horrified, horror-struck, panic-stricken, petrified, scared
terrify v = **frighten,** alarm, appall, horrify, make one's hair stand on end, scare, shock, terrorize
territory n = **district,** area, country, domain, land, patch, province, region, zone
terror n 1 = **fear,** alarm, anxiety, dread, fright, horror, panic, shock 2 = **scourge,** bogeyman, bugbear, devil, fiend, monster
terrorize v = **oppress,** browbeat, bully, coerce, intimidate, menace, threaten
terse adj 1 = **concise,** brief, condensed, laconic, monosyllabic, pithy, short,

degree, order, etc. ◆ n **2** (**T-**) geological period before Quaternary.

tes·sel·late [TES-ə-layt] vt **-lat·ed, -lat·ing 1** make, pave, inlay with mosaic of small tiles. **2** (of identical shapes) fit together exactly. **tes'ser·a** [-ər-ə] n, pl **-ae** [-ee] stone used in mosaic.

test vt **1** try, put to the proof. **2** carry out test(s) on. ◆ n (critical) examination. **3** means of trial. **test'ing** adj **1** difficult. **test case** lawsuit viewed as means of establishing precedent. **test tube** narrow cylindrical glass vessel used in scientific experiments. **test-tube baby** baby conceived in artificial womb.

tes·ta·ment [TES-tə-mənt] n **1** Law will. **2** declaration. **3** (**T-**) one of the two main divisions of the Bible. **tes·ta·men'ta·ry** adj

tes·tate [TES-tayt] adj having left a valid will. **tes'ta·cy** n [-tə-see] state of being testate. **tes'ta·tor** [-tay-tər], (fem) **tes·ta·trix** [te-STAY-triks] n maker of will.

tes·ti·cle [TES-ti-kəl] n either of two male reproductive glands.

tes·ti·fy [TES-tə-fī] v **-fied, -fy·ing 1** declare. **2** bear witness (to).

tes·ti·mo·ny [TES-tə-moh-nee] n, pl **-nies 1** affirmation. **2** evidence. **tes·ti·mo'ni·al** [-əl] n **1** certificate of character, ability, etc. **2** gift, reception, etc. by organization or person expressing regard for recipient. ◆ adj

tes·tis n, pl **-tes** [-teez] testicle.

tes'ty adj **-ti·er, -ti·est** irritable, short-tempered. **tes'ti·ly** adv

tet·a·nus [TET-n-əs] n acute infectious disease producing muscular spasms, contractions (also **lockjaw**).

tête-à-tête [TAYT-ə-TAYT] n, pl **tête-à-têtes** [-tayts] Fr private conversation.

teth·er [TETH-ər] n **1** rope or chain for fastening (grazing) animal. ◆ vt **2** tie up with rope. **be at the end of one's tether** have reached limit of one's endurance.

Teu·ton·ic [too-TON-ik] adj **1** German. **2** of ancient Teutons.

text [tekst] n **1** (actual words of) book, passage, etc. **2** passage of Scriptures, etc., esp. as subject of discourse. ◆ v **3** send text message (to). **tex'tu·al** [-choo-əl] adj of, in a text. **text'book** n book of instruction on particular subject. **text message** message, usu. in form of coded abbreviations, sent from cell phone to cell phone.

tex·tile [TEKS-tīl] n **1** any fabric or cloth, esp. woven. ◆ adj **2** of (the making of) fabrics.

tex·ture [TEKS-chər] n **1** character, structure. **2** consistency.

Th Chem. thorium.

tha·lid·o·mide [thə-LID-ə-mīd] n drug formerly used as sedative, but found to cause abnormalities in developing fetus.

thal·li·um [THAL-ee-əm] n highly toxic metallic element. **thal'lic** adj

than [than] conj introduces second part of comparison.

thank [thangk] vt **1** express gratitude to. **2** say thanks. **3** hold responsible. **thanks** pl n words of gratitude. **thank'ful** [-fəl] adj grateful, appreciative. **thank'less** [-lis] adj **1** having, bringing no thanks. **2** unprofitable. **Thanks·giv'ing Day** public holiday in US, Canada.

that [that] adj, pron **1** used to refer to

THESAURUS

succinct **2 = curt**, abrupt, brusque, short, snappy

test v **1 = check**, analyze, assess, examine, experiment, investigate, put to the test, research, try out ◆ n **2 = examination**, acid test, analysis, assessment, check, evaluation, investigation, research, trial

testament n **1 = proof**, demonstration, evidence, testimony, tribute, witness **2 = will**, last wishes

testify v = **bear witness**, affirm, assert, attest, certify, corroborate, state, swear, vouch

testimonial n = **tribute**, commendation, endorsement, recommendation, reference

testimony n **1 = evidence**, affidavit,

deposition, statement, submission **2 = proof**, corroboration, demonstration, evidence, indication, manifestation, support, verification

testing adj = **difficult**, arduous, challenging, demanding, exacting, rigorous, searching, strenuous, taxing, tough

tether n **1 = rope**, chain, fetter, halter, lead, leash **2 at the end of one's tether = exasperated**, at one's wits' end, exhausted ◆ v **3 = tie**, bind, chain, fasten, fetter, secure

text n **1 = contents**, body **2 = words**, wording

texture n = **feel**, consistency, grain,

something already mentioned or familiar, or further away. ◆ *conj* **2** used to introduce a clause. ◆ *pron* **3** used to introduce a relative clause.

thatch [thach] *n* **1** reeds, straw, etc. used as roofing material. ◆ *vt* **2** to roof (a house) with reeds, straw, etc. **thatch'er** *n*

thaw *v* **1** melt. **2** (cause to) unfreeze. **3** defrost. **4** become warmer, or more genial. ◆ *n* **5** a melting (of frost, etc.).

the [thə, thee] *adj* the definite article.

the·a·ter [THEE-ə-tər] *n* **1** place where plays, etc. are performed. **2** drama, dramatic works generally. **3** large room with (tiered) seats, used for lectures, etc. **4** surgical operating room. **the·at'ri·cal** *adj* **1** of, for the theater. **2** exaggerated, affected.

thee [thee] *pron obs* objective and dative of THOU.

theft *n* stealing.

their [thair] *adj* of or associated with them. **theirs** *pron* (thing or person) belonging to them.

the·ism [THEE-iz-əm] *n* belief in creation of universe by one god. **the'ist** *n*

them [them] *pron* refers to people or things other than the speaker or those addressed. **themselves** *pron* emphatic and reflexive form of THEY or THEM.

theme [theem] *n* **1** main idea or topic of conversation, book, etc. **2** subject of composition. **3** recurring melody in music. **the·mat·ic** [thə-MAT-ik] *adj* **theme park** leisure area designed around one subject.

theme song one associated with particular program, person, etc.

then [then] *adv* **1** at that time. **2** next. **3** that being so.

thence [thens] *adv obs* from that place, point of reasoning, etc.

the·oc·ra·cy [thee-OK-rə-see] *n, pl* **-cies** government by a deity or a priesthood. **the·o·crat'ic** [-ə-KRAT-ik] *adj*

the·od·o·lite [thee-OD-l-īt] *n* surveying instrument for measuring angles.

the·ol·o·gy [thee-OL-ə-jee] *n, pl* **-gies** systematic study of religion(s) and religious belief(s). **the·o·lo·gian** [thee-ə-LOH-jən] *n*

the·o·rem [THEE-ər-əm, THEER-əm] *n* proposition that can be demonstrated by argument.

the·o·ry [THEE-ə-ree] *n, pl* **-ries 1** supposition to account for something. **2** system of rules and principles. **3** rules and reasoning, etc. as distinguished from practice. **the·o·ret'i·cal** *adj* **1** based on theory. **2** speculative, as opposed to practical. **the'o·rize** *vi* **-rized, -riz·ing** form theories, speculate.

the·os·o·phy [thee-OS-ə-fee] *n* any of various religious, philosophical systems claiming possibility of intuitive insight into divine nature.

ther·a·py [THER-ə-pee] *n, pl* **-pies** healing treatment. **ther·a·peu'tic** [-PYOO-tik] *adj* **1** of healing. **2** serving to improve or maintain health. **ther·a·peu'tics** *n* art of healing. **ther'a·pist** *n* esp. psychotherapist.

structure, surface, tissue

thank *v* = **say thank you**, show one's appreciation

thankful *adj* = **grateful**, appreciative, beholden, indebted, obliged, pleased, relieved

thankless *adj* = **unrewarding**, fruitless, unappreciated, unprofitable, unrequited

thanks *pl n* **1** = **gratitude**, acknowledgment, appreciation, credit, gratefulness, kudos, recognition **2 thanks to** = **because of**, as a result of, due to, owing to, through

thaw *v* = **melt**, defrost, dissolve, liquefy, soften, unfreeze, warm

theatrical *adj* **1** = **dramatic**, Thespian **2** = **exaggerated**, affected, dramatic, histrionic, mannered, melodramatic, ostentatious, showy, stagy

theft *n* = **stealing**, embezzlement, fraud,

larceny, pilfering, purloining, robbery, thieving

theme *n* **1** = **subject**, idea, keynote, subject matter, topic **2** = **motif**, leitmotif

theological *adj* = **religious**, doctrinal, ecclesiastical

theoretical *adj* = **abstract**, academic, conjectural, hypothetical, notional, speculative

theorize *v* = **speculate**, conjecture, formulate, guess, hypothesize, project, propound, suppose

theory *n* = **supposition**, assumption, conjecture, hypothesis, presumption, speculation, surmise, thesis

therapeutic *adj* = **beneficial**, corrective, curative, good, healing, remedial, restorative, salutary

therapist *n* = **healer**, physician

therapy *n* = **remedy**, cure, healing,

there [*thair*] *adv* **1** in that place. **2** to that point. **there·by'** *adv* by that means. **there'fore** *adv* in consequence, that being so. **there'up·on** *conj* at that point, immediately afterward.

therm [*thurm*] *n* unit of measurement of heat. **ther'mal** [-əl] *adj* **1** of, pert. to heat. **2** hot, warm (esp. of a spring, etc.).

therm·i·on [THURM-ī-ən] *n* ion emitted by incandescent body. **therm·i·on·ic** [thur-mee-ON-ik] *adj* pert. to thermion.

thermo- *comb. form* related to, caused by or producing heat.

ther·mo·dy·nam·ics [thur-moh-dī-NAM-iks] *n* the science that deals with the interrelationship and interconversion of different forms of energy.

ther·mom·e·ter [thə-MOM-ə-tər] *n* instrument to measure temperature. **ther·mo·met·ric** [thur-mə-MET-rik] *adj*

ther·mo·nu·cle·ar [thur-moh-NOO-klee-ər] *adj* involving nuclear fusion.

ther·mo·plas·tic [thur-mə-PLAS-tik] *n* plastic that retains its properties after being melted and solidified. ♦ *adj*

ther·mos [THUR-məs] *n* double-walled flask with vacuum between walls, for keeping contents of inner flask at temperature at which they were inserted.

ther·mo·stat [THUR-mə-stat] *n* apparatus for automatically regulating temperature. **ther·mo·stat'ic** *adj*

the·sau·rus [thi-SOR-əs] *n* **1** book containing lists of synonyms and antonyms. **2** dictionary of selected words, topics.

these [*theez*] pl. of THIS.

the·sis [THEE-sis] *n, pl* **-ses** [-seez] **1** written work submitted for degree, diploma. **2** theory maintained in argument.

thes·pi·an [THES-pee-ən] *adj* **1** theatrical. ♦ *n* **2** actor, actress.

they [*thay*] *pron* the third person plural pronoun.

thick [*thik*] *adj* **-er, -est 1** having great thickness, not thin. **2** dense, crowded. **3** viscous. **4** (of voice) throaty. **5** *inf* stupid, insensitive. **6** *inf* friendly. ♦ *n* **7** busiest, most intense part. **thick·en** [THIK-ən] *v* **1** make, become thick. **2** become more involved, complicated. **thick'ly** *adv* **thick'ness** [-nis] *n* **1** dimensions of anything measured through it, at right angles to length and breadth. **2** state of being thick. **3** layer. **thick·et** [THIK-it] *n* thick growth of small trees. **thick'set** *adj* **1** sturdy and solid of body. **2** set closely together.

thief [*theef*] *n, pl* **thieves** one who steals. **thieve** [*theev*] *v* **thieved, thiev·ing** steal. **thiev'ish** *adj*

thigh [*thī*] *n* upper part of leg.

thim·ble [THIM-bəl] *n* cap protecting end of finger when sewing.

thin *adj* **thin·ner, thin·nest 1** of little thickness. **2** slim. **3** lean. **4** of little density. **5** sparse. **6** fine. **7** loose, not close-packed. **8** *inf* unlikely. ♦ *v* **thinned, thin·ning 9** make, become thin. **thin'ness** [-nis] *n*

thine [*thīn*] *pron, adj obs* belonging to thee.

treatment

therefore *adv* = **consequently**, accordingly, as a result, ergo, hence, so, then, thence, thus

thesis *n* **1** = **dissertation**, essay, monograph, paper, treatise **2** = **proposition**, contention, hypothesis, idea, opinion, proposal, theory, view

thick *adj* **1** = **wide**, broad, fat, solid, substantial **2** = **dense**, close, compact, concentrated, condensed, heavy, impenetrable, opaque **3** *Inf* = **friendly**, close, devoted, familiar, inseparable, intimate, pally (*inf*) **4** = **full**, brimming, bristling, bursting, covered, crawling, packed, swarming, teeming **5 a bit thick** = **unfair**, unjust, unreasonable

thicken *v* = **set**, clot, coagulate, condense, congeal, jell

thicket *n* = **wood**, brake, coppice, copse, covert, grove

thickset *adj* = **well-built**, bulky, burly, heavy, muscular, stocky, strong, sturdy

thief *n* = **robber**, burglar, embezzler, housebreaker, pickpocket, pilferer, plunderer, shoplifter, stealer

thieve *v* = **steal**, filch, pilfer, pinch (*inf*), purloin, rob, swipe (*sl*)

thin *adj* **1** = **narrow**, attenuated, fine **2** = **slim**, bony, emaciated, lean, scrawny, skeletal, skinny, slender, slight, spare, spindly **3** = **meager**, deficient, scanty, scarce, scattered, skimpy, sparse, wispy **4** = **delicate**, diaphanous, filmy, fine, flimsy, gossamer, sheer, unsubstantial **5** = **unconvincing**, feeble, flimsy, inadequate,

thing n **1** material object. **2** any possible object of thought.

think [thingk] v **thought** [thawt], **think·ing** ◆ vi **1** have one's mind at work. **2** reflect, meditate. **3** reason. **4** deliberate. **5** imagine. **6** hold opinion. ◆ vt **7** conceive, consider in the mind. **8** believe. **9** esteem. **think'a·ble** adj able to be conceived, considered, possible, feasible. **thinking** adj reflecting. **think tank** group of experts studying specific problems.

third [thurd] adj **1** ordinal number corresponding to three. ◆ n **2** third part. **third degree** violent interrogation. **third party** Law person involved by chance or only incidentally in legal proceedings, etc. **Third World** developing countries of Africa, Asia, Latin Amer.

thirst [thurst] n **1** desire to drink. **2** feeling caused by lack of drink. **3** craving. **4** yearning. ◆ v **5** feel lack of drink. **thirst'y** adj **thirst·i·er, thirst·i·est**

thir·teen [thur-TEEN] adj, n three plus ten. **thir'ty** n, adj, pl **-ties** three times ten.

this [this] adj, pron **1** used to refer to a thing or person nearby, just mentioned, or about to be mentioned. ◆ adj **2** used to refer to the present time, e.g. this morning.

this·tle [THIS-əl] n prickly plant with dense flower heads.

thong [thawng] n **1** narrow strip of leather, strap. **2** type of light sandal.

thor·ax [THOR-aks] n part of body between neck and belly. **tho·rac·ic** [thaw-RAS-ik] adj

tho·ri·um [THOR-ee-əm] n radioactive metallic element.

thorn n **1** prickle on plant. **2** spine. **3** bush noted for its thorns. **4** anything that causes trouble or annoyance. **thorn'y** adj **thorn·i·er, thorn·i·est**

thor·ough [THUR-oh] adj **1** careful, methodical. **2** complete, entire. **thor'ough·ly** adv **thor'ough·bred** adj **1** of pure breed. ◆ n **2** purebred animal, esp. horse. **thor'ough·fare** [-fair] n **1** road or passage open at both ends. **2** right of way.

those [thohz] adj, pron pl. of THAT.

thou [thow] pron, pl **ye** or **you** obs the second person singular pronoun.

though [thoh] conj **1** in spite of the fact that, even if. ◆ adv **2** nevertheless.

thought [thawt] n **1** process of thinking. **2** what one thinks. **3** product of thinking. **4** meditation. **5** pt./pp. of THINK. **thought'ful** [-fəl] adj **1** considerate. **2** showing careful thought. **3** engaged in

lame, lousy (sl), poor, superficial, weak

thing n **1** = **object**, article, being, body, entity, something, substance **2** Inf = **obsession**, bee in one's bonnet, fetish, fixation, hang-up (inf), mania, phobia, preoccupation **3 things** = **possessions**, belongings, effects, equipment, gear, luggage, stuff

think v **1** = **believe**, consider, deem, estimate, imagine, judge, reckon, regard, suppose **2** = **ponder**, cerebrate, cogitate, contemplate, deliberate, meditate, muse, reason, reflect, ruminate

thinker n = **philosopher**, brain (inf), intellect (inf), mastermind, sage, theorist, wise man

thinking n **1** = **reasoning**, conjecture, idea, judgment, opinion, position, theory, view ◆ adj **2** = **thoughtful**, contemplative, intelligent, meditative, philosophical, rational, reasoning, reflective

think up v = **devise**, come up with, concoct, contrive, create, dream up, invent, visualize

thirst n **1** = **thirstiness**, drought, dryness **2** = **craving**, appetite, desire, hankering,

keenness, longing, passion, yearning

thirsty adj **1** = **parched**, arid, dehydrated, dry **2** = **eager**, avid, craving, desirous, greedy, hungry, longing, yearning

thorn n = **prickle**, barb, spike, spine

thorny adj = **prickly**, barbed, bristly, pointed, sharp, spiky, spiny

thorough adj **1** = **careful**, assiduous, conscientious, efficient, exhaustive, full, in-depth, intensive, meticulous, painstaking, sweeping **2** = **complete**, absolute, out-and-out, outright, perfect, total, unmitigated, unqualified, utter

thoroughbred adj = **purebred**, pedigree

thoroughfare n = **road**, avenue, highway, passage, passageway, street, way

thoroughly adv **1** = **carefully**, assiduously, conscientiously, efficiently, exhaustively, from top to bottom, fully, intensively, meticulously, painstakingly, scrupulously **2** = **completely**, absolutely, downright, perfectly, quite, totally, to the hilt, utterly

though conj **1** = **although**, even if, even though, notwithstanding, while ◆ adv **2** = **nevertheless**, for all that, however, nonetheless, notwithstanding, still, yet meditation. **4** attentive. **thought'less** [-lis] *adj* inconsiderate, careless, heedless.

thou·sand [THOW-zənd] *n, adj* cardinal number, ten hundred.

thrall [thrawl] *n* **1** slavery. **2** slave, bondsman. **thrall'dom** [-dəm] *n* bondage.

thrash *vt* **1** beat, whip soundly. **2** defeat soundly. **3** thresh. ♦ *vi* **4** move, plunge (esp. arms, legs) in wild manner. **thrash out 1** argue about from every angle. **2** solve by exhaustive discussion.

thread [thred] *n* **1** fine cord. **2** yarn. **3** ridge cut spirally on screw. **4** theme, meaning. ♦ *vt* **5** put thread into. **6** fit film, magnetic tape, etc. into machine. **7** put on thread. **8** pick (one's way, etc.). **thread'bare** [-bair] *adj* **1** worn, with nap rubbed off. **2** meager. **3** shabby.

threat [thret] *n* **1** declaration of intention to harm, injure, etc. **2** person or thing regarded as dangerous. **threat·en** [THRET-n] *vt* **1** utter threats against. **2** menace.

three *n, adj* cardinal number, one more than two. **three-ply** [-plī] *adj* having three layers (as wood) or strands (as wool). **three'some** [-səm] *n* group of three. **three-di·men'sion·al, 3-D** *adj* **1** having three dimensions. **2** simulating the effect of depth.

thresh *v* **1** beat, rub (wheat, etc.) to separate grain from husks and straw. **2** thrash.

thresh·old [THRESH-ohld] *n* **1** bar of stone or wood forming bottom of doorway. **2** entrance. **3** starting point. **4** point at which a stimulus is perceived, or produces a response.

threw [throo] *pt.* of THROW.

thrice [thrīs] *adv* three times.

thrift *n* **1** saving, economy. **2** savings organization. **3** genus of plant, sea pink. **thrift'y** *adj* **thrift·i·er, thrift·i·est** economical, frugal, sparing.

thrill *n* **1** sudden sensation of excitement and pleasure. ♦ *v* (cause to) feel a thrill. **2**

thought *n* **1** = **thinking**, brainwork, cogitation, consideration, deliberation, meditation, musing, reflection, rumination **2** = **idea**, concept, judgment, notion, opinion, view **3** = **consideration**, attention, heed, design, regard, scrutiny, study **4** = **intention**, aim, design, idea, notion, object, plan, purpose **5** = **expectation**, anticipation, aspiration, hope, prospect

thoughtful *adj* **1** = **considerate**, attentive, caring, helpful, kind, kindly, solicitous, unselfish **2** = **well-thought-out**, astute, canny, prudent **3** = **reflective**, contemplative, deliberative, meditative, pensive, ruminative, serious, studious

thoughtless *adj* = **inconsiderate**, impolite, insensitive, rude, selfish, tactless, uncaring, undiplomatic, unkind

thrash *v* **1** = **beat**, belt (*inf*), cane, flog, paddle (*U.S. & Canad.*), scourge, spank, whip **2** = **defeat**, beat, crush, run rings around (*inf*), slaughter (*inf*), trounce, wipe the floor with (*inf*) **3** = **thresh**, flail, jerk, toss and turn, writhe

thrashing *n* **1** = **beating**, belting (*inf*), flogging, punishment, whipping **2** = **defeat**, beating, hammering (*inf*), trouncing

thrash out *v* = **settle**, argue out, debate, discuss, have out, resolve, solve, talk over

thread *n* **1** = **strand**, fiber, filament, line,

string, yarn **2** = **theme**, direction, drift, plot, story line, train of thought ♦ *v* **3** = **pass**, ease, pick (one's way), squeeze through

threadbare *adj* **1** = **shabby**, down at heel, frayed, old, ragged, tattered, tatty, worn **2** = **hackneyed**, commonplace, conventional, familiar, overused, stale, stereotyped, tired, trite, well-worn

threat *n* **1** = **warning**, foreboding, foreshadowing, omen, portent, presage, writing on the wall **2** = **danger**, hazard, menace, peril, risk

threaten *v* **1** = **intimidate**, browbeat, bully, lean on (*sl*), menace, pressurize, terrorize **2** = **endanger**, imperil, jeopardize, put at risk, put in jeopardy, put on the line **3** = **foreshadow**, forebode, impend, portend, presage

threatening *adj* **1** = **menacing**, bullying, intimidatory **2** = **ominous**, forbidding, grim, inauspicious, sinister

threshold *n* **1** = **entrance**, door, doorstep, doorway **2** = **start**, beginning, brink, dawn, inception, opening, outset, verge **3** = **minimum**, lower limit

thrift *n* = **frugality**, carefulness, economy, parsimony, prudence, saving, thriftiness

thrifty *adj* = **economical**, careful, frugal, parsimonious, provident, prudent, saving, sparing vibrate, tremble. **thrill'er** n book, motion picture, etc. with story of mystery, suspense. **thrill'ing** adj exciting.

thrive [thrīv] vi **thrived** or **throve** [throhv] **thrived** or **thriv·en, thriv·ing 1** grow well. **2** flourish, prosper.

throat [throht] n **1** front of neck. **2** either or both of passages through it. **throat'y** adj **throat·i·er, throat·i·est** (of voice) hoarse.

throb vi **throbbed, throb·bing 1** beat, quiver strongly, pulsate. ♦ n **2** pulsation, beat. **3** vibration.

throes [throhz] pl n condition of violent pangs, pain, etc. **in the throes of** in the process of.

throm·bo·sis [throm-BOH-sis] n formation of clot of coagulated blood in blood vessel or heart.

throne [throhn] n **1** ceremonial seat, powers and duties of king or queen. ♦ vt **throned, thron·ing 2** place on throne, declare king, etc.

throng [thrawng] n, v crowd.

throt·tle [THROT-l] n **1** device controlling amount of fuel entering engine and thereby its speed. ♦ vt **-tled, -tling 2** strangle. **3** suppress. **4** restrict (flow of liquid, etc.).

through [throo] prep **1** from end to end, from side to side of. **2** between the sides

of. **3** in consequence of. **4** by means or fault of. ♦ adv **5** from end to end. **6** to the end. ♦ adj **7** completed. **8** finished. **9** continuous. **10** (of transport, traffic) not stopping. **through·out'** [-OWT] adv, prep in every part (of). **through'put** [-puut] n quantity of material processed, esp. by computer. **through train** train that travels whole (unbroken) length of long journey. **carry through** accomplish.

throve [throhv] pt. of THRIVE.

throw [throh] vt **threw** [throo], **thrown, throw·ing 1** fling, cast. **2** move, put abruptly, carelessly. **3** give, hold (party, etc.). **4** cause to fall. **5** shape on potter's wheel. **6** move (switch, lever, etc.). **7** inf baffle, disconcert. ♦ n **8** act or distance of throwing. **throw'back** n **1** one who, that which reverts to character of an ancestor. **2** this process.

thrush[1] n songbird.

thrush[2] n **1** fungal disease of mouth, esp. in infants. **2** foot disease of horses.

thrust v **thrust, thrust·ing 1** push, drive. **2** stab. **3** push one's way. ♦ n **4** lunge, stab with pointed weapon, etc. **5** cutting remark. **6** propulsive force or power.

thud n **1** dull heavy sound. ♦ vi **thud·ded, thud·ding 2** make thud.

thug n brutal, violent person.

——————| THESAURUS |——————

thrill n **1** = **pleasure**, buzz (sl), kick (inf), stimulation, tingle, titillation ♦ v **2** = **excite**, arouse, electrify, move, stimulate, stir, titillate

thrilling adj = **exciting**, electrifying, gripping, riveting, rousing, sensational, stimulating, stirring

thrive v = **prosper**, boom, develop, do well, flourish, get on, grow, increase, succeed

thriving adj = **prosperous**, blooming, booming, burgeoning, flourishing, healthy, successful, well

throb v **1** = **pulsate**, beat, palpitate, pound, pulse, thump, vibrate ♦ n **2** = **pulse**, beat, palpitation, pounding, pulsating, thump, thumping, vibration

throng n **1** = **crowd**, crush, horde, host, mass, mob, multitude, pack, swarm ♦ v **2** = **crowd**, congregate, converge, flock, mill around, pack, swarm around

throttle v = **strangle**, choke, garrotte, strangulate

through prep **1** = **between**, by, past **2** =

because of, by means of, by way of, using, via **3** = **during**, in, throughout ♦ adj **4** = **finished**, completed, done, ended ♦ adv **5** **through and through** = **completely**, altogether, entirely, fully, thoroughly, totally, utterly, wholly

throughout adv = **everywhere**, all over, from start to finish, right through

throw v **1** = **hurl**, cast, chuck (inf), fling, launch, lob (inf), pitch, send, sling, toss **2** Inf = **confuse**, astonish, baffle, confound, disconcert, dumbfound, faze ♦ n **3** = **toss**, fling, heave, lob (inf), pitch, sling

throwaway adj = **casual**, careless, offhand, passing, understated

throw away v = **discard**, dispense with, dispose of, ditch (sl), dump (inf), get rid of, jettison, reject, scrap, throw out

thrust v **1** = **push**, drive, force, jam, plunge, propel, ram, shove ♦ n **2** = **push**, drive, lunge, poke, prod, shove, stab **3** = **momentum**, impetus

thud n, v = **thump**, clunk, crash, knock, smack

thumb [thum] *n* **1** first, shortest, thickest finger of hand. ♦ *vt* **2** handle, dirty with thumb. **3** make hitchhiker's signal to get ride. **4** flick through (pages of book, etc.).

thump *n* **1** dull heavy blow. **2** sound of one. ♦ *vt* **3** strike heavily.

thun·der [THUN-dər] *n* **1** loud noise accompanying lightning. ♦ *vi* **2** rumble with thunder. **3** make noise like thunder. ♦ *vt* **4** utter loudly. **thun'der·ous** [-əs] *adj* **thun'der·bolt** [-bohlt], **thun'der·clap** *n* **1** lightning flash followed by peal of thunder. **2** anything totally unexpected and unpleasant. **thun'der·struck** *adj* amazed.

thus [thus] *adv* **1** in this way. **2** therefore.

thwack [thwak] *vt, n* whack.

thwart [thwort] *vt* **1** foil, frustrate, baffle. ♦ *adv* **2** *obs* across. ♦ *n* **3** seat across a boat.

thy [thī] *adj obs* belonging to thee. **thy·self'** *pron* emphasized form of THOU.

thyme [tīm] *n* aromatic herb.

thy·mus [THĪ-məs] *n* small ductless gland in upper part of chest.

thy·roid gland [THĪ-roid] endocrine gland controlling body growth, situated (in people) at base of neck.

ti, te [tee] *n* seventh sol-fa note.

Ti *Chem.* titanium.

ti·ar·a [tee-AR-ə] *n* woman's jeweled head ornament, coronet.

tib·i·a [TIB-ee-ə] *n, pl* **-i·as** thicker inner bone of lower leg.

tic [tik] *n* spasmodic twitch in muscles, esp. of face.

tick¹ [tik] *n* **1** slight tapping sound, as of watch movement. **2** small mark (✓). ♦ *vt* **3** mark with tick. ♦ *vi* **4** make the sound. **tick·er tape** continuous paper ribbon. **tick off 1** mark off. **2** reprimand. **3** make angry. **tick over 1** (of engine) idle. **2** continue to function smoothly.

tick² *n* small insect-like parasite living on and sucking blood of warm-blooded animals.

tick³ *n* mattress case. **tick'ing** *n* strong material for mattress covers.

tick·et [TIK-it] *n* **1** card, paper entitling holder to admission, travel, etc. **2** list of candidates of one party for election. ♦ *vt* **3** attach label to. **4** issue tickets to.

tick·le [TIK-əl] *v* **-led, -ling** ♦ *vt* **1** touch, stroke, poke (person, part of body, etc.) to produce laughter, etc. **2** please, amuse. ♦ *vi* **3** be irritated, itch. ♦ *n* **4** act, instance of this. **tick'lish** *adj* **1** sensitive to tickling. **2** requiring care or tact.

tid'bit *n* **1** tasty morsel of food. **2** pleasing scrap (of scandal, etc.).

tide [tīd] *n* **1** rise and fall of sea happening twice each lunar day. **2** stream. **3** season, time. **tid'al** [-əl] *adj* of, like tide. **tidal wave** great wave, esp. produced by earthquake. **tide over** help someone for a while, esp. by loan, etc.

ti·dings [TĪ-dingz] *pl. n* news.

ti·dy [TĪ-dee] *adj* **-di·er, -di·est 1** orderly, neat. **2** of fair size. ♦ *vt* **-died, -dy·ing 3** put in order.

tie [tī] *v* **tied, ty·ing 1** equal (score of). ♦ *vt* **2**

━━━━━━ THESAURUS ━━━━━━

thug *n* = **ruffian**, bruiser (*inf*), bully boy, gangster, hooligan, tough

thump *n* **1** = **crash**, bang, clunk, thud, thwack **2** = **blow**, clout (*inf*), knock, punch, rap, smack, wallop (*inf*), whack ♦ *v* **3** = **strike**, beat, clobber (*sl*), clout (*inf*), hit, knock, pound, punch, smack, wallop (*inf*), whack

thunder *n* **1** = **rumble**, boom, crash, explosion ♦ *v* **2** = **rumble**, boom, crash, peal, resound, reverberate, roar **3** = **shout**, bark, bellow, roar, yell

thunderous *adj* = **loud**, booming, deafening, ear-splitting, noisy, resounding, roaring, tumultuous

thunderstruck *adj* = **amazed**, astonished, astounded, dumbfounded, flabbergasted (*inf*), open-mouthed, shocked, staggered, stunned, taken aback

thus *adv* **1** = **therefore**, accordingly, consequently, ergo, for this reason, hence, on that account, so, then **2** = **in this way**, as follows, like this, so

thwart *v* = **frustrate**, foil, hinder, obstruct, outwit, prevent, snooker, stymie

tick¹ *n* **1** = **mite**, bug, insect **2** = **tapping**, clicking, ticktock

tick² *n* = **credit**, account

ticket *n* **1** = **voucher**, card, certificate, coupon, pass, slip, token **2** = **label**, card, docket, marker, slip, sticker, tab, tag

tidbit *n* = **delicacy**, dainty, morsel, snack, treat

tide *n* **1** = **current**, ebb, flow, stream, tideway, undertow **2** = **tendency**, direction, drift, movement, trend

tidy *adj* **1** = **neat**, clean, methodical, orderly, shipshape, spruce, well-kept, fasten, bind, secure. **3** restrict. ◆ *n* **4** that with which anything is bound. **5** restriction, restraint. **6** long, narrow piece of material worn knotted around neck. **7** bond. **8** connecting link. **9** drawn game, contest. **10** match, game in eliminating competition. **tie'-dye-ing** *n* way of dyeing cloth in patterns by tying sections tightly so they will not absorb dye.

tier [teer] *n* row, rank, layer.

tiff *n* petty quarrel.

ti·ger [TI-gər] *n* large carnivorous feline animal.

tight [tīt] *adj* **-er, -est 1** taut, tense. **2** closely fitting. **3** secure, firm. **4** not allowing passage of water, etc. **5** cramped. **6** *inf* mean, stingy. **7** *sl* drunk. **tights** *pl n* one-piece clinging garment covering body from waist to feet. **tight'en** [-ən] *v* **tight'rope** *n* rope stretched taut above the ground, on which acrobats perform.

tile [tīl] *n* **1** flat piece of ceramic, plastic, etc. **2** material used for roofs, walls, floors, fireplaces, etc. ◆ *vt* **tiled, til-ing 3** cover with tiles.

till¹ *prep* **1** up to the time of. ◆ *conj* **2** to the time that.

till² *vt* cultivate. **till'er** *n*

till³ *n* **1** drawer for money in store. **2** cash register.

til·ler [TIL-ər] *n* lever to move rudder of boat.

tilt *v* **1** incline, slope, slant. **2** tip up. ◆ *vi* **3** take part in medieval combat with lances. **4** thrust, aim (at). ◆ *n* **5** slope, incline. **6** *Hist.* combat for mounted men with lances, joust.

tim·ber [TIM-bər] *n* **1** wood for building, etc. **2** trees suitable for the sawmill. **tim'bered** *adj* **1** made of wood. **2** covered with trees. **timber line** geographical limit beyond which trees will not grow.

tim·bre [TAM-bər] *n* quality of musical sound, or sound of human voice.

time [tīm] *n* **1** existence as a succession of states. **2** hour. **3** duration. **4** period. **5** point in duration. **6** opportunity. **7** occasion. **8** leisure. **9** tempo. ◆ *vt* **timed, tim-ing 10** choose time for. **11** note time taken by. **time'ly** *adj* at opportune or appropriate time. **tim'er** [-ər] *n* person, device for recording or indicating time. **time bomb 1** bomb designed to explode at arranged time. **2** situation resembling this. **time-honored** [-on-ərd] *adj* respectable because old. **time-lag** *n* period of time between cause and effect. **time'piece** [-pees] *n* watch, clock. **time share** *n* system of part ownership of vacation property for specified period each year. **time'ta·ble** *n* plan showing hours of work, times of arrival and departure, etc. **Greenwich Mean Time** [GREN-ich] world standard time, time as settled by passage of sun over the meridian at Greenwich, England.

well-ordered **2** *Inf* = **considerable**, ample, generous, goodly, handsome, healthy, large, sizable *or* sizeable, substantial ◆ *v* **3** = **neaten**, clean, groom, order, spruce up, straighten

tie *v* **1** = **fasten**, attach, bind, connect, join, knot, link, secure, tether **2** = **restrict**, bind, confine, hamper, hinder, limit, restrain **3** = **draw**, equal, match ◆ *n* **4** = **bond**, affiliation, allegiance, connection, liaison, relationship **5** = **fastening**, bond, cord, fetter, knot, ligature, link **6** = **draw**, dead heat, deadlock, gridlock, stalemate

tier *n* = **row**, bank, layer, level, line, rank, story, stratum

tight *adj* **1** = **stretched**, close, constricted, cramped, narrow, rigid, snug, taut **2** *Inf* = **miserly**, grasping, mean, niggardly, parsimonious, stingy, tightfisted **3** = **close**, even, evenly-balanced, well-matched

tighten *v* = **squeeze**, close, constrict, narrow

till¹ *v* = **cultivate**, dig, plow, work

till² *n* = **cash register**, cash box

tilt *v* **1** = **slant**, heel, incline, lean, list, slope, tip ◆ *n* **2** = **slope**, angle, inclination, incline, list, pitch, slant **3** *Medieval history* = **joust**, combat, duel, fight, lists, tournament **4 (at) full tilt** = **full speed**, for dear life, headlong

timber *n* = **wood**, beams, boards, logs, planks, trees

timbre *n* = **tone**, color, resonance, ring

time *n* **1** = **period**, duration, interval, season, space, span, spell, stretch, term **2** = **occasion**, instance, juncture, point, stage **3** *Mus* = **tempo**, beat, measure, rhythm ◆ *v* **4** = **schedule**, set

timeless *adj* = **eternal**, ageless, changeless, enduring, everlasting, immortal, lasting, permanent

tim'id *adj* **1** easily frightened. **2** lacking self-confidence. **ti·mid'i·ty** *n* **tim'or·ous** [-ər-əs] *adj* **1** timid. **2** indicating fear.

tim·pa·ni [TIM-pə-nee] *pl n* set of kettledrums. **tim'pa·nist** *n*

tin *n* **1** malleable metal. ◆ *vt* **tinned, tin·ning 2** coat with tin. **tin'ny** *-ni·er, -ni·est* **1** (of sound) thin, metallic. **2** cheap, shoddy.

tinc·ture [TINGK-chər] *n* **1** solution of medicinal substance in alcohol. **2** color, stain. ◆ *vt* **-tured, -tur·ing 3** color, tint.

tin·der [TIN-dər] *n* dry easily-burning material used to start fire.

tine [tīn] *n* tooth, spike of fork, antler, etc.

tinge [tinj] *n* **1** slight trace, flavor. ◆ *vt* **tinged, tinge·ing 2** color, flavor slightly.

tin·gle [TING-gəl] *vi* **-gled, -gling** feel thrill or pricking sensation. ◆ *n*

tin'ker [TING-kər] *n* **1** formerly, traveling mender of pots and pans. ◆ *vi* **2** fiddle, meddle (e.g. with machinery) oft. inexpertly.

tin·kle [TING-kəl] *v* **-kled, -kling 1** (cause to) give out series of light sounds like small bell. ◆ *n* **2** this sound or action.

tin·sel [TIN-səl] *n* **1** glittering metallic substance for decoration. **2** anything sham and showy.

tint *n* **1** color. **2** shade of color. **3** tinge. ◆ *vt* **4** dye, give tint to.

ti·ny [TĪ-nee] *adj* **-ni·er, -ni·est** very small, minute.

tip¹ *n* **1** slender or pointed end of anything. **2** piece of metal, leather, etc. protecting an extremity. ◆ *vt* **tipped, tip·ping 3** put a tip on.

tip² *n* **1** small present of money given for service rendered. **2** helpful piece of information. **3** warning, hint. ◆ *vt* **tipped, tip·ping 4** give tip to. **tip'ster** [-stər] *n* one who sells tips about races, etc.

tip³ *v* **tipped, tip·ping** ◆ *vt* **1** tilt, upset. **2** touch lightly. ◆ *vi* **3** topple over.

tip·ple [TIP-əl] *v* **-pled, -pling 1** drink (liquor) habitually, esp. in small quantities. ◆ *n* **2** drink of liquor. **tip'pler** [-lər] *n*

tip·sy *adj* **-si·er, -si·est** drunk, partly drunk.

tip·toe *vi* **-toed, -to·ing 1** walk on ball of foot and toes. **2** walk softly.

ti·rade [TĪ-rayd] *n* long speech, generally vigorous and hostile, denunciation.

tire¹ [tīr] *v* **tired, tir·ing** ◆ *vt* **1** reduce energy of, esp. by exertion. **2** bore. **3** irritate. ◆ *vi* **4** become tired, wearied, bored. **tire'some** [-səm] *adj* wearisome, irritating, tedious.

tire² *n* (inflated) rubber or synthetic rubber ring over rim of road vehicle.

———— THESAURUS ————

timely *adj* = **opportune**, appropriate, convenient, judicious, propitious, seasonable, suitable, well-timed

timetable *n* = **schedule**, agenda, calendar, curriculum, diary, list, program

timid *adj* = **fearful**, apprehensive, bashful, coy, diffident, faint-hearted, shrinking, shy, timorous

timorous *adj* = **timid**, apprehensive, bashful, coy, diffident, faint-hearted, fearful, shrinking, shy

tinge *n* **1** = **tint**, color, shade **2** = **bit**, dash, drop, smattering, sprinkling, suggestion, touch, trace ◆ *v* **3** = **tint**, color, imbue, suffuse

tingle *v* **1** = **prickle**, have goose pimples, itch, sting, tickle ◆ *n* **2** = **quiver**, goose pimples, itch, pins and needles (*inf*), prickling, shiver, thrill

tinker *v* = **meddle**, dabble, fiddle (*inf*), mess about, play, potter

tint *n* **1** = **shade**, color, hue, tone **2** = **dye**, rinse, tincture, tinge, wash ◆ *v* **3** = **dye**, color

tiny *adj* = **small**, diminutive, infinitesimal, little, microscopic, miniature, minute, negligible, petite, slight

tip¹ *n* **1** = **end**, extremity, head, peak, pinnacle, point, summit, top ◆ *v* **2** = **cap**, crown, finish, surmount, top

tip² *n* **1** = **gratuity**, gift **2** = **hint**, clue, pointer, suggestion, warning ◆ *v* **3** = **reward**, remunerate **4** = **advise**, caution, forewarn, suggest, warn

tip³ *v* **1** = **tilt**, incline, lean, list, slant **2** = **dump**, empty, pour out, unload ◆ *n* **3** = **dump**, refuse heap, rubbish heap

tipple *v* **1** = **drink**, imbibe, indulge (*inf*), quaff, swig, tope ◆ *n* **2** = **alcohol**, booze (*inf*), drink, liquor

tipsy *adj* = **drunk**, fuzzy, happy, mellow, three sheets to the wind

tirade *n* = **outburst**, diatribe, fulmination, harangue, invective, lecture

tire *v* **1** = **fatigue**, drain, exhaust, wear out, weary **2** = **bore**, exasperate, irk, irritate, weary

tired *adj* **1** = **exhausted**, drained, drowsy, fatigued, flagging, jaded, sleepy, weary, worn out **2** = **bored**, fed up, sick, weary **3** =

tis·sue [TISH-oo] *n* **1** substance of animal body, plant, etc. **2** fine, soft paper, esp. used as handkerchief, etc. **3** fine woven fabric. **4** interconnection e.g. of lies.

tit[1] *n* any of various small songbirds.

tit[2] *n sl* female breast.

ti·tan·ic [tī-TAN-ik] *adj* huge, epic.

ti·ta·ni·um [tī-TAY-nee-əm] *n* rare metal of great strength and rust-resisting qualities.

tit for tat blow for blow, retaliation.

tithe [tīth] *n* **1** esp. formerly, one tenth part of agricultural produce paid for the upkeep of the clergy or as tax. ◆ *v* **tithed, tith·ing** ◆ *vt* **2** exact tithes from. ◆ *vi* **3** give, pay tithe.

ti·tian [TISH-ən] *adj* (of hair) reddish-gold, auburn.

tit·il·late [TIT-l-ayt] *vt* **-lat·ed, -lat·ing** tickle, stimulate agreeably.

ti·tle [TĪT-l] *n* **1** name of book. **2** heading. **3** name. **4** appellation denoting rank. **5** legal right or document proving it. **6** *Sports* championship. **title deed** legal document as proof of ownership.

tit·ter [TIT-ər] *vi* **1** laugh in suppressed way. ◆ *n* **2** such laugh.

tit·tle [TIT-l] *n* whit, detail.

tit·tle-tat·tle [TIT-l-tat-l] *n, vi* **-tled, -tling** gossip.

tit·u·lar [TICH-ə-lər] *adj* **1** pert. to title. **2** nominal. **3** held by virtue of a title.

tiz·zy [TIZ-ee] *n sl pl* **-zies** state of confusion, anxiety.

Tl *Chem.* thallium.

Tm *Chem.* thulium.

to *prep* **1** toward, in the direction of. **2** as far

as. **3** used to introduce a comparison, ratio, indirect object, infinitive, etc. ◆ *adv* **4** to the required or normal state or position.

toad [tohd] *n* animal like frog. **toad·y** *n, pl* **toad·ies 1** obsequious flatterer, sycophant. ◆ *vi* **toad·ied, toad·y·ing 2** do this. **toad·stool** *n* fungus like mushroom, but usu. poisonous.

toast [tohst] *n* **1** slice of bread crisped and browned on both sides by heat. **2** tribute, proposal of health, success, etc. made by company of people and marked by drinking together. **3** one toasted. ◆ *vt* **4** crisp and brown (as bread). **5** drink toast to. **6** dry or warm at fire. **toast·er** *n* **1** electrical device for toasting bread.

to·bac·co [tə-BAK-oh] *n, pl* **-cos** or **-coes 1** plant with leaves used for smoking. **2** the prepared leaves.

to·bog·gan [tə-BOG-ən] *n* **1** sled for sliding down slope of snow. ◆ *vi* **2** slide on one.

toc·ca·ta [tə-KAH-tə] *n* rapid piece of music for keyboard instrument.

toc·sin [TOK-sin] *n* alarm signal, bell.

to·day [tə-DAY] *n* **1** this day. ◆ *adv* **2** on this day. **3** nowadays.

tod·dle [TOD-l] *vi* **-dled, -dling 1** walk with unsteady short steps. ◆ *n* **2** toddling. **tod·dler** [-lər] *n* **1** child beginning to walk.

tod·dy [TOD-ee] *n, pl* **-dies** sweetened mixture of alcoholic liquor, hot water, etc.

to-do [tə-DOO] *n inf pl* **-dos** fuss, commotion.

toe [toh] *n* **1** digit of foot. **2** anything resembling toe in shape or position. ◆ *vt* **toed, toe·ing 3** reach, touch with toe. **toe**

THESAURUS

hackneyed, clichéd, corny (*sl*), old, outworn, stale, threadbare, trite, well-worn

tireless *adj* = **energetic**, indefatigable, industrious, resolute, unflagging, untiring, vigorous

tiresome *adj* = **boring**, dull, irksome, irritating, tedious, trying, vexatious, wearing, wearisome

tiring *adj* = **exhausting**, arduous, demanding, exacting, laborious, strenuous, tough, wearing

titillate *v* = **excite**, arouse, interest, stimulate, tantalize, tease, thrill

titillating *adj* = **exciting**, arousing, interesting, lurid, provocative, stimulating, suggestive, teasing

title *n* **1** = **name**, designation, handle (*sl*), moniker *or* monicker (*sl*), term **2** =

championship, crown **3** = **ownership**, claim, entitlement, prerogative, right

titter *v* = **laugh**, chortle (*inf*), chuckle, giggle, snigger

tizzy *n Inf* = **panic**, agitation, commotion, fluster, state (*inf*), sweat (*inf*)

toady *n* **1** = **sycophant**, brown-noser (*sl*), creep (*sl*), flatterer, flunkey, hanger-on, lackey, minion, scuzzbucket (*sl*), yes man ◆ *v* **2** = **flatter**, brown-nose (*sl*), fawn on, grovel, kiss ass (*sl*), kowtow to, pander to, suck up to (*inf*)

toast[1] *v* = **warm**, brown, grill, heat, roast

toast[2] *n* **1** = **tribute**, compliment, health, pledge, salutation, salute **2** = **favorite**, darling, hero *or* heroine ◆ *v* **3** = **drink to**, drink (to) the health of, salute

DICTIONARY

the line conform.

tof·fee [TAW-fee] *n* brittle candy made of sugar and butter, etc.

to·ga [TOH-gə] *n, pl* **-gas** loose outer garment worn by ancient Romans.

to·geth·er [tə-GETH-ər] *adv* **1** in company, simultaneously. ◆ *adj* **2** *sl* (well) organized.

tog·gle [TOG-əl] *n* **1** small wooden, metal peg fixed crosswise on cord, wire, etc. and used for fastening as button. **2** any similar device.

togs [togz] *pl n* clothes.

toil *n* **1** heavy work or task. ◆ *vi* **2** labor. **toil'worn** *adj* **1** weary with toil. **2** hard and lined.

toi·let [TOI-lit] *n* **1** lavatory. **2** ceramic toilet bowl. **3** process of washing, dressing. **4** articles used for this.

to·ken [TOH-kən] *n* **1** sign or object used as evidence. **2** symbol. **3** disk used as money. ◆ *adj* **4** nominal, slight.

told [tohld] pt./pp. of TELL.

tol·er·ate [TOL-ə-rayt] *vt* **-at·ed, -at·ing 1** put up with. **2** permit. **tol·er·a·ble** *adj* **1** bearable. **2** fair, moderate. **tol'er·ance** [-əns] *n* (degree of) ability to endure stress, pain, radiation, etc. **tol'er·ant** [-ənt] *adj* **1** disinclined to interfere with others' ways or opinions. **2** forbearing. **3** broad-minded.

toll¹ [tohl] *vt* **1** make (bell) ring slowly at regular intervals. **2** announce death thus. ◆ *vi* **3** ring thus. ◆ *n* **4** tolling sound.

toll² *n* **1** tax, esp. for the use of bridge or road. **2** loss, damage incurred through accident, disaster, etc.

tom *n* male of some animals, esp. cat.

tom·a·hawk [TOM-ə-hawk] *n* **1** formerly, fighting ax of N Amer. Indians. ◆ *vt* **2** strike, kill with one.

to·ma·to [tə-MAY-toh] *n, pl* **-toes 1** plant with red fruit. **2** the fruit, used in salads, etc.

tomb [toom] *n* **1** grave. **2** monument over one. **tomb'stone** *n* gravestone.

tom·boy [TOM-boi] *n* **1** girl who acts, dresses in boyish way.

tome [tohm] *n* large book or volume.

tom·fool·er·y [tom-FOO-lə-ree] *n, pl* **-er·ies** nonsense, silly behavior.

to·mog·ra·phy [tə-MOG-rə-fee] *n* technique used to obtain an X-ray photograph of a plane section of the human body or some other object.

to·mor·row [tə-MOR-oh] *adv, n* (on) the

THESAURUS

together *adv* **1** = **collectively**, as one, hand in glove, in concert, in unison, jointly, mutually, shoulder to shoulder, side by side **2** = **at the same time**, at one fell swoop, concurrently, contemporaneously, simultaneously ◆ *adj* **3** *Inf* = **well-organized**, composed, well-adjusted, well-balanced

toil *n* **1** = **hard work**, application, drudgery, effort, elbow grease (*inf*), exertion, slog, sweat ◆ *v* **2** = **work**, drudge, labor, slave, slog, strive, struggle, sweat (*inf*), work one's fingers to the bone

toilet *n* = **lavatory**, bathroom, convenience, gents (*Brit. inf*), ladies' room, latrine, privy, urinal, water closet, W.C.

token *n* **1** = **symbol**, badge, expression, indication, mark, note, representation, sign ◆ *adj* **2** = **nominal**, hollow, minimal, perfunctory, superficial, symbolic

tolerable *adj* **1** = **bearable**, acceptable, allowable, endurable, sufferable, supportable **2** = **fair**, acceptable, adequate, all right, average, O.K. *or* okay (*inf*), passable

tolerance *n* **1** = **broad-mindedness**, forbearance, indulgence, open-mindedness, permissiveness **2** = **endurance**, fortitude, hardiness, resilience, resistance, stamina, staying power, toughness

tolerant *adj* = **broad-minded**, catholic, forbearing, liberal, long-suffering, open-minded, understanding, unprejudiced

tolerate *v* = **allow**, accept, brook, condone, endure, permit, put up with (*inf*), stand, stomach, take

toleration *n* = **acceptance**, allowance, endurance, indulgence, permissiveness, sanction

toll¹ *v* **1** = **ring**, chime, clang, knell, peal, sound, strike ◆ *n* **2** = **ringing**, chime, clang, knell, peal

toll² *n* **1** = **charge**, duty, fee, levy, payment, tariff, tax **2** = **damage**, cost, loss, penalty

tomb *n* = **grave**, catacomb, crypt, mausoleum, sarcophagus, sepulcher, vault

tombstone *n* = **gravestone**, headstone, marker, memorial, monument

tomfoolery *n* = **foolishness**, buffoonery, clowning, fooling around (*inf*), horseplay, shenanigans (*inf*), silliness, skylarking (*inf*), stupidity day after today.

tom-tom *n* drum associated with N Amer. Indians or with Asia.

ton [tun] *n* **1** measure of weight equal to 2000 pounds or 907 kilograms (short ton). **2** measure of weight equal to 2240 pounds or 1016 kilograms (long ton). **ton·nage** [TUN-ij] *n* **1** carrying capacity. **2** charge per ton. **3** ships collectively.

tone [tohn] *n* **1** quality of musical sound. **2** quality of voice, color, etc. **3** general character, style. **4** healthy condition. ◆ *vt* **toned, ton·ing 5** give tone to. **6** blend, harmonize (with). **ton'er** [-ər] *n* substance that modifies color or composition. **ton'al** [-əl] *adj* **to·nal'i·ty** *n, pl* **-ties** tone poem orchestral work based on story, legend, etc.

tongs [tongz] *pl n* large pincers, esp. for handling coal, sugar.

tongue [tung] *n* **1** muscular organ inside mouth, used for speech, taste, etc. **2** various things shaped like this. **3** language, speech, voice.

ton·ic [TON-ik] *n* **1** medicine to improve bodily tone or condition. **2** *Mus.* keynote. **3** *Mus.* first note of scale. ◆ *adj* **4** invigorating, restorative. **5** of tone. **tonic (water)** mineral water oft. containing quinine.

to·night [tə-NĪT] *n* **1** this night. **2** the coming night. ◆ *adv* **3** on this night.

ton·sil [TON-səl] *n* gland in throat. **ton·sil·li'tis** [-LĪ-tis] *n* inflammation of tonsils. **ton·sil·lec·to·my** [-sə-LEK-tə-mee] *n, pl* **-mies** surgical removal of tonsil(s).

ton·sure [TON-shər] *n* **1** shaving of part of head as religious or monastic practice. **2** part shaved. ◆ *vt* **-sured, -sur·ing 3** shave thus.

too *adv* **1** also, in addition. **2** in excess, overmuch.

took [tuuk] *pt.* of TAKE.

tool *n* **1** implement or appliance for mechanical operations. **2** servile helper. **3** means to an end. ◆ *vt* **4** work on with tool, esp. chisel stone. **5** indent design on leather book cover, etc. **tool'ing** *n* **1** decorative work. **2** setting up, etc. of tools, esp. for machine operation.

tooth *n, pl* **teeth 1** bonelike projection in gums of upper and lower jaws of vertebrates. **2** various pointed things like this. **3** prong, cog.

top¹ *n* **1** highest part, summit. **2** highest rank. **3** first in merit. **4** garment for upper part of body. **5** lid, stopper of bottle, etc. ◆ *vt* **topped, top'ping 6** cut off, pass, reach, surpass top. **7** provide top for. **top'less** [-lis] *adj* (of costume, woman) with no covering for breasts. **top'most** [-mohst] *adj* **1** supreme. **2** highest. **top dressing** layer of fertilizer spread on the surface of land. **top hat** man's hat with tall cylindrical crown. **top-heavy** *adj* **1** unbalanced. **2** with top too heavy for base. **top-notch** *adj* excellent, first-class. **top-secret** *adj* needing highest level of secrecy, security. **top'soil** *n* **1** surface layer of soil. **2** more fertile soil spread on lawns, etc.

top² *n* toy that spins on tapering point or ball bearing.

to·paz [TOH-paz] *n* precious stone of various colors.

———— THESAURUS ————

ton *n* (often plural) *Inf* = **a lot**, great deal, ocean, quantity, stacks

tone *n* **1** = **pitch**, inflection, intonation, modulation, timbre **2** = **character**, air, attitude, feel, manner, mood, spirit, style, temper **3** = **color**, hue, shade, tinge, tint ◆ *v* **4** = **harmonize**, blend, go well with, match, suit

tone down *v* = **moderate**, play down, reduce, restrain, soften, subdue, temper

tongue *n* = **language**, dialect, parlance, speech

tonic *n* = **stimulant**, boost, pick-me-up (*inf*), restorative, shot in the arm (*inf*)

too *adv* **1** = **also**, as well, besides, further, in addition, likewise, moreover, to boot **2** = **excessively**, extremely, immoderately, inordinately, overly, unduly, unreasonably, very

tool *n* **1** = **implement**, appliance, contraption, contrivance, device, gadget, instrument, machine, utensil **2** = **puppet**, cat's-paw, creature, flunkey, hireling, lackey, minion, pawn, stooge (*sl*)

top *n* **1** = **peak**, apex, crest, crown, culmination, head, height, pinnacle, summit, zenith **2** = **first place**, head, lead **3** = **lid**, cap, cover, stopper ◆ *adj* **4** = **leading**, best, chief, elite, finest, first, foremost, head, highest, pre-eminent, principal, uppermost ◆ *v* **5** = **cover**, cap, crown, finish, garnish **6** = **lead**, be first, head **7** = **surpass**, beat, best, better, eclipse, exceed, excel, outstrip, transcend

to·pee [toh-PEE] *n* lightweight hat made of pith.

to·pi·ar·y [TOH-pee-er-ee] *adj* (of shrubs) shaped by cutting or pruning, made ornamental by trimming or training. ◆ *n*

top·ic [TOP-ik] *n* subject of discourse, conversation, etc. **top'i·cal** [-ik-əl] *adj* 1 up-to-date, having news value. 2 of topic.

to·pog·ra·phy [tə-POG-rə-fee] *n, pl* **-phies** (description of) surface features of a place. **to·pog'ra·pher** *n*

top·ple [TOP-əl] *v* **-pled, -ling** (cause to) fall over, collapse.

top·sy·tur·vy [TOP-see-TUR-vee] *adj, adv* upside down, in confusion.

tor *n* high, rocky hill.

To·rah [TOH-rə] *n* parchment on which is written the Pentateuch.

torch *n* 1 portable hand light containing electric battery and bulb. 2 burning brand, etc. 3 any apparatus burning with hot flame, e.g. for welding. **torch'bear·er** [-bair-ər] *n*

tore pt. of TEAR².

tor·e·a·dor [TOR-ee-ə-dor] *n* bullfighter.

tor·ment' *v* 1 torture in body or mind. 2 afflict. 3 tease. ◆ *n* [TOR-ment] 4 suffering, torture, agony of body or mind.

torn pp. of TEAR².

tor·na·do [tor-NAY-doh] *n, pl* **-does** 1 whirlwind. 2 violent storm.

tor·pe·do [tor-PEE-doh] *n, pl* **-does** 1 cylindrical self-propelled underwater missile with explosive warhead, fired esp. from submarine. ◆ *vt* **-doed, -do·ing** 2 strike, sink with, as with, torpedo.

tor·pid *adj* sluggish, apathetic. **tor·por** [TOR-pər] *n* torpid state.

torque [tork] *n* 1 collar, similar ornament of twisted gold or other metal. 2 *Mechanics* rotating or twisting force.

tor·rent [TOR-ənt] *n* 1 a rushing stream. 2 downpour. **tor·ren·tial** [tə-REN-shəl] *adj* 1 resembling a torrent. 2 overwhelming.

tor·rid [TOR-id] *adj* 1 parched, dried with heat. 2 highly emotional. **Torrid Zone** land between tropics.

tor·sion [TOR-shən] *n* twist, twisting.

tor·so [TOR-soh] *n, pl* **-sos** 1 (statue of) body without head or limbs. 2 trunk.

tort *n Law* private or civil wrong.

tor·til·la [tor-TEE-yə] *n, pl* **-til·las** thin Mexican pancake.

tor·toise [TOR-təs] *n* four-footed reptile covered with shell of horny plates. **tor'toise·shell** *n* mottled brown shell of hawksbill turtle used commercially. ◆ *adj*

tor·tu·ous [TOR-choo-əs] *adj* 1 winding, twisting. 2 involved, not straightforward.

tor·ture [TOR-chər] *n* 1 infliction of severe pain. ◆ *vt* **-tured, -tur·ing** 2 subject to torture. **tor'tur·er** *n*

toss [taws] *vt* 1 throw up, about. ◆ *vi* 2 be thrown, fling oneself about. ◆ *n* 3 act of

——————| THESAURUS |——————

topic *n* = **subject**, issue, matter, point, question, subject matter, theme

topical *adj* = **current**, contemporary, newsworthy, popular, up-to-date, up-to-the-minute

topmost *adj* = **highest**, dominant, foremost, leading, paramount, principal, supreme, top, uppermost

topple *v* 1 = **fall over**, collapse, fall, keel over, overbalance, overturn, totter, tumble 2 = **overthrow**, bring down, bring low, oust, overturn, unseat

topsy-turvy *adj* = **confused**, chaotic, disorderly, disorganized, inside-out, jumbled, messy, mixed-up, upside-down

torment *v* 1 = **torture**, crucify, distress, rack 2 = **tease**, annoy, bother, harass, hassle (*inf*), irritate, nag, pester, vex ◆ *n* 3 = **suffering**, agony, anguish, distress, hell, misery, pain, torture

torn *adj* 1 = **cut**, lacerated, ragged, rent, ripped, slit, split 2 = **undecided**, in two minds (*inf*), irresolute, uncertain, unsure, vacillating, wavering

tornado *n* = **whirlwind**, cyclone, gale, hurricane, squall, storm, tempest, typhoon

torpor *n* = **inactivity**, apathy, drowsiness, indolence, laziness, lethargy, listlessness, sloth, sluggishness

torrent *n* = **stream**, cascade, deluge, downpour, flood, flow, rush, spate, tide

torrid *adj* 1 = **arid**, dried, parched, scorched 2 = **passionate**, ardent, fervent, intense, steamy (*inf*)

tortuous *adj* 1 = **winding**, circuitous, convoluted, indirect, mazy, meandering, serpentine, sinuous, twisting, twisty 2 = **complicated**, ambiguous, convoluted, devious, indirect, involved, roundabout, tricky

torture *v* 1 = **torment**, afflict, crucify, distress, persecute, put on the rack, rack ◆ *n* 2 = **agony**, anguish, distress, pain, persecution, suffering, torment tossing.

tot[1] *n* very small child.

tot[2] *v* **tot·ted, tot·ting 1** (with *up*) add up. **2** amount to.

to·tal [TOHT-l] *n* **1** whole amount. **2** sum, aggregate. ◆ *adj* **3** complete, entire, full, absolute. ◆ *v* **-taled, -tal·ing 4** amount to. **5** add up. **to·tal'i·ty** *n*, *pl* **-ties to·tal·i·za·tor** [TOHT-l-ə-zay-tər] *n* machine to operate system of betting at racetrack in which money is paid out to winners in proportion to their bets.

to·tal·i·tar·i·an [toh-tal-i-TAIR-ee-ən] *adj* of dictatorial, one-party government.

tote[1] [toht] *n* short for TOTALIZATOR.

tote[2] *vt* **tot·ed, tot·ing** haul, carry.

to·tem [TOH-təm] *n* tribal badge or emblem. **totem pole** post carved, painted with totems, esp. by Amer. Indians.

tot·ter [TOT-ər] *vi* **1** walk unsteadily. **2** begin to fall.

touch [tuch] *n* **1** sense by which qualities of object, etc. are perceived by touching. **2** characteristic manner or ability. **3** touching. **4** slight blow, stroke, contact, amount, etc. ◆ *vt* **5** come into contact

with. **6** put hand on. **7** reach. **8** affect emotions of. **9** deal with, handle. **10** eat, drink. **11** *sl* (try to) borrow from. ◆ *vi* **12** be in contact. **13** (with *on*) refer to. **touch'ing** *adj* **1** emotionally moving. ◆ *prep* **2** concerning. **touch'y** *adj* **touch·i·er, touch·i·est** easily offended, sensitive. **touch'down** *n* **1** *Football* crossing of goal line with football. **2** act of, moment of, landing of aircraft. **touch'stone** *n* criterion. **touch and go** precarious (situation). **touch base** make contact, renew communication.

tou·ché [too-SHAY] *interj* acknowledgment that blow (orig. in fencing), remark, etc. has been successful.

tough [tuf] *adj* **-er, -est 1** strong, resilient, not brittle. **2** sturdy. **3** able to bear hardship, strain. **4** difficult. **5** needing effort to chew. **6** rough. **7** uncivilized. **8** violent. **9** unlucky, unfair. ◆ *n* **10** rough, violent person. **tough'en** [-ən] *v* **tough'ness** [-nis] *n*

tou·pee [too-PAY] *n* man's hairpiece, wig.

tour [toor] *n* **1** traveling around. **2** journey to one place after another. **3** excursion. ◆ *v*

————————| THESAURUS |————————

toss *v* **1** = **throw**, cast, fling, flip, hurl, launch, lob (*inf*), pitch, sling **2** = **thrash**, rock, roll, shake, wriggle, writhe ◆ *n* **3** = **throw**, lob (*inf*), pitch

tot[1] *n* = **infant**, baby, child, mite, toddler

total *n* **1** = **whole**, aggregate, entirety, full amount, sum, totality ◆ *adj* **2** = **complete**, absolute, comprehensive, entire, full, gross, thoroughgoing, undivided, utter, whole ◆ *v* **3** = **amount to**, come to, mount up to, reach **4** = **add up**, reckon, tot up

totalitarian *adj* = **dictatorial**, authoritarian, despotic, oppressive, tyrannous, undemocratic

totality *n* = **whole**, aggregate, entirety, sum, total

totally *adv* = **completely**, absolutely, comprehensively, entirely, fully, one hundred per cent, thoroughly, utterly, wholly

totter *v* = **stagger**, falter, lurch, reel, stumble, sway

touch *v* **1** = **handle**, brush, caress, contact, feel, finger, fondle, stroke, tap **2** = **meet**, abut, adjoin, be in contact, border, contact, graze, impinge upon **3** = **affect**, disturb, impress, influence, inspire, move, stir **4** = **eat**, chow down (*sl*), consume,

drink, partake of **5** = **match**, compare with, equal, hold a candle to (*inf*), parallel, rival **6 touch on** = **refer to**, allude to, bring in, cover, deal with, mention, speak of ◆ *n* **7** = **feeling**, handling, physical contact **8** = **tap**, brush, contact, pat, stroke **9** = **bit**, dash, drop, jot, small amount, smattering, soupçon, spot, trace **10** = **style**, manner, method, technique, trademark, way

touch and go *adj* = **risky**, close, critical, near, nerve-racking, precarious

touching *adj* = **moving**, affecting, emotive, pathetic, pitiable, poignant, sad, stirring

touchstone *n* = **standard**, criterion, gauge, measure, norm, par, yardstick

touchy *adj* = **oversensitive**, irascible, irritable, querulous, quick-tempered, testy, tetchy, thin-skinned

tough *adj* **1** = **resilient**, durable, hard, inflexible, leathery, resistant, rugged, solid, strong, sturdy **2** = **strong**, hardy, seasoned, stout, strapping, sturdy, vigorous **3** = **rough**, hard-boiled, pugnacious, ruthless, violent **4** = **strict**, firm, hard, merciless, resolute, severe, stern, unbending **5** = **difficult**, arduous, exacting, hard, laborious, strenuous, troublesome, uphill **6** *Inf* = **unlucky**, lamentable, regrettable,

4 make tour (of). **tour·ism** n **1** tourist travel. **2** this as an industry. **tour·ist** n one who travels for pleasure.

tour de force [toor də FORS] Fr brilliant stroke, achievement.

tour·ma·line [TUUR-mə-lin] n crystalline mineral used for optical instruments and as gem.

tour·na·ment [TUUR-nə-mənt] n competition, contest usu. with several stages to decide overall winner. **tour·ney** [TUUR-nee] n, pl **-neys** tournament.

tour·ni·quet [TUR-ni-kit] n bandage, surgical instrument to constrict artery and stop bleeding.

tou·sle [TOW-zəl] vt **-sled, -sling 1** tangle, ruffle. **2** treat roughly.

tout [towt] vi **1** solicit trade (usu. in undesirable fashion). **2** obtain and sell information about racehorses, etc. ♦ n **3** one who touts.

tow¹ [toh] vt **1** drag along behind, esp. at end of rope. ♦ n **2** towing or being towed. **3** vessel, vehicle in tow. **tow'path** n path beside canal, river, orig. for towing.

tow² n fiber of hemp, flax. **tow-head·ed** [-hed-id] adj with pale-colored, or rumpled hair.

to·ward [tord], **to·wards** [tordz] prep **1** in direction of. **2** with regard to. **3** as contribution to.

tow·el [TOW-əl] n cloth for wiping off moisture after washing. **tow'el·ing** n material used for making towels.

tow·er [TOW-ər] n **1** tall strong structure often forming part of church or other large building. **2** fortress. ♦ vi **3** stand very high. **4** loom (over).

town n collection of dwellings, etc. larger than village and smaller than city. **town'ship** n small town. **towns'peo·ple** n

tox·ic [TOK-sik] adj **1** poisonous. **2** due to poison. **tox·e·mi·a** [tok-SEEM-ee-ə] n blood poisoning. **tox·ic'i·ty** [-IS-i-tee] n strength of a poison. **tox·i·col·o·gy** [tok-si-KOL-ə-jee] n study of poisons. **tox'in** n poison of bacterial origin.

toy [toi] n **1** something designed to be played with. **2** (miniature) replica. ♦ adj **3** very small. ♦ vi **4** act idly, trifle.

trace¹ [trays] n **1** track left by anything. **2** indication. **3** minute quantity. ♦ vt **traced, trac·ing 4** follow course, track of. **5** find out. **6** make plan of. **7** draw or copy exactly, esp. using tracing paper. **trace element** chemical element occurring in very small quantity in soil, etc. **tracer** bullet or shell that leaves visible trail so that aim can be checked. **tracing paper** transparent paper placed over drawing, map, etc. to enable exact copy to be taken.

trace² n chain, strap by which horse pulls vehicle. **kick over the traces** become defiant, independent.

tra·che·a [TRAY-kee-ə] n, pl **-che·as** windpipe. **tra·che·al** [-əl] adj **tra·che·ot'o·my** [-OT-ə-mee] n, pl **-mies** surgical incision into trachea.

tra·cho·ma [trə-KOH-mə] n contagious viral disease of eye.

track [trak] n **1** mark, line of marks, left by passage of anything. **2** path. **3** rough road. **4** course. **5** railroad line. **6** distance between two road wheels on one axle. **7** circular jointed metal band driven by wheels as on tank, bulldozer, etc. **8** course

unfortunate ♦ n

tour n **1 = journey**, excursion, expedition, jaunt, outing, trip ♦ v **2 = visit**, explore, go round, journey, sightsee, travel through

tourist n **= traveler**, excursionist, globetrotter, holiday-maker, sightseer, tripper, voyager

tournament n **= competition**, contest, event, meeting, series

tow v **= drag**, draw, haul, lug, pull, tug

towards prep **1 = in the direction of**, en route for, for, on the way to, to **2 = regarding**, about, concerning, for, with regard to, with respect to

tower n **= column**, belfry, obelisk, pillar, skyscraper, steeple, turret

towering adj **= high**, colossal, elevated, imposing, impressive, lofty, magnificent, soaring, tall

toxic adj **= poisonous**, deadly, harmful, lethal, noxious, pernicious, pestilential, septic

toy n **1 = plaything**, doll, game ♦ v **2 = play**, amuse oneself, dally, fiddle (inf), fool (about or around), trifle

trace v **1 = find**, detect, discover, ferret out, hunt down, track, unearth **2 = copy**, draw, outline, sketch ♦ n **3 = track**, footmark, footprint, footstep, path, spoor, trail **4 = bit**, drop, hint, shadow, suggestion, suspicion, tinge, touch, whiff **5 = indication**, evidence, mark, record, for running or racing. **9** separate section on phonograph record. **10** class, division of schoolchildren grouped together because of similar ability. ◆ *vt* **11** follow trail or path of. **12** find thus. **track record** past accomplishments of person, company, etc.

tract[1] [trakt] *n* **1** wide expanse, area. **2** *Anatomy* system of organs, etc. with particular function.

tract[2] *n* treatise or pamphlet, esp. religious one. **trac'tate** [-tayt] *n* short tract.

trac·ta·ble [TRAK-tə-bəl] *adj* easy to manage, docile, amenable.

trac·tion [TRAK-shən] *n* action of drawing, pulling. **traction engine** locomotive running on surfaces other than tracks.

trac·tor [TRAK-tər] *n* motor vehicle for hauling, pulling, etc.

trade [trayd] *n* **1** commerce, business. **2** buying and selling. **3** any profitable pursuit. **4** those engaged in trade. ◆ *v* **trad·ed, trad·ing 5** engage in trade. **6** buy and sell. **7** barter. **trade-in** *n* used article given in part payment for new. **trade'mark, -name** *n* distinctive mark (secured by legal registration) on maker's goods. **trades'man** [-mən] *n, pl* **-men 1** person engaged in trade. **2** skilled worker.

trade union society of workers for protection of their interests. **trade wind** wind blowing constantly toward equator in certain parts of globe.

tra·di·tion [trə-DISH-ən] *n* **1** unwritten body of beliefs, facts, etc. handed down from generation to generation. **2** custom, practice of long standing. **3** process of handing down.

tra·duce [trə-DOOS] *vt* **-duced, -duc·ing** slander.

traf·fic [TRAF-ik] *n* **1** vehicles passing to and fro in street, town, etc. **2** (illicit) trade. ◆ *vi* **-ficked, -fick·ing 3** trade, esp. in illicit goods, e.g. drugs. **traf'fick·er** *n* trader. **traffic lights** set of colored lights at road junctions, etc. to control flow of traffic.

trag·e·dy [TRAJ-i-dee] *n, pl* **-dies 1** sad or calamitous event. **2** dramatic, literary work dealing with serious, sad topic and with ending marked by (inevitable) disaster. **tra·ge·di·an** [trə-JEE-dee-ən] *n* actor in, writer of tragedies. **trag'ic** *adj* **1** of, in manner of tragedy. **2** disastrous. **3** appalling. **trag'i·cal·ly** *adv*

trail [trayl] *vt* **1** drag behind one. ◆ *vi* **2** be drawn behind. **3** hang, grow loosely. ◆ *n* **4** track or trace. **5** thing that trails. **6** rough ill-defined track in wild country. **trail'er** *n* **1**

remnant, sign, survival, vestige

track *n* **1** = **path**, course, line, orbit, pathway, road, trajectory, way **2** = **trail**, footmark, footprint, footstep, mark, path, spoor, trace, wake **3** = **line**, permanent way, rails ◆ *v* **4** = **follow**, chase, hunt down, pursue, shadow, stalk, tail (*inf*), trace, trail

track down *v* = **find**, dig up, discover, hunt down, run to earth *or* ground, sniff out, trace, unearth

tract[1] *n* = **area**, district, expanse, extent, plot, region, stretch, territory

tract[2] *n* = **treatise**, booklet, dissertation, essay, homily, monograph, pamphlet

tractable *adj* = **manageable**, amenable, biddable, compliant, docile, obedient, submissive, tame, willing, yielding

traction *n* = **grip**, friction, pull, purchase, resistance

trade *n* **1** = **commerce**, barter, business, dealing, exchange, traffic, transactions, truck **2** = **job**, business, craft, employment, line of work, métier, occupation, profession ◆ *v* **3** = **deal**, bargain, do

business, have dealings, peddle, traffic, transact, truck **4** = **exchange**, barter, swap, switch

trader *n* = **dealer**, merchant, purveyor, seller, supplier

tradesman *n* **1** = **craftsman**, artisan, journeyman, workman **2** = **shopkeeper**, dealer, merchant, purveyor, retailer, seller, supplier, vendor

tradition *n* = **custom**, convention, folklore, habit, institution, lore, ritual

traditional *adj* = **customary**, accustomed, conventional, established, old, time-honored, usual

traffic *n* **1** = **transport**, freight, transportation, vehicles **2** = **trade**, business, commerce, dealings, exchange, peddling, truck ◆ *v* **3** = **trade**, bargain, deal, do business, exchange, have dealings, peddle

tragedy *n* = **disaster**, adversity, calamity, catastrophe, misfortune

tragic *adj* = **disastrous**, appalling, calamitous, catastrophic, deadly, dire, dreadful, miserable, pathetic, sad, vehicle towed by another vehicle. **2** trailing plant. **3** *Motion Pictures* advertisement of forthcoming film. **trailer park** site for parking mobile homes, usu. providing facilities for trailer residents. **trailer trash** *offens* poor person or people living in trailer parks.

train [trayn] *vt* **1** educate, instruct, exercise. **2** cause to grow in particular way. **3** aim (gun, etc.). ♦ *vi* **4** follow course of training, esp. to achieve physical fitness for athletics. ♦ *n* **5** line of railroad vehicles joined to locomotive. **6** succession, esp. of thoughts, events, etc. **7** procession of animals, vehicles, etc. traveling together. **8** trailing part of dress. **9** body of attendants. **train·ee'** *n* one training to be skilled worker, esp. in industry.

traipse [trayps] *vi inf* **traipsed, traips·ing** walk wearily.

trait [trayt] *n* characteristic feature.

trai·tor [TRAY-tər] *n* one who betrays or is guilty of treason. **trai'tor·ous** [-əs] *adj* **1** disloyal. **2** guilty of treachery.

tra·jec·to·ry [trə-JEK-tə-ree] *n, pl* **-ries** line of flight, (curved) path of projectile.

tram·mel [TRAM-əl] *n* **1** anything that restrains or holds captive. **2** type of

compasses. ♦ *vt* **-meled, -mel·ing** **3** restrain. **4** hinder.

tramp *vi* **1** travel on foot, esp. as vagabond or for pleasure. **2** walk heavily. ♦ *n* **3** homeless person who travels about on foot. **4** walk. **5** tramping. **6** vessel that takes cargo wherever shippers desire.

tram·ple [TRAM-pəl] *vt* **-pled, -pling** tread on and crush under foot.

tram·po·line [tram-pə-LEEN] *n* tough canvas sheet stretched horizontally with elastic cords, etc. to frame, for gymnastic, acrobatic use.

trance [trans] *n* **1** unconscious or dazed state. **2** state of ecstasy or total absorption.

tran·quil [TRANG-kwil] *adj* **1** calm, quiet. **2** serene. **tran·quil'li·ty** *n* **tran'quil·ize** *vt* **-ized, -iz·ing** make calm. **tran'quil·iz·er** *n* drug that induces calm, tranquil state.

trans- *prefix* **1** across, through, beyond, e.g. *transnational*. **2** changing thoroughly, e.g. *transliterate*.

trans·act [tran-SAKT] *vt* **1** carry through. **2** negotiate. **3** conduct (affair, etc.). **trans·ac'tion** *n* **1** performing of any business. **2** that which is performed. **3** single sale or purchase. ♦ *pl* **4** proceedings. **5** reports of a society.

THESAURUS

unfortunate

trail *n* **1** = **path**, footpath, road, route, track, way **2** = **tracks**, footprints, marks, path, scent, spoor, trace, wake ♦ *v* **3** = **drag**, dangle, draw, haul, pull, tow **4** = **lag**, dawdle, follow, hang back, linger, loiter, straggle, traipse (*inf*) **5** = **follow**, chase, hunt, pursue, shadow, stalk, tail (*inf*), trace, track

train *v* **1** = **instruct**, coach, drill, educate, guide, prepare, school, teach, tutor **2** = **exercise**, prepare, work out **3** = **aim**, direct, focus, level, point ♦ *n* **4** = **sequence**, chain, progression, series, set, string, succession

trainer *n* = **coach**, handler

training *n* **1** = **instruction**, coaching, discipline, education, grounding, schooling, teaching, tuition **2** = **exercise**, practice, preparation, working out

traipse *v* = **trudge**, drag oneself, footslog, slouch, trail, tramp

trait *n* = **characteristic**, attribute, feature, idiosyncrasy, mannerism, peculiarity, quality, quirk

traitor *n* = **betrayer**, apostate,

back-stabber, defector, deserter, Judas, quisling, rebel, renegade, turncoat

trajectory *n* = **path**, course, flight path, line, route, track

tramp *v* **1** = **hike**, footslog, march, ramble, roam, rove, slog, trek, walk **2** = **trudge**, plod, stump, toil, traipse (*inf*) ♦ *n* **3** = **vagrant**, derelict, down-and-out, drifter **4** = **hike**, march, ramble, slog, trek **5** = **tread**, footfall, footstep, stamp

trample *v* = **crush**, flatten, run over, squash, stamp, tread, walk over

trance *n* = **daze**, abstraction, dream, rapture, reverie, stupor, unconsciousness

tranquil *adj* = **calm**, peaceful, placid, quiet, restful, sedate, serene, still, undisturbed

tranquilize *v* = **calm**, lull, pacify, quell, quiet, relax, sedate, settle one's nerves, soothe

tranquilizer *n* = **sedative**, barbiturate, bromide, downer (*sl*), opiate

tranquillity *n* = **calm**, hush, peace, placidity, quiet, repose, rest, serenity, stillness

transaction *n* = **deal**, bargain, business, enterprise, negotiation, undertaking

trans·ceiv·er [tran-SEE-vər] *n* combined radio transmitter and receiver.

tran·scend [tran-SEND] *vt* **1** rise above. **2** exceed, surpass. **tran·scend'ent** *adj* **tran·scen·den'tal** *adj* **1** surpassing experience. **2** supernatural. **3** abstruse. **transcendental meditation** process seeking to induce detachment from problems, etc. by system of meditation.

tran·scribe [tran-SKRĪB] *vt* **-scribed, -scrib·ing 1** copy out. **2** record for later broadcast. **3** arrange (music) for different instrument. **tran'script** *n* copy.

tran'sept *n* **1** transverse part of cruciform church. **2** either of its arms.

trans·fer [trans-FUR] *vt* **-ferred, -fer·ring 1** move, send from one person, place, etc. to another. ♦ *n* [TRANS-fur] **2** removal of person or thing from one place to another. **3** design that can be transferred from one surface to another by pressure, heat, etc. **trans·fer'a·ble** *adj* **trans·fer'ence** *n* transfer.

trans·fig·ure [trans-FIG-yər] *vt* **-ured, -ur·ing** alter appearance of.

trans·fix [trans-FIKS] *vt* **1** astound, stun. **2** pierce.

trans·form' *vt* change shape, character of. **trans·for·ma'tion** *n* **trans·form'er** *n Electricity* apparatus for changing voltage of alternating current.

trans·fuse [trans-FYOOZ] *vt* **-fused, -fus·ing** convey from one vessel to another, esp. blood from healthy person to one injured or ill. **trans·fu'sion** [-FYŎŎ-zhən] *n*

trans·gress [trans-GRES] *vt* **1** break (law). **2** sin. **trans·gres'sion** [-GRESH-ən] *n* **trans·gres'sor** *n*

tran·sient [TRAN-shənt] *adj* fleeting, not permanent. **tran'sience** *n*

tran·sis·tor [tran-ZIS-tər] *n* **1** *Electronics* small semiconducting device used to amplify electric currents. **2** *inf* portable radio using transistors.

tran·sit *n*, *v* **-sit·ed, -sit·ing** (make) passage, crossing. **tran·si'tion** [-ZISH-ən] *n* change from one state to another. **tran·si'tion·al** *adj* **tran'si·tive** *adj* (of verb) requiring direct object. **tran'si·to·ry** *adj* not lasting long, transient.

trans·late [trans-LAYT] *vt* **-lat·ed, -lat·ing 1** turn from one language into another. **2** interpret. **trans·la'tion** *n* **trans·la'tor** *n*

transcend *v* = **surpass**, eclipse, exceed, excel, go beyond, outdo, outstrip, rise above

transcendent *adj* = **unparalleled**, consummate, incomparable, matchless, pre-eminent, sublime, unequaled, unrivaled

transcribe *v* = **write out**, copy out, reproduce, take down, transfer

transcript *n* = **copy**, duplicate, manuscript, record, reproduction, transcription

transfer *v* **1** = **move**, change, convey, hand over, pass on, relocate, shift, transplant, transport, transpose ♦ *n* **2** = **move**, change, handover, relocation, shift, transference, translation, transmission, transposition

transfix *v* **1** = **stun**, engross, fascinate, hold, hypnotize, mesmerize, paralyze **2** = **pierce**, impale, puncture, run through, skewer, spear

transform *v* = **change**, alter, convert, remodel, revolutionize, transmute

transformation *n* = **change**, alteration, conversion, metamorphosis, revolution, sea change, transmutation

transgress *v* = **offend**, break the law, contravene, disobey, encroach, infringe, sin, trespass, violate

transgression *n* = **offense**, contravention, crime, encroachment, infraction, infringement, misdeed, misdemeanor, sin, trespass, violation, wrongdoing

transgressor *n* = **offender**, criminal, culprit, lawbreaker, miscreant, sinner, trespasser, villain, wrongdoer

transient *adj* = **temporary**, brief, ephemeral, fleeting, impermanent, momentary, passing, short-lived, transitory

transit *n* = **movement**, carriage, conveyance, crossing, passage, transfer, transport, transportation

transition *n* = **change**, alteration, conversion, development, metamorphosis, passing, progression, shift, transmutation

transitional *adj* = **changing**, developmental, fluid, intermediate, passing, provisional, temporary, unsettled

transitory *adj* = **short-lived**, brief, ephemeral, fleeting, impermanent, momentary, passing, short, temporary, transient

translate *v* = **interpret**, construe, convert, decipher, decode, paraphrase, render

translation *n* = **interpretation**, decoding,

trans·lit·er·ate [trans-LIT-ər-ayt] *vt* **-at·ed,**
-at·ing write in the letters of another
alphabet. **trans·lit·er·a'tion** *n*

trans·lu·cent [trans-LOO-sənt] *adj* letting
light pass through, semitransparent.
trans·lu'cence *n*

trans·mi·grate [trans-MĪ-grayt] *vi*
-grat·ed, -grat·ing (of soul) pass into
another body. **trans·mi·gra'tion** *n*

trans·mit [trans-MIT] *vt* **-mit·ted, -mit·ting**
1 send, cause to pass to another place,
person, etc. **2** communicate. **3** send out
(signals) by means of radio waves. **4**
broadcast (radio, television program).
trans·mis'sion *n* **1** transference. **2** gear by
which power is communicated from
engine to road wheels. **trans·mit'tal** *n*
transmission.

trans·mog·ri·fy [trans-MOG-rə-fī] *vt inf*
-fied, -fy·ing change completely esp. into
bizarre form.

trans·mute [trans-MYOOT] *vt* **-mut·ed,**
-mut·ing change in form, properties, or
nature. **trans·mu·ta'tion** *n*

tran·som [TRAN-səm] *n* **1** window above
door. **2** crosspiece separating the door and
window.

trans·par·ent [trans-PA-rənt] *adj* **1** letting
light pass without distortion. **2** that can be
seen through distinctly. **3** obvious.
trans·par'en·cy *n, pl* **-cies 1** quality of
being transparent. **2** photographic slide. **3**
picture made visible by light behind it.

tran·spire [tran-SPĪR] *vi* **-spired, -spir·ing 1**
become known. **2** *inf* happen. **3** (of plants)

give off water vapor through leaves.
tran·spi·ra'tion *n*

trans·plant [trans-PLANT] *vt* **1** move and
plant again in another place. **2** transfer
organ surgically from one body to another.
♦ *n* [TRANS-plant] **3** surgical transplanting
of organ. **4** anything transplanted.
trans·plan·ta'tion *n*

trans·port [trans-PORT] *vt* **1** convey from
one place to another. **2** enrapture. ♦ *n*
[TRANS-port] **3** means of conveyance. **4**
ships, aircraft, etc. used in transporting
supplies, troops, etc. **5** a ship, etc. so used.

trans·pose [trans-POHZ] *vt* **-posed,**
-pos·ing 1 change order of. **2** interchange.
3 put music into different key.
trans·po·si'tion [-pə-ZISH-ən] *n*

tran·sub·stan·ti·a·tion *n*
[tran-səb-stan-shee-AY-shən] doctrine that
substance of bread and wine changes into
substance of Christ's body when
consecrated in Eucharist.

trans·verse [trans-VURS] *adj* **1** lying across.
2 at right angles.

trans·ves·tite [trans-VES-tīt] *n* person
seeking sexual pleasure by wearing clothes
normally worn by opposite sex.

trap *n* **1** snare, device for catching game,
etc. **2** anything planned to deceive, betray,
etc. **3** arrangement of pipes to prevent
escape of gas. **4** movable opening, esp.
through ceiling, etc. **5** *sl* mouth. ♦ *vt*
trapped, trap·ping 6 catch, ensnare.
trap'per *n* one who traps animals for their
fur. **trap'door** *n* door in floor or roof.

THESAURUS

paraphrase, rendering, rendition, version

transmission *n* **1 = transfer**, conveyance,
dissemination, sending, shipment, spread,
transference **2 = broadcasting**,
dissemination, putting out, relaying,
sending, showing **3 = program**, broadcast,
show

transmit *v* **1 = pass on**, bear, carry,
convey, disseminate, hand on, impart,
send, spread, transfer **2 = broadcast**,
disseminate, radio, relay, send out

transparency *n* **1 = clarity**, clearness,
limpidity, pellucidness, translucence **2 =**
photograph, slide

transparent *adj* **1 = clear**, crystalline,
diaphanous, limpid, lucid, see-through,
sheer, translucent **2 = plain**, evident,
explicit, manifest, obvious, patent,
recognizable, unambiguous, undisguised

transpire *v* **1 = emerge**, become known,
come out, come to light **2** *Inf* **= happen**,
arise, befall, chance, come about, occur,
take place

transplant *v* **= transfer**, displace, relocate,
remove, resettle, shift, uproot

transport *v* **1 = convey**, bear, bring, carry,
haul, move, take, transfer **2 = exile**, banish,
deport **3 = enrapture**, captivate, delight,
enchant, entrance, move, ravish ♦ *n* **4 =**
vehicle, conveyance, transportation **5 =**
transference, conveyance, shipment,
transportation **6 = ecstasy**, bliss, delight,
enchantment, euphoria, heaven, rapture,
ravishment

transpose *v* **= interchange**, alter, change,
exchange, move, reorder, shift, substitute,
swap, switch, transfer

trap *n* **1 = snare**, ambush, gin, net, noose,

tra·peze [tra-PEEZ] *n* horizontal bar suspended from two ropes for use in gymnastics, acrobatic exhibitions, etc. **trapeze artist** one who performs on trapeze.

trap·e·zoid [TRAP-ə-zoid] *n* quadrilateral with two parallel sides.

trap·pings [TRAP-ingz] *pl n* equipment, ornaments.

trash *n* **1** rubbish. **2** nonsense. **trash'y** *adj* **trash·i·er, trash·i·est** worthless, cheap.

trau·ma [TROW-mə, TRAW-mə] *n* **1** nervous shock. **2** injury. **trau·mat·ic** *adj* of, causing, caused by trauma.

tra·vail [trə-VAYL] *vi, n* labor, toil.

trav·el [TRAV-əl] *v* **-eled, -el·ing 1** go, move from one place to another. ♦ *n* **2** act of traveling, esp. as tourist. **3** *Machinery* distance component is allowed to move. ♦ *pl* **4** (account of) traveling. **trav'el·er** *n* **trav·e·logue** [TRAV-ə-log] *n* film, etc. about travels.

trav·erse [trə-VURS] *vt* **-ersed, -ers·ing 1** cross, go through or over. **2** (of gun) move laterally. ♦ *n* [TRA-vurs] **3** anything set across. **4** partition. **5** *Mountaineering* face, steep slope to be crossed from side to side.

♦ *adj* **6** being, lying across.

trav·es·ty [TRAV-ə-stee] *n, pl* **-ties 1** farcical, grotesque imitation. **2** mockery. ♦ *vt* **-tied, -ty·ing 3** make, be a travesty of.

trawl *n* **1** net dragged at deep levels behind special boat, to catch fish, shrimp, etc. ♦ *vi* **2** fish with one. **trawl'er** *n* trawling vessel.

tray *n* **1** flat board, usu. with rim, for carrying things. **2** any similar utensil.

treach·er·y [TRECH-ə-ree] *n, pl* **-er·ies** deceit, betrayal. **treach'er·ous** [-rəs] *adj* **1** disloyal. **2** unreliable, dangerous.

trea·cle [TREE-kəl] *n* **1** cloying sentimentality. **2** *Brit* molasses.

tread [tred] *v* **trod, trod·den** *or* **trod, tread·ing 1** set foot on. **2** trample. **3** oppress. ♦ *n* **5** treading. **6** walk. **7** fashion of walking. **6** top surface of step. **8** part of motor vehicle tire in contact with ground. **tread'mill** *n* dreary routine, etc.

trea·dle [TRED-l] *n* lever worked by foot to turn wheel.

trea·son [TREE-zən] *n* **1** violation by citizen of allegiance to country or ruler. **2** treachery. **3** disloyalty. **trea'son·a·ble** *adj* constituting treason. **trea'son·ous** *adj*

pitfall **2** = **trick**, ambush, deception, ruse, stratagem, subterfuge, wile ♦ *v* **3** = **catch**, corner, enmesh, ensnare, entrap, snare, take **4** = **trick**, ambush, beguile, deceive, dupe, ensnare, inveigle

trappings *pl n* = **accessories**, accouterments, equipment, finery, furnishings, gear, panoply, paraphernalia, things, trimmings

trash *n* **1** = **nonsense**, drivel, hogwash, moonshine, rot, rubbish, tripe (*inf*), twaddle **2** = **litter**, dross, garbage, junk (*inf*), refuse, rubbish, waste ♦ *v* **3** = **destroy**, defeat, demolish, put paid to, ruin, torpedo, trounce, wreck

trashy *adj* = **worthless**, cheap, inferior, rubbishy, shabby, shoddy, tawdry

trauma *n* = **suffering**, agony, anguish, hurt, ordeal, pain, shock, torture

traumatic *adj* = **shocking**, agonizing, damaging, disturbing, hurtful, injurious, painful, scarring, upsetting, wounding

travel *v* **1** = **go**, journey, move, progress, roam, tour, trek, voyage, wander ♦ *n* **2** (usually plural) = **wandering**, excursion, expedition, globetrotting, journey, tour, trip, voyage

traveler *n* = **wanderer**, explorer, globetrotter, gypsy, holiday-maker, tourist, voyager, wayfarer

traveling *adj* = **mobile**, itinerant, migrant, nomadic, peripatetic, roaming, roving, touring, wandering, wayfaring

traverse *v* = **cross**, go over, span, travel over

travesty *n* **1** = **mockery**, burlesque, caricature, distortion, lampoon, parody, perversion ♦ *v* **2** = **mock**, burlesque, caricature, distort, lampoon, make a mockery of, parody, ridicule

treacherous *adj* **1** = **disloyal**, deceitful, double-dealing, duplicitous, faithless, false, perfidious, traitorous, unfaithful, untrustworthy **2** = **dangerous**, deceptive, hazardous, icy, perilous, precarious, risky, slippery, unreliable, unsafe, unstable

treachery *n* = **betrayal**, disloyalty, double-dealing, duplicity, faithlessness, infidelity, perfidy, treason

tread *v* **1** = **step**, hike, march, pace, stamp, stride, walk **2** = **trample**, crush underfoot, squash ♦ *n* **3** = **step**, footfall, footstep, gait, pace, stride, walk

treason *n* = **disloyalty**, duplicity,

treas·ure [TREZH-ər] n 1 riches. 2 stored wealth or valuables. ◆ vt -ured, -ur·ing 3 prize, cherish. **treas'ur·er** n official in charge of funds. **treas'ur·y** n, pl -ur·ies 1 place for treasure. 2 government department in charge of finance. **treasure-trove** [-trohv] n treasure found hidden (with no evidence of ownership).

treat n (treet) pleasure, entertainment given. ◆ vt 1 deal with, act toward. 2 give medical treatment to. 3 (with of) discourse on. 4 entertain, esp. with food or drink. ◆ vi 5 negotiate. **treat'ment** [-mənt] n 1 method of counteracting a disease. 2 act or mode of treating. 3 manner of handling an artistic medium.

trea·tise [TREE-tis] n book discussing a subject, formal essay.

trea·ty [TREE-tee] n, pl -ties signed contract between nations, etc.

tre·ble [TREB-l] adj 1 threefold, triple. 2 Mus. high-pitched. ◆ n 3 soprano voice. 4 part of music for it. 5 singer with such voice. ◆ v -bled, -bling 6 increase threefold. **tre'bly** [-blee] adv

tree n 1 large perennial plant with woody trunk. 2 beam. 3 anything (e.g. genealogical chart) resembling tree, or tree's structure. ◆ vt treed, tree·ing 4 force, drive up tree. 5 plant with trees.

tre·foil [TREE-foil] n 1 plant with three-lobed leaf, clover. 2 carved ornament like this.

trek vi, n trekked, trek·king (make) long difficult journey.

trel·lis [TREL-is] n 1 lattice or grating of light bars fixed crosswise. ◆ vt 2 screen, supply with one.

trem·ble [TREM-bəl] vi -bled, -bling 1 quiver, shake. 2 feel fear, anxiety. ◆ n 3 involuntary shaking. 4 quiver. 5 tremor.

tre·men·dous [tri-MEN-dəs] adj 1 vast, immense. 2 exciting, unusual. 3 excellent.

trem·o·lo [TREM-ə-loh] n, pl -los quivering or vibrating effect in singing or playing.

trem·or [TREM-ər] n 1 quiver. 2 shaking. 3 minor earthquake.

trem·u·lous [TREM-yə-ləs] adj 1 quivering slightly. 2 fearful, agitated.

trench n 1 long narrow ditch, esp. as shelter in war. ◆ vt 2 cut grooves or ditches in. **trench coat** double-breasted waterproof overcoat.

trench·ant [TRENCH-ənt] adj cutting, incisive, biting.

trend n direction, tendency, inclination,

THESAURUS

lese-majesty, mutiny, perfidy, sedition, traitorousness, treachery

treasonable adj = **disloyal**, mutinous, perfidious, seditious, subversive, traitorous, treacherous

treasure n 1 = **riches**, cash, fortune, gold, jewels, money, valuables, wealth 2 = **darling**, apple of one's eye, gem, jewel, nonpareil, paragon, pride and joy ◆ v 3 = **prize**, adore, cherish, esteem, hold dear, idolize, love, revere, value

treasury n = **storehouse**, bank, cache, hoard, repository, store, vault

treat v 1 = **handle**, act towards, behave towards, consider, deal with, look upon, manage, regard, use 2 = **attend to**, care for, nurse 3 = **entertain**, lay on, provide, regale, stand (inf) ◆ v 4 = **entertainment**, banquet, celebration, feast, gift, party, refreshment 5 = **pleasure**, delight, enjoyment, fun, joy, satisfaction, surprise, thrill

treatise n = **essay**, dissertation, monograph, pamphlet, paper, study, thesis, tract, work

treatment n 1 = **care**, cure, healing, medication, medicine, remedy, surgery, therapy 2 = **handling**, action, behavior, conduct, dealing, management, manipulation

treaty n = **pact**, agreement, alliance, compact, concordat, contract, convention, covenant, entente

trek n 1 = **journey**, expedition, hike, march, odyssey, safari, slog, tramp ◆ v 2 = **journey**, footslog, hike, march, rove, slog, traipse (inf), trudge

tremble v 1 = **shake**, quake, quiver, shiver, shudder, totter, vibrate, wobble ◆ n 2 = **shake**, quake, quiver, shiver, shudder, tremor, vibration, wobble

tremendous adj 1 = **huge**, colossal, enormous, formidable, gigantic, great, immense, stupendous, terrific 2 Inf = **excellent**, amazing, brilliant, exceptional, extraordinary, fantastic (inf), great, marvelous, sensational (inf), wonderful

tremor n 1 = **shake**, quaking, quaver, quiver, shiver, trembling, wobble 2 = **earthquake**, quake (inf), shock

trench n = **ditch**, channel, drain, excavation, furrow, gutter, trough

drift. **trend'y** *n, adj* **trend·i·er, trend·i·est**
consciously fashionable (person).
trend'i·ness [-nis] *n*

tre·pan [tri-PAN] *n* instrument for cutting
circular pieces, esp. from skull. ◆ *vt*
-panned, -pan·ning

trep·i·da·tion [trep-i-DAY-shən] *n* fear,
anxiety.

tres·pass [TRES-pəs] *vi* **1** intrude (on)
property, etc. of another. **2** transgress, sin.
◆ *n* **3** wrongful entering on another's land.
4 wrongdoing.

tress *n* long lock of hair.

tres·tle [TRES-l] *n* **1** board fixed on pairs of
spreading legs and used as support. **2**
structural member of bridge.

tri- *comb. form* **1** three or thrice, e.g.
trilingual. **2** occurring every three, e.g.
triweekly.

tri·ad [TRI-ad] *n* **1** group of three. **2** *Chem.*
element, radical with valence of three.

tri·al [TRI-əl] *n* **1** act of trying, testing. **2**
experimental examination. **3** *Law* conduct
of case before judge, jury. **4** thing, person
that strains endurance or patience.

tri·an·gle [TRI-ang-gəl] *n* **1** figure with
three angles. **2** percussion musical
instrument. **tri·an'gu·lar** [-lər] *adj*

tribe [trīb] *n* subdivision of race of people.
trib'al [-əl] *adj*

trib·u·la·tion [trib-yə-LAY-shən] *n* **1** misery,
trouble, affliction, distress. **2** cause of this.

tri·bu·nal [trī-BYOON-l] *n* **1** law court. **2**
body appointed to inquire into and decide
specific matter. **3** place, seat of judgment.

trib·u·tar·y [TRIB-yə-ter-ee] *n, pl* **-tar·ies 1**
stream flowing into another. ◆ *adj* **2**
auxiliary. **3** contributory. **4** paying tribute.

trib·ute [TRIB-yoot] *n* **1** sign of honor or
recognition. **2** tax paid by one country to
another as sign of subjugation.

trice [trīs] *n* moment. **in a trice** instantly.

tri·chi·na [tri-KI-nə] *n, pl* **-nae** [-nee]
minute parasitic worm. **trich·i·no·sis** *n*
[tri-kə-NOH-sis] disease caused by this.

trick [trik] *n* **1** deception. **2** prank. **3**
mannerism. **4** illusion. **5** feat of skill or
cunning. **6** knack. **7** cards played in one
round. **8** spell of duty. **9** *sl* prostitute's
customer, sexual act. ◆ *vt* **10** cheat. **11**
hoax. **12** deceive. **trick'ster** *n* **trick'y** *adj*
trick·i·er, trick·i·est 1 difficult, needing
careful handling. **2** crafty.

trick·le [TRIK-l] *v* **-led, -ling** (cause to) run,
flow, move in thin stream or drops.

tri·col·or [TRI-kul-ər] *adj* **1** three colored. ◆

———————————————— THESAURUS ————————————————

trenchant *adj* **1** = **incisive**, acerbic, caustic,
cutting, penetrating, pointed, pungent,
scathing **2** = **effective**, energetic, forceful,
potent, powerful, strong, vigorous

trend *n* **1** = **tendency**, bias, current,
direction, drift, flow, inclination, leaning
2 = **fashion**, craze, fad (*inf*), mode, rage,
style, thing, vogue

trendy *adj Inf* = **fashionable**, cool (*inf*), in
fashion, in vogue, modish, phat (*sl*),
stylish, voguish, with it (*inf*)

trepidation *n* = **anxiety**, alarm,
apprehension, consternation, disquiet,
dread, fear, nervousness, uneasiness, worry

trespass *v* **1** = **intrude**, encroach, infringe,
invade, obtrude ◆ *n* **2** = **intrusion**,
encroachment, infringement, invasion,
unlawful entry

trespasser *n* = **intruder**, interloper,
invader, poacher

trial *n* **1** = **hearing**, litigation, tribunal **2** =
test, audition, dry run (*inf*), experiment,
probation, test-run **3** = **hardship**, adversity,
affliction, distress, ordeal, suffering,
tribulation, trouble

tribe *n* = **race**, clan, family, people

tribunal *n* = **hearing**, court, trial

tribute *n* **1** = **accolade**, commendation,
compliment, eulogy, panegyric,
recognition, testimonial **2** = **tax**, charge,
homage, payment, ransom

trick *n* **1** = **deception**, fraud, hoax,
maneuver, ploy, ruse, stratagem,
subterfuge, swindle, trap, wile **2** = **joke**,
antic, jape, practical joke, prank, stunt **3** =
secret, hang (*inf*), knack, know-how (*inf*),
skill, technique **4** = **mannerism**,
characteristic, foible, habit, idiosyncrasy,
peculiarity, practice, quirk, trait ◆ *v* **5** =
deceive, cheat, con (*inf*), dupe, fool,
hoodwink, kid (*inf*), mislead, swindle, take
in (*inf*), trap

trickery *n* = **deception**, cheating,
chicanery, deceit, dishonesty, guile,
monkey business (*inf*)

trickle *v* **1** = **dribble**, drip, drop, exude,
ooze, run, seep, stream ◆ *n* **2** = **dribble**,
drip, seepage

tricky *adj* **1** = **difficult**, complicated,
delicate, knotty, problematic, risky, thorny,
ticklish **2** = **crafty**, artful, cunning,
deceitful, devious, scheming, slippery, sly,

n **2** tricolor flag.

tri·cy·cle [TRĪ-si-kəl] *n* child's three-wheeled bike.

tri·dent [TRĪD-nt] *n* three-pronged fork or spear.

tri·en·ni·al [trī-EN-ee-əl] *adj* happening every, or lasting, three years.

tri·fle [TRĪ-fəl] *n* **1** insignificant thing or matter. **2** small amount. ◆ *vi* **-fled, -fling 3** toy (with). **4** act, speak idly. **tri'fler** [-flər] *n*

trig·ger [TRIG-ər] *n* **1** catch that releases spring esp. to fire gun. ◆ *vt* (oft. with *off*) start, set in action, etc. **trigger-happy** *adj* tending to irresponsible, ill-considered behavior, esp. in use of firearms.

trig·o·nom·et·ry [trig-ə-NOM-i-tree] *n* branch of mathematics dealing with relations of sides and angles of triangles. **trig·o·no·met'ric** [-nə-MET-rik] *adj*

tri·lat·er·al [trī-LAT-ər-əl] *adj* having three sides.

trill *vi* **1** sing with quavering voice. **2** sing lightly. **3** warble. ◆ *n* **4** such singing or sound.

tril·lion [TRIL-yən] *n* number 1 followed by 12 zeroes.

tril·o·gy [TRIL-ə-jee] *n, pl* **-gies** series of three related (literary) works.

trim *adj* **trim·mer, trim·mest 1** neat, smart. **2** slender. **3** in good order. ◆ *vt* **trimmed, trim·ming 4** shorten slightly by cutting. **5** prune. **6** decorate. **7** adjust. **8** put in good order. **9** adjust balance of (ship, aircraft). ◆ *n* **10** decoration. **11** order, state of being

trim. **12** haircut that neatens existing style. **13** upholstery, accessories in automobile. **14** edging material, as inside woodwork around doors, windows, etc. **trimming** *n* **1** (oft *pl*) decoration, addition. **2** *inf* a defeat. ◆ *pl* **3** garnish to main dish.

tri·ma·ran [TRĪ-mə-ran] *n* three-hulled vessel.

trin·i·ty [TRIN-i-tee] *n* **1** the state of being threefold. **2** (T-) the three persons of the Godhead. **trin·i·tar'i·an** [-TAIR-ee-ən] *n, adj*

trin·ket [TRING-kit] *n* small ornament, trifle.

tri·o [TREE-oh] *n, pl* **tri·os 1** group of three. **2** music for three parts.

tri·ode [TRĪ-ohd] *n Electronics* three-electrode vacuum tube.

trip *n* **1** (short) journey for pleasure. **2** stumble. **3** switch. **4** *sl* hallucinatory experience caused by drug. ◆ *v* **tripped, trip·ping 5** (cause to) stumble. **6** (cause to) make false step, mistake. ◆ *vi* **7** run lightly. **8** skip. **9** dance. **10** *sl* take hallucinatory drugs. ◆ *vt* **11** operate (switch).

tri·par·tite [trī-PAHR-tīt] *adj* having, divided into three parts.

tripe [trīp] *n* **1** stomach of cow, etc. prepared for food. **2** *sl* nonsense.

tri·ple [TRIP-əl] *adj* **1** threefold. ◆ *v* **-pled, -pling 2** treble. **3** hit triple. ◆ *n* **4** *Baseball* three-base hit. **trip·let** [TRIP-lit] *n* **1** three of a kind. **2** one of three offspring born at one birth. **trip'lex** *adj* **1** threefold. **2** (of apartment) having three floors. **trip'ly**

wily

trifle *n* **1** = **knick-knack**, bagatelle, bauble, plaything, toy ◆ *v* **2** = **toy**, dally, mess about, play

trifling *adj* = **insignificant**, measly, negligible, paltry, trivial, unimportant, worthless

trigger *v* = **set off**, activate, cause, generate, produce, prompt, provoke, set in motion, spark off, start

trim *adj* **1** = **neat**, dapper, shipshape, smart, spruce, tidy, well-groomed **2** = **slender**, fit, shapely, sleek, slim, streamlined, svelte, willowy ◆ *v* **3** = **cut**, clip, crop, even up, pare, prune, shave, tidy **4** = **decorate**, adorn, array, beautify, deck out, dress, embellish, ornament ◆ *n* **5** = **decoration**, adornment, border, edging, embellishment, frill, ornamentation, piping, trimming **6** = **condition**, fettle,

fitness, health, shape (*inf*), state **7** = **cut**, clipping, crop, pruning, shave, shearing, tidying up

trimming *n* **1** = **decoration**, adornment, border, edging, embellishment, frill, ornamentation, piping **2 trimmings** = **extras**, accessories, accompaniments, frills, ornaments, paraphernalia, trappings

trinity *n* = **threesome**, triad, trio, triumvirate

trinket *n* = **ornament**, bagatelle, bauble, knick-knack, toy, trifle

trio *n* = **threesome**, triad, trilogy, trinity, triumvirate

trip *n* **1** = **journey**, errand, excursion, expedition, foray, jaunt, outing, run, tour, voyage **2** = **stumble**, fall, misstep, slip ◆ *v* **3** = **stumble**, fall, lose one's footing, misstep, slip, tumble **4** = **catch out**, trap **5** = **skip**, dance, gambol, hop

[-lee] *adv*

trip·li·cate [TRIP-li-kit] *adj* **1** threefold. ◆ *n* **2** state of being triplicate. **3** one of set of three copies. ◆ *vt* [-kayt] **-cat·ed, -cat·ing 4** make threefold.

tri·pod [TRĪ-pod] *n* stool, stand, etc. with three feet.

trip·tych [TRIP-tik] *n* carving, set of pictures (esp. altarpiece) on three panels hinged side by side.

trite [trīt] *adj* hackneyed, banal.

trit·i·um [TRIT-ee-əm] *n* radioactive isotope of hydrogen.

tri·umph [TRĪ-əmf] *n* **1** great success. **2** victory. **3** exultation. ◆ *vi* **4** achieve great success or victory. **5** prevail. **6** exult. **tri·um'phal** [-UMF-əl] *adj* **tri·um'phant** [-fənt] *adj* victorious.

tri·um·vi·rate [trī-UM-vər-it] *n* joint rule by three persons.

triv·et [TRIV-it] *n* metal bracket or stand for pot or kettle.

triv·i·a [TRIV-ee-ə] *pl n* petty, unimportant things, details. **triv'i·al** *adj* **1** of little consequence. **2** commonplace. **triv·i·al'i·ty** *n, pl* **-ties**

tro·chee [TROH-kee] *n* in verse, foot of two syllables, first long and second short. **tro·cha'ic** [-KAY-ik] *adj*

trod pt./pp. of TREAD. **trod'den** [TROD-ən] pp. of TREAD.

trog·lo·dyte [TROG-lə-dīt] *n* cave dweller.

Tro·jan [TROH-jən] *adj, n* **1** (inhabitant) of ancient Troy. **2** steadfast or persevering (person).

troll[1] [trohl] *vt* fish for by dragging baited hook or lure through water.

troll[2] *n* supernatural being in Scandinavian mythology and folklore.

trol·ley [TROL-ee] *n, pl* **-leys 1** small wheeled table for food and drink. **2** wheeled cart for moving goods, etc. **3** streetcar.

trol·lop [TROL-əp] *n* promiscuous or slovenly woman.

trom·bone [trom-BOHN] *n* deep-toned brass wind instrument with sliding tube. **trom·bon'ist** *n*

troop *n* **1** group or crowd of persons or animals. **2** unit of cavalry. ◆ *pl* **3** soldiers. ◆ *vi* **4** move in a troop, flock. **troop'er** *n* **1** cavalry soldier. **2** state police officer.

trope [trohp] *n* figure of speech.

tro·phy [TROH-fee] *n, pl* **-phies 1** prize, award, as shield, cup. **2** memorial of victory, hunt, etc. ◆ *adj* **3** regarded as highly desirable symbol of wealth or success, e.g. *a trophy wife.*

trop·ic [TROP-ik] *n* **1** either of two lines of latitude at 23½°N (**tropic of Cancer**) or 23½°S (**tropic of Capricorn**). ◆ *pl* **2** area of Earth's surface between these lines. **trop'i·cal** [-kəl] *adj* **1** pert. to, within tropics. **2** (of climate) very hot.

trot *vi* **trot·ted, trot·ting 1** (of horse) move at medium pace, lifting feet in diagonal pairs. **2** (of person) run easily with short strides. ◆ *n* **3** trotting, jog. **trot'ter** *n* **1** horse trained to trot in race. **2** foot of certain animals, esp. pig.

THESAURUS

triple *adj* **1** = **threefold**, three-way, tripartite ◆ *v* **2** = **treble**, increase threefold

trite *adj* = **unoriginal**, banal, clichéd, commonplace, hackneyed, stale, stereotyped, threadbare, tired

triumph *n* **1** = **joy**, elation, exultation, happiness, jubilation, pride, rejoicing **2** = **success**, accomplishment, achievement, attainment, conquest, coup, feat, victory ◆ *v* **3** (often with *over*) = **win**, overcome, prevail, prosper, succeed, vanquish **4** = **rejoice**, celebrate, crow, exult, gloat, glory, revel

triumphant *adj* = **victorious**, celebratory, conquering, elated, exultant, jubilant, proud, successful, winning

trivia *pl n* = **minutiae**, details, trifles, trivialities

trivial *adj* = **unimportant**, incidental, inconsequential, insignificant, meaningless, minor, petty, small, trifling, worthless

triviality *n* = **insignificance**, meaninglessness, pettiness, unimportance, worthlessness

trivialize *v* = **undervalue**, belittle, laugh off, make light of, minimize, play down, scoff at, underestimate, underplay

troop *n* **1** = **group**, band, body, company, crowd, horde, multitude, squad, team, unit **2 troops** = **soldiers**, armed forces, army, men, servicemen, soldiery ◆ *v* **3** = **flock**, march, stream, swarm, throng, traipse (*inf*)

trophy *n* = **prize**, award, booty, cup, laurels, memento, souvenir, spoils

tropical *adj* = **hot**, steamy, stifling, sultry, sweltering, torrid

troth [trawth] n fidelity, truth.

trou·ba·dour [TROO-bə-dor] n one of school of early poets and singers.

trou·ble [TRUB-əl] n 1 state or cause of mental distress, pain, inconvenience, etc. 2 care, effort. ◆ v -bled, -bling ◆ vt 3 be trouble to. ◆ vi 4 be inconvenienced, concerned (about). 5 be agitated. 6 take pains, exert oneself. **trou·ble·some** [-səm] adj

trough [trawf] n 1 long open vessel, esp. for animals' food or water. 2 hollow between two waves. 3 Meteorology area of low pressure.

trounce [trowns] vt **trounced, trounc·ing** beat thoroughly, thrash.

troupe [troop] n company of performers. **troup'er** n

trou·sers [TROW-zərz] pl n two-legged outer garment with legs reaching to the ankles.

trous·seau [TROO-soh] n, pl **-seaux** [-sohz] bride's outfit of clothing.

trout [trowt] n freshwater sport and food fish.

trow·el [TROW-əl] n 1 small tool like spade for spreading mortar, lifting plants, etc. ◆ vt **-eled, -el·ing** 2 work with or as if with trowel.

troy weight [troi] system of weights used for gold, silver and gems.

tru·ant [TROO-ənt] n one absent without leave, esp. child so absenting self from school. ◆ adj **tru'an·cy** [-ən-see] n, pl **-cies**

truce [troos] n 1 temporary cessation of fighting. 2 respite, lull.

truck[1] [truk] n wheeled (motor) vehicle for moving goods.

truck[2] n **have no truck with** refuse to be involved with.

truck·le [TRUK-əl] vi **-led, -ling** yield weakly (to).

tru·cu·lent [TRUK-yə-lənt] adj aggressive, defiant. **tru·cu·lence** [-ləns] n

trudge [truj] vi **trudged, trudg·ing** 1 walk laboriously. ◆ n 2 laborious or wearisome walk.

true [troo] adj **tru·er, tru·est** 1 in accordance with facts. 2 faithful. 3 exact, correct. 4 genuine. **tru·ism** [TROO-iz-əm] n self-evident truth. **tru'ly** adv 1 exactly. 2 really. 3 sincerely. **truth** [trooth] n 1 state of being true. 2 something that is true. **truth'ful** [-fəl] adj 1 accustomed to speak the truth. 2 accurate, exact.

truf·fle [TRUF-əl] n 1 edible fungus growing underground. 2 candy resembling this.

truism [TROO-iz-əm] n see TRUE.

———————— THESAURUS ————————

trot v 1 = **run**, canter, jog, lope, scamper ◆ n 2 = **run**, canter, jog, lope

trouble n 1 = **distress**, anxiety, disquiet, grief, misfortune, pain, sorrow, torment, woe, worry 2 = **disease**, ailment, complaint, defect, disorder, failure, illness, malfunction 3 = **disorder**, agitation, bother (inf), commotion, discord, disturbance, strife, tumult, unrest 4 = **effort**, care, exertion, inconvenience, labor, pains, thought, work ◆ v 5 = **worry**, bother, disconcert, distress, disturb, pain, perturb, plague, sadden, upset 6 = **take pains**, exert oneself, make an effort, take the time 7 = **inconvenience**, bother, burden, disturb, impose upon, incommode, put out

troublesome adj 1 = **worrying**, annoying, demanding, difficult, inconvenient, irksome, taxing, tricky, trying, vexatious 2 = **disorderly**, rebellious, rowdy, turbulent, uncooperative, undisciplined, unruly, violent

trough n 1 = **manger**, water trough 2 = **channel**, canal, depression, ditch, duct, furrow, gully, gutter, trench

trounce v = **thrash**, beat, crush, drub, hammer (inf), rout, slaughter (inf), wipe the floor with (inf)

troupe n = **company**, band, cast

truancy n = **absence**, absence without leave, malingering, shirking

truant n = **absentee**, malingerer, runaway, shirker

truce n = **ceasefire**, armistice, cessation, let-up (inf), lull, moratorium, peace, respite

truculent adj = **hostile**, aggressive, bellicose, belligerent, defiant, ill-tempered, obstreperous, pugnacious

trudge v 1 = **plod**, footslog, lumber, slog, stump, traipse (inf), tramp, trek ◆ n 2 = **hike**, footslog, march, slog, traipse (inf), tramp, trek

true adj 1 = **correct**, accurate, authentic, factual, genuine, precise, real, right, truthful, veracious 2 = **faithful**, dedicated, devoted, dutiful, loyal, reliable, staunch, steady, trustworthy 3 = **exact**, accurate, on target, perfect, precise, unerring

truism n = **cliché**, axiom, bromide,

trump n **1** card of suit temporarily ranking above others. ♦ vt **2** take trick with a trump. **trump up** concoct, fabricate.

trump·er·y [TRUM-pə-ree] adj **1** showy but worthless. ♦ n, pl **-er·ies 2** worthless finery. **3** trash. **4** worthless stuff.

trum·pet [TRUM-pit] n **1** metal wind instrument like horn. ♦ vi **2** blow trumpet. **3** make sound like one, as elephant. ♦ vt **4** proclaim, make widely known.

trun·cate [TRUNG-kayt] vt **-cat·ed, -cat·ing** cut short.

trun·cheon [TRUN-chən] n **1** police officer's club. **2** staff of office or authority. **3** baton.

trun·dle [TRUN-dəl] vt **-dled, -dling** roll, as a thing on little wheels.

trunk n **1** main stem of tree. **2** person's body without or excluding head and limbs. **3** box for clothes, etc. **4** elephant's proboscis. ♦ pl **5** man's bathing suit. **trunk line** main line of railroad, telephone, etc.

truss vt **1** fasten up, tie up. ♦ n **2** support. **3** medical device of belt, etc. to hold hernia in place. **4** pack, bundle. **5** cluster of flowers at end of single stalk.

trust n **1** confidence. **2** firm belief. **3** reliance. **4** combination of producers to reduce competition and keep up prices. **5** care, responsibility. **6** property held for another. ♦ vt **7** rely on. **8** believe in. **9** expect, hope. **10** consign for care.

trust·ee' n **1** one legally holding property on another's behalf. **2** trusty. **trust·ee'ship** n **trust'ful** [-fəl] adj **1** inclined to trust. **2** credulous. **trust'wor·thy** [-wur-thee] adj **1** reliable. **2** dependable. **3** honest. **4** safe. **trust'y** adj **trust·i·er, trust·i·est 1** faithful. **2** reliable. ♦ n, pl **trust·ies 3** trustworthy convict with special privileges.

truth [trooth] see TRUE.

try [trī] v **tried, try·ing** ♦ vi **1** attempt, endeavor. ♦ vt **2** attempt. **3** test. **4** make demands upon. **5** investigate (case). **6** examine (person) in court of law. **7** purify or refine (as metals). ♦ n, pl **tries 8** attempt, effort. **tried** adj **1** proved. **2** afflicted. **trying** adj **1** upsetting, annoying. **2** difficult.

tryst [trist] n **1** appointment to meet. **2** place appointed.

tsar [zahr] see CZAR.

tset·se [TSET-see] n Afr. bloodsucking fly whose bite transmits various diseases to

———————— THESAURUS ————————

commonplace, platitude

truly adv **1** = **correctly**, authentically, exactly, factually, genuinely, legitimately, precisely, rightly, truthfully **2** = **faithfully**, devotedly, dutifully, loyally, sincerely, staunchly, steadily **3** = **really**, extremely, greatly, indeed, of course, very

trumpet n **1** = **horn**, bugle, clarion ♦ v **2** = **proclaim**, advertise, announce, broadcast, shout from the rooftops, tout (inf)

trump up v = **fabricate**, concoct, contrive, cook up (inf), create, fake, invent, make up

truncate v = **shorten**, abbreviate, curtail, cut short, dock, lop, pare, prune, trim

truncheon n = **club**, baton, cudgel, staff

trunk n **1** = **stem**, bole, stalk **2** = **chest**, box, case, casket, coffer, crate **3** = **body**, torso **4** = **snout**, proboscis

truss v **1** = **tie**, bind, fasten, make fast, secure, strap, tether ♦ n **2** Medical = **support**, bandage **3** = **joist**, beam, brace, buttress, prop, stanchion, stay, strut, support

trust v **1** = **believe in**, bank on, count on, depend on, have faith in, rely upon **2** = **consign**, assign, commit, confide, delegate, entrust, give **3** = **expect**, assume, hope, presume, suppose, surmise ♦ n **4** = **confidence**, assurance, belief, certainty, conviction, credence, credit, expectation, faith, reliance

trustful, trusting adj = **unwary**, credulous, gullible, naive, unsuspecting, unsuspicious

trustworthy adj = **honest**, dependable, honorable, principled, reliable, reputable, responsible, staunch, steadfast, trusty

trusty adj = **faithful**, dependable, reliable, solid, staunch, steady, strong, trustworthy

truth n = **truthfulness**, accuracy, exactness, fact, genuineness, legitimacy, precision, reality, validity, veracity

truthful adj = **honest**, candid, frank, precise, sincere, straight, true, trustworthy

try v **1** = **attempt**, aim, endeavor, have a go, make an effort, seek, strive, struggle **2** = **test**, appraise, check out, evaluate, examine, investigate, put to the test, sample, taste ♦ n **3** = **attempt**, crack (inf), effort, go (inf), shot (inf), stab (inf), whack (inf)

trying adj = **annoying**, bothersome, difficult, exasperating, hard, stressful, taxing, tiresome, tough, wearisome man and animals.

T-shirt [TEE-shurt] *n* informal (short-sleeved) undershirt, sweater usu. of cotton.

T square *n* T-shaped ruler for drawing parallel lines, right angles, etc.

tsu•na•mi [tsuu-NAH-mee] *n* tidal wave, usu. caused by an earthquake under the sea.

tub *n* 1 open wooden vessel like bottom half of barrel. 2 small round container. 3 bath. 4 *inf* short, fat person. 5 old, slow ship, etc.

tu•ba [TOO-bə] *n, pl* **-bas** valved brass wind instrument of low pitch.

tube [toob] *n* 1 long, narrow, hollow cylinder. 2 flexible cylinder with cap to hold liquids, pastes. **tu'bu•lar** [-byə-lər] *adj* like tube.

tu•ber [TOO-bər] *n* fleshy underground stem of some plants, e.g. potato. **tu'ber•ous** [-əs] *adj*

tu•ber•cle [TOO-bər-kəl] *n* 1 any small rounded nodule on skin, etc. 2 small lesion of tissue, esp. produced by tuberculosis. **tu•ber•cu•lar** *adj* (tuu-BUR-kyə-lər). **tu•ber'cu•lin** *n* extraction from bacillus used to test for and treat tuberculosis. **tu•ber•cu•lo'sis** *n* communicable disease, esp. of lungs.

tuck [tuk] *vt* 1 push, fold into small space. 2 gather, stitch in folds. 3 draw, roll together. ◆ *n* 4 stitched fold. **tuck'er** *n* 1 strip of linen or lace formerly worn across bosom by women. ◆ *vt inf* 2 weary. 3 tire.

tu•fa [TOO-fə] *n* porous rock formed as deposit from springs, etc.

tuf•fet [TUF-it] *n obs* small mound or seat.

tuft *n* bunch of feathers, threads, etc.

tug *vt* **tugged, tug•ging** 1 pull hard or violently. 2 haul. 3 jerk forward. ◆ *n* 4 violent pull. 5 ship used to tow other vessels. **tug of war** 1 contest in which two teams pull against one another on a rope. 2 hard-fought contest for supremacy.

tu•i•tion [too-ISH-ən] *n* 1 teaching, instruction. 2 fee for instruction.

tu•lip [TOO-lip] *n* plant with bright cup-shaped flowers.

tulle [tool] *n* kind of fine thin silk or lace.

tum•ble [TUM-bəl] *v* **-bled, -bling** 1 (cause to) fall or roll, twist, etc. (esp. in play). 2 rumple, disturb. ◆ *n* 3 fall. 4 somersault. **tum'bler** *n* 1 stemless drinking glass. 2 acrobat. 3 spring catch in lock. **tum'ble-down** *adj* dilapidated. **tumble to** *inf* realize, understand.

tu•me•fy [TOO-mə-fī] *v* **-fied, -fy•ing** (cause to) swell. **tu•mes•cence** [too-MES-əns] *n* **tu•mes'cent** [-ənt] *adj* (becoming) swollen.

tu•mor [TOO-mər] *n* abnormal growth in or on body.

tu•mult [TOO-məlt] *n* violent uproar, commotion. **tu•mult'u•ous** [-MUL-choo-əs] *adj*

tu•na [TOO-nə] *n* large marine food and game fish.

tun•dra [TUN-drə] *n* vast treeless zone between ice cap and timber line of N America and Eurasia.

tune [toon] *n* 1 melody. 2 quality of being in pitch. 3 adjustment of musical instrument. 4 concord. 5 frame of mind. ◆ *vt* **tuned, tun•ing** 6 put in tune. 7 adjust machine to obtain most efficient running. 8 adjust radio circuit. **tune'ful** [-fəl] *adj* **tun'er** [-ər] *n* **tune in** adjust (radio, TV) to receive (a station, program).

---

tubby *adj* = **fat**, chubby, corpulent, obese, overweight, plump, portly, stout

tuck *v* 1 = **push**, fold, gather, insert ◆ *n* 2 = **fold**, gather, pinch, pleat

tuft *n* = **clump**, bunch, cluster, collection, knot, tussock

tug *v* 1 = **pull**, jerk, wrench, yank ◆ *n* 2 = **pull**, jerk, yank

tuition *n* = **training**, education, instruction, lessons, schooling, teaching, tutelage, tutoring

tumble *v* 1 = **fall**, drop, flop, plummet, stumble, topple ◆ *n* 2 = **fall**, drop, plunge, spill, stumble, trip

tumbledown *adj* = **dilapidated**, crumbling, decrepit, ramshackle, rickety, ruined

tumor *n* = **growth**, cancer, carcinoma (*Pathology*), lump, sarcoma (*Medical*), swelling

tumult *n* = **commotion**, clamor, din, hubbub, pandemonium, riot, row, turmoil, upheaval, uproar

tumultuous *adj* = **wild**, boisterous, excited, noisy, riotous, rowdy, turbulent, unruly, uproarious, wired (*sl*)

tune *n* 1 = **melody**, air, song, strain, theme 2 = **pitch**, concord, consonance, euphony, harmony ◆ *v* 3 = **adjust**, adapt, attune, harmonize, pitch, regulate

tung·sten [TUNG-stən] *n* grayish-white metal, used in lamp filaments, some steels, etc.

tu·nic [TOO-nik] *n* **1** close-fitting jacket forming part of uniform. **2** loose hip-length or knee-length garment.

tun·nel [TUN-l] *n* **1** underground passage, esp. as track for railroad line. **2** burrow of a mole, etc. ♦ *v* **-neled, -nel·ing 3** make tunnel (through).

tur·ban [TUR-bən] *n* **1** in certain countries, man's headdress, made by coiling length of cloth around head or a cap. **2** woman's hat like this.

tur·bid *adj* **1** muddy, not clear. **2** disturbed. **tur·bid'i·ty** *n*

tur·bine [TUR-bin] *n* rotary engine driven by steam, gas, water or air playing on blades.

turbo- *comb. form* of, relating to, or driven by a turbine.

tur·bu·lent [TUR-byə-lənt] *adj* **1** in commotion. **2** swirling. **3** riotous. **tur·bu·lence** [-ləns] *n* esp. instability of atmosphere causing gusty air currents, etc.

tu·reen [tuu-REEN] *n* serving dish for soup.

turf *n, pl* **turfs 1** short grass with earth bound to it by matted roots. **2** grass, esp. as lawn. **3** *sl* claimed territory of gang. ♦ *vt* **4** lay with turf.

tur·gid [TUR-jid] *adj* **1** swollen, inflated. **2** bombastic. **tur·gid'i·ty** *n*

tur·key [TUR-kee] *n* **1** large bird reared for food. **2** *sl* loser, naive person. **3** *sl* a flop.

Turk·ish [TUR-kish] *adj* of, pert. to Turkey, the Turks. **Turkish bath** steam bath. **Turkish delight** gelatin candy flavored and coated with powdered sugar.

tur·moil *n* confusion and bustle, commotion.

turn *v* **1** move around, rotate. **2** change, reverse, alter position or direction (of). **3** (oft. with *into*) change in nature, character, etc. ♦ *vt* **4** make, shape on lathe. ♦ *n* **5** act of turning. **6** inclination, etc. **7** period, spell. **8** turning. **9** short walk. **10** (part of) rotation. **11** performance. **turn'ing** *n* road, path leading off main route. **turn'coat** [-koht] *n* one who forsakes own party or principles. **turn'out** *n* **1** number of people appearing for some purpose, occasion. **2** way in which person is dressed, equipped. **turn'o·ver** *n* **1** total sales made by business over certain period. **2** rate at which employees leave and are replaced. **3** small pastry. **4** *Football, basketball* loss of ball to opponents through mistake. **turn'pike** *n* **1** *Hist.* (gate across) road where toll was paid. **2** highway. **turn'stile** *n* revolving gate for controlling admission of people. **turn'ta·ble** *n* revolving platform. **turn down** refuse. **turn up 1** appear. **2** be found. **3** increase (flow, volume).

tur'nip *n* plant with globular root used as

———— THESAURUS ————

tuneful *adj* = **melodious**, catchy, euphonious, harmonious, mellifluous, melodic, musical, pleasant

tuneless *adj* = **discordant**, atonal, cacophonous, dissonant, harsh, unmusical

tunnel *n* **1** = **passage**, burrow, channel, hole, passageway, shaft, subway, underpass ♦ *v* **2** = **dig**, burrow, excavate, mine, scoop out

turbulence *n* = **confusion**, agitation, commotion, disorder, instability, tumult, turmoil, unrest, upheaval

turbulent *adj* = **agitated**, blustery, choppy, foaming, furious, raging, rough, tempestuous, tumultuous

turf *n* **1** = **grass**, sod, sward **2 the turf** = **horse-racing**, racing, the flat

turmoil *n* = **confusion**, agitation, chaos, commotion, disarray, disorder, tumult, upheaval, uproar

turn *v* **1** = **change course**, move, shift, swerve, switch, veer, wheel **2** = **rotate**, circle, go round, gyrate, pivot, revolve, roll, spin, twist, whirl **3** = **change**, alter, convert, mold, mutate, remodel, shape, transform **4** = **shape**, fashion, frame, make, mold **5** = **go bad**, curdle, sour, spoil, taint ♦ *n* **6** = **rotation**, circle, cycle, gyration, revolution, spin, twist, whirl **7** = **shift**, departure, deviation **8** = **opportunity**, chance, crack (*inf*), go, stint, time, try **9** = **direction**, drift, heading, tendency, trend **10** *As in* **good turn** = **act**, action, deed, favor, gesture, service

turncoat *n* = **traitor**, apostate, backslider, defector, deserter, renegade

turn down *v* **1** = **lower**, lessen, muffle, mute, quieten, soften **2** = **refuse**, decline, rebuff, reject, repudiate, spurn

turn in *v* **1** = **go to bed**, go to sleep, hit the sack (*sl*) **2** = **hand in**, deliver, give up, hand over, return, submit, surrender, tender

turning *n* = **junction**, bend, crossroads,

food.

tur·pen·tine [TUR-pən-tīn] *n* **1** resin obtained from certain trees. **2** oil made from this. **turps** *n* short for turpentine.

tur·pi·tude [TUR-pi-tood] *n* depravity.

tur·quoise [TUR-kwoiz] *n* **1** bluish-green precious stone. **2** this color.

tur·ret [TUR-it] *n* **1** small tower. **2** revolving armored tower for guns on warship, tank, etc.

tur·tle [TUR-tl] *n* (esp. sea) tortoise.

tusk *n* long pointed side tooth of an elephant, walrus, etc.

tus·sle [TUS-əl] *n, v* **-sled, -sling** fight, wrestle, struggle.

tu·te·lage [TOOT-l-ij] *n* act, office of tutor or guardian. **tu'te·lar·y** [-ler-ee] *adj*

tu·tor [TOO-tər] *n* **1** one teaching individuals or small groups. ◆ *v* **2** teach thus. **tu·to'ri·al** [-TOR-ee-əl] *n* period of instruction with tutor.

tu·tu [TOO-too] *n, pl* **-tus** short, stiff skirt worn by ballerinas.

tux·e·do [tuk-SEE-doh] *n, pl* **-dos** dinner jacket.

TV television. **TV dinner** frozen meal in tray for heating before serving. **TV game** game played on TV screen using special attachment.

twad·dle [TWOD-l] *n* silly talk.

twain [twayn] *n* two. **in twain** asunder.

twang *n* **1** vibrating metallic sound. **2** nasal speech. ◆ *v* **3** (cause to) make such sounds.

tweak [tweek] *vt* pinch and twist or pull. ◆ *n*

tweed *n* **1** rough-surfaced cloth used for clothing. ◆ *pl* **2** suit of tweed.

tween *n* child of about 8 to 12 years of age.

tweet *n, vi* chirp. **tweet'er** *n* small loudspeaker reproducing high-frequency sounds.

tweez·ers [TWEE-zərz] *pl n* small forceps or tongs.

twelve [twelv] *n, adj* cardinal number two more than ten. **twelfth** *adj* the ordinal number. ◆ *n*

twen·ty [TWEN-tee] *n, adj, pl* **-ties** cardinal number, twice ten. **twen'ti·eth** [-tee-ith] *adj* the ordinal number. ◆ *n* **twenty-four-seven,** 24/7 *adj, adv inf* all the time.

twerp [twurp] *n sl* silly person.

twice [twīs] *adv* two times.

twid·dle [TWID-l] *v* **-dled, -dling 1** fiddle. **2** twist.

twig *n* small branch, shoot.

twi·light [TWĪ-līt] *n* soft light after sunset.

twill *n* fabric woven so as to have surface of parallel ridges.

twin *n* **1** one of pair, esp. of two children born together. ◆ *adj* **2** being a twin. ◆ *v* **twinned, twin·ning 3** pair, be paired.

twine [twīn] *v* **twined, twin·ing 1** twist, coil

THESAURUS

curve, side road, turn, turn-off

turning point *n* = **crossroads**, change, crisis, crux, moment of truth

turn off *v* = **stop**, cut out, put out, shut down, switch off, turn out, unplug

turn on *v* **1** = **start**, activate, ignite, kick-start, start up, switch on **2** = **attack**, assail, assault, fall on, round on **3** *Inf* = **excite**, arouse, attract, please, stimulate, thrill, titillate

turnout *n* = **attendance**, assembly, audience, congregation, crowd, gate, number, throng

turnover *n* **1** = **output**, business, productivity **2** = **movement**, change, coming and going

turn up *v* **1** = **arrive**, appear, attend, come, put in an appearance, show one's face, show up (*inf*) **2** = **find**, dig up, disclose, discover, expose, reveal, unearth **3** = **come to light**, crop up (*inf*), pop up **4** = **increase**, amplify, boost, enhance,

intensify, raise

tussle *n* **1** = **fight**, battle, brawl, conflict, contest, scrap (*inf*), scuffle, struggle ◆ *v* **2** = **fight**, battle, grapple, scrap (*inf*), scuffle, struggle, vie, wrestle

tutor *n* **1** = **teacher**, coach, educator, guardian, guide, guru, instructor, lecturer, mentor ◆ *v* **2** = **teach**, coach, drill, educate, guide, instruct, school, train

twaddle *n* = **nonsense**, claptrap (*inf*), drivel, garbage (*inf*), gobbledegook (*inf*), poppycock (*inf*), rubbish

tweak *v, n* = **twist**, jerk, pinch, pull, squeeze

twig[1] *n* = **branch**, shoot, spray, sprig, stick

twilight *n* = **dusk**, dimness, evening, gloaming (*Scot. or poetic*), gloom, half-light, sundown, sunset

twin *n* **1** = **double**, clone, counterpart, duplicate, fellow, likeness, lookalike, match, mate ◆ *v* **2** = **pair**, couple, join, link, match, yoke around. ♦ n 2 string, cord.

twinge [twinj] n 1 momentary sharp, shooting pain. 2 qualm.

twin·kle [TWING-kəl] vi -kled, -kling 1 shine with dancing or quivering light, sparkle. ♦ n 2 twinkling. 3 flash. 4 gleam of amusement in eyes. **twinkling** n 1 very brief time.

twirl [twurl] vt 1 turn or twist round quickly. 2 whirl. 3 twiddle.

twist v 1 make, become spiral, by turning with one end fast. 2 distort, change. 3 wind. ♦ n 4 thing twisted. **twist'er** n 1 person or thing that twists. 2 inf tornado, whirlwind. **twist'y** adj twist·i·er, twist·i·est

twit n inf 1 foolish person. ♦ vt **twit·ted, twit·ting** 2 taunt.

twitch [twich] v 1 give momentary sharp pull or jerk (to). ♦ n 2 such pull or jerk. 3 spasmodic jerk, spasm.

twit·ter [TWIT-ər] vi 1 giggle. 2 talk idly. 3 (of birds) utter succession of tremulous sounds. ♦ n 4 such succession of notes.

two [too] n, adj cardinal number, one more than one. **two'fold** adj, adv **two-faced** adj 1 double-dealing, deceitful. 2 with two faces. **two-stroke** [-strohk] adj (of internal-combustion engine) making one explosion to every two strokes of piston.

ty·coon [tī-KOON] n powerful, influential

businessperson.

tyke [tīk] n 1 small, cheeky child. 2 small (mongrel) dog.

tympani see TIMPANI.

type [tīp] n 1 class. 2 sort. 3 model. 4 pattern. 5 characteristic build. 6 specimen. 7 block bearing letter used for printing. 8 such pieces collectively. ♦ vt typed, typ·ing 9 print with typewriter. 10 typify. 11 classify. **type'script** n typewritten document or copy. **type'writ·er** n keyed writing machine. **typ'ist** n one who operates typewriter. **ty'po** n, pl **ty·pos** inf error in typing, printing.

ty·phoid [tī-foid] n acute infectious disease, affecting esp. intestines. ♦ adj **ty·phus** [tī-fəs] n infectious disease.

ty·phoon [tī-FOON] n violent tropical storm or cyclone.

typ·i·cal [TIP-i-kəl] adj 1 true to type. 2 characteristic. **typ'i·cal·ly** adv

typ·i·fy [TIP-i-fī] vt -fied, -fy·ing serve as type or model of.

ty·pog·ra·phy [tī-POG-rə-fee] n 1 art of printing. 2 style of printing. **ty·po·graph'i·cal** adj **ty·pog'ra·pher** [-POG-rə-fər] n

ty·rant [tī-rənt] n 1 oppressive or cruel ruler. 2 one who forces own will on others cruelly and arbitrarily. **ty·ran·ni·cal**

THESAURUS

twine n 1 = **string**, cord, yarn ♦ v 2 = **coil**, bend, curl, encircle, loop, spiral, twist, wind

twinge n = **pain**, pang, prick, spasm, stab, stitch

twinkle v 1 = **sparkle**, blink, flash, flicker, gleam, glint, glisten, glitter, shimmer, shine ♦ n 2 = **flicker**, flash, gleam, glimmer, shimmer, spark, sparkle

twirl v 1 = **turn**, pirouette, pivot, revolve, rotate, spin, twist, wheel, whirl, wind ♦ n 2 = **turn**, pirouette, revolution, rotation, spin, twist, wheel, whirl

twist v 1 = **wind**, coil, curl, screw, spin, swivel, wrap, wring 2 = **distort**, contort, screw up ♦ n 3 = **wind**, coil, curl, spin, swivel 4 = **development**, change, revelation, slant, surprise, turn, variation 5 = **curve**, arc, bend, meander, turn, undulation, zigzag 6 = **distortion**, defect, deformation, flaw, imperfection, kink, warp

twitch v 1 = **jerk**, flutter, jump, squirm ♦ n 2 = **spasm**, flutter, jerk, jump, tic

two-faced adj = **hypocritical**, deceitful, dissembling, duplicitous, false, insincere, treacherous, untrustworthy

tycoon n = **magnate**, baron, capitalist, fat cat (sl), financier, industrialist, mogul, plutocrat

type n = **category**, class, genre, group, kind, order, sort, species, style, variety

typhoon n = **storm**, cyclone, squall, tempest, tornado

typical adj = **characteristic**, archetypal, average, classic, model, normal, orthodox, representative, standard, stock, usual

typify v = **symbolize**, characterize, embody, epitomize, exemplify, illustrate, personify, represent, sum up

tyrannical adj = **oppressive**, authoritarian, autocratic, cruel, despotic, dictatorial, domineering, high-handed, imperious, overbearing, tyrannous

tyranny n = **oppression**, absolutism, authoritarianism, autocracy, cruelty, despotism, dictatorship, high-handedness, imperiousness

[ti-RAN-i-kəl] *adj* **1** despotic. **2** ruthless.
tyr·an·nize [TIR-ə-nīz] *v* **-nized, -niz·ing**
exert ruthless or tyrannical authority
(over). **tyr'an·nous** [-ə-nəs] *adj* **tyr'an·ny** *n*
despotism.
ty·ro [tī-roh] *n, pl* **-ros** novice, beginner.

———————— THESAURUS ————————

tyrant *n* = **dictator**, absolutist,
authoritarian, autocrat, bully, despot,
martinet, oppressor, slave-driver

U u

U *Chem.* uranium.

u·biq·ui·tous [yoo-BIK-wi-təs] *adj* **1** everywhere at once. **2** omnipresent. **u·biq'ui·ty** *n*

ud·der [UD-ər] *n* milk-secreting organ of cow, etc.

ug·ly [UG-lee] *adj* **-li·er, -li·est 1** unpleasing, repulsive to the sight, hideous. **2** ill-omened. **3** threatening. **ug'li·ness** [-nis] *n*

u·kase [yoo-KAYS] *n* an arbitrary command.

u·ku·le·le [yoo-kə-LAY-lee] *n* small four-stringed guitar, esp. of Hawaii.

ul·cer [UL-sər] *n* open sore on skin, mucous membrane that is slow to heal. **ul'cer·ate** *v* **-at·ed** make, form ulcer(s). **ul·cer·a'tion** *n*

ul·lage [UL-ij] *n* quantity by which a container falls short of being full.

ul·na [UL-nə] *n, pl* **-nae** [-nee] longer of two bones of forearm.

ul·te·ri·or [ul-TEER-ee-ər] *adj* **1** lying beneath, beyond what is revealed or evident (e.g. motives). **2** situated beyond.

ul·ti·mate [UL-tə-mit] *adj* **1** last. **2** highest. **3** most significant. **4** fundamental. **ul·ti·ma'tum** [-MAY-təm] *n, pl* **-tums** *or* **-ta** [-tə] **1** final proposition. **2** final terms offered.

ultra- *prefix* beyond, excessively, e.g. *ultramodern*.

ul'tra·high frequency [UL-trə-hī] (band of) radio waves of very short wavelength.

ul·tra·ma·rine [ul-trə-mə-REEN] *n* blue pigment.

ul·tra·son·ic [ul-trə-SON-ik] *adj* of sound waves beyond the range of human ear.

ul·tra·vi·o·let [ul-trə-VI-ə-lit] *adj* of electromagnetic radiation (e.g. of sun, etc.) beyond limit of visibility at violet end of spectrum.

um·bel [UM-bəl] *n* umbrella-like flower cluster with stalks springing from central point. **um·bel·lif'er·ous** [-LIF-ər-əs] *adj* bearing umbel(s).

um·ber [UM-bər] *n* dark brown pigment.

um·bil·i·cal [um-BIL-i-kəl] *adj* of (region of) navel. **umbilical cord 1** cordlike structure connecting fetus with placenta of mother. **2** cord joining astronaut to spacecraft, etc.

um·brage [UM-brij] *n* offense, resentment.

um·brel·la [um-BREL-ə] *n* **1** folding circular cover of nylon, etc. on stick, carried in hand to protect against rain, heat of sun. **2** anything shaped or functioning like an umbrella.

um·pire [UM-pīr] *n* **1** person chosen to decide question, or to decide disputes and enforce rules in a game. ◆ *v* **-pired, -pir·ing 2** act as umpire (in).

un- *prefix* **1** not, e.g. *unidentified*. **2** denoting reversal of an action, e.g. *untie*. **3** denoting removal from, e.g. *unthrone*.

un·ac·count·a·ble [un-ə-KOWNT-ə-bəl]

THESAURUS

ubiquitous *adj* = **everywhere**, ever-present, omnipresent, pervasive, universal

ugly *adj* **1** = **unattractive**, dumpy (*inf*), frowzy, hideous, homely (*U.S.*), ill-favored, plain, unlovely, unprepossessing, unsightly **2** = **unpleasant**, disagreeable, distasteful, horrid, objectionable, shocking, terrible **3** = **ominous**, baleful, dangerous, menacing, sinister

ulcer *n* = **sore**, abscess, boil, gumboil, peptic ulcer, pustule

ulterior *adj* = **hidden**, concealed, covert, secret, undisclosed

ultimate *adj* **1** = **final**, end, last **2** = **supreme**, extreme, greatest, highest, paramount, superlative, utmost

ultimately *adv* = **finally**, after all, at last, eventually, in due time, in the end, sooner or later

umpire *n* **1** = **referee**, arbiter, arbitrator, judge ◆ *v* **2** = **referee**, adjudicate, arbitrate, judge

unabashed *adj* = **unembarrassed**, blatant, bold, brazen

unable *adj* = **incapable**, impotent,

adj that cannot be explained.

u·nan·i·mous [yoo-NAN-ə-məs] *adj* **1** in complete agreement. **2** agreed by all. **u·na·nim·i·ty** [yoo-nə-NIM-ə-tee] *n*

un·as·sum·ing [un-ə-SOO-ming] *adj* not pretentious.

un·a·vail·ing [un-ə-VAY-ling] *adj* useless, futile.

un·a·ware [un-ə-WAIR] *adj* not aware, uninformed. **un·a·wares'** ['-WAIRZ] *adv* **1** without previous warning. **2** unexpectedly.

un·bear'a·ble *adj* not able to be endured.

———————— THESAURUS ————————

ineffectual, powerless, unfit, unqualified

unabridged *adj* = **uncut**, complete, full-length, unexpurgated, whole

unacceptable *adj* = **unsatisfactory**, displeasing, objectionable

unaccompanied *adj* **1** = **alone**, by oneself, lone, on one's own, solo, unescorted **2** *Mus* = **a cappella**

unaccountable *adj* **1** = **inexplicable**, baffling, mysterious, odd, puzzling, unexplainable, unfathomable **2** = **not answerable**, exempt, not responsible

unaccustomed *adj* **1** = **unfamiliar**, new, strange, unwonted **2 unaccustomed to** = **not used to**, inexperienced at, unfamiliar with, unused to

unaffected¹ *adj* = **natural**, artless, genuine, plain, simple, sincere, unpretentious

unaffected² *adj* = **impervious**, proof, unmoved, unresponsive, untouched

unafraid *adj* = **fearless**, daring, dauntless, intrepid

unalterable *adj* = **unchangeable**, fixed, immutable, permanent

unanimity *n* = **agreement**, accord, assent, concord, concurrence, consensus, harmony, like-mindedness, unison

unanimous *adj* = **agreed**, common, concerted, harmonious, in agreement, like-minded, united

unanimously *adv* = **without exception**, as one, in concert, of one mind, with one accord

unanswerable *adj* = **conclusive**, absolute, incontestable, incontrovertible, indisputable

unanswered *adj* = **unresolved**, disputed, open, undecided

unappetizing *adj* = **unpleasant**, distasteful, repulsive, scuzzy (*sl*), unappealing, unattractive, unpalatable

unapproachable *adj* **1** = **unfriendly**, aloof, chilly, cool, distant, remote, reserved, standoffish **2** = **inaccessible**, out of reach, remote

unarmed *adj* = **defenseless**, exposed, helpless, open, unprotected, weak

unassailable *adj* = **impregnable**,

invincible, invulnerable, secure

unassuming *adj* = **modest**, humble, quiet, reserved, retiring, self-effacing, unassertive, unobtrusive, unpretentious

unattached *adj* **1** = **free**, independent **2** = **single**, available, not spoken for, unengaged, unmarried

unattended *adj* **1** = **abandoned**, unguarded, unwatched **2** = **alone**, on one's own, unaccompanied

unauthorized *adj* = **illegal**, unlawful, unofficial, unsanctioned

unavoidable *adj* = **inevitable**, certain, fated, inescapable

unaware *adj* = **ignorant**, oblivious, unconscious, uninformed, unknowing

unawares *adv* **1** = **by surprise**, off guard, suddenly, unexpectedly **2** = **unknowingly**, accidentally, by accident, inadvertently, unwittingly

unbalanced *adj* **1** = **biased**, one-sided, partial, partisan, prejudiced, unfair **2** = **shaky**, lopsided, uneven, unstable, wobbly **3** = **deranged**, crazy, demented, disturbed, eccentric, insane, irrational, mad, *non compos mentis*, not all there, unhinged, unstable

unbearable *adj* = **intolerable**, insufferable, too much (*inf*), unacceptable

unbeatable *adj* = **invincible**, indomitable

unbeaten *adj* = **undefeated**, triumphant, victorious

unbecoming *adj* **1** = **unsightly**, unattractive, unbefitting, unflattering, unsuitable **2** = **unseemly**, discreditable, improper, offensive

unbelievable *adj* = **incredible**, astonishing, far-fetched, implausible, impossible, improbable, inconceivable, preposterous, unconvincing, unimaginable

unbending *adj* = **inflexible**, firm, intractable, resolute, rigid, severe, strict, stubborn, tough, uncompromising

unbiased *adj* = **fair**, disinterested, equitable, impartial, just, neutral, objective, unprejudiced

unblemished *adj* = **spotless**, flawless, immaculate, impeccable, perfect, pure,

un·bos·om [un-BUUZ-əm] *vt* tell or reveal (one's secrets, etc.).

un·can·ny [un-KAN-ee] *adj* **1** weird, mysterious. **2** extraordinary.

un·cer·tain *adj* **1** not able to be accurately known or predicted. **2** not able to be depended upon. **3** changeable.

un·cle [UNG-kəl] *n* **1** brother of father or mother. **2** husband of aunt.

un·com'fort·a·ble *adj* **1** not physically relaxed. **2** anxious or uneasy.

un·com'mon *adj* **1** not happening or encountered often. **2** in excess of what is normal.

un·com·pli·men·ta·ry [un-kom-plə-MEN-tə-ree] *adj* **1** not complimentary. **2** insulting, derogatory.

un·con·di'tion·al *adj* without conditions or limitations.

un·con·scion·a·ble [un-KON-shə-nə-bəl]

──── THESAURUS ────

untarnished

unborn *adj* = **expected**, awaited, embryonic, fetal

unbreakable *adj* = **indestructible**, durable, lasting, rugged, strong

unbridled *adj* = **unrestrained**, excessive, intemperate, licentious, riotous, unchecked, unruly, wanton

unbroken *adj* **1** = **intact**, complete, entire, whole **2** = **continuous**, constant, incessant, twenty-four-seven (*sl*), uninterrupted

unburden *v* = **confess**, confide, disclose, get (something) off one's chest (*inf*), reveal

uncalled-for *adj* = **unjustified**, gratuitous, needless, undeserved, unnecessary, unwarranted

uncanny *adj* **1** = **weird**, mysterious, strange, supernatural, unearthly, unnatural **2** = **extraordinary**, astounding, exceptional, incredible, miraculous, remarkable, unusual

unceasing *adj* = **continual**, constant, continuous, endless, incessant, nonstop, perpetual, twenty-four-seven (*sl*)

uncertain *adj* **1** = **unpredictable**, doubtful, indefinite, questionable, risky, speculative **2** = **unsure**, dubious, hazy, irresolute, unclear, unconfirmed, undecided, vague

uncertainty *n* = **doubt**, ambiguity, confusion, dubiety, hesitancy, indecision, unpredictability

unchangeable *adj* = **unalterable**, constant, fixed, immutable, invariable, irreversible, permanent, stable

unchanging *adj* = **constant**, continuing, enduring, eternal, immutable, lasting, permanent, perpetual, twenty-four-seven (*sl*), unvarying

uncharitable *adj* = **unkind**, cruel, hardhearted, unfeeling, ungenerous

uncharted *adj* = **unexplored**, strange, undiscovered, unfamiliar, unknown

uncivil *adj* = **impolite**, bad-mannered, discourteous, ill-mannered, rude, unmannerly

uncivilized *adj* **1** = **primitive**, barbarian, savage, wild **2** = **uncouth**, boorish, coarse, philistine, uncultivated, uneducated

unclean *adj* = **dirty**, corrupt, defiled, evil, filthy, foul, impure, polluted, scuzzy (*sl*), soiled, stained

unclear *adj* **1** = **indistinct**, blurred, dim, faint, fuzzy, hazy, obscure, shadowy, undefined, vague **2** = **doubtful**, ambiguous, indefinite, indeterminate, vague

uncomfortable *adj* **1** = **awkward**, cramped, painful, rough **2** = **uneasy**, awkward, discomfited, disturbed, embarrassed, troubled

uncommitted *adj* = **uninvolved**, floating, free, neutral, nonaligned, not involved, unattached

uncommon *adj* **1** = **rare**, infrequent, novel, odd, peculiar, queer, scarce, strange, unusual **2** = **extraordinary**, distinctive, exceptional, notable, outstanding, remarkable, special

uncommonly *adv* **1** = **rarely**, hardly ever, infrequently, occasionally, seldom **2** = **exceptionally**, particularly, very

uncommunicative *adj* = **reticent**, close, reserved, secretive, silent, taciturn, tight-lipped, unforthcoming

uncompromising *adj* = **inflexible**, firm, inexorable, intransigent, rigid, strict, tough, unbending

unconcern *n* = **indifference**, aloofness, apathy, detachment, lack of interest, nonchalance

unconcerned *adj* = **indifferent**, aloof, apathetic, cool, detached, dispassionate, distant, uninterested, unmoved

unconditional *adj* = **absolute**, complete, entire, full, outright, positive, total, unlimited, unqualified, unreserved

unconnected *adj* **1** = **separate**, detached, divided **2** = **meaningless**, disjointed, *adj* **1** unscrupulous, unprincipled. **2** excessive.

un·con·scious [un-KON-shəs] *adj* **1** insensible. **2** not aware. **3** not knowing. **4** of thoughts, memories, etc. of which one is not normally aware. ◆ *n* **5** these thoughts. **un·con'scious·ness** [-nis] *n*

un·couth [un-KOOTH] *adj* **1** clumsy, boorish. **2** without ease or polish.

unc·tion [UNGK-shən] *n* **1** anointing. **2** excessive politeness. **3** soothing words or thoughts. **unc'tu·ous** [-choo-əs] *adj* **1** slippery, greasy. **2** oily in manner, gushing.

un·de·cid'ed *adj* **1** not having made up one's mind. **2** (of an issue or problem) not agreed or decided upon.

un·der [UN-dər] *prep* **1** below, beneath. **2** bound by, included in. **3** less than. **4** subjected to. **5** known by. **6** in the time of. ◆ *adv* **7** in lower place or condition. ◆ *adj* **8** lower.

under- *prefix* beneath, below, lower, e.g. *underground.*

un·der·car·riage [UN-dər-ka-rij] *n* landing gear of vehicle esp. aircraft.

un·der·charge [un-dər-CHAHRJ] *vt* **-charged, -charg·ing 1** charge less than proper amount. ◆ *n* [UN-dər-chahrj] **2** too low a charge.

un·der·class [UN-dər-klas] *n* the most economically disadvantaged people, such as the long-term unemployed.

un·der·coat [UN-dər-koht] *n* coat of paint applied before top coat.

un·der·dog [un-dər-dawg] *n* person or team in a weak or underprivileged position.

un·der·go [un-dər-GOH] *vt* **-went, -gone, -go·ing** experience, endure, sustain.

un·der·grad·u·ate [un-dər-GRAJ-oo-it] *n* student at college who has not received degree.

un·der·ground [UN-dər-grownd] *adj* **1** under the ground. **2** secret. ◆ *adv* **3** secretly. ◆ *n* **4** secret but organized resistance to government in power. **5** subway.

un·der·hand [UN-dər-hand] *adj* **1** secret,

THESAURUS

illogical, incoherent, irrelevant

unconscious *adj* **1** = **senseless**, insensible, knocked out, out, out cold, stunned **2** = **unaware**, ignorant, oblivious, unknowing **3** = **unintentional**, accidental, inadvertent, unwitting

uncontrollable *adj* = **wild**, frantic, furious, mad, strong, unruly, violent

uncontrolled *adj* = **unrestrained**, rampant, riotous, unbridled, unchecked, undisciplined

unconventional *adj* = **unusual**, eccentric, individual, irregular, nonconformist, odd, offbeat, original, outré, unorthodox

unconvincing *adj* = **implausible**, dubious, feeble, flimsy, improbable, lame, questionable, suspect, thin, unlikely, weak

uncooperative *adj* = **unhelpful**, awkward, difficult, disobliging, obstructive

uncoordinated *adj* = **clumsy**, awkward, bungling, graceless, lumbering, maladroit, ungainly, ungraceful

uncouth *adj* = **coarse**, boorish, crude, graceless, ill-mannered, loutish, oafish, rough, rude, vulgar

uncover *v* **1** = **reveal**, disclose, divulge, expose, make known **2** = **open**, bare, show, strip, unwrap

uncritical *adj* = **undiscriminating**, indiscriminate, undiscerning

undecided *adj* **1** = **unsure**, dithering, hesitant, in two minds, irresolute, torn, uncertain **2** = **unsettled**, debatable, iffy (*inf*), indefinite, moot, open, unconcluded, undetermined

undefined *adj* **1** = **unspecified**, imprecise, inexact, unclear **2** = **indistinct**, formless, indefinite, vague

undeniable *adj* = **certain**, clear, incontrovertible, indisputable, obvious, sure, unquestionable

under *prep* **1** = **below**, beneath, underneath **2** = **subject to**, governed by, secondary to, subordinate to ◆ *adv* **3** = **below**, beneath, down, lower

underclothes *pl n* = **underwear**, lingerie, undergarments, undies (*inf*)

undercover *adj* = **secret**, concealed, covert, hidden, private

undercurrent *n* **1** = **undertow**, riptide **2** = **undertone**, atmosphere, feeling, hint, overtone, sense, suggestion, tendency, tinge, vibes (*sl*)

underdog *n* = **outsider**, little fellow (*inf*)

underestimate *v* = **underrate**, belittle, minimize, miscalculate, undervalue

undergo *v* = **experience**, bear, endure, go through, stand, suffer, sustain

underground *adj* **1** = **subterranean**, buried, covered **2** = **secret**, clandestine, sly. **2** *Sports* (of softball pitch, etc.) with hand swung below shoulder level.

un·der·lie [un-dər-LĪ] *vt* **-lay, -lain, -ly·ing** be situated under, lie beneath.

un·der·line [UN-dər-līn] *vt* **-lined, -lin·ing 1** put line under. **2** emphasize.

un·der·ling [UN-dər-ling] *n* subordinate.

un·der·mine [un-dər-MĪN] *vt* **-mined, -min·ing 1** wear away base, support of. **2** weaken insidiously.

un·der·neath [un-dər-NEETH] *adv, prep* **1** under or beneath. ◆ *adj, n* **2** lower (part of surface).

un·der·pass [UN-dər-pas] *n* section of road passing under another road, railroad line, etc.

un·der·stand [un-dər-STAND] *v* **-stood** [-stuud], **-stand·ing 1** know and comprehend. **2** realize. ◆ *vt* **3** infer. **4** take for granted. **un·der·stand'a·ble** *adj* **un·der·stand'ing** *n* **1** intelligence. **2** opinion. **3** agreement. ◆ *adj* **4** sympathetic.

un·der·stud·y [UN-dər-stud-ee] *n, pl* **-stud·ies 1** one prepared to take over theatrical part from performer if necessary. ◆ *vt* **-stud·ied, -stud·y·ing 2** work as understudy to (performer).

un·der·take [un-dər-TAYK] *vt* **-took** [-tuuk], **-tak·en, -tak·ing 1** make oneself responsible for. **2** enter upon. **3** promise. **un·der·tak·er** *n* one who arranges funerals. **un·der·tak·ing** *n* **1** that which is undertaken. **2** project. **3** guarantee.

un·der·tone [UN-dər-tohn] *n* **1** quiet, dropped tone of voice. **2** underlying tone or suggestion.

un·der·tow [UN-dər-toh] *n* **1** backwash of wave. **2** current beneath surface moving in different direction from surface current.

un·der·wear [UN-dər-wair] *n* (also **un'der·clothes**) garments worn next to skin.

un·der·world [UN-dər-wurld] *n* **1** criminals and their associates. **2** *Mythology* abode of

——— THESAURUS ———

covert, hidden ◆ *n* **3 the underground** = **the Resistance**, partisans

undergrowth *n* = **scrub**, bracken, briars, brush, underbrush

underhand, underhanded *adj* = **sly**, crafty, deceitful, devious, dishonest, down and dirty (*inf*), furtive, secret, sneaky, stealthy

underline *v* **1** = **underscore**, mark **2** = **emphasize**, accentuate, highlight, stress

underlying *adj* = **fundamental**, basic, elementary, intrinsic, primary, prime

undermine *v* = **weaken**, disable, sabotage, sap, subvert

underprivileged *adj* = **disadvantaged**, deprived, destitute, impoverished, needy, poor

underrate *v* = **underestimate**, belittle, discount, undervalue

undersized *adj* = **stunted**, dwarfish, miniature, pygmy *or* pigmy, small

understand *v* **1** = **comprehend**, conceive, fathom, follow, get, grasp, perceive, realize, see, take in **2** = **believe**, assume, gather, presume, suppose, think

understandable *adj* = **reasonable**, justifiable, legitimate, natural, to be expected

understanding *n* **1** = **perception**, appreciation, awareness, comprehension, discernment, grasp, insight, judgment, knowledge, sense **2** = **interpretation**, belief, idea, judgment, notion, perception, view **3** = **agreement**, accord, pact ◆ *adj* **4** = **sympathetic**, compassionate, considerate, kind, patient, sensitive, tolerant

understood *adj* **1** = **implied**, implicit, inferred, tacit, unspoken, unstated **2** = **assumed**, accepted, taken for granted

understudy *n* = **stand-in**, replacement, reserve, substitute

undertake *v* = **agree**, bargain, contract, engage, guarantee, pledge, promise

undertaking *n* **1** = **task**, affair, attempt, business, effort, endeavor, enterprise, operation, project, venture **2** = **promise**, assurance, commitment, pledge, vow, word

undertone *n* **1** = **murmur**, whisper **2** = **undercurrent**, hint, suggestion, tinge, touch, trace

undervalue *v* = **underrate**, depreciate, hold cheap, minimize, misjudge, underestimate

underwater *adj* = **submerged**, submarine, sunken

under way *adj* = **begun**, going on, in progress, started

underwear *n* = **underclothes**, lingerie, undergarments, underthings, undies (*inf*)

underweight *adj* = **skinny**, emaciated, half-starved, puny, skin and bone (*inf*), undernourished, undersized the dead.

un·der·write [un-dər-RĪT] vt **-wrote, -writ·ten, -writ·ing 1** agree to pay. **2** accept liability in insurance policy. **un'der·writ·er** n agent for insurance or stock issue.

un·do [un-DOO] vt **-did, -done, -do·ing 1** untie, unfasten. **2** reverse. **3** cause downfall of. **un·do'ing** n **un·done** adj [un-DUN] **1** ruined. **2** not performed.

un·du·late [UN-jə-layt] v **-lat·ed, -lat·ing** move up and down like waves. **un·du·la'tion** n

un·earth [un-URTH] vt **1** dig up. **2** discover.

un·eas·y [un-EE-zee] adj **-eas·i·er, -eas·i·est 1** anxious. **2** uncomfortable. **un·eas'i·ness** [-nis] n

un·em·ployed [un-im-PLOID] adj having no paid employment, out of work. **un·em·ploy'ment** [-mənt] n

---

THESAURUS

underworld n **1 = criminals**, gangland (inf), gangsters, organized crime **2 = nether world**, Hades, nether regions

underwrite v **1 = finance**, back, fund, guarantee, insure, sponsor, subsidize **2 = sign**, endorse, initial

undesirable adj **= objectionable**, disagreeable, distasteful, unacceptable, unattractive, unsuitable, unwanted, unwelcome

undeveloped adj **= potential**, immature, latent

undignified adj **= unseemly**, improper, indecorous, inelegant, unbecoming, unsuitable

undisciplined adj **= uncontrolled**, obstreperous, unrestrained, unruly, wayward, wild, willful

undisguised adj **= obvious**, blatant, evident, explicit, open, overt, patent, unconcealed

undisputed adj **= acknowledged**, accepted, certain, indisputable, recognized, unchallenged, undeniable, undoubted

undistinguished adj **= ordinary**, everyday, mediocre, unexceptional, unimpressive, unremarkable

undisturbed adj **1 = quiet**, tranquil **2 = calm**, collected, composed, placid, sedate, serene, tranquil, unfazed (inf), unperturbed, untroubled

undivided adj **= complete**, entire, exclusive, full, solid, thorough, undistracted, united, whole

undo v **1 = open**, disentangle, loose, unbutton, unfasten, untie **2 = reverse**, annul, cancel, invalidate, neutralize, offset **3 = ruin**, defeat, destroy, overturn, quash, shatter, subvert, undermine, upset, wreck

undoing n **= downfall**, collapse, defeat, disgrace, overthrow, reversal, ruin, shame

undone[1] adj **= unfinished**, left, neglected, omitted, unfulfilled, unperformed

undoubted adj **= certain**, acknowledged, definite, indisputable, indubitable, sure, undisputed, unquestioned

undoubtedly adv **= certainly**, assuredly, definitely, doubtless, surely, without doubt

undress v **1 = strip**, disrobe, shed, take off one's clothes ♦ n **2 = nakedness**, nudity

undue adj **= excessive**, extreme, improper, needless, uncalled-for, unnecessary, unwarranted

unduly adv **= excessively**, overly, unnecessarily, unreasonably

undying adj **= eternal**, constant, deathless, everlasting, infinite, permanent, perpetual, twenty-four-seven (sl), unending

unearth v **1 = discover**, expose, find, reveal, uncover **2 = dig up**, dredge up, excavate, exhume

unearthly adj **= eerie**, ghostly, phantom, spectral, spooky (inf), strange, supernatural, uncanny, weird

uneasiness n **= anxiety**, disquiet, doubt, misgiving, qualms, trepidation, worry

uneasy adj **1 = anxious**, disturbed, edgy, nervous, on edge, perturbed, troubled, twitchy (inf), uncomfortable, wired (sl), worried **2 = awkward**, insecure, precarious, shaky, strained, tense, uncomfortable

uneconomic adj **= unprofitable**, loss-making, nonpaying

uneducated adj **1 = ignorant**, illiterate, unlettered, unschooled, untaught **2 = lowbrow**, uncultivated, uncultured

unemotional adj **= impassive**, apathetic, cold, cool, phlegmatic, reserved, undemonstrative, unexcitable

unemployed adj **= out of work**, idle, jobless, laid off, redundant

unending adj **= perpetual**, continual, endless, eternal, everlasting, interminable, unceasing

unendurable adj **= unbearable**, insufferable, insupportable, intolerable

un·e·quiv'o·cal *adj* completely clear in meaning.

un·err·ing [un-ER-ing] *adj* **1** not missing the mark. **2** consistently accurate.

un·fail'ing *adj* continuous or reliable.

un·fair' *adj* not right, fair, or just.

un·fit' *adj* **1** unqualified or unsuitable. **2** in poor physical condition.

un·fold' *v* **1** open or spread out from a folded state. **2** reveal or be revealed.

un·for·get'ta·ble *adj* impossible to forget, memorable.

un·for·tu·nate *adj* **1** unlucky, unsuccessful, or unhappy. **2** regrettable or unsuitable. ◆

——— THESAURUS ———

unenthusiastic *adj* = **indifferent**, apathetic, half-hearted, nonchalant

unenviable *adj* = **unpleasant**, disagreeable, uncomfortable, undesirable

unequal *adj* **1** = **different**, differing, disparate, dissimilar, unlike, unmatched, varying **2** = **disproportionate**, asymmetrical, ill-matched, irregular, unbalanced, uneven

unequaled *adj* = **incomparable**, matchless, paramount, peerless, supreme, unparalleled, unrivaled

unequivocal *adj* = **clear**, absolute, certain, definite, explicit, incontrovertible, indubitable, manifest, plain, unambiguous

unerring *adj* = **accurate**, exact, infallible, perfect, sure, unfailing

unethical *adj* = **dishonest**, disreputable, illegal, immoral, improper, shady (*inf*), unprincipled, unscrupulous, wrong

uneven *adj* **1** = **rough**, bumpy **2** = **variable**, broken, fitful, irregular, jerky, patchy, spasmodic **3** = **unbalanced**, lopsided, odd **4** = **unequal**, ill-matched, unfair

uneventful *adj* = **humdrum**, boring, dull, ho-hum (*inf*), monotonous, routine, tedious, unexciting

unexceptional *adj* = **ordinary**, commonplace, conventional, mediocre, normal, pedestrian, undistinguished, unremarkable

unexpected *adj* = **unforeseen**, abrupt, chance, fortuitous, sudden, surprising, unanticipated, unlooked-for, unpredictable

unfailing *adj* **1** = **continuous**, boundless, endless, persistent, unflagging **2** = **reliable**, certain, dependable, faithful, loyal, staunch, sure, true

unfair *adj* **1** = **biased**, bigoted, one-sided, partial, partisan, prejudiced, unjust **2** = **unscrupulous**, dishonest, unethical, unsporting, wrongful

unfaithful *adj* **1** = **faithless**, adulterous, two-timing (*inf*), untrue **2** = **disloyal**, deceitful, faithless, false, traitorous, treacherous, untrustworthy

unfamiliar *adj* = **strange**, alien, different, new, novel, unknown, unusual

unfashionable *adj* = **passé**, antiquated, dated, dumpy (*inf*), frowzy, homely (*U.S.*), obsolete, old-fashioned, old hat

unfasten *v* **1** = **undo**, detach, let go, loosen, open, separate, unlace, untie

unfathomable *adj* **1** = **baffling**, deep, impenetrable, incomprehensible, indecipherable, inexplicable, profound **2** = **immeasurable**, bottomless, unmeasured

unfavorable *adj* **1** = **adverse**, contrary, inauspicious, unfortunate, unlucky, unpropitious **2** = **hostile**, inimical, negative, unfriendly

unfeeling *adj* **1** = **hardhearted**, apathetic, callous, cold, cruel, heartless, insensitive, pitiless, uncaring **2** = **numb**, insensate, insensible

unfinished *adj* **1** = **incomplete**, half-done, uncompleted, undone **2** = **rough**, bare, crude, natural, raw, unrefined

unfit *adj* **1** = **incapable**, inadequate, incompetent, lousy (*sl*), no good, unqualified, useless **2** = **unsuitable**, inadequate, ineffective, unsuited, useless **3** = **out of shape**, feeble, flabby, in poor condition, unhealthy

unflappable *adj* = **imperturbable**, calm, collected, composed, cool, impassive, level-headed, self-possessed

unflattering *adj* **1** = **blunt**, candid, critical, honest **2** = **unattractive**, dumpy (*inf*), frowzy, homely (*U.S.*), plain, unbecoming

unflinching *adj* = **determined**, firm, immovable, resolute, staunch, steadfast, steady, unfaltering

unfold *v* **1** = **open**, expand, spread out, undo, unfurl, unravel, unroll, unwrap **2** = **reveal**, disclose, divulge, make known, present, show, uncover

unforeseen *adj* = **unexpected**, accidental, sudden, surprising, unanticipated, unpredicted

unforgettable *adj* = **memorable**, exceptional, impressive, notable

unforgivable *adj* = **inexcusable**, deplorable, disgraceful, shameful,

n **3** unlucky person.
un·gain·ly [un-GAYN-lee] *adj* **-li·er, -li·est** awkward, clumsy. **un·gain'li·ness** [-nis] *n*
un·guent [UNG-gwənt] *n* ointment.
un·hap·py *adj* **1** sad or depressed. **2** unfortunate or wretched.
un·health·y *adj* **1** likely to cause poor health. **2** not fit or well. **3** morbid, unnatural.
uni- *comb. form* one, e.g. *unicorn; uniform.*
u·ni·corn [YOO-ni-korn] *n* mythical horselike animal with single long horn.

u·ni·form [YOO-ni-form] *n* **1** identifying clothes worn by members of same group e.g. soldiers, nurses, etc. ◆ *adj* **2** not changing, unvarying. **3** regular, consistent. **4** conforming to same standard or rule. **u·ni·form'i·ty** *n* sameness. **u'ni·form·ly** *adv*
u·ni·fy [YOO-nə-fī] *v* **-fied, -fy·ing** make or become one. **u·ni·fi·ca'tion** [-KAY-shən] *n*
u·ni·lat·er·al [yoo-nə-LAT-ər-əl] *adj* **1** one-sided. **2** (of contract) binding one party only.
un·ion [YOON-yən] *n* **1** joining into one. **2**

——— THESAURUS ———

unpardonable
unfortunate *adj* **1** = **disastrous**, adverse, calamitous, ill-fated **2** = **unlucky**, cursed, doomed, hapless, unhappy, unsuccessful, wretched **3** = **regrettable**, deplorable, lamentable, unsuitable
unfounded *adj* = **groundless**, baseless, false, idle, spurious, unjustified
unfriendly *adj* **1** = **hostile**, aloof, chilly, cold, distant, uncongenial, unsociable **2** = **unfavorable**, alien, hostile, inhospitable
ungainly *adj* = **awkward**, clumsy, inelegant, lumbering, ungraceful
ungodly *adj* **1** = **unreasonable**, dreadful, intolerable, outrageous, unearthly **2** = **wicked**, corrupt, depraved, godless, immoral, impious, irreligious, profane, sinful
ungracious *adj* = **bad-mannered**, churlish, discourteous, impolite, rude, uncivil, unmannerly
ungrateful *adj* = **unappreciative**, unmindful, unthankful
unguarded *adj* **1** = **unprotected**, defenseless, undefended, vulnerable **2** = **careless**, heedless, ill-considered, imprudent, incautious, rash, thoughtless, unthinking, unwary
unhappiness *n* = **sadness**, blues, dejection, depression, despondency, gloom, heartache, low spirits, melancholy, misery, sorrow, wretchedness
unhappy *adj* **1** = **sad**, blue, dejected, depressed, despondent, downcast, melancholy, miserable, mournful, sorrowful **2** = **unlucky**, cursed, hapless, ill-fated, unfortunate, wretched
unharmed *adj* = **unhurt**, intact, safe, sound, undamaged, unscathed, whole
unhealthy *adj* **1** = **harmful**, detrimental, insalubrious, insanitary, unwholesome **2** = **sick**, ailing, delicate, feeble, frail, infirm,

invalid, sickly, unwell
unheard-of *adj* **1** = **unprecedented**, inconceivable, new, novel, singular, unique **2** = **shocking**, disgraceful, outrageous, preposterous **3** = **obscure**, unfamiliar, unknown
unhesitating *adj* **1** = **instant**, immediate, prompt, ready **2** = **wholehearted**, resolute, unfaltering, unquestioning, unreserved
unholy *adj* = **evil**, corrupt, profane, sinful, ungodly, wicked
unhurried *adj* = **leisurely**, easy, sedate, slow
unidentified *adj* = **unnamed**, anonymous, nameless, unfamiliar, unrecognized
unification *n* = **union**, alliance, amalgamation, coalescence, coalition, confederation, federation, uniting
uniform *n* **1** = **outfit**, costume, dress, garb, habit, livery, regalia, suit ◆ *adj* **2** = **unvarying**, consistent, constant, even, regular, smooth, unchanging **3** = **alike**, equal, like, on a level playing field (*inf*), same, similar
uniformity *n* **1** = **regularity**, constancy, evenness, invariability, sameness, similarity **2** = **monotony**, dullness, flatness, sameness, tedium
unify *v* = **unite**, amalgamate, combine, confederate, consolidate, join, merge
unimaginable *adj* = **inconceivable**, fantastic, impossible, incredible, unbelievable
unimaginative *adj* = **unoriginal**, banal, derivative, dull, hackneyed, ordinary, pedestrian, predictable, prosaic, uncreative, uninspired
unimportant *adj* = **insignificant**, inconsequential, irrelevant, minor, paltry, petty, trifling, trivial, worthless
uninhabited *adj* = **deserted**, barren, desolate, empty, unpopulated, vacant

state of being joined. **3** result of being
joined. **4** federation, combination of states,
etc. **5** labor union, trade union. **un'ion·ize**
v **-ized**, **-iz·ing** organize (workers) into
labor union.

u·nique [yoo-NEEK] adj **1** being only one of
its kind. **2** unparalleled.

u·ni·son [YOO-nə-sən] n **1** Mus. singing,
etc. of same note as others. **2** agreement,
harmony, concord.

u·nit [YOO-nit] n **1** single thing or person. **2**
standard quantity. **3** group of people or
things with one purpose.

u·nite [yoo-NĪT] v **u·nit·ed, u·nit·ing ♦** vt **1**
join into one, connect. **2** associate. **3** cause
to adhere. **♦** vi **4** become one. **5** combine.
u'ni·ty [-nə-tee] n **1** state of being one. **2**

harmony. **3** agreement, uniformity. **4**
combination of separate parts into
connected whole. **5** Mathematics the
number one.

u·ni·verse [YOO-nə-vurs] n **1** all existing
things considered as constituting
systematic whole. **2** the world. **u·ni·ver'sal**
[-səl] adj **1** relating to all things or all
people. **2** applying to all members of a
community. **u·ni·ver·sal'i·ty** [-SAL-ə-tee] n

u·ni·ver·si·ty [yoo-nə-VUR-si-tee] n, pl **-ties**
educational institution for research, study,
examination and award of degrees in
various branches of learning.

un·kempt' adj of rough or uncared-for
appearance.

un·less' conj if not, except.

——————— THESAURUS ———————

uninhibited adj **1** = **unselfconscious**, free,
liberated, natural, open, relaxed,
spontaneous, unrepressed, unreserved **2** =
unrestrained, free, unbridled, unchecked,
unconstrained, uncontrolled, unrestricted

uninspired adj = **unimaginative**, banal,
dull, humdrum, ordinary, prosaic,
unexciting, unoriginal

unintelligent adj = **stupid**, braindead (inf),
brainless, dense, dull, foolish, obtuse, slow,
thick

unintelligible adj = **incomprehensible**,
inarticulate, incoherent, indistinct,
jumbled, meaningless, muddled

unintentional adj = **accidental**, casual,
inadvertent, involuntary, unconscious,
unintended

uninterested adj = **indifferent**, apathetic,
blasé, bored, listless, unconcerned

uninteresting adj = **boring**, drab, dreary,
dry, dull, flat, humdrum, monotonous,
tedious, unexciting

uninterrupted adj = **continuous**,
constant, nonstop, steady, sustained,
unbroken

union n **1** = **joining**, amalgamation, blend,
combination, conjunction, fusion, mixture,
uniting **2** = **alliance**, association, coalition,
confederacy, federation, league **3** =
agreement, accord, concord, harmony,
unanimity, unison, unity

unique adj **1** = **single**, lone, only, solitary
2 = **unparalleled**, incomparable,
inimitable, matchless, unequaled,
unmatched, unrivaled

unison n = **agreement**, accord,
accordance, concert, concord, harmony,

unity

unit n **1** = **item**, entity, whole **2** = **part**,
component, constituent, element,
member, section, segment **3** = **section**,
detachment, group **4** = **measure**,
measurement, quantity

unite v **1** = **join**, amalgamate, blend,
combine, couple, fuse, link, merge, unify
2 = **cooperate**, ally, band, join forces, pool

united adj **1** = **combined**, affiliated, allied,
banded together, collective, concerted,
pooled, unified **2** = **in agreement**, agreed,
of one mind, of the same opinion,
unanimous

unity n **1** = **wholeness**, entity, integrity,
oneness, singleness, union **2** = **agreement**,
accord, assent, concord, consensus,
harmony, solidarity, unison

universal adj = **widespread**, common,
general, total, unlimited, whole,
worldwide

universally adv = **everywhere**, always,
invariably, without exception

universe n = **cosmos**, creation,
macrocosm, nature

unjust adj = **unfair**, biased, one-sided,
partial, partisan, prejudiced, wrong,
wrongful

unjustifiable adj = **inexcusable**,
indefensible, outrageous, unacceptable,
unforgivable, unpardonable, wrong

unkempt adj **1** = **uncombed**, shaggy,
tousled **2** = **untidy**, disheveled, disordered,
messy, slovenly, ungroomed

unkind adj = **cruel**, harsh, malicious, mean,
nasty, spiteful, uncharitable, unfeeling,
unfriendly, unsympathetic

un·men'tion·a·ble *adj* unsuitable as a topic of conversation.

un·moved' *adj* not affected by emotion, indifferent.

un·or'tho·dox *adj* **1** (of ideas, methods, etc.) unconventional and not generally accepted. **2** (of a person) having unusual opinions or methods.

un·pleas'ant *adj* not pleasant or agreeable.

THESAURUS

unknown *adj* **1 = hidden**, concealed, dark, mysterious, secret, unrevealed **2 = strange**, alien, new **3 = unidentified**, anonymous, nameless, uncharted, undiscovered, unexplored, unnamed **4 = obscure**, humble, unfamiliar

unlawful *adj* **= illegal**, banned, criminal, forbidden, illicit, outlawed, prohibited

unleash *v* **= release**, free, let go, let loose

unlike *adj* **= different**, dissimilar, distinct, diverse, not alike, opposite, unequal

unlikely *adj* **1 = improbable**, doubtful, faint, remote, slight **2 = unbelievable**, implausible, incredible, questionable

unlimited *adj* **1 = infinite**, boundless, countless, endless, extensive, great, immense, limitless, unbounded, vast **2 = complete**, absolute, full, total, unqualified, unrestricted

unload *v* **= empty**, discharge, dump, lighten, relieve, unpack

unlock *v* **= open**, release, undo, unfasten, unlatch

unlooked-for *adj* **= unexpected**, chance, fortuitous, surprising, unanticipated, unforeseen, unpredicted

unloved *adj* **= neglected**, forsaken, loveless, rejected, spurned, unpopular, unwanted

unlucky *adj* **1 = unfortunate**, cursed, hapless, luckless, miserable, unhappy, wretched **2 = ill-fated**, doomed, inauspicious, ominous, unfavorable

unmarried *adj* **= single**, bachelor, maiden, unattached, unwed

unmask *v* **= reveal**, disclose, discover, expose, lay bare, uncover

unmentionable *adj* **= taboo**, forbidden, indecent, obscene, scandalous, shameful, shocking, unspeakable

unmerciful *adj* **= merciless**, brutal, cruel, hard, implacable, pitiless, remorseless, ruthless

unmistakable *adj* **= clear**, certain, distinct, evident, manifest, obvious, plain, sure, unambiguous

unmitigated *adj* **1 = unrelieved**, intense, persistent, unalleviated, unbroken, undiminished **2 = complete**, absolute, arrant, downright, outright, sheer, thorough, utter

unmoved *adj* **= unaffected**, cold, impassive, indifferent, unimpressed, unresponsive, untouched

unnatural *adj* **1 = strange**, extraordinary, freakish, outlandish, queer **2 = abnormal**, anomalous, irregular, odd, perverse, perverted, unusual **3 = false**, affected, artificial, feigned, forced, insincere, phoney or phony (*inf*), stiff, stilted

unnecessary *adj* **= needless**, expendable, inessential, redundant, superfluous, unneeded, unrequired

unnerve *v* **= intimidate**, demoralize, discourage, dishearten, dismay, faze, fluster, frighten, psych out (*inf*), rattle (*inf*), shake, upset

unnoticed *adj* **= unobserved**, disregarded, ignored, neglected, overlooked, unheeded, unperceived, unrecognized, unseen

unobtrusive *adj* **= inconspicuous**, low-key, modest, quiet, restrained, retiring, self-effacing, unassuming

unoccupied *adj* **= empty**, uninhabited, vacant

unofficial *adj* **= unauthorized**, informal, private, unconfirmed

unorthodox *adj* **= unconventional**, abnormal, irregular, off-the-wall (*sl*), unusual

unpaid *adj* **1 = voluntary**, honorary, unsalaried **2 = owing**, due, outstanding, overdue, payable, unsettled

unpalatable *adj* **= unpleasant**, disagreeable, distasteful, horrid, offensive, repugnant, unappetizing, unsavory

unparalleled *adj* **= unequaled**, incomparable, matchless, superlative, unique, unmatched, unprecedented, unsurpassed

unpardonable *adj* **= unforgivable**, deplorable, disgraceful, indefensible, inexcusable

unperturbed *adj* **= calm**, as cool as a cucumber, composed, cool, placid, unfazed (*inf*), unruffled, untroubled, unworried

un·rav·el [un-RAV-əl] *vt* **-eled, -el·ing** undo, untangle.

un·re·mit·ting [un-ri-MIT-ing] *adj* never slackening or stopping.

un·re·quit·ed *adj* not returned, e.g. *unrequited love.*

un·roll' *v* open out or unwind (something rolled or coiled) or (of something rolled or coiled) become opened out or unwound.

un·ru·ly [un-ROO-lee] *adj* **-li·er, -li·est** badly behaved, ungovernable, disorderly.

un·sa·vor·y [un-SAY-və-ree] *adj* distasteful,

───────┤ THESAURUS ├───────

unpleasant *adj* = **nasty**, bad, disagreeable, displeasing, distasteful, horrid, objectionable

unpopular *adj* = **disliked**, rejected, shunned, unwanted, unwelcome

unprecedented *adj* = **extraordinary**, abnormal, new, novel, original, remarkable, singular, unheard-of

unpredictable *adj* = **inconstant**, chance, changeable, doubtful, erratic, random, unforeseeable, unreliable, variable

unprejudiced *adj* = **impartial**, balanced, fair, just, objective, open-minded, unbiased

unprepared *adj* **1** = **taken off guard**, surprised, unaware, unready **2** = **improvised**, ad-lib, off the cuff (*inf*), spontaneous

unpretentious *adj* = **modest**, dumpy (*inf*), homely, humble, plain, simple, straightforward, unaffected, unassuming, unostentatious

unprincipled *adj* = **dishonest**, amoral, crooked, devious, immoral, underhand, unethical, unscrupulous

unproductive *adj* **1** = **useless**, fruitless, futile, idle, ineffective, unprofitable, unrewarding, vain **2** = **barren**, fruitless, sterile

unprofessional *adj* **1** = **unethical**, improper, lax, negligent, unprincipled **2** = **amateurish**, incompetent, inefficient, inexpert

unprotected *adj* = **vulnerable**, defenseless, helpless, open, undefended

unqualified *adj* **1** = **unfit**, ill-equipped, incapable, incompetent, ineligible, unprepared **2** = **total**, absolute, complete, downright, outright, thorough, utter

unquestionable *adj* = **certain**, absolute, clear, conclusive, definite, incontrovertible, indisputable, sure, undeniable, unequivocal, unmistakable

unravel *v* **1** = **undo**, disentangle, free, separate, untangle, unwind **2** = **solve**, explain, figure out (*inf*), resolve, work out

unreal *adj* **1** = **imaginary**, dreamlike, fabulous, fanciful, illusory, make-believe,

visionary **2** = **insubstantial**, immaterial, intangible, nebulous **3** = **fake**, artificial, false, insincere, mock, pretended, sham

unrealistic *adj* = **impractical**, impracticable, improbable, romantic, unworkable

unreasonable *adj* **1** = **excessive**, extortionate, immoderate, undue, unfair, unjust, unwarranted **2** = **biased**, blinkered, opinionated

unrelated *adj* **1** = **different**, unconnected, unlike **2** = **irrelevant**, extraneous, inapplicable, inappropriate, unconnected

unreliable *adj* **1** = **undependable**, irresponsible, treacherous, untrustworthy **2** = **uncertain**, deceptive, fallible, false, implausible, inaccurate, unsound

unrepentant *adj* = **impenitent**, abandoned, callous, hardened, incorrigible, shameless, unremorseful

unreserved *adj* **1** = **total**, absolute, complete, entire, full, unlimited, wholehearted **2** = **open**, demonstrative, extrovert, free, outgoing, uninhibited, unrestrained

unresolved *adj* = **undecided**, doubtful, moot, unanswered, undetermined, unsettled, unsolved, vague

unrest *n* = **discontent**, agitation, discord, dissension, protest, rebellion, sedition, strife

unrestrained *adj* = **uncontrolled**, abandoned, free, immoderate, intemperate, unbounded, unbridled, unchecked, uninhibited

unrestricted *adj* **1** = **unlimited**, absolute, free, open, unbounded, unregulated **2** = **open**, public

unrivaled *adj* = **unparalleled**, beyond compare, incomparable, matchless, supreme, unequaled, unmatched, unsurpassed

unruly *adj* = **uncontrollable**, disobedient, mutinous, rebellious, wayward, wild, willful

unsafe *adj* = **dangerous**, hazardous, insecure, perilous, risky, unreliable

unsatisfactory *adj* = **unacceptable**,

disagreeable.

un·sight·ly [un-SĪT-lee] *adj* ugly.

un·suit·a·ble *adj* not right or appropriate

for a particular purpose.

un·ten·a·ble [un-TEN-ə-bəl] *adj* (of theories, etc.) incapable of being

───────── THESAURUS ─────────

deficient, disappointing, inadequate, insufficient, lousy (*sl*), not good enough, not up to scratch (*inf*), poor

unsavory *adj* **1 = unpleasant**, distasteful, nasty, obnoxious, offensive, repellent, repulsive, revolting, scuzzy (*sl*) **2 = unappetizing**, nauseating, sickening, unpalatable

unscathed *adj* **= unharmed**, safe, unhurt, uninjured, unmarked, whole

unscrupulous *adj* **= unprincipled**, corrupt, dishonest, dishonorable, immoral, improper, unethical

unseat *v* **1 = throw**, unhorse, unsaddle **2 = depose**, dethrone, displace, oust, overthrow, remove

unseemly *adj* **= improper**, inappropriate, indecorous, unbecoming, undignified, unsuitable

unseen *adj* **= unobserved**, concealed, hidden, invisible, obscure, undetected, unnoticed

unselfish *adj* **= generous**, altruistic, kind, magnanimous, noble, selfless, self-sacrificing

unsettle *v* **= disturb**, agitate, bother, confuse, disconcert, faze, fluster, perturb, ruffle, trouble, upset

unsettled *adj* **1 = unstable**, disorderly, insecure, shaky, unsteady **2 = restless**, agitated, anxious, confused, disturbed, flustered, restive, shaken, tense, wired (*sl*) **3 = changing**, inconstant, uncertain, variable

unshakable *adj* **= firm**, absolute, fixed, immovable, staunch, steadfast, sure, unswerving, unwavering

unsightly *adj* **= ugly**, disagreeable, dumpy (*inf*), hideous, homely (*U.S.*), horrid, repulsive, scuzzy (*sl*), unattractive

unskilled *adj* **= unprofessional**, amateurish, inexperienced, unqualified, untrained

unsociable *adj* **= unfriendly**, chilly, cold, distant, hostile, retiring, unforthcoming, withdrawn

unsolicited *adj* **= unrequested**, gratuitous, unasked for, uncalled-for, uninvited, unsought

unsophisticated *adj* **1 = natural**, artless, childlike, guileless, ingenuous, unaffected

2 = simple, dumpy (*inf*), frowzy, homely (*U.S.*), plain, uncomplicated, unrefined, unspecialized

unsound *adj* **1 = unhealthy**, ailing, defective, diseased, ill, unbalanced, unstable, unwell, weak **2 = unreliable**, defective, fallacious, false, flawed, illogical, shaky, specious, weak

unspeakable *adj* **1 = indescribable**, inconceivable, unbelievable, unimaginable **2 = dreadful**, abominable, appalling, awful, heinous, horrible, monstrous, shocking

unspoiled, unspoilt *adj* **1 = perfect**, intact, preserved, unchanged, undamaged, untouched **2 = natural**, artless, innocent, unaffected

unspoken *adj* **= tacit**, implicit, implied, understood, unexpressed, unstated

unstable *adj* **1 = insecure**, precarious, shaky, tottering, unsettled, unsteady, wobbly **2 = changeable**, fitful, fluctuating, inconstant, unpredictable, variable, volatile **3 = unpredictable**, capricious, changeable, erratic, inconsistent, irrational, temperamental

unsteady *adj* **1 = unstable**, infirm, insecure, precarious, shaky, unsafe, wobbly **2 = changeable**, erratic, inconstant, temperamental, unsettled, volatile

unsuccessful *adj* **1 = useless**, failed, fruitless, futile, unavailing, unproductive, vain **2 = unlucky**, hapless, luckless, unfortunate

unsuitable *adj* **= inappropriate**, improper, inapposite, inapt, ineligible, unacceptable, unbecoming, unfit, unfitting, unseemly

unsure *adj* **1 = unconfident**, insecure, unassured **2 = doubtful**, distrustful, dubious, hesitant, mistrustful, skeptical, suspicious, unconvinced

unsuspecting *adj* **= trusting**, credulous, gullible, trustful, unwary

unswerving *adj* **= constant**, firm, resolute, single-minded, staunch, steadfast, steady, true, unwavering

unsympathetic *adj* **= hard**, callous, cold, cruel, harsh, heartless, insensitive, unfeeling, unkind, unmoved

untangle *v* **= disentangle**, extricate, unravel, unsnarl maintained, defended.

un·think·a·ble [un-THING-kə-bəl] *adj* **1** out of the question. **2** inconceivable. **3** unreasonable.

un·til' *conj* **1** up to the time that. ♦ *prep* **2** in or throughout the period before.

un·to [UN-too] *prep* to.

un·touched [un-TUCHT] *adj* **1** not touched. **2** not harmed. **un·touch'a·ble** *adj* **1** not able to be touched. ♦ *n* **2** esp. formerly, non-caste Hindu, forbidden to be touched by one of caste.

un·to·ward [un-TORD] *adj* awkward, inconvenient.

un·tram·meled [un-TRAM-əld] *adj* not confined, not constrained.

un·u'su·al *adj* uncommon or extraordinary.

un·wield·y [un-WEEL-dee] *adj* -wield·i·er, -wield·i·est **1** awkward, big, heavy to handle. **2** clumsy.

un·wit'ting *adj* **1** not knowing. **2** not

untenable *adj* = **unsustainable**, groundless, illogical, indefensible, insupportable, shaky, unsound, weak

unthinkable *adj* **1** = **impossible**, absurd, out of the question, unreasonable **2** = **inconceivable**, implausible, incredible, unimaginable

untidy *adj* = **messy**, chaotic, cluttered, disarrayed, disordered, jumbled, littered, muddled, shambolic, unkempt

untie *v* = **undo**, free, loosen, release, unbind, unfasten, unknot, unlace

untimely *adj* **1** = **early**, premature **2** = **ill-timed**, awkward, inappropriate, inconvenient, inopportune, mistimed

untiring *adj* = **tireless**, constant, determined, dogged, persevering, steady, unflagging, unremitting

untold *adj* **1** = **indescribable**, inexpressible, undreamed of, unimaginable, unthinkable, unutterable **2** = **countless**, incalculable, innumerable, myriad, numberless, uncountable

untouched *adj* = **unharmed**, intact, undamaged, unhurt, uninjured, unscathed

untoward *adj* **1** = **annoying**, awkward, inconvenient, irritating, troublesome, unfortunate **2** = **unlucky**, adverse, inauspicious, inopportune, unfavorable

untrained *adj* = **amateur**, green, inexperienced, raw, uneducated, unqualified, unschooled, unskilled, untaught

untroubled *adj* = **undisturbed**, calm, cool, peaceful, placid, tranquil, unfazed (*inf*), unperturbed, unworried

untrue *adj* **1** = **false**, deceptive, dishonest, erroneous, inaccurate, incorrect, lying, mistaken, wrong **2** = **unfaithful**, deceitful, disloyal, faithless, false, inconstant, treacherous, untrustworthy

untrustworthy *adj* = **unreliable**, deceitful, devious, dishonest, disloyal, false, slippery, treacherous, tricky

untruth *n* = **lie**, deceit, falsehood, fib, story, white lie

untruthful *adj* = **dishonest**, deceitful, deceptive, false, lying, mendacious

unusual *adj* = **extraordinary**, curious, different, exceptional, odd, queer, rare, remarkable, singular, strange, uncommon, unconventional

unveil *v* = **reveal**, disclose, divulge, expose, make known, uncover

unwanted *adj* = **undesired**, outcast, rejected, uninvited, unneeded, unsolicited, unwelcome

unwarranted *adj* = **unnecessary**, gratuitous, groundless, indefensible, inexcusable, uncalled-for, unjustified, unprovoked

unwavering *adj* = **steady**, consistent, determined, immovable, resolute, staunch, steadfast, unshakable, unswerving

unwelcome *adj* **1** = **unwanted**, excluded, rejected, unacceptable, undesirable **2** = **disagreeable**, displeasing, distasteful, undesirable, unpleasant

unwell *adj* = **ill**, ailing, sick, sickly, under the weather (*inf*), unhealthy

unwholesome *adj* **1** = **harmful**, deleterious, noxious, poisonous, unhealthy **2** = **wicked**, bad, corrupting, degrading, demoralizing, evil, immoral

unwieldy *adj* **1** = **awkward**, cumbersome, inconvenient, unmanageable **2** = **bulky**, clumsy, hefty, massive, ponderous

unwilling *adj* = **reluctant**, averse, disinclined, grudging, indisposed, loath, resistant, unenthusiastic

unwind *v* **1** = **unravel**, slacken, uncoil, undo, unroll, untwine, untwist **2** = **relax**, loosen up, take it easy, wind down

unwise *adj* = **foolish**, foolhardy, improvident, imprudent, inadvisable, injudicious, rash, reckless, senseless, silly, intentional.

un·wrap' *v* remove the wrapping from (something).

up *prep* **1** from lower to higher position. **2** along. ♦ *adv* **3** in or to higher position, source, activity, etc. **4** indicating completion. **up'ward** *adj*, *adv* **up'wards** *adv* **1** up against. **2** confronted with.

up- *comb. form* up, upper, upwards, e.g. *uproot; upgrade.*

up·braid [up-BRAYD] *vt* scold, reproach.

up'bring·ing *n* rearing and education of children.

up·date [up-DAYT] *vt* **-dat·ed, -dat·ing** bring up to date. ♦ *n*

up·front [up-frunt] *adj* **1** *inf* open, frank. ♦ *adj*, *adv* **2** *inf* (of money) paid out at beginning of business arrangement.

up·grade [up-GRAYD] *vt* **-grad·ed, -grad·ing 1** promote to higher position. **2** improve.

up·heav·al [up-HEE-vəl] *n* sudden or violent disturbance.

up·hold [up-HOHLD] *vt* **-held, -hold·ing** maintain, support, etc.

up·hol·ster [up-HOHL-stər] *vt* fit springs, padding and coverings on chairs, etc. **up·hol'ster·er** *n* one who does this work. **up·hol'ster·y** *n*

up'keep *n* act, process or cost of keeping something in good repair.

up·lift' *vt* **1** raise aloft. ♦ *n* [UP-lift] **2** a lifting up. **3** mental, social or emotional improvement.

up·load *vt Computers.* transfer data from a single computer to a server or host.

up·on [ə-PON] *prep* on.

up·per [UP-ər] *adj* **1** higher, situated above. **2** comp. of UP. ♦ *n* **3** upper part of boot or shoe. **up'per·cut** *n* short-arm upward blow. **up'per·most** [-mohst] *adj* sup. of UP.

up·right [UP-rīt] *adj* **1** erect. **2** honest, just.

stupid

unwitting *adj* **1 = unintentional**, accidental, chance, inadvertent, involuntary, unplanned **2 = unknowing**, ignorant, innocent, unaware, unconscious, unsuspecting

unworldly *adj* **1 = spiritual**, metaphysical, nonmaterialistic **2 = naive**, idealistic, innocent, unsophisticated

unworthy *adj* **1 = undeserving**, not fit for, not good enough **2 = dishonorable**, base, contemptible, degrading, discreditable, disgraceful, disreputable, ignoble, lousy (*sl*), shameful **3 unworthy of = unbefitting**, beneath, inappropriate, unbecoming, unfitting, unseemly, unsuitable

unwritten *adj* **1 = oral**, vocal **2 = customary**, accepted, tacit, understood

unyielding *adj* **= firm**, adamant, immovable, inflexible, obdurate, obstinate, resolute, rigid, stiff-necked, stubborn, tough, uncompromising

upbeat *adj* **= cheerful**, cheery, encouraging, hopeful, optimistic, positive

upbraid *v* **= scold**, admonish, berate, rebuke, reprimand, reproach, reprove

upbringing *n* **= education**, breeding, raising, rearing, training

update *v* **= revise**, amend, bring up to date, modernize, renew

upgrade *v* **= promote**, advance, better, elevate, enhance, improve, raise

upheaval *n* **= disturbance**, disorder, disruption, revolution, turmoil

uphill *adj* **1 = ascending**, climbing, mounting, rising **2 = arduous**, difficult, exhausting, grueling, hard, laborious, strenuous, taxing, tough

uphold *v* **= support**, advocate, aid, back, champion, defend, endorse, maintain, promote, sustain

upkeep *n* **1 = maintenance**, keep, repair, running, subsistence **2 = overheads**, expenditure, expenses, running costs

uplift *v* **1 = raise**, elevate, hoist, lift up **2 = improve**, advance, better, edify, inspire, raise, refine ♦ *n* **3 = improvement**, advancement, edification, enhancement, enlightenment, enrichment, refinement

upmarket *adj Inf* **= upper-class**, classy (*inf*), grand, high-class, luxurious, smart, stylish, swanky (*inf*)

upper *adj* **1 = higher**, high, loftier, top, topmost **2 = superior**, eminent, greater, important

upper-class *adj* **= aristocratic**, blue-blooded, highborn, high-class, noble, patrician

upper hand *n* **= control**, advantage, ascendancy, edge, mastery, supremacy

uppermost *adj* **1 = top**, highest, loftiest, topmost **2 = supreme**, chief, dominant, foremost, greatest, leading, main, principal

uppity *adj Inf* **= conceited**, bumptious, cocky, full of oneself, impertinent,

◆ *adv* **3** vertically. ◆ *n* **4** thing standing upright, e.g. post in framework.

up·ris·ing [UP-rī-zing] *n* rebellion, revolt.

up·roar [UP-ror] *n* tumult, disturbance. **up·roar·i·ous** [-ee-əs] *adj* rowdy.

up·set' *vt* **-set, -set·ting 1** overturn. **2** distress. **3** disrupt. **4** make ill. ◆ *n* [UP-set] **5** unexpected defeat. **6** confusion. **7** trouble. **8** overturning.

up'shot *n* outcome, end.

up·stage [up-stayj] *adj* **1** of back of stage. ◆ *vt* **-staged, -stag·ing 2** draw attention away from another to oneself.

up·start [UP-stahrt] *n* one suddenly raised to wealth, power, etc.

up·tight [up-tīt] *adj sl* **1** displaying tense nervousness, irritability. **2** repressed.

u·ra·ni·um [yuu-RAY-nee-əm] *n* white radioactive metallic element, used as chief source of nuclear energy.

U·ra·nus [YUUR-ə-nəs] *n* **1** Greek god, personification of sky. **2** seventh planet from the sun.

ur·ban [UR-bən] *adj* **1** relating to town or city. **2** describing modern pop music of African-American origin, such as hip-hop. **ur·ban·ize** *vt* **-ized, -iz·ing** change countryside to residential or industrial area.

ur·bane [ur-BAIN] *adj* elegant, sophisticated. **ur·ban'i·ty** [-BAN-i-tee] *n*

ur'chin *n* mischievous, unkempt child.

u·re·a [yuu-REE-ə] *n* substance occurring in urine.

u·re·thra [yuu-REE-thrə] *n* canal conveying urine from bladder out of body.

urge [urj] *vt* **urged, urg·ing 1** exhort earnestly. **2** entreat. **3** drive on. ◆ *n* **4** strong desire. **ur'gen·cy** [-jən-see] *n, pl* **-cies ur'gent** [-jənt] *adj* **1** pressing. **2** needing attention at once. **ur'gent·ly** *adv*

self-important

upright *adj* **1 = vertical**, erect, perpendicular, straight **2 = honest**, conscientious, ethical, good, honorable, just, principled, righteous, virtuous

uprising *n* **= rebellion**, disturbance, insurgence, insurrection, mutiny, revolt, revolution, rising

uproar *n* **= commotion**, din, furor, mayhem, noise, outcry, pandemonium, racket, riot, turmoil

uproarious *adj* **1 = hilarious**, hysterical, rib-tickling, rip-roaring (*inf*), side-splitting, very funny **2 = loud**, boisterous, rollicking, unrestrained

uproot *v* **1 = pull up**, dig up, rip up, root out, weed out **2 = displace**, exile

upset *adj* **1 = sick**, ill, queasy **2 = distressed**, agitated, bothered, dismayed, disturbed, grieved, hurt, put out, troubled, worried **3 = disordered**, chaotic, confused, disarrayed, in disarray, muddled **4 = overturned**, capsized, spilled, upside down ◆ *v* **5 = tip over**, capsize, knock over, overturn, spill **6 = mess up**, change, disorder, disorganize, disturb, spoil **7 = distress**, agitate, bother, disconcert, disturb, faze, fluster, grieve, perturb, ruffle, trouble ◆ *n* **8 = reversal**, defeat, shake-up (*inf*) **9 = illness**, bug (*inf*), complaint, disorder, malady, sickness **10 = distress**, agitation, bother, disturbance, shock, trouble, worry

upshot *n* **= result**, culmination, end, end

result, finale, outcome, sequel

upside down *adj* **1 = inverted**, backward, overturned, upturned **2 = confused**, chaotic, disordered, muddled, topsy-turvy

upstanding *adj* **= honest**, ethical, good, honorable, incorruptible, moral, principled, upright

upstart *n* **= social climber**, arriviste, *nouveau riche*, parvenu

uptight *adj Inf* **= tense**, anxious, edgy, on edge, uneasy, wired (*sl*)

up-to-date *adj* **= modern**, cool (*inf*), current, fashionable, in vogue, phat (*sl*), stylish, trendy (*inf*), up-to-the-minute

upturn *n* **= rise**, advancement, improvement, increase, recovery, revival, upsurge, upswing

urban *adj* **= civic**, city, metropolitan, municipal, town

urbane *adj* **= sophisticated**, courteous, cultivated, cultured, debonair, polished, refined, smooth, suave, well-bred

urchin *n* **= ragamuffin**, brat, gamin, waif

urge *n* **1 = impulse**, compulsion, desire, drive, itch, longing, thirst, wish, yearning ◆ *v* **2 = beg**, beseech, entreat, exhort, implore, plead **3 = advocate**, advise, counsel, recommend, support **4 = drive**, compel, force, goad, impel, incite, induce, press, push, spur

urgency *n* **= importance**, extremity, gravity, hurry, necessity, need, pressure, seriousness

urgent *adj* **= crucial**, compelling, critical,

u·rine [YUUR-in] *n* fluid excreted by kidneys to bladder and passed as waste from body. **u'ric** *adj* **u·ri·nal** [YUUR-ə-nl] *n* (place with) sanitary fitting used by men for urination. **ur·i·nar·y** *adj* **u'ri·nate** *vi* -**nat·ed**, -**nat·ing** discharge urine.

URL *Computers.* uniform resource locator: standardized address of a location on the Internet.

urn *n* **1** vessel like vase, esp. for ashes of the dead. **2** large container with tap for making and dispensing tea, coffee, etc.

ur·sine [UR-sin] *adj* of, like a bear.

us *pron,* pl. the objective case of the pronoun WE.

use [yooz] *vt* **used, us·ing 1** employ, avail oneself of. **2** exercise. **3** exploit. **4** consume. ♦ *n* [yoos] **5** employment, application to a purpose. **6** need to employ. **7** serviceableness. **8** profit. **9** habit. **us·a·ble** [YOO-zə-bəl] *adj* fit for use. **us·age** [YOOS-ij] *n* **1** act of using. **2** custom. **3** customary way of using. **used** [yoozd] *adj* secondhand, not new. **use·ful** [YOOS-fəl] *adj* **1** of use. **2** helpful. **3** serviceable. **use'ful·ness** [-nis] *n* **use'less·ness** [-lis-nis] *n* **used to** [yoost] *adj* **1** accustomed to. ♦ *vt* **2** did so formerly. **us·er friendly** [YOO-zər] (of computer, etc.) easily understood and operated.

ush·er [USH-ər] *n* **1** doorkeeper, one showing people to seats, etc. ♦ *vt* **2** introduce, announce. **3** inaugurate.

u·su·al [YOO-zhoo-əl] *adj* habitual, ordinary. **u'su·al·ly** *adv* **1** as a rule. **2** generally, commonly.

u·surp [yoo-SURP] *vt* seize wrongfully. **u·sur·pa·tion** [yoo-sər-PAY-shən] *n* violent or unlawful seizing of power. **u·surp'er** *n*

u·su·ry [YOO-zhə-ree] *n* **1** lending of money at excessive interest. **2** such interest. **u'su·rer** *n* money lender. **u·su'ri·ous** [-ZHUUR-ee-əs] *adj*

u·ten·sil [yoo-TEN-səl] *n* vessel, implement, esp. in domestic use.

u·ter·us [YOO-tər-əs] *n,* pl -**us·es** womb. **u·ter·ine** [-tər-in] *adj*

u·til·i·ty [yoo-TIL-i-tee] *n,* pl -**ties 1** usefulness. **2** benefit. **3** useful thing. **4** a public service, such as electricity. ♦ *adj* **5** made for practical purposes. **u·til·i·tar'i·an** [-TAIR-ee-ən] *adj* useful rather than beautiful. **u·til·i·tar'i·an·ism** *n* doctrine that morality of actions is to be tested by their utility, esp. that the greatest good of the greatest number should be the sole end of public action. **u·ti·li·za'tion** [-ZAY-shən] *n* **u'ti·lize** *vt* -**lized, -liz·ing** make use of.

———————— THESAURUS ————————

immediate, imperative, important, pressing

usable *adj* = **serviceable**, available, current, functional, practical, utilizable, valid, working

usage *n* **1** = **use**, control, employment, handling, management, operation, running **2** = **practice**, convention, custom, habit, method, mode, procedure, regime, routine

use *v* **1** = **employ**, apply, exercise, exert, operate, practice, utilize, work **2** = **take advantage of**, exploit, manipulate **3** = **consume**, exhaust, expend, run through, spend ♦ *n* **4** = **usage**, application, employment, exercise, handling, operation, practice, service **5** = **good**, advantage, avail, benefit, help, point, profit, service, usefulness, value **6** = **purpose**, end, object, reason

used *adj* = **second-hand**, cast-off, nearly new, shopsoiled

used to *adj* = **accustomed to**, familiar with

useful *adj* = **helpful**, advantageous, beneficial, effective, fruitful, practical, profitable, serviceable, valuable, win-win (*inf*), worthwhile

usefulness *n* = **helpfulness**, benefit, convenience, effectiveness, efficacy, practicality, use, utility, value, worth

useless *adj* **1** = **worthless**, fruitless, futile, impractical, ineffectual, pointless, unproductive, vain, valueless **2** *Inf* = **inept**, hopeless, incompetent, ineffectual, no good

use up *v* = **consume**, absorb, drain, exhaust, finish, run through

usher *n* **1** = **attendant**, doorkeeper, doorman, escort, guide ♦ *v* **2** = **escort**, conduct, direct, guide, lead

usual *adj* = **normal**, common, customary, everyday, general, habitual, ordinary, regular, routine, standard, typical

usually *adv* = **normally**, as a rule, commonly, generally, habitually, mainly, mostly, on the whole

usurp *v* = **seize**, appropriate, assume, commandeer, take, take over, wrest

utility *n* = **usefulness**, benefit, convenience, efficacy, practicality,

ut·most [UT-mohst] *adj* **1** to the highest degree. **2** extreme, furthest. ◆ *n* **3** greatest possible amount.

u·to·pi·a [yoo-TOH-pee-ə] *n* imaginary state with perfect political and social conditions, or constitution. **u·to'pi·an** [-pee-ən] *adj* ideally perfect but impracticable.

ut·ter¹ [UT-ər] *vt* **1** express, emit audibly, say. **2** put in circulation (forged bills, counterfeit coin). **ut'ter·ance** [-əns] *n* **1** act of speaking. **2** expression in words. **3** spoken words.

utter² *adj* complete, total, absolute. **ut'ter·ly** *adv*

ut·ter·most [UT-ər-mohst] *adj* **1** farthest out. **2** utmost. ◆ *n* **3** highest degree.

u·vu·la [YOO-vyə-lə] *n, pl* **-las** *or* **-lae** [-lee] pendent fleshy part of soft palate. **u'vu·lar** [-lər] *adj*

ux·o·ri·ous [uk-SOR-ee-əs] *adj* excessively fond of one's wife.

──── THESAURUS ────

serviceableness

utilize *v* = **use**, avail oneself of, employ, make use of, put to use, take advantage of, turn to account

utmost *adj* **1** = **greatest**, chief, highest, maximum, paramount, pre-eminent, supreme **2** = **farthest**, extreme, final, last ◆ *n* **3** = **greatest**, best, hardest, highest

Utopia *n* = **paradise**, bliss, Eden, Garden of Eden, heaven, Shangri-la

Utopian *adj* = **perfect**, dream, fantasy, ideal, idealistic, imaginary, romantic, visionary

utter¹ *v* = **express**, articulate, pronounce, say, speak, voice

utter² *adj* = **absolute**, complete, downright, outright, sheer, thorough, total, unmitigated

utterance *n* = **speech**, announcement, declaration, expression, remark, statement, words

utterly *adv* = **totally**, absolutely, completely, entirely, extremely, fully, perfectly, thoroughly

V v

V *Chem.* vanadium.

va·cant [VAY-kənt] *adj* **1** without thought, empty. **2** unoccupied. **va'can·cy** [-kən-see] *n, pl* **-cies** **1** state of being unoccupied. **2** unfilled position, accommodation, etc.

va·cate [VAY-kayt] *vt* **-cat·ed, -cat·ing** quit, leave empty. **va·ca'tion** [-KAY-shən] *n* **1** act of vacating. **2** holidays. **3** time when schools and courts, etc. are closed.

vac·ci·nate [VAK-sə-nayt] *vt* **-nat·ed, -nat·ing** inoculate with vaccine as protection against a specific disease. **vac·ci·na'tion** *n* **vac·cine** [vak-SEEN] *n* any substance used for inoculation against disease.

vac·il·late [VAS-ə-layt] *vi* **-lat·ed, -lat·ing** **1** fluctuate in opinion. **2** waver. **3** move to and fro. **vac·il·la'tion** *n* **1** indecision. **2** wavering. **3** unsteadiness.

vac·u·um [VAK-yoom] *n, pl* **-u·ums** **1** place, region containing no matter and from which all or most air, gas has been removed. ♦ *v* **2** clean with vacuum cleaner. **va·cu·i·ty** [va-KYOO-i-tee] *n* **vac·u·ous** [VA-kyoo-əs] *adj* **1** vacant. **2** expressionless. **3** unintelligent. **vacuum cleaner** apparatus for removing dust by suction. **vac'uum-packed** *adj* contained in packaging from which air has been removed.

vag·a·bond [VAG-ə-bond] *n* **1** person with no fixed home. **2** wandering beggar or thief. ♦ *adj* **3** like a vagabond.

va·gar·y [VAY-gə-ree] *n, pl* **-gar·ies** **1** something unusual, erratic. **2** whim.

va·gi·na [və-JÍ-nə] *n, pl* **-nas** passage from womb to exterior. **vag·i·nal** [VAJ-ə-nl] *adj*

va·grant [VAY-grənt] *n* **1** vagabond, tramp. ♦ *adj* **2** wandering, esp. without purpose. **va'gran·cy** *n, pl* **-cies**

vague [vayg] *adj* **va·guer** [-gər], **va·guest** [-gəst] **1** indefinite or uncertain. **2** indistinct. **3** not clearly expressed. **4** absent-minded.

vain [vayn] *adj* **-er, -est** **1** conceited. **2** worthless, useless. **3** unavailing. **4** foolish. **vain'ly** *adv*

vain·glo·ry [VAYN-glor-ee] *n* boastfulness, vanity. **vain·glo'ri·ous** *adj*

val·ance [VAL-əns] *n* short curtain around base of bed, etc.

vale [vayl] *n Poet.* valley.

val·e·dic·tion [val-i-DIK-shən] *n* farewell. **val·e·dic·to'ri·an** [-TOR-ee-ən] *n* **val·e·dic'to·ry** [-DIK-tə-ree] *n* farewell address. ♦ *adj*

va·lence [VAY-ləns], **va·len·cy** [-lən-see] *n Chem.* combining power of element or atom.

THESAURUS

vacancy *n* = **job**, opening, opportunity, position, post, situation

vacant *adj* **1** = **unoccupied**, available, empty, free, idle, unfilled, untenanted, void **2** = **vague**, absent-minded, abstracted, blank, dreamy, idle, inane, vacuous

vacate *v* = **leave**, evacuate, quit

vacuous *adj* = **unintelligent**, blank, inane, stupid, uncomprehending, vacant

vacuum *n* = **emptiness**, gap, nothingness, space, vacuity, void

vagabond *n* = **beggar**, down-and-out, itinerant, rover, tramp, vagrant

vagrant *n* **1** = **tramp**, drifter, hobo, itinerant, rolling stone, wanderer ♦ *adj* **2** = **itinerant**, nomadic, roaming, rootless, roving, unsettled, vagabond

vague *adj* = **unclear**, equivocal, hazy, ill-defined, imprecise, indefinite, indeterminate, indistinct, loose, nebulous, uncertain, unspecified

vain *adj* **1** = **proud**, arrogant, conceited, egotistical, narcissistic, self-important, swaggering **2** = **futile**, abortive, fruitless, idle, pointless, senseless, unavailing, unprofitable, useless, worthless ♦ *n* **3 in vain** = **to no avail**, fruitless(ly), ineffectual(ly), unsuccessful(ly), useless(ly), vain(ly)

val·en·tine [VAL-ən-tīn] *n* (one receiving) card, gift, expressing affection, on Saint Valentine's Day, Feb. 14th.

val·et [va-LAY] *n* gentleman's personal servant.

val·e·tu·di·nar·y [val-i-TOOD-n-er-ee] *adj* **1** sickly. **2** infirm. **val·e·tu·di·nar'i·an** [-NAIR-ee-ən] *n* person obliged or disposed to live the life of an invalid.

Val·hal·la [val-HAL-ə] *n* Norse mythology place of immortality for heroes slain in battle.

val·iant [VAL-yənt] *adj* brave, courageous.

val·id *adj* **1** sound. **2** capable of being justified. **3** of binding force in law. **va·lid·i·ty** [və-LID-i-tee] *n* **1** soundness. **2** power to convince. **3** legal force. **val'i·date** *vt* **-dat·ed, -dat·ing** make valid.

va·lise [və-LEES] *n* traveling bag.

Val·kyr·ie [val-KEER-ee, VAL-ker-ee] *n* one of the Norse war goddesses who chose the slain and guided them to Valhalla.

val·ley [VAL-ee] *n, pl* **-leys 1** low area between hills. **2** river basin.

val·or [VAL-ər] *n* bravery. **val'or·ous** [-əs] *adj*

val·ue [VAL-yoo] *n* **1** worth. **2** utility. **3** equivalent. **4** importance. ♦ *pl* **5** principles, standards. ♦ *vt* **-ued, -u·ing 6** estimate value of. **7** hold in respect. **8** prize. **val'u·a·ble** [-ə-bəl] *adj* **1** precious. **2** worthy. **3** capable of being valued. ♦ *n* (usu *pl*) **4** valuable thing. **val·u·a'tion** [-AY-shən] *n* estimated worth. **val'ue·less** [-lis] *adj* worthless. **value added tax** tax on difference between cost of basic materials

and cost of article made from them.

valve [valv] *n* **1** device to control passage of fluid, etc. through pipe. **2** *Anatomy* part of body allowing one-way passage of fluids. **3** any of separable parts of shell of mollusk. **4** *Mus.* device on brass instrument for lengthening tube.

va·moose [va·MOOS] *v* **moosed, -moos·ing** *sl* depart quickly.

vamp¹ *n* **1** woman who deliberately allures men. ♦ *v* **2** exploit (man) as vamp.

vamp² *n* **1** something patched up. **2** front part of shoe upper. ♦ *vt* **3** patch up, rework. **4** *Jazz* improvise.

vam·pire [VAM-pīr] *n* (in folklore) corpse that rises from dead to drink blood of the living. **vampire bat** one that sucks blood of animals.

van¹ *n* **1** large covered truck, esp. for furniture. **2** smaller such vehicle for camping, etc.

van² *n* short for VANGUARD.

va·na·di·um [və-NAY-dee-əm] *n* metallic element used in manufacture of hard steel.

van·dal [VAN-dl] *n* one who wantonly and deliberately damages or destroys. **van'dal·ism** *n* **van'dal·ize** *vt* **-ized, -iz·ing**

vane [vayn] *n* **1** weather vane. **2** blade of propeller. **3** fin on bomb, etc. **4** sight on quadrant.

van·guard [VAN-gahrd] *n* leading, foremost group, position, etc.

va·nil·la [və-NIL-ə] *n* **1** tropical climbing orchid. **2** its seed(pod). **3** essence of this for flavoring.

van·ish *vi* **1** disappear. **2** fade away.

──────| THESAURUS |──────

valiant *adj* = **brave**, bold, courageous, fearless, gallant, heroic, intrepid, lion-hearted

valid *adj* **1** = **logical**, cogent, convincing, good, sound, telling, well-founded, well-grounded **2** = **legal**, authentic, bona fide, genuine, lawful, legitimate, official

validate *v* = **confirm**, authenticate, authorize, certify, corroborate, endorse, ratify, substantiate

validity *n* **1** = **soundness**, cogency, force, power, strength, weight **2** = **legality**, authority, lawfulness, legitimacy, right

valley *n* = **hollow**, dale, dell, depression, glen, vale

valor *n* = **bravery**, boldness, courage, fearlessness, gallantry, heroism, intrepidity, spirit

valuable *adj* **1** = **precious**, costly, dear, expensive, high-priced **2** = **useful**, beneficial, helpful, important, prized, profitable, worthwhile ♦ *n* **3 valuables** = **treasures**, heirlooms

value *n* **1** = **importance**, advantage, benefit, desirability, merit, profit, usefulness, utility, worth **2** = **cost**, market price, rate **3 values** = **principles**, ethics, (moral) standards ♦ *v* **4** = **evaluate**, appraise, assess, estimate, price, rate, set at **5** = **respect**, appreciate, cherish, esteem, hold dear, prize, regard highly, treasure

vandal *n* = **hooligan**, delinquent, rowdy

vanguard *n* = **forerunners**, cutting edge, forefront, front line, leaders, spearhead, trailblazers, trendsetters, van

vanish *v* = **disappear**, dissolve, evanesce,

van·i·ty [VAN-i-tee] *n, pl* **-ties 1** excessive pride or conceit. **2** ostentation.

van·quish [VANG-kwish] *vt* **1** subdue in battle. **2** conquer, overcome.

vap'id *adj* flat, dull, insipid. **va·pid·i·ty** [və-PID-i-tee] *n*

va·por [VAY-pər] *n* **1** gaseous form of a substance more familiar as liquid or solid. **2** steam, mist. **3** invisible moisture in air. **va'por·ize** [-pə-rīz] *v* **-ized, -iz·ing** convert into, pass off in, vapor.

var'i·a·ble see VARY.

var·i·cose [VAR-i-kohs] *adj* of vein, swollen, twisted.

var·i·e·gate [VA-ree-i-gayt] *vt* **-gat·ed, -gat·ing** diversify by patches of different colors. **var'i·e·gat·ed** *adj* streaked, spotted, dappled.

va·ri·e·ty [və-RĪ-i-tee] *n, pl* **-ties 1** state of being varied or various. **2** diversity. **3** varied assortment. **4** sort or kind.

var·i·o·rum [va-ree-OR-əm] *adj, n* (edition) with notes by various commentators.

var·i·ous [VA-ree-əs] *adj* manifold, diverse, of several kinds.

var·nish [VAHR-nish] *n* **1** resinous solution put on a surface to make it hard and shiny. ◆ *vt* **2** apply varnish to.

var·y [VAIR-ee] *v* **var·ied, var·y·ing** (cause to) change, diversify, differ, deviate. **var·i·a·bil'i·ty** *n* **var'i·a·ble** *adj* **1** changeable. **2** unsteady or fickle. ◆ *n* **3** something subject to variation. **var'i·ance**

[-əns] *n* state of discord, discrepancy.

var'i·ant [-ənt] *adj* **1** different. ◆ *n* **2** difference in form. **3** alternative form or reading. **var·i·a'tion** [-AY-shən] *n* **1** alteration. **2** extent to which thing varies. **3** modification. **var'ied** *adj* **1** diverse. **2** modified. **3** variegated.

vas *n, pl* **va·sa** [VA-sə] vessel, tube carrying bodily fluid.

vas·cu·lar [VAS-kyə-lər] *adj* of, with vessels for conveying sap, blood, etc.

vase [vayz] *n* vessel, jar as ornament or for holding flowers.

vas·ec·to·my [va-SEK-tə-mee] *n, pl* **-mies** contraceptive measure of surgical removal of part of vas bearing sperm from testicle.

vas·sal [VAS-əl] *n* **1** holder of land by feudal tenure. **2** dependent.

vast *adj* **-er, -est** very large. **vast'ly** [-lee] *adv* **vast'ness** [-nis] *n*

vat *n* large tub, tank.

Vat·i·can [VAT-i-kən] *n* **1** Pope's palace. **2** papal authority.

vaude·ville [VAWD-vil] *n* theatrical entertainment with songs, juggling acts, dance, etc.

vault¹ [vawlt] *n* **1** arched roof. **2** arched apartment. **3** cellar. **4** burial chamber. **5** place for storing valuables. ◆ *vt* **6** build with arched roof.

vault² *v* **1** spring, jump over with the hands resting on something. ◆ *n* **2** such jump.

───── THESAURUS ─────

evaporate, fade (away), melt (away)

vanity *n* = **pride**, arrogance, conceit, conceitedness, egotism, narcissism

vanquish *v Literary* = **defeat**, beat, conquer, crush, master, overcome, overpower, overwhelm, triumph over

vapid *adj* = **dull**, bland, boring, flat, insipid, tame, uninspiring, uninteresting, weak, wishy-washy (*inf*)

vapor *n* = **mist**, exhalation, fog, haze, steam

variable *adj* = **changeable**, flexible, fluctuating, inconstant, mutable, shifting, temperamental, uneven, unstable, unsteady

variance *n* at variance = **in disagreement**, at loggerheads, at odds, conflicting, out of line

variant *adj* **1** = **different**, alternative, divergent, modified ◆ *n* **2** = **variation**, alternative, development, modification

variation *n* = **difference**, change, departure, deviation, diversity, innovation, modification, novelty, variety

varied *adj* = **different**, assorted, diverse, heterogeneous, miscellaneous, mixed, motley, sundry, various

variety *n* **1** = **diversity**, change, difference, discrepancy, diversification, multifariousness, variation **2** = **range**, array, assortment, collection, cross section, medley, miscellany, mixture **3** = **type**, brand, breed, category, class, kind, sort, species, strain

various *adj* = **different**, assorted, disparate, distinct, diverse, miscellaneous, several, sundry, varied

varnish *n, v* = **polish**, glaze, gloss, lacquer

vary *v* = **change**, alter, differ, disagree, diverge, fluctuate

vast *adj* = **huge**, boundless, colossal, enormous, gigantic, great, immense,

vaulting horse padded apparatus for support of hands in gymnastics.

vaunt [vawnt] v, n boast. **vaunt'ed** [-id] adj excessively praised.

VDU visual display unit, monitor.

veal [veel] n calf flesh as food.

vec•tor [VEK-tər] n **1** quantity (e.g. force) having both magnitude and direction. **2** disease-carrying organism, esp. insect. **3** compass direction, course.

veer vi **1** change direction. **2** change one's mind.

veg•e•ta•ble [VEJ-tə-bəl] n **1** plant, esp. edible one. **2** inf person who has lost use of mental and physical faculties. **3** dull person. ◆ adj **4** of, from, concerned with plants.

veg•e•tar•i•an [vej-i-TAIR-ee-ən] n one who does not eat meat. ◆ adj **veg•e•tar'i•an•ism** n

veg•e•tate [VEJ-i-tayt] vi **-tat•ed, -tat•ing 1** (of plants) grow, develop. **2** (of person) live dull, unproductive life. **veg•e•ta'tion** n **1** plants collectively. **2** plants growing in a place. **3** process of plant growth. **veg'e•ta•tive** [-tay-tiv] adj

ve•he•ment [VEE-ə-mənt] adj **1** marked by intensity of feeling. **2** vigorous. **3** forcible. **ve'he•mence** [-məns] n

ve•hi•cle [VEE-i-kəl] n **1** means of conveying. **2** means of expression. **3** medium. **ve•hic'u•lar** [-HIK-yə-lər] adj

veil [vayl] n **1** light material to cover face or head. **2** mask, cover. ◆ vt **3** cover with, as with, veil. **veiled** adj **1** disguised. **take the**

veil become a nun.

vein [vayn] n **1** tube in body taking blood to heart. **2** rib of leaf or insect's wing. **3** fissure in rock filled with ore. **4** streak. **5** distinctive trait, strain, etc. **6** mood. ◆ vt **7** mark with streaks. **ve•nous** [VEE-nəs] adj **1** of veins.

veld, veldt [velt] n elevated grassland in S Afr.

vel•lum [VEL-əm] n **1** parchment of calf skin used for manuscripts or bindings. **2** paper resembling this.

ve•loc•i•ty [və-LOS-i-tee] n, pl **-ties 1** rate of motion in given direction, esp. of inanimate things. **2** speed.

ve•lour [və-LUUR] n fabric with velvety finish.

ve•lum [VEE-ləm] n, pl **-la** [-lə] Zoology **1** membranous covering or organ. **2** soft palate.

vel•vet [VEL-vit] n silk or cotton fabric with thick, short pile. **vel•vet•een'** n cotton fabric resembling velvet. **vel'vet•y** adj **1** of, like velvet. **2** soft and smooth.

ve•nal [VEEN-l] adj **1** guilty of taking, prepared to take, bribes. **2** corrupt. **ve•nal'i•ty** n

vend vt sell. **ven•dor** [VEN-dər] n **vending machine** one that automatically dispenses goods when money is inserted.

ven•det•ta [ven-DET-ə] n bitter, prolonged feud.

ve•neer [və-NEER] n **1** thin layer of fine wood. **2** superficial appearance. ◆ vt **3** cover with veneer.

——————| THESAURUS |——————

massive, monumental, wide

vault[1] n **1** = **strongroom**, depository, repository **2** = **crypt**, catacomb, cellar, charnel house, mausoleum, tomb, undercroft

vault[2] v = **jump**, bound, clear, hurdle, leap, spring

vaulted adj = **arched**, cavernous, domed

veer v = **swerve**, change course, change direction, sheer, shift, turn

vegetate v = **stagnate**, deteriorate, go to seed, idle, languish, loaf

vehemence n = **forcefulness**, ardor, emphasis, energy, fervor, force, intensity, passion, vigor

vehement adj = **strong**, ardent, emphatic, fervent, fierce, forceful, impassioned, intense, passionate, powerful

vehicle n **1** = **transport**, conveyance,

transportation **2** = **medium**, apparatus, channel, means, mechanism, organ

veil n **1** = **cover**, blind, cloak, curtain, disguise, film, mask, screen, shroud ◆ v **2** = **cover**, cloak, conceal, disguise, hide, mask, obscure, screen, shield

veiled adj = **disguised**, concealed, covert, hinted at, implied, masked, suppressed

vein n **1** = **blood vessel 2** = **seam**, course, current, lode, stratum, streak, stripe **3** = **mood**, mode, note, style, temper, tenor, tone

velocity n = **speed**, pace, quickness, rapidity, swiftness

velvety adj = **smooth**, delicate, downy, soft

vendetta n = **feud**, bad blood, quarrel

veneer n = **mask**, appearance, façade, front, guise, pretense, semblance, show

ven·er·a·ble [VEN-ər-ə-bəl] adj worthy of reverence. **ven·er·ate** [VEN-ə-rayt] vt **-at·ed, -at·ing** look up to, respect, revere. **ven·er·a'tion** n

ve·ne·re·al [və-NEER-ee-əl] adj (of disease) transmitted by sexual intercourse. **1** infected with venereal disease. **2** of, relating to genitals or sexual intercourse.

ven·er·y [VEN-ə-ree] n obs pursuit of sexual gratification.

Ve·ne·tian [və-NEE-shən] adj **1** of Venice, port in NE Italy. ♦ n **2** native or inhabitant of Venice. **Venetian blind** window blind made of thin horizontal slats that turn to let in more or less light.

ven·geance [VEN-jəns] n **1** revenge. **2** retribution for wrong done. **venge'ful** [-fəl] adj

ve·ni·al [VEE-nee-əl] adj pardonable.

ven·i·son [VEN-ə-sən] n flesh of deer as food.

ven·om [VEN-əm] n **1** poison. **2** spite. **ven'om·ous** [-əs] adj poisonous.

venous [VEE-nəs] see VEIN.

vent[1] n **1** small hole or outlet. ♦ vt **2** give outlet to. **3** utter. **4** pour forth.

vent[2] n vertical slit in garment esp. at back of jacket.

ven·ti·late [VEN-tl-ayt] vt **-lat·ed, -lat·ing 1** supply with fresh air. **2** bring into discussion. **ven'ti·la·tor** n

ven·tral [VEN-trəl] adj abdominal.

ven·tri·cle [VEN-tri-kəl] n cavity, hollow in body, esp. in heart or brain. **ven·tric'u·lar** [-TRIK-yə-lər] adj

ven·tril·o·quist [ven-TRIL-ə-kwist] n one who can so speak that the sounds seem to come from some other person or place. **ven·tril'o·quism** n

ven·ture [VEN-chər] v **-tured, -tur·ing** ♦ vt **1** expose to hazard. **2** risk. ♦ vi **3** dare. **4** have courage to do something or go somewhere. ♦ n **5** risky undertaking. **6** speculative commercial undertaking. **ven'ture·some** [-səm] adj

ven·ue [VEN-yoo] n **1** Law district in which case is tried. **2** meeting place. **3** location.

Ve·nus [VEE-nəs] n **1** Roman goddess of love. **2** planet between Earth and Mercury. **Venus's flytrap** insect-eating plant.

ve·ra·cious [və-RAY-shəs] adj **1** truthful. **2** true. **ve·rac'i·ty** [-RAS-i-tee] n

ve·ran·da, ve·ran·dah [və-RAN-də] n open or partly enclosed porch on outside of house.

verb [vurb] n part of speech used to express action or being. **ver·bal** [VUR-bəl] adj **1** of, by, or relating to words spoken rather than written. **2** of, like a verb. **ver'bal·ize** v **-ized, -iz·ing** put into words, speak. **ver'bal·ly** adv **ver·ba·tim** [vər-BAY-tim] adv, adj word for word, literal.

ver·bi·age [VUR-bee-ij] n excess of words. **ver·bose** [vər-BOHS] adj wordy, long-winded. **ver·bos'i·ty** [-BOS-i-tee] n

ver·dant [VUR-dnt] adj green and fresh. **ver·dure** [-jər] n **1** greenery. **2** freshness.

ver·dict [VUR-dikt] n **1** decision of a jury. **2** opinion reached after examination of facts.

——— THESAURUS ———

venerable adj = **respected**, august, esteemed, honored, revered, sage, wise, worshipped

venerate v = **respect**, adore, esteem, honor, look up to, revere, reverence, worship

vengeance n = **revenge**, reprisal, retaliation, retribution

venom n **1** = **malice**, acrimony, bitterness, hate, rancor, spite, spleen, virulence **2** = **poison**, bane, toxin

venomous adj **1** = **malicious**, hostile, malignant, rancorous, savage, spiteful, vicious, vindictive **2** = **poisonous**, mephitic, noxious, toxic, virulent

vent n **1** = **outlet**, aperture, duct, opening, orifice ♦ v **2** = **express**, air, discharge, emit, give vent to, pour out, release, utter, voice

venture n **1** = **undertaking**, adventure,

endeavor, enterprise, gamble, hazard, project, risk ♦ v **2** = **risk**, chance, hazard, speculate, stake, wager **3** = **dare**, hazard, make bold, presume, take the liberty, volunteer **4** = **go**, embark on, plunge into, set out

verbal adj = **spoken**, oral, unwritten, word-of-mouth

verbatim adv = **exactly**, precisely, to the letter, word for word

verbose adj = **long-winded**, circumlocutory, diffuse, periphrastic, prolix, tautological, windy, wordy

verbosity n = **long-windedness**, loquaciousness, prolixity, verboseness, wordiness

verdant adj = **green**, flourishing, fresh, grassy, leafy, lush

verdict n = **decision**, adjudication,

ver·di·gris [VUR-di-grees] *n* green film on copper.

verdure [VUR-jər] see VERDANT.

verge [vurj] *n* **1** edge. **2** brink. ◆ *vi* **verged, verg·ing 3** come close to. **4** be on the border of.

ver·i·fy [VER-i-fī] *vt* **-fied, -fy·ing 1** prove, confirm truth of. **2** test accuracy of. **ver'i·fi·a·ble** *adj*

ver·i·si·mil·i·tude [ver-ə-si-MIL-i-tood] *n* **1** appearance of truth. **2** likelihood.

ver·i·ta·ble [VER-i-tə-bəl] *adj* actual, true, genuine. **ver'i·ta·bly** *adv*

ver·i·ty [VER-i-tee] *n, pl* **-ties 1** truth. **2** reality. **3** true assertion.

ver·mi·cide [VUR-mə-sīd] *n* substance to destroy worms. **ver'mi·form** *adj* shaped like a worm, e.g. *vermiform appendix.*

ver·mil·ion [vər-MIL-yən] *adj, n* (of) bright red color or pigment.

ver·min [VUR-min] *pl n* injurious animals, parasites, etc.

ver·mouth [vər-MOOTH] *n* wine flavored with aromatic herbs, etc.

ver·nac·u·lar [vər-NAK-yə-lər] *n* **1** commonly spoken language or dialect of particular country or place. ◆ *adj* **2** of vernacular. **3** native.

ver·nal [VUR-nl] *adj* of spring.

ver·ni·er [VUR-nee-ər] *n* sliding scale for obtaining fractional parts of subdivision of graduated scale.

ver·sa·tile [VUR-sə-tl] *adj* **1** capable of or adapted to many different uses, skills, etc. **2** liable to change. **ver·sa·til'i·ty** *n*

verse [vurs] *n* **1** stanza or short subdivision of poem or the Bible. **2** poetry. **3** line of

poetry. **ver·si·fy** [VUR-sə-fī] *v* **-fied, -fy·ing** turn into verse. **ver·si·fi·ca'tion** *n* versed in skilled.

ver·sion [VUR-zhən] *n* **1** description from certain point of view. **2** translation. **3** adaptation.

ver·so [VUR-soh] *n* back of sheet of printed paper, left-hand page.

ver·sus [VUR-səs] *prep* against.

ver·te·bra [VUR-tə-brə] *n, pl* **-brae** [-bree] single section of backbone. **ver'te·bral** [-brəl] *adj* of the spine. **ver'te·brate** [-brit] *n* animal with backbone. ◆ *adj*

ver·tex [VUR-teks] *n, pl* **-ti·ces** [-tə-seez] summit.

ver·ti·cal [VUR-ti-kəl] *adj* **1** at right angles to the horizon. **2** upright. **3** overhead.

ver·ti·go [VUR-ti-goh] *n, pl* **-goes** giddiness. **ver·tig·i·nous** [vər-TIJ-ə-nəs] *adj* dizzy.

verve [vurv] *n* **1** enthusiasm. **2** spirit. **3** energy, vigor.

ver·y [VER-ee] *adj* **1** exact, ideal. **2** same. **3** complete. **4** actual. ◆ *adv* **5** extremely, to great extent.

ves·i·cle [VES-i-kəl] *n* small blister, bubble, or cavity. **ve·sic·u·lar** [və-SIK-yə-lər] *adj*

ves·pers [VES-pərz] *pl n* **1** evening church service. **2** evensong.

ves·sel [VES-əl] *n* **1** any object used as a container, esp. for liquids. **2** ship, large boat. **3** tubular structure conveying liquids (e.g. blood) in body.

vest *n* **1** sleeveless garment worn under jacket or coat. ◆ *vt* **2** place. **3** bestow. **4** confer. **5** clothe. **vest'ment** [-mənt] *n* robe or official garment. **vested interest** strong

———————┤ THESAURUS ├———————

conclusion, finding, judgment, opinion, sentence

verge *n* **1** = **border**, boundary, brim, brink, edge, limit, margin, threshold ◆ *v* **2 verge on** = **border**, approach, come near

verification *n* = **proof**, authentication, confirmation, corroboration, substantiation, validation

verify *v* = **check**, authenticate, bear out, confirm, corroborate, prove, substantiate, support, validate

vernacular *n* = **dialect**, idiom, parlance, patois, speech

versatile *adj* = **adaptable**, adjustable, all-purpose, all-round, flexible, multifaceted, resourceful, variable

versed *adj* = **knowledgeable**, acquainted,

conversant, experienced, familiar, practiced, proficient, seasoned, well informed

version *n* **1** = **form**, design, model, style, variant **2** = **account**, adaptation, interpretation, portrayal, rendering

vertical *adj* = **upright**, erect, on end, perpendicular

vertigo *n* = **dizziness**, giddiness, light-headedness

verve *n* = **enthusiasm**, animation, energy, gusto, liveliness, sparkle, spirit, vitality

very *adv* **1** = **extremely**, acutely, decidedly, deeply, exceedingly, greatly, highly, profoundly, uncommonly, unusually ◆ *adj* **2** = **exact**, precise, selfsame

vessel *n* **1** = **ship**, boat, craft **2** = **container**, personal interest in particular state of affairs.

ves·tal [VES-tl] *adj* pure, chaste.

ves·ti·bule [VES-tə-byool] *n* entrance hall, lobby.

ves·tige [VES-tij] *n* small trace, amount. **ves·tig·i·al** [-TIJ-ee-əl] *adj*

ves·try [VES-tree] *n, pl* **-tries** room in church for keeping vestments, holding meetings, etc.

vet *n* **1** short for VETERAN. **2** short for VETERINARIAN. ◆ *vt* **vet·ted, vet·ting 3** examine. **4** check.

vet·er·an [VET-ər-ən] *n* **1** one who has served a long time, esp. in fighting services. ◆ *adj* **2** long-serving.

vet·er·i·nar·i·an [vet-ər-ə-NAIR-ee-ən] *n* one qualified to treat animal ailments. **vet·er·i·nar·y** [-ner-ee] *adj* **1** of, concerning the health of animals. ◆ *n* **2** veterinarian.

ve·to [VEE-toh] *n, pl* **-toes 1** power of rejecting piece of legislation, or preventing it from coming into effect. **2** any prohibition. ◆ *vt* **-toed, -to·ing 3** enforce veto against. **4** forbid with authority.

vex [veks] *vt* **1** annoy. **2** distress. **vex·a'tion** *n* **1** cause of irritation. **2** state of distress. **vex·a'tious** *adj* vexed *adj* **1** cross. **2** annoyed. **3** much discussed.

vi·a [VĪ-ə] *adv* by way of.

vi·a·ble [VĪ-ə-bəl] *adj* **1** practicable. **2** able to live and grow independently. **vi·a·bil'i·ty** *n*

vi·a·duct [VĪ-ə-dukt] *n* bridge over valley

for a road or railroad.

Vi·ag·ra [vī-AG-rə] *n* ® drug used to treat impotence in men.

vi·al [VĪ-əl] *n* small bottle for medicine, etc.

vi·ands [VĪ-əndz] *pl n* food esp. delicacies.

vi·bra·harp [VĪ-brə-hahrp] *n* musical instrument like xylophone, but with electronic resonators, that produces a gentle vibrato (also **vi'bra·phone**).

vi·brate [VĪ-brayt] *v* **-brat·ed, -brat·ing 1** (cause to) move to and fro rapidly and continuously. **2** give off (light or sound) by vibration. ◆ *vi* **3** oscillate. **4** quiver. **vibes** *pl n inf* **1** emotional reactions between people. **2** atmosphere of a place. **vi'brant** [-brənt] *adj* **1** throbbing. **2** vibrating. **3** appearing vigorous, lively. **vi·bra'tion** *n* a vibrating. **vi·bra·to** [vi-BRAH-toh] *n, pl* **-os** vibrating effect in music.

vic·ar [VIK-ər] *n* member of clergy in charge of parish. **vic'ar·age** [-ij] *n* vicar's house. **vi·car·i·al** [vī-KAIR-ee-əl] *adj* of vicar.

vi·car·i·ous [vī-KAIR-ee-əs] *adj* **1** obtained, enjoyed or undergone through sympathetic experience of another's experiences. **2** suffered, done, etc. as substitute for another.

vice [vīs] *n* **1** evil or immoral habit or practice. **2** criminal immorality esp. prostitution. **3** fault, imperfection.

vice- *comb. form* in place of, second to, e.g. *vice-chairman; viceroy.*

vice·roy [VĪS-roi] *n* ruler acting for king in

──────── THESAURUS ────────

pot, receptacle, utensil

vest *v* (with *in* or *with*) = **place**, bestow, confer, consign, endow, entrust, invest, settle

vestibule *n* = **hall**, anteroom, foyer, lobby, porch, portico

vestige *n* = **trace**, glimmer, indication, remnant, scrap, suspicion

vet *v* = **check**, appraise, examine, investigate, review, scrutinize

veteran *n* **1** = **old hand**, old stager, past master, warhorse (*inf*) ◆ *adj* **2** = **long-serving**, battle-scarred, old, seasoned

veto *n* **1** = **ban**, boycott, embargo, interdict, prohibition ◆ *v* **2** = **ban**, boycott, disallow, forbid, prohibit, reject, rule out, turn down

vex *v* = **annoy**, bother, distress, exasperate, irritate, plague, trouble, upset, worry

vexation *n* **1** = **annoyance**, chagrin,

displeasure, dissatisfaction, exasperation, frustration, irritation, pique **2** = **problem**, bother, difficulty, hassle (*inf*), headache (*inf*), nuisance, trouble, worry

viable *adj* = **workable**, applicable, feasible, operable, practicable, usable

vibrant *adj* = **energetic**, alive, animated, dynamic, sparkling, spirited, vigorous, vivacious, vivid

vibrate *v* = **shake**, fluctuate, oscillate, pulsate, quiver, reverberate, shudder, sway, throb, tremble

vibration *n* = **tremor**, oscillation, pulsation, quiver, reverberation, shake, shudder, throbbing, trembling

vicarious *adj* = **indirect**, delegated, substituted, surrogate

vice *n* **1** = **wickedness**, corruption, depravity, evil, immorality, iniquity, sin, turpitude **2** = **fault**, blemish, defect, failing, province or dependency. **vice·re·gal** adj

vi·ce ver·sa [VĪ-sə VUR-sə] Lat conversely, the other way round.

vi·cin·i·ty [vi-SIN-i-tee] n, pl **-ties** neighborhood.

vi·cious [VISH-əs] adj 1 wicked, cruel. 2 ferocious, dangerous. 3 leading to vice.

vi·cis·si·tude [vi-SIS-i-tood] n 1 change of fortune. 2 pl ups and downs of fortune.

vic·tim [VIK-tim] n 1 person or thing killed, injured, etc. as result of another's deed, or accident, circumstances, etc. 2 person cheated. 3 sacrifice. **vic·tim·i·za'tion** [-ZAY-shən] n **vic'ti·mize** vt **-mized, -miz·ing** 1 punish unfairly. 2 make victim of.

vic·tor [VIK-tər] n 1 conqueror. 2 winner. **vic·to·ri·ous** [vik-TOR-ee-əs] adj 1 winning. 2 triumphant. **vic'to·ry** [-tə-ree] n, pl **-ries** winning of battle, etc.

vict·ual [VIT-l] n (usu in pl) 1 food. ♦ v **-ualed, -ual·ing** 2 supply with or obtain food.

vi·cu·na [vī-KOO-nə] n 1 S Amer. animal like llama. 2 fine, light cloth made from its wool.

vi·de [VĪ-dee] Lat see. **vide in·fra** [IN-frə] see below. **vide su·pra** [SOO-prə] see above.

vi·de·li·cet [vi-DEL-ə-sit] Lat namely.

vid·e·o [VID-ee-oh] adj 1 relating to or used in transmission or production of TV image. ♦ n 2 apparatus for recording TV programs. 3 film, etc. on videocassette for viewing on this apparatus.

vid'e·o·cas·sette cassette containing video tape. **videocassette recorder** tape recorder for vision and sound signals, used for recording and playing back TV programs and films on cassette. **video game** any of various games played on video screen using electronic control. **videotape** magnetic tape on which to record TV program. **videotape recorder** tape recorder for signals for TV broadcast.

vid'e·o·tex n means of providing written or graphical representation of computerized information on TV screen for information retrieval, shopping at home, etc.

vie [vī] vi **vied, vy·ing** (foll. by with or for) contend, compete against or for someone, something.

view [vyoo] n 1 survey by eyes or mind. 2 range of vision. 3 picture. 4 scene. 5 opinion. 6 purpose. ♦ vt 7 look at. 8 survey. 9 consider. **view'er** n 1 one who views. 2 one who watches TV. 3 optical device to assist viewing of photographic slides. **view'find·er** n device on camera enabling user to see what will be included in photograph. **view'point** n 1 way of regarding a subject. 2 position commanding view of landscape.

vig·il [VIJ-əl] n 1 a keeping awake, watch. 2 eve of church festival. **vig'i·lance** [-ləns] n **vig'i·lant** [-lənt] adj watchful, alert.

vig·i·lan·te [vij-ə-LAN-tee] n one (esp. as member of group) who unofficially takes on duty of enforcing law.

vi·gnette [vin-YET] n 1 short literary essay, sketch. 2 photograph or portrait with the background shaded off.

vig·or [VIG-ər] n 1 force, strength. 2

imperfection, shortcoming, weakness

vice versa adv = **conversely**, contrariwise, in reverse, the other way round

vicinity n = **neighborhood**, area, district, environs, locality, neck of the woods (inf), proximity

vicious adj 1 = **violent**, barbarous, cruel, ferocious, savage, wicked 2 = **malicious**, cruel, mean, spiteful, venomous, vindictive

victim n = **casualty**, fatality, martyr, sacrifice, scapegoat, sufferer

victimize v = **persecute**, discriminate against, pick on

victor n = **winner**, champion, conqueror, prizewinner, vanquisher

victorious adj = **winning**, champion, conquering, first, prizewinning, successful, triumphant, vanquishing

victory n = **win**, conquest, success, triumph

vie v = **compete**, contend, strive, struggle

view n 1 (sometimes plural) = **opinion**, attitude, belief, conviction, feeling, impression, point of view, sentiment 2 = **scene**, landscape, outlook, panorama, perspective, picture, prospect, spectacle, vista 3 = **vision**, sight ♦ v 4 = **regard**, consider, deem, look on

viewer n = **watcher**, observer, onlooker, spectator

vigilance n = **watchfulness**, alertness, attentiveness, carefulness, caution, circumspection, observance

vigilant adj = **watchful**, alert, attentive, careful, cautious, circumspect, on one's guard, on the lookout, wakeful energy, activity. **vig·or·ous** [-əs] *adj* **1** strong. **2** energetic. **3** flourishing.

Vi·king [VĪ-king] *n* medieval Scandinavian seafarer, raider, settler.

vile [vil] *adj* **vil·er, vil·est 1** very wicked, shameful. **2** disgusting. **3** despicable. **vil·i·fy** [VIL-ə-fī] *vt* **-fied, -fy·ing 1** speak ill of. **2** slander. **vil·i·fi·ca'tion** [-fi-KAY-shən] *n*

vil·la [VIL-ə] *n* large, luxurious, country house.

vil·lage [VIL-ij] *n* small group of houses in country area.

vil·lain [VIL-ən] *n* **1** wicked person. **2** *inf* mischievous person. **vil'lain·ous** [-əs] *adj* **1** wicked. **2** vile. **vil'lain·y** *n, pl* **-lain·ies**

vim *n* force, energy.

vin·ai·grette [vin-ə-GRET] *n* **1** small bottle of smelling salts. **2** type of salad dressing. ◆ *adj* **3** (of food) served with vinaigrette.

vin·di·cate [VIN-di-kayt] *vt* **-cat·ed, -cat·ing 1** clear of charges. **2** justify. **3** establish the truth or merit of. **vin·di·ca'tion** *n*

vin·dic·tive [vin-DIK-tiv] *adj* **1** revengeful. **2** inspired by resentment.

vine [vīn] *n* climbing plant bearing grapes. **vine·yard** [VIN-yərd] *n* plantation of vines. **vin'tage** [-tij] *n* **1** gathering of the grapes. **2** the yield. **3** wine of particular year. **4** time of origin. ◆ *adj* **5** best and most

typical. **vint'ner** [-nər] *n* dealer in wine.

vin·e·gar [VIN-i-gər] *n* acid liquid obtained from wine and other alcoholic liquors. **vin'e·gar·y** *adj* **1** like vinegar. **2** sour. **3** bad-tempered.

vi·nyl [VĪn-l] *n* plastic material with variety of domestic and industrial uses.

vi·ol [VĪ-əl] *n* early stringed instrument preceding violin.

vi·o·la¹ [vee-OH-lə] *n* large violin with lower range.

vi·o·la² [vī-OH-lə] *n* single-colored variety of pansy.

vi·o·late [VĪ-ə-layt] *vt* **-lat·ed, -lat·ing 1** break (law, agreement, etc.), infringe. **2** rape. **3** outrage, desecrate. **vi·o·la·ble** [-lə-bəl] *adj* **vi·o·la'tion** [-LAY-shən] *n*

vi·o·lent [VĪ-ə-lənt] *adj* **1** marked by, due to, extreme force, passion or fierceness. **2** of great force. **3** intense. **vi'o·lence** [-lins] *n*

vi·o·let [VĪ-ə-lit] *n* **1** plant with small bluish-purple or white flowers. **2** the flower. **3** bluish-purple color. ◆ *adj* **4** of this color.

vi·o·lin [vī-ə-LIN] *n* small four-stringed musical instrument. **vi·o·lin'ist** *n*

vi·o·lon·cel·lo [vee-ə-lən-CHEL-oh] *n* see CELLO.

VIP very important person.

───── THESAURUS ─────

vigor *n* = **energy**, animation, dynamism, forcefulness, gusto, liveliness, power, spirit, strength, verve, vitality

vigorous *adj* = **energetic**, active, dynamic, forceful, lively, lusty, powerful, spirited, strenuous, strong

vigorously *adv* = **energetically**, forcefully, hard, lustily, strenuously, strongly

vile *adj* **1** = **wicked**, corrupt, degenerate, depraved, evil, nefarious, perverted **2** = **disgusting**, foul, horrid, nasty, nauseating, offensive, repugnant, repulsive, revolting, scuzzy (*sl*), sickening

vilify *v* = **malign**, abuse, berate, denigrate, disparage, revile, slander, smear

villain *n* **1** = **evildoer**, criminal, miscreant, reprobate, rogue, scoundrel, wretch **2** = **antihero**, baddy (*inf*)

villainous *adj* = **wicked**, bad, cruel, degenerate, depraved, evil, fiendish, nefarious, vicious, vile

villainy *n* = **wickedness**, delinquency, depravity, devilry, iniquity, turpitude, vice

vindicate *v* **1** = **clear**, absolve, acquit, exculpate, exonerate, rehabilitate **2** =

justify, defend, excuse

vindication *n* **1** = **exoneration**, exculpation, rehabilitation **2** = **justification**, defense, excuse

vindictive *adj* = **vengeful**, implacable, malicious, resentful, revengeful, spiteful, unforgiving, unrelenting

vintage *adj* = **best**, choice, classic, prime, select, superior

violate *v* **1** = **break**, contravene, disobey, disregard, encroach upon, infringe, transgress **2** = **desecrate**, abuse, befoul, defile, dishonor, pollute, profane **3** = **rape**, abuse, assault, debauch, ravish

violation *n* **1** = **infringement**, abuse, breach, contravention, encroachment, infraction, transgression, trespass **2** = **desecration**, defilement, profanation, sacrilege, spoliation

violence *n* **1** = **force**, bloodshed, brutality, cruelty, ferocity, fighting, savagery, terrorism **2** = **intensity**, abandon, fervor, force, severity, vehemence

violent *adj* = **destructive**, brutal, cruel, hot-headed, murderous, riotous, savage,

vi·per [VĪ-pər] n venomous snake.

vi·ra·go [vi-RAH-goh] n, pl **-goes** or **-gos** abusive woman.

vir·gin [VUR-jin] n **1** one who has not had sexual intercourse. ♦ adj **2** without experience of sexual intercourse. **3** unsullied, fresh. **4** (of land) untilled. **vir·gin·al** [VUR-jə-nl] adj **1** of, like virgin. ♦ n **2** type of spinet. **vir·gin'i·ty** n

vir·ile [VIR-əl] adj **1** (of male) capable of copulation or procreation. **2** strong, forceful. **vi·ril'i·ty** [-RIL-i-tee] n

virology [vī-ROL-ə-jee] see VIRUS.

vir·tu·al [VUR-choo-əl] adj so in effect, though not in appearance or name. **vir'tu·al·ly** adv practically, almost. **virtual reality** computer-generated environment that seems real to the user.

vir·tue [VUR-choo] n **1** moral goodness. **2** good quality. **3** merit. **4** inherent power. **vir'tu·ous** [-əs] adj **1** morally good. **2** chaste.

vir·tu·o·so [vur-choo-OH-soh] n, pl **-sos** or **-si** [-see] one with special skill, esp. in a fine art. **vir·tu·os'i·ty** n great technical skill, esp. in a fine art as music.

vir·u·lent [VIR-yə-lənt] adj **1** very infectious, poisonous, etc. **2** malicious.

vi·rus [VĪ-rəs] n **1** any of various submicroscopic organisms, some causing disease. **2** Computers program that propagates itself, via disks and electronic networks, to cause disruption. **vi·rol'o·gy** n study of viruses.

vi·sa [VEEZ-ə] n, pl **-sas** endorsement on passport permitting the bearer to travel into country of issuing government. **visa** vt **-saed, -sa·ing** approve visa for (someone).

vis·age [VIZ-ij] n face.

vis-à-vis [vee-zə-VEE] Fr **1** in relation to, regarding. **2** opposite to.

vis·cer·a [VIS-ər-ə] pl n large internal organs of body, esp. of abdomen. **visc'er·al** [-əl] adj

vis·cid [VIS-id] adj sticky, of a consistency like molasses. **vis·cid'i·ty** n

vis·cous [VIS-kəs] adj thick and sticky. **vis·cos'i·ty** n, pl **-ties**

vise [vīs] n appliance with screw jaw for holding things while working on them.

vis·i·ble [VIZ-ə-bəl] adj that can be seen. **vis·i·bil'i·ty** n degree of clarity of atmosphere, esp. for navigation. **vis'i·bly** adv

vi·sion [VIZH-ən] n **1** sight. **2** insight. **3** dream. **4** phantom. **5** imagination. **vi'sion·ar·y** [-er-ee] adj **1** marked by vision. **2** impractical. ♦ n, pl **-ar·ies** mystic. **3** impractical person.

vis·it [VIZ-it] v **1** go, come and see, stay

————————[THESAURUS]————————

uncontrollable, unrestrained, vicious

V.I.P. n = **celebrity**, big name, luminary, somebody, star

virgin n **1** = **maiden**, girl ♦ adj **2** = **pure**, chaste, immaculate, uncorrupted, undefiled, vestal, virginal

virginity n = **chastity**, maidenhood

virile adj = **manly**, lusty, macho, manlike, masculine, red-blooded, strong, vigorous

virility n = **masculinity**, machismo, manhood, vigor

virtual adj = **practical**, essential, in all but name

virtually adv = **practically**, almost, as good as, in all but name, in effect, in essence, nearly

virtue n **1** = **goodness**, incorruptibility, integrity, morality, probity, rectitude, righteousness, uprightness, worth **2** = **merit**, advantage, asset, attribute, credit, good point, plus (inf), strength

virtuosity n = **mastery**, brilliance, craft, expertise, flair, panache, polish, skill

virtuoso n = **master**, artist, genius, maestro, magician

virtuous adj = **good**, ethical, honorable, incorruptible, moral, praiseworthy, righteous, upright, worthy

virulent adj = **poisonous**, deadly, lethal, pernicious, toxic, venomous

viscous adj = **thick**, gelatinous, sticky, syrupy

visible adj = **apparent**, clear, discernible, evident, in view, manifest, observable, perceptible, unconcealed

vision n **1** = **sight**, eyesight, perception, seeing, view **2** = **image**, concept, conception, daydream, dream, fantasy, idea, ideal **3** = **hallucination**, apparition, chimera, delusion, illusion, mirage, revelation **4** = **foresight**, discernment, farsightedness, imagination, insight, intuition, penetration, prescience

visionary adj **1** = **prophetic**, mystical **2** = **impractical**, idealistic, quixotic, romantic, speculative, starry-eyed, unrealistic, unworkable, utopian ♦ n **3** = **prophet**, mystic, seer temporarily with (someone). ◆ *n* 2 stay. 3 call at person's home, etc. 4 official call. **vis·it·a'tion** [-ə-TAY-shən] *n* 1 formal visit or inspection. 2 affliction or plague. **vis'i·tor** *n*

vi·sor [VĪ-zər] *n* 1 front part of helmet made to move up and down before the face. 2 eyeshade, esp. on car. 3 peak on cap.

vis·ta [VIS-tə] *n* view, esp. distant view.

vis·u·al [VIZH-oo-əl] *adj* 1 of sight. 2 visible. **vis'u·al·ize** *vt* **-ized, -iz·ing** form mental image of. **vis·u·al·i·za'tion** *n*

vi·tal [VĪT-l] *adj* 1 necessary to, affecting life. 2 lively, animated. 3 essential. 4 highly important. **vi'tals** *pl n* vital organs of body. **vi·tal'i·ty** *n* life, vigor. **vi'tal·ize** [-tə-līz] *vt* **-ized, -iz·ing** 1 give life to. 2 lend vigor to. **vi'tal·ly** *adv*

vi·ta·min [VĪ-tə-min] *n* any of group of substances occurring in foodstuffs and essential to health.

vi·ti·ate [VISH-ee-ayt] *vt* **-at·ed, -at·ing** 1 spoil. 2 deprive of efficacy. 3 invalidate. **vi·ti·a'tion** *n*

vit·re·ous [VI-tree-əs] *adj* 1 of glass. 2 glassy. **vit·ri·fy** [VI-trə-fī] *v* **-fied, -fy·ing** convert into glass, or glassy substance. **vit·ri·fi·ca'tion** *n*

vit·ri·ol [VI-tree-əl] *n* 1 sulfuric acid. 2 caustic speech. **vit·ri·ol'ic** *adj*

vi·tu·per·ate [vī-TOO-pə-rayt] *vt* **-at·ed, -at·ing** abuse in words, revile. **vi·tu'per·a·tive** *adj*

vi·va·cious [vi-VAY-shəs] *adj* lively, gay, sprightly. **vi·vac'i·ty** [-VAS-i-tee] *n*

vi·va vo·ce [VĪ-və VOH-see] *Lat adj, adv* 1 by word of mouth. 2 *n* 2 in European universities, oral examination.

viv·id *adj* 1 bright, intense. 2 clear. 3 lively, animated. 4 graphic. **viv'id·ly** *adv*

viv·i·fy [VIV-ə-fī] *vt* **-fied, -fy·ing** animate, inspire.

vi·vip·a·rous [vī-VIP-ər-əs] *adj* bringing forth young alive.

viv·i·sec·tion [viv-ə-SEK-shən] *n* dissection of, or operating on, living animals. **viv·i·sec'tion·ist** *n*

vix·en [VIK-sən] *n* 1 female fox. 2 spiteful woman. **vix'en·ish** *adj*

viz. short for VIDELICET.

vi·zier [vi-ZEER] *n* (formerly) high official in some Muslim countries.

vo·cab·u·lar·y [voh-KAB-yə-ler-ee] *n, pl* **-lar·ies** 1 list of words, usu. in alphabetical order. 2 stock of words used in particular language, etc.

vo·cal [VOH-kəl] *adj* 1 of, with, or giving out voice. 2 outspoken, articulate. ◆ *n* 3 piece of popular music that is sung. **vo'cal·ist** *n* singer. **vo'cal·ize** *vt* **-ized, -iz·ing** utter with voice.

vo·ca·tion [voh-KAY-shən] *n* (urge, inclination, predisposition to) particular career, profession, etc. **vo·ca'tion·al** [-əl] *adj*

voc·a·tive [VOK-ə-tiv] *n* in some

visit *v* 1 = **call on**, drop in on (*inf*), look (someone) up, stay with, stop by ◆ *n* 2 = **call**, sojourn, stay, stop

visitation *n* 1 = **inspection**, examination, visit 2 = **catastrophe**, blight, calamity, cataclysm, disaster, ordeal, punishment, scourge

visitor *n* = **guest**, caller, company

vista *n* = **view**, panorama, perspective, prospect

visual *adj* 1 = **optical**, ocular, optic 2 = **observable**, discernible, perceptible, visible

visualize *v* = **picture**, conceive of, envisage, imagine

vital *adj* 1 = **essential**, basic, fundamental, imperative, indispensable, necessary, requisite 2 = **important**, critical, crucial, decisive, key, life-or-death, significant, urgent 3 = **lively**, animated, dynamic, energetic, spirited, vibrant, vigorous,

vivacious, zestful

vitality *n* = **energy**, animation, exuberance, life, liveliness, strength, vigor, vivacity

vitriolic *adj* = **bitter**, acerbic, caustic, envenomed, sardonic, scathing, venomous, virulent, withering

vivacious *adj* = **lively**, bubbling, ebullient, high-spirited, sparkling, spirited, sprightly, upbeat (*inf*), vital

vivacity *n* = **liveliness**, animation, ebullience, energy, gaiety, high spirits, sparkle, spirit, sprightliness

vivid *adj* 1 = **bright**, brilliant, clear, colorful, glowing, intense, rich 2 = **lifelike**, dramatic, graphic, memorable, powerful, realistic, stirring, telling, true to life

vocabulary *n* = **words**, dictionary, glossary, language, lexicon

vocal *adj* 1 = **spoken**, oral, said, uttered, voiced 2 = **outspoken**, articulate, eloquent, expressive, forthright, frank,

languages, case of nouns used in
addressing a person.

vo•cif•er•ate [voh-SIF-ə-rayt] v **-at•ed,
-at•ing** exclaim, cry out. **vo•cif'er•ous** [-əs]
adj shouting, noisy.

vod•ka [VOD-kə] n Russian spirit distilled
from grain, potatoes, etc.

vogue [vohg] n **1** fashion, style. **2**
popularity.

voice [vois] n **1** sound given out by person
in speaking, singing, etc. **2** quality of the
sound. **3** expressed opinion. **4** (right to)
share in discussion. **5** verbal forms proper
to relation of subject and action. ◆ vt
voiced, voic•ing 6 give utterance to,
express. **voice'less** [-lis] adj **voice mail**
electronic system for recording and
storage of telephone messages, which can
then be checked later or accessed
remotely.

void adj **1** empty. **2** destitute. **3** not legally
binding. ◆ n **4** empty space. ◆ vt **5** make
ineffectual or invalid. **6** empty out.

vol•a•tile [VOL-ə-tl] adj **1** evaporating
quickly. **2** lively. **3** fickle, changeable.
vol•a•til'i•ty n **vol'a•ti•lize** v **-lized, -liz•ing**
(cause to) evaporate.

vol•ca•no [vol-KAY-noh] n, pl **-noes, -nos 1**
hole in Earth's crust through which lava,
ashes, smoke, etc. are discharged. **2**
mountain so formed. **vol•can'ic** adj
vol•can•ol'o•gy [-kə-NOL-ə-jee] n study of
volcanoes and volcanic phenomena,
vulcanology.

vole [vohl] n small rodent.

vo•li•tion [voh-LISH-ən] n **1** act, power of
willing. **2** exercise of the will.

vol•ley [VOL-ee] n, pl **-leys 1** simultaneous
discharge of weapons or missiles. **2** rush of
oaths, questions, etc. **3** Tennis flight, return
of moving ball before it touches ground. ◆
v **-leyed, -ley•ing 4** discharge. **5** utter. **6** fly,
strike, etc. in volley. **vol'ley•ball** n team
game where large ball is hit by hand over
high net.

volt [vohlt] n unit of electric potential.
volt'age [-ij] n electric potential difference
expressed in volts. **volt'me•ter** n

volte-face [vohlt-FAHS] n, pl **volte-face** Fr
complete reversal of opinion or direction.

vol•u•ble [VOL-yə-bəl] adj talking easily,
readily and at length. **vol'u•bly** adv
vol•u•bil'i•ty n

vol•ume [VOL-yəm] n **1** space occupied. **2**
bulk, mass. **3** amount. **4** power, fullness of
voice or sound. **5** control on radio, etc. for
adjusting this. **6** book. **7** part of book
bound in one cover. **vol•u•met'ric** adj pert.
to measurement by volume. **vo•lu•mi•nous**
[və-LOO-mə-nəs] adj bulky, copious.

vol•un•tar•y [VOL-ən-ter-ee] adj **1** having,
done by free will. **2** done without
payment. **3** supported by freewill
contributions. **4** spontaneous. ◆ n, pl
-tar•ies 5 organ solo in church service.
vol•un•tar'i•ly adv **vol•un•teer'** n **1** one who
offers service, joins force, etc. of own free
will. ◆ v **2** offer oneself or one's services.

THESAURUS

plain-spoken, strident, vociferous

vocation n = **profession**, calling, career,
job, mission, pursuit, trade

vociferous adj = **noisy**, clamorous, loud,
outspoken, strident, uproarious,
vehement, vocal

vogue n **1** = **fashion**, craze, custom, mode,
style, trend, way **2** As in **in vogue** =
popularity, acceptance, currency, favor,
prevalence, usage, use

voice n **1** = **sound**, articulation, tone,
utterance **2** = **say**, view, vote, will, wish ◆ v
3 = **express**, air, articulate, declare,
enunciate, utter

void n **1** = **emptiness**, blankness, gap, lack,
space, vacuity, vacuum ◆ adj **2** = **invalid**,
ineffective, inoperative, null and void,
useless, vain, worthless **3** = **empty**, bare,
free, tenantless, unfilled, unoccupied,
vacant ◆ v **4** = **invalidate**, cancel, nullify,

rescind **5** = **empty**, drain, evacuate

volatile adj **1** = **changeable**, explosive,
inconstant, unsettled, unstable, unsteady,
variable **2** = **temperamental**, erratic, fickle,
mercurial, up and down (inf)

volition n = **free will**, choice, choosing,
discretion, preference, will

volley n = **barrage**, blast, bombardment,
burst, cannonade, fusillade, hail, salvo,
shower

voluble adj = **talkative**, articulate, fluent,
forthcoming, glib, loquacious

volume n **1** = **capacity**, compass,
dimensions **2** = **amount**, aggregate, body,
bulk, mass, quantity, total **3** = **book**,
publication, title, tome, treatise

voluminous adj = **large**, ample, capacious,
cavernous, roomy, vast

voluntarily adv = **willingly**, by choice,
freely, off one's own bat, of one's own

vol·up·tu·ous [və-LUP-choo-əs] *adj* of, contributing to pleasures of the senses. **vol·up·tu·ar·y** [-er-ee] *n, pl* **-ar·ies** one given to luxury and sensual pleasures.

vo·lute [və-LOOT] *n* spiral or twisting turn, form or object.

vom·it *v* 1 eject (contents of stomach) through mouth. ◆ *n* 2 matter vomited.

voo·doo *n, pl* **-doos** 1 practice of black magic, esp. in W Indies, witchcraft. ◆ *vt* **-dooed, -doo·ing** 2 affect by voodoo.

vo·ra·cious [vaw-RAY-shəs] *adj* greedy, ravenous. **vo·rac'i·ty** [-RAS-i-tee] *n*

vor·tex [VOR-teks] *n, pl* **-ti·ces** [-tə-seez] 1 whirlpool. 2 whirling mass or motion.

vo·ta·ry [VOH-tə-ree] *n, pl* **-ries** one vowed to service or pursuit. **vo·tive** [-tiv] *adj* given, consecrated by vow.

vote [voht] *n* 1 formal expression of choice. 2 individual pronouncement. 3 right to give it, in question or election. 4 result of voting. 5 that which is given or allowed by vote. ◆ *v* **vot·ed, vot·ing** 6 express, declare opinion, choice, preference, etc. by vote. 7 authorize, enact, etc. by vote.

vouch [vowch] *vi* (usu. with *for*) guarantee, make oneself responsible for. **vouch'er** *n* 1 document proving correctness of item in accounts, or to establish facts. 2 ticket as substitute for cash. **vouch·safe'** [-SAYF] *vt* **-safed, -saf·ing** agree, condescend to grant or do something.

vow *n* 1 solemn promise, esp. religious one.

◆ *vt* 2 promise, threaten by vow.

vow·el [VOW-əl] *n* 1 any speech sound pronounced without stoppage or friction of the breath. 2 letter standing for such sound, e.g. *a, e, i, o, u.*

vox pop *n* interviews with members of the public on a radio or television programme.

voy·age [VOI-ij] *n* 1 journey, esp. long one, by sea or air. ◆ *vi* **-aged, -ag·ing** 2 make voyage. **voy'ag·er** *n*

vo·yeur [vwah-YUR] *n* one obtaining sexual pleasure by watching sexual activities of others.

vul·can·ize [VUL-kə-nīz] *vt* **-ized, -iz·ing** treat (rubber) with sulfur at high temperature to increase its durability. **vul·can·i·za'tion** *n*

vul·can·ite' *n* a hard black rubber produced by vulcanizing natural rubber with sulphur. **vul·can·i·za'tion** *n* **vul·can·ol'o·gy** see VOLCANOLOGY.

vul·gar [VUL-gər] *adj* 1 offending against good taste. 2 coarse. 3 common. **vul·gar'i·an** [-GAIR-ee-ən] *n* vulgar (rich) person. **vul'gar·ism** *n* coarse, obscene word, phrase. **vul·gar'i·ty** *n, pl* **-ties** **vul·gar·i·za'tion** [-gə-ri-ZAY-shən] *n* **vul'gar·ize** *vt* **-ized, -iz·ing** make vulgar or too common.

Vul·gate [VUL-gayt] *n* fourth-century Latin version of the Bible.

vul·ner·a·ble [VUL-nər-ə-bəl] *adj* 1 capable of being physically or emotionally wounded or hurt. 2 exposed, open to

accord

voluntary *adj* = **unforced**, discretionary, free, optional, spontaneous, willing

volunteer *v* = **offer**, step forward

voluptuous *adj* 1 = **buxom**, ample, curvaceous (*inf*), enticing, seductive, shapely 2 = **sensual**, epicurean, hedonistic, licentious, luxurious, self-indulgent, sybaritic

vomit *v* = **retch**, barf (*sl*), disgorge, emit, heave, regurgitate, spew out *or* up, throw up (*inf*)

voracious *adj* 1 = **gluttonous**, greedy, hungry, insatiable, omnivorous, ravenous 2 = **avid**, hungry, insatiable, rapacious, uncontrolled, unquenchable

voracity *n* 1 = **greed**, hunger, ravenousness 2 = **avidity**, eagerness, hunger, rapacity

vortex *n* = **whirlpool**, eddy, maelstrom

vote *n* 1 = **poll**, ballot, franchise, plebiscite,

referendum, show of hands ◆ *v* 2 = **elect**, cast one's vote, opt

voucher *n* = **ticket**, coupon, token

vouch for *v* 1 = **guarantee**, answer for, certify, give assurance of, stand witness, swear to 2 = **confirm**, affirm, assert, attest to, support, uphold

vouchsafe *v* = **grant**, accord, condescend to give, confer, deign, favour (someone) with, yield

vow *n* 1 = **promise**, oath, pledge ◆ *v* 2 = **promise**, affirm, pledge, swear

voyage *n* = **journey**, crossing, cruise, passage, trip

vulgar *adj* = **crude**, coarse, common, impolite, indecent, off-color, ribald, risqué, rude, tasteless, uncouth, unrefined

vulgarian *n* = **upstart**, arriviste, boor, churl, nouveau riche, parvenu, philistine

vulgarity *n* = **crudeness**, bad taste, coarseness, indelicacy, ribaldry, rudeness, attack, persuasion, etc. **3** easily influenced or tempted. **4** financially weak and likely to fail.

vul·pine [VUL-pin] *adj* **1** of foxes. **2** foxy.

vul·ture [VUL-chər] *n* large bird that feeds on carrion. **vul'tur·ous** [-əs] *adj* **1** of vulture. **2** rapacious.

vul·va [VUL-və] *n, pl* **-vas** external genitals of human female.

vy·ing [VĪ-ing] pr. p. of VIE.

———————— THESAURUS ————————

tastelessness

vulnerable *adj* **1** = **weak**, sensitive, susceptible, tender, thin-skinned **2** = **exposed**, accessible, assailable, defenseless, unprotected, wide open

W w

W *Chem.* tungsten.

wack•y [WAK-ee] *adj* **wack•i•er, wack•i•est**
inf eccentric or funny. **wack'i•ness** [-nis] *n*

wad [wod] *n* **1** small pad of fibrous
material. **2** thick roll of paper money. **3**
sum of money. ♦ *vt* **wad•ded, wad•ding 4**
line, pad, stuff, etc. with wad. **wadding** *n*
stuffing.

wad•dle [WOD-l] *vi* **-dled, -dling 1** walk like
duck. ♦ *n* **2** this gait.

wade [wayd] *vi* **wad•ed, wad•ing 1** walk
through something that hampers
movement, esp. water. **2** proceed with
difficulty. **wad'er** *n* **1** person or bird that
wades. ♦ *pl* **2** angler's high waterproof
boots.

wa•di [WO-dee] *n, pl* **-dis** in the East,
watercourse that is dry except in wet
season.

wa•fer [WAY-fər] *n* **1** thin, crisp biscuit. **2**
thin slice of anything. **3** thin disk of
unleavened bread used in the Eucharist.

waf•fle¹ [WOF-əl] *n* kind of batter cake
with gridlike design.

waf•fle² *inf* ♦ *vi* **-fled, -fling 1** speak, write
in vague wordy manner. ♦ *n* **2** vague
speech, etc. **3** nonsense.

waft [wahft] *vt* **1** convey smoothly through
air or water. ♦ *n* **2** breath of wind. **3** odor,
whiff.

wag *v* **wagged, wag•ging 1** (cause to)
move rapidly from side to side. ♦ *n* **2**
instance of wagging. **3** humorous, witty
person. **wag'gish** *adj*

wage [wayj] *n* **1** (oft. in pl) payment for
work done. ♦ *vt* **waged, wag•ing 2** carry
on.

wa•ger [WAY-jər] *n, vt* bet.

wag•on [WAG-ən] *n* four-wheeled vehicle
for heavy loads. **off the wagon** *sl* drinking
alcoholic beverages again. **on the wagon**
sl abstaining from alcoholic beverages.

waif [wayf] *n* homeless person, esp. child.

wail [wayl] *v* **1** cry out, lament. ♦ *n* **2**
mournful cry.

wain•scot [WAYN-skət] *n* **1** wooden lining
of walls of room. ♦ *vt* **-scot•ed, -scot•ting 2**
line thus.

waist [wayst] *n* **1** part of body between
hips and ribs. **2** various narrow central
parts. **waist•coat** [WES-kət] *n* Brit vest.
waist'line *n* line, size of waist (of person,
garment).

wait [wayt] *v* **1** stay in one place, remain
inactive in expectation (of something). **2**
be prepared (for something). **3** delay. ♦ *vi*
4 serve in restaurant, etc. ♦ *n* **5** act or
period of waiting. **wait'er** *n* **1** attendant
serving diners at hotel, restaurant, etc. **2**
one who waits. **wait•ress** [WAY-tris] *n, fem.*

THESAURUS

wacky *adj Inf* = **foolish,** absurd, asinine,
crackpot (*inf*), crazy, idiotic, silly, stupid,
witless

wad *n* = **mass,** bundle, hunk, roll

waddle *v* = **shuffle,** sway, toddle, totter,
wobble

wade *v* **1** = **walk through,** ford, paddle,
splash **2 wade through** = **plow through,**
drudge at, labor at, peg away at, toil at,
work one's way through

waft *v* = **carry,** bear, convey, drift, float,
transport

wag¹ *v* **1** = **wave,** bob, nod, quiver, shake,
stir, vibrate, wiggle ♦ *n* **2** = **wave,** bob,
nod, quiver, shake, vibration, wiggle

wage *n* **1** (also **wages**) = **payment,**
allowance, emolument, fee, pay,
recompense, remuneration, reward,
stipend ♦ *v* **2** = **engage in,** carry on,
conduct, practice, proceed with,
prosecute, pursue, undertake

wager *n* **1** = **bet,** gamble ♦ *v* **2** = **bet,**
chance, gamble, lay, pledge, risk,
speculate, stake, venture

waif *n* = **stray,** foundling, orphan

wail *v* **1** = **cry,** bawl, grieve, howl, lament,
weep, yowl ♦ *n* **2** = **cry,** complaint, howl,
lament, moan, weeping, yowl

wait *v* **1** = **remain,** hang fire, hold back,
linger, pause, rest, stay, tarry ♦ *n* **2** = **delay,**

waive [wayv] *vt* **waived, waiv·ing** **1** forgo. **2** not to insist on. **waiv·er** *n* (written statement of) this act.

wake¹ [wayk] *v* **waked** or **woke, waked** or **wok·en, wak·ing** **1** rouse from sleep. **2** stir up. ◆ *n* **3** vigil. **4** watch beside corpse. **wak·en** [WAY-kən] *v* wake. **wake·ful** [-fəl] *adj*

wake² *n* track or path left by anything that has passed, as track of turbulent water behind ship.

walk [wawk] *v* **1** (cause, assist to) move, travel on foot at ordinary pace. ◆ *vt* **2** cross, pass through by walking. **3** escort, conduct by walking. ◆ *n* **4** act, instance of walking. **5** path or other place or route for walking. **6** manner of walking. **7** occupation, career. **walk'er** *n* **1** one who walks. **2** framework of metal for support while walking. **walk·ie-talk·ie** [WAW-kee-TAW-kee] *n* portable radio set containing both transmission and receiver units. **walking stick** stick, cane carried while walking. **Walk·man** [WAWK-man] *n* ® small portable cassette player, radio, etc. equipped with headphones. **walk'out** *n* **1** strike. **2** act of leaving as a protest. **walk'o·ver** *n* unopposed or easy victory.

wall [wawl] *n* **1** structure of brick, stone, etc. serving as fence, side of building, etc. **2** surface of one. **3** anything resembling this. ◆ *vt* **4** enclose with wall. **5** block up with wall. **wall'flow·er** *n* **1** garden flower, often growing on walls. **2** at dance, person who remains seated for lack of partner. **wall'pa·per** *n* paper, usu. patterned, to cover interior walls.

wal·la·by [WOL-ə-bee] *n, pl* **-bies** Aust. marsupial similar to and smaller than kangaroo.

wal·let [WOL-it] *n* small folding case, esp. for paper money, documents, etc.

wall·eyed [WAWL-īd] *adj* **1** having eyes turned outward in squint. **2** having eyes with pale irises.

wal·lop [WOL-əp] *inf* ◆ *vt* beat soundly. **1** strike hard. ◆ *n* **2** stroke or blow. **wal'lop·er** *n inf* one who wallops. **wal'lop·ing** *inf* ◆ *n* **1** thrashing. ◆ *adj, adv* **2** very, great(ly).

wal·low [WOL-oh] *vi* **1** roll (in liquid or mud). **2** revel (in). ◆ *n*

wal·nut [WAWL-nut] *n* **1** large nut with crinkled shell splitting easily into two halves. **2** the tree. **3** its wood.

wal·rus [WAWL-rəs] *n* large sea mammal with long tusks.

waltz [wawlts] *n* **1** ballroom dance. **2** music for it. ◆ *v*

wam·pum [WOM-pəm] *n* beads made of shells, formerly used by N Amer. Indians as

halt, hold-up, interval, pause, rest, stay
waiter, waitress *n* = **attendant**, server, steward *or* stewardess
wait on *or* **upon** *v* = **serve**, attend, minister to, tend
waive *v* = **set aside**, abandon, dispense with, forgo, give up, relinquish, remit, renounce
wake¹ *v* **1** = **awaken**, arise, awake, bestir, come to, get up, rouse, stir **2** = **activate**, animate, arouse, excite, fire, galvanize, kindle, provoke, stimulate, stir up ◆ *n* **3** = **vigil**, deathwatch, funeral, watch
wake² *n* = **slipstream**, aftermath, backwash, path, track, trail, train, wash, waves
wakeful *adj* **1** = **sleepless**, insomniac, restless **2** = **watchful**, alert, alive, attentive, observant, on guard, vigilant, wary
waken *v* = **awaken**, activate, arouse, awake, rouse, stir
walk *v* **1** = **go**, amble, hike, march, move, pace, step, stride, stroll **2** = **escort**, accompany, convoy, take ◆ *n* **3** = **stroll**,

hike, march, promenade, ramble, saunter, trek, trudge **4** = **gait**, carriage, step **5** = **path**, alley, avenue, esplanade, footpath, lane, promenade, trail **6 walk of life** = **profession**, calling, career, field, line, trade, vocation
walker *n* = **pedestrian**, hiker, rambler, wayfarer
walkout *n* = **strike**, industrial action, protest, stoppage
walkover *n* = **pushover** (*sl*), breeze (*inf*), cakewalk (*inf*), child's play (*inf*), picnic (*inf*), piece of cake (*inf*)
wall *n* **1** = **partition**, enclosure, screen **2** = **barrier**, fence, hedge, impediment, obstacle, obstruction
wallet *n* = **holder**, case, pocketbook, pouch, purse
wallop *v* **1** = **hit**, batter, beat, clobber (*sl*), pound, pummel, strike, thrash, thump, whack ◆ *n* **2** = **blow**, bash, punch, slug, smack, thump, thwack, whack
wallow *v* **1** = **revel**, bask, delight, glory, luxuriate, relish, take pleasure **2** = **roll**

money and for ornament.

wan [won] *adj* **wan·ner, wan·nest** pale, sickly complexioned, pallid.

wand [wond] *n* stick, usu. straight and slender, esp. as carried by magician, etc.

wan·der [WON-dər] *v* **1** roam, ramble. ♦ *vi* **2** go astray, deviate. ♦ *n* **wan·der·er** *n* **wand·er·lust** *n* irrepressible urge to wander or travel.

wane [wayn] *vi, n* **waned, wan·ing 1** decline. **2** (of moon) decrease in size.

wan·gle [WANG-gəl] *vt* **-gled, -gling** *inf* manipulate, manage in skillful way.

want [wont] *v* **1** desire. **2** lack. ♦ *n* **3** desire. **4** need. **5** deficiency. **want'ed** [-id] *adj* being sought, esp. by the police. **want'ing** *adj* **1** lacking. **2** below standard.

wan·ton [WON-tən] *adj* **1** dissolute. **2** without motive, thoughtless. **3** unrestrained. ♦ *n* **4** wanton person.

war [wor] *n* **1** fighting between nations. **2** state of hostility. **3** conflict, contest. ♦ *vi* **warred, war·ring 1** make war. **war'like** *adj* **1** of, for war. **2** fond of war. **war·ri·or** [WOR-ee-ər] *n* fighter. **war cry 1** cry used

by attacking troops in war. **2** distinctive word, phrase used by political party, etc. **war'fare** [-fair] *n* hostilities. **war'head** [-hed] *n* part of missile, etc. containing explosives. **war·mon·ger** [WOR-mung-gər] *n* one fostering, encouraging war. **war'ship** *n* vessel armed, armored for naval warfare.

war·ble [WOR-bəl] *vi* **-bled, -bling** sing with trills. **war·bler** [-blər] *n* **1** person or bird that warbles. **2** any of various kinds of small songbirds.

ward [word] *n* **1** division of city, hospital, etc. **2** minor under care of guardian. **3** guardianship. **4** curved bar in lock, groove in key that prevents incorrectly cut key opening lock. **ward'room** *n* officers' mess on warship. **ward off** avert, repel.

war·den [WOR-dn] *n* person, officer in charge of prison.

ward·robe [WOR-drohb] *n* **1** piece of furniture for hanging clothes in. **2** person's supply of clothes. **3** costumes of theatrical company.

ware [wair] *n* **1** goods. **2** articles

──────── THESAURUS ────────

about, splash around

wan *adj* = **pale**, anemic, ashen, pallid, pasty, sickly, washed out, white

wand *n* = **stick**, baton, rod

wander *v* **1** = **roam**, drift, meander, ramble, range, rove, stray, stroll **2** = **deviate**, depart, digress, diverge, err, go astray, swerve, veer ♦ *n* **3** = **excursion**, cruise, meander, ramble

wanderer *n* = **traveler**, drifter, gypsy, nomad, rambler, rover, vagabond, voyager

wandering *adj* = **nomadic**, itinerant, migratory, peripatetic, rootless, roving, traveling, vagrant, wayfaring

wane *v* **1** = **decline**, decrease, diminish, dwindle, ebb, fade, fail, lessen, subside, taper off, weaken ♦ *n* **2 on the wane** = **declining**, dwindling, ebbing, fading, obsolescent, on the decline, tapering off, weakening

wangle *v* = **contrive**, arrange, engineer, fix (*inf*), maneuver, manipulate, pull off

want *v* **1** = **desire**, covet, crave, hanker after, hope for, hunger for, long for, thirst for, wish, yearn for **2** = **need**, call for, demand, lack, miss, require ♦ *n* **3** = **wish**, appetite, craving, desire, longing, need, requirement, yearning **4** = **lack**, absence, dearth, deficiency, famine, insufficiency,

paucity, scarcity, shortage **5** = **poverty**, destitution, neediness, penury, privation

wanting *adj* **1** = **lacking**, absent, incomplete, missing, short, shy **2** = **inadequate**, defective, deficient, faulty, imperfect, lousy (*sl*), poor, substandard, unsound

wanton *adj* **1** = **unprovoked**, arbitrary, gratuitous, groundless, motiveless, needless, senseless, uncalled-for, unjustifiable, willful **2** = **promiscuous**, dissipated, dissolute, immoral, lecherous, libidinous, loose, lustful, shameless, unchaste

war *n* **1** = **fighting**, battle, combat, conflict, enmity, hostilities, struggle, warfare ♦ *v* **2** = **fight**, battle, campaign against, clash, combat, take up arms, wage war

warble *v* = **sing**, chirp, trill, twitter

ward *n* **1** = **room**, apartment, cubicle **2** = **district**, area, division, precinct, quarter, zone **3** = **dependant**, charge, minor, protégé, pupil

warden *n* = **keeper**, administrator, caretaker, curator, custodian, guardian, ranger, superintendent

ward off *v* = **repel**, avert, avoid, deflect, fend off, parry, stave off

wardrobe *n* **1** = **clothes cupboard**, closet

collectively. ◆ *pl* **3** goods for sale. **4** commodities. **5** merchandise. **ware'house** *n* **1** storehouse for goods prior to distribution and sale. ◆ *vt* **2** store for future shipment or use.

war·lock [WOR-lok] *n* wizard, sorcerer.

warm [worm] *adj* **1** moderately hot. **2** serving to maintain heat. **3** affectionate. **4** ardent. **5** earnest. **6** hearty. **7** (of color) having yellow or red for a basis. ◆ *v* **8** make, become warm. **warm'ly** *adv* **warmth** *n* **1** mild heat. **2** cordiality. **3** vehemence, anger.

warn [worn] *vt* **1** put on guard. **2** caution, admonish. **3** give advance information to. **4** notify authoritatively. **warn'ing** *n* **1** hint of harm, etc. **2** admonition. **3** advance notice of.

warp [worp] *v* (cause to) twist (out of shape). **1** pervert or be perverted. ◆ *n* **2** state, condition of being warped. **3** lengthwise threads on loom.

war·rant [WOR-ənt] *n* **1** authority. **2** document giving authority. ◆ *vt* **3** guarantee. **4** authorize, justify. **war·ran·tee'** *n* person given warranty. **war'ran·tor** [-tər] *n* person, company giving warranty. **war'ran·ty** [-tee] *n, pl* **-ties 1** guarantee of quality of goods. **2**

security. **warrant officer** officer in certain armed services holding rank between commissioned and noncommissioned officer.

war·ren [WOR-ən] *n* (burrows inhabited by) colony of rabbits.

warrior [WOR-ee-ər] *n* see WAR.

wart [wort] *n* small hard growth on skin. **wart hog** kind of Afr. wild pig.

war·y [WAIR-ee] *adj* **war·i·er, war·i·est** watchful, cautious, alert. **war'i·ly** *adv*

was [wuz, woz] *v* first and third person sing. pt. of BE.

wash [wosh] *v* **1** clean (oneself, clothes, etc.) esp. with water, soap, etc. ◆ *vi* **2** be washable. **3** *inf* be able to be proved true. ◆ *vt* **4** move, be moved by water. **5** flow, sweep over, against. ◆ *n* **6** act of washing. **7** clothes washed at one time. **8** sweep of water, esp. set up by moving ship. **9** thin coat of color. **wash'a·ble** *adj* capable of being washed without damage, etc. **wash'er** *n* **1** one who, that which, washes. **2** ring put under a nut. **wash'ing** *n* clothes to be washed. **wash'y** *adj* **wash·i·er, wash·i·est 1** dilute. **2** watery. **3** insipid. **wash'out** *n* **1** rainout. **2** *inf* complete failure.

wasp [wosp] *n* striped stinging insect

2 = clothes, apparel, attire

warehouse *n* = **store**, depository, depot, stockroom, storehouse

wares *pl n* = **goods**, commodities, merchandise, produce, products, stock, stuff

warfare *n* = **war**, arms, battle, combat, conflict, fighting, hostilities

warily *adv* = **cautiously**, carefully, charily, circumspectly, distrustfully, gingerly, suspiciously, vigilantly, watchfully, with care

warlike *adj* = **belligerent**, aggressive, bellicose, bloodthirsty, hawkish, hostile, martial, warmongering

warlock *n* = **magician**, conjurer, enchanter, sorcerer, wizard

warm *adj* **1 = heated**, balmy, lukewarm, pleasant, sunny, tepid, thermal **2 = affectionate**, amorous, cordial, friendly, hospitable, kindly, loving, tender ◆ *v* **3 = heat**, heat up, melt, thaw, warm up

warmonger *n* = **hawk**, belligerent, militarist, saber-rattler

warmth *n* **1 = heat**, hotness, warmness **2 =**

affection, amorousness, cordiality, heartiness, kindliness, love, tenderness

warn *v* = **notify**, advise, alert, apprise, caution, forewarn, give notice, inform, make (someone) aware, tip off

warning *n* = **caution**, advice, alarm, alert, notification, omen, sign, tip-off

warp *v* **1 = twist**, bend, contort, deform, distort ◆ *n* **2 = twist**, bend, contortion, distortion, kink

warrant *n* **1 = authorization**, authority, license, permission, permit, sanction ◆ *v* **2 = call for**, demand, deserve, excuse, justify, license, necessitate, permit, require, sanction **3 = guarantee**, affirm, attest, certify, declare, pledge, vouch for

warranty *n* = **guarantee**, assurance, bond, certificate, contract, covenant, pledge

warrior *n* = **soldier**, combatant, fighter, gladiator, man-at-arms

wary *adj* = **cautious**, alert, careful, chary, circumspect, distrustful, guarded, suspicious, vigilant, watchful

wash *v* **1 = clean**, bathe, cleanse, launder, rinse, scrub **2 = sweep away**, bear away, resembling bee. **wasp'ish** *adj* irritable, snappish. **wasp waist** very small waist.

waste [wayst] *v* **wast·ed, wast·ing ♦** *vt* **1** expend uselessly, use extravagantly. **2** fail to take advantage of. **3** lay desolate. **♦** *vi* **4** dwindle. **5** pine away. **♦** *n* **6** act of wasting. **7** what is wasted. **8** desert. **♦** *adj* **9** worthless, useless. **10** desert. **11** wasted. **wast·age** [WAY-stij] *n* **1** loss by use or decay. **2** losses as result of wastefulness. **waste'ful** [-fəl] *adj* extravagant. **waste'ful·ness** [-nis] *n* **waste product 1** discarded material in manufacturing process. **2** excreted urine, feces. **wast·rel** [WAY-strəl] *n* wasteful person, spendthrift.

watch [woch] *vt* **1** observe closely. **2** guard. **♦** *vi* **3** wait expectantly (for). **4** be on watch. **♦** *n* **5** portable timepiece for wrist, pocket, etc. **6** state of being on the lookout. **7** guard. **8** spell of duty. **watch'ful** [-fəl] *adj* **watch'mak·er** *n* one skilled in making and repairing watches. **watch'man** [-mən] *n, pl* **-men** person guarding building, etc., esp. at night. **watch'word** [-wurd] *n* **1** password. **2** rallying cry.

wa·ter [WAW-tər] *n* **1** transparent, colorless, odorless, tasteless liquid, substance of rain, river, etc. **2** body of water. **3** river. **4** lake. **5** sea. **6** tear. **7** urine. **♦** *vt* **8** put water on or into. **9** irrigate or provide with water. **♦** *vi* **10** salivate. **11** (of eyes) fill with tears. **12** take in or obtain water. **wa'ter·y** *adj* **water buffalo** oxlike Asian animal. **water closet** [KLOZ-it] toilet. **wa'ter·col·or** *n* **1** pigment mixed with water. **2** painting in this. **wa'ter·course** *n* stream. **wa'ter·cress** *n* plant growing in clear ponds and streams. **wa'ter·fall** *n* perpendicular descent of waters of river, stream. **wa'ter·logged** *adj* saturated, filled with water. **wa'ter·mark** *n* faint translucent design stamped on substance of sheet of paper. **wa'ter·proof** *adj* **1** not letting water through. **♦** *v* **2** make waterproof. **wa'ter·shed** *n* **1** area drained by a river. **2** important division between conditions, phases. **water-ski·ing** *n* sport of riding over water on ski towed by speedboat. **water sports** various sports, as swimming, windsurfing, that take place in or on water. **water·tight** [-tīt] *adj* **1** so fitted as to prevent water entering or escaping. **2** with no loopholes or weak points.

watt [wot] *n* unit of electric power.

carry off, move **3** *Inf* **= be plausible,** bear scrutiny, be convincing, carry weight, hold up, hold water, stand up, stick **♦** *n* **4 = cleaning,** cleansing, laundering, rinse, scrub **5 = coat,** coating, film, layer, overlay **6 = swell,** surge, wave

washout *n* **= failure,** disappointment, disaster, dud (*inf*), flop (*inf*)

waste *v* **1 = misuse,** blow (*sl*), dissipate, fritter away, lavish, squander, throw away **2 waste away = decline,** atrophy, crumble, decay, dwindle, fade, wane, wear out, wither **♦** *n* **3 = misuse,** dissipation, extravagance, frittering away, prodigality, squandering, wastefulness **4 = rubbish,** debris, dross, garbage, leftovers, litter, refuse, scrap, trash **5 wastes = desert,** wasteland, wilderness **♦** *adj* **6 = unwanted,** leftover, superfluous, supernumerary, unused, useless, worthless **7 = uncultivated,** bare, barren, desolate, empty, uninhabited, unproductive, wild

wasteful *adj* **= extravagant,** lavish, prodigal, profligate, spendthrift, thriftless, uneconomical

waster *n* **= idler,** couch potato (*sl*), good-for-nothing, loafer, shirker, wastrel

watch *v* **1 = look at,** contemplate, eye, observe, regard, see, view **2 = guard,** keep, look after, mind, protect, superintend, take care of, tend **♦** *n* **3 = wristwatch,** chronometer, timepiece **4 = lookout,** observation, surveillance, vigil

watchdog *n* **1 = guard dog 2 = guardian,** custodian, monitor, protector, scrutineer

watchful *adj* **= alert,** attentive, observant, on the lookout, suspicious, vigilant, wary, wide awake

watchman *n* **= guard,** caretaker, custodian, security guard

watchword *n* **= motto,** battle cry, byword, catch phrase, catchword, maxim, rallying cry, slogan

water *n* **1 = liquid,** H_2O **♦** *v* **2 = moisten,** dampen, douse, drench, hose, irrigate, soak, spray

water down *v* **= dilute,** thin, water, weaken

waterfall *n* **= cascade,** cataract, fall

watertight *adj* **1 = waterproof 2 = foolproof,** airtight, flawless, impregnable, sound, unassailable

watt'age [-ij] *n* electric power expressed in watts.

wat·tle [WOT-l] *n* fleshy pendent lobe on head or neck of certain birds, e.g. turkey.

wave [wayv] *v* **waved, wav·ing 1** move to and fro, as hand in greeting or farewell. **2** signal by waving. **3** give, take shape of waves (as hair, etc.). ◆ *n* **4** ridge and trough on water, etc. **5** act, gesture of waving. **6** vibration, as in radio waves, of electric and magnetic forces alternating in direction. **7** prolonged spell of something. **8** upsurge. **9** wavelike shapes in the hair, etc. **wav'y** [-ee] *adj* **wav·i·er, wav·i·est** **wave'length** *n* distance between same points of two successive sound waves.

wav·er [WAY-vər] *vi* **1** hesitate, be irresolute. **2** be, become unsteady.

wax[1] [waks] *n* **1** yellow, soft, pliable material made by bees. **2** this or similar substance used for sealing, making candles, etc. **3** waxy secretion of ear. ◆ *vt* **waxed, wax·ing 4** put wax on. **wax'y** [-ee] *adj* **wax·i·er, wax·i·est** like wax. **wax'wing** *n* small songbird. **wax'work** [-wurk] *n* lifelike figure, esp. of famous person, reproduced in wax.

wax[2] *vi* **waxed, wax·ing** grow, increase.

way *n* **1** manner. **2** method, means. **3** track. **4** direction. **5** path. **6** passage. **7** course. **8** route. **9** progress. **10** state or condition.

way'far·er [-fair-ər] *n* traveler, esp. on foot.

way'lay *vt* **-laid, -lay·ing** lie in wait for and accost, attack. **way'side** *n* side or edge of a road. ◆ *adj* **way'ward** [-wərd] *adj* capricious, perverse, willful.

way'ward·ness [-nis] *n*

we [wee] *pron* first person plural pronoun.

weak [week] *adj* **-er, -est 1** lacking strength. **2** feeble. **3** fragile. **4** defenseless. **5** easily influenced. **6** faint. **weak·en** [WEE-kən] *v* **weak'ling** *n* feeble creature. **weak'ly** *adj* **1** weak. **2** sickly. ◆ *adv*

wealth [welth] *n* **1** riches. **2** abundance. **wealth'y** *adj* **wealth·i·er, wealth·i·est**

wean [ween] *vt* **1** accustom to food other than mother's milk. **2** win over, coax away from.

weap·on [WEP-ən] *n* **1** implement to fight with. **2** anything used to get the better of an opponent. **weap'on·ry** [-ree] *n*

wear [wair] *v* **wore, worn, wear·ing** ◆ *vt* **1**

────┤ THESAURUS ├────

watery *adj* **1** = **wet**, aqueous, damp, fluid, liquid, moist, soggy **2** = **diluted**, runny, thin, washy, watered-down, weak

wave *v* **1** = **signal**, beckon, direct, gesticulate, gesture, indicate, sign **2** = **flap**, brandish, flourish, flutter, oscillate, shake, stir, swing, wag ◆ *n* **3** = **ripple**, billow, breaker, ridge, roller, swell, undulation **4** = **outbreak**, flood, rash, rush, stream, surge, upsurge

waver *v* **1** = **hesitate**, dither, falter, fluctuate, hum and haw, seesaw, vacillate **2** = **tremble**, flicker, quiver, shake, totter, wobble

wax *v* = **increase**, develop, enlarge, expand, grow, magnify, swell

way *n* **1** = **method**, fashion, manner, means, mode, procedure, process, system, technique **2** = **style**, custom, habit, manner, nature, personality, practice, wont **3** = **route**, channel, course, direction, path, pathway, road, track, trail **4** = **journey**, approach, march, passage **5** = **distance**, length, stretch

wayfarer *n* = **traveler**, gypsy, itinerant, nomad, rover, voyager, wanderer

wayward *adj* = **erratic**, capricious, inconstant, ungovernable, unmanageable, unpredictable, unruly

weak *adj* **1** = **feeble**, debilitated, effete, fragile, frail, infirm, puny, sickly, unsteady **2** = **unsafe**, defenseless, exposed, helpless, unguarded, unprotected, vulnerable **3** = **unconvincing**, feeble, flimsy, hollow, lame, pathetic, unsatisfactory **4** = **tasteless**, diluted, insipid, runny, thin, watery

weaken *v* **1** = **lessen**, diminish, dwindle, fade, flag, lower, moderate, reduce, sap, undermine, wane **2** = **dilute**, thin out, water down

weakling *n* = **sissy**, baby (*inf*), drip (*inf*), wimp (*inf*)

weakness *n* **1** = **frailty**, decrepitude, feebleness, fragility, infirmity, powerlessness, vulnerability **2** = **failing**, blemish, defect, deficiency, fault, flaw, imperfection, lack, shortcoming **3** = **liking**, fondness, inclination, partiality, passion, penchant, soft spot

wealth *n* **1** = **riches**, affluence, capital, fortune, money, opulence, prosperity **2** = **plenty**, abundance, copiousness, cornucopia, fullness, profusion, richness

wealthy *adj* = **rich**, affluent, flush (*inf*), moneyed, opulent, prosperous, well-heeled (*inf*), well-off, well-to-do have on the body. **2** show. **3** produce (hole, etc.) by rubbing, etc. **4** harass or weaken. ◆ *vi* **5** last. **6** become impaired by use. **7** (of time) pass slowly. ◆ *n* **8** act of wearing. **9** things to wear. **10** damage caused by use. **11** ability to resist effects of constant use.

wea•ry [WEER-ee] *adj* **-ri•er, -ri•est 1** tired, exhausted, jaded. **2** tiring. **3** tedious. ◆ *v* **-ried, -ry•ing 4** make, become weary. **wea'ri•ness** [-ree-nis] *n* **wea'ri•some** [-ree-səm] *adj* causing weariness.

wea•sel [WEE-zəl] *n* small carnivorous mammal with long body and short legs.

weath•er [WE*TH*-ər] *n* **1** day-to-day meteorological conditions, esp. temperature, cloudiness, etc. of a place. ◆ *adj* **2** toward the wind. ◆ *vt* **3** affect by weather. **4** endure. **5** resist. **6** come safely through. **7** sail to windward of. **weath'er•vane** [-vain] *n* rotating vane to show which way wind blows.

weave [weev] *v* **wove** or **weaved, wo•ven** or **wove, weav•ing** ◆ *vt* **1** form into texture or fabric by interlacing, esp. on loom. **2** fashion, construct. ◆ *vi* **3** become woven. **4** make one's way, esp. with side to side motion. **weav'er** [-ər] *n*

web *n* **1** woven fabric. **2** net spun by spider.

3 membrane between toes of waterfowl, frogs, etc. **the Web** short for WORLD WIDE WEB. **web'bing** *n* strong fabric woven in strips. **web'cam** *n* camera that transmits images over the Internet. **web'cast** *n* broadcast of an event over the Internet. **web'site** *n* group of pages on the World Wide Web with a single address.

web•er [WEB-ər] *n* SI unit of magnetic flux.

wed *vt* **wed•ded, wed•ding 1** marry. **2** unite closely. **wedding** *n* act of marrying, nuptial ceremony. **wed'lock** *n* marriage.

wedge [wej] *n* **1** piece of wood, metal, etc., thick at one end, tapering to a thin edge. ◆ *vt* **wedged, wedg•ing 2** fasten, split with wedge. **3** stick by compression or crowding.

weed *n* **1** plant growing where undesired. **2** *inf* tobacco. **3** *sl* marijuana. **4** thin, sickly person, animal. ◆ *vt* **5** clear of weeds. **weed'y** *adj* **weed•i•er, weed•i•est 1** full of weeds. **2** thin, weakly. **weed out** remove, eliminate what is unwanted.

weeds [weedz] *pl n obs* (widow's) mourning clothes.

week *n* **1** period of seven days, esp. one beginning on Sunday and ending on Saturday. **2** hours, days of work in seven-day period. **week'ly** *adj, adv* **1**

THESAURUS

wear *v* **1 = be dressed in**, don, have on, put on, sport (*inf*) **2 = show**, display, exhibit **3 = deteriorate**, abrade, corrode, erode, fray, grind, rub ◆ *n* **4 = clothes**, apparel, attire, costume, dress, garb, garments, gear (*inf*), things **5 = damage**, abrasion, attrition, corrosion, deterioration, erosion, wear and tear

weariness *n* **= tiredness**, drowsiness, exhaustion, fatigue, languor, lassitude, lethargy, listlessness

wearing *adj* **= tiresome**, exasperating, fatiguing, irksome, oppressive, trying, wearisome

wearisome *adj* **= tedious**, annoying, boring, exhausting, fatiguing, irksome, oppressive, tiresome, troublesome, trying, wearing

wear off *v* **= subside**, decrease, diminish, disappear, dwindle, fade, peter out, wane

weary *adj* **1 = tired**, done in (*inf*), drained, drowsy, exhausted, fatigued, flagging, jaded, sleepy, worn out **2 = tiring**, arduous, laborious, tiresome, wearisome ◆ *v* **3 = tire**, drain, enervate, fatigue, sap,

take it out of (*inf*), tax, tire out, wear out

weather *n* **1 = climate**, conditions ◆ *v* **2 = withstand**, brave, come through, endure, overcome, resist, ride out, stand, survive

weave *v* **1 = knit**, braid, entwine, interlace, intertwine, plait **2 = create**, build, construct, contrive, fabricate, make up, put together, spin **3 = zigzag**, crisscross, wind

web *n* **1 = spider's web**, cobweb **2 = network**, lattice, tangle

wed *v* **1 = marry**, get married, take the plunge (*inf*), tie the knot (*inf*) **2 = unite**, ally, blend, combine, interweave, join, link, merge

wedding *n* **= marriage**, nuptials, wedlock

wedge *n* **1 = block**, chunk, lump ◆ *v* **2 = squeeze**, cram, crowd, force, jam, lodge, pack, ram, stuff, thrust

wedlock *n* **= marriage**, matrimony

weed out *v* **= eliminate**, dispense with, eradicate, get rid of, remove, root out, uproot

weedy *adj* **= weak**, feeble, frail, ineffectual, puny, skinny, thin

happening, done, published, etc. once a
week. ♦ *n* **2** newspaper or magazine
published once a week. **week'day** *n* any
day of week except Sunday and usu.
Saturday. **week'end** *n* (at least) Saturday
and Sunday, esp. considered as rest
period.

weep [weep] *v* **wept, weep·ing 1** shed tears (for).
2 grieve. **weep'y** *adj* **weep·i·er, weep·i·est**
weeping willow willow with drooping
branches.

wee·vil [WEE-vəl] *n* small beetle harmful to
cotton, etc.

weft *n* cross threads in weaving, woof.

weigh [way] *vt* **1** find weight of. **2** consider.
3 raise (anchor). ♦ *vi* **4** have weight. **5** be
burdensome. **weight** *n* **1** measure of the
heaviness of an object. **2** quality of
heaviness. **3** heavy mass. **4** object of
known mass for weighing. **5** unit of
measurement of weight. **6** importance,
influence. ♦ *vt* **7** add weight to. **weight'y**
adj **weight·i·er, weight·i·est 1** heavy. **2**
onerous. **3** important. **4** momentous.

weir [weer] *n* **1** small dam in river or
stream. **2** fence or net in stream, etc. for
catching fish.

weird [weerd] *adj* **-er, -est 1** unearthly,
uncanny. **2** strange, bizarre.

wel·come [WEL-kəm] *adj* **1** received gladly.
2 freely permitted. ♦ *n, interj* **3** kindly
greeting. ♦ *vt* **-comed, -com·ing 4** greet
with pleasure. **5** receive gladly.

weld *vt* **1** unite metal by softening with
heat. **2** unite closely. ♦ *n* **3** welded joint.
weld'er *n* **1** person who welds. **2** machine
used in welding. **weld'ment** [-mənt] *n*
welded assembly.

wel·fare [WEL-fair] *n* well-being. **welfare**
state system in which the government
takes responsibility for the social,
economic, etc. security of its citizens.

well¹ *adv* **1** in good manner or degree. **2**
suitably. **3** intimately. **4** fully. **5** favorably,
kindly. **6** to a considerable degree. ♦ *adj*
bet·ter, best 7 in good health. **8** suitable. ♦
interj **9** exclamation of surprise,
interrogation, etc. **well-being** *n* state of
being well, happy, or prosperous.
well-disposed *adj* inclined to be friendly,
kindly (toward). **well-mannered** *adj* having
good manners. **well-off** *adj* fairly rich.
well-read [-red] *adj* having read much.
well-spoken *adj* speaking fluently,
graciously, aptly. **well-to-do** *adj*
moderately wealthy.

well² *n* **1** hole sunk into the earth to reach
water, gas, oil, etc. **2** spring. **3** any shaft
like a well. ♦ *vi* **4** spring, gush.

Welsh *adj* **1** of Wales. ♦ *n* **2** language,

weep *v* = **cry**, blubber, lament, mourn,
shed tears, snivel, sob, whimper

weepy *adj Inf* = **sentimental**,
overemotional, schmaltzy (*sl*), slushy (*inf*)

weigh *v* **1** = **have a weight of**, tip the
scales at (*inf*) **2** = **consider**, contemplate,
deliberate upon, evaluate, examine,
meditate upon, ponder, reflect upon, think
over **3** = **matter**, carry weight, count

weight *n* **1** = **heaviness**, load, mass,
poundage, tonnage **2** = **importance**,
authority, consequence, impact, import,
influence, power, value ♦ *v* **3** = **load**,
freight **4** = **bias**, load, slant, unbalance

weighty *adj* **1** = **important**, consequential,
crucial, grave, momentous, portentous,
serious, significant, solemn **2** = **heavy**,
burdensome, cumbersome, hefty (*inf*),
massive, ponderous

weird *adj* = **strange**, bizarre, creepy (*inf*),
eerie, freakish, mysterious, odd, queer,
spooky (*inf*), unnatural

welcome *v* **1** = **greet**, embrace, hail, meet,
receive ♦ *n* **2** = **greeting**, acceptance,

hospitality, reception, salutation ♦ *adj* **3** =
acceptable, agreeable, appreciated,
delightful, desirable, gratifying, pleasant,
refreshing **4** = **free**, under no obligation

weld *v* = **join**, bind, bond, connect, fuse,
link, solder, unite

welfare *n* **1** = **wellbeing**, advantage,
benefit, good, happiness, health, interest,
prosperity **2** = **benefit**, allowance, gift,
grant, handout

well¹ *adv* **1** = **satisfactorily**, agreeably,
nicely, pleasantly, smoothly, splendidly,
successfully **2** = **skillfully**, ably, adeptly,
adequately, admirably, correctly,
efficiently, expertly, proficiently, properly
3 = **prosperously**, comfortably **4** =
suitably, fairly, fittingly, justly, properly,
rightly **5** = **intimately**, deeply, fully,
profoundly, thoroughly **6** = **favorably**,
approvingly, glowingly, highly, kindly,
warmly **7** = **considerably**, abundantly,
amply, fully, greatly, heartily, highly,
substantially, thoroughly, very much ♦ *adj*
8 = **healthy**, fit, in fine fettle, sound **9** =

people of Wales. **Welsh rabbit, rarebit** dish of melted cheese, beer, spices on toast.

welsh vi inf fail to pay debt or fulfill obligation (also **welch**). **welsh'er** [-ər], **welch·er** [WELCH-ər] n

welt n 1 raised, strengthened seam. 2 weal. ◆ vt 3 provide with welt. 4 thrash.

wel·ter [WEL-tər] vi 1 roll or tumble. ◆ n 2 turmoil, disorder.

wel·ter·weight [WEL-tər-wayt] n Boxing 1 weight between light and middle. 2 boxer of this weight.

wen n obs., on scalp.

wench n obs., now facetious young woman.

wend v go, travel.

went pt. of GO.

wept pt./pp. of WEEP.

were [wur] past indicative, plural and subjunctive sing. and pl. of BE.

were·wolf [WAIR-wuulf] n, pl -**wolves** (in folklore) human being turned into wolf.

west n 1 part of sky where sun sets. 2 part of country, etc. lying to this side. 3 occident. ◆ adj 4 that is toward or in this region. ◆ adv 5 to the west. **west'er·ly** [-ər-lee] adj **west'ward** [-wərd] adj, adv **west'ward(s)** adv toward the west. **west'ern** [-ərn] adj 1 of, in the west. ◆ n 2 film, story, etc. about cowboys or frontiersmen in western US. **go west** inf die.

wet adj **wet·ter**, **wet·test** 1 having water or other liquid on a surface or being soaked in it. 2 rainy. 3 not yet dry (paint, ink, etc.).

◆ vt **wet** or **wet·ted**, **wet·ting** 4 make wet. ◆ n 5 moisture, rain. **wet blanket** one depressing spirits of others. **wet'land** [-lənd] n area of swamp or marsh. **wet nurse** woman suckling another's child. **wet suit** close-fitting rubber suit worn by divers, etc.

whack [hwak] vt 1 strike with sharp resounding blow. ◆ n 2 such blow. 3 sl share. 4 inf attempt. **whack'ing** adj inf big, enormous.

whale [hwayl] n large fish-shaped sea mammal. **whal'er** n person, ship employed in hunting whales. **whale'bone** n horny elastic substance from projections of upper jaw of certain whales. **whal'ing** n **a whale of a time** inf very enjoyable time.

wharf [hworf] n platform at harbor, on river, etc. for loading and unloading ships.

what [hwut, hwot] pron 1 which thing. 2 that which. 3 request for statement to be repeated. ◆ adj 4 which. 5 as much as. 6 how great, surprising, etc. ◆ interj 7 exclamation of surprise, anger, etc. **what·ev'er** pron 1 anything which. 2 of what kind it may be. **what'not** n 1 small stand with shelves. 2 something, anything of same kind.

wheat [hweet] n cereal plant with thick four-sided seed spikes of which bread is chiefly made. **wheat'en** [-ən] adj wheat **germ** [-jurm] embryo of wheat kernel.

whee·dle [HWEED-l] v -**dled**, -**dling** coax, cajole.

wheel [hweel] n 1 circular frame or disk

---

satisfactory, agreeable, fine, pleasing, proper, right, thriving

well² n 1 = **hole**, bore, pit, shaft ◆ v 2 = **flow**, gush, jet, pour, spout, spring, spurt, surge

well-known adj = **famous**, celebrated, familiar, noted, popular, renowned

well-off adj = **rich**, affluent, comfortable (inf), moneyed, prosperous, wealthy, well-heeled (inf), well-to-do

well-to-do adj = **rich**, affluent, comfortable (inf), moneyed, prosperous, wealthy, well-heeled (inf), well-off

well-worn adj = **stale**, banal, commonplace, hackneyed, overused, stereotyped, trite

welt n = **mark**, contusion, streak, stripe, wale, weal

welter n = **jumble**, confusion, mess,

muddle, tangle, web

wet adj 1 = **damp**, dank, moist, saturated, soaking, sodden, soggy, sopping, waterlogged, watery 2 = **rainy**, drizzling, pouring, raining, showery, teeming ◆ n 3 = **rain**, drizzle 4 = **moisture**, condensation, damp, dampness, humidity, liquid, water, wetness ◆ v 5 = **moisten**, dampen, douse, irrigate, saturate, soak, spray, water

whack v 1 = **strike**, bang, belt (inf), clobber (sl), hit, smack, thrash, thump, thwack, wallop (inf) ◆ n 2 = **blow**, bang, belt (inf), hit, smack, stroke, thump, thwack, wallop (inf) 3 Inf = **share**, bit, cut (inf), part, portion, quota 4 As in **have a whack** = **attempt**, bash (inf), crack (inf), go (inf), shot (inf), stab (inf), try, turn

wharf n = **dock**, jetty, landing stage, pier, quay

(with spokes) revolving on axle. **2** anything like a wheel in shape or function. **3** act of turning. **4** steering wheel. ◆ *v* (cause to) turn as if on axis. **5** (cause to) move on or as if on wheels. **6** (cause to) change course, esp. in opposite direction. **wheel'bar·row** [-ba-roh] *n* barrow with one wheel. **wheel'base** [-hays] *n* distance between front and rear hubs of vehicle. **wheel'chair** *n* chair mounted on large wheels, used by people who cannot walk.

wheeze [hweez] *vi* **wheezed, wheez·ing 1** breathe with difficulty and whistling noise. ◆ *n* **2** this sound. **3** story, etc.told too often. **wheez'y** [-ee] *adj* **wheez·i·er, wheez·i·est**

whelp [hwelp] *n* **1** pup, cub. ◆ *v* **2** produce whelps.

when [hwen] *adv* **1** at what time. ◆ *conj* **2** at the time that. **3** although. **4** since. ◆ *pron* **5** at which (time). **when·ev'er** *adv, conj* at whatever time.

whence [hwens] *adv* **1** from what place or source. **2** how.

where [hwair] *adv, conj* **1** at what place. **2** at or to the place in which. **where'a·bouts** *adv, conj* **1** in what, which place. ◆ *n* **2** present position. **where·as'** *conj* **1** considering that. **2** while, on the contrary. **where·by'** [-BĪ] *conj* by which. **where'fore** *adv obs* **1** why. ◆ *conj* **2** consequently. **where·up·on'** *conj* at which point. **wher·ev'er** *adv* at whatever place. **where'with·al** [-*with*-awl] *n* necessary funds, resources, etc.

whet [hwet] *vt* **whet·ted, whet·ting 1** sharpen. **2** stimulate. **whet'stone** *n* stone for sharpening tools.

wheth·er [HWE*TH*-ər] *conj* introduces the first of two alternatives, of which the second may be expressed or implied.

whey [hway] *n* watery part of milk left after separation of curd in cheese making.

which [hwich] *adj* **1** used in requests for a selection from alternatives. ◆ *pron* **2** which person or thing. **3** the thing *who*. **which·ev'er** *pron*

whiff [hwif] *n* **1** brief smell or suggestion of. **2** puff of air. ◆ *v* **3** smell.

while [hwil] *conj* **1** in the time that. **2** in spite of the fact that, although. **3** whereas. ◆ *vt* **whiled, whil·ing 4** pass (time, usu. idly). ◆ *n* **5** period of time.

whim [hwim] *n* sudden, passing fancy. **whim'si·cal** [-zi-kəl] *adj* **1** fanciful. **2** full of whims. **whim·si·cal'i·ty** [-zi-KAL-i-tee] *n, pl* **-ties whim'sy** [-zee] *n, pl* **-sies 1** whim. **2** caprice.

whim·per [HWIM-pər] *vi* **1** cry or whine softly. **2** complain in this way. ◆ *n* **3** such cry or complaint.

whine [hwin] *n* **1** high-pitched plaintive cry. **2** peevish complaint. ◆ *vi* **whined, whin·ing 3** utter this.

whin·ny [HWIN-ee] *vi* **-nied, -ny·ing** neigh softly. ◆ *n*

whip [hwip] *v* **whipped, whip·ping** ◆ *vt* **1** strike with whip. **2** thrash. **3** beat (cream, eggs) to a froth. **4** lash. **5** pull, remove, quickly. ◆ *vi* **6** dart. ◆ *n* **7** lash attached to handle for urging or punishing. **8** one who enforces attendance, voting, etc. of political party. **9** elastic quality permitting bending in mast, fishing rod, etc. **10** whipped dessert. **whip'lash** *n* injury to neck as result of sudden jerking of unsupported head. **whipping boy** scapegoat.

wheedle *v* = **coax**, cajole, entice, inveigle, persuade

wheel *n* **1** = **circle**, gyration, pivot, revolution, rotation, spin, turn ◆ *v* **2** = **turn**, gyrate, pirouette, revolve, rotate, spin, swing, swivel, twirl, whirl

wheeze *v* **1** = **gasp**, cough, hiss, rasp, whistle ◆ *n* **2** = **gasp**, cough, hiss, rasp, whistle **3** *Brit. sl* = **trick**, idea, plan, ploy, ruse, scheme, stunt

whereabouts *n* = **position**, location, site, situation

wherewithal *n* = **resources**, capital, funds, means, money, supplies

whet *v* **1** *As in* **whet someone's appetite** = **stimulate**, arouse, awaken, enhance, excite, kindle, quicken, rouse, stir **2** = **sharpen**, hone

whiff *n* = **smell**, aroma, hint, odor, scent, sniff

whim *n* = **impulse**, caprice, fancy, notion, urge

whimper *v* **1** = **cry**, moan, snivel, sob, weep, whine ◆ *n* **2** = **sob**, moan, snivel, whine

whimsical *adj* = **fanciful**, curious, eccentric, freakish, funny, odd, playful, quaint, unusual

whine *n* **1** = **cry**, moan, sob, wail, whimper **2** = **complaint**, gripe (*inf*), grouch (*inf*),

whip·pet [HWIP-it] *n* racing dog like small greyhound.

whir [hwur] *v* **whirred, whir·ring 1** (cause to) fly, spin, etc. with buzzing or whizzing sound. **2** bustle. ♦ *n* **3** this sound.

whirl [hwurl] *v* **1** swing rapidly around. **2** move rapidly in a circular course. **3** drive at high speed. ♦ *n* **4** whirling movement. **5** confusion, bustle, giddiness. **whirl'pool** *n* circular current, eddy. **whirl'wind** *n* wind whirling around while moving forward. ♦ *adj*

whisk [hwisk] *v* **1** brush, sweep, beat lightly. **2** move, remove, quickly. **3** beat to a froth. ♦ *n* **4** light brush. **5** eggbeating implement.

whisk·er [HWIS-kər] *n* **1** any of the long stiff hairs at side of mouth of cat or other animal. **2** any of hairs on a man's face. **by a whisker** only just.

whis·key [HWIS-kee] *n, pl* **-keys** alcoholic liquor distilled from fermented cereals. **whis'ky** *n, pl* **-kies** Scotch or Canadian whiskey.

whis·per [HWIS-pər] *v* **1** speak in soft, hushed tones, without vibration of vocal cords. **2** rustle. ♦ *n* **3** such speech. **4** trace or suspicion. **5** rustle.

whist [hwist] *n* card game.

whis·tle [HWIS-əl] *v* **-tled, -tling** ♦ *vi* **1** produce shrill sound by forcing breath through rounded, nearly closed lips. **2** make such a sound. ♦ *vt* **3** utter, summon, etc. by whistle. ♦ *n* **4** such sound. **5** any similar sound. **6** instrument to make it. **whis·tler** [HWIS-lər] *n* **whistle-blower** *n* person who informs on or puts stop to

something.

whit [hwit] *n* **not a whit** not the slightest amount.

white [hwīt] *adj* **whit·er, whit·est 1** of the color of snow. **2** pale. **3** light in color. **4** having a light-colored skin. ♦ *n* **5** color of snow. **6** white pigment. **7** white part. **8** clear fluid round yolk of egg. **9** Caucasian person. **whi'ten** [-ən] *v* **white ant** termite. **white-collar** *adj* denoting nonmanual salaried workers. **white elephant** useless, unwanted, gift or possession. **white flag** white banner or cloth used as signal of surrender or truce. **white hope** one (formerly, a white person) expected to bring honor or glory to his group, team, etc. **white lie** minor, unimportant lie. **white paper** government report on matter recently investigated. **white slave** woman, child forced or enticed away for purposes of prostitution. **white'wash** [-wosh] *n* **1** substance for whitening walls, etc. ♦ *vt* **2** apply this. **3** cover up, gloss over, suppress.

whith·er [HWITH-ər] *adv* **1** to what place. **2** to which.

whit·tle [HWIT-l] *vt* **-tled, -tling 1** cut, carve with knife. **2** pare away. **whittle down** reduce gradually, wear (away).

whiz [hwiz] *n* **1** loud hissing sound. **2** *inf* person skillful at something. ♦ *v* **whizzed, whiz·zing 3** move with such sound, or make it. **4** *inf* move quickly. **take a whizz** *inf* urinate.

who [hoo] *pron* relative and interrogative pronoun, always referring to persons. **who·dun'it** *n inf* detective story. **who·ev'er** *pron* who, any one or every one that.

grouse, grumble, moan

whip *n* **1** = **lash**, birch, cane, cat-o'-nine-tails, crop, scourge ♦ *v* **2** = **lash**, beat, birch, cane, flagellate, flog, paddle (*U.S. & Canad.*), scourge, spank, strap, thrash **3** *Inf* = **dash**, dart, dive, fly, rush, shoot, tear, whisk **4** = **beat**, whisk **5** = **incite**, agitate, drive, foment, goad, spur, stir, work up

whirl *v* **1** = **spin**, pirouette, revolve, roll, rotate, swirl, turn, twirl, twist **2** = **feel dizzy**, reel, spin ♦ *n* **3** = **revolution**, pirouette, roll, rotation, spin, swirl, turn, twirl, twist **4** = **bustle**, flurry, merry-go-round, round, series, succession **5** = **confusion**, daze, dither, giddiness, spin **whirlwind** *n* **1** = **tornado**, waterspout ♦ *adj*

2 = **rapid**, hasty, quick, short, speedy, swift

whisk *v* **1** = **flick**, brush, sweep, whip **2** = **beat**, fluff up, whip ♦ *n* **3** = **flick**, brush, sweep, whip **4** = **beater**

whisper *v* **1** = **murmur**, breathe **2** = **rustle**, hiss, sigh, swish ♦ *n* **3** = **murmur**, undertone **4** = **rustle**, hiss, sigh, swish

white *adj* = **pale**, ashen, pallid, pasty, wan

white-collar *adj* = **clerical**, nonmanual, professional, salaried

whiten *v* = **pale**, blanch, bleach, fade

whitewash *n* **1** = **cover-up**, camouflage, concealment, deception ♦ *v* **2** = **cover up**, camouflage, conceal, gloss over, suppress

whittle *v* **1** = **carve**, cut, hew, pare, shape, shave, trim **2** **whittle down** or **away** = **reduce**, consume, eat away, erode, wear

whole [hohl] *adj* **1** complete. **2** containing all elements or parts. **3** entire. **4** not defective or imperfect. **5** healthy. ◆ *n* **6** complete thing or system. **whol'ly** *adv* **whole-heart-ed** [-HART-id] *adj* **1** sincere. **2** enthusiastic. **whole'sale** [-sayl] *n* **1** sale of goods in large quantities to retailers. ◆ *adj* **2** dealing by wholesale. **3** extensive. ◆ *vt* **-saled, -sal-ing whole'sal-er** *n* **whole'some** [-səm] *adj* producing good effect, physically or morally. **whole-wheat** *adj* of, pert. to flour that contains the complete wheat kernel. **on the whole 1** taking everything into consideration. **2** in general.

whom [hoom] *pron* objective case of WHO.

whoop [hwuup] *n* shout or cry expressing excitement, etc.

whoop-ee [HWUUP-ee] *n inf* gay, riotous time. **make whoopee 1** participate in wild noisy party. **2** go on spree.

whoop-ing cough [HUUP-ing] infectious disease of mucous membrane lining air passages, marked by convulsive coughing with loud whoop or indrawing of breath.

whop-per [HWOP-ər] *n inf* **1** anything unusually large. **2** monstrous lie. **whop'ping** *adj*

whore [hor] *n* prostitute.

whorl [hwurl] *n* **1** ring of leaves or petals. **2** turn of spiral. **3** anything forming part of circular pattern, e.g. lines of human fingerprint.

whose [hooz] *pron* of whom or of which.

why [hwī] *adv* for what cause or reason.

wick [wik] *n* strip of thread feeding flame of lamp or candle with oil, grease, etc.

wick-ed [WIK-id] *adj* **1** evil, sinful. **2** very bad. **3** mischievous. **wick'ed-ness** [-nis] *n*

wick-er [WIK-ər] *n* woven cane, etc. basketwork (also **wick-er-work**).

wick-et [WIK-it] *n* **1** small window, gate. **2** *Croquet* wire arch.

wide [wīd] *adj* **wid-er, wid-est 1** having a great extent from side to side, broad. **2** having considerable distance between. **3** spacious. **4** liberal. **5** vast. **6** far from the mark. **7** opened fully. ◆ *adv* **8** to the full extent. **9** far from the intended target. **wi-den** [WĪD-n] *v* width *n* breadth. **wide'spread** [-spred] *adj* extending over a wide area.

wid-ow [WID-oh] *n* **1** woman whose husband is dead and who has not married again. ◆ *vt* **2** make a widow of. **wid'ow-er** *n* man whose wife is dead and who has not married again. **wid'ow-hood** [-huud] *n*

wield [weeld] *vt* **1** hold and use. **2**

away

whole *adj* **1** = **complete**, entire, full, total, unabridged, uncut, undivided **2** = **undamaged**, in one piece, intact, unbroken, unharmed, unscathed, untouched ◆ *n* **3** = **totality**, ensemble, entirety **4 on the whole: a = all in all**, all things considered, by and large **b = generally**, as a rule, in general, in the main, mostly, predominantly

wholehearted *adj* = **sincere**, committed, dedicated, determined, devoted, enthusiastic, unstinting, zealous

wholesale *adj* **1** = **extensive**, broad, comprehensive, far-reaching, indiscriminate, mass, sweeping, wide-ranging ◆ *adv* **2** = **extensively**, comprehensively, indiscriminately

wholesome *adj* **1** = **beneficial**, good, healthy, nourishing, nutritious, salubrious **2** = **moral**, decent, edifying, improving, respectable

wholly *adv* = **completely**, altogether, entirely, fully, in every respect, perfectly, thoroughly, totally, utterly

whopper *n* **1** = **giant**, colossus, crackerjack (*inf*), jumbo (*inf*), leviathan, mammoth, monster **2** = **big lie**, fabrication, falsehood, tall tale (*inf*), untruth

whopping *adj* = **gigantic**, big, enormous, giant, great, huge, mammoth, massive

whore *n* = **prostitute**, call girl, ho (*sl*), streetwalker, tart (*inf*)

wicked *adj* **1** = **bad**, corrupt, depraved, devilish, evil, fiendish, immoral, sinful, vicious, villainous **2** = **mischievous**, impish, incorrigible, naughty, rascally, roguish

wide *adj* **1** = **broad**, expansive, extensive, far-reaching, immense, large, sweeping, vast **2** = **spacious**, baggy, capacious, commodious, full, loose, roomy **3** = **expanded**, dilated, distended, outspread, outstretched **4** = **distant**, off course, off target, remote ◆ *adv* **5** = **fully**, completely **6** = **off target**, astray, off course, off the mark, out

widen *v* = **broaden**, dilate, enlarge, expand, extend, spread, stretch

widespread *adj* = **common**, broad, extensive, far-reaching, general, pervasive, brandish. **3** manage.

wife [wīf] *n, pl* **wives** a man's partner in marriage, married woman. **wife'ly** *adj*

wig *n* artificial hair for the head. **wigged** *adj*

wig·gle [WIG-əl] *v* **-gled, -gling** (cause to) move jerkily from side to side. ♦ *n*

wig·wam [WIG-wom] *n* Native American's tent.

wild [wīld] *adj* **-er, -est 1** not tamed or domesticated. **2** not cultivated. **3** savage. **4** stormy. **5** uncontrolled. **6** random. **7** excited. **8** rash. **9** frantic. **10** (of party, etc.) rowdy, unrestrained. **wild'ly** *adv* **wild'ness** [-nis] *n* **wild'cat** *n* **1** any of various undomesticated feline animals. **2** wild, savage person. ♦ *adj* **3** unsound, irresponsible. **4** sudden, unofficial, unauthorized. **wildcat strike** strike called without sanction of labor union. **wild-goose chase** futile pursuit. **wild'life** *n* wild animals and plants collectively.

wil·der·ness [WIL-dər-nis] *n* **1** desert, waste place. **2** state of desolation or confusion.

wild·fire [WĪLD-fir] *n* **1** raging, uncontrollable fire. **2** anything spreading,

moving fast.

wile [wīl] *n* trick. **wil'y** *adj* **wil·i·er, wil·i·est** crafty, sly.

will *v aux, pt* **would** [wuud] **1** forms moods and tenses indicating intention or conditional result. ♦ *vi* **2** have a wish. ♦ *vt* **3** wish. **4** intend. **5** leave as legacy. ♦ *n* **6** faculty of deciding what one will do. **7** purpose. **8** volition. **9** determination. **10** wish. **11** directions written for disposal of property after death. **will'ing** *adj* **1** ready. **2** given cheerfully. **will'ing·ly** *adv* **will'ing·ness** [-nis] *n* **will'pow·er** *n* ability to control oneself, one's actions, impulses.

will·ful [WIL-fəl] *adj* **1** obstinate, self-willed. **2** intentional. **will'ful·ness** [-nis] *n*

will-o'-the-wisp [WIL-ə-thə-WISP] *n* **1** brief pale flame or phosphorescence sometimes seen over marshes. **2** elusive person or hope.

wil·low [WIL-oh] *n* **1** tree, such as **weeping willow**, with long thin flexible branches. **2** its wood. **wil'low·y** *adj* lithe, slender, supple.

wil·ly-nil·ly [WIL-ee-NIL-ee] *adv, adj* (occurring) whether desired or not.

THESAURUS

popular, universal

width *n* = **breadth**, compass, diameter, extent, girth, scope, span, thickness

wield *v* **1** = **brandish**, employ, flourish, handle, manage, manipulate, ply, swing, use **2** *As in* **wield power** = **exert**, exercise, have, maintain, possess

wife *n* = **spouse**, better half (*humorous*), bride, mate, partner

wiggle *v, n* = **jerk**, flutter, jiggle, oscillate, shake, shimmy, squirm, twitch, wag, wave, writhe

wild *adj* **1** = **untamed**, feral, ferocious, fierce, savage, unbroken, undomesticated **2** = **uncultivated**, free, natural **3** = **uncivilized**, barbaric, barbarous, brutish, ferocious, fierce, primitive, savage **4** = **uncontrolled**, disorderly, riotous, rowdy, turbulent, undisciplined, unfettered, unmanageable, unrestrained, unruly, wayward **5** = **stormy**, blustery, choppy, raging, rough, tempestuous, violent **6** = **excited**, crazy (*inf*), enthusiastic, hysterical, raving, wired (*sl*) ♦ *n* **7** **wilds** = **wilderness**, back of beyond (*inf*), desert, middle of nowhere (*inf*), wasteland

wilderness *n* = **desert**, jungle, wasteland, wilds

wiles *pl n* = **trickery**, artfulness, chicanery, craftiness, cunning, guile, slyness

will *n* **1** = **determination**, purpose, resolution, resolve, willpower **2** = **wish**, desire, fancy, inclination, mind, preference, volition **3** = **testament**, last wishes ♦ *v* **4** = **wish**, desire, prefer, see fit, want **5** = **bequeath**, confer, give, leave, pass on, transfer

willful *adj* **1** = **obstinate**, determined, headstrong, inflexible, intransigent, obdurate, perverse, pig-headed, stubborn, uncompromising **2** = **intentional**, conscious, deliberate, intended, purposeful, voluntary

willing *adj* = **ready**, agreeable, amenable, compliant, consenting, game (*inf*), inclined, prepared

willingly *adv* = **readily**, by choice, cheerfully, eagerly, freely, gladly, happily, of one's own accord, voluntarily

willingness *n* = **inclination**, agreement, consent, volition, will, wish

willowy *adj* = **slender**, graceful, lithe, slim, supple, svelte, sylphlike

willpower *n* = **self-control**, determination, drive, grit, resolution, resolve, self-discipline, single-mindedness

wilt v (cause to) become limp, drooping or lose strength, etc.

wimp n inf feeble, ineffective person.

wim•ple [WIM-pəl] n garment worn by nun, around face.

win v **won, win•ning** ◆ vi **1** be successful, victorious. ◆ vt **2** get by labor or effort. **3** reach. **4** lure. **5** be successful in. **6** gain the support, consent, etc. of. ◆ n **7** victory, esp. in games. **winning** adj charming. **winnings** pl n sum won in game, betting, etc. **win-win** adj guaranteeing a favourable outcome for everyone involved.

wince [wins] vi **winced, winc•ing 1** flinch, draw back, as from pain, etc. ◆ n **2** this act.

winch n **1** machine for hoisting or hauling using cable wound around drum. ◆ vt **2** move (something) by using a winch.

wind¹ n **1** air in motion. **2** breath. **3** flatulence. **4** idle talk. **5** hint or suggestion. **6** scent borne by air. ◆ vt **wind•ed, wind•ing 7** render short of breath, esp. by blow, etc. **8** get the scent of. **wind•ward** [-wərd] n side against which wind is blowing. **wind'y** adj **wind•i•er, wind•i•est 1** exposed to wind. **2** flatulent. **3** talking too much. **wind'fall** n **1** unexpected good luck. **2** fallen fruit. **wind instrument** musical instrument played by blowing or air pressure. **wind'mill** n wind-driven apparatus with fanlike sails for raising water, crushing grain, etc. **wind'pipe** n passage from throat to lungs. **wind'shield** [-sheeld] n protective sheet of glass, etc. in front of driver or pilot. **wind'sock** n cone of material flown on mast at airfield to indicate wind direction. **wind•surf•ing** n sport of sailing standing up on sailboard holding special boom to control sail.

wind² [wīnd] v **wound** [wownd], **wind•ing** ◆ vi **1** twine. **2** meander. ◆ vt **3** twist around, coil. **4** wrap. **5** make ready for working by tightening spring. ◆ n **6** act of winding. **7** single turn of something wound. **8** a turn, curve.

wind•lass [WIND-ləs] n winch, esp. simple one worked by a crank.

win•dow [WIN-doh] n **1** hole in wall (with glass) to admit light, air, etc. **2** anything similar in appearance or function. **3** area for display of goods behind glass of store front. **window dressing 1** arrangement of goods in a shop window. **2** deceptive display.

wine [wīn] n fermented juice of grape, etc. **wine'press** n apparatus for extracting juice from grape.

wing n **1** feathered limb a bird uses in flying. **2** one of organs of flight of insect or some animals. **3** main lifting surface of aircraft. **4** lateral extension. **5** side portion of building projecting from main central portion. **6** one of sides of a stage. **7** flank corps of army on either side. **8** part of car body that surrounds wheels. **9** administrative, tactical unit of air force. **10** faction esp. of political party. ◆ pl **11** insignia worn by qualified aircraft pilot. **12** sides of stage. ◆ vi **13** fly. **14** move, go very fast. ◆ vt **15** disable, wound slightly. **wing'span** n distance between the wing tips of an aircraft, bird, or insect.

wink [wingk] v **1** close and open (an eye) rapidly, esp. to indicate friendliness or as

——————— THESAURUS ———————

wilt v **1** = **droop**, sag, shrivel, wither **2** = **weaken**, fade, flag, languish, wane

wily adj = **cunning**, artful, astute, crafty, guileful, sharp, shrewd, sly, tricky

wimp n Inf = **weakling**, coward, drip (inf), loser (sl), mouse, sissy, softy or softie

wimpy adj Inf = **feeble**, effete, ineffectual, soft, spineless, timorous, weak, weedy (inf)

win v **1** = **triumph**, come first, conquer, overcome, prevail, succeed, sweep the board **2** = **gain**, achieve, acquire, attain, earn, get, land, obtain, procure, secure ◆ n **3** = **victory**, conquest, success, triumph

wince v **1** = **flinch**, blench, cower, cringe, draw back, quail, recoil, shrink, start ◆ n **2** = **flinch**, cringe, start

wind¹ n **1** = **air**, blast, breeze, draft, gust, zephyr **2** = **breath**, puff, respiration **3** = **flatulence**, gas **4** = **talk**, babble, blather, bluster, boasting, hot air, humbug **5** As in **get wind of** = **hint**, inkling, notice, report, rumor, suggestion, warning, whisper

wind² v **1** = **coil**, curl, encircle, loop, reel, roll, spiral, twist **2** = **meander**, bend, curve, ramble, snake, turn, twist, zigzag

windfall n = **godsend**, bonanza, find, jackpot, manna from heaven

wind up v **1** = **end**, close, conclude, finalize, finish, settle, terminate, wrap up **2** = **end up**, be left, finish up

windy adj = **breezy**, blowy, blustery, gusty, squally, stormy, wild, windswept

wing n **1** = **faction**, arm, branch, group, section ◆ v **2** = **fly**, glide, soar **3** = **wound**,

signal. **2** twinkle. ◆ *n* **3** act of winking.
win·now [WIN-oh] *vt* **1** blow free of chaff.
2 sift, examine.

win·some [WIN-səm] *adj* charming,
winning. **win'some·ly** *adv*

win·ter [WIN-tər] *n* **1** the coldest season. ◆
vi **2** pass, spend the winter. **win'try** *adj*
-tri·er, -tri·est 1 of, like winter. **2** cold.

wipe [wīp] *vt* **wiped, wip·ing 1** rub so as to
clean. ◆ *n* **2** wiping. **wi'per** *n* **1** one that
wipes. **2** automatic wiping apparatus (esp.
windshield wiper). **wipe out 1** erase. **2**
annihilate. **3** *inf* kill. **4** *sl* beat decisively.
wiped-out *adj sl* **1** exhausted. **2**
intoxicated. **wipe'out** *n inf* **1** murder. **2**
decisive defeat.

wire [wīr] *n* **1** metal drawn into thin,
flexible strand. **2** something made of wire,
e.g. fence. **3** telegram. ◆ *vt* **wired, wir·ing**
4 provide, fasten with wire. **5** send by
telegraph. **wired** *adj sl* **1** excited or
nervous. **2** using computers and the
Internet to send and receive information.
wiring *n* system of wires. **wir'y** *adj* **wir·i·er,**
wir·i·est 1 like wire. **2** lean and tough.
wire-haired *adj* (of various breeds of dog)
with short stiff hair.

wire·less [WĪR-lis] *n* **1** obs. term for RADIO
or RADIO SET. ◆ *adj* **2** not requiring wires.

wise¹ [wīz] *adj* **1** having intelligence and
knowledge. **2** sensible. **wis·dom**
[WIZ-dəm] *n* (accumulated) knowledge,
learning. **1** erudition. **wise'ly** *adv*
wise'a·cre *n* one who wishes to seem wise.
wisdom tooth third molar usually cut
about 20th year.

wise² *n obs* manner.

wise·crack [WĪZ-krak] *n inf* flippant
(would-be) clever remark.

wish *vi* **1** have a desire. ◆ *vt* **2** desire. ◆ *n* **3**
desire. **4** thing desired. **wish'ful** [-fəl] *adj* **1**
desirous. **2** too optimistic. **wish'bone** *n*
V-shaped bone above breastbone of fowl.

wisp *n* **1** light, delicate streak, as of smoke.
2 twisted handful, usu. of straw, etc. **3**
stray lock of hair. **wisp'y** *adj* **wisp·i·er,**
wisp·i·est

wist·ful [WIST-fəl] *adj* **1** longing, yearning.
2 sadly pensive. **wist'ful·ly** *adv*

wit *n* **1** ingenuity in connecting amusingly
incongruous ideas. **2** person gifted with
this power. **3** sense. **4** intellect. **5**
understanding. **6** ingenuity. **7** humor.
wit'ti·cism [-ti-sizm] *n* witty remark.
wit'ti·ly *adv* **wit'ting·ly** *adv* **1** on purpose.
2 knowingly. **wit'less** [-lis] *adj* foolish.
wit'ty *adj* **-ti·er, -ti·est**

witch [wich] *n* **1** person, usu. female,

clip, hit

wink *v* **1** = **blink**, bat, flutter **2** = **twinkle**,
flash, gleam, glimmer, sparkle ◆ *n* **3** =
blink, flutter

winner *n* = **victor**, champ (*inf*), champion,
conqueror, master

winning *adj* **1** = **victorious**, conquering,
successful, triumphant **2** = **charming**,
alluring, attractive, cute, disarming,
enchanting, endearing, engaging, likable
or likeable, pleasing

winnings *pl n* = **spoils**, gains, prize,
proceeds, profits, takings

winnow *v* = **separate**, divide, select, sift,
sort out

win over *v* = **convince**, bring or talk round,
convert, influence, persuade, prevail upon,
sway

wintry *adj* = **cold**, chilly, freezing, frosty,
frozen, icy, snowy

wipe *v* **1** = **clean**, brush, mop, rub, sponge,
swab **2** = **erase**, remove ◆ *n* **3** = **rub**, brush

wipe out *v* = **destroy**, annihilate,
eradicate, erase, expunge, exterminate,
massacre, obliterate

wiry *adj* = **lean**, sinewy, strong, tough

wisdom *n* = **understanding**, discernment,
enlightenment, erudition, insight,
intelligence, judgment, knowledge,
learning, sense

wise *adj* = **sensible**, clever, discerning,
enlightened, erudite, intelligent, judicious,
perceptive, prudent, sage

wisecrack *n Inf* **1** = **joke**, jest, jibe, quip,
witticism ◆ *v* **2** = **joke**, jest, jibe, quip

wish *v* **1** = **want**, aspire, crave, desire,
hanker, hope, long, yearn ◆ *n* **2** = **desire**,
aspiration, hope, intention, urge, want,
whim, will

wispy *adj* = **thin**, attenuated, delicate, fine,
flimsy, fragile, frail

wistful *adj* = **melancholy**, contemplative,
dreamy, longing, meditative, pensive,
reflective, thoughtful

wit *n* **1** = **humor**, badinage, banter,
drollery, jocularity, raillery, repartee,
wordplay **2** = **humorist**, card (*inf*),
comedian, joker, wag **3** = **cleverness**,
acumen, brains, common sense, ingenuity,
intellect, sense, wisdom

believed to practice, practicing, or
professing to practice (black) magic,
sorcery. **2** ugly, wicked woman. **3**
fascinating woman. **witch'craft** *n* **witch
doctor** in certain societies, person
appearing to cure or cause injury, disease
by magic.

with [with] *prep* **1** in company or possession
of. **2** against. **3** in relation to. **4** through. **5**
by means of. **with·al** [with-AWL] *adv* also,
likewise. **with·in'** *prep, adv* in, inside.
with·out' *prep* **1** lacking. **2** *obs* outside.

with·draw [with-DRAW] *v* **-drew, -drawn,
-draw·ing** draw back or out. **with·draw'al**
n **with·drawn'** *adj* reserved, unsociable.

with·er [WITH-ər] *v* (cause to) wilt, dry up,
decline. **with'er·ing** *adj* (of glance, etc.)
scornful.

with·ers [WITH-ərz] *pl n* ridge between a
horse's shoulder blades.

with·hold [with-HOHLD] *vt* **-held,
-hold·ing 1** restrain. **2** keep back. **3** refrain
from giving.

with·stand' *vt* **-stood** [-stuud], **-stand·ing**
oppose, resist, esp. successfully.

wit·ness [WIT-nis] *n* **1** one who sees

something. **2** testimony. **3** one who gives
testimony. ◆ *vi* **4** give testimony. ◆ *vt* **5** see.
6 attest. **7** see and sign as having seen.

wiz·ard [WIZ-ərd] *n* **1** sorcerer, magician. **2**
conjurer. **wiz'ard·ry** *n*

wiz·ened [WIZ-ənd] *adj* shriveled,
wrinkled.

wob·ble [WOB-əl] *vi* **-bled, -bling 1** move
unsteadily. **2** sway. ◆ *n* **3** an unsteady
movement. **wob'bly** *adj* **-bli·er, -bli·est**

woe [woh] *n* **1** grief. **woe·be·gone**
[WOH-bi-gawn] *adj* looking sorrowful.
woe'ful [-fəl] *adj* **1** sorrowful. **2** pitiful. **3**
wretched. **woe'ful·ly** *adv*

wolf [wuulf] *n, pl* **wolves 1** wild predatory
doglike animal of northern countries. **2** *inf*
man who habitually tries to seduce
women. ◆ *vt* **3** eat ravenously. **wolf
whistle** whistle by man expressing
admiration for a woman. **cry wolf** raise
false alarm.

wolf·ram [WUUL-frəm] *n* tungsten.

wol·ver·ine [wuul-və-REEN] *n* carnivorous
mammal inhabiting northern regions.

wom·an [WUUM-ən] *n, pl* **wom·en**
[WIM-in] **1** adult human female. **2** women

——— THESAURUS ———

witch *n* = **enchantress**, crone, hag,
magician, sorceress

witchcraft *n* = **magic**, enchantment,
necromancy, occultism, sorcery, the black
art, voodoo, wizardry

withdraw *v* = **remove**, draw back, extract,
pull out, take away, take off

withdrawal *n* = **removal**, extraction

withdrawn *adj* = **uncommunicative**,
distant, introverted, reserved, retiring, shy,
taciturn, unforthcoming

wither *v* = **wilt**, decay, decline,
disintegrate, fade, perish, shrivel, waste

withering *adj* = **scornful**, devastating,
humiliating, hurtful, mortifying, snubbing

withhold *v* = **keep back**, conceal, hide,
hold back, refuse, reserve, retain, suppress

withstand *v* = **resist**, bear, cope with,
endure, hold off, oppose, stand up to,
suffer, tolerate

witless *adj* = **foolish**, halfwitted, idiotic,
inane, moronic, senseless, silly, stupid

witness *n* **1** = **observer**, beholder,
bystander, eyewitness, looker-on,
onlooker, spectator, viewer, watcher **2** =
testifier, corroborator ◆ *v* **3** = **see**, note,
notice, observe, perceive, view, watch **4** =
sign, countersign, endorse

wits *pl n* = **intelligence**, acumen, brains
(*inf*), comprehension, faculties,
ingenuity, reason, sense, understanding

witticism *n* = **quip**, bon mot, one-liner
(*sl*), pun, riposte

witty *adj* = **humorous**, amusing, clever,
droll, funny, piquant, sparkling, waggish,
whimsical

wizard *n* = **magician**, conjurer, magus,
necromancer, occultist, shaman, sorcerer,
warlock, witch

wizardry *n* = **magic**, sorcery, voodoo,
witchcraft

wizened *adj* = **wrinkled**, dried up, gnarled,
lined, shriveled, shrunken, withered

wobble *v* **1** = **shake**, rock, sway, teeter,
totter, tremble ◆ *n* **2** = **unsteadiness**,
shake, tremble, tremor

wobbly *adj* = **unsteady**, rickety, shaky,
teetering, tottering, uneven

woe *n* = **grief**, agony, anguish, distress,
gloom, misery, sadness, sorrow,
unhappiness, wretchedness

woeful *adj* **1** = **sad**, deplorable, dismal,
distressing, grievous, lamentable,
miserable, pathetic, tragic, wretched **2** =
pitiful, abysmal, appalling, bad,
deplorable, dreadful, feeble, pathetic,

collectively. **wom'an·hood** [-huud] *n*
wom'an·ish *adj* effeminate. **wom'an·ize** *vi*
-ized, -iz·ing (of man) indulge in many
casual affairs with women. **wom'an·kind**
[-kīnd] *n* **wom'an·ly** *adj* of, proper to
woman. **women's liberation** movement
for removal of attitudes, practices that
preserve social, economic, etc. inequalities
between women and men (also **women's
lib**).

womb [woom] *n* female organ of
conception and gestation, uterus.

won [wun] pt./pp. of WIN.

won·der [WUN-dər] *n* **1** emotion excited
by amazing or unusual thing. **2** marvel,
miracle. ♦ *vi* **3** be curious about. **4** feel
amazement. **won'der·ful** [-fəl] *adj* **1**
remarkable. **2** very fine. **won'der·ment**
[-mənt] *n* surprise. **won'drous** [-drəs] *adj* **1**
inspiring wonder. **2** strange.

wont [wawnt] *n* **1** custom. ♦ *adj* **2**
accustomed. **wont'ed** [-id] *adj* habitual,
established.

woo *vt* court, seek to marry. **woo'er** [-ər] *n*
suitor.

wood [wuud] *n* **1** substance of trees,
timber. **2** firewood. **3** tract of land with
growing trees. **wood'ed** [-id] *adj* having
(many) trees. **wood'en** [-n] *adj* **1** made of
wood. **2** obstinate. **3** without expression.
wood'y *adj* **wood'chuck** *n* Amer.

burrowing rodent. **wood'cut** *n* **1**
engraving on wood. **2** impression from
this. **wood'land** [-lənd] *n* woods, forest.
wood'peck·er *n* bird that searches tree
trunks for insects. **wood'wind** *adj, n* (of)
wind instruments of orchestra, orig. made
of wood.

woof [wuuf] *n* the threads that cross the
warp in weaving.

woof·er [WUUF-ər] *n* loudspeaker for
reproducing low-frequency sounds.

wool [wuul] *n* **1** soft hair of sheep, goat,
etc. **2** yarn spun from this. **wool'en** [-in]
adj **wool'ly** *adj* **-li·er, -li·est 1** of wool. **2**
vague, muddled. ♦ *n* **3** [-eez] (oft. pl)
knitted woolen garment, esp. warm
undergarment. **wool'gath·er·ing** *n*
daydreaming.

word [wurd] *n* **1** unit of speech or writing
regarded by users of a language as the
smallest separate meaningful unit. **2** term.
3 message. **4** brief remark. **5** information. **6**
promise. **7** command. ♦ *vt* **8** express in
words, esp. in particular way. **word'ing** *n*
choice and arrangement of words. **word'y**
adj **word·i·er, word·i·est** using more words
than necessary, verbose. **word processor**
keyboard, microprocessor and monitor for
electronic organization and storage of
written text.

wore pt. of WEAR.

━━━━━━━━━━ THESAURUS ━━━━━━━━━━

poor, sorry

woman *n* = **lady**, female, girl

womanizer *n* = **philanderer**, Casanova,
Don Juan, lecher, seducer

womanly *adj* = **feminine**, female, ladylike,
matronly, motherly, tender, warm

wonder *v* **1** = **think**, conjecture, meditate,
ponder, puzzle, query, question, speculate
2 = **be amazed**, be astonished, gape,
marvel, stare ♦ *n* **3** = **phenomenon**,
curiosity, marvel, miracle, prodigy, rarity,
sight, spectacle **4** = **amazement**,
admiration, astonishment, awe,
bewilderment, fascination, surprise,
wonderment

wonderful *adj* **1** = **excellent**, brilliant,
fabulous (*inf*), fantastic (*inf*), great (*inf*),
magnificent, marvelous, outstanding,
superb, terrific (*inf*), tremendous **2** =
remarkable, amazing, astonishing,
extraordinary, incredible, miraculous,
phenomenal, staggering, startling,
unheard-of

woo *v* = **court**, cultivate, pursue

wood *n* **1** = **timber 2** = **woodland**, coppice,
copse, forest, grove, thicket

wooded *adj* = **tree-covered**, forested,
sylvan (*poetic*), timbered, tree-clad

wooden *adj* **1** = **woody**, ligneous, timber
2 = **expressionless**, deadpan, lifeless,
unresponsive

wool *n* = **fleece**, hair, yarn

woolly *adj* **1** = **fleecy**, hairy, shaggy,
woollen **2** = **vague**, confused, hazy,
ill-defined, indefinite, indistinct, muddled,
unclear

word *n* **1** = **term**, expression, name **2** =
chat, confab (*inf*), consultation, discussion,
talk, tête-à-tête **3** = **remark**, comment,
utterance **4** = **message**, communiqué,
dispatch, information, intelligence, news,
notice, report **5** = **promise**, assurance,
guarantee, oath, pledge, vow **6** =
command, bidding, decree, mandate,
order ♦ *v* **7** = **express**, couch, phrase, put,
say, state, utter

work [wurk] *n* **1** labor. **2** employment. **3** occupation. **4** task. **5** toil. **6** something made or accomplished. **7** production of art or science. **8** book. **9** needlework. ◆ *pl* **10** factory. **11** total of person's deeds, writings, etc. **12** *inf* everything, full or extreme treatment. **13** mechanism of clock, etc. ◆ *vt* **14** cause to operate. **15** make, shape. ◆ *vi* **16** apply effort. **17** labor. **18** operate. **19** be engaged in trade, profession, etc. **20** turn out successfully. **21** ferment. **work'a·ble** *adj* **work·a·hol·ic** [wur-kə-HAW-lik] *n* person addicted to work. **work·ing class** social class consisting of wage earners, esp. manual. **working-class** *adj* **work·man** [WURK-mən] *n, pl* **-men 1** manual worker. **2** male worker. **work'man·ship** *n* **1** skill of workman. **2** way thing is finished. **3** style. **work'shop** *n* **1** place where things are made. **2** discussion group, seminar.
world [wurld] *n* **1** the universe. **2** Earth. **3** sphere of existence. **4** mankind, people generally. **5** society. **world'ly** *adj* **1** earthly. **2** mundane. **3** absorbed in the pursuit of material gain, advantage. **4** carnal. **World Wide Web** global computer network sharing graphics, etc., via the Internet.
worm [wurm] *n* **1** small limbless creeping snakelike creature. **2** anything resembling worm in shape or movement. **3** gear wheel with teeth forming part of screw threads. **4** *inf* weak, despised person. **5** *Computers* type of virus. ◆ *pl* **6** (disorder caused by) infestation of worms, esp. in intestines. ◆ *vi* **7** crawl. ◆ *vt* **8** work (oneself) in insidiously. **9** extract (secret) craftily. **10** rid of worms. **worm'-eaten** *adj* **1** full of holes gnawed by worms. **2** old, antiquated. **worm'y** *adj* **worm·i·er, worm·i·est**
worm·wood [WURM-wuud] *n* **1** bitter herb. **2** bitterness.
worn pp. of WEAR.
wor·ry [WUR-ee] *v* **-ried, -ry·ing** ◆ *vi* **1** be

———————| THESAURUS |———————

wording *n* = **phraseology**, language, phrasing, terminology, words
wordy *adj* = **long-winded**, diffuse, prolix, rambling, verbose, windy
work *n* **1** = **effort**, drudgery, elbow grease (*facetious*), exertion, industry, labor, sweat, toil **2** = **employment**, business, duty, job, livelihood, occupation, profession, trade **3** = **task**, assignment, chore, commission, duty, job, stint, undertaking **4** = **creation**, achievement, composition, handiwork, opus, piece, production ◆ *v* **5** = **labor**, drudge, exert oneself, peg away, slave, slog (away), sweat, toil **6** = **be employed**, be in work **7** = **operate**, control, drive, handle, manage, manipulate, move, use **8** = **function**, go, operate, run **9** = **cultivate**, dig, farm, till **10** = **manipulate**, fashion, form, knead, mold, shape
workable *adj* = **viable**, doable, feasible, possible, practicable, practical
worker *n* = **employee**, artisan, craftsman, hand, laborer, tradesman, workman
working *adj* **1** = **employed**, active, in work **2** = **functioning**, going, operative, running
workman *n* = **laborer**, artisan, craftsman, employee, hand, journeyman, mechanic, operative, tradesman, worker
workmanship *n* = **skill**, artistry, craftsmanship, expertise, handiwork, technique
work out *v* **1** = **solve**, calculate, figure out,

find out **2** = **happen**, develop, evolve, result, turn out **3** = **exercise**, practice, train, warm up
works *pl n* **1** = **factory**, mill, plant, workshop **2** = **writings**, canon, *oeuvre*, output **3** = **mechanism**, action, machinery, movement, parts, workings
workshop *n* = **studio**, factory, mill, plant, workroom
world *n* **1** = **earth**, globe **2** = **mankind**, everybody, everyone, humanity, humankind, man, the public **3** = **sphere**, area, domain, environment, field, realm
worldly *adj* **1** = **earthly**, physical, profane, secular, temporal, terrestrial **2** = **materialistic**, grasping, greedy, selfish **3** = **worldly-wise**, blasé, cosmopolitan, experienced, knowing, sophisticated, urbane
worldwide *adj* = **global**, general, international, omnipresent, pandemic, ubiquitous, universal
worn *adj* = **ragged**, frayed, shabby, tattered, tatty, the worse for wear, threadbare
worn-out *adj* **1** = **run-down**, on its last legs, ragged, shabby, threadbare, used-up, useless, worn **2** = **exhausted**, dead-tired, done in (*inf*), fatigued, ready to drop, spent, tired out, weary
worried *adj* = **anxious**, afraid, apprehensive, concerned, fearful,

(unduly) concerned. ◆ *vt* **2** trouble, pester, harass. **3** (of dog) seize, shake with teeth. ◆ *n, pl* **-ries 4** (cause of) anxiety, concern. **wor·ri·er** *n*

worse [wurs] *adj, adv* comp. of BAD, BADLY. ◆ *n* **worst** *adj, adv* sup. of BAD, BADLY. ◆ *n* **wors'en** [-in] *v* **1** make, grow worse. **2** impair. **3** deteriorate.

wor·ship [WUR-ship] *vt* **-shiped, -ship·ing 1** show religious devotion to. **2** adore. **3** love and admire. ◆ *n* **4** act of worshiping. **wor'ship·er** *n*

wor·sted [WUUS-tid] *n* **1** woolen yarn. ◆ *adj* **2** made of woolen yarn. **3** spun from wool.

worth [wurth] *adj* **1** having or deserving to have value specified. **2** meriting. ◆ *n* **3** excellence. **4** merit, value. **5** virtue. **6** usefulness. **7** price. **8** quantity to be had for a given sum. **wor·thy** [WUR-*th*ee] *adj* **-thi·er, -thi·est 1** virtuous. **2** meriting. ◆ *n* **3** one of eminent worth. **4** celebrity. **wor'thi·ness** [-*th*ee-nis] *n* **worth·less** [WURTH-lis] *adj* useless. **worth·while** [wurth-hwīl] *adj* worth the time, effort, etc. involved.

would [wuud] *v aux* **1** expressing wish,

intention, probability. **2** pt. of WILL. **would-be** [WUUD-bee] *adj* wishing, pretending to be.

wound¹ [woond] *n* **1** injury, hurt from cut, stab, etc. ◆ *vt* **2** inflict wound on, injure. **3** pain.

wound² [rhymes with *sound*] pt./pp. of WIND².

wove [wohv] pt. of WEAVE. **wo'ven** pp. of WEAVE.

wow *interj* **1** of astonishment. ◆ *n inf* **2** object of astonishment, admiration, etc. **3** variation, distortion in pitch in record player, etc.

wraith [rayth] *n* **1** apparition of a person seen shortly before or after death. **2** specter.

wran·gle [RANG-gəl] *vi* **-gled, -gling 1** quarrel (noisily). **2** dispute. **3** herd cattle. ◆ *n* **4** noisy quarrel. **5** dispute. **wran'gler** [-glər] *n* **1** cowboy. **2** disputant.

wrap [rap] *v* **wrapped, wrap·ping 1** cover, esp. by putting something around. **2** put around. ◆ *n* **3** sandwich made by wrapping filling in a tortilla, etc. **wrap'per** *n* **1** loose garment. **2** covering. **wrapping** *n* material used to wrap.

──────── THESAURUS ────────

frightened, nervous, perturbed, tense, troubled, uneasy, wired (*sl*)

worry *v* **1 = be anxious**, agonize, brood, fret **2 = trouble**, annoy, bother, disturb, perturb, pester, unsettle, upset, vex ◆ *n* **3 = anxiety**, apprehension, concern, fear, misgiving, trepidation, trouble, unease **4 = problem**, bother, care, hassle (*inf*), trouble

worsen *v* **1 = aggravate**, damage, exacerbate **2 = deteriorate**, decay, decline, degenerate, get worse, go downhill (*inf*), sink

worship *v* **1 = praise**, adore, exalt, glorify, honor, pray to, revere, venerate **2 = love**, adore, idolize, put on a pedestal ◆ *n* **3 = praise**, adoration, adulation, devotion, glory, honor, kudos, regard, respect, reverence

worth *n* **1 = value**, cost, price, rate, valuation **2 = excellence**, goodness, importance, merit, quality, usefulness, value, worthiness

worthless *adj* **1 = useless**, ineffectual, rubbishy, unimportant, valueless **2 = good-for-nothing**, contemptible, despicable, lousy (*sl*), scuzzy (*sl*), vile

worthwhile *adj* **= useful**, beneficial,

constructive, expedient, helpful, productive, profitable, valuable

worthy *adj* **= praiseworthy**, admirable, creditable, deserving, laudable, meritorious, valuable, virtuous, worthwhile

would-be *adj* **= budding**, self-appointed, self-styled, unfulfilled, wannabe (*inf*)

wound *n* **1 = injury**, cut, gash, hurt, laceration, lesion, trauma (*Pathology*) **2 = insult**, offense, slight ◆ *v* **3 = injure**, cut, gash, hurt, lacerate, pierce, wing **4 = offend**, annoy, cut (someone) to the quick, hurt, mortify, sting

wrangle *v* **1 = argue**, bicker, contend, disagree, dispute, fight, quarrel, row, squabble ◆ *n* **2 = argument**, altercation, bickering, dispute, quarrel, row, squabble, tiff

wrap *v* **1 = cover**, bind, bundle up, encase, enclose, enfold, pack, package, shroud, swathe ◆ *n* **2 = cloak**, cape, mantle, shawl, stole

wrapper *n* **= cover**, case, envelope, jacket, packaging, wrapping

wrap up *v* **1 = giftwrap**, bundle up, pack, package **2** *Inf* **= end**, conclude, finish off, polish off, round off, terminate, wind up

wrath [rath] *n* anger. **wrath'ful** [-fəl] *adj* **wrath'ful-ly** *adv*

wreak [reek] *vt* **1** inflict (vengeance). **2** cause.

wreath [reeth] *n* something twisted into ring form, esp. band of flowers, etc. as memorial or tribute on grave, etc. **wreathe** [reeth] *vt* **wreathed, wreath-ing 1** form into wreath. **2** surround. **3** wind around.

wreck [rek] *n* **1** destruction of ship. **2** wrecked ship. **3** ruin. **4** something ruined. ◆ *vt* **5** cause the wreck of. **wreck'age** [-ij] *n* **wreck'er** *n* **1** person or thing that destroys, ruins. **2** vehicle for towing disabled, wrecked, etc. automobiles, a tow truck.

wren [ren] *n* kind of small songbird.

wrench [rench] *vt* **1** twist. **2** distort. **3** seize forcibly. **4** sprain. ◆ *n* **5** violent twist. **6** tool for twisting or turning. **7** tool for gripping nut or bolt head. **8** sudden pain caused esp. by parting.

wrest [rest] *vt* **1** take by force. **2** twist violently.

wres-tle [RES-əl] *vi* **-tled, -tling 1** fight (esp. as sport) by grappling and trying to throw down. **2** strive (with). **3** struggle. ◆ *n* **wrest'ler** [-lər] *n*

wretch [rech] *n* **1** despicable person. **2** miserable creature. **wretch'ed** [-id] *adj* **-ed-er, -ed-est 1** miserable, unhappy. **2**

worthless. **wretch'ed-ly** *adv* **wretch'ed-ness** [-nis] *n*

wrig-gle [RIG-əl] *v* **-gled, -gling 1** move with twisting action, as worm. **2** squirm. ◆ *n* **3** this action.

wring [ring] *vt* **wrung, wring-ing 1** twist. **2** extort. **3** pain. **4** squeeze out.

wrin-kle [RING-kəl] *n* **1** slight ridge or furrow on surface. **2** crease in the skin. **3** fold. **4** pucker. **5** *inf* [useful] trick, hint] *v* **-kled, -kling 6** make, become wrinkled, pucker.

wrist [rist] *n* joint between hand and arm. **wrist'let** [-lit] *n* band worn on wrist.

writ [rit] *n* written command from law court or other authority.

write [rīt] *v* **wrote, writ-ten, writ-ing** ◆ *vi* **1** mark paper, etc. with the symbols that are used to represent words or sounds. **2** compose. **3** send a letter. ◆ *vt* **4** set down in words. **5** compose. **6** communicate in writing. **writ'er** *n* **1** one who writes. **2** author. **write-off** *n* **1** cancellation from accounts as loss. **2** *inf* person or thing considered hopeless. **write-up** *n* written (published) account of something.

writhe [rīth] *v* **writhed, writh-ing 1** twist, squirm in or as in pain, etc. ◆ *vi* **2** be acutely embarrassed, etc.

wrong [rawng] *adj* **1** not right or good. **2**

───────── THESAURUS ─────────

wrath *n* = **anger**, displeasure, fury, indignation, ire, rage, resentment, temper

wreath *n* = **garland**, band, chaplet, crown, festoon, ring

wreck *v* **1** = **destroy**, break, demolish, devastate, ruin, shatter, smash, spoil ◆ *n* **2** = **shipwreck**, hulk

wreckage *n* = **remains**, debris, fragments, pieces, rubble, ruin

wrench *v* **1** = **twist**, force, jerk, pull, rip, tear, tug, yank **2** = **sprain**, rick, strain ◆ *n* **3** = **twist**, jerk, pull, rip, tug, yank **4** = **sprain**, strain, twist **5** = **blow**, pang, shock, upheaval **6** = **spanner**, adjustable spanner

wrest *v* = **seize**, extract, force, take, win, wrench

wrestle *v* = **fight**, battle, combat, grapple, scuffle, struggle, tussle

wretch *n* = **scoundrel**, good-for-nothing, miscreant, rascal, rogue, swine, worm

wretched *adj* **1** = **unhappy**, dejected, depressed, disconsolate, downcast, forlorn, hapless, miserable, woebegone **2** = **worthless**, inferior, miserable, paltry,

pathetic, poor, sorry

wriggle *v* **1** = **twist**, jerk, jiggle, squirm, turn, wiggle, writhe **2** = **crawl**, slink, snake, worm, zigzag **3** *As in* **wriggle out of** = **maneuver**, dodge, extricate oneself ◆ *n* **4** = **twist**, jerk, jiggle, squirm, turn, wiggle

wring *v* = **twist**, extract, force, screw, squeeze

wrinkle[1] *n* **1** = **crease**, corrugation, crinkle, crow's-foot, crumple, fold, furrow, line ◆ *v* **2** = **crease**, corrugate, crumple, fold, furrow, gather, pucker, rumple

writ *n* = **summons**, court order, decree, document

write *v* = **record**, draft, draw up, inscribe, jot down, pen, scribble, set down

writer *n* = **author**, hack, novelist, penpusher, scribbler, scribe, wordsmith

writhe *v* = **squirm**, jerk, struggle, thrash, thresh, toss, twist, wiggle

writing *n* **1** = **script**, calligraphy, hand, handwriting, penmanship, scrawl, scribble **2** = **document**, book, composition, opus, publication, work not suitable. **3** wicked. **4** incorrect. **5** mistaken. **6** not functioning properly. ◆ *n* **7** that which is wrong. **8** harm. **9** evil. ◆ *vt* **10** do wrong to. **11** think badly of without justification. **wrong'do·er** [-doo-ər] *n* one who acts immorally or illegally. **wrong'ful** [-fəl] *adj* **wrong'ful·ly** *adv*

wrote [roht] *pt.* of WRITE.

wrought [rawt] *adj* (of metals) shaped by hammering or beating. **wrought iron** pure form of iron used esp. in decorative railings, etc.

wrung *pt./pp.* of WRING.

wry [rī] *adj* **wri·er, wri·est 1** turned to one side, contorted, askew. **2** sardonic, dryly humorous.

wuss [woos] *n, pl* **-us·ses** *sl* feeble person.

WWW World Wide Web.

THESAURUS

wrong *adj* **1** = **incorrect**, erroneous, fallacious, false, inaccurate, mistaken, untrue, wide of the mark **2** = **bad**, criminal, dishonest, evil, illegal, immoral, sinful, unjust, unlawful, wicked, wrongful **3** = **inappropriate**, incongruous, incorrect, unacceptable, unbecoming, undesirable, unseemly, unsuitable **4** = **defective**, amiss, askew, awry, faulty ◆ *adv* **5** = **incorrectly**, badly, erroneously, inaccurately, mistakenly, wrongly **6** = **amiss**, askew, astray, awry ◆ *n* **7** = **offense**, crime, error, injury, injustice, misdeed, sin, transgression, wickedness ◆ *v* **8** = **mistreat**, abuse, cheat, dishonor, harm, hurt, malign, oppress, take advantage of

wrongdoer *n* = **offender**, criminal, culprit, delinquent, evildoer, lawbreaker, miscreant, sinner, villain

wrongful *adj* = **improper**, criminal, evil, illegal, illegitimate, immoral, unethical, unjust, unlawful, wicked

wry *adj* **1** = **ironic**, droll, dry, mocking, sarcastic, sardonic **2** = **contorted**, crooked, twisted, uneven

X x Y y Z z

X 1 Christ. **2** Christian. **3** cross. **4** Roman numeral, 10. **5** mark indicating something wrong, a choice, a kiss, signature, etc. ◆ *n* **6** unknown, mysterious person, factor.

Xe *Chem.* xenon.

xe·non [ZEE-non] *n* colorless, odorless gas occurring in very small quantities in air.

xen·o·pho·bi·a [zen-ə-FOH-bee-ə] *n* dislike, hatred, fear, of strangers or aliens. **xen·o·pho'bic** *adj*

xe·rog·ra·phy [zi-ROG-rə-fee] *n* photocopying process.

Xmas [EKS-məs] *n inf* Christmas.

x-rays [EKS-rayz] *pl n* radiation of very short wavelengths, capable of penetrating solid bodies, and printing on photographic plate shadow picture of objects not permeable by rays. **x-ray** *v* photograph by x-rays.

xy·lo·carp [ZĪ-lə-kahrp] *n* hard, woody fruit. **xy·lo·carp'ous** *adj* having fruit that becomes hard or woody.

xy·lo·graph [ZĪ-lə-graf] *n* **1** wood engraving. **2** impression from wood block.

xy·loid [ZĪ-loid] *adj* **1** pert. to wood. **2** woody, ligneous.

xy·lo·phone [ZĪ-lə-fohn] *n* musical instrument of wooden bars that sound when struck.

Y *Chem.* yttrium.

yacht [yot] *n* vessel propelled by sail or power, used for racing, pleasure, etc. **yachts·man** [YOTS-mən] *n, pl* **-men**

ya·hoo [YAH-hoo] *n, pl* **-hoos** crude, coarse person.

Yah·weh [YAH-we] *n* Jehovah, God.

yak *n* shaggy-haired, long-horned ox of Central Asia.

yam *n* large edible tuber, sweet potato.

yank [yangk] *v* **1** jerk, tug. **2** pull quickly. ◆ *n* **3** quick tug.

Yank [yangk], **Yank'ee** *adj, n inf* American.

yap *vi* **yapped, yap·ping 1** bark (as small dog). **2** *sl* talk shrilly, idly. ◆ *n* **3** a bark. **4** *sl* the mouth.

yard¹ [yahrd] *n* **1** unit of length, 3 feet (36 inches, 0.9144 meter). **2** spar slung across ship's mast to extend sails. **yard'stick** *n* **1** 36-inch ruler. **2** formula or standard of measurement or comparison. **yard'age** [-ij] *n* **1** measurement of distance in yards. **2** length in yards.

yard² *n* piece of enclosed ground adjoining building and used for some specific purpose, as garden, storage, holding livestock, etc. **yard'age** *n* **1** use of yard. **2** charge made for this.

yar·mul·ke [YAHR-məl-kə] *n* skullcap worn by Jewish men and boys, esp. in synagogue.

yarn [yahrn] *n* **1** spun thread. **2** *inf* long involved story.

yash·mak [yahsh-MAHK] *n* face veil worn by Muslim women.

yaw *vi* **1** of aircraft, etc., turn about vertical axis. **2** deviate temporarily from course.

yawl *n* two-masted sailing vessel.

yawn *vi* **1** open mouth wide, esp. in sleepiness. **2** gape. ◆ *n* **3** a yawning.

yaws [yawz] *n* contagious tropical skin disease.

Yb *Chem.* ytterbium.

ye [yee] *pron obs* you.

yea [yay] *interj* **1** yes. ◆ *n* **2** affirmative vote.

year [yeer] *n* **1** time taken by one revolution

THESAURUS

Xmas *n* = **Christmas**, festive season, Noel, Yule, Yuletide

X-rated *adj* = **pornographic**, adult, dirty, graphic, hardcore (*sl*), obscene, scuzzy (*sl*)

X-rays *pl n* = **Röntgen rays** (*old name*)

yank *v, n* = **pull**, hitch, jerk, snatch, tug, wrench

yardstick *n* = **standard**, benchmark, criterion, gauge, measure, par, touchstone

yarn *n* **1** = **thread**, fiber **2** *Old-fashioned, inf* = **story**, anecdote, cock-and-bull story (*inf*), fable, tale, tall tale (*inf*)

yawning *adj* = **gaping**, cavernous, vast, wide

of Earth around sun, about 365 days. **2** twelve months. **year·ling** *n* animal one year old. **year·ly** *adv* **1** every year, once a year. ◆ *adj* **2** happening, etc. once a year.

yearn [yurn] *vi* **1** feel longing, desire. **2** be filled with pity, tenderness. **yearn·ing** *n*

yeast [yeest] *n* substance used as fermenting, leavening agent, esp. in brewing and in baking bread. **yeast·y** *adj* **yeast·i·er, yeast·i·est 1** of, like yeast. **2** frothy, fermenting. **3** (of time) characterized by excitement, change, etc.

yell *v* **1** cry out in loud shrill tone. **2** speak in this way. ◆ *n* **3** loud shrill cry. **4** a cheer, shout.

yel·low [YEL-oh] *adj* **-er, -est 1** of the color of lemons, gold, etc. **2** *inf* cowardly. ◆ *n* **3** this color. **yel·low-bel·ly** *n, pl* **-lies** *sl* coward. **yellow fever** acute infectious disease of (sub)tropical climates. **yellow jacket 1** type of wasp. **2** *sl* yellow capsule of phenobarbital.

yelp *vi, n* (produce) quick, shrill cry.

yen[1] *n* Japanese monetary unit.

yen[2] *n inf* longing, craving.

yeo·man [YOH-mən] *n, pl* **-men 1** petty officer in U.S. Navy having mainly clerical duties. **2** *Brit. hist.* farmer cultivating own land. ◆ *adj* **3** performed in valiant, thorough manner.

yes *interj* **1** affirms or consents, gives an affirmative answer. ◆ *n, pl* **yes·ses 2** affirmative reply. **yes-man** *n, pl* **-men** weak person willing to agree to anything.

yes·ter·day [YES-tər-day] *n* **1** day before today. **2** recent time. ◆ *adv, adj*

yet *adv* **1** now, still, besides, hitherto. **2** nevertheless. ◆ *conj* **3** but, at the same time, nevertheless.

yet·i [YET-ee] *n* see ABOMINABLE SNOWMAN.

yew [yoo] *n* **1** evergreen tree with dark leaves. **2** its wood.

Yid·dish [YID-ish] *adj, n* (of, in) language used by many Jews in or from Europe, orig. a form of German written in Hebrew letters, with words from Hebrew and many other languages.

yield [yeeld] *vt* **1** give or return as food. **2** produce. **3** provide. **4** concede. **5** give up, surrender. ◆ *vi* **6** produce. **7** submit. **8** comply. **9** surrender, give way. ◆ *n* **10** amount produced, return, profit, result.

Y2K *n inf* name for AD 2000 (esp. referring to the millennium bug).

yo·del [YOHD-l] *vi* **-deled, -del·ing 1** warble in falsetto tone. ◆ *n* **2** falsetto warbling as practiced by Swiss mountaineers.

yo·ga [YOH-gə] *n* Hindu philosophical system aiming at spiritual, mental and physical well-being by means of certain physical and mental exercises. **yo·gi** [-gee] *n, pl* **-gis** one who practices yoga.

yo·gurt [YOH-gərt] *n* thick, custard-like preparation of curdled milk.

yoke [yohk] *n* **1** wooden bar put across the necks of two animals to hold them together and to which plow, etc. can be attached. **2** various objects like a yoke in shape or use. **3** fitted part of garment, esp. around neck, shoulders. **4** bond or tie. **5** domination. ◆ *vt* **yoked, yok·ing 6** put a yoke on, couple, unite.

yo·kel [YOH-kəl] *n offens* person who lives

—————————————| THESAURUS |—————————————

yearly *adj* **1** = **annual** ◆ *adv* **2** = **annually**, every year, once a year, per annum

yearn *v* = **long**, ache, covet, crave, desire, hanker, hunger, itch

yell *v* **1** = **scream**, bawl, holler (*inf*), howl, screech, shout, shriek, squeal ◆ *n* **2** = **scream**, cry, howl, screech, shriek, whoop

yell at *v Inf* = **criticize**, censure, rebuke, scold, tear into (*inf*)

yelp *v* = **cry**, yap, yowl

yen *n* = **longing**, ache, craving, desire, hankering, hunger, itch, passion, thirst, yearning

yes man *n* = **sycophant**, brown-noser (*sl*), minion, timeserver, toady

yet *conj* **1** = **nevertheless**, however, notwithstanding, still ◆ *adv* **2** = **so far**, as

yet, thus far, until now, up to now **3** = **still**, besides, in addition, into the bargain, to boot **4** = **now**, just now, right now, so soon

yield *v* **1** = **produce**, bear, bring forth, earn, generate, give, net, provide, return, supply **2** = **surrender**, bow, capitulate, give in, relinquish, resign, submit, succumb ◆ *n* **3** = **profit**, crop, earnings, harvest, income, output, produce, return, revenue, takings

yielding *adj* **1** = **submissive**, accommodating, acquiescent, biddable, compliant, docile, flexible, obedient, pliant **2** = **soft**, elastic, pliable, spongy, springy, supple, unresisting

yoke *v* = **burden**, encumber, land, load, saddle

in the country and is usu. simple and
old-fashioned.

yolk [yohk] *n* **1** yellow central part of egg. **2**
oily secretion of skin of sheep.

yon *adj obs or dial* that or those over there.
yon·der [YON-dər] *adj* **1** yon. ◆ *adv* **2** over
there, in that direction.

yore [yor] *n Poet.* the distant past.

York·shire pudding [YORK-shər] baked
batter eaten with roast beef.

you [yoo] *pron* referring to person(s)
addressed, or to unspecified person(s).

young [yung] *adj* **-er, -est 1** not far
advanced in growth, life or existence. **2**
not yet old. **3** immature. **4** junior. **5**
recently formed. **6** vigorous. ◆ *n* **7**
offspring. **young'ster** [-stər] *n* child.

your [yuur] *adj* **1** of, belonging to, or
associated with you. **2** of, belonging to, or
associated with an unspecified person or
people in general. **yours** *pron* something
belonging to you. **your·self'** *pron, pl*
-selves

youth [yooth] *n* **1** state or time of being
young. **2** state before adult age. **3** young
man. **4** young people. **youth'ful** [-fəl] *adj*

yowl *v, n* (produce) mournful cry.

yo-yo [YOH-yoh] *n, pl* **-yos** toy consisting
of a spool attached to a string, by which it
can be spun out and reeled in while
attached to the finger.

yuc·ca [YUK-ə] *n* tropical plant with stiff
lancelike leaves.

Yule [yool] *n* the Christmas festival or
season.

yup·pie [YUP-ee] *n* young urban
professional. ◆ *adj*

za·ba·glio·ne [zah-bəl-YOH-nee] *n* Italian
custardlike dessert of whipped and heated
egg yolks, sugar and Marsala wine.

za·ny [ZAY-nee] *adj* **-ni·er, -ni·est 1** comical,
funny in unusual way. ◆ *n, pl* **-nies 2**
eccentric person. **3** silly person.

zap *inf* ◆ *vt* **zapped, zap·ping 1** attack, kill
or destroy. **2** *Computers* clear from screen,
erase. **3** change (TV channels) rapidly by
remote control. **4** skip over or delete sound
of (commercials).

zeal [zeel] *n* **1** fervor. **2** keenness,
enthusiasm. **zeal·ot** [ZEL-ət] *n* **1** fanatic. **2**
enthusiast. **zeal'ous** [-əs] *adj* **1** ardent. **2**
enthusiastic. **3** earnest. **zeal'ous·ly** *adv*

ze·bra [ZEE-brə] *n, pl* **-bras** striped Afr.
animal like a horse.

ze·bu [ZEE-byoo] *n* humped Indian ox or
cow.

Zen *n* Japanese school teaching
contemplation, meditation.

ze·nith [ZEE-nith] *n* **1** point of the heavens
directly above an observer. **2** point
opposite nadir. **3** summit, peak. **4** climax.

zeph·yr [ZEF-ər] *n* soft, gentle breeze.

zep·pe·lin [ZEP-ə-lin] *n* large, cylindrical,
rigid airship.

ze·ro [ZEER-oh] *n, pl* **-ros, -roes 1** nothing.
2 figure 0. **3** point on graduated
instrument from which positive and
negative quantities are reckoned. **4** the
lowest point. ◆ *vt* **-roed, -ro·ing 5** reduce
to zero. **6** adjust (instrument, etc.) to zero.

zest *n* **1** enjoyment. **2** excitement, interest,
flavor. **3** peel of orange or lemon. **zest'ful**
[-fəl] *adj*

zig'zag *n* **1** line or course characterized by

yokel *n* = **peasant**, (country) bumpkin,
countryman, hick (*inf, chiefly U.S. and
Canad.*), hillbilly, redneck (*sl*), rustic

young *adj* **1** = **immature**, adolescent,
callow, green, infant, junior, juvenile, little,
youthful **2** = **new**, early, fledgling, recent,
undeveloped ◆ *pl n* **3** = **offspring**, babies,
brood, family, issue, litter, progeny

youngster *n* = **youth**, boy, girl, juvenile,
kid (*inf*), lad, lass, teenager

youth *n* **1** = **immaturity**, adolescence,
boyhood, girlhood, salad days **2** = **boy**,
adolescent, kid (*inf*), lad, stripling,
teenager, young man, youngster

youthful *adj* = **young**, boyish, childish,
fresh-faced, girlish, immature,
inexperienced, juvenile, rosy-cheeked

zany *adj* = **comical**, clownish, crazy,
eccentric, goofy (*inf*), wacky (*sl*)

zeal *n* = **enthusiasm**, ardor, eagerness,
fanaticism, fervor, gusto, keenness,
passion, spirit, verve, zest

zealot *n* = **fanatic**, bigot, enthusiast,
extremist, militant

zealous *adj* = **enthusiastic**, ardent,
devoted, eager, fanatical, fervent,
impassioned, keen, passionate

zenith *n* = **height**, acme, apex, apogee,
climax, crest, high point, peak, pinnacle,
summit, top

zero *n* **1** = **nothing**, nada (*inf*), nil, nought,
zilch (*inf*) **2** = **bottom**, nadir, rock bottom

zest *n* **1** = **enjoyment**, appetite, gusto,
keenness, relish, zeal **2** = **flavor**, charm,

sharp turns in alternating directions. ◆ vi
-zagged, -zag·ging 2 move along in zigzag
course.

zinc [zingk] n bluish-white metallic element
with wide variety of uses, esp. in alloys as
brass, etc.

zin·ni·a [ZIN-ee-ə] n plant with daisylike,
brightly colored flowers.

Zi·on [ZĪ-ən] n 1 hill on which Jerusalem
stands. 2 modern Jewish nation. 3 Israel. 4
Christian Church heaven. **Zi'on·ism** n
movement to found, support Jewish
homeland in what now is state of Israel.
Zi'on·ist n, adj

zip n 1 short whizzing sound. 2 energy,
vigor. ◆ v **zipped, zip·ping** 3 move with
zip.

zip code [kohd] system of numbers used to
aid sorting of mail (also **ZIP code**).

zip·per [ZIP-ər] n 1 device for fastening
with two rows of flexible metal or plastic
teeth, interlocked and opened by a sliding
clip. ◆ vt 2 fasten with zipper.

zir·con [ZUR-kon] n mineral used as
gemstone and in industry.

zith·er [ZITH-ər] n flat stringed instrument.
Zn Chem. zinc.

zo·di·ac [ZOH-dee-ak] n imaginary belt of
the heavens along which the sun, moon,
and chief planets appear to move, divided
crosswise into twelve equal areas, called
signs of the zodiac, each named after a
constellation. **zo·di·a·cal** [zoh-DĪ-ə-kəl] adj

zom·bie [ZOM-bee] n 1 person appearing
lifeless, apathetic, etc. 2 corpse supposedly
brought to life by supernatural spirit.

zone [zohn] n 1 region with particular
characteristics or use. 2 any of the five
belts into which tropics and arctic and
antarctic circles divide Earth.

zoo n place where wild animals are kept,
studied, bred and exhibited.

zo·og·ra·phy [zoh-OG-rə-fee] n descriptive
zoology. **zo·og'ra·pher, zo·og'ra·phist** n
zo·o·graph'i·cal adj

zo·ol·o·gy [zoh-OL-ə-jee] n 1 scientific
study of animals. 2 characteristics of
particular animals or of fauna of particular
area. **zo·o·log'i·cal** adj **zo·ol'o·gist** n

zoom v 1 (cause to) make loud buzzing,
humming sound. 2 (cause to) go fast or
rise, increase sharply. ◆ vi 3 (of camera) use
lens of adjustable focal length to make
subject appear to move closer or farther
away. **zoom lens** lens used in this way.

zo·o·phyte [ZOH-ə-fīt] n animal
resembling a plant, such as a sea
anemone. **zo·o·phyt'ic** [-FIT-ik] adj

Zr Chem. zirconium.

zuc·chi·ni [zoo-KEEN-ee] n, pl -ni or -nis
green-skinned summer squash.

Zu·lu [ZOO-loo] n member, language of S
Afr. Bantu tribes.

zy·gote [ZĪ-goht] n fertilized egg cell.

zy·mot·ic [zī-MOT-ik] adj 1 of, or caused
by fermentation. 2 of, caused by infection.

——————— THESAURUS ———————

interest, piquancy, pungency, relish, spice,
tang, taste

zip n 1 Inf = **energy**, drive, gusto, liveliness,
verve, vigor, zest ◆ v 2 = **speed**, flash, fly,
shoot, whizz (inf), zoom

zone n = **area**, belt, district, region, section,
sector, sphere

zoom v = **speed**, dash, flash, fly, hurtle,
pelt, rush, shoot, whizz (inf)